Mrs Beeton's
Cookery and Household Management

Mrs Beeton's Cookery and Household Management

Ward Lock Limited·London

Acknowledgements

The publishers would like to thank the following firms for kindly supplying photographs:
A–Z Collection; Amtico; Armstrong Cork and Cover Plus; English Country Cheese Council; Ever Ready; Florapic; Nairn Floors and Kingfisher Vinyls; Arthur Sanderson & Sons Ltd; Harry Smith Horticultural Photographic Collection; Elizabeth Whiting; Winchmore Furniture Ltd.

The publishers would also like to thank the following people and companies for their valuable assistance:
Jane Atkinson; The Association of Barbecue Manufacturers and Suppliers; Billy Blackwell – Butcher and Edmonds Ltd; A.G.R. Bone – Wine and Spirit Education Trust Ltd; Dobeta Ltd; C.D. Figg; FMC Ltd; Ingersoll Locks Ltd; Meat and Livestock Commission; Moka Express Ltd; Moulinex Ltd; Osram (GEC) Ltd; The Pasta Information Centre; Salton Ltd; Christopher G. Smith BA, MCHIMA; Michael Sproat – Donald Sproat Ltd; Terence Walsh and G.F. Wensley – Peter Fairfax Ltd; and the many others who helped us during the course of this project.

First published in Great Britain in 1980
by Ward Lock Limited, 47 Marylebone Lane,
London W1M 6AX, a Pentos Company.

Joint editors Maggie Black and Susan Dixon
Designed by Andrew Shoolbred
Line drawings by Sue Sharples
Food photography by Sue and John Jorgenson

Colour separations by Newsele Litho Ltd, Milan and London.
Text filmset in Apollo.

Printed in Great Britain by Jolly & Barber Limited, Rugby.
Bound by Webb, Son and Co, Limited, Ferndale, Glamorgan.

British Library Cataloguing in Publication Data
Beeton, Isabella
    Mrs Beeton's cookery and household management. –
Revised ed.
1. Cookery
I. Black, Maggie
II. Dixon, Susan
III. Cookery and household management
641.5   TX717

ISBN 0–7063–5743–4

Consultant Editors

Carol Macartney – consultant home economist
Rosemary McRobert
Barbara Morrison FAHE – consultant home economist
Miss Joan Peters – consultant home economist

Contributors

Michael Beloff – legal correspondent to *The Observer*; Maggie Black; British Gas Corporation, Home Service Department; British Poultry Federation; British Turkey Federation; Mrs K.F. Broughton FAHE; Catherine Brown – Taste of Scotland food consultant; Elizabeth Chan; Robert Chase; Clive Coates MW; Lesley Connors; Maître Jean Conil – Principal, Academy of Gastronomy; A.F. Cowlard LCG – North Notts College of Further Education; Sue Cutts – Group Home Economist, The Prestige Group Ltd; Ruth Daykin; Mrs Carolyn Cheek Dehnel MA – American Women's Club, London; The Dutch Dairy Bureau; Mrs Molly Dzabala; The Electricity Council; Audrey Ellis – cookery writer; J. Audrey Ellison BSC, FSFST, FAHE, FRSH – food consultant and writer; Diana Ferguson BA; Theodora Fitzgibbon; Flour Advisory Bureau; Ruth Francis MIPR; Elizabeth Gundrey; Michael Hastin Bennett MA, MB, FRCS; Shirley Hislop; Home Laundering Consultative Council; Jan Hopcraft – cookery writer; Richard Howorth; Mrs Joyce Hughes BSC, MAHE – consultant home economist; Patricia Jacobs; Trude Johnston; Mrs Chizuko Kuroiwa; Peter Lackington – Youngs Seafoods Ltd; Margaret Leach MBE – home economist; Barbara Logan MHEA – consultant home economist; Mrs Sylvia Lyster; Carol Macartney; Rosemary McRobert; Barbara Maher; Maite Manjón – Spanish and Portuguese cookery writer; José Manser; Mrs Anne Mason; Moya Maynard; Milk Marketing Board; Mrs Iris Milutinovic; Mollie Mordle-Barnes – author and lecturer on textiles, dress and crafts; Barbara Morrison; New Zealand Lamb Information Bureau; Mary Norwak – cookery writer; Phyllis Oberman; Gabor Oliver – managing director, Cheese from Switzerland Ltd; Frances Perry – horticulturalist; Safia Racshid; Jennie Reekie; J.M. Richards MBE; Judy Ridgway; Royal Society for the Prevention of Accidents; George Schöpflin; Diana Short; Clare Slater; South African Meat Board; Textile Aftercare Staff of Derby Lonsdale College; Thorn Domestic Appliances and Hamish Hamilton; Ben Turner – Past President, National Association of Winemakers; United Kingdom Bartenders' Guild; Van den Berghs; Pauline Viola – Danish Agricultural Producers; P.C. Weedon – domestic fuel oil consultant; Dilys Wells BSC (Nutrition).

Contents

Preface to first edition

I must frankly own, that if I had known, beforehand, that this book would have cost me the labour which it has, I should never have been courageous enough to commence it. What moved me, in the first instance, to attempt a work like this, was the discomfort and suffering which I had seen brought upon men and women by household mismanagement. I have always thought that there is no more fruitful source of family discontent than a housewife's badly-cooked dinners and untidy ways. Men are now so well served out of doors, – at their clubs, well-ordered taverns, and dining houses, that in order to compete with the attractions of these places, a mistress must be thoroughly acquainted with the theory and practice of cookery, as well as be perfectly conversant with all the other arts of making and keeping a comfortable home.

In this book I have attempted to give, under the chapters devoted to cookery, an intelligible arrangement to every recipe, a list of the *ingredients*, a plain statement of the *mode* of preparing each dish, and a careful estimate of its *cost*, the *number of people* for whom it is *sufficient*, and the time when it is *seasonable*. For the matter of the recipes, I am indebted, in some measure, to many correspondents of the 'Englishwoman's Domestic Magazine,' who have obligingly placed at my disposal their formulae for many original preparations. A large private circle has also rendered me considerable service. A diligent study of the works of the best modern writers on cookery was also necessary to the faithful fulfilment of my task. Friends in England, Scotland, Ireland, France and Germany, have also very materially aided me. I have paid great attention to those recipes which come under the head of 'COLD MEAT COOKERY.' But in the department belonging to the Cook I have striven, too, to make my work something more than a Cookery Book, and have, therefore, on the best authority that I could obtain, given an account of the natural history of the animals and vegetables which we use as food. I have followed the animal from his birth to his appearance on the table; have described the manner of feeding him, and of slaying him, the position of his various joints, and, after giving the recipes, have described the modes of carving Meat, Poultry, and Game. Skilful artists have designed the numerous drawings which appear in this work, and which illustrate, better than any description, many important and interesting items. The coloured plates are a novelty not without value.

Besides the great portion of the book which has especial reference to the cook's department, there are chapters devoted to those of the other servants of the household, who have all, I trust, their duties clearly assigned to them.

Towards the end of the work will be found valuable chapters on the 'Management of Children' – 'The Doctor,' the latter principally referring to accidents and emergencies, some of which are certain to occur in the experience of every one of us; and the last chapter contains 'Legal Memoranda,' which will be serviceable in cases of doubt as to the proper course to be adopted in the relations between Landlord and Tenant, Tax-gatherer and Taxpayer, and Tradesman and Customer.

These chapters have been contributed by gentlemen fully entitled to confidence; those on medical subjects by an experienced surgeon, and the legal matter by a solicitor.

I wish here to acknowledge the kind letters and congratulations I have received during the progress of this work, and have only further to add, that I trust the result of the four years' incessant labour which I have expended will not be altogether unacceptable to some of my countrymen and countrywomen.

ISABELLA BEETON

9

Preface to new edition

When Mrs Beeton's Book of Household Management first appeared more than 120 years ago, the success it enjoyed, and has continued to enjoy ever since, was due not only to the comprehensive selection of recipes she provided, but also to the practical and often forthright advice she offered on all aspects of running a home. In preparing a new edition for the last decades of the twentieth century, we have constantly referred back to Isabella Beeton's own book and have followed her principles.

The changes since 1960, when the last new edition of this book appeared, have been at least as great as those during the whole of the previous hundred years, so that the book has received a more radical revision than ever before. Tastes in food are at once more sophisticated and more simple; mechanical aids in the kitchen are universal; the introduction of metric weights and measures is increasingly welcomed and accepted; the rights of the consumer are championed; society itself is less divided, and most social occasions are less formal. These developments have been taken into account by the many distinguished authors and advisers who have contributed to the new Mrs Beeton. We hope it will be as useful in the 1980s as was the original work in the 1860s. In making the very many necessary changes we have tried not to deviate from the original purpose of the book. We have, in particular, given recipes in a form that will be clearly understood by the inexperienced as well as the experienced cook.

Each chapter is prefaced by a quotation from the original work, as so much of the general advice Isabella Beeton gave then is still highly relevant today. They show her fundamental understanding of the arts of home-making and entertaining. We have also included a number of her own recipes, adapted only to ensure a successful result in the modern kitchen. To each of these her name has been attached.

People have always turned to Mrs Beeton to find recipes for traditional dishes, and have consulted her on social matters for both formal and informal occasions. We trust that readers of our new edition will still find all the information of this kind that they require. At the same time the new Mrs Beeton is a comprehensive modern cookery book and reference work, which can be used in a home fully equipped with modern appliances, but which is also adapted to the full and varied life-style of the modern woman.

THE PUBLISHERS

ACQUIRING A HOME

Many mistresses have experienced the horrors of house-hunting, and it is well known that " three removes are as good (or bad, rather) as a fire." Nevertheless, it being quite evident that we must, in these days at least, live in houses, and are sometimes obliged to change our residences, it is well to consider some of the conditions which will add to, or diminish, the convenience and comfort of our homes.

An ideal home is something very personal and means different things to different people. Whether buying or renting a house or flat, whether living in a bed-sitter, in 'tied' accommodation in a living-in job, or in a service room in a block of service flats or hotel, each home will be characterized by the personality and individuality of its occupants.

The first decision to make is what kind of home would suit you best, and this chapter sets out to help you make the best choice and avoid expensive mistakes.

Choosing What You Want
Renting

Before you start looking for accommodation, draw up a list of the features that you regard as important. If renting a flat, remember that they do not often stay on the market for long, and if you get a chance to rent one you may have to make up your mind quickly. But do not sign anything before you have had it checked by a solicitor, whose job it is to make sure that any lease or agreement does not contain any terms unfair to you, and that it spells out exactly what you are getting and what you are responsible for in your tenancy. This advice applies equally to renting a house.

Accommodation is advertised by word of mouth, in newspaper advertisements, in postcards in newsagents' windows, and through agencies. Sometimes a premium or capital payment is asked for a house or flat that is rented on a lease. You may

be asked to put down a deposit as a gesture of your good faith. Again, never do this without consulting a solicitor and paying the deposit formally. No one who is prepared to deal with you honestly will be surprised that you do this.

The shortage of accommodation in recent years has made renting a flat more difficult, and legislation that protects existing tenants has made landlords cautious about reletting accommodation; many former flats have been turned into 'service rooms' where the protective legislation does not bite to the same extent.

Some flats in older buildings may require tenants to take the flat on a repairing lease. This could be very expensive and a surveyor's report is a wise preliminary. A fee will have to be paid for this but it will almost certainly be worth it and could possibly save you being landed with hundreds of pounds worth of repairs.

When a flat is rented unfurnished on an agreement or lease, the lessee's responsibilities are generally limited to interior decoration and maintenance, and a flat which is held on a short-term lease or agreement is usually regarded as a more temporary accommodation than a house.

The legal formalities to renting accommodation are discussed in more detail in the chapter on The Law and You.

Sharing a flat
Sharing a flat with other people does not often involve a formal agreement, but it does help to avoid squabbles later on if there is an exchange of letters which outlines what responsibilities each

member undertakes. If one person is responsible for paying the bills, for example if the gas or electricity is in their name, it can be very difficult to get the others to pay up. For this reason, although the energy costs more, pre-payment meters may be the only answer and sharing flat-dwellers might consider installing a coin-box telephone.

In the case of sub-tenants there are legislative rulings similar to those which apply to tenants in rented flats.

Buying a Home

A very large proportion of householders in the UK own their homes, and at some stage you will almost certainly want to think about buying a house or flat. This gives you greater freedom to do what you want with your own property, as well as the chance, with a house, to have a garden of your own and to provide children with more space to play and to grow up in. (Many of the points related to renting a flat (see p11) apply to buying flats.)

Flats are not a poor alternative to houses. A lot of people prefer living in a compact flat which can be locked up and left easily, which does not need the maintenance that a house does, and which, as a rule, costs less to run.

Unless flats are extremely well built, they are often noisier than self-contained houses; you not only hear your neighbours –they hear you.

Although flats can be very convenient, one also has to consider the disadvantages of carrying everything upstairs if there is no lift, and of having to take everything, including the rubbish, down to the ground floor. Flats – especially, of course, high-rise flats – are not the ideal solution for families with children and animals.

Choosing where to live

The first thing to do, obviously, is to choose the area or areas where you want to look for a house. Buy a large-scale map and pin-point your key spots – place of work, school, relations, and so on. Draw circles round them to give the farthest distance from your key points. Study the public transport system. You may have a car but perhaps other people who are important to you do not. Fares are a

very expensive item and should be included, if they are relevant, in any budget you draw up. It may not be true that a house that is cheaper on the outskirts of a city makes better economic sense than buying something in the town.

Try to get to know the area you want to live in. Find out which neighbourhoods are more popular than others. There is usually a reason: freedom from traffic noise, near a park, no light industry, for instance.

You will also want to check that there are no plans for future developments, such as a motorway past your back garden or a complete redevelopment on a surrounding space.

A visit to the town hall to see the local planning officer is useful. You will want to have an official solicitor's search made before you finally sign the contract for your new property, but you do not need professional help to size up the district in a preliminary exercise.

Deciding what kind of house or flat you need

Your personal needs and circumstances will, of course, be very important, but consider also those of your family. How far from the shops will heavy bags have to be carried? How long will it take children to get to school; will elderly relations, visiting or living with you, find the nearest bus-stop too far away?

Consider what preferences, rooted objections, and particular requirements each member of your household has. Will stairs be a disadvantage if there is anyone with a handicap in the house? If you are going to leave someone on their own all day, is a modern house on an estate preferable to an older, more spacious house in secluded grounds? Is it more of an advantage to be within walking distance of shops than in the peaceful seclusion of a hamlet or village?

For more information, see pp30–39, pp123–129, and pp130–133.

Budgeting

Having made your own individual list of desirable features, you will have to decide what are priorities for you and then match these to the amount of money you think you will have available to buy a new property. Something at this stage will usually have to give way. The final list of essential needs will be a matter of compromise, with every member of the household airing his and her views.

You will, in fact, have to draw up a budget before you start looking for a property to buy. You will almost certainly have to borrow money to bridge the gap between your savings and the cost of buying the house. The three main ways of doing this – a mortgage from a building society, a loan from a local authority or a loan from an insurance company coupled with a life assurance policy for the same sum – are discussed on pp13–16 below. Other ways of raising smaller sums of money are detailed on pp24–29.

You will probably need more cash, or may need to raise more cash, than you thought at first. Remember that the loan you get is based on the lender's valuation of the property, which may not be the same as the price you have to pay and can often be quite a lot less.

The cost of a property – flat or house – is obviously not just a matter of mortgage repayments. There are rates, water rates, porterage in the case of flats, redecorations, and repairs. There is the cash or credit cost of furnishing the house; there are the solicitor's fees and the general charges involved in buying the house.

Finding the house or flat

As in renting accommodation, local newspapers and weekly papers that specialize in house or flat advertisements are particularly useful, as are the national Sunday newspapers. As most advertisements are put in by agents you will also get their addresses and telephone numbers through the papers. Contact estate agents in the area and ask them to send you details of property you have seen advertised. Give them a brief description of what you want, in roughly the price bracket you are aiming for. Do not ask agents to find a house for you unless you are prepared to pay them a fee, and remember that they are acting on behalf of the seller, not on your behalf.

It is also worth walking or driving around your selected area looking out for 'For Sale' notices.

Looking the property over

When you think you have found a suitable home, let the family inspect it. Some first impressions by the young can be very telling and the rest of the family might spot something about the neighbourhood that you have missed. If you have no children, ask some friends to help you inspect the possible property. What are the neighbours like? Talk to as many people in the area as you can to find out what they think about the place – its shops, schools, clubs, and so on. Have a word with customers in the nearest pub or shop.

The position and prospect of the property is worth checking. Which way does it face in relation to the sun, to the prevailing wind in an exposed place, to the road, to its own site? What does it look out on? Architectural and design features may affect resale value; a house or flat of unusual and unique design may be so unique that few buyers are attracted by it, or it may turn out to be the work of an architect who is about to become fashionable. Building societies often do not care for designs in unusual materials or with original features, and their valuation may reflect this.

In the case of a house, although you may not want to stay in the same one for ever, it is worth considering if it has possibilities for expansion as the family grows or a relation comes to live with you; on the other hand, it may have possibilities for dividing into smaller units.

All these are only suggestions. Everyone will have his own ideas to contribute. What is important is approaching the business of finding a house or flat methodically and, to a certain extent, philosophically. You have to spend a lot of time in a house or flat. No one but you can decide what is important in the property, the place, and the district where you want to live. So take time over it, and if it is necessary, pay for the best professional advice you can afford.

Types of Mortgage

There are three main kinds of mortgage:

A repayment mortgage which is paid off over a long period – up to twenty-five years. Tax relief can usually be claimed by the borrower on the interest part of the repayment.

An endowment mortgage, in which the monthly payment is part interest on the loan and part premium on an endowment insurance policy, which matures at the end of the mortgage period and pays off the loan, perhaps also providing a lump sum of money. There is a life assurance element as well, so that if the mortgagor dies before the end of the mortgage period, the loan is paid off. Tax relief can usually be claimed on the insurance policy premiums. There are several different insurance-related schemes available and you may find it helpful to take the advice of an insurance broker to find the one that is most suitable for you. If you arrange mortgage finance through an insurance broker you should not have to pay a fee for advice or the arrangement of a mortgage advance. You should choose your broker carefully; he should preferably be a member of one of the recognized bodies of insurance brokers.

An option mortgage is a government scheme to help home buyers with modest incomes whose tax bills are not large enough for them to get full benefit from tax relief available with repayment or endowment mortgages. Usually a smaller amount of money is borrowed than through other mortgage plans. Option mortgages are available for both repayment and endowment mortgages, but repayment mortgages are the most usual. If, after having an option mortgage for four years, your circumstances change, eg you earn more money and move into a different tax bracket, you can change to an ordinary mortgage if this would be more advantageous. Changing an ordinary mortgage to an option mortgage is possible in very special circumstances if your income is drastically reduced, eg through an accident or serious illness.

Borrowing Money

Building societies

Most people borrow the money to buy their home from a building society, whether it is a repayment or an endowment mortgage. Most building societies operate different policies about the kinds of property on which they lend money, so if you know what kind of home you want to look for, it is worth checking on these preferences before you invest with a society. Call on their local office and ask for the information. Some, for example, rarely lend money on older property. Similarly, if you are married and want to buy a house with your joint earnings, you will need to find a society that is prepared to take both incomes into account when lending money. Your age may be a factor too, ie policies of some societies may differ in relation to the income of an older woman with an established career, and that of a newly married wife who may be expected to leave work to start a family.

Societies will need to know in detail the amount of income you have. Some only consider the basic gross pay of the person applying for the mortgage – not overtime, or bonuses, or casual earnings. Other regular sources of income, for example, fixed income from investments or pension, might be taken into account. Most societies will not lend more than twice the gross income. Couples who are both earning may be able to have the calculations based on the higher of the two incomes.

Local authority

The terms on which local authorities will lend money for house purchase vary widely and are influenced very much by government policy at the time. A local authority is usually more ready to lend against the value of the property and the job of the borrower than the actual size of the income. When income is part of the consideration, a 'monthly outgoings' rule is often used. This means that the monthly mortgage repayment must be less than the weekly gross income. Some councils will lend 100% on their valuation of the house (which may be much less than the purchase price). The interest rate charged by local authorities is often a little higher than that charged by building societies, but local authorities will often lend money on the type of property that building societies and other lenders do not want to cover. As a rule, they will only lend money on property in their area, and only on cheaper properties. Not all local authorities grant mortgages and, when money is short, they may stop doing this altogether. Many local authorities are more flexible in their approach to lending money than building societies, however, because they regard the matter as a question of social policy.

Insurance companies

A few insurance companies lend money to buy homes through an endowment mortgage and more will lend money to supplement a building society loan. Insurance companies are as strict as building societies about their lending policies, and it is not likely that you will get a loan from an insurance company if you fail on all the counts that a building society likes you to meet.

Insurance companies may charge a higher rate of interest than the building society; however they may well be the only source of finance available for larger mortgages.

Banks

Banks do not usually grant mortgages. However, they may lend you money to buy a house if you can repay it in five years, and the sum will be on their valuation of the house. Banks will usually provide a bridging loan, for example, between the time you buy a new house and have to put down the money and the time you sell an existing house. The duration of a bridging loan tends to be only a few weeks and the bank will need to be sure that the sale of your existing home is going ahead. The rate of interest on these loans is usually the same as for an overdraft (see the chapter on Raising and Spending Money).

Employers and private lenders

Some employers make loans available to their employees for house purchase. If you leave the employment of the firm, you usually have to repay the loan (which may leave you looking for a source of mortgage) or pay the commercial rate of interest on the loan.

A relation may be able to lend you the money. Sometimes the seller of a property will offer a private loan, perhaps because no one else will advance the money. You will want to be sure that you do not take out a private loan on a property which no one else wants and which you will have difficulty in selling later.

Amounts which can be Borrowed

This is strictly related to the amount of money you can repay during the period of the loan. That is the reality of the situation. It will depend on your income and also to a certain extent on the kind of job you are in – a good steady job at a reliable income will be more attractive to a lender than an excitingly precarious one with peaks and troughs.

The lender will also take into account the kind of home you want to buy, as he will want to be sure that if you do not keep up repayments on the loan, he will be able to sell the property and recoup his money. He will probably prefer a new house or a flat in a new block, rather than an older property.

The value of the property will also be a factor. This is the value the lender puts on it, after he has had it professionally surveyed perhaps. This value may well be less than the price you are prepared to pay for it. The value of the house may, of course, increase with time, but when you are borrowing money, the only value that counts with the lender is the value at that time. It is very unusual to be able to get 100% mortgage of even *that* value.

You will almost certainly have to pay the difference between the purchase price and your loan; that is why saving up towards putting down this cash payment is an important preliminary if you are thinking of buying your home.

Repayment

When you sell your home, you have to repay the lender the amount of money you have borrowed (unless you are able to transfer the mortgage to a new property). In the early years of a mortgage, this sum will usually be almost the amount you borrowed in the first place, because most of your monthly repayment will be interest, and the capital sum you owe will only decrease slowly over the years.

In the early years of your mortgage you may find that tax relief will cover a significant amount of your repayment. If you cannot keep up with the monthly repayment, tell the lender at once, so that you can make some arrangements to extend the period of repayment and reduce the monthly sums.

Most lenders would rather get their money than go to the trouble of forcing you to put the house on the market, but you must keep them in the picture.

If you borrow money from two lenders – for example, if you get a topping-up loan from an insurance company or bank – the second lender may require the topping-up loan to be taken as a second mortgage. This then gives him rights against the proceeds after the first lender has had his loan repaid. Either of the lenders can force you to sell if you fail to keep up with the payments you have agreed to make.

Budgeting and a Mortgage

How are you going to be able to afford to spend a large proportion of your income on housing? Only you can decide whether you will be able to repay the maximum amount of money the lender will let you have. If you like to spend money on a car, holidays, clothes, meals out, hairdressing or any other theoretically 'optional' expenditure, you may find it difficult to keep up high mortgage repayments. Think carefully of any drastic cuts you may have to make before you commit yourself.

The interest rate on loans tends to go up, too, and it is sensible to try and allow yourself a margin to cope with this.

If you are buying the house on two incomes, you should assess the chances of having to repay out of one income later on – for instance, if you are a couple and one of you gives up work, perhaps in order to have a baby.

Other Expenses

Apart from the price of the property, you may incur a number of other expenses when you buy a house or flat. There may be rents; if the property is leasehold there may be ground rent; there may be service charges if the flat is in a block, and there may be contributions to a communal fund for up-keep of the fabric.

There will also be fees – for estate agents, surveyors (both your own and the building society's) and solicitors – and the cost of the move, so include these expenses too when calculating costs.

The Legal Side of Home Ownership

The facts in this section are generalities only, and some of them may change during the lifespan of the book. More detailed advice should be sought from a solicitor.

When you have found a house or a flat you like at the right price, make the seller an offer 'subject to contract'. If he accepts, contact your solicitor, who will deal with the conveyancing (transfer) of the property.

Buying a Home

The seller's solicitor first sends the buyer's solicitor a draft contract.

The next stage is to make enquiries of the seller and local council and to make searches in official registers. The purpose is to find out exactly what you are buying: to make sure that you are getting all the rights you will need, that there is nothing to interfere with your occupation of the property, and to find out what liabilities and responsibilities attach to the owner of it. Most of the important questions are the same for everyone, so they are printed on a form; but extra questions can be added. Usually searches and enquiries merely show that everything is just as it seemed. But sometimes they do reveal something important, which you should know about before buying, or which may even put you off buying altogether – and it is nobody's obligation to tell you these things unless you ask them to. If you do not like what you find out, you can still withdraw.

The buyer should also get the property surveyed, since any building society surveyor's report will not be passed on to him. He should check garden boundaries against the plans, and look for signs that anyone else has rights over the property – a track across the garden may show that the neighbours have a right of way.

Meanwhile the buyer will no doubt have arranged a mortgage. When both sides are ready, the contract will be signed and copies exchanged and the buyer will pay a deposit based on the total purchase price.

The contract

A contract is an agreement which the law will enforce. In the case of buying a house or flat, this means that the buyer can make the seller sell the property to him, and the seller can make the buyer buy the property from him, at the price which they have agreed. The law will not enforce a contract to sell land (including one to sell a house and the land it stands on) unless there is a record of it in writing or it has been partly performed by one person so that it would be unfair to allow the other to withdraw from it. (For example, the buyer may have done expensive repairs.) This means that even though the seller may have agreed orally to sell you the house or flat, if someone offers him a better price he may sell it to that person instead. This can be heartbreaking if it is just what you have been looking for; but the other side of the coin is that you can also withdraw if you find that the garden is about to be invaded by a motorway.

The contract will set a date for completion – the transfer of ownership – which is often twenty-eight days after the date of the contract. (It may take much longer than this to complete a purchase, however, particularly if the seller is in turn buying another house.) During that period the seller's title (that is, his right to sell) must be proved. This may be done by checking the title deeds – the documents which record the various transfers of the house or flat from one owner to the next down the years. To check all the transfers would take too long, so the deeds are only checked back to the last transfer which took place fifteen or more years ago. However, this system is gradually being replaced by a system of registration. One after another, areas of the country are designated 'compulsory registration areas'. After that, the next time any property in the area is sold, the title to that property, proved in the traditional way, is registered at a Land Registry. Once the title has been registered, the Register itself is the proof of ownership. This makes things much easier for the buyer. He merely has to inspect the Register to make sure that the person from whom he is buying is registered as the owner. He knows that the Government guarantees the Register to be correct; in the unlikely event that it is wrong, he will be compensated.

Finally the transaction is completed. The formal transfer of ownership takes place, the money is paid, and the keys are handed over.

Handling your own conveyancing

One consequence of registration is that conveyancing has become less complicated in the case of registered land. People often wonder whether they really need to go to a solicitor, or whether they could buy their property without one. A person who decides to do his own conveyancing with the aid of an appropriate legal reference book can save quite a lot of money in solicitors' fees, but there are several disadvantages to doing it oneself. It is impossible to tell in advance whether the transaction will be straightforward, and a solicitor has the knowledge and training to detect unusual and possibly dangerous features which the ordinary person might miss. You would have to put in more hours of work than a solicitor because you would have to find out at each stage what to do, get hold of the right forms, and so on. Finally, if a solicitor is negligent you are entitled to compensation for any loss you suffer as a result. If you yourself make a mistake, nobody will compensate you. But do not assume that compensation will be available from a solicitor for anything that goes wrong; not all defects are the result of negligence.

Co-ownership

When two or more people buy a house or flat, they may be either joint owners or owners in common. (They are confusingly called by lawyers 'joint tenants' and 'tenants in common'.) The most important difference is that when one of two joint owners dies, the entire property automatically belongs to the other; whereas when one of two owners in common dies, his share passes under his will or intestacy in the normal way. Joint ownership may be converted into ownership in common by giving written notice to the other joint owner or owners.

Even if only one person is the legal owner, he may be holding the property on trust for another person, in whole or in part. This may happen, for example, where another person has put up all or part of the money to buy the property. That person will have an equitable share, the size of which will depend on his contribution, provided that he intended to have a financial interest in the house, and not merely to make a gift or a loan of the money. A person providing half the purchase price as a loan would only be entitled to be repaid that sum and whatever interest was agreed, but a person with an equitable half-share would be entitled to half the purchase money when the property was sold, which might be much more (or less).

Mortgages

For the different types of mortgage available, see p13 above. This section describes the legal structure and consequences of a mortgage. They apply equally to leaseholds and freeholds.

A house or flat costs many thousands of pounds and most people have to borrow the money in order to buy one. They promise to pay it back; but it would be risky to lend money simply in exchange for such a promise. A house or flat is, however, worth a lot of money. So building societies and others are willing to lend a large sum of money (usually well below what they think the house is worth) in exchange for a promise to pay it back with interest *and* the right to sell the house to repay themselves if that promise is not kept.

The borrower (the property owner) is called the mortgagor. The lender is called the mortgagee. Mortgagees of ordinary dwelling-houses are now usually building societies, but anyone with the money to lend may become a mortgagee.

The mortgage will specify a 'redemption date' which is often six months from the date of the mortgage. This is the date on which, according to the mortgage, the loan becomes repayable. However, in fact, the mortgage allows for repayment over many years. The significance of the redemption date is that it is only after that date that the mortgagee will be able to recover his money by means of the house itself, instead of just suing the mortgagor for the payments. If the mortgagor defaults after a year or two and it is quite clear that he

cannot repay the mortgage, it would be unjust to make the mortgagee wait the rest of the twenty or thirty years to recover his money. Also, it is only after the redemption date that the mortgagor is entitled to pay off the mortgage in full.

If the mortgagor defaults on his repayments, several courses of action are available to the mortgagee. The most important are these. First, he has the power to sell the house (even though it belongs to the mortgagor). He will keep the amount of the original loan and the interest owing to him and hand over the remainder (if any) to the mortgagor. He must obtain the best price he can at the time he sells; he cannot agree to sell just for the amount that he is owed if the market price then is higher. But he does not have to wait until prices go up.

The traditional remedy of the mortgagee was foreclosure. This is now only possible if a court gives permission; if it does, the mortgagee becomes the owner of the property and the mortgagor loses the right to pay off the mortgage and free the property. But if the property is worth far more than the mortgage debt and outstanding interest, this will mean that the mortgagee gets a free benefit while the mortgagor loses more than he actually owes. Instead of allowing foreclosure, the court can order the property to be sold and the balance of the price after payment of the mortgage debt and interest to be paid to the mortgagor.

Unless the mortgage provides otherwise, the mortgagee has the right to possession. Normally he does not want it; but if the mortgagor breaks the terms of the mortgage, the mortgagee may wish to dispossess him in order to protect himself. He may enter peaceably without the court's permission; but if this is not possible, he must get a court order. In the case of a dwelling-house, if it appears that the mortgagor is likely to be able to remedy his default within a reasonable time, the court can adjourn the proceedings, or stay, suspend or postpone the order for possession.

SECURITY OF THE HOME

At the foot of every policy, there is rather a formidable set of conditions which are very seldom read by the insurer. Our advice is to read every word, in order that precaution may be taken to have the policy framed to meet the peculiar circumstances alluded to in the conditions.

As the owner or tenant of a house or flat you will take on the responsibilities for its safety and security. If you are buying, the property formally belongs to you when the contracts are exchanged (see the chapter on Acquiring a Home) and as soon as this is done your solicitor will insure it as a matter of course (see Insuring your Property, p22). If there is a mortgage, the lender usually insists on handling the insurance for you (to make sure that the security for his loan is covered). The landlord's responsibilities for rented property will vary according to the lease. He will almost certainly protect his interests by insurance (so to some extent you may benefit from that), but it is important to check that your belongings or responsibilities are covered even if you do not own the property.

Hazards to Consider

Your house could be hit by lightning, an aircraft, or something dropped from an aircraft. A storm could blow off a tile, the roof, the chimney, or the rain-water guttering. Rain could drive in and pour through your attic as a result and damage your furniture and furnishings. The aerial could fall, or break and damage the roof. Water tanks and pipes could burst. A car, railway train, cattle truck, runaway bus or horse (depending where you live) could crash into your house. There could be a fire or explosion. You could damage underground water or gas pipes or electricity cables by digging or excavating in the garden. Flood, earthquake, landslip or subsidence could occur. Burglars or vandals could create mess and damage.

It is at times like these that the advantages of having good neighbours and being known and respected in the community are probably a very good form of 'security'.

Hazards in relation to other people for which you could be responsible include damage by a roof tile falling on the milkman, your daily help or other employees tripping on a worn stair tread (see the chapter on Help in the Home), or the dog biting the postman.

You can insure against most of the financial consequences of these hazards, but not against the misery and inconvenience they cause. But there are precautions that are worth taking in addition to insurance. Some districts are so prone to housebreaking, for instance, that neighbours group together to provide a kind of security service when property is left unattended. Unfortunately, an epidemic of mindless, wanton vandalism can suddenly break out even in comparatively crime-free areas, and since the objective is to cause as much mess and distress as possible, the victims are often people who have taken no precautions, because they did not think they owned anything worth stealing.

Being Security-minded

It is not always easy to draw the line between being distrustful, fearful, and obsessive about security, and being sensible about what precautions to take. The best thing to do is to look your new home over for possible risks with the help of an expert. Police stations, for example, can put you in touch with a

Crime Prevention Officer who will inspect your property and advise you about necessary precautions. Firms who sell locks and burglar alarms will usually give you an estimate of your requirements free of charge.

When you buy a house, the surveyor's report should point out the building defects that might let in rain and damp. If you own a valuable property or one that is regarded as a fire risk, and if you have valuable belongings, the insurance company may require you to do certain work before they agree to cover you in full. If you are doing any building work or alterations, the new additions will have to conform with current planning and building regulations and you will have to undertake to carry out any extra security work before your plans can be approved.

Get estimates for the security work that needs to be done. Decide what is essential and how much of the rest you can afford, have the work done, and check that your insurance is adequate (see Insuring your Property, p22).

Burglaries

Few people realize that burglaries occur most often in the afternoon and evening, not at night; and during the summer (because of holiday absences or open windows). Timer switches to turn on radio and/or lights when you are out are a good deterrent. Even when away for only a day or two, be sure to cancel milk and newspapers (if these accumulate, it is obvious the house is unoccupied), and ask a neighbour to keep an eye on the house and to push letters and circulars through your letterbox. Tell the police if you are going to be away. For a modest charge, you can arrange with the telephone company to disconnect the telephone, or to disconnect it for incoming calls only for a fixed period.

Side doors should be kept locked if possible, and access for tradesmen delivering goods should not automatically mean access to the premises for every passer-by. If the house is to be left unattended all day it is often worth while to make provision for a one-way delivery hatch.

It costs little or nothing to keep valuables in your bank's strong-room, to photograph your antiques, and to list serial numbers of television, hi-fi equipment, etc, to help the police trace stolen goods.

Doors and locks

The front door is the burglar's usual entrance. Fitting a chain or a peep-hole, and asking for proof when a stranger claims to be a gas man or other official, are sensible precautions. Never leave a key under a mat or in any similar hiding-place; do not leave the door open, however briefly (most burglaries take only two minutes). Insurance rarely covers walk-in thefts.

Thief-resisting surface-mounted deadlock conforming to BS 3621

The British Standard for thief resistant locks for doors is BS 3621, and locks built to this specification are available in both mortice and rim lock (surface mounted) form. A mortice lock is preferable, but a rim lock, fitted to the inner face of the door, must be used on doors less than 4cm thick, since these are too thin to take a mortice. Rim locks all have handles or knobs which can be turned to open the locking bolt. It is essential for security that this bolt can be deadlocked by turning a key when you are going out. Some lock manufacturers use key registration systems, so that only the registered key holder can obtain keys against a signed receipt.

To prevent a door-handle being operated by means of a bent bar thrust through the letterbox, fasten a wire cage inside – and use a porch light and cut back creepers, etc so that the burglar cannot work unobserved from the street.

It is a wise precaution to fit new locks to the front door and other external doors when you move into a previously tenanted house. If you need a locksmith, choose one who is a member of the Master Locksmiths Association or who is recommended by the police.

Do not lock room doors or drawers.

Glass doors should be protected with metal grilles; ordinary bolts are best replaced with the type that has a removable key.

Windows

Even if the only really secure system for windows is metal grilles or bars, window locks are a good investment because they deter the opportunist burglar looking for an easy entry. They should be fitted to all windows, but particularly to those on the ground floor or leading off balconies. Do not forget to lock skylights leading on to the roof.

Window locks should not be visible from the outside of the house.

Some louvre windows are particularly risky. Fasteners to prevent windows (sash or casement) from being opened more than 10cm or so are inexpensive and easy to fit.

Other means of access

Access to the back of the house ought to be made difficult – locked gate, high fences, no low branches overhanging.

Child thieves get through even small windows. To prevent burglars climbing to upstairs windows, train strong creepers away from them and put special slippery paint on the upper parts of drainpipes. Do not leave ladders and tools accessible in sheds outside.

Remove the keys from the inside of locks of external doors and window locks and put them somewhere else so that it is more difficult for a thief to plan his escape route if he forces his way in. (But make sure everyone in the house knows where they are kept in case you have to get out quickly.)

Alarms

Alarms are expensive and often inconvenient because they have to sound off an unwanted intruder, yet allow the householder and his family to come and go freely without setting off a false alarm.

There is a British Standard (BS 4737) for internal alarms, and regular maintenance by the installer is essential for most systems. The National Supervisory Council for Intruder Alarms (NSCIA) will provide a list of approved installers.

There are also some do-it-yourself alarm kits that are simple to install.

If you have a lot of valuables, the insurance company may insist that you fit an alarm system connected to a telephone, which alerts the police via a 999 call or a receiving station operated by the intruder alarm company, and in some cases rings direct to the local police station. The telephone line is an out-going line with an ex-directory number and the cable should be concealed in its exit from the house so that it cannot be cut off by intruders.

Less expensive systems rely on an audible alarm bell, siren or hooter which goes off when the detection device is activated. Some alarm systems are comparatively easy to inactivate; others are concealed so that they are much more difficult to tamper with.

Flats

A flat should be less vulnerable to burglars if there is no easy ground floor access. Once thieves have entered a block of flats, however, they can often work undisturbed at breaking in, so flat doors should be as strong as main doors and the provision of locks and the general precautions should be the same as those for house doors. Communal safety measures in blocks and conversions often include remote control entry to the main doors, which should otherwise be kept closed by all tenants. Where windows are accessible, eg if there are balconies or fire escape access, the need for locks, burglar alarms, and protective grilles may be just as great as in a house.

Damage

Burglars will damage drawers and room doors if these are locked, so it is wiser not to secure them. Some thieves become violent if intercepted, so it is better simply to dial 999 for the police or yell for help through a window. Even a small dog can be an effective guard. If you are injured, apply for compensation to the Criminal Injuries Board. (For insurance claims, see below.)

Security against Fire

This is discussed in the chapter on Safety in the Home.

Insuring your Property

You need to insure your house against the cost of having to rebuild it completely in the case of disaster. If you are borrowing money to buy the house, the lender will probably want the same sort of cover. On the other hand, if the amount of the mortgage is less than the market value of the house, which is probably less than the cost of rebuilding, he might not insist on the full rebuilding costs cover as long as you have enough insurance to pay off his loan. If you own the freehold, you own the land as well, and you will have that even if the house is razed to the ground.

As the cost of building rises steadily, you should regularly adjust the sum for which your house is insured to keep it in line with inflation.

Some building societies arrange for your annual premiums to be index-linked to provide you with cover in line with building costs. It is advisable to consult an experienced insurance agent or broker.

Most policies offer the same kind of cover for buildings, and include adjacent buildings such as garages, stables, and other outbuildings; but there is no standard policy, and it is important to check carefully that the one you choose meets your particular requirements.

Leaseholds

Anyone who buys a flat or house on a leasehold basis must check what provision is made by the landlords for insurance. For a house on a lease of over twenty-one years, the property is usually insured through the ground landlord. For leasehold flats in a block or a conversion, the landlord generally arranges insurance under a 'block' policy, dividing the costs (and the cover) among the leaseholders. This may mean that individual occupiers, especially those who have made improvements

to their property, may not consider that the amount 'covered' by the landlord represents the full value of his property. In that case they may want to take out additional cover for the 'bricks and mortar' risks which are not covered by a household contents policy.

Anyone who is borrowing money to buy a leasehold property will be required by the lender of the money to ensure that the property is adequately insured.

Insurance risks and claims

Most buildings policies cover loss or damage by:

1) *Theft, fire, lightning, explosion, and earthquake.* The insurers may increase the premium for certain districts particularly vulnerable to crime; and also if the house is not made of brick, stone or concrete and roofed with slate, tiles, concrete, asphalt or metal, thus making it more of a fire risk. They may also impose particular requirements about precautions against theft or fire.
   Note Check that claims also cover damage from smoke and water used in fire fighting.

2) *Aircraft or transport damage.* This includes things dropped from aircraft and a car crashing into your house. If your house is near an airport or in a flight path you may want to insure against damage caused by sonic boom (not easy to prove).

3) *Storm and floods.* You may have to pay a small part of any damage caused and in areas prone to flooding the premiums may be higher. Storm and flood damage to fences, gates, garden sheds, etc may be excluded.

4) *Bursting or overflowing of water pipes, tanks, etc.* Again, you may have to pay a small part of the claim. You can also claim if overflowing tanks or pipes ruin wallpaper or other decoration, but probably not the cost of replacing an old or corroded tank if the reason for the failure was simply old age (though you can still claim for any damage caused).

5) *Escape of oil* from a fixed central heating installation. This might be regarded as a 'special risk' so mention it, to be sure that such an occurrence is covered.

6) *Riots or malicious damage*. Some insurers exclude damage caused by demonstrations of a non-political nature (eg students). If your house is in the path of enthusiastic demonstrators or football club fans you should check this cover; even so, you would have to pay a small part of the damage.

7) *Accidental breakage* of fixed glass in windows, doors, and sanitary fittings. This is not likely to cover the cost of replacing glass in greenhouses, conservatories or verandahs.

8) *Collapse of aerials*. Replacing the aerial should be covered by a contents policy. The buildings policy will cover any damage caused.

9) *Property owner's liability*. If you are taken to court and held to be legally liable for an accident occurring on your property in which someone (not a member of your family or staff) is hurt, you may have to pay damages. It also covers damage caused to neighbouring property while work is carried out on your own buildings. Liability is limited.

10) *Accidental damage to underground pipes and electricity cables* between your house and the mains and across your property. If this is caused by workmen, it would normally be the responsibility of their employers' insurance, but if due to you, your family or anyone you employed directly, you could claim.

11) *Alternative accommodation*. If you have to find somewhere else to live because the house is made uninhabitable by any of the insurable risks, you can claim for renting alternative accommodation for your family. The amount is usually restricted, however.

12) *Other risks*. Subsidence is a known risk in some areas of the UK and may need a higher premium. Insurers usually require householders to pay a fixed percentage of the sum insured before meeting claims for damages caused by subsidence.

Insuring the contents of your home

In addition to the insurance of buildings, you need house contents insurance. While you have a mortgage, the building is insured through the building society, but you have to insure the contents.

It is not easy to value contents; the best method is to work systematically through the house, listing everything you possess and writing down its value. This also shows how quickly the contents of even a modest modern home can add up without any particularly valuable items being owned.

You cannot normally insure your belongings against fair wear and tear, depreciation, moth, vermin, rust, war, radioactive contamination or riots.

There are two ways to insure your contents:

1) An *indemnity policy* which covers the cost of replacing your belongings with articles in similar condition. Antique furniture, pictures, oriental rugs, etc which may appreciate in value will only be compensated at the current value if you have kept up the rate of insurance to those values. Many insurers limit compensation for any one article to a small percentage of the total sum insured. If you have an item of higher value than this sum, you should list it separately when you apply for, or renew, your policy.

2) A *new-for-old policy* which covers the full cost of replacing your belongings with new ones. Naturally the premiums are accordingly higher.

Some standard contents policies are a mixture of indemnity and new-for-old. Some of your belongings will be covered by a new-for-old arrangement, with perhaps an age limit of up to five years. Other items, clothes for example, have indemnity cover only.

Your belongings are usually covered if temporarily removed from your home while you are in the UK, but theft may only be covered while they are with you at another private home or at work, or in transit to and from a bank or safe deposit.

If you want extra cover for any items you should insure them under an 'all risks' policy which, although it certainly does not cover all risks, gives much wider cover. The premiums are higher too. Make sure that a hired television set is covered.

Contents insurance premiums are about double those for buildings, and 'all risks' premiums are at least four times the cost of contents premiums. Greater risks give rise to higher charges.

Combined buildings and contents policies may be cheaper, as the minimum premium is less than for two separate policies.

RAISING AND SPENDING MONEY

The necessity of practising economy should be evident to every one, whether in the possession of an income no more than sufficient for a family's requirements, or of a large fortune, which puts financial adversity out of the question. We must always remember that it is a great merit in housekeeping to manage a little well, and it may be added, that those who can manage a little well, are most likely to succeed in their management of larger matters. Economy and frugality must never, however, be allowed to degenerate into parsimony and meanness.

Most people have to live on their earned incomes although money can also come from other sources, such as interest on savings, dividends on investments, and capital gains from selling investments or other assets. A capital gain (or loss) is the difference between the price one pays when buying something and the price one gets for selling it.

Before you can begin to manage your financial affairs you need to be in command by knowing exactly how much money you can rely on coming in throughout the year, how much you must set aside to pay for fixed and unavoidable expenses, and how you can, if necessary, supplement your income in various ways in order to meet your needs.

Where your Money Goes

Records of your earning and spending patterns over the year will help you to estimate and plan future spending.

Make a note of your regular income, including any grants or allowances you receive, once tax, pension, and insurance have been deducted. (See also the chapter on Social Welfare.) Any irregular additions to this income – a bonus, a saving bond that matures, freelance work, a windfall – should be accounted for but not relied upon in planning your finances.

Below this, list the goods and services on which you spend your money throughout the year and the estimated amount spent on each, month by month. These goods and services can be divided as follows:

Fixed expenses

Regular outgoings which cannot be varied, eg rent (or mortgage repayments), rates, insurance, house maintenance; money owed, eg credit or hire-purchase instalments; licences, eg TV or car; union dues or professional subscriptions.

Semi-fixed expenses

Living and household
Food – all food and beverages bought, meals out, school meals; cleaning materials.

Operating costs
Fuel for heating, electricity; launderette or laundry; help with cleaning the house; telephone rental and bills; replacement of household items.

Transport
Fares to work and school; car expenses; fares to shop if necessary.

Personal and family expenses
Clothes – including repairs and cleaning; health – including possible expenditure on prescriptions, special diets, teeth, glasses; gifts – birthdays, Christmas, contributions to charities; leisure – hobbies, cinema or theatre, newspapers, magazines, travel, and outings.

Reserve fund

To allow for unexpected repair bills, for car or household equipment or for an emergency.

When all the listed items above are added

together on the yearly calculation, they should be checked against the yearly income. At this point it should be possible to see where economies or reallocation of money will have to be made in order to balance the budget and create a surplus for special needs. Start by thinking out ways in which you can achieve the feat of matching your income and your expenditure so that you do not get into debt. You also need to assess what assets you have in case of an emergency. Is there anything you can sell? Do you have some savings?

Raising Money

Credit

Although the ideal is to live 'within your means', most people need some help to match their income and spending by using credit. Even people who would not dream of 'borrowing' for anything else borrow money through a mortgage to buy a house.

Credit means borrowing money from a shop, hire-purchase company, finance house or bank, to buy goods without immediate payment in full. In order to decide whether it is worth it to pay extra for using credit, one needs to ask oneself:

1) how much it will cost above the cash price and what the interest rate is
2) whether one can afford the weekly or monthly repayment instalments
3) whether it is worth borrowing now to save money (a particularly important question in times of inflation); and
4) what is the cheapest and best available source of credit.

People who lend money assess 'credit worthiness' by considering the type of employment you have, how long you have been in the same house or flat, whether or not you own it, and whether you have any 'assets' you could sell if you had to repay your debt in a hurry – shares, a diamond necklace, other valuables that you could offer as 'security'.

An established civil servant is a better credit 'risk' than a freelance journalist with approximately the same income. Indeed the cheapest form of credit, eg

a bank overdraft (see p26), goes to those who have the best credit-ratings, while the highest rates are often charged by shops in high streets where, because of the geographical location and the social and economic standing of most people in the community, interest rates for all customers are fixed at a high level to pay for the 'risk' of lending.

Inflation, a cut-back in overtime, or redundancy can, of course, entirely ruin any budget or spending plan.

When borrowing money, do not be seduced by thinking only in terms of the monthly repayment figures. It is important to check the total cost of credit and the true rate of interest.

The interest is fixed for the full period of loan and does not decrease as your debt diminishes, so that one needs to find the loan which carries the lowest true rate of interest.

Interest on bank overdrafts, however, is charged on a daily basis on what you owe; as your debt reduces so does the amount of interest, the true rate and the flat rate being the same.

Credit cards

Issued by banks and credit card organizations, these enable a credit card holder to sign for goods or services bought from shops, restaurants, etc, which have an agreement with the credit card sponsor (they usually announce this fact in the window). The credit card holder is sent a monthly account. This can either be settled in full, or paid in instalments, in which case interest is charged on the unpaid proportion of the account.

Banks usually fix lower credit limits than credit card companies, and allow longer periods for repayment. Credit card companies expect money to be repaid more quickly but often have higher credit limits. The rate of interest on bank credit cards is quite high – higher than for a bank loan or overdraft for example.

Store accounts

Many department stores will give you a credit account which works like a bank credit card. Although the interest is usually lower than that on a bank card, it is still quite high.

Some stores operate *budget accounts*. With these

you agree to pay a fixed sum monthly, and you can immediately have credit equivalent to so many times your monthly payments (it varies in different shops). You usually have to undertake to pay by monthly banker's order. Interest is normally payable on budget accounts, although it may be called a service charge or surcharge.

Mail order credits

Mail order houses which sell from catalogues and use 'agents', usually offer goods on a credit sale basis. This credit tends to be given 'free of charge' for a certain period, after which normal interest rates are charged. New customers get only a small amount of credit but this increases as they continue to buy from the firm and establish 'credit worthiness'. The firms employ good customers as 'agents', who also get a discount on the goods they sell to family and friends as a form of commission. This can be taken in cash or used to pay for goods.

The 'interest free' credit is usually reflected in the price of goods. On the other hand, it is very convenient to buy from a catalogue and have goods delivered, and unless you live in an urban area with plenty of competition, you may find that the price of goods is not much out of line with those prevailing in the shops.

Hire-purchase and credit sales

With hire-purchase agreements the goods do not belong to you until all the instalments and charges have been paid, so if the borrower allows his payments to lapse, the firm is entitled to take back the goods. With credit sales the goods belong to the borrower from the start of the agreement, even if it is going to be some time before the payments are completed. As the consumer's legal protection is slightly different in each case, it is important to realize the difference between these two methods of paying before signing an agreement.

With both systems the borrower pays an initial cash deposit. The rest of the money due, plus the interest on it and any service charges that may be incurred (mainly clerical and not always charged) is divided into equal instalments which have to be paid off regularly over an agreed period.

Anyone who buys goods on hire-purchase and on credit sale must be advised what the total price will be, ie cash price plus interest charges. If this is much higher than the cash price, it may be cheaper to draw on savings or to borrow the money in another way.

Borrowing from Banks

If you have a bank account it is worth trying to get a bank loan or overdraft, as this usually works out more cheaply than buying on hire-purchase or credit, or using a credit card.

The ease with which you can borrow from your bank depends both on your credit worthiness and the general state of the economy; government restrictions can make it difficult to obtain a loan.

Overdrafts

An overdraft enables you to borrow on your current account. The bank manager will decide on the amount, and you pay interest on this amount only. You will be expected to agree to reduce your overdraft or pay it off within a fixed period, and you may have to provide security for the loan (see p25). This is often the cheapest way of borrowing money.

Bank loans

There are two kinds – an *ordinary loan* and a *personal loan*. These loans are for an agreed length of time and are usually repaid by the bank deducting an agreed sum from your current account each month; the repayments can be spread over a period of as much as five years in certain cases. Your bank manager will want to know what the loan is for, how you intend to repay it, and with what. You may have to provide security. Interest will be higher than with an overdraft. If the loan is for an improvement to your house it may rank as a qualifying loan for income tax purposes, so that you will get tax relief on the interest payment.

A personal loan usually has to be repaid within two years and may be advanced without security; it therefore tends to be for smaller sums of money than an ordinary loan, and at a higher rate of interest.

Budget accounts

Banks offer budget account facilities. You add up all the bills you expect to have to pay in the year, excluding those that have to be paid monthly in any case. Divide the total by twelve and transfer this sum every month to your budget account. On some months you are allowed to be overdrawn. Banks charge for this facility in different ways. Some charge a fee based on the total amount passing through the account and not at all when you are overdrawn. Others charge a lower fee but a higher interest rate at times when you are overdrawn.

If you are not often overdrawn, an ordinary overdraft for a month or two when the heavy bills fall due may suit you better.

Gas and electricity boards will arrange for your estimated annual fuel account to be paid in twelve equal instalments based on your consumption. Once a year you settle up – if you have underpaid, you pay more; if you have overpaid, they refund the excess. Either way you can adjust your payments for the following year.

The Post Office sells stamps to pay for telephone bills and television licences.

Falling Behind with Payments

The level at which owing money, including a mortgage repayment, can start to lead to trouble is usually anything over about 30% of income after tax has been deducted.

If you find yourself in a situation where you either owe too much money or cannot easily pay it back, never let it drift. Most people who lend money are more concerned with getting it back than with taking action against you for falling behind in your payment. But you must either do some drastic economizing, sell some assets or inform your creditors, and ask them for extra time to pay by reducing your regular payments. If you do not do this, and fall behind with your payment, they may sue you.

If money becomes short, you may find it very difficult to get a loan if you do not have a credit rating, even if you have never been in debt. You will have to pay high rates of interest to organizations who take the risk. By law you must be told the true rate of interest; it is then up to you to decide whether you need the money badly enough to be prepared to pay the extra cost of interest.

The last resort of desperate borrowers is the 'money lender'. If you borrow a couple of hundred pounds from one, without security, the rate of interest is bound to be extremely high.

If you have temporary money problems and need a few pounds to tide you over, the pawnbroker, who will advance you money on anything that is saleable, may be tempting. If you redeem the goods (the pledge) you leave with him quickly, you may not find it too painful. However, pawnbrokers make most of their money by selling the goods left with them as security – which they have an automatic right to do if you do not claim them back within six months and one day.

Raising Money in Other Ways

You can look over your possessions and assets and see if there is anything you can sell to raise the money. You can look at any investments you may have and see if they can be reinvested to produce a better income, or be sold to produce a capital gain and then reinvested. You can check that you are getting all tax allowances and state benefit. You can look for a job that pays more or take on extra work. You can try cutting out a service you use and 'do it yourself'.

Saving or Borrowing

If you want to buy a major item you have to consider three options: whether to buy now on credit, save up and buy later from savings, or buy now, using any savings or assets you have. But at times of inflation this is not always easy to decide.

If you are sure that the rise in price will be greater than the cost of credit and you have no savings, then credit is the answer. If you think that the price will increase faster than your income and the interest your savings can earn, then use your savings. If you think the price may stay much the same, or if you are not sure that you will be able to keep up repayments on a loan, then save up until you can afford what you want to buy. You will get the advantage of buying the latest model, and you will have your savings until you buy, should you want to divert them to something more important.

If the major item is going to save you money anyway – a sewing machine for example – then it is certainly worth the extra charge of interest.

If you have to make a choice between buying goods or services on credit, choose goods; at least you have them while you are paying. There is nothing more depressing than paying for something like a holiday months after it is over.

Deciding how to save

You need to decide whether you are saving for long-term needs, eg to buy a house, or for a sum to keep against a sudden emergency. Most people who save put about 5 to 10% of their disposable income into some form of saving. Set yourself a target that you can achieve without too much difficulty.

If you want to be able to draw your money at short notice, you can choose between a bank deposit account, a building society ordinary share account, subscription shares for regular monthly savings, and National and Trustee Savings Bank Ordinary Accounts. When you have saved enough for your 'emergency account' you may want to consider other methods of saving which pay you more interest or produce capital appreciation. If you are hoping to buy a house on a mortgage you should choose a building society that will advance money on the type of property you want, and start saving with them. Building societies look more favourably at mortgage applicants who have saved with them. For more information, see p14.

Some savings have tax concessions – particularly useful for people who pay a lot of tax. Other forms of saving are specially for retired savers. Some offer security; others, such as investments, are more of a risk and some may be highly speculative. Premium bonds, for example, are safe in that you can get your purchase money back, and speculative in that instead of interest, you get a chance of winning one of the prizes.

If you have a lump sum to invest, you will be able to look at options other than those available for saving from income.

When you have saved your emergency lump sum, you may look next to assurance as a form of saving. There is a distinction between *assurance* when you pay to cover something that will happen at some time eg retirement or death, and *insurance* (see the chapter on Security of the Home) which you take out against something that might or might not happen, eg fire, theft, accident, sickness.

Annuity

If you have no ties and no responsibilities you may decide to save towards an annuity, which is a form of life assurance in reverse: instead of paying premiums until you die, you pay premiums towards a sum which is then turned into an annuity providing you with regular income until your death. How well you do out of an annuity depends on how long you live after you take it out. There are many types of annuity, including joint survivorship ones for husband and wife together. When one dies, the annuity continues, although it is reduced.

Life assurance

It is important to be quite clear whether you are treating assurance as a form of protection for yourself or your dependants, or as a form of saving.

There are two main types of life assurance. *Protection only* (or term) assurance pays out only if you die during the period for which you have insured and buys the protection your dependants need for the lowest possible outlay. The simplest form means that you insure your life for a given sum. Decreasing term assurance when the amount you get goes down year by year, is often linked to mortgage protection policies because you are assuring to cover a decreasing liability. Family income benefit provides your family with a tax-free income rather than a lump sum, should you die.

Investment-type assurance provides some life cover, but is mainly a form of saving over a long term. But you only get a poor return (surrender value) on your investment if you want to cash in early and you may not even get your premiums back if you cash in the policy during the first two years. On the other hand you can usually borrow from the insurance company up to the 'surrender value', to tide you over a bad patch.

Insurance is not easy to choose. Get information from as many companies as possible, or consult an independent broker registered with the Insurance Brokers' Registration Council. Some insurance companies lend money to buy homes (see the chapter on Acquiring a Home).

Spending your Money

If there is more than one contributor to the household budget, the allocation of financial responsibilities has to be agreed upon. Alternatively, the family income can be pooled, and added together for redistribution under the headings suggested on p24.

When a young husband and wife both work they may feel it is better not to rely on the wife's pay, in case she has children or stops working. Provided that her interests have been taken care of by something like joint mortgage, so that her contribution to the household is not frittered away or unrecognized, extra money coming in because of her work should be used for expenditure which can be cut back, eg more extravagant holidays, higher savings, or investment in more labour-saving equipment.

If more than two earners are sharing a home, whatever their relationship, it is advisable to have a joint account for the purpose of running the household and joint expenses, while all contributors keep their personal money separately. Everyone should agree to contribute a set sum to this account weekly or monthly (preferably by standing order on a bank account). It needs to be reviewed every year or if some unexpected emergency comes up.

However close the relationship, and without being mean, it is a good idea to be clear about which possessions are individually owned and which are owned jointly. Some marriages do end in separation or divorce, and few things are more embittering than dividing possessions. But things are made even worse if you have to quarrel over something belonging to you which is claimed by the other party.

Keeping Accounts

You should do this if you can. You do not have to write down an itemized account of everything you spend, but you need to have a clear idea of how much is spent on food and running expenses; you should keep fuel bills and telephone bills, and note other semi-regular expenses, so that you can check your usage one year against another. It is particularly important to keep a check on how much fuel you use, as bills can suddenly shoot up.

Always keep receipts or other proofs of purchase. You may need to produce them if anything goes wrong with the goods you have bought. When you pay bills, either ask for a receipt or make a note of the date and the amount paid, and the number of the cheque if you paid by cheque. Make sure on your bank statements that standing orders have been paid.

Consumer Protection

Standards of consumer protection are high in the UK. Banks, finance houses, and other lending institutions are controlled by a number of laws. Some laws you have to enforce yourself. Others are part of the criminal law and are enforced by trading standards officers or other enforcement authorities (see the chapter on Food Shopping Today). All credit lenders have to be registered with, and licensed by, the Office of Fair Trading; so if they do not trade properly they may lose their licence to lend money – a powerful sanction.

You have the right to know the true rate of interest and the total charge of credit. You can claim compensation from the organization lending you money if the goods are faulty; you can pay off your debt early if you wish, and get a rebate. If you sign a hire-purchase, credit agreement or other loan document at home or away from trade premises, you must be sent a second copy of the agreement by the lender within seven days. You have five days from receiving this to decide whether or not you want to be bound by the agreement. You do not have this right if you sign the agreement on business premises, if the loan is very small – this does not apply to hire-purchase agreements – or if you have arranged it entirely by post or telephone.

PLANNING YOUR HOME – DESIGN FACTORS

Cold air should never be admitted under the doors, or at the bottom of a room, unless it be close to the fire or stove; for it will flow along the floor towards the fireplace, and thus leave the foul air in the upper part of the room, unpurified, cooling, at the same 'time, unpleasantly and injuriously, the feet and legs of the inmates.

Planning, strangely enough, is something many people tend to put last, if they bother with it at all. No matter how important comfortable furniture, fine curtains, good floor coverings, paintings, ornaments, and other attractive accessories may be, none should be given a thought until the important task of planning the layout and arrangement of available space has been worked out.

Begin by thinking about the sort of life you lead during the day and during the evening: the amount of entertaining you do, the various hobbies and occupations of members of the family, the time of day when each person occupies the bathroom, the amount of noise likely to be generated at various times. Then take a careful look at the space you have available – whether that space is two small rooms with bathroom and kitchen, or a three-bedroomed semi-detached house, or something else entirely different. Then work out how your accommodation can best be arranged to fit in with your way of life.

It is wasteful, for instance, to have a separate room for dining if you invariably eat in the kitchen and rarely entertain guests; folly to make do with one bathroom/lavatory combined if you are a family of six living in a reasonably large house; and senseless to have your main living-room at the front of the house if the whole family is out until evening, when the western sun floods into the rooms at the back.

Rooms do not, after all, have to be used in a set way or as they were by the previous occupant. The bedroom level does not have to be above the living level, nor is it obligatory for a room to have one use only (such as eating, sleeping or bathing). And once these restrictive preconceptions are abandoned, planning possibilities expand enormously.

Establish at this point the amount of money you have available and the cost of what you have in mind. If the two sums do not coincide, you must set your sights lower or raise more cash. (See the chapter on Raising and Spending Money.)

Not surprisingly, the means of reorganization are as varied as the types of home available. For instance, they may involve large structural works, such as building on an extension or taking down load-bearing walls. Less ambitiously, the rearrangement may consist of simpler alterations such as enlarging windows, putting in new doorways or building cupboards. And simplest of all, you may decide merely to change the use of rooms (or parts of rooms) by rearranging the furniture, adding shelves and/or unit furniture, or transforming spaces by a little judicious decoration.

All these things, however small in scale, need to be thought about carefully before work begins. And each is best worked out on paper even where there are large-scale jobs involved and professional help is required. If you have first worked out exactly what you want, you will be able to give a clear, concise brief to your professional adviser. Make a careful scale drawing on squared graph paper of the entire area at your disposal and then you will be able to see clearly whether your ideas for rearranging furniture, room extensions, new doorways, sliding glass doors, etc are viable or not. For the legal implications of structural reorganization, see the chapter on The Law and You.

Major Structural Alterations

Something more than space can be obtained by extending a house. Often such work enables the whole place to be reorganized in a way which is much more suitable for the family concerned.

Detached houses may be extended in any direction provided there is the land space available and planning permission is obtained from the local authority. The extension can take the form of a structure specially designed for the purpose or a ready-to-erect room of the sort which is widely advertised. Some of these are simple sun-room type buildings mainly intended for summer use; some are lined and insulated and can be used in a much more comprehensive way.

Extensions for tightly packed town and suburban houses are not quite so simple to arrange. It is worth considering the space on top of the house, where a room may be contrived in a loft which had previously been used for storing junk. Lined and insulated, with windows set into the slope of the roof or even cut out in a wedge shape to form an inset terrace, such rooms can certainly add to the spaciousness of a house. At the back, ground floor rooms may be extended outwards, or new rooms added at one or two levels. The problem of light loss to existing rooms can be solved by building such extensions almost entirely of glass, enabling light to flood through to the inner rooms.

Light may also bring new vitality to a previously dismal basement if a wall of sliding glass doors is built to replace small, old-fashioned windows.

Other major work could include the removal of structural walls to throw two or three small rooms into one large open space, turning a staircase so that instead of dominating a hall it takes a less obtrusive and space-consuming position at the rear, removing part of a floor structure so that a gallery is formed over the room below, or making a second bathroom in what was once a little-used boxroom.

Professional advice

All work mentioned in this section involves tampering with load-bearing walls, altering plumbing, foundations or breaking into the main fabric of the house, and invariably professional help must be sought.

Making a scale drawing on graph paper

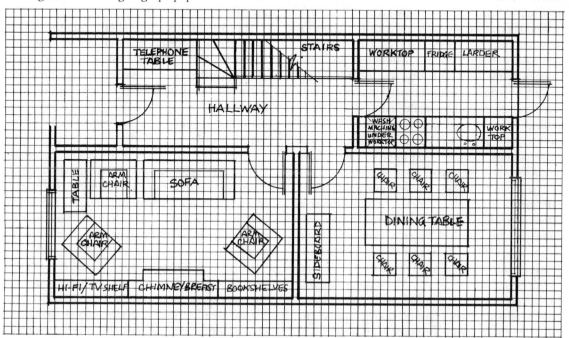

The ideal arrangement for large-scale work is to consult an architect about the design. Ask the Royal Institute of British Architects (RIBA) for a list of architects in your area doing the type of work you want. Visit examples of their previous jobs and select the one who seems most competent, imaginative, and otherwise suited to your needs. If a friend recommends an architect, check him or her in the same way and you are unlikely to be disappointed with the person you appoint.

An architect's fee is a percentage of the total cost of the job. He can simply design and do drawings of your requirements, advise you whether local authority permission is necessary (usually dependent on the size of the extension), and obtain this and building regulations approval for you. That is the first stage, and approximately a third of the total fee is payable. He can then send drawings, along with a specification, out for tender to a selection of builders, which is the second stage and entails another third of the fee. Finally, he can go on to supervise the building works for the final third of the fee. If money is short, you may decide to handle at least the second and third stages yourself. Full details of fee scales in the UK are explained in a booklet which may be obtained from the Royal Institute of British Architects (RIBA).

Another method is to dispense with an architect's services, design the extension yourself, perhaps getting a draughtsman to do drawings for submission to the local authority, and then handing the job over to a builder. The design element will not have been professionally handled and it is unlikely to be as imaginative or carefully detailed in this case, but may work well with less ambitious undertakings. More detailed information on how to go about this is given on pp40–41.

The quantity surveyor is another professional who may be involved in very large-scale and costly alterations. His job is to assess costs, and he will sometimes be called in by an architect (at your expense) to assist in costing when the specification is being prepared and to advise on which of the builders' tenders to accept. His experience and knowledge can be invaluable when inessentials have to be pared from a specification in order to cut costs. As the quantity surveyor works alongside the architect he is usually recommended by him. If, however, you want to choose your own, a list of potential candidates may be obtained from the Royal Institution of Chartered Surveyors (RICS).

For smaller alterations a building surveyor is sometimes employed to draw up plans and supervise the work rather than an architect.

Minor Structural Alterations

These can sometimes improve a house out of all proportion to the amount of work and cost involved. For instance, a window can be enlarged to bring in more light and encompass a wider view of the garden. A door can be removed between kitchen and dining-room, the opening widened and arched at the top, and the two small rooms thus transformed into one flowing and more lavish-seeming space. If the house is centrally heated, a one-time porch can have its inner door removed and the porch area can be redecorated to become part of an enlarged hall. Similarly, a cupboard under the stairs currently filled with junk may be removed, and that area can then play its part in enlarging the hall. Substantial wardrobe fittings can be built to make use of the spaces on each side of an unused, deep chimney-breast.

The possibilities are endless, and the results much easier to achieve than in a major structural alteration. As the size of the house is not increased, planning permission is not necessary. However, whenever the structure of the house is involved, building regulations permission will almost certainly be required. This permission should be sought as early as possible.

It will probably not be necessary to engage an architect (though it may be desirable if much design work is involved, such as in the construction of elaborate wardrobes) and information about building regulations can be obtained by visiting your local authority building inspector's department.

If the work is to be done by a builder (with due care taken in his choice) he will normally undertake this service on your behalf. It is advisable, even for the smallest job, to get quotations from several building firms, to pick the lowest reasonable quotation, and then to avoid adding extras as the work proceeds, or you could find yourself in a financial predicament at the end of the job.

Reorganization and Redecoration

Only two people are likely to be involved in this work: you and a local jobbing builder or tradesman. No official permission is necessary and the scope of work is limited only by the time and money available. In temporary furnished accommodation it may consist of no more than rearranging the furniture so that it works better for you: placing a chest of drawers as a half-height divider/storage/serving unit between cooking and eating areas, ranging small storage cupboards and drawer units along one wall rather than having them dispersed about the room, placing a divan bed along a wall where it can be sat on during the day rather than having it jutting out into the space of a small bed-sitting-room – and so on.

Or you may want to redecorate, build a range of shelves, hang folding louvred doors across one end wall of a bedroom to make a hanging cupboard, or line a bathroom wall with mirror tiles.

If you have no time or inclination for home decorating, small-scale joinery work and the like, then you will need to call in a local builder, and again all care should be taken to ensure his competence before work commences.

Financial arrangements should also be firmly established (see the chapter on The Law and You). Make sure it is determined beforehand who is to provide any necessary materials (you or the builder), and avoid having work done on an hourly payment basis, for that way you pay for any time lost in putting right mistakes, drinking tea, and chatting.

Colour in the Home

Colour is one of the most important aspects of home planning. Its use can effect a remarkable transformation in any part of the home; it is both rewarding and fun to use.

Often, choice of colour is restricted by what already exists, eg a stair-carpet bought from the previous owner of a house, or boldly coloured walls decorated by previous tenants of a flat and too expensive to cover. But for those lucky enough to be starting with a clean palette, there are some guide-lines worth respecting:

Bear in mind that there is a warm group of colours and a cool group and it is important to consider the aspect of the room.

The warm colours are basically orange, yellow, and red, and all variations and gradations thereof. The cool colours are blue, green, violet, and their variations. Do not use the latter group in a bleak, north-facing room which needs cheering up with colours from the former group. Cool colours could, however, look fresh and pretty in a room facing south-west which is flooded with warm afternoon sunlight (these effects would be reversed in the southern hemisphere). Electric light, which is normally used in living-rooms, emphasizes warm colours but makes cool colours even cooler, so your green or blue room can look quite bleak in the evening unless cheered by warm-toned lamp-shades and cushions.

Plan an overall colour scheme for the home rather than picking at separate areas and hoping the whole will blend. This applies whether you have a two-roomed flat or a whole house. It will give coherence to the place, make it seem more spacious, and will save you continually closing the door of the dining-room because its green walls clash dreadfully with the red and blue paper in the hall.

This does not mean there should be no contrasts, but the overall background should remain constant. For instance, you may opt for a background of dark brown carpet, cream walls, and white paintwork – a pleasant, easy combination. With that framework you could keep your brown carpet to stairs, landings, and bedrooms, have shaggy beige and brown rugs in the hall, white rugs in the living-room, and variously patterned wallpapers (keeping to a white, cream or brown background) in the bedrooms. The dining-room walls could be a deep burnt orange, those in the hallways covered in beige hessian, and the bathroom might have yellow and white blinds, with the living-room furniture upholstered in brown and apricot chintz.

Another combination might be pale green carpets, coffee-coloured walls, and white paint, and you could get marvellous effects with green and white print curtains, smart coffee upholstery, and crisp white lampshades, with perhaps lemon-yellow lamp bases and ashtrays for contrast.

There will always be small areas within which to break the overall pattern, ie a uniquely personal bedroom or a dining-room which you want to be particularly stunning and dramatic.

Consider a room in one colour. When this is used in a variety of tones, patterns, and textures, the result can be delightful. For instance, in a brown, cream, and white home, the dining-room could have brown felt-covered walls, pale beige paintwork, gingery cork floor tiles, brown, beige, and cream cotton curtains, chairs upholstered in rough beige wool, and the whole thing sparked into life by orange table linen and gilt picture frames. In a green, coffee, and white home, there could be a splendid main bedroom in shades of green, ranging from silvery green carpet, sharp green and white print curtains and bedcover to deep green silk cushions and furniture painted apple-green.

Cut colour pages of rooms you like from home interest magazines; there is nothing shameful about purloining someone else's good ideas.

Emulate the professional designers and make colour boards. When designers are preparing a scheme, they mount the colours and fabrics they are thinking of using on small boards made of thick white card, one for each room. This way, with each group of materials mounted together, you can see and correct your mistakes before they are translated to a large scale. Use samples of curtain and upholstery fabrics, clippings of paint manufacturers' samples, small pieces of carpet and floor tiles, squares of wallpaper, and so on.

Areas of the Home

In addition to colour, other important considerations when planning your home are light, warmth, visual delight, general comfort, and ease of cleaning. Neglect of any one of these is likely to cause you discomfort and increasing irritation. Light and warmth are thoroughly dealt with in the chapter on Structural Work and Essential Services, so that in the rest of this chapter they will only be alluded to in a general way. Cleaning is described in the chapters on Care and Maintenance of the Home *and* Care of Textiles and Hard Surfaces.

Entrance hall and stairs

The hall is the place where you will greet visitors and it will take heavy wear from outdoor shoes, newly delivered furniture, packages and parcels, and, since in many modern homes it is not very spacious, from trailing fingers. Make it as attractive as possible, but furnish and decorate it to cope with its arduous role.

Have as large a doormat as is practicable (preferably sunk into a well) and a shoe scraper outside if you live amidst country mud. There should be a heavy-duty floor covering such as ceramic or vinyl tiles, wood, or top quality carpet (which should also cover the stairs). Cover the walls in wipeable vinyl, patterned paper which conceals marks, or natural hessian whose texture is also a good stain concealer and which can easily be painted over if it becomes grubby. Similar wall covering should continue up the stairs.

Furniture, if there is room, could include a small table for messages, incoming mail, and a potted plant, as well as a cupboard, unobtrusive coat-stand or row of hooks. A small cupboard for family slippers and outdoor shoes would encourage much dirt to be intercepted before it even penetrated to the rest of the house.

Light should have a warm, welcoming quality, achieved by a table or hanging lamp shaded in a soft colour; the harshness of fluorescent lighting is completely out of place in an entrance hall or on a staircase. It is useful to remember that a mirror, or sheet of mirror glass, can increase the apparent size of a small hall, and if placed behind a table holding pots of plants or a vase of flowers will double their effect.

Living-room

This is the hub of the house. Not every family will use it in the same way. For some it is simply a place to relax, read or listen to music, for others it is a place for hobbies, studies or part-time work, and even a place where they also eat. Whatever its uses, its full potential as a comfortable place to be in is only realized by careful planning.

First, separate the activities into areas. If you eat in your living-room, keep the table, chairs, and all appurtenances such as serving table, trolley, and cutlery store to a corner of the room as near as possible to the door or serving-hatch leading to the kitchen. Have this area separately lit, so that when not in use it can recede into the shadows.

The seating area will be comfortably arranged around the fireplace if there is one, the television if that is your pleasure, or a large low table holding ashtrays, magazines, drinks, etc. This area should not be crossed by a traffic route, eg from door to dining-table, for it can be irritating to be constantly tripped over and brushed against when you are trying to relax. Comfortable unit seating gives more flexible arrangements than the old-style three-piece suite while retaining a pleasantly coherent appearance often lacking in an arrangement of totally different chairs and sofas.

Avoid having more than three seating positions in a row as this makes conversation awkward, and group your seats so that the company (if there are a lot of people present) will fall naturally into two conversational groups.

Bookshelves should ideally be arranged on a wall clear of the sitting area so that they can be reached without stretching across a chair and the person in it. If an area is needed for work, study or hobbies, this too should be clear of any traffic route; it could be given visual privacy by a screen or by a range of shelves and cupboards at right angles to the wall to divide off that part of the room. This would provide the general storage which is essential in a living-room. (See also the chapter on Stores and Storage.)

All the activities which occur there must be accommodated if the room is to remain tidy and presentable, so list them carefully: records, tapes, sewing and knitting materials, board and card games, writing materials, model-making equipment, drinks and glasses – these are just a few of the things many families have to stow away.

Lighting should be pleasantly low for general conversation, but there should also be adequate spot lighting in the places where people are likely to want to read or work. Consider this, therefore, when you are planning the arrangement of furniture and equipment, and make sure that there are adequate power points and lighting sockets in suitable positions.

Materials for upholstery and floor covering should be as tough as possible to cope with the wear and tear of family life. This means top quality carpet or a hard floor such as vinyl coated cork or wood, scattered with rugs which must have slip-proof underlays. Alternatively the floor could be covered with inexpensive carpet or cord, and reinforced with rugs in the places which are particularly liable to get hard wear. Upholstery too should be of as good a quality as you can afford, and if the family includes small children, cleanable loose covers are needed.

Strong, bold background colours are not normally satisfactory in a living-room. Have wallpaper, carpets, ceilings, and upholstery in soft colours of which you will not tire. This does not necessarily mean pale colours, for deep brown, deep green and so on can look excellent. But the sharp primary colours (red, yellow, and blue) should be reserved for cushions, rugs, books, and lamp bases; then they will not be too oppressive and can be changed relatively easily if you tire of them.

The living-room should be both comfortable and serene, a place where you and your guests can feel relaxed.

Dining-room

Conversely, a dining-room which is only used for brief periods can be treated in a more dramatic fashion with boldly patterned walls or curtains, or both. It should be as near the kitchen as possible, and ideally, a door or broad hatch should connect the two. If there is a good extractor fan in the kitchen to whisk away smells it sometimes makes sense to remove the dividing wall between kitchen and dining-room to increase the feeling of space, having them partially separated by a storage/serving unit.

The serving-table or sideboard should have

drawers or cupboards large enough to store table linen, cutlery, candles, etc and the table ought to be as large as the room will comfortably accommodate (allowing a metre of space behind each chair when it is drawn out to the eating position). You will then never be in the embarrassing position of crowding too many people round a tiny table. If you are using old chairs with a new table, or vice versa – which can look extremely attractive – be sure the heights marry, and that the chairs slide under the table when not in use.

The floor will not be subjected to heavy wear but should be easy to clean and not too noisy. Vinyl tiles or a medium quality carpet would be suitable.

For lighting suggestions, see the chapter on Structural Work and Essential Services.

A dining-room which is only used for evening or weekend meals can take the pressure off other rooms and be used for hobbies, homework, and sewing, in which case a polished table should be covered with a cloth for protection. (See also the chapter on Stores and Storage.)

Kitchen
See the chapter on Kitchen Planning.

Bed-sitting-room
The basic principles for planning such a room, which may be occupied by teenage children, grand-parents, newly weds or lodgers, are similar to those for sitting-rooms. Separate activities into areas, and make furnishings as hard-wearing as possible. Lighting for each area should be individually switched, and background colours should be soft and neutral, accented by bright accessories. More information on planning colour schemes can be found on pp33–34.

In addition, a bed will be fitted in and disguised in some measure. The usual divan against a wall can have a dark cover but should also have bolsters and large cushions, to make it narrower and more comfortable to sit on and to protect the wall from head-marks. A convertible sofa is an alternative, but test well for comfort before buying, as design is often of a low standard. In either case, group your bed with floor cushions and one or two chairs to make a seating area. Cooking facilities should be grouped compactly with a table for preparation and meals nearby; they can be hidden by a screen or folding louvred doors. It is also vitally important to provide adequate storage in this sort of room.

Bedrooms
Ideally, bedrooms should be in a quiet part of the house, away from road noise and overlooking a garden or other pleasant view. If this is not attainable, aim to make them as quiet and pleasant as circumstances allow. Double glazing, heavy, inter-lined curtains and a thick carpet will help to deaden traffic sounds, built-in cupboards will muffle noise from adjoining rooms or properties, and translucent curtains or blinds will partially obscure ugly views. Bedrooms being the most personal rooms in a house, decorative idiosyncracies can be indulged in, and anyone wanting to paint his room bright red will offend no one else (too much) by doing so. Floor coverings get relatively light use. Carpet tiles (laid to form unusual patterns for the individualist) or inexpensive quality fitted carpet make a warm, comfortable covering, but if this is too ambitious for young home-makers or those in rented homes, rugs or a second-hand carpet square look attractive on sanded and polished floor boards.

Colours, for the more conventionally minded, can be pale and pretty with fabrics as delicate and exotic as the occupant wishes, as this is not an area where much dirt is generated; planning colour schemes is described on pp33–34. Children's bedrooms, however, need a more serviceable treatment (see the chapter on Managing a Household with Children).

Beds should be of good quality since their long-term comfort will affect the user's daily well-being. They should also be an adequate size for their occupant and children should not suffer an out-grown bed. Place the bed so there is sufficient room all round for easy making, or use continental quilts (duvets) if this is not possible. Bedside tables should be large enough to take everything that may be needed – books, spectacles, a reading-lamp, glass of water, and possibly a telephone.

Clothes storage should be equally carefully considered. For large, old rooms the large furniture of the past is worth buying; capacious, smooth-running drawers and roomy wardrobes have much to commend them – not least the fact that they can be moved on to another home. This is not the case with built-in furniture, which would be an unwise investment for those in rented or short-term accommodation. (See also the chapter on Stores and Storage.)

Fitted furniture is for those who plan to stay in their home for a number of years, and it can be designed and custom made, or purchased from a selection of ready-made ranges. These vary from the expensive types, which are beautifully detailed and finished, to the basic arrangement of a couple of sliding-doors with which you chop off the end of a room to make hanging cupboards. The charm of ready-made ranges is that you can start with just one cupboard and a drawer unit, and then add matching units to make a wall of storage as your purse and needs grow. Units can be placed along a wall where there are chimney recesses, thus filling the recesses; later the chimney-breast itself is spanned with matching shelves.

One or two comfortable chairs are the other furniture needed, with a desk or table if the room is to be used for study.

Lighting can consist of a fairly bright overhead light for general use, possibly controlled by a two-way dimmer switch at door and bed, bedside lights and dressing-table lights.

Bathroom

When planning a bathroom in a part of the house not previously used for that purpose, aim to have it as near existing plumbing and drainage as possible to simplify the work involved and keep costs down. For the same reason, group the various items of sanitary ware, eg wash-basin, lavatory, bidet, and bath, in fairly close proximity to each other, even if the room is large. This arrangement makes the concealment of unsightly pipes easier. They can, for instance, be hidden away within a cavity formed by building a partition wall 15cm away from the wall on which they are grouped, or in built-in cupboards, or under a vanity unit.

Be careful when selecting sanitary ware to choose simple, streamlined designs without awkward nooks and crannies which collect dirt and make cleaning difficult. Consider having a wall-hung WC which makes floor cleaning an easy operation. A wash-basin set into a shelf looks attractive, and the shelf provides space for bathroom jars, bottles, and plants. If you only have room for a free-standing wash-basin make sure you have storage space in which to put spare lavatory rolls, soap, toothpaste, cleaning materials, etc. Fitted bathroom units are available which will help you to achieve a stream-lined bathroom without too much dirty construction work having to be done in a small space.

Materials used in a bathroom should be easy to wipe clean. The floor can be covered in inexpensive vinyl tiles, more expensive plastic-coated cork, or fitted with carpet or carpet tiles – preferably rubber backed nylon which will stand odd splashes. Confine tiles to the vital areas around lavatory, bath and wash-basin unless you favour a really austere, hard appearance. Cover the walls instead with paper-backed vinyl, ordinary paper coated with waterproof varnish, gloss paint in a rich colour if you are trying to do the job very economically, or tongued and grooved pine boarding finished with matt varnish for a warm, natural look.

Other washing facilities

In a family home, these will prove a great asset. A cloakroom adjacent to the kitchen, for instance, will be an excellent clean-up area for those coming in from gardening or playing. A small extension or, in older houses, a disused pantry or coal-store can often be used in this way, and if there is space to include a shower (the smallest shower tray is about one metre square) so much the better. Sometimes a small box-room, or even a deep alcove in a bedroom, will convert to make a shower-room. As long as existing plumbing and drainage are close enough to avoid long pipe runs, the building cost can be surprisingly low.

Outside arrangements

Many households have at least one member who undertakes do-it-yourself work, and the usual place to store equipment and tools is a garage if one is available. Orderly storage makes the work pleasanter and the results more likely to be successful. A decent-sized work bench with strong industrial shelving above it at one end of the garage should be sufficient for most people's needs, and good artificial lighting is vital; glare-free fluorescent lighting set on the wall or ceiling above the bench is excellent. There should be a couple of power points to operate power tools.

A home freezer could also be kept here if it is too large for the kitchen.

If the garage is small and the house large, a similar arrangement could be set up in a dry cellar or basement passageway, though it is obviously preferable to have the noise and dirt of do-it-yourself work away from the main living-room of the house. Alternatively, a garden shed could be used for this purpose.

Garden

Plan the garden, however small, as carefully as the rooms, making sensible use of all available space. Plan a sitting-out area with a hard paved surface in a sunny spot close to the house. Make hard surfaces all round the house with larger hard square areas near all the doors, so that there is less chance of mud being trampled in every time it rains. Look at the view from the various windows and bear it in mind when siting dustbin area, clothes drying area, and garden shed. Dustbins should be stowed in a ventilated brick enclosure, or at least behind a generously sized evergreen shrub, and should stand on a concrete surface. They should be as near the kitchen door as possible but easily transportable to the front gate or wherever garbage is collected. The washing line, if used, should be in a breezy, sunny place near the kitchen, but as it is not the prettiest view to enjoy, it could be partially concealed by a strategically planted hedge or group of small trees, if space allows. (Clothes dry faster over a hard surface than over grass.)

The shed which holds garden tools need not always be close to the house and will look better if it is masked by a fast-climbing plant. Try to arrange the remaining space in your back garden to meet the family's needs: a sandpit, perhaps, if there are small children, and a hard area for play (which can be grassed over later), few flower beds and plenty

of flowering shrubs if your gardening time is limited, a garden seat in the shade for the elderly, and so on.

In the front garden, aim for an effect you can maintain at all times, for this is the face your home presents to the world. Choose hedges which will only need cutting twice a year, a weeping willow tree, standard roses, tubs or stone plant containers which are all fairly easy to keep tidy and colourful. Otherwise, a simple lawn and paved path approach will look good and need only the very minimum maintenance.

Furnishing Fabrics and Floor Coverings

The principal natural and man-made fabrics suitable for furnishing and floor coverings are described on pp77–78. Many are cleverly blended to combine the best properties of more than one material.

Soft floor coverings

Other natural and man-made materials which are used as soft floor coverings include:

Coir: This is the thick fibre round the coconut shell, and is used to make coarse, inexpensive matting in a number of natural shades.

Leather: Sheepskins and goatskins can be used on the floor as rugs and are hard-wearing. If they are made from tanned skins they can be washed, but if the skins have been cured, the rugs should be dry shampooed at home using a dry shampoo intended for hair.

Rush matting: This is natural rush woven into squares, lengths or round mats, and makes an inexpensive floor covering which can be easily laid by its owner and taken up again for removal to another home. Dust and crumbs tend to drop through rush matting (which is easily brushed or vacuum-cleaned) and for this reason the floor beneath it needs to be swept regularly.

Sisal: This is a plant fibre which is used for making inexpensive and hard-wearing, but rather coarse-looking, carpet and carpet tiles in muted, natural colours.

Hard floor coverings

There are two types of sub-floor: one is made of solid concrete and any floor covering may be used on that; the other is a suspended joist and board construction which limits you to lighter tiles and covering generally. Unless they are to be sanded and sealed and used with rugs, boards should be covered with hardboard to provide a smooth base before laying your floor covering.

The following are some of the most common types of hard floor coverings:

Bricks must be laid on a solid sub-floor. They come in colours such as white, yellow, red, grey, and black, can be laid in various patterns, are easily washed, and extremely hard-wearing. Though bricks have to be tracked down, and are not cheap, they last for ever.

Ceramic tiles are most suitable for a solid sub-floor. They are fairly expensive but very hard-wearing, and can be obtained in an extensive range of colours and patterns.

Cork tiles are less hard-wearing but can be laid on any sub-floor and are warm and quiet to walk on. They should be sealed if they are to be used in a kitchen or bathroom. Some proprietary brands are pre-sealed with a vinyl coating, and can be cleaned with a damp cloth or mop.

Linoleum sheet and tiles can be laid on any floor, and come in a range of colours and patterns. The most useful type of linoleum is a heavy-duty quality, which is medium-priced and medium hard-wearing.

Marble and slate are suitable for a solid sub-floor. They are extremely expensive but have a very long life, can be washed clean, and are available in a number of colours and patterns.

Quarry tiles are suitable for a solid sub-floor and can be obtained in a range of mellow colours from buff and brown to red, blue and black. They are easy to keep clean by washing or polishing, and though they are fairly expensive, they will last a life-time.

Rubber, bought as sheet rubber with a studded or ribbed finish, is hard-wearing and quiet to walk on. It comes in an ever-increasing range of colours, including black and white, and can be washed. It is not recommended for kitchens as it is very slippery when wet and does not resist grease.

Vinyl sheet and tiles can be very hard-wearing depending on quality, but are soft and quiet to walk on. They come in a wide range of colours and patterns, and are simple to wash clean.

For more information on the care of floor coverings, see p87.

STRUCTURAL WORK AND ESSENTIAL SERVICES

The spring is the usual period set apart for sweeping of chimneys, taking up carpets, painting and whitewashing the kitchen and offices, papering rooms, when needed, and, generally speaking, the house putting on, with the approaching summer, a bright appearance, and a new face, in unison with nature.

A Builder or Doing It Yourself

If you do not use the services of an architect, you have several other options:
1) You can plan the design yourself and get several builders to tender for the job.
2) You can plan the design and act as your own builder, sub-contracting the various trades.
3) You can do both plans and building work yourself.

Whichever method you choose you must first visit your local authority building inspector's department, taking with you any existing plans of the property, and outline the alterations you have in mind. He will decide whether what you suggest is possible, advise you of any loans or grants which may be available, and tell you whether you need to get planning permission, which is necessary for extensive alterations. (See the chapter on The Law and You.)

Drawing Plans

If you are not able to obtain a plan of your home, you will need to make one or have one made by a local draughtsman (at least of that area you are intending to alter or extend). Use a metal measuring tape for absolute accuracy, squared paper to mark in the position of all windows, doors, and built-in fittings. Show which way the doors swing. Light and power points and light switches should be marked, using a different colour for clarity. Gas outlets, telephone and television aerial points, and fixed radiators should be marked, using different colours for each. An even more meticulous planner could cut out scaled shapes of all the furniture you own (or hope to own) and place that in position too. When everything is committed to paper it will be much easier to see and to work out the alterations you want. Visit building centres, local builders' merchants, and building exhibitions, and read advertisements, brochures, and magazine articles for the most up-to-date information.

List everything you want done, including details such as moving power points or hanging a door on the opposite jamb to open the other way, as well as larger jobs like removing walls, building extra rooms or enlarging windows. Then redraw your plans incorporating all the changes.

Engaging a Draughtsman

As you may have to submit your plans, together with the appropriate application forms, to your local authority for planning approval, you may feel that your own plan would be better redrawn by an expert draughtsman. The local authority may suggest names of people suitable for this work, or you can consult advertisements in your local paper. Tell the draughtsman you appoint exactly what is required, and agree on a fee.

Choosing and Briefing Builders

At this stage, if you have opted for the first method and are going to employ a contractor, you send your drawings, asking for a tender, to at least three local builders. As mentioned in the chapter on Planning Your Home – Design Factors, care should be taken over choosing builders. A strong personal recommendation from friends is reassuring. In the UK a builder should also belong to an association such as the National Federation of Building Trades Employers (NFBTE) or the Federation of Master Builders. The NFBTE, which tries to combat all forms of sub-standard building, has produced a useful pamphlet called *You and your builder* with a list of do's and don'ts. This is available from the Federation's headquarters in London.

When inviting builders to tender, tell them in writing what you want them to do, listing exact materials and fittings you want them to use, giving them a copy of your plan and also inviting them to visit the site. State that you will not necessarily accept the lowest or any other tender, inform them when you will let them know your decision, and how soon the successful tenderer will be expected to start work. It is important that each tenderer has been given identical instructions. When the tenders come in, inspect them carefully to make sure the cheapest does not have hidden snags, such as not including all the detailed work you require done, or suggesting poorer quality materials than you feel are satisfactory.

If all the tenders are too high you must start paring down your requirements, at least temporarily. You will need to negotiate with the builder of your choice to get down to the price you can afford, but you must confirm everything you arrange with him in writing so that there is no possibility of misunderstanding. It always costs more to bring back a builder on to a site to do extra work, so strive to afford as much as possible during the main building contract.

Being your own Contractor

You may opt for the second method listed above, employing all the sub-contractors direct, and thus retaining the contractor's profit for yourself if all goes well. The problems likely to arise from this course should not be under-estimated, particularly if there is a large amount of work involved, and you will need all your patience and resilience to cope.

You will also need a considerable amount of free time, so this method is not for those immersed in an arduous career. You should make a list of work to be done in the order it needs to be done, so that you can organize the various trades to appear on site at the right time and in the right sequence, and prevent workmen sitting idly waiting (at your expense) for one job to finish so that they can start on their own! You will also need to ensure that materials arrive when needed and you should organize an account with at least one local builders' merchant if you are to benefit from trade prices.

Being your own Builder

The third method, doing the building work yourself, should work out as the cheapest way of all if you have time, energy, do-it-yourself ability, and patience, all of which are essential for this sort of undertaking. Many home handymen are adept at joinery, bricklaying, plumbing, and decorating, and plenty have installed complete central heating systems with the aid of nothing more than an instruction leaflet or a book on the subject from the public library. But most handymen will know that in the UK all electrical work must be done by a certified tradesman as must all work on gas installations, and that the GPO has a rigid monopoly over all work on its telephones. Remember too that the local building inspector will require to inspect work which affects the structure of the house, the drainage system, and ventilation.

A section on being a handyman will be found at the end of this chapter.

Lighting the Home

Lighting in the home is used for two purposes – for seeing and for effect. The first should make reading, sewing, etc possible without strain. Lighting for effect is decorative, and enhances the look of the furnishing and decor.

Electric lighting is either incandescent or fluorescent. Incandescent lamps and tubes produce light from a heated tungsten filament; fluorescents have a phosphorous coating which glows when electric current passes through the gas within the tube.

Choosing Incandescent Lights

The incandescent filament is the most widely used in the home because of the warm light it gives. Best known is the General Lighting Service lamp (GLS) available in wattages from 25 to 200. Most have the familiar bayonet cap (BC) but the Edison screw (ES) is becoming more common now that more equipment with this type of fitting is being imported from the Continent or manufactured in the UK.

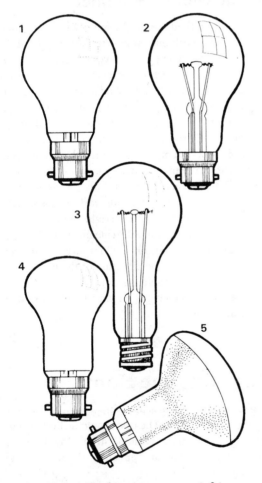

Types of light bulb: **1** *bayonet cap, pearl;* **2** *bayonet cap, clear;* **3** *Edison screw, clear;* **4** *bayonet cap, mushroom;* **5** *bayonet cap, reflector*

Lamps with clear glass give a hard light and sharp shadows but the undiffused light adds a sparkle in clear and tinted fittings. For a diffused light you need either pearl lamps which have the inner surface roughened or white lamps which have the inside coated with a silica powder.

Coiled coil lamps have a spiralled filament which gives 10% more light. Long life lamps give slightly less light but will last twice as long – about 2000 hours.

Variations on the pear shape, such as the mushroom, are used mostly where the lamp is visible. Candle shapes are for wall lights; some have a bayonet cap smaller than normal (SBC). There are also coloured lamps such as pearl pink for soft background lighting or to create a welcoming glow in a hall or patio light.

Linear filaments are slim, straight, short lamps, 35, 40 or 75 watts, for wardrobes and under work-tops, with double or single cap lamps to match the fitting.

Reflector lamps are more effective than the GLS bulb in giving a beam of light but are normally designed for special fittings. Crowned silvered bulbs of 60 or 100 watts have the front of the lamp silvered so the light is then thrown backwards against a reflector to give a smooth, narrow spotlight. The dark base of the lamp helps to cut out glare. Internally silvered lamps, in sizes of 40, 60 or 100 watts, have a built-in reflector with a choice of narrow or wide beam and different sizes to suit special fittings such as those which are recessed into the ceiling. Pressed glass (PAR38) are large lamps made of a heat-resistant glass capable of withstanding 'thermal shock', and tough enough to be used outdoors as well as indoors. Available in 100 or 150 watts, narrow or wide beam, they are more expensive to buy than GLS lamps, but have a long life of 5000 hours.

Tungsten halogen is another source of light – a variation of incandescent – which has been developed from the tiny but very efficient lamps normally used for motor car headlights.

Tungsten halogen lamps give a quarter more light than GLS lamps of the same wattage and have a life of 2000 hours. They are widely used for outdoor floodlighting, and can be used in the home in specially designed fittings; their very intense light is best controlled by a dimmer.

Choosing Fluorescent Lights

These are made in lengths from 150mm (4 watts) to 2400mm (125 watts) and in tube diameters of 16mm (miniature), 25mm (slimline), and 38mm (standard), their advantage being that they give three to four times as much light as an incandescent lamp for the same electricity consumption. Most popular fluorescent tube sizes for the home are the 40 watt (1200mm long) and the 65 and 80 watt (1500mm long), sold complete with their controls and usually a baffle or diffuser to disguise the tube.

Circular fluorescents with diameters of 300mm (32 watt) or 400mm (40 and 60 watt) are also popular as they greatly improve the light output from a ceiling point. They can be fitted flush to the ceiling and disguised with an attractive glass diffuser.

Most fluorescent fittings are supplied with a tube marked 'warm white' – this, in fact, is not as warm a colour as the incandescent lamp. A better match are the tubes giving a more yellow light.

Achieving Good Lighting

When choosing a lighting fitting consider the appearance of the fitting both when lit and unlit, how much light it produces, and how much light the shade absorbs. Consider which part of the room is to be illuminated and for what purpose. Work to a lighting plan so that the fitting is part of a scheme, and avoid placing lighting outlets at the centre of the ceiling where they often look solitary and awkward. Overhead central lighting – except in kitchens, bathrooms, bedrooms, and on staircases – usually lacks interest. It tends to be unflattering to furnishings and is not well placed for reading in comfort or, in fact, for many of the normal family activities. It is better to have several ceiling points, provided with multi and dimmer switching to allow for variations in lighting.

A good level of general lighting is about 20 watts per square metre of floor space, but if this light is evenly distributed, it can look dull. Local lights – like standard and table models – give highlights, shade and 'depth'. Try to seek a combination to suit any mood by switching lights or altering the level of illumination or angle of light. Spotlights can be angled to aim a beam of light on to a table or corner, on a favourite ornament or picture, or they can be unobtrusively fitted into the ceiling.

Individual switches help to give variety in lighting, and the door switch can be replaced by a dimmer, which not only switches the light on and off, but controls the level of illumination. The dimmer must suit the wattage of the lamps it controls. The smallest (250 watt) will control up to four 60 watt lamps or two 100 watt lamps. Candle lamps need a dimmer rated at twice the load.

Height, shape, and colour of shades for table and standard lamps are also important. A shade should look attractive unlit as well as when lit.

When watching television, it is important to have enough light to prevent too much glare from the picture. The room should be light enough to see the shape of the set and the surrounding furniture. Table or standard lamps should obviously be placed so that reflections do not show on the screen. Paintings and other pictures can be lit with linear filaments or fluorescents set out from the wall so that their light is thrown on to the canvas. Alternatively, spotlights set in the ceiling above the pictures or on an adjacent wall can be focused to aim their beam at the picture but without causing glare. Glass-covered pictures need care: the light should be placed so it flows downwards. Framing spotlights can match the size of the picture exactly.

Dining-room

The dining-table needs good lighting with something like an inverted bowl pendant fitting centred above it, or a chandelier placed to avoid interference with the view across the table and/or dazzling the diners. A pendant on a rise-and-fall cord so that height can be easily adjusted, and controlled by a dimmer switch to suit the mood, is a good idea. The dining-table light can be supplemented by wall lights, or a lamp for the serving-table or sideboard, depending on the size of the room. Spotlights can be trained on to pictures as described above.

Living-room

Most people choose central lights and standard and table lamps for the living-room. These should give decorative light and a good level of general lighting, but there should also be some concentrated light for reading and working. The ceiling light can be directional, using spotlights. If these are too modern-looking, consider the recessed eyeball spotlights which can illuminate a wall or a picture, or the curtains. A light inside a curtain pelmet, or fluorescent or tubular lights can give a good effect and might serve to illuminate shelves.

Hall and stairs

Halls should be well lit for safety, but not so brightly that eyes find it difficult to adjust to the outside darkness.

Stairs always need good lighting that does not throw glare into the eyes; there should be switches both upstairs and down. Pendant lights in groups, cylinder lights (including the recessed type), or even spotlights can be used, but there must be good light coming from overhead to make a clear distinction between the stair treads in light and the risers in shadow.

Kitchen

The kitchen should have a fluorescent lamp fitted with a diffuser parallel to, and above, the front edge of the sink. A larger kitchen may well need a second one in line with the opposite wall or at right angles to the first. A circular fluorescent fitting with a diffuser is an alternative for smaller kitchens. Small fluorescent or double cap tubular filaments can also be used fitted neatly under wall cupboards to light work surfaces. The lamp can be concealed by a wooden batten fitted to the front base of wall cupboards.

Ceiling-mounted or recessed spotlights are often used in the kitchen, though they do seem to need more regular cleaning than fluorescents. As in a dining-room, pendants with rise-and-fall fittings are useful over the eating area; cylinder down-lighters are an alternative if there is space within the ceiling to recess them. The bigger ones throw down a lot of heat as well as light, so it is best not to choose more than a 100 watt lamp.

Bedroom

Here the main ceiling light should ideally be two-way switched from the bed and the door; a two-way dimmer, for instance, is not expensive. Bedside lights may be fixed to the bedhead or wall, or suspended from the ceiling, on one or both sides of the bed. They take up less room than a table lamp which is easily knocked from a bedside table. A bedside light should always be set at eye level or slightly above, and should preferably be capable of being set to different angles. A headboard or wall fitting with a pullcord switch is the easiest to find in the dark.

For the dressing-table, one solution is to have a pair of pendant lights hanging from the ceiling each side of the mirror, just above head height. Another is a spotlight set on the wall nearby and directed across the face. Both give good light for make-up and for the room generally.

Cupboards and wardrobes are better if lit. Small push-button switches can be fitted to the inside edge of the cupboard door so the light comes on automatically when it is opened and goes off when it is shut.

Bathroom

Make sure there is one good overhead light and additional light at the mirror which will be used for shaving and for applying make-up. Fluorescent lights fitted behind a large sheet of mirror glass so that they throw light out around it, or spotlights fitted to the wall on either side are particularly good. An enclosed fluorescent light with a shaver socket (all one fitment) is ideal in the bathroom, but it must be the type with the isolation transformer designed for bathroom use.

Fittings should be made from plastic or plastic and glass, as metal will obviously be affected by the steam. Enclosed fittings flush to the ceiling or the wall look best and there are good, inexpensive textured glass styles that give a sparkling mottled-light effect on white surfaces.

Outside

A porch needs a good light if only to illuminate the name or number of the house. It should be placed to light the door and step, rather than throw glare into the eyes of anyone coming up the path. As many houses have two doors, light will be needed at the rear and side passages. The patio, if there is one, should not be left in the dark; simplest and cheapest is the light 'brick', a square of translucent material containing a GLS lamp which is screwed to an outside wall.

A garden, too, can be enhanced by lighting, which will also discourage prowlers. A control switch in the bedroom is recommended in lonely areas.

Many lighting improvements can be made without the reorganization of the existing electrical installation, but where an extension to the installation is needed, work should always be carried out by a qualified electrician.

Lighting by Oil and Bottled Gas

Although electricity is available in almost all areas, oil or 'bottled gas' lamps can be used as an alternative, or in situations such as camping and sailing where there is no electricity.

Oil lamps

In the modern, electrically equipped home, oil lamps are sometimes used as part of the décor and, if kept in working order, they can be used if the mains electricity supply is interrupted or as an alternative on special occasions when the softer light of a live flame is appropriate.

Two types of oil lamps are made: the traditional type, using a wick to carry paraffin oil from the fuel reservoir to the burner by capillary action, and the type using a hand-operated pump to pressurize the fuel and force it up through a fine nozzle in the burner. The wick-type lamp is silent in operation whereas the pressure type makes a slight noise.

Bottled gas lamps

These are very useful as emergency lighting equipment, and are rather more safe to use than oil lamps since the fuel is in a sealed container. They are also a popular and efficient means of illumination for campers and caravanners. Care should be taken, however, to avoid using the lamps in strong draughts, and to dispose of spent containers in a safe place.

Heating the Home

If you are investigating the best way to heat a new house or flat, or to put a new system in your present one, the first thing to consider is whether you want to heat all or part of it, or just individual rooms. If you own the property you may want to modernize what is already there or you may decide on a completely new system. If you are renting your home, you may not want to spend money on fitments which will become the landlord's when you go.

You will also need to decide how warm you want, and can afford, to be. For most of us being warm means an indoor temperature of between 16° and 21°C. Older people, babies, and people who are feeling ill may want a temperature nearer 20°C or even higher to feel comfortable.

You will also have to decide which fuel to use – gas, electricity, solid fuel, oil or a mixture. Your choice may be limited by what is available, cost, or by lack of storage space if the fuel needs to be stored. Before making a decision, consider the various systems which are available; collect as much information as possible about each alternative, and then start to make out your own checklist to find the heating that suits your needs, what is available to you, and what you can afford.

Insulation and ventilation also have to be considered when planning a heating system, as they have important interactions on each other. See pp56–58 below.

Radiation and Convection

While most heating equipment gives out warmth by means of both radiation and convection, each piece of equipment is designed to give heat primarily by one method or the other, and is therefore described as being either a radiant heater or a convector heater.

In radiation, heat is given out directly. It spreads in all directions from the source of the heat, warming any object on which it falls. It is not necessarily a visible heat, although the term 'radiant' heat is invariably applied to a heat that gives warm, glowing-red, direct heat – like a fire.

In convection, heat is given out by the heated object to the air in contact with it. The warmed air rises and circulates, and is replaced by cooler air which in its turn is heated and circulates. The hot air may also be circulated by a fan.

Many people like to have a fire to act as a focal point in a room. This may be the only source of heat, or it may supplement other forms of heating.

Professional Advice

You will almost certainly need to obtain professional advice before making up your mind which heating plan is best for you. Choose an engineer or installer belonging to a recognized trading organization such as the Heating and Ventilating Contractors' Association; the Institute of Domestic Heating and Environmental Engineers; the Chartered Institution of Building Services and the Institute of Plumbing. These trade associations will investigate complaints against their members if problems arise during installation.

If you are buying appliances from other sources, ensure that the dealer is a member of the National Federation of Builders' and Plumbers' Merchants. All appliances should have an appropriate safety mark such as the British Electrotechnical Approvals Board (BEAB) Mark of Safety, the BSI 'Safety Mark' for gas appliances, or the Domestic Oil Burning Equipment Testing Association (DOBETA) Seal of Approval for oil-burning equipment.

Assessing Heating Requirements

To help you decide on the best and most economical heating plan, consider both the structure of the house and its condition. A tall, narrow, detached house may need some form of heating on every floor, while a compact bungalow or flat can often be heated from one central point. An old cottage may need more heating at more points than a modern house the same size, especially if the windows and door frames do not fit well.

No two rooms have exactly similar requirements even if they are the same size and occupy the same position in a terrace of houses. Factors affecting heating requirements include the size of the room

BEAB-Mark of Safety

BS 4224

Safety marks: 1 BSI 'Safety Mark' for gas appliances; 2 British Electrotechnical Approvals Board Mark of Safety; 3 Domestic Oil Burning Equipment Testing Association Seal of Approval; 4 British Standards Institution Kitemark for safety

and the direction it faces; whether it is in an exposed position; the floor it is on; the number of windows and outside walls it has; insulation; and the presence of draughts.

The size of heating system you choose – whether it is deciding on the size of a single heater for one room or a whole house heating system – must give you the temperature you want when it is really cold outside. Most calculations are based on the equipment giving you the warmth you want inside when the temperature outside is freezing.

Before you decide to invest money in a full-scale central heating system, work out how many rooms in your house you use and how much time you spend at home each day.

There are obviously differences in running costs between heaters using different fuels. It is usually cheaper to use, say, a 2kW electric space heater on full rate electricity for up to 5 hours a day than to have a 3.75kW storage heater on reduced rate electricity running all night, while a gas room heater to give you the same amount of warmth might cost even less to run.

You can also cut down the amount of heating you need by wearing warmer clothes and you can experiment with turning the thermostats down if the room gets too warm rather than taking clothes off. It is reckoned that simply turning down thermostats by 2°C would save about 10% of the annual fuel consumption.

Choosing a Heating System

Most heating advisers agree that if you are starting from scratch it is important to decide on the type of system you want before you make up your mind about the fuel you are going to use.

The choice of heating system is dictated by how much heating you want. You may have full central heating, background central heating which you can top up as needed with room heaters, selective central heating which heats some rooms and parts of the house but not simultaneously, or partial heating (or partial cold) with some parts of the house heated (not the same as selective heating which gives you the option of deciding where and when you want the heat).

If you do not own your house or flat, you may decide that room heaters which you can take away with you are the answer.

Choosing Fuels

Solid fuel

Solid fuel needs a lot of storage space, and boilers and fires have to be stoked and the ash removed. Anyone living in rural districts is advised to stock up with as much solid fuel as possible before winter sets in; the extra cost of storing this has to be taken into account because covered storage space for solid fuel is essential. Allow 1.4 cu metres for each tonne of coal. Proprietary fuels which are less dense need about 2.5 cu metres for the same weight of fuel.

The correct size and type of fuel must be used to suit the boiler or fire if it is to operate efficiently. In a clean air zone, where soot and smoke are legally prohibited, you have to use a smokeless fuel which may be more expensive.

Solid fuel prices are usually lower during the summer, and if it is possible to buy all you need at this time there will be a saving.

It is often possible to burn logs, timber and even household rubbish in some stoves which also burn solid fuel, but it is important to check that the stove you choose will burn the fuel you prefer.

Wood-burning stoves, largely imported, are only economical if you have a good regular source of cheap wood. Newly cut woods burn poorly with a low heat output unless cut into burning size and then thoroughly weathered and dried.

Gas

Gas is a particularly good method of space heating. Like oil, it responds quickly to heat controls, and the appliances eg a boiler, need less servicing than most oil-fired units. Unlike oil, it does not need a storage tank.

Oil

Oil for central heating is either gas oil or the light kerosene, but both are now expensive in comparison with other fuels. The oil storage tank should be sited convenient to the boiler with easy access for refilling from the tanker. It should be large enough to hold at least six months' supply – about 3000 litres for a three/four bedroom detached house. The tank must comply with local by-laws and be maintained for protection against rust.

It is, however, the main alternative if a labour-saving fuel is required for central heating systems in areas where there is no mains gas. Ordering in large quantities and keeping a stock in large storage tanks can reduce the cost somewhat.

Electricity

Most sophisticated heating systems need electricity, whatever their fuel, for controls, thermostats and pumps, but the amount of current consumed is small. Storage heaters or ducted warm-air-heating need a separate supply; storage heaters need more electricity and are on a separate circuit from the normal house wiring, so extra cables or re-wiring may be necessary.

Although electricity has many advantages, ie cleanliness, controllability, automatic operation, and freedom from service problems, plus the fact that any heater can be plugged in wherever there is a suitable point, it is almost certain to be the most expensive form of fuel for space heating unless it is being used for comparatively short periods, eg up to five hours a day, or with reduced rate off-peak storage heating. Costs can be reduced by high standards of insulation and careful use of controls.

On the other hand, the installation cost is less than for other whole-house warming systems.

Bottled gas

This is a useful and convenient stand-by heater when there are no mains alternatives or when emergency heating is required.

When considering a major gas or electricity installation find out the exact cost of running cables or gas pipes to the house, and obtain in writing any estimates for connection.

If a large system is contemplated, it is not enough to presume that the existing methods of supply will be adequate: this must be confirmed before the installation is ordered.

It is always wise to make enquiries locally if you are thinking of installing a new heating system. There may be various sources of heat available to you which you might be able to tap, eg from a power station or sewage works, and which could prove cheaper to use than any traditional fuel.

Running Costs

The cost of heating a house or flat depends on the amount of heat required, the number of hours the heating system is in use, the price paid for fuel, the efficiency with which the fuel is used, and the quality and quantity of insulation. It is impossible to forecast the running costs precisely, whatever the fuel. There are many variables, starting with the price of fuel which is dependent on international and national economies. Then there are the variables such as the weather and people's changing living habits, eg young children who need an extra room for homework, older people coming to stay who need a warm room all day. Even though accurate running costs cannot be forecast, it is possible to obtain from fuel undertakings a fairly reliable estimate of the cost to you for a given system.

Wet systems

This is the most popular form of central heating. A boiler heats water which circulates through pipes to radiators which give out heat. The water is either pumped or circulates by its own pressure (gravity). The system is enclosed so the same water circulates round and round. A separate enclosed circuit usually goes to the water cylinder where it, in turn, heats domestic hot water.

Boilers are sized by their heat output measured in kilowatts (kW) or British Thermal Units (Btu). A most popular size is the 17.5 kW or 60,000 Btu per hour boiler, but a heating specialist is needed to calculate the size depending on the various factors.

Most modern wet systems use copper pipes with a small diameter, ie 22mm, but 12mm or 6mm are becoming common because they save on material cost and are less obtrusive. These two sizes are called *microbore* and *minibore* to distinguish them from *small bore*.

There is a wide choice of radiator shapes and sizes; they also come in versions that look like skirting panels, and with convectors with fans to push the air warmed by the pipes into the room.

Dry systems

The heaters of both convector and storage systems can be used as individual heaters (see pp51–52). With warm air heating the heating unit heats air which is then circulated through the house via ducts which direct the warmed air through grilles set in the floor or low in the walls. Because this involves ductwork between floors and in walls, warm air central heating is largely confined to new homes. Two systems are available:

Direct

Air is drawn to a gas, oil or electric unit where it is filtered, heated, and circulated through ducts to outlets in the house. To ensure good air circulation, delivery points are set at low level and return air grilles high on the wall. Its drawback is that hot water has to be supplied by electric immersion heater or gas circulator.

Indirect

Operates from an ordinary hot water boiler which feeds a 'heat exchanger' where air is drawn by a fan over a series of fins and hot water pipes and then carried round the house by ducting, as in the direct system. It can also provide domestic hot water.

Solar heating

Since most parts of the British Isles enjoy 1600 hours of sunshine a year, theoretically capable of providing energy equivalent to 1200 units of electricity from one square metre of solar panel, solar heating appears very attractive. Unfortunately the solar panel is at its most efficient at times when heating is least needed and the heat can only be stored in a hot water tank. This method does however allow the home to supplement its supply of hot water by courtesy of the sun, even during the time when the sun is shrouded in cloud.

The solar panels, normally mounted on the roof, are not unsightly and need little or no maintenance: rain water keeps the glass clean, though in areas of industrial dirt and dust an occasional wash with a hose is necessary. The panels have an estimated life of twenty years, and installation and plumbing take only two days. None of the various systems available involve major structural work.

The control instruments ensure that water flows through the panels as soon as there is any solar radiation. Some controllers are linked to the boiler thermostat to improve efficiency.

The panels are most efficient when sunlight is at a right angle, less efficient on overcast days, and in the evening and morning (times of maximum water demand) when the sun is low in the sky. As the design of hot water plumbing in British homes is difficult to adapt to solar heating, the result is insufficient hot water to meet demand if not enough storage space is provided.

The future for solar heating probably lies in its use in conjunction with a device called a heat pump, but this will involve drastic changes in the way we design our homes.

Central heating controls

It pays to spend money on efficient controls that will regulate the heating system automatically to give you the temperature you want when you want it. Without good controls you are liable to waste a lot of heat and a lot of money.

The *central heating boiler* should have to run only if the rooms or the hot water become too cool. Some boilers have only a control designed to keep water pumped through the system at close to peak temperature regardless of whether the rooms are chilly or warm, and even if the cylinder is full of hot water. The result is wasteful overheating.

If the boiler has a thermostat control with a temperature scale it should be set to about 66°C; this will not overheat the hot water supply if there is no thermostat in the hot water cylinder. Do not set the boiler thermostat above 82°C or below 60°C unless advised by your installer. Boilers with a numbered control should be set according to the maker's instructions; otherwise seek advice from your installer.

There are additional economy controls to regulate heat that can be fitted to the output of the boiler. *Motorized zone controls* are fitted to many new boilers to adjust water temperatures in the radiators automatically; there are also simple, small devices that can be put in by a heating specialist, together with thermostats, to regulate heat in the rooms and in the hot water cylinder automatically. There are also versions which adjust heat output according to changes in weather conditions.

If you have a wet system fit *thermostatic valves* on the radiators, other than in the living-room. These replace the normal wheel valve and control the flow of water through the radiator. All you have to do is to turn the knob to adjust the setting, which is usually a numbered scale 1–5 or 1–8 (the setting being between 8°–24°C). Use a room thermometer to find the correct temperature setting: 16°C in a bedroom and perhaps less in a dining-room if it is not used every day. Response to adjustment is fast as the valve can easily be reset, but it must be returned to its usual setting afterwards.

A *cylinder thermostat* can be fitted to the hot water tank to control the hot water temperature. Set at 60°C, it prevents wasteful overheating of hot water, as the circuit to the hot tank tends to work harder than it needs to, when the central heating is needed on cold days.

Central Heating Systems

Type	Fuels	Method
Wet systems		
Free standing boiler	Gas, oil, and solid fuel	Modern boilers are compact and a new or existing chimney can be used, or a neater balanced flue fitted where it is against an outside wall. Sophisticated controls and wide range of heat outputs with a choice of radiators, skirting heaters, etc.
Wall mounted boiler	Gas or oil	Very compact, needing no floor space as designed to contain very little water. Rapid heat response with good controls. Balanced flue only, so must be on, or close to, outside wall. Wide choice of radiators.
Back boiler	Gas, oil, and solid fuel	Fire grate and boiler combined in a cast-iron unit with glass fronted doors, capable of supplying up to six radiators in other rooms as well as hot water. With gas, an old fashioned grate can be removed altogether and a modern gas fire with wood surround substituted.
Flow heating	Electric	A compact unit containing a series of heating elements forming a jacket on the flow and return of a small bore system. Main advantage is that it needs no chimney or flue and can be sited anywhere. Disadvantage is that it uses mainly day rate electricity. Suitable for a boiler replacement.
Dry systems		
Convector system	Gas	Suitable for some homes or part of a home where it is unsuitable or too costly to install or add to an existing conventional heating system, but possible to install gas pipe connections. Separate balanced flue floor or wall mounted convector heaters are easy to install, although each heater must be placed on an outside wall. They work by either fan or natural convection. Some models have a thermostatic control to maintain the temperature you set.
Storage system	Electric	Electricity used at night at the cheaper 'off-peak' rate is converted into heat which is stored in the insulated core of a storage heater in each room or area heated and then given off slowly during the following day. Output can be controlled by dampers and some have an electric fan to push air over the heated core.
Warm air	Gas, electric, oil	Practical to install only for a new home; air is heated as it is driven by a fan over the heated core of the unit and distributed throughout ducts and grilles in the rooms that are being heated. Air is drawn into the unit by the fan and filtered before being heated.
Ceiling heating	Electric	The heating elements consist of a series of metal strips or resistance mats pressed between two sheets of special heat resistant material fixed above the ceiling surface. Thermal insulation is placed above the elements and heat is radiated downwards. No space is wasted with heating appliances and most ceiling finishes can be used. As it uses a high proportion of day time electricity it can be expensive to run, so good insulation is essential. Only suitable for a new home or one being extensively modernized.
Panel heating	Electric	Inexpensive to install compared with other systems, with a wide choice of heaters including some that fit to a skirting board, but can be expensive to run as the heaters use a high proportion of day rate electricity. Must have efficient room temperature controls and timers, and the home needs to be well insulated.
Solar heating		The heat of the sun can be used to supplement the domestic hot water supply, but domestic systems not yet (1980) practical for home heating.

Most central heating systems are controlled by a *programmer* which works like a clock, switching the boiler on and off for set periods. An economical programme in a house with good insulation where people are out during the day would be: switch on at 6am, switch off at 9am, then on again at 4.30pm and off an hour before your usual bedtime. There is a switch to over-ride the programme and to turn the boiler on or off, in or outside the chosen programme. In the summer the programmer can be set to switch the boiler on to heat the domestic hot water. A total of five hours each day usually gives enough hot water with little waste for a family; the over-ride switch can be used if more or less hot water is needed.

Make sure the *room thermostat* is sited away from any heat source or sunlight. It should be at head height on an inside wall, and easily accessible. Some thermostats work in conjunction with the programmer to give different heat settings, eg 15°C in the morning, 20°C in the evening. If you overheat your house even by one degree, your fuel costs can rise by 5% or more. If you still feel cold at 20°C then you should look at your insulation. For methods of insulation, see pp56–57 and p59.

Central and Individual Room Heating Equipment

There is a wide choice of equipment for each fuel, both for central heating and for individual room heating. Equipment is constantly being updated to make it more efficient in the way it uses fuel. So even if you do not need to change a whole system or to change fuels, you will almost certainly get better efficiency and more value for the money you spend on fuel if you install a new boiler, a new fire or simply new controls.

Many people still prefer individual room heating and even if central heating is installed, a room heater can be used to give extra heat or to provide the traditional focal point of radiant heat.

The table below summarizes available equipment. When you are making your choice you will need advice about the type and size most suitable for the area you are heating and how the equipment fits in with your house-heating plan.

Boilers:
central heating and/or hot water

Floor standing

Solid fuel: gravity feed (filled from top automatically or once every 24–36 hours); sectional (filled from front manually once or twice a day).
Oil: pressure jet for large or medium systems, efficient but noisy; Wallflame and Dynoflame similar use and efficiency, but quieter. Vaporizing with fan, quieter but less efficient; vaporizing, similar but silent.
Gas: freestanding; combined boiler and hot water system; below work-top.

Wall mounted

Gas fired with balanced flue, without or with (noisier) fan assistance. In shapes and sizes which co-ordinate with kitchen equipment.

Fireplace or hearth

Solid fuel: with openable or closed fire.
Gas: radiant/convector.
Oil: radiant/convector.

Warm air

Direct-fired systems can be run from units operated by electricity, gas or oil; indirect systems can be run from boilers fired by gas, solid fuel or oil.

Non-portable room heaters

Electric: off-peak storage heaters with or without fan booster; wall or ceiling-mounted radiant heaters; wall-mounted fan heaters and convectors; panel and skirting convectors.
Gas: built-in radiant fire; balanced flue wall convectors with or without fan.
Oil: wall-mounted paraffin convectors.

Portable heaters

Electric: fan heaters, radiant fires, radiant/convector heaters and convectors; oil filled radiators.
Low pressure gas: radiant/convectors; convectors.
Paraffin: convectors, radiant fires, radiant convectors.

Electric equipment

Electric heating equipment can be divided into two types: 'thermal storage' and 'direct acting'. Thermal storage systems and appliances are designed to work on reduced price, off-peak electricity utilizing electricity generated at times when demand is low. Direct acting appliances include radiant fires, infra-red heaters, convectors, fan heaters, radiant and convector panels, and ceiling heating.

Thermal storage heating

Storage radiators are heated during the night hours using off-peak electricity at the reduced price. The stored heat has then to provide day-long warmth which may not be achieved unless the user has anticipated very cold weather and turned up the 'charge-controller' in advance. Off-peak electricity is normally provided through a special meter. Electricity used during a night period is recorded at the low rate; at other times, when it costs just slightly more than the normal domestic tariff rate, it is recorded on a separate register.

Most storage radiators are fitted with either a booster fan or a damper mechanism so that heat left in the radiator towards the end of the day can be extracted to boost the heat output. It still needs, though, a degree of anticipation and careful control to give running costs that should compare favourably with other fuels.

Storage fan heaters are similar to storage radiators but have a fan that can be controlled by a manual switch, or an automatic thermostat, which blows air into the room. Some background heat is given out at all times which helps to maintain a background temperature, but extra heat can be provided if needed.

Direct acting heating

'Direct acting' means that heat is given out only when electricity is being consumed. Normally, direct acting heaters are connected on the standard domestic tariff but some types of heater can take advantage of an off-peak tariff.

Gas equipment

As gas equipment needs a flue, it cannot be portable. Gas wall heaters are compact, individual convectors which circulate warmth either by a fan or by natural convection. By using a high temperature setting on the heater, they give a high level of warmth quickly, and it can then be maintained at a reduced setting. An individual wall heater is ideal for heating a cold area or a cold room. Alternatively, a whole house-heating system can be built up in stages by adding wall heaters as required.

All wall heaters have a 'balanced flue'. This means that they do not require a chimney but do need to be positioned on a suitable outside wall. A flue is constructed in the wall so that fresh air can be drawn in and the burnt gases removed.

Gas fires

A gas fire can provide a focal point in a room, and like a wall heater it can give a high level of warmth quickly. With most gas fires heat is provided by glowing radiants and convected air. There are many different models, ranging from modern to traditional designs.

A gas fire can act as the only source of heat in a room, or it may supplement other forms of heating.

Most gas fires fit into an existing fireplace and can be hearth or wall-mounted. Models are also available with a 'balanced flue'.

Maintenance

It is worthwhile having a maintenance contract as an inefficient system obviously becomes expensive (see the section on Guarantees and Servicing, p74). The following points should be noted:

1) The boiler and the system should be checked once a year, making sure there is no corrosion.
2) In a 'wet system' use a scale inhibitor; this is a simple chemical, added to the water circulating in the radiators, which prevents scale and reduces the problem of air locks.
3) To get rid of air locks (which stop the water circulating so that radiators become cold, and may cause knocking noises in the pipes), first set the thermostatic valve on high. Then turn the small vent valve at the top corner of the radiator anti-clockwise with the special radiator key (which should be kept handy). Hold a jar under the valve, as water will start to spurt out with an

audible hiss once the air has escaped. Tighten up the valve again immediately. It is advisable to wear rubber gloves as the water will be hot.

Persistent air locks and knocking in the pipework should be looked at by the installer or a plumber. All pipes must be securely fixed, even if they are under a floor.

Radiators should never be boxed in. A shelf will help prevent dirt patterns appearing on the wall above, but a small space must be left between the back of the shelf and the wall to avoid the reduction of heat output. Specifically designed radiator shelves overcome this problem by slanting upwards at the front and sides.

If you have a *ducted warm air system*, make sure the grilles are clear and there are no leaks in the duct work. Try to make full use of the programmer, reducing the time periods. Keep the filter clean. Warm air systems respond quickly to demand but also lose their heat rapidly, particularly to cold surfaces like outside walls and windows. In cold areas, double glazing is a definite advantage with this kind of system. For more information on double glazing, see pp57 and 59.

If you have *solid fuel heating* make sure you have a modern grate that is not losing too much heat up the chimney. A modern grate or stove, designed for slow, controllable burning, will pay for itself in a short time, look more attractive, and be more efficient.

Pump

Most central heating systems have an electric pump to circulate the heated water from the boiler. It is sometimes fitted inside the boiler casing – a cylindrical unit with an electric flex which should be checked for signs of perishing. At the top of the pump is a small vent valve like that on a radiator. If water does not circulate when the pump is running (this sometimes happens after the system has been drained down and refilled) the cause is usually an air lock. Take a small screwdriver and make a few anti-clockwise turns to release the air, then tighten. It is important, however, that the flow adjustment which governs the amount of water passing through the pump is only carried out by the installer or a qualified heating engineer.

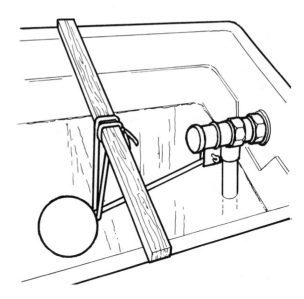

To drain the header tank of a central heating system, tie up the float

Header tank and draining

Make sure the small water tank found in the loft is free of rust and dirt, and is properly insulated. The ball valve should be working easily. In order to drain the system, first tie the float to a piece of wood laid across the tank, which will prevent fresh water from the mains entering the tank.

The drain cock is usually close to the boiler or to a nearby radiator. It has a small nipple to which a hose end can be fitted. The other end of the hose should be placed in an outside drain. Alternatively, if you want to preserve the anti-corrosion chemical for use again, the hose should be placed in a large container. A small spanner releases the nut below the nipple to allow the water in the system to flow out. Close as soon as the flow stops. To refill, you should simply release the ball valve, and then check for air locks.

Radiators

A leak from a joint connecting the pipe to the radiator can often be sealed without draining the system.
1) Turn off the boiler, or turn down the thermostat, to prevent water being pumped.
2) The radiator has two valves, one at each side;

turn off both valves, and place bowls at each side of the radiator to catch the water.

3) Loosen the hexagonal connectors between the valves and the radiator.

4) Lift the radiator off the wall carefully (it helps if there are two people to do this, as a radiator filled with water is very heavy) and tilt to allow the water to drain out.

5) Clean the threads of the connectors and smear them with a jointing compound (available from an ironmonger, together with some plumbers' hemp).

6) Wrap the hemp round the threads; rehang the radiator; then screw the connectors back into place.

7) Open the valves and, using the radiator key, open the vent valve at the top of the radiator to release the air. Close when water spurts out.

This method can also be used when redecorating a room.

Note You will need to protect your hands from hot water with a towel or rubber gloves.

Fuel tank

Every year in the autumn check the oil storage tank for leaks or signs of rust. A rust inhibitor followed by a coat of bitumastic paint (from a hardware shop) will be needed if signs of corrosion are noticed. Open the drain cock and run off any sludge or water into a bucket until clean oil appears. Clean the oil filter that connects the boiler feed pipe to the tank, by turning off the stop cock and removing the filter bowl. The bowl and the element should be cleaned carefully with petrol, and then dried before being refitted. Finally, take a short piece of wire and check that the vent pipe at the top is clear from any obstruction.

Hot Water

Where water is not provided by the boiler or heater which gives central or room heating, or in summer when the room heating is not needed, there are alternative ways of heating water. It may be more economical to use a hot water heater at the basin, eg in a bedroom, than to run pipes all over the house

to provide hot water for occasional use. The best system to choose depends on how much water is needed and in how many rooms.

Hot water quantities

A typical family (two adults, two children) can use 1,140 litres of hot water each week which is over 66,000 litres a year.

A hot bath of 114 litres needs about 60 litres of water at 70°C cooled down with about 55 litres of cold water at 12°C, which is the average temperature of cold water in the mains throughout the year. At 60°C about 73 litres are required.

Typical quantities of hot water required for various purposes

	Litres required at 60°C	Litres required at 70°C
Bath 114 litres at 43°C initial temp.	73	60
Basins for handwashing 4 litres per usage at 43°C	3	2
Dishwashing (hand) 4 litres per meal at 60°C	4	3.5
Floor washing and house cleaning 1 bucket at 9 litres per day at 60°C	9	7.5
Laundry 40–140 litres per week at 60°C	40–140	35–115

Note These figures assume a cold water temperature of 12°C which is the average over the whole year. Over the summer months the average is 18°C which reduces by approximately 5% the amount of hot water at 60°C required for a bath at 38°C.

Gas water heating

Where a gas point can be made available, gas water heating provides a direct and efficient method. Water heaters must be properly 'flued', so they need to be fixed on an outside wall or into a properly flued installation.

Instantaneous water heaters

These are connected to cold water systems. When the hot water tap is turned on, the burners light automatically and heat the water. As the burners only light when hot water is being drawn off, an instantaneous water heater is particularly economical. There are two types:

1) A single-point heater: This supplies hot water to a single unit, eg a sink or a shower unit, and is installed close to that unit.

2) A multi-point heater: This supplies hot water at several different points, such as a bath, wash-basin, and kitchen sink. The heater can be installed anywhere, providing there are facilities for connecting the heater by a flue to the outside of the house or flat and that there is access for servicing. Ideally, it should be near the point where most water is used.

Gas circulators

These are, in effect, miniature gas boilers and are used with a conventional hot water storage cylinder. All gas circulators are thermostatically controlled, and in some cases it is possible to fit a special economy valve which can be set either to heat the whole tank or just to keep a few litres at the top permanently hot. If there is an existing hot water system in need of modification, a gas circulator can often be the most economical water heater to install.

Gas storage water heater

This is a self-contained system, consisting of a well-insulated tank, holding up to 90 litres, with a built-in gas burner. It is ideal for households where there is no satisfactory hot water tank available, yet where hot water is needed regularly throughout the day.

Electric water heating

Electric water heating in a properly insulated hot water cylinder is an efficient method of heating water. The heating element is completely immersed in the water and all the heat produced by the element is transferred to the water and it is stored ready to use. Electric water heating is easy to install and has the advantages of low installation and maintenance costs. Some heaters can operate mainly on night time electricity for reduced running costs.

Immersion heaters

For simple, cheap conversion to whole-house electric water heating, an immersion heater can be fitted into an existing hot water cylinder (provided it is in good condition) to replace or supplement the boiler. If the existing cylinder is of adequate size, ie 140–230 litres, it may be well worth considering having two immersion heaters fitted for use on an off-peak tariff. With this arrangement, the lower immersion heater heats the whole cylinder at night, using the cheaper off-peak electricity. The upper immersion heater comes into operation during the day if there is a heavy demand for hot water. A 75mm glass fibre or similar lagging jacket, or a box filled with loose insulation 75mm thick should be placed round an uninsulated cylinder.

Combination cylinders are intended for houses without existing cold water cisterns. A built-in cistern supplies the hot cylinder and this enables the unit to be connected directly to the cold water main. Some smaller models suitable for a bathroom are made for mounting in situations where they will always be visible.

Open outlet heaters for on-the-spot hot water are ideal for sinks, wash-basins, and showers. Models ranging from 4.5–70 litres are available, and some are designed to be tucked out of sight below sinks and wash-basins. There are also models designed to supply hot water for a shower.

Low pressure (cistern fed) heaters are designed to supply a number of taps and are available in a range of sizes from about 90 litres upwards, including some that can be wall mounted. The Under Draining Board pressure type heater (UDB) has an upper heating element to maintain hot water for immediate use at the sink or wash-basin. The lower element is switched on to heat the whole cylinder to provide large quantities of water for baths.

Central hot water cylinders for a whole house come in a range of sizes, the most common having a capacity of 136 litres. These are usually fitted with a 3kW immersion heater, and the thermostat should be set at 70°C, especially if the maximum amount of hot water is required from an off-peak tariff. In hard water areas, the temperature setting should be reduced to 60°C to avoid excessive scale deposits and build-up on the element sheath.

In a large family house a large cylinder, up to 230 litres, is recommended in order to ensure that most of the hot water needs are met by cheaper off-peak electricity.

Instantaneous heaters provide a continuous low capacity flow of hot water where limited quantities meet the need. The water is heated as it is drawn off and models for handwashing supply hot water at the rate of approximately 1.4 litres per minute. There are small, compact models to supply ample hot water for showers; these are directly connected to the water mains.

An instantaneous electric shower heater will give 2–3 litres of water per minute at 50°C which is one way of saving energy and economizing on the fuel bill.

Insulation

Despite continued propaganda about the vital need to conserve energy and the continuing rise in the price of all kinds of fuel, very few domestic buildings are adequately insulated.

In a typical house, 25% of the heat is lost through the roof (more in a bungalow), about 35% through the walls, 10% through the windows, and 15% in draughts, while another 15% goes into the ground.

It is worth noting however that many materials commonly used for insulating houses represent a considerable fire risk, and it would be wise to consult BRE Digest 233: *Fire hazards from insulating materials* (HMSO) before making a final choice of insulating material.

Roof insulation

Make sure that your roof is weather-proof. Sheets of heavy polythene or building paper fixed to the rafters will stop snow blowing in as well as air getting out. If you wish to use your roof space for living in, you should insulate the roof. This can be done easily and fairly cheaply with glass fibre or similar insulating material, sold in rolls, which can be tacked up between the rafters before lining the roof with some type of ceiling board.

If you are not going to use this loft space, then you can insulate the floor instead; this is both easier to do and cheaper.

A 75mm layer of glass fibre, mineral wool or granular vermiculite insulation laid between joists in the loft will substantially reduce the heat loss.

Having reduced the heat loss by insulation, temperatures in the roof space will be much colder. The cold water tank and pipes in the attic must therefore be lagged as well (see the section on Frozen pipes, p70) and the underside of the cold water tank left uninsulated, to minimize the possibility of freezing in cold weather.

Other methods of roof insulation include expanded polystyrene, impregnated fibre insulation board, rigid polyurethane and laminated expanded polystyrene/plasterboard. These are sometimes fixed to the rafters, but it is recommended that they should only be installed by experts and that in any case only flame retardant or self-extinguishing materials should be used.

If your roof is inaccessible from the inside, insulate the ceilings directly under it with some of the many ceiling tiles which are available. For insulating walls and attics, see the section on Being a handyman, p59.

Wall insulation

North-facing walls, and any others which never see the sun or which are particularly exposed, are likely to benefit from insulation.

Internally, built-in cupboards and even bookshelves will help to conserve heat, as will panelling, and insulating wallpapers or lining materials such as cork tiles.

Damp-proof courses

All walls should have damp-proof courses built in about 150mm above ground level to prevent rising damp. If your home does not have these, it certainly should; the work may well be costly to have done, but should be one of your first priorities. If you apply for an improvement grant from a local authority for the property (see p160), you will almost certainly find that a damp-proof course is an essential prerequisite to being given any financial aid.

Externally, heat can be saved by hanging walls with tiles or weather-boarding backed with insulating quilting; or you can consider plastering face-brick, or replacing the existing plaster, if necessary. For carrying out damp-proofing yourself, see the section on Being a handyman, p59.

Cavity walls

Houses built in the UK since the 1920s normally have cavity walls, and the cavities can be filled with foam for extra insulation. Relaxation of building regulations must first be obtained and it is essential to use a reputable installer or you may end up with damp problems.

Cavity insulation takes about a day. Holes are drilled in the brickwork joints at regular intervals through which either *foamed ureaformaldehyde* (which sets after a few minutes) or *mineral fibre* is injected to form a low-density insulating infill. The holes are then repointed and the brickwork left with little sign of disturbance.

Floor insulation

Fifteen per cent of the total heat loss of a house is through floors; but insulation for suspended floors is often neglected. Sometimes a thick carpet with an ample underlay is satisfactory, but for really effective insulation some form of insulating material, such as glass fibre, should be placed below the floor surface.

Solid floors at ground level or below should, like walls, have built-in damp courses.

With suspended floors where there is a crawl space underneath, much can be done to cut down the heat loss by lining the underside of the floors with rolls of paper-backed glass fibre or expanded polystyrene sandwiched in building paper.

Care must be taken not to mask the natural ventilation necessary to prevent dry rot or other damage to woodwork. In a room where a carpet is not completely fitted, excessive draughts and air changes often occur through shrinkage between the skirting board and the floor. This can easily be remedied by nailing a wooden fillet to the floor close up against the skirting.

Double glazing

The main advantages of double glazing are considerable reductions in heat loss, draught, and external noise.

Factory-made double glazing units are produced for new houses or conversions and they are available in most present day window sizes. Sometimes reglazing can be as cheap as fitting a system based on screw-on inner frames. Visually, sealed units are almost indistinguishable from a single sheet of glass, and the air space between the two panes is hermetically sealed to prevent misting.

The savings on the fuel bill of a three-bedroomed house after installing double glazing could amount to something like 5%. Professionally fitted double glazing units cost about three times the cost of do-it-yourself methods; the latter – for the whole house –can often be recovered in about eight to ten years.

The important thing to note about double glazing, whether with a factory-made unit or with one of the do-it-yourself systems, is that air from the room must be prevented from entering between the panes. If humid air from the room gets between the panes there will be heavy condensation. The air gap between the panes must be at least 3mm; anything less gives virtually no heat saving. The ideal gap is between 12mm and 20mm. Anything more than this is hardly worth while, except for improving sound insulation.

For draughtproofing, see the section on Being a handyman, p58.

Ventilation

Houses and people need ventilation and there must be enough air for gas and solid fuel heaters to burn safely.

Air bricks with 'hit-and-miss' ventilators are very practical, as they make changes of air possible even in store-rooms and other places that are seldom used. Two air bricks in opposite walls are best; if this is not possible, though, they should be fitted high up and low down in the same wall. Bathrooms and separate WCs often need extra ventilation, which can be supplied by extractor fans; mechanical air-changing in bathrooms without opening windows is generally obligatory. When you install a fan, follow the manufacturer's instructions scrupulously concerning its size since this determines the amount of air it will extract. Fans built into walls are generally more efficient than those set into window panes, but the latter type (such as near a tumble drier's exhaust) can often do the job and are certainly better than nothing.

Unused chimneys should be sealed to cut down heat loss by blocking up the fireplace opening and fitting a ventilation cap at the top of the stack. A ventilation grille, either in the chimney breast or in the material blocking the fireplace, must be installed to allow air movement; this prevents the build up of condensation in the chimney.

Condensation

Lack of adequate ventilation also leads to condensation problems, though these are considerably less likely to occur in a house which is well heated, well insulated, and well ventilated as described above. It tends to be particularly bad in kitchens, bathrooms, and laundries. The harder and glossier a surface, the more likely water vapour is to condense on it, and, if this is not mopped up or absorbed, a very unpleasant mould growth (mildew) can appear. For information on how to cope with condensation and mildew, see p73.

Humidifiers

Humidifiers may be electrically operated or take the form of water troughs hanging over radiators or in other convenient places. They are designed to put back some of the moisture taken out of the air by the heating systems installed, and are sometimes necessary in thatched roof buildings, old timber framed buildings, and where antique furniture and musical instruments are kept.

If the heating system has been properly designed, humidifiers should not be necessary because a correct balance of warmth and moisture can be achieved by heating controls. A simple device called a hygrometer (usually combined with a thermometer) will allow you to check on the correct levels.

Being a Handyman
Draughtproofing

Although no room should be airtight (particularly where there is a fire or boiler, which needs air to burn properly) it is worth draughtproofing doors and windows; a lot of heat can be wasted through even narrow cracks. Gaps between floorboards can also be stopped up. Do not seal up air bricks, however. If filling in a disused fireplace, leave a few holes to keep the chimney ventilated.

Doors

Sometimes draughts enter through a loose letter-box; this may be cured by tightening the spring on the flap or gluing on a pair of small magnets to hold it closed.

Self-adhesive foam strips are easy to put round doors. Warm slightly, cut to length and press on to the sides and top of the frame (cleaned) against which the door closes. Do not stretch. For wider gaps, rubber or plastic tubing can be tacked on; a more substantial version is housed in a metal channel to screw on. Very durable are springy metal or plastic strips, V-shaped, to tack or glue on. Some systems can be used even on sliding doors or sash windows; some can be painted to match the woodwork – check when you buy.

If the draught is entering below a door, a wooden weatherboard can be screwed on outside (in the case of an outer door) or a draught excluder fitted inside. The simplest excluder consists of a plastic strip to stick or tack along the bottom of the door, with a resilient flap of foam, felt or bristle hanging down. Bristle will adjust itself to an uneven threshold and is suitable for sliding doors. If the floor is carpeted, it will be necessary to get an excluder with a spring in it which will raise the flap as the door opens, so that it can pass over the carpet. Another alternative is to screw to the threshold (if it is level) a metal strip with a resilient insert, but this can cause people to trip, and impede wheeled things like tea-trolleys.

Windows

Wood casements are dealt with like doors (apply draughtstripping at the bottom as well as round the sides and top). For metal ones, special snap-on metal strips are available. Before fitting them, rub off any rust and apply anti-rust paint.

If draughts are coming in through gaps between a window (or door) frame and the masonry, or where pipes enter the building, fill these with a resilient mastic which can later be painted.

Floorboards

Gaps can be filled with string or even shredded newspaper mashed in boiling water with wallpaper adhesive. This will set hard and can then be stained to match the boards; alternatively, you can mix stain in with the water. There are plenty of branded fillers suitable: resilient ones will do better than those which shrink as they harden. If gaps are very wide, hammer in thin strips of softwood, coated with adhesive, then smooth down with a Surform or similar tool. If the whole floor is gappy, it can be covered with roofing felt or even newspapers if it is carpeted; or with sheets of thin plywood or sealed hardboard if it is not, provided that access to the underfloor will not be needed later.

If there is a crack between the floor and the skirting board, buy quarter-round moulding and nail this to the floor. Stop up any remaining gap with filler, then paint to match the skirting.

Roof Insulation

Pour granular vermiculite between the joists or roll out fibre matting between them. The granules are easier to put down and will fill awkwardly shaped spaces, but are more trouble to take up should the need ever arise. If you use glass fibre, cut it to fit the spaces (do not put it over the joists) and wear gloves and a face mask when handling it. Do not insulate below the water tank, and remember to lag any pipes in the attic so that they do not freeze.

Wall Insulation

If doing this yourself, line the inside of the walls with insulating boards, polystyrene panels, boards backed with glass fibre or, easiest of all though not so effective, tiles or sheeting of polystyrene foam. In sheet form, this is applied just like wallpaper except that joins should overlap and then be cut with a razor-sharp craft knife so that, when the trimmings are removed, there is a perfect join. The backs of tiles should be coated all over with adhesive. Do not dab adhesive on as this leaves an airspace which can lead to an uncontrollable blaze if a fire starts. Polystyrene can be emulsion-painted or papered over. As it dents easily, an embossed or

patterned paper is desirable in order to camouflage any dents.

Weatherboarding or cladding on the exterior can help to keep an exposed wall warmer. Damp walls are, of course, cold walls: for damp-proofing see p56 and below.

Double-glazing of Windows

There are many do-it-yourself kits available at varying prices: compare the instruction sheets and you will soon see which are easiest and which involve fewest tools. The costly part is the glass itself. Where appearance is of secondary importance, transparent plastic will be both cheaper and simpler to use; it will not shatter, is light in weight, and is excellent for larger windows. Plastic can also be put up very easily with double-sided adhesive tape where a fully sealed effect is wanted.

Double glazing is sometimes better applied to the outside rather than the inside of the window but not all kits are suitable for this. For sash or other vertical windows there are sliding systems which go up and down rather than to and fro. On the whole, sliding systems are easier to put up; hinged ones need more care plus an existing frame with space to take their hinges, but they do give a closer seal.

Lagging a Hot-water System

Padded jackets are sold to fasten round cylinders. Square tanks can be insulated and pipes lagged as described on p70. There will still be a little warmth escaping – enough for an airing cupboard – but a very substantial saving on fuel bills should be achieved by the insulation. In some situations it may be easier to box round a hot tank and pour in granular vermiculite to fill the space.
Note In some circumstances, local authority grants towards the cost of installing heat- or sound-insulation may be available.

Damp-proofing

Few homes in the UK are immune from damp. Rain may penetrate either because of some defect in the structure or because brickwork is porous. (For damp caused by condensation see pp58 and 73.)

Defective gutters, etc

If the damp marks are fairly high on a wall or ceiling, look outside to see whether the cause is a leak from a cracked gutter, downpipe or flashing (the metal strips that seal joins between chimney and roof, adjacent roofs, etc). Look also for blockages, loose joints, and rust holes through which rain water may be trickling, and inspect flat roofs and bays to see whether their rain outlets have got blocked. Repairing these fittings is not difficult provided you can get at them readily, and do-it-yourself shops sell a variety of products for the purpose, ie water-proof fillers, tapes, etc. Replacing broken tiles and skylights is usually a job for the professional because clambering about on a roof can be dangerous.

Damp chimneys

If the damp marks occur on a wall behind which a chimney runs, they may be caused by wet in the flue. If it is not in use and the fireplace has been boarded up, drill holes in the board or put a ventilating panel in it to allow air to circulate inside. A builder can cap a disused chimney pot to keep rain out, and can repair defective mortar in the brickwork of a chimney stack. Flues from boilers sometimes suffer from condensation: curing this by means of a lining is also a job for a professional.

Damp around windows or doors

A resilient mastic can be used to fill any gaps around frames. Water coming in under a door may call for a new threshold or a weatherboard (see Draughtproofing p58). If the damp marks are below a window-sill, it may be that the drip groove on the underside of the sill has got blocked: its purpose is to prevent rain running back to the wall.

Defective damp course

The damp marks resulting from this will be seen on the lower part of the wall. Most walls have a narrow layer of waterproof material a little way up from the ground, visible as a grey or black line. This stops damp rising up the masonry, but if anything absorbent covers the wall and its damp course, this can provide a bypass through which wet may travel. If earth has been heaped up against the damp course, shovel it away. If rendering has been applied over it, chip it off. Sometimes water from an open gulley may splash up above the damp course. This may be deflected by adding a 'shoe' (an angled section) to the bottom of the down-pipe. Where no damp course exists, it may be possible to obtain from your local authority a grant towards the cost of having one put in.

Defective masonry

Crumbling bricks, gaps in mortar between bricks, and cracks in rendering all provide openings for rainwater to penetrate. Repairs should be carried out as soon as possible.

Porous brickwork, etc

This can be remedied by painting waterproofing liquid on the exterior of the wall. Rendering, masonry paints or liquid plastic coatings all provide a waterproof film, too – provided they are well applied (otherwise, rain penetrating through cracks will merely be trapped behind them). There are special coatings for deteriorated roofs, whether flat, corrugated, tiled or with slates.

Sometimes it is not easy to tackle the wall outside, in which case coatings or linings for the inside are worth considering. But these are only a second-best since the masonry will remain wet (and therefore cold).

As with other building materials, relevant details can be obtained by writing to your nearest Building Centre whose address will be in the telephone directory.

If in doubt whether damp on walls or floors is coming from outside or is condensation from indoors, tape a piece of plastic, glass or foil to the surface and later take it up to see on which side damp has collected.

CARE AND MAINTENANCE OF THE HOME

Included, under the general description of house-cleaning, must be understood, turning out all the nooks and corners of drawers, cupboards, lumber-rooms, lofts, &c., with a view of getting rid of all unnecessary articles which only create dirt and attract vermin.

Care and maintenance of your home is largely a matter of common sense. A house and its contents which are kept really clean and in good repair will function at maximum efficiency. This chapter sets out to show how this can be achieved.

Housework

Routine Housework

With more people out at work, and housework cut to a bare minimum, it helps to establish a daily routine, ie 'Wash up, make the beds, tidy bathroom, etc', and, ideally, a specific order of work within each particular room. Once jobs become systematic, they tend to take less time. Regular cleaning is also easier and quicker than an occasional 'blitz'.

Once a routine is established, try to complete jobs at a comfortable speed; then you can relax with a clear conscience.

The time at which various jobs are done must depend on family circumstances. But whatever time is chosen, housework should be planned for ease.

Organizing the housework

Whatever basic plan is chosen, routine housework can be divided into two kinds; *daily care* and *thorough cleaning*. Daily care is particularly important for rooms such as a hall, living-room, cloakroom and bathroom, which are likely to be seen by chance callers. This will be achieved more

easily if all the members of a family are encouraged to tidy up after themselves.

How often to do thorough cleaning depends very much on how often a room is used and by whom, the cleanliness of the atmosphere, and whether or not there are open fires. Particular attention should always be paid to bathroom, lavatory, and kitchen.

In the bathroom, daily, wipe around the basin, bath, cistern handle, and toilet seat, check the towels, tidy away any toiletries which have been left out, and clean the floor or vacuum the carpet. A quick and easy way to keep the inside of the lavatory pan clean is to sprinkle bleach or one of the proprietary powders around the bowl last thing at night and then flush it away in the morning. Otherwise, brush out the inside as often as is necessary. For more thorough cleaning, dust or wipe down the walls, clean the basin (an old toothbrush is useful to clean around taps and overflow), bath, and lavatory; wash handles, towel-rails, and other fittings, empty any waste bins, replace towels, wipe window frames, clean windows, if necessary, and clean the floor or vacuum the carpet.

Daily care in the kitchen should include wiping over work surfaces, top of cooker hob, and cupboard doors; leaving sink and draining boards clean after washing up, and mopping up any food spills or splashes from the floor. Cooker and refrigerator often need particular attention (see the chapter on Kitchen Equipment). Defrost the latter when necessary (if this is not done automatically) and wash it out with a solution of bicarbonate of soda (see the manufacturer's instructions on maintenance). Cupboards should be kept tidy and clean, walls wiped down to remove grease splashes, windows washed, and floors thoroughly cleaned. Upholstery should be regularly brushed or vacuum-cleaned, using the special tool for getting right into corners and crevices.

Main cleaning jobs

These are listed below together with hints on how they can best be done. (For the actual *cleaning materials* see the chapter on Care of Textiles and Hard Surfaces.)

Cleaning floors

Regular vacuuming, or sweeping with a stiff brush or carpet sweeper, will prolong the life of a carpet. As sweeping with a brush causes dust to fly, it should be done before dusting. When giving a room a thorough cleaning, it may help to pull all the furniture into the centre and then vacuum the edges of the carpet. If necessary, use special attachments on the cleaner to get right into the corners, close to the skirting-boards, or right under and close to furniture which cannot be moved. On stairs, the use of a stiff brush may be easier, but remember to work from the top downwards and to dust after sweeping. Spots and stains should be dealt with as soon as possible (see the section on Removing Stains, pp90–92).

Hard floors will need regular sweeping with a soft brush to remove abrasive dust or grit. If they are to be mopped or sealed, try to choose a time when the floor can be left to dry thoroughly. If possible, remove all the furniture, or at least push it to one side of the room so that a large area can be cleaned at once. Sweep up any loose dust first. Work towards an exit, or otherwise you may get marooned on a small patch of dry floor. The use of long-handled squeeze mops and detergents which do not need rinsing make washing a floor a quick and easy job.

Cleaning windows

Many people, although they clean the inside of windows themselves, prefer to employ someone else to do the outside. But even inside, when cleaning high windows, particular attention must be paid to safety. Do not balance on a chair or stool but use a sound ladder which is steadily fixed in place. There are several appliances and cleaning products available to make the job easier. If possible, choose a warm but dull day, as frost, rain or sun make window-cleaning difficult.

Dusting and polishing

Remember to plan this so that dust will not be redeposited. Shut doors and windows and work towards the door. Have an adequate supply of clean dusters, and shake them frequently out of the window. Impregnated cloths and one-stage cleaners and polishes save time. 'Feather' dusters are useful for routine dusting of ornaments and books but for more thorough cleaning it is easier to remove them all, clean them separately, and return them to the shelves when the room is finished. Do not forget to pay particular attention to mirrors, areas around handles, crevices, and awkward ledges. Use any available attachments on your vacuum cleaner to help.

Washing up

It is easier to wash dirty dishes as soon as they have been used. If you cannot wash up immediately, soaking will help.

If washing up by hand, scrape off any excess food and stack the dishes near the sink, keeping all similar items together. Start by washing the glassware, then cups and saucers, side-plates and other lightly soiled crockery, then cutlery and dinner plates, gradually working through to the greasy pots and pans. Change the water when necessary. A draining rack is useful; not only do the things drain and dry safely, but it is more hygienic than using tea-towels. When the washing up is finished, do not forget to wipe over work surfaces and to clean the sink and washing-up bowl, if used, inside and out. Rinse out brushes, dishcloths, and tea-towels, and spread them out to dry. Dishcloths need occasional soaking in a solution of household bleach (following manufacturer's instructions about concentration); alternatively, use disposable dishcloths.

Washing up using a dishwasher is covered in the chapter on Kitchen Equipment.

Shoe cleaning

Some of the materials used to make shoe uppers only need wiping over with a damp cloth, but leather shoes need to be protected with regular polishing. Proprietary polishes are quick and easy to use and the coloured ones also help to hide scuff marks.

Damp shoes should be packed with newspaper and allowed to dry slowly, as drying too quickly makes them brittle, and tends to crack the leather. If they are caked with mud, wash it off with a little warm water and a soft brush and then allow to dry before applying polish. Buffing can be done with a soft cloth or brush. Pigskin and suede should be regularly brushed and cleaned with brushes and cleaners specially designed for them. For more information on the care and cleaning of leather, see p85.

Lighting a fire

The actual method of lighting will depend on the type of fire and the fuel being used. Proprietary fire-lighter blocks or gas pokers are probably the quickest way, but crumpled newspapers and wood chips can be equally successful if laid carefully. Clear out any old ashes from the grate to ensure a good draught. When the fire has been lit, brush up any coal dust and wipe any dirty marks.

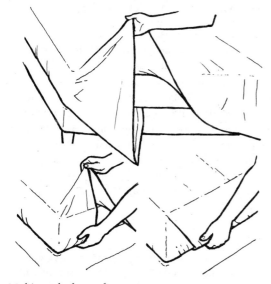

Making a bed: envelope corners

Making beds

Beds should be allowed to air before they are made each morning. Throw back the bedclothes and open a window on getting up. If possible, pull the bed away from furniture or walls so that bed-making is easier.

An underblanket provides additional warmth as well as protection for the mattress. Straighten this and the bottom sheet before replacing the top covers. When tucking in, use envelope corners. This should secure the bedclothes for even the most restless sleeper. Ideally, both sheets, or sheet and quilt cover, should be changed once a week.

The use of continental quilts (duvets) makes bed-making very much faster and easier.

Seasonal Tasks

Not many people have time for spring-cleaning nowadays and the very word may be thought old-fashioned; certainly with modern cleaning aids and equipment a drastic upheaval should not be necessary. However, there are some extra jobs which ought to be done at least once a year, and spring may well be the most suitable time to do them.

If solid fuel fires are used, have the chimneys swept when they are no longer required, and then walls, ceiling, and paintwork can be cleaned afterwards. Any necessary redecoration can also be attended to.

Cupboards and drawers should be turned out once a year; this is particularly important for medicine cupboards. Before putting anything back in place, clean and re-cover the shelves.

Carpets should be cleaned with a proprietary carpet shampoo at least once a year, preferably when the weather is warm and dry so that they will dry quickly. Shampoo the worn and dirtier parts first, then cover the whole area; this leaves a more even finish. Loose carpets should also be turned round regularly to even the wear. If they are fitted, the furniture can be rearranged, or extra rugs provided in areas where the traffic is heaviest. Stair carpets should be moved so that the carpet which covered the tread covers the riser. Upholstery should be shampooed or covers removed and washed as necessary. Clean with one of the proprietary upholstery shampoos, following the manufacturer's instructions, but always do a test area first to make sure that the fabric is suitable for the cleanser. Shampoo headrest area, arms, and projecting areas first. Treat stains as soon as possible (see p90). Curtains should be taken down for cleaning. As it gets warmer, winter clothing, including sports clothing, and any extra bedding put on for winter should also be cleaned and then stored carefully. Protect woollen items from moths by using moth crystals (see p74). For care of electric blankets, see p67.

In the spring, inspect everything you can think of; replace any picture wires that may have begun to fray, renew all electrical flexes that are at all worn, test handrails and bannisters, not forgetting external balconies or stairs which may have been weakened during the winter months; make sure all fire appliances are serviceable. Examine storage tanks and drip trays, and check the gutters and downpipes which should have been cleaned out at the beginning of winter. Try out sash windows to see that their cords are intact. Drains should be rodded through once a year, chimneys swept, boilers serviced, and any central heating system overhauled (see Servicing pp75–76). Then, make a list of all that has been done, carefully documented with dates, costs and addresses of service tradesmen and organizations; you will find it a great help as a check-list in the following years.

Do not let faults noticed throughout the year go unchecked. A gutter blocked with leaves may take only fifteen minutes to clear and cost you nothing; left as it is it can do great damage to the wall beneath it, resulting in a need for costly repairs, both to the external brickwork and to internal decoration. One loose or missing roof tile can bring down a ceiling overnight as the result of a heavy downpour.

Paint is a very good preservative; softwood windows and doors need cleaning down and repainting externally every three to five years. Hardwoods should be oiled annually, or, if painted, treated in the same way as softwoods. Metalwork should be rubbed down, treated, and repainted as soon as any signs of rust appear. Cracks should be investigated, the reasons for them sought and corrected, and they should then be repaired. Painted external walls should be repainted every five to seven years. Some people favour the longer-lasting spray painting.

Before going away on holiday, ensure that equipment, clothing, passports, and travel papers are in order, gradually run down stocks of fresh food in the kitchen, and give it a thorough clean. Empty and then turn off the refrigerator, and leave the door ajar. Before leaving, unless you have a freezer, turn off the gas and electricity and, especially in winter, turn off the water supply, and drain the tank and pipes.

Household Help

If you decide to employ someone else to help with the housework, it is important, for maximum benefit, that his or her time and work plan is well organized. Decide which jobs are to be done on each visit. The helper could, for instance, be responsible for the thorough cleaning of the various rooms in rotation while you cope with the daily tidying up. Helpers need to know exactly what is expected of them and must be given the right tools and equipment for the work. (See also the chapter on Help in the Home.)

Equipment and Materials

Housework is also made easier by carefully chosen equipment, well looked after. This is just as important for small items such as brushes or dusters as it is for large ones. Keep an eye on stocks of cleaning materials, too. Collect everything you will need before starting, thus avoiding unnecessary trips to and from the store cupboard. The items most often used, such as dusters, polishes, a mop, dustpan and brush, can be kept in a bucket, basket or even a cardboard carton so that they can easily be carried about from room to room and are readily available when needed.

Brushes

Brushes are essential tools, and are always a good standby when electrical appliances are not functioning or are not available.

Sweeping brushes: A medium stiff long-handled sweeping brush is suitable as a yard or path brush, and does not wear out as easily as a soft brush. A stiff brush is also suitable for carpets.

The head of sweeping brushes should always be well secured. If it is not, wind some electrical insulating tape around the handle until it screws in firmly. Or you can drill a small hole through the brush head in the middle of the hole where the handle fits, through into the bristles, fit the handle and secure it with a small screw.

Medium and soft hand brushes are also obtainable for more intricate jobs.

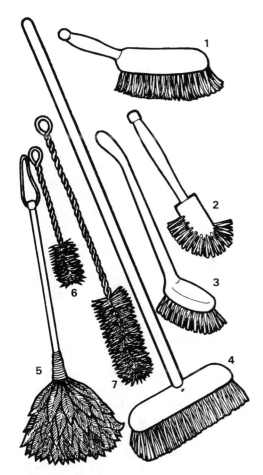

Household brushes: **1** *hand brush;* **2** *lavatory brush (Turk's head);* **3** *lavatory brush;* **4** *long-handled sweeping brush;* **5** *feather duster;* **6** *bottle brush;* **7** *flue brush*

Lavatory brushes: These will have either a curved handle or be of the 'Turk's head' type; both are ideal for brushing round the bend and under the lipped ledge.

Venetian blind brushes: These are very soft and save time; they also prevent grazed hands on the laths of the blind.

Shoe brushes: You need at least four of these, two for black and two for brown; one in each set should be fairly stiff for applying the polish and the other two should be soft to give a good shine. A duster should be used to finish off the shoes. You may also need a suede brush, with a soft metal brush part. When using this, remember to brush with even strokes, all in the same direction.

Flue brushes: Before you purchase, try to estimate how far the brush has to travel through the flues and the approximate width of the flue, so that you do not buy the wrong size.

Cobweb brushes: A feather duster with a longish handle is useful for reaching all heights in the house; it can also be used for dusting ledges.

Bottle brushes: Stubborn sediment in bottles which are intended for re-use can easily be removed with a wire-handled bottle brush. The wire in which the bristles are secured can be bent to get into awkward parts of the bottle.

Care and maintenance

A brush head should be washed fairly frequently in warm water to which a little washing-up liquid has been added. It should then be rinsed well, and dried; do this by hanging it up to drip dry. The bristles then go back into the original shape. Give the handle a wipe over to keep it clean. Never stand or lay a brush on its bristle when not in use, as this distorts the bristles.

A small rack, made and secured to a convenient wall with clips, is useful to put brushes in; alternatively drill a small hole in the handles and hang them up with string on a peg. Stand your sweeping brush upside-down, bristles upwards.

Vacuum cleaners

Although they are called vacuum cleaners, the principle on which they work is suction power. *Cylinder* models, which normally have the more powerful motors (400–700W), rely almost entirely on suction for their cleaning. Some models have the hose fitted to the top on a swivel, which makes it easy to get round the room without moving the cleaner. *Upright* cleaners usually run on 250–500W motor but have revolving brushes and often beaters as well which help to loosen and sweep up ingrained dirt – useful for large areas of carpet. But even the most powerful vacuum cleaner consumes only between half and three-quarters of a unit of electricity per hour; ie it can be used continuously for two hours for little more than one unit.

All the dirt and debris are collected in a dust bag. Uprights have a fabric or plastic outer case and almost all cleaners have a lining of porous paper composition allowing clean air to filter back into the room (the bag would burst otherwise), but dense enough to retain the dirt and dust. These bags may be disposed of when full or, in some cases, reused a few times before final disposal. Some cylinder models have useful audible or visual indicators which show when the bag is full.

When buying, one should try a selection of vacuum cleaners in the shop to see whether they are right for your height and comfortable to hold and handle. If your home has a high proportion of carpets to other floor surfaces, an upright cleaner with its integral beaters and brushes may be the wisest choice, but for homes with a variety of floor coverings such as wood blocks, tiles, and vinyls as well as carpeting, a cylinder cleaner with its wide assortment of attachments for various jobs may be the best.

Smaller versions are available for small flats, but their motors will not tackle as much as the full-size machines without eventually feeling the strain.

Small hand-held cleaners and compact cleaners are suitable for dusting and light daily cleaning jobs. They are also ideal for cleaning stairs and cupboards, car interiors, and caravans.

Most makes also offer useful refinements that may help one to decide whether it is time to replace an old model with something more efficient, with greater suction power. These include self-sealing dust bags for easy disposal, easy-release flexes on upright cleaners, self-retracting flexes on cylinder cleaners, adjustable suction power, cylinder cleaner nozzles that get right to the edge of the carpet with retractable brushes for hard floors, and reverse 'blowing' action on cylinder cleaners, obtained by fixing the hose at the opposite end of the cleaner, and used to aerate pillows and quilts, and for spraying liquids. Combined vacuum cleaners and carpet shampooers are also available.

All cleaners are fitted with a length of tough flex and can be connected to any 13 or 15 amp power socket. Almost all models are 'double-insulated' which means they do not need an earth wire as all potentially live parts are shielded from the user. When connecting the flex to a 3 pin plug, the live and neutral terminals only should be used. Make sure that the correct size of fuse is used (pp68–69).

Floor cleaners

Electric floor polishers: These are heavier than vacuum cleaners, as the weight of the machine is needed to provide sufficient pressure to remove dirt. A polisher has two or three rotary heads driven by a motor immediately above them. The handle, which in some cases can telescope for easy storage, carries the flex and the controls. In most models the action of moving the handle switches the machine on and off, and it is impossible for the machine to operate without this control. Depending on the purpose, sets of stiff-bristled brushes, softer brushes or polishing 'buffers' can be clipped on the rotary heads. Some models can also be used for scrubbing floors and shampooing carpets.

Scrubbing: If the polisher is also suitable for scrubbing floors, the floor should first be brushed to remove loose dirt. Then a recommended cleaning agent, mixed with water, should be spread or sprayed lightly on the floor. The machine, with the stiff brushes fitted, is guided over sections of the floor, each section being rinsed and dried by hand or sponge-mopped as the work proceeds.

Polishing: This is carried out by first spreading the polish over the floor and then guiding the machine slowly over the surface using the recommended brushes. The polish may be spread by hand or with a special set of brushes which fit into the machine. The polisher has an optional polish dispenser that fits at the back of the machine and releases liquid polish as required. Finally, the buffers can be used for a high-gloss shine.

Shampooing: Carpet shampooers have a detergent container fixed to the handle. The shampoo is fed to the brushes on to the carpet through a small tube and the amount controlled by a separate lever. Instructions for use of the shampoo should be followed, but usually a small square of the carpet should be completed at a time, working systematically over the whole surface. The carpet should be allowed to dry and then vacuumed to remove the loosened soil, and to raise the pile.

Other Electrical Equipment

Electric blankets

Overblankets: These can be used over the top sheet with some light covering on them; this saves bed-covering costs and laundry. The unwired sides and bottom of the overblanket can be tucked in, and it can safely be left on all night, since it has sophisticated safety devices to prevent over-heating. It has a variable thermostatic heat control so that the temperature of the blanket automatically adjusts itself to remain constant, whatever the temperature of the room.

Double overblankets are available with separate controls for each side of the bed. This is important, as two people may well want different temperatures. (Women tend to need more warmth than men.) Another advantage of an all-night overblanket compared with a pre-warming underblanket is that it can usually be washed in a machine.

Underblankets: An electric preheating underblanket is placed on the mattress under the bottom sheet. Although it, too, has a control which regulates the amount of heat, it is only intended to warm the bed. It should be turned on about an hour before bedtime. It takes about 30–60 minutes to heat up, as a

rule, and it must be switched off before the user gets into bed.

There is also a heavy-duty version of the underblanket, designed to be left on all night and all day, if required. This operates on a very low voltage, through a transformer for maximum safety. A special low wattage, low voltage blanket intended primarily for use by elderly people is also available.

Both versions are placed on top of the mattress, under the bottom sheet. As it is important that they should not be creased, they should be tied securely to the mattress with the tapes provided.

Servicing

Electric blankets should be serviced at least once every three years, or as advised by the manufacturer, and servicing should be carried out by the manufacturer. Advice about how, when, and where to send the blanket for service may be found in the manufacturer's instruction book or on a label attached to the blanket.

It is wise to have servicing done at the end of the cold season, to avoid the inevitable autumn rush.

To keep the blanket in good condition between services, the following points should be observed:
1) Never plug an electric blanket into a light fitting, as it may be switched on unintentionally. Similarly, do not fit it to an adaptor which has another appliance plugged in.
2) Never use the blanket if it is wet, and never switch it on to help it dry out either. Let it dry naturally.
3) Never use an underblanket as an overblanket, or an overblanket as an underblanket.
4) Never use a blanket folded or creased, and do not stick pins into the fabric.
5) Store blankets rolled, or folded with the minimum of creases, and keep in a dry place – or leave flat on a spare bed.
6) Check frequently for frayed edges, loose connections at the plug controls, fabric wear, scorch marks, damage to the flexible cord, and displaced heating wires. To check the wires, hold the blanket up to the light – the wires should be evenly spaced and should not touch each other. If there are signs of wear or damage, return the blanket to the manufacturer.

Time switches

Many electrical appliances can be given a delayed starting time by the use of a time switch. This is a simple device by which the plug to the appliance goes into the socket on the time switch which, in turn, goes into the wall socket. It can be set to switch on at a future given moment up to several hours ahead. Thus a television set can be made to switch on at the start of a specific programme or an electric blanket can be switched on shortly before bed-time.

Some models offer more than one on and off period in the 24-hour cycle. All must only be used where there is no risk of an appliance coming on automatically in circumstances that could cause an accident, eg an electric fire switching on when clothes or furniture have been placed directly in front of it.

Emergencies

Electrical

Blown fuses

If only one appliance or light suddenly stops working, perhaps with a bang or a flash, the likelihood is that its fuse (in the plug; or in the connecting unit on the wall if it has no plug and socket) has blown. But if several appliances stop simultaneously, an entire circuit must have gone, and a main fuse (in the fuse-box) will have to be replaced.

Causes

The first step, in either case, is to trace the cause of the trouble if you can; otherwise the replacement fuse will blow just as the original one did.

If it is only a plug fuse that has blown, the cause is likely to be in the appliance concerned, or in its flex or in the plug itself. A fault in any of these may have caused a short circuit or overheating. Disconnect the appliance and check whether plug and appliance are well connected to the flex, with no loose or fraying wires. Feel for hot spots and look for scorch marks. You may notice a smell of burnt plastic. If you cannot put matters right (for instance,

by reattaching the flex more securely) do not use the appliance again until an electrician has repaired it. In the case of a motor-driven appliance, such as an electric drill or mixer, an overload could be the cause; this is easily remedied.

If a main fuse has blown, the most likely cause is an overload of the circuit concerned – too many high-wattage appliances in use on one circuit or a heater plugged into a lighting circuit. The fuse wire will probably not have vanished completely but will merely have a gap in the middle. Disconnect at least one appliance before replacing the fuse.

If this does not solve the problem and the fuse blows again, with the wire vanishing completely, the cause may be more serious: possibly a fault in the house-wiring system, especially in homes with wiring over twenty years old, where fuses often blow or fires start because of hidden cables that have deteriorated with age. This situation should be dealt with by an electrician; on no account attempt to stop the fuse blowing repeatedly by putting thicker wire into the fuse-carrier.

Try to find an electrician who belongs to either the Electrical Contractors Association or the National Inspection Council for Electrical Installation Contracting.

Sometimes a main fuse blows when it is merely an appliance that is at fault (as described above); this can occur when there is no fuse in the plug (old round-pinned ones do not have fuses in them) or if for some reason that fuse fails to function. If the fuse blew just when you turned on a certain appliance or light, this may indicate which one has the fault; otherwise, after replacing the fuse, switch on one appliance at a time until the fuse blows again, thus pin-pointing the offender.

Some adaptors too, have fuses in them, like plug fuses. These are apt to blow, not only for the same reasons as plug fuses, but also if you are trying to use too big a load, like running two or three high-wattage heaters simultaneously by means of an adaptor.

Replacing plug fuses

To replace a fuse in a plug, disconnect it and then unscrew the cover. Prise out the old cartridge fuse and press a new one into its place. While you have the plug open, check that the wires inside are correctly and securely attached. Be sure the new cartridge is of the correct amperage; either 13A (brown) for appliances of 720–3000W, or 3A (red) for appliances under 720W, unless they have a higher initial surge of electricity when newly switched on (such as colour TV and motor-driven appliances), when they need 13A. All modern appliances carry metal plates stating their wattage.

Fuses in adaptors and in wall connectors are equally easy to replace. Wall connectors (instead of plugs and sockets) are normally used for wall clocks, fixed heaters, immersion heaters, and cookers, and the cartridge fuse inside them may be as much as 45A in the case of a high-wattage appliance like a cooker.

A rule of thumb method of ascertaining the correct size of fuse for any electrical appliance is as follows:

Divide the voltage of electricity, normally 250 volts, into the wattage of your appliance (which can usually be found on the plate bearing other details); ie for a 750W appliance, 750 ÷ 250 = 3 Amps: this is the size of fuse. Remember that the fuse is the safety valve and blows when a fault occurs.

Replacing main fuses

Start by turning off the main switch and also all appliances on the affected circuit.

Replacing a main fuse in the fuse-box involves first determining which fuse in the row of several has blown. Some main fuses are in cartridge form (like plug fuses but larger); others consist of a wire stretched along a ceramic holder.

Cartridge fuses are coloured and vary in size, which aids identification; they are usually placed in order of amperage, with the largest near the main switch. Here are the ones most commonly found:

5A	white	lighting circuits
15A, 20A	blue, yellow	immersion heater
30A	red	power circuits (or cooker)
45A, 60A	green, purple	large cooker

If still in doubt which fuse has blown (there may well be more than one 5A or 30A fuse in the box if the house has several lighting or power circuits)

you can pull out each cartridge in turn and test it with a gadget called a circuit tester or with a metal-cased torch: if the bulb lights, the fuse is intact. Otherwise, you will simply have to put in a new fuse of the same amperage at random and turn on to see whether you have found the right one.

Identifying a blown fuse of wire presents no problem: it will be broken, or even have vanished almost entirely. Pull out the ceramic holder, cut a length of wire (of the right amperage for the circuit concerned – see list above) to fit it, and insert it where the broken wire ran. Its ends are wound clockwise round two screws which are then tightened – but the wire should not be taut. Finally, turn the electricity on again.

It is worth keeping a permanent record of which circuits are controlled by which fuse.

Circuit breakers

Some houses have these instead of fuse-boxes: instead of a fuse blowing, a switch turns itself off. All that is then required is to push it on again. This is far more convenient and therefore worth acquiring if replacing a fuse-box, which should certainly be done if you have the old cast-iron 'double pole' type, now considered rather dangerous.

Power cuts

When the electricity supply to the entire house fails, as for instance, during a strike, take the following action:

1) Turn off electric fires, iron, boiling-rings, kettle or electric blankets, because when power is restored, their re-starting may not be noticed.
2) Keep the refrigerator closed. Even more important, keep the freezer closed.
3) Remember that electric door bells, burglar alarms, and clocks will not be operating; nor will the electric pump on a central-heating system, auto- timer, and greenhouse controls.

Electric shock

See the chapter on Safety in the Home.

Gas

See the chapter on Safety in the Home.

Water Supply

Extremely hot summers or cold winters may bring problems of water shortage on the one hand, or frozen (and possibly burst) pipes and tanks on the other.

Water shortage

Hardware and do-it-yourself shops sell attachments for rainwater pipes, and for down-pipes carrying away bathwater, by means of which such waste can be saved up in water-butts (preferably lidded) to use for the garden or for house-cleaning. Soapy water does no harm in the garden, provided it does not have bleach or grease in it.

Water can be siphoned out of a bath for house-cleaning or clothes-washing by means of a length of hose.

To reduce water consumption, put into the WC cistern a plastic bag of water fastened with a rubber band (this will cut down the amount used at each flush); and re-employ, as far as possible, water used for boiling vegetables or eggs, and for washing clothes and face.

Frozen pipes

Preventative measures can include providing some heat (even a light bulb) in spots much exposed to cold, draining the cold water system as described below, or lagging pipes and any stopcocks on them. The most vulnerable pipes are those on outside walls, below floors, or in attic, cellar, etc. Bends in pipes are particularly liable to freeze.

Pipe lagging is of two kinds. The bandage-type is wound round spirally and secured with string; the tubular type opens up along its length to slip on to the pipe and is then secured with plastic sticky-tape: it is important to buy a size that exactly fits the pipe. Some lagging materials are waterproof on one side, others can be protected by winding waterproof building-tape round them; this is essential outdoors or in any damp place. Overflow pipes can be temporarily plugged to prevent cold air entering, or fitted with specially made flaps.

Tank lagging helps to keep the water in the whole system above freezing point. Kits are sold to fit various sizes of tank. These may comprise a roll of glass fibre matting, paper-backed, to wind round a tank and tie with string; lay a further piece loose on the lid. Alternatively, sheets of polystyrene board can be used, secured with plastic sticky-tape. In either case, do not insulate below the tank as this would cut off useful warmth rising from the rooms below.

Drains and WC cisterns can be kept from freezing by putting salt in at nightfall.

Unfreezing pipes

If in doubt where the frozen section is, turn on various taps until you find which ones are not running. Check whether any pipes have cracked (see below).

Warmth should then be applied to the pipe wherever convenient; the heat will travel along to the frozen part. Preferably start near a tap, which should be turned on, or other outlet, so that the melting ice can escape.

Warmth could be provided by a fan heater, or hair drier, by a boiling kettle, hot water bottle or hot, wet cloths, by a blowtorch or even a candle.

For a frozen drain-pipe or WC cistern, use salt; this will also melt ice on paths, but must be kept off plants.

If the pipes of an unheated boiler have frozen, do not light the boiler nor turn on hot taps until the ice has thawed.

Burst pipes

As water turns to ice it expands, and sometimes this cracks pipes or forces joints open. If you can spot the damage before the ice melts, you will be in time to prevent a flood.

The first essential is to turn off the supply coming from the cold tank; if water is leaking on to electric fittings or cables, the electricity must be turned off. There may be a stopcock on the pipe leading from the tank to the part of the system that has frozen. Take a large screwdriver when you go up to the attic to look for it, to get some purchase on the handle if it has become stiff through disuse. For X-head cocks a spanner would be even better. If there is no stopcock, you can stop water leaving the tank by plugging the outlet hole – use a broomstick with a cloth on the end.

The best alternative is to stop water entering the tank by tying its ball float to a piece of wood laid across the tank, which closes the intake hole.

Some taps, notably the cold tap at the sink, may get their water direct from the mains and not via the cold tank. To cut off the supply in the pipe serving these, you need to use the main stopcock – usually sited below the sink.

The next step is to get rid of any water left in the pipes if you can, so turn on all taps. If you drain the pipes supplying a boiler or water heater, make sure this is turned off until the water supply is restored.

There are a number of ways to mend splits in pipes, at least until the plumber comes to do a permanent repair. Even rubbing soap into the crack may do the trick, provided you then turn the water on again very gently. Other first-aid measures include petroleum jelly- or paint-soaked rags tied round the pipe, plastic sticky-tape or sticky-plaster, or even hammering the gap together. A more lasting repair can be made with an epoxy adhesive, as used for car body repairs: rub the surface with sandpaper, smear on the resin, bind with a bandage, and wait till set before turning on the water. Epoxy putty is even easier, needing no bandage. Special pipe-mending tapes are sold to bind round split pipes and hoses of all kinds; these are a useful standby to keep in the home.

Emergency plumbing services are apt to be expensive. To find a regular plumber who is well qualified, obtain a list of registered plumbers from the Institute of Plumbing. Incidentally, damage done by burst pipes, including dry rot, can be the subject of a claim under most household insurance policies, whether the burst occurred in the claimant's own home or in a neighbour's; see the chapter on Security of the Home.

Waste-pipes and Drains

To keep drains and waste-pipes from blocking or overflowing, it is important to see that little solid matter or grease goes down them: sink tidies and wastehole strainers are sold for the purpose. So-called disposable paper goods often do not dissolve, while lint from clothes washing and hairs from shampooing are a frequent cause of trouble.

Waste-pipes and WCs

Sometimes obstruction in waste-pipes can be cleared with boiling water and washing soda or the much stronger caustic soda. The crystals are put down the pipe, followed by the hot water, and then left for 30 minutes. Caustic jelly is even more powerful: mix into cold water, pour into the pipe or WC, and leave for 30 minutes. There are proprietary products for unblocking sink outlets which are easier to use than caustic soda but still need care. (Keep caustics away from children.)

Mechanical alternatives include special flexes or steel tapes to insert down the waste-pipe while turning clockwise. The idea is to get the flex past the blockage and then pull it up. A plunger (a flexible cup on a handle) is used to suck the obstruction upwards. The overflow of the sink is plugged with a cloth, the sink partly filled with water, the rim of the plunger cup greased, and placed over the wastehole. Pump up and down. When the water starts to flow away, it means the blockage has shifted. Long-handled plungers are for use in WCs, but be careful not to pump so hard

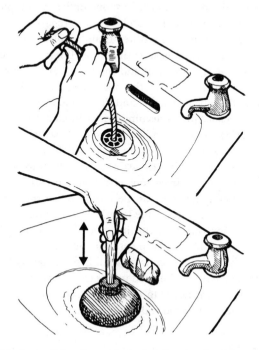

Methods of clearing a blocked sink, using (top) a flexible drain clearer, and (bottom) a plunger

as to break the pan. Forcing the obstruction down, not up, is sometimes achieved by running water through a hose into the waste-pipe; plug the overflow and the wastehole with wet cloths. Tool hire firms have liquid gas appliances to do the same thing; they are more powerful.

For severe blockages it may be necessary to undo the trap below. Place a bucket underneath and put the plug in the wastehole. In the case of a U-trap, use either a screwdriver or wrench to undo its plug (to get at a bath trap, you may need a special bath wrench: tool hire shops have them). If necessary, push a flex or steel tape up each side of the U. Some U-traps are different: they unscrew by means of two nuts at the tops of the U. Bottle traps can be unscrewed by hand. If all else fails, call a plumber.

Drains

Waste water from sinks, gutters, etc may reach the drainage system under the ground via an open gulley, while that from WCs is, of course, enclosed in soil pipes all the way; but in many houses now, all waste goes into one pipe. In either case, all waste water discharges into at least one underground pit on its way to join the public sewer in the road.

The clearing of a blocked drain involves taking the lid off the pit nearest the house; if it is dry, the blockage is between it and the house. If it is not, look for the next pit; if this one is dry, the blockage is in the pipe between it and the previous pit.

Specialist drain-cleaning firms (found in the yellow pages of the telephone directory) use powered rods or pressure jets; so do local councils who may charge you less than these firms. Similar equipment can be rented from tool hire firms, or ordinary drain-cleaning rods can be rented to do the job. These consist of flexible lengths to screw together while inserting and turning clockwise via one of the holes in the dry inspection pit, towards the blockage. A corkscrew or a rubber plunger is attached to the leading end to free the obstruction. It is important never to turn anti-clockwise or you may unscrew a rod and lose it in the pipe.

Fire

See the chapter on Safety in the Home.

Pests

Woodworm

House timbers or furniture peppered with tiny holes have been infested by woodworm, but the insect may no longer be there. You need worry only if there are traces of powdered wood nearby during summer, the time when the grubs burrow their way out after many years' life in the wood. If you live in Surrey and notice large holes up to about 10mm across, you may have a more serious problem – longhorn beetle, which in 1980 had not so far spread to other counties. An insurance policy against woodworm can be taken out before infestation occurs.

For a serious outbreak, free reports can be obtained from several firms who are members of the British Wood Preserving Association. Compare what treatment they propose, their charges, and what guarantees of non-recurrence they offer. The Association will intervene if you have a complaint.

To tackle the trouble yourself is not difficult if the wood concerned is easy to get at. An aerosol will do for small areas. If hard woods are affected, first attach a fine nozzle and inject the fluid in through some of the holes (about 10cm apart). The whole surface should then be coated, including backs, insides and undersides of furniture, staircases or cupboards. If appearance is unimportant, choose a tinted fluid so that you can easily see which areas have been done.

For large areas like attics and floors, hire a spray with a long nozzle and buy 5 litres of fluid for every 20 square metres to be done. Floorboards will have to be lifted to get at joists below, raising about one board in five; any attic insulation will have to be temporarily removed. Lay boards across attic joists to stand on. Put out any fires, cigarettes or bright lights because the vapour is explosive.

Needless to say, adjacent surfaces and electric cables must be shielded, water tanks covered, and care taken not to let any fluid penetrate to ceilings below the joists. Wear plastic gloves and a face mask while spraying, and cover your hair.

Unless the infestation is severe, an attic, unless it is draughty, can be kept free of woodworm by placing Fly-Tox units in it each spring. These release a vapour steadily for months to come.

Mildew

This is usually a consequence of condensation, caused by warm, moist air striking a cold surface. Ordinary bleach or fungicide may get rid of it but it is likely to recur if these conditions continue. Fungicidal paints do not remain immune to attack indefinitely.

To end condensation one can aim to prevent moisture in the air, or disperse it by more ventilation, or keep surfaces warmer. As the usual sources of steam are kitchen and bathroom (even if it is not in these that the mildew occurs), the kettle should be turned off as soon as it boils, outlets from washing and drying appliances plumbed in or ducted to outdoors, cold water run into bath or basin before hot, and so on. Extractor fans in window or wall will make a big difference if correctly sited, though cooker hoods do not solve the problem, while automatic oven door-closers will prevent steam spreading to other rooms. Opening windows even briefly may solve the problem.

Low even heat is better than hot and cold alternating, but do not resort to oil heaters, as these produce a lot of vapour themselves. Walls will be less cold if lined with polystyrene or other insulating material and they will then be less prone to condensation. A reason why upstairs rooms and their contents suffer from mildew is that often the attic above is uninsulated. (The whole subject of insulation is dealt with on pp56–57, and p59.)

Wet Rot

When wood is continually saturated, tiny organisms flourish, gradually eating it away. The wood appears dark, soft, and split, paintwork flakes, and there may be strands of fungus fanning out. Once the cause of the damp has been traced and remedied (see pp59–60), the wood will dry out, and once the rotted wood has been replaced with new, no further trouble should arise.

To protect wood that has to withstand damp, especially outdoors, creosote is often painted on during dry weather. This is cheap and, if made to British Standard 144, is very effective; it does, however need renewal from time to time. Inaccessible parts may be treated by drilling downward-sloping holes and pouring creosote into them. Nearby plants need protecting until the creosote is dry. If the dark colour of creosote is unacceptable, the next best thing is an oil- or spirit-based timber preservative, clear or coloured, though this costs more and does not last so long. Some of these are harmful to birds, pets or plants.

Dry Rot

This, too, infects wood that has become damp and is more destructive than wet rot because it can spread far and fast, even through masonry. Signs of dry rot include crumbling or soft wood, warping or cracks, reddish dust, fungus, a mushroomy smell, white 'wool' or strands, and bulging plaster.

The damp must be cured (see pp59–60) and the affected wood cut out (and burned); also adjacent material of any kind must be cut out to a distance of at least half a metre. Fungicide then has to be applied to this area, and also for 1.5 metres all round it (alternatively, masonry can be sterilized with a blowtorch and painted with bitumen). Replacement wood, too, should be steeped in fungicide.

All this may involve replacing entire joists, replastering walls, and other work beyond an amateur's skill. As with woodworm, quotations should be obtained from several firms that are members of the British Wood Preserving Association.

Insects and Rodents

Electric waste-disposers and even plastic garbage-bags (if sealed) are two good ways to discourage flies and other pests, which are often attracted by food scraps in dustbins. Dustbins can be sprinkled with insecticidal powder. Keeping food (including sugar) covered or in a refrigerator is, of course, essential; so is cleanliness: the grease on cookers or other fitments can attract insects.

Stop up holes at skirtings and where pipes enter, and repair broken airbricks: these gaps provide an entrance for crawling insects and mice. Use blinds to keep flies out when windows or doors are kept open in summer.

If it is a neighbour's dustbin that is bringing flies (or mice) to the area, the Environmental Health Officer of the local council can be asked to see that the nuisance is ended. His advice on your own pest problems, too, will be freely given – even to the point of identifying specimens of insects and perhaps dealing with them or with mice.

Cockroaches, like flies, are disease-carriers. It is not only food that attracts them to kitchens but the warmth. They may live in cracks, on the undersides of tables or behind cookers, crawling out only at night. Regular cleaning will help to get rid of them.

It is better to end the conditions attracting such insects than to use chemicals to kill them, as chemicals are often more harmful to man than insects are. But, if you do resort to these, read what the labels say about covering food, keeping pets away, and other precautions. Some insecticides need continual use, others leave a film which remains effective for weeks or months. There are dispensers to hang up which continually give off an insecticide. Choose a liquid in aerosol form if you want it to penetrate cracks or to coat such things as walls and light fittings; powders may be sprinkled as a band around a floor when dealing with crawling insects, or puffed into heating ducts or under floorboards. If you find a swarm of flies in the attic, suck them up in a vacuum cleaner and then suck some insecticide powder into it.

Here are ways to deal with other pests:

Ants and ant nests: Place insecticide such as *lindane* or *carberyl* on the floor across their usual trail, and along thresholds and window-sills. Paraffin or boiling water can be used to destroy nests under paths.

Carpet beetles: Clear any birds' nests in eaves or attic, as the beetles often live there. Spray carpets and curtains with insecticide or special carpet beetle killer, or use moth crystals.

Clothes moth: Spray moth repellent on textiles. Store blankets and other woollens in sealed plastic bags with moth crystals.

Mites and weevils: Occasionally found in stale flour, dried fruit, etc. Empty, clean, and dry the food cupboard, especially any cracks. Spray a contact insecticide such as *pyrethrum* on walls and floor.

Rats and mice: Effective poisons are Rodine and Alpha-Kil (humane). Chocolate may succeed as mousetrap bait if cheese fails. Report rats to the local council. But the most effective rat and mouse killer, is of course, the domestic cat!

Silverfish: Harmless. Found in cupboards under the sink, etc. Use insecticide.

Spiders: Harmless – in fact, beneficial because they eat flies.

Wasps: A jar with some jam and beer in the bottom will attract, intoxicate, and drown wasps. Use an aerosol insecticide to kill the odd one or two flying around. Some local councils will remove wasps' nests on request. Or use a spoon tied to the end of a long cane to place derris dust in the nest at dusk when the wasps have returned; then cover the entrance to the nest with a large stone so that the wasps are trapped. Take care not to prod the wasps when pouring in the insecticide.

Guarantees and Servicing

Manufacturers' Guarantees

When you buy goods and services, the person selling them to you is usually legally responsible. If you have bought goods or paid for a service on credit, you may be able to look to the firm or organization granting the credit to provide any redress if things go wrong. If you have bought goods which are faulty, you may be able to claim against the manufacturer of the goods under his guarantee, if any. If the faulty goods have caused death or personal injury, or damage to property, you can sue the manufacturer for negligence in the civil courts. But most people will be concerned with getting things put right without going to court.

Manufacturers' guarantees are in addition to the rights a purchaser enjoys under the Sale of Goods Act against the seller; in effect these guarantees involve the manufacturer in a relationship with you which he would not otherwise have.

What guarantees cover

This varies, and the terms are usually printed on a card supplied with the goods. The best guarantees cover all the costs that one might incur if things go wrong: labour charges, transport or postage, and the cost of spare parts. For some goods there may be two guarantees, one from the manufacturer of a television set, for example, and one from the manufacturer of the tube.

The guarantee card

Some manufacturers ask for the guarantee card to be filled in and returned. Usually you will have to fill in the date of purchase; this helps the manufacturer to check whether the goods are still under the guarantee period if you claim. (You should still keep some proof of the date of purchase as you might decide to claim against the seller.) Sometimes guarantee registration cards ask you to return the card within a given period of the date of purchase. Although in theory a manufacturer would be entitled to refuse to meet your claim if you have failed to return the card or took longer to do it, most will in practice honour the guarantee if you can produce some proof of the date of purchase. However, a guarantee is a commitment by a manufacturer, and it is sensible and courteous, therefore, to deal with the guarantee card promptly.

There may be a number of market research questions on the card, asking for example, where you bought the goods, or whether they were a gift; you do not have to answer them.

Claiming under a guarantee

If you have problems with goods bought, you generally have a choice between going back to the seller or to the manufacturer. Claiming against one does not affect your right to claim against the other, but you cannot accept compensation from both.

Whether you decide to claim against the seller or manufacturer often depends on when the fault occurred. If, for example, the goods are found to be defective when you get them home or if they break down very soon afterwards, you can reject them and get your money back from the retailer, or agree to change them for another model of the same thing. Manufacturers, on the other hand, usually only undertake to repair or replace goods if they are faulty –they do not usually refund you.

If you have some use out of the goods before they go wrong, then obviously, you are unlikely to be able to get your money back. But you can claim 'compensation', and a repair or replacement may suit you much better.

Before deciding whether to claim under the guarantee against the manufacturer, it is important to check what costs you would incur – heavy transport charges, for example. But it is often easier to claim under a guarantee than to persuade a retailer to accept his liability under the Sale of Goods Act. Legally, if you have a justifiable claim, the seller is liable to pay the full cost of remedying a fault. This includes the costs of parts, labour, transport, and the cost of supplying substitute goods during the period of repair. But in practice it may be quicker to send the goods back to the manufacturer than to spend time on persuading the seller to acknowledge his liability.

Strictly speaking, the manufacturer's guarantee may also be the only way you can claim against faulty goods if they were given to you, because only the actual purchaser has rights against the seller. But if you can produce a receipt you are not likely to be asked further questions. If the seller has gone out of business, or if you have moved away from his district, a manufacturer's guarantee may be the only way to get compensation.

Most multiple shops honour their responsibilities under the Sale of Goods Act at any of their branches, while gas and electricity boards also normally deal with goods bought from their showrooms in other areas. It is illegal for manufacturers to put terms in their guarantees which give the impression that you have no rights against the seller; for example, 'all conditions or warranties, whether expressed or implied by statute or otherwise, are now excluded'. Before deciding whether you want to make use of the services offered by a manufacturer's guarantee, read the small print carefully.

Servicing

Most household appliances are 'guaranteed' by the

manufacturer for a year. After this, the owner is likely to be responsible for servicing.

There are many kinds of servicing, ranging from regular maintenance calls which are a sensible precaution to avoid breakdown (such as the annual servicing of a central heating installation), or servicing due to a breakdown or fair wear and tear. Manufacturers may do servicing themselves, or they may leave it to be done by retailers and dealers.

Heating

Routine servicing of heating appliances and equipment varies from fuel to fuel. Gas-fired boilers and water heaters should be serviced once a year. The gas boards offer comprehensive regular servicing schemes. Oil-fired equipment also needs annual servicing, mainly to make sure that burners are clean and working properly and that the controls are properly set. Electric water heaters need periodic attention. Storage heaters and immersion heaters in hard water areas may need descaling every two or three years of use.

Cookers

Cookers, apart from oil-fired or solid fuel models, do not need regular servicing, though they obviously need to be cleaned regularly.

Major electrical appliances

Refrigerators and freezers do not need regular servicing, but automatic washing machines, dishwashers, and vacuum cleaners should be serviced annually to keep them in good working order.

Maintenance contracts

Regular checks can be arranged in two ways: a regular annual service visit paid for by a minimum charge for labour plus the cost of any components needing replacement, or a maintenance contract entitling you to a maintenance visit plus labour and replacement of parts for an inclusive fee.

Maintenance contracts are sometimes called service contracts or members' clubs. They are an advantage for people who do not want to face an unexpectedly large bill and who are happier paying for the maintenance contract as a form of insurance. On the other hand, the chances of paying more than the cost of the maintenance contract in repair charges is, on average, low.

Service calls

It is usual for a call-out fee to be charged for a serviceman to come and repair equipment in your home. This is charged before he even looks at the equipment and diagnoses a fault. If you then decide to have the equipment repaired, the cost of any parts replaced and the cost of fitting them will be charged in addition. As call-out fees tend to be very high, it is sensible to check on this and any minimum repair charge before you arrange a visit. Some firms charge a cancellation fee if you cancel your appointment at the last minute and they would also be entitled to charge if they turned up for an appointment and you were not in (though they would be unlikely to do so).

Standard of work

You are entitled to get the standard of work which would be provided by the average serviceman working in that line of business. If the work is not up to standard you can claim part or all of your money back, and if you have not paid you can withhold all or part of the money you owe until the job is done satisfactorily.

If you are not able to resolve a problem with the serviceman, you may need to call in the help of a trade association. Most trade associations try to resolve disputes between their members and the public. Some have Codes of Practice which include a scheme for resolving disputes. If the service is provided by a nationalized industry you can go to the relevant consumer council if you cannot get the problem resolved by the local organization. If the serviceman is not a member of a trade association, your local consumer advice centre or citizens' advice bureau will advise you, and they may approach the serviceman on your behalf. If that does not work you will have to consider taking your case to the county court (see p166) and calling in another expert to check the standard of service and give evidence on your behalf.

CARE OF TEXTILES AND HARD SURFACES

Sheets should be turned " sides to middle " before they are allowed to get very thin. Otherwise, patching, which is uneconomical from the time it consumes, and is unsightly in point of appearance, will have to be resorted to.

Types of Textiles

All fabrics to be found in the home are made from one or more of a few basic types of fibre. Without guidance, it is, however, often impossible to guess from which fibre or fibres any particular item is made.

Natural Fibres

Cotton is widely used for clothes, household textiles, and furnishings, eg cotton velvet, cotton sateen, curtain fabrics, denim, and corduroy. It is sometimes blended with viscose or polyester. Rugs can also be made from cotton. Cotton fabrics can often be recognized by their characteristic smooth, crisp handle. They are absorbent, and usually strong and hard-wearing. Being able to withstand repeated washing at high temperatures, cotton is very suitable for household items such as sheets, quilt covers and pillow-cases, though the 'easy-care' ones are 50% cotton, 50% polyester.

Linen is made from flax and is similar to cotton though a little heavier; fabrics often have slubs (thicker threads) in the yarn. When combined with cotton linen is known as linen union. Linen is used for curtains, upholstery, and loose covers.

Wool is widely used for clothes, furnishings, carpets, rugs, and blankets, mainly because of its softness, springiness, warmth, and bulk. Fabrics made from wool are absorbent, but most can felt and shrink if subjected to too much mechanical action and heat during laundering. There are some machine-washable wools available. Wool does not attract dirt nor does it burn easily. It is often combined with viscose and nylon.

Unless treated, wool is subject to attack by moths. For treatment, see p74.

Silk is used mainly for clothes, although it is also found in furnishings, eg very expensive and hard-wearing Chinese rugs. Natural tweedy-looking silk fabrics, many from India and containing a mixture of other fibres, are also available for upholstery and curtains.

Silk fabrics have a characteristic handle and are usually lustrous. They need careful treatment as they can be easily damaged. Perspiration will rot the fibre.

Man-made Fibres

These may be divided into two main classes: first, the regenerated cellulose, cellulose acetate, and cellulose tri-acetate fibres, so-called because the cellulose from which these fibres are made is obtained from fibrous natural materials such as wood, and is then regenerated in the fibre form, termed viscose (rayon); second, the synthetic fibres, so-called because they are produced from non-fibrous natural materials such as oil, eg acrylics, nylons, and polyesters. Any of these can be found mixed with natural fibres or with other man-made fibres in textiles.

Acetate has much of the aesthetic appeal of silk and is therefore used for fashion, especially in satins and brocades for evening wear, and also for furnishings, eg curtains.

Tri-acetate is similar to the acetates but a little more robust. Fabrics can be permanently creased by heat treatments. Tri-acetate fibres are used mainly for fashion fabrics and home furnishing, eg bedspreads, bath mats, etc.

Acrylic is very like wool in handle and appearance, especially in a bulked form.

Acrylic fabrics are 'easy-care' but can be distorted by even gentle heat. They are widely used for clothes, furnishings, upholstery, eg silky looking velvets and open-weave sheers, carpets, and rugs.

Nylon is a strong, easy-care fibre used for clothes and household textiles, eg velvet curtains, sheers, and stretch covers, as well as for carpets and rugs. It is also a heat sensitive fibre.

Polyester is very similar to nylon, being strong, easy-care, and heat-sensitive. It is widely used for fashion and household textiles (mixed with cotton), eg sheers, some furnishings, and carpets.

Vinyl is often made into different quality upholstery fabrics, some of which have a leather-like appearance.

Viscose (rayon) is found in all types of textiles. Some forms, termed modal, are made to resemble cotton. Like cotton, all viscose rayon fibres are absorbent, not sensitive to heat, and unless specially treated, need ironing. The principal disadvantage of viscose is that, when wet, it lacks the exceptional strength of cotton. Modified viscoses which include fibres with a permanent crimp are used to produce fabrics with a full, warm handle, cheap carpets, and fibres of low flammability. Viscose is also used in tweedy-looking and inexpensive upholstery fabrics.

When buying these or any other fabrics for the home, specific advice on care should be obtained from the retailer.

Washing, Ironing, and Dry Cleaning

Working at Home

Washing

Whether you are washing by hand or machine, it is important to choose the correct powder, bearing in mind the type of clothes being washed, the method of washing, the type of washing machine, if you use one, and the type of water.

Water in some areas is hard; some soap-based detergents contain water softening agents, but synthetic detergents are best for washing in really hard water. Follow the directions on detergent packs for the right amount to use.

Each numbered wash process on packs indicates the best wash temperature, amount of agitation, and any special instructions for rinsing, spinning or wringing for that group of fabrics. Wringing may be too harsh for some items, and for some only a minimum of spinning is advisable. Drip-drying, though suitable for some lightweight, non-absorbent fabrics, may distort heavier garments.

Guidance is given on garment labels as well as on detergent packs; see labelling symbols on p79.

Using the numbered processes as a guide, laundry can be sorted into groups which require the same treatment. (Sometimes it may be convenient to combine groups, but remember to use the gentlest process.) Strong coloured articles should be treated separately in case any dye comes off. Remove non-washable trimmings or fasteners, ensure that pockets are empty, zips are fastened, any necessary mending has been done, and any special stains have been treated (see pp90–92). See that cuffs and sleeves are turned down. A spray-on stain remover is useful for loosening heavy soiling as well as stains. When washing curtains, remove any hooks or rings which may rust, and smooth out gathers or pleats. Heavily soiled clothes will benefit from a soak before washing. Any boiling should be done after washing, since plunging dirty items straight into very hot water may 'set' stains. Fabric softeners or conditioners added to the final rinse give a fuller, softer handle to washed clothes, and also reduce the clinging tendency of nylon, polyester, and acrylic fabrics. Any items to be dip-starched should be taken out after the final rinse, starched, and then spun or wrung out. If only a small amount of starching is needed, it may be simpler to use a spray starch which is applied to the damp garment before ironing.

Drying

Drying clothes in the open air freshens them and sunlight helps to bleach white cotton items. However, strong direct sunlight causes yellowing of white nylon and woollen goods. Whiteners are available for use on nylon, and hydrogen peroxide can be used on wool (see p90). Lines and pegs should be kept clean, and garments hung so that their weight is evenly distributed over the line, as otherwise they may hang out of shape.

For those people without gardens or balconies, indoor dryers are a great help. Various types are available but the tumble dryer probably gives the best results for most things (see p82). The correct heat setting must be selected, and the garments allowed to cool before they are handled, otherwise creases may be set into the hot fabric.

Ironing

For best ironing results, any fabric should be at the particular degree of dampness which lets the creases be smoothed out most easily. Only acrylics should be ironed dry. If other fabrics get too dry, the problem can be overcome by using a steam iron, by wrapping the garment in a damp towel or by sprinkling or spraying with water immediately before ironing. Do not leave damp clothes lying around for any length of time, in case spots or mould develop. Select the appropriate iron setting and allow time for the iron to reach this temperature. Fabrics scorch or melt if the iron is too hot. Where a smooth shiny finish is required, ironing is usually done on the right side.

After ironing, the clothes should be allowed to air for a while before they are put away. Airing cupboards built round a hot water tank are useful, but not suitable for long-term storage as air currents 'pattern' the textiles with dirt.

Types of irons are described on pp83–84.

Care Labelling Symbols

Many labels on textiles, particularly clothing, carry international symbols which signify the best methods of caring for them. There are five basic symbols:

Drying: drip dry

dry flat

tumble dry

Dry cleaning: may be dry cleaned

may be dry cleaned professionally, but not in 'Coin-op' machine

do not dry clean

Washing: hand wash only

hand or machine wash at recommended temperature

do not wash

Bleaching: do not bleach

Ironing: warm iron (one dot means cool, three dots mean hot)

do not iron

Using a Laundry

If you have no time, inclination or equipment to do the washing at home, you can of course send it to a laundry, though this can be costly.

Using a Launderette

The types of machines and the cost of the wash often lead to loads being combined. Provided the safest common programme for all the articles in the wash is selected, no damage should occur, but repeated washing in less than ideal conditions will result in general dinginess of clothes.

Dry Cleaning

This is essential for fabrics which are harmed by water, and for the removal of certain stains. Many launderettes contain coin-operated dry cleaning machines which are reasonably satisfactory for most items, although some may require expert treatment and finishing. Clothes must be aired well after dry cleaning, as any solvent still clinging to the clothes will give off poisonous vapour.

Whichever way you decide to clean your clothes and household linen, remember that it is always best to do so, if possible, before they get very dirty.

Laundry Equipment and Appliances

Washing Machines

Automatic

Automatic single-tub washing machines can be left to wash clothes entirely on their own. They carry out pre-selected programmes of washing, rinsing, and spin drying; a few models will tumble-dry as well. A completely automatic sequence for heavy cotton fabrics may include a soak, pre-wash or biological wash, followed by a spin and rinse, a main wash, and several spins and rinses followed by a final spin. Most of the latest machines make use of electronic controls to improve performance

and reliability; improved spin speeds and accurate water and temperature control have produced energy saving benefits. Most washing machines indicate on their programme switch or selector guide the number corresponding to the 'wash care' labels promoted by the Home Laundering Consultative Council (HLCC) also attached to many ready-made garments (see p79). Special programmes have been developed for the washing of wool and delicate fabrics.

Almost all machines are front-opening and have a perforated inner clothes container or drum within an outer container. Most machines take in hot and cold water and select it according to the temperature required. A 2–3kW heater boosts the water temperature if necessary. Some machines will run off a cold water supply only.

Automatic washing machines should be permanently connected to the water supply, electricity supply, and main drainage. This leaves the sink free for other purposes.

Washing is by tumble or reverse tumble action. The horizontal clothes container or drum rotates slowly in one direction or first in one direction and then in the other with a periodic pause. After the soak, wash or rinse, the inner clothes container rotates at high speed, pressing the clothes to the sides by centrifugal force and throwing the water out through the holes and perforations.

The capacity of tumble machines varies from 3–5.5kg dry weight of clothes.

The water level in some front opening machines is below the door, so garments can be added during a washing programme – although for safety reasons on British Electrotechnical Approvals Board (BEAB) approved machines, the door cannot be opened after the water reaches a certain temperature. A childproof safety device is usually fitted to the door to prevent it being opened by children during the washing programme.

Where detergent dispensers are fitted they can be used to feed in fabric conditioners in some models. Some models incorporate automatic conditioner dispensers. It is important to use low-sudsing detergents as they use the minimum amount of water – a benefit in energy saving as well as in performance.

Twin-tub

These consist of a washing-tub and a spin-dryer assembled side by side in an outer casing. The washer is on the left, the spinner on the right. Unfortunately there are now very few models left on the market. Most twin-tub machines are semi-automatic. Water heating and wash cycles can be automatic, and once the clothes are transferred to the spin tub, the rinsing on most machines is carried out automatically too.

Twin-tub washers handle from 1.8–3kg dry weight of clothes. Washing water from the spinner can be pumped out of the clothes back into the wash-tub and used again. To rinse, water is introduced by a hose or jet and then spun away into the sink. Some machines provide automatic rinsing until the water is turned off.

Although they use more water than the automatics, the hot water can be used more than once unless the clothes are particularly dirty.

Twin-tub machines are free standing and have casters, so that they can be wheeled to the sink for use, but stored elsewhere in the kitchen. They have flexible hoses for filling and draining. They must be connected to a nearby power supply.

Safety

All washing machines must be earthed, and run only from an earthed 3 pin 13 amp or 15 amp socket outlet.

It is advisable to select home laundry appliances that carry the British Electrotechnical Approvals Board (BEAB) Mark of Safety. This is shown by the yellow swing ticket attached to the appliance and by a mark or rating plate. It means that a sample of the model in question has been subjected to rigorous tests to the safety standards laid down by the British Standards Institution (BSI). Continental machines are usually tested in the same way to European Safety Standards, but these do not always match those set in the UK.

Check that the machine will stand steadily on the floor in the washing position. Make certain that any transit brackets have been removed before using the machine as they may otherwise cause damage. Be sure to read the manufacturer's instructions carefully.

Care and maintenance

1) Before first using the machine, read the instruction manual carefully and keep it handy for reference.
2) Many instruction manuals contain check-lists which can be helpful if for any reason the machine does not work.
3) Have the machine serviced as advised. Some manufacturers offer service contracts (see the chapter on Care and Maintenance of the Home).
4) Regular care after each wash keeps the machine in good condition, so
   – dry all parts thoroughly before putting away
   – remove fluff and clean filters
   – keep the outside of the machine clean, and polish occasionally.

Clothes Dryers

There are three kinds: spin dryers, tumble dryers, and warm air rack dryers, either wall-hung or in a cabinet.

Spin dryers

These are of two types: those which let the water out through a spout in the bottom of the machine, and those which have a pump and a hook-ended draining hose which carries water away into a sink. All automatic washing machines incorporate a spin dryer, but they are useful for those who do not feel their laundry is sufficient to justify the high cost of an automatic and prefer to hand wash. All spin dryers are more efficient and quieter than almost all the automatic washing machines.

A spin dryer has two containers, one inside the other. The inner container rotates at high speed when the machine is switched on, creating centrifugal force which presses the clothes against its perforated sides. The perforations allow the water to escape into the outer container, from which it is either pumped away or drained into a bowl.

To prevent accidents from the fast-revolving clothes container, safety regulations demand that the spinner motor will operate only when the spinner lid is closed, and that the cover cannot be opened until the drum has completely stopped spinning.

A spin dryer will rinse soapy clothes or damp dry rinsed ones; some clothes will even be dry enough for ironing. The machine should never need to stay switched on for more than four minutes, and many fabrics dry sooner. Some spinners have an automatic cut-out which operates after four minutes. Others have timers which can be set to stop the machine at any time from one to four minutes after spinning starts.

To obtain good results the machine must be loaded properly and never overloaded. Capacity is between 2–3kg dry weight. The clothes should be evenly distributed in the machine, and well pressed down. Where a perforated mat is supplied, it should be pressed down firmly under the rim of the clothes container. An unbalanced load can cause vibrations and noise.

Tumble dryers

A tumble dryer combines movement with heat to give quick and even drying. Clothes are tumbled gently in warm air in a drum which revolves slowly in one direction, although some models have reverse tumble action. Warm dry air is passed through the gently tumbling clothes, taking up the moisture. The warm damp air is then filtered and discharged from the machine through an air outlet. A flexible venting kit is available to fit on to the air outlet and take the damp air out of a window. Since the dryer can remove a large volume of water in a short period, this is usually advisable unless the room is large, warm, and well ventilated.

Tumble dryers vary in size. Some are very small and some are designed to fit beneath a standard counter top. Others can be stacked above a matching automatic washing machine using a special stacking kit. They are generally on wheels or casters and easily moved. If the dryer is kept against the outside wall, a permanent duct for the air outlet can be installed through the wall.

The maximum dry weight clothes capacity varies from 1.5–3kg according to the machine; it is less with man-made fibres.

All tumble dryers are front-loading. Some have right or left-hand door openings, others open downwards. On some machines, door handles are removable to prevent interference from children.

For safety, tumble dryers stop as soon as the door is opened and re-start when it is closed again. A thermal cut-out prevents over-heating.

The tumble dryer is operated by two simple controls: an automatic minute timer operating from 0–90 or 0–120 minutes and a heat selection switch with two or more positions. A cool tumble to reduce creasing, particularly of man-made fibres, is introduced before the automatic switch-off on many machines; on others it is optional. Some automatic washing machines include a separate tumble-dry cycle.

Rack dryers

Rack type dryers are designed to fold away for easy storage. There are two types. The first has a convector heater base on which a concertina type rack is fitted and then extended upwards so the clothes can be hung and covered with the supplied fabric cover. As the heat rises from the convector the clothes are dried by the warm air. The heater loading is usually 1kW and this is not controllable. The second type is usually wall-mounted and incorporates a fan. In the closed position the unit looks rather like a wall heater, but when the outer casing is pulled upwards, a hood folds out supporting drying racks. The clothes are hung on the racks and the whole unit is enclosed in a bag. The 2kW fan heater, with a choice of heat positions, blows warm air down through the clothes for a drying time selected by the user on a timer control. Maximum dry weight clothes capacity varies but the average is up to 2.7kg.

Rack dryers are particularly useful in households where there are no facilities for drying clothes out-of-doors, or when natural drying is either difficult or would take too long.

Other methods of drying

The heat from a well-lagged hot water cylinder can be utilized to dry and air clothes already spun-dried (never attempt to remove the lagging jacket from the tank in order to speed drying – it will waste heat) and the airing cupboard should be planned with slatted racks and hanging fitments.

Electric Irons

Dry heat-controlled iron

This has a heat-selecting dial which is controlled by a thermostat.

Although a dry iron can weigh as little as 0.5kg, the majority weigh between 1–1.5kg. Irons of 1kg and below are loaded to about 1000 watts; heavier irons to 750 watts.

Lightweight irons have a slim, pointed soleplate and a low body to make intricate ironing easier and faster. Design variations include the position and style of rests, open handles, and special flexible cable joints adjustable for either left or right-handed users.

Steam/dry iron

This is a heat-controlled dry iron which can also be set to supply steam through holes or grooves in the soleplate.

A small valve allows water to drip from a tank on to the top of the hot soleplate, where it forms steam which is forced through the holes or grooves. There is only one steam temperature setting. The iron stops steaming when stood on its heel. It can be easily switched to dry ironing.

Steam/dry irons weigh about 2kg and usually have a loading of 1000 watts. The tubular, sheathed element is embedded in the soleplate. Some steam irons have a spray which sends a fine mist of cold water in front of the iron when a button on the handle is pressed. A water gauge is sometimes fitted. Another type sends an extra jet of steam through the soleplate when a button is pressed.

Soleplates can be of aluminium or aluminium alloy, or they may have a chromium or non-stick finish.

Rotary iron

This has a large ironing surface, and may be used on a table, or on a specially designed stand. Ironing is done sitting down.

It is particularly useful for large flat items such as bed and table-linen. Shirts and pyjamas can also be ironed quickly and easily after a little practice.

There are also flat bed models like those used by tailors and dry cleaners, with two linen-covered surfaces, one containing a heater, which are brought together on the clothes.

The usual type of ironer consists of a rotating padded roller and a thermostatically heated, curved metal 'shoe' which is pressed against it. Flat articles placed on the roller are carried round and ironed as they pass under the 'shoe'. The iron is operated by pressure on a foot control, so both hands are free to control the article being ironed.

Sometimes the two halves of the 'shoe' are separately heated and controlled and most have Home Laundering Consultative Council (HLCC) markings on the temperature selector dial.

The loading of the irons varies with their length, but a 600mm roller will probably have a loading of 1250–1500 watts, of which 50 watts may be for the motor.

Choosing an iron

First decide which of the main types of iron is most suited to your particular needs, and choose one that feels comfortable and balanced in your hand.

Have a look at the special features provided by different makes of iron, and choose which you find most useful.

Sheer weight is not necessary for good results; the essentials are the right heat for the fabric, the right amount of moisture, and a smoothly gliding iron. This has led to a reduction in the weight of irons, and to the adoption by most manufacturers of standard international temperature settings with terminology and symbols agreed by the Home Laundering Consultative Council (HLCC):

Hot (210°C)
Cotton, linen, rayon or modified rayon
Warm (160°C)
Polyester mixtures, wool
Cool (120°C)
Acrylic, nylon, acetate, tri-acetate, polyester

Use and care

1) The three-core flex of your iron should be properly wired to a 3 pin 15 amp plug or a 13 amp plug with a 13 amp fuse. Never use an electric iron connected to a lighting circuit.
2) Always stand and store a hand iron on its heelrest.

3) A flex-holder prevents undue wear on the flex and keeps it from creasing the fabric which has been ironed.

4) An iron takes longer to cool down than to heat up, so that when an adjustment is made from a high to a low setting, time must be allowed for the iron to cool to the new heat level.

5) A steam iron should be properly set and be given time to heat up from cold or to adjust from one setting to another.

6) Hard water will gradually clog a steam iron. Although some manufacturers make provisions for cleaning, and cleaning fluids can be bought, it is advisable to use demineralized or distilled water, obtainable from department stores.

7) When filling a steam iron, always follow the manufacturer's instructions, and make sure that the iron is disconnected from the electricity supply.

8) Empty the tank of water after use and while the iron is still hot.

9) To clean starch or other marks from a soleplate, rub the iron over a damp piece of coarse cloth held taut over the edge of the ironing board. For more resistant marks rub gently with the finest of wire wool. While doing this, hold a steam iron in the ironing position so that nothing becomes lodged in the steam vents.

Note Not all fabrics can be ironed or steam ironed. Heavy creases in bone-dry articles will not be removed even by a steam/spray iron.

Care of Household Goods

Ceramics

This term is used to cover all types of pottery, clay and quarry floor tiles, and items with a vitreous coating such as wash-basins, baths, sinks and vitreous enamelled saucepans and cooking pots. See the various items below.

Crockery

Wash in hot washing-up detergent solution, being careful to avoid banging pieces together. Do not use abrasive scourers as these can damage the surface, and avoid hard rubbing if the crockery is decorated or gold-rimmed. Also avoid sudden changes in temperature as this may cause cracking. Remove bad stains with a little neat detergent on a cloth. A soft tooth or nail-brush used occasionally will remove stains round handles. Make sure that decorated china is dishwasher-proof before machine washing.

Vitreous enamelled pans

Use a cleaner approved by the Vitreous Enamel Development Council and avoid harsh abrasives. Soak immediately after use. Burnt on food can be removed by using a non-abrasive pan scourer sprinkled with salt; or add biological washing powder to warm water in the pan, boil up, rinse, and wash in the usual way.

Baths, wash-basins, cookers, sinks, etc

Special non-abrasive cleaners are available. Soap, scum, and grease can be removed with a synthetic detergent or washing-up liquid.

Floor tiles

Fully vitrified clay tiles are made in a wide variety of colours and surface finishes whereas quarry tiles are usually found in natural browns, black, buff, red or sometimes dark blue. Both types are impervious to all household fluids and are very hard-wearing. They should be swept regularly and any spills mopped up immediately to avoid danger of slipping. Mop with hot detergent solution, using a scouring powder on stubborn marks.

Wall tiles

Wipe over with a cloth wrung out in one of the proprietary cleaners or in washing-up detergent.

Glass

Glassware

Wash in a warm solution of washing-up detergent. Rinse in hot water, adding a few drops of ammonia or a rinse aid for extra sparkle. Wash crystal glasses one at a time and store side by side without touching. Avoid using harsh abrasives on ovenproof glass casseroles as these can produce flaws along which they may later crack; for the same reason, never put hot dishes into cold water. Soak oven-proof glass in cold water to loosen baked-on food.

Pictures, mirrors

These can be treated in the same way as windows. There are special polishes available for mirrors which help to prevent misting.

Windows

Many proprietary window cleaners are available. Alternatively a damp leather followed by a dry cloth can be used. The dry cloth should ideally be lint free (scrim cloth is ideal). If the windows are really dirty, add a few drops of washing-up liquid or ammonia. Wash with hot water and washing-up liquid or a few drops of ammonia using scrim or a fluff-free cloth. Polish with a damp leather and finally rub up with a non-fluffing cloth.

Leather

Gloves

In the absence of specific advice, washable leather gloves should be washed in warm soapy .water or special glove shampoo. Put on the gloves and squeeze the hands together to ease out the dirt, and then rinse in the same way in clean warm water; dry away from direct heat. For gloves which cannot be washed, try sprinkling with French chalk or Fuller's earth; wrap in a cloth and leave for a few hours before brushing off powder with a clean brush. If necessary, repeat with fresh powder.

Handbags and luggage

The leather needs treating according to type and it is, therefore, best to ascertain at the time of purchase whether or not there are any special cleaners available.

Calf may have been specially treated so that it can be wiped clean; otherwise special calf cleaner should be used.

Crocodile needs little more than regular dusting and an occasional clean with a colourless shoe cream or liquid wax. Use sparingly and polish well, or residue will rub on to clothes.

Hide needs protecting and feeding by regular waxing, or use a special leather cleaner.

Suede needs careful cleaning. Normal freshening up can be accomplished by using a special suede brush; soil can be removed by rubbing with a warm, damp cloth. When using proprietary suede cleaners, follow the manufacturer's instructions. Always finish cleaning by rubbing the nap in an upward direction.

Shoes

If there is a specially recommended polish for a particular type of shoe leather, use this. Otherwise regular use of a good wax polish will feed the leather and prolong the life of the shoes. When applying polish, brush well into the welt; this gives added waterproofing and protection. Surface mud and grit should be removed first by sponging with warm water and mild soap, and damp shoes should always be allowed to dry thoroughly on shoe trees before polishing. See also p63.

Upholstery

Leather upholstery should be occasionally rubbed with a special cleaner or a liquid silicone polish. If sticky, it can be sponged down with a cloth wrung out in a solution of synthetic detergent. Really dirty leather can be treated with a solution of one part vinegar to two parts water. Saddle soap is ideal for renovation; it feeds the leather and leaves it supple. When dry, the leather needs oiling with, for example, a proprietary leather-cleaning product. After leaving the oil to penetrate for some time, rub well to remove all traces of excess oil, and then polish.

Metal

Cutlery

Most cutlery is made from silver, EPNS (electro-plated nickel silver) or stainless steel. Silver cutlery washed often in hot soapy water, dried and polished with a cloth while still hot, will stay cleaner longer. Since some types of food stain silver, it is best to wipe off food particles as soon as possible. Tarnishing, caused by sulphur in the atmosphere or by food, can be removed from small items by using a proprietary silver dip. After soaking for a short time, the silver is rinsed and dried. Alternatively a specially impregnated cloth can be used which cleans and polishes at the same time. There are a variety of silver polishes for more thorough cleaning. The foam type is particularly easy to use. Long-term polishes impart a longer-lasting shine than ordinary polishes. When storing silver, wrap it in foil and keep it in an airtight polythene bag or specially treated tissue paper or cloth. EPNS can be cleaned like silver.

Stainless steel normally only needs thorough washing and rubbing dry to keep its shine, but there are proprietary stainless steel cleaners for bad marks. Rinse or wash stainless steel cutlery as soon as possible after use especially if it has been in contact with salt. Never use household bleach in the water, and do not use silver polishes on stainless steel cutlery.

Ornaments

The most common ornamental metals are copper, silver, brass, and chromium. Proprietary cleaners are available for all of them, and the use of long-term polishes means less frequent cleaning. When using a liquid cleaner on intricate items, use an old toothbrush to get into difficult corners.

Lacquered items should not be cleaned with metal polish, but the very sparing occasional application of a silicone polish will give extra protection (see also cooking pans and cutlery).

Cooking pans

The most common metals used for pans are aluminium, copper, and stainless steel.

Frying and omelet pans should be seasoned before being used. If the manufacturer's instructions are available, follow these carefully. Otherwise, pour in enough cooking oil to cover the base of the pan, heat gently, taking care not to allow the oil to get too hot. Pour off the oil and wipe out the pan with soft kitchen paper. Non-stick pans should be washed in hot water and detergent, rinsed, dried, and then seasoned as described above.

From whatever metal a pan is made, it must be thoroughly cleaned and dried after being used. Soaking immediately after use helps to loosen food particles so that the pans can be cleaned satisfactorily with a pan scourer and detergent.

Aluminium saucepans and bakeware: Fill with cold water immediately after use; then wash in warm water and washing-up liquid using a nylon scourer or saucepan brush. If burnt, soak pan to soften burnt-on particles of food, then wash in hot soapy water using a pan scourer. Alternatively, add a little biological washing powder to hand-hot water in the pan. Whisk the solution and leave to soak for a few hours; boil up, and clean in the normal way.

Non-stick aluminium pans and bakeware: Wash in hot soapy water, and use a non-abrasive pan scourer if necessary.

To remove the brown stain from the interior of a non-stick pan, simmer a solution of 250ml water, 125ml domestic bleach, and 2 × 15ml spoons vinegar in the pan for 10 minutes. Wash the pan well and re-season.

Aluminium is harmed by alkaline cleaners. The dark stain which sometimes develops on the inside of a pan after cooking will be removed if the pan is later used for cooking acid foods such as rhubarb or apple peelings. Alternatively, boil some water containing a little cream of tartar or vinegar in the pan to clean it.

To prevent aluminium pans becoming stained when used for steaming, add a squeezed-out lemon half or 1 × 15ml spoon lemon juice to the steaming water.

The outside of a *copper* pan can be lacquered to give a long-lasting shine which only needs polishing occasionally. The inside of copper pans are usually lined with tin or nickel which can be cleaned as for aluminium. Neglected copper can be cleaned with a proprietary cleaner or with salt and vinegar followed by thorough rinsing.

Sinks

Many modern kitchen sinks are made from *stainless steel*. They should be washed regularly with hot detergent solution. Special liquid cleaners are available for removing stubborn stains. Abrasives should not be used.

Paintwork

Paintwork can be cleaned with liquid detergent, a proprietary paint cleaner, or with old-fashioned sugar soap (50g sugar soap to 1 litre warm water) if it is very dirty. The sugar soap must be thoroughly washed off with clean water as it is an alkaline solution which will soften the paint if left on. Washing from bottom to the top is correct in theory; in practice the opposite works well. Any residue from the cloth runs down the paintwork, giving an extra soaking where it is usually dirtier, and it also stops residue running over finished work. If the gloss on paint needs restoring, it means either that it needs repainting or that too harsh a cleanser has been used. If polish is used on paintwork it must be thoroughly cleaned off before repainting, or the paint will not adhere to the surface. Any painted surface may be prepared for painting by using a handful of soda in 5 litres of hot water; this removes all greasy fingermarks, etc. For lightly soiled paintwork, a spray polish/cleaner is useful as it cleans and protects the surface at the same time.

Plastics

The word 'plastics' is used to describe a number of materials, mostly synthetic, which can have very different properties and appearance and are used in the home in many ways. There are two basic types: *thermoplastics* which will soften if heated sufficiently and *thermosetting plastics* which, once they have been set, cannot be softened again by heating.

Baths and basins

Acrylic baths, basins and other sanitary fittings should be cleaned with washing-up detergent used neat on a cloth. Slight scratching can be removed with metal polish. (It should be noted that the surface of plastic baths and basins can be damaged by a lighted cigarette.)

Note Never mix bleaches, soda or lavatory cleaners in any quantity, as they can produce, and give off, harmful gases.

Floor coverings

These include thermoplastic tiles, vinyl tiles, linoleum, and sheetings.

Thermoplastic tiles are usually only obtainable in a limited range of dark flecked colours, whereas *vinyl tiles* are found in a wide range of colours and designs; they can be very hard-wearing. There are a variety of vinyl sheetings, some of which have hessian, cork or felt backings. They are soft and quiet to walk on. Sheet vinyl can be used to avoid joints.

The most useful type of linoleum is in a heavy-duty quality; it is medium hard-wearing. It should be polished to look its best.

All these floors should be swept regularly with a soft brush and mopped when necessary with hot water and one of the detergents specially formulated for them (sometimes marketed by the manufacturer). For scuff marks, first wet fine steel wool with a little detergent solution, rub off mark and then dry off; this counteracts the black mark that steel wool sometimes leaves, and is also less abrasive. Floors look better when polished, and there are a variety of products available to choose from.

Dual-purpose cleaners are combined detergents and polishes, and as the polish is usually self-shining, rubbing or buffing is unnecessary.

Two kinds of liquid floor polish are available; non-buffable types which dry to a glossy appearance and buffable ones which are normally used in conjunction with an electric polisher. Repeated use of a non-buffable liquid polish will lead to a build-up of polish on the floor which may discolour it eventually. After the initial standard has been reached it is helpful to apply polish only to the work parts. In any case it must be stripped off regularly either by adding ammonia to the normal detergent or by using special cleaners. A renovator for liquid polish is twenty parts hot water to one part polish; wash area, allow to dry, and buff up. This build-up of polish does not occur with buffable liquid polishes, if used properly.

There are also seals for some plastic floor coverings to give a long-lasting protective finish. But be sure to buy one which is suitable for the floor to be treated, and follow the manufacturer's instructions for application and removal. See also p62.

Laminated surfaces

Laminated plastics are widely used for work-tops, table tops, kitchen furniture, and trays. They are easily cleaned by washing in hot soapy water or by wiping over with a damp cloth, rinsing, and drying. Where a glossy finish is desired, give an occasional rub with a silicone polish or a spray polish cleaner. These surfaces can be scratched by sharp knives, and excess heat will damage them. See also the chapter on Care and Maintenance of the Home.

Upholstery

Vinyl upholstery or simulated leather can usually be cleaned quite satisfactorily by occasionally wiping with a cloth wrung out in a solution of synthetic detergent, or moistened with one of the non-abrasive cleaners used for baths, wash-basins, etc. Follow this by wiping with a cloth wrung out in clean water, and then polishing with a clean, dry cloth. Alternatively, one of the proprietary spray polishes which clean and polish in one operation can be used.

Rubbing gently with a cloth moistened in white spirit will remove stubborn greasy marks; surgical spirit or methylated spirit can be used on ball-point ink, and pencil marks can usually be removed with a soft eraser, although marks which have penetrated the surface of the vinyl are almost impossible to remove.

Miscellaneous plastics

The most common plastics found in the home include the acrylics, which are thermoplastics with a gloss-like appearance used for record racks, ash trays, etc; cellulose acetate, a tough resilient thermoplastic used for brush and mirror handles, lampshades, etc; polyethylene (polythene), a wax-like flexible thermoplastic used for bowls, buckets, and many other household items; polystyrene, a shiny rigid thermoplastic often used for picnic ware or in a modified form for refrigerator interiors; and melamine, a thermosetting plastic commonly used for table and picnic ware which is almost unbreakable.

In case you do not know which plastic you are dealing with, remember one or two general points. Although some plastics can stand boiling water, most are damaged by excess heat. Sharp knives and abrasives can damage the surface and make the plastic more difficult to clean, and some articles can be damaged by being dropped or banged. Plastics are easily washed in hot detergent or wiped with a damp cloth. Special melamine cleaners can be obtained for removing tea stains from plastic cups; alternatively, neat detergent on a damp cloth can be used.

One of the problems with plastic lampshades, newspaper racks, and similar items is that, when dusted, they tend to develop static electricity and so pick up more dust. This can be reduced by rubbing with a cloth moistened with synthetic detergent or fabric conditioner. Do not rinse or wipe dry.

Textiles

Carpets and upholstery

See the chapter on Care and Maintenance of the Home.

Wall coverings

Regular vacuum cleaning will remove surface dust from all wall coverings, especially fabric ones. There are special dry cleaning powders which can be used on marks on some of these; careful rubbing with the foam from a carpet or upholstery shampoo may also prove satisfactory on some fabric surfaces, but avoid overwetting. If marks are really heavy, it may be best to re-cover the affected area.

Wallpaper

If wallpaper is washable, it can be sponged down lightly with detergent, but avoid excess wetting. Always work up and down and not across which tends to push water between the joints and loosen paper. Other wallpapers should be dusted regularly with a soft dry cloth or mop; alternatively, the appropriate attachment on a vacuum cleaner can be used. Grease marks should be treated with a solvent; other odd marks can sometimes be removed by rubbing with a soft india rubber, and general grime can be cleaned with a dough, either bought or made from two parts flour to one part warm water and one part white spirit. Turn the dough frequently so that a clean portion is always in use.

Wood

Floors

There are two ways of maintaining a wood floor. One is to seal the floor first, and then polish occasionally with a wax or liquid polish; the other is to use a paste wax or liquid wax polish regularly.

If the floor is to be sealed, it must first be thoroughly cleaned and all traces of wax removed. The seal should be applied according to instructions, and when completely dry, one of the recommended polishes should be applied to give a good surface. To maintain such a floor, a dry mop, soft brush or the floor cleaning attachment of a vacuum cleaner should be used regularly to remove grit. Buffing with a soft cloth will restore lustre, and polish can be reapplied when necessary to restore the shine.

If the floor is not sealed, a paste wax will fill any pits and cracks in the surface. The whole floor may not need polishing each time; usually only the heavy traffic areas need be done. Leave the polish to dry before buffing. Scratches, marks, and build-up of polish can be removed by rubbing lightly with a cloth moistened with white spirit.

Never let an unsealed floor get wet, and wipe up spills immediately. If a mark is left, try rubbing daily with linseed oil until it disappears.

Furniture

Wood needs waxing to avoid risk of damage by damp, sunlight, central heating, and insect attack. However, if the furniture is dusted regularly, waxing need not be done very frequently. Once a month may be sufficient or even less often for French polished or cellulose-finished furniture. There is a variety of modern furniture waxes which clean off light surface dirt and are generally easy and quick to use. The soft paste waxes are especially good for antique furniture. The harder, wipe-on, wipe-off type are often available as aerosols which make the job less arduous. Those polishes which contain silicones give extra protection against water-borne stains. Since wood absorbs moisture, the best day for polishing is a dry one, irrespective of whether it is hot or cold; and remember that, as waxing is meant to feed and seal the wood, it should be done on both seen *and* unseen parts, especially areas where the grain has been cut across.

French-polished furniture which has become sticky can be wiped with a cloth wrung out in warm soapy water but it must be allowed to dry thoroughly before re-polishing. Special liquid removers are available for treating heat marks. Alternatively, rub the way of the grain with metal polish. Since alcohol dissolves French polish, any spilt drinks should be wiped up immediately. If the polish has been removed, a French polish substitute, available from hardware shops, should be applied.

Oak should be cleaned with a white wax, always applied with a scrupulously clean cloth to prevent darkening of the wood. If it does become discoloured, rub with very fine steel wool moistened in turpentine. General darkening due to smoke and dust can be cleaned by using a solution of one part vinegar to two parts warm water. Allow the wood to dry thoroughly before re-polishing.

Teak and other matt finishes should be cleaned with teak oil or cream; deal with scratches by rubbing oil well in and then oiling the entire area. Finish by rubbing with a soft cloth.

Mahogany can be cleaned using vinegar and warm water. Allow to dry before re-polishing.

In the absence of any special recommendations, the following *general tips* may be useful:

Waxing will hide many spots and blemishes; or try disguising the blemishes with wax crayon or shoe polish. Scratches on dark furniture can be hidden by using iodine. Heat and water marks are best removed with proprietary scratch-removing polishes. A build-up of polish can be removed by rubbing with a cloth soaked in turpentine. Work over a small area at a time, and use a clean cloth to rub the turpentine off while the furniture is still wet. Old furniture which has been neglected can be cleaned in a solution of 1×15ml spoon turpentine and 3×15ml spoons boiled linseed oil to 1 litre hot water. Clean one section at a time, rubbing the wood with a soft cloth dampened in the solution, and polish with a dry cloth.

Tableware

Some wooden tableware may have been specially finished so that it can be washed, but it should never be left to soak. Other tableware should be wiped clean after use and oiled occasionally with olive oil to preserve the wood. Any marks can be rubbed with fine steel wool dipped in oil. Chopping boards, which are usually unfinished, should be kept scrupulously clean by thorough scrubbing and rinsing, the final rinse being in cold water.

Removing Stains

A stain is like a dye in that it penetrates and colours the fibres of goods, and, like a dye, it takes time to set. Immediate action is, therefore, important. Many common stains can be dealt with during washing because of the various ingredients in modern detergents, but other stains need special treatment.

If a stained article is washable, immediate rinsing in cold water followed by normal washing may be all that is necessary. If it is not washable, however, or if the stain is not one which will respond to water, then various solvents have to be used. Dealing with a localized stain rather than the complete article is called 'spotting' and good spotting techniques are essential if the stain is not to look worse after treatment.

Scrape off any excess solid material first and then work from the wrong side of the fabric, first placing a clean pad or cloth underneath to absorb the stain as it comes out. Sometimes, when stains have been removed, a ring or sweal-mark can still be seen around the stained area. Avoid this by working from the outside towards the centre of the stain and dry the solvent quickly.

If the cause of the stain is unknown, try to identify it as far as possible by looking, feeling, and smelling. On unidentified stains, try the least severe treatments first. On damp stains use something to absorb the moisture, eg salt, or blotting or absorbent kitchen paper; if the article is washable, try rinsing in cold water; or, if grease is suspected, try washing at a high temperature or using a grease solvent. If a lot of colour is left, try an appropriate bleach.

Whatever stain remover is used, always test its effect on an inconspicuous part of the garment or fabric first. Check for colour fastness or weakening of the fabric.

Common stain removal agents

Washing powders

Sodium perborate, contained in heavy-duty washing powders, is often effective at high temperatures or during a long soak, particularly on stains such as tea, coffee, and fruit juice. Enzymes are most effective during a soaking period in hand-hot to hot water ($50°-60°C$), and work on protein stains such as egg, blood, and milk. However, some fabrics should not be soaked; always check the recommendations on the detergent packet before use.

Bleaches

The most common household bleaches are hypochlorite and hydrogen peroxide.

Hypochlorite is sold under various trade names and is usually referred to as household or chlorine bleach. It should never be used undiluted, and never on silk or wool or any article with a flame-resistant finish. Be careful to follow instructions relating to concentration very closely.

Hydrogen peroxide can be used on silk or wool. It is normally available as 'ten volume' hydrogen peroxide. Stained garments may be soaked in a cold solution containing one part of ten-volume hydrogen peroxide to four parts of water.

Whenever bleach has been used, the articles must be thoroughly rinsed.

Solvents

The most common solvents are perchloroethylene, trichloroethylene, turpentine, white methylated spirit (surgical spirit), and acetone.

Perchloroethylene is particularly useful for removing greasy stains, but it must be used in a well-ventilated room, preferably near an open window, or in the open air. Although it is non-flammable, it should not be used near heat or a naked flame. It is safe on most fabrics and colours, but should not be used on plastics. It is sold under trade names.

Trichloroethylene is often sold under a trade name as a dry cleaning fluid. Like perchloroethylene, it gives off dangerous vapour and so should be used in a well-ventilated room and kept away from heat or naked flames. Trichloroethylene should not be used on tri-acetate fabrics or fabrics containing even a little tri-acetate fibre.

Turpentine and *turpentine substitute* (white spirit) can be used for removing grease stains, oil paint, enamel, and varnish stains and are often used in removing dirt and accumulated polish from wood. They are suitable for use on all fabrics and colours. But they are flammable and should, therefore, not be used near a naked flame.

White methylated spirit (surgical spirit) is particularly useful for removing grass and ballpoint ink stains, and can also be used on most oils and grease. It is safe for most fabrics, but is highly flammable.

Acetone, often contained in nail varnish remover, is an excellent solvent for fats and varnishes. It will dissolve acetate fabrics and may damage other coloured materials, so it must be tested first on an inconspicuous part of the article. It will also dissolve some plastics. Acetone is also highly flammable.

After using any solvent, the article should be thoroughly rinsed if washable, or aired well.

Other common aids

Vinegar contains acetic acid and is often used in stain removal to neutralize an alkali.

Salt sprinkled on a wet stain quickly absorbs it.

Fuller's earth and *French chalk* will absorb grease stains. Fuller's earth is brown and should, therefore, not be used on white fabrics, but French chalk, being white, can be used on any colour.

Fat and *glycerine* can be used to lubricate a stain in order to make stain removal easier.

Oxalic acid is useful in removing rust and iron mould stains, if you can get it, but it is very poisonous, and must not be used on silk or wool. It is also unsuitable for some colours. It is usually available as crystals which have to be dissolved in hot water (1×2.5ml spoon to 250ml water), preparation being in a non-metallic vessel. Proprietary rust stain removers, employed in strict accordance with their instructions for use, are much safer than oxalic acid.

Ammonia is a mild alkali which can be used to remove acid stains such as fruit juice. It is however dangerous, so manufacturer's recommended precautions must be followed.

Borax is another mild alkali, used in removing acidic stains such as fruit juice, tea, and coffee. Use in a solution of 1×10ml spoon to 250ml warm water. On damp stains, stretch the stained fabric over a basin, sprinkle dry borax over the stain, and pour hot water through.

Glossary of common stains

It is impossible to list every stain and its treatment, but the following is a useful guide, if you bear the above comments in mind.

Note When removing stains from carpets or fixed upholstery, the same basic treatments can be applied, but carpet or upholstery shampoo should be used instead of normal washing powder. For enzyme treatments, make a paste with the powder and water, cover the stain, and leave for a few hours, keeping it moist with warm water.

Beer

If the fabric is suitable, wash at a high temperature or treat the stain with one part white vinegar to four parts water; rinse thoroughly.

Blood

Soak in hand-hot solution of enzyme detergent. Wash as recommended.

Butter

Scrape off any excess, then wash at a high temperature if the fabric is suitable. Otherwise, treat with a grease solvent, and air well, then rinse and wash as recommended.

Coffee and Tea

Soak in hand-hot solution of enzyme detergent. Wash as recommended. If stain is set, wash at a high temperature or use bleach.

Egg

Soak in hand-hot solution of enzyme detergent. Wash as recommended. Treat stubborn stains by soaking in a solution of one part 'ten volume' hydrogen peroxide to nine parts water to which a few drops of ammonia have been added. Rinse well.

Fruit

If fabric is suitable, wash at a high temperature, or treat with diluted hydrogen peroxide, checking first for colour fastness.

Glue

If glue is water soluble, it should come out on washing. Waterproof glue should be treated with amyl acetate.

Grass

Soak in hand-hot solution of enzyme detergent; then wash as recommended or treat with white methylated spirit. Rinse and wash normally.

Grease

As for *Butter*.

Ink (ball-point)

Treat with white methylated spirit. Rinse thoroughly and wash as recommended.

Ink (writing)

Cover stain with salt, squeeze lemon juice over and leave for an hour. Rinse thoroughly, then wash as recommended.

Iron Mould and Rust

Soak stains in lemon juice, and press under a piece of damp cotton fabric. On cotton and linen articles, oxalic acid can be used, but test for colour fastness first. Proprietary rust stain removers are also available, and are generally preferable to the traditional methods.

Lipstick

Treat the stain with a grease solvent; then wash as recommended.

Mildew

Soak white cottons and linens in one part bleach to 100 parts water with 1×15ml spoon white vinegar. For other white fabrics, soak in one part hydrogen peroxide to four parts water. Rinse well. There is no really safe home remedy for coloured fabrics, but regular washing will reduce the marks.

Milk

Soak in hand-hot solution of enzyme detergent; then wash as recommended, or use a grease solvent.

Paint (emulsion)

Treat immediately with cold, soapy water. Wash as recommended.

Paint (oil)

Treat with white spirit or other solvent before washing as recommended, or use a proprietary paint stain remover.

Perspiration

Soak in hand-hot solution of enzyme detergent; then wash as recommended. Colour removed by perspiration cannot be restored.

Scorch

Soak in hydrogen peroxide for an hour. Nothing can be done if the fibres have been melted or damaged.

Tar

Scrape off excess. Soften the remainder with margarine or butter, and wipe away with a clean rag. Remove any residue with a grease solvent or eucalyptus oil.

Urine

Soak in cold washing solution; then wash as recommended, using a synthetic detergent. If stains are not removed by normal washing, treat with a solution of hydrogen peroxide and diluted ammonia.

Vomit

Sponge with borax solution; then wash in an enzyme detergent.

Wine

If the fabric is suitable, wash at a high temperature, or treat with bleach.

Dyeing and Colour Freshening

Natural fibres, as well as a wide range of synthetics and fibre mixtures can be dyed or colour-freshened at home and given a new lease of life. There are two categories of dye:

1) Substantive dyes: These are available in powder and liquid form for use in hot water. They are suitable for use on cotton, linen, silk, wool, viscose rayon, nylon, acetate, tri-acetate, polyester, modal rayon, and elastomeric fabrics.

2) Reactive dyes: These are available in powder form for use in cold water. When used correctly, they give strong, fast colours on cotton, linen, silk, wool, viscose rayon, and elastomeric fabrics. Reactive dyes are also suitable for dyecrafts such as batik.

Although both types of dye can be used in a washing machine, a substantive dye with an added low-lather detergent has been specially formulated for machine use, making it possible to wash and dye an article in one operation.

Normally, however, an article must be clean before dyeing is started. Where possible, coloured, faded or stained fabrics should be treated with a colour and stain remover to strip them back to a light, even base colour. If the original colour cannot be removed, a darker shade of the same colour family, such as red over pink, should be chosen, or a colour that will blend to give the desired result, eg blue over yellow to make green. Patterns cannot be completely obliterated by dyeing them, so a colour should be picked which will cover the darkest shade or blend with the existing colours to bring out the design in a new, exciting way; for example, a white/yellow/green pattern dyed red will produce attractive shades of red/orange/brown.

Once the colour has been decided, it is important to choose the right type of dye for the fabric and to use the correct amount. The Fabric Guide and Dye Chart which follows is a useful guide. But it must be remembered that as different fabrics 'take' dye differently, the resulting depth of shade may vary slightly from that shown on the dye pack.

When selecting a container for dyeing, make sure that it is large enough to allow the fabric room to move freely. Cramming the article into too small a bowl will prevent the dye penetrating evenly and the result will be patchy. When using a washing machine, dye only half its maximum wash load at a time.

Fabric guide and dye chart

Fabric	Substantive dye Powder or liquid	Substantive dye Powder + detergent	Reactive dye
Acetate	*	*	
Acrylic	Do not dye	Do not dye	Do not dye
Canvas	*	*	*
Cotton	*	*	*
Elastomeric	*		*
Glass fibre	Do not dye	Do not dye	Do not dye
Linen	*	*	*
Modal rayon	*	*	*
Nylon	*	*	
Polyester	+		
Silk	*	*	*
Tri-acetate	*		
Viscose	*	*	*
● Wool	*		*

+ Polyester: not possible to obtain deep shades.
● Wool: use hot water and substitute malt vinegar for washing soda when dyeing with a reactive dye.

Mending and Simple Sewing

However careful one may be, accidental damage to clothes and household items occurs from time to time. Children's clothes are particularly prone to mishaps. A knowledge of mending and simple sewing may save an otherwise perfectly sound article from being thrown away.

Damage to Look For

Clothes

Among the most common mishaps to clothing are buttons tearing away from the garment with a scrap of material adhering to it, causing a hole or damage to the threads surrounding it. Buttons, snap fasteners, hooks and eyes often just come adrift. Zip fasteners break out or their teeth get enmeshed in the material, jamming the slider. Accidental underarm tears in magyar, kimono, and raglan-type garments are common mishaps. The rough treatment to which children's jeans and trousers are subjected may also result in breaking out at the crotch seams, fraying at leg bottoms, and in torn or worn knees. The normal wear-and-tear on shirts and jackets usually shows first in fraying edges at neck and cuffs, in thinning elbows, and 'rubbed' pocket tops. Drooping, uneven hems may occur where fabric has stretched on bias seams and this may also cause sagging over the seat on a tightly fitting but loosely woven skirt or coat.

Knitted garments are subject to pulled threads, and wearing or breaking out at ribbed edges or hems, cuffs, and neckband, with unshapely stretching at these parts. Thin places soon turn into holes at elbows, etc.

Plastic, vinyl, and coated materials, as used in rainwear, are liable to split at the seams and tear out at pockets, buttonholes, and underarms unless properly reinforced.

Leather articles, although generally strong, tend in time to split at seams and joins, especially where, as in many fur coats, the garment is made up from innumerable small pieces, joined by small seams. Although the skins have a certain natural elasticity, the thickness varies according to the part of the pelt used. With older furs, a certain drying and stiffening takes place over the years. This makes the skin brittle and more liable to split under strain. These splits can be satisfactorily repaired (see p99). If moths penetrate, however, there will be permanent damage, so precautions must be taken when storing furs to prevent moth attack. See p74 for more detailed information.

Household articles

Household linen, curtains, soft furnishings, etc can suffer accidental damage from cigarette burns, stains, cuts, and tears, and require careful repairing. Worn corners and edges of towels need attention before threads have frayed out too badly. Old curtains sometimes need their edges removed and rehemmed. Heavy curtains are often worth the trouble of relining. Similarly, large shabby lampshades can be refurbished by fresh braid or fringing. The worn parts of loose covers can sometimes be replaced with matching or toning fabric, and broken fastenings can be renewed to prolong their useful life.

The golden rule with regard to repairs to both clothing and household articles is to attend to the damage immediately it is spotted. Strengthen buttons and small fastenings as soon as they get loose; mend holes before washing the article. Mend all household articles before further use, laundering or dry cleaning.

Mending and Renovating Clothes

Buttons

When these are torn off, with threads adhering, it is often because no adequate interfacing was used between the button and its facing. This is essential; even thin materials require a suitable backing for strong anchorage of all fastenings. Where a hole has been made, place a 5cm square of fine net between the outside and its facing, and tack. Withdraw some self threads from inside hem or elsewhere. Darn across the hole, drawing up gently. Darn over the inside of hole also, if necessary. Press. Replace the button, anchoring it to a small button sewn on the inside.

*Sewing on buttons: **1** making a shank; **2** using a supporting button*

When sewing on buttons, always allow a sufficiently long shank, by placing a matchstick or pencil according to thickness of material over button to ensure stitches of even length. Remove, and pull up button. Wind thread round shank several times before finishing off inside.

Except on fine materials, it is advisable to anchor larger buttons to small ones inside. Buttons with metal loops need no shank.

Damaged buttonholes are often caused by buttons which are too large or too thick to pass easily through the holes. Square, oblong or irregularly shaped buttons will also fray and wear out buttonholes prematurely. If a worked buttonhole is stretched but sound, run fine stitches round the inside near the knotted edge, draw up, and then fasten off securely.

For worn and shapeless buttonholes in cottons and linen, apply a 5cm square of fine, iron-on interfacing, and tack into place. See that the buttonhole lies flat, with edges together. Slit interfacing at hole, and lightly rework the buttonhole, covering original stitching. Trim away surplus interfacing, and press. Use this technique for buttonholes which slit at the outer ends.

Zip fasteners

Broken zips can seldom be repaired successfully. Before buying a replacement, make sure that the opening or placket is sufficiently long to allow easy access for head, hips, etc. Breakage is often due to zips being too short. If necessary, get a longer one. Carefully unpick and remove the original one, lengthening the opening, if necessary. On skirt tops or neck openings, release tapes from facings, bands or collars.

The lapped placket: A concealed opening, used at side opening of skirts, dresses, etc. Press opening, without stretching material. Check zip length against opening. Tack one half of tape under unlapped edge of placket, with teeth just clearing fold. Stitch close to fold. With zip closed, place lap over zip, with fold edge just covering teeth and stitching of underlap. Tack, and stitch on original stitchmarks. Fold in and neaten ends of tape inside.

Centrally placed zip: Remove old zip, and press opening, leaving edges folded. Oversew fold edges together, and place new zip underneath, with teeth lying exactly below seam, with slider facing to front, and its top 5mm below seamline. Tack carefully, and stitch from right side on original stitching lines. Remove tacks and press. To strengthen opening, work a bar tack 5mm up from bottom.

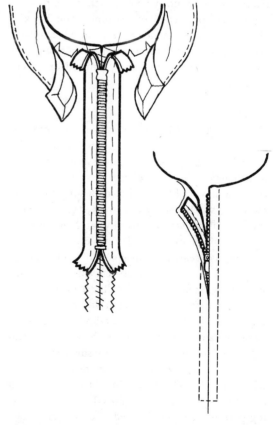

Replacing a central zip

Hooks and eyes and press-studs

Overlapping plackets: Before replacing, darn in any broken threads in material with colourless thread – or use self thread if an actual tear has been caused. See that new hooks, eyes and/or bars are of suitable size for type of material and likely amount of strain in use. Too small hooks will bend, and too large ones look clumsy. Arrange hooks, spacing fairly closely, or ugly gaps will appear in wear. Sew on hooks with bend never less than 3mm from under edge of overwrap. Completely cover eyelets with over-stitching or blanket stitch, and the shank as far as bend of hook. Stitches should be invisible on outside. Position metal bars on underwrap and stitch eyelets as above. Alternatively, work bars (bar tacks) with knotted edge facing away from opening.

Edges meeting with no overlap, eg top of skirt petersham: Use the round eye. Place so that loop projects slightly beyond edge of opening. The hook is placed the same distance back from edge, so that both sides of opening meet exactly when fastened. Avoid using hooks on loosely knitted or woven material.

Tears

Underarm tears: On magyar, raglan, and kimono-type garments these are usually due to restriction caused by tight seam allowance and lack of re-inforcement over the curved or angled seam. If stitching has broken without damaging the seam, merely restitch this, going over it twice. Slash turnings (if not done originally) at 2cm intervals. Press turnings apart, and lay a piece of crossway binding over seamline. Cut a piece of it long enough to take in entire curve, or 7cm either side of a square-angled underarm. Tack both edges of binding. From right side, stitch 3mm either side of seam. The result is a smooth, strong, and pliable reinforcement. If seam has been torn at right angles to seam, repair by turning in torn edges by smallest possible amount, and oversew finely from inside. Reinforce with net or iron-on interfacing. Stretch underarm edge to coincide with opposite edge, after unpicking part of the seam. Proceed as described above. See p97 for illustration.

Hedge tears: These are clean-cut L-shaped tears caused by catching on a sharp projection, such as a nail. The weakest part is the corner. First, from the right side, draw the edges gently together with a self thread taken from an unseen part of the garment, or invisible plastic thread. On thin materials, tack a piece of fine net on the wrong side, and work through this. Use a fishbone stitch, taking the needle over and under the edges alternately, about 3–5mm from the cut. Do not pull tight. Then, working from the right side, start beyond one arm of the L and darn to and fro across the cut, continuing to beyond the corner. Repeat from the end of the other arm of the L, so that the corner is doubly strengthened.

Tops of pleats: These tear out when garment has not enough ease, or pleats have been stitched too far down. To remedy this, unpick pleat seam to 2cm above damaged area. Place a square of fine net behind torn threads. Using self or invisible thread, darn over affected place, taking in net. Restitch seam, and reform pleat edges and tack flat. On the inside, stitch a strip of tape across top of pleat position. If liked, work an arrowhead tack on right side to make the repair stronger and conceal it.

To work arrowhead tack, use buttonhole twist, and follow the diagram on p97. On the inside, a strong bar of stitches forms a long tack (hence name).

Torn pocket corners: Unpick top of pocket 2–3cm below tear. Darn in broken threads or hole over net or interfacing. Cut a second piece of interfacing, and apply over the entire position of top of pocket inside. Restitch the pocket through all thicknesses.

Trousers or jeans torn at crotch

Unpick underleg and front-to-back seams to well beyond affected area. Trim off frayed seam edges, and restitch seams in same order as originally. On the inside, lay strips of seam binding or tape along seamlines, extending these to 7cm from crotch junction. Pin and tack. On outside, machine exactly along seamlines for length of tape; or use zig-zag, if machine can do this.

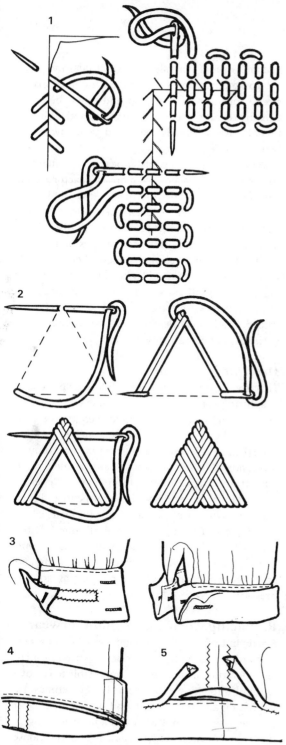

Frayed shirt cuffs

Turn-up type: Completely unpick cuff from sleeve, using pointed scissors or stitch ripper. Lay cuff flat, right side up, and apply tape over worn or frayed middle part. Tack in place and stitch, turning ends under. Gather bottom edge of sleeve, and form pleats as before; then check against cuff, drawing up to fit. With taped repair now on the outside, place bottom of sleeve between edges of cuff. Tack, leaving top edge of cuff free. Stitch. On the outside, pin the free edge so it just covers stitching on sleeve just done. Machine close to edge. When the cuff is turned up, the repair will be concealed in fold.

Single cuffs: Since the lower edge is usually curved at the bottom, cuffs cannot be reversed, as above. Unpick worn or frayed bottom edge to start of shaping, then on each edge turn folds under 6mm, and closely slip-hem folds together. If the cuff is top-stitched, follow original stitching line.

Worn collars: Unpick collar from neckband. Stitch tape over worn foldline, as for cuffs above. Replace collar with repaired side lying under when collar is folded over. Remove any tapes or slot for stiffeners, and replace on new underside.

Worn underarms: If shirt is otherwise sound, insert an underarm gusset as follows. Cut one gusset from each side of lower edge of front flap, approximately 7cm by 15cm. Re-shape and hem shirt edge. Turn under 6mm all round gussets, and press. Tack on outside of underarms, with longer points matched to underarm seams. Stitch close to edge. On the inside, neatly cut away worn material.

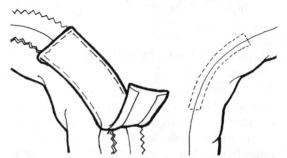

Mending techniques: **1** *repairing a hedge tear;* **2** *working an arrowhead tack;* **3** *turning a worn cuff;* **4** *repairing frayed trousers;* **5** *levelling a dropped hem of a skirt*

Repairing a curved underarm seam with crossway binding

Worn trouser bottoms, jeans, and dungarees

Trouser bottoms: At first signs of wear on bottom edge, unpick hem and turn down. On the inside, apply ready-made adhesive binding to match (after testing for heat reaction, if cloth is synthetic or mixture). Turn up hem 1cm above original crease. Slip-hem and press new foldline.

Crease edge worn right through: Unpick hem, and cut off on crease line. With right sides together, place cut-off hem over trouser bottom with worn edge away from bottom, tack and stitch 6mm up. Press turnings apart, and turn up hem with the join just concealed inside. Hem upper edge and press well.

Children's jeans and dungarees: Let these down and renovate by adding a false hem inside, or a contrast facing outside. A worn crease can also be concealed with plain or ric-rac braid.

Trousers worn or torn at knees

With cloth trousers, wear at knees is first seen as a bulge, before weakened threads actually break out. To prevent a hole appearing, first press the knee area to restore correct shape. From inside, apply iron-on interfacing, cut approximately 15cm–20cm deep, and wide enough to reach seams (test fabric first for heat resistance).

Torn knees on jeans and dungarees can be patched with contrasting cloth, ready-made patches or decorative motifs. Cut patches large enough to reach well beyond worn or torn area or these will soon tear out. Turn edges under, position patch, and stitch round the edge with straight or zig-zag stitching.

Jackets and coats: reinforcing worn elbows

When elbows begin to show wear, the pile has disappeared and threads have become thin, weak, and shiny. At this stage the weave should be filled in and strengthened, using threads drawn from inside facings, hem or seam edges. If lined, unpick at cuff, and turn it up clear of the elbow. Cut a piece of net, large enough to cover the entire elbow area,

and tack inside. Turn sleeve to right side, and place a darning mushroom (or suitable flat object) inside sleeve for support. Darn up and down between existing threads, following the weave and taking in the net. Keep threads loose and take rows well beyond weakened place.

When holes have already appeared on casual and sports jackets, patches are more satisfactory than darning. Cut oval patches, larger than holes, of material, suede, felt or even backed leather-look material. Smear underside of patch thinly with a fabric adhesive and press firmly in position. Allow to dry. If of felt or cloth, oversew edges of patch with invisible thread, or blanket stitch with matching thread. Leather, suede or vinyl patches are backstitched with strong linen or mercerized thread. Ready-made leather patches are obtainable, with spaced holes already pricked.

Dropping hemlines

This trouble often occurs only after wearing. If due to splitting seams, first restitch these with a looser tension. Unpick entire hem, and then press crease flat. Try the garment on, and get a helper to level hem. (Failing this, use a patent hem-marker, though this tends to be less accurate.) Using a ruler, place pins at an equal distance from floor at level of original fold of hem. Remove the garment, and turn hem up on line of pins. Cut off surplus material, so that depth of turn-up is the same all round. If the hem is seam-bound, unpick where necessary, and reapply binding on adjusted edge. Redo hem, and press on hem edge only, to avoid making an 'impression'.

Replacing worn elastic in underwear

Elastic in underwear, although concealed in a slot, is often inserted with an overlocking machine all in one operation, making elastic impossible to remove without unpicking entire hem also. Sometimes, by unpicking and pulling a thread of overlocking, it may be possible to pull a hem undone in one length. If so, remove elastic and restitch slot, using a loose tension. Put in new elastic to fit wearer. Alternatively, leave old elastic in, and insert the new if the slot is wide enough to permit this.

Where elastic is set on to garment edge, as with a

wide, multi-weave elastic waistband, cut this off, leaving overlocked edge only. Measure new elastic on wearer's waist, joining ends by overlapping and oversewing raw edge on both sides. Divide top of waist and elastic into equal sections, marking with a pin. Place new elastic on edge of garment, just covering overlocked edge. Stretch elastic to fit each section and tack firmly. Machine, using zig-zag or largest straight stitch, stretching elastic and holding taut while doing so.

Knitwear

Pulled threads: Never be tempted to cut these off. First, try gently pulling the fabric widthways to stretch loop, which may then disappear. Otherwise, thread the loop on to a needle and take to inside. If long enough, knot uncut loop close to fabric inside. (Use the same technique for woven fabrics.)

Worn ribbing at sleeve and hem: If self wool is available, edges may be buttonhole-stitched to strengthen. Or, if length permits, turn ribbed part under, and hem invisibly. On handknits, one can knit new ribbing in self or contrast yarn. Cut off worn ribbing, and secure loops by threading wool through. Rather than grafting, it is easier to cast off the new ribbing loosely, and place it to the garment with cast off edge of new ribbing to cut-off loops, right sides together. Stretch ribbing to fit, and blanket-stitch it to the garment.

Loosened neckbands, stretched seams, holes, etc: Tighten slack neckbands by inserting elastic in slot if band is double, or sew it behind the rib if single, using loose herringbone stitch. Support stretched seams with crossway binding sewn along seamlines (straight binding is too rigid). Thin places can be reinforced with net inside. Tack in place, and darn up and down the rows with self or matching wool. Darn across the knitting with invisible thread, drawing up slightly. For holes, prepare on inside as above, but work imitation loops down the rows, taking stitches well beyond the hole. Bind down loose threads with invisible thread.

Note This method shows up darn less than if using wool, etc across darn.

Furs and leather

Tears and splits in fur are fairly simple to repair, and will not show on fur side. Remove lining and interlining (if any) from area, and pin out of way. For split seams, place edges together, and oversew or blanket-stitch closely with strong thread, using a glover's needle. To strengthen and to prevent reoccurrence, apply adhesive surgical tape across the repair. For tears not in seams, lightly overcast edges together, apply non-woven interfacing over the tear, and stick firmly down. For thin and broken edges, do not stitch. Lay skin side up and gently position edges together. Reinforce as above, taking interfacing well beyond affected area.

Patching fur: On curly furs, eg Indian and Persian lamb, etc, a small patch of fur can be set direct on to right side. Smear patch thinly with adhesive and press down firmly. Oversew edges of patch with invisible thread. On inside, apply a square of interfacing. Brush up fur round the patch.

Handbags: Stitch broken out seams as above. New handles and fastenings are usually obtainable at craft and leather shops. A faded and shabby handbag will look like new if re-dyed with special leather paint or suede dye, obtainable from shoe repairers and department stores.

Rainwear

To mend edges in plastic and vinyl-coated garments, place torn portions together so they meet exactly, and hold securely with strips of clear adhesive tape on outside. On inside, apply wide strips of woven surgical tape, and press well down. Remove clear tape on outside. With invisible thread, work fishbone stitch at the tear, going through tape on back. Protect seams from tearing out by stitching cotton tape along seamlines inside. Pocket positions should be reinforced from behind with non-woven interfacing, stuck with suitable adhesive.

Mending and Renovating Household Items

Repairing curtains

Frayed bottom edges eventually occur where curtains have constantly rubbed against floor or sills.

Unpick hems, turn up 2cm above frayed edges, re-stitch hem, and if lined, shorten by same amount. Glass fibre curtains must never come in contact with floor, sills or walls, or the edges will disintegrate.

Curtains in sunny rooms often fade at the edges. If the faded area is extensive, the best answer is to redye them, if possible. Where fading only affects a few centimetres beyond the edges, this can be effectively hidden by applying a suitable braid down the sides. If the curtains are sufficiently generous in width, merely turn in a wider hem at sides. Undo the tape at top and sides of hem at bottom. Turn in by required amount, and restitch at new position. If lined, adjust accordingly.

Constant handling will cause holes and thin places where curtains are pulled to and fro. To repair, draw some long threads from inside hem, and place a sufficiently large piece of net underneath hole or worn place. Tack in place. Darn to and fro, following weave as closely as possible. Regularly reversing position of curtains will equalize the wear, or the use of a cording set to draw curtains will reduce wear altogether.

Lampshades

Scorchmarks are usually caused by light bulbs too powerful for the size of shade, or when the shade gets set off centre too close to the lamp. They are practically impossible to remove, but can be concealed with appliqué motifs or matching braid, balanced by a strip on the opposite side. Stick on with adhesive, tucking ends under existing braid or fringing. To renew worn binding, lift cover clear of frame, if necessary, and undo old binding. Wipe wire frame, rubbing off any signs of rust with fine glasspaper. Wind on new binding, pulling taut. Restitch cover where undone.

To renew shabby braid or fringing, remove carefully, and measure new trimming round shade, adding 4cm for turning ends. Turn ends under and stick with fabric adhesive, placing loose ends towards middle of braid. Place one end of braid to edge of shade at seam, and secure with a pin. Smear adhesive thinly inside braid, holding the braid well clear of frame and keeping to centre, and stick down. Meet ends exactly and oversew invisibly. If preferred, sew on by hand.

Loose covers, repairing worn arms, renewing fasteners, etc

If arms and edges are merely worn thin, they can be reinforced by applying iron-on interfacing underneath. Cut this to reach well beyond the weak places. Darn holes with self or matching thread. Stabilize the hole first by tacking or stitching a small piece of net or matching material underneath. On cretonnes and printed materials it may be possible to cut small patches from inside facings, and to appliqué these over the holes. Where the matching cushions are reversible, it is worth while cutting away the underside of the cushion cover, using the material to make loose arm protectors to conceal worn places on the arms of loose covers. Remove cushion cover and cut away material from underside, leaving a 2cm border all round. Replace with plain material. Cut this to exact size of cushion, plus turnings. Fold turnings under, and place over cut margin of cover.

This method saves having to take the cushion cover apart. Cut material obtained in half and hem round edges. Arrange over each chair arm, holding in place with invisible stitching or press-studs. Alternatively, shape to fit arms, and sew on.

When fastenings have broken or come off, renew with small strips of Velcro, or special tape with studs already attached. Otherwise, sew on new hooks, tapes or studs with strong thread, and back position with net or tapes where edges have become weakened.

Repairing carpets and rugs

To patch holes, burns, irremovable stains, etc:
1) Where carpet can be lifted or rolled back, cut away damaged area, following weave (or tufts, if foam-backed) using sharp handyman's knife. Smear fabric adhesive along cut edges, avoiding top of pile. If self cuttings are available, cut patch exactly to size of piece removed, smearing cut edges with adhesive to prevent fraying. If self pieces are unobtainable, cut the patch from a part of the carpet which is permanently concealed by furniture. Fill in second hole so caused with a patch cut from carpet sample of a near match. To insert a patch, cut a hessian square at least 2cm larger than hole and stick firmly over

the hole on the underside. Turn carpet down and insert patch into hole.

2) Where a hole comes near centre of a fitted carpet, the repair must be done entirely from the right side. Cut away the hole and protect the edges as described. Cut hessian larger than hole and push through to underside of carpet. Smear carpet edges around hole with adhesive, using spatula (or nail file), and press down on to hessian. Apply adhesive to back of patch and press firmly into hole.

Joining carpet pieces: Prepare edges to be joined by folding under any loose threads and sticking down. Smear all edges with adhesive and allow to dry. Place one piece, with pile down, with second piece, pile down, close up to it. Using a curved carpet needle and fine twine, stitch edges together with fishbone stitch, taking needle in 6mm from edges. Apply iron-on binding or hessian webbing stuck with adhesive along the join.

Rugs: Worn edges can be satisfactorily bound with carpet braid, either stitched or stuck on. Corners should be mitred, and oversewn with invisible thread. Unless a rug is too thick, worn edges can be turned under at both sides. Apply fabric adhesive under side edges, fold them under and hammer down. Allow to dry. Now apply iron-on carpet braid over the turned edges, or stick hessian webbing over the edges. At ends of rug, apply new fringing to complete the renovation.

Mending lace mats

Darn small holes with matching thread, following design as closely as possible. If the area is thin, place fine net underneath, and darn through this, cutting away surplus afterwards. Strengthen fraying edges with close blanket-stitching.

Techniques Used in Mending Clothing and Household Articles

1) Strengthening weak places by applying suitable reinforcements underneath, eg net, woven or non-woven interfacing, matching or self material, iron-on interfacing (where suitable). Reinforcements may be applied with stitching, using self or invisible thread, or fabric adhesive.

2) Using patches of self or other material, eg suede, felt, leather or carpet, applied to right side. Included are ready-made adhesive patches and decorative motifs.

3) Darning by machine or hand over net base, including simulated knitted stitches (Swiss darning).

4) Taping of seams to strengthen.

5) Using clear sticky tape to hold edges, zips, pockets, etc while repairing.

6) Bonding of hems on clothes and household items with fusible web.

Note When using techniques requiring the application of heat, it is essential to test the reaction of each material on cuttings, facings, etc. Many synthetic and synthetic/natural mixtures have a low melting point and may be irreparably damaged by the high temperatures required to melt the bonding agents used in fusible webbing.

Essential Stitches used in Needlework and Mending

Tacking (basting)

For holding seams, etc in place temporarily. Begin with a knot, taking longer stitches above than below. Fasten off with three overstitches. When removing, snip thread at intervals. Pulling out long lengths may mark the material.

Running

For stitching two pieces of material together, making hand seams, tucks, and gathers. Stitches are small and even on both sides.

Overcasting

Used to neaten raw edges. The needle is inserted near the edge, and the thread brought over to other side in slanting direction. All stitches should slant at same angle.

Oversewing

Method of joining folded edges together, eg lace on to material. Worked as above, but with finer, closely spaced stitches. Used also for holding a folded edge to single material.

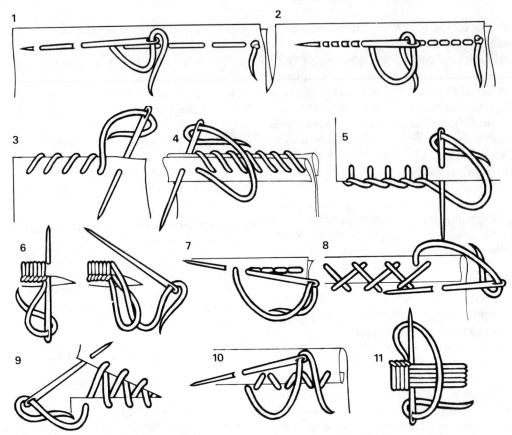

*Basic sewing stitches: **1** tacking (basting); **2** running stitch; **3** overcasting; **4** oversewing; **5** blanket stitch; **6** buttonhole stitch; **7** backstitch; **8** herringbone stitch; **9** fishbone stitch; **10** slipstitch for hemming; **11** bar tack*

Blanket (loop) stitch

For neatening edges. Worked over a loop of thread. Hold loop down with thumb, while bringing needle from under it.

Button-hole stitch

A strong, knotted stitch, giving a firm edge. Begin at the end farthest from edge of item. Start with two backstitches inside and bring needle out on right side, from under one edge of slit. Pass thread from behind needle, and back under point, working from right to left. Pull needle up, forming a figure-of-eight knot on edge. Fan stitches out at round end (nearest garment edge). At straight end, work five loop stitches across. Button-holes coming within a strap or slot, eg shirt front, are placed vertically, and have two straight ends.

Backstitch

Backstitch is very strong. It is normally worked at ends of plackets, pockets, and zips; and also when stitching heavy material, or through several layers. Start with a running stitch, then take the needle back into the end of the first stitch. Bring out one stitch ahead; repeat, keeping stitches at an even tension. It is usually worked from right side and looks like machine stitching.

Herringbone

A loose stitch worked in two lines. Used for hemming, and for keeping elastic in place where there is no slot. Begin with a backstitch and start at left, with needle pointing in opposite direction to that being worked. Take alternative small stitches from right and left, forming crosses between rows.

Fishbone stitch

For drawing together edges of hedge tears, slits, and jagged holes. Take needle into tear on inside: come through to right side in a slanting direction. Insert needle under opposite edge, coming out slightly lower. Proceed, going under and over each edge in fishbone formation, and gently drawing edges together. May be worked from right or wrong side. Hold tear on side not being worked with clear adhesive tape.

Slip-hemming

A loose stitch for turning up hems. Insert needle inside hem edge, and come out. Take a single thread from garment beside fold edge. Slip needle into fold, bringing out 5mm further on. Take another thread from garment and carry on, keeping the stitches slack.

Worked bar (bar tack)

A visible strand for strengthening ends of openings and pleats; also used instead of metal bars with hooks. Take several stitches across end of opening, about 1cm long. Work loop-stitch over these. If used with hooks, the knotted edge should lie towards edge of opening.

Decorative arrowhead

Use buttonhole twist and work as shown in the diagram on p97. This is a useful method for strengthening tops of pleats, etc.

The Sewing Machine

A sewing machine is an essential item of equipment in most homes. Whether used mainly for simple 'running up', repairing household linen, or for serious dressmaking, it deserves proper care and regular oiling and checking. Treated well, a good machine will give many years of troublefree service. The manufacturer's instruction booklet will give information on using and caring for your machine. As a check, remember that a good stitch lies flat on both sides of the work, with both threads at the same tension. The golden rule when machining is to test out needle size, stitch length, tension, and thread on each different material used.

Types of sewing machine

Zig-zag

This type of electrically powered machine which will do straight stitching and simple two-step zig-zag, satin stitching, simple embroidery, over-casting, and button-holing is considered to be the ideal choice for the average home dressmaker. Lightweight and portable models are available.

Semi-automatics

These are more expensive and in addition to the two-step zig-zag, will do a three-step zig-zag stitch which is particularly useful for sewing stretch fabrics. They offer a wider choice of embroidery stitches; some models have twin needle facilities.

Swing needle or semi-automatic

Does straight and zig-zag stitching by changing the sewing foot, and making certain adjustments. Will also make buttonholes, do darning, and a few fancy stitches. A good machine for the average home dressmaker. There are many lightweight portable models.

Fully automatic

The most expensive machine. Some models have built-in discs (cams) which are interchangeable, and will execute innumerable decorative stitches, and do most sewing techniques, eg hemming, button-holing, blind-stitching, etc. Some models incorporate an electronic control, which permits stitch selection to be done at a touch of the finger.

Hand machine

This will do straight stitching, with a reverse action for finishing off seams. Various attachments are usually included, and others can be purchased. Hand machines are not now widely used.

Straight stitch electric

As hand machine, but is electrically powered, and controlled by foot. A light is incorporated in most models. Runs off the mains.

Treadle machine

Now little used domestically in the UK but very widely in Asia and remoter areas. A treadle machine is operated by foot pressure on a platform, connected by a rod and belt to the balance wheel. In industry, these are run by electricity.

Most modern machines will tackle all kinds of materials, providing the correct needles and thread are used. Preparations are available to combat the build-up of static electricity, which can make stitching some synthetic materials troublesome. Strips of thin paper laid along seamlines help when stitching filmy or slippery fabrics.

Needles and Threads

Choosing the correct needle and thread for each sewing job is important. Synthetic threads should be used with synthetic materials, eg nylon, polyester, cotton-covered polyester (for thick materials). Silk is preferable for silks and woollens. Thread sizes vary from 24–60; the higher the number the finer the thread. Avoid using synthetic thread with materials which will be subjected to high iron temperatures or hot steam, as it may melt.

The needles most used for hand sewing are:
1) *Sharps*, which are fine in relation to their length. Popular sizes are 3–10, for most sewing jobs.
2) *Betweens*, which are thicker and shorter. Sizes are as for sharps.
3) *Straws*, which are very long, fine needles used for fine darning and running, etc. Sizes are 1–10.
4) *Carpet needles* (also known as packing needles), which have a wide, bladed point, either straight or curved. They are used for carpet and rug repairs. Various sizes are obtainable.

Machine needles are also of several different types:
1) *For general work*, available in sizes 11, 14, 16 and 18 (British), and sizes 65, 75, 90 and 100 (Continental). However, some different sizes are made by less known makers.
2) *Special 3-bladed needle* for leather, suede, etc.
3) *Ball-pointed needles* for use with knitted fabrics. These 'part but do not pierce' the threads.
4) *Anti-static needles* are specially made to combat static electricity in some synthetic materials.
The last three categories are made in usual sizes.

SAFETY IN THE HOME

When you are in the midst of cooking operations, dress suitably. In the kitchen, for instance, the modern crinoline is absurd, dangerous, out of place, and extravagant. It is extravagant, because the dress is, through being brought nearer the fire, very liable to get scorched, and when once scorched, soon rots, and wears into holes.

Home is the place where children spend most of their time until they go to school, where they learn about their surroundings by experience, a place where we constantly use dangerous knives, fire, hot cooking fat or oil, boiling water, and poisons – and where we are from time to time appallingly careless because we are tired, depressed or over-worked. Home is therefore a place where there are a great number of accidents every year.

Many of these accidents can be prevented; the purpose of this chapter is to bring common dangers to mind and suggest ways of avoiding them.

Two out of every three people who die due to domestic accidents are sixty-five years of age or more, and one out of every ten is a child under five. Three out of ten people sent to hospital as a result of such accidents are children under five, and one in every three is sixty-five or older. Children get hurt because they do not know what the dangers are; older people get injured because they no longer react to their surroundings as quickly and adequately as they once could.

Falls

Falling is the most common fatal domestic accident. Nine out of ten of the victims are sixty-five or older. Young people can fall without doing themselves much damage, and even if they suffer a fracture or some other severe injury, they have every chance of recovering without complications. But for various reasons, elderly people are both more likely to fall, and to suffer from serious complications afterwards.

Precautions against falling

The first thing to look at is the floor. Inspect it for unevenness and loose boards which could trip people up. The kitchen floor is especially important, because falling or stumbling in the kitchen can result in burns and scalds.

If the floor is satisfactory, consider the floor coverings and mats, which should be in good repair, must lie flat, and must not be slippery. The least slippery floor covering is carpet. The next best substance is flexible vinyl, with special non-slip granules incorporated to counteract its tendency to become slippery when wet. Cork has good non-slip properties, but unless treated with a special seal is adversely affected by damp. Linoleum is reasonably resistant to slipping, although like vinyl, the edges, unless fastened down, tend to curl and trip people up. Vinyl asbestos tiles are especially suitable for use on kitchen floors because they are not slippery even when wet, and are more resistant to oil and grease than thermoplastic tiles. Rubber tiles or sheets are all right when dry, but very slippery when wet, and are therefore unsuitable for kitchens and bathrooms. Any floor can be made into a skating rink by incessant polishing, but there are some polishes made from natural or synthetic resins which are less slippery than wax, if properly used.

Stairs

It is always easy to trip on the stairs, even when they are well lit, with the stair carpet in good repair and safely fastened down. Stairs without handrails are dangerous. Any handrail should be continuous, at least on one side of the staircase and must be securely fixed; the most dangerous hazard of all is something which looks safe but in fact is not. A handrail must not suddenly change height or stop, and if it is supported by railings, the bars must not be more than 90mm apart; if the gaps between them are wider, children can squeeze between them or may get their heads stuck. A winding or spiral staircase is best avoided, if possible, because the tapered steps may be too narrow to afford a secure foothold.

All types of stairs need good bright lighting (see p44). Two-way switches are needed so that the light can be switched on at the top or bottom of the staircase. Light fittings must be within easy reach, over a landing.

Single steps where floor levels change are dangerous and need bright lighting; make them as obvious as possible by using a change of colour in the floor covering, or by painting the step itself. Shallow steps are more likely to trip people up; the worst height is 75mm or under. Never leave things on the stairs, eg shoes, children's toys, etc, which might cause a fall.

Bathroom

Many falls happen in the bathroom; some in the bath and some on the wet floor. The best kind of bath has a flat bottom and a handle for people to steady themselves as they get in or out; some are made with patches of slip-resistant finish on the bottom. If the bath is old-fashioned, a bar or handle can be fitted to the wall, and non-slip mats are available which fasten by suction pads to the bottom of the bath. See also *Electricity* p110.

If you have older people living in the house, it is sensible in any case to arrange to have the sort of door lock which can be opened from the outside if there is an accident. This is also true of the door of the WC.

Other areas

Still inside the house, a number of falls are caused every year by cupboards and shelves out of easy reach. People get up on rickety chairs or lose their balance when they are stretching out, particularly if spring-cleaning.

There should always be a stout pair of steps about the house which can be used for climbing up, not only to cupboards and shelves but also to light fittings and the tops of windows; one of the commonest causes of falling at home is window-cleaning.

More than a quarter of all domestic accidents happen just outside the house. As most of these accidents involve falls, it is sensible to check whether there are any obviously dangerous traps on the way to the dustbin or clothes line, ie shallow steps, uneven surfaces, blind corners, and the single step where there is an unexpected change of level. It is important that such places are well lit; if you cannot have an outside light fitting, keep a torch by the door to take with you.

Fires

Most domestic fires are caused by carelessness, by children experimenting with matches and lighters, by unguarded fires, cigarette ends put down carelessly, smoking in bed, misused gas, paraffin, and electric equipment (especially television sets still plugged in overnight), and by clothes left to air too close to a source of heat.

Preventing fires involves keeping down the fire risks in the home. If you want to find out how to do this or advice on installing a fire escape or fire detecting system, your local fire brigade headquarters will give you free advice and may also offer to inspect your house.

Most household insurance policies cover damage by fire; make sure that yours also covers claims for damage by smoke and water used in fire fighting (see p22).

You should ensure that all room partitions, ceiling tiles, etc are made from flame-resistant materials.

You may find that the building regulations for a conversion require you to take elaborate precautions to cut down fire risk.

Fireguards

Always use a fireguard in front of open fires when there are small children in the house, preferably one made to British Standard (BS) specifications and bearing the Kitemark. Never leave an open fire alight in an empty room without an efficient fixed small mesh spark guard. It is compulsory to fit oil heaters, gas fires, and electric fires with guards which have apertures small enough to stop children poking their fingers or hands through, but there are probably still many in use with bigger apertures; check to make sure that children cannot reach the fire through such a guard. See also *Open Fires* p113.

It is illegal to sell flammable nightwear for children; if you make the children's nightclothes yourself, check that the material is not flammable. Adult's nightwear made of flammable material must by law carry a tag warning of fire risk.

Maintenance

Even appliances manufactured to the highest safety standards can cause fires if they are not correctly maintained. Electric blankets, oil stoves, boilers and chimneys should be serviced or cleaned regularly. See the chapter on Care and Maintenance of the Home.

Look out for worn flexes and plugs that are broken or cracked, or which become hot when in use; replace these immediately. If the wiring in the house is old, have it checked every five years. (See also p110.)

Exits

It is important to consider how to get out of the house in case of fire, when the normal exits may be blocked. If you live in a terrace or semi-detached house, you may be able to get out through a skylight to the next roof. The keys to security locks should be kept where the family can find them (even in the dark). If you have a choice, find out if it is easier to get out of the back of the house on to an outbuilding roof, or perhaps the front would provide a soft fall on to earth in a flower-bed. If you live in a flat, you should make sure that you know how to get to the fire escape.

If you live in a tall house or are remote from help, there are a number of devices which can be fitted to help you to escape quickly via an outside escape, and equipment is available for lowering people out of windows. It is a good idea to invest in several

strong, tested rope ladders which can be kept in the upstairs rooms. The rope ladders must be long enough to reach the ground floor level from the top window.

Fire detectors

These are commonly available and should be installed in every home. They respond to changes caused in the alarm system by smoke, thereby setting off an alarm. It may be necessary to have several installed.

Fire blankets

It is useful to have a fire blanket particularly to deal with a chip pan fire. Blankets are easier and safer to use if they have tabs on the back so that they can be held with the hands shielded from the heat. They should be kept in the kitchen in a place where they can be reached if the cooker is alight.

Extinguishers

Fire extinguishers are useful if you know how to use them. Put them in obvious places and have them serviced as the maker recommends. Water extinguishers should never be used on electrical or chip pan fires.

Buckets of earth or sand

These are useful for smothering small fires.

What to do in case of fire

Unless the fire is in its very early stages, the top priority is to get everyone out of the room concerned and – this is vital – shut the door to starve the flames of air and prevent the fire spreading; telephone 999 for the fire brigade, and leave the house (see above).

If you are trapped upstairs, stuff clothes under the door to keep out smoke (it kills more people than flames do) and shout for help from the window. Do not leap unless you really must, but prepare for this eventuality by knotting sheets together and getting a mattress ready to throw down to the ground.

Should a person's clothes catch fire, roll him in a blanket on the ground until the flames are out. Cover burnt skin with a clean cloth wrung out in water or a solution of a 1 × 5ml spoon of salt in 600ml water, and dial 999 for an ambulance. (Four-hour courses on first-aid, run by the St. John ambulance brigade, are well worth taking in readiness for such emergencies.) See also the chapter on Medical Care in the Home.

Even if a fire is only small, call the fire brigade in case it spreads (there is no charge) but tackle it yourself meanwhile. If electricity or gas is involved, turn this off. Do not carry a blazing object because the air movement will fan the flames, but smother it with a wet cloth. Throw water (from a distance of two metres) except when a chip pan is involved, or anything connected to electricity. Do not stand where the fire is between you and the door or other escape route, in case it spreads and cuts you off.

(For insurance claims dealing with damage not only from fire but also from smoke and water used in fire fighting, see the chapter on Security of the Home.)

The kitchen

The kitchen is clearly the most dangerous room in the house, and the most dangerous area is around the cooker; its position in the kitchen is all-important. In the first place, the cooker must not be near a door, as this creates a risk of collision involving boiling water or fat. Secondly, the cooker must not be in the line between two doors, so that people have to walk past it. Thirdly, it must not be under a window, for draughts can blow a gas flame out and can blow curtains across the cooker so that they catch fire.

If possible, work surfaces of the same height as the cooker should be provided on each side of it, not only for the sake of convenience, but also because this reduces the risk of saucepan handles sticking out and being knocked.

It is sensible to keep a fire extinguisher of the type to deal with burning fat fixed in a place easily accessible if the cooker is on fire. Fire blankets make good kitchen extinguishers (see p107). The pan for deep-frying should never be filled to more than one-third capacity. Never leave a pan of fat on the cooker if you go out of the room even if only for a short time, and remember that wet food like frozen chips, put suddenly into hot fat, will make it

bubble up and perhaps spill over. If the fat should catch fire, switch off the electricity or turn off the gas. Then wet a large cloth – a drying-up cloth will do – wringing it until it no longer drips, and cover the pan with it. If you have a metal cover or lid for the pan, use that, and cover any burning fat with the cloth. Leave the pan for at least two hours before uncovering it. Never try to put the flaming pan out with water or carry it outside. Take your time and keep calm, and you will be able to control the fire more effectively than if you panic.

Scalds

Scalds are caused by boiling water or steam, usually coming from a kettle, saucepan, hot-water bottle or teapot. Washing machines too can be the cause of scalds. It is only too easy to have an accident with boiling water because water is so often boiled, and boiling it is dangerous. If you are cautious, however, the dangers are minimized.

Saucepan handles must not project from the top of the cooker. Take the teapot to the kettle when making tea. Do not pass hot drinks at the table over heads or hands. Take hot-water bottles out of young children's beds before they get in. These are common-sense precautions, but they are all too often neglected. For advice on the treatment of scalds, see p141.

Oil heaters

These are quite safe if used properly, with regard for some important safety precautions.

In Britain any modern oil heater must carry the British Standards Institution Kitemark (BS 3300). Under the Consumer Safety Act, it is illegal to sell new or second-hand heaters which do not comply with the Oil Heaters (Safety) Regulations of 1977. Older heaters can sometimes be modified to comply with the above standard. This should be arranged through your dealer.

Follow the manufacturer's instructions on the correct use of an oil heater. Only use it for heating a room; do not try to cook on it or to dry clothes around it.

Never carry an oil heater when it is alight: an accident is all too likely. Do not stand an oil heater in a draught and make sure that it is kept where it cannot easily be knocked over by children or pets. Children should never be left in a room with an unguarded heater. Convector-type heaters should be fixed to the floor or wall with brackets, but well away from any flammable materials, and in an area where people passing by will not be exposed to direct or close contact with the heater.

Flammable liquids

Paraffin ought not to be stored in the home, but if it has to be, keep it in a proper container, in a different room from the heater. Some leases include restrictions on the storage of 'oil', which includes paraffin. Never keep more than 3 litres indoors, and keep the supply out of reach of children. When you want to fill the heater with paraffin, first make quite certain the heater is not alight; it is possible to turn the wick down quite a long way without the flame being wholly quenched. If the heater has a separate tank, take it out, and carry it into a separate room to fill it. If the heater has no separate tank, take it out of the room in which it is being used, to fill it. Try not to spill the paraffin on the tank, heater or floor. If you do, wipe the spilt oil completely dry before returning the heater or tank to its place. Always take the tank or heater to the paraffin, not the paraffin to the heater.

Flammable liquids, including cleaning materials, should never be used in a kitchen if a cooker is on, or if anyone is smoking. Remember that a pilot light on a gas cooker is a live flame. Make sure that the caps of all containers for flammable liquids are tightly fastened.

It is illegal to store petrol in your home, but you can store up to two 3 litre containers of petrol in your garage. It is possible to buy special metal petrol containers which are safer than ordinary petrol storage cans. If you are using portable gas heaters (LPG), never store spare cylinders in the house.

Risky materials

Modern furniture made of plastics and modern fabrics and foam fillings present more of a fire risk than traditional materials. When they ignite they may give off a lot of smoke and fumes which can quickly overcome people. Flame-retardant materials are available at an additional cost – they still burn, but more slowly.

Other items that flare most quickly are wooden ironing boards, oil paint, and old oil, electric or gas appliances made in the days before strict safety standards were implemented; get rid of them if possible.

Gas

Although natural gas is not poisonous, it is explosive, and so any suspected leak should be taken very seriously.

Never try to fit any gas appliance yourself or allow any unskilled person to do so, and do not attempt repairs yourself. Contact your Gas Board or a registered gas installer.

You should know where the main gas tap is; if not, look near the gas meter: the tap is usually next to it. Make sure the tap moves freely, and that you can shut off the gas. When the line scored across the centre of the main gas tap is at right angles to the long axis of the gas pipe the gas is off.

A slight smell may merely be due to a pilot flame having gone out, leaving a small jet of unburnt gas escaping. Turn off the pilot gas, put out any flame or fire in the room, and open windows. When the smell has disappeared, turn the pilot on and light it.

If you think that the oven burner might have gone out, make sure that all the burners on top of the cooker, including the pilot light, are out before you open the oven door. If you use a slot meter and it runs out, turn all the gas taps off before you put in another coin, and make sure that all the pilots are re-lit when the gas comes on again.

Sometimes gas may leak from joints on water heaters; all that is needed is to tighten the nuts with a spanner. A smell of burnt gas may indicate a blockage in a ventilation duct, eg a bird's nest, which you could remove yourself.

If there is a strong smell of gas, immediately turn off the main tap, put out any flame or fire in the house, and open all the windows; then phone the Gas Board.

The emergency gas service makes no charge for stopping gas leaks. (Charges are made, however, for doing repairs to prevent a recurrence.)

Electricity

Sometimes an electric fire or cooker ring looks harmless because it is black, but a good number of burns are caused by 'black heat' in an appliance like an iron or a hotplate which never becomes red hot, or by one which has just been switched off. This is the sort of accident which is very difficult to guard against, but there are other dangers from electric appliances which are quite obvious: never drape clothes over convector heaters, and never leave electric fires with exposed elements switched on when there is nobody in the room; never leave electric fires standing where people or animals can knock them over. It is worth remembering that there is a risk of fire from a radiant heater allowed to stand nearer than 900mm to a piece of furniture, and that a BS approved appliance, connected to an electric plug which complies with the appropriate British Standard by a length of British Standard flex is still a danger, if there are metres of flex lying on the carpet waiting to trip somebody up.

Defective insulation is extremely dangerous, so be careful to inspect all flexes and plugs regularly. Replace flex with a new length if it is frayed or worn – do not try to mend it with insulating tape. Replace plugs and sockets if they are cracked, and make sure that connections are not loose. Plugs with fuses should have the right value of fuse for the appliance they are supplying; if in doubt ask the Electricity Board. (See also pp68–69.) Open sockets offer a perpetual temptation to small children, so keep 'blind' plugs in the sockets when you are not using them, or fit covers if there are toddlers in the house. In any case you should have shuttered sockets, with a shutter that closes over the live hole when the plug is removed.

For electric blankets, see the chapter on Care and Maintenance of the Home.

Bathroom

A wet body is a particularly good conductor of electricity, and the bathroom is the one place in the house where there can be no compromise with safety precautions. The light must be controlled by a pull switch, and the only socket allowed is the special fitting for shavers. The light should be an enclosed fitting to prevent anything being plugged into the light socket. Electric fires must be wall-mounted, with a cord-operated switch. (See *Electric Shock* p144.) Never take any mains-operated appliance into the bathroom.

Poisoning

Every year hundreds of people die from accidental poisoning, and many thousands of people survive only after hospital treatment. Children are more liable to accidental poisoning than adults as they tend to swallow all kinds of things through curiosity or ignorance, many of which can be dangerous. Remember that alcohol is a poison and should be inaccessible to children. See also *Poisonous Plants* (p112).

There are two groups of poisons which regularly cause fatal domestic accidents: drugs and household fluids.

Drugs

The great danger with tablets, particularly if coloured, is that small children mistake them for sweets. Parents too, for the best of reasons, sometimes induce their children to take medicine by pretending that they are a type of sweet, thereby giving rise to a natural confusion in the child's mind.

Sometimes too, a child will take an overdose of an attractively flavoured preparation which has been prescribed for him or her, simply because of the appealing taste. This may prove dangerous as there is little difference between a beneficial and a poisonous dose. Additionally, few modern drugs in overdoses cause vomiting.

Precautions
1) Lock up all medicines in cupboards out of the reach of children, and make sure that the lock is childproof.
2) Do not leave medicines lying around or even in handbags or loose clothing.
3) Try not to let children see you taking medicine, as they may try to copy you later.
4) If medicines have been supplied for acute conditions, flush them down the lavatory as soon as the patient recovers.

5) If there is a chronic invalid in the house, check every few months with the doctor which preparations need to be kept.

6) Do not take medicines out of the containers in which they are supplied because the name of the drug is always clearly stated and any change may cause confusion.

7) Never take a medicine left over from a previous illness.

Domestic fluids

Disinfectants, paraffin, bleach, turpentine or turpentine substitute, and detergent solutions are nearly always found in a house somewhere near the sink, often in a cupboard at ground level. It is not surprising, therefore, that small children drink them from time to time. This is more likely to happen if the poisonous fluids are stored in an old lemonade or beer bottle; so they must be left in their own containers, which cannot be mistaken for soft drink bottles, and clearly labelled. It goes without saying that poisonous domestic fluids must be stored out of the reach of small children.

Aerosols must also be kept out of the reach of children, and in a cool place; they must never be put on a fire for disposal, for when heated the cans are liable to explode. Use aerosols at arm's length, and avoid breathing in the contents.

Suffocation

Six out of ten victims of suffocation are children under five. Children under a year old are especially liable to choke on small pieces of food, sweets or pieces of toys that have broken off. A baby's dummy must be BS approved; there must be no danger of it coming apart.

Very small babies need no pillow. When they get old enough to want their heads supported, the pillow is best put under the mattress, not on top. The dangers of plastic bags and sheets are well known, but one still finds plastic bags lying about in houses where there are toddlers.

Every year there are an increasing number of cases of asphyxia associated with the use of heating appliances. People are affected by carbon monoxide gas in rooms too poorly ventilated to get rid of the products of combustion given off by oil and gas heaters, and there have been cases where inefficient central heating installations have allowed carbon monoxide to escape in lethal quantities inside the home.

It is vital to keep rooms well ventilated in spite of the human tendency to cut out every likely source of draughts on a cold evening; for it is possible, in a small closed room, to use up the oxygen in the air while building up a concentration of carbon monoxide. Methods of adequate ventilation are described on pp57-58.

Never use gas appliances in rooms without adequate ventilation. Central heating and other gas appliances such as water heaters must be fitted by the Gas Board, or by a qualified gas installer, and regularly maintained.

The use of natural gas has eliminated the danger of gas poisoning because it contains no carbon monoxide. It can, however, cause asphyxiation and is highly flammable. It must, therefore, be treated with caution.

Heating equipment which burns solid fuel or oil must also be correctly installed, as these can otherwise result in carbon monoxide asphyxia.

Drowning

The bathroom can be a dangerous place for young children. Babies should never be left alone in the bath – even for a moment. Children in the early walking stages sometimes overbalance into a full bath and fail to keep their heads out of the water; small children and babies should never be left or allowed to play in the bathroom by themselves.

Children begin to wander outside the house by themselves by the time they are two or three years old – an age when they cannot get themselves easily out of trouble if they fall into a swimming-pool or a pond; and very small children can drown in as little as 50mm of water. This sort of accident is more liable to happen in the summer when pools are kept full, but a winter accident – especially if the water has a covering of ice – is very serious, the temperature of the water being low and the shock attendant on falling in being more severe.

In general, by the time children reach school age

they usually succeed in getting themselves out of the worst trouble, but where there are children it is only common-sense to keep water butts and tanks covered up and swimming-pools either covered, fenced in or empty.

Accidents in the Garden

A garden shed or garage usually shelters a lethal collection of weed-killers and sharp tools dangerous both to children and adults. Gardeners are advised to hang up rakes, hoes, and brooms on the wall with their heads upwards. All tools with sharp edges must be kept out of the reach of children.

It is sensible for gardeners to make sure that they are immunized against tetanus and to keep their immunity up to date, because sooner or later everyone who works in a garden is bound to cut or scratch himself and contaminate the wound with soil. If you are in doubt, consult your doctor. In some areas, poisonous snakes can be a real if rare hazard; but the bite of an adder, the only poisonous snake found naturally in the UK, is not very dangerous. If you are bitten, keep calm; wash the wound in water but do not try to cut it open or put on a tourniquet; keep the bitten limb still until you reach medical aid.

Pesticides and herbicides must be kept out of the reach of children, if possible in a locked cupboard. When you use any of these special products for the garden, always follow the instructions on the label. It is a mistake to make up more of a solution than is needed and any solutions that have not been used at the end of the job should be flushed away. Keeping herbicides and pesticides in old lemonade or beer bottles is highly dangerous.

For advice on wasp and bee stings, see the chapter on Medical Care in the Home.

Heart attacks

Although not strictly speaking accidents, a number of attacks of coronary disease of the heart are brought on in the spring by the task of mowing the lawn. Elderly people or those liable to heart disease should take it gently at first; it is a mistake to rush up and down even though the weather is marvellous and the grass long.

Poisonous Plants

Poisonous plants grow not only in the country but also in towns and parks, on vacant building sites, and on wasteland. About 200 British plants contain some sort of poison, but only a few cause serious symptoms. The best known is deadly nightshade (*Atropa belladonna*) which bears small black berries that children sometimes eat. Another quite common poisonous seed is that of the thorn apple (*Datura stramonium*) which produces the same symptoms as deadly nightshade: the child becomes 'as hot as a hare, blind as a bat, dry as a bone, red as a beet, and mad as a hen'.

The most poisonous tree in the UK is the yew; children are sometimes tempted by the berries, which produce acute, alarming, and dangerous symptoms. As yew trees are not very common in towns, this particular danger is more present in the country, perhaps threatening the town child on holiday more than the child brought up in rural surroundings.

A tree more common in towns but almost as poisonous is the laburnum. All its parts are poisonous, but there is a concentration of poison in the leaves, the seeds, and the pods which look like miniature pea pods. Other poisonous plants include holly, mistletoe, and lupin – it is the seeds or berries of these common plants which contain the poison – and also cherry, the stone of which is poisonous if broken and chewed.

Children should be trained never to eat anything growing wild except blackberries, which they can be taught to recognize easily.

Similarly, the best defence against poisoning by fungi which look like mushrooms is never to eat 'mushrooms' growing wild unless you know exactly what you are doing.

Diseases Transmitted by Pets

Zoonoses are diseases and infections naturally transmitted between vertebrate animals and man. They include worm infections, infestation with fleas or lice, infections with bacteria such as anthrax, tuberculosis, and paratyphoid, fungus infections and diseases caused by viruses such as cat-scratch fever, psittacosis from certain birds, and rabies from mad dogs. If you are unlucky enough to get bitten or scratched, let the doctor see the wound as soon as possible. For other common-sense precautions, see p128.

Summary

To summarize some important points on safety in the home:

Oil heaters

1) Make sure that the heater has the Kitemark of the British Standards Institution (BS 3300).
2) Follow the maker's instructions.
3) Store paraffin in a proper container outside the house. Never keep more than 3 litres inside the house.
4) Do not keep paraffin in the same room as the heater.
5) Before you fill the heater make sure it is not alight.
6) Take the tank or heater to the paraffin, not the paraffin to the heater.
7) Do not carry an oil heater while it is alight.
8) Do not try to cook on an oil heater.
9) Do not dry clothes on or too near it.
10) Make sure that children and animals cannot knock it over.
11) Make sure that the room is well ventilated.

Open fires

It is an offence punishable by law to allow a child under the age of twelve years old (seven years in Scotland) to be in a room containing an unguarded fire as a result of which the child is killed or injured (Children and Young Persons Act 1933).

In case of fire:

1) Get everyone out of the room.
2) Close the door.
3) Let everyone in the building know there is a fire.
4) Call 999 for the fire brigade.
5) See if the fire can be dealt with; ie what appliances are available which can be used safely.
6) Do not endanger yourself.

If you are trapped:
  i) Get into a room facing on to the street if possible.
  ii) Block up the door with a blanket or rug.
  iii) Shout for help from the window. Do not jump unless you have to.
  iv) Should a person's clothes catch fire, roll him in a blanket on the ground till the flames are out.

Gas

It is illegal to use a gas appliance if you know or suspect that it is defective or insufficiently ventilated (Gas Safety Regulations 1972).

1) Never try to fit a gas appliance yourself.
2) Make sure your gas appliances are British Gas Approved.
3) Know where your main gas tap is and how to use it, and make sure it moves properly.
4) If you use a slot meter and it runs out, make sure all the gas taps are turned off before you put in another coin, and that all pilot lights are re-lit afterwards.
5) With a strong smell of gas, turn off main tap, put out any flame or fire in the house, open windows, and phone Gas Board.
6) Maintain all appliances carefully.
7) Make sure the room is properly ventilated.
8) If in doubt, consult your Gas Board.

Electricity

1) An electric plate or iron may be 'black hot'.
2) Throw away frayed or worn flexes. Do not mend them; replace them.
3) Replace cracked plugs and sockets; fasten them securely if they are loose.
4) Make sure that plugs have the right fuses and are correctly wired.
5) Switch off at the wall socket and unplug the television set at night or when you leave the house – do not rely merely on the switch on the set.
6) Switch off the mains electricity before you try to carry out any repairs. Switch off and unplug appliances before attempting to mend them.

Medicines, poisons, and knives

Keep out of the reach of children.

HELP IN THE HOME

Good temper should be cultivated by every mistress, as upon it the welfare of the household may be said to turn; indeed, its influence can hardly be over-estimated, as it has the effect of moulding the characters of those around her, and of acting most beneficially on the happiness of the domestic circle.

Few people these days employ full-time living-in staff in the home. Those who do usually have a reason which will enable at least some of the cost to be set off against business expenses – a large house open to the public or a lot of official entertaining to do. A household with a working wife or mother who has to leave the house and family in reliable hands may have to have living-in help such as an au pair girl, particularly if there is an invalid or several small children at home.

The formal hierarchy of a fully staffed house, with servants who had a professional understanding of the jobs to be done, has gone, and with it, the rigid demarcation of who did what. There are, therefore, few clearly defined rules about what is and what is not expected from help. This makes drawing up a 'job specification' both easier and more difficult.

Any employer who recognizes that help in the home which is reliable, trustworthy, and competent deserves care, consideration, appreciation, and reward for good work willingly done, is not likely to have any need to consider what actions are 'legal'. Nevertheless, every employer does have certain responsibilities: the legal requirements relating to employment of staff and to the use of service agencies are discussed on pp120–22.

Hiring Help for the Home

The best, and possibly most reliable, way is through personal recommendation. For full-time or specialist staff, a reputable employment agency is the place to go. These tend to be found only in the largest cities, although they will, of course, consider supplying staff all over the country. Some of the large agencies specialize in recommending and placing staff from and for overseas postings. A good agency will screen applicants before sending them to you, so specify as clearly as possible the duties that are involved.

Agencies charge a fee; it may be the equivalent of your employee's salary for a month, or a percentage of the annual wage.

Advertising in national or local papers for living-in specialist staff may produce a response.

If you are looking for daily or casual help, advertising in the local paper is one of the best ways. One can also put a postcard in a local shop window, but there is a certain security risk in doing this in some neighbourhoods in large cities. Never say 'Help wanted for professional man/woman out at work all day' and never give the telephone number!

The Interview

Never take on help in the home (au pair girls excepted) unless you have had an opportunity to interview the applicant before you offer the job, preferably at the place of work.

If you call anyone for an interview from a distance, you will of course have to pay their travelling expenses.

You should have a clear idea of the duties you expect to have performed; these should be written down, or at least clearly marshalled in your own mind.

When prospective helps arrive, whether it is for work inside or outside the home, invite them in for a few moments' conversation. Ask about previous jobs, the reason for a change, etc. Explain the set-up in your household – the number of people and an outline of the work you expect them to do. If you like the person you are interviewing, you can then embark on a tour of the house or garden, including, of course, the living quarters for a living-in post, and go into more detail. If you do not like the person, explain that you are interviewing a number of people, will decide shortly, and will get in touch.

When you have shown the house or garden and explained the work, invite the applicant to sit down and discuss in more detail the wages you are offering, when and how they will be paid, what time off and leave is suggested, and how social security and tax will be dealt with.

(If you have any 'house rules' about smoking, it is best to explain these before rather than after you have engaged new staff.)

Your prospective employee will expect to ask you a few questions about your family, the amount of entertaining you do, and so on; it is important to cover in an interview any relevant points – the fact that you may be away, or that your mother-in-law lives next door, if needed in case of emergency. If you have typed out a list of duties to be performed, and you want to offer the job then and there, give her the list. Make the offer 'subject to references'. Even if the applicant has come with a written reference, you must check it carefully, either by talking to the person concerned, if that is possible, or by asking for the name of one or more further referees. Decide on a date on which work is to begin – obviously a day when you can be there yourself.

You should follow up your verbal offer in writing. This letter should spell out the terms of the agreement offered, salary, time off, paid leave, and the period of notice to be given on either side. It is a good idea to take on permanent living-in staff with an initial trial period of one month. Of course, you may not need to do this for daily or part-time help, although it is quite a good idea to set down in writing just what you have agreed.

Types of Help

Nanny or children's nurse
A living-in trained nanny or children's nurse whose sole responsibility is the general care of the children is a very rare person these days. Sometimes women are lucky enough to be able to have a professional nursery nurse for the first few weeks after the baby is born, to help the baby and mother settle into the programme of feeding and care. If you do have a trained nanny or children's nurse, it is important to remember that she is a 'professional' and whether she lives in or, as is happening more often, comes daily, perhaps for five days a week, her main job is the care of the child. What she is prepared to do in addition to help to run a house is a matter for negotiation between you, but if you are lucky enough to have this kind of help, you have to work as a 'nanny and mother' team, and the duties of looking after the child must be clearly understood between you.

Mother's help
This is a reliable, though untrained, helper in the home who is expected to look after the children rather more than doing the housework. She should be trustworthy, get on well with the children, and be able to stand in for you in your absence. Until you are satisfied that she is really capable, you should not disappear to work and leave her to cope for too long. You may have to come home early or unexpectedly for a few days. It may, of course, take several weeks to find out how you can best work together in the interest of the children.

Whether your mother's help lives in or comes for a few hours a day, it is obviously important that she knows exactly what her duties are. You should also leave clear instructions about contacts in case of emergencies (see *Baby-sitters* p118) and write down any points you particularly want her to remember in your absence.

Au pairs
This is a girl from a foreign family, here to learn English, and living with a family. She has no worker rights, being classed as a student, and is expected to work half a day, spending the rest as a

tourist or in language classes. She is paid her keep and pocket money. She nearly always helps families with children; occasionally she helps with caring for the elderly.

Most families find their au pairs through personal recommendation, and exchange information. The au pair will usually send a photograph as an aid to recognizing her when you meet her.

Au pairs are not usually interviewed before being accepted into the house, although agencies placing girls will want to know about you and your circumstances and will expect you to provide references.

Agencies also have codes of conduct to which both parties are expected to agree, but au pairs are sometimes exploited by families and sometimes families are exploited by au pairs. Living with strange people and having a stranger come to your house requires adjustments on both sides.

Different languages can make problems in communication, and situations develop which would easily be resolved if both parties could express their wishes clearly. It should be possible to spell out, with the aid of a friend or someone from the agency who speaks the same language as your au pair, the conditions that you want to make clear to her.

It is important that the au pair should like children and that she will be given some guidance on looking after them. If cleaning and other household duties are expected, this should be made clear from the beginning. Evening duties have to be settled. Her use of the telephone can create friction. If you cannot stop her, at least make it clear that calls overseas are cheaper at night and at the weekend.

If the relationship with your first au pair goes well you will probably have a stream of her friends and friends' friends applying to come to you when she leaves.

Accommodation

As the house they live in is 'home' for living-in staff, their rooms should be pleasantly and comfortably furnished. There should be easychairs as well as a bed, writing table, cupboard and drawer space,

reading light and television set. A child's nanny or nursery help who is expected to sleep in the same room as the baby should be able to retreat to another room where she can read, write, watch television or receive a visitor in private.

Indeed privacy, independence, and the possibility of inviting friends are vital for any living-in staff, whether it be a cook-housekeeper, so rare nowadays, or an au pair girl.

A helper who comes in by the day should have a place to sit and rest and some space in which to store a spare overall, shoes, and a cardigan, for example.

If you do not make considerate provision for living-in and other regular help, you will not be able to keep even a most willing employee.

Time Off

Living-in staff should be quite clear about the number of hours they are expected to work during the day, and the amount of time they have off each week. They should have at least one whole day and one half day a week and a regular slice of time to themselves each day.

Do not make a habit of expecting employees to give up their time off because of emergencies. If one arises, or a special event is planned well in advance, it is usually possible to come to some kind of arrangement with staff, but they should be compensated for giving up their time off by an extra payment, extra leave or time off. It is often a temptation when staff are living in to think that because they are on the premises they can be asked to help out; their free time must, however, be respected.

Equipping your Help

Help in the home must not be expected to work with worn-out or old-fashioned equipment. If you do not do any cleaning yourself, you may not realize that mops, brooms, and vacuum cleaners are not working efficiently, so helpers should be asked from time to time if equipment is in good order, or needs replacing.

If you have any fixed ideas about the type of

product you want to use for cleaning or washing, say so; otherwise be resigned to buying the product your daily help prefers. It will probably lead to smoother working.

Giving Notice

Terminating the employment of a member of your staff who lives in is not easy to do. As with any other relationship, the business of living under the same roof is not always plain sailing. That is why an initial trial period is recommended, since it will not be quite as difficult on either side to terminate the agreement at the end of the month and acknowledge that it has not worked out.

The employee who is in breach of agreed conditions should, in normal circumstances, be given a second chance. If the employer believes the employee has been negligent or dishonest, he or she must say so, and let the employee state her case.

If the situation cannot be resolved, any act of dismissal must be done calmly and privately after due deliberation and without anger or petulance.

You must speak directly to the employee, never through another person. It is usual to make the dismissal verbally and confirm it in writing.

If the employee has been with you for some time, and the reason for terminating employment is a change in your circumstances, you should be as generous as you can be in terms of salary and period of notice.

If, for any reason, you wish the employee to leave at once or if the employee wishes it, salary in lieu of notice should be given. If the employee wants to leave you and the circumstances are not particularly agreeable, it is usually wise to let her do so without working out the period of notice, if that is what she wants. Of course if this is very inconvenient, you can require her to stick to the terms of any contract you have made, but you may regret your insistence.

The employee may be entitled to appeal to an Industrial Tribunal for compensation for being dismissed.

Terminating the employment of part-time or casual labour is not usually as difficult, but even here it must be carried out fairly and calmly.

References

While it is not fair to give a glowing reference to an employee who does not deserve it, withholding a letter of reference is unjust. The giving of a reference is privileged in law. Anything said that is true, provided it is not malicious, is not actionable. If someone has been dishonest you should not write in her reference that she is honest, but equally you should not spell out the reason for her dismissal.

If, however, you are losing a reliable, trustworthy, and competent employee you will not find it difficult to write a reference which will make clear your regret that such a paragon is leaving you.

A typical letter of reference should be headed with your address and the date, and signed clearly with your name. You can head it 'To whom it may concern'. State how long the employee worked for you without necessarily spelling out the exact number of weeks. Write any positive statement you can make about the way she performed her work. If she got on well with the children, was honest and reliable, say so. If you can, give the reason for her leaving, but make it as positively in favour of the employee as you can. Here is an example:

'To Whom It May Concern.

. . . . worked in my employ as a housekeeper in the winter of 19 . . She was good-tempered, honest, and carried out her duties under my daily supervision willingly and efficiently. She is leaving me because she has found it difficult to fit in with the pattern of our life which involves a lot of official entertaining.' signed . . .

If a prospective employer telephones or calls to check on the reference, you can be more frank than you would be in writing, but it is important to be just. In stressing the virtues of your former employee, you could explain, for instance, that the main problem was that she did not get on with children particularly well, neither did she care for last-minute changes of plans involving entertaining. In a household without children, with a more orderly way of life, she would probably manage very well.

Being a Good Employer

A good employer has to work at the job. People who work with and for you are subject to their own ups and downs. The relationship with people who work in the home is a close and personal one and demands that both sides deal with each other in good faith.

An employer must stick by the terms of employment laid down at the first interview and perhaps confirmed in writing. If there are to be changes, these should be discussed with and agreed by the employee. It is very easy to pile extra work on willing employees without noticing that it has become a burden.

If there are problems and it is necessary to point out shortcomings, this should be done in private. But no employer should avoid being firm, if there are problems, for the sake of a quiet life.

The best relationships operate on the basis of a partnership in running the house, looking after the children, doing the garden, the cooking, the cleaning or whatever the help you have does for you. But the employer is the senior person in the relationship and holds the responsibility, which should not be delegated until it is clear that the help can and will accept it.

Other Forms of Help

Daily help

Part-time regular help for a few hours a week, or every day, is the most usual form of help for the majority of people who are able to employ help in the home.

This type of help is usually paid at an hourly rate. The rate for the job varies from district to district. Some employers also pay the fares to and from work, and to get help at all in areas with transport problems, it may be necessary to fetch and carry the daily help.

Some people do not realize that a person coming in for only a few hours a week cannot do everything, and tend to overburden their domestic help. It is important, therefore, to decide between you what duties have priority. You may have to choose between the cleaning on the one hand and the laundry and ironing on the other (though there are the commercial laundries). You may ask the daily help to clean silver and cutlery, for instance. Asking her to do the shopping can be quite an expensive use of her time, but it is your decision if that is what you want her to do above everything else.

Your insurance policy should cover the possible injury of employees in your household. (See the chapter on Security of the Home.) A daily is an employee if working directly for you. If you get your daily help through a cleaning agency who pays the cleaner and then charges you, the relationship is different. You are employing the agency as an independent contractor.

Baby-sitters

It is important to have someone looking after your children who is kind, reliable, and mature enough to cope with an emergency in your absence. If you are not happy about the ability of a baby-sitter to cope, you will have a miserable time while you are out of the house. The age of the children and the demands likely to be made on the sitter are obviously related. A young teenager able to cope with a six-year-old who can tell if something is the matter and explain what it is, may not know what to do if a small child, unable to speak, cries and is obviously distressed.

Baby-sitters are usually hired by the hour. Try and use the same sitters as often as possible, so that the children get to know and like them. Word-of-mouth recommendation is the best way to find a sitter, but if you have a school or college nearby you may find that it organizes a baby-sitter scheme. Retired people are sometimes prepared to sit in on a regular basis. Some parents join together to baby-sit for each other on a rota system. You may get a good response from advertising for an experienced baby-sitter in the local paper. You must ask for, and check references unless the sitter is known or recommended to you.

It helps to write down detailed instructions for the sitter, if necessary. If a baby has to be fed, you will obviously satisfy yourself that your sitter knows how to do this. Always leave a note of an emergency number for the doctor and a note of the number where you can be reached if necessary.

If you are likely to get back later than you said you would, try to telephone the sitter.

You should leave the baby-sitter something to eat and drink. Be specific about what it is, so that you do not find yourself short of something you need for the next day.

If you cannot get a baby-sitter, you may find, whether you are a working mother or not, that your child and you would benefit from seeing less of each other for a few hours a day. You should investigate the following:

Play-groups

Pre-school play-groups are often organized by mothers on a co-operative basis. They take children, usually from three to five, for up to three hours a morning or afternoon. Premises have to be approved by the local authority. You can get advice on how to start one and how to run it either from your local authority or from a specialized association, such as the Pre-School Playgroups Association. (See also the chapter on Social Welfare.)

Day nurseries

Some local authorities run day nurseries for working mothers who cannot get living-in help for their children. They take children from three months old for up to eight hours a day. (See also the chapter on Social Welfare.)

Nursery schools

There are local authority and private day nursery schools for three to five-year-olds. There are very rarely enough places to meet the demand, and some local authorities have to be persuaded by parental campaigns to start one. Shortage of places means that priority is usually given to the children of mothers who have to work and who can neither get nor afford home help. (See also the chapter on Social Welfare.)

Registered child-minders

These can look after children for up to eight hours a day in their own home, where they keep an eye on them and feed them. It is not wise to choose a child-minder unless one has been recommended to you by word of mouth.

Trained nurses for the sick and elderly

If you engage a trained nurse to look after an elderly or invalid member of the household, that will be her full-time occupation. She will look after the patient's bed and wants, and will prepare beverages for her patient and herself, but she cannot be expected to do any other chores, or to cook for herself or her charge. When the patient is on the mend or if the nursing duties are not demanding, she may offer her help in some other way, but it is not part of her duties to do this.

Home helps

Often help is needed to look after people too weak to take full care of themselves, usually as a result of illness; a trained nurse is not necessary. It can be very difficult to find help of this kind, even to give a member of the family a much needed regular break. Home helps are employed by local authorities to come in daily in times of illness or convalescence, to provide basic help to people who are unable to look after their homes. They also help with old people living alone, or where the person who looks after an elderly person is ill. The home help is paid by the local authority who recovers all or part of it from the householder. They are much in demand and their help is consequently made available to those most in need.

Casual help

Most people rely for their help in the home on casual help, regular or intermittent. To find the kind of help you need, ask around, look in the yellow pages of your telephone directory, read the advertisements in local papers and, if necessary, put in one yourself. If you follow up any circular put through the door, establish that the advertiser can be found at an address and is not a fly-by-night. Ask for references for anyone who works in or around your house.

Cleaners

Sometimes you may want to hire a firm of contract cleaners to come in and clean your house from top to bottom. These tend to be primarily office and commercial cleaners who may only be prepared to do domestic jobs if they involve a minimum fee, which may be quite high. They will clean paint, vacuum-clean, polish, sand floors to clean off a build-up of old polish, and wash the glass and china.

Specialist *in situ* carpet, upholstery and soft furnishing cleaners will move in to clean these, if needed.

The cleaners will want to look at the house and give you an estimate. You must specify any preparatory work you want carried out (eg covering furniture with dust-sheets) and make sure that the firm accepts responsibility for any damage caused by their workmen.

In larger cities, domestic cleaning agencies can supply cleaners regularly or intermittently by the hour, half day or day.

Window cleaners

The best way to find window cleaners is to see if your neighbours have one, check that they are satisfied with his honesty and that they do not mind your asking him to clean your windows. Window cleaners should carry their own insurance against injury and provide their own equipment and ladders. (If they have an accident because of a defect in one of your ladders, you may be liable. See *Legal Aspects* below.) They normally quote a price 'per job' and will expect to be hired on a regular basis.

Gardeners

Help in the garden is usually hired by the hour, half day or day. You should make it clear whether you are offering employment all year round, and on what basis, or whether you only need someone in the summer. You have to come to some arrangement about the days when the weather makes gardening impossible; your help may make the time up on another day or you may prefer to pay for the actual hours worked.

As there is so much work to do in a garden, you should make clear your priorities: is the gardener to concentrate on the vegetables and leave you the flower beds; do you cut the hedges, or is that his job; does he cut the lawn or is that something you and your family can cope with?

If you do not want, or cannot get a gardener on a part-time, regular basis, you may be able to arrange for a contract gardener to come in during the season to do specific jobs –the lawns, hedges, digging, etc. Some people hire contract gardeners to dig over beds, to weed, put down weed-killer, etc at the beginning of the season, and then to come again in the autumn to clear the garden for the winter. Your local garden centre may know of garden contractors who do work of this kind.

Help with entertaining

You can contract out the whole business of entertaining, whether you want a three-course dinner for four prepared, served, and washed up, or a party for hundreds of people. You can simply order the food to be prepared and delivered, or arrange for staff to move into your house for several hours and prepare, serve, and wash up your meal, leaving you free to entertain your guests. This help can come as a fully trained, professional team, or it can be a local husband and wife team who act as bartender and waitress, or a more unskilled kind of help hired for the event.

Even if the arrangement is informal, you should write down what you want – date, time, number of people, etc. If you employ an outside caterer, the relationship is between customer and contractor, not employer and employee. All the tasks you want done, the menu, ordering and serving drinks, hiring crockery, extra chairs and tables, flowers, decorations or any special requirement should be discussed in detail and included, itemized, in the quotation. You should check how much notice you need to give in the event of a cancellation and find out what cancellation charges, if any, might be incurred.

A written estimate should be provided. If you have alterations after you have agreed the arrangements, there will obviously be an extra sum on the bill. It is important to ensure that the estimate includes any taxes and service charges.

Legal Aspects

House occupiers owe the same duty to all employees and independent contractors who come to their house as that which they owe to all visitors: to take reasonable care to see that they are safe in using the premises (see p181). They also owe their employees a general duty to take reasonable care for their safety, which includes providing safe equipment, a safe system of work (eg not asking them to do things in a dangerous way), and competent fellow-employees.

An employee who works for sixteen or more hours per week is classified as full-time, and has various rights, depending on how long she has been continuously employed.

Notice

Every full-time worker who has been employed for four weeks or more is entitled to a minimum of one week's notice of the termination of her employment. After two years she becomes entitled to two weeks' notice, and thereafter to an extra week for every year worked, up to a maximum of twelve weeks. If the contract requires a longer period of notice, that period must be given. When the contract says nothing expressly about notice, it is an implied term that a reasonable period of notice must be given; in some circumstances this could be more than the statutory minimum. An employee who is guilty of gross misconduct which shows a total disregard for the contract can be dismissed without notice; but the misconduct would have to be very serious to justify this. The employer is entitled to one week's notice from the employee (unless the employer is himself in serious breach of contract).

Written particulars

A full-time employee is entitled to certain particulars of her terms of employment in writing within thirteen weeks of starting her job. These include the names of employer and employee, the date the employment began, the amount of pay and frequency of payment, the hours of work, holidays and holiday pay, sickness and sickness pay, pension (if any), period of notice, job title. If some of them do not apply, the employee has the right to be told that too. An employee is also entitled to a written breakdown of her pay (gross pay, deductions, net pay) each time she is paid.

Maternity

After a woman has worked for two years continuously full-time, she has the right to six weeks' maternity pay. The employer can reclaim the amount paid from the Department of Employment. She also has the right to return to work after up to nine months (eleven weeks before the birth and twenty-nine weeks afterwards); but her remedy for denial of this right would be a claim for unfair dismissal, which may not be available (see below). In both cases she must give prior notice to her employer of her intentions.

Redundancy

A person who has been employed full-time continuously for two years is entitled to redundancy pay if she is dismissed because she is redundant. The amount will depend upon length of service; the rules are complicated. The employer can reclaim part of any payment she makes from the Department of Employment. Domestic servants in private households are not entitled to redundancy pay if they are employed by close relatives. Men of sixty-five and women of sixty (or more) are not entitled to redundancy pay.

Unfair dismissal

An employee who has worked full-time for fifty-two weeks or more has the right not to be unfairly dismissed; if she is, she can complain to an Industrial Tribunal. In order to qualify for this right, however, the employee must have been one of at least four full-time staff.

Wrongful dismissal

All employees (including part-timers) have the right to claim against their employers if they are dismissed in breach of their employment contracts.

Part-time workers

After five years a person who works eight or more hours (but less than sixteen) is treated as a full-time worker, and thus acquires the above rights.

Foreign workers

Foreign workers need work permits (unless they are EEC nationals), which must be applied for by the employer before the employee comes to the UK. But if they are employed by an agency and contracted out to private households, the agency will normally obtain the work permit.

Au pair girls do not need a work permit; this concession applies only to girls of seventeen or more from Western Europe who come to live as a member of the family and learn English. They may only stay for a maximum of two years (including any previous period spent here as an au pair).

Agencies

The use of an agency may create two different kinds of legal relationship. Firstly, you may use an agency to find someone for a domestic vacancy. You will make a contract with the agency to pay for the introduction; your rights and obligations will depend entirely on the agreement you make, and you should make sure the agency checks references, and in what circumstances the fee is payable. If the agency introduces someone suitable, you will make a separate contract with that person, who will then become your employee and be entitled to all the rights described above.

Secondly, you may want an agency to provide their own staff to carry out a specific task, either permanently (eg contract gardeners or cleaners) or on a particular occasion (eg spring-cleaning or catering for a party). You will probably make a contract with the agency, but not with the staff who come to do the work. Therefore your rights with respect to them will depend on the contract you have made with the agency – whether you may give them direct instructions or not, whether you may send them away if they are not satisfactory, and so on. However you will owe to them, as to all visitors, the ordinary duty of taking reasonable care that they are safe in using the premises to carry out their tasks, and in using any equipment you may provide.

Note At the time of going to press (1980) the government has plans for new legislation on employment.

MANAGING A HOUSEHOLD WITH CHILDREN

It ought to enter into the domestic policy of every parent, to make her children feel that home is the happiest place in the world; that to imbue them with this delicious home-feeling is one of the choicest gifts a parent can bestow.

The arrival of a child in the home brings great change as well as pleasure whether for parents expecting a child, a couple preparing to foster or adopt, or relatives or friends helping out by taking children into their home. The financial cost can be cut by thoughtful and imaginative planning. In general, knowing what to expect is the key to the situation.

For new parents there are books on baby care, lectures, relaxation classes, classes for fathers, and, usually, helpful relatives and friends with children. Handling someone else's baby beforehand is also a valuable experience. Above all, a sensible book on child development will help parents to understand what children need at various stages, and what can be expected of them.

Full advantage should be taken of help offered during pregnancy and afterwards by the Health and Social Services. (For financial benefits, see the chapter on Social Welfare.) The choice of a general practitioner who is interested is very important. A doctor who runs an ante-natal clinic may well prove sympathetic. Health Service midwives and health visitors are invariably helpful.

Parenthood is taxing, and help, paid or unpaid, in the shape of a friend or relative is almost essential in the days following the arrival of a new baby, and very useful if available through all the pre-school years. Grandparents often prove excellent friends and aids to parents and children. Aunts and uncles, godparents, and friends of the family with or without children of their own, will want to get to know the children, and even offer to have them in their own homes.

Rearranging Your House or Flat

Few flats or houses will be ideal for children without some rearrangement. The confinement of a flat in particular can pose problems. But intelligent use of the space available and a good choice of furniture and equipment can make all the difference. (See the chapter on Planning your Home – Design Factors.)

Convenience, practicality, and safety are primary considerations. Parents have to realize, for example, that elegant furnishings and decorations, expensive carpets, and treasured ornaments are incompatible with small children. Life will be simplified if unnecessary adult trappings are removed while the children are young.

The provision of as much drawer and cupboard space as possible for storing and tidying away children's equipment and playthings should have high priority.

Perhaps the most essential item to have at the start of family life is a reliable washing machine, or at least a good spin drier. (See the chapter on Care of Textiles and Hard Surfaces.)

Below, the usual accommodation in a home is considered area by area with children in view. Day-to-day care as it relates to the planning and equipping of their environment is also discussed.

The Child's Room

The room allocated to a baby or child should obviously be as pleasant a place as possible. Children spend a lot of time there and the room should offer comfort and interest, so that from an early age it has good associations for them. A tree outside the window, a nice view, light and sunshine coming in – these things mean much to a child, and its room can be a refuge through all the stages of childhood and adolescence. Such a room may also do something to nip in the bud the desire of a toddler or small child to seek his parents' room in the very early hours, or a reluctance to retire to his room in the evening.

For the arrival of a new child, the room will probably be decorated. Walls, whether papered or painted, should be washable, and paint on furniture or woodwork must be lead-free, or a child who sucks it may get lead poisoning. Windows should be made safe, either with bars or with fastenings which limit the degree they can open. Washable flooring is practical, but may look and feel chilly except in the case of cork tiles. Washable rugs can partly protect a carpet and, with non-slip trimmings fixed underneath, can cheer a washable floor. Plenty of wide, low shelving in the room ensures that toys and books are accessible, and it will still prove its use when the adolescent sets up his hi-fi equipment. Areas of pegboard and blackboard incorporated into the wall decorations have a similarly long life.

A baby may sleep in its parents' room at first, but where possible it ought soon to be put into its own room; certainly by six months.

New babies are very vulnerable to cold and a steady temperature of 20°–21°C is needed day and night when they are dressed, and of about 29°C at bath time. After a few months a baby develops some ability to conserve heat, but throughout babyhood it is necessary to be alert to signs of chill.

The safety of the heating unit is obviously of great importance, particularly when the child becomes active. All appliances should have a British Standards Institution Kitemark. Adequate heating remains an important consideration throughout the child's life if homework and hobbies are to be carried out in comfort as well as privacy.

Until it is about four to five months old, a baby needs a cradle, Moses basket or carry-cot; it is then ready for a drop-side cot. This must meet recognized safety standards, to ensure that the

baby does not get its head stuck between the bars, trap its fingers in the fastenings, or find it too easy to climb out at a later stage. The mattress should be firm, of hair or foam. With anything soft, the baby risks suffocation, and for the same reason, no pillow is best. To raise the baby's head to give it a better view from cot or pram, a pillow can be slipped under the mattress.

Until the child is dry at night, usually some time between two and three years old, machine-washable, waterproof sheeting, nicest with a warm cloth finish on both sides, and large enough to tuck round the mattress, will be needed. A plain rubber or plastic draw-sheet should have a washable quilted pad in addition. The sheet covering will need frequent washing too, so several will have to be bought. A number of light-weight, washable blankets will allow a flexible degree of warmth. A sleeping bag like a dressing-gown with a bag bottom is a good idea, as it keeps a baby or toddler warm even if the bedclothes slip; it also makes climbing out of the cot difficult.

Some time towards three, most children are ready for the change from cot to bed, and it is sensible to get a full-sized adult bed. One can buy a temporary side-rail with feet that tuck in between mattress and bed; this gives a feeling of security at first and prevents the child from falling out.

Sleep
For the first nine months a baby will take all the sleep it needs unless it is disturbed. Adults, on the other hand, must expect to have their sleep disturbed: first by a night feed until the child is about six weeks old, then by a late night or early morning feed, and possibly by a wakeful child for some years after that. From the age of about nine months, excitement, sheer overtiredness, or a wish to stay with its parents may stop a child going to bed and to sleep when it really needs to. A peaceful atmosphere as bedtime approaches, reading aloud or making up stories, and a mixture of firmness and reassurance usually help.

Equipment and baby clothes
Feeding, bathing, and dressing a new baby can take place in the child's room or elsewhere in the house.

But some steady surface near the crib or cot for changing and dressing the baby, low enough to sit at or high enough to stand at, will prove useful; this could take the baby bath as well. You will need a box or basket to include small items such as cotton wool, soap, a hairbrush and curved safety pins, and a table or trolley to take other items for the baby's care.

Special furniture to take baby clothes is not necessary. A good-sized chest with smoothly running drawers will do throughout childhood. Provision for hanging clothes will have to be available later, and conversely, cupboards which meet an adolescent's needs can also be used for a child if the rails are adjusted to its height.

Sharing Rooms

Young children are usually quite happy to share a room and actually enjoy one another's company. Bunk beds are often used, but though they save space, they can present problems both of safety and in nursing a child who is ill. Where possible, it is probably better to give children separate beds, each with its own bedside light, together with a place for toys and important belongings within reach. Family policy on boys and girls sharing rooms will vary, or it may simply be dictated by the limits of bedrooms available. Where a child is ready for a room of its own but cannot have it, rearranging the furniture and installing a screen may give the needed sense of privacy.

Whether the children sleep in beds or bunks, continental quilts (duvets) make comfortable, easily managed, cheerful-looking bedding.

The Bathroom

A bathroom planned for children should not be carpeted, but should have washable, non-slip floor coverings. (See the chapter on Safety in the Home.) Safe heating, however, is a necessity. A unit fixed high on wall or ceiling may be the answer. Radiators and heated towel rails within reach should have efficient controls to keep the temperature at a level safe to touch.

Daily bathing is not really necessary until a child

is crawling and getting dirty. Until then, a baby can perfectly well be cleaned by 'topping and tailing'. The majority of babies do, however, revel in their evening bath, beginning to do so from the age of about three months.

A young baby can be bathed in a fixed basin or sink, though the taps may be a hazard. A safe, well-designed baby bath, used in the bathroom or another warm room, is probably the best answer.

At some time between three and six months, a baby can be introduced to the adult bath. A rubber mat in the bottom of the bath will make it less slippery. Babies must never be left alone whilst in the bath, not even for a moment.

A pot should be bought in advance, so that it becomes a familiar object. It should be stable, with a shield in front for a boy. Later, a child's lavatory seat which fits on to the adult one and a box to make a step will help children to use the lavatory by themselves.

The bathroom is a popular place for the family medicine cabinet, though there is a lot to be said for keeping it in the kitchen, high on the wall, and out of reach.

Hall and Stairs

Paintwork and walls of hall, landings, and staircase are especially vulnerable to trailing sticky fingers. When decorating with children in mind, washable, patterned wallpaper seems to be the most practical solution.

Wear on stairs will be considerable, and if they are going to be carpeted, it is wise to buy good quality. An extra length concealed at the top or bottom of a flight will allow the carpet to be moved up or down a few centimetres when it wears.

A staircase provides interesting exercise for a newly mobile child, but gates should be fitted at top or bottom, or both, as family activities dictate. Slatted staircases without risers may need a safety-net tacked behind to stop small children falling through. The design of some stairs may demand a handrail at child height if children are to manage safely. Landing windows should be checked for safety. A front door opening on to the street may need to be fitted with safety catches.

Part of the downstairs hall, if draught-free, can be provided with suitable flooring and turned into a convenient play area for a small child, easily supervized by an adult working in the kitchen. Each house, according to its layout, will offer its own solution to such a play area, often using space which might otherwise be wasted, eg space under the stairs. Make sure that play areas are safe, cheerful, and provided with storage for toys etc.

Kitchen and Living Rooms

The accommodation available and the attitude of particular families will determine whether all the living rooms are to be shared with the children. In the average house, the downstairs area will need to make provision for: kitchen activities, eating (at times formally), sitting comfortably, playing (under supervision at first), watching television, adult entertaining, storage for prams, toys, tricycles, bicycles, outdoor clothes, gumboots, etc, washing and lavatory facilities.

In most flats and many houses, activities are circumscribed and rooms made to double for more than one function. Eating often takes place in the kitchen, and a play space here is a good idea for small children who still need company and supervision. (Even if planted in a playroom, they will probably come crawling or toddling back to where interesting action is going on.) Or again, the room most devoted to play may double as a TV room or as the dining-room – though it is a good idea to keep one area for relaxation not dominated by television. For an older child content to be absorbed in play and activities on its own, its bedroom may become its main place for play. A large room for children's parties and active games is a boon where available and can give adolescents some of the scope and independence they need. Play space and playroom can always do with large stretches of pinboard and blackboard for displaying pictures, paintings, pin-ups, and all sorts of treasures and creative efforts. Hooks in ceilings or door frames will take first a baby bouncer and later gymnastic equipment.

A separate 'withdrawing room' for adults only is a welcome luxury where possible, but most families

will probably share the main living-room. Here and throughout the shared rooms, walls, floors, and furniture should be wipeable, fabrics should be washable, and plain colour schemes, which show stains and marks more easily, should be avoided.

Safety

Tippable pieces of furniture are a danger to an infant learning to stand and walk. It needs solid pieces to pull itself up by and hang on to as it makes unsteady progress round the room.

Once mobile, a child is learning by constant exploration and nothing is safe from its investigations. Some potential sources of danger should be set high and out of reach; the television set is an example.

In the kitchen, a high place should be found for the medicine chest if it is kept there, for those potentially lethal chemical cleaners and disinfectants which are too often kept at floor level under the sink, and for a magnetic knife rack to hold sharp implements.

Dummy plugs in power points within reach but not in use can frustrate curious fingers. Trailing flexes and dangling tablecloths invite disaster. Great care should be taken to choose electric fires and other heating appliances which meet recognized safety standards (see the chapter on Safety in the Home). Open fires must always be guarded with a fire screen – again, of approved design.

The cooking area presents obvious hazards (see the chapters on Kitchen Planning and Kitchen Equipment). A continuous surface between the cooker and sink lessens the danger of dropping pots, pans, and other things on to a child. A cooker guard can be fitted to keep pans out of a child's reach. Otherwise saucepan handles must always be turned away from the edge of the cooker. A telephone extension to the kitchen is not only practical but also an aid to safety, allowing uninterrupted supervision of a child.

(See also the chapter on Safety in the Home.)

Medical Care

See the chapter on Medical Care in the Home.

Additional Furniture and Equipment

Family living-rooms may need some additions with the coming of children. A large and comfortable sofa with a washable cover, built to stand much hard wear, is a sensible investment. A cabinet to hold a domestic filing system might be considered to keep records such as birth certificates, Health Service cards, immunization records, school reports, and the more general household documents.

From carry-cot or Moses basket in the living room, a child can progress to a baby chair. The kind which adjusts from lying to sitting position can be used from two months onwards. Propped up and strapped in this, the baby can survey the family scene. It is a good place, too, for giving the baby its first spoonfuls of puréed food. Some of these chairs come with stands to convert them to a high chair.

Babies also feel happy in the midst of things when put to jump in a 'baby bouncer' – a canvas seating arrangement slung with an elastic cord from a hook in door frame or ceiling. For a mobile baby, the traditional play-pen although safe, is also boring. An excellent piece of equipment for a child learning to stand and walk is a stable truck with a tall handle by which it can pull itself to a standing position, and then push the truck while walking slowly behind it. This greatly increases the toddler's mobility and will hold some of its toys.

Prams and push-chairs

These will probably be kept in the hall. A pram should have a depth of about 20cm, firm padding, anchorage points for a harness, and a clearly visible brake designed to hold at least two of the wheels. A transporter for the carry-cot may be a suitable alternative, but will not stand up to all weathers.

Once a baby can support its own head, it can be comfortably carried in front in a 'papoose' bag hung from one shoulder, or in a carrier with aluminium frame, on the back; these arrangements certainly help family mobility. When a child is sitting up, a well-designed collapsible push-chair will prove useful. A harness with reins, though sometimes frowned on as too restrictive, is in fact very suitable for a lively toddler.

Feeding equipment

A minimum of one bottle and two teats will be needed for a breast-fed baby, to give it water or juice to drink. If the baby is bottle-fed, eight bottles with teats and covers is a reasonable number to buy, together with mixing jugs marked in millilitres, and spoons and funnels for the preparation of the feed. After washing (and rubbing teats with salt inside and out to remove fatty deposits), all equipment used in connection with feeding must be sterilized, either by boiling it for ten minutes in a large saucepan or by totally submerging it in the appropriate sterilizing liquid. One or two containers should be bought for this purpose, and enough equipment sterilized at a time to last for twenty-four hours.

The feed itself should either be used as soon as it is prepared, or refrigerated until use, in which case several feeds can be prepared at a time. Before being given to the baby, the bottled feed should be warmed in hot water or in an electric bottle warmer.

At about six months a baby is ready to drink cow's milk. Over the next six months it can gradually be weaned from breast or bottle and taught to drink from a cup; a trainer beaker with a spout will help here. For solid foods which need to be puréed, a vegetable mill or blender save time.

During these first years, meal times are bound to be messy. A large bib made of towelling backed by plastic, and newspaper or a plastic sheet spread under the high chair, are the best solutions.

Toys

Play, an important first step in learning about the world, does not always require expensive toys. Thought and ingenuity can produce safe playthings at little or no cost: an eye-catching mobile for a tiny baby for example, safe objects of differing textures and shapes for a six-month-old baby to grasp, dough, silver sand, safe domestic utensils and tools for the toddler, and adult cast-offs for the pre-school child to dress up in.

With bought toys, safety, suitability for the child's age, and real play value are the things to look out for. A baby will put everything in its mouth. Teething-rings and rattles must not chip or break and should be easy to sterilize. Soft toys should be washable, made without metal or wire, and have safety-locked eyes. The stable baby-walker mentioned on p127 is a good buy for a child learning to walk, and lasts several years as a container to hold and trundle about all manner of objects. Other push-along toys may move too fast for a child until it is walking steadily. Pull-along toys come first. A good set of wooden bricks, bought, or made and carefully sanded, is an essential toy. A child in his second year will love to put one thing inside another, whether kitchenware or a bought set of coloured beakers. Co-ordination of hand and eye are helped by a posting-box, threading toys or a holed board for hammering through pegs. In the third year play becomes more imaginative, and children enjoy dressing up as other people and playing with dolls.

Play at Home

Provision for play at home for the pre-school child will very much depend on whether it goes to a play-group or nursery school. If not, considerable effort should be made to provide scope for such activities as painting, modelling, growing things, and dressing up at home, in the company of other children of the same age. Where there is room either indoors or out, apparatus for climbing, swinging, and acrobatics should be provided. A well-built wooden or metal climbing-frame is an excellent buy, giving many years of physical play; so is a paddling-pool, and young children lucky enough to have access to a swimming-pool have a head start in learning to swim. The importance of tricycles and bicycles is obvious.

Progress in language and learning are greatly helped at home through conversation, reading aloud, help with homework, and the provision of books. A good set of encyclopedias and reference books are a sound investment.

Household Pets

Pre-school-age children are unlikely to take a very active part in looking after pets. But from an early age watching and being aware of animal life in the home is instructive and a delight.

The choice of animal will obviously depend partly on the amount of time and attention the adult, and later the child, is prepared to spend on it. For example, after the initial preparation of the aquarium, fish require little beyond regular changes of water and a pinch of food every other day. A child can give this, watching carefully that all is consumed, as the decay of uneaten food is the main cause of the death of these pets. Caged birds are even less trouble. In both cases it is a kindness to make the cage or tank as large as possible.

Cats are reasonably self-sufficient creatures, and are popular partly for this reason. (A cat net over a sleeping baby is a necessity, as the cat will make for the warmth of cot or pram and its presence is unhygienic and may even cause suffocation.)

Acquiring a dog must be given very careful thought beforehand. In addition to a licence, it needs food, exercise, companionship, training, washing, and grooming. But caring for dogs and the affection they usually engender are most valuable experiences for children.

In helping to care for household pets, children can also minimize the damage they do. In stopping them scratching furniture or digging up flower-beds, children acquire a sense of responsibility themselves. Total responsibility for the daily care of small pets such as hamsters, gerbils, guinea-pigs or rabbits is an even more valuable lesson.

Young children have to be taught how to handle their pets gently. Untaught, they may suffer scratches or bites. Unless deep, these should be washed well with cold water and covered until healed. Dogs already established in a household may be jealous of a new baby, so that constant alertness is needed. Cat and dog food and excreta must obviously be kept well out of the way of a crawling baby or toddler. Disinfectant should always be used to clear up after an animal. (It is possible for worms to be transmitted to a child if this is not done.) Cats and dogs should be checked regularly for fleas. Children can also catch ringworm from dogs – a fungoid disease affecting scalp or skin. Though infectious, this can be cured by prompt medical treatment.

It need hardly be added that no child should ever be made to handle or touch household pets against its will.

Garage, Car and Garden

A garage not used as such can provide wet weather play space for children. (If in use, the inevitable oil patches make it impractical.) Again, obvious safety measures, such as putting sharp tools out of reach, must be taken.

The family car should be fitted with an approved, safely designed child's car seat for older babies and toddlers, and safety harnesses for older children. These should always be in the back of the car. A small baby can travel in its carry-cot, safely wedged on the back seat. Four-door cars should be fitted with childproof locks at the back. For safety's sake, a two-door model may be preferred.

Where there is a garden available for children, some safety measures must be taken. A lockable gate should be considered to keep in roaming toddlers, and the driveway should be made as open as possible, so that child and driver are always aware of each other. Laburnum, yew, and the nightshades are poisonous and should be removed (see p112). Even quite shallow ponds must be fenced in or covered with mesh wire until a child is old enough to be responsive to warnings. Constant supervision of small children is needed where the garden boasts a swimming-pool, or where a paddling-pool is in use; in the latter case, it should always be emptied after use. Steps may be a danger, not only to the toddler but to a child on a tricycle; more gating may be necessary.

Active play in the fresh air should be encouraged by the provision of ropes, ladders, and swings, using suitable trees where these exist, or climbing-frames and self-standing swings. For sand-pits, silver or washed sand should be used, as builders' sand tends to stain. An area for rough riding on tricycles, scooters, and bicycles is excellent where space allows.

Most children will eventually show an interest in tending a small plot of their own, and this should be encouraged by support and advice, and the provision of small suitable tools.

Beyond the Home

From an early age a child will have some contact with the world beyond the safe confines of home. Many young parents refuse to be too housebound by young children. Through competent organization of arrangements for feeding (relatively easy if the child is breast-fed), and carrying sleeping facilities for their children, parents can manage a full life of visiting and travelling as a family. Others will prefer to limit their outings to local shopping expeditions and occasional visits to family, friends, doctor or clinic.

Some thought must be given to physical safety. On local shopping trips, the use of a 'papoose' or a supermarket trolley with child seat will forestall any chance of the child being snatched from pram or push-chair outside the shop.

From three onwards some training in road safety should be given and later, when bicycles are acquired, formal lessons in riding and maintenance should be considered.

Children also need to be taught to deal firmly with approaches from strangers.

Sometimes a parent needs or wishes to delegate responsibility for a child to others. Such an arrangement can obviously be beneficial to all concerned. (See the chapters on Help in the Home, and Social Welfare.)

Working or not, many mothers choose to give their pre-school children the experience of nursery school or play-group, and this can be extremely mentally and socially enriching for the child. But children differ in their needs, and if a child does not seem to settle down in the group available, a more congenial alternative could perhaps be created with suitable playmates and activities in its own home.

When the time comes for a child to go to school, parents can help a great deal by ensuring that the child has the necessary skills such as managing the lavatory on its own, tying shoe-laces, and knowing clearly its own full name and address.

It is vital to cultivate a good relationship with the school. Co-operation between parent and teachers benefits both the child and the community.

CARE OF THE ELDERLY

The human body, materially considered, is a beautiful piece of mechanism, consisting of many parts, each one being the centre of a system, and performing its own vital function irrespectively of the others, and yet dependent for its vitality upon the harmony and health of the whole. It is, in fact, to a certain extent, like a watch, which, when once wound up and set in motion, will continue its function of recording true time only so long as every wheel, spring, and lever performs its allotted duty, and at its allotted time; or till the limit that man's ingenuity has placed to its existence as a moving automaton has been reached, or, in other words, till it has run down.

The Active Older Person

Many older people are well able to care for themselves, but need to live with younger relatives, perhaps for financial reasons. In such cases the biggest problems tend to lie in the sphere of personal relations.

Before anyone of a different generation is added to an existing household, therefore, due care and thought must be given to the way in which he or she is likely to alter the balance of family relationships. Thinking about this realistically before an additional member joins the household should make it possible to avoid some of the difficulties which very often arise.

Sometimes the family unit taking in the newcomer comprises at least husband and wife; sometimes it is an unmarried daughter and occasionally an unmarried son. When an unmarried daughter does take on this responsibility, it often means that she either has to exchange full-time for part-time work or that she gives up work altogether: problems which have to be faced beforehand. For an unmarried daughter or son to surrender independence of action, or for the family with its own pattern of life to have to change, is equally difficult. However loving the relationship may be, situations of domestic tension and tyranny can develop quite quickly and cause immense unhappiness. Sensible arrangements about the need for relative privacy for families, and for some freedom for the daughter or son, definitely have to be agreed on. Some older people quite unconsciously continue to treat younger adult members of their family as children. They do not realize that this can cause great difficulties; distortion may be produced, for instance, in the adults' parental role with their own children.

Accommodation and alterations

Where it is possible and not misconstrued as a rejection, setting aside a separate part of the house for the older relation can work most successfully. In small modern houses, however, this is not always possible.

Where there is not enough room for a 'Granny flat' it may still be practicable to set aside one room as a ground-floor bed-sitting room. The installation of a downstairs WC, unless one already exists, can make the care of an older person easier. A downstairs bathroom is also of great benefit; if there is not enough room for a full-sized bath, a hip 'sitz' bath or shower may be sensible alternatives.

Where structural alterations are needed, such as the widening of doors, the construction of ramps for wheelchairs or the addition of rails to bath or WC, the local Social Services Department should be consulted. It may be possible for some or all of the cost of the work to be grant-aided by the local authority under the provisions of the Chronically Sick & Disabled Persons Act, 1970.

Even if the newcomer is in good health, it is wise to consider the possibility of rearranging the allocation of rooms and making extra provision before he or she first comes to the household. This avoids the double upheaval of having to make special arrangements at a later date if the older relative become frail.

Television viewing

Problems often arise if there is competition and dissension over the use of a television set, so it may well be worth providing a separate set for the older person's use. This avoids the possibility of conflicts of taste with children in the household, and the kind of difficulties which can arise if the older person is hard of hearing. When this is admitted, a special fitment for the set can be obtained, but many people are defensive about the onset of deafness and may insist on having the volume turned to a level which may be intolerable for others.

Financial arrangements

People of all ages are prone to anxiety, and elderly people – very naturally – tend to worry about their finances. This is a most delicate area where great tact is required, but for this reason it is all the more important that financial arrangements should be spelled out fully, and mutually agreed from the beginning. Most people reject anything which they feel smacks of charity, so it is important that they should feel that they are paying their way; on the other hand, they should never have to feel that they are being exploited or are subsidizing the rest of the household. A right balance may be difficult to achieve, but every attempt should be made to reassure the relative that the contribution is enough, and to allow them the pleasure of giving if they are so inclined. If these arrangements can be reached in a rational and quiet way, it will be much easier to reopen the whole question if at some future date the family's situation changes and a reappraisal becomes essential. Later on, should mental confusion prevent a person from handling his or her own affairs, problems can arise if there is no clear arrangement in writing which can be used as a guide.

Grief

If the older person is admitted to the household on the death of a partner, it is important to realize that he or she still needs to work through the various stages of mourning and that this may take quite a long time. Even when the bereaved partner is apparently adjusted to the loss, there may be a sudden onset of acute grief at a later period, most commonly about six months to a year after the death of the spouse. Those who have accepted a relation into their household should be prepared for this and deal with it gently and with patience.

Apparently irrational shortness of temper and irritability at this time may be due to the onset of such feelings and the undisclosed residue of anger at the partner for having left them.

Active pursuits

For both physical and mental health, it is of prime importance to maintain activity and to foster the older people's self-respect by making sure that they still have a definite role to play. There is nothing more destructive to the psyche than the feeling of being thrust aside and of no use to anyone. Older people should, therefore, be encouraged, as soon as they arrive, to take part in active pursuits both inside and outside the home.

Some definite area of responsibility within the household will help enormously to make the older relative feel useful. What this is will depend upon the individual's capacities and may range from active work such as cooking, gardening or sewing to baby-sitting or reading to the children.

If they have previously been involved in particular hobbies and activities, they should be encouraged to form links to replace those which may have been severed by the removal from their own home area. Membership of a church may help in integrating them into a new community and forming new associations.

For the enthusiast joining a chess club, for example, one of the benefits may be people of all ages within its membership. But for those who enjoy the company of their contemporaries there are many specialized clubs and facilities which are open both to the able-bodied and to the partially or extensively disabled older citizen. The quality and diversity of such provision varies a great deal in different parts of the UK. But everywhere there are special rates for those of pensionable age who attend local adult education institutes, many of which have a wide range of handicraft and other classes. In addition, most local authorities run day centres, which provide excellent handicraft teaching for those who are disabled, and, in some cases, sheltered workshops where it is possible to earn a nominal wage. There are also many private clubs; details about them can be obtained from the local branch of Age Concern.

For the housebound person with a special interest, it may be possible to find a fellow-enthusiast who will visit and help to keep that interest alive. Help in finding such a person may be found through a local specialized society (eg a history society, embroidery guild, etc), through a Volunteer Bureau or Council of Voluntary Service, if there is one, or even by means of advertising in the specialist press.

Practical Problems

Even in the physically healthy there will inevitably be a progressive slowing-up of physical and mental responses, but it should not be assumed that these are due to age alone: there may be underlying physical causes which can be treated, and this possibility should be kept in mind.

If the older person is occupying separate accommodation and is catering for him or herself, it is essential to be sure that he or she is eating properly, and it may be wise to check that the refrigerator is being used correctly, and that food is not kept in it for too long.

While older people need less food than younger ones, it is vitally important that they should have a balanced diet and they may need help and encouragement to prepare or eat particular foods (see the chapter on Nutrition and Diet). It is well to remember also that regular care should be given to both natural and false teeth. If the latter have been worn for some years, the shrinkage of the gums will eventually result in uncomfortably loose dentures which discourage proper eating.

For those who are becoming forgetful or slightly confused, the ordinary domestic 'pinger' can be very useful indeed. This can be used as a reminder for all sorts of things such as when to take pills, prepare food, etc.

It must be remembered that people are often conservative in their tastes and only really enjoy food which is familiar. If they are sharing meals with the family, it is easier, and less likely to cause conflict and ill-feeling, if the older person's preferences can be taken into account even if it means preparing a separate dish for them. To ask them to change the habits of a lifetime may be asking more than they are capable of doing and may even, in some cases, cause digestive upsets.

Older people need less sleep than others and may want to make a hot drink during the night or an early morning pot of tea long before the rest of the household is ready to start the day; so, where the family meals are shared, it is sensible to make provision for them to be able to make hot drinks without disturbing other people.

Care of the frail older person

The problems and difficulties which arise from the addition of an older person to a household are similar but more acute in the case of a frail or sick person. The inexorable nature of the need for constant care and vigilance can wear down the most loving relationship. Those who are faced with this situation should, for their own sakes, make use of every possible means to get assistance from both official and unofficial sources. The latter may range from the involvement of other members of the family on a regular basis to the recruitment of volunteer 'granny sitters', so that the caring person can continue to enjoy some kind of social life and be given relief from being permanently on call.

It is often possible for older people to be admitted into an old people's home or hospital for a short period to enable the caring person to have a holiday. Provided that the purpose and duration of such an admission is understood, it should be possible for this to happen without it causing distress. The local Social Services Department usually has a senior officer who is responsible for the welfare of the elderly and can advise about the possibility of making such an arrangement.

When an old person is ill or failing, one of the great problems is that of keeping in touch with him or her while continuing to maintain the household. It may well be worth installing some kind of 'intercom' system, so that the old person can call for help without any particular exertion. Sophisticated systems can be used, but the basic 'baby alarm' is quite adequate and fairly inexpensive.

For the older person who is still mentally alert, a telephone at the bedside can be a boon in enabling them to keep in touch with friends and relations.

In the case of illness or final decline, the common-sense rules of medical care apply at this time; tender, loving care must be the central theme.

Safety

Since personal possessions enshrine memories which are precious, older relatives should be encouraged to bring their own furniture with them and arrange it in the way they want it, if possible, but the temptation to overcrowd a room with precious possessions is great and can lead to safety hazards.

Adding an older person to a household calls for a special approach to safety, keeping in mind not only the present but also possible future dangers when he or she becomes disabled or progressively more frail and prone to fall.

Remember that with age the circulation of blood in the brain becomes less efficient. This can cause giddiness and some loss of balance, made worse by any serious anaemia and the consequent tendency to faint. People with arthritis tend to shuffle, and therefore catch their feet in, and stumble over small obstacles, especially if their eyesight has begun to fail.

Old people tend to move about comparatively little; this lessens the risk of falling, but it can encourage a condition called osteoporosis which makes the bones brittle. If their diet is poor or they seldom go out in the sun, their bones may be weakened still more, especially in the pelvis and at the neck of the thigh bone. Thus even minor falls lead to badly broken bones.

While falls are rarely fatal themselves, fatal lung infection can easily follow the shock and immobilization after such an accident.

Dangerous points to look for include inaccessible storage (which may tempt old people to climb on chairs to reach high shelves or cupboards), uneven floors, and different levels and steps in the area they are likely to use, trailing flexes on electrical equipment, and electric points which are too low. Electric fires or oil heaters should only be used if they can be guarded by a fireguard fixed to the wall; convector-type electric heaters are safe. Open fires should have a proper, fixed fireguard. Careful lighting on landings, corridors, and stairs is important.

For elderly people, switches need to be put within easy reach, especially on the way to the bathroom or toilet; old people may have to get up at night when not properly awake and, if in darkness, may suffer from giddiness and uncertain sense of direction. There are switches that only need a slight pressure to turn them on; these are particularly useful to people whose movements are limited. Any particular hazards such as isolated steps can be picked out with a small spotlight, and outside steps can have a white painted edge to make them easier to see.

Other sensible precautions include the use of flame-resistant blankets (for the safest kind of electric blanket for the elderly, see the section on electrical equipment in the chapter on Care and Maintenance of the Home), bottles with different coloured tops for pills, the provision of a hook on which to hang a hot-water-bottle while it is being filled and non-slip mats in the bath. Other aids to bathing include the provision of handles and, if necessary, a low platform beside the bath which will make getting in and out a little easier. The sort of bath seat which fits down into the bath and is supported on the bath sides is extremely helpful.

With increasing age, the problem of getting in and out of both beds and chairs makes it important that these should be of the right height. An upright chair with tall support is more comfortable and much easier to get in and out of than a modern, low 'easy-chair'. The recommended height for beds in old people's homes is 0.65 metres. Beds should be comfortable but not too soft. (See also the chapter on Safety in the Home.)

Exercise

Regular exercise is, of course, important. Even for the partly disabled, it should be possible to devise a regimen which includes exercise within the limitations of the disability. The advice of a doctor and/or physiotherapist can be most helpful in such cases.

Foot care

It is essential that feet should be properly cared for. Tender or painful feet restrict the desire to move and the amount of exercise taken. Corns, callouses, and bunions are common and even cutting one's own toe-nails may present a problem when one is old. A side-effect of painful feet may be that the posture is thrown off balance and the resultant strains can cause muscular pain.

Chiropody services were formerly provided through the local authority but are increasingly the responsibility of the National Health Service. The general practitioner or the local Social Services Department should be consulted to discover what provision there is for old people to attend special clinics or to receive service at home.

The wearing of soft shoes should be discouraged; they do not give sufficient support to the feet, allow the feet to spread, and are liable to cause falls.

Special aids

Many older people suffer from arthritis. For this and other disabilities special furniture and a variety of aids are available. These include: clawfooted walking sticks, walking frames, and 'long-arm grabbers', easy-to-grip and turn controls for cookers and other appliances, tap-turning devices, etc and cutlery with specially thick handles or set at a particular angle to enable the disabled to feed themselves. There are also devices and specially adapted forms of clothing which aid dressing and undressing. Many of these aids can be obtained through the local authority's Social Services Department, and their specialist adviser should be consulted about any particular difficulty. If the Department does not itself supply the aids, it will certainly be able to recommend sources who do.

An additional source of help and advice is the Disabled Living Foundation. Wheelchairs are obtainable through the National Health Service on a doctor's certificate, though there may be a waiting period before delivery. Chairs may be hired from the Red Cross for a nominal fee. The Red Cross also hires out other equipment such as commodes.

Incontinence is a problem for many old people. Here again specialist help is available. For the slightly incontinent but mobile person some form of protective clothing may be suitable, while for the bed-ridden there are a number of special 'one-way' pads which make the condition easier to deal with and reduce the risk of bed sores. Most local authorities provide a special laundry service which is available to those caring for the incontinent.

The Statutory Background

See the chapter on Social Welfare.

Sources of Help

There are a number of national and local bodies with special concern for the welfare of the elderly and/or the disabled. The Social Services Department of the local authority or a local Citizens' Advice Bureau can help by referring enquirers to the proper source of help for particular difficulties. The Women's Royal Voluntary Service (WRVS) Good Companions Scheme provides helpers for people who are finding it difficult to run their own home without assistance.

Other national voluntary organizations with regional branches which can provide services or advice to help with an elderly person's problems include Age Concern, and Help the Aged, which produce useful information on subjects that concern elderly people. The National Council of Social Service has local councils for voluntary service. The British Red Cross, the St John Ambulance Organization, and the Disabled Living Foundation can help with information and advice about aids for the elderly with mobility problems.

Many elderly people go without the help they need because they do not know whom to ask for advice about taking the first steps. People with specific handicaps, such as deafness and blindness, can be helped by specialized services. The Royal National Institute for the Blind provides books in braille and Moon, and talking books. For the partially sighted, books with extra large print are increasingly available through public libraries. The Royal National Institute for the Deaf runs specialized services. The National Library of Talking Books for the Handicapped offers a service similar to that of the Royal National Institute for the Blind.

MEDICAL CARE IN THE HOME

All women are likely, at some period of their lives, to be called on to perform the duties of a sick-nurse, and should prepare themselves as much as possible, by observation and reading, for the occasion when they may be required to perform the office. The main requirements are good temper, compassion for suffering, sympathy with sufferers, which most women worthy of the name possess, neat-handedness, quiet manners, love of order, and cleanliness.

Some knowledge of minor complaints, how to nurse simple illnesses, and what to do in emergencies before professional help can arrive is part of the general knowledge needed to run a home successfully, and this chapter is written to help you deal with the simple medical problems which do arise in the home.

Calling the Doctor

If you are too ill to go to the surgery, ring up as early as practical if you want the doctor to call on you at home; otherwise he may not be able to fit you in quickly. The surgery cannot always give a precise time for a visit, but try and make sure that there is somebody to open the door when the doctor calls. (In general, country doctors expect to make more home visits than town doctors, whose patients live nearer the surgery.)

If possible, arrange the bed so that the doctor can stand on the right-hand side of the patient to make his examination; make sure that there is a good light. He will want to wash his hands, and he may need a receptacle to throw away used tissues, gloves or wooden spatulae. What he throws away should be burnt.

Visiting the Surgery

Your doctor probably has an appointment system; he may also have open surgeries for those who prefer not to wait for an appointment or who have to be seen quickly. In any case, time is set aside for urgent consultations.

When you see the doctor tell him simply and clearly what is wrong and how long it has been troubling you. The more accurate you are, the easier it will be for him to make a diagnosis.

The doctor may want to examine you, so it is best not to wear clothes that are difficult to take off or put on.

If you would like a second opinion suggest this to your doctor. If he agrees, a letter will be written to the doctor concerned. If you lose confidence in your doctor, change to another. Information on the procedure can be obtained from your local Department of Health and Social Security (DHSS) Area Health Authority.

Emergency or Accident

It is best to telephone the family doctor for his advice first, though he may tell you to go directly to the casualty department at the local hospital. If you have to ring the emergency services yourself, be ready to tell the operator which service you need, and your name and address. Give the name and address of the patient, if it is different, and describe clearly and calmly what is wrong.

Caring for a Patient in Bed

If you have to take care of a sick member of your family, put the patient in a single bed with a firm mattress. Place the bed so that it is possible to walk all round it. Ideally the bed should be by a window, so that the patient can look out. Make sure that the light is good enough to read by. The less furniture there is in a sick-room the better: a minimum of two chairs to put the bedclothes and pillows on when you make the bed, and a bedside table for books, drinks, a lamp, etc. It takes two people to make a bed easily; the aim is to leave the bed flat, clean, and unwrinkled. A sick person usually needs four pillows behind him to be able to sit up enough to eat and drink, and where there is difficulty in breathing he will need a back rest, so that he can sit upright, or a bed-table on which he can lean forwards. A foot-rest will keep him from sliding down the bed.

The areas of skin that need attention in the bedridden are over the heels, elbows, shoulders and hips, knees, buttocks, and the lower part of the back. The position of the patient must be changed at least every two hours to prevent the pressure falling on the same area of skin all the time; the skin must be kept dry and clean and must never be irritated by wrinkles in the lower sheet. If redness develops in the places mentioned above, skilled attention is necessary. In some cases bedclothes must be kept away from the legs and feet; if you cannot get a bed cradle, use a pillow at each side of the legs to raise the bedclothes.

Do not use an electric blanket or pad in a sick-bed. Never fill a hot-water-bottle with boiling water, and always use a cover on it.

Wash the patient's face and hands two or three times a day, as it is refreshing, and make sure that toe nails as well as finger nails are properly cut. Attend to the hair regularly; this is good for morale.

The doctor will tell you whether a special diet is needed. Always make sure that the sick person has enough to drink within easy reach, for in most short, acute illnesses solid food is not nearly as important as water. The patient must never become dry, especially when the bowels are upset. One can often get children to drink by making up flavoured drinks with soda water; in very difficult cases try giving plain or flavoured ice to suck. When patients improve they become hungry, and common sense suggests boiled fish, scrambled eggs, chicken, bread and butter – no fried food.

Old people and children easily become bored and lonely, and need to be kept occupied. People get better much more quickly if they are contented.

On the whole, it is best to get patients out of bed as soon as possible, but follow the doctor's instructions.

ABC of Medical Care

Abdominal pains

Pain in the abdomen may be the sign of something serious or may be due to a simple stomach upset. If in doubt, call the doctor; never let a bad abdominal pain last for more than six hours without asking for skilled advice. When the doctor comes he will want to know how long the pain has been present, exactly where it is, whether it is continuous, spasmodic, spreading, helped or made worse by anything – for example, vomiting. If there has been vomiting keep a specimen for the doctor to see, and keep specimens of the urine and motions. Note what position is most comfortable for the patient, and whether he is more inclined to move about or to lie still. A hot-water-bottle will often ease the pain.

Abortion

This is the termination of pregnancy before twenty-eight weeks. It may be induced or spontaneous, in which case it is generally called a miscarriage. If it appears likely that an abortion is threatening – the symptoms are bleeding and pain – the patient should call the doctor and lie down. The majority of miscarriages that take place during the first three months of pregnancy result in the delivery of a malformed foetus, so it appears that a miscarriage very often prevents the full-term development of a deformed child. In such cases the miscarriage will take place whatever the treatment. If, however, the pregnancy continues after an attack of bleeding, there is no increased risk of delivering an abnormal child.

The laws concerning induced or procured abortion differ from country to country, but in general in those countries where abortion is legal it is only allowed when continued pregnancy would endanger the health or mental stability of the mother or when there is reason to believe that the unborn child is likely to be physically or mentally abnormal.

Abscess

An abscess consists of a collection of pus surrounded by a zone of 'granulation tissue'; it is formed when the centre of an area of inflammation dies and becomes liquified. Usually the inflammation has been set up by bacterial infection, and when it is on the surface of the skin the abscess is called a boil. Normally the abscess bursts and the pus escapes – a process which can be helped by the use of a poultice. But a bad infection may have to be treated by antibiotics or even a surgical operation.

Do not squeeze a boil because you will force the pus through the protective wall of granulation tissue and spread the infection.

Accidents

Keep calm, because you can make an accident worse by doing the wrong thing. If you think a bone has been broken in the leg, leave the victim where he is, making him as warm and comfortable as possible without moving him until help arrives.

In the case of a bad accident, call 999 straight away; otherwise ask for advice from the doctor's surgery. (See also *Burns, Fracture,* and *Wounds.*)

Acne

This is a chronic disease of the sebaceous glands which secrete sebum, the fatty substance which normally lubricates the skin. It usually runs a fluctuating course until the patient is about twenty-five years old, and in girls it tends to be worse before their periods. The most common sort is called *acne vulgaris*, and affects the sebaceous glands of the face, chest, and back at about the time of puberty. It is a distressing disease and can cause permanent scarring and disfigurement; nobody can tell how a given case is going to progress, so that all cases should be taken seriously. The disease shows itself by the development of blackheads and pimples and may go on to the formation of cysts under the skin and infection with subsequent scarring.

The treatment is simple but has to be continued for a long time: sulphur ointment is recommended to promote drainage of the affected glands, the strength of the ointment depending on the reaction of the skin. Before the ointment is put on each night, wash the face thoroughly and express the blackheads with a special 'comedo extractor' which can be bought at a chemist's; do not try to squeeze the blackheads with the fingers because it leads to infection. The process is often made easier by putting a hot flannel on the skin for a minute or two beforehand, or wetting the skin with surgical spirit before using the comedo extractor. The sulphur paste is left on all night, and washed off in the morning.

A great number of preparations are sold for the treatment of *acne vulgaris*; as they contain fixed small quantities of sulphur they are only suitable for mild cases. More severe cases need a doctor's advice, for the strength of the sulphur ointment may have to be varied, and there are other ways of treating acne available only on prescription.

Adenoids

Overgrowth of the lymphatic tissue which lies at the back of the nose makes some children breathe through their mouths. In severe cases the middle ear is liable to become infected, and the doctor may advise removal of the adenoids. As the tonsils are often affected by chronic infection, they too may be taken away.

Air travel

Anyone in normal health should be able to fly without difficulty. Conditions which need special consideration include heart disease and anaemia; sufferers should consult their doctor before flying. So should those who suffer from high blood pressure or severe chest disease, those who have had an operation for the removal of a lung or part of a lung, and those who have a severe cold, sinus disease or ear infection. At least ten days should elapse after an abdominal operation (the surgeon may advise a longer period) while a varying time has to pass after an operation on an eye. Old age is itself no bar to air travel, but people with glaucoma should ask their doctor for advice. Pregnant women are regarded as fit to fly up to the eighth month, but during the month before labour air lines are apt to discourage flying. After a flight it sometimes happens that those near term develop false labour pains, which mean nothing. (See also *Sea sickness.*)

Allergy

Foreign matter introduced into the body provokes a reaction designed to get rid of it; alteration of this natural defensive reaction is called allergy, a condition invoked to explain a large number of diseases. Essentially, the development of an allergy depends on the presence in the body of an antibody, a substance which reacts with the antigen, the matter to which the body is allergic.

Allergy to foods

Patients are commonly allergic to shellfish, milk, eggs, and to a substance in wheat called the *gliadin* fraction. There may be an attack of asthma; weals or eczema (*urticaria*) may break out on the skin. Certain substances such as penicillin or the derivatives of benzoic acid which are sometimes found in food, may set up an allergic reaction. Once a patient finds he is allergic to a certain food he should avoid it for a number of years, and if he suffers an allergic reaction after taking penicillin or any other drug he must inform his doctor, who will enter the fact on his notes to prevent the same thing happening in the future.

Skin allergy

The skin reacts to allergic stimulation by developing dermatitis. First it becomes red, then it itches; blisters form and weep; finally the surface becomes scaly and thick. Infection may occur and obscure the basic pattern of the reaction. Substances which may set up dermatitis include house dust, cosmetics, deodorants, cloth and the dressings used on it, perfumes, rubber, nickel, soap powders, enzyme detergents, oil, petrol, dyes, and a long list of chemicals. The identification of the cause of an allergic dermatitis needs close co-operation between the doctor and the patient.

Allergy affecting the nose

There are two types. One is hay fever, which occurs in the early part of the summer, while the other occurs all year round. In both, the precipitating factor is dust, either from plants or animals, feathers, mould, and so on; there is a watery discharge from the nose, sneezing, and irritation of the eyes. Treatment depends on the doctor's advice.

Amenorrhoea

This means absence of the periods. Menstruation usually starts between the ages of twelve and fourteen, and continues at least until the fortieth birthday. The periods always stop before the sixtieth birthday. The commonest cause of amenorrhoea is pregnancy, but there are a number of others; in any case it is best to go and ask the doctor for advice if menstruation has not begun by the sixteenth birthday or if the pattern of menstruation alters.

Anaemia

This condition is frequently, but usually wrongly, blamed for tiredness, nervousness, and lack of appetite. With anaemia, the number of red blood corpuscles is too low, or the amount of haemoglobin in the blood is too small to supply enough oxygen to the tissues in order to support normal function under stress. The existence of anaemia is therefore determined by simple examination of the blood. There are a number of different types of anaemia for which various treatments are needed, but the commonest type is caused by deficiency of iron, either because the diet is deficient or because there is a loss of blood, eg from a bleeding gastric ulcer or excessive menstrual loss. The result of taking iron in cases such as these is so dramatic that iron has come to be thought of as a universal remedy for tiredness and lassitude, and a great deal of iron is uselessly swallowed every year. (See also p228.)

Angina

A word meaning choking, commonly used to describe a condition (*angina pectoris*) in which a suffocating pain is felt behind the breastbone, in the root of the neck, and down one or both arms. It is brought on by effort, large meals or exposure to cold, and is caused by narrowing of the coronary arteries of the heart which interferes with the free supply of blood to the heart muscle. This allows waste matter produced by exertion of the heart muscle to build up; pain develops which acts as an alarm to stop over-exertion. People who suffer from angina have to live within the limits set by the state of their circulation.

Antidotes

It used to be thought that each poisonous substance had its own antidote, but this is true only to a limited extent. In cases of poisoning the first thing to do is apply general measures to remove the poison and keep the patient alive. (See also *Poisons*.)

Antidotes which can be useful are white of egg for phenol or strong alkalis, raw eggs in milk for mercury poisoning, and sodium bicarbonate for aspirin and iron tablet overdoses; never try, however, to force anything down the throat of an unconscious patient.

Apoplexy

See *Stroke*.

Appendicitis

This is a common condition in childhood and those under thirty. Pain is at first felt round the navel, but after a few hours usually travels to the right lower part of the abdomen. It is accompanied by diarrhoea, nausea – the patient may vomit once or twice – and then constipation. The appetite is lost, the tongue dry. If you suspect appendicitis call the doctor, for the best treatment is surgical operation as soon as a firm diagnosis can be made.

Arthritis

Over 80% of people between the ages of fifty-five to sixty have changes characteristic of osteo-arthritis present in their joints, and about one-fifth of them have symptoms. Pain in the affected joints varies from time to time, but does not seem to be related to the degree of stiffness. Treatment includes measures to reduce the weight in cases where it is necessary, and encouragement of movement and active exercise. It is best to try to reduce the load falling on the affected hip and leg joints by using a stick on the opposite side.

Aspirin is the drug most commonly found to relieve pain. Unfortunately aspirin may cause irritation of the stomach and even bleeding, while some people are sensitive to the drug, so that it must be used with caution. Paracetamol, a safer alternative analgesic that can be bought over the counter, is somewhat less effective.

Artificial respiration

The best method, and the easiest, is the 'kiss of life'. Kneel on the patient's right. Pull the tongue well forward and the head well back, remove artificial teeth and look into the mouth and throat to make sure that nothing is blocking the way. Pinch the patient's nose with the left hand, keep his jaw up with the right, and blow into his mouth until you see his chest rise. Turn your head away to take another breath while the chest wall falls by itself and blows the air out of the patient's lungs. Repeat the process between twelve and twenty times a minute until the patient starts to breathe again or is obviously dead.

In cases of electrocution do not give up before two hours have elapsed, and in cases of drowning not one second must be wasted after the victim is recovered from the water before artificial respiration is started. Keep it up for fifteen minutes without stopping.

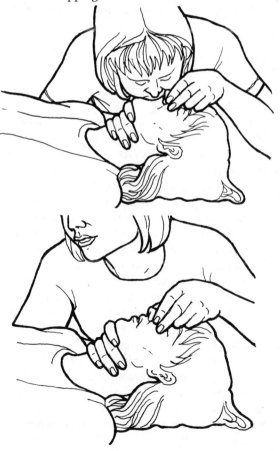

Athlete's foot

This is a fungus infection of the webs of skin between the toes, usually the fourth and fifth and to a lesser extent the third and fourth. The skin becomes soggy and irritated. Treatment is by application of ointment: Whitfield's or zinc undecenoate. When the infection has died down, the feet must be kept clean and dry. A dusting powder is useful and cotton socks which can be changed once or twice a day are recommended in bad cases.

This very common disease is picked up from the floors of showers, swimming-baths, and other places where people walk about with bare feet.

Backache

This is a common symptom of many conditions ranging from arthritis of the spine to pelvic disease in women. Most backaches are simply caused by muscular strains, and they will respond to rest, heat, and local massage with or without liniment; if the pain persists, however, a doctor's advice is necessary.

Bed-wetting

See *Enuresis*.

Blood pressure

As the heart beats, pressure in the arteries rises and falls. When the heart contracts the pressure is highest; it falls as the heart muscle relaxes. The point of highest pressure is called the *systolic pressure*, the lowest point the *diastolic pressure*. Actual figures vary from person to person, and increase with age, but there are limits beyond which the pressure can be said to be too high or too low. High blood pressures are dangerous, for they can lead to heart disease, failure of the kidneys, loss of vision, and strokes. In its early stages a high blood pressure produces little in the way of symptoms, and although it is often thought to be responsible for headaches, dizziness, fatigue, and other troubles, doctors most often detect a high blood pressure on routine examination of patients who complain of none of these things. An increasing number of drugs are used in the treatment of high blood pressure, and one thing they have in common is the need for routine regular use. You may not feel very different when your doctor starts you on treatment to lower your blood pressure, and you may wonder if there is any point in taking pills day after day; but remember that the treatment is meant to prevent serious complications rather than alter your present state of health. Keeping your weight down can often reduce a blood pressure on the high side to within normal limits.

Boils

Boils are small abscesses in the skin (see p137).

Breast-feeding

The breasts secrete milk on about the third day after delivery. Suckling is a powerful stimulus, and in a short time about a litre of milk a day is produced. In the early days of breast feeding inflammation or even an abscess may sometimes develop, but with skilled attention these disorders are soon righted.

Breasts

The breast is the site of a number of diseases but the most important is cancer, and any lump in the breast always raises the question of malignant growth. A potentially dangerous lump is hard, relatively immovable, and is usually in the upper part of the breast nearest the armpit. Women should check their breasts for lumps every month, about a week after menstruation. While it is true that the vast majority of lumps in the breast are simple and not cancerous, show any lump to the doctor as soon as possible.

Bronchitis

This often follows a winter cold in the middle aged and elderly, and shows itself by pain in the chest, shortness of breath, cough, and a fever. Antibiotics are the usual treatment. Smoking is forbidden and should not be allowed near the sick-room, where the air must be clean and at as even a temperature as possible. There is a form of bronchitis affecting children, usually in the winter, which may progress so rapidly that a child with a mild cough in the morning can, by the end of the day, be fighting for breath. Call the doctor at once if a child has the slightest difficulty in breathing.

Bruise

This is damage to the tissues by direct violence that does not break the skin but crushes the underlying fat and muscle. The blood which escapes from the small damaged vessels first colours the area red, then as the pigment breaks down the bruise turns blue and finally yellow. The pain can be helped by cold compresses. If the swelling does not go down soon, see the doctor.

Burns and scalds

Burns are caused by dry heat, scalds by boiling water or steam. Cover the damaged area with a wet, clean cloth, for example a newly laundered handkerchief, towel or part of a sheet. Never put anything on a burn or scald except cold water or a weak solution of salt (1 × 5ml spoon salt in 600ml water), and remember that burns are always accompanied by some degree of shock, so that the patient should be kept warm; if he feels faint he should be put to bed and given a warm drink while you call for skilled help. In the case of minor burns and scalds, use a light gauze dressing; do not puncture the blisters or use greasy or coagulating applications such as tannic acid jelly. Burns easily become infected, so always be scrupulously clean when dealing with them; if they show the signs of infection –redness, pus formation, swelling, pain – ask for medical advice.

Cancer

The characteristic property of cancer is its power to spread to parts of the body remote from the original tumour; it grows at the expense of the tissue where it lies and destroys the function of organs it invades. In men the disease is commonly found in the intestines, lungs, and prostate gland, while in women the commonest sites are the breast, womb, gall-bladder, and thyroid gland. There are no symptoms particular to cancer, but loss of weight, persistent cough, change in bowel habits, indigestion and changes in menstruation, as well as the presence of an obvious swelling, can enable the doctor to diagnose and treat cancer before it is too late. If you have the slightest doubt go straight to the doctor, as speed is the key to success in treating cancer. (See also *Breasts*.)

Chicken-pox

This is a disease of childhood caused by virus infection. The incubation period is 14–21 days, and the patient feels ill a day or two before the spots develop. They start as small red dots on the part of the body covered by the vest, and as the rash develops outwards to the limbs the small red bumps become blisters which eventually scab over. The patient is best kept in bed as long as he feels ill; aspirin will help the headache and calamine lotion the rash, which must be kept clean to prevent infection and subsequent scarring. The period of infectivity lasts for a week after the appearance of the rash, but the disease is very rarely severe and strict quarantine is not needed. Children are usually ready to go back to school about two weeks after the beginning of the disease. The same virus that causes chicken-pox in children causes *herpes zoster* (see p147) in adults, but the relationship between the two diseases is not quite straightforward, for while a patient with *herpes* can pass chicken-pox to a child, *herpes* does not follow exposure to chicken-pox.

Chilblains

These are red itchy swellings on the fingers or toes, nose or ears, which develop in cold weather, usually in young people. If you are susceptible, wear gloves, thick boots, and thick stockings or tights, and do not heat the fingers and toes up too quickly by plunging them into hot water, for example, when you come in out of the cold.

Choking

The gullet and the windpipe divide in the neck, and there is a mechanism whereby the top of the windpipe is shut off when anything is swallowed. If this fails and food or drink reaches the inside of the windpipe, it sets up a spasm which prevents the patient taking breath. The only remedy is to dislodge the offending substance by hitting the sufferer on the back as he coughs, and in the case of babies and small children, turning them upside down. If the choking continues, you may have to reach behind the root of the tongue with a finger to dislodge the food which has gone down the wrong way.

Colitis

This is a term used to refer to the irritable bowel syndrome (see p149).

Common cold

This is a disease caused by a virus. In itself more of a nuisance than a danger, it is often complicated by bacterial infection of the sinuses, ears, windpipe, and lungs which turns it into a more serious disease. It is, therefore, sensible to stay at home for a couple of days when you catch a cold, for by staying in the warm in a fairly controlled atmosphere you have a good chance of avoiding extra infection – and you will not spread the cold to other people.

Concussion

This is injury to the brain caused by a blow on the head which results in a loss or diminution of consciousness, usually recovering within twenty-four hours. The state is not properly understood, but from a practical point of view, it is important that everyone who suffers a blow on the head grave enough to make him unconscious should be seen by the doctor. No lasting damage follows simple concussion, although the patient often cannot remember exactly how the accident happened. Any persisting headache or pain should be reported to the doctor.

Conjunctivitis

Also called pink-eye; an inflammation of the *conjunctiva*, the membrane covering the front of the eye, usually due to infection by micro-organisms but sometimes caused by mechanical irritation, eg an eyelash growing inwards. If there is no obvious cause of irritation, the eye should be bathed with a bland solution such as sodium chloride eye lotion. If the redness persists, ask the doctor for advice.

Constipation

Suggested methods of cure are increased physical activity and the consumption of foods with a high fibre content (roughage) such as raw vegetables and fruits, whole grain products, and bran. Drinking liquids aids the effect of fibre. A person with persistent constipation should see a doctor.

Convulsions

In children severe infections may produce convulsions. The child becomes unconscious, twitches and jerks, and may cry out. During the attack it is important to see that the patient can breathe easily. The treatment is fundamentally that of the underlying fever, although the doctor may use sedative drugs. An attack of convulsions is not in itself dangerous, and it does not mean that the child has epilepsy.

Coronary thrombosis

This is a condition in which the small arteries supplying blood to the heart muscle are narrowed or blocked by clots. The victim feels severe pain in the centre of the chest, the root of the neck or down the left arm, and collapses. He must be kept lying down, quiet, and warm. He may become pale and anxious, cold, and breathless. The doctor should be called at once.

Cuts

See *Wounds*.

Deafness

This may be the result of infection, blockage of the outer passage to the ear by wax or blockage of the tube leading from the inside of the throat to the middle ear; in children it may be caused by something introduced into the ear. It may be congenital or inherited, or the penalty of increasing age. Most types of deafness can be helped by an expert, and hearing aids are supplied by the National Health Service to those who need them. Never buy a hearing aid without consulting the doctor.

Dental decay

See p232.

Dermatitis

This is inflammation of the skin; see *Skin allergy* on p138. Treatment consists of identifying the cause – allergy, external irritation, etc – and in dealing with each stage of the condition as it develops. Calamine lotion and cold water compresses are suitable for the first stage, aluminium acetate lotion for the second stage, and zinc oxide paste with or without coal tar for the third and chronic stages. Dermatitis and eczema are virtually synonymous.

Diabetes

There are two sorts of diabetes. In one the patient produces too much urine, in the other, the more common, he cannot use sugar properly because of a lack of the hormone insulin which is normally supplied by the pancreas. This type is often called sugar diabetes, and is treated with insulin by injection or by mouth or in mild cases by adjusting the diet. If an overdose of insulin is taken, or the patient misses a meal, he becomes confused and unsteady and seems to be drunk. He recovers after a dose of sugar by mouth or by intravenous injection. On the other hand, if he misses a dose of insulin or takes too much sugar he feels nauseated, may vomit, and may lose consciousness. His blood pressure falls and his pulse rate rises. This means that he needs a dose of insulin. Every diabetic should carry a card saying he is a diabetic, and a supply of sugar. (See also p236.)

Diarrhoea

This is a state in which the motions are more fluid and frequent than they should be. It is usually due to infection of the bowels by bacteria or irritation by toxins produced by bacteria, and in most cases is simple and self-limiting. In severe cases the most important measure is prevention of dehydration, especially in children, who are liable to lose water very quickly. They must be encouraged to drink as much water as possible during and after an attack.

Diverticulitis

This is a disease of the large intestine, in which the internal lining of the bowel bulges through the muscle of the bowel wall to form small protruding pouches. These diverticula may become infected and inflamed, causing pain low down on the left hand side of the abdomen. There may be diarrhoea or constipation and fever. The disease is rarely found below middle age, and is thought to be caused, at least in part, by lack of fibre (roughage) in the diet (p236). Many doctors, therefore, recommend up to 4 × 15ml spoons of bran a day, sprinkled on cereals or other food.

Dog bites

In countries where rabies is endemic, dog bites are dangerous and anyone bitten is at once started on a course of vaccine treatment if there is the slightest reason to suspect that the dog was rabid. Where rabies has been eradicated by strict quarantine regulations, there is still a danger of tetanus and infection of the wound, and dog bites must be carefully cleaned. It is best to go to the doctor so that he can give an antibiotic and an anti-tetanus injection, if necessary.

Dysentery

This is diarrhoea with the passage of mucus and blood. The onset is acute, about four days after the infecting organisms have been picked up (usually in food). There is nausea, vomiting, fever, and diarrhoea with considerable pain. The doctor will want to know exactly where the patient has been in the week before the attack, and will take a swab in order to identify the infecting bacteria. It is important for anyone doing the cooking to be careful about personal hygiene; the disease is spread by dirtiness, especially in kitchens, and is growing more common in cities and institutions.

Dysmenorrhea

Dysmenorrhea (painful periods) is a common complaint, particularly among women in the age range 15–25. The cramp-like pains in the lower abdomen are caused by spasm of the uterine muscle; the patient frequently complains of associated headache, backache, and painful legs. Aspirin, or other pain-killing drugs, and sometimes exercise, can bring relief. The doctor's advice should always be sought if dysmenorrhea becomes incapacitating, or if it occurs unexpectedly in older women, when it may be indicative of other gynaecological problems.

Dyspepsia

This is a feeling of discomfort and flatulence after meals. It may be the sign of a gastric or duodenal ulcer, or a disorder of the gall-bladder, but often means little. If it persists, ask the doctor for his advice; do not go on taking alkaline medicines for months except on his instructions.

Earache

Several conditions give rise to earache, but perhaps the most important is infection of the middle ear – the part behind the ear drum. Not long ago this sometimes spread to the mastoid bone behind the ear, but antibiotics can now be used to prevent such a dangerous complication. It is important that all children who complain of earache should be taken to see the doctor as soon as possible.

Electric shock

First make sure that the victim is not still in contact with the electrical supply. If you can, switch the electricity off; if you cannot, push him away from the live wires with a broom handle or a chair, or handle him with a cushion or thick gloves. If he is not breathing start artificial respiration quickly (see p139), and keep it up until skilled help arrives. If the victim is still near a live rail or a high voltage cable, do not go near him, but call for help.

Electric burns are treated like ordinary burns, but they often take a long time to heal.

Enuresis

This means bed-wetting. The cause is sometimes an infection of the bladder or kidneys, or diabetes, and children with this trouble should be examined to exclude disease. If none is found, the reason for bed-wetting is as likely to be found in the attitude of the parents as in the disposition of the child, but it is certain that the condition will respond to kindness and understanding. Control of the bladder is generally complete by the age of three.

Epilepsy

This is a condition in which the patient suffers from fits. In major epilepsy, *grand mal*, the fits involve loss of consciousness and convulsive movements of the whole body; in minor epilepsy, *petit mal*, there is only a momentary loss of consciousness or attention. People with epilepsy are to be encouraged to lead as normal a life as possible. While they cannot take part in occupations where a lapse of consciousness could be dangerous, they can carry out safe jobs perfectly well; but obviously they must not drive. If you see someone suffering an epileptic fit, make sure he can breathe freely and cannot hurt himself by banging against hard objects. Sometimes it is possible to slip something between the teeth to prevent the tongue being bitten.

There is no need for a known sufferer to go to the doctor every time he has a fit, but children who have fits for the first time must be taken for a medical examination. Epilepsy may be a sign of underlying disease, especially when it comes on in older people, but in most cases no underlying cause can be found. Although the incidence of epilepsy increases very slightly in the children of marriages where one or both of the parents have epilepsy, it is of very little significance.

Eye injuries

Seek medical advice for all eye injuries as soon as possible. If small particles lodge under the eyelids, or on the front of the eyeball, do not rub the eye – blink as quickly as you can. If this does not dislodge the grit, then pull the upper lid outwards and downwards over the lower lid and release it. If this fails, try blowing the nose hard; if you can see the speck, it may be taken away by the corner of a clean handkerchief. If it does not come away easily, go to the doctor. (See also *Conjunctivitis*.)

Fainting

This means temporary loss of consciousness caused by transient failure of the blood supply to the brain. The patient may have been standing up too long, the surroundings may be too hot and stuffy, and emotional shock may affect the nervous control of the circulation; or fainting may be a sign of anaemia or other underlying disease. Because the fundamental condition is a lack of blood pressure to the head, the treatment is to lie the patient flat and raise the legs. If he just feels faint, make him sit down and put his head between his knees. Do not try to force the patient to drink. (See also *Epilepsy*.)

Fever

The normal body temperature is usually said to be 36.9°C, but it varies during the day. It is lowest in the morning and rises during the day to a maximum of 37.5°C. One temperature reading, even though it is raised, is not very useful, and it is better to make up your mind whether a patient is ill or not by comparing his behaviour with normal behaviour rather than by using a thermometer; in doubtful cases, however, the temperature may help the doctor to make up his mind.

Fibrositis

This is a term used to mean an aching pain in the muscles, usually of the neck and shoulders, in which a localized area of tenderness or spasm can be found. Massage or heat applied to these areas gives relief; but no underlying pathological changes have been found and the condition remains a minor mystery.

First aid

See *Accidents, Antidotes, Artificial respiration, Burns and scalds, Electric shock, Epilepsy, Eye injuries, Fracture, Head injury, Labour, Nose bleeding, Poisons, Shock, Sprain, Stings, Stroke, Wounds.*

First aid kit

A home first aid kit should contain any items you feel are necessary to attend to likely minor accidents. The basic equipment is as follows: bandages (2–6cm wide), adhesive plasters, adhesive plaster strip, gauze dressings, gauze pads, cotton wool, cleansing tissues, calamine lotion, antiseptics, aspirin and junior aspirin, antihistamine cream (for stings), safety pins, tweezers, scissors, and eye bath.

As with all medicines, this kit should be stored out of a child's reach.

Flat foot

Usually the foot arches from side to side and from the heel to the base of the toes. Absence of arching may be connected with pain, especially on standing, but by itself is not significant. Treatment of the pain may include exercises and supports worn in the shoes, but advice should be sought from a doctor before spending money.

Flatulence

This is the presence of abnormal quantities of gas in the stomach and intestines. In nearly all cases the cause is the habit of swallowing air. Eating quickly, chewing gum, and sucking a thumb all add to the amount of air swallowed. A person suffering from flatulence can often be convinced that this is the source of their problem if they can be persuaded to keep a cork between their teeth for a few hours so that they cannot swallow unconsciously.

The other cause of flatulence is the bacterial action of digestion on certain foods, notably beans, cabbage, and turnips.

Food poisoning

The symptoms of this begin between four and forty-eight hours after ingestion, and include stomach cramps, vomiting, diarrhoea, chills, headache, and fever. The patient should get plenty of bed rest and refrain from eating or drinking anything until the vomiting stops; thin soup with salt is then suggested. A doctor should be consulted to watch for dehydration and to monitor the illness. The symptoms should disappear in one to five days.

Fracture

This means a break in a bone. If you have to deal with one, do as little as possible. Keep the affected limb still; often the best way is to keep the patient where he lies until skilled help arrives, although he will be better off if he is lying down. A broken leg may be tied to the sound one, or a broken arm to the side. If the collar bone is broken, the arm is more comfortable in a sling. If you have any reason to suppose that a patient has broken his back, keep him lying still on his front, and tell the ambulance men or the doctor why you think the back may be broken. People who have broken bones suffer from shock and must be kept warm and as comfortable as possible.

German measles

Otherwise called *Rubella*. A virus infection with an incubation period of two or three weeks, infective until the acute phase is over. It begins with a running nose, headache, and enlargement and tenderness of the glands behind the ears. A rash of small pink spots develops in a day or two over the face and trunk; the spots run together and fade in about two days, leaving a slight peeling of the skin.

The disease is virtually harmless to children, but

if a woman in the first four months of pregnancy comes into contact with a case, she should consult her doctor because it can have an effect on the baby she carries. As one attack confers immunity it is sensible to try and make sure that all girls catch the disease in childhood. Women who have not had the disease can be given a vaccine when they are of child-bearing age, but once pregnancy has started the vaccine is dangerous.

Glandular fever

This is a condition in which there is a raised temperature, the lymphatic glands at the sides of the neck are swollen and tender, and the throat is sore. There may be a skin rash like German measles. The patient, who is generally between the ages of fifteen and twenty-five, feels ill and miserable. The disease may apparently recover only to recur, and relapses may continue for weeks. There is no specific treatment, but it may be necessary to treat the sore throat when it is severe.

Growing pains

It used to be thought that pains in the limbs were normal while a child was growing, but the truth is that growth never causes pain and such pains are not normal. A doctor should be consulted.

Gumboil

This an abscess at the root of a decayed tooth which produces swelling of the gum and the skin around it. The local application of heat and a visit to the dentist are recommended.

Haemorrhoids

These are small enlarged veins near the anus, otherwise called piles. They vary from mild to quite serious, and usually start to show themselves by irritation. The best treatment is washing the area three or four times a day with cold water and cotton wool. If there is pain or bleeding, it is much better to ask the doctor for advice than rely on proprietary remedies, for very occasionally haemorrhoids are the sign of an underlying disorder.

Hay fever

See *Allergy*.

Headache

This may be caused by disease, worry, over-indulgence in smoking or alcohol – but 90% of headaches have no obvious cause. If rest and a couple of soluble aspirins do not relieve a headache, and particularly if it recurs, ask the doctor for his advice.

Head injury

Bleeding from the scalp is usually fiercer than bleeding from any other part of the body, but luckily it is easy to stop; all that is required is firm pressure against the underlying bone. Matting of hair and blood running down the face make the injury look worse than it is. (See also *Concussion*.)

Hearing aids

See *Deafness*.

Heart disease

The symptoms of heart disease do not bear a direct relationship to the anatomical position of the heart, and pain over the heart on the left-hand side of the chest is more often due to indigestion than heart disease. The pain of angina or coronary thrombosis is usually felt in the centre of the chest, in the root of the neck, or down the arm. Palpitations tend to be a sign of anxiety and tension, and in general it is found that patients who are certain there is something wrong with their heart are wrong, and it is those who do not suspect it who have heart disease. Symptoms of importance include breathlessness, swelling of the ankles, tiredness, headaches, and giddiness. The patient with heart disease has to learn to live within limits set by the onset of such symptoms. He does not have to give up all normal activities, but needs to take things easily and move with care. He may not be able to afford such luxuries as running, or losing his temper. (See also *Angina* and *Coronary thrombosis*, and p236.)

Hepatitis

See *Jaundice*.

Hernia

This is a rupture. Although the term strictly means protrusion of any organ from the compartment of the body in which it is normally contained, it is commonly used to mean the protrusion of part of the intestine from the abdominal cavity at the site of a weakness in the muscular walls of the abdomen, particularly at the groin. Do not wear a truss to try to control a hernia without taking advice from the doctor. If you suffer from a hernia, and it will not go back or becomes painful, go to the doctor at once.

Herpes

Herpes simplex is the name given to the blisters that form at the corners of the mouth in association with a cold. The treatment is to keep the area dry and clean, and to dab the blisters occasionally with surgical spirit.

Herpes zoster, or shingles, is a virus infection related to chicken-pox in which painful blisters form along the course of a sensory nerve in the skin, most often running round the chest wall. The blisters must be protected, and the best way to do this is to paint them with flexible collodion (a liquid mixture of ether, alcohol, pyroxylin and castor oil). This also reduces the pain.

Hiccough

Hiccoughs result from sudden violent contraction of the diaphragm, often caused by irritation of the stomach. Sometimes a drink of water or a biscuit will stop it, although at other times holding the breath for as long as possible is a good remedy. In intractable cases try inhaling carbon dioxide; this sounds complicated, but may be accomplished at home by breathing in and out of a paper bag.

Immunity

Active immunity to disease follows an attack of that disease, during which the blood not only produces antibodies to the disease but retains the ability to manufacture the antibodies again if they should be required in the future. Immunity can be acquired artificially, in the form of vaccination, if the organisms causing a particular disease, or in some cases the poisons they produce, are introduced into the body in amounts too small to be dangerous.

Immunization

The diseases against which children should be immunized are:

Diphtheria, tetanus, and *whooping cough*
– first injection between three and six months
– second after six weeks
– then after six months
(Not all doctors advise immunization against whooping cough.)

Tetanus – booster injections are recommended at intervals of five years following the original series. Animal bites and major cuts require a booster, if five years have lapsed since the previous injection.

Poliomyelitis – vaccine given by mouth at the same intervals as diphtheria, tetanus, and whooping cough vaccinations.

Measles – during the second year.

Smallpox – not now advised in every case. Take your doctor's advice.

Tuberculosis – given to children between ten and thirteen years old who are found by skin tests to be susceptible to the disease.

Immunization is also available in later life against *Yellow fever, German measles, Typhoid and Paratyphoid fevers, Cholera, Plague, Influenza,* and *Rabies* (see below).

German measles (Rubella) – All young women should, before they start a family, make sure that they are immune to infection. An attack in childhood will confer immunity, but if there is any doubt a blood test will give a definite answer. If such a test shows no immunity, vaccination is required, for infection with *rubella* during pregnancy, particularly in the first three months, may cause serious defects in the development of the baby.

Influenza – Immunization against influenza is often advised for the elderly, those with chronic bronchitis or other lung disease, sufferers from heart and kidney conditions, diabetics, and such people as nurses and doctors who are especially exposed to infection. The drawback is that influenza viruses change from year to year, and it is not possible to foretell exactly which type will predominate in the next epidemic. Immunization may, therefore, be only partially effective.

Rabies – see *Dog Bites*.

Smallpox and Cholera – Sometimes required before travel abroad. Your travel agent will tell you if it is necessary to obtain certificates of immunization, which will be signed by the doctor carrying out the vaccination. His signature must be authenticated by the local authority. Full immunization against cholera means two injections preferably at an interval of four weeks, so leave enough time to have the two injections before you travel. Immunity to cholera lasts for six months, after which time reinforcing vaccination is required; immunity to smallpox lasts for three years.

Typhoid and paratyphoid (TAB) – Recommended before travelling to countries where the diseases are prevalent. Your doctor will advise you, as will the travel agent. Two injections are needed at an interval of about four weeks, and immunity lasts for three years. The injections may cause constitutional or local reactions which usually disappear after thirty-six hours.

Yellow fever – Recommended or required in certain Central African countries, in Columbia and Peru. This vaccination is usually available only from the public health authorities, not from your family doctor.

Impetigo

This is a skin disease caused by superficial infection with an organism called *staphylococcus*. It is contagious, and the areas most often affected are the face, neck, and scalp. Medical advice is essential. Make sure that the patient's towel, face flannel, and linen are not used by others in the family.

Incubation period

This means the time elapsing between infection and the first symptoms of the disease.

Common incubation periods are:

Short – up to seven days: Diphtheria, meningitis, scarlet fever, influenza, plague, cholera.

Intermediate – seven to fourteen days: Smallpox, measles, glandular fever, whooping cough, typhoid fever.

Long – over fourteen days: German measles (up to twenty-one days), mumps (up to twenty-one days), chicken-pox (up to twenty-one days), infective jaundice (up to four weeks).

Infant welfare

See the chapter on *Social Welfare*.

Influenza

This is an acute infectious disease caused by a virus. It starts with a high temperature, shivering, headache, a dry cough, and aching in the bones and muscles. It lasts for about a week but is often complicated by bronchitis or pneumonia, especially in the elderly, and then the illness may take much longer to disappear. People often become depressed after influenza, and the feeling of tiredness and lassitude may last up to three weeks. For injections, see *Immunization*. No specific treatment for influenza is known, and the symptoms must be treated as they arise. Aspirin is the most generally useful drug.

Ingrowing toe nail

As it grows towards the end of the toe the great toe nail sometimes catches in one of the folds of skin at each side and sets up an inflammation. The skin folds may become infected, and the toe is often painful. The nailfold has to be kept away from the edge of the nail until the nail has grown out to its proper length, and then the nail should be cut straight across the end to prevent the same thing happening again. Make sure that shoes are not too narrow, as they can pinch the skin folds inwards. Seek medical advice if infection occurs.

Insomnia

This means inability to sleep. The cause is generally undue anxiety, and it is easy to set up a vicious circle in which the patient worries about not going to sleep and is consequently unable to do so. On the whole, it is true that people sleep as much as they need, and that many complaints about 'not being able to sleep a wink' relate to an hour or so at the beginning of the night, after which sleep is normal, or to an hour awake in the small hours – when everything assumes the worst possible aspect. If you suffer from insomnia, remember that worry is the chief cause, and that while sleeping tablets can help to regain the habit of sleep, indifference to loss of sleep is the best way of ensuring that it does not occur.

Irritable bowel syndrome

This is a common cause of symptoms referable to the large bowel –discomfort in the abdomen, diarrhoea or constipation, and the passage of thin or hard, round stools, or even mucus. The condition is not dangerous, and is often found in younger people subject to anxiety or emotional disturbance. Treatment is designed to relieve the psychological trouble, but the response may not be immediate. It is essential to stop smoking and to be very moderate in the use of alcohol, for both these habits exacerbate the disease.

Jaundice

This means yellow discoloration of the skin and the whites of the eyes, caused by diseases of the liver, gall-bladder, and in some cases the blood. By far the most common cause is infective hepatitis, which is particularly liable to attack young adults. It is a virus disease which can be passed between people by flies and contamination of food by dirty hands and dust; patients need rest in bed, plenty of fluids and a light diet without fat. In older people jaundice may follow obstruction of the bile passages. All cases need the doctor's advice.

Kaolin poultice

Used to keep an inflamed area of the body warm and wet, as well as to soothe any irritation there.

The best way of applying a kaolin paste poultice is to spread it on a piece of lint, and toast it under the grill until it is the right temperature. It is easy to burn a patient with a hot poultice, so be careful.

Labour

The onset of labour will usually be accompanied by backache, regular uterine contractions, and the appearance of blood and mucus. At this stage, the mother should be taken to hospital, or the doctor or midwife called if the birth is to take place at home.

The process of birth takes place in three stages. The first is marked by loss of the water from the membranes surrounding the baby, and is complete when the neck of the womb is fully opened. The second stage is the birth of the baby; and the third the expulsion of the afterbirth. The first labour usually takes longer than subsequent labours.

Lumbago

This is a term commonly used to mean a pain in the lower part of the back for which no obvious cause can be found. It is often due to trouble in the muscles at each side of the spinal column, and may come on during an attack of influenza or after uncommon exercise or strain. The treatment is rest on a hard bed; local heat may help, and aspirin is well worth trying.

Measles

This is a virus infection usually affecting children and occurring in epidemics. The incubation period is about fourteen days, and the disease starts with a running nose, red eyes, and a cough. There is headache and fever, and on about the fourth day a rash of small red spots breaks out on the skin behind the ears and on the face. Before this, white spots may be seen inside the mouth. The spots join up and spread all over the body; after about three days they fade to leave a brownish stain. During an attack of measles the lungs, ears, and eyes are all liable to become infected with bacteria which have nothing to do with the measles virus. The secondary infection may be damaging unless it is treated, usually with antibiotics. While a child is in the acute stages of measles, he has to be kept quiet in bed and is best given a light diet with plenty to drink. Other children should be kept away. Immunization against measles is possible, and is carried out in the second year of life. Ask your doctor for his advice.

Meningitis

This is an inflammation of the membranes covering the brain. A severe and dangerous disease, it starts with a bad headache, confusion, vomiting, a stiff neck, and dislike of light in the eyes. There may be a skin rash. Medical treatment has to be quick if it is to succeed; if you have any suspicion that the disease is present, call the doctor at once.

Menopause

This means the cessation of the monthly periods, which normally happens any time between forty and fifty-five. Many women are frightened of the 'change of life', but there is no necessary reason why trouble should arise. If you are worried, go and talk to your doctor. You can be sure that the disturbances, which include hot flushes, insomnia, joint pains, increase in weight, and general irritability, will pass; but in a number of cases the emotional upset is made worse by domestic strain or by loneliness. By the time of the menopause, children are likely to be leaving home and husbands are often absorbed to an increasing degree by the responsibilities of their occupation. In such circumstances it is sensible to try to find a new interest in life, or to resurrect an old one. Although hot flushes are unpleasant they go unnoticed by other people, and there is no reason to worry about how you look in company. As for sexual activity, the menopause need make no difference, except, obviously, that there is no longer the possibility of pregnancy.

Menstruation
See *Amenorrhoea* and *Dysmenorrhea*.

Migraine
Sometimes used to describe a severe headache, the term strictly means a particular sort of headache which starts with disturbances of vision, sensation or speech, is felt on one side of the head, and is accompanied by nausea or even vomiting. Migraine may run in families, and the frequency of attacks varies. The patient is best put to bed in a darkened room; there are a number of drugs which can be prescribed, but the doctor will treat each case individually. There is no one specific remedy. Attacks are often precipitated by known factors such as flashing lights, anxiety or certain kinds of food, eg chocolate or cheese. Some sufferers find that red wine and sherry are best avoided.

Miscarriage
See *Abortion*.

Mumps
This is an acute infective illness, usually of childhood, caused by a virus. The incubation period is between fourteen and twenty-one days, and the disease starts as a swelling in front of, and below the ears. In children mumps is virtually harmless

except in rare cases, but in adults it may progress to involve the sex glands and may prove a fairly serious matter if the testicles or ovaries are infected. It is, therefore, important that no attempt should be made to prevent children, particularly boys, from catching mumps. All patients should be kept quiet while the disease is active, but there is no known specific treatment. The swelling over the angle of the jaw is usually uncomfortable rather than painful; there is a fever but it is mild, and the disease lasts between one and three weeks.

Napkin rash
In some cases the urine of infants is broken down by bacteria into irritating ammoniacal compounds which redden the skin under the napkin and make it sore. Frequent changing of the napkins, which should be thoroughly rinsed and boiled to ensure sterilization, and the use of zinc compound paste on the skin is recommended.

Nose bleeding
This may occur without obvious cause or may follow nose-picking or injury, or be caused by high blood pressure or the presence of abnormal blood vessels; sometimes children are found to have pushed objects up their noses. The patient should be made to lie down, and a cold compress – ice, for example, wrapped in a handkerchief – should be applied to the root of the nose. The nostrils may be pinched together for about ten minutes and all clothing round the neck should be loosened. If the bleeding does not stop, call the doctor, particularly if the patient is elderly.

Obesity
See p232.

Osteoarthritis
See *Arthritis*.

Overdose
See *Antidotes* and *Poisons*.

Palpitations
Sometimes the usually imperceptible action of the heart is felt or heard, especially when the heart is

under stress or when all is quiet, as in the night. The heart beats more strongly under the stimulus of strong emotion, and the vast majority of cases in which the patient complains of palpitations are found to be examples of anxiety; only very rarely do they mean that there is anything wrong with the heart.

Phlebitis

This is inflammation of a vein, usually associated with varicose veins (see p154). There is pain and local tenderness, with redness and perhaps swelling over the affected vein. It is treated by support with an elastic stocking or bandage, and while there is no need for the patient to rest more than normal (indeed, movement will help to maintain circulation), the leg is less painful if it is kept up when he sits down.

Piles

See *Haemorrhoids*.

Pink eye

See *Conjunctivitis*.

Pneumonia

This is inflammation of the substance of the lung. The disease may mainly involve the lobes of the lung, when it is called lobar pneumonia and is usually caused by the *pneumococcus*; or it may spread from the wind passages in the lungs when it is called bronchopneumonia and occurs during an attack of bronchitis, influenza or other infection of the respiratory system. Often the first symptoms of pneumonia do not suggest trouble in the lungs, for the patient may complain of violent headache and feel very ill indeed without having any cough or pain in the chest, making it difficult to diagnose the disease in its early stages.

Pneumonia is a disease which responds well to antibiotics and can, therefore, be treated at home with success. The patient should be kept in a room at an even temperature, not too hot, well ventilated but free from draughts. He must be encouraged to drink fluids freely, although his appetite will be poor and he will not want to take more than a very light diet.

Poisons

If you think that anyone has taken poison, by mistake or on purpose, ring for the ambulance at once or, if you can, take the patient yourself to the nearest hospital casualty department – speed is important. While help is on its way telephone the hospital to say that the patient is coming. It may be possible to make him vomit by giving him salt water to drink or by tickling the back of his throat, but never do this if there is any suspicion that he has swallowed a corrosive poison. If the patient does vomit, keep the specimen, and in any case, keep whatever is left of the poison you think the patient has taken so that the doctor can identify it. It is far more important to keep the patient warm and make sure he can breathe freely than to worry about antidotes (see p139). If the patient is unconscious, turn him so that he lies half on his front with his face towards the ground so that he cannot inhale vomit.

Pregnancy

The first sign of pregnancy is usually the cessation of menstruation. Other indications include swelling and tingling of the breasts, sensitive nipples, frequent urination, and tiredness. Additionally, two-thirds of all pregnant women suffer 'morning sickness', ie a mild nausea upon rising, between the third and sixth weeks.

The average duration of pregnancy in the human being is 274 to 280 days. Although the vast majority of pregnancies are quite normal and free of trouble, it is important to consult the family doctor as soon as you think you might be pregnant, so that he can make sure that everything is as it should be and arrange for a bed to be booked at the hospital for your delivery. Regular visits to the ante-natal clinic will enable him to keep in touch with your progress. (See also *Labour*.)

Pulse rate

As the heart beats the arteries expand and contract. The change in volume and pressure can be felt particularly in the radial artery that runs across the bones of the wrist at the base of the thumb, and is called the pulse. The normal pulse rate is between about 70 and 80 beats a minute at rest.

Quarantine

This means the isolation of people who have been in contact with infectious fevers to prevent them passing on the disease. It is usually two days longer than the incubation period (see p148). The term used to be applied to the detention of ships, usually for forty days.

Rash

This is a temporary eruption on the skin which occurs very often as part of an infectious fever. Common rashes are measles, in which small raised spots start behind the ears, on the forehead, and the face, and spread over the whole body, running together to form large patches (see p149); chicken-pox, where the rash starts on the trunk and spreads to the limbs (see p141), unlike the rash of small-pox which starts on the face, hands, and feet and spreads inwards to the trunk; German measles (*rubella*) where small red spots start on the face and spread to the trunk, but do not run together (see p145); scarlet fever (*scarlatina*) where the rash is irregular and consists of red patches especially at the groins, armpits, and elbows (see below); and nettlerash (*urticaria*) with red patches and raised weals on the skin.

Respiration

The rate of breathing is normally about 18–20 a minute at rest. It is raised in fevers and maladies of the lungs.

Ringworm

This is a fungus infection of the skin. The infection spreads outwards from the centre so that the active edge is at the periphery of a circle; this gives the condition its name. It is found in the scalp, where it makes the hair brittle, and elsewhere on the body. It occurs in cattle and domestic animals, especially cats, and may be caught from them. The treatment is local application of suitable ointment or dusting powder. The patient must use his own separate washing things, comb, and towel to avoid spreading the infection.

Rubella

See *German measles*.

Rupture

See *Hernia*.

Scalds

See *Burns*.

Scarlet fever

Otherwise called *scarlatina*, this is a condition in which infection of the throat by a micro-organism (*streptococcus*) produces a skin rash which consists of red blotches tending to form at the armpits, groins, and elbows. The incubation period is two to four days. Whereas formerly scarlet fever was a very serious state which killed or incapacitated many children, it is now easily controlled by antibiotics.

Sea sickness

Travel sickness of all kinds is caused by the motion of the ship, airplane or vehicle affecting the organ of balance in the inner ear. If you are subject to travel sickness it is best to start the journey with a light meal and to keep doing something interesting during the voyage or flight. Concentration lessens travel sickness. There are a number of tablets available which help if taken before the journey, and in very bad cases the doctor will prescribe a more powerful drug. Remember, however, that drugs which lessen motion sickness are liable to make people feel sleepy.

Shingles

See *Herpes*.

Shock

After any severe injury a patient may go into a state of shock which shows itself by a low blood pressure, fast pulse, shallow breathing, and diminished consciousness; the skin feels cold to the touch. It is a dangerous condition, and the most valuable thing one can do after an accident is to treat for shock. Make the patient as comfortable as possible, keep him warm, and keep his spirits up – talking to him will help maintain consciousness. He should lie down and if he is badly shocked the legs should be higher than the head. Unless he has an abdominal wound it is sensible to offer him a warm drink, but do not give alcohol. If there are any bones broken keep the affected limbs still, as follows: the arms: tie to the sides; the legs: strap a broken leg to the sound one.

Sinusitis
The bones of the face contain air spaces above and below the eyes which are called sinuses. They connect with the inside of the nose, so that infections, such as a cold, which involve the nose, can lead to infection of the sinuses.

The symptoms of sinusitis are pain above or below the eyes, headache, a blocked or running nose, and a slight fever. In mild cases rest, inhalations of plain or medicated steam, and the sniffing of a solution of 1 × 5ml spoon salt in 600ml water will resolve the inflammation, but in severe or chronic cases the doctor's advice will be necessary.

Sleep
See *Insomnia*.

Slipped disc
Between the vertebral bones of the spine are flat circular pads of gristle which let the bones move to a certain extent upon each other and act as shock absorbers. Occasionally, part of one of these pads protrudes from its proper place as a result of injury or disease, and presses on a nerve root as it passes outwards from the spinal cord. The protrusion is usually in the lower part of the spine and the 'slipped disc' presses on one of the roots of the sciatic nerve to cause sciatica. Treatment in mild cases is rest on a hard bed; graduated exercises to strengthen the muscles of the spine are useful. In more severe cases treatment may involve surgical operation.

Snake bites
See chapter on Safety in the Home.

Sore throat
See *Tonsillitis*.

Spastic colon
See *Irritable bowel syndrome*.

Sprain
This is an injury to a joint in which the ligaments are damaged. The joint is stiff, swollen, and painful, but will recover with rest, cold compresses, and a supporting bandage. Severe sprains should be seen by the doctor, because damage to the ligaments is sometimes accompanied by damage to the bones of the joint.

Squint
Usually a new-born baby has a squint, but it should have gone by the sixth month. If it persists, expert advice is needed because the earlier treatment starts the more likely it is to be successful.

Stammer
This is a defect of speech in which there is hesitation in the free flow of words, resulting from lack of co-ordination related to control of the muscles of the voice-box. If it is present in early life it is usually due to physical causes, while its development later is likely to be due to psychological reasons. Treatment is by speech therapy and training in breath control, accompanied by a search for complicating psychological factors.

Stings
Insects when they sting usually inject an acid poison, so that the application of an alkali such as sodium bicarbonate is soothing. Some people are sensitive to stings, especially bee stings, and swell up in places far removed from the site of the sting – the tongue and throat may swell, and medical help is urgently needed. If there is any suspicion that a sting has set up a general reaction, the patient must at once be taken to the doctor.

Stroke
If a blood vessel in the brain is blocked by a clot, or bleeds through a part of its wall weakened by disease into the substance of the brain, the patient becomes weak or paralysed in an arm or leg or one side of the face, and in severe cases lapses into unconsciousness. If the damage is to the right side of the brain the left side of the body is affected, and if it is on the left, the right side of the body is weakened, and in right-handed people the power

of speech is upset. The patient may lose vision on one side, and be unable to read because writing has no meaning for him. Similarly, he may be unable to write, or to understand what is said to him. The immediate treatment in a severe case is to make sure that the patient can breathe easily. Pull the tongue forward and turn him half on his front so that he cannot inhale vomit; keep him warm. Call the doctor. In less severe cases, when the patient is conscious or partly conscious, get him into bed; watch his progress carefully until the doctor comes, because he may slowly become unconscious. Home nursing after a stroke is difficult, hard work. Dangers are bedsores and pneumonia; if the limbs are allowed to become stiff, recovery is impossible, and the paralysed parts must be moved through a full range of movement at least four times a day. Both patient and attendants need great courage during convalescence from a stroke, for it is easy to become demoralized and depressed.

Sunburn

If the skin is exposed to strong sunlight it develops a brown pigmentation, but before enough pigment is formed to protect it from the sun, there is a risk of burning from short-wave ultra-violet radiation. The burnt skin becomes red and swollen and on the second day blisters form which are followed by scaling. The patient may feel quite ill, run a temperature, and have a bad headache. Remember that you cannot tell how badly your skin is being burnt – it does not hurt while it is happening. So do not expose your skin to the direct rays of a strong sun for more than 30 minutes on the first day. If there is no reaction, increase the period day by day, but if you get burnt do not, obviously, expose your skin again until the burn is healed.

Teething

Milk teeth, which are later replaced by the permanent teeth, begin to develop in the sixth month and should be completely erupted by the end of the second year. Although 'teething' in babies is commonly held to be responsible for a large number of troubles ranging from diarrhoea to skin rashes, eruption of the teeth rarely causes anything but local irritation of the gums and dribbling.

Tonsillitis

This is an inflammation of the tonsils – two small masses of tissue that lie on each side of the throat. They normally filter off germs which might enter the wind passages and set up infection, so it is not surprising that they themselves are sometimes infected. When this happens they swell up and become painful, the patient has a sore throat, fever, and a headache, and the lymph glands associated with the tonsils (which lie just behind the angle of the jaw) are enlarged.

Treatment should be quick, for scarlet fever or kidney damage may follow infection of the tonsils; a sore throat should never be neglected. Removal of the tonsils is only advised when there have been repeated attacks of tonsillitis, and enlargement has led to complications such as blockage of the tube connecting the inside of the throat with the middle ear.

Travel sickness

See *Sea sickness*.

Ulcerative colitis

This is a serious disease of the large bowel characterized by the passage of mucus, pus, and blood in the motions. The cause is not fully understood; the condition is said to be associated with psychological disturbance, but is sufficiently unpleasant of itself to produce anxiety and emotional instability. Advances in medical and surgical treatment have made the disease less dangerous than once it was, but treatment may be prolonged and may involve admission to hospital and even surgical operation.

Vaccination

See *Immunization*.

Varicose veins

The veins which run superficially in the legs are, in the course of time, liable to become distended and painful, and are then called varicose. The condition is present in one out of two women, and one in four men after the age of forty. In severe cases there is pain and a heavy feeling in the legs, made worse by standing, swelling of the ankles, and skin trouble usually above the ankle. Mild cases are helped a great deal by putting the legs up when possible, but more severe cases may need a surgical operation. Elastic stockings can be worn to give support, but where ulcers form in the lower part of the leg the skilled application of special dressings and bandages may be necessary.

Warts

Otherwise called *Verrucae*. They are very common, small, moderately hard outgrowths on the skin, usually on the hands or the soles of the feet. Warts are thought to be caused by virus infection picked up in schools, swimming-baths, and other public places. They can be treated by the application of carbon dioxide snow (dry ice) or other mild caustics such as glacial acetic acid or silver nitrate; but they often disappear spontaneously.

Whooping cough

This is a disease less important than it used to be, for it has been almost controlled by the immunization of children. It is very infectious, the incubation period being seven to fourteen days. Children cough as if they had an ordinary cold, but the coughing grows more severe and spasmodic until at the end of an attack the child draws breath with the characteristic whoop. This is first heard about ten days after the beginning of the illness. Complications such as bronchitis or pneumonia, or infection of the ear are prevented by antibiotics. Some doctors question the wisdom of immunizing all children against whooping cough, for there have been a few tragic complications of the immunizing process. Nevertheless, it is a difficult matter to judge, and each mother should discuss the matter with her family doctor.

Worms

The most common sorts of worms to inhabit the human body are threadworms and roundworms. Flat worms are also found, eg the tapeworm. If worms are seen in motions, go and see the doctor. Signs of infestation with worms are itching and redness round the anus, loss of general health and colour, anaemia, and loss of weight. Threadworms, which come out to lay eggs at night, may cause bed-wetting.

Wounds

Whether the wound is an abrasion, cut or laceration, make sure that it is cleaned by washing it well, in running water, if possible, and then put a clean dressing on it. If bleeding is troublesome, stop it by direct pressure on the dressing; when it has stopped, change the dressing. If the wound is large or needs stitching, do not put any disinfectant or ointment on it before the doctor sees it. Antiseptics are best avoided even in small wounds if they can be washed clean, and dressings should be light and only just thick enough to exclude dirt. There are a number of good dressings sold in sterile packages; they must not be bound on with heavy bandages, but kept in place with the minimum of sticking plaster. If dressings stick, soak them off in water.

Take any infection seriously, particularly the formation of yellow pus or redness round the wound, and ask for skilled advice; wounds caused by animal bites are particularly liable to infection and should always be shown to the doctor. (See also *Rabies*.) All puncture wounds made with thin knives or instruments in the region of the chest or abdomen must also be shown to the doctor, for it is impossible to tell how far they have gone in by looking at the entry wound.

SOCIAL WELFARE

Great advantages may result from visits paid to the poor; for there being, unfortunately, much ignorance, generally, amongst them with respect to all household knowledge, there will be opportunities for advising and instructing them, in a pleasant and unobtrusive manner, in cleanliness, industry, cookery, and good management.

Social welfare services in the UK change constantly and continuously, month by month. For this reason, no guide can be definitive; this chapter attempts no more than an outline of existing welfare provisions at the time of compilation (1980).

Where leaflet numbers are given for details of statutory benefits, the leaflets can be obtained from the local offices of the Department of Health and Social Security; the numbering remains constant, the leaflets being printed with the date of issue. If in doubt about any point, a Citizens' Advice Bureau will always help; the telephone number and address of your local one can be found in the telephone directory or at any local Post Office.

Main Areas of Responsibility of Local Authorities

Service	Metropolitan area	Non-metropolitan area	Greater London	
			Inner London Borough (LB)	Outer London Borough
Education	District	County	Greater London Council (GLC)	London Borough
Careers service	District	County	Greater London Council (GLC)	London Borough
Social Services	District	County	London Borough	London Borough
Housing	District	District	GLC/LB	GLC/LB
Rent and rate rebate schemes	District	New Town corporation and District	GLC/LB	GLC/LB
Rent allowances	District	New Town corporation and District	LB	LB
Consumer Protection	County	County	LB	LB

Miscellaneous Provisions

Legal aid and advice
Civil cases: Provided by solicitors through Legal Aid and Advice scheme administered by the Law Society

Criminal cases: Provided through the Court concerned on application to the Clerk

Free legal advice may also be available through local Law Centres, voluntary Legal Advice schemes and the Citizens' Advice Bureaux.

Housing aid and advice centres
Local authority and/or voluntary organizations

Consumer advice centres
Local authority and/or voluntary organizations

Main Areas of Responsibility of the Departments of State

Department of Employment
Manpower Services Commission
 Employment Services Agency
 Training Services Agency
 Job Creation Programme
Health and Safety Commission
Advisory, Conciliation, and Arbitration Service (ACAS)
Payment of Unemployment Benefits, Redundancy Payments
Central Administration of Careers Service

Home Office
Police
Prison Service
Probation and After Care Service
Criminal Injuries Compensation
Immigration and Naturalization
Urban Programme
Voluntary Services Unit

Department of Health and Social Security (DHSS)
Central Administration of the National Health Service
Central Administration of the Personal Social Services

Social Security Service & Supplementary Benefits Commission

Department of Education and Science (DES)
Universities and Higher Education
Civil Science

The National Social Security Network

The most important element of nationally provided services is the social security scheme, comprising the two elements of national insurance and supplementary benefits.

The essential distinction between these two elements is that the first is contribution-based and entitlement to benefit is directly related to past contribution records, whereas the second is needs-based and entitlement to benefit is directly related to the provision of the means to maintain a minimum standard of life for an individual or a family.

With certain exceptions, all those over school-leaving age who work either for themselves or for an employer are required to pay contributions to the national insurance scheme according to the scheme currently adopted and at the rates statutorily laid down.

The national insurance scheme
Contributory benefits
Unemployment benefit (NI 12)
 Claimants are required to register for employment.
Sickness benefit, invalidity benefit (NI 16/16a)
 Claimants are required to produce medical certificate within specified time.
Retirement pension (NI 5/15a)
 Claimants are required to have retired from work in order to qualify (aged sixty-five for men, sixty for women) or to be over seventy or sixty-five respectively.
Earnings-related pension (NP 34, NP 31)
 All employees who have paid contributions for one or more years after April 1978 and who retired after 5 April 1979 are eligible for an additional earnings-related pension.

Widow's benefits (NI 13, NP 35, NP 36)
There are three categories of widow's benefit:
1) Widow's allowance (first twenty-six weeks of widowhood)
2) Widowed mother's allowance
3) Widow's pension.
The industrial death benefit (NI 10) also makes provision for widows.
The rates of payment of benefit are dependent upon the contribution record of the former husband, the age of the woman, and the age(s) of her child(ren), if any. Co-habitation with a man as his wife disqualifies a woman from benefit.
Guardian's allowance (NI 14)
Payable to those caring for an orphaned or abandoned child.
Child's special allowance
Payable to a woman whose marriage has been dissolved or annulled, who has not re-married, on the death of her former husband if he was paying towards the support of the child.
Maternity benefit (NI 17A)
1) Maternity grant
Lump sum payment towards the expenses of having a baby. Payable on either the woman's or her husband's contributions.
2) Maternity allowance
Weekly allowance paid for eighteen weeks, beginning eleven weeks before the expected date of confinement. Payable on the woman's contributions.
Both should be claimed on form B4, with the appropriate certificate from the doctor or midwife.
Death grant (NI 38/49)
Payable to executor, administrator or spouse of the deceased, or parent or a child. Claim should be made within six months of the date of death.

In addition to the range of contributory benefits, the national insurance scheme also administers a limited range of non-contributory benefits.

Non-contributory benefits
Attendance allowance for the disabled (NI 205)
Paid at two rates, the higher for those so severely disabled physically or mentally that they have required frequent attention or continual supervision day and night for six months or more, the lower for those needing this either by day or by night. Qualification for either benefit is decided by the Attendance Allowance Board.
Non-contributory invalidity pension (NI 210)
Paid to people of working age who have been unable to work for some time, and who do not qualify for sickness or invalidity benefit because they do not have sufficient contributions.
Child benefit (CH 1, CH 4, CH 7)
Payable for all children in a family, with a preferential rate for the first child of one-parent families. Exempt from income tax and clawback, and not taken into account as income when family income supplement is claimed, but subject to the progressive reduction of income tax allowance.
Child benefit increase (CH 11)
Additional payment for lone parents not in receipt of widow's or certain other benefits.
Old person's pension (NI 184/177A)
A special provision for claimants over eighty either not receiving a national insurance retirement pension or receiving one at a low rate.
Family income supplement (FIS 1)
Payable to those in full-time work, having at least one dependent child, whose normal gross weekly income is below a defined amount. The payment of FIS carries automatic entitlement to a number of other benefits, eg free prescriptions, etc and is not taxable.
Industrial injuries benefit (NI 5/NI 12)
Payable in place of sickness benefit for 156 days (excluding Sundays) when a worker is incapable of working owing to an industrial accident or a prescribed industrial disease.
Industrial disablement benefit (NI 6)
Payable on expiration of 156 days of industrial injury benefit according to the degree of disability. Claims may be made either when the worker returns to work or after 156 days.
Industrial death benefit (NI 10)
Payable to widows and other dependants of an employee who dies as a result of an accident at work or an industrial disease. Claims must be made within three months of the date of death.
Note The application of the Industrial Injuries

scheme is complicated, but independent advice is usually readily available through Trade Union officers or a Citizens' Advice Bureau.

Invalid care allowance (NI 212)

Payable to people unable to work because they have to stay at home to care for a severely disabled relative. Benefit is taxable but not means-tested. Married women do not generally qualify for the allowance.

Mobility allowance (NI 211)

Payable to those between five and sixty (women) or sixty-five (men) who are immobile. The inability to walk must be expected to persist for at least twelve months from the time of application. Cannot be paid in addition to a vehicle or private car allowance provided under the National Health Service or War Pensioners Vehicle Service. Those with such a vehicle can switch to mobility allowance without regard to the age limit.

It is a principle that an individual may not receive payment of more than one category of benefit under the national insurance scheme; eg a worker may not draw both industrial injury and unemployment benefits, but he may draw whichever benefit is the larger of the two.

The supplementary benefits scheme

There are two sections of the supplementary benefits scheme:

1) Supplementary pension (SB 1/SB 8). Payable to those of pensionable age.
2) Supplementary allowance (SB 1/SB 9). Payable to those below pensionable age.

Those who are not in full-time work are entitled to benefit; if they are over school-leaving and under pensionable age, they are required to register for work if they are fit to do so.

Benefit payable is calculated by taking a person's requirements according to the scale rates, plus an addition for rent and any special additions, less any income received, so that scale rate plus rent plus special additions minus income equals rate of benefit. There are two scale rates, ie ordinary and long-term. The long-term scale is subdivided into that payable when the claimant and wife are under eighty and that payable when the claimant or wife is eighty or over. In order to qualify, those under eighty must have been in receipt of supplementary allowance for two years or more without having to register for work.

Those receiving supplementary benefit are automatically entitled to a number of exemptions and other concessions.

Certain limited amounts of income are disregarded in the calculation of benefit, as is the value of an owner-occupied house. Where a house is being bought on mortgage, the interest on the mortgage is payable in lieu of the rent element in the equation above, but not instead of the principal. Capital above a certain limit is taken into account in the final calculation, according to defined rules. Special payments may be made for exceptional needs, eg the purchase of bedding, heating allowances, etc.

Appeals

Where there is a dispute about the payment of benefits under either of the above schemes, appeal in the first instance is to the relevant tribunal. Legal aid is not available for representation at a tribunal.

Benefits available through the National Health Service (NHS) and local authorities

In addition to the main benefits outlined above, there are numerous exemptions from payment which apply to those receiving various categories of benefit, eg free dental treatment for expectant mothers, or those with low incomes. The available benefits include:

drugs and appliances supplied by hospitals
dental treatment
hospital fares/hospital fares for visitors
milk and vitamins
prescription charges
school milk
spectacles

Family planning

Advice and treatment is free from NHS Family Planning Clinics, and contraceptive supplies prescribed under the NHS are free of charge.

Infant welfare

Under the National Health Service any mother can receive advice on the feeding and care of her baby from the staff of the hospital where she was delivered, her own doctor, the domiciliary midwife or the health visitor. Maternal and Child Welfare services are available until the child is five years old; after that its health becomes the concern of the School Medical Services, and the child's own doctor.

Educational maintenance allowances

These may be granted by local education authorities to parents to help them maintain children over school-leaving age who wish to stay on at school.

School meals

Free meals are available to children in families who receive supplementary benefits, a family income supplement or who have a low income.

School uniform or clothing

Local education authorities can help with clothing and footwear, including clothing for sports and physical training, and towards the cost of a school uniform when this is required by the school.

Fares to school

Children under eight who live more than two miles (3.2km), or those over eight who live more than three miles (4.8km) from their school normally get free transport. Those not attending the nearest school may get help with the cost of transport.

Rate rebates

Ratepayers not in receipt of supplementary benefits can claim a rebate on their general rates from their local authority. The granting of rebates is related to income ceiling and family size. Local authorities have the power to grant higher than minimum rebates in their own schemes if they so desire.

Rent rebates and allowances

Tenants not in receipt of supplementary benefits can obtain financial help with their rent in the form of a rebate (in the case of local authority tenants) or a rent allowance (in the case of private tenants). Like rate rebates both benefits are related to income ceiling and family size.

A general guide, *Family Benefits and Pensions (FB1)* is available from the Department of Health and Social Security. Staff from the Social Services Department of the local authority, Age Concern, the Citizens' Advice Bureau or the Child Poverty Action Group can be consulted about the benefits available, the eligibility of individuals, and how to apply for aid. Those on a low income are very often eligible for more than one form of help. Those who are trying to help someone on a low income, or who are themselves in such a position should, therefore, seek help from one of the sources quoted above.

Mortgages

See the chapter on Acquiring a Home.

Structural work

See the chapter on Structural Work and Essential Services.

Improvement grants

These are normally available from local authorities for most schemes which involve basic structural improvements, eg a first time bathroom or damp-proof course. If the improvement is for slightly better than basic structural work, it is then subject to rateable value on the house.

Legal aid and advice

Legal advice and assistance and legal aid for representation is available to those on low incomes in both civil and criminal cases. The provisions vary from time to time, and so do the income limits for those eligible.

The Law Society issues lists of solicitors operating the scheme. These are available in public libraries, Citizens' Advice Bureaux, etc, and many solicitors and other agencies display a 'logo' which indicates that they participate in the scheme.

Civil cases

The administration of the Legal Aid and Advice Scheme is carried out by the Law Society, under the general guidance of the Lord Chancellor, working through the area committees. These appoint local committees to consider applications for legal aid and issue certificates in approved cases. The provision of legal advice and assistance is subject to strictly determined limits of 'disposable capital' and 'disposable income', of which a declaration must be made.

Criminal cases

In criminal cases application for legal aid is made to the court concerned. A court may not make an order for the granting of legal aid to an applicant unless it appears to the court that it is in the interest of justice that this should be done, having regard to the applicant's means. Strict rules apply to the granting of aid in certain categories of cases; eg an order *must* be made when a person is committed for trial on a charge of murder.

Legal advice and assistance scheme

This covers any advice and assistance normally considered to be within the scope of a solicitor's practice, but does not extend to representation. Those eligible are enabled to obtain advice and assistance without the need for reference to the legal aid area committee, providing that the cost is not more than a certain sum which is determined nationally from time to time. Those not receiving supplementary benefit or family income supplement, and whose income exceeds the level set down, will be required to contribute towards costs in accordance with a scale related to their disposable income and capital.

Fixed fee scheme

Many solicitors will give a client an initial consultation of thirty minutes at a fee which is fixed nationally. The Legal Aid Solicitors list, which is issued by the Law Society, names those firms which offer this service and also quotes the current fee.

Free legal advice

A number of law centres give free legal advice, particularly to groups within their area of operation who wish to test the law. Many Citizens' Advice Bureaux and other voluntary advice agencies run free legal advice sessions.

Specialized provisions

There are special provisions designed for the benefit of categories within the general population. These can be listed under the following headings: 1) Children and young people 2) The physically handicapped, deaf and blind 3) The mentally ill and mentally handicapped 4) The elderly.

Whereas the welfare benefits listed above are in the form of monetary support of one kind or another, these benefits are mainly in the form of service provision and are, usually, the direct responsibility of the local authority Social Services Department, or the Education Department. These departments have certain statutory duties, and also some permissive powers.

1) Children and young people

Education: Local education authorities are required to provide full-time primary and secondary education for all children up to the legal school-leaving age of sixteen, and also to make special educational arrangements for children with particular needs, eg blind and partially sighted children. It is the duty of the local education authority to provide facilities for further education beyond the school-leaving age other than in schools, universities, and colleges.

Additional responsibilities of local education authorities

Recreation: the provision of facilities for recreation, social, and physical training

School health service: the medical and dental inspection and treatment of pupils in local education authority schools. This is provided by the Department of Health and Social Security Area Health Authorities

School meals and milk: the provision of midday meals for day pupils in schools maintained by local education authorities and free milk for all day pupils up to the age of seven, or up to school-leaving age in special schools

Education and welfare service: the responsibility of education welfare officers for working with children and their families, as well as for monitoring attendance

Child guidance clinics: administered usually by the local education authorities and the

Department of Health and Social Security. Children are sent to these on referral by GPs, school medical officers, head teachers, social workers, etc

Careers service: the provision by the local education authority of vocational guidance for people attending educational institutions (other than universities) and an employment service for those leaving them

Grants and awards: the statutory duty of the local education authority to make awards to first-time students attending degree courses, initial teacher training, courses leading to Dip. HE and HND, or courses comparable with first degree courses at universities and institutions for higher education. They also have discretionary powers to make awards to students attending other courses. Each award comprises the compulsory tuition fees plus a standard maintenance allowance (subject to a parental means test).

Welfare: the statutory duty of the Social Services Department of the local authority for the care of:

1) Children received into the care of the local authority because they have no parents or guardians, or because their parents or guardians are unable to look after them properly or have abandoned them
2) Children and young persons who appear before a court in either care or criminal proceedings
3) Children placed by a court in the care of a local authority in connection with matrimonial proceedings or as wards of court
4) Children who have been placed in foster homes or who have been placed privately for adoption.

Provision is made for children in residential homes, with foster parents or by arrangement with a parent, guardian, relative or friend.

Day nurseries: the provision for some children (usually those with special needs, eg those from one-parent families) under the age of five.

Childminders: the requirement is that childminders register with the Social Services Department. They are subject to inspection.

Play-groups: it is the responsibility of local authorities to oversee the work of play-groups. Most of these are members of the Pre-School Play-groups Association, and many are run by independent groups or by voluntary organizations, such as the Save the Children Fund.

Adoption: Many local authorities are registered as adoption agencies and there are also a number of independent agencies in existence. The representative body is the Association of British Adoption Agencies.

Illegitimate children: The local authority Social Services Department has responsibility for the care of the single mother and her child, but may delegate particular aspects of care to a number of voluntary agencies.

The principal bodies working in this field are the National Council for One-Parent Families, the Scottish Council for Single Parents, Committee for Social Work and Social Services of the Board for Social Responsibility of the Church of England, and the Social Welfare Commission of the Catholic Bishops' Conference (England and Wales). These provide specialized help and access to sources of help from voluntary sources.

Severely handicapped children: The Family Fund is administered by the Joseph Rowntree Memorial Trust. It is a fund set up by the government for the benefit of families who are caring for a very severely disabled child. The fund has considerable freedom of action and may give help in the form of goods, services or money grants. It exists to fill the gaps in existing provisions. Except in exceptional circumstances, children must be under sixteen to be eligible. There is no means test as such, but the general family circumstances are taken into account in considering applications.

The National Society for the Prevention of Cruelty to Children (NSPCC): The NSPCC has a special responsibility in that it is the only independent body which has the power to institute care proceedings when it believes that it will be in the interest of the child to do this. It has a nationally maintained inspectorate which works in close co-operation with local authority Social Services Departments and the police.

Other bodies working with children: There are a

number of voluntary bodies working in the field of child care. The major ones include: The Catholic Child Welfare Council, the Church of England Children's Society, The National Children's Home, Dr. Barnado's Homes, The Norwood Homes for Jewish Children, The Salvation Army, The Shaftesbury Homes, and the Thomas Coram Foundation.

2) The physically handicapped, deaf, and blind

Education: Local education authorities have a duty to provide special education for handicapped children, defined as blind, partially sighted, deaf, partially hearing, delicate, educationally subnormal, epileptic, maladjusted, physically handicapped or suffering from speech defect. This may be provided in special schools, special classes in ordinary schools, in hospitals, day centres, or elsewhere.

Welfare: The local authority Social Services Department has a duty to provide a social work service to meet the needs of the handicapped. This includes the provision of residential accommodation, day centres, home helps, free or subsidized travel, holidays, sheltered housing, and the keeping of a register of handicapped people.

Under the provisions of the Chronically Sick and Disabled Persons Act 1970, the local authority has a wide range of duties towards the handicapped, including the adaptation of the home of the handicapped person, in order to enable him to continue to live there. Special arrangements made for the disabled include the provision of either a Mobility Allowance (NI 211), see p159, or special transport, which has most usually taken the form of a three-wheeled vehicle capable of carrying only the disabled person.

There is also a voluntary organization, established by government initiative, called 'Motability', which aims to help those disabled people whose mobility needs are best met by the provision of a private motor car. It enables a disabled person to use their mobility allowance to lease a new car for a period of years. Priority was given in the first phase of the scheme for those between sixteen and nineteen and those who need a car to get to work or to an approved training course. All recipients of mobility allowance receive a leaflet from the Department of Health and Social Security explaining the scheme and how to apply to join it. Further information may be obtained from the local Disablement Resettlement Officer.

Specialized services and consultancies are provided for the benefit of the deaf and blind within the terms of reference of legislation relating to all forms of welfare provision.

Employment: Disabled persons of school-leaving age or over may apply for inclusion in the Register of Disabled Persons and, providing the Disablement Officer is satisfied that the applicant is eligible, he will register the person for from one to ten years, according to the degree of disability. The responsibility for this and other employment services for the disabled lies with the Manpower Services Commission. Provisions include employment rehabilitation, vocational training, the professional training scheme, special resettlement service, and sheltered employment. In addition, all employers of twenty or more persons have an obligation to employ a quota of disabled persons of not less than 3% of the total staff.

Voluntary agencies: Certain voluntary agencies provide additional support and assistance for the physically handicapped. In 1980 these included:

The Royal Association for Disability and Rehabilitation which provides an information service, promotes study courses, and undertakes research. The council operates an advisory mobility engineering department called Rehabilitation Engineering Movement Advisory Panels (REMAP).

Central Council for the Disabled which acts as a central co-ordinating body and information source, is concerned with the international exchange of information and is particularly active in matters concerned with access, housing problems, and leisure activities.

National Fund for Research into Crippling Diseases which promotes research into the causes, prevention, cure, and treatment of crippling conditions.

Hand Craft and Advisory Association for the Disabled which runs courses for craft teachers.

Disabled Living Foundation which maintains an exhibition of aids for disabled people and provides an information service for the disabled.

The Spastics Society which provides care, treatment, education, and employment training for spastics, and support for their parents. Sponsors research into the cause of cerebral palsy.

The British Epilepsy Association which provides an advisory service and a holiday service. Publicizes information about epilepsy.

The British Polio Fellowship which provides holiday homes, caravans, etc, residential centres, an employment scheme, and personal welfare services. Gives advice and financial help.

The Invalid Children's Aid Association which provides personal service for children in London and surrounding areas. Administers five special schools and provides an advisory information service to all those dealing with invalid, delicate or handicapped children.

Malcolm Sargent Trust which administers a fund established to alleviate the circumstances of children suffering from cancer, and their families.

3) The mentally ill and mentally handicapped

Statutory provision: General provision for psychiatric treatment and care is the responsibility of the National Health Service. This may be provided through and by GPs and general hospitals, but the greatest number of patients are referred to psychiatric hospitals. Patients may be admitted to hospital on a voluntary basis, but where the patient is judged to be a danger to himself or to others, admission may be compulsory under the terms of the National Health Act 1959. This requires an application signed by the nearest relative of the patient, or by a social worker designated by a local authority as a mental welfare officer, supported by two doctors. The local authority maintains a twenty-four hour service for this purpose.

While many hospitals for the mentally disordered also accommodate the mentally handicapped, there are some hospitals caring solely for mentally handicapped and geriatric patients.

Increasing emphasis has been given to outpatient, day hospital, and day centre care of the mentally ill and mentally handicapped, and there is a certain commitment to the principle of community care, though resources are still limited in this field. For the mentally handicapped, adult training centres provide day training and sheltered employment for those unable to comply with the normal requirements of an employer. Local authorities have a duty to provide residential accommodation for those mentally handicapped people who do not need hospital care but are unable to live at home. Provision of accommodation may be undertaken by voluntary bodies, who also run social clubs and provide recreational facilities.

Where a person is mentally incapable of managing his own affairs he cannot authorize anyone to do so on his behalf, and any authorization previously given may become legally inoperative owing to his illness. In this situation, application should be made to the Court of Protection, which exists to protect and manage the affairs of such people, and which will supply full information about the procedure to be followed.

Voluntary provision: In 1980 there were two principal bodies working in this field:

MIND (The National Association for Mental Health) which arranges training courses and conferences, and offers an advisory service to anyone with a problem related to mental illness.

The National Society for Mentally Handicapped Children which is concerned with mentally handicapped people of any age and their families. It has a large number of local groups for families with mentally handicapped members. The fields of activity include counselling, education and training, residential care and holiday facilities, hospital visiting, and recreational facilities.

4) The elderly

Statutory provision: Local authorities have the duty under Section 21 of the National Assistance Act 1948, as amended by Section 195 and Schedule 23 of the Local Government Act 1972, to provide accommodation for all who need care and attention regardless of their financial circumstances.

While a local authority is under no obligation to provide accommodation in premises other than its own, it may make use of accommodation provided by a voluntary organization or by a private person, registered under Section 37 of the National Assistance Act. Accommodation may be provided in an old person's home or in sheltered housing.

Other services provided include those which enable old people to remain in their own homes, such as home help services, home nursing, chiropody, and meals-on-wheels. In many areas the meals-on-wheels service is provided by the local authority; in others, by the Women's Royal Voluntary Service. Luncheon clubs and day centres are also provided, both by the local authority and by many different voluntary agencies. Special laundry services are widely operated for the benefit of families caring for incontinent old people.

Voluntary provision: There are a large number of voluntary agencies concerned with the welfare of old people. Of these, the most important in 1980 were:

Age Concern which relates to a network of local groups throughout the country, and acts as a forum in all matters connected with the welfare of the elderly. It collects evidence and makes representation to government on matters of concern, and acts as an information and casework service on a local basis, promoting and running old people's clubs, and selling welfare foods.

The Pre-Retirement Association which is primarily concerned with those approaching retirement; it promotes and advises on pre-retirement courses, and trains tutors for such courses.

National Corporation for the Care of Old People, an offshoot of the Nuffield Foundation, which has two main functions: grant-aid to voluntary bodies and research. It publishes discussion documents and other reports, including an annual compilation of research in progress in the UK.

The Elderly Invalids Fund which provides an information and advisory service on accommodation and services for elderly people. It makes grants towards the cost of the care of elderly people who cannot be cared for at home or in a welfare home, but who do not need hospital treatment.

National Federation of Old Age Pensions Associations which is primarily a pressure group for the improvement of pensions.

Help the Aged which is mainly devoted to fund raising and the provision of housing.

Charities, Trusts, and Associations

Many agencies, trusts, etc cater for special needs within closely defined terms of reference. Every local authority is required to keep a list of local charities, but this is often incomplete. A local Council of Social Service/Council for Voluntary Service may have better information about local trusts.

Support groups and specialist associations

For specialist needs, reference to a Citizens' Advice Bureau will reveal whether or not there is an association which can help. Many medical conditions have societies or associations of people who concern themselves with research into causes, act as pressure groups, and/or undertake casework support and services for sufferers, eg the Ileostomy Society.

There are also a number of mutual support groups ranging from the well-known ones such as Alcoholics Anonymous and Gamblers Anonymous, to small, specialized ones concerned with specific phobias, etc.

Counselling services

A wide variety of counselling services exist, some of which, such as the Marriage Guidance Council and The Samaritans, are nationally available, though organized through local groups or branches, while others are purely local. Many of these small groups are linked with churches, eg the Westminster Pastoral Foundation.

THE LAW AND YOU

Humorists tells us there is no act of our lives which can be performed without breaking through some one of the many meshes of the law by which our rights are so carefully guarded; and those learned in the law, when they do give advice without the usual fee, and in the confidence of friendship, generally say, " Pay, pay anything rather than go to law."

This chapter describes, as comprehensively as possible in a book of this kind, some ways in which the law affects the life of the ordinary citizen. Where it provides an answer to some particular question, check this with a qualified adviser as there may be some details of your situation which alter its legal consequences and the law may have changed since this book was published. For information on consumer law, see the chapters on Care and Maintenance of the Home, Raising and Spending Money, and Food Shopping Today.

Lawyers and Legal Proceedings

There are two kinds of lawyers in the UK – barristers and solicitors – but most lawyers are solicitors. If a member of the public needs any kind of legal help, a solicitor will give advice on any matter that has a legal aspect, draw up legal documents such as wills, contracts, and house conveyances (see p17). He will also prepare and, in the lower courts, conduct court proceedings. But a solicitor cannot represent his client in the High Court.

Barristers have two main functions. If the problem which the client brings to his solicitor is particularly difficult or unusual, the solicitor may ask the advice of a barrister who is a specialist in the subject. Barristers are also the only people who have the right to represent people in the High Court. They specialize in advocacy (putting forward a case in court) and in the procedure of the courts. Because of this, they often represent people in county courts, magistrates' courts, and tribunals, but solicitors can also do this.

A non-lawyer cannot consult a barrister directly; he must first consult a solicitor, who will bring the barrister into the case, if necessary. Of course, anyone may conduct his own case in any court in the land; but barristers (in all courts) and solicitors (in all except the superior courts) are the only people allowed to conduct someone else's case for a fee.

Legal aid
Those who cannot afford lawyers' fees may still be able to obtain their services by getting legal aid. There are two kinds of legal aid: (a) for legal advice and assistance, and (b) for court proceedings. For more information, see the chapter on Social Welfare.

How the courts work
Civil proceedings can be brought in the High Court, in a county court, or, in the kinds of cases which Parliament has specifically assigned to it, in a tribunal. Any claim, except one which Parliament has said must be brought in some other way (such as claims for unfair dismissal, which must be in an industrial tribunal) can be started in the High Court. But if it is the kind of case which can be brought in a county court, this is usually better; the county court is a local court and is less expensive. Also, if you bring a case in the High Court which should have been in the county court, you may not get your costs paid even if you win. Any claim for a sum of money or damages of less than £2000 (1980) can be brought in the county court and one for a small claim will probably be heard by a county

court Registrar. In addition, a county court Registrar can act as an arbitrator in small claims; when he does this he is really acting as an umpire whose decision both parties have agreed to accept, and it will be more difficult to appeal if you do not like his decision. But the advantage is that the matter is dealt with informally, not in open court, and the rules of evidence and procedure are relaxed.

Claims arising from legislation dealing with employment, equal pay, race and sex discrimination, rent assessment, national insurance, and supplementary benefits are dealt with by tribunals, where procedure is simple and which are designed to be used by people conducting their own case. If you are in one of these, the court officials will tell you what official documents are needed and will help you with procedure, but they cannot give you legal advice or tell you the best way to put your case. The judge or members of the tribunal will help you with the procedure in the court itself.

In the High Court, court proceedings are normally started by a writ in a county court, by summons in an industrial tribunal, and by originating application. The Plaintiff then sends to the Defendant a written statement of what he is complainant about, and the Defendant replies in writing saying how he disagrees. These documents are called 'pleadings'; their purpose is to tell the other party exactly what he will have to prove at the trial in order to win. Before the trial, each party has the right to see any documents the other party has which are relevant to the case (except privileged ones, such as letters between solicitor and client). The following are the main kinds of remedies for which a court can be asked:

1) *Payment of a fixed sum of money:* If a person has failed to pay the price he agreed to pay for goods or services, the court may demand payment.

2) *Damage:* When one person's unlawful action has caused another person's injury or loss, the wrongdoer must pay the injured party the amount that he has lost, or (if he has suffered otherwise than financially) a sum of money to make up for what he has lost. For example, if your new car is delivered six weeks later than it was promised, or if someone crashes into it and it takes six weeks to repair, you may have to hire a car while you are waiting. You can claim the cost of that as damages. Sometimes a person may be able to say exactly how much he has lost; at other times the court will have to work out how much it thinks he should be compensated, for example, where someone is hurt in a car accident.

3) An *injunction:* This is a court order telling someone to stop doing something he has no right to do, or (less usually) to do something he is obliged to do.

4) *Specific performance:* This is an order that a person is to perform his obligations under a contract. If someone promises to sell you a house, for example, you may want to make him sell you that very house rather than pay you damages for breaking his promise.

5) *Possession:* The court orders someone to leave land (including a building) which he has no right to occupy. If someone is in your house who never had the right to be there (eg a squatter, but *not* an ex-tenant who refuses to leave), there is a special quick procedure for getting such an order.

6) *Restitution of property:* The court can order a person to give property which does not belong to him back to its true owner.

The Family

Getting married

Marriage, according to English law, is a voluntary union for life of one man and one woman to the exclusion of all others. Although such a union can now be dissolved, its nature has not changed; an agreement to live together which was non-exclusive or limited as to time would not be a marriage, and would probably be void as being contrary to public policy. This does not mean, of course, that unmarried people cannot live together, merely that such an agreement would not be enforced by the courts.

A person domiciled in England has no capacity to contract a polygamous marriage even outside England.

Any two persons may marry provided they are sixteen or over and not too closely related. The prohibited degrees of relationship include half-blood and illegitimate relationships. A man may not marry his mother, daughter, grandmother, granddaughter, sister, aunt, niece, the wife of his father, son, grandfather or grandson, or his wife's mother, daughter, grandmother or granddaughter. A woman may not marry her corresponding male relations. An adopted child remains within the prohibited degrees in relation to his natural relatives; and in addition, he (or she) and the person or persons who have adopted him are deemed to be within the prohibited degrees. But the prohibition does not extend to the rest of his adopted family; so an adopted boy could, for instance, marry the natural daughter of his adopted parents. Any marriage within the prohibited degrees is void.

Consent

Those between sixteen and eighteen require the consent of their parents or guardian to marry. Where the parents are divorced, only the consent of the one having custody is required, though that is not always the one with whom the child lives; normally divorced parents have joint custody. However, the marriage will not be invalid in the absence of consent, unless the person whose consent is required has formally objected (either at the reading of the banns or by lodging a caveat against the grant of a licence), and the parties have proceeded in knowing and wilful disregard of the objection. If a necessary consent is refused, application may be made to the court to authorize the marriage without it. Most such applications are dealt with by the magistrates in private, though the High Court and county court also have jurisdiction.

Formalities of marriage

These are complicated. The following are the available preliminaries:

1) *Superintendent Registrar's certificate:* Each party must give notice to the Superintendent Registrar of the district where he or she has lived for seven days beforehand and must make a solemn declaration that there are believed to be no lawful impediments to the marriage, that the residential requirements have been satisfied, and that any consent needed has been given or dispensed with. It is a criminal offence to make a wilfully false declaration. Notice is entered in a book which is available for public inspection for twenty-one days, during which time objections may be lodged. After twenty-one days the Registrar must (in the absence of objection) issue a certificate authorizing the marriage; the certificate lasts three months from entry of the notices in the book. This certificate may be used for both Anglican (Church of England) and other marriages.

2) *Superintendent Registrar's certificate and licence* (known unofficially as a *special licence*): Notice, together with a declaration as above, must be given to the Superintendent Registrar of the district in which *one* of the parties has lived for the previous fifteen days. It is entered in the book. The marriage may take place after the expiry of one whole day (ie two days after notice was given). The certificate and licence costs more than 1). It is not available for Anglican weddings.

3) *Registrar General's licence:* This permits a 'death-bed' marriage to take place at any hour at a place not normally authorized for marriages. It requires evidence that one of the parties is too ill to be moved and is not expected to recover, also that there is no impediment, that any requisite consents have been given, and that there is sufficient reason for the licence to be granted. No waiting period is prescribed. It is not available for Anglican weddings (which, in similar circumstances, would require a special licence from the Archbishop of Canterbury).

4) *Banns* (Anglican weddings only): These must be published on three Sundays in the churches of the parishes where each party resides and in the church where they intend to be married (if different). If a person whose consent is required publicly objects in the church, the publication of the banns is void. Otherwise the parties may marry immediately after the third publication. A clergyman may (but need not) insist on seven days' notice in writing before calling the banns. No declaration is required. The parties must marry in one of the churches where the banns have been called.

5) *Common licence* (Anglican weddings only): This permits a marriage to take place either in the church of the parish where one of the parties has lived for the preceding fifteen days, or in the church which is the usual place of worship of either or both parties. The marriage may take place immediately (but it may take a little time to obtain the licence). A declaration is required (see **1)** above). This costs more than banns.

6) *Special licence* (Anglican weddings only): The Archbishop of Canterbury may licence marriages at any hour of the day or night in any church or chapel or other meet and convenient place, whether consecrated or not. This is the most expensive; such licences are mainly granted to allow marriages to take place in chapels not normally authorized for marriages, eg college chapels.

Ceremony

The marriage ceremony must normally take place between the hours of 8am and 6pm with open doors. The rules governing the ceremony fall into four categories.

i) *Anglican religious ceremony* (preliminaries **1)**, **4)**, **5)** or **6)**): This must be according to the rite currently authorized by the Church of England celebrated in the presence of two witnesses. A clergyman may refuse to marry anyone whose former spouse is still living, but may not refuse on the ground of the parties' religion (or lack of it).

ii) *Jewish and Quaker marriages* (preliminaries **1)**, **2)** or **3)**): The place, celebrant, and form of the ceremony are entirely a matter for the rules of the respective religions. It need not take place within the normal hours, or in public.

iii) *Other non-Anglican religious ceremonies* (preliminaries **1)**, **2)** or **3)**): These must take place in a registered building (except where a Registrar General's licence has been obtained) and be attended by a Registrar or authorized person (usually a minister of the religion concerned). The doors must be open, two witnesses must be present, and the parties must at some stage declare (in the prescribed form) that they know of no impediment to the marriage, and call upon those present to witness that they take each other as lawful wedded

spouse. Otherwise, the ceremony may be in any form the parties (with the consent of the religious authorities who own the building) see fit to adopt. (This applies to non-Christian as well as Christian ceremonies.)

iv) *Civil ceremony* (preliminaries **1)**, **2)** or **3)**): The ceremony takes place (except where there is a Registrar General's licence) in a register office with the doors open, in the presence of the Superintendent Registrar and a Registrar. It must be entirely secular; the parties must declare that they know of no impediment to the marriage and call upon those present to witness that they take each other as lawful wedded wife or husband.

Rights and obligations of married people

Spouses are under a duty to cohabit. This duty will not be enforced directly by the courts, nor will they permit it to be enforced by violence. But it may have indirect consequences: a spouse who refuses to cohabit without proper excuse will be in desertion, will not be entitled to be maintained, and after two years will have provided grounds for divorce. While the duty to cohabit exists, the wife is assumed to consent to sexual intercourse with her husband (even if she in fact does not), so the husband cannot be guilty of rape. He may, however, be guilty of assault.

Spouses have a duty to keep each other's secrets; they can be prevented from disclosing marital confidences. One spouse cannot be compelled to give evidence against the other except in criminal proceedings where the offence has been committed by one spouse against the other. But they may give evidence against each other if they want to do so.

Maintenance

A wife is normally entitled to be maintained by her husband, but this right also cannot be enforced while the parties are living together. The High Court, county court, and the magistrates' court all have jurisdiction to order maintenance payments, but the normal procedure is a complaint to the magistrates on one of a number of grounds, among which are wilful neglect to maintain, desertion, adultery, and persistent cruelty. As well as ordering maintenance, the magistrates may relieve the parties of the duty to cohabit and make an order for custody of any children. It is exceptional for a husband to be able to claim maintenance from his wife; he must show that his earning capacity is impaired *and* that it is reasonable for her to maintain him.

If the parties make a formal separation agreement without mentioning maintenance, it will normally not be payable; the law assumes that the obligation to cohabit and the obligation to maintain go together.

Anyone considering making a separation agreement should obtain legal advice.

Property rights

English law has no concept of community property; the property rights of married people (except where they are rearranged on divorce) are decided in the same way as anybody else's.

Wedding presents are not assumed to belong to both spouses jointly. Who owns them depends on the intention of the giver, as inferred if not explicit. Anything bought out of the housekeeping money will belong to both parties unless they agree otherwise. The money in a joint account will be presumed to be jointly owned if the parties pool their incomes in it, but property bought with money from the account will belong to the person in whose name it was bought.

All these presumptions are only used to decide ownership when there is no indication of what the spouse actually intended.

The matrimonial home

During the marriage, both spouses are entitled to occupy the matrimonial home, even if it belongs to only one of them. Either may have this right enforced against the other by a court order. A spouse may register the right at any time when the other spouse still owns the property, whether or not he or she is in occupation; but once the house is sold it is too late to register and the right will be lost. If the right is registered as a charge on the property, it is binding on third parties; so that if one spouse sells the house, the other still has the fair claim to live there. The right cannot be exercised against the owner-spouse's creditors if he or she goes bankrupt or dies insolvent. If the owner-spouse defaults in the mortgage payments, the non-owner spouse is entitled to require the mortgage company to accept payments from him or her rather than sell the house.

Finally, if it is necessary for the protection of one spouse or the children, the court can exclude the other from the home. If there is a real danger of violence, the court can attach to the order a power of arrest which enables a policeman to arrest the excluded spouse if he disobeys the order. This power of exclusion is also available to unmarried people living together as husband and wife.

Parents and children

The mother and father of a legitimate child have equal rights and authority, and either parent may exercise them without the other. Parents may restrict the liberty of their children in a reasonable way and may inflict reasonable corporal punishment on them. They are responsible for maintaining and looking after their children; neglect and ill-treatment are criminal offences and may result in the child being removed from his parents' custody. In addition, each parent has an obligation to ensure that each of his children of school age (five to sixteen) receives suitable full-time education. This does not have to be at a school, but if the parents fail in the duty, the local authority can serve a school attendance order requiring the parents to send the child to a specified school; failure to comply is a criminal offence. When they send their child to school, parents are taken to delegate their rights to the teacher, including that of reasonable corporal punishment. But this assumed permission can be withdrawn.

Local authorities have wide powers to take into care children who are neglected, abandoned, ill-treated, out of control, delinquent or not receiving suitable education. In some cases they have the power to extinguish the parents' rights altogether. For more information, see the chapter on Social Welfare.

The mother of an illegitimate child has full parental rights unless a court or local authority has ruled otherwise. She may apply to the magistrates for an order that the father maintain her and the child, provided she does so within three years of the birth (unless he has been making payments and then ceases, in which case the period is not so restricted). A married woman may not apply for such an order unless she is no longer living with her husband and has lost the right to be maintained by him (which she would probably have done as a result of the adultery resulting in the illegitimate birth). The father of an illegitimate child has the right to apply to the court for custody.

Adoption

This is only possible by court order (High Court, county court or juvenile court); all proceedings are in private. The effect of an adoption order is that the child ceases for all legal purposes to be the child of his natural parents and becomes the child of his adoptive parents. Normally the consent of the natural parents is required; but in some circumstances it may be dispensed with (eg if it cannot be obtained or is unreasonably withheld, or if the parent has very badly failed in his duties to the child). The first (but not the only) consideration the court must take into account is the welfare of the child; his wishes and feelings must be considered (in so far as is possible and appropriate). Normally the child must have lived with the prospective adopters for a year before the order, but in some circumstances the period may be reduced to thirteen weeks. Only those under eighteen may be adopted. Once an adopted child reaches the age of eighteen, he has the right to a copy of his original birth certificate; but counselling must be made available to any adopted child who seeks information from the registrar about his natural parentage.

Disputes about children

Divorce proceedings are dealt on pp172–173. But disputes about children may arise and be dealt with in other ways.

1) If a matrimonial complaint (eg of adultery, persistent cruelty to spouse or children, wilful neglect to maintain spouse or children) is made in a magistrates' court, the magistrates must consider whether any order should be made concerning the children. Amongst other things, the order may provide for legal custody of a child under sixteen, grant access to the father or mother, order either or both to maintain the child, or commit the child to the care of the local authority (see p162). The exercise of these powers does not depend on whether the complaint is successful.

2) A parent or guardian of a child may apply under the Guardianship of Minors Acts to the High Court, county court or magistrates' court either for a decision on a particular matter in dispute or for custody of, or access to, the child in general. The father of an illegitimate child may apply for custody of, or access to, the child under these provisions.

3) Anyone interested in the welfare of a child under eighteen may apply to the High Court to have the child made a ward of court. If the application is granted, the court will exercise a wide and, if necessary, detailed control over the ward's upbringing; all important matters affecting the ward must be brought before the court. If the court feels the ward should be separately represented it will appoint the Official Solicitor to do this; he will make a thorough investigation but is not bound to accept the ward's views.

4) Under the Children Act 1975, a person with whom a child has been living for a specified period (three years unless the person with legal custody consents) may apply to the High Court, county court or magistrates' court to be made the custodian of the child. This provides a simpler procedure for foster parents and relations who have been caring for a child and who do not want it taken away from them. Notice of the application must be given to the local authority, who will report to the court. As long as it is in force, a custodianship order gives the custodian legal custody of the child; this is defined as 'so much of the parental rights and duties as relate to the person of the child (including the place and manner in which his time is spent)'. But the order can be revoked; the parental rights are merely suspended during its existence.

Note At the time of writing (1980) this provision has not been brought into force.

Ending the marriage

A marriage will be void in the following circumstances: the parties are within the prohibited degrees of relationship (see p168); one or both was under sixteen; they have disregarded certain of the formalities; one or both were already lawfully married; they are not male and female respectively.

A void marriage is not a marriage at all; it is not necessary for the parties to obtain a decree of annulment before marrying again. However they are entitled to such a decree if they wish; and if they obtain one, they are entitled to financial provision orders in the same way as divorced people. Children of a void marriage are to be treated as legitimate if at the time of the intercourse resulting in their conception (or the marriage ceremony, if later) both or either of the parties reasonably believed the marriage to be valid.

Certain marriages are voidable; they are valid until annulled. A decree of nullity has no retrospective effect but only ends the marriage from that day forward. As a consequence, the children of such a marriage are legitimate and do not become illegitimate when the decree is granted.

A marriage may be annulled on the following grounds: incapacity or wilful refusal of either party to consummate it; lack of valid consent to the marriage by either party (eg because of duress, mistake as to the identity of the other party or the nature of the ceremony, or insanity); mental disorder of one party which unfits him or her for marriage; communicable venereal disease of either party, or pregnancy of the wife by another man at the time of the marriage (provided, in both cases, that the other party was in ignorance).

Except in the case of non-consummation, a party wanting the marriage annulled must apply to the court within three years of the marriage ceremony. And if one spouse, knowing that he could have the marriage annulled, leads the other spouse to think he would not do so and the court feels it would be unjust to grant a decree, it will not do so. If a decree is granted, the parties may seek financial provision in the same way as after divorce.

A decree of divorce dissolves a marriage rather than declaring it not to exist; but because a voidable marriage is, both before and after the decree of annulment, treated as a valid marriage up to the time the decree is granted, there is little practical difference between annulment of such a marriage and divorce. The main practical difference is in the time limits for applying to the court; in the case of most voidable marriages, application must be made *within* three years of marriage, whereas there can be no divorce until *after* three years from the marriage except in cases of exceptional hardship or depravity.

Divorce

A person who wants a divorce must present a petition to the county court. There is now only one ground for divorce: that the marriage has broken down irretrievably. But in order to satisfy a court that this is so, the petitioner must prove one (or more) of five things:

1) That the other party (called 'the respondent') has committed adultery and the petitioner finds it intolerable to live with him (or her).
2) That the respondent has behaved in such a way that the petitioner cannot reasonably be expected to live with him.
3) That the respondent has deserted the petitioner for the previous two years.
4) That the two have lived apart for the previous two years and the respondent consents to a divorce.
5) That the two have lived apart for the previous five years.

If the respondent wants to contest the case it will be heard in the High Court.

The court has very wide powers to rearrange the spouses' financial affairs by ordering periodical payments or a lump sum payment to be made by one to the other, transferring the ownership of property from one to the other, or ordering one to settle property on the other. The court must aim to place the parties, so far as it is practicable and just to do so, in the same financial position they would have been in if the marriage had not broken down, and if each had properly discharged his or her financial obligations towards the other. But it will not normally penalize one party financially for misconduct, unless it has been particularly gross.

The court also has a duty to make sure that the

best possible arrangements are made for any children. It has very wide powers and will do what it thinks is in the child's best interests. It will direct with whom the child is to live (care and control), and who is to have the right to make decisions about its upbringing (custody). Custody or care and control may be given to someone other than the parents if the court considers this would be in the best interests of the child; but parents are normally given access. The court also has power to commit a child to the care of a local authority, and wide powers to vary or discharge previous orders and make fresh ones while the child is under eighteen.

Divorce is granted in two stages, a *decree nisi* and a *decree absolute*; the decree absolute is usually granted six weeks after the decree nisi. Only after the decree absolute can the parties marry again.

Separation

A decree of judicial separation may be obtained if any of the five states of affairs listed above is established; it is not necessary to show that the marriage has broken down irretrievably. The effect of this decree is to relieve the spouses of the obligation to cohabit, and to prevent one from succeeding to the other's property if he dies intestate. But they are not free to marry again.

Formalities of Death

A death should be registered with the local registrar within five days by a relative who was present or who is in the district where the death took place. If there is no such relative, it should be done by someone present at the death, or the head of the household, or anyone living in the house who knew of the death, or the person who is making the funeral arrangements. Before a death can be registered, medical evidence of the cause of death must be provided to the registrar in one of three forms:

1) *Doctor's certificate:* This is the normal method. The doctor who attended the dead person will either give the certificate to the person who is to register the death or send it direct to the registrar.

2) *Coroner's notification:* Some deaths have to be reported to the coroner; for example, the death of someone who has not been attended by a doctor in his last illness, a sudden or accidental or suspicious death, one where the cause is unknown, death during an operation, suicide, death from abortion, drugs or poisoning. The coroner may (but need not) order a post mortem; if he does, the relatives cannot prevent it. If the coroner is satisfied, he notifies the registrar and the death can be registered.

3) *Coroner's certificate after inquest:* The coroner may hold an inquest on any death reported to him, and must do so if he has reason to suspect that the death was violent or unnatural. An inquest is a formal investigation to establish the facts necessary for registration of the death, ie who the dead person is and how he died. Evidence is taken on oath; sometimes there is a jury. The coroner's certificate is sent direct to the registrar, and in this case it is not necessary for anyone else to register the death.

When the death has been registered, the registrar can issue certified copies of the entry in the register (ie death certificates) and a certificate authorizing burial (ie the disposal certificate). If there has been an inquest, it is for the coroner to authorize burial (and if the inquest is adjourned, he may do so before it is completed). Nobody can lawfully be buried without a disposal certificate.

Because cremation destroys evidence of the cause of death, more evidence is required before it can take place. Two doctors must certify the cause of death; if the death has been reported to the coroner, his authority is required for cremation. If not, the registrar authorizes cremation in the disposal certificate (so he must be told if cremation is intended).

Wills

To be valid, a will must be in writing, signed by the testator, and witnessed by two witnesses. No witness may receive any gift or benefit from a will, nor may anyone married to the witness at the date of the will. If a will does make a gift to one of its witnesses, that gift will be void but the rest of the will will be valid.

A person under eighteen cannot make a will (except in special circumstances – see below). The testator's signature must be at the end of the will. Anything written below his signature, or anything inserted after he has signed, is not part of the will. He must sign in the presence of the witnesses, who should see him do so (though they need not, of course, read the will). Thus a blind person cannot witness a will. If the testator cannot sign it himself, his hand may be guided or he may make a mark, or someone may sign his name for him; but this must be done in his presence and the will should state that it has been done at his direction. The witnesses must sign in the presence of the testator and of each other, preferably opposite a statement that they have done so. If the testator has already signed the will before the witnesses come in, he may acknowledge his signature (ie indicate it and tell them that it is his signature) in their presence, and they may then witness the acknowledgement; the witnesses must actually sign in each other's presence.

A member of the armed forces on active service or a mariner or seaman at sea may make a will which does not conform to the above rules; he or she need not be eighteen; the will need not be in writing, nor witnessed. Any clear expression of intention about what is to happen to his property when he is dead will be a valid will, enforceable by the courts. (Of course it will be much easier to prove what his intention was if he writes it down and has it witnessed.)

Revoking a will

A will only revokes a previous will to the extent that it is inconsistent with it, unless it expressly says otherwise. To make matters clear, any will should state that it revokes all previous wills and should set out all the desired provisions (even if they are the same as in a previous will). A testator may revoke a will by any writing which is signed and witnessed in the manner required for wills (see above); it need not contain any new gifts. Apart from this method, a will may be revoked by marriage and by destruction:

Marriage revokes any previous will except one made in contemplation of marriage. But such a will must be in contemplation of a particular marriage to

a particular person, and should say that it is. Divorce does not revoke a will. *Destruction of a will* revokes it, provided it is done by the testator or at his direction, and with the intention of revoking the will. It is not enough to draw a line through it; it must actually be torn up or burnt. If a will is destroyed without an intention on the part of the testator to revoke it, it is still a valid will, and may be proved by other evidence (eg a copy). But if a will was kept in the testator's possession and cannot be found when he dies, he is presumed (in the absence of evidence to the contrary) to have revoked it by destruction.

The courts aim to put into effect the intentions of a testator. But there are technical rules for deciding what these were, so it is wise to have a will drawn up by a solicitor, if possible. A person who wants to make a will without legal advice should, however, use the simplest words and sentences he can find to make his intentions clear. He should never use words and phrases which he thinks sound more 'legal', in case the courts have attached meanings to them of which he is not aware.

Intestacy

When a person dies intestate – that is, without having made a will – his property passes to his next of kin according to certain rules, depending on what relations he has when he dies. If there are a spouse and children, all the personal belongings and a lump sum of money go to the spouse. The rest of the assets are divided in two; the income from one half goes to the spouse until his or her death and then that half passes to the children; the other half goes to the children immediately. If there are no children, the spouse receives personal belongings, a larger lump sum, and half the remaining assets; the other half goes to the deceased's parents, or if they are dead, to his brothers and sisters or their children. If there is no spouse, the next of kin inherit as follows: if there are children or grandchildren, everything passes to them. Otherwise the property passes to parents; if none, to brothers and sisters or their children; if none, to half-brothers and sisters or their children; if none, to grandparents; if none, to uncles and aunts or their children.

Children adopted since the beginning of 1976 have the same rights as natural children in relation to deaths since that date. An illegitimate child may share in the intestacy of both his parents and they in his, but he has no rights in respect of more remote relations, nor they in respect of him. Children do not receive their share until they are eighteen or marry with consent.

Certain people may, after someone dies, apply to the court on the grounds that the will, or the intestacy rules, do not make reasonable provision for them. The people who may apply are a spouse, an unmarried former spouse, a child of the deceased or one treated by him as a child of his family, or anyone who was being maintained by the deceased before his death. Except in the case of a spouse, the court can only give the claimant enough to maintain him. Claims should be brought within six months of probate.

Probate

A deceased person's property cannot be distributed until his will has been officially accepted as valid. This process is called 'probate'; in London it is done through the Principal Registry of the Family Division of the High Court, elsewhere by local Probate Registries. It takes time, and the executor (the person appointed by the deceased to carry out the instructions in his will) may leave it to his solicitors. But in order to save money an executor may decide to do it himself; the Probate Registry has a Personal Application Department to help him if he does. He will have to pay a larger fee than a professionally qualified person because the Registry staff will have to do more work, but it will be cheaper in the long run. Principally, obtaining probate involves giving the Registry the will and a list of the assets and debts of the deceased, and when these have been checked, taking an oath to deal with the deceased's property according to his will, and paying any capital transfer tax. In return, the Probate Registry sends the executor a document which enables him to have the assets transferred to him and to distribute them in accordance with the will. The Registry keeps the original will and gives him a copy.

If there is no will, or the will does not appoint executors, the next of kin must apply to the Probate Registry for a grant of letters of administration.

Citizenship

National status

Citizens of any country in the Commonwealth have the status of British Subjects and Commonwealth Citizens (the two terms are interchangeable). But since 1948 the primary national status for the people of the UK has been Citizenship of the UK and Colonies (called 'UK Citizenship' for short). Anyone born in the UK or whose father was born here is a UK citizen. Wives of UK citizens are entitled to register as citizens, and Irish or Commonwealth citizens can normally register as UK citizens if they have lived in the UK for five years. Aliens can acquire citizenship by naturalization if they have lived here for five (not necessarily consecutive) years. Citizens by birth or descent cannot be deprived of their citizenship. A person who obtains a naturalization or registration certificate by fraud may be deprived of citizenship, as can naturalized citizens who have shown disloyalty or disaffection, traded with an enemy in wartime, been imprisoned for a year or more within five years of naturalization, or lived abroad for seven years.

Patrials

UK citizens with the right to live in this country are called 'patrials'. They are:

1) UK citizens who acquired their citizenship by birth, adoption, naturalization or registration in the UK.
2) UK citizens who at the time of their birth, had a parent within category 1).
3) UK citizens born to or adopted by a UK citizen who, at the time of his or her birth, had a parent within category 1).
4) UK citizens who have been settled in the UK for five years (ie who have lived here legally and without being subject to immigration control).
5) Commonwealth citizens born to, or adopted by, a UK citizen who was born here.
6) Women who are Commonwealth citizens and who are, or were, married to a patrial.

Patrials in categories 1) to 4), and their wives, do not require leave to enter the country (but will have to establish their identity and nationality). All other patrials require leave to enter (which is given by an Immigration Officer at the port of entry) unless they have a certificate of patriality, which is issued by the Home Office or a British Government representative overseas. People with British passports issued in the UK should be admitted without further proof of their right unless the passport is endorsed to show that they are subject to immigration control; so should people with a British passport issued anywhere, who can show that they have previously been admitted for settlement. But any other patrial without a certificate of patriality will have to prove his or her status each time he or she returns to the country.

Commonwealth citizens who were settled in the UK before 1 January 1973 (and their wives and children), and Commonwealth citizens one of whose grandparents was born here, can enter freely even if they are not patrials.

Immigrants

All non-patrials require leave to enter and remain in the UK. Leave is given by an Immigration Officer at the port of entry to those entering the country and by the Home Office to those already here who want to prolong their stay. Leave may be given for a limited time and may be subject to conditions (eg a prohibition on taking employment). A person who wants to make sure in advance that he will be admitted to the UK can apply for an entry clearance to a representative of the British government in the place where he is living. Those wishing to come as dependants of a person already here must obtain an entry clearance before coming; so must fiancés, or men wishing to join their fiancées or wives. The categories of people who will be admitted, and under what conditions, are set out in the immigration rules according to the purpose for which they come, such as visitors, working holiday-makers (young Commonwealth citizens only), students (who must have been accepted for a full-time course), au pair girls (maximum of two years), businessmen (who must bring money of their own into the country to put into a viable business), and people with enough money to support themselves without working. People who want to take a job in the UK must have a work permit issued by the Department of Employment before they come; the permit is applied for by the prospective employer. Those given leave to enter subject to a condition prohibiting employment will not normally be allowed to stay on in order to take a job. Those who have been here for four years in approved employment or in business can apply to have the conditions and time limit attached to their stay removed; they will still be subject to immigration control but, as persons settled here, will normally be able to go in and out of the country freely and to have their families here, provided they can support them.

EEC nationals

By Common Market law the right of EEC nationals to come to the UK and work cannot be restricted; the immigration rules provide for this. They are also entitled to bring their families. But they have no general right to live here. An EEC national will normally be admitted for six months, and if he finds employment he will be granted a residence permit for five years; this may be refused or revoked if he is a charge on public funds or unable to support himself. Normally the time limit and any conditions on his leave will be removed after four years.

Voting

British subjects (ie all Commonwealth citizens) and Irish citizens over eighteen are entitled to vote in both parliamentary and local government elections, provided that they are on the appropriate electoral register, and resident in the constituency (or electoral area in the case of local government elections) on the qualifying date. People who are under eighteen may be registered as electors if they are going to be eighteen during the twelve months after the register is published. Peers may not vote in parliamentary elections. People who are severely mentally ill may not vote, nor may those who are in prison at the time of an election. In addition, people convicted of certain offences of corruption may be disqualified for five years.

Normally electors must vote in person at the particular polling station to which they are assigned. But those who for certain recognized reasons cannot attend in person may vote by post or by appointing a proxy to do it for them, provided they apply in advance to the registration officer. This applies to members of the armed forces, those too ill to attend, those the nature of whose occupation makes personal attendance impossible, those who no longer live at their qualifying address, and those who cannot attend by reason of religious observance (these must produce a certificate to that effect from their minister). If a proxy does not live in the same area as the elector who has appointed him, he may vote by post.

Jury service

Since the abolition of National Service, jury service is the only remaining duty to which the state can require a citizen to devote his time whether he likes it or not. But the duty is not enforced oppressively. Jurors are summoned by the Lord Chancellor to attend at a particular court on a particular date; he must have regard to their convenience and try to select jurors within a reasonable daily travelling distance of the court. Jurors are entitled to be reimbursed for travelling and subsistence and for financial loss resulting from their attendance at court.

Anyone on the electoral register who is between eighteen and sixty-five and who has been resident in the UK for any period of five years since reaching the age of thirteen, is qualified to serve on a jury provided he is not ineligible or disqualified. Those who have been sentenced to imprisonment for five years or more, and those who have been sentenced to imprisonment for three months or more in the previous ten years, are disqualified. (But if such a person does serve on a jury, the verdict is still valid.) Judges, lawyers, court staff, police, probation officers, forensic scientists, clergymen, monks, and nuns are ineligible because their opinions might carry too much weight (the jury are there to decide matters of fact, not questions of law or morals). The mentally ill are also ineligible.

Certain kinds of qualified people may, if they wish, be excused from serving on a jury; ie MPs, peers and peeresses, members of the armed forces, doctors, nurses, vets, and pharmacists. This is because it may be against the public interest that they should leave their work. In addition, there is a discretion to excuse a juror on one of the following grounds: he has served on a jury within the last two years (in some long or burdensome case the court may specify a longer time); he shows a good reason to be excused, such as personal hardship or personal knowledge of the facts or people in the case; he appears to be incapable of acting effectively as a juror due to physical disability or insufficient understanding of English.

If it appears to the court that the jury is likely to be incomplete, it can summon qualified persons in or near the court to make up the number. The twelve jurors who are to try any particular case are chosen by ballot in open court from a larger group called a panel. Before they take the oath they may be challenged, ie one of the parties may object to their being on the jury. In a criminal case the accused (either personally or by his counsel) may challenge three jurors without giving a reason. Those challenged in this way are excluded from the jury. The prosecution does not have this right, but may ask a juror to step aside to see if a jury can be made up without him. Either party may challenge any juror if he gives a reason for his objection; for example, that the juror is not qualified to serve on a jury, or that there is some reason to think he might not be impartial. It is then for the judge to decide whether to uphold the challenge. No challenge may be made once the juror has taken the oath, in which he swears to faithfully try the several issues and to give a true verdict according to the evidence.

Home Ownership

Freeholds and leaseholds

There are two types of home ownership: freehold and leasehold. If you buy a freehold property, you become the absolute owner. If you buy a leasehold property you become the owner of a valuable bundle of rights over the property for a limited period.

A lease is a grant of ownership rights by one person (the freeholder, lessor or landlord) to another (the leaseholder, lessee or tenant) for a period of years (called the term of the lease) in return for the periodical payment of a sum of money (the rent). Unless the lease prohibits him, the lessee may, during the term, himself grant a lease (called a sub-lease) of the property for part or all of the remaining term; or he may sell the rights he has to someone else (this is called an assignment). If the rent is at least two-thirds of the rateable value, the tenant is probably protected by the Rent Act (see p179). Sometimes the rent is very low (normally where the lease was granted for at least ninety-nine years and has at least thirty-five years left to run); it is then called ground rent, and the leaseholder pays a lump sum called a premium either to the landlord or to the previous leaseholder in return for the rights under the lease. Where the term granted is a number of years, the words 'lease', 'lessor', and 'lessee' are used, and where the term granted is a year or less (even if it is constantly renewed so that the tenant keeps his rights for a number of years) it is called a tenancy rather than a lease, and the parties are called landlord and tenant. But this is a matter of usage only.

Most flats are leasehold, but flat owners can sometimes arrange between themselves to buy the freehold of the block.

There are two main differences between a leasehold and a freehold ownership. First, a tenant has many obligations to his landlord. Second, a lease will run out eventually and then (unless the lessee can exercise certain rights mentioned below) the property will belong entirely to the landlord again. An owner would have neither of these concerns.

Covenants

A tenant usually has to make a lot of promises to the landlord called 'covenants'. If you are the original tenant you will remain liable for any breach of these covenants by a later tenant (eg a flatmate who joins you). Normally the landlord will sue the tenant who actually breaks the covenant; but if he is bankrupt this remedy will not be of much use. If the original tenant is then sued, he is entitled to get back from the actual covenant-breaker any damages he has to pay the landlord. A person who takes an assignment of a lease, however, is only liable for

breaches of covenant committed while he is actually in the position of tenant.

All leases contain a covenant to pay the landlord a sum of money at fixed intervals.

Repairing covenants: Apart from the rent, the most important obligations of the tenant are repairing covenants. These vary considerably from lease to lease. If a tenant covenants to 'keep' the premises in repair, this will be construed by the courts as including an obligation to *put* them in repair; so if they were dilapidated to start with, the tenant will have to return to the landlord something better than was let to him. However, there are various statutory restrictions on the landlord's right to enforce the tenant's repairing obligations. For example, if you have a lease of seven years or more, the landlord will probably not be entitled to make you do repairs or pay compensation for not doing them until the lease has less than three years to run; and if the house is going to be pulled down or so altered as to make repairs pointless, you may not have to do any repairs or pay any compensation at all. Landlords of leases of dwelling-houses of less than seven years have certain statutory obligations. They must repair and maintain the structure and exterior of the building, the drains, external water pipes, fixed heating and water heating installations, and sanitary equipment.

If the landlord fails to carry out his repairing obligations, the tenant cannot simply refuse to pay rent; the two obligations are quite separate. But he may do the repairs himself and deduct the cost from the rent. He may also be able to get a court to order the landlord to do the repairs. And he can claim damages for any loss resulting from non-repair.

Other covenants: In residential property there will usually be one covenant prohibiting business use. There may be one prohibiting alteration to the premises or assignment of the lease, either completely or without the landlord's consent. For his part, the landlord will promise the tenant 'quiet enjoyment' of the property. (If he does not do so expressly, the law will imply the promise.) This does not mean absence of noise but that the landlord and anyone to whom he transfers the property will not try to drive the tenant out (either by eviction or by cutting off the water supply, for instance). Nor can they prevent him from using it for the purpose for which it was let to him.

Leases of flats usually have very detailed covenants, which may include such things as not keeping pets and not putting milk bottles out for the milkman. The landlord will have to look after the common parts – the staircases, passages, etc. If there is a service charge, tenants have the right to see accounts showing them how it is made up, and they may not have to pay the charge if the standard and price of what is provided is unreasonable.

Service agreements

Where flats or houses are bought on a co-ownership basis or where there is a management committee formed by all the owners of the property, repainting and decorating may have to be carried out at specified periods, and the responsibilities for maintenance and servicing of 'common parts', eg staircases and entrances, may also be a joint responsibility. It is important to establish just how responsibility, insurance, etc for 'common parts' is apportioned. Any communally provided services, such as heating, should also be clearly defined in any agreements. If this is not settled when the property is bought, it will be very difficult, if not impossible, to achieve any sensible arrangements afterwards.

Other considerations are disposal of rubbish, and responsibility for the maintenance of common service parts, eg the area where dustbins are kept, the road in front of a block of garages, gardens, and drives.

A solicitor should always be consulted about the terms of any service agreement.

Forfeiture

Any lease will almost certainly provide that if the tenant breaks his covenants the landlord can forfeit the lease. This means that the lease comes to an end before its time and the landlord takes back the property. But the courts may give the tenant relief against forfeiture. A tenant whose lease is forfeited because he has not paid his rent can get the lease back if he applies to the court within six months and pays all the arrears and the landlord's expenses. In the case of other breaches of covenant, the landlord must serve notice on the tenant telling him what the breach is, telling him to put it right if this can be done, and asking him to pay compensation. Only if it is not or cannot be put right within a reasonable time, can the landlord forfeit the lease.

The traditional remedy for non-payment of rent was 'distress' –the landlord could seize and sell enough of the tenant's goods to pay the arrears. This remedy is still available. In the case of Rent Act tenants (see below), but not council tenants, the landlord must get a court order first. The landlord can, of course, simply sue the tenant on his promise to pay the rent.

End of lease

Normally when a lease comes to an end the tenant must leave. But under statute law, tenants under long leases at low rents may be able to stay on in one of three ways: they may be able to become protected tenants under the Rent Act 1977, or get another lease at a low rent, or buy the freehold (this is called 'enfranchisement').

The Rent Act 1977

Tenants paying higher rents (at least two-thirds of the rateable value) are usually protected by the Rent Act 1977. Only very expensive properties are now outside this legislation. The Act has two main consequences: rent control and security of tenure. In addition, it is illegal to charge a premium for a property which is protected by the Rent Act. If a premium is charged, the tenant can get it back.

If no rent is registered, the landlord can charge what he likes. But the tenant is entitled to ask a Rent Officer to assess and register a fair rent. He is not allowed to take into account the scarcity value of the premises, so a landlord does not benefit from the fact that many people want accommodation in the same area. The register can be inspected by the public. Once a fair rent has been registered by the Rent Officer, the landlord cannot charge any more for those premises (even to a new tenant). However, if the rent agreed with the tenant was less than the fair rent, he can charge only the agreed rent until the end of the contractual tenancy (unless the agreement allows an increase). Any rent increase must be registered; it usually has to be spread over three years. The landlord is not allowed to charge a lump sum for letting the premises; if he does, the tenant can claim it back after he has moved in. This also applies to a tenant who has been made to pay an inflated price for fixtures and fittings or furniture.

The Rent Act applies to furnished tenancies as well as unfurnished ones.

When a tenancy protected by the Rent Act comes to an end, the tenant will probably have the right to stay on. A residential tenant is entitled to at least four weeks' notice. He can only be made to leave by an order of the court, and this will only be made if the circumstances fit into one or other of the categories specified in the Act. These fall roughly into three classes. First, the landlord can show that suitable alternative accommodation is available; second, the tenant has misbehaved in some way (eg not paying rent, sub-letting at more than the fair rent); third, the landlord wants the premises for one of the listed reasons. A tenant who stays on after the end of his lease under this protection is called a 'statutory tenant' because his right to stay depends entirely on the Rent Act and not on any agreement between himself and the landlord.

Sub-tenants are also protected by the Rent Act. Normally, if a tenancy comes to an end, any sub-tenancies that tenant has granted come to an end. But in many cases, if a sub-tenant is protected in his relations with his own landlord (the original tenant who granted him his tenancy), then if the middle tenancy comes to an end he will become the tenant of the head landlord directly.

Certain people are not fully protected by the Rent Act. The most important category of these are those who live in the same house as their landlords. They may ask a Rent Tribunal to fix a reasonable rent, and they may get limited security of tenure by asking the Tribunal to suspend a notice to vacate for up to six months. This also applies to a person who shares living accommodation with his landlord and to one whose rent includes a payment for services. But a tenant who takes a room in a flat in a purpose-built block will be fully protected even if the landlord lives there too, unless he shares some living accommodation with his landlord. (Living accommodation includes a kitchen but not a bathroom.)

Council tenancies: Leases for under three years do not have to be in writing. Most council tenancies are weekly tenancies. There may, nevertheless, be a proper tenancy agreement; but often a tenant is merely given a list of conditions which he is deemed to accept by moving in. The council, as landlord, has certain obligations too, but these may not be stated. Like any landlord of a short lease, it will be responsible for the structure and exterior, including drains and pipes, and for the installations for the supply of water, gas, electricity, sanitation, heating, and hot water; it must take reasonable care to keep the common parts safe. Unless extra obligations are imposed in his tenancy agreement, the tenant's obligation is to use the property in a tenant-like manner. This (an obligation of any tenant) means taking ordinary care of it, eg by cleaning chimneys, mending fuses, and keeping it in good condition generally.

If the council does not carry out its repairing obligations, the council tenant has the same remedies as other tenants. If he considers the house unfit for human habitation he can complain to a local JP, parish or community council, who in turn can complain to the council's medical officer of health who must inspect the house and report to the council. In addition, council tenants can complain to a local councillor or to a Local Commissioner if the council's behaviour amounts to maladministration.

Council tenants do not have the right under the Rent Act 1977 either to a fair rent or to become statutory tenants. Councils may charge a reasonable rent; in theory, a tenant can challenge the rent in court as being unreasonable, but they are unwilling to interfere with a council's discretion.

Since council tenants cannot become statutory tenants, their tenancies (if weekly) can be brought to an end by four weeks' notice (unless the agreement provides for more). They cannot be evicted without a court order.

Boundaries

The deeds or lease of your house may impose an obligation on you to build and maintain a fence or wall, or they may prohibit you from doing so. If they do not say anything about it, you have no duty to fence unless there is something particularly dangerous about your property. Fences, walls, hedges, etc belong to the person on whose land they are. But it is not always easy to tell. A fence or wall with supports on one side is presumed to belong to the person on whose side of the fence the supports are.

There are general planning restrictions on the height of boundary walls and fences; those on a road frontage may be up to about one metre high and others up to about two-and-a-half metres.

Party walls, ie walls dividing two semi-detached or terraced houses, belong to both owners. Theoretically, each owns the half of the wall on his own side and has the right to have it supported by the other half. Each must usually pay half of the costs of repairing and maintaining the wall.

If the roots or branches of your neighbour's tree encroach on your property you may cut them off at the boundary. But they are still his property, so you must give them back. The roots of a tree may grow slowly and do damage, eg to the foundations of your house, before anyone realizes what has happened. If you can prove that the roots are responsible, the owner of the tree will have to pay for the damage. You may not eat the apples that dangle over your garden. If you cut off an offending branch, it must be returned to the owner.

Neighbours

Neighbours (including neighbours living in flats above and below) can make life a burden to each other. The law expects a certain amount of give and take but if one person's activities seriously interfere with another's use and occupation of his own property, they may amount to a nuisance. If they do, a court will give the aggrieved person damages, and probably – which is usually much more important to him – an injunction to stop the offending activity. If your property is being damaged by your neighbour's activities (for example, a large machine which makes your house vibrate and

causes the walls to crack) you have the right to stop him. But where your neighbour disturbs and annoys you without doing any physical damage, your rights will depend on what the courts think is reasonable in all the circumstances. If, for example, you are complaining about noisy neighbours, a court will take into consideration the type of area you live in, whether it is quiet or noisy in general, what time of day or night the noise is made and for how long, why the noise is made, and so on. A noise which might be reasonable at 8pm may not be so after midnight. The same volume of noise may be reasonable in a busy commercial area and unreasonable on a quiet housing estate; it may be reasonable if made by a child practising a musical instrument but unreasonable if made simply in order to annoy the neighbours. Anything which makes you especially vulnerable is not relevant; if you work at night and have to sleep during the day, you cannot expect the neighbours to keep quiet on that account.

If you want to take legal steps to stop a nuisance, you can ask either a county court for an injunction and damages or a magistrate for an order under the Control of Pollution Act 1974. The second procedure is simple and quick, but you cannot get damages from the magistrate; if the person against whom the order is made disobeys it, he will be fined. Your local council has some duties under this Act to stop or prevent nuisances.

Visitors

The occupier of a house or flat has a statutory duty to take reasonable care to see that his lawful visitors and their property are reasonably safe when they are on his property. The duty covers all the people you ask to your house – dinner guests, workmen, an au pair girl or cleaner, lodgers, the milkman and other delivery men; it covers anyone who comes to your door (the postman, canvassers, salesmen) unless you specifically put up a notice excluding him, either by name or as a member of a group (eg 'No hawkers'). The duty also covers certain people whom you have no right to exclude, such as policemen with a warrant, and in certain circumstances gas and electricity men and some local authority officials – you can, of course, always ask to see their credentials and authority. You must do what is reasonable in all the circumstances; for example, you must be more careful to see that children and old or disabled people are safe. If you call workmen in to repair something, you should not just leave them to find out the dangers for themselves; you should tell them all you know or suspect.

If a tenant's visitor is injured as a result of the landlord's failure to fulfil his repairing obligations, he may be able to get damages from the landlord (so may the tenant). This may also apply if the injury results from the tenant's failure to repair, provided the landlord has the right to enter the property and do repairs which the tenant has failed to do. But in this case the landlord will be able to get back from the tenant the damages he pays to the visitor.

Trespassers

Occupiers also have some duty to take care for the safety of trespassers, though it is not so onerous as the duty owed to visitors. The courts call it the 'duty of common humanity'. You must not set traps for trespassers. Beyond that, the duty depends very much on whether you had any way of knowing that trespassers, or trespassers of that particular kind, were likely to come. For example, if you know very well that children come and play in your garden, and you also know that one of the trees is rotten, you must take steps to prevent them from climbing it and hurting themselves. Putting up notices or chasing them away will not be enough to relieve you of liability if you know that they will probably come back. But what you are bound to do depends also on your resources; if you are relatively poor you need not spend a lot of money removing a danger to trespassers. And you will only be liable for dangers you actually know about, whereas in the case of visitors you will be liable for dangers you would have known about if you had taken reasonable steps to find out.

Extending or altering your home

You will usually need two different kinds of permission from your local authority: planning permission and building regulations consent. Planning permission is required for change of use (eg starting up a play-group) as well as for building work. Internal alterations which do not extend your home or alter its external appearance do not need planning permission *unless* you are converting a house into flats or in any way sub-dividing the premises to create more than one residential unit. There are certain other works for which you *may* not need planning permission, for example, building a garage. But it is important to check with the council before you begin work, because the various rules contain detailed qualifications, which are changed from time to time, and very often building regulations consent is needed even when planning permission is not. Also, you may be able to get a council grant to help with the cost.

If you go ahead without planning permission, you can be made to undo all the work. After four years any building works you have done will be safe; but there is no time limit for stopping an unauthorized change of use. You can appeal against the refusal of planning permission, and also against a local authority's order stopping you from going ahead without permission. In some cases the authority can make you stop the contravention until the appeal is decided (if it turns out not to have been a contravention, they will pay compensation); but usually you need not stop until or unless you lose the appeal.

Restrictions: Planning control and the building regulations do not provide the only kinds of restriction on building works. Most leases will contain restrictions; so may the title deeds of a freehold property. The latter restrictions will have been agreed by previous owners of adjoining properties, but they can bind subsequent owners. They are very common on estates. There will always be someone who is entitled to the benefit of the restriction in his capacity as owner for the time being of certain other property; restrictions of this kind cannot be imposed in the abstract simply because some past owner thought they were a good idea. You may find that the person entitled to the benefit does not object to your plans. Even if he does, you can sometimes get the restriction modified or annulled by the Lands Tribunal, if it is unreasonable, obsolete, or if changing or cancelling it would not hurt those entitled to the benefit. If you go ahead in defiance of a restrictive covenant you can be forced to undo the work or pay damages (or both); but you can insure against the risk that the covenant will be enforced.

You must make sure that your plans do not infringe your neighbours' rights, for example, to have their drains running under your land, or to take a short cut across your garden, or to have a bit of their house supported by the bit of your house you want to alter. If you interfere with their rights, they can get an injunction to stop you, and damages.

A neighbour may have a long-held right to light to certain windows of his house. This arises if at some time in the past he was granted the right, or if he has enjoyed light to those windows for twenty years or more. (There are still some signs by windows saying 'ancient lights'. This is what they mean.) However, he is not thereby entitled to all the light he has previously enjoyed, but only to a reasonable amount. Plans may, therefore, be able to be carried out without infringing his rights, even though the amount of light flowing to the windows is cut down.

Arrangements with the builder: No special legal rules apply to this; you will simply be making a contract to pay him for doing certain work. But do make sure that both sides understand and agree exactly what the arrangement is before the work starts. You cannot alter the contract once it is made.

Builders usually submit an estimate, but there will probably be provision in the contract for the price to be increased if costs increase. This does not mean that the builder can charge you what he likes; you can always ask him to prove that the costs have increased in such a way as to justify his increase in price. Unless the contract provides otherwise, you will have no obligation to pay anything until the work is finished; but it will probably provide for instalment payments. You may want to consider keeping back a small portion of each payment until a few months after the work is finished, in order to make sure that the builder puts right any defects. This is a fairly normal provision, but you cannot keep anything back unless it is provided for in the contract.

If the builder does not finish when he promised he would, you can claim damages for any loss you have suffered; for example, this might include the value of any room you are prevented from using. You will, however, be wise to make it a term of the contract that the builders will work continuously on your house once they have started. Then if they disappear for weeks when the work is half done, they will be in breach of contract and you may end your contract with them, call someone in to finish the work, and make the original builders pay the extra cost. (You can only do this if they disappear for a substantial time; not if they take two or three days off.)

Finally, find out, or specify in the agreement, who is to be responsible for the equipment and materials they leave on the premises. It may be you, even though it was the builders who brought them there. If it is, make sure you are insured for this. Your ordinary household policy may not cover it.

KITCHEN PLANNING

It must be remembered that the kitchen is the great laboratory of every
household, and that much of the " weal or woe," as far as regards bodily health,
depends upon the nature of the preparations concocted within its walls.

So much advertising is directed at the home owner
by manufacturers of kitchen furniture and equipment, that many people feel they are deprived or
inadequate if their kitchen is not of a standard
shape and expensively equipped with new wall-to-
wall cupboards and glittering machinery. With a
little money and some thought, imagination, time,
and hard work, a pleasant and workable kitchen
can be created from even the most unpromising
beginnings.

Using Space

The space you have available may be too small, too
big, awkwardly shaped or cluttered with someone
else's misconceived arrangements, but any of these
drawbacks can be overcome by good planning. If
you are not being advised by an architect, designer, or professional kitchen planner, there are
certain rules worth following.

Kitchen work-flow should follow the sequence:
work-surface/cooker/work-surface/sink/work-sur-
face, and the same in reverse. There should be no
gap or obstruction between sink and cooker. This
applies to both hob and oven, though in many
modern kitchens they are sited separately.

Make a scale drawing of your kitchen on squared
graph paper and fit this work-flow into it, with the
refrigerator placed so that it is easily accessible to
the main work-surface. Then arrange storage cupboards and larder (if you are lucky enough to have
one), and fit such items as refrigerator, dishwasher
or washing machine into the remaining spaces.
Cupboards near the cooker can be used for dry

stores at high level, saucepans at low level; cupboards under the largest work area can contain
mixing-bowls, and so on. The flow need not be
along one wall: it can be L-shaped along two
adjoining walls, or U-shaped around three walls.
Alternatively, to overcome the difficulties of a
large kitchen (and these do exist), sink or hobs can
be built into a peninsular unit which stretches at
a right angle into the room. The main point to
remember is that someone working in a kitchen
should be able to move round in sequence from
cooker to sink and back, using an unbroken stretch
of work-surface.

Work-surfaces should be at a suitable height for
the cook if she is not to find her activities awkward
and tiring. British Standard 1195 specifies a work-
top height of 900mm, but for the very tall or the
very short it may be necessary to go another 50mm
higher or lower. The height also depends on the
height of cooker, fridge, etc which the standard
takes into account. Adjustment can be achieved by
cutting off, or adding to the plinth of floor-standing
units, and some manufacturers offer a range of
variable plinth heights.

If you are lucky enough to be building a completely new kitchen (perhaps an extension to an
existing house) try to have a separate laundry or
laundry area with its own sink.

Try to site your window to take advantage of an
attractive view and to have one door leading to the
outside, another to the dining-room.

Even if you are planning a new kitchen, not
everything in it need be new. You can fit in your
older equipment and repaint or put new work

surfaces on existing cupboards, remembering that kitchens with the most character and visual appeal have often been designed in this way.

Neither does everything have to be purchased at once. The appropriate space for a dishwasher can be left to one side of the sink, gloss paint can go on walls which will eventually be covered in ceramic tiles, and so on. The important thing is to have everything planned from the outset.

Layouts

Here are suggested layouts for some common kitchen shapes. They all keep to the rule for sensible work-flow mentioned on p184 and they include suggested arrangements for cupboards and basic equipment. In the larger ones there is provision for eating and laundry.

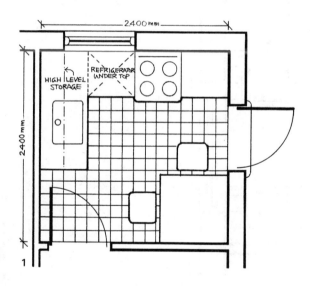

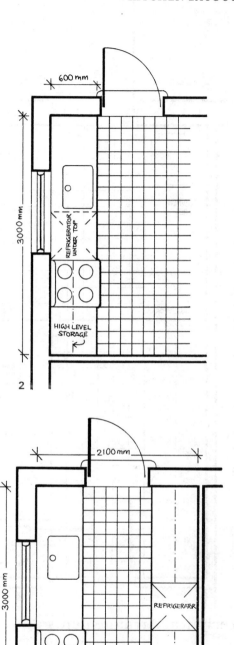

1) Small square kitchen where L-shaped arrangement is best and there is room for a table for eating.
2) Kitchen area for bed-sitter or combined kitchen/dining room.
3) Small galley with door into garden on one end wall, and door into dining-room on the opposite end wall.

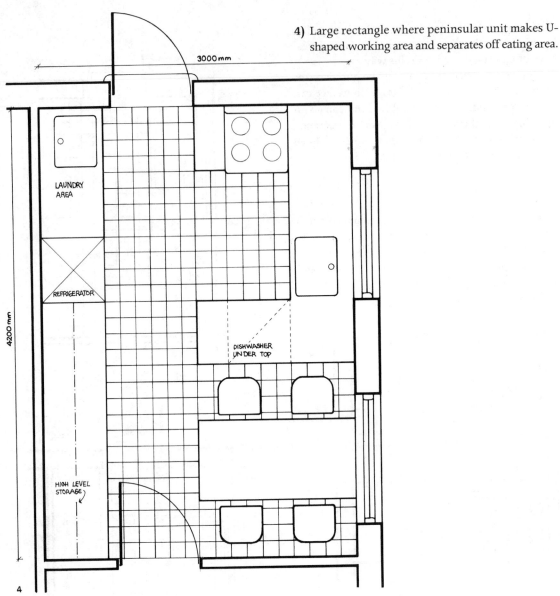

4) Large rectangle where peninsular unit makes U-shaped working area and separates off eating area.

3000 mm

4200 mm

LAUNDRY AREA

REFRIGERATOR

DISHWASHER UNDER TOP

HIGH LEVEL STORAGE

4

Technical Arrangements

These apply whether you are dealing with a new kitchen, a conversion of an existing kitchen or an inexpensive rearrangement of an existing kitchen.

Adequate water, drainage and electrical services are essential for an efficient and safe kitchen, so where compromises have to be made because of shortage of finance, these should not involve cutting back on services. Alterations to services should be carried out by qualified tradesmen.

Water

An abundant supply of hot water is essential. This may come from a central heating boiler; otherwise other types of gas or electric water heaters are available (for more information, see the chapter on Structural Work and Essential Services). Cold water for drinking and cooking should come from the mains. If water pipes can be concealed (but remain accessible in case of leaks) the kitchen will look much neater; a suitable place for them is under the work-tops of floor units.

5) Large square kitchen with central table for both working and eating.

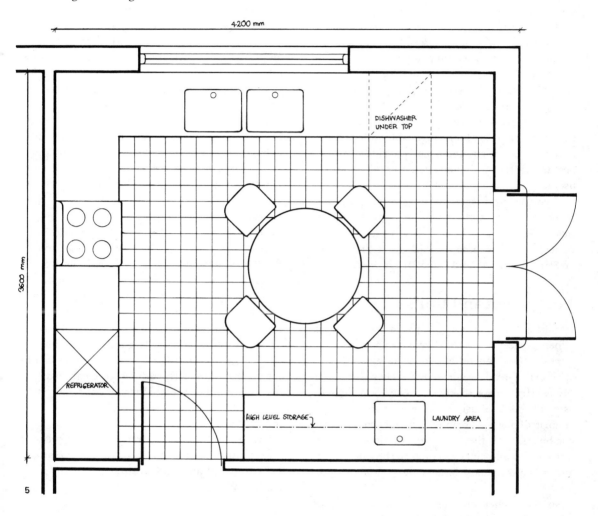

Drainage

A competent plumber will ensure that there is adequate slope on the waste pipes, and separation for individual appliances to avoid any risk of back flow. Waste disposal outlets should enter the drain beneath the external grid cover.

Power

There should be power outlets for the main appliances: cooker, refrigerator, and dishwasher, and also double sockets in appropriate positions above the work-surface for all the small appliances. For example: food mixer behind the preparation area, kettle adjacent to the sink, or electric toaster near the eating area.

Note Your electrician will certainly advise you that it is dangerous to install a point immediately behind the cooking rings or taps.

Lighting

If a kitchen is to be a pleasant and safe place in which to work, there must be a good level of both natural and artificial light (see pp41–44).

Heating

If you have a central heating system, a boiler is best sited in a utility room, cellar or hall cupboard, but as it needs a flue and ventilator, a cupboard may not be suitable. If you are forced to house it in the kitchen and need something larger than an unobtrusive wall-hung model, arrange for it to be concealed behind ventilated doors (ready-made louvre doors are excellent for the purpose) and use the warm, enclosed space as a drying or airing-cupboard. There are boilers available which fit into a work sequence and these may provide sufficient heat for a kitchen, though a radiator might also be useful.

If you have no central heating, a radiant heater or wall-fixed blow heater is both quick and efficient. For more information on central heating boilers and other forms of heating, see the chapter on Structural Work and Essential Services.

Equipment and Units

If units are not home-made or custom-made by a joiner to meet the special requirements of your kitchen, they can be bought from an extensive selection of ready-made ranges. They are either pre-constructed or in knock-down form for self-assembly. Door finishes can be of natural wood, laminated plastics, painted whitewood or some combination of these. There are floor-standing units, wall-hung units, tall units for broom storage, and tall units to house larders, ovens, and refrigerators.

Special kitchen units are available for disabled people with knee space allowed under the work-top for those in wheelchairs.

Interior fitments

A variety of fitments are available, and can include a pop-up waste-bin, vegetable baskets, bread drawer, food mixer or slicer swing-out platform, cutlery drawer dividers, bottle storage, and pull-out storage. Corner units can have revolving or pull-out storage. If the ironing is done in the kitchen, a built-in ironing board is useful.

Interior fitments can also be bought separately for fitting into existing units.

Work-tops

Laminated plastic work-tops are reasonably priced and easy to clean, especially if they have a smooth rather than textured surface; they may have a curved 'post-formed' edge rather than a right-angled edge. Hardwood surfaces, which need to be oiled periodically, give a traditional look. Stainless steel is impervious to heat but is expensive and scratches easily. Ceramic tiles make a hard, handsome surface but must be expertly laid. A marble inset for rolling pastry, though increasingly difficult to obtain, and a hardwood insert for chopping and cutting are luxury items to add, and the latter would need renewing after hard use.

Sinks

A sink should be at least 55 × 350mm and about 175mm deep in order to hold an oven shelf, one of the largest items likely to need washing. (Ideally there should be twin sinks for food preparation and washing up, and a third in the laundry area.) Stainless steel is easily cleaned, vitreous enamel may chip, and ceramic is liable to chip and crack if knocked by heavy pots (see also the chapter on Care of Textiles and Hard Surfaces). Sinks can be set directly into work-surfaces, or combined with drainers and then set into the work-surface.

Taps

The choice is between separate or mixer-type taps; either can be set into the work-surface or project from the wall above. The latter makes an easily cleaned arrangement.

Appliances and equipment

See the chapters on Kitchen Equipment, and Care of Textiles and Hard Surfaces.

Ordering equipment

If you are planning your kitchen without assistance from an architect or designer, do seek advice and guidance from either the manufacturer or supplier. For instance, work-tops deeper than standard size may be needed to obtain a clean, straight line with your appliances. This would bring the units out from the wall, and if backs are not normally included, these would have to be added.

When appliances are placed in a corner arrangement, make sure that there is enough room for the door or drawer of the unit on the return to clear any protrusion.

Work-tops should be specified approximately 25mm longer and deeper than required so that they can be cut to shape if walls are not square.

Enquire about delivery times when making your plans; self-assembly units can often be bought off the shelf and taken away immediately, but ready-made units sometimes take weeks to be delivered, and custom-built units tend to take a considerable time to complete.

Decoration

This is something to consider at the outset with the rest of your planning, because it will – or should – have a direct effect on everything you choose. Decide from the start whether you want a stream-lined kitchen with shiny plastic surfaces, clear colours, and little clutter; or whether, on the other hand, you are going to have a homely, country-style kitchen with a lot of wood, gentle colours, natural surfaces and the sort of pots, jugs, and crockery that go with it. Everything you choose – the units, floor covering, paint colours, curtains – will then be appropriate for the type of kitchen you prefer.

Other factors will affect your choices; for further information on these, see the chapter on Planning Your Home – Design Factors.

Ceilings and walls

These can be gloss-painted – an excellent, easily cleaned, and inexpensive treatment for kitchen surfaces. Or they can be covered with a patterned, washable paper; vinyl covering is even harder-wearing but more expensive and not generally available in such a good range of designs. Tongued and grooved boarding lasts many years, gives a warm, friendly look to a kitchen, and can be treated with a matt or gloss varnish to make it easy to clean.

Keep your scheme simple with not more than two types of surface covering in one kitchen. Ceramic tiles, the traditional kitchen wall covering,

are expensive (though DIY ones are available) and give a clinical effect if used in quantity; but they are good as an impervious and cleanable surface around sink and cooker, and are made in very attractive designs and colours. Stainless steel tiles would make an alternative for a cool, clinical type of kitchen.

Floor

For coverings see the chapter on Planning Your Home – Design Factors. A sanded and sealed boarded floor with washable cotton rugs by sink and cooker is inexpensive to contrive and would give a pleasant, farmhouse look to the kitchen. It is, however, hard work to maintain, and would not stand up to too much water and grease.

Windows

Curtains and blinds tend to become dirty quickly because of greasy fumes, so they should be easy to clean. Unlined cotton curtains look crisp and fresh, especially in a small print, and could be combined with complementary blinds of spongeable fabric; or blinds could be used alone. Venetian blinds are difficult to clean but might be necessary to combat glare in a hot, sunny kitchen.

Installation

The co-ordination and timing of the various jobs which go to the building of a new or converted kitchen is important if the work is to go smoothly. The following sequence is recommended:

1) Prepare the electric power points, lighting, woodwork, wall surfaces, and ceiling.
2) Remove any high cupboards to enable the ceiling surface to be completed.
3) Remove existing units and appliances and install new ones, at the same time carrying out work to any of the services. Care must be taken to provide sufficient air circulation for built-in ovens, refrigerators, and freezers.
4) Complete woodwork and all wall surfaces.
5) Lay floor up to the units and under the appliances, with the exception of a ceramic tiled floor, which should be laid between removing existing items and installing new ones.

KITCHEN EQUIPMENT

Of the culinary utensils of the ancients, our knowledge is very limited; but as the art of living, in every civilized country, is pretty much the same, the instruments for cooking must, in a great degree, bear a striking resemblance to each other. On referring to classical antiquities, we find mentioned, among household utensils, leather bags, baskets constructed of twigs, reeds, and rushes; boxes, basins, and bellows; bread-moulds, brooms, and brushes; caldrons, colanders, cisterns, and chafing-dishes; cheese-rasps, knives, and ovens of the Dutch kind; funnels and frying-pans; handmills, soup-ladles, milk-pails, and oil-jars; presses, scales, and sieves; spits of different sizes, but some of them large enough to roast an ox; spoons, fire-tongs, trays, trenchers, and drinking-vessels; with others for carrying food, preserving milk, and holding cheese.

This chapter gives detailed information on the appliances referred to in the previous chapter.

Cookers

As the work of a kitchen is usually planned round the cooker, one needs to consider its basic shape and size in relation to present and planned kitchen equipment. Most electricity and gas undertakings and many kitchen equipment suppliers offer free advice on planning the arrangement of a kitchen in relation to a smooth, time- and effort-saving work sequence (see the chapter on Kitchen Planning).

Choosing a cooker

Many people have no definite idea about the kind of fuel they want to cook with. Most new houses are wired for an electric cooker point. If there is also a gas supply to the house, there will probably be a point for a gas cooker. Bottled gas cookers are available – a viable choice where there is no mains supply. Some people favour solid fuel or oil cookers, though these are more expensive to buy.

Choice of fuel

Electric cookers are commended for their cleanliness, good design, and the availability of special features, eg spit-roasters, auto-timers, ceramic hobs, and fan-assisted ovens.

Gas cookers have the advantage of burners with visible flames, and may also have auto-timers, spit-roasters and fan-assisted ovens.

Solid fuel advocates usually own one of the larger heat storage cookers (as made by Aga, Raeburn, etc) because they have more than one oven and provide useful background heat as well as, usually, heating the hot water supply. These also come in gas and oil versions.

Paraffin (domestic kerosene) cookers are inexpensive to buy and kerosene is obtainable almost anywhere in the world.

Important check-points

Whatever fuel is used, four important factors should be considered when choosing a cooker:

1) The size of the household and/or the amount of cooking that is going to be done at home. This influences the number of burners or hotplates and the size of the oven or ovens needed. It is better to have a cooker which is bigger than is strictly needed than to be frustrated by the limitations of one which is too small.

2) Individual preferences for particular features of cookers, eg eye-level grill, spit-roaster, plate warmer, second oven, ceramic hob.

3) The available space in the kitchen. Although there is some degree of standardization (see p191), cookers, like other kitchen units, vary in width, depth, and height.

4) How much you can afford. Before buying a cooker, try to see as many different models as possible. Make your own check-list of the features you like and want. Your final choice may have to be a compromise, but it is important to satisfy yourself that you have chosen from what is available and not simply from what is put in front of you.

Styles

Basically there are three styles of cooker – the 'range', where the cooker is wider than its depth (this design is available for all fuels); the free-standing upright, where the hob or hot-plate is over the oven; and the relatively expensive though undoubtedly convenient 'built-in' separates, where oven and grill, and rings and burners are separated from each other.

Size

The dimensions, in particular the hot-plate (hob) height of modern cookers, should be compared with the British Standard for kitchen units (see p184). There is a good deal of variation in the size of cookers, particularly among those with two ovens, so it is very important to check that the cooker selected will match the space it is to occupy. In addition, cookers with special features, eg spit-roasters or eye-level grills, may need space for clearance which is outside the stated cooker dimensions. This can create problems if not considered when planning a fitted kitchen.

People who find it tiring to bend or stoop should notice that the height of ovens varies even in cookers that look the same. On cookers with eye-level grills there may be a warming drawer or pan below the oven, for example, and the oven will therefore be higher. 'Baby' or table-top cookers, which stand on the table or their own stand and are widely used for small kitchens, boats, and caravans, and the various built-in units, are often a sensible answer for people who are elderly or handicapped and who want to cook at the level that suits them best.

Choice of finish

Most cookers are finished in smooth, hard materials so that they can be wiped clean with a damp cloth and should only need gentle scouring if there has been a major spill. Decoration is usually limited to fascia panels and trim and control knobs. The basic cooker colour is white or cream, but coloured finishes are available on some models.

Cleaning

Modern cookers are easy to keep clean. Most models have removable spillage trays, so that anything that has boiled over can be mopped up before burning on to the enamel. Spills on solid plates are burned off and both gas burners and electric rings burn themselves clean. Well-designed gas and electric cookers are equally good in this respect.

Ovens usually have continuous cleaning (catalytic) oven linings which prevent dirt building up by vaporizing away any splashes. Removable catalytic linings are easier to get at for thorough cleaning and they can be replaced. Solid fuel and heat-storage cookers have ovens which are virtually self-cleaning.

A few electric cookers have pyrolytic ovens, which means that the oven is cleaned by setting it at a very high temperature with the door locked automatically. All that is left when it has had time to cool is a little dry ash, which can be brushed out.

Shelves, spillage trays, and glass doors may need special attention from time to time and most manufacturers recommend the type of cleaner they judge suitable for their ovens.

Controls

Heat controls on modern cookers range from quite simple air controls on solid fuel cookers, to the positive heat settings of electric and gas cookers, which have thermostatically-controlled ovens to maintain the heat selected.

Auto-timers

Auto-timers are a standard fitting on almost all full-size electric cookers and are available on some gas models. They switch the oven on and/or off without the user having to be present. They consist basically of a clock which can be set ahead to start cooking at any time the user wants, as long as the cooking can be finished before the cooker switches off automatically at a pre-set time (which is not usually later than twelve hours ahead). Some clocks have conventional hour and minute hands on a circular face; others are of the digital type with the time given in numbers.

Instructions on how to use the clock are usually more complicated than the operation itself, which consists of five simple steps:

1) Check that the clock is showing the right time.
2) Select your starting time and set it.

3) Decide how long you want the cooking to take (the minimum is 30 minutes) and set the stopping time.
4) Put the food in the oven.
5) Set the oven to the required heat.

When the cooking time is over the control has to be turned back to the 'manual' position, as the oven will otherwise not heat up the next time the cooker is turned on.

Remember that the control can be used just to switch the oven off – a very useful facility if you have to go out unexpectedly while something is cooking, or do not want to remain indoors after preparing a meal.

It is a good idea to use the automatic oven timer for the first time while you are at home, so that you can watch it click itself on and off, or even try a 'dummy-run' with nothing in the oven, just to reassure yourself that it will work.

Timing

Almost any dish which takes longer than 30 minutes to cook can be auto-timed. There is no need to allow extra cooking time for the warming-up period for anything which takes over an hour to cook. Cakes need a little more care than meat dishes, but they can generally be started in a cold oven.

Choose foods which take approximately the same time to cook, at approximately the same temperature. However, as food is far more tolerant than generally supposed, items requiring different times and temperatures can be evened up by
1) wrapping small quick-cooking quantities in foil, or standing inner utensils in large tins of water, to slow them down.
2) cooking several small containers of longer-cooking foods instead of one big quantity, to hurry it up.
3) cutting vegetables accordingly.
4) using enamel or aluminium containers for speed and pottery ones to slow things down.

Some suitable dishes for auto-timed cooking

1) Casseroles, stews, hot pots, braised meat, and curries
2) Roast joints and poultry, with or without stuffing

3) Potatoes: roast, baked in jackets, 'boiled' (to be mashed before serving)
4) Rice
5) Root vegetables, sweetcorn, soaked pulses
6) Pies (both plate pies and deep pies); pasties (savoury and sweet)
7) Crumbles, charlottes, baked sponges, and suet puddings
8) Baked apples and poached fruit
9) Milk puddings, baked custards, bread and butter puddings
10) Breakfasts, including porridge, sausages, potato cakes.

Warning

In very hot or humid weather, or if your kitchen is very warm, it is not advisable to leave food in the oven for a long delay period before cooking, so transfer any meat dishes from a refrigerator to the oven at the last moment.

Safety

Most of the accidents involving cookers are caused by the cook, but points to check are whether children can reach the controls, and whether these turn on or off with a positive movement that discourages accidental switching. If the controls are out of reach of children, they may, however, be difficult to reach for the elderly or handicapped. Oven shelves should allow dishes to be withdrawn to a safe distance for turning food over or round without tipping.

Cookers sold by the gas and electricity boards must conform to their own requirements for safety as well as any statutory minimum standards. They may refuse to service any cooker not approved by them as safe. There is also an approvals scheme for British oil and solid fuel cookers.

Spares and reliability

Gas and electric cooker manufacturers who supply the British fuel undertakings usually agree to maintain a supply of spare parts for a specified period after a cooker has been withdrawn from the market. The manufacturers of heat storage and solid fuel cookers also reckon on a long life for their cookers and plan their spare parts policies accordingly.

Most cookers have to be serviced by specially trained servicemen. See also pp75–76.

Installation

Gas and electric cookers can be put almost anywhere in the kitchen convenient to the user, though it may be necessary to move the cooker point. They should not, however, be placed near a door or window. Unless there are hob and oven lights, cookers should be put in a good light, and it is an advantage to have a cooker near the sink. (See also the chapter on Kitchen Planning.)

Gas cookers with auto-timers, electric ignition, etc will need to be near an electric point. Any gas cooker with a high-level grill must have a clear space of at least 460mm above and 310mm on either side of the grill. Bottled gas cookers can go anywhere, provided the fuel containers can be accommodated nearby or, if more convenient, outside the kitchen and piped to the cooker.

Any electric cooker, except a 'baby' one, must be connected to its own separate cooker circuit by a special flexible cable. This circuit and the separate control panel are usually provided as standard in new houses. One cooker control can serve a separate oven and hob if they are within 2m of the switch. A small cooker can be used from a 13 amp socket outlet. It is controlled either so that the plug cannot be overloaded or it is in two separate parts (oven/grill and hob), each of which can be run off separate 13 amp socket outlets.

Heat storage and solid fuel cookers must be provided with a flue.

Energy efficiency

There are variations in energy efficiency between models of cooker. As a general rule, though, it is more economical to cook with the fuel you use to heat space and water.

The type of fuel used is unlikely to be as significant in cost as the way it is used.

Using the oven economically

To save fuel, and therefore money, plan meals which use only oven space to cook, rather than the oven and the hob; plan cake baking to coincide with cooking other oven-baked foods. If cooking small quantities of food, enclose foods in foil parcels, and cook on the same baking sheet or in the same tin. Remember that stock can be left simmering in the oven just as well as on the hob.

Using the hob economically

All the vegetables for a meal can be placed in separate boiling bags or in foil and then added to a single pan of boiling water. Vegetables which need a longer cooking time should go in first. Alternatively, foods can be cooked in separate containers of a tiered steamer or in perforated separators of a pressure cooker.

If you are using liquids to cook food, use the least possible amount. It is more economical to bring water to the boil in an electric kettle than in a pan over heat. If you do use a pan on the hob, turn the heat down once the liquid has boiled so that it is only just boiling.

Electric Cookers

Types and sizes of cooker

Most British electric cookers are upright and floor-standing. The height from floor to hob is usually 900mm. Overall heights are 1000–1200mm to the top of the control panel (up to 1600mm on high-level grill cookers). Width and depth of 550–600mm is usual. Separate units for building-in can be obtained. Range-type cookers are also available.

The hob

Three or four radiant boiling rings are standard on all British cookers. Most imported cookers have flat circular metal discs enclosing an element. Discs are also available for building into heat-resistant work-tops so that personal hob layout can be planned. Both types of ring are controlled by 'energy regulator' switches which give steady, precise control of the selected setting from simmer to boil. Control knobs show which rings are in use.

To use fuel most economically, pan sizes should match the size of the rings. For disc rings, a perfectly flat, preferably ground base pan is recommended. Any good quality pan is suitable for use on radiant rings. Dual radiant rings have two coils, separately controlled, so that the small centre coil can be used alone for small pans. If fuel economy is important, it is sensible to insist on at least one dual radiant ring on a cooker.

Ceramic hobs

Ceramic hobs are made of a flat piece of virtually unbreakable, opaque glass. The position of the heating elements underneath is shown by a circular pattern on top of the hob. Ceramic hobs are found on standard floor-standing cookers and can also be bought for building into a work surface. They make an attractive feature in the kitchen, but they tend to be expensive.

The heating area changes colour when in use but returns to normal when cold. Spills are easily mopped up but should be tackled before they burn on the surface. Initial heating takes slightly longer than on a conventional boiling ring but overall cooking times are approximately the same. Good quality saucepans with flat bases should be used as it is important to make good all over contact with the ceramic surface.

The hob may be used as an ordinary work surface when not being used for cooking.

The grill

Most floor-standing electric cookers have the grill immediately under the hob at waist level, above the main oven, in a separate compartment which can be used for warming dishes. On all but basic models this compartment can be used as a special small oven. All have drop-down doors.

A few cookers have high-level grills. Some of these are in an enclosed compartment which can be used as a small oven and/or rotisserie. High-level grills are usually a little smaller than the waist-level ones, which take up the whole width of the cooker. Dual grills have two elements, so that one side or the central part only may be used for small quantities of food.

The oven

An electric oven is virtually an enclosed box with only a small vent to allow steam to escape. It is heated by convected hot air from two elements low on either side of the cooker, behind the side racks which hold the shelves. The heat in an electric oven is much the same in every part, without the zones of heat to be found in a gas oven.

Use can be made of almost all the shelf space. (Some models even have a hook in the oven roof from which to suspend a large turkey for roasting.)

Fan ovens are heated by a simple circular element which surrounds a small fan in the back wall of the oven. These ovens are designed to give even heat distribution for a full load of food without the need for turning or changing food round to get the benefit of the same temperature. Cooking times in fan ovens are up to a quarter less than in other ovens and the recommended cooking temperatures are slightly lower. The overall fuel consumption is, therefore, more economical if full use is made of the oven.

Most electric ovens have a light, and a removable glass door. Other features may include a meat thermometer, shelves which can be moved up and down from outside, and toughened coloured-glass outer doors. Cookers with micro-processors which compute when cooking should start and finish and check temperatures throughout are also available. Touch controls which do away with protruding control knobs are available on some models. A light finger touch on a marked square adjusts the control.

The second oven

A second or small oven has an upper radiant (grill) element and an enclosed element in the base. In some cookers it can only be used as an oven for moderate-temperature cooking of casseroles, milk puddings, etc and for keeping food hot. Some of these ovens are fully heat-controlled and can be controlled by the auto-timer.

Controls

British electric cookers all have a thermostat which controls oven temperature. The range of temperatures is 100°C to 250°C.

Most electric ovens have automatic time control.

Microwave cookers

Microwaves are electromagnetic waves similar to radio waves. Cookers work and look completely different from conventional ovens.

Microwaves, within a confined space and

operating at a very high frequency, agitate the molecules in food or liquid, which then vibrate against each other; friction between the molecules produces heat within the food. (Familiar comparisons with this are rubbing one's hands together to warm them, or the scout's well-known way of starting a fire by rubbing two sticks together.)

Mains electricity is passed through a magnetron which generates the high frequency waves and distributes them evenly through the cooker. The cooker interior is made of metal which reflects the waves through the food. To get the best results, the food needs to be turned during cooking, and some ovens incorporate a revolving platform. The food is put in its container on the platform and automatically turns throughout cooking. The magnetron must only work when the oven door is closed, and the oven door and its surrounding frame have a special seal. Safety standards require the oven door to have at least two interlocks, so that if one fails it is impossible to operate the cooker with the door open.

Microwaves are transmitted through materials such as glass, china, and paper without heating them. Any material which microwaves can pass through can therefore be used to hold food. (Metal reflects microwaves and so cannot be used for food containers.) Although food is hot when it comes out of the oven, the containers are warmed only by contact with the heated food.

The major advantage of microwave cooking is speed. The more powerful the cooker the faster it will be. A 2kg chicken would be cooked in anything from fifteen to fifty minutes.

Frozen food Microwave cookers are particularly useful for defrosting and heating up frozen food; a bread roll will thaw in fifteen seconds; a frozen shepherd's pie will be ready to eat in fifteen minutes. The cookers boil, steam, and poach. They also 'bake', but without browning food on the outside; it comes out looking as if it has been boiled. Special browning dishes are available, which are preheated in the cooker and brown the food by contact. Alternatively, food can be finished off under a conventional grill.

Steaming and boiling Almost any food which is normally steamed or boiled can be cooked in a fraction of the usual time by microwaves. Because microwaves cook so quickly, and little additional liquid is needed, they cook vegetables and fish especially well.

Deep frying This is not possible in a microwave cooker and shallow frying is not advised. As there is no temperature control, it is possible to overheat fat.

Microwave cookers come within the scope of the Electrical Equipment (Safety) Regulations 1975 made under the Consumer Protection Act, 1961. These regulations require domestic electrical equipment to be so designed and constructed that when in use it does not emit any kind of radiation which could be dangerous. The safety limit for microwave leakage is set out in a British Standard (BS 5175); in addition the cookers are tested for electrical safety to the requirements of BS 3456 Part II (Section 2.33). (Microwave cookers for domestic use that conform to the standards carry the British Electrotechnical Approvals Board [BEAB] label.)

Installation
Microwave ovens can be connected to any convenient 13 or 15 amp plug. They have to be put a short distance away from surrounding walls or cupboards and from anything that produces a lot of heat. Although they are portable in the sense that they can be moved from room to room, they are quite heavy and need a secure flat base to stand on.

Servicing
To keep within the safety limit, it is important that the door seal should be in good condition; that is, free from excessive contamination and undamaged. The British Standard requires instructions on maintenance for the user to be included in the manufacturer's instruction sheets. These should include their recommended method for cleaning door seal areas as well as instructions for inspecting these areas for damage. A warning has to be included to the effect that if door seal areas are damaged, the appliance should not be operated

until it has been repaired by a service technician trained by the manufacturers.

Controls

The speed of development with these cookers is too fast to be sure that every feature is covered in a book like this, but manufacturers supply instruction books for their particular models. There is always a basic on/off switch, a 'start', and a 'cook' button, and a timer dial on the simple models. More sophisticated ones have different power levels: low for cooking eggs, cheese dishes, and pastries, medium for defrosting, and high for typical microwave cookery.

Gas Cookers

Types and sizes of cooker

Gas cookers come as freestanding, range-type or with grill, hot-plate, and oven sections available separately for building in to kitchen units. Most cookers are designed to fit in with standard kitchen units. Freestanding cookers are usually between 460 and 610mm wide; range cookers are more than 640mm wide. Freestanding cookers may have either a drop-down or side-opening door, usually hinged on the left, but built-in ovens can be bought with a left-hand or a right-hand hinged door.

The hot-plate

This is the top of the gas cooker and has either two or four burners. Many models have burners of different sizes – large ones for fast cooking and smaller burners for simmering. Gas is easy to ignite, by either a piezo spark or an electric spark ignition. This operates automatically or by pushing a button when the control knob is turned. If this ignition is mains-operated, the cooker will have to be near an electric socket. Some ignition systems have a re-ignition device, so that if the burner goes out accidentally it will automatically relight.

The controls have visual indicators which show which boiling ring is on and at what setting. Some models have a preset simmer position, which means that there is no need to judge the height of the flame by eye to be sure that the pan is only simmering.

Flame height on gas burners is easily adjustable up or down, and there is no residual heat when the burner has been turned off.

The grill

Most gas cooker grills are at eye level, although waist-level grills are available. The heat is adjusted by turning the flame up or down, and on 'surface combustion' grills the heat is even over the whole of the grill at half-heat. Some grills have extra features such as electrically operated rôtisseries, snack turners or kebab attachments. Most grills have at least two grilling positions and room for warming plates. Many have a device which allows the grill pan to be drawn forward and held in position safely so that food can be turned over.

The oven

This is a box of sheet steel heated directly by a burner along the back. As the heat is instant there is no need to preheat before use except for a few dishes where temperature is very critical. The heat in the gas oven of a British cooker is 'zoned', which means that it is hotter at the top than at the bottom. Dishes which need different temperatures can, therefore, be cooked together and the whole of the oven can be used. The position of the burners in North American and continental ovens is not the same and in these ovens the heat is even throughout. Cookers with fan-assisted ovens are also available (see Electric ovens, p194).

All British gas cookers are fitted with a thermostat which controls the heat to give a wide range of steady temperatures. The thermostat setting is given in numbers, not temperatures, and refers to the temperature at the middle of the oven. There are usually two shelves in a British gas cooker oven and up to six shelf runners. The runner positions are counted from the top downwards. Some cookers have oven lights, viewing windows, and time switch controls which need an electric point.

Solid Fuel Cookers

There are two types: the heat storage cooker and the freestanding insulated cooker. Both types will heat domestic hot water, and have the added advantage that they keep the kitchen warm.

Heat storage cookers

These are designed to retain the heat from a continuously burning fire distributed through a specially designed burner. A heat reserve is stored up during the night and this is called on during the day to heat hot water, a fast and slow boiling plate, and two ovens, one for roasting and baking and one for slow cooking, keeping food warm, or plate warming.

Most models have a guaranteed fuel consumption if the maker's recommendations about the correct fuel to use are followed. (Heat storage cookers can also be bought in versions which use gas and oil. But how long these will be available depends on fuel prices.)

The cookers need little cleaning. The ovens and hot-plates burn off spills to a dry powder which is easy to brush away and the enamelled exterior needs no more attention than other cookers. Refuelling may create a little dust.

The oven

A good range of temperatures for family cooking is given by maintaining the hot oven at 220°C and the slow oven at 160°C. It is possible to roast a joint of beef and Yorkshire pudding in one oven and bake a meringue in the other.

Hob

To get the best results from the solid hot-plates, use good quality pans with flat, ground bases, as these provide the best contact for conducting the heat.

Grilling

Grilling can be carried out on the top of the fast oven, using the heat which radiates from the roof of the oven. The alternative is to 'sear' food on the hot side of the hot-plate in a form of griddle cooking. A special toaster attachment is used for toasting on the hot-plate.

Freestanding insulated cookers

These more modestly priced cookers provide continuous warmth, good cooking facilities, and constant hot water. They are not as heavily insulated as heat storage cookers and are much lighter in construction. Versions can be obtained to run on solid fuel, oil or gas, and in some cases wood or peat.

Installation

Freestanding cookers vary in size from a one oven, one hot-plate model with dimensions of 762mm width, 457mm depth, and 762mm height to one with four ovens, two large hot-plates and a warming/serving plate with dimensions of 148mm width, 679mm depth and 851mm height.

Those cookers using solid fuels or other fuels must have a flue.

Controls

These are few and simple. Heat storage cookers are controlled by a thermostat which is set when the cooker is installed. This thermostat is automatically responsive to the demands made on the cooker.

On freestanding cookers the temperature is controlled by an air inlet and a flue damper. When the temperature needed for cooking or hot water is reached, the damper has to be closed and the air inlet partially closed to allow only enough air in to maintain combustion.

Maintenance

Cookers which use solid fuel, peat or wood have to be filled by the user, and the firebox has to be emptied of ashes, etc regularly. Chimney sweeping is recommended every year if burning smokeless fuels, and twice a year if burning bituminous coal.

Bottled Gas Cookers

Bottled gas describes the petroleum refinery gases – propane and butane – which are supplied as liquids in pressurized containers. The liquid turns to gas as it is released from the container. Most bottled gas is butane, but propane has the virtue of standing freezing temperatures and is, therefore, useful for camping, etc in cold weather.

Bottled gas cookers vary almost as much as mains gas models. Small single burner units are useful for picnic and overnight camping and as a 'standby' against mains failure. They use small disposable containers. The household-sized appliances run off large metal containers supplied for a fee 'on deposit' and exchangeable by any bottled gas supplier.

The running cost of a bottled gas cooker is higher than that of a mains gas cooker of similar size, but as these cookers are normally used when other forms of power are not a practical alternative, the cost is not usually the primary consideration in choosing this type of fuel. Where mains gas supplies are not available, bottled gas cookers are often used as a supplement to an oil, solid fuel or electric cooker when the fire is not lit or the electricity supply is interrupted, for instance.

These cookers are made on the same lines as mains gas cookers and give the same facilities. It is essential to make sure that the connection between the gas container and the cooker is tight before turning on the gas; additionally, gas jets and burners must be kept clean as otherwise there will be poor or incomplete combustion.

Refrigerators

In temperatures below 10°C, micro-organisms such as bacteria, yeasts or moulds, which cause food to deteriorate, develop much less quickly, so a refrigerator is an important piece of kitchen equipment.

A refrigerator also helps by making meal planning and shopping easier, and by enabling the cook to produce a wider variety of meals and dishes which need to be chilled to be at their best.

Choosing a refrigerator

The choice of a refrigerator, its overall size, and the size of the frozen food storage compartment depend on a number of factors, ie the size of the household, the distance from shops and the amount of time available for shopping, the availability of other cool storage, and the kind of food and drink the household likes.

Refrigerators normally have two compartments, a small ice-making/frozen food storage compartment at the top which has a normal temperature of −6°C to −18°C according to size and design, and a main compartment which operates at 4–7°C.

Refrigerators work on the principle that when a liquid vaporizes it draws heat from its surroundings. The liquid which does this is called the refrigerant and it works in a sealed system which includes the tubes forming the 'evaporator' in a refrigerator.

There are two types of refrigerator; these are the *compressor* which uses an electric motor and is more widely used, and the *absorption* model which operates without motor or other moving part.

Because the refrigeration cycle is achieved by heating only, absorption models can operate from electricity, gas or bottled gas, and models using paraffin (kerosene) can still be found.

The compressor model cools more quickly than the absorption; it also uses about half the amount of energy. On the other hand, absorption models are completely silent and make refrigeration possible where there is no mains supply.

Star markings

Refrigerators are described both by capacity and by ability to store frozen foods in good condition for a particular length of time. BS 3739 sets out the system of 'star marking' which indicates the depth of temperature maintained inside the frozen food storage compartment.

Celsius

4°–7°	Average temperature range in main cabinet of refrigerator
0°	Freezing point of water
−6°	Temperature of frozen food storage compartment in * ('one star') refrigerator: frozen food can be kept for one week.
−12°	Temperature of frozen food storage compartment in ** ('two star') refrigerator: frozen food can be kept for one month.
−18°	Temperature of frozen food storage compartment in *** ('three star') refrigerator: frozen food can be kept for three months.

In order to buy the most practical and economical type of refrigerator ('one', 'two' or 'three' star) the anticipated turnover of frozen food should be taken into account. A 'two star' refrigerator is usually considered the most practical for normal household use.

Running costs
These are nominal, varying from model to model. Most refrigerators use on average between 1 and 2 units of electricity or 0.1 to 0.2 gas therms per day, but absorption models use more energy, size for size, than compressor refrigerators.

Sizes
Experience shows that once a refrigerator has been installed, maximum use is made of it; it is wise, therefore, to choose the largest suitable model. Refrigerators range from 30–350 litres capacity, 100 litres being about the smallest practical size for a small family. It is sensible to allow at least 30/50 litres capacity per person, but if a freezer is also used by the family, a slightly smaller refrigerator may be practical.

The small models below 100 litres in capacity are useful in flatlets, bed-sitters, caravans or where extra refrigeration (say, a house 'bar') is needed. Very small refrigerators which can be stood on a working surface or hung on a wall are useful for elderly or disabled people. These often use bottled gas and some have the added advantage of being portable.

Styles
Modern insulating materials allow maximum storage capacity without increasing overall dimensions. There are several styles to choose from, such as the models with work-tops, up to about 150 litres in capacity, which provide useful additional working space, and tall, slim refrigerators to fit in where floor space is at a premium. 'Fridge-freezers' are increasingly popular; these incorporate a proper food freezer, capable of freezing fresh food as distinct from merely storing ready-frozen foods. The ratio of freezer to fridge space in these models varies but is usually about 4:5. Separate, matching refrigerators and freezers are available. The refrigerators are usually 'larder fridges' without ice-making compartments. The units can be stacked one above the other, by means of a special stacking kit, or they can stand side by side.

Construction and finish
The external finish on a refrigerator or 'fridge-freezer' is usually white, sometimes with a chrome or coloured trim. Coloured models are occasionally available and some have wood effect finishes. Most of the interiors are made of a moulded strong plastic material in white or a pastel colour.

Doors are front-opening, generally right-hand hinged, and have magnetic fastenings. A few models are available with an alternative left-hand hinge.

Interior design
While litre capacity is an indication of the amount of internal space, this space can be divided in a number of ways. The design and positioning of shelves, frozen food storage compartment, vegetable drawers, bottle racks, and other special containers vary from model to model. The design of the interior should be assessed according to your needs, and you should, therefore, inspect as many models as possible before making a final choice.

Installation
An electrically powered refrigerator simply needs plugging into a 13 amp earthed socket outlet. Other types are equally easily connected to the gas supply or paraffin or bottled gas containers. Any refrigerator should stand on a level surface and be positioned to allow free air circulation around it. Models are available for building into a fitted kitchen. If this is done, careful attention should be paid to the manufacturer's instructions with regard to allowing circulation of air around the refrigerator.

Controls
Control of temperature within a refrigerator is very simple. A dial on one of the inside walls controls a thermostat which keeps the temperature constant. A domestic refrigerator is designed to maintain a temperature of between 4°C and 7°C within the main body of the cabinet. Manufacturers usually indicate the normal setting for each model in the appropriate instruction book and this setting should be adjusted only in very hot and humid weather.

Methods of defrosting

The defrost control is usually linked with the thermostat. If ice is allowed to build up on the evaporator, the refrigerator works less efficiently, so that when ice has collected to a thickness of about 1cm it should be removed. There are three methods of defrosting.

Manual defrosting

The control dial must be set to 'off' or 'defrost'. The food should be removed from the refrigerator and from the frozen food storage compartment. Any packets of frozen food should be wrapped closely together in clean newspaper and put in a cool place during the defrosting process; they should then be returned, as soon as possible after defrosting is completed.

As the ice melts during defrosting, water collects in the drip tray beneath the evaporator. A bowl of hot water on a shelf in the refrigerator speeds up this process. When all the ice has melted, the interior, the evaporator, and the cabinet should be dried with a clean cloth; the controls can then be reset and the food replaced.

'Push-button' defrosting

This is sometimes known as 'semi-automatic' defrosting, and is carried out by pressing the special 'defrost' button. The refrigeration system stops and the ice melts as above. When the defrosting is over, the refrigeration cycle starts up again automatically. There is sometimes a rapid defrosting device in the refrigerator whereby heat is introduced into the evaporator. The manufacturer's instructions with regard to the removal of food should be carefully followed.

Fully automatic defrosting

This takes place at frequent intervals, so that there should be no build-up of ice, nor any need to remove food. Any melted ice is usually absorbed by a wick at the back or base of the refrigerator, from which it slowly evaporates.

Cleaning

A refrigerator needs very little other attention. Any inside spills should be mopped up at once, and the cabinet should be washed out occasionally after defrosting with warm water with a little bicarbonate of soda or detergent dissolved in it. The outside can be washed with warm soapy water and given a polish from time to time to keep it in good condition. Occasionally one may find that the cabinet develops an odour from food accidentally left uncovered or spilled, or if the refrigerator has been switched off for a period for some reason. Washing the interior with water and bicarbonate of soda usually removes the smell, but it may be necessary to leave it turned off, with the door open, until the smell has gone.

Wrapping or covering food

When food is put in a refrigerator it loses its heat and a certain amount of moisture. For this reason it is advisable to wrap or cover all food before placing it inside. This prevents evaporation and excessive build-up of ice. Foods can be stored either in their own containers, if suitable, or in clean bowls or polythene boxes, or on plates, after being covered with clingfilm wrapping or foil. Commercially frozen foods and ice creams should be left in their own containers and put into the frozen food storage compartment as soon as possible.

Where to store food

The coldest part of the refrigerator is the shelf immediately below the frozen food storage compartment, and wet fish, raw meat, and offal are best kept there (take care that they do not drip on to food below). Cooked food, cooking fats, cheese, leftovers and any prepared cold desserts can be placed anywhere in the main section of the refrigerator: milk, butter, and drinks should be placed in their special racks; salad vegetables, fruit, and mushrooms should go in the vegetable drawer. Fruits with a strong flavour such as melon, strawberries or pineapple will soon pass on their flavour to dairy foods in the refrigerator; so if these need chilling, they should be wrapped well or put in a container with a tightly fitting lid. They should be left in the refrigerator for as short a time as possible. Eggs can be stored at the bottom of the refrigerator, where they should keep for two months.

Hot food which is still steaming will raise the

temperature inside the cabinet unduly, and soon cause excess frosting on the evaporator. It is wise, therefore, to cool food thoroughly, and as quickly as possible, *before* putting it in the refrigerator.

More detailed guidance about storage and the correct use of a refrigerator can be obtained from the manufacturer's instruction booklet.

Going away

If anticipating a period of disuse, run down stocks, then turn off, defrost and dry the refrigerator. Leave with the door slightly open, otherwise a musty smell may develop inside. Wedge a folded tea-towel in the door, and then, with a piece of adhesive tape, fix it so as to prevent the door swinging wide open.

Home Freezers

Methods of freezing and storage are discussed in the chapter on Home Freezing. This section covers buying and using a freezer.

Frozen food symbol

A food freezer can be identified by the food freezing symbol – a large six-pointed star enclosed in a rectangular frame together with the three-star symbol for frozen food storage in refrigerators. It distinguishes between appliances designed merely for the storage of frozen foods, normally called conservators, and those designed to freeze as well as to store it. The weight of food which can be frozen in the cabinet, within 24 hours, without lowering the quality of frozen food already inside it, is shown in the instructions supplied with the freezer and on the rating plate fixed to it.

Styles and sizes of freezer

There are three basic types of freezer, the first two operating off electricity only.

1) The chest type has a top opening lid. Sizes range from about 120 litres to over 600 litres capacity. Removable wire baskets or trays are available, which facilitate easier packing. Larger models have counter-balanced lids and interior lights. Some have a lock and key, and some have laminated work-tops on their lids. Chest freezers offer easier storage than upright freezers for large items like joints of meat and whole salmon.

2) The upright type has a front opening door and takes up less floor space. It is easier to place, pack, unpack, and defrost, and makes stock-taking easy. The fittings usually include one or more fixed shelves through which the refrigerant medium circulates in fine pipes, and some shelves which are removable. Some models contain baskets which slide in and out and others may have drop-down guards on the front of the shelves. Sizes range from 120 litres to around 300 litres; there are also some small 60 litre models which may be stood on a working surface. Some of the bigger upright freezers have two doors.

3) A combination freezer/refrigerator comprises an upright freezer and matching refrigerator of approximately the same capacity (150–200 litres). They are usually housed in the same cabinet with separate doors, the freezer being underneath or beside the refrigerator. Some models are also available with a smaller refrigerator and a larger freezer, and others with a large refrigerator and small freezer.

Controls

The controls of a freezer hardly vary from one model to another. They generally consist of:

1) An 'ON' light which glows all the time to show that the freezer is working.

2) A warning light that comes on only if, for any reason, the temperature inside the freezer rises too high. As soon as this light is seen to be on, the cause must be established and qualified help enlisted if necessary.

3) A 'fast freezing' light which shows that the 'fast freezer' is operating.

Note To avoid a plug being accidentally pulled out or switched off, either have the freezer specially wired to a spur plug, or cover the complete plug top and switch with adhesive tape.

Timing

The time required to freeze individual packs of food cannot be assessed as they vary greatly in size, shape, and consistency, but once each pack is frozen solid it can be stacked in the storage zone. The manufacturer's instructions should always be followed when putting food in the freezer (see also the chapter on Home Freezing).

A 'fast freezing' switch (which may be called by another name) is available on some freezers, and its function is to override the thermostat so that the internal temperature does not stay at the storage temperature of −18°C, but goes on falling lower. It is recommended that the switch is turned on about two hours before any large quantity of fresh food is introduced into the freezer and left on until that batch of food is frozen hard (usually about 24 hours), after which the switch may be returned to the normal setting. As the main purpose of this switch is to safeguard the food already in the freezer by keeping its temperature at or below −18°C, it is not necessary to use it when introducing only a small quantity of food, up to about 0.5kg in weight.

Running cost

Food freezers use, on average, about 1 unit of electricity per week for each 15 litres capacity, although larger models may well use a little less. For the most economical running, keep the freezer in cool, dry surroundings, do not open it too often, try to keep it about three-quarters full, and defrost it regularly according to the manufacturer's instructions. Chest freezers are slightly cheaper to buy and fractionally cheaper to run.

Siting a freezer

A freezer can be kept almost anywhere, even in a garage or corridor, provided there is adequate air circulation around the cabinet so that it remains cool and dry. It should be run from a suitable 13 or 15 amp three-pin earthed electric socket outlet where it can remain permanently connected. If the freezer is sited in a garage or an outhouse it should be raised on wooden blocks to encourage air circulation all round it and to prevent rust. In particularly damp situations it may be advisable to have the base of the cabinet undersealed like a car; and in the case of upright freezers the floor should be tested before installation, to make sure that it will bear the weight of the fully loaded cabinet. Wherever it is kept, the cabinet must stand level.

Defrosting

Chest freezers should be defrosted at least once or twice a year on average. Upright models (unless they have fully automatic defrost) may need to be defrosted two or three times a year. In either case it should obviously be done when stocks are fairly low; perhaps after Christmas or a school holiday. Follow the manufacturer's instructions and bear in mind a few general guidelines:

1) Switch off the electricity and empty the freezer completely. Stack all the packs of food tightly together in a large box or other suitable container. Cover closely with sheets of clean newspaper and a blanket. Spread a towel at the bottom of the cabinet to catch the ice and facilitate its removal.

2) Bowls of hot water can be placed on the shelves of an upright freezer to hurry the thawing of the ice. Do this in a chest freezer only if the manufacturer recommends it.

3) As soon as the ice begins to loosen, scrape it off with a blunt wooden or plastic spatula. Never use a metal scraper.

4) When all the ice has melted and has been removed, wash the inside walls of the freezer with warm water in which a little bicarbonate of soda has been dissolved and dry it thoroughly before closing the lid or door.

5) Switch on the electricity and return the food to the cabinet immediately. Take the opportunity to bring the inventory up to date, and note which stocks you need to replace and which packs should be used first.

6) Polish the outside of the freezer with a little silicone polish.

Servicing

When buying a freezer, make sure to find out the address and telephone number for service calls. (The supplier will tell you whether to contact him or the manufacturer.) The number should be written on an adhesive label and stuck on the freezer in an obvious place. Most freezers, however, function for years unimpaired.

Service contracts are sometimes available, but you may consider this facility unnecessary. A large freezer ought to have its contents insured against loss in the event of a breakdown. Most insurance companies offer this extra cover within a general household policy; if not, brokers who specialize in this type of insurance offer nominal premium rates. See also the section on Guarantees and Servicing, pp74–76.

Power cuts

If the electricity supply has to be interrupted for any reason, and due warning has been given, turn the freezing control on to get the internal temperature of the freezer as low as possible before the supply is cut. Also take out any stocks required during this preliminary period. Do *not* open the freezer again until power is restored. All food will remain in perfect condition for at least six to eight hours with these precautions, and few planned cuts last as long as this.

Some localized accidental interruptions may last longer, or a breakdown or accidental switch-off of your own freezer may occur, so that there is a longer inoperative period. In this case, estimate how long food normally takes to thaw; the close-packed mass of food in the freezer will certainly take longer. Even then it does not immediately go bad but is simply thawed naturally and is perfectly edible.

After a cut, check through the contents of the freezer, use up immediately the most perishable items such as ice cream, offal, fish, and any food in sauce, and treat the rest as follows: Some foods – fruit in syrup, bread, and cakes – soften quickly but will not necessarily suffer if refrozen. Some foods which are slightly thawed can be frozen again, provided that the packs are fully sealed, and are used fairly quickly. There will be no health risk in this but the texture and flavour of the food may have suffered somewhat. Meat and fish usually remain frozen for the longest periods, but check through the individual packs. If they are still solidly frozen, all should be well. If the worst happens and a breakdown is not discovered for some days, it is usually very obvious that none of the food is safe to eat, and it should be destroyed, preferably

by burning. If the smell of decomposed food is very persistent, it is wise to defrost again and then to wash the inside of the cabinet thoroughly, leaving the lid or door open for some days until the smell has vanished; do not attempt to switch on and repack the freezer until all appears to be normal.

Removal

Most removal contractors have experience of moving food freezers and will probably explain that there is no need to empty a freezer unless one is travelling a considerable distance. Before moving, be certain where the freezer will stand in the new home. Check that the electricity supply will be turned on there, have the right size of plug ready to connect to the freezer, turn the freezing control as low as it will go for a few hours before the time of removal and try to get the freezer loaded on to the van last of all so that it will be the first off. Check that the overall weight can be moved by the removal men.

If you know your moving date well enough in advance, you can, of course, run down the contents of the freezer and have it moved empty.

Dishwashers

Dishwashers provide an efficient, labour-saving method of washing tableware and kitchen utensils. Most models are fully automatic and simple to operate. They do demand a revision of established kitchen routine, but once this is accepted they save both time and trouble.

A dishwasher will wash, rinse, and dry a full load of dishes in an average time of 80–90 minutes, depending on the type. Manual operations are restricted to loading, setting the controls, and unloading, and scraping off heavily encrusted dirt. The machine gets on with the job on its own once the controls have been set, so the only time spent with it is the few minutes needed to load and unload the machine. Because of the high water temperature used, glass, china, and cutlery are left clean and hygienic, and saucepans, especially those with non-stick finishes, can also be put in. It is most economical only to use the machine when it is full, so it may be necessary to buy enough tableware for a day's requirements.

Machines are front-loading and usually designed to fit into a run of standard kitchen units, but some are small enough to stand on a work surface. Space is needed at the back of the machine for pipes and at the front for opening the door.

Choosing a dishwasher

The size chosen will depend on the space available, the size of the household, the number of meals eaten at home, and the amount of entertaining done. A small family would do best with one of the small models standing on a work space. In order to fill a standard machine it would need duplicate sets of crockery. The capacity of a dishwasher is usually indicated by the number of standard place settings a machine will hold and wash at once. The number varies between four and fourteen place settings. Most people find that it is more practical to choose one which will take ten or twelve place settings at a time.

A British Standard place setting consists of: 1×25cm dinner plate, 1 soup plate, 1 side plate, 1 cup, 1 saucer, 1 glass, 1 knife, 1 fork, 1 teaspoon, 1 dessertspoon, 1 soup spoon plus a few additional serving pieces and utensils.

It is a good idea to take a dinner plate when choosing a dishwasher to ensure that the model you want holds your largest plate size.

Finish

The external finish is usually white smooth or vitreous enamel, stainless steel or PVC coated steel. Most machines have the control panel across the front, at the top.

Fittings

1) Racks: Much of the success of a dishwasher depends on the size and shape of its racks. Hot water must be able to reach all surfaces of the utensils. There are usually two plastic-coated wire racks, in sections. Generally they are mounted on nylon rollers to allow them to slide partially out of the machine when being loaded. The sections are designed to hold specific items, so study the variations carefully, since each

machine is different. Choose yours as far as possible in relation to the utensils and crockery used in your household.

2) Built-in water softeners: These are an advantage in hard water areas to help economize on detergent and to leave a sparkling finish on the dishes. Alternatively, a water softener can be fitted to the water inlet. Water softeners have to be recharged regularly with coarse salt, but this is simple.

3) Sound-absorbing insulation: Dishwashers can be rather noisy and some include acoustic insulation to keep noise to a minimum.

4) Plate warming: Some models offer a separate hot air cycle for drying or plate warming.

Installation and water supply

A dishwasher must be connected to the water supply and drainage system, and to the electricity supply by a separate earthed 13 or 15 amp socket. It can either be plumbed in or connected to taps by hose pipes. Plumbing-in is recommended as this leaves the taps free for other purposes. Local water board regulations should be checked to find out if a permanent connection is permitted. Follow the manufacturer's instructions when having the machine connected up. Most dishwashers are connected to the cold water supply; some can be connected to the household hot water supply which makes the cycle quicker, and may also reduce the running cost of the dishwasher.

Drainage

Dishwashers are emptied into the drainage system either by pump or by gravity. For pump emptying, the discharge hose should rise at least above the level of water in the machine; for gravity emptying, the discharge hose should never be raised above the bottom of the washing chamber. Check local regulations before installation.

The washing cycle

There are four basic steps to a washing cycle:

1) Heating: Water from the hot or cold water supply is heated to a thermostatically controlled temperature of about 65°C.

2) Washing: All dishwashers make use of water pressure to carry out the cleaning process. The water may be sprayed round the dishes from above or below through revolving or rotating arms. Some models incorporate sprays from above and below the dishes. But however it is done, the object is to cascade water round the dishes from every direction in order to wash them thoroughly. During the cycle, food particles from the dirty dishes are trapped by a filter which may be self-cleaning – if not, this needs regular attention. Some models disperse food particles automatically without the use of filters.

3) Rinsing: According to the programme, the dishes are rinsed in hot, warm or cool water to which a rinse aid is added by an automatic dispenser.

4) Drying: This is carried out either by a fan-assisted heater or by the residual heat of the hot water after the washing cycle.

All this is controlled automatically by a rotary selector switch and an on/off switch. The machine will stop if the door is opened during the operating cycle.

What to put in

Most household crockery and cutlery can be washed in a dishwasher, but any encrusted dirt must first be scraped off. Pots and pans can be cleaned successfully, providing that there is no burnt-on food.

It is advisable not to put the following things into a dishwasher:

Pans and cutlery with wooden, plastic or bone handles

Hand-painted porcelain and any old, precious china

Painted or lead crystal glass ware

Narrow-necked vessels

Wooden or non-heat-resistant plastic utensils

Many manufacturers make utensils and tableware specially suited for washing in a dishwasher, so look for this assurance when buying new pots, pans, and tableware.

Loading the machine

Always follow the manufacturer's instructions,

because dishes and cutlery should be placed correctly to obtain the best cleaning effect and to make the best use of the racks. Cups and glasses should face downwards to allow water to drain away from them during the drying cycle.

Some machines have a short rinsing programme which can be used as soon as the dishes are put inside to prevent food hardening on the surface.

Detergents

Specially formulated detergents must be used in a dishwasher. Some machines have a built-in detergent dispenser which adds the necessary amount of detergent at the correct point in a washing cycle. Other machines require the detergent to be added by hand before they are switched on. Most well known dishwashing detergents are approved for safe performance by the British Ceramics Research Association. It is safest to use the one specially recommended by the manufacturer of your machine.

Rinse aids

A rinse aid (wetting agent) is used to reduce the surface tension of the water at the end of the operation. It may be in liquid or powder form and its purpose is to help the water drain away quickly, and to reduce spotting, streaking, and filming, which may be especially noticeable in hard water areas. Most machines have a rinse aid dispenser, which only needs filling occasionally, and which injects rinse aid automatically into the water during the rinsing cycle.

Programmes

Some dishwashers have one all-purpose washing programme. Others have different programmes to deal with different types of load, such as a special one for glass. Others may be switched on simply for a cold rinse or for heating clean plates.

Running costs

A twelve-setting dishwasher uses about 2.5 units of electricity per full load, plus the cost of the detergent (usually about 25–40 grams).

Care and maintenance

Dishwashers need little daily care as they are

self-cleaning inside. Clean the food filters when necessary. Wipe the outside with a damp cloth when required and use a little silicone polish occasionally. Make sure you have the name and telephone number of a contact in case of a breakdown. As with freezers, service contracts are sometimes available; ask your supplier at the time of purchase.

Washing Machines, Spin Dryers, and Electric Irons

See the chapter on Care of Textiles and Hard Surfaces.

Waste Disposers

A waste disposer offers an effective and hygienic – though expensive – way of disposing of most kinds of household waste. Almost all kitchen waste is accepted, the few exceptions being string, bacon rinds, bandages, metal, plastic and large pieces of glass. (Stringy waste twists round the grinder, and paper and plastic pulps into a solid ball unless first torn up.) Small bones can go down, but not large joint bones or large hard stones from peaches or avocado pears. If the waste is to drain into a septic tank it may be necessary to enlarge this.

Installation

Most waste disposal units measure 45×20cm and have to be fixed permanently to a 7cm diameter outlet in the kitchen sink. Most modern stainless steel sinks are fitted with these outlets, but although they can be cut into an existing stainless steel sink, an old ceramic sink nearly always has to be replaced before the waste disposer can be fixed. The unit fits into the average cupboard below a sink and the electric socket outlet with control switch is usually fixed nearby. This should still leave plenty of room for cleaning materials, as long as easy access is available for servicing the disposer when necessary.

As installation costs vary, estimates from more than one contractor should be considered.

How they work

Waste matter is spun at high speed against a shredding ring which pulverizes it and the resulting 'slurry' is washed away with cold water in the main drainage system. In the continuous-feed type the waste is fed in after turning on the cold water and switching on the electricity, while in 'batch-feed' models waste is fed in and the cover fixed before the electricity and water are turned on. Some people consider this is the safest type as the machine will not operate unless the cover is in position. Waste disposers are noisy, but as they are normally used for only 30 seconds at a time to grind away rubbish, the noise level is never likely to be intolerable.

Safety

A model which is constructed to British Standards conforms not only to electrical safety but also ensures that the machine cannot be switched on when hands are near the blades. Sometimes, however, things slip down past the guard. If a teaspoon or a vegetable knife accidentally falls into the grinder, the overload switch on the body of the waste disposer cuts out. Once the jam is cleared, it is a simple matter to press the reset button that brings it back into use. On some models, the grinders are set to revolve in the opposite direction when the disposer is switched off, so a jam can often be cleared by simply switching the unit on and off again. Most makers supply a grinder cleaning tool – a large turncock which enables the grinders to be moved in a reverse direction to clear the object jammed between the grinder and the sides.

Running cost

Most units are powered by a 220 watt motor, and the running cost is very small – about 50kg for a unit of electricity.

Smaller Labour-saving Appliances

The appliances described below all need a 13 amp socket. They are listed in alphabetical order, rather than in fixed order of importance. A household which often eats large roast joints may find an electric carving knife invaluable, whilst a vegetarian household will have less use for it, but may rely a great deal on a juice extractor. Every family has slightly different priorities and must choose which aids suit its needs best.

Servicing and guarantees are dealt with in the chapter on Care and Maintenance of the Home.

Blenders
These are described in the chapter on Mixer, Blender and Processor Cookery.

Can opener
Some can openers are designed for wall mounting, others are table models, and some large mixers carry one as an optional attachment. All models work in the same way: a magnet holds the can against the cutting wheel, a lever is pulled over to grip the can edge, and a motor drives a cutter round the top edge of the can.

Carving knife
An electric carving knife essentially is a pair of swiftly moving blades which slide backwards and forwards in opposite directions, rubbing against each other. Hand pressure makes the blades cut downwards through the fibres.

Coffee grinder and coffee mill
In a coffee *grinder* the beans fall from a container on to two discs or cones – one rotating, one fixed. The size of coffee can be varied by altering the clearance between the discs. In a coffee *mill* the beans are broken by cutting blades at high speeds and the contents remain in this container.

A coffee mill will also make breadcrumbs, grind spices, chop nuts, and some can make caster sugar from granulated sugar. After grinding spices, thorough cleaning is necessary.

For information on making coffee, see the chapter on Beverages.

Contact grill
Previously called an infra-red grill, this has two heavy aluminium heating plates which make direct

Portable contact grill

contact with the food, above and below it, thereby ensuring rapid cooking by both conduction and the penetrating infra-red heat. The cooking area ranges from approximately 18 × 20cm to approximately 30 × 30cm. The upper plate has an adjustable open hinge to accommodate foods of varying thickness; it is also useful when using a shallow baking tin in which soft foods are cooked. Both upper and lower plates are ribbed, giving an attractive pattern to the food. The ribs seal the food quickly, while the depressions allow infra-red heat to radiate backwards and forwards between the plates, cooking the food quickly and thoroughly. As both plates are usually coated with a non-stick material, sticking does not often occur. In a few models it is possible to open the lid through 180° so that twice the area is available either as a griddle, or for heating dishes. In this case, the handles act as a firm support. On some models the plates can be removed for washing in the sink; some have alternative plates with sealed edges for small toasted sandwiches or waffles.

Cooker hood
This is a metal hood placed over a cooker to trap grease, smells, and steam. A fan collects these as they rise, and passes them through filters of aluminium or plastic foam to catch the grease, while a bed of charcoal traps the steam and smells. The

main filter is usually easy to remove for cleaning, which should be done at least once a month when a cooker is in normal family use. Some cooker hoods can be fitted with a vent through an outside wall, which makes them more effective.

A cooker hood should never be more than 915mm above a hob; between 560mm and 770mm is the best height. With an eye-level grill it is best if the canopy is brought out 127mm from the wall. Space between the eye-level grill and the hood should be no more than 458mm. The 610mm hood suits most cookers and the most practical arrangement is to fit one below wall cupboards, flanked by cupboards on either side.

Deep fat fryer

The electric fat fryer has thermostatic control, normally with settings between 130°–190°C, and is therefore always at the right temperature. It is fitted with a basket which on some models can be gradually lowered into the fat by an elevator lever. Some also have a lid fitted with a filter which degreases and deodorizes the steam given off – about 0.5kg of steam containing oil droplets from every 1kg of chips. The grease filter is removable and needs to be replaced after about a hundred fryings. The steam diffuser can be removed and washed in the sink. Other fat fryers cook with their lids open.

Deep fat fryers take about twelve minutes to heat the oil or fat up to the correct temperature. A red signal light goes on during heating and goes out when the correct temperature is reached. The light comes on again as the food is immersed, as this lowers the oil temperature, and it will continue to go on and off during the cooking period as the temperature of the oil varies.

Cooking times vary depending on the degree of crispness required, but about four to six minutes is an average.

Electric kettle

This provides a very efficient method of heating water: 1.7 litres will boil in approximately 3.75 minutes, which is much quicker than boiling a kettle on a ring or plate.

Kettles are filled either through a removable lid or through the spout. In use, they should neither be overfilled nor underfilled; they should always contain sufficient water to cover the element. There is a mark inside all British Electrotechnical Approvals Board (BEAB) approved kettles showing the maximum filling level, and usually one showing the minimum level as well.

All BEAB approved kettles are fitted with safety devices which cut off the current before the kettle boils dry. The safety device acts when the temperature of the kettle begins to rise, as happens when there is too little water to carry off the heat. The safety device may cut the current off in one of two ways:

1) by a switch which is thermostatically controlled
2) by releasing a spring plugger which ejects the connector from the kettle.

In some kettles the vapour from the boiling water causes the current to be automatically switched off, the heat operating a small thermostat.

Wall kettles are water heaters which fill from a cold tap, and can boil up to 4 litres of water at a time. They have a 2.5–3 kW heater.

Extractor fan

An extractor fan is sited on an outside wall to collect and expel cooking smells from the air of the kitchen as a whole. The amount of air a fan can handle depends entirely on the size of its blades, not the size of its casing. Any kitchen needs a fan which can change the air between twelve and sixteen times an hour if cooking smells are to be disposed of as they are created. To work out the size of fan needed, first calculate the size of the room in cubic metres, multiplying its height by its length by its width. Then multiply the total by fifteen to get the cubic metres per hour extraction rate. Consult the manufacturer's brochures to find a fan which can achieve this rate. Given that it is the right size, a fan need only be switched on for a short time, as this cuts down the heat wastage which occurs if too much warm air is sucked out of the kitchen with the smells.

To prevent cold air from outside getting into the kitchen, any extractor fan must have louvres on the outside, and some kind of automatic or manually operated baffle to close when the fan is not switched on. There are fans with a reversing action for drawing in cool air deliberately – a simple kind of air conditioning – which can be useful if the kitchen gets over-hot; they have a choice of two speeds, and the switching is on a control box. Most smaller fans have only a pull-cord switch and operate at only one speed, but this is adequate for the average kitchen.

The position of the extractor fan is important. It should be placed as high as possible and near the cooker – if possible between the cooker and the door leading to the rest of the home. The aim of this is to avoid a short circuit of the air, by not siting the extractor opposite the main source of replacement air.

Food mixer

These are described in the chapter on Mixer, Blender and Processor Cookery.

Food processor

These are described in the chapter on Mixer, Blender and Processor Cookery.

Frypan

This is a shallow plug-in cooker which will fry, stew, poach, or act as a griddle for making scones; it is also useful for keeping food hot, and for warming plates, and costs less to run than using the oven for the same jobs. Models with a lid can be used for roasting, and even for baking cakes, so the appliance is sometimes called a 'multi-cooker'.

Hot trolley and tray

This appliance simplifies serving hot food and keeps it piping hot. Food can be served in the dining-room at the table, and kept hot for second helpings (see the chapter on Presenting a Meal).

Dishes can be placed on it ready for serving, which allows time for saucepans to be washed up before a meal.

The best heat retention is provided by a model with glass dishes set into a heated surround. However, a hot tray with heated surface allows one to use one's own serving dishes, and also to keep plates warm.

Using a hot tray costs less than keeping an oven on a low heat to do the same work.

Ice cream maker

The essential parts are slow-moving paddles which churn the ice cream mixture when it is in the ice-making compartment of a refrigerator, or in a home freezer, thus preventing the formation of large ice crystals. The paddles stop automatically as soon as the ice cream is the right consistency. More information and recipes for making home made ices are given in the chapter on Ices and Frozen Desserts.

Juice extractor

There are two kinds:

A *citrus press* has a juice cone, sieve, and juice container in one unit; the cone revolves when a half piece of fruit is pressed down on it.

A *centrifugal juice extractor* makes juice from any fruit or vegetable. It works like a miniature spin dryer. The fruit is pulped and pushed against a sieve revolving at high speed. Some machines have filter papers which act like a jelly bag, trapping solid matter and giving a clearer juice.

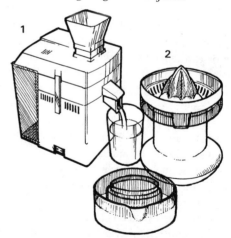

*Juice extractors: **1** centrifugal extractor; **2** citrus press*

Knife sharpener

This is a useful tool, as all cooking knives should be kept sharp. The knife is placed between two grinding wheels at the correct angle. The wheels rotate at speed and produce a very fine edge on the knife when it is pulled against them.

Most knife sharpeners also sharpen scissors and small chisels, and screwdrivers can be honed too.

Rôtisserie and grill

This cooks meat and poultry very evenly, and requires little attention. Some electric ovens contain a rôtisserie or turning spit. There are separate rôtisserie units, both table and wall-mounted models, which will also grill, bake, and cook kebabs. Gas-fired models are also available.

Slow cooking pot

The electric low-temperature cooking pot or casserole simply applies a modern fuel to traditional long cooking of food at low temperatures.

Some delicate foods are cooked in about five hours, but most recipes need between eight and twelve hours cooking time. Few of the pots are thermostatically controlled, but because of the low heat level, they may safely be left unattended for long periods during the day. The food can be prepared and set to cook before one leaves home and is ready on return. Once cooked, a dish can be kept at serving temperature without spoiling.

Although the design, size, and colour of these cookers vary, there are basic features common to all. Each consists of an internally glazed stoneware or earthenware pot with a lid. Some of the pots are removable from their base, which contains a tubular heating element; others have an element wound round their sides behind a protective casing. Capacity of the standard cooking pot is between 1.5 and 3.5 litres. Loading of the electric element is between 60 and 180 watts, so even the largest is extremely inexpensive to operate. There is usually one control with two settings – high and low – and a neon indicator light which comes on as soon as the mains switch is turned on.

The flex connector may be unplugged from some models, so that the cooker can be taken to the table. With most of them, the interior pot is simply lifted out to be taken to the table, and cleaning in the sink afterwards is simple.

This method of cooking is particularly suitable for cuts of meat which need long, gentle cooking to tenderize them; for offal, fish, soups, and sauces; and for poached fruit and steamed puddings.

Careful laboratory tests have proved that if the basic instructions are followed, food reaches the required temperatures for destroying any micro-organisms which may be present. Some foods and liquids should be put into the casserole hot and some manufacturers recommend that for some recipes the pot should be preheated.

Preparatory cooking such as browning vegetables and meat in fat is done first, in a separate pan.

Teamaker

The bedside teamaker has a clock that can be set for the time early morning tea is wanted. In some, tea or tea bags are placed in a basket which drops into the hot water when it reaches the right temperature. In most, water heated in a separate container bubbles through a spout into the teapot. The alarm sounds when the tea begins to brew.

Toaster

This holds two slices of bread (a few models can hold four) and toasts both sides of each slice simultaneously. A dial is set to determine the length of time the current is switched on, and when the current is automatically switched off, the toast springs up. Some models have a browning control which adjusts itself automatically to the moisture content of the bread. Since the toaster does its work so quickly, it is the most economical way of making toast, especially when only one or two slices are needed.

Yoghurt maker

This provides very low, controlled heat at the right temperature to encourage the rapid development of a yoghurt-making culture in prepared milk. It makes about a litre of yoghurt, for use at once or for refrigerator storage.

Making yoghurt is described on p876.

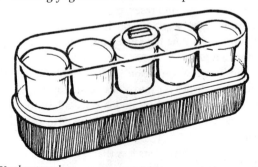

Yoghurt maker

Pots, Pans, Dishes, Tools, and Containers

As kitchen tools, pots, and pans have to stand up to hard wear and you will expect them to last a long time, it is wise to buy well-designed, good-quality equipment. Look for such things as hanging rings, neatly designed storage racks, and stackability. You will want pots and pans that are easy to clean and in some cases dishwasher-proof. Draw up a list of essentials and be prepared to pay a good price for items which you will use frequently and over a long period of time.

Small kitchen equipment in vitreous enamel and plastic can be both colourful and serviceable.

Choice of material

Aluminium conducts heat evenly so that food does not hot-spot (ie burn on certain areas of the base). Its main disadvantage is its tendency to discolour and pit in use, but with care pitting can be avoided (and discoloration can be removed, see p86). Pans of medium or heavy gauge quality will keep their shape and last well and are certainly worth buying. Lightweight pans are only suitable for gas cookers and are not worth buying for long-term use. If plain aluminium seems dull, look for pans coated with coloured vitreous enamel or a sprayed-on polyimide finish. The vitreous enamel finish is slightly more durable than polyimide, which tends to scratch.

Vitreous enamelled steel pans are available in a good choice of colours and patterned designs, though they are less efficient than other metals. They heat quickly but food tends to stick in them. Some pans have a special metallic coating on the base which, it is claimed, reduces hot-spotting. Pans with a metal rim round the top and lid are a good choice, as the metal protects the pan against chipping in the most vulnerable areas. Vitreous enamel does chip if carelessly handled.

Stainless steel, though expensive, is easy to look after, and good quality pans will give a lifetime of wear. Stainless steel does not conduct heat evenly, so most manufacturers overcome the problem of hot-spotting by bonding on or sandwiching into the base a layer of another metal which is a good conductor of heat – usually aluminium or copper. In some pans the sandwich construction extends up the sides of the pan and this cuts down spluttering when you are pouring from the pan. Stainless steel pans with a sprayed-on copper coating are less good value.

Cast iron and *cast aluminium* make heavy pans which are excellent for long, slow cooking. They are usually coated in vitreous enamel, which makes them easy to clean and attractive to look at. Cast iron pans treated with oil have a pleasant, natural look and do not rust in the way old fashioned untreated ones do.

Both cast iron and aluminium pans are the best choice for use on ceramic hobs, sealed electric hot plates, and solid fuel burners.

Copper conducts heat beautifully and evenly and is often the professional cook's choice for pans, but it is expensive. Although it looks attractive, copper takes a lot of cleaning, and the interior of the pan must be coated with tin, nickel or aluminium to prevent the copper reacting with foods to produce an unpleasant taste. Good quality copper pans should last a lifetime.

Non-stick coatings are often used on aluminium and vitreous enamel steel pans. They make pans easier to clean and are, obviously, very good on frying pans, milk pans, and other pans used for foods which stick. Manufacturers have improved the techniques used to make the coating adhere to the metal, thereby producing a much harder-wearing finish.

Care must be taken not to scratch the finish with metal utensils – use wooden spoons and spatulas instead. Avoid putting a non-stick pan on the heat without food or liquid in it.

Note For information on care of the above utensils, see pp84 and 86.

Choosing saucepans and frying pans

When buying these, watch the following points:
1) Choose pans which will fit exactly over the gas burner or electric ring, and which will suit your cooker (see above).
2) Ground base pans are necessary for use on ceramic tops and sealed (solid) electric hot-plates and solid fuel cookers.

3) Lids should fit well but move just enough to allow steam to escape. Be sure that the rim is easy to clean.

4) Handles need to be comfortable to hold and heat-resistant. Good plastic is the most practical material. Wood looks attractive but tends to char over heat. Metal handles should be hollow, as otherwise they become too hot to hold. Pans with a capacity of over three litres should have a short handle opposite the usual long one, to facilitate lifting. Check whether handles are dishwasher-proof.

5) Knobs and their collars also need to be heat-resistant, to prevent burning one's knuckles when raising the lid.

6) A continuous pouring rim ensures satisfactory pouring from every point; two pouring lips are an advantage on any pan, but essential on milk pans.

7) The pan should be curved slightly on the inside where the sides meet the base. This makes cleaning easier.

8) Stacking pans are useful where storage space is limited.

Frying pans

These need to be reasonably heavy with a good flat base. Aluminium with or without a non-stick coating heats evenly and is probably the most practical choice. Sloping sides make it easier to turn food over, though some people prefer the straight-sided traditional sauté pan. A lid is useful when sautéing or poaching food and a pouring lip is also an asset.

Casseroles

The most versatile casseroles are those which can be used in the oven or over direct heat, and are good-looking enough to bring to the table. Remember that very bulgy or tall pots take up a lot of oven and storage space.

Look for the following design points: handles which will stand up to oven heat and which can be easily gripped; a well-fitting lid but not too tight fitting unless it has a steam vent; easy clean lines.

Casseroles are available in the materials listed above for saucepans, all suitable for use in the oven and over direct heat.

Glass ceramic has the advantage of resisting extreme changes of temperature; casseroles of this material can be used over direct heat, in the oven, and can even be taken from a freezer and put straight in a hot oven without fear of cracking. The material conducts heat unevenly, however, so that hot-spotting occurs when pans are used on the hob. Lids are normally of ordinary ovenglass. Some casseroles have a detachable handle, doubling up as a saucepan.

Porcelain is used for expensive casseroles. It is tough, but should not be used over direct heat unless marked clearly as flameproof. Earthenware, pottery, and stoneware are attractive materials for oven-to-table casseroles, but can only be used in the oven.

Ovenglass, for use in the oven only, provides a very wide range of inexpensive casseroles and other oven dishes.

Bakeware

The most practical choice is aluminium. Cake, bun tins, etc can have a non-stick coating of *PTFE* or silicone which facilitates turning out cakes.

Tinware, though cheaper, needs special care to keep it free from rust.

Tools and cutlery

Sharp knives and other cutting tools are essential, so buy the best you can afford and take care of them. The blades of knives should always be protected not only to prevent them being damaged but also for your safety. A slotted or magnetic rack provides an easy method of storage and keeps knives handy for use. Failing this, keep them in a baize-lined drawer with divisions so that they are kept separate.

Other cutting tools such as scissors, graters, etc should be equally well protected during storage. Those in constant use are best kept on a hanging rack along with frying or basting spoons and ladles. For tools which are used less often, arrange a drawer with divisions.

Knives

Most kitchen knives have stainless steel blades. Some are hollow ground, straight or scalloped edged. This type retains its sharpness well. But there is nothing to beat a non-stainless steel blade for a really fine, sharp edge, and many people like to have at least one of this type for chopping and slicing.

Handles are usually of plastic or wood. It is important to test them for a comfortable grip and good balance. Check for dishwasher-proof quality, if required.

Start with a basic set of knives (see p214) and buy the more specialized ones as required.

Storage containers

Lids must fit well; storage jars should take for example 500g or 1kg of sugar or rice: they should be easy to grip and easy to clean.

Bread-bins should have ventilating holes in the side or lid.

Spice or dried herb containers should have screw-tops. Ideally they should be of dark glass, as spices and herbs deteriorate in strong light.

Plastic containers with airtight lids are excellent for cakes, biscuits, breakfast cereals, etc. If space is limited, choose the stacking variety.

Lidded plastic containers for use in store cupboard, refrigerator, and freezer are made in many practical shapes and sizes, and a selection of these is indispensable for every household.

See also the chapter on Stores and Storage.

List of Useful Kitchen Equipment

Note Equipment for bathroom and bedrooms etc, can be found in the chapter on Stores and Storage.

Pots and pans

Basic selection

4 saucepans with lids: 2 × 1.5 litres for vegetables, soups, and stews

1 × 3.4 litres for boiling joints, steaming puddings, etc

1 × 4.5 litres for larger quantities. A wire basket would be useful for blanching vegetables prior to freezing

1 × 1 litre non-stick milk pan

1 kettle – stainless steel, vitreous enamel or aluminium

1 × 20–23cm lidded frying-pan

Additional equipment

1 omelet pan: the even heating quality of copper and cast iron is an asset

1 steamer: this should be designed to fit over a pan of water; tiered steamers are also available, enabling two or three foods to be cooked over one burner or hot-plate

1 double boiler

1 deep fat fryer: this should be heavy quality with a removable basket

1 egg poacher, preferably non-stick, with little pans deep enough to hold a large egg each

1 fish kettle: a removable grid facilitates easy lifting of cooked fish

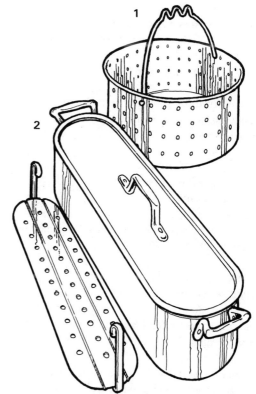

1 Steaming basket designed to fit into a saucepan;
2 fish kettle with perforated steaming platform for steaming fish whole

1 preserving pan: this should be made of medium to heavy quality aluminium, stainless steel, or enamel; sloping sides, and either two side handles or one on the side and one over the top, are design points to watch

1 colander: metal is a better choice than plastic

1 pressure cooker

Ovenware and bakeware
Basic selection

3 casseroles: two (2.5–3 litres) with lids and one shallow lidded casserole

1 au gratin dish: round or rectangular, and shallow enough to fit under the grill

3 pie dishes: 750ml, 1 litre, or 1.5 litre with rims

1 pie plate: 18–20cm diameter

1 roasting tin preferably with a non-stick finish

1 double roaster; non-stick

1 soufflé dish

6 ramekins

3 pudding basins: various sizes

1 cake tin: 15–20cm; a loose base is useful

2 sandwich tins: 20cm diameter

1 bun or tartlet (patty) tin (12 hole)

1 Swiss roll tin

1 gingerbread tin: square or rectangular

2 loaf tins: $20 \times 10 \times 6$cm, or $23 \times 13 \times 7$cm

1 baking sheet

Additional equipment

1 flan ring or loose base flan tin

1 fluted flan ring

1 ring tin

1 hinged pie mould: for raised meat or game pies

cream horn tins

Cookery utensils
Basic selection

2 wooden spoons

1 mixing bowl: preferably a pouring lip and a ridge for gripping

1 rolling-pin

2 wire cooling trays

1 pastry brush: nylon bristles are practical

1 chopping board/carving board/bread board

2 strainers, wire or nylon. Nylon have a finer mesh. May be drum-shaped, round or conical

1 nylon sieve

1 coffee strainer

1 tea strainer

1 metric measuring jug

1 set metric measuring spoons

1 set metric scales

1 whisk: choose between rotary for ease and speed, and the balloon type for small quantities and maximum volume

1 funnel: plastic or metal

1 lemon squeezer: those designed to catch the pips in the top and the juice in the base are particularly good

cutters, plain and fluted: metal tends to be sharper than plastic

1 plastic/rubber spatula: for scraping mixing bowls

1 pepper mill

Additional equipment

1 pastry blender

1 pastry wheel for fancy edges

icing nozzles and nylon piping bag: large bag and nozzles for cream, meringue, and potato; metal nozzles give the best definition

1 fat frying thermometer

1 sugar/jam thermometer

1 pestle and mortar

1 flour dredger

1 salad shaker

Knives and other tools
Basic selection

1 cook's knife: tapering pointed blade, for cutting and chopping

1 vegetable knife: pointed blade, about 7–8cm long

1 serrated knife: about the same size as above

1 carving knife: long, strong, pointed blade; those intended for poultry have a blade which curves towards the pointed end

1 carving fork: the guard prevents the knife slipping and cutting the carver's hand

1 bread knife: with serrated or scalloped edge

1 pair kitchen scissors

1 potato/apple peeler

1 nut mill

1 can opener: wall-fixed is the most practical; otherwise choose rotary wheel or claw type

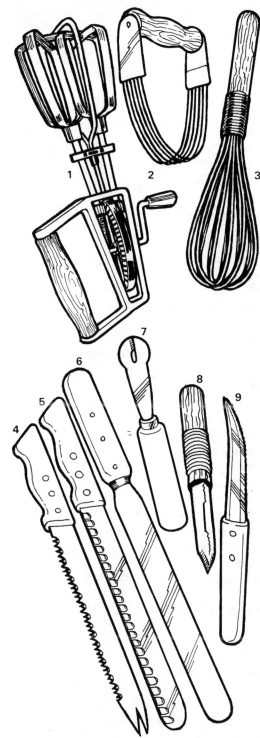

1 *Rotary whisk;* 2 *pastry blender;* 3 *balloon whisk;*
4 *freezer knife;* 5 *ham carver;* 6 *palette knife;*
7 *canelling knife;* 8 *potato peeler;* 9 *grapefruit
knife*

1 corkscrew
1 bottle opener
1 grater: the most practical are cylindrical or square
   and stand firmly on a flat surface; these incorporate several sizes of grating holes
1 perforated spoon
1 fish slice
1 basting spoon
1 ladle
1 vegetable masher
1 pair kitchen tongs
skewers

Additional equipment
1 paring knife
1 ham slicer: a long knife with a slightly flexible
   blade and a rounded end
1 palette knife: beware of the cheaper ones with
   very flexible blades
1 grapefruit knife
1 tomato knife
1 canelling knife: for taking a fine layer of skin off
   vegetables or fruits
1 frozen food knife: has a long, deeply serrated
   blade, usually with a two-pronged point
1 knife sharpener or hone
1 chopper
1 apple corer
1 cherry stoner
1 ball scoop: for cutting melon and potato balls
1 mandoline
1 egg slicer
1 bean slicer
1 herb chopper: this may have a curved blade with
   two handles, or it may have one central handle
   for chopping herbs in a wooden bowl; or it may
   be a simple mouli-type gadget
1 garlic press
1 nutcracker
1 pair poultry shears: need to be very strong with
   sharp curved blades and comfortable grip
1 mincer
1 nutmeg grater

Storage containers
storage jars: in a variety of sizes for dried fruit,
   dried vegetables, pulses, spices, herbs, etc

1 bread bin
1 vegetable rack
1 tea caddy and scoop
1 coffee container (airtight)
1–2 cake/biscuit tin/box
1 bacon box
1 cooking salt container

China
Everyday selection
1 dinner service comprising 6 each of:
  side plates
  soup/cereal bowls
  pudding plates
  dinner plates; plus:
  2 vegetable dishes
  2 meat plates (1 large, 1 small)
  1 gravy boat with stand
1 tea service comprising 6 each of:
  tea plates
  cups
  saucers; plus:
  1 large plate
  cream jug
  sugar bowl
1 teapot
3 jugs (varying capacities)
1 water jug
1 coffee pot (if no percolator)
1 salad bowl (may also be used for fruit)
6 mugs
6 egg cups
cruet set
1 butter dish
1 toast rack

Additional equipment
coffee service
cheese board/dish
Another set may be reserved as best china, etc

Table cutlery
Everyday selection
6 each of:
  table knives
  table forks
  dessert forks

  dessert spoons
  dessert knives
  soup spoons
  serving spoons
12 teaspoons
1 carving set
1 bread knife
1 butter knife

Additional equipment
6 each of:
  fish knives and forks
  steak knives
  coffee spoons
2 sugar spoons
2 pickle spoons/forks
1 cheese knife
salad servers
Another set may be reserved for best.

Glass
Everyday selection
6 small wine glasses
6 large wine glasses
6 tumblers
1 water jug

Additional equipment
6 sherry glasses (copitas)
6 liqueur glasses
6 brandy glasses
decanter
insulated ice container (ice bucket)

Kitchen linen, etc
6 napkins
6 tea-towels
6 dusters
2 chamois leathers
3 dish cloths
soft cloths (eg roll of stockinette)
length of muslin (for straining)
3 floor cloths
oven gloves
3 kitchen towels

Cleaning and laundry equipment

1 washing-up bowl
pan scourers
1 sink tidy
1 washing-up mop
1 laundry bowl
1 dish drainer
2 buckets
1 laundry basket
clothes pegs and container
clothes line/rotary clothes dryer (check that line posts are available: they are seldom supplied with new houses)
ironing board
1 clothes airer

Brushes, etc

1 sweeping brush
1 dustpan
1 handbrush
1 yard broom (if outside areas need to be swept)
1 sponge-headed mop
1 carpet sweeper
1 hearth brush (if using open fires)
1 carpet shampooer
1 scrubbing brush
1 vegetable brush
1 laundry brush
1 bottle brush
1 lavatory brush and container

Appliances

Most useful:

cooker
kettle
steam iron
vacuum cleaner
refrigerator
washing machine
food mixer or processor
blender (liquidizer)

Additional equipment

freezer
dishwasher
toaster
coffee-making machine
coffee grinder
tumble dryer/spin dryer
floor polisher
extractor fan
sewing machine

Miscellaneous

trays (assorted sizes – small ones may be used for sandwich platters, etc)
mats, small
1 kitchen timer
1 pedal bin
1 dustbin (galvanized, if it is to take hot ashes)
indoor step-ladder

STORES AND STORAGE

Nothing shows more, perhaps, the difference between a tidy thrifty housewife and a lady to whom these desirable epithets may not honestly be applied, than the appearance of their respective store-closets. The former is able, the moment anything is wanted, to put her hand on it at once; no time is lost, no vexation incurred, no dish spoilt for the want of " just a little something,"—the latter, on the contrary, hunts all over her cupboard for the ketchup the cook requires, or the pickle the husband thinks he should like a little of with his cold roast beef or mutton-chop, and vainly seeks for the Embden groats, or arrowroot, to make one of her little boys some gruel.

Life will run more easily for every member of the household if storage is properly organized from the start. The word storage can encompass many things: a second-hand chest of drawers or wardrobe, an old seaman's chest or a brightly coloured plastic trolley incorporating a range of drawers, shelves, and a tray. It can be built-in cupboards of all kinds, ready-to-hang shelving, knock-down wardrobe units for home assembly, expensively fitted out wall units for use in the kitchen, living-room or bedroom, or a range of fitted furniture for the bathroom.

Start by making lists of the things you and your family need to store, bearing in mind that most people's belongings accumulate to fill the space available; try to provide just sufficient for each room and each person, but not too much. Remember also that if you fit your entire home with built-in furniture you will find, if you move, that you have virtually nothing apart from beds, tables, and chairs.

The following is a list of basic requirements for each of the main rooms in an average household, together with a guide to the options available. Flat or bed-sitter dwellers will need to telescope their requirements.

Kitchen

There should be good-sized food cupboards, with an air vent in at least one, cupboards for kitchen utensils (bowls, jugs, etc), one for crockery and glassware (with hooks for hanging cups fixed to the undersides of shelves), and one for saucepans and baking tins. If you prefer to make a decorative arrangement with handsome saucepans and other utensils, do not have your shelves over the hob for safety reasons and do not forget the greasy fumes which gather on everything exposed in a kitchen.

There should be two cupboards under or near the sink for washing powders and liquids, and for buckets and bowls. Poisonous household chemicals should be kept out of the reach of children (see the chapter on Safety in the Home).

There should be drawers for kitchen knives and other small pieces of equipment (unless these are hung on racks over the work surface), for cutlery, tea-towels, greaseproof paper, cooking foil, and plastic bags. If you own a freezer, you need cupboard space or a deep drawer for freezer packaging material. A tall cupboard with shelves above is useful for brooms, vacuum cleaner and polisher, as well as such small cleaning items as polishes, brushes, dusters, etc. Even if you have no other open shelves you will probably want one for your collection of cookery books.

A larder is, of course, a most useful storage place, if you are fortunate enough to have one.

A kitchen can be fitted from the many standard ranges which vary in quality according to the price. (See the chapter on Kitchen Planning.)

On the other hand, you can build up an adequate and unusual arrangement of kitchen storage from second-hand cupboard and shelf units. A dresser, a small chest of drawers, a waist-height cupboard, and a set of glass-fronted bookshelves could all be decorated and linked with a home-made work surface.

Whatever type of storage you choose, aim to store as much as possible on narrow shelves. The widest shelves in the china cupboard should be just wide enough to take your largest dinner plate; this will avoid catastrophes caused by reaching across to get things at the back of a deep shelf.

Similarly, in the food storage cupboards, 127mm is sufficiently wide for most items, and there could be narrower shelves for herbs, spices, and essences. Information on types of containers can be found on p213.

Bathroom

This is a room which often has too little storage space, so that quantities of jars, bottles, and dangerous medicines stand around on window-sills and ledges.

There should be a unit of furniture with shelves for storing spare soap, lavatory paper, talcum powder, bath salts, cotton-wool, and any cosmetics used in the bathroom. The medicine cupboard, which may be either here or in the kitchen, should be locked against children and out of their reach. There should also be a box or bin for soiled linen.

Ideally, the general linen storage cupboard should not be in the bathroom which is steamy, but on a landing or in a corridor where it is easily accessible.

Some attractive pieces of bathroom storage furniture are available, but a second-hand dresser or cabinet would be perfectly suitable. Built-in furniture has also entered the bathroom market; one or two ranges incorporate every bathroom need with refinements such as built-in seats, rubbish bins, etc. These are streamlined and easy to keep clean.

Hallways

Where there is room, the entrance hall should contain a tall cupboard for coats. If you need to substitute a coat-stand or even a row of hooks, these should be in as unobtrusive a position as possible; a huddle of coats and wet raincoats is not the most attractive of sights. There should also be a small cupboard for outdoor shoes and slippers belonging to the family; the cupboard under the stairs would serve well for these, fitted out with shelves and racks.

An upper landing or corridor is a suitable place for linen storage, with a built-in or free-standing tall cupboard fitted out with slatted wood shelves.

Living-room

This will certainly need bookshelves and there are several excellent ranges of proprietary shelving which are easily fitted and have adjustable shelves made of wood, glass or plastic faced chipboard. Alternatively, you can have shelves specially built. You will probably need to store drinks and glasses, records and cassettes, games such as chess, and sewing materials, including perhaps a portable sewing machine. All these can go into free-standing pieces of furniture, such as an old-fashioned chest, a modern chest of drawers, a Victorian chiffonier, a circular library table or one of the plastic trolleys mentioned on the first page of this chapter.

For do-it-yourself enthusiasts, many attractive ranges of fitted furniture are available. These are mostly made of blockboard (which does not succumb so easily to the rigours of central heating) with wooden or laminated plastic veneers. One could build up, by easy stages, a whole wall of fittings to take all the items listed above – and indeed some of the more luxurious ranges have wooden panelling to line the wall itself. One could incorporate shelves, solid-fronted cupboards, glass-fronted cupboards, drawers, and even a pull-down writing table. A neat sewing corner could be arranged with the sewing machine on a pull-down flap, and cottons, scissors, etc stowed in shallow drawers.

Dining-room

Here you may need to store your glass, china, cutlery, and table-linen. You may like to do this in a chest of drawers and a low cupboard, with perhaps a couple of open shelves for displaying pretty china, or in the traditional sideboard, of which there are well fitted modern versions; or you may opt for fitted furniture like that which may be used in the living-room. Be sure that one of the shelves incorporates an impervious surface for resting hot dishes, especially if you have no separate serving-table, and that the finish you have chosen, be it wood or veneer, laminated plastic veneer or painted wood, goes well with the rest of your dining-room furniture.

Bedrooms

Storage here can consist of the traditional wardrobes and chests of drawers – furniture not to be despised if yours is an old house with large rooms and high ceilings since it is often of good quality and relatively inexpensive: it is simply too large for most people's homes. If your house has special architectural quality, with ceiling mouldings, panelling and beautiful doors, such furniture will look well.

If you live in a house or flat where this consideration does not apply, however, and you would like fitted furniture, it can be of the utmost simplicity. One 'system', for instance, consists of no more than sliding doors fitted from floor to ceiling which slice off an area of the room for storage space. These are invaluable in a small bedroom as no space need be allowed for door opening, though access is restricted to some extent since doors must overlap at the centre. Then the interior has to be fitted out with hanging rails, shelves, and drawers. Other space-savers would be blinds fixed to the ceiling which pull down over the storage space; or even curtains if you do not wish to spend more money than is necessary. There are, however, immensely elaborate and beautifully fitted systems with sliding, hinged or folding doors (some mirrored), shoe racks, sliding trays, stacks of drawers, and hanging spaces. Prices are as variable as quality. Many manufacturers, given the dimensions of your room, will plan your arrangements for you (using their own fittings, of course), and so will some retailers.

Besides storage for hanging clothes, indoor and out, make provision for sweaters, shirts, underwear, small personal items such as scarves, belts, tights, and socks. Everything except boots and shoes can go into drawers or racks; boots and shoes can go on stands at the bottom of cupboards. Large items such as luggage can go into dead storage high up above hanging cupboards.

Some bedrooms will also need shelves and cupboards for sports equipment, hobbies, books, and jewellery. Beds incorporating large storage drawers, though expensive, are useful for storing blankets, pillows, etc, and are very practical in small bedrooms. A desk with adjacent shelving and a filing trolley may be required for home study or work – or even for doing the household accounts.

If you are making your own storage, remember that an adequate wardrobe depth is about 600mm, which is slightly deeper than the normal alcove formed on either side of a chimney-breast. If you are building a wardrobe into a space too shallow to take the width of a clothes-hanger, use the type of hanging rods which are fitted from front to back of the wardrobe and which slide out to give easy access to the hanging garments.

Children's Rooms

Babies' and children's requirements change rapidly, so furniture and units should be kept simple and inexpensive.

For the nursery, adequate drawer space for clothes, nappies, and spare bed-linen, some shelves for toys, and a table to take feeding equipment and a basket of mending things, are sufficient. After that, children have the same storage requirements as adults except for toys (see below). It is pointless to have scaled-down furniture because when children are small they are helped with their clothing and as they get older they are soon able to reach fittings of normal height.

Keep the furniture bright and easy to clean (laminated plastic surfaces, wood with a coat of polyurethane, and hard gloss paint are all ideal). See also the chapter on Managing a Household with Children.

Toys

Any of the following are suitable for storing toys: a capacious cupboard with deep shelves such as is often found in older houses, a large old-fashioned chest, a big trunk painted in a bright colour, a wicker log basket, plastic laundry baskets, open shelves, or some industrial storage which consists of steel wall panels on to which are hung brightly coloured plastic bins of various sizes. Some beds, and some children's bunks, incorporate storage drawers; these too would be useful for stowing away larger toys.

Safety

Safe storage is of particular importance where children are concerned, but what follows applies to every room in the house.

Do not store heavy items high up, as a child – or anyone else – trying to reach them is in danger of pulling them down on his head. Store them at a low level.

Make sure that shelves and hanging cupboards are firmly attached to the wall so that there is absolutely no possibility of them coming away under the weight of a heavy load.

Do not fix heavy storage items to non-structural walls which might not be able to bear the weight.

Store fragile objects such as precious glassware in high cupboards which are beyond the reach of small children.

Store medicines, drugs, alcohol, and other potentially dangerous items in locked cupboards out of reach. This has already been mentioned in relation to the medicine cupboard, but there are other less obvious hazards which should be remembered where there are small children: alcohol bottles in the living-room, bleach in the kitchen and bathroom, methylated spirits and soda in the cleaning cupboard. (See also the chapter on Safety in the Home.)

Accessibility

Things which are to be in daily use should always be conveniently accessible. Obviously high-level cupboards are a useful way of obtaining extra storage space, but they should be reserved for things one only uses occasionally, eg suitcases, etc. For getting at such high-level items there should be a small, light, indoor step-ladder stowed in a hall cupboard (accessible for upstairs and downstairs).

Additional Storage

Make use of other spaces in the house for additional storage:

Industrial racking in the garage or cellar can take tools for the handyman, spare paint cans and decorating equipment, heavy sports gear (such as skis), and so on.

Fit any recesses in hallways and on landings with shelving to take books or decorative collections of china and pottery.

Unused space on the top landing will often accommodate quite a lot of useful storage.

A laundry-room will have shelves for soap powders, etc. This might be the place to keep a box containing all the shoe-cleaning equipment for family use, if it cannot be stored elsewhere.

Children's bicycles and prams should be stored in a dry place, but preferably not the entrance hall. The problem can sometimes be resolved by parking them neatly in a glazed closed-in porch. Bicycles can be hung from sturdy nails fixed at a suitable height in the garage or in a covered passageway at the side of the house. An unused outside lavatory, stripped down, might also be a suitable storage place for them.

List of Useful Equipment

Note Kitchen equipment can be found on pp213–217.

Bed-linen
Per bed: traditional
   3 pairs of sheets
   3 sets of pillowcases
   3–4 blankets
   eiderdown
   bedcover
Per bed: using continental quilts (duvets)
   1 continental quilt
   3 continental quilt covers
   3 fitted sheets
   3 valances
   3 sets of pillowcases
Per bed in either case:
   1 electric blanket
   pillows (number according to preference)

Table-linen

12 table napkins
1 set of tablemats
tablecloths (if required)

Towels, etc

3 bath towels per person
3 bath towels for guests
3 hand towels
3 hand towels for guests
3 face cloths per person
2 hand towels for cloakroom

Bathroom

1 bathroom cabinet
1 toilet roll holder
1 lavatory brush and holder
1 set of bathroom scales
1 nailbrush
2 bathmats
2 pedestal mats

Shoe cleaning equipment

2 brushes for brown polish
2 brushes for black polish
2 brushes for neutral colour polish
4 polishing cloths
suede brush
mud-removing brush
large wooden or plastic container

Miscellaneous household items

The following is a list of items which are not essential, but which add to the comfort and convenience of the home.

cushions
coffee/occasional tables
vases or other flower containers
waste paper bins
ashtrays
magazine rack
radio and/or television
tool kit
garden and/or paint equipment (if appropriate)
electric fire (additional to central heating)

NUTRITION AND DIET

The regime most favourable to health is found in variety: variety pleases the senses, monotony is disagreeable. The eye is fatigued by looking always on one object, the ear by listening to one sound, and the palate by tasting one flavour. It is the same with the stomach: consequently, variety of food is one of the essentials for securing good digestion.

A Well-balanced Diet

This term describes a choice of food which satisfies all the body's nutritional needs in the correct proportions.

Our whole body is made from substances derived from food. Food is also the body's only source of energy. Every one of its cells, whatever its function, needs energy. For healthy growth and development during childhood and for continued good health during adult life, it is therefore essential that food should supply all the energy and nutrients the body needs, in the right proportions.

Amounts of Food Needed

Investigations show that certain people need two, three or even four times as much energy from food compared with others of the same age, sex, and body size, who appear to be equally active. This is because metabolic rates vary, and explains, of course, why some people eat enormous amounts and never put on weight, while others eat sparingly and still have a weight problem.

Nutritionists think that individuals also vary in the amount of protein, minerals, and vitamins they need for health.

To cover these individual variations, nutrition and medical experts have devised lists of recommended daily intakes of energy and different nutrients calculated to satisfy the needs of the majority of healthy people.

As to whether certain foods ought to be eaten daily, there are no hard and fast rules. As long as the chosen diet satisfies the body's needs for growth, development, health, and energy, it is adequate.

Palatability

The most desirable kind of diet is often seen as a succession of juicy, tender steaks, chops, and prime white fish. But a simple, inexpensive diet can be just as nourishing as an elaborate and costly one. Cheap cuts of meat, for example, have as much food value as the most expensive joints and steaks, but they need longer and more gentle cooking, and more nutrients may be lost than in brief cooking methods. Cheap and homely cabbage provides much more vitamin C than expensive exotic fruits like peaches, nectarines, and pineapples. A very rich diet, which is usually high in sugar and animal fat content, may even be harmful to health. A frugal, plainer diet may prove to be healthier in the long term.

We have to eat in order to live, and most of us obviously choose to eat the foods we like best: a well-balanced diet, therefore, needs to be attractive and palatable as well as nutritious.

Variety

As a general rule, the more varied the diet, the better the chance that it will be a well-balanced one. Provided an individual has a wide variety of foods to choose from, and is not inhibited by food fads, he will usually select an adequately balanced diet.

In order to choose wisely, it is important to know what nourishment and energy is supplied by the more usual foods. These are as follows:

Basic Nutrients

Protein

This is the body's basic cell-building and repair material, and is vital for growth. The faster the growth rate, the more rapid the cell-building process, and the greater the need for protein. Protein needs are highest of all during late adolescence and, for women, during the last months of pregnancy and the time of breast feeding.

But protein is important throughout the adult years; all body cells have a limited life, and worn-out cells need to be replaced by new ones to keep the body healthy and efficient.

Proteins come from a variety of foods derived from both plants and animals. In the UK, about two-thirds of total protein in the national average diet is obtained from animal foods, including meat, fish, poultry, milk, cheese, and eggs. The remaining third of protein is supplied by plant foods, including cereal foods like bread, rice, and pasta, pulses such as peas and beans, nuts, and other vegetables. Proteins from animal foods have the highest nutritional value. Practically any animal protein contains all the materials we need for building our own body cells; so we do not need to eat fish and eggs or meat and cheese at the same meal.

Proteins in plants are more limited in their nutritional value. If two or more plant protein foods are eaten in the same meal, however, the nutritional value of the combined protein is much better than if the protein were eaten at separate meals. Two vegetable protein foods eaten together (for example, a peanut butter sandwich or baked beans on toast) may have a nutritional value comparable with a single animal protein food.

The nutritional value of vegetable protein is also enhanced when it is eaten with an animal protein. Traditional food combinations such as Yorkshire pudding with beef, dumplings with meat stew, bread and milk or bread and cheese, in which the vegetable protein is eaten with animal protein make nutritional sense. The combined protein not only has good food value, but is cheaper than that derived solely from the more expensive animal protein food.

Energy from protein

One gram of pure protein gives the body 17 kilojoules (kJ). If the protein intake from food exceeds the body's requirement for either building or repair of tissues, the surplus protein is broken down and used for energy. This is an uneconomical use of protein as a rule since the body's energy needs can be met more cheaply by carbohydrate foods. Protein is also used for energy if the overall energy value of the diet does not satisfy the body's needs.

If, however, the protein and energy value of the diet exceed the body's requirements, the surplus protein is converted into body fat.

This fact should be remembered by those who think that protein foods like meat, eggs, and cheese are 'not fattening'. These excellent sources of protein also contain fats. Like excess protein, excess fat can be converted into body fat and hence be responsible for a gain in weight.

To derive the best value from protein, the total daily amount should be divided between the three meals of the day. It is important to remember that an adequate amount of protein should be eaten early in the day, normally at breakfast (see p230).

Carbohydrates

These are the body's main source of energy for physical activity, metabolism, and warmth. In the average UK diet, about one-half of the total energy value of the diet is supplied by carbohydrates. There are two major groups: starches and sugars. One gram of pure carbohydrate equals 16kJ.

Starch is provided by a number of foods produced from grains: flour, and bread, biscuits etc made from flour; spaghetti, macaroni, and other pasta; semolina, rice, barley, oats, sago and tapioca. Potatoes and, to a lesser extent, other root vegetables, are another source of starch.

Most of the sugar added at table or during cooking is derived from cane or beet sugar, and nutritionally known as sucrose. Other sugars occur naturally in food. Lactose is the sugar in milk, and is the only carbohydrate found in an animal food.

Maltose is the sugar in malt, while fructose, the sweetest of all sugars, occurs in fruit and vegetables. Glucose occurs in honey, grapes, and a few other fruits.

Sorbitol is a carbohydrate sweetener made from glucose. It is sometimes used in diabetic foods because it is absorbed more slowly into the blood stream following digestion than the true sugars. Sorbitol has the same energy value as glucose and must be regarded as an alternative to sugar, not as an energy-free sugar substitute like saccharin.

Sugar consumption

Since the 1950s consumption of sugar and sweet foods in general has gradually increased, with a corresponding decrease in the consumption of starchy foods, eg bread.

The increased consumption of sugar in the post-war years has been matched by an increase of overweight and dental decay. Sugar has also been associated by some research workers with the increase in coronary heart disease (CHD).

Because unwise sugar consumption can have adverse effects on health, carbohydrates as a whole are often regarded as undesirable food items. This reputation is undeserved, as they remain important staple foods in the Western diet. Potatoes supply more vitamin C in the average diet than any other single food. Bread alone contributes one-fifth of most people's total protein intake, as well as important quantities of calcium, iron, and B group vitamins.

Fats (including oils)

Fats and oils are also energy-giving foods. They are a more concentrated source of energy than protein; one gram of pure fat supplies 38kJ. In the average Western diet, fats as a whole supply roughly 40% of the body's total energy intake. People in the higher income groups consume rather more fat, and tend to compensate for this by a decrease in consumption of carbohydrate foods.

Certain components of fats, known as essential fatty acids, are vital for healthy growth and development. And it is only in association with fat that some vitamins – the fat-soluble ones – are found in various foods (see p226).

The commonly eaten fats are derived from both animal and plant foods. Butter, dripping, lard, suet, fat meat, and fat or 'oily' fish like herring are the most obvious sources of animal fats. Although less apparent, these are present in so-called lean meat and poultry. Animal fats are also supplied by eggs and dairy foods – milk, cream, cheese, and butter.

Fats from plants are usually described as oils rather than fats because they are liquid at room temperature. Oil seeds such as sunflower, soya, cottonseed, groundnut, coconut, and palm kernel give the vegetable oils used for cooking and for salad dressings. These oil seeds also provide the raw materials from which much margarine is made. Olive oil is another vegetable oil widely used, especially in southern Europe. All nuts contain oil too.

Fats may be made of either saturated, unsaturated or polyunsaturated fatty acids. Many fats are a combination of these. In general, fats derived from animals have a high proportion of saturated fatty acids, while oils derived from plants have more unsaturated fatty acids. (There are exceptions. For example, coconut and cashew nuts have a higher proportion of saturated fatty acids.) The polyunsaturated fats come from the oil seeds listed above, and from the specially formulated soft margarines.

Satiety value

A meal which contains a fairly high proportion of fat stays in the stomach for a longer time than a meal largely consisting of carbohydrate. The fat in the meal also inhibits the movement of the stomach and thus delays the onset of hunger pangs between meals. These two effects give fat a satiety value, ie they make us feel full, and satisfied. The fact that there is a limit to the amount of fat one individual can eat augments its satiety value. It is easy to overeat on carbohydrate foods, particularly the sweet foods, which do not 'fill one up', but one is much less likely to eat too much of fatty foods. Because of this, it is helpful to include a certain amount of fat in a slimming diet to add richness and palatability, even though fats have a higher energy value than sugar.

Vitamins

A variety of different substances called vitamins occur naturally in the food we eat. Vitamins are essential for growth and development during childhood and for general good health throughout life. About twenty different vitamins are known to exist. Most of them are chemically unrelated, but they have one common feature: the body cannot function without minute quantities of each of them. If we do not take in these small amounts of all the different vitamins regularly, ill health is inevitable. In fact, death or permanent crippling can result from a long-term vitamin deficiency, through diseases like scurvy and rickets.

There is no need to take vitamin pills if you eat a normal diet.

Vitamins are needed mainly to regulate the building and repair of body tissues or to set into action and maintain the complex chain of chemical reactions by which we derive energy from food. Vitamins A, C, and D belong to the 'structural vitamins' group, while members of the B complex group of vitamins are the chief 'energy release vitamins'.

Vitamin A

The body's internal tracts, including the digestive, respiratory, and urinary tracts, are lined with mucous membranes. Vitamin A is needed to keep these delicate linings moist and free from infection. It keeps the eyes and eyelids healthy, it enables the eyes to see in dim light and it is also needed for a smooth and healthy skin.

Vitamin A is contained in a great many of the different foods we normally eat. It is also made within the body from carotene, the plant pigment found in yellow, orange, and green fruits and vegetables. In the average UK diet, vitamin A comes mainly from butter, margarine (vitamin A is added to margarine to make its vitamin content equivalent to that in butter), liver, green vegetables, and carrots. Cheese, eggs, milk, fat fish, fish liver oils, and other fruits and vegetables also contribute to the daily intake of vitamin A. Because it is unaffected by cooking and most other food processing techniques, a dietary shortage of vitamin A in the UK is extremely unlikely.

B Vitamins

There are thirteen or more different B vitamins. We continue to class them as B vitamins, often described as the B complex group of vitamins, because these different substances perform similar tasks in the body and are often found together in the same foods. One of the vital roles of the B group vitamins is the release of energy from food. This energy is stored within the molecular structure of carbohydrates, fats, and proteins. To release it, the food molecules enter a complex chain of chemical reactions which requires a constant supply of several B vitamins in order to proceed.

The B group vitamins also overlap into the 'structural vitamins' category because some of them have an important role to play in building blood. Vitamin B_{12} and another B vitamin called folic acid are required for this purpose. B vitamins are also needed for transmission of impulses along nerves, and for the general good health of all the body tissues.

Meat (in particular liver, kidney, heart, and other offal), cereal foods (including breads), eggs, milk, potatoes, and other vegetables are the main sources of B vitamins in our diet.

Enrichment At present, white flour is required by law to be enriched with calcium, iron, and two B vitamins, thiamin and nicotinic acid. The miller has to add enough of these nutrients to bring them to the same level as in less highly refined flour of 80% extraction. Various breakfast cereals are also enriched with B vitamins to replace those lost during manufacture.

Stability All B vitamins dissolve in water and may be washed out of food or dissolved out in cooking liquids. For this reason, unsalted meat should not be washed or left to soak. Any juices which exude from meat during cooking should be used as gravy or in sauces, since they may contain B vitamins which might otherwise be lost. Some B vitamins, notably thiamin, are easily destroyed by cooking heat. To conserve them, care must be taken to avoid overcooking; keeping food hot for long periods and re-heating foods should also be avoided, if possible.

Vitamin C

Scientists are still not sure about the precise role of vitamin C in the body. It seems to be essential for the building of connective tissue, the material which joins together all body cells. Vitamin C is also known to be required for healthy blood and efficient wound healing. In recent years theories have been put forward about the value of vitamin C in preventing colds and lowering the blood cholesterol level, but these theories have not yet been sufficiently substantiated.

The richest sources of vitamin C in the diet are blackcurrants, Brussels sprouts, other green vegetables, soft berry fruits, and citrus fruits. In practice, potatoes provide more vitamin C than any other single food, simply because most people eat a lot of them.

Milk is the only animal food which contains vitamin C, but much of this is lost when milk is heated.

Stability Vitamin C is the most easily destroyed nutrient of all. The vitamin content of fruits and vegetables begins to diminish the moment they are harvested. Vitamin C loss continues during storage, especially if fruits and vegetables are kept in a warm place. It is destroyed by exposure to air when vegetables are cut. The more finely they are chopped, sliced or grated, the greater the cut surface area exposed to air, and so the greater the loss of vitamin C.

Vitamin C loss is also hastened when soda is added to cooking water, when copper lined pans are used, and when food is kept hot or is re-heated. As vitamin C is dissolved out of foods as they are being washed, it is advisable to wash vegetables and salads quickly, and before slicing or cutting them. Vitamin C also dissolves in any cooking liquids; whenever possible these should be used to make stock, sauces, and gravy.

Vitamin D

The function of vitamin D is closely related to the body's use of the mineral calcium (see p228). It is needed for the absorption of calcium from food after it has been digested.

Some vitamin D is made by the body itself when the ultraviolet rays of the sun fall on the skin. It is thought that most adults make all the vitamin D they need in this way. Children, adolescents, pregnant women, and nursing mothers need extra vitamin D to meet the demands of growth, so they should have foods to supply this in addition to the vitamin made on their skins. Elderly people, invalids, and housebound adults, may also need a regular dietary intake of vitamin D. These groups do not spend much time in the fresh air, and may be heavily clothed when they do, so that their skin is seldom exposed to the sun, and thus the amounts of vitamin D which they can synthesize on their skin surfaces is negligible.

The main sources of vitamin D in the average person's diet are margarine, fat fish, eggs, and butter. Fish liver oils, including cod and halibut liver oils, are very rich sources of vitamin D. Like vitamin A, it is added to all margarines during their manufacture; this is required by law. Vitamin D is also added to some infant foods, including dried milk products.

Vitamin D is a very stable vitamin: it is unaffected by most food processing methods, including cooking, and does not dissolve in water.

Vitamin E

The precise role of vitamin E in the body has, as yet, not been clearly established. Some scientists hold that vitamin E may not even be required by man, although experiments have shown that it is essential for many animals.

The popular name for vitamin E is the 'fertility vitamin', as experiments have shown that it is needed to ensure male rat fertility and for female rats to be able to produce live young.

Unsubstantiated claims have been made that the vitamin can delay the ageing process, improve physical performance, and may prevent muscular dystrophy.

Vitamin E is very widely distributed in plant foods, especially vegetable oils, nuts, and dark green vegetables; butter and eggs are the best sources of vitamin E among the animal foods.

Vitamin E is unaffected by cooking, food processing techniques and temperature, but it is gradually destroyed by exposure to air.

Minerals

Small quantities of about twenty different minerals are required for good health, though some in only minute quantities. Two important minerals needed in larger quantities are iron and calcium.

Iron

Iron is an essential constituent of hæmoglobin, the red pigment of blood cells which carries oxygen to every cell in the body. The best sources of iron in food are meat, especially liver and kidney, and vegetables, notably green vegetables and potatoes. Some other foods are extremely rich in iron, such as curry powder, cocoa, black treacle, dried fruit, cockles, corned beef, and some game such as hare, pigeon, and grouse. These rich sources of iron can be valuable in meals for people needing a high iron intake (see p138).

Not all the iron we eat can be absorbed. Normally the body extracts just enough for its immediate needs. When it has a special need for iron, it steps up the absorption rate. But absorption can be prevented or depressed by certain organic constituents of food. Vitamin C makes absorption easier, so one should eat a vitamin C-rich food with an iron-rich one if possible. For example, have a glass of orange juice before a boiled egg at breakfast or serve sprouts or cabbage with liver at lunchtime, or include a tomato salad as a side dish with curry.

Calcium

Calcium is one of the main building materials for bones and teeth. It is also needed in the blood, to aid clotting if bleeding occurs from a wound. Muscles need calcium too, in small quantities, in order to contract and move the body.

The most important foods containing calcium are cheese, milk, bread, and green vegetables. In some parts of the UK, the dissolved calcium salts which give the 'hardness' to water also help to satisfy the body's calcium needs.

The same organic substances which interfere with iron absorption may also prevent absorption of calcium from food in the intestine. For this reason, calcium in milk is absorbed more easily than calcium in cabbage. (For the value of vitamin D in helping the absorption of calcium, see p227.)

Growing children, pregnant women, and nursing mothers have a high calcium requirement. Adults continue to need calcium for strong healthy bones and teeth. The bones of elderly people become weaker and more liable to fracture with increasing age. There is no evidence that extra calcium can prevent these changes, but it is still very important that elderly people should satisfy their calcium requirements.

Phosphorus

This mineral is combined with calcium in bones and teeth. Phosphorus is very widely distributed in food and dietary deficiency is unknown in man.

Potassium and sodium

These two minerals help to maintain the concentration of the various fluids inside and outside the body cells. This function is very closely related to the body's water requirements. It is essential that the sodium chloride or salt content of the blood be maintained. Excessive amounts of salt may be lost by sweating in extreme heat or during very strenuous exercise. The loss should be made good immediately by drinking salt water (1 ×5ml spoon salt in 500ml water) as otherwise muscular cramps may occur.

In normal life more salt is added to food to improve its flavour than the body needs. The average adult leading a sedentary life needs about 4g of salt daily, but people eat between 5–20g. The excess is excreted in the urine.

Unlike salt, potassium is not lost in sweat. But purgatives, if used too frequently, can cause excessive loss of potassium. Most common foods contain it, however, so there should be no deficiency in a normal mixed diet.

Trace minerals

Many minerals are needed by the body in such small quantities that they are described as 'trace' elements or 'trace' minerals. (Larger quantities could even be poisonous.)

Some of the more important trace minerals required for good health are:

Iodine, needed to make the hormone thyroxin which plays a very important part in controlling metabolic rate. Iodine may be found dissolved in drinking water and is also present in sea fish, shellfish, and any vegetables grown in coastal areas. To avoid any possible shortage of iodine, it is added to some varieties of table salt, which are then said to be 'iodized'.

Fluorine, one of the constituents of bones and teeth. It gives children's teeth a certain resistance to decay. Fluorine is sometimes added to drinking water by certain local authorities. In areas where no fluorine occurs naturally or is added to the water, fluorine tablets and fluorine toothpastes appear to give the teeth an added resistance to decay while they are developing.

Tea is the only other dietary source of fluorine.

Magnesium is needed for healthy bones and teeth also, while *copper*, with iron, is needed to make the red pigment of blood.

Zinc, manganese, cobalt, selenium, molybdenum, and *chromium* are also known to be necessary to good health. All are adequately supplied by an average Western diet.

Water

Another essential constituent of a good diet is water. Approximately two-thirds of the total weight of the body is made up by water, its function being to transport foods to the body cells and to carry away the waste products. The body is always balancing the water intake and output. If too little water is taken, results are more serious than with too much, for excess is readily excreted through the kidneys. At least 750ml of water or other (non-alcoholic) fluid should be taken daily in addition to the water taken as an integral part of most foods. Care must be taken to see that a sick person receives sufficient fluid, especially if he has a raised temperature or an infection of the throat or a cold.

Planning Meals

Meals for children

As children grow fast and are usually very active, they need proportionally more protein and energy for their size than adults do. They may not be able to eat as much at each meal, but most children need to have breakfast, a main meal at mid-day, afternoon tea, and a light supper at bed time. Alternatively, if family meals are spaced with adult appetites in mind, younger children may need well-planned snack meals in between the formal meal pattern; a mid-morning drink of milk plus cheese and fruit may provide the necessary stopgap, for instance.

Many children are too tired to eat a heavy meal at night, but most of them need a substantial meal in the middle of their busy, energetic day.

Fads and fancies

Some children are so fussy that they seem able to exist on a very limited selection of foods. However irritating a fussy child can be with his strange eating habits, there is usually no reason for concern, if he is healthy, active, and growing well. It seldom helps for parents to cajole, bribe or even threaten to get him to eat. It is best not to make an issue out of it. The child should be offered the food everyone else is eating, given very small helpings of anything he thinks he would like, and then left alone. Alternatives should not be offered at every meal, and the child should not be allowed sweets or biscuits between meals. A normal child does not let him- or herself starve, and provided no-one makes a fuss and draws attention to his not eating, he usually conforms to family eating habits sooner or later.

Nowadays nearly all children eat practically the same food as their parents as soon as they can eat solid foods. In fact, the baby can be weaned on to normal family foods, sieved or puréed in an electric blender. Commercially prepared infant foods are convenient at times, but expensive.

Seasoning foods for children

Highly spiced and seasoned foods, those with a high fat content or any recipe containing alcohol are not suitable for very young children. Simpler alternatives can usually be offered to them when adults are eating such dishes as curry, jugged hare or roast goose. Some young children, however, have been known to relish such dishes. If they like them, there is no reason why children should not try a small helping of any food.

Extra salt should not be added to young children's food. This is particularly important for babies who cannot excrete surplus salt. They may become seriously ill if the sodium content of their blood rises.

Meals for adults

Breakfast

Many people either miss breakfast completely or just have a small snack. Nutritionally this is not wise. On rising, the body is at a low ebb, and its blood sugar level is at the 'fasting rate'. A well-balanced breakfast boosts the flagging blood sugar level and maintains it until lunchtime; a very light breakfast gives it a quick boost, but it falls back to fasting level by mid-morning. When the blood sugar level is low, an individual feels tired and listless, often irritable, and mentally sluggish. With a raised blood sugar level a person becomes more energetic, alert, and quick to react mentally and physically. Having a good breakfast, therefore, makes very good sense.

Breakfast should provide one-quarter of an individual's total daily requirement for both energy and protein. A meal consisting of orange juice, breakfast cereal with milk, a boiled egg with bread or toast, butter and marmalade, and either tea or coffee with milk satisfies these criteria.

For young children, cereal with milk, a glass of milk, bread or toast with preserves makes an adequate meal. Older children, who need more protein should have a high-protein dish, eg bacon or cheese with extra milk or yoghurt.

There are also many excellent, traditional breakfast dishes, with good food value (see the chapter on Breakfasts and Suppers). But a well-balanced breakfast is not necessarily an expensive or elaborate cooked meal.

The main meal

Whether eaten at lunchtime or in the evening, this usually consists of meat and vegetables followed by a dessert or cheese. Meat can be replaced by fish, poultry or a cheese or egg dish.

Vegetarians may serve a first course made with peas, beans, lentils or nuts. In any vegetarian diet, the main meal should include two or more different protein-rich foods to ensure that any nutritional deficiency in one vegetable protein is made up by the other.

Bread, pastry, dumplings, pasta or legumes such as peas, beans, and lentils all contain vegetable protein. When these foods are served, less meat is needed. The same is true of textured vegetable protein (TVP) products, usually derived from seed beans such as soya or wheat.

Potatoes, rice, and pasta have a similar energy value, but potatoes are also an important source of vitamin C. One or two other vegetables, or a salad, usually complete the central part of the main meal. Vegetables are vital as a source of fibre (roughage) in the diet.

Sweet course In labour-saving urban life, sedentary people do not need stocking up with high-energy desserts. Traditional puddings such as treacle sponge, roly-poly, and Spotted Dick should be kept for very active people such as teenage boys, who have high energy requirements. The urge to eat great quantities of sweet foods is rarely based on real nutritional needs. Light puddings, such as jellies, mousses, puddings made with fruit and ice cream are more suitable for most people.

The light meal

This meal, whether it be lunch, high tea or supper, should be just as well planned as the others.

Salads and cuts of cold meat are light to carry and make convenient packed lunches as a change from sandwiches. Hard-boiled eggs, patés, savoury flans, and pasties are ideal for light summer meals. Soup, toasted savouries, pasta, and egg dishes are popular light meals in the winter. Salads or simply cooked vegetables such as grilled tomatoes and mushrooms add interest. Fruit, served fresh or lightly stewed, makes a very good dessert.

Snacks

Ideally, between-meal snacks should be restricted to cups of tea and coffee, or milk and fruit juice for children. If a more substantial snack is required, fruit, cheese with bread or crispbread, crisps or nuts should take the place of sweet foods.

Food for the elderly

For many house-bound old people, or for those whose failing eyesight or hearing limits their pleasures, meal-times become the highlight of the day so appearance is particularly important.

Although elderly people still require all the essential nutrients, proteins, minerals, and vitamins, they need slightly smaller helpings of most foods, and meals have to be prepared to suit their physical ability.

The digestive system of ageing people may become less robust, so that they suffer from indigestion if they eat very rich or highly seasoned dishes. However, as the sense of taste tends to diminish with age, food should be well flavoured. They often prefer foods which are grilled instead of fried, while fatty meats such as pork or goose, and rich creamy pastries, may not be a wise choice for them.

Food for old people needs to be easy to eat, since poor teeth or dentures can make eating raw fruit, vegetables, and salads difficult. But the elderly are also prone to constipation, and they need a diet containing adequate fibre (see pp236–37). Fortunately vegetable fibre softens with cooking, while retaining its value as a source of roughage; plenty of cooked vegetables and stewed fruit should, therefore, be included in meals for the elderly.

For very old people, minced meat is easier to eat than slices of roast meat or chops. Toast should be cut into fingers, which are easy to hold, and sandwich fillings should be firm, so that they do not slip out from between the bread. Meat and vegetables can be puréed and served as soup; vegetables can also be diced, so that they can be eaten with a spoon. Lightly cooked dishes with eggs and milk are easy to eat, and easily digested (see the chapter on Light Dishes for One or Two). Cheese is another nourishing food for the elderly, provided care is taken not to overcook it.

Enjoyment of food

Reaction to food is strongly influenced by its smell, colour, and general appearance. When food is served attractively, well garnished, on good-looking plates, it stimulates the appetite because we can imagine how pleasant it will taste. This is particularly important for the ill. An attractive blend of colours and textures on the plate is also important. (See the chapter on Presenting a Meal.)

Variety enhances our enjoyment of food and helps the digestion, as the sight, smell, and taste of good food stimulate secretion of digestive juices.

Regular or over-liberal use of a few favourites can make every dish taste much the same. Take advantage of fresh fruits and vegetables when they are in season. They are cheapest then, and also at their freshest and most nutritious. If you have a freezer, frozen seasonal fruits and vegetables can give a lift to winter meals with out-of-season foods. Use herbs, spices, and seasonings with discretion.

Dietary Problems

Planning a special diet

When, for example, a slimmer has to cut down on total energy intake or a diabetic needs to keep a close watch on carbohydrates, special diets are needed. In preparing these, one has to make sure that they contain enough proteins, minerals, and vitamins. Thus a slimmer has to get the vitamin C normally eaten in potatoes from an extra helping of green vegetables. On the other hand, for anyone on a low animal fat diet, extra bread, potatoes, and pasta help to maintain the body's energy.

There are some illnesses during which the body's nutritional requirements are, in fact, slightly increased; especially those in which some physical damage has occurred. These include severe infections and fevers, burns, accidents, and surgical operations.

In certain illnesses, notably jaundice, a special diet is an essential part of the treatment of the disease. In conditions like diabetes and coeliac gloss disease, a carefully planned and modified eating pattern is necessary throughout life.

Anaemia

Anaemia, normally caused by a dietary shortage of iron, is fairly common. Women are more susceptible to anaemia than men because of their regular loss of blood during menstruation. (See *Anaemia* in the chapter on Medical Care in the Home.)

To avoid anaemia, iron-rich foods should be eaten regularly (see p228). Liver or kidney should be included once or twice in each week's menus, and one portion of meat should be eaten on every other day of the week. Enriched cereal products and green vegetables should also be eaten regularly.

Dental decay

It has been estimated that as much sugar is now consumed in two weeks as was eaten in a whole year one hundred years ago. One effect of this has been an increase in dental decay among children, especially those who eat a lot of refined sugar in the form of sweets, biscuits, ice cream, and sweetened drinks. Decay is found most often among children who regularly eat between meals and then fail to brush their teeth properly.

To reduce the risk of decay, children should learn not to regard sweets or any food as reward for good behaviour or as comfort when they are hurt or upset. Sweets in particular should be strictly limited, to encourage a savoury rather than a sweet tooth. The texture of hard, crisp foods like raw apple, celery, cucumber, and carrot also have a direct part to play in good dental hygiene.

Obesity

Causes Normally the body keeps a perfect balance between energy taken in from food and drink and energy used for physical activity, warmth, and metabolism. Adults should keep a steady weight varying only a kilogram or two between the ages of twenty and sixty, though an individual eats several tonnes of food during this period. But the balance between energy taken in and energy used can be upset in many people. When their daily food regularly provides more energy than they need, they put on weight, because any surplus energy is converted into body fat. To reduce weight, it is this stored fat which needs to be mobilized to provide energy. So the only way to slim is to eat a diet which forces the body to do this. Taking more exercise, and being more energetic than usual is helpful too.

To lose weight and feel well, one needs to be on a properly balanced slimming diet. The body's store of nutrients like iron, for instance, can soon be depleted on a badly planned slimming programme. Many so-called crash diets provide such a poor intake of vital nutrients that they make one feel exhausted if followed for more than a few days, and destroy one's will to go on dieting.

Eating less The recommended daily intake of energy for most women is about 9200kJ, and for men, 11300kJ. If a woman eats only 5000kJ in food daily, she utilizes 4200kJ from her fat stores and this can give her a weight loss of just less than 1kg each week. Men keeping to 6250kJ a day can expect to lose rather more than 1kg in a week. See the chart on p234.

These figures are average ones which suit most people. Anyone who does not lose weight on the recommended energy allowance may in fact need less than average amounts of food. If this is the case, a woman can safely reduce energy intake further to 4200kJ daily and a man to 5000kJ daily.

Which foods to choose A well-balanced slimming scheme must contain all the essential nutrients required for good health, even though the total energy value of the foods eaten is reduced. This is neither complicated nor difficult to plan, as foods which supply all the necessary protein also satisfy the body's needs for minerals and vitamins *and* provide almost all the slimmer's daily energy allowance. For example, the average woman's daily protein needs would be provided by the following:

100–125g meat or fish

0.25 litre milk

1 egg

25g cheese

100g bread

The total energy value of these foods in the above quantities is between 3500 and 3750kJ depending mainly on the kind of meat or fish chosen.

Men need a little more protein, and should have the foods above with an extra 25–50g of either meat, fish or cheese; these would provide a total energy value of 4250–4500kJ.

It is obvious, therefore, that a crash diet supplying as little as 2000kJ can prove harmful if followed for more than two or three days. Most nutritionists agree that a slimmer should not attempt to reduce energy intake to less than 4000kJ. A slimming diet based on a daily intake of between 5000 and 6250kJ is normally considered to be the best. With this food allowance, the slimmer usually has a satisfactory rate of weight loss without becoming ravenously hungry. One should aim at a small regular weight loss of about 1kg a week.

Kilojoules (kJ) Slimming diets are usually of two kinds. Both effectively reduce the total amount of food eaten. Slimmers can either estimate the energy value (or kilojoules) of everything they eat or concern themselves only with the carbohydrate content of their food. See the Table on p234.

On an energy or joule-controlled diet, the slimmer estimates the energy value of everything he eats and drinks, and keeps his total daily consumption of food to within a given limit, as described above. Besides the foods listed there a slimmer may choose to have 15g of butter (468kJ), two pieces of fresh fruit (420kJ), a selection of salads and leafy vegetables (450kJ) or a medium-sized potato (450kJ).

Low carbohydrate diet For a low carbohydrate diet the slimmer needs to know only the carbohydrate content of his foods. He has to limit his consumption of carbohydrate very rigidly, usually to between 50–60g a day. As an example, this amount of carbohydrate is contained in two thin slices of bread, plus one medium-sized potato, 0.75 litre of milk, and one small apple. The table on p234 shows the carbohydrate content of certain foods and also lists those that are carbohydrate-free.

Foods for slimmers

Sweet foods It is easy to overeat on sweet foods as they have little satiety value. Most of them are high in energy value but low in essential nutrients. One of the simplest ways to reduce weight, therefore, is to cut out all sweetened foods from normal meals. As sugar and similar sweeteners supply roughly 2000kJ in the average diet, cutting out sweet foods alone can give a steady weight loss, provided, of course, that they are not replaced by an equivalent amount of savouries.

Many overweight people admit to having a very sweet tooth, and find sweet foods the most difficult to give up. But if they can be strong-willed enough to forego them, they do eventually lose their taste for excessive sweetness.

Starchy foods Bread, potatoes, rice, and pasta have less high energy value than sweet foods. They also contain some essential nutrients, although animal protein foods contain much more. Except on a very low carbohydrate diet, most slimming diets allow a small intake of these starchy foods daily. Two thin slices of bread plus a medium-sized potato, supplying about 850kJ, is a reasonable daily allowance. Small helpings of crispbreads, rice, pasta, peas, beans or sweetcorn, can be eaten instead, to add variety. Using the table on p234, which shows the comparative energy value of these foods, it is easy to substitute, say, 35g crispbreads for 50g bread, or 100g boiled rice for 150g boiled potatoes.

Alcohol This is another source of energy, used in the body in much the same way as carbohydrate. Alcoholic drinks have little if any other food value, and they should be severely restricted by those trying to slim. If an occasional drink is taken, compensate by eating a portion less of starchy foods. Again, the table on p234 shows how to make the necessary substitution.

Fats These are a very concentrated source of energy. If the amount of fat eaten is restricted, the overall energy value of a diet falls considerably. When slimming, butter or margarine consumption should be limited to about 15g or 2 ×10ml spoons daily. Rich cakes, pastries, and puddings made with fat and sugar are obviously unsuitable for the slimmer. Cream and cream cheese should be eaten in only very small quantities, if at all. Milk, cheese, and eggs, also being rich in fat, should only be consumed in small quantities. Fried foods of all kinds should be avoided by the slimmer. Fat should be trimmed off meat. Fat is even present in lean meat, and more so in rich meats like duck, goose, and pork, and in fat fish.

A certain amount of fat is, however, desirable in a slimming diet. It makes meals more palatable, and

Table of Kilojoules and Carbohydrates

This chart shows the energy value, measured in kilojoules, and the carbohydrate content of 25g of different foods.

	kJ	carbohydrate (g)
cream		
double	470	0.6
single	198	1.0
milk	68	1.2
yoghurt		
natural	60	1.3
fruit	83	3.0
cheese		
Cheddar	480	0
cottage	120	1.1
cream	856	0
bacon (average)	498	0
beef (average)	337	0
chicken	193	0
ham	441	0
kidney	110	0
lamb (average)	347	0
liver	145	0
pork	425	0
pork sausage	387	4.3
white fish such as cod, haddock	88	0
fried in batter	208	1.9
fish fingers	201	5.2
herring	199	0
kipper	230	0
salmon (canned)	139	0
sardines (canned in oil)	298	0
eggs	165	0
butter, margarine	780	0
lard, cooking fat, vegetable oils	940	0
sugar	412	26.5
golden syrup	311	20.0
jam	274	17.5
honey	302	19.0
marmalade	276	17.5
beans (canned in tomato sauce)	96	4.3
beans (broad)	72	2.5
beetroot	46	2.5
carrots	24	1.4
peas	51	2.6

	kJ	carbohydrate (g)
potato		
boiled	82	4.9
fried	247	9.3
roast	129	7.0
sweetcorn	50	0
apple	48	3.0
banana	80	4.8
grapefruit	23	1.4
orange	37	2.1
peach	39	4.3
pear	43	2.6
plum	33	2.0
raspberries, strawberries	21	1.5
biscuits		
plain, semi-sweet	420	15.0
rich, sweet	519	18.7
chocolate	520	16.9
bread		
brown	248	11.2
white	265	12.4
starch reduced	245	11.4
cornflakes	382	21.3
crispbread (rye)	333	17.7
rice (boiled)	128	21.7

Note Unless otherwise stated, energy values are given for meat and fish served grilled, poached, roasted or boiled; for boiled vegetables and for fresh fruit.

Values are for edible portions after the usual trimming of bones, skin, stones, etc have been removed.

Alcoholic drinks

	kJ	carbohydrate (g)
beer		
brown ale 250ml	335	20
draught bitter 250ml	380	22
draught mild 250ml	295	17
lager 250ml	305	19
pale ale 250ml	380	22
stout 250ml	420	26
strong ale 250ml	585	33
spirits		
70 proof 100ml	910	56
wine (medium)		
red 100ml	284	8
rosé 100ml	294	18
white 100ml	311	19
sherry		
dry 100ml	481	29
sweet 100ml	568	34
port 100ml	655	40
cider		
dry 250ml	420	26
sweet 250ml	505	31

Non-alcoholic drinks

	kJ	carbohydrate (g)
orange juice canned unsweetened 100ml	145	9
tomato juice canned unsweetened 100ml	65	3
tea 150ml		
black unsweetened	4	0
with 1 × 10ml milk, unsweetened	85	0
with milk and sugar	185	7
coffee 100ml		
black unsweetened	4	0
coffee 150ml		
with milk, half and half, unsweetened	335	7
with milk and sugar	425	13
cocoa 150ml		
with milk and 10g sugar	590	23
malted milk drink 150ml		
unsweetened	565	14

because of its satiety value, helps to make slimming meals more satisfying, and to keep hunger pangs at bay between meals.

Animal protein foods Foods which contain enough protein to cover the average woman's daily recommended intake are listed on p232. Included in this list are 100–125g meat or fish, 0.25 litre milk, an egg, and 25g of cheese. Lighter meats and poultry such as lamb and chicken, and white fish in preference to oily or fat fish are obviously better for the slimmer. They contain less fat than, for example, pork, goose, and herring. Meat, poultry, and fish should be roasted, grilled, stewed or braised, and for the slimmer, should be served without a pastry crust, stuffing, a coating of batter or a heavy layer of breadcrumbs, nor in fact, with any additional ingredients which increase the energy value. This includes the addition of wine or cream to sauces which make up part of the main course. Eggs, too, should be cooked simply, without any extra high energy value ingredients like cream or butter. They should never be fried.

Because milk is a rich source of calcium, slimmers are usually allowed 0.25 litre fresh, whole milk, or 0.5 litre made-up low fat milk powder. Cheese is another important source of calcium. Cottage cheese is an excellent food for weight control because it is very low in fat. Yoghurt, especially the low fat variety without added fruit and sugar, is another good food for the slimmer. A small carton of yoghurt may be substituted for half the day's allowance of milk.

Fruit and vegetables: Fruit contains sugar and has a higher energy value than many people realize; two servings of fresh fruit are allowed daily. Count as one serving: an apple, orange, banana or pear, or 100g of stoned fruit, or soft fruit such as peaches or plums, strawberries or raspberries. No sugar or cream is to be served with the fruit. Canned or dried fruit have a very high energy value and should not be included in slimming meals. Other fruits like apples, rhubarb, blackcurrants, and gooseberries can be lightly stewed, without sugar, in a little water, and the cooked fruit sweetened with a few drops of liquid synthetic sweetener.

Potatoes, dried peas, beans, and lentils have more carbohydrate and a higher energy value than other kinds of vegetables. A small portion of those listed above can be served daily on all but the most strict slimming diets.

Frying or serving vegetables with butter or a rich sauce should be avoided.

The following vegetables, being very low in energy value, can be eaten in large quantities by the slimmer: globe artichokes, asparagus, French and runner beans, broccoli, Brussels sprouts, spinach, cabbage, cauliflower, lettuce, cucumber, radishes, tomatoes, watercress, mustard and cress, endive, chicory, and green peppers. An average serving of each provides only 100kJ or even less.

Beverages Unless there is a medical reason why fluid intake should be restricted, the slimmer may drink as much water, and low-energy drinks as he wishes. Tea and coffee are almost energy-free until milk and sugar are added. Even then, provided the daily milk allowance is not exceeded and synthetic sweetener is used in place of sugar, the slimmer can have as many cups of tea or coffee as he likes. Clear soups, consommé, yeast and meat extracts may be served as hot savoury drinks, though they tend to stimulate the appetite. Soft drinks made without sugar can be taken freely; so can tomato juice.

For alcoholic drinks, see p235.

Heart disease and overweight

Statistics show that overweight people are more likely to suffer from coronary heart disease (CHD) than people of normal weight. If an overweight person reduces to the average weight for his height, his chances of developing CHD are reduced. As overweight people are often less physically active than slim people, lack of exercise is another risk factor where CHD is concerned. Investigations have shown that regular physical exercise has a protective effect against the development of CHD.

High blood pressure is another condition commonly found among overweight people, and it also seems to predispose an individual to heart disease. It is important, therefore, to maintain a normal, slim weight, to avoid unnecessary strain on the heart. Any overweight person who has suffered a heart attack, or anyone with high blood pressure, or with a high blood cholesterol or fat level, will always be advised to shed his excess weight. A good diet with a sensible balance of animal and vegetable fat, which maintains a normal figure, will help to guard against coronary heart disease.

Diabetes

In diabetes, little or no insulin is produced, which means that the body is unable to use carbohydrates for energy in the usual way (see the chapter on Medical Care in the Home).

It is important for the person who prepares the diabetic's meals to know the carbohydrate content of most commonly eaten foods. With this knowledge, a portion of one food can be substituted for another without upsetting the overall carbohydrate content of the day's meals. Substitutions make the meals more varied and attractive. The British Diabetic Association have various charts, lists, and games which can be used for learning the carbohydrate content of foods.

Weight control Diabetics are also recommended to keep to a lighter than normal weight. As is clear from the recommendations for diet, a low carbohydrate slimming diet is suitable (see p233).

CHD and diabetes

Unfortunately diabetics are more inclined to develop coronary heart disease than other people. To avoid the dangers of CHD, diabetics are often advised to keep to a low animal fat diet as well as to their own specialized low carbohydrate diet.

Low fibre dietary problems

A number of disorders, mainly of the digestive system, have been attributed to a shortage of vegetable fibre in the diet. Fibre (roughage) is derived from those plant tissues which cannot be broken down in the human digestive system. The value of fibre is that it gives bulk to food as it passes along the digestive system.

In the last hundred years there has been a marked change in the source of dietary fibre in the West. In developing countries where natural or lightly processed cereals still form a major part of

diet, diseases like cancer of the large bowel, appendicitis, gall bladder disease, haemorrhoids, and
diverticular disease are very rare. By contrast, in
highly developed countries cancer of the bowel is
second only to lung cancer as the cause of death
from cancer; appendicitis is the most common
emergency abdominal operation, and 70% of all
those over sixty are thought to suffer from diver-
ticulitis. Although it is difficult to make direct
comparisons among people in countries with vastly
different life styles, many doctors now consider
that the varying incidence of the diseases mentioned can be explained by the difference in consumption of dietary fibre.

Whole grain foods Wholemeal bread should be
chosen in preference to white or ordinary brown
bread. Many bakers offer a wheatmeal bread made
with a mixture of white and wholemeal flours, but
this has considerably less fibre than real wholemeal
bread which is made from 100% wholemeal flour
with nothing added or taken away. If other sources
fail, wholemeal bread can be obtained from health
food stores. It can, of course, be made at home as
easily as white bread.

Other whole grain cereal foods, breakfast cereals,
and crispbreads should also be eaten. Wholemeal
flour or oatmeal can be used in place of white flour
in making cakes, tea breads, scones, and biscuits;
wholemeal flour also makes excellent pastry.

Breakfast cereals containing a high proportion of
bran are helpful, especially as they can be used in
cooking as well as a breakfast food. Wholemeal
breadcrumbs or crushed wholemeal cereals can be
used in place of white breadcrumbs in stuffings
and coatings.

Bran Plain bran can be bought at most health food
stores and many good supermarkets, and can be
added to usual recipes for bread, cakes, tea breads,
and biscuits in place of a small proportion of white
flour. It can be mixed with cheese and breadcrumbs to make an 'au gratin' topping for vegetables and other savoury dishes. It can also be
added to a savoury crumble, mixed into soup, or
added to breakfast cereals; or it can be used as an
ingredient in home-made muesli, or stirred into
yoghurt.

Fruits, vegetables, and nuts These should be eaten in
quantity. Dried fruits, such as prunes and figs,
have a well-known laxative property of their own
and should be served regularly.

Note Figures of food values in this chapter have
been reproduced with the permission of the con-
troller of Her Majesty's Stationery Office, and taken
from *The Composition of Foods* by McCance and
Widdowson, published by HMSO.

FOOD SHOPPING TODAY

In marketing, that the best articles are the cheapest, may be laid down as a rule; and it is desirable, unless an experienced and confidential housekeeper be kept, that the mistress should herself purchase all provisions and stores needed for the house. If the mistress be a young wife, and not accustomed to order " things for the house," a little practice and experience will soon teach her who are the best tradespeople to deal with, and what are the best provisions to buy.

The way people choose to spend their money on food is very personal; every family has different skills in shopping and preparing food, different tastes, likes, and dislikes. The nutritional properties to be considered are discussed in the chapter on Nutrition and Diet. But it is, of course, quite possible to be both an economical cook and a good cook.

You are bound to spend quite a lot of money on food, and if you have a comparatively small income it will account for a large percentage of your spending. It is vital, therefore, to establish friendly relationships with your local shopkeepers who will then give you their advice on what is of best value at any one time.

When there is a choice of shops, each will tend to specialize in some products, and although it may be very convenient to do all your shopping under one roof in the supermarket, it does not always mean that you will get the best choice in all the goods available.

Other factors you will want to take into account include cleanliness of the shops and the people who work there, the service, accessibility, availability of parking, whether it is possible to pay by cheque or credit card, and if there is a delivery service.

Though shopping without any plan can lead to overspending, flexibility is all-important. When you are shopping for the week, or the weekend, look out for any seasonal bargains and plan the rest of your shopping around them. It must be emphasized, however, that quality also matters (see p240 below): in the long run it is often more economical to pay a little more, as there is less waste.

Information on Labels

You expect to buy food that is clean and safe to eat. Choosing from thousands of items in a supermarket, you need to be able to rely on labels for information about the kind of product you are buying, what is in it, and how much you are going to get. Most of the legislation that relates to food exists:

1) to prevent the sale of adulterated, impure or bad quality food.
2) to prevent short weight or measure in the sale of food.
3) to prevent extravagant claims or misdescription on labels and in advertisements.
4) to ensure a good standard of hygiene where food is prepared, distributed or sold.
5) to provide standards of composition to ensure food value and quality, particularly where it is difficult to judge for oneself, as with processed or packaged foods. (For example, you want to know that a tin of meat loaf has got meat in it and that however different brands may taste, when they say 'meat loaf' it basically means the same thing.)
6) to inform consumers about the quantity of food being offered.

In some cases the law also requires the price to be displayed and the price per unit of weight (g, kg, etc) to be given (see p239).

Pre-packed foods must by law carry on the label a full list of the ingredients, which has to include any additives used and be given in descending order of weight. (Water does not have to be listed as an ingredient.)

Reading the labels can be very instructive if one is trying to decide which brand of food to buy, or to check that it is still made from the same ingredients.

Cutting the Cost

It is a good idea to keep a simple record of the money you spend on food and drink. Check on how much you spend on groceries, bread, biscuits, cake, fruit and vegetables, meat and fish. This will help you to cut expenditure when you are short of money, because it will show you where you can cut back.

For certain regular staple items you may be able to save 10% if you visit the shop that consistently sells these items at the lowest price.

Buying in Bulk

You may find that you can cut down your food bills by 10–15% on average, through buying in quantity – a sack of potatoes, for example, or 5 litres of cooking oil. Unless you can reach a 'bulk buy' store, you can probably save almost as much by buying goods on 'special offer'; you may get more variety that way too. Perishable foods like fruit and vegetables usually offer the biggest savings. If you do not have a freezer or a very large family, it is sometimes a good idea to share the buying with a group of friends. (This type of bulk buying is sometimes called a food co-op.)

You may find that your local trader will meet you half way by ordering, for example, a case of oranges for you and splitting the difference between his usual profit on a case and a discount to you. It is always worth asking.

Value for Money

If you do not know how much food costs (and it is surprising how few items most people can cost accurately) you will find it difficult to judge whether you are getting good value for money and whether an apparent bargain really is a bargain. Prices for thousands of food products do vary, in fact, from shop to shop.

Price on its own should not necessarily be regarded as the most important factor in your choice. It must be related to both quantity and quality and to your own personal taste.

Quantity

Most foods have, by law, to be sold by weight – for example, meat, fish, cheese, poultry, and most fresh fruit and vegetables. Almost all pre-packaged food (except in very small sizes) has to be marked with its weight, though some fruit and vegetables can be sold pre-packed by 'count', provided there are scales on which you can check-weigh them. Some pre-packaged foods, butter for example, are sold only in prescribed quantities.

The importance of quantity is that it gives you a measure against which you can judge price. One should always check the weight or quantity marked. For example, a tea producer will mark the weight of his packet of tea (which has to be sold in prescribed quantities) quite clearly, but he may use quite a different approach for his tea bags. The law requires him to mark the weight and to sell the tea in the same prescribed quantities, but he will emphasize the number of bags. This number may appear on five of the six sides of the packet, and the weight on only two, in much smaller letters. In fact, the price of tea in tea bags is about 50% more than tea of similar quality sold in a packet. This is useful to remember when one is short of money and looking for ways to cut down on food spending.

It is an offence to give short weight or measure.

A number of products are not sold in standard quantities. This often makes comparisons between brands, sizes and relative prices difficult when one is trying to work out which represents the best value for money. One needs to work out the unit price.

Unit price

The unit price is the price per kg, per litre, and so on. The 'unit' of measurement is divided by the price to show you the comparative cost of the 'unit' (whatever quantity you are buying).

As working out the unit price is a nuisance, there

are moves to oblige retailers to mark it on odd or fractional pre-packs. But we do it every day when we buy goods in irregular quantities by reference to a marked price per kg and pay for just that amount.

Many people do not order by weight when they are buying, say, meat; they order simply by telling the butcher how much money they want to spend. Reference to the unit price, however, can help you judge exactly what value for money you are getting.

Quality

Good quality in food is something one soon learns to recognize by experience when buying on a regular basis.

For some foods which are of nutritional importance or which have expensive main ingredients, such as meat, that lead to the possibility of 'stretching' by the addition of less expensive substitutes, the law steps in with standards which lay down the minimum acceptable 'composition of the good'. Sausages, for example, have to contain a given percentage of meat. Bread, butter, margarine, milk, canned meat products, fish pastes, and ice cream are some of the food products which have these compulsory standards; with products which contain well above the standard, the manufacturer often displays the exact percentage of the pure ingredients on the package.

Modern methods of distribution and selling involve much more centralized buying and packaging. Symptoms of the mass market include food grown with high yield per hectare rather than flavour at a premium, tomatoes developed with thick skins for protection against damage in travelling, rather than for taste, apples graded for uniformity of size to help pre-packing, for crispness rather than flavour. Vegetables are trimmed and washed, fish skinned and filleted; chickens eviscerated and sold without giblets; colour added to canned peas.

If you wish and can afford to buy fresh foods with all their natural qualities intact, it may, therefore, be necessary to look for specialist shops and pay accordingly.

Grading

Very few products which are 'graded' by producers reach the shops with any indication to the consumer to declare their grade. Fruit and vegetables are exceptions. The European Economic Community (EEC) has strict regulations designed to ensure that only good quality produce reaches the shops (which is not, of course, the same as saying that it reaches the consumer). The grower grades his produce for quality and size, and each package carries his name or trademark, the class, weight or number of the contents, and the country of origin. Any product which does not reach the requirements of its class must be removed to a lower grade.

Some retailers indicate that their fruit and vegetables are suitable for particular purposes and offer produce which is 'ripe for eating', or which should be kept for a few days. This is particularly true of supermarkets without trained assistants who are prepared to underwrite the quality of their fresh fruit and vegetables.

For the grading of eggs, see the chapter on Eggs. As for meat, expressions such as 'prime quality' and 'top class' are no guarantee in themselves.

So, whatever grading schemes there may be, there is no substitute for personal examination by the customer and the reputation of a retailer or manufacturer who stands to lose business if his produce is not 'up to standard'. Here again a good relationship with local shops will prove to be helpful.

'Sell by' Dates

Most perishable and semi-perishable food carries a 'sell by' date, which indicates that if it has been held at the proper temperature and in the right condition it will be at its best until this date. Cooked meat products such as pies, made-up dishes like fish cakes, and delicatessen products should in any case only be bought from refrigerated displays. They deteriorate quickly at ordinary temperatures.

Usually there is a 'safety margin' of a few days built in, but few retailers will keep products on sale after this date, and will often offer them at a reduced price on the 'sell by' date, to clear them.

Provided one takes food home in reasonable time, the 'sell by' date is a most useful guide for the shopper. Some producers add the advice 'eat by' or 'best eaten before' to ensure that you use their products at their best. (For more information, see the Chart of Storage Life on pp1398–99.)

Complaints and Food Poisoning

If you have complaints about food going bad or containing a 'foreign body', or if you have been given short weight or measure, you can go back to the shop and complain and get a refund, or go to your local authority who will look into the matter for you – in which case you may not get any compensation. If you are suffering from food poisoning which you think may be caused by contaminated food, report this to the Department of Environmental Health of the local authority so that they can investigate and prevent others from suffering. If you have a really bad time, you may want to sue the food supplier, in which case the evidence of the local authority will be important to you. But remember that a great deal of food poisoning is caused by bad domestic storage of food (see the chapter on Stores and Storage).

Shopping Wisely

The check-list which follows sums up the advice given in this chapter.

1) Know what food costs. If you intend to use convenience foods or ready-made dishes because they save time, remember that nearly all of them cost more than making them at home.

2) Plan ahead in outline, if not in detail. Keep a list on the back of a door so that you can add what you need when you think of it.

3) Always think in terms of price per unit of weight, measure or serving, not per tin or pack.

4) Loose foods are often cheaper than packaged goods, and many dry goods do not need expensive packaging.

5) Buy the quantity which suits you best. Some apparent bargains are so large that the contents will lose their freshness before you get around to using them, for instance. This is a question of experience.

6) Compare the prices of different versions of the same food, eg fresh, frozen or dried vegetables, before you decide which is the best buy at the time.

7) Consider if a freezer would help you to shop more economically or prepare meals of greater variety for less work, or give you the benefit of out-of-season foods (see the chapter on Home Freezing).

8) If this appeals to you, you might find that you could save money by buying in bulk, or joining with friends to buy large quantities and sharing the goods out between you.

9) Always take advantage of seasonal bargains and special offers when they occur.

10) Consider buying 'own brands'. They usually work out from 10% cheaper than branded equivalents.

HOSPITALITY AND SOCIAL CUSTOMS

Hospitality is a most excellent virtue; but care must be taken that the love of company, for its own sake, does not become a prevailing passion; for then the habit is no longer hospitality, but dissipation. In giving an entertainment, the mistress should remember that it is her duty to make her guests feel happy.

Hospitality

The giving and receiving of hospitality is at the root of all social behaviour, and in many cultures there is an almost sacred relationship between host and guest. In Mrs Beeton's England the laws of hospitality were more complicated and stricter than they are today, but the principles have remained unchanged: both host and guests have an obligation to each other to ensure that their company helps to create a happy and relaxed atmosphere. Today's freer social structure makes thoughtfulness no less important; rules of etiquette still govern behaviour on formal occasions, and the most important of these are outlined in the section on Social Customs (pp248–256); there are, however, many matters to be considered by host and guests on all social occasions.

Entertaining can be very enjoyable, but it is hard work to entertain well. A good host does this with pride and pleasure, not with polite resentment, for it is no kindness to your friends to return their hospitality out of a sense of duty. Nor will they find it pleasant if you invite them in order to show off or try and outdo them. If you make some extra personal effort to please your guests, and enjoy yourself doing this, your hospitality will be appreciated. However, try not to let the effort show. If you are attempting something too ambitious, you will make your guests ill at ease, for your anxiety will quickly communicate itself.

When you are entertaining family or close friends you may feel more relaxed, but do not, even then, forget that as host or hostess you should always be sensitive to your guests' comfort and enjoyment, and give some special thought to making the time they spend in your home enjoyable.

Do not ask more guests than can be accommodated comfortably at your dining table if you are serving a sit-down meal, or who have space to circulate easily if you are giving a buffet or drinks party. It is usual to invite roughly equal numbers of men and women, but it is not necessary to be too rigid about this. It may not be a good idea to invite groups of people who will stick too closely together, excluding outsiders, but it can also be unwise to invite people without any common interest. Never use a party to try and affect a reconciliation between people who have quarrelled with one another – they will not thank you for it and you are unlikely to provide a relaxed atmosphere for your other guests.

Preparing for Guests

When you invite guests to your home, you will want to see that it is clean, tidy, and comfortable. It helps to think in turn of each room your guests may use. Guests wanting to change when they arrive should be shown to a bedroom with a good mirror, and a clothes brush should be provided. You may want to prepare another bedroom in which your guests can leave their coats. In the bathroom, provide hand towels and soap. (Any guests who have not been to your home before should be shown where the bathroom and lavatory are when they arrive.) In the rooms where you are entertaining, you may need to re-arrange furniture and lighting, lay the table, arrange flowers, check there are ashtrays. Remember to ensure that the rooms are a comfortable temperature, cool and airy enough in hot weather and warm enough in cold weather (even if you yourself are hot from working in the kitchen). Old people are especially sensitive to the cold, and it is always a good idea to see that they are sitting in the warm away from draughts. When you have elderly visitors, think carefully about any hazards in the home, particularly polished floors or loose rugs that might cause a fall. Warn your visitors about these if they cannot be removed or avoided. You will need to take the same care with young children, watching especially for electrical appliances and fires. Keep anything precious or breakable out of children's reach. They will probably be happiest if they can be left to play in the garden or a playroom.

If you invite a guest who is disabled or in a wheelchair make sure that the car can be parked as near the front door as possible, even if it means asking other guests to park well away so as to leave space. Entry to the house should be made as easy as possible. If the chair will need lifting up steps, see that you have someone on hand who will be able to do this. Finally, make sure there is enough space at the dining table to accommodate the wheelchair.

If you have pets, do not assume that all your guests will share your love of animals. Some people are allergic to cat fur, while others may be frightened of cats, dogs or birds. Try to find out tactfully about this, and keep your pets away from visitors, if necessary.

Do not assume either that guests will want to spend all their time admiring your children. Young children can often be very tiresome among a party of adults, and older children will usually want to keep out of the way.

One side of traditional hospitality is inviting guests to share the intimacy of your own home, the other is the offer of food and drink. Here, particularly, you must consider your own means and capabilities, and also your guests' comfort and tastes. Many people are unable to eat certain foods for reasons of health or conviction, and others may not take alcoholic drinks. Never press a guest if a firm refusal has been given. You can get to know

people socially without finding out if they are diabetic, vegetarian, or require special consideration in some other way, and no one should ever feel the slightest embarrassment about asking when unsure. Once you do know, do not single out one guest, giving him or her a very different menu from the rest. You can serve delicious slimming or vegetarian meals which all your guests will enjoy, and you can include a few optional extra dishes. You should always have some fruit juice, mineral water or other soft drink available as an alternative to wine, beer or spirits.

Invitations

In the past the etiquette associated with all types of entertaining ensured that guests knew what degree of formality or informality to expect. Today it is just as important when inviting guests to be explicit.

For formal occasions it is usual to send out printed cards, which clearly specify the event, the time and place, and generally include a note on dress. Standard invitation cards may be bought at a stationer's, or you can have cards printed for a special event. For parties it is often simplest to send an 'At Home' invitation, which should state 'Drinks', 'Sherry', 'Buffet' or 'Dinner', as appropriate. It is a good idea too to include a note on dress, even if this is to be 'informal'. 'Black tie' on an invitation means that men wear dinner jackets and women long evening dresses.

If you are planning a small party, such as a dinner party, and want to be certain to get guests who will mix well, telephone first to see if they are available on the date you have planned, or discuss alternatives. Fix a time which will suit your guests, not too late for those who have a long journey home or a train to catch, but leaving yourself enough time for preparation. After any telephone invitation, it is sensible to send a brief confirmation by letter or postcard. Otherwise try to telephone again to confirm the date nearer the time. For children's parties it is important to state the finishing as well as the starting time, and this is also usual for drinks parties where a meal is not to be served. It is popular among young people to ask guests to bring a bottle of wine to a party and this can be stated on the invitation; guests may also be asked to bring a partner, and this should always be clearly stated.

For any formal or semi-formal occasion send out invitations in good time, allowing six weeks before a wedding, a ball or other special celebration, three or four weeks before a cocktail or buffet party and two or three weeks before a lunch or dinner party.

The earlier you can send out invitations the likelier you are to get together the guests you want. Inviting people late may give the impression that other guests were invited first but have refused, and nobody likes to believe he is a second choice.

If your home is hard to find, it is worth drawing a simple map, photocopying it, and sending a copy with each invitation.

Introductions

When guests arrive always introduce them to the people already there; if there is too big a crowd to effect introductions all round, introduce them to one group of fellow guests. When performing introductions, the general rule is to introduce men to women, the younger person to the older person, and the non-titled to the titled. If possible, introduce a husband and wife together as Mr and Mrs, so that there is no doubt. It may be a good idea to say briefly what each person does, where they live, or some such thing, in order to initiate a conversation. Except on very informal occasions, do not introduce people just by their first names, as this could cause embarrassment or offence.

If you have invited foreign visitors, make a special effort to ensure they feel at ease, and are not left out of conversations and discussions. Explain any social customs with which they may be unfamiliar and encourage them to talk about their own country.

The Perfect Guest

The qualities of the perfect guest complement those of the perfect host. It is important to be relaxed, gracious in your acceptance of hospitality, considerate of the tastes and pleasures of your hosts. Never try to outshine your hosts or your fellow guests. Respond quickly to invitations and do not hesitate to ask about dress, etc if you are in any doubt. If you are vegetarian or are unable to eat certain foods, you must let your hostess know beforehand. Arrive punctually – but not too early; nothing is more likely to create panic than guests who arrive before preparations are complete. (If you have accepted an invitation, but are unavoidably prevented from coming, try to give as much notice as you can.)

It is not necessary to bring a gift whenever you are invited, but chocolates or a bottle of wine will often be appreciated, and some such gift would be only courteous if you are staying overnight. Flowers or a house-plant can be taken – particularly to people living in town – but it is no kindness to present your dinner party hostess with an unmanageably large bunch of flowers. Do not make a gift too lavish, or you may embarrass your hosts and make fellow-guests feel at a disadvantage. It is not usual to bring a gift when invited to a formal occasion.

Do not spend all the time talking to the people you know best, but try and help your hosts by mixing with fellow-guests who may be new to you.

There are no fixed rules nowadays as to how long guests should stay, but a good guest will always be sensitive to the inconvenience that may be caused by overstaying one's welcome. This is true even of the most informal visits. On the other hand, having accepted hospitality, you should not leave too soon, as this might cause offence.

How much assistance a guest should offer his host or hostess with those jobs which need to be done during the party is mostly a matter of commonsense. Follow the lead given by your host. Helping with drinks or passing dishes at a party will always be useful, but you should never, for instance, insist on helping to clear up in a small kitchen. On a longer visit, there are often jobs where you could be useful, and you should offer help tactfully. Only help in the kitchen if it does not look as if you are taking over responsibility.

It is always good manners to thank for hospitality received – by telephone or postcard if the occasion was informal, and by letter for any formal occasion or overnight visit. You should try to do this as soon as possible after the occasion; it becomes more and more difficult to do this with each day it is left.

Many people feel that hospitality should be returned before a guest is invited again, but no strict obligation should be placed. There are many circumstances which may make it difficult for you to return hospitality at a particular time.

Parties

For the principles of planning a menu, see the chapter on Menus; for advice on preparing food in quantity, see the chapter on Party Food; and for ideas and information on serving the food and drink, see the chapter on Presenting a Meal.

Once you get down to detailed planning of a party, it is almost always worth making lists. Make a guest list which you can up-date as acceptances and refusals come in. Write out the menu plan with drinks to be served, and from this make a shopping list and a list of items you will prepare in advance. List the household chores to be done and add to your shopping list any cleaning or polishing materials you may need for glasses, silver, etc. It is also very useful to draw up a timetable for the last few hours before your guests are due to arrive, to make sure nothing gets forgotten. Try and leave yourself enough time to bath or shower, change, and sit down to relax for a few minutes before the doorbell rings.

Do not be too ambitious in your choice of menu. Plan within your capabilities and your budget. Try to stick to recipes which you know can be relied upon to succeed. A simple meal, well presented in a relaxed way, is infinitely preferable to an array of elaborate dishes that have not quite worked, served in an atmosphere of suppressed panic. If you are working during the day, plan a meal for which most of the preparation can be done in advance.

Of course, if you decide to use professional caterers, they will do all the buying and preparation and will be responsible for serving the food and drink. Some caterers are also able to supply extra chairs etc, should you need them.

Dinner Parties

Dinner parties can be one of the most enjoyable ways of entertaining a small group of friends. When you are planning a dinner party, think first what you yourself would hope for if invited out to dinner; good food and drink, stimulating conversation, the opportunity of seeing old friends and making new ones. Whether this is achieved or not depends on good preparation and well-chosen company. Eight people will often make a better party than six, but larger numbers than this are more difficult to cope with, particularly if you are preparing and serving all the food yourself, for it is easy to find yourself left out of your own party.

A celebration dinner can consist of up to five or six courses; however, you will usually want to serve three or four courses, possibly with cheese to follow the dessert.

Work out a seating plan, using place cards only if you have ten or more guests. It is usual to separate couples, and alternate men and women around the table.

If you invite guests for 8.00pm, expect to start eating at about 8.45pm; if you invite them for 8.15pm or 8.30pm, plan to start at 9.00pm or a little after. When guests arrive, offer them a drink. Canapés, dips, nuts, olives, etc may be served with the aperitif, but be careful not to spoil your guests' appetites.

When you are ready to serve the meal, show everybody to their places at the table. Serve the food and wine simply and without elaborate ceremony, allowing your guests to enjoy conversation, and trying to ensure that no one is left out. Coffee is usually served at the end of the meal, but you may want to offer tea or decaffeinated coffee as an alternative.

Port is traditionally served with the cheese course and guests will continue drinking it with nuts and sweetmeats; when coffee is served, liqueurs and brandy may be offered. Less formally, however, the port, brandy, and liqueurs are brought in with the coffee, and a choice is offered. Alternatively, if the party adjourns to another room for coffee, the brandy and liqueurs can be offered there; it is not usual to serve port on such occasions. Port is passed round the table from right to left and people help themselves. Sticklers for etiquette will not allow the bottle to be put down on the table until it has completed the round. The tradition that ladies leave the gentlemen over their port and brandy is seldom observed nowadays, except on very formal occasions.

Attitudes have changed very much towards smoking, and many people today dislike any smoking during a meal. Both smokers and non-smokers need to show consideration, but certainly if fine wines are being served, there should be no smoking until the meal is finished. At a formal dinner there is no smoking before the loyal toast. Cigars may be offered with the coffee.

Lunch Parties

Weekend lunch parties can be a convenient way for busy people to entertain, and they are often easier than dinner parties for elderly people and parents with young children to attend to. A lunch party will usually be less formal than dinner, so that, if space allows, you can entertain a larger number of people.

Drinks are served before the meal; the main course may be quite substantial, but the starter can be very simple, and you may serve either a dessert (or fruit) or cheese, rather than both. Beer or cider are often offered as alternatives to wine. Nevertheless, the same planning is required as for a dinner party and the same thought and consideration for your guests. This is particularly true if guests are invited to join a family lunch, when they can only too often feel like intruders. Children need to be entertained and will easily get bored sitting at table for too long. They should be allowed to get down from the table early if the rest of the party is lingering.

Drinks Parties and Buffet Parties

When you want to entertain a larger number of people than can be satisfactorily seated at table, a buffet or drinks party is the best idea. This can take place at midday during a weekend or holiday, or in the evening.

A drinks party should normally last one-and-a-half or two hours, generally starting at noon or at 6.00pm. You can serve a fairly full range of alcoholic drinks, including whisky, vodka, gin, rum, brandy, dry and sweet vermouth, sherry, and red and white wine; in addition, you may want to have some liqueurs for mixing cocktails (see the chapter on Table Wines and Other Drinks). For soft drinks and mixers you will need soda water, Indian tonic water, dry ginger ale, bitter lemon, bitters, fresh fruit juices, and squashes. Garnishes should include sliced lemon, cocktail cherries, and olives.

If you do not want to provide the full range of drinks, you can offer a more restricted choice if this includes something special, such as champagne or a champagne cocktail, a wine or cider cup, or a Pimms. Another very good alternative is a sherry party, where a variety of sherries and perhaps vermouths is served.

Many drinks should be served chilled, so make sure you start the party with a good supply of ice (see p1368).

The choice of food for a drinks party should not be neglected. It should not be elaborate, but should look attractive and be easy to eat with the fingers. Cold canapés (see pp1284–88), nuts, olives, etc can be set out in advance and, perhaps, some hot cocktail sausages served half-way through the party. Make sure there are plenty of napkins around for wiping greasy fingers.

A drinks party demands less preparation than other parties, but it is expensive and the hosts will need to work hard to circulate among their guests. It is important not to let glasses stay empty for long, and if one or two guests offer help, do not refuse it. This also helps to keep people moving about, thereby meeting other guests. A garden provides an ideal setting for a drinks party if the weather is fine, and the extra space this gives will make a great difference to the occasion.

At a buffet party the food is more important than the drink, and you are in effect giving a full meal to your guests without the formality of serving it at table. As always, adequate planning and preparation is essential and everything possible must be done in advance. Providing food for large numbers of people is taxing and you should refer to the guide to party quantities on pp1580–84. Keep it simple – neither too many different dishes, nor anything too elaborate. Provide food that can be eaten easily with a fork or with the fingers. Soups and runny desserts are difficult to eat standing up, so avoid serving these.

Arrange, if you can, for two buffet lines or serving tables. Although this means presenting the food in two sets of dishes, it will make the serving much quicker and easier. Guests can either help themselves, or you may prefer to serve them yourself. Consider using disposable tableware as an alternative to hiring or borrowing extra plates and cutlery. Matching paper plates and napkins can be very attractive and will save you a lot of washing-up after the party.

When guests arrive, offer them a drink and do not start serving food until virtually everyone expected has come. After the dessert and cheese, serve plenty of coffee.

Outdoor or Barbecue Parties

When arranging any party out of doors, you must have a contingency plan in case the weather is bad. Do not ask more people than you can accommodate indoors if you have to.

It is almost essential to make a list of what to take on a picnic as it is too late to remember the salt or mustard, or the corkscrew for the wine, once you have left home.

The barbecue is an informal kind of party where guests can not only serve themselves, but can also do some of their own cooking. Pin up a guide to cooking times and make sure there is a good supply of salads, sauces, chutneys, etc. Serve cider, beer, punch or wine. (See the chapter on Packed and Outdoor Meals for recipes and further ideas.)

Children's Parties

The success of a children's party depends on really careful planning and organization. Decide how many children you can cope with, invite them in good time, and be specific about what time the party starts and what time the children should be collected.

Most children's parties are given for birthdays, and the time of year may well influence the type of party chosen. Fine summer weather and a garden open up a whole range of possibilities, but they do not make the need for thorough organization any less crucial. A party for younger children (up to nine or ten years old) generally starts at 3.00 or 3.30pm and finishes at 5.30 or 6.00pm, and you will probably plan a continuous programme of games, interrupted only for tea in the middle of the afternoon. Alternatively, you may want to have a professional entertainer, who will amuse the children with conjuring tricks and so on, for part of the afternoon.

Many children are shy to start with, and it is important to see that no one is left out. If the birthday child has a brother or sister, it is a good idea to invite a friend of the same age so that he or she does not feel left out either.

Allow time between groups of games for children to go to the lavatory and make sure as many as possible go after tea, although even then you may not always be able to prevent accidents when you have very young children.

Tea itself will take a surprisingly short time. Food should be chosen to please the children rather than their mothers. Children's tastes are relatively unsophisticated – sausages and fish fingers could be their idea of a good party. Choose savoury rather than sweet things; they tend to be more popular and healthier. Serve orange and lemon squash to drink. Remember to cover the carpet around the tea-table, and think about using disposable tableware.

Have plenty of small gifts to give as prizes to the winners of the games, and to each child at the end of the party.

For older children, an outing to a film, pantomime or children's show is often preferred to party games. Assemble the children at your home in good time, and have a party tea when you get back. Plan to have a couple of short games after tea, before the children are collected.

The mothers or fathers of some of the children may stay for part or all of the afternoon, in which case you will need to provide plenty of tea to drink and some extra sandwiches and cakes.

Informal Parties

Every group of friends develops its own social conventions, but principles of hospitality always apply, and special thought has to be given to making outsiders who join the group feel welcome. There are many ways of sharing the responsibilities of entertaining within a group of friends – each family contributing a part of the meal, or moving from one household to another during the course of the day, for example.

Tea parties may seem old-fashioned but they are an excellent way of entertaining informally, particularly if you want to invite friends and neighbours who might be embarrassed by more lavish hospitality.

If you invite friends to play cards or for some special entertainment, do not let food or drink intrude too much on the main purpose of the occasion, but make sure it is available when required.

Business Entertaining

It is never worth undertaking business entertainment at home unless you feel sure you can do it successfully; at the same time, business colleagues and associates will be flattered to be invited to your home, particularly if they are visiting from overseas.

Business conversation at a social dinner party is boring for your other guests. If the aim of the evening is to provide a relaxed atmosphere in which to discuss business affairs, it is therefore best not to invite any guests unconnected with that business.

Overnight and Weekend Guests

If your home is large enough, it is enjoyable to have guests to stay overnight. Try and make the rooms where they are to stay as welcoming as possible; clear some space in cupboards or on the dressing table, make sure there is something to read, that there is a reading light that works, and put out fresh towels. Keep one or two new toothbrushes and disposable razors in case these are needed. A small vase of flowers is a charming touch. If the weather is cold, make sure the heating is adequate, and if the bed has not been used recently, air it with a hot-water-bottle or electric blanket.

Find out when your guests will want to be called in the morning, use the bathroom, and have breakfast. Explain what your plans and the usual routines of the household are, so that your guests can fit in without inconvenience. Try to allow guests some time to themselves if they want it.

Breakfast should be simple. If weekend guests have arrived on Friday night, a cold lunch on Saturday allows everyone to plan independently if they want to. Thought and consideration of your guests' interests will make all the difference between convenience and hospitality.

Longer-staying Guests

If a relative stays for a longer period, or a child comes on an exchange visit, it is even more important to make them familiar with the household routines, and not give the impression that you are having to put yourself out all the time on their behalf. Make them feel that their time with you is a pleasure to you, not an imposition and a nuisance. Include them in your plans wherever possible, but make sure to allow them enough time on their own, so that they are not smothered with well-meaning hospitality.

Social Customs

However informal personal entertaining has become, there are still many formal occasions and functions where the rules of etiquette apply. A knowledge of what to do, and what not to do on such occasions can add immeasurably to everyone's enjoyment of a family affair such as a wedding or christening. You may even receive an invitation to Buckingham Palace – to receive honours or to attend a garden party for instance – and knowing exactly how to behave in the presence of royalty will give you the self-confidence to make this a relaxed and happy occasion.

Births

A baby's birth may be announced in the appropriate column of a daily paper; family and close friends like, however, to be informed personally of the event. Birth announcement cards can be bought from any good stationer's or you can have them specially printed. If the baby is born in hospital, it is usual to give a present to the nursing staff, such as chocolates or a bottle of wine which they can share. In a private nursing home, a rather more expensive present may be appropriate.

Friends and relations should not be in too great a hurry to visit the mother and baby. It is tactful to enquire beforehand when a visit would be welcomed, and in the meantime a card or telegram of congratulations should be sent.

Christenings

The baby's birth having been registered in the usual way, the time and place of the christening, if there is to be one, depends on the wishes and religious beliefs of the parents. Most christenings take place between the ages of six weeks and four months, although in churches where total immersion pertains, baptism is usually performed at a later age. The christening is a simple, informal ceremony held around the font where the holy water is poured over the baby's head. It is attended only by family and close friends, although other members of the congregation will be present if the vicar chooses to perform the christening during the course of a regular service. It is possible to arrange for a christening to take place at home, and this is sometimes preferred in the case of mixed marriages or when the health of mother or child precludes a visit to church.

It is customary for a girl child to have two godmothers and one godfather, while a boy child has two godfathers and one godmother. Godparents are expected to keep a friendly and watchful eye over the child to see that it is brought up as a believer. This is a role to be undertaken seriously or not at all, and anyone who cannot conscientiously accept the invitation to be a godparent should tactfully decline to do so.

The simple christening party which follows the ceremony can consist of a buffet, luncheon or tea, depending on the time of day. A cake with white icing is traditional fare. The priest who officiated at the ceremony should be invited to the party, although official commitments may prevent him coming. Godparents traditionally give a small silver item such as a mug, spoon or napkin ring, or a piece of jewellery such as a bracelet or locket, as a christening present. (Pewter is an excellent, less expensive alternative to silver.) Other guests may give something smaller, such as a toy or baby garment.

Confirmation/Barmitzvah

At confirmation, which takes place in early teenage, the religious duties of the godparents are ended. They should be invited to the service, and there may be a simple family party afterwards. It is usual for the godparents to give a present, often of a religious nature such as a Bible or prayer book.

In the Jewish faith the barmitzvah, which takes place at the age of thirteen, is a more formal occasion, the religious ceremony being followed by a large party.

The child is now considered to be taking responsibility for his own beliefs and behaviour, and should be able to take an active role in looking after the guests at his party.

Engagement

When a couple decide to marry, they often wish to make a formal announcement of their intention in the appropriate column of the local or national press. The announcement should be as simple as possible, and make the identities of the couple quite clear. The man's name always comes first, thus: 'The engagement is announced between (man's name) son of (parents' names and address) and (girl's name) daughter of (parents' names and address)'. If one or both parents are no longer living, they are referred to as 'the late Mr or Mrs . . .' In the case of divorced parents where the mother has remarried, both parents' names should be given. If the bride-to-be is a widow, then her

late husband's name can be substituted for her parents' names in the announcement, but a previous marriage that ended in divorce need not be referred to. If the date of the wedding has already been decided upon, this can be included in the announcement.

An engagement party may be given by either or both sets of parents, or by the couple themselves. Invitations to this can also serve the purpose of informing relations and close friends of the engagement before the official announcement appears. At the party a speech can be made by the prospective bride's father, godfather, or a close family friend, and replied to by the groom.

Guests at an engagement party are not expected to bring a gift (as this would have to be returned if the engagement was subsequently broken off). The party does, however, offer a good opportunity to consult the bride about the choice of wedding present.

The giving of an engagement ring as a token of a binding contract is a very old custom, and many couples still like the ring as a symbol of their love and their promise to marry. The ring is bought by the man and worn by the girl on the third finger of her left hand. It is traditionally – but not necessarily – a diamond ring, and most couples choose it together, although the man might present it to his fiancée more formally at a party. Alternatively, a man may wish to give his fiancée a ring which has become a family heirloom, or, if his mother has died, a ring which once belonged to her. If she wishes, the girl can give him in return an engagement present such as a tie-pin, pen or cuff-links.

Some couples decide to dispense with the engagement ring, and put the money instead towards furniture for their house or flat.

Though not essential, it is a pleasant custom for parents to write to their future son- or daughter-in-law if they have not already met, just to say welcome, and, if they live some distance away, perhaps to invite them for a visit.

Once a couple are engaged, it is generally thought to be bad manners for either to go out alone with someone of the opposite sex, quite apart from any hurt or jealousy it might cause.

If the engagement is broken off, it might be wise to give notice of this in the newspaper, if the engagement itself was so announced. There is no need for explanation – the simple statement that the marriage will not now take place, is all that is required. The girl should return her ring and any other presents she has received from her fiancé, unless he specifically asks her to keep them. At one time, both would automatically have severed relationships with each other and with the prospective in-laws, but this does not always happen nowadays, and all parties may remain friends.

Weddings

When planning a wedding, the first thing to decide is whether to have a civil or religious ceremony. (See also the chapter on The Law and You.) The civil ceremony takes place in a registrar's office and is usually only attended by a few close relatives and friends because of lack of space.

Marriage in a church allows for a larger number of guests. It is a basically simple ceremony which can be rendered more elaborate by having, for instance, a choir or bell-ringers. The various fees to be paid in connection with the wedding ceremony are the responsibility of the groom. A church wedding needs to be arranged well in advance to make sure that church and vicar are free, and to allow for the calling of banns (unless an ecclesiastical licence is used), discussion of the service, and the choice of music. Weddings are not always allowed during Lent or Advent, and ceremonies performed at these times are kept very simple.

Having established what kind of wedding it is to be, the bride must decide what to wear. She can choose between an ordinary dress or suit and the full, white, bridal gown. If she chooses to have a white wedding, she may also wish to have bridal attendants, and will consult with them as to what they should wear. Each bridesmaid, page or matron of honour will bear the expense of their own costume, but the groom will be expected to give each one a present after the ceremony.

The groom chooses his best man, and, if there is to be a large congregation, friends of the bride and the groom can be asked to act as ushers to show the guests to their seats. The bride's mother enters the church first and sits on the left of the aisle, followed by the groom's parents who sit on the right. Other relatives and friends follow, sitting on the left or right according to whether they have been invited by the bride or the groom.

The bride is led up the aisle by her father on his right arm, or by an older close male relative if her father is no longer living, after the groom has taken his place near the altar. If sisters marry together, the father can call on any other male relative to give away the younger daughter, as, according to custom, he himself should give away the elder. He and the elder daughter walk up the aisle first. At the chancel steps, the bride stands to the left of the groom, while the best man stands on his right.

After the ceremony, the congregation waits while the couple sign the register in the vestry and remains seated as bride and groom walk solemnly back down the aisle to the waiting photographers and cars.

Before throwing confetti over the heads of the bridal pair, guests should remember that this is not allowed in some churches and is an offence if the church opens directly on to the street.

Obviously, elaborate weddings rarely take place if the family is in mourning, and, more often than not, a wedding is postponed for a short time under such circumstances. If it must go on because there is no time to rearrange it, then the bereaved appear in dark clothes rather than wedding attire, with the exception of the bride and groom themselves and the bridal attendants. It is not nowadays thought wrong to conduct a wedding soon after a member of the close family has died, and at such weddings it is customary to allow a moment's silence in his or her memory during the speeches at the reception party.

A widow marrying again rarely has a white wedding (although she may do so if she wishes) and, unless she is still very young, will wear simple clothes rather than the elaborate gown and veils of a first-time bride. A girl marrying a widower can have all the veils, whiteness and froth of a first wedding, since it is, after all, her first.

Divorced people cannot usually be married in church, although there are some churches where they will be accepted. This is a matter to be discussed with the vicar. Once a civil marriage has taken place many clergymen will conduct a simple religious ceremony to bless the union, either in church, if this is allowed, or in a private home.

Roman Catholic weddings

The Catholic marriage service can take two principal forms, depending at what time in the religious calendar the wedding takes place. Normally, the couple take their solemn vows immediately before a nuptial mass at which the priest dispenses special blessings. However, such marriages may not be performed during Lent or between Advent Sunday and Boxing Day, at which times the service is duly simplified and the bride and groom go separately to Holy Communion before the marriage.

In other respects, the procedure for a Catholic wedding is very much the same as in the Church of England. In both churches, the bride's promise to obey her husband is not an obligatory part of the service and is frequently omitted these days, and the groom can choose whether to 'endow' or 'share' his worldly goods.

A Catholic may obtain special dispensation from the church to marry a non-Catholic, but such dispensation is usually only given upon certain conditions; for instance, that even if the wedding service is held elsewhere, it will be followed by a ceremony in the Roman Catholic church; that all children be brought up in the Catholic faith; and that the non-Catholic partner promises never to interfere with the faith of the Catholic.

The Roman Catholic church admits no divorce.

Weddings in other churches and religions

Most *Nonconformist* church buildings are registered for the solemnization of marriages, and the ceremony is similar to that in the Church of England. If their own church or chapel is not registered for marriages, the couple must either choose another church in which to be married, or they must have a registry office wedding and a religious celebration in their church afterwards. In Nonconformist churches, brides are never expected to give the promise to obey, and all marriages are regarded as totally equal partnerships.

Quaker weddings take place in the Friends Meeting House. The meeting usually starts with a brief explanation of the procedure. Early in the course of the meeting the bridal pair will stand, take each other by the hand, and each in turn will make a solemn declaration of marriage. The marriage certificate is signed and witnessed and is then read aloud by the local Registering Officer of the Society of Friends. At the end of the meeting all present may be invited to sign as witnesses. At both the beginning and end of the meeting there is a period of silence and spoken prayers or messages. Wedding rings play no formal part in Quaker marriages, but are sometimes exchanged after the spoken declaration.

Jewish weddings normally take place in a synagogue, although they may be performed at home or in any suitable building. In Orthodox synagogues, men and women occupy separate places during the service. Dress is the same as for a Christian wedding, but it is essential for all men and married women to cover their heads. The bridal pair stand beneath a silken canopy – a symbol of God's protective love and their future home together. Vows are exchanged and a ring is placed on the bride's finger. A glass is placed on the floor to be crushed by the bridegroom's foot – symbolizing the difficulties to be encountered through life.

At *Greek* or *Russian Orthodox* weddings, the congregation stands throughout the ceremony. If rings are exchanged, this will be done at the beginning of the service. The high point of the ceremony comes at the end when crowns are placed on the heads of the bridal couple.

A *Moslem* wedding can take place in the mosque or at home, usually that of the bride. Men and women may assemble in separate rooms, in which case the wedding is conducted before the male part of the congregation. The ceremony itself will be planned according to the Moslem calendar, and the reception often takes place the following weekend in a hotel or a restaurant.

Hindu marriage rites vary enormously between the different castes and sects and according to local custom. The ceremony may take place in a temple or in the home, and generally lasts very much longer than a church wedding. Non-Hindu guests should present their gifts as they would for any other kind of wedding, and should dress as for a church wedding. At some weddings, such as those in the Sikh religion, heads must be covered. The bride's party frequently remains apart from the groom's party throughout the ceremony, and men and women may be required to assemble in different parts of the room.

The Wedding Reception

It is customary for the wedding reception to follow immediately upon the marriage ceremony. The bride's parents are hosts for the occasion and, as they bear the expense, they are the ones who decide where it should be held, how many guests should be invited, and how lavish the affair should be. They should send out the invitations about six weeks before the wedding to their own and to the groom's family and friends.

Wedding gifts are always sent or taken to the bride's home some time before the wedding if this is possible, and not presented on the day itself. If one cannot accept an invitation to a wedding, it is customary to send a telegram of congratulations on the day.

On arrival at the reception, guests may be received by the bride's parents; beside them stand the groom's parents, and next to them the bridal couple. Although this formal procedure is sometimes dispensed with these days, it does make it simple for the two families to introduce their friends and relations to each other at the outset. A buffet or a full sit-down meal can be served, and, while it is traditional to serve champagne either throughout the party or at least for drinking the toasts, a variety of drinks can be offered. The wedding cake, a central feature of the celebrations, is cut by the bride with the assistance of the groom just before the toasts and speeches. If the groom is in military uniform, complete with sword, his sword is used for cutting the cake. Once the couple have cut the first slice, the cake is removed and cut into small pieces for distribution – perhaps by the bridesmaids – to the guests. (Small pieces of cake are often boxed and sent to guests who were unable to attend and with thank-you letters for gifts.)

There is a traditional order for the speeches. The bride's godfather, uncle, or an old family friend proposes the health of the bridal pair. The bridegroom replies, remembering to thank his new in-laws for the reception and the guests for their presents and attendance. The best man replies on behalf of the bridesmaids, and if the telegrams are to be read, he will do this at the same time. The order in which members of the wedding party should be addressed by the speaker is as follows: bride, bridegroom, host and hostess, groom's parents, priest or minister, ladies and gentlemen. Most social speeches, such as those at weddings, require a maximum of four or five minutes. The party ends after the departure of the bride and groom for their honeymoon, although often there is a dinner dance for the guests in the evening.

Anniversaries

Wooden, pearl, silver, ruby, golden or diamond weddings may or may not be celebrated, but, if they are, it is usually only among family and close friends so that the couple chooses whatever entertainment they prefer. Normally only husband and wife exchange presents, but close friends may take along an appropriate anniversary gift – glass or pewter are often given on silver weddings now that silver is so expensive. Ideas about which anniversary is associated with which material or gem vary slightly, but the following is a general guide:

1 year Paper	13 years Lace
2 years Cotton	14 years Ivory
3 years Leather	15 years Crystal
4 years Linen	20 years China
5 years Wood	25 years Silver
6 years Iron	30 years Pearls
7 years Wool	35 years Jade
8 years Bronze	40 years Rubies
9 years Pottery	45 years Sapphires
10 years Tin	50 years Gold
11 years Steel	55 years Emeralds
12 years Silk	60 years Diamonds

Funerals and Mourning

When a death occurs, there is usually much to be decided and done in a very short time. If there is to be a cremation (and the wishes of the deceased on this point are often known beforehand) two medical certificates will be necessary, and it saves time and trouble if the family doctor is notified and asked to bring a colleague with him.

Relatives and friends can be advised of the death and of the date of the funeral by letter, and an announcement can be placed in the paper. Placing the press announcement is just one of the many aspects of the procedure which can be done by the undertaker. The funeral takes place as soon as possible after death, unless, for some reason, there is to be an inquest. The private service is usually held before the funeral and there are very few rules as to procedure, although the official and emotional next-of-kin normally follow the coffin into the church or chapel. If the coffin is already there, all mourners and guests wait outside until the next-of-kin have entered, then proceed inside and sit as they wish. The next-of-kin are the first to leave the chapel at the end of the service. It is customary for the bereaved to offer the funeral party some refreshment at their home after the ceremony.

A memorial service, often organized by the employer of the deceased, may be held at any time up to a month or so after death. It is advertised in newspapers so that anyone who wishes can attend; all business and personal friends should be invited.

Black dress is not obligatory for a funeral, and if you do not already possess a black outfit, any dark clothing will be quite adequate. Requests by the deceased or the bereaved for no flowers or no letters to be sent should always be respected. If it is suggested that the price of the flowers can be sent instead to a particular charity, this should be done quietly. If the bereaved do not ask specifically that no letters of condolence should be sent, then these will have to be answered. Black-edged stationery is not often used these days.

For the many people who dislike or do not wish to have a funeral service, an undertaking firm will arrange simply for a burial or cremation.

Jewish funerals

Orthodox Jews do not allow cremation, although in the Reform synagogue cremations do sometimes take place. The funeral service is conducted at the cemetery or crematorium within forty-eight hours of death. No flowers are taken to the funeral. For the week which follows, the next-of-kin are in official mourning at the home of the deceased or other member of the family. During this time it is customary for those acquainted with the deceased to pay their condolences.

Quaker funerals

Quaker funerals always involve cremation. The Friends gather in the chapel of the crematorium for a meeting which takes the usual form of a period of silent prayer during which any Friend can speak who is moved to do so.

Moslem funerals

Moslem funerals always involve burial, and take place in the open air, usually outside the mosque, and it is the custom for those who attend to remove their shoes. A funeral feast at the home of the bereaved follows the ceremony.

Hindu funerals

The Hindus always cremate their dead, and the funeral service is held in the crematorium chapel.

General Points of Etiquette

The Professions

Each profession has rules of etiquette which exist primarily for the protection of its members.

In the National Health Service, the procedure for changing one's doctor can be found on the medical card issued to every patient. If you wish to change your dentist, this can be done whenever you are about to start a new session of treatment. In the field of private medical practice, it is correct procedure to approach your regular doctor about any changes you wish to make, and he will not wish to retain you as a patient against your will. It is also his job to advise you about seeking a second opinion or to make arrangements for you to consult a specialist in a particular field.

Similarly, in the legal field, consult first the solicitor with whom you have dealt in the past, even though he may refer you to another solicitor better able to deal with the current matter.

The clergy are bound by very few rules of professional etiquette. However, a breach of etiquette is often committed when a family wish a priest other than the incumbent himself to officiate, for example at a wedding, in the parish church, or when they want somebody other than the church's own organist to play the organ at the ceremony. It is essential to explain the situation at the outset to the parish priest and/or the organist and seek his permission. It is most unlikely that this will be refused, but fees due to both vicar and organist must be paid whether or not they are involved in the ceremony. It is a usual courtesy to ask the incumbent to take some part, if not the major one, in the service.

Tipping

The bothersome business of tipping has been greatly eased by the widespread practice of including a service charge on the bill. There is no need to tip over and above the service charge unless you have received some extra personal service. Where the service charge does not pertain, 10% of the bill is considered to be the minimum that can be offered.

In a restaurant, tip the waiter and the wine waiter separately. In an hotel the amount should be divided between the dining-room staff and the chambermaids, not forgetting the porter; but it is quite acceptable to give the entire amount to the receptionist to be allocated on your behalf. In many establishments tips are pooled, each member of the staff drawing a percentage.

At the hairdresser the more attendants you have, the more tipping you will be expected to do: the shampooer, the stylist, the manicurist, the girl who brings you a cup of coffee. Roughly 10% of the individual cost of each treatment would be correct.

In a hospital, if you have a private room, you may tip the ward maids when you leave. Nurses are professional people and should not be tipped, but a small present in the form of a book, tights, chocolates or a bottle of sherry will be readily accepted.

A minimum of 10% of the fare is normally given to a taxi driver. If a commissionaire calls you a cab, he will expect a small tip for his services. An airline porter is tipped according to the amount of luggage he carries for you, but it is incorrect to tip other members of airline staff.

When travelling by sea, rules for tipping are much the same as in an hotel, the money being divided between deck stewards, dining-room stewards, and cabin stewards.

Committees

The committee is the basis of public life; so much so that you may well find yourself sitting on your first committee while you are still at school, perhaps organising a school dance or charity appeal, and you may still be much occupied with committee work long after you have reached retirement age. Committee members are expected to do the jobs allocated to them and to attend regular meetings. The chairman will be an experienced committee member. At the start of a meeting, he makes sure there are enough people present to form a quorum and that the secretary is ready to take the minutes. He will then bring the meeting to order. The first item on the agenda will be the approval by the committee of the minutes of the previous meeting, which are signed by the chairman. All remarks throughout the meeting should be addressed to the chair.

Public speaking

There are a few basic rules of public speaking to be borne in mind on all types of occasion. At the time the invitation to speak is issued and accepted, ascertain from your host how long the speech is expected to be and take great care not to exceed this time. Prepare and rehearse your speech thoroughly – do not memorize it word for word but have the script or notes to refer to if and when necessary; particular attention should be paid to making both the introduction and the conclusion striking in some way. Make the speech as light-hearted as the occasion will allow, without resorting to jokes which might be found offensive by any members of the audience. Do not use complicated language or difficult words where simple ones

would suffice. Speak as naturally as possible – not too fast, and project your voice towards the audience.

Except on occasions when royalty is present, the chairman of the meeting is always mentioned first in addressing one's audience before a speech. If the chairman is a Lord, he is addressed as 'My Lord Chairman'. The preamble to the speech should also include the head of the organization responsible for the occasion, eg 'Mr President', 'Mr Vice-Chancellor', etc. If it has not been possible to ascertain in advance exactly who is present, refer to the toastmaster or to the chairman for guidance.

Royal and other Formal Occasions

An invitation to Buckingham Palace itself, or to one of the official buildings used for royal or government functions, will include instructions about what to wear, when to arrive, and where to park if parking is available. On arrival your path will be smoothed by officials who will furnish you with any information as to procedure that you may need.

Ladies normally wear gloves when shaking hands with the Queen, as a courtesy and no longer as a bounden duty. The gloves should be thin and light but do not need to be white as once was the custom. They are worn for the Queen's comfort since she can get hot and painful hands from too much handshaking. Never grasp her hand firmly, for the same reason, merely lay your hand in hers while making a 'bob' curtsey. For men, gloves are optional but preferred. Again, the handshake should be very light and be accompanied by a slight bow.

When royalty is present at a private function, formalities are more relaxed. If you are to be presented, you will be warned and briefed in advance.

At other formal occasions, banquets, receptions, and so on, be prepared to meet a reception committee. Your name and that of your escort, if you have one, will be taken by an attendant or toastmaster who will announce your arrival. You then shake hands with those who are there to receive you before proceeding to join the party. If the occasion is a formal dinner with speeches to follow, remember that it is incorrect to smoke before the loyal toast is drunk.

Styles of Address

When speaking to royalty, the address 'Your Majesty' or 'Your Royal Highness' should not be used more than once, and, indeed, may be omitted altogether in favour of the simpler 'Ma'am' (pronounced to rhyme with Pam) for The Queen and 'Madam' or 'Sir' for other members of the Royal Family.

Letters to The Queen should be addressed to the Private Secretary to Her Majesty the Queen. Begin the letter 'Dear Sir', and ask him, for instance, 'to submit for Her Majesty's approval/consideration . . .'. Never refer to The Queen as 'she', but always as 'Her Majesty'. Close the letter 'Yours faithfully'. If you do wish to write to The Queen direct, the opening style is 'Madam, With my humble duty'. Use 'Your Majesty' and 'Your Majesty's' instead of 'you' and 'your', and close the letter 'I have the honour to be/remain, Madam, Your Majesty's most humble and obedient servant'.

Letters to other members of the Royal Family should be addressed to their Equerry, Private Secretary or Lady-in-Waiting. Begin '(Dear) Sir' or '(Dear) Madam'. Refer to the member of the Royal Family first as 'His/Her Royal Highness' and subsequently as 'Prince/Princess . . .' or 'The Duke/Duchess of . . .' as appropriate. End the letter 'Yours faithfully'. When writing direct, open the letter 'Sir' or 'Madam', use 'Your Royal Highness' instead of 'you', and end 'I have the honour to be, Sir/Madam, Your Royal Highness's most humble and obedient servant'.

When writing to royalty or people of title, the envelope should bear their most important title.

When addressing a person of title, either verbally or in writing, the form of address varies according to whether the communication is formal or social. Thus, when writing formally to a Duke, the style of address is 'My Lord Duke', and the formal verbal address is 'Your Grace'; but socially, the written form of address is 'Dear Duke', and the verbal form simply 'Duke'. A Duchess is written to formally as 'Madam' or 'Dear Madam', and spoken to as 'Your Grace', but socially she is addressed in writing as 'Dear Duchess'.

A Marquis, Earl, Viscount or Baron is addressed formally as 'My Lord' and socially as 'Lord . . .' both verbally and in writing.

The wife of a peer is addressed formally in writing as '(Dear) Madam' and verbally as 'Madam'; socially she is addressed as 'Lady (surname)'. Style of address for a Peeress in her own right is the same as that for the wife of a Peer, although she may choose to be known as 'Baroness (surname)' rather than 'Lady (surname)'. A Baroness in her own right and the wife of a Baron are also addressed in the same way.

A Baronet or Knight is written to formally '(Dear) Sir', and addressed socially as 'Sir (Christian name)'. The surname should be added if the acquaintance is only slight. Formal and social verbal address is 'Sir (Christian name)'. His wife is written to formally '(Dear) Madam', but for all other purposes the style of address is 'Lady (surname)'.

An Archbishop, like a Duke, is addressed formally as 'Your Grace', and socially as 'Archbishop'. Bishops, Deans and Archdeacons are addressed simply using these titles. Vicars and Rectors are addressed formally as 'The Reverend (Christian name + surname), Vicar/Rector of . . .', and socially as 'Mr . . .' or 'Father . . .' according to his preference. Wives of all clergymen are addressed simply as 'Mrs . . .', unless they have a title in their own right.

The formal style of address for a Lord Mayor is 'My Lord Mayor', and his wife is 'My Lady Mayoress'; socially the style is 'Lord Mayor' and 'Lady Mayoress'. A mayor is formally addressed 'Mr Mayor'; a woman mayor may prefer to be addressed 'Madam Mayor'. Socially the style is Dear Mr/Madam Mayor.

Management

This bathroom with its restful tones of green is a good example of how an awkwardly situated room can be put to good use

1

2

3

4

Different types of flooring

1 Cork tiles are warm and quiet to walk on
2 Ceramic tiles are very hard-wearing
3 Cushioned vinyl is very easy to wash clean
4 Vinyl tiling comes in a wide range of designs
*5 A sealed wooden floor is inexpensive yet gives a warm
   country look to the kitchen*

RIGHT *Furnishings, decorations and a sensible use of
space can transform a room out of all proportion*

5

1

2

3

4

5

Different forms of lighting

1 *This type of dressing table light gives excellent light for make-up*

2 *An inverted bowl pendant fitting is particularly useful over the eating area in both kitchen and dining-room*

3 *The positioning of this table lamp and armchair makes good use of an otherwise wasted area*

4 *Hall lighting must be such that no glare is thrown into the eyes*

5 *Recessed spotlights and a pendant light are attractive and unusual ways of lighting a hall, and putting a corner to good use*

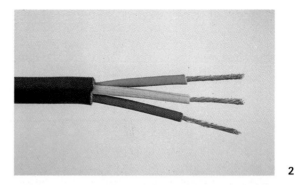

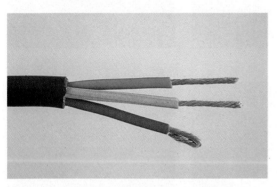

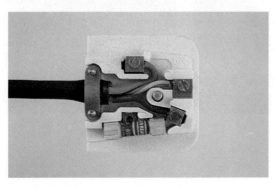

Wiring a plug

1 *Strip off about 3cm of outside cable covering so that the 3 internal wires are exposed*
  Yellow/green striped wire is Earth
  Blue wire is Neutral
  Brown wire is Live
2 *Strip off about 1cm of cover on each of the 3 wires exposed and twist the strands together*
3 *Fold each exposed portion of wire in half*
  Remove the plug cover, loosen the cable grip screws and insert the cable. Tighten the cable grip screws to ensure that the cable is securely gripped
4 *Loosen the screws on each of the 3 brass pins. These are marked E ⊥ for Earth, L for Live and N for Neutral. Insert the correct wires into the holes as shown*

5 *Retighten the screws to lock the wires into position.*
  DO NOT *tighten screws on to the wire covering – ensure that the bared wire ends are trapped by screws only and that there are no loose strands to be seen*
  Check that correctly rated fuse to BS nr 1362 is fitted for the appliance to be used
6 *Replace the plug cover and secure firmly by tightening the centre screw*
Note *If the terminals have a nut and washer instead of holes, remove these. Wind each wire in a clockwise direction around the screw thread. Replace the washer and nut and tighten firmly*
If in any doubt, consult an electrical dealer

1

2

3

4

5

6

7

Poisonous Plants

1 *Deadly Nightshade*
2 *Thorn Apple*
3 *Holly berries*
4 *Laburnum tree*
5 *Lupin seed pods*
6 *Yew berries*
7 *Mistletoe*

Children's Rooms

TOP RIGHT *This room makes good use of wall areas and encourages creative activity by the positioning of the blackboard. In addition to being a bedroom, it serves as a very practical playroom*

BELOW RIGHT *This room uses colour in an exciting and stimulating way. When children have grown too old for this particular décor, it only needs to be painted over*

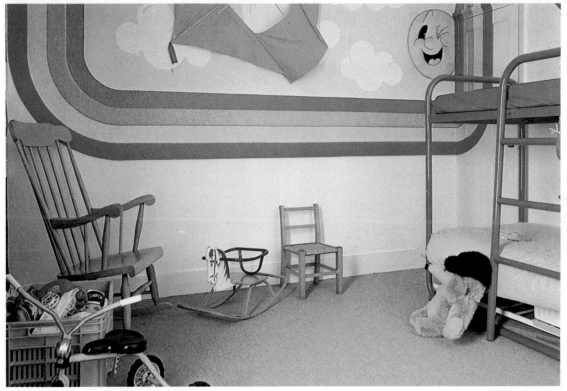

Kitchens

TOP *A fitted kitchen, light, practical and very cosy*

LEFT *A compact fitted kitchen making the best use of very little space*

PRESENTING A MEAL

The elegance with which a dinner is served is a matter which depends, of course, partly upon the means, but still more upon the taste of the master and mistress of the house. It may be observed, in general, that there should always be flowers on the table, and as they form no item of expense, there is no reason why they should not be employed every day.

Good food deserves good presentation as well as careful cooking. No matter how much trouble you take over choosing ingredients and following a recipe, the food will only look appetizing if it is correctly and attractively served. Time spent in learning how to present food to the best advantage, both when entertaining and for everyday meals, is time well spent. There are certain basic rules. Menus should be planned to include foods which contrast in colour and texture. No one finds an 'all white' meal appetizing, and a three-course meal with too many cream-based dishes is cloying. With a little imagination, contrasts of colour and texture can be introduced. For example, a crisp side salad could be served with a soft, creamy dish. (See the chapter on Menus for more information.)

Garnishes and Decorations

Attractively garnished or decorated dishes are far more tempting than those served without thought for their presentation. Suggestions for suitable trimmings are incorporated in the individual recipes. Instructions for preparing these can be found in the chapters on Stuffings, Garnishes and Accompaniments, and Icings, Fillings and Decorations.

A *garnish* should be chosen to complement the food in colour, flavour, and texture. It should always be edible and can be simple or elaborate. Parsley, for instance, adds an attractive touch of green to many dishes; a small sprig may be placed in the centre of the potato crust on a Shepherds' Pie or a trail of chopped leaves on top of a bowl of soup. A few sprigs of watercress bunched together and placed at the leg end of roast poultry add extra colour and texture to the dish. Lemon can be cut in wedges, or in thin slices twisted into butterflies, and used to garnish fish, veal, and poultry dishes. When squeezed over the food it also supplies a valuable added flavour.

Various brilliantly hued spices make a quick, easy, and effective garnish when sprinkled over meat or vegetable dishes. The most commonly used are paprika, red pepper, yellow curry powder and turmeric. Be careful not to spoil the flavour of the dish by using too much of these spices. Piped mashed potato is an excellent trimming for many dishes, especially those like fricassée of veal or chicken arranged on a flat dish. Pipe round the edges and add colour with parsley or a dusting of paprika. Some garnishes, such as sliced canned pimento, which tend to dry and discolour when exposed to the air can be coated with aspic jelly to prevent this. A good general rule is to garnish food on a flat dish round the edges and in a deep dish across the top. Garnishes should always be used sparingly or the effect is worse than no garnish at all.

For sweet dishes, decorations such as piped whipped cream, sliced canned fruit, chocolate drops, and chopped nuts are often also an essential part of the recipe. Simple decorations include a dusting of icing sugar or a sprinkling of grated chocolate. Be careful not to put highly coloured decorations on too long before serving a moist dish as the colour may run; beware, too, of using heavy decorative items on soft dishes into which they might sink. Toasted nuts are often used to better effect than plain shelled ones. Fresh fruit decorations remain attractive if coated with an arrowroot glaze (see Raspberry Yoghurt Cheesecake p1043). As with garnishes, the rule is never to be heavy-handed with decorations.

Laying the Table

If soup is to be served, round soup spoons or tablespoons should be provided. Special fish knives and forks can be laid for the fish course; the knives are blunt with a slightly pointed end which enables the bones to be eased out of the fish without cutting the flesh. Large knives and forks are laid for the main meat course, with a small knife for bread and butter and cheese. Steak knives with a serrated cutting edge are often used for grilled steak or chops. A dessert spoon and fork are provided for the sweet course, or a teaspoon if the dessert is to be served in small dishes or glasses. If fresh fruit is being served, knives and forks should be provided. A cake slice with one sharp edge is useful for cutting and serving fragile gâteaux, while a two-pronged fork with one flat-blade prong is practical for eating the cake.

The correct way of setting out the cutlery, glass, etc facilitates easy and efficient serving. These are the basic rules for formal place settings. Allow, if possible, 50–60cm for each place setting (measuring from the centre of one plate to the centre of the next). Lay the knives, blades pointing inwards, on the right of the dinner plate and the forks on the left in the order in which they will be used (first to be used on the extreme right or left and the last next to the plate). The dessert spoon and fork can either be laid in neat alignment across the top of the setting, with the spoon handle to the right and the fork handle to the left, or at the sides of the plate, spoon on the right, fork on the left; either arrangement is correct. Fruit knives and forks can be laid across the top of the setting with the dessert spoon and fork, or at the side. Alternatively, they can be handed round with the dessert plates. The small knife for bread may go next to the dinner plate, on the right-hand side or vertically across the side plate, which should be on the left of the place setting. The soup spoon is placed on the extreme right-hand side as this is the first implement to be used. Line up the cutlery neatly and as closely together as practical, with the handles about 1cm from the edge of the table.

Glasses should be arranged in a straight line across the top of the right-hand cutlery, in the order of use; for example, a glass for white wine on the right, then one for red, and a port or liqueur glass on the left of the row. If you include a tumbler or stemmed glass for water, place this before the liqueur glass. The last glass should be placed just above the meat knife (for information on suitable glasses, see p263 below and p1363). If you are laying a single wine glass, put it anywhere above the right-hand cutlery.

Allow one cruet set for each four places and the same number of butter dishes, each with its own small butter-knife. Finger-bowls, if used, are placed to the left just above the line of forks. Table napkins can be put in the centre of the place setting, on the side plate or in one of the glasses. The choice is entirely yours and will depend on the overall design of the table decorations. It is quite in order to use paper table napkins, but for formal occasions it is hard to beat crisply laundered linen or cotton ones – in white or a suitable colour. Size is important; 400 × 400cm is really the minimum and paper napkins should always be the two-ply absorbent quality. The larger 550 × 550cm damask napkins are less common nowadays but they are easier to fold into decorative shapes, and of course they cover the lap well. The classic shapes for folding table napkins include the Fan, the Mitre, the Lily and the Candle (see diagrams). If you have not got the large size linen napkins, try folding the paper ones – they hold their shape well and you will often find directions on the packet. For less formal occasions, smaller coloured cotton or non-iron fabric napkins, 350 × 350cm, can be used. If the food is to be served on the table rather than from a sideboard, arrange the appropriate serving implements at each side of the mats placed to receive the dishes.

The rest of the table setting is decorative rather than functional. Remember that the enjoyment of food and wine is of first importance and that no decorations should detract from this. Table linen should be crisply laundered or, if mats are pre-ferred, make sure that the dining table is well pol-ished. Flower arrangements should be low so as not to inhibit conversation across the table, and flowers must not be overpoweringly scented or they will detract from the flavour of the food. Wine should be placed ready on the sideboard or side table together with a jug of iced water and soft drinks for those who prefer them. Sauce-boats should have a stand or saucer to avoid drips on the tablecloth. Remove cruets and savoury accompaniments from the table before serving the dessert. Keep butter and salt at hand if cheeses are to be served.

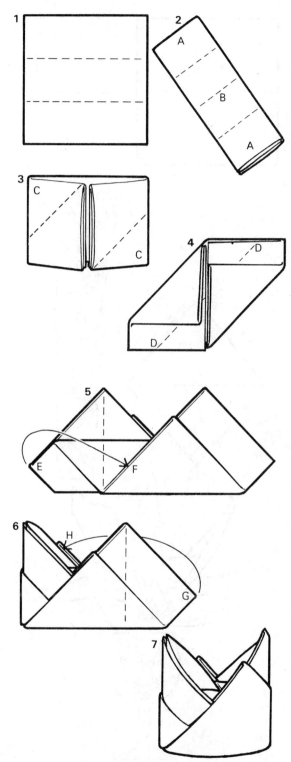

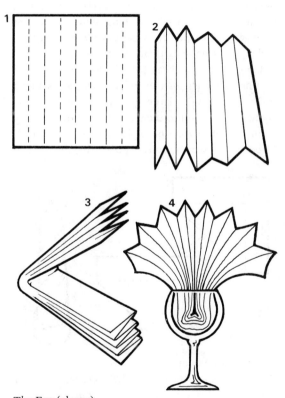

The Fan (above)

The Mitre (right)
1 Fold the napkin into three; 2 Fold ends (AA) over to centre line (B); 3 Fold corners (CC) to the centre; 4 Fold the back across at dotted line (D); 5 Tuck point (E) into pleat (F); 6 And point (G) into pleat (H) on the reverse side; 7 Complete

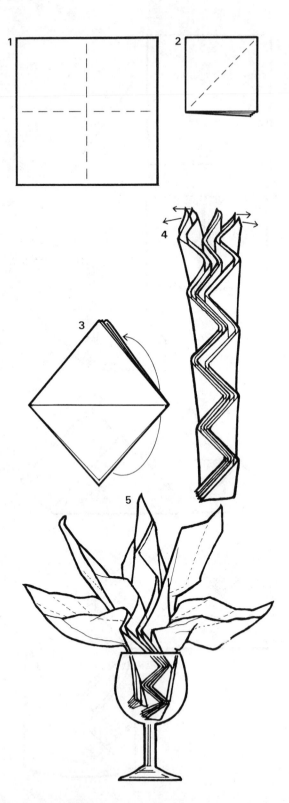

Serving the Correct Way

When food is served the right way, the meal is invariably more pleasant for the guests and easier for the host and hostess. On the whole, it is better to avoid self-service from a sideboard at a dinner party. The following notes are a guide to smooth service of some foods which may seem difficult to handle. When handing a dish at table, always hand at the left of the person and hold the dish low enough to make it easy to transfer food on to the plate.

Choose serving dishes which complement the food. A hearty soup looks well in a pottery bowl but consommé should be served in a china soup-plate or cup. Poached Salmon (p451) or Chaudfroid of Chicken (p644) need fine china, silver or stainless steel platters to look their best, whereas casseroles look appetizing in earthenware dishes.

Light dishes such as fruit fools, custards, and creams look delicious in individual glasses but a dish containing a large golden-brown fruit pie should be brought to the table for cutting. Serving dishes should always be well filled if food is to look its best. If, however, you are presenting the food on

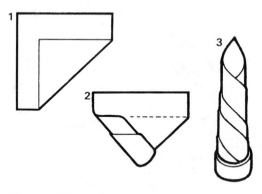

The Candle (above)
1 Fold the napkin diagonally; 2 Turn over and roll along the fold; 3 Stand napkin upright in a napkin ring to complete

The Lily (left)
1 Fold the napkin into four; 2 Then diagonally across; 3 Turn two loose leaves on to either side; 4 Pleat and pull down two loose leaves from either side of centre; 5 Complete

individual plates, do not make the mistake of serving over-large portions; a piled plate can be off-putting. It is always better to keep some food in reserve for second helpings. Be careful to avoid colour clashes between food and crockery.

Roasts: Carve, if possible, on the side table and arrange the slices of meat or poultry and stuffing to one side of the plate. Vegetables and accompaniments such as Yorkshire pudding should be handed separately to each diner or placed on the table for the guests to help themselves. Detailed descriptions of how to carve are given in the chapters on Meat, Poultry, and Game.

Fish: See p412.

Asparagus: Lay the heads pointing to the left. Special asparagus plates with a shallow dip at one side to hold butter are convenient (these plates are also practical for globe artichokes, see below). Finger-bowls and extra paper napkins should be provided.

Avocado Pears: Serve in individual shallow dishes with a teaspoon. Dishes in the shape of avocados are useful; each dish holds half a fruit and keeps the pear steady while the diner scoops out the flesh.

Corn on the Cob: Spiked holders, pushed into each end of the cob, make the eating of this vegetable much more manageable. The cob can be picked up easily and rotated as the corn is eaten. Again, finger-bowls and extra table napkins should be provided, if possible.

Fondues: This kind of meal is not practical on a large table or for more than 5–6 people. Both meat and cheese fondues are described in detail in the chapter on Table Cookery.

Globe Artichokes: Serve individually on a dessert plate making sure that the base of the artichoke is cut level so that it stands upright on the plate. Give each person a small side plate for the discarded outside leaves and, ideally, a finger-bowl.

Oysters: Raw oysters are always served in their shells, preferably on a bed of crushed ice. Arrange them in a circle round the plate and provide small forks with which to eat them. Special oyster plates are available with an indentation or dip to hold each oyster and a shallow well in the centre for the sauce.

Snails: Plates for serving snails are similar to oyster plates with indentations to hold the snail shell and a shallow well in the centre for any sauce. Even if you have not got special plates, it is convenient to have snail holders. These are tongs with which to hold the shell steady while removing the snail with a fork, preferably a two-pronged one.

Salad: When serving salad as a side dish, provide small plates or bowls; crescent shaped plates which fit against the dinner plate are practical. Guests can either help themselves, or an individual salad can be arranged on each plate before the course is served.

The Buffet Table

The art of laying a buffet table is to show off the food to its best advantage while making serving easy. Whether you choose a formal style with fine china and linen, cut crystal and silver, or an informal setting with pottery, wooden bowls, and gingham, the arrangement of dishes, plates, and cutlery is the same.

For buffets to serve 50 people or more, place plates and cutlery at each end of the buffet table so that there are at least two serving points. This means that there must be two platters (at least) of each dish so that guests may help themselves from either end of the table. Drinks, and later coffee, should be served from a side table. Depending on the space available, the dessert can be displayed ready on a side table, or served from the main table when the main course is finished. Use cake stands for gâteaux-type desserts to vary the height of the display. The most convenient way to lay cutlery is to wrap a set for each person in a table napkin. Distribute cruets along the table, and accompaniments, eg salad dressing or sauce, near the appropriate dishes. Place bread or rolls with butter at each end of the table. Cheese boards (see p262) should be brought in with the dessert and placed at each end of the buffet with celery, biscuits and butter, and, of course, small plates and knives. For smaller buffets, it is usually possible to lay everything on one table with cutlery and plates at one end only.

Keeping Food Hot

A variety of appliances is available to simplify the problem of keeping food hot at the table. These range from electrically heated trolleys to small hot-plates heated by a night light, all of which are effective. The most elaborate trolleys have individual dishes for vegetables, gravy, etc in a heated top surface with a hot cupboard below for a joint or pie, which will keep food hot and moist for 2–3 hours. Others have one or two heated surfaces only on which food and plates are placed. Hot-plates for standing on the sideboard are made in all sizes.

Bread and toast can be kept warm while the meal is being served if it is wrapped in a napkin and placed in a basket.

Cheese

For a simple meal a single cheese can be selected to complement the rest of the meal. Even for a dinner party, or a larger party, it is a mistake to serve too many cheeses, as their flavours may conflict or cross-flavouring occur.

If the main course has been a light one, such as fish, Camembert can be served, with a semi-firm mild cheese such as Port Salut, and a white crumbly Lancashire or gentle blue Pipo Crème. If, however, roast beef or game has been the main course, the cheeses should be stronger, perhaps a Pont l'Evêque, a mature Double Gloucester, and a robust blue Cheshire.

Many British and foreign cheeses are described in the chapter on Dairy Foods, Fats and Oils.

Preparing a Cheese Board

Cheeses are best served on a wooden board or tray, not on a metal, glass or ceramic surface which will blunt the cheese knives. It can be garnished with a small bunch of fruit or salad ingredients such as tomato, celery, etc. The cheeses should be placed well apart, each with its own knife, slicer or spoon, to prevent cross-flavouring. For hard and semi-hard cheeses, cheese knives with pronged ends for picking up the portions are useful. Semi-soft cheeses can be cut in slivers with a continental cheese slicer; Scandinavian and Dutch breakfast cheeses are cut in this way.

Dry biscuits, which should be neither very salty nor cheese-flavoured themselves, should be served with slightly salted butter. Bread can be offered as an alternative. Some people may prefer the continental system of eating cheese alone, using a knife and fork.

Apéritifs

It is customary to offer a choice of apéritif before a main meal; this can be dry or medium sherry, dry or sweet vermouth or spirits. It is quite in order, however, to offer just sherry, particularly if you are serving clear soup as the first course of the meal; guests can then continue drinking sherry during the soup course. Wine on its own is also a viable alternative. Always provide tomato or fruit juice for non-drinkers.

For a largish dinner party it is a good idea to offer a dry white wine or Champagne instead of a choice of apéritifs. Alternatively, you may like to serve a cocktail (see the chapter on Table Wines and Other Drinks).

Serve apéritifs in the appropriate glasses, sherry in copitas, vermouth in small wine glasses, and gin and tonic in small tumblers or large wine glasses.

A selection of cocktail snacks, eg nuts, crisps, small savoury biscuits, etc can be handed around with the drinks, but be sure not to spoil your guests' appetites.

Wine

While it is important not to be tied rigidly to rules concerning suitable wines for particular foods, the following can be used as general guide-lines:

1) With most first course, cold, and fish dishes and white meat dishes in a white sauce, serve a dry or medium white wine or rosé.

2) With red meat dishes, casseroles and stews, roasts and grills, serve red wine.

3) The richer, the fuller, and the spicier the food, the richer and fuller the wine must be. Do not let the delicacy of a light wine be killed by an over-assertive food flavour, or vice versa.

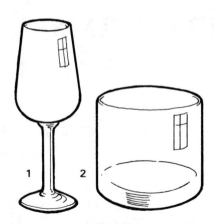

Apéritif Glasses
1 Sherry copita; 2 Whisky

Liqueur Glasses
1 Brandy; 2 Liqueur; 3 Port

Suggested wines for certain dishes:
1) Cold fish dishes such as oysters or fish mousse: Muscadet, Pouilly Blanc Fumé, Chablis.
2) Hot fish dishes: as 1) but also Bourgogne Aligote, Pouilly Fuissé, Sylvaner, Alsace Riesling, and other light, dry wines.
3) Crustaceans – lobster, crab, etc generally in richer sauces: serve one of the better white Burgundies or Alsace wines, although the four mentioned above will not be out of place, especially if the dish is cold.
4) Cold meat dishes, pâtés and pies, and smoked fish: as 2) or 3), according to taste. The more flavoured and spicy the dish, the more assertive the wine should be; the fruity Alsace wines are generally very good. With ordinary cold meat and salad, German wine is suitable.
5) White meat in white sauces: as 2) or 3), also dry white Bordeaux. Many people prefer German wines. When veal or chicken is served in a brown sauce or one containing Madeira or sherry, one has the choice of white or red wines, of which the best would be a light, young claret or a Beaujolais.
6) Roasts and grills: all red wines, except the very richest and heaviest.
7) Casseroles and stews: red wines, of a weight and richness approximating to the dish.

It is usual to allow at least half a 70cl bottle (three glasses) of wine per head at a main meal. This gives one the chance to serve a glass of white wine with the first course, and two glasses of red with the main course. However, one may well find that more is needed, so it is wise to have a bottle or two in reserve, if possible.

If serving more than one wine, it is wise to abide by the following rules:
1) White wine before red
2) A light wine before a heavy one
3) A young wine before an old one
4) Dry wine before sweet.

Once a bottle has been broached, it will keep quite well for several days in a cool place (for red wines), or in a refrigerator (for whites). Alternatively, it can be used for cooking. More information on serving wine can be found in the chapter on Table Wines and other Drinks.

Liqueurs and Coffee

Port, brandy and liqueurs can be served after an evening meal. For more information, see the chapter on Hospitality and Social Customs.

Port glasses are small, and should ideally curve slightly inwards at the top to hold the bouquet of the wine. Liqueurs are served in standard liqueur glasses although brandy may be served in brandy balloon glasses or small stemmed glasses which curve inward at the top. Brandy glasses should be warmed very slightly before the spirit is poured in.

Coffee is served black, in small cups; cream or milk and brown sugar are offered separately.

GLOSSARY OF COOKERY TERMS AND TECHNIQUES

Modern cookery stands so greatly indebted to the gastronomic propensities of our French neighbours, that many of their terms are adopted and applied by English artists to the same as well as similar preparations of their own. A vocabulary of these is, therefore, indispensable in a work of this kind.

Key

(Am) American
(Aus) Austrian
(Bel) Belgian
(Can) Canadian
(Fr) French
(Ger) German
(Gr) Greek
(Hun) Hungarian
(It) Italian
(Pol) Polish
(Port) Portuguese
(Mex) Mexican
(N Afr) North African
(Rus) Russian
(S Afr) South African
(Scot) Scottish
(Sp) Spanish
(Sw) Swedish
(Tur) Turkish

Cookery Terms

Absorption method Method of cooking rice with twice its volume of liquid, until the liquid has been absorbed.

Acidulated water Cold water mixed together with lemon juice or vinegar, and used to soak certain fruits and vegetables, eg apples and potatoes, to prevent them from discolouring. Also used in the base of an aluminium pressure cooker for recipes to be cooked in a container.

Agar-agar Setting agent obtained from certain seaweed; often used as an alternative to a meat-based jelly.

Agro-dolce (It) Sweet and sour sauce based on sugar, vinegar, wine, garlic, onion, and chocolate. Can also contain carrots, mint, raisins and candied orange peel.

Aiguillettes, en (Fr) Manner in which fish, meat or poultry is cut into long or small thin strips.

Aïle (Fr) Wing of poultry or game bird.

Aïoli, aïlloli (Fr) Garlic mayonnaise.

À la, au, aux (Fr) **Alla** (It) In the style of, or made with.

Albumen White of egg.

Al dente (It) Term meaning tender, but still firm to the bite. Used to describe cooked pasta, rice, and blanched vegetables.

Allemande, à l' (Fr) In the German style, eg with smoked sausages, or garnished with buttered noodles and mashed potatoes.

All-in-one Method of preparing sauces and cakes using all the basic ingredients simultaneously. Also known as the 'One-stage method'.

Allumettes (Fr) 1) Small strips of vegetables cut like matchsticks, eg potato straws.
2) Puff pastry cut into strips and baked. Can be sweet or savoury.

Américaine, à l' (Fr) 1) Lobster dissected (usually while live) and baked with lobster coral over herbs and tomatoes, then served with a fish Velouté sauce or mayonnaise.
2) Braised chicken in a cream sauce with port, button onions, and mushrooms.
3) Poached fish in white wine sauce with parsley, butter, onions, and mushrooms.

Andalouse (Fr) 1) Cold mayonnaise sauce mixed with tomato purée and garnished with red peppers.
2) Garnish for meat and poultry consisting of halved peppers stuffed with rice à la Grecque and slices of cooked tomato and aubergine.

Anglaise, à l' (Fr) 1) In the English style; usually plainly boiled or steamed.
2) Food dipped in egg, coated with breadcrumbs and fried or grilled.

Aperitifs (Fr) **Aperitivi** (It) Pre-meal drinks.

Arrowroot Thickening agent used in clear sauces and soups; gives a translucent appearance.

Artois, d' (Fr) 1) Garnish of potato croquettes and peas for meat, or vegetables and artichoke hearts for poultry; both served with a Madeira wine sauce.
2) Savoury pastry made from a mixture of cheeses and flour.

Aspic Jelly made from meat, fish or poultry stock and either gelatine or calf's foot. Used as a setting agent, for coating food, or chopped, as a garnish.

Aurore, à l' (Fr) Sauce for chicken, fish and eggs made from a Béchamel, Velouté or Hollandaise sauce with either tomato sauce, tomato purée or tomato juice added to give it a pink colour.

Avgolemono (Gr) Egg and lemon soup or sauce.

Baba (Fr) **Babka** (Pol) Small or large round cake made from a basic savarin mixture with sultanas, raisins or currants. Usually soaked in a rum or kirsch syrup.

Bacalao (Sp) **Bacalhau** (Port) Dried salt cod.

Bagna cauda (It) Warm garlic and anchovy sauce into which raw vegetables are dipped.

Bain-marie (Fr) Large shallow pan filled with hot water into which smaller pans, etc can be placed allowing their contents to keep warm, or to cook without boiling or reducing. Also called Water-bath.

Baking powder Raising agent made from bicarbonate of soda and cream of tartar.

Baklava (East Med) Dessert made from phyllo pastry, walnuts or almonds, and a honeyed syrup.

Ballottine, de (Fr) 1) Meat or poultry boned and shaped into a bundle or roll. Served hot or cold.
2) Boned, stuffed duck or turkey rolled like a galantine, but served hot or cold.

Baron Large joint of beef including both sirloins with the backbone intact. Can also include the saddle and hind legs of mutton or lamb, or the hindquarters of lamb. Baron of hare is the body section without head, neck or limbs.

Bâton (Fr) Pastry, biscuit or bread loaf made in the form of a stick.

Bavarois, à la crème (Fr) Bavarian cream. Rich cold dessert made with custard and cream, and set with gelatine. Can have many flavours.

Béarnaise, à la (Fr) Thick sauce made with vinegar or wine, herbs, eggs, shallots or onions, and butter.

Béchamel (Fr) Classic foundation French white sauce, more flavoured than British white sauce.

Beef Wellington Fillet of Beef en croûte.

Beignet (Fr) Fritters both sweet and savoury.

Bercy, au (Fr) Sauce of white wine, shallots, Velouté sauce made with fish or chicken stock, butter, and parsley. Served with fish or meat.

Beurre, au (Fr) Cooked or dressed with butter.

Beurre à la Meunière (Fr) Browned butter with seasonings, parsley and lemon juice, usually poured over fish which has been fried in butter.

Beurre manié (Fr) Butter and flour kneaded into a paste; added to soups and sauces as a thickening agent. An alternative to a roux.

Beurre noir, au (Fr) Butter heated until rich brown in colour, then mixed with vinegar. Parsley and capers are often included. Generally served over skate or brains.

Bigarade (Fr) Brown sauce made with Seville oranges.

Biscuit glacé (Fr) Different kinds of ice cream or water ice layered together in a box-shaped mould.

Bisque (Fr) Thick, creamy soup made with shellfish.

Bitok (Rus) Small meat patty made from raw minced beef and breadcrumbs, and bound with an egg.

Bivalve mollusc Shellfish enclosed by two shells, eg mussel, cockle, oyster, scallop.

Blaeberry Another name for bilberry or whortleberry.

Blanquette (Fr) White stew, usually of veal or chicken in a white sauce enriched with cream and sometimes egg yolks.

Blatjang (S Afr) Chutney made from dried apricots.

Bleu, au (Fr) 1) Term applied to freshly caught fish, usually trout, cooked in boiling water, vinegar and seasonings, giving the skin a blue tinge.
2) Very rare steak.

Blini, bliny (Rus) Pancakes, generally yeasted, traditionally made with a mixture of plain and buckwheat flour. Served with caviar and soured cream.

Blintz (Rus) Pancake stuffed with a cheese or other filling, and fried until crisp.

Bombay duck (Indian, S Asian) Dried and salted small fish. Served with curry.

Bombe glacé (Fr) Moulded ice cream dessert usually round or cone shaped, and of two or more different flavours, or an outer layer of ice cream around a mousse or parfait centre.

Bonne femme (Fr) Fillets of fish, generally sole, in a white wine sauce with mushrooms, shallots, and parsley.

Bordelaise, à la (Fr) Applies to a variety of dishes, but most commonly to a sauce for grilled meats consisting of red wine, shallots, seasoning, and herbs, often finished with a meat glaze.

Borsch (Rus) Beetroot soup served hot or chilled and garnished with soured cream.

Bouchée (Fr) Mouthful. Small, filled puff pastry patty or vol-au-vent case.

Bouillabaisse (Fr) Mixed fish soup/stew from the French Mediterranean.

Boulangère, à la (Fr) Baker's style. Sliced potatoes and onions cooked in stock. Often served with a roast joint such as lamb.

Bourguignonne à la (Fr) Cooked with red wine, onions, and mushrooms. This is a speciality of Burgundy. Boeuf Bourguignonne is the best known example.

Bran Flaked outer husks of grain separated from flour during the milling process. Supplies fibre (roughage) necessary to a diet.

Brandade (Fr) Pounded fish pâté; *Brandade de Morue* made from salt cod is the most common.

Brawn Meat from a pig or boar's head, encased in jelly made from the broth in which it has simmered.

Bretonne, à la (Fr) Brittany style. 1) Garnished with haricot beans.
2) White wine sauce for eggs or fish garnished with shredded leeks, carrots, and celery.

Brine Salt water solution used for pickling and preserving.

Brioche (Fr) Rich yeasted dough baked in a variety of shapes and sizes; the most common is a rounded loaf with a knob on top.

Brisling Small sprats.

Brochette (Fr) Method of grilling small chunks of meat or fish on skewers.

Broiled-on topping Grilled topping of nuts, shredded coconut, brown sugar, etc on plain and light fruit cakes.

Brulé (Fr) Burnt. Glaze formed by grilling sugar until caramelized on top of a custard base dessert.

Brun, au (Fr) Cooked in brown sauce.

Brunoise, à la (Fr) Garnish for soup and other dishes of finely chopped spring vegetables, eg carrots, onions, leeks, celery, turnips, etc.

Brut (Fr) Dry wine.

Burghul, Bulgur (Mid East) Cracked wheat.

Butter muslin Thin, open-weave cotton cloth. Used for straining dairy products, jellies, stocks, etc; should be scalded before use.

Byssus Filaments of a mollusc used for attaching itself to rocks.

Caille (Fr) Quail.

Calabrese (It) Variety of broccoli.

Calyx Leaves at the base of fruits or flowers.

Campden tablets Sodium metabisulphite. In solution this produces sulphur dioxide.

Canard (Fr) Duck.

Caneton (Fr) Duckling.

Caper Pickled flower bud of the caper bush. Used in sauces and as a garnish.

Capon Castrated cockerel.

Caquelon (Fr) Open ceramic or earthenware pan. Used for cheese fondues.

Caramel Sugar dissolved in water and then boiled until brown. Used for lining moulds, colouring sauces, in confectionery, etc.

Carbonnade 1) (Bel) Beef stew made with beer.
2) Method of grilling meat so that the outside is well done and the inside very rare.
3) (Fr) Braised lamb or mutton dish.

Cardinal, à la (Fr) 1) Red-tinted sauce of fish stock, Béchamel sauce, lobster butter, and Cayenne pepper.
2) Fish dishes garnished with lobster.

Carob Ground pod of an evergreen tree; used as an alternative to chocolate.

Carolines (Fr) Small savoury éclairs.

Carré d'Agneau (Fr) Loin of lamb.

Casein Protein in milk which is coagulated by rennet. Used in making cheeses.

Cassata alla Siciliana (It) 1) Mould of two or more different coloured layers of ice cream with fruits, nuts or small macaroons as a filling.
2) Rich gâteau surrounded by green almond paste.

Casserole 1) Deep lidded cooking pot made of flameproof or ovenproof materials for cooking stews or meat, poultry or vegetables.
2) Name for dishes cooked in a casserole pot.

Cassolette (Fr) 1) Special flameproof dish used for serving various hot or cold hors d'oeuvres, entrées or sweets.
2) A fried case used as a container for a savoury filling.

Cassoulet (Fr) Stew of haricot beans, pork, sausages, vegetables, and herbs. Lamb and goose or duck are also used.

Caul Animal membrane often used as a casing for minced offal.

Cèpe Edible fungus with sponge-like gills.

Cereal Farinaceous food such as wheat, oats, barley, rye, millet, rice, Indian corn, and buckwheat.

Cervelas (Fr) Smoked sausage made with pork meat and fat, garlic and seasonings.

Cervelat (Ger) Smoked, highly spiced sausage made from minced pork and beef.

Chafing-dish Metal dish or frying pan placed on a trivet over a spirit lamp which allows food to be either cooked at the table or kept warm.

Chambord, à la (Fr) Fish, often carp or trout, cooked in wine, and garnished with fish quenelles, mushrooms, soft roes, shrimps, crayfish tails, and truffles.

Chantilly (Fr) Sweetened whipped cream flavoured with vanilla essence; often lightened with a whisked egg white.

Chapatti (Indian) Unleavened round Indian bread.

Charlotte (Fr) 1) Cold moulded dessert lined with biscuits and filled with a cream or custard, eg Charlotte Russe.
2) Hot pudding lined with bread and filled with fruit, eg Apple Charlotte.
3) A similar savoury dish.

Charlotte mould (Fr) A deep, round, straight-sided mould that tapers in slightly at the base. Used for moulded desserts.

Chasseur, à la (Fr) Hunter's style, ie game, poultry or meat which is cooked in white wine with shallots.

Châteaux [pommes de terre] (Fr) Potatoes cut into olive shapes, blanched and roasted.

Chaudfroid (Fr) Classic French sauce, cooked but served cold. Prepared from a foundation sauce, into which gelatine dissolved in aspic is blended. It is poured over cold joints, poultry cutlets, fish, eggs, etc, and allowed to set.

Cheesecloth Butter muslin.

Chiffonade, Chiffonnade (Fr) 1) Salad dressing of hard-boiled eggs, red pepper, parsley, shallots, and French dressing.
2) Shredded sorrel or lettuce leaves sautéed in butter.

Chinois, à la (Fr) Chinese style.

Chipolata (It) 1) Small sausage.
2) Garnish of spicy sausages, chestnuts, and various vegetables.

Chorizo (Sp) Spicy, smoked sausage flavoured with paprika.

Choron (Fr) 1) Béarnaise sauce, without tarragon and chervil, blended with tomato purée.

2) Type of mustard made with tomato purée.

Chourico (Port) Sausage spiced with paprika.

Chowder Thick soup made with fish or shellfish; vegetables are often added.

Chrane (Jewish) Bitter-sweet preserve made with beetroot, horseradish, vinegar, and sugar.

Citric acid Acid which occurs naturally in citrus fruits. Bottled commercially, it is used as a preservative or alternative to lemon juice.

Civet (Fr) Game casserole using a marinade and generally the blood of the animal.

Clafouti (Fr) Pastry or thick pancake baked with a topping of fruit, usually black cherries.

Clamart, à la (Fr) Garnished with peas.

Clarified butter/fat Butter or fat cleared of water and impurities through slow heating and straining.

Cochineal Natural red food colouring. Carmine is also a cochineal extract, but of a deeper colour.

Cocotte (Fr) Small ramekin dish of porcelain or earthenware in which eggs, mousses, soufflés, etc are baked.

Coeur à la crème (Fr) Light cream or curd cheese from which the whey has been drained; usually set in heart-shaped moulds and served with fresh fruit or cream.

Colbert, à la (Fr) 1) Food, generally fish and especially sole, dipped in egg and breadcrumbs, then fried.

2) Classic French sauce made from butter, meat stock and glaze, lemon juice, and chopped parsley or tarragon.

3) Clear soup.

Collop Sliced or minced meat or offal; similar to French escalope.

Compôte (Fr) 1) Dish of stewed fruit served cold.

2) Pigeon or partridge stew.

Concasse, concasser (Fr) To pound, grind or chop roughly.

Condé (Fr) 1) Dish with a rice base, usually sweet, but can be savoury.

2) Cake with almond icing.

3) Red haricot bean soup or garnish.

Condiment Seasonings added to dishes at the table, eg mustard, salt, pepper, various relishes.

Conservation method Method of cooking carrots and similar root vegetables to retain flavour, colour and vitamins.

Conserve 1) Whole fruit preserve with a thick syrup.

2) Meat preserved in its own fat so that air cannot penetrate, eg confit d'oie – preserved goose, confit de porc – preserved pork.

Consistency Term describing the texture of a cake, pudding or similar mixture.

Coquille St. Jacques (Fr) Scallops. Also describes a recipe for scallops served in their shells with a sauce.

Coral Ovaries of a hen lobster used in various sauces and as a garnish.

Cornflour Finely ground kernel of Indian corn or maize. Used in puddings and cakes, or as a thickening agent in sauces.

Corn syrup Obtained from maize. Used to make various biscuits and sweets.

Côtelette (Fr) Chop, cutlet.

Cotriade (Fr) Fish soup or stew.

Coulibiac, kulebyaka (Rus) Fish pie (originally sturgeon) with other ingredients; usually encased in a brioche paste.

Coupe (Fr) 1) Stemmed, round goblet used for serving ice cream, fruit or shellfish cocktails.

2) Ice cream sundae.

Coupe Jacques (Fr) Fresh fruits soaked in liqueur and served with ice cream in a coupe (goblet).

Couronne, en (Fr) Meat or pastry preparations shaped in a ring or piled like a crown, eg crown roast of lamb.

Court bouillon (Fr) Liquid flavoured with herbs, vinegar or lemon juice and vegetables in which fish, meat or vegetables can be cooked or poached.

Couscous (N Afr) 1) Ground wheat meal, usually semolina, mixed with salted water and formed into pellets; cooked in a special steaming pan called a couscousier.

2) A meat stew served with couscous.

Couverture (Fr) Cooking chocolate containing a high proportion of cocoa butter; has excellent flavour and glossy finish.

Crécy, à la (Fr) With carrots.

Crème, à la (Fr) With a creamy or cream-based sauce.

Crème Anglaise (Fr) Basic egg custard used either as a sauce or as a dessert.

Crème brûlée (Fr) Baked egg custard made with cream and a crisp caramel topping.

Crème fraiche (Fr) Cream which has ripened and thickened naturally, but not soured.

Crème renversée (Fr) 1) Moulded custard inverted on to a dish when cold.
2) Moulded custard flavoured with vanilla, fruit, etc, and served cold.

Créole (Fr) Of southern USA or Caribbean origin. Refers to dishes with a spicy sauce, red and green peppers, tomatoes, okra, rice, etc.

Crêpe (Fr) Thin pancake.

Crêpe Suzette (Fr) Thin pancake heated in an orange sauce and flamed with orange liqueur or brandy.

Crépinette (Fr) Small flat pork sausage.

Crevette (Fr) Shrimp; **crevette rouge**, prawn.

Croissant (Fr) Crescent shaped roll made with a light butter- and egg-enriched dough.

Croquembouche (Fr) 1) Madeira cake topped with custard-filled profiteroles mounted on a paper cone and glazed with caramelized sugar.
2) Oranges or other fruits dipped in caramel and mounted on a cone or mould.

Croque Monsieur (Fr) Fried, grilled, toasted or baked sandwich with a ham and cheese filling.

Croquette (Fr) Minced or chopped food bound together, formed into various shapes, coated, and fried.

Croustades (Fr) Cases of fried or baked bread, rice, noodles, potatoes or pastry which are filled with savoury mixtures.

Croûtes (Fr) 1) Pastry case for savoury fillings.
2) Shapes of fried or toasted bread. Used as a base for either small, whole or portioned game birds or poultry, or for spreads such as canapés.
3) Dice of fried or toasted bread served with soup or egg dishes (now usually called croûtons).
4) Small round or triangular shapes of fried or toasted bread used to garnish fricassées and other sauced dishes as an alternative to fleurons of puff pastry.

Croûton (Fr) Small dice of fried or toasted bread used as a garnish.

Crudités (Fr) Small raw or blanched vegetables, eg carrots, tomatoes, courgettes, fennel, cucumber, etc, cut up or grated, and served with an oil and vinegar dressing, French dressing or dip.

Crustacea Shellfish. Crustacean (sing).

Curd 1) Solids remaining after coagulated milk separated from whey.
2) Fruit custard made with citrus fruit, and used in the same way as jam.

Cushion Topside of veal.

Dal, Dhal (Indian) Lentils and tomatoes spiced with chillis, garlic, and various herb and spice seasonings.

Dariole mould (Fr) Small, smooth sided cylindrical mould used for making puddings, sweet and savoury jellies, and creams.

Darne (Fr) Thick slice cut from the middle of a fish, eg salmon, and cooked on the bone.

Daube (Fr) Meat, vegetables, and herbs cooked very slowly.

Déglacer (Fr) To add wine, stock, cream or other liquid to juices left in the pan after roasting or sautéeing.

Délice (Fr) Fillet of fish, poultry or meat.

Demi-glace (Fr) Well reduced Espagnole sauce with the juices from roasted meat added. Also the basis for a Madeira sauce.

Dieppoise, à la (Fr) Garnished with shrimps, mussels, and mushrooms.

Digestifs (Fr) **Digestivi** (It) Drinks including some liqueurs served either before or, more often, after a meal to aid digestion.

Dobos torte (Hun) Layered cake with thick layers of sweet or savoury filling. Sweet cakes are topped with crisp caramel.

Dolma, dolmades, dolmas, dolmadakia (Gr, Tur, Rus) Stuffed vine leaves. Can also be cabbage leaves.

Doner Kebab (Gr and Tur) Pounded minced lamb or mutton, formed into a roll and grilled. Slices are put into a piece of pitta, together with chopped cabbage, onion, lettuce, tomato, etc.

Duchesse [pommes de terre] (Fr) Purée of potatoes blended with eggs and butter, and piped into whorled shapes or into a border, and then baked. Used as a garnish.

Duxelles (Fr) Basic preparation of chopped mushrooms, spring onions, seasonings, and sometimes Madeira. Used as a flavouring.

Éclair (Fr) Choux pastry oblong in shape, filled with flavoured cream, and topped with chocolate or coffee fondant icing.

Écrevisse (Fr) Crayfish.

Egg wash Mixture of beaten egg and water used for glazing pastries, breads and buns to give them a shiny surface.

Elver Young eel about 5cm long; cooked whole.

Émincé (Fr) 1) Finely sliced or shredded meat.
2) Dish using cooked meat.

Emulsion 1) Liquid of milky appearance containing minute drops of fat or oil.
2) Butter or oil mixed with egg yolks.

Enchilada (Mex) Pancake softened in hot oil, then rolled up with grated cheese and chilli sauce.

Épigramme, Epigram (Fr) Small slice of poultry, game or breast of lamb dipped in egg, rolled in breadcrumbs, and deep fried.

Escalope (Fr) Small thin slice of lean meat, generally veal, but may be pork, turkey, etc.

Espagnole Classic French foundation brown sauce.

Essence 1) Concentrate of natural juices from meat, poultry, and fish.
2) Extraction from the distillation of herbs, spices and flowers, eg essence of anise, cinnamon, orange, rose, etc.

Faggot 1) Dish of minced pork offal shaped into squares or balls, and baked until brown.
2) Bunch of herbs used for flavouring.

Farce (Fr) Stuffing.

Farci (Fr) Stuffed.

Farmed Animal or vegetable bred or grown for the table.

Fermière, à la (Fr) Farmer's style, ie garnished with vegetables, usually carrots, onions, celery and turnips.

Fibre Roughage; fibrous products which are not digestible, but essential for a healthy digestive and alimentary system.

Fillet 1) Underside of a sirloin of beef; the same cut of lamb, pork or beef.
2) Small, thin slice of poultry or game.
3) Side, whole or halved, of fish taken off the bone.

Filo see *Phyllo*.

Financière (Fr) Rich garnish consisting of some or all of the following: cock's combs, veal or poultry quenelles, olives, truffles, mushrooms, etc.

Flambé (Fr) Flamed; sprinkled with warm alcohol and set alight.

Flameproof Cookery utensils which can withstand direct heat, ie gas flame, electric ring.

Flan Open flat tart.

Flapjack 1) Bar- or square-shaped oat biscuit.
2) (Am) Griddle scone.

Flead Membrane of a pig's stomach containing pieces of lard. Used in pastry making.

Fleurons (Fr) Small, half-moon shapes of puff pastry. Used as a garnish.

Florentine, à la (Fr) 1) Made or garnished with spinach.
2) Flat thin biscuit containing dried fruits, nuts, and candied peel, and coated on one side with dark chocolate.

Flummery Pudding based on oatmeal or custard with regional variations of dried or stewed fruit, wine, etc added.

Foie d'agneau, de veau (Fr) Lamb's or calf's liver.

Foie gras (Fr) Goose liver from specially fattened geese.

Fondant (Fr) Solution of sugar, glucose, and water boiled to soft ball stage and worked until pliable. Diluted with a stock syrup, it is used as an icing, or flavoured, as a sweetmeat.

Fonds d' (Fr) 1) Round fleshy bases beneath the choke of an artichoke.
2) Broths and stocks made from veal, fowl or beef. Used as the basis for a variety of sauces.
3) Any basic cooking preparation, eg flavoured vinegar, pastry or roux.

Fondue (Swiss) 1) Cheese melted with white wine and Kirsch, and served at the table in the dish in

which it is cooked. Cubes of bread are dipped into it.
2) Puréed vegetables cooked in butter.

Fondue Bourguignonne (Fr) Cubed steak cooked briefly at the table in hot oil, then dipped in various seasonings before being eaten.

Fool Cold dessert consisting of fruit purée, whipped cream and/or custard.

Forcemeat Stuffing.

Forestière, à la (Fr) Garnish for small cuts of meat and poultry consisting of mushrooms, diced lean bacon and diced potatoes, fried until browned.

Four, au (Fr) Cooked in the oven.

Frappé (Fr) Iced or chilled.

Fricadelles (Bel) Meat balls made from finely minced pork or veal, herbs, spices, breadcrumbs, milk or cream, and eggs, then poached in stock and fried.

Fricassée (Fr) Velouté or white stew, usually of chicken, rabbit, lamb or veal.

Frit (Fr) Fried in shallow or deep fat.

Frites [pommes de terre] (Fr) Chipped potatoes.

Fritot (Fr) Fritter made with pieces of poultry, lamb or veal sweetbreads, brains or calves' heads.

Frittata (It) Flat omelet.

Fritter Variety of foods coated in batter, or chopped and mixed with batter, and fried.

Fritto misto (It) Small mixed pieces of coated and deep-fried food.

Friture (Fr) Fried food.

Fromage à la crème (Fr) Sweet cheese dessert made with fromage blanc.

Fromage blanc (Fr) Light, soft curd cheese, usually home-made.

Frosting (Am) Icing.

Fruits de mer (Fr) Seafood, usually shellfish.

Fry 1) Small fish, very young, only a few cms long.
2) Pig's and lamb's offal.

Fumé (Fr) Smoked.

Fumet (Fr) Fish or vegetable stock reduced by heating, uncovered, until thick and shiny.

Galantine (Fr) Boned poultry or meat cooked and pressed or moulded with aspic.

Galette (Fr) 1) Flat cake of sliced or mashed potato.
2) Traditional, flat, round puff or choux pastry cake.

Game chips Thin slices of potato fried until crisp.

Ganache paste (Fr) Melted chocolate and warm cream well mixed and cooled until firm. Used for decorations, fillings, and to make truffles.

Garam masala (Indian) Mixture of various ground spices used as a base for curries.

Garbure (Fr) Thick vegetable broth.

Garni, -e (Fr) Garnished with.

Gâteau (Fr) 1) Rich, elaborate sweet cake.
2) Round, square or oval shape of pâté, sliced meat, etc.

Gâteau Saint-Honoré (Fr) Cake made with short-crust and choux pastry, and filled with a pastry cream mixed with whisked egg whites.

Gelatine Setting agent made from animal bones, skin and tissues.

Genoese sponge Light, rich cake made with melted butter and eggs. Used as a base for desserts, for petits fours, etc.

Ghee (Indian) A form of clarified butter made from the milk of the water buffalo or goat.

Gherkin Small fruit from a plant of the cucumber family; gathered green, pickled and used as a condiment or garnish.

Giblets Neck, gizzard, liver, and heart of poultry or game. Can also include head, pinions, feet, and kidney.

Gigot (Fr, Scot) Whole leg of lamb.

Gizzard Small second stomach in birds and poultry. Part of the giblets.

Glacé (Fr) 1) Glazed.
2) Frozen or iced.

Glucose Sugar found in its natural form in honey, grapes and a few other fruits. Not very sweet. Available also in liquid and powdered form.

Gluten Substance in flour which gives it elasticity and strength.

Glycerine A syrup used as a sugar substitute in diabetic foods and in confectionery.

Gnocchi (It) Small dumplings made from semolina, maize, flour, choux pastry or potatoes.

Goujon, en (Fr) Small strips of deep-fried fish, eg plaice or sole.

Goulash (Hun) Thick soup or meat casserole often containing tomatoes and paprika.

Gram flour Flour made from chick-peas.

Granité (Fr) **Granita** (It) Water ice with a crystalline texture.

Gras, au (Fr) Served with a rich gravy or sauce.

Gratin, au (Fr) Dishes prepared with a sauce; usually sprinkled with breadcrumbs and/or grated cheese, baked in the oven or put under the grill until browned.

Grecque, à la (Fr) Greek style, ie vegetables such as courgettes and aubergines, cooked in stock, olive oil, and herbs.

Green bacon Unsmoked bacon.

Grenadins (Fr) Small fillets of veal or fowl, larded and braised.

Griddle, girdle Flat iron pan used for making scones, soda bread, etc.

Griskin 1) Backbone, spine or chine of pig cut away when preparing a side for bacon.
2) Shoulder of pork stripped of fat; top of the spare rib.

Grissini (It) Long sticks of hard-baked bread dough.

Groats Crushed hulled oat grains. Used generally to make porridge or gruel or for thickening broths, etc.

Guglhupf, Gugelhopf (Ger) Sweetened yeast cake with raisins, almonds, and lemon rind, traditionally baked in a fluted dish of pottery or metal known as a guglhupf mould.

Gumbo (West Indian, Am) Okra; also okra soup or various dishes made with okra.

Halva (East Med) Sweet paste used as a sweetmeat, dessert or cake; made with almonds or sesame seeds, and sweetened with honey or syrup. Pale gold in colour.

Hard sauce Whipped butter sauce such as brandy or rum butter.

Haricot (Fr) 1) Bean.
2) Different dried white beans.

Haricot de mouton (Fr) Mutton stew. Often served with potatoes and turnips.

Haricots verts (Fr) Green or French beans.

Heatproof Surface or material which can withstand a minimum amount of indirect heat, but not a direct flame or a high temperature.

Homard (Fr) Lobster.

Hongroise, à la (Fr) Hungarian style, ie prepared with paprika and fresh or soured cream.

Horse mushroom Common edible fungus, larger and coarser than a field mushroom, and of a stronger flavour.

Hough (Scot) Shin of beef boiled in stock.

Hummus (Mid East) Paste or dip consisting of pounded, cooked chick-peas flavoured with tahina, oil, garlic, and lemon juice.

Hydrometer Instrument used in wine-making. Called a saccharometer if used for sweet making.

Impératrice, à la (Fr) Desserts with a rice base.

Impériale, à la (Fr) Dishes garnished with foie gras, truffles, kidneys, etc.

Indienne, à la (Fr) Indian style, ie usually curry flavoured.

Infusion Liquid in which herbs or other flavouring agents have been boiled, heated or steeped until their flavour has been absorbed.

Italienne, à la (Fr) Italian style, ie garnished with pasta, cooked or garnished with mushrooms and artichoke bases.

Jalopeno pepper (West Indian) Hot red chilli.

Jambalaya (West Indian) Rice dish made with pork, chicken or shellfish, vegetables, garlic, and herbs.

Japonaise, à la (Fr) 1) Japanese style, ie garnished with croustades containing Japanese artichokes and croquette potatoes.
2) Bombe of peach ice cream and a mousse.

Jardinière, à la (Fr) 1) Garnished with mixed spring vegetables cut into small shapes or bâtons.
2) Vegetables stewed in their own juice.

Jugged dishes 1) Game cooked in a covered earthenware pot. The sauce or gravy can be thickened with the blood of the animal.

2) Kippers placed in a jug and covered with boiling water.

Julienne, à la (Fr) Vegetables cut into fine strips. Used as a garnish or added to consommé, etc.

Junket Milk with enough rennet added to set the milk to a soft curd. Flavouring and sweetening can be added.

Jus (Fr) Meat or fruit juice.

Jus, au (Fr) In its own juice, broth or gravy, seasoned, but without thickening.

Kale Type of cabbage with green curled leaves.

Kascha, kasha (Rus) Cooked buckwheat, semolina or rice.

Kebab, kebob, shish kebab (East Med) Cubes of meat or fish cooked on skewers.

Keffedes, kephtethakia, keftethes (Gr) Meat balls.

Knödel (Ger, Aus) Light dumplings either sweet or savoury.

Köfta (Tur) Meat balls.

Kosher (Jewish) Food prepared according to Orthodox Jewish Law.

Kromeski, Cromesqui (Pol, Fr) Savoury croquette often wrapped in a pancake, bacon rasher, etc before being coated and deep fried.

Kulich (Rus, Eastern European) Easter cake made of yeasted dough, usually tall and cylindrical in shape.

Lait, au (Fr) With milk, or cooked in milk.

Laitance (Fr) Soft fish roe used for garnishing or as a savoury.

Langouste (Fr) Crawfish.

Langoustine (Fr) Dublin Bay prawn.

Larding bacon Fat bacon or pork cut from the belly or flank of the pig.

Lardoons Strips of larding fat or bacon threaded through lean meat, poultry and game with a larding needle.

Lasagne al forno (It) Flat broad sheets of pasta layered with a savoury mixture and sauce, and then baked.

Laver Edible seaweed.

Leaven Raising agent.

Légumes (Fr) 1) Vegetables.
2) Podded vegetables, eg peas, beans.

Leveret (Fr) A hare, up to 1 year old.

Liaison (Fr) Any thickening or binding agent for soups, sauces and stews, eg roux, batter, beurre manié, arrowroot, tapioca, egg or blood.

Liègoise, à la (Fr) Cooked or garnished with juniper.

Lights, lites Lungs of certain animals.

Lockshen (Jewish) Vermicelli.

Lumpfish Large seafish. Its roe, either red or black, is an inexpensive alternative to caviar.

Lyonnaise, à la (Fr) Lyons style, ie fried, shredded onion usually added to the preparation.

Macédoine (Fr) Mixture of various kinds of vegetables or fruits cut into even-sized dice.

Mâche (Fr) Lamb's lettuce or corn salad.

Madère, au (Fr) Cooked or flavoured with Madeira wine.

Madrilène, à la (Fr) Madrid style, ie with tomato juice added.

Maison à la (Fr) Cooked to a recipe of the house or restaurant.

Maître d'Hôtel, à la (Fr) Dishes usually plainly cooked and garnished with parsley, or accompanied with Maître d'Hôtel butter, or Maître d'Hôtel sauce.

Maltaise, à la (Fr) Maltese style. Usually indicates oranges have been used.

Mange-tout Sugar peas; peas eaten with their pods.

Maple syrup (Am, Can) Natural syrup tapped from the trunks of maple trees. Used as a sweet flavouring for desserts, cakes, sweatmeats, etc, or as a syrup poured over pancakes, etc.

Maraichère, à la (Fr) Large joints of roasted or braised meat garnished with salsify, Brussels sprouts and potatoes.

Marbling Flecks of fat in the best quality cuts of meat.

Maréchale, à la (Fr) Small cuts of meat and poultry dipped in egg and breadcrumbs, fried in butter, and garnished with truffles and asparagus tips.

Marinière, à la (Fr) Fisherman's style, ie with mussels.

Marmite (Fr) Large metal or earthenware casserole. Dishes cooked *à la Marmite* are usually slow cooking casseroles.

Marsala, au (Fr) Cooked in or with Marsala wine.

Masséna, à la (Fr) Tournedos, fillets and noisettes of lamb garnished with artichokes, filled with Béarnaise sauce and strips of poached beef marrow.

Matelote (Fr) Sailor's style, ie fish stew made with wine or cider.

Matzo (Jewish) Flat cake or biscuit made of unleavened wheat flour and water. Traditionally eaten at Passover festival.

Médaillons (Fr) Fillets, meat mixtures, etc, cut or shaped into a round form.

Melts Animal's spleen.

Meunière, à la (Fr) Fish lightly dusted with flour, fried in butter and sprinkled with parsley and lemon juice.

Mignon (Fr) 1) Thin end of the fillet of beef.
2) Small oval steak.

Milanaise, à la (Fr) 1) Milanese style, ie escalope or poultry traditionally garnished with strips of tongue, mushrooms and ham in a tomato sauce with spaghetti or macaroni.
2) Food dipped in egg and crumbs mixed with Parmesan cheese, then fried.
3) Sweet soufflé flavoured with lemon.

Mille feuille (Fr) Puff pastry cake, or small pastry made of layers of cooked puff pastry, whipped cream, raspberry or strawberry jam, and a glacé icing on the top.

Mimosa (Fr) Garnish of sieved, hard-boiled egg yolks sprinkled over salads.

Minute, à la (Fr) Quickly prepared dishes, usually meat, eg fillet steak, escalopes, which can be served with a variety of sauces.

Miroton (Fr) Stew made from small thin slices of cooked meat, flavoured with onions.

Mocha (Fr) Mixture of coffee and chocolate flavours in desserts, cakes, beverages, etc.

Mode, à la (Fr) 1) In the style of.
2) Basic braised large joint, eg beef, strictly cooked with calves' feet and onions.
3) (Am) Any sweet dish with ice cream.

Mollusc Edible shellfish, both univalve and bivalve. The snail, too, is a mollusc.

Montmorency (Fr) 1) Type of cherry.
2) Flavoured with cherries.
3) A vegetable garnish for noisettes or tournedos.

Mornay (Fr) With a cheese sauce.

Moussaka (Gr) Minced meat, tomatoes, aubergines (sometimes potatoes) layered with a cheese sauce or savoury egg custard.

Mousse (Fr) Light sweet or savoury cold dish with a base of whipped cream and, sometimes, egg whites.

Must The name given to any liquid about to be converted into wine.

Nantua, à la (Fr) Sauce or garnish using crayfish tails.

Napolitaine, à la (Fr) 1) Neapolitan style.
2) Spaghetti bound with tomato sauce, butter, cheese, and roughly chopped tomatoes.
3) Ice cream and sweet cake layered in 3 different colours and flavours; pink, green, and white.

Naturel, au (Fr) Uncooked or plainly cooked food which is served simply.

Navarin (Fr) Mutton or lamb stew.

Nibbed Finely chopped nuts, especially almonds.

Niçoise (Fr) 1) In the style of Nice, ie cooked with tomatoes, garlic and oil.
2) Salad of beans, tomatoes, tuna, lettuce, hard-boiled eggs, black olives, and anchovy fillets.

Noisettes (Fr) 1) Pommes noisettes. Potatoes scooped out with a melon scoop and browned in butter.
2) Neatly trimmed round or oval shapes of boneless lamb or beef.

Noix (Fr) 1) Nut.
2) Walnut.
3) Cushion of veal.

Normande, à la (Fr) 1) With apples or apple flavour. Refers to dishes often cooked with cider or Calvados.
2) Cooked with cream.
3) Shellfish garnish.

Norway lobster Dublin Bay prawn.

Nougatines (Fr) Small cakes of Genoese sponge

layered with praline cream and iced with chocolate fondant.

Noyau (Fr) 1) Nut or kernel.

2) Liqueur made from the stones of fruits.

One-stage method see *All-in-one.*

Orange flower water Liquid flavouring distilled from the oil of orange flowers.

Oven brick Terracotta container of various sizes and shapes that completely encases fish, game or poultry to seal in flavours and juices while baking.

Ovenproof Cooking utensils which can withstand oven heat but not direct heat, eg a hob.

Paella (Sp) Dish of saffron or plain rice with chicken and shellfish; named after the flat dish with handles in which it is cooked.

Pailles (Fr) Fried potato or cheese straws.

Pain d'épice (Fr) Spiced gingerbread made with honey and rye flour.

Palmiers (Fr) Small or large pastries made from a sheet of puff pastry sprinkled with sugar; each side is rolled up towards the centre and then the whole is cut into slices and baked.

Panada Thick mixture made of flour, butter, seasonings, and milk, stock or water. Used for binding meat, poultry or fish.

Pannequet (Fr) Sweet or savoury pancake folded into a 'packet' round a filling.

Papillote, en (Fr) Food wrapped, cooked, and served in greased paper or foil.

Parfait (Fr) Chilled or frozen dessert made with egg white and fruit purée or other flavourings.

Parma ham see *Prosciutto.*

Parmentier, à la (Fr) With potatoes.

Parson's Nose Extreme end portion of the carcass of a bird.

Pasty Boat-shaped filled pastry case, or a double crust patty.

Pâté (Fr) 1) Cold meat pie or pasty.

2) A cooked meat paste generally made of pork, chicken, game or offal coarsely or finely ground.

Pâte (Fr) General term for sweet and savoury pastry, ie pâte à chou, pâte sucrée.

Pâtisserie (Fr) **Pasticceria** (It) 1) Fancy cakes and pastries.

2) Shop selling these items.

Patty 1) Small, double crust pie.

2) Puff or flaky pastry case with a recessed centre for savoury or sweet fillings.

3) Small shaped cake of food, eg hamburger.

Paupiettes (Fr) Thin slices of meat rolled around a savoury filling and served with a sauce.

Paysanne, à la (Fr) Garnish of bacon and buttered vegetables.

Pectin Gum-like substance in certain fruits and vegetables which acts as a natural setting agent. Also available commercially in bottles.

Peperonata (It) Cooked vegetable dish of peppers, onions, tomatoes, and seasoning. Served as a garnish, on its own or as a filling.

Pérsillade, à la (Fr) Garnished with chopped parsley to which a little crushed garlic is sometimes added.

Pesto (It) Sauce made with basil, garlic, pine kernels and Parmesan cheese.

Petits pois (Fr) Small, tender, young peas.

Phyllo pastry (Gr) Flour and water dough worked until paper-thin. Used for pastries, eg baklava, or in savoury dishes.

Pikelet Yeasted variation of a crumpet or pancake cooked without rings on a griddle.

Pilaf, pilau (East Med, Indian) Rice cooked in the Eastern manner, usually a savoury dish to which meat, fish or vegetables are added.

Pinion 1) Tip of a bird's wing.

2) Bone in the fin of a fish.

Pissaladière (Fr) Flan containing anchovies, olives and onion; a speciality of Nice.

Pistou (Fr) 1) Soup of vegetables, vermicelli, garlic, tomatoes, olive oil, and basil.

2) A variation of pesto, served with soup.

Pita, Pitta (Mid East and Yugoslavian) 1) (Mid East) Flat disc-shaped bread which rises when baked to create a pocket in the centre.

2) (Yugoslavian) Flour and water dough baked with savoury fillings.

3) (Yugoslavian) Sweet cake layered with almonds and honey.

Pith White lining in the rind of citrus fruits.

Pizza (It) Round of yeast dough on which a variety of fillings may be spread and baked.

Pizzaiola, alla (It) Meat or chicken cooked in a tomato and red wine sauce flavoured with garlic.

Plombière (Fr) Rich ice cream mixture with almonds or chestnuts and cream, either frozen in a single mould or formed into a pyramid and topped with a sweet sauce. It may also be flavoured with fruit.

Pluck Lungs, heart, liver, and sometimes entrails, of a slaughtered animal.

Poivrade, au poivre (Fr) 1) With pepper, generally either freshly ground black pepper or green peppercorns.
2) Meat or game served with a Poivrade sauce, eg foundation brown or Espagnole sauce with added shallots, herbs, red wine, vinegar and pepper.

Pommes de terre (Fr) Potatoes.

Portugaise, à la (Fr) Portuguese style; usually indicates tomatoes, onions and olive oil.

Poussin (Fr) Baby chicken.

Praline (Fr) Nut and sugar mixture, usually crushed and used as a flavouring or decoration. Can also be a caramel covered almond sweetmeat.

Presunto (Port) Cooked ham which is highly cured.

Printanière, à la (Fr) Spring style, ie with a garnish of spring vegetables.

Profiteroles (Fr) Small balls of choux pastry filled with various sweet creams, Chantilly, confectioners' custard, or savoury fillings. If sweet, can be glazed and covered with a chocolate sauce.

Prosciutto (It) Parma ham, ie raw smoked ham served thinly sliced.

Provençale, à la (Fr) Provençal style, ie, generally garlic, onions, tomatoes, olive oil, red and green peppers, etc.

Ptarmigan Game bird of the grouse family which has white feathers in the winter and brown feathers in the spring.

Pudding cloth Scalded cloth, which is floured and used for wrapping suet pudding before boiling or steaming.

Pulled sugar Boiled sugar mixture which has been manipulated with oiled hands and palette knives.

Pumpernickel (Ger) Dark yeasted rye bread.

Purée (Fr) Smooth pulp of fruit or vegetables; occasionally of meat or fish.

Puris (Indian) Deep-fried unleavened wholemeal bread.

Putu, mealie meal (Central Afr) Type of cornmeal porridge.

Quenelles (Fr) Smooth light oval-shaped dumplings of fish, poultry, game, meat or vegetables. Served as a garnish or as a main course.

Quiche (Fr) Open pastry flan filled with a savoury egg custard and other solid additions, eg vegetables, meats.

Ragoût (Fr) Well-seasoned, slowly cooked stew of meat and vegetables.

Raised pie Moulded hot water crust pastry enclosing a meat or game filling.

Raita (Indian) Vegetables in curd, usually yoghurt.

Ramekin Small, round ovenproof dish.

Rascasse Fish found in Mediterranean water; essential part of authentic bouillabaisse.

Raspings Bread or crusts dried and browned in a moderate oven, and crushed or rolled to make fine breadcrumbs for coating purposes.

Ratafia 1) Small biscuit made with almond flavouring.
2) Almond extract flavouring.
3) Liqueur made by infusing fruit kernels, eg peach, cherry, almond, in spirit.

Ratatouille (Fr) Vegetable stew made with aubergines, onions, tomatoes, peppers, courgettes. Can be eaten hot or cold.

Reform Sauce based on Poivrade sauce, with port, gherkins, tongue, mushrooms, and hard-boiled egg white.

Relish Vinegar-based pickle or sauce.

Rennet Enzyme extracted from the stomach of a calf. Used as a coagulant for junket and curds.

Rhizome Underground stem, eg ginger, stem ginger, which grows horizontally. Distinguished from a root by its leaves and buds.

Rice paper Made from pith of Chinese tree. Used for macaroon and other similar bases.

Ricotta (It) Soft whey cheese.

Rillettes (Fr) Pounded pork, rabbit, etc, sealed with pork fat; similar to pâté.

Rind Thin layer of skin of some fruits, vegetables, cheeses, and pork.

Risotto (It) Savoury rice dish in which the rice is fried, then cooked in stock; meat, poultry or fish is sometimes added.

Romaine, à la (Fr) 1) Garnish of gnocchi browned with Parmesan cheese.
2) Mould of chicken or spinach.

Root vegetable Vegetable with an underground main root, eg carrot, parsnip, beetroot.

Rossini, à la (Fr) Garnished strictly with foie gras and truffles.

Rôtisserie (Fr) Rotating spit used for grilling or roasting meat, poultry or game.

Roughage see *Fibre*.

Roulade (Fr) 1) Rolled meat, veal or pork.
2) Galantine of veal or pork.
3) Baked soufflé mixture rolled up like a Swiss roll.

Roux (Fr) Equal quantities of fat and flour cooked together. There are 3 kinds – white, blond and brown, depending upon the length of time of the preliminary cooking. A roux is used to thicken soups and sauces, and as an alternative to beurre manié.

Rubané (Fr) Ribbon-like or layered.

Ryjsttavel, rijsstafel (Dutch-Indonesian) 30–40 side dishes consisting of meat, fish and vegetables, sometimes curried. Served with a large bowl of rice and a variety of sweet and sour relishes and sauces.

Sabayon (Fr) 1) Hot or cold sweet egg sauce with alcohol flavouring; served with desserts.
2) French version of Italian zabaglione dessert made with white wine.

Saccharometer Sugar boiling thermometer.

Sago Thickening agent derived from the sago palm tree. Also made into a hot pudding.

Saignant (Fr) Very rare or underdone meat, especially steak.

Saint-Germain (Fr) 1) Thick pea soup.
2) Garnished with peas.

Salamander Metal utensil which, when heated until red-hot, is used to brown the tops of puddings.

Salame, salami (It) Beef and pork sausage which is spiced, salted, and smoked or air dried.

Salmi, salmis (Fr) Casserole made from game or poultry in which the birds have usually been partially roasted.

Salpicon (Fr) Vegetables, poultry or game finely cubed or diced, and bound together with a white or brown sauce.

Saltpetre Potassium nitrate. Used for curing and preserving meats.

Sanieh (Mid East) A large shallow pan used for cooking.

Sates, sateh (Dutch-Indonesian) Highly seasoned, small pieces of meat, poultry or fish marinated and roasted on a skewer. Served hot with a sweet-sour sauce containing peanuts or peanut oil.

Saturiana (Sp) Black pudding.

Savarin (Fr) Light yeasted cake made in a ring mould. It is usually soaked in a rum syrup, or the centre is filled with fruit, fruit purée or a flavoured whipped cream.

Savoy cake or finger Small, bar-shaped sponge cake.

Scallop Bivalve mollusc with white flesh and orange coral or roe.

Scallopine (It) Small escalopes of meat, generally served with a sauce.

Schnitzel (Ger) A thin slice of veal. See also *Escalope*.

Scone Quick bread made from a variety of flours, a small proportion of fat to flour, and fresh milk, soured milk or buttermilk. Cheese, nuts, currants, potatoes, treacle, etc can be added. Usually round or wedge shaped.

Seasoned flour Flour flavoured with salt and pepper, and occasionally other spices.

Sediment Solid residue left in the bottom of the pan after roasting meat or poultry.

Shashlik, Shashlek, Shashlyk (Rus) Marinated lamb or mutton grilled on skewers.

Sippets Pieces of toast cut into 'fingers', triangles and other shapes. Used as a garnish.

Skillet Frying pan.

Slack consistency Mixture which falls off the spoon almost of its own accord.

Smetana (Rus) Soured cream.

Smörgasbord (Swed) Sandwich table literally, but is actually a large display of small hot and cold dishes.

Smørrebrød (Danish) Open sandwiches.

Sodium metabisulphite Campden tablet.

Soubise (Fr) 1) With onions.

2) Sauce based on a Béchamel sauce made with onions, butter, and nutmeg.

Spätzli (Ger) Small noodles.

Spring chicken Young chicken, 2–4 months old.

Springform mould Baking tin with hinged sides held together by a metal clamp or pin. Has a loose base.

Sprue Thin stalks of asparagus.

Spurtle (Scot) Wooden stick used for stirring porridge.

Squab Young pigeon.

Stollen (Ger) Traditional Christmas and holiday bread made from yeasted dough and dried fruits.

Strudel (Aus) Thin leaves of pastry dough rolled around a sweet or savoury mixture.

Sugar nibs Small pointed crystals of sugar.

Sugar pea see *Mange-tout*.

Sulphur dioxide see *Campden tablet*.

Sundae (Am) Ice cream combined with fruit or other flavourings, nuts, crumbs, etc.

Suprême (Fr) 1) Boned wing and breast of a bird; can also apply to the choicest pieces of fish, veal, etc.

2) Sauce or liaison of cream and egg.

Syllabub Cold dessert of sweetened thick cream with alcohol and other flavourings.

Szechwan (Chinese) 1) Method of cookery practised in the province of Szechwan.

2) Very hot peppercorn.

Tahina (Mid East) Sesame seeds pounded to a paste.

Tamarind (Asian, West Indian) Leaves, flowers and fruit pods of the tamarind tree. Pod used for making curries, relishes, chutney, etc.

Tarte (Fr) see *Tourte*.

Terrine (Fr) 1) Earthenware dish in which pâtés are cooked.

2) Strictly a cold pâté, but now generally interchangeable with all types of pâtés.

Timbale (Fr) 1) Rounded cup-shaped, plain or fluted mould in earthenware or metal.

2) Any of the many dishes prepared in such a mould. Can be sweet or savoury.

Tisane (Fr) Medicinal drink prepared by soaking or infusing herbs or flowers.

Torte (Ger, Am) A flan or an elaborate gâteau.

Tortilla (Mex) 1) Thin pancake made from cornmeal.

2) (Sp) Flat omelet which can have a variety of meats or vegetables mixed in with the eggs.

Tourte (Fr) Round savoury or sweet tart. A sweet tourte is also called a tarte.

Trail Intestines of small game birds.

Trivet 1) Metal tripod, bracket or rack used for supporting utensils or food above the heat.

2) Raised, perforated plate fitted into the base of a pressure cooker.

Tronçon (Fr) Slice of flat fish, including the bone.

Truffle 1) Edible fungus.

2) Chocolate sweetmeat.

Tuber Swollen edible underground stem of a plant, eg potato, Jerusalem artichoke.

Turban (Fr) 1) Food arranged on a dish in a circle.

2) Forcemeats of poultry, game, etc cooked in a border mould.

Tutti frutti (It) 1) Mixture of fruits, generally candied or crystallized.

2) Vanilla ice cream mixed with such fruits.

TVP (Textured Vegetable Protein, TSP) Commercially prepared protein substance made of soya beans (soybean) or wheat. Can be flavoured to taste like various meats or fish.

Univalves Shellfish which live in a single shell, eg whelks, winkles.

Unleavened bread Bread made without a raising agent.

Vacherin (Fr, Swiss) 1) Full flavoured soft cheese. 2) Layered cake made with circles of meringue, cream, fresh fruit or chestnut purée.

Vanilla sugar Sugar stored with a vanilla pod.

Vegan Person who excludes from the diet not only meat, poultry, and fish, but also related products such as butter, cheese, milk, and eggs.

Vegetable extract Product obtained by evaporating vegetable juice. Commercial preparations may have yeast added.

Vegetable parchment Product similar to grease-proof paper but with non-stick properties. Used for lining baking tins, etc.

Velouté (Fr) Basic French sauce, with a rich fawn colour, usually made with fish or chicken stock.

Venison Deer or buck meat.

Véronique, à la (Fr) Garnished with white grapes.

Viennoise, à la (Fr) Viennese style, ie garnished with anchovy fillets, olives, capers, and chopped hard-boiled eggs.

Vinaigrette, à la (Fr) Oil and vinegar based dressing, generally used for vegetables.

Vol-au-vent (Fr) Round or oval puff pastry case. Usually filled with small pieces of meat, game, fish or vegetables in a creamy sauce.

Waterbath see *Bain-marie*.

Whey Liquid left after draining coagulated milk.

Whey butter Butter manufactured from the fat solids in whey.

Wishbone A 'Y' shaped bone between the neck and breast of a chicken or turkey.

Wok (Chinese) Round-bottomed pan with gently sloping sides. Used over a spirit lamp or burner with a trivet. Excellent for stir frying food.

Yeast In cookery, a raising agent, and an agent of fermentation in brewery and wine making.

Yeast extract Derived from fresh brewer's yeast through a process in which the soluble and insoluble materials are separated and the liquid is reduced to a sticky brown substance which is rich in B group vitamins.

Zabaglione, Zabaione (It) Dessert made from whipped egg yolks, sugar and Marsala wine. Usually served warm.

Zéphire (Fr) Light preparation.

Zest Outer rind of citrus fruits which contains the flavoured oils from the skin. Obtained by rubbing a sugar lump against the rind, or by using an implement known as a zester.

Zucchini (It) (Am) Courgette.

Zuppe Inglese (It) Sweet dish similar to an English trifle.

The Menu

General

À la carte (Fr) **Alla carta** (It) List of the available dishes on the menu; each dish is individually priced.

Carte du jour (Fr) **Carta del giorno** (It) Menu of the day. This may change daily or periodically.

Plat du jour (Fr) **Piatti del giorno** (It) Dish of the day.

Table d'hôte (Fr) **Menu del giorno** (It) 1) Set meal of two or more courses offered at a fixed price.
2) Selection of dishes from the à la carte menu offered at a slightly cheaper price.

Diners fixes au choix (Fr) **Menu a prezzo fisso** (It) When a choice of alternative dishes is offered for one or more courses in a table d'hôte menu, this term may replace or follow the heading: table d'hôte.

Carte du vin (It) **Lista dei vini** (It) List of all wines available at the restaurant.

Courses

Hors d'oeuvre (Fr) **Zakuski** (Rus) **Antipasti** (It) Light hot or cold dishes, served as a starter.

Mezze (It) 2) Assorted small hot or cold dishes. Sometimes chosen as an alternative to the above or to soup. Normally referred to as *hors d'oeuvre variés*.

Potage (Fr) **Minestre** (It) Soup. 1) May be alternative choice to the above.
2) In a formal dinner, the second course, ie coming after the hors d'oeuvre.

Farineuses (Fr) **Farinacei** (It) Pasta dishes. 1) An alternative to hors d'oeuvre.
2) Main course.

Oeufs (Fr) **Uova** (It) Egg dishes. Offered in some restaurants as a light main-course dish.

Poissons (Fr) **Pesci** (It) Fish dishes. 1) Main course alternative to meat.
2) Course before the meat.
3) In a formal dinner, the third course, ie coming after the soup.

Entrée (Fr) **Pietanze** (It) 1) Main course.
2) In a formal dinner, light dishes served after the fish and before the solid meat course. May consist of eggs, pasta, or very light meat or fish dishes such as quenelles.

Relevé (Fr) In a formal dinner, the main meat or poultry dish, served after the entrée; almost obsolete.

Rôti (Fr) **Arrosti** (It) Roasts. 1) Often used as a heading to distinguish from grillades and other meat courses.
2) When occasionally two meat courses are served in a formal dinner, the relevé consists of butcher's meat, the rôti of poultry or game.

Grillades (Fr) **Grigliati** (It) Steaks and any other items from the grill.

Buffet froid (Fr) **Piatti Freddi** (It) Choice of cold cooked meat and fish, usually served with salads.

Légumes (Fr) **Legumi** (It) Vegetables served with an entrée, rôti, grillade or relevé.

Salades (Fr) **Insalata** (It) Salad. 1) Main course.
2) An alternative or addition to hot vegetables.
3) In a formal dinner, part of the buffet or eaten after the roast or other main course.

Sorbet (Fr) **Sorbetto** (It) Half-frozen water ice often with liqueur. 1) Served in the middle of a formal dinner to refresh the palate.
2) Served as a dessert on an à la carte menu.

Entremets (Fr) French term originally used to indicate sweet and savoury dishes; now generally refers to all sweet dishes, hot or cold.

Tramessi (It) Italian term equating to original French term, entremets. *Dolci* generally used nowadays.

Desserts (Fr) Last course of a meal; can consist either of sweet desserts, cheese, and/or fruit.

Glaces (Fr) **Gelati** (It) Iced and frozen desserts.

Fromages (Fr) **Fromaggi** (It) Cheese(s) available.

Café (Fr) **Caffé** (It) Coffee.

Friandises (Fr) **Frivolezze** (It) Sometimes called Petits Fours (Fr) or Lecornie (It). Very small sweetmeats, biscuits, etc, served with coffee.

Cookery Techniques

Bake To cook by dry heat in the oven.

Bake blind To bake pastry cases either partially or completely before a particular filling or preparation is added. The dough is rolled out, placed in a tin, pressed well into the sides, and trimmed. The base is pricked with a fork and lined with greaseproof paper, cut slightly larger than the pastry case. The case is filled with dried beans, bread crusts or rice to prevent the pastry rising. For both partially and fully cooked cases the paper and weights are removed at the end of the cooking time, and the case returned to the oven for 5–7 minutes to dry out the inside.

Bard To cover delicate parts of lean meat, poultry or game with thin rashers of fat bacon, held in place with string, and removed before serving. When cooking birds, barding keeps the breast moist, and protects it while other parts of the bird, such as the legs, require further cooking.

Baste To pour, spoon or brush melted fat, pan juices, milk or other liquids over meat, poultry or game while cooking to keep in moisture.

Bat To beat out a thick slice of meat into a larger, thinner slice, tenderizing the meat in the process. The slice is usually placed between two thicknesses of greaseproof or waxed paper, and beaten from the centre outwards on both sides with a cutlet bat or rolling-pin.

Beat To turn over a cake mixture, egg or batter with firm, quick strokes of a spoon, fork or wooden spoon, lifting the mixture a little with each stroke to incorporate air in order to make the food lighter or more liquid. An electric mixer or food processor can also be used.

Bind To add moist ingredients, eg cream, egg, melted fat, a sauce or panada, to dry, eg breadcrumbs, stuffings, forcemeats, etc, in such proportions that the dry ingredients are held together.

Blanch 1) To place food in a saucepan of cold water, bring to the boil, then strain off the water. 2) To pour boiling water over the food.

Both methods are used to preserve the colour of certain foods, to remove strong, undesirable flavours, or to loosen the skin of nuts before skinning. Blanching also halts enzyme activity prior to freezing. For blanching vegetables before home freezing, see p1387.

Blend To mix evenly one ingredient with another, using a spoon, electric blender or liquidizer.

Braise To cook vegetables alone or with meat, poultry, fish, or game, by first browning the vegetables and meat in hot fat. The vegetables are then put in a heavy-based saucepan or ovenproof casserole and the meat placed on top. A little stock or water is added, the pan covered, and the food simmered over low heat or in a warm oven until tender.

Brand To burn the surface of a finished dish, such as a steak or omelet, with a hot skewer, or to place on a red-hot grill so that the food is seared at points of contact.

Broil (Am) To grill or spit roast.

Brown 1) To seal in the juices of meat or fish by searing the surface.
2) To finish cooking a dish by letting its outer surface cook uncovered under a grill or in a hot oven, until it becomes brown.

Bruise To beat with a weight or heavy object in order to release flavour, as when using root ginger.

Caramelize 1) To heat sugar and water to 177°C, until they turn a rich golden colour; see p1079.
2) To coat a mould with sugar and water heated to caramel point.

Carve To cut up meat, poultry or other food for serving. For carving meat, see pp474–80, and poultry, see pp625–26.

Casserole To cook meat, game, poultry, fish and/or vegetables slowly, generally with stock or other liquid added, in a covered pan, either over heat or in the oven.

Chill To cool food, preferably in a refrigerator, until it is thoroughly cold, but not frozen.

Chine To sever the backbone from the ribs of joints such as loin or best end of neck of lamb, before cooking, so that the joint can be divided easily into chops or cutlets when carving.

Chip To cut potatoes or root vegetables into sticks.

Cut the vegetables into sticks 1cm thick and 8cm long.

Chop To divide food into very small pieces. On a board, slice or cut the food up roughly. Use a heavy knife with a very sharp blade and keep one hand on the top of the knife blade, near the point, and the other hand on the handle. Cut the food into small pieces with sharp up and down movements.

Clarify 1) To remove the impurities from fat used for frying or roasting. Heat an equal quantity of fat and cold water in a large pan until the water begins to boil. Simmer for about 5 minutes, then strain into a bowl and leave the fat to solidify. Remove in one piece, dry, and scrape any sediment off the bottom. Heat the fat gently until bubbling ceases to drive off any water.

2) Butter and margarine can be clarified to remove any milk solids, salt, and water by heating gently until melted. The water is expelled when the fat ceases to bubble. Remove from the heat and strain the fat into a bowl through a fine sieve or muslin, which catches the salt; or skim off any scum that has risen to the top. Leave for a few minutes, then pour off the clear or clarified fat into a clean container, leaving the sediment behind.

Clear 1) To remove impurities and opaque matter from stocks, consommés or jellies. Add beaten egg white and crushed shell to the liquid, and bring it to the boil without stirring. When cooked, the egg white rises to the top of the liquid, taking with it the unwanted particles, which are then strained off.

2) Jelly preserves are cleared by pouring the fruit juice through a jelly bag, felt or flannel cloth which has been scalded first with boiling water. The juice is allowed to drip for 45 minutes–1 hour.

Coat 1) To cover fish fillets, slices of liver, cubes of meat, slices of fruit, etc, completely in flour, egg and breadcrumbs or batter. This is most frequently done before frying. The coating protects the food, and keeps in all the juices and flavour during cooking.

2) To cover food with a sauce or icing before serving.

Core 1) To remove the core from fruit such as apples, pears, pineapples, etc, usually leaving the fruit in one piece. Use an apple corer, or a long, narrow, sharp knife. Place the fruit upright on a board, and push the corer or knife through the fruit, then twist, and remove the core.

2) To snip out the cores in kidneys.

Cream 1) To beat to a creamy consistency.

2) To mix fat and sugar by beating the fat first, then adding the sugar and beating until the mixture is light, fluffy, and pale in colour.

Crimp To decorate the edge of a tart or pie by pressing the layers of pastry together and pinching with the thumb and first finger of both hands, then twisting in opposite directions.

Crumb To crumble bread for fresh or soft breadcrumbs. Remove the crusts from white bread which is at least 1 day old, and either grate the bread on a grater, rub it through a wire sieve or between the palms of the hand, or process in an electric blender. Soft crumbs can be stored in a sealed container for 2–3 days in a refrigerator or up to 3 months in a freezer.

Cube To cut food into evenly sized, cube-shaped pieces. Small cubes, 5mm–1cm across, are referred to as dice.

Deep fry To fry food, generally coated with batter or egg and breadcrumbs, by immersing in deep hot fat or oil. For detailed instructions, see p932; a temperature chart can be found on pp302–3.

De-seed To remove the seeds or pips from food such as peppers, tomatoes or marrows. Cut the tomatoes and marrows in half, and scoop out the seeds with a spoon. If the vegetable is required whole, eg stuffed peppers, cut round the stem end only, and lift this out, then scoop out any remaining membranes and seeds.

Devil To spread food, usually fish or meat, either with hot, dry seasonings, or with a strongly flavoured sauce, before grilling or frying.

Dice see *Cube*.

Dot To place small pieces or knobs of butter or fat over the surface of food before cooking, to prevent it from drying up.

Drain To remove surplus liquid or fat from food by pouring the food into a colander or sieve placed over a basin, or by lifting small quantities of food out of the liquid on a perforated spoon and placing it on soft kitchen paper.

Draw To remove the head, neck, feet, and viscera from poultry and game. For detailed instructions, see pp617–18.

Dredge To sprinkle food with flour or sugar so that it is evenly coated.

Dress 1) To pluck, draw and truss poultry or game.
2) To arrange cooked shellfish in the shell.
3) To add an oil-based dressing to a salad.
4) To decorate food with a garnish.
5) To blanch tripe.

Dust To distribute flour, sugar or other finely ground ingredients very sparingly, eg icing sugar over a cake, or flour over a greased tin.

Fillet To remove whole pieces of flesh from the main carcass of meat, poultry or fish. For detailed instructions on filleting fish, see p407.

Flake 1) To break up cooked fish or shellfish into pieces with a fork.
2) To cut fat into thin slivers.
3) To mark pastry edges with horizontal lines, using a knife blade.

Flame 1) To ignite alcohol poured over food during or after cooking. This burns off some of the excess fat and drives off the alcohol content, leaving only the essential flavour of the spirit or liqueur used. Dishes prepared in this way are described as *flambéd*.
2) To singe poultry or game before cooking, to burn off small hairs.

Flute To decorate the edges of a pastry pie by pressing the thumb on the top outer edge, and drawing the pastry about 1cm towards the centre of the pie with the back of a knife, repeating the process at intervals of 2cm for savoury pies and 5mm for sweet pies.

Fold in To combine an aerated ingredient with other ingredients, so that the entrapped air is retained, as when combining sifted flour with other ingredients, or combining two whisked mixtures. Gently sift or pile the ingredient to be folded in on top of the other ingredient. If folding in whisked egg whites, first stir in up to a quarter of the foam into the main mixture to lighten it. Cut down through the centre of the mixture with a metal spoon, and round half the bowl, then spoon up half the mixture and lay it lightly on the other half, thus trapping the added ingredient between two layers of the main mixture. Turn the bowl and repeat the process until the ingredient has been folded in.

Frick To spread glacé icing or an icing sugar glaze over another icing of contrasting colour or flavour so that the top coating trickles down over the edges of a cake revealing the base icing.

Frothing To dredge meat or poultry with flour and baste it with cooking juices or fat shortly before the end of cooking time, before returning it to the oven at a high heat until it appears brown and glazed.

Fry To cook in hot fat or oil.

Glaze To brush or coat food with beaten egg, egg white, milk, sugar syrup, sweet or aspic jellies, or meat glaze, to give it a glossy surface.

Grate To reduce food to coarse or fine shreds, crumbs or powder, by rubbing them against a grater. The food to be grated should be firm, and the correct sized grater used. Apples and onions should be grated coarsely, otherwise they produce more liquid than pulp. Hard cheese can be grated coarsely for cooking, or finely for a garnish. Nutmegs are grated finely.

Grill To cook food over or under direct, dry heat.

Grind 1) To reduce hard foods to granules or powder by working in a mortar with a pestle, or by processing in an electric blender, mill or grinder.
2) (Am) To mince.

Gut To remove the entrails from a fish and clean it before cooking; see p406.

Hang To suspend meat, poultry, and game in a cool, airy place, which tenderizes the meat and gives it the characteristic gamey flavour. To hang venison, see p673; to hang game birds, see p656.

Hull To pluck or twist off the calyx and stalk from soft berry fruits.

Ignite To set fire to brandy, sherry or liqueur, previously warmed in a chafing-dish, saucepan or ladle, before or after pouring it over crêpes, Christmas pudding, etc. (See also *Flame*.)

Infuse To pour boiling liquid over herbs, spices, vegetables, tea or coffee, allowing the liquid to draw off and absorb the flavour. Alternatively, the ingredients can be brought to the boil with a liquid, eg water, milk, sugar syrup, alcohol or fruit juices, then removed from the heat and allowed to stand in a warm place.

Joint To divide poultry, game, or small animals such as rabbit, into suitable pieces for serving by severing the cartilage between the joints. For detailed instructions on jointing, see pp619–20.

Knead To press and stretch dough with the heel of the hand or an electric dough hook, until it is smooth and elastic. For details, see p1154.

Knock Back To knead yeast dough after the first rising, in order to knock out the air bubbles and ensure an even texture. (See also *Prove*.)

Knock Up To make a raised edge to double crust pastry pies or tarts by lifting up the sealed pastry edges with the back of a knife blade, before baking.

Lard To thread long, thin strips of pork fat or lardoons into game or very lean meat, to prevent them drying up during roasting.

Liquidize To reduce moist foods to a smooth liquid in an electric blender or liquidizer.

Macerate To soften food by soaking it in a liquid. Lentils and other dried pulses are macerated in water or stock to soften before cooking. Dried fruits are macerated in water, fruit juice, wine or liqueur, then cooked if required.

Marinate To steep meat or fish in a mixture usually containing oil or lemon juice, acid in the form of vinegar or wine, and herbs and spices, to tenderize and improve the flavour of the food, before or instead of cooking. For more information see pp729–30.

Mash To reduce food to a smooth consistency with a fork or an instrument called a masher.

Mask 1) To cover food with a thin layer of jelly, glaze, sauce or icing.
2) To coat the inside of a mould with jelly.

Mince To reduce foods to pieces by passing them through a mincing machine. Both electric and hand-operated machines have different sized blades to mince food finely or coarsely.

Parboil To cook food partially by boiling for only part of the usual time. The cooking is then often completed by another method, eg frying.

Pare To remove the thin outer layer of skin from vegetables or fruit with a sharp knife.

Peel To remove the outer layer of skin (and sometimes pith) from vegetables, fruit, shrimps etc.

Pick Over To discard any damaged fruit.

Pipe To force soft foods through a forcing bag and nozzle to make a particular shape.

Pit To remove stones from fruits and vegetables.

Pluck To remove the feathers from poultry and game birds. For detailed instructions, see p616.

Poach To cook food gently in liquid which is kept just below boiling point. The liquid should be moving gently, but not bubbling.

Polish To give a shine to food, such as apples for dessert, by rubbing gently with a soft cloth.

Pot roast To cook a smaller, less tender joint of meat by first browning it in hot fat, then placing it on a wire rack or a bed of root vegetables in a heavy-based pan. Cover with a tight-fitting lid and slowly cook either over low heat or in a warm oven.

Prove To leave a yeast dough to rise for a second time after it has been knocked back and shaped ready for baking. (See also *Knock back*.)

Purée To reduce raw or cooked food to a smooth pulp by pounding, sieving, or processing in an electric blender or food processor.

Reduce To evaporate surplus liquid, usually from soups, sauces, and syrups, by fast boiling in an uncovered pan, to obtain a concentrated, well-flavoured, final mixture.

Refresh To rinse vegetables in cold water after blanching, to preserve their colour.

Render To extract fat from bacon rinds or small fatty meat trimmings, by heating gently either in the oven or over low heat, until the fat runs and the pieces of skin, etc are crisp. Strain through a fine metal strainer into a clean basin, pressing the crisp pieces against the strainer to extract all the fat.

Roast To cook food by dry heat, either in an oven or over or under dry heat, generally using a small amount of fat and usually with frequent basting.

Roll out To flatten pastry or dough smoothly with a cylindrical object. The process prepares the dough for cutting into shapes, for lining a mould or baking tin, or for covering a pie.

Roll up To turn in one end of a strip or other piece of food, and continue rolling to make a cylindrical shape, as for a Swiss Roll.

Rub in To combine fat and flour for shortcrust pastry, plain cakes, etc. First cut the fat into small pieces with a knife, then, using the tips of the fingers, rub the fat into the flour, lifting the hands up from the bowl so that as the flour falls back into the bowl the mixture becomes aerated. When all the lumps of fat have been worked in, the mixture should resemble breadcrumbs.

Sauter (Sauté) To fry food rapidly in shallow fat, turning or shaking it all the time to prevent burning. For more detailed information, see p932.

Scald 1) To dip vegetables or fruit into boiling water, usually to make it easier to remove the skins.

2) To heat milk or cream to near boiling point.

3) To clean a pan or other utensil thoroughly with boiling water.

Scallop see *Flute*.

Score To make cuts in the surface of food, eg the skin on pork joints before roasting, to facilitate carving, and to make the outside skin crisper.

Scrape To shave away the top layer of a vegetable, eg carrot, without actually peeling it, using a sharp knife drawn quickly across the surface.

Seal or Sear To brown the surface of meat, poultry, game or fish in hot fat or in a hot oven to keep in the juices during cooking.

Season To add salt, pepper and other flavourings to food, if recipe requires, to bring out the flavour. See also p287.

Shallow fry To fry food in a small amount of fat or in no fat at all. For detailed instructions, see p931.

Shred To reduce vegetables, fruit or fruit peel to fine pieces or shavings, either with a sharp knife or a grater or mandoline. Shredding produces a coarser texture than grating.

Sieve To rub or pass food through a sieve to reduce it to very fine crumbs, pulp or purée, or to separate the pips and skin from fruit and vegetables. The process is also used to separate unwanted solid matter.

Sift To shake a dry ingredient through a sieve, sifter or dredger to remove lumps and to incorporate air.

Simmer To heat liquid until boiling point, then reduce the heat to keep the liquid just below boiling point, over a gentle heat. The surface of the liquid should be moving gently with only occasional slow bubbles.

Singe see *Flame* (2).

Skewer To pass a metal or wooden spike through meat to hold it in a neat shape while cooking, or to thread small pieces of food on metal skewers for cooking under the grill.

Skim To remove surface fat, scum or cream from a liquid.

To remove fat, lay a piece of soft kitchen paper on the surface, and lift off when saturated.

For scum, pass a shallow or perforated metal spoon slowly across the surface.

To remove cream from milk, use a shallow metal spoon.

Skin To remove the outer layer of peel or membrane from vegetables, fruit, meat or fish.

Slake To mix a starchy material with liquid before adding it to a hot liquid for thickening.

Slash To make shallow cuts across raw foods, such as herrings and sausage rolls, to allow heat to penetrate and steam to escape during cooking. Slashing can also be decorative.

Snip 1) To cut into the edge of the fat round cuts of meat such as gammon rashers, to prevent the meat curling while cooking.

2) To cut up food, using kitchen scissors.

Souse To immerse and cook food, usually fish or pork, in a vinegar and spiced pickling solution. The food should be allowed to cool in the liquid.

Spit roast To cook meat, uncovered, by rotating it on a metal skewer, over or in front of direct heat, or under a grill. Some cookers are equipped with a 'rôtisserie', which revolves so that the food is roasted evenly on all sides.

Steam To cook food in the steam rising from boiling liquid.

Steam fry To cook moist food in a very little fat in a covered pan, so that the food gives off its own liquid and is actually steamed rather than fried.

Steep To soak food in liquid, either to soften it or extract the flavour.

Stew To cook food, eg tougher cuts of meat or vegetables, fish, fruit etc, with a liquid by simmering it in a covered pan, either over heat or in the oven.

Stir fry To fry finely chopped food quickly in a very little fat, stirring to prevent burning. Use a wok, or frying pan with curved base and sides. For details, see p932.

Stone To remove the stone from fruit such as plums, olives, etc.

Strain To separate liquids from solids by pouring the mixture through a colander, sieve or muslin.

Stud To stick cloves into onions, the skin of bacon, or other meat and vegetables, to impart flavour.

Sweat To release the juices from vegetables to be used in soups or as a base for casseroled or stewed meat. Melt a little fat in a pan, add the vegetables, cover, and leave over low heat until the juices run.

Tammy To force soups or sauces through a fine woollen cloth, to produce a smooth, glossy finish. Nowadays, nylon or fine-meshed metal sieves are generally used instead of a tammy cloth.

Thicken To give a thick consistency to sauces, gravies and soups usually by adding cream, egg and cream or farinaceous substances blended with fat or cold liquid. For detailed instructions on thickening processes, see pp327–28.

Top and tail To remove the stubs and stems at both ends of gooseberries, currants, and green beans before cooking.

Toss To turn meat in flour, or salad in a dressing, so as to coat the food evenly.

Truss To tie poultry, meat or game into a neat shape before cooking, either with string or with string and a skewer. For detailed information on trussing poultry, see pp618–19.

Weight or Press To place a weight over a piece of meat, tongue, pâté or home made cheese, to expel excess moisture and condense the texture of the food before serving. Cover the food with greaseproof paper, and place a plate or piece of cardboard on top. Put a weight or heavy object on the plate, and leave for several hours or overnight. For details on weighting pâtés, see p731.

Whip To beat with a whisk, rotary beater, electric blender or liquidizer to incorporate air and so make the ingredient(s) thick, stiff or light-textured.

Whisk To beat with light, rapid strokes, using a balloon or rotary whisk, to incorporate air into an ingredient.

SEASONINGS AND FLAVOURINGS

The sweet herbs most usually employed for purposes of cooking, such as the flavourings of soups, sauces, forcemeats, &c are the thyme, sage, mint, marjoram, savory, and basil. Other sweet herbs are cultivated for purposes of medicine and perfumery: they are most grateful both to the organs of taste and smelling; and to the aroma derived from them is due, in a great measure, the sweet and exhilarating fragrance of our " flowery meads."

Seasonings are usually added to food before cooking, and are adjusted afterwards. A seasoning should not give its own flavour to the food, but merely heighten or temper the flavour of the food to which it is added.

Flavourings are generally added during or after cooking. A flavouring agent is used in food to give it added or improved flavour.

The general title 'flavourings' includes herbs, spices, purées, natural and synthetic essences, meat and yeast extracts, wines and spirits. Any of these can be mixed with other ingredients in making a dish, added to them temporarily, as in the case of a bay leaf infused in milk, or added to a marinade in which the food is soaked before cooking. Some can be rubbed on the surface of the food before cooking, or used to baste it while it is cooking, eg garlic can be rubbed over meat and poultry before grilling or frying, and a barbecue sauce containing different flavourings can be used to baste the meat while cooking.

Herb flavourings can be used fresh or dried; generally, fresh herbs give a better, cleaner flavour. Dried herbs tend to be more aromatic, so must be used more sparingly; as a general rule, half to two-thirds of the quantity given for fresh herbs is sufficient. If dried herbs are left unused for any length of time they become flavourless or musty. Once opened, store in a dry jar for up to six months, and replace them when they are past their best. Most fresh herbs can be frozen, and if well sealed in airtight containers, or chopped and frozen in cubes of ice, will keep their aroma for up to six months.

Many spices are derived from herbs and other plants. They are used in various forms: whole leaves (eg bay leaves), husks or seeds (eg blades of mace, whole peppercorns), stems, flowers or leaves. Some are available both whole and ground in powder form: ginger, nutmeg, and cloves are common examples. Whole spices are generally infused in one of the ingredients for a dish, or are cooked with the dish and removed before serving. Powdered spices are mixed in direct, or sprinkled over the finished dish. Most spices are strongly flavoured, and should therefore be used sparingly; it is best to add them to a dish gradually, tasting between each addition. Curry powder, being a mixture of spices, must be cooked long and slowly to let the flavours develop and blend. Highly spiced mixtures can develop unpleasant flavours when frozen, so spices are best added to frozen dishes after thawing, if possible. Since spices, like herbs, deteriorate with long keeping, they should be bought in small quantities, and stored in airtight containers.

Essences include concentrated extracts and purées, and natural and synthetic bottled concentrates. Most of these are strong, and should be used very sparingly. Bottled colourings are equally potent, and unless used with care will make foods look unnatural. Gravy browning, which is made from caramelized sugar, is a common and useful colouring not only for savoury dishes, but also to darken the colour of fruit cakes. Some spices, such as saffron and turmeric, colour the food as well as flavour it, as do coffee, cocoa, and powdered drinking chocolate.

Common Herbs, Spices, and Essences used in Cookery

Name	Form in which generally used	Descriptions and accepted uses
Allspice (Jamaica pepper, Myrtle pepper)	Dried berries (like large peppercorns), whole or ground	Flavour is similar to a compound of cloves, juniper, and cinnamon. Used in a variety of savoury and sweet dishes, especially as an ingredient in pickling spice and in fruit cakes.
Almond	Nut, whole, flaked, ground, nibbed, or as essence	*Sweet almonds* have a very subtle, bland flavour, and are widely used, especially in sweet foods, such as cakes and desserts, and as a garnish or decoration. Ground sweet almonds are used for sweetmeats, to add body to flours, and for flavouring. *Bitter almonds* have a quite different, stronger flavour, and are used sparingly in sweet dishes and biscuits. They should not be used raw, as the nut contains the substance used as a basis for prussic acid. *Almond essence* is a commercial preparation of varying strength, made from bitter almonds. *Ratafia*, is, strictly speaking, a liqueur made by infusing various substances in spirit, but the term is now generally used of an almond-flavoured infusion, ie a subtler form of almond essence. Ratafia biscuits are flavoured with ratafia essence, made from oil of bitter almonds.
Angelica	Stem, candied; leaf, fresh	Candied angelica is used to decorate cakes, biscuits and desserts, but in Scandinavia the plant is eaten as a vegetable, and the leaves can be used in salads, or to flavour rhubarb or marmalade.
Anise (Aniseed)	Seed, whole or as essence	Used for fish and shellfish, and in curries, but mainly for flavouring sweets, cakes and breads; also in liqueurs such as Anis and Pastis.
Asafoetida	Dried resinous juice from stem, usually ground	A powerful, rank flavour, used in curry powder and South Indian vegetable dishes.
Basil	Leaf, fresh or dried, crushed	Flavour varies slightly according to variety, and only the leaf tips of bush basil should be used. Popular in Southern European cookery, and used with well-flavoured savoury foods, especially tomatoes, eggs, and cheese. A traditional flavouring for turtle soup. An essential ingredient for Pesto Genovese (p1532).
Bay	Leaf, fresh or dried	Essential ingredient of a bouquet garni, and used as an infused flavouring for many savoury and sweet dishes, especially casseroles and milk puddings. Also used in chutneys, pickles, and marinades.
Bergamot	Leaf or flower, fresh	Little used in cooking, but can be used to flavour drinks, or in salads.
Borage	Leaf or flower, fresh	Used mainly to impart a flavour of cucumber to drinks, but can also be used in salads or as fritters.
Bouquet garni	Herbs and spices, fresh or dried	Sprigs of fresh herbs and whole spice berries tied in a square of muslin or cheesecloth, and dropped into stocks, soups, stews and other dishes. The bouquet garni is removed before serving. The classic herb bundle consists of 3 parsley stalks to 1 sprig of thyme and 1 bay leaf, or 1 × 10ml spoon mixed dried herbs and 1 bay leaf. Other ingredients, eg sprigs of marjoram, basil, chervil, tarragon or rosemary, can vary to suit the dish. Black peppercorns, juniper berries, whole cloves, nutmeg fragments or orange peel may also be included.

Name	Form in which generally used	Descriptions and accepted uses
Burnet	Leaf, fresh	Several varieties, when crushed, have an aroma similar to cucumber. An important ingredient in certain classic butters and sauces; also used in salads and for flavouring drinks.
Caper	Bud, pickled	Used as a garnish for hors d'oeuvres and fish, and in salads and stuffings, but especially important in sauces, such as Caper Sauce (p693) for mutton.
Capsicum (see Peppers)		
Caraway	Seed, fresh	A dominant flavour, used extensively in German and Austrian dishes and in cakes, bread, cheeses, cabbage, and sauerkraut. Kümmel liqueur is flavoured with caraway.
Cardamom	Seed and seed pods, dried	Ground cardamom is an ingredient of curry powder, and is widely used in Indian and Middle Eastern cookery. It is also used to flavour drinks. In the UK it is used in pickling spice, and sometimes in cakes.
Cassia (see Cinnamon)		
Cayenne pepper (see Peppers)		
Celery	Seed, dried	A flavouring for salt, also used in pickles, sauces, and soups (especially those containing tomato), and with shellfish.
Chervil	Leaf, fresh	When fresh, the flavour is similar to parsley, but more delicate; dried chervil has little flavour. Used in seasonings of chopped, mixed herbs to flavour sauces and butters, and with soups, fish and white meats.
Chicory	Leaf, fresh; root, fresh or dried	Leaves are eaten raw in salads, or cooked as a vegetable. Roots are eaten raw, as a vegetable, or dried, ground and added to coffee.
Chilli (see Peppers)		
Chive	Leaf, fresh	Chopped chives can be used in any dish, especially salads, when a delicate onion flavour is needed; chives are also an important garnish.
Chocolate (see Cocoa)		
Cinnamon	Bark, dried, whole or ground	A flavouring for spice or fruit puddings, gingerbread, cakes, and apple dishes, also some savoury stews and curries; is delicious sprinkled on hot buttered toast. *Cassia* has a similar but less subtle flavour.
Citron	Peel, candied, dried, or as essence	The fruit is like a large lemon, but the peel has a peculiar aromatic taste unlike other citrus fruits. Used in candied peel mixtures, and for making flavouring essences. Candied citron peel is the traditional decoration for Madeira cake (p1199).
Clove	Bud, dried whole or ground	A strong, intrusive flavour, used sparingly in dishes containing apples and pears, and infused in milk for Bread Sauce (p713). Also inserted in onions to flavour stews and casseroles. Whole cloves are used to garnish ham, and as a pickling spice or in a marinade.
Cocoa	Seed, processed	Seeds of the cacao tree are dried, partially fermented, roasted and processed in various ways to make cocoa, chocolate, and drinking chocolate powder. Used in numerous sweet recipes, and to flavour certain savoury ones. Cocoa is also used for flavoured drinks, and in a liqueur, Crème de Cacao.

Name	Form in which generally used	Descriptions and accepted uses
Coffee	Bean, whole, roasted and ground, or as essence	Ground, or processed 'instant' coffee is used not only as a drink, but to flavour cakes, confectionery, puddings, and desserts. Commercial coffee essences are inferior in flavour to the strained liquid from a strong infusion of ground coffee, or instant coffee powder. To obtain a particularly delicate coffee flavour for a dish containing cream, infuse whole or cracked beans in the cream before cooking (see White Coffee Ice Cream, p1058).
Coriander	Leaf, fresh; seed, dried, whole or ground	Leaves are used in curries, chutney and some casseroles and salads. Seeds have a different flavour, and are used in curries, chutney, cheese and vegetable dishes, and some spiced fruit recipes. Also made into a flavoured vinegar.
Cumin	Seed, dried, whole or ground	Used widely in curries and Eastern and Mexican dishes.
Curry	Leaf, fresh or dried	Gives the characteristic smell to curry powder, though it imparts less flavour than the other ingredients.
Dill	Leaf, fresh; seed, dried	An essential flavouring in many Scandinavian and Northern European recipes, especially fish dishes. Can be used in salads, soups and sauces, and as a flavouring for pickles, particularly those containing cucumber.
Duxelles	Vegetable, fresh, cooked	Flavouring made with 200g whole mushrooms or mushroom stalks, 2 × 15ml spoons chopped spring onion, 25g butter, 1 × 10ml spoon cooking oil, salt and pepper, and 65ml beef stock or Madeira (optional). The mushrooms are wrung in a towel to remove as much juice as possible; they are then fried in the butter and oil with the spring onion until the mushroom pieces are separate and lightly browned. Seasoning is added. The mushrooms can then be boiled rapidly in the stock or Madeira until the liquid has evaporated. After being cooled, the duxelles should be stored in a screw-top jar and used to flavour stuffings, soups, and sauces.
Fennel	Leaf, stalk and seed, fresh or dried; bulb of Florence fennel, fresh	A subtle, aniseed-like flavour especially effective with fish. Fish can be flamed over dried fennel stalks (see Haddock and Fennel Flambé, p1450) or cooked with the chopped leaves or seeds. Also used with pork or veal, and in salads. The bulb can be eaten cooked as a vegetable or raw as a salad, and the leaves used as a garnish.
Fenugreek	Leaf, fresh; seed, dried	Ground fenugreek seed is an ingredient in curry powder, and can be used in other spiced Eastern dishes. The fresh leaf can be curried, or used when young as a salad.
Fines herbes	Leaves, fresh	Finely chopped, mixed fresh herbs, used extensively in French cookery, especially omelets. The usual herbs are chervil, chives, parsley, and tarragon.
Garlic	Root (bulb), composed of sections (cloves), fresh	Used for almost any type of savoury dish when a fairly strong flavour is needed; raw garlic is more pungent than cooked, and is used for salads, garlic mayonnaise, and butters.
Geranium (scented leaf varieties only)	Leaf, fresh	The leaves can be used to line the baking tin for sponge cakes, and to flavour custards, jellies, and preserves.

Name	Form in which generally used	Descriptions and accepted uses
Ginger	Root, fresh or dried, whole or ground	One of the most widely used flavourings for jams, chutneys, gingerbread and cakes, also in many Eastern savoury recipes. Fresh ginger root is generally bruised with a rolling-pin to release its flavour for use in jams and preserves. It can also be grated for salads and curries, and preserved in syrup ('stem' ginger), and candied as a sweetmeat or for use in cakes, etc. The root, when dried with the skin on, is called 'green' or 'black' ginger. Ground ginger is used in cakes, biscuits, puddings, fruit dishes, and for sprinkling on melon or grapefruit.
Horseradish	Root, fresh or dried, grated	Has a very strong flavour when fresh, and must be used sparingly. Use in horseradish sauces, savoury butters, and some stuffings.
Hyssop	Leaf, fresh or dried	A Biblical 'bitter herb'; used to flavour liqueurs, and sparingly in salads.
Juniper	Berry, fresh or dried, whole or crushed	Used often as a flavouring for game dishes, but also for pork, poultry stuffings, pâtés, and marinades. Principal flavouring agent for gin.
Ketchup	Extract of fish or vegetables	Name given to a salty, pungent and well-reduced extract for flavouring savoury dishes. Anchovy and oyster ketchup are the most common fish extracts, mushroom and walnut the best-known vegetable ketchups. 'Tomato ketchup' is in fact a sauce.
Lemon	Juice and rind	Lemon juice is a widely used souring and tenderizing agent, also used to prevent the discoloration of fruit and vegetables after peeling. It is particularly important for accentuating the flavour of fish, and some fruit and vegetables. Lemon rind, grated or in strips, is infused in both sweet and savoury dishes. See also p1070.
Lemon balm	Leaf, fresh or dried	Used with fish, mushrooms, salads, for drinks and with strawberries.
Lime (fruit)	Juice and rind	Used in the same way as lemon, when a sourer flavour is needed, especially in West Indian cookery; popular as marmalade and for flavouring drinks.
Lime (tree)	Flower, dried	Made into herbal teas, and used in sweet creams and desserts.
Liquorice	Root, extract of root juice	Extract of liquorice is used in flavouring stout and other drinks; the prepared root is eaten as a sweetmeat.
Lovage	Stem, leaf and seed, fresh or dried	A warm, aromatic flavour, reminiscent of both celery and angelica; the stems can be candied, like angelica. The leaves are used fresh in salads, and fresh or dried in soups and casseroles. The seeds are baked in biscuits for cheese.
Mace	Husk, dried, whole or ground	Dried outer husk of nutmeg. Whole 'blades' of mace are used as an infused flavouring; ground mace is used like nutmeg, especially in fish dishes and for pâtés and sausages.
Marigold	Flower	Can be used as a substitute for saffron in colouring butter and cheese, also as a flavouring in fish soups, salads, and cakes.
Marjoram	Leaf, fresh or dried	Very widely used for savoury dishes, particularly lamb, veal, sausages, some fish dishes, mushrooms, and tomatoes.

Name	Form in which generally used	Descriptions and accepted uses
Mint	Leaf, fresh	Flavour varies according to variety, but is always best used fresh. *Spearmint* is the type most commonly grown, but some prefer *apple mints*, which have larger, rounded leaves. Both are used for the traditional Mint Sauce (p403), in vegetable dishes and salads, and for flavouring drinks. *Cologne mint* has a slightly orange flavour and is used for drinks; *Pennyroyal* is used in black puddings and in peppermint essence, of which the principal ingredient is *peppermint*. Peppermint, in the form of oils, essences, certain cordials or liqueurs, is the type of mint flavouring most used in sweet dishes and confectionery.
Mustard	Seed (black, brown or white), dried, whole, ground, or as a prepared paste	Whole mustard seeds are used in chutneys and pickles, and the ground seeds for seasoning meat, fish, salad dressings, vegetable dishes, and particularly cheese dishes. English and French mustards, in which the mustard seeds are mixed with various herbs and spices, are widely used as condiments, especially with beef.
Myrtle	Leaf and berry, fresh	Used as a substitute for bay leaves, especially with lamb and pork, and in marinades.
Nasturtium	Leaf and berry, fresh	Home-grown leaves and buds can be used as an alternative to capers, and in salads, salad dressings, and to flavour vinegar.
Nutmeg	Seed, dried, whole or ground	Used in a variety of sweet and savoury dishes, as a flavouring for spinach, in fruit cakes, mincemeat and for drinks.
Onion	Bulb	Onion in all its varieties, including shallots and spring onions, are by far the most common vegetable flavouring, used raw or cooked.
Orange	Juice and rind	The juice and rind are used for flavouring in the same way as lemon. Orange is also used for orange flower water and in many liqueurs. See also p1072.
Oregano	Leaf, fresh or dried	The milder variety grown in the UK is used fresh in the same way as marjoram, as are the stronger Southern European varieties, generally used dried. Widely used for cheese dishes and pizzas, and in Greek and Mexican cooking.
Paprika (see Peppers)		
Parsley	Leaf and stalk, fresh	The leaves and stalks of fresh parsley are an essential ingredient of a bouquet garni, and are also used in sauces, salads and many other savoury dishes. Dried parsley has little flavour or aroma.
Peppers or capsicum 1) Chilli peppers	Fruit (green – unripe, yellow or red – ripe), fresh or dried, whole, ground (chilli powder and Cayenne pepper), or as a paste	A very pungent flavour, used for hot, spicy dishes, in pickles and chutneys, and in a variety of Eastern, Mexican and West Indian recipes. Fresh green chillis have an interesting capsicum flavour, but red chillis should be used sparingly, and are usually added in the form of Tabasco sauce. *Chilli powder* is usually sold with other spices added. *Cayenne pepper* is finer ground, and used more often as a seasoning in European cooking. The yellow *Nepal pepper* is less pungent.
2) Sweet or bell peppers	Fruit (green or red), fresh	These are used as a vegetable and in salads. *Paprika* or *Hungarian pepper* is a powder ground from a pointed variety of capsicum, and is fairly mild; much used in Spanish and Hungarian cooking. It should be bought in small quantities as it deteriorates very rapidly with keeping.

Name	Form in which generally used	Descriptions and accepted uses
3) Vine peppers	Berry (unripe – black pepper, ripe – white pepper), dried, whole or ground	The most important seasoning spice after salt, used with almost all savoury dishes, and in some rich fruit cakes and puddings. Whole peppercorns can be included in a bouquet garni, and in many marinades, chutneys, and pickles. Whole peppercorns should be freshly ground for use in cooking and at the table; the flavour of ground pepper deteriorates rapidly. *Mignonette pepper* is a mixture of black and white peppercorns ground together.
Pickling spice	Spices, dried	A mixture of spices such as black peppercorns, red chillis, allspice berries, mustard seed, cardamom, coriander, and mace. Used for pickling, brining, and in marinades.
Poppy	Seed, fresh	A nutty flavour when baked; often sprinkled on bread and cakes.
Purslane	Leaf, fresh	Can be cooked as a vegetable, or used in salads and pickled in vinegar.
Rocket	Leaf, fresh	Can be cooked as a vegetable or used in salads; much used in Italian and other Mediterranean cookery.
Rose	Petals, fresh or as essence (rose water); fruit (hips)	Fresh petals are used for candied sweetmeats and decorating sweet dishes, and rose water is used as an alternative to vanilla in old recipes for desserts, cakes and biscuits, and in Eastern cookery. Rose-hips are used for preserves, jellies, syrups, and drinks.
Rosemary	Leaf and sprig, fresh or dried	Used especially with lamb, either sprinkled over the meat or inserted in it, and with oily fish, pork, veal or game. Rosemary is also included in stuffings, apple jams and jellies, and with drinks.
Rue	Leaf, fresh	A strong, bitter flavour; large quantities can be poisonous. Rue is used in Southern European cookery, and to make the liqueur Grappa.
Safflower (Bastard saffron)	Seed and flower, fresh	The seeds are used to make cooking oil with a high polyunsaturated fat content; yellow food colouring is made from the flowers.
Saffron	Stamens of the saffron crocus, whole or powdered	The cost of saffron prevents its extensive use; it is essential for a classic Bouillabaisse, and can be used as an infusion to flavour breads, cakes and rice dishes, and in Middle Eastern meat dishes and Spanish paellas.
Sage	Leaf, fresh or dried, powdered	Sage and onion stuffing (p378) is traditional with pork, duck and goose, and sage can also flavour lamb, veal and sausages. Some cheeses, such as Sage Derby, are flavoured with sage.
Salad burnet	Leaf, fresh or dried	With a flavour similar to borage, salad burnet is used in salads, cream soups and omelets, and for flavouring drinks.
Salt	Granulated mineral	The most common of all seasonings, used in virtually all savoury and many sweet dishes. *Rock salt* is obtained from underground deposits, and *sea salt* is evaporated from sea water. Both these have large granules, and must be ground in a mill for use at the table, but their flavour is better than *table salt*, which is finely ground and has magnesium carbonate added to prevent caking. Sea salt and table salt are the salts most commonly used in cookery. *Kitchen salt* or *common salt* is mined by a process slightly different from rock salt, and has finer granules. *Flavoured salt*, with added spices or herb flavourings such as garlic, onion or celery, is used for some dishes.

Name	Form in which generally used	Descriptions and accepted uses
Savory	Leaf, fresh or dried	*Summer* and *winter savory* are two different plants with a similar flavour; summer savory has the stronger taste. In Mediterranean cooking it is traditionally used with beans and peas, and is also used with trout and liver, and in sausages and stuffings.
Sesame	Seed, fresh	The seeds are an important source of vegetable oil, and are used extensively in Greek and Middle Eastern cookery. In the UK they are used in breads, cakes, and biscuits.
Sorrel	Leaf, fresh	There are many varieties of sorrel. It can be cooked as a vegetable, or used in a salad, or used with fish, eggs and veal. The flavour is sour but pleasant, and makes excellent soups and sauces.
Soy	Bean, fresh or dried, whole or processed	Soy beans can be eaten fresh or dried, and are made into *soy sauce* by fermentation with salt, water and barley or wheat flour. There are many varieties of soy sauce. It has a strong, slightly meaty flavour, and is essential in Far Eastern cookery. It is also an ingredient of Worcestershire sauce and Harvey's sauce, and is used in marinades, barbecue sauces, and with meat and vegetable dishes.
Star anise	Fruit, dried	The flavour is similar to anise; star anise is used in some Chinese dishes, and for making drinks.
Sunflower	Seed, fresh or dried	These seeds are an important source of vegetable oil, and are also eaten alone, raw or toasted.
Sweet cicely (anise chervil)	Whole herb and root, fresh; leaf, fresh or dried	The whole herb can be boiled and used as a vegetable, or the cooked root dressed as a salad. Fresh or dried leaves are used to flavour soups, sauces, salad dressings, herb butters and stewed fruit.
Tamarind	Pod, partly dried	An infusion made from the pod is an essential souring agent for authentic Indian curries.
Tansy	Leaf, fresh	A strong, bitter flavour used in old recipes for cakes, puddings, custards and herb teas, but little used today.
Tarragon	Leaf, fresh	*French tarragon* is an essential ingredient in fines herbes mixtures, some bouquets garnis, and as a flavouring for vinegar. It is used in numerous dishes, particularly with chicken and fish, and in many classic French sauces. It does not dry well; *Russian tarragon*, often used as a substitute, has an inferior flavour.
Thyme	Leaf, fresh or dried	*Garden thyme* is used in a bouquet garni, and with almost every kind of savoury dish. It has a strong but delicate flavour. *Lemon thyme* is similar, but with a taste of lemon. It is used especially with eggs and in cream sauces, and with drinks.
Turmeric	Root, dried, ground	Turmeric has a powerful yellow colour, but not a very strong flavour. It can be used as an inferior substitute for saffron, to colour rice, curries and mustard pickles, and in some Indian sweet dishes, but should not be used where a saffron flavour is required.
Vanilla	Pod, dried, whole or as essence	Vanilla has a subtle and distinctive flavour, suitable for almost all sweet dishes, particularly those containing chocolate. Whole pods can be used to infuse the flavour, or *vanilla essence* can be added. Vanilla pods are also used to flavour sugar.

INGREDIENT SUBSTITUTES

Although haricots and lentils are not much used in this country, yet in France, and other Catholic countries, from their peculiar constituent properties, they form an excellent substitute for animal food during Lent and maigre days.

Every cook sometimes finds that, having decided on a particular recipe, certain ingredients are not available. This table lists some basic ingredients with acceptable substitutes.

It is important to remember, however, that a substitute can never give precisely the same result as the original ingredient. The recipe may work successfully, but the taste will not be exactly the same. It is, for example, possible to substitute cottage cheese for some of the eggs in a scrambled egg mixture, but the result will be different from that of a recipe using just eggs. Marshmallows, as another example, will make an agreeable but not an exact substitute for a meringue topping on a cake or pudding.

Finally, it is always possible to substitute a convenience food such as packet stuffing, packet or canned soup, or frozen pastry for the home-made equivalent. Some convenience substitutes are given here, but the subject is covered more fully in the chapter on Convenience Foods.

Table of Ingredient Substitutes

Ingredient	Substitute
Fish	
Canned salmon	Canned tuna fish, well drained
Canned tuna fish	Canned pink salmon, well drained
Caviar	Canned or bottled red or black lumpfish roe for garnishing, or for open sandwiches Tubes of Scandinavian 'caviar' paste for canapés
Cod	Fresh haddock
Dover sole	Fillets of dab or witch sole or lemon sole
Kipper	Kippered mackerel for all kippered herring recipes which require cooking Smoked mackerel for pâtés and spreads
Pilchard	Fresh or canned mackerel
Scampi	Monkfish cut in short strips for cooking in batter Huss, skinned and cut to resemble scampi
Smoked haddock fillet	Smoked fillet of cod

Table continues over.

Ingredient	Substitute
Meat	
Bacon	Trimmings of raw or boiled ham for cooked dishes Smoked ham sausage Gammon Pickled pork
Chicken	Boned legs of tame rabbit soaked in water with a few drops of lemon juice before cooking
Guinea-fowl	Chicken or pheasant
Liver pâté	Equal quantities of liver sausage and full-fat soft cheese mashed together and lightly flavoured with Worcestershire sauce
Minced meat	Textured vegetable protein (TVP) ready-flavoured with meat flavouring TVP bought unflavoured and yeast extract or stock then added Crumbled hamburgers Canned minced meat, well drained
Pheasant	Small chickens or guinea-fowl
Rabbit	Chicken
Turkey	Chicken for pies, casseroles, and dishes with sauce
Veal	Lean pork beaten flat for escalopes, or cubed for casseroles, pies, and goulash (**Note** Pork needs a longer cooking time than veal.)
Venison	Lean beef marinated in red wine for 24 hours for casserole dishes (**Note** Venison and beef roasting cuts are not the same and cannot be interchanged.)
Dairy products	
Blue cheeses	Most blue cheeses are interchangeable (**Note** If the substitute cheese is saltier than the original required in the recipe, use a small amount of mild flavoured semi-soft cheese mixed well with cottage cheese for a small part of the cheese ingredient.)
Cream cheese	Sieved cottage cheese, or sieved full-fat curd cheese with a little dried skimmed milk powder or thick cream added for richer consistency

Ingredient	Substitute
Gruyère cheese	A cheese of similar texture and flavour, eg Emmental or Jarlsberg
Mozzarella cheese	Thin slices of Gruyère or Bel Paese for pizza; add extra herbs and seasoning
Butter	Block margarine for cakes and pastry Soft tub margarine for spreading Oil or lard for frying
Cream, clotted	Frozen or bottled clotted cream Double cream that has been scalded and left to stand for 24 hours
Cream, double	Canned sterilized cream, or frozen whipping cream, or UHT whipping cream Powdered dessert topping reconstituted with milk 75g unsalted butter or margarine whipped with 150ml milk
Cream, single	Top of milk, preferably from Channel Islands variety, which can be blended with a little dried skimmed milk powder for a thicker consistency
Cream, soured	1×15ml spoon lemon juice mixed into 1×150ml carton single or double cream and left to stand for 30 minutes; or substitute unsweetened natural yoghurt for the lemon juice
Mayonnaise	High quality bottled mayonnaise (**Note** A few spoonfuls of whipped cream folded in will lighten texture and offset acidity.)
Milk	Reconstituted dried skimmed milk for baking, drinks, puddings, and sauces Canned evaporated milk diluted with water to the consistency of fresh milk
Yoghurt	Single cream or soured cream in recipes where the kilojoule content is not critical (**Note** The fat content will be higher.) Dried skimmed milk powder made up with just enough water to give a creamy consistency, with a few drops of lemon juice added

Ingredient	Substitute
Eggs	
Egg white	Milk brushed lightly for glazing pastry or biscuits
Egg yolk	Milk brushed thickly for glazing pastry or scones
Scrambled eggs	25g cottage cheese for 1 egg in 4
Fats and oils	
Corn oil	Sunflower seed, vegetable or nut oil for frying or baking Olive or walnut oil for salad dressing
Lard	White vegetable shortening, clarified dripping or block margarine for baking Corn, sunflower seed, vegetable or nut oil for frying
Olive oil	Corn, sunflower seed, vegetable or nut oil for frying, with 1 part butter added to 2 parts oil Any of the above oils or walnut oil for salad dressing
Vegetables	
Celeriac	The nutty core of a celery heart raw, in salad, or cooked in a casserole
Celery	Finely chopped fresh or dried lovage leaves
Courgettes	Cucumbers cut in lengths and quartered Small, young marrows
Leek	Finely sliced spring onions in soups and pies
Lovage	Finely chopped fresh or dried celery leaves
Potatoes, mashed	Instant dried potato reconstituted according to directions
Pumpkin	Steamed vegetable marrow in pies and soups, with a pinch of sugar and yellow vegetable colouring, turmeric, or ground saffron added
Shallot	A small quantity of mild onion
Split peas	Yellow or green lentils
Sweet red or bell pepper	Canned pimentos, except for salads

Ingredient	Substitute
Tomato purée	Tomato ketchup, but adjust seasoning in recipe to counteract acidity, if required Skinned and de-seeded fresh or canned tomatoes that have been simmered until the flesh and juice are soft and thick
Pasta	
Macaroni	Broken spaghetti or pasta shapes
Vermicelli	Small pieces of broken spaghetti or pasta shapes in soups
Moulded desserts	
Blancmange powder	Equal quantity of cornflour, plus flavouring, eg vanilla essence, and food colouring
Custard powder	Cornflour with vanilla flavouring and yellow food colouring (optional)
Jelly	Fruit juice or strained fruit squash and gelatine (**Note** 2 × 10ml spoons powdered gelatine will set 500ml liquid.)
Garnishes, decorations, and glazes	
Angelica	Quartered or sliced green glacé cherries Sliced candied peel tinted with green vegetable coating
Apricot jam	Sieved yellow plum jam, sieved sweet jelly, marmalade or redcurrant jelly for glazing fruit in tarts, or for brushing cakes to be covered with almond icing
Aspic jelly	Equivalent quantity made up with water and gelatine (**Note** 2 × 10ml spoons powdered gelatine will set 500ml liquid. For this quantity, flavour with 1 × 10ml spoon beef extract and 1 × 15ml spoon dry sherry.)
Candied peel	Residue of strained chunky marmalade with the peel cut into small pieces Fresh orange peel cut in strips, boiled in sugar and drained

Table continues over.

INGREDIENT SUBSTITUTES

Ingredient	Substitute
Meringue topping	Chopped marshmallows spread on the pudding or cake, placed under a moderate grill until half-melted and golden
Ratafias	Macaroons broken into 2cm pieces for trifles and other sweet dishes

Raising agents

Ingredient	Substitute
Baking powder	1 part bicarbonate of soda sifted together with 2 parts cream of tartar and 1 part filler, eg rice flour, and made up to the quantity required by the recipe
Cream of tartar	Soured milk or buttermilk in place of milk in a recipe for cake making Baking powder in the same quantity as the combined weight of cream of tartar and bicarbonate of soda in a recipe
Yeast, fresh	Half the quantity of dried yeast, reconstituted according to directions

Sweetening agents

Ingredient	Substitute
Caster sugar	Ground, granulated sugar
Corn syrup (American)	Sugar syrup
Golden syrup	Clear honey with a small pinch of ground cinnamon or mixed spice
Icing sugar	Powdered granulated or caster sugar for butter or water icings, but not for fine royal icing

Thickening agents

Ingredient	Substitute
Arrowroot	Equivalent quantity of cornflour, rice or potato flour (Note These agents will thicken but not clear in the same way as arrowroot, and sauces made with cornflour or potato flour may be re-heated, unlike those made with arrowroot.)
Cornflour (or Cornstarch, American)	Arrowroot for clear sauces and puddings Plain flour for soups and gravies

Flours, grains, and nuts

Ingredient	Substitute
Bran	Crushed or crumbled proprietary bran breakfast food for sweet dishes Bran sifted from wholemeal flour
Ground almonds	Semolina and a drop or two of almond essence for up to one-third of the required quantity of almonds
Ground rice	Semolina in milk puddings, cakes or biscuits
Pecan nuts	Walnuts A few blanched, chopped almonds added to chopped walnuts
Potato flour	Arrowroot or cornflour
Rice flour	Cornflour, potato flour or ground rice
Self-raising flour	Plain flour with 3×5ml spoons of baking powder, or 1×5ml spoon bicarbonate of soda and 2×5ml spoons cream of tartar, added to 200g plain flour (Note The flour and raising agents must be sifted together 3 times before using.)
Semolina	Equivalent quantity of ground rice for milk puddings, cakes or biscuits

Coatings and stuffings

Ingredient	Substitute
Breadcrumbs	Crushed cornflakes, potato crisps, water biscuits, crispbread or crackers for coating food Oatcake crumbs for wholemeal breadcrumbs
Forcemeat	Commercial stuffing mix reconstituted as directed (Note Add extra flavouring such as grated lemon rind, minced parsley or nuts.)
Raspings	Finely crushed water biscuits, cream crackers, cornflakes, potato crisps or medium oatmeal

Ingredient	Substitute

Vinegars and other acids

Ingredient	Substitute
Cider vinegar	Dry still cider with a few drops of lemon juice added
Citric acid	Lemon juice, tartaric acid or fruit juice from cooking apples, redcurrants or gooseberries for jam and marmalade making (**Note** 1 × 2.5ml spoon citric acid is equivalent to 2 × 15ml spoons lemon juice, 1 × 2.5ml spoon tartaric acid, and 150ml acid fruit juice.)
Fresh lemon juice	Commercially processed and packaged lemon juice Citric acid or tartaric acid for jam or marmalade making Cider vinegar or white wine vinegar in salad dressings
Herb vinegar	White or wine vinegar with the appropriate fresh or dried herb added to taste and steeped before use
Vinegar	Unsweetened lemon juice, or dry red or white wine

Herbs, flavourings, and essences

Ingredient	Substitute
Bouquet garni	1 × 15ml spoon dried mixed herbs and 2 whole cloves in a piece of clean, thin cloth
Brandy	Dry sherry or cold milkless tea in fruit cakes
Chocolate	25g cocoa powder mixed to a paste with 1 × 15ml spoon butter or lard for 25g plain chocolate in baking
Coffee essence	1 × 15ml spoon instant coffee blended with 1 × 15ml spoon boiling water, sweetened if liked

Ingredient	Substitute
Garlic	Garlic powder or salt (**Note** If using garlic salt, omit salt from recipe.)
Gravy browning	Roux well browned before adding liquid when making thickened gravy Washed brown onion skin added to stews when cooking (**Note** Remove before serving.) Beef bones browned in a roasting tin in a hot oven with enough liquid added to make gravy for roast meat A small quantity of meat or yeast extract to colour gravy
Lime juice	Lemon juice Lime juice cordial in sweet dishes
Orange or lemon essences	Grated fresh orange or lemon rind A few drops of concentrated orange or lemon squash, or sweetened lime juice
Oregano	Marjoram or thyme
Saffron	A pinch of turmeric powder or a few drops of yellow vegetable colouring (**Note** There is no substitute for the scent and taste of saffron.)
White wine	For cooking purposes use equivalent quantity of dry cider, or one-half quantity dry white vermouth with one-half quantity water

WEIGHTS, MEASURES, TEMPERATURES AND EQUIVALENTS

In these pages all those indecisive terms expressed by a bit of this, some of that, a small piece of that, and a handful of the other, shall never be made use of, but all quantities be precisely and explicitly stated. With a desire, also, that all ignorance on this most essential part of the culinary art should disappear, and that a uniform system of weights and measures should be adopted, we give an account of the weights which answer to certain measures.

Metric quantities are easy to weigh and measure; all you need are weighing scales giving metric quantities, a metric measuring jug, and a set of metric measuring spoons for small quantities.

Metric Units used in Cookery

Weight	gram	(g)
	kilogram = 1000g	(kg)
Capacity	millilitre	(ml)
	centilitre	(cl)
	decilitre	(dl)
	litre = 1000ml	(litre)
	100cl	
	10dl	
Length	millimetre	(mm)
	centimetre	(cm)
	metre = 1000mm	(m)
	100cm	
Temperature	degree Celsius (Centigrade)	(°C)

Measuring by Weight

Spring balance and loose weight metric scales are available in various sizes and designs. Those calibrated in 10g divisions for small amounts and 25g or 50g for larger amounts are the most useful.

Measuring by Capacity

Using a metric jug
Measuring jugs are available in 500ml, 1 litre and 2 litre sizes calibrated in divisions of 50ml, 100ml and 200ml, and sometimes, in decimals or fractions of a litre.

Using metric measuring spoons
These spoons are used for measuring small quantities of both dry and liquid ingredients, and are available in sets containing the following sizes:

*1.25ml
2.5ml
5ml
10ml
15ml
*20ml

* These two spoons are not as widely available as the others and are not used in the recipes in this book.

Metric spoons are described by capacity rather than as teaspoons, dessertspoons or tablespoons to avoid confusion with domestic spoons which vary considerably.

Guide to spoon measures

This table gives 10g, 15g, 25g and 40g quantities of many common ingredients which you may find easy to measure using standard spoons. Results are, however, only approximate as measuring is not as accurate as weighing. The quantities for dry ingredients refer to full spoons levelled with a knife edge.

Ingredient	Spoons equivalent to			
	10g approx	15g approx	25g approx	40g approx
almonds, ground	2 × 10ml	3 × 10ml	5 × 10ml	5 × 15ml
butter, margarine, lard	1 × 15ml	2 × 10ml	2 × 15ml	3 × 15ml
chocolate, grated	3 × 15ml	4 × 15ml	6 × 15ml	9 × 15ml
cocoa	2 × 10ml	2 × 15ml	4 × 15ml	6 × 15ml
cornflour, custard powder	2 × 10ml	3 × 10ml	3 × 15ml	7 × 10ml
desiccated coconut	2 × 15ml	3 × 15ml	5 × 15ml	8 × 15ml
drinking chocolate	3 × 5ml	4 × 5ml	4 × 10ml	7 × 10ml
flour, unsifted	2 × 10ml	3 × 10ml	3 × 15ml	5 × 15ml
gelatine	2 × 10ml	5 × 5ml	3 × 15ml	6 × 10ml
golden syrup, clear honey, black treacle, molasses, corn syrup, maple syrup, etc	1 × 10ml	1 × 15ml	1 × 15ml	2 × 15ml
ground rice	1 × 15ml	2 × 10ml	4 × 10ml	4 × 15ml
jam (eg raspberry)*	1 × 10ml	1 × 15ml	2 × 10ml	2 × 15ml
mixed peel	1 × 15ml	2 × 10ml	2 × 15ml	4 × 15ml
oats, rolled	2 × 15ml	3 × 15ml	5 × 15ml	7 × 15ml
rice	1 × 15ml	2 × 10ml	2 × 15ml	5 × 10ml
salt	1 × 10ml	3 × 5ml	2 × 10ml	7 × 5ml
sugar – granulated, caster	5 × 2.5ml	2 × 10ml	2 × 15ml	3 × 15ml
sugar – Demerara	5 × 2.5ml	2 × 10ml	2 × 15ml	3 × 15ml
sugar – soft brown	1 × 15ml	2 × 10ml	2 × 15ml	5 × 10ml
sugar – icing	1 × 15ml	3 × 10ml	3 × 15ml	7 × 10ml
Crumbs				
breadcrumbs, fresh white	3 × 15ml	7 × 10ml	7 × 15ml	12 × 15ml
bread raspings, dried white breadcrumbs	2 × 10ml	3 × 10ml	3 × 15ml	7 × 10ml
plain sponge cake crumbs	2 × 15ml	3 × 15ml	5 × 15ml	8 × 15ml
crispbread, oatcake, digestive biscuits, cornflake crumbs	2 × 15ml	3 × 15ml	4 × 15ml	7 × 15ml
dried yeast	5 × 2.5ml	2 × 10ml	2 × 15ml	3 × 15ml
Cheese				
Cheddar, coarsely grated	2 × 10ml	2 × 15ml	3 × 15ml	5 × 15ml
finely grated	1 × 10ml	1 × 15ml	4 × 15ml	5 × 15ml
Parmesan, grated	3 × 10ml	4 × 10ml	4 × 15ml	6 × 15ml
soft paste or soft (without rind)	1 × 10ml	1 × 15ml	5 × 5ml	4 × 10ml

* varies according to how much whole fruit jam contains

Cookware

The size of cookware varies from manufacturer to manufacturer, so sizes given in recipes should be treated as approximations only. The following range of measurements will help you select the appropriate-sized piece of cookware:

Dimension

Metric	imperial equivalent
2cm	$\frac{3}{4}$ inch
5cm	2 inches
7cm	$2\frac{3}{4}$ inches
10cm	4 inches
15cm	6 inches
20cm	8 inches
25cm	10 inches
30cm	12 inches
35cm	14 inches
40cm	16 inches
45cm	18 inches
50cm	20 inches

Capacity

Metric	imperial equivalent
125–150ml	$\frac{1}{4}$ pint
250–300ml	$\frac{1}{2}$ pint
375–450ml	$\frac{3}{4}$ pint
500 (0.5 litre)–600ml	1 pint
625–700ml	$1\frac{1}{4}$ pints
750–900ml	$1\frac{1}{2}$ pints
1 litre–1.25 litres	$1\frac{3}{4}$–2 pints
1.4–1.75 litres	3 pints
1.8–2 litres	4 pints
3 litres	6 pints

Dimension is used most frequently to describe the length of straight edge tins or the diameter of round cookware. Height and depth are used where they are particularly important.

Capacity measurements apply largely to pans, ovenproof dishes, bowls, moulds, and basins, and soufflé or pie dishes. The exact equivalent depends on the other ingredients in the recipe.

Note Some cookware, such as loaf tins, can also be described by the average weight of the contents, the most common weights being 1kg (2lb) and 500g (1lb).

Temperatures

Deep fat frying temperatures

These are basic guidelines only, since the temperature depends so much on the thickness of the food to be cooked, whether more is added during frying, whether it is frozen, etc. Deep frying is described in detail in the chapter on Batters and Fried Foods.

Using a thermometer

Temperatures are given for the principal types of food to be deep fried, and should be used as a guide for all similar recipes.

VEGETABLES, PASTA AND CEREALS	°C	Approx. frying time (minutes)
Potatoes		
chips		
cook from raw	185	4–6
final browning	190	1–2
small cut		
cook from raw	185	3
final browning	190	1
potato puffs		
cook from raw	175	soft
second cooking	190	well puffed
game chips, potato ribbons	190	3
croquettes	190	4–5
with choux pastry	190	golden-brown
Other vegetables (raw)		
sliced and coated	175–180	2–3
sliced uncoated	175–180	1–2
Other vegetables (parboiled) in batter	175–180	3–4
Onion rings		
dipped in milk and flour	180–185	2–3
Parsley	190	5–10 secs
Crisp noodles	175–180	2–3
Rice croquettes	180–185	2–3
Bean croquettes, Lentil rissoles, Vegetarian Forcemeat Balls	170–175	3–4

FISH AND SHELLFISH

	°C	Approx. frying time (minutes)
Fish fillets, thin		
in batter or		
breadcrumbed	175–180	3–5
goujons (eg plaice)	175	2–3
Fish portions, thick		
in batter or		
breadcrumbed	170–175	3–5
Fish, whole		
sole 250–350g	170–175	5–6
smelts, sprats	180–185	1–2
whitebait	190–195	$\frac{1}{2}$–1
whiting 250–300g	170–175	6–8
Fish cakes, croquettes,		
rissolettes	175–180	2–3
Shellfish		
(eg scampi, oysters)	175–180	2–3

MEAT AND POULTRY

	°C	
Cooked meat and poultry		
croquettes, etc	175–180	2–4
cutlets	175–180	2–5
fritters, other batters	175–180	2–4
kromeskies, rissoles,		
pancakes, etc	180–185	3–4
Uncooked meat and poultry		
Sweet and sour pork	175–180	4–6
Poultry/Game portions		
breadcrumbed large	160–165	8–12
small	175–180	6–10
cooked in batter	175–180	4–7

Note Sausages, hamburgers and similar raw meat items are better shallow fried as they exude animal fat which contaminates the frying medium.

DAIRY FOODS AND EGGS

	°C	Approx. frying time (minutes)
Scotch Eggs	170–175	5–6
egg croquettes	175–180	2–3
choux fritters, meringues	170–175	6–7

SWEET ITEMS

	°C	
Fruit fritters		
in batter		
apple	175–180	3–4
other fruits	180–185	2–3
Bread and butter fritters }		
Custard fritters	180–185	2–3
Doughnuts	185–190	3–4

Bread Test

The other method of testing the temperature of deep fat or oil is by lowering a 2cm square of day-old thickly sliced bread into the hot fat as follows:

To reach temperature of	Time in which bread turns brown
160°C	2 minutes
170°C	1$\frac{1}{2}$ minutes
180°C	1 minute
190°C	$\frac{1}{2}$ minute

Sugar boiling temperatures

	°C
thread	102 to 103
pearl	104 to 105 (seldom used)
blow	110 to 112 (seldom used)
soft ball	115
hard ball	120
small crack	140
large crack	155
caramel	177

Ambient and cooking temperatures

	°C
home freezer	−18 to −20
frozen food storage compartment of refrigerator	−6 to −18
freezing (water)	0
refrigerator interior	4 to 7
a cold place	10
average room temperature (with central heating)	21
a warm place	27
tepid/lukewarm	30 to 35
blood–heat	37
simmering (water)	88 to 90
boiling (water)	100

Oven temperatures

°C	°F	Gas mark	Oven heat
70	150		
80	175		
100	200		
110	225	$\frac{1}{4}$	very cool
120	250	$\frac{1}{2}$	very cool
140	275	1	very cool
150	300	2	cool
160	325	3	warm
180	350	4	moderate
190	375	5	fairly hot
200	400	6	fairly hot
220	425	7	hot
230	450	8	very hot
240	475	9	very hot
260	500		
270	525		
290	550		

Quantity Guide to Processed and Unprocessed Ingredients

Where recipes include processed ingredients, it is useful to know the quantities of basic foodstuffs needed to produce them. The table below gives an approximate guide to some common foods.

Ingredient	Process	Quantity obtained
Broad beans		
500g in pods	shelled	175g beans
Peas		
500g in pods	shelled	175g peas
Chestnuts		
500g in shells	shelled	300g chestnuts
Dried milk		
50g or 8 × 15ml spoons	reconstituted	500ml milk
Butter/hard-block margarine/lard		
25g	melted	2 × 15ml spoons butter/margarine/lard
Cream		
125ml double	whipped	225–250ml whipped cream
125ml whipping	whipped	250–275ml whipped cream
Eggs		
1 grade 3 or 4 (standard)	separated	2 × 15ml spoons egg white
1 grade 1 or 2 (large)	separated	4 × 10ml spoons egg white

Metric/Imperial Equivalents

25g = 0.875oz	500g = 1.1lbs	1kg = 2.2lbs
25ml = 0.875fl oz	500ml = 0.88 pint	1 litre = 1.76 pints

The figures above link metric and imperial quantities exactly. As these are very inconvenient to use, the following approximate conversions should be used to convert British imperial recipes to metric, if the following points are borne in mind:

1) The fundamental proportions in metric recipes are the same as imperial ones, so that a rich pastry will use half fat to flour in both metric and imperial versions.

2) *Always* convert all ingredients, solid and liquid.

3) *Never* use both metric and imperial in the same recipe.

4) Using the 25g/ounce equivalent you will decrease all quantities by approximately 10% when converting imperial quantities to metric. When using small quantities, the reduction will be insignificant, so existing cookware can still be used and the baking time will be the same. For large recipe quantities, smaller tins and shorter baking times will be needed.

Note If you wish to convert metric measures to imperial ones, remember that metric measures based on the 25g/ounce give 10% more of any goods weighed in oz/lb than the equivalent gram/kg.

Weight

Metric	Approx. imperial equivalent
10–15g	$\frac{1}{2}$oz
25g	1oz
50g	2oz
75g	3oz
100–125g	4oz
150–175g	6oz
200–250g	8oz
300–375g	12oz
400–500g	1lb
600–750g	$1\frac{1}{2}$lb
800–1000g (1kg)	2lb
1.5kg	3lb

Capacity

25ml	1 fl oz
50ml	2 fl oz
125–150ml	$\frac{1}{4}$ pint (5 fl oz/1 gill)
250–300ml	$\frac{1}{2}$ pint
375–450ml	$\frac{3}{4}$ pint
500–600ml	1 pint (20 fl oz)
750–900ml	$1\frac{1}{2}$ pints
1–1.25 litres	$1\frac{3}{4}$–2 pints
1.4–1.75 litres	3 pints

Where alternative metric figures are shown, the weight or capacity used depends on the type of recipe, and the proportion of other ingredients. For large-scale recipes such as those for breads or jams, the larger figure is more suitable. For $\frac{1}{2}$oz, 10g or 15g may be selected according to the importance of the ingredient in the recipe.

Using Recipes from other Countries

When recipes are given in cup and spoon measurements, it is important to know the country of origin as the capacities vary from country to country. The following countries use metric measures:

	standard cup	table- spoon	tea- spoon
Canada	250ml	15ml	5ml
Australia	200ml	20ml	5ml
New Zealand	250ml	15ml	5ml
UK	250ml	15ml	5ml

At the time of publication (1980) the USA was not yet using metric quantities. The differences between US and imperial British cup and spoon measures can be clarified as follows:

	UK	USA
pint	20 fl oz	16 fl oz
cup	10 fl oz	8 fl oz
tablespoon	17.7ml	14.8ml
teaspoon	5.9ml	4.9ml

American cookery terms and their British equivalents

US term	British term/ nearest equivalent

Basic ingredients

baking soda	bicarbonate of soda
biscuit	scone
bouillon cube	stock cube
cake batter	cake mixture
cornstarch	cornflour
cream, heavy	double cream
cream, light	single cream
extract/flavouring	essence
flour, all purpose	plain flour
bread flour	strong flour
cake flour	no exact equivalent; replace a small amount of the stated quantity with cornflour to give the required finer, shorter texture.
graham/wholewheat	wholemeal or wholewheat
meat, ground beef	minced beef
tenderloin steak	fillet steak
corned beef	salt beef
shortening	cooking (baking) fats
sugar, superfine/granulated	caster sugar
light brown	soft brown sugar
confectioner's/powdered	icing sugar
white/golden raisin	sultana

Vegetables

eggplant	aubergine
rutabaga	swede
scallion/green onion	spring onion
zucchini	courgette

Utensils

bowl	basin
broiler	grill
layer cake pan	sandwich tin
pastry bag	piping bag
pie shell	pastry case
skillet	frying pan
wax paper	greaseproof

The Americans also use the term 'stick' or 'cube' of butter, meaning (4oz) 100g butter, and a 'square' of chocolate, meaning (1oz) 25g chocolate.

Using the Recipes in this Book

Ingredients
1) are listed in order of use
2) are listed as purchased for most items
3) are listed as prepared if:
   a) a small quantity, eg chopped parsley
   b) available commercially prepared, eg grated Parmesan cheese, chicken stock. Where these comprise a recipe in their own right, refer to the Index.
   c) can be easily prepared in advance, eg hard-boiled eggs.
4) White flour has been used in testing the recipes, unless otherwise indicated. In recipes requiring simply 'flour', either plain or self-raising can be used.
5) Egg sizes are specified only if important to the final result.

Cross-references
A complex process or made-up ingredient, eg sauces, pastry, weighting a pâté, which forms part of a recipe is cross-referred to the page which describes it in full. Where ingredients are available commercially prepared, it is possible to substitute these for the relevant ingredient.

Quantities
1) are always specified for ingredients unless:
   a) a question of taste
   b) a particular ingredient is dependent upon processes or other ingredients in the recipe
   c) the ingredient itself comprises a separate recipe, in which case the full quantity is generally required.
2) Metric sizes of canned and other packaged foods are those used by manufacturers at the date of publication (1980). In the event of commercial variations, select the nearest equivalent.
3) Helpings, yields, etc can be adapted by proportionately changing the quantities of the main ingredients, and by adjusting the cooking time where necessary. (See the chapter on Party Foods for information on cooking in quantity.)

Oven Temperatures
Instructions for preheating are given in those recipes which need to rise very rapidly, or which need a very short cooking time, eg soufflés and certain baked goods. This is indicated by the phrase 'heat the oven' at the appropriate stage within the recipe. If you prefer, you may turn the oven on 15–20 minutes before the food is put in.

Before you start
First, read through the recipe carefully, checking a) that you have all the necessary ingredients and equipment; b) that you understand all the processes involved (if in doubt, see if they are described in more detail earlier in the same chapter, or refer to the Glossary of Cookery Terms and Techniques or the Index); and c) that you have allowed yourself enough time to prepare the whole recipe, including any ready-prepared ingredients.

Keeping food hot
Cooked or partly cooked food waiting to be added to a dish can either be left at room temperature or put in a container in a bain-marie.

Leave casseroles and oven-baked dishes in the oven with the heat turned right down, or off if there is sufficient residual heat.

Leave cooked garnishes in a container in a bain-marie.

Open-baked dishes should be lightly covered with greaseproof paper or foil which can be greased, if necessary. Cover pastry goods and stacked pancakes (separated with rounds of greaseproof paper) in the same way.

Place pasta, rice and plainly cooked vegetables in a steamer or in a strainer over very hot water.

Sauces, and dishes in sauces, are best kept hot in a bain-marie. The food container should be sufficiently deep and/or lightly covered to prevent water splashing or dripping into it.

Fried food should be served at once, but if it must be kept hot it should be put on soft kitchen paper on a baking tray, uncovered, in a cool oven.

Electrically heated trolleys and hotplates can be used for keeping food and plates hot at the table (see p209).

FIRST-COURSE DISHES

It is generally established as a rule, not to ask for soup or fish twice, as, in so doing, part of the company may be kept waiting too long for the second course, when, perhaps, a little revenge is taken by looking at the awkward consumer of a second portion.

Strictly, the term 'hors d'oeuvre' should be kept for assorted very small vegetable, fish, and meat snacks offered before the soup at dinner. In the last century, a selection of these hors d'oeuvres or a choice of soups was the standard way to begin a formal dinner.

Today, however, dinners are much shorter – only one main course instead of three or four – so a first course can be chosen from a much wider range of dishes, both light and more substantial. Pâtés, quiches, soufflés, mousses, and various fruit and vegetable dishes are all used to begin a meal, and are sometimes (although not correctly) called hors d'oeuvre for lack of a better term.

In this chapter there are various light, small, hot and cold dishes, any of which can be used as a first course to stimulate the appetite at the beginning of a meal. They are grouped together here because some are seldom used for any other purpose, although others can also be served as a summer lunch main course or as side salads. Many dishes in other chapters make equally suitable first-course dishes, however, including those in the chapter on Soups.

Offer a classic mixed hors d'oeuvre (p315) as a first course when a fairly substantial main course will follow. If the main course will be light, choose a soup, an egg dish, a substantial salad, pâté or savoury pastry dish as a first course. Try to achieve a balance of hot and cold dishes in choosing courses.

Fruit Dishes

Grapefruit

4 helpings

2 large firm grape-
    fruit
white **or** brown sugar

4 × 10ml spoons
    medium-dry sherry
    (optional)

Decoration

2 maraschino **or** glacé
    cherries

angelica (optional)

Choose sound, ripe fruit and wipe them. Cut them in half crossways, and remove the pips. Snip out the cores with scissors. With a stainless steel knife (preferably with a saw edge) or a grapefruit knife, cut round each half between the flesh and the pith, to loosen the flesh. Cut between the membranes which divide the segments, but leave the flesh in the halved skins as if uncut. Sweeten to taste with sugar, or, if preferred, pour 1 × 10ml spoon sherry over each half grapefruit, and serve sugar separately. Decorate the centre of each half fruit with a halved cherry and with angelica, if liked. Chill before serving. Serve 1 half fruit per person.

Hot Yoghurt and Grapefruit
See p876.

Grapefruit Baskets

4 helpings

2 large firm grapefruit
1 × 5cm segment ripe
  Charentais **or** Ogen
  melon
1 × 227g can pineapple
  cubes

1 orange
4 maraschino cherries
white **or** brown sugar
  or 4 × 10ml spoons
  medium-dry sherry

Decoration
mint sprigs

Cut the grapefruit in half crossways and prepare as in the recipe for Grapefruit. Remove the flesh from the halved skins, and snip out the membranes in the skins. Keep the halved skins aside, and put the flesh in a basin. Cut the melon flesh into 2cm cubes, drain the pineapple, and prepare the orange like the grapefruit. Halve the cherries. Mix all the fruit with the grapefruit flesh in the basin. Sweeten slightly if desired, or add the sherry. Pile the fruit (with any juice or sherry) back into the grapefruit skins. Chill before serving. Serve decorated with mint sprigs.

Grapefruit Cocktail

6 helpings

3 grapefruit
50g sugar
3 × 15ml spoons boiling
  water

2 × 15ml spoons
  medium-dry sherry

Decoration
6 maraschino cherries

6 mint sprigs

Cut the grapefruit in half crossways and prepare as in the recipe for Grapefruit. Put the flesh in a basin. Dissolve the sugar in the water, add the sherry and pour the mixture over the fruit. Cover and chill until ready to serve. Spoon into suitable glasses, and decorate with the cherries and sprigs of mint before serving.

Spiced Grapefruit

4 helpings

2 large grapefruit
25g softened butter
25–50g brown sugar

½–1 × 5ml spoon ground
  mixed spice

Decoration
4 glacé **or** maraschino
  cherries

Cut the grapefruit in half crossways and prepare as in the recipe for Grapefruit. Spread the butter over the grapefruit and sprinkle with the sugar and spice. Put under a hot grill for 4 minutes, or in a fairly hot oven at 200°C, Gas 6, for 10 minutes. Decorate with the cherries and serve at once.

Melon

Melon makes a refreshing starter throughout the year. The varieties most often used are the Cantaloup, honeydew, Ogen, Charentais, and watermelon. Melon should always be served lightly chilled, but it should not be too cold or it loses its delicate flavour.

To serve a large Cantaloup or honeydew melon, cut it in half lengthways, then cut into segments and remove the seeds with a spoon. Serve 1 segment per person; a large melon should supply 8 segments.

Serve the melon with the flesh attached to the skin, or cut the flesh from the skin with a sharp knife but leave the skin underneath the melon segment. The melon flesh can then also be cut into small pieces which are easier to eat.

Smaller melons, such as Ogen and Charentais, should just be cut in half crossways, and the pips scooped out with a spoon. They serve 2 people as a rule, although they can be cut into quarters, to serve four.

Watermelon should be cut into suitably sized segments. Small spoons should be provided for removing the seeds, as well as knives and forks for cutting up the melon.

Ripe melons may not require any sugar, but sugar can be served separately, with chopped stem ginger or ground ginger, or with lemon or lime.

Melon with Parma Ham

This is a more elaborate dish using paper-thin slices of Parma or other smoked ham. For each person, serve 3 loosely rolled slices of ham arranged in a line alternately with 7 × 2cm sticks of firm, ripe, green-fleshed melon.

Marinated Melon

4 helpings

2 Ogen **or** Charentais melons	4 × 15ml spoons maraschino liqueur **or** port

Cut the melons in half crossways and scoop out the seeds. Spoon 1 × 15ml spoon of maraschino liqueur or port into the centre and chill for 1 hour before serving. Sugar can be served with the melons as well, if desired.

Avocado Pears Vinaigrette

4 helpings

2 large, firm, ripe avocado pears	vinaigrette sauce
2 × 15ml spoons lemon juice	

Make sure the pears are firm but ripe, and are not discoloured. If they show any signs of over-ripeness such as being soft or blackened, use them for a cooked dish.

Halve the pears lengthways and remove the stones. Brush the halved pears with lemon juice immediately to prevent discoloration. Serve 1 half pear per person, cut side uppermost on a small plate, with a special avocado spoon, stainless steel or silver teaspoon or a grapefruit spoon. Serve the vinaigrette sauce separately.

Avocado Pears with Prawns or Avocado Royale

4 helpings

2 × 15ml spoons olive oil	a pinch of sugar (optional)
2 × 15ml spoons distilled vinegar	½ clove of garlic (optional)
a pinch each of salt and pepper	100g peeled prawns, fresh, frozen **or** canned
a little mixed French mustard (not Dijon)	crisp lettuce leaves
2 large avocado pears	

Garnish
lemon wedges

Blend the oil, vinegar, and seasonings together. Halve and stone the pears, and brush all over with a little of the dressing. Add the sugar and crush and add the garlic to the remaining dressing, if used. Toss the prawns in this; then spoon into the pear halves. Place on crisp lettuce leaves. Garnish with lemon wedges.

Note Frozen prawns should be squeezed gently before using to get rid of any excess moisture.

Avocado and Cheese Slices

4 helpings

2 large slices brown bread	50g Emmental cheese
butter for spreading	2 × 5ml spoons browned breadcrumbs (p375)
French mustard	melted butter
lemon juice	
2 large, firm, ripe avocado pears	

Cut the bread slices in half. Toast both sides lightly under the grill. Spread one side of each slice with butter and a little French mustard. Sprinkle lightly with lemon juice.

Cut the avocado pears in half, remove the stones, and peel off the skins. Cut the flesh into even slices, and sprinkle at once with lemon juice. Grate the cheese finely. Lay the slices of avocado in a neat pattern on the toast and coat with cheese. Sprinkle lightly with browned breadcrumbs and with melted butter. Grill under moderate heat until the cheese bubbles and browns slightly. Serve at once, very hot.

Avocado Pears and Soured Cream

4 helpings

2 avocado pears	1 × 2.5ml spoon dry
1 × 5ml spoon lemon	mustard
juice	a pinch of paprika
1 × 5ml spoon salt	150ml soured cream **or**
2 × 5ml spoons caster	smetana
sugar	

Halve the pears lengthways and remove the stones. Scoop all the flesh out of the skins, and mash it with the lemon juice and 1 × 2.5ml spoon salt. Replace the flesh in the shells. To make the dressing, mix all the remaining ingredients together until smooth. Top the pears with the dressing.

Hot Stuffed Avocado Pears

4 helpings

2 large avocado pears	dried white **or** buttered
100g cooked smoked	breadcrumbs for
haddock **or** cod	coating (p375)
lemon juice	butter
salt and pepper	

Garnish
parsley sprigs

Cut the avocado pears in half lengthways and remove the stones. Flake the fish, and fill the hollows of the pears with it. Sprinkle the surface of the pear and fish with lemon juice, and season the pear only with a sprinkling of salt and pepper. Cover the pears with breadcrumbs. Dot with a very little butter. Bake in a fairly hot oven at 200°C, Gas 6, for 15–20 minutes. Garnish with parsley sprigs. Serve at once with dry toast.

Note This is a good way to use avocado pears which are past their best. It does not matter if they are slightly discoloured, but they should not be mushy.

Pears with Stilton

4 helpings

2 hard cooking pears	salt
50–75g Stilton cheese	fat for greasing
juice of 1 lemon	pepper

Peel the pears, cut in half lengthways, and remove the core and any pips. Cut each half pear into 3 or 4 thin slices lengthways. Cut the cheese into thin slices. Trim the cheese slices to fit the pears. Put to one side together with the trimmings. Simmer the pear slices in water with the lemon juice and a little salt. Remove them when softened at the edges but still firm in the centre.

Grease a flat flameproof dish. Lay the pear slices in a circle with the narrower ends to the centre. Lay the cheese slices on top, and sprinkle with any cheese trimmings. Season very lightly with pepper (no salt). Grill under moderate heat for 3–5 minutes or until the cheese begins to bubble and brown. Serve at once, either as a hot first course or as a last-course savoury.

Note Another rich blue cheese can be used if desired, provided it is not very salty.

Salads and Vegetable Dishes

Salads

A salad makes an attractive first course, by itself or as an item in a mixed hors d'oeuvre platter. It can contain meat, fish or eggs, or be composed simply of raw, blanched or cooked vegetables. It can be simple, made of just a single dressed vegetable, such as the Cabbage Salad on p819; or it can be a decorative, elaborate salad such as the Apple, Celery and Nut Salad on p830.

A salad for a first course should complement the main course to follow. Like a soup, it should stimulate the palate rather than take the edge off hunger. For this reason, a salad dressed with a plain French dressing or vinaigrette sauce is preferable to one dressed with mayonnaise. Small individual salads are a good choice.

Suitable salads can be chosen from the chapter on Salads and Dressings.

Dressed Artichoke Bases or Fonds

6 helpings

12 small cooked **or**	*200g macédoine of*
canned artichoke bases	*cooked vegetables*
2–3 gherkins	*(p398)*
1 × 15ml spoon capers	*125ml mayonnaise*

Garnish
strips of canned pimento   *4–6 sliced stuffed olives*

Trim the artichokes neatly. Chop the gherkins finely and mix with the capers, vegetables, and enough mayonnaise to moisten. Fill the hollow parts of the artichoke with the mixture. Arrange on a serving plate and spoon the remaining mayonnaise over the vegetables. Garnish with the pimento and olives.

Note Artichoke bases are the round fleshy parts of the artichoke found under the hairy choke.

VARIATION

The stuffing mixture is also good as a filling for avocado pears. Use the quantities above to fill 4 halved pears, to serve four.

Hot Stuffed Artichoke Bases

4 helpings

8 small cooked **or**	*round slices of fried*
canned artichoke bases	*bread* **or** *toast*
butter for greasing	
1–2 × 15ml spoons	
stuffing (see below) for	
each base	

Re-heat the artichoke bases by steaming for 6–8 minutes, or bake in a shallow dish in a cool oven under buttered paper for 15–18 minutes. Pile the hot stuffing in the bases and serve immediately on the fried bread or toast.

STUFFINGS

The following stuffing mixtures should be heated before use.

1) Mix together 200g cooked short-grain rice, 4 × 15ml spoons grated Parmesan cheese, 2 × 15ml spoons pine nut kernels, a little lemon juice, and seasoning to taste.
2) Mix together 100g cooked sausage-meat, 1 × 5ml spoon oregano or basil, 2 sieved hard-boiled egg yolks, a little finely chopped, cooked onion, chopped parsley, and seasoning to taste.
3) Mix together 300g finely chopped or creamed cooked spinach, 200ml Béchamel sauce (p704), 75g finely grated mild cheese, and seasoning to taste.
4) Mix together 75g soft white breadcrumbs, 4 finely chopped or crumbled cooked bacon rashers, 1 small chopped fried onion; season well with salt, pepper, and a pinch of mixed herbs.

Aubergine Pâté

3–4 helpings

1 large aubergine	1 × 5ml spoon
1 × 2.5ml spoon salt	concentrated tomato
a pinch of pepper	purée
1 × 15ml spoon	3 × 2.5ml spoons
mayonnaise	chopped chives **or**
1 × 5ml spoon lemon	spring onions
juice	

Garnish
tomato slices	cucumber slices
olives	

Wash and dry the aubergine. Pierce it in several places with a fork. Grill on all sides until the skin begins to split and the flesh is soft. Peel the flesh and mash it in a bowl with the rest of the ingredients. Chill, well covered, for a few minutes before serving. Serve on lettuce leaves, on small saucers, garnished with tomato slices, olives, and cucumber slices.

Eat with thin crackers or rye bread.

Bean Salad with Tuna

4 helpings

500g dry flageolet beans	1 clove of garlic
150g tomatoes	1 × 15ml spoon chopped
2 spring onions	parsley
6 × 15ml spoons salad	1 × 212g can tuna fish
oil	
50ml white wine vinegar	

Soak the beans in warm water overnight. Put into fresh water, and boil gently for about 1 hour or until tender. Meanwhile, skin, de-seed, and chop the tomatoes, and chop the onions finely. Drain the beans, and mix with the tomatoes and onions while still hot. Mix together the oil and vinegar, chop the garlic finely, and add it with the parsley. Drain and flake the tuna, and mix with the hot beans. Pour the cold oil and vinegar dressing over the salad. Serve on small, warmed plates.

Note This dish originated in Italy. Haricot peas or beans can be used instead of flageolets.

Stuffed Tomato Salad

4 helpings

4 large firm tomatoes	stuffing (see below)
salt	

Cut the tops off the tomatoes, and remove the cores, seeds, and juice with a small spoon, leaving a firm cup of skin and flesh. Keep the tops if desired. (The cores and juice can be sieved for use in a sauce or added to tomato juice.)

Sprinkle the tomato cups inside with salt, and turn upside-down on a plate to drain for 30 minutes. Fill with the stuffing. Remove the stalks from the tops and replace them on the stuffed tomatoes if desired. Serve the tomatoes on a bed of lettuce leaves.

Note A large platter of tomatoes with assorted, variously coloured stuffings makes an attractive dish for an informal buffet party.

STUFFINGS FOR
STUFFED TOMATO SALAD

Stuffing (1)

½ small tomato	½ clove of garlic
3 × 2.5ml spoons olive	3 × 2.5ml spoons
oil	chopped ham
3 × 2.5ml spoons	salt and pepper
chopped onion	2 eggs
3 × 2.5ml spoons	2 × 15ml spoons butter
chopped pimento	

Skin, de-seed, and chop the tomato. Heat the oil in a saucepan, add the onion and pimento, and simmer, covered, for a few minutes until they soften. Meanwhile, crush the garlic. Add it to the pan with the chopped ham and tomato, and simmer, uncovered, until the liquid has evaporated. Season with salt and pepper and leave to cool. Scramble the eggs in the butter. Leave to cool under buttered paper. When cold, mix with the onion and pimento mixture.

Stuffings continued over.

Stuffing (2)

75g cottage cheese with
  chives
½ clove of garlic

salt
white **or** *Cayenne pepper*

Drain any free liquid from the cheese. Crush the garlic, and mix it thoroughly with the cheese, adding salt to taste, and either white pepper or a few grains of Cayenne pepper for a hotter flavour.

Stuffing (3)

2 hard-boiled eggs
1 small gherkin
1 × 10ml spoon chopped
  onion

salt and pepper
mayonnaise

Chop the hard-boiled eggs and gherkin. Mix with the onion, season to taste, and moisten with mayonnaise.

Stuffing (4)

100g peeled prawns **or**
  shrimps
2–3 young lettuce leaves
  or *leaves from a lettuce*
  heart

salt and pepper
a few drops Tabasco
  sauce
mayonnaise

Chop the prawns or shrimps. Shred the lettuce leaves. Sprinkle both with salt and pepper. Mix the Tabasco sauce into 1 × 10ml spoon mayonnaise; then add just enough extra mayonnaise to bind the shellfish mixture.

Stuffing (5)

50g cooked carrots
50g cooked garden peas
1 × 15ml spoon natural
  yoghurt

a pinch of white sugar
  (optional)
salt and pepper

Dice the carrots and mix with the peas. Bind with the yoghurt. Mix in a pinch of sugar if the yoghurt is sharp, and season with salt and pepper to taste.

Note 1 × 5ml spoon chopped mint can be added with the sugar, if used.

VARIATION

Tomato Baskets

Instead of making cups, shape the tomatoes into baskets. Take off any stalk. Make 2 vertical parallel cuts on each side of the other end of the tomatoes, each slightly to one side of the centre, and reaching down to the centre of the fruit to form the handle. Make 2 horizontal cuts at right angles to the first 2 and remove the 2 segments of tomato, leaving a handle of tomato flesh in the centre. Hollow out; then fill the baskets like the cups.

Russian Salad

4 helpings

1 small cooked
  cauliflower
3 boiled potatoes
2 tomatoes
50g ham **or** tongue
  (optional)
3 gherkins
a few lettuce leaves
4 × 15ml spoons peas

2 × 15ml spoons diced
  cooked carrot
2 × 15ml spoons diced
  cooked turnip
50g peeled prawns **or**
  shrimps (optional)
salt and pepper
3 × 15ml spoons
  mayonnaise

Garnish

1 small diced cooked
  beetroot
50g smoked salmon, cut
  into strips (optional)

4 olives
1 × 15ml spoon capers
4 anchovy fillets
  (optional)

Break the cauliflower into small sprigs. Peel and dice the potatoes. Skin, de-seed, and dice the tomatoes. Cut the ham or tongue into small strips, if used. Chop the gherkins and shred the lettuce leaves. Put the vegetables, meat, and fish, if used, in layers in a salad bowl, sprinkling each layer with salt, pepper, and mayonnaise. Garnish with the remaining ingredients.

Note If using Russian Salad as part of a mixed hors d'oeuvre or for stuffing items such as eggs, omit the lettuce and garnish, and mix all the ingredients together lightly.

Crudités

These are small raw or blanched vegetables, cut up or grated, and served as a first course with an oil and vinegar dressing, French dressing or a dip. They are usually arranged in a decorative pattern on a large flat dish or tray, from which people help themselves. Suitable items to include are:

1) apples (cubed, dipped in lemon juice)
2) black or green olives
3) carrots (cut into matchsticks)
4) cauliflower florets (blanched)
5) celery (raw or blanched, sliced thinly)
6) courgettes (unpeeled, cut into matchsticks)
7) cucumber (cubed or sliced thickly)
8) fennel (raw or blanched, sliced thinly)
9) green or red pepper (cut in rings or strips)
10) radishes (small, whole)
11) spring onions
12) tomatoes (thin wedges, slices, or if small, halved)

Soured Cream Dip for Crudités

3–4 helpings

½ clove of garlic	½ × 2.5ml spoon dry
1 × 15ml spoon chilli	mustard
sauce	a pinch of Cayenne
1 × 5ml spoon creamed	pepper
horseradish	1 × 5ml spoon lemon
1 × 15ml spoon	juice
Worcestershire sauce	250ml soured cream

Crush the garlic. In a small basin, combine all the ingredients. Chill for 2–3 hours to allow the flavours to develop.

Serve with crudités or with cream crackers or potato crisps.

VARIATIONS
Onion Dip

To the 125ml of soured cream, add 2 × 15ml spoons dried onion soup mix. Chill and serve as above.

Crab Dip

To the 125ml of soured cream, add 25g finely chopped onion, 1 × 15ml spoon lemon juice, and 125g fresh, frozen or canned crabmeat. Chill and serve as above.

Mixed Hors d'Oeuvre Wheel

4–6 helpings

6–8 anchovy fillets	200g Celeriac in
150g liver pâté	Mustard Dressing
100–150g Cucumber in	(p316)
Soured Cream (p316)	2 medium-sized carrots
2 medium-sized red-	oil
skinned dessert apples	4 or 6 Stuffed Russian
lemon juice	Eggs, using 2 or 3
75g black and stuffed	whole eggs (p320)
green olives	grated orange rind
	salt and pepper

Garnish
parsley sprigs

Use a large, flat, round hors d'oeuvre wheel. Drain the anchovy fillets and wind them round the black olives using cocktail sticks, if necessary. Arrange with the stuffed olives in the centre. Cut the pâté in neat slices, 1 per person. Prepare the cucumber and soured cream but keep the fennel and egg garnish aside. Core and cube the apples and sprinkle with lemon juice. Prepare the celeriac for serving. Grate the carrots and mix with a little oil. Prepare the Russian Eggs.

Arrange all these ingredients in triangular sections on the wheel. Sprinkle the cucumbers with their fennel and egg garnish, and the carrots with grated orange rind and seasoning. Garnish with parsley sprigs.

Offer small spoons for people to help themselves. Serve slices of dark rye bread separately.

Note Instead of a wheel a 25–30cm platter with a small dish in the centre, can be used.

Cucumber in Soured Cream

4 helpings

3 cucumbers	pepper
salt	150ml soured cream
1 × 5cm piece fennel stem **or** 1 thick slice of the bulb	1 × 10ml spoon cider vinegar **or** white wine vinegar
1 hard-boiled egg yolk	

Slice the cucumbers very thinly, sprinkle with the salt; then leave for 30 minutes. Drain and pat dry. Slice the fennel thinly. Crumble the egg yolk coarsely and mix it with the fennel. Just before serving, sprinkle the cucumber with pepper, mix the soured cream with salt and the vinegar, and pour it over the cucumbers. Sprinkle with the fennel and egg.

Note This can also be served with meat rissoles, fish cakes, grilled meat or fried fish.

Stuffed Cucumber Salad

6 helpings

1 large cucumber	1 × 15ml spoon chopped parsley
3 large tomatoes	salt and pepper
150g macédoine of cooked vegetables (p398)	
4 × 15ml spoons mayonnaise **or** salad dressing	

Garnish
mustard and cress

Peel the cucumber if desired and cut it into 2cm slices. Scoop out the seeds and dry the pieces thoroughly. Skin and slice the tomatoes, allowing 1 slice for each piece of cucumber. Remove the seeds from any tomato remaining, chop the pulp, and add to the macédoine. Stir the mayonnaise or salad dressing into the macédoine with the parsley. Season to taste. Place 1 cucumber ring on each tomato slice and arrange on a serving dish. Spoon the macédoine into the cucumber rings and garnish with small bunches of mustard and cress.

Celeriac in Mustard Dressing

4 helpings

450g **or** 1 medium-sized celeriac	3 × 15ml spoons boiling water
3 × 2.5ml spoons salt	100ml olive oil **or** as needed
3 × 2.5ml spoons lemon juice	2 × 15ml spoons white vinegar
4 × 15ml spoons French mustard	salt and pepper

Garnish
2 × 15ml spoons
  chopped mixed herbs
  or parsley

Peel the celeriac, and cut it into matchsticks. Toss the sticks in a bowl with the salt and lemon juice, and leave to stand for 30 minutes. Rinse in a strainer under cold running water, drain well, and pat dry. Put the mustard into a warmed bowl, and very gradually whisk in the boiling water. Then whisk in the oil drop by drop as when making mayonnaise (p843), using enough to make a thick sauce. Whisk in the vinegar in the same way. Season with salt and pepper. Fold in the celeriac matchsticks, cover loosely with a cloth, and leave in a cool place for several hours or overnight. Sprinkle the herbs over the dish before serving.

Vegetables à la Grecque

4 helpings

500g vegetables (see **Note**)	2 × 15ml spoons lemon juice
½ × 2.5ml spoon coriander seeds	150ml water
1 clove of garlic	1 bay leaf
400g tomatoes	1 sprig of thyme
4 × 15ml spoons olive oil	salt and pepper

Prepare the vegetables. Slice courgettes, celery, fennel, and leeks; skin onions; leave button mushrooms whole or cut into halves or quarters; dice cucumber or aubergines.

Crush the coriander seeds, skin and crush the garlic, and skin and chop the tomatoes. Put the oil, lemon juice, water, bay leaf, thyme, coriander seeds, garlic, and seasoning into a saucepan. Bring to the boil. Add the tomatoes and cook, uncovered, over moderate heat for 25 minutes. If the vegetables are to be cooked and served hot, add for the appropriate time according to the type of vegetable. If they are already cooked and only need re-heating, or they are to be served raw but hot, add to the sauce for the final 2–3 minutes. If they are to be served cold, pour the hot sauce over the raw vegetables and leave to cool. Remove the bay leaf and thyme before serving.

Note Many different vegetables can be cooked *à la Grecque* and can be served hot or cold. Small portions are often served cold as a first course or as part of a mixed hors d'oeuvre. The most usual ones are courgettes, celery, fennel, button onions and mushrooms, and red and green peppers. Cucumber, aubergines, and leeks are also popular.

Asparagus with Hot Lemon Sauce

4–8 helpings

50 heads asparagus	*25g butter*
250ml milk	*25g flour*
1 small lettuce	*1 egg*
1 small onion (75g approx)	*pepper*
1 bay leaf	*1 × 5ml spoon lemon juice*
1 sprig of thyme	*8 slices toasted **or** fried bread*
salt	

Garnish
chopped parsley *cucumber strips*

Prepare the asparagus heads and tie them into bundles. Put the milk into a deep saucepan or asparagus pan. Shred the lettuce finely and skin and chop the onion. Add to the pan with the bay leaf, thyme, and a little salt. Bring the milk to the boil and put in the asparagus. Simmer gently for about 15 minutes or until the asparagus is tender. Remove from the pan and trim off all the inedible parts of the stalks. Untie, and keep the asparagus warm. Strain the milk.

Melt the butter in a small clean saucepan, stir in the flour, and cook gently for 1 minute. Draw off the heat and gradually stir in the strained milk. Return to the heat and stir all the time until the sauce thickens. Cool slightly, beat the egg until liquid, and stir it into the sauce. Season to taste, and add the lemon juice. Arrange the slices of fried or toasted bread on a warmed serving dish, and pile the asparagus on them. Coat with the sauce and garnish with chopped parsley and cucumber strips.

Corn on the Cob
See p802.

Egg and Cheese Dishes

Eggs Courtet

4 helpings

4 tomatoes (75g each approx)	*salt and pepper*
4 eggs	*25g butter*
4 × 15ml spoons milk	*150ml aspic jelly*

Garnish
chopped parsley

Cut the tomatoes in half and scoop out the centres. Leave upside-down to drain. Beat the eggs, milk, salt, and pepper together lightly. Melt the butter in a small pan, add the beaten egg, reduce the heat and cook gently, stirring all the time, until the eggs are just set and creamy. Fill the tomato cups with the eggs and leave until cold.

Melt the aspic jelly; then chill it until at setting point but still liquid. Coat each filled tomato half with jelly. Chill the remaining jelly until set; then chop it roughly. Serve the tomato cups surrounded by the chopped jelly on a platter of salad, and garnish with parsley.

Note The scrambled egg mixture can be flavoured in any of the ways given in the Scrambled Egg recipe (p916).

Eggs Rémoulade

4 helpings

4 hard-boiled eggs
4 ×15ml spoons thick mayonnaise

1 × 2.5ml spoon anchovy essence

Garnish
tomato
gherkin

4 crisp lettuce leaves

Cut the eggs in half lengthways. Pat dry with kitchen paper. Mix together the mayonnaise and anchovy essence. Turn the eggs, cut side down and coat the white outside with the mayonnaise mixture. Arrange small pieces of tomato or gherkin on top. Place 2 egg halves, cut side down, on each lettuce leaf.

Poached Eggs Belle Hélène

6–8 helpings

50 heads asparagus
500ml milk
1 large lettuce
1 medium-sized onion (125g approx)
1 bay leaf
3 sprigs thyme

salt
50g butter
50g flour
7–9 eggs
pepper
1 × 5ml spoon lemon juice

Scrape the white stalks of the asparagus and cut off the points. Put the milk into a saucepan and bring to the boil. Shred the lettuce finely and skin and chop the onion. Add to the pan with the bay leaf, thyme, and a little salt; then put in the asparagus stalks. Simmer gently for about 15 minutes or until the stalks are tender. Drain the asparagus, and rub through a fine stainless steel or nylon sieve. Melt the butter in a second pan, add the flour and cook for 1 minute. Remove from the heat and stir in the asparagus purée. Return to the heat and bring to the boil, stirring all the time until the sauce thickens. Beat one of the eggs lightly, stir it into the sauce and continue stirring over very gentle heat, without boiling, until the sauce is very thick. Season the sauce well and add the lemon juice. Cook the asparagus points in boiling salted water for 5 minutes or until tender. Drain well. Poach the eggs and trim neatly to a round shape. Chop the trimmings finely and add them to the sauce. Spoon the sauce in a line down the centre of a heated serving dish. Arrange an equal number of eggs on each side and garnish the top of the sauce, between the eggs, with the asparagus points.

Serve as a first course at dinner, as a light lunch or supper dish.

Cased Eggs and Mushrooms

6 helpings

125g butter
6 medium thick slices white bread
2 sticks celery or 1 onion (50g approx)

50g mushrooms
5 eggs
75ml milk
salt and pepper
100g continental sausage

Garnish
lettuce leaves

watercress sprigs

Melt 100g of the butter, and let it cool but not solidify. Cut the crusts off the bread. Brush the butter generously on to both sides of each slice so that the bread is saturated, especially at the corners. Press into individual bun tins so that the corners stick upwards, and trim neatly, if necessary. Bake in a fairly hot oven at 200°C, Gas 6, for 15–20 minutes until golden-brown. Take care that the tips do not brown too much. Leave to cool.

Slice the celery or skin and chop the onion finely. Slice the mushrooms. Melt half the remaining butter in a pan and sauté the celery or onion for 3–4 minutes until softened. Add the mushrooms and cook for 2–3 minutes until tender. Drain.

Beat the eggs, milk, salt, and pepper together lightly. Melt the remaining butter, pour in the beaten egg, reduce the heat and cook gently, stirring all the time, until the mixture is just set and creamy. Cut the sausage into 5mm dice and add to the scrambled egg with the sautéed vegetables. Stir lightly. Leave to cool. Spoon the cold egg into the bread cases.

Serve on lettuce leaves, garnished with small watercress sprigs.

Anchovy Eggs

4 helpings

4 hard-boiled eggs	2 × 15ml spoons coating
1 × 65g can anchovy	white sauce (p692) or
fillets	mayonnaise
1 × 5ml spoon anchovy	Cayenne pepper
essence	

Garnish
watercress leaves

Cut the eggs in half lengthways. Remove the yolks carefully. Trim a thin slice off the rounded side of each half white so that they stand firmly. Chop or pound the anchovies, and pound with the egg yolks until smooth. Gradually add the anchovy essence and the white sauce or mayonnaise to make a moist paste. Add Cayenne pepper to taste. Fill the egg whites with the mixture. Garnish with watercress leaves.

Stuffed Eggs (cold)

4 helpings

4 hard-boiled eggs	salt and pepper
25g softened butter	½ × 15ml spoon
1 × 15ml spoon	Worcestershire sauce
mayonnaise	(optional)

Garnish
parsley sprigs, tomato,
sliced gherkin, stuffed
olives, radishes

Cut the eggs in half lengthways. Remove the yolks carefully and press through a fine sieve into a bowl, or mash with a fork. Trim a small slice off the rounded side of each half white so that they stand firmly. Mix the yolks with the butter, mayonnaise, salt, and pepper. Add Worcestershire sauce, if liked. Beat until smooth and creamy, put into a forcing bag with a 1.5cm star nozzle and pipe into the egg whites. Garnish with a small piece of parsley or tomato, a slice of gherkin, stuffed olive or a radish.

Serve on curled lettuce leaves or watercress sprigs.

VARIATIONS

1) To the creamed yolk filling above, add one of the following:
   a) 25g finely grated cheese; garnish with paprika pepper
   b) 25g finely minced tongue or ham
   c) 50g liver sausage and a little top of the milk; garnish with a slice of olive
   d) 1 × 5ml spoon anchovy essence; garnish with parsley; omit the Worcestershire sauce
   e) 50g shrimp or salmon paste; omit the Worcestershire sauce
   f) 60g mashed sardines, a little lemon juice, and top of the milk; omit the Worcestershire sauce
   g) 50g very finely chopped shrimps; garnish with whole shrimps; omit the Worcestershire sauce
   h) 1 × 5ml spoon curry powder; garnish with a raisin
   i) 2 × 5ml spoons concentrated tomato purée; garnish with a slice of stuffed olive.

2) Omit the mayonnaise and Worcestershire sauce from the basic filling, cream the yolks with 50g butter, seasoning, and one of the following:
   a) 2 × 15ml spoons chopped chives and a little top of the milk
   b) 50g cream cheese, 1 × 15ml spoon top of the milk, and either a stick of celery finely chopped or 1 × 15ml spoon chopped chives
   c) 50g chopped crabmeat and 1 × 15ml spoon single cream.

3) Cream the yolks and seasoning without butter or mayonnaise, with one of the following:
   a) 2 × 15ml spoons soured cream; garnish with cress
   b) the flesh of an avocado pear creamed with a little garlic; garnish with paprika.

Stuffed Russian Eggs

6 helpings

6 hard-boiled eggs
1 × 100g jar lumpfish roe
3 × 15ml spoons mayonnaise

2–3 even-sized tomatoes
oil
vinegar
salt and pepper
chopped parsley

Garnish
chopped parsley

Cut the eggs in half lengthways, remove the yolks, and trim a small slice off the rounded side of each half white to make them stand firmly. Fill the egg whites with lumpfish roe. Rub the yolks through a sieve, blend with the mayonnaise, and using a forcing bag with a star nozzle, pipe the mixture on to the stuffed egg whites. Cut the tomatoes into slices, and season with oil, vinegar, salt, and pepper. Sprinkle with chopped parsley. Serve the eggs on the slices of tomato and garnish with extra chopped parsley.

Dijon Eggs

4 helpings

4 hard-boiled eggs
100g cooked ham

50g cooked mushrooms
salt and pepper

Garnish
small pieces of tomato

Cut the eggs in half lengthways, remove the yolks and trim a thin slice off the rounded side of each half white to make them stand firmly. Mince the ham finely. Mix with the egg yolks and mushrooms, and season with salt and pepper. Fill the egg whites with the mixture. Garnish with small pieces of tomato.

Individual Hot Soufflés

See p921.

Eggs in Aspic

4 helpings

4 eggs

500ml liquid aspic jelly

Decoration
1 or 2 of the following:
  prawns, shrimps,
  chervil, tarragon,
  cress, watercress,
  cooked peas

Garnish
cress or watercress
  sprigs

The eggs can be hard-boiled, cooked by the *oeuf mollet* method (p909), or poached as follows: poach the eggs in water until the whites are firm and the yolks semi-set. Drain on soft kitchen paper and leave to cool. Trim the eggs with a pastry cutter or sharp knife so they will fit into dariole moulds. Chill the eggs and 4 moulds in the refrigerator. Put a little of the jelly in each mould. Rotate, tilting the mould so that the inside becomes entirely coated with a thin layer of jelly. Chill until set. Arrange a decoration of prawns, leaves or peas on the set jelly, using a long pin or fine skewer to set them in place. Add another layer of jelly carefully. Return to the refrigerator to set. Place 1 egg in each mould and add enough jelly to cover it. Return the moulds and any remaining jelly to the refrigerator. When the jellied eggs are firmly set, turn them out on to a dish. Chop the remaining jelly and arrange round the eggs. Garnish with cress or watercress sprigs.

Note 1 × 15ml spoon Madeira or dry sherry can be added to the aspic jelly for an extra rich flavour.

VARIATIONS

1) Use hard-boiled eggs and slice them crossways, discarding the curved end pieces. Put 1 slice of egg into each mould on the set jelly, and pour in enough liquid jelly to cover it. Return to the refrigerator to set. Continue in this way, setting each slice of egg in aspic until all the egg has been used. Finish with a layer of aspic jelly. Turn out and garnish as above.

2) If dariole moulds are not available, put the cooked eggs into a dish just large enough to hold them side by side, with about 1.5cm between each egg and between the side of the dish and the eggs. Pour the aspic over them and leave to set. When the aspic is firm, use a pastry cutter to cut out the eggs with 5mm jelly round the edge of each. Lift on to a serving dish. Chop the remaining jelly and use it to garnish the eggs with some cress or watercress sprigs.

3) An attractive dish for a buffet table can be made by setting eggs in aspic jelly in a ring mould. Coat the mould with jelly and decorate with prawns and cress. Arrange the eggs in the mould, leaving just enough space between the eggs for serving. Fill the mould to the brim with aspic jelly. When firm, turn out on to a plate and garnish with quartered or sliced hard-boiled eggs and some more prawns. Lemon-flavoured mayonnaise (p843) is a good accompaniment.

Cheese Cream

4 helpings

50g Cheddar **or** Gruyère cheese	25g grated Parmesan cheese
dry English mustard	4 × 15ml spoons aspic jelly
a pinch of Cayenne pepper	125ml double cream
a pinch of salt	

Garnish

watercress sprigs	Cayenne pepper

Grate the Cheddar or Gruyère cheese very finely. Season it with a little mustard, a pinch of Cayenne pepper, and a good pinch of salt. Mix in the Parmesan cheese. Warm the aspic jelly until just liquid if set; cool it until quite cold but still liquid. Meanwhile, whip the cream until semi-stiff. Stir the liquid aspic jelly into the whipped cream, blending lightly but thoroughly. Fold in the cheeses lightly, a little at a time; do not beat or the mixture will lose its lightness. Turn the mixture into a 400ml glass bowl or individual bowls, and leave to set. When cold, garnish with watercress sprigs which have been dusted lightly with Cayenne pepper.

Cheese Pâté

6–8 helpings

125g Roquefort **or** other blue cheese	1 × 2.5ml spoon Worcestershire sauce
125g full-fat soft cheese	1 × 2.5ml spoon paprika
1 × 15ml spoon softened butter	a pinch of Cayenne pepper
125g Cheddar cheese	chopped parsley
75g walnuts	

Crumble the blue cheese. Blend together with the soft cheese and butter with the back of a spoon. Grate the Cheddar cheese finely and work it in. Chop the walnuts finely. Add them to the mixture with the Worcestershire sauce, paprika, and Cayenne pepper and mix well. Shape the cheese mixture into a ball. Roll in enough parsley to cover completely. Cover with clingfilm and chill.

Serve in small wedges on lettuce leaves, with slices of Fairy Toast (p385) or pumpernickel.

Zéphire of Cheese

4–6 helpings

25g gelatine	50g grated Parmesan cheese
4 × 15ml spoons cold water	salt and pepper
325ml milk	a good pinch of grated nutmeg
50g Cheddar cheese	
125ml double cream	

Garnish

250ml chopped aspic jelly	watercress sprigs
	strips of pimento

Soften the gelatine in the cold water in a small heatproof container. Stand the container in a pan of hot water and stir until the gelatine dissolves. Cool slightly, and mix into the milk. Chill until cold but not set. Meanwhile, grate the Cheddar cheese and whip the cream until semi-stiff. Mix both cheeses, the cream, and seasoning to taste into the cold milk when it is beginning to thicken. Pour the mixture into wetted individual moulds or one 625ml fluted jelly mould. Chill until set, then turn out, and garnish with the chopped jelly, watercress, and pimento.

Fish and Meat Dishes

Herring Rolls

4 helpings

4 salted **or** rollmop herrings	25g butter
2 hard-boiled eggs	Cayenne pepper
8 anchovy fillets	lemon juice

Garnish

8 lemon slices	1 small diced beetroot
4–6 sliced gherkins	chopped parsley

If using salted herrings, soak them in cold water for several hours, then fillet, and remove all the bones. If using rollmop herrings, divide each into 2 fillets. Separate the egg yolks and whites. Chop the anchovy fillets and egg yolks finely, and mix them with the butter and pepper. Spread most of the anchovy mixture on the herring fillets and roll up firmly. Spread the remaining mixture thinly on the round ends of each roll. Chop the egg whites finely and use to coat the spread end of the rolls. Sprinkle the rolls with a little lemon juice and garnish with lemon slices, gherkins, beetroot, and parsley.

Chopped Herring

6–8 helpings

3 salted herrings	1 slice white bread
1 small mild onion	1 × 15ml spoon white
1 large cooking apple	wine vinegar (approx)
2 hard-boiled eggs	25g sugar (approx)

Soak the herrings overnight. Skin and bone them; then rinse well. Skin the onion and peel the apple. Separate the egg yolks from the whites. Cut the crusts off the bread. Mince together the herrings, onion, apple, both egg whites, 1 yolk, and the bread. Add vinegar and sugar to taste. Mash well and serve decorated with the remaining egg yolk, sieved.

Soused Herrings

6 helpings

6 herrings	4 bay leaves
salt and pepper	2 small onions (150g
150ml malt vinegar	approx)
100ml water	
1 × 15ml spoon pickling spice	

Scale, de-head, and bone the herrings; then season well. Roll up the fillets, skin side inwards from the tail end. Place neatly and fairly close together in an ovenproof dish. Pour the vinegar and water over the fish, sprinkle with pickling spice, and add the bay leaves. Skin the onion, cut into rings, and lay on top. Cover the fish loosely with greaseproof paper, and bake in a cool oven at 150°C, Gas 2, for about 1½ hours. Leave to cool completely.

Serve as a first course or summer main course with any suitable salad.

Mrs Beeton's Dressed Whitebait

3–4 helpings

50g flour	milk
salt and pepper	fat for deep frying
100g whitebait	Cayenne pepper

Garnish

parsley sprigs	lemon wedges

Season the flour with salt and pepper. Wash the whitebait, dip in milk, and coat with flour, by shaking them together in a tea-towel or plastic bag. Make sure that the fish are separate. Heat the fat (p303), and fry the fish in small batches until crisp. Check that the fat is at the correct temperature before putting in each batch. When all the fish are fried, sprinkle with salt and Cayenne pepper. Serve immediately, garnished with parsley and lemon wedges, with thinly cut brown bread and butter.

Note Whitebait are eaten whole.

Cucumber Cassolettes

4 helpings or 8 small savouries

1 large or 2 thin cucumbers	*200g crabmeat **or** cooked **or** canned red salmon*
olive oil	*3 ×15ml spoons mayonnaise*
vinegar	*Tabasco sauce*
salt and pepper	*1 ×65g can anchovy fillets*

Garnish
chopped parsley

Peel the cucumbers and cut them into 5cm thick pieces. Remove the seeds with an apple corer or potato peeler. Place the rings on a dish and pour a little oil and vinegar over them; season well. Pound the crabmeat or salmon and mix it with the mayonnaise and a few drops of Tabasco sauce. Drain the cucumber pieces and fill the centres with the fish mixture. Drain the anchovy fillets and twist one round the top of each cucumber ring. Garnish with parsley. Serve on small round croûtes or biscuits if desired.

Camargue Mussels

5–6 helpings

2kg live mussels	*100ml salad oil*
1 egg yolk	*1 × 5ml spoon white wine vinegar*
1 × 5ml spoon French mustard	*2 ×10ml spoons lemon juice*
salt	
Cayenne pepper	

Garnish
chopped parsley

Clean and prepare the mussels as for Moules Marinière (p462). Arrange the cooked mussels on their half shells on a large flat dish. Strain the juice from the mussels, and cool. Make a very thick mayonnaise (p843) with the egg, mustard, salt, Cayenne pepper, oil, and vinegar. Stir in the lemon juice, and the cold cooking liquid from the mussels. Pour over the mussels and sprinkle with chopped parsley. Serve chilled.

Oysters Rockefeller

2 helpings

24 oysters	*1 ×15ml spoon Worcestershire sauce*
100g shallots	*100g butter*
100g spinach	*25ml pastis*
2 stalks celery	*50g soft white breadcrumbs*
1 sprig thyme	
100ml water	

Open the oysters (p426) and leave on the half shell. Reserve the liquid. Place the oysters on an oven-proof dish.

Skin the shallots, clean the celery, and chop the shallots, spinach, celery, and thyme finely. Put in a saucepan, add the oyster liquid and water. Boil for 5–7 minutes. Add the Worcestershire sauce and butter. Beat until all the ingredients are well-blended. Add the pastis and mix in well. Pour the sauce over the oysters. Sprinkle with the breadcrumbs. Bake in a hot oven at 220°C, Gas 7, for 5–10 minutes.

Asparagus and Prawn Salad

4 helpings

1 small or ½ large bundle green asparagus or 1 ×397g can asparagus	*75g peeled prawns **or** shrimps*
	4 ×15ml spoons mayonnaise

Garnish
4 hard-boiled eggs	*paprika*
salt	

Prepare and cook the asparagus (p746) or drain canned asparagus thoroughly. When cold, cut the points and the tender parts of the stem into small pieces, and put them into a bowl with the prawns or shrimps. Mix lightly with just enough mayonnaise to bind. Serve piled on a small dish or on individual plates, garnished with a border of thinly sliced hard-boiled eggs sprinkled with salt and paprika.

Note Frozen prawns can be used for this dish. Squeeze gently before using to get rid of excess moisture.

Prawn Cocktail

4 helpings

4 lettuce leaves
200g peeled prawns
5 × 15ml spoons
  mayonnaise
1 × 15ml spoon
  concentrated tomato
  purée **or** tomato
  ketchup

a pinch of Cayenne
  pepper **or** a few drops
  Tabasco sauce
salt (optional)
1 × 5ml spoon chilli
  vinegar **or** tarragon
  vinegar (optional)

Garnish
4 shell-on prawns

Shred the lettuce leaves. Place a little shredded lettuce at the bottom of 4 glass dishes. Put the prawns on top. Mix the mayonnaise with the tomato purée or ketchup and add a pinch of Cayenne pepper or a few drops of Tabasco sauce. Season with salt and vinegar if required. Pour the mayonnaise over the prawns and garnish each dish with an unshelled prawn.

Serve with rolled brown bread and butter.

Spanish Prawns

5–6 helpings

75ml cooking oil
1 clove of garlic
a small bunch of chives
500g cooked shell-on
  prawns

2 × 15ml spoons dry
  sherry
salt and black pepper

Pour the oil into a large flat pan, and heat for a few minutes. Crush the garlic, chop the chives, and add to the oil. Put the prawns (with the shells) in the pan with the sherry. Season with salt and black pepper. Cover the pan and cook for 5 minutes, turning the prawns once.

Serve in small bowls, with crusty French bread. Hand paper napkins and fingerbowls separately.

Smoked Salmon

See p419.

Other Smoked Fish

Apart from smoked salmon there are many kinds of smoked fish to choose from, including buckling (smoked herring), kipper, hot or cold smoked mackerel, oysters, sprats, and trout.

All smoked fish should be served with the head and skin removed and the bones too, if possible. For buckling and trout, the tail should be left on. As mackerel are often too large to serve whole, a fillet is generally enough for 1 helping. Oysters are generally served on toast or speared with cocktail sticks as part of a mixed seafood platter. Smoked sprats vary considerably in quality; the best have a firm oily texture. Provide 3–4 sprats per person.

Smoked fish should be served accompanied by horseradish sauce or lemon slices, Cayenne pepper, and brown bread and butter or pumpernickel.

Kipper Mousse

4 helpings

600g kipper fillets
1 small onion
50g butter
250ml Velouté sauce
  (p708)
250ml mayonnaise

15g gelatine
75ml dry white wine
250ml double cream
salt and black pepper
lemon juice
butter for greasing

Garnish
lemon slices

parsley sprigs

Skin the kipper fillets and cut into 2–3cm pieces. Skin the onion and slice it finely. Fry the fish and onion gently in the butter for 7 minutes. Mix in the Velouté sauce and mayonnaise. Pound, or process in an electric blender to make a smooth purée. Soften the gelatine in the wine in a small heatproof container. Stand the container in hot water and stir until the gelatine dissolves. Add it to the purée and mix very thoroughly. Blend in the cream and season to taste. Add a squeeze of lemon juice. Spoon into a lightly buttered soufflé dish or oval pâté mould and chill for 2 hours. Serve from the dish, or turn out the mousse on to a serving dish and garnish with lemon slices and parsley sprigs.

Serve with hot toast and lemon slices.

Salmon Mousse (1)

6–8 helpings

400g cut of salmon	*50g butter*
1 litre court bouillon	*50ml double cream*
(p429)	*1 × 15ml spoon medium-*
250ml Béchamel sauce	*dry sherry*
(p704)	*oil for greasing*

Garnish
cucumber slices

Put the salmon in a large pan and cover with court bouillon. Bring to the boil, reduce the heat and simmer for 15 minutes. Drain, cool, remove the skin and bones; then pound or process in an electric blender until smooth. Put the cold Béchamel sauce into a bowl, add the salmon and mix until completely blended. Cream the butter until soft, whip the cream until semi-stiff, and add to the mixture. Stir well, and put the mousse mixture into an oiled glass fish mould. Smooth the top and leave to set in a refrigerator. Before serving, dip the base of the mould into warm water and turn out the mousse on to a large platter. Garnish with cucumber slices.

Note For other savoury mousses, see pp881–84.

Creamed Ham and Egg Toasts

6 helpings

3 hard-boiled eggs	*salt and pepper*
150g cooked ham	*6 slices white bread*
250ml coating white	*butter for spreading*
sauce (p692)	
½ × 2.5ml spoon dry	
mustard	

Garnish
stuffed olives

Slice the eggs. Dice the ham and add it to the white sauce with the eggs and mustard. Season to taste. Toast the bread and butter it. Cover with the ham mixture and garnish with stuffed olives. Serve hot.

Ham and Egg Tartlets

6 helpings

150g cooked ham	*75ml milk (approx)*
50g soft white	*fat for greasing*
breadcrumbs	*browned breadcrumbs*
a good pinch of grated	*(p375)*
nutmeg	*6 eggs*
salt and pepper	*15g butter*

Chop the ham finely. Mix together the ham and white breadcrumbs. Add a good pinch of nutmeg, season well with salt and pepper, and moisten gradually with milk to make a stiff paste. Grease six 6–8cm patty tins, coat them thickly with browned breadcrumbs, and line them with the meat mixture. Break an egg carefully into each, sprinkle lightly with browned breadcrumbs, and dot with the butter. Bake in a moderate oven at 180°C, Gas 4, for 15 minutes or until the eggs are set. Remove carefully from the tins and serve hot.

Ham Ramekins

8 helpings

225g lean cooked ham	*½ × 2.5ml spoon dry*
2 eggs	*mustard*
4 × 15ml spoons milk	*salt and pepper*
½ × 5ml spoon dried	*fat for greasing*
mixed herbs	*paprika*

Chop the ham finely. Separate the eggs. Whisk the egg yolks lightly, add the ham, milk, herbs, mustard, salt and pepper, and mix together well. Divide the mixture equally between 8 well-greased ramekin dishes, filling each about three-quarters full. Cook in a fairly hot oven at 190°C, Gas 5, for 15 minutes until set. Meanwhile, whisk the egg whites until stiff, and add a little salt. Divide the meringue between the dishes, piling it up roughly. Sprinkle with paprika, return the dishes to the oven, and bake them for another 10–15 minutes until crisp and lightly browned. Serve at once.

Ham Rolls

See p1287.

Platter of Pork Meats

Choose 4–6 varieties of bought sausage and other pork meats, ready to eat, allowing 100–125g per person. Arrange them in a decorative pattern on a bed of lettuce leaves. Serve with small forks, and offer rolled sandwiches of dark rye bread or pumpernickel.

Some suitable meats to offer are, for instance:

1) salami
2) thin slices of Italian raw smoked ham, loosely rolled
3) cooked British sausages, thinly sliced diagonally
4) very small slices of cooked pork fillet
5) thin slices or 2cm cubes of pickled pork or pork luncheon meat

Chopped Liver

4–5 helpings

1 medium-sized onion	*2 hard-boiled eggs*
225g chicken or calf's	*salt and freshly ground*
liver	*pepper*
4 × 10ml spoons chicken	
fat	

Garnish

lettuce leaves	*tomato slices*

Skin and chop the onion. Remove any gristle or tubes from the liver. Heat the chicken fat in a frying pan. Fry the onion with the liver until soft but not brown. Mince the liver, onion, and hard-boiled eggs very finely. Season with salt and freshly ground pepper, and mix to a paste.

Serve on a bed of lettuce leaves, garnished with tomato slices as a first course or use as a spread for canapés or sandwiches.

Pâtés

A pâté is always popular as a first course, and it is easy to serve. It should not, however, be rich or heavy; a light, mousse-like pâté is ideal. Fish pâtés, particularly those made with smoked fish are increasingly popular for this reason, and are a good choice, especially if the main course is red meat or game.

Instead of offering at table a large terrine or dish of pâté, it is wiser to serve individual portions, dressed with a small salad garnish. They should be accompanied by small slices of hot dry toast or brown bread and butter, not by large bread rolls or chunks of bread. Alternatively tiny individual jars of pâté or potted meat accompanied by hot dry toast fingers can be served.

Most of the fish and meat pâtés in this book are in the chapter on Pâtés and Potted Foods. For others, refer to the Index.

SOUPS

The principal art in composing good rich soup, is so to proportion the several ingredients that the flavour of one shall not predominate over another, and that all the articles of which it is composed, shall form an agreeable whole. To accomplish this, care must be taken that the roots and herbs are perfectly well cleaned, and that the water is proportioned to the quantity of meat and other ingredients.

The Menu

The choice of soup depends entirely on its role in the menu. A soup that is the forerunner of a meal should stimulate the appetite for the enjoyment of the latter courses. Clear soups and consommés are ideal for this purpose. If a soup is to be served as a main course, it should contain quite a large proportion of solid foods, like a stew, eg Lamb or Mutton Broth (p333).

The quantity of soup served can vary from 125ml before a generous meal to over 250ml if the soup is a main course. Consommés and jellied soups are best served in soup bowls or two-handled cups. Thick soups can be served in bowls or deep plates, others are often brought to the table in a soup tureen to display their garnishing.

Soups are usually served hot, but, in hot weather, certain soups can be served very cold or even iced, making them cooling and refreshing.

PRINCIPAL TYPES OF SOUP

Clear Soups

These are usually made from Brown Stock (p329) and, if cleared with egg white, are generally known as consommés. Consommés may vary in colour from pale fawn to deep golden-brown, according to the meat used, but they must always be clear. Clear soups made from stock take their distinguishing names from their garnishes, which are immensely varied.

Broths

These are the uncleared liquids in which meat, poultry or vegetables have been cooked. Other vegetables, rice or barley are usually added. They are not thickened, but may contain so many solid ingredients that they are easily confused with thick soups.

Puréed Soups

The basic ingredients for these soups are made into a smooth pulp or purée, either by sieving them, or by processing them briefly in an electric blender.

Although the pulp or purée is the main thickening agent, these soups, like thickened soups (see below), often contain a starch ingredient (liaison) such as flour, cornflour or arrowroot. Purées can be garnished with dice or shreds of the main ingredient; they are often served with fried, toasted or baked croûtons.

Thickened Soups

Various ingredients can be added to soups to thicken and enrich them.

Fine cereals: Flour, cornflour, arrowroot, barley, rice flour, semolina or fine tapioca. These are usually first blended with a little cold stock, water or milk, before being stirred into the rest of the soup. The soup must be boiled for a few minutes to thicken the starchy cereal and to remove its raw flavour.

White or brown roux: White roux in which the flour is not allowed to turn colour, is the usual thickening for vegetable purées made from green vegetables, such as spinach, Brussels sprouts, and watercress (which are not fried before processing). Brown roux is used for some meat purées; in this case, the flour is browned slowly in the fat before the purée or stock is added.

Beurre manié: This is whisked into the hot, but not boiling soup, a small piece at a time. The soup must be reboiled to thicken it.

Cream: This is used both to thicken and enrich soups. It is best added by beating a little hot soup into the cream in a small bowl before folding it into the hot mixture, off the heat. The soup may be re-heated gently, but it must not reach boiling point or it will curdle. Use single cream to thicken or to garnish hot soups, sauces, and most other hot liquids. It curdles less easily than richer cream.

Egg yolks and milk or cream: Egg yolks are also used to thicken and enrich soups, but they are always mixed thoroughly with a little cream or milk first. The method of adding egg yolks to hot soup is the same as that for adding cream (see above). Soups are less likely to curdle when a cream or egg yolk liaision is added, if they already contain flour or some other starch.

Potato: The starch in potatoes cooked in a soup is usually enough to thicken it, so that no additional starch thickening is needed.

Bread: Some soups have a slice of bread or breadcrumbs as an ingredient. During cooking, the starch in the bread swells and thickens the soup.

Blood: This is seldom used except for Hare Soup (p342). The blood must be added at the end of the cooking time. The soup can be re-heated gently but must not reach boiling point or it will curdle.

Note A soup made from starchy vegetables, such as dried peas, beans or potatoes, can easily produce a soup which is too thick. It can be thinned to the right consistency by adding stock, water or milk.

Cream Soups

A cream soup is any thick soup, including purées and thickened soups, which has cream and/or egg yolks added. Shellfish-based cream soups are called bisques (see pp349–50).

EQUIPMENT FOR SOUP-MAKING

Various labour-saving devices make the preparation of soups easy and quick.

1) To minimize cooking time, an electric blender/ liquidizer or food processor can be used to process raw vegetables.
2) Pressure cookers enable well-cooked and well-flavoured soups to be produced in a very short time. See p1427.
3) Stainless metal and nylon sieves are easier to clean than the older hair sieves which they have replaced. They do not stain and, having a harder mesh, make sieving quicker and easier.
4) Various food mills are also available which grate, shred or sieve raw or cooked vegetables with very little labour. A hand mill gives a less bland texture than an electric one.

Garnishes and Accompaniments for Soups
See pp384–88.

STOCK FOR SOUP-MAKING

Most home-made soups should be made with fresh stock using the bones and flesh of meat, poultry or fish, and with vegetables, herbs, and spices; these should blend with the ingredients for the particular soup to be made.

There are six basic stocks: brown stock, general household stock, white stock, chicken or game stock, fish stock, and vegetable stock. Stock made from raw meat and bones is essential for a consommé, but for most other soups, a general household stock is quite suitable, using the skin and gristle of raw meat, scraps and trimmings of cooked meat, and raw or cooked bones.

Most of the flavour is extracted from meat in the first 2–3 hours of cooking a meat stock, and body is given by the gelatine released by the chopped bones. Extra flavour is obtained from vegetables, although swedes, turnips, and other roots should be used with care, and starchy vegetables, such as potatoes, should not be used as they will cloud the stock.

STOCKS

Brown Stock
(Beef stock)

Makes 1.5 litres (approx)

500g beef **or** *veal marrow bones*	*1 medium-sized carrot (50g approx)*
500g lean shin of beef	*1 stick of celery*
1.5 litres cold water	*(50g approx)*
1 × 5ml spoon salt	*bouquet garni*
1 medium-sized onion	*1 × 2.5ml spoon black*
(100g approx)	*peppercorns*

Ask the butcher to chop the bones into manageable pieces. Wipe them thoroughly. Trim off any fat and cut the meat into small pieces. Put the bones and meat in a roasting tin in a hot oven at 220°C, Gas 7, for 30–40 minutes to brown, turning them occasionally.

Put the browned bones and meat in a large saucepan with the water and salt. Prepare and slice the vegetables. Add them to the pan with the bouquet garni and peppercorns. Heat slowly to boiling point, skim well, and cover the pan with a tight-fitting lid. Reduce the heat and simmer very gently for 4 hours. Strain through a fine sieve and leave to cool. When cold, remove any fat from the surface.

General Household Stock

Makes 1 litre (approx)

1kg cooked **or** *raw bones of any meat* **or** *poultry, cooked* **or** *raw meat trimmings, giblets, and bacon rinds*	*500g onions, carrots, celery, and leeks*
	salt
	1 bay leaf
	4 black peppercorns

Break or chop the bones into manageable pieces. Wipe thoroughly. Prepare and slice the vegetables, retaining a piece of brown onion skin if a brown stock is required. Put the bones and meat trimmings into a saucepan. Cover with cold water and add 1 × 2.5ml spoon salt for each litre of water used. Heat slowly to simmering point. Add the other ingredients. Simmer, uncovered, for at least 3 hours. Strain and cool quickly by standing the pan in chilled water. When cold, skim off the fat. If the stock is not required at once, keep it cold. Use within 24 hours, or within 3 days if kept in a refrigerator. Reboil before use.

White Stock

Makes 2 litres (approx)

1kg knuckle of veal	*1 × 10ml spoon white*
1 medium-sized onion	*vinegar* **or** *lemon juice*
(100g approx)	*1 × 2.5ml spoon white*
1 stick of celery	*peppercorns*
(50g approx)	*a small strip of lemon*
2 litres cold water	*rind*
1 × 10ml spoon salt	*1 bay leaf*

Chop the knuckle into manageable pieces. Scrape the bones, trim off any fat, and wipe the bones thoroughly. Prepare and slice the onion and celery. Put the bones in a large pan with the cold water, salt, and vinegar or lemon juice. Heat to boiling point and skim. Add the vegetables and the other ingredients. Bring back to the boil, cover, reduce the heat, and simmer gently for 4 hours. Strain the stock through a fine sieve and cool it quickly by standing the pan in chilled water. When cold, skim off the fat. Store as for General Household Stock.

Chicken or Game Stock

Makes 1 litre (using 1 litre water)

1 medium-sized onion (100g approx)	cleaned feet of bird (optional)
1 stick of celery (50g approx)	1 × 10ml spoon salt
carcass of 1 chicken or game bird, including the giblets	4 white peppercorns bouquet garni

Prepare and slice the vegetables. Break or chop the carcass into manageable pieces. Put the carcass, giblets, and feet, if used, in a large saucepan, cover with cold water, and add the salt. Heat to boiling point. Draw the pan off the heat and leave to stand for 2–3 minutes, then skim off any fat. Add the vegetables, peppercorns, and bouquet garni. Reheat to boiling point, cover, reduce the heat, and simmer very gently for 3–4 hours. Strain the stock through a fine sieve and cool it quickly by standing the container in chilled water. When cold, skim off the fat. Store as for General Household Stock (p329).

Fish Stock (1)

Makes 1 litre (using 1 litre water)

bones, skin, and heads from filleted fish or fish trimmings or cod's or other fish heads or any mixture of these	1 small onion (50g approx)
	1 stick of celery (50g approx)
	4 white peppercorns
1 × 5ml spoon salt	bouquet garni

Break up the bones and wash the fish trimmings, if used. Prepare and slice the vegetables. Put the bones, fish trimmings, or heads in a saucepan and cover with cold water. Add the salt. Heat to boiling point. Add the vegetables, the peppercorns, and bouquet garni. Cover, and simmer gently for 40 minutes. Strain the stock through a fine sieve.

Note If cooked for longer than 40 minutes, fish stock tastes bitter. It does not keep unless frozen, and should be made only as required.

Fish Stock (2)

Makes 1 litre (using 1 litre water)

1 litre water or as required	1 large onion
	1 large carrot
100ml dry white wine or dry cider for each litre of water	a few mushroom stalks
	a blade of mace
	6 peppercorns
750g white fish heads, trimmings, and bones for each litre of water	1 bouquet garni for each litre of water

Put the liquids into a large saucepan. Wash the fish heads and trimmings, and break up the bones. Add them to the pan. Prepare the onion and carrot and slice them thinly. Add them to the pan with the rest of the ingredients. Heat to simmering point, cover, and simmer for 30 minutes. Leave to cool, then strain the stock through a fine sieve.

Use for cooking fish or shellfish, for poaching fish quenelles, or as a base for sauces or fish soups.

Court Bouillon

See p429.

Vegetable Stock (1)

Makes 2 litres (approx)

2 large carrots (200g approx)	1 × 2.5ml spoon yeast extract
2 medium-sized onions (200g approx)	bouquet garni
	1 × 5ml spoon salt
3 sticks celery (150g approx)	6 black peppercorns
2 tomatoes (100g approx)	a blade of mace
	outer leaves of 1 lettuce or ¼ small cabbage (100g approx)
25g butter or margarine	
2 litres boiling water	

Slice the carrots, onions, and celery thinly and chop the tomatoes. Melt the fat in a large saucepan and fry the carrots, onions, and celery for 5–10 minutes until the onions are golden-brown. Add the tomatoes and fry for a further minute. Add the water and the rest of the ingredients, except the lettuce or cabbage. Cover, and simmer for 1 hour.

Shred the lettuce or cabbage, and add to the pan. Simmer for a further 20 minutes. Strain through a fine sieve. Use the same day, if possible, or cool quickly and store in a refrigerator for up to 2 days.

Vegetable Stock (2)

Makes 2 litres (approx)

2 medium-sized onions (200g approx)	2 tomatoes (100g approx)
2 leeks (100–200g approx)	2 litres cold water
2 medium-sized carrots (100g approx)	bouquet garni
1 small turnip (50g approx)	1 × 5ml spoon salt
1 small beetroot (50g approx)	6 black peppercorns
1 small head of celery (200g approx)	2 cloves
	a few sprigs watercress
	a few lettuce leaves
	25g spinach
	1 × 2.5ml spoon yeast extract (optional)

Cut the first six types of vegetables into small pieces; chop the tomatoes. Put in a large saucepan or casserole with the water, and heat to simmering point. Add the bouquet garni, salt, peppercorns, and cloves. Cover, and simmer gently for 1 hour.

Meanwhile, wash and shred the watercress, lettuce leaves, and spinach. After the stock has simmered for 1 hour, add the shredded vegetables and simmer for a further 30 minutes. Strain the stock through a fine sieve. Add the yeast extract, if used, for flavour.

Coconut Infusion

Makes 700ml (approx)

4 × 15ml spoons desiccated coconut	750ml boiling water

Put the coconut in a bowl, and pour over the boiling water. Leave to infuse for 15–20 minutes. Strain through a fine sieve.

Use as part or all of the liquid in West Indian and Eastern dishes, especially curries and sweet dishes.

THIN SOUPS

Broths

Beef Broth

4–6 helpings

1 medium-sized carrot (50g approx)	1 × 2.5ml spoon salt
1 small turnip (50g approx)	½ small cabbage (250g approx)
1 medium-sized onion (100g approx)	a sprig of parsley
1 clove of garlic (optional)	a few chives
25g butter or margarine	salt and pepper
1 litre brown stock (p329) or general household stock (p329)	grated nutmeg
	6 thin slices French bread

Prepare the carrot, turnip, and onion, and slice them thinly. Skin and crush the garlic, if used. Melt the fat in a large saucepan, add the vegetables, cover, and fry gently for 10 minutes. Heat the stock to boiling point and add to the vegetables in the pan with the salt. Cover, and simmer for 30 minutes.

Meanwhile, shred the cabbage and chop the parsley and chives. Add the cabbage to the broth, cover, and simmer for a further 20 minutes. Season to taste with salt, pepper, and a little nutmeg. Add the parsley and chives. Keep over very low heat while toasting the bread slices until golden. Put one in each soup bowl or cup and pour the broth over them.

Serve with grated cheese, if liked.

Chicken Broth

8 helpings

1 small boiling fowl (1.5kg approx) **or** 1 chicken carcass with some flesh left on it	1 stick of celery (50g approx)
giblets of the bird	$\frac{1}{2}\times 2.5ml$ spoon ground pepper
1.5–2 litres water	a blade of mace
1 × 5ml spoon salt	bouquet garni
1 medium-sized onion (100g approx)	a strip of lemon rind
2 medium-sized carrots (100g approx)	25g long-grain rice (optional)
	1 × 15ml spoon chopped parsley

Joint the boiling fowl or break up the carcass bones, and wash the giblets. Put them into a large saucepan and cover with the cold water. Add the salt, and heat slowly to simmering point. Cut the onion in half, and dice the carrots and celery. Add the vegetables to the pan with the pepper, mace, bouquet garni, and lemon rind. Cover, and simmer gently for 3–3½ hours if using a raw boiling fowl, or for 1½ hours if using a chicken carcass. Strain the broth through a colander. Skim off the fat.

Return the broth to the pan and re-heat to simmering point. Wash the rice, if used, and sprinkle it into the broth. Cover, and simmer for a further 15–20 minutes until the rice is cooked.

Some of the meat can be chopped finely and added to the broth, the rest can be used in made-up dishes, eg a fricassée. Just before serving the broth, re-season if required, and add the chopped parsley.

Cabbage and Bacon Broth

4–6 helpings

½ small cabbage	1.5 litres water in which vegetables have been cooked **or** general household stock (p329)
125g carrots	
150g onions	
50g lean bacon, without rinds	salt and pepper
bouquet garni	4–6 slices French bread

Shred the cabbage, cut the carrots into julienne strips (p384); slice the onions thinly. Cut the bacon into small strips. Put the vegetables and bacon into a large, heavy saucepan and fry gently until the bacon fat runs and the vegetables are well coated. Add the bouquet garni. Pour in the water or stock, cover, and heat to boiling point. Cook for 20 minutes at just above simmering point.

Remove the bouquet garni and season to taste. Keep over very low heat while toasting the bread slices until crisp and golden. Put one into each soup bowl or cup, and pour the broth over them.

Serve with grated cheese.

Veal Broth

4–5 helpings

1 knuckle of veal (600–750g approx)	1 leek **or** medium-sized onion (100g approx)
1.5 litres water	1 stick of celery (50g approx)
1 × 10ml spoon lemon juice	bouquet garni
3 × 2.5ml spoons salt	a strip of lemon rind
25g pearl barley **or** rice	4 white peppercorns
2 medium-sized carrots (100g approx)	1 × 10ml spoon chopped parsley
1 small turnip (50g approx)	

Wipe the knuckle and put it into a pan with the water. Heat slowly to simmering point, and add the lemon juice and salt. Blanch the pearl barley or rice and add it to the pan. Cover, and simmer gently for 2 hours. Cut the vegetables into 5mm dice. After the broth has simmered for 2 hours, add the vegetables, bouquet garni, lemon rind, and peppercorns. Cover, and simmer for a further hour. Lift out the knuckle of veal. Remove all the meat from the bone and cut it into 5mm dice. Strain the broth through a colander and return it to the pan; keep hot. Remove the bouquet garni, lemon rind, and peppercorns from the vegetables. Return the meat and vegetables to the broth and add the parsley. Re-season if required. Re-heat before serving.

Note The bone can be used again for stock.

Calf's Foot Broth

4–6 helpings

1 calf's foot	salt and pepper
1.5 litres water	egg yolks
2–3 strips lemon rind	milk

Wash the foot thoroughly. Put it into a large saucepan with the water, heat to simmering point, cover, and simmer gently for 3 hours. Strain through a colander or a sieve into a basin and leave to cool. When cold, skim the fat. Re-heat the broth with the lemon rind until sufficiently flavoured. Remove the lemon rind. Season to taste. For each 250ml broth, allow 1 egg yolk and 4×15ml spoons milk. Beat together the egg yolks and milk with a fork until well blended. Beat into a little hot soup, and fold into the rest of the soup. Stir over low heat until thickened. Do not allow the broth to boil or it will curdle. Serve hot.

Hotch Potch (1)

8 helpings

1kg scrag and middle neck of lamb **or** mutton	1 small lettuce (100g approx)
1.25 litres water	100g shelled young broad beans **or** runner beans
1 × 10ml spoon salt	
bouquet garni	100g cauliflower florets
1 medium-sized carrot (50g approx)	150g shelled peas
1 small turnip (50g approx)	salt and pepper
	1 × 15ml spoon chopped parsley
6 spring onions	

Wipe the meat and trim off any excess fat. Remove the meat from the bone and cut the meat into small pieces. Put the bone and meat into a large saucepan, add the water, and heat very slowly to simmering point. Add the salt and the bouquet garni, cover, and simmer very gently for 30 minutes.

Meanwhile, cut the carrot and turnip into 5mm dice and the spring onions into thin rings; shred the lettuce and runner beans, if used. Add the carrot, turnip, and spring onions to the pan, cover, and simmer for $1\frac{1}{2}$ hours. Add the rest of the vegetables to the soup, cover, and simmer for a further 30 minutes. Season to taste. Skim off the fat and remove the bouquet garni and the bones. Add the chopped parsley just before serving.

Note The vegetables can be varied according to the season.

For Hotch Potch (2), see p369.

Lamb or Mutton Broth

4–6 helpings

600g neck of lamb **or** mutton	1 small turnip (50g approx)
1 litre water	1 stick of celery (50g approx)
1 × 5ml spoon salt	salt and pepper
1 × 15ml spoon pearl barley	1 × 15ml spoon chopped parsley
1 medium-sized carrot (50g approx)	
1 medium-sized onion **or** leek (100g approx)	

Wipe the meat and trim off any excess fat. Put the meat and the bones, water, and salt into a large saucepan and heat very slowly to boiling point.

Meanwhile, blanch the barley in a small saucepan. Lift the meat and bones out of the broth, or strain the liquid and return it to the pan. Remove the meat from the bones and cut it into 5mm dice. Return the meat to the broth. Allow the broth to stand while preparing the vegetables. Cut all the vegetables into 5mm dice. Skim the fat off the broth. Add the vegetables and the blanched barley. Re-heat to simmering point, cover, and simmer for 1 hour. Season to taste; add the parsley just before serving.

Scots or Scotch Broth

See p1459.

Sheep's or Lamb's Head Broth

6–8 helpings

1 sheep's **or** lamb's head	1 medium-sized carrot (50g approx)
2–3 litres cold water	1 stick of celery
salt	(50g approx)
50g pearl barley **or** rice	pepper
1 small turnip (50g approx)	1 × 10ml spoon chopped parsley
1 medium-sized onion (100g approx)	

Prepare the head as for Boiled Sheep's Head (p555). Remove the brains and use for another recipe (pp551–52).

Put the head into a large saucepan with the cold water (2 litres for the lamb's head and 3 litres for the sheep's head), and add 1 × 5ml spoon salt for each litre of water used. Heat slowly to boiling point, skim, cover, and simmer gently for 1 hour. Blanch the pearl barley or rice. Cut the vegetables into 5mm dice. After the broth has simmered for 1 hour, add the pearl barley or rice and the vegetables, and continue to simmer gently for 2–3 hours until the meat is tender. Lift out the head. To serve the broth, skim off the fat, season carefully, and add the chopped parsley.

Note Some of the broth can be strained off for stock.

Spanish Country Broth

4–6 helpings

2 Spanish onions	1 leek
2 cloves garlic	2 × 15ml spoons olive oil
1 red pepper (100g approx)	1 litre boiling water
200g tomatoes	bouquet garni
¼ small cabbage (100g approx)	salt and pepper
	4–6 thin slices brown bread

Prepare and chop the onions, garlic, red pepper, tomatoes, and cabbage. Cut the leek into thin slices. Heat the olive oil in a saucepan, add the onions, garlic, and leek, and fry very gently for 10 minutes. Add the red pepper and the tomatoes, and fry for a further 10 minutes. Add the boiling water, bouquet garni, and cabbage. Cover, and simmer for 1½ hours. Remove the bouquet garni and season lightly. Place the bread slices in the soup bowls or a soup tureen and pour the hot soup over them.

Spring Broth

4–6 helpings

12 spring onions	2 × 10ml spoons olive oil **or** butter
4 young carrots (100g approx)	1 litre white stock (p329) **or** general household stock (p329)
1 small turnip (50g approx)	
a few heads sprue asparagus	salt and pepper
100g shelled green peas	1 × 10ml spoon chopped parsley

Cut the spring onions and carrots into thin rings and the turnip into 5mm dice. Remove the tips of the asparagus and reserve. Cut the tender parts of the stalks into 5mm lengths. Heat the oil or butter in a pan, add all the vegetables, cover, and cook over gentle heat for about 10 minutes. Do not let them brown. Heat the stock to boiling point, add to the pan, cover, and simmer gently for 30 minutes. Add the asparagus tips, cover, and simmer for a further 15 minutes. Season to taste, and add the chopped parsley just before serving.

CONSOMMÉS AND CLEAR SOUPS

Consommé

Makes 1 litre (approx)

100g lean shin of beef	*1.25 litres cold brown*
125ml water	*stock (p329)*
1 small onion	*bouquet garni*
(50g approx)	*$\frac{1}{2} \times 2.5$ml spoon salt*
1 small carrot	*4 white peppercorns*
(25g approx)	*white and crushed shell*
1 small stick of celery	*of 1 egg*
(25g approx)	

Shred the beef finely, trimming off all the fat. Soak the meat in the water for 15 minutes. Prepare the vegetables. Put the meat, water, and the rest of the ingredients into a deep saucepan, adding the egg white and shell last. Heat slowly to simmering point, whisking all the time, until a froth rises to the surface. Remove the whisk, cover, and simmer the consommé very gently for $1\frac{1}{2}$–2 hours. Do not allow to boil or the froth will break up and cloud the consommé. Strain slowly into a basin through muslin or a scalded jelly bag. If necessary, strain the consommé again. Re-heat, re-season if required, and serve plain or with a garnish (see below).

Consommé Brunoise

4–6 helpings

1 litre consommé	*1 × 15ml spoon sherry*
1 × 2.5ml spoon lemon	*(optional)*
juice	

Garnish
1 × 15ml spoon finely	*1 × 15ml spoon finely*
diced carrot	*diced green leek*
1 × 15ml spoon finely	*1 × 15ml spoon finely*
diced turnip	*diced celery*

Cook the diced vegetables for the garnish very carefully in boiling salted water until just tender. Drain and rinse the vegetables; then put them into a warmed tureen.

Meanwhile, heat the consommé to boiling point and add the lemon juice and sherry, if used. Pour the hot consommé over the diced vegetables, and serve.

VARIATION

Consommé Brunoise au Riz

Make as for Consommé Brunoise but add 2 × 15ml spoons of cooked Patna rice, well rinsed, to the tureen with the vegetables.

Consommé Jardinière

4–6 helpings

1 litre consommé

Garnish
1 × 15ml spoon turnip,	*1 × 15ml spoon tiny*
cut in pea shapes	*cauliflower florets* **or**
1 × 15ml spoon carrot,	*1 × 15ml spoon finely*
cut in pea shapes	*diced cucumber*
1 × 15ml spoon small	
green peas	

Cook the vegetables for the garnish separately in boiling salted water until just tender. Drain and rinse the vegetables; then put them into a warmed tureen.

Meanwhile, heat the consommé to boiling point. Pour the hot consommé over the vegetables, and serve.

Note Pea shapes can be formed from the turnip and carrot, using a very small ball scoop.

Consommé Julienne

4–6 helpings

1 litre consommé (p335)

Garnish (see **Note**)

*1 × 15ml spoon julienne
   carrot*

*1 × 15ml spoon julienne
   turnip*

*1 × 15ml spoon julienne
   leek*

Cook the vegetables for the garnish separately in boiling salted water until just tender. Drain and rinse them; then put them into a warmed tureen.

   Meanwhile, heat the consommé to boiling point. Pour the hot consommé over the vegetables, and serve.

Note For the method of preparing julienne strips, see p384.

Consommé Madrilène

4–6 helpings

100g lean shin of beef
125ml water
*500g fresh or canned
   tomatoes*
*1 medium-sized green
   pepper (100g approx)*
*1 small onion
   (50g approx)*

*1 small carrot
   (25g approx)*
*1 small stick of celery
   (25g approx)*
1 litre chicken stock
bouquet garni
*white and crushed shell
   of 1 egg*

Garnish

*2 × 15ml spoons diced
   fresh tomato, skinned*

Shred the beef finely, trimming off all the fat. Soak the meat in the water for 15 minutes. Prepare and chop the vegetables. Put the meat, water, vegetables, stock, and bouquet garni into a deep saucepan. Whisk the egg white slightly and add it to the pan with the egg shell. Heat gently until just below boiling point. Cover, and simmer very gently for 1 hour. Strain through muslin or a scalded jelly bag. Serve the consommé hot, or iced, with the garnish. If iced, it should be almost liquid and may, therefore, need whisking a little just before serving.

Consommé Princesse

4–6 helpings

*1 × 15ml spoon pearl
   barley*
salt and pepper
1 litre consommé (p335)

50g cooked diced chicken
*50g canned asparagus
   tips*

Wash and blanch the barley; then cook it in boiling salted water for 20 minutes. Drain, and put it into a warmed tureen. Heat the consommé to simmering point, add the chicken meat, and heat through for 10 minutes. Season with salt and pepper. Pour the hot consommé over the pearl barley, add the drained asparagus tips, and serve.

Consommé Printanier

4–6 helpings

1 litre consommé (p335)

Garnish

*1 × 15ml spoon green
   peas*
*1 × 15ml spoon French
   beans, cut in 1cm
   lengths*

*1 × 15ml spoon young
   carrot, cut in pea
   shapes*
*1 × 15ml spoon shredded
   outer lettuce leaves*

Cook the vegetables for the garnish separately in boiling salted water until just tender. Drain and rinse the vegetables; then put them into a warmed tureen.

   Meanwhile, heat the consommé to boiling point. Pour the hot consommé over the vegetables, and serve.

Consommé Royale

4–6 helpings

1 litre consommé (p335)

Garnish (Royale Custard)
1 egg yolk   *butter for greasing*
salt and pepper
1 × 15ml spoon white
  stock (p329) **or** *milk*
  or *cream*

Mix the egg yolk, seasoning, and stock or milk or cream. Strain into a small greased basin and cover with buttered greaseproof paper or foil. Stand the basin in a pan of simmering water and steam the custard for about 8 minutes or until firm. Leave until cold and turn out. Cut into thin slices and then into tiny fancy shapes. Rinse the custard shapes in hot water, and drain.

Heat the consommé to boiling point and add the custard garnishes just before serving.

VARIATION

Consommé Dubarry

Make as for Consommé Royale but add 4 blanched, finely chopped almonds to the Royale Custard before steaming it. Add 2 × 15ml spoons cooked Patna rice, well rinsed, with the Royale Custard garnish, to the hot consommé.

Consommé with Pasta

4–6 helpings

1 litre consommé (p335)

Garnish
25g pasta (tiny fancy
  shapes **or** *macaroni,*
  spaghetti, home-made
  noodles (p852) **or**
  vermicelli)

Cook the pasta for the garnish in boiling salted water. Tiny fancy shapes of Italian pasta require 4–8 minutes cooking time; macaroni requires 12–20 minutes and should be cut with scissors into 5mm rings after boiling; spaghetti requires 7–12 minutes and should be broken into 2cm lengths before boiling; noodles or vermicelli require only 5 minutes and should be broken into 2cm lengths before boiling. Drain the pasta and put it into a warmed tureen.

Heat the consommé to boiling point. Pour the hot consommé over the pasta, and serve.

Consommé with Rice

4–6 helpings

1 litre consommé (p335)

Garnish
25g Patna rice

Cook the rice in boiling salted water until just tender. Rinse and drain. Heat the consommé to boiling point, add the rice, and heat through.

Consommé with Sago or Tapioca

4–6 helpings

1 litre consommé (p335)

Garnish
25g sago **or** *tapioca*

Cook the grain in boiling salted water until just tender. Drain. Heat the consommé to boiling point, sprinkle in the grain, and serve.

VARIATION

Consommé with Semolina

Use 25g coarse semolina instead of sago or tapioca.

Iced Consommé

(Consommé Frappé)

6 helpings

*1 litre brown stock
    (p329) or chicken stock
    (p330) made with veal
    bones*

*1 × 15ml spoon dry
    sherry (approx)*
ice (optional)

Garnish
*chopped parsley, chives,
    and tarragon or
    chervil*
*finely diced raw
    cucumber*

*finely chopped hard-
    boiled egg white*
*small squares of skinned
    tomato*

Make the stock with veal bones to give a firmer jelly when it is iced. Clear the stock as for Consommé (p335). Season it carefully before cooling the consommé. When cool, add the sherry. Chill in a refrigerator, or in a bowl surrounded by ice, for 1–2 hours. The chilled consommé should be a soft jelly. Just before serving, whip the jelly lightly with a fork so that it is not quite solid. Serve in chilled soup bowls with one of the above garnishes.

Note Canned consommé can also be served iced. Check that it will 'jelly' by chilling it. Heat the canned consommé until liquid. Add a little dissolved gelatine, if necessary. Check the seasoning, leave to cool, then add sherry to taste. Chill, and serve as above.

Vegetable Consommé

4–6 helpings

*1 litre vegetable stock
    (p330)*
*25g piece each of carrot,
    celery, onion, and leek*

*white and crushed shell
    of 1 egg*
*1 × 5ml spoon yeast
    extract*

Garnish
*chopped fresh parsley,
    chives or tarragon*
diced raw cucumber

chopped skinned tomato
*cooked julienne or diced
    vegetables*

Put all the ingredients, apart from the garnish, into a deep saucepan. Heat slowly to simmering point,

whisking all the time, until a froth rises to the surface. Remove the whisk and simmer gently for 15 minutes. Strain the consommé slowly into a basin through a double layer of muslin or a scalded jelly bag. Return the consommé to the pan, re-heat, and garnish with one of the garnishes listed above.

Green Herb Consommé

6 helpings

*2 medium-sized
    tomatoes
    (100g approx)*
*1 litre white stock
    (p329) or chicken stock
    (p330)*
*a bunch of fresh mixed
    herbs (marjoram,
    basil, thyme)*

*white and crushed shell
    of 1 egg*
*1 × 2.5ml spoon lemon
    juice*
*50ml dry white wine
    (optional)*

Garnish
*1 × 15ml spoon shredded
    lettuce leaves*
*1 × 15ml spoon shredded
    spinach or sorrel
    leaves*
*1 × 15ml spoon small
    green peas*

*1 × 10ml spoon shredded
    cucumber rind*
extra white stock
6 mint leaves
6 chives
6 chervil leaves

Skin the tomatoes and dice the flesh. Heat the stock to boiling point and add the tomatoes and herbs. Add the white and shell and heat slowly to simmering point, whisking all the time, until a froth rises to the surface. Remove the whisk, cover, and simmer very gently for 30 minutes only. Strain slowly into a basin through muslin or a scalded jelly bag.

Meanwhile, cook the vegetables for the garnish separately in a little boiling stock until just tender. Chop the mint and the chives.

Heat the consommé to boiling point and add the cooked vegetables for the garnish with the stock in which they were cooked. Re-heat for 1 minute only. Just before serving, add the lemon juice, wine, if used, and chopped mint and chives. Float 1 chervil leaf on top of each helping.

Clear Tomato Soup

4–6 helpings

2 medium-sized tomatoes (150g approx)	1 litre consommé (p335) white and crushed shell of 1 egg

Garnish (optional)
orange **or** *lemon slices*   *1 × 15ml spoon each of diced carrot, celery, and green leek*

Skin the tomatoes and cut them into small pieces. Add to the consommé, heat to simmering point, and simmer for 10 minutes. Strain the consommé, then return it to the pan. Add the egg white and shell, re-heat slowly to simmering point, whisking all the time, until a froth rises to the surface. Strain slowly into a basin through muslin or a scalded jelly bag; if necessary, strain again.

Garnish, if liked, with orange or lemon slices. Alternatively, cook the diced vegetables separately in boiling salted water until tender. Drain and put in a warmed tureen. Re-heat the consommé and pour over them.

Clear Beetroot Soup

4 helpings

1 small raw beetroot (50g approx)	$\frac{1}{2} × 2.5ml$ spoon salt 4 black peppercorns
1 small onion (50g approx)	white and crushed shell of 1 egg
1 stick of celery (50g approx)	a few drops red food colouring
1 litre white stock (p329)	2 × 15ml spoons sherry

Garnish
1 egg white   *butter* **or** *margarine for greasing*

Prepare and slice the vegetables. Put into a saucepan with the stock, salt, and peppercorns, and heat to simmering point. Cover, reduce the heat, and simmer for 1 hour. Strain the soup through a sieve, and then return it to the pan. Add the egg white and shell, heat slowly to simmering point, whisking all the time, until a froth rises to the surface. Strain slowly into a basin through muslin or a scalded jelly bag; if necessary, strain again.

Put the egg white for the garnish in a small greased basin. Stand the basin in a pan of simmering water and steam the egg white until just firm. Turn out and cut it into tiny dice or fancy shapes. Rinse them in hot water.

Add the colouring to the cleared soup to give a pink colour. Re-heat the soup, add the sherry and garnish, and serve.

Serve with soured cream or yoghurt.

Mock Turtle Soup (1)

(clear)

8 helpings

2 litres white stock (p329), *made with* $\frac{1}{2}$ *calf's head* **or** 2 calf's feet instead of veal bones	white and crushed shell of 1 egg 75ml sherry 2 × 5ml spoons lemon juice

Prepare and soak the head, if used, as for Sheep's Head Broth (p334). Remove the brains and tongue and use for another dish. Wrap the head in clean muslin and tie firmly. If using calf's feet, scrub, scrape and blanch them, or have them prepared by the butcher. Make as for White Stock (p329).

Remove the head or feet, strain the soup through a sieve, leave to cool; then skim. Return it to the pan and add the egg white and shell. Heat slowly to simmering point, whisking all the time, until a froth rises to the surface. Strain slowly into a basin through muslin or a scalded jelly bag; if necessary, strain again. For each litre of the cleared soup, add 2 × 15ml spoons neat cubes of meat from the head, if used, the sherry, and lemon juice. Re-heat and serve.

Note For thick Mock Turtle Soup, see p344.

THICK SOUPS

Meat-based Soups

Chicken Purée Soup

4–6 helpings

1 litre chicken stock (p330)	*a pinch of grated nutmeg*
100g cooked chicken	*salt and pepper*
25g butter or margarine	*50ml single cream*
25g plain flour	
1 × 10ml spoon lemon juice	

Skim all the fat from the stock. Purée the chicken with a little of the stock. Melt the fat in a saucepan and add the flour. Stir for 1–2 minutes until cooked but not browned. Gradually add the rest of the stock and stir until boiling. Reduce the heat and simmer for 3 minutes, then gradually stir it into the chicken purée. Add the lemon juice and nutmeg, and season to taste. Return the mixture to the pan, add a little to the cream, fold into the rest of the soup, and re-heat without allowing it to boil.

Chicken Soup with Almonds

4–6 helpings

1 litre chicken stock (p330)	*a pinch of grated nutmeg*
25g ground almonds	*salt and pepper*
25g soft white bread	*2 egg yolks*
100g cooked chicken	*50ml milk*
1 × 10ml spoon lemon juice	*75ml single cream*

Heat the stock to boiling point, add the almonds and bread, reduce the heat, and simmer for 5 minutes. Rub the mixture through a metal sieve. Purée the chicken with a little of the stock mixture; then add it to the rest of the stock with the lemon juice. Re-heat. Add the nutmeg, and season to taste. Beat the yolks with the milk and cream and strain into the hot soup. Heat until the soup thickens, but do not allow it to boil.

Cream of Chicken Soup

4–6 helpings

25g cornflour	*1 × 5ml spoon lemon juice*
125ml milk	*a pinch of grated nutmeg*
1 litre chicken stock (p330)	*2 egg yolks*
50g cooked chicken	*2 × 15ml spoons single cream*
salt and pepper	

Blend the cornflour with a little of the milk. Heat the stock to boiling point and stir into the blended cornflour. Return the mixture to the pan and re-heat to boiling point, stirring all the time. Reduce the heat, cover, and simmer for 20 minutes. Cut the chicken into 5mm dice and heat these in the soup. Season to taste, and add the lemon juice and nutmeg. Beat the yolks with the rest of the milk and the cream; beat in a little hot soup, and fold into the rest of the soup. Heat until it thickens, but do not allow it to boil.

Cow-Heel Soup

4–6 helpings

1 cow-heel	*salt and pepper*
1.5 litres water	*25g fine tapioca or sago*
1 medium-sized onion (100g approx)	*1 × 5ml spoon lemon juice*
1 large carrot (100g approx)	*a pinch of grated nutmeg*
1 stick of celery	*1 × 15ml spoon chopped parsley*
bouquet garni	

Scrape and clean the cow-heel. Put in a saucepan, cover with cold water, and heat slowly to boiling point to blanch. Pour off the water. Divide the cow-heel into pieces. Put in a large saucepan with the water and heat to boiling point. Prepare the vegetables and cut into 5mm dice. Add to the pan with the bouquet garni. Cover, and simmer for 3½ hours. Remove the cow-heel and strain the soup. Remove some meat from the bone and cut into 5mm dice. Season the soup to taste. Re-heat to boiling point and sprinkle in the tapioca or sago. Cook until the grain is quite clear and soft. Add the pieces of meat, the lemon juice, nutmeg, and parsley.

Game Soup

4 helpings

remains of 1 roast pheasant **or** 2–3 smaller game birds	bouquet garni
	a blade of mace
50g lean bacon, without rinds	1 chicken's liver **or** 50g calf's liver
25g butter **or** margarine	25g flour
1 medium-sized onion (100g approx)	4 × 10ml spoons port **or** sherry (optional)
1 large carrot (100g approx)	salt and pepper
1 litre general household stock (p329) **or** game stock (p330)	

Cut any large pieces of meat from the carcass of the game birds and cut the bacon into small cubes. Melt the fat in a frying pan and fry the game pieces and bacon lightly. Put to one side. Prepare and slice the vegetables. Put the stock and game bones in a large stewpan and add the vegetables, bouquet garni, and mace. Heat to boiling point, cover, and simmer for 2–2½ hours.

Remove any skin and tubes from the liver; add the liver to the pan and simmer for another 15 minutes. Lift out the liver; then strain the soup through a colander into a clean pan. Discard the bones. Purée the liver and reserved meat and bacon with a little of the fat in the pan if a rich purée is wanted. Re-heat the rest of the fat in the pan, stir in the flour, and cook for 4–5 minutes, stirring all the time, until nut brown. Stir the roux gradually into the meat purée. Heat the soup to boiling point; then draw the pan off the heat. Stir in the purée mixture in small spoonfuls. Return to gentle heat and stir until the soup thickens to the preferred consistency. Add the port or sherry, if used, and season to taste.

Serve with fried bread croûtons or sprigs of watercress.

VARIATIONS

Game Soup with Chestnuts

4–6 helpings

Score 400g chestnuts on the rounded side of the shells. Boil them for 15 minutes. Drain, cool slightly, and remove the shells and skins. Follow the recipe as for Game Soup. Add the chestnuts with the stock and game bones, etc. Continue as for Game Soup, but omit the liver. Purée the chestnuts with the meat, and finish as for Game Soup.

Note If the soup is too thick, thin it to the required consistency with more general household (p329) or game stock (p330).

Game and Lentil Soup

4 helpings

Replace the carrot with 1 leek and omit the liver and flour. Follow the recipe as for Game Soup to the point where the soup is strained into a clean pan. Add 100g lentils to the soup and cook for 1 hour or until tender. Strain the lentils from the soup, mix them with the reserved meat, and purée the mixture. Stir one spoonful of the purée at a time into the soup, off the heat. Re-heat to boiling point, and season to taste. Remove from the heat, stir in 2 × 15ml spoons single cream, and serve at once.

Game Soup with Mushrooms

4 helpings

Follow the recipe as for Game Soup, but fry 100g prepared mushrooms with the pieces of game and bacon. After straining the soup, purée half of the mushrooms with the meat. Cut the rest of the mushrooms into thin strips and add them at the end when re-heating the soup.

Giblet Soup

4 helpings

2–3 sets chicken giblets	*1 stick of celery*
or *1 set of turkey* **or**	*bouquet garni*
goose giblets	*1 clove*
1 litre water	*a small blade of mace*
1 medium-sized onion	*6 black peppercorns*
(100g approx)	*1 × 5ml spoon salt*
1 medium-sized carrot	*25g butter* **or** *margarine*
(50g approx)	*25g flour*

Prepare the giblets if required (p624). Put them in a saucepan and add the cold water. Heat gently to simmering point. Prepare the vegetables and either leave them whole or chop coarsely. Add them to the pan with the bouquet garni, spices, peppercorns, and salt. Cover, and simmer for 2½ hours. Strain the stock. Melt the fat in a saucepan, stir in the flour, and brown very slowly, stirring all the time. Gradually add the stock and stir until boiling. Boil for 5 minutes, stirring all the time. Dice the best pieces of giblets finely and add to the soup. Re-season if required. Re-heat and serve.

Hare Soup

6 helpings

1 hare	*1 stick of celery*
1.5 litres general	*3 × 10ml spoons*
household stock (p329)	*dripping* **or** *lard*
or *water*	*bouquet garni*
1 medium-sized onion	*3 × 2.5ml spoons salt*
(100g approx)	*8 black peppercorns*
1 large carrot	*4 × 15ml spoons flour*
(100g approx)	*4 × 10ml spoons port*
½ turnip (25g approx)	
1 small parsnip	
(50g approx)	

Prepare and paunch the hare (p671) or ask the butcher to do it for you. Fillet the meat from the back and legs, and use for another recipe. Only the head, flaps, bones, and blood of the hare are used for the soup.

Split the head, break the bones, and put them and the meat trimmings into a large saucepan.

Cover with stock or water, and leave to stand for 1 hour. Prepare and slice the vegetables.

Heat the fat in a saucepan, add the vegetables, and fry until golden-brown. Lift out the vegetables and reserve the fat in the pan. Heat the bones and liquid very slowly to simmering point. Add the fried vegetables, bouquet garni, salt, and peppercorns. Cover, and simmer very gently for 3–4 hours.

Meanwhile, add the flour to the fat in the saucepan and fry gently, until golden-brown, stirring all the time. Strain the soup. Remove all pieces of meat from the bones and cut them into small dice. Whisk the fried flour into the soup and heat to boiling point, whisking all the time. Stir in the diced meat, blood, and port. Re-season if required. Re-heat gently without boiling.

Note Hare Soup can be served with Forcemeat Balls (p376 and p377).

For Mock Hare Soup, see p345.

Kidney Soup

4 helpings

200g ox kidney	*1 stick of celery*
25g plain flour	*1 litre general household*
25g dripping **or** *lard*	*stock* (p329)
1 medium-sized onion	*bouquet garni*
(100g approx)	*6 black peppercorns*
1 large carrot	*salt*
(100g approx)	*a little extra stock*
1 small turnip	**or** *cold water*
(50g approx)	

Skin, core, and cut the kidney into small pieces. Coat with flour. Keep any remaining flour to thicken the soup at the end. Heat the fat in a large saucepan. Fry the kidney lightly until just browned, then remove from the pan. Prepare and slice the vegetables. Fry them in the fat for about 5 minutes until they begin to brown. Drain off any excess fat. Add the stock, bouquet garni, and seasoning. Heat to boiling point, cover, reduce the heat, and simmer gently for 2 hours.

Remove the bouquet garni and strain the soup. Reserve a few pieces of kidney for the garnish.

Purée the rest of the kidney and add to the soup. Blend any remaining flour with a little stock or water, add it to the soup, and stir until boiling. Reduce the heat and simmer for 5 minutes. Chop the reserved kidney pieces and add to the soup. Re-season if required.

Note Kidney Soup can be served with Herb Dumplings (p386).

Liver Soup

4 helpings

1 medium-sized carrot (50g approx)	*½ × 2.5ml spoon yeast* **or** *meat extract*
1 medium-sized onion (100g approx)	*salt and pepper*
25g butter **or** *margarine*	*2 tomatoes (100g approx)*
25g flour	*200g calf's, ox* **or** *lamb's liver*
1 litre general household stock (p329)	*1 × 5ml spoon lemon juice*
a blade of mace	

Prepare and slice the carrot and onion. Melt the fat in a large saucepan, and fry the vegetables until they begin to brown. Add the flour, and fry gently until browned, stirring occasionally. Gradually add the stock and stir until boiling. Add the mace, yeast or meat extract, and seasoning. Cover, reduce the heat and simmer the soup for 1 hour.

Meanwhile, skin and chop the tomatoes. Add to the soup, cover, and continue simmering for another 30 minutes. Rub the soup through a fine sieve. Remove the skin and tubes from the liver, and mince or chop it finely. Whisk it into the soup with the lemon juice. Re-heat the soup and simmer until the liver just loses its red colour. Re-season if required.

Mulligatawny Soup

4 helpings

400g lean mutton, rabbit, stewing veal **or** *shin of beef*	*1 large carrot (100g approx)*
1 medium-sized onion (100g approx)	*¼ small parsnip (50g approx)*
1 small cooking apple (100g approx)	*bouquet garni*
25g butter **or** *margarine*	*1 × 2.5ml spoon lemon juice*
2 × 15ml spoons curry powder	*1 × 2.5ml spoon salt*
25g plain flour	*½ × 2.5ml spoon black treacle* **or** *extra lemon juice*
1 litre water	

Trim off any fat and cut the meat into small pieces. Prepare the onion and apple and chop them finely. Melt the fat in a deep saucepan and fry the onion and apple quickly for 2–3 minutes. Add the curry powder, cook gently for 2 minutes, then stir in the flour. Gradually add the water and stir until boiling. Add the meat. Prepare and slice the carrot and parsnip, and add to the pan with the bouquet garni, lemon juice, and salt. Simmer until the meat is very tender. This will take 2 hours for rabbit, 3 hours for stewing veal and mutton, and 4 hours for shin of beef.

Taste the soup, and add black treacle or more lemon juice to obtain a flavour that is neither predominantly sweet nor acid. Strain the soup. Dice some of the meat finely, add to the soup and re-heat.

Serve with boiled long-grain rice.

Note The amount of curry powder can be varied to taste; the quantity given above is for a mild-flavoured soup.

Mock Turtle Soup (2)

(thick)

8–12 helpings

½ calf's head **or**	3 cloves
1 sheep's head	a blade of mace
50g lean bacon, without	6 black peppercorns
rinds	2.5 litres water
1 medium-sized onion	1 × 10ml spoon salt
(100g approx)	flour **or** cornflour
1 large carrot	salt and pepper
(100g approx)	lemon juice
1 stick of celery	4 × 10ml spoons sherry
1 bay leaf	(optional)
bouquet garni	

Prepare the head as for Sheep's Head Broth (p334). Chop the bacon. Prepare and slice the vegetables. Put them into a large saucepan with the head, bacon, herbs, and spices. Add the water and salt. Heat to boiling point, cover, and simmer for 3–4 hours.

Strain the soup. Cut some of the meat from the head into 1cm dice. Measure the soup. Blend 25g flour or cornflour with a little cold water for each litre of soup. Stir it into the soup and re-heat to thicken. Season, add lemon juice to taste and the sherry, if used. Add the pieces of meat to the soup and heat through before serving.

Note For clear Mock Turtle Soup, see p339.

Ox Cheek Soup

6–8 helpings

½ ox head and 4 litres	1 stick of celery
water **or** 1 ox cheek	3 × 10ml spoons
and 2 litres water	dripping
1 medium-sized onion	bouquet garni
(100g approx)	1 bay leaf
1 large carrot	3 × 2.5ml spoons salt
(100g approx)	8 black peppercorns
½ turnip (25g approx)	4 × 15ml spoons flour
1 small parsnip	4 × 10ml spoons port

Prepare the ox head or cheek as for Sheep's Head Broth (p334) or Stewed Ox Cheek (p513). Split the head, if used, and separate the bones. Put them or the ox cheek in a large saucepan, cover with the water, and soak for 1 hour. Prepare and slice the vegetables. Heat the dripping in a saucepan and fry the vegetables until they begin to brown. Remove the vegetables and reserve the fat in the pan. Heat the pan with the ox head or cheek very slowly to simmering point. Add the fried vegetables, bouquet garni, bay leaf, salt and peppercorns; cover, and simmer very gently for 3–4 hours.

Meanwhile, add the flour to the dripping in the saucepan and fry gently until golden-brown. Strain the soup. Remove any meat from the bones. Dice the pieces of meat and return these to the soup. Whisk in the browned flour. Re-heat the soup to boiling point, whisking all the time. Add the port. Re-season if required.

Oxtail Soup

4–6 helpings

1 oxtail	1 stick of celery
25g beef dripping	1 litre water **or** general
1 medium-sized onion	household stock (p329)
(100g approx)	1 × 5ml spoon salt
1 large carrot	bouquet garni
(100g approx)	6 black peppercorns
1 turnip (25g approx)	25g plain flour

Wash, trim off any fat, and joint the tail. Heat the dripping in a saucepan. Add half the jointed tail and fry until the meat is browned. Lift out the meat and reserve the fat in the pan. Prepare and slice the vegetables. Fry in the hot dripping until golden-brown, then remove. Put all the oxtail and the fried vegetables into a deep saucepan. Add the water or stock, and heat very slowly to boiling point. Add the salt, bouquet garni, and peppercorns. Cover, and simmer very gently for 3–4 hours.

Meanwhile, stir the flour into the dripping in the saucepan and fry gently until golden-brown. Strain the soup. Remove all the meat from the bones. Return some of the smaller pieces of meat and any small slices of carrot to the soup. Whisk in the browned flour. Re-heat the soup to boiling point, whisking all the time. Re-season if required.

Rabbit and Bacon Soup

6–8 helpings

1 rabbit	*2 medium-sized onions*
100g lean bacon **or**	*(200g approx)*
pickled pork	*2 cloves*
2 litres water **or** *general*	*4 × 15ml spoons plain*
household stock (p329)	*flour*
bouquet garni	*125ml milk* **or** *75ml*
1 bay leaf	*milk and 50ml cream*
a blade of mace	*salt and pepper*
1 small turnip	*1 × 5ml spoon lemon*
(25–50g approx)	*juice*
2 sticks celery	

Prepare and joint the rabbit (pp671–72). Blanch it by covering it with cold water in a saucepan and heating to boiling point. Drain and rinse. Put the rabbit and whole piece of bacon or pork in a large saucepan. Cover with the water or stock. Add the bouquet garni, bay leaf, and mace. Heat to boiling point, cover, and simmer very gently for 1 hour.

Meanwhile, cut the turnip and celery into 5mm dice. Skin the onions and press a clove in each. Add the vegetables to the soup, cover, and simmer for a further 1½ hours. Strain the soup. Remove and dice some meat from the bones. (The rest of the rabbit meat can be used for a fricassée or similar dish.) Dice the bacon or pork. Add the diced meat to the soup. Blend the flour with the milk or milk and cream and stir it into the soup. Heat until the soup is thickened, stirring all the time. (If cream is used, add it to the hot soup, off the heat, and serve at once.) Season to taste and add the lemon juice.

Note The internal organs of rabbit have a strong flavour and so can be used or left out, as preferred.

Shin of Beef Soup

6 helpings

500g lean shin of beef	*1 stick of celery*
25g beef dripping	*1 litre water* **or** *general*
1 medium-sized onion	*household stock* (p329)
(100g approx)	*1 × 5ml spoon salt*
1 large carrot	*bouquet garni*
(100g approx)	*6 black peppercorns*
a piece of turnip	*25g plain flour*
(25g approx)	

Slice the meat very finely across the fibres. Heat the dripping in a frying pan. Add half the meat, and fry until browned on all sides. Remove the meat and reserve the fat in the pan. Prepare and slice the vegetables. Add them to the hot fat and fry until golden-brown. Lift out the vegetables and put them into a deep saucepan with all of the meat and the water or stock. Heat very slowly to boiling point. Add the salt, bouquet garni, and pepper-corns, cover, and simmer very gently for 3–4 hours.

Meanwhile, stir the flour into the dripping and fry until golden-brown. Strain the soup. Add some of the very small pieces of meat to the soup. Whisk in the browned flour. Heat to boiling point, whisking all the time. Re-season if required.

Note The rest of the meat can be minced and served with another dish.

VARIATION

Mock Hare Soup

After thickening the soup, add 1 × 5ml spoon red-currant jelly, 1 × 10ml spoon Worcestershire sauce, and 25–50ml port. Simmer for 10 minutes. Garnish, if liked, with tiny Forcemeat Balls (p376) poached in a little of the soup for 20 minutes.

Note For Hare Soup, see p342.

Turkey Soup

4–6 helpings

carcass and trimmings of 1 turkey	1 stick of celery
25g lean bacon, without rinds	25g plain flour
25g butter **or** margarine	1 litre water for each 400g cooked turkey remains
1 medium-sized onion (100g approx)	bouquet garni
1 large carrot (100g approx)	1 clove
½ parsnip (50g approx)	25–50g breast of turkey
	salt and pepper

Weigh the carcass and trimmings. Break the carcass into pieces. Dice the bacon. Heat the fat in a saucepan. Add the carcass pieces, meat trimmings, and bacon, and fry until browned. Remove them and reserve the fat in the pan. Prepare and slice the vegetables. Add them to the pan and fry until golden-brown. Add the flour and fry gently until golden-brown. Stir in the water and heat to boiling point. Add the bouquet garni and clove. Return the turkey carcass, trimmings, and bacon to the pan. Cover, and simmer for 1½–2 hours.

Meanwhile, cut the pieces of breast meat into 5mm dice. Strain the soup. Add the diced meat, and re-heat. Season to taste.

Note Leftover pieces of stuffing improve the flavour and help to thicken the soup.

Fish Soups, Bisques, and Chowders

Bouillabaisse

This famous French dish is a mixed fish pot-au-feu stew, made in different ways in different areas, and often served as soup. It originated in Marseilles whose people still claim to make the only authentic bouillabaisse. It is almost impossible to make this dish further north than the Mediterranean area because its essential ingredients are fresh Mediterranean sea and shellfish (preferably cooked alive). They always include the *rascasse* and, almost always, angler fish, John Dory, red mullet, and crawfish. Other fish include weever, gurnard, and whiting; mussels or baby crabs are sometimes added in their shells. The stew is based on a stock made with vegetables such as onions, tomatoes, etc, well flavoured with fresh herbs such as fennel leaves, and with olive oil and saffron. The shellfish are put in first, the firm-fleshed fish a few minutes later. The stew is boiled fast for 12–20 minutes so that the fish do not disintegrate and each flavour remains distinct. Plenty of seasoning, especially pepper, is added. The fish broth is strained over slices of dried (not toasted) bread, and the fish is served separately.

A bouillabaisse-style stew can be made by following the recipe for Fisherman's Hot Pot (p347). Omit the cabbage, leek and potato; add tomatoes and fresh fennel leaves, and use an assortment of small shellfish as well as white fish. The fish must be very fresh and olive oil should be used for the cooking.

Crab Soup

4–6 helpings

200g onions	1 × 10ml spoon lemon juice
600g fresh **or** canned tomatoes	a pinch of grated nutmeg
1 clove of garlic	salt and pepper
25g butter	50ml dry white wine
a bunch of herbs (parsley, basil, fennel **or** tarragon)	1 medium-sized cooked fresh crab (1.5kg approx) **or**
a pinch of powdered saffron	1 × 150g can crabmeat
a small strip of lemon rind	1 litre water
	125ml single cream

Prepare and slice the onions and fresh tomatoes, if used. If using canned tomatoes, drain off the juice, use it to replace an equal quantity of the measured water, and slice the tomatoes. Skin the garlic. Melt the butter in a deep saucepan. Add the onions and whole garlic clove and fry gently for 10 minutes. Add the tomatoes, herbs, lemon rind and lemon juice, nutmeg, and seasoning to taste. Heat to simmering point, cover, and simmer for 20 minutes.

Add the wine and boil for 2 minutes. Pick the crabmeat from the shell (p423) or drain the canned crabmeat. Add the crabmeat and the water to the pan. Re-heat to boiling point, cover, reduce the heat, and simmer for 20 minutes. Remove the herbs, garlic, and lemon rind. Rub the soup through a wire sieve, or process in an electric blender. Re-season if required. Stir in the cream; re-heat carefully without boiling the soup.

Eel Soup

6 helpings

500g eels	a strip of lemon rind
1 large onion	1 × 5ml spoon lemon
(200g approx)	juice
25g butter	salt and pepper
1.25 litres water	25g flour
bouquet garni	25ml milk
a blade of mace	100ml single cream

Wash, dry, and skin the eels and cut them into small pieces. Skin and slice the onion. Melt the butter in a saucepan, add the eel and onion, and fry gently for 10 minutes without browning them. Add the water and heat to boiling point. Add the bouquet garni, mace, lemon rind and lemon juice, and seasoning to taste. Cover the pan and simmer very gently until the eel is tender.

Strain the soup. Transfer the pieces of eel to a warmed dish and keep warm. Blend the flour with the milk. Stir it into the soup, re-heat, and boil for 2–3 minutes until the flour thickens the soup. Re-season if required. Draw the pan off the heat and stir in the cream and the pieces of eel. Re-heat without boiling the soup.

Note The eels take about 1 hour to cook altogether.

Fisherman's Hot Pot

4 helpings

50g white cabbage	150ml Muscadet **or**
100g leek	other dry white wine
250g potatoes	1 litre water
100g onions	50g concentrated tomato
25g red pepper	purée
2 slices white bread	1 chicken stock cube
50ml cooking oil	bouquet garni
25g butter	1 clove of garlic
250g cod **or** other white	salt and pepper
fish fillets (see **Note**)	

Garnish
1 × 15ml spoon chopped
  parsley

Shred the cabbage, slice the leek and potatoes, chop the onion and pepper. Remove the crusts from the bread, cut into 1cm cubes, and dry in the oven for 10 minutes.

Heat the oil and butter in a large saucepan, add the vegetables, cover, and cook gently for 7–8 minutes; do not let them colour. Skin the fish, cut them into 3cm cubes, and fry for 3 minutes with the vegetables, turning them over to firm the surface of the cubes. Pour in the wine, water, and tomato purée. Crumble in the stock cube. Skin and crush the garlic. Add the bouquet garni and garlic, and season to taste. Heat to simmering point and simmer for 20 minutes. Discard the bouquet garni. Pour into a soup tureen and sprinkle with the chopped parsley.

Serve with sippets of bread (p385).

Note Any white fish can be used for the hot pot, eg haddock, hake, whiting, ling, etc.

Haddock, Cod or Skate Soup

4–6 helpings

600g haddock, cod,
  skate **or** any available
  white fish
2 large onions
  (400g approx)
1 large carrot
  (100g approx)
2 sticks celery
200g potatoes
25g butter
2 × 10ml spoons olive oil

1 × 5ml spoon curry
  powder
750ml boiling water
bouquet garni
salt and pepper
50ml white wine
  (optional)
25g flour
125ml milk
75ml single cream

Prepare the fish and cut them into small pieces. Prepare the onions, carrot, and celery and slice thinly. Peel and dice the potatoes. Heat the butter and olive oil in a deep saucepan. Add all the vegetables and fry gently for 10 minutes. Stir in the curry powder and cook for 3 minutes. Add the boiling water, bouquet garni, and seasoning to taste. Add the fish and re-heat the soup to simmering point; cover, and simmer until the fish is tender.

Transfer the best pieces of fish from the soup and keep them hot in a little of the liquid. Simmer the rest of the soup, uncovered, for 15 minutes until it is reduced. Remove the bouquet garni and rub the soup through a sieve, or process in an electric blender. Add the wine, if used, and re-heat the soup. Blend the flour with a little of the cold milk and then stir in the rest of the milk. Stir it into the soup and heat to boiling point. Add the pieces of fish and the cream to the soup at boiling point, but do not reboil.

Mussel Soup

4–6 helpings

800g live mussels
125ml white wine
1 × 10ml spoon lemon
  juice
750ml fish stock (p330)
25g butter

2 × 15ml spoons flour
salt and pepper
2 × 10ml spoons
  chopped parsley
1 egg yolk
75ml single cream

Scrub and beard the mussels (p425). Put them in a deep saucepan. Add the wine, lemon juice, and 250ml of the fish stock. Heat the mussels in the liquid until they open. Strain the liquid through muslin into the rest of the fish stock. Shell the mussels. Melt the butter in a deep saucepan. Stir in the fish stock, and heat to boiling point; boil for 2 minutes, stirring all the time. Season to taste and add the parsley. Mix the egg yolk with the cream, and add with the mussels to the soup at just below boiling point. Re-heat gently, without boiling the soup, to cook the egg.

Note Other shellfish can be cooked in the same way.

Spiced Fish Soup

6 helpings

500g white fish, eg cod
  or haddock
25g cornflour
2 × 15ml spoons soy
  sauce

1 shallot (25g approx)
1.5 litres water
a pinch of salt (optional)

Wash, skin, and bone the fish and cut them into small pieces. Blend the cornflour with the soy sauce. Coat the fish pieces in the mixture. Skin and chop the shallot. Put the water in a saucepan and heat to boiling point. Add the shallot, seasoned fish, and salt, if needed. Re-heat to simmering point and simmer for 15 minutes.

Crayfish Bisque

4–6 helpings

750ml fish stock (p330)	a pinch of grated
3 × 15ml spoons soft	nutmeg
white breadcrumbs	100ml white wine **or**
12 crayfish	cider
salt and pepper	1 egg yolk
50g butter	125ml single cream **or**
6 canned anchovy fillets	milk **or** half cream and
1 × 5ml spoon lemon	half milk
juice	

Heat 250ml of the fish stock to boiling point. Pour it over the breadcrumbs and allow to soak for 10 minutes. Rinse the crayfish and remove the intestinal tract (p424). Drop the fish into fast boiling, salted water and boil for 10 minutes. Drain, and remove the shells.

Melt half the butter in a deep saucepan. Add the shelled crayfish and anchovies, and toss in the butter over gentle heat for 5 minutes. Add the lemon juice, nutmeg, and breadcrumbs in stock; heat gently for 5 minutes. Beat in the rest of the butter. Pound this paste and rub it through a metal sieve. Return to the pan and gradually stir in the wine or cider and the rest of the fish stock. Heat to boiling point. Draw off the heat and season the soup to taste. Mix the egg yolk with the cream or milk or both. Blend a little of the hot bisque into the egg mixture. Add to the rest of the bisque and stir over low heat, without boiling, to thicken the egg.

Crab and Corn Bisque
See p1411.

Lobster Bisque

4–6 helpings

shell, trimmings, and a	1 × 5ml spoon anchovy
little of the flesh of a	essence
small **or** medium-sized	125ml white wine
lobster	750ml fish stock (p330)
1 medium-sized onion	salt
(75g approx)	1 × 15ml spoon cooked
1 medium-sized carrot	lobster coral
(50g approx)	50g butter
1 clove of garlic	25g flour
1 bay leaf	125ml single cream
a blade of mace	pepper
1 × 5ml spoon lemon	a few drops red food
juice	colouring (optional)

Crush the lobster shell. Flake the rough pieces of flesh finely, keeping the neat pieces for a garnish. Prepare the onion, carrot, and garlic and slice them thinly. Put the shell, flaked lobster, vegetables, bay leaf, mace, lemon juice, anchovy essence, and wine into a deep saucepan. Heat quickly to boiling point and cook briskly for 3–5 minutes. The alcohol in the wine extracts much of the flavour from the lobster and vegetables. Add the fish stock and a little salt. Heat to boiling point, cover, reduce the heat, and simmer for 1 hour.

Strain the soup through a metal sieve and rub through any pieces of firm lobster. Pound the lobster coral with half the butter and rub through a sieve. Melt the rest of the butter in a saucepan and stir in the flour. Gradually add the strained soup and stir until boiling. When at boiling point, whisk in the lobster coral butter. Remove the pan from the heat and stir in the cream. Add salt and pepper to taste. Add the food colouring, if necessary, to obtain a deep orange-pink colour. Add any neat pieces of lobster. Re-heat without boiling the soup.

Note Live lobsters can be used. See p424 for the methods of killing lobsters.

Prawn Bisque

4–6 helpings

100g butter	1 egg yolk
250g cooked shelled prawns	125ml single cream **or** milk **or** half cream and half milk
25g flour	salt and pepper
750ml fish stock (p330) in which prawn shells have been cooked	lemon juice
125ml white wine	a pinch of grated nutmeg
125ml court bouillon (p429)	

Melt 25g of the butter in a saucepan. Add the prawns, and toss over gentle heat for 5 minutes. Pound the prawns, gradually working in another 50g of the butter. Rub the pounded prawn and butter mixture through a sieve, or process briefly in an electric blender. Melt the remaining 25g butter in a deep saucepan. Stir in the flour and cook gently for 1–2 minutes. Strain the fish stock and gradually stir it into the flour with the wine and court bouillon. Heat to boiling point. Mix the egg yolk with the cream or milk or both. Season the soup and add lemon juice and nutmeg to taste. Whisk the prawn butter into the soup, at just below boiling point, adding a small pat at a time. Add the egg yolk and cream mixture and stir over low heat, without boiling, to thicken the egg.

VARIATION

Shrimp Bisque

Substitute shrimps for the prawns.

Shrimp Bisque with Wine

4–6 helpings

750ml fish stock (p330) in which the shells of the shrimps have been cooked	1 × 5ml spoon lemon juice
3 × 15ml spoons soft white breadcrumbs	100ml white wine **or** cider
50g butter	salt and pepper
250g cooked shelled shrimps	1 egg yolk
a pinch of grated nutmeg	125ml single cream **or** milk **or** half cream and half milk

Heat 250ml stock to boiling point. Pour it over the breadcrumbs and soak for 10 minutes. Melt 25g butter in a pan. Add the shrimps and toss over gentle heat for 5 minutes. Add the nutmeg, lemon juice, and breadcrumbs in their stock, and heat gently for 5 minutes. Beat in the rest of the butter. Pound the paste and rub through a metal sieve, or process in an electric blender. Gradually add the wine or cider and the rest of the stock. Heat to boiling point. Remove from the heat and season to taste. Mix the yolk with the cream or milk or both. Blend a little hot bisque into the egg mixture. Add to the rest of the bisque and stir over low heat to thicken the egg.

VARIATION

Substitute prawns for the shrimps.

White Fish Chowder

4 helpings

125ml dry white wine	75g leek
1 litre water	75g carrot
bouquet garni	50g butter
salt and pepper	50g flour
400g skinned coley fillets **or** other coarse-fleshed white fish	1 × 5ml spoon turmeric
	3 × 15ml spoons chopped parsley

Put the wine, water, bouquet garni, and seasoning in a pan and poach the fish gently in the liquid until tender. Meanwhile, prepare and dice the leek and carrot. Strain the soup into a clean pan. Remove the bouquet garni and cut the fish into 1.5cm cubes. Return the pan to the heat and heat to simmering point. Cream the butter and flour to a smooth paste, then add it gradually to the soup, whisking in each addition. Stir in the turmeric. Add the diced vegetables and simmer gently for 7 minutes. Add the fish and the parsley. Simmer for a further 5 minutes.

Serve hot with crusty bread.

Channel Chowder

4 helpings

400g onions	400g tomatoes
½ green pepper	1 bay leaf
75g streaky bacon, without rinds	salt and pepper
	100ml fish stock (p330)
25g butter	
400g skinned dogfish fillets or similar white fish	

Garnish
chopped parsley

Prepare and chop the onions and pepper. Chop the bacon. Melt the butter in a frying pan and fry the vegetables and bacon gently for 4–5 minutes. Put them in a casserole with the fish. Skin the tomatoes, remove the seeds, and chop the flesh roughly. Add to the casserole. Place the bay leaf on the top, season well, and pour the fish stock over the ingredients. Cover, and bake in a moderate oven at 180°C, Gas 4, for 45 minutes. Serve hot, garnished with the parsley.

Puréed Vegetable Soups

Vegetable Soup (1)

Basic recipe

4 helpings

500g vegetables (approx)	salt and pepper
	125ml milk
15–25g butter, margarine or other fat	2 × 10ml spoons thickening (flour, cornflour, ground rice, tapioca, or potato) for each 500ml puréed soup
500ml–1 litre white stock (p329) or general household stock (p329)	
bouquet garni or flavouring herbs	cold stock, water or milk
lemon juice	

For Cream of Vegetable Soup (1)
add
4–8 × 15ml spoons
single cream and/or 1 egg yolk

Prepare and chop the vegetables. Melt the fat in a deep saucepan, add the vegetables, and fry gently for 5–10 minutes without browning them. Add the stock, bouquet garni or herbs, lemon juice, and seasoning to taste. Heat to boiling point, reduce the heat, and simmer gently until the vegetables are quite soft. Do not overcook.

Remove the bouquet garni. Purée the vegetables and liquid by either rubbing through a fine sieve, or by processing in an electric blender. Add the milk, measure the soup, and return it to a clean pan. Weigh the thickening in the correct proportion and blend it with a little cold stock, water or milk. Stir it into the soup. Bring to the boil, stirring all the time, and cook for 5 minutes. Re-season if required.

Serve with croûtons, Melba or fairy toast (p385).

Note To make a cream of vegetable soup, remove the pan from the heat after the soup has been thickened and leave to cool slightly. Add a little of the hot soup to the single cream (which can replace some of the milk in the main recipe) and egg yolk, if using, and beat well. Whisk the mixture into the rest of the soup. Return the soup to gentle heat and re-heat, without boiling, stirring all the time.

For Vegetable Soup (2), see p359.

Jerusalem Artichoke Soup

(Palestine Soup)

4 helpings

500g Jerusalem artichokes	lemon juice
white vinegar	salt and pepper
1 medium-sized onion (100g approx)	125ml milk
25g butter **or** margarine	2 × 10ml spoons cornflour for each 500ml puréed soup
500ml white stock (p329)	cold stock, water **or** milk

For Cream of Jerusalem Artichoke Soup
add
4 × 15ml spoons single
  cream

Scrape the artichokes and put each one into water acidulated with a little vinegar. Rinse and dry them. Proceed as for Vegetable Soup (1) (p351) for both Jerusalem Artichoke and Cream of Jerusalem Artichoke Soup.

Note The lemon juice improves the flavour and whiteness of the soup.

Celeriac Soup

4 helpings

300g celeriac	salt and pepper
1 medium-sized onion (100g approx)	125ml milk
25g butter **or** margarine	2 × 10ml spoons cornflour for each
500ml white stock (p329)	500ml puréed soup
lemon juice	cold stock, water **or** milk

For Cream of Celeriac Soup
add
4 × 15ml spoons single
  cream

Make as for Vegetable Soup (1) (p351) for both Celeriac Soup and Cream of Celeriac Soup. The celeriac will take 45–60 minutes to cook.

Carrot Soup

(Potage à la Crecy)

4 helpings

400g carrots	bouquet garni
1 medium-sized onion (100g approx)	a little meat **or** yeast extract
2 sticks celery	lemon juice
½ small turnip **or** swede (25g approx)	salt and pepper
a few bacon scraps, without rinds	125ml milk
15g butter **or** margarine	2 × 10ml spoons cornflour for each 500ml puréed soup
500ml general household stock (p329)	cold stock, water **or** milk

For Cream of Carrot Soup
add

4–8 × 15ml spoons single cream	1 egg yolk

Make as for Vegetable Soup (1) (p351) for both Carrot Soup and Cream of Carrot Soup.

Cream of Cauliflower Soup

4 helpings

1 medium-sized cauliflower (300–400g after trimming)	salt and pepper
	125ml milk
1 medium-sized onion (100g approx)	2 × 10ml spoons cornflour for each 500ml puréed soup
25g butter **or** margarine	cold stock, water **or** milk
500ml white stock (p329)	4 × 15ml spoons single cream
bouquet garni	1 egg yolk
lemon juice	

Remove the green leaves from the cauliflower but keep all the stalk. Remove the end of the stalk and cut the rest into small, even-sized pieces. Break the head of the cauliflower into florets, and then proceed as for Vegetable Soup (1) (p351). The cauliflower should be cooked for the shortest possible time or its flavour will be spoilt.

Starters

Mixed Hors d'Oeuvre Wheel (p315)

TOP *Platter of Pork Meats* (p326)

LEFT *Kipper Mousse* (p324)

RIGHT *Eggs Courtet* (p317)

Hotch Potch (p333),
a broth made with
vegetables which can be
varied according to
season

Green Pea Soup (p354) *with Liver Dumplings* (p387)

The base of the globe artichoke (back of picture) is the tenderest part of this starter (see pp744–45)

Celery Soup

4 helpings

400–500g outer sticks celery	salt and pepper
1 medium-sized onion (100g approx)	125ml milk
25g butter **or** margarine	2 × 10ml spoons cornflour for each
500ml white stock (p329)	500ml puréed soup
25ml lemon juice	cold stock, water **or** milk

For Cream of Celery Soup
add
4 × 15ml spoons single cream

Make as for Vegetable Soup (1) (p351) for both Celery Soup and Cream of Celery Soup. Cook the celery without boiling or it will become stringy and difficult to sieve.

Chestnut Soup

4 helpings

400g shelled chestnuts **or** 600g in shells (approx)	salt and pepper
1 medium-sized onion (100g approx)	a little meat **or** yeast extract
25g butter	a pinch of sugar
1 litre white stock (p329)	a pinch of ground cinnamon
lemon juice	a pinch of grated nutmeg

For Cream of Chestnut Soup
add
125ml single cream
(optional)

Shell the chestnuts, if necessary. Make as for Vegetable Soup (1) (p351) for both Chestnut Soup and Cream of Chestnut Soup. Add the spices very sparingly so that they enhance but do not overpower the chestnut flavour. No thickening is required for Chestnut Soup; add the cream for Cream of Chestnut Soup, if liked.

Cucumber and Potato Soup

4–6 helpings

400g potatoes	salt and pepper
1 medium-sized onion (100g approx)	1 pickled dill cucumber (75g approx)
25g butter	½ small bunch of chives
500ml white stock (p329) **or** water	a sprig of mint
125ml milk	a sprig of parsley
2 ridge cucumbers **or** 1 long cucumber	

Make as for Vegetable Soup (1) (p351). Peel and grate the raw cucumbers and add them to the soup after it has been puréed. Season to taste. Heat to boiling point. Chop finely the pickled cucumber, chives, mint, and parsley. Add to the soup and simmer gently for 5 minutes. Serve hot.

Cream of Cucumber Soup

4 helpings

500g cucumber	cold stock, water **or** milk
25g butter	a sprig of mint
6 spring onions	a sprig of parsley
500ml white stock (p329)	a few drops green food colouring
salt and pepper	4 × 15ml spoons single cream
lemon juice	
2 × 10ml spoons cornflour for each 500ml puréed soup	

Peel the cucumber. Reserve a 5cm length for a garnish and slice the rest. Melt the butter in a deep saucepan and cook the onions gently, without browning them, for 10 minutes. Add the stock, sliced cucumber, seasoning, and lemon juice to taste. Proceed as for Vegetable Soup (1) (p351).

Cut the reserved cucumber into 5mm dice, boil these in a little stock or water until just tender and add them to the finished soup. Five minutes before serving the soup, add the mint and parsley, and tint the soup pale green. Stir in the cream and serve at once.

French or Runner Bean Soup

4 helpings

400g young beans	a few parsley stalks
100g potatoes	a sprig of savory
1 medium-sized onion	salt and pepper
(100g approx)	125ml milk
25g butter	
500ml water or white	
stock (p329)	

Reserve 2 or 3 beans for a garnish. Make as for Vegetable Soup (1) (p351), cooking the beans, potatoes, and onion in the stock for not more than 30 minutes, before sieving them. No thickening is required.

Cut the reserved beans into diamond-shaped sections, boil in a little stock or water until just tender, and add them to the finished soup.

Green Pea Soup

4 helpings

600g green peas in the pod	2 × 10ml spoons cornflour for each 500ml puréed soup
1 medium-sized onion (100g approx)	cold stock, water or milk
a few spinach leaves	salt and pepper
1 × 10ml spoon butter	sugar
500ml white stock (p329)	a few drops green food colouring (optional)
a sprig of mint	
a few parsley stalks	

For Cream of Green Pea Soup
add
4 × 15ml spoons single
cream (see Method)

Garnish
a few shelled peas	4 × 15ml spoons chilled whipping cream

Shell the peas and wash half the pods. Trim off any hard parts. Skin and slice the onion. Wash the spinach leaves and chop them roughly. Melt the butter in a deep saucepan, add the washed pods and onion, and fry very gently for 10 minutes. Add the stock and heat to boiling point. Add the peas, spinach leaves, and herbs. Simmer for 10–20 minutes or until the peas are just cooked. Proceed as for Vegetable Soup (1) (p351). Season to taste with salt, pepper, and sugar; add the colouring, if liked. Stir in the cream, if used, at boiling point, off the heat.

Meanwhile, cook the peas for the garnish in boiling salted water until just tender. Whip the cream until stiff. Add the cooked peas and blobs of whipped cream to the soup just before serving.

Note Instead of the garnish above, the soup may be served with Liver Dumplings (p387).

VARIATION

Saint Germain Soup

Add 1 whole garlic clove, 1 small diced carrot, and 1 small diced potato with the peas and herbs. Remove the garlic clove before thickening the soup. Thicken it with cornflour and cream.

Herb Soup

6 helpings

400g mixed lettuce and spinach or sorrel leaves	1 clove of garlic or 4 spring onions
5cm piece of cucumber	1 litre boiling water
a sprig each of parsley, thyme, marjoram, tarragon, savory, basil and mint, or a selection of at least 4 different types	salt
	lemon juice
	6 chopped chives leaves

Wash the lettuce and spinach or sorrel leaves and chop them roughly, reserving a few leaves for a garnish. Peel and chop the cucumber. Tie the herbs in a bunch, reserving a few leaves of each for the garnish. Skin the garlic, if used. Drop the chopped leaves, cucumber, herbs, and garlic or onions into the fast boiling water. Cover, reduce the heat, and simmer for 20 minutes. Rub the soup through a fine sieve. Add salt and lemon juice to taste. Shred the leaves and herbs for the garnish and add them with the chives. Boil for 1 minute. Serve hot, or chill and serve iced. If served iced, the garnish should only be chopped and added just before serving.

Note This soup is not suitable for use as a cream soup.

Hot Vichyssoise Cream Soup

4 helpings

250g leeks, white parts only	salt and pepper
250g potatoes	125ml milk
25g butter	4–8 × 15ml spoons
500ml white stock (p329)	single cream

Make as for Vegetable Soup (1) (p351). No thickening is required.

VARIATION

Iced Vichyssoise

Make as above but chill the soup well before serving it.

Italian Tomato Soup

4 helpings

600g fresh tomatoes	a pinch of dried
1 × 15ml spoon olive oil	marjoram
500ml white stock (p329)	salt and pepper
1 clove of garlic	2 × 10ml spoons ground rice
a sprig of parsley	4 × 15ml spoons single cream (optional)
a pinch of dried basil	1 egg yolk (optional)

Chop the tomatoes finely to shorten their cooking time. Proceed as for Vegetable Soup (1) (p351), but cook the tomatoes in the stock for 5 minutes only before sieving them.

Note This soup can be iced if it is not thickened. Sprinkle in 4 × 10ml spoons finely sieved brown breadcrumbs before chilling it.

Broad Bean Soup

4 helpings

400g shelled broad beans	125ml milk
1 medium-sized onion (100g approx)	2 × 10ml spoons cornflour for each 500ml puréed soup
1 × 10ml spoon butter	cold stock, water or milk
25g lean bacon scraps, without rinds	salt and pepper
500ml white stock (p329)	caster sugar
a sprig of savory	lemon juice
	chopped parsley

For Cream of Broad Bean Soup
add

4–8 × 15ml spoons single cream	1 egg yolk

Unless the beans are young, cook them for 10 minutes in boiling salted water; then drain, and remove the skins. Skin and slice the onion. Melt the butter in a deep saucepan, add the onion and bacon scraps, and fry gently for 10 minutes. Add the stock and savory, heat to boiling point, then add the beans. Re-heat to boiling point and simmer gently for about 20 minutes or until the beans are softened. Proceed as for Vegetable Soup (1) (p351) for both Broad Bean and Cream of Broad Bean Soup. Add salt, pepper, sugar, and lemon juice to taste. Sprinkle with the parsley just before serving.

Cream of Leek Soup

4–5 helpings

400g thick leeks, white parts only	4 × 15ml spoons single cream (optional)
300g potatoes	250ml milk
1 × 10ml spoon butter or margarine	salt and pepper
500ml water or white stock (p329)	1 egg yolk (optional)

Make as for Vegetable Soup (1) (p351). The leeks should be cut into 1cm lengths to make them easier to sieve. No thickening is required.

Lettuce Soup

4 helpings

400g lettuce	1 × 10ml spoon butter
1 medium-sized onion	bouquet garni
(100g approx)	salt and pepper
200g potatoes	125ml milk
1 clove of garlic	sugar
500ml white stock	
(p329)	

Wash and shred the lettuce. Prepare and slice the onion and potatoes. Skin and crush the garlic. Heat the stock to boiling point and pour it over the lettuce. Melt the butter in a deep saucepan. Add the onion, potato, and garlic, and fry them gently for 10 minutes. Add the lettuce and stock, bouquet garni, and seasoning to taste. Heat to boiling point; then simmer gently for 2 minutes until the lettuce is tender. Remove the bouquet garni. Rub the soup through a sieve. Add the milk. Re-heat, and add extra seasoning and sugar to taste.

VARIATION

Cream of Lettuce Soup

Omit the milk, mix 125ml single cream and 1 egg yolk together, and blend with a little of the hot soup. Whisk the mixture into the rest of the soup. Return to gentle heat and re-heat without boiling, stirring all the time.

Marrow Soup

4–6 helpings

400g vegetable marrow,	bouquet garni
peeled and seeded	salt and pepper
2 medium-sized onions	125ml milk
(200g approx)	2 × 10ml spoons
1 stick of celery	cornflour for each
25g butter **or** margarine	500ml puréed soup
500ml white stock	cold stock, water **or**
(p329)	milk

Make as for Vegetable Soup (1) (p351).

Mixed Vegetable Soup

6–8 helpings

800g mixed vegetables	bouquet garni
(onions, carrots,	salt and pepper
turnip, leeks,	125ml milk
1 tomato, 2 medium-	2 × 10ml spoons flour
sized potatoes)	for each 500ml puréed
25g butter, margarine	soup
or dripping	cold stock, water **or**
1 litre white stock	milk
(p329) **or** 1 litre water	
and 1 × 5ml spoon	
meat **or** yeast extract	

For Cream of Mixed Vegetable Soup
add

4 × 15ml spoons single	2 egg yolks
cream	

Make as for Vegetable Soup (1) (p351) for both Mixed Vegetable and Cream of Mixed Vegetable Soup.

Nettle Soup

4–6 helpings

400g nettle tops	750ml white stock
a few sorrel **or** spinach	(p329)
leaves	lemon juice
1 medium-sized onion	salt and pepper
(100g approx)	125ml milk **or** single
25g butter	cream

Make as for Vegetable Soup (1) (p351).

Parsnip Soup

6 helpings

800g parsnips
2 medium-sized onions
  (200g approx)
2 sticks celery
25g butter, margarine
  or dripping
1 litre white stock
  (p329)
bouquet garni

lemon juice
salt and pepper
125ml milk
2 × 10ml spoons
  cornflour for each
  500ml puréed soup
cold stock, water or
  milk

For Cream of Parsnip Soup
add
4–8 × 15ml spoons
  single cream
1 egg yolk

a pinch of grated
  nutmeg

Make as for Vegetable Soup (1) (p351) for both
Parsnip Soup and Cream of Parsnip Soup.

VARIATION

Turnip Soup

Substitute 800g turnips for parsnips.

Potato Soup

6 helpings

800g potatoes
2 medium-sized onions
  or the white part of
  2 leeks (200g approx)
2 sticks celery
50g dripping, bacon fat
  or margarine

1 litre white stock
  (p329) or water
bouquet garni
salt and pepper
125ml milk
a pinch of grated
  nutmeg

Make as for Vegetable Soup (1) (p351). No thickening is required.

Potato and Onion Soup

(Flemish Soup)

6 helpings

500g potatoes
2 leeks or 2 medium-
  sized onions (200g
  approx)
3–4 outer sticks celery
2 × 15ml spoons bacon,
  pork or pork sausage
  fat

1 litre white stock
  (p329) or water
bouquet garni
salt and pepper
125ml milk
a pinch of grated
  nutmeg

Make as for Vegetable Soup (1) (p351). No thickening is required.

Potato and Watercress Soup

4 helpings

500g potatoes
1 medium-sized onion
  (100g approx)
25g butter, margarine
  or dripping
500ml white stock
  (p329) or water

100g watercress
salt
Cayenne pepper
125ml milk

For Cream of Potato and Watercress Soup
add
4 × 15ml spoons single
  cream (see Method)

1 egg yolk

Make as for Vegetable Soup (1) (p351). Prepare the
watercress, plunge it into the boiling soup for a
second, then remove and chop it. Add the chopped
cress to the sieved soup and re-heat to boiling
point. Mix the cream and yolk together, if used,
and add to the soup at below boiling point. Stir
over gentle heat to thicken the yolk.

Spring Purée Soup

4–6 helpings

400g shelled green peas	6 young carrots
pods from shelled peas	1 × 10ml spoon butter **or** margarine
a few asparagus heads	1 litre white stock (p329)
a few lettuce, spinach, and watercress leaves	salt and pepper
200g potatoes	125ml milk
6 young spring onions	

For Cream of Spring Purée Soup
add

4 × 15ml spoons single cream	1 egg yolk

Garnish

chopped parsley	chopped chives

Make as for Vegetable Soup (1) (p351) for both Spring Purée Soup and Cream of Spring Purée Soup. Boil the stock before adding it, and cook the vegetables in it for 20 minutes at the most. Garnish the finished soup with the parsley and chives.

Sweetcorn Soup

4 helpings

3 young sweetcorn cobs **or** 1 × 350g can sweetcorn kernels (approx)	500ml white stock (p329)
	salt and pepper
	a pinch of grated nutmeg
1 × 10ml spoon butter	

Remove the husks, silks, and tassels from the fresh cobs, and cut off the kernels. Melt the butter in a deep saucepan, add the kernels and scraped cobs, and fry gently for 10 minutes. Add the stock, heat to boiling point, reduce the heat, cover, and simmer gently for 1–1½ hours or until the kernels are quite soft. Remove the scraped cobs and reserve 2 × 15ml spoons kernels for the garnish. Rub the rest of the kernels and the liquid through a sieve. Add salt, pepper, and nutmeg to taste. Re-heat the soup to boiling point. Add the reserved kernels.

VARIATION
Cream of Sweetcorn Soup

Stir in 4 × 15ml spoons single cream. Do not allow the soup to boil after adding it.

White Onion Soup

6 helpings

3 large Spanish onions (800g approx)	bouquet garni
25g butter, margarine **or** dripping	2 × 10ml spoons flour for each 500ml puréed soup
1 litre white stock (p329) **or** 500ml white stock and 500ml milk	cold stock, water **or** milk
	salt and pepper

For Cream of White Onion Soup
add

125ml milk **or** cream

Make as for Vegetable Soup (1) (p351) for both White Onion Soup and Cream of White Onion Soup. Do not brown the onions when cooking them in the butter.

VARIATION
Brown Onion Soup

Use brown stock (p329) or general household stock (p329) and cook the onions in the butter for about 20 minutes, or until browned, before adding the stock.

Thick Tomato Soup

4 helpings

400g fresh or canned	*a pinch of grated nutmeg*
tomatoes	*lemon juice*
1 medium-sized onion	*salt and pepper*
1 medium-sized carrot	*bouquet garni*
1 × 10ml spoon	*2 × 10ml spoons*
margarine	*cornflour or minute*
25g bacon scraps	*tapioca for each 500ml*
500ml white stock	*puréed soup*
(p329) or juice from	*sugar*
canned tomatoes made	*a few drops red food*
up with water	*colouring (optional)*

Make as for Vegetable Soup (1) (p351). Just before serving, add the food colouring, if liked.

Note For Cream of Tomato Soup, see p360.

Vegetable Soup (2)

Basic recipe

3–4 helpings

250–500g vegetables	*25g flour*
250–500ml white stock	*250ml milk*
(p000)	*salt and pepper*
25g butter or margarine	

For Cream of Vegetable Soup (2)
add

50–125ml single cream	*1 egg yolk*

Prepare and chop the vegetables. Bring the stock to the boil and add the vegetables. Cover, and boil the vegetables until tender. Purée them. Melt the fat in a deep saucepan. Add the flour and stir over gentle heat for 2–3 minutes, without allowing it to colour. Gradually add the milk, stirring well to prevent lumps forming. Heat to boiling point and simmer for 2–3 minutes, stirring all the time. Stir in the vegetable purée, re-heat to boiling point, and season to taste.

Note To make a cream of vegetable soup, proceed as for Vegetable Soup (1) (p351).

Cream of Asparagus Soup

4 helpings

1 bundle (25 heads)	*25g flour*
sprue or young	*250ml milk*
asparagus	*salt and pepper*
500ml white stock	*lemon juice*
(p329)	*sugar*
1 small onion	*4 × 15ml spoons single*
(50g approx)	*cream*
25g butter or margarine	

Cut off the points of the asparagus and cook them in a little of the stock for about 10 minutes or until just tender. Strain the liquid and reserve the asparagus points for the garnish. Add the strained liquid to the rest of the stock. Cut the rest of the asparagus into 2cm lengths. Skin and slice the onion. Proceed as for Vegetable Soup (2). Just before serving, season with salt and pepper, and add lemon juice and sugar to taste. Stir in the cream at boiling point; do not reboil. Garnish with the asparagus points.

Cream of Beetroot Soup

4 helpings

1 cooked beetroot	*25g flour*
(200g approx)	*250ml milk*
1 stick of celery	*salt and pepper*
500ml white stock	*4 × 15ml spoons single*
(p329)	*cream*
25g butter or margarine	

Peel and chop the beetroot. Wash the celery and cut it into short lengths. Proceed as for Vegetable Soup (2).

Cream of Mushroom Soup

4 helpings

200g mushroom stalks	*25g butter* **or** *margarine*
or large mushrooms	*25g flour*
1 medium-sized onion	*500ml milk*
(100g approx)	*salt and pepper*
250ml white stock	*125ml single cream*
(p329)	*1 egg yolk (optional)*

Make as for Vegetable Soup (2) (p359). Reserve a few pieces of mushroom for the garnish before sieving the soup. Chop these pieces and add them to the soup just before stirring in the cream and egg yolk, if used.

Pea Pod Soup

4 helpings

800g young pea pods	*25g butter* **or** *margarine*
1 medium-sized onion	*25g flour*
(100g approx)	*salt and pepper*
a few sprigs mint	*sugar*
a few sprigs parsley	*8 × 10ml spoons small*
1 litre white stock	*peas*
(p329) **or** *water*	

Garnish

a sprig of mint

Wash the pods. Skin and slice the onion. Put the pods, onion, mint, and parsley in a deep saucepan with 750ml of the stock or water. Bring to the boil, cover, and boil until the outer flesh of the pods is soft. Discard the sprigs, and purée the pods and liquid. Proceed as for Vegetable Soup (2) using the rest of the white stock.

Just before serving, cook the peas in a little boiling water until tender. Drain. Season the soup with salt, pepper, and sugar to taste. Chop the mint for the garnish. Add the peas and mint, and serve at once.

Note For Green Pea Soup, see p354.

Cream of Spinach Soup (1)

4 helpings

500g spinach	*250ml milk*
1 small onion	*salt and pepper*
(50g approx)	*a few drops green*
500ml white stock	*colouring (optional)*
(p329)	*125ml single cream*
25g butter **or** *margarine*	*1 egg yolk*
25g flour	

Wash and shred the spinach, and skin and chop the onion. Proceed as for Vegetable Soup (2) (p359). Add a little food colouring, if liked, before thickening the soup.

Note For Cream of Spinach Soup (2), see p363.

Cream of Tomato Soup

4 helpings

600g tomatoes	*500ml white stock*
1 small onion	*(p329)*
(50g approx)	*bouquet garni*
1 medium-sized carrot	*salt and pepper*
(50g approx)	*25g flour*
1 stick of celery	*250ml milk*
25g lean bacon, without	*4 × 10ml spoons single*
rinds	*cream*
50g butter **or** *margarine*	

Prepare and chop the tomatoes, onion and carrot; slice the celery. Chop the bacon. Melt 25g of the fat in a deep saucepan, add the vegetables and bacon, and fry gently for 5 minutes. Add the stock and bouquet garni, and season to taste. Heat to boiling point and simmer gently until the vegetables are soft. Remove the bouquet garni. Rub through a fine sieve. Proceed as for Vegetable Soup (2) (p359), using the rest of the fat.

Cream of Watercress Soup (1)

4 helpings

2 bunches watercress | 25g flour
  (250g approx) | 250ml milk
500ml white stock | salt and pepper
  (p329) | 50ml single cream
25g butter **or** margarine

Wash the watercress and remove the coarse stalks. Reserve a few sprigs as a garnish. Proceed as for Vegetable Soup (2) (p359).

Note For Cream of Watercress Soup (2), see p1412.

Other Thick Vegetable Soups

Bonne Femme Soup

6 helpings

½ lettuce | 2 × 10ml spoons flour
a few sorrel leaves | 125ml milk
a few chervil leaves | salt and pepper
a few watercress **or** | lemon juice
  tarragon leaves | 2 egg yolks
5cm piece of cucumber | 4 × 15ml spoons single
1 × 10ml spoon butter | cream
1 litre white stock
  (p329)

Wash and finely shred the lettuce and other leaves. Peel the cucumber and cut it into matchstick-like strips. Melt the butter in a deep saucepan, add the vegetables, and fry very gently for 3 minutes. Heat the stock to boiling point, add to the vegetables, and simmer for 10 minutes. Blend the flour with half the milk. Stir into the soup and cook until the flour thickens. Add salt, pepper, and lemon juice to taste. Mix the rest of the milk with the egg yolks and cream. Pour a little hot soup on to this mixture, beating well, then whisk the mixture into the rest of the soup. Return to gentle heat and re-heat, without boiling, to thicken the yolks.

Pimento Soup

4–6 helpings

3–4 sweet red peppers | salt
  (300–400g approx) | Cayenne pepper
1 medium-sized onion | 2 × 10ml spoons
  (100g approx) | cornflour for each
1–2 tomatoes | 500ml puréed soup
  (100g approx) | cold stock **or** water
1 litre white stock | sugar
  (p329)

Prepare and slice the vegetables. Put the stock in a deep saucepan and heat to boiling point. Add the vegetables and simmer until soft. Rub the soup through a fine sieve, measure it, and return to the pan. Season to taste. Blend the required amount of cornflour with a little cold stock or water. Stir the cornflour paste into the soup and re-heat until the cornflour has thickened. Add sugar to taste.

Sorrel Soup

4–6 helpings

200g sorrel leaves | 200g potatoes
100g lettuce **or** spinach | 25g butter
  leaves **or** turnip tops | 1 litre white stock
1 small onion | (p329) **or** water
  (50g approx) | salt and pepper

Wash and shred the leaves, skin and chop the onion, and peel and slice the potatoes. Melt the butter in a deep saucepan, add the vegetables, and fry gently for 10 minutes. Heat the stock or water to boiling point, add to the pan, and simmer for 10–15 minutes. Rub the soup through a fine sieve and return it to the pan. Season to taste and heat to boiling point.

VARIATION

Cream of Sorrel Soup

Stir in 4–8 × 15ml spoons single cream at boiling point; do not reboil.

Cabbage Soup

6 helpings

500g firm young cabbage
1 medium-sized onion
  (100g approx)
1 large tomato
  (100g approx)
50g fat bacon, without
  rinds
1 clove of garlic
  (optional)
750ml white stock
  (p329) **or** water in
  which vegetables **or**
  mild pickled pork **or**
  bacon have been cooked

a few caraway **or** dill
  seeds (optional)
25g minute tapioca
salt and pepper
a very little grated
  horseradish
250ml milk **or** 150g
  yoghurt

Shred the cabbage, and chop the onion and tomato. Chop the bacon. Skin and crush the garlic, if used. Fry the bacon slowly in a deep saucepan until the fat runs. Add the vegetables, and shake them over gentle heat for 5 minutes. Heat the stock to boiling point, add to the vegetables with the caraway or dill seeds, if used, and simmer until the cabbage is soft. Rub through a sieve and return it to the pan. Sprinkle in the tapioca and stir and cook until it is clear and soft. Season and add horseradish to taste. Stir in the milk or yoghurt and re-heat without boiling.

Sweet and Sour Cabbage Soup

4–6 helpings

200g cabbage
200g cooking apples
1 medium-sized onion
  (125g approx)
1 litre vegetable stock
  (p330)

125ml tomato juice **or**
  sieved tomato pulp
25g sultanas
salt and pepper
juice of 1 lemon
sugar

Trim and shred the cabbage finely. Prepare and grate the apples and onion. Pour the stock and tomato juice or pulp into a saucepan. Add the cabbage, apple, onion, sultanas, and seasoning to taste. Heat to boiling point, cover, reduce the heat, and simmer gently for 30 minutes. Add the lemon juice and sugar to taste just before serving the soup. Re-season if required.

Catalan Soup

4–6 helpings

50g bacon, without rinds
2 Spanish onions
  (500g approx)
1 sweet pepper
  (100g approx)
1 stick of celery
2 large potatoes
  (500g approx)
2 large tomatoes
  (200g approx)

1 litre white stock
  (p329)
100ml white wine
a pinch of thyme
chopped parsley
salt and pepper
a pinch of grated nutmeg
2 egg yolks
4 × 15ml spoons milk

Chop the bacon. Skin and slice the onions very thinly. Fry the bacon in a deep saucepan until the fat runs. Add the onions, and fry until the onions and bacon are golden-brown.

Meanwhile, prepare the pepper and celery and slice them very finely. Peel the potatoes and slice them thickly; skin and slice the tomatoes. Add all the vegetables to the pan and shake over gentle heat for 5 minutes. Add the stock, wine, and herbs. Heat to boiling point, cover, and simmer gently for 30–45 minutes or until all the vegetables are soft. Add salt, pepper, and nutmeg to taste. Mix the egg yolks and milk together. Pour a little hot soup on to this mixture and stir until blended. Add the mixture to the rest of the soup and heat gently, without boiling, to thicken the yolks, stirring all the time.

French White Onion Soup

3–4 helpings

4 medium-sized onions
  (400g approx)
50g butter
1 large slice of white
  bread

500ml milk
250ml white stock
  (p329) **or** water
salt and pepper

Skin and chop the onions. Melt the butter in a deep saucepan, add the onions, cover with a tight-fitting lid, and cook very gently for 1 hour, without allowing the onions to brown. Crumble the bread. Add to the pan with the milk, and stock or water. Heat to boiling point, reduce the heat, cover, and simmer for 45 minutes. Rub the soup through a fine sieve. Return to the pan and re-heat. Season to taste.

Note For White Onion Soup, see p358.

Country Soup

6 helpings

600g mixed vegetables
(carrot, turnip, onion,
leek, celery, tomato)
2 × 15ml spoons bacon
fat
500ml white stock
(p329), water **or** water
in which vegetables
have been cooked

25g brown bread
250ml milk
salt and pepper

Garnish
chopped parsley **or** other
fresh herbs

Grate the carrot and turnip coarsely, and chop the onion, leek, celery, and tomato. Melt the bacon fat in a deep saucepan, add all the vegetables except the tomato, and fry gently until they begin to brown. Add the stock or water and the tomato. Toast the brown bread, break it up roughly, and add it to the soup. Heat to boiling point, cover, and simmer for 45 minutes or until the vegetables are quite soft. Rub the soup through a fine sieve. Stir in the milk, and season to taste. Re-heat before serving. Garnish each portion with chopped herbs.

Serve with bread croûtons.

All-in-one Vegetable Soup

See p1399.

Cream of Spinach Soup (2)

6 helpings

300g frozen whole leaf
spinach
50g butter
100ml boiling water
25g onion

3 × 10ml spoons plain
flour
500ml milk
salt and pepper

Put the thawed spinach and 25g of butter in a pan. Add the boiling water and cook for 5 minutes. Rub the spinach and liquid through a sieve, or process in an electric blender. Skin and grate the onion. Melt the rest of the butter in a saucepan and cook the onion for 2 minutes. Stir in the flour. Gradually add the milk, and heat to boiling point, stirring all the time. Reduce the heat and simmer gently for 5 minutes. Stir in the spinach purée and heat gently, stirring well. Season to taste and serve hot.

Note For Cream of Spinach Soup (1), see p360.

Midsummer Soup

4–6 helpings

5 small carrots
(125g approx)
a bunch of radishes
1 small cauliflower
100g mange-tout peas
1.5 litres water
50g shelled green peas

4 × 15ml spoons flour
1 × 5ml spoon meat
extract
salt and pepper
1 egg yolk
100ml single cream

Slice the carrots and radishes, break the cauliflower into florets, and top and tail the mange-tout peas. Heat the water to boiling point in a large saucepan. Add all the vegetables and simmer until tender. Blend the flour with a little cold water and stir it into the soup. Simmer gently for another 5 minutes to thicken the soup. Add the meat extract and seasoning to taste. Mix together the yolk and cream. Pour a little hot soup on to the mixture and stir until blended. Add the mixture to the rest of the soup and heat gently, without boiling, to thicken the yolk.

Serve hot with cheese biscuits.

Hollandaise Soup

6 helpings

1 large carrot	1 litre white stock
10cm piece of cucumber	(p329)
4 × 10ml spoons small	2 egg yolks
green peas	75ml milk
white stock (p329) **or**	50ml single cream
water	salt and pepper
25g butter **or** margarine	a sprig of tarragon
4 × 10ml spoons flour	

Cut pea shapes from the carrot and cucumber to give 4 × 10ml spoons of each. Cook the vegetables in a little boiling stock or water until just tender. Put to one side. Melt the fat in a deep saucepan and stir in the flour. Gradually add the 1 litre stock, and stir until boiling. Boil for 2–3 minutes, stirring all the time. Remove from the heat and leave to cool slightly. Mix the egg yolks, milk, and cream in a basin. Pour a little hot soup on to the egg yolk mixture, beating well, then whisk the mixture into the rest of the soup. Stir over gentle heat to thicken the yolks, without boiling the soup. Season to taste. Chop the tarragon and add to the soup with the cooked vegetables; add the cooking liquid also, if liked.

Milk and Onion Soup

4–5 helpings

1 Spanish onion **or**	bouquet garni
3 medium-sized onions	a little grated lemon
(300g approx)	rind
25g butter **or** margarine	salt and pepper
25g flour	4 × 10ml spoons sherry
625ml milk	(optional)

Skin the onion and chop it finely. Melt the fat in a deep saucepan, add the onion, and fry gently for 10 minutes. Stir in the flour. Add the milk and heat to boiling point, stirring all the time. Add the bouquet garni and lemon rind, and simmer until the onion is just tender. Remove the bouquet garni. Season to taste and add the sherry, if used.

Okra Soup

4 helpings

400g fresh okra **or**	a few bacon scraps **or** a
1 × 400g can okra	bacon bone
2 large tomatoes	a bunch of parsley stalks
(200g approx)	100g Lima **or** fresh
750ml general household	haricot beans
stock (p329)	salt and pepper

Garnish
chopped parsley

Prepare and slice the okra pods and tomatoes. Put the stock in a deep saucepan and heat to boiling point. Add the okra, tomatoes, bacon scraps or bone, parsley stalks, and beans, and cook until tender. Discard the bacon bone, if used, and rub the soup through a fine sieve. Re-heat and season to taste. Sprinkle a little chopped parsley over the soup before serving.

Onion and Turnip Soup

6 helpings

200g onions	1 litre vegetable stock
200g turnips	(p330)
200g potatoes	1 bay leaf
25g margarine	salt and pepper

Garnish
1 × 10ml spoon chopped
parsley

Prepare and dice the vegetables. Melt the margarine in a saucepan, add the vegetables, and fry gently for 5 minutes, without browning them. Add the stock, bay leaf, and seasoning to taste. Heat to simmering point, cover, and simmer gently for about 30 minutes or until the vegetables are soft. Remove the bay leaf, and re-season if required. Serve garnished with the parsley.

Vegetable, Cheese, and Rice Soup

6 helpings

¼ cabbage (200g approx)	50g butter
1 leek (100g approx)	25g long-grain rice
1 large carrot (100g approx)	1 × 2.5ml spoon sugar
1 small turnip (50g approx)	1.25 litres white stock (p329)
1 small onion (50g approx)	salt and pepper
	2 × 15ml spoons grated Cheddar cheese

Shred the cabbage, slice the leek thinly, and dice the carrot, turnip, and onion. Melt the butter in a deep saucepan, add the vegetables and fry gently for 10–15 minutes, without browning them. Add the rice and sugar, and continue cooking, stirring all the time, until all the butter has been absorbed. Stir in the stock and seasoning. Heat to boiling point, cover, and simmer gently for 40 minutes. Sprinkle with grated cheese and serve.

Brown Vegetable Soup

4–6 helpings

2 medium-sized onions (200g approx)	2 × 10ml spoons oil or 25g butter
1 cabbage	1 slice of brown bread
2 large carrots (200g approx)	2 litres water
1 turnip (50g approx)	salt and pepper
2 potatoes (300g approx)	chopped parsley

Slice the onions, shred the cabbage, and dice the carrots, turnip, and potatoes. Heat the oil or butter in a deep saucepan, add the onions, and fry gently until golden-brown. Toast the bread. Add the water, toast, and vegetables to the pan. Heat to boiling point and season to taste. Cover, and simmer gently for 1–1¼ hours.

Mash the vegetables in the pan with a potato masher, or process with a little of the stock in an electric blender; return to the liquid in the pan, and simmer for another 10 minutes. If the soup is too thick, add more water and boil for another 10 minutes; if too thin, boil rapidly, uncovered, until the soup is thick enough. Sprinkle a little chopped parsley into the soup before serving.

Note Any other vegetables, such as French beans, green peas with their pods, celery, and parsnips, can be added to the vegetables above.

Winter Vegetable Soup

6 helpings

1 medium-sized onion (100g approx)	bouquet garni
1 leek	a trace of grated nutmeg
1 large carrot (100g approx)	½ × 2.5ml spoon meat or yeast extract
¼ turnip (25g approx)	500ml general household stock (p329) or water
½ winter cabbage	25g rice
25g dripping or bacon fat	500ml milk
	salt and pepper

Chop the onion and leek, grate the carrot and turnip coarsely, and shred the cabbage. Heat the dripping or bacon fat in a deep saucepan, add the onion, leek, carrot, and turnip, and fry gently until they begin to brown. Add the cabbage to the pan with the bouquet garni, nutmeg, and meat or yeast extract, and cook gently for 3 minutes. Heat the stock or water to boiling point and pour it on to the vegetables. Add the rice, and simmer until the vegetables are soft. Remove the bouquet garni. Add the milk and re-heat the soup. Season to taste.

Serve with grated cheese.

Pulse Soups

Basque Bean Soup

4 helpings

100g haricot beans	*50g bacon or pork fat*
1 litre water	*1 clove of garlic*
2 medium-sized onions	*salt and pepper*
(200g approx)	*a few drops white wine*
200g white cabbage	*vinegar*

Garnish
2 × 15ml spoons
 crumbled cooked bacon

Soak the beans in the water overnight. Skin and slice the onions and shred the cabbage. Heat the bacon or pork fat in a saucepan, add the onions, and fry gently for about 10 minutes until browned. Add the cabbage, and shake the pan over gentle heat for 2–3 minutes. Skin and crush the garlic and add to the pan with the soaked beans and water. Heat the soup to simmering point, cover, and simmer for 1½–2½ hours until the beans are quite soft. Season and add the vinegar to taste. Just before serving, sprinkle the bacon on top.

Butter Bean Soup

6 helpings

150g butter beans	*1 medium-sized potato*
1 litre water or general	*(100g approx)*
household stock (p329)	*1 × 10ml spoon bacon*
a few bacon scraps or	*fat*
rinds or a bacon bone	*bouquet garni*
1 medium-sized onion	*a blade of mace*
(100g approx)	*250ml milk*
2 sticks celery	*salt and pepper*
½ small turnip	
(25g approx)	

Wash the beans. Heat the water or stock to boiling point, pour it over the beans, and leave to soak overnight. Chop the bacon, if used. Prepare and slice the vegetables. Heat the bacon fat in a deep saucepan, add the bacon or bone, and vegetables, and fry gently for 10 minutes. Add the soaked beans and the liquid, the bouquet garni, and mace. Heat to boiling point, cover, and simmer for 2 hours or until the beans are quite soft. Remove the bouquet garni and bone, if used, and rub the vegetables and cooking liquid through a sieve, or process in an electric blender. Return to a clean pan and add the milk. No starch thickener other than the potato should be needed. Re-heat and season to taste.

VARIATIONS
Dried Pea Soup

Substitute 150g dried, whole or split peas for the butter beans, and add a sprig of mint or a little dried mint.

Haricot Bean Soup

Substitute 150g haricot beans for the butter beans.

Lentil Soup

Substitute 150g red or brown lentils for the butter beans, and add 50g carrot to the flavouring vegetables.

Split Pea and Ham Soup

Substitute 150g split peas for the butter beans, and add a ham or bacon bone to the soup.

Haricot Bean and Tomato Soup

6 helpings

150g haricot beans	*1 medium-sized potato*
750ml water or half	*(100g approx)*
water and half stock	*1 × 10ml spoon butter,*
200g tomatoes	*margarine or bacon fat*
1 medium-sized onion	*bouquet garni*
(100g approx)	*a blade of mace*
1 medium-sized carrot	*salt and pepper*
(50g approx)	

Soak the beans overnight in water. Drain, and put them in a pan with the water or water and stock; heat to boiling point, and simmer for 1 hour.

Meanwhile, prepare and slice the vegetables. Heat the fat in a deep saucepan, add the vegetables, and fry gently for 10 minutes. Add the beans and the cooking liquid, the bouquet garni and mace. Cover, and simmer until the beans are quite soft. Remove the bouquet garni and mace, and rub the soup through a fine sieve. Return to a clean pan and re-heat. Season to taste.

Lentil and Bacon Soup

6 helpings

*150g red **or** brown lentils*	*a sprig of parsley*
	salt and pepper
1 litre water	*200g piece of bacon*
1 clove of garlic	*400g potatoes*
1 clove	

Soak the lentils in the water overnight. Put the beans and water into a deep saucepan. Skin and crush the garlic and add to the pan with the clove, parsley, and seasoning. Dice the bacon and add to the pan. Heat to boiling point, cover, and simmer for 1 hour or until the lentils and bacon are cooked.

Meanwhile, peel and dice the potatoes. Add to the soup and cook for a further 10–20 minutes or until just soft. Remove the clove and re-season if required.

Lentil and Parsley Soup

4 helpings

2 medium-sized carrots (100g approx)	*500ml water*
	250ml milk
2 × 15ml spoons margarine	*salt and pepper*
	2 × 15ml spoons chopped parsley
*2 × 15ml spoons finely chopped leek **or** onion*	
	2 × 15ml spoons chopped Brussels sprouts (optional)
6 × 15ml spoons red lentils	

Prepare and dice the carrots. Melt the margarine in a saucepan, add the carrots and leek or onion, and fry gently for 2–3 minutes, stirring or tossing frequently. Add the lentils, water, milk, and seasoning. Heat gently to simmering point, cover, and

simmer for 30–45 minutes or until the lentils are soft. Re-season if required. Add the chopped parsley, and the sprouts, if used, and serve.

Green Lentil Soup

4–6 helpings

250g green lentils	*bouquet garni*
1 litre water	*salt*
1 medium-sized onion (100g approx)	*125ml single cream **or** 250ml milk*
1 large carrot (100g approx)	*pepper*
½ small turnip (25g approx)	*a few drops green food colouring **or** spinach juice*
1–2 sticks celery (50–100g approx)	

Garnish
*toasted **or** fried bread croûtons*

Soak the lentils in the water overnight. Rinse and drain them. Put the water in a saucepan, heat to boiling point, and add the lentils. Prepare and slice the vegetables. Add to the pan with the bouquet garni and 1 × 2.5ml spoon salt. Re-heat to simmering point; then cover and simmer for 3½ hours or until the lentils are soft. Rub the soup through a fine sieve, or process in an electric blender. Return the soup to the pan and add the cream or milk. Season to taste. Re-heat gently to just below simmering point, stirring all the time. If cream has been added, do not allow to boil. Stir in the colouring or juice to improve the colour. Serve hot, garnished with the bread croûtons.

Rich Lentil Soup
See p1427.

Other Thick Soups

Almond Cream Soup

4 helpings

50g whole **or** ground almonds	2 × 10ml spoons flour
500ml white stock (p329)	salt and pepper **or** Cayenne pepper
2 × 15ml spoons soft white breadcrumbs	lemon juice
1 × 10ml spoon butter	3 drops almond essence
	4 × 10ml spoons single cream

Blanch the whole almonds, if used. Dry and toast them until light golden-brown. Chop them or grind them coarsely in a coffee or nut-mill. If ground almonds are used, toast them as for whole almonds. Put the almonds in a saucepan with the stock, heat to boiling point, and simmer until soft. Add the breadcrumbs and simmer for a further 10 minutes. Rub the soup through a fine sieve. Melt the butter in a pan and stir in the flour. Gradually add the almond and crumb purée and heat to boiling point, stirring all the time; then simmer for 2–3 minutes to cook the flour. Add seasoning, lemon juice to taste, and almond essence. Re-heat to boiling point, add the cream, and serve at once.

Broad Bean and Ham Soup

4–6 helpings

625g young shelled broad beans	1 × 15ml spoon chopped parsley
125g ham **or** bacon in 1 piece	1 × 15ml spoon concentrated tomato purée
4–5 finely chopped sage leaves	750ml water
2 small onions (100g approx)	4–6 slices brown **or** white bread

Cook the broad beans in boiling salted water until tender; then drain. Meanwhile, cut the ham or bacon into very small pieces, about 5mm square. Skin and chop the onions finely. Heat the ham or bacon gently in a saucepan until the fat begins to run. Add the sage, onions, and parsley, and fry quickly for 2–3 minutes to brown the onion a little.

Add the tomato purée and fry gently for a further 2–3 minutes. Add the water, and heat to boiling point. Add the broad beans to the soup, return to simmering point, partly cover the pan, and simmer for 15 minutes. Toast the slices of bread until golden-brown, and place 1 slice in the bottom of each soup bowl. Pour the hot soup over them, and serve quickly.

Note See also Broad Bean Soup (p355).

Caraway Soup

6 helpings

50g bacon **or** pork fat	a pinch of salt
1 × 10ml spoon caraway seeds	1 litre brown stock (p329)
50g flour	salt and pepper

Heat the bacon or pork fat in a deep saucepan, add the caraway seeds, and fry gently for 3–5 minutes. Add the flour and salt, and fry very gently until browned. Add the stock, heat to boiling point, stirring all the time; then simmer gently for 30 minutes. Strain the soup and season to taste.

Cream of Chicken Soup
See p340.

Cottage Soup

4 helpings

500g mixed vegetables (onion, carrot, celery, etc)	1 × 2.5ml spoon yeast extract
2 × 10ml spoons butter	1 × 10ml spoon salt
750ml water	50g grated cheese
2 × 10ml spoons flour	1 × 10ml spoon chopped parsley
250ml milk	

Prepare the vegetables and grate them coarsely. Melt the butter in a deep saucepan, add the vegetables, cover, and shake over gentle heat for 1 minute. Add the water, heat to boiling point, cover, and simmer for 10 minutes. Blend the flour with the milk. Add to the soup with the yeast extract and salt, re-heat to boiling point, then simmer for 5 minutes. Add the cheese and parsley, and serve at once.

Garlic Soup

(Pistou)

4–6 helpings

100g potatoes	salt and pepper
2 tomatoes	50g vermicelli
400g French beans	3 cloves garlic
4 onions	1 × 10ml spoon olive oil
2 green peppers	½ × 2.5ml spoon dried
200g vegetable marrow	basil
1 litre water	

Dice the potatoes, and chop the tomatoes, French beans, onions, green peppers, and marrow. Put the water in a saucepan and heat to boiling point; add the vegetables, and simmer for 15–20 minutes. Add the salt, pepper, and vermicelli and cook for a further 8–10 minutes.

Meanwhile, skin and crush the garlic. Pound it with the oil and basil. Add a little hot soup to the garlic and basil, and return the mixture to the saucepan. Stir well and heat through for 2–3 minutes.

Serve with grated Gruyère cheese.

Hotch Potch (2)

6–8 helpings

75g pearl barley	2 medium-sized onions
3 litres water	(200g approx)
2 large carrots	bouquet garni
(200g approx)	50g butter
1 small cabbage	salt and pepper
1 turnip (50g approx)	

Put the barley and water into a large, deep saucepan and heat to boiling point. Reserve 1 carrot, and chop the rest of the vegetables into very small pieces. Add the vegetables, bouquet garni, butter, and seasoning to the pan. There should be enough vegetables to make the soup rather thick. Re-heat to boiling point, cover, and simmer for 2 hours.

Grate the reserved carrot coarsely. Add to the soup and simmer for another 30 minutes. Remove the bouquet garni before serving.

Note Other vegetables such as lettuce, green peas, and celery can be added.

For Hotch Potch (1), see p333.

Minestrone (1)

4–6 helpings

75g butter beans **or**	150g white cabbage
haricot beans	25g butter
2 rashers streaky bacon,	1 bay leaf
without rinds	1 × 10ml spoon
1 clove of garlic	concentrated tomato
1 leek	purée
1 onion	1.25 litres white stock
2 carrots	(p329)
50g French beans	salt and pepper
3 sticks celery	50g pasta rings
2 potatoes	

Garnish
grated Parmesan cheese

Soak the beans overnight in cold water. Drain thoroughly. Chop the bacon. Skin and crush the garlic. Slice the leek, onion, carrots, and French beans, chop the celery, dice the potatoes, and shred the cabbage. Fry the bacon in a saucepan for 2–3 minutes, add the garlic and butter, and fry for 2–3 minutes. Add all the vegetables and cook for 3–4 minutes. Add the bay leaf, tomato purée, stock, salt, and pepper. Heat to boiling point, cover, then simmer for 45–50 minutes. Add the pasta rings and cook for a further 6–8 minutes.

Serve hot, garnished with grated Parmesan cheese.

Note For Minestrone (2) see p1411.

Crème Royale

6 helpings

25g macaroni	$\frac{1}{2} \times 2.5ml$ spoon meat **or**
1 × 15ml spoon butter	yeast extract
2 × 15ml spoons flour	salt and Cayenne pepper
750ml white stock	2 egg yolks
(p329)	75ml milk
a trace of grated nutmeg	50ml single cream
1 bay leaf	

Cook the macaroni in boiling water until very soft. Drain, and cut it into 5mm lengths. Melt the butter in a saucepan, add the flour, and fry gently for 3 minutes without browning it. Gradually add the stock and stir until boiling. Add the nutmeg, bay leaf, meat or yeast extract, and macaroni. Season to taste. Mix together the egg yolks, milk, and cream in a basin. Stir in a little of the hot soup and then beat the mixture into the rest of the soup. Heat gently to thicken the yolks but do not boil the soup.

Serve with grated cheese.

Rice and Tomato Soup

4–6 helpings

100ml olive oil	4 tomatoes
200g long-grain rice	(200g approx)
1 clove of garlic	1 litre general household
400g lean bacon	stock (p329)
3 medium-sized Spanish	
onions (300g approx)	

Heat the oil in a pan, add the rice, and fry until golden-brown. Skin and crush the garlic and stir it into the rice. Chop the bacon into small pieces about 1cm square. Skin and slice the onions and tomatoes. Fry the bacon gently in a deep saucepan until the fat begins to run. Add the onions and tomatoes, and fry gently until the onion is transparent. Stir in the rice. Add the stock, heat to boiling point, cover, and simmer gently for about 1 hour.

Rich Gravy Soup

4 helpings

1 litre vegetable stock	1 × 5ml spoon arrowroot
(p330)	salt and pepper
white and crushed shell	a few drops gravy
of 1 egg (optional)	browning
1 × 15ml spoon	2 × 15ml spoons sherry
mushroom ketchup	(optional)
1 × 5ml spoon walnut	
ketchup	

Garnish
shredded vegetables **or**
cooked macaroni,
vermicelli **or** *other*
soup pasta

If the stock is cloudy, clear it first as for Consommé (p335), then heat to boiling point. Blend the mushroom and walnut ketchups with the arrowroot. Pour a little of the hot stock on to the blended arrowroot and mix well, then stir it into the rest of the stock. Season to taste. Add the gravy browning to give a rich brown colour, and the sherry, if used. Re-heat the soup and simmer for 3–4 minutes, stirring all the time. Serve garnished with shredded vegetables or cooked macaroni, vermicelli, etc.

Vegetable Stock Soup

6–7 helpings

1 medium-sized carrot	1 litre vegetable stock
(50g approx)	(p330) **or** 1 × 10ml
1 medium-sized onion	spoon yeast extract
(100g approx)	dissolved in 1 litre
1 stick of celery	water
1 tomato (50g approx)	2 cloves
25g butter	1 bay leaf
2 × 10ml spoons flour	salt and pepper

Garnish
12 tiny fried forcemeat	1 × 5ml spoon chopped
balls (p376)	parsley

Prepare and dice the vegetables or slice them thinly. Melt the butter in a deep pan, add the vegetables, cover, and fry very gently for 15 minutes. Stir in the flour and cook until the flour is slightly browned. Add the rest of the ingredients and stir until boiling. Cover, and simmer gently for 20 minutes.

Put the forcemeat balls into a tureen and pour the soup over them. Garnish with the parsley. Serve at once.

Serve with redcurrant jelly.

Note A few mushrooms can be added to the vegetables for extra flavour.

Velvet Soup

4 helpings

25g butter	1 × 15ml spoon Patna
25g flour	rice
1 × 10ml spoon curry	salt and pepper
powder	4 × 10ml spoons single
500ml milk	cream

Melt the butter in a saucepan, add the flour and curry powder, and fry very gently for 3–5 minutes without hardening the flour. Gradually add the milk, heat to boiling point, and simmer for 5 minutes, stirring all the time.

Meanwhile, cook the rice in boiling water until tender. Drain, and add to the hot soup. Season to taste. Remove the soup from the heat and stir in the cream.

COLD SOUPS

Chilled Avocado Soup

6 helpings

4 ripe avocado pears	250ml soured cream
juice of 1 lemon	salt and pepper
500ml consommé (p335)	
or canned consommé	

Garnish
chopped chives **or** green
part of spring onions

Scoop out the flesh from the avocado pears, and mix with the lemon juice. Rub through a sieve. Mix the avocado, consommé, and soured cream until blended, and season to taste. Chill in a refrigerator for 2–3 hours. Just before serving, add the chives or spring onions.

Chicken and Beetroot Broth

6 helpings

400g young uncooked	6 hard-boiled eggs
beetroots	salt and pepper
1 litre water	a little made English
400g cooked chicken **or**	mustard
veal	250ml soured cream
200g cooked ham	1 × 15ml spoon chopped
2–3 lettuce hearts	fennel leaves **or** stem
(75g approx)	6 ice cubes
2 long **or** 5 small	
cucumbers	
(800g approx)	

Garnish
2 × 15ml spoons
chopped green part of
spring onion **or** chives

Wash and peel the beetroots. Heat the water to boiling point, add the beetroots, cover, and simmer gently for 1 hour. Strain off the liquid and leave to cool. Chop the chicken or veal, the ham, and lettuce hearts into small pieces. Peel and dice the cucumbers. Separate the hard-boiled egg yolks from the whites and sieve the yolks into a bowl. Add salt, pepper, and the mustard to the yolks and gradually stir in the soured cream. Add the chicken, ham, lettuce, and cucumbers, and stir well. Pour the cold beetroot juice over them, and mix well. Chill in a refrigerator for 2–3 hours.

Just before serving, chop the egg white and add it to the soup with the fennel. Put an ice cube in each bowl and pour the soup over it.

Serve with the chopped spring onion tops or chives.

Note The beetroots can be puréed and added to the liquid if liked, to make a very thick soup.

Cucumber and Yoghurt Soup

4 helpings

1 small onion
 (50g approx)
½ cucumber
 (200g approx)
1 × 15ml spoon butter
400g natural yoghurt
250ml chicken stock
 (p330)

grated rind and juice of
 ½ lemon
½ × 15ml spoon finely
 chopped mint
salt and pepper

Garnish
sprigs of mint

Skin and chop the onion finely. Peel the cucumber and cut the flesh into 5mm dice. Melt the butter in a saucepan and cook the onion and cucumber gently, without browning them, for 8–10 minutes. Leave to cool. Whisk the yoghurt until the curd is evenly broken down and add to the soup with the stock. Add the lemon rind and juice, and the mint. Season to taste. Chill for several hours. Serve garnished with sprigs of mint.

Note Another cold cucumber soup can be found on p1411.

Iced Vichysoisse
See p355.

Iced Consommé
See p338.

Chilled Pea Soup with Yoghurt

4 helpings

150g potatoes
1 medium-sized onion
 (100g approx)
3–4 lettuce leaves
250g frozen green peas

500ml chicken stock
 (p330)
275g natural yoghurt
salt and pepper
a pinch of sugar

Peel and slice the potatoes and onion, and shred the lettuce leaves. Put most of the peas into a saucepan with the stock and heat to boiling point. Reduce the heat and simmer for 10 minutes. Rub the soup through a fine sieve, or process in an electric blender. Whisk the yoghurt until the curd is evenly broken down, and add to the soup, reserving 4 × 15ml spoonfuls as a garnish. Chill for several hours. Add salt, pepper, and a little sugar to taste. Serve garnished with the remaining peas and yoghurt.

Summer Soup with Buttermilk

4 helpings

½ green pepper
 (75g approx)
½ cucumber
 (200g approx)
250ml buttermilk

250ml tomato juice
grated rind and juice of
 ½ lemon
salt and pepper

Garnish
chopped parsley

Prepare and dice the vegetables. Put the green pepper into a saucepan with a little cold water and heat to boiling point. Drain, and leave to cool. Mix together the buttermilk and tomato juice and add the pepper, cucumber, lemon rind and juice. Season with salt and pepper. Chill for several hours. Serve sprinkled with the chopped parsley.

Jellied Tomato Soup with Soured Cream

4 helpings

375–450g piece
  honeydew melon
250ml chicken stock
  (p330)
2 spring onions
2–3 celery leaves
250ml tomato juice
a few drops
  Worcestershire sauce

3 cloves
a pinch of sugar
a few drops lemon juice
salt
Cayenne pepper
1 × 15ml spoon gelatine
2 × 15ml spoons water

Garnish

4 × 10ml spoons soured
  cream

freshly ground black
  pepper

Remove the seeds from the melon and scoop out the flesh with a ball scoop. Chill the melon balls and the chicken stock while preparing the other ingredients.

Chop the onions finely and shred the celery leaves. Put into a large saucepan with the tomato juice, Worcestershire sauce, cloves, sugar, and lemon juice. Season to taste, half cover, and simmer for 10 minutes. Remove from the heat and strain into a bowl.

Soften the gelatine in the water in a small heat-proof basin. Stand the basin in a pan of hot water and stir until it has dissolved. Add a little of the strained tomato liquid and stir well. Pour the gelatine into the rest of the tomato liquid and mix well. Add the chilled chicken stock, stir until well blended, and leave to set.

To serve, whisk the jellied soup until frothy. Spoon into 4 chilled bowls, and gently mix in the melon balls. Garnish with soured cream and the black pepper.

Curried Chicken Soup

4–6 helpings

600ml chicken stock
  (p330)
1 × 2.5ml spoon curry
  paste
1 clove of garlic
1 × 2.5ml spoon ground
  coriander
1 × 2.5ml spoon ground
  cumin

a pinch of ground
  allspice
a pinch of ground
  turmeric (optional)
1 × 418g can condensed
  cream of chicken soup
salt and pepper

Garnish

3 × 15ml spoons diced
  unpeeled cucumber

Pour the stock into a large saucepan. In a separate container, cream the curry paste with 1 × 15ml spoon of the stock. Skin and crush the garlic, and add it with the ground spices to the curry. Mix well and add to the chicken stock. Stir in the canned soup and season to taste. Bring to the boil over moderate heat, stirring all the time; then reduce the heat and simmer until smooth and well blended. Remove from the heat, half cover, and leave to cool. Chill for several hours. Serve garnished with the diced cucumber.

STUFFINGS, GARNISHES, AND ACCOMPANIMENTS

The French are noted for their skill in making forcemeats; one of the principal causes of their superiority in this respect being, that they pound all the ingredients so diligently and thoroughly. Any one with the slightest pretensions to refined cookery, must, in this particular, implicitly follow the example of our friends across the Channel.

Stuffings or Forcemeats

Stuffings are sometimes called forcemeats or farce-meats, a name derived from the French word for stuffing – *farce*. They are a useful way of moistening or adding extra flavour or interest to meat, poultry, fish, and vegetables. They can also be an economical way of using up small quantities of food, and of extending the bulk, variety, and flavour of a main dish without buying expensive, extra protein foods. A stuffed vegetable or croustade with a sauce can be a satisfying yet cheap main dish on its own.

For the best results, a stuffing should be fairly loose and crumbly before cooking, yet firm with enough binding to hold it together when served.

Food should only be stuffed just before it is cooked to avoid bacterial infection. It is important not to stuff a joint or bird too tightly, because almost all stuffings expand during cooking and may burst the skin of the bird or seep out of a joint. Surplus stuffing can be cooked separately in a greased baking dish, or shaped into a roll and baked.

Alternatively, stuffing mixtures can be made into small balls, and either baked round a vegetable, joint or bird, or fried in shallow or deep fat. If necessary, they should be bound with an egg, and can be coated with egg and crumbs.

Almost all stuffings are adaptable concerning their cooking temperature and time. If cooked separately in a greased dish, 200–300g stuffing, containing solid raw food, will generally cook through in 35–40 minutes at a temperature of between 180°C, Gas 4 – 200°C, Gas 6. If containing cooked ingredients only, the stuffing will be heated through in 20–30 minutes. A roll of stuffing, wrapped in foil, may take 10–15 minutes longer than these times in each case. Stuffing or forcemeat balls will usually take 6–9 minutes to fry, depending on whether they include raw ingredients; they will bake in 15–20 minutes. They should be basted well and turned at least once during baking.

If substituting dried herbs for the fresh herbs in the recipes which follow, halve the quantity suggested in the particular recipe.

Note For other stuffings, see the chapters on Fish, Meat, Poultry, Game, and Vegetables.

BREADCRUMB-BASED STUFFINGS

Breadcrumbs
(to make)

Soft breadcrumbs: Remove the crusts from white or brown bread that is at least 1 day old. Either process in an electric blender, or grate coarsely. Alternatively, rub through a wire sieve, or between the palms of the hand until fine crumbs are obtained.

Note Soft crumbs can be stored in a clean polythene bag or sealed polythene container for 2 to 3 days in a refrigerator, or up to 3 months in a freezer. Frozen breadcrumbs remain separate and the required quantity can be removed from the container easily.

Dried breadcrumbs: Prepare soft breadcrumbs and dry them slowly without colouring in a very cool oven, or in a warm place, until thoroughly dry.

Note Dried breadcrumbs can be stored in an airtight jar or tin for 2–3 weeks in a cool place. However, they develop a strong stale taste if kept longer.

Browned breadcrumbs (raspings): Put crusts or any pieces of stale bread in a moderate oven, 180°C, Gas 4, and bake them until golden-brown and crisp. Crush with a rolling-pin or process in an electric blender. These crumbs are not used for stuffings, but for coating croquettes, fish cakes, rissoles, etc or for covering *au gratin* dishes.

Note They can be stored in an airtight jar or tin for 2–3 weeks in a cool place. Like dried breadcrumbs, they develop a strong stale taste if kept longer.

Buttered breadcrumbs: Lightly fork 125g soft breadcrumbs with 25g melted butter. When the crumbs have absorbed the fat, spread them on a baking sheet and dry them without browning, in a very cool oven, 110°C, Gas ¼. Buttered crumbs can be used as they are for coating meat, fish or croquettes, or for covering *au gratin* dishes.

To use in place of soft crumbs, soak buttered crumbs in a little hot water (100g buttered crumbs to 5 × 15ml spoons water) for 5 minutes. Soaked buttered crumbs can be used for bread sauce and stuffings.

Note Buttered crumbs keep better and longer than either soft crumbs or raspings (unless these are frozen). They can be stored in an airtight container in a cool place for up to 2 months.

Basic Herb Stuffing or Forcemeat

Enough for a 1.5–2kg chicken, a boned joint of veal or eight 75g thin fish fillets; use double the quantity for the neck end of a 5–6kg turkey

50g shredded suet **or** margarine
100g soft breadcrumbs
a pinch of grated nutmeg
1 × 15ml spoon chopped parsley
1 × 5ml spoon chopped fresh mixed herbs
grated rind of ½ lemon
salt and pepper
1 egg

Melt the margarine, if using. Mix the breadcrumbs with the suet or margarine. Add the nutmeg, herbs, and lemon rind. Season, beat the egg until liquid and stir into the mixture to bind it.

Use as above, or for vegetables. Alternatively, form the mixture into 12 or 16 balls, and bake in a moderate oven at 180°C, Gas 4, for 15–20 minutes, or fry in deep or shallow fat until golden.

VARIATIONS

Thyme and Parsley Stuffing

Substitute 1 × 5ml spoon thyme for the mixed herbs and omit the grated nutmeg.

Ham Stuffing

Mince or shred 100g lean ham or bacon, and add to the breadcrumbs before mixing with the fat. Use a little milk or chicken stock with the egg to bind the mixture if necessary.

Use for veal, poultry or rabbit. When made with suet, the stuffing can also be used for hare.

Prawn or Shrimp Stuffing

Enough for four 450g whole fish, 6 fish cutlets or eight 75g thin fish fillets

Add 100g prawns or shrimps to the breadcrumbs before mixing with the fat. Chop large prawns roughly, leave small fish whole. Add a little milk with the egg, if necessary, to bind.

For further **variations** see over.

Glazed Forcemeat Balls

Brush the balls with egg wash before baking them.

Crumbed Forcemeat Balls

Coat the balls with beaten egg yolk; then roll in dried or browned breadcrumbs before baking or frying them.

Nut Forcemeat Balls

Coat the balls with beaten egg yolk; then roll in finely chopped or ground nuts before baking them.

Apple and Celery Stuffing

Enough for a 4–5kg goose; half the quantity will stuff a 2.5kg duck or a boned joint of pork

50g bacon, without rinds
  or *pork sausage-meat*
1 medium-sized onion
1 stick celery
3 large cooking apples

75g soft white
  breadcrumbs
1 × 15ml spoon grated
  lemon rind
salt and pepper

Chop the bacon, if used. Fry the bacon or sausage-meat in a pan, turning it over, until browned. Remove, and put to one side, leaving the fat in the pan. Prepare the onion and celery and chop them finely. Fry them in the pan for 5 minutes. Remove and put to one side. Peel, core, and dice the apples finely and fry them in the pan until softened and lightly browned. Mix together the meat, onion, celery, apples, breadcrumbs, lemon rind, and seasoning to taste.

Use as above, or for turkey or wild rabbit.

Note Any kind of bacon can be used, eg scraps off the end of a bacon joint or trimmings left after slicing. Knuckle end scraps of ham can be used as an alternative. Adapt the quantity of salt used to suit the saltiness of the meat.

Apple and Walnut Stuffing

Enough for a 2.5kg duck; double the quantity will stuff a 4–5kg goose

1 small onion
15g butter
1 large cooking apple
12 whole shelled walnuts
  or *24 halves*
50g pork sausage-meat
50g soft white
  breadcrumbs

1 × 2.5ml dried mixed
  herbs
salt and pepper
1 egg
a little milk
  (optional)

Skin the onion and chop it finely. Melt the butter in a pan, add the onion, and fry very gently until softened and light golden. Peel, core, and chop the apple. Chop the walnuts and mix together with the onion, apple, sausage-meat, breadcrumbs, and herbs. Season to taste. Beat the egg until liquid and stir into the stuffing mixture to bind it, adding a little milk if necessary.

Use for roast goose or duck.

Chicken Herb Stuffing

Enough for a 1.5kg chicken

1 chicken liver
4 × 10ml spoons soft
  white breadcrumbs
1 × 5ml spoon chopped
  shallot
1 × 5ml spoon chopped
  fresh tarragon

1 × 5ml spoon chopped
  parsley
1 × 5ml spoon chopped
  fresh chervil
salt and pepper
25g butter (approx)

Remove the skin and tubes, and chop the liver finely. Mix it with the breadcrumbs, shallot, herbs, and seasoning. Melt the butter and stir in enough to moisten the stuffing.

Use for roast chicken.

Note Do not use dried herbs for this delicately flavoured stuffing.

Chicken Giblet Stuffing

Enough for a 2kg chicken or the neck end of a 5–6kg turkey

1 set of chicken giblets	1 × 2.5ml spoon dried
1 medium-sized onion	mixed herbs
100g soft white	grated rind of ¼ lemon
breadcrumbs	salt and pepper
50g butter **or** margarine	1 egg
1 × 15ml spoon chopped	
parsley	

Prepare the giblets if required. Skin the onion and slice it thickly. Put into a saucepan with the giblets, cover with water, heat to boiling point, reduce the heat, and simmer for 45 minutes or until the giblets are cooked. Strain, and reserve 125ml of the cooking liquid; use the rest to make a gravy, soup or sauce.

Pick all the meat off the neck bones, and cut out the lining of the gizzard; chop or mince the flesh of all the giblets. Soak the crumbs in the reserved stock to moisten them. Melt the butter or margarine, and mix together with the giblets, breadcrumbs, herbs, and lemon rind. Season to taste. Beat the egg until liquid and stir into the stuffing mixture.

Use as above, or for pasta (eg cannelloni) or vegetables such as peppers.

VARIATION

Turkey Giblet Stuffing

Substitute turkey giblets for chicken giblets, and use double the quantity of breadcrumbs, stock, and butter or margarine.

Duck Liver Stuffing

Enough for a 2.5kg duck

heart and liver of duck	1 × 5ml spoon chopped
to be stuffed	parsley
1 small onion	25g butter
50g soft white	salt and pepper
breadcrumbs	

Prepare the heart and liver if required. Skin the onion and slice it thinly. Put it in a pan with a little water and simmer for 5–7 minutes until softened. Drain, and chop it finely with the duck heart and liver. Mix with the breadcrumbs and parsley. Melt the butter and stir it into the mixture. Season to taste.

Use for roast duck.

Mrs Beeton's Forcemeat or Forcemeat Balls for Hare

Enough for a large hare

50g ham **or** bacon,	salt
without rinds	a few grains Cayenne
100g shredded suet	pepper
grated rind of 1 lemon	a pinch of ground mace
1 × 5ml spoon chopped	150g soft white
parsley	breadcrumbs
1 × 5ml spoon chopped	3 eggs
fresh mixed herbs	lard for frying (optional)

Shred the ham or bacon. Put it in a bowl with the suet, lemon rind, herbs, and seasonings. Mix well with a fork, then mix in the breadcrumbs. Beat the eggs lightly until liquid and stir gradually into the dry ingredients, adding enough egg to make a smooth firm mixture.

Use as above, or for veal or poultry.

VARIATION

Roll the mixture into small balls. Either fry them in hot lard until browned on all sides, or place them in the roasting tin with the hare for the last 30 minutes of the cooking time.

Veal Stuffing

Enough for 1 partridge, 4 aubergines or 4 marrow rings; double the quantity will stuff a 1.5–2kg chicken

100g veal	*1 × 5ml spoon chopped*
50g ham **or**	*parsley*
bacon, without rinds	*a good pinch of dried*
25g soft white	*mixed herbs*
breadcrumbs	*salt and pepper*
25g shredded suet	*1 egg*

Chop the veal and ham or bacon finely. Add the breadcrumbs, suet, and herbs, and season to taste. Beat the egg until liquid and stir into the stuffing mixture to bind it.

Wholemeal Stuffing or Filling

Enough for a 1.5–2kg chicken, eight 75g thin fish fillets or a boned joint of veal

50g margarine	*1 × 2.5ml spoon chopped*
100g soft wholemeal	*thyme*
breadcrumbs	*grated rind of $\frac{1}{2}$ lemon*
2 × 15ml spoons chopped	*salt and pepper*
parsley	

Melt the margarine and mix with the breadcrumbs, herbs, and lemon rind; season to taste.

Tomato Stuffing

Enough for 1 wild duck, 2 pigeons or 1.5kg coarse white fish

2 large ripe tomatoes	*50g soft brown*
1 sweet red pepper **or**	*breadcrumbs (approx)*
2 canned pimentos	*salt and pepper*
1 clove of garlic	

Skin, de-seed, and chop the tomatoes. Remove the membranes and seeds from the pepper and chop the flesh of the pepper or pimentos finely. Skin and crush the garlic. Mix the ingredients together, using enough breadcrumbs to absorb the juice of the tomatoes. Season to taste.

Use as above, or for other small game birds.

Sage and Onion Stuffing

Enough for a 2.5kg duck; double the quantity will stuff a 4–5kg goose

2 small onions	*50g butter* **or** *margarine*
4 young sage leaves **or**	*salt and pepper*
1 × 2.5ml spoon dried	*1 egg (optional)*
sage	
100g soft white	
breadcrumbs	

Skin the onions and slice them thickly. Put them in a pan with a little water and parboil. Drain and chop the onions finely. Scald the fresh sage leaves, if used, and chop them finely. Mix together with the onions and breadcrumbs. Melt the butter or margarine, add to the stuffing, and season to taste. Mix together thoroughly. If the stuffing is to be shaped into balls, beat the egg until liquid and add enough to the stuffing to bind it.

Use as above, or for pork.

Mushroom Stuffing

Enough for 4 pigeons, eight 75g thin fish fillets, 6 aubergines or 6 medium marrow rings

100g button mushrooms	*1 × 15ml spoon butter*
1 rasher of streaky	*or margarine*
bacon, without rinds	*a pinch of grated nutmeg*
100g soft white	*salt and pepper*
breadcrumbs	*1 egg*

Clean and chop the mushrooms including the stalks. Chop the bacon, and fry in a pan for 2 minutes or until the fat runs. Add the chopped mushrooms and fry very gently for 3–5 minutes, turning them frequently. When the mushrooms soften, remove the pan from the heat and stir in the breadcrumbs, fat, nutmeg, and seasoning. Beat the egg until liquid and stir into the mixture to bind it.

Garlic Stuffing
See p1400.

Oyster Stuffing (1)

Enough to fill the neck end of a 4kg turkey or the body cavity of a 2–2.5kg boiling fowl

*6 fresh **or** canned oysters*
100g soft white
  breadcrumbs
*50g shredded suet **or***
  butter

1 × 5ml spoon chopped
  fresh mixed herbs
a pinch of grated nutmeg
salt and pepper
1 egg

Open fresh oysters (p426) and simmer them very gently in their own liquor for 10 minutes. Canned oysters need no cooking. Drain, and reserve a little of the liquor. Cut the oysters into small pieces. Mix the breadcrumbs with the suet or with melted butter. Add the oysters, herbs, and nutmeg, and season to taste. Beat the egg until liquid and stir into the oyster mixture, adding a little oyster liquor if necessary to bind it.

Oyster Stuffing (2)

Enough for 1 carp or similar fish

*8 fresh **or** canned oysters*
6 anchovy fillets
25g soft white
  breadcrumbs
1 shallot

1 × 5ml spoon chopped
  parsley
salt and Cayenne pepper
1 egg yolk

Open fresh oysters (p426) and simmer them very gently in their own liquor for 10 minutes. Canned oysters need no cooking. Drain, and reserve the liquor. Cut the oysters and the anchovy fillets into small pieces, and mix together with the breadcrumbs. Skin the shallot and chop it finely. Add to the stuffing with the parsley, and season to taste. Stir in the egg yolk and enough of the oyster liquor to bind the mixture.

Marrowfat Forcemeat

See Russian Veal Escalopes, p561.

Egg Stuffing

Enough for two 75g sliced thin white fish fillets or chicken breast meat, rolled

1 hard-boiled egg
1 × 15ml spoon softened
  butter
7 × 10ml spoons soft
  white breadcrumbs

1 × 2.5ml spoon chopped
  parsley
salt and pepper
milk

Chop the egg finely. Cream the butter and mix thoroughly with the chopped egg, breadcrumbs, and parsley. Season to taste. Add just enough milk to bind the mixture.

PANADA-BASED STUFFINGS

Flour Panada

Basic recipe

125ml water, stock
  or milk
25g butter

25g plain flour
salt and pepper

Put the liquid and butter in a small pan, and heat to boiling point. Sift the flour and add to the pan, stirring briskly with a wooden spoon. Continue to stir over heat until the panada forms a stiff ball and leaves the sides of the pan clear. Season to taste. Spread the panada on a plate, and when cool, use to bind pancake fillings and croquette mixtures.

Veal Panada or Farce

Enough for 20 small pastry cases or 8 pancakes

400g raw veal,
  preferably from the
  fillet
100g panada using white
  stock (p329)

2 eggs
salt and pepper

Mince or chop the veal very finely. Mix the veal and cooled panada, and pound together. Add the eggs, one at a time, and beat well after each addition. Season to taste.

Chicken Panada or Farce

Enough for 20 cocktail vol-au-vents or 8 pancakes

200g raw white chicken meat or 1 large chicken joint or quarter (wing and breast) weighing 200–250g (approx)
butter for greasing

salt and pepper
1 egg
100g panada (p379), using chicken stock or milk

Skin and bone the chicken meat or joint. Mince the meat finely. Grease the inside of a heatproof pot or jar with butter and put in the minced meat. Cover tightly, stand in a pan of simmering water at least 10cm deep, and cook for 1 hour. Top up with more boiling water if required during cooking.

Let the pot or jar cool for 5 minutes. Remove the chicken meat and pound it with any liquid in the jar, or process it briefly in an electric blender. Season to taste.

Beat the egg until liquid, and mix most of it slowly and thoroughly into the cooled panada. Mix with the pounded chicken. Re-season if required.

Use as above, or for filling other small pastry cases.

Fish Forcemeat

Enough for twelve 75g thin fish fillets, 8 fish cutlets or 4 whole fish weighing 350–450g

1 egg
100g panada (p379), using fish stock (p330) or milk
salt and pepper

200g raw white fish, without skin or bone
grated rind and juice of ½ lemon

Beat the egg until liquid. Add it gradually to the cooled panada, beating well after each addition. Season to taste. Flake the fish and beat it into the panada. Add the grated lemon rind and juice to taste.

Use as above, or for vegetables.

Smelt and Shrimp Farce

Enough for four 75g thin fish fillets or 1 whole fish

2 smelts
100g cooked shelled shrimps
50ml fish stock (p330) or water
1 × 15ml spoon butter

1 × 15ml spoon plain flour
1 × 5ml spoon anchovy essence
1 egg
salt and pepper

Remove the heads and back bones from the smelts. Pound the smelts and shrimps together or process in an electric blender until quite smooth. Make a panada (p379) using the fish stock or water, the butter, and flour. Spread the panada on a plate and leave to cool. Add the smelt and shrimp mixture and anchovy essence to the panada. Beat the egg until liquid and stir in. Mix together thoroughly. Season to taste.

Note Rub through a sieve if to be used for quenelles.

OTHER STUFFINGS

Apricot Stuffing

Enough for 1 boned joint of pork or a 2.5kg duck; double the quantity will stuff a 4–5kg goose

75g dried apricots
75g boiled long-grain rice **or** *soft white breadcrumbs*
25g butter
1 × 2.5ml spoon salt
1 × 2.5ml spoon ground pepper

a pinch each of dried thyme, ground mace and grated nutmeg
1 stick celery **or** *50g green pepper*
white stock (p329) **or** *water from soaked apricots*

Soak the apricots overnight in cold water. Drain and reserve the liquid. Chop the apricots and mix with the rice or breadcrumbs. Melt the butter and stir it into the stuffing with the seasoning, herbs, and spices. Prepare the celery or green pepper, chop finely, and add to the mixture. Moisten the stuffing with a little stock or water reserved from the soaked apricots.

Use as above, or for roast chicken, turkey, guinea-fowl, and lamb.

Calf or Chicken Liver Stuffing

Enough for a 2kg chicken

200g calf **or** *chicken liver*
4 thick bacon rashers, without rinds **or** *100g pork sausage-meat*
1 small onion
25g butter

2 × 15ml spoons beaten egg
1 × 2.5ml spoon chopped fresh herbs
1 × 5ml spoon chopped parsley
salt and pepper

Remove the skin and tubes, and cut the liver into 5mm dice together with the bacon rashers, if used. Skin the onion and chop it finely. Melt the butter in a frying pan and stir in the liver, bacon or sausage-meat, and the onion. Fry gently for 10 minutes, stirring the mixture and turning it over often. Leave to cool; then chop the liver mixture more finely. Mix in the beaten egg, herbs, and seasoning.

Use as above, or for game.

Chestnut Stuffing

Enough for the neck end of a 5–6kg turkey; half the quantity will stuff a 1.5kg chicken

800g chestnuts **or** *500g shelled* **or** *canned chestnuts (approx)*
125–250ml stock
50g butter

salt and pepper
a pinch of ground cinnamon
1 × 2.5ml spoon sugar

Make a slit in the rounded side of chestnuts in their shells and bake or boil them for 20 minutes. Remove the shells and skins while hot. Put the chestnuts in a pan with just enough stock to cover them. Heat to boiling point, reduce the heat, cover, and stew until the chestnuts are tender. Drain and reserve the stock. Rub the chestnuts through a fine wire sieve into a bowl. Add the butter, seasoning, cinnamon, and the sugar. Stir in enough stock to make a soft stuffing.

Chestnut and Onion Stuffing

Enough for a 2.5kg duck

500g chestnuts **or** *300g shelled* **or** *canned chestnuts (approx)*
stock **or** *water*

1 large mild onion
salt and pepper
1 egg

Prepare the chestnuts as above, and cook in stock or water until tender. Drain off the liquid. Mince or chop the chestnuts finely. Skin the onion and slice it thickly. Put the onion in a pan with a little water and boil for 10 minutes; drain and chop finely. Mix together the chestnuts and onion, and season to taste. Beat the egg until liquid and mix in to bind the stuffing.

Mousseline Forcemeat
(for fish)
See p885.

Oatmeal Stuffing

Enough for a 2–2.5kg boiling fowl

200g medium oatmeal   *salt and pepper*
2 medium-sized onions   *a pinch of grated nutmeg*
100g shredded suet

Toast the oatmeal, shaking the pan occasionally, until it is a light golden colour. Skin the onions and slice them thickly. Put in a pan with a little water, and simmer for 7–8 minutes. Drain and chop finely. Mix together with the toasted oatmeal and the suet. Add the seasoning and nutmeg.

Buckwheat Stuffing

See p869.

Prune and Apple Stuffing

Enough for 1 boned joint of pork or a 2.5kg duck; double the quantity will stuff a 4–5kg goose

100g prunes   *50g shredded suet* **or**
4 × 10ml spoons long-   *butter*
  grain rice **or** *125g*   *salt and pepper*
  cooked rice   *grated rind and juice of*
1 large cooking apple   *$\frac{1}{2}$ lemon*
50g shredded almonds   *1 egg*

Soak the prunes overnight in cold water. Drain off the liquid. Cook the rice in boiling salted water until tender; then drain. Stone and chop the prunes. Peel, core, and chop the apple roughly, and mix together with the prunes, rice, apple, almonds, and suet or butter. Season to taste and add the lemon rind and juice. Beat the egg until liquid and mix into the stuffing to bind it.

Rice Stuffing

Enough for a 2kg chicken

50g long-grain rice **or**   *25g butter*
  150g cooked rice   *2 × 15ml spoons chopped*
1 chicken liver   *parsley*
1 small onion   *a sprig of thyme*
50g seedless raisins   *salt and pepper*
50g ground almonds   *1 egg*

Cook the rice in boiling salted water until just tender; then drain. Remove the skin and tubes, and chop the liver. Skin the onion and chop it finely. Mix together with the rice, liver, raisins, and almonds. Mash in the butter with a fork. Add the herbs, and season to taste. Mix well. Beat the egg until liquid and mix into the stuffing to bind it.

Use for roast chicken, other meats, fish or vegetables.

Wild Rice Stuffing

Enough for a brace of pheasants or 1 large guinea-fowl

giblets of the bird to be   *1 small stick of*
  stuffed   *celery*
750ml water   *100g mushrooms*
1 × 5ml spoon salt   *50g butter*
150g wild rice   *4 × 15ml spoons*
2 shallots   *concentrated tomato*
15g green pepper   *purée*

Prepare the giblets, if required (p624), and cut into small pieces. Put them into a pan with the water, and salt. Heat to boiling point, reduce the heat, cover, and simmer for 15 minutes. Remove the giblets from the liquid. Re-heat to boiling point and stir in the wild rice. Reduce the heat, cover, and simmer for about 30 minutes until the rice is nearly tender; then drain. Prepare and chop the vegetables. Melt the butter in a pan, add the vegetables, and fry gently for 3 minutes. Remove from the heat, add the rice and tomato purée, and mix well.

Use as above, or for other roast game birds.

Rice and Olive Stuffing

Enough for a 1–1.5kg fresh haddock

4 × 10ml spoons long-grain rice **or** 125g cooked rice	50g stuffed olives
50g butter	¼ × 2.5ml spoon dried sage
1 medium-sized onion	¼ × 2.5ml spoon dried thyme
2 sticks celery	salt and pepper

Cook the rice in boiling salted water until tender; then drain. Melt the butter in a small pan. Prepare the onion and celery and chop them finely. Fry gently in the butter for 3 minutes. Chop the olives, and add to the pan with the rice and herbs; cook gently for 3 minutes. Season to taste.

Use for baked fish.

Brown Rice and Fruit Stuffing

Enough for 2.5kg chicken or 1 large marrow

50g dried apricots	25g pine kernels
50g prunes	25g butter
40g brown rice	salt and pepper
1 large **or** 2 small cooking pears	1 egg
juice and grated rind of ¼ lemon	

Put the apricots and prunes into a large bowl and cover with boiling water. Soak for about 4 hours until tender and swollen. Put the rice into a saucepan, drain the liquid from the dried fruit into it, add extra water if required, and bring slowly to the boil. Reduce the heat, cover, and simmer gently for about 40 minutes until the rice is tender.

Meanwhile, chop the fruit finely and discard any stones. Peel, core, and chop the pears, and mix with the lemon rind and juice. Chop the nuts coarsely. Drain the rice and add the fruit and nuts. Melt the butter and add to the rice, mixing it in well. Beat the egg until liquid and mix into the stuffing to bind it.

Sausage-meat Stuffing

Enough for a 1.5–2kg chicken; triple the quantity will stuff a 5–6kg turkey

liver of the bird to be stuffed	1 × 15ml spoon chopped parsley
500g pork sausage-meat	1 × 5ml spoon dried mixed herbs
50g soft white breadcrumbs	1 egg
	salt and pepper

Remove the skin and tubes, and chop the liver finely. Mix together with the sausage-meat and breadcrumbs. Add the herbs. Beat the egg until liquid and mix into the stuffing to bind it. Season to taste.

Soyer's Apple and Herb Stuffing

Enough for a 4–5kg goose

300g potatoes	a pinch of bruised fresh thyme (see **Note**)
2 medium-sized onions	salt and pepper
2 medium-sized cooking apples	
a pinch of finely rubbed fresh sage (see **Note**)	

Prepare the potatoes and cook them in boiling salted water until tender. Drain and mash. Skin the onions and slice them thickly. Put them in a pan with a little water, and simmer for 7–8 minutes. Drain and chop the onion finely. Mix all the ingredients together, and season to taste.

Use for roast goose.

Note The original recipe for this stuffing called for 4 large fresh sage leaves and 4 thyme leaves. The leaves were rubbed, bruised, and crushed between the fingers so that their aromatic oils would flavour the stuffing, but the small quantity of leaves would not be noticeable.

Garnishes and Accompaniments

A garnish is best described as an edible decoration added to a savoury dish to improve its appearance, and to provide complementary flavour and texture. The quantity used is very much a matter of personal choice and convenience, although it should be simple rather than elaborate.

A garnish should generally be added just before the dish is served; it is, therefore, important to prepare it in advance, and to keep it fresh, whether a crisp or moist raw garnish or one that should be served hot.

A soup accompaniment such as dumplings or quenelles can make a first course into a main course, whilst certain main course accompaniments are a traditional part of a meal, eg Roast Beef with Yorkshire Pudding.

GARNISHES FOR SOUPS

A garnish gives character to a clear soup or consommé. Some consommés derive their name from the garnish added; Consommé Julienne, for example, is garnished with julienne strips of vegetables, and Consommé with Pasta is garnished with tiny fancy shapes of macaroni or vermicelli. For consommés and their garnishes, see pp335–38.

Chopped Fresh Herbs

Wash and dry the herbs and chop them finely. Squeeze in muslin or soft kitchen paper to remove excess moisture. Sprinkle them over the soup just before it is served.

The herbs most often used are parsley or mint in green pea soup, chervil or basil in tomato soup, and chives in potato soup.

Cucumber

Cut some very thin slices or julienne strips of cucumber and add to chicken or other hot soups.

Fried Onion Rings

Skin an onion and slice thinly. Dip the rings in egg white, or milk and flour, and fry in a little fat until golden-brown and crisp. Add to a thick soup just before it is served.

Julienne Vegetables

Finely shred vegetables into strips about 2–3cm in length. Use as required.

Mushroom Slices

Slice mushrooms thinly and fry gently in a little butter for a few minutes, until softened. Add to thick soups.

Orange and Lemon Slices

Cut thin slices. Serve in clear soups, some cold soups, and in tomato soup.

Pasta

Pasta, such as macaroni and tagliatelli, can be added, in short lengths, to thin soups. Cook the pasta separately so that the soup is not clouded. Add the hot, drained pasta to the soup preferred, just before it is served.

Chopping fresh herbs

Rice

Dry boiled rice can be added to soup just before it is served, or it can be cooked in the soup. In this case, it should be added about 15 minutes before the end of the cooking time.

Watercress

Wash, dry, and break into small sprigs. Keep in a polythene bag in a refrigerator until needed. Add to thick soups, especially chicken or vegetable purée soups, just before serving.

ACCOMPANIMENTS FOR SOUPS

Accompaniments are generally handed separately when the soup is served. Many of them can be served with main-course dishes as well as with soups. For instance, dumplings are a standard accompaniment for boiled beef.

Bread Croûtons

Cut bread slices into 5mm–1cm dice and fry in deep or shallow fat until golden-brown. Alternatively, butter a 5mm thick slice of crustless bread, cut into dice, and place, buttered side up, in a shallow tin. Bake in a moderate oven at 180°C, Gas 4, until golden-brown and crisp.

Serve hot in a separate dish or sprinkle over any kind of soup.

Grissini

Follow the recipe on p1164. Serve with thin or thick soups.

Cheese Croûtes

Cut rounds from a thin slice of bread, using a 3–4cm cutter. Toast these on one side, spread the other with butter and a little grated cheese, and toast under a grill until golden-brown. Either serve separately or add to tomato or onion soup.

Fairy Toast

Bake very thin slices of bread in a cool oven at 150°C, Gas 2, until golden and very crisp. Serve hot, separately, with most soups.

Grated Hard Cheese

Serve separately with Minestrone (p369) and other mixed vegetable soups. Can also be sprinkled over the soup just before it is served. Finely grated Parmesan is usually served with these soups.

Melba Toast

Toast thin slices of white bread, then split carefully through the middle and toast the untoasted surfaces under a hot grill, or bake in a cool oven until crisp and golden. Serve with any hot soup.

Pulled Bread

Break apart a fresh French loaf, pull out the inside, and dry in a very cool oven until pale golden and crisp. Serve with soup or pâté.

Rusks

Cut thick slices of bread into 'fingers', dip in milk or gravy and place on a baking sheet in a cool oven until dry, crisp, and golden. A little beaten egg can be added to the milk or gravy. Serve, separately, with any hot soup.

Sippets or Toasted Croûtons

Toast thin slices of bread until crisp and golden. Cut into triangles, 'fingers' or small dice. Serve hot, separately, with thick soups.

Soured Cream or Thick Yoghurt

Serve separately, or add to, Russian, Polish, or Hungarian Soups.

Quenelles

Dip 2 dessertspoons in hot water, and form oval shapes by filling each with the quenelle mixture. Cover the first spoonful with the second. Scrape the loose mixture from the sides. Loosen each quenelle from the spoons with a knife dipped in hot water, and drop gently into simmering water or soup as required. Alternatively, poach the quenelles.

As they are so delicate, quenelles are generally only added to soup or any other dish at the point of serving.

Small quenelles made with a light forcemeat or fish forcemeat, are traditionally served in Mock Turtle Soup (p339). If made with fish, they are sometimes served in fish soups, but more frequently used to garnish sole or chicken dishes. They can also form a main course if served with a suitable sauce.

For specific quenelle recipes, see Beetroot Quenelles (p387); Poached Chicken Quenelles (p400); Liver Dumplings (p387); Veal Quenelles (p400); Mousseline Quenelles (p884); Pike Quenelles (p446).

Dumplings

Basic recipe

Makes 16 (approx)

100g self-raising flour   *50g shredded suet*   *salt and pepper*

Mix together the flour, suet, and seasoning to taste. Bind with enough cold water to make a soft smooth dough. With floured hands, divide the dough into 16 portions and roll into balls. Drop into simmering salted water, stock, soup or into a stew, and simmer for 15–20 minutes.

Serve with the liquid or with boiled meat, stew or vegetables.

Note See also Boiled Beef with Vegetables and Dumplings (p500).

VARIATIONS

Herb Dumplings

Add 25g finely grated onion and 1 × 2.5ml spoon chopped fresh herbs to the flour and suet.

Meat Dumplings

Add 2 × 15ml spoons finely minced or puréed meat to the flour and fat, and bind the dumplings with meat stock instead of water.

Soya Dumplings

Substitute 1 × 15ml spoon soya flour for 1 × 15ml spoon flour, and add 1 × 2.5ml spoon dried mixed herbs.

Liver Dumplings

Makes 30–36

2 slices white bread
a little milk **or** water
500g calf **or** chicken
  liver
1 small onion
grated rind of $\frac{1}{2}$ lemon
1 × 5ml spoon chopped
  parsley
salt and pepper

a pinch of grated nutmeg
2 × 15ml spoons plain
  flour
2 eggs
1.5 litres general
  household stock (p329)
  or water
50g butter (optional)

Cut the crusts off the bread and soak the bread in milk or water. Remove the skin and tubes from the liver and chop or mince the liver finely. Squeeze the bread as dry as possible and add it to the liver. Skin the onion and chop it finely. Add to the liver and bread with the lemon rind, parsley, seasoning, nutmeg, and flour. Mix together well. Beat the eggs until liquid, and mix with the other ingredients. Form the mixture into quenelles (p386).

Meanwhile, heat the stock or water to boiling point in a large pan and gently lower the quenelles into the liquid. Simmer for 15 minutes.

Serve in meat purées and other thick soups. Alternatively, drain, and serve with melted butter poured over them or with sautéed onions.

Note It is advisable to test the first dumpling before forming the others. If it crumbles, add a little more egg to the rest of the mixture. It is important not to have the mixture too stiff. It should be of a dropping consistency and not possible to form the dumplings with the hands.

Beetroot Quenelles

Makes 20 (approx)

1 cold cooked beetroot
200g cooked chicken **or**
  beef
$\frac{1}{2}$ × 2.5ml spoon salt
4 × 15ml spoons double
  cream

1 egg white
1.5 litres water
1 × 10ml spoon salt

Peel the beetroot and grate it finely. Mince the chicken or beef; then pound it with $\frac{1}{2}$ × 2.5ml spoon of salt, or process it with the salt in an electric blender, to make a smooth purée. Rub the meat through a sieve to make it smoother, if necessary. Beat the cream into the purée. Whisk the egg white until stiff but not dry, and fold it into the meat and cream mixture. Form quenelles (p386), adding a little grated beetroot to the first spoonful of each quenelle, so that each has beetroot in the centre.

Meanwhile, heat the water in a large pan to boiling point and add the salt. Reduce the heat to simmering point, lower the quenelles gently into the liquid, and simmer for 10 minutes. Serve in soups, eg Clear Beetroot Soup (p339).

Vegetarian Forcemeat Balls

Makes 12 (approx)

1 × 15ml spoon pine
  kernels
100g soft white **or**
  wholemeal
  breadcrumbs
1 × 15ml spoon plain
  flour
1 × 15ml spoon
  vegetable cooking fat

1 × 2.5ml chopped
  parsley
1 × 2.5ml spoon dried
  mixed herbs
1 × 2.5ml spoon grated
  lemon rind
salt and pepper
1 egg
fat **or** oil for frying

Chop the pine kernels, and mix together with the breadcrumbs, flour, fat, herbs, and lemon rind. Season to taste. Beat the egg until liquid, add to the breadcrumbs, and mix to a stiff paste. Roll into balls. Fry them in deep fat or oil (p302), or in shallow fat until golden-brown. Serve hot.

Serve in soups.

Devilled Biscuits

Makes 12 biscuits or 'fingers'

12 small water biscuits
  or *3 large slices white*
  bread from a tin loaf
butter for spreading
2 × 15ml spoons
  anchovy essence
½ × 2.5ml spoon Cayenne
  pepper

½ × 2.5ml spoon curry
  powder
½ × 2.5ml spoon ground
  allspice
1 × 5ml spoon mixed
  English mustard

Warm the water biscuits, if used, in a low or moderate oven. If using bread, cut off the crusts and toast the slices lightly on both sides. Spread one side with butter and cut into 2 × 6cm 'fingers'. Keep warm. Blend together the rest of the ingredients, and use to spread on the biscuits or toasted 'fingers'. Re-heat, flavoured side up, under a high grill or in a hot oven for 2–3 minutes or until thoroughly heated. Serve in a warmed, folded napkin, with soups.

Farfel

3–4 helpings

1 egg
1 × 2.5ml spoon salt

ground pepper
100g flour (approx)

Beat the egg until liquid, and season with salt and pepper. Add enough flour to make a stiff dough. Put to one side until hard, then grate into coarse shreds. Cook in boiling salted water for 5 minutes, then drain thoroughly. Sprinkle into thin soups or serve with vegetables and grated cheese.

Note Farfel can be stored uncooked and used as required.

TRADITIONAL ACCOMPANIMENTS FOR OTHER DISHES

The traditional accompaniments for white fish are whole boiled potatoes (called 'fish' potatoes), melted butter sauces (p715) or a sauce with a foundation white or Béchamel Sauce base (pp692–98, pp704–6), and lemon wedges. Oily fish, if plainly poached, grilled or fried, are served with sprigs of fried parsley (p398) and with Hollandaise (p712) or Tartare Sauce (p706 and p846).

The traditional accompaniments for poultry, game birds, and animals are given on p624, p657 and p674.

Most other traditional accompaniments are described in the main recipes concerned, eg Mackerel with Gooseberry Sauce (p445).

Accompaniments for Curries

bombay duck
chapatti (small, flat cake of unleavened bread)
chilli sauce or paste
chopped salted nuts, usually almonds or peanuts
desiccated coconut
diced fresh pineapple
fresh or dried dates or other dried fruits (often mixed with chopped apple or other tart fruit dipped in lemon juice)
hard-boiled eggs cut in sections
lemon wedges
mango or other fruit chutney (a sharp-flavoured and a sweet chutney can be offered as alternatives)
okra
poppadoms (thin, crisp pancakes)
sliced banana dipped in lemon juice
sliced cucumber
sliced cucumber in soured cream
sliced tomato sprinkled with oil, vinegar, and chopped chives or mint
small strips of red and green sweet peppers
thick natural yoghurt or curd cheese
thin rings of finely sliced raw onion

Apart from rice, certain accompaniments for curries have become traditional and a selection of those listed here is usually served with curries in Europe, even though they may not form part of Eastern cuisines.

Serve them in small dishes or bowls, placed on the table so that diners can help themselves.

Most of these accompaniments are also served with Indonesian, Malaysian and other South East Asian curries and similar dishes such as *satés*; also with grain-based dishes such as the Indonesian *ryjsttavel* (rice table).

UNCOOKED GARNISHES

Anchovy Fillets

Well-drained anchovy fillets are used to garnish pizzas and some salads such as Anchovy Chequerboard Salad (p835). Savouries such as Scotch Woodcock (p1284) also carry a garnish of anchovy fillets; so do some veal escalopes – the fillets are laid flat in the form of a cross on each escalope, or 1 fillet is rolled up like a small rosette and placed on each escalope.

Artichoke Hearts

Canned artichoke hearts which are already neatly trimmed can be bought ready for use as a garnish. They are set upright; the small hollow in the centre can be filled with a halved olive or a small spoonful of pâté, stuffing, or a creamy filling of the type made for vol-au-vents. The hearts then look like small, pale green flowers with the filling as the centre.

The hearts can be served cold with a dish such as cold salmon, or may be gently steamed and used on a mild fish, veal or chicken dish in a rich creamy sauce.

Caviar

This luxury roe has been largely superseded by lumpfish roe when only a sprinkling may be needed for garnishing. The black or red 'caviar' is served on fish salads and cold fish dishes, on egg dishes such as Stuffed Russian Eggs (p320), open sandwiches, and on hot Russian-style dishes such as blinis (p942) with a suitable filling.

Celery Curls

Wash a young tender stick of celery and cut it into 5cm lengths. Slice lengthways into very fine strips, or shred by drawing the pieces lengthways over a coarse grater or mandoline. Put the shreds into very cold water (iced if possible) and leave for 30 minutes. Drain the curls thoroughly, first in a colander and then on soft kitchen paper. Use chiefly for garnishing plates of cocktail snacks or for mixed hors d'oeuvres and salads. Can also garnish hot dishes containing celery.

Cucumber

(sliced)

Peel or score lengthways with the prongs of a fork or with a canelling knife. Slice thinly on to a plate. Sprinkle with salt and leave for 30 minutes with the plate slightly tilted. Drain off the liquid.

Thinly sliced cucumber, laid in overlapping lines, is used to garnish a great many cold dishes and salads. It is the classic garnish or accompaniment for cold poached salmon (p451).

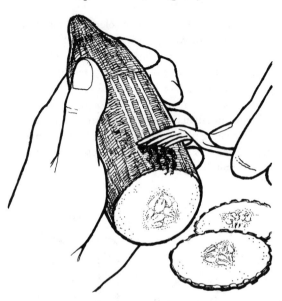

Edible Flowers and Leaves

Small flowers, such as marigolds or nasturtiums, were often used in the past for garnishing salads. Such flowers can make a fresh looking, colourful and cheap garnish. Choose flowers known to be edible and of types which do not wilt quickly.

Many common herbs have attractive flowers which can serve as a garnish. Borage flowers and leaves are a well-known garnish for salads and cold fruit cups.

Foie Gras

Foie gras or good liver pâté is used to garnish various grilled or fried steaks, such as Tournedos Rossini (p490), and similar dishes. Slice the pâté, cut out circles with a pastry cutter and chill them well before garnishing the dish.

Gherkin Fans

Make about 6 cuts from the top almost to the base of each gherkin, taking care not to cut right through the base. Spread the gherkins out carefully into fan shapes, with the base as a hinge.

Use to garnish cocktail snacks and salads.

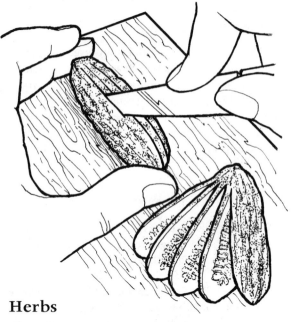

Herbs

Fresh herbs, chopped and sprinkled over a dish, are one of the simplest yet most attractive garnishes. They should be chopped and put on the dish just before it is served, so that their aroma and flavour are at their strongest. No addition is needed except perhaps a few grains of salt or 1–2 drops of lemon juice. Chives are particularly good for their fresh sharp flavour. Use chopped basil, marjoram, mint, parsley or thyme. The feathery sprays of dill and fennel make a delicately attractive garnish.

Dried herbs have little appeal as a garnish and should not be substituted for fresh herbs.

Lemon, Orange or Grapefruit Baskets

Take a clean lemon, orange or grapefruit and, with a sharp knife, cut out almost a whole quarter segment. Leave a strip of rind wide enough for the handle (about 5mm) and then cut out the corresponding segment on the other side. Carefully cut out the pulp from the handle and then remove the pulp from the lower half.

Alternatively, proceed as for Tomato Lilies (p394); then cut out the flesh from each half. Fill with any cold savoury or sweet mixture which has lemon, orange or grapefruit in its flavouring.

Note For melon and pineapple baskets and containers, see p1005.

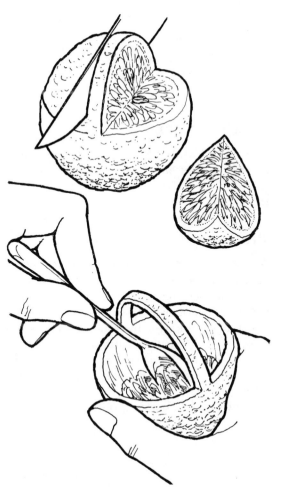

Lemon Butterflies

Take a clean lemon and, with a sharp knife, cut it into thin slices, discarding the end pieces. Depending on the size of 'wings' required and the size of the lemon, cut the slices either into halves or quarters. Cut through the rind in the middle of each piece and gently pull into 2 wings without breaking into 2 pieces. A piece of parsley may be placed in the centre to represent the 'butterfly's' body.

Lemon 'butterflies' can garnish both savoury and sweet dishes. They are served on breadcrumbed, fried or grilled meats, such as veal escalopes, and on several fish dishes.

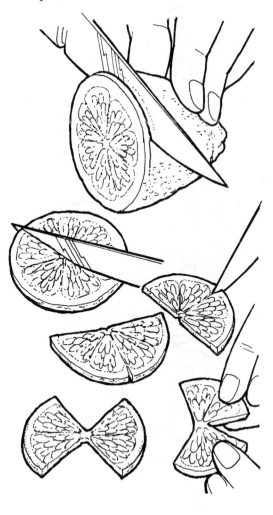

Lemon and Orange Twists

Take a clean lemon, and slice thinly, discarding the end pieces. Cut through the rind in the middle of each piece up to the centre, then gently twist each half in opposite directions. Use to garnish savoury dishes.

Crimped Lemon Slices

Using a canelling or other knife, score from the top to the bottom of a whole lemon to give a serrated edge. Cut into slices. Use to garnish escalopes and other savoury dishes.

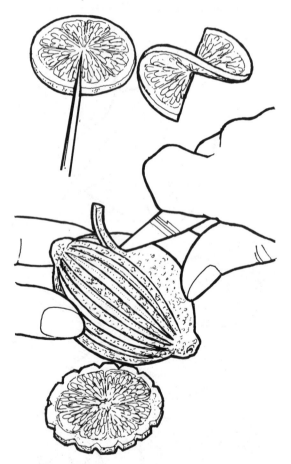

TOP *Making lemon twists*
BOTTOM *Crimping a lemon*

Olives

Green, ripe (black) and stuffed olives all make quick garnishes for many hot or cold savoury dishes. Black olives are used to garnish pizzas and cold chicken dishes; green olives are used to garnish salads and poultry dishes; and stuffed olives are often sliced to garnish cold dishes.

Both Spanish and French green olives are suitable for hors d'oeuvres, although the Spanish are considered better. Choose them large and firm and a good green colour. They can be tossed in a little oil or vinegar, but this is not essential. Any green olives left over from a meal should be rebottled at once or they may turn black.

As for black olives, the Southern Greek ones are the largest and juiciest of those generally available.

Onion Rings

Thin rings of sliced, raw onion, sometimes lightly blanched, can garnish a number of salads and spicy savoury dishes.

Pickled Onions

Very small pickled onions can be bought in various colours for garnishing cocktails. They can also be served as a colourful garnish for salads such as cole slaw (p820).

Prawns

Cooked shelled prawns are often scattered over a hot fish dish or cold fish salad. Unshelled prawns may be arranged round the edge of a hot dish, eg Sweet and Sour Prawns (p463). Use one unshelled prawn to garnish an individual dish such as fish cooked *au gratin* and presented in a scallop shell. Unshelled prawns also make an attractive garnish for a cold fish dish such as a prawn cocktail or a salad.

Many dishes for sole are garnished with prawns.

Prunes
(stuffed)

Soak prunes overnight; then drain, split and stone them. The stuffing should be pale, eg cottage or a full fat soft cheese, as a contrast to the dark prunes, and a line of the stuffing should show when the prune has been re-formed. Prunes stuffed with soft cheese are a well-known garnish for Russian, Polish and Hungarian spicy meat stews.

Radish Roses

Wash the radishes, cut off the stalks and a very thin slice of the root end. Cut thin petals from the root to the stem, taking care not to cut right through; then place the radishes in cold water (preferably iced) until they open out like roses.

Radish Water Lilies

Wash the radishes and cut off the stalks and the roots. Make 4–6 cuts from the root to the stem, taking care not to cut right through. Place in cold water (preferably iced) and leave until the radishes open out like lilies.

Savoury Butters

Smooth savoury butter of any suitable flavour can be piped in ribbons or rosettes on any cold dish with a smooth surface. This type of garnish is often used on fish or meat masked with aspic jelly or on cold savoury mousses. It looks particularly attractive if the colour of the butter contrasts with that of the dish. For savoury butters, see pp1297–1301.

Seeds and Spices

A pale coloured dish such as one masked with mayonnaise or a chaudfroid sauce can be sprinkled with dill, fennel, sesame or other suitably flavoured seeds. They can be arranged over the surface in lines or in a decorative pattern.

A brightly coloured ground spice such as paprika or turmeric can be sprinkled on a dish in the same way. Paprika gives interest as well as a spicy flavour to meat stews, and turmeric makes a vivid garnish for pasta and rice dishes. Saffron, although expensive, is only used in very small quantities and gives a beautiful touch of colour to rice and dishes masked with a white sauce, such as a blanquette of chicken, veal or rabbit. A table of herbs and spices and their uses can be found on pp287–94.

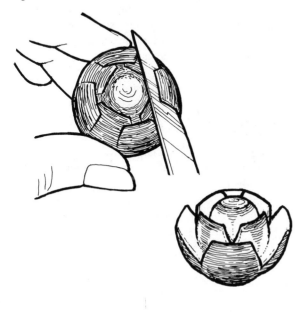

Making radish roses

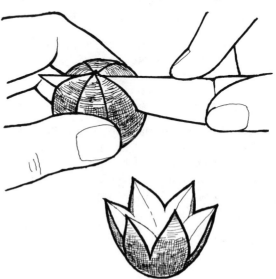

Making radish lilies

Tomato Lilies

Take a clean, firm tomato and, using a sharp knife, halve it by making a series of zigzag cuts. When you have gone right round the tomato, gently pull the halves apart. Alternatively, use a potato peeler to make the zigzag cuts.

Besides being a decorative way of presenting tomatoes as part of a large salad, small cherry tomatoes made into 'lilies' can also garnish hot or cold sliced meats.

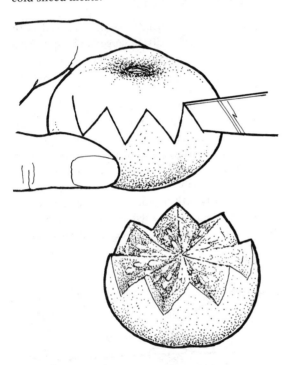

Watercress

Wash, dry, and cut the stalks short. Keep in a polythene bag in the refrigerator until needed.

Watercress can be used to garnish many different dishes. In particular, it is a classic garnish for roast game birds and cold poultry.

NUT GARNISHES

Almonds

Roasted almonds are used for garnishing grilled or fried fish or poultry. Plain or roasted almonds can make quick decorations for savoury and sweet dishes. Skinned almonds are sold whole, halved, flaked or nibbed (finely chopped).

To blanch, skin and roast almonds, see p1185.

Hazelnuts

Chopped hazelnuts are often sprinkled over vegetable dishes.

To skin hazelnuts, see p1185.

Peanuts

Chopped or whole peanuts can be used in salads and on various savoury dishes, or they can be salted and roasted like almonds.

To skin peanuts, proceed as for hazelnuts.

Pistachio Nuts

Finely chopped pistachio nuts make a colourful green garnish on savoury and sweet dishes. They can be served (salted) with drinks or used in various Middle Eastern lamb dishes and as a decorative layer in pâtés.

To skin pistachio nuts, proceed as for hazelnuts.

Walnuts and Other Nuts

Shelled and halved or chopped walnuts are used to garnish cold meats, salads, and some hot lamb and pork dishes and poultry.

Other nuts which can be chopped for garnishes are Brazil nuts, boiled or roasted glazed chestnuts (used whole or halved), cobs and filberts, macadamia or Queensland nuts, pecan nuts and pine kernels.

COOKED GARNISHES

Apple Slices

(fried)

4 helpings

2 large cooking apples	*salt and ground black*
sugar (optional)	*pepper*
flour for coating	*fat for shallow frying*

Peel and core the apples and cut each apple into 4 round slices. Discard the rounded ends. Sprinkle the slices with a little sugar if very sour. Season the flour with salt and pepper and coat the slices quickly before they discolour. Heat a little fat in a frying pan and fry the slices gently, turning once, until golden and just tender but not yet soft.

Use as a garnish for any fried or grilled pork dish.

Artichoke Hearts

See p389.

Aspic Jelly

Makes 1 litre (approx)

1 litre brown or white	*2 × 15ml spoons white*
stock (p329)	*wine vinegar*
125ml white wine or	*40–50g gelatine*
4 × 15ml spoons white	*bouquet garni*
wine and 4 × 15ml	*whites and crushed*
spoons dry sherry (for	*shells of 2 eggs*
use with red meats or	
game)	

Leave the stock to cool completely, if necessary. Skim off the fat. Put into a scalded enamel or tin-lined (not aluminium) pan with the rest of the ingredients. Stir with a scalded whisk until the gelatine softens; then bring almost to boiling point whisking all the time. Remove the whisk and leave for a few minutes. Let the liquid rise to the top of the pan, and remove from the heat.

Strain the crust and liquid very gently into a basin through muslin or a scalded jelly bag; do not break the crust as it acts as an extra filter. If it is cloudy, strain again to obtain a sparklingly clear jelly.

Note It is possible, but seldom economic or practical today, to make the jellied stock with 2 calf's feet or 500g cracked veal knuckles and 100g pork rind, instead of using the gelatine. The long, slow boiling of the large quantity of stock needed to make 1 litre of jellied stock is costly and time consuming.

Asparagus Points

See p746.

Bacon Rashers

These can be fried or grilled and served as they are. The rinds can be removed before cooking if a plain garnish is required, but the rashers curl and look more decorative if the rinds are left on. The bacon should be cooked until crisp.

Uncooked rashers are used to line a terrine to form a 'jacket' for certain pâtés. They can also be wrapped round prunes, then cooked and served as a garnish for hot savoury dishes. Long, narrow strips of bacon can be wrapped in spirals round food such as sausages, and cooked with them. Small, narrow strips of bacon can be used to bard the surface of a piece of meat for a decorative effect.

Crumbled Cooked Bacon

Crisp bacon makes an excellent garnish if it is crumbled finely and evenly. It can then be scattered over any meat or vegetable dish, or combined with grated cheese, browned breadcrumbs or hard-boiled egg yolk.

Bacon Rolls

(fried or grilled)

Cut the rinds off the rashers of streaky bacon, if required. Roll up each rasher. If frying, secure the outer end with a wooden toothpick inserted along each roll. If grilling, thread the rolls on short skewers. Put in a dry frying pan or under moderate grilling heat, and fry or grill for 3–5 minutes, turning frequently, until crisp.

Crescents of Fried Bread

Remove the crusts, and cut each slice of bread into crescents. Fry in shallow fat until golden-brown. Use to garnish blanquettes or fricasseés and various fish dishes.

Croûtons

Fried or toasted croûtons (p385) are suitable garnishes for hot fish and game dishes as well as for soups. A small pile is placed on the side of each diner's plate.

Fried Breadcrumbs

Heat a little butter in a frying pan or baking tin, add some soft white breadcrumbs, season to taste with salt and pepper, and either fry or bake until well browned. Drain well on soft kitchen paper.

Serve hot with roast game.

Gnocchi

See p867.

Hard-boiled Egg

Crumbled or sieved hard-boiled egg yolk makes an attractive, colourful garnish sprinkled over hot or cold dishes. When sprinkled over a vegetable salad, it is known as a Mimosa salad.

It can be mixed with about half its quantity of fried breadcrumbs, crumbled, crisply fried bacon, grated hard cheese or finely chopped fresh parsley.

Another way of using hard-boiled yolks is in strips or bands, either alone or alternating with bands of chopped egg white or parsley. To make the bands, cut strips of paper the same width as the bands you want to make; lay them with the same spaces between each, across the dish. Scatter the egg yolk over the spaces between the paper strips. Remove the strips carefully and serve.

Alternatively, cover the yolk bands with the paper strips and scatter chopped egg white or parsley over the spaces previously covered by paper. When the paper is removed, the dish has a topping of alternate stripes.

Whole hard-boiled eggs, sliced or cut into wedges, make an attractive garnish for many salads. Run cold water over the eggs as soon as their cooking time is up, and before shelling them, to prevent a dark line developing round the yolk.

Ham and Tongue Forcemeat Balls

See p1400.

Meat Glaze

This can be made from any strong, dark, meat stock made with lean meat and bones. It is strained, then boiled steadily until syrupy. When cooled, it should set like a rich, shiny, brown jelly. If the stock has been made without bones, gelatine is sometimes added to make it set, but it lacks the clarity of flavour of reduced bone stock and it does not keep as well.

Meat glaze is used to augment and improve the flavour of gravy and sauces, and it is sometimes added to vegetables for the same purpose. It can also be brushed over meats, such as roast beef or tongue, or over a galantine or pâté to improve its appearance, although it will not give it an aspic coating.

No set recipe can be given for making this meat glaze since stock varies in consistency and flavour whenever it is made.

Meat glaze can be made a short time in advance and stored in a heat-proof jar in the refrigerator. It can then be liquefied to a brushing consistency by standing the container in hot water. The time it can be kept will vary with the ingredients used to make the stock; if any starchy or green vegetables have been used, the glaze should be used as soon as it is made.

Meat Glaze

(made with gelatine)

Makes 150ml (approx)

4 × 15ml spoons gelatine
125ml cold water
1 × 5ml spoon beef extract **or** *yeast extract*
a few grains onion salt (optional)

a few drops dry sherry (optional)
1–2 drops gravy browning (optional)

Using a metal spoon, stir the gelatine into the cold water in a heatproof container. Stand the container in a pan of hot water and stir until dissolved; then stir in the extract and chosen flavouring. Add gravy browning if a darker colour is wanted. Brush the glaze at once, while still hot, over cold meats, galantines or pâtés. If it starts to set in ridges or lumps while brushing, replace the bowl in hot water to keep it warm.

Note Do not store the glaze for more than 48 hours. Keep covered in a refrigerator.

Other Glazes

1) *Hot meat and poultry:* Brush very lightly with butter or oil just before serving.

2a) *Crackling on roast pork:* Brush with apricot glaze (p1234) or smooth apricot jam 7–10 minutes before the end of the cooking time. Return to the oven to finish cooking and to set the glaze.

b) Melted, cooled redcurrant jelly can be used in the same way; so can clear honey flavoured with lemon juice or mixed English mustard.

c) Sieved fine-cut marmalade is sometimes used as a glaze and can be flavoured with whisky.

d) A fruit syrup glaze, eg from canned fruit, has less colour than a jam glaze, but gives a clear crisp coating.

e) If a non-sweet glaze is wanted for the crackling, brush with lightly salted butter or oil, with a little extra salt added. Raise the oven heat for a short time so that the crackling is, in effect, 'fried'.

3) *Frothing:* Dredge meat or poultry with flour and baste thoroughly with its cooking juices or with fat, shortly before the end of the cooking time. Return to the oven at a high heat to give a well-browned glazed appearance.

4) *Glazes for Pastry:* See p1248.

Macédoine of Vegetables

Makes 500g (approx)

1 turnip	*200g shelled peas*
100g carrot	*750ml water*
200g potatoes	*1 × 5ml spoon salt*
a few runner beans	*3–4 × 15ml spoons*
a few cauliflower	*butter*
florets	*pepper*

Prepare all the vegetables. Cut the turnip, carrots, and potatoes into 1cm dice. Cut the beans into 1cm diamond shapes. Bring the water to the boil, and add the salt. Put in the turnip and carrots, and boil for 3 minutes. Add the beans, and boil for another 3 minutes; then add the remaining vegetables. Boil for 5–10 minutes until the vegetables are tender but not broken. Drain thoroughly and toss in the butter. Season to taste, and use as a border or in small piles round a dish of meat. Serve hot.

Mushrooms

The most decorative way of garnishing or trimming a dish with mushrooms is to use whole, button mushroom caps. They should be steamed gently, or they can be sautéed, rather than grilled or fried, so that they keep their shape.

Large mushrooms can be cut into neat slices if care is taken in arranging the garnish.

Mushroom Purée

Makes 100g (approx)

200g mushrooms	*2 × 15ml spoons soft*
salt and pepper	*white breadcrumbs*
a pinch of grated nutmeg	*2 × 15ml spoons milk*
or *dried mixed herbs*	

Clean and blanch the mushrooms, including the stalks, in lightly salted boiling water for 1–2 minutes, or steam them over simmering water for 4–6 minutes until softened. Drain or squeeze out excess water and season with salt, pepper, and grated nutmeg or herbs. Chop the mushrooms very finely, then mix in the breadcrumbs and milk. Pound the mixture until fairly smooth, or process briefly in an electric blender.

To use the purée for garnishing, mix it with a panada (p379) and a beaten egg until it reaches the consistency of creamed potato. Use to make mushroom quenelles or a piped border for garnishing fish or meat dishes.

Onions

(glazed)
See p782.

Fried Onion Rings

Serve as a garnish for grilled or fried meat dishes such as steak, hamburgers, and sausages. Serve also on hot steamed vegetables such as spinach and with some savoury pasta and rice dishes.

Parsley

(fried)

Unless the parsley is very dirty, do not wash it before frying as parsley is difficult to dry and the moisture causes the fat to bubble and spit, which can be dangerous. Allow 4 good sprigs of parsley for each person and cut off the main stalks. Heat a pan of deep oil or fat (p302), place the parsley sprigs in the frying basket and put it into the pan. Remove from the pan immediately the hissing noise stops. Drain and serve.

Use to garnish grilled or fried fish and steaks.

Pastry

Small choux puffs and éclairs (p1251) can be used to garnish fish or meat dishes. As a rule, these small, savoury pastries are filled with a savoury butter flavoured to suit the main dish or its sauce.

Cocktail-sized vol-au-vents (p1253) are used in the same way, and are often filled with small quantities of colourful vegetables.

Fleurons of Puff Pastry

Roll out the pastry, 5cm thick, and cut out circles with a 6cm cutter. Move the cutter half-way across the circle and cut it again, making a half moon and an almond shape. Lay the half moon shapes on a baking sheet, brush the tops with egg wash, and bake in a fairly hot oven at 200°C, Gas 6, for 8–10 minutes. Roll out and re-cut the almond shapes, or bake and serve them as small biscuits.

Use to garnish dishes in a white or creamy sauce.

Spiced Pears, Peaches or Apricots

4 helpings

2 (fresh or canned) pears **or** peaches **or** 8 apricots	$\frac{1}{2} \times 2.5ml$ spoon ground cinnamon
25g butter	$\frac{1}{2} \times 2.5ml$ spoon grated nutmeg
1 × 15ml spoon soft light brown sugar	

Peel the pears, if using fresh ones, cut in half and remove the cores. Halve fresh peaches or apricots and remove the stones. If using canned fruit drain off the syrup. Arrange the fruit, cut side up, in a shallow tin. Place a small nut of butter in each hollow and sprinkle lightly with the brown sugar, cinnamon, and nutmeg. Bake in the oven for 5–10 minutes with the meat or joint.

Serve with baked ham or with roast pork.

Potatoes

Whole boiled potatoes are so often used to garnish fish dishes that they are called 'fish potatoes'. Boiled new potatoes topped with butter and chopped parsley are a common garnish for fish, white meats, poultry, and rabbit. Potato ribbons or straws, or game chips (p792) are a classic garnish for roast game birds.

Potatoes Parisienne

4–6 helpings

1kg potatoes	3 × 15ml spoons finely chopped fresh mixed
25g butter	herbs (parsley, chives,
1 × 15ml spoon oil	tarragon)
$\frac{1}{2} \times 2.5ml$ spoon salt	pepper
3 × 15ml softened butter	

Peel the potatoes and cut into small, round balls, using a potato ball scoop. Dry in a clean cloth. Heat the butter and oil in a frying pan large enough to hold all the potatoes in 1 layer. Put in the potatoes and coat evenly in the fat. Fry them gently until the potatoes are a light golden colour all over. Reduce the heat, sprinkle with the salt and cover the pan. Continue frying very gently for 12–15 minutes, shaking the pan frequently, until the potatoes are tender. Drain off the fat. Raise the heat and shake the potatoes in the pan until sizzling. Remove from the heat, add the softened butter and herbs, season well with pepper, and roll the potatoes round the pan until coated with herbs. Arrange round a meat dish or serve separately in a warmed dish.

Note Carrots, turnips, and similar vegetables can be cooked in the same way as the potatoes.

Potato as a Border

Make up 500g Duchesse potato mixture (p793). Put the mixture into a forcing bag with a large star nozzle and pipe it round the edge of a serving dish; if the dish is not heatproof, pipe it on to a greased baking sheet and transfer to the serving dish after baking. Brush with beaten egg for a golden border, or leave plain for a white border. Re-heat in a fairly hot oven at 200°C, Gas 6.

Alternatively, form the potato into a long, narrow roll with your hands and, using as little flour as possible, arrange the roll on the serving dish or baking sheet in the shape you want. Glaze it with beaten egg, if liked, and bake as above.

Use to garnish fish and meat dishes in sauces. A border of creamed potato is often used to garnish fish dishes in scallop shells and *au gratin* dishes.

Poached Chicken Quenelles

Makes 20–25

125ml chicken stock **or** *water*	*125ml single cream* **or** *milk (approx)*
1 × 10ml spoon butter	*salt and pepper*
50g flour	*fat for greasing*
300g raw chicken	*boiling water*
2 eggs	*chopped parsley*

Make a panada (p379) using the chicken stock or water, butter, and flour. Spread it on a plate and leave to cool. Chop or mince the chicken very finely. Beat the eggs until liquid and add very gradually to the chicken with the panada. Add enough cream or milk to form a moist but pliable mixture. Season well. Form the mixture into quenelles (p386). Put them in a wide, greased, shallow pan. Gently pour in enough boiling water to cover the quenelles and cover with a sheet of greased greaseproof paper. Poach very gently, without boiling, for about 20 minutes until firm. Drain, and sprinkle with chopped parsley.

Use to garnish Chicken Broth (p332) or Cream of Chicken Soup (p340), and poached chicken dishes.

Note These chicken quenelles make an excellent, light main dish. Cover them with 375ml Béchamel Sauce (p704) or Velouté Sauce (p708) and garnish with cooked green peas.

VARIATION

Poached Rabbit Quenelles

Chop or mince rabbit meat instead of chicken.

Pike Quenelles
See p446.

Veal Quenelles

Makes 24–30

500g fillet of veal	*2 eggs*
125ml white stock (p329)	*salt and pepper*
25g butter	*1 × 15ml spoon single*
50g flour	*cream (optional)*

Mince or chop the veal very finely. Make a panada (p379) using the white stock, butter, and flour. Spread it on a plate and leave to cool. Pound the panada and veal together. Beat in the eggs one at a time, and pound well. Season to taste. Rub the mixture through a sieve. Add the cream, if used. Form the mixture into quenelles (p386).

Place them in a greased, wide, shallow pan. Gently pour in enough boiling water to cover, and cover with a sheet of greased greaseproof paper. Poach very gently, without boiling, for about 20 minutes until firm. Drain. Use to garnish clear or cream soups, or delicately flavoured veal dishes.

Note Like Poached Chicken Quenelles, Veal Quenelles make a beautiful, light main-course dish. Coat them with 375ml of any delicately flavoured sauce based on Béchamel Sauce (pp704–6) and sprinkle with finely chopped parsley or hard-boiled egg yolk.

Serve garnished with green peas.

Rice as a Border
See p860.

Savoury Parsley Balls
(for stew)
See p498.

Timbales of Veal with Mushrooms

Makes 18

Panada
125ml water   *50g plain flour*
1 × 10ml spoon butter

Mushroom Purée
200g mushrooms   *2 × 15ml spoons milk*
25g butter   *salt and pepper*
2 × 15ml spoons soft
  white breadcrumbs

Meat Farce
150g lean veal   *2 × 15ml spoons*
50g cooked ham **or**   *foundation white sauce*
  tongue   *(coating consistency)*
25g butter   *(p692)*
                         2 eggs
                         oil for greasing

Make a panada (p379) using the water, butter, and flour. Spread it on a plate and leave to cool.

Make the mushroom purée. Clean the mushrooms and chop them. Melt the butter in a pan, add the chopped mushroom caps and stalks, and fry gently for 4–5 minutes, turning them over several times. Add the breadcrumbs, milk, and seasoning to taste. Mix well, then pound until smooth, or process briefly in an electric blender. Cool.

Make the meat farce. Mince or chop the veal and ham or tongue very finely. Add to the panada, and pound well. Add the butter and white sauce, and beat well. Beat in the eggs one at a time. Rub the farce through a wire sieve.

Grease eighteen 75ml timbale moulds and fill them with meat farce, leaving a 1–2cm space at the top. Make a well in each with the handle of a teaspoon previously dipped in hot water. Fill the well with mushroom purée. Cover the top with a little extra meat farce. Cover the moulds securely with oiled greaseproof paper or foil. Steam in a pan or bain marie for 20–35 minutes or until the farce is firm. Turn out on to a warmed dish and serve as soon as possible.

Use as a garnish round a party dish of veal or chicken, eg a roasted joint stuffed with mushrooms

or a dish of sliced meat in a sauce. Serve one timbale per helping.

Tomatoes

Small, whole baked tomatoes, halved baked or grilled tomatoes, or sliced, grilled or fried tomatoes are often used as a garnish for grilled and fried meat dishes, especially a mixed grill, kebabs or chops. They are also used to garnish grilled chicken or game birds.

Roast joints are sometimes presented with a garnish of small tomatoes stuffed with basic herb forcemeat (p375).

Tomato Aspic

Makes 275ml (approx)

5 × 5ml spoons gelatine   *1 × 15ml spoon meat*
2 × 15ml spoons cold   *glaze (optional) (p397)*
  water   *1 × 15ml spoon extra*
250ml fresh tomato pulp   *aspic jelly*
4 × 15ml spoons aspic   *salt and Cayenne pepper*
  jelly

Soften the gelatine in the water in a small heatproof container. Put the tomato pulp, aspic jelly, and meat glaze, if used, in a saucepan, and heat to boiling point. Remove from the heat, stir well, add the gelatine and the extra spoonful of aspic jelly, if needed (eg in hot weather). Stir until the gelatine dissolves. Season to taste with salt and Cayenne pepper. Strain through muslin or a fine nylon sieve. Cool to the consistency required; then use for masking or coating cold, white fish dishes, red meats, salmon or ham mousses.

Aspic Mayonnaise
See p844.

Sweet Glazes and Garnishes
See pp1234–35 and pp1238–41.

RELISHES, MUSTARDS, AND MUSTARD DRESSINGS

For pickles, chutneys, sauces, and ketchup, see the chapter on Bottled and Dried Preserves.

Cold Horseradish Cream

Makes 150ml (approx)

125ml double cream
2 × 15ml spoons fresh
  grated horseradish
1 × 15ml spoon white
  wine vinegar **or** lemon
  juice

1 × 10ml spoon caster
  sugar
½ × 2.5ml spoon made
  English mustard
salt and pepper

Whip the cream lightly until semi-stiff. Carefully fold in the other ingredients. Chill until ready to use.

Serve with beef.

Chrane

Makes 500g (approx)

400g cooked beetroot
150g fresh horseradish
red wine vinegar **or**
  malt vinegar

sugar

Peel and grate the beetroot and horseradish finely. Mix together, and pour over as much vinegar as the mixture will absorb. Add sugar to taste. Put into pots and secure with vinegar-proof covers or lids. Chill and use as required.

Serve with fritters or rissoles, or with cold fried fish, cold meat or poultry.

Soured Cream Relishes

See p881.

Sharp Sauce

(hot or cold)

Makes 200ml (approx)

1 shallot
2 hard-boiled egg yolks
4 anchovies
1 × 2.5ml spoon made
  English mustard

1 × 10ml spoon vinegar
1 × 5ml spoon chopped
  capers
salt and pepper
caster sugar

For a Cold Sauce
125ml single cream

For a Hot Sauce
125ml thin gravy (p727)

Skin and chop the shallot finely. Rub the egg yolks through a sieve. Pound the shallot, egg yolks, and anchovies together to form a paste. Add the mustard, vinegar, and capers, and blend together.

For a cold sauce, whip the cream until it forms soft peaks, and fold it carefully into the other ingredients.

For a hot sauce, heat the gravy to boiling point and add to the other ingredients. Return to the pan and heat to just below boiling point.

Serve with roast or grilled meats, or grilled or baked fish.

Sharp Wine Sauce

Makes 100ml (approx)

2 × 15ml spoons dry
  English mustard
4 × 15ml spoons
  medium-sweet red wine
1 × 5ml spoon
  Worcestershire sauce

1 × 15ml spoon chutney
a pinch of Cayenne
  pepper
25g butter

Blend the mustard with a little of the wine. Add the rest of the wine, the sauce, chutney, and Cayenne pepper. Melt the butter in a saucepan. Pour in the wine mixture and heat to boiling point, beating well. Use at once.

Serve with grilled meat.

Mint Sauce

Makes 125ml (approx)

*4 × 15ml spoons chopped
  fresh mint
1 × 10ml spoon sugar*

*1 × 15ml spoon boiling
  water
2 × 15ml spoons vinegar*

Put the mint into a sauce-boat. Sprinkle with the sugar. Add the boiling water, and stir until the sugar dissolves; then add the vinegar. Leave the sauce for 1–2 hours for the flavours to infuse.

Serve with roast lamb.

Note For Bottled Mint Sauce, see p1149. For Mint Jelly, see p1112.

Choron Mustard

Makes 75ml (approx)

*3 × 15ml spoons mild
  French mustard
2 × 15ml spoons
  concentrated tomato
  purée*

*a few drops lemon juice
freshly ground black
  pepper*

Mix together the mustard and tomato purée. Add the lemon juice and a grinding of black pepper.

Serve with hamburgers, sausages or fried pork chops.

Devilling Mustard for Cold Meats

Devilling Pepper
*1 × 2.5ml spoon Cayenne
  pepper
1 × 5ml spoon salt*

*1 × 5ml spoon ground
  black pepper*

Mustard
*dry English mustard
Worcestershire sauce*

water

Make up the devilling pepper by mixing all 3 ingredients thoroughly. Store in an airtight jar for use when required.

Make the mustard, using equal quantities of Worcestershire sauce and water. Season to taste with the devilling pepper.

Score cuts in any cooked cold joint of dark meat. Rub the mustard well into the cuts. Dot the meat with butter, then grill or bake, turning as required, until very hot and aromatic.

Serve at once with savoury or plain rice.

Note The devilling mustard is very good with marrow bones.

FISH AND SHELLFISH

It will be seen, from the number and variety of the recipes which we have been enabled to give under the head of FISH, that there exists in the salt ocean, and fresh-water rivers, an abundance of aliment, which the present state of gastronomic art enables the cook to introduce to the table in the most agreeable forms, and oftentimes at a very moderate cost.

Fish and shellfish are well known as a rich source of protein and minerals; but besides their value as nourishment, the many different types available today provide a wide choice of interesting dishes. Conveniently prepared fillets, cutlets, and steaks offer dishes of many different styles and textures, while the natural shapes of whole fish such as mackerel, herring, and trout look good on the plate, and are a lighter alternative to meat.

Fish is easy to cook and, having a delicate and tender texture, only needs brief cooking, thereby helping the family budget in saving fuel costs.

These factors have created an ever-widening market for seafood; this has led to forms of preservation such as freezing being used more and more to supplement untreated or wet fish. Freezing has made many seasonal fish and shellfish available all the year round as well as distributing them widely and conveniently to purchasers.

Fish

The time taken to reach the consumer largely governs the condition in which one buys fresh, wet fish, but quality also depends on the health of the fish, and on when they were caught. Depending on their breeding cycle, fish vary in weight and natural oil content with the seasons, and freezing allows fish caught at their best to be sold in the same condition throughout the year.

CLASSES OF FISH

Fish are usually classified as flat fish or round fish, and, more importantly, as white fish or oily fish.

The stronger-tasting sea fish like mackerel, herring, sprats, sardines, and salmon have their natural oil distributed throughout their bodies, whereas white fish which include the most popular sea-water fish, cod, haddock, plaice, sole, halibut, etc store this valuable fat content, along with the important vitamins A and D, in their livers.

FOOD VALUE OF FISH

Besides supplying these vitamins and minerals, fish provide an excellent source of easily digested protein. The lean white fish contain a minimum of fat, and most fish contain no carbohydrate. Steamed white fish fillets contain only about 350kJ per 100g flesh. (Naturally, a 100g fillet of plaice breadcrumbed and shallow-fried contains many more.)

BUYING FISH

All fish should be fresh. When buying whole fish look for clear shining eyes and a bright skin or scales. A recently caught mackerel is iridescent, but its colour dulls as the fish goes stale. The dark skin on plaice should show up its vivid pinky-orange spots, and the cut just behind the head, where the fish has been gutted, should show thick white flesh. For smoked fish, check for a skin that is dry to touch and has a healthy, bright bloom.

Although many fishmongers still give advice

and fillet fish to suit your needs, many shops now show only fillets ready for sale. Look for firm, translucent, close-grained flesh which looks moist and natural, not waterlogged, flabby or discoloured. Some fillets will have been frozen and defrosted before being displayed but it should not have altered their quality or food value.

Frozen Fish

It is not easy to judge quality when buying frozen fish. However, a known brand name should give the same reassurance that you expect from a good tradesman. The frozen seafood supplier is only a large fishmonger, using the best available method to preserve a delicate food.

Fillets in larger packs are usually individually quick-frozen, although block packs, some interleaved with polythene for easy separation, give good protection to the fish and take up less space in the freezer. If you can check the fish through a clear window in the film bag, see that the fillets have not dried and choose the sizes and shapes which suit you best.

The normal pieces in a frozen fish pack may be whole fillets from a small fish, or cuts from a larger unskinned fillet. The skin need not be discarded. It helps to keep the fish together when cooking and preserves a lot of the natural moisture.

As a final rule, when buying frozen fish, look for packs in good condition which indicate that they have been stored properly and for only a short time.

SALTED AND SMOKED FISH

Salting and smoking are still important in preserving fish. However, since the introduction of freezing, the heavy brining and lengthy smoking techniques have been modified. Salted cod, a standby in much old European cookery, is now more widely used elsewhere.

Smoked fish however, has become very popular in recent years. From salmon to sprats, there is a style and type of smoking to suit every fish. Two different processes are used – hot and cold smoking. Hot-smoked fish are cooked during smoking and need no further cooking. (Trout, mackerel, sprats, sole, eel, buckling, and Arbroath Smokies are examples.) Cold-smoking (at or under 35°C), simply gives a smoky flavour, reduces the moisture content, and 'sets' the flesh. (Kippers, haddock, bloaters, and smoked salmon are cold-smoked.) Kipper fillets can be marinated in oil or vinegar and eaten without further cooking, and salmon can be sliced for immediate use, but all other cold-smoked fish must be cooked.

PREPARING FISH

Except for small round fish, most fish caught by commercial fishermen are gutted at sea. Only fish such as herrings, mackerel, and red mullet have to be gutted by the fishmonger or in the kitchen.

Scaling Fish

If the scales are thick and coarse and need to be taken off, eg from sea bream, herring, or red mullet, this job must be done first. Lay the fish on soft kitchen paper to make cleaning up easier. With sharp scissors, cut off the fins; then, holding the tail, scrape both sides of the fish towards the head with the back of the knife. Rinse occasionally to remove the loose scales.

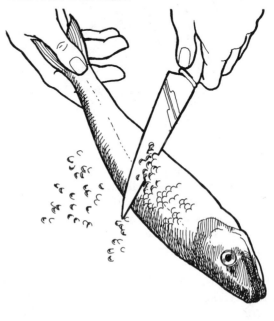

Cleaning Fish

Some small fish, like fresh sardines and whitebait, are cooked and served complete, but most have to be gutted. This simply means making a cut in the right place, removing the intestines and cleaning the cavity of blood, membrane, and black skin. At some seasons, the roe takes up a lot of the cavity space, and both hard and soft roes should be kept as they make good eating. After cleaning, lightly rinse the cut area with cold water and pat dry.

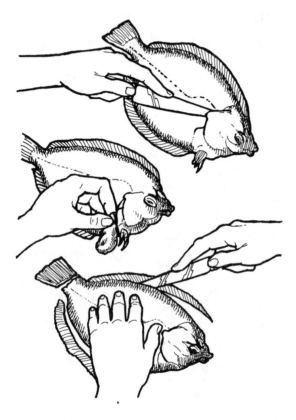

Flat fish: Place the fish, dark skin up, on soft kitchen paper and locate the gill cover, positioned just behind the head. Make a deep cut from the centre line of the fish out to the fin just at the rear of the gill opening. Remove the intestines, but if the fish is to be cooked whole, leave the roe in place. To complete the cleaning, trim the 'frill' fins and tail back to the body. You can cut off the heads of plaice and lemon sole, but the head of a Dover sole is normally left on.

Large round fish: Cut the belly lengthways, from the gills to a point about two-thirds the length of the fish from the head. Remove the entrails, saving the roe if required, rinse thoroughly, and pat dry.

Small round fish: Clean most white fish and trout as described above. It is usual to remove mackerel heads before preparing, which makes cleaning easier. Herring are different because the entrails to be disposed of are minimal. Just make a downward cut behind the gills and pull the head back; then clean the area before rinsing. Leave the roe in place if grilling or cooking whole.

Skinning Fish

Removing the skin from a slippery fish can be tricky and it may be simpler to cook the fish first. Dover soles should have at least the dark skin removed because it is coarser than that of lemon sole or plaice.

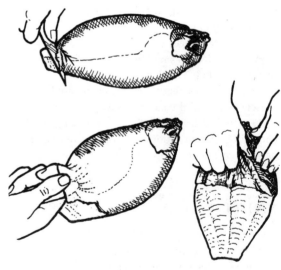

Flat fish: Lay the fish on a wooden board, white side down. With a sharp knife or scissors cut the 'frill' fins and tail back to the fish, if not already done, and scrape the tail end until the skin starts to lift. It is then easy to free a piece of skin; now slip the thumb or the end of a round-bladed knife under it and loosen the skin from the flesh, working towards the head. When enough has been loosened like this, pull it off from the tail to head end. Repeat the process on the white side if required.

Work cautiously on soft-skinned fish, so as not to tear the flesh.

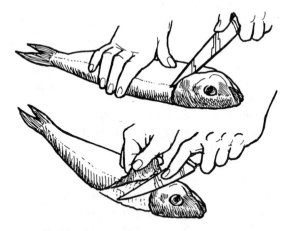

Round fish: Remove all the fins and make a cut in the skin all around the fish behind the head. It also helps to make a thin cut along the backbone of the fish. Starting on one side, loosen the skin from the belly flap and gradually pull towards the tail. Take care not to remove the flesh at the same time. It may help to hold the flesh down with the flat of a knife blade, and to dip your fingers in dry salt to give a firmer grip. Then skin the other side of the fish.

Filleting Fish

Filleting means removing the flesh in two or four whole slices from the head and central bone structure. The head, bones, and skin of white fish are the basis for natural fish stock and should not be thrown away. If the fishmonger is filleting the fish, always ask him for the bones and trimmings. You have paid for them, and are entitled to them.

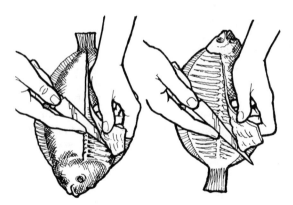

Flat fish: Lay the fish on a flat surface with its tail towards you. With a sharp, pointed knife, make a cut down the centre of the back right down to the backbone, from just behind the head to the tail. Then, turning the knife so that it lies flat against the bones, cut the flesh free from the bone, using the bone structure as a guide. Cut and loosen the fillet all the way to the edge of the fish and lift free.

Repeat the process with the other top fillet; then turn the fish over, and remove the two fillets from the other side in the same way.

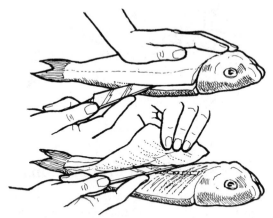

Round fish: Lay the gutted fish on its side and cut round behind the head. Then insert the point of the knife into the back of the fish, just behind the head, and cut right down the backbone all the way to the tail. Keeping the knife flat, and pressed against the rib bones, slice the fillet free along the length of the fish. Turn the fish over and remove the second fillet in the same fashion. Rinse, check for bones, and cut off the fins.

Boning Fish

Herring, mackerel or trout: Remove the head and cut the belly right to the tail. Open the fish flat, and set aside the roe; then place the fish, skin side up, on a board and press both sides of the backbone all the way down the fish. Turn over and pull the backbone clear, cut off end of bone and tail. Rinse and check for any remaining bones. (For boning sprats, see p420.)

Other Specialized Preparations

Skate: Fish other than the two main types may require a more specialized filleting technique. For instance, when preparing skate or any of the other rays, only the 'wings' are used for cooking. The skate wings are cut from either side of the backbone and cooked whole or cut into portions, depending on size; skate bones are large and pliable, so there is no need to fillet the wings. However, the dark skin is a problem and the sharp hooks embedded in the skin should be carefully cut out after skinning. Skate carry a good deal of natural slime

and this should be scrubbed off first; then nick out the flesh along the thick side, just under the skin, to provide a purchase point. Use a strong pair of pliers to grip the skin and pull it off in one piece.

Dog fish or tope: These members of the shark family present the same sort of problem. The fish has a soft-boned (cartilaginous) structure so there is no need to fillet it. The skin, however, is very tough and needs to be removed before cooking. Gut the fish as for round fish and remove the fins and tail. To skin, follow the method described for eel (below).

Monkfish: Of the remaining soft-boned fish, the monkfish is the most common. At first sight the fish seems unattractive but the flesh is white, close-textured, and has much flavour. The large head should be removed where the definite shape of the tail commences. The meaty tail portion is easy to skin and cut into portions before cooking.

Eels: Both fresh-water and conger eels pose a slightly different problem in preparation. The larger sea-water species are difficult to skin, and are best cooked gutted and cut into steaks or fillets. The skin can then be removed after cooking.

Fresh-water eels, unlike other fish, live for a long time out of water. They are sold live, killed at the point of sale, and then skinned if necessary. If large, hang the eel up by a string round the 'neck', and make a cut through the skin all round the eel, just behind the head. Loosen the skin with a knife and pull the skin downwards over the tail. If small, just secure the head and proceed in the same way. Clean the eel after skinning and cut into sections across the body before cooking. The very small young eels called elvers can, however, be cooked whole.

FREEZING FISH

For detailed information, see the chapter on Home Freezing.

COOKING FISH

Fish is as delicate as egg white and must not be cooked for long, or at high temperatures. There are only a few tough fish which can be tenderized in a casserole. Once the fish has turned opaque, ie from raw translucent to a solid white, it is ready and should be served as quickly as possible. Further cooking only leads to shrinking and toughening. In general, oily fish lend themselves better than white sea fish to smoking or sousing. Lean white sea fish, with their more subtle taste and texture, are more often poached or used in delicately sauced dishes. River fish are sometimes thought to taste muddy, and are therefore often marinated or cooked with stronger flavourings. Fish steaks, thick fillets, and whole small fish, whether white or oily, from sea or river, are popular plainly grilled or fried, and served simply with plain or seasoned butter.

Frying

The most popular method of cooking fish is by deep or shallow frying.

Deep frying: For deep frying, the fish is normally first coated with batter, egg and breadcrumbs, or flour, and then fried in a properly designed, thick-bottomed pan with a suitable basket. The pan should contain enough clean vegetable oil or fat to cover the fish completely.

In deep frying fish the temperature should be between 170°–195°C, depending on the fish to be fried (p303). Use a frying basket for small, flour-dusted fish, to minimize spluttering.

Fish are particularly well suited to frying in batter. A good batter protects the natural flavour and texture from the hot oil, while the fish is cooked by the steam sealed inside the batter coating.

Do not use a basket for fish in batter because the uncooked batter will stick to the wires and spoil the look of the cooked fish. Use a large perforated spoon or broad slice to lift out the cooked fish. Always check that the fish is cooked through, especially any thicker pieces in a heavy batter. Test by piercing with a fine skewer to check that both the batter and fish are firm but tender right through. After frying, drain the fish on soft kitchen paper, and serve immediately.

Shallow frying: Shallow-fried fish are often coated first. The coating can be egg and breadcrumbs, flour, or, for scaled herrings, milk or beaten egg, then fine oatmeal. For the best results, use a heavy

frying pan with a thick flat base. Oil or fat can be used, or equal quantities of oil and butter. Cook the fish slowly, letting the coating brown before turning the fish so it only needs to be turned once, which minimizes the risk of breaking it. Shallow frying takes 5–15 minutes, depending on the size of the fillet or whole fish being cooked. When shallow frying fillets, cook the flesh side first, and the skin side afterwards.

Cooking *à la meunière* is a well-known method of shallow frying suitable for some whole fish such as sole or trout. The basic method is given on p430.

Fried fish should always be garnished and served with a piquant sauce to offset any oiliness. Garnish with sprigs of parsley, fresh or deep fried, and with lemon wedges. Tartare (p846) or Rémoulade sauce (p845) is good with most fish, Mustard sauce (p442) with grilled or fried herrings, and Gooseberry sauce (p445) with mackerel.

Grilling

Cooking in dry heat is a simple way of preparing whole fish, cutlets or fish steaks, and thick fillets. Oily fish respond particularly well to the heat from a kitchen grill or outside barbecue. In the kitchen, cover the grill pan with foil for easy cleaning. The grill must be preheated and the fish brushed or sprinkled with melted butter, margarine, or cooking oil, and seasoned inside and out. Make 3 diagonal slits in the skin of larger whole fish on each side, to prevent them curling.

Whole fish should be turned over once during grilling but fish steaks and fillets, unless very thick, will cook right through without being turned. Cook under moderate heat. Allow 7–8 minutes for thin fillets, 10–15 minutes for steaks and thicker fish. If you wish, baste fish with a savoury or herb butter while grilling.

Alternatively, marinate the fish before grilling. A simple marinade can be made up from oil and vinegar (or lemon juice) with grated onion or garlic seasoning, and a suitable herb such as dill, fennel, rosemary, thyme, sage or tarragon. Allow the fish to steep in the marinade for 1–2 hours before grilling. See also pp729–30.

After grilling, garnish the fish with chopped parsley and lemon wedges for flavouring, and serve with plain melted butter or a sauce such as Tartare (p846), or Rémoulade sauce (p845).

A colourful dish can be made with small chunks of fish used as seafood kebabs. Really thick pieces of fish or shellfish such as bacon-wrapped scallops are threaded on long skewers with small tomatoes or onions, pieces of courgette, green pepper or other similar vegetables. Blanch the vegetables before making up the kebabs, to make sure they cook as quickly as the seafood.

Baking and Sousing

Baking: Cooking smells are kept to a minimum when baking in the oven, and this helps to preserve flavour. There are many suitable ovenproof dishes with lids, including fish bricks in terracotta. For cooking in most ovenproof ware, the fish should be dotted with flakes of butter and then seasoned; add a generous squeeze of lemon juice and moisten with a very little fish stock or milk to prevent the fish sticking to the dish. Cover with the lid and bake in a moderate oven at 180°C, Gas 4. For cooking times see the table on p411.

A good way to bake fish is to use the *en papillote* method of wrapping in foil. Even very large fish, like whole salmon, can be cooked in this way if the oven is big enough. Lay the fish on a sheet of foil which will enclose it completely. Add seasoning, butter, and a few drops of lemon juice, but no other liquid. Fold up the foil to make a parcel, and place on a baking tray in the preheated oven. Cook as above but check for readiness by piercing the thickest part of the fish through the foil with a clean skewer. A defrosted Pacific salmon cooked in this fashion, then skinned and decorated when cold, will be acceptable on any buffet.

Sousing: This is a simple method of oven-baking fish with vinegar to eat cold with salad. Oily fish, such as herrings, mackerel, and sardines are best. Herrings should be scaled and boned, then rolled up starting with the head end. Mackerel can be soused whole or filleted, but sardines can be cooked, and served whole. See Soused Herrings (p322).

The usual garnishes for baked fish are parsley or watercress for colour, lemon wedges for a tang, and Maître d'Hôtel butter (p1300). For information on barbecuing, see pp1308–10.

Poaching

Cooking fish in liquid gives a bonus in the form of well-flavoured fish stock. The liquid should never boil except when cooking live shellfish or trout in *au bleu* style, and then only gently, not a rolling boil. Poaching at just under boiling point, with the water only shivering, is enough for most fish; a higher heat will ruin their texture and flavour and create a smell. The fish should be poached in a suitable-sized pan with a well-fitting lid, either in the oven or over direct heat. Larger fish should be cooked in a fish kettle with a plate or rack inside on which to lift the fish out in one piece. Alternatively, line an oval, flameproof, pot-roaster or similar dish with a net of clean muslin, leaving the ends hanging over the side of the pot. Preheat the poaching liquid, making sure there is just enough to cover the fish, before adding small pieces or fillets; but put whole fish into cool liquid, and judge the cooking time from when the liquid starts to tremble. (See the table on p412.) For fish to be eaten cold, just heat the liquid gently and maintain it for 5 minutes; then turn off the heat and allow the fish to cool in the liquid.

There is a two-way exchange of flavour in poaching. A well-flavoured and seasoned liquid will add to the flavour of the fish, and the fish will give up flavour to the liquid, making a particularly well-flavoured fish stock. It is important, especially for fresh-water fish, and fish which have been in the freezer for some time, not to use water or salted water alone, except for cooking shellfish. For simple dishes using white fish fillets or smoked haddock, poach in a half-and-half mixture of milk and water with a knob of butter, seasoning, and a bouquet garni. Use salt sparingly (no salt or herbs for smoked fish) because it may become concentrated in the cooking; it is better to taste and add later when the sauce is being prepared.

Other poaching liquids are court bouillon (p429) or fish stock (p330), both of which need preparation beforehand.

Reducing the fish stock (until it becomes thick and shiny) by heating it in an uncovered saucepan makes a strong fish fumet or glaze for use in sauces, and as a coating aspic. Take care not to reduce the liquid too drastically, because overcooking will spoil the fresh flavour and colour. Add salt to taste after reducing the stock. Fish stock or fumet can be frozen in any suitable container and preserved for later use.

Steaming

This is a good way to cook fish without fat, yet without making it too moist. It also avoids any risk of overcooking small thin fillets. It is useful for those on a light diet, or for precooking fish which will be finished in a sauce or served cold.

Take a plate which fits neatly on top of a saucepan, half fill the pan with water and heat until it boils; then reduce the heat so that the water only simmers. Place the plate on the saucepan and, if wished, warm a knob of butter on the plate until it melts, and add just a little water, wine, milk or lemon juice. Add any seasoning required; then put the prepared fish fillet on the plate and cover with another plate. Serve with a little of the liquid. See the table on p412 for cooking times.

The Chinese style of steaming fish in a properly perforated steamer has much to recommend it. See Sole with Sherry and Bean Sauce (p456).

Stewing

This is a specialized casseroling method for fish which is the basis of fish soups, stews, and chowders. The fish is cooked in a seasoned liquid with vegetables and herbs to make a delicious basis for such dishes.

Home Smoking

There are several makes of home smoking equipment available. Whole fish like trout and pieces of fillet can be hot or cold smoked, but for hot smoking they must be small. Most home smoking kits come complete with fuel, and the instructions cover the fish that are suitable.

Cooking Fish and Shellfish at the Table

See pp1445 and 1450.

Cooking Times for Fish

Cooking times for fish depend largely on the thickness of whole fish or fillets and on whether they are frozen or stuffed, or on the size of small pieces or cubes. The following times should therefore be taken as a general guide only.

Baking White and Oily Fish

1) Whole large fish and cuts   *25–35 minutes per 500g*
   If frozen or stuffed   *35–45 minutes per 500g*
2) Small whole fish, steaks, and thick fillets   *15–20 minutes*
   If frozen or stuffed   *20–30 minutes*
3) Small thin fillets   *8–12 minutes*
   If frozen or stuffed   *15–20 minutes*
   If stuffed and rolled   *20–30 minutes*
Treat fish *wrapped in foil* like frozen or stuffed fish.

Frying and Grilling White and Oily Fish

1) Thin fillets and pieces, and kebab cubes
   Coated and deep fried   *5–10 minutes*

Coated and shallow fried *10–15 minutes*
Uncoated and shallow fried *5–10 minutes*
Grilled *7–8 minutes*
2) Steaks and thick whole fish or pieces
Grilled *10–15 minutes*

Poaching White and Oily Fish

1) Small thin fillets and portions *3–5 minutes*
2) Medium and thick fillets *6–10 minutes*
3) Steaks and thick portions and small whole fish *8–15 minutes*
4) 700g–1kg whole fish or cut *8–15 minutes*
5) 1.8–2.6kg *15–18 minutes*
6) Larger fish *5–12 minutes per 500g*

These times are also suitable for smoked fish. Allow 5–8 minutes extra if the fish is frozen, stuffed or rolled. Allow 5–10 minutes extra for *steaming* fish.

Stewing White and Oily Fish

1) Cubes and thick small pieces of coarse fish *8–10 minutes*
2) Cubes and thick small pieces of soft fish *4–7 minutes*

Casseroling White and Oily Fish

1) Thick whole fish, thick cuts and steaks *20–30 minutes*
2) Thin whole fish, fillets *15 minutes (approx)*

Allow 5–8 minutes extra if the fish is frozen.

PRESENTING FISH AT THE TABLE

As with all food, a colourful garnish and a suitable sauce can greatly enhance a simple fish dish. The sauces can be a rich Hollandaise, or a simple Béchamel flavoured with shellfish, egg or parsley for serving with hot poached fish, or a chaudfroid for cold fish, or perhaps one of the sauces suggested above for fried or grilled fish.

For conventional garnishing, use parsley, dill or watercress sprigs, and lemon wedges. For variety, choose from fennel, bay, basil, rosemary, tarragon, and from curry, paprika, and allspice.

Fish can be prepared for the table in individual dishes or served complete. A whole salmon presented on a large dish looks splendid, and, using fish servers, can soon be neatly portioned. Fish in a sauce or other made-up dish usually needs no 'carving' and can be served with ordinary serving utensils. For family meals, it is useful to offer a spare plate for bones, skin, heads, and tails.

TYPES OF FISH

The supply of fish varies with weather conditions and the seasons. However, many white fish, and some others, are interchangeable in cooking; so if the particular fish you want is scarce or expensive, you can easily substitute another.

Fish products range from caviar (sturgeon roe), probably the most expensive food in the world, to fish and chips, still one of the most popular ready-prepared 'take away' foods. You can also find fish dried to an almost unrecognizable shape like Bombay Duck (a curry condiment) or in a strongly flavoured liquid like anchovy essence.

Note The illustrations of fish in this chapter have not been drawn to scale.

Anchovy

Small fish related to the herring. Caught mainly in the Mediterranean, although sometimes found with sprats round the south-west coast of Britain. Heavily salted whole fish or fillets are sold in cans or bottles. Anchovies are very strongly flavoured. Soak preferably for 2–3 hours in milk before use as a garnish.

Bass (Sea)

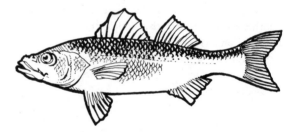

With its silvery scales and salmon shape, bass makes excellent eating. In season from May to August but only available from specialist fish-mongers. Best grilled (with fennel) or baked.

Bream (Red Fish, Ocean Perch)

Instantly recognized by its bright red colour, large scales, and dangerous, spiny dorsal fin. It is of the same family as the popular Mediterranean fish dorada and dentex. In prime condition from June to December.

This delicately flavoured white fish gives a deep fillet when large, or can be cooked whole when small. Cook like other white sea fish.

Fresh-water bream are deep-bodied, with a reddish tinge to the scales. Soak in salt water for 30–45 minutes; then cook as for other river fish.

Brill

A large flat fish resembling turbot, but more elongated. In season all the year, but reaches its best condition from April to July. Good flavour, but not as firm as turbot. Soak well in salted water; then cook like carp, but handle the soft flesh carefully.

Brisling
See Sprats (p420).

Carp

A fresh-water fish, at its best from November to January. There are several types, but the common carp (scales all over), and mirror carp (olive colour

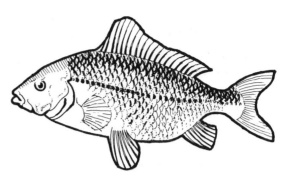

and isolated large scales) are most valued for the table. The fish should be cleaned, soaked in salt water, and rinsed in vinegar and water before cooking. Cook as for other river fish.

Catfish (Wolf-fish, Rock-fish)

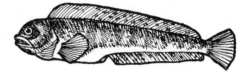

The wolf-fish, a variety of catfish, commonly sold in the UK under the name of rock-fish, has a large head, with strong jaws and striped body. The flesh is pinkish white with a small amount of bone. Bake or grill with a sprinkling of lemon juice.

Cod

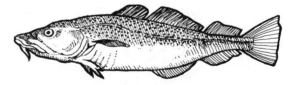

The most popular of the round white fish, principally because the larger specimens offer heavy fillets of bone-free flesh for deep frying. Younger fish are called codling. Cod is available everywhere, wet or frozen. Smoked fillets and roe are also popular. Cod has firm, flaky white flesh, and can be cooked in all the accepted ways for white fish. Take care not to overcook.

413

Coley (Saithe)

A close relation of cod but has darker coloured skin and flesh. In cooking, the fish turns white and can be used as an alternative to cod and haddock. Available everywhere, wet or frozen.

Dab

A smaller member of the plaice family, in season all year round. Gut, trim fins, and fry or grill whole. Larger dabs can be cooked like plaice.

Dogfish (Huss, Flake, Tope)

One of the shark family, and free of small bones. Available all the year. It is most popular in batter and deep fried but is even better grilled, baked or in kebabs, soups, and fish stock, because of its firm flesh.

Eel

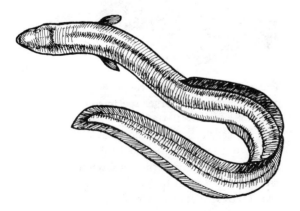

Fresh-water eels are olive in colour, with very rich, oily flesh. Though always in season, they are less good in summer. Available live from specialist fishmongers, also cooked and jellied. Because of their fat content, eels are excellent smoked for eating raw. Unsmoked eels are poached and sauced, baked or grilled, and are an essential ingredient in continental fish hot-pots, chowders, and cotriades.

Conger eel, a sea-water fish, can grow up to 3 metres in length. Dark-grey in colour, the medium-sized ones are best for eating. Can be used in recipes for monkfish or dogfish, or instead of fresh-water eels in most recipes.

Flounder

See Lemon Sole (p420).

Garfish

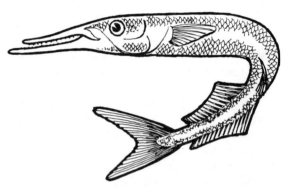

Has a long narrow iridescent coloured body with a protruding snout. Caught among mackerel in south-west fishing grounds, and available from specialist fishmongers in its short season (March–May). Has good white flesh with brightly tinted emerald bones (colour harmless). Excellent grilled, or cut into 5cm pieces, dipped into seasoned flour, and shallow fried.

Grayling

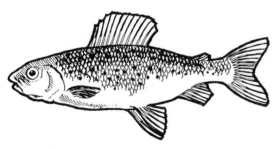

A fresh-water fish of the salmon and trout family. Rarely sold commercially, but the firm white flesh and trout flavour make the fish excellent eating if you can find it. Best in winter. Cook like trout.

Grey Mullet

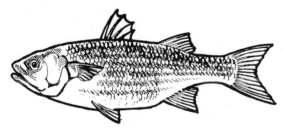

Plentiful in summer when shoals move inshore to live in shallow waters and estuaries. A handsome round fish with large scales. Try to make sure that the fish have come from wholesome water areas. Best from July to February. Clean and soak in several changes of salt water before cooking. Cook like mackerel or red mullet.

Gudgeon

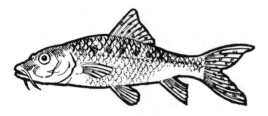

A small fresh-water fish with silvery to brown skin. Gut the fish and remove gills, dip in egg and breadcrumbs and deep fry. Serve whole, 3–4 per person depending on size.

Gurnet (Gurnard)

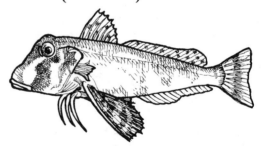

These colourful fish can be grey, red or yellow, depending on the type. They are easily identified by their large angular bony heads. The red-coloured fish is the best for eating, and is available at good fishmongers. Most seasonable from July to April. Cook whole or filleted. Try poaching in court bouillon and serving cold with mayonnaise.

Haddock

A close relation to cod, but with a black spot on either side of the body and a black lateral line beneath it which makes this very popular fish easy to identify. In season all year round, but best from November to February. Available everywhere, wet or frozen. Cook wet fish gently to appreciate its sweet fresh flavour.

Finnan haddock are either split or left on the bone; they are lightly cold smoked. They have a delicious, mild flavour. *Smoked haddock cutlets* (boned), unlike finnan haddock, have been dyed and quite heavily smoked. *Arbroath smokies* are headless and hot smoked, so can be eaten cold or heated in the oven.

Poach smoked fish in half milk and half water, and serve with a generous pat of plain or savoury butter.

Hake

This fish is of the same family as haddock and cod, but has a longer, slimmer shape. In best condition from June to January when it is quite widely available from fishmongers, especially in the west and south western areas of the country.

Frozen hake usually comes from South Atlantic fishing grounds, and has a drier, more fibrous texture than the silver hake from more northerly waters.

Halibut

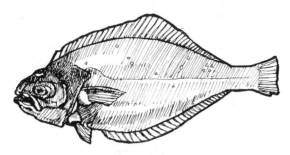

A very large flat fish, rich in vitamins A and D. Widely available from fishmongers as whole fish (up to 1.5kg, it is called chicken halibut) or in steaks from larger fish. The pre-sawn frozen steaks of Pacific halibut make a good alternative to the Atlantic ones. Both types are available fresh and frozen.

Greenland halibut is grey-brown with rather more watery flesh than the Atlantic or Pacific fish. This has led to it being called 'mock' halibut.

Herring

Perhaps the most perfectly shaped of all fish. With its smooth silvery scales, large bright eyes and tasty flesh, the herring is also the most nourishing fish available, weight for weight.

This excellent fish is found in many guises, and also provides both hard and soft roes. It can be split, boned, and cold smoked to produce a *kipper*. Most kippers are now in fact, salted and dyed to give a pleasant traditional taste and tint. (Uncoloured kippers are also available though.) Kippers are also sold as cutlets, with the head and backbone removed, or as fillets.

Bloaters are ungutted herrings lightly smoked. They must be cooked as soon as they are purchased. *Buckling* are the same fish hot smoked, and can be used as an alternative to smoked trout without further cooking.

Red herrings are heavily smoked and salted, but are rarely seen in Britain, most of them being exported. They need long soaking before cooking.

Herrings are also available in various sauces and continental styles. *Matjes herrings* are preserved in a light brine, *Bismarck herrings* in a marinade of white wine and vinegar with onions and juniper berries, and the most popular preserved herrings, *rollmops*, are packed with gherkins and onions in a vinegar marinade.

Herrings are oily fish and a little mustard or horseradish sauce helps to offset the richness. They can be grilled, baked or fried without adding fat.

John Dory

A deep-bodied fish that is easily recognized by its large head and extravagant fin formation. When

Fish

Stuffed Whole Plaice (p447)

LEFT *Golden Grilled Cod*
(p433)

BELOW *Sweet and Sour Prawns* (p463)

RIGHT *Sole Véronique*
(p456)

Moules Marinière (p462)

LEFT *Skate in Black Butter* (p453)

BELOW *Halibut, Orange and Watercress Salad* (p835)

RIGHT *Lobster on the Half-Shell* (p425) *filled with Russian Salad* (p314)

BELOW RIGHT *Red Mullet Baked in Foil* (p448)

headless and gutted, the fish is reduced to two-thirds of its original weight. In eating quality, the flesh is as good as turbot for flavour and texture and should be more popular. Not widely available. At its best from January to April. Grill, poach or cook, and serve cold with salad and mayonnaise.

Kippers

See Herring (p416).

Ling

This is another member of the cod family, with a distinctive elongated body and an underchin barbel. Fairly widely available, and in best condition from September to May. Cook as for other white fish.

Mackerel

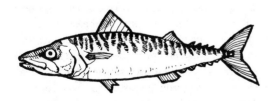

A well proportioned fish, with greenish-blue colouring. The upper part of the body is patterned with black bands and the belly is silvery. Available everywhere wet or frozen; at its best in the winter and spring. Grill, souse, or stuff and bake *en papillote*.

Smoked mackerel is also widely available either as whole fish or fillets; it is popular in salads and as a pâté. It is available hot smoked and therefore cooked and ready to eat, or cold smoked and vacuum packed.

Kippered mackerel is cold smoked and needs cooking, like kippers. Like herring, the flesh is savoury and rich, so horseradish, mustard or some other piquant condiment or side dish should be served with the fish.

Megrim

Closely related to brill and turbot. Cook in the same ways.

Monkfish

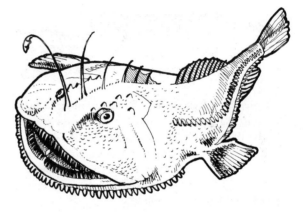

As a rule only the tail of this strange-looking fish is seen on the fishmonger's slab. The firm white meat is delicious and can be cooked in all the ways suggested for halibut or turbot; it is excellent eaten either hot or cold.

Perch

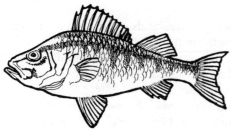

A fresh-water fish, olive-green above with vertical black stripes. Has a large spiny dorsal fin with a sting. Good eating quality although bony. Fillet and poach in court bouillon; then remove the skin and scales. Alternatively, fillet, skin, and cook *à la meunière*.

Pike

A large, fierce fresh-water fish. Medium-sized fish of up to 3kg are best for cooking. Gut and remove the head, tail, and fins; then soak for 5–6 hours in salt water. Rinse in vinegar before poaching in court bouillon or fish stock. The flesh breaks easily, making it good for quenelles (p446). Alternatively, grill long fillets with bacon.

Pilchards
See Sardines (p419).

Plaice

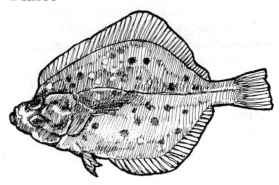

Easily recognized flat fish with dark coloured upperside dotted with orange spots. Widely available as whole fish or fillets, wet or frozen; when frozen, plaice are often sold ready-prepared in breadcrumbs or sauced. In best condition from May to January. The flesh is white and distinctive in flavour; it should not be overcooked. Frozen prepared fish or fillets are suitable for deep or shallow frying, steaming or poaching, and for baked dishes with a sauce.

Red Mullet

A most attractive fish, red in colour and with a heavy scale formation. Available from specialist fishmongers from May to September. Frozen supplies, usually from the Mediterranean, are on sale all year round. Scale and grill whole, or bake with butter, lemon, and seasoning *en papillote*, depending on size.

Salmon

Although usually caught in rivers, the salmon is conditioned by long spells at sea before returning to its home waters. The fish from the Scottish, Irish, and English rivers are best known in Europe. Many rivers have their own seasons, but in general the Scottish and English seasons are from February to August, and the Irish from January to September.

For appearance and flavour, salmon is the king of all fish. The deep red flesh turns pink when cooked. Frozen Pacific salmon is less expensive than European fresh salmon, and with careful

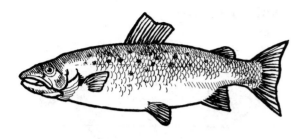

defrosting and cooking makes an attractive, more economical alternative.

Poach salmon whole in court bouillon, cook *en papillote*; poach, grill or fry steaks or cutlets cut across the fish.

Smoked salmon is the cold smoked fillet or flank of the fish, either Atlantic or Pacific, the latter being cheaper. Slice very thinly and serve with lemon wedges, Cayenne pepper, and brown bread and butter. Alternatively, form thicker slices into cornets and secure with cocktail sticks, if necessary. Smoked salmon can also be served on canapés. Trimmings can be made into a mousse (p882).

Canned salmon, containing Pacific fish, is a useful standby, but because the fish is already cooked, its culinary uses are restricted.

Salmon Trout (Sea Trout)

Salmon trout looks very like true salmon, but is a smaller fish related to the brown trout. Sea-going, but river-breeding, the fish do not undertake the long journeys which salmon do. Since it has the colour of salmon and the texture of trout, the salmon trout has the attributes of both fish, and can truly be called the finest fresh-water fish. At its best in spring and summer, and available from most good fishmongers. When *rainbow trout* (see trout) are sea-farmed and fed on shellfish, the flesh turns pink, making an acceptable, cheaper alternative to true salmon trout.

Sardines

The formal title *Sardina pilchardus* is a clue to the fact that large sardines are called pilchards. *Pilchards* are very widely available canned with various sauces, and although a useful standby, this limits their use. Fresh sardines make a stylish first course when grilled or floured and shallow fried. There is no need to gut or head the fish. Cook through and serve 4–5 fish per person with lemon wedges.

Canned small sardines in oil from Spain, Portugal or France are a delicacy in their own right. The best quality packs use good olive oil, and the sardines are allowed to mature in the can. Serve with lemon and a crisp green salad or as part of a mixed hors d'oeuvre platter.

Shad

Closely related to herring, but differs in its habitat as the fish enter estuaries to spawn. The same size as a herring. Cook in the same way.

Skate

A long-tailed, flat fish with its mouth on the underside of the body. Skate and rays propel themselves by a waving movement of the outer edges of the body known as the 'wings'. Only the wings are eaten, the best part being the fleshier centre cut. The flesh is firm and delicate with a simple, soft bone formation. It is available everywhere from fishmongers. Portions of the wing can be deep or shallow fried, or used in the classic Skate in Black Butter (p453).

Smelt (Sparling)

Although rounder in body, smelts look like herring, but in fact belong to the salmon family. Not always easy to find at fishmongers. In season from June to September, the fish has a sweet smell that has been described as resembling that of violets or cucumber. To cook, gut and coat with egg and breadcrumbs before deep frying.

Snapper (Red)

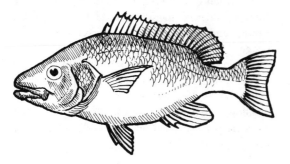

Red snapper is normally imported frozen from Caribbean or South Atlantic fishing grounds. It has a blunt head with large eyes and the body scales are pinky-silver in colour. The flesh is firm and suitable for grilling or for barbecuing with herbs and spices.

Sole (Dover)

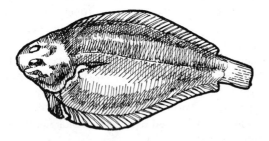

The finest flat fish of all. The 'tear drop' shape of this fish differentiates it from distant relations like *lemon sole*. Available everywhere, wet or frozen, but always relatively expensive. Has firm white flesh, with a succulent flavour, easy to separate from bones. Remove the dark skin; then grill, cook *à la meunière*, or use in any of the recipes on pp454–56.

Sole (Lemon)

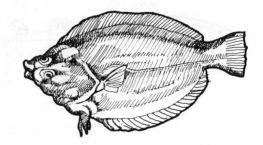

Part of a large family of flat fish including plaice, dab, flounder, and witch (Torbay sole). Widely available wet and frozen, comes between Dover sole and plaice in flesh, texture, and flavour, and is a pleasant alternative to either. Fry or poach fillets, or cook whole to retain the natural juices.

Sprats

Bright little silvery fish widely available during the winter months. Can be grilled, deep-fried or home-smoked. Allow 500g for 3 portions. Cut off the head and split the fish by running the thumb-nail down the belly to the tail. Open out and pull the backbone out starting at the head end.

Commercially smoked sprats are also available and make a good first course.

Brisling are small sprats canned and ready to serve in the same way as sardines.

Tench

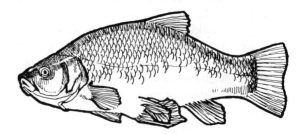

A river fish of reasonable eating quality. Treat like carp or pike. Gut and steep in salt water before cooking.

Trout (Rainbow)

With the advance of modern fish farming, trout is now as popular as some of the better-known sea fish. It can be cooked plainly *à la meunière*, yet also lends itself well to more elaborate cooking and to various sauces. Gut and remove the gills before cooking. Grilled, baked (especially *en papillote*), poached, or fried *à la meunière*, the fish is easy to bone, and with good presentation adds style to any meal.

Tunny (Tuna)

Not an important fish in Britain but much prized in warmer areas. A much larger relation of the mackerel, the tunny's flesh is darkish red but becomes fawn coloured after cooking. It is best baked or braised for an hour in a warm oven at 160°C, Gas 3, with wine and suitable vegetables. Canned tuna is popular. Serve it like canned salmon, or use it in cooked dishes such as Vitello Tonnata (p1527).

Turbot

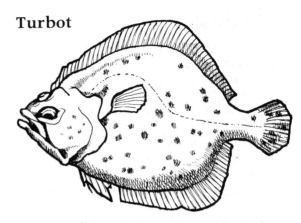

A large flat fish, available most of the year. Rated next to Dover sole for quality of flesh. Large fish must be sliced into cutlets, but the smaller (chicken turbot) fish can be foil-wrapped and cooked whole with butter and seasoning. Serve with a savoury herb butter or a shrimp sauce, or serve grilled cutlets with Maître d'Hôtel butter (p1300) or Béarnaise sauce (p712).

Whitebait

These are the fry (young fish) of herring and sprats. Certainly the smallest fish eaten, but with a long gastronomic history and always a fashionable dish. Caught in several large estuaries round British coasts, the bulk of the catch is now frozen because the little fish deteriorate quickly. They should be floured and deep fried whole.

Whiting

Another member of the great cod family. The flesh is white, flaky, very soft, and tender. Available everywhere, the gutted and headed fish can be egg and breadcrumbed before frying. Opened and with the backbone removed, the whiting can be grilled or poached in milk with seasoning and is an easily digested dish suitable for invalids.

Blue whiting are slimmer and less well fleshed than the true whiting; these fish are caught in deep water. The flesh is darker though quite pleasant when cooked. Cut off the head, gut, and skin; then fry. As the fish are small, allow 2–3 per portion.

Shellfish

There are 3 main types of shellfish:

1) Crustaceans, ie lobsters, crabs, prawns, and shrimps, all of which moult and re-grow their shells as they grow larger.
2) Bivalve molluscs such as mussels, cockles, oysters, and scallops, which have two shells to enclose the shellfish.
3) Univalves like the ormers, whelks, and winkles, which live in a single shell.

Although most shellfish have only a limited season, the problem of seasonal supply has partly been solved by modern freezing techniques, which now make shellfish available year round.

Oysters and some clams are eaten raw. Most other shellfish are cooked live to ensure their freshness.

Whole shellfish add drama and glamour to any fish dish, especially to a party or buffet centrepiece.

TYPES OF SHELLFISH

Abalone (Ormer)

A single-shelled relation of the limpet, this is not a very tender shellfish. In Europe it is caught mainly round the Channel Islands and French coasts. Once plentiful but now scarce. Tenderize by pounding gently; then marinate and stew slowly with onions and seasoning. The shell is attractive and valuable, having a mother of pearl interior which is used a good deal for costume jewellery and *objets d'art*.

Clam (Palourde)

Two grey, finely lined shells enclose this bivalve mollusc. Not freely available in Britain but very popular in France and USA. Clams can be eaten like oysters after removing the small tube-like feeding mechanism and sandy parts. Very good cooked in soups, stews, and as a clam chowder (p1567).

Cockle

A bivalve mollusc, dug or dredged from tidal sand flats. Rarely sold uncooked. However, if supplies are available, keep alive for 24 hours in sea water to clear sand from the intestine, and wash in several changes of water; then boil in salt water for 5–6 minutes until the shells open. Cool, and discard the shells. Eat with salad or in a mixed fish dish.

Shelled cockle meat is quite widely available loose, or in frozen packs, and canned or bottled. Fresh or frozen cockles are better than canned or bottled ones for cooked dishes because they are vinegar-free. Wash well before cooking to remove any particles of grit.

Crab

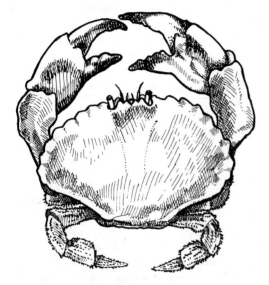

Available live, cooked or as frozen crabmeat, crabs are plentiful. Choose a crab by weight rather than size, and if bought ready-cooked make sure that the shell is fresh and dry, and the legs and claws tight against the body.

British crabs produce white meat from the claws and legs and spicy brown meat from inside the main shell. Frozen or canned crab packs usually contain foreign *Pacific King* crab or the smaller *Atlantic Queen* crab. Both are closer to spider crabs which have large legs containing good white meat, but have very little meat in the body.

Crabmeat has many uses from conventional salad dishes to seafood flans, stuffings, and soups. The brown meat (the liver and roe) of the female is particularly good as a flavouring for sauces or savoury butters.

To cook a live crab: Choose a good-sized heavy crab and kill it either by piercing it through the shell above the mouth, or by drowning it in tepid fresh water for 2 hours. It is wise to kill the crab before boiling it to prevent water entering the body.

Place in a large pan of boiling water containing 2×15ml spoons of salt per litre. Boil for 3 minutes, then lower the heat and simmer for a further 25 minutes; remove and leave to cool.

To pick and dress a cooked crab: Turn the crab on its back. Male crabs have a slim flap on the underside, the females have a broader one. Twist off the legs and claws. Press firmly on the 'crown' where the legs join the body, and remove in one piece. Discard the grey finger-like gills and pick out the meat. Remove the meat from the main shell, keeping dark meat and pink coral separate from the white meat. Crack the claws and legs with nutcrackers or a clean hammer, and pick out the white meat. The crab should give 25–30% of its total cooked weight in meat; males usually give more white meat.

Scrub and dry the main shell inside and out, and break off the undershell to the dark line around the perimeter. Flake the white meat from the legs and claws. Cream together the darker meat, liver and coral, and add 2×15ml spoons of fresh brown breadcrumbs and a little seasoning. Mix thoroughly and fill both ends of the shell. Place the white meat in the centre.

Crawfish (Spiny Lobster, Langouste)

This is a big lobster-like crustacean, but without large claws. It is thought by gourmets to be equal to lobster in flavour, and its larger body makes up for the lack of claw meat. Cook and serve as for lobster. Since large specimens can weigh 2.5kg, a crawfish can make a splendid table centrepiece. For this presentation, cook it like lobster, and when cool, cut out the soft shell on the underside of the tail, and remove the meat in one piece. Slice into medallions and display on the back of the suitably mounted whole shellfish. Garnish the cut meat with dill, small pieces of cucumber or slivers of tomato, and glaze with an aspic jelly.

Frozen crawfish are generally sold ready-cooked but the tails are sometimes available uncooked. Poach in fish stock or split and grill.

Crayfish (Ecrevisse)

These are small fresh-water crustaceans, closely resembling the lobster. Greenish-brown in colour, the crayfish turns bright red on being cooked. Rinse the crayfish and remove the intestinal tract by pulling out the middle tail fin. To serve cold with salad, boil the crayfish for 2 minutes in well-flavoured fish stock; then simmer for a further 10 minutes. Cool. Allow at least 8 fish per person, and serve on a large dish, suitably garnished. Offer mayonnaise and a spare plate for the shells, as well as a finger bowl for each person.

Crayfish can be served hot in any made-up dish designed for large prawns or lobster meat. It is excellent cooked at the table in a chafing-dish, like prawns.

Frogs

Not strictly within the world of fish, although amphibians. The legs alone are used, and are sometimes sold deep-frozen. They are a great delicacy with a taste like chicken. After thawing, the legs are usually rolled in seasoned flour and shallow fried. Serve 4–6 legs per portion, garnished with parsley and lemon wedges, as a first course.

Lobster

Live lobsters can be obtained from fishermen at some harbours or, in towns, from specialist fishmongers. As a rule, however, these regal, distinctive shellfish are sold cooked.

Available all year round, the most popular sizes are between 500g and 1.5kg in weight. When live they should feel heavy for their size and be lively when picked up. The dark shells turn bright red on being cooked; if buying a ready-cooked lobster look for a dry firm shell and tightly curled tail. Lobsters are often dressed and eaten cold with mayonnaise, but there are also many superb hot lobster dishes; many of them call for the meat to be prepared, then returned to the shell for presentation.

To boil a lobster: There are several methods of cooking a live lobster. The simplest is to half fill a suitably sized pan with salt water (2 × 15ml spoons salt per litre), bring the water to the boil and drop the lobster in quickly. Place a lid on the pan and weight it down, then lower the heat to keep the water just under boiling point. Cook for 15–20 minutes, depending on the lobster's size.

An alternative method is to put the live lobster into cool, salted water or court bouillon, and bring to the boil, then to cook as described. Perhaps a less harrowing method is to drown the lobster by leaving it in tepid fresh water for 2–3 hours before cooking.

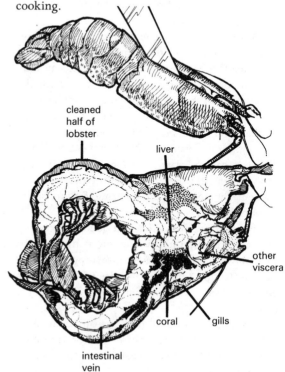

cleaned half of lobster

liver

other viscera

coral

gills

intestinal vein

Splitting a lobster

After cooking, allow the lobster to cool, then place on a cutting board, with the tail spread behind. Take a large, sharp, broad-bladed knife and insert the point in the middle of the head. Lower the blade of the knife and cut through the shell, along the centre line, splitting the shellfish into 2 equal parts. Pull out the intestinal tract that runs from the head to the tail and clear out the head cavity. Remove the sponge-like gills also. The dark, mustard-coloured meat is the liver and is good for flavouring sauces. The pink coral sometimes found in the female is also valuable for lobster butter, a luxurious accompaniment for grilled fish.

To dress a lobster to eat cold: Place the half lobster, cut side up, on a suitable plate. Crack the claws and arrange them round the half-shell. (Offer a suitable thin fork or lobster pick to get all the meat out of them.) Garnish the half lobster by filling the head cavity with Russian salad (p314) and serve chilled with mayonnaise and salad. A half lobster is generally thought enough for a single portion as a first course.

For hot lobster dishes, see p461.

Mussels

These under-valued, black bivalve molluscs are abundant around northern European coastlines. If you collect them personally, make sure that it is in a pure water area. They are of better quality when there is an 'R' in the month. Mussels are farmed commercially in carefully selected sea-water areas. Buy from a reliable dealer, and make sure that the mussels have tightly closed shells. This shows that they are alive. Mussel meat can also be bought frozen, bottled or canned; the frozen ones are better for cooked and mixed seafood dishes since they have not been preserved in salt or vinegar. When adding any cooked shellfish, but particularly mussels, to a recipe, cook for as short a time as possible, to avoid making them tough.

To prepare mussels: Wash the mussels in several changes of clean water; then scrape off the byssus threads (the beard), found near the hinge of the two shells, using a sharp knife. These threads are the anchors which hold the shellfish to the rocks. Check again that each mussel is tightly shut before

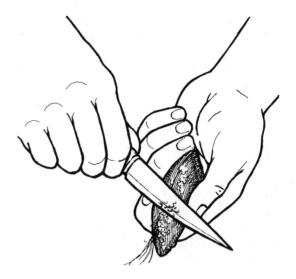

cooking. For the basic cooking, follow the Moules Marinière recipe (p462) as it produces a valuable bonus of delicious mussel liquor.

Oysters

Among several types available, the native oyster is the most highly prized. An oyster is enclosed by one concave and one flat shell, roughly circular and greyish-brown. Portuguese and Pacific oysters are cheaper, and easily distinguished by their deeper, longer, and more irregular shaped shells.

All oysters are farmed. This ensures that the shellfish are pure, a vital point since they are most often eaten raw.

Native oysters can be bought fresh from specialist fishmongers when there is an 'R' in the month; like any shellfish they must be inspected to ensure that the shells are tightly closed.

To open, use a proper oyster knife; work the blade between the shells and cut the ligament hinge which keeps the shells shut. Pass the knife under the oyster to free it from the shell. Serve on the deep half shell (6–12 per portion) on a bed of crushed ice with lemon wedges and brown bread and butter.

To keep oysters alive for up to 24 hours before opening, put them in a wet sack and keep in a cool, dark place.

Fresh, frozen or canned unsmoked oysters are suitable for Steak and Oyster Pie (p502) and other cooked dishes. Smoked oysters are only suitable for use cold, as part of a mixed hors d'oeuvre platter or as cocktail snacks. They are particularly popular in the USA.

Prawns

The word prawn is only used in Britain to distinguish the larger members of the shrimp family. There are many varieties of prawns around the world. Prawns turn from a translucent grey to reddish-pink when boiled briefly in salted water.

Prawns from cold water fishing grounds in the North Atlantic and North Sea are of better eating quality than those from warmer climates. The northern prawns from Canada, Greenland, Iceland, Norway, and Great Britain have a delicate pink colour with a soft, pleasant texture. Warm-water prawns are usually tightly curled with a much firmer texture, and bands of reddish-orange around the body.

For cocktails, salads, and cold dishes, shell-on or peeled cold-water prawns are best. The warm-water prawns are more suitable for cooked dishes and curries, and are usually cheaper.

Nearly all prawns sold in Britain, whether shell-on or peeled, are imported ready-cooked; they are sold widely, fresh or in frozen packs. Always allow a reasonable defrosting time; never defrost quickly in water. The best method is to sprinkle the prawns lightly with salt and then to defrost them on a plate overnight in a refrigerator.

Both shell-on and peeled prawns are used in a great many recipes for cooked and cold dishes, and garnishes.

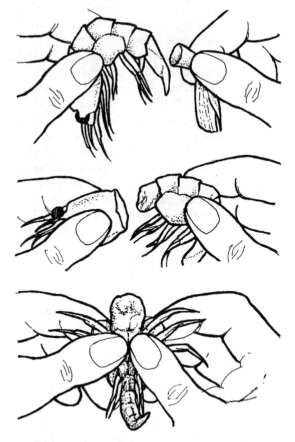

Peeling a prawn

King Prawns: These larger prawns come from various warm water fishing areas round the world. All supplies in Britain are frozen raw, headless, but with the shells. Packs of 1kg contain 16–20 prawns, depending on size. King prawns should be marinated before cooking, and their size and texture then make them well suited to grilling or barbecuing. If the prawns are wanted for a cold dish, poach in fish stock and allow to cool in the liquid. Chill well before serving.

Crystal Prawns: These come from Middle East or Far East fishing grounds. The large whole prawns are sold ready-cooked, and are pink to orange in colour. Defrost overnight in a refrigerator.

Scallop

This mollusc has two heavily ribbed shells, one flat, the other concave. The shellfish itself is in two parts, a large white muscle which opens and closes the shell and the orange and fawn coloured roe (coral). Just the muscle and roe are offered for sale, usually on the flat shell.

When buying scallops on the half shell, always ask for the deep shells to hold the many 'scalloped' cooked fish dishes, for example the well-known Coquilles St Jacques (p464).

Large scallops can be bought frozen all year round, but fresh only from November to March. The scallop is very tender, with a high natural liquid content, and great care should be taken when cooking. Just let the shellfish turn from translucent to solid white over a low heat in a little white wine or seasoned milk; if they must be heated in a sauce, add them at the last possible moment to prevent toughening and shrinkage.

Queen Scallops: These smaller versions are usually sold shelled and frozen. Cook in the same way as larger scallops, using minimal heat. Queen scallops are excellent dipped in batter or egg and breadcrumbs, and briefly deep fried.

Scampi

These are often referred to as Dublin Bay Prawns. They are closely related to lobster and crawfish, but do not change colour when cooked. Widely distributed from Iceland to the Mediterranean, they are popular everywhere.

Scampi (from Italian *scampo*) is, properly, the

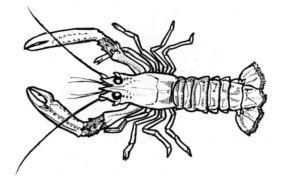

term for the tail meat from shellfish de-headed at sea, and is most often fried. However, the whole shellfish can be poached, and then served cold or grilled.

Scampi flesh is sweet and tender, but deteriorates quickly, so most supplies are frozen. Like scallops, scampi should be cooked briefly. In dishes using a sauce, the defrosted shellfish should be added at the last moment to prevent overcooking.

Shrimps

Smaller and rounder-bodied than prawns, shrimps are caught in shallow sandy water and turn from grey to pinkish-brown when cooked in salted water. They must be boiled alive to have the characteristic springy curled shape.

Peeled shrimps have a particularly good and sweet shellfish flavour, and are used in mixed seafood dishes, as stuffings or fillings, in sauces, and as a garnish.

Fresh shell-on shrimps are widely available and so are frozen and potted shrimps.

Pink Shrimps: These are smaller relatives of a certain type of prawn. They are slim in body like cold-water prawns but the size of brown shrimps. They are caught in the same areas, and turn pink when boiled. Very colourful for display. Use like brown shrimps.

Snails

Preparing snails for human consumption is a long process which involves starving the snail to clear its system, then cooking in several stages before returning the snail to its shell and packing the opening with parsley and garlic butter. Snails are therefore usually best bought canned with separate shells, or frozen ready-prepared.

Special equipment should be used at the table, ie an indented dish to hold the snails, plus tongs and a special fork.

Squid (Ink Fish, Calamares)

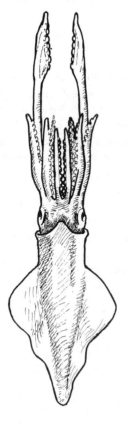

This is the most popular of the tentacled, soft-bodied molluscs. Small squid are tender, but larger ones (30cm and over) need quite long cooking. Before cooking, cut off the heads (eyes) and tentacles, remove the transparent central 'bone' and pull out the dark coloured ink sac at the same time. Wash and pull off any visible outer skin.

Squid is well suited to stuffing; it is also good thinly sliced (body and tentacles), coated, and deep fried. Alternatively, slice and poach in a little white wine or seasoned milk, chill and mix with peeled prawns, cockles, mussels, and white crabmeat as a seafood salad.

Whelks and Winkles

Whelks are boiled in salt water and shelled before sale. The firm, cream-coloured flesh can be eaten with vinegar or in a mixed seafood hors d'oeuvre. It can also be minced or diced for adding to stuffings, sauces, and soups.

Winkles live on a diet of seaweed which makes them nutritious, if not attractive to look at. When collecting winkles, make sure that the sea is unpolluted.

The whelk and winkle are the only shellfish which need steady boiling in salted water for 5–10 minutes. Wash in several changes of fresh water beforehand, and allow the shellfish to cool in the boiling liquid.

The winkle has a flat black cover to the shell opening and this should be discarded before removing the shellfish entire with a pin or needle. They can make an interesting contribution to a mixed shellfish platter.

Basic Recipes for Cooking Fish

In the following recipes the fish are assumed to be gutted and filleted where required.

Court Bouillon

(for salmon, salmon trout, and other whole fish)

water	2 large onions
500ml dry white wine **or** dry cider to each litre water	2–3 sticks celery
	parsley stalks
	1 bouquet garni to each litre water
2 × 15ml spoons white wine vinegar to each litre water	a few peppercorns
	salt and pepper
2 large carrots	

Put the liquids in a large pan. Slice the carrots and onions, chop the celery, and crush the parsley stalks. Add to the liquid with the remaining ingredients. Simmer for 30 minutes, leave to cool, then strain and use as required.

Fish Stock

See p330.

Basic Recipe for Grilling Fish

fish fillets	2 × 10ml spoons salad oil
salt and pepper	
1 × 5ml spoon chopped gherkins (optional)	1 × 10ml spoon white wine vinegar **or** lemon juice
1 × 5ml spoon chopped capers (optional)	

Garnish
chopped parsley

Remove the rack of the grill pan. Wipe the fish and season it with salt and pepper. Mix the gherkins and capers, if used, with the oil and vinegar. Heat the grill to give a medium cooking heat. Snip or slash the skin of the fish to prevent curling, if necessary. Lay it in the bottom of the grill pan, skin side up. Pour most of the liquid mixture over it.

Grill, basting frequently. Turn the fish over and pour the remaining liquid over it. Grill for about another 5 minutes. Calculate the total grilling time from the table on p411. Sprinkle with chopped parsley and serve immediately.

Note Use gherkins and capers for fairly large thick fillets and for most river fish. Thin, delicately flavoured fillets can be grilled with just a sprinkling of lemon juice instead of vinegar.

Basic Recipe for Poaching Fish

1 small whole fish **or** fillets	juice of $\frac{1}{2}$ lemon
	court bouillon

Garnish
lemon wedges	parsley sprigs

Allow 100–150g fish for each helping. Clean a whole fish inside, rinse the cavity and wipe both inside and outside dry. Cut off the fins. Wipe fillets, if used. Sprinkle the fish or fillets with a little lemon juice.

Put the fish into a large deep frying pan, and add enough court bouillon to cover 1–2cm of the pan depth when the fish is in it. Cover with a spatter-proof lid or a plate, and poach gently, with the liquid barely shivering. Calculate the cooking time from the table on p412. Lift out the cooked fish gently with a broad slice, drain, and slide it on to a warmed serving dish. Garnish with lemon wedges and parsley sprigs.

Note Keep the cooking liquid to make the sauces recommended for fish on p412. Shrimp sauce (p697) is particularly suitable for a plainly flavoured white fish like brill. Serve the fish with the sauce. If you wish to serve the sauce over the fish, scrape off any skin after cooking it and before garnishing.

If the fish is to be served cold, just heat the liquid gently and maintain it for 5 minutes; then turn off the heat and leave the fish to cool in the liquid.

Basic Recipe for Baking Fish

1 whole fish
salt and pepper
butter for greasing

water or *fish stock*
(p330) (optional)
50g butter

Wash the cleaned fish inside and out and pat dry. Season with salt and pepper and place in a well-greased baking dish. Add enough water or stock to cover 5mm of the dish, if desired. Dot with small pieces of butter. Cover loosely with greased paper and bake in a fairly hot oven at 190°C, Gas 5. Calculate the cooking time from the table on p411.

Basic Recipe for Deep Frying Fish in Batter

fish fillets
flour for coating

salt and pepper
oil or *fat for deep frying*

Batter
100g plain flour
½ × 2.5ml spoon salt

1 egg
125ml milk

Make the batter first. Sift the flour and salt into a bowl. Make a well in the centre of the flour and add the egg and a little of the milk. Gradually work in the flour from the sides, then beat until smooth. Stir in the rest of the milk.

Cut the fish into serving portions, if required; the pieces should all be of a similar size. Season the flour with salt and pepper. Dry the pieces of fish well and coat in the flour. Stir the batter well and dip the pieces of fish into it. Heat the oil or fat (p303) and fry until golden-brown. Drain on soft kitchen paper and serve immediately.

Note Do not use a basket when frying fish in batter as it will stick. Use a perforated spoon or broad slice to lift it out.

For Fish and Chips use the basic recipe above with any suitable fish, eg cod, haddock or plaice, and the recipe for potato chips on p792.

Basic Recipe for Shallow Frying Fish

small whole fish or *fish*
fillets
flour for coating
salt and pepper

1 egg
dry white breadcrumbs
for coating
fat for shallow frying

Garnish
lemon wedges

Cut the fish into serving portions, if required. Season the flour with salt and pepper and beat the egg lightly. Coat the fish with flour, then dip in the egg, and coat with breadcrumbs. Heat the fat in a frying pan and fry the fish, turning once, for the time given in the table on p411, until the coating is golden-brown. Serve immediately with lemon wedges.

Basic Recipe for Frying Fish
(à la meunière)

small whole fish or *fish*
fillets
flour for coating
salt and pepper

50g butter
1 × 10ml spoon chopped
parsley
juice of ½ lemon

Trim off the fins if necessary, rinse the fish, and dry well with soft kitchen paper. Season the flour with salt and pepper and coat the fish with the flour. Heat the butter in a frying pan. When foaming, place the fish in the pan. Cook gently for the time given in the table on p411, turning once. When the fish is golden-brown and cooked through, arrange on a serving dish and keep hot. Season the butter left in the pan and heat until it is nut-brown. Add the parsley and lemon juice, pour over the fish, and serve at once.

Recipes for Sea and River Fish

For main-course fish salads, see the chapter on Salads and Dressings.

Baked Sea Bream

4 helpings

1 bream (900g approx)
salt and pepper
butter for greasing
water or fish stock
* (p330) (optional)*

50g butter
1 × 5ml spoon Cayenne
* pepper*

Wash the cleaned fish inside and out and pat dry. Season with salt and pepper and place in a well-greased baking dish. Add enough water or stock to cover 5mm depth of the dish, if liked. Dot with small pieces of butter. Sprinkle with Cayenne pepper. Bake, loosely covered with greased paper, in a fairly hot oven at 190°C, Gas 5, for 35 minutes.

Savoury Grilled Sea Bream

4 helpings

400g sea bream fillets
salt and pepper
2 × 10ml spoons salad
* oil*
1 × 10ml spoon white
* wine vinegar*

1 × 5ml spoon chopped
* gherkins*
1 × 5ml spoon chopped
* capers*

Garnish
chopped parsley

Remove the rack of the grill pan. Wipe the fish and season it with salt and pepper, Place, skin side up, in the bottom of the grill pan. Heat the grill to give a medium heat. Mix together all the other ingredients except the parsley, and pour over the fish. Grill steadily for 15 minutes, turning once and basting frequently with the sauce. Sprinkle with chopped parsley and serve immediately.

Poached Brill

4–6 helpings

1 small brill
* (600g approx)*

juice of ½ lemon
court bouillon (p429)

Garnish
lemon wedges

parsley sprigs

Clean the brill inside and out. Cut off the fins and rub a little lemon juice over the flesh. Put the fish into a large deep frying pan and cover with court bouillon. Cover with a lid and poach gently for 10 minutes. Lift out the fish gently with a broad fish slice, drain, and slide on to a warmed serving plate. Garnish with lemon wedges and parsley.

Serve with Shrimp (p697) or Hollandaise Sauce (p712).

Brill and Potato Mornay

6 helpings

800g potatoes
75g butter
600g brill fillets
salt and pepper

juice of 1 lemon
500ml cheese sauce
* (p693)*
50g Cheddar cheese

Boil the potatoes in their skins and keep them hot. Use a little of the butter to grease a shallow oven-to-table baking dish and a sheet of greaseproof paper. Lay the fish in the buttered dish, season with salt and pepper, dot with butter, and sprinkle with lemon juice. Cover the dish with the sheet of buttered greaseproof paper and bake in a moderate oven at 180°C, Gas 4, for 15 minutes. Meanwhile, make the cheese sauce. Peel the potatoes, cut into rounds, and cover the fish with them in a neat pattern. Pour the cheese sauce over the fish, then grate the cheese, and sprinkle it evenly on top. Brown under the grill.

Fried Carp

2–4 helpings

1 small **or** medium-sized carp	salt
flour for coating	Cayenne pepper
	oil for shallow frying

Garnish
lemon wedges

Clean, scale, and soak the fish for 1 hour in salted water; then split open and lay flat. Season the flour with salt and Cayenne pepper. Pat the fish dry, and coat with the flour. Heat the oil in a frying pan and shallow fry the fish for 15–20 minutes, turning once, until browned. Garnish with the lemon. Serve with Anchovy Sauce (p692).

Note It is sometimes possible to strip off the thin outer skin together with the heavy scales.

Stuffed Carp

4 helpings

1 carp (1.4kg approx)	1 litre court bouillon
salt and pepper	(p429)

Stuffing
50g butter	100g soft white breadcrumbs
1 medium-sized onion	
1 × 15ml spoon chopped parsley	3 eggs
	300g mushrooms
1 × 5ml spoon chopped chives	125ml red wine

Garnish
lemon wedges   parsley sprigs

Clean the fish inside and scale it. Sprinkle with salt and pepper and put to one side. Melt the butter, skin and dice the onion, and fry gently for a few minutes until soft. Add the herbs. Mix in the breadcrumbs. Beat the eggs until liquid and add them. Dice the mushrooms and add to the stuffing, moisten with the wine, season well, and mix thoroughly. Stuff the cavity of the fish, skewer the opening to close it, and wrap the fish in greaseproof paper. Place in a fish kettle or flameproof pot-roaster lined with muslin and cover with court

bouillon. Bring almost to the boil and cover the container. Reduce the heat and poach for 25 minutes. Lift out the fish, unwrap from the paper, and serve garnished with lemon wedges and parsley sprigs.

Note For other stuffings for fish, see the chapter on Stuffings, Garnishes and Accompaniments.

Stuffing a fish

Carp with Mushrooms

6 helpings

1.2kg carp fillets	150g mushrooms
butter for greasing	1 × 15ml spoon chopped parsley
salt and pepper	
150ml dry white wine	25g flour
100g butter	150ml double cream
1 medium-sized onion	

Cut the fillets into large pieces and arrange in a buttered ovenproof dish; sprinkle with salt and pepper. Add the wine. Cover with a sheet of buttered greaseproof paper and poach in a warm oven at 160°C, Gas 3, for 25–35 minutes. Remove the fish to a serving platter and keep hot. Reserve the poaching liquid.

Melt the butter in a frying pan, skin and chop the onion finely, and fry gently until transparent. Slice the mushrooms, add to the onions, and continue to fry gently. Add the chopped parsley, sprinkle with flour, and moisten with the poaching liquid. Add the cream and mix well. Cook for 3–4 minutes without boiling. Taste and re-season if required. Coat the fish with the sauce.

Golden Grilled Cod

4 helpings

4 cod cutlets **or** steaks (2cm thick approx)	margarine for greasing

Topping
50g mild Cheddar **or** Gruyère cheese	2 × 15ml spoons milk (optional)
25g soft margarine	salt and pepper

Garnish
grilled tomatoes	watercress sprigs

Trim and rinse the fish and pat dry. Place the fish in a greased shallow flameproof dish and grill under moderate heat for 2–3 minutes on one side only. Meanwhile, grate the cheese and cream the margarine with it. Work in the milk, a few drops at a time, if used, and season to taste.

Turn the fish over, spread the topping on the uncooked side, and return to the grill. Reduce the heat slightly and cook for 10–12 minutes until the fish is cooked through and the topping is golden-brown. Serve garnished with grilled halved tomatoes and watercress sprigs.

VARIATIONS
Devilled Grill

25g margarine	1 × 5ml spoon anchovy essence
1 × 5ml spoon chutney	
1 × 5ml spoon curry powder	salt and pepper
1 × 5ml spoon dry mustard	

Combine these ingredients and substitute for the topping in Golden Grilled Cod.

Surprise Grill

25g margarine	3 × 5ml spoons grated onion
2 × 5ml spoons lemon juice	salt and pepper

Combine these ingredients and substitute for the topping in Golden Grilled Cod.

Cod à la Maître d'Hôtel

5–6 helpings

800g cod fillets (cold leftovers can be used)	1 × 15ml spoon chopped parsley
100g butter	juice of ½ lemon
2 × 15ml spoons chopped onion	salt and pepper

Poach the cod if required, and remove the skin when cool. Separate the flesh into large flakes. Melt the butter in a saucepan, add the onion, and fry for 2–3 minutes without browning. Add the fish and sprinkle it with the chopped parsley, lemon juice, and a good pinch of salt and pepper. Cook over low heat for 5 minutes, stirring gently all the time.

Serve with boiled potatoes.

Flaking a fish

Cod Fillets in Beer Batter
See p936.

Cod with Cream Sauce

6 helpings

6 cod steaks **or** *portions*
  (100g each)
75g butter
250ml fish stock (p330)
  or *milk*
25g flour

2 × 15ml spoons single
  or *double cream*
1 × 5ml spoon lemon
  juice
salt and pepper

Rinse the fish and pat dry. Heat half the butter in a frying pan, put in the cod, and seal by frying quickly on both sides, without browning. Add the stock or milk, cover, and simmer gently for 20 minutes. Drain the fish, place on a warmed dish, and keep hot. Melt the remaining butter in a clean pan, add the flour, and stir together for 2 minutes. Gradually add the fish cooking stock and enough milk to make up 250ml. Bring to the boil, reduce the heat and simmer for 4 minutes. Remove from the heat, add the cream and lemon juice, season to taste, and pour the sauce over the fish.

Cod au Gratin

4 helpings

50g butter
4 cod fillets (100–125g
  each)
butter for greasing
200g onion
1 green pepper

400g tomatoes
100g mushrooms
salt and pepper
50g Cheddar cheese
75g soft white
  breadcrumbs

Heat the butter in a frying pan and fry the cod portions for 2 minutes on each side. Lift out and put in a single layer into a buttered, fairly deep ovenproof dish. Skin and chop the onion and fry gently in the butter until soft. Place on top of the fish. De-seed and dice the pepper and blanch in boiling salted water for 2 minutes. Drain and add to the fish. Skin, de-seed, and slice the tomatoes. Clean and slice the mushrooms and fry gently for 2–3 minutes. Arrange these ingredients in layers on top of the fish. Sprinkle with salt and pepper. Grate the cheese, mix with the breadcrumbs, and sprinkle over the dish. Bake in a fairly hot oven at 190°C, Gas 5, for 30 minutes.

Curried Cod

5–6 helpings

800g cod fillets
50g butter
100g onion
1 × 15ml spoon flour
1 × 10ml spoon curry
  powder

500ml fish stock (p330)
1 × 15ml spoon lemon
  juice
salt and pepper
Cayenne pepper

Rinse the fish and pat dry. Cut into pieces about 3cm square. Melt the butter in a saucepan and fry the cod lightly. Remove the fish and keep hot. Skin and slice the onion. Add the sliced onion, flour, and curry powder to the butter and fry for 15 minutes, stirring all the time to prevent the onion becoming too brown. Pour in the stock and stir until on the boil; reduce the heat and simmer gently for 20 minutes. Strain and return to the saucepan, add the lemon juice and seasoning to taste, bring nearly to boiling point, and then put in the fish.

Cover and heat gently until the fish has absorbed the flavour of the sauce. Stir occasionally to avoid sticking.

Serve with boiled rice.

Note Remains of cold fish can be used, in which case omit the preliminary frying.

Cod Portugaise

4 helpings

75ml cooking oil
100g onion
25g flour
200g tomatoes
75g green pepper

125ml dry white wine
125ml water
salt and pepper
600g cod fillets
10–12 stuffed olives

Heat 25ml of the oil in a saucepan. Skin and finely dice the onion and fry gently until soft. Stir in half the flour. Skin, chop, and de-seed the tomatoes, and add to the mixture. De-seed and chop the green pepper and add this to the sauce. Then gently stir in the wine and water. Cover the pan and simmer while frying the fish, stirring occasionally. Season the remaining flour. Cut the fish into 4 pieces, and coat each with the flour. Heat the remaining oil in a frying pan, and fry the fish gently for 10 minutes, turning once. Add the stuffed olives to the sauce and heat through. Place the fish in a serving dish and pour the sauce over it.

Cod Steaks with Shrimp Stuffing

4 helpings

4 cod steaks (centre cut)	1 × 15ml spoon cooking oil

Stuffing
25g butter	150g peeled shrimps **or**
1 medium-sized onion	prawns
50g soft breadcrumbs	juice of ½ lemon
1 × 15ml spoon chopped parsley	salt and pepper

Garnish
lemon wedges	watercress sprigs

Make the stuffing first. Melt the butter, skin and chop the onion, and fry gently until soft. Remove from the heat, and add the breadcrumbs and chopped parsley. Chop the shrimps and add to the other ingredients. Add the lemon juice, and season with salt and pepper.

Rinse the fish, pat dry, and remove the centre bones. Arrange the fish neatly on a flameproof platter or baking sheet and fill the centre spaces with the stuffing. Brush with a little oil, and grill, using medium heat, for 10 minutes. Serve garnished with lemon wedges and watercress sprigs.

Smoked Cod and Corn Casserole

3–4 helpings

1 × 326g can sweetcorn kernels	salt and pepper
	25g butter
400g smoked cod fillets	125ml single cream

Drain the corn and spread a layer on the bottom of an ovenproof dish. Cut the fish into 1cm wide strips and place a few on top. Season with salt and pepper and dot with butter. Repeat these layers until all the ingredients are used, then pour the cream on top. Cover and cook in a moderate oven at 180°C, Gas 4, for 25 minutes.

Scalloped Cod's Roe

3–4 helpings

400g uncooked cod's roe	375ml parsley sauce (p696)
salt	
white wine vinegar	butter for greasing
a little milk **or** single cream	browned breadcrumbs (p375)

Wash and wipe the cod's roe, then poach it for 10 minutes in water sharpened with a little salt and vinegar. Cool the roe to tepid to let it firm up. Add the milk or cream to the parsley sauce. Dice the roe and put it into the sauce. Butter 3–4 clean scallop shells, put in the roe, cover with breadcrumbs, and heat in a fairly hot oven at 200°C, Gas 6, for a few minutes until the sauce bubbles and the crumbs are crisped. If scallop shells are not available, serve on buttered toast.

Note Cod's roe can be purchased ready-cooked or in cans. If these are used, omit the initial poaching.

Coley Provençale

4–5 helpings

2 onions	salt and pepper
1 green pepper	600g coley fillets
300g tomatoes	margarine for greasing
1 clove of garlic	8 green olives
1 × 15ml spoon cooking oil	

Garnish
stoned black olives

Skin and chop the onions, and de-seed and chop the pepper. Skin the tomatoes, de-seed and chop the flesh. Skin and crush the garlic. Heat the oil in a frying pan, add the onion and pepper, and fry gently for 5 minutes, stirring often. Add the tomatoes and garlic, and simmer for another 10 minutes, stirring occasionally. Remove from the heat, and season.

Skin the fish fillets, and cut them into 2cm cubes or pieces. Grease a shallow oven-to-table baking dish, and put in the fish. Stone and add the green olives; then pour the tomato mixture over the dish. Cover loosely with oiled greaseproof paper or greased foil, and bake in a moderate oven at 180°C, Gas 4, for 30 minutes. Garnish with black olives.

Eel Casserole

4–5 helpings

800g eels	100g button mushrooms
100g onions	cooking oil for shallow
1 clove of garlic	frying
bouquet garni	50g butter
salt and pepper	50g flour
250ml red wine	gravy browning

Garnish
fried croûtons   *peeled prawns*

Skin the eels and cut into 5–7cm lengths. Skin and slice the onions into rings and put them in a saucepan with the garlic, bouquet garni, salt, and pepper; then put the fish on top. Add the wine to cover, and simmer for 20 minutes. Meanwhile, clean the mushrooms and fry gently in a little oil until soft. Remove the fish and mushrooms to a warmed serving dish and keep hot. Blend the butter and flour together. Reduce the cooking liquid to the desired flavour, then thicken as liked with most or all of the butter and flour mixture. Darken the sauce with a little gravy browning, and pour it over the fish. Garnish with fried croûtons and prawns.

Stewed Eels

4 helpings

1kg eels **or** 4 × 200g conger eel steaks (5cm thick approx)	75ml port **or** Madeira
	50ml double cream
	50g flour
salt and pepper	Cayenne pepper
1 large onion	a few drops lemon juice
3 cloves	
1 strip lemon rind	
500ml general household stock (p329)	

Wash, dry, and skin the eels, if used. Cut into pieces about 7cm long. Lay the pieces of eel or the steaks in a stewpan which will just hold them in one layer. Season lightly. Skin the onion and press the cloves into it; put it on the fish. Add the lemon rind. Mix together the stock and port or Madeira, and pour this over the fish. Cover the pan and bring to boiling point; then reduce the heat and simmer for 30 minutes.

Remove the pieces of eel with a perforated spoon, drain them, and place on a warmed serving dish; keep hot. Strain the cooking liquid into a clean pan. Mix the cream and flour to a smooth paste, and blend in enough liquid from the pan to make it semi-liquid. Add the mixture to the rest of the liquid in the pan. Stir over moderate heat until the sauce thickens. Add Cayenne pepper and lemon juice to taste, and pour the sauce over the eels. Serve at once.

Fried Eels

5–6 helpings

1–2 medium-sized eels (800g approx)	beaten egg for coating
salt and pepper	breadcrumbs for coating
1 × 15ml spoon flour	fat for shallow frying

Garnish
fried parsley (p398) **or**
  whole capers

Wash, dry, and skin the eels. Cut into 5–7cm pieces. Season the flour and roll the pieces of eel separately in the mixture. Coat well with egg and breadcrumbs. Heat the fat in a frying pan and fry the eels for 15–20 minutes or until brown. Drain well. Pile on a warmed serving dish, and garnish with fried parsley or whole capers.

Matelote of Eels

4–5 helpings

flour for coating	125ml claret
salt and pepper	25g flour
800g eels	12 fresh **or** canned
50g butter	button mushrooms
375ml fish stock (p330)	

Season the flour with salt and pepper. Wash, dry, and skin the eels. Cut into pieces 7–8cm long. Coat in the seasoned flour. Heat 25g butter in a frying pan, add the eels, and fry until lightly browned, turning as required. Drain off any butter that remains. Pour in the stock and wine, bring to the boil, cover, reduce the heat, and simmer for 30 minutes. Meanwhile, melt the remaining butter in a small saucepan, add the 25g flour, and cook gently until nut-brown; put to one side.

Drain the pieces of eel and keep hot in a serving dish. Strain the stock and add it gradually to the browned flour. Stir until boiling. Slice and add the mushrooms and simmer for 3–4 minutes. Season to taste and pour the sauce over the fish.

Fried Grayling

4 helpings

4 small grayling (250g each approx)	salt and pepper
flour for coating	fat for shallow frying

Garnish
lemon wedges

Remove the fins from the fish. Rinse thoroughly and pat dry inside and out. Season the flour with salt and pepper and coat the fish lightly. Heat the oil in a frying pan and fry the fish for 8–9 minutes or until browned, turning once. Drain and serve immediately with lemon wedges.

Baked Grayling

2 helpings

25g butter	2 medium-sized grayling (500g each approx)
300g onions	175ml dry white wine
2 × 15ml spoons chopped parsley	175ml double cream
salt and pepper	juice of ½ lemon

Garnish
watercress sprigs

Butter an ovenproof dish with half the butter. Skin and slice the onions, and cover the bottom of the dish with the slices. Sprinkle with the chopped parsley, and season. Clean the fish, remove the heads and fins, then lay the fish in the dish, side by side. Melt the remaining butter and brush it over the fish. Bake in a fairly hot oven at 200°C, Gas 6, for 10 minutes. Add the wine, baste with the juices, and bake for a further 15 minutes. Add the cream and cook for a further 5 minutes. Squeeze the lemon juice over the fish just before serving. Garnish with watercress sprigs.

Baked Grey Mullet

4 helpings

4 small grey mullet (250g each)	*1 lemon*
200g onions	*salt and pepper*
butter for greasing	*1 × 15ml spoon chopped*
200g tomatoes	*tarragon **or** 1 × 10ml*
100ml dry white wine	*spoon dried tarragon*

Garnish
sippets (p385)

Scale and rinse the fish. Skin and slice the onions into rings and place in a buttered oven-to-table dish. Skin, de-seed, and slice the tomatoes, and lay them on the onions. Lay the fish on top and pour the wine over it. Slice the lemon. Season the fish well with salt, pepper, and tarragon. Cover the fish with lemon slices. Cover loosely with buttered greaseproof paper and bake in a fairly hot oven at 190°C, Gas 5, for 30 minutes. Serve from the dish, garnished with sippets.

Poached Gurnet

2–3 helpings

*1 **or** 2 gurnet (1kg approx)*	*court bouillon* (p429)

Clean the fish and cut off the head and fins. Place the fish in a suitable pan, half cover with court bouillon, and heat until nearly boiling; then cover with a lid, reduce the heat, and poach gently for 20 minutes.

Serve hot with Anchovy Sauce (p692).

Note To serve cold, follow the instructions for poaching above, then leave the fish to cool in the cooking liquid. Serve with salad.

Poached or Grilled Smoked Haddock

4 helpings

450–600g smoked haddock fillets	*pepper*
milk	*butter **or** oil*

Garnish (optional)
4 pats parsley butter (p1301)

To poach: Cut the fins off the fish, and cut it into serving portions if required. Place the fish in one layer in a large frying pan. Add just enough milk, or milk and water mixed, to cover all but the top of the fish. Dust lightly with pepper. Simmer for 10–15 minutes or until tender. Lift each piece in turn on to a fish slice, drain well, and place on a heated dish or plate. Brush lightly with butter, and serve topped with a pat of chilled parsley butter if desired.

To grill: Cut off the fins and portion the fish as above. Place the portions in a large frying pan and cover with boiling water. Leave to stand for 5 minutes. Lift each piece on to a fish slice, drain well, and place the pieces, skin side up, in the grill pan. Grill under medium heat for 3–5 minutes, depending on the thickness of the fish. Turn, brush the fish lightly with butter or oil, dust with pepper, and grill for another 4 minutes or until tender. Serve topped with pats of chilled parsley butter.

Kedgeree

4 helpings

150g long-grain rice	*1 × 15ml spoon curry*
400g smoked haddock	*powder*
100ml milk	*salt and pepper*
100ml water	*Cayenne pepper*
50g butter	*2 hard-boiled eggs*

Garnish

1 × 15ml spoon chopped parsley	*butter*

Boil the rice for 12 minutes and drain thoroughly. Keep warm. Poach the haddock in equal quantities of milk and water in a covered pan for 4 minutes. Remove from the pan and drain. Remove the skin and tail, and break up the fish into fairly large flakes. Melt half the butter in a saucepan. Blend in the curry powder and add the flaked fish. Warm the mixture through. Warm the rice in the rest of the butter. Season both the fish mixture and the rice with salt, pepper, and a few grains of Cayenne pepper. Chop the hard-boiled eggs coarsely. Add them to the fish and combine the mixture with the rice. Pile on a heated dish and sprinkle with chopped parsley. Dot with butter and serve immediately.

Cooking time – 25 minutes (approx)

Scalloped Smoked Haddock

4 helpings

250ml milk	2 ×15ml spoons
2 ×15ml spoons	chopped parsley
chopped onion	2 ×15ml spoons double
1 blade of mace	cream
200g smoked haddock	browned breadcrumbs
50g butter	(p375) for topping
25g flour	400g creamed potato
salt and pepper	

Garnish
watercress sprigs

Put the milk, onion, and mace into a deep frying pan. Poach the fish gently in the milk. When cooked, remove any skin and flake the fish. Reserve the cooking liquid. Butter 4 scallop shells or other suitable dishes and divide the fish between them. Melt 25g butter, stir in the flour, and gradually add the cooking liquid, stirring all the time. Season, add the parsley and the cream, and pour the hot sauce over the fish. Sprinkle with breadcrumbs and pipe a border of creamed potato around the edge of the shells. Dot with butter and place under a low grill or in a fairly hot oven at 200°C, Gas 6, for a few minutes until the breadcrumbs are crisped and the potato browned. Garnish with the watercress sprigs and serve at once.

Cooking time 20 minutes (approx)

Haddock in Cider

4 helpings

600g haddock fillets	2 ×15ml spoons
butter for greasing	chopped parsley
200g tomatoes	25g Cheddar cheese
150g mushrooms	(approx)
125ml dry cider	2 ×15ml spoons soft
salt and pepper	white breadcrumbs

Cut the fish into cubes, and place them in an even layer in a buttered oven-to-table baking dish. Skin and slice the tomatoes and clean and slice the mushrooms; lay them on top of the fish. Pour the cider over the fish, season, and sprinkle with chopped parsley. Grate the cheese. Mix the crumbs and cheese together and scatter over the fish. Bake in a hot oven at 220°C, Gas 7, for 20–25 minutes.

Haddock Florentine

4 helpings

1kg haddock fillets	salt and pepper
100ml fish stock (p330)	a pinch of ground
100ml dry white wine	nutmeg
1kg raw spinach or 500g	50g grated Parmesan
frozen leaf spinach	cheese
50g butter	
500ml Mornay sauce	
(p706)	

Poach the fish in the stock and wine for 7–10 minutes. If using fresh spinach, tear the leaves from the stalks and place in a large saucepan with half the butter and seasoning. Cover with a tight-fitting lid and cook gently for about 15 minutes, shaking occasionally. Cook frozen spinach according to the directions on the packet. Drain the spinach well and press out all free liquid. Use half the butter to grease a shallow oven-to-table baking dish. Put the spinach in the bottom of the dish, drain the fish fillets, and lay them on top. Reduce the fish cooking liquid to half by boiling uncovered. Add it to the Mornay Sauce, season with salt, pepper and nutmeg, and pour the sauce over the fish. Sprinkle with cheese and dot with the remaining butter. Brown under the grill. Serve hot from the dish.

Baked Haddock Fillets

4 helpings

1 medium-sized onion	*800g haddock fillets*
150g mushrooms	*100ml dry white wine*
butter for greasing	*50g soft white*
1 × 15ml spoon chopped	*breadcrumbs*
parsley	*50g butter*

Skin and chop the onion, clean and slice the mushrooms, and spread them evenly over the bottom of a buttered ovenproof dish. Sprinkle with the parsley. Cut the fish into 4 portions, place in the dish and add the wine. Sprinkle with breadcrumbs, dot with butter, and cook in a fairly hot oven at 190°C, Gas 5, for 30–35 minutes.

French Fried Haddock

4–5 helpings

1kg haddock fillets	*100g flour*
250ml milk	*oil **or** fat for deep frying*
salt and pepper	

Garnish
fried parsley (p398)   *lemon wedges*

Skin the fillets if necessary. Cut the fish into 4–5 portions. Season the milk with salt and pepper and dip the fish first into the milk and then into the flour, shaking off any excess. Heat the oil (p303) and fry the fish until evenly browned. Garnish with fried parsley and lemon wedges.

Haddock with Soured Cream

4 helpings

1 lemon	*1 × 125ml carton soured*
butter for greasing	*cream*
600g haddock fillets	*salt*
salt and pepper	*paprika*

Garnish
watercress sprigs

Slice the lemon and place the slices in an even layer in a buttered baking dish large enough to hold the fish in one layer. Skin the fish if necessary, cut into serving portions, and lay them on the lemon. Season lightly, cover closely with foil, and bake in a fairly hot oven at 200°C, Gas 6, for 20–25 minutes. Uncover, and pour the cream over the fish. Sprinkle with salt and paprika. Grill until lightly browned on top. Garnish with watercress.

Hake with Sweet and Sour Sauce

3–4 helpings

400g hake fillets	*cornflour for coating*
1 green pepper	*oil for deep frying*

Marinade
2 spring onions	*1 × 15ml spoon chopped*
1 × 15ml spoon medium-	*ginger root*
dry sherry	
2 × 15ml spoons soy	
sauce	

Sauce
6 × 15ml spoons	*1 × 5ml spoon white*
pineapple juice	*wine **or** malt vinegar*
2 × 5ml spoons cornflour	*1 × 5ml spoon cooking*
2 × 15ml spoons soy	*oil*
sauce	*1 × 227g can pineapple*
1 × 15ml spoon medium-	*pieces*
dry sherry	

Skin the fillets if necessary. Cut the fish into 2cm cubes. Chop the spring onions. Mix together the sherry, soy sauce, ginger, and spring onions; marinate the fish in this mixture for 1–2 hours. De-seed and chop the green pepper finely.

Make the sauce. Mix the pineapple juice with the cornflour. When blended add all the other sauce ingredients except the pineapple pieces. Bring to the boil, stirring all the time, reduce the heat, and simmer for 3 minutes.

Drain the fish and roll in cornflour. Heat the oil (p303) and fry the fish until well and evenly browned. Dry the fish with soft kitchen paper. Place in a warmed serving dish and sprinkle with the chopped green pepper. Add the pineapple pieces to the sauce, heat through, and pour the sauce over the fish.

Hake Mornay

4 helpings

1kg hake fillets
100ml dry white wine
100ml fish stock (p330)
butter for greasing
500ml Mornay sauce
  (p706)

50g grated Parmesan
  cheese
25g butter

Cut each fillet into 3 portions and poach gently for 10 minutes in the wine and stock. Drain the fillets and arrange in a greased oven-to-table baking dish. Reduce the cooking liquid to half its volume by heating, and add to the Mornay sauce. Cover the fish with the sauce. Sprinkle with the cheese, dot with butter, and brown lightly under the grill.

Scalloped Halibut

4 helpings

butter for greasing
100g Gruyère cheese
250ml Mornay sauce
  (p706)
100g mushrooms
400g halibut

500ml court bouillon
  (p429)
400g soft white
  breadcrumbs
400g creamed potato
25g butter

Grease lightly 4 deep scallop shells or other suitable oven-to-table individual dishes. Grate the cheese and add half to the Mornay sauce. Clean and slice the mushrooms. Poach the fish in the court bouillon for 10 minutes, add the mushrooms for the last 5 minutes. Leave to cool; then remove the bones from the fish and flake the flesh. Divide the fish and mushrooms between the shells or dishes and cover with the sauce. Mix together the remaining cheese and breadcrumbs and sprinkle over the dishes. Pipe the creamed potato around the rims. Dot with the butter and bake in a fairly hot oven at 190°C, Gas 5, for 15–20 minutes.

Halibut Bristol

4 helpings

400g halibut (centre cut)
butter for greasing
salt and pepper
250ml fish stock (p330)

1 × 15ml spoon butter
1 × 15ml spoon flour
50g grated Parmesan
  cheese

Garnish
12 cooked mussels on the
  half shell (p462)

Place the halibut in a buttered oven-to-table baking dish, season well, and add the fish stock. Cover and cook in a fairly hot oven at 190°C, Gas 5, for 20 minutes. Drain off the liquid and reserve it. Skin the fish and remove the centre bone. Melt the butter, stir in the flour, and gradually add the fish stock, stirring all the time until the sauce thickens. Add half the cheese and season well. Pour the sauce over the fish and sprinkle with the remaining cheese. Return the dish to a very hot oven at 230°C, Gas 8, for 7–8 minutes. Arrange the mussels around the dish and serve.

Baked Herrings

4 helpings

4 herrings
salt and pepper
150g onions
25g butter

400g tomatoes
butter for greasing
2 × 15ml spoons malt
  vinegar

Garnish
chopped parsley

Clean and scale the herrings. Make 3 shallow cuts in each side and season well. Skin the onions and slice finely. Melt half the butter and fry the onions lightly for 5 minutes. Skin and slice the tomatoes and place in the bottom of a buttered oven-to-table baking dish with the onions. Season well and sprinkle with vinegar. Arrange the fish on top and brush with the remaining butter. Cover and bake in a fairly hot oven at 190°C, Gas 5, for 45 minutes. Garnish with chopped parsley.

Herrings with Mustard Sauce

4 helpings

4 herrings	50g butter
2 × 5ml spoons lemon juice	2 × 15ml spoons double cream
salt and pepper	1 × 15ml spoon chopped capers
1 × 10ml spoon dry mustard	1 × 15ml spoon chopped gherkin
2 egg yolks	

Scale the herrings, cut off the heads, and bone the fish. Sprinkle the flesh with lemon juice and season well. Grill, using moderate heat, for 3–5 minutes on each side. Keep hot. Put the dry mustard and egg yolks in a basin and whisk over a pan of hot water until creamy. Divide the butter into small pieces, and whisk into the sauce one by one. When the sauce thickens, remove from the heat and stir in the cream. Add the finely chopped capers and gherkin. Season well. Serve the sauce hot with the herrings.

Herrings Stuffed with Shrimps

4 helpings

4 herrings	browned breadcrumbs (p375)
salt and pepper	25g butter
1 egg	

Stuffing

1 × 15ml spoon soft white breadcrumbs	Cayenne pepper
1 × 15ml spoon milk	a few drops anchovy essence
50g peeled shrimps	

Scale the herrings, cut off the heads, and bone them; then season well. Make the stuffing. Soak the breadcrumbs in the milk. Chop the shrimps finely, mix with the breadcrumbs, season with Cayenne pepper and a few drops of anchovy essence. Spread this filling on the flesh side of the fillets and roll up tightly. Fasten with a small skewer. Place, packed tightly together, in an ovenproof dish. Beat the egg until liquid. Brush the fish with the egg, sprinkle with the browned breadcrumbs, dot with the butter, and bake in a fairly hot oven at 190°C, Gas 5, for 30–35 minutes.

Stuffed Herrings

4 helpings

4 large herrings	butter for greasing

Stuffing

200g onions	1 × 15ml spoon cider or white wine vinegar
50g butter	
200g cooking apples	salt and pepper

Scale the herrings, cut off the heads, open out the fish, and bone without breaking the skin. Make the stuffing. Skin the onions and chop finely. Melt the butter and fry the onions gently until soft. Peel, core, and grate the apples. Mix with the onion, and add the vinegar and seasoning. Divide the stuffing between the herrings and fill the cavities. Reshape the fish. Lay them on a flat ovenproof dish. Cover loosely with lightly greased foil and bake in a fairly hot oven at 190°C, Gas 5, for 25 minutes.

Herrings Tails-in-air

4 helpings

4 herrings	salt and pepper
50g soft white breadcrumbs	a little milk
2 small onions	1 green pepper
1 tomato	150ml ready-to-serve tomato soup
1 × 10ml spoon chopped parsley	

Scale the herrings, cut off the heads, but leave the tails on, and bone the fish. Keep the roes. Trim the tails neatly, and cut off the fins. Chop the roes and mix with the breadcrumbs. Skin and grate 1 onion. Skin, de-seed, and chop the tomato. Mix into the breadcrumb mixture with the parsley, and season well. Bind together using a little milk, if required. Lay the herrings on a board. Put 1 × 15ml spoon of the mixture on the head end of each and roll up towards the tail. Place the rolled herrings in an ovenproof dish with the tails sticking up in the centre. Skin the second onion, de-seed the green pepper, and cut both into rings. Scatter these over the fish. Pour the soup over them. Cover and bake in a fairly hot oven at 200°C, Gas 6, for 30 minutes.

Soused Herrings

See p322.

John Dory in White Wine

3–4 helpings

8 John Dory fillets	*1 × 15ml spoon flour*
butter for greasing	*125ml water*
50g butter	*2 egg yolks*
salt and pepper	*125ml double cream*
350ml dry white wine	

Garnish
50g peeled prawns

Roll up the fish fillets and place in a greased oven-to-table baking dish. Dot with half the butter and season well. Pour over half the wine, cover with buttered greaseproof paper, and bake in a fairly hot oven at 190°C, Gas 5, for 20 minutes.

Melt the remaining butter in a pan, add the flour and cook without colouring for 2–3 minutes. Gradually add the rest of the wine, and the water. Cook, stirring all the time, until the mixture thickens. Drain the fillets, and add the cooking liquid to the sauce. Mix the egg yolks with the cream, and add them slowly to the sauce, stirring all the time. Do not allow to boil. Pour the sauce over the fish and garnish with the prawns.

John Dory au Gratin

3–4 helpings

8 John Dory fillets	*50g Gruyère cheese*
butter for greasing	*100g dry white*
salt and pepper	*breadcrumbs*
50ml milk	*25g butter*

Lay the fillets in a buttered ovenproof dish as for John Dory in White Wine. Season well and add the milk. Grate the cheese. Sprinkle with the breadcrumbs and cheese. Dot with butter, and bake in a fairly hot oven at 190°C, Gas 5, for 20 minutes.

Jugged or Poached Kippers

4 helpings

4 kippers

Garnish (optional)
4 pats chilled Maître
 d'Hôtel butter (p1300)

Put the kippers, tail end up, in a tall, heatproof jug. Pour boiling water over the whole fish except the tails. Cover the jug with a cloth, and leave to stand for 5 minutes. Tilt the jug gently over a sink, and drain off the water. Do not try to pull the kippers out by their tails. Serve them on warmed plates, topped with pats of Maître d'Hôtel butter, if liked.

Kipper and Tomato Bake

4 helpings

4 kippers	*50g butter*
milk	*lemon juice*
200g tomatoes	*salt and pepper*
25g parsley (approx)	*butter for greasing*
1 × 15ml spoon soft	
white breadcrumbs	

Garnish
chopped parsley

Poach the kippers in a little milk. Skin and bone them, and flake the flesh. Skin and slice the tomatoes. Chop the parsley. Mix the kippers with 2 × 15ml spoons of the poaching milk, the breadcrumbs, butter, and parsley. Add a little lemon juice, and season to taste. Spread in a lightly greased shallow ovenproof dish and top with the tomato slices. Bake in a warm oven at 160°C, Gas 3, for 20 minutes. Sprinkle with chopped parsley before serving.

Grilled Kippers

4 helpings

4 kippers	*4 × 5ml spoons butter* **or** *margarine*

Garnish

4 pats chilled butter	*chopped parsley*

Lay the kippers flat, skin side up, on the grill pan base (not on the rack). Grill under medium heat for 3 minutes. Turn, dot each kipper with 1 × 5ml spoon butter or margarine, and grill for another 3 minutes. Serve on warmed plates, topped with pats of chilled butter and sprinkled with parsley.

Casserole of Ling

4 helpings

600g ling fillets	*25g flour*
150g onions	*375ml tomato juice*
25g butter	*a pinch of mixed herbs*
100g button mushrooms	*salt and pepper*

Cut the fish into 5cm pieces and place in an oven-proof dish. Skin and slice the onions. Melt the butter in a deep pan and fry the onions and mushrooms; sprinkle in the flour when the onions begin to colour. Add the tomato juice, and bring to the boil, stirring all the time. Add the herbs and seasoning; then pour the sauce over the fish. Cover and bake in a fairly hot oven at 200°C, Gas 6, for 30 minutes.

Grilled Mackerel

4 helpings

2 large **or** *4 small mackerel*	*milk for brushing*
	salt and pepper

Garnish

4 pats Maître d'Hôtel butter (p1300)	*watercress sprigs*

Split the fish, and remove the heads, tails, and backbones. Score the skin without cutting through the flesh, and nick it at the edges in a few places. Heat the grill to give moderate cooking heat. Brush the fish with milk on both sides, season, and lay, skin side up, on the grill pan. Grill for the time given in the table on p411, turning once. Arrange on a warmed serving dish and garnish with pats of chilled Maître d'Hôtel butter and watercress sprigs.

Mackerel Niçoise

4 helpings

4 small mackerel	*1 × 10ml spoon*
1 large onion	*concentrated tomato*
1 clove of garlic	*purée*
2 × 15ml spoons olive oil	*a pinch of powdered*
25g butter	*saffron*
125ml medium-dry	*salt and pepper*
white wine	*200g tomatoes*

Garnish

parsley sprigs	*lemon slices*
stoned olives	

Rinse the fish inside and out, and pat dry. Skin and chop the onion finely. Crush the garlic. Heat the oil and butter together in a large frying pan. Fry the onion and garlic until soft, then place the fish on top. Pour the wine and tomato purée over the fish and season with the saffron, salt, and pepper. Poach together for 10 minutes. Take out the fish, arrange on a plate, and keep warm. Skin, de-seed, and chop the tomatoes, add to the sauce and boil briskly for 5 minutes. Pour the sauce over the fish. Garnish with parsley, olives, and lemon slices.

Mackerel with Gooseberry Sauce

4 helpings

flour for coating	*50g butter*
salt and pepper	*25g parsley (approx)*
8 mackerel fillets	*juice of 1 lemon*

Sauce

400g gooseberries	*1 × 15ml spoon caster*
50ml dry still cider	*sugar*
25g butter	

Make the sauce first. Wash and prepare the gooseberries, and poach in the cider and butter until tender. Sieve to make a smooth purée. Add the sugar. Put into a saucepan and put to one side.

Meanwhile, season the flour with salt and pepper. Dip the fish fillets in the flour. Heat the butter in a frying pan and fry the fillets gently for 5–7 minutes, turning once. Remove them, arrange on a serving plate and keep hot. Reserve the butter in the pan. Chop the parsley.

Heat the gooseberry sauce and keep hot. Add the remaining butter to the pan, and heat until light brown. Add the lemon juice and chopped parsley, and pour this over the fish.

Serve the gooseberry sauce separately.

Dipping fillets in flour

Baked Mackerel Parcels

4 helpings

4 small mackerel	*salt and freshly ground*
150g mushroom stuffing	*black pepper*
(p378)	*juice of 1 lemon*
25g butter	

Garnish (optional)
8 grilled button
  mushrooms

Rinse the fish and pat dry. Fill the cavities with the mushroom stuffing. Lay each fish on a separate piece of buttered foil large enough to enclose it completely. Dot the tops of the fish with any remaining butter. Sprinkle lightly with salt, pepper, and lemon juice. Enclose the fish in the foil, and bake in a fairly hot oven at 200°C, Gas 6, for 20 minutes or until tender when pierced through the foil with a fine skewer. Serve in the parcels, still closed, or open the parcels just enough to show the tops of the fish, and place 2 mushrooms on top of each.

Mackerel with Soured Cream Sauce

4 helpings

2 × 10ml spoons flour	*50g butter*
8 mackerel fillets (50g	*salt and pepper*
each approx)	*2 egg yolks*
butter for greasing	*125ml milk*
25g parsley (approx)	*125ml soured cream*

Flour the fillets and place in a buttered ovenproof dish. Chop the parsley and sprinkle it over them. Dot with the butter and season well. Cover loosely with foil and bake in a fairly hot oven at 190°C, Gas 5, for 20 minutes. Place the fish on a warmed serving dish and keep hot. Reserve the cooking liquid.

Mix the yolks, milk, and soured cream into the reserved liquid in a pan. Heat very gently until the mixture thickens; do not allow it to boil. Pour the sauce over the fish and serve immediately.

Fried Perch

6 helpings

flour for coating	100g butter
salt and pepper	3 × 15ml spoons cooking
2 eggs	oil
12 perch fillets	
dry breadcrumbs for	
coating	

Marinade

1 spring onion	juice of 1 lemon
6–8 × 15ml spoons olive	salt and pepper
oil	

Garnish
lemon wedges

Make the marinade first. Chop the spring onion. Mix all the ingredients for the marinade together and steep the fillets for at least 1 hour. Drain. Season the flour. Beat the eggs until liquid. Dip the fish into the flour, shaking off any excess, then into the egg and breadcrumbs. Heat the butter and oil together and fry the fish gently for 6–8 minutes, turning once, until evenly browned on both sides. Garnish with lemon wedges.

Baked Perch

4 helpings

4 small perch	25g parsley (approx)
50g butter	
300ml fish stock (p330)	
or stock and white wine	

Garnish

lemon wedges	parsley sprigs

Plunge the fish into boiling water for a few minutes to help remove the scales. Trim and clean the fish. Place in a buttered oven-to-table baking dish and dot with butter. Pour the stock and wine over it. Chop the parsley and sprinkle it over the dish. Cover and bake in a fairly hot oven at 190°C, Gas 5, for 15–20 minutes. Drain the liquid into a saucepan and reduce it by boiling, uncovered, for 7–10 minutes. Serve the fish with the sauce poured over it, and garnish with lemon wedges and parsley.

Braised Pike

4 helpings

1 small pike	1 × 10ml spoon lemon
(1kg approx)	juice
75g butter	salt and pepper
200g streaky bacon	50g flour
250ml fish stock (p330)	

Garnish
chopped parsley

Clean and fillet the fish, and cut into 5cm cubes. Melt 25g of the butter in a saucepan and add the fish. Cut the rinds off the bacon, cut it into small squares, and place in the saucepan. Pour the stock and lemon juice over it and season well. Cover and simmer for 15 minutes. Remove the fish and bacon, place on a warmed serving dish and keep hot. Strain the cooking liquid into a clean saucepan. Blend the remaining butter with the flour and gradually whisk it into the cooking liquid. Cook over gentle heat until the sauce thickens. Pour it over the fish and sprinkle with parsley.

Pike Quenelles

(Quenelles de Brochet)

4–6 helpings

400g pike fillets	a pinch of grated nutmeg
4–5 egg whites	1 litre court bouillon
500ml double cream	(p429)
salt and pepper	

Skin the fillets if necessary. Dice the fish finely, add the egg whites, and process in an electric blender to a smooth purée. Rub the mixture through a sieve. Whip the cream to the same consistency as the fish purée. Fold it in lightly but thoroughly. Season the mixture with salt, pepper and nutmeg, and chill in the refrigerator for several hours.

Heat the court bouillon until just simmering. Shape the chilled fish mixture into quenelles with warmed rounded dessertspoons, and gently lower into the liquid. Simmer for 8–10 minutes. Drain with a perforated spoon.

Serve immediately with 500ml of either hot Aurora (p704) or Mushroom Sauce (p695).

Plaice Portugaise

4 helpings

2 shallots	8 plaice fillets (75g each
300g tomatoes	approx)
25g butter	100ml medium-dry
100g button mushrooms	white wine
butter for greasing	salt and pepper

Skin and slice the shallots. Skin, de-seed, and chop the tomatoes, and fry in the butter with the shallots. Add the mushrooms and heat gently for 4–5 minutes. Pour into a buttered oven-to-table baking dish. Fold each fillet into three, skin side in, and lay on the tomato mixture. Pour the wine over the fish, season well, and cover loosely. Bake in a fairly hot oven at 190°C, Gas 5, for 25 minutes. Baste the fish with the mixture on the dish before serving.

Plaice in Red Wine

4 helpings

1 onion	salt
1 plaice (500–750g)	250ml red wine
1 × 10ml spoon chopped	250ml fish stock (p330)
parsley	25g flour
4 cloves	25g butter
pepper	100g mushrooms
1 bay leaf	butter for shallow frying

Skin and chop the onion finely. Skin and fillet the plaice. Put the parsley and onion in a saucepan. Add the cloves, pepper, and bay leaf. Put the prepared fish on top, season with salt, and pour on the wine and stock. Cover, bring to boiling point, reduce the heat, and simmer for 15–20 minutes. Drain off the liquid. Keep the fish fillets hot on a warmed serving dish.

Boil the wine and stock until reduced to about 250ml. Mix the flour and butter to a smooth paste, and moisten to a cream with a little of the stock. Off the heat, add the mixture in small spoonfuls to the reduced liquid, and stir until the sauce begins to thicken. Taste and re-season with salt if required. Fry the mushrooms in a little butter until tender. Place 1 or 2 mushrooms on each slice of fish and pour the sauce over the dish.

Goujons of Plaice

6 helpings

12 plaice fillets (100g	salt and pepper
each approx)	100ml milk
flour for coating	oil or fat for deep frying

Garnish
fried parsley (p398)   lemon wedges

Cut the fillets lengthways into short strips about 3–4cms wide. Season the flour with salt and pepper. Dip the fish in the milk and coat with the flour, shaking off any excess. Heat the oil (p303) and fry the strips until golden-brown. Arrange on a dish and serve hot, garnished with fried parsley and lemon wedges.

Serve Tartare Sauce (p846) separately.

Stuffed Whole Plaice

4 helpings

4 small plaice (300g	25g butter
each approx)	

Stuffing

100g mild Cheddar	salt and pepper
cheese	1 × 10ml spoon mixed
50g soft white	dried herbs
breadcrumbs	juice of $\frac{1}{2}$ lemon
1 × 5ml spoon dry	2 × 15ml spoons beaten
mustard	egg

Garnish
lemon wedges   parsley sprigs

Make a cut down the centre of the entire length of the fish as for filleting. Loosen the flesh from the bone on each side of the cut, but do not detach it. Make the stuffing. Grate the cheese and mix with the crumbs, together with the mustard, seasoning, herbs, lemon juice, and beaten egg. Raise the 2 loose flaps of the fish and fill the pockets with the stuffing. Place the stuffed fish in a buttered oven-to-table baking dish, dot with the rest of the butter, and cover loosely with foil. Bake in a fairly hot oven at 190°C, Gas 5, for 20–30 minutes. Garnish with lemon wedges and parsley sprigs.

Plaice Stuffed with Prawns

4 helpings

8 plaice fillets (75g each approx)	75g butter
butter for greasing	50g flour
100ml dry white wine	juice of 1 lemon
250ml fish stock (p330)	salt and pepper
100g button mushrooms	100ml double cream

Stuffing

50g soft white breadcrumbs	50g softened butter
	50g peeled prawns

Garnish

fleurons of puff pastry (p399)	chopped parsley

Skin the fillets. Make the stuffing. Mix the breadcrumbs with the butter, chop the prawns, and mix with the butter and breadcrumbs. Spread the stuffing on the fillets and roll up. Place in a buttered oven-to-table baking dish. Pour the wine and fish stock over them. Cover loosely and bake in a fairly hot oven at 190°C, Gas 5, for 20 minutes.

Meanwhile, slice the mushrooms and cook gently in 25g of the remaining butter. Blend the rest of the butter with the flour. Drain the fish and keep hot, reserving the liquid. Pour it into a saucepan. Whisk in the flour and butter slowly, then heat gently, stirring all the time until the sauce thickens. Add the lemon juice, mushrooms, and seasoning. Draw off the heat, mix in the cream, and pour the sauce over the fish. Garnish with the fleurons of puff pastry and sprinkle with chopped parsley.

Fried Plaice with Herbs

See p936.

Plaice Mornay

4 helpings

350ml milk	butter for greasing
1 onion	50g butter
1 carrot	50g flour
1 stick of celery	100g Gruyère cheese
bouquet garni	50g grated Parmesan cheese
salt and pepper	
8 plaice fillets (75g each approx)	1 × 2.5ml spoon dry mustard

Pour the milk into a saucepan. Skin the onion, scrape the carrot, and clean the celery. Chop them finely and add them to the milk, with the bouquet garni and seasoning. Bring to the boil, reduce the heat, and simmer for 10 minutes; then leave to cool. Strain the milk into a deep frying pan.

Fold the fillets into three, skin side inwards, and poach in the milk for 6–8 minutes. Put the fish into a buttered, shallow oven-to-table flameproof dish. Keep hot in the oven under buttered paper. Reserve the cooking liquid.

Make a roux using the butter and flour, add the liquid gradually, and whisk until the sauce thickens. Grate the Gruyère cheese, mix with the Parmesan cheese, and add half to the sauce. Add the mustard, and stir until the cheese is just melted. Pour the sauce over the fish and sprinkle with the remaining cheese. Brown briefly under a low grill.

Red Mullet Baked in Foil

(en papillote)

6 helpings

6 red mullet	salt and pepper
50g butter	juice of ½ lemon

Garnish

lemon wedges	parsley sprigs

Lay each mullet on a piece of foil large enough to enclose it completely. Dot with butter, sprinkle with salt and pepper, and add a little lemon juice. Fasten the packages by pressing the edges of the foil firmly together over the fish. Bake in a fairly hot oven at 190°C, Gas 5, for 20–30 minutes.

Remove from the foil and place on a warmed plate. Pour the liquid from the foil packages over the fish, and garnish with lemon wedges and parsley sprigs.

Red Mullet with Mushrooms

6 helpings

6 small red mullet

Stuffing
1 large onion	*25g parsley (approx)*
50g butter	*salt and pepper*
250g mushrooms	
50g soft white breadcrumbs	

Garnish
chopped parsley	*lemon wedges*

Clean the fish. Skin and chop the onion. Melt half the butter and fry the onion gently until soft. Clean and chop the mushrooms finely and mix with the breadcrumbs and onion. Chop and add the parsley, and season well. Stuff the fish with this mixture, and place in an oven-to-table baking dish greased with the remaining butter. Cover and bake in a fairly hot oven at 190°C, Gas 5, for 30 minutes. Garnish with parsley and lemon wedges.

Red Mullet Niçoise

4 helpings

1 onion (150g approx)	*bouquet garni*
1 clove of garlic	*salt and pepper*
25g parsley (approx)	*4 small red mullet (250g each approx)*
150ml olive oil	
200g tomatoes	*8 black olives*
1 × 5ml spoon concentrated tomato purée	*75ml dry white wine*

Garnish
lemon slices

Skin and chop the onion, crush the garlic, and chop the parsley. Heat 100g of the olive oil and brown the onion lightly. Add the garlic and parsley. Skin,

de-seed, and chop the tomatoes, and add to the onions with the tomato purée, bouquet garni, and seasoning. Simmer for 15 minutes.

Meanwhile, clean and scale the mullet and fry gently in the remaining oil in a deep frying pan for 5 minutes, turning once. Stone the olives. When the sauce is cooked, remove the bouquet garni and add the wine and olives. Pour the sauce over the fish. Cover and cook for a further 10 minutes. Transfer to a warmed serving dish. Serve hot, garnished with lemon slices.

Baked Salmon

6–8 helpings

800g middle cut salmon	*1 × 15ml spoon chopped parsley*
salt and pepper	
grated nutmeg	*25g butter*
2 small shallots	*100ml dry white wine*

Wash and dry the fish and lay on a sheet of foil large enough to enclose it completely. Lift the edges of the foil and pinch the corners together to make a shallow case. Season the fish with salt, pepper, and a little grated nutmeg. Skin and chop the shallots and sprinkle with the parsley over the fish. Dot with the butter, and pour over the wine.

Carefully raise the edges of the foil and pinch them together to enclose the fish and the wine. Place the foil parcel in an ovenproof dish. Cook in a fairly hot oven at 190°C, Gas 5, for 25 minutes.

Serve hot with Hollandaise Sauce (p712), or leave to cool and serve with a green salad (p812), cucumber salad (p815), and mayonnaise.

Grilled Salmon Steaks

clarified butter (p886) salt and pepper
  for brushing
1 salmon steak per
  person (150–200g each
  approx)

Garnish
Maître d'Hôtel butter
  (p1300)

Melt the butter. Season each salmon steak well
with salt and pepper. Brush liberally with melted
butter. Grill, using moderate heat, for 4–5 minutes
on each side, turning once. Serve garnished with
Maître d'Hôtel butter.

Salmon Aurore

4 helpings

1 shallot 50g beurre manié
butter for greasing 2 ×10ml spoons butter
4 salmon steaks 125ml Hollandaise
salt and pepper sauce (p712)
125ml dry white wine 1 × 5ml spoon chopped
125ml tomato juice chives

Garnish
fleurons of puff pastry
  (p399)

Skin and chop the shallot, and sprinkle over the
bottom of a buttered oven-to-table baking dish.
Put the fish steaks on top, in one layer, and sprinkle
with salt and pepper. Pour the wine and tomato
juice over them. Cover loosely with buttered greaseproof paper or foil, and bake in a fairly hot oven at
190°C, Gas 5 for 20 minutes. Drain off the cooking
liquid, and keep the fish hot under the paper or
foil. Strain the liquid into a small saucepan, reduce
it slightly by boiling, and remove from the heat.
Stir the beurre manié into the sauce in small spoonfuls. Put the pan over gentle heat, and stir until the
sauce thickens. Stir in the remaining butter, the
Hollandaise sauce, and chives. Pour the sauce over
the fish. Serve at once, garnished with fleurons of
puff pastry.

Marinated Salmon Steaks with Avocado Butter

6 helpings

6 salmon steaks
  (300–400g each)

Marinade
1 clove of garlic 1 ×15ml spoon
50g onion Worcestershire sauce
125ml olive oil salt and pepper
3 ×15ml spoons lemon
  juice

Avocado Butter
2 ripe avocado pears 1 ×15ml spoon
1 ×15ml spoon lemon Worcestershire sauce
  juice Tabasco sauce
100g unsalted butter salt and pepper
1 clove of garlic

Prepare the marinade first. Skin the garlic and
onion and slice thinly. Mix together with the rest
of the marinade ingredients. Put in the salmon
steaks and turn them over to coat thoroughly.
Marinate them in a refrigerator for at least 6 hours.
Drain 15 minutes before cooking.

  For the avocado butter, scoop out the flesh of the
avocado pears from their skins. Discard the stones.
Mash the flesh with the lemon juice to prevent
discoloration; cream it with the butter, blending
thoroughly. Skin and crush the garlic and add
it also. Add the Worcestershire sauce, a dash of
Tabasco, and a little salt and pepper.

  Grill the salmon steaks for 8–10 minutes, turning once. Serve with the avocado butter.

Salmon Provençale
See p890.

Poached Salmon

1 salmon (1.6–3.2kg)   *3–4 litres (approx) court bouillon (p429)*

Weigh the fish to determine the cooking time (see p412), if it is to be served hot. Put the fish into a fish kettle and pour over the court bouillon. Bring gently to the boil. If the salmon is to be served cold, simmer for 5 minutes, then leave to cool in the cooking liquid before draining. If the fish is to be served hot, bring the liquid to boiling point, reduce the heat and simmer for the required time. Drain and skin.

Hot salmon can be served with Hollandaise (p712) or Shrimp (p697) Sauce.

Cold salmon is served glazed with fish fumet or aspic jelly, and garnished with a line of cucumber slices along each side of the fish.

Allow about 150g salmon per helping.

Creamed Salmon in Pastry

4–6 helpings

1 onion	*50g butter*
125ml dry white wine	*25g flour*
125ml water	*150g button mushrooms*
bouquet garni	*75ml double cream*
salt and pepper	*500g prepared puff*
*500g salmon (pieces **or***	*pastry (p1243)*
small steaks can be	*flour for rolling out*
used)	*1 egg*

Garnish
lemon wedges

Skin and slice the onion. Pour the wine and water into a saucepan, add the bouquet garni, onion, and seasoning. Bring to the boil, reduce the heat, and simmer gently for 5 minutes. Strain into a clean pan. Put the salmon into the liquid and poach gently for 10–15 minutes, depending on the size of the pieces. Remove the fish from the pan, skin, remove any bones, and flake the flesh. Reserve the cooking liquid.

Make a roux using 25g of the butter and the flour; then add the cooking liquid gradually, stirring all the time until the sauce thickens. Simmer

for 3–4 minutes. Add the flaked salmon and take off the heat. Clean and slice the mushrooms and cook in the remaining 25g butter. Drain and add to the sauce and the salmon. Stir in the cream. Let the mixture cool under damp greaseproof paper.

Roll out the pastry on a lightly floured surface into a 25cm square 2mm thick, and place the salmon mixture in the middle. Beat the egg until liquid. Brush the edges of the pastry with egg, lift the corners into the middle and join them to form an envelope. Brush the pastry with egg. Place on a baking sheet and bake in a fairly hot oven at 200°C, Gas 6, for 15 minutes, then reduce the temperature to 190°C, Gas 5, and bake for a further 20 minutes. Serve hot, garnished with lemon wedges.

Scandinavian Pickled Salmon

(Gravad Lax)

4–6 helpings

2 unskinned salmon	*200g salt*
fillets (1kg approx)	*100g caster sugar*
50g white peppercorns	*100g fresh dill*

Garnish
fresh dill

Keep the fillets separate and cut them into pieces about 12cm square. Score the skin on each piece in 4 places. Crush the peppercorns or grind them coarsely. Mix the salt, sugar, and peppercorns together. Sprinkle a third of the mixture on the base of a shallow dish. Place the pieces of 1 fillet, skin side down, on the mixture and cover with a third more dry mixture and half the dill. Place the pieces of the second fillet, skin side up, on top and cover with the remaining dry mixture and dill.

Place a heavy plate on top of the fish and weight it down. Leave at room temperature for 6 hours; then transfer to a refrigerator. Leave for 48 hours, in which time the dry mixture will turn to a brine solution. Drain off the brine before serving.

Slice the pickled salmon as for smoked salmon and serve garnished with dill, sweet mustard, and mayonnaise (p843) made with vinegar.

Angevin Salmon Trout

4 helpings

1 salmon trout (1kg approx)	1 × 15ml spoon plain flour
butter for greasing	25ml double cream
1 medium-sized onion	salt and pepper
375ml rosé wine	125ml Hollandaise
100ml water	sauce (p712)
1 × 15ml spoon butter	

Garnish

fleurons of puff pastry (p399) **or** crescents of fried bread	watercress sprigs

Remove the fins and place the fish in a buttered fairly deep ovenproof dish or baking tin. Skin, chop, and add the onion. Pour the wine and water over the fish. Poach in a warm oven at 160°C, Gas 3, for 30 minutes. Skin the trout, and keep it hot.

Strain the cooking liquid into a pan and reduce by a third, by boiling uncovered. Make a roux with the butter and flour. Add the reduced liquid gradually, stirring all the time until it comes to the boil. Take off the heat, then add the cream and seasoning, and beat in the Hollandaise sauce.

Fillet the salmon trout and place the 2 fillets on a suitable serving dish. Coat with half the sauce, saving the rest to serve with the dish. Garnish with the fleurons or bread and the watercress sprigs, and serve immediately.

Baked Fresh Sardines

6 helpings

100g onions	butter for greasing
50ml olive oil	900g sardines
50ml medium-dry white wine	50g soft white breadcrumbs
250g tomatoes	25g butter
salt and pepper	

Garnish
parsley sprigs

Skin and chop the onions. Heat the oil and brown the onion lightly. Add the wine and boil until the volume is reduced by two-thirds. Skin, de-seed, and chop the tomatoes. Add to the onions and season to taste. Cook gently for 3–4 minutes. Pour the mixture into a buttered oven-to-table baking dish, arrange the sardines on top, sprinkle with the breadcrumbs and dot with the butter. Bake in a moderate oven at 180°C, Gas 4, for 25 minutes. Serve hot, garnished with sprigs of parsley.

Baked Shad

4 helpings

2 shad (1kg approx)	2–3 rashers bacon
100g basic herb forcemeat (p375)	

Scale and clean the fish. Stuff it with the forcemeat and place in an ovenproof dish or on a baking tray. Lay the slices of bacon on the top and bake in a moderate oven at 180°C, Gas 4, for 25–30 minutes. Transfer to a warmed serving dish.

Serve with boiled potatoes and a suitable sauce.

Grilled Shad

6 helpings

2 shad (1kg approx)	150g butter

Marinade

100ml walnut **or** olive oil	2 bay leaves parsley stalks
juice of 1 lemon	salt and pepper
thyme leaves, fresh **or** dried	

Garnish
parsley sprigs

Clean the fish and make several slashes through the skin on each side. Mix together the ingredients for the marinade and marinate the fish for 1 hour; then drain. Melt the butter and brush it over the fish. Place the fish on a grill rack, and grill gently for 15 minutes, turning once, and basting frequently. Serve very hot, garnished with parsley sprigs.

Fried Skate

3–4 helpings

600g skate wing	*dry white breadcrumbs*
flour for coating	*for coating*
salt and pepper	*fat for shallow frying*
1 egg	

Garnish
lemon wedges

Cut the skate into serving portions if required. Season the flour with salt and pepper, and beat the egg lightly. Coat the portions of fish with flour, dip in the egg, and coat with breadcrumbs. Heat the fat in a frying pan and shallow fry the fish for 5 minutes on each side, until all the pieces are golden and cooked through. Garnish with lemon wedges and offer Tartare Sauce (p846) separately.

Skate in Black Butter

3–4 helpings

1–2 skate wings	*salt and pepper*
(800g approx)	*2 ×15ml spoons capers*
1 litre court bouillon	*2 ×10ml spoons*
(p429)	*chopped parsley*
25g butter	*75ml wine vinegar*

Rinse and dry the skate and cut it into serving portions. Put the fish in a deep frying pan and cover with the court bouillon. Bring to the boil, reduce the heat, cover, and simmer for 15–20 minutes. Lift out the fish, drain on soft kitchen paper, and gently scrape away the skin. Place in an oven-proof dish and keep hot.

To make the black butter, pour off the stock, put in the butter and heat until it is a rich golden-brown colour. Spoon it quickly over the fish, season with salt and pepper, and scatter the capers and chopped parsley over the fish. Add the vinegar to the pan, heat quickly, and pour over the dish. Serve immediately.

Baked Smelts

3 helpings

12 smelts	*50g butter*
dry white breadcrumbs	*salt and Cayenne pepper*
for coating	*a squeeze of lemon juice*

Garnish
fried parsley (p398)   *lemon wedges*

Clean the fish. Arrange in a flat oven-to-table baking dish, cover with breadcrumbs, and dot with butter. Season, and bake in a fairly hot oven, 190°C, Gas 5, for 15 minutes. Just before serving, add a squeeze of lemon juice. Serve garnished with fried parsley and lemon wedges.

Fried Smelts

6 helpings

1 egg	*3 ×15ml spoons milk*
200g flour	*18 smelts*
salt	*fat for deep frying*
1 ×15ml spoon olive oil	

Garnish
parsley sprigs

Separate the egg. Mix together the flour, salt, oil, and egg yolk with enough milk to make a stiff batter. Allow to stand for 15–20 minutes. Just before using, whisk the egg white until stiff and fold it into the batter. Remove the heads of the fish and dip in the batter. Heat the fat (p303) and deep fry the fish. Drain and garnish with the parsley sprigs.

Serve with Fresh Tomato Sauce (p715).

Fillets of Sole Anthony

6 helpings

125g butter
6 Dover sole fillets (125g
  each approx)
salt and pepper
250g dry white
  breadcrumbs

6 slices pineapple (fresh
  or canned)
25g sugar
75g button mushrooms
250ml White Wine
  sauce (p698)

Garnish
parsley sprigs

Melt the butter. Season the fillets and coat with
some of the butter and the breadcrumbs. Place on a
shallow buttered flameproof dish and grill for
5 minutes on each side. Drain the pineapple, if
canned, brush with melted butter, sprinkle with
sugar and brown under the grill. Clean and chop
the mushrooms, and mix into the white wine sauce.
Coat the bottom of a flameproof serving dish with
the sauce. Arrange the fillets on top and place a
slice of pineapple on top of each. Grill for 5 minutes. Serve very hot, garnished with parsley sprigs.

Fillets of Sole Bonne Femme

4 helpings

8 lemon sole fillets
butter for greasing
150g mushrooms
1 shallot
1 × 10ml spoon chopped
  parsley

salt and pepper
125ml dry white wine
125ml Velouté sauce
  (p708)
25g butter

Put the fish in a greased oven-to-table baking dish.
Clean and slice the mushrooms. Skin and slice the
shallot. Sprinkle them over the fish, add the parsley,
and season well. Add the wine and cover the dish
loosely with greased paper or foil. Bake in a moderate oven at 180°C, Gas 4, for 20 minutes.

Remove the fish and keep hot. Strain the liquid
into a clean saucepan and boil it rapidly until
reduced by half. Stir in the hot Velouté sauce and
the butter. As soon as the butter has melted, pour
the sauce over the fillets, and place under a hot grill
until lightly browned. Serve at once.

Sole Colbert

6 helpings

6 Dover soles
2 eggs
100g flour
salt and pepper
soft white breadcrumbs
fat for deep frying

200g Maître d'Hôtel
  butter (p1300)
2 × 5ml spoons finely
  chopped tarragon
2 × 15ml spoons meat
  glaze (p397)

Garnish
fried parsley (p398)   *lemon wedges*

Remove the dark skin of the fish. Cut down the
backbone on the skinned side and slice under the
flesh, following the bones to make a pocket on each
side. Cut the backbone in 3 places with sharp
scissors, to allow removal after cooking.

Beat the eggs until liquid. Season the flour with
salt and pepper. Coat the fish with flour, then with
egg and breadcrumbs. Heat the fat and deep fry the
fish (p303) until golden-brown. Drain, then remove the bone where cut and arrange on a serving
dish. Keep hot. Mix together the Maître d'Hôtel
butter, tarragon, and meat glaze to make Colbert
butter. Fill the pockets of the fish with the Colbert
butter. Serve immediately, garnished with fried
parsley and lemon wedges.

Fillets of Sole Meunière

4 helpings

50g flour
salt and pepper
4 large sole fillets
75g butter

2 × 15ml spoons
  chopped parsley
juice of 1 lemon

Garnish
lemon wedges

Season the flour with salt and pepper and coat the
fish fillets lightly. Heat the butter in a frying pan
and fry the fillets for about 7 minutes, turning
once, until golden-brown. Arrange the fillets on a
warm dish and keep hot. Continue heating the
butter until it is nut-brown. Add the parsley. Pour
the butter over the fish. Sprinkle with lemon juice,
garnish with lemon wedges, and serve at once.

Fillets of Sole Orly

6 helpings

6 lemon sole fillets (175g each approx)	fat **or** oil for deep frying

Marinade

2 ×15ml spoons chopped parsley	1 ×15ml spoon lemon juice
2 ×15ml spoons chopped onion	1 ×15ml spoon salad oil
salt and pepper	

Batter

50g flour	1 ×15ml spoon salad oil
salt	1 egg white
4 ×15ml spoons water	

Garnish
fried parsley (p398)

Mix all the ingredients for the marinade together and steep the fillets in this for 1 hour. Drain and pat dry.

Meanwhile, mix the flour and salt with the water and oil to make a smooth batter. Whisk the egg white until stiff and fold it into the batter. Heat the fat (p303). Dip the fillets into the batter, and fry until golden-brown. Garnish with the fried parsley.

Serve with Fresh Tomato Sauce (p715).

Sole Dieppoise

2 large or 4 small helpings

1 × 750g Dover sole	1 ×15ml spoon softened butter
bouquet garni	
150ml dry white wine	1 ×15ml spoon flour
25g onion	1 egg yolk
12 live mussels	6 ×15ml spoons single cream
150ml water	
1 ×15ml spoon white wine vinegar	salt and pepper
	a pinch of grated nutmeg
25g butter **or** margarine	juice of $\frac{1}{2}$ lemon
12 peeled cooked shrimps **or** prawns	a pinch of Cayenne pepper **or** paprika

In this classic international dish the fish is poached in white wine with mussels and shrimps.

Skin and fillet the sole. Put the bones, skin, and head in a saucepan with the bouquet garni and white wine. Skin the onion, slice it thinly, and add it to the fish trimmings. Scrub and beard the mussels and add them. Bring to boiling point and simmer for 6 minutes. Remove the mussels and shell them. Put to one side. Add the water and vinegar to the cooking liquid and boil gently, un-covered, for 15 minutes until reduced. Strain and reserve the liquid.

Flatten and beat the sole fillets with a cutlet-bat. Fold in half. Grease a shallow ovenproof dish with butter or margarine. Place the folded fish fillets in the dish in one layer. Pour in the stock and arrange the shelled mussels and shrimps or prawns around the fish. Cover with well-greased paper and bake in a fairly hot oven at 190°C, Gas 5, for 20 minutes; then drain the cooking liquid into a saucepan and keep the fish hot.

Mix the butter and flour to a smooth paste. Off the heat, add the mixture in small spoonfuls to the cooking liquid. Stir until it dissolves; then boil for 10 minutes. In a basin, blend the egg yolk and cream and add about 100ml of the thickened sauce. Pour this mixture into the rest of the sauce in the pan. Bring almost back to the boil. Season to taste with salt and pepper, and a pinch of grated nutmeg. Coat the fish fillets evenly with the sauce. Sprinkle with lemon juice and a pinch of Cayenne pepper or paprika.

Note The sole can be poached whole if preferred. In this case the sauce can be made with other white fish bones and trimmings.

Sole with Sherry and Bean Sauce

3–4 helpings

1 lemon sole (400–600g approx)	2cm ginger root
50ml dry sherry	200ml canned bean sauce (see **Note**)
3 cloves garlic	2 × 15ml spoons sugar
4 spring onions	50ml corn oil

Garnish

crisp noodles (p852)   browned almonds (p1185)

Leave the head and tail on the fish, but trim the fins and remove the gills. Rinse the fish inside and out with the sherry. Place it in the perforated top section of a large steamer, or cook between 2 plates over a saucepan of boiling water for 10–15 minutes.

Meanwhile, skin and crush the garlic, chop the spring onions finely, and mince or grate the ginger. Combine with the bean sauce and sugar. Heat the oil in a saucepan and add the bean sauce mixture. Cook until the sauce boils, stirring all the time. Strain if liked, and pour the liquid over the fish. Serve garnished with the noodles and almonds.

Note Canned bean sauce is available from stores specializing in Chinese foods.

Sole Véronique

4 helpings

4 large lemon sole fillets	100g small white grapes
2 shallots	25g butter
50g button mushrooms	2 × 15ml spoons flour
parsley sprigs	125ml milk
1 bay leaf	juice of ½ lemon
salt and pepper	2 × 15ml spoons single cream
125ml dry white wine	
125ml water	

Garnish

fleurons of puff pastry   chopped parsley
  (p399)

Lay the fillets in a shallow ovenproof dish. Skin and chop the shallots and clean and chop the mushrooms. Sprinkle them over the fish. Add the herbs, season well, and pour the wine and water over the dish. Cover and bake in a fairly hot oven at 190°C, Gas 5, for 15 minutes.

Meanwhile, peel and de-pip the grapes. Drain the fish, and keep it hot. Reserve the cooking liquid, and reduce it to half by boiling uncovered. Melt the butter and stir in the flour. Cook for 2–3 minutes without colouring. Add the cooking liquid and milk gradually, stirring all the time, and heat the sauce until it thickens. Stir in the grapes, saving a few to garnish the dish. Add the lemon juice and cream. Pour over the fish, garnish with the reserved grapes, the fleurons and parsley, and serve immediately.

Sole with Prawns

6 helpings

100g prawns	125ml dry white wine
50g soft white breadcrumbs	125ml fish stock (p330)
1 egg	500ml fish sauce (p694) made with the cooking liquid (optional)
salt and pepper	
12 Dover **or** lemon sole fillets	

Chop the prawns finely and mix with the breadcrumbs, egg, and seasoning. Spread the mixture over each fillet and roll up. Place the rolled fillets in an ovenproof dish, and pour the stock and wine over them. Cover and cook in a fairly hot oven at 190°C, Gas 5, for 20 minutes.

Place the fish on a hot serving dish. If liked, reduce the cooking liquid and use to make a prawn sauce. Pour the sauce over the fish and place under the grill for 2–3 minutes before serving.

Grilled Tench

4 helpings

4 tench	1 × 15ml spoon chopped
salt	parsley
vinegar	1 × 5ml spoon dried
1 small onion	mixed herbs
2 shallots	2 × 15ml spoons oil
pepper	fat for greasing

Clean the fish thoroughly, removing the gills and scales. Soak in salted water for 2 hours; then rinse in vinegar. Skin and chop the onion and shallots. Place the fish in a deep dish, with the seasoning, onion, shallots, parsley, mixed herbs, and oil. Leave to steep for 2 hours, basting frequently. Drain the fish.

Enclose each fish in a piece of well-greased foil, and grill, using a hot grill heat, for 10–15 minutes. Test for readiness by opening 1 package and piercing the fish with a fine skewer. It should be tender right through. When the fish are ready, remove the foil and place them on a heated dish.

Serve with Piquant Sauce (p702).

Baked Trout with Olives and Tomatoes

4 helpings

4 river trout (250g each)	25g stuffed olives
50g flour	250g tomatoes
salt and pepper	25ml white wine vinegar
125ml oil for shallow	juice of 1 lemon
frying	1 × 15ml spoon capers
125g onions	50g butter

Garnish

4 thin lemon slices	6 parsley sprigs

Wash, scale, and cut off the fins of the trout. Wipe with a cloth. Season the flour with salt and pepper, and coat the trout with it. Heat the oil in a large frying pan and brown the trout on both sides without cooking through. Drain, and place in one layer in a shallow oven-to-table baking dish. Reserve the cooking oil.

Skin and slice the onions and olives. Sauté quickly in the oil remaining in the pan for 4 minutes. Drain, and sprinkle them over the fish. Skin, de-seed, and chop the tomatoes, and spread on top of the fish. Sprinkle with the vinegar and lemon juice. Scatter the capers on top. Season the fish to taste, and bake in a moderate oven at 180°C, Gas 4, for 15 minutes.

Meanwhile, melt the butter in a pan until it foams; pour it over the fish when they are cooked. Garnish with lemon slices and parsley sprigs.

Note Any other whole, round, small fish can be prepared in the same way, eg mackerel, whiting, herrings, etc.

Stuffed Trout

6 helpings

6 trout	salt and pepper
200g apricot stuffing	250ml dry white wine
(p381)	50g butter
2 medium-sized onions	375ml White Wine
butter for greasing	sauce (p698)

Garnish
chopped parsley

Clean the fish and trim the fins and tail. Fill the fish with the apricot stuffing. Skin and chop the onions and sprinkle them over the bottom of a buttered ovenproof dish. Lay the fish on top. Season well. Pour the wine over the dish. Dot with the butter, cover, and poach in a moderate oven at 180°C, Gas 4, for 25 minutes. Drain the fish and skin them. Arrange on a heated flameproof serving dish. Strain the cooking liquid into a clean pan, boil until it is reduced by a quarter, and add to the white wine sauce. Coat the trout with the sauce, and place under the grill for 4–5 minutes to brown lightly. Garnish with chopped parsley.

Trout with Almonds

4 helpings

4 trout	50g flaked blanched
100g butter	almonds
salt and pepper	125ml double cream
juice of ½ lemon	3 egg yolks

Garnish
parsley sprigs

Clean the trout and remove the fins. Melt the butter in a grill pan under medium heat. Lay the trout in the pan, season, and sprinkle with lemon juice. Grill for 5 minutes, and then turn the fish. Sprinkle the trout with most of the almonds, spread the rest at the side of the pan, and continue grilling for a further 3–5 minutes until the trout are tender and the almonds are browned. Drain the trout and almonds on soft kitchen paper. Put the almonds to one side.

Mix the cream with the egg yolks and put into a small pan with any juices from the grill pan. Heat gently, stirring well, until thickened; do not let the mixture boil. Lay the trout on a serving dish, and spoon the cream sauce over them. Garnish with the reserved almonds and with parsley.

Trout Meunière

4 helpings

4 trout	juice of ½ lemon
flour for coating	1 × 10ml spoon chopped
salt and pepper	parsley
50g butter	

Garnish
lemon wedges

Trim off the fins, rinse the fish inside, and dry well with soft kitchen paper. Season the flour, and coat the fish. Heat the butter in a frying pan. When foaming, place the trout in the pan. Cook slowly for 6–7 minutes on each side, until the skin is golden and crisp. When the fish is cooked, arrange on a serving dish and keep hot. Season the butter left in the pan and heat until it is nut-brown. Add the lemon juice and chopped parsley, and pour it over the trout. Garnish with lemon wedges.

Poached Trout with Prawn Sauce

4 helpings

1 clove	25g butter
125ml red wine	25g flour
1 bay leaf	100g peeled prawns
salt and pepper	3 × 15ml spoons double
4 trout	cream
milk	

Garnish
chopped parsley

Make a poaching liquid with the clove, red wine, bay leaf, salt, and pepper. Poach the trout gently in this mixture in a warm oven at 160°C, Gas 3, for 15–20 minutes. Remove the trout to a warmed serving dish, skin, and keep hot. Strain the cooking liquid and make up to 250ml with the milk.

Melt the butter in a saucepan, and add the flour to make a roux. Stir thoroughly and cook over moderate heat for 1 minute. Gradually add the fish liquid, whisking all the time. Bring the sauce gently to the boil, then reduce the heat and simmer for 2–3 minutes. Remove from the heat and stir in the prawns and cream. Pour the hot sauce over the trout, sprinkle with chopped parsley, and serve at once.

Trout Hollandaise

6 helpings

6 trout	250ml Hollandaise
1 litre court bouillon	sauce (p712)
(p429)	

Garnish
chopped parsley

Clean the fish and trim the fins. Cover with court bouillon and poach for 15 minutes. Arrange on a serving dish, garnish with parsley, and serve with Hollandaise Sauce.

Baked Turbot

6 helpings

3 shallots	250ml fish stock (p330)
6 turbot fillets (150g each approx)	juice of 1 lemon
	250ml double cream
150g mushrooms	3 egg yolks
salt and pepper	

Garnish
12 fleurons of puff
   pastry (p399)

Skin and chop the shallots, put in an ovenproof dish, and lay the fish on top. Clean and slice the mushrooms, sprinkle them on the fish, and season well. Pour the fish stock and lemon juice over the dish. Cover, and bake in a fairly hot oven at 190°C, Gas 5, for 30 minutes. Drain the fish and mushrooms, and arrange on a dish. Strain the cooking liquid into a clean pan. Mix the cream with the egg yolks, add to the cooking liquid, and heat very gently until thickened; do not boil. Pour the sauce over the fish and garnish with the fleurons.

Turbot Dugléré

4 helpings

1.5kg turbot	butter for greasing
25g onion	salt and pepper
250g tomatoes	bouquet garni
25ml cooking oil	1 × 10ml spoon softened
25g butter	butter **or** margarine
25ml white wine vinegar	2 × 10ml spoons flour
200ml dry white wine	

Garnish
1 parsley sprig   juice of ¼ lemon
4 tarragon leaves

Skin and fillet the turbot. Reserve the trimmings. Rinse and dry the fish well. Skin and chop the onion and tomatoes. Heat the oil and butter in a sauté pan and fry the onions for 2–3 minutes, without colouring, until soft. Add the chopped tomatoes, vinegar, and white wine. Simmer for 10 minutes. Allow to cool. Grease a shallow ovenproof dish. Place the fish fillets in the dish. Season

and cover with the wine mixture. Cover the dish with a lid or greaseproof paper. Bake in a fairly hot oven at 190°C, Gas 5, for 20 minutes.

Boil the fish trimmings in 300ml water with the bouquet garni for 15 minutes. Strain the liquid into a small saucepan. Mix the butter and flour to a smooth paste. Off the heat, add this in small spoonfuls to the fish stock and stir until dissolved. Heat until the sauce thickens. Season to taste, and pour over the fish. Chop the parsley and tarragon leaves and sprinkle them over the fish with a squeeze of lemon just before serving.

Turbot Marengo

4 helpings

4 slices turbot (1cm thick approx)	dried mixed herbs
	50g butter
325ml fish stock (p330)	50g flour
1 onion	175g concentrated
1 carrot	tomato purée
1 turnip	salt and pepper
25g lard	

Garnish
stuffed olives   lemon slices
chopped parsley

Put the fish into an ovenproof dish, pour 75ml of the stock over it, cover, and bake in a moderate oven at 180°C, Gas 4, for 20 minutes.

Meanwhile, prepare and slice the onion, carrot, and turnip. Heat the lard in a saucepan and fry the vegetables. Add the herbs, pour on the remaining stock, and cover the pan. Simmer for 20 minutes. Strain off the stock and reserve it. Melt the butter in a clean pan, add the flour, and cook together for 2–3 minutes without browning. Add the stock to the roux gradually, stirring all the time. Add the tomato purée and seasoning. Cook for a further 10 minutes. Arrange the fish in a serving dish, pour the sauce over it, and garnish with stuffed olives, chopped parsley, and lemon slices.

Mrs Beeton's Dressed Whitebait
See p322.

Baked Whiting

4 helpings

50g butter	dry white breadcrumbs
4 medium-sized whiting	for coating
salt and pepper	

Garnish
lemon wedges

Melt the butter. Brush the whiting with the butter, season, and sprinkle with breadcrumbs. Place in a buttered oven-to-table baking dish and bake in a fairly hot oven at 190°C, Gas 5, for 20 minutes. Serve hot, garnished with lemon wedges.

Fried Whiting

6 helpings

2 eggs	fat for deep frying
12 whiting fillets	
dry white breadcrumbs	
for coating	

Garnish
fried parsley (p398)

Beat the eggs until liquid. Coat the fish with egg, and then with breadcrumbs. Roll up the fillets and keep in shape with a skewer or cocktail stick. Heat the fat (p303) and deep fry the fish. Arrange on a serving dish and garnish with fried parsley. Serve with Fresh Tomato (p715) or Tartare (p846) Sauce.

Fried Whiting with Prawns

6 helpings

salt and pepper	juice of 1 lemon
12 whiting fillets	125g shelled prawns
flour for coating	50g capers
150g butter	

Season the fillets and coat with flour. Heat the butter in a frying pan and cook the fish gently for 4–5 minutes on each side. Place on a serving dish. Continue to heat the butter until brown, add the lemon juice, prawns, and capers, pour over the fish, and serve immediately.

Recipes for Shellfish

For shellfish salads, see the chapter on Salads and Dressings.

Crab Au Gratin

4 helpings

400g white crabmeat	salt and pepper
100g Gruyère cheese	50g soft white
25g butter	breadcrumbs
25g plain flour	grated Parmesan cheese
250ml milk	

Garnish
2 sliced tomatoes *parsley sprigs*

Flake the crabmeat. Grate the cheese. Make a roux with the butter and flour, add the milk gradually, and stir until the sauce thickens. Season well. Add the crabmeat and the Gruyère cheese and stir into the sauce. Re-season if required. Put the mixture into empty crab shells or an ovenproof dish, and sprinkle with the breadcrumbs and Parmesan cheese. Brown under the grill for 2–3 minutes. Garnish with slices of tomato and parsley sprigs.

Crawfish with Chicken

4 helpings

1 small chicken	1 × 15ml spoon
(1kg approx)	concentrated tomato
flour for coating	purée
salt and pepper	bouquet garni
2–3 × 15ml spoons oil	75ml dry white wine
2 cloves garlic	1 × 5ml spoon flour
100g butter	1 × 2.5ml spoon white
1 onion	wine vinegar
3–4 shallots	1 × 15ml spoon chopped
3 crawfish tails	almonds **or** hazelnuts
2 tomatoes	

Cut the chicken into 4 pieces. Season the flour with salt and pepper, and coat each quarter lightly. Heat the oil, crush and add the garlic, and brown the chicken lightly on all sides. Put to one side and keep warm. Melt 75g butter in a large flameproof casserole. Skin and dice the onion and shallots finely and cook gently in the butter. Cut the crawfish tails into round slices, including the shells, and add to the pan. Sauté gently for 5–6 minutes until the shells turn red. Add the chicken quarters. Skin and chop the tomatoes, and add to the chicken mixture with the tomato purée, bouquet garni, and wine. Season well, cover, and simmer for 30 minutes.

Place the chicken on a dish, and surround it with the crawfish slices. Remove the bouquet garni from the casserole. Work together the remaining butter and the flour and slowly whisk into the sauce. Stir in the vinegar. Simmer until the sauce thickens. When well thickened, pour the sauce over the chicken, and sprinkle with the nuts.

Serve with boiled rice.

Spanish Lobster

3–4 helpings

2 × 15ml spoons oil	300g lobster meat
1 large onion	(canned or frozen meat
4 tomatoes	can be used)
125ml medium-dry	125ml fish stock (p330)
sherry	1 small bunch chives
salt and pepper	juice of ½ lemon

Heat the oil in a saucepan or deep frying pan. Skin and chop the onion, and fry gently for 2–3 minutes. Skin, chop, and de-seed the tomatoes, and add to the onion with the sherry. Season well, and cook to a soft consistency.

Dice the lobster meat roughly, put into the pan with the vegetables, and add enough stock to moisten thoroughly. Simmer down to a semi-solid consistency; this takes 6–7 minutes. Chop the chives finely and add to the lobster stew with the lemon juice.

Serve hot with boiled rice.

Lobster Thermidor

4 helpings

2 shallots	125ml double cream
3 × 15ml spoons butter	2 × 15ml spoons French
150ml dry white wine	mustard
(approx)	2 × 15ml spoons grated
1 × 5ml spoon chopped	Parmesan cheese
tarragon	salt and pepper
1 × 5ml spoon chopped	2 cooked lobsters (p424)
chervil	
200ml Béchamel sauce	
(p704)	

Garnish
watercress sprigs

Skin and finely chop the shallots. Melt the butter and fry them gently until soft. Add the wine and herbs and boil, uncovered, until the liquid is reduced by half; then add the Béchamel sauce. Remove from the heat. Stir well, and mix in the cream, mustard, and half the cheese. Season well and put to one side.

Split the lobsters in half lengthways. Remove the meat from the claws and body and chop coarsely. Mix with most of the sauce, keeping a little sauce separate to complete the dish; return the sauced lobster meat to the shells. Place the shells on a flat dish, cut side up, and coat the surface of the shellfish with the remaining sauce. Sprinkle with the rest of the cheese and brown in a fairly hot oven at 200°C, Gas 6, for 10–15 minutes. Garnish with watercress sprigs and serve very hot.

Lobster Newburg
See p1445.

Moules Marinière

4–6 helpings

1.6kg live mussels	125ml water
1 onion	125ml white wine
1 carrot	25g butter
1 stick of celery	1 × 15ml spoon flour
bouquet garni	pepper

Garnish
chopped parsley

Scrub and beard the mussels, making sure that all are tightly closed, and put them into a large pan. Peel and slice the vegetables and tuck them among the mussels with the bouquet garni. Pour the water and wine over the mussels and place over moderate heat. Leave until the liquid boils up over them. Shake the pan 2 or 3 times and put to one side.

Blend the butter and flour together into a smooth beurre manié and put to one side. Strain the liquid from the pan of mussels, through muslin, into a smaller pan. Keep the mussels warm. Add the butter and flour mixture to the liquid in small pieces, whisking well. Heat until boiling, then season well with pepper. Put the mussels into a deep dish and pour the cooking liquid over them. Sprinkle with chopped parsley.

Serve with pieces of crusty bread.

Cooking time 10–15 minutes

Mussels in White Sauce

3–4 helpings

1.6kg live mussels	2 × 15ml spoon double
50g butter	cream
25g flour	lemon juice
1 egg yolk	

Garnish
chopped parsley

Prepare and cook the mussels as for Moules Marinière. Strain and keep 250ml of the mussel liquid. Heat half the butter in a saucepan and simmer the flour in it without letting it colour. Remove from the heat, and add the mussel liquid gradually,

whisking well. Return to the heat, bring to the boil, then reduce the heat and simmer for 5 minutes. Beat the egg yolk and cream together and add to the sauce with lemon juice to taste. Add the rest of the butter. Shell the mussels and add to the sauce. Heat through, but do not boil. Pour into a serving dish, and sprinkle with chopped parsley.

Cooking time 20 minutes (approx)

Prawn Céleste

4 helpings

100g button mushrooms	125ml milk
50g butter	125ml single cream
50g plain flour	200g peeled prawns
salt and pepper	25ml dry sherry

Garnish
chopped parsley   *triangles of fried bread*

Clean and slice the mushrooms, melt the butter, and cook the mushrooms gently for 4 minutes. Stir in the flour and seasoning. Mix in the milk and cream, and stir all the time until the sauce thickens; then add the prawns and sherry. Garnish with chopped parsley and triangles of fried bread.

Prawn Curry

4 helpings

1 clove of garlic	250ml fish stock (p330)
1 large onion	2 × 15ml spoons oil
1 × 15ml spoon crushed	2 × 15ml spoons
coriander seeds	concentrated tomato
1 × 2.5ml spoon ground	purée
cumin	2 tomatoes
1 × 2.5ml spoon chilli	1 × 10ml spoon coconut
powder	cream (optional)
1 × 2.5ml spoon	400g peeled prawns
turmeric	juice of ½ lemon

Skin and crush the garlic. Skin and chop the onion finely. Mix all the spices and the garlic into a paste with a little of the stock. Heat the oil and fry the onion until brown. Add the tomato purée and cook for 1–2 minutes. Skin, de-seed, and chop the tomatoes. Add to the pan with all the remaining ingredients, except the prawns and lemon juice. Simmer gently for 20 minutes, then add the prawns and lemon juice. Cook for a further 5 minutes.

Serve with boiled rice and any suitable curry accompaniments (p388).

Note Canned coconut cream is available from some health food stores and oriental delicatessens.

Sweet and Sour Prawns

4 helpings

200g peeled prawns	*1 × 15ml spoon*
1 × 15ml spoon medium-	*cornflour*
dry sherry	*2 × 15ml spoons soy*
salt and pepper	*sauce*
2 onions	*125ml white wine*
2 green peppers	*vinegar*
2 × 15ml spoons oil	*75g sugar*
125ml chicken stock	
1 × 227g can pineapple	
pieces	

Garnish
unpeeled prawns

Marinate the prawns in the sherry for 30 minutes and season well. Skin the onions and de-seed the green peppers. Slice them into rings. Heat the oil in a saucepan and fry the onions and peppers gently until tender. Add the stock, and drain; then add the pineapple. Cover and cook for 3–5 minutes. Blend the cornflour, soy sauce, vinegar and sugar together, and add to the mixture. Stir until thickened. Add the prawns, and cook for 1 minute.

Serve hot on boiled rice garnished with prawns.

Prawn Quiche
See p1255.

Scallops on Skewers

4 helpings

12 small onions	*16 scallops*
2 courgettes	*12 button mushrooms*
8 rashers streaky bacon,	*butter*
without rinds	*salt and pepper*

Skin the onions and cover with cold water in a pan. Cut the courgettes into 2cm cubes. Bring the water to the boil, reduce the heat, and simmer for 4 minutes; then add the courgettes and simmer for a further 2 minutes. Stretch the bacon and cut each rasher in half. Wrap half a rasher round each scallop. Spear the vegetables and scallops alternately on 4 skewers. Melt the butter and brush it over the kebabs. Season well. Grill under a moderate heat for 5–7 minutes, turning frequently.

Serve on a bed of savoury rice with Barbecue Sauce (p1312).

Scallops Thérèse

4–5 helpings

75g butter	*salt and pepper*
25ml dry white wine	*4 hard-boiled eggs*
16–20 queen scallops	*1 × 15ml spoon single* **or**
5 × 15ml spoons flour	*double cream*
a pinch of paprika	*1 egg yolk*
250ml milk	

Melt half the butter in a large frying pan. Add the wine and scallops and cook very gently for 5 minutes without boiling. Put to one side. Melt the remaining butter in a saucepan, stir in the flour and paprika, then add the milk slowly. Cook, stirring all the time, until the sauce thickens. Season well. Add most of this sauce to the scallops and shake the pan well to blend the ingredients. Spoon the reserved sauce into a shallow dish. Cut the eggs lengthways into 8 segments each and put them on the dish. Beat together the cream and the yolk. Add to the scallops and sauce, and mix in well. Spoon the mixture over the eggs. Place under a hot grill briefly, to colour.

Coquilles St Jacques Mornay

4 helpings

1 small onion	125ml milk
400g scallops	75ml single cream
salt and pepper	butter for greasing
1 bay leaf	200g mashed potato
50ml dry white wine	3 × 15ml spoons dry
75ml water	white breadcrumbs
juice of ½ lemon	4 × 15ml spoons grated
25g butter	Parmesan cheese
25g flour	

Skin and slice the onion. Wash the scallops and place in a pan with the sliced onion, seasoning, and bay leaf. Pour the wine, water, and lemon juice over them. Poach gently for 5 minutes. Strain off the liquid and put to one side with the scallops.

Melt the butter in a pan, then stir in the flour. Blend in the liquid strained from the scallops, and stir over gentle heat until the sauce starts to thicken. Add the milk and simmer for 2–3 minutes. Stir in the cream. Slice the scallops and divide between 4 lightly greased scallop shells or suitable small flameproof dishes. Coat with the sauce. Pipe the mashed potato around the edge of each shell. Sprinkle lightly with the breadcrumbs and Parmesan cheese. Bake in a fairly hot oven at 200°C, Gas 6, for 10–15 minutes.

Fried Scampi

2 helpings

flour for coating	225g peeled scampi
salt and pepper	oil **or** fat for deep frying

Batter
1 egg	1 × 15ml spoon cooking
100g plain flour	oil
salt	2–3 × 15ml spoons milk

Garnish
lemon wedges

Season the flour with salt and pepper in a plastic bag and toss the scampi in the flour. Separate the egg. Mix the flour, salt, oil, egg yolk, and milk to a stiff batter. Just before cooking, whisk the egg white until stiff and fold it into the batter. Heat the oil (p303). Dip the scampi in the batter and fry, a few at a time, until golden-brown. Drain, and serve garnished with lemon wedges.

Offer Tartare Sauce (p846) separately.

Creamed Scampi

4 helpings

25g butter	3 egg yolks
450g peeled scampi	200ml double cream
1 × 5ml spoon paprika	4 small tomatoes
100ml medium-dry sherry	salt and pepper

Heat the butter in a saucepan and cook the scampi gently; then add the paprika and sherry. Boil, uncovered, to reduce the liquid by half. Blend the egg yolks with the cream, strain into the pan, and heat slowly until the sauce coats the back of a wooden spoon; do not boil. Skin, quarter, and de-seed the tomatoes. Add to the scampi, heat, and season. Turn on to a warmed serving dish.

Serve with boiled rice.

Cooking time 20 minutes (approx)

Scampi Provençale

4 helpings

flour for coating	25g butter
salt and pepper	75g button mushrooms
450g peeled scampi	3 tomatoes

Sauce
2 shallots	2 × 15ml spoons flour
bouquet garni	1 clove of garlic
150ml dry white wine (approx)	1 × 10ml spoon concentrated tomato purée
25g butter	250ml fish stock (p330)

Garnish
chopped parsley

Make the sauce first. Skin and finely chop the shallots, put in a saucepan with the bouquet garni and the wine. Boil, uncovered, until the liquid is reduced by half. Put to one side. Melt $1 \times 15ml$ spoon of the butter in another saucepan, add the flour, and cook for 2–3 minutes, stirring all the time. Chop the garlic finely, and add it to the roux with the tomato purée and stock. Simmer for 10–15 minutes, then pour in the wine and cook for a further 5 minutes. Add the remaining butter and keep warm.

Season the flour with salt and pepper. Roll the scampi in the seasoned flour and fry gently in the 25g butter for 4–5 minutes. Remove with a perforated spoon. Place in a serving dish and keep hot. Clean and slice the mushrooms and skin and slice the tomatoes. Sauté these in the fat left in the pan and add them to the sauce. Boil the sauce for 2 minutes and spoon it over the scampi. Sprinkle with chopped parsley.

Serve with boiled rice.

Scampi Jambalaya

4 helpings

25g butter	Cayenne pepper
$1 \times 15ml$ spoon cooking oil	$1 \times 5ml$ spoon Worcestershire sauce
2 onions	250g long-grain rice
100g ham	125ml chicken stock
3 tomatoes	450g peeled scampi
1 green pepper	100g shelled cooked mussels
1 clove of garlic	
1 bay leaf	$2 \times 15ml$ spoons medium-dry sherry
a pinch of thyme	
salt and pepper	

Heat the butter and oil in a deep frying pan. Skin and chop the onions finely and fry gently until soft. Dice and add the ham. Skin and chop the tomatoes, de-seed and chop the pepper finely, and add both to the onions. Crush and add the garlic, with the herbs, seasonings, and rice. Stir well. Pour in the chicken stock. Cover, and cook for 12 minutes. Add the scampi and mussels, cover, and simmer for a further 5 minutes. Stir in the sherry, and serve at once, very hot.

MEAT

Of the various methods of preparing meat, roasting is that which most effectually preserves its nutritive qualities. In roasting meat, the heat must be strongest at first, and it should then be much reduced. To have a good juicy roast, therefore, the fire must be red and vigorous at the very commencement of the operation.

About Meat in General

Look for a butcher who sells good quality meat from a clean and well-equipped shop. If you buy most of your meat from a supermarket, do not hesitate to ask the butchery department for the cut of meat you want if it is not on the counter, or for advice on how to cook an unfamiliar cut.

As there are many different cuts and cooking methods, it is wise to learn as much as possible about them. Some cuts, particularly the cheaper ones, are better braised than roasted, otherwise the meat can be dry and tough to eat.

Family preference for roasted, fried, and grilled meats can empty your purse fast, but the less expensive joints and cuts, properly roasted at a low temperature or pot-roasted, often make better eating and are more economical because there is less shrinkage in the meat.

Stews and casseroles can cost less in preparation time, cooking fuel and meat than, for instance, a fried rump steak. The secret is that, once in the oven or slow-cooking casserole, the meat can be left on a low heat completely unattended. A fried meal requires the constant presence of the cook.

QUALITY OF MEAT

Young Animals

Meat from young animals is mostly lean and the bones are supple and pliant. This can be tested by bending a rib bone from a young lamb, ie a bone from a best end chop, and a rib bone from a sheep, ie a bone from a mutton chop.

The meat from very young animals, such as veal, spring lamb, and suckling-pig, is light-coloured and tender, but it has little flavour. When cooked, it often needs a sauce or stuffing to make it more palatable.

As the animal grows older and bigger, its bones grow and harden, and the quantity of muscle or meat increases. The ratio of meat to bone changes considerably with the muscular growth. Light deposits of fat are evident. Examples of such carcasses are the large veal calves, especially Dutch calves, lambs, and small pork pigs. The meat of these animals is very tender but still lacks flavour and can be rather dry if cooked by dry heat methods.

Mature Animals

Quality is not found in meat until the animal has reached maturity. At that stage, fat has been deposited internally within the muscular structure and under the animal's skin. Marbling fat, the creamy white flecks of fat between the muscle fibres, is always an indication of quality. When the meat is cooked, the marbling fat bastes the meat internally and keeps it moist.

Flavour and Tenderness

The greater the development of the animal's muscle the stronger will be the flavour of the meat. An example of full-flavoured meat is lean hill mutton. It is an acquired taste, and many people find its flavour too strong, and prefer meat from an animal which has been suitably fattened and not over-exercised. The marbling fat in the muscle structure has a mellowing effect on the flavour of the meat when it is cooked. It is largely the fat which gives the meat its characteristic flavour.

Tenderness depends on the age of the animal, the development and general condition of the muscle, the period of 'hanging' after slaughter, and the cut of the meat. The proportion of connective tissue (fibrous tissue) in the muscle is dependent on the activity of the muscle in the live animal. The more the muscles of the animal are exercised the less tender the meat will be. The hardest working muscles are those which the animal uses for walking, ie in the legs and, consequently, the amount of connective tissue is much greater in these muscles than in the psoas muscle (fillet), which has comparatively little work to do.

Where there is little connective tissue, the meat can be roasted, grilled or fried. Where there is a high proportion of connective tissue, the meat should be boiled or stewed, since the combined action of heat and moisture softens the connective tissue and converts it into gelatine.

The colour of the meat in the butcher's shop is no indication as to quality. Although many peeople prefer to buy meat which has a brighter colour, this means only that the meat is freshly cut. As soon as the cut surface is exposed to the atmosphere, the red colour becomes dull, and begins to turn brown, but the quality does not deteriorate, and may actually improve. Some butchers nonetheless display their produce under red tinted lights to make it appear red; it is illegal to add any artificial colouring to meat.

IMPORTED MEATS

Imported meat is chilled or carcass-frozen, depending on the distance it must travel. Chilled meat is kept as near as possible to freezing point without ice formation taking place. In either case, whole carcasses are wrapped in cloth, and quarters or joints in polythene before being packed in cartons. Both are stored under refrigeration and then loaded into the refrigerated cargo holds. The meat remains frozen or chilled until it reaches the retailer.

TRAY MEATS

Nowadays, a self-service, fresh meat department is a feature of most supermarkets. Large joints are enveloped in transparent film, while chops, smaller joints, offal, mince or cut-up pie meat are usually presented in film-covered trays and are known in the trade as tray meats. A particular cut of meat packed in this way may be hard to identify and its label is, therefore, important. All packed meat should carry the name of the country of origin and the cut.

CONTINENTAL CUTS

There are many methods of cutting a carcass, and the demand for particular cuts determines the principal methods used in each country and even in adjacent regions. However, if you know the part of the carcass from which an unfamiliar cut is taken, refer to the information on 'Methods of Cooking Meat' (pp469–73), to make the best use of the meat.

OFFAL

For many people, the word 'offal' means the organs of an animal which are usually discarded. This is a pity since offal, when properly cooked, produces very good, inexpensive dishes full of flavour.

Offal are the parts cut off the main carcass of an animal when it is prepared for food. In trade terms it comprises: brains, feet, head, heart, liver, kidneys, lights, sweetbreads, tail, tongue, tripe, caul, melts, and marrow bones. By extension, it also includes sausages and meat drippings.

Most offal is quite as nutritious as meat, has an excellent flavour and, apart from calf's liver, kidneys, and sweetbreads, is much cheaper than meat. Liver, kidneys, and heart are rich in minerals and are especially valuable as a source of iron. Sweetbreads, brains, and tripe are easily digested and are, therefore, valuable as food for invalids or the elderly.

Some offal may be hard to find in butchers' shops and supermarkets, although you can usually buy liver, kidneys, heart, oxtail, and tripe quite easily. However, you can generally get other offal from a butcher if you order it a few days in advance. Many butchers will also salt a tongue and prepare other items, eg split a sheep's head, if asked well in advance.

Liver: Most people like calf's liver best, followed by lamb's, pig's, and ox liver respectively. Calf's liver is tender and delicately flavoured. Lamb's liver has a stronger flavour. Both are excellent for grilling and frying. Pig's liver has a very pronounced flavour and a soft texture; therefore, for most people, it needs mixing with mild-flavoured ingredients in a casserole or stew (it is also excellent in a pâté). Ox liver has a strong flavour and is often rather tough and coarse textured. Marinating it before using in casseroles or stews is a good way of tenderizing it. When heating soups, stews or other dishes containing liver, heat gently without allowing the dish to boil, otherwise the smooth rich gravy separates into ragged shreds of solid material and thin tasteless stock.

Kidneys: These are the only kind of offal which can be purchased as part of the carcass as well as on their own. They have a marked flavour, and look and taste interesting in a mixed grill, and are delicious devilled or made into a rich stew. Lamb's kidneys are the best for grilling, while pig's and calf's kidneys can be grilled or fried, and ox kidney should be used in stewed or braised dishes or in steak pies and puddings.

Hearts: Ox, calf's and lamb's or sheep's hearts all make good eating. A heart is a hard, tightly packed muscle containing very little fat, so it is best served stuffed and pot-roasted, braised or stewed. Ox heart is tough and is better cut up and used in casseroles and braised dishes although a whole heart can be stuffed and baked slowly.

Sweetbreads: This name describes the two portions of the thymus gland distinguished as the throat bread and the heart bread. They take time to prepare, but the results are worth the effort. Fried, baked, braised or steamed, they are always delicious. Ox, calf's and lamb's sweetbreads are sold in pairs and one pair will serve 2 people.

Oxtail: This is sold skinned and is often jointed. The meat is bright red and the fat creamy white. The flavour is good, but the meat is tough and must be braised or casseroled or used as a basis for soups.

Tongues: Ox and lamb's tongues are the easiest kinds to obtain. Ox tongues are often sold salted or pickled, and need less cooking time than a fresh tongue. An ox tongue weighs 1.5–3kg; a calf's tongue (which is rare) weighs 0.5–1kg and a lamb's tongue weighs 125–225g. Salted tongues are usually boiled, pressed, and eaten cold.

Tripe: Lamb's tripe is delicate and good for making a small haggis, but ox tripe is more commonly available. Tripe is the inner lining of the stomach. 'Blanket' tripe comes from the first stomach and is the smoothest. 'Honeycomb' tripe comes from the second stomach, and is more often rucked and uneven in thickness. Both kinds of tripe should be firm and white. Tripe is usually sold 'dressed', ie cleaned and partly boiled. Butchers vary in the amount of pre-cooking which they give tripe and you should, therefore, ask the butcher how much longer it should be cooked for. The additional cooking time can vary from 30 minutes to 2 hours. Undressed tripe should be blanched and partly cooked as follows: put into cold water and heat to boiling point, then drain off the water. Repeat this twice more. Boil the tripe in clean water or stock for 2 hours, then follow your chosen recipe for dressed tripe.

Brains: Lamb's and calf's brains are interchangeable in most recipes, although you should allow for the fact that lamb's brains are small and break up more easily. Both are delicately flavoured and can be steamed, poached, braised, grilled or fried. The classic way of serving them with capers and 'black' butter is one of the best (see Brains in Black Butter, p575).

Heads: The use of head meat varies with the animal and the region. The cheek and tongue of an ox head are the most popular meat. Pig's head is the traditional meat for making brawn. The cheek and lower jaw are sometimes cured and boiled as for Bath Chap (p1471). Sheep's or lamb's heads are split in half and boiled or stewed; the stock is used for broth and the meat is used for brawn. Calf's head, when available, is sold fresh or salted. A salted calf's head is used also for making brawn.

Feet: Pig's trotters are available in most butchers' shops. Cow-heel and calf's foot are rare and must usually be ordered well in advance. The main use of any of these is for making jellied stock for consommés, brawns, etc, although they are also added to casseroles which are to be served hot, to give gelatinous body to the stock and extra flavour.

Bones: The leg or shin bones from beef contain delicately flavoured marrow and are chopped into short, neat lengths for preparation as on p516. Any bones are excellent in a stock-pot. The stock from veal bones, when properly clarified, produces the best base for jellies and aspics.

Other offal: Lights, melts, and other minor offal are used in thrifty household cooking in various ways. Melts, for instance, are used as an economic substitute for kidneys in steak and kidney puddings, and caul is used for wrapping items such as faggots (p595).

STORAGE OF MEAT

Fresh (ie, unchilled) meat should be cooked and eaten within 24 hours of buying. However, it can be wiped, covered, and kept in a refrigerator immediately below the freezing unit for 2–3 days.

Chilled pre-cut and pre-packed meat available from supermarkets can be re-wrapped and stored in a domestic refrigerator for up to a week. For information on freezing, see pp1386–87.

Methods of Cooking Meat

Since meat is an expensive item on the food budget, it is most important to choose the correct cooking method for the cut of meat being used to gain the maximum nutritional and palatability value from it. By choosing the most suitable cooking method, a poorer cut of meat can be made tender, palatable, and just as nutritious as an expensive cut.

There are two basic methods of cooking meat: the first is dry heat cooking (roasting, baking or grilling), where the food is in direct contact with the heat; the second is moist heat cooking (pot-roasting, stewing, braising or boiling), where the food is cooked in liquid. The tender cuts are usually roasted, grilled or fried while the cheaper, tougher cuts are better suited for pot-roasting, braising, casseroling, and boiling. Dry heat and moist heat methods do, in fact, overlap. For example, roasting usually takes place with some moisture in the oven if only from the joint itself.

These basic meat cooking methods are described in the following pages and should be followed accordingly.

The recipes which follow them have been arranged in line with these methods. Because of the way in which they have evolved, however, it will be seen that some do not conform precisely to any one of the basic processes as described.

ROASTING

Roasting originally meant cooking on a roasting spit before a steadily burning fire. A spit-roaster or *rôtisserie* can be attached to a cooker or to a separate, free-standing grill or barbecue. It is a horizontal, rotating shaft or spit, which can hold joints of meat, game, poultry, fish or kebabs.

The process usually now called roasting or oven-roasting is in fact baking. There are two methods of roasting meat in the oven:

Method 1 – Quick roasting: The meat is cooked in a very hot oven, 230°C, Gas 8, for about 10 minutes to sear or brown the outside of the meat and seal in the juices. The temperature is then reduced to fairly hot, 190°C, Gas 5, to finish the cooking. (See Meat Roasting Chart opposite.) This method preserves the full flavour of prime joints. However, it is not very suitable for a small joint because it will shrink.

Method 2 – Slow roasting: The meat is cooked in a warm or moderate oven, 160°–180°C, Gas 3–4, for a longer time. (See Meat Roasting Chart opposite.) This method is best suited to the poorer quality roasting joints and small joints, since it causes less shrinkage and provides a more tender joint.

Whichever roasting method is used, any joint must be weighed in order to calculate its cooking time. Both its size and shape influence this also. The larger the joint, the shorter the time per kg; joints on the bone cook faster than boned ones because the bone conducts heat more quickly than muscle fibres. Roasting in foil also affects the cooking time, see below.

The cooking times given in the Meat Roasting Chart are, therefore, only approximate. If you roast varied types of joints, it is worth investing in a meat thermometer which registers the internal temperature of the meat and takes a great deal of the guesswork out of roasting times. The meat thermometer should be inserted into the thickest part of the meat before it is cooked, taking care that it does not touch bone or fat as they will affect the reading. When the right temperature is reached, the joint is cooked. A meat thermometer is particularly useful for calculating the cooking time for beef according to whether you want the meat to be lightly cooked, still pink inside (known as 'rare'), or fully cooked ('well-done').

Where a meat thermometer is not available, a good indication of readiness is the colour of the juice which seeps out of the meat when a skewer is pushed into the centre and withdrawn. The juice from a well-done joint or piece of meat will be colourless, juice from a rare joint will be pinkish-red, and there will be various shades of pink in between.

Joints for roasting should be placed, fat side up, on a wire rack in a shallow roasting tin. If the outside covering of fat varies in thickness, then the thickest part should be uppermost. A rib, cooked on the bone, should be prepared by the butcher so that it will stand upright. A rolled piece of beef should be slightly flattened on one side so that it will stand level. It is advisable to rub a lean joint with dripping or lard before putting it in the oven. Place the roasting tin in the centre of the oven so that air circulates round it freely. During roasting, enough fat should come from the meat to baste it naturally. However, basting the joint from time to time will give an improved flavour and moistness.

Roasting in foil or clear plastic roasting bags is popular, mainly because it keeps the oven cleaner. It is also particularly beneficial when roasting slightly tough joints because the moist heat tenderizes the meat; when roasting small joints of 1.5kg or less, it reduces the shrinkage and any drying out. When using foil, the joint should be wrapped loosely in it and the edges sealed; this does away with the need to baste the joint during cooking. However, it is advisable to remove the foil for the last 15–30 minutes of cooking time to brown the surface of the joint. Foil deflects the heat, and so the oven temperature should be raised by 10°–20°C or by one Gas mark; alternatively the cooking time should be increased.

Follow the manufacturer's instructions when using clear plastic roasting bags. The bag need only be removed when the joint has finished cooking since the meat browns whilst in the bag.

Meat Roasting Chart

Meat	Method 1 – Quick Roasting 230°C, Gas 8, reducing to 190°C, Gas 5, after 10 mins	Method 2 – Slow Roasting at 160°–180°C, Gas 3–4	Meat thermometer temperatures
Beef (with bone)	15 minutes per 0.5kg plus 15 minutes extra	25 minutes per 0.5kg plus 25 minutes extra	rare – 60°C
Beef (without bone – rolled)	20 minutes per 0.5kg plus 20 minutes extra	30 minutes per 0.5kg plus 30 minutes extra	medium – 68°–70°C well-done – 75°–77°C
Lamb (with bone)	20 minutes per 0.5kg plus 20 minutes extra	25 minutes per 0.5kg plus 25 minutes extra	80°–82°C
Lamb and Mutton (without bone – rolled)	25 minutes per 0.5kg plus 25 minutes extra	30 minutes per 0.5kg plus 30 minutes extra	
Mutton (with bone)	20–25 minutes per 0.5kg plus 25 minutes extra	30–35 minutes per 0.5kg plus 35 minutes extra	
Veal (with bone)	25 minutes per 0.5kg plus 25 minutes extra	30 minutes per 0.5kg plus 30 minutes extra	80°–82°C
Veal (without bone – rolled)	30 minutes per 0.5kg plus 30 minutes extra	40 minutes per 0.5kg plus 30 minutes extra	
Pork (with bone)	25–30 minutes per 0.5kg plus 25–30 minutes extra	35 minutes per 0.5kg plus 35 minutes extra	85°–88°C
Pork (without bone – rolled)	35 minutes per 0.5kg plus 35 minutes extra		

Note The above cooking times are approximate. The exact time will depend on the form and thickness of the joint, its age and condition, and its preparation.

GRILLING

Grilled meat is cooked by radiant heat under a hot grill, usually preheated. It is an ideal cooking method for small, tender cuts, and other items: prime steak, chops, sausages, liver, kidney, bacon and gammon rashers or steaks, if you do not want to use much fat. The meat is only lightly brushed with oil or fat before placing it under the grill; this prevents the high heat from drying the meat out. The grill bars or grid must also be greased to prevent the meat sticking to them. The meat is cooked on one side until it is lightly browned. It is then turned over (using a palette knife and spoon to avoid piercing the meat and letting its juices run out) to brown the other side quickly. The heat is reduced, if necessary, after browning, to allow the meat time to cook through. Beef is usually cooked using high heat throughout, while other meats are cooked more slowly.

Grilling and Frying Chart

Cuts	Approx cooking time
Beef	
Steaks	see Steak Grilling and Frying Chart, p488.
Lamb and Mutton	
Chops (loin and chump)	8–15 minutes
Cutlets	7–10 minutes
Veal	
Cutlets	12–15 minutes
Escalopes (beaten and crumbed)	7–10 minutes
Pork	
Chops (loin, chump and spare rib)	15–20 minutes
Bacon and Gammon	
Bacon chops	10–15 minutes
Bacon rashers (thin)	5 minutes
Gammon steaks	10–15 minutes
Offal	
Kidney	5–10 minutes
Liver (1cm thick)	8–10 minutes
Sausages	
Large	10–15 minutes
Chipolata	7–10 minutes

FRYING

Frying is used for the same cuts of meat as grilling. Frying times are the same as grilling times. In addition, some meats, notably mutton, lamb and veal, are often coated with egg and breadcrumbs before frying.

Meat is almost always shallow-fried. Use just enough fat and/or oil to cover the base of the pan. Dripping can be used for beef, or lard for pork; butter gives the best flavour to other meats. Add the meat to the hot (but not smoking) fat or oil. Fry it over high heat, turning once only, again taking care not to puncture the surface. For thick cuts, the heat should be reduced considerably after the outside has been seared, and the cooking continued until the meat is well-done.

For cooking times, see the Chart below and the Steak Grilling and Frying Chart on p488.

POT-ROASTING

This is best for smaller and less tender joints of meat. The meat is browned all over in hot fat in a deep, heavy-based pan. It is then put in the bottom of the pan, on a wire rack or a bed of root vegetables, covered with a tight-fitting lid and cooked slowly over low heat or in a warm oven, 160°C, Gas 3, for 45 minutes per 0.5kg or until tender.

BRAISING

This method combines pot-roasting and stewing. The meat is browned all over in hot fat. It is then placed on a bed of fried vegetables called a mirepoix (see p809), in a casserole or heavy-based pan. Stock or water is added to cover the vegetables. The casserole or pan is covered with a tight-fitting lid and the meat cooked slowly over low heat or in a warm oven, 160°C, Gas 3, for 2–3 hours or until tender.

CASSEROLING AND STEWING

These are long, slow, moist methods of cooking suitable for tougher cuts of meat. Solid cuts or small pieces of meat are browned quickly in hot fat and then cooked in liquid, with vegetables, in a pan covered with a tight-fitting lid or in a heat-proof casserole over gentle heat; or they are cooked in a warm oven, 160°C, Gas 3, for 1½–4 hours until tender.

BOILING

This is a moist method of cooking whole joints, but a rather more tender cut is used for boiling than for stewing. The meat is totally or almost covered with stock or water. Herbs, spices, seasonings, and onions may be added for extra flavour. The liquid is heated to boiling point, skimmed well, then reduced to simmering point until the meat is tender. A little of the liquid may be served with the meat, and the rest used as a basis for a sauce, to make broth or, where suitable, as a general stock.

USING DRIPPING AND OTHER MEAT-FLAVOURED FAT

This makes an appetizing spread on hot toast. It can also be used for flavouring vegetables, for making plain cakes (p1188) and in various other ways, especially if it is cleared, or clarified. Hard fat or suet cut off raw meat can also be used if all skin and gristle are removed. This can be done by melting (rendering) the fat.

To Clarify Fat

To clean fat which has been used for cooking meat, eg for frying, put the fat into a large saucepan and add about the same volume of cold water. Heat very gently until the water begins to boil, removing the scum as it rises. Allow to simmer for about 5 minutes, then strain into a bowl and leave the fat to cool and solidify. Remove the fat in one piece, dry it on soft kitchen paper and scrape away the sediment from underneath. Heat the fat very gently until all bubbling ceases, to drive off any water.

To Render Fat or Suet

Cut the fat into small pieces, and heat very gently in a frying pan or in a cool oven, 150°C, Gas 2, until the fat has melted and the pieces of tissue or skin are quite crisp. While hot, strain the fat through a fine metal strainer into a clean basin, pressing the pieces of tissue and skin against the strainer to extract all the fat. The crispy bits left are called by different names in different parts of the UK, eg mammocks, scraps, scratchings or scruggins, and are used sometimes in old recipes. When crushed, they make a good topping for baked meat or vegetable dishes.

Carving

Carving is an acquired skill requiring practice and a really sharp knife. A sharp knife is essential since it can be used lightly and is always under control. Carving knives should be sharpened before use either with a hone, steel, patent sharpener or an oil-stone. When a knife fails to produce a good edge with a domestic sharpener, take it to an iron-monger or send it to the manufacturer for regrinding.

Note Some modern, stainless steel knives have a hollowed-out grooved blade; these seldom require sharpening.

SHARPENING A CARVING KNIFE

Hold the steel in your left hand (if you are right-handed), with your thumb on top of the handle. Hold the carving knife in your right hand. Angle both the steel and the knife upwards. Place the heel of the blade on the handle end of the steel, almost flat against it, and draw the blade sharply along the steel with a stroking movement. Repeat, but start with the blade *under* the steel, and sharpen the other side of the knife. Go on doing this, alternately holding the knife on top of the steel and under it, until the knife has a sharp, tapered, cutting edge. About 6 strokes on each side should be enough to sharpen any good quality knife.

Carving knives can also be sharpened on a fine

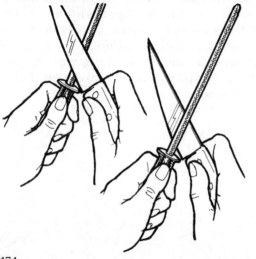

oil-stone or carborundum stone. First dip the stone in water, then sharpen the knife as above.

Another method of using an oil-stone, which may be easier, is to lay the knife almost flat on the stone, with the cutting edge towards you. Draw the knife along the stone, away from you; then turn the knife over, lay it on the far end of the stone and draw it towards you. Repeat several times.

HOW TO CARVE

A knife should be used in the same way as a saw, ie drawn back and forth through the meat. Never try to push even a sharp knife through meat without using a sawing movement. If the knife is sharp, keep the backward and forward movements long and light, and the knife will cut through the meat quickly and smoothly. Try to hold the knife slanted at the same angle all the way through the joint, and to make each slice equally thick when cutting slices of meat from a partly carved joint.

When cutting slices from the top of a rolled joint which is standing on end, always try to cut from right to left (if you are right-handed), not towards you, so that there is no danger of the knife slipping and cutting you. Protect the left hand by using a proper carving fork with a thumb guard. A modern carving dish studded with small, sharp prongs which hold the joint steady can be a great help.

Boned and rolled joints rarely present carving problems since the bones have already been removed, so a beginner learning to carve should start on them. When carving rolled joints, leave some strings and skewers in place until you have carved down to them and then only remove the one which impedes further carving. Anyone who carves meat on the bone should, however, know how the bones lie in the meat, and where the knuckle ends are.

Meat is usually carved across the grain or run of muscle in the UK, because this makes it more tender to cut and eat. The thickness of the slices varies with each type of meat. In general, carve thin slices of beef from a boneless joint and thicker slices from fillet or sirloin. Carve moderately thick slices of pork and veal, and still thicker slices of lamb and mutton.

Beef

Joints on the bone are carved from the outside fat towards the bone after making a vertical cut at the edge of the chine bone. At the base bone, the knife

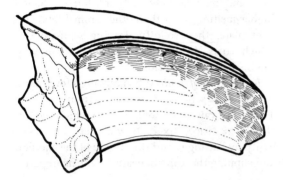

Carving the fillet

Then turn the sirloin over, so that it rests on the bone, and carve the meat across the width of the joint and straight down towards the blade of the bone. These slices are cut thicker than slices from a boneless joint.

Round of beef: Use a thin-bladed and very sharp knife. Cut a thick slice first from the outside of the joint, at its top, leaving the surface smooth; then carve thin, even slices to leave a level-topped joint.

is turned parallel with it and the slices are gently eased off the bone. When dealing with a sirloin or ribs, try to carve the outside rib muscles first as these are better eaten really hot. Save the least cooked meat in the centre for eating cold.

Brisket of beef on the bone: The joint should be cut in even slices across the whole width of the joint, across the bones.

Ribs of beef: Loosen the meat from the ribs by inserting the knife between the meat and bones. Cut thin slices off the sides, starting at the thick end and carving through to the thin end.

Sirloin of beef: A sirloin is carved on the bone. First cut out the fillet or undercut. Carve it into a suitable number of slices. It is best eaten hot.

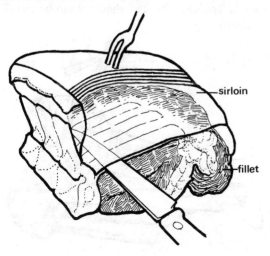

Note The drawings in this chapter are not to scale.

Beef tongue (pressed): Carve thinly across the top, parallel to the round base.

Beef tongue (unpressed): Cut across the tongue at the thickest part, all the way through it. Cut out and serve a fairly thick slice. Continue carving in this way towards the tip of the tongue until all the best meat on the upper side has been served. The fat which lies around the root of the tongue can be turned over, sliced, and served.

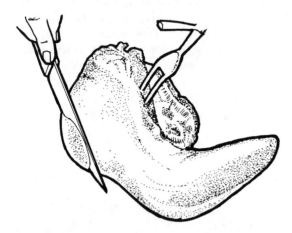

Lamb and Mutton

Mutton and, to a lesser extent, lamb, should always be served as quickly as possible and on very hot plates. This is because the flavour of mutton is soon lost, and because lamb and mutton fat have a higher melting point than other animal fats. On a cold plate, they solidify, leaving semi-solid fat which coats the palate, producing a 'furry' or diminished sense of taste.

Forequarter of lamb: When carving a forequarter of lamb, first separate the shoulder from the breast. To do this, raise the shoulder, into which the fork should be firmly fixed. It will then come away easily by cutting round the outline of the shoulder and slipping the knife beneath it. The main part of

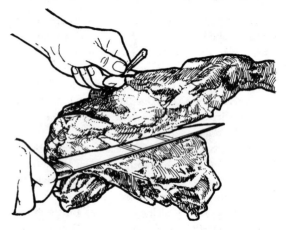

the joint is then turned over and served as cutlets carved from the ribs. The shoulder can be served cold later.

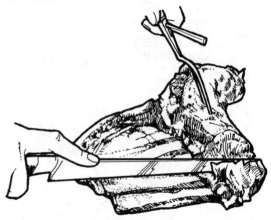

Leg of lamb or mutton: Turn the meatiest side of the joint uppermost. Begin the carving by cutting a V-shaped piece down to the bone close to the knuckle end. Cut slices at a slant up to the thicker

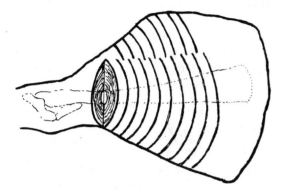

end. Those from the knuckle end will be the most fully cooked. Turn the joint over, discard any unwanted fat and carve horizontal slices along the leg.

Loin of lamb or mutton: Loin, and other similar pieces, should be well-jointed before cooking. Ask the butcher to chine or saw it across the blade parts of the bone or to chop it through the joints for serving in cutlets. If this has not been done, use an old knife and knock the blade through between the joints where they are separated by white discs of gristle, before trying to carve. Carve the loin downwards, in thick slices or in chops, following the

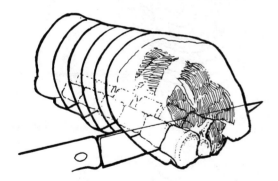

natural division of the bones. If boned and rolled, the loin can be carved in thinner slices, like any other boned and rolled joint.

Saddle of lamb or mutton: There are two ways of carving a saddle, either by carving the slices at right angles to the backbone (spine), or by cutting the slices parallel to it.

For the first method, cut down one side of the spine, and then slip the knife under the meat and cut slices at right angles to the spine, separating the meat from them. Repeat this on the other side of the spine.

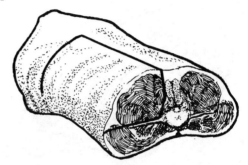

Cut down one side of the spine

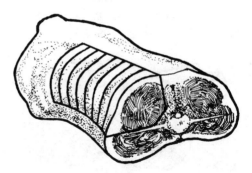

Cut slices at right angles to the spine

See over for **second method**.

For the second method, cut down each side of the spine and separate the meat from the rib bones as in the first method. Make a cut, parallel to the spine a few centimetres up from the lower edge of the meat, then cut slices off downwards parallel to the spine and the cut line. This can be done in the kitchen; the slices can then be put back in place for serving at the table.

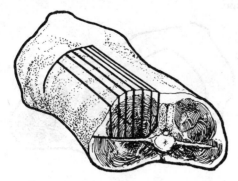

Cut slices parallel to the spine

To finish both methods, carve the chops at the chump end from each side in turn, slanting the knife towards the centre of the joint.

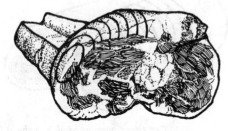

Turn the joint over and slice the fillet along the length of the joint.

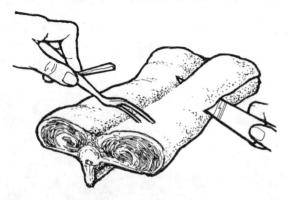

Shoulder of lamb or mutton: Before cooking, insert a sharp knife and ease the meat away from the whole surface of the bladebone, to make carving easier. Turn the joint over, if necessary, so that the thickest part is on top. When cooked, carve a vertical slice at the narrow end of the bladebone right down to the bone. Then carve thick slices along the length of the bladebone until all the shoulder meat on top has been carved, leaving only the shank of the foreleg.

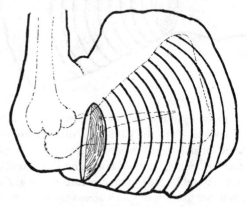

Carve this in horizontal slices along the shank bone until all the meat has been cut from the top of the joint.

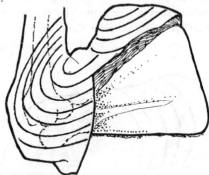

Turn the joint over, and carve the remaining meat in horizontal slices.

Veal

Breast of veal: A breast of veal consists of two parts – the rib bones and the gristly brisket. Separate these first by passing the knife sharply through the centre of the joint. Then cut off each rib bone and serve it. The brisket can be served by cutting pieces from the centre part of the joint. If the veal is boned and stuffed, carve it by cutting downwards across the end of the rolled joint.

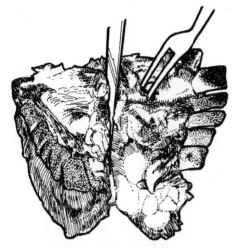

Calf's head: A calf's head is nearly always boned before serving, and is then cut into slices like any other boned and rolled joint. If the bones have not been removed, cut strips from the ear to the nose, and with each of these serve a piece of the throat sweetbreads, cut in a half-moon shape from the throat. The tongue and brains should be served on a separate dish.

Fillet of veal: The carving of this joint is very like that of a round or roll of beef. A stuffing is inserted between the flap and the meat.

Loin of veal: As in the case of a loin of lamb, the careful jointing of a loin of veal greatly lessens the difficulty in carving it. Ask the butcher to do this. When properly jointed, there should be little difficulty in separating the chops from each other. Each helping should include a piece of the kidney and kidney fat.

Pork and Cured Pig Meat

When carving a joint with crackling, first take off a small section of crackling, but only enough to serve one or two people. Cut it into serving portions.

Leg of pork: This joint, a favourite with many people, is easy to carve. Having removed some of the crackling, begin to carve by cutting a V-shaped piece down to the bone close to the knuckle end. Cut slices at a slant up to the thicker end, as when carving a leg of lamb.

Loin of pork: Like a loin of lamb, a loin of pork must be properly chined before roasting, and the crackling must be scored. Ask the butcher to do both. Cut through the cooked meat between the

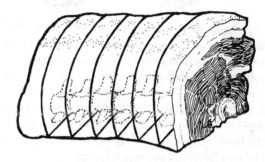

bones into neat, even chops. A boned and rolled loin of pork can be carved in thinner slices, but remove more of the crackling first to make carving easier.

Hand and spring of pork: Using a sharp, thin-bladed knife, remove the rib bones from the underside and the crackling from the top.

Carving a hand and spring of pork continues over.

Carve the meat from each side of the bone in downward slices until the bone is reached. Turn the joint over and carve the rest of the meat across the grain.

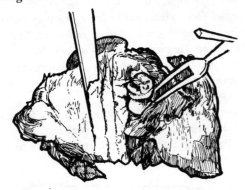

Suckling-pig: A suckling-pig seems, at first sight, an elaborate dish to carve. Like poultry, it is mainly jointed rather than sliced. It is usually prepared by splitting it in half lengthways; the head is then separated from the body. Detach the shoulders from the carcass in the same way as a shoulder is separated from a forequarter of lamb. Then take off the hind legs; the ribs are then ready to be cut up and may be served as 2 or 3 helpings.

Whole gammon or ham: Turn the meatiest side of the joint uppermost. Using a very sharp and thin knife, begin carving at the knuckle end. Make a V-shaped cut into one side of the joint, down to the bone. Take out the slice of meat. Then take thin slices down the side of the joint. Repeat this on the other side of the joint until all the gammon or ham has been carved.

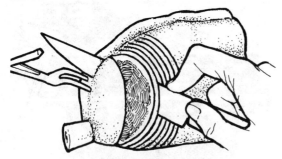

Middle gammon: Using a sharp, thin knife, cut thin slices through to the bone. Because this joint narrows towards the bone end, make the cuts into the joint opposite the bone thicker at the outside, then taper them towards the bone.

Note All pot-roasted and braised whole joints are carved in the same way as the roasted joints above.

Meat

Fillet of Beef en Croûte (p487)

TOP *Steak and Kidney Pie* (p502)

LEFT *Tournedous Rossini* (p490)

RIGHT *Marinated Roast Beef* (p486),
with Yorkshire Puddings, Roast
Potatoes, Demi-Glace Sauce and
Horseradish Cream

TOP *Lamb Shish Kebab* (p527) *showing alternate chunks of tomato, lamb and green peppers before cooking*

BELOW *Holstein Schnitzel* (p559)

RIGHT *Crown Roast of Lamb with Saffron Rice* (p524)

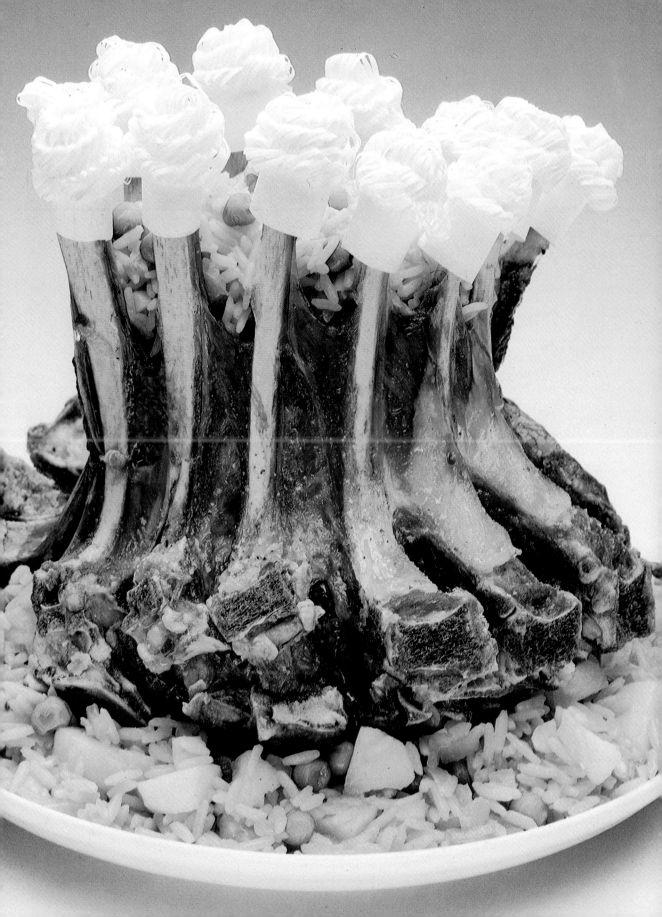

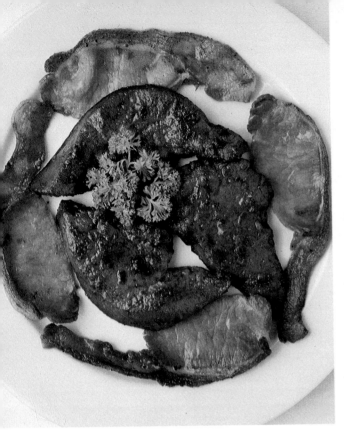

LEFT *Lamb's Liver and Bacon* (p548)

TOP RIGHT *Brains in Black Butter* (p575) *and* BELOW *Sautéed Kidneys* (p1322)

Roast Savoury Loin of Pork (p583) with Red Cabbage and Apple Sauce

Honey-glazed Ham with Pineapple (p605)

Beef

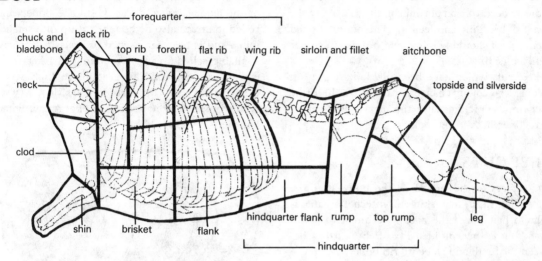

The word beef comes from the old French word *boeuf* meaning an ox. Beef has been eaten in Britain since ancient times, but until the eighteenth-century, beef cattle were small, tough and, as a rule, only slaughtered when elderly. New, small-boned and heavily fleshed animals began to be bred in Britain in the early eighteenth-century and Britain became the beef stock market of the world, providing its inhabitants with some of the best beef available.

Today, most of our beef comes from bullocks (castrated males) and heifers (female calves), reared specifically for meat. The average animal is reared in only 15–30 months, depending on the system used. The young male animals produce a better proportion of lean to fat, but the females have a lighter bone structure. Heifer beef is indistinguishable from bullock beef to the lay person.

QUALITY OF BEEF

All beef must be matured or 'hung' after slaughtering. The ideal time for hanging any beef is 10–14 days at a constant humidity and at a steady temperature of 1°–3.5°C. During this time, certain enzymes break down the connective tissue, making the meat more tender and improving its keeping quality.

Long hanging is expensive. The meat must be stored under specially controlled conditions and there is no quick turnover for the retail butcher who hangs fresh meat himself. Largely for these reasons, the specially bred young animals now slaughtered are hung for as short a time as possible, and fully matured beef has become an expensive purchase. However, fully matured beef needs less cooking time than lightly hung meat of the same quality since it has less connective tissue, so not only is the final product better but the power costs to the consumer are lower.

The colour of beef changes after cutting and exposure to air. Freshly cut beef should be bright red, but after exposure to air for a short time, the lustre is lost and the colour darkens; in fact, a certain dullness is usually an indication that the meat has matured. The lean meat should also have a slightly moist appearance and, in the case of prime cuts for roasting or grilling, should have a smooth and velvety texture. Coarse lean meat in a prime cut is usually an indication that the meat is suitable only for slow, moist cooking. Dark red, lean, and sinewy beef in any cut indicates that it comes from an older animal or one not of prime quality and that it is likely to be tough. Such meat is suitable only for slow, moist cooking but makes a good dish if it is well-marbled with fat.

Fresh lean beef should be surrounded by a layer of firm, cream-coloured fat. At some times of the year the fat can be almost yellow; this does not indicate beef from an old animal, but is usually the result of breeding and feeding. The bones of good quality beef should be shiny and pinkish in colour with a blue tinge.

Beef cuts which have been pickled are grey in colour. The colour change is caused by the brine used in the pickling and the meat will turn an attractive pink during cooking.

BEEF CUTS

The carcass of the animal, ie the body after the removal of head, feet, skin and internal organs, is split in half down the backbone into two sides. Each side is then divided in half by cutting between the tenth and eleventh rib bones. The piece that contains the forelimb and first 10 rib bones is called the forequarter, and the other half of the side is called the hindquarter.

Beyond this, the cuts of beef vary considerably in different parts of Great Britain. Those described are the most widely used British cuts, but they are by no means standard and reference is made to some of the other terms used. The cuts will be better understood from the diagram on p481.

Forequarter
(Average weight 66.25kg)

1) *Shin* comes from the foreleg, has much gristle, and is relatively cheap. It is an excellent soup meat and when cooked on the bone provides a good, jellied stock and is ideal for making brawn. (Av wt boneless shin 2–2.5kg)

Part cut of shin of beef

2) *Brisket* is the muscular extension of the belly of the animal towards the chest. The boned and rolled joint can also be bought cut up into smaller joints and is best pot-roasted or braised. It is also available salted, ready for boiling. Brisket is an economical, yet well-flavoured joint which, when properly cooked, is little fattier than sirloin. (Av wt whole brisket on the bone 9–13.5kg; Av wt boneless joint 7–10.5kg)

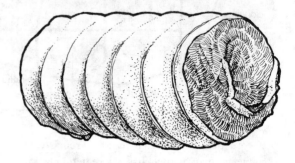

3) *Flank* is also from the belly of the animal. It is a cheaper cut which deserves wider recognition. It provides a more fatty joint than brisket and is ideal for pot-roasting, braising or boiling. It is sometimes salted or pickled before being boiled, for pressed beef. (Av wt 1–2.25kg)

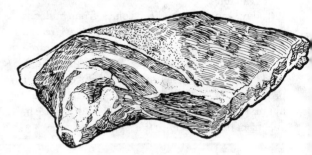

4) *Flat rib* comes from between the flank and foreribs. Like the forerib, this joint should be slowly roasted. (Av wt 5kg)

5) *Wing rib* is a rib joint cut from between the forerib and sirloin. It is one of the most expensive cuts and is particularly good when roasted. (Av wt 2–6kg)

6) *Forerib* is merely an extension of the sirloin, but it requires slower cooking at a lower temperature than the sirloin because the muscles of the live animal were more fully exercised. The forerib can be bought either on the bone, or boned and rolled. (Av wt on the bone 1.4–2.6kg; Av wt boneless 1–2kg)

7) *Top rib* along with the *back rib* is also known as middle rib or thick ribs or leg-of-mutton cut, and comes from the ribs between the foreribs and shoulders. In other words, it is an extension of the foreribs. The joint is often divided into two (top and back ribs) and partly boned and rolled which makes it easier to carve. There is less bone in these joints than in forerib joints and they are very good when slow roasted or pot-roasted. (Av wt 7–11.5kg)

8) *Chuck* and *bladebone* are similar types of beef; the meat is removed from the bone and sold as chuck steak for braising, stewing, and as fillings for puddings and pies. Though sold for stewing, chuck steak needs a shorter cooking time than any other cut of stewing meat. Many butchers cut blade of beef into dice and mix it with chopped kidney, ready for filling puddings and pies. Chuck is known in the north of England as a chine, and in Scotland the chuck and blade together is known as a shoulder. (Av wt boneless chuck – 4.5kg; Av wt boneless bladebone – 3kg)

9) *Clod* or *front chest* and

10) *Sticking* or *neck* of the animal provide meat suitable for casseroling or stewing. These cuts contain less connective tissue than the shin or leg and less marbling fat than chuck steak and bladebone. Both clod and sticking are usually cheap. There is, however, a little wastage due to gristle. (Av wt clod (de-fatted) – 4.5kg; Av wt sticking – 3.5kg)

Hindquarter

(Average weight 71.5–72kg)

11) *Leg of beef* is the name used for the hind leg only. The leg meat is only suitable for long, slow cooking and is best used for stews, casseroles, pies, and soups. It can be cut in two ways. Cut in strips, it shows clearly the structure of the working muscle as it is sheathed with white or transparent connective tissue gathered together at the ends into thick pieces of white gristle. Cut in slices, it reveals 'lines' where the various sheaths of connective tissue have been cut across. There is little to choose between the leg and the foreleg, except that the leg is larger and so provides bigger pieces of meat for stewing. In Scotland, the leg and shin are called the hough. (Av wt boneless leg – 4kg)

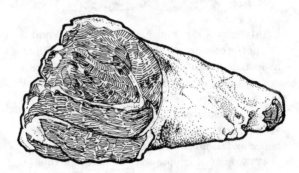

12) *Topside* is the muscle of the inside of the leg. This is a lean joint without bones. It can be slow roasted but a piece of barding fat must be tied round the joint to keep it moist during cooking. It is really better pot-roasted or braised. (Av wt 8.5–8.75kg)

13) *Silverside* is the muscle of the outside of the thigh and buttock. It is common for this joint to be roasted but it is best suited to salting and boiling, as in the past (Av wt boneless silverside – 5.5kg)

14) *Top rump* or *thick flank* is the muscle of the front of the thigh, which is usually cut into 2 joints and barded with fat. This makes an acceptable joint for slow roasting or, better still, for moist cooking such as pot-roasting. It may also be sold sliced, ready for frying or braising. (Av wt boned and trimmed 5.25–5.5kg)

15) *Aitchbone* is the cut lying over the rump bone. It is a large joint on the bone which can be roasted or braised. Can be boned and cut into smaller joints. Not cut very often nowadays. (Av wt on the bone – 5.4kg)

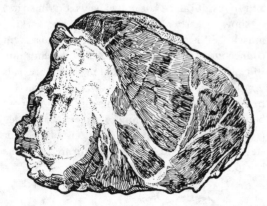

16) *Rump* is the joint next to the sirloin and is one of the commonest cuts for frying and grilling. In Scotland rump steak is sometimes called 'pope's eye'. Although not as tender as fillet, it is preferred by many people for its fuller flavour. The meat should be close-grained and should have about 5mm fat on the outside edge and no gristle. (Av wt boned and trimmed rump 8.25–8.5kg)

17) *Sirloin* (which properly includes the fillet) is the traditional joint for roast beef. It is tender and full of flavour, but is also the most expensive joint. It is often sold without the fillet which makes it slightly cheaper. Sirloin is also sold sliced as steaks for grilling or frying. (Av wt sirloin with bone and fillet – 12.25kg)

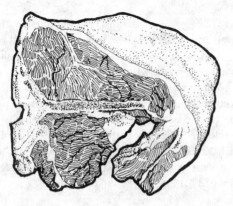

18) *Fillet* is found on the inside of the sirloin bone, and fillet and sirloin may be boned and rolled together to provide a luxury roast. If the sirloin is bought on the bone, the fillet can be removed for roasting by itself in the piece, or for slicing into fillet steaks, which are the most tender steaks for grilling or frying. (Av wt fillet 1.5–2.25kg)

19) *Hindquarter flank* is the belly of the animal, which provides a cheap and delicious joint for pot-roasting, braising or boiling. It is, however, rather fatty. It is not suitable for dry heat cooking methods. (Av wt with bone – 6.25kg)

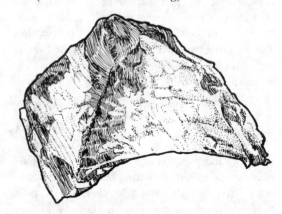

Steaks

Several terms are used for various types of beef steaks. They are not new terms and some have already been mentioned.

Fillet (undercut) is a lean and boneless piece lying below the ribs of the sirloin. It is the most expensive steak meat and is usually sliced for grilling or frying. The tiny flecks of fat running through the meat are evidence that the steak will grill or fry well. Fillet steak can be served in several ways and under several names.

Tournedos is a slice from the fillet, weighing about 125–150g, usually 2cm thick and a neat round shape. It is sometimes tied to preserve its shape.

Châteaubriand is a piece of fillet enough for 2 people, ideally about 4cm thick and cut from the centre of the fillet. A popular and delicious steak. Its average weight is 250g.

Rump is the best flavoured steak, particularly good for grilling and frying. It is not as tender as fillet steak but has a good texture. This steak should have about 5mm fat on the outside edge.

Sirloin (contre-fillet) provides tender steaks with a good flavour. However, the texture is not as good as fillet or rump. Sirloin, like fillet, is cut in several ways and served under several names.

Porterhouse is a thick steak about 2–2.5cm thick, cut from the wing end (thick end) of the sirloin. Excellent for grilling.

T-bone is a steak cut through the sirloin so that it contains, on one side at least, the T-shaped loin bone. It has 2 'eyes', that of the loin meat and that of the fillet.

Entrecôte is a sirloin steak without the undercut (fillet) and without the bone. In other words, it is the eye meat of the loin cut into steaks. Each steak is usually cut 2–3cm thick.

Minute steak is a very thin steak from the upper part of the sirloin or occasionally from the fillet, weighing 125–150g without any trimmings or fat.

ROASTED AND BAKED DISHES

Roast Beef

Basic recipe

a joint of beef suitable for roasting
salt and pepper

beef dripping (25g per 0.5kg meat approx)

Select the method of roasting, ie quick or slow-roasting (p470). Weigh the meat to calculate the cooking time (p471). Wipe, trim, and tie the meat into a neat shape. Place the joint, fat side up, on a wire rack if available, in a shallow roasting tin. Season the meat, and rub or spread it with the dripping. Place the roasting tin in the oven and cook for the required time.

Transfer the cooked meat to a warmed serving dish, remove any string and secure with a metal skewer if necessary. Keep hot. Drain off the fat from the roasting tin and make a gravy from the sediment in the tin, if liked.

Serve with Yorkshire Pudding (pp934–35) and Cold Horseradish Cream (p402) if using traditional accompaniments.

Mrs Beeton's Roast Ribs of Beef

6–8 helpings

2.5kg forerib of beef
flour for dredging

50–75g clarified
 dripping (p473)
salt and pepper

Garnish
shredded horseradish

Ask the butcher to trim the thin ends of the rib bones so that the joint will stand upright. Wipe the meat but do not salt it. Dredge it lightly with flour. Melt 50g dripping in a roasting tin and brush some of it over the meat. Put the meat in the tin and roast it in a very hot oven, 230°C, Gas 8, for 10 minutes. Baste well, reduce the heat to moderate, 180°C, Gas 4, and continue to roast for $1\frac{3}{4}$ hours for rare meat, or $2\frac{1}{4}$ hours for well-done meat. Baste frequently during cooking, using extra dripping if required.

When cooked, salt the meat lightly. Transfer the joint to a warmed serving dish and keep hot. Pour off almost all the fat in the roasting tin, leaving the sediment. Pour in enough water to make a thin gravy, then heat to boiling point, stirring all the time. Taste, and season with salt and pepper. Strain the gravy into a warmed gravy-boat. Garnish the dish with 1 or 2 small heaps of shredded horse-radish.

Serve with Yorkshire Pudding (pp934–35) and Cold Horseradish Cream (p402).

Marinated Roast Beef

6–8 helpings

750g–1kg fillet or boned
 sirloin or topside of
 beef
fat for greasing

2 × 5ml spoons meat
 glaze (p397)
250ml Demi-glace sauce
 (p708)

Marinade
2 × 15ml spoons olive oil
1 × 15ml spoon lemon
 juice or vinegar
1 × 5ml spoon chopped
 onion
1 × 5ml spoon chopped
 parsley

a pinch of dried mixed
 herbs
a pinch of ground cloves
a pinch of ground pepper
$\frac{1}{2}$ × 2.5ml spoon salt

Make the marinade first by mixing all the ingredients together. Wipe, trim, and tie the meat into a neat shape. Place the meat in a bowl, pour the marinade over and leave it to soak for 2–3 hours, turning and basting frequently.

Cut a sheet of foil large enough to form a parcel round the meat, and grease it well. Lay the foil in an ovenproof dish with sides so that it forms a container, and place the meat in the centre of it; use the marinade also. Fold the foil round the meat and seal the edges to form a parcel. Roast the beef in a fairly hot oven, 190°C, Gas 5, for 1 hour for fillet, and $1\frac{1}{2}$ hours for sirloin or topside. Open the foil for the last 15 minutes of the cooking time to let the meat brown. Lift out the meat, place it on a warmed serving dish and remove the string. Brush with Demi-glace Sauce. If liked, a little of the sauce can also be poured round the dish, the rest being served separately.

Serve with Cold Horseradish Cream (p402), as well as the Demi-glace Sauce.

Note For other marinades, see p730.

Stuffed Rolled Fillet of Beef

6 helpings

800g fillet of beef
125ml port (optional)
150ml malt or red wine
  vinegar
150g basic herb stuffing
  (p375) or ham stuffing
  (p375) or mushroom
  stuffing (p378)
1 × 2.5ml spoon ground
  allspice
375ml Espagnole (p707),
  Piquant (p702) or
  Demi-glace (p708)
  sauce

Wipe and trim the meat. Put in a bowl and pour the port, if used, and vinegar over it; leave to stand for 2 days. Baste frequently and turn once or twice during this time. Drain the meat thoroughly and reserve the liquid.

Flatten the beef slightly with a cutlet bat or rolling-pin and cover it with the stuffing. Roll it up tightly and tie securely. Place in a roasting tin. Add the allspice to the marinade and pour it over the meat. Cook in a moderate oven, 180°C, Gas 4, for about 45 minutes, basting frequently.

When cooked, remove the string and serve the meat with the chosen sauce and redcurrant jelly.

Fillet of Beef Dauphin

6–8 helpings

750g–1kg fillet or boned
  sirloin or topside of
  beef
salt and pepper
50g larding bacon
1 × 15ml spoon plain
  flour
2 × 15ml spoons beef
  dripping
2 × 5ml spoons meat
  glaze (p397)
250ml Madeira sauce
  (p708)

Garnish
12 potato croquettes
  (p796)

Wipe, trim, and season the meat with salt and pepper. Cut the larding bacon into strips 5mm × 4cm (approx) and use them to lard the meat. Sprinkle the meat with flour and tie it into a neat shape.

Melt the dripping in a roasting tin over gentle heat, add the prepared meat and baste it with the dripping. Cover with foil, and put into a hot oven, 220°C, Gas 7, for 10 minutes, then reduce the heat to moderate, 180°C, Gas 4, and cook for a further 35 minutes, basting twice. Remove the foil and return the meat to the oven for 15 minutes to brown and complete the cooking. Transfer the meat to a warmed serving dish, remove the string, and brush the fillet with meat glaze. Garnish with potato croquettes.

Pour away the fat from the roasting tin and add any of the brown sediment to the Madeira sauce. Serve the hot sauce separately.

Fillet of Beef en Croûte

6 helpings

750g–1kg fillet of beef
ground pepper
25g butter
1 × 15ml spoon oil
100g button mushrooms
1 × 5ml spoon fresh
  mixed herbs, chopped
1 × 5ml spoon chopped
  parsley
450g prepared puff
  pastry (p1253)
flour for rolling out
beaten egg for glazing

Wipe, trim, and tie the meat into a neat shape. Season with pepper. Heat the butter and oil in a large pan, add the fillet and brown it quickly all over. Reserve the fat in the pan and draw it off the heat. Transfer the fillet to a roasting tin and roast it in a very hot oven, 230°C, Gas 8, for 10 minutes. Remove the fillet, and leave it to get cold.

Meanwhile, clean and slice the mushrooms. Sauté them in the remaining oil and butter in the pan for 2–3 minutes. Remove from the heat, add the herbs, and leave to cool.

Roll out the puff pastry on a lightly floured surface to make a rectangle large enough to enclose the fillet. Put the mushroom mixture on one half of the pastry. Lay the beef on top of the mushroom mixture. Wrap the pastry round the beef to form a neat parcel, sealing the edges well. Place the parcel on a baking tray with the cut edges underneath. Decorate with leaves cut from the pastry trimmings and brush the pastry with the beaten egg. Bake in a hot oven, 220°C, Gas 7, for 20–30 minutes, or until the pastry is well-browned. Serve hot or cold.

STEAKS

Steak Grilling and Frying Chart

	Fillet	Tournedos	Châteaubriand	Rump	Sirloin	Porterhouse	T-bone	Entrecôte	Minute
Thickness of meat	2cm	2–3cm	4cm	2cm	2–2.5cm	4–5cm	4–5cm	2–3cm	1cm
Helpings	1	1	2	4	1	2	2–3	1	1
Cooking times (in minutes):									
Rare	6	6–7	15–17	6–7	5	7–8	7–8	5	1–1.5
Medium-rare	7	8	18–20	8–10	6–7	9–12	9–12	6–7	2–3
Well-done	8	9–10	21–24	12–14	9–10	14–16	14–16	9–10	4–5

Grilled Steak

Basic recipe

150–200g steak per person   *oil **or** melted butter*
   freshly ground pepper

Garnish
Maître d'Hôtel butter
 (p1300)

Wipe the steaks and trim off any excess fat. Beat each steak lightly on both sides with a cutlet bat or rolling-pin. Brush with oil or melted butter and, if possible, leave for 1 hour before cooking.

Season with pepper. (Do not salt steaks before grilling because it makes the juices run.) Heat the grill to a high heat and oil the grid, or brush with melted butter. Place the meat on the grid and cook under the grill until the steak has browned lightly on one side. Turn the meat over, using a palette knife or spoons. Grill quickly to brown the other side. If the steaks are required medium-rare or well-done, lower the grid or the grill heat and continue cooking as required (see Steak Grilling Chart above). Serve at once with a pat of Maître d'Hôtel butter on the top of each helping.

Serve with chipped potatoes, grilled mushrooms, and/or grilled tomatoes, and a sprig of watercress.

Châteaubriand Steak

2 helpings

*a double fillet steak, not less than 4cm thick olive oil **or** melted butter*   *freshly ground pepper*
   fat for greasing

Garnish
Maître d'Hôtel butter
 (p1300)

Wipe, trim the fillet and, if necessary, flatten it slightly with a cutlet bat or rolling-pin. Brush both sides with oil or melted butter and season with pepper. Place the steak on a greased grid and cook under a very hot grill until browned and sealed. Turn the steak over, using a palette knife or spoons, and grill until browned. Reduce the heat slightly and continue grilling for 4–5 minutes, turning it once or twice, until the steak is well-browned on the outside but slightly underdone on the inside. Garnish with pats of Maître d'Hôtel butter and serve at once.

Serve with Potato Straws (p792) and Demi-glace Sauce (p708), Fresh Tomato Sauce (p715) or Béchamel Sauce (p704).

Note To serve, slice downwards at a slight angle, into 4–6 even slices.

Fried Steaks

Basic recipe

150–200g steak, 2cm
  thick, per person
freshly ground pepper
1 × 15ml spoon oil,
  dripping **or** butter
  (approx)

a pinch of onion salt
  (optional)
1– 2 × 5ml spoons flour
  for gravy (optional)
100ml boiling water
  (optional)

Garnish
Maître d'Hôtel **or** other
  savoury butter
  (pp1297–1301)

Wipe the steaks and trim off any excess fat. Beat each steak lightly on both sides with a cutlet bat or rolling-pin. Season with pepper. (Do not salt steaks before frying because it makes the juices run.) Heat a thick, heavy frying pan on full heat until hot. Add enough oil, dripping or butter just to cover the bottom of the frying pan and, when hot, put in the prepared steaks. Keep on full heat until they are well-browned on one side; then turn them over with a palette knife or spoons, and brown the other side. Reduce the heat if necessary to complete the cooking time (see Chart opposite). Serve at once garnished with a pat of Maître d'Hôtel or other butter.

If serving gravy with the steak, drain any fat from the frying pan, keeping back the sediment. Add a pinch of ground black pepper and onion salt, and stir in the flour. Gradually add the water, and stir until boiling. Skim and strain the gravy.

Serve with chipped potatoes, grilled mushrooms and/or grilled tomatoes, and a sprig of watercress.

Steaks with Mustard Sauce

4 helpings

4 fillet **or** sirloin steaks
  (150–200g each)
freshly ground pepper
25g unsalted butter
2 × 15ml spoons oil
150ml soured cream

1 × 5ml spoon lemon
  juice
2 × 5ml spoons French
  mustard
salt

Prepare the steaks as for Fried Steaks. Heat the butter and oil in a heavy-based frying pan. When hot, put in the steaks and fry quickly on both sides for the required cooking time (see Steak Grilling and Frying Chart p488). Lift out the steaks, transfer them to a warmed serving dish, and keep hot. Stir the soured cream into the juices in the pan and cook gently, without boiling. Stir in the lemon juice, mustard, and salt to taste. Pour the mustard sauce over the steaks and serve at once.

Steak au Poivre

4 helpings

4 steaks (fillet, sirloin
  or entrecôte, 150–200g
  each)
2 × 10ml spoons whole
  black and white
  peppercorns, mixed

1 clove of garlic
4 × 15ml spoons olive oil
50g unsalted butter

Garnish
50g parsley butter
  (p1301)

Wipe the steaks and trim off any excess fat. Crush the peppercorns coarsely in a mortar or in a paper or polythene bag, using a rolling-pin. Skin and cut the garlic in half and rub the steaks on both sides with the garlic. Brush each steak on both sides with 1 × 15ml spoon of olive oil. With the heel of your hand, press the crushed peppercorns into the surface of the meat on each side.

Heat the butter in a frying pan and fry the steaks over high heat for 1 minute on both sides until sealed and browned. Reduce the heat and fry the steaks for 4–5 minutes for rare, 7 minutes for medium-rare, and 9 minutes for well-done steaks, turning them 2 or 3 times. Remove with a palette knife or spoons, and place on a warmed serving dish. Garnish with pats of parsley butter and serve at once.

Steak Diane
See p1449.

Tournedos Rossini

4 helpings

4 tournedos steaks (175g each approx)
4 slices white bread
50g butter
1 × 15ml spoon cooking oil
50g unsalted butter

50ml Madeira **or** dry Marsala (see **Note**)
75ml brown stock (p329)
100ml Espagnole sauce (p707)
salt and freshly ground black pepper

Garnish

4 rounds good quality liver pâté (5mm thick)
4 small flat mushrooms

4 × 5ml spoons chilled butter
sprigs of watercress

Wipe, trim, and tie the tournedos into a neat shape. Cut 4 rounds from the bread slices, a little wider than the tournedos' bases. Heat the butter and oil in a large, deep frying pan, and fry the bread rounds over moderate heat until light gold and crisp on both sides. Transfer them to a warmed serving dish and keep warm under buttered paper.

Put half the unsalted butter into the pan. Pat the tournedos dry, add them to the pan, raise the heat, and fry the steaks quickly, turning as required, until they are well seared and browned all over but rare inside. Remove them with a palette knife or spoons. Place them on the fried bread rounds and keep warm.

Lower the heat and stir the wine and stock quickly into the pan, scraping up all the drippings. Simmer for 3 minutes, then stir in the sauce and simmer until reduced to the desired consistency.

Meanwhile, heat the remaining 25g unsalted butter in a small frying pan, and turn the pâté slices and mushrooms in it for 2–3 minutes over high heat, until the mushrooms are soft and the pâté is lightly browned but not melted.

Place a slice of pâté on each tournedos and cap it with a mushroom, gill side down. Garnish the top of each mushroom with 1 × 5ml spoon chilled butter. Serve at once, with the sauce in a warmed sauce-boat. Garnish the dish with watercress and offer a peppermill of black pepper with the steaks.

Note Good quality medium-sweet sherry can be used instead of Madeira or Marsala. If using Madeira, use Sercial, not Bual Madeira.

Fillet Steak Chasseur

4 helpings

65g butter
1 shallot (25g approx)
50g button mushrooms
125ml dry white wine
1 × 10ml spoon concentrated tomato purée

250ml Demi-glace sauce (p708)
4 fillet steaks (150–200g each)

Melt 15g of the butter in a small saucepan. Skin the shallot and chop it finely. Cook gently in the butter until softened but not browned. Clean and slice the mushrooms. Add them to the pan and shake over the heat for 2–3 minutes. Add the wine and boil it rapidly, uncovered, to reduce it by half. Stir in the tomato purée and Demi-glace Sauce, heat to simmering point, and simmer for 2–3 minutes.

Prepare the fillet steaks and fry them in the remaining 50g butter (see Fried Steaks p489). Arrange the steaks on a warmed serving dish and pour the hot Chasseur sauce over them.

Fillet Steak with Wine Sauce

4 helpings

50g butter
75ml dry white wine
50ml white stock (p329) **or** water
2 shallots **or** 25g onion

100g button mushrooms
50g cooked ham
4 fillet **or** sirloin steaks (150–225g each)

Heat 25g of the butter in a saucepan and add the wine and stock or water. Skin and chop the shallots or onion finely. Clean and slice the mushrooms. Dice the ham. Add the shallots or onion, the mushrooms and ham to the pan and simmer, uncovered, for 5 minutes.

Prepare the steaks and fry them in the remaining butter (see Fried Steaks p489). Arrange the steaks on a warmed serving dish and pour the sauce over them.

Carpet-bag Steak

6 helpings

1–1.5kg piece of rump steak **or** *topside, not less than 5cm thick*	*150g soft white breadcrumbs*
100g mushrooms	*1 × 15ml spoon chopped parsley*
12 raw oysters	*salt and paprika*
3 × 10ml spoons butter	*1 egg*
grated rind of ½ lemon	*fat for roasting*

Wipe the meat and trim off any excess fat, then slit it through the centre horizontally, leaving 3 edges joined, to make a deep pocket. Clean and slice the mushrooms. Open the oysters (p426). Heat the butter gently in a frying pan, add the oysters and mushrooms, and cook for 3 minutes. Transfer the oysters and mushrooms to a bowl and mix in the grated lemon rind, breadcrumbs, parsley, salt and paprika to taste. Beat the egg until liquid and stir it into the stuffing. Stuff the pocket of the steak, and stitch or skewer the open edge to close it. Heat a little fat in a roasting tin, add the steak and baste it. Roast in a warm oven, 160°C, Gas 3, for 1½ hours or until the meat is tender.

Serve with roast potatoes and roast pumpkin or any other suitable vegetables.

BRAISED DISHES

Beef à la Mode

8 helpings

1kg rump of beef	*salt and pepper*
25g butter **or** *dripping*	*2 rashers streaky bacon, without rinds*
10 button onions	
25g plain flour	*2 medium-sized carrots (100g approx)*
750ml brown stock (p329)	

Marinade

1 small onion (50g approx)	*2 cloves*
	salt and pepper
100ml claret	*bouquet garni*
juice of ½ lemon	

Wipe, trim, and tie the meat into a neat shape if necessary.

Make the marinade first. Skin and chop the onion finely. Mix all the ingredients for the marinade, put in the meat, and leave it to stand for 2 hours, basting frequently. Drain the beef thoroughly, and strain and reserve the marinade.

Heat the butter or dripping in a large stewpan and fry the meat in the hot fat, turning it until browned on all sides. Skin the button onions and fry at the same time, turning them so that they brown evenly. Remove the beef and onions and put to one side. Stir the flour into the fat in the pan and cook until browned. Gradually add the stock and the marinade and stir until boiling. Replace the meat and onions. Season to taste. Cover the top of the meat with the bacon. Slice the carrots thinly, then add them to the pan. Cover with a tight-fitting lid and cook gently for 2½ hours, stirring occasionally, or transfer to an ovenproof dish, cover, and cook in a warm oven, 160°C, Gas 3, for 2 hours. When tender, transfer the meat to a warmed serving dish and keep hot. Strain the liquid in the stewpan or casserole, and pour it over the meat.

Note If liked, the bacon, onions, and carrots can be served with the meat although they will have given up most of their food value during the long, slow cooking.

Mrs Beeton's Beef à la Mode

4 helpings

2 rashers back bacon (100g approx)	100ml red wine vinegar
1kg thick flank of beef (see **Note**)	75ml port
	salt and pepper

Seasoning

1 clove	1 sprig of fresh thyme **or**
4 black peppercorns	a good pinch of dried
3 allspice berries	thyme
3 sprigs parsley	1 bay leaf

Mirepoix

1 medium-sized onion (100g approx)	½ turnip (50g approx)
2 sticks celery	50g clarified dripping (p473)
1 medium-sized carrot (50g approx)	250ml water

Cut the bacon into strips 2cm wide crossways, including lean and fat in each strip. Wipe the meat and make deep slits in the flesh with a sharp-pointed knife. Make the same number of slits as strips of bacon.

Make the seasoning mixture. Pound the clove, peppercorns, and allspice berries in a mortar. Chop the parsley and thyme finely and crumble the bay leaf finely. Mix the ingredients together to make 1 × 5ml spoon seasoning.

Dip the bacon strips in the vinegar, then coat them with about one-third of the seasoning mixture. Insert 1 bacon strip into each slit in the meat. Rub the meat all over with the remaining seasoning and tie the meat into a neat shape.

Prepare the vegetables for the mirepoix. Slice the onion and celery, and chop the carrot and turnip. Melt the dripping in a flameproof casserole or stewpan. Add the onion and fry gently until softened and golden-brown. Add the celery, carrot, and turnip. Place the meat on the vegetables. Pour the vinegar and water gently over the vegetables, then cover the pan closely. Heat to boiling point, reduce the heat, and simmer very gently for 1 hour 40 minutes. Turn the meat over after 40 minutes cooking time, and again after a further 30 minutes.

When cooked, transfer the meat to a warmed serving dish and keep hot. Strain the cooking liquid into a pan, skim off the fat, and add the port. Heat gently to boiling point. Taste, and season if required. Remove the strings from the meat and pour a little of the sauce over the meat. Serve the rest separately in a warmed sauce-boat.

Note Thick flank or top rump, as it is often called, is usually sold with extra fat tied round it. In this recipe the weight of the meat is without the added fat.

Italian Braised Beef

4–6 helpings

1kg topside of beef (approx)	200g canned tomatoes
salt and pepper	2 × 10ml spoons concentrated tomato purée
1 medium-sized onion	
1 clove of garlic (optional)	1 bay leaf
1 × 15ml spoon olive oil	a sprig of parsley
75ml dry red wine	50g mushrooms
2 small carrots	100ml beef stock **or** water
1 stick of celery	

Wipe, trim, season, and tie the meat into a neat shape. Weigh it to calculate the cooking time, allowing 1 hour 40 minutes per kg. Skin and chop the onion, and skin and crush the garlic, if used. Heat the olive oil in a large stewpan. When warm, add the onion, garlic, if used, and the meat. Brown the meat on all sides. Pour in the wine and cook, uncovered, over high heat until it is reduced by half. Prepare and chop the carrots and celery, and add to the pan with the canned tomatoes, tomato purée, bay leaf, and parsley. Clean the mushrooms, chop them finely, and add them to the pan with the stock or water. Cover with a tight-fitting lid and cook gently for the calculated cooking time. Transfer the cooked meat to a warmed dish and keep hot.

Rub the contents of the pan through a fine sieve to make a purée. Return the purée to the pan and boil briskly for 5 minutes. Slice the meat, place it in a shallow serving dish and pour the sauce over it.

Braised Brisket of Beef

10–12 helpings

1.25–1.5kg brisket of beef	25g dripping

Mirepoix

1 large carrot (100g approx)	25g streaky bacon, without rinds
1 small turnip (50g approx)	bouquet garni
1 large onion (200g approx) **or** 15 button onions	salt and pepper
2 sticks celery (100g approx)	125–150ml general household **or** brown stock (p329)

Gravy

1–2 × 15ml spoons dripping **or** oil	1 × 5ml spoon concentrated tomato purée
1 × 5ml spoon plain flour	
375ml general household **or** brown (p329) stock	

Wipe, trim, and tie the meat into a neat shape if necessary. Heat the dripping in a large stewpan. Put in the meat and brown it on all sides. Put the meat to one side.

Prepare the vegetables for the mirepoix and slice them thickly. Chop the bacon and cook in the stewpan until the fat runs. Add the vegetables and fry gently. Add the bouquet garni and season with salt and pepper. Place the meat on top of the mirepoix and pour the stock over it. Cover with a tight-fitting lid and cook over gentle heat for 2 hours, or until the meat is tender. Baste occasionally and add more stock if necessary. Alternatively, cook in a warm oven, 160°C, Gas 3, for 2 hours or until tender.

Meanwhile, prepare the gravy. Heat the dripping or oil in a saucepan. Stir in the flour, and cook gently until the roux is lightly browned. Add extra dripping or oil, if necessary. Gradually add the stock, then the tomato purée, and stir until boiling. Reduce the heat and simmer, uncovered, for 15–20 minutes.

When cooked, transfer the meat to a warmed serving dish, remove the string and keep hot. Add any stock left in the stewpan to the gravy, or reserve for cooking other vegetables (see Braised Beef with Peppers p494). Garnish the meat with some of the vegetables from the mirepoix. Serve the gravy separately.

Paupiettes of Beef

4 helpings

500g rump **or** chuck steak	½ small turnip (25g approx)
150g beef **or** pork sausage-meat	125–250ml general household **or** brown stock (p329)
salt and pepper	bouquet garni
3 × 15ml spoons dripping	500ml Fresh Tomato (p715) **or** foundation brown (p698) sauce
1 large onion (200g approx)	
1 large carrot (100g approx)	

Wipe the steak and trim off any excess fat. Cut the meat into 4 slices measuring 5 × 12cm (approx). Mince or chop the trimmings finely, and mix with the sausage-meat. Season the beef slices with salt and pepper, and spread with the sausage-meat mixture. Roll up the beef slices and tie them securely with fine string or cotton. Heat the dripping in a large saucepan and fry the beef rolls, turning them frequently until browned. Transfer to a warmed dish and keep hot. Reserve the fat in the pan.

Prepare and slice the onion, carrot, and turnip. Fry the vegetables gently in the hot fat until just beginning to brown. Add just enough stock to cover the vegetables, and add the bouquet garni. Place the beef rolls on top and cover with a tight-fitting lid. Cook over gentle heat for 1½ hours, basting and adding more stock if necessary; or cook in a moderate oven, 180°C, Gas 4, for 1½ hours, removing the lid for the last 20 minutes of cooking time. Remove the strings from the beef rolls and place the rolls on a warmed serving dish. Pour some of the tomato or brown sauce round the rolls and serve the rest separately.

Serve with Savoury Rice (p863).

Beef Olives(1)

4 helpings

500g rump **or** chuck
  steak
100g basic herb stuffing
  (p375)
3 × 15ml spoons
  dripping
1 large onion
  (200g approx)
3 × 15ml spoons plain
  flour

625ml general household
  or brown stock (p329)
1 tomato
1 medium-sized carrot
  (50g approx)
1 × 15ml spoon
  Worcestershire sauce
salt and pepper

Wipe, trim, and flatten the slices of meat with a cutlet bat or rolling-pin. Cut the meat into 4 slices. Divide the stuffing into 4 portions. Spread 1 portion on each slice of meat, roll up tightly and tie securely with fine string or cotton.

Heat the dripping in a large saucepan and fry the beef olives, turning them frequently until browned. Transfer to a warmed dish and keep hot. Skin and slice the onion, and fry in the fat until golden-brown. Remove with a perforated spoon and keep hot with the beef olives. Add the flour to the fat, stir, and cook until golden-brown. Draw the pan off the heat and gradually stir in the stock. Return to the heat and stir until boiling, then reduce the heat and simmer for 5 minutes. Skin the tomato, scrape the carrot, and slice them. Return the beef olives and onion to the pan. Add the tomato, carrot, Worcestershire sauce, and seasoning to taste. Cover the pan with a tight-fitting lid and simmer for 1½–2 hours; or cook in a moderate oven, 180°C, Gas 4, for 1½ hours.

Remove the strings from the beef olives, and serve the meat arranged in a row on a bed of mashed potatoes. Strain the sauce and pour it over the beef olives.

Note For Beef Olives (2), see p497.

Braised Beef with Peppers

6 helpings

1kg topside **or** brisket of
  beef

25g dripping

Mirepoix

25g streaky bacon,
  without rinds
1 large carrot (100g
  approx)
1 small turnip (50g
  approx)
18 button onions
  (150–200g approx)
2 sticks celery (100g
  approx)

2 leeks (200g approx)
bouquet garni
salt
6 black peppercorns
125–250ml general
  household **or** brown
  stock (p329)

Gravy

1 × 15ml spoon oil **or**
  dripping
1 × 10ml spoon plain
  flour
250ml general household
  or brown stock (p329)

1 × 5ml spoon
  concentrated tomato
  purée

Garnish

3 green **or** red peppers
  (125g each approx)

12 small black olives
  (optional)

Follow the recipe for Braised Brisket of Beef (p493) to the point where the meat is cooked and the gravy prepared. Take out the meat and reserve the braising liquid. Put the meat on a board, remove the string, and carve the meat into neat slices. Arrange the slices in an overlapping row on a warmed serving dish, cover with foil and keep hot.

Remove the membranes and seeds from the peppers, and slice the flesh lengthways into strips 5mm–1cm wide. Simmer the strips in the reserved stock for 10 minutes. Garnish the meat with the pepper strips, button onions from the mirepoix, and the black olives if used. Pour the gravy over the slices, and serve at once.

German Braised Beef

4–6 helpings

1kg topside of beef
50g unsalted butter
salt

1 × 15ml spoon flour
125ml soured cream

Marinade
1 medium-sized onion
4 black peppercorns
2 cloves
1 bay leaf
1 × 5ml spoon caster
  sugar

salt and pepper
250ml red **or** white wine
  vinegar
375ml water

Wipe, trim, and tie the meat into a neat round shape and put it into a large bowl.

Make the marinade. Skin and slice the onion and add it to the meat, together with the peppercorns, cloves, bay leaf, sugar, and seasoning to taste. Mix the vinegar and water and pour it over the meat. Cover, and leave in a cold place for 2 days, turning the meat twice a day.

Remove the meat from the marinade and drain thoroughly. Reserve the marinade. Heat the butter in a deep pan, add the meat, and brown it quickly all over. Season to taste with salt, and strain 250ml of the marinade over the dish. Cover the pan with a tight-fitting lid and simmer over low heat for 1½ hours or until the meat is tender. Add a little extra strained marinade if required. Transfer the meat to a warmed dish and keep hot.

Strain 250ml of the cooking liquid through a fine sieve into a pan, making it up with extra strained marinade if required. Mix the flour to a smooth paste with a little water and stir it into the gravy. Heat to boiling point, stirring all the time. Re-season if required and stir in the soured cream. Slice the meat, pour a little of the sauce over it and serve the rest separately.

Serve with boiled potatoes, dumplings or boiled noodles.

CASSEROLED AND STEWED DISHES

Carbonnade of Beef

Basic recipe

6 helpings

700g stewing steak
  (chuck, blade, skirt **or**
  thin flank)
50g dripping
2 large onions (400g
  approx)
1 clove of garlic
1 × 15ml spoon plain
  flour
250ml beef stock **or**
  water
375ml brown ale
salt and pepper

bouquet garni
a pinch of grated nutmeg
a pinch of light soft
  brown sugar
1 × 5ml spoon red wine
  vinegar
6 thin slices from a
  French bâton loaf
1 × 15ml spoon French
  mustard **or** 1 × 15ml
  spoon English mustard
  mixed with vinegar to
  taste

Wipe the meat and trim off any excess fat. Cut the meat into 3–4cm cubes. Heat the dripping in a large pan. Fry the meat quickly until browned on all sides. Transfer to a casserole and keep warm. Skin and slice the onions and fry them in the fat in the pan until lightly browned. Skin and crush the garlic, add it to the onions and fry gently for 1 minute. Pour off any excess fat. Sprinkle the flour over the onion and garlic and cook, stirring until just beginning to brown. Gradually stir in the stock or water, and the ale. Add the salt and pepper, bouquet garni, nutmeg, sugar, and vinegar. Heat to boiling point and pour the liquid over the meat in the casserole. Cover, and cook in a warm oven, 160°C, Gas 3, for 1½–2 hours.

When cooked, remove the bouquet garni, spread the slices of bread with mustard, and press them well down into the gravy. Return the casserole, uncovered, to the oven, for about 15 minutes to allow the bread to brown slightly. Serve from the casserole.

Curried Beef

6 helpings

700g chuck steak
65g butter, lard **or**
 dripping
1 large onion (200g
 approx)
1 cooking apple (150g
 approx)
2 × 5ml spoons curry
 powder
1 × 15ml spoon plain
 flour

750ml brown stock
 (p329) **or** coconut
 infusion (p331)
2 × 5ml spoons curry
 paste
2 × 5ml spoons mango
 chutney
salt and pepper
juice of ½ lemon
1 × 5ml spoon brown
 sugar (optional)
300g Patna rice

Garnish
6 small gherkins

Wipe the meat and trim off any excess fat. Cut the meat into 2cm cubes. Heat the fat in a large pan and fry the meat lightly, turning to brown all sides. Transfer to a warmed dish and keep hot, leaving the fat in the pan. Prepare and chop the onion and apple. Fry them in the fat until the onion is golden-brown. Add the curry powder and flour, and fry gently, stirring all the time, for 1 minute. Draw the pan off the heat and quickly stir in the stock or coconut infusion, the curry paste, mango chutney, and salt and pepper to taste. Return to the heat and stir until simmering. Return the meat to the pan, half cover, and simmer gently for 1½–2 hours. Add the lemon juice and sugar, if used, and re-season if required.

Meanwhile, boil the rice in salted water for 15–20 minutes until tender. Drain through a sieve and separate the grains by pouring boiling water over them. Arrange in a border on a warmed serving dish, and pour the curry into the middle. If preferred, the rice can be served separately. Garnish the curry with the gherkins.

Note Traditional accompaniments for curries can be found on p388.

Hot Beef Pie

6 helpings

700g stewing steak
 (chuck, blade **or** neck)
3 medium-sized onions
 (300g approx)
3 large carrots (300g
 approx)

1kg potatoes
salt and pepper
beef stock **or** water as
 required

Wipe the meat and trim off any excess fat. Cut the meat into 2cm cubes. Prepare the vegetables. Slice the onions and carrots thinly, and cut the potatoes into slices about 5mm thick. Arrange the meat, onion, carrot, and potato slices in layers in a 2 litre casserole, finishing with a neat layer of potatoes. Season with salt and pepper. Three-quarters cover the meat and vegetables with stock or water (add more during cooking if the dish seems dry). Cover the pan with a tight-fitting lid and cook in a warm oven, 160°C, Gas 3, for 2 hours.

Uncover 30 minutes before the end of the cooking time to allow the top layer of potato to brown. Serve from the casserole.

Scotch Collops

6 helpings

700g stewing steak
 (chuck, blade, neck **or**
 shin)
50g dripping **or** lard
1 × 10ml spoon finely
 chopped onion **or**
 shallot
1 × 10ml spoon plain
 flour

250ml beef stock
salt and pepper
1–2 drops gravy
 browning
1 × 5ml spoon
 Worcestershire sauce
 or mushroom ketchup

Garnish
sippets of toast

1 × 10ml spoon chopped
 parsley

Wipe the meat and trim off any excess fat. Cut the meat into 1cm cubes. Heat the dripping or lard in a stewpan. Add the onion or shallot and fry gently until softened but not browned. Stir in the flour, and cook for about 5 minutes, stirring all the time.

Gradually add the stock, then the seasoning, gravy browning, sauce or ketchup, and the meat. Heat slowly to boiling point, stirring all the time. Reduce the heat to simmering point, cover the pan, and simmer slowly for 1 hour or until the meat is tender. Re-season if required; then pour the meat and its sauce into a warmed serving dish. Garnish with sippets of toast and chopped parsley.

Mock Hare

4 helpings

500g chuck steak **or** *neck* **or** *shin of beef*
100g fairly fat bacon, without rinds
2 × 15ml spoons plain flour
1 × 2.5ml spoon salt
½ × 2.5ml spoon ground pepper
1 medium-sized onion (100g approx)
3 cloves

375ml general household **or** *brown stock* (p329)
bouquet garni
1 × 15ml spoon redcurrant jelly
4 × 15ml spoons port (optional)
1 × 10ml spoon chopped pickled gherkins **or** *mixed pickled vegetables*
salt and pepper

Garnish
8 fried **or** *baked basic herb forcemeat balls* (pp375–76)

1 × 15ml spoon chopped parsley

Wipe the meat and trim off any excess fat. Cut the meat into 2cm cubes. Cut the bacon into 1cm cubes, and fry in a large flameproof casserole until the fat runs; then remove the bacon. Season the flour with salt and pepper, and toss the meat in it. Fry the floured meat in the bacon fat, turning it until evenly browned. Skin the onion and press the cloves into it. Add to the casserole with the stock and bouquet garni. Heat to boiling point, reduce the heat, cover with a lid, and simmer for 1½–2 hours until tender. Remove the onion and bouquet garni. Add the redcurrant jelly, port, if used, and the pickle. Simmer, uncovered, until the jelly melts. Re-season if required. Serve the beef from the casserole, garnished with forcemeat balls and parsley.

Beef Olives (2)
(Coolgardie Beef Olives)

4 helpings

750g rump steak
2 hard-boiled eggs
1 medium-sized onion
2 × 15ml spoons plain flour
salt and Cayenne pepper
1 egg
200g streaky bacon, without rinds

flour for dredging
fat **or** *oil for browning*
400g canned **or** *fresh tomatoes*
juice of 1 lemon
500ml beef stock **or** *water*

Wipe the steak and trim off any excess fat. Cut the meat into 8 thin slices, 12cm long. Chop the hard-boiled eggs. Skin and chop the onion. Mix the egg and onion with the flour and season with salt and Cayenne pepper to taste. Beat the egg until liquid and mix it into the hard-boiled egg mixture. Cut each rasher into 7cm lengths. Roll a 5ml spoonful of the egg mixture in each strip of bacon, making sausage or cork shapes, and then roll each bacon 'sausage' in one of the slices of steak. Secure with a small skewer or toothpick. Dredge with flour.

Heat enough fat or oil to cover the bottom of a frying pan, then add the beef olives. Fry gently turning frequently, until browned all over. Drain the canned tomatoes, or skin and slice the fresh ones. Transfer the beef olives to a casserole and add the tomatoes, lemon juice, and stock or water. Cook in a moderate oven, 180°C, Gas 4, for 2 hours. Remove the skewers or toothpicks from the cooked beef olives.

Serve with a macédoine of vegetables and creamed potatoes.

Note For Beef Olives (1), see p494.

Brown Stew

6 helpings

*700g stewing steak
(chuck, blade or neck)
1 large onion (200g
approx)
2 large carrots (200g
approx)
1 large turnip (100g
approx)*

*25g dripping
3 × 15ml spoons plain
flour
750ml general household
or brown stock (p329)
or water
salt and pepper
bouquet garni*

Wipe the meat and trim off any excess fat. Cut the meat into neat pieces 2–3cm thick. Prepare the vegetables; then slice the onion and carrots, and dice the turnip.

Heat the dripping in a stewpan. Put in the meat, and fry quickly until browned on all sides. Take the meat out of the pan, and put in the onion. Reduce the heat, and fry the onion gently until lightly browned. Stir in the flour and cook slowly until it turns a rich brown colour. Gradually add the stock or water, and heat to boiling point, stirring all the time. Add the seasoning and bouquet garni. Return the meat to the pan, cover with a tight-fitting lid, and simmer for 1½ hours. Skim off any fat on the surface. Add the carrot and turnip, replace the lid and simmer for another hour or until the meat and vegetables are tender. Again skim off any fat. Re-season if required, and remove the bouquet garni before serving.

Note If preferred, the stew can be cooked in a warm oven, 160°C, Gas 3, for 1½–2 hours. Add the carrots and turnip for the last hour of cooking.

Exeter Stew

6 helpings

*700g chuck steak or
blade or neck of beef
3 × 10ml spoons
dripping
3 medium-sized onions
(300g approx)*

*3 × 15ml spoons plain
flour
625ml water
1 × 5ml spoon vinegar
salt and pepper*

Savoury Parsley Balls
*100g plain flour
½ × 2.5ml spoon baking
powder
4¼ × 15ml spoons
shredded suet
1 × 15ml spoon finely
chopped parsley*

*1 × 2.5ml spoon dried
mixed herbs
1 × 5ml spoon salt
1 × 2.5ml spoon ground
pepper
1 egg or 3 × 15ml
spoons milk*

Wipe the meat and trim off any excess fat. Cut the meat into 5cm cubes. Heat the dripping in a stewpan and fry the meat in it until browned on all sides. Remove the meat and put to one side. Skin and slice the onions. Put them in the pan, and fry gently until light brown. Add the flour, and cook, stirring until browned. Mix in the water and stir until boiling. Reduce the heat to simmering point. Add the vinegar and seasoning to taste. Return the meat, cover the pan, and simmer gently for 1½ hours.

To make the parsley balls, sift the flour and baking powder into a bowl. Add the suet, herbs, salt and pepper, and mix together. Beat the egg, if used, until liquid and bind the dry ingredients together with the beaten egg or milk to form a stiff dough. Divide the dough into 12 equal pieces and roll each into a ball.

Heat the stew to boiling point and drop in the balls. Reduce the heat and simmer for a further 30 minutes with the pan half-covered. Pile the meat in the centre of a warmed serving dish, pour the gravy over it and arrange the balls neatly round the base.

Leg of Beef Stew

6 helpings

700g leg **or** shin of beef	1 small turnip
2 ×15ml spoons	(50g approx)
vinegar	bouquet garni
2 small onions	1 × 5ml spoon salt
(100g approx)	1 × 2.5ml spoon ground
2 small carrots	pepper
(50g approx)	

Wipe the meat and trim off any excess fat. Remove the meat from the bones, if necessary. Keep the bones. Cut the meat into neat pieces, 2–3cm thick. Put them into a casserole with the vinegar and leave for about 1 hour; turn them over 2 or 3 times while steeping. Prepare the vegetables and chop or slice them roughly. Add to the meat with the bouquet garni, salt and pepper. Pour over just enough water to cover the meat. Add any bones which may have been cut out of the meat. Cover the casserole with a tight-fitting lid and cook in a warm oven, 160°C, Gas 3, for 2½–3 hours, until the meat is tender.

Before serving, remove the bouquet garni and bones, and serve hot with freshly cooked vegetables.

Beef Creole

6–8 helpings

1kg topside **or** rump **or**	500g onions
brisket of beef	500g tomatoes
1 × 5ml spoon salt	1 green pepper (125g
1 × 5ml spoon ground	approx)
pepper	a little beef stock **or**
75g streaky bacon,	water (optional)
without rinds	

Wipe, trim, and tie the meat into a neat shape, if necessary. Season with salt and pepper. Lay the rashers in the bottom of an ovenproof casserole. Place the meat on the bacon. Skin and slice the onions and tomatoes. De-seed and slice the pepper. Cover the meat with the vegetables. Cover the casserole with a tight-fitting lid and cook in a warm oven, 160°C, Gas 3, for about 2½ hours, until the meat is tender. Lift out the meat, remove the string, and cut the meat into slices. Arrange the slices on a warmed serving dish and keep hot.

Rub the onions, tomatoes, and pepper through a sieve into a saucepan and re-heat to form a sauce, thinning with a little stock or water, if necessary. Pour the sauce round the beef slices.

Beef Creole with Chillies

6 helpings

4 rashers back **or**	salt and pepper
streaky bacon, without	2 small chilli peppers
rinds	600g onions
1kg rump steak	600g tomatoes

Lay the rashers in the bottom of an ovenproof casserole. Wipe the meat and trim off any excess fat. Place the beef on top of the bacon and season lightly with salt and pepper. Chop the chilli peppers very finely and sprinkle them over the meat. Skin and slice the onions and tomatoes, and put them on top of the beef. Cover with foil and a tight-fitting lid and cook in a warm oven, 160°C, Gas 3, for 3½–4 hours.

Note No extra fat or water is used for this recipe; the meat cooks in its own juices and the tomato and onion juice.

Beef Stroganoff

See p1446 for Beef Stroganoff cooked at the table and p1552 for Beef Stroganoff cooked in the kitchen.

Beef Goulash

6 helpings

700g chuck steak **or** *blade of beef*	*200g fresh* **or** *canned tomatoes*
2 medium-sized onions (200g approx)	*1 × 2.5ml spoon salt*
	1 × 15ml spoon paprika
50g dripping	*bouquet garni*
40g flour	*500g potatoes*
3 × 15ml spoons brown stock (p329)	*2 × 15ml spoons soured cream (optional)*
125ml red wine (optional)	

Wipe the meat and trim off any excess fat. Cut the meat into 2cm cubes. Skin and slice the onions. Heat the dripping in a stewpan and fry the meat in it until browned on all sides. Remove the meat from the pan. Add the onions to the pan and fry gently until just beginning to brown. Add the flour, and cook, stirring until browned. Draw the pan off the heat and gradually stir in the stock, and the wine, if used. Skin and dice the fresh tomatoes, if used, or chop the canned tomatoes roughly. Add the tomatoes, salt, paprika, and bouquet garni to the pan. Return the pan to the heat and stir until boiling. Reduce the heat to simmering point, cover, and cook gently for 1½–2 hours, until the meat is tender. Alternatively, transfer the goulash to a casserole and cook in a warm oven, 160°C, Gas 3, for 1½–2 hours.

Meanwhile, prepare and cut the potatoes into 2cm cubes. Add to the goulash for the last 30 minutes of the cooking time. They should be cooked but not broken. Remove the bouquet garni. Stir in the soured cream, if used, just before serving.

BOILED DISHES

Boiled Beef with Vegetables and Dumplings

Basic recipe

8–10 helpings

1–1.25kg brisket **or** *silverside* **or** *aitchbone of beef*	*bouquet garni*
	3 medium-sized onions (300g approx)
1 × 5ml spoon salt	*4 large carrots (400g approx)*
3 cloves	
10 peppercorns	*2 small turnips (100g approx)*

Suet Dumplings

200g self-raising flour	*½ × 2.5ml spoon salt*
100g suet	

Weigh the meat and calculate the cooking time, allowing 25 minutes per 0.5kg plus 20 minutes over. Wipe, trim, and tie the meat into a neat shape with string, if necessary. Put the meat into a large stewpan, cover with boiling water, and add the salt. Bring to the boil again and boil for 5 minutes to seal the surface of the meat. Reduce the heat to simmering point, and skim. Add the cloves, peppercorns, and bouquet garni. Cover the pan and simmer for the rest of the calculated cooking time.

Meanwhile, prepare the vegetables and cut them into serving-sized pieces. About 45 minutes before the end of the cooking time, add the vegetables to the meat and re-heat to simmering point.

Prepare the dumplings. Mix the flour, suet, and salt in a bowl. Add enough cold water to make a fairly stiff dough. Divide this mixture into walnut-sized pieces and roll them into balls. Drop them into the pan with the beef, so that they simmer for the final 20–30 minutes of the cooking time. Keep the pan covered and turn the dumplings over once during this time.

To serve, remove the bouquet garni. Take out the dumplings and vegetables with a perforated spoon, and arrange them as a border on a large warmed serving dish. Remove any strings from the meat, skewer if necessary, and set it in the centre of the dish. Serve some of the liquid separately in a sauce-boat.

Note When adding the dumplings, make sure they have plenty of room to swell. If the pan is very full, it is better to cook them separately in stock.

For other dumpling recipes, see pp386–87.

Boiled Brisket of Beef(1)

10–12 helpings

1.25–1.5kg boned and
  rolled brisket of beef
1 × 15ml spoon vinegar
1 × 5ml spoon salt
2 medium-sized carrots
  (100g approx)
2 medium-sized onions
  (200g approx)

1 turnip (100g approx)
2–3 sticks celery (150g
  approx) (optional)
1 blade of mace
10 black peppercorns
bouquet garni

Sauce
25g butter **or**
  dripping

25g plain flour
salt and pepper

Wipe the meat. Mix the vinegar with 1 × 2.5ml spoon salt, rub it over the meat and leave for 2–3 hours. Put the meat in a stewpan, just cover with water, add 1 × 2.5ml spoon salt, heat to boiling point, and skim well. Reduce the heat to simmering point, cover the pan with a tight-fitting lid, and simmer gently for 30 minutes.

Meanwhile, prepare the vegetables and cut them into thick slices. Add to the pan at the end of the 30 minutes, together with the mace, peppercorns, and bouquet garni. Re-heat to simmering point, replace the lid and simmer very gently for another 2 hours. When cooked, take the meat and the vegetables out of the pan, transfer them to a warmed serving dish, and keep hot.

Make the sauce. Strain the stock left in the pan and make it up to 375ml with water if necessary. Melt the butter or dripping in a small saucepan. Stir in the flour and cook gently until browned. Draw the pan off the heat and gradually stir the stock into the roux. Return to the heat, bring to the boil, stirring all the time, and boil for 2–3 minutes. Season to taste with salt and pepper. Serve the

vegetables with the meat, and offer the sauce in a sauce-boat.

Boiled Brisket of Beef(2)

10–12 helpings

1.25–1.5kg boned and
  rolled brisket of beef
150g streaky bacon,
  without rinds
2 medium-sized onions
  (200g approx)
bouquet garni

2 cloves
1 blade of mace
4 allspice berries
10 black peppercorns
brown stock (p329) **or**
  water to cover

Sauce
25g butter **or** dripping
25g plain flour

salt and pepper

Garnish
2 medium-sized carrots,
  diced and cooked (100g
  approx)

Wipe the meat. Cover the bottom of a stewpan with half the bacon rashers. Place the meat on them and lay the remaining rashers on top of the meat. Skin and slice the onions thickly. Add the onions, bouquet garni, spices, and peppercorns to the stewpan and just enough stock or water to cover. Heat to boiling point and skim well. Reduce the heat to simmering point, cover the pan with a tight-fitting lid, and cook very gently for 2½ hours. Add more boiling stock or water during cooking, if necessary. When cooked, take the meat out of the pan and place it on a warmed serving dish. Remove any strings and keep the meat hot.

Make the sauce as for Boiled Brisket of Beef (1) above. Garnish the meat with the diced, cooked carrots, and serve the sauce separately in a sauce-boat.

PIES AND PUDDINGS

Mrs Beeton's Steak Pie

6 helpings

*600g lean stewing steak
(chuck, blade or neck)*
*3 × 15ml spoons plain
flour*
1 × 5ml spoon salt
*¼ × 2.5ml spoon ground
pepper*
*2 medium-sized onions
(200g approx)*
*250ml beef stock or
water (approx)*

*flaky or rough puff
pastry (p1252) using
100g flour or
shortcrust pastry
(p1249) using 200g flour
flour for rolling out
beaten egg or milk for
glazing*

Wipe the meat and trim off any excess fat. Cut the meat into 1–2cm cubes. Mix the flour with the salt and pepper in a bag or deep bowl. Toss the cubes of meat in the seasoned flour and put them in a 1 litre pie dish, piling them higher in the centre. Skin and chop the onions, and sprinkle them between the pieces of meat. Pour in stock or water to quarter-fill the dish.

Roll out the pastry on a lightly floured surface and use to cover the dish. Trim the edge, knock up with the back of a knife and flute the edge. Make a small hole in the centre of the lid, and decorate round with leaves of pastry. Make a pastry tassel or rose to cover the hole after baking, if liked. Brush the pastry with the beaten egg or milk.

Bake the pie in a very hot oven, 230°C, Gas 8, until the pastry is risen and light brown. Bake the tassel or rose blind, if made. Reduce the oven heat to moderate, 180°C, Gas 4, and, if necessary, place the pie on a lower shelf. Cover with greaseproof paper to prevent the pastry over-browning, and continue cooking for about 2 hours until the meat is quite tender when tested with a skewer. Heat the remaining stock and pour in enough to fill the dish by funnelling it through the hole in the pastry. Insert the pastry tassel or rose, if made, and serve.

VARIATIONS

Steak and Kidney Pie

Follow the recipe for Steak Pie, but add 2 sheep's or 150g ox kidneys. Skin, core, and cut the kidneys into slices before mixing with the steak and onions.

Steak and Mushroom Pie

Follow the recipe for Steak Pie, but add 100g mushrooms, cleaned and sliced, to the meat in the pie dish.

Steak and Oyster Pie

Follow the recipe for Steak Pie but add 12 fresh or canned oysters to the ingredients and slice the steak thinly instead of cubing it. Open the fresh oysters (p426), if used, and reserve the oyster liquor. (This liquor can be heated, seasoned, strained and added to the pie just before it is served.) Place an oyster on each slice of meat and roll up tightly. Place the rolls on end in the pie dish. Proceed as for Steak Pie.

Steak and Potato Pie

Follow the recipe for Steak Pie, but add about 300g potatoes. Slice the meat and dip in seasoned flour. Prepare and slice the potatoes thinly. Place a layer of sliced potatoes on the bottom of the pie dish, season, and cover with a layer of meat. Add a little of the chopped onion. Repeat the layers of potato, meat, onion, and seasoning until the dish is full. Add enough stock or water to fill one-third of the dish. Proceed as for Steak Pie.

Steak Pudding

6 helpings

600g stewing steak
  (chuck, blade **or**
  neck)
3 × 15ml spoons plain
  flour
1 × 5ml spoon salt
¼ × 2.5ml spoon ground
  pepper

suet crust pastry (p1250)
  using 200g flour
flour for rolling out
fat for greasing
3 × 15ml spoons beef
  stock **or** water

Wipe the meat and trim off any excess fat. Cut the meat into 1cm cubes. Mix the flour with the salt and pepper in a bag or deep bowl. Toss the cubes of meat in the seasoned flour.

Reserve one-quarter of the pastry for the lid. Roll out the rest on a lightly floured surface so that it is 1cm larger than the top of a greased 750ml basin, and 5mm thick. Press well into the basin to remove any creases. Half fill the basin with the prepared meat and add the stock or water; then add the rest of the meat. Roll out the pastry reserved for the lid to fit the top of the basin. Dampen the edges, place the lid in position, and seal. Cover with greased greaseproof paper or foil.

Place the basin in a steamer, or on a saucer in a pan with water coming half-way up the basin's sides. Steam, or half-steam, for 3–3½ hours, topping up the steamer or pan with boiling water when it is reduced by a third. Serve from the basin or turn out on to a warmed serving dish. Serve with a thin beef gravy.

VARIATION

Steak and Kidney Pudding (1)

Follow the recipe for Steak Pudding, but add 2 sheep's kidneys or 150g ox kidney. Cut the meat into thin slices about 8 × 5cm. Dip them in the seasoned flour. Skin, core, and cut the kidneys into thin slices a little smaller than the meat. Dip them in the seasoned flour. Place a slice of kidney on each slice of meat, roll up tightly, and place the rolls on end in the pastry-lined basin. Proceed as for Steak Pudding.

Note For Steak and Kidney Pudding (2), see p1430.

Cornish Pasties (1)

Makes 6

300g chuck steak **or**
  blade of beef
1 large potato (150g
  approx)
1 small onion (50g
  approx)
salt and pepper

2 × 15ml spoons water
  or beef stock
shortcrust pastry
  (p1249) using 200g
  flour
flour for rolling out
beaten egg **or** milk for
  glazing (optional)

Wipe the meat and trim off any excess fat. Cut the meat into 5mm dice. Prepare and dice the potato; skin and chop the onion finely. Mix together the meat, potato, onion, and add seasoning to taste. Add the water or stock to moisten.

Divide the pastry into 6 portions. Roll each portion on a lightly floured surface into a circle 12–14cm in diameter (approx). Trim the edges neatly. (A saucer or small plate can be used to cut the rounds.) Divide the meat filling into 6 portions and pile one portion on one half of each circle of pastry. Dampen the edges of the pastry and fold over to cover the mixture. Press the edges of the pastry together. Turn the pasties so that the sealed edges are on the top. Flute the sealed edges with the fingers. Brush with beaten egg or milk, if liked. Place the pasties on a baking tray. Bake in a hot oven, 220°C, Gas 7, for about 10 minutes, then reduce the heat to moderate, 180°C, Gas 4, and cook for 30–40 minutes.

Note See also Cornish Pasties (2) (p1305) and Cornish Pasties (3) (p1472).

Steak and Kidney Batter Pudding

6 helpings

600g lean rump **or** *chuck steak*	*2 eggs*
200g ox kidney	*400ml milk* **or** *water*
3 × 10ml spoons dripping	*175g plain flour*
	salt and pepper

Wipe the meat and trim off any excess fat. Cut the meat into oblong pieces. Skin, core, and cut the kidney into thin slices. Heat 2 × 10ml spoons of the dripping in a large pan or frying pan, and fry the steak, turning frequently, to seal the surface. Mix the eggs, milk or water, and flour into a smooth batter. Season the batter and the meat to taste.

Melt the remaining dripping in an oval or oblong-shaped ovenproof dish, casserole or pie dish. Pour in half the batter and bake in a hot oven, 220°C, Gas 7, for about 15 minutes until set. Remove from the oven, place the steak and kidney on top of the set batter, and pour the remaining batter over them. Return the dish or casserole to the oven and bake for 10 minutes; then reduce the heat to moderate, 180°C, Gas 4, for about 1 hour, until the batter is well-browned and the meat is tender when tested with a skewer.

Serve with a thin gravy.

Sea Pie (1)

6 helpings

600g stewing steak (chuck, blade **or** *neck)*	*1 large carrot (100g approx)*
3 × 15ml spoons plain flour	*2 small turnips (100g approx)*
2 × 5ml spoons salt	*brown stock* (p329) **or**
¼ × 2.5ml spoon ground pepper	*water to cover*
1 medium-sized onion (100g approx)	*suet crust pastry* (p1250) *using 200g flour*
	flour for rolling out

Wipe the meat and trim off any excess fat. Cut the meat into thin slices about 5cm square. Mix the flour with the salt and pepper in a bag or deep bowl. Toss the pieces of meat in the seasoned flour. Skin and slice the onion and dice the carrot and turnips. Put the meat and vegetables into a pan. Heat to boiling point just enough stock or water to cover the meat and vegetables and pour into the pan. Re-heat, cover with a tight-fitting lid, and simmer very gently for about 1½ hours.

Roll out the pastry on a lightly floured surface to a round a little smaller than the top of the stewpan. Place the pastry on top of the meat and vegetables. Cover with the pan lid and continue cooking for 1 hour. Cut the pastry into portions and serve with the meat.

Note For Sea Pie (2), see p1431.

MINCED DISHES

Minced Beef

Basic recipe

4–5 helpings

1 large onion (200g approx)	*1 × 15ml spoon chopped parsley* **or** *1 × 5ml spoon dried parsley*
1 clove of garlic	
2 × 15ml spoons oil	*a pinch of dried mixed herbs*
500g raw minced beef	
salt and pepper	*1 bay leaf*
250g canned tomatoes	

Skin and chop the onion and garlic. Heat the oil in a stewpan. Add the onion and garlic, and fry gently until softened. Add the minced meat and fry until browned, stirring all the time. Season, and add the tomatoes and herbs. Stir well, and heat to boiling point. Reduce the heat and simmer, uncovered, for about 30 minutes, stirring from time to time.

Serve with vegetables, pasta or rice, or use as a filling for green peppers, baked potatoes, etc.

Note Minced beef from the butcher may be prepared from coarse cuts and trimmings or from good quality braising or stewing steak. The price is often the only indication of the quality. If you want to be certain of the type of meat, buy the cut first, then ask the butcher to mince it, or mince it yourself.

Hamburgers

Basic recipe

4 helpings

500g raw blade **or** *chuck*   *coarse salt*
* steak, minced*   *4 × 5ml spoons butter*
2 × 5ml spoons grated   *Tabasco sauce*
* onion (optional)*   *Worcestershire sauce*
freshly ground black   *lemon juice*
* pepper*

Garnish
chopped parsley   *chopped chives*

Mix together the minced beef and onion, if used, and season with pepper. Shape the meat lightly into 4 flat round cakes about 1cm thick. Sprinkle a thin layer of salt in a cold frying pan. Place the frying pan over high heat and put in the patties. Cook for about 5 minutes until well browned underneath. Turn the patties over and cook to the degree of rareness wanted. For a rare hamburger, cook for 1–2 minutes only, lowering the heat to medium after 30 seconds. When cooked, top each patty with 1 × 5ml spoon butter, and sprinkle with Tabasco and Worcestershire sauce and lemon juice. Transfer to a warmed serving dish, pour any pan juices over them, and serve garnished with parsley and chives.

VARIATIONS

1) Add 1 × 2.5ml spoon salt, a pinch of paprika and 2 × 15ml spoons double cream to the meat mixture. Brush the pan lightly with melted bacon fat instead of using salt. Brown the patties on both sides over high heat, then reduce the heat and cook slowly as required.

2) Prepare the patties as for variation 1. Wrap each in a rasher of bacon secured with a toothpick before cooking.

3) After cooking the patties as for the basic recipe, transfer them to a warmed serving dish but omit the sauces and lemon juice. Instead, add to the pan 50ml red wine or soured cream or 2 × 15ml spoons sherry or brandy; swill round, scraping up the pan juices, and pour the sauce over the patties.

4) Prepare the patties as for the basic recipe. Brush them lightly with melted butter, then grill under high heat for 5 minutes. Lower the heat and cook the second side for 1–2 minutes, or longer for well-done patties. Season and garnish as for the basic recipe.

5) Prepare and cook the patties and serve on buttered toast seasoned with the pan juices.

6) Garnish each cooked hamburger with a fried onion ring and 1 × 5ml spoon tomato ketchup or chutney instead of parsley and chives.

7) Split 4 round soft dinner rolls in half horizontally. Prepare the patties as for the basic recipe, brush lightly with butter, then grill them on one side only. Place them on the bottom halves of the rolls, cooked side down, then grill the second side. Top each with a fried onion ring and 1 × 5ml spoon tomato ketchup or chutney and replace the top halves of the rolls.

8) Add a few sprigs of watercress or a small lettuce leaf to the onion and tomato ketchup topping in variations 7 and 8.

9) Substitute raw onion rings and raw tomato slices for the fried onion rings and ketchup or chutney in variation 7.

10) Mix together the minced beef with 50g finely chopped onion, 50g soft white breadcrumbs, 100ml milk, salt and pepper. Form it into 6 patties, then fry as for variation 1.

Vienna Steaks

6 helpings

700g raw rump steak
  or any lean stewing
  steak, minced
1 × 5ml spoon chopped
  parsley
1 × 5ml spoon dried
  mixed herbs
a little grated nutmeg

salt and pepper
2 eggs
1 × 15ml spoon plain
  flour for dredging
75g butter **or** dripping
  or 75ml oil
250–350ml Espagnole
  sauce (p707)

Garnish
2 medium-sized onions
  (200g approx)

flour for coating

Put the meat into a bowl. Add the herbs, nutmeg, and salt and pepper to taste, and mix well. Separate one of the eggs, reserve the white, and add the yolk to the other egg. Beat the whole egg and yolk until liquid, add to the meat and mix well to bind the mixture. Divide the mixture into 6 portions and shape into round cakes 7cm in diameter. Dredge lightly with flour. Heat 25g of the fat or 25ml oil in a frying pan and fry the 'steaks' for about 7 minutes on each side or until cooked through; then drain. Transfer to a warmed serving dish and keep hot.

Skin the onions for the garnish, and slice them thinly. Separate the onion rings and coat them with flour. Whisk the remaining egg white until stiff. Dip the onion rings into the egg white and then again into the flour. Heat the remaining fat in the frying pan and fry the onion rings until golden-brown and crisp. Remove with a perforated spoon and drain on soft kitchen paper.

Serve the Vienna Steaks garnished with the onion rings. Serve the Espagnole Sauce separately.

Baked Minced Beef Loaf

4–6 helpings

1 medium-sized onion
  (50g approx)
1 clove of garlic
1 × 10ml spoon dripping
  or oil
500g raw chuck steak **or**
  blade **or** neck of beef,
  minced
50g white breadcrumbs
salt and pepper

1 × 15ml spoon chopped
  parsley
1 × 15ml spoon
  Worcestershire sauce
1 egg
milk
375–500ml Espagnole
  (p707) **or** Fresh
  Tomato (p715) sauce

Skin and chop the onion and garlic. Heat the dripping or oil in a pan and fry the onion and garlic gently until softened but not coloured. Mix together in a large bowl with the meat, breadcrumbs, seasoning, parsley, and Worcestershire sauce. Beat the egg until liquid and add to the meat mixture with enough milk to bind it well. Press into a 1kg loaf tin and cover with foil. Bake in a moderate oven, 180°C, Gas 4, for 1 hour or until cooked through. Turn out on to a warmed serving dish and serve with Espagnole Sauce or Fresh Tomato Sauce.

Collops of Minced Beef

6 helpings

1 large onion (200g
  approx)
2 × 15ml spoons oil
700g raw rump steak **or**
  any lean stewing steak,
  minced
2 × 10ml spoons plain
  flour

250ml brown stock
  (p329) **or** water
salt and pepper
1 × 15ml spoon lemon
  juice **or** vinegar **or**
  Worcestershire sauce

Garnish
toasted **or** fried bread
  croûtons

sprigs of parsley

Skin and chop the onion finely. Heat the oil in a small stewpan. Add the onion and fry until lightly browned. Add the minced meat and fry quickly until lightly browned, stirring all the time. Add the flour, stirring it in well, then stir in the stock or water. Add salt and pepper, lemon juice or vinegar or Worcestershire sauce, and continue to stir until boiling. Reduce the heat and simmer gently for about 30 minutes, stirring occasionally. Serve in a fairly deep meat dish, garnished with bread croûtons and sprigs of parsley.

Beef Cream Moulds

6–8 helpings

3 × 10ml spoons butter, margarine, dripping **or** oil
3 × 15ml spoons plain flour
200ml brown stock (p329)
700g raw chuck steak **or** blade of beef, minced
salt and pepper
2 eggs

1 × 5ml spoon Worcestershire sauce **or** mushroom ketchup
1 × 5ml spoon chopped parsley
4 × 15ml spoons single cream
fat for greasing
375ml Espagnole (p707) **or** Fresh Tomato (p715) sauce

Garnish
3 medium-sized carrots   100g green peas

Heat the fat in a large saucepan. Add the flour and cook gently for about 3 minutes, stirring all the time. Add the stock gradually and stir until boiling. Cook for 3 minutes. Remove from the heat and add the minced meat, salt and pepper to taste, eggs, and sauce or ketchup, and beat well. Pound until soft, then rub the mixture through a wire sieve into a bowl. Add the parsley and cream, and stir in lightly. Turn the mixture into a well-greased 1.5 litre ring mould or 12 well-greased dariole moulds, and cover with greased greaseproof paper. Steam gently until firm; the ring mould will need 45 minutes–1 hour, the dariole moulds about 30 minutes.

Meanwhile, cut very small ball shapes from the carrots with a small potato ball scoop. Cook the carrots and peas separately in boiling salted water until tender. Turn out the meat from the ring or dariole moulds on to a warmed serving dish. Coat with a little of the chosen sauce and garnish with the vegetables. Serve the rest of the sauce separately.

Meatballs in Spicy Sauce

4 helpings

1 small onion (50g approx)
1 small clove of garlic
400g raw minced beef
50g soft white breadcrumbs

2 × 15ml spoons chopped parsley
salt and pepper
2 eggs
3 × 15ml spoons cooking **or** olive oil

Spicy Sauce
2 × 15ml spoons oil
2 small onions (100g approx)
1 stick of celery
2 × 15ml spoons concentrated tomato purée

1 × 15ml Worcestershire sauce
Tabasco sauce
1 × 15ml spoon vinegar
1 × 5ml spoon made mustard
300ml water
salt and pepper

Make the sauce first. Heat the oil in a saucepan. Skin and chop the onions. Wash and chop the celery finely. Fry the onions and celery gently in the oil until softened. Add the tomato purée, and mix well. Stir in the Worcestershire and Tabasco sauces, the vinegar, mustard, and water. Season with salt and pepper. Heat to boiling point, reduce the heat, cover with a lid, and simmer for about 25 minutes.

Prepare the meat balls. Skin and chop the onion finely and skin and crush the garlic. Mix together the onion, garlic, meat, breadcrumbs, parsley, and seasoning. Beat the eggs until liquid and use to bind the meat mixture. Divide into 16 pieces and shape into balls. Heat the oil in a frying pan. Add the meat balls and fry, turning frequently, until browned all over. Drain the excess oil and fat from the pan. Pour in the spicy sauce, cover the pan with a tight-fitting lid, and cook for about 45 minutes.

Steak Tartare
See p1497.

Chilli con Carne

6 helpings

400g dried red kidney
  beans **or** *1 × 430g can*
  red kidney beans
1 large onion (200g
  approx)
1 clove of garlic
2 × 15ml spoons
  vegetable oil

750g raw minced beef
1 × 396g can tomatoes
1 × 10ml spoon chilli
  powder
salt and pepper

Soak the kidney beans, if used, overnight, then cook them gently in boiling salted water until tender. Drain and leave to cool. Skin the onion and chop it coarsely; skin the garlic and slice it thinly. Heat the oil in a large saucepan, add the onion and garlic, and cook until softened. Add the meat, break up any lumps with a fork, and stir until browned all over. Add the tomatoes, kidney beans, and chilli powder. Cover the pan with a lid, heat to simmering point and simmer for 2 hours. Season with salt and pepper to taste. For a spicier Chilli con Carne, add extra chilli powder. The mixture should be very thick. If possible, keep it for 24 hours before use to let the flavours blend and mellow; then re-heat.

Beef Galantine (1)

6–8 helpings

200g lean bacon,
  without rinds
500g chuck steak **or**
  blade of beef, minced
150g soft white **or**
  brown breadcrumbs
salt and pepper
1 egg

125ml brown stock
  (p329)
margarine **or** *lard for*
  greasing
2 × 15ml spoons
  raspings (p375) **or**
  1 × 15ml spoon meat
  glaze (p397)

Garnish
125ml chopped aspic
  jelly

Mince the bacon. Put into a bowl with the meat, breadcrumbs and seasoning to taste, and mix together well. Beat the egg until liquid, add the

stock, and stir into the meat mixture to bind. Shape the mixture into a short, thick roll, wrap it in greased greaseproof paper, wrap in a scalded pudding cloth, and secure the ends. Steam for $2\frac{1}{2}$–3 hours or, if preferred, boil gently in stock for about 2 hours.

When cooked, remove the meat, unwrap it, and then roll it up tightly in a clean dry cloth. Press the roll between 2 plates until cold. When cold, remove the cloth and roll the meat in the raspings, or brush all over with melted meat glaze. Garnish with aspic jelly.

Beef Galantine (2)

6–8 helpings

500g chuck steak **or**
  blade of beef, minced
250g beef **or** *pork*
  sausage-meat
50g soft white
  breadcrumbs
1 small onion (50g
  approx)
1 × 15ml spoon chopped
  parsley
a pinch of dried mixed
  herbs

a pinch each of mixed
  spice and ground mace
2 × 5ml spoons salt
$\frac{1}{2}$ × 2.5ml spoon ground
  pepper
2 eggs
2 × 15ml spoons
  raspings (p375) **or**
  1 × 15ml spoon meat
  glaze (p397)

Garnish
125ml chopped aspic
  jelly

Put the minced meat, sausage-meat, and breadcrumbs into a large bowl. Skin the onion and chop or mince it finely. Add to the meat with the herbs, spices, and seasoning. Beat the eggs until liquid, add to the meat mixture and mix well to bind. Continue as for the previous recipe.

Shepherd's Pie
(Cottage Pie)

4–6 helpings

600g lean beef mince	700g potatoes
2 medium-sized onions	a pinch of grated nutmeg
25g dripping	milk
1 × 15ml spoon flour	1–2 × 15ml spoons
150ml strong beef stock	butter (optional)
salt and freshly ground	butter for greasing
black pepper	

Break up any lumps in the meat with a fork. Skin and slice the onions. Melt the dripping in a saucepan, and fry the onions until softened but not coloured. Stir in the flour, and cook gently for 1–2 minutes, stirring all the time. Gradually add the stock, without letting lumps form, and stir until boiling. Reduce the heat, and simmer for 2–3 minutes until the sauce thickens. Stir in the mince, cover the pan, and simmer for 20 minutes. Season well, replace the lid, and simmer for 10 minutes longer or until the mince is cooked through and tender.

Meanwhile, prepare the potatoes and boil them in salted water until tender. Mash them until smooth with a seasoning of salt, pepper, nutmeg, enough milk to make them creamy, and butter, if liked. Put the meat and sauce into a greased pie dish or shallow oven-to-table baking dish. Cover with the potato, smooth the top, then flick it up into small peaks or score a pattern on the surface with a fork. Bake for 10–15 minutes in a hot oven, 220°C, Gas 7, until browned on top. Serve hot.

VARIATIONS

Spicy Shepherd's Pie

Add 3 × 2.5ml spoons curry powder with the flour, and 1 × 15ml spoon mango chutney with the salt and pepper.

Cheesy Shepherd's Pie

Mix 75g grated mild Cheddar cheese into the mashed potato before covering the pie, and sprinkle another 2 × 15ml spoons grated cheese over the potato just before baking.

OFFAL DISHES

Baked Stuffed Ox Heart

6 helpings

1 ox heart	50–75g dripping
150g sage and onion	25g flour
stuffing (p378) **or**	500ml strong general
basic herb **or** ham	household **or** brown
stuffing (p375)	stock (p329)

Wash the heart thoroughly under running water or in several changes of cold water. Cut off the flaps and lobes, and remove any gristle. Cut away the membranes which separate the cavities inside the heart and see that it is quite free from blood inside. Soak in cold water for 30 minutes. Drain and dry the heart thoroughly and fill it with the stuffing. Sew up the top with fine string or cotton, or skewer securely.

Heat the dripping in a roasting tin, and put in the heart. Baste well and bake in a warm oven, 160°C, Gas 3, for 3 hours. Baste frequently and turn it occasionally. When tender, remove the string, cotton or skewer, place the heart on a warmed serving dish and keep hot. Pour off most of the fat from the baking tin, retaining about 1 × 15ml spoon of the sediment. Stir in the flour and cook until browned. Gradually add the stock and stir until boiling. Boil for 3 minutes. Pour a little round the heart and serve the rest separately.

Serve redcurrant jelly with the heart if stuffed with basic herb stuffing; serve Cranberry or Boar's Head Sauce (p717) if it is stuffed with ham or sage and onion stuffing.

Mock Goose

8 helpings

1 ox **or** 2 calf's hearts
1.5 litres brown **or**
  general household stock
  (p329)
2 bay leaves

4 cloves
salt and pepper
dripping
2 × 15ml spoons flour

Stuffing

1 large onion
1 stick of celery
50g margarine
100g brown rice
125ml brown **or** general
  household stock (p329)
125ml medium-dry
  white wine **or** cider

1 cooking apple (150g
  approx)
6–8 finely chopped sage
  leaves
50g seedless raisins
salt and pepper

Prepare the heart(s) (p509). Put in a large flame-proof casserole with the stock, bay leaves, cloves, and seasoning to taste. Cover with a tight-fitting lid. Either heat gently to simmering point, or cook in a cool oven, 150°C, Gas 2, until tender. Cook an ox heart for $4\frac{1}{2}$ hours (approx), calf's hearts for $2\frac{1}{2}$ hours. Leave in the stock, covered, until tepid.

Meanwhile, make the stuffing. Prepare and chop the onion and celery. Melt the margarine in a large frying pan and sauté the onion and celery until softened but not browned. Stir in the rice, stock, and wine or cider. Cover, heat to simmering point, and simmer for 15 minutes. Meanwhile, peel and chop the apple, and mix with the sage and raisins. Remove the pan from the heat, stir in the apple, sage, raisins, and seasoning to taste. Leave until cool enough to handle.

Remove the heart(s) from the stock and wipe off any fat. Reserve 850ml of the stock. Fill the heart(s) with a little of the stuffing, leaving room for it to swell. Sew up or skewer the openings. Spread with dripping and wrap in foil. Make the remaining stuffing into 16–20 forcemeat balls (see p375).

Put the heart(s) and forcemeat balls into a baking tin with a little extra dripping, and bake in a fairly hot oven, 190°C, Gas 5, for 30 minutes. Remove the foil for the last 10 minutes of the baking time, and baste well.

Meanwhile, make the gravy. Melt 4 × 15ml spoons dripping in a saucepan. Stir in the flour and cook until lightly browned. Gradually add the reserved stock and stir until it simmers and the gravy thickens. Re-season if required.

Place the heart(s) on a warmed serving dish; calf's hearts should be placed with the openings facing each other. Remove the skewers or strings. Pour some of the gravy over the meat, and surround with the forcemeat balls.

Serve the remaining gravy, and a sauce-boat of apple sauce, separately.

Casseroled Ox Heart

6 helpings

1 ox heart (1.25–1.5kg)
25g flour
salt and pepper
50g dripping **or**
  2 × 10ml spoons oil
2 medium-sized onions
  (200g approx)

2 sticks celery (100g
  approx)
250ml beef stock
2 large carrots (200g
  approx)
$\frac{1}{4}$ turnip (25g approx)
juice and grated rind of 1
  orange

Prepare the heart as for Baked Stuffed Ox Heart (p509). Cut it into 1.5cm slices. Season the flour with salt and pepper and toss the slices in it until well coated. Heat the dripping or oil in a large pan and fry the slices of heart, turning once, until they are lightly browned on both sides. Lift them out and put them into a casserole. Prepare and slice the onions and celery. Fry them in the fat until lightly browned, then add them to the casserole. Pour the stock into the pan and stir until boiling; then strain it into the casserole. Cover, and cook in a cool oven, 150°C, Gas 2, for $3\frac{1}{2}$–4 hours.

Meanwhile, prepare and grate the carrots and turnip. Add the vegetables to the casserole for the last hour of the cooking time. Add the orange juice and grated rind to the casserole 15 minutes before the end of the cooking time.

Liver Hot Pot

6 helpings

650g ox liver	*900g–1kg potatoes*
25g flour	*3 × 2.5ml spoons dried*
salt and pepper	*sage*
100g streaky bacon,	*beef stock or water to*
without rinds	*cover*
3 large onions	*dripping*

Garnish
chopped parsley

Remove the skin and tubes, and cut the liver into 5mm slices. Season the flour with salt and pepper in a bag or bowl, and toss the liver slices in it. Cut the bacon into small squares. Skin the onions and slice them thinly. Prepare and slice the potatoes.

Place alternate layers of liver, bacon, onion and potatoes in a pie dish or casserole, sprinkling each layer with a little sage and seasoning. End with a thick layer of potatoes. Pour in just enough stock or water to cover the contents of the dish, cover with a lid, and cook in a moderate oven, 180°C, Gas 4, for about 2 hours. Remove the lid 30 minutes before serving, dot the top of the dish with dripping, and leave to cook, uncovered, to brown the potatoes. Sprinkle with parsley, and serve from the dish.

Baked Liver

6 helpings

600g ox liver	*25g plain flour*
fat for greasing	*salt and pepper*
150g streaky bacon,	
without rinds	
250ml (approx) general	
household stock (p329)	
or water	

Garnish
chopped parsley

Remove the skin and tubes, and cut the liver into slices about 1cm thick. Lay them in a deep, greased baking tin or dish. Lay the bacon on top of the liver. Add enough stock or water to half-cover the liver. Cover the tin or dish with a lid or foil. Bake in a moderate oven, 180°C, Gas 4, for about $1-1\frac{1}{4}$ hours until the liver is cooked and tender.

Lift out the liver, arrange the slices on a warmed serving dish and keep hot. Reserve the liquid. Chop the bacon rashers and sprinkle them over the liver.

Mix the flour to a smooth paste with a little cold stock or water. Gradually mix in the reserved stock. Pour into a pan and heat to boiling point, stirring all the time. Reduce the heat and simmer for 2–3 minutes. If too thick, add more stock or water. Season with salt and pepper to taste and strain the sauce round the liver. Garnish with parsley.

VARIATION
Calf's, sheep's and lamb's liver can be used equally well.

511

Stuffed Baked Liver

6 helpings

600g ox liver
fat for greasing
200g basic herb **or** ham
  stuffing (p375)
150g streaky bacon,
  without rinds

200ml (approx) general
  household stock (p329)
  or water
25g plain flour
salt and pepper

Garnish
chopped parsley

Prepare the liver as for Baked Liver (p511). Lay the slices in a greased dish and cover each with the stuffing. Lay the bacon on the stuffing. Add enough stock or water to half-cover the liver. Cook and serve as for Baked Liver (p511).

VARIATION
Calf's, sheep's and lamb's liver can be used equally well.

Kidney Hot Pot

4 helpings

500g ox kidney
2 large onions (200g
  approx)
3 tomatoes
800g potatoes
salt and pepper

500ml general household
  or brown stock (p329)
6 rashers streaky bacon,
  without rinds

Prepare the kidney as for Kidney in Italian Sauce. Prepare the vegetables and slice them finely. Proceed as for Liver Hot Pot (p511), adding alternate layers of sliced tomatoes, onion and bacon.

Kidney in Italian Sauce

4 helpings

500g ox kidney
3 × 15ml spoons plain
  flour
1 × 2.5ml salt
pepper
1 small onion (50g
  approx)
3 × 10ml spoons beef
  dripping

25g butter **or** margarine
375ml general household
  or brown stock (p329)
100g mushrooms
1–2 × 15ml spoons
  sherry (optional)

Garnish
100g cooked green peas

Skin, core, and cut the kidney into slices about 1cm thick. Season the flour with the salt and a generous pinch of pepper in a bag or bowl and toss the kidney in it until well-coated. Skin and chop the onion. Heat the dripping in a sauté pan and fry the kidney quickly on both sides. Add the onion, reduce the heat, cover, and fry gently for 20 minutes.

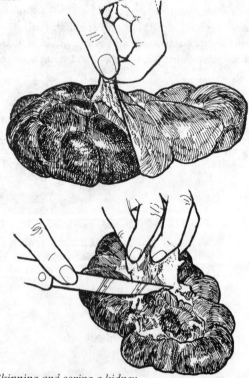

Skinning and coring a kidney

Meanwhile, melt the butter or margarine in a saucepan. Stir in the flour left after coating the kidney, and cook until a nut-brown colour. Gradually add the stock and stir until boiling. Reduce the heat and simmer for 5 minutes. Drain the kidney and onion from the fat, add them to the sauce, half cover the pan and simmer for about 45 minutes. Clean and slice the mushrooms and add them to the pan with the sherry, if used, and extra seasoning, if liked. Simmer for a further 15 minutes. Serve hot, garnished with green peas.

Note For another Italian sauce, see p700.

Stewed Ox Kidney and Rice

4 helpings

500g ox kidney
3 × 15ml spoons plain
 flour
1 × 2.5ml spoon salt
pepper
1 small onion (50g
 approx)

3 × 10ml spoons beef
 dripping
500ml water **or** beef
 stock
2 × 5ml spoons tomato
 or mushroom ketchup
200g long-grain rice

Garnish
100g cooked green peas

Prepare the kidney as for Kidney in Italian Sauce (p512). Season the flour with the salt and a generous pinch of ground pepper in a bag or bowl, and toss the kidney in it until well-coated. Skin and chop the onion. Heat the dripping in a sauté pan and fry the kidney and onion, turning the kidney until browned. Add the water or stock and the ketchup, and stir until boiling. Reduce the heat, cover the pan, and simmer very gently for about 2 hours. If cooked too quickly, the kidney will be tough. When cooked, re-season if required.

Meanwhile, wash the rice and cook it in boiling salted water until tender. Drain thoroughly and arrange as a border on a warmed serving dish. Pour the stewed kidney into the centre, and garnish with green peas.

Mrs Beeton's Stewed Ox Cheek

6 helpings

1 boned ox cheek
2 medium-sized onions
 (200g approx)
2 large carrots (200g
 approx)
1 turnip (50g approx)
12 peppercorns
2 cloves
bouquet garni
2 × 5ml spoons salt

2 × 10ml spoons butter
 or margarine
4 × 10ml spoons plain
 flour
2–3 × 15ml spoons
 sherry (optional)
2 × 5ml spoons lemon
 juice
salt and pepper

Garnish
diced **or** julienne strips
 of cooked carrot and
 turnip

Wash the ox cheek well in cold water. Soak for at least 12 hours in salted water, changing the water 2 or 3 times; then wash it well in warm water. Cut the cheek into convenient-sized pieces. Put them into a stewpan and cover with cold water. Heat to boiling point and skim well. Prepare the vegetables and slice them thickly. Add to the pan with the peppercorns, cloves, bouquet garni, and salt. Re-heat to boiling point, reduce the heat, cover with a tight-fitting lid, and simmer very gently for $1\frac{1}{2}$–2 hours, or until the meat is tender, keeping it just covered with liquid the whole time.

When cooked, strain the liquid from the meat into a measuring jug. Put the meat to one side. Melt the butter or margarine in a saucepan, stir in the flour and cook over gentle heat until lightly browned. Gradually add 625ml of the reserved liquid and stir until boiling; reduce the heat and simmer for 10 minutes. Add the sherry, if used, the lemon juice, and seasoning to taste. Add the pieces of meat to the sauce, and re-heat briefly. Serve on a warmed dish, and garnish with the carrot and turnip.

Note The rest of the cooking liquid will make an excellent soup stock.

Stuffed Ox Cheek

6 helpings

1 ox cheek	*browned breadcrumbs*
150g basic herb stuffing	*(p375)*
(p375)	*fat for baking*
1 egg	

Follow the recipe for Mrs Beeton's Stewed Ox Cheek (p513), but leave the cheek whole. When the bones (if left in) can be easily separated from the meat, or when the meat is tender, remove the cheek from the pan. Reserve the liquid. Remove the bones carefully to keep the meat in one piece. Spread the stuffing over the cheek, roll up tightly, and tie it securely with thin string. Beat the egg until liquid and coat the stuffed cheek with the egg, then with the browned breadcrumbs. Heat a little fat in a baking tin, add the cheek and baste it well. Cook in a moderate oven, 180°C, Gas 4, for 45 minutes, basting it frequently.

Serve with a gravy made from the liquid in which the cheek was cooked.

Beef Sausages

6 helpings

500g lean raw beef (skirt	*25g stale white*
or neck or clod	*breadcrumbs (optional)*
trimmings)	*natural or synthetic*
200g shredded suet	*sausage casings (skins)*
1 × 5ml spoon salt	*(optional)*
freshly ground black	*fat or oil for frying,*
pepper	*grilling or baking*
½ × 2.5ml spoon ground	*(optional)*
allspice	

Mince the beef. Mix thoroughly with the suet, and mince again. Add the seasoning and allspice, and mix well. Mix in the breadcrumbs, if used. Fill the sausage skins, if using, with the mixture (see p591). Alternatively, shape the mixture into patties.

Cook the sausages or patties by grilling or frying them gently, turning from time to time, until they are well-browned and cooked through; or bake them in a moderate oven, 180°C, Gas 4, for about 20 minutes.

Braised Oxtail

4–6 helpings

1.5kg oxtail	*salt and pepper*
50g beef dripping	*bouquet garni*
2 medium-sized onions	*2 cloves*
(200g approx)	*1 blade of mace*
25g plain flour	*juice of ½ lemon*
500ml water or beef	
stock	

Garnish

fried bread croûtons	*diced or julienne strips*
	of cooked carrot and
	turnip

Wash the oxtail, dry it thoroughly, and trim off any excess fat. Cut into joints, if not already jointed by the butcher, and divide the thick parts in half.

Heat the dripping in a stewpan. Fry the pieces of oxtail until browned all over, then remove them from the pan and put to one side. Skin and slice the onions. Fry them slowly in the fat until browned. Stir in the flour and cook for 1–2 minutes. Gradually add the water or stock, then add the seasoning, bouquet garni and spices, and stir until boiling. Return the pieces of oxtail to the pan, cover with a tight-fitting lid, reduce the heat, and simmer gently for 2½–3 hours. Remove the meat and arrange it on a warmed serving dish. Add the lemon juice to the sauce and re-season if required. Strain the sauce and pour it over the oxtail. Garnish with the bread croûtons, carrot and turnip.

Oxtail Hot Pot

4 helpings

1kg oxtail	*1 × 5ml spoon dried*
2 × 15ml spoons plain	*mixed herbs*
flour	*general household or*
1 × 2.5ml spoon salt	*brown stock (p329) to*
a pinch of ground pepper	*cover*
800g potatoes	*6 rashers streaky bacon,*
2 large onions	*without rinds*
salt and pepper	

Prepare the oxtail as for Braised Oxtail. Follow the recipe for Liver Hot Pot (p511), using just enough stock to cover the meat. Season, and sprinkle the herbs between the layers of meat and vegetables. Cook in a moderate oven, 180°C, Gas 4, for 2½–3 hours. Remove the lid 30 minutes before the end of the cooking time, lay the bacon rashers on top of the dish, and finish the cooking with the dish uncovered.

Boiled Cow-Heel

6 helpings

2 cow-heels	25g butter or dripping
water or general	25g flour
household stock (p329)	1 × 10ml spoon chopped
to cover	parsley
fat for greasing	salt and pepper

Wash the heels and blanch them for 6–8 minutes in boiling water. Drain, and put them in a large saucepan. Cover with fresh cold water or stock. Heat to boiling point, reduce the heat, cover the pan with a tight-fitting lid, and simmer very gently for about 3 hours.

Just before the end of the cooking time, melt the butter or dripping in a saucepan, add the flour, and cook without colouring for 2–3 minutes, stirring all the time. Pour off 500ml of the liquid in which the cow-heels have cooked and gradually stir it into the roux. Put the pan containing the cow-heels to one side. Heat the stock in the saucepan to boiling point, stirring all the time, then reduce the heat and simmer for 5 minutes. Add the parsley and seasoning to taste. Leave the pan over the lowest possible heat.

Drain the cow-heels, then remove the bones, holding each heel in a cloth. Arrange the pieces of meat on a warmed serving dish. Pour the hot sauce over them and serve at once.

VARIATION
Boiled Calf's Feet

Cook as for Boiled Cow-Heel, but reduce the simmering time to 1½ hours.

Fried Cow-Heel

6 helpings

2 cow-heels	1 egg
water or general	1 × 15ml spoon milk
household stock (p329)	1 × 5ml spoon chopped
to cover	parsley
2 × 15ml spoons plain	grated rind of ½ lemon
flour	dried white breadcrumbs
1 × 2.5ml spoon salt	oil for deep frying
a pinch of ground pepper	

Garnish
sprigs of parsley

Wash and blanch the heels as for the previous recipe. Put them in a large saucepan and cover with cold water or stock. Heat to boiling point, reduce the heat, cover the pan with a tight-fitting lid and simmer very gently for about 3 hours. Drain the cow-heels. Remove the bones, and press the meat between 2 plates until cold. Cut into pieces about 4cm square. Season the flour with the salt and pepper and toss the pieces of meat in it. Beat the egg with the milk. Add the parsley and lemon rind. Dip the pieces of meat in the egg mixture, then toss them in the breadcrumbs making sure they are well-coated.

Heat the oil (p303), and fry the coated meat pieces until golden-brown. Lift them out with a perforated spoon on to crumpled, soft kitchen paper. Serve hot, garnished with parsley sprigs.

VARIATION
Fried Calf's Feet

Cook as for Fried Cow-Heel, but reduce the simmering time to 1½ hours.

Boiled Ox Tongue

9–12 helpings

1 fresh ox tongue	*1 turnip*
(2kg approx)	*bouquet garni*
1 medium-sized onion	*6 black peppercorns*
1 medium-sized carrot	

Hot Garnish
boiled sprigs of
  cauliflower **or** *Brussels*
  sprouts

Cold Garnish

chopped parsley	*savoury butter*
	(optional)
	(pp1297–1301)

Weigh the tongue, then wash it thoroughly. Soak for 2 hours. Drain, and put in a large pan. Cover with cold water, heat to boiling point, then drain thoroughly.

Return to the pan and cover a second time with fresh cold water. Prepare and dice the vegetables. Add to the pan with the bouquet garni and peppercorns. Heat to boiling point, cover with a tight-fitting lid, reduce the heat and simmer gently, allowing 30 minutes per 0.5kg plus 30 minutes over. When cooked, lift out the tongue and plunge it into cold water. Drain. Remove the skin carefully, and the small bones at the root of the tongue, together with any excess fat, glands, and gristle.

To serve hot: Garnish the tongue with sprigs of cauliflower or Brussels sprouts.

To serve cold: **(1)** Place the tongue on a board and stick a fork through the root and another through the top to straighten it. Leave to cool completely, then trim. Glaze with meat glaze (p397) or aspic jelly and garnish with parsley. Decorate with rosettes of a smooth savoury butter, if liked.

(2) Bend and roll the tongue into a round shape and press it into a deep round cake tin, just big enough to hold it (18cm in diameter approx). Spoon over a little of the strained stock in which the tongue was cooked to fill up the crevices. Put a flat plate on the tongue and then a heavy weight. Leave to set, then turn out and serve in slices.

VARIATION

Pickled, Rolled Ox Tongue

Follow the recipe for Boiled Ox Tongue but use a pickled (salted) ox tongue. Soak overnight in cold water before proceeding with the recipe. Finish by the method given under *To serve cold* **(2)**.

Mrs Beeton's Boiled Marrow Bones

2 pieces of marrow bone per helping

marrow bones	*flour*
(150g approx each)	

Choose marrow bones from the leg or shin. Ask your butcher to saw them across into pieces 7cm long, or do it yourself. Shape the thick ends by chopping them so that the bones will stand upright. Mix some flour to a stiff paste with water, and plaster this paste over the open end of each bone to seal in the marrow. Tie each bone in a floured cloth.

Stand the bones upright in a deep saucepan containing enough boiling water to come half-way up the bones. Cover the pan with a tight-fitting lid, reduce the heat, and simmer gently for about $1\frac{1}{2}$ hours. Refill the pan with boiling water, if necessary. When cooked, remove the bones from the cloth and scrape off the paste. Fasten a paper napkin round each one and serve with a pointed teaspoon to extract the marrow.

Serve with Melba or hot dry toast and a seasoning of pepper.

Tripe and Onion

4 helpings

500g dressed tripe   *25g butter **or** margarine*
500ml milk   *25g flour*
salt and pepper
3 medium-sized onions
  (300g approx)

Garnish
1 × 15ml spoon chopped   *toasted croûtons*
  parsley

Wash the tripe and cut it into pieces 5cm square (approx). Put into a stewpan, pour over the milk and, if necessary, add some water to cover. Add salt and pepper to taste. Skin and chop the onions. Add them to the pan. Heat to boiling point, cover with a tight-fitting lid, reduce the heat and simmer gently until the tripe is tender (the length of time should be suggested by the butcher).

Knead the butter or margarine and flour together until evenly blended, and add it in small pieces to the contents of the pan. Stir until smooth, then continue cooking for another 30 minutes. Serve the tripe on a warmed dish and garnish with chopped parsley and toasted croûtons.

Tripe Lyonnaise

4 helpings

500g dressed tripe   *6 black peppercorns*
bouquet garni   *1 × 5ml spoon salt*
2 medium-sized onions   *50g butter **or** margarine*
  (200g approx)   *1 × 10ml spoon chopped*
1 large carrot (100g   *parsley*
  approx)   *1 × 10ml spoon vinegar*
1 leek   *salt and pepper*
1 stick of celery (50g
  approx)

Wash the tripe. Put in a stewpan, cover with water, and add the bouquet garni. Heat slowly to boiling point. Meanwhile, prepare one of the onions and the rest of the vegetables, and slice them thinly. Add to the pan with the peppercorns and salt. Cover with a tight-fitting lid, reduce the heat and simmer gently until the tripe is tender (the length of time should be suggested by the butcher). Drain thoroughly (the stock can be used in a soup or casserole). Leave to cool slightly, then cut the tripe into pieces 5cm square (approx).

Skin and slice the second onion. Melt the butter or margarine in a frying pan and fry the onion until soft and golden-brown. Add the tripe, parsley, vinegar, and seasoning. Toss in the pan for a few minutes until heated through. Serve at once.

Lamb and Mutton

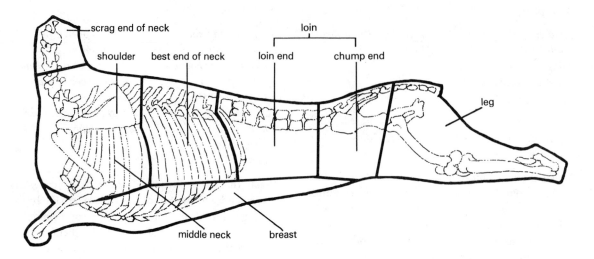

Lamb is meat from a sheep less than 1 year old, after which it becomes mutton, although occasionally mutton may be sold as 'old' or 'well-aged' lamb. The first of the new season's home-produced lambs reaches the British market at the end of March or early April and is available until October or November. Imported, chilled, and frozen lamb is available all year round. A home-produced lamb carcass weighs between 13.5–18kg, an imported chilled lamb carcass usually weighs between 11–13kg.

Mutton should also be available all year round but, partly because of a lack of demand for mutton, many butchers no longer sell it. A mutton carcass weighs between 20–23kg.

QUALITY OF LAMB AND MUTTON

There can be a lot of difference in the size, fat covering, and flavour of lamb between the various breeds of sheep. Lambs bred in hilly districts and salty grass areas are usually smaller and have less fat than the lowland pasture lambs. Perhaps for this reason, experts say that lamb and mutton from hilly districts are sweeter-eating and have more flavour than those from lowland areas. Most of the lamb sold today, especially foreign, frozen, and chilled lamb, is 'fat' pasture lamb. These carry more meat to the amount of bone. As they must often be pared of some fat before cooking, however, there is some weight loss which makes the meat more expensive.

LAMB AND MUTTON CUTS

English lamb and mutton and most imported, chilled and frozen lamb and mutton are usually cut in a similar way to beef, ie into sides and quarters before jointing. As with beef, cuts vary in different parts of Great Britain. The diagram above shows the most usual ones.

1) *Leg* or hind limb, also known as gigot in Scotland, is an excellent roasting joint on the bone or boned, stuffed and rolled. The leg is often

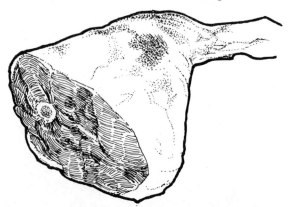

divided into fillet and shank end. Leg is leaner (tougher and slightly drier) than the shoulder (forelimb) and is also more expensive. (Av wt leg of lamb – 2kg; Av wt leg of mutton – 2.5kg.)

2) *Loin* can be roasted whole on the bone or boned, stuffed, and rolled. However, it is usually divided into loin end and chump end, and is cut into loin chops and chump chops (see p520). (Av wt loin of lamb – 1.5kg; Av wt loin of mutton – 2kg)

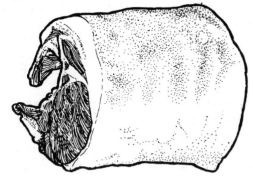

3) *Saddle* is the whole loin from both sides of the animal, left in one piece. (Av wt saddle of lamb – 3.5kg; Av wt saddle of mutton – 4.5kg.)

4) *Best end of neck* can be roasted on the bone or boned, stuffed, and rolled. It is often sold as chops or cutlets for grilling and frying. These chops or cutlets are sometimes served as noisettes which are prepared by removing the backbone (chine bone) and trimming away some of the meat at the rib end. Two best ends of neck are used to make a Crown Roast (p524) or Guard of Honour (p525). (Av wt best end of neck of lamb – 1kg; Av wt best end of neck of mutton – 2.5kg)

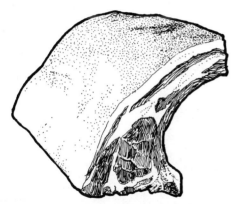

5) *Breast* is the most economical cut for roasting or braising and for tasty stews. Because of its high fat content it is best roasted with a stuffing to which no fat has been added so that much of the lamb fat is absorbed, making it a more palatable dish. (Av wt breast of lamb – 675g; Av wt breast of mutton – 1kg)

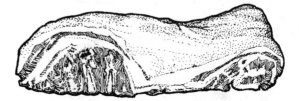

6) *Shoulder* is an economical roast on the bone or boned, stuffed, and rolled. It is fattier than the leg and is more moist after roasting. It is often divided into two smaller cuts: the blade or best end and the knuckle end. Both are ideal for roasting, braising, and casseroling. In Scotland, shoulder is not cut as a separate joint. The entire forequarter is usually divided in half, boned and rolled, then cut into smaller rolled joints. (Av wt shoulder of lamb – 1.75kg; Av wt shoulder of mutton – 2.5kg)

7) *Middle neck* is usually cut into chops for casseroles and stews. It is possible to cut 2 or 3 chops suitable for grilling or frying from the meat closest to the best end of neck.

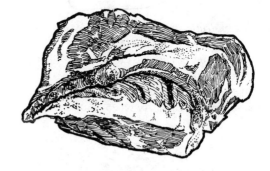

8) *Scrag end of neck* is a very economical cut for stews and soups. To avoid splinters of bone, look for scrag which has been cut into neat rings and not chopped roughly. (Av wt middle neck and scrag end of lamb – 0.75kg; Av wt of mutton – 1.5kg)

9) *Lamb chops* are cut from the loin or from the leg. Good for grilling, frying or braising.

Chump: 4–6 per carcass. (Av wt 125–150g each)

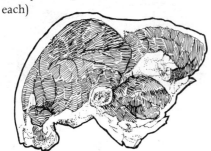

Loin: 6 (approx) per carcass. (Av wt 100–150g each)

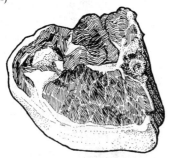

Neck (cutlet with rib bone removed): 4–6 per cut. (Av wt 75–125g each)

Leg (chops or cutlets): Cut from the fillet end. (Av wt 100–150g each)

10) *Lamb cutlets* are cut from the best end of neck. 4–6 per carcass. (Av wt 75–150g each)

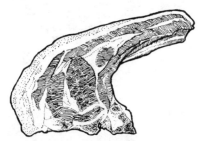

Mutton chops and cutlets are thicker and weigh more than lamb chops and cutlets.

ROASTED AND BAKED DISHES

Roast Leg of Lamb or Mutton

Basic recipe

*a leg of lamb **or** mutton*   *oil **or** fat for basting*
salt and pepper

Select the method of roasting, ie quick or slow roasting (p470). Weigh the leg joint to calculate the cooking time (p471). Wipe the meat. Place the leg on a wire rack, if available, in a shallow roasting tin. Season the meat, and either pour over it a little oil or rub it with a little fat. Place the roasting tin in the oven, and cook for the required time.

Transfer the cooked meat from the oven to a warmed meat dish, and keep hot. Prepare a gravy, if liked, from the sediment in the roasting tin.

Serve roast leg of lamb with Mint Sauce (p403), and roast leg of mutton with Onion Sauce (p695) and redcurrant jelly.

Roast Shoulder of Lamb or Mutton

Basic recipe

*a shoulder of lamb **or***   *salt and pepper*
mutton

Follow the method for Roast Leg of Lamb of Mutton. No additional fat should be required for basting, since a shoulder joint usually contains enough fat of its own.

French Leg of Lamb

6–8 helpings

a leg of lamb (2kg approx)
1 medium-sized carrot (50g approx)
1 medium-sized onion (100g approx)

1 shallot
1 clove of garlic
1 × 5ml spoon chopped parsley
salt and pepper
50g dripping

Bone the leg of lamb or ask the butcher to bone it. Wipe the meat. Prepare the carrot and onion and slice them thinly. Skin and chop the shallot finely and skin and crush the clove of garlic. Mix together the shallot, garlic, parsley, salt and pepper, and then sprinkle the mixture on the inner surface of the meat. Tie the meat into a neat shape.

Weigh the joint to calculate the cooking time, allowing 20 minutes per 0.5kg plus 20 minutes over. Heat the dripping in a baking tin, put in the meat, carrot and onion, and baste the meat with the dripping. Season the meat well with salt and pepper. Cover the baking tin and bake for 20 minutes in a fairly hot oven, 200°C, Gas 6, then reduce the heat to moderate, 180°C, Gas 4, for the rest of the calculated cooking time. For the last 15 minutes of the cooking time, remove the cover and allow the meat to brown and become crisp.

Serve on a warmed dish with gravy made from the sediment in the baking tin.

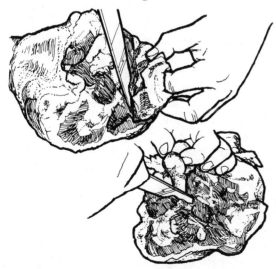

Bone a leg of lamb by removing the knuckle bone and working the main bone out

Stuffed Roast Leg of Lamb or Mutton

6–12 helpings

a leg of lamb or a small leg of mutton (2–2.5kg approx)
2 shallots (25g approx)
50g bacon or ham
4 × 15ml spoons soft white breadcrumbs
2 × 15ml spoons shredded suet
1 × 5ml spoon chopped parsley

1 × 2.5ml spoon dried mixed herbs
1 × 2.5ml spoon grated lemon rind
a pinch of grated nutmeg
salt and pepper
1 egg
a little milk
oil or fat for basting

Bone the leg of lamb or ask the butcher to bone it. Wipe the meat. Skin the shallots. Chop the shallots and bacon or ham finely. Mix together well with the breadcrumbs, suet, herbs, lemon rind, and nutmeg. Season to taste. Beat the egg until liquid and add it to the stuffing mixture with enough milk to bind the mixture lightly together. Press the stuffing into the cavity, taking care not to pack tightly since the stuffing will swell during cooking. Tie the meat into a neat shape with thin string.

Weigh the meat and calculate the cooking time, allowing 30 minutes per 0.5kg plus 30 minutes over for lamb, and 35 minutes per 0.5kg plus 35 minutes over for mutton. Place the leg on a wire rack in a shallow roasting tin. Pour a little oil over it or rub it with fat. Roast the meat in a moderate oven, 180°C, Gas 4, for the calculated cooking time or until cooked through. Baste the meat occasionally.

Serve with a slightly thickened gravy or Foundation Brown Sauce (p698).

521

Stuffed Roast Shoulder of Lamb or Mutton

6–10 helpings

a shoulder of lamb **or**
  mutton
salt and pepper

150–200g basic herb
  (p375) **or** *sage and*
  onion (p378) stuffing
dripping

Remove all the bones from the meat. Wipe the meat and trim off any skin and excess fat. Flatten the meat with a cutlet bat or rolling-pin. Season the inner surface of the meat well with salt and pepper and spread on the stuffing. Roll it up and tie securely with fine string.

Weigh the meat to calculate the cooking time, allowing 30 minutes per 0.5kg plus either 30 minutes over for lamb, or 35 minutes over for mutton. Heat the dripping in a roasting tin, put in the meat, and baste with the dripping. Cover the roasting tin and roast in a moderate oven, 180°C, Gas 4, until tender. Baste occasionally during the cooking time.

Serve on a warmed dish with lamb gravy (p728) or Foundation Brown Sauce (p698).

Leg of Lamb Provençale

6–10 helpings

4 canned anchovy fillets
2 cloves garlic (optional)
a leg of lamb (2.5–3kg)

lardoons of fat bacon
a few sprigs parsley
butter for greasing

Marinade

1 small onion
a few sprigs each of
  fresh thyme and
  parsley
2–3 bay leaves

salt and freshly ground
  pepper
250ml olive oil
2 × 15ml spoons vinegar

Cut the anchovy fillets in half lengthways, then across into 4 thin, narrow strips. Skin and crush the garlic, if used. Weigh the meat to calculate the cooking time, allowing 25 minutes per 0.5kg plus 25 minutes over. Wipe the leg of lamb and lift the skin a little without damaging the meat. Tuck under the skin the lardoons, strips of anchovy fillet, parsley, and garlic.

Make the marinade. Skin and chop the onion. Put the onion, thyme, parsley, and the bay leaves into a large bowl and season to taste. Pour the olive oil and vinegar over them. Marinate the leg of lamb for 2–3 hours, turning frequently.

Remove the meat, and spread it with the onion and herbs from the marinade. Wrap the leg in buttered foil or greaseproof paper, put it in a roasting tin and roast in a moderate oven, 180°C, Gas 4, for the calculated cooking time. Remove the foil or paper from the cooked meat.

Serve on a warmed dish, with gravy made from the sediment in the tin.

Greek Easter Lamb

(Arnaki Sti Souvia)

8–10 helpings

a very young spring
  lamb **or** *leg of lamb* **or**
  2 legs of baby lamb
3 lemons
salt and freshly ground
  black pepper
1kg new potatoes **or** *2–3*
  new potatoes for each
  helping

250ml olive oil
300g broad beans **or**
  parboiled butter beans
  (optional)
2 cloves garlic

Wipe the meat. Cut the lamb into large serving pieces. Cut the lemons in half, and rub the meat generously all over with them. Make small slits in the lamb, and rub the meat with salt and pepper, pressing it well into the slits. Place the meat in a large baking tin or oven-to-table baking dish with room to spare for the potatoes. Cut the potatoes in half and pack them between the meat pieces. Pour the oil over the dish. Bake in a cool oven, 150°C, Gas 2, for $1\frac{1}{2}$ hours.

Add the beans, if used. Skin the garlic and arrange among the potatoes. Re-season if required. Raise the heat to moderate, 180°C, Gas 4, and cook for 35 minutes. Add a little extra hot oil during the cooking if the dish appears to be dry. Serve very hot, from the tin or dish.

Lamb Cutlets en Papillotes

6 helpings

6 lamb cutlets	*1 × 10ml spoon chopped*
4–6 slices cooked ham	*parsley*
1 medium-sized onion	*salt and pepper*
(100g approx)	*grated rind of ½ lemon*
25g flat or button	*oil or butter for greasing*
mushrooms	
1 × 10ml spoon oil or	
butter	

Wipe and trim the cutlets neatly. Cut 12 small rounds of ham just large enough to cover the round part of the cutlet. Prepare the onion and mushrooms and chop finely. Heat the oil or butter in a small pan, and fry the onion until tender and lightly browned. Remove from the heat and stir in the mushrooms, parsley, salt and pepper to taste, and the grated lemon rind. Leave to cool.

Cut out 6 heart-shaped pieces of strong white paper or double thickness greaseproof paper or foil large enough to hold the cutlets. Grease them well with oil or butter. Place a slice of ham on half of each paper or foil, and spread on top a little of the cooled onion mixture. Then arrange the cutlet, a little more of the onion mixture, and a round of ham in layers on top. Fold over the paper or foil and twist the edges well together. Lay the cutlets in a greased baking tin and cook in a fairly hot oven, 190°C, Gas 5, for 30 minutes. Arrange the cutlets in the paper or foil on a warmed serving dish.

Foundation Brown Sauce (p698) or gravy can be served separately.

Baked Lamb or Mutton Cutlets with Mushrooms

6 helpings

6 cutlets from best end	*fat for greasing*
of neck of lamb or	*200g button mushrooms*
mutton	*1 × 10ml spoon oil or*
salt and pepper	*butter*

Wipe and trim the cutlets neatly. Season the cutlets on both sides and place them in a single layer in a greased casserole or ovenproof dish. Clean the mushrooms and scatter them over the cutlets. Season to taste with salt and pepper, and sprinkle with oil or dot with pats of butter. Cover with a tight-fitting lid and bake in a cool oven, 150°C, Gas 2, for 1–1½ hours, until the cutlets are tender.

Rolled Loin of Lamb or Mutton

6–12 helpings

a loin of lamb (1kg	*3 × 15ml spoons soft*
approx) or mutton	*white breadcrumbs*
(1.5kg approx)	*a pinch of grated nutmeg*
general household stock	*salt and pepper*
(p329) to cover	*1 egg*
25g bacon or ham	*a little milk*
2 × 15ml spoons	*3 rashers streaky bacon,*
shredded suet	*without rinds*
1 × 5ml spoon finely	*meat glaze (optional)*
chopped parsley	*(p397)*
½ × 2.5ml spoon grated	
lemon rind	

Remove all the bones from the meat. Put the bones in the bottom of a baking tin and just cover with stock. Chop the bacon or ham finely and mix with the suet, parsley, lemon rind, breadcrumbs, and nutmeg. Season to taste. Beat the egg until liquid, and add it to the stuffing with enough milk to bind the mixture lightly together. Spread the stuffing on the inner surface of the meat, roll up, and tie the meat securely with string.

Weigh the meat and calculate the cooking time, allowing 30 minutes per 0.5kg plus 30 minutes over for lamb, and 35 minutes per 0.5kg plus 35 minutes over for mutton. Cover the top of the meat with the rashers. Wrap the meat in 3 thicknesses of greaseproof paper. Place the meat on top of the bones, cover the baking tin and cook in a moderate oven, 180°C, Gas 4, for the calculated cooking time or until a meat thermometer registers the required internal temperature. When cooked, remove the paper and bacon. If liked, brush with meat glaze and return to the oven for a further 10 minutes.

Serve hot with Fresh Tomato (p715) or Foundation Brown (p698) Sauce.

Crown Roast of Lamb with Saffron Rice

6 helpings

2 best ends of neck of lamb (6 cutlets each)	oil for brushing salt and pepper

Saffron Rice

1 stick of celery (50g approx)	150g long-grain white rice
1 medium-sized onion (100g approx)	$4 \times 15ml$ spoons dry white wine
500ml chicken stock	25g blanched almonds
$\frac{1}{2} \times 2.5ml$ spoon powdered saffron	2 dessert apples (250g approx)
50g butter	50g frozen green peas

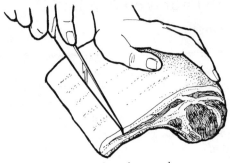

Remove fat and meat from bone ends

Ask the butcher to prepare the crown roast or prepare it as follows. Wipe the meat. Remove the fat and meat from the top 4–5cm of the thin ends of the bones and scrape the bone ends clean. Slice the lower half of each best end of neck between each bone, about two-thirds up from the base. Trim off any excess fat. Turn the joints so that bones are on the outside and the meat is on the inside, and sew the pieces together with a trussing needle and fine string. The thick ends of the meat will be the base of the crown, so make sure they stand level.

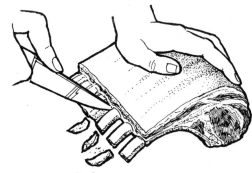

Scrape bone ends clean

Place the prepared crown roast in a roasting tin. Brush it with oil and season well with salt and pepper. Wrap a piece of foil round the top of each cutlet bone to prevent it from scorching. Cook in a fairly hot oven, 190°C, Gas 5, for $1\frac{1}{4}$–$1\frac{1}{2}$ hours.

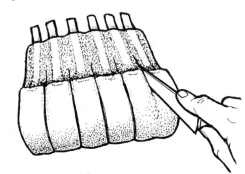

Slice between each bone

About 30 minutes before the end of the cooking time, make the saffron rice. Prepare and chop the celery and onion. Heat the chicken stock in a saucepan with the powdered saffron. Heat 25g of the butter in a saucepan and fry the celery and onion gently until softened but not browned. Wash the rice, stir it into the vegetables and cook for 1–2 minutes. Pour on the wine and cook gently until the rice has absorbed it. Add 250ml of the hot stock and cook, uncovered, stirring occasionally, until almost all the liquid is absorbed. Pour the remaining stock into the rice and cook gently until it has been completely absorbed and the rice is just tender. Chop the almonds and peel, core, and dice the apples. Remove the rice from the heat and add

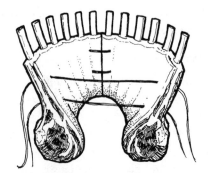

Sew pieces to form a crown roast

the almonds, diced apple, peas, and butter. Cover the pan with a tight-fitting lid, and leave to cook in its own steam until the peas are thawed and heated through, and the roast is ready.

When cooked, place the crown roast on a warmed serving dish. Remove the foil from the cutlet bones. Fill the hollow centre of the roast with the hot saffron rice. Top each cutlet with a cutlet frill and serve. Any extra rice can be served separately.

Guard of Honour

6 helpings

2 best ends of neck of lamb (6–7 cutlets each)	2 × 15ml spoons oil

Stuffing

1 small onion (50g approx)	1 × 15ml spoon chopped parsley
50g mushrooms	grated rind of 1 lemon
25g butter **or** margarine	salt and pepper
100g soft white breadcrumbs	1 egg
	a little milk

Gravy

1 × 15ml spoon plain flour	salt and pepper
250ml vegetable stock (pp330–31)	gravy browning (optional)

Garnish

sprigs of parsley

Ask the butcher to chine the joints. Remove the fat and meat from the top 5cm of the thin end of the bones and scrape the bone ends clean. Wipe the meat and score the fat with a sharp knife in a lattice pattern. Place the joints together to form an arch.

Make the stuffing. Prepare the onion and mushrooms. Melt the butter or margarine in a frying pan and fry the onion gently for 5 minutes until softened but not browned. Mix together the fried onion, mushrooms, breadcrumbs, parsley, lemon rind, and seasoning to taste. Beat the egg until liquid and add it to the stuffing with enough milk to bind it together. Stuff the cavity of the Guard of Honour.

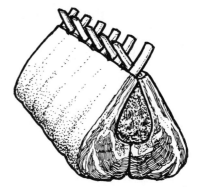

Best ends of neck placed together to form an arch

Close the joints together at the top, by criss-crossing the bones. Cover the bones with foil to prevent them from scorching. Heat the oil in a baking tin and put in the Guard of Honour. Bake in a fairly hot oven, 190°C, Gas 5, for $1\frac{1}{4}$–$1\frac{1}{2}$ hours or until the lamb is tender. When cooked, transfer the lamb to a warmed serving dish, and allow to rest in the turned-off oven.

Meanwhile, make the gravy. Pour off most of the fat from the roasting tin. Stir in the flour, and cook gently for a few minutes. Gradually add the stock and stir until boiling. Reduce the heat and simmer for 2 minutes. Season to taste and add gravy browning if liked. Pour into a warmed gravy-boat.

Remove the foil from the bones of the Guard of Honour and replace with cutlet frills. Garnish with sprigs of parsley.

GRILLED AND FRIED DISHES

Grilled Lamb or Mutton Cutlets or Chops

Basic recipe

6–8 helpings

6–8 lamb **or** *mutton*   *salt and pepper*
  cutlets **or** *chops*   *oil*

Garnish (optional)
pats of any savoury
  butter (pp1297–1301)

Choose plump cutlets or chops with the nut of meat 2–2.5cm thick so that they not will curl up when grilled. Wipe and trim the cutlets or chops into a neat shape. Season with salt and pepper and brush them all over with oil. Cook on the grid or base of the grilling pan, turning once or twice; keep well-brushed with oil. Cutlets require 7–10 minutes in all, and chops require 8–15 minutes, according to their thickness. When cooked, the cutlets or chops should be well-browned with crisp fat on the outside, and slightly pink on the inside when cut. Garnish with pats of any savoury butter, if liked. The ends of the cutlet bones can be covered with cutlet frills before serving.

Suitable accompaniments are green peas, baby carrots, new, creamed or chipped potatoes, and lamb gravy (p728) or Demi-glace Sauce (p708).

Grilled Crumbed Lamb or Mutton Cutlets

6 helpings

6 cutlets from best end   *75g mushrooms*
  of neck of lamb **or**   *oil as required*
  mutton   *500g mashed* **or**
salt and pepper   *creamed potatoes*
3 × 15ml spoons oil   *250ml Demi-glace*
5–6 × 15ml spoons dried   *(p708)* **or** *Fresh*
  white breadcrumbs   *Tomato (p715) sauce*
6 small tomatoes (300g
  approx)

Wipe and trim the cutlets neatly. Flatten the meat with a cutlet bat or rolling-pin. Season on both sides and brush them all over with oil. Cover lightly with the breadcrumbs and press them on firmly with a knife.

Slice the top off each tomato; reserve the tops for 'lids'. Remove most of the flesh and the seeds from the tomatoes, using a small spoon. Clean and chop the mushrooms finely. Season to taste with salt and pepper. Stuff the tomatoes with the mushrooms, and put on the 'lids'. Place in a greased ovenproof dish and brush them all over with oil. Bake in a moderate oven, 180°C, Gas 4, for 15–20 minutes until tender.

Meanwhile, grill the crumbed cutlets under high heat, turning them 2 or 3 times, until cooked evenly and browned. Spoon or pipe the hot mashed or creamed potatoes in a border on a warmed serving dish. Arrange the cutlets with the bone ends resting on the potato border, and place the stuffed tomatoes in the centre. Pour a little of the hot sauce round the cutlets and serve the rest separately.

Lamb Shish Kebab

6 helpings

1kg boned lean lamb,
  preferably from the leg

6 firm tomatoes
3 small green peppers

Marinade
1 large onion (200g
  approx)
1½ × 15ml spoons olive
  oil
3 × 15ml spoons lemon
  juice

5 × 5ml spoons salt
1 × 2.5ml spoon ground
  black pepper

Wipe the meat and trim off any excess fat. Cut the meat into 2cm cubes.

Make the marinade. Skin the onion and slice it thinly. Put it in a deep bowl. Sprinkle the olive oil, lemon juice, salt and pepper over the onion slices. Add the meat and stir well to coat the pieces of meat thoroughly. Marinate the meat at room temperature for several hours, turning it occasionally.

Remove the lamb from the marinade and drain thoroughly. Cut the tomatoes crossways into slices. Cut the green pepper into chunks and remove the membranes and seeds. Thread tomato slices, meat, and chunks of pepper on each skewer. Grill the skewers of meat and vegetables under high heat, or over a charcoal fire, turning the skewers occasionally, until the vegetables are well-browned and the lamb is done to taste. For pink lamb, allow about 10 minutes; for well-done lamb, allow about 15 minutes. Slide the lamb and vegetables off the skewers on to warmed individual plates.

Serve with boiled rice.

Lamb or Mutton Shashlik

4 helpings

500g boned leg of lamb
  or *mutton*
50g butter
200g lean bacon

8 button onions (200g
  approx)
8 bay leaves
salt and pepper

Wipe the meat and trim off any excess fat. Cut the meat into 2cm cubes. Heat 25g of the butter in a pan and brown the meat on all sides. Cut the bacon into slightly smaller cubes. Skin the onions and parboil them in lightly salted water for 3 minutes. Drain. Divide the meat, bacon, onions, and bay leaves into 4 portions and thread each portion on to a long skewer. Season with salt and pepper. Melt the remaining butter and brush it over the meat, bacon, and onions on the skewers. Grill under high heat, or over a charcoal fire, turning the skewers occasionally, for 8–10 minutes until the meat is well browned.

Serve with boiled rice.

Grilled Lamb or Mutton Slices

6 helpings

6 slices lamb **or** *mutton*
  (2cm thick approx), cut
  from the middle of the
  leg

3 × 15ml spoons oil **or**
  melted butter

Marinade
2 × 10ml spoons malt
  vinegar
1 × 5ml spoon very
  finely chopped onion
1 × 2.5ml spoon salt

1 × 5ml spoon finely
  chopped parsley
a pinch of dried mixed
  herbs
a pinch of ground pepper

Wipe and trim the slices of meat, if necessary.

Mix together the ingredients for the marinade. Lay the slices of meat in a dish and cover with the marinade. Leave for at least 2 hours, turning occasionally. Drain and dry the slices, then brush with the oil or melted butter. Cook them under a hot grill, turning 2 or 3 times, for 10–15 minutes or until well-browned on the outside and pink inside.

Suitable accompaniments are Fresh Tomato Sauce (p715) and chipped potatoes, or Mushroom Sauce (p695), baked tomatoes, and chipped potatoes, or grilled mushrooms and Foundation Brown Sauce (p698).

Grilled Breast of Lamb or Mutton

3–6 helpings for lamb
6–8 helpings for mutton

a breast of lamb **or** *mutton (0.5–1kg approx for lamb, 1–1.5kg for mutton)*	*oil for grilling* *250ml Fresh Tomato (p715)* **or** *Piquant (p702) sauce*
salt and pepper	

Wipe the meat and divide the breast into portions convenient for serving. Trim off the excess fat and skin. Season the meat well. Brush the grill rack and the meat with oil. Sear the meat quickly under a hot grill to seal the surfaces. Then reduce the heat, turn the meat frequently and grill for 15–20 minutes until thoroughly cooked.

Serve with Fresh Tomato Sauce or Piquant Sauce.

Fried Lamb or Mutton Cutlets or Chops

Basic recipe

6–8 helpings

6–8 lamb **or** *mutton cutlets* **or** *chops*	*6 × 15ml spoons dried white breadcrumbs*
salt and pepper	*2 × 15ml spoons oil*
1 × 15ml spoon plain flour	*25g butter*
1 egg	*250ml Fresh Tomato sauce (p715)*

Garnish
200g cooked green peas

Wipe and trim the cutlets and scrape clean about 2cm of the thin end of the bones, or wipe and trim the chops neatly. Season well on both sides. Dust lightly with the flour. Beat the egg until liquid and brush the cutlets or chops all over with the beaten egg; then coat them lightly with the crumbs.

Heat the oil and butter together in a frying pan and fry the meat until golden-brown on both sides and cooked through; this takes 7–10 minutes for cutlets and 8–15 minutes for chops, depending on their thickness. Drain thoroughly. Arrange the fried cutlets or chops on a warmed serving dish, and garnish with the peas. Pour some of the tomato sauce round and serve the rest separately.

Note If liked, the cutlets or chops can be fried without the egg and breadcrumb coating.

VARIATION

Lamb or Mutton Cutlets with Spinach

Prepare and fry the cutlets as above. Arrange them in a close circle on a warmed round dish. Heat 375g canned or frozen spinach purée and pile it in the centre of the cutlets. Pour a little of the 250ml lamb gravy or tomato sauce round the cutlets and serve the rest separately.

Note Peas, green beans or creamed potatoes can be substituted for the spinach.

Lamb or Mutton Chops with Mushrooms

6 helpings

6 lamb **or** *mutton loin* **or** *chump chops*	*25g butter*
200g mushrooms	*25g plain flour*
salt and pepper	*250ml general household* **or** *brown stock (p329)*
2 × 15ml spoons oil	

Wipe and trim the chops neatly. Clean the mushrooms. Season the chops well on both sides. Heat the oil and butter together in a frying pan, and fry the chops until golden-brown on both sides. Transfer them to a warmed dish and keep hot. Drain off the fat, reserving 2 × 15ml spoons in the pan. Stir the flour into the fat in the pan and cook gently until browned. Gradually add the stock and seasoning to taste, and stir until boiling. Replace the chops, and reduce the heat to simmering point. Add the mushrooms and simmer for 10 minutes. Arrange the chops and mushrooms on a warmed serving dish, and serve the gravy separately.

Serve with creamed potatoes and peas.

Lamb or Mutton Cutlets Doria

6 helpings

6 *lamb* **or** *mutton*
  cutlets from best end of
  neck
2 *large cucumbers (400g*
  approx)
75g *butter* **or** *margarine*
salt and pepper
1 × 15ml *spoon plain*
  flour
1 *egg*

6 × 15ml *spoons dried*
  white breadcrumbs
2 × 15ml *spoons oil*
25g *butter*
500g *mashed* **or**
  creamed potatoes
125ml *foundation brown*
  sauce (p698) **or** *lamb*
  gravy (p728)

Wipe and trim the cutlets neatly. Peel and dice the cucumbers, discarding the seeds. Melt the butter or margarine in a saucepan and put in the diced cucumber. Season with salt and pepper to taste. Cover the pan with a tight-fitting lid and cook very gently for 10–15 minutes, or until the pieces are tender but unbroken. Drain thoroughly. Transfer the cucumber to a warmed dish and keep hot.

Season the flour with salt and pepper and dust the trimmed cutlets with the seasoned flour. Beat the egg until liquid and brush the cutlets all over with beaten egg. Immediately coat them lightly with the breadcrumbs. Heat the oil and butter together in a frying pan and fry the cutlets until golden-brown on both sides. Spoon or pipe the mashed or creamed potatoes in a border on a warmed serving dish. Arrange the cutlets with the bone ends resting on the potato border and place the cucumber in the centre. Pour the hot sauce or gravy round the cutlets and potatoes.

Italian Lamb or Mutton Cutlets

6 helpings

6 *lamb* **or** *mutton*
  cutlets from best end of
  neck
4 × 15ml *spoons dried*
  white breadcrumbs
1 × 15ml *spoon finely*
  chopped mushrooms
1 × 2.5ml *spoon finely*
  chopped shallot
1 × 5ml *spoon chopped*
  parsley

$\frac{1}{2}$ × 2.5ml *spoon grated*
  lemon rind
a pinch of ground mace
salt and pepper
1 *egg*
2 × 15ml *spoons oil*
25g *butter*
250ml *Italian sauce (1)*
  (p700)

Marinade

2–3 × 15ml *spoons oil*
1 × 15ml *spoon lemon*
  juice

1 × 2.5ml *spoon dried*
  mixed herbs
salt and pepper

Wipe and trim the cutlets neatly. Place them in a dish. Mix together the ingredients for the marinade, pour it over the cutlets and leave to stand for 1 hour, turning 2 or 3 times.

Mix together the breadcrumbs, mushrooms, shallot, parsley, grated lemon rind, and mace; season with salt and pepper. Drain the cutlets thoroughly. Beat the egg until liquid, and brush the cutlets all over with the beaten egg. Coat the cutlets carefully with the breadcrumb mixture. Heat the oil and butter together in a frying pan and fry the cutlets gently until cooked through and browned on both sides. This takes 7–10 minutes, depending on the thickness of the cutlets. Drain thoroughly. Arrange the cutlets on a warmed serving dish and pour a little Italian sauce round them. Serve the rest of the sauce separately.

Spanish Lamb Cutlets

6 helpings

6 lamb cutlets from best
  end of neck
2 × 15ml spoons oil
25g butter
salt and pepper
2 rashers streaky bacon,
  without rinds

2 medium-sized onions
  (200g approx)
400g tomatoes
12 pork chipolata
  sausages

Wipe and trim the cutlets into a neat shape. Heat the oil and butter together in a frying pan, and fry the cutlets quickly until golden-brown on both sides. Remove the cutlets, place them in a casserole and season with salt and pepper. Cut the bacon into 1cm pieces and fry in the same pan until just cooked. Add the bacon to the casserole. Skin and slice the onions and tomatoes. Put them into the frying pan and cook gently for 5 minutes. Then add the onions and tomatoes to the casserole. Season with salt and pepper to taste. Cover the casserole and cook in a moderate oven, 180°C, Gas 4, for 30 minutes.

Meanwhile, fry or grill the chipolata sausages, turning them frequently, until browned and cooked through. Serve the cutlets and vegetables from the casserole and top each helping with the chipolata sausages.

Lamb or Mutton Cutlets Maintenon

6 helpings

6 thick lamb or mutton
  cutlets from best end of
  neck
50g mushrooms
25g margarine or
  2 × 15ml spoons oil
1–2 × 15ml spoons finely
  chopped shallot

1 × 15ml spoon chopped
  parsley
salt and pepper
a little gravy or stock
  (optional)
oil for brushing
250ml Espagnole sauce
  (p707)

Wipe and trim the cutlets neatly. Insert a thin, sharp knife at the outer edge of the meat and split the meat horizontally nearly through to the bone, forming a 'pocket'.

Clean and chop the mushrooms finely. Heat the margarine or oil in a small frying pan and fry the shallot until tender and lightly browned. Stir in the mushrooms and parsley. Season to taste. Add a little gravy or stock if the mixture is too dry. Fill the 'pockets' made in the cutlets with the mushroom mixture and press the edges firmly together. Season the cutlets with salt and pepper, and brush them all over with oil. Grill under high heat, turning once or twice, until well-browned on both sides.

Arrange the grilled cutlets in an ovenproof dish and coat them with some of the Espagnole sauce. Sprinkle with any remaining mushroom mixture. Cook in a fairly hot oven, 200°C, Gas 6, for 5–6 minutes. Serve the rest of the sauce in a warmed sauce-boat.

Noisettes of Lamb Jardinière

6 helpings

1kg boned best end of
  neck of lamb
salt and pepper
2 × 15ml spoons oil for
  grilling or frying

500g creamed potatoes
250ml lamb gravy
  (p728) or Demi-glace
  sauce (p708)

Garnish
2 × 15ml spoons diced
  green beans
2 × 15ml spoons diced
  carrot

2 × 15ml spoons diced
  turnip
2 × 15ml spoons diced
  celery

Wipe the meat. Roll it up and tie with fine string at 2–3cm intervals. Cut through the roll between the string to make noisettes. Season the noisettes on both sides. Either brush them with oil and grill for 6–7 minutes, turning once or twice, or heat the oil in a frying pan and fry them, turning once or twice, until cooked through and browned on both sides.

At the same time, cook each vegetable for the garnish separately in boiling salted water until tender. Drain, and mix together.

Spoon or pipe the hot creamed potatoes in a border on a warmed serving dish and arrange the noisettes on top. Garnish with the vegetables, pour a little of the hot gravy or Demi-glace sauce round the noisettes, and serve the rest in a warmed sauce-boat.

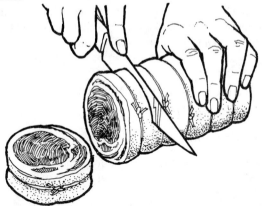

Cutting noisettes

Noisettes with Stuffed Artichokes

6 helpings

1kg boned best end of neck of lamb	*½ × 2.5ml spoon chopped chervil*
12 button mushrooms (100g approx)	*½ × 2.5ml spoon chopped chives*
25g margarine **or** *2 × 10ml spoons oil*	*½ × 2.5ml spoon chopped tarragon*
6 fresh **or** *canned artichoke hearts*	*1 × 5ml spoon beef* **or** *yeast extract*
125ml white stock (p329) **or** *water*	*salt and pepper*
juice of ½ lemon	*2 × 15ml spoons oil for grilling* **or** *frying*
1 × 5ml spoon chopped parsley	*250ml Demi-glace sauce (p708)*

Prepare the noisettes as for Noisettes of Lamb Jardinière (p530); then trim off all the fat. Clean and chop the mushrooms. Heat the margarine or oil in a pan and fry the mushrooms lightly. Warm the artichoke hearts in the stock or water or, if canned, in a little of the liquid; then drain. Add the lemon juice, parsley, herbs, and beef or yeast extract to the mushrooms in the pan. Season to taste. Fill the artichoke hearts with this mixture, transfer them to a warmed dish and keep hot.

Grill or fry the noisettes as for Noisettes of Lamb Jardinière. Arrange them neatly on a warmed serving dish and place an artichoke heart on each. Pour some of the Demi-glace sauce round the noisettes and serve the rest in a warmed sauce-boat.

Epigrams of Lamb or Mutton

4–6 helpings

a breast of lamb **or** *mutton (500g approx)*	*15g gelatine*
1 litre water **or** *brown stock (p329)*	*1 × 15ml spoon hot water*
1 medium-sized onion (100g approx)	*500ml thick Béchamel sauce (p704)*
½ turnip (25g approx)	*1 egg*
1 medium-sized carrot (50g approx)	*6 × 15ml spoons soft white breadcrumbs*
bouquet garni	*oil for deep frying*
salt and ground black pepper	*300ml Soubise sauce (p704)*

Wipe the meat. Put the water or stock in a large pan and bring to the boil. Add the meat and boil for 5 minutes. Prepare the onion, turnip and carrot, and slice them thickly. Add the vegetables to the meat with the bouquet garni and salt. Cover the pan and simmer gently for about 1 hour until the meat is tender.

Meanwhile, dissolve the gelatine in the hot water. Mix it with the Béchamel Sauce and leave the sauce until cold, and beginning to thicken.

When cooked, take the meat out of the pan. Remove the skin, bones, and gristle, and press the meat between 2 plates until cold and firm. Then cut the meat into neat pieces for serving. Season the meat well with salt and pepper, then coat it completely with the Béchamel Sauce. Repeat the coating if necessary to give a thick covering of sauce. Chill the cutlets until the sauce is set.

Beat the egg until liquid and pour on to a flat dish. When the sauce is set and firm, dip the epigrams into the beaten egg and coat them with the breadcrumbs. Heat the oil (p303) and fry the epigrams quickly until golden-brown. Lift them out and drain thoroughly. Arrange in a circle on a warmed serving dish, with the Soubise sauce in a sauce-boat in the centre.

531

BRAISED DISHES

Braised Leg of Lamb or Mutton

6–10 helpings

a leg of lamb **or** a small leg of mutton (2–2.5kg)	3 × 10ml spoons butter **or** margarine
fat for greasing	3 × 15ml spoons plain flour
2 shallots (25g approx)	salt and pepper

Mirepoix

2 medium-sized onions (200g approx)	general household stock (p329) **or** water to cover
1 turnip (75g approx)	bouquet garni
2 medium-sized carrots (100g approx)	10 black peppercorns
25g dripping	

Wipe and trim the meat.

Prepare the vegetables for the mirepoix and slice them thickly. Heat the dripping in a large stewpan, add the vegetables, cover the pan and fry (sweat) them gently for 5–10 minutes. Put enough stock or water into the pan almost to cover the vegetables. Add the bouquet garni and peppercorns. Place the meat on top, and lay a piece of greased greaseproof paper on top of the pan, greased side down. Cover with a tight-fitting lid. Cook over low heat for $2\frac{1}{2}$–3 hours for lamb, or 3–$3\frac{1}{2}$ hours for mutton, basting occasionally with the stock, and adding more stock or water if necessary.

About 30 minutes before serving, skin and chop the shallots very finely. Melt the butter or margarine in a small pan, add the shallots and fry gently until softened. Then stir in the flour and cook until it is well-browned. Draw the pan off the heat.

Transfer the meat to a warmed serving dish and keep hot. Strain the stock into a measuring jug, and make up to 500ml with more stock if necessary. Stir the stock gradually into the browned flour. Return to the heat and stir until boiling. Season to taste. Pour a little of the sauce over the meat and serve the rest in a sauce-boat.

Serve with cooked tomatoes, mushrooms, peas, diced turnips or carrots.

VARIATION

Bone the leg and fill the cavity with a stuffing of equal quantities of ham and trimmings from the leg, chopped finely; add 1 onion, skinned and chopped finely, and a little crushed garlic if liked. Allow 30 minutes extra cooking time.

Braised Lamb or Mutton Provençale

8–12 helpings

a leg **or** shoulder **or** loin of lamb **or** mutton	fat for greasing
	meat glaze (p397)

Stuffing

50g lean ham	1 × 5ml spoon chopped parsley
50g pork **or** veal	1 × 2.5ml spoon dried mixed herbs
6 button mushrooms	
1 shallot	1 × 2.5ml spoon grated lemon rind
1 egg	
50g soft white breadcrumbs	salt and pepper

Mirepoix

2 medium-sized onions (200g approx)	75g dripping
	bouquet garni
2 medium-sized carrots (100g approx)	10 black peppercorns
1 turnip (75g approx)	1 litre beef stock (approx)
2 sticks celery (100g approx)	

Provençale Sauce

500ml foundation brown sauce (p698)	25g butter **or** margarine
1 tomato (50g approx)	1 × 2.5ml spoon chopped parsley
1 small onion (50g approx)	1 × 2.5ml spoon lemon juice
2 large mushrooms (25g approx)	

Garnish

baked tomatoes	baked mushrooms

Wipe the meat. Bone it, or ask the butcher to do it for you.

Make the stuffing. Mince the meat. Prepare the mushrooms and shallot and chop them. Beat the egg until liquid. Mix together all the stuffing ingredients. Press the mixture lightly into the cavity left by the bone and sew up the opening.

Prepare the vegetables for the mirepoix and slice them thickly. Heat the dripping in a large stewpan and fry the vegetables gently for 3–5 minutes. Add the bouquet garni and peppercorns. Pour in enough stock to come three-quarters of the way up the vegetables. Place the meat on top. Lay a piece of greased greaseproof paper on top of the pan, greased side down, and cover with a tight-fitting lid. Cook over low heat for 2 hours for lamb or 2½ hours for mutton, basting frequently and making up the volume of stock as it reduces.

Transfer the meat to a baking tin and cook in a fairly hot oven, 200°C, Gas 6, for another 30 minutes, basting with a little stock as needed.

Meanwhile, strain the braising liquid from the stewpan and use it to make the brown sauce if not already made. Prepare and slice the tomato, onion, and mushrooms. Melt the butter or margarine in a saucepan. Add the vegetables and chopped parsley, half cover and cook gently for 15–20 minutes. Add the brown sauce to this mixture and simmer for another 10 minutes. Season carefully and strain through a sieve. Re-heat without boiling, add the lemon juice, and keep hot.

When cooked, transfer the meat to a warmed serving dish. Brush it over with warm meat glaze. Garnish with baked tomatoes and baked mushrooms. Serve the Provençale sauce separately.

Braised Lamb or Mutton Cutlets

6 helpings

6 cutlets from best end of neck of lamb **or** mutton	meat glaze (p397) (optional)
larding bacon	500g mashed **or**
fat for greasing	creamed potatoes

Mirepoix

1 medium-sized carrot (50g approx)	3 × 10ml spoons dripping
1 small turnip (50g approx)	bouquet garni
2 sticks celery (100g approx)	250ml beef stock
	salt and pepper

Garnish
cooked diced vegetables

Wipe and trim the cutlets neatly. Flatten them with a cutlet bat or rolling-pin. Insert 3 strips of larding bacon into the lean part of each lamb cutlet, and 5 strips if using mutton cutlets.

Prepare the vegetables for the mirepoix and slice them thickly. Heat the dripping in a large stewpan, add the vegetables, and fry them gently for 3–5 minutes. Add the bouquet garni and enough stock almost to cover the vegetables. Season to taste. Place the cutlets on top. Lay a piece of greased greaseproof paper on top of the pan, greased side down, and cover it with a tight-fitting lid. Cook over low heat for about 40 minutes for lamb cutlets and 50 minutes for mutton cutlets, adding more stock during cooking if necessary.

Lift out the cooked cutlets and brush the larded side of each cutlet with meat glaze, if liked. Put the cutlets, larded side up, into a hot oven, 220°C, Gas 7, to crisp the larding bacon. Make a bed of the mashed or creamed potatoes on a warmed serving dish. Arrange the cutlets on the potatoes, and garnish with the diced vegetables.

Serve with Fresh Tomato Sauce (p715) or Caper Sauce (p693).

Oxford John

6 helpings

600g boned leg of lamb **or** mutton	1 × 2.5ml spoon dried mixed herbs
salt and pepper	50g butter **or** margarine
1 × 15ml spoon finely chopped ham **or** bacon	25g plain flour
1 × 5ml spoon chopped parsley	250ml beef stock
1 × 5ml spoon finely chopped onion	1 × 5ml spoon lemon juice

Wipe and trim the meat. Cut it into neat, thin, round slices about 10cm in diameter. Season with salt and pepper. Mix together the ham or bacon, parsley, onion, herbs, and a little salt and pepper. Divide this mixture equally between the number of rounds of meat and sprinkle it over one side of them. Pile the slices on top of each other and leave for 1 hour to absorb the flavours.

Melt the butter or margarine in a pan and fry each slice of meat lightly and quickly. Transfer the slices to a warmed dish and keep hot. Stir the flour into the pan and cook until it is well-browned. Gradually add the stock, stir until boiling, and boil for 2 minutes. Season to taste. Add the lemon juice and put the meat in again. Cook gently for 10 minutes at just below simmering point. Serve hot.

Braised Neck of Lamb with Paprika

6 helpings

1kg middle neck of lamb, divided into cutlets	1 clove of garlic
50g dripping	1 × 10ml spoon paprika
1 large onion (200g approx)	1 × 226g can tomatoes
	250ml chicken stock
	salt and pepper

Garnish
100g cooked green beans

Wipe the cutlets and trim off any excess fat. Heat the dripping in a frying pan and fry the cutlets for 3–4 minutes, turning once, to brown both sides.

Remove the cutlets from the pan and drain. Place them in a large casserole.

Skin and slice the onion and skin and crush the garlic. Fry the onion and garlic gently in the remaining dripping in the pan until softened but not browned. Stir in the paprika and add the tomatoes and stock. Heat the sauce to boiling point, season to taste, and pour the sauce over the cutlets. Cook, uncovered, in a moderate oven, 180°C, Gas 4, for 1¾ hours. Serve garnished with cooked green beans.

Braised Breast of Lamb or Mutton

4–6 helpings

a breast of lamb **or** mutton	salt and pepper
	dripping for greasing

Mirepoix

2 medium-sized onions (200g approx)	25g fat bacon
2 medium-sized carrots (100g approx)	1 × 10ml spoon dripping
2 sticks celery (100g approx)	bouquet garni
1 small turnip (50g approx)	1 tomato (50g approx) (optional)
	general household **or** brown stock (p329) to cover

Wipe the meat. Bone the breast of lamb or mutton without cutting right through the flesh, or ask the butcher to do it for you. Season well with salt and pepper. Roll up tightly, and tie the meat with string.

Prepare the onions, carrots, celery, and turnip for the mirepoix and slice them thickly. Chop the bacon roughly. Heat the dripping in a stewpan. Add the vegetables and bacon, cover the pan, and fry gently for 10 minutes. Add the bouquet garni. Skin and slice the tomato, if used, and add it to the pan. Add enough stock almost to cover the vegetables. Heat to boiling point. Place the meat on the mirepoix, lay a piece of greaseproof paper greased with dripping on top of the pan, and cover with a tight-fitting lid. Cook over low heat for about 2 hours until the meat is tender, basting frequently and adding more stock as required.

Turkish Breast of Lamb

6 helpings

a breast of lamb (750g approx)	300g beef **or** pork sausage-meat
salt and pepper	

Mirepoix

1 large carrot (100g approx)	15g dripping
1 small turnip (50g approx)	bouquet garni
	salt and pepper
1 large onion (200g approx)	250ml general household **or** brown stock (p329)
25g streaky **or** fat bacon, without rinds	

Turkish Rice

150g Patna rice	a pinch of powdered saffron (optional)
1 large onion (200g approx)	salt and pepper
40g butter **or** margarine **or** 3 × 10ml spoons oil	250ml Fresh Tomato sauce (p715)
750ml white stock (p329)	a pinch of curry powder

Wipe the meat and remove all the bones. Flatten the meat with a cutlet bat or rolling-pin. Season well with salt and pepper and spread the sausage-meat all over it. Roll up tightly, and tie the meat neatly with thin string.

Prepare the vegetables for the mirepoix. Chop the bacon. Heat the dripping in a frying pan and cook the bacon until the fat runs. Add the vegetables to the bacon and fry them quickly until lightly browned. Drain thoroughly and put them in the bottom of a heavy-based pan or an oven-proof casserole. Add the bouquet garni, seasoning, and just enough stock to cover the vegetables. Place the stuffed, rolled breast of lamb on top of the mirepoix and cover the pan or casserole with a tight-fitting lid. Cook slowly over low heat for about 2½ hours, basting often, or cook in a moderate oven, 180°C, Gas 4, for 2–2½ hours until the meat is tender.

Meanwhile, prepare the rice border. Wash the rice well under running water, and drain. Skin and chop the onion finely. Heat the butter, margarine or oil in a saucepan. Add the onion, cover, and fry very gently for about 15 minutes until softened but not browned. Heat the stock and add to the onion with the rice and saffron, if used. Stir well and season to taste. Replace the lid, heat to boiling point, reduce the heat, and simmer gently for 15–20 minutes, until the rice is tender and dry.

When cooked, place the meat on a warmed serving dish and arrange the rice in a border round the meat. Mix together the tomato sauce and curry powder. Pour it over the meat, and serve hot.

CASSEROLED AND STEWED DISHES

Lancashire Hot Pot

6 helpings

1kg middle neck of lamb **or** mutton	fat for greasing
	salt and pepper
3 sheep's kidneys	250ml general household stock (p329)
1kg potatoes	25g lard **or** dripping
1 large onion (200g approx)	

Wipe the meat, cut it into neat cutlets, and trim off any excess fat. Skin, core, and slice the kidneys. Prepare the potatoes, slice half of them, and cut the rest into chunks or in half, if small, for the top of the casserole. Skin and slice the onion.

Put a layer of potatoes in the bottom of a greased, large, deep casserole. Arrange the cutlets on top, slightly overlapping each other, and cover with the kidneys and onion. Season well. Arrange the remainder of the potatoes (halves or chunks) neatly on top. Pour in the hot stock. Melt the lard or dripping and brush it over the top layer of potatoes. Cover the casserole with a tight-fitting lid and bake in a moderate oven, 180°C, Gas 4, for about 2 hours or until the meat and potatoes are tender. Remove the lid, increase the oven temperature to hot, 220°C, Gas 7, and cook for another 20 minutes or until the top layer of potatoes is brown and crisp. Serve from the casserole.

Crumbed Neck of Mutton

6 helpings

*a best end of neck of
    mutton (6 cutlets)
    (1.25kg approx)
general household stock
    (p329) to cover
1 egg
1 × 5ml spoon chopped
    parsley*

*$\frac{1}{2}$ × 2.5ml spoon dried
    mixed herbs
salt and pepper
2 × 15ml spoons soft
    white breadcrumbs
dripping
50g butter* **or** *margarine
50g plain flour*

Ask the butcher to remove the chine bone and short bones from the best end of neck, or do it yourself (see below). Fold the flap of meat over and secure it neatly. Put the meat in a stewpan and almost cover it with stock. Heat to simmering point, cover the pan, and simmer gently for 1 hour.

Remove the meat and drain thoroughly. Reserve the stock. Beat the egg until liquid and add the parsley, herbs, and seasoning. Coat the meat thickly with this mixture. Cover it lightly with the breadcrumbs. Heat a little dripping in a baking tin, put in the meat and bake it in a moderate oven, 180°C, Gas 4, for $1\frac{1}{4}$–$1\frac{1}{2}$ hours until well-browned. Baste often with the hot fat.

Melt the butter or margarine in a saucepan. Stir in the flour and cook until browned. Then gradually add 500ml of the reserved stock and stir until boiling. Season to taste. Serve the meat and the sauce separately.

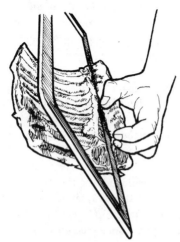

1 Saw through chine bone at the base of rib bones

Crumbed Scrag of Lamb or Mutton

6 helpings

*1–1.5kg scrag end of
    neck of lamb
2 medium-sized onions
    (200g approx)
2 medium-sized carrots
    (100g approx)
$\frac{1}{4}$ turnip (25g approx)
100g streaky bacon,
    without rinds*

*bouquet garni
10 black peppercorns
general household stock
    (p329)* **or** *water to
    cover
1 egg
5–6 × 15ml spoons soft
    white breadcrumbs
50g dripping*

Ask the butcher to cut the meat into neat rings, or cut it up yourself. Wipe the meat and trim off any excess fat. Prepare and slice the vegetables. Put them in a stewpan and lay the meat on top. Cover the meat with the bacon. Add the bouquet garni, peppercorns, and enough stock or water almost to cover the vegetables. Cover the pan with a tight-fitting lid, heat to simmering point, and simmer gently for $2\frac{1}{2}$ hours. Check the level of the stock from time to time and, if necessary, top up with more boiling stock. Alternatively, cook in a moderate oven, 180°C, Gas 4, for 2–$2\frac{1}{2}$ hours.

When cooked, remove the meat and drain thoroughly. Beat the egg until liquid and coat the meat with the beaten egg and then with the breadcrumbs. Heat the dripping in a baking tin. Put the meat in the baking tin and cook in a fairly hot oven, 200°C, Gas 6, for about 30 minutes until well-browned; baste occasionally.

Serve with a brown gravy made from the stock in which the meat was cooked.

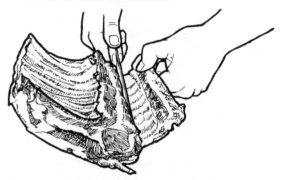

2 Cut through any remaining bone with a knife

Collared Lamb

6–10 helpings

2 breasts of lamb
(1.25–1.5kg approx)
2–3 × 15ml spoons
softened lamb fat
1 × 10ml spoon grated
lemon rind
salt and pepper
a pinch of ground
allspice
1 × 10ml spoon anchovy
essence

50g gherkins
2 × 15ml spoons
chopped parsley
1 × 5ml spoon dried
thyme
1 × 5ml spoon fresh
chives
100g soft white
breadcrumbs
750ml general household
stock (p329)

Wipe the meat, then remove the bones without piercing through the flesh. Reserve the bones. Brush the boned sides of the lamb with the fat, and sprinkle with lemon rind, salt and pepper, allspice, and anchovy essence. Chop the gherkins and mix with the herbs and breadcrumbs. Use a little of the stock to bind it. Spread the mixture over the seasoned sides of the lamb.

Place the breasts end to end, overlapping slightly, and roll them up together like a Swiss roll. Tie with string at regular intervals. Cover the meat tightly with muslin and secure it with string.

Put the meat into a casserole, add the bones and the rest of the stock. Cover with a lid and cook in a warm oven, 160°C, Gas 3, for 3 hours.

Serve hot with green peas or cold with an orange salad flavoured with chopped fresh mint.

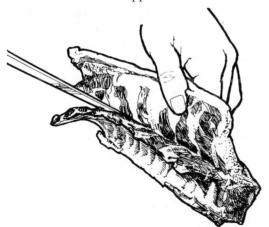

3 Cut rib bones away from meat in one piece

Fricassée of Lamb

4–6 helpings

a breast of lamb
(650–700g approx)
1 medium-sized onion
(100g approx)
50g dripping **or** lard **or**
margarine
2 bay leaves
2 cloves

1 blade of mace
6 white peppercorns
salt and pepper
500ml white stock
(p329) **or** water
25g plain flour
500g creamed potatoes

Garnish
1 × 10ml spoon roughly
chopped capers

Wipe the meat, bone it, if not already done by the butcher, and trim off any excess fat. Cut the meat into 5cm squares. Skin and slice the onion. Melt the fat in a stewpan, add the meat, onion, bay leaves, cloves, mace, peppercorns, and salt and pepper to taste. Half cover the pan and cook very gently for about 30 minutes, stirring often. Meanwhile, heat the stock or water to boiling point. Add it to the pan, and simmer, covered, for about 1½ hours or until the meat is tender.

Blend the flour to a smooth paste with a small quantity of cold water in a saucepan. Strain the liquid from the meat, measure off 250ml liquid, and gradually stir it into the blended flour. Bring to the boil, stirring all the time, and boil for 2–3 minutes. Add this sauce to the meat and re-heat if necessary. Spoon or pipe the hot creamed potatoes in a border on a warmed serving dish and arrange the meat in the centre. Sprinkle the chopped capers over the meat.

Squab Pie

4–6 helpings

1kg middle neck **or** scrag end of neck of lamb	1 × 15ml spoon mushroom ketchup (optional)
salt and pepper	boiling water
1kg cooking apples	125ml brown stock (p329) (optional)
2 large onions (400g approx)	
1 × 10ml spoon caster sugar	

Ask the butcher to cut the meat into cutlets or neat rings, or cut it up yourself. Wipe the meat and trim off any excess fat. Place the meat in the bottom of a large pie dish or casserole. Season well with salt and pepper. Peel and core the apples, skin the onions, and slice them both. Arrange layers of apples and onions sprinkled with the sugar on top of the meat. Sprinkle over the mushroom ketchup, if used. Pour enough boiling water into the dish to half cover the meat and vegetables. Cover the dish with a lid or with foil. Bake in a moderate oven, 180°C, Gas 4, for 1½ hours. Before serving, skim off any fat, and check that there is enough gravy in the dish. If necessary, add some boiling stock to increase the quantity of gravy.

Stewed Lamb or Mutton

6 helpings

1kg middle neck or scrag end of neck **or** breast of lamb	bouquet garni
	2 sprigs mint
200g young **or** small carrots	general household stock (p329) **or** water to cover
1 medium-sized onion (100g approx)	200–225g green peas
25g dripping	25g plain flour
	salt and pepper

Wipe the meat, cut it into portions convenient for serving, and trim off any excess fat and bone. Prepare and dice the carrots and onion.

Heat the dripping in a stewpan and put in the meat, diced vegetables, bouquet garni, and mint. Cover the pan with a tight-fitting lid and cook over low heat for 10 minutes, stirring occasionally. Add just enough stock or water to cover the meat. Heat to boiling point, reduce the heat, cover with the lid, and simmer gently for about 2 hours until tender. Shortly before the end of the cooking time, add the peas, return to simmering point and finish the cooking. Blend the flour to a smooth paste with a little cold water and stir in some of the hot liquid from the pan. Return to the stewpan, stir until boiling and cook for 2–3 minutes. Remove the bouquet garni and sprigs of mint. Season to taste. Serve hot.

Navarin of Lamb

6 helpings

1kg middle neck of lamb **or** mutton	a pinch of sugar (optional)
2 medium-sized carrots (100g approx)	2 × 10ml spoons plain flour
a piece of swede **or** turnip (25g approx)	375ml general household stock (p329) **or** water
2 medium-sized onions (100g approx)	salt and pepper
2 × 15ml spoons dripping	bouquet garni

Wipe the meat, cut it into neat cutlets and trim off any excess fat and bone. Prepare the vegetables, then cut the carrots and swede or turnip into short, thick strips and quarter the onions.

Heat the dripping in a stewpan and fry the cutlets quickly on both sides until browned. Lift out the cutlets, add the vegetables and fry more slowly until they are just coloured. A pinch of sugar can be added to help this colouring process. Stir in the flour, and cook for 1 minute, stirring all the time. Then gradually add the stock or water and stir until boiling. Replace the meat in the pan and check that the liquid comes just level with the meat. Season to taste, add the bouquet garni, cover the pan, and simmer gently for about 1 hour until the meat is tender. Turn the cutlets from time to time during the cooking.

Serve with creamed potatoes.

Dutch Stew

4–6 helpings

650–700g middle neck of
  lamb **or** mutton
2 medium-sized onions
  (200g approx)
25g dripping
250ml (approx) water
  or white stock (p329)

salt and pepper
1 small cabbage (500g
  approx)
6 small potatoes (500g
  approx)

Wipe the meat and cut it into cutlets or slices. Skin and chop the onions. Melt the dripping in a stewpan and fry the meat and onions for 5 minutes, turning the meat until browned on both sides. Add the water or stock, and season to taste. Heat to boiling point, reduce the heat, cover the pan with a tight-fitting lid, and simmer gently for 1 hour.

Lift out the meat and put to one side. Shred the cabbage; prepare and slice the potatoes. Put the cabbage and potatoes into the pan. Add more water or stock, if necessary, to come three-quarters of the way up the vegetables. Place the meat on the vegetables, cover with the lid, and simmer gently for about 30 minutes until the cabbage and potatoes are tender. Strain off the stock. Serve the meat and vegetables from the pan or from a dish. Serve the stock as gravy, either as it is, or thickened slightly with flour.

Haricot of Lamb or Mutton

6 helpings

1kg middle neck of lamb
  or scrag end of mutton
25g butter **or** dripping
1 large onion (400g
  approx)
2 cloves garlic

25g plain flour
800ml general household
  or brown stock (p329)
  or chicken stock (p330)
bouquet garni
salt and pepper

Garnish
2 carrots

1 turnip

Wipe the meat and trim off any skin and excess fat. Cut the meat into serving-sized pieces or cutlets. Melt the fat in a large saucepan and fry the meat quickly until sealed and lightly browned. Skin and chop the onion, and skin and crush the garlic. Fry them in the fat until softened but not coloured. Stir in the flour and cook gently until browned. Draw the pan off the heat and gradually add the stock. Return to the heat and stir until boiling. Add the bouquet garni, seasoning, and meat. Cover with a lid and simmer over gentle heat for about 2 hours until the meat is tender.

Meanwhile, prepare the carrots and turnip for the garnish and cut them into 5mm dice. Add the vegetable trimmings to the meat whilst it is cooking. Cook the diced vegetables separately from the meat in boiling salted water until just tender.

When cooked, arrange the meat on a warmed serving dish. If necessary, boil the stock in the saucepan rapidly to reduce it, then strain it over the meat. Garnish the meat with the cooked diced vegetables.

Irish Stew

4–6 helpings

1kg middle neck **or** scrag
  end of neck of lamb **or**
  mutton
2 large onions (400g
  approx)

1kg potatoes
salt and pepper
water **or** general
  household stock (p329)
  as required

Garnish
2 × 15ml spoons
  chopped parsley

Wipe the meat, cut it into neat cutlets or pieces, and trim off any excess fat. Skin the onions and slice them thinly; prepare and slice the potatoes. In a stewpan, place layers of meat, onions, and potatoes, adding seasoning between each layer, and finishing with a layer of potatoes. Add enough water or stock to come half-way up the meat and vegetables. Cover the pan with a lid, heat to simmering point, and simmer gently for 2½ hours. Alternatively, cook the stew in a casserole, covered with a lid, in a fairly hot oven, 190°C, Gas 5, for 2–2½ hours. Serve garnished with chopped parsley.

Lamb or Mutton with Rice

4–6 helpings

*500g middle neck or
 scrag end of neck of
 lamb or mutton*
*6 medium-sized carrots
 (300g approx)*
3 turnips (200g approx)

*6 medium-sized onions
 (600g approx)*
salt and pepper
*1–2 litres white (p329)
 or chicken (p330) stock*
250g long-grain rice

Garnish
*1 × 15ml spoon chopped
 parsley*

Ask the butcher to cut the meat into cutlets or neat rings, or cut it up yourself. Wipe the meat and trim off any excess fat. Prepare and slice the vegetables. Put the meat and vegetables in a casserole. Season well and cover with stock. Cover the casserole and cook in a moderate oven, 180°C, Gas 4, for about $1\frac{1}{4}$ hours. Wash the rice well, stir it into the contents of the casserole, and cook for a further $1–1\frac{1}{4}$ hours, until all the contents are tender. The rice will absorb the stock, so check the level and add extra stock as needed. When cooked, place the meat on a warmed serving dish and arrange the rice and vegetables in a neat border. Sprinkle with chopped parsley.

Pilaf of Mutton or Lamb

4–5 helpings

*600g mutton or well-
 aged lamb*
2 large onions
1 green pepper
50g butter
1 × 5ml spoon salt
200g long-grain rice
*1 × 2.5ml spoon ground
 cumin*

*1 × 2.5ml spoon
 powdered turmeric*
*1 × 2.5ml spoon fennel
 seeds*
*750ml–1 litre general
 household stock (p329)*
*1 × 100g pkt frozen
 green beans*

Wipe the meat and trim off any fat or gristle. Cut the meat into 2cm cubes. Skin and slice the onions. De-seed and slice the pepper thinly. Heat the butter in a saucepan, add the mutton, and fry for 12–15 minutes, turning the meat until browned all over. Add the vegetables and cook for 5 minutes.

Stir in the salt, rice, cumin, turmeric, and fennel seeds. Add 750ml stock and heat to boiling point. Reduce the heat, cover, and simmer for about 20 minutes, or until the mutton is cooked and the rice is tender. Add the frozen beans 7–9 minutes before the end of the cooking time. Add more stock during cooking, if necessary, to prevent the mixture from sticking to the bottom of the saucepan. Place the pilaf on a warmed serving dish.

Lamb Pilaf with Eggs

6–8 helpings

1kg lean lamb
*2 medium-sized onions
 (200g approx)*
15g ginger root
*a good pinch of ground
 coriander*
salt
800g long-grain rice
*100g clarified butter
 (p886)*
*$\frac{1}{2}$ × 2.5ml ground
 cinnamon*

*a good pinch each of
 ground cardamom and
 cloves*
*a good pinch of cumin
 seeds*
*a good pinch of black
 pepper*
25g pistachio nuts
25g dried apricots
25g seedless raisins
25g blanched almonds
1 egg

Garnish
4 fried or poached eggs

Wipe the meat. Mince 250g of the meat finely, and cut the rest into slices convenient for serving. Skin and slice the onions, and slice the ginger root. Put the sliced meat into a stewpan, add the onions, ginger, coriander, and 1 × 5ml spoon salt. Cover with cold water, heat to simmering point, cover the pan, and cook over low heat for $1\frac{1}{2}–1\frac{3}{4}$ hours until the meat is tender.

Meanwhile, wash the rice thoroughly. Put it in a pan of water, bring to the boil, and boil fast for 5 minutes, then drain. When the meat is cooked, strain and reserve the stock, and put the meat to one side. Put the parboiled rice into the stewpan, add the stock, heat to simmering point, and simmer until the rice is tender and the stock has been absorbed or has evaporated.

Heat about one-third of the butter in another stewpan, add the slices of meat, sprinkle with the spices and black pepper, and toss over heat for a few minutes. Spread the cooked rice over the meat. Melt another third of the butter and pour it over the rice. Cover the pan with a tight-fitting lid and cook very gently for 30 minutes.

Heat the remaining butter in another pan, add the minced lamb with a little salt, and toss it over heat until lightly browned. Blanch and skin the pistachio nuts and slice the apricots. Add the pistachio nuts, apricots, raisins, and almonds to the mince. Beat the egg until liquid, add it to the pan, and stir it in over gentle heat for a few minutes.

Arrange the slices of meat and the rice in a shallow, warmed serving dish, spread the minced mixture on top and garnish with the eggs. Serve at once.

Curried Lamb

6 helpings

650–700g lean leg **or** loin of lamb	1 × 10ml spoon plum jam
50g dripping	1 × 10ml spoon desiccated coconut
2 medium-sized onions (200g approx)	6 black peppercorns
1 clove of garlic (optional)	4 allspice berries
2–3 × 5ml spoons curry powder	Cayenne pepper salt
25g ground rice	50g concentrated tomato purée
1 cooking apple (150g approx)	675ml white (p329) **or** chicken (p330) stock
25g tamarind **or** mango chutney	lemon juice (optional)

Wipe the meat and cut it into 2cm cubes. Heat the dripping in a stewpan and fry the meat lightly, then put the meat to one side. Skin and slice the onions thinly, and skin and crush the garlic, if used. Fry the onion and garlic in the fat until pale golden. Add the curry powder and ground rice, and fry for 6 minutes. Peel, core, and chop the apple. Add the apple and the rest of the ingredients, except the lemon juice, to the pan. Heat to boiling point, stirring all the time. Return the meat to the pan, cover with a tight-fitting lid, and simmer gently for about 1½ hours, stirring frequently.

Lift the meat out on to a warmed serving dish. Add the lemon juice, if used, to the sauce and re-season if required. Strain the sauce over the meat.

Serve in a border of plain boiled rice and serve extra rice separately.

Note Another recipe for Curried Lamb can be found on p568.

Traditional curry accompaniments can be found on p388.

Curried Lamb Bake

4–6 helpings

400g raw **or** cooked mutton **or** lamb	juice of 1 lemon
1 slice of white bread	1 × 10ml spoon ground almonds
1 medium-sized onion (100g approx)	salt and pepper
2 × 15ml spoons butter	fat for greasing
1 × 10ml spoon curry powder	2 eggs
	200ml milk

Wipe and mince the meat. Cover the bread with water and leave to stand for 5 minutes. Squeeze the bread dry and add it to the minced meat. Skin and chop the onion finely. Melt the butter in a pan and fry the onion gently until softened but not browned. Mix the curry powder with the lemon juice and add to the meat with the onion and almonds. Stir and season to taste. Put the mixture in a greased casserole and cook, uncovered, in a moderate oven, 180°C, Gas 4, for about 20 minutes. Beat the eggs with the milk, add a pinch of salt and pepper, and pour the liquid over the meat mixture. Continue to cook for another 20 minutes or until the custard has set.

Serve with rice and apricot chutney.

BOILED DISHES

Boiled Leg of Lamb or Mutton with Caper Sauce

8–10 helpings

a leg of lamb (2kg
  approx) **or** a small leg
  of mutton (2.5kg
  approx)
1 × 5ml spoon salt
10 black peppercorns
2 medium-sized onions
  (200g approx)

4 medium-sized carrots
  (200g approx)
2 turnips **or** 1 large
  parsnip (100g approx)
1–2 leeks
375–500ml Caper sauce
  (p693)

Wipe the meat and trim off any excess fat. Put the meat in a large stewpan with the salt, peppercorns, and enough cold water to cover. Heat to boiling point. Skim, reduce the heat, cover the pan with a tight-fitting lid, and simmer over gentle heat for 2½–3 hours or until the meat is tender.

Meanwhile, prepare the vegetables and leave whole if small, or cut them into large neat pieces. Add the vegetables 45 minutes before the end of the cooking time. When cooked, drain the meat and vegetables from the cooking liquid. Place the meat on a warmed serving dish, coat with the Caper sauce, and arrange the vegetables round the meat.

Boiled Knuckle of Mutton

4 helpings

a knuckle end of leg of
  mutton (1kg approx)
1 medium-sized onion
  (100g approx)
1 medium-sized carrot
  (50g approx)
¼ small turnip (25g
  approx)

brown **or** general
  household stock (p329)
  or water to cover
1 × 5ml spoon salt
bouquet garni
8 black peppercorns

Wipe and trim the meat. Prepare and slice the onion, carrot, and turnip. Put the meat and vegetables in a large stewpan and cover with stock or water. Add the salt, bouquet garni and peppercorns. Heat to simmering point, cover the pan with

a tight-fitting lid, and simmer very gently for about 1¾ hours until tender. Remove the bouquet garni and peppercorns. Serve the meat with the vegetables.

If liked, the stock in which the mutton is cooked can be used for making a slightly thickened gravy or onion sauce, to serve with the meat.

Boiled Breast of Lamb or Mutton

8 helpings

a breast of mutton **or** 2
  breasts of lamb
salt and pepper
1 small onion (50g
  approx
1 medium-sized carrot
  (50g approx)
½ small turnip (25g
  approx)

brown **or** general
  household stock (p329)
  or water to cover
bouquet garni
10 black peppercorns

Stuffing
2 × 15ml spoons soft
  white breadcrumbs
1 × 15ml spoon shredded
  suet
1 × 10ml spoon chopped
  parsley

1 × 2.5ml spoon dried
  mixed herbs
salt and pepper
milk

Wipe the meat, remove all the bones and trim off any excess fat. Flatten the meat with a cutlet bat or rolling-pin. Season with salt and pepper.

Make the stuffing by mixing the breadcrumbs, suet, herbs, and seasoning together. Moisten with a little milk. Spread the stuffing on the meat, roll up the meat lightly and tie it securely with string.

Prepare and slice the vegetables. Put the meat and vegetables in a large stewpan and cover with stock or water. Add 1 × 5ml spoon salt, the bouquet garni, and peppercorns. Heat to simmering point, cover the pan, and simmer gently for 2 hours for breast of lamb and 2½–3 hours for breast of mutton, depending on its weight. Transfer the meat to a warmed serving dish and keep hot. Strain the stock and use it to prepare a slightly thickened gravy to serve with the meat.

Blanquette of Lamb

5–6 helpings

1kg lean best end of neck
  or middle neck or
  breast of lamb
salt and pepper
white stock (p329) *or*
  water to cover
1 large onion
  (200g approx)
bouquet garni

6 black peppercorns
a pinch of grated nutmeg
2 × 15ml spoons butter
  or margarine
2 × 15ml spoons plain
  flour
1 egg yolk
2 × 15ml spoons single
  cream or milk

Garnish
100g baked button
  mushrooms

Wipe the meat. Bone it and cut into pieces about 5cm square. Put the meat into a stewpan with the salt, and stock or water to cover. Heat to boiling point. Skin and slice the onion and add it to the pan with the bouquet garni, peppercorns, and nutmeg. Reduce the heat, cover the pan with a tight-fitting lid, and simmer for 1½–2 hours until the meat is tender. When cooked, transfer the meat to a warmed serving dish, cover, and keep hot. Strain the liquid from the meat and measure off 250ml.

Melt the butter or margarine in a saucepan, stir in the flour, and cook gently for 2–3 minutes without browning it. Gradually add the stock and stir until boiling, then reduce the heat and simmer for 3 minutes. Beat together the egg yolk and the cream or milk. Stir a little of the hot sauce into the egg yolk mixture, then add the mixture to the rest of the sauce off the heat. Return to the heat, stir, and cook very gently until the egg yolk thickens the sauce, but do not allow the sauce to boil or it may curdle. Season to taste. Strain the sauce over the meat. Garnish with the button mushrooms.

PIES AND PUDDINGS

Lamb Pie

4–6 helpings

1kg best end or middle
  neck or breast of lamb
salt and pepper
1–2 sheep's kidneys
stock or water

shortcrust pastry
  (p1249) using 150g
  flour or puff pastry
  (p1253) using 100g
  flour
flour for rolling out

Wipe the meat and remove the fat and bones. Boil the bones to make stock for the gravy. Cut the meat into 2cm cubes and put them in a 750ml pie dish. Sprinkle each layer with salt and pepper. Skin, core, and slice the kidneys thinly. Add them to the meat in the pie dish. Half fill the dish with stock or water. Roll out the pastry on a lightly floured surface and use to cover the dish. Make a hole in the centre of the lid for the steam to escape. Bake in a moderate oven, 180°C, Gas 4, for 1½–2 hours, until the meat is tender (test with a skewer).

Strain the liquid off the bones. Season it to taste. Just before serving, pour enough of this gravy stock through the hole in the centre of the pie to fill the dish.

Lamb or Mutton Pudding

5–6 helpings

500g lean lamb or
  mutton
3 × 15ml spoons plain
  flour
salt and pepper
1–2 sheep's kidneys

suet crust pastry (p1250)
  using 200g flour
flour for rolling out
fat for greasing
3 × 15ml spoons general
  household stock (p329)
  or water

Follow the directions for Steak and Kidney Pudding (p503).

Barbecued Lamb Pie with Cider

4–6 helpings

675g lean leg **or** shoulder of lamb	shortcrust pastry (p1249) using 200g flour flour for rolling out

Marinade

2 × 15ml spoons medium-dry sherry	$\frac{1}{2}$ × 2.5ml spoon dried mixed herbs
2 × 15ml spoons Worcestershire sauce	150ml water

Sauce

1 large onion	50g Demerara sugar
2 rashers bacon, without rinds	salt and pepper
50g hard block margarine	275ml dry still cider
4 × 15ml spoons concentrated tomato purée	3 × 15ml spoons plain flour
	2 × 15ml spoons cold water

Wipe the meat, remove any skin and gristle, and cut the meat into 2cm cubes. Put into a bowl.

Mix together all the ingredients for the marinade, and pour it over the lamb. Cover, and chill for at least 2 hours, turning the meat over occasionally.

Make the sauce. Skin and chop the onion. Chop the bacon. Melt the margarine in a saucepan, and sauté the onion and bacon for 3–4 minutes, until the onion is transparent but not browned. Add all the remaining sauce ingredients, except the flour and water. Blend the flour with the water, and put to one side. Heat the sauce to boiling point, reduce the heat, and simmer for 15 minutes, then stir in the blended flour and water. Simmer for a further 2–3 minutes until the sauce is thick and smooth. Stir in the lamb and the marinade. Reboil, then remove from the heat, and leave to cool completely.

When cold, put the filling in a 1 litre pie dish. Roll out the pastry on a lightly floured surface and use to cover the dish. Make a small hole in the centre of the lid and, from the trimmings, form a small rose to fill it after baking. Bake both pie and rose in a fairly hot oven, 200°C, Gas 6, for 35–45 minutes until the pastry is cooked through and golden, and the meat filling is thoroughly heated. The rose must be baked blind. When cooked, insert the pastry rose. Serve hot, with apricot chutney.

Pot Pie of Lamb or Mutton

6 helpings

650–700g middle neck of lamb **or** mutton	salt and pepper
1 medium-sized onion (100g approx)	suet crust pastry (p1250) using 100g flour flour for rolling out
general household **or** brown stock (p329) to cover	

Wipe the meat and cut it into neat chops. Remove the bones and any excess fat. Place the meat in a casserole so that it is about half-full. Skin and slice the onion thinly and put it on top of the meat. Pour in just enough stock to cover the meat and onions. Season well. Cover the casserole with a lid, and cook in a moderate oven, 180°C, Gas 4, for 1–1$\frac{1}{2}$ hours or until the meat is tender.

Roll out the suet crust pastry on a lightly floured surface so that it is a little smaller than the top of the casserole. Lay it on top of the meat, replace the lid, and cook gently for a further 1 hour. Before serving, divide the pastry crust into serving portions.

Note This dish can also be cooked over heat.

Pembrokeshire Mutton Pie

6 helpings

400g lean mutton	100g sugar
hot water crust pastry (p1250) using 300g flour	salt and pepper
flour for rolling out	general household stock (p329)
100g currants	beaten egg **or** milk for glazing

Wipe and mince the meat. Line a 15cm pie mould with three-quarters of the pastry, or use a container to mould the pie as described on p1250, keeping it about 5mm thick. Use the remaining quarter for the lid. Alternatively, line 6 small moulds with the pastry. Put a layer of minced mutton into the case(s) followed by currants, sugar, salt and pepper, until all the filling ingredients have been used up. Moisten the fillings with a little of the stock. Put on the lid(s), and make a hole in the centre of the pie(s) to allow steam to escape.

Bake in a fairly hot oven, 200°C, Gas 6, for 10 minutes, then reduce the heat to moderate, 180°C, Gas 4, and continue to bake for 1¼ hours. Brush the top of the pie(s) with beaten egg or milk about 15 minutes before the end of the cooking time. Before serving, fill the pie(s) with hot stock through the hole in the lid(s) and serve hot.

Cumberland Mutton Pies

6 helpings

300g lean mutton	salt and pepper
1 medium-sized onion	shortcrust pastry
(100g approx)	(p1249) using 300g
1 × 10ml spoon dripping	flour
100g mushrooms	flour for rolling out
1 × 10ml spoon chopped	6 × 10ml spoons general
parsley	household stock (p329)
a pinch of dried thyme	beaten egg or milk for
	glazing

Wipe and mince the meat. Skin and chop the onion. Heat the dripping in a pan and fry the onion lightly. Remove the onion and mix it with the mutton. Clean and chop the mushrooms, and add them to the meat with the parsley, thyme, and seasoning to taste.

Roll out half the pastry on a lightly floured surface, and cut out 6 circles to line 6 small round tins or saucers. Divide the mixture between the tins. Add to each 1 × 10ml spoon stock to moisten. Roll out the rest of the pastry and cut out 6 lids for the pies. Dampen the edges of the pies, put on the lids and seal well. Brush with beaten egg or milk. Make a hole in the lid of each pie to allow steam to escape. Bake in a moderate oven, 180°C, Gas 4, for 40–45 minutes.

MINCED DISHES

Lamb or Mutton Roll

6 helpings

650g lean lamb **or** mutton	salt and pepper
200g ham **or** bacon	1 egg
1 × 2.5ml spoon finely chopped onion	2 × 15ml spoons chicken stock (p330) **or** lamb gravy (p728)
3 × 15ml spoons soft white breadcrumbs	1 × 15ml spoon plain flour **or** beaten egg and
1 × 5ml spoon chopped parsley	2 × 15ml spoons breadcrumbs
½ × 2.5ml spoon dried mixed herbs	2 × 15ml spoons dripping
a pinch of grated nutmeg	
1 × 2.5ml spoon grated lemon rind	

Wipe the lamb or mutton. Finely chop or mince all the meat. Put in a bowl and mix it well with the onion, breadcrumbs, herbs, nutmeg, and grated lemon rind. Season to taste. Beat the egg until liquid, and add it with the stock or gravy to moisten the mixture. Shape it into a short thick roll. Wrap the roll in foil or several thicknesses of greaseproof paper to keep it in shape and to protect the meat. Bake in a moderate oven, 180°C, Gas 4, for 1½ hours.

Remove the foil or paper and lightly dredge the roll with the flour, or brush it with the beaten egg and coat it with breadcrumbs. Heat the dripping in a baking tin and place the roll in the tin. Baste well and return it to the oven for a further 30 minutes until browned.

Serve with gravy.

Note Under-cooked cold lamb or mutton can be used. The roll should then be cooked for only 1 hour before browning it.

DISHES USING COOKED MEAT

Baked Lamb or Veal

4–6 helpings

600g cold roast lamb **or**
  veal
1 medium-sized onion
1 × 15ml spoon butter
  or *dripping*
1½ × 15ml spoons plain
  flour
375ml general household
  (p329) **or** *chicken*
  (p330) *stock*

salt and pepper
1 × 2.5ml spoon finely
  grated lemon rind
1 × 2.5ml spoon chopped
  parsley
50–100g buttered
  breadcrumbs (p375)

Trim off any fat and gristle and slice the meat thinly. Skin and slice the onion. Melt the fat in a pan, and fry the onion lightly. Stir in the flour and cook gently until well-browned. Gradually add the stock and stir until boiling. Season, reduce the heat and simmer gently for 10 minutes.

Cover the bottom of a casserole or pie dish with some of the sauce. Put in some slices of meat and seasoning, and add a little lemon rind and parsley. Continue to add all the ingredients in layers. Cover the top thickly with the breadcrumbs. Bake in a hot oven, 220°C, Gas 7, for 15 minutes.

Collops of Lamb and Asparagus

4 helpings

400–450g cold
  undercooked lean lamb
1 × 15ml spoon plain
  flour
¼ × 2.5ml spoon salt
a pinch of ground pepper
a pinch of grated lemon
  rind
¼ × 2.5ml spoon dried
  mixed herbs

1 × 340g can asparagus
  tips
3 × 10ml spoons butter
  or *dripping*
1 × 15ml spoon plain
  flour
250ml lamb gravy
  (p728) **or** *general*
  household stock (p329)
  or *water*

Cut the meat into slices 7cm in diameter, and 1cm thick. Mix together the flour, salt, pepper, grated lemon rind and herbs, and sprinkle them over both sides of each collop. Leave to stand for about 1 hour.

Heat the asparagus tips in their liquid and keep warm. Heat the butter or dripping in a frying pan and cook the collops lightly and quickly until lightly browned on both sides. Arrange them in a close circle on a warmed serving dish and keep hot. Stir the flour into the fat in the pan and cook until browned. Gradually add the gravy, stock or water and stir until boiling. Season to taste. Drain the asparagus tips, and place them in the centre of the circle of collops. Strain the sauce round the dish.

Bordered Lamb

4 helpings

400g cold cooked lamb
1 small onion (50g
  approx)
1 × 15ml spoon dripping
  or *lard*
1 × 15ml spoon plain
  flour
375ml lamb gravy
  (p728) **or** *stock made*
  with bones and
  trimmings from cooked
  meat

1 × 15ml spoon
  mushroom ketchup **or**
  Worcestershire sauce
salt and pepper
400g creamed potatoes
  or *boiled rice*

Garnish (optional)
sippets of toast

Cut the meat into 2cm cubes. Skin and chop the onion finely. Melt the dripping or lard in a saucepan. Add the onion and fry gently until softened but not browned. Stir in the flour and fry gently until browned. Gradually add the gravy or stock, ketchup or sauce, season to taste, and stir until boiling. Reduce the heat and simmer for 10 minutes. Put in the meat and return to simmering point. Cover the pan and simmer very gently for 30 minutes.

Spoon or pipe hot creamed potatoes or arrange boiled rice in a border on a warmed serving dish. Pour the cooked lamb into the centre and garnish, if liked, with sippets of toast.

COLD DISHES

Chaudfroid of Lamb or Mutton Cutlets

6–8 helpings

6–8 cutlets from best
  end of neck of lamb
salt and pepper
fat for greasing
$\frac{1}{2} \times 15$ml spoon gelatine
1×15ml spoon water
125ml Béchamel sauce
  (p704)

250ml aspic jelly
50ml double cream
50ml Fresh Tomato
  sauce (p715) **or**
2×15ml spoons
  concentrated tomato
  purée

Mirepoix

1 medium-sized onion
  (100g approx)
1 medium-sized carrot
  (50g approx)
1 small turnip (50g
  approx)

2 sticks celery
2×10ml spoons
  dripping
bouquet garni
250ml brown stock
  (p329)

Garnish

green salad vegetables   French dressing

Wipe and trim the cutlets neatly. Flatten them with a cutlet bat or rolling-pin.

Prepare the vegetables for the mirepoix. Heat the dripping, add the vegetables, and fry gently for 3–5 minutes. Add the bouquet garni and enough stock almost to cover the vegetables. Season to taste.

Season the cutlets and lay them on top of the mirepoix. Place a piece of greased greaseproof paper on top of the pan and cover with a tight-fitting lid. Cook over gentle heat for about 40 minutes, basting frequently, and adding more stock if necessary. Lift out the cooked cutlets and press them between 2 plates until cold.

Dissolve the gelatine in the water. Heat the Béchamel sauce and melt the aspic jelly. Mix together the dissolved gelatine, hot Béchamel sauce, and half the melted aspic jelly. Divide in half. To 1 portion add the cream and to the other the tomato sauce or purée. Season both portions to taste. Coat half the cutlets with the white sauce and the rest

with the red. Leave the cutlets in a cool place until the sauce is set; then pour the rest of the cold liquid aspic jelly over the cutlets. Arrange the cutlets in a circle on a round dish, using the colours alternately. Fill the centre of the plate with the dressed salad.

Lamb Cutlets in Aspic

8 helpings

8 cutlets from best end
  of neck of lamb
salt and pepper

250ml aspic jelly

Garnish

100g cooked green
  peas
100g cooked sliced green
  beans

2×15ml spoons
  mayonnaise **or** French
  dressing
$\frac{1}{2}$ lettuce

Wipe and trim the cutlets neatly. Season with salt and pepper. Either grill, shallow fry or braise the cutlets. Although grilling and frying are simpler and quicker methods, braising is recommended because it imparts extra flavour. When cooked, leave the cutlets until cold, covered with a light cloth.

Melt the aspic jelly and pour a thin layer of it into a large dish rinsed with cold water. Leave to set. Cool the remaining jelly until cold but not set. Brush the cutlets with the cold, liquid aspic and lay them about 1cm apart on the jelly, with each bone curving the same way. Pour the remaining jelly gently over the cutlets and leave to set. Then turn out on to a sheet of greaseproof paper laid on a chilled metal tray.

Mix the cooked peas and beans with the mayonnaise or French dressing and spoon them into the centre of a round dish. With a sharp knife dipped in hot water, cut out the cutlets and arrange them in a circle around the dish, with the bones pointing inwards. Shred the lettuce and arrange it outside the circle of cutlets. Chop the aspic remaining in the dish and use to garnish the cutlets.

OFFAL DISHES

Baked Stuffed Sheep's or Lamb's Hearts

4 helpings

2 sheep's **or** 4 lamb's
 hearts
basic herb stuffing
 (p375)
50g soft lamb **or** mutton
 fat

butter for greasing
250ml any strong stock
1 × 15ml spoon flour
salt and pepper

Prepare the hearts (p509). Dry thoroughly and fill with the stuffing. Skewer or sew together the thin flaps at the top to hold in the stuffing.

Heat the fat in a small baking tin and put in the hearts. Baste well, and bake them in a moderate oven, 180°C, Gas 4, for 1 hour for sheep's hearts, 45 minutes for lamb's hearts. Baste them several times during cooking. When cooked, transfer them to a warmed serving dish, remove the skewers, if necessary, and keep hot under buttered grease-proof paper.

Drain most of the fat from the tin but keep any meat juices. Blend a little stock into the flour to make a paste. Mix the paste into the pan juices, then gradually stir in the remaining stock. Heat to simmering point, stirring all the time, and simmer until thickened. Season well. Pour a little of this gravy round the hearts and serve the rest in a warmed sauce-boat.

Note The hearts can be cooked in a covered sauce-pan over gentle heat. Allow 1½ hours for sheep's hearts and 1¼ hours for lamb's hearts.

VARIATION

Use sage and onion (p378) or thyme and parsley (p375) stuffing instead of the basic herb stuffing.

Sheep's or Lamb's Hearts

(cooked without fat)

4 helpings

2 sheep's **or** 4 lamb's
 hearts
8 small gherkins **or**
 3 × 15ml spoons capers
4 × 10ml spoons cottage
 cheese

250ml any strong stock
butter for greasing
2 × 15ml spoons tomato
 juice

Garnish
chopped parsley

Prepare the hearts (p509). Dry thoroughly. Chop the gherkins or capers finely, and mix them with the cottage cheese. Use the mixture to stuff the hearts. Close the tops of the hearts with small metal skewers.

Heat the stock in a flameproof casserole. When simmering, put in the hearts and cover the pan with a tight-fitting lid. Cook over gentle heat for 1–1½ hours until tender, or in a moderate oven, 180°C, Gas 4, for the same time. When cooked, transfer the hearts to a warmed serving dish, remove the skewers, and keep hot under buttered greaseproof paper. Add the tomato juice to the stock, and boil rapidly over heat until it is almost reduced to a glaze. Pour this sauce over the hearts, sprinkle with parsley and serve very hot.

Lamb's Liver and Bacon

4–6 helpings

500g sheep's **or** lamb's
 liver
50g flour
salt and pepper

250g back bacon
 rashers, without rinds
400ml brown stock
 (p329)

Garnish
sprigs of parsley

Remove the skin and tubes, and cut the liver into 1cm thick slices. Season the flour with salt and pepper. Dip each slice of liver in the seasoned flour. Cook the bacon rashers in a frying pan. Transfer the bacon to a warmed dish and keep hot. Fry the slices of liver lightly and quickly in the fat from the bacon until browned on both sides, without hardening or over-cooking them. Transfer the liver to a warmed serving dish, arrange the bacon around it and keep hot.

Drain off all but about 1 × 10ml spoon of fat, stir in the remaining seasoned flour and cook until browned. Gradually add the stock and stir until boiling. Re-season if required. Garnish the liver and bacon with sprigs of parsley and serve the sauce separately.

Note Calf's liver can be used equally well.

Seasoned Liver

4 helpings

700g lamb's **or** *calf's liver*	*4 × 15ml spoons malt* **or** *red wine vinegar*
75g flour	*1 bay leaf*
salt and pepper	*a pinch of dried rosemary*
150ml frying oil	*500ml tomato juice*
2 cloves garlic	
1 × 5ml spoon light soft brown sugar	

Garnish
chopped parsley

Remove the skin and tubes, and cut the liver into slices about 1cm thick. Season the flour with salt and pepper. Dip each slice of liver in the seasoned flour. Put the oil into a frying pan and fry the liver slices over medium-high heat, quickly browning both sides (do not overcook). Transfer to a warmed serving dish and keep hot.

Add the remaining seasoned flour to the frying pan and stir until golden. Skin and crush the garlic and stir in with the rest of the ingredients. Heat to simmering point and let the sauce simmer for about 5 minutes until thick. Pour the sauce over the fried liver slices, sprinkle with the chopped parsley and serve.

Note This is a Greek dish by origin. In Greece it is often made in advance and served cold. It can be served cut in strips, as *mezze* (hors d'oeuvre) or as a main meat dish.

Liver with Savoury Rice

4 helpings

250g sheep's **or** *lamb's liver*	*200ml general household* **or** *brown stock* (p329)
a few strands of saffron	*fat for greasing*
4 × 15ml spoons hot water	*100g piece of streaky bacon, without rinds*
1 small onion (25g approx)	*juice of ½ lemon*
50g butter **or** *margarine*	*200ml Espagnole sauce (p707)*
100g Patna rice	
1 × 2.5ml spoon salt	
a pinch of Cayenne pepper	

Remove the skin and tubes, and cut the liver into 1cm cubes. Infuse the saffron in the hot water for 30 minutes, then strain. Skin and chop the onion. Heat 25g of the butter or margarine in a flameproof casserole and sauté the onion. Wash the rice and add it to the casserole. Mix well, and cook for 2 minutes. Add the salt, Cayenne pepper, and saffron liquid. Heat the stock and add it. Cover, and cook in a moderate oven, 180°C, Gas 4, for 30 minutes. (The rice should have completely absorbed the stock.) Add the remaining 25g butter or margarine to the rice. Spoon the rice mixture into a greased 600ml border mould and press it down with the back of a spoon. Keep hot.

Dice the bacon, and fry in a small saucepan until crisp, then remove and put to one side. Add the liver to the hot bacon fat and cook lightly, turning often. Remove the liver and put to one side. Add the lemon juice to the bacon fat and sediment, and stir well. Pour in the Espagnole sauce and heat to boiling point. Return the liver and bacon to the saucepan and re-heat without boiling.

Unmould the rice on to a warmed serving dish. Pile the liver and bacon mixture into the centre of the rice ring and serve.

Liver Hot Pot

6 helpings

500g sheep's **or** lamb's liver	fat for greasing
3 × 15ml spoons plain flour	500ml general household **or** brown stock (p329)
salt and pepper	6 rashers streaky bacon, without rinds
800g potatoes	
2 large onions (200g approx)	

Remove the skin and tubes from the liver. Season the flour with salt and pepper. Dip each slice of liver in the seasoned flour. Prepare the potatoes and onions and slice them thinly. Arrange layers of liver, onion, and potatoes in a greased casserole, ending with a neat layer of potatoes. Heat the stock and pour in just enough to cover the potatoes. Cover the casserole with a lid. Bake in a moderate oven, 180°C, Gas 4, for about 1 hour or until the liver is tender.

Remove the lid and arrange the bacon rashers on top. Continue cooking without a lid until the bacon is crisp. Serve from the casserole.

Note Calf's, ox or pig's liver can be used equally well.

Liver with Red Bell Peppers

4–6 helpings

500g sheep's **or** lamb's liver	4 red peppers (400g approx)
3 × 15ml spoons plain flour	4 tomatoes (200g approx)
50g dripping **or** lard **or** bacon fat	25g plain flour
fat for greasing	250ml general household **or** brown stock (p329)
2 medium-sized onions (200g approx)	salt and pepper

Remove the skin and tubes, and dip each slice of liver in the flour. Heat the dripping or fat in a frying pan and fry the liver quickly until lightly browned on both sides. Remove the liver and put it in a greased casserole. Prepare and slice all the vegetables. Fry the onions and peppers in the fat in the frying pan until softened but not browned. Add the tomatoes and fry gently for 2–3 minutes. Remove the fried vegetables from the pan with a perforated spoon and place them on top of the liver in the casserole.

Make a gravy by stirring the flour into the fat in the pan and cooking gently until browned. Gradually add the stock and stir until boiling. Season to taste. Pour the gravy over the liver and vegetables. Cover the casserole with a lid and bake in a moderate oven, 180°C, Gas 4, for 1 hour. Re-season if required. Arrange the liver, vegetables, and sauce neatly on a warmed serving dish.

Serve with a border of piped potato or boiled rice.

Devilled Kidneys

4 helpings

4 sheep's **or** 8 lamb's kidneys	2 × 5ml spoons lemon juice
3 × 10ml spoons dripping **or** oil	1 × 2.5ml spoon prepared mustard
1 × 15ml spoon chopped onion	125ml brown **or** general household stock (p329)
1 × 2.5ml spoon salt	2 egg yolks
$\frac{1}{2}$ × 2.5ml spoon Cayenne pepper	soft white breadcrumbs
1 × 15ml spoon chutney	

Skin, core, and cut the kidneys in half lengthways, then cut them into neat pieces. Heat the dripping or oil in a small pan, add the onion, and cook gently until softened but not browned. Add the kidney, salt, Cayenne pepper, chutney, lemon juice, mustard, and stock. Heat to boiling point, reduce the heat, cover the pan, and simmer gently for 15–20 minutes, until the kidney is cooked. Cool slightly. Beat the egg yolks lightly and stir them in. Sprinkle in enough breadcrumbs to make the mixture a soft consistency. Re-season if required.

Serve on buttered toast or in a border of hot creamed potatoes.

Note For other basic kidney recipes, see pp1321–22.

Lamb's Fry

6 helpings

650–700g lamb's fry (liver, heart, lights, melts, sweetbreads)	1 × 15ml spoon lemon juice
1 small onion (50g approx)	1 egg 4–6 × 15ml spoons soft white breadcrumbs
1 small carrot (25g approx)	75g dripping **or** lard 25g plain flour
bouquet garni	1 × 5ml spoon finely chopped parsley
salt and pepper	

Garnish
6 grilled bacon rolls
  (p396)

Prepare the fry as for Fried Pig's Fry (p594). Prepare the onion and carrot, and slice them thinly. Put the fry, onion, carrot and bouquet garni into a stew-pan, and cover with cold water. Heat to boiling point, reduce the heat, cover the pan, and simmer gently for about 30 minutes. Allow the meat to cool in the stock. When cold, strain and reserve the stock, and divide the meat into 2 portions.

Cut 1 portion of the meat into thin slices. Season with salt and pepper. Sprinkle with the lemon juice. Beat the egg until liquid and coat the slices with beaten egg and then with the breadcrumbs, and put to one side. Dice the rest of the meat.

Melt 25g of the dripping or lard in a saucepan. Stir in the flour and cook for 3 minutes. Gradually add 250ml of the strained stock and stir until boiling. Season to taste. Add the diced meat and parsley. Cover the pan and keep hot without boiling. Heat the remaining 50g dripping or lard in a frying pan. Fry the breadcrumbed slices of fry quickly on both sides until browned. Drain thoroughly.

Pile the diced meat and sauce from the saucepan into the centre of a warmed serving dish. Arrange the slices of fried meat round the outside and garnish with the bacon rolls.

Mutton Sausages

6 helpings

500g lean raw **or** under-cooked mutton	salt and pepper 2 eggs
50g ham **or** bacon	chicken stock
100g shredded suet	sausage casings (skins) (optional)
1 × 2.5ml spoon finely chopped onion	flour for rolling out (optional)
100g soft white breadcrumbs	2 × 15ml spoons dripping **or** lard
1 × 2.5ml spoon dried mixed herbs	

Mince all the meat finely, then mix with the suet, onion, breadcrumbs and herbs, and season well. Beat the eggs until liquid and stir in with just enough stock to moisten the mixture. Fill the sausage skins, if using, with the meat mixture. (See p591 for directions.) Alternatively, shape the mixture into patties.

Heat the fat in a frying pan. Fry the sausages or patties for 8–10 minutes, turning them often, until cooked through and well-browned.

Brains on Toast

6 helpings

3 sheep's **or** lamb's brains	25g butter 1 × 5ml spoon chopped parsley
salt and pepper	
1 hard-boiled egg	

Soak the brains in lightly salted cold water for 30 minutes to remove all traces of blood; then cut off any membranes. Wash thoroughly but very gently. Tie the brains in muslin. Heat a pan of water to boiling point, add 1 × 2.5ml spoon of salt and the brains, and cook gently for 15 minutes.

Drain the brains and remove them from the muslin. Chop the brains and the egg roughly. Melt the butter in a pan, add the brains and egg, and heat through. Season to taste and add the parsley.

Serve hot on buttered toast.

Note This recipe can also be used for calf's or pig's brains.

Stewed Brains

6 helpings

3 sheep's **or** 6 lamb's
  brains
1 × 15ml spoon vinegar
salt and pepper
3 rashers streaky bacon,
  without rinds
1 small onion (50g
  approx)
2 cloves
a small bunch of parsley

white (p329) **or** chicken
  (p330) stock to cover
oil **or** dripping **or** butter
  for frying
6 slices bread
2 × 5ml spoons lemon
  juice
250ml White Wine
  sauce (p698)

Prepare the brains (p551). Heat a pan of water to boiling point. Add the vinegar and 1 × 2.5ml spoon of salt. Tie the brains loosely in muslin, add them to the pan, reduce the heat, and simmer for 5 minutes.

Lift out the brains, remove the muslin, and place the brains in another saucepan. Cover with the rashers. Skin the onion and press the cloves into it. Add to the pan the onion, parsley, and salt and pepper to taste. Just cover the brains with stock. Heat to boiling point, reduce the heat to simmering point, cover the pan, and simmer gently for about 25 minutes.

Meanwhile, heat the oil, dripping or butter in a frying pan. Cut the crusts off the slices of bread and fry until golden-brown on both sides; drain. Transfer to a warmed serving dish and keep hot.

When cooked, drain the brains and divide them between the 6 slices of fried bread. Cut each rasher of bacon in half and put 1 piece on each portion of brains. Add the lemon juice to the White Wine sauce and spoon it over the brains.

Note This recipe can also be used for calf's or pig's brains.

VARIATION

Parsley sauce (p696) with lemon juice can be served instead of white wine sauce. Add a carrot and bay leaf to the other vegetables in the stock, and omit the bacon and cloves.

Brain and Tongue Pudding

6 helpings

3 sheep's **or** 6 lamb's
  brains
salt and pepper
3 sheep's **or** lamb's
  tongues
1 hard-boiled egg
1 shallot
suet crust pastry (p1250)
  using 150g flour

flour for rolling out
fat for greasing
1 × 5ml spoon chopped
  parsley
1 × 5ml spoon flour
125ml milk
fat for greasing

Prepare the brains (p551) and the tongues (p554).

Cover the tongues with cold, lightly salted water in a saucepan, and heat to boiling point. Reduce the heat to simmering point, and simmer for about 2 hours until the skin can be removed. Top up with water during cooking, if necessary. Tie the brains in a square of muslin. Add them for the last 20 minutes of the cooking time. Drain the tongue and brains. Slice the hard-boiled egg. Chop the brains coarsely. Skin the shallot and chop it finely. Strip the skin from the cooked tongue, remove the small bones at the root, together with the excess fat and gristle, and slice the tongue.

Reserve one-quarter of the pastry for the lid. Roll out the remaining pastry on a lightly floured surface so that it is 1cm larger than the top of a greased 1 litre basin, and 5mm thick. Press well into the basin to remove any creases. Fill with layers of sliced tongue, chopped brains, and sliced egg. Sprinkle the parsley, shallot, flour, salt and pepper between each layer. Add the milk. Roll out the remaining pastry to fit the top, dampen the edges, place in position and seal. Cover with greased greaseproof paper or foil. Place the basin in a steamer, or on a saucer in a pan with water coming half-way up the basin's sides. Steam, or half steam, for 3–3½ hours, topping up the steamer or pan with boiling water when it is reduced by a third.

Note This recipe can also be used for calf's or pig's brains.

Sweetbreads Bourgeoise

6 helpings

*3 pairs lamb's
    sweetbreads (650–675g
    approx)*
25g butter **or** *margarine*
white (p329) **or** *chicken*
    (p330) *stock to cover*
salt and pepper
2 × 15ml spoons peas

*2 × 15ml spoons diced
    turnip*
*2 × 15ml spoons diced
    carrot*
250ml foundation brown
    (p698) **or** *Espagnole*
    (p707) *sauce*

Soak the sweetbreads in cold water for 1–2 hours to remove all the blood. Drain, and put them in a pan with cold water to cover. Heat to boiling point and pour off the liquid. Rinse the sweetbreads under cold water. Remove the black veins and as much as possible of the membranes which cover them.

Heat the butter or margarine in a saucepan and toss the sweetbreads in it. Then barely cover them with the stock. Season to taste with salt and pepper. Heat to simmering point, cover the pan, and cook gently for 45 minutes–1 hour, until tender. Transfer to a warmed dish and keep hot.

Prepare the vegetables and cook them separately in boiling salted water until just tender. Drain, and add them to the hot brown or Espagnole sauce. Divide the sweetbreads between 6 soup bowls and pour the sauce over them. Serve very hot.

Fried Lamb's Sweetbreads

6 helpings

*3 pairs lamb's
    sweetbreads (650–675g
    approx)*
white stock (p329) *to
    cover*
1 × 5ml spoon butter
*1 × 2.5ml spoon lemon
    juice*
*2 × 15ml spoons plain
    flour*

salt and pepper
1 egg
*soft white breadcrumbs
    for coating*
25g butter **or** *bacon fat
    for frying*
*250ml Cucumber sauce
    (p705)*

Prepare the sweetbreads as for Sweetbreads Bourgeoise. Put them in a pan, with just enough stock to cover them; add the butter and the lemon juice.

Heat to boiling point, cover the pan, reduce the heat, and simmer gently for 15–20 minutes. Leave the sweetbreads to cool in the stock. When cool, drain.

Season the flour with salt and pepper. Beat the egg until liquid. Dip the sweetbreads in the seasoned flour, then coat them with the beaten egg and breadcrumbs. Heat the butter or bacon fat in a frying pan and fry the crumbed sweetbreads for about 8 minutes until golden-brown on all sides. Lift them out and drain.

Serve the fried sweetbreads with sautéed mushrooms and the Cucumber sauce.

Note Calf's sweetbreads can be used for this and the previous recipe.

Croustades of Sweetbreads

8 helpings

*3 pairs lamb's
    sweetbreads (650–675g
    approx)*
25g butter **or** *margarine*
white (p329) **or** *chicken*
    (p330) *stock to cover*
salt and pepper

*8 baked vol-au-vent
    cases (7cm in diameter
    approx) (p1253)*
250ml Béchamel (p704)
    or *Suprême (p710)
    sauce*

Prepare and cook the sweetbreads as for Sweetbreads Bourgeoise until the sweetbreads have been cooked for 1 hour, and are tender. Drain the sweetbreads and dry thoroughly. Fill the hot vol-au-vent cases with the sweetbreads and cover them with Béchamel or Suprême sauce. Serve hot.

Boiled Sheep's or Lamb's Tongues

4 helpings

2 sheep's **or** 4 lamb's
 tongues
500ml general household
 stock (p329)
salt and pepper
25g butter

1 ×15ml spoon plain
 flour
1 ×15ml spoon capers
 (optional)
1 ×15ml spoon dry
 sherry (optional)

Soak the tongues in cold salted water for 1 hour, then drain them. Place them in a pan, cover with cold water, and heat to boiling point. Pour off the water, and dry the tongues.

Put them back in the pan, cover with stock, and season with salt and pepper. Heat to boiling point, reduce the heat, cover the pan with a tight-fitting lid and simmer for about 2 hours until tender. Drain, and reserve 250ml stock. Strip the skin and remove the small bones at the root of the tongue, together with the excess fat and gristle. Divide the sheep's tongues lengthways into three, and the lamb's tongues lengthways in half. Transfer to a warmed dish and keep hot.

Melt the butter in a saucepan. Stir in the flour and cook for 3 minutes. Gradually add the reserved stock and stir until boiling, then reduce the heat and simmer for 2 minutes. Season to taste. Chop and add the capers, and the sherry, if used; then add the sliced tongues and re-heat.

Serve hot in a border of cooked spaghetti, creamed potatoes or chopped spinach.

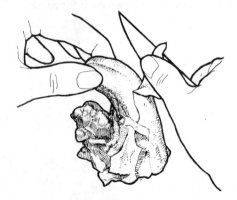

1 Strip the skin from the tongue

Braised Tongues

4 helpings

2 sheep's **or** 4 lamb's
 tongues
25g dripping **or** lard
1 medium-sized onion
 (100g approx)
1 turnip (50g approx)
1 medium-sized carrot
 (50g approx)
2 sticks celery (100g
 approx)

bouquet garni
6 black peppercorns
250ml general household
 stock (p329)
2 rashers streaky bacon,
 without rinds
butter for greasing
meat glaze (p397)

Prepare the tongues as for Boiled Sheep's or Lamb's Tongues. Heat the dripping or lard in a stewpan. Prepare and slice the vegetables. Add to the pan, cover with a tight-fitting lid and simmer for 10 minutes, shaking the pan several times to prevent sticking. Remove the lid and lay the tongues on top of the vegetables. Add the bouquet garni, peppercorns, and enough stock almost to cover the vegetables. Place the rashers on top of the tongues. Cover with buttered greaseproof paper and the lid, and cook gently for about 2 hours or until the tongues are tender.

When cooked, strip the skin from the tongue and remove the small bones at the root, together with the excess fat and gristle. Cut the tongues in half lengthways. Brush them with warm meat glaze. Place the tongues on buttered greaseproof paper in a baking tin and re-heat in a warm oven for a few minutes.

Serve on a bed of hot creamed potatoes or spinach purée.

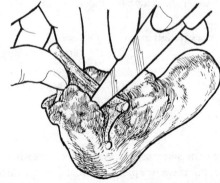

2 Remove the bones at the root of the tongue

Boiled Sheep's Head

Basic recipe

3–5 helpings

a sheep's head　　　*2 medium-sized carrots*
salt　　　　　　　　*(100g approx)*
2 medium-sized onions　*10 black peppercorns*
　(200g approx)　　　*bouquet garni*

Garnish
1 × 10ml spoon chopped
　parsley

Ask the butcher to split the head if not already done. Remove the brains and put to one side. Snip off any remaining hairy bits of skin, scrub the teeth and jaw bones with salt and scrape the bones from the nostrils. Rinse the head and soak it in cold water, adding 1 × 15ml spoon salt to each litre of water. Put the brains in the water with the head and soak both for 30 minutes to remove all traces of blood; then cut off any membranes. Wash thoroughly but very gently. The brains can be used separately or tied in muslin, cooked for part of the time with the head, and used with the meat of the head.

Cover the head with cold water, heat to boiling point, and pour the water away. Cover the head with fresh cold water. Prepare the onions and carrots and add them to the pan with 2 × 5ml spoons salt, the peppercorns, and bouquet garni. Heat to boiling point, reduce the heat, cover the pan with a tight-fitting lid, and simmer gently for 2 hours until the meat is tender.

If the brains are not to be used separately, tie them in muslin and add them to the pan for the last 10–15 minutes of the cooking time. Remove the head and brains, if cooked, from the pan and put to one side until they are cool enough to handle. Strain the liquid into a clean pan. Reserve a little for serving with the meat. Alternatively, reserve 375ml to make brain sauce to serve with the meat.

Put the head on a board. Remove and slice the meat from the bones. Strip the skin from the tongue, remove the small bones at the root, together with the excess fat and gristle. Remove the brains from the muslin. Slice the tongue and the brains, if they are to be served with the meat. Reheat the meats in the strained stock in the pan. Season to taste.

Serve garnished with chopped parsley and with either the reserved stock or brain sauce.

Note A calf's head can be prepared in the same way.

VARIATION

Boiled Sheep's Head with Brain Sauce

3–5 helpings

ingredients as for Boiled　*375ml cooking liquid*
　Sheep's Head　　　　*from boiling sheep's*
*25g butter **or** dripping*　*head*
25g plain flour　　　　*salt and pepper*

Garnish
1 × 15ml spoon chopped
　parsley

Follow the recipe for Boiled Sheep's Head, cooking the brains with the head for 10–15 minutes. Remove the cooked brains from the muslin, drain, then chop them coarsely.

Melt the butter or dripping in a saucepan. Stir in the flour and cook without browning for 3 minutes. Gradually add the cooking liquid and stir until boiling. Boil for 2 minutes. Season to taste and add the chopped brains. Leave this sauce over very low heat while dealing with the head meat. Arrange the sliced meat neatly on a warmed serving dish. Pour the sauce over it. Garnish with the sliced tongue and chopped parsley.

Note Another recipe for Brain Sauce can be found on p692.

Veal

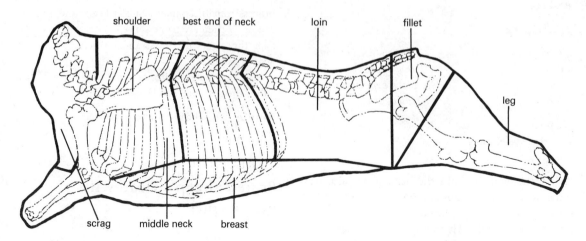

Veal is the flesh (meat) of a calf. Calves are slaughtered at any age between 10 days and 12 weeks old. 'Bobby calves' are calves from dairy herds, usually those unsuitable for rearing. They are slaughtered 7–10 days after birth, yielding a carcass of 17–28kg. Veal calves reared specially for good quality meat, and slaughtered at 10–12 weeks old yield a much larger carcass of 81–99kg; but in spite of this the meat is more expensive than that of bobby calves. The most delicate veal comes from a specially reared calf, fed on milk, usually imported from Holland or France. Although it lacks flavour, the meat is tender and a very delicate pale pink. English calves are generally partly grass-fed and the meat is less tender and pale, but it has more flavour, especially veal from older calves.

QUALITY OF VEAL

There is very little fat on veal except in the largest carcasses, and even in these the ratio of fat to meat is much smaller than in other meat. Veal bones are soft and, in most cases, can be cut through easily with a sharp knife. Air bubbles may be present in and around the knuckle end of the shoulder and along the breast continuing into the hind leg. These are formed by inflating the carcass prior to skinning, a process which aids easy stripping.

Due to the lack of fat, veal can be dry and may be tasteless unless cooked with a moist, fatty stuffing, or served with a sauce. Calf's offal is more tender and delicately flavoured than that of any other animal.

VEAL CUTS

Veal is cut in the same way as lamb and the cuts are usually described by the same names. See the diagram above.

Taking an average carcass weight of 22kg, the approximate weights of the cuts are as follows:

1) *Leg* is a large and expensive joint. The hind knuckle or shin is removed at the knee joint and used for Ossi Buchi (p564), or boned for pie veal. The rest of the leg can be roasted on the bone. Because of the continental method of cutting a leg

Part cut of leg of veal

of veal lengthways along the muscles, escalopes are usually taken from the topside (cushion) of veal or *noix*. This cut gives solid slices of meat cut across the grain, which do not curl in cooking. British butchers do not usually cut a leg in this way, so escalopes are often cut from the fleshy part of the leg, and must be snipped at the edges to prevent curling. They should be cut 1cm thick, and beaten out to 5mm thick, then left to regain resilience before cooking. (Av wt boneless leg – 3.5kg)

2) *Fillet* is the most expensive of the veal cuts. Usually cut into fillet steaks or escalopes but can be larded and roasted whole. (Av wt bobby calves 225–300g; Av wt veal calves – 900g)

3) *Loin* is suitable for roasting as a joint on the bone or as a boned, stuffed and rolled joint. It can also be cut into loin chops, suitable for grilling and frying. The end of the loin closest to the leg is often called the chump end. (Av wt 1.5–1.75kg)

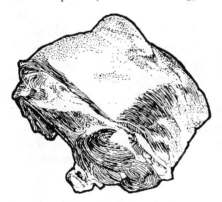

4) *Best end of neck* is suitable for roasting or braising. Also available cut into cutlets for grilling, frying or baking. (Av wt – 1kg)

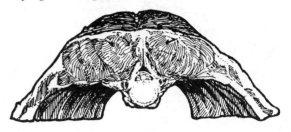

Two best ends of neck

5) *Breast* when boned, stuffed and roasted is a most tasty and economical cut of veal. (Av wt – 675g)

6) *Shoulder* (also called Oyster of Veal after the fore knuckle has been removed) is suitable for roasting on the bone or boned and rolled. (Av wt – 2.5kg)

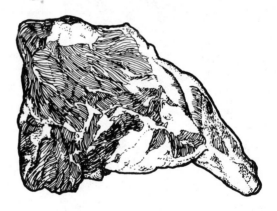

7) *Middle neck* and

8) *Scrag* are economical cuts, but there is a high proportion of bone. Middle neck is usually sold in cutlets for braising or stewing or is boned for pie veal. Scrag is mainly sold for boiling, stewing or casseroles. (Av wt both joints – 1.5kg)

9) *Cutlets* are obtained from the best end of neck. 6 per carcass. (Av wt – 175g each)

10) *Chops* from the loin (with or without kidney) can be cut to any size, so the number varies. (Av wt – 225g each)

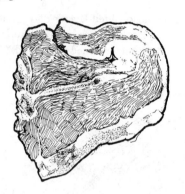

ROASTED AND BAKED DISHES

Roast Veal

Basic recipe

a joint of veal suitable for roasting	*grated lemon rind*
salt and pepper	*strips of bacon* **or** *pork fat*

Choose the method of roasting, ie quick or slow roasting (p470). Weigh the joint to calculate the cooking time (p471). Wipe the meat. Place the joint on a wire rack, if available, in a shallow roasting tin. Season the meat well with salt, pepper, and a light sprinkling of grated lemon rind. Cover the top of the joint with strips of bacon or pork fat, and cook for the required time.

Transfer the cooked meat from the oven to a warmed serving dish and keep hot. Prepare gravy from the sediment in the roasting tin.

Serve roast veal with basic herb stuffing or forcemeat balls (pp375–76) and with bacon rolls (p396) and lemon wedges.

Barded Roast Best End Neck of Veal

4 helpings

a best end of neck of veal (1kg approx)	*bouquet garni*
larding bacon	*10 white peppercorns*
2 medium-sized carrots	*125–250ml white* (p329)
1 medium-sized onion	*or chicken* (p330) *stock*
1 small turnip	*butter for greasing*
2 sticks celery	*fat* **or** *oil for basting*
salt	*25g butter* **or** *margarine*
	25g plain flour

Wipe the meat. Fold the flap of meat under the joint. Bard the upper surface (flesh side) in close rows with thin 4cm strips of fat bacon. Prepare and slice the carrots, onion, turnip, and celery. Put the vegetables in a large pan with the salt, bouquet garni, peppercorns, and just enough stock to cover them. Lay the meat on top, cover with buttered greaseproof paper and a tight-fitting lid, and cook gently for 2 hours. Add more stock, if needed.

When cooked, remove the meat from the pan. Heat some fat or oil in a roasting tin. Put the meat into the hot fat or oil, baste well and bake in a moderate oven, 180°C, Gas 4, for 30 minutes, basting after 15 minutes. Transfer the meat to a warmed dish and keep hot. Strain and measure the stock in which the meat was cooked and make up to 375ml with water.

Heat the butter or margarine in a pan. Stir in the flour and cook gently until browned. Gradually add the stock to the roux and stir until boiling. Reduce the heat and simmer for 5 minutes. Season to taste. Serve the sauce separately.

FRIED AND GRILLED DISHES

Escalopes of Veal
(Wiener Schnitzel)

6 helpings

6 thin escalopes of veal (13 × 8cm approx)	2–3 drops oil
plain flour	dried white breadcrumbs for coating
salt and pepper	butter **or** oil and butter for frying
1 egg	

Garnish
6 crimped lemon slices (p392)	1 × 15ml spoon chopped parsley

Wipe the meat. Season the flour with salt and pepper. Dip the escalopes in the seasoned flour. Beat the egg until liquid with the oil. Brush the escalopes with the egg mixture and coat with breadcrumbs, pressing them on well. Heat the butter or mixture of oil and butter in a large frying pan. Put in the escalopes and fry over moderate to gentle heat for 7–10 minutes, turning them once only.

Remove the escalopes and place them, overlapping slightly, on a warmed, flat serving dish. Garnish the middle of each escalope with a crimped slice of lemon sprinkled with parsley.

Note Escalope of veal or schnitzel is a German and Austrian speciality by origin, although its more popular garnishes now make several dishes famous in the international cuisine. The usual sauce for plain schnitzel (Naturschnitzel) consists of the pan juices mixed with a little stock and a walnut of butter; but the French often serve their escalopes with Beurre Noisette (p715), and the Swiss, with cream and lemon juice mixed with the pan juices.

VARIATION

Holstein Schnitzel

Cook as for Wiener Schnitzel, but serve with a fried, poached or chopped hard-boiled egg. Garnish with small heaps of chopped gherkin and beetroot, whole capers, whole green olives, and drained anchovy fillets. Place a crimped slice of lemon or 'lemon butterfly' (pp391–92) on the schnitzel, and pour a little Beurre Noisette (p715) over the schnitzel before serving.

Parisian Veal

3–4 helpings

300g fillet of veal	200ml Madeira sauce (p708)
salt and pepper	
1 × 15ml spoon olive oil	1 × 5ml spoon chopped parsley
1 × 10ml spoon finely chopped onion	

Garnish
potatoes Parisienne (p399)	fried bread croûtons

Wipe, trim, and cut the meat into 3 or 4 slices 1cm thick (approx). Season each slice well. Heat the oil in a frying pan and fry the fillets gently, turning once until lightly browned on both sides. Add the onion and continue frying gently until the onion is transparent. Add the sauce, cover the pan loosely, and cook gently for about 30 minutes until the meat is tender. Add the chopped parsley and arrange on a warmed serving dish. Garnish with potatoes Parisienne and bread croûtons.

Escalopes with Ham and Cheese

6 helpings

6 thin escalopes of veal	butter **or** oil and butter
plain flour	for frying
salt and pepper	6 thin slices lean ham
1 egg	6 thin slices Gruyère
2–3 drops oil	cheese **or** 6 × 15ml
dried white breadcrumbs	spoons grated
for coating	Parmesan cheese

Wipe the escalopes and flatten them with a cutlet bat or rolling-pin. Season the flour with salt and pepper. Dip the escalopes in the seasoned flour. Beat the egg until liquid with the oil. Brush the escalopes with the egg mixture and coat with breadcrumbs, pressing them on well. Heat the butter or oil and butter in a large frying pan. Put in the escalopes and fry over moderate to gentle heat for about 3 minutes on each side.

Remove the escalopes and place them side by side in a flat ovenproof dish. Cover each escalope with a slice of ham, and top with a slice or spoon of cheese. Spoon a little of the juices from the pan over the cheese. Place in a fairly hot oven, 200°C, Gas 6, and cook until the cheese melts. Serve at once.

Veal Cutlets Maintenon

6 helpings

600–700g best end **or**	25g plain flour
middle neck of veal, cut	375ml white stock
into cutlets	(p329)
butter **or** oil and butter	a few strips lemon rind
for frying	salt and pepper
25g ham	oil **or** softened butter for
1 shallot (25g approx)	greasing
25g butter	

Allow 2 cutlets per person. Wipe and trim the cutlets. Heat the butter or oil and butter in a large frying pan and fry the cutlets until lightly browned on both sides. Remove, drain, and put the cutlets to one side.

Shred the ham, and skin and chop the shallot finely. Melt the butter in a stewpan. Add the ham

and shallot and sauté for 3 minutes. Stir in the flour and cook gently until light brown. Gradually add the stock, lemon rind and seasoning, and stir until boiling. Reduce the heat and simmer gently for 15 minutes. Add the cutlets. Cover the pan loosely, and cook very gently, just below simmering point, for about 20 minutes until the meat is tender. Test with a skewer. Remove the cutlets and keep warm. Strain the sauce and leave to cool.

Place each cutlet on a sheet of foil greased with oil or softened butter. Cover with the sauce and seal the foil so that the sauce cannot escape. Put the cutlets in a baking tin and bake in a fairly hot oven, 190°C, Gas 5, for 15 minutes. Serve in the foil cases.

Fried Fillets of Veal with Lemon Sauce

3–4 helpings

300g fillet of veal	1 × 5ml spoon lemon
1 egg	juice
1 × 2.5ml spoon chopped	dried white breadcrumbs
parsley	for coating
½ × 2.5ml spoon chopped	50g butter
fresh thyme	creamed potatoes
1 × 5ml spoon grated	
lemon rind	

Lemon Sauce

1 × 15ml spoon plain	a little gravy browning
flour	salt and pepper
250ml white stock (p329)	1–2 × 15ml spoons
1 × 2.5ml spoon lemon	single cream (optional)
juice	

Garnish
6 grilled bacon rolls
(p396)

Wipe, trim, and cut the meat into 3 or 4 slices about 1cm thick. Flatten each slice with a cutlet bat or rolling-pin. Beat the egg until liquid and add the herbs, lemon rind and juice. Soak the fillets in this mixture for about 30 minutes; then coat them with breadcrumbs, pressing them on well. Heat the butter in a frying pan and fry the fillets over moderate heat until golden-brown on both sides; then reduce the heat and cook more slowly for 7–10 minutes in all. Remove the fillets and drain thoroughly. Reserve the fat in the pan. Transfer the fillets to a warmed dish and keep hot, together with the grilled bacon rolls for the garnish.

To make the sauce, stir the flour into the fat in the pan and cook gently for about 2 minutes. Gradually add the stock and stir until boiling. Add the lemon juice, enough gravy browning to make the sauce a pale brown colour, and seasoning to taste. Reduce the heat and simmer the sauce for 3 minutes. Remove from the heat and stir in the cream, if used.

Pipe or spoon a border of creamed potatoes on a warmed serving dish. Arrange the fillets in the centre and place the bacon rolls diagonally on the potato border. Strain the sauce and pour a little over the fillets. Serve the rest separately.

Grilled Veal Cutlets

6 helpings

600–700g best end **or** middle neck of veal, cut into cutlets	a little melted butter **or** oil
1 egg	375ml Italian (p705),
salt and pepper	Fresh Tomato (p715),
dried white breadcrumbs for coating	**or** Demi-glace (p708) sauce

Garnish
sprigs of parsley   slices of lemon

Wipe and trim the cutlets. Beat the egg lightly until liquid and season to taste. Brush the cutlets with the beaten egg and coat with breadcrumbs, pressing them on well; then brush the cutlets carefully with a little melted butter or oil. Place them on the rack of a grill pan and cook under a hot grill for about 10–15 minutes, basting occasionally with more melted butter or oil to prevent the breadcrumbs burning, until the cutlets are golden-brown on both sides and cooked through. Arrange them on a warmed serving dish and garnish with parsley and slices of lemon. Pour some of the chosen sauce round the cutlets and serve the rest separately.

Russian Veal Escalopes

6 helpings

1kg fillet **or** topside leg of veal cut into 6 escalopes	1 × 213g can small mushrooms
75g butter	250ml Demi-glace sauce (p708)
fat for greasing	salt and pepper

Stuffing

75g pork	1 egg yolk
75g beef marrow	salt and pepper
1 × 5ml spoon dried mixed herbs	4 × 15ml spoons soft white breadcrumbs
25–50g anchovy paste	

Garnish
sprigs of parsley   stoned green olives

Wipe the escalopes and flatten them with a cutlet bat or rolling-pin. Heat 50g of the butter in a frying pan. Put in the escalopes and fry until lightly browned on both sides. Remove the escalopes and drain thoroughly. Draw the pan off the heat. Reserve the fat in the pan for sautéing the mushrooms. Press the escalopes between 2 plates until cold.

Make the stuffing by mincing or chopping the pork and beef marrow into very small pieces. Add the herbs, anchovy paste, egg yolk, seasoning, and half the breadcrumbs, mix well, and rub through a wire sieve or process in an electric blender to make a fairly smooth paste. Spread the stuffing on one side of each escalope and sprinkle with the remaining breadcrumbs. Place the escalopes in a lightly greased baking tin, melt the remaining butter and pour it over them. Bake in a fairly hot oven, 190°C, Gas 5, for 20 minutes.

Meanwhile, drain the mushrooms and sauté them in the fat in the frying pan. Add the Demi-glace sauce. Season to taste and simmer very gently for 10 minutes. Arrange the escalopes in a circle on a warmed serving dish and spoon the mushrooms and sauce into the centre. Garnish with sprigs of parsley and stoned olives.

Fried Veal Cutlets

6 helpings

600–700g best end **or**
  middle neck of veal, cut
  into cutlets
1 egg
2 × 15ml spoons milk
1 × 5ml spoon chopped
  parsley
½ × 2.5ml spoon dried
  thyme
1 × 2.5ml spoon grated
  lemon rind

salt and pepper
1 × 10ml spoon melted
  butter
dried white breadcrumbs
  for coating
butter **or** oil and butter
  for frying
375ml Fresh Tomato
  (p715), Demi-glace
  (p708) **or** Piquant
  (p702) sauce

Garnish
sprigs of parsley   slices of lemon

Wipe and trim the cutlets. Beat the egg and milk together and mix with the parsley, thyme, lemon rind, seasoning, and melted butter. Brush the cutlets with the egg mixture and coat with breadcrumbs, pressing them on well.

Heat the butter or oil and butter mixture in a frying pan, and fry the cutlets over moderate heat, turning once, until golden-brown on both sides; then reduce the heat and cook more slowly for 10–15 minutes in all. Remove the cutlets from the pan and drain thoroughly. Arrange on a warmed serving dish. Garnish with sprigs of parsley and lemon slices.

Serve with Fresh Tomato Sauce, Demi-glace Sauce or Piquant Sauce.

Collops of Veal

6 helpings

600g fillet of veal
6 rashers streaky bacon,
  without rinds
salt and pepper
100g basic herb stuffing
  (p375)
1 egg
soft white breadcrumbs
  for coating

butter **or** oil and butter
  for frying
2 × 10ml spoons plain
  flour
250ml white stock
  (p329) **or** water
1 × 15ml spoon lemon
  juice
a pinch of ground mace

Garnish
slices of lemon   fried forcemeat balls
sprigs of parsley   (p376) (optional)

Wipe the meat and cut it into very thin slices about 8cm × 5cm. Lay the rashers on a board and stretch each one with a palette knife. Cover each slice of meat with a piece of bacon. Season well and spread thinly with stuffing. Roll up and secure with a short metal skewer, if necessary. Beat the egg until liquid and season. Brush the collops with beaten egg and coat with breadcrumbs, pressing them on well.

Heat the butter or mixture of oil and butter in a large frying pan. Gently fry the collops and the forcemeat balls for the garnish, if used. Turn often until cooked through and golden-brown all over. Test for readiness with a skewer. Drain, and arrange the collops on a warmed serving dish; keep hot. Pour any excess fat out of the pan, leaving about 1 × 15ml spoon in addition to any sediment. Stir in the flour and cook until lightly browned. Meanwhile, heat the stock or water to boiling point. Stir it into the sauce gradually with the lemon juice, mace, and seasoning to taste. Simmer gently for 5 minutes, then strain. Garnish the collops with lemon slices, parsley sprigs, and the fried forcemeat balls, if used. Serve the sauce separately.

BRAISED DISHES

Braised Neck of Veal

4–6 helpings

1kg best end neck of veal	1 blade of mace
2 × 15ml spoons lard **or** dripping	12 black peppercorns
	salt and pepper
50g streaky bacon, without rinds	white **or** general household stock (p329) to cover
2 medium-sized onions (200g approx)	
2 medium-sized carrots (100g approx)	butter for greasing
	2 × 10ml spoons plain flour
1 small turnip (50g approx)	1 × 15ml spoon capers
bouquet garni	1 × 5ml spoon lemon juice
2 cloves	meat glaze (p397)

Wipe the meat. Cut off the short pieces or rib bones which should have been sawn across, and fold under the flap of meat. Melt half the lard or dripping in a stewpan. Chop the bacon. Prepare the vegetables and chop them roughly. Fry them gently in the fat for about 5 minutes. Add the bouquet garni, spices, peppercorns, and seasoning. Pour in enough stock almost to cover the vegetables. Heat to boiling point, then reduce the heat, and place the meat on top of the vegetables. Cover with buttered greaseproof paper and a tight-fitting lid, and cook gently for about 2¼ hours, adding more stock as necessary and basting occasionally. When cooked, put the meat in a greased baking dish, and bake in a moderate oven, 180°C, Gas 4, for 15 minutes.

Meanwhile, melt the remaining lard or dripping in a small pan. Stir in the flour and fry gently until nut-brown. Strain the liquid from the vegetables in the stewpan. Gradually add the liquid to the roux and stir until the sauce boils and thickens. Pour in more stock if it is too thick, and simmer for 5 minutes. Add the capers and lemon juice. Season to taste. Place the meat on a warmed serving dish, brush with meat glaze and garnish with some of the vegetables. Serve the sauce separately.

Escalopes of Veal Milanaise

6 helpings

6 thin escalopes of veal	2 large tomatoes (200g approx)
salt and pepper	
olive oil and butter for frying	500ml foundation brown sauce (p698)
3 rashers streaky bacon, without rinds	2 × 15ml spoons sherry (optional)
1 shallot **or** 25g onion	75g spaghetti

Garnish
12 stoned green olives

Wipe and trim the escalopes. Season well on both sides. Heat the oil and butter in a large frying pan and fry the escalopes quickly on both sides until lightly browned. Remove them from the pan and drain. Place in a shallow casserole or ovenproof dish with a lid. Chop the bacon. Skin and finely chop or grate the shallot or onion, and skin and slice the tomatoes. Add the bacon and vegetables to the veal in the casserole or dish, and season to taste. Heat the brown sauce to boiling point, add the sherry, if used, and pour it over the veal. Cover, and bake in a moderate oven, 180°C, Gas 4, for 1 hour.

Meanwhile, cook the spaghetti in a large pan of boiling salted water for 5 minutes, then drain. Rinse the spaghetti with cold water and add it to the casserole or dish 15–20 minutes before the end of the cooking time. Garnish with the stoned olives. Serve from the casserole or dish.

Fricandeau of Veal

6 helpings

800–900g fillet of veal	bouquet garni
larding bacon	2 cloves
2 medium-sized onions	6 black peppercorns
(200g approx)	salt and pepper
2 medium-sized carrots	white **or** general
(100g approx)	household stock (p329)
1 small turnip	to cover
(50g approx)	butter for greasing
2 sticks celery	meat glaze (p397)
(100g approx)	600g spinach **or** sorrel
25g margarine **or** lard	purée
25g bacon cut in	375ml Espagnole sauce
pieces, without rinds	(p707) (optional)

Wipe and trim the meat. Flatten the meat slightly with a cutlet bat or rolling-pin. Bard one side closely with strips of larding bacon. Skin and slice the onions thickly. Prepare the carrots and turnip, and cut them into large dice. Wash and chop the celery. Melt the margarine or lard in a large flame-proof casserole and fry the bacon and vegetables for about 5 minutes. Lay the meat on top, baste with the fat, cover, and fry gently for a further 15 minutes. Add the bouquet garni, cloves, pepper-corns, seasoning, and enough stock to cover the vegetables. Cover with buttered greaseproof paper and a tight-fitting lid and cook gently for about 1 hour, adding more stock if necessary. When cooked, remove the lid and paper, and put the casserole into a fairly hot oven, 200°C, Gas 6, for 15 minutes to crisp and brown the lardoons. Brush with meat glaze.

Place the meat, barded side uppermost, on a bed of spinach or sorrel purée, and serve the rest of the purée separately. The liquid from the braising pan should be strained, reduced, skimmed to remove all fat, and poured round the meat. Alternatively, it can be added to hot Espagnole sauce, a little of the sauce poured over the meat, and the rest served separately.

Ossi Buchi

(Braised Veal Knuckles in Wine)

4 helpings

50g flour	2 cloves garlic
salt and pepper	150g tomatoes
4 veal knuckles **or**	25g concentrated tomato
shanks sawn across the	purée
bone (175g each	200ml beef stock
approx)	juice of 1 lemon
4 × 15ml spoons cooking	150ml dry white wine
oil	Saffron rice (p524)
2 medium-sized carrots	1 × 15ml spoon
(50g each approx)	cornflour
1–2 sticks celery	3 × 15ml spoons water
(75g approx)	
1 medium-sized onion	
(100g approx)	

Garnish

1–2 × 15ml spoons	grated rind of 1 lemon
finely chopped fresh	
herbs (oregano, basil,	
chervil, mint, parsley,	
or as available)	

Season the flour with salt and pepper and toss the knuckles or shanks in it. Shake off any surplus flour. Heat the oil in a large frying pan and fry the meat for 8 minutes, turning as required, until browned all over. Put the meat into a shallow ovenproof baking dish.

Prepare and chop the carrots, celery and onion finely, and put into the frying pan. Fry for 5 minutes, turning them over. Skin and crush the garlic, and add to the pan. Fry for 2 minutes. Put to one side.

Prepare and chop the tomatoes, and mix with the tomato purée, stock, and salt and pepper to taste. Stir the mixture into the frying pan and cook over moderate heat until boiling, scraping in any sediment in the pan. Remove from the heat. Add the lemon juice and wine. Pour the sauce over the veal, cover tightly with foil, and bake in a moderate oven, 180°C, Gas 4, for 1½–2 hours, or until the meat is very tender.

When cooked, place the meat on a bed of Saffron rice on a warmed serving dish and keep hot. Strain the sauce into a small saucepan. Blend the corn-flour with the water, and stir it into the sauce. Heat the sauce to boiling point and cook until it thickens, stirring all the time. Pour it over the veal. Sprinkle with the garnish of chopped fresh herbs and grated lemon rind.

French Fillets of Veal

6 helpings

600g fillet of veal	*bouquet garni*
larding bacon	*6 peppercorns*
1 medium-sized onion	*1 clove*
(100g approx)	*500ml white or general*
1 medium-sized carrot	*household stock* (p329)
(50g approx)	*butter for greasing*
½ turnip (25g approx)	*25g plain flour*
2 sticks celery	*500g creamed potatoes*
(100g approx)	*meat glaze* (p397)
50g butter or margarine	

Garnish
100g cooked peas or
asparagus tips or
macedoine of
vegetables (p398)

Wipe the meat and cut it into slices 1cm thick. Cut each slice into rounds 5cm in diameter (approx). Bard them on one side with thin strips of bacon 4cm long (approx). Prepare and slice the onion, carrot, and turnip. Wash and chop the celery. Heat 25g butter or margarine in a large pan, put in the vegetables, bouquet garni, peppercorns and clove, and fry gently for 2–3 minutes, turning the vegetables over several times. Lay the fillets on the vegetables, cover the pan, and fry gently for 10 minutes.

Meanwhile, heat the stock to simmering point. Pour enough stock into the pan to cover the vegetables. Cover the meat with buttered greaseproof paper, replace the lid, and cook gently for 1 hour, adding more stock as necessary.

When cooked, remove the fillets. Reserve the stock. Place the meat in a greased baking dish, barded side up, and cook in a fairly hot oven, 200°C, Gas 6, for 10–15 minutes to crisp the bacon.

Meanwhile, melt the remaining butter or margarine in a small pan. Stir in the flour and cook gently until nut-brown. Strain the braising stock and gradually add 375ml of it to the brown roux, and stir until boiling. Reduce the heat and simmer for 5 minutes. Season to taste.

Pipe or spoon a border of the hot creamed potatoes on a warmed serving dish. Brush the fillets with meat glaze and arrange in a circle inside the potato border.

Fill the centre of the dish with the peas, asparagus tips or macédoine of vegetables. Pour some of the sauce round the fillets and serve the rest separately.

Escalopes of Veal Talleyrand

6 helpings

6 thin escalopes of veal	*500g creamed potatoes*
oil and butter for frying	*1 egg yolk*
1 small onion or	*2 × 5ml spoons lemon*
2 shallots	*juice*
50g mushrooms	*2 × 5ml spoons chopped*
375ml foundation white	*parsley*
sauce (pouring	*salt and pepper*
consistency) (p692)	

Wipe the escalopes and flatten them with a cutlet bat or rolling-pin. Trim them into a neat shape. Heat the oil and butter in a large frying pan. Fry the escalopes quickly, without browning, for 2–3 minutes, turning them once. Prepare the vegetables and chop them finely. Add to the meat and continue cooking for 3–4 minutes. Drain off any excess fat. Add the white sauce, heat to boiling point, reduce the heat, cover the pan with a tight-fitting lid, and simmer gently for about 1 hour. Lift out the escalopes and place them in a single row on a bed of creamed potatoes on a warmed serving dish. Keep hot.

Mix the egg yolk and lemon juice. Blend with a little of the sauce, then stir into the remaining sauce. Cook gently, without boiling, until the egg yolk thickens the sauce. Stir in the parsley. Season to taste. Pour the sauce over the escalopes.

Stuffed Breast of Veal

6 helpings

a thick end of breast of
  veal (1kg approx)
salt and pepper
300g pork **or** beef
  sausage-meat
1 large onion
  (200g approx)
1 large carrot
  (100g approx)
½ turnip (25g approx)

bouquet garni
6 black peppercorns
white stock (p329) **or**
  water to cover
butter for greasing
225g short-grain rice
50g grated Parmesan
  cheese
meat glaze (p397)
  (optional)

Garnish
slices of lemon

Remove all bones and tendons from the meat. Wipe, and tie into a neat shape. Season well. Spread the sausage-meat evenly over the inner surface of the meat, roll up and tie securely with fine string. Prepare and slice the vegetables. Put them with the bones and trimmings in a large pan. Add the bouquet garni, peppercorns, salt and pepper, and enough stock or water to cover the vegetables. Place the meat on top, cover with buttered grease-proof paper and a tight-fitting lid. Heat to boiling point, reduce the heat and simmer gently for about 2½ hours. Baste occasionally and add more stock or water if necessary. Transfer the meat to a warmed dish and keep hot.

Strain off the liquid and make it up to 750ml with stock or water. Put the stock in a pan and bring to the boil. Wash the rice and cook it in the stock until the stock is absorbed. Season to taste and stir in the cheese. Place the rice in a layer on a warmed serving dish and put the meat on top. Brush the meat with glaze, if used, and garnish with slices of lemon.

Daube of Veal

6 helpings

chump end of loin of veal
  (1.25kg approx)
100g basic herb stuffing
  (p375)
500ml white stock
  (p329) **or** water
4 rashers lean bacon,
  without rinds

1 medium-sized onion
  (100g approx)
bouquet garni
1 blade of mace
10 black peppercorns
salt and pepper
375ml Fresh Tomato
  (p715) **or** Espagnole
  (p707) sauce

Ask the butcher to bone the meat, or bone it yourself. Wipe the meat. Fill the cavity with the stuffing and tie the meat into a neat shape. Put the stock or water into a large pan, bring to the boil and put in the meat. Cover the meat with the bacon rashers. Skin and slice the onion, and add with the bouquet garni, mace, peppercorns, and seasoning. Boil for 5 minutes, then reduce the heat, cover, and simmer gently for 2½ hours, basting the meat with stock several times. Do not add more liquid unless essential. When cooked, transfer the meat to a warmed dish and keep hot.

Strain the liquid from the pan into a small saucepan and boil rapidly until reduced to a glaze. Brush the meat thickly with the glaze.

Serve with Fresh Tomato Sauce or Espagnole Sauce.

STEWED AND CASSEROLED DISHES

Stewed Breast of Veal

6 helpings

1–1.25kg breast of veal
2 medium-sized onions
  (200g approx)
2 small carrots
  (50g approx)
1 small turnip
  (25g approx)

12 black peppercorns
salt
500ml Parsley sauce
  (p696) for a mild dish
  or Piquant sauce
  (p702) for a spicy one

Wipe the meat, put in a pan and just cover with cold water. Heat to boiling point and skim well.

Prepare and dice the vegetables. Add them to the pan with the peppercorns and salt to taste. Cover with a tight-fitting lid, reduce the heat and simmer gently for 2½–3 hours. Make the Parsley or Piquant sauce, using some of the veal stock. Transfer the veal to a warmed serving dish, pour over enough sauce to cover the meat, and serve the rest in a sauce-boat.

Stewed Rolled Breast of Veal

6 helpings

1.25–1.5kg breast of veal	1.5–2 litres white (p329) or chicken (p330) stock
salt and pepper	250ml slightly thickened
200g basic herb stuffing (p375)	gravy (p727)

Garnish
6 fried bacon rolls   slices of lemon
(p396)

Wipe and bone the meat, and flatten it with a cutlet bat or rolling-pin. Season, and spread with a thin layer of stuffing. Roll up the meat and skewer or tie it securely. Form the rest of the stuffing into balls for frying. Heat enough stock to cover the rolled meat in a large saucepan. When boiling, place the meat in it, re-heat to boiling point, and skim. Cover the pan with a tight-fitting lid, reduce the heat, and simmer gently for about 3 hours.

Place the veal on a warmed serving dish, remove the skewers or string, and pour a little gravy over it if liked. Garnish with the bacon rolls, forcemeat balls, and lemon slices. Serve the rest of the gravy separately.

Note If liked, the bones can be simmered with the meat. In this case, use half veal liquor and half milk to make Parsley sauce (p696) to coat the meat. Use cooked, diced carrot as an additional garnish.

Stewed Knuckle of Veal

6 helpings

1 large knuckle of veal (2kg approx)	2 sticks celery (100g approx)
1 medium-sized onion (100g approx)	bouquet garni salt and pepper
2 small carrots (50g approx)	50g long-grain rice 500ml Parsley sauce
1 small turnip (50g approx)	(p696)

Garnish
6 grilled bacon rolls   slices of lemon
(p396)

Wipe the meat and cut out the shank bone. Put the meat and shank bone in a large pan and cover with cold water. Heat to boiling point and skim well. Prepare and dice the onion, carrots, and turnip. Wash and slice the celery. Add the vegetables to the pan with the bouquet garni and salt to taste. Cover the pan with a tight-fitting lid and simmer gently for about 3 hours until the veal is tender. Wash the rice and add it to the pan for the last 20 minutes of the cooking time.

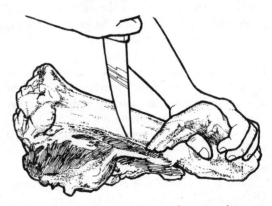

Cutting out the shank bone by gently easing the meat away from the bone

Transfer the meat to a warmed serving dish and keep hot. Take out the bone and bouquet garni and season the broth to taste. Serve the broth separately. Pour a little Parsley sauce over the meat and serve the rest in a sauce-boat. Garnish the meat with bacon rolls and slices of lemon.

Curried Veal or Lamb

6 helpings

600g lean stewing veal or lamb	4 × 5ml spoons curry paste
50g butter **or** margarine	4 × 5ml spoons mango chutney
1 × 15ml spoon oil	salt
2 medium-sized onions (200g approx)	300g cooked long-grain rice
2 cooking apples (400g approx)	2 × 10ml spoons redcurrant jelly
1 clove of garlic (optional)	lemon juice
25g plain flour	a pinch of Cayenne pepper
2–4 × 5ml spoons curry powder	
750ml white stock (p329) **or** coconut infusion (p331)	

Garnish

a few grains of chilli powder **or** a sprinkling of paprika	3 sliced gherkins
	1 sliced lemon
	sprigs of parsley

Wipe, trim, and cut the meat into 2cm cubes. Heat the fat in a stewpan and fry the meat lightly until sealed and browned. Lift out the meat and put to one side. Skin and chop the onions; peel, core, and chop the apples. Skin and crush the garlic, if used. Fry the onion, apple, and garlic over low heat for about 7 minutes until lightly browned. Add the flour and curry powder and cook, stirring, for another 5 minutes. Gradually add the stock or coconut infusion, curry paste, chutney and salt, and stir until boiling. Replace the meat, cover, and simmer gently for about 2 hours, stirring occasionally.

Arrange the cooked rice as a border on a warmed serving dish. Keep hot. Add to the curry the redcurrant jelly, lemon juice and Cayenne pepper, and simmer until the jelly melts. Spoon the curry into the centre of the rice border. Sprinkle with the chilli powder or paprika and garnish with the gherkins, lemon, and parsley sprigs.

Note A list of curry accompaniments can be found on p388.

Another recipe for Curried Lamb can be found on p541.

Casserole of Veal

6 helpings

600g lean stewing veal	200g button mushrooms
500ml thick Velouté sauce (p708)	salt and pepper
	2 × 5ml spoons lemon juice

Garnish

6 grilled bacon rolls (p396)	crimped lemon slices (p392)

Wipe the meat and trim off any skin or fat. Cut the meat into neat pieces and put them into an oven-proof dish or casserole. Heat the sauce to boiling point and pour it over the veal. Clean the mushrooms and add them to the casserole. Season to taste. Cover the dish or casserole with a tight-fitting lid and stand it in a pan of hot water. Cook in a moderate oven, 180°C, Gas 4, for about 1½ hours until the meat is tender. When cooked, stir in the lemon juice. Garnish with the bacon rolls and lemon slices. Serve from the casserole.

Haricot of Veal

6 helpings

100g haricot beans	3 × 15ml spoons plain flour
1–1.25kg neck of veal	750ml white (p329) **or** chicken (p330) stock
2 medium-sized onions (200g approx)	salt and pepper
3 × 10ml spoons dripping	

Garnish

2 cooked and diced carrots	1 small cooked and diced turnip

Soak the beans overnight in plenty of cold water. Drain them, put in a pan, and cover with plenty of fresh water. Heat to boiling point, cover, reduce the heat, and simmer for about 1½ hours or until tender but not mushy. Add more water if necessary. Drain, and put to one side.

Meanwhile, wipe and trim the meat, and cut it into convenient serving pieces. Skin and slice the onions. Heat the dripping in a flameproof casserole and fry the meat and onion lightly. Remove the meat and onion. Sprinkle the flour over the fat and cook slowly, stirring until well browned. Gradually add the stock and stir until boiling. Season to taste. Put in the meat and onion, and any trimmings from the vegetable garnish. Cover the pan and simmer gently for 1½ hours. Pour off and strain the sauce. Return it to the meat in the casserole with the cooked haricot beans, and simmer for another 15 minutes. Serve from the casserole or lift out the meat, place it on a warmed serving dish, and pour the sauce and haricot beans over it. Garnish each helping with cooked, diced carrot and turnip.

Veal Olives

6 helpings

6 thin slices fillet of veal (600g approx)	40g butter
75g streaky bacon, without rinds	2 tomatoes (100g approx)
100g thyme and parsley stuffing (p375)	250ml white **or** general household stock (p329)
grated rind and juice of 1 lemon	salt and pepper
2 medium-sized onions (200g approx)	500g creamed potatoes

Garnish

slices of lemon	sprigs of parsley

Flatten each slice of fillet with a cutlet bat or rolling-pin. Chop the rashers and add to the stuffing with the lemon rind. Skin and chop the onions, add half to the stuffing and mix well. Sprinkle the lemon juice over the veal and spread the slices with the stuffing. Roll up the fillets tightly and tie securely with string.

Melt the butter in a large pan or flameproof casserole and fry the rest of the onion until transparent. Add the veal olives, and brown them all over. Pour off any excess fat. Skin and chop the tomatoes, and add them to the pan with the stock. Season to taste. Cover the pan with a tight fitting lid and simmer over gentle heat, or bake in a warm oven, 160°C, Gas 3, for 1 hour.

Remove the strings from the veal olives when cooked, and place the olives on a bed of creamed potatoes. Pour the sauce over them and garnish with slices of lemon and sprigs of parsley. Serve very hot.

BOILED AND STEAMED DISHES

Steamed Veal

6 helpings

600–800g topside leg of veal	25g plain flour
	250ml milk
salt and pepper	1–2 egg yolks
3 sticks celery (150g approx)	1–2 × 5ml spoons lemon juice
25g butter	

Garnish (optional)

6 grilled bacon rolls (p396)	sprigs of cooked cauliflower

Wipe, trim, and tie the veal into a neat shape. Season well. Wash the celery and cut it into 2cm lengths. Put the meat and celery in the top of a steamer. Steam for 1½–2 hours or until tender.

When the veal is nearly ready, heat the butter in a small saucepan. Stir in the flour and cook for 2–3 minutes over low heat, stirring well. Do not allow to brown. Gradually add the milk and any liquid in the steamer and stir until boiling. Reduce the heat and simmer for 5 minutes. Remove the pan from the heat. Beat the egg yolks in a bowl and stir into them a little of the hot sauce. Return the egg yolk mixture to the rest of the sauce in the pan, stirring well. Add the lemon juice and season to taste. Place the veal on a warmed serving dish, remove the string, and pour the sauce over the meat. Garnish, if liked, with bacon rolls and sprigs of cooked cauliflower.

Galantine of Veal

6 helpings

a breast of veal
  (600g approx)
salt and pepper
600g sausage-meat
3 rashers streaky bacon,
  without rinds
1–2 hard-boiled eggs
a pinch of ground mace
a pinch of grated nutmeg

1 litre white stock
  (p329), chicken stock
  (p330) or water
2 medium-sized onions
  (200g approx)
1 turnip (50g approx)
1 medium-sized carrot
  (50g approx)
6 black peppercorns
meat glaze (p397)

Garnish
sprigs of parsley

Wipe the meat and remove the bones. Reserve the bones. Flatten the meat with a cutlet bat or rolling pin. Season well with salt and pepper. Spread half the sausage-meat over the veal in an even layer. Cut the rashers into narrow strips. Slice the hard-boiled eggs. Place the strips of bacon and slices of egg on top of the sausage-meat and sprinkle with the seasoning, mace, and nutmeg. Cover with the rest of the sausage-meat and roll up the meat tightly. Wrap in a scalded pudding cloth and secure the ends.

Put the stock or water in a large pan with the veal bones and heat to boiling point. Prepare and slice the vegetables. Add to the pan with the peppercorns and seasoning. Put the meat roll on top. Cover with a tight-fitting lid, reduce the heat, and simmer gently for 3 hours. Remove the meat, unwrap it, and then roll it up tightly in a clean, dry cloth or greaseproof paper. Press the meat between 2 plates under a light weight until cold. When cold, remove the cloth, brush the meat with meat glaze and garnish with parsley.

Pressed Veal

6 helpings

a breast of veal
  (600–700g approx)
salt and pepper
1 large onion
  (200g approx)
1 medium-sized carrot
  (50g approx)
$\frac{1}{2}$ turnip (25g approx)
2 sticks celery
  (100g approx) or
$\frac{1}{2}$ × 2.5ml spoon celery
seeds

bouquet garni
10 black peppercorns
butter for greasing
  (optional)
gravy browning
  (optional) ·

Wipe the meat and remove the skin, bones, and gristle. Trim the meat neatly. Reserve the bones and trimmings. Season well, then roll up the meat and tie with string. Prepare and slice the vegetables. Put them into a large pan with the bones and trimmings, celery seeds, if used, bouquet garni, peppercorns and salt to taste, and put the meat on top. Pour in just enough water to cover the vegetables. Cover the meat with buttered greaseproof paper or a tight-fitting lid. Heat to boiling point, reduce the heat, and simmer gently for 3 hours, basting occasionally and adding more water if necessary.

When cooked, remove the meat from the pan and place it between 2 plates or boards with weights on top, until quite cold. Strain the stock from the pan and, when the meat is cold, boil the stock rapidly until reduced to a glaze. Add gravy browning to the glaze if it is too pale. Trim the pressed meat and brush the glaze over it.

PIES AND PUDDINGS

Veal and Ham Pudding

6 helpings

600–800g lean pie veal
150g ham **or** bacon **or**
  salt (pickled) pork
suet crust pastry (p1250)
  using 200g flour
flour for rolling out

fat for greasing
salt and pepper
4 × 15ml spoons general
  household stock (p329)
375ml thickened gravy
  (p727)

Garnish
chopped parsley

Wipe the veal and cut it into small neat pieces. Cut the ham, bacon or pork into narrow strips. Reserve one-quarter of the pastry for the lid. Roll out the rest on a lightly floured surface so that it is 1cm larger than the top of a greased 1 litre basin, and 5mm thick. Press well into the basin to remove any creases. Fill with alternate layers of veal and ham, bacon or pork, seasoning each layer well. Add the stock when the basin is half full. Roll out the reserved pastry to fit the top of the basin. Dampen the edges, place the lid in position, and seal. Cover with a round of greased greaseproof paper, then cover tightly with foil.

Place the basin in a steamer, or on a saucer in a pan with water coming half-way up the basin's sides. Steam, or half steam the pudding for 3 hours, topping up the steamer or pan with boiling water when it is reduced by a third.

Remove the foil and paper from the pudding when ready. Serve in the basin, garnished with chopped parsley. Serve the gravy separately.

Veal and Ham Pie

See p1305.

Pot Pie of Veal

6 helpings

500g lean pie veal
200g salt (pickled) pork
salt and pepper
white **or** general
  household stock (p329)
  to cover
500g potatoes

puff pastry (p1253) **or**
  rough puff pastry
  (p1252) using 150g
  flour
flour for rolling out
beaten egg **or** milk for
  glazing

Wipe the veal and cut it into 3–5cm cubes, and the pork into thin strips. Place the veal and pork in layers in a 1.5 litre pie dish, seasoning each layer well with salt and pepper. Fill the dish three-quarters full with stock. Cover with a lid and cook in a moderate oven, 180°C, Gas 4, for 1½ hours.

Meanwhile, prepare and parboil the potatoes in salted water. Drain, and cut them in thick slices. Remove the meat from the oven and let it cool slightly. Add extra stock to the dish to bring it back to its original level, if necessary. Arrange the potatoes evenly on top of the meat. Roll out the pastry on a lightly floured surface to cover the top of the pie dish. Brush the pastry with the beaten egg or milk. Make a hole in the centre to let the steam escape. Bake in a very hot oven, 230°C, Gas 8, for 10–15 minutes until the pastry is set, then reduce the heat to fairly hot, 190°C, Gas 5, and continue cooking for 25–30 minutes. Add more hot stock through the hole in the top to fill the pie.

Raised Veal, Pork, and Egg Pie

6 helpings

hot water crust pastry
  (p1250) using 400g
  flour
400g pie veal
400g lean pork
25g plain flour
$1\frac{1}{2} \times 5ml$ spoons salt
$\frac{1}{2} \times 2.5ml$ spoon ground
  pepper

3 hard-boiled eggs
$2 \times 15ml$ spoons water
beaten egg for glazing
125ml (approx) well-
  flavoured, cooled and
  jellied stock **or** canned
  consommé

Line a 20cm round pie mould with three-quarters of the pastry, or use a round cake tin to mould the pie as described on p1250. Use the remaining quarter for the lid.

Cut the meat into small pieces, removing any gristle or fat. Season the flour with salt and pepper, and toss the pieces of meat in it. Put half the meat into the pastry case and put in the whole eggs. Add the rest of the meat and the water. Put on the lid, brush with beaten egg, and make a hole in the centre to allow steam to escape. Bake in a very hot oven, 230°C, Gas 8, for 15 minutes. Reduce the heat to very cool, 140°C, Gas 1, and continue cooking for $2\frac{1}{2}$ hours. Remove the greaseproof paper or mould for the last 30 minutes of the cooking time and brush the top and sides of the pastry with beaten egg.

Heat the stock or consommé until melted and, when the pie is cooked, funnel it through the hole in the lid until the pie is full. Leave to cool completely before serving.

Note If preferred, the ingredients can be made into 6 individual pies. The eggs should be sliced and divided between the smaller pies.

MINCED DISHES

Fladgeon of Veal

4 helpings

300g lean pie veal
100g shredded suet
75g soft white
  breadcrumbs
$1 \times 5ml$ spoon grated
  lemon rind
a pinch of grated nutmeg

salt and pepper
2 eggs
milk
fat for greasing
125ml white **or** general
  household stock (p329)

Garnish
$1 \times 15ml$ spoon chopped
  parsley

Mince the veal finely. Mix with the suet, breadcrumbs, lemon rind, nutmeg, and salt and pepper to taste. Stir in one egg and as much milk as required to moisten the mixture thoroughly without making it sloppy. Half fill a greased 1.5 litre pie dish with the mixture and bake in a fairly hot oven, 190°C, Gas 5, for 1 hour. Beat the second egg with the stock and season to taste. Pour the egg and stock over the contents of the pie dish and continue to bake for about 20 minutes until set. Garnish with the chopped parsley and serve from the dish.

Timbales of Veal with Mushrooms

See p401.

Veal Quenelles

See p400.

Fricadelles of Veal

4–6 helpings

500g boned lean veal (see **Note**)	3 eggs
75g white bread	750ml white stock (p329) **or** salted water
50ml milk	soft white breadcrumbs for coating
200g shredded suet	oil for deep frying
1 × 5ml spoon grated lemon rind	375ml foundation brown sauce (p698)
a pinch of grated nutmeg	
salt and pepper	

Garnish	
slices of lemon	chopped parsley

Wipe and trim the meat. Cut the crusts off the bread. Soak the bread in the milk for 5 minutes, and then squeeze it as dry as possible and rub out any lumps. Mince the veal. Mix it with the bread, suet, lemon rind, nutmeg, and salt and pepper. Beat two of the eggs until liquid, and stir into the veal mixture. Shape into balls about the size of a large walnut. Bring the stock or salted water to the boil in a pan. Drop the balls into it and cook for 6 minutes. Drain, and dry thoroughly.

Beat the remaining egg until liquid. Coat the balls with beaten egg, then with breadcrumbs. Heat the oil (p303) and fry the fricadelles until golden-brown. Drain, and add them to the brown sauce in a saucepan. Heat to simmering point and simmer very gently for 30 minutes. Serve in the sauce, garnished with lemon and chopped parsley.

Note If the meat is boned by the butcher, make sure he gives you the bones. These, together with the meat trimmings, can be used to make the white stock and the brown sauce.

VARIATION

Fricadelles of Veal with Tomato Sauce and Olives

Prepare and cook the fricadelles as for the main recipe. Use 375ml Fresh Tomato sauce (p715) instead of foundation brown sauce. Serve garnished with slices of lemon and black olives.

DISHES USING COOKED MEAT

Mrs Beeton's Baked Veal

3–4 helpings

200g cold roast veal	1 × 2.5ml spoon grated lemon rind
4 rashers streaky bacon, without rinds	1 × 2.5ml spoon ground mace
175g soft white breadcrumbs	a few grains Cayenne pepper
250ml general household stock (p329)	salt
	4 eggs

Mince the veal and bacon together finely. Mix the meat with the breadcrumbs, stock, grated lemon rind, mace, and seasonings. Beat the eggs until liquid and mix in. Put the mixture into a shallow 750ml baking dish, and bake in a warm oven, 160°C, Gas 3, for 1 hour.

Serve hot, with a thickened gravy, if liked.

Garnished Veal

4 helpings

500g cold cooked veal	1 × 10ml spoon lemon juice
375ml foundation white sauce (pouring consistency) (p692)	grated rind of ½ lemon
	salt and pepper

Garnish	
4–8 small fried **or** baked forcemeat balls (p376)	slices of lemon
4–8 fried **or** baked bacon rolls (p396)	sprigs of parsley

Trim off any fat and gristle from the meat. Cut the meat into very small pieces. Put the white sauce into a pan big enough to hold the meat as well. Add the lemon juice and rind to the white sauce and season to taste. Add the meat, and cover the pan with a lid. Heat gently for 30 minutes but do not allow to boil. Transfer the meat and sauce to a warmed serving dish, and garnish with the forcemeat balls, bacon rolls, slices of lemon, and sprigs of parsley.

Veal Scallops

6 helpings

500g cold roast veal	1 × 5ml spoon lemon
50–75g butter **or**	juice
margarine	salt and pepper
25g plain flour	butter for greasing
375ml white stock	6 × 15ml spoons fine
(p329)	dried white
	breadcrumbs

Garnish
sprigs of parsley   6 slices lemon

Trim off any fat and gristle from the meat. Mince the meat finely. Melt 25g of the butter or margarine in a saucepan, stir in the flour, and cook slowly until pale brown. Gradually add the stock and stir until boiling. Add the lemon juice and season to taste. Reduce the heat and simmer gently for 20 minutes. Mix the meat into the sauce. Butter 6 scallop shells well and divide the meat mixture between them. Cover with the breadcrumbs and dot with the remaining butter or margarine cut in flakes. Cook in a hot oven, 220°C, Gas 7, until browned. Serve garnished with sprigs of parsley and slices of lemon.

Veal Loaf or Mould

4 helpings

fat for greasing	1 × 5ml spoon grated
2 × 15ml spoons	lemon rind
raspings (p375)	a pinch of grated nutmeg
300g cold cooked veal **or**	2–3 × 15ml spoons
veal and ham mixed	gravy **or** milk
1 small onion	salt and pepper
1 egg	250ml thickened gravy
75g soft white	(p727) **or** Fresh Tomato
breadcrumbs	sauce (p715) **or**
3 × 2.5ml spoons	foundation brown sauce
chopped parsley	(p698)

Garnish
sprigs of parsley

Grease a 15cm round cake tin or a 500g loaf tin, and coat it well with raspings. Trim off any fat and

gristle from the meat. Chop or mince the meat finely. Skin the onion and chop it finely. Beat the egg lightly until liquid and add it to the meat with the onion, breadcrumbs, parsley, lemon rind, nutmeg, and just enough gravy or milk to moisten the mixture well. Season to taste. Press the mixture into the tin and cover with buttered greaseproof paper. Bake in a fairly hot oven, 200°C, Gas 6, for about 40 minutes.

When cooked, turn out on to a warmed serving dish. Pour some of the gravy or sauce round it, and garnish with sprigs of parsley. Serve the rest of the gravy or sauce separately.

OFFAL DISHES

Fried Calf's Brains

4 helpings

2 sets calf's brains	50g plain flour
1 × 15ml spoon vinegar	1 × 15ml spoon oil
or lemon juice	2 × 15ml spoons tepid
1 small onion	water
(50g approx)	1 egg white
a pinch of dried sage	oil for deep frying
salt	

Garnish
sprigs of parsley

Prepare the brains (p551). Put in a saucepan, cover with fresh cold water, and add the vinegar or lemon juice. Skin and slice the onion, and add it to the pan with a pinch of sage and salt. Heat to boiling point, reduce the heat, and simmer for 10 minutes or until firm. Drain, discarding the flavourings. Pat the brains dry and cut into fairly thin slices.

Make a batter by sifting the flour with a pinch of salt and blending it with the oil and water until smooth. Whisk the egg white until stiff, then fold it lightly into the batter. Heat the oil (p303). Dip each slice of brain into the batter, and fry in the hot fat, turning 2 or 3 times, until golden-brown on both sides. Drain thoroughly, place on a warmed serving dish and garnish with parsley.

Brains in Black Butter

(Cervelles au Beurre Noir)

4 helpings

2 sets calf's brains	bouquet garni
salt	flour for dusting
1 × 5ml spoon lemon	ground pepper
juice	2 × 15ml spoons butter
1 small onion	butter for greasing
1 litre water	
2 × 15ml spoons white	
wine vinegar	

Black Butter

4 × 15ml spoons butter	2 × 15ml spoons capers
1 × 15ml spoon white	(optional)
wine vinegar	

Garnish
sprig of parsley

Soak the brains for 30 minutes in lightly salted cold water sharpened with the lemon juice to remove all traces of blood. Meanwhile, skin and halve the onion, and put it in a saucepan with the water, vinegar, and bouquet garni. Heat to simmering point and simmer for 30 minutes. Leave the stock to cool.

Drain the brains, and cut off any membranes. Wash thoroughly but very gently. Put the brains into the stock, heat slowly to simmering point, and poach for 20 minutes. Drain thoroughly, and put into very cold water to cool. Drain again and pat dry. Season the flour with salt and pepper, and dust the brains with it. Heat the 2 × 15ml spoons butter in a frying pan, and fry the brains lightly, turning them over, until just browned on all sides. Put them in a shallow serving dish, and keep them warm under buttered paper.

Take any bits of brain out of the frying pan, add the butter for the Black Butter and heat until golden-brown. Add the vinegar, and let it boil up. As soon as it foams, pour the mixture over the brains, adding the capers, if used. Serve at once, garnished with a sprig of parsley.

Note Another recipe for Black Butter can be found on p715.

Calf's Brains with Maître d'Hôtel Sauce

4 helpings

2 sets calf's brains	1 × 15ml spoon finely
salt	chopped parsley
1 × 15ml spoon vinegar	1½ × 5ml spoons lemon
or lemon juice	juice
1 small onion	15–25g butter
(50g approx)	ground pepper
a pinch of dried sage	
375ml foundation white	
sauce (pouring	
consistency) (p692)	

Garnish
fried **or** *toasted bread croûtons*

Prepare the brains (p551). Cook as for Fried Calf's Brains (p574). After draining the brains, cut them into small, thick slices. Heat the white sauce in a saucepan, put in the brains, and cook gently for 10 minutes until the brains are heated through. Add the parsley and heat for a further 2 minutes. Add the lemon juice and butter, and season to taste. Serve on a warmed serving dish garnished with the croûtons.

Note Another recipe for Maître d'Hôtel Sauce can be found on p695.

Hungarian Calf's Liver

6 helpings

600g calf's liver	*2 ×15ml spoons finely*
plain flour	*grated onion*
salt	*100ml fresh or soured*
paprika	*cream*
50g butter	

Remove the skin and tubes, and cut the liver into 1cm slices. Season some flour with salt and paprika. Dip the slices of liver in the flour, then shake off the excess. Heat the butter in a frying pan and fry the liver quickly on both sides until browned, then more slowly until tender. Fry the onion with the liver for about 5 minutes. Remove the liver, arrange the slices down the centre of a warmed serving dish, and keep hot. Pour any excess fat out of the pan, add the cream, and heat gently without boiling. Season to taste. Pour this sauce over the liver. Sprinkle with paprika, and serve very hot.

Calf's Liver with Savoury Rice

6 helpings

500g calf's liver	*salt and pepper*
1 medium-sized onion	*¼–1 × 2.5ml spoon*
(100g approx)	*powdered saffron*
2 cloves garlic (optional)	*plain flour*
40g butter or margarine	*butter or oil for*
150g Patna rice	*frying*
375ml well-flavoured	*250ml foundation brown*
white stock (p329)	*sauce (p698)*
	juice of ½ lemon
	butter for greasing

Garnish
6 baked or fried bacon	*paprika*
rolls (p396)	

Remove the skin and tubes, and cut the liver into thin slices. Skin the onion and garlic cloves, if used, and chop them finely. Heat 25g of the butter or margarine in a pan and sauté the onion and garlic without colouring for 2–3 minutes. Wash the rice and add it to the pan. Mix well and cook for about 3 minutes. Add the stock, salt and pepper to taste, and the saffron. Cover the pan, and cook for 30–45 minutes over gentle heat, or in a moderate oven, 180°C, Gas 4, until the rice is tender and has absorbed all the stock. Add the remaining butter or margarine, mix well, and press into a border mould. Put to one side until set.

Season some flour with salt and pepper and dip the slices of liver in it. Heat a little butter or oil in a frying pan and fry the liver, turning once, until browned and cooked through. Drain thoroughly. Heat the brown sauce in a saucepan to boiling point, add the lemon juice and the liver, and heat through. Turn the rice on to a warmed dish, cover with buttered greaseproof paper, and heat in a warm oven, 160°C, Gas 3, for 10–12 minutes. Place the liver and sauce in the centre of the mould, and garnish with the bacon rolls and paprika.

Stewed Calf's Kidneys

6 helpings

3 calf's kidneys	*100g mushrooms*
flour	*250ml brown stock*
salt and pepper	*(p329) or thin gravy*
1 medium-sized onion	*(p727)*
(100g approx)	*1 ×15ml spoon sherry*
50g margarine or	*(optional)*
dripping	*1 ×10ml spoon chopped*
	parsley

Garnish
bread croûtons

Skin and core the kidneys, and cut them in halves lengthways. Cut each half into slices about 3mm thick. Season the flour with salt and pepper, and toss the veal kidney slices in it. Skin and chop the onion finely. Heat the margarine or dripping in a pan, add the onion, and cook until lightly browned. Clean and slice the mushrooms and add them with the kidney to the pan; cook quickly until the kidney is browned. Pour off any excess fat, and gradually stir in the stock or gravy, sherry, if used, and salt and pepper to taste. Stir until boiling, cover the pan, reduce the heat, and simmer gently for 30 minutes. Add the chopped parsley, stir well, and turn into a warmed serving dish. Garnish with bread croûtons.

Serve with plain boiled rice.

Braised Veal Sweetbreads

6 helpings

3 pairs veal sweetbreads	*6 black peppercorns*
1 small onion	*salt*
(50g approx)	*white or general*
1 small carrot	*household stock (p329)*
(25g approx)	*to cover*
½ small turnip	*butter for greasing*
(25g approx)	*1 slice of white bread*
25g butter or margarine	*5cm thick*
bouquet garni	*fat or oil for frying*

Prepare the sweetbreads (p553). Press between 2 plates until quite cold.

Prepare and slice the vegetables. Melt the fat in a flameproof casserole, and fry the vegetables for about 10 minutes. Add the bouquet garni, peppercorns, salt to taste, and enough stock almost to cover the vegetables. Place the sweetbreads on top of the vegetables, cover with buttered greaseproof paper, and heat to boiling point. Baste the sweetbreads well, cover the casserole and cook in a moderate oven, 180°C, Gas 4, for about 1 hour. Add more stock, if necessary, and baste occasionally.

Meanwhile, cut a croûte from the slice of bread and fry it in shallow fat or oil, turning once, until golden-brown on both sides. Drain thoroughly. Place the croûte on a warmed serving dish and serve the sweetbreads on top.

Note Use the stock and vegetables for soup.

VARIATIONS

Braised Sweetbreads with Italian Sauce and Mushrooms

Serve the sweetbreads with Italian Sauce (p700) and stewed or fried mushrooms.

Braised Sweetbreads with Tomato Sauce and Vegetables

Brush the cooked sweetbreads with meat glaze (p397) or Fresh Tomato sauce (p715) and serve with peas or a macédoine of vegetables. Extra tomato sauce can be served separately.

Escalopes of Sweetbreads

Prepare and braise the sweetbreads as for the main recipe, reducing the braising time to 40 minutes. Remove the sweetbreads. Cut into neat slices and place in a shallow casserole or baking tin. Brush with meat glaze (p397) and half cover with some of the braising liquid. Cook in a fairly hot oven, 190°C, Gas 5, for 10 minutes. Serve the sweetbreads in a border of creamed potatoes, garnished with fried mushrooms.

Serve with peas or spinach purée and Fresh Tomato Sauce (p715), if liked.

Fried Veal Sweetbreads

See Fried Lamb's Sweetbreads (p553).

Baked Calf's Heart

3 helpings

1 calf's heart	*fat for greasing*
100g basic herb stuffing	*(optional)*
(p375)	*flour for dredging*
50g margarine or	*250ml thin gravy (p727)*
dripping	

Garnish

2 grilled or fried rashers	*sprigs of parsley*
streaky bacon	

Prepare the heart (p509). Pat the outside dry. Fill with the stuffing, and sew up or skewer the top.

Heat the margarine or dripping in a roasting tin, and put in the heart. Baste well and cover with greased greaseproof paper or foil. Bake in a fairly hot oven, 190°C, Gas 5, for about 1½ hours, turning and basting every 15–20 minutes. Remove the paper or foil 30 minutes before serving, and dredge the heart well with flour. Baste again, and return to the oven.

When cooked, transfer the heart to a warmed serving dish, and keep hot while preparing the gravy and garnish. Use the fat and flour in the tin to enrich or form the base of a brown gravy. Serve the heart garnished with the bacon rashers and sprigs of parsley. Serve the gravy separately.

Boiled Calf's Head

Basic recipe

10 helpings

½ calf's head
2 × 5ml spoons salt
1 × 15ml spoon vinegar
 or lemon juice
 (optional)

500ml Parsley (p696)
 or Fresh Tomato
 (p715) sauce

Stock

1 medium-sized onion
 (100g approx)
1 medium-sized carrot
 (50g approx)
1 small turnip
 (50g approx)

1 stick of celery
 (50g approx)
bouquet garni
6 black peppercorns
salt

Garnish

10 grilled bacon rolls
 (p396)

lemon wedges

Remove the brains and tongue and put them to one side. Make sure the ear and nostril are clean; singe off any hairs. Rinse the head well to free it of blood. Soak it in cold water for 3–4 hours, changing the water 3 or 4 times.

Blanch the head by putting it in a pan and covering with cold water. Add the salt, and vinegar or lemon juice, if liked. Bring to the boil, and boil for 10 minutes. Drain, and wash well in cold water. Put to one side.

Prepare and dice the onion, carrot, and turnip for the stock. Wash and slice the celery. Put the head and tongue into a large pan with the vegetables, bouquet garni, peppercorns and salt to taste, and cover with boiling water. Cover the pan and simmer gently for 3 hours, removing any white scum; top up with boiling water at intervals, if necessary.

Prepare the brains (p551). Tie them in a muslin bag and add them to the stock in the pan 15 minutes before the end of the cooking time.

When cooked, lift out the tongue and the brains, and put them to one side. Place the head on a board. Put the parsley or tomato sauce in a pan large enough to hold the meat as well, and heat it gently. Cut the meat from the bone in neat pieces.

Skin and slice the tongue. Chop the brains. Add the meat from the head to the hot sauce, and re-heat briefly but thoroughly. Serve on a warmed dish, garnished with bacon rolls, sliced tongue, chopped brains, and lemon wedges.

Serve with Poulette Sauce (p710).

Note Keep the stock in which the head is boiled; it makes an excellent, jellied white stock.

Collared Calf's Head

10–12 helpings

½ calf's head
2 × 5ml spoons salt
1 × 15ml spoon vinegar
 or lemon juice
 (optional)

stock as for Boiled
 Calf's Head **or** boiling
 water

Stuffing

cooked tongue and
 brains from head
50g soft white
 breadcrumbs
2 × 5ml spoons chopped
 parsley

1 × 5ml spoon dried
 mixed herbs
grated rind of 1 lemon
salt and pepper
1 egg
milk

Gherkin Sauce

2 × 15ml spoons butter
 or margarine
3 × 15ml spoons plain
 flour
1 × 15ml spoon chopped
 gherkins

1 × 15ml spoon lemon
 juice
salt and pepper

Cold Collared Head

meat glaze (p397)

Garnish

chopped parsley

slices of lemon

Prepare and cook the head, brains, and tongue as for Boiled Calf's Head. Put the head to one side and reserve the stock.

Make the stuffing. Skin the tongue while still hot, and mince or chop it finely with the brains. Mix with the breadcrumbs, herbs, lemon rind, and seasoning to taste. Beat the egg until liquid, mix with a little milk, and use to bind the stuffing.

Bone and flatten the head without breaking the skin. Spread the meat out flat, skin side down, and spread with the stuffing. Season well. Roll up tightly, and tie it securely with string. Wrap tightly in butter muslin and tie again, leaving ends of string which will hang over the side of the pan and can be used to lift the meat out of the hot stock when cooked.

Put the reserved stock into a large pan. Heat to boiling point. Put in the roll, cover the pan, and simmer for 2 hours.

To serve hot: When the collared head is cooked, strain 500ml stock from the pan. Melt the butter or margarine for the Gherkin Sauce in a saucepan, stir in the flour, and cook gently until the flour is pale brown. Gradually stir the stock into the roux and cook for 5 minutes. Add the gherkins and heat through. Add the lemon juice and season to taste. Remove the butter muslin from the head and serve the collared meat on a warmed dish, garnished with parsley and slices of lemon. Serve the sauce separately.

To serve cold: Leave the cooked collared head in the butter muslin to cool; then remove the cloth, roll the meat up very tightly in a clean cloth or in greaseproof paper, and press between 2 dishes with a light weight on top until quite cold. When cold, remove the cloth or paper, and brush the roll with 2 coats of meat glaze. Garnish with parsley and slices of lemon.

Note A cold collared calf's head is an excellent economical dish for parties or picnics. It can be made decorative by setting watercress leaves or halved, stoned olives in the first coat of glaze, and brushing the second coat over them.

Another recipe for Gherkin Sauce can be found on p698.

Calf's Foot Jelly

3–4 helpings

1 calf's foot	a pinch of ground
1 litre water	cinnamon
salt and pepper	2 cloves
pared rind and juice of	25ml dry sherry
1 large lemon	(optional)
1 egg white and shell	

Cut the foot into convenient-sized pieces to fit into a stewpan. Wash and blanch them by putting them in the stewpan, covering with cold water and heating to boiling point, then skimming and draining.

Put the pieces back in the pan with 1 litre water, and add salt and pepper to taste. Heat to boiling point, cover with a tight-fitting lid, reduce the heat, and simmer gently for 3–4 hours, removing any scum which rises. Strain, and measure the stock. If more than 500ml, return to the pan and boil until reduced to 500ml. Leave to cool completely, then remove any fat.

Return the stock to the pan with the lemon rind and juice, egg white and shell, cinnamon, and cloves. Heat to simmering point and simmer for 10 minutes, then allow to stand for 10 minutes. Strain through a fine sieve or jelly bag. Stir in the sherry, if used. Store in a refrigerator or very cool place.

Fried Calf's Tripe

4–6 helpings

600g dressed calf's tripe	salt and pepper
coating batter	oil for deep frying
(pp933–34) *using*	
100g plain flour	

Garnish
fried onion rings (p398)	1 × 15ml spoon chopped
	parsley

Wash the tripe and cut it into 7cm squares. Prepare a thick coating batter and season well. Heat the oil (p303). Dip the tripe into the batter, and fry until crisp and brown. Drain thoroughly. Serve hot, garnished with fried onion rings and parsley.

Pork

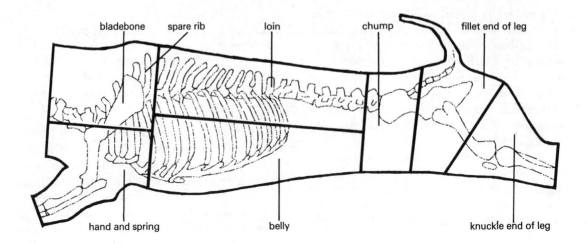

bladebone   spare rib   loin   chump   fillet end of leg

hand and spring   belly   knuckle end of leg

Pork has been part of the British national diet for centuries. Before the days of refrigeration, it was thought wise to avoid eating pork in summer but this is no longer relevant. Today, because of modern methods of breeding, feeding and refrigeration, pork is available and perfectly safe throughout the year.

Most pork comes either from young pigs (or porkers) with a carcass weight of 31.5–45kg or from 'heavy hogs' with a carcass weight of 50kg or above. Pigs slaughtered for fresh pork meat are usually between $4\frac{1}{2}$ and 8 months old. Other pigs used for pork are bacon pigs (baconers) which have failed to make the bacon grade or which are not needed for bacon. Baconers are lean pigs. Hams are cut from heavy hogs (pigs which have been fattened as quickly as possible) as a rule.

QUALITY OF PORK

The general quality considerations which apply to beef and lamb also apply to pork. Pork flesh, however, should be a light pink colour. The fat should be firm (not oily) and milky-white in colour. Fresh pork with soft, oily fat and greyish tinges must be rejected. Some cuts are sold pickled ready for boiling and these are an overall grey colour. The colour change is caused by the brine, and the meat, like beef, turns pink during cooking.

There is an old saying that nothing but the squeak need be wasted in pigs. Unlike other meats, all parts of the pig carcass can be roasted or (except for the loin) boiled, especially if salted. Even the head and trotters are good cooked.

Young porker meat has a distinctive flavour but can be indigestible. Heavy hogs yield more succulent and digestible meat although they may not be much older than the porker. Because pork is a rich meat, it needs very little or no added fat in its garnishes. But it lends itself well to many different plain or sharp accompaniments, sweet or savoury.

When buying a roasting joint, ask the butcher to score the rind to make the joint easier to carve. Just before putting the joint into the oven, rub oil and salt over the rind to make the crackling crisp.

For other glazes for crackling, see p397.

PORK CUTS

English and Scottish cuts of pork vary considerably. Those noted below are the most widely used English cuts. See also the diagram on p580.

1) *Leg* is a succulent and popular roasting joint. In Scotland a leg is known as a gigot. Often divided into fillet end and knuckle end.

> *Fillet end:* The top of the leg which is ideal for roasting or for slicing into steaks for grilling and frying. (Av wt – 2.5kg)
>
> *Knuckle end:* The lower half of the leg which can be roasted whole or boned and stuffed. (Av wt – 2.5kg)

2) *Loin* is a popular roast on the bone or boned, stuffed and rolled. It is often divided into loin and chump chops. (Av wt – 4–5.5kg)

Tenderloin is the lean cut found on the inside of the loin bone. It is sometimes called 'pork fillet' but it must not be confused with 'fillet end' from the leg. Ideal for roasting, braising, grilling, and frying. (Av wt 0.5–2.5kg)

3) *Belly* (also called draft or flank pork) is suitable (fresh or pickled) for braising, stewing or boiling. Sliced belly is a very economical cut for grilling and frying. Thick end of belly can make an economical and tasty roast, particularly when stuffed. (Av wt 1.5–2.25kg)

4) *Bladebone* is a roasting joint, tasty when boned and stuffed. It is also ideal for boiling, either fresh or pickled. (Av wt 1.75–2kg)

5) *Spare rib* is almost a parallel cut to the middle neck of lamb. It is a lean and economical roasting joint with little top fat. Meat from this cut makes the best filling for home-made pork pies. It can also be cut into spare rib chops. (Av wt 2.75–3.25kg)

6) *Spare ribs* (American-style) are cut from the belly and are removed in 1 sheath or slab, leaving the meat between the sections of rib bones. (They may also be sold under the name of pork rib bones.) They are usually barbecued. Chinese-style spare ribs are cut from the rib cage and have little meat on them. They are served roasted or braised in a sweet-sour sauce. (Av wt 2.7–3.2kg; Av wt Chinese – 2.3kg)

American-style spare ribs

7) *Hand* and *spring* is cut from the foreleg of the pig and, in bone structure, is similar to knuckle half shoulder of lamb. It is a large economical roasting joint. However, it is often too large for a small family, so it is sometimes sold divided into hand and shank. The hand can be boned and roasted or boiled. The shank is most suitable for casseroles and stews. (Av wt hand and spring 3–3.25kg)

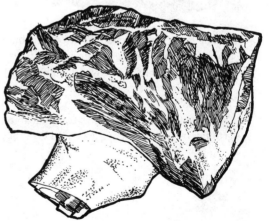

In Scotland, a shoulder of pork includes hand and spring, blade and ribs. The shoulder is usually cut in half, and boned and rolled. The amount required is cut to order. The shank end of the foreleg is called the hough end. The hand and spring, minus the shank, is called the runner.

8) *Head:* The pig carcass is usually delivered to the butcher with the head on, so a pig's head is easier to obtain than a sheep's or ox head. The head contains a considerable quantity of meat, plus the tongue and brain. The lower jaw and cheek is known as a chap or Bath Chap (p1471) when it is salted and boiled, and the meat, which is then very easy to remove, can be used for making Boiled Pig's Head (p596), Pork Brawn (p596) or galantines. (Av wt 1.75–2kg)

9) *Trotters* or *pettitoes* can be boiled, then boned, crumbed, and fried or fricasséed. The stock is used to make aspic jelly or jellied stock. (Av wt trotter – 200g; Av wt pettitoe – 150g)

10) *Chops* are thick slices of meat cut from the loin or spare rib joints.

> *Chump:* First 2–3 chops cut from the end of loin where the leg is removed. Chump chops are large and meaty and are good for grilling, frying or baking. (Av wt 200–300g each)

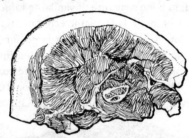

> *Middle loin:* Sometimes sold with the kidney and, occasionally, with the tenderloin (fillet). All cut from the loin. (Av wt 125–300g each)
> *Fore loin:* Similar to neck of lamb chops. (Av wt 125–175g)
> *Spare rib:* Cut from the spare rib and ideal for grilling, frying or braising. (Av wt 125–175g)

ROASTED AND BAKED DISHES

Roast Pork

Basic recipe

a joint of pork on the bone suitable for roasting	salt and pepper oil **or** fat for basting

Ask the butcher to score the rind in narrow lines, or do it yourself with a sharp knife. Select the method of roasting, ie quick or slow roasting (p470). Weigh the joint to calculate the cooking time (p471). Wipe the meat. Place the joint on a rack in a shallow roasting tin. Season the meat with salt and pepper and pour over a little oil or rub it with a little fat. Rub some salt into the scored rind to produce crisp crackling. Place the roasting tin in the oven, and cook for the required time.

If liked, brush the joint with apricot jam or glaze or with syrup from canned peaches, 10 minutes before the end of the cooking time. Alternatively, sprinkle the rind with brown sugar mixed with a little dry mustard. These mixtures give a sweeter crisp crackling.

Transfer the cooked meat to a warmed meat dish and keep hot. Prepare the gravy from the sediment in the roasting tin.

Serve roast pork with sage and onion stuffing (p378) and apple sauce.

Roast Suckling-Pig

8 helpings

a suckling-pig not more than 3 weeks old (4.5kg approx)	500g sage and onion stuffing melted butter **or** oil 2 × 15ml spoons salt

Garnish
1 red eating apple	1 green olive

Wipe the piglet. Remove the eyes. Stuff the piglet with the stuffing, then sew up the opening with fine string. Stretch the legs out and tie in a neat shape. Curl up the tail, and secure it with a small metal skewer. Cover the tail and ears with foil to protect them from scorching. Place a wooden plug in the piglet's mouth to hold it open. Brush the piglet all over with melted butter or oil, then rub the skin with salt. Put the piglet on a rack in a large roasting tin and cook in a warm oven, 160°C, Gas 3, allowing 35 minutes per 0.5kg. Baste well with more melted butter or oil.

When cooked, remove the skewer, foil, and wooden plug. Place the apple in the piglet's mouth. Halve the olive lengthways, and put half in each eye-socket, skin side out. To carve, see instructions on p480.

The usual accompaniments are a thickened gravy and apple sauce.

Note For fancy preparation, gild the ears and tail with edible gold paint.

Roast Savoury Loin of Pork

6–7 helpings

1.5kg loin of pork on the bone	*$\frac{1}{2} \times 2.5ml$ spoon freshly ground pepper*
1 × 15ml spoon finely chopped onion	*a pinch of dry mustard glaze (p397) (optional)*
1 × 2.5ml spoon dried sage	*125ml apple sauce*
1 × 2.5ml spoon salt	*250ml thickened gravy (p727)*

Ask the butcher to chine the pork and score the rind in narrow lines, or do it yourself with a sharp knife. Wipe the meat. Mix the onion with sage, salt, pepper, and mustard. Rub the mixture well into the surface of the meat. Roast the pork in a hot oven, 220°C, Gas 7, for 10 minutes, then reduce the heat to moderate, 180°C, Gas 4, for the rest of the calculated cooking time, allowing 30 minutes per 0.5kg plus 30 minutes over. About 30 minutes before serving, cover with glaze, if liked, and continue cooking to crisp the crackling. Serve hot apple sauce and gravy separately.

Mrs Beeton's
Roast Griskin of Pork

4 helpings

1kg neck end of chine of pork **or** *griskin (see* **Note***)*	*1 × 15ml spoon dried sage*
flour for dredging	*2 × 10ml spoons flour*
50g lard	*250ml water*
fat for greasing	*salt and pepper*

Wipe the meat and dredge it lightly with flour. Melt the lard in a roasting tin and brush some of it over the meat. Put the meat in the tin and roast it in a hot oven, 220°C, Gas 7, for 10 minutes. Baste well and cover the meat loosely with greased grease-proof paper. Reduce the heat to moderate, 180°C, Gas 4, and continue to roast the meat for a further $1\frac{3}{4}$ hours, basting it often. Ten minutes before the end of the cooking time, take out the meat, sprinkle it with the sage, and return to the oven, uncovered, to complete the cooking.

When cooked, transfer the meat to a warmed serving dish and keep hot. Pour off all but 1 × 15ml spoon fat in the roasting tin and retain the sediment. Stir in the flour and cook gently over low heat for 3–4 minutes until the flour is lightly browned. Gradually add the water and stir until the gravy thickens slightly. Taste and season with salt and pepper. Simmer for 1 minute, then strain the gravy into a warmed sauce-boat.

Serve with apple sauce.

Note The griskin is the backbone, spine or chine of a pig cut away when preparing a side for bacon; or it can be a shoulder of pork stripped of fat. As it is sold without rind or fat, it needs frequent basting.

Savoury Pork Chops

6 helpings

6 pork chops from the
middle loin, fore loin
or spare rib
800g Spanish onions
salt and pepper
a pinch of dried sage

125ml cold water
25g lard
a pinch of dried mixed
herbs
1 × 15ml spoon plain
flour

Wipe the chops, trim off any excess fat, and put to one side. Skin and dice the onions. Mix them with 1 × 5ml spoon salt and a pinch each of pepper and sage. Put the seasoned onions in a flameproof casserole with the water. Cover the pan, and cook over gentle heat for 30 minutes, stirring occasionally, or bake in a moderate oven, 180°C, Gas 4, for 45 minutes.

After 15 minutes' cooking time, melt the lard in a roasting tin and add the chops. Season with salt, pepper, and herbs. Bake in a moderate oven, 180°C, Gas 4, for 15 minutes, then turn them over, season the other side, and bake for another 15 minutes. Arrange the chops on a warmed serving dish and keep hot.

Pour off all the fat in the tin, leaving the sediment. Stir in the flour and cook gently, stirring until browned. Add the onions and their liquid to the flour, mix well together and re-heat. Pour the onion gravy in the centre of the chops.

Roast Pork Stuffed with Prunes

6 helpings

200g prunes
1.25–1.5kg boned loin of
pork

juice of 1 lemon
25g lard **or** butter
salt and pepper

Cover the prunes with boiling water and soak them for 2 hours. Drain, and remove the stones.

Wipe the meat and weigh it to calculate the cooking time. Spread the prunes over the flesh; roll up the meat and tie it securely. Pour the lemon juice over the joint and rub it well in. Melt the lard or butter in a roasting tin, put in the joint, season with salt and pepper, and baste. Roast in a moderate oven, 180°C, Gas 4, allowing 35 minutes per 0.5kg

plus 35 minutes over. Baste occasionally. Serve on a warmed dish and accompany with a thickened gravy made from the sediment in the roasting tin.

Note The meat can be garnished with stewed prunes, if liked.

Roast, Boned, Stuffed Pork

6 helpings

1.5kg boned bladebone
of pork

3 × 15ml spoons oil

Stuffing
1 medium-sized onion
(100g approx)
1 stick of celery (50g
approx)
100g flat mushrooms
25g butter **or** margarine
50g canned **or** frozen
sweetcorn

50g white breadcrumbs
1 × 15ml spoon chopped
parsley
salt and pepper
1 × 2.5ml spoon ground
mace
1 × 5ml spoon lemon
juice

Wipe the meat and deeply score the rind of the meat if not done by the butcher.

Make the stuffing. Prepare the onion, celery and mushrooms, and chop them finely. Melt the butter or margarine in a small pan and fry the onion and celery until lightly browned. Remove from the heat. Add the mushrooms, sweetcorn, breadcrumbs and parsley, and mix well. Season to taste, and add the mace and lemon juice.

Spoon the stuffing evenly into the 'pocket' left after the meat was boned. Roll up the joint and tie with thin string at regular intervals. Heat 2 × 15ml spoons oil in a roasting tin, then put in the joint. Brush the rind with the remaining oil and sprinkle generously with salt. Roast in a fairly hot oven, 200°C, Gas 6, for 20–30 minutes, until the crackling is browned. Reduce the heat to moderate, 180°C, Gas 4, and continue to cook for 1½ hours or until the internal temperature reaches 85°–88°C on a meat thermometer. Transfer the joint to a warmed serving dish, remove the string, and keep the meat hot. Pour off the fat in the roasting tin, then prepare a gravy using the sediment left in the tin.

FRIED AND GRILLED DISHES

Fried Pork Chops

Basic recipe

6 helpings

6 chump **or** *middle loin* **or** *fore loin* **or** *spare rib pork chops*	*salt*
ground pepper	*1 × 15ml spoon plain flour*
dried sage	*250ml general household stock* (p329)
1 × 15ml spoon oil **or** *butter* **or** *lard*	

Wipe the chops and trim off any excess fat. Sprinkle each chop with pepper and sage. Heat the oil, butter or lard in a frying pan. Add the chops and fry until sealed and browned on the underside. Turn the chops with a palette knife and continue to fry until the other side is browned. Reduce the heat and continue to fry, turning once or twice, until the meat is cooked through. The total frying time is 15–20 minutes, or longer for thick chops. Transfer the chops to a warmed serving dish, sprinkle with salt, and keep hot.

Pour the fat from the pan, reserving the sediment. Stir in the flour, and cook. Gradually add the stock and stir until boiling. Season to taste. Serve the gravy separately in a sauce-boat.

Fried Pork Chops with Peaches

Follow the recipe for Fried Pork Chops until the chops are cooked through. Arrange the fried chops on a warmed serving dish and keep hot. Pour off the fat and sediment from the frying pan and reserve for making gravy, if liked. Melt 25g butter and add 6 drained, canned peach halves. Fry gently until golden on both sides. Top each chop with a peach half, cut side down. Garnish with mustard and cress. If serving gravy, make it as for Fried Pork Chops.

Grilled Pork Chops

Basic recipe

6 helpings

6 chump **or** *middle loin* **or** *fore loin* **or** *spare rib pork chops*	*caster sugar*
	salt
2 × 15ml spoons oil **or** *melted butter*	*1 × 15ml spoon plain flour*
ground pepper	*250ml general household stock* (p329)
dried sage	*125ml apple sauce*
dried marjoram	

Wipe the chops and trim off any excess fat. Brush the grill rack with oil or melted butter and place the chops on it. Brush the upper surface of the chops with oil or melted butter and sprinkle with pepper, sage, marjoram, and sugar. Cook under a hot grill until one side is lightly browned. Draw off the heat and turn the chops over with a palette knife and spoon. Brush the second side with oil or melted butter and sprinkle with pepper, herbs, and sugar. Return to the heat and brown quickly. Reduce the heat and grill until the chops are cooked through. The total grilling time is 15–20 minutes for loin and spare rib chops, a little longer for the larger chump chops. Arrange the chops on a warmed serving dish, sprinkle with salt and keep hot.

Pour the fat from the grill pan and scrape the sediment into a small pan. Stir in the flour, then gradually add the stock and stir until boiling. Season to taste. Serve the gravy and hot apple sauce separately.

VARIATIONS

Grilled Pork Chops with Apple Slices

Follow the recipe for Grilled Pork Chops. When cooked, transfer the chops to a warmed serving dish and keep hot. Peel, core, and cut 6 slices (1cm thick) of a sharp apple. Put the slices on to the grill rack, brush them with the fat in the pan, and brown them lightly on both sides. Place 1 apple slice on each chop and garnish with sprigs of parsley.

For a second **variation**, see over.

Grilled Pork Chops with Pineapple Rings

Follow the recipe for Grilled Pork Chops until the chops are cooked through. Transfer the chops to a warmed serving dish and keep hot. Place 6 drained, canned pineapple rings on the grill rack. Brush them lightly with the fat in the pan and sprinkle them lightly with soft brown sugar. Cook under the grill until the sugar has melted and the pineapple rings are hot. Arrange the pineapple rings with the chops. Drain the fat from the grill pan and scrape the sediment into a small pan. Stir 125ml pineapple juice into the sediment and heat to boiling point. Cook over high heat until it has reduced slightly. Serve separately in a sauce-boat.

Fried Crumbed Pork Chops or Cutlets

6 helpings

6 pork chops or cutlets   *soft white breadcrumbs*
1 egg   *3 × 15ml spoons oil,*
1 × 5ml spoon dried sage   *butter or lard*
salt and pepper

Wipe the chops or cutlets and trim off any excess fat. Beat the egg until liquid and mix with the sage, salt and pepper. Brush the chops or cutlets on both sides with the beaten egg, then coat them carefully with the breadcrumbs. Heat the oil, butter or lard in a frying pan, and fry the chops or cutlets gently for about 20 minutes, turning often, until golden-brown and cooked through.

VARIATION

Grilled Crumbed Pork Chops or Cutlets

Follow the basic recipe but brush the crumbed chops or cutlets carefully with oil or melted butter. Brush the grill rack with the melted oil or fat before cooking the meat. Cook under a moderate grill for about 20 minutes, turning often, until golden-brown and cooked through.

Grilled or Fried Marinated Pork Chops

6 helpings

6 loin or spare rib pork chops

Marinade
2 × 15ml spoons olive or   *1 × 5ml spoon wine*
  corn oil   *vinegar*
1 × 2.5ml spoon dried   *salt and pepper*
  sage

Wipe the chops and trim off any excess fat. Mix all the ingredients for the marinade. Pour it over the chops. Leave to marinate for 1 hour, turning the chops often.

Drain the chops, then grill or shallow fry them for 15–20 minutes, turning until browned on both sides and cooked through.

Serve with Robert (p703) or Soubise (p704) Sauce.

BRAISED AND CASSEROLED DISHES

Braised Pork

Basic recipe

8–10 helpings

a bladebone or a spare   *1 clove of garlic*
  rib joint of pork (2kg   *125ml dry cider*
  approx)   *125ml general household*
50g lard or 3 × 15ml   *stock (p329)*
  spoons cooking oil   *bouquet garni*
1 large onion (200g   *salt and pepper*
  approx)
2 large carrots (200g
  approx)

Wipe and trim the meat. Weigh it to calculate the cooking time. Heat the lard or oil in a large, deep frying pan and fry the joint, turning often, until browned all over. Remove the meat and put to one side. Prepare and slice the onion and carrots. Skin and crush the garlic. Add the vegetables and garlic to the pan and fry gently for 5 minutes. Pour in the cider and stock and add the bouquet garni. Return the meat to the pan and season well with salt and pepper. Heat to boiling point, cover the pan, reduce the heat, and simmer gently, allowing 35 minutes per 0.5kg meat. Turn the meat occasionally. When cooked, transfer to a warmed serving dish.

Strain the liquid from the pan, skim off the fat, re-heat, and serve in a sauce-boat.

Braised Pork Chops in Cider

4 helpings

4 middle loin **or** fore loin pork chops	a pinch of ground cinnamon
4 × 15ml spoons dry cider	salt and pepper
bouquet garni	100g flat mushrooms
2 medium-sized onions (200g approx)	200g shelled fresh peas
	200g canned whole small beetroots
2 cooking apples (400g approx)	150–200g noodles

Wipe the chops and trim off the rind and excess fat. Heat the rind and fat trimmings in a frying pan until the fat runs. Add the chops and fry, turning once, until golden-brown on both sides. Remove the chops and place them in a casserole. Pour off the excess fat in the frying pan and reserve the rest. Pour the cider over the chops and add the bouquet garni. Cover the casserole and cook over gentle heat or in a warm oven, 160°C, Gas 3.

Meanwhile, prepare and chop the onions and apples. Put them into the frying pan and fry gently for 5 minutes. Add the cinnamon and just enough water to cover the onions and apples. Cover the pan, heat to simmering point, and simmer for about 15 minutes, until soft. Rub through a sieve, season to taste, and spoon the apple and onion mixture over the chops in the casserole. Replace the lid and cook for $1\frac{3}{4}$–2 hours in all.

Clean the mushrooms and slice thickly; add them and the peas for the last 30 minutes of the cooking time. Heat the beetroot separately. Cook the noodles in boiling salted water until, when tested, the centre is still slightly firm. Drain the noodles and

beetroot. Serve the noodles on a warmed serving dish with the chops on top, and arrange the mushrooms, peas, and beetroots round them.

Braised Pork Spare Ribs with Fruit

6 helpings

100g prunes	400g cooking apples
1.25–1.5kg pork spare ribs	375ml general household (p329) **or** chicken (p330) stock
salt and pepper	
$\frac{1}{2}$ × 2.5ml spoon ground ginger	

Soak the prunes in cold water overnight. Break or crack the bones in the spare ribs, then wipe off any splinters of bone. Sprinkle the meat with salt, pepper, and ginger. Place the ribs on a rack in a roasting tin, and bake in a moderate oven, 180°C, Gas 4, for 45 minutes.

Remove the meat and pour off the fat. Peel, core and slice the apples. Drain, then halve and stone the prunes. Layer the apples and prunes in the bottom of a casserole, and place the spare ribs on top, bone side up. Heat the stock to boiling point and pour it over the meat. Bake in a moderate oven, 180°C, Gas 4, for 30 minutes. Turn the ribs over and increase the heat to fairly hot, 200°C, Gas 6; bake for a further 30 minutes to brown the spare ribs well. Remove the meat, cut it into serving portions, and place them on a warmed serving dish. Drain the apples and prunes and arrange them around the meat. Strain the gravy and serve it separately.

Pork Fillets Stuffed with Prunes

6 helpings

100g prunes	*100ml boiling water*
800g fillet of pork	*200ml single cream*
2 small cooking apples	*salt and pepper*
(200g approx)	*2 × 10ml spoons butter*
50g butter **or** *margarine*	*(approx)*

Soak the prunes in cold water overnight, or cover them with boiling water and soak for 2 hours. Wipe the fillets and trim off any skin and fat, then slice them down the middle almost but not quite right through. Drain and stone the prunes; peel, core and slice the apples. Put the prunes and apple slices into the slits in the fillets, press the fillets back into shape, and tie them with thin string.

Heat the butter or margarine in a large pan, put in the fillets and brown them all over. Add the boiling water, 100ml of the cream, and salt and pepper to taste. Cover the pan, and cook gently for 30 minutes. Transfer the fillets to a warmed serving dish, remove the string, and keep hot. Add the rest of the cream to the pan, whisk well, then add a little cold butter. Pour the sauce over the fillets and serve hot.

Pork and Rice Casserole

4 helpings

250g boned hand and	*salt and pepper*
spring **or** *blade of pork*	*2 × 5ml spoons chopped*
1 medium-sized onion	*parsley*
(100g approx)	*400g tomatoes*
50g lard	*375ml general household*
150g long-grain rice	*stock* (p329) **or** *water*

Remove the rind of the pork, if necessary. Wipe the pork and cut it into very thin slices. Skin and chop the onion. Heat the lard in a saucepan and fry the onion until softened but not coloured. Wash the rice and add it with the seasoning and parsley. Continue cooking gently, stirring all the time, until the rice begins to look transparent. Skin and slice the tomatoes.

Put the rice mixture in the bottom of an oven-proof casserole, cover with half the tomatoes; then add the meat and finish with a layer of tomatoes. Heat the stock and pour it over the contents of the casserole. Cover the casserole and cook in a moderate oven, 180°C, Gas 4, for 2–2¼ hours. If necessary, add more hot stock during cooking. Serve from the casserole.

Pork and Apple Hot Pot

4 helpings

4 loin **or** *spare rib chops*	*100g mushrooms*
1 medium-sized cooking	*fat for greasing*
apple (200g approx)	*1 × 2.5ml spoon dried*
1 medium-sized onion	*sage* **or** *savory*
(100g approx)	*500g potatoes*
50g lard **or** *oil*	*salt and pepper*

Garnish
chopped parsley

Wipe the chops and trim off any excess fat. Prepare the apple and onion and slice them thinly. Heat the lard or oil in a pan and fry the apple and onion until golden-brown. Clean and slice the mushrooms.

Grease a casserole and put the mushrooms in the bottom. Lay the chops on the mushrooms and cover with the apple and onion. Sprinkle the herb over the top. Prepare the potatoes and cut them into 1.5cm cubes. Top the casserole with the potatoes and brush them with the fat remaining in the pan. Season with salt and pepper. Pour in enough water to come half-way up the meat and vegetables. Cover the pan with a tight-fitting lid and cook in a moderate oven, 180°C, Gas 4, for 1½ hours. Remove the lid 30 minutes before the end of the cooking time to allow the potatoes to brown. Garnish with chopped parsley and serve from the casserole.

PIES AND PUDDINGS

Raised Pork Pie

6 helpings

400g pork bones
  (approx)
1 small onion
salt and pepper
150ml cold water **or**
  stock
hot water crust pastry
  (p1250) *using 250g
  flour*

500g lean pork
$\frac{1}{2} \times 2.5ml$ *spoon dried
  sage*
beaten egg **or** *milk for
  glazing*

Put the pork bones in a saucepan. Skin and chop the onion finely. Add it to the pan with salt, pepper, and the water or stock. Cover the pan, heat to simmering point, and simmer for 2 hours. Leave to cool until jellied.

Line a 1kg pie mould with three-quarters of the pastry, or use a round cake tin to mould the pie as described on p1250, keeping it about 5mm thick. Use the remaining quarter for the lid. Wipe and dice the pork. Season with salt, pepper, and sage. Put into the prepared pie crust and add $2 \times 15ml$ spoons of the jellied stock. Put on the lid, brush with beaten egg or milk, and make a hole in the centre to allow steam to escape. Bake in a hot oven, 220°C, Gas 7, for 15 minutes. Reduce the heat to moderate, 180°C, Gas 4, and cook the pie for a further $1\frac{1}{2}$ hours. Remove the greaseproof paper or mould for the last 30 minutes of the cooking time and brush the top and sides of the pastry with egg or milk.

When cooked, remove from the oven and leave to cool. Warm the remainder of the jellied stock and funnel it through the hole in the pastry lid until the pie is full. Leave to cool for 2 hours until the stock sets to a jelly.

Note If preferred, small individual pies can be made. Cook for 1 hour (approx).

French Pork Pie

6 helpings

300g boned hand and
  spring **or** blade of
  lean pork
200g belly **or** salt belly
  of pork
100g lean bacon,
  without rinds
salt and pepper
a pinch of ground mace
a pinch of dried thyme

$1 \times 15ml$ spoon chopped
  parsley
$4 \times 15ml$ spoons soft
  white breadcrumbs
puff pastry (p1253)
  using 200g flour
flour for rolling out
1 egg
$1 \times 15ml$ spoon water

Remove the rind of the pork if necessary. Wipe the meat. Mince all the meat together finely. Season to taste with salt and pepper, add the mace, thyme, and parsley, and mix in the breadcrumbs.

Cut off one-third of the pastry for the lid. Roll out the rest on a lightly floured surface. Line a deep 23cm pie plate with the pastry. Separate the egg, and brush the white over the surface of the pastry. Cover with the meat filling. Roll out the remaining pastry to form a lid. Dampen the pie edge with cold water, put the lid in position and press the edges together to seal. Mix the egg yolk with the water and brush it over the top of the pie. Bake in a hot oven, 220°C, Gas 7, for 15 minutes, then reduce the heat to moderate, 180°C, Gas 4, and cook for a further 45 minutes.

Pork and Onion Roll

6 helpings

400g lean pork	*flour for rolling out*
3 small onions (150g	*fat for greasing*
approx)	*250ml thickened gravy*
salt and pepper	*(p727) or Espagnole*
a pinch of dried sage	*sauce (p707)*
suet crust pastry (p1250)	
using 300g flour	

Wipe the meat. Chop the pork finely or mince it coarsely. Skin and chop or mince the onions finely. Mix together the pork, onion, seasoning, and sage.

Roll out the suet crust pastry on a lightly floured surface into a rectangle 24 × 40cm. Spread the pork mixture over the rectangle leaving a 1cm margin all round the edge. Roll up from the narrow side, like a Swiss roll, and press the end and sides to seal in the filling. Wrap the roll firmly in a sheet of greased greaseproof paper and then in foil or a pudding cloth. Steam for 3 hours. Turn out on to a dish and serve with hot gravy or Espagnole sauce.

DISHES USING COOKED MEAT

Holiday Pork

4 helpings

400g cold roast or boiled	*1 × 10ml spoon*
pork	*Worcestershire sauce*
salt and Cayenne pepper	*1 × 5ml spoon mixed*
3 × 10ml spoons butter	*English mustard*
or dripping	*1 × 5ml spoon lemon*
	juice

Cut the meat into small neat pieces and sprinkle them with salt and a little Cayenne pepper to taste. Heat the butter or dripping in a pan and add the Worcestershire sauce, mustard, and lemon juice. When hot, add the meat, and toss over heat for 15–20 minutes, until heated through and impregnated with the flavours.

Serve with rice.

Pork Cheese

4–6 helpings

400g cold lean pork	*1 × 2.5ml spoon grated*
1 × 10ml spoon chopped	*lemon rind*
parsley	*a pinch of grated nutmeg*
½ × 2.5ml spoon dried	*salt and pepper*
sage	*250ml cooled and jellied*
¼ × 2.5ml spoon dried	*brown or white stock*
mixed herbs	*(p329)*

Cut the pork into small pieces, 5mm thick (approx). Add the herbs, lemon rind, nutmeg, salt and pepper to taste, and mix together. Press the seasoned meat tightly into an ovenproof mould or basin. Heat the jellied stock and fill up the mould or basin with it. Bake in a moderate oven, 180°C, Gas 4, for about 1½ hours. Leave until cold, and then turn out to serve. Cut in slices.

Note Pork head meat can be used if not too fat.

Pork and Fruit Stew

4 helpings

400g cold roast pork	*3 × 10ml spoons butter*
150ml stock made with	*or margarine*
bones, trimmings, and	*1 × 10ml spoon plain*
bouquet garni or	*flour*
general household stock	*a pinch of dry mustard*
(p329)	*salt and pepper*
2 medium-sized onions	*1 × 5ml spoon lemon*
(200g approx)	*juice*
1 medium-sized cooking	
apple (200g approx)	

Garnish (optional)
toasted croûtons

Cut the meat into neat cubes. If making stock, use any bones and trimmings from the meat and boil them for at least 1 hour with some trimmings of root vegetables and a bouquet garni. Strain and measure the stock. Skin and chop the onions finely; peel and core the apple and chop it coarsely. Melt the fat in a saucepan and fry the onions until lightly browned. Add the apple, cover the pan loosely with a lid, and cook gently until the apple is tender but not pulped. Sprinkle over the flour and mustard and cook gently for 3–4 minutes, stirring all the time. Gradually add the stock and stir until boiling. Season to taste. Put in the meat and lemon juice, replace the lid and simmer for about 30 minutes. Do not allow to boil.

The meat can be served in a border of rice or mashed potatoes, or garnished with toasted croûtons.

Pork Mould

4–6 helpings

400–500g cold roast **or** *boiled pork*	*125ml single cream* **or** *milk*
1 × 5ml spoon grated onion	*fat for greasing*
2 × 15ml spoons mashed potato	*browned breadcrumbs (p375)*
salt and pepper	*250ml thickened gravy (p727)*

Trim off the skin, fat, and bone from the meat, and mince or chop the pork very finely. Add the onion and mashed potato, and season to taste. Stir in enough cream or milk to bind the mixture. Grease an ovenproof mould or pie dish well and coat it thickly with browned breadcrumbs. Spoon the mixture carefully into the mould or pie dish and bake in a moderate oven, 180°C, Gas 4, for 45 minutes. Turn out and serve hot. Serve the gravy, which can be made from the bones and trimmings, separately in a sauce-boat.

VARIATION

Pork Cakes

4 helpings

Use the mixture prepared in the previous recipe to shape into small round cakes. Coat them with beaten egg and soft white breadcrumbs and fry them for 5–7 minutes in shallow fat until browned on both sides.

SAUSAGES

Sausage-meat for making sausages can be forced into casings (skins) or shaped into cylindrical rolls, patties or balls.

With casings: A family butcher may be willing to sell a few metres of sausage casings (pig's or sheep's large or small intestines) or you can buy cellulose casings for your sausage-meat. Process and prepare the casings as instructed by the butcher or other supplier. Rinse them in lukewarm water, then open them in turn by pushing one end of the casing on to the end of the cold tap and turning on the water. Fill the casings (not too tightly) with the sausage-meat mixture, using domestic sausage-filling equipment (see **Note**). Moisten the casings and twist to form links.

Do not prick cased sausages before cooking. Moisten before cooking and cook gently to prevent the skin bursting. The sausage will be more moist since there will be less loss of fat and meat juices.

Note Sausage-filling attachments are available for some electric mixers. Do not attempt to make cased sausages without such an attachment as it is difficult to fill the casings evenly by hand without leaving air spaces.

Skinless: Skinless pork sausages are best made with Pork Sausage-meat with Egg (p592). Divide the mixture into equal portions of the weight you want. Roll into sausage shapes, using wet hands. Coat the sausages with flour or beaten egg and breadcrumbs which will help to hold them together during cooking. Alternatively, form into round cakes and cook as for Hamburgers (p505).

591

Pork Sausage-meat

Basic recipe

Makes 650–700g

450g lean pork (see **Note**)	freshly ground black pepper
1 slice of dry white bread	a pinch of dried thyme
200g hard pork fat	25g dry white breadcrumbs
1 × 2.5ml spoon ground mace **or** allspice	1 × 5ml spoon salt (see **Note**)

Wipe the meat. Remove the crusts from the bread. Mince the pork very finely together with the fat and bread. Season thoroughly with the spice, pepper, and thyme. Mix in the breadcrumbs, and add salt as needed. Use as required.

Note Cured pork can be used instead of fresh pork but the salt must be used sparingly or not at all.

VARIATION

Pork Sausage-meat with Egg

Make the recipe for Pork Sausage-meat using 1 × 5ml spoon ground allspice. Add 1 × 2.5ml spoon ground coriander and 1 × 5ml spoon chopped parsley. Add 1 lightly beaten egg to the mixture. This sausage-meat can be used for making skinless sausages, stuffings and patties, as the egg will bind the mixture.

Note Sausage-meat made with egg is not suitable for freezing or long storage. It should be eaten on the day it is made.

Cocktail Sausages
See p1280.

Sausage Rolls
See p1306.

Pork Sausages

Makes 50 sausages or 100 chipolatas

500g bread (3 days old)	500g hard pork fat
1.5kg lean pork	sausage casings

Seasoning

75g salt	15g ground ginger
25g ground pepper	10g dried sage
20g ground mace	

Mix together all the ingredients for the seasoning. Use 25g seasoning per kg of meat. Store the rest in an airtight jar for future use.

Cut any crisp crust off the bread and cut the bread into large cubes. Put into water to soak. Wipe the meat and cut up the pork and pork fat roughly. Mince them coarsely. Add the correct quantity of seasoning. Squeeze out the bread, which should have doubled its weight, and mix thoroughly into the other ingredients. Mince the mixture finely, then fill it into skins with a sausage filler. Leave to mature in a cool place for 12–24 hours before use.

Sausages, with or without skins, can be baked, grilled or fried gently.

1) Bake in an ungreased baking tin for about 30 minutes in a moderate oven, 180°C, Gas 4, turning once half-way through the cooking.
2) Grill under a moderate grill for about 15 minutes for a 50–75g sausage, turning 2 or 3 times until evenly browned and cooked through.
3) Fry gently in a small quantity of hot fat, turning 2 or 3 times until evenly browned and cooked through.

Mrs Beeton's Oxford Sausages

Makes 36 sausages or 60–70 chipolatas

1.5kg pork **or** 0.5kg lean
 pork, 0.5kg lean veal
 and 0.5kg beef dripping
500g soft white
 breadcrumbs
1 × 5ml spoon ground
 pepper
grated rind of ½ lemon
grated nutmeg
6 chopped sage leaves
1 × 2.5ml spoon chopped
 winter savory
1 × 2.5ml spoon dried
 marjoram

Choose pork which consists of two-thirds lean meat to one-third fat, without skin and gristle. Cut it up roughly and mince it finely or coarsely, according to taste; for a fine cut, however, it must be put through the coarse plate first, otherwise it will clog the machine. Mix the rest of the ingredients into the sausage-meat and mince again. Fill the sausage-meat into skins, using a sausage-filler, or make it into little cakes or cork shapes. Allow to mature for 12–24 hours in a cool place, to develop flavour and texture.

Pork Sausages with Cabbage

4 helpings

1 hard white cabbage
 (1kg approx)
1 small onion
 (50g approx)
75g butter
salt and pepper
125ml white stock
 (p329) **or** water
500g pork sausages
 (50g each)

Trim the cabbage, and cut it into quarters. Shred it finely lengthways. Skin and chop the onion finely. Melt the butter in a large saucepan, and fry the onion in it until transparent. Add the cabbage, salt and pepper, and stock or water. Cover the pan with a tight-fitting lid and cook over gentle heat for 1 hour.

   Meanwhile, fry, bake or grill the sausages until cooked through. Drain any liquid from the cooked cabbage and pile the vegetable on a warmed serving dish. Arrange the hot sausages on or around the cabbage.

Black and White Puddings

These are traditional sausages, made in some form in most European countries. By custom, they are made in horse-shoe shapes, but modern synthetic sausage skins are now used to make sausages in straight shapes.

   Black puddings of various types, ie with different spicing, are made of pig's blood mixed with grain, usually oatmeal, and with small dice of pure white pig's fat. Although they used to be made on farms at the winter pig killing time, they are not a practical proposition for anyone to make today unless the pig is slaughtered at home instead of at a local slaughter-house. Black puddings are, however, made commercially on a large scale as well as by private butchers, and are fairly widely available. They can be bought whole or in cut lengths, and are then usually boiled and served with mashed potatoes, or fried or grilled and served like ordinary pork sausages.

   White puddings are made, in the UK, from various pig offal such as the cooked brain, tongues or sweetbreads, mixed with pearl barley, oatmeal or breadcrumbs, seasoned and flavoured, then fried or grilled like sausages. The traditional Irish white pudding is made just with leaf pork fat mixed with toasted oatmeal, and seasoned with cloves, black pepper and salt. It is cased and cooked like a black pudding. White puddings are less readily available than black puddings.

OFFAL DISHES

Braised Pig's Liver

6–8 helpings

1kg pig's liver in 1 piece	1 clove
200g streaky bacon, without rinds	bouquet garni
8 small carrots (200g approx)	1 × 5ml spoon salt
	freshly ground pepper
1 medium-sized onion (100g approx)	100ml dry white wine **or** dry cider
	chicken stock to cover

Remove the skin and tubes, but leave the liver whole. Put 100g of the bacon rashers in the bottom of a casserole and place the liver on top. Prepare the vegetables and press the clove into the skinned onion. Add the carrots, onion, and bouquet garni to the casserole, and season with salt and pepper. Pour the wine or cider over them. Add enough stock to come to the top of the liver. Put the rest of the bacon on top of the liver. Cover the casserole with a lid and bake in a moderate oven, 180°C, Gas 4, for about 45 minutes or until the liver is cooked through. Transfer the liver and bacon to a warmed serving dish and keep hot.

Strain the sauce into a clean pan. Bring to the boil over high heat until the sauce is reduced by half. Pour the sauce over the liver, and serve hot.

Note Lamb's or calf's liver can be cooked in the same way.

Fried Pig's Fry

6 helpings

800–900g pig's fry (sweetbreads, heart, liver, lights, melts)	flour for coating
	ground pepper
salt	1 × 5ml spoon dried sage
1 small onion (50g approx)	fat for shallow frying

Prepare the sweetbreads (p553) and the heart (p509). Remove the skin and tubes of the liver. Lights need no preparation. Trim excess fat and skin off the melts.

Put the fry in a saucepan with just enough water to cover it. Salt lightly. Skin and add the onion. Heat to boiling point, skim, reduce the heat, and simmer for 30 minutes. Drain, dry thoroughly, and cut all the meats into thin slices. Season the flour with salt, pepper and sage, and use it to coat the slices lightly. Heat the fat in a frying pan, put in the slices, and fry gently, turning once, until browned on both sides.

Serve with a well-flavoured thickened gravy or with fried apple slices (p395) and crab-apple jelly.

Baked Pig's Fry

6 helpings

600–800g pig's fry (sweetbreads, heart, liver, lights, melts)	2 medium-sized onions (200g approx)
	1.25kg potatoes
butter for greasing	general household stock (p329) **or** water as required
salt and pepper	
1 × 2.5ml spoon dried sage	1 × 15ml spoon butter
flour for dredging	

Prepare the fry as for Fried Pig's Fry. Cut the fry into slices about 1cm thick. Place a layer of the fry in the bottom of a large, well-greased pie dish. Season with salt and pepper and half the sage. Dredge liberally with flour. Prepare and slice the onions and potatoes, and heat the stock or water to boiling point. Cover the fry with layers of onions and potatoes, ending with a layer of potatoes. Three-quarters fill the dish with the boiling stock or water. Cover with buttered greaseproof paper and bake in a moderate oven, 180°C, Gas 4, for 1½–2 hours. About 30 minutes before the end of the cooking time, remove the paper and dot the dish with butter so that the potatoes brown.

Faggots or Savoury Ducks

4–6 helpings

800g pig's liver **or** *fry (sweetbreads, heart, liver, lights, melts)*	*a pinch of dried basil (optional)*
100g fat belly of pork	*salt and pepper*
2 medium-sized onions (200g approx)	*a pinch of grated nutmeg*
a pinch of dried thyme	*1 egg*
1 × 2.5ml spoon dried sage	*100g soft white breadcrumbs*
	caul fat **or** *flour, as preferred*
	fat for greasing

Prepare the liver or fry as for Fried Pig's Fry (p594). Slice the liver or fry and pork belly. Skin and slice the onions. Put the meat and onions in a saucepan with just enough water to cover them. Heat to boiling point, cover the pan, reduce the heat, and simmer for 30 minutes. Strain off the liquid and reserve it for the gravy.

Mince the meat and onions finely. Add the herbs, salt, pepper, and nutmeg. Beat the egg until liquid and stir it in. Mix in enough breadcrumbs to make a mixture which can be moulded. Divide it into 8 equal portions and shape them into round balls. Cut squares of caul fat, if used, large enough to encase the balls and wrap each ball in a piece of fat. Alternatively, roll each ball in flour. Lay the faggots side by side in a greased baking tin. Cover the tin loosely with foil. Bake in a moderate oven, 180°C, Gas 4, for 25 minutes. Remove the foil and bake for 10 minutes to brown the tops of the faggots.

Serve hot, with a thickened gravy made from the cooking liquid or with Fresh Tomato Sauce (p715).

Fried Pig's Kidneys

4 helpings

4 pig's kidneys	*1 × 10ml spoon chopped parsley*
2 small onions (100g approx)	*1 × 10ml spoon plain flour*
50g butter **or** *oil*	*125ml general household (p329)* **or** *chicken (p330) stock*
salt and pepper	
2 × 15ml spoons mushroom ketchup	

Skin, core, and cut the kidneys into thin slices. Skin and chop the onions finely. Heat the butter or oil in a frying pan and fry the onions until lightly browned. Add the kidney slices, seasoning, and mushroom ketchup. Toss gently over heat for 3–4 minutes. Add the parsley and lift out on to a warmed serving dish. Sprinkle the flour into the pan and cook until browned. Gradually add the stock and stir until boiling. Re-season if required. Pour the sauce round the kidney slices and serve hot.

Grilled Pig's Kidneys

4 helpings

4 pig's kidneys	*a pinch of dried sage*
melted butter **or** *oil*	*salt and pepper*

Garnish
Maître d'Hôtel butter
  (p1300)

Skin and split the kidneys lengthways without separating the halves. Remove the cores. Stick a skewer through the ends of each kidney to hold it flat. Brush the kidneys with melted butter or oil and sprinkle with sage, salt and pepper. Cook the cut side first under a high grill until sealed, then reduce the heat, and turn several times for 5–10 minutes until cooked through. Serve hot with a small pat of Maître d'Hôtel butter in the centre of each kidney.

Stewed Pig's Kidneys

4 helpings

4 pig's kidneys	*100ml medium-dry*
150g streaky bacon,	*white wine* **or** *dry cider*
without rinds	*150ml chicken* **or** *beef*
1 small onion	*stock*
(50g approx)	*bouquet garni*
25g butter **or** *margarine*	*salt and pepper*
100g button mushrooms	

Skin, core, and cut the kidneys into 2cm slices. Cut the bacon into small dice. Skin and chop the onion. Heat the fat in a saucepan and fry the bacon and onion for 3 minutes. Put in the kidney slices and cook for 1–2 minutes. Clean the mushrooms and add them to the pan with the wine or cider and stock. Heat to boiling point, reduce the heat and add the bouquet garni and seasoning. Cover the pan and simmer for 10–15 minutes. Drain, reduce the sauce until syrupy, and serve with the kidneys on a warmed, flat serving dish in a ring of rice.

Pork Brawn

10–12 helpings

½ pig's head	*2 small carrots*
400g shin of beef on the	*(50g approx)*
bone	*½ × 2.5ml spoon ground*
1 × 5ml spoon salt	*mace*
2 medium-sized onions	*6 black peppercorns*
(200g approx)	*bouquet garni*
4 cloves	*salt and pepper*

Ask the butcher to remove the hair, eye and snout, and to chop the half head into 2 or 3 manageable pieces and the shin beef bone in half crossways. Remove the brains and tongue from the head and use these for another dish. Scald and clean the ear and wash the head well in cold water. Soak the head meat in salted water for 2 hours, changing the water 3 or 4 times. Drain thoroughly.

Put all the meat and the salt in a large pan. Skin the onions, and press 2 cloves in each. Scrape the carrots. Add the onions and carrots to the pan with the mace, peppercorns, and bouquet garni. Cover with cold water. Heat to boiling point, skim carefully, cover with a lid, reduce the heat, and simmer gently for 2–3 hours until the meat is tender.

Lift the meat out of the stock and drain thoroughly. Reserve the stock in the pan. Remove all the meat from the bones, trimming off the skin and fat, and dice the meat finely. Put the meat in a wetted mould, basin or cake tin.

Return the bones to the pan of stock. Bring the stock to the boil and boil rapidly, uncovered, to reduce it by about half. Strain the stock and season to taste. Pour just enough stock over the meat to cover it. Stir gently to distribute the meat evenly. Allow to cool. Cover, and leave in a refrigerator or cold place until set. Turn out to serve.

VARIATION

A pickled head can be bought from a butcher which gives additional flavour to brawn. Treat in the same way as the unpickled head, but reduce the cooking time to $1\frac{1}{2}$–$1\frac{3}{4}$ hours.

Boiled Pig's Head

a pig's head	*bouquet garni*
salt	*6–10 black peppercorns*
2 medium-sized onions	
(200g approx)	

Ask the butcher to remove the hair, eyes and snout, and to chop the head in half, then each half into 2 or 3 manageable pieces. Remove the brains from the head and use these for another dish. Cut off the ears, scald them and wash thoroughly. Cut out the tongue if whole. Soak the head, ears, and tongue in salted water for 2 hours, changing the water 3 or 4 times.

Drain thoroughly. Skin the onions. Put the head in a large pan with the ears, tongue, onions, bouquet garni, peppercorns, and 1–2 × 2.5ml spoons salt. Cover with cold water. Heat to boiling point, skim carefully, cover with a tight-fitting lid, and simmer very slowly for 2–3 hours, until the meat is tender.

Note Use for making Pork Brawn, Lincolnshire Haslet (p1470), Pork Cheese (p590) or Collared Pig's Head (p610).

Spiced Pig's Cheek (chap)

3–4 helpings

½ pig's jaw and cheek   raspings (p375)

Pickling Brine

2.5 litres water	5 juniper berries
300g coarse salt	(optional)
300g soft light brown	small pieces of nutmeg
sugar	1 bay leaf
1 × 2.5ml spoon	1 × 5ml spoon black
saltpetre	peppercorns
2–3 sprigs dried thyme	3 cloves

Stock

2 medium-sized onions	2 bay leaves
(200g approx)	6–8 black peppercorns
2 medium-sized carrots	2 × 15ml spoons wine
(100g approx)	vinegar
1 clove of garlic	500ml dry white wine or
a few parsley stalks	cider
2–3 sprigs dried thyme	
or basil	

Prepare the jaw and cheek as for Bath Chap (p1471).

Make the pickling brine. Put the water into a large pan and add the rest of the ingredients. Heat to boiling point, skim the brine, then remove from the heat and allow to cool completely. When cold, soak the meat in it for 2–3 days, depending on the flavour you want.

Drain the meat, place it in a pan, and cover with cold water. Heat to boiling point. Drain the meat and wipe off as much salt as possible. Tie the meat tightly in muslin and string.

Slice the onions and carrots for the stock and chop them roughly. Put the vegetables and the rest of the stock ingredients into a large pan. Add the meat and enough water to cover the meat. Heat gently to boiling point, cover the pan with a tight-fitting lid, reduce the heat, and simmer very gently for about 3½ hours until the meat is tender.

Lift out the meat and, when it is cool enough to handle, untie the string and muslin, and remove the bones and rind carefully. Form into the shape of a cornet, and retie. Leave to cool completely. When cold, untie and coat with raspings.

Fricasséed Pig's Trotters or Pettitoes

4–6 helpings

4 pig's trotters or	6 white peppercorns
8 pettitoes (see Note)	salt and pepper
100g pig's liver	a thin strip of lemon
100g pig's heart (1 small	rind
or ½ large heart)	25g butter or margarine
white stock (p329) to	1 × 15ml spoon flour
cover	1 × 15ml spoon single
½ small onion	cream or milk
(25g approx)	
1 blade of mace	

Wash the trotters or pettitoes thoroughly in salted water. Remove the skin and tubes from the liver and prepare the heart (p509). Put the trotters or pettitoes, liver and heart in a large pan and cover with stock. Skin the onion and add it with the mace, peppercorns, salt and pepper to taste, and lemon rind. Heat to boiling point, cover the pan with a tight-fitting lid, reduce the heat, and simmer for 1 hour. Remove the liver and heart, chop them finely, and put to one side. Allow the trotters or pettitoes to continue cooking for another 1–2 hours until the meat can be easily removed from the bones. (Pettitoes may take less time to cook than trotters.) Lift out the trotters or pettitoes, split them open, remove the bones and cut the meat into neat pieces. Put to one side with the liver and heart. Strain the stock and measure 250ml.

Melt the butter or margarine in a saucepan. Stir in the flour and cook for 2–3 minutes. Gradually add the 250ml stock, stir until boiling, and cook for 2–3 minutes. Season to taste. Add the meat. Heat through and stir in the cream or milk. Turn at once into a warmed dish and serve very hot.

Note Pig's trotters are the feet and leg up to the knuckle of a pig. Pettitoes are the same as trotters but taken from a suckling pig and, therefore, smaller.

Pig's Trotters in Jelly

3–4 helpings

4 pig's trotters
2 pig's ears
1 × 10ml spoon chopped
  parsley
1 × 2.5ml spoon chopped
  fresh sage
salt and pepper

Singe off the hairs. Wash the trotters and ears thoroughly in salted water. Scald the ears. Put the trotters and ears in a large pan with just enough cold water to cover them. Heat to boiling point, cover the pan with a tight-fitting lid, reduce the heat, and simmer gently for about 3 hours until the bones can be removed easily. Lift out the trotters and ears, reserving the liquid in the pan. Cut the meat into neat dice and replace it in the liquid. Add the herbs, and season to taste. Simmer gently for 15 minutes. Turn into a mould or basin and leave until cold and set.

Spiced Pig's Trotters

4 helpings

Follow the recipe for Spiced Pig's Cheek (p597) using 4 pig's trotters. After coating them in raspings, re-heat in a moderate oven, 180°C, Gas 4, for 20–30 minutes.

Pig's Tongues

Soak the tongues in cold salted water for 1 hour, then drain them. Follow the recipes for Sheep's or Lamb's Tongues (p554). A pig's tongue is bigger than a lamb's tongue, so allow for this when estimating quantities.

Bacon, Gammon and Ham

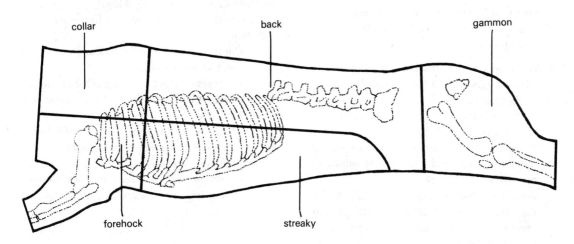

collar   back   gammon

forehock   streaky

Bacon is cured meat from the back, sides and belly of a bacon pig. Gammon is the hind leg, cured with the side, and square cut at the top. Ham, traditionally, is also the hind leg, but cut off and cured separately from the side; it is round cut at the top. Ham is usually purchased ready cooked although raw hams are also available. Smoked ham, eg Parma and Westphalian, is generally eaten raw.

While ham and gammon are traditionally defined as above, bacon shoulder is often cured and sold as ham, gammon is frequently taken to be synonymous with uncooked ham, and cooked ham can be used to describe gammon sold ready cooked, particularly since both ham and gammon can often be prepared in the same way.

The ideal bacon pig carcass should give a dressed side of 22–26kg with a good lean to fat ratio. To produce this economically, the breeding, housing and feeding of the pig are carefully controlled so that it reaches a weight of 90kg in 6–6½ months. After slaughter, the carcass is dehaired, eviscerated and thoroughly cooled. The head and feet are removed and then the carcass is cut down the backbone and trimmed into two sides which can be cured whole or subdivided before curing.

Modern, economical curing is based on a cure which originated in Wiltshire and is now used throughout the world. Brine is pumped into the carcass, then it is given a short period in extra brine and is matured before drying and marketing. The mild flavour of the bacon rashers and small joints is popular.

By contrast, a long cut Yorkshire ham is dry salted, and has a deep cream-coloured exterior and pale pink meat. It should develop a blue-green mould on its surface during storage. Bradenham hams are sweet-cured with molasses and are a very dark 'coal black'. Hams can be cured in many other ways. A good delicatessen almost always offers a selection of hams from several countries prepared from various cures.

See also pp608–12 for information on cured meats in general, and home curing of bacon, gammon and ham.

QUALITY OF BACON, GAMMON AND HAM

When choosing bacon, gammon and ham, look for a firm, lean piece of good colour, deep pink or bright red. Avoid any dark, dry cuts or meat with yellow or green stains. The fat should be white and firm, not discoloured or soft and oily. The colour of the rind will be darker on smoked bacon than on unsmoked (green) bacon, but both should be thin, smooth and resilient to touch.

BACON PIG CUTS

Cuts vary in different parts of Great Britain. The following are the most usual ones. See also the diagram on p599.

1) *Forehock* can be cooked whole. It bakes well or can be boiled. (Av wt – 3.5kg) It can be cut into three smaller joints.

> *Butt:* The leanest end of the forehock, usually boiled. (Av wt – 1.7kg)
>
> *Small hock:* Not recommended as a joint. Remove the bone, and casserole or mince the meat. (Av wt – 1.3kg)
>
> *Fore slipper:* Fat but good taste, usually boiled. Forehock joints are cheaper than gammon because their muscle structure is less regular. (Av wt – 0.5kg)

2) *Streaky* is usually divided into smaller cuts. (Av wt – 3.7kg)

> *Top streaky* can be boned and boiled or cut into thin rashers for frying or grilling. (Av wt – 2.5kg)
>
> *Prime streaky* can be boiled in a piece or cut into rashers for frying or grilling. (Av wt – 2.5kg)
>
> *Thin streaky* is sliced to make crisp small rashers or bacon rolls. (Av wt – 0.7kg)

3) *Back* is usually divided into smaller cuts. (Av wt – 8.7kg)

> *Flank* is sliced and can be served with liver and kidneys. Economical. (Av wt – 1.2kg)
>
> *Long back* and *oyster* are sliced for grilling or frying. (Av wt – 1.2kg)
>
> *Short back* is cut into prime rashers for grilling or frying. (Av wt – 2.3kg)
>
> *Back and ribs* can be boiled in a piece or cut into lean, economical rashers. (Av wt – 3kg)
>
> *Top back* can be boiled or braised or cut into bacon chops. (Av wt – 1kg)

4) *Collar* can be bought whole and is most suitable for boiling. (Av wt – 3.6kg) It is often divided into smaller cuts.

> *Prime collar* is a good boiling joint whole or cut into smaller joints. (Av wt – 2.7kg)
>
> *End collar* is economical. Skin and press after boiling or baking. (Av wt – 0.9kg)

5) *Head* can be boiled for brawn or cooked whole for an occasion. (Av wt half head – 3kg)

6) *Chap* is the lower jaw and cheek of a pig. Boiled for Bath Chap. (Av wt 350–450g)

7) *Gammon* can be divided into four cuts. (Av wt 6.5–8kg)

> *Gammon slipper* is a small, lean joint for boiling. (Av wt – 0.7kg)
>
> *Gammon hock* is boiled or parboiled and then baked. Very good cold. High proportion of bone. (Av wt – 2kg)
>
> *Middle gammon* is the best joint for boiling. Can be sliced into rashers for grilled gammon with eggs, etc. (Av wt – 2.3kg)
>
> *Corner gammon* is a lean joint for boiling or for cutting into rashers for grilling. (Av wt – 1.8kg)

STORAGE OF BACON, GAMMON AND HAM

Unwrapped joints or rashers should be kept in a refrigerator in an unsealed polythene bag or bacon box. They should be used within the storage period indicated on the chart. If using home-cured bacon, slice only enough for a week's supply. Packaged bacon may need special attention.

1) *Clingfilm* keeps bacon clean but does not prolong its storage period. Undo the wrap enough to ventilate but not expose the bacon and store in a refrigerator.

2) *Vacuum pouches* containing rashers should already be date stamped when purchased. The pouch should be kept in a refrigerator and the bacon used within the period stated.

3) *Sealed plastic bags or nylon nets* are useful because joints of bacon, gammon and ham can be both stored and cooked in them. Follow the instructions on the bag or cook for the same time as unwrapped bacon. A plastic bag usually has to be punctured before cooking to prevent the joint falling apart. If possible, keep the joint in the bag until cold and keep a net on while carving.

Bacon is seldom worth freezing since its refrigerator storage life is long. Unless very tightly wrapped, the bacon dries out during freezer storage and its flavour soon deteriorates due to its high salt content. If left in the freezer for longer than the recommended storage time, it rapidly turns rancid when thawed. It is better to freeze uncured joints and to cure them when thawed. The cure will penetrate in about half to two-thirds of the usual time.

If you do freeze a joint of cooked bacon, slice the meat and pack the slices in gravy.

STORAGE PERIOD

	In refrigerator (covered) days	In cool larder (covered) days	In freezer (wrapped and sealed)
Joint of boiling bacon (uncooked)	7–8	2	up to 3 months
Joint of boiling bacon (cooked)	3	2	up to 1 month (in slices)
Bacon (rashers)	5–7	2	up to 1 month

COOKING BACON, GAMMON AND HAM

Cured pig meat which has been dried or smoked must generally be boiled before it can be used. After boiling, it can be used hot, but it is often reboiled or baked before it is served. Home-cured bacon, if very salty, can be soaked for 30 minutes in cold water or covered in boiling water and allowed to stand for 1 minute.

The small, family-sized bacon, gammon and ham joints in the shops have either been precooked before being cut, or they have been cut with special instruments which do not tear or spoil the meat. They can be boiled as for Boiled Pickled Pork (p609).

A whole raw gammon or ham weighs at least 6.5kg and may weigh as much as 10kg. It is possible to cook a whole, bought or home-cured raw gammon or ham at home, but only given certain conditions. These are:

1) The whole gammon or ham can be boiled, parboiled or baked, in 1 piece and in a very large container in both cases. An average joint measures about 56 × 30 × 13cm and so a boiling pan and an oven of at least this size, is needed if the joint is to be baked.

2) There are several hours available in which to cook the gammon or ham. A solid fuel cooker cuts the fuel costs.

3) There is a hook or similar appliance, hanging above the cooker, to suspend the joint in its cooking pot. During the initial boiling, the knuckle end of the gammon or ham should be out of the water for the first part of the cooking time, otherwise it will cook before the bulkier part of the meat, and will be sodden and partly wasted through shrinkage.

An economic factor to be considered before boiling a bought or home-cured raw gammon or ham is the wastage. An average-sized joint will lose up to 1kg during its first boiling. In a joint smaller than 6.5kg, the ratio of bone to meat is too high to make it economic to cure the joint. These smaller joints are, therefore, normally used as fresh meat.

Because a gammon or ham can vary so much in size, in the ratio of bone to meat, in the uses to which the meat is put, and on the thickness of the slices cut, it is impossible to give an average number of helpings per joint. As a rule, cold meat can be cut more thinly than hot meat.

BACON, GAMMON AND HAM DISHES

Fried Bacon

rashers of back, streaky **or** *long cut bacon* **or** *thin slices from any suitable bacon joint*

Cut the rinds off the bacon rashers to prevent the bacon curling. Heat a frying pan for 1–2 minutes, then lay the rashers or slices in the pan in 1 layer. Cook until the fat is becoming transparent and the underside of the bacon is lightly browned. Turn the rashers or slices over with tongs or a palette knife, and fry the second side to the preferred degree of crispness. The total frying time is 3–4 minutes. Drain thoroughly. Serve quickly before the fat congeals.

Grilled Bacon

rashers of back, streaky
  or long cut bacon or
  thin slices from any
  suitable bacon joint or
  thick slices or steaks
  from a joint or
  gammon steaks

Cut the rinds off the bacon rashers or snip them at intervals to prevent the bacon curling. Heat the grill for 1–2 minutes. Lay the rashers, slices or steaks on the grill rack or pan in 1 layer. Place under the grill, and cook for 2–3 minutes until the fat is bubbling and the meat is beginning to brown. Turn the bacon or gammon over with tongs or a palette knife, reduce the heat and continue cooking to the degree of crispness preferred (for rashers and slices) or until thoroughly heated and cooked through (for steaks). The total grilling time is 4–8 minutes. Drain thoroughly. Serve quickly before the fat congeals.

Boiled Bacon

Basic recipe

any bacon joint suitable
  for boiling
cider (optional)
sugar (optional)
ginger root (optional)

4 cloves (optional)
1 onion (optional)
6–8 black peppercorns
  (optional)
1 bay leaf (optional)
2–3 juniper berries
  (optional)

Garnish (optional)
raspings (p375)   *Demerara sugar*

A bought or home-cured bacon joint will probably need soaking for 1–12 hours before cooking, depending on the saltiness of the meat. Packaged and similar joints do not need soaking as a rule. They can be put into a pan, covered with boiling water, then drained.

Weigh the joint and measure its thickness. Calculate the cooking time according to the thickness of the joint. As a guide, allow 30 minutes per 0.5kg meat plus 30 minutes over for any joint more than 10cm thick, eg cook a 1kg joint for $1\frac{1}{2}$ hours. Do not undercook the meat, but on no account cook it fast or it will shrink and be tough.

Scrape the underside and rind before boiling any bacon joint. Choose a pan large enough to hold the meat comfortably with a little space to spare, especially if boiling more than 1 joint at a time. Add enough cold, fresh water to cover the meat, or use a mixture of cider and water, if preferred. Add sugar, ginger root or other spices, if liked (see **Note**). Cloves can be pressed into a whole onion, or tied in a square of muslin with the peppercorns, bay leaf and juniper berries, if preferred. Heat to simmering point, then simmer steadily for the calculated time. Test for tenderness by piercing the meat, near the bone if it has one, with a skewer.

Alternatively, shorten the cooking time by 15 minutes, and let the meat lie in the hot cooking liquid, off the heat, for 30 minutes. This gives an easier, firmer joint to carve.

Lift out the joint, pat dry, place it on a board and remove the rind. It should come off easily, in one piece. Coat the skinned area thoroughly with raspings, mixed with a little Demerara sugar, if liked. Serve hot or cold.

As a rule, the cooking liquid is too salty to use for stock.

Note Optional spices include coriander seeds, cumin seeds, allspice berries, a blade of mace, small pieces of nutmeg, or a whole, small, red chilli pepper.

VARIATIONS

Boiled Gammon or Bacon with Olives

any gammon or bacon
  joint suitable for
  boiling

Garnish
apricot jam or treacle   *chopped parsley*
stoned black olives,
  chopped

Cook the joint as for the basic recipe but without the flavouring ingredients. When cooked, lift out the meat, drain thoroughly, and remove the rind. Spread the meat all over with apricot jam or treacle. Put it in a meat tin and bake in a very hot oven, 230°C, Gas 8, for 2–4 minutes to glaze. Sprinkle with the olives and parsley.

Serve with Piquant Sauce (p702) and boiled potatoes or with Pease Pudding (p787).

Bacon with Fruit

any bacon joint suitable   *brown sugar*
 for boiling

Garnish
3 ripe pears   *a few cloves*
juice of 1 lemon   *12 grapes*
2 small oranges

Cook the joint as for the basic recipe. Meanwhile, peel, halve and core the pears, and dip them at once in the lemon juice. Peel, de-pip, and cut the oranges into wedges.

When cooked, lift out the bacon, drain thoroughly, and remove the rind. Cool the meat quickly by placing it in a chilled container standing in a pan of chilled water. When cold, spread the brown sugar over the skinned area. Press the cloves into the rounded sides of the pear halves and arrange the pears on the meat. Cut some of the grapes in half, de-pip, and lay them in a pattern between the pears. Put the remaining grapes in a small cluster in the centre. Place the meat on a serving dish and surround it with the orange wedges.

Boiled Ham

a raw ham **or** *gammon*

Garnish
raspings (p375)   *Demerara sugar*

To ensure that the ham is sweet before cooking, insert a sharp knife close to the bone; when withdrawn, it should not give off any unpleasant odour or be slimy.

If the ham or gammon has been hung for a long time, and is very dry and salty, soak it for 24 hours at least, changing the water every 6–8 hours. For most hams, about 12 hours soaking or less is enough.

Drain; then weigh the ham and calculate the cooking time after soaking the ham (see Boiled Bacon p602). Clean and trim off any 'rusty' parts. Put the ham into a boiling pot big enough to hold it, but keep the knuckle end out of the water. Add enough cold water to cover the joint when laid flat, and cover the pan with a cloth to prevent undue evaporation. Heat to simmering point and simmer gently until tender or until parboiled, if to be baked after boiling. Do not let the water level sink below the surface of the ham when it is laid flat. Top up the pot with boiling water when required. Calculate the cooking time for the knuckle end on the thickness of the meat, and lay the ham flat in the pot to cook it (usually for about three-quarters of the total cooking time).

When cooked, lift out the ham and remove the rind. If to be eaten hot, immediately cover the skinned side with equal quantities of raspings and Demerara sugar. If to be eaten cold, put it back in its cooking liquid until cold, then drain, and cover the ham with the raspings and sugar mixture. If the ham is to be reboiled or baked, leave the coating until ready to serve.

Note If preferred, the ham can be glazed as for Boiled Gammon or Bacon with Olives (p602). Instead of garnishing a ham with olives, it is more usual to score the fat surface with a diamond pattern and to insert a clove in the centre of each diamond before glazing the ham.

Boiled Dressed Ham

a whole raw ham
1 large onion
3–4 sticks celery
1 large turnip

1 large carrot
cider or white wine
    (optional)
bouquet garni

Garnish
raspings (p375)
Demerara sugar
cloves

small bunches of
    watercress

Prepare and boil the raw ham as for Boiled Ham (p603) but cook it for only 20 minutes per 500g soaked meat. Leave it to cool in the cooking liquid for 1½ hours.

Prepare the vegetables and chop them roughly. Pour off the cooking liquid from the ham, and replace it with fresh tepid water mixed with cider or wine, if liked. Add the vegetables and bouquet garni. Half cover the pan and heat to simmering point, then simmer gently for 10 minutes per 500g soaked meat.

When cooked, lift out the meat and remove the rind. Score the fat in a pattern of diamonds. Cover the fat with equal quantities of raspings and sugar. Press a clove in the centre of each diamond pattern. Put small bunches of watercress at each end of the ham, and cover the knuckle with a pie frill. Serve hot.

Baked Ham

a whole raw ham
flour

1–2 ×15ml spoons
    brandy or apricot
    brandy (optional)

Garnish
apricot jam
canned pineapple cubes
    and maraschino
    cherries

Prepare and boil the ham as for Boiled Ham (p603) but cook for only 20 minutes per 500g soaked meat. Calculate the rest of the time required to cook the meat fully.

While boiling the ham, make a flour and water paste as firm as a pastry dough to cover the whole ham. Roll it out on a lightly floured surface. (If more convenient, prepare a foil 'jacket' instead, using 3 thicknesses of foil.)

When boiled, lift out the ham and remove the rind. Place the ham in the centre of the paste or foil sheet and fold the paste or foil over to enclose it completely. Put the ham in a baking tin and bake in a fairly hot oven, 200°C, Gas 6, for 15 minutes. Reduce the heat to cool, 150°C, Gas 2, for the rest of the calculated cooking time.

When cooked, carefully take off the covering. Score the fat in a pattern of squares, then brush it all over with apricot jam. Arrange pineapple cubes and maraschino cherries at regular intervals on the ham. Brush over with a little more jam. Cook, uncovered, in a hot oven, 220°C, Gas 7, for 5–8 minutes until the glaze is set. Serve hot or cold.

Note If it is to be eaten cold, the ham's flavour is improved by opening the top of the crust or foil half-way through the cooking time and pouring in the brandy. Alternatively, make 2 small holes in the crust or foil when the meat is fully cooked. Pour the brandy through a funnel into the holes. Leave the crust or foil on the meat until the next day; then remove it, score the fat in a pattern of squares or diamonds, and cover with raspings (p375) instead of jam and fruit.

American Spoon Bread (p866) is excellent with this dish.

VARIATION

Before covering the ham with a crust or foil, arrange a pattern of bay leaves on the fat, and sprinkle the surface with dried basil or thyme. Do not add the brandy.

Serve with Raisin Sauce (p718).

Honey-glazed Ham with Pineapple

8–10 helpings

1.5–2kg parboiled York
  or Virginia ham
500ml dry cider
4 × 5ml spoons softened
  butter

1 × 15ml spoon double
  cream

Garnish

1 × 5ml spoon mixed
  English mustard
3 × 15ml spoons stiff
  honey
a good pinch of ground
  cloves

1 × 226g can pineapple
  chunks or rings
maraschino cherries
sprigs of watercress

Put the ham in a baking tin with the cider. Cover the tin tightly with foil. Bake the ham in a moderate oven, 180°C, Gas 4, for 30 minutes.

Meanwhile, mix together the mustard, honey, and cloves for the glaze. Drain the pineapple, reserving the juice. Cut pineapple rings into cubes, if used. Halve the cherries.

When the ham is baked, remove the foil and pour off the cider into a measuring jug. Remove the rind. Score the fat in a pattern of 4–5cm squares, then brush it all over with the mustard and honey glaze. Place pineapple pieces and halved cherries, cut side down, in alternate squares on the ham. Brush over with a little more glaze. Bake, loosely covered with the foil, in the oven for 20–30 minutes until the glaze is set.

Meanwhile, measure the cider and make it up to 500ml with the reserved pineapple juice, if required. Heat to simmering point in a saucepan. Stir in the butter, in small pieces, and melt. Simmer until well reduced and flavoured. Remove from the heat, and stir in the cream. Pour the sauce into a warmed sauce-boat and keep warm.

Place the ham on a carving dish and garnish with watercress. Serve the sauce separately.

Ham with Raisin Sauce

8–10 helpings

1.5–2kg parboiled York
  ham
250g dark soft brown
  sugar

cloves
100ml white wine
  vinegar

Raisin Sauce

50g soft dark brown
  sugar
1 × 2.5ml spoon English
  mustard
1 × 15ml spoon
  cornflour

75g seedless raisins
1 × 15ml spoon grated
  orange rind
100ml fresh orange
  juice
200ml water

Put the ham in a shallow baking tin and bake, uncovered, in a warm oven, 160°C, Gas 3, for 10 minutes per 450g meat. Thirty minutes before the end of the cooking time, lift out the meat and remove the rind. Score the fat in a pattern of diamonds. Cover the fat with brown sugar, and press in cloves at the points of the diamond pattern. Trickle the wine vinegar gently over the ham. Continue baking, basting with the juices, until the ham is fully cooked.

Make the Raisin Sauce. Mix together in a saucepan the brown sugar, mustard, and cornflour. Add the rest of the ingredients and cook very gently for 10 minutes or until syrupy.

Transfer the cooked ham to a warmed serving dish and serve the sauce separately in a sauce-boat.

Note Another recipe for Raisin Sauce can be found on p718.

Baked Ham Loaf

6 helpings

fat for greasing
100g raspings (p375)
50g sultanas
1 large cooking apple
200g cooked ham
  (knuckle end **or** scraps)
100g corned beef
1 × 15ml spoon chopped
  parsley

1 × 5ml spoon grated
  lemon rind
a pinch of ground
  allspice
a pinch of grated nutmeg
salt and pepper
2 eggs
milk (optional)

Grease a loaf tin and coat it with some of the raspings. Wash the sultanas well. Peel, core and grate the apple. Mince the ham and corned beef, and mix with the remaining raspings, the sultanas, apple, parsley, lemon rind, allspice, nutmeg, and seasoning. Beat the eggs until liquid, and bind the mixture with the beaten egg and a little milk, if necessary. Put the mixture carefully into the loaf tin and bake in a cool oven, 150°C, Gas 2, for about 40 minutes.

Serve hot with gravy, or cold with salad.

Baked Ham Steaks

6 helpings

6 ham **or** gammon
  steaks (3–4cm thick)
1 × 2.5ml spoon dry
  mustard
½ × 2.5ml spoon ground
  cinnamon

2 × 15ml spoons soft
  dark brown sugar
fat for greasing
milk

Remove the rind from the steaks and snip the fat at intervals to prevent curling. Mix together the mustard, cinnamon, and sugar, and coat the steaks with the mixture on both sides. Place them in a shallow, lightly greased ovenproof baking dish, in one overlapping layer. Pour in just enough milk to cover them. Bake, uncovered, in a cool oven, 150°C, Gas 2, for 45 minutes. Cover the dish loosely with foil if the milk dries up during this time, or trickle in a very little more milk. The dish should be moist.

Serve from the dish.

Stuffed Ham Slices

6–8 helpings

6–8 dried apricots **or**
  2 sharp dessert apples
750g–1kg slices of ham
  (1cm thick approx)
75g soft white
  breadcrumbs

salt and pepper
sugar (optional)
1 egg
flour
300ml milk
150ml water

Garnish
fried apple slices
(p395)

If dried apricots are used, soak them in cold water overnight. Drain, then stew them gently in a very little water, if required; they may be soft enough not to need it.

Trim off any excess fat from the ham. Chop the apricots, or peel, core, and grate the apples. Mix the fruit with the breadcrumbs, seasoning, and a little sugar, if needed. Beat the egg until liquid and bind the fruit mixture with it lightly. Spread the mixture over half the ham slices, and make into 'sandwiches' with the rest of the slices. Cut the sandwiches in half. Coat them lightly with flour, and put them in a shallow, ovenproof baking dish. Pour the milk and water over them, and bake, uncovered, in a warm oven, 160°C, Gas 3, for 30–40 minutes.

Garnish the ham with fried apple slices and serve with Brussels sprouts topped with almonds.

Ham Slices with Fruit

3 main-course or 6 light first-course or supper helpings

6 ham or gammon slices or steaks (1cm thick approx)	75g soft white breadcrumbs
150g soft light brown sugar	200ml pineapple juice

Garnish

3 apples	75g margarine

Remove the rind from the ham or gammon and snip the fat at intervals to prevent curling. Put the slices or steaks in a frying pan with a very little water, heat to simmering point, and simmer for 10 minutes, turning them once. Drain. Lay the slices or steaks in an overlapping layer in a large, shallow, ovenproof baking dish. Mix together the sugar and breadcrumbs, and spread it over the slices or steaks, then trickle the pineapple juice over them. Bake, uncovered, in a moderate oven, 180°C, Gas 4, for 25 minutes.

Meanwhile, peel, core, and cut the apples into rings, 2cm thick (approx). Melt the margarine in a frying pan, and fry the rings until tender but not soft. Decorate the cooked dish with the apple rings, and serve at once.

VARIATIONS

1) *Apricots:* Soak 100g dried apricots in hot water for 20 minutes, then spread them over the prepared ham, and bake. Use the apricot water with the juice of an orange instead of the pineapple juice.

2) *Pineapple:* Spread 6 pineapple slices (canned or fresh) over the ham and breadcrumbs, add the pineapple juice, and bake for 20 minutes. Add the sugar, dot with butter, and continue baking for 15 minutes until the pineapple is glazed.

3) *Bacon chops:* Substitute chops for slices to make a more substantial meal. Fry the chops until browned on both sides, then continue as above.

Gammon Steaks with Marmalade

4 helpings

4 medium-sized gammon steaks	4 × 15ml spoons medium-cut orange marmalade
ground pepper	
1 small onion	2 × 5ml spoons vinegar
1 × 5ml spoon butter or margarine	

Garnish

chopped parsley

Remove the rind from the gammon steaks and snip the fat at intervals to prevent curling. Place on a grill rack and season with pepper to taste. Cook under a moderate grill, turning once, for 10–15 minutes depending on the thickness of the steaks. When cooked, transfer the steaks to a warmed serving dish and keep hot.

Skin the onion and chop it finely. Melt the fat in a pan and cook the onion gently for 5 minutes without browning it. Draw the pan off the heat and stir in the marmalade and vinegar, with any fat and juices left in the grill pan. Return to the heat and heat to boiling point, to reduce slightly.

Spoon the sauce over the gammon steaks. Garnish with chopped parsley and serve at once.

Cured Meats

Curing is the general term used for preserving meat. The process gives a range of products, of which bacon, gammon and ham are the ones most used in Great Britain (see pp599–607).

The long keeping quality of heavily cured meats, especially pig meats, has now been replaced almost entirely by milder, brine cured meats. Improved refrigeration facilities have made hard cures unnecessary. Besides this, the fat pig in particular, which is needed for hard curing does not appeal to modern tastes.

Home curing, once very popular, has become more hazardous where central heating is installed, and freezing has largely replaced it. It is, however, certainly worth doing if the circumstances are right.

Selecting Meat for Curing

Fresh raw meat can be home pickled but the process is only safe if carried out under the right conditions, using the correct ingredients. Pickle the meat soon after it has been jointed if possible to avoid any risk of contamination. The shape and thickness of the meat is more important than the weight in choosing joints for pickling. Thick pieces take longer to pickle than thin pieces because the salt takes longer to reach the centre of the meat. Do not try to pickle large joints at home. It is wiser and more practical to pickle 1–2kg pieces of meat.

Meat can be salted in a dry salt pack or in brine. Strictly, the term 'pickling' refers to brining, but it is usually extended to include dry salting. The meat can be used straight from the salt 'bed' or brine bath, or can be dried and stored for later use.

Choose meat with a good proportion of fat. Fat absorbs less salt than lean meat, which may harden and be very salty to taste when pickled. If the meat is removed from the pickle before it is fully cured, it must be used at once or within a very short time.

Curing Ingredients

Salt is the primary, essential ingredient for curing. Various types are available, and as a rule, a combination of coarse and fine salt is used, especially for dry salting. Saltpetre (potassium or sodium nitrate) has slight antiseptic properties but its chief use in curing is to give the meat a characteristic pink colour. Only a tiny quantity of saltpetre is needed and no more should be used than is strictly necessary since it hardens the meat. Various other ingredients can also be used in a cure, either to help preserve the meat or for flavour. Sugar, treacle, vinegar, beer, spices, mustard and pepper are among these ingredients.

Many, if not most, curers try to create a unique flavour in their products which others cannot copy. It may derive from the feeding of the animal as in 'peach-fed hams', from the flavours or proportions of spices used for curing, or from the use of a particular type of wood for smoking.

Smoking

Besides being salt cured, meats can be dried or smoked for long-term storage. Smoked meats have an attractive, distinctive flavour, and some of the constituents of smoke have a preservative effect too. For centuries, meats and sausages were hung from staples on the walls of wide chimneys and smoked in the home or in specially built smokehouses, but today the smoking of large pieces of meat for long storage is most safely and effectively done commercially. Small pieces of meat can be smoked at home in smoke boxes, either 'cold' smoked (at a temperature not higher than 32°C) or 'hot' smoked. 'Hot' smoked meat is not salted before smoking but is cooked briefly while being smoked. It must be treated like fresh cooked meat, and eaten very soon after smoking. Large joints 'cold' smoked at home should also be eaten quickly.

Note Although curing is a general term for preserving, it is also used more specifically to denote any method of salting, flavouring and drying which will preserve meats, whether or not they are smoked afterwards. The term pickling is sometimes used for the process of salting in brine, and meat used straight from the brine bath without being dried can be described as pickled.

PICKLED PORK

Boiled Pickled Pork

4–6 helpings

a joint of pickled **or** salted pork **or** bacon forehock (1.8–2kg approx)	½ turnip (50g approx) 10 black peppercorns 1–2kg broad beans salt
1 medium-sized carrot (50g approx)	250ml Parsley sauce (p696)
1 medium-sized onion (100g approx)	

Soak the meat in cold water for at least 2 hours, or overnight, if very salty. Drain and weigh the meat to calculate the cooking time. Prepare the carrot, onion and turnip, and cut them into thick slices. Put the meat, vegetables and peppercorns in a large pan, cover with fresh cold water, and heat to boiling point slowly. Skim, half cover, reduce the heat, and simmer gently for 30 minutes per 0.5kg plus 30 minutes over.

About 30 minutes before the end of the cooking time, cook the beans until tender. Salt them lightly, and coat them with hot Parsley sauce. Transfer the pork to a warmed serving dish. Serve with the broad beans.

Note Pease Pudding (p787) can be served instead of beans. The liquid in which the pork is cooked can be used to make Green Pea Soup (p354).

Salt Pork with Sauerkraut

4–6 helpings

750g salted belly of pork	50g unsalted butter (approx)
1 medium-sized onion (100g approx)	750g sauerkraut
1 clove of garlic	3 × 15ml spoons general household stock (p329)
1 medium-sized carrot (50g approx)	**or** water salt and pepper

Cover the pork with cold water and soak for 1 hour. Meanwhile, prepare the onion, garlic, and carrot. Drain the salt pork, then put it into a large pan and cover with cold water. Heat slowly to boiling point and skim well. Add the vegetables and garlic, half cover the pan, reduce the heat, and simmer gently for 1 hour. Remove from the heat and leave to cool in the liquid.

Grease an ovenproof casserole with 25g butter. Put the sauerkraut in the bottom of the casserole and the pork on top. Pour the stock or water over the meat and season with salt and pepper. Cover the meat with buttered greaseproof paper and cover the casserole with a tight-fitting lid. Cook in a moderate oven, 180°C, Gas 4, for about 1½ hours. The stock should then have evaporated. Take out the pork and put to one side. Stir the remaining butter into the sauerkraut. Slice the pork and serve on the sauerkraut.

Note The onion and carrot boiled with the pork can be sliced and mixed with the sauerkraut, if liked.

Salt Pork with Lentils

4 helpings

200g green **or** brown lentils	1 clove of garlic bouquet garni
750g salted belly of pork	750ml cold water
1 small onion	salt

Soak the lentils in water for 1–2 hours. Cut the pork into 5cm cubes and discard the bones. Put into a bowl and cover with cold water. Leave for about 2 hours and then drain. Skin and chop the onion, and skin and crush the garlic. Put the onion, garlic, lentils, and bouquet garni into a saucepan. Pour in the 750ml water and heat to boiling point. Add the pork, cover, reduce the heat, and simmer gently for about 1¼ hours or until the lentils and pork are very tender. About 20 minutes before the end of the cooking time, check how much water is left in the pan. If there is still a considerable amount, leave the pan uncovered for the rest of the cooking period. By the time the lentils and pork are tender, all the liquid should have been absorbed. Remove the bouquet garni and season to taste. Turn into a warmed serving dish and serve hot.

Galantine of Pork

6 helpings

750g belly of pork, preferably salted	white stock (p329) or water to cover
salt and pepper	2 onions (200g approx)
2 large or 3 small gherkins	1 carrot (50g approx)
	½ turnip (50g approx)

Garnish (optional)

green stuffed olives, sliced	aspic jelly or meat glaze (p397)
	chopped parsley

Lay the meat flat, rind side down. Season the flesh side well with salt and pepper. Slice the gherkins thinly and scatter them over the meat. Roll up the meat and secure it with string at 4–5cm intervals, then wrap it tightly in scalded butter muslin and secure the ends. Put the roll in a saucepan and just cover with the stock or water. Prepare the vegetables and add them to the pan. Heat to simmering point and skim, if necessary. Half cover the pan and simmer gently for about 3 hours.

When cooked, drain thoroughly. Press the meat between 2 plates with a light weight on top until cold, then remove the weight, plates, and the muslin. The meat can be garnished with sliced olives, and then brushed with aspic jelly or meat glaze, or garnished simply with chopped parsley.

Collared Pig's Head

a pig's head	general household stock (p329) to cover

Forcemeat

250g ham or bacon	1 × 15ml spoon chopped parsley
1 × 5ml spoon mixed spice	
100g lard	6 spring or pickling onions (optional)

Garnish

lettuce or sprigs of parsley	aspic jelly (optional)

Ask the butcher to remove the hair, eyes, snout, ears, and tongue. Remove the brains from the head and use for another dish. Scrape and wipe the head carefully. Make a straight, deep cut down the centre of the face and open out, lifting and scraping the meat from the skull and other bones without puncturing the skin. Ease out the bones with a sharp knife. Scrape clean, and put back any loose scraps of meat into the hollowed head. Put the 2 sides of the face together, skin side outside. Cure the meat for 8–10 days with either dry salt (p611) or brine (p611) spiced with juniper berries, cloves, and bay leaves.

Mince and pound together all the ingredients for the forcemeat.

Remove the head from the cure, rinse well in cold water, and drain thoroughly. Soak in cold water for 4–6 hours. Dry thoroughly. Lay the meat, skin side down, and spread an even layer of forcemeat on top. Roll up the stuffed meat tightly in a cloth and secure it with broad tape rather than string. Put it into a saucepan and cover with stock. Heat to simmering point, and skim well. Cover the pan with a tight-fitting lid and simmer steadily for 4 hours. Add extra boiling stock as required. Remove the roll of meat from the saucepan, drain, and press it between 2 dishes with a heavy weight on top. When cold, unwrap it carefully.

Note In the past, a Collared Head was left whole, ie with the ears and snout on, and it was served on a napkin. Today, it is usually laid on a carving dish, garnished with lettuce or sprigs of parsley, and served in slices. For special occasions, the roll can be garnished and glazed with aspic jelly as for a Galantine of Pork.

A Mock Boar's Head can be produced in a similar way, using a whole head with the ears and snout left on. However, it takes a lot of care and patience to shape, stitch up, and tie the meat into the original form of the head, and to cook it thoroughly without overcooking the ears, which should be erect when the head is served.

HOME CURING OF BACON, GAMMON AND HAM

Home curing is not difficult but it does require space, time, and a controlled temperature.

Temperature

Meat must be cured in a cold place. This is important from the moment of slaughter to the completion of the cure. The ideal temperature is 2°–5°C, so slaughtering and home curing should only be carried out in winter.

Cutting

After slaughtering, any animal must be cut up into joints and smaller pieces before curing. This is best done at the slaughter-house or by an expert butcher who has the necessary heavy tackle and cutting saws.

Curing

Curing can be done by dry salting or brine curing.

Dry salting

Weigh each joint and measure its thickness.
  Allow:
  Salt – 1/10th of the weight of the meat
  Saltpetre – 1/50th of the weight of the salt
  Sugar (if liked) – 1/20th of the weight of the salt
  Example: For 10kg meat, take 1kg salt, 20g saltpetre, and 50g sugar.

  Mix the salt, saltpetre and sugar together thoroughly, and divide into 3 portions. Rub one-third of the mixture into the meat's rind until it sweats. Place the joints, rind side down, on a 2cm layer of salt, and sprinkle one-third of the cure on the flesh side. Pack it carefully and tightly round the bones and veins. Scatter a little common salt over the joints and leave in a cool place protected from flies for 5 days. Remove and replace any spent (wet) salt. Re-bed the joints, and sprinkle the last portion of the curing mixture on the flesh side. If using a cure which includes beer, treacle, spices or similar flavouring ingredients, add them to it at this stage.

Pat the cure gently into the meat, then cover it lightly with plain salt.
Sample curing times:
  hams to be stored for 8–10 months: leave the meat in the cure for 5 days for each 2cm of its thickness.
  loins and bellies to be stored for up to 6 months: leave the meat in the cure for 3 days for each 2cm of its thickness.

  Inspect the meat from time to time. Replace any spent salt. If using a cure containing beer, etc, baste it over the meat daily.

  Within these limits, the length of time the meat stays in the cure is a matter of personal taste and convenience. The longer the meat is left in the cure, the longer it will keep afterwards; but it will go on getting harder and saltier and will need longer soaking before cooking.

  At the end of the curing period, wash the joints well in cold, running water, and drain thoroughly before drying (or smoking) and storing.

Brine curing

A plain brine can be made by adding 1kg salt and 20g saltpetre to 5 litres of water. Dissolve the saltpetre in a little warm water before adding it to the brine and stir until all the salt is dissolved. Add 500g brown sugar and 30g peppercorns (bruised and tied loosely in a muslin bag) for added flavour.
Sample curing times:
  trotters and chaps: 3–5 days
  tongues: 5 days
  a head or small joints: up to 10 days
  a 4kg joint: up to 14 days.

  Place a weighted board on the meat to keep it immersed in the brine. Keep it in a very cool place. After curing, wash and drain as for dry salting.

Drying and Storing

Hang the meat in a current of air at an even temperature of 15°–18°C for about 5 days for thin joints and 3 weeks for hams. When dry, the surface of the joints will look 'frosty'. Pepper the joints, especially round the bones, wrap them first in greaseproof paper and then completely with muslin. Hang in a cool place.

Alternatively, dried joints can be stored in metal bins filled with wood ash or corn. Protection from pests is essential. Do *not* enclose cured meats in polythene for storage.

USING HOME-CURED JOINTS

Remove the joint from its wrapping and wash it well in tepid water. Soak thin cuts for 6 hours only, but soak whole hams for 24–48 hours, changing the water every 6–12 hours. Put a small or medium-sized joint into a pan of cold water. Cover it, leaving a small space uncovered, and heat to boiling point. Skim, reduce the heat, and simmer for the calculated cooking time.

Lightly cured small joints do not need soaking for long, if at all. Put them into a pan of cold water and heat to boiling point. Drain off the water, replace with fresh cold water, and cook like any other boiled meat.

Cooking Time for Joints

Small joints require about $1\frac{1}{2}$ hours per kg but the cooking time per kg decreases as the weight increases. For whole hams, support the shank bone above the water level, if possible.

Weight in kg	Cooking time in hours
5	$3\frac{1}{2}$
7	4
9	$4\frac{1}{2}$
11	5

At the end of the cooking time, remove the pan from the heat and leave for 30 minutes–1 hour. Remove the meat, take off the rind, and coat the exposed surfaces of bacon and ham with raspings (p375).

Spanish Smoked Bacon Stew
(Cocido)

6 helpings

500g smoked pork **or** *home-cured bacon*	*1 green pepper*
500g butter beans **or** *other dried beans*	*6 tomatoes*
6 small onions	*salt*
6 medium-sized carrots	*2.5 litres water*
2 small turnips	*250g brown rice* **or** *lentils* **or** *dried split*
1 cabbage heart	*peas*

Soak the meat, if required. Soak the beans overnight. Cut the meat into 2cm cubes and put them in a large thick pan. Drain the beans and add them to the pan. Prepare the onions, carrots and turnips, and chop coarsely. Cut the cabbage and pepper into strips. Slice the tomatoes. Add all the vegetables and a little salt to the pan. Pour in the water, cover tightly, heat to simmering point and simmer gently for $2\frac{1}{4}$ hours. Sprinkle in the rice, lentils or peas and cook for another 45 minutes.

Note Fresh peas or beans can be added for the last 45 minutes of the cooking time, if liked.

PICKLED BEEF

Pickled, ie salted beef cooked immediately after brining, is much more common in the UK than dried or smoked (ie fully cured) beef. Most salt beef is purchased already brined from a butcher.

Drying and Storing Meat

The original reason for pickling meat was to preserve it if it could not be used immediately although some meat is now pickled just for the flavour. Meat to be stored must be fully pickled (left in pickle for at least 8–9 days for each 3cm of its thickness), and then dried. First rinse off any salt attached to the meat with cold water, then dry it thoroughly. Hang it in an airy place, at a temperature between 14°–16°C. Place a tray underneath to catch any drips. Inspect it often, wipe off any salt which appears on the surface and check that the meat is neither musty nor slimy. Keep flies out of the room, but do not use a spray fumigant.

After the meat has been properly dried it can be stored. It is wise to protect the meat by tying it tightly in a cotton or linen bag. Hang it in a fairly dark and dry place at an even temperature not above 16°C. If pests attack the meat, dust it all over with black pepper. Check from time to time that the meat has not become slimy or mouldy. Remove any meat which grows a mould before it has been cut.

Note Occasionally, meat which has been cut and put back into storage develops a harmless white mould smelling of ammonia on the cut surface. This mould can be cut off and the rest of the meat safely used. If you are in any doubt, however, about the type of mould, throw the meat away at once.

Using Meat from Pickle at Intervals

It is worthwhile pickling several pieces of meat at a time. You can take a piece out of the salt bed or brine before it is fully pickled, provided you use it at once. Take small, thin pieces out first, as these may be tough and salty if left as long as thick pieces. Soak them, if needed, and cook without delay.

Dry Salt Pack
(for beef)

joints of fresh brisket **or** *silverside of beef, up to 3kg each and 15cm thick*	*common salt for pickling tray*

Brine

10 litres water	*25g saltpetre*
3kg salt	

Dry Salting Mixture

50g mixed coarse and fine salt for each 500g meat	*a small pinch of saltpetre for each 40–50g salt*

Trim the meat neatly, leaving no ragged ends of flesh and skin. Measure the meat and calculate how long to leave it in the salt. Allow 8–9 days in pickle for each 3cm thickness of meat.

Prepare the brine. Put the water in a pan, add the salt and saltpetre, and heat to boiling point. When the ingredients have dissolved, remove from the heat and leave the brine to cool to 10°C. Place the meat in the brine and leave for about 20 minutes. Remove the meat and drain thoroughly.

Meanwhile, prepare the dry salting mixture. Divide the mixed coarse and fine salt into 3 equal portions. Crush the saltpetre and sprinkle it equally over the 3 portions of salt.

Rub one portion of the salt mixture all over the meat, taking care to rub it thoroughly round and in the hollow of any bones.

Line a shallow box or deep tray large enough to take the pieces of meat in one layer with common salt to a depth of at least 5cm. Lay the pieces of meat on the salt, skin side down, pressing them well into it. Sprinkle them with the second portion of the salt mixture; then cover them with a layer of common salt (5cm deep approx). Pack it tightly round the meat at the sides. Leave to cure for 5 days at a temperature between 2°–10°C; then remove any stained salt covering the meat. Make a fresh 'bed' of common salt, repack the meat, sprinkle it with the third portion of salt and saltpetre, and cover with common salt as before. Leave the meat in the salt until the end of the calculated curing time.

Meat cured in this dry salt pack has to be soaked before cooking. Soak the meat in fresh water, changing the water several times. Small, lightly cured pieces of meat may only need 1–2 hours' soaking, whilst heavily salted or thick pieces of meat may take up to 36 hours. It depends on the length of time it has spent in salt and on the thickness and fattiness of the meat. After soaking, weigh the meat and boil it as for Boiled Salt Beef (p614).

VARIATION
Pickled Beef Round

Use 6–6.5kg round (topside and silverside) of well marbled beef. Pickle it in a dry salt pack. When ready, rinse it and hang it up to dry overnight as described above. Next day, roll up the meat very tightly and secure with string at 5cm intervals. Complete the drying, and store as described.

Basic Pickling Brine
(for beef)

1.25–1.75kg fresh
  brisket **or** silverside of
  beef
common salt
2.5 litres water
225g coarse salt

$\frac{1}{2} \times 2.5ml$ spoon
  saltpetre
$1 \times 2.5ml$ spoon sugar,
  if needed
50g common salt, if
  needed

Wipe and trim the meat neatly, leaving no ragged ends of flesh or skin. Measure it and calculate how long to leave the meat in the pickle. Allow 8–9 days for each 3cm of its thickness for fully pickled meat. Rub the meat well with common salt and leave in a cool place for 24 hours.

Boil the water with the coarse salt and saltpetre. Skim thoroughly. Leave the pickle to cool completely. Put the meat in a deep basin and cover it completely with the pickle. Weight it down with a board or plate with a heavy object on top. Leave the meat in the pickle for the calculated time. Thick pieces of meat can be left in the pickle for up to 5 weeks except in hot summer weather. If the meat is to be pickled for longer than 5 weeks or if white mould appears on the pickle before then, lift out the meat and reboil the pickle with $1 \times 2.5ml$ spoon sugar and 50g common salt. Skim as before, then leave the pickle to get cold and place the meat in it, well weighted down, to finish curing.

After pickling, rinse the joint of meat or soak it in cold water to remove the excess salt. To cook it, follow the recipe for Boiled Salt Beef.

Note The flavour of pickled beef can be varied by adding to the brine one or more of the following ingredients: sugar, vinegar, cloves, peppercorns, wine, spices.

The pickle can be used for up to 3 batches of meat, provided you reboil it with $1 \times 2.5ml$ spoon sugar and 50g common salt each time you take out a batch of meat or if any white mould appears; do not, however, reboil it more than twice.

Suitable curing places for wet pickling are a cellar, larder or garage, or an outhouse in cold weather.

Boiled Salt Beef

12–16 helpings

1–1.5kg salt silverside
  or topside of beef
3 cloves
10 black peppercorns
bouquet garni
3 medium-sized onions
  (300g approx)

4 large carrots
  (400g approx)
2 small turnips
  (100g approx)

Salted beef needs a slightly longer boiling time than fresh beef. Allow 30–35 minutes per 0.5kg plus 30 minutes over. Put the meat into a large stewpan, cover with cold water and heat slowly to boiling point. Keep the liquid skimmed while it is coming to the boil. A dash or two of cold water will help to bring the scum to the surface. This, along with the gentle simmering, will keep the cooking liquid clear. Continue as for fresh meat (see Boiled Beef with Vegetables and Dumplings p500), allowing the extra time for cooking.

Pressed Beef

salt brisket of beef
  (allow 100g raw boned
  meat and 150g raw
  meat on the bone per
  helping)
1 large onion (200g
  approx)

1 large carrot (100g
  approx)
$\frac{1}{4}$ turnip (50g approx)
bouquet garni
10 black peppercorns
meat glaze (optional)
  (p397)

Weigh the meat and calculate the cooking time, allowing 30 minutes per 0.5kg plus 30 minutes over. Wash the meat well or, if very salty, soak for about 1 hour in cold water. Put the meat in a stewpan, cover with cold water, and heat slowly to boiling point. Skim well. Prepare the vegetables and cut them into large pieces. Add them to the meat with the bouquet garni and peppercorns. Reheat to simmering point, then cover the pan with a tight-fitting lid, and simmer gently for the calculated cooking time. Take the meat out, remove any bones, and press it between 2 boards or plates until cold. Brush with meat glaze, if liked.

Hot Collared Beef

12–16 helpings

1.5–2kg brisket or
silverside of beef
salt and pepper
½ × 2.5ml spoon ground
cloves
½ × 2.5ml spoon ground
mace
½ × 2.5ml spoon grated
ginger root
2 × 15ml spoons
vinegar

½ × 2.5ml spoon
saltpetre
½ × 2.5ml spoon ground
allspice
½ × 2.5ml spoon ground
pepper
½ × 2.5ml spoon dried
sage
½ × 2.5ml spoon dried
thyme
1 bay leaf

Season the meat with salt and pepper and sprinkle it with the cloves, mace and ginger. Roll up the meat tightly and tie it with string at regular intervals. Wrap it in muslin.

Put the meat in a stewpan, just cover with water and add the vinegar and saltpetre. Heat gently to boiling point. Skim well, add the rest of the spices and herbs, cover with a tight-fitting lid, and simmer gently for 3½ hours until tender.

Serve with boiled butter beans and Parsley Sauce (p696).

VARIATION

Cold Collared Beef

Follow the recipe for Hot Collared Beef. Remove the meat from the stewpan and leave to cool completely under a light weight. It will keep, wrapped in clingfilm, for 2–3 days in a cold larder or for 3–5 days in a refrigerator.

Serve with baked potatoes stuffed with soft cheese, and pickled walnuts, or green tomato chutney.

CURED LAMB AND MUTTON

Home pickling and smoking of large joints can be hazardous and it is wise, therefore, to take the pickled joint to a local bacon factory and arrange for it to be cured there under controlled conditions. Store the smoked mutton ham wrapped in a calico or linen bag and hang in a dry room at a temperature not above 16°C.

Mutton Ham

(to cook)

a cured and smoked
mutton ham
2 medium-sized carrots
(200g approx)

1 small turnip (50g
approx)
1 × 5ml spoon dry
mustard

Wash the piece of mutton ham and then calculate the cooking time, allowing 30 minutes per 0.5kg. Prepare and dice the carrots and turnip. Place the mutton ham in a large pan, cover with cold water, and heat to boiling point. Pour off this water. Cover again with cold water and bring to the boil. Add the vegetables to the pan with the mustard. Cover the pan, and simmer the meat for the calculated cooking time.

If serving hot, serve with Caper Sauce (p693). If serving cold, leave the meat in the cooking liquid until quite cold, then drain.

POULTRY

A Christmas dinner, with the middle classes of this empire, would scarcely be a Christmas dinner without its turkey; and we can hardly imagine an object of greater envy than is presented by a respected portly paterfamilias carving, at the season devoted to good cheer and genial charity, his own fat turkey, and carving it well.

Poultry birds are domestic fowl as opposed to wild birds. They include chickens, ducks, geese, turkeys, and guinea-fowl. No domestic or wild bird is known to be poisonous, although a bird's flavour may be unpleasant because of the food it has eaten; eg some waterfowl may have a fishy taste.

In recent years there has been an enormous increase in the quantity of poultry bred specially for the table; this has been greatest in the case of chickens. Whereas at one time chicken was considered a luxury, it is now an economical purchase which can be used in a great many dishes, both hot and cold.

PREPARING POULTRY

With the exception of some very small birds (see p656), the following instructions for preparing poultry apply to game birds as well.

Plucking

Plucking of any poultry should be done as soon as possible after the bird has been killed, preferably while it is still warm. If you have a strong hook in the wall, tie the two feet together and hang them over it. Otherwise, put the bird breast downwards on a large sheet of paper or clean cloth. Whichever method is used, first draw out one wing and pull out the under-feathers, taking a few at a time. Work towards the breast and then down to the tail. Repeat on the other side. Only pluck the lower half of the neck; the rest is cut off. The flight feathers (large quilled feathers at the ends of the wings) are

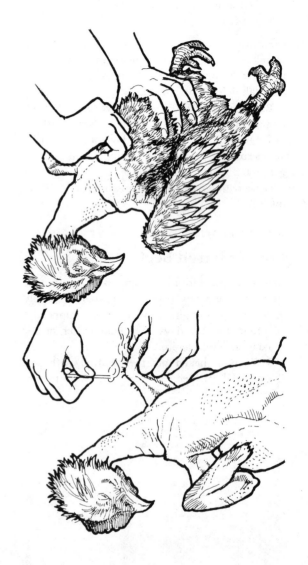

best snapped, away from the direction of growth. Small hairs can be singed off with a taper; burnt feathers, however, will give the bird an unpleasant flavour. Scoop the feathers and down into a plastic bag as you pluck. If left lying about, they can irritate the nasal membranes, and they become difficult to clear up.

Drawing

Half-way along the neck cut a ring round the outer skin, and pull or cut off the head. Slip the knife under the skin and cut it loose from the neck all round, without puncturing it.

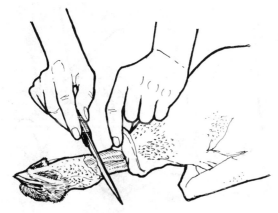

Holding the neck in a dry cloth, pull the skin back from it, leaving it bare. At the base of the neck, cut through the meat only.

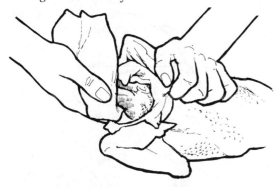

Then, still holding the neck in a dry cloth, twist it around, to break the bone. Cut through the broken bone; then withdraw the neck from the skin, and keep it for stock. Push one finger into the crop cavity to loosen the crop and gizzard.

With a sharp knife, cut the skin around each leg joint, place over the edge of a board or table, and snap the bone. Grasp the foot in one hand and the thigh of the bird in the other and pull off the foot with the tendons.

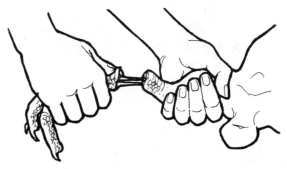

To remove the viscera, make a slit 5–7cm wide just above the vent, taking care not to cut into the rectal end of the gut. Insert the first two fingers of one hand, knuckles upwards, and feel round the inner cavity wall, loosening the contents.

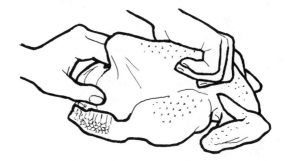

Draw out the intestines. Try to remove all the organs at once. The crop has to be pulled with the gizzard out of the back of the bird. When they are free, trim the end of the intestines and the vent.

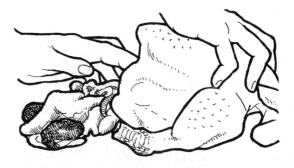

The liver can now be separated from the gall bladder; take care not to break the latter.

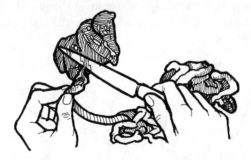

The meaty outside of the crop can be skinned or cut away from the gritty contents, for use as stock meat.

The lungs, which are bright red, lie close to the ribs. They are best removed by wrapping your index finger in a dry cloth and pushing in turn down from the backbone and out along each rib.

Destroy the inedible waste (head and feet usually, intestines, lungs, crop, container of grit from gizzard, etc) immediately. Keep the giblets (neck, gizzard, liver, and heart) away from the bird so that its flesh will not be discoloured. Wipe the inside of the bird, but do not wash it unless it is to be cooked immediately.

Trussing

The object of trussing a bird is to make it look attractive and to secure the stuffing.

The easiest way to truss is with a large needle and stout thread. Needles designed specifically for trussing can be bought at most shops selling kitchen equipment.

Put the bird on its back, and hold the legs together to form a V-shape pointing towards the neck end. Insert the threaded needle into one leg, just above the thigh bone; pass it through the body and out at the same point the other side. Leave a good length of thread on either side.

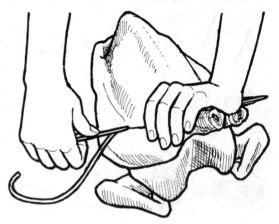

Turn the bird breast downwards and carry the thread through the elbow joint of the wing on each side.

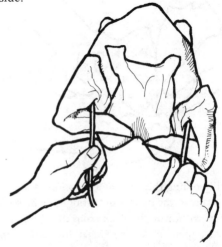

Twist the end of the wing under the neck to hold the flap of skin in place; tie the ends of the thread together, not too tightly.

Loop the thread over the ends of the drumsticks and draw them together, tying off round the 'parson's nose'. To make this easier, a slit may be cut in the flesh above the original vent cut and the 'parson's nose' pushed through.

When the bird is trussed, the skin should still be complete if possible, to prevent any loss of fat from the bird during cooking, as this can result in over-dry and unpalatable meat.

Jointing

Pull the leg away from the body; cut through the skin; break leg from body at joint; cut through the joint.

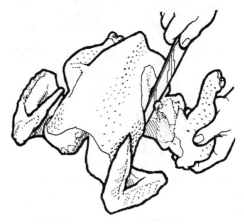

Cut the thigh from the drumstick at the joint.

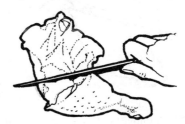

Cut the breast meat straight down to the wing joint; break the joint and cut so that the piece of breast meat and the wing are all in one piece.

With a heavy knife, cut down the back of the carcass, from vent to neck end.

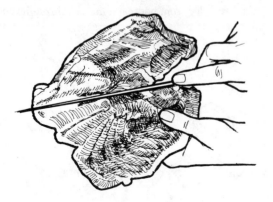

Cut the breast into two or four pieces, according to size.

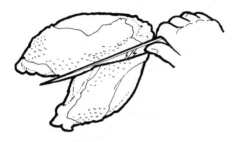

Cut off the pinions (extreme tips) of the wings (these can be cooked with the giblets); remove all small bones.

Boning

See Stuffed Boned Duck (p648).

Skinning

Loosen skin at the neck end exposing the wishbone. Using the fingertips and working under the skin, gradually loosen the skin from both sides of the breastbone. Slit the skin carefully along the length of the breastbone.

With a tugging movement and a firm grip, pull the skin off thigh and wing joints. Use a sharp knife if necessary to separate skin where it adheres to the bone. Chop away the last two sections of the wing joints and the last leg joint on the drumstick. Pull off the last remaining skin.

TYPES OF POULTRY

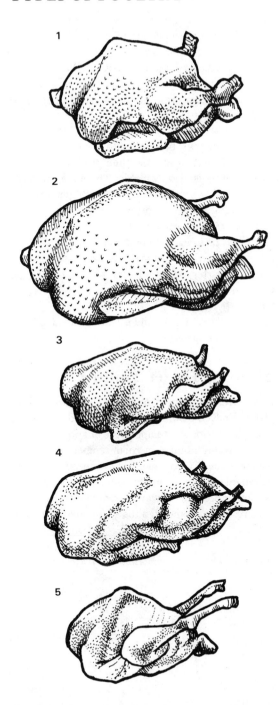

1 Chicken; 2 Turkey; 3 Duck; 4 Goose;
5 Guinea-fowl

Chickens

Chicken is a most nutritious meat, lean, and with a high percentage of protein. It is one of the easiest meats to digest and is therefore very useful in cooking for elderly people, children and invalids, as well as being a popular choice for the Sunday roast.

In a young chicken, the tip of the breastbone should be soft and pliable and the feet smooth and soft with small scales. The skin should be white and soft, the breast plump with a little fat on it. The size of the bird does not necessarily indicate its age or toughness; a capon (a castrated male bird) usually grows heavier than other birds but remains tender and can be roasted.

Fresh chickens: There are two choices in buying fresh birds. The more common type are roasters which are 6–12 months old, and usually average 1.5–2kg in weight. Boiling fowl are birds over 12 months old, and weigh 2–2.5kg.

When buying any bird, make sure the giblets are included with it. Frozen oven-ready birds usually contain the giblets, packed in a small bag in the neck end or body cavity. Oven-ready fresh birds bought from a poulterer may or may not contain the giblets, depending on whether the supplier has a ready sale for them separately. Giblets have many uses. They make excellent stock, form an important part of many stuffings, flavour and extend stews and other dishes, and can be used for pies, pâtés, omelet fillings, etc.

Fresh joints and pieces of various sizes can also be bought, usually unpackaged, from most butchers.

Capons are specially fattened, and usually weigh 2.5–3.5kg. Excellent for a large roast.

Spring chickens range from 8 weeks to 4 months old, and usually weigh 1–1.5kg.

Poussins are baby chickens, 4–8 weeks old, usually sufficient for one person; they are best roasted or grilled.

Turkeys

Turkeys are obtainable all year round, either fresh or frozen, weighing from about 3–8kg or in packs of turkey portions. A hen bird is often preferred to a cock as the meat is usually more tender, although the meat to bone ratio is slightly smaller. A small turkey can often be a more economical purchase than a chicken, since the proportion of meat to bone is greater.

Ducks and Ducklings

Duck is normally sold when weighing 2–3kg. But a bird of this size is only big enough to serve 4 because of the large carcass and quantity of fat. Choose a larger bird if possible, because the ratio of flesh to bone is higher, and any leftover meat makes excellent pâtés and other cold dishes. Duck is usually roasted, allowing 300–400g per person.

Duck is available all year round. Well-known breeds of duck are the French Rouennais, Landais, and Nantes, and the English Aylesbury and Norfolk.

A duckling weighs 1.5–2kg, and serves 2–4 people.

Geese

Although it is a fatty bird, goose has a slight gamey flavour, is expensive, and not readily available everywhere. It has a large carcass, giving a comparatively small yield of meat. The average trussed weight is 3–7kg.

Guinea-fowl

Guinea-fowl is available all year round in specialist shops, and the weight varies from 500g for young chicks to 2kg for the fowls. It should be hung for several days so that the flavour slightly resembles that of pheasant.

FROZEN POULTRY

It is difficult to assess the characteristics of frozen birds when purchasing because the skin colour and texture are both changed by the freezing process. Look for a fairly large bird with a plump breast, and make sure the wrapping is undamaged. Avoid a chalky or icy appearance or a partially defrosted bird.

For freezing poultry at home, see p1386.

Frozen chickens: In addition to oven-ready whole birds, sold with or without their giblets, a range of frozen joints is also available. These may include special packs of either drumsticks, thighs, breasts, quarter chicken joints or even half chickens, and stew-packs of assorted pieces.

Frozen turkeys: Whole turkeys, turkey roast (pieces of dark and/or light meat rolled and barded), thighs, quarter or half turkeys, breasts, wings, thigh and drumsticks, and breast scallops, are available.

Frozen ducks: Ducks and ducklings are available whole or in quarters.

Thawing Frozen Poultry

It is extremely important that all poultry is completely thawed before cooking. It should be thawed in a refrigerator at a temperature of approximately 5°C. Thawing poultry at room temperature is not recommended. Once thawed, frozen poultry is as perishable as fresh poultry, and should be cooked as soon as possible. Never re-freeze once thawed.

Here are recommended thawing times for frozen birds:

Weight (kg)	Thawing time in refrigerator (hrs)
1.00	28
1.50	38
2.00	42
2.50	48
3.00	50
4.00	60
5.00	66
6.00	70
9.00	76
over 9	76–82

CHILLED POULTRY

Chicken, turkey and duck are available prepacked from refrigerated cabinets of supermarkets. This is a convenient way of buying for immediate use whole birds, quartered birds, joints of various kinds and sizes, and boned breast.

GENERAL INSTRUCTIONS FOR ROASTING WHOLE BIRDS

Chickens, capons, and small turkeys: Traditionally chicken is stuffed at the neck end with forcemeat or other stuffing, or just with fresh herbs; turkey with basic forcemeat, or chestnut stuffing in the crop and sausage-meat in the body. Nowadays, however, the stuffing is almost always put into the body cavity; and only a large turkey for a festive dinner has 2 stuffings.

Put the bird in a roasting tin, preferably on a trivet or upturned saucer, and brush with melted fat or oil. Cover the breast with streaky bacon, if liked, or with foil. Cook for 20 minutes per 500g and 20 minutes over, until the thickest parts of the thigh, when pricked, give out a clear liquid without any blood.

The bird can be roasted on its side to start with and turned over half-way through the cooking to keep the breast moist. The final cooking should be breast side uppermost.

When the bird is cooked, place it on a warmed serving dish and keep hot. Serve with the traditional or other accompaniments (see p624, and gravy made with giblet stock if possible).

Large turkeys: Stuff the neck end and body cavity with the chosen stuffings. Place in a roasting tin and prepare as for smaller birds. (The bird can also be started on its side if liked.) Cover the breast with foil to prevent excess browning. This should be removed for the last 30 minutes – 1 hour.

For birds which are fully stuffed, cook for 15–20 minutes in a fairly hot oven, 200°C, Gas 6, then reduce to moderate, 180°C, Gas 4, and cook until tender. For unstuffed birds or ones with only the neck stuffed, cook in a warm oven, 160°C, Gas 3, until tender.

Approximate cooking times:

weight	unstuffed or with neck end only stuffed, at 160°C, Gas 3	fully stuffed, at 180°C, Gas 4 (after 20 mins at 200°C, Gas 6)
2.5 kg	$2\frac{1}{2}$–3 hrs	$2\frac{1}{2}$–3 hrs
2.75–3.5 kg	3 –$3\frac{1}{4}$ hrs	3 –$3\frac{3}{4}$ hrs
3.5–4.5 kg	$3\frac{1}{2}$–4 hrs	$3\frac{3}{4}$–$4\frac{1}{2}$ hrs
4.5–5.5 kg	4 –$4\frac{1}{2}$ hrs	$4\frac{1}{2}$–5 hrs
5.5–13.5 kg	20 mins per 500g +20 mins	20 mins per 500g +20 mins

Ducks: These are usually, although not always, stuffed before roasting. They are normally roasted in a fairly hot oven, 190–200°C, Gas 5–6, allowing 15–20 minutes per 500g for a young bird, 20–25 minutes per 500g for an older one, a few minutes longer if fully stuffed. Allow about 300g stuffing for an average-sized bird.

The skin of a duck is sometimes pricked all over with a fork before roasting to encourage the fat to run, and some cooks pour boiling water over the bird to encourage this further. The bird is roasted on a trivet with buttered paper over the breast. An average-sized bird takes 1–$1\frac{1}{2}$ hours.

Geese: These are generally stuffed, and are usually roasted in a moderate oven, 180°C, Gas 4, for 20–25 minutes per 500g, although this may vary slightly with the age and size of the bird. A buttered paper is put over the breast instead of bacon; apart from this, it is roasted like turkey. An average-sized bird, when stuffed, takes 2–$2\frac{1}{2}$ hours to roast. Allow 1.3–1.5kg stuffing for a 4–4.5kg goose.

Guinea-fowl can be treated either like chicken or like pheasant.

Roasting in Foil

This is a more convenient and cleaner method of roasting poultry than open roasting, since the bird is completely enclosed in foil and no basting is required; the juices are kept within the parcel and can be poured off and used for gravy, leaving the roasting tin clean. Use a piece of foil large enough to enclose the bird. Put the foil in the roasting tin, place the bird on top, and fold up the foil to enclose the bird, making a loose parcel. Open the foil for the last 15–20 minutes of the cooking time, to brown the bird.

Cook in a hot oven, 220°C, Gas 7, for approximately the following times:

Chicken up to 1.75kg	30–35 mins per 500g
1.75–3.5kg	25 mins per 500g
Turkey over 3.75kg	23 mins per 500g

For ducks, allow 10 minutes per 500g more than the times shown on p623, and for geese, 20 minutes extra per 500g when roasting in foil.

Preparing Giblets for Cooking

The giblets usually kept and used are the liver, heart, neck, and gizzard. If bought from a poulterer or obtained with a frozen bird they are ready prepared for cooking. If using giblets from a bird bought before eviscerating, cut the small greenish gall-bladder away from the liver, taking care not to break it; it will give the giblets a very bitter flavour. Cut any small sinews from the liver, and cut excess fat off the heart and gizzard. Break the neck into 2 or 3 pieces (a turkey neck into 4 or 5 pieces). Rinse the giblets in cold water briefly if necessary, then use them as the recipe directs.

Note Once the bones and meat have been removed, the skin of the neck of larger birds is sometimes used to contain a stuffing mixture in the same way as sausage skins.

WHAT TO SERVE WITH ROASTED POULTRY

Any stuffing, sauce, garnish, and vegetable can be served with a plainly cooked bird, but some trimmings are traditional because they have proved particularly good. Duck and goose, which are fatty and strongly flavoured, need a dryer stuffing than chickens or guinea-fowl, and a thickened, less sharp gravy. The following are the traditional accompaniments to serve with roasted birds:

Roast Chicken

1) Thin gravy (p727)
2) Basic herb stuffing (p375)
3) Bacon rolls (p396)
4) Bread sauce (p713)
5) Watercress to garnish

Roast Turkey

1) Thickened gravy (p727)
2) For the crop: chestnut stuffing (p381) or basic herb stuffing (p375)
3) For the body: sausage-meat stuffing (p383)
4) Bacon rolls (p396)
5) Grilled chipolata sausages
6) Bread sauce (p713) or cranberry sauce (p717)

Roast Duck

1) Thickened gravy (p727)
2) Sage and onion stuffing (p378)
3) Apple sauce (p717) or cranberry sauce (p717) or Cumberland sauce (p718)
4) Watercress to garnish

Roast Goose

1) Thickened gravy (p727)
2) Sage and onion stuffing (p378)
3) Apple sauce (p717)

Roast Guinea-fowl

As for roast chicken.

CARVING

Good carving, skilfully done, can make a bird much more economical.

Chicken, Small Turkey, Capon, Guinea-fowl

Insert a carving fork firmly in the breast of the bird. On each side, make a downward cut with a sharp knife between the thigh and the body, then turn the blade outward so that the joint is exposed. Cut it through with either poultry shears or a sharp carving knife. Put the legs to one side.

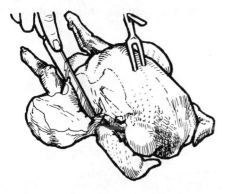

With the fork still inserted in the breast, remove the wings by cutting widely, but not too deeply, over the adjacent part of the breast, to give the wing enough meat without depriving the breast of too much flesh.

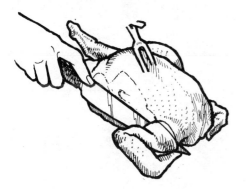

The breast of a large fowl can be sliced from the carcass as a whole.

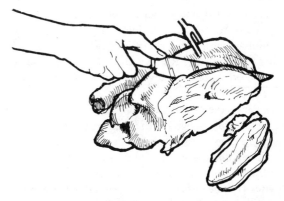

Alternatively, it can be separated from the back by cutting through the rib bones with poultry shears or a sharp knife. The breast of a small bird is detached from the carcass whole, thus providing two portions.

Carve the brown meat off the legs, if liked, working downwards in thin slices, following the direction of the bone. Serve some breast and some dark meat to each person.

To complete the carving of a large bird whose breast and back have been separated, place the back on the dish with the rib bones facing downwards; press the knife firmly across the centre of it, and raise the neck end at the same time with the fork to divide the back into two pieces.

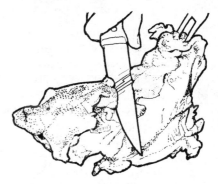

Remove the two 'oysters' (choice morsels of dark-coloured flesh) from the shallow hollows beside the thigh sockets. To do this, the tail part of the back must be stood on end and held firmly with the fork.

Large Turkey

Holding the bird steady with one carving fork, use a second one to bend each leg outward and downward, exposing the joint. Cut it through with poultry shears or a sharp carving knife. Put the legs to one side. Remove the wings in the same way. Do not take off any breast meat with the wing joints.

Carve the breast meat on the carcass, cutting downwards, parallel with the breastbone.

The legs (thighs and drumsticks) should be carved downwards in thin slices, following the direction of the bone. Alternatively, the drumsticks can be reserved for another meal. Serve both white and dark meat to each person, together with a portion of each of the stuffings. To obtain these, slit the skin vertically down the centre of the vent and neck ends, open out the slits and serve the stuffings with a spoon.

When the breast meat has been cleared, remove any remaining stuffing to a warmed plate. Detach the wishbone. With the knife or shears, cut horizontally all round the bird through the thinnest part of the rib bones, and lift off the top part of the carcass. Turn the back part of the bird over, and carve any remaining meat off the back and sides parallel with the bone. Serve with the remaining stuffings.

Duck

Cut off the legs, and then the wings with a little breast meat attached to each. The breast is carved in quite thick, wedge-shaped slices: make the first cut down along the breastbone, and, with the blade of the knife slanted slightly towards the centre, make a series of cuts down the breast, parallel to the first cut. Remove the slices by cutting upwards towards the breastbone.

Duckling

To split the bird in half, cut down along the breastbone. Use poultry shears to cut through the bone. To divide each half into leg and wing portions, cut between the ribs so that some breast meat is attached to each joint.

Goose

Goose can be carved in the same way as duck. The breast is the best part. If the bird is large, carve only the breast and save the legs and wings for cold or re-heated dishes.

Note A boned and stuffed bird is usually cut across in slices.

Chickens and Small Turkeys

ROASTED BIRDS

Roast Chicken

4–6 helpings

1 roasting chicken
oil **or** *fat for basting*
salt and pepper
2–3 rashers streaky
bacon (optional)

1 × 15ml spoon plain
flour
275ml chicken stock
gravy browning

Truss the chicken if liked. Put the oil or fat in a roasting tin and place for a few minutes in a fairly hot oven, 190°C–200°C, Gas 5–6. Remove from the oven. Place the chicken in the roasting tin, on a trivet if liked. Baste, sprinkle with salt and pepper, and place the bacon rashers, if used, over the breast. Cover the breast with a piece of foil or buttered greaseproof paper, if liked. Return the tin to the oven and cook the bird for the recommended time (p623), until tender. (Prick the thigh to test for tenderness; if there is any trace of blood, the chicken is not cooked.) The bacon and foil or greaseproof paper should be removed 10–15 minutes before serving, to allow the breast to brown.

When cooked, place the chicken on a hot carving dish, remove trussing strings or skewers, and keep hot. Pour out and discard the excess fat from the tin, keeping back the sediment for gravy. Sprinkle in the flour, stir well with a metal spoon, and add the stock gradually. Bring to the boil and boil for 2–3 minutes. Season to taste, add a little gravy browning, and strain into a hot sauce-boat.

Serve with chicken accompaniments (p624).

French Roast Chicken

4–6 helpings

1 roasting chicken with
giblets
50g butter **or** *margarine*
1 small onion
1 carrot
2 rashers streaky bacon,
without rinds

salt and pepper
200ml chicken stock **or**
water (optional)

Truss the chicken if liked. Spread the breast with half the butter or margarine. Prepare and slice the onion and carrot. Chop the bacon, chicken liver and heart. Place the remaining butter in a roasting tin, heat gently, add the vegetables, bacon, liver, and heart, and fry for a few minutes. Season well. Place the chicken on top and roast in a hot oven, 220°C, Gas 7, for 1–1¼ hours, until tender. Cover with greased foil or greaseproof paper if it becomes too brown. Baste occasionally. Remove the chicken from the tin, remove the string or skewers, and keep hot. Drain off the juices in the roasting tin, and serve as a thin pan-juice gravy; add extra stock or water if required.

Roast Chicken

(quick)

6 helpings

1 roasting chicken **or**
6 chicken joints
a little oil **or** *fat*

2 rashers streaky bacon,
without rinds
salt and pepper

Joint the chicken if using a whole bird. Heat the oil or fat in a roasting tin in a fairly hot oven, 190–200°C, Gas 5–6, for a few minutes. Meanwhile, chop the bacon into small pieces. Remove the tin from the oven, lay the joints in it, season, and sprinkle with the chopped bacon. Bake in the oven for 40–50 minutes, basting occasionally. Cover with greased foil or greaseproof paper if it becomes too brown or dry.

Serve with any suitable gravy.

Roast Chicken with Honey and Almonds

4–6 helpings

1 roasting chicken	50g blanched almonds
½ lemon	a pinch of powdered
salt and pepper	saffron (optional)
3 × 15ml spoons honey	2 × 15ml spoons oil

Truss the chicken. Rub all over with the cut lemon, then sprinkle with salt and pepper. Line a roasting tin with a piece of foil large enough to cover the bird and to meet over the top. Put the bird on the foil, and rub it all over with honey. Slice the almonds and sprinkle them and the saffron, if used, over the bird. Pour the oil over the bird very gently. Wrap it completely in the foil, keeping it clear of the skin. Seal by folding over the edges. Roast in a moderate – fairly hot oven, 180°–190°C, Gas 4–5, for about 1½ hours, until tender. Unwrap the foil for the last 10 minutes to allow the breast to brown.

GRILLED AND FRIED BIRDS

Grilled Chicken Joints

1 helping

1 breast and wing **or** leg of chicken	salt and pepper
	1 × 15ml spoon butter

Garnish
Maître d'Hôtel butter
(p1300) **or** sauce
(p695)

Remove the pinion from the wing, if used, and any excess skin. Trim away the bone end while still keeping the joint in a neat shape. Season it lightly with salt and pepper. Melt the butter and brush it over the chicken. Grill under high heat, turning 2 or 3 times during grilling to ensure even cooking. It should take 10–15 minutes to cook, depending on size.

Serve with a little Maître d'Hôtel butter or sauce.

Note Pheasant or grouse can be cooked in the same way.

Grilled Chicken with Mushroom Sauce

4–6 helpings

1 × 200g can grilling mushrooms	salad oil **or** softened butter for frying and grilling
250ml Espagnole sauce (p707)	1 large slice of white bread
salt and pepper	
1 chicken	200g lean ham

Garnish
bacon rolls (p396)   grilled mushrooms

Drain the mushrooms, mix with the Espagnole sauce, and season with salt and pepper. Keep the sauce warm by standing the container in a bain marie.

Divide the chicken into convenient pieces for serving. Brush the pieces with some of the oil or softened butter. Cut the crusts off the bread. Heat a little oil or butter and fry the bread lightly on both sides; keep warm. Cut the ham into 3–4cm strips and fry gently in the same pan until cooked; keep warm. Grill the chicken for 15–20 minutes or until tender, turning frequently to cook both sides evenly. Place the chicken and ham on the fried bread in a serving dish, pour the sauce over them, and garnish with bacon rolls and grilled mushrooms.

Barbecued Chicken

2–4 helpings

2 spring chickens **or**
  2 large chicken leg
  quarters
75g butter
4 ×15ml spoons vinegar
1 ×15ml spoon
  Worcestershire sauce
1 ×15ml spoon
  concentrated tomato
  purée

1 ×15ml spoon
  foundation brown
  sauce (p698)
1 × 5ml spoon grated
  onion
1 × 5ml spoon paprika
1 × 2.5ml spoon salt

Split the whole spring chicken, if used, through the breastbone, and cut in half lengthways. Cut the legs in half at the joints. Skewer the chicken halves to hold them flat. Melt the butter in a small pan, and brush some of it over the chicken halves or pieces, to coat them well. Arrange in a grill pan, placing the chicken halves skin side down. Add the remaining ingredients to the butter left in the pan, and simmer for 2 minutes. Brush a little of the sauce over the chicken. Grill the chicken gently for 12–15 minutes, then turn the halves or pieces over, brush with some more sauce, and grill for a further 15–20 minutes or until cooked through.

Serve with any remaining sauce poured over the meat.

Chicken Kiev

4 helpings

4 chicken breast and
  wing joints
salt and pepper
flour for coating

1 egg
100g soft white
  breadcrumbs (approx)
fat **or** oil for deep frying

Butter filling
finely grated rind of
  $\frac{1}{2}$ lemon
1 ×15ml spoon chopped
  parsley
100g softened butter

salt and freshly ground
  black pepper
2 small cloves garlic

Garnish
lemon wedges

parsley sprigs

Make the butter filling first. Work the lemon rind and parsley thoroughly into the butter, and season to taste. Crush and work in the garlic. Form the butter into a roll, wrap in clingfilm and chill.

To prepare the chicken, cut off the wing pinions. Turn the joints, flesh side up, and cut out all bones except the wing bone which is left in place. Do not cut right through the flesh. Flatten out the boned meat, cover with greaseproof paper, and beat lightly with a cutlet bat or heavy knife. Cut the seasoned butter into 4 long pieces and place one on each piece of chicken. Fold the flesh over the butter to enclose it completely, and secure with wooden cocktail sticks. The wing bone should protrude at one end of each cutlet. Season the flour with salt and pepper and roll each piece of chicken in it. Beat the egg lightly on a plate. Roll or dip the chicken in the egg, coating each cutlet completely; then roll each in the breadcrumbs. Heat the fat or oil (p303) and deep fry 2 cutlets at a time until they are golden-brown and cooked through. Drain thoroughly and keep hot while frying the remaining two. Place the cutlets on a warmed serving dish with the bones overlapping in the centre. Remove the cocktail sticks and garnish with lemon wedges and parsley before serving.

Spatchcocked Chicken

2 helpings

1 spring chicken	*salt and pepper*
25g butter	

Garnish
bacon rolls (p396)   *parsley sprigs*

Split the bird in half, cutting through the back only. Flatten out the bird, removing the breast-bone if necessary. Break the joints and remove the pinions from the wings, to make flattening easier. Use skewers to keep it in shape while cooking.

Melt the butter and brush it on both sides of the chicken; season lightly. Grill for 20 minutes, or until cooked. Brush the chicken with more butter and turn while grilling to ensure even cooking. Remove the skewers when done.

Serve garnished with bacon rolls and parsley sprigs, and accompanied by Tartare Sauce (p846) or Piquant Sauce (p702).

Devilled Chicken

1 helping

1 poussin **or** *chicken joint*	*1 × 5ml spoon chopped*
salt and pepper	*parsley*
a pinch of ground ginger	*1 × 5ml spoon chopped*
a pinch of mustard	*shallot*
powder	*1 × 10ml spoon cooking*
	oil

Split the poussin, if used, along the back, open it out, and skewer it into a neat flattish shape. Season to taste with salt, pepper, ginger and mustard, and sprinkle the parsley and shallot over it. Allow to stand for about 1 hour, turning occasionally so that the meat absorbs the various flavours. Brush with oil. Grill for 20–30 minutes or until tender, turning 2 or 3 times while cooking so that the outside is lightly browned. Serve very hot.

Viennese Chicken in Breadcrumbs

4–6 helpings

1 chicken	*100g dry white*
salt	*breadcrumbs*
2 eggs	*200g lard*
2 × 15ml spoons flour	

Garnish
lemon wedges

Cut the chicken into 4–6 joints. Sprinkle each joint with salt and leave for 30 minutes. Beat the eggs until liquid. Dip each joint first into flour, then into beaten egg, and finally into the breadcrumbs. Leave to firm up for 30 minutes.

Heat the lard in a pan for deep frying (p303). Fry the chicken joints until tender inside and crisp outside. Drain on soft kitchen paper. Garnish with lemon wedges, and serve with a green salad.

Chicken Chasseur

4–6 helpings

1 roasting chicken	*25g onion* **or** *shallot*
salt and pepper	*175g button mushrooms*
25g flour	*150ml dry white wine*
1 × 15ml spoon cooking	*275ml chicken stock*
oil	*1 sprig each of fresh*
50g butter	*tarragon, chervil, and*
3 tomatoes **or** *1 × 15ml*	*parsley*
spoon concentrated	
tomato purée	

Divide the chicken into 8 serving portions. Season the flour with salt and pepper, and use to dust the portions. Heat the oil and butter in a frying pan, and fry the chicken pieces until tender and browned all over, allowing 15–20 minutes for dark meat (drumsticks and thighs), 10–12 minutes for light meat (breast and wings). When tender, re-move from the pan, drain on soft kitchen paper, and transfer to a warmed serving dish. Cover loosely with buttered paper and keep hot.

Skin and chop the tomatoes if used, and the onion or shallot. Put the onion or shallot into the pan, in the fat in which the chicken was cooked, and fry gently without colouring. Meanwhile, slice the mushrooms, add them to the pan, and continue frying until they are tender. Pour in the wine, and add the chopped tomatoes or the tomato purée and the stock. Stir until well blended, then simmer gently for 10 minutes. Chop the herbs and add most of them to the sauce. Season to taste.

Pour the sauce over the chicken, sprinkle with the remaining herbs, and serve very hot.

Chicken or Turkey with Walnuts

4 helpings

300ml cooking oil	25g cornflour
200g shelled walnuts (whole or pieces)	a pinch of salt
	a pinch of sugar
4 whole chicken breasts or thick turkey breast fillets	2 × 15ml spoons soy sauce
	100g button mushrooms

Garnish
fingers of toast

Heat the oil in a heavy-bottomed saucepan. Fry the walnuts in the oil for 2–3 minutes until golden-brown. Remove them, and drain on soft kitchen paper.

Skin and dice the chicken or turkey breasts. Fry the meat in the pan, turning gently until light golden on all sides. Mix the cornflour, salt, sugar, and soy sauce to a smooth paste, and add the mixture to the pan. Slice the mushrooms and add them. Cook all these ingredients together very gently for about 10 minutes or until the meat is just tender. Stir the mixture during cooking, to prevent it sticking to the bottom of the pan. Remove from the heat, stir in the walnuts, and serve immediately. Garnish with fingers of toast.

Fritot of Chicken

4–6 helpings

1 cold cooked chicken	fat or oil for deep frying

Marinade

a slice of onion	1 × 2.5ml spoon dried mixed herbs
a sprig of parsley	salt and pepper
2 × 15ml spoons olive oil	
1 × 15ml spoon lemon juice	

Batter

100g flour	1 × 15ml spoon vegetable oil
125ml tepid water	
a pinch of salt	2 egg whites

Garnish
parsley sprigs

Cut the chicken into joints. Remove the skin and any excess fat, and place the joints in a deep bowl.

Make the marinade. Chop the onion finely with the parsley, and mix together with the other marinade ingredients. Pour it over the chicken joints and allow to stand for 1½ hours, turning them occasionally.

Make the batter by mixing the flour, water, salt, and oil together until smooth. Beat well, and allow to stand for 1 hour. Then whisk the egg whites until stiff, and fold into the batter.

Drain the chicken joints, dry well with soft kitchen paper, and dip each piece in the batter. Fry the joints in hot fat or oil (p303) until golden on all sides. Drain on soft kitchen paper.

Garnish with parsley, and serve with Fresh Tomato Sauce (p715) or Tartare Sauce (p846).

Chicken or Turkey Wings in Ginger Sauce

4 helpings

12 chicken wings **or** *8 turkey wings*	*flour for dredging*
salt and pepper	*oil for shallow frying*

Sauce
juice of ½ lemon	*2 × 15ml spoons*
4 × 15ml spoons	*medium-dry sherry*
chopped stem ginger in	*25g butter*
syrup	

Remove and discard the pinions from the wings. Skin the wings by holding them firmly in soft kitchen paper or a cloth, and peeling off the skin. Season the flour with salt and pepper. Roll the wings in the flour. Heat the oil in a frying pan to a depth of 1cm. Fry them gently, turning as required, until tender and golden-brown on both sides. This will take about 10 minutes for chicken wings, 17–20 minutes for turkey wings. Remove from the pan, drain on soft kitchen paper, and keep hot while making the sauce.

Put the lemon juice, stem ginger, sherry, and butter in a small saucepan, and bring to the boil. Place the chicken or turkey wings on a heated serving platter and pour the sauce over them.

Serve with buttered noodles or plain boiled rice.

BRAISED AND CASSEROLED DISHES

Braised Chicken with Chestnuts and Sausages

4–6 helpings

1 chicken	*150ml chicken stock* **or**
salt and pepper	*water*
flour for coating	*25g flour*
3 × 15ml spoons oil	*25g butter*
1 onion	
3 rashers streaky bacon,	
without rinds	

Stuffing
450g chestnuts	*grated rind of 1 lemon*
250ml chicken stock	*salt and pepper*
(approx)	*a few sprigs parsley*
50g ham	*25g butter*
100g fine soft white	*1 egg*
breadcrumbs	

Garnish
450g fried chipolata	*lemon slices*
sausages	

Make the stuffing first. Remove the shells and skins of the chestnuts. Place the cleaned nuts in a saucepan, just cover with stock, and bring to the boil. Cover, reduce the heat until the liquid is only just boiling, and cook for about 1 hour or until the nuts are tender. Drain and mash them or put them through a fine sieve. Chop the ham finely. Mix the nuts, ham, breadcrumbs, and lemon rind together, and season with salt and pepper. Chop the parsley finely. Melt the butter slowly, and add the chopped parsley. Beat the egg until liquid. Mix all the ingredients for the stuffing together well. Stuff the bird with the mixture, and truss it.

Season the flour and roll the bird in it. Heat the oil in a large, heavy-bottomed flameproof casserole or pan with a lid. Fry the bird on all sides until lightly browned, then remove it. Skin and slice the onion, and cut the bacon into strips. Fry the onion and bacon lightly in the pan. Place a trivet or inverted saucer in the pan and place the chicken on it. Pour in the stock or water. Cover the pan, bring to the boil, then lower the heat until the liquid is just simmering. Cook for about 1½ hours, or until the chicken is tender. Add a little more stock if necessary before the end of the cooking time.

Remove the chicken. Sieve the pan juices or process in an electric blender. Knead the flour and butter into a beurre manié for the sauce. Heat the juices, then remove from the heat and add the beurre manié in small balls, stirring all the time. Return to the heat and stir until the mixture boils. Cook for a few minutes, then season to taste.

Garnish with fried sausages and lemon slices. Offer the sauce separately.

Chicken with Rice

4 helpings

1 chicken or 4 chicken
  quarters
chicken giblets or 2
  chicken stock cubes
2 × 15ml spoons oil
40g butter
225g button onions

100g button mushrooms
1 bay leaf
50ml dry white wine
1 × 200g can red peppers
175g long-grain rice
salt and pepper

Garnish
Béchamel sauce (p704)   *chopped parsley*
  (optional)

If using a whole chicken, cut into quarters. Cook the giblets in 1 litre of water for 40 minutes, or make stock with the cubes. Put the oil and 25g of the butter in a large pan, add the chicken, and brown gently all over. Remove to a plate. Prepare the onions and mushrooms. Place them in the pan with the oil, bay leaf, wine, and 150ml of the stock. Cover, and cook for 15 minutes. Remove, measure the stock, and make up to 550ml with the remaining stock.

Drain the peppers and cut them into strips. Heat the remaining 15g butter in a frying pan and cook the rice in it gently for about 2 minutes. Add the onions, mushrooms, stock, wine, and peppers. Season well. Place in a casserole, arrange the chicken on top, cover, and cook in a moderate oven, 180°C, Gas 4, for 1 hour, by which time most

of the stock will have been absorbed. Arrange the rice on a heated serving dish with the chicken on top and sprinkle with parsley.

If liked, some Béchamel sauce can be spooned over the chicken before sprinkling with the parsley.

Chicken Casserole

6 helpings

1 chicken or 6 small
  chicken joints
salt and pepper
25g flour
125g streaky bacon,
  without rinds

50g mushrooms
25g shallots
50g butter or fat
500ml chicken stock

Joint the chicken. Season the flour, and dip the joints in it. Cut the bacon into strips 1cm wide, slice the mushrooms, and skin and chop the shallots. Heat the fat in a flameproof casserole and fry the bacon, mushrooms, and shallots gently. Add the chicken joints and fry them until golden on all sides, turning them as required.

Add enough hot stock just to cover the chicken pieces. Simmer for 1–1½ hours or until tender. Re-season if required. Serve from the casserole.

Ragoût of Chicken

4–6 helpings

1 chicken
1 onion
125g ham or bacon
50g butter

50g flour
500ml chicken stock
salt and pepper

Joint the chicken. Skin and slice the onion. Dice the ham or bacon. Melt the butter in a saucepan and fry the joints in it until lightly browned; then remove and keep hot. Fry the sliced onion lightly in the same fat. Sprinkle in the flour and brown it slowly. Add the stock, season carefully, and stir until boiling. Replace the joints in the sauce, add the diced ham or bacon, cover with a tight-fitting lid, and cook gently for 1 hour or until the chicken is tender. Re-season if required.

Serve the chicken with the sauce poured over it.

Chicken Braised with Chestnuts

4–6 helpings

400g chestnuts	*125ml soy sauce*
1 small chicken	*425ml water*
25g butter	*4 slices ginger root*
1 ×15ml spoon olive oil	*2 spring onions*
or other good vegetable	*a pinch of salt*
oil	

Remove the shells and skins of the chestnuts. Wipe the chicken and halve it. Cut each half into 4 pieces without removing any bones. Heat the butter and oil in a saucepan and fry the chicken until golden-brown. Add the soy sauce and water, and bring just to the boil. Remove the pan from the heat. Mince or grate the ginger and chop the onions. Add them to the saucepan with the skinned chestnuts and salt. Cover, and simmer for 1 hour or until the chicken is tender and the chestnuts have broken up and are thickening the sauce.

Chicken Casserole with Lemon

6 helpings

6 chicken joints or 3	*4 ×15ml spoons plain*
chicken quarters	*flour*
salt and pepper	*250ml chicken stock*
50g butter	*2–3 bay leaves*
1 ×15ml spoon oil	*1 × 5ml spoon caster*
1 medium-sized onion	*sugar*
1 lemon	

Halve the chicken quarters, if used. Season the joints well with salt and pepper. Heat the butter and oil in a frying pan, and fry the joints until golden-brown all over. Transfer to a casserole.

Skin and slice the onion and slice the lemon. Put the onion in the frying pan and cook gently for about 5 minutes until tender. Sprinkle in the flour and cook for 1 minute. Blend in the stock and bring to the boil, stirring all the time. Add the sliced lemon, bay leaves, sugar, and salt and pepper to taste. Pour into the casserole and cover. Cook in a fairly hot oven, 190°C, Gas 5, for about 1 hour until the chicken is tender. Remove the casserole lid 5 minutes before the end of the cooking time.

Coq au Vin

4–6 helpings

1 chicken with giblets	*1 ×15ml spoon oil*
bouquet garni	*2 ×15ml spoons brandy*
salt and pepper	*575ml Burgundy or*
125g belly of pickled	*other red wine*
pork or green bacon	*2 ×5ml spoons*
rashers	*concentrated tomato*
175g button mushrooms	*purée*
125g button onions	*25g butter*
1 clove of garlic	*25g plain flour*
50g unsalted butter	

Garnish

croûtes of fried bread	*chopped parsley*

Joint the chicken. Place the giblets in a saucepan, cover with water, and add the bouquet garni, salt, and pepper. Cook gently for 1 hour to make 275ml stock.

Remove the rind from the belly of pork or bacon rashers. Clean the mushrooms if necessary, skin the onions, and skin and crush the garlic. Heat the 50g butter and the oil in a flameproof casserole, add the pork or bacon, and the onions, and cook slowly until the fat runs and the onions are lightly coloured. Remove them to a plate.

Brown the chicken lightly all over in the same fat, then pour off any surplus fat. Warm the brandy, set alight, and pour it over the chicken. When the flame dies down, add the wine, stock, pork or bacon, onions, mushrooms, garlic, and tomato purée. Cover with a lid and cook over low heat, or in a cool oven, 150°C, Gas 2, for 1 hour or until the chicken is tender.

Remove the chicken to a serving dish and keep hot. Using a perforated spoon, remove the onions, bacon, and mushrooms, and arrange over the chicken. Simmer the liquid until reduced by about one-third. Meanwhile, make a beurre manié by kneading together the 25g butter and flour. Lower the heat of the liquid to below boiling point and gradually whisk in the beurre manié in small pieces. Continue to whisk until the sauce thickens. Pour it over the chicken. Arrange croûtes of fried bread round the dish and sprinkle with chopped parsley.

Braised Chicken with Parsley

4 helpings

50g parsley sprigs
100g butter
salt and pepper

2 spring chickens
150ml water
275ml double cream

Garnish
lemon wedges

parsley sprigs

Cut the stalks off the parsley sprigs and chop the leaves coarsely. Soften 50g of the butter, season, and mix with half of the parsley. Place half the mixture in the body of each bird. Melt the remaining butter in a large pan, put the chickens in the pan, and brown them lightly all over. Add the water, cover, and cook gently for 40 minutes or until tender. Remove the chickens and halve them. Put in a serving dish and keep hot. Add the cream to the stock in the pan and cook over low heat, stirring until the sauce is smooth. Add the remaining parsley, and re-season if required. Pour the sauce over the chicken and garnish with lemon wedges and extra parsley sprigs.

Note If spring chickens are not available, use 1 roasting chicken, stuff it with the butter and parsley mixture, and cut it into quarters after cooking. Allow 10–15 minutes extra cooking time.

POACHED AND STEWED DISHES

Chicken with Suprême Sauce

4–6 helpings

1 chicken
1 litre white stock
 (p329)

425ml Suprême sauce
 (p710)

Garnish
chopped truffle **or**
 macédoine of
 vegetables (p398)

Truss the chicken, poach it in the stock for 1½–2 hours or until tender, then divide into neat joints. Arrange the joints on a hot dish, pour the sauce over, and garnish with chopped truffle or a macédoine of vegetables piled at either end of the dish.

Chicken with Macaroni

4–6 helpings

1 chicken
1 litre (approx) chicken
 or vegetable stock
 (p330)
150ml Fresh Tomato
 sauce (p715)
150ml Espagnole sauce
 (p707)

lemon juice **or** tarragon
 vinegar
salt and pepper
100g quick-cooking
 macaroni

Truss the chicken, put it in the stock, and poach or boil it for about 45 minutes until half cooked. Drain well, and cut it into convenient pieces for serving. Heat the sauces together in a heavy pan, put in the chicken pieces, and add lemon juice or tarragon vinegar and seasoning to taste. Simmer very gently for 30–45 minutes until the chicken is fully cooked. Meanwhile, add the macaroni to fast-boiling salted water, and cook for 8–10 minutes. Drain well. Put the macaroni in a heated serving dish, pile the chicken on top, pour the sauce over it, and serve hot.

Poultry Hot Pot

4–6 helpings

1 boiling fowl with	*nutmeg*
giblets	*2 onions*
3 rashers streaky bacon,	*2 carrots*
without rinds	*275ml chicken stock*
salt and pepper	*3 × 10ml spoons flour*

Garnish
*2 × 15ml spoons
chopped parsley*

Joint the fowl and remove the skin. Place the joints, with the liver and heart, in a casserole or saucepan with a tight-fitting lid. Cut the bacon into strips, and add with the salt, pepper, and nutmeg. Prepare and slice the onions and carrots, and add with the stock. Cover, then either cook in a fairly hot oven, 190–200°C, Gas 5–6, or simmer for about 2–2½ hours until tender. Blend the flour with a little water, add some of the chicken stock, and return to the pan. Stir it in, and cook until thickened. Serve sprinkled with parsley.

Boiled rice makes a good accompaniment.

Chicken with Curried Rice

4–6 helpings

1 chicken with giblets	*150g long-grain rice*
1 carrot	*2 large mild onions*
2 sticks celery	*100g butter*
1 litre (approx) chicken	*1 × 15ml spoon curry*
stock **or** *water*	*paste*
1 blade of mace	*salt and pepper*
6 black peppercorns	*50g small onions* **or**
	shallots

Place the chicken in a large saucepan with the giblets. Slice the carrot and celery, and add them to the pan with enough stock or water to cover the chicken. Add the mace and peppercorns, and cover with a lid. Simmer gently for 2 hours or until the bird is tender. Drain well. Reserve the stock.

Strip the flesh from the chicken, and slice it. Wash and drain the rice. Skin and slice the large onions. Heat 50g of the butter in a pan and fry the onions until lightly browned. Add the curry paste, mix well, and fry gently for 2–3 minutes. Add the rice and 750ml of the reserved stock. Season to taste, cover, and simmer for 15–30 minutes until the rice is tender and the stock is absorbed. When ready, remove the rice from the heat, and keep warm.

Heat the remaining butter in a frying pan and add the chicken pieces; fry gently until browned on all sides. Leave the butter in the pan. Add the chicken to the rice mixture and cook slowly until the rice is heated through again. Stir in a little more stock if necessary, and re-season if required. Place on a serving dish and keep hot. Skin and slice the small onions or shallots into rings. Fry quickly in the butter used for the chicken, and pile on top of the rice. Serve very hot.

Poached Chicken with Oysters

4–6 helpings

24 raw oysters	*2 × 15ml spoons cream*
1 chicken	*or milk*
1 blade of mace	*1 egg*
salt and pepper	
550ml foundation white	
sauce (coating	
consistency) (p692)	

Open the oysters (p426). Place about 12 inside the chicken. Truss the chicken and put it in a large saucepan with a tight-fitting lid. Add about 2cm depth of cold water, and the mace, salt, and pepper. Cover, and cook for 1–1¼ hours until tender, adding a little extra water during cooking if required.

Remove the trussing string from the chicken. Strain off the cooking liquid, make it up to 550ml, and use it to make the white sauce. Meanwhile, keep the chicken hot.

Blend the cream or milk with the egg, stir into the hot sauce, and re-heat very gently until well thickened. Do not allow it to boil. Blanch the remaining oysters in their liquor. Pour some sauce over the chicken, add the oysters and their liquor to the rest, and serve it separately.

Chicken with Cucumber Sauce

4–6 helpings

1 chicken	1 cucumber
1 lemon	25g butter
1 bay leaf	25g plain flour
salt and pepper	2 ×15ml spoons single
1 small onion	cream

Garnish
1 ×15ml spoon chopped
  parsley

Place the chicken in a large pan with just enough water to cover it. Pare the lemon rind thinly and add to the pan with the bay leaf, salt, and pepper to taste. Bring to the boil, cover, and simmer for 1½–2 hours until the chicken is tender. Skin and chop the onion. Dice the cucumber. Lift the chicken from the pan, cool slightly, and strip away the skin. Strain 250ml stock from the pan for the sauce. Return the chicken to the pan and keep hot.

Melt the butter in another pan, add the onion and cucumber, and cook for 1 minute. Stir in the flour, gradually blend in the stock, and simmer gently for 10–15 minutes. Cool slightly. Squeeze a little juice from the lemon, and add to the sauce with the cream and salt and pepper to taste.

Lift the chicken on to a serving dish and coat with sauce. Sprinkle with parsley.

Chicken Jelly

6–8 helpings

1 chicken (1.2kg)	5 peppercorns
1.5 litres water **or**	white and crushed shell
vegetable stock (p330)	of 1 egg
salt	1–2 ×15ml spoons
1 ×15ml spoon vinegar	gelatine (see Method)
2 bay leaves	chopped parsley

Joint and skin the chicken. Bring the water or stock to the boil in a pan. Put in the chicken pieces, salt, vinegar, bay leaves and peppercorns. Bring back to the boil, and skim well. Reduce the heat, cover the pan, and simmer the chicken for 35 minutes until tender. Remove the chicken pieces

and cool slightly. Cut the meat off the bones in small pieces. Return the bones to the pan, and boil the stock down to about 700ml. Remove the bones and leave to cool completely.

Clear the stock with the egg white and shell as for Consommé (p335). Put 2 ×15ml spoons of the clarified stock in a saucer, and chill to test for setting quality. If it does not form a firm jelly, soften enough gelatine in cold water to give a firm set; re-heat the stock and dissolve the gelatine in it.

Arrange the chicken meat in a wetted 1 litre mould. Pour the stock over it gently, leave to cool, then chill until set. Sprinkle with the parsley before serving.

PASTRY DISHES

Chicken Liver Patties

4 helpings

225g chicken livers	flour for rolling out
25g butter **or** margarine	150ml foundation brown
2 ×15ml spoons grated	sauce (p698)
onion	beaten egg **or** milk for
salt and pepper	glazing
rough puff pastry (p1252)	
using 125g flour	

Remove the skin and tubes from the livers, then cut into small pieces. Heat the butter or margarine in a small saucepan, and cook the onion and livers gently for 5 minutes, turning all the time. Season well. Roll out the pastry on a lightly floured surface and cut out 4 bases and 4 tops for the patties. Line four 10cm patty tins with the base pastry, divide the livers between them, and pour a little brown sauce over each. Cover with the pastry tops. Brush the pastry with egg or milk, prick, and bake in a fairly hot oven, 190°C, Gas 5, for 20–30 minutes. Serve hot or cold.

Chicken and Bacon Patties

See p1306.

Mrs Beeton's Chicken or Fowl Pie

6–8 helpings

1 chicken **or** boiling fowl with giblets	6 slices lean cooked ham
250ml water	150g basic herb forcemeat (p375) **or**
1 onion	250–300g sausage-meat
salt and pepper	
bouquet garni	3 hard-boiled eggs
1 blade of whole mace	150–200ml water
chicken fat **or** margarine for greasing	flour for dredging
	puff pastry using 150g flour (p1253)
1 × 2.5ml spoon grated nutmeg	beaten egg for glazing
1 × 2.5ml spoon ground mace	

Skin the chicken or fowl and cut it into small serving joints. Put the leftover bones, neck, and gizzard into a small pan with the water. Split the onion in half and add it to the pan with the seasoning, bouquet garni, and mace. Half cover and simmer gently for about 45 minutes until the liquid is well reduced and strongly flavoured. Put to one side.

Grease lightly a 1.5 litre pie dish or oven-to-table baking dish. Put a layer of chicken joints in the bottom. Season lightly with salt, pepper, nutmeg, and ground mace. Cover with a layer of ham, then with forcemeat or sausage-meat; re-season. Slice the eggs, place a layer over the forcemeat, and season again. Repeat the layers until the dish is full and all the ingredients are used, ending with a layer of chicken joints. Pour 150–200ml water into the dish and dredge lightly with flour.

Roll out the pastry on a lightly floured surface to the same shape as the dish but 3cm larger all round. Cut off the outside 2cm of the pastry. Lay the pastry strip on the rim of the dish. Dampen the strip and lay the lid on top. Knock up the edge, trim, and use any trimmings to decorate the crust with pastry leaves. Make a pastry rose and put to one side. Brush the pastry with the beaten egg. Make a small hole in the centre of the pie. Bake in a hot oven, 220°C, Gas 7, for 15 minutes to set the pastry, then reduce the temperature to moderate, 180°C, Gas 4, and cover the pastry loosely with greaseproof paper. Bake for 1–1¼ hours if using forcemeat, for 1½–2 hours if using sausage-meat. Bake the pastry rose with the pie for the final 20 minutes but bake it blind. Test whether the joints are cooked through by running a small heated skewer into the pie through the central hole. It should come out clean with no trace of blood or smell of raw meat on it.

Just before the pie is cooked, re-heat the stock and strain it. When the pie is cooked, pour the stock in through the central hole, and cover with the pastry rose. Serve hot or cold.

Note For serving cold the joints can be boned. In this case sausage-meat should be used. Add the bones to the saucepan when making stock, and use a smaller dish. The cooking time will be the same.

Chicken Vol-au-vent and Chicken Patties
See p1259.

BAKED DISHES

Chicken Ramekins

8 small helpings

175g raw chicken **or** turkey meat	50g mushrooms
2 eggs	milk
3 × 15ml spoons double cream	butter **or** margarine for greasing
salt and pepper	

Chop or mince the chicken or turkey very finely. Separate the eggs and add the yolks to the meat gradually to make a very smooth mixture. Sieve if liked. Whip the cream lightly. Season well. Chop the mushrooms and add them to the meat with the cream. Fold in. Whisk the egg whites until stiff and fold in. Add a little extra milk if very stiff. Divide the mixture between 8 small well-greased ramekins, individual soufflé dishes or paper cases; fill only three-quarters full. Cook in a fairly hot oven, 190°C, Gas 5, for 45 minutes until well risen, firm to the touch, and well browned. Serve at once.

Hot Chicken Liver Mousse

4 helpings

1 × 15ml spoon butter **or** *margarine*	*1 egg*
2 × 15ml spoons plain flour	*1 egg yolk*
150ml milk	*3 × 15ml spoons double cream*
salt and pepper	*1 × 15ml spoon dry sherry*
225g chicken livers	*butter for greasing*

Garnish
chopped chives

Put the butter or margarine in a medium-sized saucepan with the flour and milk. Whisking all the time over a moderate heat, bring to the boil and cook for 2–3 minutes until thickened and smooth. Season to taste. Leave the sauce to become cold, stirring from time to time.

Remove the skin and tubes from the livers. Either process in an electric blender, or mince twice to obtain a purée. Beat in the egg and egg yolk. Add the sauce, cream, and sherry. Pour into 4 well-buttered 150ml cocotte dishes. Place in a baking tin, and fill it with enough boiling water to come half-way up the sides of the dishes. Cook in a moderate oven, 180°C, Gas 4, for 25–30 minutes until a fine skewer inserted in the centre comes out clean. Allow to stand for a few minutes before turning out. Sprinkle with chives and serve hot.

Turkey

TRADITIONAL ROAST AND OTHER TURKEY DISHES

Mrs Beeton's Roast Turkey

1 turkey	*2–3 rashers fat bacon*
450g basic herb forcemeat (p375)	*fat for basting*
500g–1.5kg seasoned sausage-meat	

Stuff the neck of the bird with basic forcemeat and put the sausage-meat inside the body. Truss, and lay the bacon rashers over the breast. Roast in a hot oven, 220°C, Gas 7, for 15–20 minutes, then reduce the heat to moderate, 180°C, Gas 4. (For the overall cooking time see p623.) Baste frequently. About 20 minutes before serving, remove the bacon to allow the breast to brown. Remove the trussing string. Serve on a hot dish.

Serve with the traditional accompaniments (p624) and with roast potatoes and Brussels sprouts.

Note A 6kg bird will just fit comfortably into an oven with an interior capacity of 0.07 cubic metres (42 × 40 × 40cm). If the oven is smaller than this, or if one wishes to cook a larger bird, it can sometimes be done by removing the legs and cooking them separately. In any recipe for a whole roast turkey, the quantity of stuffing and the accompaniments, should be adapted to fit the size of the bird.

The breast meat of a large turkey may become dry before the legs are cooked. To avoid this problem, remove the legs either before roasting the bird or when the breast is cooked, and use them for another meal.

The quantity of stuffing required will vary to some extent with the type of stuffing. One uses less of a light fluffy stuffing which needs room to swell than of a dense stuffing such as sausage-meat. As a very general guide, 700g sausage-meat and 450g basic forcemeat will stuff an average-sized (6kg) turkey.

Roast Turkey with Chipolata Garnish

1 turkey	775g sausage-meat
450g basic herb forcemeat (p375)	2–3 rashers bacon, without rinds

Garnish

100g carrots parisiennes (p399)	225g sausage-meat
100g turnips parisiennes (p399)	flour for dredging
1 × 15ml spoon butter	fat for frying
150ml stock	1 × 200g can grilling mushrooms

Stuff the crop of the bird with the basic forcemeat and the body with seasoned sausage-meat; then truss. Lay the bacon rashers over the breast, and weigh. Cook as for Mrs Beeton's Roast Turkey (p639). Thirty minutes before the turkey is ready, sweat the balls of carrot and turnip in the butter, until all the fat has been absorbed. Add the stock, and cook until just tender.

Meanwhile, roll the sausage-meat for the garnish into small chipolatas and dredge them lightly with flour. Fry them in a little fat.

Drain the mushrooms and add them to the stock for a few minutes or until heated. Drain the vegetables. Remove the trussing string from the cooked bird. Garnish with the vegetables and chipolatas.

Serve Espagnole Sauce (p707) separately.

Roast Young Turkey

(Turkey poult)

5–6 helpings

1 young turkey	fat for basting

Truss the bird. Cover the breast with 2 layers of buttered greaseproof paper or 1 layer of buttered foil, and roast in a hot or very hot oven, 220–230°C, Gas 7–8, for about 1 hour, or until tender, basting if necessary. Remove the paper to allow the skin to brown lightly. Remove the trussing string.

Serve with thin gravy (p727) and fried bacon or boiled ham.

Roast Turkey with Chestnuts

1 turkey	single cream or milk
salt and pepper	500g sausage-meat or 500g basic herb forcemeat (p375)
1kg chestnuts	
275ml stock	
50g butter	2–3 slices fat bacon
1 egg	fat for basting

Season the turkey inside with salt and pepper, but do not truss it. Remove the shells and skins of the chestnuts. Stew them in the stock for 1 hour, then drain and chop or sieve them. Melt the butter and beat the egg, and add both to the chestnuts with seasoning and enough cream or milk to moisten the mixture. Fill the neck end of the bird with this chestnut stuffing, and the body of the bird with seasoned sausage-meat or basic forcemeat. Truss, and cover the bird with bacon. Roast for 15–20 minutes in a hot oven, 220°C, Gas 7, then reduce to moderate, 180°C, Gas 4, and cook until tender. (For cooking times see p623.) Baste well. Remove the bacon towards the end of the cooking time to allow the breast to brown. Remove the trussing string, and transfer the bird to a warmed serving dish.

Serve gravy separately.

Turkey Breasts in Pastry

8 helpings

2 turkey breasts (500g each approx)	50g sage and onion stuffing mix
175g mushrooms	salt and pepper
50g onion	flour for rolling out
25g butter	1 × 420g pkt frozen puff pastry, thawed
1 egg	
225g belly of pork	

Remove the skin from the turkey breasts, and cut each across to make 2 thinner slices. Place each slice between sheets of greaseproof paper and flatten with a cutlet bat or rolling-pin.

Chop the mushrooms finely. Skin the onion and chop it finely. Melt the butter and fry the mushrooms and onion gently until the onion is soft but not brown. Remove from the heat. Beat the egg until liquid. Trim and mince the belly of pork, and add it to the pan with the stuffing mix, salt, pepper, and half the beaten egg. Allow to stand for a few minutes for the crumbs to swell.

On a lightly floured surface, roll out the pastry into a 30cm square. Place 2 turkey pieces in the centre and spread the stuffing over them. Lay the remaining 2 turkey breasts on top of them to enclose the stuffing. Dampen the edges of the pastry lightly and fold it over the turkey. Place on a baking sheet with the seam underneath, brush with the remaining egg, and decorate with any pastry trimmings. Bake in a hot oven, 220°C, Gas 7, for 20 minutes, then reduce the heat to moderate, 180°C, Gas 4, and bake for a further 35 minutes. Serve hot, in slices.

Casserole of Turkey Legs

4 helpings

2 turkey thighs **or** drumsticks	1 large clove of garlic
flour for dredging	125g mushrooms
50g butter **or** margarine	1 × 400g can tomatoes
1 × 15ml spoon cooking oil	2 chicken stock cubes
1 medium-sized onion	2 × 5ml spoons dried marjoram
	salt and pepper

Sprinkle the turkey legs with flour. Heat the fat in a large flameproof casserole, add the oil, and when hot, put in the turkey joints. Fry gently, turning as required, until browned on all sides. Drain on soft kitchen paper. Skin and chop the onion, add to the fat remaining in the casserole, and fry gently for about 5 minutes, until softened. Skin, crush, and add the garlic. Quarter the mushrooms, and add to the pan with the tomatoes and their liquid. Add the crumbled stock cubes, marjoram, and seasoning to taste. Return the turkey joints to the casserole, cover, and simmer, or cook in a warm oven, 160°C, Gas 3, for 1½ hours or until the meat is very tender.

Remove the meat from the bones, and serve from the casserole.

Braised Turkey

12–14 helpings

1 turkey (5-6 kg approx)	1.5 litres chicken stock
2 onions	125ml red wine
2 carrots	a pinch of dried thyme
1 leek	1 bay leaf
4 sticks celery	6 parsley sprigs
1 small turnip	salt and pepper
2 rashers streaky bacon, without rinds	25g flour
100g butter **or** margarine	2 × 15ml spoons double cream

Garnish
chopped parsley

Choose a large pan which will hold the turkey, or halve the bird lengthways, and place each half in a large deep roasting tin. (In this case, divide the other ingredients equally between the tins.)

Prepare and chop all the vegetables and the bacon. Melt the butter or margarine in the pan, and fry the chopped vegetables and bacon, turning as required, until lightly browned all over. Add the turkey, pour the stock and wine over the bird, and add the herbs and seasoning. Cover tightly with a lid or foil, and simmer very gently for 3½–4 hours. (If cooking the halved bird in 2 tins, reduce the cooking time to 2–2½ hours.) Baste occasionally with the liquid in the pan while cooking.

When the bird is tender, remove it from the pan, and keep hot. Strain the remaining cooking liquid into a smaller pan. Discard the vegetables and herbs. Blend the flour to a smooth paste with a little cold water, and stir it into the stock in the pan. Place over gentle heat, and stir until the sauce thickens. Stir in the cream, and re-heat, but do not boil. Place the bird on a heated serving platter and sprinkle with chopped parsley. Serve the sauce separately.

DISHES USING COOKED CHICKEN AND TURKEY

The recipes in this section are for main dishes, hot and cold, using cooked chicken or turkey meat. Many other recipes using cooked poultry, including salads, can be found elsewhere in the book, by reference to the Index.

Chicken à la King

4 helpings

350–450g cooked	*4 × 15ml spoons whisky*
chicken meat	*salt and freshly ground*
1 red pepper	*black pepper*
175g button mushrooms	*a pinch of garlic powder*
225g long-grain rice	*200ml double cream*
50g butter	*1 egg yolk*

Dice the chicken meat and put to one side. De-seed the pepper and slice it thinly. Trim and slice the mushrooms. Boil the rice for 12–15 minutes until tender, drain thoroughly, and keep hot.

Melt 25g of the butter in a frying pan and, when foaming, add the pepper and fry quickly for 2–3 minutes. Stir in the mushrooms, and cook gently for another 2 minutes. Put to one side. In a second pan, melt the remaining butter, add the diced chicken meat, and fry gently, turning as required, until well heated through. Pour on the whisky, set alight, and shake the pan to distribute the flames. When they die down, season the chicken well with salt, pepper, and garlic powder, and simmer until nearly all of the juices have evaporated. Stir in most of the cream, and bring gently to boiling point, stirring all the time. Blend the egg yolk into the remaining cream, and add a little of the cooking liquid from the pepper and mushrooms. Add the pepper and mushrooms to the chicken, then stir in the yolk and cream. Re-heat gently without boiling until the sauce thickens a little. Pile on to a warmed serving dish, and surround with a ring of the rice. Serve hot.

Chicken Soufflé (1)

3–4 helpings

1 small onion	*200g cooked chicken **or***
4 cloves	*turkey meat*
250ml milk	*4 drops Tabasco sauce*
1 bay leaf	*4 × 10ml spoons*
50g butter	*chopped parsley*
50g plain flour	*salt*
4 eggs	*fat for greasing*

Skin the onion and stud with the cloves. Put the milk in a saucepan with the onion and the bay leaf. Heat until almost boiling, cover with a lid, and draw off the heat. Leave to infuse for 20 minutes, then strain, reserving the milk.

Melt the butter in another pan and stir in the flour. Remove from the heat and stir in the milk gradually. Return to the heat and bring to the boil stirring all the time until the sauce is thick. Remove from the heat and cool slightly.

Separate the eggs. Mince the chicken or turkey meat. Beat the egg yolks into the sauce. Add the chicken, Tabasco, parsley, and salt to taste. Whisk the egg whites until stiff but not dry. Fold half into the chicken mixture, and then fold in the remainder. Heat the oven to fairly hot, 200°C, Gas 6. Turn the mixture into a greased 1.25 litre soufflé dish. Bake for about 40 minutes until well risen and golden-brown. Serve immediately.

Note For other chicken soufflés, see p922 and p1403.

Devilled Poultry or Game
See p1311.

Curried Chicken or Turkey

4 helpings

50g butter **or** *margarine*	*1 × 5ml spoon chutney*
1 onion	**or** *redcurrant jelly*
1 × 15ml spoon flour	*2 × 5ml spoons lemon*
1 × 15ml spoon curry	*juice*
powder	*salt and pepper*
425ml chicken stock	*350g cooked chicken* **or**
1 eating apple	*turkey meat*

Melt the butter or margarine in a medium-sized saucepan. Skin and slice the onion and fry lightly. Stir in the flour and curry powder. Cook for 3 minutes. Stir in the stock gradually. Peel and slice the apple. Bring the curry sauce to the boil, then add the apple with the chutney or jelly, lemon juice, and seasoning. Simmer gently for 30 minutes. Add the chicken. Keep hot but not simmering for 30 minutes.

Serve separately with plain boiled rice and chutney, or any other traditional accompaniments (p388).

Quick Curried Chicken or Fowl

(Country Captain)

4–6 helpings

1 cooked chicken **or** *fowl*	*1 large sweet apple*
2 large onions	*1 × 10ml spoon chutney*
50g chicken fat **or** *butter*	*1 × 15ml spoon lemon*
1 × 15ml spoon curry	*juice*
powder	*salt and pepper*
1 × 10ml spoon curry	*50g whole blanched*
paste	*almonds*
1 × 15ml spoon flour	*fat for frying*
375ml stock	

Garnish
lemon butterflies (p391)

Cut the bird into neat pieces. Keep any bones and trimmings for stock. Skin and chop the onions. Heat the chicken fat or butter, and fry the onions slowly until lightly browned. Add the curry powder, paste, and flour, and fry gently for 3 minutes. Stir in the stock gradually and bring to the boil. Peel, core, and dice the apple, and add to the mixture, together with the chutney, lemon juice, and seasoning. Simmer gently for 30 minutes, stirring occasionally. Add the chicken pieces and heat through slowly. Re-season if required.

Fry the almonds for a few minutes until golden-brown. Serve the chicken curry on a hot dish with the almonds sprinkled on top. Garnish with lemon butterflies.

Plain boiled rice and chutney should be served separately as accompaniments.

Stuffed Chicken Legs

4 helpings

4 cooked drumsticks	*1 × 5ml spoon chopped*
salt and Cayenne pepper	*parsley*
1 × 15ml spoon	*1 small onion*
vegetable oil	*1 × 2.5ml spoon grated*
2 × 15ml spoons soft	*lemon rind*
white breadcrumbs	*1 egg*
1 × 2.5ml spoon mixed	*4 gammon rashers*
herbs	*fat for greasing*

Garnish
parsley sprigs

Season each drumstick with salt and Cayenne pepper and moisten with oil. Mix the breadcrumbs, herbs, and finely chopped parsley in a basin. Skin, blanch, and chop the onion finely and add it to the basin together with the lemon rind. Moisten the mixture with the egg. Spread each gammon rasher with this stuffing, and wrap one rasher around each drumstick. Tie or skewer the rasher securely in place. Put the drumsticks on a greased baking tray and cook in a moderate oven, 180°C, Gas 4, for 20 minutes; then cover them with foil, and cook for a further 20 minutes. Garnish with parsley sprigs.

Serve at once on trimmed slices of hot buttered toast.

Chicken Cutlets

4 helpings

225g cold cooked chicken	*nutmeg*
1 small shallot	*salt and pepper*
25g butter	*1 egg*
1 × 15ml spoon flour	*egg and breadcrumbs for*
150ml foundation white	*coating*
sauce (coating	*fat for deep frying*
consistency) (p692)	

Garnish
fried parsley (p398)

Chop the chicken finely. Skin and chop the shallot. Melt the butter and fry the shallot without browning. Add the flour and cook for 2 minutes without colouring. Add the sauce and bring to the boil. Boil for 2 minutes, stirring all the time. Put in the chicken. Add nutmeg and seasoning to taste. Stir over low heat until thoroughly heated. Add the egg. Cook for 3 minutes longer stirring all the time. Cool. When firm, divide into 6 or 8 equal pieces, shape into cutlets, and coat with egg and crumbs. Heat the fat (p303) and fry the cutlets until golden-brown. Drain, arrange in a circle on a warmed dish, and garnish with the parsley. Serve hot.

Blanquette of Turkey or Chicken

4 helpings

1 small onion	*40g flour*
turkey or chicken bones,	*350–450g cooked turkey*
raw or cooked	*or chicken meat*
1 blade of mace	*a pinch of nutmeg*
salt and pepper	*2 × 15ml spoons cream*
600ml water (approx)	*or top of milk*
40g butter	*1 egg yolk*

Skin and slice the onion. Place the turkey bones, onion, mace, and seasoning in a pan. Add about 600ml water, cover the pan, and simmer for at least 1 hour. Strain, and reserve 400ml of the stock.

Melt the butter in a pan, stir in the flour, and cook for 2 minutes without browning. Gradually stir in the reserved stock. Bring to the boil, stirring all the time, and cook for 10 minutes. Dice the chicken or turkey meat. Add the nutmeg and turkey pieces to the sauce, and re-season if required. Heat thoroughly for about 20 minutes. Mix the cream or milk with the egg yolk, and stir in a little of the hot sauce. Return the mixture to the pan, and heat gently without boiling for about 5 minutes.

Serve hot with boiled rice.

Chaudfroid of Chicken

6 helpings

6 cooked chicken joints	*lettuce leaves*
125ml aspic jelly	*3 sticks celery*
375ml mayonnaise	*2 hard-boiled eggs*

Garnish

stoned olives or gherkins	*tomato wedges or slices*

Remove the skin, excess fat, and bones from the chicken joints, keeping the pieces in neat shapes. Melt the aspic jelly, and leave to cool. Just before it reaches setting point, while still tepid, add half the mayonnaise, and whisk in. Blend to a smooth consistency. Place the chicken joints on a wire cooling tray and coat with the mayonnaise sauce as soon as it reaches a good coating consistency. Arrange the lettuce leaves on a serving dish and place the chicken joints on top. Prepare and chop the celery, slice the eggs, and arrange these round the chicken. Spoon the remaining mayonnaise over the celery and egg. Garnish with the olives or gherkins and the tomatoes.

Devilled Turkey (1)

3–4 helpings

350g cold roast turkey

Devilling Butter

25g butter	*1 × 2.5ml spoon curry*
1 × 2.5ml spoon	*paste*
Cayenne pepper	*a pinch of ground ginger*
1 × 2.5ml spoon ground	
black pepper	

Mix together all the ingredients for the devilling butter. Divide the turkey into convenient portions for serving, remove the skin, and score the flesh deeply. Spread lightly with the butter and leave for 1 hour (longer if a highly seasoned dish is wanted). Grill the meat for about 8 minutes, turning once, until crisp and brown.

Serve with Piquant Sauce (p702).

Note For Devilled Turkey (2), see p1311.

Turkey Loaf

6–8 helpings

50g long-grain rice	25g (approx) thyme and
225g cooked turkey meat	parsley stuffing mix
4 rashers streaky bacon,	grated rind of ½ lemon
without rinds	1 × 5ml spoon paprika
salt and pepper	fat for greasing
1 egg	

Cook the rice in boiling salted water for 10 minutes. Mince the turkey and the bacon rashers, and mix with the salt, pepper, and egg. Drain the rice and add to the turkey mixture. Mix thoroughly.

Make up the stuffing according to the directions on the packet. Add the lemon rind and paprika. Mix well. Place half the turkey mixture in a greased tin, and spread with stuffing; cover with the remaining turkey mixture. Cook in a fairly hot oven, 190°C, Gas 5, for 35 minutes. Serve hot or cold.

Chicken or Turkey Mousse

4 helpings

225g cooked chicken **or**	1 × 15ml spoon gelatine
turkey breast meat	3 egg yolks
275ml double cream	salt and pepper
275ml chicken stock **or**	4 × 10ml spoons
broth with fat removed	mayonnaise

Garnish

watercress sprigs	small lettuce leaves

Remove any skin, gristle, and fat from the poultry. Mince the meat finely. Whip the cream until semi-stiff, then chill. Put 100ml of the stock or broth in a heatproof container, and sprinkle on the gelatine. Leave until softened. Meanwhile, beat the egg yolks

lightly and stir into the rest of the stock or broth. Season if required, and cook gently in the top of a double boiler until the custard thickens. Remove from the heat, and turn into a chilled bowl. Dissolve the softened gelatine by standing the container in a pan of hot water. Stir until dissolved; then stir it into the egg custard, blending well. Blend the minced poultry meat in thoroughly. Stand the bowl in a basin of cold water or crushed ice, or chill until the mousse mixture begins to thicken at the edges. Fold in the chilled whipped cream and the mayonnaise at once. Turn into a wetted 1 litre mould and chill until set. Turn out on to a platter, and garnish with watercress sprigs and small lettuce leaves.

Chicken Mayonnaise

6 helpings

1 cold cooked chicken **or**	275ml aspic jelly
6 cooked chicken joints	425ml mayonnaise

Garnish

pickled walnuts	pieces of red and green pepper

Joint the whole chicken, if used; remove the skin, excess fat, and as much bone as possible, and trim the joints to a neat shape. Melt the aspic jelly. When almost cool, blend 150ml of it carefully into the mayonnaise. Beat well to blend thoroughly. Place the pieces of chicken on a wire cooling rack, and when the sauce is a good coating consistency, coat the pieces, using a large spoon. Cut the pickled nuts and the pieces of red and green pepper into attractive shapes for garnishing, dry well on soft kitchen paper, and stick on the chicken with dabs of half-set mayonnaise. Melt the remaining aspic jelly again if necessary; cool until it is on the point of setting, and use to coat the chicken thinly.

Chicken or Turkey Salad
See p839.

Galantine of Chicken

8–10 helpings

1 cooked boiling fowl	*450g sausage-meat*
salt and pepper	*750ml chicken stock*
*100g ham **or** tongue*	* (approx)*
2 hard-boiled eggs	*1 chicken stock cube*
6 mushrooms	*500ml White*
10–15g pistachio nuts	* Chaudfroid sauce*
* **or** almonds*	* (p711)*
	125ml aspic jelly

Garnish
chopped pimento	*sliced hard-boiled egg*
strips of lemon rind	

Cut down the back of the fowl, then remove all the bones neatly. Spread out the boned bird like a spatchcocked chicken (p630), distributing any loose pieces of meat evenly over the surface. Season well. Cut the ham or tongue into 1 × 3cm strips, slice the eggs, and chop the mushrooms. Blanch, skin, and chop the nuts. Spread 225g of the sausage-meat on the bird. Arrange the ham or tongue, egg slices, mushrooms, and nuts on top. Season well, then cover with the remaining sausage-meat.

Lift the 2 halves of the bird, and bring them together so that it is as near its original shape as possible. Wrap the bird in foil. Heat the chicken stock and add the cube. Put in the chicken in foil, and simmer gently for 2½ hours. Allow to cool slightly in the stock. Remove and drain. Tighten the foil to allow for any shrinkage while cooking. Press the 'parcel' between 2 large plates or boards and leave until quite cold.

Unwrap, remove the skin, and wipe away any excess grease. Spoon the Chaudfroid sauce over the chicken. Chop the aspic coarsely and place round the chicken. Garnish in a decorative pattern with the pimento, lemon rind, and egg.

Duck and Goose

ROAST DUCK AND GOOSE DISHES

Roast Goose with Fruit Stuffing and Red Cabbage

6–8 helpings

350g prunes	*salt and pepper*
1 goose with giblets	*450g cooking apples*
1.5 litres water	*1 × 15ml spoon*
½ lemon	* redcurrant jelly*

Red Cabbage
1.5kg red cabbage	*75ml malt **or** cider*
50g butter	* vinegar*
50g Demerara sugar	*salt and pepper*
75ml water	

Soak the prunes overnight. Remove the giblets from the goose and simmer them in 1.5 litres water until the liquid is reduced by half. Weigh the goose and calculate the cooking time at 20 minutes for every 500g. Remove the excess fat usually found around the vent. Rinse the inside of the bird, then rub the skin with lemon. Season with salt and pepper. Remove the stones from the prunes and chop the flesh. Peel and core the apples and chop them roughly. Mix with the prunes and season to taste. Stuff into the body of the bird. Place in a very hot oven, 230°C, Gas 8, reduce the temperature immediately to moderate, 180°C, Gas 4, and cook for the calculated time.

Meanwhile, prepare the red cabbage, shred finely. Melt the butter in a large flameproof casserole. Add the sugar and cabbage and stir well. Add the water, vinegar, and seasoning, cover and cook in the bottom of the oven for about 2 hours, stirring occasionally.

When the goose is cooked, drain off the excess fat, retaining the juices in the pan. Add the redcurrant jelly and stir until it melts.

Serve the gravy and red cabbage separately.

English Roast Duck

4–5 helpings

1 duck	*3 ×10ml spoons flour*
sage and onion stuffing	*275ml stock*
(p378)	*salt and pepper*
fat for basting	

Fill the duck with sage and onion stuffing, and truss for roasting. Heat the fat and baste the duck well. Roast in a fairly hot oven, 190–200°C, Gas 5–6, covered with buttered paper, for 1–1½ hours or until tender, basting frequently. Uncover for the last 30 minutes. Keep the duck hot. Pour off the fat from the roasting tin, sprinkle in the flour, and brown it. Stir in the stock, simmer for 3–4 minutes, season, and strain. Remove the trussing string from the duck.

Serve hot with traditional accompaniments (p624) and Fennel and Cucumber Salad (p823).

Roast Duck with Orange

4–5 helpings

1 duck	*3 ×10ml spoons flour*
basic herb forcemeat	*275ml stock*
(p375)	*salt and pepper*
fat for basting	

Garnish
1 large orange	*1 ×15ml spoon brandy*

Truss and roast the duck as for English Roast Duck, but use basic forcemeat instead of sage and onion stuffing. Meanwhile, pare the rind of the orange and remove all the pith. Cut the orange into segments, discard the membranes, and soak the segments in the brandy. Cut the rind into thin strips, boil in a little water for 5 minutes, then drain. Heat the orange segments gently in the brandy. Serve the cooked duck with the strips of rind and hot orange segments as a garnish.

Fillets of Duck Bigarade

2 helpings

1 duck	*275ml Bigarade sauce*
300g Duchesse potatoes	*(p707)*
(p793)	*1 × 5ml spoon salad oil*
2 small oranges	

Truss the duck, and roast in a fairly hot oven, 190–200°C, Gas 5–6, for 1–1½ hours or until tender, basting when necessary. Pipe the potato mixture in a border around the serving dish, brown it in the oven, and keep hot. Grate the rind of the oranges, add to the Bigarade sauce, and keep hot. Peel the orange and divide it into segments; heat these in a basin over hot water, and mix with the salad oil. Remove the breast from the duck. Cut it into neat strips while still hot, and arrange them overlapping each other within the potato border. Pour the sauce over the duck and garnish with the orange segments.

Salmi of Duck

4 helpings

1 Spanish onion	*25g flour*
*1 duck **or** trimmings*	*350ml brown stock*
from 2 cold roast ducks	*(p329)*
fat for basting	*12 stoned green olives*
40g butter	*salt and pepper*

If using a whole duck, skin and slice the onion into a roasting tin, put the prepared duck on top, baste with hot fat, and roast in a fairly hot oven, 190–200°C, Gas 5–6, for 1–1½ hours or until tender.

Melt the butter in a small saucepan, add the flour, and cook slowly until the flour browns. Stir in the stock and simmer until thick. Keep warm. Remove the trussing string from the roast duck and cut it into small joints. Add either the freshly roasted or the cold duck to the sauce with the olives; season, and re-heat thoroughly. Sieve the onion or chop it finely, and add to the duck. Drain off the fat from the roasting tin and add the sediment to the sauce.

The salmi can be served on a croûte of fried bread with the sauce and olives poured over it.

Duck with Green Olives

4–5 helpings

500ml water	2 × 15ml spoons goose,
giblets of 1 duck	duck **or** chicken fat
2 carrots	2 slices stale white bread
2 medium-sized onions	24 stuffed green olives
bouquet garni	3 small carrots
salt and pepper	
1 duck	

Put the water in a saucepan with the duck giblets but reserve the liver (this can be used for another dish). Cut up the carrots and onions roughly and add them to the pan with the bouquet garni and seasoning to taste. Simmer uncovered for about 40 minutes to obtain about 375ml well-flavoured stock. Put to one side.

Meanwhile, season the inside of the duck. Heat the fat in a heavy flameproof casserole, put in the duck, and brown it on all sides. Reduce the heat, cover the casserole, and cook slowly for 15 minutes. Remove the duck, joint it, and return the joints to the casserole. Grate or crumble the bread, sprinkle it over the duck, and strain the stock over the dish. Plunge the olives into boiling water for 1 minute, then add them to the casserole. Slice the small carrots thinly, and add them also. Cover the casserole, place over low heat, and simmer for 45 minutes.

Serve with plain boiled rice or saffron rice (p524).

Stuffed Boned Duck

6–8 helpings

100g onion	1 egg
25g butter **or** margarine	50g peanuts
100g long-grain rice	225g ham
275ml chicken stock	50g seedless raisins
1 bay leaf	1 duck
salt and pepper	2 × 15ml spoons corn oil
1 small red pepper	

Skin and chop the onion finely. Melt the butter or margarine, and fry the onion without browning. Stir in the rice and cook until it is translucent. Pour on the stock, add the bay leaf, salt and pepper, and cook for 12–15 minutes or until the rice is tender and the stock has been absorbed. Drain if necessary, and remove the bay leaf.

Wash the pepper, remove the membranes and seeds. Place in cold water, bring to the boil, and cook for 5 minutes. Drain well and cool under cold water. Beat the egg until liquid. Chop the peanuts coarsely. Mince the ham, raisins, pepper, peanuts, and rice together, add the egg, and stir in. Add salt and pepper.

Remove any trussing string from the duck. Use a small pointed knife to loosen and remove the wishbone. Slit the skin right along the backbone. Ease the flesh away from the bones either side of the backbone and down as far as the leg joints. Place the breast meat flat, skin side down, on a board. At the leg joints, cut the sinew joining them to the body; then, holding the leg firmly, gradually scrape and push the flesh away from the bones. Remove the bones. Repeat the process on the other leg. Cut away the first 2 joints of the wing, scrape the flesh down so that the bones can be pulled out. Repeat the process on the other wing. Continue carefully cutting away the flesh from the breastbone, being careful not to puncture the skin. Carefully remove the breastbone. If serving the duck hot, cover the bones with water, cook, and make stock for the gravy.

Put the stuffing in the body of the bird, make it a good shape, and sew the skin together. Heat the oil in a roasting tin in a fairly hot oven, 190–200°C, Gas 5–6. Place the duck in the tin, breast side up, and baste with the hot oil. Cook for 1–1½ hours. Serve hot or cold.

Note The above directions for boning can be followed for any poultry or game bird.

BRAISED AND SIMILAR DISHES

Braised Duck

4–5 helpings

1 duck	40g flour
2 onions	575ml brown stock
2 sage leaves	(p329)
bouquet garni	salt and pepper
40g butter	mushrooms (optional)

Truss the duck, and roast it for 20 minutes in a hot oven, 220–230°C, Gas 7–8. Skin and slice the onions. Place the duck in a saucepan with the onions, sage, and bouquet garni, cover tightly, and cook slowly for 45 minutes. Melt the butter in a saucepan, add the flour, and brown well, then stir in the stock. Simmer for 20 minutes, then strain. When the duck is tender, remove the trussing string. Season the sauce and serve in a sauce-boat. Some mushrooms may be added to the sauce, if liked.

Note Since the skin of a duck is fatty, it is often open-roasted in a hot oven instead of being sealed in fat as the first stage in braising.

Duck Casserole

4–5 helpings

1 duck	425ml (approx) brown
salt and pepper	stock (p329)
25g flour	225g shelled green peas
4 shallots	1 × 5ml spoon chopped
100g mushrooms	mint

Joint and skin the duck. Season the flour, and dip the joints in it. Prepare and chop the shallots and mushrooms finely, and put them with the duck in a casserole. Just cover with stock, put on a tight-fitting lid, and cook in a fairly hot oven, 190–200°C, Gas 5–6, for 45 minutes. Add the peas and mint, and continue cooking for about 30 minutes until the duck is tender. Re-season if required. Serve from the casserole.

Braised Duck with Chestnuts

4–5 helpings

1 duck	425ml Espagnole sauce
larding bacon (optional)	(p707)
50g butter	100ml (approx) port
bouquet garni	(optional)
6 black peppercorns	1 × 10ml spoon
2 cloves	redcurrant jelly
575ml (approx) general	salt and pepper
household stock (p329)	

Stuffing

450g chestnuts	salt and pepper
1 Spanish onion	1 egg

Mirepoix

2 onions	2 carrots
1 small turnip	1 stick of celery

Garnish

watercress sprigs	forcemeat balls (p375)

Make the stuffing first. Slit the rounded sides of the chestnuts. Boil them for 15–20 minutes, then remove the shells and skins, and chop or mince all but 6 nuts. Skin the onion and cook in water until tender, chop it finely, and add it to the chestnuts. Season well, and bind with egg. Stuff the duck with the chestnut mixture; then truss, and lard it with bacon, if liked.

Prepare and slice the vegetables for the mirepoix. Put them in a large saucepan with the butter, lay the duck on the vegetables, and cover the pan; fry gently for 20 minutes, then add the bouquet garni, spices, and enough stock to cover three-quarters of the mirepoix. Cover with buttered paper, put on a lid, and simmer gently for about 2 hours or until the duck is tender. Add more stock if necessary during cooking to prevent it burning.

Heat the Espagnole sauce, add the 6 chestnuts, the port if used, and the jelly. Re-heat and re-season if required. When the duck is ready, remove the paper and trussing string, and place it in a hot oven, 220°C, Gas 7, to crisp the bacon. Serve on a hot dish, garnished with watercress sprigs and forcemeat balls. Serve the sauce separately.

Braised Duck with Turnips

4–5 helpings

1 duck
mirepoix and other
  braising ingredients
  for Braised Duck with
  Chestnuts (p649)
meat glaze (p397)
  (optional)

basic forcemeat (p375)
  (optional)
3 young turnips
575ml general household
  stock (p329)
75ml (approx) medium-
  dry sherry (optional)
salt and pepper

Braise the duck on a mirepoix of vegetables as in Braised Duck with Chestnuts, and brush it with warm meat glaze if liked, before crisping it in the oven. It can be braised with or without forcemeat.

Meanwhile, peel the turnips, dice them, and boil until tender. Drain, keep them hot, and strain the stock. Boil it quickly until reduced by half; add the sherry if used, and season to taste. Serve the duck on a hot dish with turnips piled at either end. Serve the sauce separately.

Duck and Orange Curry

4–5 helpings

1 duck
salt
2 × 15ml spoons ghee or
  clarified butter (p886)
  or margarine or
  vegetable oil
2 large onions
2 cloves garlic
1 × 2.5ml spoon
  cardamom seeds
1 × 10ml spoon finely
  chopped ginger root

1 × 5ml spoon ground
  cumin
1 × 5ml spoon turmeric
1 × 10ml spoon ground
  coriander
1 × 5cm piece cinnamon
  bark
6 cloves
freshly ground black
  pepper
750ml unsweetened
  orange juice

Joint the duck into 4 or 6 pieces, removing any surplus fat. Season well with salt. Heat the ghee, fat or oil, add the duck, and fry for 15–20 minutes, turning frequently. Remove the duck from the pan and put to one side. Skin and chop the onions and cloves of garlic, add them to the fat left in the pan, and fry until transparent. Add all the spices and the orange juice and bring to the boil, stirring all the time. Replace the duck in the pan, cover, and simmer for $1\frac{1}{4}$–$1\frac{1}{2}$ hours. Season with a little extra salt if required.

Serve with rice and other curry accompaniments (p388).

Duck with Green Peas

4–5 helpings

1kg fresh peas
12 button or spring
  onions
225g rashers streaky
  bacon
50g butter
1 duck

425ml chicken stock
bouquet garni
salt and pepper
sugar
1 small round lettuce
  (optional)

Shell the peas and put to one side. Prepare the onions, and parboil them with the bacon. Drain. In an ovenproof casserole or saucepan large enough to hold the duck, melt the butter, add the onions and bacon, and toss quickly until light brown in colour. Remove from the pan. Put the duck in the pan and brown it well all over, then remove it.

Put a third of the stock into the pan and boil down to half its quantity, then add the remainder of the stock with the duck, onions, bacon, peas, and bouquet garni. Season lightly with salt and pepper and a pinch of sugar. Bring to the boil, then cover the pan and cook in a fairly hot oven, 190°C, Gas 5, for about 45 minutes. Baste from time to time.

Remove the duck and place on a serving dish; surround with the peas, onions, and bacon. Reduce the cooking liquor by boiling, then pour it over the duck.

A quartered lettuce may be added to the duck and peas when cooking; in this case, cut and serve the duck in quarters, and garnish with lettuce leaves as well as the other vegetables.

Duck Stuffed with Liver

4–5 helpings

50g butter	275ml brown stock
1 large duck	(p329)
2 × 10ml spoons	100ml (approx) claret
chopped shallot	(optional)
1 × 10ml spoon flour	bouquet garni
	lemon juice

Stuffing

duck's heart and liver	1 × 5ml spoon chopped
1 small onion	parsley
25g butter	salt and pepper
4 × 10ml spoons soft	
white breadcrumbs	

Prepare the stuffing first. Chop the liver and heart finely. Skin and parboil the onion and chop it finely. Melt the butter and add to the liver and heart with the onion, breadcrumbs, parsley, and seasoning. Stuff the duck with this mixture, then truss it.

Melt the butter and fry the duck with the chopped shallot until brown. Remove the duck. Stir the flour into the butter and brown it. Stir in the stock gradually, bring to boiling point, and add the claret, if used. Replace the duck in the pan and add the bouquet garni and lemon juice to taste. Cover with a tight-fitting lid. Cook in a moderate oven, 180°C, Gas 4, for 1–1½ hours or until the duck is tender. Remove the trussing string, and joint the duck. Arrange it on a warmed serving dish and pour the sauce over it.

Duckling in Red Wine

4 helpings

1 duckling	400ml stock
salt and pepper	1 medium-sized carrot
2 medium-sized onions	2 sticks celery
1 bay leaf	grated rind of 1 orange
250ml red wine	**or** lemon
100g bacon	100g button mushrooms
1 × 10ml spoon cooking	
oil	

Cut the duckling into quarters and season well. Skin and chop the onions finely, and put into a bowl with the duck quarters, bay leaf, and red wine. Cover, and leave to marinate for 2 hours. Remove the duck portions from the wine and dry on soft kitchen paper; strain and reserve the liquid.

Chop the bacon. Heat the oil in a pan and cook the bacon gently for 3–4 minutes. Add the duckling and brown it all over. Drain well, and put in a casserole. Heat the stock and pour it into the casserole. Cook in a moderate oven, 180°C, Gas 4, for 15 minutes.

Meanwhile, prepare and slice the carrot and celery. Add to the casserole with the grated rind, mushrooms, and the reserved marinade. Cover, and cook for 1½–2 hours until tender. Skim off any surplus fat before serving.

DISHES USING COOKED DUCK AND GOOSE

Duck in Brown Sauce

4 helpings

500g shelled peas or
* young broad beans*
1 sprig of mint
1 × 5ml spoon sugar
400g (approx)
* trimmings of 2 cold*
* roast ducks*

300–400ml foundation
* brown sauce (p698)*
salt and pepper
lemon juice

Parboil the peas or beans with the mint and sugar; drain well. Shred the duck meat, cutting larger pieces into neat dice. Heat the brown sauce, add the meat and the peas or beans, re-season if required, and simmer for 10 minutes. Add a little lemon juice to taste just before serving.

Duck in Orange and Claret

4–5 helpings

1 cold roast duck
25g butter
1 onion
25g flour
550ml brown stock
* (p329)*

1 orange
100ml claret
salt and pepper

Carve the duck ready for serving. Melt the butter in a saucepan, skin and chop the onion finely, and fry it in the butter. Stir in the flour and cook gently until brown. Add the stock, stir until boiling, and simmer for 10 minutes. Pare the rind of the orange, cut it into very thin strips, and squeeze out the juice from the orange. Add the rind to the sauce with the orange juice, claret, and pieces of duck. Season to taste. Simmer very gently for 30 minutes. Arrange the meat on a serving dish and pour the sauce over it.

Duck and Red Cabbage

4–6 helpings

450g red cabbage
50g butter
good gravy or stock
salt and pepper
400g (approx)
* trimmings of 2 cold*
* roast ducks*

1 × 15ml spoon vinegar
1 × 15ml spoon
* Demerara sugar*

Wash and drain the cabbage, shred it finely, and cook gently with the butter for 1 hour in a tightly covered pan. Add gravy or stock if necessary to prevent burning, season well, and shake the pan occasionally. Shred the duck meat and heat in a little of the gravy or stock. Add the vinegar and sugar to the cabbage and turn it on to a hot dish. Arrange the duck on top.

Duck or Goose on Croûtes

4 helpings

350g trimmings of roast
* goose or duck*
2 onions
50g butter
25g flour
550ml brown stock
* (p329)*
2 cloves

1 blade of mace
6 allspice berries
6 small mushrooms
salt and pepper
8 croûtes fried bread,
* 9cm in diameter*

Cut the meat into neat pieces. Skin and chop the onions finely, melt the butter in a saucepan, and fry the onions until lightly browned. Stir in the flour and cook slowly until nut-brown. Stir in the stock and boil for 10 minutes. Tie the spices in muslin and add with the mushrooms to the pan. Season to taste, and simmer gently for 20 minutes. Arrange the pieces of meat neatly on the croûtes, remove the spices from the sauce, re-season if required, and pour the sauce over the meat.

Serve apple sauce separately.

Guinea-fowl

Roast Guinea-fowl

4–5 helpings

1 guinea-fowl	*2 rashers fat bacon*
50g butter	*flour for dredging*
salt and pepper	

Garnish
watercress sprigs   *French dressing*

Wipe the bird, mix the butter and seasoning, place it in the body of the bird, and on the thighs. Lay rashers of bacon over the breast, and roast in a moderate oven, 180°C, Gas 4, for 1–1½ hours, basting frequently. When the bird is almost cooked, dredge the breast with flour, baste, and finish cooking.

Wash and dry the watercress, and toss it lightly in French dressing. Remove any trussing strings from the bird, and garnish with the watercress.

Serve with browned breadcrumbs (p375), Bread Sauce (p713), and Espagnole Sauce (p707).

Guinea-fowl with Grapes

4–6 helpings

1 guinea-fowl with	*1 sprig of parsley*
giblets	*6 rashers streaky bacon*
250ml water	*25g flour*
bouquet garni	*125ml dry white wine*
salt and pepper	*225g white grapes*
50g butter	*lemon juice*

Put the guinea-fowl giblets in a pan with 250ml water, the bouquet garni, salt and pepper. Cook gently for 40 minutes to make a good stock. Put a knob of butter and the parsley in the body of the bird; spread the remaining butter thickly over the breast and cover with the rashers of bacon. Roast as for Roast Guinea-fowl. Remove the bird from the oven, and take off the trussing string. Transfer to a warmed serving dish and keep hot.

Drain the fat from the tin, leaving only a thin layer, just enough to absorb the flour. Stir round to scrape up the pan juices. Scatter in the flour and brown it lightly. Stir in the wine and 150ml of the giblet stock, bring to the boil, stirring all the time, and cook for 5 minutes. Skin and de-pip the grapes, and add them. Heat through, add a little lemon juice to bring out the flavour, and re-season if required.

GAME BIRDS AND ANIMALS

It is difficult to define any exact time to " hang " a pheasant; but any one
possessed of the instincts of gastronomical science, can at once detect the right
moment when a pheasant should be taken down, in the same way as a good cook
knows whether a bird should be removed from the spit, or have a turn or two more.

Game birds and animals are those hunted for sport
and for food. In the UK, the killing of game is
restricted by the British Game Laws and by the
Wild Life Protection Act. A game licence is required to shoot any game animal protected by the
law, and it is an offence to shoot during the closed
season, which varies according to the nesting and
mating patterns of the particular species. Rabbits
and woodpigeons are not protected by the law and
have no closed season. Rabbits are also farmed and
imported into the UK on a large scale, and are
therefore easily available all year round.

Game Birds

The flavour of game is always best in unfrozen,
well-hung birds, and young birds are the most
tender and therefore the best for roasting and
grilling. In selecting a bird, you should look for one
with a firm, plump breast, and if it is unplucked,
soft plumage and supple feet and beak are good
indications that the bird is young.

Capercailzie

A very large bird of the grouse family, now rare in
the UK. In season October 1 to January 31.

Grouse

The most common and popular grouse is the red or
Scottish type. It is in season between August 12
and December 10. The best birds for the table are
those shot from mid-August to mid-October. An
average-sized grouse serves 1 or 2 people.

A *blackcock*, sometimes known as heathpoult, is
a larger type of grouse, known for its unusually
good flavour. It is in season from August 20 to
December 10.

Partridge

There are two varieties, the grey which is fairly
plentiful in East Anglia, and the larger red-legged
French partridge. Both are in season from
September 1 to February 1. The best table birds
are obtained in October and November.

Pheasant

This is the best known game bird, and (with grouse)
the most widely available in its season. An unplucked cock bird is easily identified by its colourful plumage, but the smaller, undistinguished grey
hen bird is usually better-flavoured and more
tender. A hen bird will serve 3 people, a cock
should serve 4. Pheasants are sold and served
either singly or, often, as a brace (a pair). They are
in season from October 1 to February 1. The
best months for table birds are November and
December.

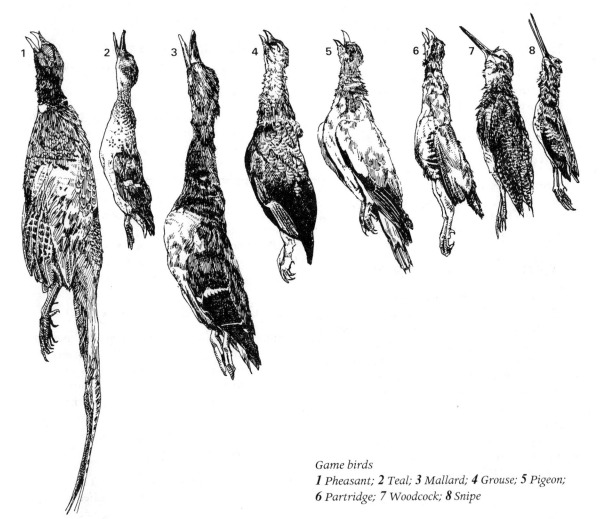

Game birds
1 Pheasant; 2 Teal; 3 Mallard; 4 Grouse; 5 Pigeon;
6 Partridge; 7 Woodcock; 8 Snipe

Mallard, Pintail, Teal, and Widgeon

There are many varieties of wild duck but these are the most common. The largest is the mallard, which should serve 2 or 3 people. The teal, being the smallest, only serves 1 person. All these birds are in season from September 1 to January 31 (to February 20 on the foreshore), and they are all cooked in the same way. The best months for eating are November and December.

Pigeon

There are two types of pigeon. Woodpigeons are the larger, and have a stronger flavour and dark flesh. Tame pigeons have pale flesh and are cooked like young chickens. Both are available all year round but are at their best from August to October.

Quail

A very small bird, related to the partridge, weighing about 50g when plucked. Wild quail, common in the US and elsewhere, have a delicate flavour, much esteemed by gourmets. All quail sold in Britain are farmed, and they are often sold pre-packed and frozen. Two birds are usually served per person. Available all year round.

Ortolans, which are not generally available in Britain but may be found abroad, are treated like quail.

Snipe

These small birds are seldom found in shops. They serve 1 person and are in season from August 12 to January 31. The flavour is generally best in November.

Woodcock

Related to snipe, and also seldom found in shops, woodcock is prized for its flavour. Heavy for its size, a 150g bird serves 1 person. In season from October 1 to January 31.

HANGING GAME BIRDS

All water birds should be eaten as fresh as possible. Most other game birds of any size should be hung before being eaten to tenderize the meat, and to give it the characteristic gamey flavour. The birds should hang in a cool place where air can circulate freely. The time for which it should be hung depends on the type of bird, the weather, and on individual taste. A pheasant may mature in 3–4 days in warm weather but only after 10 days in cold weather. Small birds such as woodcock need only 2–3 days hanging, if any.

Most game birds should be hung by the neck, unplucked, and undrawn. They are ready for cooking when the tail feathers come out easily. If there is a distinct bluish or greenish tinge to the skin, they have probably been hung too long for most tastes. In this case, they should be washed with salted water containing a little vinegar, then rinsed. Fresh powdered charcoal tied in muslin and left in the crop during cooking will also help to remove any over-strong flavour.

PLUCKING, DRAWING, TRUSSING, AND JOINTING GAME BIRDS

For most birds, follow the general procedures for poultry (pp616–20).

Very small birds, such as snipe and woodcock, are cooked without being drawn. They are traditionally dressed with their heads left on, and skewered with the bird's own long beak. If the head is removed, the bird is just skewered into a neat shape for cooking.

Traditionally, pheasant is roasted with its head left on, but the modern style is to truss as for chicken.

COOKING GAME BIRDS

Unless they are old or badly damaged by shot, most game birds are plainly roasted. The basic recipe for roast grouse on p657 can be used for any other tender, unblemished, and unstuffed bird, by adjusting the cooking time to the appropriate one in the chart below.

Roasting Time Chart

These roasting times are for unstuffed birds. Allow up to 10 minutes extra for a small stuffed bird up to 375g, 15–18 minutes extra for a bigger bird.

Blackcock   *40–50 minutes*
Grouse   *25–35 minutes*
Pheasant   *45–60 minutes*
Partridge   *20–30 minutes*
Teal   *15–20 minutes*
Widgeon   *25–35 minutes*
Pintail   *20–30 minutes*
Mallard   *30–45 minutes*
Tame pigeon   *30–40 minutes*
Squab (young pigeon)   *15–25 minutes*
Woodpigeon   *35–45 minutes*
Other small birds   *10–15 minutes*

Note If you joint or cut up a game bird before cooking, eg for a pie, always cut off and discard the vent end of the body, since it may give the dish a bitter flavour.

WHAT TO SERVE WITH GAME BIRDS

Since most game birds are plainly roasted, the same traditional accompaniments are served with all of them. These are:

1) A croûte of fried or toasted bread to fit under medium-sized and small birds or fried bread-crumbs (p396) for larger birds
2) Thin gravy (p727) or giblet gravy (p728)
3) Game chips (p792) or potato straws (p792)
4) Bread Sauce (p713) for grouse, pheasant, and partridge; Cumberland Sauce (p718) for wild duck; Piquant Sauce (p702) for woodpigeon
5) Redcurrant or other sharp fruit jelly
6) Watercress sprigs as garnish
7) A green vegetable such as Brussels sprouts or a green salad is usually the only other accompaniment.

In all the following recipes, the birds are assumed to be ready for marinating or other cooking preparations.

GROUSE AND BLACKCOCK

Roast Grouse

2 helpings

a brace of grouse
red wine marinade (p730) (see Method)
50g butter
salt and pepper
2 rashers fat bacon, without rinds

fat for basting
2 croûtes fried bread, each big enough to put under 1 bird
flour for dredging

Garnish
watercress sprigs

Marinate the birds if home-shot or at all tough (birds sold as oven-ready need not be marinated as a rule).

Cream the butter with enough salt and pepper to give a good flavour, and put half into the body of each bird. Truss for roasting. Cover the breast of each bird with a bacon rasher. Place on a trivet or rack in a roasting tin, and roast in a fairly hot oven, 190°C, Gas 5, for about 30 minutes, until tender. Baste with fat several times while cooking.

Half-way through the cooking time, put the croûtes in the tin, under the birds. Remove the bacon 7–8 minutes before the end of the cooking time, dredge the birds lightly with flour, baste well, and return to the oven to finish cooking and to brown. Serve the birds on the croûtes and garnish with watercress sprigs.

Serve thin gravy (p727), Bread Sauce (p713), and fried breadcrumbs (p396) separately.

Note A grouse can be cut in half lengthways through the breast-bone and spine, to make 2 helpings. Each half is served cut side down. If necessary, a third helping can be carved by removing the legs and thighs with a small portion of extra meat such as the 'oyster' on the back, before splitting the bird.

Highland Grouse

4 helpings

250g raspberries	*salt and pepper*
2 young grouse	*grated rind of 1 lemon*
50g butter	

Prepare the raspberries. Place half the butter inside each bird and sprinkle well with salt and pepper. Mix the raspberries and lemon rind together and fill the cavities in the birds with the mixture. Put 5mm water in a deep flameproof dish with a lid which will just hold the birds. Place the birds and any remaining raspberry mixture in the dish, and cover. Cook in a fairly hot oven, 200°C, Gas 6, for 35–45 minutes. Remove the lid, and cook for a further 10 minutes, to brown the birds.

Serve with creamed potatoes and a green vegetable.

Note For other game stuffings, see the chapter on Stuffings, Garnishes and Accompaniments.

Grilled Young Blackcock

6 helpings

2 young blackcock	*1 × 5ml spoon lemon*
50g butter (approx)	*juice*
salt and pepper	*anchovy essence*
250ml foundation brown	
sauce (p698)	

Split the birds down the back, cut off the legs at the first joint, and skewer as flat as possible as for Spatchcocked Chicken (p630). Melt the butter. Brush the birds on both sides with melted butter. Season lightly and grill under high heat for 5 minutes, then reduce the heat, and cook for 25–30 minutes, turning frequently. Brush with more butter during cooking if necessary. Make or re-heat the sauce as required, and add the lemon juice, anchovy essence, and seasoning to taste.

Serve the birds with game chips (p792) or potato straws (p792), and offer the sauce separately.

Roast Blackcock

6 helpings

50g butter	*2 croûtes fried bread,*
salt and pepper	*each big enough to put*
2 blackcock	*under 1 bird*
4 rashers fat bacon	

Garnish
watercress sprigs **or**
lemon wedges

Cream the butter with salt and pepper to taste. Put the seasoned butter in the birds, truss them, and cover the breasts with bacon. Roast on a rack in a fairly hot oven, 190°C, Gas 5, for 45–50 minutes, basting frequently. Half-way through the cooking time, put the croûtes in the tin, under the birds. When the birds are almost cooked, remove the bacon, and raise the heat to brown the breasts. Serve garnished with watercress sprigs or lemon wedges, on the croûtes of fried bread.

Serve thin gravy (p727), Bread Sauce (p713), and fried breadcrumbs (p396) separately.

Note The breast and thighs are the best meat on a blackcock. Carve the breast into thin slices as for chicken, or, if the bird is small, detach the breast whole, and slice it in half.

Young Blackcock or Grouse Fillets Financière

5–6 helpings

2 young blackcock **or**	*250ml foundation brown*
grouse	*sauce (p698)*
1 medium-sized onion	*butter for frying*
1 small carrot	*12 button mushrooms*
½ turnip	*75ml (approx) sherry* **or**
3 rashers streaky bacon,	*Madeira (optional)*
without rinds	*salt and pepper*
100ml game stock	
(p330)	

Joint the birds and cut the meat into fillets. Prepare and slice the vegetables and place them in a sauté or frying pan with the bacon; put the fillets on top.

Add the stock, cover with a buttered paper and a tight-fitting lid, and simmer gently for 30 minutes.

Meanwhile, heat the brown sauce. Melt the butter, fry the mushrooms, and keep them hot. Add the wine to the sauce, if used. Season to taste and keep the sauce hot.

When the fillets are cooked, arrange them on a hot dish, strain the sauce over them, and use the mushrooms and bacon as a garnish.

French Game Pie

6–8 helpings

1 blackcock **or** cock pheasant **or** 2 large partridges **or** 2–3 pigeons, depending on size	2–3 rashers bacon, without rinds
350g lean veal	sage and onion stuffing (p378)
350g lean pork	125ml game stock (p330)
1 × 2.5ml spoon dried mixed herbs	100g prepared puff pastry (p1253)
salt and pepper	flour for rolling out
8 mushrooms	beaten egg **or** milk for glazing

Cut the bird or birds into neat joints and season the pieces lightly. Mince the veal and pork. Season well with the mixed herbs, salt, and pepper. Chop the mushrooms finely and mix them in. Chop the bacon rashers. Form the stuffing into balls.

Put a layer of minced meat in the bottom of a 1.5 litre pie dish, then a layer of game, then one of bacon and the stuffing balls. Repeat these layers until the dish is full. Moisten with the stock.

Roll out the pastry on a lightly floured surface, to make a lid for the dish. Moisten the rim of the dish and fit on the lid. Decorate with the trimmings. Glaze, and bake in a fairly hot oven, 200°C, Gas 6, for 30 minutes. Reduce the heat to moderate, 180°C, Gas 4, and bake for a further 1–1¼ hours. Serve hot or cold.

Grouse Pie

6–8 helpings

2 grouse	flour for rolling out
350g rump steak	100g prepared puff pastry (p1253)
2 hard-boiled eggs	beaten egg **or** milk for glazing
2–3 rashers bacon, without rinds	
salt and pepper	
250ml game stock (p330) **or** general household stock (p329)	

Joint the birds. Slice the steak thinly and slice the eggs. Cut the bacon rashers into strips. Season the steak and eggs to taste. Line the bottom of a 1 litre pie dish with some of the pieces of seasoned steak, cover with a layer of grouse, and pack round them some bacon, egg, and seasoning. Repeat the layers until the dish is full. Add enough stock to fill three-quarters of the pie dish. Roll out the pastry on a lightly floured surface to make a lid. Moisten the rim of the dish and fit on the lid. Trim, crimp the edge, and make a small hole in the centre to allow steam to escape. Decorate with the trimmings. Bake the pie in a hot oven, 220°C, Gas 7, for 20 minutes, then lower the heat to moderate, 180°C, Gas 4, and cook for another 1¼–1½ hours. Glaze the pastry with the egg or milk 30 minutes before the cooking is complete.

Meanwhile, simmer the necks and trimmings of the birds in the remaining stock; strain and season. Pour the hot stock into the pie through the hole just before serving.

Note Finely chopped mushrooms, parsley, and shallots can be added to the pie, if liked.

PHEASANT

Roast Stuffed Pheasant

6 helpings

2 pheasants	50g butter
½ onion	

Stuffing
100g onion	salt and pepper
25g butter **or** margarine	1 × 15ml spoon game
100g mushrooms	stock (p330) *(optional)*
50g ham	
75g soft white	
breadcrumbs	

Garnish
watercress sprigs	French dressing

Wash the pheasant giblets, cover with cold water, add the half onion, and simmer gently for 40 minutes to make stock for the gravy.

Make the stuffing. Skin the onion and chop it finely. Melt the butter or margarine and cook the onion until soft. Chop the mushrooms and add them to the onion; cook for a few minutes. Chop the ham, and add with the breadcrumbs. Stir, add salt and pepper, and the stock if the stuffing is too crumbly.

Divide the stuffing between the birds, filling the body cavities only. Truss the birds neatly and put in a roasting tin; spread with the 50g butter. Roast in a fairly hot oven, 190°C, Gas 5, for 45 minutes– 1 hour, depending on the size of the birds; baste occasionally while roasting. Transfer the birds to a heated serving dish, and remove the trussing strings. Garnish with watercress tossed very lightly in French dressing.

Serve with gravy (p728), Bread Sauce (p713), and fried breadcrumbs (p396).

Note A pheasant trussed in modern style should be carved like chicken; if trussed in traditional style with its head on, cut it off before carving.

Salmi of Pheasant

4–5 helpings

50g butter	1 bay leaf
1 pheasant	250ml foundation brown
½ × 2.5ml spoon grated	sauce (p698)
lemon rind	100ml (approx) Madeira
2 shallots	(optional)
½ × 2.5ml spoon dried	salt and pepper
thyme	6–8 button mushrooms

Garnish *(optional)*
croûtons of fried bread

Melt the butter in a roasting tin. Baste the bird well with the hot butter and roast it on a rack in a fairly hot oven, 200°C, Gas 6, for 40–45 minutes, basting frequently. When cooked, pour the butter used for basting into a saucepan, and add the lemon rind. Skin, chop, and add the shallots with the thyme and bay leaf. Remove from the heat, joint and bone the bird, and put the flesh on one side. Add the bones to the saucepan and fry well. Drain off and reserve any excess butter. Add the brown sauce and the wine, if used, to the bones, season to taste, and simmer for 10 minutes. Strain the sauce, add the meat, and simmer for 20 minutes.

Re-heat the reserved butter and fry the mushrooms in it. Re-season the sauce if required. Serve the pheasant with the mushrooms on top; strain the sauce over it. Garnish with croûtons, if liked.

Pheasant with Oysters

4–5 helpings

1 pheasant	½ small turnip
oyster stuffing (p379)	bouquet garni
550ml chicken stock	400ml oyster sauce
1 onion	(p696)
1 carrot	

Fill the cavity of the bird with oyster stuffing. Truss the bird for roasting. Bring the stock to boiling point. Skin and slice the onion. Peel and slice the carrot and turnip. Wrap the bird securely in well greased foil, then put the bird into the boiling stock. Bring back to boiling point, add the sliced vegetables and bouquet garni to the pan, reduce the heat, and simmer gently for about 1 hour. Remove the trussing strings and serve the bird on a hot dish with a little oyster sauce poured round. Serve the rest of the sauce in a sauce-boat.

VARIATIONS

Chestnut stuffing (p381) can be substituted for oyster stuffing. Alternatively, the bird can be cooked with chopped vegetables in the body cavity instead of stuffing, and served with Celery (p714) or Oyster (p696) Sauce.

Pheasant Véronique

4–6 helpings

225g white grapes	4 ×15ml spoons double
2 pheasants	cream
salt and pepper	1 × 5ml spoon lemon
75g butter	juice
550ml chicken stock	
1½–2 × 5ml spoons	
arrowroot	

Peel and de-pip the grapes. Wipe the pheasants, season, and rub well all over with butter. Put a knob of butter inside each bird. Place the pheasants, breast side down, in a deep pot roaster or flame-proof casserole; cover with stock and buttered paper. Cook in a moderate oven, 180°C, Gas 4, for 1–1¼ hours until tender; turn the birds breast side up after 25 minutes.

When cooked, remove the pheasants from the stock, and cut into convenient portions for serving; keep hot. Boil the liquid in the casserole to reduce it a little. Strain into a saucepan. Blend the arrowroot with a little water, then stir it into the hot stock. Bring to the boil and stir until the sauce thickens and clears. Add the grapes, cream and lemon juice, and heat through without boiling. Re-season if required. Arrange the pheasants on a serving dish with the sauce spooned over them.

Pheasant Pilaf

4 helpings

75g dried apricots	2 eggs
75g prunes	2 ×15ml spoons clear
1 cold roasted pheasant	honey
250g long-grain rice	2 ×15ml spoons
50g butter	chopped parsley
75g blanched almonds	salt and pepper
75g seedless raisins	

Soak the apricots and prunes overnight. Stone the prunes. Remove the pheasant meat from the bones, and dice it. Cook the rice in boiling salted water for 12–15 minutes until tender. Drain well. Heat the butter in a frying pan and brown the almonds lightly. Drain and add the soaked fruits and raisins. Add the pheasant meat and heat through for 5 minutes. Beat the eggs until liquid, and add them with the cooked rice and all the remaining ingredients. Cook, stirring frequently, until the eggs are lightly set. Serve at once.

PIGEON

Grilled Spatchcocked Pigeons

6 helpings

3 young tame pigeons	salt and pepper
3 ×15ml spoons butter	

Split the birds down the back, lay them out, skin side down, and skewer them flat. Melt the butter, and brush them all over with butter. Season to taste. Grill for 20 minutes, turning frequently.

Serve very hot, and offer Fresh Tomato Sauce (p715) or Mushroom Sauce (p695) separately.

Roast Pigeons

3 helpings

3 young woodpigeons **or**
  older tame pigeons
75g butter
lemon juice
salt and pepper
3 small rashers streaky
  bacon, without rinds

3 croûtes fried bread,
  each big enough to put
  under 1 bird

Garnish
watercress sprigs

Wipe the birds with a damp cloth. Mix the butter, lemon juice, and seasoning to taste. Insert 25g butter in each bird. Truss for roasting, and cover each bird with a bacon rasher. Roast the pigeons in a fairly hot oven, 190°C, Gas 5, for 20–30 minutes or until tender. Baste while cooking, if necessary. Remove the bacon 10 minutes before the end of the cooking time to allow the birds to brown. When they are done, remove the trussing strings, and replace the bacon. Serve each bird on a croûte of fried bread, and garnish with watercress.

Offer Espagnole Sauce (p707), Fresh Tomato Sauce (p715), or Piquant Sauce (p702) separately.

Note Pigeon can be cut in half lengthways through the breast-bone and spine to make 2 portions.

Jugged Pigeons

6 helpings

3 woodpigeons
75g butter
1 small onion
500ml beef stock

salt and pepper
25g flour
100ml (approx) port **or**
  claret (optional)

Garnish
fried balls of basic herb
  forcemeat (p376)

croûtons of fried bread
parsley sprigs

Truss the pigeons for roasting. Heat 50g of the butter, and fry them in it until well browned. Remove the birds to a casserole, preferably earthenware. Skin and chop the onion and brown it in the same butter as the pigeons. Add the onion to the

pigeons, together with the stock and seasoning to taste. Cover, and cook in a warm oven, 160°C, Gas 3, for 1¾ hours.

Knead together the flour and remaining 25g butter to make a beurre manié and drop small pieces into the stock, stirring all the time. Continue cooking for a further 15 minutes. Add the wine, if used, and cook for another 15 minutes. Serve the pigeons with the sauce poured over them, and garnish with forcemeat balls, croûtons, and parsley.

Pigeon Cutlets with Espagnole Sauce

6 helpings

3 tame pigeons
salt and pepper
3 ×15ml spoons butter
  or *corn oil*
200g (approx) chicken
  liver stuffing (p381)

2 eggs
breadcrumbs for coating
butter for greasing
250ml Espagnole sauce
  (p707)

Garnish
Duchesse potatoes
  (p793) *(optional)*
beaten egg for glazing
  (optional)

450g cooked green
  vegetables, eg peas,
  green beans, asparagus
  tips

Cut the feet off the pigeons. Split the birds in half lengthways and remove all the bones except the leg bones. Season the meat well and fold each half bird into a neat cutlet shape. Heat the butter or oil in a frying pan. Fry the birds lightly on both sides to seal them and press between 2 plates until cold. Spread one side of each half pigeon with the stuffing. Beat the eggs until liquid and coat the portions twice with egg and breadcrumbs. Leave to set.

Place in a shallow greased tin, cover with buttered paper, and cook in a moderate oven, 180°C, Gas 4, for 20–30 minutes. If liked, pipe a border of Duchesse potato mixture round a dish, glaze, and brown it. Place the cutlets in the centre, pour the Espagnole Sauce round them, and garnish with small piles of green vegetables.

Duchesse Pigeons

4 helpings

2 tame pigeons	breadcrumbs for coating
40g butter	oil **or** fat for deep frying
salt and pepper	250ml Espagnole sauce
100g sausage-meat	(p707)
2 eggs	

Garnish

500g Duchesse potatoes	macédoine of vegetables
(p793) (optional)	(p398)

Prepare, shape, and fry the cutlets in the butter as for Pigeon Cutlets with Espagnole Sauce. Season the sausage-meat well. Spread one side of each cutlet with the seasoned sausage-meat. Beat the eggs until liquid and coat the cutlets with egg and breadcrumbs twice (the second coating prevents the sausage-meat from splitting away). Heat the oil or fat (p303) and fry the cutlets until well browned and cooked through.

Serve very hot, in a Duchesse potato border, if liked. Pour the Espagnole Sauce over the cutlets and garnish with a macédoine of vegetables.

Cooking time 30 minutes (approx)

Compôte of Pigeons

6 helpings

3 woodpigeons **or** large tame pigeons	40g butter
100g ham **or** bacon	500ml general household stock (p329)
3 shallots **or** 1 large onion	bouquet garni
1 carrot	25g flour
½ turnip	salt and pepper

Truss the pigeons for roasting. Cut the ham or bacon into small pieces. Skin the shallots, or skin and slice the onion. Slice the carrot and turnip. Heat the butter in a large pan and fry the pigeons, ham or bacon, and onions until well browned. Add the stock and bring to boiling point. Add the bouquet garni, carrot, and turnip. Cover, reduce the heat, and simmer steadily for 1–1½ hours or until the pigeons are tender.

Blend the flour with a little cold water and add a little of the hot cooking liquid; blend well and add to the pan. Bring to boiling point, stirring all the time; re-cover, and simmer for 10 minutes. Skim off any excess fat and season to taste. Remove the pigeons, cut off the trussing strings, and split the birds in half. Serve them on a hot dish with the sauce poured over them.

Pigeon Casserole

6–8 helpings

225g button onions	40g plain flour
4 rashers streaky bacon, without rinds	275ml beef stock
4 young pigeons	1 × 15ml spoon concentrated tomato
50g butter **or** margarine	purée
225g button mushrooms	salt and pepper

Garnish

chopped parsley

Skin the onions and leave them whole. Cut the bacon into strips. Wipe and dry the pigeons. Heat the butter or margarine in a frying pan and brown the pigeons all over.

Put the pigeons in a 2 litre casserole. Clean the mushrooms. Put the onions and bacon in the frying pan, and brown lightly. Stir in the flour, and gradually add the stock; bring to the boil. Stir in the tomato purée, blend in thoroughly, then add the mushrooms and season well. Pour the mixture over the pigeons, cover, and cook in a moderate oven, 180°C, Gas 4, for 1–1½ hours, until the pigeons are tender. Lift them out and arrange on a heated serving dish. Spoon the sauce over them, and sprinkle with chopped parsley.

Pigeon with Olives

6 helpings

3 woodpigeons
50g butter
500ml Espagnole sauce
  (p707)

24 stuffed olives

Split each pigeon into quarters. Heat the butter and fry the pigeon quarters until well browned on all sides. Heat the Espagnole sauce to simmering point in a flameproof casserole. Put the birds into the hot Espagnole sauce, cover, and simmer for about 45 minutes or until they are cooked and tender. Add the olives and cook for 4–5 minutes to heat them through. Serve the pigeons with the sauce and olives poured over them.

Stewed Pigeons

6 helpings

50g butter
3 woodpigeons
500ml foundation brown
  sauce (p698)
150ml (approx) red wine
  (optional)

salt and pepper
1 large onion **or**
  3 shallots
butter for frying

Heat the butter and fry the pigeons, turning as required, until browned on all sides. Heat the brown sauce to simmering point in a saucepan. Put the pigeons into the hot brown sauce and simmer with the pan half-covered for about 45 minutes or until the birds are tender. Add the wine, if used, and season just before serving.

    Meanwhile, skin and slice the onion, if used, or skin the shallots. Melt the butter and fry the shallots or onion. Drain well and keep hot. Split the cooked pigeons in half and serve half to each person with the onions and the sauce poured over them.

    Serve with new carrots and garden peas.

Pigeon Pie(1)

4 helpings

3 small woodpigeons
salt and pepper
200g grilling steak
100g ham **or** bacon
2 hard-boiled eggs
350ml general household
  stock (p329)

puff pastry (p1253)
  using 175g flour
flour for rolling out
beaten egg **or** milk for
  glazing

Remove the feet from the pigeons and cut each bird into quarters. Season well. Cut the steak in small thin slices, the ham or bacon in strips, and slice the eggs. Layer all the ingredients in a 1 litre pie dish, seasoning the layers well. Three-quarters fill the dish with stock. Roll out the pastry on a lightly floured surface to fit the dish. Moisten the rim of the pie dish and cover the pie with the pastry, leaving a small hole in the centre. Brush with the egg or milk to glaze it. Cook in a hot oven, 220°C, Gas 7, for 20 minutes, until the pastry is risen and set; then lower the heat to moderate, 180°C, Gas 4, and bake for 1 hour longer. Heat the remaining stock. Before serving the pie, fill it with the remaining hot stock poured through the central hole.

VARIATION

Make the pie with 1 jointed pheasant or 2 partridges.

Pigeon Pie(2)

4–5 helpings

2 tame pigeons
salt and pepper
3 × 15ml spoons plain
  flour
3 × 15ml spoons corn oil
100g chuck steak
100g button onions
2 × 15ml spoons sage
  and onion stuffing mix

1 small cooking apple
225ml beef stock
225g prepared puff
  pastry (p1253)
flour for rolling out
beaten egg for glazing

Cut the pigeons into quarters. Remove the feet and backbone. Season the flour with salt and pepper. Coat the pigeon joints with seasoned flour. Heat the oil and fry the joints in the oil for about 10 minutes, turning as required, until lightly browned all over. Cut the steak into cubes and dip in the seasoned flour. Skin the onions, and leave whole. Remove the pigeons from the pan and drain on soft kitchen paper. Put the steak and onions in the pan and cook for 5 minutes, turning frequently. Make up the stuffing according to the packet directions. Make into small balls and fry in the pan to brown them lightly all over. Remove and drain. Peel, core, and slice the apple.

In a large casserole or pie dish, layer all the filling ingredients, adding salt and pepper to taste. Pour in the stock. Roll out the pastry on a lightly floured surface to fit the dish. Moisten the rim of the pie dish and cover the pie with the pastry. Brush the crust with the egg. Cook in a hot oven, 220°C, Gas 7, for 20 minutes until the pastry is risen and golden. Reduce the heat to moderate, 180°C, Gas 4, and cook for a further 2 hours or until the pigeons are tender when pierced with a skewer through the crust. Cover the pie crust with buttered paper if necessary to prevent it over-browning or drying out.

Pigeon or Rabbit Pudding

6 helpings

3 woodpigeons **or** 1kg boneless rabbit meat	2 hard-boiled eggs suet crust pastry (p1250) using 350g flour
200g chuck steak	150ml general household stock (p329)
salt and pepper	
25g flour	

Skin the pigeons, if used. Cut pigeons into quarters or rabbit meat into 6–7cm pieces. Cut the steak into small pieces. Season the flour with salt and pepper to taste. Dip the pieces of meat in the seasoned flour. Cut the eggs into sections. Line a greased 1 litre basin with two-thirds of the suet crust pastry, then put in the prepared meat and eggs. Add the stock and cover with the remaining pastry. Cover with greased paper or foil. Steam the pudding for at least 3½ hours.

Serve with thin gravy (p727).

VARIATION
Make the pudding with an old or badly shot grouse.

QUAIL

Roast Quail

4 helpings

8 oven-ready quail	4 large slices bread from a tin loaf
8 fresh **or** canned vine leaves	butter for spreading
8 rashers streaky bacon, without rinds	

Garnish
lemon wedges	watercress sprigs

Wrap each quail in a vine leaf. Wrap 1 rasher of bacon round each quail. Secure with thread or wooden cocktail sticks. Place on a rack in a roasting tin, and roast in a fairly hot oven, 200°C, Gas 6, for 10–12 minutes. Meanwhile, cut the crusts off the bread, cut each slice in half, and toast lightly on both sides. When the quail are roasted, spread the toast with drippings from the quail and a little butter. Serve each quail on toast, and garnish with lemon wedges and watercress sprigs.

Note Quail should always be plainly roasted or grilled. Their flavour is lost in a rich sauce or with a strongly flavoured garnish.

VARIATION
Stuffed Quail

Make a stuffing with the chopped livers of the quail, if available, 4 × 15ml spoons diced cooked bacon, and 6–8 × 15ml spoons soft white bread-crumbs. Season with a little brandy or lemon juice. Roast the quail for 14–18 minutes to heat the stuffing through. When the quail are cooked, make a slightly thickened gravy with the pan juices, adding a little more brandy and 200g seedless or de-pipped green grapes to the gravy.

PARTRIDGE

Roast Partridges Stuffed with Juniper

4 helpings

4 young partridges
juice of 1 lemon
a thin sheet of pork fat
 for barding
50g butter
50ml dry white wine
150ml game stock
 (p330)

flour for dredging and
 for making gravy
4 large slices white
 bread from tin loaf
butter for shallow frying
extra game stock for
 gravy

Stuffing
12 juniper berries
100g ham
2 medium-sized onions
grated rind of 1 lemon
100g butter
2 eggs

a pinch of dried
 marjoram
75g soft white
 breadcrumbs
salt and pepper

Garnish
watercress sprigs
potato straws (p792) or
 fried breadcrumbs
 (p396)

lemon wedges

Make the stuffing first. Crush the juniper berries, shred the ham, and skin and chop the onions. Mix the crushed berries, ham, onions, and lemon rind in a bowl. Melt the butter and add it to the bowl. Beat the eggs lightly, and mix them in with the marjoram and breadcrumbs. Season well with salt and pepper. Use the mixture to stuff the birds.

Truss the birds for roasting, sprinkle with a little of the lemon juice, and bard them with the pork fat. Put into a roasting tin. Melt the butter and brush it over the birds. Add the wine and game stock to the tin, and roast in a fairly hot oven, 190°C, Gas 5, for 45 minutes, basting often with the pan juices. About 15 minutes before the end of the cooking time, remove the pork barding fat. Dredge the birds lightly with a little flour, and return them to the oven to finish cooking, and to brown. Fry the bread slices in butter until golden and lightly crisped, cut off the crusts, and keep aside.

When the birds are cooked, place each on a croûte of fried bread, and arrange them on a serving dish with their drumsticks in the centre. Keep warm under buttered paper while making the gravy. Skim the fat off the pan juices, sprinkle in a little flour, and place over moderate heat. Stir for 2 minutes, scraping in any sediment. Stir in enough stock to make a thin, well-flavoured gravy.

Garnish the birds with a bunch of watercress sprigs in the centre of the dish. Place small piles of potato straws or fried crumbs between them, and lemon wedges on top.

Serve the gravy separately in a warmed sauceboat, with Bread Sauce (p713) and redcurrant jelly or Cumberland Sauce (p718).

Note A partridge may be cut in half lengthways through the breast-bone and spine. Although a partridge is seldom large enough to serve more than 2 people, a third portion can be carved; if necessary, in the same way as grouse (p657). As the wings of the partridge and other small birds are often dry and bony, they are usually cut off before serving.

Grilled Partridge

4 helpings

2 partridges
salt

Cayenne pepper
50g butter

Garnish
grilled tomatoes

grilled mushrooms

Split the birds in half and wipe the insides thoroughly with a damp cloth. Season with salt and Cayenne pepper. Melt the butter, and brush the birds with it. Grill for 20–30 minutes, turning frequently. Garnish quickly with grilled tomatoes and mushrooms, which can be cooked during the birds' cooking time.

Serve with Mushroom Sauce (p695) or Foundation Brown Sauce (p698) handed separately.

Normandy Partridges

2 helpings

100g unsalted butter	*700g dessert apples*
2 young partridges	*100ml double cream*
salt and pepper	*2 × 15ml spoons*
2 rashers streaky bacon,	* Calvados or brandy*
* without rinds*	*chopped parsley*

Heat half the butter in a flameproof casserole, add the partridges, and brown them on all sides. Sprinkle with salt and pepper. Place a bacon rasher on each bird's breast. Peel, core, and cut the apples into wedges. Melt the remaining butter in a pan, add the apples, and cover the pan. Cook gently for 5 minutes, then add to the casserole. Cook in a moderate oven, 180°C, Gas 4, for 20–30 minutes. Transfer the partridges and apples to a hot serving dish.

Mix the cream and the Calvados or brandy, season to taste, and heat the mixture, stirring well. Do not boil. Pour this sauce over the apples, and sprinkle with chopped parsley.

Casserole of Partridges

2 helpings

butter	*2 small or 1 large carrot*
2 partridges	*1 small onion*
1 lemon	*bouquet garni*
4 rashers streaky bacon,	*100ml dry white wine*
* without rinds*	*salt and pepper*
550ml general household	*25g butter*
* stock (p329)*	*25g flour*

Garnish
potato straws (p792) or	*purée of mushrooms or*
* sautéed potatoes (p792)*	* green peas (optional)*

Place a knob of butter inside each bird. Cut 4 slices from the lemon. Truss the partridges and cover the breast of each bird, first with 2 lemon slices, then with 2 bacon rashers. Heat the stock. Dice the carrot and skin and slice the onion. Put the birds into a flameproof casserole with the stock, vegetables, bouquet garni, wine, salt, and pepper. Cover closely, and cook very gently for 1 hour. Remove the bacon and slices of lemon. Transfer the birds to a fairly hot oven, 190°C, Gas 5, for 6–10 minutes, to brown the breasts.

Meanwhile, melt the 25g butter and cook the flour in the butter until nut-brown. Strain the stock from the casserole and add it gradually to the roux, stirring until it boils.

Place the birds on a heated serving dish. Garnish with crisply fried potato straws or with thin slices of sautéed potato; add a purée of mushrooms or green peas, if liked. Serve the sauce separately.

Mrs Beeton's Hashed Partridges

3–4 helpings

3 cooked partridges or	*375ml game stock*
* 1 cooked grouse or*	* (p329)*
* pheasant*	*bouquet garni*
1 × 25g slice ham	*4 whole cloves*
75g carrots	*4 black peppercorns*
50g mild onion or	*100ml medium-dry*
* shallots*	* sherry or Madeira*
25g butter	*1 lump of sugar (if using*
oil for frying	* sherry)*
25g button mushrooms	

Garnish
fried bread croûtons

Joint the bird or birds. Skin the wings, legs, and breasts; keep the skin and carcasses. Dice the ham. Prepare the carrot and onion or shallots, and slice them thinly. Heat the butter and a little oil in a large, heavy-bottomed stewpan, and fry the ham and vegetables gently for 6–8 minutes until softened but not browned. Add the stock and bouquet garni. Tie the spices in muslin and add them, with the skin and carcasses. Simmer for 15 minutes. Strain the sauce and chill it.

When cold, take off all the fat. Add the wine and sugar, if used. Return to the pan with the joints. Heat thoroughly to boiling point, then turn into a heated serving dish. Scatter the croûtons over the dish and serve very hot.

Partridges with Cabbage

3–4 helpings

1 medium-sized cabbage	*200g frankfurter*
100g bacon rashers,	*sausages*
without rinds	*2 juniper berries*
2 partridges	*salt and pepper*
50g butter	*a pinch of ground*
2 small onions	*nutmeg*
2 cloves	*450ml general household*
2 carrots	*stock (p329)*
	beurre manié (optional)

Prepare and slice the cabbage, then parboil in boiling salted water for 5 minutes. Drain well. Cut the bacon into small pieces. Prepare the birds for casseroling by tying or skewering the limbs to the body in a neat shape. Melt the butter in a pan and brown the birds all over. Skin the onions and stick a clove in each one. Put an onion in the body of each bird. Cook the bacon lightly in the pan. Slice the carrots, and cut the frankfurters into 2cm pieces. Crush the juniper berries.

Place a layer of cabbage in the base of a deep casserole, and arrange the partridges on top with the bacon, sliced carrots, frankfurters, and crushed juniper. Season with salt, pepper, and nutmeg. Cover with the remaining cabbage, and pour in enough stock to come half-way up the casserole. Cover with buttered paper and a lid. Cook in a very cool oven, 140°C, Gas 1, for 3–4 hours.

Arrange the birds on a bed of cabbage, on a heated serving dish with the other ingredients from the casserole. Skim and strain the liquid from the casserole into a clean pan. Reduce it by boiling to the desired strength; or if preferred, measure the skimmed, strained liquid, stir in enough beurre manié to thicken it, then stir it over moderate heat until it boils and thickens.

Note This is an excellent way of serving partridges which are not tender enough to be roasted.

WILD DUCK

To prevent water birds tasting fishy, pour boiling water over them before roasting; drain and pat dry with kitchen paper.

Roast Wild Duck

(Mallard, Pintail or Widgeon)

3 helpings

1 wild duck	*1 large slice of white*
butter for basting	*bread to fit under the*
flour for dredging	*bird*

Garnish
watercress sprigs

Cut off the toes of the bird, and scald and scrape the feet. Truss the bird with the feet twisted underneath the body. Warm the butter until melted, and brush the bird all over with melted butter. Dredge lightly with flour. Place on a trivet in a roasting tin, baste with any remaining butter, and roast in a fairly hot oven, 190°C, Gas 5, for 20–30 minutes. Baste often during cooking.

As soon as the bird is in the oven, cut the crusts off the bread, and toast it lightly on both sides. Place it while still warm in the roasting tin, under the bird.

Remove the bird and the bread croûte from the oven as soon as it is tender. Serve it slightly underdone, or the flavour will be lost. Place on a heated serving dish, and garnish with watercress sprigs just before serving.

Serve game chips (p792), Cumberland Sauce (p718) and redcurrant jelly with the bird. Bread Sauce (p713) can also be served, if liked.

Note Carve the breast like that of farmed duck. Remove the wings without any extra meat above the joint, and discard them. Remove the legs in the same way as a chicken's, and cut in half at the joint. Serve only the thighs.

Roast Teal with Orange Salad

2 helpings

2 teal	lemon juice
1 orange	flour for dredging
50g unsalted butter	watercress sprigs
2 slices white bread	
Cayenne pepper	

Orange Salad

2 small sweet oranges	1 × 15ml spoon French
1 × 5ml spoon caster	dressing
sugar	brandy (optional)

Prepare the birds as for Roast Wild Duck. Before trussing them, halve the orange, and put half inside each bird. Truss with the feet twisted underneath the body. Melt the butter, and brush the birds with it. Place them on a trivet in a roasting tin, baste them, and pour any remaining butter into the tin. Roast them in a hot oven, 220°C, Gas 7, for 20 minutes, basting often.

As soon as the birds are in the oven, cut the crusts off the bread, toast lightly on both sides, and place the slices under the birds in the tin. At the same time, sprinkle the birds lightly with Cayenne pepper and lemon juice.

Five minutes before the end of the cooking time, sprinkle the birds with flour, baste well, and return them to the oven until the flour froths and the breasts are well coloured.

Make the salad. Let the oranges stand in boiling water for 2 minutes, turning them over once. Peel them and remove all the white pith. Cut into segments, discarding the pips and membranes. Sprinkle the segments with sugar, French dressing, and a very little brandy, if liked.

Serve the birds on the croûtes of bread, and garnish with orange salad and watercress sprigs. Serve Bigarade sauce (p707) separately.

CAPERCAILZIE

Casserole of Capercailzie

5 helpings

1 young capercailzie, well hung	300ml general household stock (p329)
red wine marinade, uncooked (p730)	2 × 15ml spoons redcurrant jelly
3 × 15ml spoons olive oil	soured cream (optional)

Marinate the bird for 2–3 days, depending on how high it is after hanging. Turn several times in the marinade. Remove the bird and dry well on soft kitchen paper; reserve the marinade.

Heat the oil in a heavy casserole just large enough to take the bird, and brown it all over. Strain the marinade over the bird, and add enough stock to come half-way up its sides. Cover the casserole and cook the bird, breast side downwards in a cool oven, 150°C, Gas 2, for 2½ hours or until tender.

Pour off the juices, skim off any fat, add the redcurrant jelly, and a little soured cream if liked.

Carve the bird and spoon the sauce over it.

Devilled Poultry or Game

See p1311.

SMALL GAME BIRDS

Roast Snipe or Other Small Game Birds

3 helpings

3 snipe or other small game birds	*250ml foundation brown sauce (p698)*
40g butter	*juice of 1 lemon*
3 thin rashers bacon	*100ml (approx) port or*
3 slices toast	*other red wine*
butter for basting	*(optional)*
flour for dredging	

Garnish

watercress sprigs	*lemon wedges or slices*

Truss the birds as for wild duck or as described on p656. Do not draw them. Melt the butter and brush the birds with it. Tie a bacon rasher over each bird's breast. Place the slices of toast in a roasting tin to catch the juices (the trail) as they drop from the birds. Place a roasting rack or trivet over them and put the birds on it. Roast in a fairly hot oven, 190°C, Gas 5, for 15–20 minutes, depending on the type of bird; white-fleshed birds such as quail should be well cooked; dark-fleshed birds and waders such as snipe should be served underdone. Baste the birds frequently with butter while cooking.

Shortly before serving, remove the bacon, dredge the birds lightly with flour, and baste well to brown the breasts lightly. Return to the oven to finish cooking.

Meanwhile, heat the brown sauce; add the lemon juice, and the wine, if used.

Serve the birds on the toast, and garnish with watercress and lemon wedges or slices. Serve the sauce separately.

Note Melted clarified butter (p886), flavoured with lemon juice, can be served instead of brown sauce.

Snipe can be divided into 2 portions by cutting lengthways through the breast-bone and spine, after removing the head.

Game Animals

HARE

Two types of hare are fairly common in the UK, the English or brown hare and the Scots or blue hare. The brown hare is thought to have the better flavour. The male hare is called a buck and the female a doe. A young hare (up to 1 year old) is called a leveret. A leveret has a small bony knot near the foot which disappears when it is older. Young hares also have short, stumpy necks, long joints, smooth sharp claws, a narrow lip cleft, and soft ears which tear easily.

A hare is usually bought ready hung, but if freshly killed should be hung for 7–10 days, depending on the weather. It should hang by the hind legs unskinned and unpaunched in a cool, dry well-ventilated place, with the head in a tin mug to catch the blood. If buying a pre-hung hare from a butcher, make sure that you also get its blood. Add 1–2 drops of vinegar to the blood to prevent it clotting and keep it in a refrigerator for use in casseroled and jugged dishes.

The best parts of the meat are the back or saddle, as it is also called, and the hind legs, which can be sautéed or roasted. The shoulders and forelegs are usually divided into 3 or 4 pieces and braised or jugged; if the hare is not young, and fairly small, it can be jugged whole.

RABBIT

A rabbit for the table may be wild, or specially bred and farmed for the table; it is then usually called tame rabbit. Wild rabbit meat is darker, with a more gamey flavour, and can be cooked in several of the ways suggested for hare. The meat of a tame rabbit is more like that of chicken, and can be cooked in the same ways. Both wild and tame meat is available frozen, whole, in joints or (mostly tame rabbit) in boneless blocks.

In both freshly killed and frozen animals, the back and legs give the best, most fleshy meat. The remaining meat, including the forelegs, is usually kept for casseroled dishes, stews, and stock.

A newly killed rabbit is treated much like a hare,

but it should be paunched immediately it is killed. There is no need to hang rabbit as the flavour will not improve by so doing. It can, however, hang for about a day. Some experts say that if a rabbit is skinned as soon as it is killed, the meat will not have the musty flavour often associated with it.

A rabbit is best for eating between 3 and 4 months old, when it has thick foot joints, smooth claws, a flexible jaw, and ears which tear easily. The eyes should be bright, the fat whitish, and the liver bright red. Tame rabbits, especially, vary widely in weight according to type; a big Ostend rabbit can weigh as much as 4kg, although an average tame rabbit weighs 2–2.25kg.

Preparing Hares and Rabbits

Paunching: Make a slit the length of the stomach. Slide out all the entrails except the kidneys. Leave them in their fat attached to the back. Carefully detach and discard the greenish gall-bladder from the liver. Throw away all but the liver and heart. Reserve these for cooking.

Skinning: Cut off the feet at the foot joint with a small thin-bladed knife.

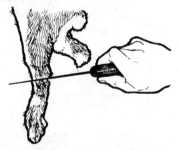

Cut the skin of a hare straight down the belly without penetrating the gut. (A rabbit will already have been paunched.)

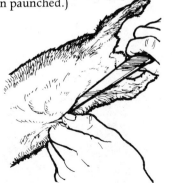

Loosen the skin from the meat on each side of the slit, then ease it away from the flesh, up towards the spine on both sides, until the centre of the body is completely free from its skin. Now push forward

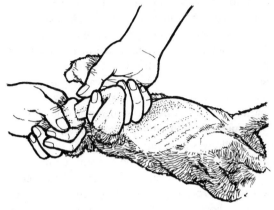

one hind leg and work the skin free. Repeat the process on the other leg, then pull the skin up and over to free the tail.

Holding the skinned hindquarters in the left hand,

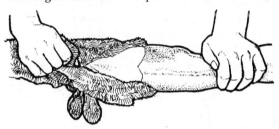

gently pull the skin up the back and over the shoulders, working each foreleg through in turn. The skin must now be eased with a knife from the neck and head so that the skin can be rolled back and pulled off like a jumper.

If the ears are being left on, as in a traditional roast, cut round the base of each before skinning the head. (Skinning the head is a difficult process, usually best done by the butcher. For this reason, the head is often left with its skin on and covered with foil to be roasted.) A hare is now ready to be paunched, as described above.

Cleaning and Marinating: A hare should only be wiped clean, but a rabbit can be washed in salted water. The meat will be lighter-coloured if it is left to soak in salted water with a few drops of lemon juice for 20–30 minutes. If its flavour is strong, it can be blanched; put it into cold water, bring to the boil, and simmer for 2 minutes. Drain and wipe dry.

A young hare can be marinated in a little oil and brandy with chopped fresh herbs; it needs only a few hours soaking. Older hares can be marinated for 1–2 days in a red wine marinade; if a venison marinade is used, dilute it with a little water.

An older or wild rabbit, in particular, will taste more delicate and be more digestible if steeped for 12 hours in water containing 1×5ml spoon white wine vinegar per 500ml water. Change the water at least once. Frozen whole rabbit can be steeped for up to 24 hours, but joints and boneless pieces for 30–60 minutes at most. For extra flavour, marinate a tame rabbit in white wine sharpened with a little lemon juice. Wild rabbit benefits from a herbal marinade, especially if it includes herbs the animal has fed on. See the red wine marinades on p730.

Trussing: The simplest method of trussing is to cut off the head and neck of the hare or rabbit, leaving a flap of skin which can be skewered over the cut surface like the skin over the neck end of a chicken. The limbs are tied or skewered as above. Roast the hare or rabbit on its belly; or cook it for half its cooking time on one side, and then turn it over to complete the cooking.

A hare for roasting is traditionally trussed with the head raised, and is balanced to lie on its belly as if alive and just alerted. (Any barding fat or stuffing should be put in place and secured before trussing.) To truss, hold the animal in this position. Crook the forelegs with the lower part lying on the plate level with the breastbone, evenly balanced to hold the rib cage steady. Tie or skewer. Crook and skewer the hind legs in the same way. Remove the eyes. If the head has been left unskinned, cover with foil while cooking. In any case, the ears must be covered with foil.

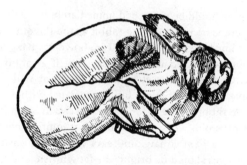

Jointing: Remove the head, cutting straight down at the base of the neck. Cut off each foreleg in one piece. Cut off the hind legs at the pelvic joint. A rabbit's hind legs are usually left whole, except for a pie; but when jointing a hare, separate the thigh from the lower leg. Separate the rib cage from the saddle by cutting through the spine (about a third of the way down the back). Split the forepart of a hare along the spine to give two joints. Separate the saddle from the rump. The saddle can be split into two parts, if liked.

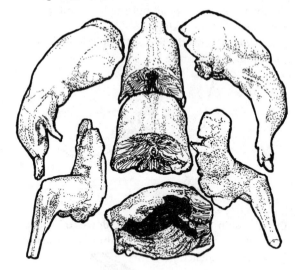

Poultry and Game

Hindle Wakes (p1466)

LEFT *Spatchcocked Chicken* (p630)

BELOW *Stuffed Chicken Legs* (p643)

RIGHT *Galantine of Chicken* (p646)

LEFT *(back) Mrs Beeton's Roast Turkey* (p639) *with forcemeat balls, chipolata sausages, Brussels Sprouts, and accompanied by Bread Sauce and Cranberry Sauce (front) Braised Duck with Turnips* (p650) *and Redcurrant Jelly*

BELOW *Roast Goose with Fruit Stuffing* (p646)

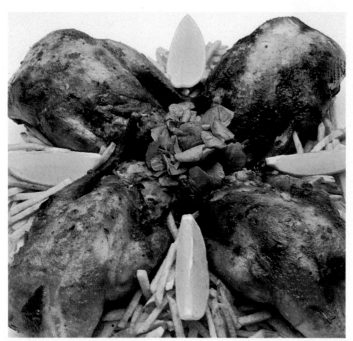

LEFT *Roast Partridges Stuffed with Juniper* (p666)

BELOW *Jugged Pigeons* (p662) *with forcemeat balls and croûtons*

RIGHT *Roast Baron of Hare* (p676)

BELOW RIGHT *Rabbit Casserole* (p683) *with crescents of fried bread*

Roast Shoulder of Venison (p687) with chipolata sausages, bacon rolls and redcurrant jelly

VENISON

Almost any wild animal used for food was once called venison, but today in the UK, the word is used only for deer meat. In North America, it includes the flesh of moose, elk, and caribou, and in France and elsewhere on the Continent it still includes the meat of hares and various other animals.

The types of deer found in the UK are red deer, roe deer, and fallow deer.

The red deer is the largest and most splendid beast, the roe deer meat is whiter and less gamey, and the fallow deer is considered to have the finest flavour. The flesh of any type should be fine-grained and dark, with firm white fat. The meat of young animals or fawns up to 18 months old is delicate and should not be marinated. The meat of male deer is preferred to that of female deer.

The best parts of the meat in an animal of any age are the haunch, saddle, loin, and shoulder. These can be roasted or cut into chops and cutlets for grilling or frying. The rest of the meat is best made into stews.

This is also true of the many types of buck found in the Middle and Far East, in India and Africa. Recipes for European deer can equally well be used for them.

Venison may only be hunted in the UK at certain seasons which vary according to the type of deer and its sex. During the twentieth century, hunting has become progressively more expensive and deer have become rarer; these factors have led to venison becoming more costly, so that it is now classed as a luxury meat.

Hanging Venison

Unless bought ready for cooking, venison must always be hung; it has little flavour otherwise. When buying fresh venison, always ask the supplier whether it needs further hanging; venison frozen commercially can be assumed to be fully hung.

Whole venison should be hung from 10–14 days, depending on the weather and on the strength of gamey flavour wanted. Pieces need only be hung from 5–7 days. The meat must hang in a cool, dry well-ventilated place.

Before hanging, the meat should be inspected thoroughly. If there is any musty smell, it should be washed in lukewarm water and dried thoroughly. It should then, in any case, be rubbed with a mixture of ground ginger and black pepper. While hanging, it should be inspected daily and any moisture seeping from it should be wiped off.

To test whether the meat is ready for cooking, run a small sharp knife into the flesh near the bone. If it smells over-strong, cook the meat at once or wash it with warm milk and water, dry thoroughly, and cover with more of the preserving mixture. Wash this off before cooking.

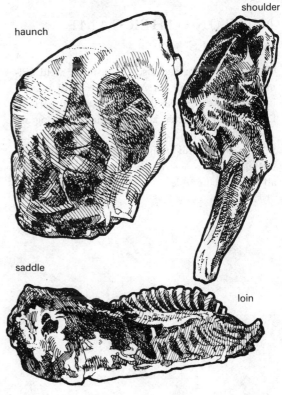

haunch

shoulder

saddle

loin

Preparing Venison

Marinades for venison and other game meat are given on p730. Marinate the meat for as long as required; this will depend on its age and quality. The older and tougher it is, the longer it needs. The marinating time also depends on the strength of gamey flavour wanted. Meat marinated for 24 hours will be tenderized but will have more or less its natural flavour; after 48 hours it will have a distinct gamey flavour which will get progressively stronger thereafter.

Although it is a dry meat, the fat should be cut off as it is unpleasant and makes the venison taste like goat's meat. Barding fat should be used instead. Sinews and gristle must also be removed; the meat tends to be sinewy in any case, and they add to the risk of toughness.

NOTE ON OTHER GAME ANIMALS

On the Continent and elsewhere, other wild animals are killed and eaten as game. Wild boar is hunted and eaten as a delicacy in several parts of Europe. Badger, otter, squirrel, and hedgehog are also used for food in some areas, and outside Europe, other wild animals, such as buck, beaver, buffalo, kangaroo, even the meat of elephant, are all considered edible.

COOKING GAME ANIMALS

Game animals lend themselves to more varied cooking methods than birds. Venison can be cooked in any of the ways suggested for mutton or lamb, depending on its age, condition, and the cut of meat available. The rich, strongly flavoured meat of hare can be compared with that of goose or duck. Wild rabbits can be treated like grouse or pigeons, whereas farmed (tame) rabbits can be cooked in any of the ways given for chicken.

To counteract dryness and toughness in venison, always bard well. Pork fat or fat bacon wrapped round it helps to keep it moist and supple. Wrapping it in well-greased foil before cooking is an alternative.

Roasted, grilled, and fried venison, especially, must be served immediately after cooking, while still really hot; the meat cools quickly and any fat then has a tallowy taste.

WHAT TO SERVE WITH HARE, RABBIT AND VENISON

Plainly roasted game meat is served with:
1) Basic herb stuffing (p375) or forcemeat balls (p376)
2) Thickened gravy (p727)
3) Roast potatoes for venison; potato straws (p792) for hare, rabbit; sautéed potatoes for rabbit
4) Bacon rolls (p396)
5) Redcurrant, cranberry or other sharp jelly.

Grilled or fried game meat is served with:
1) Game chips (p792) or potato crisps
2) Any grilled or fried garnish such as mushrooms or halved tomatoes, and watercress sprigs
3) Redcurrant or rowan-berry jelly or cranberry sauce (p717)

Note Cumberland (p718), Boar's Head (p717) or a similar sauce can be served with roasted, grilled or fried game instead of gravy and jelly, if preferred. Cherry salad (p834) can be served with plain roasted game.

CARVING GAME ANIMALS

Hare

If serving roasted hare, which has been trussed in the traditional way (p672), place it on its belly on a carving dish, remove the foil from the head and ears, and snip through the spine in 2 or 3 places with game shears, to make carving at table easier. At table, cut along the spine from the centre of the back to the buttock end.

Cut across through the middle, and remove one hind quarter. This releases any stuffing.

Divide the thigh and lower leg from the body meat, to make 2 portions; do the same using the second hind quarter.

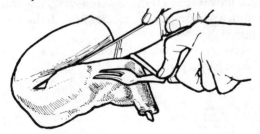

Traditionally, hare meat is served sliced off the bones, but this takes time, and hare meat is best served really hot.

Now cut through the spine just behind the shoulders, and divide the saddle (the centre back) into 2 or more joints.

If the drier forequarter meat is being served, remove any skewer through the neck, cut off the head, and divide the forequarter into 2 portions along the spine. Cut off the lower forelegs before serving.

If the hare has been trussed headless in modern style, 'seat' it, joint, and carve it as above; alternatively, lay it on its side, and carve as above.

Rabbit
(roasted or boiled)

Treat a large tame whole rabbit like hare. If serving a small wild rabbit whole, carve it in the same way, but serve the whole saddle as 1 portion or divided into 2 portions by cutting along the backbone instead of across it.

Venison

Haunch: Place the joint with the thick end facing you. Carve fairly thick slices parallel to the dish on which the joint rests.

Saddle: Carve as for saddle of mutton or lamb (p477).

HARE

Roast Baron of Hare

3 helpings

1 hare	*400ml foundation brown*
basic herb forcemeat	*sauce* (p698)
(p375)	*100ml port (approx)*
6 rashers streaky bacon	*(optional)*
butter or game dripping	

Cut off the head, neck, and limbs of the hare. Use only the body. The legs, neck, and head can be used for soup or pâté, or a civet (p678).

Prepare the hare's liver and parboil it; chop it finely, and add it to the forcemeat. Stuff the hare with the mixture and sew up securely. Lard the hare with the bacon, then wrap it in well-greased foil or greaseproof paper. Roast in a fairly hot oven, 200°C, Gas 6, for 40–50 minutes, basting frequently with hot butter or dripping. Remove the foil or paper about 15 minutes before the end of the cooking time. Meanwhile, heat the brown sauce and add the wine, if used. When the meat is ready, remove the sewing thread, and place the hare on a heated platter for serving.

Serve the sauce separately with redcurrant jelly.

Roast Leveret

5–6 helpings

2 leverets	*flour for dredging*
butter or margarine for	*250ml general household*
basting	*stock* (p329)

Truss the leverets as for hare using the simpler method (p672), but do not stuff them. Roast them in a fairly hot oven, 190°C, Gas 5, for 50–60 minutes, basting them often with butter or margarine. Dredge with flour 10–15 minutes before serving, baste again, and leave to brown. When ready, remove the trussing strings. Keep hot, while making gravy with the stock and pan drippings. Serve the leverets with the gravy.

Serve redcurrant jelly separately. A purée of chestnuts or braised red cabbage makes a good accompaniment.

Roast Hare

5–6 helpings

1 hare	*1 × 5ml spoon chopped*
basic herb forcemeat	*parsley*
(p375)	*a pinch of thyme*
4 rashers streaky bacon	*40g flour*
milk for basting	*400ml general household*
butter for basting	*stock* (p329)
(optional)	*salt and pepper*
1 small shallot	*100ml port (approx)*
50g butter	*(optional)*
	flour for dredging

Garnish
1 stuffed olive

Stuff the hare with the forcemeat and sew up securely. Truss the hare for traditional roasting (p672). Place on a rack in a roasting tin. Cover it with the streaky bacon and roast in a fairly hot oven, 200°C, Gas 6, for $1\frac{1}{2}$–2 hours or until tender. Baste frequently with milk and a little butter, if liked.

Meanwhile, prepare the liver, put it into cold water, bring to the boil, and boil for 5 minutes. Chop it very finely. Skin and chop the shallot. Melt the butter, add the liver, shallot, parsley, and thyme. Fry for 10 minutes. Remove the liver mixture from the butter. Stir in the flour and brown the roux well. Stir in the stock gradually. Bring to boiling point, add the liver mixture, season to taste, and simmer for 10 minutes. Add the wine, if used.

Remove the bacon from the hare, dredge with flour, baste, and return to the oven to continue cooking for 10–15 minutes, to allow the hare to brown. Remove the trussing strings and skewers. Take the covering off the head and ears. Place half a stuffed olive in each eye socket. Serve the hare on a heated dish.

Serve the liver sauce, forcemeat balls, and redcurrant jelly separately.

Jugged Hare

6 helpings

1 hare
liver of the hare (optional)
blood of the hare (if obtainable)
1 × 5ml spoon vinegar (if required)
salt and pepper
2 × 15ml spoons flour
100g butter or margarine
100g onion (approx)
3 whole cloves

bouquet garni
a good pinch of ground mace
a good pinch of grated nutmeg
beef stock to moisten
125ml port or claret
50g redcurrant jelly
1 × 15ml spoon butter (optional)
1 × 15ml spoon flour (optional)
lemon juice (optional)

Garnish

heart-shaped or triangular sippets (p385)

forcemeat balls (p376)

Joint the hare. Reserve the liver and the blood. Mix the blood with the vinegar to prevent it coagulating. Season the flour with salt and pepper, and dust the hare joints with it. Heat the butter or margarine in a frying pan and brown the hare joints all over. Put to one side. Skin the onion, and press the cloves into it. Put the hare joints into a deep ovenproof pot or cooking jar, preferably earthenware. Add the onion, bouquet garni, spices, and just enough stock to cover about a quarter of the joints. Cover the dish very securely with foil, and stand it in a pan of very hot water. Cook in a moderate oven, 180°C, Gas 4, for about 3 hours, depending on the age and toughness of the hare.

Meanwhile, prepare the liver. When the hare is cooked, remove the meat to a serving dish, and keep hot. Pour off the juices into a smaller pan. Mash the hare's liver into the hot liquid, if using it. Add the port or claret, and redcurrant jelly. If using the hare's blood to thicken the sauce, add it to the liquids in the pan and re-heat, stirring all the time; do not allow it to boil. If not using the blood, mix the butter and flour to make a beurre manié, heat the liquids in the pan to simmering point, remove from the heat, and stir in the beurre manié in small spoonfuls. Return the pan to the heat and stir gently until the beurre manié is dissolved and the mixture boils and thickens. Sharpen with a few drops of lemon juice, if liked.

Pour the thickened sauce over the hare joints and serve garnished with the sippets and forcemeat balls.

Hare in Soured Cream

6 helpings

saddle and hindquarters of 1 large hare
200ml vinegar
1 large onion
1 bay leaf
a few peppercorns

25g lard
4 rashers streaky bacon, without rinds
250ml milk
250ml soured cream
salt and pepper

Garnish

forcemeat balls (p376) *or small liver dumplings* (p387)

chopped parsley

Put the hare in a bowl with the vinegar and enough water to cover. Skin the onion, add it with the bay leaf and peppercorns, and leave for several hours or overnight.

When ready to use the hare, remove it from the marinade, and dry it. Melt the lard and brush the hare with it. Chop the onion and put it with the bay leaf into a roasting tin; chop and add the bacon. Put in the hare and roast in a fairly hot oven, 200°C, Gas 6, for 1½–2 hours until tender. After the first 10 minutes, baste the hare with the milk; then baste it every 20 minutes.

When the meat is tender, remove the hare and cut it up. Place it on a hot dish. Strain the sauce into a pan and add the soured cream, salt, and pepper. Bring almost to the boil, and pour it over the hare.

Serve with cranberry or apple jelly, and garnish with forcemeat balls or small liver dumplings, and with chopped parsley.

Civet of Hare

4 helpings

forequarters, neck, and
  breast of 1 hare
100g ham **or** bacon
50g butter
2 ×15ml spoons flour
1 clove of garlic
bouquet garni

1 × 2.5ml spoon sugar
salt and freshly ground
  black pepper
10 very small **or**
  pickling onions
200g mushrooms
liver and blood of the
  hare

Marinade

1 onion
1 litre red wine
2 cloves
2 bay leaves
salt and freshly ground
  black pepper

1 × 5ml spoon chopped
  parsley
1 × 5ml spoon rosemary
  leaves
1 × 10ml spoon wine
  vinegar

Make the marinade first. Skin and split the onion, then mix together all the marinade ingredients. Put in the hare and leave overnight.

Remove the hare and dry it thoroughly. Strain the marinade and reserve the liquid. Cut the hare into small pieces. Cut the ham or bacon into 2cm cubes. Melt the butter in a deep flameproof casserole or pot, add the cubed ham or bacon, and fry gently until well browned. Remove the cubed meat, put in the hare pieces, and fry until browned on all sides. Sprinkle with the flour and cook for 2 minutes, stirring all the time. Add the marinade liquid. Skin and add the garlic clove with the bouquet garni, sugar, salt, and pepper. Return the ham or bacon to the casserole, cover it, and simmer gently for 2 hours. Skin and add the onions, cook for 10 minutes longer, then add the mushrooms including their stalks. Cook for 15 minutes. Chop the hare's liver very finely or pound it until almost smooth. Stir the liver and the hare's blood into the civet, reduce the heat so that the sauce does not boil, and let it steam for 3–4 minutes until the sauce thickens slightly. Remove the bouquet garni.

Serve the hare from the casserole with fried bread croûtons instead of potatoes.

Baked Hare with Mushroom Stuffing

5–6 helpings

1 shallot
200g pickled **or** salt
  pork
200g pie veal
a little general household
  stock (p329)
salt and pepper

75ml sherry (approx)
  (optional)
200g flat well-flavoured
  mushrooms (horse
  mushrooms can be
  used)
1 young hare
lard for basting

Skin the shallot and mince with the pork and veal. Moisten with a little stock, season to taste, and add the sherry if used. Clean and chop the mushrooms and add them to the stuffing. Press the stuffing lightly into the body of the hare, sew up the opening, and truss into shape. Heat the lard in a roasting tin in a fairly hot oven, 200°C, Gas 6. Baste the hare well with the hot fat, cover with 2–3 sheets of greased paper, and bake for 1–1¼ hours. Baste frequently while cooking. About 20 minutes before serving, remove the paper and allow the hare to brown. When the meat is cooked, remove any skewers and string.

Serve Espagnole (p707) or Port Wine (p729) Sauce with the hare.

Haricot of Hare

5–6 helpings

1 hare
3 ×15ml spoons butter
100g onions
100g turnips
200g carrots
salt and pepper

1 ×15ml spoon chopped
  parsley
1 × 2.5ml spoon dried
  thyme
1 litre general household
  stock (p329)

Joint the hare. Melt the butter in a saucepan and fry the joints until well browned on all sides. Prepare and dice the vegetables and add them to the hare with the seasoning, herbs, and stock. Cover tightly and stew gently for 2½–3 hours. Re-season if required.

Serve with apple or blackcurrant jelly.

Hashed Hare

remains of cold roast
*   hare*
400ml foundation brown
*   sauce (p698)*
100ml (approx) port,
*   claret **or** cider*
*   (optional)*
salt and pepper

Trim the hare meat into neat pieces. Make a stock with the bones and trimmings, to use for the sauce or for another game dish. Heat the brown sauce, add the wine if used, put in the pieces of hare, and heat thoroughly for 15–20 minutes. Re-season if required.

Serve with a chestnut purée or mashed potatoes, and offer redcurrant jelly separately.

Note The forelegs and ribs of 1 hare will serve 4 people.

Hare Pie

4–5 helpings

250–300g cooked hare
200g streaky bacon,
*   without rinds **or** a*
*   piece of boiling*
*   bacon*
100g soft white
*   breadcrumbs*
*gravy **or** stock made*
*   from the bones*
salt and pepper
Worcestershire sauce
fat for greasing
500g creamed potato
25g butter

Cut the hare meat off the bone, and cut it into small pieces. Cut the bacon into small squares or cubes, and fry it gently until just tender. Mix with the pieces of hare, the breadcrumbs, and just enough gravy or stock to moisten. Season, and add a few drops of Worcestershire sauce. Place half the meat mixture in the bottom of a greased pie dish, and cover with half the creamed potato. Repeat these 2 layers. Dot the top potato layer with the butter. Cook in a hot oven, 220°C, Gas 7, for 30 minutes or until the top is golden-brown.

Serve hot, with Cumberland Sauce (p718) or Prune Sauce (p719) and with sweet-sour pickles or chutney.

RABBIT

Sandringham Rabbit

3–4 helpings

1 tame rabbit
salt and pepper
2 large tomatoes
1 small shallot
1 × 5ml spoon grated
*   lemon rind*
50g soft white
*   breadcrumbs*
1 × 5ml spoon chopped
*   parsley*
1 × 2.5ml spoon thyme
50g shredded suet
1 egg
1 rasher of bacon
2 ×15ml spoons cooking
*   oil for basting*

Garnish
bacon rolls (p396)

Season the rabbit well. Skin the tomatoes and chop them finely. Skin and chop the shallot. Mix the tomatoes with the shallot, lemon rind, bread-crumbs, parsley, thyme, and suet. Bind the mixture with the egg. Stuff the rabbit with the mixture and truss it using the simpler method (p672). Lay the bacon rasher on top of the rabbit. Brush with some of the oil. Roast the rabbit in a fairly hot oven, 200°C, Gas 6, for 50–60 minutes, basting with the oil from time to time. Remove the bacon about 10 minutes before serving to let the meat brown. At the same time, put the bacon rolls in the oven in a small baking tin to cook until crisp. When the meat is cooked, remove the trussing strings or skewers. Serve the rabbit garnished with the bacon rolls.

Serve Fresh Tomato Sauce (p715) or Foundation Brown Sauce (p698) separately.

Roast Rabbit with Espagnole Sauce

4 helpings

1 tame rabbit	fat for basting
basic herb forcemeat (p375)	400ml Espagnole sauce (p707) (see **Note**)
4 rashers streaky bacon	

Garnish

cubed roasted potatoes (see Method)	4–8 bacon rolls (p396)
	watercress sprigs

Prepare the garnish first. Cut 4 medium-sized potatoes into 2cm cubes and put in salted water to prevent them discolouring.

Stuff the rabbit with the forcemeat, skewer up the cavity opening, and truss using the simpler method (p672). Cover the back with the bacon rashers. Heat the oven to fairly hot, 200°C, Gas 6. Heat the fat in the oven, in the roasting tin to be used for the rabbit. Baste the rabbit with the hot fat, and put the rabbit into the tin; roast it for 1–1½ hours, depending on its size. Baste it often while cooking.

About 30 minutes before the end of the cooking time, drain and dry the potatoes, and put into the roasting tin with the meat. Baste them well, and cook with the meat until tender and browned, turning them over often while cooking. Ten minutes before the rabbit is ready, remove the bacon rashers from the back, to let the meat brown. At the same time put the bacon rolls in a small baking tin, and place in the oven on the rack below the rabbit to bake-fry in their own fat. While they cook, heat the sauce.

When the rabbit is cooked, remove the skewers. Place it on a heated dish, and pour a little of the sauce round it. Garnish with small piles of the potato and with the bacon rolls and watercress sprigs. Serve the sauce separately.

Note To make carving easier, the rabbit can be garnished only with watercress, and the potatoes and bacon rolls served on a separate dish.

Foundation Brown (p698) or Robert (p703) Sauce can be served instead of Espagnole sauce, if preferred.

Epigrams of Rabbit

4–6 helpings

2 rabbits	1 egg
fat for shallow frying	breadcrumbs for coating
chicken liver stuffing (p381)	oil **or** fat for deep frying

Garnish
fried parsley (p398)

Use only the back flesh. Remove it from the bones keeping the meat from each side whole. Divide each piece of meat into 2 or 3 portions. Flatten them slightly with a cutlet bat. Heat the oil or fat and fry the rabbit gently for 10–15 minutes, turning 2 or 3 times. When tender, press between 2 plates until cold.

Cover one side of each portion with stuffing, beat the egg until liquid, and coat the portions with egg and breadcrumbs twice. Heat the oil or fat (p303) and fry until crisp and golden-brown. Drain the epigrams. Garnish with the parsley.

Serve with Foundation Brown Sauce (p698).

Barbecue of Rabbit

3–4 helpings

1 large tame rabbit	1 × 5ml spoon French mustard
salt and pepper	
butter **or** olive oil	2 ×15ml spoons Demerara sugar
150ml tomato ketchup	
1 ×15ml spoon lemon juice	a few drops Tabasco sauce

Garnish

lemon slices	fried parsley (p398)

Leave the rabbit in salted water for 1 hour; then dry it thoroughly. Make slits with a knife point in the flesh of the back and legs, and rub salt and pepper into them. Melt the butter, if used. Brush the rabbit all over with butter or oil. Heat the ketchup and mix in the remaining ingredients. Re-season. Grill the rabbit for 20–25 minutes, basting it with the sauce and turning it often. When tender and brown, divide it into neat joints, and place them on a hot dish. Pour any remaining sauce over them. Garnish with the lemon and parsley.

Farmer's Braised Rabbit

8 helpings

*1 large tame rabbit
(2.5kg approx before
skinning)
liver, heart, and kidneys
of the rabbit
8 prunes
500ml dry red, white* **or**
rosé wine **or** *dry cider
flour for coating
50ml cooking oil
1 small onion
150g carrots
2 sticks celery*

*2 cloves garlic
25g concentrated tomato
purée
bouquet garni
salt and ground black
pepper
a pinch of ground mace
8 olives, green* **or** *black
8 button mushrooms
8 button* **or** *pickling
onions
3 × 10ml spoons
cornflour
100ml water*

Garnish
chopped parsley

crescent **or** *heart-shaped
sippets (p385)*

Keep the liver, heart, and kidneys to one side. Soak the rabbit in cold water for 1 hour to whiten the flesh. Meanwhile, steep the prunes in the wine or cider.

Dry the rabbit thoroughly. Cut it into 8 serving portions, and toss them lightly in the flour. Heat the oil in a large frying pan, and fry the meat until the pieces are golden-brown all over, turning them as required. Transfer them to a heavy, ovenproof casserole. Keep the remaining oil in the frying pan.

Prepare and dice the onion and carrots, and slice the celery. Skin the garlic and chop it finely. Fry the vegetables gently in the oil, turning them over to brown them slightly. Add them to the casserole with the tomato purée, bouquet garni, seasoning, and mace. Prepare the liver, heart, and kidneys; chop and add them to the casserole. Stone and add the olives. Stone the soaked prunes and add them with the liquid they have soaked in. Cover the casserole tightly, and cook in a moderate oven, 180°C, Gas 4, for 1½ hours.

Meanwhile, sauté the button mushrooms in the frying pan. Skin and boil the onions for 5 minutes in lightly salted water. Add both to the casserole 5 minutes before the end of the cooking time.

When the meat is done, strain the cooking liquid into a small saucepan, and remove the bouquet garni. Cover the casserole and keep hot. Blend the cornflour and water, stir into the cooking liquid, and heat gently, stirring, until the sauce thickens. Re-season if required. Pour the sauce over the meat, and sprinkle with the chopped parsley. Serve from the casserole with crescents or heart-shaped sippets.

Note In some versions of this old dish, beer or tea is used instead of wine or cider.

Rabbit with Tomato and Lemon

4 helpings

*50g dripping
4 tame* **or** *wild rabbit
joints
400ml chicken stock
(approx)
40g butter
25g flour*

*200g concentrated
tomato purée
salt and pepper
a pinch of caster sugar
1 × 5ml spoon lemon
juice*

Melt the dripping in a saucepan and fry the pieces of rabbit until well browned on all sides. Drain off any surplus fat, add enough stock just to cover the rabbit, cover with a tight-fitting lid, and cook for about 1–1¼ hours or until tender. Meanwhile, melt the butter in a small saucepan, stir in the flour, and cook gently until the roux is nut-brown; then stir in the tomato purée.

When the rabbit is cooked, remove it from the pan, drain and keep hot. Strain the stock and stir it into the tomato mixture. Stir until boiling, season to taste, and add a pinch of sugar and the lemon juice. Put the rabbit joints in the sauce, heat thoroughly, and serve at once.

Rabbit in Lager

4–5 helpings

1 tame rabbit	125g button mushrooms
salt and pepper	2 × 5ml spoons made
3 × 15ml spoons flour	English mustard
50g butter **or** margarine	2 × 5ml spoons made
1 × 15ml spoon oil	French mustard
1 large onion	250ml lager (approx)
125g streaky bacon,	salt and pepper
without rinds	sugar (optional)

Garnish
chopped parsley

Joint the rabbit. Soak the joints in a bowl of cold water for 30 minutes; then dry them thoroughly. Season the flour with salt and pepper. Coat the joints lightly with the seasoned flour, shake off the excess, and put the unused flour to one side.

Heat 25g of the butter or margarine in a frying pan, add the oil, and fry the rabbit lightly. Remove, drain off any excess fat, and place in a casserole. Skin and chop the onion, add it to the pan, and cook very gently without browning for 10 minutes. Chop the bacon, and add to the onion. Quarter the mushrooms if large, and add them to the pan, with both mustards and the lager. Season to taste. Spoon the mixture over the rabbit in the casserole. Cover the casserole and cook in a moderate oven, 180°C, Gas 4, for 1½ hours or until the rabbit is tender; the time will vary, depending on the age and size of the rabbit.

When the rabbit is cooked, strain off the liquor from the casserole into a saucepan, bring to the boil, and boil rapidly to reduce it by one-third. Remove from the heat. Blend the remaining flour and butter together on a plate to make a beurre manié and add in small pieces to the saucepan. Stir well, return to the heat, and bring to the boil. Cook for 2 minutes to thicken and clear the sauce. Re-season if required. If liked, add a little sugar to remove any bitterness from the lager. Pour the sauce over the rabbit and serve sprinkled with a little chopped parsley.

Ragoût of Rabbit

3–4 helpings

1 wild rabbit	400ml chicken stock
100g streaky bacon,	salt and pepper
without rinds	1 carrot
50g butter	½ small turnip
1 small onion	6 peppercorns
40g flour	½ clove of garlic

Garnish
macédoine of vegetables
 (p398)

Joint the rabbit. Discard the lower forelegs and rib-cage, or keep for stock. Dice the bacon. Heat the butter in a large saucepan and fry the rabbit joints in it until well browned on all sides. Remove the joints and keep hot under greased paper. Skin, chop, and fry the onion with the bacon, stir in the flour, and fry gently until the onion and bacon are well browned. Bring the stock to the boil and add to the bacon and onion. Boil for 10 minutes. Return the rabbit to the pan. Add seasoning to taste. Peel, dice, and add the carrot and turnip. Tie the peppercorns and garlic in muslin, and add them. Cover the pan tightly. Stew gently for about 2 hours until the rabbit is tender. Re-season if required. Remove the muslin bag.

Serve the rabbit on a hot dish with the sauce spooned over it. Garnish both ends of the dish with a macédoine of vegetables.

VARIATIONS
1) A little dried thyme can be added with the peppercorns.
2) 225ml dry cider can be substituted for 225ml stock.

Larded Rabbit

3–4 helpings

1 tame rabbit	bouquet garni
larding bacon	1 onion
50g dripping	25g butter
300ml chicken stock	25g flour
salt and pepper	

Joint the rabbit. Lard each piece with strips of chilled fat larding bacon. Heat the dripping in a saucepan, and fry the rabbit joints until lightly browned. Pour off any excess fat and add the stock, seasoning, and bouquet garni. Skin, slice, and add the onion. Cover the saucepan tightly. Bring to the boil and stew very gently for $1\frac{1}{4}$–$1\frac{1}{2}$ hours or until the rabbit is tender. Knead the butter and flour together to make a beurre manié. Remove the saucepan from the heat and add the beurre manié in small pieces 20 minutes before serving. Stir well, then return to the heat to finish the cooking and to thicken the sauce.

When the rabbit is tender, remove it from the sauce, and drain it well over the saucepan. Pile the joints on a hot dish and strain the sauce over them.

Rabbit Casserole

4 helpings

1 wild rabbit	1 onion
salt and pepper	225g cooking apples
4 × 15ml spoons plain	1 × 213g can prunes
flour	1 chicken stock cube
65g butter	

Garnish

chopped parsley	crescents of fried bread
	(p385)

Joint the rabbit, and discard the lower forelegs and rib-cage, or keep for stock. Season half the flour lightly with salt and pepper and coat the rabbit lightly. Melt 50g butter in a flameproof casserole or frying pan, add the rabbit, and brown lightly on all sides. Remove the joints to a plate. Skin and slice the onion and fry in the butter until soft but not brown. Peel, core, and slice the apples, and add

them to the onion. Drain the prunes and make the juice up to 250ml with water. Add the stock cube, crumbling it finely. Return the rabbit to the casserole with the prunes and stock. Cover and cook in a moderate oven, 180°C, Gas 4, for $1\frac{1}{2}$ hours or until the rabbit is tender.

When the rabbit is cooked, arrange the joints on a warmed serving dish with the apples and prunes; keep hot. Blend the remaining butter and flour together on a plate to make a beurre manié and add in small pieces to the liquid in the casserole. Bring to the boil and stir all the time until the sauce thickens. Re-season if required and pour the sauce over the rabbit. Sprinkle with chopped parsley. Surround with the crescents of fried bread, and serve at once.

Scotch Rabbit

4 helpings

1 wild rabbit	2 tomatoes
125g pork or bacon	1 small onion
(25g optional)	bouquet garni
1 cabbage	275ml chicken stock
salt and pepper	(approx)

Cut the flesh from the rabbit bones (these can be used to make stock). Chop the rabbit meat and 100g of the pork or bacon, and mix together. Separate and wash the cabbage leaves, cut out the stems, blanch the leaves, and season them. Line a saucepan with some of the cabbage leaves. Skin and chop the tomatoes, and skin and chop the onion. Put the meat, tomato, onion, seasoning, and bouquet garni into the lined pan. Cover closely with more cabbage leaves and put the extra piece of pork or bacon on top, if liked. Heat enough stock in a separate pan to cover the dish. Bring to boiling point and pour it into the saucepan. Cover tightly, and simmer for about $2\frac{1}{2}$ hours, adding more stock if necessary. Re-season if required, remove the bouquet garni, and serve.

VARIATION
Kale can be used instead of cabbage.

Hunter's Rabbit Casserole

4 helpings

100g streaky bacon rashers, without rinds	1 × 2.5ml spoon mixed herbs
3 medium-sized onions	salt and pepper
2 carrots	500ml chicken stock
750g–1kg wild rabbit joints	

Trim the bacon, and cut each rasher into 3 pieces. Prepare and slice the onions and carrots. Layer the rabbit, bacon, and vegetables in a casserole, sprinkle with herbs and seasoning, and pour in the stock. Cover, and cook in a warm oven, 160°C, Gas 3, for 1½–2 hours or until the rabbit is tender.

Stewed or Poached Rabbit

4 helpings

1 rabbit	bouquet garni
1 onion	6 peppercorns
1 carrot	1 × 5ml spoon salt
½ turnip	onion sauce (1) (p695)
2 sticks celery	

Garnish

chopped parsley	grilled bacon rolls (p396) (optional)

Truss the rabbit and put it into boiling, lightly salted water. Prepare the vegetables and cut them into pieces. When the water comes to the boil, add them together with the bouquet garni, peppercorns, and 1 × 5ml spoon salt. Poach gently for 45–60 minutes until the rabbit is tender.

Meanwhile, heat the sauce. When the rabbit is tender, remove the skewers. Drain the rabbit. (Keep the cooking liquid for stock or broth.)

Lay the rabbit on a hot dish, and pour the hot sauce over it. Serve very hot, sprinkled with the chopped parsley. Serve any extra sauce separately.

Garnish, if liked, with bacon rolls.

Curried Rabbit

3–4 helpings

1 tame or wild rabbit	1 × 10ml spoon mango chutney
50g butter	
1 small onion	1 × 15ml spoon lemon juice
1 × 10ml spoon flour	
1 × 15ml spoon curry powder	salt and pepper
	25g sultanas
1 × 10ml spoon curry paste	25g blanched almonds
	2 × 15ml spoons single cream or top of milk (optional)
1 × 10ml spoon desiccated coconut	
1 apple	
400ml white stock (p329)	

Garnish

paprika	gherkin fans (p390)
lemon wedges	(optional)

Joint the rabbit. Heat the butter in a saucepan and fry the joints lightly. Remove the meat and drain it. Skin, chop, and fry the onion lightly in the same fat. Add the flour, curry powder and paste, and continue frying, stirring occasionally for 3–4 minutes. Tie the coconut in a piece of muslin. Peel, core, and chop the apple. Stir the stock into the pan and bring to the boil. Put in all the other ingredients except the cream or milk, and lay the rabbit joints on top. Simmer for 15 minutes, then remove the coconut. Simmer gently for a further 1½ hours, adding a little extra stock if necessary. Stir in the cream or milk, if used. Remove the rabbit to a heated serving dish. Pour the sauce over it. Sprinkle lightly with paprika and garnish with lemon wedges and gherkin fans, if used.

Serve with a selection of the traditional accompaniments listed on p388.

Rabbit Stewed in Milk

3–4 helpings

500g boneless rabbit
1 small onion
salt and pepper

1 small blade of mace
225ml milk (approx)
1 × 5ml spoon cornflour

Garnish
chopped parsley

Cut the rabbit into small pieces. Place them in a casserole. Skin and chop the onion finely and add it with the seasoning and mace. Three-quarters fill the dish with milk, cover, and cook in a fairly hot oven, 190°C, Gas 5, for 1–1¼ hours. Blend the cornflour with a little cold milk, and add to the liquid in the casserole, stirring all the time. Bring to the boil, and cook for another 10 minutes. Sprinkle with chopped parsley before serving.

Rabbit Creole

4–5 helpings

450g boneless rabbit
1 onion
1 clove of garlic
1 small green pepper
1 × 400g can tomatoes
25g unsalted butter
1 × 15ml spoon corn oil

1 × 5ml spoon sugar
1 × 15ml spoon
  concentrated tomato
  purée
salt
1 × 2.5ml spoon
  Tabasco sauce
10 stuffed olives

Cut the rabbit meat into small strips. Skin and slice the onion; skin and crush the garlic. Halve the pepper, remove the membranes and seeds, and slice it. Drain and cut up the tomatoes roughly. Put the butter and oil in a saucepan with the onion, garlic and pepper, and fry for 2–3 minutes without colouring. Add the rabbit and cook gently for 15 minutes until the onion is soft, taking care not to brown it. Stir in all the remaining ingredients, cover, and simmer gently for 25 minutes.

Serve with plain boiled rice or buttered noodles.

Rabbit Pilaf

4–5 helpings

225g boneless rabbit
550ml chicken stock
1 small onion
2 sticks celery
225g long-grain rice
50g sultanas
25g butter

100g streaky bacon,
  without rinds
1 green pepper
25g blanched almonds
  (optional)
salt and pepper

Garnish
paprika   celery leaves

Cut the rabbit into serving portions, place in a saucepan with the stock, and cook gently for about 40 minutes until tender. Remove with a perforated spoon, and put to one side. Meanwhile, skin and chop the onion, and slice the celery finely. Bring the stock to the boil, add the rice and sultanas, and cook for 12–15 minutes until the rice is tender. The rice should have absorbed almost all the liquid when cooked; add a little more stock if necessary.

Melt the butter in a large pan, add the onion and celery, and cook gently until soft. Cut the bacon into pieces, and add to the onion and celery; cook for a few minutes until crisp. Halve the pepper and remove the seeds and membranes. Cut the flesh into shreds, and add it to the onion, celery, and bacon. Cook for 5 minutes. Brown the almonds, if used, under the grill. Stir the rice and sultanas into the onion, celery, and bacon mixture with the rabbit and the almonds. Heat gently but thoroughly. Add salt and pepper to taste. Place in a warmed dish, sprinkle with paprika, and garnish with celery leaves.

Marbled Rabbit

8 helpings

2 wild rabbits
salt
500g pickled pork **or**
    boiling bacon
chicken stock
1 × 2.5ml spoon mixed
    herbs
salt and pepper

1 × 5ml spoon chopped
    parsley
soft white breadcrumbs
    (see Method)
1 egg
fat for shallow frying
5 × 5ml spoons gelatine
2 hard-boiled eggs

Joint the rabbits, reserving the liver and kidneys. Leave the joints for at least 1 hour in strongly salted water. Slice the pork or bacon, and chop half of it finely. Keep the chopped portion aside. Pack the rabbit joints in a saucepan with the sliced pork or bacon on top; barely cover with stock. Cover tightly, and simmer gently for $1\frac{1}{4}$–$1\frac{1}{2}$ hours until the rabbit is tender.

Lift out the joints, drain them over the pan, and remove the bones, leaving the flesh in large pieces. Trim into neat shapes. Chop the trimmings finely. Mix them with the herbs, seasoning, and parsley; then weigh the mixture and add half its weight in breadcrumbs. Add some of the chopped pork or bacon and bind with egg. Mix thoroughly. Form into small balls and poach them for 10 minutes in the stock. Drain, and put to one side. Fry the livers and kidneys in a little fat and slice them thinly.

Strain 125ml of the stock into a small pan. Soften the gelatine in it, and then heat until dissolved. Slice the hard-boiled eggs. Allow the gelatine mixture to cool but not set. Pour a little into a wetted mould, and let it set. Cover with pieces of rabbit, layered with the remaining chopped pork or bacon, the forcemeat balls, slices of liver and kidney, and slices of hard-boiled egg. Do not pack down tightly; leave spaces to be filled with stock. Fill up the mould with the remaining stock, covering the rest of the ingredients completely.

Leave for 3–4 hours to set, turn out on to a serving dish, slice, and serve with salad.

Rabbit Pie

4–5 helpings

450g boneless rabbit
1 small onion
salt and pepper
150ml water
2 × 15ml spoons
    cornflour
3 × 15ml spoons milk

2 × 15ml spoons
    chopped parsley
shortcrust pastry
    (p1249) using 250g
    flour
flour for rolling out
2 hard-boiled eggs
milk for glazing

Cut the rabbit into large pieces and place in a saucepan. Skin and chop the onion, and add it to the pan with salt, pepper, and the water. Cover and simmer slowly for $1\frac{1}{4}$ hours or until the rabbit is tender. Remove the rabbit meat. Blend the cornflour with the milk, and stir into the rabbit stock. Bring slowly to the boil, stirring all the time, and cook until the sauce thickens and clears. Stir in the parsley and rabbit meat. Leave the sauce to cool.

Roll out the pastry on a lightly floured surface, and use half of it to line a 23cm shallow pie plate. Arrange the rabbit mixture in the centre. Slice the hard-boiled eggs and place on top. Dampen the edges of the base pastry lightly with milk, cover with the remaining pastry, seal, and crimp the edges. Glaze the top crust with milk, and make a small hole in the centre. Cook the pie in a hot oven, 220°C, Gas 7, for 15 minutes; then reduce the heat to fairly hot, 190°C, Gas 5, and bake for a further 25–30 minutes. Serve hot or cold.

Durham Rabbit Pie

See p1255.

Pigeon or Rabbit Pudding

See p665.

All meat in the following recipes is assumed to be prepared ready for cooking.

VENISON

Roast Haunch of Venison

a haunch of venison
clarified butter (p886)
  or dripping
flour for dredging

Saw off the knuckle-bone (or wrap the foot, if left on, in several layers of foil). Melt the clarified butter or dripping and brush the joint well all over; then wrap in well-greased aluminium foil or a sheet of greaseproof paper. If using paper, make a stiff paste of flour and water and cover the joint with it; then cover with another well-greased sheet of paper, and tie securely with string.

Roast the joint on a rack in a moderate oven, 180°C, Gas 4 (see below). Twenty to 30 minutes before the cooking time is completed, remove the foil or paste and papers, dredge lightly with flour, and baste well with hot butter. Continue cooking until the joint is tender and a good brown colour.

Have the traditional or other accompaniments ready before removing the venison from the oven. Transfer to a heated carving dish; serve at once.

Cooking time 15 minutes per 500g for large joints, 20 minutes per 500g for smaller joints weighing 1.5kg or less.

Note The haunch can be replaced by a shoulder of venison.

Grilled Fillets of Venison

4 helpings

4 slices fillet of venison,
  1cm thick
2 ×15ml spoons olive oil
freshly ground pepper
2 ×15ml spoons
  chopped fresh mixed
  herbs

Flatten the fillets a little, brush well with the olive oil, and sprinkle with pepper and fresh herbs. Leave to stand for about 1 hour. Grill under medium heat for 3–5 minutes on each side.

Serve Cumberland Sauce (p718) separately.

Roast Venison with Baked Apples

4–6 helpings

4 small sharp cooking
  apples
juice of 1 lemon
2 × 10ml spoons
  gooseberry, rowan-
  berry **or** *redcurrant*
  jelly
1 ×15ml spoon butter
1 ×10ml spoon soft
  brown sugar
1kg piece young venison
3 ×15ml spoons oil
  (approx)

Sauce
125ml general household
  stock (p329)
2 ×15ml spoons
  gooseberry, rowan-
  berry **or** *redcurrant*
  jelly
a small pinch of ground
  cloves
salt and pepper
1 ×10ml spoon
  cornflour
1 ×15ml spoon cold
  water
2 ×15ml spoons sherry

Peel and core the apples but leave them whole; simmer them gently in a little water with the lemon juice for 10–15 minutes. Drain and arrange in an ovenproof dish. Fill the core holes with the gooseberry, rowan-berry or redcurrant jelly. Dot each apple with a small piece of butter, and sprinkle with the brown sugar. Brush the venison with 2 ×15ml spoons oil and roast with the apples for 40 minutes in a fairly hot oven, 190°C, Gas 5; baste with extra oil from time to time.

Meanwhile, make the sauce. Put the stock, jelly, ground cloves, salt, and pepper in a small pan. Heat gently to dissolve the jelly. Blend the cornflour with the water, add to the stock, and bring to the boil, stirring all the time. Cook for 2 minutes to thicken and clear the sauce.

Slice the meat and arrange it on a warm dish with the apples; keep both hot. Place the pan in which the meat was cooked, over the heat, add the sauce and the sherry, and scrape together with the pan drippings. Strain over the meat.

Fried Venison Cutlets

8 helpings

8 cutlets of venison from leg **or** loin	75g butter
75ml olive oil	8 large mushrooms
salt and pepper	100g redcurrant jelly
4 × 15ml spoons flour	2 × 5ml spoons red wine vinegar
1 egg	1 × 5ml spoon Demerara sugar
75g fine dry breadcrumbs	

Soak the cutlets in the oil for about 1 hour. Drain well. Season the flour with salt and pepper and use to coat each cutlet. Beat the egg until liquid and coat each cutlet first in the egg and then in the crumbs, pressing them on well. Heat 40g of the butter and fry the cutlets for about 10–12 minutes, adding more butter if necessary, and turning once or twice. Drain and keep hot. Heat the remaining butter and fry the mushrooms; place a mushroom on each cutlet. Mix the jelly, vinegar, and sugar with the pan juices. Heat the jelly to melt it, and reduce it a little. Serve with the cutlets.

Polish Fried Venison

6 helpings

6 juniper berries	salt and pepper
4 × 15ml spoons wine vinegar	40g butter
1 × 15ml spoon meat extract	6 × 1cm thick slices leg of venison
250ml Velouté sauce (p708)	

Crush the juniper berries and simmer them in the vinegar until the liquid is reduced by half; add the meat extract and the sauce, and cook gently for 15 minutes. Strain the sauce, season it, stir in 15g of the butter, and keep hot under damp paper.

Flatten the venison slices with a cutlet bat, heat the rest of the butter, and fry them for 10–15 minutes, turning once. Arrange the steaks on a hot dish and pour some of the sauce over them. Serve the rest separately in a heated sauce-boat.

Chafing Dish Venison

3–4 helpings

500g venison	1 egg
3 small onions	salt and pepper
1 × 5ml spoon chopped parsley	flour for coating
a pinch of grated nutmeg	25g butter
	1 × 15ml spoon oil

Garnish
fried tomato halves   watercress sprigs

Cut the meat into small pieces. Skin and quarter the onions and mince both meat and onions coarsely. Stir in the parsley, nutmeg, egg, and seasoning. Form into 4 flat cakes, the size and shape of cutlets, and coat lightly with flour. Heat the butter and oil in a frying pan, put in the cutlets, and fry gently for 10 minutes. Turn over and fry for another 7–10 minutes. Drain, and serve at once, garnished with the tomatoes and watercress sprigs.

Collared Venison

10–12 helpings

100ml port (approx) (optional)	750ml game stock (p330)
8 thin slices lamb **or** pork fat	1 × 2.5ml spoon black peppercorns
shoulder of venison	1 × 2.5ml spoon ground allspice
salt and pepper	

Garnish
forcemeat balls (p376)

If port is used, soak the lamb or pork fat in it for 2–3 hours. Bone the venison, flatten it with a cutlet bat, and season well. Cover with the slices of lamb or pork fat. Roll it up tightly and tie securely with tape. Bring the stock to simmering point in a large pan and add the meat with the venison bones, peppercorns, allspice, and the port in which the fat was soaked. Simmer gently with a lid on the pan for 3–3½ hours.

Serve garnished with forcemeat balls and offer redcurrant jelly separately.

Braised Venison

6–8 helpings

1–1.25kg haunch **or**
shoulder of venison
red wine marinade
(p730)
25g dripping
1 orange
general household stock
(p329)

fat for greasing
2 ×15ml spoons
redcurrant jelly
salt and freshly ground
black pepper
25g butter
25g flour

Mirepoix
1 onion
2 carrots

2 sticks celery

Garnish
watercress sprigs

forcemeat balls (p376)

Place the venison in a deep dish. Cover with the red wine marinade and leave for about 12 hours, basting and turning occasionally. Dry on soft kitchen paper and trim if required. Reserve the marinade. Heat the dripping and brown the venison on all sides. Remove and keep on one side.

Cut the vegetables for the mirepoix into thick slices, and fry for a few seconds in the hot dripping; then place in the bottom of a large casserole. Pare off a few thin strips of rind from the orange. Strain the marinade into the casserole. Add the rind and enough stock just to cover the vegetables. Place the venison on top, cover with a well-greased piece of greaseproof paper, and cover with a lid. Cook in a fairly hot oven, 190°C, Gas 5, allowing 20 minutes for every 500g plus 20 minutes.

When cooked, carve the meat into slices. Arrange on a heated serving dish and keep hot. Strain the liquor from the vegetables into a pan. Squeeze the orange and strain the juice into the pan. Add the redcurrant jelly, salt and pepper, and bring to the boil, stirring to dissolve the jelly. Blend the butter and flour together on a plate to make a beurre manié. Remove the pan from the heat and add the beurre manié in small pieces; stir until blended in. Return the pan to the heat, bring to the boil, and cook for 2–3 minutes until the sauce thickens. Pour the sauce over the venison and serve hot, garnished with watercress and forcemeat balls.

Serve with a purée of chestnuts or celeriac.

Braised Venison Steaks

6–8 helpings

4 slices venison (from
haunch) (300g each
approx)
salt and ground black
pepper
25g flour

butter **or** *dripping*
1 small onion
6–8 juniper berries
125ml game (p330) **or**
brown stock (p329)

Marinade
300ml red wine (approx)
bouquet garni
6 peppercorns
4 slices onion

2 ×15ml spoons olive oil
1 ×10ml spoon red wine
vinegar

Garnish
chopped parsley

Make the marinade first. Boil together all the ingredients for it for 1 minute. Allow to cool completely. Lay the venison steaks in a shallow dish, and pour the marinade over them. Leave overnight.

Take the venison out of the marinade, and pat dry. Snip the edges of the slices with scissors to prevent curling. Season the flour with salt and pepper, and rub it over both sides of the venison steaks. Heat the fat in a large flameproof pan or roasting tin until it hazes. Sear the steaks on both sides in the fat. Skin and chop the onion and add it when searing the second side. Crush the juniper berries. Pour off all but a film of fat. Sprinkle the steaks with the crushed juniper. Pour the stock and a little of the marinade round them, covering about 1cm of the depth of the dish. Cover tightly with foil and bake in a moderate oven, 180°C, Gas 4, for 30 minutes or until the steaks are tender. Drain and serve sprinkled with chopped parsley.

Remove the grease from the stock and serve as a sauce, or serve Port Wine Sauce (p729), or Boar's Head Sauce (p717), if preferred.

Note For other marinades, see p730.

Civet of Venison

4–6 helpings

*750g pieces **or** | 125g button mushrooms*
trimmings of venison | 1 ×15ml spoon
for stewing | concentrated tomato
cooked red wine | purée
marinade (p730) | 25g butter
2 ×15ml spoons oil | 25g plain flour
120g streaky bacon | salt and pepper
rashers, without rinds | 1 × 5ml spoon sugar

Garnish
croûtons of fried bread

Place the venison in a bowl, cover with the marinade, and leave for 24 hours. Drain the meat and reserve the marinade. Dry the meat well on soft kitchen paper.

Place 1 ×15ml spoon of the oil in a saucepan. Cut the bacon rashers into small pieces. Add to the saucepan with the mushrooms and cook for a few minutes until the bacon is lightly browned. Remove the bacon and mushrooms with a perforated spoon; put to one side. Add the remaining oil to the pan and heat it. Add the meat, and cook fairly quickly to brown it all over. Return the bacon and mushrooms to the saucepan. Add the marinade, stir in the tomato purée, cover with a lid, and simmer gently for 2–2½ hours until the meat is tender.

Meanwhile, soften the butter and blend together with the flour to make a beurre manié. Off the heat, add this to the stew in small pieces. Return to the heat and stir until the beurre manié melts and the stew thickens. Add salt, pepper, and sugar to taste. Garnish with croûtons of fried bread.

Serve with boiled rice.

Hashed Venison

3–4 helpings

300g cold roast venison | 50ml port (approx)
400g general household | (optional)
stock (p329) | 4 ×15ml spoons
40g butter | redcurrant jelly
3 ×15ml spoons flour | salt and pepper

Garnish
croûtons of fried bread

Slice the meat neatly. Break up any bones and put them with any meat trimmings into the stock. Simmer the stock gently for 45 minutes, then strain it. Melt the butter and stir in the flour. Brown together slowly. Stir in the strained stock, and continue stirring until the sauce comes to the boil. Put in the meat, port, if used, and the jelly. Bring quickly to the boil and re-heat thoroughly. Season to taste. Garnish with the croûtons.

Serve at once, very hot, and offer extra redcurrant jelly separately.

SAUCES, GRAVIES AND MARINADES

The preparation and appearance of sauces and gravies are of the highest consequence, and in nothing does the talent and taste of the cook more display itself. Their special adaptability to the various viands they are to accompany cannot be too much studied, in order that they may harmonize and blend with them as perfectly, so to speak, as does a pianoforte accompaniment with the voice of the singer.

Sauces

Sauces are used to add flavour, colour or moisture, but they must never overpower or disguise the flavour of the food with which they are served.

Making them is one of the most interesting forms of cookery because of the innumerable variations in flavour, texture, and consistency. Most, although not all, are distinctly savoury or sweet. They may be either cooked or uncooked.

The main ingredient of all sauces is a liquid or a semi-liquid purée. It can be thin, or thickened either by boiling down to the preferred consistency, or by adding a thickening agent (liaison), such as flour, cornflour, egg or cream.

The two largest groups are the starch-thickened white and brown sauces, whose counterparts in French savoury cookery are Béchamel and Espagnole sauce. Velouté sauce, which is fawn in colour, is the third basic French sauce. Mayonnaises based on egg and oil emulsions, are also French in origin, as is Tomato sauce. Recipes for mayonnaises and salad dressings can be found on pp843–49.

In starch-thickened savoury sauces, the thickening agent is added in one of three ways:

1) *Roux method:* Fat and flour (or another starch) are cooked together to make a roux, and the liquid is then added to it.
2) *Beurre manié method:* Standard quantities of fat and flour are kneaded together to a paste which is whisked into the very hot, but not boiling, liquid in small spoonfuls, and is dissolved to thicken the sauce before it is boiled. Equal quantities of fat and flour are sometimes used or 2 parts fat to 1 part flour. The paste can be stored in a refrigerator for a few days before use.
3) *All-in-one method:* The basic ingredients are all put in a pan and heated together.

With all three methods, care must be taken to see that the sauce cooks for long enough to burst the starch grains, otherwise the sauce will have the flavour of uncooked starch. In the roux method, the fat and flour are partly cooked together before the liquid is added to prevent this happening but, in the other two methods, all the cooking of the starch is done after being mixed with the liquid.

A sauce must sometimes be whisked to make it smooth. A hand-held wire whisk is ideal except in a non-stick pan which it may scratch. An electric blender can be used to beat out lumps but it alters the consistency of the sauce, making a thickened sauce foamy, and a brown one lighter coloured. It is better to prevent lumps forming in the first place by careful stirring and gentle heating.

Starch-thickened sauces are simmered, ie at boiling point, but sauces thickened with egg yolks and/or cream must never come to the boil, or they will curdle. They are best cooked in a double boiler, or in a basin over a pan of simmering water. The water must not be allowed to boil.

Thickened sauces which are to be served hot can be made in advance if a piece of wet greaseproof paper is placed on the surface to prevent a skin forming. Just before serving, remove the paper and re-heat the sauce gently without boiling, beating briskly to keep it smooth.

ENGLISH FOUNDATION SAUCES

Foundation White Sauce

Basic recipe

Makes 500ml coating or pouring sauce

Coating Sauce

50g butter **or** *margarine*	*500ml milk* **or** *fish stock*
50g plain flour	*(p330)* **or** *white stock*
	(p329) **or** *a mixture of*
	stock and milk
	salt and pepper

Pouring Sauce

35g butter **or** *margarine*	*500ml liquid as for*
35g plain flour	*coating sauce*
	salt and pepper

1) *Roux Method*

Melt the fat in a saucepan, add the flour, and stir over low heat for 2–3 minutes, without allowing the mixture (roux) to colour. Draw the pan off the heat and gradually add the liquid, stirring all the time. Return to moderate heat, and stir until the sauce boils and has thickened. Reduce the heat, and simmer for 1–2 minutes, beating briskly. (This helps to give the sauce a gloss.) Season to taste.

2) *Buerre Manié Method*

Knead the fat and flour, or work them together with a fork or spoon until they are blended smoothly. Heat the liquid in a saucepan and, when at just below boiling point, gradually whisk in the kneaded butter and flour in small pieces. Continue to whisk the sauce until it boils, by which time all the beurre manié must be smoothly blended in. Season to taste.

3) *All-in-one Method*

Put the fat, flour, and liquid in a saucepan. Whisk over moderate heat until the sauce comes to the boil. Reduce the heat and cook for 3–4 minutes, whisking all the time, until the sauce has thickened, and is smooth and glossy. Season to taste.

Note A coating sauce should coat the back of the spoon used for stirring, A pouring sauce should barely mask the spoon and should flow freely.

Sauces based on Foundation White Sauce

A foundation white sauce made by any of the three methods above can be used as the basis of many other savoury sauces. The quantities of the ingredients in the following recipes are for adding to 250ml Foundation White Sauce of either coating or pouring consistency. In most cases, this will give about 250ml completed sauce, the extra ingredients making up the small quantity lost by evaporation.

Anchovy Sauce

250ml foundation white	*1–2 × 5ml spoons*
sauce made with fish	*anchovy essence*
stock (p330) **or** *half*	*½ × 2.5ml spoon lemon*
milk and half fish	*juice*
stock	*1–2 drops red colouring*

Heat the sauce, if necessary; then stir in the anchovy essence to taste. Add the lemon juice and stir in enough red colouring to tint the sauce a dull pink.

Serve with fish.

Brain Sauce

1 set of sheep's brains	*1 × 2.5ml spoon lemon*
1 large onion (200g	*juice*
approx)	*1 × 10ml spoon chopped*
250ml white stock	*parsley*
(p329)	*salt and pepper*
250ml foundation white	*(optional)*
sauce made with white	
stock	

Prepare the brains (p551). Skin and slice the onion. Put in a saucepan with the brains. Add the stock. Heat to boiling point, cover, reduce the heat and simmer gently for 30 minutes. Strain off the stock. Heat the sauce, if necessary. Chop the onion and brains. Add them to the white sauce with the lemon juice and parsley. Stir well, and re-season if required.

Serve with steamed or boiled meats.

Note Another recipe for Brain Sauce can be found on p555.

Caper Sauce(1)
(white)

250ml foundation white sauce (p692) made with white stock (p329) **or** half milk and half white stock

1 × 15ml spoon chopped capers
1 × 5ml spoon vinegar in which the capers were pickled

Heat the sauce, if necessary. Add the capers and vinegar, and stir well.

Serve with boiled mutton or fish.

Note See also Caper Sauce (2) (p699)

Cheese Sauce

75g Cheddar cheese **or** other hard cheese
250ml foundation white sauce (p692) made with milk **or** half milk and half white stock (p329)

a pinch of dry English mustard
a pinch of Cayenne pepper
salt and pepper

Grate the cheese finely. Heat the sauce to boiling point, then remove the pan from the heat. Add the grated cheese, mustard, Cayenne pepper, and seasoning to taste. Stir well. Do not reboil the sauce; use at once.

Serve with vegetables, fish, ham, poultry, eggs or pasta.

Note See also Mornay Sauce (p706).

Chicken Liver Sauce

1 chicken liver
125ml chicken stock (approx)
250ml foundation white sauce (p692) made with chicken stock **or** half milk and half chicken stock

juice and grated rind of $\frac{1}{2}$ lemon
1 × 15ml spoon chopped parsley

Remove any skin and tubes from the liver. Put in a pan with the chicken stock and simmer for 5–10 minutes. Remove the liver and chop it. Heat the sauce, if necessary. Add the chopped liver and grated lemon rind and simmer for 3 minutes. Just before serving, stir in the lemon juice and chopped parsley.

Serve with boiled chicken.

Crab Sauce

1 small cooked crab (750g approx)
250ml foundation white sauce (p692) made with fish stock (p330) in which the crab shell, claws, and legs have been simmered

$\frac{1}{2}$ × 2.5ml spoon lemon juice
a pinch of Cayenne pepper
salt (optional)

Pick the meat from the cooked crab (p423). Chop the white crabmeat. Heat the sauce, if necessary. Stir the soft brown and chopped white crabmeat into the sauce. Add the lemon juice and Cayenne pepper and simmer for 5 minutes. Season with salt, if liked.

Serve with fish.

Creamy Mustard Sauce

(Flemish Sauce)

*250ml foundation white
   sauce* (p692) *made
   with half milk and half
   fish stock* (p330)
1–2 egg yolks

*1 × 2.5ml spoon made
   English mustard* **or**
*1 × 10ml spoon French
   mustard*
a few drops lemon juice

Cool the sauce slightly, if necessary. Stir 1 × 15ml spoon of the cooled sauce into the egg yolks. Beat the egg yolk mixture and the mustard into the sauce. Re-heat the sauce, stirring carefully, but do not boil. Stir in the lemon juice.

Serve with fish.

Dutch Sauce

*250ml foundation white
   sauce* (p692) *made
   with milk*

*1 egg yolk
a few drops lemon juice*
   or *vinegar*

Cool the sauce slightly, if necessary. Stir 1 × 15ml spoon of the cooled sauce into the egg yolk. Beat the egg mixture into the sauce. Re-heat the sauce gently, stirring carefully; do not let it boil. Stir in the lemon juice or vinegar.

Serve with poultry or fish.

Egg Sauce

*250ml foundation white
   sauce* (p692) *made
   with milk*
1 hard-boiled egg

*1 × 5ml spoon chopped
   chives (optional)
salt and pepper
   (optional)*

Heat the sauce, if necessary. Chop the egg and stir with the chives, if used, into the sauce. Re-season if required.

Serve with fish, poultry or veal.

Fennel Sauce

*3–4cm piece green fennel
   stem*
*250ml foundation white
   sauce* (p692) *made
   with milk* **or** *fish stock*
   (p330)

a few drops lemon juice

Plunge the fennel stem into boiling water. Drain, squeeze dry, and chop. Heat the sauce, if necessary. Add the fennel to the sauce with the lemon juice. Stir well.

Serve with white fish or mackerel.

Fish Sauce

*250ml foundation white
   sauce* (p692) *made
   with concentrated fish
   stock* (p330)

*a few drops lemon juice
salt and pepper*

Heat the sauce, if necessary. Stir the lemon juice into the sauce. Season to taste.

Serve with fish.

Herb Sauce

*250ml foundation white
   sauce* (p692) *made
   with milk*

*1–2 × 15ml spoons
   chopped fresh mixed
   herbs (parsley, chives,
   tarragon, sorrel,
   thyme, marjoram, and
   savory)*

Heat the sauce, if necessary. Add the herbs and simmer for 5 minutes.

Serve with fish, poultry, veal or eggs.

Hot Horseradish Sauce

*250ml foundation white
  sauce (p692) made
  with milk or half milk
  and half white stock
  (p329)*

*2 × 15ml spoons grated
  horseradish
1 × 5ml spoon vinegar
1 × 2.5ml spoon sugar*

Heat the sauce, if necessary. Add the horseradish, vinegar and sugar, and stir well.

Serve with beef, trout, mackerel or herring.

Note For cold Horseradish Cream, see p402.

Maître d'Hôtel Sauce

*juice of ½ lemon
250ml foundation white
  sauce (p692) made
  with milk*

*2 × 15ml spoons finely
  chopped parsley
25g butter*

Strain the lemon juice. Heat the sauce, if necessary, and add the lemon juice and parsley. When heated to just below boiling point, whisk the butter into the sauce, adding a small pat at a time.

Serve with fish, poultry or vegetables.

Note Another recipe for Maître d'Hôtel Sauce can be found on p575.

Mushroom Sauce(1)
(white)

*50–100g button
  mushrooms
15–25g butter*

*250ml foundation white
  sauce (p692) made
  with milk*

Clean the mushrooms and slice them thinly. Melt the butter in a pan, add the mushrooms, and cook gently for 15–20 minutes. Heat the sauce, if necessary. Stir the mushrooms and their cooking juices into the sauce.

Serve with most fish and meat entrées, poultry, ham, egg, and vegetable dishes.

Note For Mushroom Sauce (2), see p701.

Mustard Sauce

*1 × 5ml spoon dry
  English mustard or
1 × 15ml spoon French
  mustard
1 × 5ml spoon tarragon
  vinegar*

*250ml foundation white
  sauce (p692) made
  with milk or fish stock
  (p330) or half milk
  and half stock
1 × 5ml spoon sugar
15–25g butter*

Mix the mustard with the tarragon vinegar. Heat the sauce, if necessary. Whisk the mustard mixture and the sugar into the sauce. When heated to just below boiling point, whisk the butter into the sauce, adding a small pat at a time.

Serve with fish, especially herrings, or with lamb, mutton, or rabbit.

Onion Sauce(1)
(white)

*2 medium-sized onions
  (200g approx)
250ml foundation white
  sauce (p692) made
  with half milk and half
  liquid in which onions
  were cooked*

a few drops lemon juice

Skin and chop the onions. Put them in a saucepan and cover with salted water. Heat to boiling point, reduce the heat, and simmer for 10–15 minutes until softened. Drain thoroughly, and reserve the liquid to make the white sauce. Stir the onion into the sauce. Add the lemon juice.

Serve with lamb or mutton, rabbit or tripe.

Note For Onion Sauce (2), see p702.

Oyster Sauce

8–10 large fresh oysters
or 1 × 225g can oysters
(not smoked oysters)
250–275ml fish stock
(p330)
milk **or** top of the milk,
if needed

250ml foundation white
sauce (p692) made
with fish stock after
cooking the oysters
salt and pepper
a few drops lemon juice

Open the fresh oysters, if used (p426). Strain the liquor from the shells and add it to the fish stock. Reserve 6 oysters. Heat the stock gently to simmering point, add all except the 6 oysters, and simmer for 10 minutes. Strain the stock and make it up to 250ml with milk, if necessary. Use to make the white sauce. Cut the reserved oysters into 3–4 pieces. Add them to the hot sauce and simmer for 3–4 minutes until they just begin to stiffen. Season, and add lemon juice to taste.

If using canned oysters, drain the liquid from the can and add it to the fish stock. Simmer the stock until reduced to 250ml. Strain, and use to make the white sauce. Cut 6–8 oysters into 3–4 pieces. Add them to the hot sauce and simmer for 2–3 minutes. Season, and add lemon juice to taste.

Serve with fish or boiled chicken.

Savoury Lemon Sauce

juice and rind of 1 lemon
250ml foundation white
sauce (p692) made
with milk **or** half milk
and half white stock
(p329) **or** half milk
and half fish stock
(p330)

1–2 × 15ml spoons
single cream (optional)
1 × 15ml spoon chopped
parsley (optional)
1 × 2.5ml spoon sugar
(optional)

Add the lemon rind to the milk or stock which is to be used to make the sauce, and simmer for 10 minutes. Strain the liquid and use it to make the white sauce. Carefully stir the lemon juice and the cream, if used, into the hot sauce. Do not reboil. Stir in the parsley and sugar, if used.

Serve with fish, chicken or rabbit.

Parsley Sauce

250ml foundation white
sauce (p692) made
with white stock (p329)
or fish stock (p330) **or**
half milk and half
stock

1–2 × 15ml spoons finely
chopped parsley
25g butter

Heat the sauce, if necessary. Add the parsley and heat to just below boiling point. Whisk the butter into the sauce, adding a small pat at a time.

Serve with fish, lamb or mutton, or light dishes such as quenelles or vegetables.

Roe Sauce

200g fresh cod's roe
1 × 2.5ml spoon made
English mustard
1 × 5ml spoon anchovy
essence
1 × 10ml spoon white
vinegar **or** lemon juice

250ml foundation white
sauce (p692) made
with half milk and half
fish stock (p330)

Poach the cod's roe in a little salted water for 10–15 minutes until firm. (This water can be used to prepare the sauce, if not made ahead.) Drain, skin the roe, and crush it with the back of a wooden spoon. Blend the mustard, anchovy essence, and vinegar or lemon juice into the crushed roe. Heat the sauce, if necessary, add to the roe mixture, and blend together. Return the sauce to the pan, reheat, and simmer for 10 minutes.

Serve with fish.

Spiced Mustard Sauce

250ml foundation white
sauce (p692) made
with fish stock (p330)
1 × 5ml spoon made
English mustard

1 × 10ml spoon lemon
juice
1 × 5ml spoon
Worcestershire sauce

Heat the sauce, if necessary. Whisk the mustard, lemon juice, and Worcestershire sauce into the sauce.

Serve with fish.

Shrimp or Prawn Sauce

250ml foundation white
   sauce (p692) made
   with half milk and half
   fish stock (p330)
50g fresh, frozen **or**
   canned shrimps **or**
   prawns

a few drops anchovy
   essence
a few drops lemon juice
a few grains Cayenne
   pepper

Heat the sauce, if necessary. Add the shrimps or prawns, and stir in the anchovy essence, lemon juice, and Cayenne pepper.

Serve with fish.

Sorrel Sauce (1)
(white)

100g sorrel leaves
15g butter
250ml foundation white
   sauce (p692) made
   with half milk and half
   vegetable stock
   (pp330–31)

a small pinch grated
   nutmeg
2 × 15ml spoons single
   cream (optional)

Wash and chop the sorrel. Melt the butter in a saucepan, add the sorrel, and cook gently for 5 minutes. Rub through a fine nylon sieve. Heat the sauce, if necessary. Whisk the sorrel purée into the sauce at boiling point. Add the nutmeg, and stir in the cream, if used. Do not reboil.

Serve with veal or poultry; without the cream, it can be served with goose.

Note For brown Sorrel Sauce, see p703.

Soyer Sauce

2 shallots (25g approx)
15g butter
1 × 15ml spoon chopped
   fresh mixed herbs
   (thyme, marjoram,
   tarragon, fennel,
   sorrel, and parsley)

a few drops lemon juice
250ml foundation white
   sauce (p692) made
   with fish stock (p330)
1–2 egg yolks
2 × 15ml spoons single
   cream

Skin the shallots and chop them finely. Melt the butter in a saucepan, add the shallots, and cook until softened. Add to the sauce with the herbs and lemon juice. Re-heat the sauce for 2–3 minutes, then cool it. Mix a little of the cooled sauce with the egg yolks and cream, and beat this mixture into the rest of the sauce. Re-heat the sauce gently, stirring carefully; do not let it boil.

Serve with fish.

Venetian Sauce

2 shallots (25g approx)
6 × 15ml spoons
   tarragon vinegar
250ml foundation white
   sauce (p692) made
   with white stock (p329)
   or fish stock (p330)

1 × 5ml spoon chopped
   fresh chervil
1 × 5ml spoon chopped
   fresh tarragon

Skin and chop the shallots finely. Put in a saucepan with the tarragon vinegar, and bring to the boil. Boil rapidly until the vinegar has reduced by half its volume. Strain the vinegar. Heat the sauce, if necessary. Add the flavoured vinegar and the herbs to the sauce.

Serve with chicken, veal or fish.

Note This sauce can also be made with Béchamel Sauce (p704).

Watercress and Fennel Sauce

(Xavier Sauce)

½ bunch of watercress
a few leaves fennel or
  tarragon

250ml foundation white
  sauce (p692) made
  with fish stock (p330)
  or white stock (p329)
a few drops lemon juice

Plunge the watercress and fennel or tarragon leaves into boiling water. Drain, dry, and chop them. Heat the sauce, if necessary. Stir the chopped leaves into the sauce and simmer for 1–2 minutes. Add lemon juice to taste.

Serve with fish or poultry.

White Wine Sauce

250ml foundation white
  sauce (p692) made
  with white stock (p329)
  or fish stock (p330)
4 × 15ml spoons white
  wine

1–2 egg yolks
juice of ½ lemon
25g butter
salt and pepper

Heat the sauce, if necessary, add the wine and simmer for 10 minutes. Blend the egg yolks and lemon juice together. Whisk the butter into the sauce at just below boiling point, adding a small pat at a time. Draw the pan off the heat, and mix a little of the sauce with the egg yolk mixture. Beat this mixture into the rest of the sauce. Re-heat the sauce, stirring carefully, without allowing it to boil. Season to taste.

Serve with fish or white meat.

Foundation Brown Sauce

Basic recipe

Makes 300ml (approx)

1 small carrot
1 medium-sized onion
  (100g approx)
25g dripping or lard

25g plain flour
500ml general household
  stock (p329)
salt and pepper

Prepare and slice the carrot and onion. Melt the dripping or lard in a saucepan. Fry the carrot and onion slowly until the onion is golden-brown. Stir in the flour, reduce the heat, and cook the flour very gently until it is also golden-brown. Draw the pan off the heat and gradually add the stock, stirring all the time to prevent lumps forming. Return to moderate heat and stir the sauce until boiling. Reduce the heat, cover, and simmer for 30 minutes. Strain the sauce. Season to taste.

Note For extra flavour, add mushroom trimmings or a piece of celeriac to the carrot and onion. For extra colour add a piece of brown onion skin, a little gravy browning, meat or vegetable extract before the sauce is simmered.

Sauces based on Foundation Brown Sauce

The quantities of the ingredients in the following recipes are for adding to 300ml Foundation Brown Sauce. In most cases, this will give about 300ml completed sauce, the extra ingredients making up the small quantity lost by evaporation.

Gherkin Sauce

300ml foundation brown
  sauce
1 × 15ml spoon chopped
  gherkins

1 × 15ml spoon vinegar
  in which the gherkins
  were pickled
caster sugar

Heat the sauce, if necessary. Add the chopped gherkins, gherkin vinegar, and sugar to taste. Re-heat.

Serve with meat and poultry entrées or grills.

Bordelaise Sauce

1 medium-sized carrot
  (100g approx)
2 small onions (100g
  approx) **or** 2 shallots
  (25g approx)
1 clove of garlic
150ml general household
  stock (p329)
6 black peppercorns
1 bay leaf
a sprig of thyme

a few parsley stalks
a sprig of tarragon
150ml red **or** white wine
300ml foundation brown
  sauce (p698)
lemon juice
Cayenne pepper
1 × 5ml spoon chopped
  fresh chervil
1 × 5ml spoon chopped
  parsley

Prepare and chop the carrot and onions or shallots. Skin and crush the garlic. Put the stock, vegetables, garlic, peppercorns, bay leaf, thyme, parsley stalks, and tarragon into a small saucepan. Heat slowly to simmering point and simmer until the liquid is reduced to a sticky consistency. Add the wine. Re-heat, and cook until the liquid is reduced slightly. Add the brown sauce and heat to boiling point. Strain the sauce. Add the lemon juice and Cayenne pepper to taste. Stir in the chervil and parsley just before serving.

    Serve with beef, pork, ham or duck.

Note This sauce can also be made with Espagnole Sauce (p707).

Christopher North's Sauce

300ml foundation brown
  sauce (p698) in which
  mushroom trimmings
  have been cooked
75ml juices from roast
  game
2 × 10ml spoons
  mushroom ketchup

50–75ml port
caster sugar
Cayenne pepper
2 × 15ml spoons lemon
  juice
1 × 2.5ml spoon salt

Put the brown sauce, roast game juices, mushroom ketchup, and port in the top of a double boiler, or in a basin placed over a pan of simmering water. Add sugar and Cayenne pepper to taste, and the lemon juice and salt. Heat, but do not allow to boil.

    Serve with meat or game.

Caper Sauce (2)
(brown)

1 small onion (50g
  approx) **or** 1 shallot
  (15g approx)
300ml foundation brown
  sauce (p698)
1 × 15ml spoon capers
1 × 5ml spoon vinegar in
  which capers were
  pickled

1 × 5ml spoon anchovy
  essence
Cayenne pepper
lemon juice

Skin and chop the onion or shallot. Add to the brown sauce and simmer for 10 minutes; then strain it. Halve the capers, and add to the sauce with the caper vinegar, anchovy essence, Cayenne pepper, and lemon juice to taste. Re-heat the sauce.

    Serve with steak, kidneys or fish.

Note This sauce can also be made with Espagnole Sauce (p707).

    See also Caper Sauce (1) (p693).

Game Sauce

trimmings and carcass
  of strong-flavoured
  roast game
1 medium-sized onion
  (100g approx)
2 shallots (25g approx)
a blade of mace
4 black peppercorns

1 clove
a bunch of parsley stalks
a sprig of thyme
1 bay leaf
125ml sherry **or** general
  household stock (329)
300ml foundation brown
  sauce (p698)

Break the game carcass into small pieces. Skin and chop the onion and shallots. Put the carcass and trimmings, chopped vegetables, spices, and herbs into a saucepan with the sherry or stock. Heat to boiling point, reduce the heat, half cover, and simmer very slowly for 30 minutes. Heat the brown sauce, if necessary. Strain the liquid into the brown sauce. Re-heat, and cook until the sauce is reduced slightly.

    Serve with game.

Note This sauce can also be made with Espagnole Sauce (p707).

Cider Sauce

300ml foundation brown
  sauce (p698)
150ml cider
½ bay leaf
1 clove
salt and pepper

Heat the sauce, if necessary. Add the cider, bay leaf and clove, and season to taste. Simmer the sauce to reduce it to the preferred consistency and then strain it.

Serve with braised ham, pork or duck.

Geneva Sauce

75g mushrooms
300ml foundation brown
  sauce (p698) made
  with fish stock (p330)
  and mushrooms above
4 × 10ml spoons sherry
  or Madeira
1 × 5ml spoon lemon
  juice
1 × 5ml spoon anchovy
  essence

Clean and slice the mushrooms. Add them with the stock when making the brown sauce. Strain the sauce and chop the cooked mushrooms. Return the mushrooms to the sauce. Add the sherry or Madeira, re-heat the sauce and simmer for 10 minutes. Add the lemon juice and anchovy essence.

Serve with fish.

Ham Sauce

3 shallots (50g approx)
  or 1 × 15ml spoon
  chopped chives
15g butter
50g lean cooked ham
300ml foundation brown
  sauce (p698)
juice of ½ lemon
pepper
1 × 15ml spoon chopped
  parsley

Skin and chop the shallots, if used. Melt the butter in a saucepan, add the shallots or chives, and cook gently for 10 minutes. Chop the ham. Add to the pan and heat through for 2–3 minutes. Stir in the brown sauce, lemon juice, and pepper to taste. Heat to boiling point. Stir the parsley into the sauce.

Serve with fried or grilled meat.

Italian Sauce (1)
(brown)

a bunch of parsley stalks
a sprig of thyme
1 bay leaf
4 shallots (50g approx)
6 mushrooms (50g
  approx)
1 × 15ml spoon olive oil
4 × 15ml spoons general
  household stock (p329)
4 × 15ml spoons white
  wine (optional)
300ml foundation brown
  sauce (p698)
salt and pepper

Tie the herbs in a small square of cotton or muslin. Prepare and chop the shallots and mushrooms. Heat the olive oil in a small saucepan, and fry the chopped vegetables very gently for 10 minutes. Add the stock, wine, if used, and the herbs. Heat to boiling point, reduce the heat, and simmer gently until reduced by half. Add the brown sauce. Re-heat and simmer gently for 20 minutes. Remove the herbs. Season to taste.

Serve with fish or meat.

Note This sauce can also be made with Espagnole Sauce (p707).

For white Italian Sauce, see p705. For another Italian Sauce, see Kidney in Italian Sauce (p512).

Kidney Sauce

50–100g ox kidney
300ml foundation brown
  sauce (p698)

Skin, core, and chop the kidney into small pieces. Fry for 2–3 minutes in the hot fat to be used for frying the vegetables and flour for the brown sauce. Remove the kidney from the fat with a perforated spoon and reserve. Return the kidney to the sauce when the liquid has been added, and simmer for 30 minutes with the other sauce ingredients. Complete the sauce as in the basic recipe (p698).

Serve with fried or grilled meat.

Marsala Sauce

2 shallots	1 clove
4 button mushrooms	1 bay leaf
50g raw ham	300ml foundation brown
25g butter	sauce (p698)
125ml Marsala	125ml Fresh tomato
125ml brown stock	sauce (p715)
(p329)	

Skin the shallots and clean the mushrooms. Chop the vegetables and ham finely. Melt the butter in a saucepan and fry the vegetables and ham gently for 10 minutes. Add the Marsala, stock, clove, and bay leaf. Bring to the boil and boil rapidly until the liquid is reduced by half. Stir in the brown and tomato sauces. Heat gently for 3–4 minutes; then strain and serve.

Serve with pigeon, ham, or small game birds.

Mushroom Sauce (2)
(brown)

50–100g mushrooms	300ml foundation brown
	sauce (p698)

Clean the mushrooms and remove the stalks. Fry the mushroom stalks with the other vegetables when making the brown sauce. Slice the mushroom caps and add with the stock when making the brown sauce. After straining the sauce, remove and chop the mushrooms. Return them to the sauce and re-heat.

Serve with poultry or veal.

Note This sauce can also be made with Espagnole Sauce (p707).

For Mushroom Sauce (1), see p695.

Mushroom and Pepper Sauce

1 medium-sized onion	25g butter
(100g approx)	300ml foundation brown
4 mushrooms (25g	sauce (p698)
approx)	salt and pepper
1 green pepper	1 × 15ml spoon chopped
½ sweet red pepper	parsley

Prepare the onion and mushrooms, and chop them finely. De-seed the peppers and cut the flesh into thin strips. Melt the butter in a saucepan, and fry all the vegetables very gently for 10 minutes. Add the brown sauce, and heat to boiling point. Reduce the heat and simmer very gently for 1 hour. Stir the parsley into the sauce.

Serve with grilled steak or ham.

Note This sauce can also be made with Espagnole Sauce (p707).

Pepper Sauce
(Poivrade Sauce)

2 shallots (25g approx)	2 × 15ml spoons wine
a sprig of thyme	vinegar
1 bay leaf	300ml foundation brown
12 black peppercorns	sauce (p698)
4 × 15ml spoons red	freshly ground pepper
wine	

Skin the shallots and chop them finely. Put into a saucepan with the herbs, peppercorns, wine, and vinegar. Heat to boiling point, reduce the heat, and simmer until the liquid is reduced by half. Heat the sauce, if necessary. Strain the liquid into the brown sauce. Season to taste with pepper.

Serve with roast or grilled beef or game.

Note This sauce can also be made with Espagnole Sauce (p707).

Onion Sauce (2)
(brown)

300ml foundation brown sauce (p698) made with 2 medium-sized onions (200g approx) and omitting the carrot
a pinch of grated nutmeg
1 × 5ml spoon wine vinegar
1 × 2.5ml spoon made English or French mustard
salt and pepper

Prepare the sauce in the usual way, but do not strain it. Add a little grated nutmeg, the vinegar, and mustard. Season to taste.

Serve with beef or offal.

Note For Onion Sauce (1), see p695.

Piquant Sauce

1 small onion (50g approx) or 2 shallots (25g approx)
25g mushrooms
1 bay leaf
a blade of mace
2 × 15ml spoons vinegar
300ml foundation brown sauce (p698)
1 × 15ml spoon capers
1 × 15ml spoon gherkins
1 × 10ml spoon mushroom ketchup
1 × 2.5ml spoon sugar (optional)

Skin the onion or shallots and chop finely. Clean the mushrooms and chop coarsely. Put the onion or shallots, bay leaf, mace, and vinegar in a saucepan. Heat to boiling point, reduce the heat and simmer for 10 minutes. Heat the sauce, if necessary. Add the onion mixture and the mushrooms to the brown sauce, and simmer for about 15 minutes until the mushrooms are softened.

Meanwhile, halve the capers and chop the gherkins. Remove the bay leaf and mace from the sauce, and add the capers, gherkins, mushroom ketchup, and sugar, if used. Re-heat if required.

Serve with pork, mutton or vegetables.

Note This sauce can also be made with Espagnole Sauce (p707).

Reform Sauce

2 mushrooms (15g approx)
a little brown stock (p329)
6 cocktail gherkins
15g cooked tongue
white of 1 small hard-boiled egg
300ml Pepper sauce (p701)
2 × 15ml spoons port
1 × 15ml spoon redcurrant jelly

Clean the mushrooms, then poach them in a little stock. Drain. Shred the mushrooms, gherkins, tongue, and egg white. Heat the sauce, if necessary. Add the port and redcurrant jelly to the Pepper sauce, then add the shredded ingredients. Re-heat the sauce.

Serve with lamb cutlets.

Rich Brown Sauce

2 shallots (25g approx)
15g butter
300ml foundation brown sauce (p698)
1 × 5ml spoon meat glaze (p397)
1 × 5ml spoon lemon juice
1 × 10ml spoon chopped parsley

Skin the shallots and chop them finely. Melt the butter in a saucepan, add the shallots, and fry gently until softened. Add the brown sauce, meat glaze, and lemon juice. Re-heat the sauce. Stir the parsley into the sauce.

Serve with fried or grilled steak or chops.

Sage and Onion Sauce

2 medium-sized onions (200g approx)
25g butter or pork or goose dripping
1 × 2.5ml spoon chopped fresh sage
1 × 15ml spoon soft white or brown breadcrumbs
300ml foundation brown sauce (p698)

Skin the onions and chop them finely. Melt the fat in a saucepan, add the onion and fry until tender but not browned. Stir into the brown sauce with the sage and breadcrumbs. Heat to boiling point, reduce the heat, and simmer gently for 10 minutes.

Serve with pork, goose or duck.

Robert Sauce

1 small onion (50g approx)	*1 × 2.5ml spoon sugar*
15g butter	*4 × 15ml spoons white wine*
½ × 2.5ml spoon made English mustard	*300ml foundation brown sauce* (p698)

Skin and chop the onion. Melt the butter in a saucepan, add the onion, and fry until golden-brown. Stir in the mustard, sugar and wine, and simmer for 10 minutes. Add the brown sauce. Re-heat, and simmer for a further 10 minutes.

Serve with roast or grilled beef, lamb or mutton, pork or goose.

Note This sauce can also be made with Espagnole Sauce (p707).

Venison Sauce

1 shallot (15g approx)	*2 × 15ml spoons vinegar*
12 black peppercorns	*300ml foundation brown sauce* (p698)
a sprig of thyme	*1 × 10ml spoon redcurrant jelly*
a few parsley stalks	
1 bay leaf	
2 × 15ml spoons port (optional)	

Skin and chop the shallot. Crush the peppercorns. Put the shallot, peppercorns, and herbs into a saucepan with the port, if used, and the vinegar. Heat to simmering point and simmer very gently for 2 minutes. Add the brown sauce. Re-heat, half cover the pan, and simmer for 10 minutes. Strain the sauce. Add the redcurrant jelly, and re-heat.

Serve with venison or mutton.

Walnut Sauce

4 pickled walnuts	*1 × 15ml spoon vinegar in which walnuts were pickled*
300ml foundation brown sauce (p698)	*sugar (optional)*

Chop the pickled walnuts. Heat the sauce, if necessary. Add the walnuts and vinegar to the brown sauce. Add sugar to taste, if liked, and re-heat.

Serve with ham and bacon.

Sorrel Sauce (2)

(brown)

100g sorrel leaves	*salt and pepper*
15g butter	*lemon juice*
4 × 15ml spoons water	*sugar*
300ml foundation brown sauce (p698)	

Wash and chop the sorrel leaves. Melt the butter in a saucepan. Add the sorrel leaves and water, and cook until tender. Rub the sorrel through a fine nylon sieve. Heat the sauce if necessary. Add the sorrel and its cooking juices to the brown sauce. Re-heat, and season with salt and pepper. Add lemon juice and sugar to taste.

Serve with goose.

Note For white Sorrel Sauce, see p697.

Salmi Sauce

2 shallots (25g approx)	*a sprig of thyme*
25g mushroom stalks	*1 bay leaf*
1 × 15ml spoon olive oil	*300ml foundation brown sauce* (p698)
125ml game stock (p330) or chicken stock	*1 × 10ml spoon redcurrant jelly*
4 × 15ml spoons red wine (optional)	

Prepare and chop the shallots and mushroom stalks. Heat the olive oil in a saucepan, add the vegetables, and fry them until golden-brown. Add the stock, wine, if used, and herbs. Heat to boiling point, reduce the heat, and simmer until reduced by half. Add the brown sauce, and simmer very gently for 10 minutes. Strain the sauce. Add the redcurrant jelly and re-heat.

Serve with game or duck.

Note This sauce can also be made with Espagnole Sauce (p707).

FRENCH FOUNDATION SAUCES

Béchamel Sauce

(French Foundation White Sauce)

Basic recipe

Makes 500ml (approx)

1 small onion (50g approx)	a sprig of thyme
	salt
1 small carrot (25g approx)	1 clove
	6 white peppercorns
a piece of celery (15g approx)	a blade of mace
	50g butter
500ml milk	50g flour
1 bay leaf	4 × 15ml spoons single
a few parsley stalks	cream (optional)

Prepare the vegetables and heat gently to simmering point with the milk, herbs, salt, and spices. Cover with a lid, and stand the pan in a warm place on the cooker to infuse for 30 minutes. Do not allow to boil. Strain the milk.

Melt the butter in a saucepan, add the flour, and stir until smooth. Cook over gentle heat, without allowing it to colour, for 2–3 minutes, stirring until the mixture (roux) begins to bubble. Draw the pan off the heat, and gradually add the flavoured milk, stirring to prevent lumps forming. Return to moderate heat and bring the sauce to the boil, stirring all the time. When the sauce has thickened, simmer for 3–4 minutes, beating briskly. (This helps to give the sauce a gloss.) Re-season if required. If cream is used, add it to the sauce just at boiling point, and remove from the heat immediately. Do not let the sauce reboil.

Note This sauce can be made with half white stock (p329) and half milk; it will have a good flavour, but will be less creamy in texture.

Sauces based on Béchamel Sauce

The quantities of the ingredients in the following recipes are for adding to 125ml or 250ml Béchamel Sauce. In most cases, this will give about 125ml or 250ml completed sauce, the extra ingredients making up the small quantity lost by evaporation.

Aurora Sauce

250ml Béchamel sauce made from fish stock (p330)	paprika
	2 × 15ml spoons single cream (optional)
2 × 15ml spoons concentrated tomato purée **or** 1 × 15ml spoon sieved, canned pimento	

Heat the sauce, if necessary. Carefully stir the tomato purée or sieved pimento into the sauce. Add paprika to taste and the cream, if used. Re-heat the sauce without allowing it to boil.

Serve with eggs, chicken or fish.

Note This sauce can also be made from Velouté Sauce based on fish stock (p330). Serve with fish.

Soubise Sauce

200g onions	250ml Béchamel sauce
40g butter	salt and pepper
1–2 × 15ml spoons white stock (p329)	sugar
	grated nutmeg

Skin and slice the onions. Heat 15g of the butter in a saucepan. Add the onions and enough stock to moisten them. Cook gently until tender. Sieve the onions. Add the onion purée to the Béchamel sauce and re-heat. Season with salt and pepper, and add sugar and nutmeg to taste. When heated to boiling point, whisk the rest of the butter into the sauce, adding a small pat at a time. Do not allow the sauce to reboil. Use at once.

Serve with fish, poultry or vegetables.

Cucumber Sauce

15g butter
½ cucumber
1 × 15ml spoons white
  stock (p329) **or** *chicken*
  stock (p330)
125ml Béchamel sauce
  (p704)
salt and pepper

lemon juice
sugar
grated nutmeg
1–2 drops green
  colouring
2 × 15ml spoons single
  cream

Melt the butter in a saucepan. Slice the cucumber, and cook it gently in the butter for 10 minutes. Add the stock and continue cooking until the cucumber is softened. Rub the cucumber through a fine nylon sieve. Return the purée to the saucepan, and simmer until reduced a little. Heat the Béchamel Sauce, if necessary. Stir into the cucumber purée, and season with salt and pepper. Add lemon juice, sugar, and nutmeg to taste. Colour the sauce with a little green colouring. Heat the sauce to boiling point and stir in the cream. Remove at once from the heat. Do not allow the sauce to reboil.

Serve with salmon or other fish, veal or poultry.

Italian Sauce (2)

(white)

2 shallots (25g approx)
50g button mushrooms
1 × 15ml spoon butter
250ml Béchamel sauce
  (p704)
50ml dry white wine
  (optional)

125ml chicken stock
salt and pepper
lemon juice
1 × 10ml spoon chopped
  parsley
2 × 15ml spoons single
  cream

Prepare the shallots and mushrooms and chop them finely. Melt the butter in a saucepan. Add the vegetables and cook very gently for 10 minutes. Stir in the sauce, wine, if used, and stock. Heat to simmering point, and simmer steadily until the mushrooms are softened and the sauce is reduced to a creamy consistency. Season with salt and pepper and add lemon juice to taste. Stir in the parsley. Just before serving, stir in the cream.

Serve with chicken, veal or fish.

Note For brown Italian Sauce, see p700.

Lobster Sauce

50g cooked **or** *canned*
  lobster meat
250ml Béchamel sauce
  (p704)

15g butter
salt and pepper
paprika (optional)

Chop the lobster meat finely. Heat the sauce, if necessary. Add the lobster and the butter to the sauce. Season with salt and pepper, and a little paprika, if liked.

Serve with white fish or shellfish.

Mock Béarnaise Sauce

125ml Béchamel sauce
  (p704)
2 shallots (25g approx)
2 sprigs tarragon
2 sprigs chervil
4 × 15ml spoons white
  wine **or** *wine vinegar*

6 black peppercorns
2–3 egg yolks
100g butter
1 × 10ml spoon lemon
  juice
salt and pepper

Cool the sauce, if necessary. Skin and chop the shallots. Chop the tarragon and chervil. Put the wine or vinegar in a small saucepan with the shallots, half the herbs, and the peppercorns. Heat to simmering point and simmer gently until reduced by half. Strain the liquid. Stir the egg yolks into the cool Béchamel Sauce. Heat the sauce in a double boiler or in a basin placed over a pan of simmering water, stirring carefully. Add the strained liquid. Whisk in the butter, adding a small pat at a time, until it is all absorbed. Add the lemon juice. Season with salt and pepper and add the rest of the herbs. Use at once.

Serve with grilled meat or shellfish.

Note For Béarnaise Sauce, see p712.

Mock Hollandaise Sauce

250ml Béchamel sauce
(p704)
1–2 egg yolks
2 × 15ml spoons single
cream

1 × 10ml spoon lemon
juice **or** white wine
vinegar
Cayenne pepper
salt

Cool the sauce, if necessary. Mix the egg yolks and cream. Stir a little of the cooled sauce into the yolk and cream mixture. Add this to the rest of the Béchamel Sauce. Heat gently, stirring carefully, to cook the egg yolk, taking care not to let the sauce boil. Add the lemon juice or vinegar, and season with Cayenne pepper and salt to taste. Use at once.

Serve with salmon or other fish, or with delicately flavoured vegetables such as asparagus and seakale.

Note For Hollandaise Sauce, see p712.

Mornay Sauce

250ml Béchamel sauce
(p704)
1 egg yolk
40g grated Parmesan
and Gruyère cheese,
mixed

4 × 15ml spoons single
cream (optional)
a few grains Cayenne
pepper

Cool the sauce, if necessary. Stir a little into the yolk, and blend together. Add to the rest of the Béchamel Sauce. Heat the sauce gently, stirring carefully, to cook the egg yolk; do not let it boil. Stir the cheeses into the sauce. Add the cream, if used, and season with Cayenne pepper.

Serve with fish, chicken, ham, eggs or vegetables.

Savoury Cream Sauce

250ml Béchamel sauce
(p704)
Cayenne pepper
salt

lemon juice
4 × 15ml spoons single
cream

Heat the sauce, if necessary. Add Cayenne pepper, salt, and lemon juice to taste. Heat to just below boiling point, then stir in the cream. Do not allow the sauce to boil. Use at once. Serve with chicken, veal, fish or delicately flavoured vegetables.

Cardinal Sauce

1 × 15ml spoon coral
and spawn of 1 lobster
3 × 10ml spoons butter
125ml Béchamel sauce
(p704)
125ml well-reduced fish
stock (p330)

4 × 15ml spoons single
cream
1 × 10ml spoon lemon
juice
salt
Cayenne pepper
a few drops red food
colouring (optional)

Pound together the lobster coral and spawn, then beat into the butter. Put the sauce and stock in a saucepan and heat to just below boiling point. Stir in the cream and lemon juice, and whisk in the lobster butter, a small pat at a time. Do not allow the sauce to boil. Add salt and Cayenne pepper to taste. The sauce should be bright scarlet. Red food colouring can be added if necessary.

Serve with lobster or other fish.

Note The Béchamel Sauce and fish stock can be replaced by Velouté Sauce (p708) made from fish stock.

Tartare Sauce (1)
(hot)

250ml Béchamel sauce
(p704)
1–2 egg yolks
1 × 15ml spoon single
cream
1 × 5ml spoon chopped
gherkins

1 × 15ml spoon chopped
capers
1 × 10ml spoon chopped
parsley
lemon juice **or** white
wine vinegar

Cool the sauce, if necessary. Mix the egg yolks and cream, and stir in a little of the sauce. Add this to the rest of the sauce. Heat the sauce gently, without boiling, to cook the egg yolk. Stir the gherkins, capers, and parsley into the sauce. Add lemon juice or vinegar to taste. Use at once.

Serve with salmon or other fish.

Note For Tartare Sauce (2), see p846.

Espagnole Sauce

(French Foundation Brown Sauce)

Basic recipe

Makes 350ml (when using tomato purée and omitting the sherry); makes 500ml (when using tomato pulp and sherry)

1 small onion (50g approx)	*bouquet garni*
1 small carrot (25g approx)	*6 black peppercorns*
50g mushrooms **or** *mushroom trimmings*	*1 bay leaf*
50g lean raw ham **or** *bacon*	*125ml tomato pulp* **or** *1 × 15ml spoon concentrated tomato purée*
50g butter	*salt*
50g flour	*4 × 15ml spoons sherry (optional)*
500ml brown stock (p329)	

Prepare and slice the vegetables. Chop the ham or bacon into small pieces. Melt the butter in a saucepan and fry the ham or bacon for 2–3 minutes. Add the vegetables, and fry very slowly for 8–10 minutes until golden-brown. Add the flour and stir until smooth. Cook over gentle heat, stirring frequently, for about 10 minutes or until the flour is a rich brown colour. Draw the pan off the heat and gradually add the stock, stirring all the time to prevent lumps forming. Add the bouquet garni, peppercorns, and bay leaf. Return to moderate heat and stir until boiling. Half cover the pan, reduce the heat and simmer the sauce gently for 30 minutes. Add the tomato pulp or concentrated tomato purée. Simmer the sauce for a further 30 minutes. Rub through a fine nylon sieve. Season to taste with salt. Add the sherry, if used. Re-heat the sauce before serving.

VARIATION

Substitute 1 large tomato for the mushrooms. Add the vegetables and flour to the ham or bacon in the saucepan and fry them together for 10 minutes. Add 1 × 10ml spoon mushroom ketchup with the stock instead of using tomato pulp or purée. Makes 425ml sauce.

Sauces based on Espagnole Sauce

The quantities of the ingredients in the following recipes are for adding to 250ml Espagnole Sauce. In most cases, this will give about 250ml completed sauce, the extra ingredients making up the small quantity lost by evaporation.

Bigarade Sauce

½ Seville orange	*1 × 5ml spoon redcurrant jelly*
juice of ½ lemon	
250ml Espagnole sauce	*salt*
4 × 15ml spoons red wine (optional)	*Cayenne pepper*
	sugar

Pare the orange rind and cut into neat, thin strips. Put them in a saucepan and cover with a little cold water. Heat to simmering point and cook until just tender. Drain. Squeeze the juice from the orange. Add to the Espagnole Sauce with the orange rind and lemon juice. Re-heat the sauce. Stir in the wine, if used, and the redcurrant jelly. Add salt, Cayenne pepper, and sugar to taste.

Serve with roast duck, goose, wild duck, pork or ham.

Brittany Sauce

2 medium-sized onions (200g approx)	*250ml Espagnole sauce*
15g butter	
2 × 15ml spoons cooked haricot beans **or** *mashed potato*	

Skin and chop the onions. Melt the butter in a saucepan. Add the onions and cook gently until softened but not browned. Rub the cooked beans or potato through a sieve. Add the onions and beans or potato to the Espagnole Sauce, and re-heat.

Serve with meat.

Chasseur Sauce

See p630 and p490.

Demi-Glace Sauce

125ml juices from roast
  meat **or** 125ml bone
  stock (p329) and
  1 × 5ml spoon beef
  extract **or** meat glaze
  (p397)

250ml Espagnole sauce
  (p707)

Add the meat juices, stock or meat glaze to the sauce. Bring to the boil, and boil until the sauce is well reduced. Skim off any fat.

    Serve with meat, poultry or game.

Madeira Sauce

250ml Demi-glace sauce
4 × 15ml spoons
  Madeira

salt and pepper
1 × 5ml spoon meat
  glaze (p397)

Heat the sauce, if necessary. Add the Madeira, and simmer together until well reduced. Season to taste. Add the meat glaze and stir until dissolved. Strain the sauce.

    Serve with meat, poultry or game.

Olive Sauce

12 green olives
250ml Espagnole sauce
  (p707)

lemon juice

Rinse the whole olives to remove the preserving vinegar, then stone them. Add the olives to the Espagnole sauce and cook over a gentle heat for 10 minutes. Add lemon juice to taste.

    Serve with roast duck or goose.

Velouté Sauce

(French Foundation Fawn Sauce)

Basic recipe

Makes 500ml (when using 100ml cream)

50g butter
6 button mushrooms **or**
  25–50g mushroom
  trimmings
12 black peppercorns
a few parsley stalks
50g flour

500ml white stock
  (p329) (fish, vegetable
  or meat)
salt and pepper
lemon juice
4–8 × 15ml spoons
  single cream

Melt the butter in a saucepan, and add the mushrooms, peppercorns, and parsley stalks. Cook gently for 10 minutes. Add the flour, and stir over gentle heat for 2–3 minutes, without allowing it to colour. Draw the pan off the heat and add the stock gradually, stirring well to prevent lumps forming. Return to gentle heat and heat the sauce to simmering point, stirring all the time. Simmer for 3–4 minutes. Rub the sauce through a sieve. Season to taste with salt and pepper, and add lemon juice to taste. Re-heat the sauce to boiling point and stir in enough cream to give the desired flavour and consistency. Do not reboil. Use at once.

    Serve with meat, poultry, fish or vegetables.

Sauces based on Velouté Sauce

The quantities of the ingredients in the following recipes are for adding to 250ml Velouté Sauce. In most cases, this will give about 250ml completed sauce, the extra ingredients making up the small quantity lost by evaporation.

Allemande Sauce

*250ml Velouté sauce
(p708)
1 egg yolk
1 × 15ml spoon single
cream*

*1 × 15ml spoon butter
a few drops lemon juice
a pinch of grated nutmeg
salt and pepper*

Cool the sauce, if necessary. Mix the egg yolk and cream. Stir a little of the cooled sauce into the yolk and cream mixture. Add this to the rest of the Velouté sauce. Heat the sauce gently, stirring carefully, to thicken the egg yolk; do not let it boil. Whisk in the butter. Add the lemon juice and nutmeg, and season to taste. Use at once.

Serve with any meat, poultry, fish or vegetables.

Bercy Sauce

*2 shallots (25g approx)
4 × 15ml spoons white
wine
250ml Velouté sauce
(p708) made with fish
stock (p330) or chicken
stock*

*25g butter
1 × 10ml spoon chopped
parsley*

Skin and chop the shallots. Put into a small saucepan with the wine, and cook until the wine is reduced by half. Add the sauce, and re-heat without allowing it to boil. Whisk in the butter, adding a small pat at a time. Add the parsley to the sauce.

Serve with fish or meat.

Onion and Mushroom Sauce

(Tournée Sauce)

*6 spring onions, white
parts only
4 button mushrooms
250ml Velouté sauce
(p708)*

*bouquet garni
1 × 15ml spoon chopped
parsley*

Prepare and chop the onions and mushrooms. Add to the Velouté sauce with the bouquet garni. Heat to simmering point and simmer the sauce very gently until the onions and mushrooms are quite tender. Remove the bouquet garni. Stir the parsley into the sauce.

Serve with meat or fish.

Mushroom and Soured Cream Sauce

See p880.

Paprika Sauce

*1 small sweet red
pepper or canned red
pimento
paprika*

*250ml Velouté sauce
(p708)
2–4 × 15ml spoons
single cream*

De-seed and cut the pepper or pimento into neat strips of equal length. If a raw pepper is used, simmer it in water for 10 minutes. Drain. Remove the skin, if necessary. Add enough paprika to the sauce to give it a pink colour and the desired flavour. Add the pepper strips and re-heat the sauce carefully. When heated to just below boiling point, stir in the desired amount of cream. Use at once.

Serve with veal or beef.

French Egg and Lemon Sauce

(Sauce Normande)

250ml Velouté sauce (p708) *made with fish stock* (p330) *(See* **Note***)*

1 egg yolk
15–25g butter
lemon juice

Cool the sauce, if necessary. Stir a little into the egg yolk. Add this to the rest of the Velouté sauce. Heat the sauce gently, stirring carefully, to thicken the egg yolk; do not let it boil. Whisk in enough butter, adding a small pat at a time, to give the desired consistency and flavour. Add lemon juice to taste. Use at once.

Serve with sole or other white fish.

Note The Velouté sauce should be made with fish stock containing liquor from oysters or mussels to give the correct flavour.

Poulette Sauce

250ml Velouté sauce (p708)
1 egg yolk
1 × 15ml spoon single cream

1 × 15ml spoon chopped parsley
1 × 10ml spoon lemon juice
salt and pepper

Cool the sauce, if necessary. Mix the egg yolk and cream. Stir a little of the cooled sauce into the yolk and cream mixture. Add this to the rest of the Velouté sauce. Heat the sauce gently, stirring carefully, to thicken the egg yolk; do not let it boil. Add the parsley, lemon juice, and seasoning. Use at once.

Serve with vegetables or some meat dishes, eg calf's head.

Ravigote Sauce

(hot)

250ml Velouté sauce (p708)
1 × 15ml spoon wine vinegar
grated nutmeg

sugar
salt and pepper
25g Ravigote butter (p1301)

Heat the sauce, if necessary. Add the vinegar, nutmeg, sugar, and seasoning to taste. When heated to just below boiling point, whisk in the Ravigote butter, adding a small pat at a time. Do not allow the sauce to boil. Use at once.

Serve with meat, boiled fish or poultry.

Suprême Sauce

250ml Velouté sauce (p708)
2–4 × 15ml spoons single cream
1 egg yolk

15–25g butter
grated nutmeg
lemon juice
salt and pepper

Cool the sauce, if necessary. Mix the cream and egg yolk, using the larger quantity of cream for a rich sauce. Stir a little of the cooled sauce into the cream and yolk mixture. Add this to the rest of the Velouté sauce. Heat the sauce gently, stirring carefully, to thicken the egg yolk; do not let it boil. Whisk in the butter, adding a small pat at a time. Add nutmeg, lemon juice, and seasoning to taste. Use at once.

Serve with any meat, poultry, fish or vegetables.

Note Adjust the proportions of cream, butter, and seasoning in this classic sauce to give the flavour and richness you want.

Soured Cream or Yoghurt Sauce

(Polonaise Sauce)

250ml Velouté sauce (p708)
2cm piece green fennel stem
1 × 5ml spoon grated fresh horseradish
1 × 5ml spoon lemon juice
4 × 15ml spoons soured cream **or** yoghurt

Heat the sauce, if necessary but do not allow to boil. Plunge the fennel stem into boiling water. Drain, squeeze dry, and chop. Stir the fennel, horseradish, and lemon juice into the Velouté sauce. Blend the soured cream or yoghurt into the sauce. Use at once.

Serve with grilled cutlets or steaks.

CHAUDFROID SAUCES

Chaudfroid sauces are so called because the sauces are cooked but are served cold. They are prepared from foundation savoury sauces, into which gelatine dissolved in aspic is blended. They are used when cold, but still liquid, to mask cold cooked meat, poultry, and fish.

White Chaudfroid Sauce

Makes 375ml (approx)

250ml Béchamel sauce (p704)
125ml aspic jelly
1 × 10ml spoon gelatine
salt and pepper
1 × 5ml spoon white wine vinegar **or** lemon juice
1 × 15ml spoon double cream

Cool the Béchamel sauce until tepid. Melt the aspic jelly in a basin placed over hot water. Add the gelatine to the melted aspic. Continue to stir over heat until the gelatine dissolves. Cool the aspic jelly until tepid, then fold it into the sauce. Season to taste. Add the vinegar or lemon juice. Rub the sauce through a fine sieve. Fold in the cream. Leave the sauce to cool completely but use while still liquid. Use the sauce to mask poultry, veal or fish served *en chaudfroid*.

VARIATIONS

Brown Chaudfroid Sauce

Make as for White Chaudfroid Sauce, substituting Espagnole Sauce (p707) for Béchamel Sauce.

Use for masking beef, mutton or game.

Fawn Chaudfroid Sauce

Make as for White Chaudfroid Sauce, substituting Velouté Sauce (p708) for Béchamel Sauce.

Use for masking lamb, veal or poultry.

Green Chaudfroid Sauce

Make as for White Chaudfroid Sauce, using 1 × 15ml spoon spinach purée (p801) or green colouring with the Béchamel Sauce.

Use for masking veal or poultry.

Tomato Chaudfroid Sauce

Make as for White Chaudfroid Sauce, substituting Fresh Tomato Sauce (p715) for Béchamel Sauce.

Use for masking fish, veal, poultry or lamb.

Note See also Chaudfroid of Chicken (p644).

OTHER THICKENED SAVOURY SAUCES

Béarnaise Sauce

Makes 200ml (approx)

1 shallot **or** *25g onion*	*4 peppercorns*
1 × 15ml spoon chopped fresh tarragon	*4 × 15ml spoons wine* **or** *tarragon vinegar*
1 × 15ml spoon chopped fresh chervil	*2 egg yolks*
a small piece of bay leaf	*100g softened butter*
	salt and pepper

Prepare and chop the shallot or onion finely. Put in a saucepan with the herbs. Crush the peppercorns and add with the vinegar. Bring to the boil, and boil gently until reduced by half. Leave to cool, then strain. Heat the sauce in a basin placed in a pan of hot water to avoid boiling the sauce. Whisk in the yolks, one at a time. Stir until thickened. Whisk in the butter, adding a small pat at a time. It should be as thick as mayonnaise. Season to taste.

Serve the sauce, lukewarm, as soon as possible. Keep warm, if necessary, over hot water and re-whisk before serving. This sauce is thicker and sharper in flavour than Hollandaise Sauce.

Serve with steaks, shellfish or grilled fish, poultry or eggs.

Note 1 × 5ml spoon finely chopped tarragon and 1 × 5ml spoon finely chopped chervil can be added to the completed sauce, if liked.

For Mock Béarnaise Sauce, see p705.

VARIATION

Choron Sauce

Omit the tarragon and chervil, and stir 1 × 15ml spoon (approx) concentrated tomato purée into the completed sauce.

Serve with chicken or pork chops.

Hollandaise Sauce (1)

Makes 125ml (approx)

3 × 15ml spoons white wine vinegar	*a blade of mace*
6 peppercorns	*3 egg yolks*
½ bay leaf	*100g softened butter*
	salt and pepper

Put the vinegar, peppercorns, bay leaf, and mace into a small saucepan and boil rapidly until the mixture is reduced to 1 × 15ml spoon. Strain, and leave to cool. Add the yolks and a nut of butter to the vinegar and beat well. Heat the sauce in a basin over a pan of hot water to avoid boiling the sauce. Beat the egg yolk mixture until thick. Add the rest of the butter, a small pat at a time, beating well between each addition. When all the butter has been added, the mixture should be thick and glossy. Season lightly with salt and pepper.

This is the classic sauce to serve with poached fish, asparagus or broccoli. Serve lukewarm.

Note If the sauce curdles, whisk in 1 × 10ml spoon cold water. If this fails to bind it, put an egg yolk in another basin and beat in the sauce gradually.

For mock Hollandaise Sauce, see p706.

Hollandaise Sauce (2)

Makes 125ml (approx)

2 × 15ml spoons white wine vinegar	*2 egg yolks*
2 × 15ml spoons water	*100g softened butter*
4 peppercorns	*salt and pepper*
a small piece of bay leaf	*Cayenne pepper*
	lemon juice (optional)

Put the vinegar and water into a small saucepan. Crush the peppercorns and add to the pan with the bay leaf. Bring to the boil, and continue boiling gently until the liquid is reduced by half. Leave to cool. Strain the liquid into a double boiler or a basin over a pan of hot water to avoid boiling the sauce. Whisk in the egg yolks, one at a time. Cook until the mixture is thick, whisking all the time. Whisk in the butter, adding a small pat at a time. The sauce should be thick enough to just hold its shape. Each addition must be thoroughly worked in before the next is added. Season lightly with salt, pepper, and Cayenne pepper. Add a little lemon juice, if liked, to give a slightly piquant flavour.

Note A Hollandaise Sauce with a more delicate flavour can be made by using 1×15ml spoon strained lemon juice and 1×15ml spoon water instead of the reduced vinegar.

VARIATION

Mousseline Hollandaise Sauce

Just before serving, fold in $2-3 \times 15$ml spoons lightly whipped double cream. Re-season if required.

Savoury Mousseline Sauce
See p884.

Cold Mousseline Sauce
See p846.

Yoghurt Sauce for Vegetables
See p877.

Bread Sauce

Makes 250ml (approx)

1 large onion (200g approx)	*1 bay leaf*
250ml milk	*50g dried white breadcrumbs*
2 cloves	*1 × 15ml spoon butter*
a blade of mace	*salt and pepper*
4 peppercorns	*2 × 15ml spoons single cream (optional)*
1 allspice berry	

Skin the onion. Heat the milk very slowly to boiling point with the spices, bay leaf, and onion. Cover the pan and infuse over gentle heat for 30 minutes. Strain the liquid. Add the breadcrumbs and butter to the flavoured milk. Season to taste. Heat the mixture to just below simmering point and keep at this temperature for 20 minutes. Stir in the cream, if used.

Serve with roast chicken or turkey.

Chestnut Sauce

Makes 375ml (approx)

200g chestnuts	*a small strip of lemon rind*
375ml chicken stock (p330) **or** *white stock (p329)*	*25g butter*
a pinch of ground cinnamon	*salt and pepper*
	75ml single cream (optional)

Make a slit in the rounded side of the shells of the chestnuts, and boil or bake them for 15–20 minutes. Remove the shells and skins while hot. Put the chestnuts in a saucepan with the stock, cinnamon, and lemon rind. Heat to simmering point, and simmer gently for 30 minutes or until the chestnuts are very tender. Remove the lemon rind. Rub the chestnuts and the liquid through a sieve, or process in an electric blender. Return the purée to the pan, add the butter, and season to taste. Heat gently for 2–3 minutes. Stir in the cream, if used, just before serving.

Serve with roast chicken or turkey.

Celery Sauce

Makes 250ml (approx)

6 large sticks celery	salt and pepper
250ml water	1–2 drops lemon juice
25g butter **or** margarine	1–2 × 15ml spoons
25g plain flour	single cream (optional)

Wash the celery and cut into short lengths. Heat the water to boiling point, add the celery, reduce the heat, cover, and simmer for 20 minutes or until the celery is softened. Drain, and reserve the liquid. Rub the celery through a fine nylon sieve, or process in an electric blender and then sieve. Measure the purée and make it up to 250ml with the reserved liquid.

Melt the fat in a saucepan and add the flour. Stir over gentle heat, without allowing the flour to colour, for 2–3 minutes, or until the mixture begins to bubble. Draw the pan off the heat and gradually stir in the celery purée. Return to moderate heat and bring the sauce to the boil, stirring all the time to prevent lumps forming. When it has thickened, simmer for 3–4 minutes, beating vigorously. Season to taste. Remove from the heat, and stir in the lemon juice and the cream, if used.

Serve with lamb, mutton or rabbit.

MISCELLANEOUS SAVOURY SAUCES

Agro-Dolce
(Bitter-sweet Sauce)

Makes 250ml (approx)

1 onion	125ml red wine
1 carrot	75ml wine vinegar
1 clove of garlic	50g sugar
(optional)	2 × 15ml spoons water
1 bay leaf	125ml good thin gravy
6 black peppercorns	(p727)
1 × 15ml spoon olive oil	

Sweetening

1 × 5ml spoon chopped mint	1 × 10ml spoon chopped nuts
1 × 5ml spoon finely shredded candied orange peel	1 × 10ml spoon sultanas
	1 × 15ml spoon grated bitter chocolate

Prepare and chop the onion and carrot. Skin and crush the garlic, if used. Put them into a saucepan with the bay leaf, peppercorns and oil, and cook very gently, half covered, for 15–20 minutes. Drain off the oil, and add the wine and vinegar. Simmer gently for 30 minutes; remove the bay leaf and peppercorns.

Put the sugar and water into a separate pan. Beat gently until the sugar has dissolved; then boil rapidly, without stirring, until the sugar becomes a golden caramel. Remove from the heat immediately. Stir into the wine mixture with the gravy. Add any one, or a mixture, of the sweetening ingredients to taste.

Serve with braised meat or vegetables.

Black Butter

(Beurre Noir)

Makes 200ml (approx)

150g butter
2 × 15ml spoons chopped parsley

1 × 15ml spoon chopped capers
1 × 10ml spoon vinegar (approx)

Heat the butter in a saucepan until nut-brown but not burned. Add the parsley and capers. Pour into a heated container. Heat the vinegar in the same pan and mix it with the butter.

Serve poured over brains, fish, and some vegetables.

Note Use also with eggs. Omit the parsley and capers.

See also Brains in Black Butter (p575) and Skate in Black Butter (p453).

VARIATION

Brown Butter

(Beurre Noisette)

Heat the butter until a light hazelnut colour. Add lemon juice to taste.

Serve poured over eggs, brains, skate, soft roes, or various vegetables.

Meunière Butter

butter
chopped parsley

a few drops lemon juice
salt and pepper

Heat the butter to a light hazelnut colour. Add the parsley, lemon juice, and seasoning to taste. Use sizzling hot.

This butter is used mainly for cooking fish or other ingredients, but it can be made and served separately.

Fresh Tomato Sauce (1)

Makes 500ml (approx)

1 medium-sized onion
1 clove of garlic (optional)
1 rasher of streaky bacon, without rinds
750g tomatoes

2 × 15ml spoons olive oil
salt and pepper
a pinch of sugar
1 × 5ml spoon chopped fresh basil (optional)

Skin the onion and chop it finely. Skin and crush the garlic, if used. Chop the bacon rasher. Skin and chop the tomatoes. Heat the oil in a saucepan, and fry the onion, garlic, and bacon over gentle heat for 5 minutes. Add the rest of the ingredients, cover, and simmer gently for 30 minutes. Rub through a sieve or process in an electric blender until smooth. Re-heat and re-season if required.

Serve with meat, some fish, and pasta.

Fresh Tomato Sauce (2)

Makes 375ml (approx)

1 small onion
400g ripe tomatoes
a pinch of Barbados sugar or ¼ × 2.5ml spoon molasses

salt and pepper

Skin the onion and chop roughly with the tomatoes. Put them into a saucepan with just enough water to prevent them from burning. Cover, and simmer gently for 30 minutes. Rub through a sieve. Re-heat, adding the sugar or molasses, and season to taste.

Serve with meat, some fish, and pasta.

Mint Sauce

See p403.

Creole Sauce

Makes 500ml (approx)

500g tomatoes
1 medium-sized onion
1 clove of garlic
1 green pepper (75g
 approx)
75g butter **or** margarine

a pinch of ground cloves
salt and pepper
1 × 5ml spoon chilli
 powder
1 × 5ml spoon sugar
1 bay leaf

Skin and chop the tomatoes, onions, and garlic. De-seed the pepper and chop the flesh. Melt the fat in a saucepan, add the onion, garlic, and green pepper, and fry for 5 minutes. Add the rest of the ingredients including the tomatoes. Cover, and simmer gently for 45 minutes. Remove the bay leaf and re-season if required before serving.

Shallot Sauce

Makes 250ml (approx)

6 shallots (50g approx)
1 × 10ml spoon dripping
 or butter
2 × 10ml spoons flour
250ml brown stock
 (p329)

salt and pepper
lemon juice
1 × 10ml spoon chopped
 parsley

Skin and chop the shallots finely. Heat the fat in a saucepan. Add the shallots and fry until golden-brown. Stir in the flour and cook over gentle heat for 2–3 minutes. Draw the pan off the heat and gradually add the stock, stirring well to prevent lumps forming. Return to the heat and stir until boiling. Reduce the heat, half cover, and simmer gently for 30 minutes. Add seasoning and lemon juice to taste. Stir the parsley into the sauce.

Serve with meat, fish, ham or game.

Thick Vegetable Sauce

Makes 250ml (approx)

2 sticks celery (100g
 approx)
2 tomatoes (100g
 approx)
1 small onion (50g
 approx)
25g dripping **or**
 margarine

25g flour
250ml brown stock
 (p329) **or** strong
 vegetable stock
 (pp330–31)
salt and pepper

Wash and chop the celery. Skin the tomatoes and onion and chop them. Melt the fat in a saucepan or frying pan, add the vegetables, and fry gently until softened but not browned. Stir in the flour. Gradually add the stock, and stir until boiling. Reduce the heat and simmer for 3–4 minutes. Season to taste.

Serve with rissoles and vegetable dishes.

Sharp Sauce
See p402.

Sharp Wine Sauce
See p402.

FRUIT SAUCES FOR SAVOURY DISHES

Apple Sauce

Makes 375ml (approx)

500g apples   *rind and juice of ½ lemon*
2 × 15ml spoons water   *sugar*
15g butter **or** *margarine*

Peel, core, and slice the apples. Put them into a saucepan with the water, fat, and lemon rind. Cover, and cook over low heat until the apple is reduced to a pulp. Beat until smooth, rub through a sieve, or process in an electric blender. Re-heat the sauce with the lemon juice and sugar to taste.

    Serve hot or cold with roast pork, duck or goose.

Note Apple sauce is also excellent served as a sweet sauce with ginger pudding.

VARIATION

Apple Sauce with Horseradish

Add 1–2 × 15ml spoons grated horseradish.
    Serve with pork or beef.

Boar's Head Sauce

Makes 250ml (approx)

2 large oranges   *25g sugar*
1 shallot   *½ × 2.5ml spoon made*
200g redcurrant jelly   *English mustard*
2 × 15ml spoons port   *Cayenne pepper*

Grate the rind of the oranges. Squeeze the juice from 1 orange. Skin and chop the shallot. Put the rind, shallot, jelly and port into a small saucepan. Heat slowly to boiling point, cover, and infuse for 30 minutes over very gentle heat. Add the orange juice, sugar, mustard, and Cayenne pepper. Stir well, then strain and leave to cool.

    Serve with game, venison or mutton.

Note This sauce can be bottled and stored for future use.

Cranberry Sauce

Makes 300ml (approx)

125ml water   *200g cranberries*
150g sugar

Put the water and sugar in a saucepan and stir over gentle heat until the sugar dissolves. Add the cranberries, and cook gently for about 10 minutes until they have burst and are quite tender. Leave to cool.

    Serve with roast turkey, chicken or game.

VARIATIONS

1) For economy, use half cranberries and half sour cooking apples.
2) Add 2–3 × 15ml spoons sherry with the cranberries.
3) Add 2–3 × 15ml spoons seedless raisins with the cranberries.

Cherry Sauce

Makes 375ml (approx)

200g freshly stewed,   *pepper*
* bottled* **or** *canned*   *1 × 5ml spoon vinegar*
* cherries (preferably* *2 × 15ml spoons red*
* Morellos)*   *wine*
125ml juice in which   *1 × 2.5ml spoon*
* cherries were cooked,* *arrowroot (optional)*
* bottled or canned*   *1 × 15ml spoon cold*
sugar   *water (optional)*
2 × 15ml spoons
* redcurrant jelly*

Stone the cherries, if necessary. Put all the ingredients, except the arrowroot and water, into a saucepan and simmer for about 20 minutes, or until the liquid is slightly syrupy.

    If preferred, put all the ingredients in a pan, except the arrowroot and water, and simmer for 5 minutes only; then blend the arrowroot with the cold water. Add to the pan and cook, stirring until the sauce thickens.

    Serve with roast or braised game or rabbit.

Cumberland Sauce

Makes 250ml (approx)

grated rind and juice of 1 orange	100g redcurrant jelly
grated rind and juice of 1 lemon	$\frac{1}{2} \times 2.5ml$ spoon made English mustard
75ml water	salt
75ml port	a pinch of Cayenne pepper
$2 \times 15ml$ spoons vinegar	

Put the orange and lemon rind into a small saucepan with the water and heat to simmering point. Simmer gently for 10 minutes. Add the port, vinegar, redcurrant jelly and mustard, and heat gently until the jelly melts. Add the orange and lemon juice to the pan with the seasoning. Simmer for 3–4 minutes.

Serve hot or cold with roast game, mutton or ham.

Currant Sauce

Makes 375ml (approx)

25g butter	juice of $\frac{1}{2}$ lemon
25g flour	a pinch of ground cloves
250ml water	a pinch of ground ginger
75ml red wine	50g currants
a pinch of grated nutmeg	sugar

Melt the butter in a saucepan, add the flour, and cook until the flour is golden-brown. Draw the pan off the heat and gradually stir in the water and wine. Return to the heat and stir until boiling. Add the rest of the ingredients, reduce the heat, and simmer gently for 10 minutes.

Serve with roast pork, hare or venison.

VARIATION

Sultana Sauce

Substitute sultanas for the currants.

Fruit Curry Sauce

Makes 500ml (approx)

$\frac{1}{2}$ small onion (25g approx)	50g flour
$\frac{1}{2}$ cooking apple (100g approx)	$1 \times 10ml$ spoon curry powder
1 banana (150g approx)	salt
6 seedless raisins	500ml vegetable stock (p330–31)
1 tomato (50g approx)	lemon juice
25g butter **or** margarine	
$1 \times 5ml$ spoon desiccated coconut	

Prepare the onion and apple, and chop them finely. Slice the banana. Chop the raisins. Skin and chop the tomato. Melt the fat in a saucepan, add the vegetables and fruit, and fry gently for 5 minutes. Add the coconut, flour, curry powder and salt to taste, and stir well. Stir in the stock. Heat to simmering point, cover, and simmer gently for 20 minutes. Add lemon juice to taste.

Serve with vegetables or eggs.

Raisin Sauce

Makes 400ml (approx)

75g soft dark brown sugar	salt and pepper
25g flour	350ml boiling water
$1 \times 15ml$ spoon dry English mustard	50ml vinegar
	50g seedless raisins
	25g butter

Mix the dry ingredients in the top of a double saucepan or in a basin placed over simmering water. Stir in the boiling water and the vinegar gradually to prevent lumps forming. Cook slowly for 15–20 minutes. Add the raisins, and continue to cook for 5 minutes. Beat in the butter, a small pat at a time. Use at once.

Serve with hot ham dishes.

Note See also Ham with Raisin Sauce (p605).

Gooseberry Sauce

Makes 375ml (approx)

200g gooseberries
125ml water
15g butter
25g sugar
1 × 15ml spoon lemon juice

a pinch of grated nutmeg
1 × 2.5ml spoon chopped chives (optional)
1 × 15ml spoon chopped sorrel (optional)
salt and pepper

Top and tail the gooseberries and put into a saucepan with the water and butter. Cover, and cook over low heat until they are reduced to a pulp. Rub through a sieve or process in an electric blender. Re-heat the sauce, and stir in the sugar, lemon juice, nutmeg, chives and sorrel, if used. Season to taste.

Serve with mackerel. This sauce is also good with roast or braised pork.

Note See also Mackerel with Gooseberry Sauce (p445).

Quince Sauce

Makes 375ml (approx)

200g quinces
250ml water
a good pinch of grated nutmeg
a good pinch of ground cloves

1 × 15ml spoon lemon juice
75ml red wine (optional)
sugar

Peel, core, and slice the quinces. Put them into a saucepan with the water. Cover, and cook over low heat until reduced to a pulp. Beat, rub through a sieve, or process in an electric blender until smooth. Re-heat the sauce, and add the rest of the ingredients with sugar to taste.

Serve with roast pork or game.

Prune Sauce

Makes 375ml (approx)

200g prunes
250ml water
a strip of lemon rind
25g sugar
a pinch of ground cinnamon

*1 × 15ml spoon rum **or** brandy (optional)*
lemon juice

Soak the prunes in the water overnight. Put them into a saucepan with the lemon rind, and stew until tender. Remove the stones and lemon rind, and rub the prunes and liquid through a sieve, or process in an electric blender until smooth. Re-heat, and add the sugar, cinnamon, rum or brandy, if used, and lemon juice to taste.

Serve with roast pork, goose, venison or mutton.

Note This sauce can also be served with some hot milk and custard puddings or with Apple Pudding (steamed) (p983).

Redcurrant Sauce

Makes 150ml (approx)

100g redcurrant jelly   *3 × 15ml spoons port*

Put the jelly and port in a small saucepan and cook over gentle heat until the jelly melts.

Serve with game, venison or mutton.

Note This sauce can also be served as a sweet sauce with hot milk or steamed puddings.

SWEET SAUCES

Most sweet sauces look better if they are translucent and they should have a more delicate texture than savoury sauces. This means that thickeners such as cornflour and arrowroot which make them clear and light must be used. To produce a smooth sauce both must be blended with cold liquid before being added to a hot liquid.

Cornflour-based sauces should not be over beaten because this thins them. Arrowroot-based sauces should be used soon after they have been made because they will thin if left to stand, and they do not re-heat satisfactorily.

Sweet sauces also include egg-based and fruit purée sauces. Egg-based sauces must never be boiled as this will make them curdle.

Sweet sauces, like savoury ones, must complement the dish with which they are served; for instance, serve a bland sauce such as Vanilla Sauce (p721) with tart, stewed fruit, or a sharp lemon sauce with a bland milk pudding.

Sweet Cornflour Sauce or Sweet White Sauce

Basic recipe

Makes 250ml (approx)

2 × 10ml spoons cornflour	*1–2 × 15ml spoons sugar*
250ml milk	*vanilla essence **or** other flavouring*

1) *Blended Method*

Blend the cornflour to a smooth, thin paste with a little of the cold milk. Put the rest of the milk in a saucepan and heat to boiling point. Stir the boiling milk into the blended cornflour. Return to the pan and stir until boiling. Reduce the heat and cook for 3 minutes. Add the sugar and flavouring to taste.

2) *All-in-one Method*

Put the cornflour, milk, and sugar in a medium-sized saucepan. Whisk over moderate heat until the sauce comes to the boil. Reduce the heat, and cook for 2–3 minutes, whisking all the time, until the sauce is thickened and smooth.

Note If the sauce must be kept hot for a short time, cover it with wet greaseproof paper and a lid. Just before serving, beat again to remove any lumps that may have formed.

VARIATIONS

The following ingredients can be added to 250ml hot Sweet Cornflour Sauce after it has been cooked:

Almond Sauce

Add 1 × 10ml spoon ground almonds to the cornflour when blending to a paste with the milk. Add 2–3 drops of almond essence, and vanilla essence to taste after the sauce has been cooked.

Brandy Sauce

Add 1–2 × 15ml spoons brandy.

Chocolate Sauce (1)

Add 1 × 15ml spoon cocoa powder and 1 × 15ml spoon sugar dissolved in 1 × 15ml spoon boiling water.

Note For Chocolate Sauce (2), see p725.

Coffee Sauce

Add 1 × 10ml spoon instant coffee dissolved in 1 × 10ml spoon boiling water **or** 1 × 15ml spoon coffee essence.

Ginger Sauce

Add 1 × 10ml spoon ground ginger and 50g finely chopped crystallized ginger (optional).

Lemon or Orange Sauce(1)

Add the grated rind of half an orange or lemon and a drop of orange or yellow colouring (optional).

Note For Lemon Sauce (2), and Orange Sauce (2), see below.

Rich Sauce

Add 1 egg yolk and 2 × 15ml spoons cream. Re-heat the sauce but do not boil.

Rum Sauce

Add 1–2 × 15ml spoons rum.

Sweet Spice Sauce

Add 1 × 5ml spoon mixed spice **or** grated nutmeg.

Vanilla Sauce

Add ½ × 2.5ml spoon vanilla essence and a drop of yellow colouring (optional).

Sweet Arrowroot Sauce

Basic recipe

Makes 175ml (approx) using 125ml liquid

125–250ml water
thinly pared rind of
  lemon **or** *other*
  flavouring
100g sugar, golden syrup
  or *honey*

lemon juice
2 × 5ml spoons
  arrowroot

Put the water in a pan and add the lemon rind or other flavouring. Heat to boiling point, reduce the heat, and simmer gently for 15 minutes. Remove the lemon rind, if used. Add the sugar, syrup or honey. Re-heat to boiling point and boil for 5 minutes. Add lemon juice to taste. Blend the arrowroot with a little cold water until smooth and stir into the hot liquid. Heat gently for 1–2 minutes, stirring all the time until the arrowroot thickens.

VARIATIONS

Lemon Sauce(2)

Make as above, using 125ml water, the rind of half a lemon and the juice of 2 lemons.

Rich Lemon Sauce

Add a small glass of sherry and an egg yolk when the sauce is just below boiling point. The sauce must not be allowed to boil once the egg yolk has been added.

Orange Sauce(2)

Make as above, using 125ml water, the rind of half an orange and the juice of 1 orange instead of the lemon rind and juice.

SWEET CUSTARD SAUCES

Crème Anglaise(1)
(Egg Custard Sauce)

Makes 300ml (approx)

250ml milk
a few drops vanilla
  essence **or** *a strip of*
  lemon rind

3 egg yolks
50g caster sugar

Put the milk and flavouring in a pan and warm gently but do not let it boil. Beat the egg yolks and sugar together until creamy. Remove the lemon rind, if used, and add the milk. Strain the custard into a double boiler or a basin placed over a pan of simmering water. Cook, stirring all the time with a wooden spoon, until the custard thickens and coats the back of the spoon. Take care not to let the custard curdle. Serve hot or cold.

Note For Crème Anglaise (2), see p965.

VARIATIONS
Stir 125ml lightly whipped double cream and 2 × 15ml spoons Grand Marnier into the completed sauce.

Chocolate Custard Sauce

Grate 100g plain chocolate coarsely and add to the milk with vanilla essence instead of lemon rind. Warm until the chocolate melts, stir, and add to the egg yolks. Complete the recipe as above.

Caramel Custard Sauce

Put 25g sugar and 1 × 15ml spoon water in a small pan. Heat gently until the sugar dissolves; then boil the syrup until it is golden-brown. Remove from the heat, quickly add 2 × 15ml spoons cold water, and leave in a warm place to dissolve. Add enough caramel to the finished custard sauce to give a good flavour.

Cornflour Custard Sauce

Makes 250ml (approx)

1 × 15ml spoon
  cornflour
250ml milk
1 egg yolk

1 × 15ml spoon sugar
a few drops vanilla
  essence

Blend the cornflour with a little of the cold milk in a large bowl. Put the rest of the milk in a pan and heat to boiling point. Stir the milk into the blended mixture. Rinse the pan and return the sauce to it. Bring to the boil, and boil for 3 minutes to cook the cornflour. Leave to cool; then stir in the yolk and sugar. Cook over low heat, stirring carefully, until the egg thickens. Do not let it boil. Add a few drops of vanilla essence.

Cream Custard Sauce

Makes 250ml (approx)

4 egg yolks **or** *2 whole*
  eggs
50g caster sugar

125ml milk
grated rind of 1 orange
125ml single cream

Beat together the egg yolks or the whole eggs with the sugar and milk. Add the orange rind and cream. Pour into a double boiler or into a basin placed over a pan of simmering water. Cook, stirring all the time, until the sauce thickens. It must not boil or the sauce will curdle. Serve hot or cold.

Sweet Mousseline Sauce

Makes 300ml (approx)

2 eggs
1 egg yolk
40g caster sugar

75ml single cream
1 × 15ml spoon medium-
  dry sherry

Put all the ingredients in a double boiler or in a basin placed over a pan of simmering water. Cook and whisk until pale and frothy and of a thick, creamy consistency.

Serve at once over light steamed or baked puddings, fruit desserts or Christmas pudding.

Sabayon Sauce
(hot)

Makes 200ml (approx)

3 egg yolks
25g caster sugar
50ml Marsala,
  Madeira, sweet sherry
  or *sweet white wine*

a small strip of lemon
rind

Beat the yolks and sugar together in a basin until thick and pale. Whisk in the chosen wine gradually. Add the lemon rind. Pour into a double boiler or stand the basin over a pan of simmering water. Cook until thick and creamy, whisking all the time. When the whisk is lifted out of the mixture it should leave a trail that lasts for 2–3 seconds. Remove the lemon rind.

Serve at once, with steamed puddings.

Sabayon Sauce
(cold)

Makes 400ml (approx)

50g caster sugar
75ml water
2 egg yolks
1 × 15ml spoon medium-
  sweet sherry **or** *brandy*

3 × 15ml spoons double
cream

Warm the sugar and water gently in a pan until the sugar is completely dissolved. Bring to the boil and boil for 3 minutes. Mix together the yolks and sherry or brandy in a basin. Whisk in the syrup gradually, and continue whisking until the mixture is cool, and thick and foamy. Whip the cream lightly and fold it in gently. Chill.

Serve with fruit desserts.

Simple Custard
See p964.

SWEET FRUIT SAUCES

Apricot Sauce

Makes 375ml (approx)

200g fresh **or** *canned*
  apricots (see **Note***)*
125ml water (approx)
25–50g brown sugar
1 × 15ml spoon lemon
juice

1 × 10ml spoon
  maraschino **or** *apricot*
  brandy (optional)
1 × 5ml spoon arrowroot
1 × 15ml spoon cold
  water

Stone the apricots and reserve the stones. Put the fruit and water into a pan. Simmer gently in a covered pan until softened. Rub through a sieve, or process in an electric blender until smooth. Crack the apricot stones and remove the kernels. Cover the kernels with boiling water and leave for 2 minutes. Drain, and when cool enough to handle, skin them. Add to the apricots with sugar to taste, lemon juice, and liqueur, if used. Re-heat the sauce. Blend the arrowroot with the water. Add to the sauce and bring to the boil, stirring until the sauce thickens.

Note If using canned apricots use 125ml of the syrup from the can instead of sugar and water. Purée the apricots with the syrup, and re-heat as above.

Prune Sauce
See p719.

Redcurrant Sauce
See p719.

Cold Chantilly Apple Sauce

Makes 500ml (approx)

500g cooking apples
2 × 15ml spoons cold
* water*

25g butter
50g sugar
125ml double cream

Peel, core, and slice the apples. Put them into a pan with the water, butter, and sugar. Simmer gently in a covered pan until reduced to a pulp. Beat, rub through a sieve, or process in an electric blender until smooth. Leave to cool. Whip the cream until stiff, and fold into the apple purée.

Apple Sauce

See p717.

Melba Sauce

Makes 100–125ml

200g fresh raspberries
3 × 15ml spoons icing
* sugar*

white wine (optional)

Crush the raspberries in a sieve over a heatproof bowl. Add the sugar and rub through the sieve into the bowl. Place the bowl over a pan of simmering water, and stir for 2–3 minutes to dissolve the sugar. Remove from the heat, and add a little white wine if a thinner consistency is preferred. The sauce should only just coat the back of a spoon. Chill before use.

Serve over Peach Melba (p1062), meringues, or any hot or cold raspberry-flavoured dessert.

Thickened Fruit Sauce

Basic recipe

fresh fruit (damsons,
* plums, raspberries,*
* blueberries **or***
* blackberries)*
sugar

lemon juice
1 × 5ml spoon arrowroot
* for every 250ml fruit*
* purée*
1 × 5ml spoon water

Put the fruit into a pan with a very little water. Heat to simmering point and simmer until softened. Stone the fruit; then rub through a sieve, or process in an electric blender until smooth. Measure the fruit to calculate the quantity of arrowroot needed. Pour the fruit purée back into the saucepan and add sugar and lemon juice to taste. Blend the correct quantity of arrowroot with the water. Add to the fruit purée and bring to the boil, stirring all the time until the sauce thickens.

Note Canned or bottled fruit can be used, in which case it will be unnecessary to add extra sugar.

Fruit and Yoghurt Sauce

Makes 375ml (approx)

250ml fruit purée
* (p1002)*

150g natural yoghurt
sugar

Fold the fruit purée into the yoghurt. Sweeten to taste. Serve cold.

Fruit Syrups as Sauces
See pp1135–38.

MISCELLANEOUS SWEET SAUCES

Chocolate Sauce (2)

Makes 150ml (approx)

100g plain chocolate
200g sugar
125ml water

salt
1 × 2.5ml spoon vanilla essence

Break up the chocolate and put it into a saucepan with the other ingredients. Stir over gentle heat until the chocolate and sugar melt and blend together.

Serve hot over ice cream, profiteroles, or stewed pears.

Note Black coffee can be substituted for water.

For Chocolate Sauce (1), see p720.

Chocolate Cream Sauce

Makes 125ml (approx)

75g plain chocolate
1 × 15ml spoon butter
4 × 15ml spoons water
1 × 15ml spoon single cream

1 × 5ml spoon vanilla essence

Grate the chocolate coarsely. Put it in a heatproof basin with the butter and water. Stand the basin over a pan of simmering water and stir until the chocolate and butter melt. Remove from the heat and immediately stir in the cream and vanilla essence.

Serve at once over rice desserts, chilled, stewed, or canned pears, or ice cream. When cold, the sauce thickens enough to be used as a soft filling for éclairs or profiteroles.

Chocolate or Cocoa Liqueur Sauce

Makes 400ml (approx)

75g plain chocolate **or** *cooking chocolate* **or** *1 × 15ml spoon cocoa powder*
250ml water
1 × 10ml spoon custard powder **or** *cornflour*

1 × 15ml spoon Cointreau **or** *Grand Marnier*
1 × 15ml spoon sugar

If using chocolate, break it into small pieces and put into a basin with a little of the 250ml cold water. Stand the basin over a saucepan of simmering water and stir until the chocolate melts. When melted, beat the chocolate until smooth, gradually adding the rest of the water. Blend the custard powder or cornflour with 2 × 15ml spoons more water, then stir into the chocolate and cook for 3–4 minutes. Add the liqueur and the sugar.

Note If using cocoa, add it to the cornflour before blending with the water.

Rich Chocolate Sauce

Makes 500ml (approx)

350g bitter-sweet dessert chocolate
200ml water
4 × 10ml spoons butter

2 × 15ml spoons double cream
1 × 5ml spoon whisky

Grate the chocolate coarsely. Put it in a saucepan with the water and heat gently, stirring all the time, until the chocolate melts. Do not let the sauce boil. Add the butter, a spoonful at a time, and continue stirring until it melts. Remove from the heat and stir in the cream and whisky.

Serve at once over ice cream, a chocolate Swiss roll, or plain cake.

Note The sauce can be poured into a heatproof container with a lid, cooled, and then stored in a refrigerator for up to 1 week. To use, bring to room temperature, then stand the container in a pan of very hot water.

Rum and Raisin Chocolate Sauce

Makes 250ml (approx)

50g seedless raisins	175ml milk
25g cocoa	2–3 × 15ml spoons rum
25g cornflour	2–3 × 15ml spoons
25g caster sugar	single cream

Chop the raisins. Blend the cocoa, cornflour, and sugar to a smooth paste with a little of the milk. Put the rest of the milk in a saucepan and heat to boiling point. Stir it into the cocoa paste. Return the mixture to the saucepan and stir until boiling. Add the raisins, rum and cream, and stir. Serve hot or cold.

Ginger Syrup Sauce

Makes 300ml (approx)

a strip of lemon rind	1 × 5ml spoon lemon
a piece of fresh ginger	juice
root	1 × 10ml spoon
250ml water **or** 125ml	arrowroot
syrup from preserved	1 × 2.5ml spoon ground
ginger and 125ml	ginger
water	1 × 15ml spoon
100g brown sugar,	preserved ginger
golden syrup **or** honey	

Put the lemon rind, ginger root, and water or syrup and water into a saucepan. Heat to boiling point, reduce the heat, and simmer gently for 15 minutes. Remove the lemon rind and ginger root. Add the brown sugar, syrup or honey, bring to the boil and boil for 5 minutes. Add the lemon juice. Blend the arrowroot and ground ginger with a little cold water until smooth. Stir the arrowroot mixture into the hot liquid. Heat gently until the arrowroot thickens, stirring all the time. Chop the preserved ginger and add to the sauce. Simmer the sauce for 2–3 minutes.

Serve over steamed puddings such as Ginger Pudding (p985) or over ice cream.

Butterscotch Sauce

Makes 500ml (approx)

400ml evaporated milk	1 × 2.5ml spoon vanilla
100g soft brown sugar	essence
100g caster sugar	a pinch of salt
50g butter	
1 × 15ml spoon clear	
honey	

Put the evaporated milk, sugar, butter, and honey into a thick saucepan, and stir over gentle heat until the sugar is dissolved. Stir in the vanilla essence and a pinch of salt.

Serve hot with steamed puddings such as Ginger Pudding (p985) or Lemon Pudding (p986) or over ice cream.

Jam Sauce

Makes 300ml (approx)

4 × 15ml spoons seedless	1 × 10ml spoon
jam	arrowroot
250ml water	a few drops food
sugar	colouring (optional)
lemon juice	

Put the jam and the water in a saucepan and heat to boiling point. Add sugar and lemon juice to taste. Blend the arrowroot with a little cold water until smooth. Stir into the hot liquid and heat gently until the arrowroot thickens, stirring all the time. Colour if necessary.

Serve with steamed or baked puddings, ice cream or cold cornflour desserts.

VARIATION

Marmalade Sauce (1)

Substitute marmalade for jam.

Serve with Marmalade Custard Pudding (p970), other hot puddings or cold cornflour desserts.

Marmalade Sauce (2)

Makes 125ml (approx)

4 × 15ml spoons   *75ml white wine*
  marmalade

Heat the marmalade and wine gently for 5 minutes in a saucepan.

Serve over steamed or baked puddings containing dried fruit.

Sweet Sherry Sauce

Makes 150ml (approx)

75ml water   *sugar*
75ml sherry   *lemon juice*
2 × 15ml spoons seedless
  jam or jelly

Heat the water, sherry, and jam in a saucepan. Add sugar and lemon juice to taste. Bring to the boil and boil for 2–3 minutes. Strain, if necessary, before serving. If liked, the sauce can be thickened with arrowroot as for Jam Sauce (p726).

Serve with steamed puddings or fruit desserts.

Gravies

Thin Gravy
(for roast beef)

Makes 250ml (approx)

pan juices   *salt and pepper*
250ml hot water from   *(optional)*
  cooking vegetables **or**   *gravy browning*
  beef stock   *(optional)*

After roasting a joint, carefully pour off the fat from the roasting tin, leaving all pan juices and sediment behind. Add the vegetable water or beef stock to the juices. Bring to the boil, stirring well until all the sediment dissolves, and boil for 2–3 minutes to reduce the liquid slightly. Season to taste. If the gravy is pale, add a few drops of gravy browning. Strain, and serve very hot.

Thickened Gravy
(for roast pork and roast veal)

Makes 250ml (approx)

pan juices   *salt and pepper*
1 × 15ml spoon plain   *(optional)*
  flour
250ml hot water from
  cooking vegetables **or**
  general household stock
  (p329) made with pork
  meat trimmings and
  vegetables

After roasting a joint, pour off most of the fat from the roasting tin leaving 2 × 15ml spoons of fat and sediment in the tin. Sift the flour over the fat and blend thoroughly with the pan juices. Stir and cook until browned. Gradually add the hot liquid, and stir until boiling. Boil for 3–4 minutes. Season to taste. Strain, and serve very hot.

Lamb Gravy

(for roast lamb)

Makes 250ml (approx)

pan juices
1 × 5ml spoon plain
   flour
250ml hot water from
   vegetables or general
   household stock (p329)
   made with lamb meat
   trimmings and
   vegetables

salt and pepper
   (optional)
gravy browning
   (optional)

Make as for Thin Gravy (p727) but, after pouring off the fat, stir the flour into the pan juices. Add the hot vegetable water or stock gradually to prevent lumps forming, and stir until boiling. Season to taste, if required. If the gravy is pale, add a few drops of gravy browning. Strain, and serve very hot.

Giblet Gravy

(for roast poultry)

Makes 300ml (approx)

1 set of giblets
1 medium-sized onion
   (100g approx)
   (optional)
400ml water

pan juices
gravy browning
   (optional)
salt and pepper
   (optional)

Prepare the giblets (p624) and skin the onion, if used. Put the giblets and the onion in a pan and cover with cold water. Heat to boiling point, cover, reduce the heat, and simmer gently for 1 hour. Pour off the fat from the tin in which the bird has been roasted, leaving any sediment. Add the liquid from the giblets and stir until boiling. Boil for 2–3 minutes. If the gravy is pale, add a few drops of gravy browning. Season to taste, if required. Strain and serve very hot.

Note The gravy can be thickened slightly, if liked, by adding 1 × 5ml spoon plain flour for each 250ml giblet stock. Blend the flour with the sediment before adding the stock. Boil for 3–4 minutes.

Gravy

(for roast game)

Makes 400ml (approx)

200g bones, giblets, and
   game trimmings
500ml water
1 bay leaf
a sprig of thyme
1 clove

6 white peppercorns
50g onion for each
   500ml water
pan juices
salt and pepper
   (optional)

Put the bones, giblets, and game trimmings in a saucepan and cover with the water. Heat to boiling point, add the herbs, clove, peppercorns, and onion. Reduce the heat, cover, and simmer gently for about 1 hour. Strain the stock. Pour off the fat from the tin in which the game has been roasted, leaving any sediment. Add the stock and stir until boiling. Boil for 2–3 minutes to reduce the gravy slightly. Skim off any fat. Serve very hot.

Vegetable Gravy

(brown)

Makes 400ml (approx)

1 medium-sized onion
   (100g approx)
1 small carrot (25g
   approx)
½ small turnip (25g
   approx)
25g butter or margarine
1 × 15ml spoon plain
   flour

500ml water
bouquet garni
1 × 10ml spoon vinegar
1 × 2.5ml spoon sugar
2 cloves
¼ blade of mace
salt and pepper
1 × 5ml spoon
   Worcestershire sauce

Prepare and chop the vegetables. Melt the fat in a saucepan, add the vegetables, and fry for about 10 minutes or until well browned. Stir in the flour. Gradually add the water and stir until boiling. Add the rest of the ingredients except the sauce. Reduce the heat, cover, and simmer gently for 1 hour. Strain. Add the Worcestershire sauce and re-season if required.

Port Wine Gravy or Sauce

Makes 175ml (approx)

*125ml lamb gravy
(p728)* **or** *venison
gravy made as for thin
gravy (p727)*

*1 × 15ml spoon
redcurrant jelly
4 × 15ml spoons port*

Put all the ingredients in a saucepan and cook over gentle heat for about 5 minutes until the jelly melts.

Serve hot with roast lamb, mutton or venison.

Walnut Gravy

Makes 250ml (approx)

*2 pickled walnuts
250ml vegetable stock
salt and pepper*

*2 × 15ml spoons walnut
ketchup
gravy browning
(optional)*

Chop the walnuts coarsely. Pour the stock into a saucepan, season to taste, and stir in the walnut ketchup and walnuts. Heat gently for 2–3 minutes. If the gravy is pale, add a few drops of gravy browning.

Marinades

A marinade is a flavoured and seasoned liquid in which fish, meat, and game are steeped or soaked before being cooked. Dry mixtures of herbs rubbed into the flesh are sometimes called marinades but, strictly, the term should apply only to liquids.

The object of marinating is to tenderize, moisten, and flavour the flesh. A marinade, therefore, contains an acid which tenderizes and preserves the flesh, herbs and spices for flavour, and an oily ingredient to combat dryness.

A marinade may be uncooked or cooked. An uncooked marinade has a slower but more subtle effect. A cooked marinade has the advantage that it can often be reboiled and used several times depending on individual recipes. Both types of marinade can be strained and added to any sauce served with the fish, meat or game.

The length of time fish, meat, or game is steeped in a marinade depends on the age and condition of the flesh and on the surrounding temperature. As a general rule, fish and small pieces of meat need only a few hours, whereas a large piece of meat or game may profit from between 2 and 4 days' soaking (the longer time in winter). Small game birds seldom need marinating. The food should be marinated in a cool place out of direct sunlight.

A glazed earthenware vessel and a wooden spoon should be used, if possible. Alternatively, mix the marinade ingredients in a polythene bag, put in the meat and place the bag in a bowl. Whilst flesh is being marinated, it should be turned from time to time and even basted, to ensure that each part is soaked and impregnated. If left out of the marinade for any length of time, the flesh may dry off and the surface become tough.

There are a great many different marinades. Most fish marinades consist of onions or shallots, herbs, oil, lemon juice, white wine, salt and pepper, in varying proportions. Meat and game marinades, however, are more varied. White meats are usually steeped in a white wine marinade which is more often uncooked than a red wine one. Red meats and game are usually soaked in a red wine mixture; a marinade for game is often seasoned with coriander or juniper.

Uncooked White Wine Marinade

(for fish or white meat)

Makes 325ml (approx)

1 onion	1 bay leaf
6–10 parsley stalks	juice of 1 lemon
1 × 5ml spoon fennel	50ml salad oil
seeds (for fish)	250ml white wine **or**
1 × 5ml spoon dried	wine mixed with water
thyme	salt and pepper

Skin and slice the onion and chop the parsley stalks. Tie very loosely in butter muslin with the fennel seeds, if used, and the herbs. Put the herb bag into a basin with the fish or meat and pour the liquids over them. Season to taste. Marinate for as long as required, turning over the contents of the dish occasionally.

Uncooked Red Wine Marinade

(for red meat or game)

Makes 650ml (approx)

1 medium-sized onion	1 × 2.5ml spoon ground
1 medium-sized carrot	coriander (for game)
1 stick of celery	1 × 2.5ml spoon juniper
6–10 parsley stalks	berries (for game)
1 clove of garlic	salt and pepper
1 × 5ml spoon dried	250ml brown stock
thyme	(p329)
1 bay leaf	125ml red wine
6–8 black peppercorns	125ml water
1–2 cloves	125ml salad oil

Chop the vegetables and parsley stalks. Skin and crush the garlic. Mix the ingredients in a basin as for the uncooked white wine marinade.

Devilling Marinade or Sauce

See p1311.

Barbeque Basting Sauce

See p1312.

Cooked Red Wine Marinade

(for red meat or game)

Makes 1.25 litres (approx)

1 carrot	250ml red wine
1 onion	juice of 1 lemon
1 litre water	1 × 5ml spoon
3 bay leaves	granulated sugar
12 black peppercorns	6 juniper berries (for
1 × 15ml spoon salt	game)

Prepare the carrot and onion and slice them thinly. Put in a saucepan with the water, bay leaves, peppercorns and salt, and cook until the vegetables are tender.

When cooked, add the rest of the ingredients. Put the meat or game in a basin and pour the hot marinade over it. Marinate for as long as required, turning over the meat frequently. For a large piece of meat left to soak for 36 hours or longer, strain off the marinade on the second day, reboil it, and leave to cool completely; then pour it back over the meat. This can be done a second time over a 4–5 day period, if required. The marinade should not be reboiled more than twice.

Note More information on marinating game can be found on p672 and p674.

Dry Spice Mixture

(for game birds)

Enough to cover 4 small birds

1 large clove of garlic	1 × 5ml spoon paprika
1 × 5ml spoon salt	**or** dry mustard
1 × 2.5ml spoon freshly	
ground black pepper	

Skin and crush the garlic. Combine all the ingredients, and rub well into game birds. Leave at room temperature for at least 1 hour.

Note This should be used instead of a marinade.

VARIATION

For quail, replace the paprika or mustard with 10 crushed juniper berries.

PÂTÉS AND POTTED FOODS

If well seasoned, potted ham will keep a long time in winter, and will be found very convenient for sandwiches, &c. The butter used for potted things will answer for basting, or for paste for meat pies.

Pâtés and terrines, potted meats, cheeses, and fish, are all savoury foods either minced, chopped or pounded prior to or after some form of cooking. They are frequently sealed under fat to make them last longer.

The distinction between a *pâté*, meaning paste, and *terrine*, which takes its name from a fairly shallow earthenware dish used by the French for baking and serving certain pâté mixtures, has diminished to such an extent that they are virtually synonymous. Together with potted foods, which are a British tradition, most are popular as first or last-course dishes or as part of a packed or outdoor meal.

TEXTURES

Luxury pâtés, such as chicken liver pâté made with cream, must be as smooth as velvet, like the world-famous *pâté de fois gras*. Other pâté mixtures such as a *terrine de campagne* (which means, in French, a household dish of the local region) or a *pâté maison* (a pâté made to the cook's personal recipe) are likely to be fairly coarse, crumbly mixtures using cheap ingredients, cooled under a weight after being baked. The recipes which follow contain a selection of both smooth and coarse pâtés.

Weighting and Cooling a Pâté

If a pâté needs to be weighted, first cut a piece of stout card to fit the top of the dish, inside the rim, and cover it with foil. Place this cover over the dish and put a weight on top, eg a can of fruit, a large stone, flat iron or brick. A light weight should be used at first, especially if there is any melted fat round the sides of the pâté which may well up and spill over if a heavy weight is used. As the dish cools, the pressure can be increased by substitut-

ing or adding a heavier weight. The heavier the weight, the more solid or condensed the pâté will be.

Cool the pâté by standing the dish in a pan of iced or very cold water which comes half-way up its sides, for between 12–24 hours, or as indicated in the recipe. Leave on a cold surface such as a stone slab or floor, or a metal table, in a cool place. Remove the weight, take out of the water, cover with clingfilm, and chill in a refrigerator or very cool place to allow the flavours to blend and mature. Pâtés should be eaten as soon as possible, so should not be stored for very long.

Note Whether or not a pâté needs to be weighted, any melted fat should be removed from the sides before serving.

BAKED PÂTÉS AND TERRINES

Liver Pâté

Makes 700g (approx)

*200g calf's **or** pig's liver*
200g poultry livers
1 small onion
*100g very lean ham **or** bacon*
75g butter
a few gherkins (optional)

1–2 hard-boiled eggs
salt and pepper
1–2 × 5ml spoons dried mixed herbs
butter for greasing
melted clarified butter (p886)

Remove any skin and tubes from the livers. Skin the onion. Chop the liver, onion, and ham or bacon into small pieces. Melt the butter in a pan and cook the meats and onion for 5–6 minutes. Mince finely twice or process in an electric blender to make a smooth paste. Chop the gherkins, if used, and the hard-boiled eggs and add to the liver mixture together with the seasoning and herbs. Put into an ovenproof terrine or similar dish and cover with buttered greaseproof paper. Stand the dish in a pan of hot water which comes half-way up the sides. Bake in a moderate oven at 180°C, Gas 4, for about 30 minutes.

When cooked, either cover immediately with a layer of clarified butter and leave to cool, then chill before serving; or place under a light weight (p731) and cover with clarified butter as soon as cold. Serve the pâté in the dish in which it has been cooked, or cut it into slices and place on a bed of crisp lettuce.

Serve with hot dry toast or brown bread rolled sandwiches.

VARIATION

Use 500g pig's or calf's or chicken's livers instead of 200g pig's or calf's liver and 200g poultry livers. Add 2–4 × 15ml spoons double cream to the mixture for a softer texture.

Liver Pâté with Mushrooms

Makes 2.3kg (approx)

*1kg lamb's **or** pig's liver*
1kg green bacon, without rinds
1 × 5ml spoon salt
freshly ground pepper
*a pinch of ground cinnamon **or** grated nutmeg*

1 small onion
125g small cup mushrooms
*125g butter **or** margarine*
2 eggs
a pinch of dried thyme

Garnish
3 bay leaves

Remove any skin and tubes from the liver. Chop the bacon. Mince together finely or process in an electric blender. Add the salt, pepper, and cinnamon or nutmeg. Skin the onion and chop it finely; clean and slice the mushrooms. Melt the butter or margarine in a pan and fry the onion and mushrooms gently for 4–5 minutes, turning frequently. Remove from the heat and stir in the liver and bacon. Beat the eggs lightly until liquid and stir them into the mixture.

Put the mixture into a shallow ovenproof casserole or dish with a lid. Sprinkle the surface with thyme and put the bay leaves in a trefoil pattern on top. Cover the dish and stand it in a pan of hot water which comes half-way up the sides. Bake in a cool oven at 150°C, Gas 2, for 3 hours. When cooked, leave to cool, keeping the lid on the dish. Chill before serving from the dish.

Household Pâté

(Pâté Maison)

Makes 1kg (approx)

8–10 back bacon rashers, without rinds	25g soft white breadcrumbs
100g pig's liver	1 egg
100g fresh belly of pork	1 × 15ml spoon milk
200g sausage-meat	75ml brandy
200g cold cooked rabbit	salt and pepper
1 medium-sized onion	

Garnish
3 bay leaves

Place the garnish of 3 bay leaves in a trefoil pattern in the bottom of a 1.25 litre oblong, ovenproof dish. Line the dish with bacon rashers, reserving 2 or 3 to cover the top of the dish. Remove any skin and tubes from the liver. Chop the liver and pork coarsely and mix with the sausage-meat. Chop the rabbit meat finely and add to the mixture. Skin and chop the onion and add it with the breadcrumbs. Beat the egg until liquid and blend with the milk and brandy. Mix them into the dry ingredients and season to taste. Turn the mixture into the lined dish, cover with the reserved bacon rashers, and then with a lid or foil. Stand the dish in a pan of hot water which comes half-way up its sides. Bake in a moderate oven at 180°C, Gas 4, for 1 hour.

When cooked, weight the pâté (p731), and leave to cool. Chill for 12–24 hours. To serve, remove the top bacon rashers and turn out of the dish.

Smooth Pork Pâté

See p1400.

Terrine of Duck

Makes 1.5kg (approx)

500g raw boneless duck meat **or** wild duck meat	a pinch each of dried thyme and savory
100ml brandy	salt and pepper
2 shallots	3 eggs
200g fresh belly of pork	450g thin slices pork back fat **or** streaky bacon rashers
300g raw chicken meat	
rind of 1 orange	

Garnish
3 bay leaves

Use only fleshy meat and discard any sinewy fibres. Mince or shred the meat finely. Put it into a bowl with the brandy, and leave to marinate for 4–6 hours.

Skin the shallots and chop them. Mince the pork and chicken meat. Mix them with the duck meat in the bowl. Cut the orange rind into thin shreds and add with the herbs and seasoning. Beat the eggs lightly until liquid, stir them in, and mix together thoroughly.

Line a 1.4 litre ovenproof dish with slices of pork fat or bacon, reserving enough to cover the top of the dish. Put in the meat mixture. Smooth and level the top and arrange the bay leaves in a trefoil pattern in the centre. Cover with the reserved slices of fat, then with foil. Stand the dish in a pan of hot water which comes half-way up the sides of the dish. Bake in a moderate oven at 180°C, Gas 4, for $1\frac{1}{4}$ hours or until the pâté shrinks slightly from the sides of the dish, and any melted fat on the top is clear. Fifteen minutes before the end of the cooking time, remove the foil and fat to let the pâté brown slightly.

When cooked, weight the terrine (p731) and cool it. Chill for 12 hours. Serve, cut in slices, from the dish.

Rabbit Terrine

Makes 2.3kg (approx)

1kg rabbit **or** *450g*	*450g belly of pork*
boneless rabbit meat	*2 × 15ml spoons brandy*
2 pigeons	*ground pepper*
100g pig's liver	*275g unsmoked streaky*
150ml red wine	*bacon rashers, without*
1 bay leaf	*rinds*
1 clove of garlic	

Remove the rabbit and pigeon meat from the bones. Remove any skin and tubes from the liver. Place the liver and meat in a bowl with the wine and bay leaf. Cover and leave in a cold place to marinate overnight.

Drain and reserve the wine. Skin and crush the garlic. Remove the rind from the belly of pork. Mince the pork, marinated meats, and garlic. Mix in the wine and brandy and season with pepper. Stretch the bacon rashers slightly with the back of a knife and line a 2 litre terrine or pie dish with them. Put in the pâté mixture, cover with foil or a lid, and stand the dish in a pan of hot water which comes half-way up the sides of the dish. Bake in a warm oven at 160°C, Gas 3, for about 2 hours.

When cooked, pour off any excess liquid and weight the pâté (p731). Cool it until quite cold. Chill before serving. Serve either in wedges from the terrine, or turned out of the dish.

Baked Hare Pâté

Makes 300g (approx)

450g cooked boneless	*2 egg yolks*
hare meat	*4–6 × 15ml spoons*
50g flat mushrooms	*cooking brandy* **or**
butter for frying	*Marsala* **or** *Madeira*
1 thick slice of white	*rich gravy (preferably*
bread	*game) if necessary*
1 × 15ml spoon milk	*salt and pepper*
50g slightly salted butter	*butter for greasing*

Garnish
1 bay leaf

Chop the meat. Clean and slice the mushrooms. Melt a little butter in a pan and fry the mushrooms gently until softened. Remove the crust, and soak the bread in the milk until well moistened, then mash thoroughly. Mix together the meat, mushrooms, and bread, and mince or process in an electric blender. Add the butter, egg yolks, and liquor, and mix together thoroughly. Moisten with a little gravy if necessary. Season to taste.

Grease a terrine or pie dish with butter. Put the bay leaf in the bottom, turn in the hare mixture and cover tightly. Stand the dish in a pan of hot water which comes half-way up the sides of the dish. Bake in a warm oven at 160°C, Gas 3, for 2 hours.

When cooked, weight the pâté (p731) and cool it. Chill for 12 hours. Turn out to serve, so that the bay leaf is on top of the pâté.

Serve in thin slices with rye bread.

Note Cut in small blocks, this pâté makes a good last-course savoury with a glass of Madeira or port. It is too rich for a first course.

Pâté En Croûte

Makes 1.5kg (approx)

600g chicken livers	*3 eggs*
450g lean pork	*salt and pepper*
a pinch of ground	*shortcrust pastry* (p1249)
allspice	*using 300g flour*
2–3 drops mushroom	*flour for rolling out*
ketchup	*beaten egg for glazing*
125ml double cream	

Remove any skin and tubes from the livers. Chop the livers and the pork together finely, or mince coarsely, and mix with the allspice and ketchup. Beat the cream and eggs together until blended and add to the meat mixture. Season to taste.

Roll out the pastry thinly on a lightly floured surface and use three-quarters of it to line the base and sides of a 17–18cm spring-form cake tin. Turn the meat and cream filling into the pastry case. Roll out the remaining pastry into a circle to fit the top of the tin. Dampen the edges of the pastry, and cover with the lid, sealing the edges well. Flute the edges with the back of a knife. Make a small hole in the centre of the lid to let the steam escape. Re-roll any trimmings and use them to make decorative pastry leaves for the lid. Glaze the lid with beaten egg.

Bake in a warm oven at 160°C, Gas 3, for 1½ hours. Remove the pie from the oven, loosen the spring-form clip and remove the sides. Brush the sides of the pie with beaten egg; then return it to the oven, on its base, and bake for a further 30 minutes. Serve hot.

OTHER PÂTÉS, POTTED FOODS, AND PASTES

Jellied Chicken Liver Pâté

Makes 1.5kg (approx)

1 small onion	a pinch of ground mace
1 clove of garlic	a few grains ground
100g slightly salted	cloves
butter	salt and pepper
450g chicken livers	50ml (approx) aspic jelly
3 × 15ml spoons brandy	or jellied canned
1 × 15ml spoon port or	consommé
Madeira	
1 × 10ml spoon French	
mustard	

Skin and chop the onion and skin and crush the garlic. Melt 50g of the butter in a large frying pan, add the onion and garlic and fry gently until softened but not coloured. Remove any skin and tubes from the chicken livers. Add to the pan and continue frying, turning them over gently for 6 minutes, until browned but not crisp. Scrape the contents of the pan into a bowl. Pour the liquor into the frying pan, and cover the livers with it. Add the rest of the butter, the mustard, and spices. Season well. Mash or pound the mixture or process in an electric blender to a smooth paste. If mashed or pounded, the mixture should be sieved afterwards. Re-season if required.

Turn the pâté into an earthenware dish or pot. Leave 1cm headspace. Cover loosely with greaseproof paper and refrigerate or leave in a cool place until firm.

Meanwhile, measure enough aspic jelly or consommé to cover the dish completely. Melt the jelly or consommé and let it cool until almost setting. Spoon it gently over the firmed up pâté. Leave in a cool place until set, then refrigerate or leave in a very cool place for at least 24 hours. Use within the following 4–5 hours. Serve from the dish.

Potted Beef

Makes 550g (approx)

500g raw lean beef	butter for greasing
a blade of mace	75g butter
a pinch of ground ginger	salt and pepper
2 × 15ml spoons beef	melted clarified butter
stock	(p886)

Wipe the meat and trim off any fat and gristle. Cut the meat into small cubes. Put it in an ovenproof casserole with the mace, ginger, and stock. Cover tightly with buttered greaseproof paper and foil. Bake in a cool oven at 150°C, Gas 2, for 3–3½ hours until the meat is very tender. Remove the mace. Mince the meat twice, then pound it well with the butter and any meat juices left in the casserole to make a smooth paste. Season with salt and pepper. Turn into small pots and cover with clarified butter. Leave until the butter is firm.

Note When sealed with clarified butter, this meat will keep for at least a week in a refrigerator or for 2 days in a cool place.

Potted Game

Makes 400g (approx)

300g cooked boneless
  game meat
100g cooked ham **or**
  boiled bacon, without
  rinds
8 × 15ml spoons game
  stock (p330) **or**
4 × 15ml spoons butter

a pinch of Cayenne
  pepper
salt
½ × 2.5ml spoon ground
  black pepper
melted clarified butter
  (p886)

Trim off any skin and fat from the meat, and chop or mince very finely with the ham or bacon; then pound, gradually adding the stock or butter to make a smooth paste. Add the Cayenne pepper and seasoning to taste. Turn into small pots and cover with clarified butter. Leave until the butter is firm.

Potted Gammon

Makes 200–300g

1 gammon knuckle
1 small onion
25g butter
2 × 15ml spoons chopped
  parsley

a small pinch each of
  ground mace, pepper,
  and grated nutmeg
melted clarified butter
  (p886)

Wipe the gammon knuckle, then weigh it to calculate the cooking time, allowing 20 minutes per 0.5kg, plus 20 minutes over. Place the knuckle in a saucepan, cover with cold water, and heat slowly to boiling point. Drain, cover with fresh cold water, heat slowly to boiling point, reduce the heat, and simmer gently for the calculated cooking time. Drain and leave to cool.

When cool enough to handle, cut off the rind, then remove the meat from the bone. Cut into pieces and mince twice. Skin and chop the onion finely. Heat 25g butter in a pan and cook the onion until softened but not browned. Stir in the parsley, spices, and meat. Turn into small pots and cover with clarified butter. Leave until the butter is firm.

Potted Ham

Makes 900g–1kg

1kg lean ham
250g fat ham
½ × 2.5ml spoon ground
  mace
½ × 2.5ml spoon grated
  nutmeg
a pinch of Cayenne
  pepper

½ × 2.5ml spoon ground
  pepper
butter for greasing
melted clarified butter
  (p886)

Mince both hams 2–3 times or chop very finely; then pound well and rub through a fine sieve. Add the spices and pepper and mix well together. Put into a well-greased pie dish and cover with buttered greaseproof paper. Bake in a moderate oven at 180°C, Gas 4, for about 45 minutes.

When cooked, leave to cool. Turn into small pots and cover with clarified butter. Leave until the butter is firm.

Potted Hare

Makes 800g (approx)

1 hare
4 rashers streaky bacon,
  without rinds
bouquet garni
6 juniper berries
½ × 2.5ml spoon ground
  cloves
½ × 2.5ml spoon ground
  mace
2 bay leaves

salt
½ × 2.5ml spoon ground
  black pepper
a pinch of Cayenne
  pepper
game (p330) **or** rich
  brown (p329) stock to
  cover
melted clarified butter
  (p886)

Prepare the hare (p671) and cut into small neat pieces. Line the base of a casserole with the bacon rashers. Pack the pieces of hare closely on top, and add the herbs, spices, and seasoning. Just cover with stock. Cover the casserole with a tight-fitting lid and cook in a very cool oven at 140°C, Gas 1, for about 3 hours. Add more stock while cooking, if necessary.

When cooked, remove the meat from the bones; chop and mince the meat together with the bacon. Moisten with a little of the stock and re-season if required. Turn into small pots and cover with clarified butter. Leave until the butter is firm.

Note When minced, the hare meat may weigh nearly 1kg. Since 500g potted hare is enough for 8–10 people, you may wish to keep the saddle for roasting, and to pot the legs only. Cold remains of cooked hare can be potted, as above, if well moistened with good stock.

Potted Ox Tongue

Makes 450g (approx)

400g cooked ox tongue
75g clarified butter
  (p886)
$\frac{1}{2}$ × 2.5ml spoon ground
  mace
$\frac{1}{2}$ × 2.5ml spoon ground
  cloves
$\frac{1}{2}$ × 2.5ml spoon grated
  nutmeg

a pinch of Cayenne
  pepper
salt
$\frac{1}{2}$ × 2.5ml spoon ground
  black pepper
additional melted
  clarified butter (p886)
  for sealing

Chop the tongue while still warm or re-heat cold cooked tongue, and chop. Pound it well or mince it. Slowly work in 75g clarified butter and reduce the tongue to a smooth paste. Add the spices, Cayenne pepper, and seasoning. Rub through a fine sieve. Turn into small pots and cover with clarified butter. Leave until the butter is firm.

Note If a rough texture is preferred, do not sieve the tongue.

Potted Veal

Makes 500g (approx)

400–500g lean pie
  veal
100g ham
butter for greasing
2 × 15ml spoons water
1 bay leaf
6 black peppercorns
a blade of mace

butter **or** margarine
salt and pepper
a pinch of Cayenne
  pepper
a pinch of ground mace
melted clarified butter
  (p886)

Chop the veal and ham finely. Put into a well-greased earthenware jar or casserole with the water. Tie the bay leaf, peppercorns, and mace in a piece of muslin and add to the meat. Cover the jar or casserole with buttered greaseproof paper, and either stand it in a pan of boiling water or bake in a moderate oven at 180°C, Gas 4, for 2½ hours.

Remove the muslin bag and pound the meat finely, adding enough liquid from the jar or casserole together with a little butter or margarine to make a very smooth paste. Season with salt, pepper, Cayenne pepper, and mace. Rub the meat through a wire sieve. Turn into small pots and cover with clarified butter. Leave until the butter is firm. Store in a cold place and use within 3 days.

Potted Venison

Makes 1.2kg (approx)

1kg cooked venison (any
  cut **or** trimmings)
125g butter (approx)
4 × 15ml spoons port **or**
  brown stock (p329) **or**
  gravy (p728)
$\frac{1}{2}$ × 2.5ml spoon grated
  nutmeg

$\frac{1}{2}$ × 2.5ml spoon ground
  allspice
salt
$\frac{1}{2}$ × 2.5ml spoon ground
  black pepper
melted clarified butter
  (p886)

Cut the meat into pieces and mince it finely. Melt the butter in a saucepan and add the minced venison, liquid, spices, and seasoning. Cooked venison can be very dry so, if necessary, add a little extra melted butter. Simmer until blended. While still hot, turn into small pots and leave to cool. Cover with clarified butter. Leave until the butter is firm.

Potted Lobster

Makes 600g (approx)

500g boiled lobster
125ml single cream
$\frac{1}{2} \times 2.5$ml spoon ground
  white pepper
a pinch of ground mace

a pinch of Cayenne
  pepper
salt
melted clarified butter
  (p886)

Pick the lobster meat from the shell and put it in a saucepan with the cream, white pepper, mace, Cayenne pepper, and salt to taste. Heat gently to boiling point, then turn at once into small pots. Leave to cool. Cover with clarified butter. Leave until the butter is firm.

Potted Shrimps or Prawns

Makes 500g (approx)

200g unsalted butter
400g cooked, peeled
  shrimps **or** prawns
$\frac{1}{2} \times 2.5$ml spoon ground
  white pepper
$\frac{1}{2} \times 2.5$ml spoon ground
  mace

$\frac{1}{2} \times 2.5$ml spoon ground
  cloves
melted clarified butter
  (p886)

Melt the butter in a pan and heat the shellfish very gently, without boiling, with the pepper, mace and cloves. Turn into small pots with a little of the butter. Leave the remaining butter until the residue has settled, then pour the butter over the shellfish. Chill. When firm, cover with clarified butter. Store in a refrigerator for not more than 48 hours before use.

Potted Salmon

Makes 400g (approx)

400g cold cooked salmon
salt and pepper
a pinch of Cayenne
  pepper

a pinch of ground mace
anchovy essence
melted clarified butter
  (p886)

Skin and bone the fish and pound the flesh thoroughly. Gradually add the seasoning, Cayenne pepper, and mace, and the anchovy essence. Blend in 2×15ml spoons clarified butter. Rub through a fine sieve. Turn into small pots and cover with clarified butter. Leave until the butter is firm.

Smoked Mackerel Pâté

Makes 450g (approx)

2 shallots
25g clarified butter
  (p886)
75g concentrated tomato
  purée
1×5ml spoon soft light
  brown sugar
juice of $\frac{1}{2}$ lemon
8 crushed peppercorns
1×5ml spoon chopped
  fresh basil

$\frac{1}{2} \times 2.5$ml spoon dried
  tarragon
a few drops Tabasco
  sauce
400g skinned smoked
  mackerel fillets
75ml double cream
additional melted
  clarified butter (p886)
  for sealing

Skin and chop the shallots very finely. Melt the clarified butter in a pan and cook the shallots gently until softened. Add the purée, sugar, lemon juice, peppercorns, and herbs, and cook gently for 4–5 minutes to make a sauce. Add the Tabasco sauce, remove from the heat and leave to cool. Process the sauce, mackerel, and cream in an electric blender or pound to a smooth paste. Turn into a suitable dish or mould and leave to cool. Cover with clarified butter. Leave until the butter is firm.

Serve with hot dry toast.

Sprat Paste

Makes 400g (approx)

400g sprats
2 × 10ml spoons butter
a pinch of Cayenne
   pepper
freshly ground pepper
$\frac{1}{2}$ × 2.5ml spoon ground
   mace

1 × 5ml spoon anchovy
   essence
1 × 15ml spoon lemon
   juice
melted clarified butter
   (p886)

Place the sprats on a large sheet of foil on a baking tray. Dot with butter and fold the foil over the fish, making a parcel. Bake in a moderate oven at 180°C, Gas 4, for 10–15 minutes. While still warm, remove the heads, tails, skin, and backbones. Pound the flesh well, then rub through a sieve. Season with Cayenne pepper, black pepper, and mace; add the anchovy essence and the lemon juice. Turn into small pots and cover with clarified butter. Leave until the butter is firm.

Herring Roe Pâté

Makes 175g (approx)

100g soft herring roes
salt and pepper
75g butter

2 × 15ml spoons lemon
   juice
15g chopped parsley

Season the herring roes with salt and pepper. Heat a little of the butter in a pan, add the roes, and fry gently for 10 minutes. Pound the roes or process in an electric blender to make a smooth paste. Soften the rest of the butter and mix it in with the lemon juice and parsley. Turn into a small mould and leave to set in the refrigerator or in a very cool place for 2 hours.

Turn out of the mould, garnish as liked, and serve with fingers of hot dry toast.

Potted Herring Fillets

Makes 200g (approx)

1 × 198g can herring
   fillets (in any sauce)
25g butter
a pinch of Cayenne
   pepper (optional)

a pinch of ground mace
salt and pepper
melted clarified butter
   (p886)

Mash the herring fillets. Melt the butter in a small saucepan and add the fillets, spices, and seasoning. Stir until heated through but not fried. Cool slightly, then turn into small pots and cover with clarified butter. Leave until the butter is firm.

Use as a pâté or a sandwich filling.

Potted Cheese with Mustard

Makes 500g (approx)

2 eggs
200g strong hard cheese
   or mixed cheeses
1 × 15ml spoon butter
2 × 15ml spoons made
   English mustard
4 × 15ml spoons single
   cream

a pinch of Cayenne
   pepper
salt
melted clarified butter
   (p886)

Beat the eggs until liquid. Grate the cheese. Mix together the cheese, butter, mustard, cream, Cayenne pepper, and salt to taste. Put the mixture into a saucepan slowly and heat to simmering point. Add the beaten eggs and cook gently until the mixture thickens. Turn into a chilled container or small pots, and cool quickly. Cover with clarified butter. Leave until the butter is firm.

Store for use as a spread.

Note This potted cheese will keep for 2–3 weeks in a refrigerator. It is a good way of using up scraps of hard British cheeses after a wine and cheese party.

Potted Cheese with Sherry or Port

Makes 500g (approx)

500g grated mature Cheddar or Cheshire cheese
100g softened unsalted butter
salt
a good pinch of ground mace

50–75ml medium sweet or cream sherry or tawny port
melted clarified butter (p886)

Pound about one-third of the cheese with the butter until smooth, or process in an electric blender. Add the rest of the cheese, salt, mace, and liquor, and pound or blend to a smooth paste. Turn into small pots and cover with clarified butter. Leave until the butter is firm.

Use as a sandwich spread or as a filling for savoury choux, or serve instead of a block of cheese as a last course at dinner.

VARIATION

Potted Stilton

Prepare as above. Use tawny or ruby port to moisten, but add it with discretion. A good Stilton should need very little.

This is a useful way to keep the remains of a large piece of Stilton, after Christmas for instance. The cheese will keep well in a refrigerator for several weeks.

Potted Beans

Makes 400g (approx)

200g haricot beans
50g strong Cheddar cheese
50g soft white breadcrumbs
50g butter

a pinch of Cayenne pepper
salt and black pepper
a pinch of grated nutmeg
melted clarified butter (p886)

Soak the beans in cold water overnight, then cook in plenty of boiling water. Drain, put them into a bowl, and crush finely. Grate the cheese finely, then beat it gradually into the beans with the rest of the ingredients, except the clarified butter. Turn into small pots and cover with the clarified butter. Leave until it is firm.

Potted beans make a very good filling for sandwiches. Store in a cool, dry place, because dried beans quickly ferment; use within 48 hours.

Note Dried split peas or lentils can be potted in the same way as beans.

Potted Mushrooms

Makes 300g (approx)

450g button mushrooms
50g butter
salt and freshly ground black pepper
a good pinch of ground allspice

2 anchovy fillets
melted clarified butter (p886)

Chop the mushrooms coarsely. Simmer gently in a covered pan until the juice runs freely. Raise the heat slightly, and cook, uncovered, until all the juice evaporates. Add the butter, and season with salt and pepper to taste. Sprinkle with the allspice. Continue cooking for 15–20 minutes, until all the fat is absorbed. Meanwhile, chop or mince the anchovy fillets finely. When the mushrooms are dry, stir the anchovies into the pan, and cook for a further 5 minutes. Remove from the heat, turn into small pots, and leave to cool. Cover with clarified butter. Leave until the butter is firm, then cover with a second coat of clarified butter. Use within 21 days.

VEGETABLES

If you live in the country, have your vegetables gathered from the garden at an early hour, so that there is ample time to make your search for caterpillars, &c. These disagreeable additions need never make their appearance on table in cauliflowers or cabbages, if the vegetable in its raw state is allowed to soak in salt and water for an hour or so.

Vegetables have long been underestimated as an essential or interesting part of any meal. They provide vitamins, minerals, carbohydrate, protein, and fibre (roughage); they both complement and give a contrasting texture and flavour to a main meat, fish or egg dish, and are, in addition, a suitable main course themselves. This chapter describes vegetables suitable for cooking; many of them, and others, are also used either raw or cooked in salads.

Buying Vegetables

The buying of vegetables is important since no amount of care and attention during preparation and cooking will improve the flavour of a wilted yellow cabbage or of tough, dry peas. The decision as to which vegetables to serve is often best left until you arrive at the greengrocers' or supermarket and see what looks fresh and in good condition and what is at a reasonable price. As with most other shopping, it is sometimes worth paying a little extra for a better quality vegetable, rather than buying an inferior one which may largely be wasted through being blemished. Prices of vegetables fluctuate rapidly from week to week, and careful buying can save a considerable amount of money. When buying prepacked vegetables, check very carefully that they are in prime condition. Shop-stored vegetables in polythene bags, especially root vegetables, can be rather soft and slimy, particularly in hot weather.

Preserving Food Value

In order to preserve the maximum amount of flavour and their vitamin and mineral content, vegetables must be stored, prepared, and cooked correctly. Apart from root vegetables, such as potatoes, carrots, parsnips, onions, and turnips, which keep well for several months during the late autumn and winter, most vegetables should either be picked from the garden, or cooked as soon as possible after buying. Vitamin C, in particular, is lost very quickly after the vegetable is picked, especially in a warm atmosphere; spinach, for example, will lose as much as 40% of its vitamin C in one day.

Vegetables should not be prepared too long before cooking, since this, again, causes vitamin and mineral loss. Cabbage and similar vegetables should be shredded only just before cooking because vitamins and minerals are lost rapidly when the cut surfaces are exposed to the air. Vitamin C and minerals such as calcium and phosphorous are water soluble; green vegetables should therefore not be left soaking for any length of time.

To obtain maximum food value, vegetables should not be overcooked. Root vegetables, especially young ones, and some other vegetables, should be cooked and eaten with their skins. This may not always be as aesthetically pleasing, but the nutrient value is much greater since much of the vitamin and mineral content is just under the skin.

The Nutritional Value of Vegetables

Green Vegetables

Vitamin C is present in all green vegetables, but is particularly high in turnip tops, Brussels sprouts, cabbage, cauliflower, and watercress. There is also more vitamin C present in all vegetables when they are growing most rapidly, that is, in the spring and summer. Vitamin A in the form of carotene is present in all green vegetables – the amount of carotene present being proportional to the depth of colour of the vegetable. Therefore, provided they are not coarse and tough, the outside leaves of vegetables such as cabbage, endive, and lettuce should always be used. Vitamin B_1 and thiamine are also found in these vegetables, as are mineral elements. Watercress and sprouting broccoli are good sources of calcium, and parsley, turnip tops, spinach, and endive all contain iron and a small amount of protein.

Green vegetables also provide fibre which is essential to the body for healthy digestion and is too often lacking in the Western diet.

Roots and Tubers

Potatoes are one of our staple foods and are a valuable source of vitamin C, particularly in the case of new potatoes. Potatoes also provide fibre, a small amount of protein, and, most important of all, carbohydrate in the form of starch. While carbohydrates are fattening, a certain amount is important for a well-balanced diet and is essential for young growing children.

Beetroot, carrots, swedes, parsnips, and onions all contain energy-giving sugar. This sugar is easily soluble and is therefore lost if the vegetables are cooked for any length of time in boiling water. These root vegetables should therefore be cooked by the conservation method (p762) to retain maximum food value. Beetroots retain their sweet flavour if they are baked or cooked in a pressure cooker, rather than boiled in the usual way. Carrots are an extremely rich source of vitamin A (in the form of carotene).

Fresh Peas and Beans

Fresh peas and beans contain the vitamin and mineral salts found in green vegetables, but their vitamin B_1 content is higher. Peas and broad beans contain sugar and a rather higher percentage of protein than most other vegetables: usually about 6% as compared with 3% or much less in some other vegetables.

Pulses

Dried peas, beans, and lentils have a high protein content and are therefore an extremely useful addition to the diet, generally providing a cheaper source of protein than meat or fish. They form one of the chief sources of protein for vegetarians. They do not, however, contain any vitamin C and only a very little vitamin A.

Availability of Vegetables

Some indication of the times at which home-grown vegetables are available in the UK is given for each vegetable in this chapter. This can only be a guide, however, because seasons have been lengthened by the ever-increasing use of hot-houses and by imports of foreign vegetables. This second factor has also meant that some previously rare vegetables such as courgettes, aubergines, bean sprouts, okra, and mange-tout peas, have become more popular. Tropical vegetables, such as breadfruit, yams, and sweet potatoes, can also be found in the UK, both in markets and in Afro-Asian stores.

Freezing techniques have also changed our eating patterns considerably, by making vegetables such as peas, beans, and asparagus available throughout the year. The nutritional value of frozen vegetables is almost equal to that of fresh vegetables, and they can generally be cooked and served by any of the methods suitable for fresh vegetables, although they need cooking for a much shorter time. Techniques of home freezing are described on pp1387–89. Frozen vegetables have to a large extent replaced canned vegetables although these (together with freeze-dried vegetables) still make extremely useful standbys.

COOKING VEGETABLES

Most vegetables should only be cooked until just tender, and in the case of green vegetables, such as cabbage and Brussels sprouts, they should be served still slightly crisp. A small piece of green vegetable should be removed from the pan and eaten to test this, while root vegetables should be pierced with a skewer to see if they are cooked. Both should then be drained, turned into a warmed serving dish and served as quickly as possible.

Basic Cooking Methods

Boiling

At one time it was said that vegetables growing above the ground should be put into boiling water and vegetables growing below the ground into cold water. In fact, all vegetables should be put into boiling salted water to preserve both the flavour and the vitamin and mineral content. Although the quantity of water used obviously depends on the type of vegetable and the quantity being cooked, all vegetables should be cooked in the minimum amount of water. Fresh herbs, such as parsley, mint sprigs and dill, can be added to the cooking water to give flavour and interest. Although boiling is suitable for most vegetables, carrots and similar root vegetables are better cooked by the conservation method (p762), and vegetables which have a very high water content, such as marrows, are better steamed. The flavour of some vegetables is improved if they are cooked in stock rather than water.

Note The liquor from boiling vegetables should never be discarded, but should be kept for use in gravies, sauces or vegetable soups.

Parboiling

Whereas boiling is a total cooking process, parboiling involves boiling a vegetable until is it only semi-cooked, prior to processing it by another method, eg deep frying, which will fully cook it. Cooking times vary according to the vegetable and are indicated where appropriate.

Steaming

The flavour and nutritional value of many vegetables is improved if they are steamed rather than boiled.

Put in the top of a steamer, season with salt, and cook over boiling water until they are just tender. Drain thoroughly and serve.

Baking

Baking is an easy method of cooking. Even green vegetables can be baked if wrapped in foil, and this method ensures that any vegetable retains its maximum food value. Vegetables to be baked can be prepared in advance which is an advantage if using an auto-timer. Baking is also a practical way of saving fuel if the oven is being used to cook the main dish.

Roasting

Roasting is suitable for root vegetables, such as potatoes, parsnips, and swedes and for a few other vegetables such as pumpkin. The vegetables can be parboiled before roasting and, in the case of potatoes, this will give a crisper result. They can either be roasted around a joint in the oven or in a separate pan. If the meat is being roasted slowly at 190°C, Gas 5, it is generally better to put potatoes in a separate pan and to roast them at a higher temperature, so that they cook as quickly as possible.

Grilling

Not many vegetables are suitable for full cooking by grilling, although most vegetables topped with a sauce are good if 'finished' under the grill. The vegetables most commonly grilled are mushrooms, tomatoes, and courgettes; mushrooms, in particular, should be basted well with fat or oil before and during cooking.

Frying

Shallow frying is suitable for mushrooms, tomatoes, cooked potatoes, courgettes, aubergines, peppers, etc, but is not generally suitable for raw green vegetables. However, some vegetables, such as mange-tout peas and finely shredded white cabbage, can be cooked very quickly by the Chinese stir-fry method. Heat a little oil in a frying pan and fry the vegetables for just a few minutes, turning all the time until cooked but still crisp. Deep frying is particularly suitable for potatoes.

Fritters can be made from various vegetables, such as artichokes, courgettes, salsify, cauliflower, fennel, mushrooms, and sweetcorn. Basic recipes for fritters can be found on p945.

Stewing

This is a good method of cooking vegetables which have a high water content, such as courgettes, leeks, and cucumber.

Melt a little butter or margarine in a heavy-based pan. Add the vegetables, season with salt and pepper, cover the pan, and cook over low heat, shaking the pan frequently to prevent the vegetables from sticking to the bottom. The vegetables can then be served in the cooking liquor.

Braising

Braising vegetables as a mirepoix (p809) with a small amount of stock is a delicious way of cooking them. Celery is the vegetable which is most often braised, but endive, lettuce, chicory, and fennel are also excellent served in this way.

After cooking, remove the vegetables from the pan, and rapidly boil the liquid that is left until it forms a glaze. Spoon this over the vegetables.

Puréeing

Puréeing is an easy method of preparing many hard and some softer vegetables, eg carrots and spinach. Most are cooked first, then rubbed through a sieve, mashed, or processed in an electric blender, until thick and smooth. Cream, butter or a creamy sauce is often added, together with seasoning. Puréed vegetables are also very popular as a basis for soups (see pp351–61).

GLOSSARY OF VEGETABLES
Description – Usage – Recipes

Artichokes – *Globe*

Globe artichokes are available all year round, but are generally at their cheapest in the late summer. Although the artichoke bases, or *fonds* as they are also called, are served as a vegetable side dish, whole artichokes are generally served as a starter either hot or cold.

An artichoke base is the small fleshy part of the artichoke which is left after all the leaves and the furry 'choke' (the undeveloped flower) have been removed. It is sometimes served on its own with melted butter, Hollandaise sauce (p712) or a stuffing; or it can be deep fried. Artichoke hearts, which are the centres of very small, young artichokes, are also available frozen and in cans.

To buy: Allow 1 medium to large artichoke per person or 2 small ones. When fresh, the leaves of the artichoke should be stiff and have a slight bloom on them.

To store: Artichokes should be bought as fresh as possible, but they can be stored for several days in a cool vegetable rack or larder or in the bottom of a refrigerator.

To prepare: Wash the artichokes thoroughly in cold water. Cut the stalk level with the base of the artichoke and trim off any very coarse outer leaves. (The tops of the outer leaves are often also trimmed with scissors which gives a more attractive appearance.) Brush the cut surface of the artichokes with lemon juice to prevent discoloration.

To boil: Put the artichokes into a pan with just enough boiling salted water to cover them; if liked, a bouquet garni can be added to the pan. Cover and cook for 30–45 minutes, depending on the size of the artichokes; cooking is complete when one of the lower leaves can be easily pulled out. Remove from the pan and turn upside-down for a minute to drain thoroughly. (The 'choke' in the centre of the artichoke can be removed before serving the artichoke, if liked; it is best removed with a teaspoon.) Serve the artichokes either hot with melted butter or Hollandaise sauce (p712), or cold with vinaigrette sauce or mayonnaise.

To steam: Season with salt and cook in the top of a steamer over boiling water for 40–55 minutes. Serve as for boiled artichokes

To eat: Using your fingers, pull off each leaf, dip the soft fleshy end in the melted butter, sauce or mayonnaise and suck both together. When all the leaves have been pulled off in this way, the choke will be revealed if it has not previously been removed. Cut this off and eat the base (*fond*) beneath with a knife and fork.

To deep fry: Use only the artichoke bases. Cut 6–8 artichoke bases into 3–4 pieces according to size. Coat with batter and fry as for Jerusalem artichokes.

Artichokes – *Jerusalem*

These white tubers are not, in fact, artichokes at all; they belong to the sunflower family. They are a winter vegetable and are usually available from October to April. Jerusalem artichokes can be served in a variety of ways and in particular make an excellent soup (p352).

To buy: Allow 150–200g per person. The tubers should be hard and firm. Prime tubers are fairly regular in shape and measure about 10 × 5cm. Try to avoid buying artichokes which are very misshapen because they are difficult to peel and consequently cause a lot of wastage.

To store: Artichokes will store for a few weeks in a cool vegetable rack or larder.

To prepare: Wash the artichokes thoroughly, then peel thinly or scrape, and put at once into acidulated water; this helps to keep the vegetables white. Cut into slices or pieces convenient for serving just before cooking.

To boil: Cook in just enough boiling, salted, acidulated water to cover for about 20 minutes or until tender. Drain thoroughly and serve either with melted butter and seasoned with freshly ground black pepper, or with a white, Béchamel or Hollandaise sauce.

To steam: Scrub the artichokes, but leave them whole and unpeeled. Season with salt and cook in the top of a steamer over a pan of boiling water for about 40 minutes. Peel and slice them and serve as for boiled artichokes.

To roast: Parboil the artichokes, as above, for 5 minutes. Drain thoroughly. Put into hot dripping in a roasting tin, or in the tin containing a roast joint. Roll in the fat and cook in a fairly hot oven, 190°C, Gas 5, for about 1 hour, turning 2–3 times during cooking. The colour of artichokes cooked in this way is not very good but the flavour is excellent.

To stew: Heat 50g butter for every 750g–1kg artichokes. Add the peeled and sliced artichokes and season to taste; cover tightly and cook for about 30 minutes, shaking the pan from time to time. Serve in the cooking liquor or add this to a white or Béchamel (p704) sauce.

To deep fry Method (1): Peel and slice the artichokes very thinly and soak in acidulated water for 10 minutes. Dry thoroughly and fry in deep fat or oil (p302) until golden-brown. Drain on soft kitchen paper and season with salt and pepper.

To deep fry Method (2): Peel the artichokes and cut into 1cm slices. Parboil for 5 minutes, drain, and dry thoroughly. For 750g artichokes, make up a double quantity of coating batter (1) (p933). Dip the artichoke slices into the batter and fry in deep fat or oil (p302) until golden-brown, turning once during cooking. Drain thoroughly and serve very hot with fried parsley (p398).

To purée: Mash, sieve or blend steamed or boiled artichokes, and to every 1kg artichokes (weight before cooking) add 2 × 15ml spoons milk and 25–50g butter. Season to taste with salt and pepper and serve sprinkled with plenty of chopped parsley.

Artichokes au Gratin

4 helpings

750g Jerusalem artichokes	50g Cheddar cheese
375ml cheese sauce (p693)	25g soft white breadcrumbs

Prepare and boil or steam the artichokes. Drain thoroughly and stir into the cheese sauce. Turn into a flameproof dish. Grate the cheese and mix with the breadcrumbs; sprinkle this mixture over the artichokes. Place the dish under a moderate grill or in a hot oven, 220°C, Gas 7, for 10 minutes and cook until the top is golden-brown. Serve at once.

Asparagus

The season for home-grown asparagus is a short one, only May and June, but imported asparagus can be bought from March to July. It is also possible to buy asparagus at other times, but from only a few shops and usually at a premium price. Asparagus can also be bought frozen and canned. It can be served in many ways, but one of the best is to boil it, and then serve it with melted butter or Hollandaise sauce (p712) as a starter.

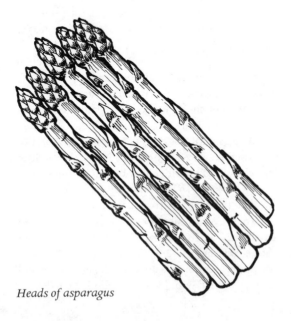

Heads of asparagus

To buy: Fresh asparagus is generally sold in bundles and is graded according to the thickness of the stem and plumpness of the buds. The heads should be tight and well formed, and the stems should not be dry and woody. Allow 6–8 medium-sized heads per person, 150–200g approx.

To store: Asparagus is best bought on the day or the day before it is needed, although it will keep for a couple of days in the bottom of a refrigerator, if necessary.

To prepare: Cut the woody parts evenly from the base of the stems. Scrape the white part of each stalk with a knife. Tie into bundles and put into cold salted water until ready to cook.

To boil: The asparagus must stand upright in the saucepan because if it lies in the water, the heads will be overcooked and will drop off before the stems are tender. It is therefore important to use a deep saucepan (it is possible to buy special asparagus pans). The water in the saucepan should come to just below the heads of the asparagus. Salt the water and bring to the boil. Stand the asparagus in a jam jar or other heatproof pot, if not using an asparagus pan. Put into the water, and cover the pan with a tight-fitting lid. Cook gently until the stems are tender; this will take 14–20 minutes depending on the thickness of the stems. Drain thoroughly and serve either with melted butter, seasoned and lightly flavoured with lemon juice, or with Hollandaise sauce (p712). Asparagus can also be served cold with vinaigrette sauce.

Asparagus Points or Tips

Sometimes, the thinner stalks of asparagus, or *sprue* as they are called, are sold loose. Cut the points and the tender green parts into short pieces. Cook in a small amount of gently boiling salted water for 5–10 minutes according to their size and age. Drain thoroughly, toss in butter, and season with salt and pepper. Serve as a garnish or as a main vegetable, or use as a filling for omelets.

Note It is a mistake to add anything which will impair the delicate flavour of asparagus, but a little chopped shallot and parsley may be fried in the butter before tossing with the asparagus.

Asparagus Croustades

6–8 helpings

50 heads asparagus
6–8 small French rolls
1 egg
250ml foundation white
  sauce (p692)

salt and pepper
1 × 5ml spoon strained
  lemon juice

Prepare and cook the asparagus. Cut off the tops of the rolls and scoop out the soft crumb inside. (This can be kept and made into breadcrumbs.) Put the rolls, together with the tops, on a baking sheet, and put into a hot oven, 220°C, Gas 7, for 5 minutes or until they are very crisp. Cut off the asparagus points and keep warm. Either rub the stalks through a fine stainless metal or nylon sieve, or trim off and discard all the inedible parts of the stems and process the rest in an electric blender to give a smooth purée. Beat the egg until liquid and add to the white sauce with the asparagus purée. Put over gentle heat, but do not boil the sauce or the egg will curdle. Season well and add the lemon juice. Spoon the sauce into the hot rolls, garnish with the asparagus points, and replace the tops on the rolls. Serve immediately.

Serve as a hot first-course dish, or as a light lunch or main vegetarian dish.

Cooking time 30 minutes (approx)

Mrs Beeton's Asparagus Pudding

3–4 helpings

100g asparagus points
25g ham
50g flour
salt and pepper

2 eggs
25g softened butter
milk
fat for greasing

Chop the asparagus points until they are the size of peas. Mince the ham very finely. Put into a bowl with the flour, asparagus, and seasoning. Beat the eggs well, and add with the butter to the asparagus with enough milk to make the mixture the consistency of a thick batter. Pour into a greased 750ml mould or pudding basin. Cover securely with a double layer of buttered greaseproof paper or foil.

Steam gently for 2 hours. Turn out on to a warmed serving dish and serve with melted butter poured round, but not over, the pudding.

Garlanded Asparagus

4 helpings

30 heads asparagus
100g butter
salt and pepper
50g grated Parmesan
  cheese

4 unbroken egg yolks
butter or fat for frying

Prepare and cook the asparagus. Drain thoroughly. Untie and place in an ovenproof dish. Melt the butter and spoon it over the asparagus. Season with salt and pepper and sprinkle the Parmesan cheese over it. Cook in a fairly hot oven, 200°C, Gas 6, for 15 minutes or until the cheese is golden-brown.

Meanwhile, fry the egg yolks in a little butter or fat. Drain them free of fat, arrange round the asparagus, and serve.

Aubergines

Aubergines, also known as *eggplants*, are obtainable all year round, but are generally at their cheapest in late summer. They are used extensively in Mediterranean cooking and, in addition to being served as a vegetable on their own (often stuffed), are an important ingredient in such well-known dishes as Ratatouille (p811) and Moussaka (p1515).

To buy: Allow 100–150g per person (an average aubergine weighs about 250g). Fresh aubergines are firm to the touch and have a firm, glossy skin, whereas those that have been in the shop for some time will be slightly soft and have a rather wrinkled skin.

To store: Aubergines can be kept for several days in a cool vegetable rack or larder or in the bottom of a refrigerator.

To prepare: Aubergines are used in a variety of ways, and preparation will vary according to the dish. They can be rather bitter, and in order to avoid this, cut them into 5mm–1cm slices, sprinkle salt over the cut surfaces, and leave in a sieve for

30 minutes to 1 hour, during which time a great deal of liquid will drain off. Rinse under cold water and dry thoroughly. If the aubergines are left whole for cooking, the skin should be scored with a knife in a few places and sprinkled with salt.

Deep-fried Aubergines

4–6 helpings

600g aubergines (approx)	soft white **or** dried white breadcrumbs
salt	fat **or** oil for deep frying
2 eggs	

Cut the aubergines into slices about 8mm thick. Lay the slices flat on a large dish, sprinkle with salt, and leave for 30 minutes. Rinse and dry thoroughly. Beat the eggs until liquid. Dip the aubergine slices first in the egg and then in the breadcrumbs. Press the crumbs on firmly. Heat the fat or oil (p302) and fry the aubergine slices, a few at a time, until crisp and brown. Drain thoroughly on soft kitchen paper and serve very hot.

Baked Aubergines with Cheese

6 helpings

800g aubergines (approx)	salt and pepper
2 × 15ml spoons grated Parmesan cheese	1 × 15ml spoon crisp breadcrumbs
250ml Béchamel sauce (p704)	2 × 10ml spoons butter

Parboil the whole aubergines in boiling salted water for 10 minutes. Drain and cut into slices about 8mm thick. Lay the slices in an ovenproof dish. Stir the cheese into the Béchamel sauce, season to taste, and pour it over the aubergines. Sprinkle the breadcrumbs on top. Cut the butter into very small flakes, and dot them on top. Bake in a fairly hot oven, 190°C, Gas 5, for 30 minutes.

Serve as a starter or a light main dish.

Stuffed Aubergines

4 helpings

2 large aubergines	1 × 15ml spoon grated Parmesan cheese
salt	
4 × 15ml spoons oil	

Stuffing

100g mushrooms	1 × 15ml spoon chopped parsley
1 medium-sized onion	
1 large tomato	pepper
50g soft white breadcrumbs	

Cut the aubergines in half lengthways. Score the flesh with a knife, sprinkle with salt and leave for 30 minutes for the excess water to drain off. Rinse and dry thoroughly on soft kitchen paper. Brush the aubergines with oil and cook under a low grill for about 20 minutes or until tender. Remove the aubergine pulp to within 5mm–1cm of the skin, and chop this finely. Reserve the skins and pulp.

To make the stuffing, clean the mushrooms, skin the onion, and chop both finely. Heat 2 × 15ml spoons of the oil in a small saucepan and fry the mushrooms and onion gently for 5 minutes. Skin and chop the tomato. Add to the mushrooms and onion with most of the breadcrumbs, the parsley, aubergine pulp, and seasoning.

Pile the mixture back into the aubergine cases and place in an ovenproof dish. Mix the remaining breadcrumbs with the cheese. Sprinkle this over the stuffing and moisten with a little oil. Bake in a fairly hot oven, 200°C, Gas 6, for 20 minutes.

Serve as a starter or a light main dish.

VARIATIONS

1) Top the stuffed aubergines with a poached egg before serving.
2) Add 50g Ricotta or other soft cheese to the stuffing.
3) Chop and add 50g ham to the stuffing.
4) Chop and add 50g olives to the stuffing.

Note For other stuffings, see the chapter on Stuffings, Garnishes and Accompaniments.

Fried Aubergines with Onion

6 helpings

600g aubergines (approx)	a pinch of Cayenne pepper
salt	1 onion
flour	oil for frying

Cut the aubergines into slices about 8mm thick. Lay the slices flat on a large dish, sprinkle with salt, and leave for 30 minutes. Rinse and dry thoroughly. Season the flour with Cayenne pepper and salt, and use to coat the aubergine slices lightly. Skin the onion and chop it finely. Heat a little oil in a frying pan and fry the onion until golden. Remove from the pan, drain thoroughly, put to one side, and keep warm. Fry the aubergines, a few at a time, in the oil, until lightly browned, turning once during cooking. Remove from the pan, drain, transfer to a warmed serving dish, and keep warm. When all the aubergines have been fried, sprinkle with the fried onion, and serve.

Note Fresh Tomato Sauce (p715) goes well with this dish.

Cooking time 15 minutes (approx)

Beans – *Broad*

Broad beans are generally available from April to September, but can also be bought in cans; frozen beans are particularly good. Fresh beans are generally shelled before cooking although very small, young beans can be cooked in their pods.

To buy: Allow 300g per person. The pods should be full and a good green colour with no black markings; do not buy beans whose pods are shrivelled and yellow.

To store: Beans are best eaten on the day or day after they are bought, but they can be kept for a few days in a cool vegetable rack or larder or in the bottom of a refrigerator.

To prepare: Shell the beans unless using very young beans. These are cooked whole in the pod, in which case top and tail the pods and remove any strings as with runner beans. Shelled beans should be covered either with clingfilm or with some of the washed pods to prevent them drying out. If the beans are very mature, they may need to be skinned after cooking because the outer skin can be tough and unpalatable.

To boil: Add the beans to about 2cm boiling salted water, cover, and cook for 15–20 minutes for young beans in their pods or young shelled beans, or for about 30 minutes for more mature beans. If liked, a few leaves of summer savory or a sprig of parsley can also be added to the water. Drain the beans thoroughly and serve either tossed in butter with chopped parsley or savory, or with a white or Hollandaise sauce.

To steam: Season the beans with salt and cook in a steamer over a pan of boiling water for about 25–45 minutes, depending on the age of the beans. Serve as for boiled beans.

Broad Beans with Cream Sauce

4 helpings

1kg broad beans	1 × 5ml spoon sugar
250ml chicken stock	1 egg yolk
a bunch of herbs (thyme, sage, savory, marjoram, parsley stalks)	125ml single cream
	salt and pepper

Shell the beans. Put the stock, herbs, and sugar into a saucepan. Bring to the boil, add the beans and cook for 15–20 minutes, or until tender. Remove the herbs. Beat the egg yolk with the cream in a basin. Add 2 × 15ml spoons of the hot stock to the cream, then pour the cream into the pan. Heat gently, stirring all the time, until slightly thickened, but do not allow the mixture to boil or it will curdle. Season to taste and serve.

Note If preferred, the herbs may be chopped finely before cooking and left in the sauce.

Broad Beans with Spanish Sauce

4 helpings

1kg broad beans	50g butter
1 small onion	25g flour
375ml brown stock	1 × 5ml spoon chopped
(p329)	parsley
2–3 sprigs thyme	1 × 5ml spoon lemon
1 bay leaf	juice
100g button mushrooms	salt and pepper

Shell the beans. Skin and chop the onion finely, and put into a saucepan with the stock, thyme, and bay leaf. Bring to the boil, add the beans, and cook for 15–20 minutes, or until tender. Drain and reserve the stock but discard the herbs.

Meanwhile, clean and slice the mushrooms. Melt the butter in a pan and fry the mushrooms; then remove from the pan with a perforated spoon, and add to the beans when cooked. Stir the flour into the remaining butter and cook for 1 minute, stirring all the time. Draw off the heat and gradually stir in the stock from the beans. Return to the heat and bring to the boil, stirring all the time. Add the beans and mushrooms, the parsley and the lemon juice, and season to taste.

Beans – *French*

There are several varieties of French bean. The commonest is the straight bean, usually about 10–15cm long with no strings, which is also known by its French name, *haricot vert*. Other beans include kidney beans, which are more heavily podded, with the kidney-shaped bean showing through; and pea beans, or bobby beans, which also have a heavier pod but round pea-like beans. Home-grown beans are available in the summer, but imported beans are available all year round. Frozen beans are also available, both whole and sliced.

To buy: Allow 100–150g per person. Choose beans which are a good colour, appear crisp and fresh, and are of an even size.

To store: French beans should be used as fresh as

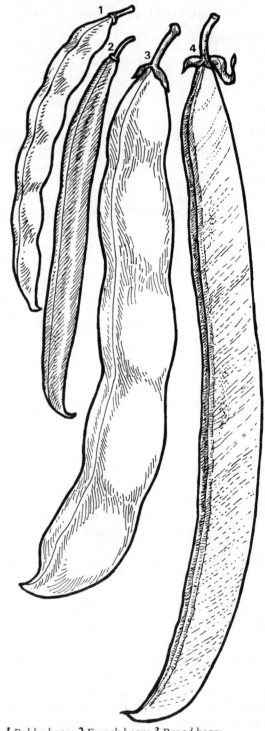

1 Bobby bean; 2 French bean; 3 Broad bean; 4 Runner bean

possible, but they can be stored for 2–3 days in a cool, dry place or in the bottom of a refrigerator.

To prepare: Top and tail the beans and remove any strings. Leave the beans whole.

To boil: Cook the beans in the minimum of boiling salted water for 5–10 minutes or until just tender. Drain thoroughly and toss in butter. Season with black pepper, preferably freshly ground, and top with chopped summer savory or tarragon, or a little crushed garlic, if liked.

To steam: Season the beans with salt and cook in a steamer over boiling water for 10–15 minutes or until just tender. Drain and serve as for boiled beans.

French Beans with Cream Sauce

6 helpings

600g French beans	*125ml single cream*
50g butter	*1 × 10ml spoon lemon*
1 egg	*juice*
1 × 10ml spoon grated	*a pinch of grated nutmeg*
Parmesan cheese	*salt and black pepper*

Prepare the beans and boil or steam them until almost tender. Drain thoroughly. Heat the butter in a saucepan, add the beans, cover, and cook over gentle heat, shaking the pan frequently, until they are quite tender.

Meanwhile, beat the egg in a small pan until liquid. Add the cheese, cream, lemon juice, nutmeg and seasoning, and heat gently, without boiling. Spoon the beans into a serving dish, pour the cream sauce over them, and serve as soon as possible.

Cooking time 20–30 minutes

Beans – *Runner*

Runner beans are the type most often found in the UK, and are available from mid-July until the end of September. They are much larger than French beans and can vary in length from 15–30cm. Frozen runner beans are also easily obtainable.

To buy: Allow 150g per person. The beans should be a bright green colour and it should be possible to snap them in half. The long beans are just as tender as the smaller ones but, especially early in the season, the pods should not be fat; if so, the bean inside has had time to develop, and the outside of the bean is likely to be tough. Avoid buying beans which are at all discoloured or are limp or mis-shapen.

To store: Runner beans can be kept for 2–3 days in a cool vegetable rack or larder or in the bottom of a refrigerator.

To prepare: Top and tail the beans and remove any strings, then cut into thin, oblique slices, about 3–5cm long.

To boil: Add the beans to about 2cm boiling salted water, cover, and cook for 5–10 minutes or until just tender. Drain thoroughly. Serve tossed with butter and a little chopped savory and well seasoned with black pepper.

To steam: Season the beans with salt and cook in a steamer over a pan of boiling water for about 10–15 minutes. Drain and serve as for boiled beans.

Beans with Soured Cream

3–4 helpings

400g runner beans	*salt and pepper*
125ml soured cream	*50g butter*
$\frac{1}{2}$ × 2.5ml spoon grated	*50g soft white*
nutmeg	*breadcrumbs*
1 × 2.5ml spoon	
caraway seeds	

Prepare the beans and boil or steam them until just tender. Drain thoroughly. Mix the soured cream with the nutmeg, caraway seeds, and seasoning. Add the beans and toss well together. Grease a 1 litre ovenproof dish with some of the butter and spoon in the beans. Melt the rest of the butter and toss the breadcrumbs in it. Sprinkle them on top of the beans. Bake in a moderate oven, 180°C, Gas 4, for 30 minutes or until the topping is crisp and golden.

Cooking time 45 minutes (approx)

Braised Beans with Savory

4 helpings

600g runner beans	*1 × 10ml spoon chopped*
salt	*savory*
1 small onion	*125ml brown stock*
25g butter	*(p329)*

Prepare the beans and parboil in boiling salted water for 3–4 minutes. Drain thoroughly. Skin and chop the onion finely. Melt the butter in a saucepan and fry the onion for 2–3 minutes. Add the beans and savory, and pour the stock over them. Cover with a tight-fitting lid and cook gently for 1 hour. Re-season if required before serving. Remove the beans from the pan with a perforated spoon and transfer to a warmed serving dish. Boil the liquid in the pan rapidly until it is reduced to about 60ml; then spoon it over the top of the beans.

Beans – *Dried*

Dried beans, like other pulses, have a high protein content and can be used to make excellent, nourishing, and comparatively inexpensive meals. As well as being used as a hot vegetable, or in composite dishes, they are also very good when served cold in salads. Cooked beans are available in cans, and these can be especially useful for dishes such as Cassoulet de Toulouse (p1501) and Chilli Con Carne (p508). There are many varieties of dried beans and a lot of them are known by different names according to the country of origin, but in most cases, these beans are interchangeable, and so where haricot beans are given in the recipes below, butter or lima beans or black-eyed peas can equally well be used instead.

Aduki or azuki beans: Small round, red beans which are used extensively in Japanese cookery for both sweet and savoury dishes.

Black-eyed peas: Despite their name, these are in fact beans, small and white in colour and similar to a haricot bean, but, at the point of attachment to the pod, they have a small black 'eye'. They are used a great deal in South American cooking.

Borlotti beans: Red or mottled pink beans used in salads and stews.

Butter beans: Large, white, kidney-shaped beans.

Brown beans: Medium-sized, kidney-shaped beans used extensively in Mediterranean cooking.

Haricot beans: There are several varieties of small white beans whose shape can vary from almost round to very long and thin, according to the variety and where it is grown.

Flageolet beans: Pale green haricot beans; a very choice variety.

Lima beans: A green American bean.

Pinto beans: These are similar to red kidney beans, but are a dappled pink in colour.

Red kidney beans: Kidney-shaped beans, traditionally used in Chilli Con Carne; deep purplish red and larger than haricot beans.

Soya beans: Creamy white and almost round. They have a very high protein content and are of particular value in a vegetarian diet.

To buy: Allow 40–50g dried beans per person.

To prepare: Soak the beans in cold water for 6–12 hours, preferably changing the water once during this time to prevent them fermenting.

To boil: Drain the beans and put them into a pan. Cover with fresh cold salted water and bring to the boil. Cover the pan and simmer gently for $1\frac{1}{2}$–$3\frac{1}{2}$ hours until tender.

The cooking time of beans varies with the type of bean and its age; freshly dried beans need a much shorter cooking time than older ones. If preferred, the beans can be cooked in stock to improve the flavour; alternatively or in addition, a chopped onion, a peeled clove of garlic, and sprigs of fresh herbs can be added to the water.

To serve: Drain off the excess liquid, toss in a little butter, season to taste, and sprinkle with chopped parsley.

To purée: Puréed beans, especially haricot and soya beans, are used in vegetarian cooking. Drain the beans, reserving the cooking liquor, then sieve or process in an electric blender with a little of the liquor to give a smooth purée. Season to taste and add a little butter and/or top of the milk.

Haricot Beans and Minced Onions

4–6 helpings

200g haricot beans	*salt and pepper*
2 medium-sized onions	*chopped parsley*
25g butter **or** *margarine*	

Prepare and cook the beans. Drain. Skin and chop the onions finely. Melt the fat in a frying pan and fry the onions for about 7 minutes until just transparent. Add the beans, toss together, and season to taste. Serve hot, sprinkled with the parsley.

Haricot Beans with Parsley Sauce

4–6 helpings

200g haricot beans	*lemon juice*
250ml parsley sauce	
(p696) using all milk	
or *half milk and half*	
bean water	

Prepare and cook the beans. Heat the parsley sauce, and add lemon juice to taste. Drain the beans. Mix them into the sauce, and heat gently for a few minutes.

VARIATION

Haricot Beans with Parsley Butter

Cook the beans as above, and top with a good knob of parsley butter (p1301).

Boston Roast

6 helpings

300g haricot beans	*1 egg*
1 onion	*100g soft white*
1 × 15ml spoon oil	*breadcrumbs*
150g Cheddar cheese	*salt and pepper*
2 × 15ml spoons meat	*fat for greasing*
or *vegetable stock* **or**	
water	

Prepare and cook the beans. Drain and mash them finely. Skin and chop the onion. Heat the oil in a frying pan and fry the onion until golden-brown. Grate the cheese. Put all the ingredients into a bowl and mix well. Shape the mixture into a loaf, place in a greased baking tin, and cover with buttered greaseproof paper. Bake in a moderate oven, 180°C, Gas 4, for 45 minutes.

Serve with gravy and vegetables.

Cooking time 2½ hours (approx)

Breton Haricot Beans

4 helpings

200g haricot beans	*salt and pepper*
1 clove of garlic	*25g butter*
1 rasher streaky bacon	*1 × 15ml spoon*
2 onions	*concentrated tomato*
2 cloves	*purée*
a bunch of herbs (thyme,	
sage, savory,	
marjoram, parsley	
stalks)	

Garnish
1 × 15ml spoon chopped
  parsley

Cover the beans with cold water and leave to soak overnight. Skin and crush the garlic, and chop the bacon. Drain the beans, put into a saucepan, and cover with fresh cold water. Skin 1 onion, press the cloves into it, and add to the pan with the garlic, bacon, herbs, and seasoning. Cover and simmer for 1½ hours or until the beans are tender. Drain the beans, reserving 250ml of the liquid, and discard the herbs, bacon, and onion. Skin and chop the remaining onion finely. Melt the butter in a pan and fry the onion gently for about 5 minutes. Add the tomato purée and the reserved bean stock. Cover and simmer gently for 10 minutes. Add the drained beans and simmer for a further 10 minutes. Garnish with the chopped parsley before serving.

Curried Beans

4 helpings

200g haricot beans	*1 × 10ml spoon ground*
1 medium-sized onion	*coriander*
1cm piece fresh root	*1 × 2.5ml spoon*
ginger	*turmeric*
2 cloves garlic	*2 × 15ml spoons brown*
2 × 15ml spoons	*sugar*
vegetable oil	*400g tomatoes* **or**
1–2 × 2.5ml spoons	*1 × 400g can tomatoes*
Cayenne pepper	*salt and pepper*

Prepare and cook the beans. Skin the onion and chop finely with the ginger. Skin and crush the garlic. Heat the oil in a pan and fry the onion, ginger, and garlic for about 10 minutes. Stir in the Cayenne pepper to taste, with the coriander, turmeric, and sugar. Continue frying for 5 minutes, stirring all the time. Skin the tomatoes if using fresh ones, chop, and add with any juice to the beans. Season to taste. Cover the pan and simmer gently for 1 hour.

Cooking time 3 hours (approx)

Baked Soya Beans and Vegetables

6 helpings

1 medium-sized onion	*3 × 15ml spoons*
½ green pepper	*chopped parsley*
1 medium-sized carrot	*1 × 2.5ml spoon dried*
1 stick of celery	*thyme*
2 × 15ml spoons	*1 × 2.5ml spoon dried*
margarine	*savory*
450g cooked soya beans	*salt and pepper*
2 × 15ml spoons	*50–75ml tomato juice*
molasses	*medium oatmeal*

Skin the onion and chop it finely with the pepper. Grate the carrot coarsely, and slice the celery thinly. Grease a medium-sized ovenproof casserole with a little of the margarine. Mix together the vegetables and soya beans. Warm the molasses and stir it into the vegetables. Add the herbs and salt and pepper to taste. Turn the mixture into the dish and pour over 50ml tomato juice. Sprinkle thickly with oatmeal. Melt the remaining margarine and sprinkle it over the oatmeal. Cover the dish, and bake in a moderate oven, 180°C, Gas 4 for 45 minutes. Pour over a little extra tomato juice if the contents seem dry during this time. Remove the lid and bake for a further 15 minutes. Serve hot from the dish.

Bean Sprouts

Bean sprouts are available in many greengrocers' shops and supermarkets or can be grown at home. They are served both raw in salads and cooked. Excellent canned bean sprouts are also obtainable.

To buy: Allow 50g bean sprouts per person. Choose crisp fresh looking bean sprouts.

To sprout beans: Use young mung beans as old ones will not sprout. Discard any discoloured or decayed beans and soak the rest in plenty of cold water. Drain and place either on damp muslin stretched over a tray or in a jar with muslin or cheesecloth stretched over it, and placed on its side.

Pour cold water over the beans to keep them moist and tilt the container to let the water run off. Repeat twice daily for 6–8 days until the beans have sprouted and the sprouts are 4–5cm long. Keep the beans well ventilated and at a fairly warm even temperature over 18°C and, if sprouting them in the dark, bring into the light for 24 hours before use.

To store: Bean sprouts do not keep well and should preferably be eaten on the day of purchase; if not, they can be kept for a day in the bottom of a refrigerator.

To prepare: Pick over the bean sprouts, remove any withered or brown stalks and wash in cold water.

To steam: Prepare as above and season with salt. Cook in the top of a steamer over a pan of boiling water for about 5–8 minutes or until just soft. Drain and serve as soon as possible.

To stir-fry (Chinese method): Heat 2 × 15ml spoons olive, corn or soya oil in a pan. Add the bean sprouts and cook, stirring all the time, for about 5 minutes or until the bean sprouts are just cooked, but are still slightly crisp. Serve as soon as possible after cooking.

Beetroot

Small, young beetroots make an excellent hot vegetable as well as being good in salads. Beetroot is available all year round, but the young ones are at their best in mid-summer. At this time of year, the leaves can be used as well as the roots and these should be cooked as for spinach (p800). For salads, the beetroots should be baked, boiled or steamed, or they can be bought already cooked.

To buy: Allow 100–150g per person. Uncooked beetroots should be firm, the skins smooth and unbroken, and in the summer any leaves which have been left on should look fresh. If buying cooked beetroots, avoid buying any with a wrinkled skin which does not look moist because these tend to be hard and 'woody'.

To store: Young beetroots are best cooked and eaten as soon as possible after purchase, but older ones can be stored for several weeks in a cool airy place. Cooked beetroots can be wrapped in clingfilm and stored in the bottom of a refrigerator for 2–3 days.

To prepare: Raw beetroot 'bleeds' so it is important that the skin is not damaged in any way. Cut off the leaves and trim the stalks to within 2cm of the top of the root. Wash thoroughly to remove any dirt.

To boil: Cook in a large pan of boiling salted water for 45 minutes–1 hour for small beetroots, or for up to 2 hours for large, older ones. Drain thoroughly if serving hot, or allow to cool in the cooking water. To serve beetroot hot, peel off the skin and either season with pepper and top with melted butter and chopped parsley or mint, or serve with a white, parsley or caper sauce.

To steam: Season the beetroots with salt. Cook in the top of a steamer over a pan of boiling water for 1½ hours if small, or for up to 2½ hours if large. Serve as for boiled beetroot.

To bake: If the skin of the beetroot has been damaged in any way, seal the damaged part with a little flour and water paste. Place each beetroot in a piece of buttered greaseproof paper and enclose it completely. Bake in a moderate oven, 180°C, Gas 4, for 1 hour (for young beetroots) or for up to 2 hours for older beetroots. Serve as for boiled beetroot.

Beetroot is also excellent cooked in a pressure cooker.

Polish Beetroot

6 helpings

800g cooked beetroot	*2 × 15ml spoons finely*
1 small onion	*grated horseradish*
15g butter **or** *margarine*	*salt and pepper*
2 × 15ml spoons flour	*sugar (optional)*
150g natural yoghurt	

Garnish
1 × 15ml spoon chopped parsley

Peel and grate the beetroot and skin and finely chop or grate the onion. Melt the fat in a saucepan and fry the onion gently for about 5 minutes. Stir in the flour and cook gently for 1 minute, stirring all the time. Draw off the heat and gradually stir in the yoghurt. Return to the heat, and bring to the boil, stirring all the time, until the sauce thickens. Add the beetroot and horseradish and heat thoroughly. Season to taste, and add sugar to taste, if liked. Serve hot, garnished with the parsley.

Cooking time 15 minutes (approx)

Broccoli

There are three different kinds of broccoli, and this often causes confusion.

1) Many of the winter cauliflowers available are, in fact, broccoli, because the broccoli plant is much hardier than the cauliflower; this broccoli should be cooked and treated exactly like cauliflower.

2) Heads of purple sprouting and white sprouting broccoli are found in the shops at the end of the winter and in early spring. After this central head has been removed, the plant gives out leafy side shoots with a small head which are available in the late spring.

3) The third and choicest type of broccoli is the green or Italian *Calabrese* variety. Home-grown *Calabrese* is in the shops from July to December, but if imported it is available at other times of the year. *Calabrese* also freezes well and is fairly widely obtainable in this form.

To buy: Allow 100–200g per person depending on the amount of leaf and consequent wastage. The heads of both Calabrese and purple sprouting broccoli should be a good colour. The leaves should appear fresh, and the stalks should be firm and not limp.

To store: Purple sprouting broccoli does not store well and should be kept for only 1–2 days in a cool, dry vegetable rack or larder or in a polythene bag in the bottom of a refrigerator. Calabrese will keep for 2–3 days in a polythene bag in a refrigerator, but should be eaten as fresh as possible.

To prepare: Calabrese does not generally require very much preparation since it is usually separated into small heads when bought. Simply trim the stalks to within 7–10cm of the head and wash thoroughly. The whole heads of purple sprouting broccoli should be trimmed and either left whole if they are small, or broken up into smaller heads if large. The leafy side shoots should be trimmed and any tough stalks discarded. It is often neater to tie the shoots in bundles before cooking.

To boil: Cook the broccoli in the minimum of boiling salted water for 10–15 minutes or until just tender. Drain thoroughly and turn into a serving dish. Season with pepper, preferably freshly ground, and either spoon melted butter over it or serve with Hollandaise (p712) or Béarnaise (p712) sauce.

To steam: Season the broccoli with salt. Cook in the top of a steamer over a pan of boiling water for 15–20 minutes. Drain thoroughly and serve as for boiled broccoli.

Broccoli
1 Purple; 2 Calabrese

Broccoli au Gratin

4 helpings

600–800g broccoli	*1 egg yolk*
1 small onion (optional)	*salt and pepper*
butter **or** *margarine for*	*a pinch of grated nutmeg*
shallow frying	*25g grated Parmesan*
250ml cheese sauce	*cheese*
(p693)	*25g dry breadcrumbs*

Prepare and cook the broccoli until just tender. Drain thoroughly. Skin and chop the onion, if used. Melt the fat in a pan and fry the onion until just transparent. Add to the cheese sauce and whisk in the egg yolk; season to taste, and add the nutmeg. Spread a little of the sauce in the bottom of a flameproof dish and arrange the broccoli on top. Pour the remaining sauce over the broccoli and sprinkle with the cheese and breadcrumbs. Cook under the grill until golden; or put into a fairly hot oven, 200°C, Gas 6, for 20 minutes until golden-brown.

Brussels Sprouts

Brussels sprouts are in season from August to March, although the flavour is generally better after the first frosts. The best sprouts to buy are the small hard ones, also known as button sprouts, since these have the best flavour and texture and freeze well. Sprout tops, when available, should be cooked as for spinach.

To buy: Allow 150–200g sprouts per person. Choose sprouts which are small, firm, and green and which do not have a great many loose outside leaves. These should also be a good green colour and not yellow or wilted.

To store: Sprouts can be kept for 1–2 days in a cool, dry vegetable rack or larder, or for 2–3 days in a polythene bag in a refrigerator, but they are best eaten as fresh as possible.

To prepare: Cut a slice off the bottom of each sprout and remove the outer leaves. Soak the sprouts for 10 minutes in cold salted water and drain thoroughly. To cook large sprouts more quickly and evenly, cut a cross in the base.

To boil: Add the sprouts, a few at a time, to the minimum of boiling salted water so that the water does not leave the boil. Cook for 7–10 minutes according to size or until they are just tender. Do not overcook. Drain thoroughly and season with black pepper, preferably freshly ground. Toss in melted butter or soured cream or sprinkle with a little crumbled crisply fried or grilled bacon.

The sprouts can also be boiled in stock. Prepare 750g sprouts and cook in 500ml beef stock. Drain, reserving the cooking liquor, and keep warm. Boil the cooking liquor rapidly until it is reduced to a thin glaze. Pour over the sprouts and serve as soon as possible.

To steam: Season the sprouts with salt. Cook in the top of a steamer over a pan of boiling water for about 15 minutes or until the sprouts are just tender. Drain and serve as for boiled sprouts.

To braise: Parboil the sprouts in boiling salted water for 5 minutes. Fry a chopped onion in 25g butter until it is just soft. Pour 500ml stock over it, season, and simmer for 5 minutes. Add the sprouts and simmer for a further 10 minutes.

Brussels Sprouts in Cream

6 helpings

1kg Brussels sprouts	*a pinch of grated nutmeg*
75g butter	*salt and pepper*
1 × 15ml spoon flour	
125ml milk **or** *single*	
cream	

Prepare and cook the sprouts. Drain thoroughly. Heat 50g of the butter in a saucepan and fry the sprouts gently until lightly browned.

Meanwhile, melt the remaining butter in a smaller pan, stir in the flour, and cook gently for 2–3 minutes without colouring; stir all the time. Gradually stir in the milk or cream. Add the nutmeg and seasoning, and cook the sauce gently for about 10 minutes. Pile the sprouts on a hot dish, pour the sauce over them, and serve.

Cooking time 40 minutes (approx)

Brussels Sprouts with Chestnuts

6 helpings

1kg Brussels sprouts　　*4 ×15ml spoons single*
12 cooked chestnuts　　　*cream*
*　(p766)*　　　　　　　*salt and pepper*
75g cooked ham

Prepare and cook the sprouts. Drain thoroughly. Cut each chestnut into quarters and chop the ham finely. Put the sprouts, chestnuts, and ham in a casserole. Stir in the cream and season with salt and pepper. Cover and cook in a moderate oven, 180°C, Gas 4, for 15 minutes.

Cooking time 25 minutes (approx)

Breadfruit

Breadfruit are not widely available because they do not travel well, but they can sometimes be found in markets and Afro-Asian stores. They can be peeled and steamed and/or boiled in the same way as potatoes, but it is generally better to puncture the skin with a fork or skewer and bake them in a moderate oven, 180°C, Gas 4, for 1–1½ hours or until they are tender.

Breadfruit

Cabbage

There are many varieties of cabbage, but the most common are:
1) the Savoy
2) the pale green, hard or 'white' (Dutch) cabbage
3) red cabbage
4) spring and summer cabbage.

To buy: Allow 200g per person. Always choose cabbages that are crisp and a good colour. They should never be limp with yellow edges; this indicates that they were picked some time ago and so probably lack both flavour and valuable vitamin C.

To store: Apart from red and white cabbage, which can be stored for some time, it is inadvisable to store cabbage for more than a few days. It should be kept in a cool dry vegetable rack or larder. If only part of a cabbage is needed, wrap the rest and store in the bottom of a refrigerator.

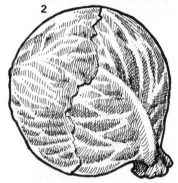

1 Summer cabbage; 2 'White' (Dutch) cabbage

To prepare: Remove the coarse outer leaves and trim off the stem. Cut the cabbage into half, cut out the hard part of the stalk, then cut into quarters. Spring and summer cabbage is usually left in quarters, but other varieties are generally finely shredded. This should not be done until shortly before the vegetable is to be cooked because mineral salts and vitamin C are rapidly lost. Wash the cabbage well in cold water; a little salt added to the water helps to draw out any small insects which may be between the leaves. Drain in a colander.

To boil: Add the cabbage, a little at a time, to boiling salted water so that the water does not leave the boil. Cover the pan and cook for 5–12 minutes or until the cabbage is just tender but not soggy; do not overcook. Drain thoroughly and season with a little pepper, preferably freshly ground, and any other flavouring desired; grated nutmeg or a few caraway seeds are popular. Toss in butter just before serving.

To steam: Season the cabbage with salt and cook in the top of a steamer over boiling water for 5–12 minutes or until just tender. Serve as for boiled cabbage.

To braise: Parboil wedges of cabbage for 10 minutes. Drain and dry thoroughly. Fry a chopped onion and carrot in a little lard or dripping. Add a bouquet garni and place the cabbage on top. Pour over just enough beef stock to cover the cabbage and cook for 1 hour. Remove from the pan with a perforated spoon and serve.

Bavarian Cabbage

6 helpings

1.25kg white cabbage	*½ × 2.5ml spoon*
1 medium-sized onion	*caraway seeds*
1 cooking apple	*1 × 15ml spoon*
75g butter	*cornflour*
salt and pepper	*4 × 15ml spoons white*
1 × 10ml spoon sugar	*wine* **or** *white vinegar*
125ml stock **or** *water*	

Wash, quarter, and shred the cabbage. Skin the onion, peel and core the apple, and chop both finely. Melt the butter in a thick saucepan and fry the onion gently for 5 minutes. Add the cabbage, apple, seasoning, sugar, stock or water, and caraway seeds and mix together. Cover the pan with a tight-fitting lid and simmer very gently for 1 hour. Blend the cornflour with the wine or vinegar and pour it over the cabbage. Bring to the boil, stirring all the time. Re-season if required before serving.

Polish Cabbage

4–5 helpings

25g bacon, without rinds	*125ml boiling water*
1 × 15ml spoon bacon	*salt and pepper*
fat	*1 medium-sized cooking*
1 small onion	*apple* **or** *150g tomatoes*
500g cabbage heart	*1 × 10ml spoon flour*

Chop the bacon into small pieces, and fry it gently in a saucepan with the bacon fat. Skin and chop the onion finely, add to the pan, and cook for a further 5 minutes. Wash and shred the cabbage finely and add to the bacon and onion, stirring well. Add the boiling water and seasoning and simmer gently until the cabbage is almost soft. Peel, core, and chop the apple, or skin and chop the tomatoes. Add to the cabbage and cook for a further 10 minutes. Sprinkle the flour over the cabbage, bring to the boil, and cook for 2–3 minutes, stirring, until the liquid has thickened. Serve very hot.

Cooking time 45 minutes (approx)

Cabbage with Soured Cream

4–6 helpings

1 small white cabbage	*125ml soured cream*
(1kg approx)	*1 × 2.5ml spoon*
2 egg yolks	*caraway seeds*
1 × 10ml spoon lemon	*salt and pepper*
juice	

Prepare and boil or steam the cabbage. Transfer to a warmed serving dish and keep warm. Blend the egg yolks with the lemon juice, cream, caraway seeds, and seasoning in the top of a double saucepan or in a basin over a pan of hot water. Cook over a pan of gently simmering water until the sauce thickens. Re-season if required. Pour it over the cabbage and serve as soon as possible.

Cooking time 20 minutes (approx)

Stuffed Cabbage Leaves

4 helpings

8 large cabbage leaves	*fat for greasing*

Stuffing

1 medium-sized onion	*½ × 2.5ml spoon dried*
1 × 15ml spoon oil	*mixed herbs*
400g minced beef	*1 × 15ml spoon chopped*
1 × 400g can tomatoes	*parsley*
1 × 10ml spoon	*salt and pepper*
cornflour	
1 × 15ml spoon	
Worcestershire sauce	

Sauce

juice from the canned	*2 × 10ml spoons*
tomatoes	*cornflour*
1 × 15ml spoon	*a pinch of sugar*
concentrated tomato	*salt and pepper*
purée	

Remove the thick centre stems from the cabbage leaves, blanch in boiling water for 2 minutes, and drain thoroughly.

To make the stuffing, skin and chop the onion finely. Heat the oil in a pan and fry the onion gently for 5 minutes. Add the beef and cook, stirring until the beef has browned. Drain the tomatoes and reserve the juice. Add the tomatoes to the meat mixture. Blend the cornflour with the Worcestershire sauce and stir into the meat mixture with the herbs and seasoning. Cover and simmer for 20 minutes, stirring occasionally.

Divide the stuffing between the cabbage leaves and roll up, folding over the edges of the leaves to enclose the meat completely. Place in a greased, shallow ovenproof dish, cover with foil, and bake in a fairly hot oven, 190°C, Gas 5, for 20 minutes.

Prepare the sauce while the cabbage leaves are cooking. Blend the reserved juice from the tomatoes with the tomato purée and make up to 250ml with water. Blend the cornflour with 1 × 15ml spoon of the sauce. Pour the rest of the sauce into a pan and bring to the boil. Pour in the blended cornflour and bring to the boil, stirring all the time, until the sauce has thickened. Add the sugar and season to taste. Pour the sauce over the cabbage leaves just before serving.

Cooking time 1 hour (approx)

Savoy Cabbage and Apples in Curry Sauce

4 helpings

1 savoy cabbage	*400g leeks*
(800g–1kg approx)	*500ml fruit curry sauce*
2 dessert apples	*(p718)*

Wash and quarter the cabbage. Either steam the cabbage for 10 minutes or parboil in boiling salted water for 5 minutes. Drain thoroughly and leave to cool, then cut the cabbage into thick slices. Peel, core, and slice the apples thinly. Wash the leeks and cut lengthwise into four. Place a layer of cabbage in the bottom of a casserole, then add a layer of apple, and a layer of leeks. Continue these layers until all the ingredients are used, ending with a layer of cabbage. Pour the curry sauce over the vegetables and cover the casserole. Cook in a fairly hot oven, 200°C, Gas 6, for 30 minutes.

Red Cabbage

Red cabbage can be cooked as for ordinary green cabbage but is more usually braised gently for about 1½ hours until very tender.

Red Cabbage with Apples

6 helpings

1kg red cabbage (approx)	*1 × 15ml spoon golden syrup*
1 medium-sized onion	*juice of ½ lemon*
300g cooking apples (approx)	*2 × 15ml spoons vinegar*
25g butter **or** *margarine*	*salt and pepper*

Prepare and shred the red cabbage finely. Skin and chop the onion finely and peel, core, and slice the apples. Melt the fat in a saucepan, add the onion and fry gently for 5 minutes. Add the cabbage, apples, and syrup and cook over very gentle heat for 10 minutes, shaking the pan frequently. Add the lemon juice, vinegar, and seasoning. Cover and simmer gently for 1½ hours, stirring occasionally. Re-season if required before serving.

Stewed Red Cabbage

6 helpings

1 small red cabbage (1kg approx)	*500ml beef stock*
1 slice of ham (50g approx)	*125ml vinegar*
2 × 10ml spoons butter **or** *margarine*	*1 × 15ml spoon granulated sugar*
	salt and pepper

Prepare and shred the cabbage finely and dice the ham. Put the cabbage, ham, fat, half the stock, and the vinegar in a heavy-based pan. Cover, and cook over gentle heat, stirring from time to time, for 1½ hours. Add the rest of the stock and the sugar and seasoning. Increase the heat and cook for about another 15 minutes, stirring frequently, until almost all the liquid has evaporated. Serve at once.

This is an excellent dish to serve with sausages or frankfurters.

Sauerkraut

Sauerkraut is made from fermented cabbage leaves. It is sometimes possible to buy sauerkraut loose from a large barrel in delicatessens, but it is more generally sold in cans or jars. It can simply be heated and served as a vegetable but is more usually simmered with wine, herbs, and spices to give additional flavour.

Sauerkraut with Juniper

4 helpings

1 can **or** *jar sauerkraut (400g approx)*	*1 clove of garlic*
50g streaky bacon (approx)	*50g butter*
	2 bay leaves
1 large onion	*1 × 5ml spoon celery seeds* **or** *caraway seeds*
6 juniper berries	*250ml chicken stock*

Soak the sauerkraut in cold water for 15 minutes. Drain and squeeze dry in your hands. Chop the bacon, skin and chop the onion, crush the juniper berries, and skin and crush the garlic. Melt the butter in a pan, add the bacon and onion and fry gently for 10 minutes. Add all the remaining ingredients. Cover the pan and simmer gently for 1 hour. Re-season if required before serving.

Note If liked, frankfurters, knackwurst or Polish sausage can be cooked in the pan with the sauerkraut.

Cardoon

The cardoon is a member of the thistle and artichoke family. It is not used extensively although it has an excellent flavour. Both the stalks and the leaves can be used; the leaves should be cooked as for spinach. Cardoons are in season from October to March.

To buy: Although cardoons are not readily available in most greengrocers' shops, they can be found in some speciality stores. They should appear fresh, and the stalks should be firm and crisp.

To store: They can be kept for 1–2 days in a cool, dry vegetable rack or larder, or for 2–3 days in a polythene bag in the bottom of a refrigerator.

To prepare: Discard the outer stems which are very tough. Remove the strings and prickles from the remainder, cut into 12cm lengths and wash thoroughly in acidulated water.

To boil: Cook in boiling, salted, acidulated water for about 20 minutes or until they are very tender. Drain thoroughly and turn into a serving dish. Season with pepper, preferably freshly ground, and pour over melted butter and some chopped herbs (parsley, chives or tarragon) or a light Béchamel or cream sauce. To improve the flavour, the cardoons can be drained and then cooked for a further 20 minutes in the sauce.

Cardoon

Carragheen

See Seaweed (p799).

Carrots

Carrots are a most useful vegetable since they are used extensively as a flavouring for all kinds of soups, casseroles, and sauces. They are available throughout the year, although young carrots, which have the best flavour for serving as a vegetable, are usually only obtainable during the late spring and summer. Frozen young carrots are also available, and both young and old carrots can be bought in cans.

To buy: Allow 100–150g per person. The tops of young carrots should appear fresh and green, and the carrots should be of an even size. If the head of the carrot is green, however, the carrot is insufficiently mature. Older carrots should be firm and smooth and not broken or pitted. Care should be taken when buying prepacked carrots because they are sometimes not in prime condition and can be slimy.

To store: For the maximum flavour, young carrots should be eaten as fresh as possible, preferably on the day they are bought, although they can be stored for 1–2 days in a cool, dry vegetable rack or larder. Older carrots can be kept for several weeks, provided they are in a cool, dry place.

To prepare: Young carrots need only to be topped and tailed and scrubbed with a stiff brush. More mature carrots need to be either scraped with a knife or thinly peeled, depending on age. Young carrots should be left whole, but older carrots should be sliced and cut into strips or fancy shapes.

To boil (conservation method): Carrots should be cooked in the minimum of water to give the best flavour and to preserve all the vitamins. For 600g carrots, melt 25g butter or margarine in a heavy-based pan. Add the carrots and cook very gently for 10 minutes, shaking the pan frequently so that the carrots do not stick to the bottom. Pour over approximately 100ml boiling salted water, cover the pan, and cook the carrots gently for a further 10–15 minutes depending on their age. Serve the carrots with the cooking liquor and sprinkle them liberally with chopped parsley, mint, chervil or marjoram, and a little lemon juice, if liked. The carrots can also be served with a parsley sauce, or 1–2 ×15ml spoons cream can be added to the carrots in the pan just before serving.

To steam: Young carrots are particularly good steamed. Season with salt and cook in the top of a steamer over boiling water for 10–30 minutes, depending on the age of the carrots. Serve as for boiled carrots.

To deep fry: This is suitable for old carrots. Parboil the carrots for 5 minutes, drain, and dry thoroughly. Coat with batter and fry as for Jerusalem artichokes.

To purée: Older carrots make a good purée and can be mixed with an equal quantity of puréed potatoes. Cook the carrots as above and sieve, mash or process in an electric blender together with the cooking liquor. Add 25g butter, season with salt and pepper, preferably freshly ground, and add a little cream or top of the milk, if liked. Sprinkle with chopped parsley before serving, or add a little grated orange rind for a more unusual flavour.

Glazed Carrots

6 helpings

600g young carrots
50g butter
3 sugar lumps

½ × 2.5ml spoon salt
beef stock

Garnish
1 × 15ml spoon chopped
 parsley

Prepare the carrots but leave them whole. Heat the butter in a saucepan. Add the carrots, sugar, salt, and enough stock to half cover the carrots. Cook gently, without a lid, for 15–20 minutes or until the carrots are tender, shaking the pan occasionally. Remove the carrots with a perforated spoon and keep warm. Boil the stock rapidly in the pan until it is reduced to a rich glaze. Replace the carrots, 2–3 at a time, and turn them in the glaze until they are thoroughly coated. Place on a serving dish and garnish with parsley before serving.

Cooking time 30–40 minutes

German Carrots

6 helpings

600g carrots
½ small onion
50g butter **or** margarine
500ml stock
extra stock
25g flour

a good pinch of grated
 nutmeg
1 × 15ml spoon chopped
 parsley
salt and pepper

Prepare the carrots, and skin and chop the onion finely. Melt half the fat in a heavy-based pan. Add the carrots and the onion and cook very gently for 10 minutes, shaking the pan frequently so that the vegetables do not stick to the bottom. Pour the stock over the carrots, cover the pan, and simmer gently for 10–15 minutes or until the carrots are tender. Drain the carrots, reserving the cooking liquor, and keep them warm. Make the cooking liquor up to 375ml with extra stock, if necessary. Melt the remaining fat in a saucepan. Add the flour and cook gently for 1 minute, stirring all the time. Draw off the heat and gradually stir in the stock. Return to the heat and bring to the boil, stirring all the time. Add the carrots, nutmeg and parsley, and season to taste. Serve as soon as possible.

Carrots with Cider

6 helpings

600g young carrots
75g butter
100ml boiling water
salt
4 × 15ml spoons double
 cream

125ml dry cider
a few drops lemon juice
pepper

Prepare the carrots and cook them by the conservation method (p762) using 25g of the butter, the water, and the salt. Drain the carrots and keep them warm. Melt the remaining butter in a pan. Gradually stir in the cream and cider. Add the lemon juice and seasoning to taste. Place the carrots in the sauce, cover, and cook gently for 10 minutes. Serve at once.

Cooking time 35 minutes (approx)

Cauliflower

Cauliflower is one of our most useful green vegetables because it is available throughout the year. Served with a cheese sauce, cauliflower is a popular and substantial supper dish, but it is also excellent as a side vegetable or when used for soup. Some supermarkets also sell prepacked cauliflower florets, and these can be a good buy because there is no waste. Frozen cauliflower florets are also available.

To buy: Allow 100g per person if buying florets, but 150g per person if buying a whole cauliflower. The head or curds of the cauliflower should be a good creamy white and should have no marks or blemishes. The leaves round the cauliflower should be a good green colour and should not appear yellow or wilted.

To store: Cauliflower will keep for 2–3 days in a cool, dry vegetable rack or larder, or in a refrigerator. To save space in a refrigerator it is usually easier to divide the head into florets first.

To prepare: Fresh florets should simply be washed in cold salted water. Whole cauliflower should be trimmed of most of the outside leaves and the stalk cut so that the cauliflower will stand upright. To ensure the stalk cooks quickly, either make a cross in the base, or cut out the first 2cm of the stalk with an apple corer. Soak the whole cauliflower for 10 minutes in salted water before cooking, to draw out any insects.

To boil: Florets should be cooked in the minimum of boiling salted water for 8–10 minutes, or until just tender; they should then be drained. Put a whole cauliflower head, stalk down, in 2cm boiling salted water in a large pan, season with salt, and bring back to the boil. Cover, and cook over fairly high heat for about 15 minutes or until tender. Cauliflower should never be overcooked. Drain thoroughly and place on a serving dish with the head uppermost. Season with pepper, preferably freshly ground black pepper, and spoon over some melted butter and chopped chives or parsley; alternatively, sprinkle with crumbled, crisply fried or grilled bacon or a few chopped and lightly fried almonds; or pour a white or light cream sauce over the cauliflower.

To steam: Steaming is particularly good for cauliflower florets. Season with salt and cook in the top of a steamer over boiling water for 15 minutes for florets, or for up to 40 minutes for a large, whole head. Do not overcook. Drain thoroughly and serve as for boiled cauliflower.

To deep fry: Divide the cauliflower into florets and parboil for about 8 minutes. Drain and dry thoroughly. For a medium-sized cauliflower or 600g florets, make up a double quantity of coating batter (1) (p933) and coat and fry as for Jerusalem artichokes. Serve deep-fried cauliflower with Tartare Sauce (p706).

Cauliflower with Rich Mushroom Sauce

4–6 helpings

1kg cauliflower (approx)	*1 × 15ml spoon lemon*
50g butter	*juice*
25g flour	*salt and black pepper*
*375ml chicken **or***	*a pinch of grated nutmeg*
*vegetable stock **or** milk*	*4–6 slices bread*
100g button mushrooms	*butter*
3 egg yolks	

Prepare the cauliflower. Break it into medium-sized florets and boil or steam them until just tender. Drain thoroughly and keep hot. Melt the 50g of butter in a pan, stir in the flour, and cook for 1 minute. Draw off the heat and gradually stir in the stock or milk. Return to the heat and bring to the boil, stirring all the time, until the sauce thickens. Clean and chop the mushrooms finely, add to the sauce, and simmer gently for 5 minutes. Beat the egg yolks lightly, beat in the lemon juice and 2 × 15ml spoons of the hot sauce, then stir into the sauce. Heat gently, but do not allow the sauce to boil after the egg yolks have been added or it will curdle. Season to taste and add the nutmeg.

Toast the bread, cut into rounds, and butter each. Arrange the cauliflower neatly on the rounds, and pour the sauce over. Serve as soon as possible.

Cooking time 30 minutes (approx)

Polish Cauliflower

4 helpings

1 large cauliflower
50g butter **or** *margarine*
50g soft white
  breadcrumbs

2 hard-boiled eggs
1 × 15ml spoon chopped
  parsley

Prepare and cook the cauliflower. Meanwhile, heat the fat in a frying pan and fry the breadcrumbs until they are crisp and golden. Chop the egg whites finely and sieve the yolks. Drain the cauliflower thoroughly and place on a serving dish. Sprinkle the breadcrumbs and then the egg yolk and parsley over the cauliflower. Arrange the chopped egg white round the edge of the dish.

Cooking time 30 minutes (approx)

Cauliflower Cheese

See p1324.

Celeriac

This large swede-like root has a flavour very like that of celery and can be used in the same way for flavouring soups, stews, and casseroles. It can also be used raw, shredded, in salads. For a more delicate flavour it can be blanched in acidulated water for 2 minutes before shredding. Celeriac is available from October to April.

To buy: Allow 150g celeriac per person. The root should be firm to the touch and not caked in too much mud and earth.

To store: Celeriac, like other root vegetables, will keep well for several weeks in a cool, dry place.

To prepare: Celeriac can be cooked either whole or cut into slices 1cm thick. Unfortunately, celeriac is not easy to peel because it is rather knobbly. Wash it first in cold water to remove all the mud and earth. If it is to be cooked in slices, slice and then peel it; if it is to be cooked whole, peel thickly with a small sharp knife. As soon as the celeriac has been peeled, it should be put into acidulated water to preserve the colour.

To boil: Cook the whole or sliced celeriac in boiling, salted, acidulated water for 25–30 minutes for sliced celeriac, or for 45 minutes–1 hour for whole celeriac. Drain thoroughly, season with pepper, preferably freshly ground, and either spoon melted butter and/or a squeeze of lemon juice over it, or serve with a white, cheese or Hollandaise sauce.

To steam: Season the celeriac with salt and toss in lemon juice to preserve the colour. Cook in the top of a steamer over boiling water for 30–35 minutes if sliced or for 1–1½ hours if whole.

To bake: Cut the celeriac root in half lengthways without peeling it. Heat 5mm depth of bacon fat or dripping in a roasting tin. Put the celeriac into the fat, cut side down, and bake in a moderate oven, 180°C, Gas 4, for 1–1½ hours. The celeriac is cooked when a skewer pierces it easily. Turn it cut side up for serving, and cut in wedges as with melon.

To shallow fry: Cut the celeriac into slices and parboil for 10 minutes. Drain and dry thoroughly. Fry in some butter or margarine until they are golden-brown. Drain thoroughly, sprinkle with chopped parsley, and serve as soon as possible.

To deep fry: Cut the celeriac into slices and parboil for 10 minutes. Drain and dry thoroughly. Coat in batter and fry as for Jerusalem artichokes.

To purée: Boil or steam the celeriac, drain, and then sieve, mash or process in an electric blender. Because it has a very strong flavour, celeriac purée is best mixed with an equal quantity of potato purée. Season with salt and pepper and add a good knob of butter and a little cream or top of the milk.

Celery

Celery is generally served braised as a side vegetable, but is also used extensively as a flavouring in soups, stews, and casseroles (for which the tough outer stalks can be used), as well as raw in salads, or with cheese. Celery is available all year round, although the best home-grown celery comes in November after the first frosts. Celery hearts (the tender inner part of the vegetable), are also available in cans.

To buy: Allow 1 small head per person if braising or half a head if boiling, steaming or frying. The celery should be crisp and white, without too many thick outer stalks.

To store: Celery can be kept for 2–3 days in a cool, dry vegetable rack but is best separated into stalks and stood in a jug of cold water to keep it crisp and fresh. Outer celery stalks, which you may wish to reserve for flavouring, can be kept for several days in a polythene bag in a refrigerator until they are required.

To prepare: Remove the outer leaves of the celery and put on one side to use as flavouring. Either separate the celery into stalks or leave the head whole. Wash or wipe the celery if required. Leave the stalks whole, or cut in half lengthways if very wide. Cut the whole head or the stalks crossways into halves or quarters.

To boil: Cut the celery stalks into 2cm pieces and cook in the minimum of boiling salted water for 15–20 minutes or until just tender. Drain, season with pepper, preferably freshly ground, and spoon over some melted butter or a white or cheese sauce.

To steam: Cut the celery stalks into 2cm pieces and season with salt. Cook in the top of a steamer over boiling water for 20–30 minutes until tender. Drain and serve as for boiled celery.

To deep fry: Cut the celery into 2cm pieces and parboil for 5 minutes. Drain thoroughly. Coat in batter and fry as for Jerusalem artichokes.

To braise: Trim the celery, but leave it whole. For 4 small heads of celery make a mirepoix (p809) and add enough stock to half cover the vegetables. Bring to the boil and place the celery on top. Baste some of the stock over the celery. Cover the pan

with a piece of greaseproof paper or foil and then with the lid. Cook over gentle heat for 1½ hours or until the celery is very tender, basting with the stock from time to time. Remove the celery from the pan with a perforated spoon and place in a serving dish. Drain the cooking liquor into a small pan and add 1 × 5ml spoon meat glaze (p397) if available. Boil the liquor rapidly until it is reduced to a thin glaze, and then pour it over the celery. The mirepoix can be served as a separate vegetable dish, sprinkled with chopped parsley.

Chard
See Swiss Chard (p803).

Chestnuts

Chestnuts make an excellent winter vegetable, either served on their own, or added to other vegetables (see Brussels Sprouts with Chestnuts, p758). They are available from October to January.

To buy: Allow 150–200g per person. Choose chestnuts which are a good size and are dark brown with a smooth skin.

To store: Chestnuts can be stored for several weeks in a cool, dry vegetable rack or larder.

To prepare: For all recipes, chestnuts must first be peeled. Using a sharp knife, make a small slit in

the rounded side of the shell of each chestnut. Put into a pan of boiling water for 5 minutes, drain, and peel while still very hot. Alternatively, the chestnuts can be put on a baking tray in a hot oven, 220°C, Gas 7, for 5–10 minutes and then peeled.

To boil: Chestnuts can be boiled in salted water, but most frequently veal, chicken or beef stock is used. Put the chestnuts into a pan of stock and cook gently for about 20 minutes or until tender. Drain thoroughly, turn into a serving dish, and season with pepper, preferably freshly ground. Toss in butter and sprinkle with chopped parsley.

To purée: Boil the chestnuts in stock, as above, and drain, reserving the cooking liquor. Sieve the chestnuts or process in an electric blender. To 1kg unpeeled chestnuts, add 2 × 10ml spoons butter, 2 × 15ml spoons single cream, and enough cooking liquor to give a smooth purée. Season to taste and pile into a vegetable dish. If the purée is not to be eaten immediately, dot the top surface with butter to prevent a crust forming. The purée can also be mixed with an equal quantity of potato purée.

Chestnuts with Sweet and Sour Sauce

4 helpings

600g chestnuts	*1 × 15ml spoon sugar*
25g butter **or** *margarine*	*2 × 15ml spoons*
25g flour	*sultanas*
2 × 15ml spoons white	*salt and pepper*
vinegar	

Peel the chestnuts and boil in plenty of water until tender. Drain, reserving the cooking liquor. Transfer the chestnuts to a serving dish and keep warm. Melt the fat in a pan, stir in the flour, and cook for 1 minute, stirring all the time. Draw off the heat and gradually stir in 250ml of the reserved cooking liquor. Return to the heat and bring to the boil, stirring all the time, until the sauce thickens. Add the vinegar, sugar, and sultanas. Season to taste, and heat gently for 5 minutes. Pour the sauce over the chestnuts and serve hot.

Cooking time – 35 minutes (approx)

Braised Chestnuts

6 helpings

1kg chestnuts	*1 blade of mace*
1 small onion	*salt*
2 cloves	*a pinch of Cayenne*
1 stick of celery	*pepper*
500ml brown stock	*1 × 10ml spoon meat*
(p329)	*glaze (p397) if*
1 bay leaf	*available*

Garnish
fleurons of puff pastry
(p399)

Peel the chestnuts. Skin the onion and press the cloves into it. Wash or wipe the celery and chop it roughly. Bring the stock to the boil, add the chestnuts, onion, celery, bay leaf and mace, season with salt, and add the Cayenne pepper. Cover and simmer for about 30 minutes or until the chestnuts are tender. Strain the chestnuts, reserving the cooking liquor, and keep hot. Return the liquor to the pan, add the meat glaze if available, and boil the liquor rapidly until it is reduced to a thin glaze. Pour it over the chestnuts and garnish with fleurons of puff pastry.

Chicory

People sometimes confuse chicory with endive because its French name is *endive*. Chicory is, however, a clump of fleshy white leaves with yellow tips, widely used raw in salads. It is also served as a side vegetable and is available from September to May.

To buy: Allow 1 large or 2 small heads per person (75–100g approx). Buy chicory which looks fresh and has no withered stems. The ends should be yellow, not green; green ends tend to be very bitter.

To store: Chicory can be kept for 2–3 days in a cool, dry vegetable rack or larder, or for up to a week in a polythene bag in the bottom of a refrigerator.

To prepare: Cut a slice off the base and remove a few outer leaves. Wash thoroughly in cold water. To reduce the bitterness, first blanch the chicory for 5 minutes in boiling water, and then drain and cook as required. Do not leave chicory standing once it has been cut because it tends to discolour.

To boil: Blanch the chicory as above. Cook in a very little boiling salted water for 15–20 minutes or until just tender. Drain thoroughly and season with pepper. Spoon a little melted butter over it or serve with a white or cheese sauce.

To braise: Blanch the chicory as above. Cook as for braised celery.

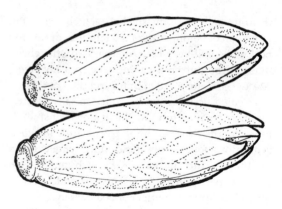

Chicory and Ham

6 helpings

12 small heads chicory	50g Cheddar cheese **or** grated Parmesan cheese
12 thin slices ham	
fat for greasing	25g dried white breadcrumbs
375ml cheese sauce (p693)	25g butter **or** margarine

Prepare the chicory, blanch, and cook in boiling salted water until tender. Drain and dry each head in a cloth. Wrap each head in a slice of ham and place in a lightly greased 1.5 litre ovenproof dish. Pour the cheese sauce over it. Grate the Cheddar cheese, if used. Mix the cheese with the breadcrumbs, and sprinkle it over the sauce. Melt the fat and spoon it over the top. Bake in a fairly hot oven, 190°C, Gas 5, for 20–30 minutes until golden-brown and piping hot.

Cooking time 1 hour (approx)

Chinese Leaves

Sometimes called Chinese cabbage, this vegetable is in fact more closely related to a swede than a cabbage. It can be used like spinach or lettuce or can be stir-fried. Its merit compared with winter lettuce is that it is crisp and well-hearted, and keeps excellently in a refrigerator for several days or even longer.

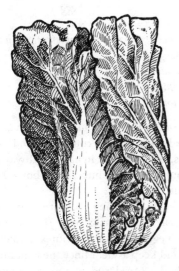

Corn *and* Corn on the Cob

See Sweetcorn (p802).

Courgettes

Courgettes, or *zucchini* as they are also called, are small vegetable marrows, produced by using special strains of seed. They are available all year round, but are generally at their cheapest and best from June to September. Besides being served as a side vegetable, they are also excellent stuffed and served hot or cold as a main course or starter.

To buy: Allow 100–150g per person. Courgettes vary considerably in size from almost finger thickness and length, to 4–5cm in diameter and 25cm long. If they are too thick, however, the flavour will not be as good. The courgettes should be a good green colour, firm to the touch, and not limp.

To store: Courgettes can be kept for several days in a cool, dry vegetable rack or larder.

To prepare: Very small courgettes can be cooked whole. Simply trim off each end, and wash in cold water. Larger courgettes should be trimmed at either end and cut into 1–2cm slices; or they can be trimmed, and then sliced after cooking. To remove some of the excess liquid from slightly older courgettes, especially if frying, place them in a colander, sprinkle with salt, and leave for 30 minutes. Drain and dry thoroughly.

To boil: Cook the courgettes in the minimum of boiling salted water for about 10 minutes or until just tender. Drain thoroughly, season with pepper, and spoon melted butter and some chopped parsley, thyme or tarragon over them. Courgettes can also be served with a white, parsley, or cheese sauce or topped with crisply fried or grilled and roughly chopped or crumbled bacon.

To steam: Courgettes are generally best left whole for steaming. Season with salt and cook in the top of a steamer over a pan of boiling water for 10–20 minutes, depending on the size of the courgettes, until they are just tender. Drain and cut into slices, if large. Serve as for boiled courgettes.

To bake: Leave the courgettes whole and parboil for 5 minutes in boiling salted water. Drain thoroughly. For 500g courgettes, melt 50g butter in an ovenproof dish. Add the courgettes, roll in the butter and season with salt and pepper. Bake for 25 minutes in a fairly hot oven, 190°C, Gas 5.

To shallow fry: Cut the courgettes into slices. For 500g courgettes, melt 50g butter in a frying pan and fry a little chopped onion, if liked, until golden. Add the sliced courgettes and fry until golden-brown, turning frequently. Drain and serve topped with chopped tarragon, thyme or parsley.

To deep fry: Cut the courgettes into slices and parboil for 5 minutes. Drain and dry thoroughly. Coat in batter and fry as for Jerusalem artichokes.

To stew: Cut the courgettes into slices. For 500g courgettes, melt 50g butter in a pan, add the sliced courgettes, and season. Cover the pan and cook over gentle heat for 10–15 minutes, shaking the pan frequently to prevent the courgettes sticking to the bottom. Sprinkle with chopped herbs before serving in the cooking liquor.

Courgettes with Tomatoes

4 helpings

500g courgettes	1 bay leaf
6 spring onions	1 × 15ml spoon chopped
1 clove of garlic	basil
2 × 15ml spoons olive oil	2 × 15ml spoons white
200g tomatoes	wine
1 × 15ml spoon	salt and pepper
concentrated tomato	
purée	

Trim the courgettes and cut into slices. Trim and chop the onions and skin and crush the garlic. Heat the oil in a pan, add the courgettes, spring onions, and garlic, and cook for 5 minutes. Skin the tomatoes, cut in half, and remove the pips. Add to the pan with the tomato purée, bay leaf, basil, white wine, and seasoning. Bring to the boil, cover, and simmer gently for 15 minutes.

Courgettes Stuffed with Bacon

4 helpings

8 courgettes	25g butter **or** margarine
1 large onion	1 × 2.5ml spoon dried
400g collar **or** streaky	mixed herbs
bacon, without rinds	salt and pepper
300g tomatoes (approx)	fat for greasing

Cut a quarter out of each courgette lengthways, making a V-shaped slit; these pieces can be put aside to serve as a vegetable or added to soup. Skin and chop the onion finely. Mince the bacon and skin and chop the tomatoes. Melt the fat in a saucepan and fry the onion for 5 minutes. Add the bacon to the pan and cook for a further 10 minutes. Add the tomatoes, herbs and seasoning, and pile the mixture into the courgettes. Place in a greased ovenproof dish. Cover and bake in a moderate oven, 180°C, Gas 4, for about 45 minutes.

Stuffed Courgettes

4 helpings

1 × 10ml spoon	25g butter for greasing
salt	100g grated Parmesan
1 litre water	cheese
1kg courgettes	chopped herbs

Stuffing

50g onion	1 egg
1 clove of garlic	salt
150g button mushrooms	a pinch of ground mace
50ml cooking oil	black pepper
150g lean ham	
50g soft white	
breadcrumbs	

Add the salt to the water in a saucepan and bring it to the boil. Add the courgettes and cook for 8 minutes. Drain and cut in half lengthways. Scoop out the pulp and put it into a small bowl. Keep the skins aside.

To make the stuffing, prepare and chop the onion, garlic, and mushrooms. Heat the oil and sauté the vegetables for 5 minutes. Remove from the heat and keep aside. Mince the ham finely and mix with the breadcrumbs and courgette pulp. Add to the pan, return to the heat and cook for 3 minutes. Turn the mixture into a large bowl. Beat the egg until liquid and season well with salt, mace, and pepper; then add enough egg to the main mixture to make a paste soft enough to be spooned. Season generously.

Fill the courgette skins with the mixture and level the surfaces. Place on a baking tray well greased with soft butter. Sprinkle the stuffed courgettes with the cheese and bake in a moderate oven, 180°C, Gas 4, for 15–20 minutes until the cheese is melted and golden-brown. Brush once or twice with butter while baking. Sprinkle with chopped herbs, and serve hot.

Serve alone, or with rice or Indian Lentils (p775).

Note Rings of a large marrow, halved small squash, or halved aubergines can be cooked in the same way.

Cucumber

Cucumbers are usually eaten raw in salads or pickled, but they are extremely useful as a side vegetable, and this is a particularly good way of using the outdoor or ridge cucumbers. Cucumbers should not be boiled because they contain a very high percentage of water; they should be either steamed or fried.

To buy: Allow 150–200g per person, or one-third of a large cucumber. Make sure the cucumbers are firm and the skin is not tough and wrinkled.

To store: Cucumbers keep for several days in a cool vegetable rack or larder or in a refrigerator.

To prepare: Hot-house cucumbers can be peeled or not, according to personal choice, but the skin contains much of the flavour and minute amounts of the substances which help the body to digest the cucumber flesh. Outdoor cucumbers generally have a rather tough skin, and these should be peeled. Cut the cucumber into slices or leave whole.

To steam: Either cut the cucumber into slices 5cm thick or leave whole. Season and place in the top of a steamer over a pan of boiling water for 10 minutes, if sliced, or for up to 20 minutes, if whole. Drain thoroughly and cut into slices if the cucumber has been left whole. Season with pepper, preferably freshly ground, and serve topped with melted butter and chopped herbs (dill, tarragon, parsley, mint), with a plain white or cheese sauce or with chopped tarragon, dill or celery seed added, or with Hollandaise sauce (p712).

To bake: Cut the cucumbers into 5cm pieces. Put in an ovenproof dish and cover. Dot the cucumber with butter and sprinkle with a few chopped herbs, if liked. Bake in a fairly hot oven, 190°C, Gas 5, for 30 minutes.

To fry: Cut the cucumbers into slices 2cm thick. Steam as above for 5 minutes, drain, and dry thoroughly. Dredge the cucumber slices lightly with flour and fry in butter or margarine until golden-brown, turning frequently. Drain thoroughly, season with salt and pepper, and serve at once.

Stuffed Cucumbers

6 helpings

2 large cucumbers	*fat* **or** *oil for frying*
salt	*1 × 15ml spoon chopped*
4 slices bread (approx)	*parsley*

Stuffing

200g cooked meat (ham,	*1 egg*
veal, beef **or** *chicken)*	*general household* (p329)
25g butter **or** *margarine*	**or** *chicken stock* (p330)
3 × 15ml spoons soft	*(depending on the meat*
white breadcrumbs	*used)*
1 × 15ml spoon chopped	*pepper*
parsley	*a few drops*
¼ × 5ml spoon dried	*Worcestershire sauce*
mixed herbs	

Cut the cucumbers into 5cm lengths. Scoop the seeds from the centre with a small spoon. Season the cucumbers with salt and steam for 10 minutes until just tender.

Meanwhile, prepare the stuffing. Mince the meat finely. Heat the fat in a pan. Add the meat, breadcrumbs, parsley and mixed herbs, and heat thoroughly. Beat the egg until liquid and add to the pan, together with enough stock to give a soft stuffing. Season well with salt, pepper, and Worcestershire sauce.

Cut the bread into circles, a little larger than the diameter of the cucumber, and allow 1 circle of bread for each piece. Fry the bread in the fat or oil until crisp and golden. Drain thoroughly. Drain the cucumber and stand a piece on each croûte of bread. Pile the hot stuffing into each piece and sprinkle with the parsley.

Serve with Fresh Tomato Sauce (p715).

VARIATIONS
Stuff the cucumbers with one of the following:
1) 3 hard-boiled eggs, chopped and mixed with 250ml thick cheese sauce (p693)
2) 200g macédoine of vegetables (p398) in 250ml thick cheese sauce (p693)
3) For a vegetarian main meal, replace the meat with 200g finely chopped mushrooms and a finely chopped onion, and use vegetable stock.

Dandelion Leaves

Dandelion leaves must be young and tender and are at their best in the spring. If the leaves are growing in your garden, they should be covered with a pot 2–3 days before they are to be picked; this blanching avoids bitterness. Prepare and cook the leaves as for spinach.

Dulse

See Seaweed (p799).

Endive

Endive, pronounced in the English way, should not be confused with chicory which is known in France as *endive*. Endive is a green vegetable, resembling a curly lettuce, which is generally used in winter salads. It is in season from November to March.

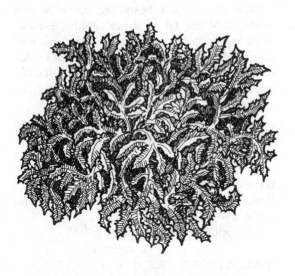

To buy: Allow 1 small or half a large endive per person. Choose endive with a good yellow heart and not too many discoloured, tough outer leaves.

To store: Endive is best stored for 2–3 days in a polythene bag in the bottom of a refrigerator.

To prepare: Cut off the stumps and discard any tough, discoloured outer leaves. The very centre of the endive can be removed and served as a salad.

Wash the endive thoroughly in plenty of cold water to remove any dirt, grit, and sand. Because endive tends to be bitter, blanch it for 10 minutes in boiling water and drain thoroughly.

To braise: Blanch the endive as above. Cook as for braised celery.

Stewed Endive

6 helpings

3 large **or** *6 small endive*	*1 × 15ml spoon lemon*
25g butter **or** *margarine*	*juice*
25g flour	*salt and pepper*
375ml white stock	
(p329)	

Prepare and blanch the endive. Drain thoroughly and chop finely. Melt the fat in a saucepan, stir in the flour, and cook for 1 minute, without browning. Draw off the heat and gradually stir in the stock. Return to the heat and bring to the boil, stirring all the time, until the sauce thickens. Add the lemon juice and seasoning. Add the endive, cover, and cook gently for 30 minutes or until the endive is very tender.

Fennel

The bulbous Florence fennel can be used raw in salads or braised; it has a slight aniseed flavour. The part eaten is the swollen stem base, although the leaves can be used in soups and make an attractive feathery garnish for salads.

To buy: Allow 1 small bulb (about 150g) per person. Choose clean white fennel on which any leaf tips are still fresh and green.

To store: Fennel can be stored for 2–3 days in a cool, dry vegetable rack or larder or in the bottom of a refrigerator.

To prepare: Remove the coarse outer sheaths and trim the stalks.

To deep fry: Parboil the fennel for 10 minutes. Drain, dry thoroughly, and cut into slices. Dip the slices in batter and fry as for Jerusalem artichokes. Drain thoroughly and serve with lemon juice.

To braise: Parboil the fennel in boiling salted water for 5 minutes. Drain thoroughly and cook as for braised celery.

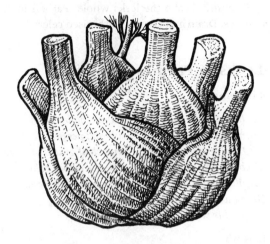

Fungi other than Mushrooms

There are a great many edible fungi besides mushrooms. Some look very like mushrooms, others quite different. Ceps, for instance, have spongy fine tubes instead of gills, and look like glossy buns. All ceps are edible, although any with red or purple on the spores or stalks should be avoided on the whole, since they can cause gastric disorders.

Besides edible fungi, there are many which are poisonous, and some which are extremely dangerous to eat. Like edible fungi, these poisonous ones may look very like mushrooms. *Before gathering and eating any unknown wild fungi, it is wise to consult some knowledgeable person who has used them.*

Kelp
See Seaweed (p799).

Kohlrabi

Kohlrabi, although a root, is really a swollen-stemmed cabbage. It has a flavour between that of a turnip and a swede, and is in season from July to April.

To buy: Allow 150g per person. Choose kohlrabi which is a good purple colour with a smooth skin. Avoid large kohlrabi because it has a coarse flavour, and reject any on which the skin is shrivelled or the leaves are withered.

To store: Kohlrabi does not store well and should be used as soon as possible after buying or picking.

To prepare: Kohlrabi can either be thinly peeled and sliced or diced before cooking, or it can simply be washed, trimmed, and cooked in the skin, which preserves the maximum flavour.

To boil: Cook in boiling salted water for 30 minutes–1 hour, depending on size. Drain, and peel if cooked in the skin. Serve either seasoned with pepper, preferably freshly ground, and with melted butter, or with a cream or Hollandaise sauce.

To steam: Season with salt and cook in the top of a steamer over a pan of boiling water for 45 minutes–1½ hours depending on size. Drain and serve as for boiled kohlrabi.

To braise: Parboil the kohlrabi for 5 minutes. Drain, peel, and cut into quarters. Cook as for braised celery.

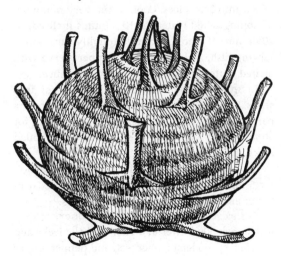

Laver

See Seaweed (p799).

Leeks

Leeks are in season from August to May and as well as being served as a vegetable are also used extensively to flavour soups and casseroles. They can also be served cooked and cold, or blanched and raw in salads.

To buy: Allow 150–200g leeks per person. Choose leeks that are of an even size with fresh-looking green tips and a firm white stem.

To store: Leeks can be kept for 2–3 days in a cool, dry vegetable rack or larder.

To prepare: Leeks need to be cleaned thoroughly because dirt and grit gets between the leaves. First, trim off the leaves, leaving only about 5cm of the green stem. Trim the roots and remove the outer leaves. Push the point of the knife through each leek about 5cm from the top and cut through to the top. Do this a second time, then peel back the leaves and wash the leeks thoroughly under running cold water to remove every speck of dirt. Leeks can also be cut into slices, in which case the vertical cuts are omitted; after slicing, wash thoroughly under running cold water.

To boil: Boiled leeks are apt to be watery so they must be drained thoroughly. Leave the leeks whole or cut into 2cm slices. Cook in the very minimum of boiling salted water for 10 minutes if sliced, or 20 minutes if whole. Drain thoroughly, turn into a serving dish, and season with pepper. Serve with melted butter or with a cheese or white sauce.

To steam: Leave the leeks whole or cut into slices. Season with salt and place in a steamer over a pan of boiling water for 15 minutes if sliced, or for 30 minutes if whole. Drain and serve as for boiled leeks.

To deep fry: Cut the leeks into 2cm slices. Parboil for 5 minutes. Drain and dry thoroughly. Coat in batter and fry as for Jerusalem artichokes.

To stew: Cut the leeks into slices. For every 750g leeks, melt 50g butter in a pan. Add the leeks and 1 × 15ml spoon lemon juice, salt and pepper. Cover the pan and cook the leeks very gently, shaking the pan from time to time, for about 30 minutes or until the leeks are very tender. Serve in the cooking liquor. If liked, 3–4 chopped rashers of bacon can also be cooked with the leeks.

To braise: Leave the leeks whole. Parboil for 5 minutes. Drain and cook as for braised celery.

Leeks in Parmesan Sauce

4 helpings

1kg leeks	150ml single cream
1 litre water	salt and pepper
1 × 10ml spoon salt	a pinch of grated nutmeg
25g butter **or** margarine	1 chicken stock cube
25g plain flour	50g grated Parmesan
300ml well-flavoured	cheese
vegetable stock	

Garnish
1 × 15ml spoon chopped
 parsley and chives,
 mixed

Prepare the leeks and keep them whole; tie up in a bundle. Bring the water and salt to the boil in a saucepan and cook the leeks for 20 minutes, then drain well. Put to one side.

Meanwhile, melt the fat in a small pan, add the flour, and cook for about 4 minutes, stirring until the mixture looks like wet sand. Add the stock gradually, stirring all the time, to make a sauce. Bring to the boil, lower the heat, and stir until the mixture thickens. Stir in the cream, a little salt and pepper, and the nutmeg. Lower the heat, and simmer gently for 5 minutes. Crumble the stock cube into the sauce. Boil for 5 minutes longer. Remove from the heat, and scatter in half the grated cheese. Untie the bundle of leeks. Put in a long, shallow, flameproof dish and cover with the sauce. Sprinkle with the remaining cheese, and brown under the grill for 5–6 minutes. Sprinkle the herbs on top just before serving.

Baked Leek Casserole

4 helpings

8 large leeks	*a few drops lemon juice*
1 small onion	*a pinch of sugar*
75g butter **or** *margarine*	*salt and pepper*
tomato juice	
a few drops	
Worcestershire sauce	

Prepare the leeks and keep them whole. Skin the onion and chop it finely. Melt 50g of the fat and fry the leeks and onion until the leeks are just gilded and the onion is transparent. Transfer to an oven-proof casserole which will hold the leeks in 2 layers. Pour enough tomato juice into the casserole to half cover the leeks. Stir in the Worcestershire sauce, lemon juice, and sugar. Season well. Dot with the rest of the fat. Cover the casserole securely, and bake in a fairly hot oven, 190°C, Gas 5, for 1 hour. Serve with the cooking liquor.

Note This recipe can also be used for small heads of celery.

Lentils

There are several kinds of lentils. The most common are pink or red; these form a purée as soon as they are cooked. If whole lentils are required, the green or brown variety must be used. The best (and most expensive) lentils are the black *lentilles de Puy* which come from the Auvergne in France.

Lentils are excellent served cold in salads.

To buy: Allow 50g lentils per person.

To prepare: Lentils do not need long soaking like peas and beans, but they can profitably be soaked for 1–2 hours before cooking.

To boil: Put the lentils into a pan and cover with cold water or stock. A small skinned onion, a few parsley stalks, or a bouquet garni, a ham bone, or a few bacon rinds can be added to give extra flavour. Bring the water to the boil and simmer gently for about 1 hour or until the lentils are quite tender. Drain and remove any herbs and flavouring. Re-season if required, and serve hot. If using the pink lentils, drain and purée them before serving.

Boiled Lentils

4–6 helpings

1 onion	*1 × 2.5ml spoon salt*
1 clove	*½ × 2.5ml spoon pepper*
375g lentils	*25g butter* **or** *margarine*
bouquet garni	*a few grains of chilli*
1 bacon bone	*powder (optional)*

Skin the onion, press the clove into it, and put into cold water with the lentils, bouquet garni, bone, salt, and pepper. Bring to the boil and cook for about 1 hour or until the lentils are soft. Strain the lentils and remove the bouquet garni, bone, and onion. Heat the fat in a pan, add the lentils and chilli powder, if used, and stir for 2–3 minutes.

Note If preferred, the lentils can be sieved before adding to the fat.

Indian Lentils

4 helpings

225g red, black **or** *green lentils*	*50g clarified butter* **or** *margarine* (p886)
375ml (approx) vegetable stock	*1 × 15ml spoon curry powder*
2 medium-sized onions	

Put the lentils into a pan and cover with the stock. Bring to the boil, reduce the heat and simmer gently until they are tender; add a little more stock, if necessary, but the lentils should absorb it all by the end of the cooking time. Skin and slice the onions. Melt the fat in a large frying pan, and fry the onion slices until they are lightly browned all over; stir and turn them while cooking. Sprinkle in the curry powder, stir for a few minutes, then add the lentils. Cover and cook very gently for about 20 minutes, stirring from time to time.

Note This is an attractive dish to use instead of potatoes or pasta, for plain grilled or fried meats or for plainly cooked mixed green and root vegetables. Choose lentils which contrast in colour with the other foods served with them.

Cooking time 1¼ hours (approx)

Spiced Lentils

4–6 helpings

450g red lentils
1 litre water
1 × 2.5ml spoon sea salt
  or *1 × 5ml spoon table*
  salt
1 onion
1 × 5ml spoon turmeric
1 × 5ml spoon crushed
  ginger root **or** *ground*
  ginger

3 tomatoes
2 whole cardamoms
3 × 15ml spoons cooking
  oil
1 × 5ml spoon crushed
  garlic
1 × 5ml spoon ground
  coriander
a pinch of chilli powder

Garnish
chopped fresh coriander
  leaves

finely chopped **or** *grated*
  onion

Put the lentils into a large pan and cover with the water and salt. Bring to the boil, reduce the heat, and simmer for 30–45 minutes until tender. Drain and put to one side.

Meanwhile, skin and chop the onion, and mix with the turmeric and ginger. Chop the tomatoes, and crush the cardamoms in a pestle and mortar, or grind in a coffee or nut mill. Heat the oil in a large deep frying pan, add the onion, ginger and turmeric, and fry gently until soft and lightly browned. Add the tomatoes and all the remaining ingredients, and fry for 3–4 minutes, stirring all the time. Remove from the heat.

Add the lentils to the mixture in the pan, and mix thoroughly to coat them with oil. Replace over moderate heat, and cook until well heated through and quite mushy. Serve very hot, sprinkled with the coriander leaves and onion.

Note Although hot and spicy, this dish is not as hot as a curry. It can be served as an accompaniment to any pasta, pulse or plainly cooked root vegetable dish, or with a green vegetable salad as a main-course dish.

Lettuce

Although generally used raw as a salad ingredient, lettuces can also be served as a cooked vegetable, provided they are well-hearted or have crisp outer leaves. Cos lettuce is particularly good.

1

2

To buy: Choose fresh, green lettuces and allow 1 small lettuce per person. Alternatively, use the outside leaves of 2 lettuces and reserve the hearts for salads.

To store: Lettuces can be kept for 1–2 days in a cool, dry vegetable rack or larder or in a polythene bag in a refrigerator.

To prepare: Remove the very outside leaves of the lettuce. Trim off the root and wash the lettuce well in plenty of cold water to remove all the dirt and sand.

To stew: For 4 lettuces, melt 50g butter or margarine in a wide pan. Add the lettuces and season with salt. Cover the pan and stew for about 30 minutes or until the lettuces are very tender. Season to taste with salt and pepper before serving.

To braise: Make each lettuce into a neat bundle by tying the loose leaf tops together with fine string. Blanch the bundles for 5 minutes in boiling salted water and drain thoroughly. Cook as for braised celery.

1 Soft-leaved lettuce; 2 Cos lettuce; 3 Webb's Wonderful lettuce

Lettuce with Herb Sauce

6 helpings

6 small lettuces	*1 × 10ml spoon chopped*
salt	*chives*
25g butter or margarine	*1 bay leaf*
25g flour	*1 × 10ml spoon chopped*
250ml chicken or	*parsley*
vegetable stock	*pepper*

Trim and wash the lettuces. Plunge into boiling salted water for 2 minutes and then drain. Refresh in cold water and drain thoroughly. Melt the fat in a saucepan. Stir in the flour and cook for 1 minute without browning, stirring all the time. Draw off the heat and gradually stir in the stock. Return to the heat and bring to the boil, stirring all the time, until the sauce thickens. Add the herbs and seasoning and then add the lettuces. Cover and cook gently for 30 minutes, stirring from time to time. Remove the bay leaf. Re-season if required before serving.

Marrow
See Vegetable Marrow (p806); Courgettes (p769).

Mooli
See Radishes (p798).

Mushrooms

Cultivated mushrooms are available throughout the year. There are three main types which are all grown from the same spore, the only difference being their age. The youngest mushrooms are the small round button ones in which the underneath of the mushroom touches the stalks; cup mushrooms are slightly larger and flatter but still have a lip on the underside; the larger, flat mushrooms are the oldest and have the strongest flavour. For pale sauces, it is always best to use button or cup mushrooms because the black underside of flat mushrooms will discolour a sauce.

As for wild mushrooms, field mushrooms are similar to cultivated mushrooms. They can be cooked in all the same ways and are particularly good grilled or stuffed.

Although the whole of any mushroom can be used, the stalks are sometimes removed for appearance's sake or for easier cooking (eg stuffed mushrooms) and are used separately for flavouring sauces, casseroles, or for duxelles (p290).

Button mushrooms are also available in cans and make a very useful standby. Button and cup mushrooms can be bought frozen.

For fungi other than mushrooms, see p773.

To buy: Allow 50–75g per person. Mushrooms should look fresh and moist, and the tops should be creamy white.

To store: Mushrooms should be eaten on the day of purchase, but they can be kept for a day in the bottom of a refrigerator.

To prepare: Cultivated mushrooms should not be peeled. Simply wipe with a damp cloth, or wash if they are very dirty, and trim a slice off the stalk ends. Either leave the mushrooms whole or cut them into slices, halves or quarters, depending on their size and how you wish to serve them.

To boil: Mushrooms are not generally boiled because their flavour is better when fried, grilled or baked, but this is a good method for slimmers. Cook the mushrooms in the minimum of boiling salted water, with a good squeeze of lemon juice, for about 5 minutes. Drain thoroughly and serve seasoned with black pepper, preferably freshly ground, and sprinkled with chopped parsley or chives.

To bake: Place the mushrooms in a greased oven-proof dish and dot with butter or margarine. Season with salt and pepper and a little powdered mace, grated nutmeg or chopped lemon thyme. Cover, and bake in a fairly hot oven, 190°C, Gas 5, for 25–30 minutes. Serve the mushrooms either in the dish in which they were cooked, or transfer them to a serving dish together with all the juices.

To grill: Grilling is suitable for flat or large cup mushrooms. Remove the stalks; these can be put into the grill pan under the rack and will cook in the juices from the caps. Brush both surfaces of the mushrooms with oil or dot with butter or margarine; season with salt and pepper. Place the mushrooms on the rack of the grill pan and cook under a moderate grill for about 5 minutes or until the mushrooms are very tender, turning once, and basting with fat several times to prevent them drying out. Serve with the juices collected in the grill pan.

To fry: For every 100g mushrooms, heat 25g butter, margarine or lard, or 2 × 15ml spoons oil in a frying pan. Fry the mushrooms for about 5 minutes or until they are very tender. Season with salt and black pepper, preferably freshly ground. Serve together with the cooking liquid, sprinkled with chopped parsley, chives or lemon thyme. A squeeze of lemon juice added to the pan also improves the flavour.

To deep fry: Whole button mushrooms are excellent deep-fried. Using 125g mushrooms, coat in batter, and fry as for Jerusalem artichokes.

Note For mushroom purée, see p398.

Mushrooms with Wine

6 helpings

400g button mushrooms
6 rashers streaky bacon,
  without rinds
1 × 5ml spoon chopped
  chives
1 × 5ml spoon chopped
  parsley

1 × 10ml spoon flour
5 × 15ml spoons white
  wine **or** *cider*
salt and pepper

Clean the mushrooms and leave whole or cut into halves or quarters. Chop the bacon and cook gently in a pan for 10 minutes or until the fat has run out and the bacon is pale golden. Add the mushrooms, chives and parsley, and toss in the bacon fat. Sprinkle the flour over the mushrooms, then add the wine or cider. Cook gently for a further 10 minutes, stirring from time to time. Season to taste before serving.

Mushrooms with Brown Sauce

4–6 helpings

300g mushrooms
1 medium-sized onion
50g dripping
25g flour

250ml vegetable **or** *beef*
  stock
1 × 15ml spoon sherry
salt and pepper

Garnish
1 × 15ml spoon chopped
  parsley

Clean and slice the mushrooms and skin and chop the onion. Melt the dripping in a saucepan and fry the mushrooms and onion together for 10 minutes. Remove the vegetables from the pan with a perforated spoon and put to one side. Stir the flour into the fat remaining in the pan and cook over low heat, stirring all the time, until the flour is well browned. Draw off the heat and gradually stir in the stock. Return to the heat and bring to the boil, stirring all the time, until the mixture thickens. Replace the mushrooms and onion, add the sherry, and season to taste. Simmer gently for 5 minutes. Turn into a serving dish and garnish with the parsley.

Mushrooms with Cheese

6 helpings

400g flat mushrooms
butter **or** *margarine for*
  greasing
salt and pepper
1 × 15ml spoon chopped
  chives
1 × 15ml spoon chopped
  parsley

1 × 15ml spoon soft
  white breadcrumbs
2 × 15ml spoons grated
  Parmesan cheese
25g butter

Clean the mushrooms and remove the stalks. These can be cooked with the caps or kept and used as a flavouring in another dish. Place the mushrooms, gills uppermost, in a greased ovenproof dish and season. Sprinkle with the chives and parsley. Mix the breadcrumbs and cheese together and sprinkle them over the mushrooms. Melt the butter and sprinkle it over the top. Bake, uncovered, in a fairly hot oven, 190°C, Gas 5, for 25 minutes.

Stewed Mushrooms with Cream

6 helpings

400g button mushrooms
50g butter **or** *margarine*
1 × 10ml spoon
  arrowroot
125ml chicken **or**
  vegetable stock

1 × 15ml spoon lemon
  juice
2 × 15ml spoons double
  or *single cream*
salt and pepper

Garnish
1 × 15ml spoon chopped
  parsley

fleurons of puff pastry
  (p399)

Clean the mushrooms and leave them whole. Melt the fat in a pan and fry the mushrooms very slowly without browning for 10 minutes. Blend the arrowroot with the stock. Add to the pan and bring the mixture to the boil, stirring all the time. Simmer gently for 20 minutes. Stir in the lemon juice, cream and seasoning, and heat gently without boiling. Re-season if required before serving. Garnish with the parsley and fleurons of puff pastry.

Note This mixture may be used to fill small French rolls, as with Asparagus Croustades (p747).

Stuffed Mushrooms

6 helpings

12 large flat mushrooms	1 × 10ml spoon grated
fat for greasing	Parmesan cheese
1 medium-sized onion	1 × 10ml spoon chopped
25g butter **or** margarine	parsley
50g cooked ham	white wine
1 × 15ml spoon soft	salt and pepper
white breadcrumbs	

Clean the mushrooms and remove the stalks. Place the caps in a well-greased ovenproof dish, gills uppermost, and chop the stalks finely. Skin and chop the onion finely. Melt the fat in a pan and fry the mushroom stalks and onion gently for 5 minutes. Chop the ham finely and add to the onion mixture together with the breadcrumbs, cheese, and parsley. Add enough white wine to just bind the mixture together, and season well. Divide the stuffing mixture between the mushroom caps. Cover and bake in a fairly hot oven, 190°C, Gas 5, for 25 minutes.

Note If liked, the mushrooms can be served on croûtes of toast or fried bread.

Nettles

Young nettles make an excellent summer vegetable, but gloves must be worn for both collecting and preparing them. Choose only the young, tender tops of the nettles, wash thoroughly, and cook as for spinach. Use also to make Nettle soup (p356).

Okra

This is an aromatic bean, native to the West Indies where it is known as Gumbo or Ladies' Fingers. It is now grown in other parts of the world, however, including India, West Africa, and the Mediterranean countries. The young green pods are sometimes pickled and the older pods preserved in cans for export. Okra has an unusual flavour and a large amount of gum exudes from the pods when they are cooked. Okra is used extensively in Indian curries.

To buy: Allow 75–100g per person. Choose young okra which are bright green in colour. They should not appear at all yellowed or limp.

To store: Okra should be eaten as fresh as possible, but can be stored for 2–3 days in a cool vegetable rack or larder or in the bottom of a refrigerator.

To prepare: Wash the okra in cold water, but do not trim or remove the stems.

To boil: Cook the okra in boiling salted water for about 15 minutes until just tender. Drain thoroughly and turn into a serving dish. For every 400g okra, melt 50g butter in a pan, add 2 × 15ml spoons single cream and pour this over the okra. Season with salt and pepper and serve. Canned okra can be served in the same way, or simply heated, tossed in melted butter, and seasoned to taste.

To braise: Parboil for 5 minutes. Drain thoroughly and cook as for braised celery.

Scalloped Okra and Tomatoes

6 helpings

300g okra	*25g flour*
milk	*2 × 15ml spoons soft*
200g tomatoes	*white breadcrumbs*
salt and pepper	
3 × 15ml spoons butter	
or *margarine*	

Wash the okra and cook in boiling salted water for 15 minutes. Drain, reserving the cooking liquor. Make the liquor up to 250ml with milk, if necessary. Cut the okra into small pieces and slice the tomatoes. Divide the okra and tomatoes between 6 scallop shells or small ramekin dishes. Season with salt and pepper. Melt 2 × 15ml spoons of the fat in a pan. Stir in the flour and cook for 1 minute without browning, stirring all the time. Draw off the heat and gradually stir in the cooking liquor and milk. Return to the heat and bring to the boil, stirring all the time, until the sauce thickens. Re-season if required. Pour this over the okra and tomatoes. Sprinkle with the breadcrumbs and dot with the remaining fat. Bake in a fairly hot oven, 190°C, Gas 5, for 15–20 minutes. Serve hot in the scallop shells or ramekin dishes.

Okra and Aubergine

6 helpings

400g okra	*salt*
150g aubergine (approx)	*1 × 15ml spoon chopped*
100g tomatoes	*parsley*
1 medium-sized onion	*pepper*
25g butter **or** *margarine*	

Wash the okra and cut into slices. Peel the aubergine and cut into 2cm cubes. Skin and slice the tomatoes and skin and chop the onion finely. Melt the fat in a pan. Add the okra, aubergine, tomatoes, onion, and salt. Cover and simmer gently for 40 minutes, stirring frequently to prevent the mixture sticking to the bottom. Add the parsley, re-season if required, and serve.

Onions

Onions are used mostly as a flavouring for sauces, soups, stews, casseroles and stuffings, although they make an excellent vegetable dish and can be cooked in various ways. Small pickling onions, or button onions as they are also called, are available from July to October, while main-crop onions grown in the UK are in season from September to March. Imported onions are available during the summer, and Spanish onions are generally available throughout the year. These are large onions with a mild flavour which originally came from Spain, although they are now grown in many other parts of the world. Spring onions, which are a mild small onion used mainly in salads, are also available throughout the year, although they are much scarcer in winter.

To buy: When serving as a side vegetable, allow 1 large or 2 medium-sized onions (150–200g) per person. Choose onions which are firm with a smooth skin. They should not have wrinkled skins or be at all soft since this generally indicates that they are bad inside. Avoid buying onions which have already begun to sprout.

To store: Onions keep well for several months in a cool, dry vegetable rack or larder, especially in winter. If you have sufficient storage space, it can be quite economical to buy a sack of onions in the autumn, when they are generally cheaper, so that some are always to hand.

To prepare: For certain methods of cooking, onions are cooked in their skins, but they are generally skinned and either left whole, chopped, or cut into rings.

To chop an onion, first cut it in half lengthways. Lay the flat surface on a chopping board and make 3 or 4 horizontal cuts, stopping about 1cm from the root. Holding the root end, make about 6 cuts at right angles to the root, but stopping 1cm short, then cut the onion across into small pieces. To prevent onions making you cry while preparing them, either skin the onions under running cold water or skin them under water, and then place them in cold water straight away.

To boil: Skin the onions but leave them whole. If you do not like a very strong flavour, blanch the onions first by putting them into a pan of cold water. Bring to the boil, boil for 1 minute, and then drain. Cook the onions in the minimum of boiling salted water for 20–25 minutes for button onions, for 45–50 minutes for medium-sized onions, and for up to $1\frac{1}{4}$ hours for large onions. Drain the onions thoroughly and serve topped with melted butter or with a white sauce made from half milk and half stock from cooking the onions. Onions can also be boiled in their skins, which colours the cooking water pale pink and helps to preserve the nutritional value of the onion.

To bake (Method 1): Skin medium-sized or large onions, but leave them whole. Parboil in boiling salted water for 20 minutes. Drain thoroughly. Place in a shallow, greased ovenproof dish. Season with salt and pepper and dot with butter. Pour in enough milk to come half-way up the onions. Cover and bake in a moderate oven, 180°C, Gas 4, for 45 minutes–1 hour or until the onions are very tender. Serve with the cooking liquor, which can be thickened with a little cornflour or arrowroot, if liked.

To bake (Method 2): Top and tail medium-sized or large onions, but leave the skins on. Parboil, if very large, for 20 minutes; drain and dry thoroughly. Wrap each onion in a piece of well-buttered greaseproof paper and place in an ovenproof dish. Bake in a moderate oven, 180°C, Gas 4, for $1–1\frac{1}{4}$ hours. Peel the onions before serving with butter and grated nutmeg.

To bake (Method 3): Place unpeeled medium-sized to large onions on a baking tray and bake in a fairly hot oven, 200°C, Gas 6, for $1\frac{1}{2}$ hours or until tender. Remove from the oven and carefully skin. Place in a serving dish and dot with butter, salt, pepper, and a little grated nutmeg, if liked.

To shallow fry: Skin the onions and cut into rings. For every 400g onions, melt 25g butter, margarine or lard, or heat 2×15ml spoons oil in a pan. Fry the onions gently for about 30 minutes, turning them frequently until they are golden-brown. Season well, drain, and serve hot. A little chopped thyme or sage or a few caraway seeds can also be fried with the onions.

To deep fry: Skin the onions, slice into rings, and separate. Dip the onion rings in a little milk and then toss in seasoned flour. Fry the onion rings in deep oil or fat (p302) until golden-brown and crisp. Drain on soft kitchen paper and serve hot. Onion rings can also be dipped in batter and fried as for Jerusalem artichokes.

To stew: Skin and blanch the onions as above. Put into a pan just large enough to hold them all upright. For 6 large onions, pour over 500ml brown stock (p329) and add a bouquet garni. Cover and simmer gently for $1\frac{1}{2}$ hours. Re-season if required, and serve the onions with the cooking liquor.

To braise: Skin the onions but leave them whole. Parboil for 5 minutes. Drain thoroughly. Cook as for braised celery.

Glazed Onions

4 helpings

400g button onions	*25g butter*
chicken stock	*a pinch of grated nutmeg*
salt and pepper	
1 × 15ml spoon light soft brown sugar	

Skin the onions and put them in a saucepan into which they just fit in one layer. Add just enough stock to cover them. Heat to simmering point, and simmer for 15–20 minutes until the onions are just tender, adding a very little extra hot stock if needed. When the onions are ready, the stock should be reduced almost to a glaze. Remove from the heat, and add the rest of the ingredients. Turn the onions over with a spoon to blend the extra seasonings well with the stock and to coat the onions. Return to the heat, and shake the onions in the pan, until the glaze and fat give them a shiny brown coating. Serve at once, with the remaining syrupy glaze.

Note Glazed onions are often used as a garnish.

Onions and Apples

4 helpings

300g onions	1 × 10ml spoon sugar
400g cooking apples	salt and pepper
3 × 15ml spoons butter	
or margarine	

Skin and blanch the onions. Drain and cut them into rings. Peel, core, and slice the apples. Melt the fat in a pan and add the onions, apples and sugar. Cover and simmer gently for about 30 minutes or until tender. Season to taste and serve.

Stuffed Onions

6 helpings

6 large onions	salt and pepper
75g cooked liver, ham **or**	beaten egg
any other cooked meat	2 × 10ml spoons butter
2 × 15ml spoons soft	**or** margarine
white breadcrumbs	375ml foundation brown
1 × 2.5ml spoon finely	sauce (p698)
chopped sage	

Parboil the onions in their skins for 45 minutes or until they are almost tender. Drain, skin, and remove the centres with a teaspoon. Chop the onion centres finely. Chop or mince the cooked meat finely and add to the chopped onion with the breadcrumbs, sage, and seasoning. Bind the stuffing together with enough beaten egg to give a fairly firm mixture. Divide between the hollows in the onions. (A band of stiff paper can be tied round each onion to prevent it splitting, but this is not essential.) Dot the tops of the onions with the fat and bake, uncovered, in a moderate oven, 180°C, Gas 4, for 45 minutes, or until tender. Serve with the brown sauce poured round them.

Creamed Onions

6–8 helpings

1kg small onions	salt and pepper
100ml double cream	50g butter
Béchamel sauce (p704)	50g dried white
using 300ml milk	breadcrumbs
grated nutmeg	chopped parsley

Skin the onions and cook in salted water for 10–15 minutes until just tender. Drain well. Add the double cream to the Béchamel sauce, and reheat gently without boiling. Add the nutmeg and salt and pepper to taste. Grease a 2 litre casserole with a little of the butter, put the sauce and the onions in the casserole, and mix well. Dot the top of the mixture with the remaining butter and the breadcrumbs, and bake in a warm oven, 160°C, Gas 3, for 20 minutes. Serve hot, sprinkled with chopped parsley.

Italian Onions

6 helpings

600g button onions	4 white peppercorns
2 × 15ml spoons olive oil	2 × 15ml spoons white
2 bay leaves	wine vinegar
2 cloves	1 × 15ml spoons sugar

Cook the onions in their skins in boiling salted water until they are just tender. Drain and skin them. Heat the oil in a saucepan and add the bay leaves, cloves, and peppercorns. Shake these in the oil for a few minutes. Add the skinned onions and cook very gently for 5 minutes. Stir in the vinegar and sugar and continue cooking until the liquid is reduced to a syrup. Serve hot.

Cooking time 40–45 minutes

Onions in Cheese Sauce

6 helpings

6 large onions
375ml thick cheese sauce
  (693) using half milk
  and half onion stock

2 × 15ml spoons grated
  Cheddar cheese

Skin the onions and cook them in boiling salted water until tender; drain thoroughly. Put into a serving dish and pour the cheese sauce over them. Sprinkle with the cheese. Brown under a moderate grill or put into a hot oven, 220°C, Gas 7, for 10 minutes. Serve hot.

Onions in Cider with Tomatoes

6 helpings

6 large onions
200g tomatoes
50g butter **or** margarine
2 bay leaves

2 cloves
2 × 15ml spoons cider
250ml vegetable stock
salt and pepper

Skin and blanch the onions. Drain and cut them into rings. Skin and slice the tomatoes. Melt the fat in a pan. Add the onion rings and fry gently until golden. Add the tomatoes, bay leaves, cloves, cider, and stock. Cover and simmer gently for 45 minutes. Season to taste and serve with the cooking liquor.

Onions in Sherry

4–6 helpings

1kg onions
500g tomatoes
200g green peppers

4 × 15ml spoons olive oil
salt
125ml dry sherry

Skin and chop the onions and tomatoes. Remove the membranes and seeds from the peppers and chop the flesh. Heat the oil in a pan, add the onions, and fry gently for 10 minutes or until pale golden. Add the peppers and fry for a further 5 minutes. Add the tomatoes, salt, and sherry. Cover and cook gently for 45 minutes.

Parsnips

Parsnips are in season from September to April, but are generally better when there has been a slight frost on the ground. They are an extremely useful winter vegetable and are excellent roasted with potatoes around a joint, or puréed and served on their own.

To buy: Allow 150g parsnips per person. Choose parsnips that are firm to the touch; the skins should not appear shrivelled and wrinkled.

To store: Parsnips can be stored for several days in a cool larder or vegetable rack, but are better eaten as soon as possible after purchase.

To prepare: Peel and trim the parsnips and either cut into slices, or cut into quarters lengthways according to the method of cooking. Remove any hard core from the quarters.

To boil: Like carrots, parsnips should be cooked in the minimum of water to give the best flavour and to preserve all the vitamins. For 600g parsnips, melt 25g butter or margarine in a heavy-based pan. Add the thinly sliced parsnips and cook very gently for 10 minutes, shaking the pan frequently so that they do not stick to the bottom. Pour approximately 100ml boiling salted water over them, cover the pan, and cook the parsnips for a further 15–20 minutes or until they are very tender. Serve with the cooking liquor and sprinkle liberally with chopped parsley or chopped lemon thyme.

To steam: Steam only young parsnips. Cut into quarters, season with salt, and steam in the top of a double saucepan over a pan of boiling water for 35 minutes or until very tender. Drain and season with black pepper, preferably freshly ground, spoon melted butter over them, and sprinkle with chopped parsley.

To roast: Cut the parsnips into quarters lengthways. Parboil in boiling salted water for 10 minutes. Drain and dry thoroughly. Heat a little dripping in a roasting tin. Add the parsnips and roll in the hot dripping or put into the dripping in a pan around a roast joint. Roast in a fairly hot oven, 190°–200°C, Gas 5–6, for 45 minutes–1 hour or until tender and golden-brown.

To deep fry (Method 1): Cut the parsnips into thin slices. Parboil for 10 minutes and drain thoroughly.

Coat in batter and fry as for Jerusalem artichokes.

To deep fry (Method 2): Cut the parsnips into paper-thin slices. Dry thoroughly and fry in deep fat as for game chips (p302).

To purée: Parsnips make an excellent purée, either on their own or mixed with carrots or mashed potato. Boil or steam the parsnips as above and sieve, mash, or process in an electric blender together with the cooking liquor. Add 25g butter, season with salt and pepper, preferably freshly ground, and add a little cream or top of the milk, if wished. Sprinkle with plenty of chopped parsley before serving.

Parsnip and Apple Casserole

6 helpings

400g parsnips	*1 × 15ml spoon lemon*
200ml apple sauce	*juice*
fat for greasing	*75g butter*
75g brown sugar	*75g soft white*
salt	*breadcrumbs*
1 × 2.5ml spoon grated	*½ × 2.5ml spoon paprika*
nutmeg	

Prepare and boil or steam the parsnips. Mash or sieve them. Arrange with the apple sauce in layers in a greased casserole. Sprinkle each layer with brown sugar, salt, nutmeg, lemon juice, and flakes of butter. Top with the breadcrumbs and sprinkle with paprika. Cook in a fairly hot oven, 190°C, Gas 5, for 30 minutes.

Cooking time 1 hour (approx)

Peas

Fresh peas are in season from May to September, although imported peas can be found at other times and mange-tout peas are available throughout the year. Peas freeze extremely well, and both frozen and canned peas are easily obtainable.

To buy: When buying fresh peas, allow 300–400g per person, depending on the fullness of the pods. It is not always easy to buy good, fresh peas because the majority of the best crops are bought straight from the fields by large food companies for freezing. The peas should be a good green colour and the pods should appear moist. The peas should be starting to fill the pod and, if eaten raw, should taste sweet and juicy. Do not buy peas which have been allowed to grow too large because they will be dry and unpleasant.

To store: Peas should be eaten as fresh as possible, but can be kept for 1–2 days in a cool vegetable rack or larder or in the bottom of a refrigerator.

To prepare: Shell the peas and, if preparing them in advance, cover with the washed pods to keep them moist. The pods can be kept to make soup.

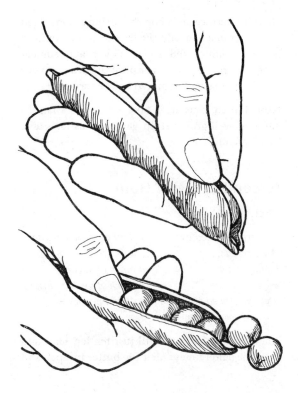

To boil: The peas should be cooked in the minimum of boiling salted water. Bring a pan of salted water to the boil and add a sprig of mint or chervil and a pinch of sugar, if liked. Add the peas and cook gently for about 10 minutes or until the peas are just tender. Do not overcook peas because this toughens them. Drain thoroughly and turn into a serving dish. Season with black pepper, preferably freshly ground, and dot with butter. Serve as soon as possible after cooking.

To steam: Shell the peas and season with salt. Cook in the top of a steamer over a pan of boiling water for 15–20 minutes or until tender. Drain and serve as for boiled peas.

Petits Pois à la Française

6 helpings

1 lettuce heart	*salt and pepper*
1 bunch spring onions	*a pinch of sugar*
50g butter	
750g fresh shelled **or**	
frozen peas	

Shred the lettuce and chop the spring onions. Melt the butter in a pan, add the lettuce, spring onions, peas, seasoning, and sugar. Cover and simmer gently for 10–15 minutes or until the peas are very tender. Re-season if required before serving.

Note Frozen peas may take even less than 10 minutes; well-grown fresh garden peas may take 20–25 minutes.

Green Peas with Ham

6 helpings

750g fresh shelled **or**	*250ml general household*
frozen peas	*stock* (p329)
½ small onion	*a pinch of sugar*
25g butter	*a pinch of grated nutmeg*
50g lean cooked ham	*salt and pepper*
1 × 5ml spoon flour	

Boil or steam the peas until just tender. Skin and chop the onion finely. Melt the butter in a pan and fry the onion gently until golden. Chop the ham finely and add to the pan with the flour. Cook, stirring, for 1–2 minutes. Add the peas, stock, sugar, and nutmeg. Cover the pan and simmer gently for 10 minutes. Season to taste before serving.

Cooking time 30 minutes (approx)

Mange-tout Peas

These flat pea pods are widely available throughout the year. The word literally means 'eat all' which is what you do; mange-tout can therefore be extremely economical because there is no wastage.

To buy: Allow 50–75g per person. Choose mange-tout that are a good green colour and appear bright and fresh.

To store: They should be eaten as fresh as possible, but can be kept for 1–2 days in the bottom of a refrigerator.

To prepare: Remove the tops and tails of the mange-tout and any strings from the sides of older pods.

To boil: Cook the mange-tout in the very minimum of boiling salted water for about 2–3 minutes or until just tender. Drain thoroughly, turn into a serving dish, and season with pepper, preferably freshly ground. Spoon plenty of melted butter over them and serve as soon as possible.

To steam: Season the mange-tout with salt and cook in the top of a steamer over a pan of boiling water for 5 minutes. Drain and serve as for boiled mange-tout.

To stew: For every 200g mange-tout, heat 50g butter in a pan. Add the pea pods, season with salt and pepper, and cover. Cook for about 5 minutes or until they are quite tender, shaking the pan frequently to prevent the peas sticking to the bottom. Serve with the juices from the pan.

Peas – *Dried*

With the popularity of deep freezing, dried green peas are not used as widely as they used to be, although they can be a useful standby. Like other pulses, such as lentils and dried beans, they have a high protein content. The following are the main types of dried peas.

Green peas: These are dried garden peas which are used mainly for soups and purées.

Green and yellow split peas: Green split peas are traditionally used for Pease Pudding, but are also used in soups, stews, and purées.

Chick-peas or *garbanzos:* These are large round peas which are used extensively in Spanish, Greek, Middle Eastern, and American cooking.

To buy: Allow 40–50g per person.

To prepare: Soak the peas for 6–12 hours in cold water, preferably changing the water once during this time to prevent the peas fermenting.

To boil: Drain and cover with fresh cold water. Season with salt and add a chopped onion, a few parsley stalks or a bouquet garni if liked. A few bacon rinds or bacon trimmings can also be added to the cooking liquor for extra flavour. Bring the water to the boil and cook for about 2–2½ hours or until the peas are very tender.

To purée: Cook the peas as above and drain thoroughly, reserving the cooking liquor. Sieve the peas or process in an electric blender, then add enough of the cooking liquor to give a thick purée, or add a little cream or top of the milk. Season to taste. Pea purée is excellent served with grilled or fried sausages, bacon, or bacon and eggs. If liked, the pea purée can be served garnished with crisply fried or grilled bacon or bacon rinds, which have been roughly chopped or crumbled.

Pease Pudding

6 helpings

600g split peas	*salt and pepper*
1 small onion	*50g butter* **or** *margarine*
bouquet garni	*2 eggs*

Soak the peas overnight. Drain, put into a pan, and cover with fresh cold water. Skin the onion and add to the pan with the bouquet garni and seasoning. Cover and simmer the peas slowly for about 2–2½ hours or until they are tender. Drain thoroughly and sieve or process in an electric blender. Cut the fat into small pieces, beat the eggs until liquid, and add both to the pea purée with the seasoning. Beat well together. Place the mixture in a floured cloth and tie tightly. Simmer gently in boiling salted water for 1 hour. Remove from the pan, take out of the cloth, and serve very hot.

Serve with sausages or pickled pork.

Chick-pea Casserole

4–6 helpings

300g chick-peas	*1 × 15ml spoon oil*
1 medium-sized onion	*1 × 2.5ml spoon ground*
1 clove of garlic	*ginger*
1 green pepper	*a pinch of ground cloves*
400g tomatoes	*salt and pepper*
200g cabbage	

Soak the chick-peas overnight and drain. Cook and drain again, reserving the cooking liquor. Skin and chop the onion, skin and crush the garlic. Remove the membranes and seeds from the pepper and slice the flesh. Skin and slice the tomatoes and wash and shred the cabbage. Melt the oil in a large saucepan and fry the onion, garlic, green pepper, tomatoes, and cabbage for 10 minutes. Add the chick-peas, together with 250ml of the cooking liquor, the ginger and the ground cloves, and season with salt and pepper. Cover the pan and simmer gently for 1 hour. Re-season if required before serving.

Cooking time 3 hours (approx)

Savoury Peas and Rice

4 helpings

200g split peas	salt
1½ × 2.5ml spoons ground ginger	200g Basmati rice
¼ × 2.5ml spoon ground mace	

Garnish

2 small boiled **or** fried onions, sliced	4 hard-boiled eggs, quartered

Soak the peas overnight and drain. Put into a pan with fresh cold water and add the ginger, mace, and salt to taste. Cover and cook gently for about 1¾ hours or until the peas are almost tender. Wash and drain the rice well. Add to the peas, cover, and cook for a further 20–30 minutes or until the rice and peas are tender and nearly all the liquid has evaporated. Garnish with the onion slices and the hard-boiled eggs.

Peppers

Large, sweet or bell peppers, often called pimentos, are used raw in salads and form an important part of such dishes as Ratatouille (p811) and Peperonata (p811). Red peppers are the sweetest, followed by yellow and then green. Red and green peppers are available all year round, but yellow ones are less easy to obtain. The very small chilli peppers, which are extremely hot, are used as a seasoning in curries and for other highly spiced dishes. As some varieties are much hotter than others, they should always be used with caution.

To buy: Choose peppers with smooth firm skins and a good bright colour.

To store: Peppers will keep for 2–3 days in a cool vegetable rack or larder or, preferably, in the bottom of a refrigerator.

To prepare: Whether the pepper is to be used raw or cooked, the membranes and seeds must first be removed. Cut a slice off the top of the pepper, and discard the membranes and seeds. If liked, the skins of the peppers can also be removed. Heat the pepper over an open flame on a fork or skewer or under a grill until the skin blackens and splits, then skin as for a tomato. To reduce the slight bitterness of green peppers, it is sometimes preferable to blanch them before use. Plunge into boiling water for 2–3 minutes. Drain, rinse in cold water, and drain again.

To fry: Slice the peppers into rings. For 400g peppers, heat 4 × 15ml spoons olive oil in a frying pan. Add the peppers and fry gently over low heat for 30 minutes or until they are very tender. Season to taste with salt and pepper and serve with the cooking liquor. A few coriander seeds can also be added with a little chopped fennel, thyme or marjoram. A crushed clove of garlic can also be added, if liked.

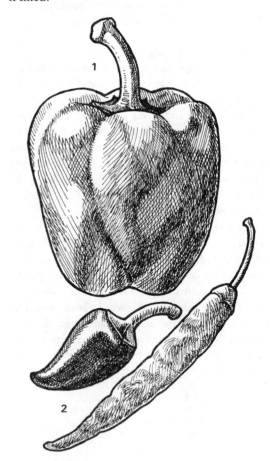

1 Pimento; 2 Chillies

Baked Stuffed Peppers(1)

4 helpings

4 medium-sized green peppers	salt and pepper
1 small onion	a good pinch of dried marjoram
400g raw lean beef, minced	butter or margarine for greasing
100g cooked rice	250ml tomato juice

Garnish
strips of pepper

Cut a slice off the top of the peppers, remove the membranes and seeds, and blanch. Skin and chop the onion finely. Mix together the onion, beef, rice, seasoning, and marjoram. Stand the peppers upright in a greased ovenproof dish; if they do not stand upright easily, cut a thin slice off the base. Divide the stuffing mixture between the 4 peppers. Pour the tomato juice around the base of the peppers. Cover and bake in a moderate oven, 180°C, Gas 4, for 1 hour. Garnish with strips of pepper.

Baked Stuffed Peppers(2)

6 helpings

6 small or 3 large peppers	3 × 15ml spoons dried white or brown breadcrumbs
stuffing – see Stuffed Cabbage Leaves (p760), Stuffed Onions (p783), Stuffed Tomatoes Provençale (p804), or Baked Stuffed Marrow (p807)	2–3 × 15ml spoons melted butter or margarine
	fat for greasing

Halve the peppers lengthways and remove the membranes and seeds. Place in boiling salted water and parboil for 5 minutes. Remove from the water and drain thoroughly. Fill the halved peppers with the stuffing, sprinkle with a few breadcrumbs, and spoon the melted butter or margarine over them. Pack tightly into a greased ovenproof dish and bake for 35 minutes in a fairly hot oven, 190°C, Gas 5.

Mexican Stuffed Peppers
(Pimientos Rellenos)

4 helpings

2 large green peppers	100–150g Mozzarella or other semi-soft cheese

Sauce

375ml tomato pulp from fresh stewed tomatoes or canned tomatoes	1 onion
	2 cloves garlic
$\frac{1}{4}$ × 5ml spoon dried oregano	3 × 15ml spoons butter
	3 × 15ml spoons flour
	salt and pepper

Batter

2 eggs	fat for shallow frying
3 × 15ml spoons flour	

Make the sauce first. Sieve the tomato pulp, and put into a pan with the oregano; simmer for 10 minutes. Meanwhile, skin the onion and garlic and chop both finely. Melt the butter in a large deep frying pan, add the onion and garlic, and fry until soft. Add the flour and fry until lightly browned. Stir in the tomato pulp, and season well. Simmer for 3 minutes. Put to one side until required.

Halve the peppers lengthways, remove the membranes and seeds, and skin. Cream the cheese with a little salt and pepper and fill the pepper halves with it. Fold the peppers to enclose the cheese completely.

To make the batter, separate the eggs. Beat 2 × 15ml spoons of the flour and a pinch of salt with the yolks until well blended. Whisk the egg whites until stiff, and fold them in. Heat the fat. Dust the stuffed peppers with the remaining flour, then dip them in the batter, coating well. Fry, turning once, until lightly browned. Drain on soft kitchen paper and put to one side until required.

Just before serving, reheat the sauce in the frying pan. Put in the peppers and heat, turning once, for 5–7 minutes, until heated through and well puffed. Serve hot.

Cooking time 40 minutes (approx)

Roast Stuffed Peppers

6 helpings

6 medium **or** *large peppers*	*50–75g butter* **or** *margarine*
stuffing – see Stuffed Cabbage Leaves (p760), Stuffed Onions (p783), Stuffed Tomatoes Provençale (p804), **or** *Baked Stuffed Marrow (p807)*	

Remove the membranes and seeds from the peppers, taking care not to split them. Fill the peppers with the stuffing. Melt the fat in a roasting tin in a fairly hot oven, 190°C, Gas 5; then stand the peppers upright in the tin and baste them. Roast for 50 minutes or longer if they are very large, until the filling is 'set' and the peppers are tender. Baste from time to time while cooking. When cooked, place the peppers in a warmed serving dish, and pour any remaining butter over them.

Note Instead of melted fat, the peppers can be served with Fresh Tomato Sauce (p715).

Peppers with Apple

3–4 helpings

1 large cooking apple	*250ml milk*
100g Gruyère cheese	*salt and freshly ground black pepper*
3–4 large green peppers	
1 small green pepper	*butter* **or** *margarine for greasing*
25g butter **or** *margarine*	
25g flour	

Garnish (optional)

1 thickly sliced tomato	*3–4 button mushroom caps*

Peel, core, and chop the apple into small pieces. Grate the cheese. Wash the large peppers and cut off the tops. Discard the membranes and the seeds, but keep the caps. Blanch the peppers and their caps. Drain. Chop the small pepper finely. Melt the fat, stir in the flour, and cook together over gentle heat for 2–3 minutes, stirring all the time. Do not let the flour colour. Draw off the heat and gradually stir in the milk, without letting lumps form. Return to the heat, bring to the boil, and simmer until very thick, stirring occasionally. Season to taste. Mix in the chopped apple, grated cheese, and chopped pepper. Trim the bases of the other peppers so that they stand steadily, cut sides uppermost. Spoon the stuffing mixture into the peppers and replace the caps. Place the peppers, cut side uppermost on a lightly greased baking tray. Bake in a cool oven, 150°C, Gas 2, for 25–30 minutes. Garnish, if liked, with the sliced tomato and mushroom caps before serving.

Plantains

Plantains, which resemble bananas, can be used when they are green or ripe. Unlike bananas, however, they must be cooked. For boiling, steaming or baking they should be left in their skins. They can also be parboiled and roasted, or they can be peeled and cut into thin slices and fried as for game chips (p302).

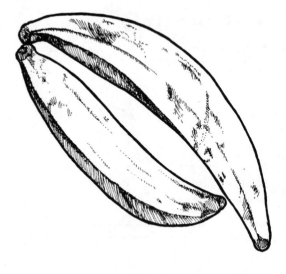

Potatoes

Potatoes are a staple food in the UK, and they are certainly the most versatile of all vegetables. Different varieties of potato vary considerably, some being more suitable for boiling and mashing, and others better for frying or roasting. Home-grown new potatoes are available from May to August, and imported Jersey and other continental potatoes can be found a little earlier than this. These are generally best served boiled or steamed, although they can be sautéed or used for chips. Generally, the best potatoes to buy in the summer for chips or for roasting are Cyprus potatoes. Of the main-crop potatoes, King Edward, Redskin, Maris Piper, Pentland Hawk, and Pentland Ivory are some of the best varieties for boiling, mashing, and baking in their jackets, while Desirée and Majestic are better for roasting and frying.

To buy: Allow 150–200g per person for new potatoes and 200–250g per person for old potatoes because of the greater wastage. New potatoes should be bought as fresh as possible every few days. To test that they are fresh, make sure the skins rub off easily and the potatoes are damp to the touch. When buying main-crop potatoes from September onwards it is practical to buy in larger quantities, and, if suitable storage space is available, a large sack of potatoes can save a considerable amount of money, but the potatoes must be stored in a cool, dark place. Never buy potatoes which are green or which have been exposed to the light.

To prepare: New potatoes should, preferably, not be peeled because the maximum amount of flavour and vitamin C is found just under the skin and is lost when the potatoes are scraped or peeled. Simply wash thoroughly to remove all the dirt and mud. If the potatoes are scraped put into cold water immediately to prevent them browning. If the skin is not too thick on older potatoes, it can be left on for boiling or steaming and removed after cooking. Otherwise, older potatoes should be peeled using a small sharp knife or vegetable peeler. Small and medium-sized potatoes are generally left whole, and large potatoes are cut into halves or quarters.

To boil: Prepare the potatoes as above. Cook in the minimum of boiling salted water until just tender, about 15 minutes for small new potatoes or up to 30 minutes for larger old potatoes. Particularly when boiling larger, old potatoes, do not allow the water to boil rapidly or the outsides will start to break up before the inside of the potatoes are cooked through. Drain the potatoes thoroughly, turn into a serving dish, and spoon plenty of melted butter over them. Sprinkle with chopped parsley or chives before serving.

To steam: Both new and old potatoes can be steamed, but this method is particularly good for small new potatoes. Prepare the potatoes as above, but do not peel them. Season with salt and cook in the top of a steamer over a pan of boiling water for 20 minutes for small new potatoes, or up to 45 minutes to 1 hour for larger old potatoes. Peel, if liked, after cooking and serve as for boiled potatoes.

Mashed potatoes: Boil or steam old potatoes as above. Drain thoroughly and either mash with a potato masher, or sieve or beat with an electric hand mixer until smooth. To every 1kg potatoes (weight before cooking), beat in 25–50g butter or margarine, a little milk or single cream, and salt and pepper to taste. A little grated nutmeg can also be added, if liked. Turn into a serving dish and garnish with a sprig of parsley before serving.

For creamed potatoes, add more butter and cream to give a very smooth, creamy texture.

To bake: **Jacket potatoes** – Choose medium-sized to large old potatoes. Wash thoroughly, dry, and prick lightly with a fork. For a very crisp skin, brush the outside of the potatoes with oil and place on a baking tray. Bake in a fairly hot oven, 190°–200°C, Gas 5–6, for 1–1½ hours depending on the size of the potatoes. Test with a skewer to make sure the centre of the potato is cooked. Split the potatoes in half, or make a cross in the top and push with your fingers to open up the potato. Serve with plenty of butter and coarse salt, with soured cream and chopped chives or with cream cheese. Baked potatoes can also be stuffed in a variety of ways (see p793). Baking is an excellent way of cooking potatoes if using an automatic oven.

To roast (Method 1): Peel old potatoes and cut into even-sized pieces (halves or quarters). Parboil in boiling salted water for 5 minutes and drain thoroughly. Return the potatoes to the pan and stand over low heat for 1–2 minutes until the potatoes are quite dry. Heat a little lard or dripping in a roasting tin, add the potatoes, and turn in the fat so that they are evenly coated, or put the potatoes in the dripping around a joint of roast meat. Roast in a fairly hot to hot oven, 190°–220°C, Gas 5–7, for 40 minutes to 1 hour or until crisp and golden-brown. Baste the potatoes with some of the fat several times during cooking. The cooking time will vary according to the size of the potatoes and the oven temperature, which will depend on the type of joint being roasted. Parboiling helps to give a very crisp roast potato.

To roast (Method 2): Peel the potatoes and cut into even-sized pieces. Put into a roasting tin containing hot dripping or fat, coat evenly with fat, and roast as above for $1-1\frac{1}{4}$ hours depending on the size of the potatoes and the oven temperature.

To fry: 1) **Chips** – Peel old potatoes and cut into sticks about 1cm thick and 8cm long. *For small French fried potatoes*, cut into small sticks about 5mm thick and 5cm long. *For potato straws*, cut into matchsticks. Leave the potatoes in cold water to remove some of the excess starch before frying; then drain and dry thoroughly. Heat the oil or deep fat in a chip pan (p302), put a layer of chips in the bottom of the wire basket and lower into the pan. Fry until the chips are pale golden. Remove from the pan and drain on soft kitchen paper. Repeat this with the remaining chips. Just before serving, reheat the oil, and fry all the chips, French fried potatoes or potato straws until they are very crisp and golden.

2) **Game chips** – Peel old potatoes and cut into very thin slices, using either a very sharp knife or a mandoline. Rinse in cold water to remove the excess starch, then dry thoroughly. Heat the deep fat or oil (p302) and fry the chips until crisp and golden. Drain well on soft kitchen paper and sprinkle with salt before serving. Serve with roast game or poultry. These chips can also be served cold and will keep for several days in an airtight tin.

3) **Potato puffs** – Peel old potatoes and cut into slices 5mm thick. Trim into neat ovals and drop into cold water. Drain and dry them. Heat the oil or deep fat in a pan (p302), put the potato slices into the bottom of the basket and cook until they begin to rise to the surface. Drain on soft kitchen paper. Just before serving, reheat the fat (p302) and fry the potato slices until they are well puffed. Drain again, and sprinkle with salt.

4) **Potato ribbons** – Peel old potatoes and cut across into slices 1cm thick. Trim the edges so that the potatoes have a smooth edge; then, with a sharp knife or potato peeler, cut round and round, making long ribbons. Fry as for Game Chips above.

To sauté: Boil or steam old potatoes as above, until they are just tender. Drain thoroughly and cut into 8mm slices. Heat some lard or dripping in a frying pan and fry the potato slices on both sides until crisp and golden. Drain thoroughly and serve garnished with chopped parsley.

Anna Potatoes

6 helpings

fat for greasing	*melted clarified butter*
1kg even-sized potatoes	**or** *margarine* (p886)
salt and pepper	

Thoroughly grease a 20cm round cake tin and line the base with greased greaseproof paper. Peel and trim the potatoes so that they will give equal-sized slices. Slice them very thinly using either a sharp knife or a mandoline. Arrange a layer of potatoes, slightly overlapping, in the base of the tin. Season, and spoon a little clarified fat over them. Make a second layer of potatoes, season, and spoon some more fat over them. Complete these layers, until all the potatoes have been used. Cover the tin with greased greaseproof paper and foil. Bake in a fairly hot oven, 190°C, Gas 5, for 1 hour. Check the potatoes several times during cooking and add a little more clarified fat if they become too dry. Invert the tin on to a warmed serving dish to remove the potatoes, and serve as soon as possible.

Baked Stuffed Potatoes

6 helpings

6 large old potatoes
oil for brushing
beaten egg for brushing
  (optional)

watercress sprigs

Stuffing

75g grated Cheddar
  *cheese, 25g butter **or***
  margarine, milk,
  seasoning, nutmeg
or
75g chopped fried bacon
  or *cooked ham, milk,*
  seasoning
or
75g flaked, cooked
  smoked haddock,
  1 × 15ml spoon
  chopped parsley,
  1 × 10ml spoon lemon
  juice, milk, seasoning,
  nutmeg
or
75g flaked, cooked
  kipper, 1 chopped
  hard-boiled egg, milk,
  seasoning

or
50g grated Cheddar
  cheese, 25g butter,
  1 × 15ml spoon
  chopped parsley, milk,
  seasoning, 2 egg yolks
  stirred into the filling,
  2 egg whites folded in
  at the end
or
50g grated Cheddar
  *cheese, 25g butter **or***
  margarine,
  50g chopped, cooked
  mushrooms, milk,
  seasoning
or
50g crumbled blue
  cheese, 25g chopped
  *fried bacon **or** cooked*
  *ham, 25g butter **or***
  margarine, milk,
  seasoning

Prepare the potatoes. Brush their jackets with oil, and bake until soft. Leaving the skin intact, carefully remove the soft inside by either cutting the potatoes in half or cutting a thin slice off the top of each.

Mash the potato in a basin and beat in the stuffing ingredients. Mix thoroughly and season well. Replace the stuffing mixture in the potato skins, piling it up well. Fork the tops, and brush with a little beaten egg, if liked, or sprinkle with a little extra grated cheese if it is an ingredient of the stuffing. Replace in the oven and bake for 20 minutes or until golden-brown, or put under a moderate grill. Garnish with the watercress and serve hot.

Note A stuffing consisting of cooked minced meat in a sauce or gravy, or of cooked mixed vegetables, or flaked fish in a sauce may entirely replace the mashed potato from the inside. In this case, the inside of the potato should be mashed and served separately, or mashed and piped round the opening of the potato after it has been stuffed and before returning it to the oven.

Cooking time $1\frac{1}{2}$–$1\frac{3}{4}$ **hours**

Duchesse Potatoes

Makes 500g (approx)

500g old potatoes
*25g butter **or** margarine*
*1 egg **or** 2 egg yolks*
salt and pepper
a little grated nutmeg
  (optional)

*butter **or** margarine for*
  greasing
a little beaten egg for
  brushing

Prepare the potatoes, and boil or steam them. Drain thoroughly, and sieve. Beat in the fat and egg or egg yolks. Season to taste with salt and pepper and add the nutmeg, if used. Spoon the mixture into a piping bag fitted with a large rose nozzle and pipe rounds of potato on to a greased baking tray. Brush with a little beaten egg. Bake in a fairly hot oven, 200°C, Gas 6, for about 15 minutes or until the potatoes are a good golden-brown.

Note The potatoes can be piped on to the baking tray and then baked when required. If a piping bag is not available, shape the potato into diamonds, rounds or triangles. Criss-cross the tops with a knife, brush with the egg, and bake as above.

Duchesse potatoes are a popular garnish for certain fish and meat dishes. For instructions on how to present them, see p399.

Mousseline Potatoes
See p884.

French Mashed Potatoes

6 helpings

1kg potatoes	*milk*
25g butter **or** *margarine*	*salt and pepper*

Garnish
1 × 15ml spoon chopped
  parsley

Peel the potatoes and cut them into slices. Put into a pan, add the fat and just cover with cold milk. Cover the pan and cook the potatoes very gently for about 30 minutes or until they are tender. Mash the potatoes in the pan, season with salt and pepper, and beat well. Turn into a serving dish and garnish with the parsley before serving.

Potato Pie

4 helpings

600g potatoes	*salt and pepper*
1 medium-sized onion	*milk* **or** *water*
1 stick of celery	*shortcrust* (p1249) **or**
50g shelled nuts	*cheese pastry* (p1251)
25g butter	*using 150g plain flour*
25g sago **or** *tapioca*	*flour for rolling out*

Peel the potatoes and cut them into slices. Put into a pan, add the fat and just cover with cold milk. butter in a small pan and fry the onion gently for 5 minutes. Arrange the potatoes, onion, celery, and nuts in a 500ml pie dish and sprinkle the sago or tapioca over them. Season with salt and pepper and pour in enough milk or water to come to within 2cm of the top of the dish. Roll out the pastry on a lightly floured surface and use to cover the filling. Bake towards the top of a fairly hot oven, 190°C, Gas 5, for about 1 hour, or until the pastry is golden-brown and the potatoes are tender. Cover the pastry with a piece of foil if it becomes too brown.

Potatoes Baked in Soured Cream

4 helpings

1kg potatoes	*salt*
250ml milk	*3 onions*
50g butter	*250ml soured cream*
2 eggs	

Peel the potatoes and boil them. Drain thoroughly and sieve. Heat the milk to scalding point and melt 25g of the butter. Add the hot milk, melted butter, eggs and salt to taste, and mix thoroughly.

Skin and slice the onions. Melt the remaining 25g butter in a large flameproof baking dish or small roasting tin, and fry the onions until soft and transparent. Remove from the dish or tin. Put half the potato mixture into the tin and flatten it into an even layer. Top with the onions, and cover with the remaining potato. Level the surface. Coat with the soured cream. Bake in a fairly hot oven, 200°C, Gas 6 for 20–25 minutes.

Potato Rolls

Makes 6–8 rolls

500g potatoes	*a pinch of dried mixed*
1 small turnip	*herbs*
1 small onion	*salt and pepper*
1 stick of celery	*shortcrust pastry* (p1249)
25g Cheddar cheese	*using 200g plain flour*
25g butter	*flour for rolling out*
1 × 15ml spoon chopped	
parsley	

Peel and dice the potatoes and turnip. Skin and chop the onion, chop the celery. Grate the cheese and cut the butter into flakes. Mix the potatoes, turnip, onion, celery, cheese, butter and herbs in a bowl, and season with salt and pepper. Roll out the pastry on a lightly floured surface, and cut into rounds or squares 10cm across. Put some of the vegetable mixture on one half of each piece of pastry, dampen the edges, fold over the other half, pinch the edges together, and flute. Place on a baking tray and bake in a fairly hot oven, 190°C, Gas 5, for 30 minutes.

Potatoes Byron

4–6 helpings

1kg potatoes	125ml single cream **or**
salt and pepper	thin foundation white
a good pinch of grated	sauce (p692)
nutmeg	50g grated Parmesan
100g butter	cheese
flour	

Wash and bake the potatoes in their skins. When cooked, cut them in half and scoop the pulp into a basin. Season with salt, pepper, and nutmeg. Add 75g of the butter and beat the mixture well with a wooden spoon. Divide into 6 or 8 portions and mould into medallion shapes, 1–2cm thick, on a floured surface. Heat the remaining butter in a frying pan and fry the potatoes gently on both sides until golden-brown. Remove from the pan and put in an ovenproof dish. Either spoon the cream over each potato medallion and sprinkle with the cheese, or add half the cheese to the white sauce, spoon it over the potatoes, then sprinkle with the remaining cheese. Place the dish under a moderate grill until the cheese is golden-brown.

Cooking time 1¼ hours (approx)

Mashed Potatoes with Cheese

4 helpings

750g potatoes	salt and pepper
150g Cheddar cheese	milk

Peel, cook, and mash the potatoes. Grate the cheese finely and beat into the potato with the seasoning and enough milk to make a creamy mixture.

Serve with a green vegetable or tomatoes.

Cooking time 25 minutes (approx)

VARIATION

Cheese and Potato Pie

Make the mixture as above, put into an ovenproof dish, and sprinkle with 25g extra grated cheese. Put under a moderate grill until golden-brown.

Potatoes with Cheese and Bacon

6 helpings

1kg potatoes	75g Cheddar cheese
1 medium-sized onion	salt and pepper
75g streaky bacon **or**	125ml boiling milk
bacon pieces, without	125ml boiling water
rinds	1 × 15ml spoon chopped
2 sticks celery	parsley

Peel and dice the potatoes. Skin the onion and chop very finely. Cut the bacon into small pieces. Wash or wipe the celery and chop it finely. Grate the cheese. Fry the onion and bacon together in a pan over gentle heat, shaking frequently, for about 5 minutes. Add the potatoes and celery, cover, and heat for a few minutes, shaking frequently. Sprinkle with a little salt and pepper. Add the milk and water and cook very gently for about 20 minutes until the potatoes are quite soft. Stir the cheese into the potatoes with the parsley. Re-season if required, and serve at once.

Potatoes Savoyarde

6 helpings

1kg potatoes	1 small clove of garlic
salt and pepper	40g butter
grated nutmeg	375ml (approx) white
75g Gruyère cheese	stock (p329)

Peel the potatoes and cut into thin slices about 4mm thick. Place in a mixing bowl. Season with salt, pepper, and a little nutmeg. Grate the cheese, add most of it to the potatoes, and mix thoroughly. Cut the garlic in half and rub a 2 litre ovenproof dish with it. Flake the butter and rub a little over the inside of the dish. Put in the potatoes and cheese and add barely enough stock to cover. Sprinkle with the remaining flaked butter and grated cheese. Bake in a fairly hot oven, 190°C, Gas 5, for 1 hour or until the top is golden-brown and the potatoes are tender. Serve the potatoes in the dish in which they were cooked.

Potatoes Lyonnaise

6 helpings

1kg potatoes	*salt and pepper*
250g onions	*1 × 15ml spoon chopped*
75g butter **or** *margarine*	*parsley*

Scrub the potatoes, but do not peel them. Boil or steam them in their skins until tender. Drain, peel, and cut into slices 5mm thick. Skin and slice the onions thinly. Melt the fat in a frying pan and fry the onions gently until they are just golden. Remove from the pan, put on one side, and keep warm. Add the potatoes to the pan and fry on both sides until crisp and golden. Replace the onions in the pan and mix with the potatoes. Season to taste with salt and pepper, turn into a serving dish, and sprinkle with the parsley.

Cooking time 45 minutes (approx)

Mrs Beeton's Potato Rissoles

Makes 12 (approx)

325–350g hot mashed	*browned breadcrumbs*
* potato*	* (p375)*
salt and pepper	*butter* **or** *margarine*
1 × 5ml spoon chopped	*lard* **or** *oil for shallow*
* parsley*	* frying*
beaten egg for coating	

Season the mashed potato well and mix in the parsley. Allow the mixture to cool completely. When cold, shape into small balls. Coat thoroughly with egg, and then roll in breadcrumbs. Allow to stand for 15 minutes to firm up. Heat a little butter or margarine with the lard or oil in a frying pan. Put in the rissoles, and turn them in the hot fat for about 6–9 minutes until golden-brown all over. Drain on soft kitchen paper and serve hot.

Potato Croquettes

Makes 12–15

500g old potatoes	*2 eggs*
25g butter **or** *margarine*	*flour for dusting*
1 egg **or** *2 egg yolks*	*dried white breadcrumbs*
salt and pepper	* for coating*
1 × 5ml spoon chopped	*fat* **or** *oil for deep frying*
* parsley* **or** *2 × 15ml*	
* spoons grated*	
* Parmesan* **or** *Cheddar*	
* cheese (optional)*	

Prepare the potatoes and boil or steam them. Drain thoroughly, and sieve. Beat in the fat and egg or egg yolks, and season to taste. Add the parsley or grated cheese, if used. Beat the eggs until liquid, form the potato into balls or cylindrical rolls, dust with flour, and coat twice with egg and breadcrumbs. If possible, chill for 1 hour before frying. Heat the fat or oil (p302) and fry the potato croquettes or balls. Drain thoroughly and serve as soon as possible.

Potatoes Dauphine

4–6 helpings

500g potatoes	*oil* **or** *fat for deep frying*
salt and pepper	
choux pastry (p1251)	
* using 75g flour*	

Scrub the potatoes, but do not peel them. Boil or steam them until tender. Drain thoroughly, peel, and sieve. Season well with salt and pepper. Beat the potato purée into the choux pastry. Heat the oil or fat (p302). Drop small spoonfuls of the mixture into the hot fat, a few at a time, and cook until they are golden-brown and puffed up. Remove from the pan and drain on soft kitchen paper. Serve as soon as possible after cooking.

Cooking time 40 minutes (approx)

Potato Soufflé

See p923 and p1335.

Scalloped Potatoes with Onions

4–6 helpings

750g potatoes　　　　*125ml milk*
500g onions　　　　*2 × 10ml spoons butter*
fat for greasing　　　　**or** *margarine*
salt and pepper

Peel the potatoes and cut into slices 5mm thick. Skin and slice the onions into rings. Put a layer of potatoes into a greased ovenproof dish, season with salt and pepper, and cover with a layer of onions. Repeat these layers, seasoning each, and end with a layer of potatoes. Pour the milk over the top. Dot with the fat and cover with foil or a lid. Bake in a fairly hot oven, 190°C, Gas 5, for 1½ hours. Remove the lid for the last 20 minutes of cooking so that the potatoes on the top can brown.

Potatoes Parisienne

See p399.

Pumpkin

Pumpkins, which belong to the same family as marrows, can be used for both sweet and savoury dishes. They are in season from July to November and are generally sold in wedges, so that you can buy as much of the pumpkin as you wish. Pumpkin purée is available in cans.

To store: A whole pumpkin will keep for a couple of weeks in a cool larder, but a cut piece of pumpkin is best used as soon as possible. It can, however, be wrapped in clingfilm and stored for 1–2 days in the bottom of a refrigerator.

To prepare: Remove the seeds from the pumpkin, peel off the skin, and, unless roasting, cut into pieces about 5cm square.

To boil: Although pumpkin can be boiled, it is really better steamed because of the very high water content. Boil in the very minimum of boiling salted water for 20–30 minutes or until tender. If cooking the pumpkin for Pumpkin Pie (p1572) or other sweet dishes, use less salt in the cooking water. Drain the pumpkin thoroughly, turn into a serving dish, and season very well with salt and freshly ground black pepper. Dot liberally with butter and serve as soon as possible.

To steam: Season the pumpkin with salt, unless using for a sweet dish. Cook in the top of a steamer over a pan of boiling water for 35–40 minutes or until it is very tender. Drain and serve as for boiled pumpkin.

To roast: Remove the seeds from the pumpkin, peel, and cut into wedges. Roll the pumpkin in the dripping round a joint of meat and roast in a fairly hot oven, 200°C, Gas 6, for 45 minutes–1 hour.

To fry: Parboil or steam the pumpkin for 10 minutes. Drain and dry thoroughly. Coat in batter and fry as for Jerusalem artichokes.

To purée: Boil or steam the pumpkin as above. Drain thoroughly, then mash or sieve and to every 1kg pumpkin (weight before cooking) beat in 25g butter or margarine and 2 × 15ml spoons cream or milk. If serving as a savoury purée, season to taste with salt and plenty of freshly ground black pepper and serve garnished with chopped parsley.

Radishes

Although generally eaten raw, either in salads or as a garnish, radishes can also be used very successfully cooked, as a flavouring or as an alternative to turnips. Red radishes, the large French white radishes or mooli, and black radishes can all be used in this way.

Radish tops are a valuable source of vitamin C and can be cooked in the same way as spinach.

To buy: Choose firm, equal-sized radishes of a good colour.

To prepare: Wash, top, and tail the radishes.

Radishes
1 Black; 2 Regular; 3 White

Salsify and Scorzonera

These roots, which are in season from October to May, have a delicate and unusual flavour. Salsify is a white root, resembling a long thin parsnip, whereas scorzonera has a black skin and is generally considered to have a superior flavour. The young leaves can be used in salads or they can be cooked as for spinach.

To buy: Allow 150g per person. Choose roots that are of a good size and are not shrivelled. Any leaves which have been left on the roots should appear fresh.

To store: Salsify and scorzonera can be kept in a cool vegetable rack or larder for 3–4 days.

To prepare: If possible, scorzonera should not be scraped before cooking because much of the flavour lies just below the skin. Simply scrub and cut into 5cm lengths. Drop the scorzonera quickly into acidulated water to prevent it browning. Salsify can be scraped before cooking and cut into 5cm lengths, but it must be put immediately into acidulated water.

To boil: Cook in the minimum of boiling salted water for about 30 minutes or until just tender. If liked, a little lemon juice can also be added to the cooking water to preserve the colour. Drain the salsify or scorzonera and serve, seasoned with a little pepper and with melted butter spooned over it and/or lemon juice and chopped herbs, such as parsley, dill or tarragon. Boiled salsify can also be served in a white or cream sauce.

To shallow fry: Prepare the salsify or scorzonera but do not scrape. Boil in the skins until just tender. Drain thoroughly, peel, and cut into slices 1cm thick. Heat some butter or margarine in a pan and fry the slices until golden-brown, turning several times. Season with salt and pepper and serve hot.

To deep fry: Parboil the salsify or scorzonera for 15 minutes. Drain and dry thoroughly, coat in batter and fry as for Jerusalem artichokes.

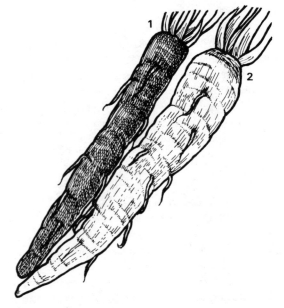

1 Salsify; 2 Scorzonera

Salsify (or Scorzonera) au Gratin

4 helpings

1kg salsify **or** *scorzonera*	*1 × 15ml spoon grated Cheddar cheese*
375ml cheese sauce (p693)	*1 × 15ml spoon soft white breadcrumbs*

Prepare and boil the salsify or scorzonera. Drain thoroughly. Stir into the cheese sauce, and turn into an ovenproof dish. Mix together the grated cheese and breadcrumbs and sprinkle them on top. Brown under a moderate grill for 5 minutes or in a hot oven, 220°C, Gas 7, for 10 minutes. Serve at once.

Seakale

This is an excellent vegetable resembling celery stalks; it can be used raw in salads or cooked. Seakale grows wild on the beaches of South East England and in Western Europe but is also cultivated, although it is not often seen in greengrocers' shops. It is in season from December to May and the leaves can be cooked as for spinach.

To buy: Allow 100g per person. Choose fresh-looking stalks which can be snapped in half.

To store: Seakale should be used as fresh as possible but can be stored for 1–2 days in a cool vegetable rack or larder or in the bottom of a refrigerator.

To boil: Cook in the minimum of boiling salted water for about 20 minutes or until just tender. It is important not to overcook seakale because it hardens if cooked for too long. Drain thoroughly and turn into a serving dish. Pour melted butter over it or serve with a white, cream, Béchamel or Hollandaise sauce. If preferred, the seakale stems can be simmered in stock.

To steam: Season the seakale with salt and cook in the top of a steamer over a pan of boiling water for about 25 minutes; do not overcook. Serve as for boiled seakale.

Seakale Beet

See Swiss Chard (p803).

Seaweed

(Dulse, Kelp, Carragheen, Laver)

Seaweed is rich in mineral salts; it can be eaten as a vegetable, added to stocks, soups or sauces, or used to make a substitute fish stock. Most seaweeds need lengthy preparation and boiling before use, and are usually sold ready-prepared and dried or as a gelatinous purée.

For a sea-flavoured stock, soak a dried seaweed such as laver for about 3 hours in just enough water to cover. Then add a small chopped onion and salt and pepper to taste, and simmer the seaweed for $1\frac{1}{2}$–2 hours or longer, to obtain the desired flavour. The liquid is then drained off for use. The seaweed itself can be chopped and simmered in milk with tomato or saffron, butter, and any other seasoning desired (eg a bay leaf) for use as a vegetable. No set quantities can be given since the seaweed varies in flavour according to type and quality.

Dulse and Kelp need very little cooking. Dulse, in particular, needs simmering for only a few minutes. Kelp has little flavour but is added to dishes for its B vitamin content.

Sorrel

Sorrel is used as both a vegetable and a herb. There are several different varieties, of which wild sorrel, which has the smallest leaves, is the most bitter. Sorrel is generally served as a purée and it should be prepared, cooked, and puréed in exactly the same way as spinach. To counteract the acidity of the sorrel, a little sugar can be added while it is cooking. Sorrel is excellent served with eggs, veal or white fish.

Soya Beans
See Beans – *Dried* (p752).

Spinach

Spinach is in season almost throughout the year because there are both winter and summer varieties. It is an extremely valuable source of iron and is generally a particularly good vegetable to serve to invalids and convalescents. Spinach can also be eaten raw in salads. It freezes well and can be bought frozen as either leaf spinach or chopped spinach; it is also available in cans.

To buy: When cooked, spinach reduces considerably because of its very high water content, so allow 250–300g per person. Choose spinach that is a good green colour and appears fresh without any withered yellow leaves.

To store: Once picked, spinach does not keep well and should preferably be eaten on the day of purchase, but it can be kept for 1–2 days in a cool vegetable rack or larder or in the bottom of a refrigerator.

To prepare: Remove any thick stalks from the spinach. (These can be kept and cooked as a separate vegetable. Wash them and tie together in a bundle; then boil or steam as for seakale until they are tender. Drain and serve with melted butter.) Spinach must be washed thoroughly because it can be gritty; wash in at least 3 changes of cold water.

To boil (Method 1): For 1kg spinach, melt 25g butter or margarine in a pan, then add the wet spinach leaves to the pan. Season with salt and stir for a few minutes, until all the leaves are limp. Cover and cook slowly for about 10 minutes or until the spinach is tender. Drain the spinach thoroughly, pressing out the water. Heat 2×15ml spoons cream in the pan, replace the spinach, and cook for a minute. Season to taste with salt, pepper, and nutmeg. A small, crushed clove of garlic added to spinach helps to remove some of the iron tang, and the cream can be omitted, if preferred.

To boil (Method 2): Cook the spinach in 1cm depth of boiling salted water, adding the leaves a few at a time so that the water does not leave the boil. Cover, and cook for a further 10 minutes or

until tender. Drain thoroughly, pressing all the water out and serve as for boiled spinach (1).

To purée: Cook the spinach as above. Drain thoroughly and either chop finely, sieve or process in an electric blender. For every 1.5kg spinach, melt 25g butter or margarine in a pan with 3×15ml spoons cream. Stir in the chopped or sieved spinach and heat gently. Season to taste with salt, pepper and nutmeg. Alternatively, thicken 125ml of the spinach liquor with 1×10ml spoon cornflour, and add the sieved or chopped spinach to this panada; or add 125ml thick foundation white (p692) or Béchamel (p704) sauce to the chopped or sieved spinach. The spinach purée can be served garnished with fleurons of puff pastry (p399), sieved hard-boiled egg yolk or crescents of fried bread.

Italian Spinach

4 helpings

1kg spinach	*2 × 15ml spoons olive oil*
25g sultanas	*salt and pepper*
1 clove of garlic	*25g pine kernels*

Prepare and cook the spinach, drain thoroughly, and chop coarsely. Cover the sultanas with boiling water for 1 minute to plump them; then drain thoroughly. Skin and crush the garlic. Heat the oil in a wide pan. Add the spinach, garlic, and seasoning. Turn the spinach over and over in the pan to heat it thoroughly without frying. Add the sultanas and nuts and serve hot.

Cooking time 20 minutes (approx)

Spring Onions

See Onions (p781).

Sprue

See Asparagus Points (p746).

Swedes

Swedes are generally an inexpensive root vegetable, yet very good, especially when puréed. They have a similar flavour to turnips but are milder; they are in season from September to May.

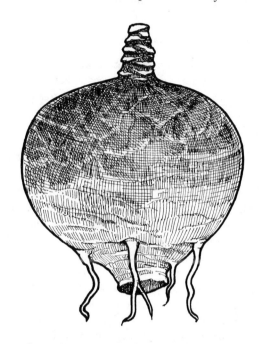

To buy: Allow 200g per person. Choose swedes of a good size, but not too large: the smaller roots have a better flavour. The skin should be firm and not wrinkled.

To store: Like other root vegetables, swedes will keep for several weeks in a cool, dark place.

To prepare: Peel the swedes thickly and cut into pieces about 8cm square or into wedges.

To boil: Cook swedes in the minimum of boiling salted water for about 30 minutes or until quite tender. Drain thoroughly, return to the pan, and put over gentle heat for 1–2 minutes to dry them out. Turn into a serving dish and season with pepper, preferably freshly ground black pepper, and a little nutmeg if liked. Spoon melted butter over the swedes and garnish with chopped parsley.

To steam: Season with salt and cook in the top of a steamer over a pan of boiling water for about 40 minutes or until tender. Drain thoroughly and serve as for boiled swedes.

To purée: Swedes can be served on their own in a purée, or mixed with potatoes, turnips or carrots. Cook the swedes as above, then mash or sieve. To every 1kg swede (weight before cooking), beat in 25g butter or margarine, 1–2 × 15ml spoons cream if liked, seasoning, and nutmeg.

Sweetcorn (Corn)

Hot, boiled corn on the cob makes an excellent starter, or can be served as a vegetable main dish. Home-grown corn is available from July to November, but imported corn can be bought at other times of the year. Frozen and canned corn is obtainable, both on the cob and as kernels.

To buy: Allow one cob per person or 100g kernels. Once corn has been picked, the sugar in the kernels converts to starch, making the vegetable tough rather than sweet and juicy; corn should therefore be eaten as soon as possible after picking. Choose only cobs on which the kernels are a pale yellow; if they are a bright yellow they are likely to be over-ripe and hard. When pressed, the kernels should exude a milky liquid. Check also that the kernels go right to the tip of the cob and do not finish half-way up.

To store: Corn should not be stored and should be cooked as quickly as possible.

To prepare: Peel off the green husks of corn and reserve some of them if boiling the cobs. Take off the silks (threads), and trim the base end. To remove the kernels from the cob, use a sharp knife, and cut off the kernels in long strips from the centre to one end, then from the centre to the other end. Any flesh and juice which remains on the cob can also be scraped off.

To boil: **1) Cobs** – Place some of the husks in the bottom of a pan. Lay the cobs on top, cover with boiling water, and cook for 5–8 minutes, or until a kernel can easily be removed from the cob. Salt should not be added to the water because this tends to toughen the corn. Drain the cobs and serve hot with salt, freshly ground black pepper, and plenty of melted butter.

2) Kernels – Corn kernels should be cooked in boiling unsalted water for 3–5 minutes or until just tender. Drain, and serve like the cobs or with a white or parsley sauce.

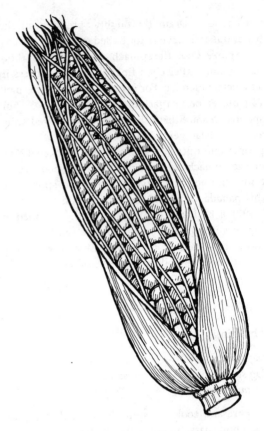

To steam: Place the cobs or kernels in the top of a steamer over a pan of boiling water and steam for 10–15 minutes for cobs, or 5–10 minutes for kernels.

To bake: Put the cobs into a roasting tin and just cover with milk. Bake in a fairly hot oven, 190°C, Gas 5, for 35 minutes or until a kernel can easily be removed from the cob. Drain the cobs, toss in melted butter, and place under a hot grill for 2–3 minutes before serving, seasoned with salt and pepper.

To roast: For 6 cobs, melt 50g butter in a roasting tin. Roll the cobs in this so that they are lightly coated with butter. Roast in a fairly hot oven, 190°C, Gas 5, for about 20 minutes, turning them frequently, until a kernel can easily be removed from the cob. Season with salt and pepper and serve with the butter in which they have been cooked.

Corn Pudding

6 helpings

100g plain flour
1 × 5ml spoon salt
1 × 2.5ml spoon black
* pepper*
2 eggs

500ml milk
*400g fresh **or** frozen*
* sweetcorn kernels*
fat for greasing

Sift the flour, salt, and pepper. Beat the eggs until liquid and add them to the flour, stirring well. Beat together with the milk and then the corn to form a batter. Turn into a greased 1.5 litre pie or ovenproof dish and bake in a moderate oven, 180°C, Gas 4, for 1 hour. Serve hot.

Swiss Chard

Swiss chard belongs to the beet family, and is sometimes called seakale beet. Its top leaves which are dark green, can be cooked and served as for spinach. They have a sweeter, less earthy flavour, and are very rich in vitamins. The stalks, which resemble celery stalks can be prepared as for celery.

Sweet Potatoes

Sweet potatoes are available most of the year. They can be served as a savoury dish or as a dessert. When served as a vegetable, they can be prepared in any of the ways suitable for potatoes, but are usually baked or roasted.

See also Yams (p808).

Tomatoes

Tomatoes are available throughout the year, although home-grown ones are in season only from March to November. In addition to the standard round tomatoes, large Mediterranean tomatoes and small Italian plum tomatoes can be bought, both of which have an excellent flavour.

To buy: When serving as a side vegetable allow 100g, ie 1 large or 2 medium-sized tomatoes, per person. For baking and stuffing, choose tomatoes of an even size and make sure that the skins are not cracked.

To store: Tomatoes keep well for several days in a cool, dry vegetable rack or larder.

To prepare: The preparation of tomatoes depends largely on the method of cooking. To skin tomatoes, either hold each tomato on a fork over a gas flame or under a grill until the skin blackens and splits, then skin; or place the tomatoes in a basin, cover with boiling water, leave for 1 minute, and then drain and skin.

To bake: Halve the tomatoes. Brush with oil or dot with butter or margarine and season with salt and pepper. If liked, the tomatoes can be sprinkled with a little finely chopped tarragon or basil. Place in a greased ovenproof dish, cover, and bake in a moderate oven, 180°C, Gas 4, for about 20 minutes or until soft.

To grill: Halve the tomatoes, or if very small, leave whole and mark a cross in the bottom with a sharp knife. Dot with a little butter or margarine or brush with oil and season with salt and pepper. Cook under a fairly hot grill, turning once. Serve hot.

To fry: Halve the tomatoes, season with salt and pepper, and fry in hot fat for about 5 minutes, turning once. Remove from the fat with a fish slice and serve hot.

Tomato and Onion Pie

4 helpings

400g onions, preferably Spanish	fat for greasing
50g butter	salt and pepper
800g tomatoes	50g soft white breadcrumbs
50g Cheddar cheese	

Skin the onions, put into a bowl, and cover with boiling water. Leave for 5 minutes, drain, dry thoroughly, and cut into slices. Melt half the butter in a pan and fry the onions until golden-brown. Skin and slice the tomatoes, and grate the cheese. Place the onions and tomatoes in alternate layers in a greased pie dish, sprinkle each layer lightly with salt and pepper and liberally with cheese and some of the breadcrumbs. Cover the whole with a layer of breadcrumbs and dot with the remaining butter. Bake in a fairly hot oven, 190°C, Gas 5, for 45 minutes.

Scalloped Tomatoes

6 helpings

400g ripe tomatoes	a pinch of sugar
25g butter **or** margarine	a pinch of grated nutmeg
½ small onion	salt and pepper
3 × 15ml spoons soft white breadcrumbs	fat for greasing

Blanch the tomatoes. Drain them, slice roughly, and sieve. Melt 15g of the fat in a pan. Skin and chop the onion finely and fry in the fat for about 5 minutes or until golden-brown. Add the tomato pulp and cook gently for 5 minutes. Stir in 1 × 15ml spoon of the breadcrumbs. Add the sugar, nutmeg, and seasoning. Pour the tomato mixture into 6 deep, greased scallop shells or small ramekin dishes. Sprinkle with the rest of the breadcrumbs. Melt the rest of the butter and sprinkle it over the top. Bake in a fairly hot oven, 190°C, Gas 5, for 15 minutes or place under a hot grill until golden-brown.

Tomato Ragoût

6 helpings

800g tomatoes	1 × 5ml spoon sugar
1 small onion	1½ × 5ml spoons cornflour
25g fat for frying	3 × 15ml spoons milk **or** water
bouquet garni	
salt and pepper	

Skin and quarter the tomatoes. Skin and chop the onion finely. Melt the fat in a pan and fry the onion gently for 5 minutes. Add the tomatoes, bouquet garni, seasoning, and sugar. Cover and simmer gently for about 20 minutes. Combine the cornflour with the milk or water and stir into the tomato mixture. Bring to the boil, stirring all the time, until the mixture has thickened. Re-season if required.

Serve with haricot or butter beans or with cooked macaroni or spaghetti.

Stuffed Tomatoes Provençale

4 helpings

8 medium-sized tomatoes	25g butter
salt and pepper	75–100g soft white breadcrumbs
50g onions **or** shallots	1 × 15ml spoon chopped parsley
1 small clove of garlic	
1 × 15ml spoon olive oil	

Halve the tomatoes crossways. Remove the pips and juice and place the tomatoes in an ovenproof dish. Season lightly with salt and pepper. Skin and chop the onion or shallots finely. Skin and crush the garlic. Heat the oil in a pan and fry the onion and garlic gently without browning. Add the butter and heat until melted; then add the breadcrumbs and parsley. Season to taste and mix well together. Spoon this mixture into the tomato halves. Bake in a hot oven, 220°C, Gas 7, for 15 minutes or until the breadcrumbs are lightly browned.

VARIATION
Add 4 finely chopped anchovy fillets and 1 × 5ml spoon finely chopped capers to the stuffing.

Turnips

There are two varieties of turnip: the young summer or early turnip and the main-crop turnip. The former has a milder flavour than the main-crop vegetable. Early turnips are in season from April to July while main-crop turnips are found from August to March.

To buy: Allow 200g turnips per person. Early turnips should be a good white colour, with a hint of green and purple, and any remaining stalks should appear fresh. Older turnips should have a smooth, unwrinkled skin and be hard; do not buy turnips which appear spongy.

To store: Early turnips should be eaten as soon as possible after purchase, although they will keep for 1–2 days in a cool vegetable rack or larder. Main-crop turnips keep well for several weeks in a cool, dark place.

To prepare: Both early and main-crop turnips should be peeled thickly. Early turnips can be left whole or cut into halves or quarters; main-crop turnips should be cut into quarters or chunks about 8cm square.

To boil (Method 1): Cook the turnips in the minimum of boiling salted water for 20–30 minutes, depending on the size of the pieces and the age of the turnip. Drain thoroughly, turn into a serving dish, and season with pepper, preferably freshly ground, and spoon melted butter over them. Serve garnished with parsley or chopped chives. Turnips, particularly early turnips are excellent served in a cream or Béchamel sauce.

To boil (Method 2 – conservation method): For 800g turnips, heat 25g butter or margarine in a heavy-based pan. Add the turnips and cook very gently for 10 minutes, shaking the pan frequently so that the turnips do not stick to the bottom. Pour approximately 100ml boiling salted water over them, cover the pan, and cook the turnips gently for a further 15–20 minutes depending on their age. Serve the turnips with the cooking liquor and garnish with chopped parsley before serving, or serve in a sauce as in method (1). Stir 1×15ml spoon cream into the cooking liquor before serving.

To steam: Season the turnips with salt, and cook in the top of a steamer over a pan of boiling water for 30–40 minutes, depending on the size and age of the turnips. Drain and serve as for boiled turnips.

To purée: Boil or steam the turnips as above and drain if boiling by method (1) or steaming. If cooking by the conservation method, retain the cooking liquor. Mash or sieve the turnips and to every 1kg turnips (weight before cooking) add 25g butter or margarine, $1–2 \times 15$ml spoons cream or top of the milk, and seasoning.

Note Turnips can also be glazed in the same way as Glazed Carrots (p763).

Turnip Greens

These, when young, are a most pleasant green vegetable, very rich in vitamin C. Turnip greens should be used as soon as they are picked. The stalks should be removed and the leaves shredded and cooked as for cabbage.

Vegetable Marrow

Together with pumpkins and courgettes, vegetable marrow is part of the *gourd* family, known in the USA as *squash*. Other varieties are sometimes available in the UK in markets; they can also be grown in gardens. They include *acorn squash* which is pale coloured and a similar, though smaller shape to marrow; *crookneck squash* which is yellow and the shape of an elongated pear; *custard marrow* which has deep ribbing and is the size of a small football; and *hubbard squash* which has a rough green skin and is melon shaped. They are all cooked in the same way as marrow, the length of cooking time depending on size.

Marrows have a very high water content and are best suited to steaming or stewing. They are in season from July to October. The biggest marrow may win the local horticultural show, but the flavour of smaller marrows is far superior.

To buy: Choose marrows not more than 30cm long. This serves 3–4 people.

To store: Marrows keep well for a week or two in a cool, dry vegetable rack or larder.

To prepare: For baking and stuffing, the marrow is often halved and the skin left on, but for steaming, stewing, and baking, cut the marrow into rings, peel thickly, and remove the seeds. Cut into halves or leave as rings.

To boil: Cook in the very minimum of boiling salted water for about 10 minutes or until just tender. Drain thoroughly. A slice of slightly stale bread put in the base of the serving dish will help to absorb excess water. Turn the marrow into a serving dish, season with pepper, preferably freshly ground, and spoon plenty of melted butter over it, or serve with a white or cheese sauce.

To steam: Season the marrow with salt and cook in the top of a steamer over a pan of boiling water for about 20 minutes, depending on the size of the marrow pieces. Serve as for boiled marrow.

To bake: Cut the marrow into rings. Place in a greased ovenproof dish, season with salt and pepper, and dot with 25g butter or margarine. Cover and bake in a fairly hot oven, 190°C, Gas 5, for 45 minutes. Serve with the cooking liquor.

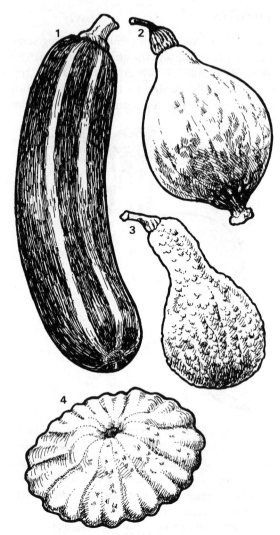

1 Marrow; 2 Hubbard squash; 3 Crookneck squash; 4 Custard marrow

To stew: Melt 25g butter or margarine in a pan. Add the pieces of marrow, and season with salt and pepper and a little chopped thyme and lemon juice, if wished. Coat the pieces of marrow with the fat, cover with a lid, and cook over gentle heat for about 30 minutes, shaking the pan from time to time. Serve the marrow together with the juices in the pan, or add these to a white or cheese sauce.

To purée: Marrow can also be served as a purée. Steam as above, drain thoroughly, and mash. Then beat 25g butter or margarine, 1 × 15ml spoon beaten egg, and 1 × 15ml spoon cream (if liked) into the hot sauce. Season very well with salt, pepper, and nutmeg.

Marrow with Tomatoes

4–6 helpings

400g tomatoes	1 medium-sized marrow
25g butter **or** margarine	salt and pepper

Garnish
1 × 10ml spoon chopped parsley   1 × 10ml spoon chopped chives

Skin the tomatoes and cut into slices. Melt the fat in a saucepan. Add the tomatoes and cook gently for 10 minutes. Peel the marrow, discard the seeds, and cut the flesh into 2cm squares. Add to the tomatoes and season with salt and pepper. Cover the pan with a tight-fitting lid and cook the marrow gently for 20 minutes or until tender. Re-season if required before serving. Garnish with the parsley and chives.

Marrow with Cheese

4 helpings

1 medium-sized marrow	salt and pepper
1 very small onion **or**	1 × 15ml spoon browned
1 clove of garlic	breadcrumbs (p375)
100g Cheddar cheese	

Prepare the marrow and steam until tender. Drain thoroughly. Cut the onion or clove of garlic and rub the inside of a casserole with it. Grate the cheese finely. Place a layer of marrow in the bottom of the casserole. Season lightly and sprinkle with cheese. Continue in this way, finishing with a good 15ml spoon cheese mixed with the breadcrumbs. Bake in a hot oven, 220°C, Gas 7, for 15 minutes or until brown.

Cooking time 40 minutes (approx)

Baked Stuffed Marrow

4–6 helpings

1 medium-sized marrow	1 × 15ml spoon chopped
fat for greasing	chives
1 small onion	1 × 5ml spoon
200g minced beef	Worcestershire sauce
100g pork sausage-meat	salt and pepper
or 100g extra minced	1 egg
beef	250ml cheese sauce
25g soft white	(p693)
breadcrumbs	
1 × 15ml spoon chopped	
parsley	

Halve the marrow lengthways and scoop out the seeds. Lay each half side by side, in a well-greased, large, shallow casserole. Skin and chop the onion finely or grate it. Put into a basin with the beef, sausage-meat, if used, breadcrumbs, parsley, chives, Worcestershire sauce, and seasoning. Mix well. Beat the egg until liquid and use it to bind the mixture.

Divide the stuffing between each marrow half. Cover the dish and bake in a moderate oven, 180°C, Gas 4, for 1 hour. Strain off most of the liquid in the casserole. Pour the cheese sauce over the marrow and bake for a further 20 minutes, uncovered, or until the sauce is golden-brown.

Note If preferred, the marrow can be cut into rings, peeled, the seeds removed, and then stuffed as above.

Marrow or Crookneck Squash

4–6 helpings

1kg young marrow **or**　　*salt and pepper*
　crookneck squash　　*2 × 15ml spoons butter*
1 medium-sized onion

Top and tail the marrow or squash; cut it crossways into 2cm slices, discarding any seeds. Skin the onion and chop it finely. Put the marrow and onion in a medium-sized saucepan, and just cover with water. Add the salt and pepper and bring to the boil. Cook for 7–10 minutes until the marrow just yields to pressure. Drain off the water and add the butter. Cook for an additional 3–5 minutes until the marrow is tender.

Yams

The yam resembles the potato, but has a thicker skin and often weighs as much as 1kg. The flesh is very white and floury when cooked and has a sweeter flavour. It can, however, be boiled, steamed, baked, roasted, etc in the same way. Yams are not widely available, but can be found in markets and shops specializing in West Indian, African, and Asian food.

　See also Sweet Potatoes (p803).

MIXED VEGETABLE DISHES

Mixed Vegetables

6 helpings

750g mixed vegetables　　*25g butter* **or** *margarine*
　parsnips, turnips,　　*100–150ml boiling*
　carrots, leeks,　　　*water*
　cauliflower **or**　　*salt and pepper*
　broad beans, peas,
　spring onions,
　tomatoes, new carrots,
　new turnips

Garnish
1 × 15ml spoon chopped
　parsley

Prepare the vegetables; then thinly slice the parsnips, turnips, carrots, and leeks, if used, splitting the slices into halves or quarters if large. Break the cauliflower into florets. Leave most of the other vegetables whole, cutting the larger carrots into thick slices, trimming the spring onions rather short, and cutting the tomatoes into wedges. Melt the fat in a heavy-based saucepan. Add the vegetables at intervals, starting with those which take the longest time to cook. Put the lid on the pan after each addition and toss the vegetables in the fat. (Do not add the tomatoes until 5 minutes before serving.) Add the boiling water and salt; use very little water with the beans and new carrots, etc. Simmer gently until the vegetables are tender. Season with pepper and serve hot, garnished with the parsley.

Note These cooked vegetables can also be used to make a salad. Leave to cool and serve either tossed in French dressing or in mayonnaise.

Cooking time
Parsnips, etc 30–35 minutes
Broad beans, etc 20–25 minutes

VARIATIONS

Mixed Vegetables with Cheese

Cook the vegetables as above and drain off any cooking liquor. Make up 375ml cheese sauce (p693), using the cooking liquor. Coat the vegetables with the sauce in a heatproof dish and sprinkle with 1 × 15ml spoon grated Cheddar cheese. Put under a hot grill to brown or into a hot oven, 220°C, Gas 7, for 10 minutes or until golden-brown.

Note This mixture can also be used to stuff peppers or marrows for a vegetarian main course.

Curried Mixed Vegetables

Cook the vegetables as above and drain off any cooking liquor. Make up 375ml Fruit Curry sauce (p718), using the cooking liquor, and simmer the sauce for at least 2 hours. Add the cooked vegetables and reheat gently.

Serve with boiled rice and the usual curry accompaniments.

Mirepoix of Vegetables

A mirepoix is used in the base of a pan when braising meat and vegetables to give flavour. It is generally discarded after cooking, although it can be kept and served as a vegetable, or puréed and used as a base for a soup. The ingredients can be varied according to the time of year and whatever is being braised. The proportions below give a well-flavoured mirepoix. Keeping these proportions, use larger or smaller quantities of the ingredients as the individual recipes require.

2 medium-sized onions (250g approx)	$\frac{1}{2}$ turnip (50g approx)
1 carrot (50g approx)	25g fat bacon
	15g dripping

Skin and chop the onions, carrot, and turnip. Chop the bacon. Melt the dripping in a pan, add the vegetables and bacon, cover, and fry gently for 10 minutes. Use as required.

VARIATION

Add a chopped stick of celery, some peppercorns, and 1–2 cloves to the basic mirepoix. A little chopped leek can also be added, if liked.

Macédoine of Vegetables

See p398.

Vegetable Casserole

4–6 helpings

400g onions	2 bay leaves
2 cloves garlic	1 × 15ml spoon chopped
2 green peppers	parsley
400g courgettes	1 × 5ml spoon chopped
2 medium-sized	marjoram
aubergines	1 × 5ml spoon chopped
400g tomatoes	thyme
2 × 15ml spoons oil	salt and pepper
200g mushrooms	250ml vegetable stock
1 × 70g can	or water
concentrated tomato	400g potatoes
purée	25g butter

Skin and chop the onions and skin and crush the garlic. Remove the membranes and seeds from the peppers and chop the flesh. Slice the unpeeled courgettes and aubergines and skin and slice the tomatoes. Heat the oil in a frying pan and fry the onions, garlic, and peppers for 5 minutes. Turn into a 3 litre casserole with the courgettes, aubergines, tomatoes, mushrooms, tomato purée, herbs, and seasoning. Mix well and pour in the stock or water. Peel and slice the potatoes thinly, and arrange on the top. Dot with the butter, and cover. Bake in a moderate oven, 180°C, Gas 4, for 1 hour. Remove the lid and bake for a further 30 minutes or until the potatoes are golden-brown.

Vegetable Pie

6 helpings

750g mixed cooked vegetables (p808)	200g cooked haricot beans
1 × 5ml spoon yeast extract	shortcrust pastry (p1249) or cheese pastry (p1251) using 200g flour
1 × 5ml spoon dried mixed herbs	flour for rolling out

Turn the cooked vegetables into a 1–1.5 litre pie dish and add the yeast extract, herbs, and haricot beans, if used. Roll out the pastry on a lightly floured surface and use to cover the pie. Use the pastry trimmings to make leaves to decorate the top of the pastry, and flute the edges. Bake in a fairly hot oven, 200°C, Gas 6, for 40 minutes. Serve hot.

VARIATION

750g mashed potato with 2 × 10ml spoons butter or margarine can be used instead of pastry. Make a pattern on top of the potato with a fork or knife and dot with the butter or margarine. Bake for 25 minutes.

Vegetable Flan

See p1256.

Vegetable and Nut Fricassée

3–4 helpings

1 medium-sized onion	75g cashew nuts **or** pine kernels
2 sticks celery	salt and pepper
25g margarine	2–3 × 15ml spoons single cream
50g flour	
500ml milk	

Garnish

cooked spinach **or** green peas	cooked carrots

Skin the onion, and chop finely with the celery. Melt the margarine in a pan and fry the onion and celery gently for a few minutes, without browning. Stir in the flour and cook for 1 minute. Draw off the heat and gradually stir in the milk. Return to the heat and bring to the boil, stirring all the time, until the sauce thickens. Add the nuts and seasoning. Cover the pan, reduce the heat, and simmer gently for 15 minutes. Stir in the cream and re-season if required.

Make a border of the spinach or peas on a hot dish. Pour the fricassée into the centre of the dish and garnish with the carrot, cut into matchsticks. Serve hot.

Potato and Pepper Casserole with Tomatoes

6 helpings

200g onion	750ml chicken stock
250g green peppers	salt and pepper
150g red peppers	1 × 15ml spoon chopped mixed herbs (oregano, basil, mint, parsley)
250g tomatoes	
1kg potatoes	
50g celery	a pinch of saffron (optional)
50ml oil	150g grated Parmesan cheese
1 × 15ml spoon grated garlic	
50g lean bacon	
50g concentrated tomato purée	

Prepare the vegetables; then chop the onion and celery finely. De-seed the peppers and tomatoes and chop them coarsely. Dice the bacon. Heat the oil in a large saucepan, and sauté the onion, garlic, and bacon for 5 minutes without browning. Add the chopped celery, tomato purée, stock and seasoning, and bring to the boil. Cut the potatoes into quarters or large cubes, and add them to the pan; then stir in the tomatoes, herbs, and saffron, if used. Cook gently for 15 minutes or until the potatoes are tender but not mushy; then transfer to an ovenproof casserole. Sprinkle the vegetables with the cheese, and brown in a fairly hot oven, 190°C, Gas 5, for 15 minutes. Serve at once.

Ratatouille

4 helpings

250g onions (approx)
1 clove of garlic
100g green pepper
  (approx)
200g aubergine (approx)
200g courgettes

400g tomatoes
4 × 15ml spoons olive oil
salt and pepper
1 × 2.5ml spoon
  coriander seeds

Garnish

1 × 15ml spoon chopped
  parsley

Skin the onions and slice in rings. Skin and crush the garlic. Remove the membranes and seeds from the pepper and cut the flesh into thin strips. Cut the unpeeled aubergine and courgettes into 1cm slices. Skin and chop the tomatoes roughly.

Heat 2 × 15ml spoons of the oil in a pan and gently fry the onions, garlic, and pepper for about 10 minutes. Add the remaining oil, the aubergine, and the courgettes. Cover and simmer gently for 30 minutes, stirring occasionally to prevent the vegetables from sticking to the bottom. Add the tomatoes, seasoning and coriander seeds, and simmer for a further 15 minutes. Serve hot or cold, garnished with the parsley.

Nut Mince

6 helpings

200g shelled nuts
1 medium-sized onion
25g margarine
150g dried breadcrumbs
1 × 15ml spoon
  mushroom ketchup or
  any similar sauce

375ml (approx)
  vegetable stock
salt and pepper

Pass the nuts through a nut mill, process them in an electric blender, or chop very finely. Skin and grate the onion. Melt the margarine in a frying pan and fry the nuts, onion, and breadcrumbs until pale golden. Stir in the ketchup and stock, adding a little extra stock if the mixture is too dry. Season to taste and simmer gently for 20–30 minutes. Serve hot.

Peperonata

4 helpings

300g tomatoes
1 large onion
1 large red pepper
2 large green peppers
1 large yellow pepper or
  1 extra red pepper

3 × 15ml spoons olive oil
1 × 2.5ml spoon
  coriander seeds
  (optional)
salt and pepper

Skin the tomatoes, cut into quarters, and remove the seeds. Skin and slice the onion. Skin the peppers, remove the membranes and seeds, and chop the flesh. Heat the oil in a frying pan, add the onion, and fry for 5 minutes. Lightly crush the coriander seeds, if used. Add the tomatoes, peppers, coriander seeds, and seasoning to the pan. Cover and cook gently for 1 hour, stirring from time to time. Re-season if required before serving. Serve hot or cold.

Nut Galantine

6–8 helpings

75g pine kernels
75g cashew nuts
1 clove of garlic
200g soft white or
  brown breadcrumbs
salt and pepper

1 egg
foundation white sauce
  (coating consistency)
  (p692) or Béchamel
  (p704) sauce
meat glaze (p397)

Pass the nuts through a nut mill, process them in an electric blender, or chop very finely. Skin and crush the garlic. Put the nuts and garlic into a basin and add the breadcrumbs and seasoning. Beat the egg until liquid and use to bind the nuts with enough white or Béchamel sauce to form a stiff paste. Shape the mixture into a roll. Tie the galantine in a floured cloth and steam for 1½ hours. Remove from the steamer and place between 2 boards with a light weight on top. Leave for 24 hours.

Heat the glaze and brush over the galantine. Serve with salad.

Note Agar-agar (which comes from seaweed) can be used in place of gelatine for glazing.

SALADS AND DRESSINGS

In making salads, the vegetables, &c., should never be added to the sauce very long before they are wanted for table; the dressing, however, may always be prepared some hours before required. Where salads are much in request, it is a good plan to bottle off sufficient dressing for a few days' consumption, as, the reby much time and trouble are saved.

Salads

Although many salads are simple and easy to make, care must be taken both in preparing the vegetables, fruit, meat, etc and in flavouring the dressing; otherwise the result can be unattractive and unpalatable.

Making Green Salad

The simplest and most usual salad is a tossed green salad, but even this must be carefully prepared. The salad consists of green leaves of one type, or a mixture such as lettuce, watercress, chicory, and endive. The leaves must be fresh and crisp, and they must be dried thoroughly or the salad will be watery and tasteless. The vegetables should be tossed in a French dressing (p849) or vinaigrette sauce (p849) just before serving with chopped herbs, such as parsley, chervil, chives, savory, and marjoram, if liked. If you like garlic, a small crushed clove can be added to the dressing; or a *châpon* of bread can be put in the salad bowl, as is often done in France. To make a *châpon*, rub a crust of French or ordinary white bread all over with crushed garlic. Place the crust in the bottom of the salad bowl with the salad vegetables on top. Pour the dressing over it and toss the bread with the salad, so that the flavour of the garlic gently permeates the whole dish. Although the bread is only meant as a flavouring, garlic addicts will enjoy eating it afterwards!

Making Cooked Vegetable Salads

Not only raw vegetables are used in salads, although nutritionally this is the best way to eat them so that their full vitamin and mineral content is retained. Cooked vegetables of all kinds are also excellent served in a French dressing (p849) or in mayonnaise (p843) with other herbs and seasonings added. Ideally, most vegetables should be cooked especially for the salad and tossed in the dressing while they are still warm, but very good salads can be made from cooked, leftover vegetables, particularly root vegetables. Basic cooking methods are described in the chapter on Vegetables.

Making Salads with Pulses, Pasta, and Rice

Dried pulses – peas, beans, lentils etc, make appetising salads, especially in winter when good fresh vegetables are scarce. They should be tossed in their dressing while still warm, and left to cool and marinate for at least 2–3 hours. For maximum flavour, they can be cooked in stock rather than water; fresh herbs can be added with the dressing.

For more filling and economical salads, pasta and rice provide a good basis, to which can be added a wide variety of fruits and vegetables such as peppers, celery, chicory, carrots, cooked peas, apples, oranges, dried fruit, and nuts. While good for family meals, these salads are particularly useful for buffet parties, since they are easy to prepare in large quantities and are easy to eat with a fork.

Making Salads with Fruit

Adding fruit to mixed salads, or using it as a salad on its own, is an American custom which is now extremely popular in the UK. Fresh fruit is preferable, but frozen or canned can be used if it is not too sweet. Fruits which discolour quickly, such as apples, pears, bananas and peaches, must be quickly dipped in lemon juice or in the dressing in which they will be served – usually mayonnaise (p843) or French dressing (p849) to preserve their colour. Apples can be peeled, but the bright green or red skins often give an attractive colour and texture contrast to other ingredients in the salad. Citrus fruit, such as oranges and grapefruit, should be stripped of every scrap of white pith; they are then generally cut into segments or slices and the thin skin between the segments is removed. Dried fruit, such as apricots, raisins and sultanas, and nuts (usually walnuts, hazelnuts, and almonds) can also be added to rice and pasta salads, coleslaw, and other mixed vegetable salads.

Note Most salads are delicious just with plain mayonnaise (p843) or French dressing (p849). Different ways of making these salad dressings are given on pp843–45 and p849. Any version can be used when a recipe calls for one of the dressings; each will give a slightly different flavour or texture to the salad.

Most other salad dressings and sauces are variations on the basic dressings. Try experimenting with them sometimes instead of using one of the basic dressings.

COMMON SALAD VEGETABLES

Artichokes

Whole globe artichokes are often used in salads, as are the hearts or the bases (*fonds*). Artichokes are always used cooked, and instructions on cooking them can be found on pp744–45.

Jerusalem artichokes are not often used in salads, but small amounts of the cooked vegetable can be mixed with other cooked root vegetables.

Asparagus

Cold cooked asparagus is excellent in salads, and instructions on cooking it can be found on p746. Although fresh asparagus is firmer and has much more flavour, well-drained, frozen or canned asparagus can also be used.

Avocado Pears

These make a very pleasant salad as well as an hors d'oeuvre (see pp310–11). To prepare, first strip or break off the skin, cut the fruit in half, and remove the stone. The flesh can then be either sliced, diced or mashed, but it must first be coated quickly in lemon juice or French dressing (p849) to preserve the colour.

Batavia

Batavia is an open lettuce, rather like endive but not as curly, and with less bitter leaves. It is generally available in winter and should be prepared like lettuce.

Beans – *Fresh*

Broad beans and French beans are the ones most often used in salads, although runner beans can also be used. All these beans are generally cooked but are occasionally used raw.

Beans – *Dried*

Dried beans provide excellent, inexpensive winter salads. Most beans must first be soaked overnight and then cooked until they are tender. They are best if tossed in a dressing while still warm and then left in it to cool. All kinds of beans, including haricot, flageolet, red kidney, Lima and pinto, can be used in this way.

Bean Sprouts

Bean sprouts make a delicious crisp addition to a salad and are easily grown indoors (p754). They should be picked over, washed and dried thoroughly, then mixed with any desired dressing; they are particularly good with French dressing or vinaigrette sauce (p849).

Beetroot

Beetroot are usually used cooked for salads, and instructions on cooking can be found on p755. They can be served in any of the oil and vinegar, cream or mayonnaise dressings given on pp843–49. Beetroot can also be served raw and finely grated.

Brussels Sprouts

Brussels sprouts can be used both cooked and raw. For using raw, they should be prepared as on p757; any coarse outside leaves should be discarded and the sprouts finely shredded. There is therefore no need to choose small compact sprouts when using them raw in salads.

Cabbage

The best cabbage to use for salads is the hard 'white' or Dutch cabbage, but when it is unobtainable, other firm cabbages can be used; salads made with red cabbage look particularly attractive. Cabbage salads are good in the winter when cabbages are generally cheap and other green salad vegetables, such as lettuces and cucumber, are expensive. To prepare, remove any coarse outer leaves, cut the cabbage into quarters, and remove any tough stalks. Shred very finely, using either a small knife or a coarse grater. Blanch for 2–3 minutes, wash in cold water, then dry thoroughly before mixing with the required dressing.

Carrots

Carrots can be used either cooked or raw. If using raw, scrape or peel them, grate finely, and toss quickly in French dressing (p849) or lemon juice to preserve the colour. If cooking the carrots especially for a salad, cook them unpeeled, as on p762 to preserve the maximum food value; then peel.

Cauliflower

Both cooked and raw cauliflower florets make excellent salads. If using raw, break the cauliflower into small florets, discarding all the green leaves and the coarse central stalk. Wash in salted water, dry thoroughly, and blanch.

Celeriac

Celeriac is very good in salads, both raw and cooked. Prepare as on p765. Because raw celeriac discolours quickly, toss it in its dressing as soon as it has been cut.

Celery

Only the inside stalks or heart of the celery can be used for salads. Remove the coarse outer stalks and keep these for flavouring soups, stews, and casseroles. Cut off most of the celery leaves, wash well under running cold water to remove all the earth, then prepare as the recipe describes. Celery is sometimes blanched for 1 minute in boiling water to bring out the flavour.

Chicory

Chicory is a very useful salad ingredient, and is generally available throughout the year. It should be washed in cold water, and can then be cut into thin rings, sliced lengthways, or broken into individual leaves.

Chinese Leaves

Chinese leaves, sometimes called Chinese cabbage, are widely available and, during the winter, make a good alternative to lettuce in a green salad. Wash in cold water, dry thoroughly, then shred finely.

Corn Salad

Corn salad, or lamb's lettuce, is more common in France, where it is known as *Mâche*, than in the UK, but it can sometimes be found and is a most excellent green salad vegetable. Wash, dry thoroughly, and prepare like lettuce.

Courgettes

Lightly cooked courgettes make a very pleasant salad tossed in French dressing or vinaigrette sauce (p849); they can also be eaten raw.

Cress

Cress, or mustard and cress, is frequently used for garnishing salads but can also be added to green salads. Trim from its box, hold in your fingers under running cold water, then dry thoroughly. Mustard and cress are easily grown indoors.

Cucumber

Although cucumber is more digestible if the skin is left on, many people prefer it peeled. For most recipes, it is best to salt the cucumber to drain off the excess liquid. Slice the cucumber thinly and place in a large colander. Sprinkle over 1×5ml spoon salt and leave for 30–40 minutes to drain. Remove from the colander, pat dry with a clean tea-towel or piece of soft kitchen paper, and use as required.

Dandelion Leaves

Dandelion leaves must be young and tender and they should be blanched several days before by placing an inverted pot or other cover over each plant. Prepare like lettuce and toss in French dressing or vinaigrette sauce (p849).

Endive

Endive is an extremely good winter salad vegetable. Advice on buying and storing can be found on p772; endive should be prepared like lettuce.

Fennel

Florence fennel, with its slight flavour of aniseed, can be served on its own or added to a mixed green salad. It is best if served in a French dressing made with lemon juice rather than vinegar (p849).

Kohlrabi

Finely chopped or grated raw kohlrabi is a pleasant addition to winter salads, or it can be blanched with a little mayonnaise (p843) and served as a salad on its own.

Leeks

Leeks can be used either raw or cooked. If using raw, it is best to use very small, young leeks because these have a milder flavour; they should be shredded very finely. Blanched or fully cooked leeks in a vinaigrette sauce (p849) make an excellent winter hors d'oeuvre.

Lentils

Cooked lentils, tossed in French dressing (p849) or mayonnaise (p843), make an unusual and pleasant salad. It is important, however, to use only brown, green or black lentils, since orange ones quickly cook down to a mush.

Lettuce

Lettuce is the most usual basis of any salad and is, of course, the essential ingredient in most green salads. There are two principal types of lettuce: the round cabbage lettuce which is either soft-leaved or crisp (eg Webb's Wonderful), and the cos lettuce, which is tall and crisp. (See also pp776–77.) All lettuces should be as fresh as possible. Avoid buying any with wilted or yellow leaves; they will never taste crisp and fresh. Remove any tough outside leaves (these can be braised or used for soup). Wash the lettuce in cold water to remove all dirt and grit. Dry thoroughly, first in a salad shaker, then in a clean, dry tea-towel, patting lightly without breaking the leaves until quite dry. To ensure that it is really crisp, the lettuce should then be put into a polythene bag in a refrigerator for 1 hour. If the leaves are too large to be left whole, tear them roughly with your fingers (do not use a knife unless shredding) just before adding to the salad. Toss the lettuce in the dressing only just before it is to be served because the acid in the dressing will cause the lettuce to wilt.

Mushrooms

Mushrooms can be served either raw or cooked, but in either case it is best to use the small button ones. They should be prepared as described on p778.

Onions

Spring onions improve the flavour of many salads. To prepare, the root and outside skin of the onion should be removed and the green end trimmed down.

If using large, *whole onions*, it is best to use the mild, Spanish variety, unless only a very small quantity is required.

Parsnips

Cooked, finely diced parsnips can be added with other root vegetables to a mixed salad.

Peas

Cooked fresh or frozen peas are a pleasant addition to both summer and winter salads, and also make an attractive garnish. They should be well coated in French dressing (p849) or mayonnaise (p843) so that they do not dry out, and are particularly good if chopped chervil and/or tarragon has been added to the dressing.

Peppers

Green, yellow, and red peppers can all be used, both raw and cooked, in salads. Green peppers can be blanched in boiling water for 1 minute; this brightens the colour, softens them slightly, and helps to remove some of the slightly bitter taste. The membranes and seeds should be removed, and the flesh is generally finely sliced or diced.

Potatoes

Cooked potatoes, coated in a dressing while they are still warm, make one of the most delicious salads. The potatoes should be cooked in their skins for maximum food value and, if using new potatoes, the skins can be left on (if they are very small they can be left whole). Older potatoes should be peeled and diced.

Radishes

The slightly peppery flavour of radishes and their attractive red colour improves many salads. They should be scrubbed, the root and stem neatly trimmed, and the radishes then very thinly sliced or diced. Instructions for making radish roses and lilies are given on p393. White radishes, or mooli, which are not as strong as red radishes, are another good salad vegetable and it is sometimes possible to buy black radishes as well.

Salsify

Cooked salsify makes an unusual winter salad.

Spinach

Spinach is excellent eaten raw. Choose only the young leaves, wash thoroughly to remove all the dirt and grit, then prepare like lettuce. Raw spinach retains maximum food value, and is extremely economical since no bulk is lost in cooking.

Swedes

Cooked swedes can be added to mixed root vegetable salads.

Sweetcorn (Corn)

Cooked, frozen or canned sweetcorn makes a colourful addition to many salads. It should be drained thoroughly. It can be served on its own in French dressing (p849) or mayonnaise (p843), but is more often added to cooked rice, pasta, potatoes or other ingredients for a composite salad.

Tomatoes

Tomatoes are one of the most common salad vegetables. They are frequently skinned (p803) or the seeds and pulp removed.

Turnips

Turnips can be used both raw and cooked. If raw, use only young turnips; peel and grate or chop them very finely before mixing with the dressing.

Watercress

Watercress can be used both as a garnish and as an addition to green salad. It does not keep well, so choose watercress that looks fresh and green and keep it in a jug of water or in a polythene bag in the refrigerator until it is required. Trim off the coarse stalks, pick over the watercress, then wash in cold water. Dry first in a salad shaker, then pat dry in a clean tea-towel. Put into a polythene bag in the refrigerator and leave to crisp for 1 hour before using.

VEGETABLE SALADS

Artichoke Salad

6 helpings

6 globe artichokes   *vinaigrette sauce* (p849)

Boil or steam the artichokes. Trim the bases so that they stand upright. When cold, trim off the tips of the leaves, if liked. Place the artichokes on individual dishes and serve the vinaigrette sauce separately.

Artichokes are generally served as a starter by themselves.

Artichoke and Asparagus Salad

6 helpings

6 globe artichokes   *100ml French dressing*
500g sprue asparagus   (p849)

Boil or steam the artichokes. When cold, remove the choke and the centre leaves. Cook the asparagus. Leave to cool, then cut the points and green stalks into 1.5cm lengths. Pile into the centres of the artichokes and spoon 1 × 15ml spoon French dressing over each one. The remaining French dressing can be served separately.

Asparagus Salad

6 helpings

50 heads asparagus   *100ml mayonnaise*
2 × 15ml spoons French   (p843)
 dressing (p849)

Boil the asparagus. Leave to cool, then chill lightly. Arrange on a serving dish, with all the points facing the same way. Stir the French dressing into the mayonnaise, and pour it over the points of the asparagus. Serve as soon as possible.

Asparagus and Cauliflower Salad

6 helpings

30 heads asparagus   *1 × 10ml spoon chopped*
1 medium-sized   *parsley*
 cauliflower   *1 × 5ml spoon chopped*
100ml mayonnaise   *tarragon*
 (p843) **or** *salad*   *1 × 5ml spoon chopped*
 dressing (p845)   *chervil*

Boil the asparagus. Cut off the points (the rest of the tender part of the asparagus should be eaten as a hot vegetable). Break the cauliflower into florets and boil or steam until just tender. When the vegetables are quite cold, put into a bowl, add the mayonnaise or salad dressing, and toss lightly. Pile into a serving dish and sprinkle with the chopped herbs before serving.

Avocado Pear Salad

4 helpings

2 avocado pears
4 × 15ml spoons French
  dressing (p849)
1 lettuce

1 medium-sized orange
2 tomatoes
¼ cucumber

Peel the pears, cut them in half, and remove the stones. Cut the flesh into neat slices. Dip quickly in the dressing to preserve the colour. Wash the lettuce, dry thoroughly, and arrange on a serving plate. Peel the orange and cut into segments, discarding all the white skin and pith. Skin and slice the tomatoes and slice the cucumber thinly. Toss all the ingredients lightly in the dressing, then arrange attractively on the bed of lettuce.

Broad Bean Salad

4 – 6 helpings

500g young broad beans
250g young carrots
3 × 15ml spoons French
  dressing or vinaigrette
  sauce (p849)

1 × 10ml spoon chopped
  savory or 1 × 15ml
  spoon chopped chives

Boil or steam the beans and the carrots. While the beans are still warm, toss in the dressing and pile into a serving dish. Leave to become quite cold. Slice the carrots and arrange them neatly round the edge of the dish. Sprinkle with the chopped herbs before serving.

Flageolet Bean Salad

4–6 helpings

250g flageolet beans
salt
a bunch of herbs (thyme,
  sage, savory,
  marjoram, parsley
  stalks)

150ml mayonnaise
  (p843)
1 medium-sized onion
1 × 15ml spoon chopped
  parsley

Soak the beans in cold water overnight. Drain and put into a saucepan with salt and the herbs. Cover with fresh cold water. Bring to the boil, cover, and simmer gently for 1½ hours or until the beans are just tender. Drain thoroughly and, while still warm, stir in the mayonnaise. Skin the onion and chop it finely. Add to the salad with the parsley and toss lightly together. Leave to stand for at least 3 hours before serving for the flavours to blend.

French Bean and Tomato Salad

4 helpings

250g French beans
1 clove of garlic
4 × 15ml spoons
  French dressing or
  vinaigrette sauce
  (p849) or Cambridge
  sauce (p846)

3 tomatoes
salt and freshly ground
  black pepper
1 × 15ml spoon chopped
  chives

Boil or steam the beans until just tender. Skin and crush the garlic, mix with the dressing, and toss the beans in it while still warm. Leave to cool. Skin and quarter the tomatoes and remove the seeds. Add to the beans, season with salt and pepper, and toss lightly. Turn into a bowl and sprinkle with the chives before serving.

Lima Bean Salad

4–6 helpings

250g Lima beans
salt
1 bay leaf
1 sprig of parsley

4 × 15ml spoons French
  dressing (p849)
3 sticks celery

Soak the beans overnight in cold water. Drain, put into a pan and cover with fresh cold water. Add salt, the bay leaf, and parsley. Cover, bring to the boil, and simmer gently for 2 hours or until the beans are quite tender. Drain thoroughly and toss in the French dressing while the beans are still warm. Chop the celery finely, add to the beans, and mix thoroughly. Leave to cool in the dressing for 2 hours before serving.

Bean Sprout Salad

4 helpings

250g bean sprouts
100g Chinese leaves
2 sticks celery
1 small orange

3 × 15ml spoons
French dressing **or**
vinaigrette sauce
(p849)
salt and pepper

Pick over the bean sprouts, wash well, and dry thoroughly. Shred the Chinese leaves and chop the celery finely. Peel the orange, discarding all the white pith. Cut into slices, then cut each slice across into quarters. Put the sprouts, cabbage, celery, and orange into a bowl. Pour the dressing over the salad and toss lightly. Season to taste.

Beetroot and Celery Salad

6 helpings

500g cooked beetroot
1 medium-sized celery
  heart
50g shelled walnuts
2 eating apples,
  preferably with green
  skins

5 × 15ml spoons French
  dressing (p849)
1 × 15ml spoon chopped
  parsley
salt and pepper

Garnish
watercress

Peel the beetroot and cut a few neat rounds for the garnish. Dice the remainder neatly. Use 1 stick of the celery to make celery curls (p389) and chop the remainder. Chop the walnuts coarsely. Quarter the apples, core and dice them. Quickly pour the French dressing over the apples to preserve the colour. Add the beetroot, chopped celery, walnuts and parsley, and toss lightly. Season to taste. Pile into a serving dish. Garnish the salad with small bunches of watercress, the reserved beetroot, and the celery curls.

Beetroot Salad

4–6 helpings

500g cooked beetroot
1 × 10ml spoon grated
  horseradish

4 × 15ml spoons French
  dressing (p849)

Peel the beetroot and slice or dice it neatly. Place in a serving dish. Mix the horseradish with the dressing and spoon over the top of the salad. Chill for 1 hour before serving.

VARIATION

Omit the horseradish, add 1 × 2.5ml spoon dry mustard to the French dressing, and sprinkle with 1 × 10ml spoon chopped chives.

Winter Flemish Salad

4–6 helpings

1 cooked beetroot
  (200g approx)
2 cooked potatoes
  (250g approx)

1 celery heart
4 × 15ml spoons French
  dressing (p849)

Garnish
6 anchovy fillets

watercress sprigs

Peel the beetroot and potatoes and cut them into 5mm dice. Chop the celery finely. Mix the vegetables with the French dressing and toss lightly. Pile into a salad bowl and garnish with anchovy fillets and watercress sprigs before serving.

Cabbage Salad

6 helpings

500g white cabbage
1 × 2.5ml spoon salt

4 × 15ml spoons French
  dressing (p849)

Discard any tough stalks or outside leaves of the cabbage and shred very finely. Sprinkle with the salt. Pour the dressing over the cabbage and toss lightly.

Cabbage, Beetroot, and Carrot Salad

6 helpings

250g white cabbage
1 celery heart
1 cooked beetroot
2 carrots
25g seedless raisins **or**
  sultanas
100ml salad dressing
  (p845)

salt and pepper
½ box mustard and cress
1 × 10ml spoon lemon
  juice
1 × 15ml spoon chopped
  parsley

Discard any tough stalks or outside leaves of the cabbage and shred very finely. Chop the celery finely, peel and dice the beetroot finely, and grate the carrots coarsely. Reserve half the beetroot and carrot for the garnish, and put the rest into a bowl with the cabbage, celery, and raisins or sultanas. Add the salad dressing, toss lightly, and season to taste. Pile on a serving dish. Arrange small piles of beetroot and carrot around the edge of the dish, with small bunches of cress in between. Sprinkle the beetroot and carrots with lemon juice and chopped parsley before serving.

Red Cabbage and Apple Salad

6 helpings

500g red cabbage
3 eating apples,
  preferably with green
  skins

75ml French dressing
  (p849)
1 × 5ml spoon made
  mustard

Garnish
½ box mustard and cress

Discard any tough stalks or outside leaves of the cabbage and shred finely. Quarter the apples, core, and slice thinly. Toss quickly in the dressing to preserve the colour. Add the mustard and mix well, then add the cabbage and toss lightly. Pile into a salad bowl and garnish with cress before serving.

Coleslaw

4–6 helpings

500g firm white cabbage
100g carrots
150ml mayonnaise
  (p843)

salt and freshly ground
  black pepper

Shred the cabbage very finely, scrape the carrots and grate coarsely. Put into a bowl with the mayonnaise and seasoning, and toss well together.

VARIATIONS

1) Core and dice 1 eating apple, toss in 1 × 15ml spoon lemon juice to preserve the colour, and add to the slaw with 25g seedless raisins or sultanas and 25g chopped walnuts, hazelnuts or almonds.
2) Add 100g chopped canned pineapple.
3) De-seed a green pepper, chop the flesh finely, and add to the slaw.
4) Substitute soured cream or yoghurt for mayonnaise.

Marinated Carrot Salad

6 helpings

750g young carrots

1 × 10ml spoon French
  mustard

Marinade
1 clove of garlic
125ml water
125ml wine vinegar
125ml white wine
1 × 5ml spoon salt
1 × 5ml spoon sugar

1 sprig of parsley
1 sprig of thyme
1 bay leaf
a good pinch of Cayenne
  pepper
125ml olive oil

Scrape the carrots and cut into quarters lengthways. Crush the garlic and put it into a pan with the other ingredients for the marinade. Bring to the boil, add the carrots, and cook gently for 15 minutes or until the carrots are just tender. Drain, reserving the liquor. Place the carrots in a deep serving dish. Strain the cooking liquor, stir in the mustard, and pour over the carrots. Serve cold; ideally they should be left to marinate for 24 hours.

Carrot Salad

4–6 helpings

500g carrots	*1 small lettuce*
4 × 15ml spoons French dressing (p849)	*1 × 15ml spoon chopped parsley*

Scrape the carrots, grate finely, and place in a bowl. Pour over the dressing and toss lightly. Wash the lettuce leaves, dry thoroughly and place around the edge of a salad bowl. Pile the carrot into the centre and sprinkle with the chopped parsley before serving.

Cooked Cauliflower Salad

6 helpings

1 large cauliflower	*100ml vinaigrette sauce* (p849)

Remove all the leaves from the cauliflower and boil or steam it until just tender. Drain thoroughly and divide the head neatly into florets. Place the florets in a serving bowl and pour over the sauce while the cauliflower is still warm. Toss very lightly and leave to become quite cold before serving.

Cooked Brussels Sprouts Salad

6 helpings

750g small Brussels sprouts	*75ml French dressing* (p849) **or** *salad dressing* (p845)

Garnish
1 cooked beetroot, peeled and diced finely

Boil or steam the Brussels sprouts. Drain thoroughly and toss in the dressing while still warm. Leave to cool, then pile into a salad bowl. Arrange the beetroot round the edge of the bowl.

Chicory Salad

6 helpings

6 heads chicory	*100ml French dressing made with lemon juice* **or** *vinaigrette sauce* (p849)

Wash the chicory and discard any damaged outside leaves. Cut each head into quarters lengthways. Arrange in a serving dish and pour the dressing over the salad.

Grapefruit and Chicory Salad

6 helpings

3 grapefruit	*3 × 15ml spoons corn* **or** *vegetable oil*
3 small heads chicory	*1 × 2.5ml spoon French mustard*
50g seedless raisins	*salt and pepper*
1 × 15ml spoon grapefruit juice	

Garnish
½ box mustard and cress

Cut the grapefruit in half. Cut the fruit into segments and remove all the pulp and pith from the shells. Shred the chicory, reserving some neat rounds for the garnish, and add to the grapefruit segments, together with the other ingredients. Toss the mixture lightly together, then pile back into the grapefruit shells. Chill lightly for 1 hour, garnish with cress and the reserved pieces of chicory, and serve at once.

Mimosa Salad
See p396.

Celeriac Salad

6 helpings

1 medium-sized celeriac
200ml mayonnaise
  (p843)

1 × 15ml spoon capers
salt and pepper

Peel the celeriac, cut into matchstick-sized pieces, and blanch for 1 minute in boiling acidulated water. Drain, rinse quickly in cold water, drain again and dry thoroughly. Turn into a bowl and add the mayonnaise and capers; season to taste.

Celery Salad

6 helpings

2 celery hearts
125ml mayonnaise
  (p843) **or** *tomato*
  mayonnaise (p845)

1 × 10ml spoon chopped
  chervil
1 × 10ml spoon chopped
  tarragon

Use 1 stick of celery to make celery curls (p389). Chop the rest finely. Stir in the mayonnaise and herbs, and mix well. Leave the salad to stand for 1 hour for the flavours to blend. Garnish with the celery curls before serving.

Celery and Chestnut Salad

4–6 helpings

250g cooked chestnuts
1 celery heart
1 eating apple

100ml mayonnaise
  (p843)
1 small lettuce

Halve or quarter the chestnuts. Use 1 stick of celery to make celery curls (p389). Chop the rest finely. Quarter, core, and dice the apple, and mix quickly with the mayonnaise to preserve the colour. Add the chestnuts and celery and toss lightly. Wash the lettuce, dry thoroughly, and place round the edge of a salad bowl. Pile the chestnut mixture into the centre and garnish with the celery curls before serving.

Cucumber Salad

4–6 helpings

1 large cucumber
1 × 5ml spoon salt
3 × 15ml spoons French
  dressing (p849)

1 × 15ml spoon chopped
  parsley
1 × 5ml spoon chopped
  tarragon

Slice the cucumber thinly and salt it (p815). Rinse and place in a serving dish. Pour over the dressing and sprinkle with the herbs before serving.

Russian Cucumber Salad

6 helpings

4 hard-boiled egg yolks
250ml soured cream
a few drops vinegar

1 large cucumber **or**
  500g small ridge
  cucumbers
salt and pepper

Sieve the egg yolks into a basin. Stir in the cream and vinegar and blend well. If using ridge cucumbers, peel and dice them; it is not necessary to peel the large cucumber. Season the cucumber, and stir in the soured cream mixture. Chill well before serving.

Spanish Cucumber Salad

4 helpings

1 large **or** *2 small*
  cucumbers
1 large red pepper
2 × 15ml spoons olive **or**
  corn oil
1 × 15ml spoon vinegar

salt and pepper
1 × 10ml spoon chopped
  chervil
1 × 15ml spoon chopped
  parsley **or** *chives*

Peel the cucumber thinly, halve lengthways, and remove the seeds with a small spoon. Cut the cucumber into very thin slices or dice finely. Remove the membranes and seeds from the red pepper and cut the flesh into fine strips. Mix the pepper with the cucumber in a basin and add the oil, vinegar, seasoning, and chervil. Toss lightly, turn into a serving dish, and sprinkle with the parsley or chives.

Cucumber and Yoghurt Salad

4–6 helpings

1 large cucumber
1 × 5ml spoon salt
300g natural yoghurt
1 × 15ml spoon vinegar

2 × 15ml spoons
  chopped mint
a pinch of sugar
pepper

Slice the cucumber thinly and salt it (p815). Drain thoroughly, turn into a bowl, and add the yoghurt, vinegar, mint, and sugar. Season, and pile into a serving bowl.

Endive, Celery, and Beetroot Salad

4–6 helpings

1 endive
4 × 15ml spoons salad
  dressing (p845)

2 sticks celery

Garnish
150g cooked beetroot,
  peeled and sliced

Wash the endive and dry thoroughly. Separate the tufts. Place it in a bowl, pour the salad dressing over it, and mix well together. Turn into a salad bowl. Use the sticks of celery to make celery curls (p389). Arrange the beetroot in a border round the salad and scatter the celery curls over the salad.

Endive Salad with Bacon

4–6 helpings

2 small endive
4 rashers streaky bacon,
  without rinds

salt and pepper
2 × 5ml spoons white
  wine vinegar

Use only the white hearts of the endive (the outside of the endive can be braised); divide the tufts into pieces. Place in a salad bowl. Chop the bacon finely. Put into a small frying pan and fry until the bacon is crisp and golden. Add the bacon, with its fat, to the endive. Season, add the vinegar and toss well together.

Fennel Salad

4 helpings

2 Florence fennel bulbs
4 × 15ml spoons French
  dressing (p849) made
  with lemon juice

salt and pepper

Discard any tough outside sheaths of the fennel. Slice very thinly and place in a serving dish. Pour over the French dressing, and season to taste. Leave to marinate for 1 hour before serving.

Fennel and Cucumber Salad

6 helpings

$\frac{1}{2}$ large cucumber
6 radishes
1 Florence fennel bulb
1 clove of garlic
1 × 5ml spoon chopped
  mint

salt and pepper
2 × 15ml spoons olive oil
1 × 15ml spoon lemon
  juice

Garnish
2 hard-boiled eggs

Dice the unpeeled cucumber, slice the radishes and fennel thinly, skin and crush the garlic. Mix the vegetables and garlic together. Add the mint, seasoning, olive oil and lemon juice, and toss together. Pile the salad into a bowl and garnish with quartered hard-boiled eggs before serving.

Cooked Leek Salad

4 helpings

8 small leeks
  (500g approx)
4 × 15ml spoons
  vinaigrette sauce
  (p849)

2 × 15ml spoons
  chopped parsley

Clean and trim the leeks. Boil or steam until just tender, and then drain thoroughly. Arrange in a serving dish and pour the sauce over them while they are still warm. Leave to stand for at least 2 hours. Sprinkle with the parsley before serving.

Lentil Salad

4–6 helpings

250g brown or green lentils	*salt and pepper*
a bunch of herbs (thyme, sage, savory, marjoram, parsley stalks)	*4 × 15ml spoons French dressing (p849)*
	1 medium-sized onion
	2 × 15ml spoons chopped parsley

Put the lentils into a saucepan with the bunch of herbs and the seasoning. Cover with cold water and bring to the boil. Cover, and simmer gently for 1 hour or until the lentils are tender but not mushy. Drain, remove the herbs, and toss the lentils in the dressing while still warm. Skin and chop the onion finely and add to the lentils with half the parsley. Leave to cool. Sprinkle with the remaining parsley before serving.

Lettuce with Soured Cream

4 helpings

1 large crisp lettuce	*salt and pepper*
2 × 5ml spoons sugar	*250ml soured cream*
2 × 5ml spoons vinegar	

Garnish
2 hard-boiled eggs

Wash the lettuce, dry thoroughly, and place the leaves in a salad bowl. Mix the sugar, vinegar, and seasoning into the cream and pour over the lettuce. Garnish with the hard-boiled eggs.

Roman Salad

4–6 helpings

2 cos lettuces	*1 × 5ml spoon clear honey*
1 onion	
3 × 15ml spoons wine vinegar	

Wash the lettuces and dry thoroughly. Skin the onion and chop it finely. Arrange the lettuce leaves in a salad bowl. Blend the vinegar with the honey, pour over the lettuce, and sprinkle with the onion.

Raw Mushroom Salad

4 helpings

350g button mushrooms	*100ml French dressing (p849) made with lemon juice*
1 × 5ml spoon French mustard	*1 × 15ml spoon chopped chives*

Clean the mushrooms but do not peel them. Cut into thin slices. Add the mustard to the dressing and pour over the mushrooms; toss lightly. Leave the mushrooms to marinate in the dressing for at least 30 minutes before serving. Sprinkle with the chopped chives.

VARIATION

Add a thinly sliced red or green pepper to the salad.

Fried Mushroom Salad

6 helpings

500g button mushrooms	*2 × 15ml spoons vinegar or lemon juice*
1 medium-sized onion	*salt and freshly ground black pepper*
3 × 15ml spoons corn or vegetable oil	

Clean the mushrooms, but do not peel them. Leave them whole if small, or cut into halves or quarters if large. Skin the onion and chop it finely. Heat the oil in a wide frying pan and fry the onion gently for 10 minutes. Remove from the pan with a perforated spoon. Add the mushrooms to the oil remaining in the pan, and fry gently for a further 10 minutes or until the mushrooms are cooked. Turn into a salad bowl. Add the onion and vinegar or lemon juice, and toss together. Season to taste. Leave to become quite cold before serving.

Onion Salad

6 helpings

3 large Spanish onions
3 large firm tomatoes

4 × 15ml spoons
French dressing **or**
vinaigrette sauce
(p849)

Parboil the onions for 30 minutes. Leave to cool, then slice as finely as possible. Skin and slice the tomatoes. Arrange the onions and tomatoes in a salad bowl and pour over the dressing. Leave for 1 hour before serving for the flavours to blend.

Pasta Slaw

4–6 helpings

100g pasta rings
300g white cabbage
½ green pepper
¼ cooking apple
1 small carrot
lemon juice
a pinch of sugar

4 × 15ml spoons
mayonnaise (p843)
2 × 15ml spoons soured
cream
1 × 10ml spoon cider
vinegar
salt and pepper

Cook the pasta in boiling salted water until tender. Drain thoroughly and leave to cool. Shred the cabbage very finely. Remove the membranes and seeds from the pepper and slice the flesh finely. Peel the apple and carrot and grate both coarsely. Dip in lemon juice. Put all the ingredients into a bowl and toss lightly. Season to taste before serving.

Rice Salad

5–6 helpings

75g long-grain rice
2 × 15ml spoons olive oil
2 × 15ml spoons white
* wine vinegar*
25g carrots

25g peas
1 small green pepper
2–3 gherkins
chives
salt and pepper

Garnish
watercress sprigs

Cook the rice in boiling salted water for 18–20 minutes. Drain, and stir in the oil and vinegar while the rice is still hot. Scrape and dice the carrots. Cook with the peas in enough salted water to cover until tender; drain thoroughly. De-seed the green pepper and chop the flesh finely. Chop the gherkins and chives. Season well. Mix all the ingredients together and pile on to a dish. Garnish with watercress sprigs before serving.

Rice Salad with Apricots

4 helpings

100g dried apricots
200g long-grain rice
100ml French dressing
* (p849)*

½ bunch spring onions
25g seedless raisins
50g blanched almonds

Soak the apricots in cold water for 6 hours. Drain thoroughly and chop. Cook the rice in boiling salted water until just tender. Drain thoroughly, put into a bowl, and mix in the dressing while the rice is still hot. Chop the spring onions. Add to the rice with the apricots and raisins. Toss well together and leave to cool. Toast the almonds until golden-brown, if liked, and sprinkle over the top of the salad before serving.

Rice and Artichoke Salad

4 helpings

200g long-grain rice
100ml vinaigrette sauce
* (p849)*
1 clove of garlic

400g canned artichoke
* hearts*
2 × 15ml spoons
* chopped chives*

Cook the rice in boiling salted water until just tender. Drain thoroughly, put into a bowl, and mix in the dressing while the rice is still hot. Skin and crush the garlic, add to the rice, toss lightly, and leave to cool. Drain the artichoke hearts, cut them in half, and add to the rice. Mix lightly and sprinkle with the chopped chives before serving.

Potato Salad

6 helpings

6 large new potatoes **or**
  waxy old potatoes
100ml French dressing
  or vinaigrette sauce
  (p849)
3 × 15ml spoons
  chopped parsley

1 × 5ml spoon chopped
  mint
1 × 5ml spoon chopped
  chives **or** spring onions
salt and pepper

Boil or steam the potatoes in their skins until just tender. Drain thoroughly. When cool enough to handle, peel and dice the potatoes. Turn into a bowl and pour over the dressing. Add the herbs and seasoning and toss the mixture together while the potatoes are still warm. Leave to become quite cold before serving.

VARIATIONS

1) Substitute 150ml mayonnaise (p843) or salad dressing (p845) for the French dressing and use 3 chopped spring onions and 2 × 15ml spoons chopped parsley. Omit the mint. Mix together with the potatoes while still warm.
2) Add 2 sticks of celery, finely chopped, to Variation (1).
3) Add 1 red-skinned apple, cored and diced, and tossed in a little lemon juice, to Variation (1).

Hot Potato Salad

6 helpings

6 large new potatoes **or**
  waxy old potatoes
butter **or** margarine for
  greasing
2 × 15ml spoons
  chopped parsley

1 × 15ml spoon chopped
  chives **or** spring onions
1 × 15ml spoon lemon
  juice
4 × 15ml spoons French
  dressing (p849)

Boil or steam the potatoes in their skins until just tender. Drain thoroughly. When cool enough to handle, peel off the skins and cut the potatoes into slices 5mm thick. Put a layer of potatoes into the base of a greased ovenproof dish. Sprinkle with some of the parsley, chives or spring onions, and the lemon juice. Repeat these layers until all the potatoes have been used. Put the French dressing into a small saucepan, bring to the boil, and pour over the potatoes. Cover the dish and cook the potatoes in a moderate oven, 180°C, Gas 4, for 15 minutes or until they are very hot.

German Potato Salad

4 helpings

600g potatoes
1 × 5ml spoon finely
  chopped parsley
1 × 5ml spoon finely
  chopped onion
4 × 15ml spoons stock

1 × 15ml spoon wine
  vinegar
2 × 15ml spoons salad
  oil
salt and pepper

Boil or steam the potatoes in their skins until just tender. Drain thoroughly. When cool enough to handle, peel and cut the potatoes into thick slices Place half in a salad bowl, sprinkle with the parsley and onion, then cover with the remaining potatoes. Heat the stock. Beat in the vinegar, oil, and seasoning. Pour over the potatoes and mix well together, turning lightly over and over. Serve hot or cold.

Potato and Bacon Salad

6 helpings

6 large new potatoes **or**
  waxy old potatoes
2 spring onions
salt and pepper
2 × 15ml spoons white
  wine vinegar

150g lean bacon,
  without rinds
125ml mayonnaise
  (p843)
1 × 15ml spoon chopped
  parsley

Boil or steam the potatoes in their skins until just tender. Drain thoroughly. When cool enough to handle, peel off the skins and cut the potatoes into 1cm dice. Put into a basin. Chop the onions finely, add to the potatoes, and mix lightly. Season, and spoon over the vinegar. Chop the bacon into small pieces, fry slowly until crisp and golden. Drain the bacon of any fat and add to the potatoes, with the mayonnaise. Mix lightly, turn into a serving dish, and sprinkle with the parsley before serving.

Pepper Salad

6 helpings

4 large peppers preferably yellow **or** red	1 celery heart
	3 tomatoes
	salt and pepper
1 bunch of radishes	100ml olive oil

Remove the membranes and seeds from the peppers and cut the flesh into thin strips. Slice the radishes thinly and chop the celery finely. Skin and slice the tomatoes. Mix the vegetables together and arrange in a serving dish. Season, and sprinkle with the oil before serving.

Sweetcorn, Pepper, and Celery Salad

4 helpings

400g cooked, canned **or** frozen and thawed sweetcorn kernels	3 spring onions
	4 × 15ml spoons French dressing (p849)
1 green pepper	
1 celery heart	1 × 15ml spoon chopped parsley

Drain the cooked or canned sweetcorn. Cook the frozen sweetcorn for a few minutes and drain. Blanch the pepper in boiling water for 2 minutes. Drain thoroughly, remove the membranes and seeds, and cut the flesh into 5mm dice. Chop the celery and onions finely. Put the vegetables in a bowl with the dressing and toss lightly. Turn into a serving bowl and sprinkle with the parsley before serving.

Salsify Salad

6 helpings

750g salsify	1 × 10ml spoon chopped dill
125ml tomato mayonnaise (p843) **or** salad dressing (p845)	

Prepare and cook the salsify. Drain thoroughly. Pile into a salad bowl and coat with the mayonnaise or salad dressing. Leave to cool, and sprinkle with the chopped dill before serving.

Spinach Salad(1)

6 helpings

500g fresh spinach	1 × 5ml spoon French mustard
1 clove of garlic	
100ml French dressing (p849) **or** Gloucester sauce (p846)	1 medium-sized onion

Remove the stalks from the spinach, wash the leaves well in cold water, and dry thoroughly. Skin and crush the garlic and add to the dressing with the mustard. Pour over the spinach and toss lightly. Skin the onion, cut about 3 slices into rings, and chop the rest finely. Add the chopped onion to the salad and toss again. Turn into a salad bowl and garnish with the onion rings before serving.

Spinach Salad(2)

4 helpings

500g fresh young spinach	125g button mushrooms
	1 small onion
4 rashers streaky bacon, without rinds	French dressing (p849) made with 100ml oil

Prepare the spinach as above. Fry the bacon until crisp; then drain and crumble it. Wipe the mushrooms and trim the end of the stalks; slice thinly. Skin the onion and slice it thinly. Tear the spinach into large pieces and put into a large salad bowl. Add the bacon, mushrooms, and onion. Pour over the dressing and toss well. Serve immediately.

Tomato Salad

4–6 helpings

500g firm tomatoes
salt and pepper
3 × 15ml spoons French
dressing (p849)

1 × 5ml spoon chopped
basil

Skin the tomatoes and cut into slices. Place in a serving dish and season lightly with salt and pepper. Pour over the dressing and sprinkle with the chopped basil before serving.

VARIATIONS

1) Omit the basil.
2) Omit the basil and sprinkle with 1 × 15ml spoon chopped chives or spring onions.
3) Rub the salad bowl with a cut clove of garlic before putting in the tomatoes.
4) Add 25g stoned black olives.

Tomato and Artichoke Salad

6 helpings

500g firm tomatoes
6 cooked or canned
artichoke bases (fonds)

4 × 15ml spoons
mayonnaise (p843) or
salad dressing (p845)
a pinch of paprika

Skin the tomatoes and cut into slices. Split the artichoke bases in half crossways. Arrange the tomato and artichoke slices in a serving dish. Spoon the mayonnaise or salad dressing over the top and sprinkle with the paprika before serving.

Tomato and Onion Salad

4–6 helpings

1 large Spanish onion
500g firm tomatoes

4 × 15ml spoons French
dressing (p849)

Parboil the onion for 30 minutes. Leave to cool, then chop finely. Skin and slice the tomatoes. Arrange the tomatoes in a serving dish, sprinkle with the onion, and pour over the dressing.

MIXED SALADS

Chef's Salad (1)

4 helpings

½ clove of garlic
½ lettuce
8 anchovy fillets
8 black olives
4 small tomatoes
5cm length cucumber

2 hard-boiled eggs
50g Gruyère cheese
salad dressing for Crab
and Mandarin Salad
(p837)

Rub the cut side of the garlic round the inside of a salad bowl. Wash the lettuce, dry thoroughly and shred; lay it in the bottom of the bowl. Chop the anchovy fillets. Halve and stone the olives. Quarter the tomatoes but do not skin them. Dice the cucumber without peeling it. Cut the eggs into 6 or 8 segments each and the cheese into 5mm strips. Jumble all these ingredients together, taking care not to break the egg segments. Arrange on the lettuce so that red, black, and yellow ingredients are all showing. Just before serving, trickle a little of the dressing over the salad. Serve the rest of the dressing separately.

Note For Chef's Salad (2), see p837.

Fruit, Cheese, and Yoghurt Salad

3–4 helpings as a main course

6–8 helpings as a side salad

200g black grapes
4 red dessert apples
juice of 1 lemon

200g Wensleydale cheese
250g natural yoghurt
lettuce leaves

Halve and de-pip the grapes. Core the apples but do not peel them. Cut them into 1.5cm cubes, and toss at once in the lemon juice. Cut the cheese into 1.5cm cubes. Toss the grapes, apple, and cheese cubes lightly in the yoghurt, taking care not to break the cheese cubes. Make a bed of lettuce leaves on a salad platter, and pile the salad on top. The red tints of the apple skin and the black grapes supply colourful touches through the white dressing. No other garnish is needed.

Mixed Vegetable Salad(1)

(using cooked summer vegetables)

4–6 helpings

3 large new potatoes	*1 × 5ml spoon chopped*
3 young turnips	*mint*
½ bunch young carrots	*125ml mayonnaise*
(250g approx)	*(p843)*
250g shelled peas	*salt and pepper*
1 × 15ml spoon chopped	*a pinch of paprika*
parsley	

Boil or steam the potatoes, turnips, and carrots in their skins. Drain thoroughly, then peel and dice neatly. Boil or steam the peas. Add to the remaining vegetables with the parsley, mint, mayonnaise and seasoning, and mix well. Turn into a serving dish and sprinkle with a little paprika before serving.

Mixed Vegetable Salad(2)

(using cooked winter vegetables)

6 helpings

2 large carrots	*4 × 15ml spoons*
2 young turnips	*mayonnaise* (p843)
1 medium-sized	*salt and pepper*
cauliflower	*2 × 15ml spoons French*
1 cooked beetroot	*dressing* (p849)
250g frozen peas	

Garnish
½ bunch watercress

Boil or steam the carrots and turnips in their skins. Boil or steam the cauliflower. Peel and dice the carrots, turnips, and beetroot. Break the cauliflower into florets. Cook the peas according to the directions on the packet. Drain thoroughly. Put all the vegetable trimmings and uneven pieces into a bowl with half the peas. Add the mayonnaise, mix well, and season. Pile on to a serving plate. Arrange the remaining vegetables in neat rows over the mixture, with suitable colours adjoining. Garnish the edges with small sprigs of watercress and sprinkle the French dressing over the vegetables.

Italian Salad

4 helpings

500g potatoes	*1 shallot*
1 large carrot	*125ml mayonnaise*
1 turnip	*(p843)*
250ml stock	*salt and pepper*
1 cooked beetroot	

Garnish
watercress sprigs

Boil or steam the potatoes in their skins until tender, then drain thoroughly. Peel and slice the carrot and turnip, and cook in the stock until just tender. Drain thoroughly. Slice the potatoes, peel and slice the beetroot and cut into strips, and skin and chop the shallot finely. Mix all the ingredients together and season to taste. Pile the salad on to a serving plate and garnish with watercress sprigs before serving.

Pasta Salad with Sweetcorn and Anchovy

4–6 helpings

150g pasta shells	*150g cooked or canned*
4 × 15ml spoons	*sweetcorn kernels*
mayonnaise (p843) *or*	*100g cooked peas*
salad dressing (p845)	*2 × 15ml spoons*
1 × 15ml spoon chutney	*chopped parsley*
50g canned anchovies	*pepper*

Cook the pasta in boiling salted water until just tender. Drain thoroughly, and while still warm, stir in the mayonnaise or salad dressing, and the chutney. Cool. Drain the anchovies and chop finely. Add to the pasta with the drained sweetcorn, peas, half the parsley, and seasoning. Toss all the ingredients together. Turn into a salad bowl and sprinkle with the remaining parsley before serving.

Spanish Salad

4–6 helpings

6 firm tomatoes	salt and pepper
3 cooked potatoes	4 ×15ml spoons French
2 cooked **or** canned red	dressing (p849)
peppers	
250g cooked French	
beans	

Skin the tomatoes, peel the potatoes, and slice both. Remove the membranes and seeds from the peppers and slice the flesh. Arrange the vegetables in neat rows on a serving dish. Season, and sprinkle with the dressing.

Summer Salad

6 helpings

1 large lettuce	3 tomatoes
½ small cucumber	½ bunch radishes

Garnish
2 hard-boiled eggs,	watercress sprigs **or**
thickly sliced	mustard and cress

Wash the lettuce and dry thoroughly. Reserve the best leaves and shred the rest. Slice the cucumber thinly. Skin and slice the tomatoes and slice the radishes. Mix the shredded lettuce leaves with half the cucumber, tomatoes, and radishes. Line a salad bowl with the lettuce leaves and pile the salad into the centre. Garnish with the reserved cucumber, tomatoes and radishes, the eggs, and the watercress or mustard and cress.

Serve with whole spring onions and 100ml salad dressing (p845).

Russian Salad

See p314.

SALADS WITH FRUIT

Apple, Celery, and Nut Salad

6 helpings

2 large green eating	1 large **or** 2 small celery
apples	hearts
4 ×15ml spoons	about 6 crisp lettuce
mayonnaise (p843) **or**	leaves (preferably cos)
salad dressing (p845)	
100g black **or** white	
grapes	

Garnish
a few walnut halves

Quarter the apples, core, and cut into thin slices. Stir into the mayonnaise or salad dressing to preserve the colour. Halve and de-pip the grapes. Chop the celery finely. Add to the apple and mix lightly. Arrange the lettuce leaves round the edge of a salad bowl. Pile the apple mixture into the centre and garnish with the walnuts before serving.

VARIATION

Use 2 oranges, peeled and segmented, in place of the grapes.

Apple and Cucumber Salad

6 helpings

1 small cucumber	3 ×15ml spoons single
3 eating apples,	cream **or** evaporated
preferably with red	milk
skins	salt and pepper
1 ×15ml spoon lemon	1 ×15ml spoon finely
juice	chopped mint

Slice the cucumber thinly and salt it (p815). Dry thoroughly and put into a basin. Quarter the apples, core, and cut into thin slices. Toss quickly in the lemon juice to preserve the colour. Add to the cucumber, then stir in the cream or milk and toss lightly. Season to taste. Pile into a salad bowl and sprinkle with the mint before serving.

Apple, Banana, and Nut Salad

6 helpings

6 medium-sized red
  eating apples
2 × 15ml spoons lemon
  juice
2 bananas
1 small lettuce heart
1 × 15ml spoon coarsely
  chopped nuts (walnuts,
  almonds **or** hazelnuts)

4 × 15ml spoons
  mayonnaise (p843) **or**
  salad dressing (p845)
salt and pepper

Garnish
a few watercress sprigs

Polish each apple with a soft cloth. Cut off the top, then scoop out the core and seeds and most of the apple flesh, leaving a shell approximately 1cm thick. Discard the core and seeds. Chop about half the apple pulp and toss quickly in the lemon juice to preserve the colour. Cut the bananas into thin slices, then add to the chopped apple and toss together. Wash the lettuce heart, shred finely and add to the fruit with the nuts and mayonnaise or salad dressing. Toss lightly and season to taste, then pile this mixture back into the apple cases. Garnish each with a sprig of watercress before serving.

Waldorf Salad

4 helpings

4 sharp red dessert
  apples
2 sticks celery
25g chopped **or** broken
  walnuts

75ml mayonnaise (p843)
2 × 15ml spoons lemon
  juice
a pinch of salt
lettuce leaves (optional)

Core the apples and chop them coarsely; if unblemished, the peel should be left on. Slice the celery thinly. Mix the walnut pieces with the apples and celery. Mix together the mayonnaise, lemon juice and salt, and fold into the apple mixture. Chill before serving. Serve on a bed of lettuce leaves, if liked.

Apple and Potato Salad

4–6 helpings

1 × 5ml spoon French
  mustard
100ml French dressing
  (p849)
4 eating apples,
  preferably with red
  skins

3 cooked potatoes
1 × 10ml spoon chopped
  chives
1 × 10ml spoon chopped
  parsley

Blend the mustard into the dressing in a basin. Quarter and core the apples, and cut into 5mm dice. Toss quickly in the dressing to preserve the colour. Cut the potatoes into 5mm dice and add to the apples. Mix lightly, then pile into a serving dish and sprinkle with the chives and parsley before serving.

Grapefruit and Asparagus Salad

4 helpings

20 heads asparagus
2 grapefruit
2 × 15ml spoons lemon
  juice
1 × 15ml spoon
  Worcestershire sauce

2 × 15ml spoons tomato
  ketchup
salt and pepper

Boil the asparagus. Cut off the points and leave to cool. (The rest of the tender part of the asparagus can be eaten as a hot vegetable.) Cut the grapefruit in half. Cut the fruit into segments and remove. Cut all the pith and skin out of the shells. Mix the grapefruit segments with the asparagus points. Put the rest of the ingredients into a screw-topped jar and shake well to mix. Pour over the grapefruit and asparagus. Toss lightly, then pile into the grapefruit shells. Chill for 1 hour before serving.

Banana Salad

6 helpings

6 bananas
2 ×15ml spoons lemon juice
4 ×15ml spoons mayonnaise (p843) **or** *salad dressing* (p845)

1 ×15ml spoon chopped parsley
1 small bunch watercress
1 ×15ml spoon French dressing (p849)

Cut the bananas into slices about 5mm thick. Put into a basin, sprinkle with the lemon juice, and toss lightly. Pile into a serving dish and spoon over the mayonnaise or salad dressing. Sprinkle with the chopped parsley. Arrange the watercress neatly round the edge of the dish and sprinkle lightly with the French dressing.

VARIATION

Add 25g coarsely chopped walnuts to the sliced bananas.

Banana and Celery Salad

6 helpings

6 bananas
2 ×15ml spoons lemon juice
1 small celery heart
25g shelled walnuts

4 ×15ml spoons mayonnaise (p843) **or** *salad dressing* (p845) (approx)*
salt and pepper

Garnish
orange segments from 1 orange
a few watercress sprigs

Cut the bananas into thin slices. Put into a basin, sprinkle with the lemon juice, and toss lightly. Chop the celery and walnuts finely. Add to the bananas with the mayonnaise or salad dressing, toss lightly, and season to taste. Pile the mixture into a salad bowl. Garnish with orange segments and watercress sprigs.

Banana, Raisin, and Carrot Salad

6 helpings

6 bananas
2 ×15ml spoons lemon juice
25g blanched almonds
2 large carrots
50g seedless raisins

3 ×15ml spoons French dressing (p849) *made with lemon juice*
1 ×15ml spoon chopped parsley

Cut the bananas into thin slices. Put into a basin, sprinkle with the lemon juice, and toss lightly. Chop the almonds and grate the carrots coarsely. Add to the bananas with the raisins. Pour over the dressing and toss lightly. Turn into a serving dish and sprinkle with the parsley before serving.

Carrot and Orange Salad

4 helpings

300g carrots
3 ×15ml spoons French dressing (p849)
2 oranges

Garnish
watercress sprigs

Scrape the carrots and grate finely. Pour over the dressing and toss lightly. Peel the oranges, discarding all the white pith, and cut into slices. Pile the grated carrot into the centre of a serving dish. Arrange the orange slices round the edge and garnish with watercress sprigs before serving.

Orange Salad for Game

See p669.

Vegetables, Salads and Dairy Foods

Spinach Soufflé (p924)

TOP *Baked Stuffed Potatoes* (p793)

LEFT *Baked Stuffed Peppers* (p789)

RIGHT *(clockwise from top) Cooked French Bean Salad* (pp812–13), *Rice Salad with Apricots* (p825), *Tomato Salad* (p828), *Waldorf Salad* (p831), *Beetroot Salad* (p819), *Sweetcorn, Pepper and Celery Salad* (p827), *Potato Salad* (p826), *Orange and Celery Salad* (p833)

English Cheeses
1 *Wensleydale*
2 *Leicester*
3 *Caerphilly*
4 *Derby*
5 *English Cheshire*
6 *Lancashire*
7 *Double Gloucester*
8 *English Cheddar*
9 *Stilton*

Pulses, Pasta and Rice

LEFT *Stacked Omelet* (p927) *filled with prawns, mushrooms and tomatoes*

BELOW *Cauliflower Cheese* (p1324), *Spinach Pancakes* (p938), *and Eggs in Cocottes* (p906)

Orange and Celery Salad

4 helpings

6 oranges	*4 × 15ml spoons French*
6 sticks celery	*dressing* (p849)
50g shelled walnuts (can	*8 crisp lettuce leaves*
be broken pieces)	*(optional)*

Peel the oranges and cut into segments, discarding all the white skin and pith. Chop the celery and walnuts. Put the oranges, celery, and walnuts into a bowl, pour over the dressing, and toss together. Arrange the lettuce leaves, if used, on individual plates and spoon the salad on top just before serving.

Pineapple Salad

4–6 helpings

1 small pineapple **or**	*4 × 15ml spoons*
400g canned pineapple	*mayonnaise* (p843) **or**
1 celery heart	*salad dressing* (p845)
	salt and pepper

Garnish
½ lemon, thinly sliced

If using a fresh pineapple, peel, removing all the eyes, and cut out the core. Cut the fresh or canned pineapple into 5mm pieces. Shred the celery finely and add to the pineapple with the mayonnaise or salad dressing and the seasoning. Toss the mixture lightly, then chill for at least 2 hours. Garnish with lemon slices just before serving.

Indian Pineapple Salad

4–6 helpings

1 small pineapple	*1 celery heart*
1 sharp apple	*250ml mayonnaise*
1 × 15ml spoon lemon	*(p843)*
juice	*salt and pepper*

Garnish
1 small sweet red pepper

Peel the pineapple, removing all the eyes, and cut out the core. Cut into 5mm pieces. Peel and core the apple, cut into small pieces, and toss quickly in the lemon juice. Cut the celery into fine strips, reserving the leaves. Mix the pineapple, apple, and celery in a bowl, add the mayonnaise and seasoning, mix well, and turn into a serving bowl. Remove the membranes and seeds from the red pepper and slice the flesh thinly. Garnish with the pepper and the celery leaves. Serve chilled.

Pineapple and Cheese Salad

4 helpings

8 crisp lettuce leaves	*4 × 15ml spoons*
4 slices fresh **or** *canned*	*Thousand Islands*
pineapple	*dressing* (p847)
100g full-fat soft cheese	

Garnish

4 × 5ml spoons chopped	*gherkin slices*
parsley	*4 pieces chilli pepper*

Arrange the lettuce leaves on a small plate and place the pineapple in the centre. Pile the cheese on top of the pineapple, then spoon over the dressing and garnish with chopped parsley, gherkin slices, and chilli pepper.

Carrot and Pineapple Salad

4 helpings

350g young carrots	*3 × 15ml spoons French*
150g white cabbage	*dressing* (p849)
150g crushed pineapple,	
fresh **or** *canned*	

Garnish

1 small lettuce	*canned pimento strips*

Scrape the carrots and grate coarsely. Shred the cabbage finely. Drain the pineapple if required. Mix the vegetables with the pineapple. Pour over the dressing and toss lightly. Wash the lettuce and dry thoroughly. Pile the salad into a serving dish and garnish with lettuce and pimento strips.

Note Fresh pineapple will be sharper in flavour than canned pineapple.

Melon Salad

6 helpings

¼ medium-sized honeydew melon	1 bunch watercress
salt and pepper	3 × 15ml spoons French dressing (p849)
a pinch of paprika	3 × 15ml spoons mayonnaise (p843)
1 × 5ml spoon caster sugar	
1 × 10ml spoon lemon juice	

Garnish

3cm length cucumber, sliced	½ sliced lemon

Peel the melon and cut into 1cm cubes. Put into a basin and add the salt, pepper, paprika, caster sugar, and lemon juice. Pile into a salad bowl and chill for 1 hour. Wash the watercress thoroughly, dry, and toss lightly in the French dressing. Arrange the watercress round the edge of the melon salad. Spoon the mayonnaise over the melon mixture. Garnish with cucumber and lemon slices just before serving.

Cherry Salad

4–5 helpings

500g black cherries	1 × 5ml spoon finely chopped tarragon
1 × 15ml spoon olive oil	
1 × 5ml spoon lemon juice	1 × 5ml spoon finely chopped chervil
1 × 2.5ml spoon tarragon vinegar	1 × 5ml spoon caster sugar
1 × 10ml spoon brandy or Kirsch	salt and pepper

Stone the cherries. Crack some of the stones and mix the kernels with the cherries. Put the other ingredients into a screw-topped jar and shake well. Pour over the cherries. Leave for at least 1 hour before serving.

Serve with roast game or duck.

Strawberry and Tomato Salad

6 helpings

300g firm strawberries	1 × 10ml spoon lemon juice
450g firm tomatoes	
salt	3 × 15ml spoons mayonnaise (p843)
a pinch of paprika	

Garnish

1 lettuce heart	3cm length cucumber, thinly sliced

Hull the strawberries and cut them into quarters. Skin the tomatoes, cut in half, remove the seeds and pulp, and cut the remaining tomato into thin slices (the seeds and pulp can be sieved and used for cocktails, etc). Season the tomato slices with salt and paprika, and sprinkle with the lemon juice. Just before serving, mix with the strawberries and pile into a salad bowl. Spoon over the mayonnaise and place the lettuce heart in the centre. Use the cucumber slices to encircle the base of the platter on which the salad bowl stands.

Pear, Nut, and Date Salad

6 helpings

3 ripe dessert pears or 6 canned pear halves	50g shelled walnuts
	1 × 10ml spoon chopped parsley
1 × 15ml spoon lemon juice	3 × 15ml spoons French dressing (p849) or salad dressing (p845)
1 small crisp lettuce	
100g stoned dates	

If using fresh pears, peel and halve them, and remove the cores with a small spoon. Sprinkle lightly with the lemon juice to preserve the colour. If using canned pears, drain off the juice, and dry thoroughly. Wash the lettuce and dry thoroughly. Reserve 6 outside leaves and shred the rest. Mix with the dates, walnuts, and parsley. Add the dressing and toss lightly. Arrange a lettuce leaf on each of 6 individual plates and place the pear in the centre, with the cut side uppermost. Pile in the date mixture and chill lightly for 1 hour before serving.

Grape Salad

4–6 helpings

500g green grapes   *4 × 15ml spoons French dressing (p849)*

Skin the grapes, halve and de-pip them. Place in a salad bowl, pour over the dressing, and toss lightly. Chill for 1 hour before serving.

MAIN-COURSE SALADS

Anchovy Chequerboard Salad

4 helpings

400g cod fillet
2 × 15ml spoons water
2 × 15ml spoons lemon juice
1 × 15ml spoon chopped parsley
1 × 15ml spoon chopped chives

salt and pepper
1 large lettuce heart
1 hard-boiled egg
1 × 100g can anchovy fillets

Garnish
radish roses (p393)   *parsley sprigs*

Put the cod fillet in an ovenproof dish with the water. Cover and cook in a fairly hot oven, 190°C, Gas 5, for 20 minutes. Leave to cool. Remove any skin and bones, and flake the fish. Moisten it with the lemon juice, and stir in the parsley and chives with seasoning to taste. Shred the lettuce, and arrange in a flat layer on a platter. Arrange the fish neatly on the bed of shredded lettuce, and smooth the surface. Slice the egg. Drain the anchovy fillets and place in a grid pattern on top of the fish mixture. Fill the spaces with rings of hard-boiled egg. Garnish with radish roses and parsley sprigs.

Dressed Lobster to Eat Cold

See p425.

Halibut, Orange, and Watercress Salad

4 helpings

4–6 halibut steaks
500ml court bouillon (p429)

1 lettuce
mayonnaise (p843)

Garnish
orange twists (p392)   *watercress sprigs*

Poach the fish steaks in the court bouillon for 7–10 minutes. Lift out, drain well and leave to cool. Remove the skin. Wash the lettuce, dry thoroughly and shred the outer leaves; arrange them on a salad dish. Coat the fish with mayonnaise, and arrange on the lettuce. Garnish with orange twists, the remaining lettuce, and watercress sprigs.

Mackerel Salad

4 helpings

8 mackerel fillets
500ml court bouillon (p429)

1 × 15ml spoon gelatine
50ml cider vinegar
50ml mayonnaise (p843)

Garnish
sprigs of tarragon, chervil or parsley

tomato wedges
watercress sprigs

Wash and dry the fillets, then poach them gently for 15 minutes in the court bouillon. Drain and leave to cool. Skin neatly.

While the fish is cooking, soften the gelatine in the vinegar, then stand the container in hot water, and stir until the gelatine dissolves. Mix with the mayonnaise, and chill until almost at setting point. Coat the skinned side of each fillet with the semi-set mayonnaise. Garnish each fillet with tarragon, chervil or parsley, and with tomato wedges and watercress sprigs.

Prawn or Shrimp Salad

4 helpings

½ cucumber	200g cooked shelled
salt	prawns **or** shrimps,
2 lettuce hearts **or** 1	fresh **or** frozen and
large well-hearted	thawed
lettuce	2 hard-boiled eggs
4 × 15ml spoons	freshly ground black
mayonnaise (p843)	pepper
2 × 15ml spoons natural	
yoghurt **or** buttermilk	

Slice the unpeeled cucumber thinly and salt it (p815). Drain for 30 minutes, then rinse lightly and pat dry. Use the slices to line a glass salad bowl, placing them side by side, touching but not overlapping. Wash the lettuce, dry thoroughly, and shred finely. Sprinkle with salt, and lay in the lined bowl. Mix together the mayonnaise and yoghurt or buttermilk, and spoon this over the lettuce. Pile the prawns or shrimps in the centre of the dish. Slice or halve the hard-boiled eggs lengthways, and arrange the slices in a circle round the shellfish. Sprinkle with freshly ground black pepper just before serving.

Salmon and Aspic Moulded Salad

6–8 helpings

25g gelatine	100g cooked salmon **or**
500ml fish stock (p330)	1 × 400g can salmon
salt and pepper	

Garnish
½ unpeeled cucumber,	a few slices tomato
sliced	

Dissolve the gelatine in the stock, and season to taste. Drain the oil from the salmon, if using canned fish, and remove all skin and bones. Cover the bottom of a 600ml mould with the stock and leave to set; then garnish with slices of cucumber and tomato. Add a little more jelly and leave to set. Add a layer of salmon, cover with jelly, and leave on one side until set. Repeat these layers until the mould is full. Keep in a cool place until required, then turn out on to a wetted serving plate and garnish with cucumber and tomato slices.

Serve cold with Potato Salad (p826) and Cucumber Salad (p822).

Red Fish Salad or Sea Bream Mayonnaise (Red Fish)

4 helpings

600g sea bream fillets	1 hard-boiled egg
butter **or** margarine for	125ml mayonnaise
greasing	(p843)
lemon juice	1 × 10ml spoon chopped
salt and pepper	parsley

Garnish
lettuce leaves	tomato wedges

Skin the fillets and place in a greased ovenproof dish. Sprinkle with lemon juice and seasoning. Cover loosely with greaseproof paper and bake in a fairly hot oven, 190°C, Gas 5, for 20 minutes. When cooked, flake with a fork, remove any bones, and leave to cool. Meanwhile, chop the hard-boiled egg. Just before serving, mix the fish with the mayonnaise, chopped parsley, and chopped egg. Serve on a bed of lettuce leaves and garnish with tomato wedges.

Salad Niçoise

4–6 helpings

250g French beans	225g canned tuna
2 hard-boiled eggs	50g black olives
3 tomatoes	4 × 15ml spoons French
1 large lettuce	dressing (p849)
1 clove of garlic	salt and pepper

Garnish
50g canned anchovy	
fillets	

Boil or steam the beans until just tender. Cut the eggs into quarters. Skin and quarter the tomatoes. Wash the lettuce and dry thoroughly. Skin and crush the garlic, and drain and flake the tuna. Line a large salad bowl with the lettuce leaves. Put the beans, eggs, tomatoes, garlic, tuna, most of the olives, and the dressing into a bowl and toss lightly. Season to taste. Pile into the centre of the salad bowl and garnish with the remaining olives and the anchovy fillets before serving.

Crab and Mandarin Salad

4 helpings

100g canned mandarin orange segments	*lettuce leaves*
75g celery	*400g white crabmeat, canned or frozen and thawed*
50g shelled whole walnuts or walnut halves	

Dressing

125ml soured cream	*salt and pepper*
50g blue cheese (see Note)	*75ml salad oil*
1 × 2.5ml spoon grated lemon rind	*25ml fresh or bottled lemon juice*

Drain the mandarin segments. Slice the celery into fine rings, and chop 25g of the walnuts coarsely. Reserve the rest for garnishing. Lay the lettuce leaves on a flat salad platter. Drain the crabmeat well. Toss together the crabmeat, mandarin orange segments, celery and chopped walnuts, breaking up any large chunks of crabmeat with a fork. Arrange on the lettuce leaves.

For the dressing, gradually work the soured cream into the cheese to make a smooth mixture. Add the remaining ingredients and beat or whisk until completely blended. Leave to chill.

Serve by trickling a very little dressing over the crabmeat. Stud with the reserved walnuts. Serve the rest of the dressing separately.

Note Use Dolcelatte, Pipo Crème or any other mild blue cheese with a white ground colour which is not too salty or pungent for this salad dressing.

Chef's Salad (2)

4 helpings

½ cos lettuce	*2 hard-boiled eggs*
French dressing (p849)	
50–75g each of:	
cooked chicken or turkey	
cooked ham	
cooked tongue	
Gruyère cheese	

Wash the lettuce, dry thoroughly, and shred. Toss with a little of the dressing, and place in the bottom of a salad bowl. Cut the meats and cheese into julienne strips. Jumble them on top of the lettuce. Halve the eggs and place on the salad. Serve the remaining dressing separately.

Note For Chef's Salad (1), see p828.

Cooked Meat Salad

4 helpings

200g small potatoes	*1 hard-boiled egg*
300g cold roast lamb, mutton, beef or veal	*4 × 15ml spoons salad dressing (p845), soured cream or natural yoghurt*
6 gherkins	
25g canned mushrooms in brine	*salt and pepper*
½ small onion	*1 lettuce*
3 sprigs pickled cauliflower	*1 × 10ml spoon chopped parsley*

Boil the potatoes in their skins and leave until cold before peeling them. Cut the meat into small neat pieces. Slice the gherkins and mushrooms, and chop the onion, cauliflower, and egg. Mix all together with the salad dressing, soured cream or yoghurt. Season to taste. Wash the lettuce, dry thoroughly and arrange a border of leaves in a salad bowl; spoon the salad into the centre. Sprinkle with the chopped parsley.

Cold Meat Salad

6 helpings

450g cold roast meat
  (beef, lamb **or** veal)
200g cooked green peas
celery salt
pepper
6 crisp lettuce leaves
150ml mayonnaise
  (p843)

1 × 2.5ml spoon mixed
  English mustard
  (optional)
1 × 10ml spoon chopped
  mint (optional)

Cut the meat into 2cm cubes and mix with the cooked peas. Season to taste with celery salt and pepper. Wash the lettuce leaves and leave to crisp in the refrigerator, if necessary. Place the lettuce leaves on a salad plate and divide the meat mixture between them, forming a small pyramid on each lettuce leaf. Flavour the mayonnaise or salad dressing with the mustard and/or chopped mint, if liked. Spoon the mayonnaise or salad dressing over the meat salad.

Jellied Ham Salad

2–3 helpings

125g cooked ham
50g cooked macaroni
1 medium-sized tomato
salt and pepper
1 × 5ml spoon chopped
  parsley

150ml aspic jelly
2 hard-boiled eggs
2 × 10ml spoons gelatine
75ml white stock (p329)

Garnish
green salad (p812)

Chop or mince the ham, chop the macaroni, skin and chop the tomato. Mix together and add seasoning and a little of the chopped parsley. Line a small, flat roasting tin with half the aspic jelly. Slice the hard-boiled egg and lay the slices on the jelly with the remaining chopped parsley. Leave to set. Dissolve the gelatine in the stock with the rest of the aspic jelly, and when cool, add to the mixed ingredients. Pour into the prepared tin when cold and leave until set. When set, unmould and cut into strips. **Surround** with the green salad.

Ham Salad and Pineapple

4–6 helpings

250g cooked ham
1 small fresh pineapple
  or 1 × 212g can
  pineapple chunks

6 × 15ml spoons
  mayonnaise (p843) **or**
  salad dressing (p845)

Garnish
gherkin slices

Cut the ham into short strips. If using a fresh pineapple, peel, removing all the eyes, and cut out the core. Drain and dice the canned pineapple. Toss lightly with the mayonnaise or salad dressing and garnish with gherkin slices.

Veal and Tuna Salad

6 helpings

1kg leg of veal
1 medium-sized carrot
1 small onion

1 stick of celery
4 black peppercorns
1 × 5ml spoon salt

Sauce
100g canned tuna fish
4 anchovy fillets
125ml olive oil
2 egg yolks

black pepper
1–2 × 15ml spoons
  lemon juice

Garnish
capers
sliced gherkins

fresh tarragon (optional)

Bone the meat and tie it in a neat roll. Cut the carrot and onion into quarters. Chop the celery. Put the meat into a large saucepan with its bones. Add the vegetables, peppercorns, salt, and enough water to cover the meat. Bring quickly to the boil, reduce the heat, cover, and simmer for about $1\frac{3}{4}$ hours or until the meat is tender. Carefully lift the meat from the pan and leave on one side to cool. Boil the cooking liquid rapidly to reduce it by half, strain through a fine sieve, and reserve.

To make the sauce, drain the tuna fish and anchovy fillets and put them in a bowl with 15ml of the oil. Mash with a fork until thoroughly mixed. Blend in the egg yolks and season with pepper.

Rub this paste through a sieve into a small bowl. Stir in 15ml of the lemon juice, then add the remaining oil, little by little, beating thoroughly after each addition. When the sauce has become thick and shiny, add more lemon juice to taste. Stir in about 30ml of the reserved veal liquid to give the sauce the consistency of thin cream.

Cut the cold meat into thin slices and arrange them in a dish. Cover completely with the sauce, then cover the dish with a lid or clingfilm, and leave to stand in a cold place for up to 24 hours. Before serving, garnish with capers, sliced gherkins, and a sprig of fresh tarragon, if liked.

Serve with a salad of green beans dressed with a little oil.

Veal, Salami, and Olive Salad

4–6 helpings

200g cold roast veal	*1 × 15ml spoon capers*
200g cold boiled potatoes	*salt and pepper*
100g boiled beetroot	*100ml mayonnaise*
100g gherkins	*(p843)*

Garnish
lettuce leaves	*12 stoned green olives*
lemon slices	*12 slices salami*

Dice the veal, potatoes, and beetroot. Slice the gherkins. Mix them together with the capers, and season to taste. Pile the mixture into a salad dish and pour the mayonnaise over it. Garnish with lettuce leaves, lemon slices, olives, and salami.

Chaudfroid of Chicken

See p644.

Chicken or Turkey Salad(1)

4 helpings

350g cold cooked chicken	*1 × 15ml spoon vinegar*
or turkey	*salt and pepper*
1 hard-boiled egg	*6 × 15ml spoons*
2 sticks celery	*mayonnaise (p843)*
1 × 15ml spoon corn	*lettuce leaves*
salad oil	

Garnish
*selection of gherkins,
  capers, anchovy fillets,
  radishes, and
  watercress*

Cut the chicken or turkey into neat pieces. Separate the egg white and yolk. Chop the celery and egg white. Mix all these together with the corn oil, vinegar, and seasoning. Leave to stand for 1 hour. Stir in the mayonnaise. Sieve the egg yolk. Pile the chicken or turkey, celery and egg white on a bed of lettuce, sprinkle with the sieved yolk, and garnish as liked. Chill before serving.

Chicken or Turkey Salad(2)

6 helpings

350g cooked chicken **or**	*salt and pepper*
turkey meat	*150ml mayonnaise*
1 large lettuce	*(p843)*
1 celery heart	
1 × 10ml spoon tarragon	
vinegar	

Garnish
lettuce leaves	*stoned olives* **or** *gherkin*
2 hard-boiled eggs,	*strips*
sliced	

Cut the chicken or turkey into neat, small pieces. Wash the lettuce and dry thoroughly. Shred the outer leaves with the celery. Mix all these lightly with the vinegar and a little salt and pepper. Pile into a salad bowl and coat with the mayonnaise. Garnish with lettuce leaves, egg slices, and olives or gherkin strips.

Sweet and Sour Turkey Salad

4–5 helpings

1 × 226g can pineapple rings	*1 × 15ml spoon cider vinegar*
a pinch of salt	*1 × 453g can bean sprouts*
a pinch of pepper	*225g cold cooked turkey*
a pinch of dry English mustard	*1 small green pepper*
a pinch of caster sugar	*100g carrots*
4 × 15ml spoons corn oil	*50g whole blanched almonds*
1 × 5ml spoon soy sauce	

Drain the juice from the pineapple and reserve 1 × 15ml spoon for the dressing. Put the salt, pepper, dry mustard, and sugar in a mixing bowl and add the corn oil. Blend together. Gradually add the reserved pineapple juice, the soy sauce and vinegar, and beat well. Drain the bean sprouts and add them to the dressing. Cut the turkey meat into pieces and add it to the bowl. Remove the membranes and seeds from the pepper and cut the flesh into thin strips. Scrape the carrot, and cut into thin strips. Add both to the bowl. Toast the almonds lightly. Cut the pineapple into segments and stir into the salad with the almonds. Transfer to a salad bowl or dish. Chill before serving.

Curried Turkey or Chicken Salad

6–8 helpings

1 small cooked turkey or large chicken	*500g (approx) natural yoghurt*
150ml mayonnaise (p843)	*salt and pepper*
25g curry powder	*paprika*

Garnish
parsley sprigs   *thin green pepper rings*

Remove the cooked meat from the bones. Take off any skin or fat, and cut into small pieces. Mix the mayonnaise with the curry powder, stir in the yoghurt, and season to taste. Mix half the sauce with the turkey or chicken, arrange on a serving dish, and spoon the remaining sauce over. Sprinkle with a little paprika and garnish with the parsley and pepper rings.

Duck Salad

6 helpings

½ cold duck	*mayonnaise (p843) as required*
1 small celery heart	*1 × 10ml spoon chopped parsley*
salt and pepper	*1 × 10ml spoon chopped olives (optional)*
3 × 15ml spoons French dressing (p849)	
1 lettuce	
½ bunch watercress	

Garnish
2 slices unpeeled orange

Cut the duck into 2cm cubes and the celery into fine strips. Mix in a basin with the seasoning and 2 × 15ml spoons of the French dressing, and leave to stand. Line a flat salad platter with lettuce leaves and watercress sprigs, and spoon over the rest of the French dressing. Place the duck mixture in the centre of the platter and cover with a thin layer of mayonnaise. Sprinkle with the parsley and olives, if used. Garnish with orange sections, cut into quarters.

Game Salad

6 helpings

450g cold game	*mayonnaise (p843) as required*
1 lettuce	*Cayenne pepper and salt*
2 hard-boiled eggs	

Garnish
chopped beetroot

Dice the meat finely. Wash the lettuce, dry thoroughly and shred. Chop one of the eggs. Mix the meat and egg together. Arrange with the lettuce and mayonnaise in alternate layers in a salad bowl, seasoning each layer with Cayenne pepper and salt. Cover the surface with a thin layer of mayonnaise. Separate the second egg, sieve the yolk and chop the white. Garnish with alternate rows of finely chopped beetroot, sieved egg yolk, and chopped egg white.

Jellied Game Salad

4 helpings

4 hard-boiled eggs	*500ml aspic jelly*
350g lean cooked ham	*450g cold cooked game*
¼ cucumber (approx)	*meat (bird or animal)*

Cut the eggs into round slices. Cut the ham into slices, then into rounds of the same size as the eggs. Peel the cucumber and cut into thin slices.

Rinse a plain 1 litre jelly mould with cold water, and line it with aspic jelly. Decorate the base of the mould with some of the ham and all the egg sandwiched together. Pour a little cold liquid aspic jelly over them and allow to set. Cut the game meat into neat small pieces. Sandwich together the remaining ham and cucumber slices. Arrange pieces of seasoned game and rounds of ham and cucumber on the set jelly, pour more jelly on top and allow this to set. Repeat the layers until the mould is full; chop and include any extra egg white from the ends of the eggs, if liked. Allow each layer of jelly to set firmly before adding the next layer of meat.

When the jelly has set firmly, unmould. Any remaining jelly can be chopped on a wet board and used for decoration.

Cheese Salad

6 helpings

1 large mild onion	*blue cheese salad*
1 small cucumber	*dressing (p847)*
6 large firm tomatoes	*3 ×15ml spoons grated*
salt and pepper	*Parmesan cheese*

Garnish

6 stoned black olives or
 2 large gherkins, sliced

Skin the onion and slice it finely. Slice the cucumber finely without peeling it, and cut the tomatoes into slightly thicker slices. Arrange these 3 ingredients in layers, sprinkling each layer with seasoning, dressing, and some of the cheese. Garnish with olives or gherkins and the remaining cheese.

Cheese and Pasta Salad

4–6 helpings

100g pasta shells or	*150g natural yoghurt*
rings	*1 clove of garlic*
1 celery heart	*salt and pepper*
1 green pepper	*a few drops Tabasco*
100g full-fat soft cheese	*sauce*

Cook the pasta in boiling salted water until just tender. Drain thoroughly. Chop the celery finely, remove the membranes and seeds from the pepper, and slice the flesh finely. Beat the cheese in a bowl, then beat in the yoghurt. Skin and crush the garlic and add to the cheese mixture; then add the pasta, celery and pepper, and mix well. Season to taste with salt, pepper, and Tabasco sauce. Chill lightly before serving.

Caesar Salad

6 helpings

3 cloves garlic	*1 ×65g can anchovy*
4 large thick slices bread	*fillets*
2 cos lettuces	*50g grated Parmesan*
150ml olive oil	*cheese*
1 egg	*salt and freshly ground*
juice of 1 lemon	*black pepper*

Cut the garlic cloves in half. Cut the bread into 1cm cubes. Wash the lettuces, dry thoroughly, and tear into small pieces. Heat 4 ×15ml spoons olive oil in a frying pan with 2 cloves of garlic. Add the bread cubes and fry until crisp and golden on all sides. Remove from the pan and drain on soft kitchen paper. Discard the garlic and oil. Rub the remaining garlic clove all round the salad bowl. Add the lettuce and the rest of the olive oil, and toss until every leaf is coated. Cook the egg in boiling water for 1 minute, then remove from the pan and break over the lettuce. Add the lemon juice to the lettuce with the anchovies, cheese, and seasoning. Toss lightly, and re-season if required. Add the croûtons of fried bread, toss the salad again, and serve as soon as possible, while the croûtons are still crisp.

Harlequin Salad

4 helpings

75g Cheddar cheese	½ cucumber
75g red Leicester cheese	1 small bunch of
75g blue Stilton cheese	watercress
75g white Wensleydale	100ml soured cream
cheese	milk
1 lettuce	1 × 15ml spoon chopped
4 medium-sized	chives
tomatoes	

Cut the cheeses into small cubes, and mix together without breaking them. Wash and dry the lettuce, slice the tomatoes and cucumber, and chop the watercress. Place the lettuce and watercress on a flat oval platter, in a flat layer. Pile the cheeses into the centre of the platter. Mix the cream with a little milk if required, to obtain a thick pouring consistency. Pour it round the cheeses, trickling a little over them. Arrange the tomato and cucumber in a decorative pattern round the cheeses, and sprinkle the dish with chives.

Note The cubes can be cut more easily if each cheese is bought in a block.

Egg and Carrot Salad

4–6 helpings

4 hard-boiled eggs	4 × 15ml spoons French
1 bunch of young carrots	dressing **or** vinaigrette
(500g approx)	sauce (p849)
salt and pepper	

Garnish
½ box mustard and cress

Slice the eggs thickly. Boil or steam the carrots in their skins until just tender. Drain thoroughly, leave to cool, then peel and slice thinly. Arrange the carrots and eggs alternately in overlapping slices. Season, and pour over the dressing. Garnish with small bunches of cress before serving.

Egg Salad

6 helpings

6 hard-boiled eggs	1 × 15ml spoon chopped
2 × 15ml spoons double	parsley
cream (optional)	1 small lettuce
125–150ml mayonnaise	salt and pepper
(p843)	

Garnish

1 cooked beetroot, peeled	1 × 15ml spoon capers
and sliced	

Slice the eggs thickly. Lightly whip the cream, if used, and fold into the mayonnaise with 1 × 5ml spoon of the parsley (use the larger amount of mayonnaise if not using the cream). Wash and dry the lettuce thoroughly. Arrange a layer of lettuce leaves in a salad bowl, spread with a layer of mayonnaise, then add a layer of egg slices. Season each layer with salt and pepper. Continue these layers, piling the centre high, until all the ingredients have been used. Garnish with beetroot slices and capers just before serving.

Salad Dressings and Sauces

EGG AND OIL-BASED SAUCES

Mayonnaise(1)

Basic egg and oil sauce

Makes 300ml (approx)

2 egg yolks
1 × 2.5ml spoon dry English mustard
1 × 2.5ml spoon salt
pepper

2 × 15ml spoons white wine vinegar, tarragon vinegar, or lemon juice
250ml oil, preferably either olive or corn oil

Blend the egg yolks with the mustard, salt, pepper, and 1 × 15ml spoon of the vinegar or lemon juice in a basin. Using either a balloon whisk, a wooden spoon, or an electric blender, beat in the oil very gradually, drop by drop, until about half of it has been added and the mixture looks thick and shiny. At this stage, the oil can be added in a slow thin stream. Add the remaining vinegar or lemon juice when all the oil has been incorporated.

If the mayonnaise curdles while making, beat a fresh egg yolk in another basin and beat the mixture into this gradually, 1 × 5ml spoonful at a time.

To store the mayonnaise, put it into a basin or jar, cover, and store in the least cold part of the refrigerator; if the mayonnaise becomes too cold, it will separate.

Note For the best results, all the ingredients should be at room temperature. If the eggs are used straight from the refrigerator, the mayonnaise is much more likely to curdle.

For Mayonnaise (2), made in an electric blender, see p1414.

Cooked Mayonnaise(1)

Makes 300ml (approx)

1 × 5ml spoon caster sugar
1 × 2.5ml spoon salt
1 × 2.5ml spoon dry mustard
a pinch of pepper
1 × 15ml spoon corn or vegetable oil

3 egg yolks
4 × 15ml spoons wine vinegar
1 × 5ml spoon tarragon vinegar
250ml milk or single cream

Mix the sugar, salt, mustard, and pepper. Stir in the oil, then the egg yolks. Beat well. Add the vinegars gradually and finally the milk or cream. Turn into the top of a double boiler, or into a basin placed over a pan of gently simmering water. Cook the sauce, stirring all the time until it thickens. Do not allow the sauce to boil or it will curdle. Remove from the heat and leave to cool, stirring frequently to prevent a skin forming. Re-season if required when cold.

Cooked Mayonnaise(2)

Makes 250ml (approx)

1 × 15ml spoon flour
1 × 5ml spoon caster sugar
1 × 5ml spoon salt
1 × 5ml spoon dry mustard
a good pinch of pepper

1 × 15ml spoon butter or margarine
1 egg yolk
4 × 15ml spoons malt or wine vinegar
250ml milk

Mix the flour with the sugar, salt, mustard, and pepper. Melt the fat and beat into the flour. Beat in the egg yolk, then gradually beat in the vinegar and milk. Turn into a small saucepan and bring to the boil, stirring all the time, until the sauce is smooth and thick. Remove from the heat, cover with a circle of damp greaseproof paper to prevent a skin forming, and leave to cool. Beat, and re-season if required when cold.

Aspic Mayonnaise(1)

Makes 300ml (approx)

1 × 5ml spoon gelatine
2 × 15ml spoons water
4 × 15ml spoons liquid
  aspic jelly

2 × 15ml spoons double
  cream
250ml mayonnaise
  (p843)

Soften the gelatine in the water in a heatproof container. Stand the container in very hot water, and stir until the gelatine dissolves. Let the gelatine mixture cool until quite cold but not yet set. Cool the aspic jelly until quite cold. Meanwhile, whip the cream until it just holds soft peaks.

Put the mayonnaise in a bowl, and beat in the aspic jelly drop by drop as lightly as possible; then beat in the gelatine little by little. Fold in the cream. Use at once for masking fish or chicken; or use when just at setting point in the same way as aspic jelly for making a savoury mould.

Aspic Mayonnaise(2)

Makes 250–375ml

125–250ml aspic jelly

125ml thick mayonnaise
  (p843)

If necessary, melt and cool the jelly. It should be cold but still liquid. Fold it little by little into the mayonnaise. Allow to come almost to setting point before use; it should just be thickening.

Use the smaller quantity of jelly for an aspic mayonnaise for piping, ie for garnishing. Use the larger quantity for coating meats, fish, etc.

Curry Mayonnaise

Makes 125ml (approx)

1 clove of garlic
125ml mayonnaise
  (p843)

1 × 2.5ml spoon curry
  powder

Crush the garlic and fold it into the mayonnaise with the curry powder.

Serve with cold meat or fish; this sauce is particularly good with cold chicken.

Green Mayonnaise

Makes 150ml (approx)

25g mixed leaves of
  watercress, spinach,
  chervil, tarragon,
  parsley, and chives

salt
125ml mayonnaise
  (p843)

Cook the leaves in a very little boiling salted water until just tender. Drain thoroughly and sieve, or process in an electric blender to a smooth purée. Fold into the mayonnaise just before serving. Do not add the purée to the mayonnaise too early or it will lose its colour.

Serve with fish and fish salads.

Red Mayonnaise

Makes 150ml (approx)

25g canned red salmon
a few drops lemon juice
125ml mayonnaise
  (p843)

red food colouring
salt and pepper

Remove any skin and bones from the fish. Pound it with the lemon juice until a smooth paste is obtained; this may be easier if 1–2 small spoonfuls of the mayonnaise are added. When smooth, blend it into the remaining mayonnaise gently. Colour, and season to taste.

Serve with fish or shellfish.

Escoffier's Mayonnaise

Makes 125ml (approx)

1 × 2.5ml spoon bottled
  horseradish cream
125ml mayonnaise
  (p843)

1 × 5ml spoon chopped
  parsley
1 × 5ml spoon chopped
  chervil

Fold the horseradish cream into the mayonnaise, then the chopped parsley and chervil. Leave to stand for 1 hour before serving for the flavours to blend.

Tomato Mayonnaise

Makes 150ml (approx)

2 × 15ml spoons thick fresh tomato purée **or** *1 × 10ml spoon concentrated tomato purée* **or** *2 × 10ml spoons tomato ketchup*

125ml mayonnaise (p843)

Fold the tomato purée or ketchup into the mayonnaise.

Serve with meat, fish or shellfish salads.

VARIATION

Add a few drops of Worcestershire sauce.

English Salad Dressing **or** Cream

Basic recipe

Use the ingredients below in the proportions of:

1 hard-boiled egg yolk
¼ × 2.5ml spoon mixed English mustard
1 × 5ml spoon Worcestershire sauce **or** *to taste*
salt and pepper
a pinch of caster sugar

1 × 10ml spoon cider **or** *white wine vinegar*
1 × 15ml spoon olive oil
2 × 15ml spoons double cream **or** *evaporated milk prepared for whipping (p872)*

Sieve the egg yolk. Work into it gradually the seasonings, vinegar, and oil. Whip the cream or evaporated milk lightly, and fold into the mixture. Use at once.

Andalusian Sauce

Makes 150ml (approx)

1 small red pepper
125ml mayonnaise (p843)

2 × 15ml spoons concentrated tomato purée

Remove the membranes and seeds from the pepper and cut the flesh into thin strips. Fold into the mayonnaise with the tomato purée.

Epicurean Sauce

Makes 500ml (approx)

½ cucumber
salt
4 × 15ml spoons aspic jelly **or** *good stock and 1 × 2.5ml spoon gelatine*
1 × 15ml spoon tarragon vinegar
4 × 15ml spoons double cream

125ml mayonnaise (p843)
2 gherkins
1 × 10ml spoon chutney
1 × 5ml spoon anchovy essence
pepper
sugar

Peel and dice the cucumber. Cook in 5mm depth of salted water until tender, or steam. Sieve, or process in an electric blender to make a smooth purée. If using stock and gelatine, sprinkle the gelatine over the stock in a basin and leave for 5 minutes to soften. Stand the basin over a pan of hot water and leave until the gelatine dissolves. Allow to cool. Stir the cucumber purée and the vinegar into the stock or aspic jelly. Whip the cream until it holds its shape, then fold it into the mayonnaise. Finely chop the gherkins and any large pieces in the chutney. Fold into the mayonnaise with the anchovy essence, and finally fold in the aspic jelly and cucumber mixture. Season with salt and pepper and add sugar to taste.

Serve with fish salads, asparagus or globe artichokes.

Remoulade Sauce

Makes 125ml (approx)

1 × 5ml spoon French mustard
1 × 5ml spoon chopped capers
1 × 2.5ml spoon chopped parsley

1 × 2.5ml spoon chopped tarragon
1 × 2.5ml spoon chopped chervil
125ml mayonnaise (p843)

Fold the mustard, capers, and herbs into the mayonnaise. Leave the sauce to stand for at least 1 hour before serving for the flavours to blend.

Serve with grilled meat or fish, or with salads.

Cambridge Sauce

Makes 200ml (approx)

3 hard-boiled egg yolks
125ml salad oil
*white wine **or** cider*
* vinegar*
1 × 2.5ml spoon capers
12 anchovy fillets
1 × 2.5ml spoon French
* mustard*
1 × 5ml spoon chopped
* chervil*

1 × 5ml spoon chopped
* parsley*
1 × 2.5ml spoon chopped
* tarragon*
1 × 2.5ml spoon chopped
* chives*
salt
a pinch of Cayenne
* pepper*

Sieve the egg yolks into a basin. Beat in the oil very gradually as for mayonnaise (p843). When all the oil has been incorporated, add enough vinegar to make the sauce a thin cream. Chop the capers and anchovy fillets finely and stir into the sauce with the mustard and herbs. Season to taste with salt and Cayenne pepper.

Serve with cold fish, pork or Pork Brawn (p596). On the Continent, Cambridge Sauce is popular with fatty boiled meats such as pig's trotters.

Cold Mousseline Sauce

Makes 150ml (approx)

2 × 15ml spoons double
* cream*

125ml mayonnaise
* (p843)*

Whip the cream lightly until it holds its shape, then fold into the mayonnaise.

Serve with fish.

VARIATION

Green Mousseline Sauce

Fold 1 × 15ml spoon of cooked spinach purée into the mayonnaise with the cream.

Gloucester Sauce

Makes 150ml (approx)

1 × 15ml spoon soured
* cream **or** yoghurt*
125ml mayonnaise
* (p843)*
½ × 2.5ml spoon
* Worcestershire sauce*

1 × 2.5ml spoon chopped
* chives*
1 × 10ml spoon lemon
* juice*
Cayenne pepper

Fold the soured cream or yoghurt into the mayonnaise with the Worcestershire sauce, chopped chives, and lemon juice. Season with a little Cayenne pepper.

Serve with meat salads.

Tartare Sauce (2)

Makes 150ml (approx)

1 × 5ml spoon each of
* chopped gherkins*
* chopped olives*
* chopped capers*
* chopped parsley*
* chopped chives*

125ml mayonnaise
* (p843)*
½ × 2.5ml spoon French
* mustard*
1 × 10ml spoon wine
* vinegar **or** lemon juice*

Fold the chopped ingredients into the mayonnaise with the mustard, then add the vinegar or lemon juice. Leave the sauce to stand for at least 1 hour before serving for the flavours to blend.

Serve with grilled or fried fish and meat.

Note For Tartare Sauce (1), see p706.

Aïoli

Makes 200ml (approx)

*4–6 cloves garlic **or***
* 4 shallots*
1 egg yolk
a pinch of salt
125ml olive oil
1 × 15ml spoon lemon
* juice **or** wine vinegar*

1 medium-sized potato
a pinch of Cayenne
* pepper*

Crush the garlic or shallots and pound to a smooth pulp. Add the egg yolk and salt; then proceed as for mayonnaise (p843). Cook the potato for 20 minutes in enough boiling salted water to cover it. Drain, rub through a sieve, and leave to cool. Gradually work the sauce into the potato, beating thoroughly. Season to taste with Cayenne pepper.

Serve with salads, vegetables, fish or meat.

Roquefort Salad Cream

Makes 375ml (approx)

200ml soured cream
100ml mayonnaise
  (p843)
2 × 15ml spoons grated
  onion
2 × 15ml spoons mild
  white vinegar
50g Roquefort cheese
1 clove of garlic

Combine the cream, mayonnaise, onion, and vinegar in a bowl or the goblet of an electric blender. Crumble the cheese, and add it to the mixture. Split the garlic clove and rub a salad bowl thoroughly with the cut sides. Discard the garlic. Whisk or blend the other ingredients until smooth. Use over a green salad placed in the bowl.

Note If to be stored, rub the garlic clove round the inside of the storage container before putting in the dressing. Store chilled.

Thousand Islands Dressing

Makes 300ml (approx)

250ml mayonnaise
  (p843)
1 × 15ml spoon chopped
  parsley
1 × 15ml spoon finely
  chopped capers
1 × 15ml spoon finely
  chopped olives
1 × 15ml spoon finely
  chopped pickles
1 × 15ml spoon lemon
  juice
tomato juice

Put the mayonnaise into a basin and add the parsley, capers, olives, pickles, and lemon juice, and mix well. Stir in enough tomato juice to make a dressing of pouring consistency.

OTHER DRESSINGS AND SAUCES

Cream Salad Dressing

Makes 100ml (approx)

1 × 2.5ml spoon made
  English mustard
$\frac{1}{2}$ × 2.5ml spoon salt
$\frac{1}{2}$ × 2.5ml spoon caster
  sugar
4 × 15ml spoons double
  cream
1 × 15ml spoon malt **or**
  wine vinegar
1 × 5ml spoon tarragon
  vinegar

Mix the mustard, salt, and sugar together. Stir in the cream. Add the vinegars, drop by drop, beating the mixture all the time.

Blue Cheese Salad Dressing

Makes 300ml (approx)

200ml olive oil
a good pinch of salt
50ml mild vinegar
$\frac{1}{2}$ × 2.5ml spoon dried
  thyme (optional)
50g blue cheese

Put the oil, salt, and vinegar in a bowl or in the goblet of an electric blender. Crush the thyme if required, and crumble the cheese. Add to the other ingredients, and whisk or blend until smooth.

Cream and Potato Salad Dressing

Makes 100ml (approx)

1 small cooked floury
  potato
$\frac{1}{2}$ × 2.5ml spoon salt
pepper
a good pinch of caster
  sugar
$\frac{1}{2}$ × 2.5ml spoon made
  mustard
2 × 15ml spoons double
  cream **or** oil
1 × 15ml spoon malt **or**
  wine vinegar

Sieve the potato and beat in the salt, pepper, sugar, and mustard. Beat in the cream or oil and then the vinegar drop by drop. Re-season if required.

Cream and Egg Salad Dressing

Makes 150ml (approx)

2 egg yolks
*½ × 2.5ml spoon made
   mustard*
salt and pepper
*2 × 15ml spoons
   vegetable or corn oil*
*2 × 15ml spoons double
   cream*
*1 × 15ml spoon malt or
   wine vinegar*
*1 × 15ml spoon tarragon
   vinegar*
*1 × 2.5ml spoon finely
   chopped chives, spring
   onions or shallots*

Tip the egg yolks into a basin. Add the mustard, salt and pepper, and beat with a wooden spoon. Add the oil, drop by drop, beating the mixture briskly. Stir in the cream, then beat in the vinegars slowly. Stir in the chives, spring onions or shallots. Re-season if required.

Evaporated Milk Dressing

Makes 100ml (approx)

*4 × 15ml spoons
   unsweetened
   evaporated milk*
*1 × 15ml spoon malt or
   wine vinegar*
*½ × 2.5ml spoon made
   mustard*
*a good pinch of caster
   sugar*
½ × 2.5ml spoon salt

Whisk the milk until it forms soft peaks. Beat in the vinegar, drop by drop, then the mustard, sugar, and salt.

Salad Dressing
(made with Béchamel Sauce)

Makes 250ml (approx)

1 egg or 2 egg yolks
*250ml Béchamel Sauce
   (p704) made with all
   milk*
*2 × 15ml spoons malt or
   wine vinegar*
*1 × 15ml spoon tarragon
   vinegar*
salt and pepper
*a good pinch of caster
   sugar*

Beat the egg or egg yolks until liquid. Cool the sauce until lukewarm. Stir in the egg and beat well. Beat in the vinegars, seasoning, and sugar. Cover the sauce with a circle of damp greaseproof paper to prevent a skin forming, and leave to cool. Remove the greaseproof paper and beat well. Re-season if required when cold.

Soured Cream Dressing

Makes 125ml (approx)

125ml soured cream
salt and pepper
*1 × 5ml spoon French
   mustard or 1 × 2.5ml
   spoon made English
   mustard*
a pinch of caster sugar
*milk or top of the milk
   (optional)*

Stir the cream, then add the seasoning, mustard, and sugar. If liked, the dressing can be thinned down with a little milk or top of the milk.

VARIATION
Yoghurt Dressing

Use thick natural yoghurt instead of soured cream.

Soured Cream Cooked Dressing

Makes 250ml (approx)

1 × 10ml spoon flour
1 × 10ml spoon sugar
*1 × 5ml spoon dry
   mustard*
1 × 5ml spoon salt
*a pinch of Cayenne
   pepper*
1 egg yolk
*3 × 15ml spoons white
   vinegar*
*1 × 15ml spoon melted
   butter*
125ml soured cream

Put all the dry ingredients into the top of a double boiler or in a basin over a pan of hot water. Add the egg yolk and vinegar, and beat well. Cook gently for 7–8 minutes, stirring all the time. Add the butter. Remove from the heat and leave to cool. Fold into the soured cream before serving.

Note For other yoghurt and soured cream dressings, see p877 and p881.

Swedish Sauce

Makes 150ml (approx)

125ml double cream **or**
evaporated milk
1 hard-boiled egg yolk
1 raw egg yolk
1 × 10ml spoon sugar

½ × 2.5ml spoon dry
English mustard
salt and pepper
1 × 15ml spoon wine
vinegar

Boil and cool the evaporated milk if used, as described on p872. Sieve the hard-boiled egg yolk into a basin. Beat into it the raw egg yolk, sugar, mustard, seasoning, and vinegar. Whip the cream or evaporated milk until it holds its shape, then fold it carefully into the vinegar mixture.

Serve with hot fish, or with fish or other salads.

French Dressing(1)

Basic recipe

Use the ingredients in the proportions of:

2–3 × 15ml spoons olive
oil
salt and freshly ground
black pepper
a pinch of dry English
mustard (optional)

a pinch of caster
sugar (optional)
1 × 15ml spoon wine
vinegar

Mix together the oil and seasonings. Add the vinegar gradually, stirring all the time with a wooden spoon so that an emulsion is formed. Alternatively, put all the ingredients into a small screw-topped jar, and shake vigorously until well blended.

The standard basic French dressing is made with oil, salt and pepper and vinegar alone, but it can be varied in other ways, eg
1) Use ½ × 2.5ml spoon French or mixed English or German mustard instead of dry mustard.
2) Use white wine instead of some of the vinegar.
3) Use lemon juice instead of some or all of the vinegar.
4) In recipes which contain grapefruit or orange, use grapefruit or orange juice instead of the vinegar.
5) Add a little skinned garlic, crushed without salt, to the basic ingredients.

Note French dressing keeps well, so a large quantity can be made and stored in a screw-topped jar or bottle in a cool place. Shake well before use.

For French Dressing (2), made in an electric blender, see p1414.

Vinaigrette Sauce

Makes 100ml (approx)

4 × 15ml spoons French
dressing
1 × 5ml spoon finely
chopped gherkin
1 × 2.5ml spoon finely
chopped chives **or**
shallot

1 × 2.5ml spoon finely
chopped parsley
1 × 5ml spoon finely
chopped capers
1 × 2.5ml spoon finely
chopped tarragon
and/**or** *chervil*

Mix all the ingredients together and leave for at least 1 hour before using for the flavours to blend.

Chiffonade Dressing

Makes 150ml (approx)

2 hard-boiled eggs
¼ small red pepper
2 × 15ml spoons finely
chopped parsley

1 × 5ml spoon very
finely chopped shallot
French dressing

Chop the eggs and red pepper very finely. Mix with the parsley and shallot, then add enough dressing to give the desired consistency. Use very cold.

Claret Dressing

Makes 150ml (approx)

1 clove of garlic
125ml claret
1 × 5ml spoon lemon
juice

1 × 5ml spoon finely
chopped shallot
salt and pepper

Crush the garlic. Mix all the ingredients together and leave to stand overnight. Strain, and pour over a salad previously tossed in a little salad oil.

PASTA, RICE, AND OTHER GRAINS

Macaroni is composed of wheaten flour, flavoured with other articles, and worked up with water into a paste, to which, by a peculiar process, a tubular or pipe form is given, in order that it may cook more readily in hot water. That of smaller diameter than macaroni (which is about the thickness of a goose-quill) is called *vermicelli;* and when smaller still, *fidelini.*

Pasta

Pasta is an Italian word meaning a flour and water paste, which is cut or extruded through a nozzle into various shapes such as rods, ribbons or shells, rings, and wheels.

In addition to those in this chapter, there are many other pasta and rice recipes in the chapter on Foreign Cookery.

Commercially, pasta is made from Durum wheat, grown mainly in North America but also around the Mediterranean. The kernel of the grain is coarsely ground to form semolina. Durum is a 'hard' wheat with a high protein content which, as in breadmaking, forms gluten when mixed with water. This produces a strong dough which keeps its shape, texture, and flavour when cooked, whereas pasta made from softer flours loses colour in cooking, clouds the water it is boiled in, and goes soft and sticky.

Pasta is made from two types of dough – *pasta secco* and *pasta all'uovo. Pasta secco* (dry pasta) is made from Durum semolina and water. The dough is then dried carefully and evenly so that it is hard; it will then keep for a long time. It is hardly ever home-made; macaroni, spaghetti, and the other shapes of *pasta secco* are all commercial products.

Pasta all'uovo is also made from Durum semolina and water but has egg added. Many Italian housewives make their own *pasta all'uovo* daily; or they buy it from shops which produce it freshly made every morning. Fresh *pasta all'uovo* is pliant, not hard. However, factories do make dried *pasta all'uovo* in the same shapes, with the same names as home-made pasta. Purists say that dried *pasta all'uovo* can never be as good as home-made pasta; but few people outside Italy have the skill, time or tools to make their own pasta, and the dried *pasta all'uovo* makes excellent dishes when accompanied by a good sauce.

Pasta verde (green pasta) is made by adding cooked sieved spinach to the basic pasta recipe. It can be bought already prepared as *tagliatelle verdi* and *lasagne.*

Pasta secco provides 13–14% protein together with 70% carbohydrate; other nutrients are always added in the form of a sauce or other accompaniment. *Pasta all'uovo* contains the extra protein of the eggs. Wholemeal pasta is also available; unlike the other types this contains fibre.

Pasta Shapes

Pasta secco and *pasta all'uovo* each have their own traditional shapes. *Pasta secco* is frequently made in new shapes for novelty products. However, since *pasta all'uovo* is by tradition home-made with only simple equipment, it is always just cut into flat ribbons or noodles of varying width, each with its own Italian name. Tagliatelle and lasagne are the best known.

Any pasta shape can be used for any dish; but some are more practical to use for certain dishes than others. Any of the large-sized and medium-sized rods and ribbons (except lasagne) can be used for what, in Italy, is called *pasta asciutta*, meaning first and main-course dishes of boiled pasta. Short lengths of these pasta shapes can also be used. The curved or twisted shapes are used most often when the pasta is served simply with a sauce, because their curves and twists hold the sauce, making it easy to mop up.

Most oven-cooked pasta dishes *(pasta al forno)* consist of alternate layers of pasta and a stuffing with sauce. Large pasta such as extra broad noodles, lasagne or rigatoni are nearly always used for these dishes because they do not let the stuffing and sauce seep down to the bottom of the dish.

As tiny pasta shapes do not hold sauce well, they are nearly always used in soups and broths *(pasta in brodo)* in the same way as croûtons or pearl barley.

It is useful to remember that *pasta all'uovo* is richer than *pasta secco*; so when serving pasta with just a sauce, choose *pasta all'uovo*. Keep *pasta secco* for dishes with a protein addition.

Cooking Pasta

All pasta can be cooked simply in fast-boiling, well-salted water. However, for some dishes such as lasagne, the pasta is removed after a few minutes only, when it will have just softened, and the dish is finished in the oven *(pasta al forno)*.

Basic method

1) Provide 50–75g pasta (uncooked weight) per person for a first-course dish, 75–100g for a main dish.
2) Use 1 litre water and 1 × 5ml spoon table salt or 1 × 2.5ml spoon household salt per 100g pasta. The addition of 2 × 15ml spoons of oil to the cooking water will help prevent the pasta sticking together.
3) Bring the water, salt and oil, if used, to a fast boil. Break long pasta into 15–25cm lengths. Put them into the water and push them gently below the surface as they soften. Drop round pasta shapes into the water a few at a time, and stir once. Slide large pasta such as sheets of lasagne into the water individually to prevent them sticking together. Drop bundled (folded) pasta into the water, leave for 2 minutes, then stir with a fork to separate the strands. Do not let the water go off the boil.

4) Cook for the appropriate time (see table below), stirring once or twice with a fork to prevent the pasta sticking to the bottom of the pan. The pasta, when cooked, should have no floury taste, but should be *al dente*, firm to the bite, apart from dishes which are also to be baked in the oven.
5) Drain into a colander; then return to the dry pan, off the heat, if making a sauce. If the pasta must wait more than 4 minutes, place it on a damp cloth in a strainer or sieve, over simmering water.

Cooking Times for Pasta

The cooking time for dried pasta depends partly on the size of the shapes and partly on the flour used. Manufacturers usually state the cooking times for their pasta on each packet, and their directions should be followed. If none are given, use the following general guide:

String or tubular and flat ribbons, eg

cappellini, vermicelli, spaghettini	5 minutes
spaghetti, tagliatelle	7–12 minutes
macaroni	12–20 minutes

Fancy shapes and short lengths, eg

shells, bows, cocks-combs	8–10 minutes

Ridged, large, eg

cannelloni, rigatoni	16–20 minutes

Stuffed

ravioli	15–20 minutes

Soup

alphabets, stars, small wheels, small rings, small shells	4–8 minutes

Re-heating Pasta

Pasta is best served as soon as it is cooked, but if this is not possible it can be re-heated by:
1) putting it into boiling water for 30 seconds
2) putting it into a saucepan with melted butter and simmering for 2–3 minutes
3) putting it into a colander over a saucepan of boiling water for 10 minutes.

Freezing Pasta

Undercook the pasta by about 2 minutes. Prepare the pasta dish in a foil container. Cover with any lightly spiced sauce and a lid, and freeze. To serve, place the unthawed covered dish in a fairly hot oven to heat through. See also p1391.

Storing Pasta

Pasta must be stored in a dry place. Good quality dry pasta can be stored unopened for up to two years without losing its flavour. *Pasta secco* lasts longer than *pasta all'uovo*.

Egg Noodles
(Pasta all'uovo)

Makes 400g (approx)

400g strong white flour	*2 eggs*
$\frac{1}{2}$ × 2.5ml spoon salt	*a little milk **or** water*
40g softened butter	*cornflour for dusting*

Sift the flour and salt into a basin. Make a well in the centre and put in the butter and eggs. Mix thoroughly and add a little milk or water, if necessary, to make a stiff paste. Knead well for about 15 minutes or until the paste is perfectly smooth and elastic. Dust a little cornflour on to a pastry board and roll out the dough as thinly as possible; then dust with cornflour again. Fold the dough neatly into pleats leaving 2cm unfolded. Cut across the pleats with a sharp knife making each strip about 5mm wide. Hold each strip by the unfolded end and shake out. Drop the noodles into boiling salted water and cook for about 5–8 minutes. Drain in a colander, and fork over the ribbons to separate them. Use as required.

VARIATION

Green Pasta
(Pasta Verde)

Add 100g well-drained spinach purée to the basic ingredients with the eggs, then continue making the pasta as above.

Crisp Noodles

4–6 helpings

400g noodles	*fat for deep frying*

Cook the noodles in boiling salted water as directed; drain well. Leave to cool completely. Heat the fat (p302), put some noodles in a wire basket and cook in the fat until crisp and golden-brown. Drain on soft kitchen paper, and keep hot while cooking the rest of the noodles.

Fried Chinese Noodles with Vegetables

4 helpings

6 × 15ml spoons oil	*50g mushrooms*
2 eggs	*1 × 15ml spoon*
100g canned bamboo	*cornflour*
shoots	*4 × 15ml spoons soy*
200g noodles	*sauce*
*200g fresh **or** canned*	*125ml water*
bean sprouts	

Heat 2 × 15ml spoons oil in a large frying pan. Beat the eggs until liquid and pour into the pan. Fry lightly on both sides, to form a thin omelet. Leave to cool; then cut into strips. Drain and slice the bamboo shoots. Cook the noodles in boiling salted water as directed; then drain. If using fresh bean sprouts, pour boiling water over them, and drain at once. Drain canned bean sprouts. Prepare and slice the mushrooms.

Heat the rest of the oil in the pan, add the noodles and fry for 2–3 minutes. Add the omelet strips, bamboo shoots, bean sprouts, and mushrooms to the frying pan and cook for a further 2–3 minutes. Blend the cornflour with a little of the soy sauce, then add the remaining soy sauce and the water. Pour into the pan, bring to the boil, stirring all the time, and simmer for 2–3 minutes.

Stewed Noodles

2 helpings

100g noodles	375ml chicken stock
75g raw chicken meat	1 × 15ml spoon soy
2 leeks	sauce
50g mushrooms	

Cook the noodles in boiling salted water as directed; drain well. Remove any skin and bones from the chicken and mince the meat. Prepare and slice the leeks and mushrooms. Heat the stock in a saucepan, add all the ingredients and simmer for 10 minutes.

Noodles with Eggs

4 helpings

150g tagliatelle **or** other plain noodles	$\frac{1}{2}$ × 2.5ml spoon grated nutmeg
200g button mushrooms	50g strong Cheddar cheese
4 hard-boiled eggs	
75g butter	125ml foundation white sauce (p692)
$\frac{1}{2}$ × 2.5ml spoon pepper	

Cook the noodles in boiling salted water as directed; drain well. Prepare and slice the mushrooms. Slice the eggs. Melt 50g of the butter in a frying pan, add the mushrooms and cook for 4–5 minutes. Season the noodles with pepper and nutmeg. Grate the cheese. Butter a 700ml pie dish with most of the remaining butter. Place a layer of noodles in the bottom of the pie dish, sprinkle with cheese, and cover with slices of egg and mushrooms. Repeat the layers twice, reserving 1 × 15ml spoon of cheese. Pour the sauce over the dish, sprinkle with the remaining cheese and dot with the rest of the butter. Bake in a hot oven, 220°C, Gas 7, for 15–20 minutes.

Mrs Beeton's Macaroni with Cheese

4–6 helpings

200g thick pipe macaroni	50g red **or** white Cheshire cheese
500ml milk	salt and pepper
1 litre water	25g dry white breadcrumbs
1 × 10ml spoon salt	
100g butter (approx)	

Break the macaroni into 15cm lengths. Put the milk and water in a large pan with the salt. Bring to the boil, put in the macaroni and stir round once. Reduce the heat to just above simmering point, and cook the macaroni for 14 minutes or until tender.

Meanwhile, use some of the butter to grease a 1 litre pie dish or flameproof oven-to-table dish, and reserve some of it for sprinkling over the completed dish. Grate the cheese coarsely. When the macaroni is ready, drain it in a colander or sieve. Place a layer of hot macaroni in the dish, and sprinkle it with some of the cheese. Dot with some of the remaining butter and sprinkle lightly with a little salt and pepper. Repeat the layers until the ingredients are used, apart from 25g cheese, and ending with a layer of macaroni. Sprinkle with the remaining 25g cheese and the breadcrumbs. Melt the reserved butter and sprinkle it over the dish. Place under a moderate grill heat for a few minutes, until the cheese melts and begins to brown. Serve at once.

Note If the dish is not served immediately, it can be placed in a *bain marie* of simmering water. This method of re-heating melts the cheese more gently and gives the dish a better flavour than heating in the oven.

Macaroni Cheese

(Macaroni Au Gratin)

3–4 helpings

125g long or elbow cut
  macaroni
500ml foundation white
  sauce (p692)

100g Cheddar cheese
salt and pepper
25g butter

Break long macaroni into 2cm pieces. Cook in boiling salted water as directed; then drain well. Meanwhile, heat the white sauce and grate the cheese. Mix together in a pan the macaroni, sauce, 75g of the cheese, and season to taste. Heat thoroughly for 1–2 minutes, and put the mixture in a greased 700ml pie dish. Sprinkle with the remaining cheese, and dot with the rest of the butter. Grill for 2–4 minutes to melt and brown the cheese. Alternatively, bake in a hot oven, 220°C, Gas 7, for 20 minutes.

VARIATIONS

Substitute 125g noodles or 125g spaghetti for the macaroni.

Macaroni with Bacon

2–3 helpings

250ml white stock
  (p329)
100g long or elbow cut
  macaroni
100g streaky bacon,
  without rinds

25g butter
$\frac{1}{2} \times 2.5$ml spoon grated
  nutmeg
salt and pepper

Bring the stock to the boil. Break long macaroni into 2cm lengths. Cook in the boiling stock as directed; drain well. Chop the bacon and fry it in a saucepan for 3–4 minutes. Add the macaroni, butter, nutmeg, and seasoning. Stir over low heat for a few minutes until the macaroni is slightly browned. Turn on to a warmed dish for serving.

Macaroni with Ham and Cheese

4 helpings

200g long or elbow cut
  macaroni
1 shallot
$\frac{1}{2}$ clove of garlic
25g unsmoked streaky
  bacon, without rinds
  or tongue
25g butter
125ml Béchamel sauce
  (p704)

125ml Fresh Tomato
  sauce (p715)
50g strong grated cheese
  (Pecorino or Parmesan
  if possible)
salt and pepper
2×15ml spoons
  chopped fresh basil

Garnish
fried croûtons

Break long macaroni into 2cm lengths and cook in boiling salted water as directed; drain well and return to the dry pan. Skin and finely chop the shallot and garlic. Chop the bacon or tongue finely. Melt the butter in a saucepan, add the shallot and garlic and fry for 2–3 minutes without browning. Add the chopped meat and continue cooking for a further 2–3 minutes. Add the macaroni, Béchamel sauce and tomato sauce, and heat well. Stir half the cheese into the pan with the seasoning. Mix the other half with the basil and put to one side. Serve the macaroni piled on a warmed dish, and garnish with the croûtons. Serve the cheese and basil mixture separately.

Macaroni with Mushrooms and Meat

3–4 helpings

150g long **or** elbow cut macaroni	2 × 15ml spoons concentrated tomato purée
100g mushrooms	salt and pepper
50g butter	1 × 10ml spoon flour
25g cooked ham	75g grated Parmesan cheese
25g cooked tongue	
175ml dry white wine **or** white stock (p329)	

Break long macaroni into 2cm lengths. Cook in boiling salted water as directed; drain well. Prepare and slice the mushrooms. Melt 25g of the butter in a saucepan, add the mushrooms and cook for 2–3 minutes. Cut the ham and tongue into 5mm strips and add to the saucepan with the wine or stock; simmer for 5 minutes. Stir a little of the wine or stock into the tomato purée and return the mixture to the pan. Add the macaroni, and salt and pepper to taste. Cook gently, stirring occasionally, for 10–15 minutes. Mix together the remaining butter and flour to form a smooth paste and stir it into the saucepan. Stir with a fork and heat for 5 minutes. Stir the cheese into the mixture.

Macaroni with Tomato Sauce and Cheese

2–3 helpings

100g long macaroni	250ml Fresh Tomato sauce (p715)
25g butter	salt and pepper
25g flour	25g grated Parmesan cheese
1 × 5ml spoon caster sugar	

Cook the macaroni in boiling salted water as directed; drain well and return to the dry pan. Melt the butter in a small pan, add the flour and cook for a few minutes. Stir in the sugar, tomato sauce, and seasoning to taste. Bring to the boil and simmer for 2–3 minutes. Add to the cooked macaroni, and heat for 2 minutes. Pour into a warmed serving dish and serve with the cheese sprinkled on top.

Steamed Macaroni Pudding

3–4 helpings

50g elbow cut macaroni	2 eggs
200g grated Parmesan cheese	250ml Fresh Tomato (p715) **or** well-flavoured Béchamel sauce (p704)
100g shredded suet	
salt and pepper	

Cook the macaroni in boiling salted water as directed; drain well. Mix the grated cheese with the macaroni, suet, and seasoning. Beat the eggs until liquid and mix them in thoroughly. Put the mixture into a greased 600ml basin, cover with greased paper or foil and steam for 1–1½ hours. Heat the sauce. Turn out the pudding on to a warmed serving dish and pour the hot sauce over the dish.

Macaroni and Onion Fritters

2–3 helpings

2 onions	75g soft white breadcrumbs
50g elbow **or** short cut macaroni	salt and pepper
2 eggs	oil for shallow frying

Skin and slice the onions. Boil in lightly salted water for 10–15 minutes; drain well and chop finely. Cook the macaroni in boiling salted water as directed; drain well. Beat the eggs until liquid. Mix together the onion, breadcrumbs, macaroni, eggs, and seasoning. Heat the oil in a frying pan and carefully drop in large spoonfuls of the mixture. Cook for 3–4 minutes; then turn and cook for 2–3 minutes on the second side. Drain well on soft kitchen paper before serving.

Spaghetti Bolognese

4 helpings

75g unsmoked streaky bacon, without rinds	1 × 15ml spoon concentrated tomato purée
1 medium-sized onion	125ml dry white wine
1 medium-sized carrot	salt and pepper
½ stick celery	a pinch of grated nutmeg
200g lean beef mince	200ml beef stock
100g chicken livers	300g spaghetti
15g butter	a knob of butter
1 × 15ml spoon olive oil	

Chop the bacon into small pieces. Prepare and chop finely the onion, carrot, and celery. Break down any lumps in the mince with a fork. Cut the chicken livers into small shreds. Heat the butter and oil in a saucepan, and cook the bacon gently until brown. Add the vegetables and fry until tender and browned. Stir in the mince, and turn it until browned all over. Add the chicken livers and continue cooking for 3 minutes, turning the livers over to brown them. Mix in gradually the tomato purée and then the wine. Season with salt, pepper, and nutmeg. Lower the heat so that the sauce just simmers. Stir in the stock, cover the pan, and simmer for 30–40 minutes or until the sauce is the desired consistency. Meanwhile, boil the spaghetti as directed. Drain it and pile on a warmed serving dish. Pour the sauce over the spaghetti. Top with a knob of butter and serve Parmesan cheese separately.

Spaghetti with Oil and Garlic

4 helpings

2–3 cloves garlic	300g spaghetti
1 large sprig of parsley	100ml olive oil
1 small green pepper	

Skin the garlic cloves and cut them into thin slivers. Chop the parsley finely, discarding the stems. Remove the seeds of the pepper, and chop the flesh finely. Boil the spaghetti as directed. Meanwhile, heat the oil, add the garlic and fry for 3–4 minutes until lightly browned. Add the parsley and chopped pepper and fry for 4–5 minutes until they

are lightly browned. Stir frequently while frying. Drain the pasta when just tender. Put it in a warmed serving bowl, add the hot dressing, toss well together, and serve at once.

Note Do *not* serve cheese with this classic Italian dish.

Wholewheat Spaghetti and Tomatoes

4 helpings

100g mince-style textured vegetable protein (TVP) **or** quick-cooking red lentils	a good pinch of grated nutmeg
2–3 cloves garlic	1 × 70g can concentrated tomato purée
2 medium-sized onions	250ml red wine (approx)
450g fresh **or** canned tomatoes	1 × 15ml spoon cornflour (optional)
1 × 15ml spoon vegetable oil	1 × 15ml spoon water (optional)
2 × 5ml spoons dried basil	300g wholewheat spaghetti

Soak the TVP or lentils for about 20 minutes in cold water. Skin and crush the garlic. Skin the onions, and fresh tomatoes if used, and chop both onions and tomatoes roughly. Heat the oil in a large pan, and fry the garlic and onions until soft and light golden. Drain off the fat, and add to the pan the tomatoes, basil, nutmeg, and tomato purée. Drain, and add the TVP or lentils. Cover the pan and simmer gently for 30 minutes if using TVP, or 45 minutes if using lentils, adding red wine as required to prevent any drying out. If you wish to thicken the sauce, blend the cornflour and water, and add to the tomato mixture 3–4 minutes before serving.

While simmering the sauce, cook the spaghetti in fast-boiling salted water as directed. Drain the spaghetti and pile it in the centre of a serving dish. Surround it with the hot sauce. Serve grated Parmesan cheese separately.

Stuffed Baked Cannelloni

4 helpings

16–20 cannelloni	butter for greasing
1 × 15ml spoon olive oil	75g any strong hard
300g frozen chopped	cheese
spinach	500ml foundation white
50g ham	sauce (p692)
salt and pepper	25g dry white
½ × 2.5ml spoon grated	breadcrumbs
nutmeg	25g grated Parmesan
150g Ricotta **or** cottage	cheese
cheese	

Cook the cannelloni as directed in boiling salted water with the oil; drain well. Cook the spinach and drain thoroughly. Chop the ham finely. Mix together the spinach, salt, pepper, nutmeg, soft cheese, and ham. Hold each cannelloni tube upright and open, and spoon the mixture into the tubes. Place in a buttered ovenproof dish. Grate the hard cheese and stir it into the white sauce. Pour it over the cannelloni. Bake in a moderate oven, 180°C, Gas 4, for 15–20 minutes. Mix together the crumbs and Parmesan cheese and sprinkle over the dish. Place under a hot grill for 2–3 minutes to brown the top.

Cannelloni with Mushroom Stuffing

4 helpings

16–20 cannelloni	50g Gruyère cheese
1 × 15ml spoon olive oil	50g Parma ham
750ml Béchamel sauce	1 × 15ml spoon fine
(p704)	dried breadcrumbs
200g button mushrooms	1 × 15ml spoon single
50g butter	cream **or** top of the
50g grated Parmesan	milk
cheese	

Cook the cannelloni as directed in boiling salted water with the oil; drain well. Simmer 500ml of the Béchamel sauce until well reduced and very thick. Put to one side. Prepare and slice the mushrooms thinly. Melt 25g of the butter in a pan and sauté the mushrooms gently for 2 minutes. Add to the sauce with 25g of the Parmesan cheese. Leave to cool for 10 minutes. Grate the Gruyère cheese and shred the ham very finely. Fill the cannelloni with the cooled mixture and place in a buttered shallow ovenproof dish. Sprinkle the Gruyère cheese and ham over the cannelloni, and sprinkle with the breadcrumbs. Add the cream or top of the milk to the remaining sauce and pour over the pasta. Sprinkle with the remaining Parmesan cheese and dot with the rest of the butter. Bake in a fairly hot oven, 200°C, Gas 6, for 15–20 minutes until lightly browned. Cover with greased foil if browning too much before the end of the cooking time. Serve very hot, from the dish.

Lasagne with Tomatoes, Meat, and Cheese

4 helpings

6 sheets lasagne	salt and pepper
3 × 15ml spoons oil	100g Mozzarella cheese
2 onions	butter for greasing
300g lean beef mince	500ml foundation white
1 × 410g can plum	sauce (p692)
tomatoes	50g grated Parmesan
½ × 2.5ml spoon dried	cheese
crushed marjoram	

Cook the lasagne as directed in boiling salted water with 1 × 15ml spoon oil; drain well. Skin and chop the onions. Heat the rest of the oil in a frying pan, add the onions and mince, and fry for 10 minutes. Add the tomatoes, marjoram, and seasoning to taste. Simmer for 3–4 minutes, mashing in the tomatoes to make a sauce. Slice the Mozzarella cheese thinly. Butter the sides only of a square or oblong oven-to-table dish, and spread the bottom with a little white sauce. Cover with 2 sheets of the cooked lasagne, some meat mixture, a few slices of Mozzarella, more white sauce, and a little Parmesan cheese. Repeat the layers, finishing with white sauce and Parmesan cheese. Bake in a moderate oven, 180°C, Gas 4, for 20–30 minutes.

Lasagne with Sausages and Cheese

4–6 helpings

200g lasagne	salt and ground black
1 × 15ml spoon oil	pepper
1 × 15ml spoon salt	200g Mozzarella cheese
400g Ricotta **or** cottage	100g fried pork
cheese	chipolata sausages
2 eggs	25g butter
50g grated Parmesan	125ml strong beef stock
cheese	

Cook the lasagne as directed in boiling salted water with 1 × 15ml spoon oil; drain well.

Sieve the Ricotta or cottage cheese into a bowl. Mix in the eggs, 35g of the Parmesan cheese, and seasoning to taste. Cut the Mozzarella cheese into thin slices. Slice the sausages across into thin rounds. Use one-third of the butter to grease the inside of a large oven-to-table baking dish. Put aside enough Mozzarella slices to cover the top. There will be only a few left.

Place one-third of the cooked lasagne in a flat layer in the bottom of the greased dish. Trim them to fit the dish if required, and use the trimmings as part of the pasta layer. Spread half the soft cheese mixture over the pasta. Put half the remaining Mozzarella slices on top, with half the sausage slices. Sprinkle with a little stock. Repeat the pasta layer, using another third of the lasagne. Cover with the rest of the soft cheese mixture, Mozzarella, and sausage slices. Sprinkle with stock. Cover the cheese and sausage with the last third of the pasta. Place the reserved Mozzarella slices in a flat layer on top. Sprinkle with the remaining Parmesan and dot with the rest of the butter. Trickle all the rest of the stock over the dish. Cover the top loosely with greased foil and bake in a moderate oven, 180°C, Gas 4, for 30 minutes. Uncover and bake for another 10 minutes or until the surface is browned. Serve from the dish while still very hot.

Ravioli with Chicken and Ham

4–6 helpings

100g cooked chicken	½ × 2.5ml spoon grated
25g cooked ham	nutmeg
1 × 15ml spoon chopped	200g egg noodle paste
parsley	(p852)
50g grated Parmesan	cornflour for rolling out
cheese	1 × 5ml spoon salt
1 × 15ml spoon double	25g butter
cream	250ml Fresh Tomato
salt and pepper	sauce (p715)

Mince the chicken and ham together. Mix together with the parsley, 25g Parmesan cheese, cream, salt and pepper to taste, and nutmeg; pound well together. Rub through a coarse sieve or process briefly in an electric blender until almost smooth. Divide the noodle paste into 2 equal portions and, on a lightly floured surface, roll out each piece as thinly as possible. Brush cold water over 1 sheet and place small spoonfuls of the stuffing on it, about 2cm apart. Cover with the other sheet of paste and press down well round each mound of filling. Press the sides of each mound with a ruler to get an even grid of straight lines. Using a pastry wheel or small fluted cutter, cut out squares, circles, etc, using the lines as a guide.

Place on a tray and leave to dry out for 1½–2 hours. Drop the ravioli into a large saucepan of boiling salted water; boil for 10–15 minutes. Drain the ravioli and place a layer in a greased 700ml baking dish; cover with tomato sauce and some of the remaining Parmesan cheese. Repeat until all the ingredients are used, finishing with a layer of cheese. Dot with the remaining butter and bake in a moderate oven, 180°C, Gas 4, for 20–25 minutes.

Rice

Rice is the seed of an annual grass (*Oryza sativa*) which has been the staple food of many peoples for centuries. Western people, however, still eat very little rice indeed, compared with those in the Orient, and in the case of plainly cooked rice, tend to use it as an alternative to potatoes or pasta.

Types of Rice

White rice contains the highest proportion of starch and the lowest proportions of protein, fat and minerals of any cereal, because it has been polished to remove the bran. It therefore contains little fibre and is almost completely absorbed during digestion. The many varieties of white rice available are as follows:

Carolina: Round thick grain for puddings; becomes soft and creamy with long slow cooking.

Patna: Long, cylindrical, thin, hard grain, used when grains must remain separate and dry since it absorbs less liquid than a thicker grain.

Basmati: Narrow long grain with distinct aroma and flavour. Used like Patna rice. It should be soaked for 30 minutes in salted water, then tossed in butter and simmered in fresh salted water for 20 minutes.

Javanese: Long, flat, thick grain, transparent and shiny.

Spanish: Thick short grain.

Italian: Large, thick, white or golden grain used a great deal for risotto – usually sold husked but not polished; sometimes called 'red' because of the pinkish line running through the husk.

Pre-cooked, 'Instant' or Quick: Sold already cooked, it only requires 5 minutes or less in boiling water to be ready to use. Do not overcook.

Flaked: Use in the same way as a medium grain, ie, mainly for hot or cold puddings and porridge-type dishes.

Ground: Rice grain ground to a medium or fine powder, mainly for use in puddings and cakes. It can be used instead of rice flour in shortbread to give a slightly grainy texture.

Other types of rice are:

Brown: Unpolished rice with a nutty flavour. It contains significant quantities of vitamins B and E. It is good for risotto, but takes longer to cook than white rice.

Wild Rice: Is not in fact a rice but the seed of an aquatic grass found in muddy swamps, along shores, streams, and lakes in central North America where it has always been the main food of certain Indian tribes. Wild rice is very expensive and in short supply. The grain is long and purplish-black in colour and takes 40–50 minutes to cook.

Cooking Rice

Everybody has their own way of cooking rice, especially boiled rice. But the differences are slight, and generally the results are the same if the preparation and cooking are done correctly.

Before cooking, wash the rice well under running cold water in a sieve or colander. This removes the loose surface starch which prevents rice drying out into separate grains when cooked. Remove also any dark or discoloured grains.

Do not overcook the rice. Something between 12–20 minutes is a basic guide, depending on the type of rice used. Test it after 10 minutes; it should be tender to the touch but still have a slight 'bite' for savoury dishes. Toss lightly with a fork before serving.

As rice almost trebles its bulk when boiled, 25–50g of dry rice is usually enough for one average helping.

Boiled Rice (white)

Basic recipe

3–4 helpings

METHOD 1

Put 125g long-grain rice into a saucepan, pour in 375ml cold water and add 1×5ml spoon salt. Bring to the boil, stir once with a fork, reduce the heat, cover with a lid, and simmer for 12–15 minutes by which time the liquid should all be absorbed.

Method 2 follows over.

METHOD 2

Put 3 litres of water into a large saucepan, add 1 × 5ml spoon salt and bring to the boil. Sprinkle in 125g long-grain rice and stir two or three times with a fork until the water is at boiling point again. Reduce the heat so that the water is just boiling and cook for 15–18 minutes. Test for readiness after 10 minutes. Drain thoroughly before use.

The juice of half a lemon, added to the water, will help to keep the rice white.

Boiled Rice (brown)

Basic recipe

4 helpings

Put 275g brown rice into a large saucepan, pour in 400ml water, and add 1 × 2.5ml spoon salt. Bring slowly to the boil. Reduce the heat, cover with a lid, and simmer gently for about 20 minutes. Do not stir. If the pan is dry, add a little more water. After 30 minutes, add a few drops more water if the rice is not yet cooked. When ready, the liquid should all be absorbed and the rice should just be beginning to stick to the bottom. Remove from the heat and let it stand, covered, for 10–15 minutes before use.

Note Brown rice keeps well for 4–5 days in a refrigerator, so it is worth cooking a fairly large quantity at one time.

Sautéed Rice

Rice for risotto and pilaf dishes is usually cooked in this way. The rice is sautéed in oil or butter before the liquid (usually stock) is added to the saucepan. Sometimes the rice is half covered with very little liquid, and cooked until tender.

Using Rice as a Border

Plain boiled rice can be pressed into a well-buttered ring or border mould, standing in a pan of hot water, and heated gently for 7–10 minutes. It can then be turned out by placing a serving plate on the mould and turning both plate and mould over together. The rice should come away from the mould easily, without breaking. The centre can then be filled with any savoury or sweet mixture.

Keeping Rice Hot

If the cooked rice cannot be used at once it can be kept hot in one of the following ways:
1) Put the well-drained rice in a colander or sieve over a saucepan of hot water.
2) Put it into an oiled dish, cover with greased foil or greaseproof paper and place in a warm oven until required. Toss lightly with a fork before serving.

Re-heating Rice

Plain boiled rice can be re-heated by placing it in a colander or sieve lined with thin damp muslin or similar cloth, covering it loosely with a damp cloth or paper, and heating it over simmering water for 5–7 minutes; the rice should be forked over to loosen the grains at least once while re-heating. Risotto or other savoury rice can be placed in a lightly greased heatproof dish with a very little extra stock or a small pat of extra fat on top, and then heated over simmering water or stood in a pan of hot water in the oven for 5–8 minutes.

Risotto

Basic recipe

4–5 helpings

1 × 2.5ml spoon saffron	*75ml dry white wine*
375–425ml white (p329)	*1 × 5ml spoon salt*
or *chicken* (p330)	*pepper*
stock	*50g grated Parmesan*
200g Italian rice	*cheese*
1 onion	
50g butter	

Mix together the saffron and 2 ×15ml spoons stock, and leave to stand until the stock is a deep golden colour. Wash and drain the rice. Skin and chop the onion. Melt the butter in a saucepan, add the onion and fry until soft. Add the rice and stir over gentle heat for about 10 minutes. Pour in the wine, stir, and simmer until the liquid is absorbed. Add the saffron mixture to the pan with 375ml stock, and season with the salt and pepper. Bring to the boil, reduce the heat and simmer, uncovered, for 15–20 minutes until the stock has been absorbed. Add more stock if necessary while the rice is cooking. Just before serving, stir in the cheese.

VARIATIONS

Chicken Risotto

Add 200g chopped cooked chicken meat to the rice 6–7 minutes before the end of the cooking time.

Prawn Risotto

Add 200g peeled prawns or shrimps to the rice 3 minutes before the end of the cooking time. Use white stock.

Moist Brown Risotto

4–6 helpings

1 litre vegetable stock (p330)	2 × 15ml spoons sultanas
1 × 10ml spoon white wine or dry white vermouth or water	2 × 15ml spoons finely chopped sweet red pepper
300g brown rice	2 × 5ml spoons chopped fresh thyme leaves or
1 small onion	1 × 5ml spoon dried thyme
50g margarine	
1 × 5ml spoon concentrated tomato purée	salt and pepper
25g button mushrooms	3 × 15ml spoons natural yoghurt
2 × 15ml spoons shelled young peas	

Warm the stock with the wine, vermouth or water, and put to one side. Wash and drain the rice. Skin and chop the onion. Melt 25g of the fat in a saucepan and fry the onion gently until soft but not browned. Add the rice and tomato purée, and stir until well coated and blended with the fat. Prepare

and chop the mushrooms and add to the pan with the peas, sultanas, pepper, and thyme. Stir in 500ml of the stock, 100ml at a time, letting the rice absorb the liquid each time before adding more. Add the rest of the stock, season, and half cover the pan. Reduce the heat and simmer gently, covered, for about 40 minutes until most of the liquid has been absorbed. The rice should be tender but not mushy. Stir in the remaining fat and the yoghurt. Re-season if required. Serve very hot.

Tuscan Rice

2–3 helpings

100g Patna rice	50g butter
1 onion	salt and pepper
1 clove	a pinch of Cayenne pepper
bouquet garni	
125ml white stock (p329)	$\frac{1}{2}$ × 2.5ml spoon ground mace
250ml Fresh Tomato sauce (p715)	25g grated Parmesan cheese
2 shallots	3 small tomatoes
2 thick slices salami	

Wash and drain the rice. Skin the onion. Stick the clove in the onion. Put the rice, onion, bouquet garni, stock, and tomato sauce into a saucepan and cook for about 20 minutes or until the rice is just tender. Add more stock during cooking if necessary, to prevent the rice from becoming too dry. Draw off the heat, remove the onion and bouquet garni and keep the rice warm.

Meanwhile, skin and chop the shallots and dice the salami. Melt 25g butter in a frying pan, add the shallots and salami and fry for 4–5 minutes. Add to the rice the shallots, salami, salt and pepper to taste, Cayenne pepper, mace, and cheese; stir well. Slice the tomatoes and fry in the remaining butter. Pile the rice on to a warmed serving dish and garnish with the tomatoes.

Polish Rice

2–3 helpings

100g Patna rice	50g ham
500ml chicken stock	salt and pepper
(approx)	1 × 15ml spoon
2 onions	Parmesan cheese
50g butter	

Garnish
chopped parsley

Wash and drain the rice. Put it in a saucepan with the stock. Cover and simmer gently for 20–25 minutes or until all the liquid is absorbed and the rice is just soft. Add more stock if necessary while cooking. Skin and thinly slice the onions. Melt the butter in a saucepan, add the onion and fry for 2–3 minutes. Cut the ham into thin strips. Add the ham and rice to the saucepan, season with salt and pepper, and stir in the cheese. Heat for 2–3 minutes. Pile the rice on to a warmed serving dish and sprinkle with the parsley.

Rice with Tomatoes

4–5 helpings

200g Patna rice	1 onion
50g butter	5 small tomatoes
3 shallots	3 cloves
2 rashers streaky bacon,	salt and pepper
without rinds	25g grated Parmesan
1 litre white stock	cheese
(p329)	

Wash and drain the rice. Melt the butter in a saucepan, put in the rice, half cover and simmer gently for 4–5 minutes. Skin and chop the shallots and chop the bacon; add to the rice and fry a further 3–4 minutes. Add the stock. Skin the onion and tomatoes. Stick the cloves in the onion. Slice and de-seed the tomatoes. Add the onion and tomatoes to the saucepan. Season with salt and pepper. Cook gently for about 20 minutes or until the rice is tender and the stock has been absorbed. Remove the onion and stir in the cheese. Pile on a warmed serving dish.

Fried Rice(1)

2–3 helpings

100g long-grain rice	salt and pepper
1 onion	2 eggs
50g ham	2 × 15ml spoons soy
4 × 15ml spoons cooking	sauce
oil	

Garnish
chopped parsley

Wash and drain the rice and cook it in boiling salted water for about 12 minutes. Drain well. Skin and chop the onion. Cut the ham into thin strips. Heat the oil in a frying pan, add the cooked rice and onion, and fry for about 5–6 minutes. Stir in the ham and seasoning. Beat the eggs until liquid, and pour them into the pan. Stir the mixture over low heat until the eggs are just beginning to set. Stir in the soy sauce quickly. Pile the rice on to a warmed serving dish and sprinkle with parsley.

Fried Rice(2)

2–3 helpings

100g long-grain rice	4 × 15ml spoons cooking
1 onion	oil
50g mushrooms	1 × 10ml spoon soy
50g ham	sauce
2 eggs	salt and pepper

Wash and drain the rice and cook it in boiling salted water for about 12 minutes. Drain well. Skin and chop the onion. Slice the mushrooms. Cut the ham into thin strips. Beat the eggs until liquid. Heat half the oil in a frying pan, pour in the eggs and make a thin omelet; lift it out of the pan with a palette knife and cut it into strips. Add the onion to the pan, with a little more oil if required, and fry for 2 minutes. Add the mushrooms and fry for a further 2–3 minutes. Stir in the rice with any remaining oil and fry for 5 minutes. Add all the other ingredients, heat well, and pile on a warmed serving dish.

Curried Rice

2–3 helpings

100g Patna rice	250–300ml stock
1 onion	1 × 15ml spoon single
50g butter	cream
1 × 5ml spoon curry	salt and pepper
powder	½ × 2.5ml spoon grated
1 tomato	nutmeg

Garnish

1 sliced hard-boiled egg   *watercress sprigs*

Wash and drain the rice. Skin and chop the onion. Melt the butter in a saucepan, add the onion and curry powder and fry for 2–3 minutes. Stir in the rice, half cover the pan, and cook over moderate heat for 5–6 minutes. Skin and chop the tomato. Add with 250ml stock, the cream, seasoning and nutmeg to the saucepan, and cook gently for about 15 minutes or until the rice is just soft; add more stock if necessary to prevent the rice from becoming too dry. When the rice is cooked, pile it on to a warmed serving dish, and garnish with the sliced egg and watercress.

Savoury Rice

3–4 helpings

200g long-grain rice	1 × 2.5ml spoon dried
1 onion	mixed herbs
50g mature Cheddar	a pinch of Cayenne
cheese	pepper
3 × 15ml spoons Fresh	½ × 2.5ml spoon salt
Tomato sauce (p715)	50g butter
2 × 15ml spoons	
chopped parsley	

Wash and drain the rice. Skin and chop the onion. Cook the rice and onion in boiling salted water for 18–20 minutes; drain well. Put the rice back into the dry saucepan. Grate the Cheddar cheese and stir it into the mixture with the tomato sauce. Add the parsley, herbs, Cayenne pepper, salt, and butter to the saucepan. Stir well and heat for 3–4 minutes. Pile on to a warmed serving dish.

Serve hot with grated Parmesan cheese.

Oven-cooked Rice

2–3 helpings

1 medium-sized onion	250ml water or white
2 × 15ml spoons	stock (p329)
margarine	1 × 5ml spoon salt
125g long-grain rice	

Skin and chop the onion. Melt the fat in a shallow flameproof baking dish and fry the onion gently until soft. Wash and drain the rice and add it to the dish. Bring the water or stock plus the salt to the boil and pour the liquid over the rice; stir with a fork. Cover the dish and bake in a moderate oven, 180°C, Gas 4, for 30–40 minutes.

Note Alternatively, the onion can be fried in a deep flameproof casserole, the rice stirred in and the stock added to the ingredients and brought to the boil before transferring to the oven.

Rice with Shrimps

2–3 helpings

100g long-grain rice	100g peeled shrimps
50g ham	salt and pepper
50g butter	

Wash and drain the rice. Cook in boiling salted water for 15–18 minutes; drain well. Return the rice to the dry pan. Cut the ham into thin strips. Melt the butter in a frying pan, add the rice and fry for 4–5 minutes. Stir in the ham and shrimps and heat for 2–3 minutes. Season to taste with salt and pepper. Pile on to a warmed serving dish.

Saffron Rice
See p524.

Rice Stuffings
For stuffings made with rice, see pp382–83.

Other Grain Cereals

Many whole grain cereals with husks and processed grains are used for food, and they can often be substituted for pasta or rice. Any grain left wholly or partly unprocessed is particularly nutritious, and also usually contains some fibre. Some of these grain cereals are:

Buckwheat: The seed of a plant (*Fagopyrum esculentum*) which is rather like beechmast. It is sometimes called beech wheat. The seeds are usually sold hulled and roasted, but they must still be cooked before being used in a recipe. To cook them, put twice the volume of water as buckwheat into a pan with the grain, bring to the boil and simmer for 10–15 minutes. The grain can then be used for making porridge, or stuffings, etc. Buckwheat flour is used to make the Russian pancakes called Blini, and can also be used for scones.

Oats: Often sold as flaked or rolled oats, which are made by crushing pre-steamed pinhead oatmeal. They are cooked in the same way as whole, small, and powdered grains in puddings (pp957–58) and are also used for many baked goods. Groats (grain with the husk removed) are also available. Rolled oats and groats are used more frequently for porridge than for puddings.

Maize: The kernel of Indian corn. Yellow or white maize meal (cornmeal) is very much like semolina and is cooked in the same way. It is used for making the Italian polenta and in many American and African dishes.

Wheat: Whole grain, kibbled wheat, and wheat flakes are the forms most usually sold. The whole grain can be ground into flour or coarser meal, and then used for making bread, cereals and pasta products. Semolina is obtained from the first milling of wheat. Couscous is a similar form.

Barley: Usually sold as Scotch barley, pearl barley or barley flakes. Use pearl barley in soups and casseroles; barley flakes make good puddings. It is also used commercially in the making of whisky and beer.

Rye: Often milled and used in making a number of dark, firm-textured breads, especially popular in northern European countries. The grain is also used in the fermentation and distillation of rye whisky.

OATS AND OATMEAL

Muesli (1)
(to store)

4–6 helpings

200g mixed grains (eg natural wheat bran, maize meal, wheat meal, oat flakes etc)
2 × 15ml spoons chopped mixed nuts
2 × 15ml spoons raisins
2 × 15ml spoons dried apple and apricots
2 × 15ml spoons brown sugar

Mix all the ingredients together and store in an airtight jar until required.

Serve for breakfast or as a dessert with milk, yoghurt, stewed fruit or honey.

Muesli (2)
(made with fresh fruit)

4 helpings

1 large dessert apple
unstrained fresh lemon juice
100g rolled oats
15g natural wheat bran
25g sultanas
25g seedless raisins
25g clear honey **or** *soft light brown sugar*
250g natural yoghurt
25g chopped mixed nuts

Core and dice the apple without peeling. Toss at once in the lemon juice and put to one side. Mix together the oats, bran, sultanas, and raisins. Warm the honey, if used. Stir the honey or sugar into the muesli. Drain and add the apple. Serve in 4 individual bowls, cover with yoghurt, and sprinkle with nuts.

VARIATIONS
1) Add 25–50g other dried fruit (eg dates or apricots) well chopped, with the sultanas.
2) Add 50g chopped fresh fruit with the apple.

Porridge

4 helpings

850ml water	salt
125g rolled oats (not quick-cooking)	Demerara sugar **or** golden syrup (optional)

Bring the water to a fast boil in a heavy pan. Sprinkle in the oats gradually, stirring with a wooden spoon. Reduce the heat, cover the pan, and simmer for 8 minutes. Add salt to taste, cover, and simmer for another 8 minutes or until the porridge is the required consistency.

Spoon into cold bowls (to stop the porridge cooking). Serve at once sprinkled either with extra salt or with Demerara sugar or golden syrup. Add hot or cold milk to taste. Alternatively, top the porridge with a knob of salted butter.

Note For Oatmeal Porridge, see p1463.

Oatmeal Herb Pudding

4–6 helpings

100g self-raising flour	1 × 5ml spoon chopped fresh sage leaves
100g fine oatmeal	salt and pepper
100g shredded suet **or** pork dripping	fat for greasing
young leaves of spinach, beet, parsley, and spring onion green to taste	2 rashers bacon, without rinds
1 small onion	foundation brown sauce (p698)

Mix together the flour, oatmeal, and suet. Chop the leaf vegetables finely. Skin and chop the onion finely. Add to the flour mixture with the sage leaves and seasoning to taste. Mix thoroughly, and then mix to a stiff dough with cold water.

Turn the mixture into a well-greased pudding basin, cover closely with greased paper or foil and steam for 3 hours. Leave to stand for 7–10 minutes in the basin and then turn out. Meanwhile, fry the bacon rashers until crisp. Crumble the bacon and sprinkle it on to the pudding. Heat the sauce and pour it over.

Honesty Pudding

4 helpings

50g fine oatmeal	a pinch of salt
1 × 15ml spoon plain flour	1 × 2.5ml spoon grated orange rind
750ml milk	fat for greasing
1 egg	

Blend the oatmeal and flour to a smooth paste in a basin with a little of the milk. Bring the rest of the milk to the boil, and pour it over the mixture, stirring all the time. Return the mixture to the pan and cook over low heat for 5 minutes, stirring all the time. Remove from the heat, and cool for 5 minutes. Beat the egg until liquid, and then beat it into the cooled oatmeal mixture. Flavour with the salt and orange rind. Pour the mixture into a greased 750ml pie dish, and bake in a moderate oven, 180°C, Gas 4, for 35–40 minutes.

Serve hot from the dish, with cream and brown sugar.

Oatcakes
See p1222.

Oatmeal Stuffing
See p382.

POLENTA AND MAIZE MEAL (cornmeal)

Polenta with Cheese

3–4 helpings

500ml water	*50g butter*
1 × 5ml spoon salt	*50g grated Parmesan*
200g polenta	*cheese*

Put the water and salt into a saucepan and bring to the boil. Pour in the polenta and stir well with a wooden spoon. Cook for 20–30 minutes, stirring all the time. When the mixture leaves the sides of the saucepan cleanly, stir in the butter and cheese quickly and thoroughly. Put the mixture on a dish which has been sprinkled with cold water. Cut into slices to serve.

VARIATION

Cut cold polenta into pieces, 1.5cm thick, place in a pie dish, and cover with a thick layer of grated cheese. Continue layering the polenta and cheese until all the polenta has been used up. Top with a thick layer of cheese, dot with butter and bake in a fairly hot oven, 190°C, Gas 5, for 20–25 minutes.

Polenta with Smoked Sausage

3–4 helpings

500ml water	*50g grated Parmesan*
400g polenta	*cheese*
salt and pepper	*25g dry white*
400g chorizo, cabanos	*breadcrumbs*
or other small smoked	*25g butter*
sausages	
200g concentrated	
tomato purée (approx)	

Bring the water to the boil in a large saucepan and stir in the polenta and seasoning. Cook, stirring all the time, for 10–15 minutes. Leave to cool. Cook the sausages in boiling water for 10 minutes, remove from the pan and leave to cool. Remove the skins and cut into 2cm slices. Put a layer of polenta in the bottom of an ovenproof dish, cover with a layer of sausages, some tomato purée, cheese, salt, and pepper. Repeat the layers until all the ingredients have been used. Sprinkle the breadcrumbs over the mixture. Dot with the butter. Bake in a moderate oven, 180°C, Gas 4, for 25–30 minutes.

American Spoon Bread

8 helpings

200ml water	*25g butter*
400ml milk	*4 eggs*
125g cornmeal	*fat for greasing*
1 × 2.5ml spoon salt	

Bring the water and 200ml of the milk to boiling point. Add the cornmeal and salt slowly, stirring all the time. Cook, still stirring, for 1 minute. Remove from the heat and add the butter; beat well. Beat the eggs until liquid, and add them to the cornmeal mixture with the remaining milk. Mix well. Pour into a greased 23cm pie dish and bake in a fairly hot oven, 200°C, Gas 6, for 25 minutes. When cooked, the spoon bread should be firm to the touch and brown on top.

Serve from the dish, instead of potato, pasta or a pulse purée, with grilled or fried meats or with roast chicken or turkey. Serve with a spoon.

SEMOLINA

Spinach Gnocchi

4–6 helpings

500g fresh spinach **or**	40g plain flour
1 × 375g pkt frozen	25g semolina
leaf spinach	75g grated Parmesan
100g butter	cheese
150g Ricotta **or**	salt and pepper
Mozzarella cheese	½ × 2.5ml spoon grated
2 eggs	nutmeg
2 × 15ml spoons double	butter for greasing
cream	

Wash the fresh spinach several times and remove any coarse stalks. Put into a saucepan with just the water that clings to the leaves, cover, and cook gently for a few minutes until just cooked. Cook frozen spinach according to the directions on the packet. Drain thoroughly. Chop the spinach and cook for 2–3 minutes with 50g of the butter until it is quite dry, stirring all the time. Rub the Ricotta or Mozzarella cheese through a sieve, add to the spinach and cook for a further 2–3 minutes. Remove the saucepan from the heat. Beat the eggs until liquid and stir into the mixture with the cream, flour, 15g semolina, and 25g Parmesan cheese. Add seasoning to taste and the nutmeg. Put the mixture on a flat dish and chill for 1–2 hours.

Shape the gnocchi into small balls and drop into a large saucepan of simmering salted water. Cook only a few at a time, and as soon as they puff up and rise to the surface, remove them carefully from the saucepan with a perforated spoon. Place in a buttered ovenproof dish. Melt the remaining butter and pour it over the gnocchi. Sprinkle with the rest of the Parmesan cheese and remaining semolina, and place under a hot grill for a few minutes until the cheese has melted and is golden-brown.

Russian Gnocchi

4–5 helpings

250ml milk	½ × 2.5ml spoon paprika
100g butter	100g grated Parmesan
100g flour **or** semolina	cheese
2 eggs	125ml Béchamel sauce
½ × 2.5ml spoon salt	(p704)

Heat the milk in a saucepan, add 50g butter and bring to the boil. Stir in the flour or semolina and, beating all the time, cook the mixture gently until it leaves the sides of the pan cleanly. Leave to cool. Beat the eggs until liquid and gradually work them into the mixture. Add the salt, paprika, half the cheese, and the remaining butter. Shape the mixture into quenelles and poach in boiling salted water for 10–15 minutes. Drain well and place on a warmed dish. Heat the sauce, mix it with the remaining cheese and pour over the gnocchi. Serve immediately.

VARIATION

Chop 50g ham and add it to the gnocchi with the cheese.

Semolina Gnocchi

4 helpings

500ml milk	1 egg
100g semolina	100g grated Parmesan
salt and pepper	cheese
½ × 2.5ml spoon grated	fat for greasing
nutmeg	25g butter

Bring the milk to the boil, sprinkle in the semolina and stir over low heat until the mixture is thick. Mix in the salt, pepper, nutmeg, egg, and 75g of the cheese; beat the mixture well until smooth. Spread on a shallow dish and leave to cool. Cut into 2cm squares or shape into rounds. Place in a shallow greased ovenproof dish and sprinkle with the remaining 25g cheese; dot with butter. Brown under the grill or in a fairly hot oven, 200°C, Gas 6, for 8–10 minutes.

Baked Semolina

6–8 helpings

25g butter	*1 × 2.5ml spoon salt*
375ml milk	*1 × 2.5ml spoon baking*
40g fine semolina	*powder*
3 eggs	*fat for greasing*

Melt the butter in a saucepan. Add the milk and heat until warm. Add the semolina and mix well. Cook over gentle heat until thick, stirring all the time. Remove from the heat and put to one side. Separate the eggs. Beat the yolks until light with the salt, and add to the semolina. Whisk the egg whites until stiff, and fold into the semolina with the baking powder. Pour into a greased 1.8 litre pie or soufflé dish. Bake in a moderate oven, 180°C, Gas 4, for 40 minutes or until golden-brown.

Serve at once with plenty of butter, instead of potatoes or pasta.

COUSCOUS

This is generally served as part of a main-course dish also known as Couscous (see p869). It is very popular in the Middle East. The cereal is steamed over a stew or broth until dry and fluffy. It must never be cooked in the stew, nor even touch the liquid throughout the steaming.

The traditional pot, the *couscousier*, is in two parts. The bottom part is a large, round pan in which the stew or broth cooks; the top is a sieve which holds the couscous. A double steamer or a metal sieve which fits over a large saucepan can, however, be substituted.

To prepare the couscous: About 1 hour before the stew is cooked, moisten 375g couscous slightly with a little cold water, working it in with the fingers to prevent lumps forming. Put into the couscousier, or into the top of a double steamer, or into a sieve over the saucepan holding the stew. Steam for 20–30 minutes. Rub the grain with your fingers from time to time to air it and help it to swell better. Do not cover the cereal.

Turn the couscous into a large bowl and sprinkle well with cold water. Stir to break up any lumps. Add salt to taste. Return to the couscousier, steamer or sieve and place over the stew for a further 30 minutes.

Couscousier

Couscous

6–8 helpings

50g chick-peas	2 × 5ml spoons ground
1 × 5ml spoon salt	ginger
1kg lean stewing lamb	salt and pepper
2 onions	650ml water
100g turnips	375g couscous
100g carrots	75g seedless raisins
1 green pepper	1 × 5ml spoon paprika
200g courgettes	½ × 2.5ml spoon finely
200g tomatoes	chopped chilli
25g parsley	50g butter
2 × 15ml spoons cooking	
oil	

Soak the chick-peas in plenty of cold water overnight. Strain the water into a large saucepan, bring to the boil, put in the chick-peas and salt, reduce the heat, cover closely, and simmer for 2½ hours or until the chick-peas are nearly cooked. Strain, and reserve the chick-peas in the pan.

Remove any fat from the lamb and cut it into 2cm cubes. Prepare and slice the onions, turnips and carrots. Cut the pepper in half, remove the seeds and chop finely. Slice the courgettes. Skin and chop the tomatoes. Chop the parsley. Heat the oil in a saucepan, add the meat, and fry for 5 minutes. Add the onions, turnips, carrots and green pepper, and fry for a further 2–3 minutes. Add the ginger, salt and pepper, and stir the water into the mixture. Turn it into the saucepan with the chick-peas, bring back to the boil, reduce the heat, cover, and simmer for about 1 hour.

Meanwhile, prepare the couscous as described on p868, but before replacing the sieve and cooking for another 30 minutes, add the raisins, courgettes, tomatoes, and parsley to the stew. Mix together the paprika and chilli and stir in 125ml liquid from the stew; keep hot for serving with it.

Pile the couscous on to a large dish; cut the butter into small pieces and fork into the dish. Pour the stew over the grain and serve the peppery sauce on top.

BUCKWHEAT

Savoury Buckwheat or Buckwheat Stuffing

3–4 helpings

200g roasted buckwheat	50g butter
1 egg	1 × 15ml spoon oil
½ × 2.5ml spoon salt	1 onion

Prepare the buckwheat as on p864. Beat the egg until liquid, add the buckwheat and the salt. Melt the butter in a double boiler, stir in the buckwheat mixture and cook for 1½–2½ hours. Heat the oil in a frying pan. Skin and chop the onion, and fry in the oil for a few minutes until soft. When the buckwheat is cooked, stir in the onion.

Serve as a stuffing or as an accompaniment to meat instead of potatoes.

Buckwheat and Cheese Pudding

3–4 helpings

200g roasted buckwheat	75g grated Parmesan
1 egg	cheese
75g butter	fat for greasing
250ml boiling salted	salt
water	

Prepare the buckwheat as on p864. Put into a bowl, add the egg and beat well. Add 25g butter and the boiling water. Put the mixture into a double boiler and simmer for 1½–2½ hours or until the buckwheat is tender. Melt the rest of the butter. Put layers of the buckwheat and cheese into a greased 700ml ovenproof dish, sprinkling each layer with melted butter and a little salt, until all the mixture is used. Bake in a fairly hot oven, 190°C, Gas 5, for 20–30 minutes, until the top is browned.

DAIRY FOODS, FATS, AND OILS

From no other substance, solid or fluid, can so great a number of distinct kinds of aliment be prepared as from milk; some forming food, others drink; some of them delicious, and deserving the name of luxuries; all of them wholesome, and some medicinal: indeed, the variety of aliments that seems capable of being produced from milk, appears to be quite endless.

Recipes using dairy foods etc. are located throughout the book. This chapter includes a selection which use them as a principal ingredient. Others may be found by reference to the Index.

Milk

FOOD VALUE OF MILK

Whole milk is an important food for everyone as it is nutritionally one of the most complete foods. It is rich in protein, calcium, vitamin A and some B vitamins, and is therefore especially good for people who need extra nutrients, such as children, pregnant and nursing mothers, and the elderly. It is, however, low in iron and vitamins C and D; and small losses of some B vitamins and vitamin C may result during processing and distribution.

All milks must contain a legal minimum of 8.5% non-fatty solids and milk must contain a legal minimum of 3% fat unless it is sold as skimmed or separated milk. Milk fat is suspended in many tiny globules throughout the milk so it is easy to digest.

TYPES OF MILK

Most of the milk consumed in the UK comes from cows, although milk from goats, sheep, buffalo, reindeer, and camels is widely used in other countries. Goats' milk is available in the UK in some health food stores. It has a similar composition to ordinary cows' milk, but has a higher percentage of fat and protein. The fat globules are smaller, and are, therefore, easier to digest. These small globules rise very slowly, so only a very small amount of cream, if any, forms on the top of the milk. Goats' milk can be used in all the same ways as cows' milk. Its flavour is, however, slightly sweeter and stronger.

Attested Milk

All milk herds in the UK are now attested, that is, they have been examined and found free of tuberculosis.

Untreated Milk

Untreated milk straight from the cow (or goat) is called raw milk and is the produce of tuberculin and brucellosis accredited herds. It is sometimes bottled and sold under licence from a farm or dairy (1980). It has a visible cream line and a slightly different flavour from pasteurized milk. The harmless lactic acid bacteria contained in raw milk convert the lactose (milk sugar) into lactic acid. In small quantities this gives the milk a slightly acid taste; in larger quantities it causes it to curdle or turn sour.

Raw milk is also an ideal food for pathogenic bacteria. Some of these cause the milk to putrefy (go bad) and some cause disease. Bacteria multiply quickly in warm conditions so it is essential to keep all raw milk cool. It should be used on the day it is produced or within 2 days if refrigerated.

Heat-treated Milk

Of the milk sold in the UK, 95% is heat-treated before sale to ensure that all disease-causing bacteria are destroyed. Various heat treatments are used and the milk is graded accordingly. Dairies usually use different coloured metal caps to denote the various grades.

Pasteurization: This is the most common and mildest of processes, and is the usual treatment for milk sold for domestic use. In the UK the milk is heated to 72°C for 15 seconds and then rapidly cooled to 10°C, which destroys all the disease-causing bacteria. Some of the lactic acid bacteria are also destroyed, so the keeping quality of the milk after pasteurization is improved to 1–2 days in a cool place, 2–3 days in a refrigerator. There is also a slight loss of vitamin B_1 (thiamin) and vitamin C. The flavour is not affected.

Homogenization: The milk is processed so that the cream is evenly distributed throughout to give a uniform product. Warm raw milk is forced through fine apertures so that the fat globules are broken down into such tiny particles that they do not rise to the top of the milk. The milk is then pasteurized. Homogenized milk has a richer, creamier taste than ordinary milk. The keeping qualities and food value are the same as for ordinary pasteurized milk.

Ultra-heat-treated milk (UHT): Homogenized milk is heated for a longer time at a lower temperature to stabilize the protein, then heated to 132°C for 1–2 seconds. It is then packed in sterile, usually foil-lined, cardboard containers, which should be date-stamped. The milk will keep unopened and unrefrigerated for several months, but once opened it should be treated like ordinary pasteurized milk. There is little change of flavour when the milk is first processed but the flavour gradually deteriorates during storage. Only small losses of vitamins occur during processing but a good deal of vitamins B and C is lost if the milk is stored for a long time.

Sterilization: Homogenized milk is bottled, sealed with an hermetic cap, and heat-treated to above boiling point for 30–40 minutes, then allowed to cool. Sterilization is designed to produce a sterile milk which will keep unrefrigerated for a minimum of 7 days, if unopened; it can however be up to several weeks. The milk appears rich and creamy as the cream does not separate out, but there is a slight caramel or 'boiled-milk' flavour due to the high temperature at which it was processed. This process reduces the vitamin C and B_1 (thiamin) content considerably.

Channel Island and South Devon Milk

The milk from all the farms is usually combined when it reaches the dairy, so the milk in a bottle may be a blend from all breeds of cow. However, if it comes from Jersey, Guernsey or South Devon cows, it has been bottled separately, and is usually sold at a higher price than other milk. Channel Island milk must have a 4% butterfat content. The extra fat gives a rich, creamy flavour.

This milk is normally pasteurized and has the same keeping qualities as ordinary pasteurized milk. Its food value is about the same, although its energy content is greater.

STORING FRESH MILK

Throughout its production, the greatest care is taken to ensure that milk arrives pure and fresh at the retail outlet or (in the UK) on the doorstep. But this care will have been wasted if it is not looked after properly in the home.

1) If milk is delivered to the house take it indoors as soon as possible. Do not leave it out in the sunlight as the flavour is spoiled and some of the vital vitamins are destroyed.

2) Store milk in a clean container. It will keep best in the bottle in which it is delivered as this is sterilized before filling.

3) Keep milk in a cool place, dark if possible. A refrigerator is best, but if not available, put it in the coolest part of the larder; and on warm days stand the container in a basin of cold water and cover it with a damp cloth that reaches down into the water.

4) Any milk jug should be covered so that dust and flies do not carry harmful bacteria into the milk. Even in a refrigerator, it is best to keep milk away from strongly flavoured foods, such as onions, which can easily taint it.

5) Any jug which has contained milk should be rinsed in cold water and then scalded with boiling water, then left to cool and drain. This is to remove stale, dried milk in which bacteria can multiply.

6) Use milk in the same order as you receive it, the oldest first. Never mix several days' milk.

Soured Milk

Untreated milk sours naturally and may be used in cooking, whereas milk which has been heat treated will putrefy; it can be used for a very short time only once it has passed its freshness.

OTHER MILKS AND MILK PRODUCTS

Skimmed Milk

This is milk from which most of the cream has been removed; it has a maximum butterfat content of 0.3%. Skimmed milk must be heat treated either by pasteurization, sterilization or the UHT process. It is not suitable for infant feeding.

Canned and Dried Milk

The most common forms in which these are sold are evaporated milk, condensed milk, and powdered or dried (usually skimmed) milk. Dried milk, with a storage life of 6 months, is best stored in a cool, dry cupboard, but cans of liquid milk can be stored for 1 year in an ordinary cupboard. As a large percentage of the liquid has been removed during processing, the volume is reduced so they take up less storage space too. These milks are, therefore, ideal for keeping as a stand-by in an emergency or for use where space is limited, eg camping, caravanning or boating. Once reconstituted, canned or dried milk should be treated as fresh milk.

Evaporated Milk

Evaporated milk is whole milk from which water has been removed by heat so that it is $2\frac{1}{2}$ times as concentrated as fresh milk. It is then homogenized, canned, and sterilized at 116°C. The processing gives the milk a slight caramel flavour and darkens the colour. There is a considerable loss of vitamins C and B_1 (thiamin), but extra vitamin D is added by the manufacturers. This milk is quite suitable for weaned infants.

Cans may become dirty during storage, and great care must be taken to see that the outside is clean, especially the top, or the milk may be contaminated when the can is opened or poured out. Once opened, the can should be kept covered in a cool place or refrigerator, like fresh milk.

Undiluted evaporated milk is often used as a substitute for cream or custard. It can also be whisked until thick and frothy and double in volume. The process is considerably speeded up if the milk is treated beforehand in one of the following ways:

1) Store the unopened can in a refrigerator for at least 24 hours before using.

2) Put the unopened can in a saucepan, cover with water, bring to the boil, and simmer for 20 minutes. Cool before using.

3) Add 2×15ml spoons lemon juice to a large can of milk before whisking.

Condensed Milk

This is whole or skimmed milk which has been heat-treated to remove the water and make it even more concentrated than evaporated milk. Sugar has also been added so that the finished product contains at least 55% sugar. This sugar acts as a preservative, so it is not necessary to sterilize the canned milk. The high energy value produced by the sugar makes it unsuitable for infants, however.

Once opened, condensed milk will keep for several days without refrigeration due to its low proportion of water and high proportion of sugar; in all other ways, it should be stored and used like evaporated milk.

Dried Milk

This can be made from whole, half-cream (partially skimmed), or skimmed milk. In each case it is roller-dried or spray-dried to remove 95–98% of the moisture, and is then reduced to powder or granule form. The milk is sold in airtight and moisture-proof containers. Once opened, the milk gradually deteriorates as it absorbs moisture from the air. Resealing the lid firmly after use helps to keep the milk in good condition.

When reconstituted, whole milk powder has a similar food value to fresh milk, although some vitamins are lost. Skimmed milk powder, however, contains virtually no fat, and therefore no fat soluble vitamins; it does, however, contain protein, calcium, and riboflavin. It is often used in slimming diets. Some skimmed milk powder has extra fat added, from vegetable sources, to replace the milk fat and is known as filled milk. It may be fortified with vitamins A, D and sometimes C, so that its food value is similar to that of fresh milk.

Whey

If whey is produced commercially, the milk is ripened with a bacterial starter and rennet is added. To obtain whey at home, see p874. Whey butter made from commercial whey, therefore, has a lactic flavour. Whey butter can be prepared at home by separating off the fat with a cream separator.

Buttermilk

Buttermilk is a by-product from the manufacture of butter. If the butter is made from fresh cream, the buttermilk is similar to skimmed milk, but if the butter is made from ripened cream lactic acid will give the buttermilk a sour taste. Modern buttermilk is mostly used dried for bakery goods or animal feed, but some is available for domestic use. Commercially cultured buttermilk is, however, usually made from skimmed milk rather than buttermilk. It makes a refreshing milk drink with a fermented sharp taste. As buttermilk has a low fat content (only 0.1–1.5%), it is low in vitamins A and D.

Ways of Using Buttermilk

1) Chilled plain buttermilk makes a refreshing, nutritious drink.
2) Flavour it with fruit juice: eg add 2 × 15ml spoons blackcurrant syrup to 250ml buttermilk; or use equal quantities of orange or tomato juice and buttermilk.
3) Flavour it with coffee, ie dissolve 2 × 5ml spoons instant coffee and sugar to taste in a very little hot water and add 250ml buttermilk.
4) Use it to make milk shakes.
5) Use it in milk jellies.
6) Use it to make soda bread, scones or teabread.
7) Make sauces for fish and vegetables with it.

Pineapple Buttermilk Whip

4 helpings

400ml unsweetened pineapple **or** *orange juice*

1 × 15ml spoon gelatine
150ml buttermilk

Put 4 × 15ml spoonfuls of fruit juice into a heat-proof basin and sprinkle in the gelatine. When the gelatine has softened, stand the basin in a pan of hot water, and stir until completely dissolved. Add the rest of the juice and put a little into each of 4 stemmed glasses. Chill the rest for about 1 hour and when it is on the point of setting, whisk in the buttermilk until frothy. Spoon into the glasses and chill.

Note This is a very good dessert for slimmers. If using fresh pineapple juice, it must be boiled for 2–3 minutes first as it contains an enzyme which destroys the setting power of gelatine.

Curds and Whey (1)

4 helpings

500ml milk	*1 × 15ml spoon rennet essence*

Heat the milk to blood-heat (37°C approx) and pour into a bowl. Stir in the rennet and leave to stand at room temperature for 1 hour. Cut the curd to release the whey.

Note Rennet is a natural extract derived from the lining membrane of a calf's stomach. It should be stored in a cool, dark place and kept tightly covered.

Curds and Whey (2)

4 helpings

200ml fresh milk	*400ml buttermilk*

Heat the fresh milk until it is hot but not boiling (65°C approx). Pour quickly into the buttermilk and leave the mixture to stand until cold and firm; do not move it. This gives a slightly softer curd than Method 1. Cut the curd to release the whey.

Curds and Whey (3)

4 helpings

500ml milk	*2 × 15ml spoons lemon juice*

Heat the milk with the lemon juice to blood-heat (37°C approx). Pour into a bowl and leave to stand for 15 minutes. This gives a curd of a less smooth texture.

Note Curds and whey can be eaten as they are, sweetened, and flavoured with cinnamon or nutmeg.

Draining Curds and Whey

If using curds and whey separately, eg Curd Cheesecake (p1042), Whey Drink (see below), line a sieve or colander with a scalded, dampened, thin cloth and stand it over a bowl or shallow dish.

Spoon the curds carefully into the cloth. Bring the corners of the cloth together, tie securely with string and hang above the bowl for 18 hours. By this time, all the whey will have run out and the curd will be firm.

Soft Cheese

See p898.

Whey Drink

4 helpings

juice of 1 lemon	*1 × 15ml spoon sugar (approx)*
whey from 500ml milk (400ml approx)	

Strain the lemon juice into the whey. Add sugar to taste. Serve chilled.

Note If the whey has been made by adding lemon juice to milk it will already be acidic in flavour; taste it before adding any extra lemon juice, and flavour accordingly.

Junket

4 helpings

600ml milk	*1 × 5ml spoon rennet essence*
1 × 15ml spoon sugar	
a few drops vanilla essence	*grated nutmeg or ground cinnamon*

Warm the milk to blood-heat (37°C approx) with the sugar and vanilla essence. Stir in the rennet essence and pour into 1 large or 4 small dishes. Cover and leave to stand in a warm place, for about 1 hour or until set. Do not move it. Sprinkle with spice and serve cold but not chilled.

Note The type of milk and the temperature are very important in the making of junket. The milk must *not* be sterilized nor must it be UHT milk, and it must be at the correct temperature; if it is too hot or too cold, it will not set. The junket should be left to set in a warm room; it should not be put in a refrigerator.

VARIATIONS

Almond or Rum Junket

Instead of the vanilla essence, add 1×2.5ml spoon almond or rum essence to the milk.

Coffee Junket

Add 2×5ml spoons instant coffee to the warmed milk and decorate with chopped nuts. Use vanilla essence and ground cinnamon, if liked.

Chocolate Junket

Grate 50g plain chocolate into the milk and dissolve it. Decorate with grated chocolate. Use vanilla essence and ground cinnamon, if liked.

Lemon or Orange Junket

Infuse the pared rind of 1 lemon or orange in the milk. Tint the junket pale yellow or orange. Do not use any other flavouring.

Rich Junket

Run a layer of single cream, flavoured with brandy, if liked, over the top of the junket. Flavour in any of the ways given above.

Yoghurt

Yoghurt is milk which is thickened by the addition of a culture of certain bacteria *(Lactobacillus bulgaricus* and *Streptococcus thermophilus)*.

The food value of plain yoghurt is virtually the same as that of the milk from which it is made. Most commercial yoghurts in the UK are made from skimmed milk, so are low-fat (1.5% fat) or fat-free (0.3%) and consequently have a low energy (joule) value. Fruit-flavoured yoghurt and whole fruit yoghurt have more energy value however.

When made commercially, the milk is first pasteurized and then homogenized. After cooling, it is inoculated with the yoghurt culture. For stirred yoghurt, eg fruit yoghurt, the mixture is incubated in large vats. When the desired level of acidity is reached, the yoghurt is broken and cooled; flavouring and permitted thickeners may then be added. It is then packaged in cartons. *Set yoghurt*, eg plain yoghurt, is packaged before incubation and then cooled rapidly.

Some yoghurt is labelled 'live' or 'true' yoghurt. This is yoghurt made with heat-treated milk and, in fact, applies to all yoghurts which are not heat-treated after being made. This covers most commercial ones.

BUYING AND STORING YOGHURT

1) Always buy yoghurt from a shop that stores it in a properly controlled chilled cabinet.
2) Check the date stamp to make sure that the yoghurt will be eaten within the recommended time.
3) Keep yoghurt in a cool place, unopened, until it is required.

As the organisms are still live, they gradually increase in activity and so make the yoghurt more and more acidic. This is not harmful in any way, in fact the yoghurt bacteria inhibits the growth of harmful bacteria, but it may become too acid to be palatable.

Fruit yoghurt may begin to bubble and give off a yeasty smell. This is due to yeasts fermenting the fruit and sugar. Again, this is quite harmless but the flavour may be unpleasant. Sometimes, there is a watery liquid or whey on top of set yoghurt; this is caused by the carton being shaken so that the yoghurt curd is broken and the whey is released. Its flavour may become too acidic for consumption.

Making Yoghurt at Home

Yoghurt can easily be made at home if a slightly less consistent result is acceptable.

The yoghurt can be incubated in one of three ways:

1) In an electric, thermostatically controlled incubator. These are very useful if a lot of yoghurt is consumed regularly.
2) In a wide-necked vacuum flask (a narrow-necked flask is not suitable as the yoghurt is broken up when it is removed). This is suitable for smaller quantities of yoghurt.
3) In a home-made incubator made from a large biscuit or cake tin with a lid. Line the base and sides with an insulating material such as woollen fabric or cotton wool and have a piece of material large enough to fit inside the top. Use 4 or 5 screw-topped glass jars that will fit inside the incubator.

Method

1) Sterilize all equipment to be used by immersion in boiling water or by using a commercial sterilizing solution. Dry afterwards.
2) Heat 500ml UHT or sterilized milk to 43°C (use a cooking thermometer) and blend in 1 × 5ml spoon *fresh* natural yoghurt; or use a yoghurt starter culture (obtainable with full instructions from dairy laboratories).
3) Pour into the prepared incubator, seal, and leave for 6–8 hours.
4) Turn the yoghurt into a cold basin and cool rapidly, standing the basin in cold water and whisking the yoghurt.
5) Cover the basin and chill for about 4 hours; the yoghurt will have thickened further.
6) When serving, gently stir in flavouring or fruit if liked, eg sugar, cinnamon, stewed fruit or jam.

Note The yoghurt will keep for 4–5 days in a refrigerator. A new carton of commercial yoghurt will be needed for the next incubation.

Ways of Using Yoghurt

1) Use natural yoghurt instead of soured milk when making scones.
2) Substitute natural yoghurt for cream to give a lighter texture and sharper flavour.
3) Add natural yoghurt to a meat or chicken casserole just before serving.
4) Stir natural or lemon yoghurt into sauces for fish, chicken or veal, just before serving.
5) Try a yoghurt topping on baked pasta or vegetable dishes. Mix 300g natural yoghurt with 2 eggs and 25g flour. Season well. Pour the topping over the dish and sprinkle with grated cheese. Bake uncovered in a fairly hot oven at 190°C, Gas 5, for 20–25 minutes, until the top is golden-brown.
6) Serve natural yoghurt as a snack food or dessert well chilled and flavoured, eg stir in a little jam, marmalade or blackcurrant syrup; mix in Demerara sugar, desiccated coconut, and a pinch of ground ginger; sprinkle ground mixed spice or cinnamon and brown sugar on top; stir in fruit purée or chopped stewed fruit.

Note For curdling, see p880.

Hot Yoghurt and Grapefruit

4 helpings

2 grapefruit
150g natural yoghurt
2 × 15ml spoons brandy (optional)

2 × 15ml spoons brown sugar
2 maraschino cherries

Cut the grapefruit in half crossways and cut out the segments with a sharp knife, removing all the pith and membranes. Put the segments into a bowl and stir in the yoghurt, and brandy if used. Return the mixture to the grapefruit shells and sprinkle with brown sugar. Heat under a hot grill for 2–3 minutes or until the sugar bubbles. Decorate with the maraschino cherries.

Serve as a dessert or as a first course for dinner.

Yoghurt Sauce for Vegetables

**Enough to cover 1 head of cauliflower or
4 large onions**

50g Cheddar cheese
150g natural yoghurt
1 egg yolk
1 × 5ml spoon made
  mustard
salt and pepper

Grate the cheese. Mix all the ingredients together
in a saucepan and heat gently without boiling until
the sauce thickens. Stir all the time.

Serve over boiled cauliflower, onions or similar
vegetables.

Yoghurt Salad Dressings

1) Mix 150g natural yoghurt, 1 × 15ml spoon
   chopped mint, a pinch of dried fennel leaves,
   and garlic salt.
2) Mix 150g natural yoghurt, the grated rind of 1
   orange, and 2 × 5ml spoons chopped mint.
3) Mix 150g natural yoghurt, ½ crushed clove of
   garlic, 2 × 5ml spoons made mustard, 1 × 15ml
   spoon lemon juice, and 1 × 15ml spoon chopped
   chives; season with salt and pepper. Use on
   coleslaw.
4) Mix 150g natural yoghurt, 2 × 5ml spoons caster sugar, 1 × 5ml spoon vinegar, and a pinch of
   Cayenne pepper. Good with beetroot.
5) Mix 150g natural yoghurt, 1 × 15ml spoon
   single cream, 2 × 15ml spoons oil, 1 × 15ml
   spoon wine vinegar, and 1 × 5ml spoon sugar.
   Season with salt and pepper, and sprinkle with a
   little chopped parsley.

Yoghurt Drink

2 long or 4 short drinks

300g natural yoghurt
250ml fruit juice
  (orange, grapefruit,
  pineapple **or** tomato)

Whisk the yoghurt in a jug until the curd is evenly
broken down. Mix in the juice, and chill.

Serve as a breakfast drink or as a first course at
dinner.

Fruit Yoghurt Whip

4 helpings

1 × 500ml pkt fruit jelly
150ml hot water
300g fruit yoghurt (the
  same flavour as the
  jelly)
1 egg white

Dissolve the jelly in the hot water. Cool, then stir in
the yoghurt. Whisk the egg white until stiff and
fold it into the mixture when it is on the point of
setting. Spoon into glasses and put in a cool place to
set.

Raspberry and Yoghurt Delight

4 helpings

1 × 425g can raspberries
  or strawberries in
  syrup
1 × 15ml spoon gelatine
300g natural yoghurt

Drain the syrup from the fruit and make it up to
250ml with water. Put 4 × 15ml spoons syrup into a
small heatproof basin and sprinkle on the gelatine.
When the gelatine has softened, stand the basin in
a pan of hot water and stir until completely dissolved. Add the rest of the syrup. Whisk the yoghurt until the curd is broken down evenly, and mix
with the syrup. Put in a cool place. When the
mixture is on the point of setting, fold in the
drained fruit. Place in a serving dish. Serve cool
but not chilled.

Raspberry Yoghurt Cheesecake
See p1043.

Cottage Yoghurt Ice Cream
See p1059.

Cream

Cream consists of the fat of milk together with some proportion of the other milk constituents and water.

The traditional method of separating cream from milk was to leave fresh milk to stand for 24 hours, and then to skim off the cream which had risen to the top, by hand, using a skimmer. This process is now mechanized and the cream is extracted by centrifugal force in a separator, which removes the skimmed milk until the cream has the desired butterfat content.

There are strict government regulations concerning the description and the minimum fat content of cream, and it is illegal to add preservatives to it.

TYPES OF CREAM

Half-cream

Half-cream has a minimum of 12% fat (it may be called top of the milk). It is homogenized to thicken the cream slightly and to distribute the fat globules evenly. It is then pasteurized, packed, and sealed. It will keep for 2–3 days in summer and 3–4 days in winter or in a refrigerator. It is a thin pouring cream suitable for cereals, fruit or coffee.

Sterilized half-cream is homogenized, canned or bottled, then heated to 115°C for 20 minutes and cooled rapidly. It will keep for up to 2 years if unopened, but once opened it must be treated as fresh cream. This is a pouring cream with a slightly distinctive flavour due to the processing.

UHT half-cream has a minimum fat content of 12% and is sometimes known as enriched milk. It is used mainly by caterers, and will keep for 3 months.

Single Cream

Single cream has a minimum of 18% fat. It is processed like half-cream and will keep in the same way. It is a thicker pouring cream which is used like half-cream; it is also used in sauces and savoury dishes.

Sterilized single cream is processed in the same way as sterilized half-cream and keeps in the same way. It is thicker than single cream, with a minimum of 23% fat, and will whip if treated in the following way. Put the unopened can in the refrigerator for several hours, then carefully turn it upside down and open it. Pour off any whey and whip the cream gently.

UHT single cream has a minimum of 18% fat. It is homogenized, heated to 132°C for 1 second, and then cooled immediately. It is usually packed into sterile foil-lined cardboard containers. This cream will keep for 6 weeks if unopened and need not be stored in a refrigerator. It is a pouring cream.

Whipping Cream

Whipping cream has a minimum of 35% fat. It is only pasteurized, not homogenized, and is then packed like half-cream. It keeps in the same way. When whipped it becomes light and fluffy, and doubles in volume. It is good for pastry fillings and ice cream. Whipping cream also holds its shape when piped.

Double Cream

Double cream has a minimum of 48% fat. It is slightly homogenized to keep it thick, especially in hot weather. It is then pasteurized and packed as above, and keeps in the same way. This is a rich pouring cream which will float on coffee or soup. It can also be whipped and piped and is frequently used to decorate puddings, gâteaux etc.

Extended life double cream has a minimum of 48% fat. It is heated to 82°C for 15 seconds and cooled before being homogenized. The cream is then bottled, vacuum-sealed, heated to 65.5°C for 30 minutes and cooled quickly. It will keep for 2–3 weeks under refrigeration. It is a thick cream which will whip lightly.

Clotted Cream

Clotted cream has a minimum of 55% fat. It is heat-treated so that the liquid is reduced and the fat percentage increased. Clotted cream is very thick, and has a special nutty flavour, crumbly texture, and a golden-yellow colour. It can be spread on scones, splits, and pastries, and served with fruit pies.

Fresh clotted cream keeps just like fresh ordinary cream, but a long-keeping clotted cream is available in jars or cans which will keep for 4–10 weeks.

Soured Cream

Soured cream has a minimum of 18% fat. It is made from fresh, single pasteurized cream which has had a special lactic acid-forming culture added to it under controlled conditions, in a similar way to yoghurt. It has a clean, piquant flavour and a similar consistency to that of double cream as the acid causes the protein to precipitate.

It can be made at home by adding lemon juice to fresh cream.

Ways of Using Soured Cream

1) Stir into cream soups just before serving, or float a spoonful on the top of each helping.
2) Add to casseroles or other meat dishes just before serving, for example, Beef Stroganoff (p1446 and p1552).
3) Add chopped chives and seasoning, and serve on split jacket potatoes.
4) Toss cooked vegetables, eg broad beans, in soured cream for a tangy flavour.
5) Soured cream is delicious with sweet fruit, eg strawberries or dried apricots, fruit compôte, or any very sweet flan, pie or gâteau.

Non-dairy Creams

Various non-dairy creams are made from vegetable oils and emulsifiers; these give a creamy flavour and consistency to beverages.

STORING CREAM

1) Keep cream in a cool place and always cover it when opened.
2) Keep cream away from strong smelling foods as it readily absorbs both odours and flavours.
3) If cream is transferred to a new container, make sure that it is perfectly clean.

How to Whip and Pipe Cream

1) Whipping or double cream should be at least 24 hours old after separation.
2) The bowl, whisk, and cream must be really cold to keep the fat globules firm.
3) Whip quickly at first until the cream looks matt, then slowly until it stands in smooth peaks.
4) Take care not to overwhip, or the cream will turn to butter and cannot then be reconstituted.

If double cream seems especially thick before whipping, add 1 × 15ml spoon milk to 125ml cream to help prevent overwhipping.

If the cream is not to be used immediately, do not whip until required.

If piping cream, always use a vegetable nozzle and not a tiny icing nozzle, or the cream may turn to butter as it is forced through the small hole. Do not hold the piping bag with warm hands. The bag should be held above the cream and pressure exerted with the fingers.

Note By adding 4 × 15ml spoons single cream or 1 egg white to 125ml double cream before whipping, double cream can be extended and yet still produce a stiff or piping cream.

Curdling

When cream or yoghurt is added to a hot dish, eg soup or sauce, it may curdle, ie small white specks may appear in the food and prevent an even, creamy appearance. To avoid this, remove the dish from the heat, pour a little of the liquid into a basin and add the cream or yoghurt; then return this mixture to the dish and stir in well. It is most important not to reboil.

Chantilly Cream

4 helpings

250ml double cream
25g caster sugar
vanilla essence

Chill the cream for several hours. Whip it lightly. Just before serving, whip in the sugar and a few drops of vanilla essence to taste.

Crème Fraîche

Enough to fill 2 layers, or to fill and coat one 20cm sponge cake

250ml double cream
2 × 5ml spoons buttermilk

Pour the cream into a small basin or glass jar. Gently stir in the buttermilk. Cover, and leave it to stand at 25°C for 6–8 hours. Stir, and chill until needed.

This French cream has a slightly sharp taste, and is delicious served with rich desserts or gâteaux.

Mrs Beeton's Sherry or Liqueur-flavoured Whipped Cream

4 helpings

grated rind and juice of
½ lemon
1–2 × 15ml spoons sweet
sherry **or** brandy-based
liqueur (see **Note**)
2 × 15ml spoons caster
sugar
250ml double cream
1 egg white (optional)

Put the lemon rind, juice, sherry or liqueur, and sugar into a bowl. Stir until the sugar is dissolved. Add the cream and whip lightly, gradually increasing speed until the cream is firm but not very stiff. Whisk the egg white, if used, until it holds soft peaks, and fold it gently into the cream.

Note A fruit-flavoured liqueur should be used, eg apricot brandy or Grand Marnier. Alternatively, brandy or a strong sweet white wine give a good flavour.

Mushroom and Soured Cream Sauce

Makes 600ml (approx)

100g button mushrooms
75g butter
25g flour
2 × 15ml spoons paprika
500ml chicken stock
125ml soured cream
salt and pepper

Slice the mushrooms finely, and fry gently in the butter until soft. Remove the mushrooms from the pan, and stir the flour and paprika into the remaining butter. Cook slowly for 2–3 minutes, then add the chicken stock gradually, stirring briskly. Bring to the boil, stirring all the time, and cook until thick, still stirring. Add the mushrooms. Re-heat, then add the soured cream. Season to taste, and serve at once over chicken, tripe, or other delicately flavoured foods.

Soured Cream Relishes

1) Mix 125ml soured cream with 1×2.5ml spoon made mustard. Serve with gammon or steak.
2) Mix equal quantities of soured cream and grated Stilton or other strong-flavoured blue cheese. Serve on grilled steak.

Soured Cream Salad Dressings

1) Mash the yolks of 2 hard-boiled eggs with $\frac{1}{2} \times 2.5$ml spoon pepper and 1×15ml spoon dry mustard. Work in 125ml soured cream.
2) Mix 125ml soured cream, 1×15ml spoon made mustard, 1×15ml spoon wine vinegar, 2×15ml spoons finely chopped chives and salt and pepper to taste.
3) Mix 125ml soured cream, 2×15ml spoons lemon juice, 1×15ml spoon chopped parsley, $\frac{1}{2} \times 2.5$ml spoon curry powder, and salt and pepper to taste.
4) Mix 125ml soured cream, 125ml mayonnaise, and 3×15ml spoons finely chopped onion.

Banana and Soured Cream Dessert

4 helpings

4 bananas (500g approx)
1 × 15ml spoon lemon juice
2 × 15ml spoons soft brown sugar
150ml soured cream
2 × 15ml spoons top of the milk

Decoration
grated chocolate

Mash the bananas with the lemon juice. Stir in the sugar, cream, and top of the milk. Serve decorated with grated chocolate.

Mousses and Mousseline Mixtures

A mousse, savoury or sweet, is a very light, smooth, creamy mixture. It is usually served cold or iced.

A savoury mousse can be made with fish or shellfish (smoked fish mousses are excellent), with chicken, cheese, hard-boiled eggs or a light pâté. It can be served as a first course at dinner, or as a light main course at lunch.

A savoury mousse can be served in a dish or turned out on to a plate. When it is to be served in the dish in which it is set, a little aspic jelly is often run over its surface and allowed to set. A decoration is then arranged on it. More aspic jelly is carefully spooned over the decoration, just enough to cover it, and the mousse left until quite set.

If it is to be turned out, a ring mould or a decorative mould is used. A little aspic jelly is poured in and the mould turned until the whole of the inside is evenly coated with a thin layer. Any excess is poured out. If the mould is turned in a bowl of ice cubes the jelly will set more quickly. When the aspic is set, a decoration is arranged on the base and a little more jelly carefully spooned over to cover it.

For sweet mousses, see pp1019–20.

Mousseline mixtures can be of many different kinds; they are most frequently made with whipped cream. The term is used generally to describe moulds made from fish, poultry or game, enriched with cream, and served hot or cold; but it can also be used to describe certain sauces, stuffings and delicate cakes.

Fish Mousse

4 helpings

50g onion	grated rind and juice of
1 celery stick	½ lemon
250ml milk	1 × 15ml spoon chopped
1 bay leaf	parsley
3–4 peppercorns	salt and pepper
500g haddock **or** cod	1 × 10ml spoon gelatine
fillets	2 × 15ml spoons water
25g butter	125ml double cream
25g flour	

Garnish
125ml aspic jelly	thin strips of lemon rind
watercress leaves	

Slice the onion and celery thickly. Put into a pan with the milk, bay leaf, peppercorns and fish. Bring to the boil slowly, cover, and draw off the heat for 10 minutes. Lift out the fish, remove any skin or bones, and flake the flesh. Strain the milk.

Melt the butter, stir in the flour, and cook for 1–2 minutes. Add the flavoured milk gradually. Bring to the boil and cook for 1–2 minutes, stirring all the time. Remove from the heat and stir in the flaked fish, lemon rind and juice, chopped parsley, and a generous amount of salt and pepper.

Soften the gelatine in the water in a small heat-proof basin. Stand the basin in a pan of hot water and stir until it has dissolved. Add a little of the fish mixture, stir, then mix into the rest. Stir in well. Put in a cool place.

When it is on the point of setting, whip the cream until it forms soft peaks and fold in until evenly distributed. Put into an 800ml dish, level the top, and chill until set.

Spoon sufficient liquid aspic jelly on to the mousse to cover it by 2mm. When the aspic has set, arrange the watercress and lemon rind cut into shapes on the top, and spoon over enough liquid jelly to cover the garnish. Leave to set.

Note Fish mousses can be made more piquant by substituting 100ml home-made mayonnaise (p843) for the double cream and adding 2 × 15ml spoons double cream, lightly whipped.

VARIATIONS

Salmon Mousse (2)
(using fresh salmon)

Prepare the mousse as above using a 350g cutlet of fresh salmon, and omitting the chopped parsley. The salmon can be cooked in a buttered foil parcel, with 2 slices of lemon and a piece of bay leaf. Bake in a warm oven at 160°C, Gas 3, for about 15 minutes. Discard the lemon and bay leaf, and remove the skin and bones before adding the flaked fish to the sauce. Add 2 × 15ml spoons dry sherry, if liked. Garnish the top with cucumber and aspic jelly.

Smoked Haddock Mousse

Prepare the mousse as above using 350g smoked haddock. Alternatively, use 200g smoked haddock and 2 chopped hard-boiled eggs instead of flaked fish alone. Garnish the top with slices of hard-boiled egg and aspic jelly.

Smoked Salmon Mousse

Prepare the mousse as above but omit the parsley, and add 75g finely chopped smoked salmon trimmings to the sauce. Fold in 125ml soured cream, instead of fresh cream, then add the gelatine. When on the point of setting, fold in 1 stiffly whisked egg white. Garnish the top with chopped parsley, lemon, and aspic jelly.

Chicken Mousse

Prepare the mousse as above using 350g minced cooked chicken; add 50g softened butter to the sauce. Garnish the top with sliced tomato and aspic jelly.

Salmon Mousse (3)

(using canned salmon)

4 helpings

1 × 200g can red **or** pink salmon	1 × 15ml spoon lemon juice **or** cider vinegar
15g butter	a pinch of dry mustard
15g flour	salt and pepper
200ml milk	100ml double cream
2 eggs	a few drops pink food colouring (optional)
1 × 15ml spoon concentrated tomato purée	1 × 15ml spoon gelatine
	2 × 15ml spoons water

Garnish

125ml aspic jelly	mustard and cress
cucumber slices	

Drain the liquid from the can of salmon into a large bowl. Remove any dark skin or bone from the fish. Add the flesh to the liquid and mash with a fork.

Melt the butter in a saucepan, stir in the flour and cook for 1–2 minutes. Add the milk gradually, bring to the boil, and cook for a further 1–2 minutes, stirring all the time. Remove from the heat and leave to cool slightly.

Separate the eggs and beat the yolks into the sauce, one at a time. Stir in the salmon, with the tomato purée, lemon juice or cider vinegar, mustard, and salt and pepper. Whip the cream until it forms soft peaks and fold into the fish. Re-season if required; it should be generously flavoured. Tint pink with the colouring, if necessary. Soften the gelatine in the water in a small heatproof basin. Stand the basin in a pan of hot water. Add a little of the mixture, stir, then mix into the rest and stir until it has dissolved. Stir in well. Put in a cool place. When the mixture is on the point of setting, whisk the egg whites until stiff and fold in until evenly distributed. Put into an 800ml dish, level the top, and chill until set. Spoon sufficient liquid aspic jelly on to the mousse to cover it by 2mm. When the aspic has set, arrange the cucumber slices and mustard and cress on the top, and spoon over enough liquid jelly to cover the garnish. Leave to set.

Note For Salmon Mousse (1), see p325.

VARIATION

Prawn Mousse

Chop 250g peeled prawns, reserving a few. Make the mousse as for salmon mousse, but use 25g butter and flour. Flavour the milk with a sliced onion and celery stick, a bay leaf, 3–4 peppercorns, and the prawns. Bring to the boil, remove the fish and strain the milk. Continue as above but omit the tomato purée and mustard, and replace the cream with 100ml dry white wine or stock. Use the reserved prawns as the garnish.

Ham Mousse (1)

4 helpings

250g lean ham	1 × 5ml spoon gelatine
200ml cold Espagnole sauce (p707)	100ml aspic jelly
100ml double cream	1 egg white

Garnish

125ml aspic jelly	slices of hard-boiled egg

Mince the ham twice finely. Add the sauce. Whip the cream until it is the same consistency as the sauce mixture and stir it in. Sprinkle the gelatine on to the liquid aspic, and when dissolved, add to the ham mixture. When it is on the point of setting, whisk the egg white until stiff and fold in until evenly distributed. Pour into an 800ml dish, level the top, and chill until set. Spoon enough liquid aspic jelly on to the mousse to cover it by 2mm. When the aspic has set, arrange the slices of hard-boiled egg on top and spoon over enough liquid jelly to cover the decoration. Leave to set.

Serve with green salad.

Note 200ml Béchamel sauce (p704), flavoured with 1 × 15ml spoon concentrated tomato purée and paprika, can be used instead of Espagnole Sauce.

For Ham Mousse (2), see p1414.

VARIATION

Ham and Tongue Mousse

Use 125g minced ham and 125g minced tongue.

Egg Mousse

4 helpings

6 eggs	Cayenne pepper
1 × 5ml spoon anchovy	Worcestershire sauce
essence	1 × 10ml spoon gelatine
200ml thick home-made	2 × 15ml spoons water
mayonnaise (p843)	125ml double cream
salt and pepper	

Garnish
anchovy fillets	watercress sprigs

Hard boil the eggs. When they are cool, chop them. Mix the anchovy essence and mayonnaise. Stir in the eggs. Season generously with the salt, pepper, and Cayenne pepper. Add a few drops of Worcestershire sauce. Soften the gelatine in the water in a small heatproof basin. Stand the basin in a pan of hot water and stir until it has dissolved. Add a little of the egg mixture, stir, then mix into the rest. Stir in well. Put into a cool place.

When it is on the point of setting, whisk the cream until stiff and then fold in until evenly distributed. Pour into a 700ml dish, level the top and chill until set.
Garnish with anchovy fillets and watercress.

Mousseline Potatoes

4 helpings

500g potatoes	salt and pepper
75ml double cream	grated nutmeg
75g butter	butter for greasing
2 egg yolks	beaten egg for glazing

Scrub the potatoes and bake them in their jackets. When cooked, scrape all the flesh out of the skins and rub through a sieve. Whip the cream lightly. Warm the potato in a pan over low heat, stirring occasionally. Beat in the butter, egg yolks, salt, pepper, and a little grated nutmeg, using a wooden spoon. When the potato is thoroughly heated through, remove from the heat, beat vigorously until smooth and creamy, then gradually beat in the whipped cream. Put into a buttered ovenproof dish and mark the top with a pattern. Brush with the beaten egg, and brown in a fairly hot oven at 190°C, Gas 5, for 15–20 minutes. Alternatively, brown under a hot grill.

Note The potatoes can be boiled, drained, and dried thoroughly before sieving. This method saves time but the flavour is not as good.

VARIATION
Mousseline Quenelles

Form the prepared potato mixture into quenelle shapes using 2 rounded dessertspoons; put on a greased baking sheet, brush with beaten egg, and brown in the oven.

Savoury Mousseline Sauce

4 helpings

15g butter	salt and pepper
2 eggs	grated nutmeg
1 egg yolk	75ml single cream
1 × 15ml spoon fish	1 × 15ml spoon lemon
stock (p330), chicken	juice
stock (p330), or	
vegetable stock (p331)	
or water	

Cut the butter into dice. Put all the ingredients except the butter and lemon juice in a basin over a pan of hot water, and whisk until pale, frothy, and of a thick creamy consistency. This will take 8–10 minutes. Remove from the heat and whisk in the butter; then whisk in the lemon juice gradually, mixing well between each addition to prevent the sauce curdling.

Serve at once with fish, poultry or vegetables.

Note For other savoury mousseline sauces, see p846.

Sweet Mousseline Sauce
See p722.

Zéphire of Cheese
See p321.

Mousseline Forcemeat

Makes 150–175g

200g whiting **or** *see*	*a pinch of grated nutmeg*
Note	*1 egg white*
salt and pepper	*50–75ml double cream*

Poach the fish for about 10 minutes in just enough water to cover it. Drain, and remove the skin and bones. Mash the fish with a pestle and mortar or a wooden spoon until it is a smooth paste. Season generously with salt, pepper, and a pinch of grated nutmeg. Beat in the egg white. Sieve the mixture to obtain a really smooth result. Beat again thoroughly and chill for 2 hours until very cold.

Put ice cubes in a bowl and stand the basin of fish purée in it to keep the mixture cold. Blend in the cream gradually until it is of a soft consistency which will just hold its shape. The amount of cream used varies with the temperature and the texture of the fish. Use the forcemeat to stuff large braised or baked fish, such as salmon.

Note This delicate forcemeat can be made from any white fish, salmon, shellfish, lightly cooked chicken or game.

Mousseline Pudding

4 helpings

50g butter	*grated rind and juice of*
50g icing sugar	*½ lemon* **or** *a few drops*
3 eggs	*vanilla essence*
	butter for greasing

Cream the butter and icing sugar together. Separate the eggs and beat the yolks into the creamed mixture, one at a time. Add the lemon rind and juice to the mixture, or add a few drops of vanilla essence. Stand the bowl over a pan of hot water or use a double boiler. Heat for 10–12 minutes, stirring all the time, until the mixture is thick enough to hold the mark of a trail for 1–2 seconds. At first it may curdle, and will become runny as the butter melts, but the mixture will rebind and thicken as the egg yolks cook. Remove from the heat. Continue stirring until the mixture is cold. Whisk the egg whites until stiff and fold them in. Put the mixture into a greased 1 litre basin, cover with buttered greaseproof paper or foil, and steam for 45 minutes.

Turn out, and serve with cream if lemon flavoured, or with a fruit sauce if vanilla flavoured. The pudding will collapse if not served immediately.

Mousseline Cake

fat for greasing	*4 eggs*
caster sugar for dusting	*100g caster sugar*
50g plain flour	*vanilla essence* **or** *grated*
50g cornflour	*rind of ½ lemon*

Decoration

125ml double cream	*liqueur-flavoured glacé*
100ml fruit (see	*icing* (p1225)
Method)	

Line the base of an 18cm cake tin with greaseproof paper. Grease the tin and dust with caster sugar. Sift the flour and cornflour together. Separate the eggs. Whisk the yolks and sugar together in a bowl until thick, creamy, and pale, adding the essence or grated lemon rind. Whisk the whites until they form soft peaks and add to the yolk mixture. Whisk together over a pan of hot water until the volume is greatly increased and the mixture is thick enough to hold the mark of a trail for 2–3 seconds. Remove from the heat and whisk until cool. Fold in the sifted flours. Put into the tin, and bake in a moderate oven at 180°C, Gas 4, for 30–35 minutes, until well risen and browned. Leave in the tin for 1–2 minutes, then turn out. Cool on a wire rack.

Whip the cream lightly. Fill a measuring jug up to the 100ml mark with fresh fruit or well-drained canned fruit. Strawberries, raspberries, pineapple or peaches are good. Chop most of the fruit and mix it with two-thirds of the cream. Split the cake in half, spread with the fruit and cream mixture, and replace the top of the cake. Ice with the glacé icing. Pipe the remaining cream in whirls around the edge, and decorate with the reserved whole fruit.

Note The cake mixture can be baked in two 18cm sandwich cake tins. Bake in a fairly hot oven at 190°C, Gas 5, for 20–25 minutes.

Butter

Butter is made from the fat in milk. It takes 10 litres of milk to make 450g butter. The cream is separated from the milk and pasteurized. It is then churned at 7°C for about 40 minutes until it separates, and butter grains are formed in the buttermilk. The buttermilk is poured off and the grains washed. They are then worked to remove any surplus water or air pockets, until they become a solid block of butter. Salt is sometimes added to improve the keeping quality of the butter and enhance the flavour, but it must be worked in evenly or the texture and appearance will be spoilt.

The quality and purity of butter are strictly controlled. Most butters contain over 80% milk fat and the maximum moisture content allowed is 16%. If salt is added, it is usually 1–2%; this raises the mineral content. Butter contains vitamins A and D, but the amount depends on the amount of natural sunlight. The actual composition of the butter, as well as the texture, flavour, and colour, varies with the district, climate, and breed of cow. As butter is almost all fat, it is a valuable energy food.

TYPES OF BUTTER

Two main kinds of butter are sold in the UK: sweet cream butter made from fresh or sweet cream, and lactic butter made from ripened, acidic cream.

Sweet cream butter comes mainly from Australia, New Zealand, the UK, and Eire. It has a mild delicate flavour, a firm smooth texture, and is usually bright in colour. It is best for pastry and biscuits.

Creamery butter is cheaper, a blend of sweet cream butters, suitable for general use in cooking; but the flavour and texture is inferior, so it is less good for the table.

Lactic butter comes mainly from France, Holland, Denmark, and other Scandinavian countries. The cream is ripened by the addition of a starter of acid-producing bacteria (*lactic streptococci*) before being churned. Lactic butter has a rich full flavour with a mild acidity and a very fine texture. As it is soft, it creams easily and is good for cake-making.

Lactic butter makes well-flavoured fudge, caramels or toffee due to its strong flavour. This butter matures on keeping, and is at its best when 6 weeks old. It does not, however, keep for as long as sweet cream butter.

Lactic butter can be bought with or without added salt; sweet cream butter is generally salted. Use unsalted butter for cakes, butter creams, and cold desserts that have a high proportion of butter. It should also be used in recipes that call for melted butter, as the residue in salted butter may affect the texture or flavour, and it burns more easily. If only salted butter is available, it should be clarified before use.

Clarified Butter

This is used when a clear butter, free from any milk solids, salt or water is required. It is used to fry white fish, chicken and veal, as it gives a light golden colour; to moisten the surface of food to be grilled; to seal potted meats; to oil moulds or baking tins; and to add to Genoese sponge mixtures.

Hot clarified butter, or as it is sometimes called, oiled or melted butter, is often served instead of sauce with fish, meat or vegetables.

To clarify butter, put the butter in a saucepan, heat it gently until it melts, then continue to heat slowly without browning, until all bubbling ceases (this shows the water has been driven off). Remove from the heat and skim off any scum that has risen to the top. Let it stand for a few minutes for any sediment to settle, then gently pour off the clear butter into a basin or jar, leaving the sediment behind. If there is a lot of sediment, it may be necessary to strain the fat through a fine sieve or muslin.

Whey Butter

See p873.

Savoury Butters

See pp1297–1301.

Butter Curls

Use a block of well chilled butter and a short sharp knife with a plain (not serrated) cutting edge. Starting at one end of the butter block, draw or scrape the knife blade along the surface, taking off a thin layer 1–2cm wide. As it comes off it will curl over in the same way as chocolate.

Butter curls can also be made with a special small tool which is grooved so that the butter curls have ridged lines on them.

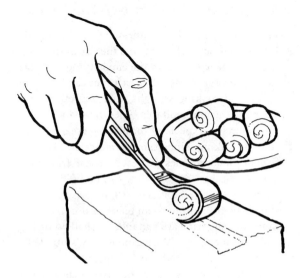

Desalted Butter

To desalt butter, put the butter into a basin and pour boiling water over it. Leave until cold. The butter will then have risen to the top of the water and can be lifted off. The water will have washed out the salt.

This is quite adequate for any recipe calling for salt-free butter but will not replace clarified butter as the milk solids and a lot of moisture are still present.

STORING BUTTER

1) Keep butter in its wrapper until required.
2) Keep in a cool, dark place. If a refrigerator is not available keep the butter in a special earthenware butter cooler, or put it on a rack standing in a dish of water and cover the butter with a damp cloth that reaches down into the water. Keep butter in a dark place as light destroys the vitamin content, and warmth and air will make it rancid.
3) Keep butter away from strong flavours and smells as it absorbs them readily.
4) If properly stored it will keep for up to 1 month. It can also be deep-frozen, eg in the form of butter curls. It will keep in a home freezer for up to 6 months (unsalted) and 3 months (salted). Allow to thaw completely in the refrigerator before use or it may be grainy.

Margarine

Although not a dairy fat, margarine is used in so many ways as an alternative to butter that it is most conveniently classed with it. Unlike lard or dripping, both animal fats, margarine may or may not contain animal fat.

Invented over 100 years ago, all margarine was originally made from beef fat and milk. Today, however, vegetable oils can be used instead of animal fats and this has added to the ways in which margarine can be used instead of, or with butter. This can be important for anyone whose diet forbids the use of animal fats, for any reason.

FOOD VALUE OF MARGARINE

The energy values of butter and margarine are about the same. Each contributes about 451 kJ per 15g fat on average. Both also contribute a significant amount of vitamins A and D. The levels of vitamins A and D in margarine are controlled by legislation in the UK; a daily intake of 25g margarine will supply about one-quarter of the vitamin A and almost all the vitamin D recommended as an adult's daily requirement. The vitamin D content of margarine is greater than that of butter.

TYPES OF MARGARINE

Margarine may consist of various different blends of oils; some margarines are made up of vegetable oils and animal fats mixed, and sometimes marine oils may be included. Vegetable oils commonly included are: coconut, groundnut, palm, palm kernel, rape seed, corn, cottonseed, soya bean, and sunflower. Some margarines may include up to 10% butter. Margarines usually also include emulsifiers (derived from vegetable oils). To improve the texture, whey, salt, and water are also added, although no margarine may contain more than 16% water. The colouring of most margarines derives from natural sources, and the flavourings are often those found in butter. Some are as firm as butter, others stay soft even in a refrigerator.

Several different types of margarine are available, although some may not always be easy to obtain. They are:

1) Margarines containing vegetable oils only. These are labelled as containing 'edible vegetable oils'.
2) Margarines containing both vegetable and other edible oils. These are labelled as containing 'edible oils'.
3) Margarines containing a large proportion of polyunsaturated oils. These are labelled 'high in polyunsaturates' and are available for people on low saturated-fat diets.
4) All-vegetable, milk-free margarines suitable for those who require an animal fat- or milk-free diet. These are suitable for a strict kosher or vegan diet, for instance.

5) Margarines containing up to 10% butter. These are labelled as containing a proportion of butter. There are also low-fat spreads. They cannot be classed as margarines, since they contain only half the fat of margarine or butter and more water, but they are similar in appearance and flavour. They are used for spreading in slimming and other low-fat diets, and can also be used for cooking if special recipes are used.

COOKING WITH MARGARINE

Margarine varies in hardness depending on the blend of fats and oils used, and the size of the water droplets incorporated in the emulsifying and plasticizing process. Soft tub margarines can be spread or used in cooking straight from the refrigerator. They are the most suitable types to use for any all-in-one recipe, especially for making creamed mixtures in baking, since they aerate easily. Hard or firm block margarines are best for use in traditional pastry-making; for this, they can be used straight from the refrigerator. For all other uses, they should be brought to room temperature first. Both kinds of margarine are suitable for shallow frying, making sauces, etc. Margarine is only suitable for deep frying if it is first clarified (p886).

In the recipes below, the particular type of margarine most suitable is indicated wherever relevant.

STORING MARGARINE

Ideally, margarine should be used fresh, soon after purchase. Properly sealed, and stored under favourable conditions, however, it can be kept for up to 3 months. All margarines should be stored closely wrapped, in a cool, dark place such as a refrigerator or cool larder; if exposed for long to warmth or sunlight, they become rancid.

Margarine can be deep-frozen and stored for up to 6 months in a home freezer. Before use, it should be allowed to thaw fully in the refrigerator.

SOFT TUB MARGARINE

The recipes which follow use the all-in-one method of making pastry. For one-stage cakes, see p1211.

Hawaiian Chicken with All-in-one Pastry

4–5 helpings

All-in-one Shortcrust Pastry

225g plain flour	*flour for rolling out*
150g soft tub margarine	*beaten egg* **or** *milk for*
2 × 15ml spoons cold	*glazing*
water	

Filling

1 large onion	*2 × 15ml spoons soft*
1 × 198g can pineapple	*light brown sugar*
cubes	*1 × 2.5ml spoon ground*
¼ cucumber	*ginger*
3 tomatoes	*a pinch of salt and*
25g soft tub margarine	*pepper*
25g plain flour	*350g cooked chicken*
2 × 15ml spoons malt	
vinegar	

Make the pastry first. Sift the flour. Put the margarine, water, and one-third of the flour in a mixing bowl. Cream with a fork for about 30 seconds until well mixed. Stir in the remaining flour and mix to form a firm dough. Place in a polythene bag and chill until the filling is ready.

To make the filling, skin and chop the onion. Drain the pineapple and reserve the juice. Dice the cucumber and chop the tomatoes. Sauté the onion in the margarine for 3–4 minutes until soft but not browned. Add the flour and 150ml liquid from the reserved pineapple juice. Stir in the remaining filling ingredients. Bring to the boil, stirring all the time over moderate heat, and cook for 2–3 minutes until smooth and thickened. Pour into a 1 litre pie dish.

Roll out the chilled pastry on a lightly floured surface into an oval 2cm larger than the top of the pie dish. Cut off a narrow strip from the edge of the pastry. Dampen the rim of the dish with water, and cover it with the pastry strip. Brush the strip with water. Cover with the remaining pastry and press the layers together to seal; trim and flute the edges. Make a hole in the centre of the pie, and decorate with leaves made from the pastry trimmings. Glaze with the egg or milk. Bake in a fairly hot oven at 200°C, Gas 6, for 30–40 minutes. Serve hot.

All-in-one Turkey and Mushroom Flan

4–5 helpings

All-in-one shortcrust	
pastry	

Filling

1 small onion	*25g blanched, chopped*
50g mushrooms	*almonds*
225g cooked turkey	*a pinch of tarragon*
breast	*salt and pepper*
25g soft tub margarine	*25g grated Parmesan*
25g plain flour	*cheese*
275ml milk	

Garnish

tomato slices	*parsley sprigs*

Make the pastry as for Hawaiian Chicken above.

To make the filling, skin and chop the onion, slice the mushrooms, and dice the turkey meat. Melt the margarine and sauté the onion and mushrooms for 2–3 minutes until soft but not browned. Add the flour and stir in the milk gradually. Bring to the boil, still stirring, and cook for 2–3 minutes until smooth and thickened. Stir in the turkey, almonds, tarragon, and seasoning.

Roll out the pastry on a lightly floured surface into a round large enough to line a 20cm plain flan ring placed on a baking sheet. Line the flan ring with the pastry. Bake blind in a fairly hot oven at 200°C, Gas 6, for 15 minutes. Remove the dry filling and flan ring. Put the hot filling into the flan case, and sprinkle with the cheese. Bake for a further 15–20 minutes. Garnish with overlapping tomato slices round the edge of the flan, and put a sprig of parsley in the centre. Serve hot.

MILK-FREE MARGARINE

The following recipes contain no milk product whatsoever.

Salmon Provençale

4 helpings

1 medium-sized onion	2 × 5ml spoons
1 clove of garlic	concentrated tomato
25g milk-free margarine	purée
350g cooked **or** canned	1 × 5ml spoon thyme
salmon	1 bay leaf
1 × 5ml spoon sugar	salt and freshly ground
1 × 397g can tomatoes	black pepper
150ml dry white wine	

Skin and chop the onion and crush the garlic. Melt the margarine, and sauté the onion and garlic for 2–3 minutes until soft but not browned. Flake the salmon and add it to the onion with the sugar; sauté for another 3 minutes. Add all the remaining ingredients and simmer for 10 minutes, stirring occasionally.

Serve with boiled rice.

Curried Steak Pie

4–5 helpings

Shortcrust Pastry

225g plain flour	2 × 15ml spoons very
125g milk-free	cold water
margarine	flour for rolling out

Filling

1 medium-sized onion	1 × 15ml spoon plain
1 small cooking apple	flour
25g milk-free margarine	25g sultanas
350g minced beef	1 × 10ml spoon lemon
2 × 15ml spoons curry	juice **or** vinegar
powder	4 × 15ml spoons water

To make the pastry, sift the flour into a bowl and rub in the margarine until the mixture resembles fine breadcrumbs. Mix to a stiff paste with the cold water. Place in a polythene bag and chill.

Make the filling. Skin and chop the onion. Peel, core, and chop the apple. Melt the margarine, and sauté the onion over moderate heat for 3–4 minutes until soft but not browned. Stir in the minced beef and cook for 10 minutes until browned. Add the remaining ingredients and simmer for 30 minutes, stirring occasionally. Leave to cool completely.

Cut off just over half the pastry, roll it out on a lightly floured surface to a large round and use it to line a 20cm ovenproof pie plate. Put in the cold meat mixture, spreading it evenly to within 2cm of the edge. Dampen the uncovered edge of the pastry. Roll out the remaining pastry into a round large enough to cover the top. Press the layers to seal; trim and flute the edges. Make a hole in the centre of the top crust and decorate with leaves made from the pastry trimmings. Bake in a fairly hot oven at 200°C, Gas 6, for 40–50 minutes. Serve hot.

Apricot Meringue Flan

4–6 helpings

Rich Shortcrust Pastry

225g plain flour	2 × 15ml spoons cold
150g milk-free	water
margarine	flour for rolling out

Filling

2 eggs	1 × 5ml spoon cornflour
1 × 340g can apricots	2 × 15ml spoons brandy
25g milk-free margarine	75g caster sugar
150ml water	

To make the pastry, sift the flour into a bowl and rub in the margarine until the mixture resembles fine breadcrumbs. Mix to a stiff paste with the cold water. Roll out on a lightly floured surface to a round large enough to line a 20cm fluted flan ring placed on a baking sheet. Line the flan ring with the pastry. Bake blind in a fairly hot oven at 200°C, Gas 6, for 15 minutes until golden-brown.

Meanwhile, make the filling. Separate the eggs. Sieve the apricots with their liquid to form a purée, or process in an electric blender. Put the margarine, water, and cornflour in a small saucepan. Whisking all the time over moderate heat, bring to simmering point; then simmer gently for 2–3 minutes until thickened and smooth. Cool slightly. Stir in the egg yolks, brandy, and apricot purée. Pour the mixture into the cooked flan case. Whisk the egg whites until stiff, then whisk in the sugar gradually until stiff peaks form. Pile the meringue on top of the apricot mixture, covering it completely. Bake in a fairly hot oven at 200°C, Gas 6, for 25–35 minutes until the meringue is set and the peaks are tinged golden.

White Fats and Oils

WHITE FATS (SHORTENINGS)

White fats, which are sometimes called shortenings, are made from various blends of lard, soya bean oil, palm oil, tallow, and marine oils. Some are aerated or whipped to make rubbing in and creaming easier. To make white fats react in the same way at different seasonal temperatures, the melting point of these oils is sometimes changed in the manufacturing process.

Uses of White Fats

White fat is especially good for making flaky or puff pastry because it is plastic at room temperature and can be moulded; this means that it keeps its shape when rolled into thin sheets between the dough layers.

If used for making creamed cakes, it will produce a light-textured cake, but one that is very bland. It is therefore best for strongly flavoured cakes.

Follow manufacturer's instructions for use.

White fat is good for both deep and shallow frying. The bland flavour lets the food's own flavour predominate, and reduces the risk of frying odours.

Note For further information on frying, see the chapter on Batters and Other Fried Foods.

OILS

The most important types of oil used in the UK are blended vegetable oils, such as soya bean, corn, groundnut, olive, and sunflower oil.

Uses of Oils

The two most important uses of oils are for making emulsions such as salad dressings (see pp843–47), and for frying, especially deep frying (see pp929–31). They can, however, also be used when making cakes and pastries. The oil can just be beaten in, thus doing away with rubbing in or creaming fat. However, only recipes which specify oil should be used, because the proportions of the ingredients and the methods of mixing vary from traditional recipes which use solid fat.

Confectioners' Custard or Pastry Cream
(made with oil)

Makes 200ml (approx)

2 × 15ml spoons cooking oil
25g plain flour
150ml milk
25g caster sugar
1 egg
2–3 drops vanilla essence **or** *1 × 15ml spoon sweet sherry*
2 × 15ml spoons double cream (optional)

Heat the oil gently until very hot but not smoking. Beat in the flour; then add the milk gradually, beating well between each addition. Bring the mixture slowly to the boil, stirring all the time. Cook until very thick and smooth; it will be almost solid. Add the sugar, and remove from the heat. Separate the egg, and beat the yolk into the mixture with the flavouring. Leave to cool slightly. Whisk the egg white until stiff, and fold it into the thickened pastry cream when still warm. Whip the cream, if used, until semi-stiff and fold it into the pastry cream when quite cold.

Note Recipes for Confectioners' Custard made with solid fat can be found on p1237.

Gingerbread

(made with oil)

fat for greasing	*225g plain flour*
100ml cooking oil	*1 × 2.5ml spoon*
100g soft dark brown	*bicarbonate of soda*
sugar	*1 × 2.5ml spoon salt*
100g golden syrup	*3 × 15ml spoons ground*
100g black treacle	*ginger*
150ml milk	*1 egg*

Grease and line a shallow 18cm square tin. Put the oil, sugar, syrup, treacle, and milk into a small saucepan and melt gently. Sift together the flour, soda, salt, and ginger. Beat the egg lightly in a small bowl. Pour the melted mixture gradually into the dry ingredients, beating well between each addition. Beat in the egg. Pour the mixture into the tin, and bake in a warm oven at 160°C, Gas 3, for $1\frac{1}{4}$–$1\frac{1}{2}$ hours. Cool in the tin for 10 minutes, then turn on to a wire rack to finish cooling. When cold, wrap in greaseproof paper and leave for at least 24 hours before cutting.

Note Recipes for gingerbread made with solid fat can be found on pp1191–93.

Cheese

FOOD VALUE OF CHEESE

Cheese is one of our most nourishing foods. Full-fat cheese contains almost all the nourishment of whole milk except the milk sugar (lactose), and a few vitamins and minerals. It consists of the solid parts of the milk solidified into clots or curd, separated from the whey, which is drained off. The curd is usually pressed or heated, or both, to expel more whey, and as it dries becomes firm and will keep for some time without spoiling.

Depending on how much whey is removed from it, cheese may be classed as hard, semi-hard, semi-soft or soft.

Cheese of any type is most valuable for its protein content. It contains more protein, weight for weight, than prime raw beef. It is a good source of calcium, and contains vitamins A and D, and some B vitamins. Most cheeses, certainly the hard and semi-hard ones, are also rich in fat. A hard cheese like Cheddar is made up of about one-third fat, one-third protein, and one-third water. Cheese made from skimmed or defatted milk contains less fat and therefore a higher proportion of protein.

Cheese does not contain any carbohydrate, but is generally eaten with foods which supply carbohydrate, eg bread and biscuits, vegetables or pasta.

HOW CHEESE IS MADE

Most cheese in the UK is now made from cows' milk, although the milk of goats, sheep, asses, and other animals is also used in some parts of the world.

Commercially, it is made from fresh milk which is first heat-treated. It is then cooled before being pumped into vats where a starter culture is added. When the acidity in the ripened milk reaches 0.02% lactic acid, the milk is heated to 30°C and rennet is added to clot the milk.

Most semi-hard and hard cheeses are made in much the same general way as soft ones; but they are drained more thoroughly, pressed, and moulded in a variety of ways which all help to give them an individual character. Some are heat-treated a second time. Some are quick-ripening, others are hard pressed and matured for several months after being made. Some are made from skimmed or partly skimmed milk, others have cream or herbs added. Moulds are another way of making cheese.

Soft cheeses such as Camembert and other soft-paste cheeses, are made like hard cheeses, but are less fully drained and may have a mould added which gives them their particular flavour and rind.

Besides these different ways of making cheese, the variations in climate, pasture, temperature, the breed of cow or goat, even the time of milking, all affect the final product, so cheeses can be almost infinitely varied in flavour and texture.

Many are farmhouse cheeses made by hand, or local cheeses, made only in one particular area. Most British hard and semi-hard cheeses are now made for mass sale in big creameries, although the most full-flavoured and individual in style are still made on farms. Both the creamery and farmhouse-made cheeses were traditionally large, drum-shaped, rinded, and matured in cloth bandages. But, increasingly, both kinds have come to be made in a block for easier storage, and are waxed instead of having a rind and bandages. There is said to be no loss in the quality and flavour of these cheeses compared with rinded, round ones of the same age.

Soft, fresh, and slightly salted curd cheeses are the ones most frequently made at home (see p898). They consist of curds (sometimes with cream added), and are drained so that some of the liquid whey has run off; they may be lactic cheeses made with a starter alone, or renneted. They all still contain a good deal of whey, and must therefore be refrigerated and eaten soon after production.

Cottage cheese is more difficult to make than curd cheese because it is heat-treated and washed, and is made from ripened milk which has stood for some time.

BUYING AND STORING CHEESE

It is much easier to assess the quality of cheese in the block, free of wrappings, as both the texture and condition can be seen.

The cut surface of any cheese is a good guide to its quality and condition. A hard or semi-hard cheese for eating raw (or for grating) should be firm, even slightly flaky in a cheese such as Cheddar, but must not have cracks in the surface. Equally, it must not be sweaty or show beads of fat, which indicate it has been kept too long in a warm place, uncovered. It should be more or less the same colour throughout; a darker colour near the rind may be a sign that the cheese is old; any white specks or blue sheen indicate mould and a musty flavour. Even a strong cheese should not taste harsh or acidic.

A milder cheese for eating or cooking should be firm or crumbly and still have a definite cheesy taste; it should not be soapy.

The blander semi-soft cheeses such as Edam or Port Salut should be velvety when cut, neither moist nor flaky, and should be the same creamy colour throughout. They should yield slightly when pressed with the finger.

Soft cheeses such as Camembert and Brie can quickly ripen and spoil but are tasteless when under-ripe. The crust of Brie should be white and even with signs of red at the edges; the curd pale yellow and creamy throughout, although not spilling out. If it is running when purchased, it may well be inedible by the time it is needed. A hard cake-like white strip in the centre is unlikely to ripen before the outer cheese goes bad.

The same applies to soft-paste cheeses, such as the creamy French cheeses. Like soft fresh cheeses, they spoil within a few days. They should be clean and well-shaped, neither discoloured nor dented, and the inside should be even in texture, without seeping moisture but soft enough to cut with a spoon.

Blue cheeses should also be even-coloured, without greyish patches, and with clear-cut veins of colour. They should be crumbly or moist, not grainy. Milder ones such as Dolcelatte may look creamy. All blue cheeses are fairly pungent, and may become unpleasantly harsh with age, so that colour and texture should be noted carefully before buying.

None of these pointers to quality can be checked in the case of prepacked cheeses. There are, however, one or two ways of telling whether they are good value and have been well cared for:

On any cheese counter, or in a chilled cabinet, cheeses should be in their own shelf or rack, separate from other foods so that cross-flavouring cannot occur. Ideally, each cheese should have its separate place; strong and mild cheeses should not be stacked together.

Any semi-soft cheese should yield to the touch. It should always fill its box or wrapping, and never be sunken in the middle. All cheese wrappings should be fresh and clean. Sticky, stained or torn wrappings are always a warning not to buy.

Whenever possible, cheese should be bought in a compact block, not a long, thin slice or section. A thin slice is less easy to package, and keeps less well.

Cheese should be bought in small quantities, preferably just enough for 1 or 2 servings. Although the harder cheeses keep well, and it is tempting to keep a quantity in stock, any cheese tends to lose surface texture and flavour in storage, especially in a refrigerator. If it must be stored in a refrigerator, it should be kept in the least cold part, closely wrapped in clingfilm or foil, and with an outer polythene wrapping; and it must be removed and unwrapped at least 1 hour before use, to let it regain its full flavour. Any refrigerator-stored hard or semi-hard cheese should be used within 2 weeks, semi-soft and blue cheeses within 1 week. Soft cheeses must be used as soon as possible. To prevent ripe, soft, crusted cheeses oozing when a wedge has been cut out, wrap closely in clingfilm.

Any blue mould which develops on the surface of a hard or semi-hard cheese may be cut off; the cheese itself is unharmed; the flavour, especially of mature cheeses, will however become stronger the longer they are kept.

For information on freezing cheese, see p1396.

Note Serving cheese, see p262.

COOKING CHEESE

Cheese must always be cooked gently and as briefly as possible. Even if cooked with extra fat, it should never spit, or bubble quickly.

Gentle cooking prevents the cheese becoming rubbery or ropey. If the fat globules melt due to quick or fierce heating, the fat runs off, leaving a stringy mass of curd and separate fat instead of a creamy mass.

Hard and semi-hard cheeses are most often used for cooking. Cheeses with a high fat content and well-aged, mature cheeses melt and blend better with other ingredients than low-fat or less ripened cheeses. Less is needed too, since they are richer and better flavoured. Matured Cheddar and Parmesan cheeses are good for this reason. Processed cheeses melt easily but their flavour is usually very bland.

Most cheese keeps a creamier texture if it is first grated and mixed with breadcrumbs, flour or extra fat. This coats the fat globules and will absorb some of the cooking heat, thereby preventing the fat melting too soon.

A good way to melt cheese by itself is to place it in a basin over a pan of simmering water. Another way is to add it to a hot mixture after the main cooking is completed, eg to sprinkle it into a cooked omelet just before folding and serving it.

When grilling cheese, it should be kept 10–12cm below the heat which should be as low as possible. When the cheese is being used as a topping, it should be grated; it can be mixed with breadcrumbs before being sprinkled on the dish.

When cheese is mixed into a casserole or similar dish, whether cooked over heat or in the oven, the heat should also be kept as low as possible throughout the cooking time.

TYPES OF CHEESE

British Cheeses

Caerphilly is a mild, white, close-textured, slightly salty cheese. The new cheese is lightly brined, then dried, and allowed to ripen for about 14 days. Caerphilly is good with salads and in packed meals and sandwiches, but is not an ideal cooking cheese. It can be crumbled instead of grated.

Cheddar is the best known and most widely used British cheese, and is copied in many parts of the world. Its flavour varies in strength a great deal. British Cheddar is of two main kinds: farmhouse and creamery. Farmhouse Cheddar is still made by individual families and small dairies, usually from a single herd of cows, although creameries do produce it also. It is of high quality, is matured slowly for at least 6 months, preferably much longer, and is slightly more expensive than creamery Cheddar. This may be a quickly ripened, quite mild cheese; or it may be sold as mature, having been allowed to ripen for 6–8 months. Like most British cheeses, Cheddar is a full-fat, hard cheese made from cows' milk only. All Cheddar should be gold in colour, close in texture, with a clean, nutty flavour. It is a first-class eating cheese, but is also excellent for grating and cooking.

Cheshire may also be farmhouse or creamery-made. It is more salty than Cheddar, due to the salt in the Cheshire soil where most of it is still made. It is also slightly more acid, and more crumbly. It is naturally white, but a reddish type, dyed with a harmless vegetable dye, is also popular. There is also a fuller-flavoured, creamy-textured *blue Cheshire*, yellow in colour with broad blue streaks. Modern Cheshire cheese has a 48% fat content, and is usually medium-ripened for 4–8 weeks. It is a good eating cheese, especially with gingerbread, cake or apples. It is also widely used for cooking.

Derby is a pale honey-coloured, smooth-textured cheese, mild when young but with a certain tang when mature at 4–6 months old. It is good with biscuits, as a lunch cheese, and with fruit. *Sage Derby* has green threads or a broad band of green through it, and a flavour of the sage leaves which provide the colouring.

Double Gloucester is akin to Cheddar. It is straw-coloured or light red, close in texture, and mellow or pungent in flavour when mature; it ripens in 3–4 months as a rule. It is good after a meat meal or with beer, and is also good for cooking.

Dunlop is a Cheddar-style cheese from Scotland; so are the small *Orkney* and *Islay* cheeses.

Lancashire is a semi-hard cheese which may be farmhouse-made. It is the strongest farmhouse cheese in flavour, although the creamery-made cheese is mild. Both are white and crumble easily, and are good for toasted dishes (it was once called the 'Leigh Toaster'). It is also good crumbled into stews, or eaten, uncooked, with sharp salads or with sweet fruits.

Leicester, a rich orange-red cheese, is fairly mild, but with a tang when mature at about 2 months old. It is soft and crumbly, and may be slightly flaky. It makes a good cooking as well as an eating cheese.

Stilton is considered the king of British cheeses. It is rich and creamy, and slowly matured to let the blue veins develop properly. It is best eaten with bread or plain biscuits, and is an excellent accompaniment to wine, especially Madeira or port. The rind is wrinkled and crusty, and the creamy interior is slightly darker near the crust. Top-quality Stilton is still made, as a rule, in large drums although smaller drums and jars of Stilton are widely available; it is sold too in film-wrapped or vacuum-packed wedges. Aged Stilton, past its prime, can be potted for storage, and used later as a spread (see p740).

If you buy a whole Stilton or part of a round, do not scoop the cheese out of the centre or pour port into the cheese. It will be difficult to store and may go sour. The correct way to care for a Stilton is to cut off the top crust in a thin layer; keep this aside. When serving the cheese, cut wedges of equal depth from all round the cheese so that it keeps a flat top. To store the cheese, replace the top crust, wrap in clingfilm, and keep in a cool place.

The younger *white Stilton* is crumbly, with a strong aroma, and a mild, slightly sour flavour.

Wensleydale is a white, softish, close-textured cheese, not unlike Caerphilly in taste when young, being mild and slightly salty. It matures in 12–14 days. On the whole, it is better for eating than for cooking. *Blue Wensleydale* has finer, more diffuse threads of blue veining than blue Cheshire, and, as a rule, is less creamy and more salty than either blue Cheshire or Stilton.

Soft cheeses of various kinds are made on farms and at home as well as in creameries. *Colwick* cheese and *York* cheese are both now made only on farms, for private use. *Caboc* and *Crowdie* are creamery cheeses. They differ in appearance, flavour, and texture according to the area in which they are made, the type of moulds used, and the method of making. They may be lactic (sweet milk) or acid-curd cheeses, and are normally graded according to their butterfat content as follows:

skimmed milk soft cheese (less than 2% fat)
low-fat soft cheese (2–10% fat)
medium-fat soft cheese (10–20% fat)
full-fat soft cheese (20–45% fat)
cream cheese (46–65% fat)
double cream cheese (at least 65% fat)

Curd cheeses of various types which are often made in the home, may be low-fat or full-fat. Like cream cheese, they have a closer texture than cottage cheese which contains about 4% butterfat but also more whey. All these cheeses keep for only about 4 days chilled.

Other cheeses available include *Red Windsor* which is based on Cheddar and flavoured with an English red wine. It has a creamier paste and a slightly more acid flavour than mature Cheddar. *Ilchester*, another Cheddar-based cheese, flavoured with beer and garlic, is a soft-textured cheese with a full flavour; the garlic is well subdued. *Walton* is a softer cheese based on Cheddar mixed with Stilton, with walnuts added; the taste of Stilton is only mild. *Cotswold* is based on Double Gloucester and is flavoured with chives. *Blue Shropshire* cheese has a deep golden paste and clear-cut blue veining. It is lighter in flavour than blue Cheshire or Stilton, but fuller than blue Wensleydale, with its own character.

Foreign Cheeses

Bel Paese is one of the best known Italian cheeses. It is a full-fat, ivory-coloured cheese, semi-soft and bland. It is used mostly as a table cheese although it melts easily, and is therefore useful in cooked dishes and for toasted sandwiches.

Boursin is French fresh cheese. The basic light-flavoured cheese can have either garlic added or a coat of crushed black peppercorns.

Brie, with a recorded history from 1217, is the most famous French cheese. It is often sold in pre-packed wedges, so that its quality cannot be checked; it is best to buy it cut to order, from a whole 35cm wheel, since Brie must be eaten in peak condition. Brie varies widely in flavour, depending on how long it is ripened. *Brie de Coulommiers*, for instance, generally has a delicate, mild flavour whereas *Brie de Melun* is well-ripened and tastes much stronger, more like Camembert.

Camembert is France's most plentiful and popular cheese. It is widely sold prepacked, in whole or half rounds, or in small sections. One has to take a chance on its quality, since it is usually kept very cool in a store and is firmer than it will be when eaten. An unwrapped Camembert should have an even, light brownish crust level with the rim, with no sunken centre. Inside, it should be creamy-yellow throughout, like Brie. Its aroma and flavour is, however, a good deal stronger. Camembert matures and becomes inedible even more quickly than Brie, and is distinctly unpleasant when over-ripe.

Chèvre is the term for small, rich, French goats' milk cheeses, often shaped like small cylinders. Unless the words *pur chèvre* appear on the label, the cheese may be made from a mixture of goats' and cows' milk. Goats' milk cheeses vary in flavour with their type and area of origin; but they should all have a pale crust with only a light mould, and should be crumbly or creamy inside, not grainy.

Danish Blue is of two types: the usual type, sometimes called *Danablu*, is white with bluish-green veins; *Mycella*, which is less common, is yellowish with green veins, more aromatic and subtle. Both are rich in cream, buttery in texture, and are table cheeses. Danablu is sometimes over-salted for export.

Demi-sel and *Petit-Suisse* are two of the family of French soft cream cheeses. Rich and mild in flavour, all these cream cheeses should be eaten as soon as possible after purchase.

Dolcelatte is a mild, creamy, Italian cheese using milk from valley herds, and made in a similar way to Gorgonzola.

Edam is Holland's most widely exported cheese. It is made from partly skimmed cows' milk, and has a cannonball shape and a bright red rind or wax coating. Its texture is smooth, and its flavour bland. It is not good for cooking, but is popular for eating, especially with slimmers. It tastes fuller when cut in thin slivers or slices.

Emmental is Swiss in origin, and the best Emmental cheese still comes from Switzerland. It is one of the most difficult cheeses to make, requiring high-quality raw milk and considerable skill in manufacture. It has a hard golden-brown rind, and a yellow-ivory curd with cherry-sized holes. It has a sweet, dry flavour, and an aroma like hazelnuts. Famous as a cooking cheese, it is often used with Parmesan; and it is one of the cheeses traditionally used for a classic cheese fondue (see p1453). It takes 7–10 months to mature fully.

Esrom, *Havarti*, and *Samsøe* are hard Danish cheeses, all versatile, with a pale or golden-yellow paste, mild when young but gaining piquancy with age. All have tiny holes, yet are distinctly different; Esrom is the sweetest and most fragrant.

Feta is a Greek fresh sheeps' milk cheese or mixed milk cheese. It ripens in its own whey mixed with brine, so tastes piquant and salty. It should be eaten as soon as it is purchased, with salads, cold meats or black olives.

Gorgonzola is an ancient Italian blue cheese, widely exported. The curd varies from cream to straw-yellow with blue-green veining, and it should be elastic rather than crumbly. It is used mainly as a table cheese although its mildness makes it suitable for a number of cooked dishes.

Gouda is a full-fat Dutch cheese, made in both farmhouses and creameries. There is a good deal of difference between the two products, although both are good. Factory-made Gouda is relatively bland, not unlike Edam, although cartwheel in shape with a yellowish rind. Farmhouse Gouda has a noticeably variable flavour depending on where it comes from. An old one has a hard rind, a firm paste, and a full flavour. A farmhouse Gouda may be matured for as much as 12–14 months.

Gruyère is another Swiss cheese, although it is now widely copied because it is so popular. It is a classic cooking cheese, used for fondues and quiches. Wheel-shaped, with a warm brown rind, its curd is ivory-yellow, pocked with small holes, moister than that of Emmental, and therefore still better for hot dishes.

Jarlsberg is an old Norwegian full-fat cheese, revived and popularized in modern times. Its curd is pale and smooth with large, cherry-sized holes; its flavour is slightly sweet, mild, and nutty.

Mozzarella is a soft, fresh Italian cheese, originally made from buffalo milk, now more usually from cows' milk. Its shape varies, but the commonest is an oval ball. It should be very moist and yield slightly when bitten; it should be eaten as soon as possible after purchase.

Parmesan is the most famous and widely used Italian cheese. It is piquant, hard, and grainy due to long, slow maturing, although a milder, elastic, younger Parmesan is sold for table use in Italy. The Parmesan which reaches foreign markets, either in the block or ready-grated for cooking use, is at least 2–3 years old. The flavour of Parmesan bought ungrated is very much better than that of the factory-grated product.

Pipo Crème is a mild, creamy, fairly modern French blue cheese.

Pont l'Évêque is a semi-hard French cheese from Normandy, with a fat content of 50%. The cheese has a smooth, creamy consistency, golden rind, a savoury taste and some bouquet.

Port Salut is a small, round, French cheese with a pale yellow rind and a mild flavour. It is closely related to *St Paulin*. Both are mild table cheeses, not generally well suited to cooking.

Roquefort is easily the best known French blue cheese, with an old and noble history. Originally a sheeps' milk cheese, it is not always so today. Genuine Roquefort cheeses still come from the same Tarn area and are matured in mountain caves where the bacteria *penicillium roqueforti* give them their particular mould veining and flavour. The rind of a

Roquefort cheese is wrinkled, its paste white and fairly crumbly, its veining dark blue-green and delicate. Matured in a thin coating of salt, its high but fine flavour can only be tasted fully when it is mature. Exported Roquefort cheeses, sometimes prepacked in wedges, are often too young and salty.

Soft Cheese

(to make)

Makes 400g (approx)

2.5 litres fresh **or** slightly soured milk	salt
4 × 5ml spoons rennet essence	double **or** single cream (optional)
	flavouring (see below)

Warm the milk to tepid (30–35°C approx) and pour into a bowl. Stir in the rennet essence and leave at room temperature until a curd forms; the time will depend on the temperature of the milk and the surroundings. Line a metal sieve with a scalded piece of muslin about 25cm square, and stand it over a bowl. Tip the curded milk gently into the cloth. Bring the corners of the cloth together, tie securely with string, and hang above the bowl to catch the dripping whey. Leave for 6–8 hours, or longer if a fairly thick cloth is used.

Open the bag, and scrape down any curd on the sides of the cloth into the main mass. Cut any solid curd into small pieces. Retie the bag, and rehang it to continue draining. Repeat the scraping down and cutting once or twice more until the cheese reaches the required consistency. This can be judged by pressing the bag gently.

Turn the curd into a bowl, and mix in salt to taste lightly but thoroughly. Blend in any cream and flavouring used. If the cheese is then softer than required, return it to the cloth bag and rehang for 2–3 hours. Form the cheese into pats or turn into pots or cartons. Cover, and chill until required. Use within 36 hours or within 24 hours if flavoured with fresh solid flavourings such as herbs.

Flavouring

1) Finely ground, coarsely ground or crushed whole spices.
2) Finely chopped herbs, eg chives.
3) Well-drained chopped fruit.

The quantity used will depend on the flavour of the cheese and on how it will be used. As a general rule, 1 × 2.5ml spoon ground or crushed spice or 1 × 5ml spoon solid flavouring is sufficient to flavour 200g cheese.

If desired, the cheese can be coated with ground or crushed spice instead of mixing it in.

Cheese Pudding

4 helpings

100–150g Cheddar **or** Gruyère cheese	100g soft white breadcrumbs
2 eggs	salt (optional)
250ml whole **or** skimmed milk	butter for greasing

Grate the cheese. Beat the eggs until liquid, and add the cheese and milk. Add the breadcrumbs with a little salt, if needed. Mix thoroughly, and pour into a greased 500ml dish. Bake in a moderate oven at 180°C, Gas 4, for 25–30 minutes, or until set in the centre and browned on top. Serve hot.

Cheese Ramekins

4 helpings

25g Cheshire cheese	25g softened unsalted butter
50ml milk (approx)	1 egg
25g soft white breadcrumbs (approx)	salt and pepper
25g grated Parmesan cheese	a pinch of ground mace
	butter for greasing

Grate the Cheshire cheese finely. Heat the milk and pour just enough over the breadcrumbs to cover them. Leave to stand for 5–10 minutes. Stir in both cheeses and the butter. Separate the egg, and mix the yolk into the cheese mixture. Season well with salt, pepper and mace. Whisk the egg white until very stiff. Stir one spoonful into the cheese mixture, then fold in the rest. Turn the mixture gently into 4 small greased ovenproof pots or ramekins. Bake in a fairly hot oven at 200°C, Gas 6, for 15–20 minutes, or until risen and slightly browned. Serve as soon as possible before they sink.

Camembert or Brie Soufflé

4 helpings

100g ripe Camembert **or** Brie cheese	125ml whole **or** skimmed milk
100g cottage **or** curd cheese	salt
1 × 10ml spoon gelatine	2 egg whites

Cut the crusts off the Camembert or Brie cheese. Sieve or mash with the cottage or curd cheese until both are smooth and well-blended. Soften the gelatine in the milk in a small heatproof container. Stand the container in very hot water, and stir until the gelatine dissolves. Leave to cool, then mix with the cheeses and seasoning. Chill. Whisk the egg whites until stiff but not dry. When the cheese mixture is beginning to set at the edges, fold in the egg whites lightly but thoroughly. Turn into a wetted 500ml soufflé dish, and chill until set.

Cheese Meringues

Makes 14–16

2 egg whites	a pinch of Cayenne pepper
50g finely grated Parmesan cheese	oil **or** fat for deep frying
a pinch of salt	

Garnish
grated Parmesan cheese	Cayenne pepper

Whisk the egg whites until stiff. Season the cheese, and fold it lightly into the whisked egg whites. Heat the fat (p303), and gently lower the mixture from a rounded spoon into it; or, using a forcing bag with a 1cm nozzle, squeeze out the meringue and cut off small pieces with a knife. Fry until golden-brown. Drain well. Serve sprinkled with cheese and pepper.

Welsh Rarebit

For this and numerous variations, see pp1325–26.

Cream Cheese Flan

6–8 helpings

200g prepared shortcrust pastry (p1249)	pepper
flour for rolling out	a few grains Cayenne pepper
3 × 2.5ml spoons gelatine	100g full-fat soft cheese
2 × 15ml spoons cold water	½ × 2.5ml spoon grated lemon rind
4 × 15ml spoons milk	1 × 15ml spoon lemon juice
1 egg yolk	125ml soured cream
2 × 5ml spoons sugar	2 × 15ml spoons grated Parmesan cheese
½ × 2.5ml spoon salt	

Roll out the pastry on a lightly floured surface into a round large enough to fit a 20cm flan ring placed on a baking sheet. Line it with the pastry and bake blind in a fairly hot oven at 200°C, Gas 6, for 15 minutes. Remove the dry filling and flan ring, and bake for a further 10–15 minutes until golden-brown. Leave to cool.

Soften the gelatine in the water in a small heatproof container for 2–3 minutes, then place the container over a pan of very hot water, and stir until the gelatine has dissolved. Warm the milk. Whisk the egg yolk, sugar, and seasonings together until light, then stir in the milk and gelatine. Mix thoroughly with the soft cheese, adding the lemon rind and juice. Leave to cool. When cold but not yet set, stir in the soured cream and Parmesan cheese. Re-season if required. Turn the mixture into the flan case, and chill for at least 2 hours. Serve cold.

Note Recipes for cheesecakes may be found on pp1041–43.

EGGS

In choosing eggs, apply the tongue to the large end of the egg, and, if it feels warm, it is new, and may be relied on as a fresh egg. Another mode of ascertaining their freshness is to hold them before a lighted candle, or to the light, and if the egg looks clear, it will be tolerably good; if thick, it is stale; and if there is a black spot attached to the shell, it is worthless.

FOOD VALUE OF EGGS

Eggs are one of our most useful basic foods as they are high in food value, are easily digested, and can be cooked in many different ways.

They are rich in protein, contain fats, some carbohydrate, and vitamins A, B, D, and E, as well as certain minerals (iron and calcium). The energy value of an average-sized (55–60g Grade 3–4) egg is 360–396kJ.

A raw egg is assimilated by the body in $1\frac{1}{2}$ hours. When beaten into light dishes or liquids such as milk puddings or clear soup, it is an ideal way of giving nourishment to someone on a light diet or unable to take solid food.

The colour of the egg shell, which varies from white to deepest brown, with an occasional speckled one, depends on the breed of the bird, and in no way affects nutritional value or flavour. (The diet, environment, and laying age of the bird does however affect the thickness and strength of the shell.)

The method used to rear the chickens does not affect the food value either, so free-range or farm chickens do not lay more nutritious eggs than battery chickens.

The colour of the egg yolk varies from pale yellow to deep gold and is determined by the hen's diet. If the hen has been fed with food rich in carotene, such as the residue and seeds of tomatoes, the yolk will be deep yellow.

FRESHNESS OF EGGS

If the egg is fresh, the white is thick, viscous, and transparent, except for two little white cords which hold the yolk in the centre of the white. In a good egg, the yolk is well centred in the white and round in form. The membrane should not break too easily.

The white usually divides into two parts: a more watery part, and a more jelly-like part near the yolk. Summer eggs are more watery than winter eggs, and some hens just lay watery eggs.

In a newly laid egg, the yolk and white fill the shell, but as the egg cools and the contents contract, an air space forms at the rounded end of the shell. Long storage, or storage in warm conditions may make some of the water in the egg evaporate and let carbon dioxide escape through the porous shell, so that the air space becomes larger. The yolk membrane becomes thinner, so it cannot hold the yolk in a round shape and it therefore breaks easily. The white becomes thinner and translucent.

With age, an egg still contains its nutrients, but it loses flavour and moisture, which makes it leathery when cooked. The yolk breaks easily, and is at one end instead of in the centre in a boiled or a hard-boiled egg. This makes it less pleasant to eat; also it is then unsuitable for stuffing or garnishing.

Home Tests for Freshness

1) Put the unbroken egg in the bottom of a bowl of warm water. If the egg lies on its side in the bottom of the bowl, it is fresh. If the rounded end rises or the egg floats, it is probably stale, since the air space at the round end has become enlarged.

2) Crack the egg open, and pour the contents on to a plate. The yolk should be firm and round, lying in the centre of a thick, viscous white. If the yolk is flat, and the white so thin that it spreads, the egg is probably stale.

POINTS TO NOTE WHEN BUYING EGGS

The vast majority of British hens' eggs in retail shops have been quality-tested and graded by weight at egg packing stations. These eggs are labelled on the containers accordingly. Details are given below. Others are obtained directly from producers and are usually called farm eggs.

Eggs that have been kept in a warm place, such as a shop window, should not be bought, as changes within the egg will occur very quickly. The same applies to dirty eggs, as dirt and germs may have been absorbed through the porous shell.

Eggs are generally sold in packs containing 6 eggs. The packs must have the following information on them:

1) A number indicating the country of packing (9 stands for the UK) followed by a number indicating the region of that country, and then the packing station's registered number.
2) Quality and weight grading marks.
3) Name and address of enterprise which graded or arranged for the grading of eggs (and its trade mark, with some limitations).
4) Number of eggs packed.
5) Week number (1–52), or date of packing. The actual date need only be shown when the pack carries the optional 'Extra' label.
6) Egg packs may also show an 'Extra' label if applicable (see below).

All producers must conform with these regulations except for those who sell their own eggs direct to the consumer (at farm gates, on delivery rounds or on their own stalls).

These regulations also apply to eggs sold loose or in trays holding 30 eggs. A label must be displayed near the eggs showing the quality, classification, and weight grade.

Grading Systems

The European Economic Community (EEC) has one grading system based on the weight of the egg and one based on its quality.

The first ranges between Grade 1 and Grade 7:
Grade 1 – 70g and over
Grade 2 – 65g–69g
Grade 3 – 60g–64g
Grade 4 – 55g–59g
Grade 5 – 50g–54g
Grade 6 – 45g–49g
Grade 7 – below 45g

Eggs of Grades 1 and 2 correspond approximately to the old-style large eggs, Grade 3 and 4 to standard eggs, Grade 5 and 6 to medium eggs, and Grade 7 to small and extra small eggs.

The second grading system, based on quality, ranges between Grade A and Grade C. Grade A eggs are fresh, with clean unstained shells, sound texture, and a good shape. The egg content should be free of any visible blemish or discoloration when tested. The yolk should be positioned centrally and defined clearly. The white should be translucent with the two parts visible. The air space should not exceed 5mm in depth.

Some packs containing Grade A eggs have a red band, with the word 'Extra' around them. This means superior quality with air cells of less than 4mm in depth at the time of packing, which itself has been less than 7 days. In addition, they will have come from a producer from whom the packer collects at least twice a week. (Once a week is sufficient for other eggs.) The shopkeeper is expected to remove this band if the eggs have not been sold within 7 days.

Grade B are second quality eggs which have been downgraded because they may have enlarged air cells, indicating age, or they may have been stored or refrigerated.

Grade C eggs are only suitable for manufacturers. They are neither graded by weight nor available in retail shops.

STORING EGGS

Whole eggs should be stored in cool conditions, but should not be frozen because ice formed inside splits the shells; when thawed, the yolks remain semi-solid or pasty and the white may be amber coloured.

The best storage temperature is 10–12°C, at the bottom of a refrigerator or on a cool shelf in a larder. Keep a few at room temperature for quick use. Eggs keep for up to 2 months in a refrigerator.

Store eggs rounded end up. The yolk then rises in the white and rests against the air space which helps protect the yolk from jolts and from some contamination through the shell.

As the shell is porous, strong smells and flavours are easily absorbed by eggs, so they should not be stored near such foods as onions, cheese or fish. If eggs are rattled or knocked about, the shells may develop small cracks and the yolks may be bumped against the shells; the eggs keep less long, and may crack badly if boiled. For this reason, an egg rack situated in the door of the refrigerator is not a good place to store eggs.

The best container in which to keep eggs is the box in which they were purchased. The eggs do not dry out by evaporation through the shell, nor absorb smells or flavours from nearby foods. They are also protected against accidental knocks.

Eggs should be taken out of the refrigerator at least 30 minutes before use, to give them time to reach room temperature. A cold egg will crack when put into hot water for boiling, it may curdle a creamed cake mixture, and it will not have as much volume or be as light when whisked. Eggs will, however, separate more easily when cold.

In an emergency, warm eggs by holding them under warm water for a moment or two.

Storing Eggs Without Shells

Whole eggs: Beat whole eggs lightly, and add a pinch of salt or 1 × 2.5ml spoon of sugar per egg. Keep in a covered container in a refrigerator for up to 1 week. The salt or sugar prevents the yolks from becoming sticky during storage.

Yolks: Beat the yolks lightly, add a pinch of salt or 1 × 2.5ml spoon of sugar per 2 yolks. Store as for whole eggs.

If the yolks are whole, pour them into a container and gently cover with milk, cold water or oil (if to be used for mayonnaise). Drain before using. Store as for whole eggs.

Whites: Store in a covered container with a pinch of salt added, and use within 2 days.

Note Label the container with the number of eggs it holds and the quantity of sugar or salt added.

For methods of preserving eggs for long-term storage, see p905.

SEPARATING EGGS

1) Crack the egg and pour on to a saucer. Place an egg-cup over the yolk and hold it firmly in place; then tilt the saucer to let the egg white slide off into a basin.
2) Crack the shell sharply with the blade of a knife or against the side of a basin or cup. (Do not tap it as this may crush the shell and break the yolk instead of breaking it cleanly.) Hold the egg over a cup or basin and, using the thumbs, prise the crack open just enough to allow the white to slip out. Break the shell into two halves, tipping one half so that it holds the yolk. Tip the yolk carefully into the other half to release all the white. Repeat if necessary. Then put the yolk in a second cup or basin.

If separating more than one egg, use a third basin for cracking the eggs, so that only one white is spoilt if any yolk breaks.

Some Uses for Surplus Egg Whites and Yolks

Whites:
1) Add an extra white to a meringue, mousse or soufflé mixture.
2) Make into a meringue topping for an oven-baked pudding.
3) Whisk 1 egg white until very stiff with 50g caster sugar. Poach in flavoured, simmering milk for 3 minutes. Drain, and float on cooled custard desserts.

4) Whisk until stiff and fold into fruit purée for a light dessert.

5) Make double cream go further by adding an egg white to 125ml cream before whipping.

6) For a light, crisp egg and crumb coating, brush fish cakes or croquettes with egg white; then roll in very fine dry white crumbs. Leave for 20 minutes, and shallow fry.

7) Whisk 1 egg white lightly with 1×10ml spoon caster sugar and brush on sweet breads, pastry or cakes as a glaze; or brush the food with the egg white, and sprinkle with granulated, crushed lump or caster sugar.

Yolks:

1) Use 2 yolks instead of 1 whole egg in custards.

2) Use 2 yolks with 1×15ml spoon water instead of 1 whole egg in yeast mixtures, cakes, buns or biscuits.

3) Mix with 1×10ml spoon milk and add instead of 1 whole egg when scrambling eggs.

4) Mix 1 egg yolk with 1×10ml spoon water and use on baked goods to give a glossy rich brown glaze.

5) Use to enrich and thicken sauces or soups. Beat with a little milk, water or lemon juice, and add a little of the hot sauce or soup. Return the egg mixture to the pan, and re-heat without boiling, stirring all the time.

6) Use hard-boiled yolks for Mrs Beeton's Fairy Butter (p1303) or as a garnish by crumbling or sieving the yolks over soup, a salad or vegetables.

COOKING EGGS

What Heat Does

When an egg is heated, its protein changes in chemical composition and gradually becomes solid. The protein in egg yolk differs from that in egg white and they thicken at different temperatures. The yolk coagulates at about 68°C and the white at about 60°C, at which temperature it is jelly-like and tender; above this temperature it becomes dense and firm. When the yolk and white are well beaten together, the egg usually coagulates at approximately 63–65°C. However, if heated very slowly, it needs a higher temperature to set it. If ingredients such as milk, cream or sugar are added, it needs a still higher temperature of 82–85°C.

Above 85°C, the protein toughens, so that it becomes unappetising and indigestible. If heated any more the eggs appear to 'weep'; this happens when they are scrambled too quickly or when a baked custard is cooked at too high a temperature. The protein fibres shrink, squeezing the liquid out from between them. This also happens when an overheated 'boiled' custard curdles. Take care, therefore, never to overheat egg dishes.

Another change takes place inside a whole egg during cooking. The white releases some sulphur (hydrogen sulphide) near the shell, and the yolk releases some iron. If the sulphur and iron combine, a greyish-black ring forms around the outside of the yolk because iron sulphide is formed. If a boiled egg is not being served at once, put it under cold running water as soon as it is taken out of hot water, to prevent this happening. The ring is harmless but looks unattractive.

Uses of Eggs in Cooking

Eggs are one of the most versatile of cooking ingredients. They can be:

1) eaten by themselves boiled, poached, fried, baked, scrambled, in omelets and set custards.

2) hard-boiled for salads, for making stuffed savouries (as containers), and for garnishing.

3) blended with liquid and heated very gently to thicken custards and sauces.

4) blended into cake and sponge mixtures to make them richer and lighter.

5) whisked to entrap air, then folded into soufflés and similar mixtures, omelets, and other dishes to make them very light; and also to make meringue desserts.

6) used for binding a panada, for coating ingredients before frying, and to hold a crumb coating in place to prevent food absorbing hot fat and becoming soggy.

7) used for glazing pastry, cakes, and other baked goods.

8) used as the basic ingredient in many sauces such

as Hollandaise sauce and mayonnaise), and in fruit curds (eg lemon curd).

9) used for making nourishing drinks and soups.
10) used for clarifying consommé and jellies.

Cooking Terms

Beating eggs: When whole eggs or egg yolks are beaten, they become more liquid at first. Whole eggs *beaten lightly* have been beaten with a fork only just enough to blend the yolks and whites together as a liquid. When they are *beaten well*, they are frothy. When egg yolks alone are *well beaten*, they are thick and lemon-coloured.

Whisking egg whites: Egg whites consist of albumen in water; when whisked, large air bubbles are formed in the albumen. As whisking continues, these break down, forming smaller bubbles. The shiny white becomes opaque, increases in volume as it stiffens, and finally becomes a matt, stiff foam; properly beaten egg white should more than triple its volume.

Whites will not whisk properly if they contain any speck of grease, yolk or moisture, so the bowl and whisk must be clean and dry.

They whisk better and more quickly at room temperature; so refrigerated eggs should be separated, and the whites left to stand for 1 hour before whisking, if possible.

A pinch of bicarbonate of soda, cream of tartar or salt will give a firmer, smoother meringue.

When egg whites are *whisked until stiff*, they stand in soft peaks when the whisk is lifted, so that the tips of the peaks droop. The foam is moist and glossy, and clings to the whisk. It is then suitable for folding into dishes such as soufflés. If any stiffer, the foam breaks up when folded in, and cannot be blended in without losing air and lightness.

If the whites are *whisked until very stiff*, the foam looks dry and lumpy. The basin can be turned upside down without it falling out. It is then suitable for meringues.

Whisked eggs must be used quickly because the albumen becomes stretched and frail during whisking, and if the foam is left to turn watery, it will not stiffen again.

To fold in whisked egg whites: Stir up to a quarter of the foam into the main mixture, to lighten it. Then pile the remaining foam on top, and using a metal spoon, cut down through the mixture, across the base, then up the side, turning the mixture over the foam. Turn the bowl a little, and repeat the process. Fold in slowly; quick folding breaks down the foam.

Whisking whole eggs: Whole eggs only make a permanent foam like egg whites if sugar is added and the mixture is whisked in a bowl over a pan of hot water. A soft foam can be produced in this way which leaves a trail from the lifted whisk for about 3 seconds. The temperature must be kept low. Over high heat, the egg protein hardens instead of foaming.

EGGS FROM BIRDS OTHER THAN HENS

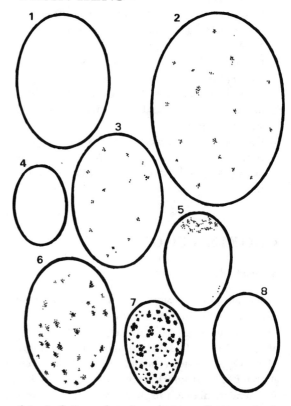

1 Duck; 2 Goose; 3 Turkey; 4 Pigeon; 5 Guinea-fowl; 6 Herring gull; 7 Plover; 8 Fulmar.

Duck eggs are larger than hens' eggs, contain more fat, and have a richer flavour. Since ducks often lay their eggs in wet or dirty places, they may contain bacteria and must be cooked thoroughly. They should not be eaten boiled, or be made into meringues or any dish which is only cooked briefly or lightly heated. Nor should they be stored or preserved.

When using duck eggs for baking, 2 can be used instead of 3 hens' eggs. Add 1 × 15ml spoon water to each egg to prevent the mixture being heavy.

Duck eggs make very good custards.

Goose eggs are similar to duck eggs in being larger and richer than hens' eggs. They can be used in any way and are particularly good for cakes and puddings. Goose eggs are quite safe to eat boiled, but take 7 minutes to soft boil. One goose egg will make scrambled egg for 4 people.

Turkey eggs are larger than hens' eggs but have the same delicate flavour. They may be cooked in all the usual ways. Two turkey eggs are equivalent to 3 hens' eggs. It takes 7 minutes to soft boil a turkey egg.

Pigeon, guinea-fowl, gull and fulmar eggs are all eaten in places where they are available. They are slightly smaller than hens' eggs. These eggs are sometimes served hard-boiled as an hors d'oeuvre at dinner parties. Cook for 10–15 minutes.

Plovers' eggs were once considered a great delicacy, but the taking and selling of these eggs is now prohibited in the UK.

PRESERVING EGGS

Eggs are plentiful all year round, so there is normally no need to preserve them for winter use. However, an unusually cheap supply may be worth preserving for longer than eggs can be kept in a refrigerator. There are two methods:

1) Freezing (see p1396).
2) Making the shell impervious, and so stopping bacteria from entering the egg or moisture evaporating from it.

Only preserve hens' eggs. Duck and goose eggs may contain *salmonella* bacteria.

The eggs must be free from cracks, smooth, clean, and at least 12 hours old. They must be fresh

however, so make sure that bought eggs are from the latest delivery.

Do not wash the eggs, since this removes a thin natural varnish from the shell surface. Just brush off loose dirt, and wipe them with a damp cloth.

Preserving Methods

1) Brush or rub melted paraffin wax or white petroleum jelly all over the shell, taking care to cover it completely. Let melted wax dry thoroughly before storing. Store the eggs in egg trays, rounded end up, not touching each other.

   In some places, commercially made solutions can be bought and used like paraffin wax. Follow the manufacturers' instructions scrupulously.

2) Eggs can be preserved in waterglass (sodium silicate) although it is hard to get in the UK. Pour the diluted waterglass into an earthenware crock, enamel or galvanized pail. Pack the eggs in layers in the cooled solution, rounded end up. They must be entirely covered by the solution and the container must be kept covered to prevent evaporation.

   Before boiling an egg preserved in waterglass, prick the shell with a needle to prevent it cracking when heated.

BAKED EGGS

Eggs are traditionally baked in individual, ovenproof china or earthenware dishes called ramekins or cocottes. These are round dishes shaped like small soufflé dishes or tartlet tins, sometimes with a handle. However, any small shallow ovenproof dish will do. Alternatively, a flat ovenproof dish which is large enough to hold all the helpings can be used; care must be taken to see that it is not too big, or the egg whites will spread out thinly and be overcooked.

Remember that the eggs will continue cooking after the dish has been taken from the oven, so do not overcook them.

EGGS

Baked Eggs

25g butter   *salt and pepper*
1–2 eggs per person

Heat 4 individual or 1 large ovenproof dish, put a
knob of butter into each, and add the eggs and
seasoning. Bake in a moderate oven at 180°C, Gas 4,
for 8–10 minutes (12–15 minutes if the dishes are
ovenproof glassware) until the eggs are just set.

VARIATIONS

1) Grill 4 rashers of rindless bacon lightly and put
   them in the dishes before adding the eggs. Alternatively, put the uncooked bacon in the dishes
   and bake in the oven for 3–4 minutes before
   adding the butter, eggs, and seasoning.
2) Put thin slices of cheese, or grated cheese, into
   the dishes before adding the eggs.
3) Arrange halved or quartered tomatoes round
   the eggs before cooking.
4) Add sliced sautéed mushrooms, onions, chopped
   kidney or shrimps to the cooked egg.

Eggs in Cocottes
(Oeufs en Cocottes)

4 helpings

25g butter   *4 ×15ml spoons milk* **or**
4 eggs   *cream*
salt and pepper

Butter 4 ramekins or cocottes at least 3cm deep, and
stand them in a baking tin containing enough warm
water to come half-way up their sides. Break an egg
into each warm dish, and season with salt and
pepper. Top with any remaining butter cut into
flakes and with 1 ×15ml spoon milk or cream. Bake
in the centre of a moderate oven at 180°C, Gas 4, for
6–10 minutes, depending on the thickness of the
dishes. The whites of the eggs should be just set.
Wipe the outsides of the dishes and serve at once.

VARIATIONS

1) Shake ground nutmeg or Cayenne pepper over
   the eggs before cooking.
2) Sprinkle the eggs with very finely grated cheese
   before cooking.

3) Put sliced, fried mushrooms, chopped ham,
   cooked diced chicken or lightly sautéed, diced
   Italian sausage in the bottom of each dish before
   adding the eggs.
4) Put 1–2 ×15ml spoons spinach purée in the
   dishes before adding the eggs.

Moulded Eggs

4 helpings

50g butter   *4 eggs*
2 ×15ml spoons finely   *4 slices white bread*
  chopped parsley

Butter 4 dariole moulds generously. Reserve the
butter not used. Coat the insides of the moulds
lightly with the parsley. Break an egg into each,
and put them in a baking tin. Pour on enough warm
water to come half-way up the sides of the moulds.
Cook in a moderate oven at 180°C, Gas 4, for 10–12
minutes until the whites are just firm.

Meanwhile, cut a circle 7cm in diameter from
each slice of bread and fry in the remaining butter
until golden-brown on each side. Loosen the
cooked eggs in the moulds, turn out on to the fried
bread, and serve immediately.

VARIATIONS

1) 1 ×15ml spoon finely chopped chives can be
   used instead of the parsley.
2) 25g mushrooms, finely chopped, cooked in
   butter and drained can be used instead of the
   parsley.
3) 25g minced ham mixed with 1 ×10ml spoon
   chopped parsley can be used instead of the
   parsley alone.
4) The bread can be toasted and buttered instead of
   fried.
5) The eggs can be turned out on to rounds of
   pastry or into shallow pastry cases.
6) Large flat mushrooms, lightly cooked in butter,
   can be used instead of the bread.
7) Tomatoes, skinned, cut in half, and de-seeded,
   can be used instead of the bread.

Shirred Eggs

4 helpings

4 eggs	½ × 2.5ml spoon paprika
salt	chopped chives **or**
butter for greasing	parsley

Separate the eggs. Whisk the whites until very stiff with a little salt. Butter the inside of a shallow oven-to-table baking dish which will hold the egg white in a layer about 5cm deep. Turn in the egg white lightly. Make 4 hollows in the meringue mixture, not too near the edge and equally spaced apart. Slip 1 yolk into each hollow. Bake in a moderate oven at 180°C, Gas 4, for 10 minutes or until the eggs are set. Sprinkle with paprika and with chopped chives or parsley before serving.

Alpine Eggs

4 helpings

50g butter	1 × 15ml spoon finely
100g Gruyère cheese	chopped parsley
4 eggs	salt and pepper

Butter 4 cocottes or 1 ovenproof dish generously. Slice 75g cheese thinly and line the base of the dishes with it. Break the eggs over the cheese, keeping the yolks whole. Grate the rest of the cheese and mix it with the parsley. Season the eggs generously, sprinkle the cheese and parsley on top, and add the rest of the butter in small pieces. Stand the dishes in a baking tin, and pour in enough hot water to come half-way up the sides of the dishes. Bake in a moderate oven at 180°C, Gas 4, for 12–15 minutes until lightly set.

Serve at once with hot rolls or crisp toast.

Eggs Baked in Tomatoes

4 helpings

4 large tomatoes	4 eggs
salt and pepper	1 × 15ml spoon butter

Cut the tops off the tomatoes and remove the centre cores and seeds. Leave them upside-down on a plate for a few minutes to drain. Season the tomatoes inside with salt and pepper. Break an egg into each tomato case, season again, and add a knob of butter. Put into cocotte dishes or a large ovenproof dish and bake in a moderate oven at 180°C, Gas 4, for 12–15 minutes until the egg is lightly set.

Tomato Meringues

4 helpings

4 medium-sized	4 eggs
tomatoes	50g Cheddar **or** Cheshire
salt and pepper	cheese

Skin the tomatoes, cut the tops off, and remove the centre cores and seeds. Leave them upside down on a plate for a few minutes to drain. Season the tomatoes with salt and pepper and put into individual cocotte dishes or 1 ovenproof dish. Separate the eggs, and drop 1 yolk into each tomato shell. Grate the cheese finely. Whisk the egg whites until stiff, fold in the cheese, and pile the meringue mixture on top of the tomatoes, completely covering them. Bake in a fairly hot oven at 200°C, Gas 6, for 10–12 minutes, until the meringue is browned. Serve hot.

Indian Buttered Eggs

4 helpings

1 × 15ml spoon butter	3 eggs
4 hard-boiled eggs	50g browned
1 × 2.5ml spoon curry	breadcrumbs (p375)
powder	salt and pepper

Grease a deep 1 litre ovenproof dish with some of the butter. Slice the hard-boiled eggs and arrange in layers in the dish. Sprinkle the curry powder over the slices. Beat the 3 remaining eggs lightly and season. Pour into the dish, cover with the browned breadcrumbs, dot with the remaining butter, and cook in a moderate oven at 180°C, Gas 4, for 13–15 minutes until the egg is lightly set.

Eggs in Nests
(Oeufs Parmentier)

4 helpings

600g potatoes	butter for greasing
150g Cheddar cheese	4 eggs
salt and pepper	ground nutmeg
2 ×15ml spoons milk	

Peel the potatoes, cut into small pieces, and cook in boiling salted water for 10–15 minutes until tender. Drain and mash. Grate the cheese. Add most of the cheese, salt, pepper, and the milk to the potatoes, and beat with a wooden spoon until creamy. Using a forcing bag with a large star nozzle, pipe 4 nests of potato on to a greased baking tray. Alternatively, pile the potato mixture into 4 heaps and, using a fork, make into nest shapes. Break an egg into each nest. Mix the remaining cheese with a pinch of ground nutmeg, and sprinkle on the eggs. Bake in a fairly hot oven at 190°C, Gas 5, for 12–15 minutes until the egg whites are lightly set and the potato is browned.

Ox Eyes

4 helpings

4 slices stale white bread (2cm thick)	4 eggs
1 ×15ml spoon butter	salt and pepper
4–6 ×15ml spoons soured cream	

Toast the bread on both sides. Cut into 8cm rounds with a biscuit cutter. Using a 5cm cutter, take out the centre of each round, cutting through the top of the bread only, leaving the bases whole. Butter the bottom of an ovenproof dish well, and arrange the bread cases in it. Spoon over them as much soured cream as they will absorb without becoming soggy. Break an egg into each case, season, and bake in a moderate oven at 180°C, Gas 4, for 12–15 minutes until the eggs are lightly set.

Eggs Florentine(1)

4 helpings

1kg fresh spinach **or**	1 ×15ml spoon butter
2 ×225g pkts frozen leaf spinach	salt and pepper
100g Fontina **or** Cheddar cheese	4 eggs

Wash the fresh spinach several times and remove any coarse stalks. Put into a saucepan with just the water that clings to the leaves, then cover, and heat gently. Cook for 10–15 minutes, turning the spinach occasionally. Cook frozen spinach according to the directions on the packet. Grate the cheese finely. When the spinach is tender, drain thoroughly, and cut through several times with a knife to chop it. Grease an ovenproof dish with a little of the butter. Re-heat the spinach with the remaining butter and a little salt and pepper. Put into the dish, and make 4 hollows in the surface. Break an egg into each hollow, season, and sprinkle the cheese over the eggs. Bake in a fairly hot oven at 190°C, Gas 5, for 12–15 minutes until the eggs are lightly set.

Note For Eggs Florentine (2), see p915.

BOILED, CODDLED, AND STEAMED EGGS

Boiled Eggs

Eggs should be simmered rather than actually boiled ideally at 88–90°C. Hotter water does not speed the cooking, it only makes the white tough before the yolk is ready. Rapidly boiling water may also jostle the eggs together, and crack the shells.

The eggs should be at room temperature before cooking; hot water may crack a cold shell. If eggs are taken straight from the refrigerator, hold them under the hot tap for a few minutes before cooking or use the cold water start method of boiling (see p909).

If the eggs are cracked, some of the white will escape into the water. If you suspect that an egg is cracked, add 1 ×15ml spoon vinegar or lemon juice to the water and the white will coagulate as it escapes from the shell, so preventing any more white getting into the water.

The consistency of a soft-boiled egg is a personal choice, so the times that are given can only be a general guide. Generally speaking, a soft-boiled egg means that the white is soft and the yolk is runny, a medium-boiled egg means that the white is firm and the yolk is soft but set, and a hard-boiled egg means that both the white and the yolk are firm. Really fresh eggs take $\frac{1}{2}$–1 minute longer to cook than eggs which are some days old.

Eggs can be boiled in two ways, by putting into boiling water or into cold water at the start. The water must completely cover the eggs, otherwise they cook unevenly.

1) Put enough water into a pan to cover the eggs. Bring to the boil, and lower in the eggs one at a time, using a spoon. Reduce the heat so that the water is just bubbling. Time the cooking from the moment the eggs are put into the water.

	soft minutes	medium minutes	hard minutes
Grade 5 eggs	3	$4\frac{1}{2}$	10
Grades 3 and 4	$3\frac{1}{4}$	$4\frac{3}{4}$	11
Grades 1 and 2	$3\frac{1}{2}$	5	12

2) Place the eggs carefully in a pan and just cover with cold water. Bring slowly to the boil and then boil gently. Start timing from the moment the water boils gently.

	soft minutes	medium minutes	hard minutes
Grade 5 eggs	$2\frac{1}{2}$	$3\frac{1}{2}$	8
Grades 3 and 4	$2\frac{3}{4}$	4	9
Grades 1 and 2	3	$4\frac{1}{2}$	10

Whichever method is used, correct timing is crucial since eggs can easily overcook. Once cooked, the eggs must be served immediately, as they continue cooking inside the shell. If they are not to be eaten straightaway, take them out of the water just before the cooking time is up, and tap the pointed end to break the shell and so release the steam, preventing any further cooking.

Alternatively, cool quickly, and re-heat in hot (not boiling) water. Once cooked and removed from the heat, later heating will not harden soft or medium-boiled eggs.

Hard-boiled eggs must be plunged into cold water for at least 5 minutes immediately after cooking, to prevent a dark ring forming round the yolk. It also makes the shell easier to remove. To shell hard-boiled eggs, crack the shell by tapping all over on a hard surface; then roll gently between the hands and peel off the shell. Rinse in cold water to remove any small pieces of shell.

Soft-boiled eggs, especially if still hot, must be shelled more delicately. Hold the egg under a cold tap for 1–2 minutes to cool the outside. Grasp it, using a cloth, and crack the shell by using a pointed knife; then remove any small pieces of shell by wiping with kitchen paper.

Always keep shelled boiled eggs in a bowl of water to keep the whites supple. Pat dry before using.

Coddled Eggs

Coddled eggs are very soft-boiled eggs, with a soft white and the yolk just set. Being easily digested, they are ideal for invalids. Place the eggs in boiling water, cover with a lid, and remove from the heat, but keep the water hot without simmering for about 6 minutes for a grade 5 egg, and 8–9 minutes for grades 1 and 2 eggs.

Alternatively, put the eggs into cold water, bring slowly to the boil, and remove them immediately.

Oeufs Mollets

Oeuf mollet is the French term for a shelled soft-boiled egg. These eggs are very often used in made-up dishes, such as Eggs Mornay (p911) when a soft-boiled egg is preferable to a hard-boiled or poached egg.

Put the eggs into boiling water and cook them for 5 minutes. Plunge them into cold water, leave for 5 minutes, and then remove the shell carefully under the water. If the eggs are to be served cold, leave them in the water. If they are to be served hot, re-heat them in hot salted water, stock or milk well under the boil. Drain before using.

Steamed Eggs

Eggs can be steamed in heatproof dishes or small moulds, such as cocottes or dariole moulds.

A steamer gives the best results as the eggs are cooked more gently and do not toughen. However, the dishes or moulds can be placed in a saucepan with hot water coming half-way up the sides.

Put the bottom part of a steamer or a saucepan of water on to boil. Butter the egg containers generously, crack an egg into each and season with salt and pepper. Cover with foil or greased grease-proof paper. Put the containers in the top part of the steamer, cover with the lid, and place the steamer on top of its pan. If using a saucepan, stand the egg dishes in the hot water in the saucepan, making sure that the water only comes half-way up the sides of the dishes. Cover the pan with a lid. The eggs will take 8–10 minutes to cook in a pan of water and 10–12 minutes in a steamer.

Eggs Maître d'Hôtel

4 helpings

100g butter	2 ×15ml spoons finely
25g flour	chopped parsley
250ml milk	salt and pepper
1 ×15ml spoon lemon	6 hard-boiled eggs
juice	

Melt 50g of the butter in a saucepan, add the flour, and stir with a wooden spoon until smooth. Cook over gentle heat without colouring for 2–3 minutes, stirring all the time. Remove from the heat and add the milk gradually, stirring all the time. Return to moderate heat and bring the sauce to the boil, stirring all the time. When it has thickened, reduce the heat and simmer for 1–2 minutes, beating vigorously to give the sauce a good gloss. Remove from the heat, and beat in the rest of the butter, adding it gradually in small pieces. Stir in the lemon juice, parsley, and season to taste. Slice the eggs and arrange them on a warmed dish. Re-heat the sauce if necessary, but take care not to let it boil. Pour it over the eggs and serve at once with hot toast.

Fricassée of Eggs

4 helpings

50g mushrooms	250ml foundation white
2 ×10ml spoons butter	sauce (p692)
6 hard-boiled eggs	2 ×15ml spoons single
salt and pepper	cream

Garnish
chopped parsley

Clean and slice the mushrooms. Heat the butter and cook the mushrooms slowly until tender. Drain. Slice the eggs. Arrange the eggs and mushrooms on a hot dish, and season with salt and pepper. Heat the sauce thoroughly, remove from the heat, and stir in the cream. Pour the sauce over the eggs and mushrooms. Sprinkle with a little chopped parsley.

Serve with triangles of fried or toasted bread.

Curried Eggs

4 helpings

2 onions	1 chicken stock cube
50g lard or 4 ×15ml	2 ×15ml spoons mango
spoons oil	chutney
1 cooking apple	1 ×15ml spoon brown
(200g approx)	sugar
1–2 ×15ml spoons	2 ×15ml spoons lemon
curry powder	juice
2 ×15ml spoons flour	salt
2 × 5ml spoons	6 hard-boiled eggs
concentrated tomato	2 ×15ml spoons single
purée	cream or top of the
500ml water	milk

Skin and chop the onions. Heat the lard or oil in a saucepan and sauté the onions gently for 5 minutes, until soft but not coloured. Peel, core, and chop the apple. Add to the onions and continue cooking for 5 minutes. Stir in the curry powder and flour and fry for 5 minutes. Add the tomato purée, water, stock cube, chutney, sugar, lemon juice, and a pinch of salt. Bring to the boil, stirring all the time. Reduce the heat, cover with a lid and simmer for 30 minutes, stirring occasionally. Cut the eggs into quarters. Re-season the sauce with more salt if required. Remove from the heat and stir in the cream or top of the milk. Add the eggs and heat through.

Serve with boiled rice.

Eggs Mornay

4 helpings

500g potatoes	*6 oeufs mollets* (p909)
50g Cheddar cheese	*1 × 2.5ml spoon French*
50ml milk	*mustard*
2 × 10ml spoons butter	*250ml Béchamel sauce*
salt and pepper	*(p704)*

Peel the potatoes and cook them in boiling salted water for 15–20 minutes, until tender. Grate the cheese. Mash the potatoes, adding the milk, butter, and seasoning. Beat well with a wooden spoon until smooth. Using a forcing bag with a large nozzle, pipe or fork the creamed potatoes round the edge of a pie plate. Arrange the whole eggs on the plate. Add most of the cheese and the mustard to the Béchamel sauce and re-heat gently. Do not boil the sauce as the cheese may go stringy. Re-season if required. Coat the eggs with the sauce, sprinkle with the remaining cheese, and brown under the grill.

Scotch Eggs

4 helpings

250g sausage-meat	*4 hard-boiled eggs*
1 × 15ml spoon flour	*50g soft white*
1 egg	*breadcrumbs*
2 × 5ml spoons water	*oil for deep frying*
salt and pepper	

Garnish
parsley sprigs

Divide the sausage-meat into 4 equal pieces. On a lightly floured surface, roll each piece into a circle 12cm in diameter. Beat the egg with the water. Season the remaining flour with salt and pepper and toss the hard-boiled eggs in it. Place an egg in the centre of each circle of sausage-meat and mould evenly round the egg, making sure it fits closely. Seal the joins with the beaten egg and pinch well together. Mould each Scotch egg into a good shape, brush it all over with beaten egg, and then toss it in the breadcrumbs, covering the surface evenly. Press the crumbs well in. Put enough oil to cover the Scotch eggs into a deep pan and heat it (p303). Fry the eggs until golden-brown. Drain them on soft kitchen paper. Cut in half lengthways and garnish each half with a small piece of parsley.

Serve hot with Fresh Tomato Sauce (p715) or cold with salad.

Note As the sausage-meat is raw, it is important that the frying should not be hurried.

Hot Stuffed Eggs

4 helpings

1 onion	*salt and pepper*
3 × 15ml spoons butter	*a pinch of dried oregano*
or margarine	*6 hard-boiled eggs*
50g mushrooms	*1 × 10ml spoon*
250ml tomato juice	*cornflour*
1 × 5ml spoon sugar	*2 × 15ml spoons water*

Skin the onion and chop it finely. Melt the butter or margarine in a saucepan. Fry the onion gently for 5 minutes until softened but not browned. Clean and chop the mushrooms, add to the onion, and fry for a further 2 minutes. Remove half the onion and mushroom mixture, drain well, and put into a bowl. Add the tomato juice, sugar, salt, pepper, and oregano to the saucepan and bring to the boil. Reduce the heat and simmer for 5 minutes.

Meanwhile, cut the hard-boiled eggs in half lengthways. Remove the yolks, put into the bowl with the onions and mushrooms, and mix thoroughly with a fork. Stuff the halved egg white with this mixture and arrange on a warm serving dish. Keep hot.

Blend the cornflour with the water, add a little of the tomato juice mixture, pour into the saucepan, and stir well. Bring to the boil, stirring all the time, and boil for 1–2 minutes. Re-season the sauce if required. Pour it round the eggs.

Serve with boiled rice or creamed potatoes.

Hot Stuffed Eggs in Mornay Sauce

4 helpings

100g mushrooms	*250ml milk*
3 ×15ml spoons butter	*50g Cheddar cheese*
* or margarine*	*6 hard-boiled eggs*
2 ×15ml spoons flour	*salt and pepper*

Garnish
watercress sprigs

Clean and chop the mushrooms. Melt 2 ×10ml spoons of the butter or margarine and fry the mushrooms for about 5 minutes, or until all the moisture has evaporated. Melt the rest of the butter or margarine in a clean saucepan, add the flour, and stir until smooth. Cook over gentle heat for 2–3 minutes, stirring all the time. Remove from the heat and add the milk gradually, stirring all the time. Return to the heat, bring to the boil, stirring all the time, and cook for 1–2 minutes. Grate the cheese. Cut the hard-boiled eggs in half lengthways. Remove the yolks and put them into a bowl. Add the fried mushrooms and mix well together. Stuff the halved egg whites with this mixture and arrange on a warm serving dish. Bring the sauce to the boil again, stirring all the time. Remove from the heat and add most of the cheese, and the salt and pepper. Mix in well. Pour the sauce over the stuffed eggs, sprinkle with the remaining cheese and brown under a hot grill until golden-brown. Garnish with the watercress and serve at once.

Cold Stuffed Eggs

See p319.

FRIED EGGS

There are two basic methods of frying. The first involves shallow-frying and the second, deep-frying.

1) Melt a little fat, dripping, lard, butter, bacon fat or cooking oil in a frying pan. Allow about $\frac{1}{2}$ ×15ml spoon per egg. The fat should be just hot, not sizzling. Break the eggs, one at a time, into a cup or saucer and slide them into the fat. Cook over gentle heat for 2–3 minutes until the white is no longer transparent; high heat toughens the egg whites and makes them crisp round the edges. Lift the eggs out of the pan, using a fish slice or a broad palette knife. Hold for 1–2 seconds above the pan to allow any surplus fat to drain off before putting them on the dish. Fried eggs can be blotted with soft kitchen paper to remove any excess fat. If liked, the eggs can be basted with the hot fat during cooking, using a spoon or wooden spatula. This makes a film over the yolk, and cooks the top of the white more thoroughly. The egg is usually cooked in 1–2 minutes.

Some people prefer fried eggs which are turned over during cooking, so that both sides are fried. The eggs cook in 1–2 minutes. In America, eggs served with the yolk upwards are known as 'sunny side up', and eggs fried on both sides are known as 'once over lightly'.

2) Half fill a small, deep pan with lard or oil. Heat it to 180°C (when a square of white bread sizzles immediately without browning) and then maintain this temperature. Break one egg into a cup or saucer and slide it carefully into the fat. With a wooden spatula pull the white over the yolk so as to cover it completely. Turn the egg over in the oil. The egg cooks very quickly, in 30–60 seconds from the moment it touches the fat. Have a perforated spoon ready and lift out the egg as soon as the white is set. Blot on soft kitchen paper to remove any excess fat, and serve quickly.

Eggs Colbert

4 helpings

4 eggs	*fat or oil for shallow*
salt and pepper	* frying*
4 ×15ml spoons grated	
* Parmesan cheese*	

Break 1 egg into a cup or saucer, season well and sprinkle 1 × 2.5ml spoon of cheese over it. Slide the egg into hot fat or oil. Repeat with the other eggs. Fry the eggs until golden-brown, turning them over often with a wooden spatula. Drain on soft kitchen paper, sprinkle with the remaining cheese, and serve immediately.

Framed Eggs

4 helpings

4 thick slices white bread	*4 eggs*
fat or oil for shallow frying	

Cut each slice of bread into a circle 10cm in diameter; then cut a second round 6cm in diameter from the centres, so that 4 bread rings are left. Fry the rings in hot fat until brown and crisp on one side; turn them over, reduce the heat and break an egg into the centre of each. Fry gently until the eggs are set. Lift out with a broad slice and drain before serving.

Piedmont Eggs

4 helpings

100g long-grain rice	*2 ×15ml spoons grated Parmesan cheese*
250ml chicken or vegetable stock	*salt and pepper*
3–4 ripe firm tomatoes	*butter for greasing and shallow frying*
2 rashers bacon, without rinds	*4 eggs*

Garnish
ground black pepper

Put the rice and stock into a saucepan, bring quickly to the boil, stir well and cover with a tight-fitting lid. Reduce the heat and simmer gently for 14–15 minutes, until the grains are soft and the stock has been absorbed. Remove from the heat.

Meanwhile, skin and de-seed the tomatoes. Cut the flesh into 5mm dice. Cut the bacon rashers into strips and fry until crisp. Add the tomatoes, bacon, and cheese to the rice. Season well and stir thoroughly. Butter a 1 litre flat dish and spoon the rice mixture into it. Press down firmly into an even layer and keep hot.

Fry the eggs on 1 side only. Trim off any uneven or overcooked parts. Turn the rice mould out on to a hot dish, arrange the eggs round the rice and decorate each with a small pinch of black pepper in the centre of the yolk. Serve at once.

Buttered Anchovy Eggs

4 helpings

4 slices white bread	*4 eggs*
75g butter	*1 ×10ml spoon tarragon vinegar*
anchovy paste	

Garnish
chopped parsley

Toast the bread on both sides and cut off the crusts. Spread each slice with some butter and a little anchovy paste. Melt the remaining butter in a frying pan, and fry the eggs. Put 1 egg on each slice of toast and keep hot. Continue heating the butter with the vinegar until it browns, and pour it over the eggs. Garnish with the parsley and serve at once.

Peasant's Eggs

4 helpings

600g potatoes	*2 ×15ml spoons chopped parsley*
8 rashers bacon, without rinds	*salt and pepper*
4 ×15ml spoons oil	*4 eggs*
1 onion (50g approx)	*oil*

Peel and cut the potatoes into 7mm dice. Put into boiling salted water and blanch for 1–2 minutes; then drain. Cut the bacon rashers into strips. Heat the oil and fry the bacon for 2–3 minutes until crisp; remove and drain on soft kitchen paper. Skin and chop the onion. Fry the onion gently in the oil for 3–4 minutes until golden-brown and tender; then drain. Put the bacon and onion in an oven-proof dish and keep hot. Add the potatoes to the pan and fry gently for 5–6 minutes until cooked and brown. Drain and add to the bacon and onion with the parsley and seasoning. Mix lightly together and keep hot. Fry the eggs, adding more oil if necessary, arrange on the potato mixture, and serve at once.

POACHED EGGS

To poach an egg perfectly needs careful attention. Do not try to poach very fresh or stale eggs as the yolks break easily.

Eggs can be poached in water, stock or milk. Water is the usual medium. The liquid should simmer, not boil, as the movement will break up the egg white. Salt can be added to the water, to raise the temperature at which it simmers. A little vinegar or lemon juice can also be added to water or stock since the acid makes the egg white coagulate quickly and not break away from the yolk. Care must be taken when adding salt or acid, however, because too much will flavour the eggs.

Stock is used to poach an egg when extra flavour is wanted, but this flavour is delicate and should not be masked by a strongly flavoured accompaniment.

Eggs are poached in milk when the liquid is wanted for making a sauce.

Basic Method

Put 5cm water into a shallow pan and bring to simmering point. (The eggs are easier to remove from a shallow pan.) Break an egg into a cup or on to a saucer and slide the eggs into the water, holding the cup or saucer near the surface of the liquid. If necessary, gather the white together gently with a spoon and roll the egg over after a few seconds. This gives a more compact shape to the poached egg. Simmer gently, with the water hardly moving, for 2–3 minutes. Lift out the egg, using a perforated spoon or fish slice and drain well. Blot on soft kitchen paper to remove any excess liquid before serving. Providing the pan is big enough for them to cook without touching each other, 2 or 3 eggs can be poached at the same time.

More evenly shaped eggs can be produced by using plain pastry cutters as moulds. Put the required number of buttered 8cm cutters into the simmering water and break an egg into each. When the eggs are just set, remove the cutters and lift the eggs out.

Eggs can be poached in swirling water to give a neatly rounded shape. For this method, half fill a small pan with water, and when it is simmering, stir the water vigorously in one direction with a spoon. Slip the eggs into the centre of the whirlpool and the moving water should fold the white over the yolk.

If eggs are poached one at a time for serving together, slip each poached egg into a bowl of hand-hot water as soon as it is cooked to keep warm until all the eggs are ready. If the eggs are wanted cold, put them straight into cold water after poaching, to prevent them toughening. Cold poached eggs can be re-heated in fairly hot water; but it must not be very hot or the eggs will harden. Leave for a few minutes to warm through, drain, and serve.

Eggs can also be poached in a special egg poacher, although technically speaking they are steamed. The poacher consists of a shallow container, shaped like a frying pan, which is half filled with water. A tray fits on top, holding 1–4 cups made from metal or heat resisting material, and is covered by a lid. Put a small piece of butter into each cup, heat the pan and, when the water boils, break the eggs into the cups; season them lightly and cover with the lid. Simmer gently for 3–5 minutes until the eggs are lightly set. Loosen them round the edge with a knife and lift them out on to a serving dish with a spoon.

Poached Eggs in Potato Nests

4 helpings

600g potatoes	*salt and pepper*
400g onions	*ground nutmeg*
25g butter **or** *margarine*	*4 eggs*
1 × 15ml spoon top of	
the milk	

Peel the potatoes and cut them into fairly small pieces. Skin and slice the onions. Cook the potatoes and onions in boiling salted water for 10–12 minutes until tender. Drain, and return the pan to the heat for 1–2 minutes to dry them off. Mash the potatoes and onions together. Add the fat, milk, salt, pepper, and a little nutmeg. Beat with a wooden spoon until creamy. Divide the mixture between 4 individual dishes and make a hollow in the centre of each one. Keep hot with buttered paper. Poach the eggs. Drain and serve in the potato nests at once.

Alternatively, put the potato and onion mixture into 1 serving dish and make 4 hollows in which to place the eggs.

VARIATION

The potato can be flavoured with cheese. Omit the onion, add 150g grated cheese to the mashed potatoes, and cream them together.

Poached Eggs with Western Sauce

4 helpings

1 × 15ml spoon sugar	1 clove of garlic
1 × 15ml spoon paprika	3 × 15ml spoons butter
salt and pepper	or margarine
250ml tomato juice	1 × 5ml spoon cornflour
3 × 15ml spoons vinegar	200g rice
1 × 15ml spoon	8 eggs
Worcestershire sauce	1 × 5ml spoon water
1 onion	

Garnish
chopped parsley

Mix together the sugar, paprika, salt, pepper, tomato juice, vinegar, and Worcestershire sauce in a saucepan. Skin the onion and grate coarsely or chop very finely. Chop the garlic. Add the onion, garlic, and butter or margarine to the saucepan. Bring to the boil, stir well, reduce the heat, cover, and simmer for 20 minutes, stirring occasionally. Blend the cornflour with the water, and add a little of the sauce. Pour the blended mixture into the remaining sauce and stir well. Bring to the boil, stirring all the time, and boil for 1–2 minutes. Re-season if required, and keep hot.

Cook the rice in boiling salted water for 12–15 minutes, until tender. Meanwhile, poach the eggs.

Drain the rice and arrange on 4 individual dishes. Drain and blot the eggs with soft kitchen paper and put them on the rice. Pour the sauce over the eggs and garnish with the chopped parsley.

Eggs Florentine (2)

4 helpings

1kg fresh spinach **or**	salt and pepper
2 × 225g pkts frozen	mild French mustard
leaf spinach	4 eggs
50g butter	75g Gruyère cheese
25g flour	ground nutmeg
250ml milk	

Wash fresh spinach well and remove any coarse stalks. Put into a saucepan with just the water that clings to the leaves, cover, and cook gently for 10–15 minutes until tender, turning the spinach over occasionally. Cook frozen spinach according to the directions on the packet.

Melt 25g of the butter in a saucepan, add the flour, and stir with a wooden spoon until smooth. Cook over gentle heat for 2–3 minutes without colouring. Draw off the heat and add the milk gradually, stirring all the time. Bring to the boil and continue to stir until the sauce thickens. Season to taste with salt, pepper, and a little mustard.

Poach the eggs. Grate the cheese. Drain the spinach well, chop roughly, and re-heat with salt, pepper, a little nutmeg, and the remaining butter. Mix well and put into a hot serving dish. Re-heat the eggs if necessary, drain, and arrange on top of the spinach. Bring the sauce to the boil, remove from the heat, and stir in 50g of the cheese. Cover the eggs with the hot cheese sauce, sprinkle with the remaining grated cheese, and brown the surface under the grill.

Note For a more substantial dish, poach 8 eggs and put them close together on the spinach. Serve 2 eggs per person.

For Eggs Florentine (1) see p908.

Eggs Benedict

4 helpings

2 muffins **or** *4 slices*	*4 eggs*
white bread	*4 ×15ml spoons*
3 ×15ml spoons butter	*Hollandaise sauce*
4 slices ham	*(p712)*

Split the muffins in half and toast them, or toast the slices of bread on both sides and remove the crusts. Butter the hot muffins or toast. Trim the slices of ham to fit the bread. Put the trimmings on the hot muffins or toast and cover with the slices of ham. Keep warm. Poach the eggs, drain, and blot carefully with soft kitchen paper. Put 1 egg on each slice of ham and cover with 1 ×15ml spoon of Hollandaise sauce. Serve at once.

SCRAMBLED EGGS

Soft, creamy scrambled eggs are a delicate dish which must be cooked slowly over low heat, as the eggs become dry and granulated or watery through overcooking. When they thicken, remove from the heat at once, as they continue cooking in their own heat.

Scrambled Eggs

Basic recipe

4 helpings

50g butter	*2–3 ×15ml spoons top*
8 eggs	*of the milk* **or** *single*
salt and pepper	*cream*

Heat the butter in a heavy-bottomed frying or omelet pan. Beat the eggs, salt, and pepper together lightly. Before the butter begins to sizzle, pour the eggs into the pan. Reduce the heat to very low. Allow the eggs to set slightly round the sides and on the bottom of the pan. Then, using a wooden spoon or spatula, stir slowly and constantly. Run the spoon round the edge of the pan and draw the cooked egg into the centre. Draw the cooked egg up from the base of the pan. When most of the egg has set, remove the pan from the heat, add the milk or cream (which will stop any further cooking), and stir carefully until the eggs are evenly set into a soft, creamy mixture. Serve immediately.

Note 8 ×15ml spoons milk can be beaten in with the eggs and seasoning. Cook as above but do not add the milk or cream afterwards. Take particular care not to overcook the eggs using this method. Remove the pan from the heat while some of the egg is still liquid, since no cold milk is added to stop any further cooking.

VARIATIONS

Many flavourings can be added to scrambled egg to make a more substantial or tasty dish. If the flavouring does not need cooking, add it to the beaten egg before pouring into the pan. If the flavouring needs cooking, sauté it in the butter before adding the egg.

Add one or more of the following to the beaten eggs:
1) 1 ×15ml spoon chopped parsley
2) 1 ×10ml spoon chopped chives
3) 1 ×10ml spoon chopped spring onion
4) 1 × 5ml spoon dried herbs, eg tarragon or chervil
5) 1 × 5ml spoon curry powder
6) 100g grated cheese
7) 100g chopped cooked ham or tongue
8) 50g cooked shrimps
9) 50g flaked smoked salmon
10) 1 × 5ml spoon anchovy essence (omit the salt and garnish with anchovy fillets).

Add one or more of the following to the butter in the pan:
1) 4 rashers of bacon, without rinds and chopped (use less butter)
2) 100g sliced mushrooms
3) 4 peeled tomatoes, chopped.

Scrambled egg can also be served on buttered toast spread with a little meat extract or fish paste, on fried bread, in pastry cases, tomato cups or baked potatoes.

Fish Scramble

4 helpings

250g smoked haddock	4 eggs
150ml milk	salt
pepper	25g butter

Put the haddock into a pan, pour the milk over it, and add some pepper. Bring to the boil, reduce the heat and simmer for 10 minutes, until the fish will separate into flakes easily. Drain, remove the skin and bones, and flake the flesh.

Beat together lightly the eggs, 4 × 15ml spoons of the milk, and a little salt. Melt the butter in a pan, add the haddock, and re-heat the fish. Pour the beaten eggs over the haddock, reduce the heat, and cook gently, stirring all the time, until the mixture is just set and creamy. Serve at once on buttered toast.

VARIATION

Use 250g of any white fish instead of the smoked haddock. This gives a dish with a more delicate flavour suitable for someone on a light diet.

Pipérade Basque

4 helpings

2 onions	50g butter
2 red or green peppers	salt and pepper
or 1 × 175g can	6 eggs
pimentos	3 × 15ml spoons milk
400g tomatoes	
1 clove of garlic	
(optional)	

Skin the onion and slice it thinly. Cut the peppers into quarters and remove the seeds and membranes. Slice the flesh thinly. Drain canned pimentos and dice them. Skin the tomatoes, cut them into quarters, de-seed and chop the flesh roughly. Crush or chop the garlic, if used. Melt the butter and fry the peppers (if used) for about 5 minutes, add the onions and garlic, and continue cooking gently for 5 minutes until softened. Add the tomatoes and pimentos (if used) and cook for a further 2–3 minutes. Season generously. Beat the eggs lightly together with the milk, and when the vegetables are mushy, pour in the eggs. Reduce the heat and cook gently, stirring all the time, until just set and creamy. Serve at once with chunks of bread.

Note Pipérade, a famous dish from the Basque country, is often served topped with fried rashers of bacon.

SAVOURY CUSTARDS

Baked and steamed custards are familiar as sweet dishes, but a savoury set custard makes an unusual and tasty lunch or supper dish. As it has a high food value and is easily digested, a plain savoury custard is ideal for many people on a light diet. Savoury custards are baked or steamed in the same way as sweet custards (see p963).

Beef Tea Custard

4 helpings

butter for greasing	4 eggs
500ml water	pepper
2 × 10ml spoons beef	
extract	

Grease four 200ml ovenproof dishes or custard cups. Warm the water and stir in the beef extract until it is completely dissolved. Beat the eggs together lightly and season with pepper. Stir in the dissolved beef extract. Strain the custard mixture into the dishes or cups, cover with greased foil or greaseproof paper, and place on a heatproof plate or in a steamer over simmering water. Cover and steam very gently for about 20 minutes until just firm in the centre. Serve in the dishes or cups.

Note Beef tea custard can be cut into dice and added to clear soups.

Chicken Custard

4 helpings

butter for greasing
300g cooked chicken
500ml milk

4 eggs
salt and pepper

Grease a 750ml ovenproof dish. Remove any bones from the chicken and mince the flesh. Put the minced chicken into the dish. Warm the milk. Beat the eggs, salt, and pepper together lightly and stir in the milk. Strain the custard into the dish. Stand the dish in a shallow tin containing enough warm water to come half-way up the sides of the dish. Bake in a cool oven at 150°C, Gas 2, for 1½ hours or until the custard is set in the centre.

Alternatively, put the chicken custard into a greased basin, cover with greased foil or grease-proof paper and steam very gently for 45–50 minutes until just set in the centre.

Cheese and Asparagus Custard

4 helpings

1 bundle small **or** sprue
  asparagus **or** 225g
  canned **or** frozen
  asparagus
100g cheese

butter for greasing
4 eggs
salt and pepper
500ml milk

Cook fresh asparagus as directed on p746. Drain canned asparagus or cook frozen asparagus according to the directions on the packet. Grate the cheese. Cut the asparagus into short lengths and put into a greased 750ml ovenproof dish, with the tips arranged on the top. Sprinkle the grated cheese over the asparagus. Beat the eggs, salt, and pepper together lightly and stir in the milk. Strain the custard into the dish. Stand the dish in a shallow tin containing enough warm water to come half-way up the sides of the dish. Bake in a cool oven at 150°C, Gas 2, for 1½ hours or until the custard is set in the centre.

Alternatively the custard can be steamed.

Bacon and Mushroom Custard

4 helpings

200g bacon rashers,
  without rinds
oil for shallow frying
fat for greasing
100g onions
200g mushrooms

4 eggs
salt and pepper
500ml milk
4 × 15ml spoons
  chopped parsley

Chop the bacon rashers into small pieces. Heat the oil and fry the bacon until crisp. Drain well and put into a greased 750ml ovenproof dish. Skin and chop the onion finely and fry for about 5 minutes until tender, adding a little oil if necessary. Drain and add to the bacon. Clean and slice the mushrooms finely and sauté them in the same pan. Drain well and mix with the bacon and onion. Beat the eggs, salt, and pepper together lightly and stir in the milk. Strain the custard into the dish. Stand the dish in a shallow tin containing enough warm water to come half-way up the sides of the dish. Bake in a cool oven, 150°C, Gas 2, for 1½ hours, or until the custard is set in the centre.

Alternatively the custard can be steamed.

Cheese, Bacon, and Chive Custard

4 helpings

200g bacon rashers,
  without rinds
butter for greasing
200g cheese
4 eggs

salt and pepper
500ml milk
4 × 15ml spoons
  chopped chives

Cut the bacon rashers into small pieces and fry until crisp. Drain well and put into a greased 750ml ovenproof dish. Grate the cheese and add to the bacon. Beat the eggs, salt, and pepper together and stir in the milk. Strain the custard into the dish and add the chives. Stand the dish in a shallow tin containing enough warm water to come half-way up the sides of the dish. Bake in a cool oven at 150°C, Gas 2, for 1½ hours or until the custard is set in the centre.

Alternatively the custard can be steamed.

Fish Custard

4 helpings

500g sole **or** *plaice fillets*	*4 eggs*
butter for greasing	*1 × 2.5ml spoon grated lemon rind*
500ml milk	*salt and pepper*

Skin the fish fillets, if liked. Arrange the fillets in the bottom of a greased 750ml ovenproof dish. Warm the milk but do not boil it. Beat the eggs, lemon rind, salt, and pepper together lightly and stir in the milk. Strain the custard into the dish. Stand the dish in a shallow tin containing enough water to come half-way up the sides of the dish. Bake in a cool oven at 150°C, Gas 2, for 1½ hours or until the custard is set in the centre.

Alternatively the custard can be steamed.

Note 500g fresh or smoked cod or haddock can be used instead of sole or plaice.

VARIATION

Put the fish and milk into a pan, bring to the boil and simmer gently for 10 minutes. Drain the fish, remove any skin or bones, and flake the flesh. Use the warm, not hot, fish-flavoured milk to make the custard, making the amount up to 500ml if necessary. Put the flaked fish into the dish, strain the custard over it, and proceed as above.

Spinach Custard

4 helpings

1kg fresh spinach **or** *2 × 225g pkts frozen leaf spinach*	*2 × 150g cartons natural yoghurt*
salt and pepper	*100g cheese*
ground nutmeg	*200ml milk*
butter for greasing	*2 eggs*
	a pinch of dry mustard

Wash fresh spinach thoroughly. Cook gently, with only the water that clings to the leaves, for 10–15 minutes, until tender. Chop the spinach and drain well. Thaw frozen spinach and drain well. Flavour the spinach with salt, pepper, and a little ground nutmeg. Grease a 750ml ovenproof dish and put in the spinach. Tip the yoghurt into a basin and mix with a fork until the curd is evenly broken down. Grate the cheese. Stir the cheese, milk, eggs, and mustard briskly into the yoghurt. Pour on to the spinach. Stand the dish in a shallow tin containing enough warm water to come half-way up the sides of the dish. Bake in a cool oven at 150°C, Gas 2, for 1½ hours or until the custard is set in the centre.

HOT SOUFFLÉS

A soufflé is a feather-light dish consisting, basically, of a well-flavoured panada and stiffly whisked egg whites. Its lightness derives from the air trapped by whisking the egg whites, and is held by 'setting' the egg white by heating it. A true soufflé is a hot dish and is usually baked, although steamed soufflés (more like very light steamed puddings) are an alternative. A cold soufflé, whether savoury or sweet, is really a mousse or mousseline; it can be made in various ways, but always contains stiffly whisked egg whites set with gelatine. Cream and other preparations are sometimes very stiffly whisked so that they look like (and are named) soufflés, but they are in fact mousses and should be so called.

A soufflé is usually cooked and served in a special china soufflé dish with straight sides, although any fairly deep ovenproof dish or tin of the right size can be used, provided it will look good on the table. It is prepared by tying a band of paper tightly round it (see below). This supports a hot soufflé as it rises, and a cold mixture until it has set. It is removed for serving so that the soufflé has a distinctive appearance, rising 7–8cm above the rim of the dish. The dish must always be prepared before starting to make a soufflé so that the mixture can be turned into it as soon as it is ready.

To Prepare a Soufflé Dish or Tin

Cut a strip from two thicknesses of greaseproof paper or vegetable parchment 8cm taller than the dish and long enough to go right round the dish with an overlap. Tie the paper round the dish with string. If the dish has sloping sides or a projecting rim, secure the paper above and below the rim with gummed tape or pins. Make sure that the paper is uncreased and forms a neat round shape. Grease the inside of the dish and paper collar for a hot soufflé with clarified butter or oil. Oil the inside of the collar for a cold soufflé. When the soufflé is ready for the table, ease the paper away from its sides with the blade of a knife.

Preparing a soufflé dish can be tricky, and it is not essential to use a paper collar. A soufflé can be baked without one, although it will not rise as much as when a collar is used. A cold soufflé can be set in a dish big enough to hold all the mixture.

If a paper collar is used, put any of the following hot soufflés into an 800ml dish; otherwise use a 1 litre dish. Use a paper collar if the recipe tells you to prepare a soufflé dish before making the soufflé.

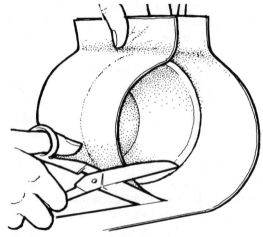

Cutting a strip to go round a soufflé dish with an overlap.

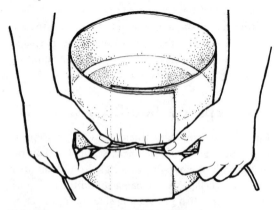

Tying the paper round the dish with string.

Making a Hot Soufflé

First set the oven to heat or get a steamer ready to use. Then prepare the soufflé dish or tin. Grease the inside and dust it with fine dried breadcrumbs or grated Parmesan cheese for a savoury soufflé, and with caster sugar for a sweet soufflé. Put the dish on a baking tray or plate to make handling easier.

Hot soufflés are usually made from a very thick white sauce or panada, which must be free from lumps. To make the panada, add the milk gradually to the roux, beating well after each addition. Cook thoroughly, remove from the heat, then beat until the sauce leaves the sides of the pan. If undercooked, the flavour will be poor; if overcooked, the soufflé will be greasy and heavy. The sauce must be cooled enough for the egg yolks to be beaten in without coagulating, but not so cool that the yolks are difficult to mix in and the mixture becomes lumpy. Flavourings and seasoning are added at this stage, and must be strong because the bland flavour of the whisked egg whites will dilute them. Taste the mixture carefully.

Sometimes the panada is replaced by a thick semolina or vegetable purée.

The panada is lightened by adding egg whites whisked very stiffly until they stand in peaks but are not dry. Stir a small quantity of the whites into the main mixture first, to lighten it. Then fold in the rest carefully, using a metal spoon. Fold lightly and quickly, cutting down through the mixture. Do not overmix, beat or stir rapidly as the light fluffy whites will release their air and the soufflé will not rise.

Put the soufflé mixture into the prepared dish; it must not be more than three-quarters full if not using a collar.

Instead of using a collar, the dish can be about seven-eighths full and a deep incision made in the mixture, 2cm from the edge. The centre of the soufflé will then rise above the rest. The soufflé must be served immediately it is cooked. The mixture falls very quickly after removal from the heat.

Baked Soufflés

Baked soufflés are served in the dish in which they

are cooked; this can be one large dish or individual ovenproof dishes. Preheat the oven and cook the soufflé in the centre of the oven. The heat circulating all round the soufflé makes the air in the mixture expand evenly, so causing the soufflé to rise. A cold draught or jolting the oven may make the mixture fall, so avoid opening the oven door needlessly during cooking. If it must be opened, always close it very gently. When cooked, the soufflé should have risen 5–7cm, be browned and firm on the outside, and creamy inside. To test whether the soufflé is ready, open the oven door after 30 minutes and give the dish a slight shake without removing it. If the crust moves much in the centre, leave for 4–8 minutes longer.

Steamed Soufflés

Steamed soufflés may be old-fashioned but are still very good. The dish must have a collar and a well-greased circle of greaseproof paper for the top, to prevent water drops falling on the surface of the soufflé. Simmer the water very gently; too much heat will make the soufflé rise too quickly and then collapse before it is cooked. A two-tiered steamer is the best pan, but if this is not available, put an inverted saucer in the bottom of a pan and stand the soufflé on this.

Steamed soufflés are usually turned out after cooking. Metal charlotte moulds, wider at the top than at the bottom, are ideal; or a cake tin with the base lined with greased greaseproof paper can be used. These soufflés are very delicate. Remove the paper and string, and allow the soufflé to stand for 2–3 minutes to shrink slightly from the sides. Ease it away gently from the tin, using the flat of a knife and very light pressure. Turn it over on to a hot dish and draw the tin off very carefully so as not to damage the soufflé. Serve with a sauce.

If preparing a soufflé for a dinner party, the base can be made up earlier in the day. Make the sauce, add the flavouring and egg yolks, and leave covered with damp greaseproof paper or foil until required. Re-heat until just warm, whisk the egg whites, and finish the dish.

The completed mixture can be left to stand for up to one hour, provided it is protected from draughts. Cover with a large bowl. It will stand up to 4 hours in the refrigerator. (Remember that a chilled soufflé will take 5–10 minutes longer to cook.)

Note Other soufflé recipes can be found in the chapter on Light Dishes for One or Two.

For hot sweet soufflés, see pp975–77.

Savoury Soufflé

Basic recipe

4 helpings

50g butter	salt and pepper
5 × 15ml spoons flour	4 eggs
250ml milk	1 egg white

Heat the oven to fairly hot, 190°C, Gas 5, or put the steamer on to heat. Prepare the soufflé dish (pp919–20). Melt the butter in a pan, stir in the flour, and cook slowly for 2–3 minutes, stirring all the time. Add the milk gradually and beat until smooth. Cook for another 1–2 minutes, still stirring all the time. Remove the pan from the heat and beat hard until the sauce comes away from the sides of the pan cleanly. Put into a bowl, season well, and add any flavouring (see variations). Separate the eggs and beat the yolks into the mixture one by one. Whisk all the egg whites until stiff. Using a metal spoon, stir 1 spoonful into the mixture and then fold in the rest until evenly distributed. Put into the prepared dish. Bake in the centre of the oven for 30–35 minutes, until well risen and browned; or cover with greaseproof paper and steam for one hour until just firm to the touch.

Serve immediately with hot buttered toast.

Note Individual hot soufflés make a very good starter, a light main course or a savoury finish to a meal. The quantity of mixture above will make 6 individual soufflés in 200ml dishes, and will take 20 minutes to bake, 25–30 minutes to steam.

The flavour of some soufflés, such as those made with fish or white meat, can be very bland, so it is wise to infuse the milk with plenty of flavouring as when making a Béchamel sauce (p704).

For **Variations**, see over.

VARIATIONS

Asparagus Soufflé

Cook 200g frozen asparagus according to the directions on the packet or drain 200g canned asparagus. Chop it, and fold into the savoury soufflé mixture.

Cheese Soufflé

Reduce the flour to 25g and add 100–150g grated Cheddar cheese or 75–100g mixed grated Parmesan and Gruyère cheese, and $\frac{1}{2} \times 2.5$ml spoon dry mustard or a pinch of Cayenne pepper.

Cheese and Onion Soufflé

Add 50g very finely chopped onion sautéed in the butter for 2–3 minutes until transparent, to the cheese flavouring in the above variation.

Cheese and Watercress Soufflé

Chop the leaves from half a bunch of watercress and add to the cheese flavouring for the Cheese Soufflé.

Layered Cheese Soufflé

Put half the mixture into the dish and add a layer of 75g sautéed mushrooms, or 100g cooked flaked fish, or 3×15ml spoons spinach purée and then the remaining mixture.

Oeufs Mollets en Soufflé

Soft boil 4 small eggs (Oeufs Mollets p909). Put one-third of the cheese soufflé mixture into the dish. Arrange the eggs on top. Add the remainder of the mixture and bake.

Chicken Soufflé(2)

Add 200g cooked minced chicken, 25g chopped sautéed onion, 2×15ml spoons lemon juice, and 1×5ml spoon chopped parsley.

For other chicken soufflé recipes, see p642 and p1403.

Crab Soufflé

Add 200g flaked crabmeat, a few drops of Tabasco sauce, and 2×15ml spoons dry white wine.

Ham or Ham and Tongue Soufflé(1)

Make a sauce using 125ml stock and 125ml tomato juice. Add 150g minced meat, 1×10ml spoon chopped parsley, grated nutmeg, and Cayenne pepper.

Salmon Soufflé

Add 150g cooked salmon to 100ml Béchamel sauce (p704).

Smoked Haddock Soufflé

Cook 200g smoked haddock in the milk. Use the milk to make the sauce and then add the flaked fish, 50g grated mild cheese such as Gruyère, and a pinch of ground nutmeg. (Do not add too much salt.)

Smoked Salmon Soufflé

Add 100g chopped smoked salmon trimmings, 100g full-fat soft cheese, and 1×15ml spoon lemon juice.

Soufflé Panache

Divide the sauce into 2 portions. Flavour 1 portion with 50g cheese and the other portion with 2×15ml spoons spinach purée. Add 2 egg yolks and half the whisked white to each part. Spoon the mixtures alternately into the prepared dish.

Tomato Soufflé

Use tomato juice or fresh tomato pulp in place of the milk.

Ham and Tongue Soufflé(2)

3–4 helpings

75g cooked ham	200ml brown stock
75g cooked tongue	(p329)
200g fresh **or** canned	2 × 5ml spoons chopped
tomatoes	parsley
3 × 15ml spoons butter	salt and pepper
or margarine	3 eggs
5 × 15ml spoons flour	fat for greasing

Remove all the skin and bone from the meat, and mince it. Chop the tomatoes and rub them through a sieve to make a purée. Heat the oven to moderate, 180°C, Gas 4. Melt the fat in a saucepan, add the flour, and cook for 2–3 minutes; then add the stock, puréed tomatoes, and parsley, and heat to boiling point, stirring all the time. Sprinkle in the meat, season to taste, and cook for a further 3 minutes. Cool slightly. Separate the eggs. Add the yolks to the sauce one at a time. Whisk the whites until stiff and fold them in lightly. Pour the mixture into a well-greased soufflé dish. Bake in the centre of the oven for 30–45 minutes or until it is well-risen and firm. Serve immediately.

Potato Soufflé(1)

4 helpings

500g potatoes	125ml top of the milk
3 eggs	2 × 15ml spoons
100g Cheddar cheese	chopped parsley
salt and pepper	1 egg white
grated nutmeg	butter for greasing
50g butter	

Peel the potatoes and cook in boiling salted water until tender. Separate the eggs. Grate the cheese finely. Mash the potatoes and put them through a sieve. Add a generous amount of salt, pepper, and nutmeg, and the rest of the ingredients except the egg whites. Beat well with a wooden spoon until smooth.

Heat the oven to fairly hot, 190°C, Gas 5. Whisk all the egg whites until stiff. Using a metal spoon, stir 1 spoonful into the potato mixture and then fold in the rest carefully. Put into a greased 1 litre soufflé dish and bake in the centre of the oven for 30–35 minutes, until well risen and browned.

Serve with grilled bacon and tomatoes.

Note For Potato Soufflé (2), see p1335.

VARIATIONS

Meat and Potato Soufflé

Make as for Potato Soufflé using 350g potatoes. Omit the cheese, and stir in 150g minced cooked beef or lamb and 1 × 15ml spoon brown table sauce.

Fish and Potato Soufflé

Make as for Potato Soufflé using 350g potatoes. Poach 200g white fish, cod or haddock, for 10 minutes in the milk. Drain, remove any skin or bone from the fish, and flake the flesh. Omit the cheese and add the flaked fish, the milk made up to 125ml if necessary, and a few drops of anchovy essence, if liked.

Fish and Rice Soufflé

4 helpings

500g cod **or** haddock	a piece of lemon rind
fillets	50g rice
500ml milk	salt and pepper
a slice of onion	3 eggs
6 peppercorns	1 egg white
1 small bay leaf	butter for greasing

Poach the fish in half the milk with the onion, peppercorns, bay leaf, and lemon rind for 10–15 minutes or until tender. Simmer the rice in the remaining milk for 15 minutes. Strain the milk from the fish and add it to the rice. Skin and bone the fish, flake the flesh, and add it to the rice and milk. Season generously. Heat the oven to fairly hot, 190°C, Gas 5. Separate the eggs and stir the yolks into the fish and rice mixture. Whisk all the whites until stiff, and fold in. Put into a greased 1 litre soufflé dish and bake in the centre of the oven for 30–35 minutes until well risen and browned.

Shrimp and Parmesan Soufflé

4 helpings

4 eggs
250ml coating white sauce (p692)
150g peeled shrimps or small prawns
50g grated Parmesan cheese

1 × 5ml spoon concentrated tomato purée
1 × 2.5ml spoon mixed English mustard
butter for greasing

Separate the eggs. Make or re-heat the white sauce. Add the shrimps, cheese, tomato purée, and mustard to the hot sauce. Heat the oven to fairly hot, 200°C, Gas 6. When the sauce has cooled slightly, beat in the egg yolks. Whisk the whites until stiff. Fold the egg whites into the sauce as lightly as possible. Pour the mixture very gently into a prepared soufflé dish. Bake in the centre of the oven for 30–35 minutes. Serve immediately.

Spinach Soufflé

4 helpings

25g butter
3 × 10ml spoons flour
125g spinach purée
125ml single cream

50g finely grated cheese
salt and pepper
4 eggs
1 egg white

Garnish (optional)
grated Parmesan cheese

Heat the oven to fairly hot, 190°C, Gas 5, or put a steamer on to heat. Melt the butter in a saucepan, stir in the flour, and cook slowly for 2–3 minutes, stirring all the time. Stir in the spinach purée, and add the cream gradually, still stirring. Cook for another 1–2 minutes. Remove the pan from the heat, stir in the cheese, and beat hard until the panada comes away from the sides of the pan cleanly. Put into a bowl and season generously. Separate the eggs, and beat the yolks into the mixture one by one. Whisk all the egg whites until stiff. Using a metal spoon, stir 1 spoonful of the whisked white into the mixture, and fold in the rest until evenly distributed. Put into a prepared soufflé dish. Bake in the centre of the oven for 30–35 minutes, until well risen and browned.

Alternatively, cover lightly with greaseproof paper, and steam for 1 hour until just firm to the touch. Sprinkle with grated Parmesan cheese, if liked.

Serve immediately with crisp cheese-flavoured biscuits, or cheese straws (p1290).

OMELETS

There are two basic kinds of omelet. A savoury omelet is usually made with beaten whole eggs, and folded into 3 layers or into half, depending on the filling. A Spanish omelet is generally unfolded, the top surface being lightly browned under a grill. A sweet omelet is usually made with separated eggs, the whites being whisked until stiff to give a puffed or soufflé omelet. It is always folded in half.

Making an Omelet

The general method is identical for both savoury and sweet omelets. Before starting, have all the equipment and ingredients to hand, ready-prepared, including the chosen filling and a plate on which to serve the omelet. An omelet must never be kept waiting.

Do not overcook an omelet. It should be just set but still moist, the texture soft and creamy, yet with no part still distinctly liquid and raw. It should never resemble scrambled eggs or pancakes. Rapid cooking, and quick, deft manipulation of the egg mixture as it sets are the keys to success; slow cooking or overcooking make an omelet tough and leathery.

Equipment

The ideal omelet pan is a small, thick-based aluminium or cast iron pan, used only for omelets or pancakes. A pan with sloping sides is the best shape as the omelet can be loosened more easily. But any *thick*, *flat* frying pan will do. It must be thick to hold enough heat to cook the omelet quickly as the mixture should not be over the heat for longer than 2 minutes, and the pan must be flat to produce an even omelet. Use a pan 15cm in diameter for a 2–3 egg omelet, 18–20cm for a 4 egg omelet. If it is too big, the omelet will be thin and tough, if too small, the eggs will cook unevenly.

Many frying pans are non-stick and easy to use, but they are not really suitable for omelets as the pan has to be heated before adding the egg mixture and this is not recommended for non-stick pans. Keep one special well-seasoned pan for omelets. Any new aluminium or iron frying pan has to be seasoned anyhow before use. If using a frying pan which is used for general frying, it is also a good idea to season it, before cooking an omelet in it, to prevent sticking.

To season a pan for omelets, put a knob of butter or a little cooking oil into the pan and heat it slowly; sprinkle in a little salt, and rub the inside of the pan vigorously with a pad of soft kitchen paper.

To heat the pan before cooking an omelet, place it over very gentle heat a few minutes beforehand and heat it evenly right to the edges. Avoid using a fierce heat, as this causes it to heat unevenly. When the pan is ready, it will feel comfortably hot if you hold the back of your hand about 3cm away from the surface.

Use a flat tool such as a spatula or palette knife for folding the omelet.

Do not wash an omelet pan after using it. Rub it over with soft kitchen paper, then wipe it with a clean cloth. If egg is still sticking to the pan, put it over gentle heat, add a little salt and rub vigorously with a small pad of soft kitchen paper. The salt, being gritty, cleans and smooths the surface perfectly.

Ingredients

The best fat to use for frying omelets is clarified butter, but unsalted butter or margarine can be used. (Salt makes the omelet stick.) Clarified bacon fat is good and gives added flavour to a savoury omelet.

Water is usually added to the beaten egg to make a light omelet. Milk makes the omelet rich and creamy.

The following recipes are for one or two helpings only, since a large, unwieldy pan is needed to make a simple omelet for more than two people. If more than two helpings are needed, make two or more omelets.

For sweet omelets, see pp977–78.

Plain Omelet

Basic recipe

1 helping

2 eggs	1 × 15ml spoon unsalted
salt and pepper	butter **or** margarine
1 × 15ml spoon water	

Break the eggs into a basin, season with salt and pepper, add the water, and beat lightly with a fork. Place the pan over gentle heat and when it is hot, add the butter or margarine. Tilt the pan so that the whole surface is greased lightly. Do not overheat or let the butter brown. Without drawing the pan off the heat, pour the beaten eggs on to the hot fat. Leave to stand for 10 seconds; then with the back of the prongs of a fork, or with a spatula, draw the mixture gently from the sides to the centre as it sets and let the liquid egg from the centre run to the sides. Repeat this once or twice more, as necessary. Do not stir round, or it will become scrambled eggs. In about 1 minute, the egg will have set softly. Leave it to cook for a further 4–5 seconds until it is golden underneath. Remove the pan from the heat. Loosen the edges by shaking the pan or using a round-bladed knife. Tilt the pan slightly towards you, and as the omelet slides up the side of the pan towards the handle, use a palette knife or spatula to fold this third of the omelet towards the centre. Raise the handle of the pan, slide the omelet up the side furthest from the handle, and fold over the opposite third, also towards the centre.

Change your grip on the pan so that your hand is underneath the handle and it runs across the palm between the thumb and forefinger. Hold the plate in the other hand, and with a quick movement, tip the omelet on to it, folded sides underneath.

For **filled omelets**, see over.

Filled Omelets

Any plain omelet can be filled. Some flavourings are added to the beaten eggs and some are added to the omelet just before it is folded.

Add to the beaten eggs one of the following:

Cheese Omelet

Grate 50g cheese and mix 40g with the eggs; sprinkle the rest over the omelet just before serving it.

Omelette Fines Herbes

Add 1 × 2.5ml spoon chopped tarragon, 1 × 2.5ml spoon chopped chervil, 1 × 5ml spoon chopped parsley, and a few chopped chives or 1 × 5ml spoon mixed dried herbs.

Fish Omelet

Add 50g flaked cooked fish.

Ham or Tongue Omelet

Add 50g chopped meat and 1 × 5ml spoon chopped parsley.

Onion Omelet

Chop 25g onion and sauté in butter in a saucepan until tender, ie about 5 minutes.

Put one or more of the following into the centre of the omelet before folding. Fold in half, rather than in thirds.

Bacon Omelet

Chop 2 rashers of rindless bacon; fry in a saucepan until crisp.

Mushroom Omelet

Clean and slice 50g mushrooms and cook in butter, in a saucepan, until soft.

Omelette Provençale

Mix together one skinned and chopped tomato, a little garlic, 50g finely chopped onion, 1 × 15ml spoon chopped parsley, a little chopped fresh tarragon, salt and pepper. Sauté in a little butter for 5 minutes, until the onion is tender.

Shrimp or Prawn Omelet

Sauté 50g shrimps or prawns in a little butter in a saucepan; add a squeeze of lemon juice.

Tomato Omelet

Peel and chop 1–2 tomatoes and fry in a little butter for 5 minutes, until soft and pulpy. Add $\frac{1}{2}$ × 15ml spoon chopped parsley.

If a 3-egg omelet is filled with a substantial filling it will make 2 helpings. Omelets of this type are:

Chicken Omelet

Chop 50g cooked chicken and heat gently in a little white sauce.

Fish and Cheese Omelet

Flake 50g cooked fish and heat gently in a little cheese sauce.

Kidney Omelet

Skin, core, and chop 1–2 lamb's kidneys; add 1 × 15ml spoon finely chopped onion and fry lightly in a saucepan until tender.

Prawn and Mushroom Omelet

Melt 25g butter, and sauté 25g chopped mushrooms; remove from the butter, and keep hot. Make a sauce using the butter, 3 × 10ml spoons flour, and 125ml milk. Add the mushrooms and 50g coarsely chopped prawns. Re-heat and season before filling the omelet.

Stacked Omelets

These serve four or more people. Make up three or four types of filling, such as shrimps mixed with a little cream, chopped mushrooms fried with onions, and grated cheese. Make a plain omelet and slide it on to a plate standing over hot water. Top with a filling. Make a second omelet and lay it over the first. Top with another type of filling. Repeat, allowing at least 1 omelet per person. To serve, cut the stack into wedge-shaped pieces.

Breadcrumb Omelet

2 helpings

25g soft white	*4 eggs*
breadcrumbs	*salt and pepper*
50ml milk	*2 ×10ml spoons butter*

Put the crumbs in a basin, add the milk, and leave to stand for 10 minutes. Separate the eggs. Stir the yolks into the crumb mixture and season. Whisk the whites until stiff and fold in. Heat the pan and melt the butter. Make an omelet in the usual way (pp924–25).

Note Some people find this omelet more digestible than an ordinary omelet as it is less rich. It can be filled in any of the same ways.

Polish Omelet

4 helpings

2 slices white bread	*1 × 5ml spoon finely*
butter for shallow frying	*chopped parsley*
4 eggs	*1 × 5ml spoon finely*
2 ×15ml spoons milk	*chopped chives*
salt and pepper	

Cut the crusts off the bread and cut the slices into 1cm dice. Heat the butter in a pan and fry the bread until golden-brown and crisp. Drain on soft kitchen paper. Beat the eggs until liquid and add the fried bread and the other ingredients. Melt 2 ×15ml spoonfuls butter in the pan. Add the egg mixture and cook over gentle heat as for a plain omelet (p925). Serve unfolded.

Omelette Paysanne

2 helpings

4 rashers bacon, without	*1 × 5ml spoon chopped*
rinds	*chives*
25g butter	*4 eggs*
2 cooked potatoes	*salt and pepper*
1 × 5ml spoon chopped	
parsley	

Chop the bacon and fry it until crisp in an 18–20cm frying pan. Drain well and put on to a plate to keep warm. Heat the butter in the pan. Dice the potatoes and fry in the fat until golden-brown. Return the bacon to the pan, with the parsley and chives. Beat the eggs lightly, season, and pour into the pan. Stir once or twice, and leave to cook slowly, shaking the pan from time to time to prevent the omelet sticking. When the underside is lightly and evenly browned, brown the second side under the grill or turn the omelet over and cook the other side.

Omelet Arnold Bennett

2 helpings

150g smoked haddock	*2 eggs*
2 ×15ml spoons	*salt and pepper*
clarified (p886) *or*	*2 ×15ml spoons grated*
unsalted butter	*Parmesan cheese*
50ml single cream	

Poach the haddock in water for 10 minutes. Drain, remove any skin or bones, and flake the flesh into a bowl. Add 1 ×15ml spoon of butter and 1 ×15ml spoon of cream. Mix well together. Separate the eggs. Beat the yolks with $\frac{1}{2}$ ×15ml spoon cream and season to taste. Mix together the yolks, haddock, and half the cheese. Whisk the egg whites until stiff, and fold them into the fish mixture. Heat half the remaining butter in an omelet pan. Heat the grill. Pour half the mixture into the hot pan and cook quickly until golden-brown underneath. Sprinkle over half the remaining cheese, spoon over 1 ×15ml spoon cream, and brown quickly under the grill. Do not fold. Very quickly, make a second omelet in the same way. Serve at once.

Spanish Omelet

(Tortilla)

2 helpings

1 onion	*1 × 15ml spoon chopped*
2 tomatoes	*parsley*
2 cold boiled potatoes	*4 eggs*
2 canned pimentos	*salt and pepper*
oil or unsalted butter for frying	

Skin and chop the onion and tomatoes. Dice the potatoes. Chop the pimentos. Heat the oil or butter in an 18–20cm frying pan. Fry the onion for about 5 minutes until soft but not coloured. Add the tomatoes, potatoes, pimentos, and parsley. Heat through thoroughly. Beat the eggs, and season well. Pour over the vegetables, stir once or twice, and then leave to cook slowly, shaking the pan from time to time to prevent the omelet sticking. When the underside of the omelet is lightly and evenly browned, brown the second side under a moderate grill. Alternatively, turn the omelet and fry the second side.

Note To turn a very thick omelet, use a plate. When the first side is browned, cover the omelet with a plate and turn the pan, omelet, and plate over together so that the omelet falls on to the plate. Slide the omelet off the plate back into the pan, browned side uppermost.

Friday Omelet

2 helpings

200g smoked haddock	*50g Gruyère cheese*
100ml milk	*125ml cheese sauce*
2 eggs	*(p693)*
pepper and salt	

Poach the smoked haddock in the milk; then drain and flake it. Beat the eggs, season with pepper, but very little salt, and add the fish. Cook as for a plain omelet (p925), but do not fold it. Slide it on to a warm plate. Grate the Gruyère cheese. Pour the cheese sauce over the omelet, top with the grated cheese, and brown quickly under a hot grill.

Oven Omelet

2 helpings

4 rashers streaky bacon, without rinds	*4 eggs*
	125ml milk
½ onion	*salt and pepper*
2 × 15ml spoons chopped parsley	*100g strong cheese*

Chop the bacon and fry until crisp. Drain well and put it in a deep 23cm pie plate. Skin and chop the onion. Fry it in the bacon fat for about 5 minutes until tender. Add to the bacon with the chopped parsley. Beat the eggs and milk together, season, and pour on to the plate. Grate the cheese and sprinkle over the top. Bake in the centre of a moderate oven at 180°C, Gas 4, for 30 minutes, until golden-brown.

Mushroom Oven Omelet

2 helpings

200g mushrooms	*2 × 15ml spoons double cream*
50g unsalted butter or margarine	
	1 × 15ml spoon dry sherry
salt and pepper	
1 × 15ml spoon flour	*4 eggs*
250ml milk	

Clean and slice the mushrooms. Heat the butter, and sauté the mushrooms for about 3 minutes until tender. Season with salt and pepper. Add the flour and stir over heat for 1 minute. Stir in 125ml of the milk gradually, bring to the boil, and cook for 1–2 minutes, stirring all the time. Remove from the heat, allow to cool slightly, and then stir in the cream and sherry. Put into a deep 23cm pie plate. Beat the eggs and remaining milk together and pour this over the mushroom mixture. Bake in the centre of a moderate oven at 180°C, Gas 4, for 30 minutes until golden-brown.

BATTERS AND FRIED FOODS

Do not scrub the inside of your frying-pan, as, after this operation, any preparation fried is liable to catch or burn in the pan. If the pan has become black inside, rub it with a hard crust of bread, and wash in hot water, mixed with a little soda.

Frying

Frying is a method of cooking food rapidly, at a high temperature, in fat or oil. The heat should be high enough to seal the surface of the food immediately it comes in contact with the hot fat, so that very little juice, mineral content or flavour are lost. As the cooking is quick, not all foods are suitable for frying. The best are good quality meat, fish, eggs, vegetables, and made-up dishes such as pancakes, fritters or croquettes.

It is important to use the right equipment and a good quality fat or oil, to maintain the correct cooking temperature steadily, and to have the food prepared in a suitable way. Above all, care is needed because the high temperature at which fats are used can be dangerous.

TYPES OF FATS AND OILS

The choice of fat is important; it must be able to reach a temperature of at least 200°C without burning or disintegrating, and it must not contain impurities or water which may make it spit and splutter dangerously.

Butter gives the best flavour but is expensive to use and breaks down at high temperatures. A slight blue haze rises from the pan when it is hot enough for frying. If it is overheated, it will produce dark smoke, discolour, and develop an unpleasant flavour. Clarified (p886) or unsalted butter is best for frying. Adding 1 × 15ml spoon cooking oil per 50g butter will enable it to reach a higher temperature. It is not suitable for deep frying.

Only foods which cook quickly or at relatively low temperatures are suitable for frying in butter, eg eggs, fillets of fish, mushrooms.

Margarine (especially soft tub margarine) contains water and non-fatty materials such as salt and milk solids. It also breaks down at high temperatures, so is unsuitable for deep frying unless clarified (p886). Different types of margarine are described on p888.

Lard should be 100% pure fat, and will heat to a high temperature, so is suitable for frying. Occasionally, lard contains water or impurities, so make sure that it is of high quality.

Dripping, the fat from roast meat, can be heated to a high temperature; it has a decided savoury flavour however, which limits its use to frying savoury foods. Dripping often contains impurities or water, which cause the fat to spit, so it should be clarified (p473) before use.

White cooking fats are mostly made from vegetable oils. Unlike margarine they do not contain colouring, vitamins or salt, so are free from impurities. They reach a high temperature without disintegrating and are quite suitable for frying any food. White fat should be broken into small pieces before being melted for frying, and must be heated gently so that it does not burn before it has all melted.

Cooking oils also have a vegetable source but they are liquid at room temperature, and have not been hydrogenated, ie made into a solid mass.

For frying, especially deep frying, oils which reach a high temperature without burning should be used. A pure oil such as corn, maize, safflower or sunflower, is ideal, although expensive. Cheaper oils are blended rather than pure but if very cheap, often have a distinctive taste and disintegrate at high temperatures, which makes them unsuitable for frying. Always use a refined oil, such as groundnut oil, since these have a blander taste than unrefined oils; they also reach higher temperatures.

Olive oil, besides being very expensive, will not reach a high temperature, and has a distinctive flavour, so is not ideal for frying. If you have to fry with olive oil, or any other strongly flavoured oil, fry and discard a small piece of bread first. This will get rid of any over-strong flavour.

Food cooked in oil should be light and crisp with no aftertaste. It need never be greasy, pallid or distinctively flavoured if it is cooked correctly and at the right temperature.

METHODS OF TESTING TEMPERATURES FOR FRYING

These depend on the type of fat used. In the case of animal fat, the correct temperature can be gauged by the appearance of a faint blue haze above the hot fat. This is known as the smoking point. If the fat is heated any more, it begins to break down and gives off an acrid blue smoke. It may also darken and develop an unpleasant flavour. To avoid this, heat the fat slowly and evenly. While cooking, check that the temperature does not fall below the correct level or rise above it.

This is not, however, the case with the majority of oils or white fats; the correct temperature must be gauged by other methods. This is because a smoke or haze, formed only at temperatures above 210°C, indicates that the fat or oil is far too hot for frying.

When shallow frying, the temperature can be tested by putting a small piece of food or a 2cm square of thickly sliced bread into the pan; the oil or fat should sizzle immediately.

When deep frying, a thermometer should be used. Heat the thermometer with the oil or fat to the required temperature and cool it slowly after use. Alternatively, test the temperature using a square of bread. The time it takes to turn brown in the fat indicates the required temperature. A third, though less accurate, test can be carried out using a small piece of food or a square of bread. It should sink to the bottom of the pan, then rise immediately to the surface; bubbles should appear round it. If it remains on the bottom of the pan or rises to the surface slowly, the fat or oil is still too cool; if the oil froths round the food, it is too hot.

Frying at a higher temperature than that indicated will not make the food cook more quickly; it will only burn the outside before the centre is done. The oil will also break down more quickly.

Raw foods are usually fried at a lower temperature than cooked foods to ensure thorough cooking; cooked foods are only heated through. Equally, the thickness of the food to be deep fried will affect the frying time and temperature; ie the larger the item the longer the frying time and the lower the temperature.

A general guide to deep fat frying temperatures is given on pp302–3.

CARE OF FRYING FATS AND OILS

When food is cooked at the right temperature, the outside is sealed immediately, so that very little fat or oil is absorbed and the volume is not much decreased. However, during cooking, water may have escaped into the fat or oil and fragments of coating may have fallen off and charred. These must be removed, or the fat or oil may begin to decompose.

After cooking, warm the fat or oil gently until any bubbling ceases; this drives off any water. Leave to cool, then strain it through a fine metal sieve or a piece of muslin, to remove any crumbs. Pour the cleaned fat into a sturdy, lightproof container, and cover securely. Oil can be poured back into its bottle, using a funnel, provided it is kept in a cool, dark place (not the refrigerator). Fat, but not oil, can be clarified from time to time (p473).

Note Do not mix different fats or oils.

Oil is often used for deep frying as it is easier to handle and store than solid fat. A good oil should serve for 9 or 10 fryings. However, it may deteriorate sooner under the following conditions:

1) If it is heated to a very high temperature.
2) If it is not heated enough, or if large batches of food are put in and moisture from the food gets into the oil.
3) Long exposure to air and light will make the oil oxidize, and give it an unpleasant smell and taste. It should be stored in an airtight container, out of the light.
4) Sediment left in the oil will char during later frying. Oil keeps better if cooled and then strained after frying.
5) Salt, soap, detergent, acid or copper make an oil deteriorate quickly. Make sure that pans are rinsed, clean, and dry.

You can tell when an oil has broken down if it:

1) foams too much: small white bubbles form all over the surface. They may rise, and if they reach the top of the pan, can be a serious fire hazard. Do not confuse them, however, with the bubbles given off when wet food is put into the pan.
2) darkens: some oils darken quite quickly, but if an oil thickens as well as darkens, it is usually spent. If dark, spent oil is used, food may seem cooked because it is stained, but it will still be half-raw inside.
3) sinks into the food: if food tastes greasy even though cooked at the right temperature, the oil is spent.
4) smells and tastes unpleasant: when an oil gets an unpleasant smell and taste, it is probably spent and should be thrown away.

PREPARING FOOD FOR FRYING

All food, both coated and uncoated, must be dried before being put into hot fat. Use a clean tea-towel or soft kitchen paper, or dust with flour.

Some meats, such as steak or chops, and some vegetables, such as courgettes, can be shallow fried without any other preparation, but almost all other foods, especially foods like rissoles, made from reheated ingredients, must be given a crisp coating, especially if they are being deep fried, to prevent moisture escaping into the fat. The food is usually brushed with egg or milk, and then rolled in the coating. Milk and seasoned flour are usually used for fish; egg and breadcrumbs for Scotch eggs and croquettes. Soft white crumbs or browned crumbs can also be used, on their own or mixed with grated cheese, or with herbs such as chopped parsley. A packeted stuffing mix can be used as a substitute. Oatmeal makes a good coating for oily fish. Crushed cornflakes are another alternative. A thick batter can also be used.

When making pancakes, beignets or other stiff batter mixtures which need turning or dropping into hot fat, always use wooden spatulas and metal spoons; contact with very hot fat may melt plastic ones.

FRYING METHODS

Shallow Frying

Use a strong, thick-based frying pan which stands level on the heat source so that the food will cook evenly. The pan must be big enough to hold easily all the food to be fried.

There are three types of shallow frying:

1) Food containing a lot of fat, such as bacon or sausages, can be put into a moderately hot pan without any extra fat or oil at all. Fry gently, turning the food over to prevent it burning. This method is called dry frying.
2) A very small amount of fat or oil, just enough to grease the surface, is added to the pan, warmed and run over the base. When it is heated, very thin foods which cook quickly can be fried, eg eggs, pancakes, and omelets.
3) Enough fat or oil is put into the pan to give a depth of 1.5cm. Food fried in this fat must not be more than 3cm thick, since the fat should cover half its thickness. If necessary, cut large portions of food into smaller pieces. Lower the food gently into the hot fat, waiting a moment or two between adding each piece, to let the fat

re-heat. When the food is golden-brown underneath, turn it over carefully, to avoid piercing the sealed food surface. When the food is cooked, it should be lifted out of the fat or oil with a perforated spoon or slice. Drain on soft kitchen paper to remove any fat still clinging to it; otherwise it will taste greasy.

Fried food should be served at once, very hot. If it must be kept hot, do not cover it or it will go soggy. Put on soft kitchen paper on a baking tray in a warming drawer or cool oven.

Deep Frying

Use a strong, thick-based pan. A good size holds 2.8 litres, is about 10cm deep and 23cm in diameter. The basket should be about 2cm smaller in diameter than the pan, and fit into it comfortably. Use oil or 100% fat without any added impurities. Heat the basket with the fat, to prevent it cooling the fat, and so that the food does not stick to it.

The pan should only be one-third filled with fat or oil. Do not fill it more than this, or the fat may spill over when the food is put in. The fat must be deep enough to cover the food, but only a single layer of food should be put in at one time or it will stick together.

All foods fried in deep fat must be coated (see above) unless they are starchy, eg potatoes and doughnuts. Raw foods only need coating once, but cooked foods need two coats, to prevent the contents from drying out.

Uncoated foods and foods coated with batter may stick to a frying basket, so put these straight into the hot fat, using a perforated spoon. These foods float, and need turning with the spoon to brown the second side.

In deep frying, the food is sealed immediately and no flavours should escape; so the fat can be used to cook sweet and savoury foods one after another. Drain all deep-fried foods on soft kitchen paper.

Sautéing

This is a French term which means shaking food in fat while it is frying; it comes from *sauter* to jump.

A well-flavoured fat, such as butter and oil mixed, should be used, since it will be absorbed by the food. If the food is raw, a lid should be kept on the pan, to keep in the steam which helps the cooking. The cooked food should be soft and moist, not crisp. Sautéing is very often the first step in making soups or sauces, because it brings out the flavour of food. However, sautéing can also be a complete method of cooking some foods, eg kidneys. If the food to be sautéed is already cooked, such as potato, it can be tossed in an open pan or turned with a fork, which gives a golden finish and soft inside texture.

Oven Frying or Bake Frying

This is an easy way to cook food so that it seems to have been fried. Put enough fat or oil in a baking tin to give a depth of 5mm. Heat it in a fairly hot oven at 190°C, Gas 5, for 10 minutes. Put in the food, prepared as for other frying, baste with the hot fat, then cook until golden and tender. Drain on soft kitchen paper.

Stir Frying

This is a method of cooking used a great deal in the East, especially in China. The food must be of top quality. Cut it into thin slices so that it cooks very quickly. Slice, shred or dice meat, and slice vegetables crossways or diagonally. Prepare all the ingredients before starting to cook. Heat a little oil in a large frying pan, and when it is very hot, add the food at intervals, according to the length of time each takes to cook. Fry for 1–2 minutes only, stirring all the time. The various ingredients should be ready together, cooked through but still crisp, with a firm texture. Season with salt and pepper. Serve at once.

If meat and a green vegetable are used, cook the vegetable first for a minute, until it turns bright green. Remove it from the pan and re-heat the oil, adding a little more if necessary. Then fry the meat and return the vegetable to the pan when the meat is nearly cooked. Stir the mixture together for 1 minute until it is hot.

Soy sauce, stock, water or some other liquid can

be added to the pan when the meat is half cooked. Cover the pan and cook over medium heat for 3–5 minutes, shaking it frequently. The liquid may be thickened with cornflour.

SAFE FRYING

Frying can be dangerous, so remember:
1) Use a clean pan every time.
2) Warm the pan up slowly; do not use a high heat, and see that a gas flame does not come up the sides of the pan.
3) Never leave a hot frying pan unattended.
4) Never allow water to splash into hot fat since this makes the fat spit; do not have a kettle or any other pan nearby when frying.
5) Do not let the fat get too hot. If it does, turn off the heat immediately and leave it to cool. Always retest before using.
6) Do not let the pan handle jut out over the edge of the cooker.
7) Keep children away.
8) Never carry a pan of hot fat or oil from the heat source to another spot.
9) Do not have a lid on the pan when deep frying.
10) Turn off heat source when frying is finished.

If fat or oil does catch fire, turn off the heat source, wet a large cloth, wringing it until it no longer drips, and cover the burning fat with it. Cover the pan with a lid if you have one. Leave the pan for at least 2 hours before uncovering it. *Never* move the pan or pour on water. Oil, in particular, may splash, and water will have no effect on it except to spread the flames.

Batters

A batter is a mixture of egg, flour, and a liquid, usually milk or water. As a rule, use plain flour since the batter will be raised by air entrapped by the eggs, and by steam created by the high temperature used in cooking. If the batter is made some time before it is needed, cover it, and leave it to stand in a cold place such as a refrigerator.

When making a batter, the flour, eggs, and some of the liquid are beaten with a wooden spoon or a whisk until smooth and well blended. When the spoon or whisk is removed from the batter, bubbles will rise to the surface. The rest of the liquid should then be stirred in.

An electric blender makes batters very easily and quickly. Put the liquid and the egg into the goblet first, then add the flour. Hold the lid on firmly, switch on, and mix according to the manufacturer's instructions.

A thin batter is used to make pancakes, drop scones or batter puddings, including Yorkshire pudding. A thicker batter is used to coat food such as fish before frying, and to make dishes such as fritters or kromeskies, and a thicker one still, eg a panada, is used for binding small or loose pieces of food. The cooked batter should be crisp, light, and well-risen.

Coating Batter(1)

Makes 250ml (approx)

100g plain flour
½ × 2.5ml spoon salt
1 × 15ml spoon cooking oil **or** *melted butter*

125ml water **or** *milk and water*
2 egg whites

Sift the flour and salt into a bowl. Make a well in the centre of the flour and add the oil or butter and some of the liquid. Gradually work in the flour from the sides, then beat well until smooth. Stir in the rest of the liquid. Just before using, whisk the egg whites until stiff. Give the batter a final beat and fold in the egg whites lightly.

Alternatively, use an electric blender. Put the water and oil into the goblet. Add the flour and salt and blend until smooth. Just before using, whisk the egg whites until stiff in a separate bowl. Give the batter a quick mix, then pour it down the sides of the bowl containing the egg whites. Fold the egg whites into the mixture lightly.

This makes a crisp, light batter suitable for fruit fritters, small fish fillets, and kromeskies.

Note The egg yolks can be added to the flour but then only 100ml liquid should be added. This makes a thicker, richer batter.

Coating Batter(2)

Makes 175ml (approx)

100g plain flour	*1 egg*
½ × 2.5ml spoon salt	*125ml milk*

Sift the flour and salt into a bowl. Make a well in the centre of the flour, and add the egg and a little of the milk. Gradually work in the flour from the sides, then beat until smooth. Stir in the rest of the milk. Just before using, stir well.

Alternatively, use an electric blender. Put the milk and egg into the goblet. Add the flour and salt and blend until smooth.

This makes a firmer batter suitable for fish fillets, fish and meat cakes, and meat.

Coating Batter(3)

Makes 175ml (approx)

100g plain flour	*125ml warm water*
½ × 2.5ml spoon salt	*1 × 5ml spoon baking*
1 × 15ml spoon oil **or**	*powder*
melted butter	

Sift the flour and salt into a bowl. Make a well in the centre of the flour, and add the oil or butter and a little of the water. Gradually work in the flour from the sides, then beat until smooth. Stir in the rest of the water. Alternatively, use a blender. Make in the same way as Batter (2). Just before using, sprinkle on the baking powder and give the batter a final beat. Use as for Batter (2).

Coating Batter(4)

Makes 400ml (approx)

125ml milk	*½ × 2.5ml spoon caster*
25g butter	*sugar*
1 × 5ml spoon dried	*100g plain flour*
yeast **or** *10g fresh*	*a pinch of salt*
yeast	

Warm the milk and butter until the butter melts. Do not let it get hot. Mix the yeast and sugar into the milk. Leave for 15 minutes in a warm place until frothy.

Put the flour and salt into a bowl, make a well in the centre, and pour in the yeast and milk. Gradually work in the flour from the sides to form a thick batter, the consistency of double cream. Cover and leave to stand in a warm place for 30–35 minutes, until the mixture doubles in size.

This makes a crisp, well-flavoured batter, suitable for meat and fish.

Basic Thin Batter

(for puddings and pancakes)

Makes 375ml (approx)

100g plain flour	*1 egg*
½ × 2.5ml spoon salt	*250ml milk*

Sift the flour and salt into a bowl, make a well in the centre and add the egg. Stir in half the milk, gradually working the flour down from the sides. Beat vigorously until the mixture is smooth and bubbly. Stir in the rest of the milk. Use as below, and for pancakes pp937–42.

Note Half milk and half water can be used. Some cooks claim this gives a lighter batter.

VARIATIONS

Baked Batter Pudding

Heat the oven to hot, 220°C, Gas 7. Put 25g cooking fat or 25ml oil into a 17 × 27cm baking tin. Heat in the oven for 15 minutes. Pour in the batter quickly and bake for 30–35 minutes, until brown and well risen.

Serve immediately, cut into squares, either with a savoury sauce or gravy, or as an accompaniment to roast beef, sausages or braised vegetables. The batter can also be served as a sweet pudding; sprinkle with sugar and serve with jam or with Ginger Syrup Sauce (p726).

Yorkshire Pudding

Plain baked batter is eaten most often as Yorkshire Pudding. It is the traditional British accompaniment to roast beef. In the north of England, the meat is roasted on a grid placed in the meat tin.

Thirty minutes before the meat is cooked, the joint is basted for the last time, and then the batter is poured into the meat tin below the grid, where it cooks in the meat dripping. The pudding is served either with the meat or, more traditionally, as a first course with gravy.

Very often Yorkshire Pudding is cooked in a separate tin, using beef dripping for the flavour; the tin is placed on the shelf above the meat, and cooked as in the basic Baked Batter Pudding.

Individual Yorkshire Puddings

These should be baked in deep individual patty tins. Put a small knob of lard (about 1 × 5ml spoon) in each tin. Place in a preheated oven, 220°C, Gas 7, until the fat is smoking hot. Half fill the tins with basic thin batter and bake for at least 20–25 minutes, depending on the depth of the tins. The puddings will rise high above the tins, and will be almost hollow shells. Do not underbake or they will collapse when taken out of the oven.

Cheese Batter

Add 50g grated cheese to the batter and sprinkle another 50g on the top before baking.

Onion Batter

Sauté 50g onion in a little fat and put into the tin before adding the batter.

Bacon Batter

Fry 2–3 chopped bacon rashers and put into the tin before adding the batter.

Herb Batter

Add ½ × 5ml spoon dried mixed herbs to the batter.

Steamed Batter Pudding

Grease a 750ml pudding basin or 4 small basins. Pour in the basic thin batter. Cover securely with greased foil or doubled greaseproof paper. Steam a 750ml pudding for 2 hours, individual puddings for 30 minutes.

Beer Batter

Makes 375ml (approx)

100g plain flour	1 × 15ml spoon oil or
a pinch of salt	cool melted butter
1 egg	250ml light beer

Sift the flour and salt into a bowl. Make a well in the centre of the flour, and add the egg and oil or butter. Stir in half the beer, gradually working the flour down from the sides. Beat vigorously until the mixture is smooth and bubbly. Stir in the rest of the beer. Let the batter rest for about 30 minutes to allow the beer froth to settle.

Use for savoury dishes such as Toad-in-the-hole.

Toad-in-the-hole

4 helpings

500g skinless sausages	375ml beer batter
25g cooking fat or	
dripping	

Heat the oven to hot, 220°C, Gas 7. Cut each sausage into 3 pieces. Put the sausages and fat into a 17 × 27cm baking tin and heat in the oven for 5 minutes. Pour the batter round the sausages quickly, and bake for 30–35 minutes until brown and well-risen.

Serve cut into 4 pieces, with gravy.

Note 500g sausage-meat can be used instead, rolled into 8 sausage shapes on a floured board.

VARIATIONS
1) Steak: The original Toad-in-the-hole recipe used 500g frying steak cut into small pieces.
2) Chops: Use 4 small chops instead of sausages.
3) Steak and kidney: Cut 500g steak and kidney into small pieces.
4) Ham: Use 250g cooked ham cut into small pieces.
5) Frankfurter: Cut 4 large frankfurters into pieces, and stir a little chopped parsley into the batter.

Cod Fillets in Beer Batter

(deep-fried)

4 helpings

100g plain flour	oil **or** fat for deep
salt and pepper	frying
800g skinned cod fillets	

Batter

250g plain flour	200ml light beer
1 × 15ml spoon oil	150ml water
salt and pepper	2 egg whites

Prepare the batter first. Sift the flour and mix with the oil, salt, pepper, beer, and water. Whisk well for 3–5 minutes. Leave to stand for at least 30 minutes. Before coating the fish, whisk the egg whites until stiff and fold into the batter.

Season the remaining flour with salt and pepper, and cut the fish into serving portions. Roll each portion in the flour, shake off any excess, then dip immediately into the batter. Heat the fat (p303) and fry the fish until golden-brown. Drain on soft kitchen paper, and serve immediately.

Fried Plaice with Herbs

(shallow-fried)

4 helpings

500g plaice fillets	juice of ½ lemon
50g lettuce, sorrel, beet	1 × 15ml spoon
tops **or** other salad	vegetable oil
greens	oil **or** fat for shallow
salt and pepper	frying

Batter

100g flour	150ml warm water
a pinch of salt	2 egg whites
2 × 15ml spoons	
vegetable oil	

Garnish

parsley sprigs

Prepare the batter first. Mix the flour, salt and oil, add the water and beat well to remove any lumps. Cover, and leave to stand for 30 minutes.

Cut the fish fillets into slices 1cm thick and 5–7cm long. Wash and chop the salad greens finely. Sprinkle the fish with salt, pepper, and the chopped greens. Pour the lemon juice over the fish, add the oil and leave to stand for 15–20 minutes.

Whisk the egg whites until fairly stiff, and fold into the batter. Dip each piece of fish in the batter. Heat the fat in a frying pan and put in the fish. Tilt and shake the pan to cover the fish with fat. Fry for 10–15 minutes, turning once, until crisp and golden-brown. Drain on soft kitchen paper. Serve the fish in a pyramid on a heated dish. Garnish with sprigs of parsley.

Serve with a mayonnaise sauce with chopped gherkins, or a hot tomato sauce.

Note Any white fish fillets may be used.

Other recipes for fried fish may be found in the chapter on Fish and Shellfish.

Sweet Batters

Apple Batter Pudding

4 helpings

25g cooking fat **or** oil	50g sugar
500g cooking apples	grated rind of ¼ lemon
basic thin batter (p934)	

Heat the oven to hot, 220°C, Gas 7. Put the fat or oil into a 17 × 27cm baking tin and heat in the oven for 5 minutes. Peel, core, and slice the apples thinly. Prepare the batter. Remove the tin from the oven, arrange the apple slices in an even layer on the bottom, and sprinkle with the sugar and lemon rind. Pour the batter over the apples and bake for 30–35 minutes until brown and well-risen.

Serve cut into 4 pieces, with golden syrup or a lemon sauce.

VARIATIONS

Apricot Batter Pudding

Just cover 100g dried apricots with water and soak until soft, preferably overnight. Put the apricots and water into a pan and simmer for 15 minutes. Drain. Heat the tin and put the apricots in an even layer on the bottom. Continue as for Apple Batter Pudding. Serve with an apricot jam sauce.

Dried Fruit Batter Pudding

Spread 50g mixed dried fruit over the bottom of the tin and sprinkle with $\frac{1}{2} \times 5$ml spoon mixed spice or ground cinnamon. Continue as for Apple Batter Pudding. Serve with a lemon sauce.

Black Cap Pudding

Grease 12 deep patty tins and divide 50g currants between them. Pour in enough batter to half fill each tin and bake for 15–20 minutes. Turn out to serve, and offer Ginger Syrup Sauce (p726).

PANCAKES

Pancakes are very versatile. They can be served with a sweet or savoury sauce or filling, and are suitable at many times of the day. Different forms of pancakes are known in most countries, adapted to local ingredients and cooking methods. In the UK, the commonest way of serving them is with lemon, as on Shrove Tuesday. Savoury stuffed pancakes make an economical main dish since they are satisfying and leftovers can be used for the filling.

Pancakes should, ideally, be eaten straight from the pan, but if cooking more than 4, keep them warm by putting each pancake as it is made between 2 plates over a pan of hot water or into a warm oven.

Cooked pancakes can be stored for a week in a refrigerator and they freeze excellently. Stack the cold pancakes alternately with 15cm squares of clingfilm. Wrap the whole in greaseproof paper, foil or a polythene bag and put in a refrigerator or freezer. Re-heat in a hot frying pan with a very little fat, turning once; if frozen, heat in a cool oven, 150°C, Gas 2, for 15 minutes (see also p1391).

Serve pancakes hot. They can be rolled or folded in half and then half again to form a quarter circle; or flat pancakes can be piled up alternately with filling and cut into wedges for serving.

Note When making pancakes, always use a well-seasoned or non-stick frying pan or omelet pan; it should preferably be used only for pancakes and omelets.

Plain Pancakes

Basic recipe

Makes 8 pancakes

Prepare a basic thin batter (p934). Pour it into a jug. Heat a little cooking fat or oil in a clean 18cm frying pan or omelet pan. Pour off any excess fat or oil, as the pan should only be coated with a thin film of grease. Stir the batter and pour in 2–3×15ml spoons batter, just enough to cover the base of the pan thinly. Tilt and rotate the pan to make sure that the batter runs over the whole surface evenly. Cook over moderate heat for about 1 minute until the pancake is set and golden-brown underneath. Make sure the pancake is loose by shaking the pan, then either toss it or turn over with a palette knife or fish slice. Cook the second side for about 30 seconds until golden. Slide out on to a warmed plate so that the first side fried will be on the outside when the pancake is rolled up or folded.

Repeat this process until all the batter has been used, greasing the pan when necessary.

VARIATIONS
Rich Pancake Batter

Add 15g butter, melted and cooled, or 1×15ml spoon oil, and an egg yolk to the batter. Alternatively, add 1 whole extra egg.

Cream Pancake Batter

Use 150ml milk and 50ml single cream instead of 250ml milk. Add 2 eggs and 25g cooled butter. The mixture should only just coat the back of a spoon as the pancakes should be very thin. For sweet pancakes, 1×15ml spoon brandy can be added and 2×15ml spoons caster sugar.

Yeast Pancake Batter
See Blini p942.

Soured Milk Pancake Batter
See p940.

Savoury Pancakes

Basic recipe

Add salt and pepper to the batter. Make the consistency a little thicker by using slightly less liquid than for sweet pancakes.

Savoury pancakes are usually rolled round a thick filling and arranged in an ovenproof dish. They are then heated in a moderate oven at 180°C, Gas 4, for 30 minutes if they have a cold filling and for 20 minutes if the filling is hot. Alternatively, pancakes with hot fillings can be browned lightly under the grill.

VARIATIONS

Beef Pancakes

Brown 500g minced beef in 2×15ml spoons oil. Add 2×5ml spoons chopped parsley, 4×15ml spoons cooked rice, 1×15ml spoon grated onion, salt and pepper, a pinch of herbs, and 125ml beef stock. Simmer for 5 minutes until the stock is absorbed. Fill the pancakes, sprinkle with 25g grated cheese and re-heat. (Cheddar, Cheshire, Lancashire or a mixture of Gruyère and Parmesan can be used.)

Beef and Kidney Pancakes

Fry 75g chopped onion in 25g butter, until soft. Reserve 25g onion. Add 1 chopped lamb's kidney to the rest and fry lightly. Stir in 1×15ml spoon flour, 125ml beef stock, and bring to the boil. Add 375g minced cooked beef and 1×15ml spoon tomato ketchup. Fill the pancakes, sprinkle with the reserved onion, and re-heat.

Smoked Haddock Pancakes

Poach 300g smoked haddock fillets in a little water for 10–15 minutes. Drain and flake the fish. Make 250ml white sauce (p692). Add the fish and 2 chopped hard-boiled eggs, 1×5ml spoon chopped capers, 1×15ml spoon chopped parsley, 2×15ml spoons lemon juice, salt and pepper. Fill the pancakes, sprinkle with 25g grated cheese and re-heat.

Chicken Pancakes

Mix 100g minced cooked chicken, 50g finely chopped red or green pepper, 50g grated onion, salt and pepper. Fill the pancakes and arrange in a dish. Mix 1×15ml spoon concentrated tomato purée with 125ml soured cream, pour over the pancakes, sprinkle with 1×15ml spoon grated cheese and re-heat.

Curried Turkey Pancakes

Fry 50g chopped onion in 50g fat for 5 minutes, until tender. Add 1×5ml spoon curry powder and cook for 1 minute. Stir in 25g flour and 250ml chicken stock to make a sauce. Add 300g chopped cooked turkey and 1×15ml spoon cream. Fill the pancakes, sprinkle with 25g grated cheese and re-heat.

Spinach Pancakes

Cook 300g frozen spinach and drain well. Add 200g cottage cheese, 3 lightly beaten eggs, 50g grated strong cheese, 100ml double cream, a pinch of ground nutmeg, salt and pepper. Fill the pancakes. Sprinkle with 25g grated cheese and re-heat.

Tomato and Mushroom Pancakes

Chop 8 mushrooms and sauté in a little butter until tender. Add 6 skinned chopped tomatoes, and heat for 1 minute. Make 500ml white sauce (p692). Add 2×15ml spoons sauce to the vegetables, and fill the pancakes. Add 75g grated cheese to the rest of the sauce and pour over the pancakes. Sprinkle with 1×15ml spoon grated cheese and re-heat.

Cheese Pancakes

Add 50g grated strong cheese to 375ml thick white sauce (p692). Fill the pancakes, sprinkle with 25g grated, hard cheese and 1×15ml spoon chopped parsley. Dot with butter and re-heat.

Meat Pancake Stack
See p1320.

Sweet Pancakes

Basic recipe

Add 2 ×5ml spoons caster sugar to the batter. Cook as for Plain Pancakes. Slide the pancakes on to sugared paper and roll or fold as preferred.

VARIATIONS

Apple Pancakes

Mix together 250ml sweetened, thick apple purée, 50g sultanas, and a pinch of powdered cinnamon. Spoon on to the pancakes when made, and roll up. If liked, sprinkle the rolled pancakes with caster sugar, and glaze in a very hot oven or under the grill.

Apricot Pancakes

Add 1 ×15ml spoon powdered cinnamon to the batter. Soak 50g dried apricots in 4 ×15ml spoons water, and then simmer with 50g sugar and a good squeeze of lemon juice, until soft and pulpy. Add 25g almonds, lightly browned and chopped. Fill the pancakes as for Apple Pancakes.

Banana Pancakes

Mash 4 bananas with 50g softened butter, 2 ×15ml spoons sugar, and the grated rind and juice of 1 lemon. Fill the pancakes as for Apple Pancakes.

Cherry Pancakes

Spread soured cream on the pancakes and, when rolled up, spoon canned cherry pie filling over them.

Chocolate Pancakes

Sprinkle each pancake with grated plain chocolate and dredge with icing sugar when made. Stack the flat pancakes and dredge the top one with sugar. Serve cut in wedges, with cream.

Currant Pancakes

Scatter a few currants or sultanas on each pancake as it is cooking in the pan. Allow 50g in all. Do not add them to the batter because the fruit will sink to the bottom. Serve the pancakes with lemon and sugar.

Dried Fruit Pancakes

Simmer 100g chopped raisins, dates and cut mixed peel in 100ml fruit juice, until syrupy. Fill the pancakes as for Apple Pancakes.

Fruit Pancakes

Fill the pancakes with any canned pie filling.

Fruit and Nut Pancakes

Mix 3 ×15ml spoons golden syrup, 1 ×15ml spoon lemon juice, 50g chopped glacé cherries, 25g sultanas, and 25g chopped walnuts. Fill the pancakes, roll up and put in an ovenproof dish. Drizzle with more syrup, sprinkle with Demerara sugar and bake in a moderate oven at 180°C, Gas 4, for 20 minutes. Serve with cream.

Ginger and Banana Pancakes

Add 1 ×15ml spoon ground ginger to the batter. Mash 4 bananas with 2 ×15ml spoons double cream, and add a few pieces of chopped preserved ginger. Fill the pancakes as for Apple Pancakes.

Jam Pancakes

Spread the pancakes with warmed jam before rolling up.

Lemon Pancakes

Sprinkle with lemon juice, roll up, and sprinkle with caster sugar. Serve with wedges of lemon. Serve on Shrove Tuesday.

Variations continue over.

Lemon Curd Pancakes

Spread lemon curd on the pancakes and stack the flat pancakes in a pile. Completely cover with meringue made from 2 egg whites and 100g caster sugar, and bake in a fairly hot oven at 190°C, Gas 5, for 15–20 minutes, until crisp and lightly browned. Serve cut in wedges.

Orange Pancakes

Make as for lemon pancakes, substituting orange juice.

Pineapple Pancakes

Drain 1 × 227g can crushed pineapple. Mix the fruit with 250ml soured cream, and fill the pancakes. Heat the fruit syrup, add a few drops of lemon juice, and serve poured over the pancakes.

Surprise Pancakes

Spoon some ice cream into the centre of each pancake and fold it in half like an omelet. Serve with Jam Sauce (p726).

Sweet Cheese Pancakes

Beat 100g curd cheese with 3 × 15ml spoons double cream, 2 × 15ml spoons caster sugar, and the grated rind of ½ lemon. Add 40g sultanas. Fill the pancakes as for Apple Pancakes.

Layered Pancakes

Stack the pancakes in layers, and fill each layer with the following: 100g curd cheese mixed with 1 egg yolk, 1 × 10ml spoon sugar and the grated rind of ½ lemon; warmed apricot jam; 50g finely chopped nuts mixed with 50g grated plain chocolate. Make a meringue from 2 egg whites and 100g caster sugar, and use to cover the pile of pancakes completely. Bake in a fairly hot oven at 190°C, Gas 5, for 15–20 minutes, until crisp and lightly browned. Serve cut in wedges.

Other Pancakes
Breakfast Pancakes

4 helpings

1 egg	100g plain flour
250ml milk	2 × 5ml spoons baking
2 × 15ml spoons melted	powder
butter **or** oil	1 × 2.5ml spoon salt
1 × 15ml spoon caster	fat **or** oil for frying
sugar	

Beat the egg until liquid, add the remaining ingredients and whisk until smooth. Heat a little fat or oil in a frying pan. Pour off any excess. Put 2 × 15ml spoons batter into the pan to make a pancake about 10cm in diameter. Bubbles will appear on the surface of the pancake. As soon as it is brown underneath but before the bubbles break, turn the pancake over and fry the other side until brown. Transfer to a clean tea-towel, fold the towel over it, and keep warm.

Cook the rest of the batter in the same way, greasing the pan when necessary.

Serve in piles of 3 with butter and maple syrup or marmalade, or with grilled sausages and bacon.

Soured Milk Pancakes

4 helpings

100g plain flour	½ × 2.5ml spoon
a pinch of salt	bicarbonate of soda
1 egg	1 × 10ml spoon hot
125ml soured milk	water
1 × 10ml spoon melted	fat **or** oil for frying
butter	caster sugar

Filling
250ml mashed
  sweetened ripe fruit
  (see **Note**)

Sift the flour and salt into a bowl, make a well in the centre, and add the egg. Stir in the milk, gradually working the flour down from the sides. Beat vigorously until the mixture is smooth and bubbly. Add the butter. Dissolve the bicarbonate of soda in the hot water and stir into the mixture. Pour the batter into a jug. Heat a little fat or oil in a frying pan, and pour off any excess. Pour a little batter into the pan to make a pancake about 7cm in diameter. As soon as it rises and is brown underneath, but before the bubbles break, turn the pancake over and fry the other side until golden-brown. Keep each cooked pancake warm in a tea-towel. Cook the rest of the batter in the same way, greasing the pan when necessary. The cooked pancakes will be thick and fluffy.

For each person, sandwich 3 pancakes together with the fruit. Sprinkle with caster sugar.

Note Use any soft fruit except currants, eg skinned, stoned peaches, apricots or plums, or well-drained stewed fruit or crushed pineapple.

Blintzes

4 helpings

250ml basic thin batter (p934)	50g butter
1 egg	caster sugar
oil for frying and greasing	ground cinnamon soured cream

Filling

500g cottage cheese	$\frac{1}{2} \times 2.5ml$ spoon salt
1 × 15ml spoon double cream	1 × 15ml spoon sugar 1 egg

Prepare the batter and beat in an extra egg. Make 8 pancakes, turn on to oiled greaseproof paper and leave to cool. Make the filling by mixing the cottage cheese, cream, salt, and sugar together. Beat the egg lightly and add it to the mixture. Divide the filling between the pancakes. Brush round the edges of the pancakes with leftover batter or beaten egg. Fold in the sides and roll up to form loose parcels. Brush the end flaps with more batter or egg if necessary, to make a good seal. Heat the butter in a frying pan and fry the blintzes quickly until crisp.

Serve very hot, sprinkled with caster sugar and cinnamon, and with soured cream.

VARIATIONS

1) Dice 100g smoked salmon, mix with 500g cottage cheese, 1 × 15ml spoon lemon juice, and chopped chives. Use to fill the pancakes instead of the sweet cheese filling.
2) Mix together 200g cooked minced beef, 1 egg and 100g grated raw onion; season with salt and pepper, and a pinch of garlic powder. Use to fill the pancakes. Brush the pancakes with oil. Instead of frying, bake in a greased shallow dish at 200°C, Gas 6, for 30 minutes.

Kaiserschmarrn

(Emperor's Pancakes)

4 helpings

75g plain flour	4 × 15ml spoons caster sugar
4 eggs	
a pinch of salt	2 × 5ml spoons ground cinnamon
125ml milk	
fat **or** oil for frying	

Put the flour into a bowl and make a well in the centre. Separate the eggs. Put the yolks, salt, and half the milk into the flour. Gradually work in the flour, then beat vigorously until smooth and bubbly. Stir in the rest of the milk. Whisk the whites until stiff. Beat the batter again and fold in the whites. Heat a little fat or oil in a frying pan, and pour off any excess. Pour one-quarter of the batter into the pan and fry over moderate heat for about 1 minute until light brown underneath. Turn and cook the other side for about 30 seconds until golden. Turn out on to a plate or greaseproof paper. Tear into 6 or 8 pieces, using 2 forks. Return to the pan and re-heat for 30 seconds, turning the pieces over carefully. Turn on to greaseproof paper, add 1 × 15ml spoon sugar and 1 × 2.5ml spoon ground cinnamon and toss together. Put on to a warm plate and keep warm.

Cook the rest of the batter in the same way, greasing the pan when necessary. Work as quickly as possible, and serve the pancakes as soon as they are all ready.

Serve with stewed fruit or jam.

Blini

(Basic yeast batter)

5–6 helpings

250ml milk	2 × 10ml spoons butter
1 × 10ml spoon dried	$\frac{1}{2}$ × 2.5ml spoons salt
yeast	2 eggs
150g plain flour	fat for greasing

Warm half the milk slightly. Sprinkle the yeast into the milk and whisk with a fork. Leave for 15 minutes in a warm place until frothy. Put half the flour into a bowl, make a well in the centre and pour in the yeast and milk. Gradually work in the flour from the sides to form a thick batter. Cover and stand the bowl in a warm place for about 30 minutes, until the mixture is bubbly and risen.

Warm the rest of the milk and the butter to melt it, but do not let it get too hot. Mix the melted butter and milk into the risen batter with the salt and the remaining flour. Separate the eggs. Add the yolks to the mixture and beat well to form a smooth thick batter. Cover and leave to rise in a warm place for about 1 hour, until twice the original size.

Whisk the egg whites until stiff and stir into the batter. Leave to rise for a third time, for 30 minutes.

Heat a heavy-based frying pan and grease it lightly. Pour 2 × 15ml spoons batter into the pan to make a pancake about 10cm in diameter. Bubbles will appear on the surface. As soon as it rises and is brown underneath, but before the bubbles break, turn the pancake over and fry the other side until golden-brown. Keep each cooked pancake warm in a tea-towel. Cook the rest of the batter in the same way, greasing the pan when necessary.

Note Blinis, which are of Russian origin, are traditionally made with a mixture of plain and buckwheat flour. They are served on special days in Russia and other East European countries, spread with butter and soured cream, and topped with caviar and lemon wedges. They are also good with smoked salmon and cottage cheese; lumpfish roe can be used instead of caviar.

Crêpes Suzette (1)

(Orange Brandy Pancakes)

4 helpings

250ml basic thin batter (p934)	butter or oil for frying
1 × 15ml spoon butter	50ml brandy

Filling

100g unsalted butter	1 × 15ml spoon liqueur
75g caster sugar	(Kirsch or Grand
grated rind and juice of	Marnier)
1 orange	
1 × 5ml spoon lemon	
juice	

Prepare the batter. Melt the butter, cool, and beat it into the batter. Make the filling by creaming the butter and sugar together. Beat the orange rind, lemon juice, and liqueur into the creamed mixture. Beat in enough orange juice to give a soft creamy consistency.

Make 8 very thin pancakes and keep them warm until all are cooked. Spread the filling over the pancakes, dividing it evenly between them. Fold each one in half, then in half again to make a quarter circle.

Return half the pancakes to the pan and re-heat them for 1–2 minutes. As the orange butter melts and runs out, spoon it over the pancakes. Pour in half the brandy, tip the pan to one side and increase the heat. Ignite the brandy and serve at once with the orange sauce poured over the pancakes.

Re-heat and serve the other pancakes in the same way. If you have a large enough pan, re-heat all the pancakes at once.

Note See also Crêpes Suzette (2) (p1451).

FRITTERS AND BEIGNETS

A fritter, known in France as *beignet*, is generally a small piece of food coated in batter, or chopped food mixed with batter, which is then fried in hot fat. It can also consist of a flavoured panada or choux pastry, deep-fried in small spoonfuls; it is not coated. Fritters can be sweet or savoury.

Although fritters are usually fried in deep fat, some can be fried in shallow fat if more convenient, eg the Meat Fritters on p944.

Small pieces of food are first mixed with a thicker batter than is used for coating to hold them together. The batter is made in the same way as a coating batter, the liquid being added gradually until it has the consistency of double cream.

General Points to Note

If deep frying fritters, heat enough fat to give a depth of 6cm. It should be hot enough to seal the batter immediately, to prevent the food inside becoming greasy, but not hot enough to burn the coating before the filling is cooked or heated through. A cooking thermometer is very useful. Spear each piece of food in turn on a skewer or fork, dip it into the batter, lift it to let the excess batter drip off, then lower into the hot fat, using a perforated spoon. Only cook a few fritters at a time because they will swell and need room to move. A lot of cold fritters put in at once will also cool the fat below the correct frying temperature, and they will be soggy. When frying, let fritters which float cook completely on one side before turning them over to cook the second side. Make sure that the fat returns to the correct heat for frying before putting in another batch of fritters.

Lift the fritters out with a perforated spoon and drain on soft kitchen paper. Turn them over two or three times to blot off all excess fat or it will be absorbed by the cooling food and make it greasy and soggy instead of light and crisp. For the same reason do not let the paper become soggy with fat.

Savoury Fritters
Chicken or Turkey Fritters

4 helpings

400g sliced cold cooked chicken **or** turkey	50g soft white breadcrumbs
50g ham **or** boiled bacon	2 × 5ml spoons chopped parsley
1 egg	oil **or** fat for deep frying

Cut the turkey into neat pieces. Mince the ham or bacon very finely. Beat the egg until liquid. Mix together the minced ham, breadcrumbs, and parsley. Dip the turkey in the beaten egg and coat with the breadcrumb mixture. Press the coating on firmly. Heat the fat (p303), and fry the fritters. Drain and serve immediately.

Madras Fritters

4–5 helpings

20 × 5cm rounds brown bread	10 × 4cm rounds canned **or** cooked ham
butter **or** margarine for spreading	coating batter (1) (p933)
mango chutney	oil **or** fat for deep frying

Spread the bread with butter or margarine. Chop the chutney finely, and spread a thin layer on the bread. Place a round of ham on 10 rounds of the bread, cover with the remaining rounds, and press together. Prepare the batter. Heat the oil or fat (p303). Dip the bread into the batter, and fry in the hot fat, turning if necessary until golden-brown. Drain on soft kitchen paper. Serve hot.

VARIATION
Madras Rissoles

Peel, core, and chop 2 sharp dessert apples. Spread 6–7cm bread rounds with butter or margarine and chutney as above, then press apple chips over the surface of 10 rounds before putting on the ham. Cover with the remaining bread rounds. Coat well with egg and breadcrumbs instead of batter. These rissoles can be shallow-fried or deep-fried.

Meat Fritters

(shallow-fried)

4 helpings

250g cold cooked beef **or** lamb
salt and pepper

1 × 5ml spoon chopped parsley
fat for frying

Batter
50g plain flour
a pinch of salt

2 eggs
4 × 15ml spoons milk

Prepare the batter first. Sift together the flour and salt, and separate the eggs. Mix the yolks and milk into the flour and beat well to form a thick batter.

Mince the meat, season well and add the parsley. Whisk the egg whites until stiff and fold into the batter. Add the meat. Heat a little fat in a frying pan. Drop spoonfuls of the mixture into the hot fat and fry until golden-brown underneath. Turn and fry the other side, about 5 minutes in all. Drain on soft kitchen paper.

Savoury Meat Fritters

4 helpings

250g cold cooked meat (see **Note**)
450–500g mashed potatoes
salt and pepper

milk
coating batter (2) (p934)
oil **or** fat for deep frying

Cut the meat into thick slices, about 4cm square. Season the mashed potatoes generously and add a little milk. Beat with a wooden spoon to a smooth creamy texture which spreads easily. Cover both sides of the meat with potato, smoothing it with a knife. Chill for at least 30 minutes. Prepare the batter. Heat the fat (p303). Dip the meat and potato in the batter and fry in the hot fat. Drain well.

Note The cold meat can be slices of ham, under-done beef spread with Worcestershire sauce, or lamb with slices of tomato.

Oyster Fritters

2 helpings or 10 small savouries

10 small oysters
5 rashers back bacon, without rinds
lemon juice
Cayenne pepper
coating batter (2) (p934)

1 × 5ml spoon grated onion
2 × 5ml spoons chopped parsley
oil **or** fat for deep frying

Open the oysters and dry gently. Cut each rasher of bacon into 4 square pieces. Season each oyster with lemon juice and Cayenne pepper. Place between 2 squares of bacon and press together firmly. Prepare the batter and add the onion and parsley. Heat the fat (p303), dip the fritters into the batter, and fry slowly until crisp and golden-brown. The oysters must be fully cooked, although not toughened.

Serve piled on lettuce leaves with lemon wedges.

Note To serve as small savouries, place each fritter on a small round of toast spread with parsley butter (p1301) or on crisply fried bread.

Scampi Fritters(1)

2 helpings

flour for coating
salt and pepper
225g peeled scampi

oil **or** fat for deep frying

Batter
1 egg
100g plain flour
a pinch of salt

1 × 15ml spoon oil
2–3 × 15ml spoons milk

Prepare the batter first. Separate the egg, mix the plain flour, salt, oil, and egg yolk with the milk to make a stiff batter; beat it until smooth. Just before cooking, whisk the egg white until stiff and fold it into the batter. Heat the oil (p303), and season the coating flour with salt and pepper. Dip the scampi in the seasoned flour, then in the batter. Deep fry the scampi, a few at a time, until golden-brown.

Drain, and serve with Tartare Sauce (p706) and lemon wedges.

Scampi Fritters(2)

4 helpings

500g fresh or frozen scampi	*coating batter (1) or (4) (p933 and p934)*
flour for coating	*oil or fat for deep*
salt and pepper	*frying*

If fresh scampi are used, discard the heads, remove the flesh from the shells, and remove the dark veins. If they are frozen, defrost, then drain well. Season the flour with salt and pepper, and dip the scampi in the seasoned flour. Prepare the batter. Heat the fat (p303), dip the scampi in the batter and fry in the hot fat, a few at a time, until golden-brown. Keep each batch warm while frying the rest.

Serve with Tartare Sauce (p706) or Fresh Tomato Sauce (p715) as soon as the last batch is fried.

Note The scampi can be coated with beaten egg and breadcrumbs if preferred.

Cheese Soufflé Fritters
(Beignets)

4 helpings

choux pastry (p1251) using 100g flour	*a pinch of Cayenne pepper*
50g grated Parmesan or other strong cheese	*a pinch of dry mustard*
salt and pepper	*oil or fat for deep frying*

Garnish
grated Parmesan cheese

Prepare the choux pastry, adding the cheese, salt, pepper, Cayenne pepper, and mustard with the flour. Heat the fat (p303). Dip a metal dessertspoon in the hot fat and use it to drop spoonfuls of the mixture gently into the fat, a few at a time. Fry slowly until crisp, puffed, and golden-brown. Drain well on soft kitchen paper. Serve at once, sprinkled with the extra Parmesan cheese.

Vegetable Fritters

Method 1 (using raw vegetables)

Prepare and slice or quarter the vegetables. Dry well on soft kitchen paper. Heat deep fat or oil (p302). Dip the pieces of vegetable one by one into coating batter (1) (p933) using a skewer or fork. Put a few pieces into the fat and fry, turning once, until crisp and golden. Drain well. Keep hot in a single layer on a baking sheet in a cool oven at about 150°C, Gas 2.

Method 2 (using parboiled vegetables)

Prepare the vegetables, half cook in boiling salted water, drain, dip into cold water, and drain again. Dry well on soft kitchen paper. They will have more flavour if marinated for 30 minutes in a mixture of olive oil, lemon juice, salt, pepper, and a pinch of herbs. Dip the vegetables in coating batter (1) (p933) and fry as above.

Method 3 (using chopped or very small vegetables)

Prepare the vegetables, eg sweetcorn or peas, mix with the batter used for Gooseberry Fritters (p946) and fry in the same way.

Note Specific recipes for deep-fried vegetable fritters, and for chips, game chips, potato puffs and ribbons can be found in the Vegetables chapter.

Sandwich Fritters
See p1294.

Potatoes Dauphine
See p796.

Sweet Fritters
Fruit Fritters

Prepare the fruit as below. Dry well on soft kitchen paper. Heat deep fat or oil (p303). Test the consistency of the batter to make sure that it coats the back of a spoon. Using a skewer or fork, dip the pieces of fruit, one by one, in coating batter (1) (p933). Put a few pieces into the fat and fry, turning once, until crisp and golden. Drain the fritters well on soft kitchen paper. Keep hot in a single layer on a baking sheet in a cool oven at about 150°C, Gas 2.

Serve while hot, sprinkled with caster sugar and with a suitable fruit sauce or cream.

Apples: Peel and core 500g apples, and cut into 5mm slices. Put into water containing a little lemon juice until needed. Drain well and dry with soft kitchen paper before coating. Coat, and fry. Serve with Lemon Sauce (p721) or Ginger Syrup Sauce (p726).

Apricots: Sprinkle canned apricot halves with rum and leave for 15 minutes. Coat, and fry. Serve dredged with caster sugar and cinnamon, and with custard or cream.

Bananas: Peel 4 small bananas, cut in half lengthways, then in half across. Coat, and fry. Serve with Simple Custard (p964) flavoured with rum.

Oranges: Remove the peel and pith from 4 oranges. Divide them into pieces of 2 or 3 segments each. Carefully cut into the centre to remove any pips. Coat, and fry. Serve with custard or sweetened cream flavoured with an orange-flavoured liqueur.

Pears: Peel and core 4 pears. Cut into quarters, sprinkle with sugar and Kirsch, and leave to stand for 15 minutes. Crush 4 macaroons finely, and toss the pear pieces in the crumbs. Coat, and fry. Serve with Lemon Sauce (p721) or warmed apricot jam flavoured with Kirsch.

Pineapple: Drain 1 × 566g can pineapple slices, pat dry and sprinkle with 4 × 5ml spoons Kirsch; leave for 15 minutes before coating. Coat, and fry. Serve with the pineapple juice thickened with arrowroot or cornflour.

Gooseberry Fritters

4 helpings

400g gooseberries
oil **or** fat for deep frying
caster sugar

Batter
50g plain flour
a pinch of salt
1 × 15ml spoon caster sugar
2 eggs
3 × 15ml spoons milk

Prepare the batter first. Sift together the flour and salt. Add the sugar. Separate the eggs. Mix the yolks and milk into the flour and beat well to form a thick batter. Prepare and dry the gooseberries. Heat the fat (p303). Whisk the egg whites until stiff and fold into the batter. Add the gooseberries. Dip a metal tablespoon in the hot fat, and then lift 3 coated gooseberries on to it. Lower them into the hot fat, without separating them. As the batter cooks, the berries will fuse together. Fry until golden-brown, turning once. Drain well.

Serve sprinkled with plenty of sugar.

VARIATIONS
Hulled strawberries, stoned cherries, red and blackcurrants can be cooked in the same way. Canned fruit can also be used but it must be drained very thoroughly. Alternatively, add 50g currants to the batter instead of the gooseberries. Serve sprinkled with sugar, and with Lemon Sauce (p721).

Almond Fritters

4 helpings

2 eggs	*1 × 15ml spoon milk*
25g caster sugar	*a few drops vanilla*
oil **or** *fat for deep frying*	*essence*
15g cornflour	*caster sugar*
50g ground almonds	

Separate the eggs. Cream the yolks and sugar together until well blended and the consistency of thick custard. Heat the fat (p303). Mix the cornflour, almonds, milk, and vanilla essence into the creamed yolks and sugar to make a soft batter. Whisk the egg whites until stiff and fold into the mixture. Drop the mixture in small spoonfuls into the hot fat and fry until golden-brown underneath. Turn the fritters over, and fry the other side. Drain well.

Serve dredged with caster sugar.

Poor Knights

(shallow-fried bread fritters)

4 helpings

4 thick slices white	*1 × 15ml spoon sugar*
bread	*oil* **or** *clarified butter*
2 eggs	*(p886) for shallow*
200ml milk **or** *white*	*frying*
wine	*caster sugar and ground*
½ × 2.5ml spoon ground	*cinnamon* **or** *red jam*
cinnamon	

Cut the crusts off the bread, then cut each slice into quarters. Put into a deep dish. Beat the eggs until liquid, add the milk or wine, cinnamon, and sugar. Pour the liquid over the bread, cover, and leave to soak for 2–3 minutes. Heat enough oil or clarified butter in a frying pan to give a depth of 5mm. Using a palette knife or fish slice, drain a piece of bread from the dish. Drop the fritter in the hot fat. Add 1 or 2 more, drained in the same way. Fry until golden-brown on both sides, turning once. Drain on soft kitchen paper, then keep uncovered in a warm place until needed. Fry the rest of the bread squares in the same way.

Serve sprinkled with caster sugar and cinnamon.

Alternatively, decorate with a dab of red jam, and serve with custard or cream.

Note 'Poor Knights' originated in England, in the Middle Ages, but soon became popular all over Europe. Every country has its own traditional variation, and some have more elaborate versions called 'Rich Knights'. Some are made with sweet bread or stale cake, others are moistened with red wine.

Cake Sandwich Fritters

4 helpings

25g glacé cherries	*oil* **or** *fat for deep*
2 × 15ml spoons Kirsch	*frying*
confectioners' custard	*8 thin slices stale sponge*
(p1237)	**or** *plain cake*
coating batter (1) (p933)	*caster sugar*

Wash the cherries in hot water to remove the excess syrup and cut into pieces. Soak in the Kirsch for 10 minutes. Drain, and mix with the confectioners' custard.

Prepare the batter. Heat the fat (p303). Spread the slices of cake with the cherry and custard mixture. Sandwich together in pairs. Cut in half and leave to soak in the remaining Kirsch. Lift the cake sandwiches carefully with a fish slice and dip into the batter. Drain, and fry in the hot fat until golden-brown, turning once. Drain again, and put on a baking tray or flat ovenproof dish; sprinkle with caster sugar and put under a hot grill until the fritters are glazed.

VARIATION

Pieces of plain cake about 5 × 2 × 1cm can be dipped in batter and fried as above. Sprinkle lightly with a sweet liqueur first, if liked.

Bread and Butter Fritters

4 helpings

coating batter (1) (p933)	*butter for spreading*
oil **or** *fat for deep frying*	*jam*
8 thin slices white bread	*caster sugar*
(from a tin loaf)	*ground cinnamon*

Prepare the batter. Heat the fat (p303). Cut the crusts off the bread, spread with butter and jam, and make into sandwiches. Cut each sandwich into 4 neat squares or triangles. Dip in the batter, and drain. Drop into the hot fat, a few at a time. Fry until golden-brown on both sides, turning once. Drain on soft kitchen paper. Dredge with caster sugar and cinnamon.

Serve at once, with Simple Custard (p964).

Custard Fritters or Fried Creams

4 helpings

4 egg yolks	*1 × 15ml spoon liqueur*
40g plain flour	*or brandy (optional)*
40g cornflour	*butter for greasing*
500ml milk	*coating batter (1)* (p933)
40g caster sugar	*or 1 egg and 50g fine*
a pinch of salt	*cake crumbs*
a few drops vanilla	*oil* **or** *fat for deep frying*
essence	*caster sugar (optional)*

Beat the egg yolks until liquid. Blend the flour and cornflour with a little of the milk. Bring the rest of the milk to the boil. Add slowly to the blended mixture, stirring all the time. Return to the pan and bring to the boil, still stirring. Cook for 2–3 minutes. (It is important to cook the flour thoroughly.) Stir in the sugar, salt, and egg yolks slowly. The mixture will be very thick, so take care to stir thoroughly to keep it smooth. Let it warm through, but do not let it come near the boil. Add the vanilla essence and liqueur or brandy, if used.

Spread the mixture in a greased 500ml dish to a depth of 2cm, and leave to set. Prepare the batter. When the custard is cold, cut into neat shapes about 3cm across. Heat the fat (p303). Dip the shapes in the batter, and drain, or dip in the beaten egg, then roll in the fine cake crumbs. Fry in the hot fat until golden-brown.

If coated in batter, spread on a baking tray or flameproof oven dish, sprinkle with caster sugar and put under a hot grill until the sugar has melted. If egged and crumbed, serve dredged with caster sugar.

Serve with Jam Sauce (p726), or sprinkle with the warmed liqueur or brandy used to make the custard.

Lexington Apples

4 helpings

4 cooking apples (600g	*25g plain flour*
approx)	*25g caster sugar*
1 × 375g can pineapple	*1 egg*
pieces	*25g cake crumbs*
2 × 5ml spoons	*oil* **or** *fat for deep*
arrowroot	*frying*

Peel and core the apples and steam them for about 10 minutes until they are half cooked. Drain the pineapple. Blend 125ml of the syrup with the arrowroot. Bring gently to the boil, stirring all the time, until the sauce thickens and clears. Keep hot. Chop the pineapple. Leave the apples to cool.

Mix the flour and sugar together and roll each apple in the mixture. Beat the egg until liquid. Brush the apples carefully with the egg and roll in the cake crumbs. Heat the fat (p303) and fry the apples until browned. Meanwhile, heat the pineapple. Fill the centres of the apples with the pineapple and serve with the hot pineapple syrup poured round.

Polish Fritters

4 helpings

basic thin batter (p934), using *50g flour*
4 × 5ml spoons apricot jam (approx)
75g macaroons
50g white breadcrumbs
1 egg
oil **or** *fat for deep frying*
caster sugar
ground cinnamon

Prepare the batter and fry 4 pancakes. Spread each one with apricot jam and roll up firmly. Trim off the ends and cut each pancake in half across. Crush the macaroons finely and mix with the breadcrumbs. Beat the egg until liquid. Heat the fat (p303). Dip each piece of pancake in the egg and then roll it in the crumbs. Fry the pancakes in the hot fat until browned. Drain well. Sprinkle with caster sugar and ground cinnamon.

Spanish Fritters

4 helpings

choux pastry (p1251), using *100g flour*
1 × 15ml spoon caster sugar
vanilla essence
oil **or** *fat for deep frying*
caster sugar
ground cinnamon

Prepare the choux pastry, adding 1 × 15ml spoon caster sugar and vanilla essence to taste. Heat the fat (p303). Put the mixture into a forcing bag with a 1cm star nozzle. Press out 7cm lengths of pastry, and let them drop into the fat. They will form various twisted shapes. Fry slowly until crisp and golden-brown. Drain well. Dredge thoroughly with caster sugar and ground cinnamon.

Indian Fritters

4 helpings

choux pastry (p1251), using *100g flour*
oil **or** *fat for deep frying*
jam **or** *jelly*
caster sugar

Prepare the choux pastry. Heat the fat (p303). Fill a dessertspoon with the mixture, make a hollow in the centre, put $\frac{1}{2}$ × 5ml spoonful of jam or jelly in the hollow, and cover with some more of the choux mixture. Make sure that the jam or jelly is completely covered or it will leak out into the hot fat. Slide this from the spoon into the fat, using a palette knife. Make the other fritters in the same way. Fry until golden-brown, turning once. Drain well.

Dredge with caster sugar and serve with the same warmed jam or jelly used in the filling.

Sweet Soufflé Fritters

(Beignets)

4 helpings

choux pastry (p1251), using *100g flour*
vanilla essence
oil **or** *fat for deep frying*
icing sugar

Prepare the choux pastry, adding vanilla essence to taste. Heat the fat (p303). Dip a metal dessertspoon in the hot fat and use it to drop spoonfuls of the mixture gently into the hot fat, a few at a time. Fry slowly until crisp, puffed, and golden-brown. Drain well on soft kitchen paper.

Dredge with icing sugar and serve with Brandy (p720), Orange or Rum (p721) Sauce.

VARIATION

Ring Fritters

Put the mixture into a forcing bag with a 1cm star nozzle. Pipe the paste into rings 4–5cm in diameter on to oiled greaseproof paper. Holding the edges of the paper, slip the rings into the hot fat. Keep the fritters moving with a spoon; they will then rise to the surface.

When drained, split the fritters, and fill with jam or very thick confectioners' custard (p1237). Serve very hot, dusted with icing sugar.

WAFFLES

Waffles are crisp, light, fried wafers, made from a leavened or raised batter, and cooked in a waffle iron, which can either be heated electrically or over direct heat. The iron has a hinged top which opens and closes. Inside, the metal surface is divided into small raised squares separated by a grid of indented lines or grooves. This surface usually has a non-stick coating, although older irons may need light greasing before use. Like an omelet pan, a waffle iron should never be washed.

Follow the manufacturer's instructions on how to use the iron. As a rule, it is heated, then just enough batter is poured on to cover the surface. The iron is closed, and, when steaming stops, the waffle should be sufficiently cooked. Take care not to overfill the iron, or the mixture will seep out at the sides.

A waffle should be easy to lift out of the iron, but if it seems to stick, cook it for $1-1\frac{1}{2}$ minutes longer.

Serve waffles immediately they are cooked. If they must be kept warm, do not pile them up or they will go soggy, but put them on a wire rack in a cool oven.

Waffles are good with either savoury or sweet accompaniments. They can be served with bacon and egg, grilled ham or small fried sausages. Bacon and marmalade makes a surprising but pleasant combination. For sweet waffles suitable as a dessert, try golden syrup, jam or honey with butter, a fruit purée, or stewed fruit and cream. In North America, maple syrup is popular.

Waffles

Makes 8

75g butter	2 eggs
250g self-raising flour	375ml milk
$\frac{1}{2} \times 5ml$ spoon salt	
$1 \times 5ml$ spoon baking powder	

Melt the butter and cool it. Sift the flour, salt, and baking powder into a bowl. Separate the eggs. Make a well in the centre of the flour. Add the egg yolks, cooled butter, and some of the milk. Gradually work in the flour from the sides and then beat well until smooth. Beat in the rest of the milk. Whisk the egg whites until stiff, and fold into the batter. It should be the consistency of thick cream.

Heat the waffle iron, pour in the batter, and cook for about 5 minutes until the steaming stops.

Serve hot with butter and golden or maple syrup.

VARIATIONS

Buttermilk Waffles

Substitute buttermilk for the milk. Add the whole eggs to the batter instead of separating them.

Spice Waffles

Add $1 \times 2.5ml$ spoon mixed spice to the flour.

Nut Waffles

Sprinkle $1 \times 15ml$ spoon chopped nuts over the batter as soon as it has been poured into the iron.

Cheese Waffles

Add 100g grated cheese to the batter. Serve with grilled bacon.

CROQUETTES AND KROMESKIES

Croquettes are made of minced or chopped food mixed with a binding agent, such as egg, a very thick sauce or a panada. They are formed into small cork or roll shapes 4–6cm long, coated with egg and breadcrumbs, and generally fried in deep fat like fritters. Alternatively, they can be coated with finely chopped nuts, fine oatmeal, crushed corn-flakes or rolled oats.

Kromeskies of French-East European origin are virtually identical to croquettes, the only difference being that they are often wrapped in a pancake, thin bacon rasher, or piece of caul fat, depending on their country of origin. The wrapping can be secured with a cocktail stick before coating with egg and crumbs.

Beef Croquettes

4 helpings

250g cooked beef	*1 × 5ml spoon any*
25g cooking fat	*bottled savoury sauce*
25g finely chopped onion	*flour for dusting*
25g flour	*2 eggs*
150ml beef stock	*50g dry white*
salt and pepper	*breadcrumbs*
1 × 5ml spoon chopped	*oil* **or** *fat for deep*
parsley	*frying*

Remove any fat, skin or gristle, and mince the meat. Melt the fat in a large frying pan and fry the onion for 2–3 minutes. Stir in the flour and cook for 1–2 minutes. Stir in the stock and bring to the boil, stirring all the time. Cook for 2 minutes until the sauce thickens. Add the meat, seasoning, parsley, and sauce. Stir over the heat for a moment. Turn the mixture on to a plate, level the surface, cover with a second plate, and leave to cool completely.

When cold, divide into 8 equal-sized portions. On a floured surface, form into neat cork or roll-shaped pieces. Beat the eggs until liquid. Scatter the crumbs on a sheet of greaseproof paper. Dip each croquette into the egg, brushing it all over to make sure it is evenly covered, then roll it in the crumbs until it is completely covered. Press the crumbs on lightly. Heat the fat (p303). Coat each croquette a second time. Fry in the hot fat, a few at a time, until crisp and browned all over. Drain well. Keep the first batches hot while cooking the rest.

Note The filling should have a soft creamy texture, contrasting with the crisp coating.

VARIATIONS

Lamb Croquettes

Use 250g cooked lamb instead of beef.

Pork Croquettes

Use 250g lean, cooked pork instead of beef. Use chicken or vegetable stock. Flavour with a pinch of marjoram and $\frac{1}{2}$ × 2.5ml spoon powdered sage.

Omit the bottled savoury sauce from all the following variations:

Veal Croquettes

Use 250g cooked veal instead of beef. Flavour with 1 × 5ml spoon chopped parsley, grated rind of $\frac{1}{2}$ lemon, and a pinch of nutmeg. Use chicken or vegetable stock.

Chicken Croquettes(1)

Use 200g cooked chicken and 50g cooked ham instead of beef. Add 50g chopped mushrooms and 1 × 5ml spoon lemon juice. Use chicken stock.

Note For Chicken Croquettes (2) see p1415.

Hare Croquettes

Use 100g minced cooked hare instead of 250g beef. Flavour with a pinch of powdered cloves. Do not mince a second time. Use game stock (p330) if possible.

Variations continue over.

Ham and Egg Croquettes

Use 100g minced ham and 2 chopped hard-boiled eggs instead of beef. Do not mince a second time. Use milk instead of stock.

Bacon or Ham Croquettes

4 helpings

250g cooked bacon joint **or** ham	salt and pepper
75g soft white breadcrumbs	1 egg
	50g breadcrumbs
2 × 15ml spoons mashed potato	oil **or** fat for deep frying
4 × 15ml spoons coating white sauce (p692)	

Mince the bacon or ham with the breadcrumbs and potato. Heat gently in a pan and stir in the white sauce. Season well. Turn the mixture on to a plate and complete as for Beef Croquettes (p951).

Note Tough outside pieces of bacon or ham can be used for the croquettes.

Egg Croquettes

4 helpings

50g button mushrooms	1 × 5ml spoon chopped parsley
25g finely chopped onion	
4 hard-boiled eggs	a pinch of grated nutmeg
25g butter	2 eggs
25g flour	50g dry white breadcrumbs
150ml milk	
salt and pepper	oil **or** fat for deep frying

Prepare and chop the mushrooms; chop the onion finely. Mix both together. Chop the hard-boiled eggs and put them to one side. Melt the butter in a pan large enough to hold all the ingredients, and fry the mushrooms and onion lightly until soft. Stir in the flour and cook for 1 minute. Stir in the milk gradually, and bring to simmering point, stirring all the time. Simmer, still stirring, for 3 minutes or until the sauce thickens. Mix in the chopped hard-boiled eggs, seasoning, parsley, and nutmeg. Stir

over gentle heat for 1 minute. Turn the mixture on to a plate and complete as for Beef Croquettes (p951).

Mackerel Croquettes

See p1402.

Bean Croquettes

4 helpings

200g haricot beans	grated rind of $\frac{1}{2}$ lemon
salt	salt and pepper
25g onion	50g soft white breadcrumbs
oil for shallow frying	
1 × 5ml spoon chopped parsley	1 egg
	oil **or** fat for deep frying

Soak the beans overnight, then simmer for about 2 hours in lightly salted water until tender. When the beans are cooked, chop the onion finely, and fry in a little oil for 5 minutes until tender. Mash or sieve the beans, and stir in the onion, parsley, lemon rind, and plenty of salt and pepper. Mix in sufficient breadcrumbs to make the mixture stiff enough to mould. Form into cork shapes or balls and complete as for Beef Croquettes (p951).

Serve with a tomato sauce or brown gravy.

VARIATIONS

Split peas or lentils can be used instead of beans. Lentils do not need long soaking.

Potato Croquettes

See p796.

Savoury Rice Croquettes

4 helpings

25g onion	25g butter
100g long-grain rice	3 eggs
1 bay leaf	50g dry white
bouquet garni	breadcrumbs
1 × 5ml spoon salt	oil **or** fat for deep
pepper	frying
500ml milk	

Chop the onion finely and put in a saucepan with the rice, bay leaf, bouquet garni, salt, pepper to taste, and milk. Bring to the boil, stir well, and cover with a tight-fitting lid. Reduce the heat and simmer gently for about 15 minutes, when the rice should be tender and all the milk absorbed. Remove the bay leaf and bouquet garni. Stir in the butter. Beat 2 of the eggs lightly and add them to the rice. Stir over gentle heat for 1 minute to let the egg thicken. Turn on to a plate and complete as for Beef Croquettes (p951).

VARIATION

Rice and Cheese Croquettes

Omit the bay leaf and bouquet garni. Mix 50g strong grated cheese and a few grains of Cayenne pepper into the rice with the eggs.

Chicken Kromeskies

6 helpings

chicken croquette	soft white breadcrumbs
mixture (p951)	for coating
1 egg	oil **or** fat for deep frying

Batter

125g plain flour	1 egg
1 × 5ml spoon salt	275ml milk

Garnish
fried parsley (p398)

Make the croquette mixture; then make the batter. Sift the flour and salt, add the egg, and half the milk; beat until smooth. Add the rest of the milk, and leave to stand for 30 minutes. Make very thin pancakes, and when each is cooked, spread it with the chicken mixture. Roll up tightly and leave to cool. Beat the egg until liquid. Cut the rolls in 4cm pieces, and coat with egg and breadcrumbs. Heat the fat (p303) and fry the kromeskies until golden-brown. Drain well. Serve very hot, garnished with fried parsley.

Veal Kromeskies

4 helpings

200g cooked veal	salt and pepper
50g cooked ham	a pinch of grated nutmeg
25g butter	flour for dusting
25g flour	6 long rashers streaky
150ml chicken stock	bacon, without rinds
25g mushrooms	oil **or** fat for deep
1 × 15ml spoon double	frying
cream	coating batter (1)
1 × 5ml spoon chopped	(p933)
parsley	

Mince the veal and ham. Melt the butter in a saucepan, add the flour and cook for 1–2 minutes, stirring all the time. Mix in the stock gradually, bring to the boil, and boil for 1–2 minutes, still stirring. Remove from the heat. Chop the mushrooms and add to the sauce with the cream, parsley, salt, pepper, nutmeg, and meat. Mix well together. Turn the mixture on to a plate, level the top, cover with a second plate and leave to cool completely. Divide into 12 equal-sized portions, and roll into cork shapes on a floured surface. Cut each rasher of bacon in half. Wrap a piece of bacon round each kromeski. Heat the fat (p303). Dip the kromeskies in the batter, drain, and fry in the fat until golden-brown. Drain well.

Serve with Fresh Tomato Sauce (p715).

RISSOLES AND RISSOLETTES

Rissoles are generally like large croquettes, either cork-shaped or round. Before being egged and crumbed, they are usually wrapped in a pastry case or pancake; the pancakes can be prepared ahead of time.

Rissolettes are small rissoles, used as cocktail savouries for a buffet or as a savoury course at a formal dinner.

Madras Rissoles

See p943.

Chicken Rissoles

4 helpings

100g cooked chicken	*shortcrust* (p1249) **or**
50g cooked ham **or**	*rough puff pastry*
tongue	*(p1252), using 200g*
25g button mushrooms	*flour*
25g butter	*flour for rolling out*
25g flour	*oil* **or** *fat for deep frying*
150ml chicken stock	*1 egg*
1 × 15ml spoon double	*fine dry white*
cream	*breadcrumbs for*
salt and pepper	*coating*

Chop the chicken and ham finely. Chop the mushrooms. Melt the butter gently in a fairly large pan, add the mushrooms and cook for 1–2 minutes. Stir in the flour, add the stock gradually, and bring to the boil, stirring all the time. Cook for 1–2 minutes. Add the meat, cream, and seasoning. Leave to cool completely between 2 plates.

Roll out the pastry very thinly on a lightly floured surface, and cut into eight 12cm rounds. Divide the filling between the rounds, dampen the edges, and fold over to form half circles. Press the edges together and seal firmly. Heat the fat (p303). Beat the egg until liquid. Coat the rissoles with the beaten egg and breadcrumbs. Fry in the fat until golden-brown on both sides. Drain well.

VARIATION

Lentil Rissoles

Instead of cooked chicken and ham or tongue, boil 200g lentils until soft; mash them with 25g butter and season with salt, pepper, and a pinch of grated nutmeg. Use well-flavoured vegetable stock instead of chicken stock, then complete as above.

Savoury Nut Rissoles

4 helpings

50g hazelnuts	*1 × 15ml spoon milk*
50g margarine	*100g soft wholemeal*
50g wholemeal flour	*breadcrumbs*
250ml vegetable stock	*1 × 15ml spoon finely*
or water	*grated Gruyère cheese*
salt and pepper	*flour for dusting*
a pinch each of dried	*1 egg*
thyme and powdered	*fat* **or** *oil for deep frying*
sage	
1 × 15ml spoon thick	
tomato sauce	

Skin the hazelnuts, grate them coarsely, and put to one side. Melt the margarine in a saucepan, add the flour and cook together gently for 4–5 minutes until lightly coloured. Stir in the stock or water gradually, and simmer for 5 minutes. Add the seasoning, herbs, tomato sauce and milk, and cook for another 5 minutes, stirring gently. Re-season if required. Remove from the heat and stir in 75g of the breadcrumbs, all the nuts and the cheese. Mix thoroughly, and leave to cool.

On a floured surface, form the mixture into large cork or round shaped pieces. Beat the egg lightly, dip the rissoles in it, then coat them with the remaining crumbs. Heat the fat or oil (p303) and fry the rissoles until golden-brown on all sides. Drain well and serve at once.

Liver Sausage Rissolettes

Makes 18–24 small savouries

basic thin batter (p934)
200g firm liver sausage
1 × 2.5ml spoon grated
 onion
salt and freshly ground
 black pepper

2 egg yolks
fine dry white
 breadcrumbs for
 coating
oil or fat for deep frying

Prepare the batter and make small, thin pancakes about 8cm in diameter. Turn on to oiled grease-proof paper and leave to cool.

Mash the liver sausage with the onion, and season to taste. Beat the yolks lightly. Roll each pancake round enough of the mixture to enclose it completely, and tuck the open end of each under the joined edge like envelope flaps. Seal the edges with a little egg yolk. Roll the pancakes in egg yolk, then in breadcrumbs. Heat the fat (p303) and fry the rissolettes until lightly crisped and brown on both sides. Drain thoroughly and serve at once.

Sardine Rissolettes

Makes 12 or 24 savouries

1 × 120g can sardines
2 hard-boiled eggs
15g grated Parmesan
 cheese
shortcrust pastry (p1249),
 using 150g flour

flour for rolling out
oil or fat for deep frying
1 egg
50g dry white
 breadcrumbs for
 coating

Drain the sardines and remove the fins, tails and bones. Chop the hard-boiled eggs. Mix the sardines, eggs, and cheese together. Roll out the pastry very thinly on a lightly floured surface and cut out twenty-four 5cm rounds. Put a spoonful of the mixture into the centre of 12 of the rounds, dampen the edges and cover with the remaining rounds. Alternatively, divide the filling between all the rounds, dampen the edges and fold them over to form half circles. Press the edges together and seal.

Heat the fat (p303). Beat the egg until liquid. Coat the risolettes with the beaten egg and the breadcrumbs, and fry in the hot fat until crisp and brown on both sides. Drain well. Serve hot or cold

as a savoury, sprinkled with grated Parmesan cheese.

VARIATIONS

Veal and Ham Rissolettes

For the filling mixture, make a sauce from 15g fat, 15g flour, and 125ml stock. Add 1 × 5ml spoon finely grated lemon rind, a pinch of mace, 125g finely minced cold cooked veal, 75g finely minced, lean cooked ham, salt and pepper. Stir over low heat until well mixed.

Egg Rissolettes

For the filling mixture, make a sauce from 15g fat, 15g flour, and 125ml milk. Add 4 chopped hard-boiled eggs, 25g finely chopped ham or tongue, salt and pepper. Stir over low heat until well mixed.

HOT PUDDINGS AND DESSERTS

Souffles, omelets, and sweet dishes, in which eggs form the principal ingredient, demand, for their successful manufacture, an experienced cook. They are the prettiest, but most difficult of all entremets. The most essential thing to insure success is to secure the best ingredients from an honest tradesman.

Milk Puddings

Milk puddings are generally thought of as starch-based, with added sweetening and milk. Beaten eggs and flavourings are sometimes added.

Most milk puddings are simmered or baked; but they can be steamed and turned out provided they contain at least 2 eggs per 500ml liquid. All milk puddings must be cooked very slowly so that they stay moist and creamy.

Grains

Rice: Carolina rice, the type most often used for puddings, is a round thick grain. Flaked rice is a processed form. Ground rice can be a medium or fine powder; it is used for puddings, cakes, and as a thickening.

Semolina: This is the endosperm of wheat in the form of coarse particles derived from the first grinding process in flour milling. It is used mainly for hot puddings and cold moulds.

Sago: Made from the pith of the sago palm; the starch is washed, dried and granulated as round 'pearls'. It is used for hot puddings.

Tapioca: Made from the root of the cassava plant after the bitter, poisonous juice has been washed out. The starch is dried, then granulated, ie made into 'pearls' or finer 'seeds', or crushed into rough flakes. It is used mostly for hot puddings.

Cornflour: The finely ground kernel of Indian corn or maize. It can be used not only for puddings but with flour in cake making, and to thicken sweet and savoury sauces.

Arrowroot: Made from the rhizomes of a plant called maranta, found mainly in the West Indies. It is crushed, mixed with water and dried as a fine powder. It only needs a short cooking time and is used for milk puddings as well as for thickening sauces and glazes.

Wheat, barley, oats and similar grains can also be used for puddings, either whole or flaked, rolled, crushed or ground. Follow the basic recipes for the type of grain.

Milk

Dried skimmed milk can be used in most puddings, and 25g of butter or suet can be added per 500ml, to make up the fat. Alternatively, evaporated or sweetened, condensed milk can be used, made up with water to the fluid content of fresh milk; the sugar in the recipe must be reduced if you use sweetened milk.

Eggs

Eggs make a milk pudding richer. If the whites are whisked before being added, the pudding becomes lighter. To prevent curdling, never add eggs until the grain is fully cooked, and always cool the pudding somewhat before adding them. In baked puddings, eggs need only 30 minutes in a warm oven to set a 500ml pudding and to brown the top.

Flavourings

Grated lemon or orange rind, ground cinnamon, allspice or nutmeg, a flavouring essence or liqueur can be mixed into milk puddings. Pared orange or lemon rind or a bay leaf can be infused in the milk, but must be removed before making the pudding. A vanilla pod can be stored in a jar of caster sugar, and the flavoured sugar used for sweetening. A pinch of salt improves the flavour of all puddings.

Cooking Milk Puddings

Boiling and steaming: Puddings cooked directly in a saucepan, not in a mould, must only be allowed to simmer. The saucepan must be thick, and it should be rinsed with cold water, or greased, before putting in the pudding mixture. Stir the mixture well, from the bottom of the saucepan, as it cooks. A pudding cooked in the top of a double boiler needs no stirring but takes longer to cook. For moulded (shaped) puddings, prepare the mould or basin and a cover of greased paper or foil first. Grease them well with unsalted butter, margarine or cooking fat. Turn in the pudding, cover closely, and steam very gently until set.

Baking: The dish in which a baked pudding is cooked must be well greased and ready for use before making the pudding. It should stand in a shallow tray of water, so that it cooks evenly and slowly. Stand the tray of water on a baking sheet, for easy removal from the oven. Wipe round the rim of the dish after filling it, to remove any drops of spilt pudding. Finely shredded suet, flaked butter or margarine dotted over the top of the pudding before baking improves its appearance, flavour and texture. An oven-to-table baking dish may be substituted for a pie dish.

BASIC RECIPES

Large Grain Milk Puddings

(eg whole or flaked rice, sago, flaked tapioca)

4–5 helpings

butter for greasing	*15g butter (optional)*
100g grain	$\frac{1}{2} \times 2.5ml$ *spoon grated*
1 litre milk	*nutmeg* **or** *similar*
a pinch of salt	*flavouring (see* **Note***)*
50–75g caster sugar	

Butter a 1.75 litre pie dish. Wash the grain in cold water, and put it into the dish with the milk. Leave to stand for 30 minutes. Add the salt and sugar, and sprinkle with flakes of butter and nutmeg, if used. Bake in a cool oven at 150°C, Gas 2, for 2–2½ hours or until the pudding is thick and creamy, and brown on the top. The pudding is better if it cooks even more slowly, for 4–5 hours.

Note If using a flavouring essence, mix it into the milk before cooking. If using dried or canned milk, reduce the grain to 75g, use the quantity of milk product to make up 1 litre, and cook at 140°C, Gas 1, for at least 3½–4 hours.

Large Grain Milk Puddings with Eggs

6 helpings

100g grain	*50–75g caster sugar*
1 litre milk	*flavouring*
2–3 eggs	*butter for greasing*
a pinch of salt	

Wash the grain in cold water and put it into the top of a double boiler with the milk. Cook slowly for about 1 hour, or until the grain is tender. Remove from the heat and leave to cool slightly. Separate the eggs. Stir the egg yolks, salt, sugar and flavouring into the grain. Whisk the egg whites to the same consistency as the pudding, and fold into the mixture. Pour into a buttered 1.75 litre pie dish and bake in a warm oven at 160°C, Gas 3, for 40–45 minutes until the top is brown.

Medium and Small Grain Milk Puddings

(eg coarsely ground rice, semolina or oatmeal, small sago, cornmeal)

6 helpings

1 litre milk
flavouring (p957)
75g grain
a pinch of salt

50–75g caster sugar
butter for greasing
(optional)

Warm the milk. Infuse any solid flavouring, if used, in the milk for about 10 minutes; then remove. Sprinkle the grain into the milk, stirring quickly to prevent lumps forming. Bring to simmering point, stirring all the time. Continue stirring, and simmer for 15–20 minutes or until the grain is transparent and cooked through. Add the salt, sugar, and any flavouring essence used.

The pudding can then be served as it is, hot or cold; alternatively, it can be poured into a well-buttered 1.75 litre pie dish, and baked in a moderate oven at 180°C, Gas 4, for 20–30 minutes until the top has browned.

Serve with stewed fruit, or with warmed jam or marmalade.

VARIATION

Medium and Small Grain Milk Puddings with Eggs

Cook the grain as above, but add the salt with the grain. Leave to cool slightly. Separate 2–3 eggs. Stir the yolks, 50–75g sugar, and any flavouring essence into the grain. Whisk the egg whites to the same consistency as the pudding, and fold into the mixture. Pour the mixture into a well-buttered 1.75 litre pie dish, and bake in a warm oven at 160°C, Gas 3, for 30–40 minutes until the top has browned.

Serve with stewed fruit, or with warmed jam or marmalade.

Powdered Grain Puddings

(eg arrowroot, cornflour, custard powder, finely ground rice, fine oatmeal)

6 helpings

1 litre milk
flavouring (p957)
65g grain
a pinch of salt

50–75g caster sugar
butter for greasing
(optional)

Warm the milk. Infuse any solid flavouring, if used, in the milk for 30 minutes; then remove. Blend the grain with a little of the milk. Bring the rest of the milk to boiling point with the salt, and pour on to the blended paste, stirring briskly to prevent lumps forming. Return the mixture to the saucepan, heat until it thickens, and simmer for 2–3 minutes to cook the grain completely, stirring all the time. Add the sugar and any flavouring used.

The pudding can then be served as it is, hot or cold or poured into a well-buttered 1.75 litre pie dish, and baked for 20–30 minutes in a moderate oven at 180°C, Gas 4, until the top has browned.

Serve with stewed fruit, or with warmed jam or marmalade.

VARIATION

Powdered Grain Puddings with Eggs

Cook the grain as above, but do not add the flavouring or the salt. Leave to cool slightly. Separate 2–4 eggs. Stir the egg yolks, salt, sugar, and any flavourings into the grain. Whisk the egg whites to the same consistency as the pudding, and fold into the mixture. Pour into a well-buttered 1.75 litre pie dish, and bake in a warm oven at 160°C, Gas 3, for about 30 minutes until the top has browned. Sprinkle with brown sugar and/or butter flakes before baking, if liked.

Serve with stewed fruit, or with warmed jam or marmalade.

OTHER MILK PUDDINGS

Rice Puddings

Geneva Pudding

6 helpings

75g Carolina **or** similar rice	50g butter
750ml milk	$\frac{1}{2} \times 2.5$ml spoon ground cinnamon
a pinch of salt	3×15ml spoons water
75g caster sugar	butter for greasing
1kg cooking apples	

Wash the rice and simmer it in the milk, with the salt, for about 1 hour or until tender. Add 25g of the sugar. Peel, core, and chop the apples. Put them into a second saucepan with the butter, cinnamon, and water. Simmer gently until soft, then sieve. Add the rest of the sugar. Arrange the rice and apple in alternate layers in a buttered 1.5 litre pie dish, with rice on the top and bottom. Bake in a moderate oven at 180°C, Gas 4, for 20–30 minutes.

Lemon Rice

6 helpings

50g Carolina **or** similar rice	2 eggs
500ml milk	butter for greasing
a pinch of salt	3×15ml spoons smooth seedless jam
pared rind and juice of 1 lemon	50g caster sugar
75g granulated sugar	caster sugar for dredging

Wash the rice and put it in a double boiler with the milk, salt and lemon rind; simmer for about 1 hour or until tender. Remove the rind and stir in the granulated sugar. Cool slightly. Separate the eggs. Stir the yolks and lemon juice into the rice. Pour into a buttered 1 litre pie dish and bake in a warm oven at 160°C, Gas 3, for 20–25 minutes. Spread the jam on top of the pudding. Whisk the egg whites until stiff, and fold in the caster sugar. Pile on top of the pudding, dredge with a little extra caster sugar, and bake in a very cool oven at 140°C, Gas 1, for 20–30 minutes until the meringue is set and coloured.

Empress Pudding

6–7 helpings

100g Carolina **or** similar rice	butter for greasing
1 litre milk	75g prepared shortcrust pastry (p1249)
a pinch of salt	flour for rolling out
50g butter **or** margarine	200g jam **or** stewed fruit
50g caster sugar	

Wash the rice and simmer it in the milk, with the salt, for about 1 hour or until tender. Add the fat and sugar. Butter the base of a 1.25 litre oven-to-table baking dish. Roll out the pastry on a lightly floured surface and line the sides of the dish with it. Spread a layer of rice on the bottom and cover with jam or fruit. Repeat the layers until the dish is full, finishing with a layer of rice. Bake in a moderate oven at 180°C, Gas 4, for 25–30 minutes.

Serve with any suitable sweet sauce.

Rice Meringue Pudding

6 helpings

75g Carolina **or** similar rice	25g butter
750ml milk	2 eggs
a pinch of salt	butter for greasing
1 bay leaf	50g caster sugar
40g granulated sugar	caster sugar for dredging

Wash the rice and simmer it in the milk with the salt and bay leaf for about 1 hour, until the rice is tender. Remove the bay leaf. Add the granulated sugar and butter. Cool slightly. Separate the eggs and stir the yolks into the rice. Pour into a buttered 1.5 litre pie dish. Whisk the egg whites until stiff, and fold in the caster sugar in spoonfuls. Pile on top of the rice, dredge with a little extra caster sugar and bake in a very cool oven at 140°C, Gas 1, until the meringue is crisp and golden-brown.

VARIATION

Pears and Rice

Arrange 6 pear halves, cut side down, on the rice in the dish, cover with the meringue and bake.

Caramel Rice Pudding

6 helpings

125g Carolina **or** similar rice	75g lump sugar
750ml milk	75ml water
a pinch of salt	2 eggs
	40g caster sugar

Wash the rice, and put it into a saucepan with the milk and salt. Bring to simmering point and simmer for about 1 hour or until the rice is soft and all the milk has been absorbed.

Meanwhile, prepare a thickly folded band of newspaper long enough to encircle a 1 litre charlotte mould (it can then be held firmly in one hand when heated). Heat the mould in boiling water or in the oven and wrap the newspaper round it. Prepare the caramel by heating the sugar and water together, stirring until it boils. Remove the spoon and leave it to boil, without stirring, until golden-brown. Immediately, pour the caramel into the warmed charlotte mould; twist and turn it until the sides and base are evenly coated. Leave to harden for a few minutes.

Beat the eggs until liquid and stir them into the cooked rice with the sugar. Turn into the prepared mould, cover with greased greaseproof paper or foil, and steam for 1 hour or until firm. Turn out, if liked. Serve hot or cold.

Swedish Rice

6 helpings

300g Carolina **or** similar rice	75g caster sugar
a pinch of salt	$\frac{1}{2} \times 2.5$ml spoon ground cinnamon
600g cooking apples	100ml sweet sherry
pared rind of 1 lemon	100g raisins
375ml milk	

Wash the rice and cook it in boiling salted water for 3 minutes; drain well. Peel and core the apples and slice them thinly. Put the rice, apples, lemon rind, and milk into a saucepan and simmer gently for about 45 minutes until tender. Remove the rind. Add the sugar, cinnamon, sherry, and raisins, and cook for a further 4–5 minutes. Serve with cream.

Windsor Pudding

6 helpings

40g Carolina **or** similar rice	grated **or** pared rind and juice of $\frac{1}{2}$ lemon (see Method)
375ml milk	50g caster sugar
1kg cooking apples	3 eggs
	butter for greasing

Wash the rice and simmer it in the milk for 45 minutes –1 hour or until the rice is tender and all the milk has been absorbed. Cool slightly. Peel, core, and chop the apples roughly, and stew in a covered pan until soft. Shake the pan from time to time to prevent them sticking. Rub the apples through a sieve, then add the grated rind and juice of the lemon. Alternatively, process the apples in an electric blender with the pared rind and juice. Stir the cooked rice into the apples with the sugar. Separate the eggs; whisk the whites until fairly stiff and fold them into the mixture. Put the mixture into a buttered 1 litre basin, cover with greased greaseproof paper or foil, and steam very gently for 40–45 minutes.

Serve with Pouring Cup Custard made from the egg yolks (p964).

Semolina Puddings

Chocolate Semolina

4–5 helpings

800ml milk	50g caster sugar
65g semolina	a few drops vanilla essence
75g plain chocolate	

Heat 750ml of the milk, sprinkle in the semolina, stir well, and simmer for 15–20 minutes or until the semolina is cooked. Meanwhile, grate the chocolate into a pan, add the remaining milk and heat until the chocolate has melted. Stir into the semolina with the sugar and essence, and serve at once.

Hasty Pudding

6 helpings

750ml milk	25g caster sugar
65g semolina **or** sago **or** ground rice	

Heat the milk almost to boiling point. Sprinkle in the grain and stir briskly. Simmer for 10–15 minutes until the grain is cooked, and the mixture has thickened. Stir in the sugar.

Serve with cream, jam or golden syrup.

Honey Pudding (1)

5–6 helpings

125ml milk	1 × 2.5ml spoon ground ginger
25g semolina	
2 eggs	150g stale white breadcrumbs
25g butter	
100g honey	fat for greasing
grated rind of ½ lemon	

Heat the milk, sprinkle in the semolina, and cook for 10 minutes, stirring all the time. Separate the eggs. Add the yolks to the semolina with the butter, honey, lemon rind, ground ginger, and breadcrumbs. Beat well. Whisk the egg whites until fairly stiff and fold into the mixture. Put into a greased 600–750ml basin, cover with greased greaseproof paper or foil, and steam gently for 1¾–2 hours.

Serve with Almond Sauce (p720).

Note For Honey Pudding (2), see p987.

Semolina Soufflé
See p977.

Hot Timbale of Semolina

6 helpings

butter for greasing	2 eggs
500ml milk	2 × 15ml spoons single cream
75g semolina	
50g caster sugar	
a few drops vanilla essence	

Decoration

6 canned apricot halves	3 glacé cherries
250ml apricot syrup from can	1 × 10ml spoon chopped almonds
1 strip angelica	

Butter a 750ml timbale mould or 6 small dariole moulds. Heat the milk, sprinkle in the semolina, stirring all the time, and simmer for 10–15 minutes until it is cooked. Cool slightly. Add the sugar and vanilla essence. Separate the eggs, and stir the yolks into the mixture. Beat with an electric or rotary whisk until it is nearly cold. Whisk the egg whites until just stiff, and fold into the mixture with the cream. Three-quarters fill the timbale mould or small moulds with the mixture. Cover with greased greaseproof paper or foil. Steam a large mould for about 45 minutes and small moulds for 30 minutes or until set.

Meanwhile, heat the apricots between 2 plates over simmering water. Boil the apricot syrup until well reduced. When the pudding is cooked and set, turn out on to a hot dish and decorate with halved apricots, angelica, glacé cherries and chopped almonds. Pour the syrup round and serve.

Note For a Timbale of Semolina served cold, see p1000.

Other Grain Puddings
(tapioca, cornmeal, etc)

Tapioca Cream Pudding

6 helpings

75g tapioca	*½ × 2.5ml spoon almond*
750ml milk	*essence*
a pinch of salt	*3 eggs*
*15g butter **or** margarine*	*butter for greasing*
1 × 15ml spoon caster	*75g ratafias **or** small*
sugar	*macaroons*

Wash the tapioca and soak it in the milk for 1–2 hours with the salt. Heat to simmering point, and simmer for about 1 hour until the grain is soft and all the milk has been absorbed. Add the butter, sugar, and essence. Cool slightly. Separate the eggs and stir the yolks into the tapioca. Pour the mixture into a buttered 1 litre pie dish, and bake in a moderate oven at 180°C, Gas 4, for 15–20 minutes. Crush the ratafias or macaroons. Whisk the egg whites until stiff, and fold in the biscuits. Pile on top of the tapioca. Bake in a very cool oven at 140°C, Gas 1, for 20–30 minutes.

American Indian Pudding

4 helpings

750ml milk	*½ × 2.5ml spoon ground*
*75g white **or** yellow*	*cinnamon **or** nutmeg*
cornmeal	*25g butter*
100g caster sugar	*fat for greasing*

Heat the milk until it comes to the boil, and pour in the cornmeal. Cook over gentle heat for 5 minutes, stirring all the time, until thickened. Remove from the heat and stir in the sugar, spice, and butter. Pour into a greased 1 litre pie dish and bake in a very cool oven at 140°–150°C, Gas 1–2, for 1 hour until browned on top.

Serve with maple syrup.

Cornmeal Pudding

4 helpings

500ml milk	*grated rind and juice of*
*75g white **or** yellow*	*½ lemon*
cornmeal	*2 eggs*
75g caster sugar	*fat for greasing*
50g seedless raisins	

Heat the milk until it just comes to the boil, and pour in the cornmeal. Cook over gentle heat for 5 minutes, stirring all the time, until thickened. Remove from the heat and stir in the sugar and raisins. Add the lemon rind and juice. Cool slightly. Beat the eggs thoroughly and add to the mixture. Put into a greased 750ml pie dish, level the top, if necessary, and bake in a moderate oven at 180°C, Gas 4, for 50–60 minutes until risen and browned on top.

Serve with cream or ice cream.

Honesty Pudding

See p865.

Oatmeal Flummery

4–6 helpings

150g fine oatmeal	*juice of 1 orange*
500ml water	*1 × 15ml spoon caster*
extra water	*sugar **or** honey*

Soak the oatmeal in the 500ml water for 24 hours. Put the mixture into a large measuring jug. Measure an equal volume of water. Place the oatmeal mixture and extra water in a large container, and soak for another 24 hours. Strain through a fine sieve into a pan, squeezing or pressing to extract as much floury liquid as possible. Add the orange juice and sugar or honey to the mixture in the pan. Stir over gentle heat for 15–20 minutes or until the mixture boils and is very thick.

Serve warm.

Sweet Custards and Custard Puddings

These are traditionally made from a mixture of eggs and milk, cooked just enough to set the egg in the mixture. If used as a sauce the custard may still be liquid; or it may be firm enough to turn out (eg Caramel Custard), depending on the proportion of eggs to milk. Great care must be taken not to overcook a custard; it should be smooth and creamy rather than grainy, and must therefore be cooked very slowly.

The egg mixture is frequently strained prior to cooking; a very fine nylon sieve should be used for this purpose.

A custard can be served alone, as an accompaniment to other dishes or as an integral part of such cold dishes as trifles (pp1033–36).

Cup or 'Boiled' Custard

This custard is cooked over heat, eg in a saucepan. In spite of its name, it should never be boiled but kept at a temperature *below* boiling point until all the egg has set evenly and smoothly. Ideally, the custard should be cooked over hot or simmering water rather than over direct heat. Using a double boiler lessens the risk of curdling considerably but a heatproof bowl or basin placed over a pan of simmering water is a good substitute. If the custard is made directly in a saucepan, the pan must have a thick base and should be heated very gently. It should be rinsed out with cold water before being heated.

This type of custard is often called a 'cup' custard because it used to be served cold in individual glass custard cups.

Although a pouring custard for use as a sauce is traditionally made in this way, it is frequently made nowadays from a proprietary custard powder or cornflour, with, or instead of, eggs. Recipes for custard sauces may be found on pp722–23.

Baked Custard

For this custard, the eggs should be beaten until liquid and blended well with the milk and any flavouring used, but should not be whisked until frothy. Air bubbles in the froth produce holes in the cooked custard, spoiling the smooth consistency.

To make the custard, the egg and milk mixture is poured into a well-greased, ovenproof dish which is put into a baking tin containing enough hot water to come half-way up the sides of the dish. This is to ensure that the custard cooks without boiling. The custard is then baked in a cool oven until set. The dish should be removed from the oven and from the water immediately the custard is set to prevent any further cooking.

Steamed Custard

Although steamed custard is cooked over simmering water like a cup custard, it contains more eggs since it is meant to be firm. It is usually made and served in the same dish, although some steamed custards contain enough eggs to be turned out.

The basin or dish in which the custard is cooked must be well greased, and the custard must be closely covered with greaseproof paper or foil to prevent any condensed steam dripping on to it. It must be steamed very gently to prevent overcooking.

BASIC RECIPES

Cup or 'Boiled' Custard
(Coating custard)

4 helpings or 500ml (approx)

500ml milk
*4 eggs **or** 3 eggs and*
* 2 yolks*

25g caster sugar
flavouring (see below)

Warm the milk to approximately 65°C. Mix the eggs and sugar together well, and stir in the milk. Strain the custard into a saucepan or into a heat-proof bowl placed over a pan of simmering water. Alternatively, use a double boiler, but make sure the water does not touch the upper pan. Cook over very gentle heat for 15–25 minutes, stirring all the time with a wooden spoon, until the custard thickens to the consistency of single cream. Stir well round the sides as well as the base of the pan or basin to prevent lumps forming, especially if using a double boiler. Do *not* let the custard boil. If it shows the slightest sign of curdling, put the pan or bowl into a bowl of cold water, or turn the custard into a clean basin and whisk rapidly.

As soon as the custard thickens, pour it into a jug to stop further cooking. Keep it warm by standing the jug in a basin of hot water. If it is to be served cold, pour into a basin and cover with a piece of dampened greaseproof paper to prevent a skin forming. When cold, pour into a serving dish.

Note A mixture of whole eggs and yolks gives a richer, smoother custard.

Flavourings

Vanilla: Add a few drops of vanilla essence with the sugar.

Lemon: Infuse strips of lemon rind in the warm milk for 30 minutes, then remove before adding the milk to the eggs.

Bay: Infuse a piece of bay leaf in the warm milk for 30 minutes, then remove before adding to the eggs.

Nutmeg or cinnamon: Sprinkle the top of the cooked custard with grated nutmeg or ground cinnamon.

VARIATIONS

Pouring Custard

Make as above but use only 3 eggs or 2 eggs and 2 yolks. The custard will thicken only to the consistency of thin single cream or top of the milk.

Rich Custard

Stir 2 × 15ml spoons double cream into the custard when it is cooling.

Simple Custard

4 helpings or 500ml (approx)

1 × 10ml spoon
* cornflour*
500ml milk

25g caster sugar
2 eggs
flavouring (see above)

This custard will not curdle as easily as a cup custard but still keeps the delicious creamy flavour of an egg custard.

Blend the cornflour to a smooth paste with a little of the cold milk. Heat the rest of the milk, and when hot pour it on to the blended cornflour, stirring well. Return to the saucepan, bring to the boil and boil for 1–2 minutes, stirring all the time, to cook the cornflour. Remove from the heat and add the sugar. Leave to cool. Beat the eggs together lightly. Add a little of the cooked cornflour mixture, stir well, then pour into the saucepan. Heat gently for a few minutes until the egg has thickened, stirring all the time. Do not boil.

Serve hot or cold as an accompaniment to a pudding or pie.

Baked Custard

4 helpings or 500ml (approx)

500ml milk
2 eggs (for a softly set
* custard)* **or** *3 eggs (for*
* a firmer custard)*

25g caster sugar
fat for greasing
grated nutmeg **or** *other*
* flavouring (see* **Note***)*

Warm the milk to approximately 65°C. Mix the eggs and sugar together and stir in the milk. Strain the custard into a greased 700ml ovenproof dish. Sprinkle nutmeg on top, if used. Stand the dish in a tin containing enough hot water to come half-way up the sides of the dish, and bake in a very cool oven at 140°–150°C, Gas 1–2, for 1 hour or until the custard is set in the centre.

Note If preferred, the nutmeg can be omitted and the custard flavoured by infusing a bay leaf or thinly cut strips of lemon rind in the milk for a few minutes; they must, however, be removed before adding the milk to the eggs.

Steamed Custard

4 helpings or 500ml (approx)

500ml milk
4 eggs **or** *3 eggs and*
* 2 yolks*

25g caster sugar
fat for greasing
flavouring (p964)

Warm the milk to approximately 65°C. Mix the eggs and sugar together and stir in the milk. Strain the custard into a greased 750ml heatproof dish, cover with greased foil or oiled greaseproof paper, and steam very gently for about 40 minutes until just firm in the centre.

Serve hot or cold with fruit or Jam Sauce (p726).

Note The custard can be turned out on to a warm plate for serving, but when it is removed from the steamer, leave it to stand for a few minutes before attempting to turn it out.

Crème Anglaise (2)

(Thick custard)

4 helpings or 500ml (approx)

500ml milk
a few drops vanilla
* essence* **or** *other*
* flavouring (see below)*

8 egg yolks
100g caster sugar

Warm the milk gently without letting it boil, and infuse any solid flavouring used; then remove. Beat the egg yolks and sugar together until creamy. Add the milk. Strain the custard into a double boiler or a basin placed over a pan of simmering water. Cook, stirring all the time with a wooden spoon, for 20–30 minutes or until the custard thickens and coats the back of the spoon. Take care not to let the custard curdle.

Use hot, or pour into a basin and cool, stirring from time to time to prevent a skin forming.

Note The recipe given here can be used as a basis for ice cream or for a Bavarian Cream p1028.

Flavourings

Lemon: Infuse a thin strip of lemon rind in the milk, then remove before adding the eggs.

Orange: Add orange rind in the same way as lemon rind.

Liqueur: Add 1 × 15ml spoon Kirsch, curaçao or rum at the end of the cooking time.

Praline: Top with crushed praline (p1241).

VARIATIONS

A simpler Crème Anglaise can be made in an ordinary saucepan without curdling too easily. Use 6 egg yolks and blend them and the sugar with 2 × 5ml spoons cornflour or arrowroot. Continue as above.

To make Crème Anglaise as a sauce and to make other sweet custard sauces, see pp722–23.

OTHER CUSTARD PUDDINGS AND DESSERTS

Apple Snow (1)

6 helpings

1kg cooking apples	2 eggs
pared rind of 1 lemon	250ml milk
75ml water	butter for greasing
175g caster sugar	

Peel, core, and slice the apples into a saucepan. Add the lemon rind and water. Cover and cook until the apples are pulped. Remove the lemon rind and beat the apple purée until smooth. Add 100g of the sugar. Separate the eggs and beat the yolks until liquid in a basin. Heat together the milk and 25g of the sugar and pour on to the egg yolks. Return the mixture to the saucepan and cook, stirring all the time, until the mixture coats the back of the spoon. Do not allow the mixture to boil. Put the apple purée into a buttered 1 litre pie dish, pour the custard over it, and bake in a warm oven at 160°C, Gas 3, for 30–40 minutes. Whisk the egg whites until stiff, fold in the remaining 50g sugar and pile on top of the custard. Return to the oven and bake for a further 10 minutes until the meringue is just set.

Serve with Simple Custard (p964) or cream.

Note For Apple Snow served cold, see p1005.

Banana Custard

4 helpings

500ml Coating Cup Custard (p964)	3 bananas (400g approx)

Decoration (optional)
4 × 5ml spoons crushed butterscotch **or** grated chocolate **or** browned flaked almonds

Make the custard. Peel and slice the bananas. Add to the custard and leave to stand for 5 minutes. Spoon into a serving dish or 4 glasses. Decorate before serving.

Banana Meringue

4 helpings

Crème Anglaise (p965) using 500ml milk and 4 egg yolks only	50g caster sugar a few drops lemon juice 2 egg whites
4 bananas	

Decoration
glacé cherries — angelica

Make the Crème Anglaise. Peel and mash the bananas and put into 4 individual ovenproof dishes, adding a little of the sugar and the lemon juice. Pour the custard over the bananas. Whisk the egg whites until stiff, add half the remaining sugar and whisk again. Fold in nearly all the remaining sugar. Pile the meringue on top of the custard, making sure it covers the surface of the pudding entirely. Arrange in decorative peaks and sprinkle with the remaining sugar. Bake in a very cool oven at 120°C, Gas ½, for 40–45 minutes until the meringue is set. Decorate with the cherries and angelica. Serve hot or cold.

Bread and Butter Pudding

4 helpings

butter for greasing	a pinch of nutmeg **or**
4 thin slices bread (100g approx)	cinnamon
25g butter	400ml milk
50g sultanas **or** currants	2 eggs
	25g granulated sugar

Grease a 1 litre pie dish. Cut the crusts off the bread and spread the slices with the butter. Cut the bread into squares or triangles and arrange in alternate layers, buttered side up, with the sultanas or currants. Sprinkle each layer lightly with spices. Arrange the top layer of bread in an attractive pattern. Warm the milk to approximately 65°C; do not let it come near the boil. Beat together the eggs and most of the sugar with a fork and stir in the milk. Strain the custard over the bread, sprinkle some nutmeg and the remaining sugar on top, and leave to stand for 30 minutes. Bake in a moderate oven at 180°C, Gas 4, for 30–40 minutes until set and lightly browned.

Cabinet Pudding (1)

(plain)

4 helpings

fat for greasing	*3 eggs*
75g seedless raisins	*25g caster sugar*
3–4 slices white bread	*1 × 5ml spoon grated*
(100g approx)	*lemon rind*
400ml milk	

Grease a 1 litre pudding basin and halve the raisins. Decorate the sides and base of the basin by pressing on some of the dried fruit. Chill. Remove the crusts from the bread and cut the slices into 5mm dice. Warm the milk to approximately 65°C; do not let it come near the boil. Beat the eggs and sugar together with a fork and stir in the milk. Add the lemon rind to the bread with the rest of the raisins. Strain the custard over the bread, stir, and leave to stand for 30 minutes. Pour into the prepared basin and cover with greased foil or greaseproof paper. Steam gently for 1 hour or until the pudding is firm in the centre. Remove the cooked pudding from the steamer, leave to stand for a few minutes, and turn out on to a warmed dish.

Serve with Jam Sauce (p726).

Cabinet Pudding (2)

(traditional)

4 helpings

50g glacé cherries **or**	*9 ratafias* **or**
seedless raisins	*2 macaroons*
2 × 15ml spoons	*400ml milk*
medium-sweet sherry	*3 eggs*
fat for greasing	*25g caster sugar*
4 individual trifle	*a few drops vanilla*
sponges (5 × 7cm	*essence*
approx)	

Decoration
glacé cherries	*angelica*

Soak the glacé cherries or raisins in the sherry. Grease a 13cm round cake tin and line the base with oiled greaseproof paper. Cut up the cherries and angelica for the decoration. Decorate the bottom of the tin with them. Cut the sponges into 1cm dice, crumble the ratafias or macaroons and mix them together. Drain the dried fruit. Put alternate layers of cake and fruit in the tin. Warm the milk to approximately 65°C; do not let it come near the boil. Beat the eggs and sugar together with a fork and stir in the milk. Add a few drops of vanilla essence. Strain the custard into the tin slowly, so as not to disturb the decoration. Leave to stand for 1 hour. Cover with greased foil or greaseproof paper and steam gently for 1 hour. Remove the pudding from the steamer, leave to stand for a few minutes, turn out on to a warmed dish and peel off the paper.

Serve with Sabayon Sauce (p723) or Jam Sauce (p726).

Note For Cabinet Pudding served cold, see p1037.

Crème Brûlée (1)

4 helpings

1 × 15ml spoon	*3 eggs*
cornflour	*50g caster sugar*
250ml milk	*fat for greasing*
250ml single cream	*ground cinnamon*
a few drops vanilla	*(optional)*
essence	

Blend the cornflour to a smooth paste with a little of the milk, and bring the rest of the milk to the boil. Pour the boiling milk on to the blended cornflour, stirring well. Return the mixture to the pan, bring to the boil, and boil for 1 minute, stirring all the time. Remove from the heat and leave to cool. Beat together the cream, vanilla essence, and eggs. Stir into the cooled mixture. Whisk over low heat for about 30 minutes or until the custard thickens; do not boil. Add 25g sugar and pour into a greased 600ml flameproof dish. Sprinkle the pudding with the rest of the sugar and a little cinnamon, if used. Place under a hot grill for 10 minutes or until the sugar has melted and turned brown. Keep the custard about 10cm from the heat. Serve hot or cold.

Alternatively, bake in a fairly hot oven at 200°C, Gas 6, for about 15 minutes until the pudding is browned.

Crème Brûlée (2)

4 helpings

250ml single cream **or** milk
250ml double cream
1 vanilla pod **or** a few drops vanilla essence **or** 1 × 15ml spoon brandy

6 egg yolks
25g caster sugar
4 × 15ml spoons caster sugar (approx)

Warm the cream or milk and the double cream slowly, with the vanilla pod, if used, in a double boiler or a basin over a pan of hot water. Beat the egg yolks and 25g caster sugar together thoroughly. When the cream feels just warm to the finger, remove the pod, if used, pour the cream on to the yolks, stir, and return to the double saucepan or basin. Continue to cook gently for about 40 minutes, stirring all the time with a wooden spoon, until the custard thickens to the consistency of single cream. Scrape down the sides of the pan frequently to prevent lumps forming, and do not let the custard come near boiling point. If a vanilla pod has not been used, add a few drops of vanilla essence or the brandy. Strain the custard into a shallow 600ml flameproof dish, stand it on a baking sheet and bake in a warm oven at 160°C, Gas 3, for 5–10 minutes until a skin has formed on the top. Do not allow it to colour. Leave to cool, then refrigerate for at least 2–3 hours, or preferably overnight.

Heat the grill. Sprinkle enough caster sugar over the surface of the custard to cover it entirely with an even, thin layer. Place under the hot grill for 10–15 minutes or until the sugar melts and turns to caramel. Keep the top of the custard about 10cm from the heat. Serve hot or cold.

If serving cold, tap the caramel sharply with the back of a spoon to break it up.

Caramel Custard

4 helpings

100g lump **or** granulated sugar
150ml water
400ml milk **or** 300ml milk and 100ml single cream

2 eggs and 2 yolks **or** 3 eggs
25g caster sugar
a few drops vanilla essence

Prepare a thickly folded band of newspaper long enough to encircle a 13cm round cake tin or charlotte mould. Heat the tin or mould in boiling water or in the oven and wrap the newspaper round it. Prepare the caramel by heating the sugar and water together, stirring occasionally, until the sugar dissolves completely. Bring to the boil gently, and boil, without stirring, for about 10 minutes until the syrup turns golden-brown. Do not let it turn dark brown as it will have a bitter taste. Pour a little of the caramel on to a metal plate and put to one side. Pour the remaining caramel into the warmed, dry tin, tilt and turn it, holding it by the paper, until the base and sides are evenly coated. Leave until cold and set.

Warm the milk and cream to approximately 65°C; do not let it come near the boil. Beat the eggs and sugar together with a fork and stir in the milk. Add a few drops of vanilla essence. Strain the custard into the tin and cover with greased foil or greaseproof paper. Steam very gently for about 40 minutes or until the custard is firm in the centre.

Alternatively, stand the custard in a shallow tin containing enough warm water to come half-way up the sides of the dish, and bake in a very cool oven at 140°–150°C, Gas 1–2, for 1 hour.

Remove the cooked custard and leave it to stand for a few minutes, then turn it out carefully on to a warmed dish. The caramel will run off and serve as a sauce. Break up the reserved caramel by tapping sharply with a metal spoon, and decorate the top of the custard with the pieces of broken caramel.

Note Individual caramel custards can be made in four 150ml ovenproof moulds. Steam for 20 minutes, or bake for 30 minutes.

Cornflour Custard Pie

4 helpings

shortcrust pastry   500ml milk
  (p1249) using   2 eggs
  125g flour   50g caster sugar
flour for rolling out   a few drops vanilla
2 × 15ml spoons   essence **or** a pinch of
  cornflour   grated nutmeg

Roll out the pastry on a lightly floured surface and use it to line an 18cm flan ring or pie plate; prick the base. Blend the cornflour to a smooth paste with a little of the milk, and bring the rest of the milk to the boil. Pour the boiling milk on to the blended cornflour, stirring well. Return the mixture to the pan, bring to the boil, and boil for 1 minute, stirring all the time. Remove from the heat and leave to cool; stir from time to time or cover with dampened greaseproof paper to prevent a skin forming. Mix the eggs and sugar together and stir in the cooled cornflour mixture gradually. Add a few drops of vanilla essence, if liked. Pour the custard into the flan case. If vanilla essence has not been used, sprinkle grated nutmeg on top. Bake in a fairly hot oven at 190°C, Gas 5, for 10 minutes, then reduce the temperature to very cool, 140°–150°C, Gas 1–2, and bake for a further 20–25 minutes or until the custard is set in the centre.

Custard Tart

4 helpings

shortcrust pastry   250ml milk
  (p1249) using   2 eggs
  125g flour   50g caster sugar
flour for rolling out   a pinch of grated nutmeg

Put an 18cm flan ring on a heavy baking sheet or line an 18cm sandwich tin with foil. Roll out the pastry on a lightly floured surface and use it to line the flan ring or cake tin, taking care not to stretch the pastry. Warm the milk to approximately 65°C; do not let it come near the boil. Beat the eggs and sugar together with a fork and add the milk. Strain the mixture into the pastry case and sprinkle the top with grated nutmeg. Bake in a fairly hot oven at 190°C, Gas 5, for 10 minutes, reduce the temperature to cool, 150°C, Gas 2, and bake for a further 15–20 minutes or until the custard is just set. Serve hot or cold.

Floating Islands

4 helpings

3 eggs   a few drops vanilla
200g caster sugar   essence
500ml milk

Separate the eggs. Whisk the egg whites until very stiff. Fold in 150g caster sugar. Pour the milk into a frying pan and add a few drops of vanilla essence. Heat gently until the surface of the milk is just shivering. It must not boil or the milk will discolour and form a skin. Using 2 dessertspoons, mould egg shapes from the meringue and slide them into the milk. Make only a few at a time, and leave plenty of space between them in the pan as they swell when cooking. Cook slowly for 5 minutes, then turn them over, using a palette knife and a spoon, and cook for a further 5 minutes. They are very delicate and must be handled with care. Remove from the milk gently and place on a cloth or soft kitchen paper to drain. Continue making shapes from the meringue and poaching them in the milk, until all the meringue is used. Arrange the 'islands' in a flat serving dish.

Blend the egg yolks with the rest of the sugar, then stir in the milk gradually. Strain the mixture into a saucepan and cook gently, stirring all the time, until the sauce thickens slightly. Do not let it come near the boil or it will curdle. Pour the custard round the 'islands' and serve at once.

Forest Pudding

4 helpings

3 pieces plain cake **or**
  individual trifle
  sponges (5 × 7cm
  approx)
jam
fat for greasing

1 × 5ml spoon grated
  lemon rind
500ml milk
2 eggs
25g caster sugar

Cut the cake vertically into 1cm slices, spread half the slices with jam, and sandwich in pairs with the remaining slices. Place the cake in a greased 750ml pie dish and sprinkle with the lemon rind. Warm the milk to approximately 65°C; do not let it come near the boil. Beat the eggs and sugar together with a fork and add the milk. Strain the custard into the dish and leave to stand for 1 hour. Bake very slowly in a very cool oven at 140°–150°C, Gas 1–2, for 1–1¼ hours until the custard is set and the pudding browned on top.

Lemon Delicious Pudding

4 helpings

3 eggs
1 × 15ml spoon self-
  raising flour
75g caster sugar
200ml milk
juice and grated rind of 2
  large lemons

a pinch of salt
1 × 15ml spoon icing
  sugar
butter for greasing

Separate the eggs. Sift the flour. Beat the yolks with the caster sugar until light, pale, and creamy. Whisk the milk, flour, lemon juice, and rind into the egg yolks. Whisk the egg whites with the salt, adding the icing sugar gradually. Continue to whisk until stiff but not dry. Fold into the lemon mixture. Grease a deep 1 litre ovenproof dish and pour the mixture into it. Stand the dish in a shallow pan of cold water and bake in a moderate oven at 180°C, Gas 4, for 1 hour.

Note This pudding has a light spongy top with lemon sauce underneath.

Lemon Meringue Pie

See p1264.

Marmalade Custard Pudding

4 helpings

3 × 15ml spoons
  marmalade
fat for greasing
75g soft white
  breadcrumbs

400ml milk
25g butter
2 eggs
75g caster sugar

Warm the marmalade so that it spreads easily. Grease a 750ml pie dish and spread half the marmalade over the bottom. Dry the crumbs slightly by placing in a cool oven for a few moments. Warm the milk and butter in a saucepan. Separate the eggs and stir 25g of the sugar into the yolks. Pour the warmed milk on to the yolks and stir well. Add the crumbs, mix thoroughly and leave to stand for 30 minutes. Pour half the breadcrumb mixture into the dish, add another layer of marmalade in small spoonfuls, and put the rest of the breadcrumb mixture on top. Smooth the top of the mixture, if necessary. Bake in a warm oven at 160°C, Gas 3, for 40–45 minutes until the pudding is lightly set.

Remove the pudding from the oven and reduce the temperature to very cool, 120°C, Gas ½. Whisk the egg whites until stiff, add half the remaining sugar and whisk again. Fold in nearly all the remaining sugar, then pile the meringue on top of the pudding, making sure it is entirely covered. Arrange in decorative peaks and sprinkle with the remaining sugar. Return the pudding to the oven for 40–45 minutes until the meringue is set and the peaks are brown.

Orange Custard

4 helpings

pared rind and juice of 3
  oranges
50g caster sugar

500ml boiling water
4 eggs

Put the orange rind, sugar, and boiling water into a basin, cover and leave for 2 hours. Strain the liquid into a pan and warm but do not boil it. Beat the eggs together and stir in the liquid. Strain the custard into the pan and heat very gently, stirring all the time with a wooden spoon until the custard thickens. Do not boil or the mixture will curdle. Strain the orange juice into the custard, and stir. Pour into 4 glasses and serve warm or chilled, topped with cream.

Pudding à l'Ambassadrice

4 helpings

1 savarin (p1048) *using
    half quantities*

Custard Filling
25g butter   *1 × 15ml spoon caster*
25g plain flour   *sugar*
150ml milk   *rum* **or** *brandy essence*
1 egg yolk
*3 × 15ml spoons single
    cream*

Caramel
100g granulated sugar   *150ml water*

Cream Custard
200ml milk   *1 × 15ml spoon caster*
2 eggs   *sugar*
100ml single cream

Make the savarin using half quantities. Bake in a fairly hot oven at 200°C, Gas 6, for about 20 minutes. Leave to cool.

Make the custard filling. Melt the butter, stir in the flour and cook for 1 minute. Stir in the milk gradually and bring to the boil, stirring all the time. Cool slightly. Beat the egg yolk, cream, and sugar together with a fork, and add to the cooled mixture. Re-heat, and cook gently, stirring all the time, until the mixture thickens. Add enough essence to give a definite flavour. Cool.

Prepare a thickly folded band of newspaper long enough to encircle a 13cm round cake tin. Heat the tin in boiling water or in the oven and wrap the newspaper round it. Prepare the caramel by heating together the sugar and water, stirring occasionally, until the sugar dissolves completely.

Bring to the boil, and boil without stirring until the syrup turns golden-brown. Do not let it turn dark brown or it will have a bitter taste. Pour the caramel into the warmed, dry tin, and tilt and turn, holding it by the paper, until the base and sides are evenly coated. Leave until cold and set.

Cut the savarin into 2cm slices, spread thickly with the custard filling and arrange in layers in the tin.

Make the cream custard. Warm the milk to approximately 65°C; do not let it come near the boil. Beat the eggs, cream, and sugar together with a fork, and stir in the milk. Strain the custard into the tin, making sure all the pieces of savarin are covered. Cover with greased foil or greaseproof paper and steam gently for 1 hour. Remove the cooked pudding from the steamer, leave to stand for a few minutes, then turn out on to a warmed plate.

Serve with cream.

Newmarket Pudding

4 helpings

fat for greasing   *400ml milk*
4 individual trifle   *3 eggs*
    sponges (5 × 7cm   *a few drops vanilla*
    approx)   *essence*
50g cut mixed peel   *3 × 15ml spoons*
50g seedless raisins   *redcurrant jelly*
25g currants

Grease a 13cm round cake tin. Cut the cake vertically into 1cm slices. Mix together the peel, raisins, and currants. Put the cake and fruit in the tin in layers. Warm the milk to approximately 65°C; do not let it come near the boil. Beat the eggs with a fork, add a few drops of vanilla essence and stir in the milk. Strain the custard over the cake and leave to stand for 1 hour. Cover with greased foil or greaseproof paper, and steam gently for 1 hour. Warm the redcurrant jelly over low heat until it melts. Remove the cooked pudding from the steamer, leave to stand for a few minutes and turn out on to a warmed dish. Pour the jelly over the pudding just before serving.

Pineapple Custard

4 helpings

1 × 375g can crushed pineapple	400ml milk
25g cornflour	2 eggs
	25g caster sugar

Drain the juice from the pineapple into a basin. Put the fruit into a 750ml ovenproof dish and spread it flat. Blend the cornflour to a smooth paste with a little of the milk. Heat the rest of the milk until it is almost boiling, and pour on to the blended cornflour. Stir in well. Return the mixture to the saucepan and bring to the boil, stirring all the time. Boil gently for 1–2 minutes. Remove from the heat and stir in the juice from the can. Separate the eggs and add the yolks to the cornflour sauce. Stir well. Return to the heat and cook very gently, without boiling, stirring all the time, until the mixture thickens. Remove from the heat and leave to cool; stir from time to time to prevent a skin forming.

Pour the custard over the pineapple. Whisk the egg whites until stiff, then whisk in most of the sugar. Spread the meringue over the custard, making sure that it is completely covered. Sprinkle with the rest of the sugar. Bake in a very cool oven at 140°C, Gas 1, for 30 minutes until the meringue is crisp and browned.

Queen's Pudding

4 helpings

oil for greasing	400ml milk
100g stale sponge cake	1 × 15ml spoon brandy
2 eggs	**or** sherry **or** a few
25g caster sugar	drops vanilla essence

Decoration

1 × 425g can apricot halves	sugar
	glacé cherries

Grease a 13cm round cake tin and line the base with oiled greaseproof paper. Crumble the sponge cake finely. Mix together the eggs and most of the sugar and stir in the milk. Add the flavouring, strain the custard mixture on to the crumbs, stir, and leave to stand for 10–15 minutes. Sprinkle the base of the tin with the rest of the sugar. Beat the crumb mixture until smooth, and pour it carefully into the tin. Cover with greased foil or greaseproof paper. Stand it in a shallow pan or tin containing enough warm water to come half-way up the sides of the cake tin, and bake in a very cool oven at 140°–150°C, Gas 1–2, for 75–80 minutes, or until firm in the centre.

Meanwhile, drain the apricot halves and boil the juice with sugar to taste until it is slightly reduced. Leave the cooked pudding to stand for a few minutes, then carefully unmould on to a warmed dish. Remove the paper, arrange the apricot halves on top of the pudding and decorate with glacé cherries. Serve with the apricot syrup sauce.

Queen of Puddings

4 helpings

75g soft white breadcrumbs	2 eggs
400ml milk	75g caster sugar
25g butter	fat for greasing
2 × 5ml spoons grated lemon rind	2 × 15ml spoons red jam

Dry the breadcrumbs slightly by placing in a cool oven for a few moments. Warm the milk with the butter and lemon rind, to approximately 65°C; do not let it come near the boil. Separate the eggs and stir 25g of the sugar into the yolks. Pour the warmed milk over the yolks, and stir in well. Add the crumbs and mix thoroughly. Pour the custard mixture into a greased 750ml pie dish and leave to stand for 30 minutes. Bake in a warm oven at 160°C, Gas 3, for 40–45 minutes until the pudding is lightly set.

Remove the pudding from the oven and reduce the temperature to 120°C, Gas ½. Warm the jam and spread it over the pudding. Whisk the egg whites until stiff, add half the remaining sugar and whisk again. Fold in nearly all the remaining sugar. Spoon the meringue round the edge of the jam and sprinkle with the remainder of the caster sugar. (The piled-up meringue and the red jam centre then suggest a crown.) Return the pudding to the oven for 40–45 minutes or until the meringue is set.

Ring of Pears or Other Fruit

4 helpings

fat for greasing	*25g caster sugar*
3 pieces plain cake **or**	*1 × 5ml spoon grated*
individual trifle	*lemon rind*
sponges (5 × 7cm	*1 × 425g can pear halves*
approx)	**or** *other fruit (see*
400ml milk	**Note)**
25g butter	*a few drops cochineal*
2 eggs	*(optional)*
1 egg yolk	

Grease a 500ml ring mould. Cut the cake vertically into 1cm slices and arrange them in the mould. Warm the milk and butter together until the butter just melts. Beat together the eggs, sugar, and grated lemon rind with a fork. Stir in the warmed milk and butter, and pour the mixture over the sponge cakes. Cover with greased foil or greaseproof paper. Stand the mould in a shallow pan or tin containing enough warm water to come half-way up the sides of the mould. Bake in a cool oven at 150°C, Gas 2, for about 1 hour or until set.

Strain the juice from the can of fruit and boil for 15 minutes until it is syrupy. Add a few drops of cochineal to make the syrup pink if using pale coloured fruit. Turn the ring out on to a hot dish, arrange the fruit in the centre and pour the syrup over the fruit.

Note If using other fruit, tint the syrup a suitable colour, and add extra sugar if necessary.

Savoy Pudding

4 helpings

125g stale plain cake	*2 eggs*
40g cut mixed peel	*fat for greasing*
40g butter	*50g caster sugar*
300ml milk	
50ml sweet sherry **or**	
Marsala	

Crumble the cake finely. Chop the peel even more finely. Melt the butter. Put the crumbs, peel, butter, milk, and sherry or wine into a basin. Separate the eggs and add the yolks to the mixture. Beat well and leave to stand for 10–15 minutes. Pour into a greased 750ml pie dish and bake in a warm oven at 160°C, Gas 3, for 35–40 minutes until lightly set.

Remove from the oven and reduce the temperature to very cool, 120°C, Gas ½. Whisk the egg whites until stiff, add half of the sugar and whisk again. Fold in nearly all the remaining sugar, then pile the meringue on top of the pudding, making sure it is entirely covered. Arrange in decorative peaks and sprinkle with the remaining sugar. Return the pudding to the oven for 40–45 minutes or until the meringue is set.

Saxon Pudding

4 helpings

25g flaked almonds	*12 ratafias*
oil for greasing	*2 eggs*
glacé cherries	*100ml single cream*
angelica	*25g caster sugar*
3 pieces plain cake **or**	*300ml milk*
individual trifle	*50ml medium-sweet*
sponges (5 × 7cm	*sherry* **or** *1 × 5ml*
approx)	*spoon grated lemon*
4 macaroons	*rind*

Brown the almonds in a cool oven. Grease a 13cm round cake tin and line the base with oiled greaseproof paper. Decorate the sides of the tin with the almonds. Cut the cherries and angelica into small pieces, and arrange in a pattern on the bottom of the tin.

Crumble the cake and macaroons and put with the ratafias into a bowl. Beat together the eggs, cream, and sugar with a fork and stir in the milk. Strain on to the cake. Add the sherry or lemon rind. Stir, and leave to stand for 1 hour. Stir again, making sure the ratafias are properly soaked. Spoon into the tin, taking care not to disturb the decoration. Cover with greased foil or greaseproof paper and steam gently for 1–1¼ hours. Remove the cooked pudding from the steamer, leave to stand for a few minutes, turn out on to a warmed dish and peel off the paper.

Serve hot with fruit syrup or sauce, or cold with whipped cream.

Viennese Pudding

4 helpings

50g granulated sugar	*2 × 5ml spoons grated*
100ml water	*lemon rind*
300ml milk	*50g sultanas*
4 pieces plain cake **or**	*25g caster sugar*
individual trifle	*2 eggs*
sponges (5 × 7cm	*2 × 15ml spoons*
approx)	*medium-sweet sherry*
25g cut mixed peel	*(optional)*
25g blanched almonds	*fat for greasing*

Heat together the granulated sugar and water, stirring until the sugar dissolves completely. Bring to the boil, and boil without stirring until the syrup turns golden-brown. Do not let it turn dark brown or it will have a bitter taste. Remove from the heat and cool slightly. Add the milk quickly. Re-heat gently, stirring until the caramel has dissolved in the milk. Cool.

Cut the cake into 1cm dice. Chop the peel a little more finely. Shred or chop the almonds. Brown them slightly in a cool oven, if liked. Put the cake, peel, almonds, lemon rind, sultanas, and sugar into a bowl. Beat the eggs until liquid and add the sherry, if used. Mix in the caramel and milk mixture, and strain it over the cake mixture. Leave to stand for 1 hour. Stir, and pour into a greased 750ml basin. Cover with greased foil or greaseproof paper and steam gently for 1–1¼ hours. Remove the cooked pudding from the steamer, leave to stand for a few minutes, then turn out on to a warmed plate. Serve with cream.

Winter Pudding

4 helpings

500g cooking apples	*2 pieces plain cake* **or**
75g cooking dates	*trifle sponges*
75g seedless raisins	*(5 × 7cm approx)*
25g cut mixed peel	*2 eggs*
1 × 5ml spoon grated	*300ml milk*
nutmeg	*fat for greasing*

Peel, core, and slice the apples. Chop the dates. Put with the raisins, peel, nutmeg, and a little water into a saucepan, cover, and simmer gently until tender. Crumble the cake finely. Beat the eggs lightly with a fork and stir in the milk. Add the crumbs, stir, and leave to stand for 10 minutes. Drain the stewed fruit, put it into a greased 750ml pie dish and level the top. Pour the custard mixture over the fruit. Bake in a warm oven at 160°C, Gas 3, for 1–1¼ hours until the top of the pudding is browned.

Serve with cream.

Zabaglione (1)

4 helpings

4 egg yolks	*4 × 15ml spoons*
40g caster sugar	*Marsala (Bual)* **or**
	Madeira **or** *sweet*
	sherry

Put the egg yolks into a deep heatproof basin and whisk lightly. Add the sugar and wine, and place the bowl over a pan of hot water. Whisk for about 10 minutes or until the mixture is very thick and creamy. When the whisk is lifted out of the bowl, a trail of the mixture from the whisk should lie on top for 2–3 seconds. Pour the custard into individual glasses and serve at once while still warm.

Serve with Mrs Beeton's Savoy Cakes (p1208).

VARIATION

Cold Zabaglione

Dissolve 50g caster sugar in 4 × 15ml spoons water, and boil for 1–2 minutes until syrupy. Whisk with the egg yolks until pale and thick. Add 2 × 15ml spoons Marsala (Bual), Madeira or sweet sherry and 2 × 15ml spoons single cream while whisking. The finely grated rind of half a lemon can be added, if liked. Chill before serving.

Zabaglione (2)
See p1533.

Wine Trifles
See p1036.

Sweet Soufflés

Sweet soufflés are made in exactly the same way as savoury soufflés. For the method of preparing a soufflé dish and making the soufflé, see pp919–20.

Note For cold sweet soufflés, see pp1016–18.

Vanilla Soufflé

Basic recipe

4 helpings

35g butter	$\frac{1}{2}$ × 5ml spoon vanilla
35g plain flour	essence
250ml milk	1 egg white
4 eggs	caster **or** icing sugar for
50g caster sugar	dredging

Heat the oven to moderate, 180°C, Gas 4, or put the steamer on to heat. Prepare a 1 litre soufflé dish (p919). Melt the butter in a saucepan, stir in the flour and cook slowly for 2–3 minutes, without colouring, stirring all the time. Add the milk gradually and beat until smooth. Cook for another 1–2 minutes, still stirring all the time. Remove from the heat and beat hard until the sauce comes away from the sides of the pan cleanly. Cool slightly and put into a bowl.

Separate the eggs and beat the yolks into the mixture one by one. Beat in the sugar and vanilla essence. Whisk all the egg whites until stiff. Using a metal spoon, stir 1 spoonful of the whites into the mixture, then fold in the rest until evenly distributed. Put into the dish and bake for 45 minutes until well risen and browned; alternatively, cover with greased greaseproof paper and steam slowly for 1 hour until just firm to the touch.

Dredge with caster or icing sugar and serve immediately from the dish, with Jam Sauce (p726).

VARIATIONS

A hot sweet soufflé can be flavoured in many different ways. Unless otherwise stated below, stir in the flavouring before adding the egg yolks. Omit the vanilla essence.

Almond Soufflé

Add 100g ground almonds, 1 × 15ml spoon lemon juice, and a few drops of ratafia essence. Reduce the sugar to 40g.

Coffee Soufflé

Add 2 × 15ml spoons instant coffee dissolved in a little hot water, or use 125ml strong black coffee and only 125ml milk.

Ginger Soufflé

Add a pinch of ground ginger and 50g preserved stem ginger, chopped. Serve each portion topped with double cream and a spoonful of ginger syrup. 1 × 15ml spoon brandy can also be added.

Lemon Soufflé

Add the thinly grated rind and juice of 1 lemon. Serve with Lemon Sauce (p721).

Liqueur Soufflé

Add 2 × 15ml spoons Cointreau, Kirsch or curaçao and make as for Soufflé au Grand Marnier below. Serve with sweetened cream flavoured with the liqueur, or with the same orange sauce.

Orange Soufflé

Pare the rind of 2 oranges thinly. Put in a pan with the milk and bring slowly to the boil. Remove from the heat, cover, and leave to stand for 10 minutes, then remove the rind. Make up the sauce using the flavoured milk. Reduce the sugar to 40g. Add the strained juice of half an orange.

Soufflé au Grand Marnier

Add 2–3 × 15ml spoons Grand Marnier to the orange soufflé mixture. Serve with the following orange sauce: boil 125ml orange juice and a few drops of liqueur with 50g caster sugar until syrupy. Add very fine strips of orange rind.

Praline Soufflé

Dissolve 2–3 × 15ml spoons almond praline (p1241) in the milk before making the sauce, or crush and add just before the egg yolks.

Soufflé Ambassadrice

Crumble 2 macaroons and soak them in 2 × 15ml spoons rum with 50g chopped blanched almonds. Stir into a vanilla soufflé mixture.

Soufflé Harlequin

Make up 2 half quantities of soufflé mixture in different flavours, eg chocolate and vanilla, or praline and coffee. Spoon alternately into the dish.

Soufflé Rothschild

Wash 50g mixed glacé fruit in hot water to remove any excess sugar. Chop the fruit and soak it in 2 × 15ml spoons brandy or Kirsch for 2 hours. Put half a vanilla soufflé mixture into the dish, add the fruit, and then the rest of the soufflé mixture.

Soufflé Surprise

Crumble 3 sponge fingers or macaroons and soak them in 2 × 15ml spoons Grand Marnier or Cointreau. Add 2 × 15ml spoons of the same liqueur to an orange soufflé mixture. Put half the mixture into the dish, sprinkle the biscuits on top, and add the rest of the soufflé mixture.

Fruit Soufflés

For fruit-flavoured soufflés a thick, sweet purée is added. It is important that the purée should have a strong flavour, otherwise the taste will not be discernible. If extra purée is added, the soufflé will be heavy and will not rise.

Apple Soufflé

Add 125ml thick sweet apple purée, 1 × 15ml spoon lemon juice, and a pinch of powdered cinnamon. Dust with cinnamon before serving.

Apricot Soufflé

Add 125ml thick apricot purée and 1 × 15ml spoon lemon juice, if using fresh apricots. If using canned apricots (1 × 400g can makes 125ml purée) use half milk and half syrup to make the sauce. A purée made from dried apricots makes a delicious soufflé.

Pineapple Soufflé

Add 125ml crushed pineapple or 75g chopped pineapple, and make the sauce using half milk and half pineapple juice.

Raspberry Soufflé

Add 125ml raspberry purée (1 × 400g can makes 125ml purée) and 1 × 10ml spoon lemon juice.

Strawberry Soufflé

Add 125ml strawberry purée, and make the sauce using half milk and half single cream. Add a little pink food colouring, if necessary.

Other Soufflés

Chocolate Soufflé

4 helpings

fat for greasing	*1 × 15ml spoon butter*
100g plain chocolate	*3 eggs*
400ml milk	*1 egg white*
50g caster sugar	*icing sugar for dusting*
40g flour	

Heat the oven to moderate, 180°C, Gas 4. Prepare a 1 litre soufflé dish (p919). Break the chocolate into pieces. Put into a saucepan with most of the milk and the sugar. Warm over low heat until the chocolate begins to melt. Remove from the heat and leave to stand until the chocolate is completely melted, stirring occasionally. Blend the flour to a smooth paste with the reserved cold milk, stir in the chocolate-flavoured milk, return to the pan, bring to the boil and cook for 1–2 minutes, stirring all the time.

Remove from the heat and add the butter. Leave to cool slightly.

Separate the eggs, and beat the yolks into the chocolate mixture one at a time. Whisk the egg whites until stiff. Stir one spoonful of the white into the mixture and then fold in the rest, until evenly blended. Put into the dish and bake for 45 minutes.

Dust with icing sugar and serve with hot chocolate sauce.

VARIATION
Chocolate Rum Soufflé

Add 1–2 ×15ml spoons rum with the milk.

Semolina Soufflé

4 helpings

pared rind of ½ lemon   50g caster sugar
400ml milk   3 eggs
50g semolina

Heat the oven to moderate, 180°C, Gas 4, or put a steamer on to heat. Prepare a 750ml soufflé dish (p919). Put the lemon rind into the milk, bring to the boil, remove from the heat, and leave to stand for 10 minutes. Remove the rind and sprinkle in the semolina. Cook for 2–3 minutes, stirring all the time, until the semolina thickens. Stir in the sugar and leave to cool.

Separate the eggs and beat the yolks into the mixture one by one. Whisk the egg whites until stiff, and fold in. Put into the prepared dish and bake for 45 minutes. Alternatively, cover with greased greaseproof paper and steam for 30–40 minutes.

Serve with Apricot Sauce (p723).

Sweet Soufflé Omelets

For the general method of preparing and making plain omelets, see p924.

Sweet Soufflé Omelet

Basic recipe

1 helping

2 eggs   2 × 15ml spoons water
1 × 5ml spoon caster   1 × 15ml spoon unsalted
  sugar   butter or margarine
a few drops vanilla   icing sugar for dredging
  essence

Separate the eggs. Whisk the yolks until creamy, add the sugar, vanilla essence and water, and whisk again. Whisk the egg whites until stiff and matt. Place an 18cm omelet pan over gentle heat and when it is hot add the butter or margarine. Tilt the pan so that the whole of the inside of the pan is greased. Pour out any excess. Fold the egg whites into the yolk mixture carefully until evenly distributed, using a metal spoon. Do not overmix, as it is most important not to break down the egg white foam. Pour the egg mixture into the pan, level the top very lightly, and cook for 1–2 minutes over a moderate heat until the omelet is golden-brown on the underside; the top should still be moist. (Use a palette knife to lift the edge of the omelet to look underneath.)

Put the pan under a moderate grill for 5–6 minutes until the omelet is risen and lightly browned on the top. The texture of the omelet should be firm yet spongy. Remove from the heat as soon as it is ready, as overcooking tends to make it tough. Run a palette knife gently round the edge and underneath to loosen it. Make a mark across the middle at right angles to the pan handle but do not cut the surface. Put any filling on one half, raise the handle of the pan and double the omelet over. Turn gently on to a warm plate, dredge with icing sugar and serve at once.

Note For **Variations** to the basic recipe, see over.

VARIATIONS

Soufflé omelets can have many different fillings:

Apricot Omelet

Add the grated rind of 1 orange to the egg yolks. Spread 2 × 15ml spoons warm, thick apricot purée over the omelet.

Cherry Omelet

Stone 100g dark cherries, or use canned ones. Warm with 2 × 15ml spoons cherry jam and 1 × 15ml spoon Kirsch. Spread over the omelet.

Jam Omelet

Spread the cooked omelet with 2 × 15ml spoons warmed jam.

Lemon Omelet

Add the grated rind of $\frac{1}{2}$ lemon to the egg yolks. Warm 3 × 15ml spoons lemon curd with 1 × 10ml spoon lemon juice, and spread over the omelet.

Raspberry Omelet

Spread 2 × 15ml spoons warm, thick, sweetened raspberry purée or Melba Sauce (p724) over the omelet.

Rum Omelet

Add 1 × 15ml spoon rum to the egg yolks.

Strawberry Omelet

Hull 5 ripe strawberries, and soak in a little Kirsch. Mash slightly with icing sugar. Put in the centre of the omelet.

Surprise Omelet

Put ice cream into the centre of the omelet before folding.

Flambé Omelet

Warm 2 × 15ml spoons rum or brandy. Put the cooked omelet on to a warm plate, pour the warmed spirit round it, ignite, and serve immediately.

Branded Soufflé Omelets

Soufflé omelets are sometimes served 'branded' for a special occasion. A lattice decoration is marked on the top using hot skewers. Heat the pointed ends of 3 metal skewers until red-hot. When the omelet is on the plate, dredge with icing sugar, then quickly press the hot skewers, one at a time, on to the sugar, holding them there until the sugar caramelizes. Make a diagonal criss-cross design. Each skewer should make 2 marks if you work quickly.

Note Remember to hold the skewers in an oven cloth.

Baked Soufflé Omelet

2 helpings

fat for greasing	*2 × 15ml spoons water*
4 × 15ml spoons jam **or**	*a pinch of salt*
stewed fruit	*caster* **or** *icing sugar for*
4 eggs	*dredging*
50g caster sugar	

Heat the oven to fairly hot, 190°C, Gas 5. Grease a shallow 23cm ovenproof dish and spread the jam or fruit over the base. Separate the eggs. Beat the yolks with the sugar and add the water. Whisk the egg whites and salt until stiff and fold into the yolk mixture. Pour over the jam or fruit and bake for 15–20 minutes. Dredge with sugar, and serve at once.

Fritters, Pancakes and Waffles

Recipes for these may be found in the chapter on Batters and Fried Foods.

Boiled, Steamed and Baked Puddings

Boiled, steamed, and baked puddings are made from flour, breadcrumbs or cake crumbs, mixed with fat (usually butter, margarine or suet), and a raising agent such as baking powder. These are usually mixed with sugar and often with eggs.

In suet mixtures, a lighter pudding is obtained if breadcrumbs or cake crumbs are substituted for some of the flour. If 1×15ml spoon of baking powder to 250g plain flour is suggested, self-raising flour can be used as an alternative. A good pinch of salt should be added to each 250g flour used.

General Method

The fat can be worked into the pudding in various ways:

Chopped-in method (suet): If using fresh beef suet, remove any skin, gristle, and fibres. Sprinkle a little flour over the suet, cut the fat into flakes and chop it finely. When the suet is ready, mix in all the other dry ingredients.

Ready-prepared shredded suet needs no preparation and can be used straight from the packet.

Rubbed-in method (all fats): Sift the flour, salt, and raising agent into a mixing bowl. Cut the fat into small pieces. Rub the fat into the flour with the tips of the fingers, lifting it so that it becomes aerated as it falls back into the bowl. Continue until the mixture is like fine breadcrumbs.

Creamed method (all fats except suet): This method is used for puddings with too much fat to rub in, or which contain no flour. Use caster sugar because the small crystals dissolve easily. Work the fat with a wooden spoon and work or beat in the sugar little by little as the fat becomes soft. Beat the mixture until it is pale, soft and creamy. Beat the eggs together, and add a little at a time to the creamed mixture, beating well after each addition.

To complete the pudding, either mix with water to a soft but not sticky dough, or mix together the flavouring, beaten egg, and liquid and add this last (to chopped-in and rubbed-in methods). Alternatively, mix dry flavouring, flour, salt, and the raising agent and sift them together into a creamed mixture, followed by any other ingredients.

Consistency of Mixture

A *dropping consistency* means the mixture should just drop from the spoon when shaken lightly.

A *soft dropping consistency* means that the mixture drops from the spoon easily.

A *slack consistency* means that it falls off the spoon almost of its own accord.

Preparing Containers

Always prepare the containers and a greased paper or foil cover before making the pudding. The inside of the container should be well greased with clarified butter or margarine, cooking fat or oil.

Note A charlotte mould, cake tin or foil container can be used instead of a pudding basin for a baked pudding. For individual puddings, small dariole moulds, ceramic cocottes or ramekins are useful.

To Line a Basin with Suet Crust

Cut off one-quarter of the pastry for the lid. Roll the remaining pastry 1cm larger than the top of the basin, and put the pastry into the greased basin. By pressing with the fingers, work evenly up the sides of the container to the top. Put in the required filling. Roll out the pastry for the lid to the same size as the top of the basin. Dampen the rim, and place it on top of the filling. Press the rim of the lid against the edge of the lining to seal the crust.

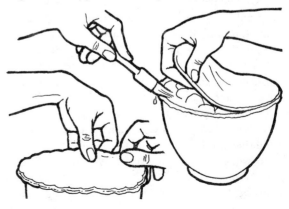

General Hints on Cooking

Steamed puddings: Only three-quarters fill the basin before putting on the pastry lid. Cover with greased paper or foil, to prevent steam getting in. Put the cover on greased side down. Either twist the edges under the rim of the basin, or tie them.

If you have a steamer, put the pudding in the perforated top part and have the water underneath boiling. If, however, a recipe calls for gentle steaming, only let the water simmer. Cover closely and steam for the time directed.

If you have no steamer, stand the pudding basin on an old saucer or plate in a saucepan, with water coming half-way up the basin's sides. Put a tight-fitting lid on the pan, and simmer gently. This method is called 'half-steaming'.

With either method, always top up the water with more boiling water when the water in the pan is reduced by a third.

After taking the pudding out of the steamer, let it stand for a few minutes to shrink and firm up before turning it out on to a dish. To turn out a steamed or boiled pudding, loosen the sides from the basin with a knife. Place the warmed serving dish upside-down over the basin and turn them over together. Do not use a plate for fruit puddings in case juice seeps out.

Boiled puddings: If you wish, you can boil a pudding in a basin covered with a floured cloth, or in a well-floured cloth only. Roly-poly puddings can be rolled in a scalded floured cloth, forming a sausage shape; tie loosely at each end, leaving room for the pudding to swell. If you use a basin, fill it completely and cover securely as for steamed puddings.

Have enough rapidly boiling water ready in a large saucepan to cover the pudding completely. Put the pudding into the fast-boiling water, and reduce the heat so that the water only simmers. Top up with boiling water when required, as above.

Let the pudding stand for a few moments after removing it from the water to let it shrink and firm up.

Baked puddings: Use a well-greased basin, pie dish, oven-to-table baking dish or a foil container with a really clean edge. Baked puddings are easier to handle if placed on a flat baking sheet in the oven.

BOILED PUDDINGS

Suet Pudding
(unsweetened)

Basic recipe

6–7 helpings

300g plain flour
½ × 2.5ml spoon salt
2 × 5ml spoons baking powder

150g shredded suet
cold water
flour for dusting

Sift the flour, salt, and baking powder together. Add the suet, and enough cold water to make a soft but not sticky dough. Shape into a roll. Lay the dough on a scalded, well-floured pudding cloth and roll up loosely. Tie up the ends of the cloth. Put into a saucepan of fast-boiling water, reduce the heat and simmer for 2–2½ hours. Drain well and unwrap.

Serve sliced, with meat or gravy or with any sweet sauce.

VARIATIONS

Roly-poly Pudding

Make the suet crust as in the basic recipe. Roll out the dough into a rectangle about 5mm thick. Spread with jam almost to the edge. Dampen the edges and roll up lightly. Seal the edges. Cook as in the basic recipe.

Fruit Roly-poly

Mix into the basic recipe 150g chopped dates, currants, sultanas, raisins or figs. Shape into a roll, and cook as in the basic recipe. Drain, unwrap, slice, and serve with any custard or sweet sauce, or with warmed golden syrup and cream.

Spotted Dick

Mix into the basic recipe 150g caster sugar and 150g currants. Use milk instead of water. Shape into a roll and cook as in the basic recipe. Drain, unwrap, slice, and serve with any custard or sweet sauce, or with warmed golden syrup and cream.

Apple and Blackberry Pudding

6 helpings

200g plain flour	*75g shredded suet*
1 × 5ml spoon baking	*cold water*
powder	*fat for greasing*
a pinch of salt	*flour for dusting*

Filling
300g cooking apples	*2 × 15ml spoons cold*
75g granulated sugar	*water*
300g blackberries	

Sift the flour, baking powder, and salt together. Add the suet and enough cold water to make a soft, but not sticky dough. Grease and line a 750ml basin with the crust (p979).

To make the filling, peel, core, and slice the apples, and stir in the sugar. Clean the blackberries. Put the fruit into the prepared basin and add the cold water. Put on the top crust and seal well. Cover with a well-floured cloth, greased paper or foil and boil for 2½–3 hours. Serve from the basin, or leave for 5–10 minutes at room temperature to firm up, then turn out.

Serve with Pouring Cup Custard (p964).

VARIATIONS

Use 600g apples, blackcurrants, damsons, gooseberries, plums or rhubarb instead of apples and blackberries. Prepare the fruit as for stewing (p1001). If using blackcurrants or rhubarb, steam for 2 hours instead of boiling.

Boiled Apple Dumplings

6 helpings

6 cooking apples	*flour for dusting*
300g prepared suet crust	*75g Demerara sugar*
pastry (p1250)	*6 cloves*

Core and peel the apples. Divide the pastry into 6 portions and, on a lightly floured surface, roll each into a round. Put an apple in the centre of each round of pastry and work the pastry round the apple until it almost meets at the top. Fill the core hole with sugar and stick a clove upright in the middle of each apple. Dampen the edges of the pastry, work it up to meet over the apple, and seal well, leaving the clove exposed. Tie each dumpling in a small well-floured pudding cloth. Put the dumplings into a saucepan of boiling water and boil gently for 40–50 minutes.

Drain well and serve with Apple Sauce (p717) and Pouring Cup Custard (p964).

Note For baked Apple Dumplings, see p995.

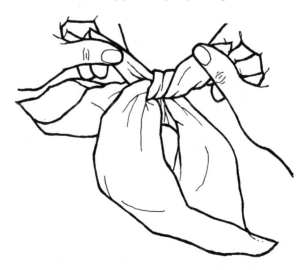

Dried Fruit Pudding

6 helpings

fat for greasing	*100g currants*
100g stale white	*100g brown sugar*
breadcrumbs	*½ × 2.5ml spoon ground*
100g plain flour	*mace*
a pinch of salt	*½ × 2.5ml spoon grated*
2 × 5ml spoons baking	*nutmeg*
powder	*1 egg*
100g shredded suet	*125ml milk (approx)*
100g raisins	

Grease a 1 litre basin. Mix together all the ingredients, using enough milk to make a dropping consistency. Put into the prepared basin, cover with greased paper or foil, and a floured cloth. Put into deep boiling water and boil steadily for 4–5 hours. Leave for 5–10 minutes at room temperature to firm up, then turn out.

Serve with warmed golden syrup and whipped cream, or with Pouring Cup Custard (p964).

Christmas Pudding (1)

(rich boiled)

6 helpings per pudding

fat for greasing	*250g shredded suet*
200g plain flour	*250g sultanas*
a pinch of salt	*250g currants*
1 × 5ml spoon ground	*200g seedless raisins*
ginger	*200g cut mixed peel*
1 × 5ml spoon mixed	*175g stale white*
spice	*breadcrumbs*
1 × 5ml spoon grated	*6 eggs*
nutmeg	*75ml stout*
50g chopped blanched	*juice of 1 orange*
almonds	*50ml brandy or to taste*
400g soft light or dark	*125–250ml milk*
brown sugar	

Grease three 600ml basins. Sift together the flour, salt, ginger, mixed spice, and nutmeg into a mixing bowl. Add the nuts, sugar, suet, sultanas, currants, raisins, peel, and breadcrumbs. Beat together the eggs, stout, orange juice, brandy, and 125ml milk. Stir this into the dry ingredients, adding more milk

if required, to give a soft dropping consistency. Put the mixture into the prepared basins, cover with greased paper or foil, and a floured cloth. Put into deep boiling water and boil steadily for 6–7 hours, or half steam for the same length of time.

To store, cover with a clean dry cloth, wrap in greaseproof paper and store in a cool place until required. To re-heat, boil or steam for 1½–2 hours. Serve with Brandy Butter (p1302) or Pouring Cup Custard (p964).

Note For a steamed Christmas pudding see p984.

Christmas Pudding or Plum Pudding (2)

(vegetarian)

6 helpings per pudding

fat for greasing	*100g soft light brown*
200g dried figs	*sugar*
200g blanched almonds	*100g cut mixed peel*
25g shelled Brazil nuts	*a pinch of salt*
100g pine nut kernels	*grated rind and juice of*
100g cooking apples	*1 lemon*
100g currants	*100g butter or*
200g seedless raisins	*margarine*
175g stale white	*100g honey*
breadcrumbs	*3 eggs*
1 × 5ml spoon mixed spice	

Grease two 750ml basins. Chop the figs and nuts. Peel, core, and chop the apples. Mix together the dried fruits, nuts, apple, breadcrumbs, spice, sugar, peel, salt, and rind and juice of the lemon. Warm the butter and honey together until the butter melts. Beat the eggs until liquid and add to the honey mixture. Stir into the dry ingredients; mix all thoroughly together. Put into the prepared basins, cover with greased paper or foil, and a floured cloth. Put into deep boiling water and boil steadily for 3 hours, or half steam for 3½–4 hours.

Store as for Christmas Pudding (rich boiled). To re-heat, boil or steam for 1½ hours.

Note The Christmas pudding of today is also frequently known as Plum pudding, largely as a result of the popularity of prunes (ie dried plums) in Tudor times, when they were first used in boiled puddings. The name became a portmanteau label for all dried fruits.

STEAMED PUDDINGS
(made with suet)

Apple Pudding
(steamed)

5–6 helpings

150g cooking apples	$\frac{1}{2} \times 2.5ml$ spoon grated
100g shredded suet	nutmeg
100g stale white	a pinch of salt
breadcrumbs	2 eggs
100g soft light brown	125ml milk (approx)
sugar	fat for greasing

Peel, core, and chop the apples coarsely. Mix together the apples, suet, breadcrumbs, sugar, nutmeg, and salt. Beat the eggs until liquid and stir into the dry ingredients with enough milk to make a soft dropping consistency. Leave to stand for 1 hour to allow the bread to soak. If very stiff, add a little more milk. Put the mixture into a greased 1 litre basin, cover with greased paper or foil and steam for $1\frac{3}{4}$–2 hours. Serve from the basin, or leave for 5–10 minutes at room temperature to firm up, then turn out.

Serve with Pouring Cup Custard (p964).

VARIATIONS

Cumberland Pudding

Use 250g apples, and substitute 200g sifted plain flour with $2 \times 5ml$ spoons baking powder for the breadcrumbs. Add 150g currants with the flour. Reduce the sugar to 75g and the milk to 75ml. Steam in a 750ml basin. Serve turned out, dredged with soft light brown sugar.

Other Fruit Puddings

Instead of apples, use the same quantity of prepared damsons, gooseberries, greengages, plums or rhubarb.

Baroness Pudding

6 helpings

200g plain flour	100g shredded suet
$2 \times 5ml$ spoons baking	150g raisins
powder	125ml milk (approx)
a pinch of salt	fat for greasing
50g caster sugar	

Sift together the flour, baking powder, and salt into a bowl. Stir in the sugar, suet, and raisins. Add enough milk to make a soft dropping consistency. Put into a greased 750ml basin, cover closely with greased paper or foil and steam for $1\frac{1}{2}$–2 hours. Serve from the basin, or leave for 5–10 minutes at room temperature to firm up, then turn out.

Serve with Pouring Cup Custard (p964), Lemon Sauce (p721) or well dredged with caster sugar.

VARIATIONS
1) Instead of raisins, use 150g figs, sultanas or currants.
2) Omit the fruit and put $2 \times 15ml$ spoons jam, lemon curd or marmalade in the bottom of the basin.

Brown Bread Pudding

4–6 helpings

175g stale brown	75g caster sugar
breadcrumbs	2 eggs
75g raisins	milk
75g sultanas	fat for greasing
100g shredded suet	

Mix together all the ingredients, adding enough milk to make a dropping consistency. Leave to stand for 30 minutes. Add more milk if the pudding is too stiff, to give a dropping consistency. Put the mixture into a greased 750ml basin, cover with greased paper or foil and steam for $2\frac{1}{2}$–3 hours. Serve from the basin, or leave for 5–10 minutes at room temperature to firm up, then turn out.

Serve with Pouring Cup Custard (p964) or Simple Custard (p964).

Christmas Pudding (3)

(economical)

12 helpings

fat for greasing	200g shredded suet
1 cooking apple	150g mixed cut peel
100g plain flour	grated rind and juice of
25g self-raising flour	1 lemon
a pinch of salt	2 eggs
100g stale white	125ml milk (approx)
breadcrumbs	1 × 5ml spoon almond
400g mixed dried fruit	essence
100g soft light **or** dark	1 × 5ml spoon gravy
brown sugar	browning

Grease two 600ml basins or one 1 litre basin. Peel, core, and chop the apple. Sift together the flours and salt into a bowl. Add the breadcrumbs, dried fruit, sugar, suet, peel, lemon rind, and juice. Beat together the eggs, milk, and almond essence and stir into the dry ingredients, adding more milk if required, to give a soft dropping consistency. Add the gravy browning to darken the mixture. Mix well, then put the mixture into the basins. Cover with greased paper or foil, and a floured cloth, and steam for 5 hours.

Store, re-heat and serve as for Christmas Pudding (rich boiled) (p982).

Mrs Beeton's Delhi Pudding

5–6 helpings

fat for greasing	150g currants
suet crust pastry	75g soft light brown
(p1250) using 400g	sugar
flour	$\frac{1}{2}$ × 2.5ml spoon grated
flour for rolling out	nutmeg
400g cooking apples	grated rind of 1 lemon

Grease a 750ml basin. Cut off half the pastry and, on a lightly floured surface, roll out in a circle 2cm larger than the diameter of the basin. Put this into the basin and, pressing with the fingers, work the pastry evenly up the sides to the top. Roll out 3 more circles of pastry from the remaining pastry to fit inside the basin at 3 different levels.

Peel, core, and slice the apples and mix with the remaining ingredients. Put layers of fruit and pastry in the basin, finishing with a layer of pastry. Seal the pastry edges firmly by pinching together. Cover with greased paper or foil or a pudding cloth, and steam or boil for $2\frac{1}{2}$–3 hours. Serve from the basin, or leave at room temperature for 10 minutes to firm up, then turn out.

Serve with Pouring Cup Custard (p964).

Treacle Layer Pudding

6–7 helpings

fat for greasing	grated rind of 1 lemon
65g stale white	200g treacle **or** golden
breadcrumbs	syrup **or** a mixture

Suet Crust Pastry

300g plain flour	150g shredded suet
a pinch of salt	cold water
2 × 5ml spoons baking	flour for rolling out
powder	

To make the pastry, sift together the flour, salt, and baking powder. Add the suet and enough cold water to make an elastic dough. Divide the dough into 2 equal portions, and use 1 portion to line a greased 1 litre basin as described on p979. From the other portion cut off enough to make the lid. On a lightly floured surface, roll out the rest thinly and cut 2 circles to fit the basin at 2 different levels.

Mix together the breadcrumbs and lemon rind. Put a layer of treacle or golden syrup in the basin and sprinkle well with the breadcrumbs. Cover with the smaller round of pastry, moisten the edges and press to join them to the pastry at the side of the basin. Continue in this way, finishing with the rolled-out lid of pastry. Cover with greased paper or foil and steam for $2\frac{1}{4}$–$2\frac{1}{2}$ hours. Serve from the basin, or leave for 10 minutes to firm up, then turn out.

Serve with warmed golden syrup and Simple Custard (p964) or single cream.

Fruit Pudding with Suet Crust

6 helpings

400–500g fresh fruit
(see below)
50g caster sugar
fat for greasing
suet crust pastry (p1250)
using 200g flour

flour for rolling out
2 ×15ml spoons cold
water

Prepare the fruit as for stewing (p1001) and mix with the sugar. Grease and line a 750ml pudding basin with the pastry as described on p979. Fill to the top with fruit and add the cold water. Put on the top crust, cover with greased paper or foil and steam for 2½–3 hours. Serve from the basin, or leave at room temperature for 10 minutes to firm up, then turn out.

Serve with Pouring Cup Custard (p964).

Fillings

Apples, blackberries and apples, blackcurrants, cranberries, damsons, gooseberries, plums, rhubarb.

Ginger Pudding

6 helpings

200g plain flour
1 × 5ml spoon ground
ginger
a pinch of salt
1 × 5ml spoon
bicarbonate of soda
100g shredded suet

75g caster sugar
1 ×15ml spoon black
treacle
1 egg
75–100ml milk
fat for greasing

Sift together into a bowl the flour, ginger, salt, and soda. Add the suet and sugar. Beat together the treacle, egg, and about 50ml milk. Stir into the dry ingredients, adding more milk if required, to give a soft dropping consistency. Put into a greased 1 litre basin, cover with greased paper or foil and steam for 1¾–2 hours. Serve from the basin, or leave at room temperature for 5–10 minutes to firm up, then turn out.

Serve with warmed golden syrup.

VARIATION

Spice Pudding

Substitute the same quantity of mixed spice, grated nutmeg or ground cinnamon for the ginger.

Snowdon Pudding

6 helpings

25g glacé cherries
100g raisins
100g stale white
breadcrumbs
100g shredded suet
25g ground rice
grated rind of 1 lemon

100g caster sugar
a pinch of salt
2 ×15ml spoons
marmalade
2 eggs
75ml milk (approx)
fat for greasing

Halve the cherries. Decorate the bottom of the basin with some of the raisins and cherry halves. Mix together the breadcrumbs, remaining raisins, cherries, suet, ground rice, grated rind, sugar, salt, and marmalade. Beat the eggs until liquid and stir into the dry ingredients with enough milk to make a dropping consistency. Put into a greased 1 litre basin, cover with greased paper or foil and steam for 2–2½ hours. Leave for 5–10 minutes, then turn out.

Serve with Marmalade Sauce (2) (p727).

VARIATION

Marmalade Pudding

Use 100g sultanas instead of glacé cherries and raisins, 100g self-raising flour instead of ground rice, and only 50g sugar. Add 4 ×15ml spoons marmalade. Steam for 1½–2 hours.

Golden Syrup Pudding

6–7 helpings

fat for greasing
3 × 15ml spoons golden
  syrup
150g plain flour
1 × 5ml spoon
  bicarbonate of soda
a pinch of salt
1 × 5ml spoon ground
  ginger

150g stale white
  breadcrumbs
100g shredded suet
50g caster sugar
1 egg
1 × 15ml spoon black
  treacle
75–100ml milk

Grease a 1 litre basin, and put 1 × 15ml spoon of golden syrup in the bottom. Sift together the flour, bicarbonate of soda, salt, and ginger. Add the breadcrumbs, suet, and sugar. Beat together the egg, remaining syrup, treacle, and 75ml of the milk. Stir this mixture into the dry ingredients, adding more milk if required, to make a soft dropping consistency. Put into the basin, cover with greased paper or foil and steam for $1\frac{1}{2}$–2 hours. Leave for 5–10 minutes to firm up, then turn out.

Serve with warmed golden syrup and whipped cream.

Lemon Pudding (1)

6–7 helpings

50g plain flour
a pinch of salt
1 × 5ml spoon baking
  powder
175g stale white
  breadcrumbs
100g caster sugar

100g shredded suet
grated rind and juice of
  2 lemons
2 eggs
150–175ml milk
fat for greasing

Sift together the flour, salt, and baking powder. Stir in the breadcrumbs, sugar, suet, and lemon rind. Beat together the eggs, lemon juice, and about 50–75ml of the milk. Stir into the dry ingredients, adding more milk if required, to make a soft dropping consistency. Put into a greased 750ml basin, cover with greased paper or foil and steam for $1\frac{1}{2}$–2 hours. Leave for 5–10 minutes, then turn out.

Serve with Lemon Sauce (p721).

Note For a baked lemon pudding, see p992.

STEAMED PUDDINGS
(made with butter or margarine)

Steamed Sponge Pudding
(Canary Pudding)

Basic recipe

6 helpings

150g butter **or**
  margarine
150g caster sugar
3 eggs
grated rind of $\frac{1}{2}$ lemon

150g plain flour
1 × 5ml spoon baking
  powder
fat for greasing

Work together the fat and sugar until light and creamy. Beat in the eggs gradually. Add the lemon rind. Sift together the flour and baking powder and fold lightly into the mixture. Put into a greased 750ml basin, cover with greased paper or foil and steam for $1\frac{1}{4}$–$1\frac{1}{2}$ hours. Leave in the basin at room temperature for 3–5 minutes, then turn out.

Serve with Pouring Cup Custard (p964) or Jam Sauce (p726).

Note For a baked sponge pudding, see p990.

VARIATIONS
1) Add to the basic recipe one of the following: 50g desiccated coconut, 150g chopped stoned dates, 150g dried fruit, 75g glacé cherries, 25g cocoa, 50g chopped preserved ginger, grated rind of 1 orange or lemon.
    Serve with Simple Custard (p964).
2) Before putting the basic mixture into the basin, put in 2 × 15ml spoons golden syrup, jam, marmalade or lemon curd. Serve with the same preserve used in the recipe.

Washington Pudding

Stir into the basic mixture 2 × 15ml spoons raspberry jam. Serve with warmed raspberry jam.

Alma Pudding

Add to the basic mixture 50g currants, 50g sultanas, and the grated rind of 1 lemon. Serve with golden syrup.

Apricot Pudding

Use only 75g flour and sugar, only 2 eggs, and $\frac{1}{2} \times 2.5$ml spoon baking powder. Stir in 6 drained and chopped canned apricot halves after adding the flour. Serve with Apricot Sauce (p723).

Almond Puddings

4–8 helpings

fat for greasing	150g ground almonds
75g butter **or** margarine	3 × 15ml spoons single
75g caster sugar	cream
3 eggs	

Grease 8 dariole moulds. Cream together the fat and sugar. Separate the eggs and beat the yolks into the creamed mixture. Stir in the ground almonds and cream. Whisk the egg whites until as stiff as the main mixture, and fold them in lightly. Three-quarters fill the moulds; cover with greased paper or foil, and steam for 45–60 minutes until firm to the touch. Leave in the moulds for a few minutes, then turn out.

Serve with warmed apricot or strawberry jam.

Mrs Beeton's Bachelor's Pudding

5–6 helpings

150g cooking apples	$\frac{1}{2} \times 2.5$ml spoon grated
100g stale white	nutmeg
breadcrumbs	2 eggs
grated rind\of $\frac{1}{2}$ lemon	milk
100g currants	1 × 5ml spoon baking
75g caster sugar	powder
a pinch of salt	fat for greasing

Peel, core, and chop the apples coarsely. Mix together the breadcrumbs, apples, grated lemon rind, currants, sugar, salt and nutmeg. Beat the eggs until liquid and add to the dry ingredients with enough milk to form a soft dropping consistency. Leave to stand for 30 minutes. Stir in the baking powder. Put the mixture into a greased 1 litre basin, cover with greased paper or foil and steam for $2\frac{1}{2}$–3 hours. Leave in the basin for a few minutes, then turn out.

Serve with Simple Custard (p964) or Vanilla Sauce (p721).

Coconut Pudding

4–6 helpings

150g plain flour	50g caster sugar
a pinch of salt	50g desiccated coconut
2 × 5ml spoons baking	1 egg
powder	50ml milk (approx)
50g butter **or** margarine	fat for greasing

Sift together the flour, salt, and baking powder. Rub in the fat, then add the sugar and coconut. Beat the egg and milk together, stir into the dry ingredients, and mix to a soft dropping consistency. Put the mixture into a greased 750ml basin, cover with greased paper or foil and steam for $1\frac{1}{2}$–2 hours. Leave in the basin for a few minutes, then turn out.

Serve with Jam Sauce (p726).

VARIATIONS
Orange or Lemon Pudding

Substitute the grated rind and juice of 1 orange or 1 lemon for the coconut. Serve with Orange Sauce or Lemon Sauce (p721).

Honey Pudding (2)

Put 1 × 10ml spoon honey in the bottom of the prepared basin. Use 75g fat and add 1 × 10ml spoon honey with the milk. Omit the coconut.

Note For Honey Pudding (1), see p961.

Chocolate Pudding (1)

5–6 helpings

fat for greasing	2 eggs
50g plain chocolate	100g stale white
125ml milk	breadcrumbs
40g butter **or** margarine	$\frac{1}{2} \times 2.5ml$ spoon baking
40g caster sugar	powder

Grease a 750ml basin or 6 dariole moulds. Grate the chocolate into a saucepan, add the milk and heat slowly to dissolve the chocolate. Cream together the fat and sugar. Separate the eggs and beat the yolks into the creamed mixture. Add the melted chocolate, breadcrumbs, and baking powder. Whisk the egg whites until fairly stiff and fold into the mixture. Put into the basin or moulds, cover with greased paper or foil, and steam for 1 hour for a large pudding, and 30 minutes for dariole moulds. Leave in the basin for a few minutes, then turn out.

Serve with Chocolate Sauce (p720 or p725).

Chocolate Pudding (2)

6 helpings

200g plain flour	100g caster sugar
$1 \times 5ml$ spoon baking	2 eggs
powder	$\frac{1}{2} \times 2.5ml$ spoon vanilla
a pinch of salt	essence
25g cocoa	milk
100g butter **or**	fat for greasing
margarine	

Sift together the flour, baking powder, salt, and cocoa. Rub in the fat, and stir in the sugar. Beat the eggs and essence together. Add to the dry ingredients with enough milk to form a soft dropping consistency. Put the mixture into a greased 1 litre basin, cover with greased paper or foil, and steam for $1\frac{3}{4}$–2 hours. Leave in the basin for a few minutes, then turn out.

Serve with Chocolate Sauce (p720 or p725).

Finger Pudding

5–6 helpings

40g sponge fingers	$\frac{1}{2} \times 2.5ml$ spoon ground
3 eggs	cinnamon
125g caster sugar	50g butter **or** margarine
125g ground almonds	grated rind of $\frac{1}{2}$ lemon
a pinch of ground cloves	fat for greasing

Crush the biscuits to fine crumbs. Separate the eggs. Beat the yolks and sugar together until light and creamy. Stir in the ground almonds, cloves, cinnamon, and biscuit crumbs. Melt the fat, and stir it into the mixture with the lemon rind. Whisk the egg whites until fairly stiff and fold into the mixture. Put into a greased 750ml basin, cover with greased paper or foil, and steam for 1–$1\frac{1}{4}$ hours. Leave in the basin for a few minutes, then turn out.

Serve with Lemon Sauce (p721).

Guards Pudding

4–6 helpings

100g butter **or**	a pinch of salt
margarine	100g brown
100g soft light **or** dark	breadcrumbs
brown sugar	$1 \times 2.5ml$ spoon
$3 \times 15ml$ spoons	bicarbonate of soda
raspberry **or**	$1 \times 10ml$ spoon warm
strawberry jam	water
2 eggs	butter for greasing

Cream together the fat and sugar, and beat in the jam. Mix in the eggs, salt, and breadcrumbs. Dissolve the bicarbonate of soda in the warm water and stir into the mixture. Put into a buttered 1 litre basin, cover with greased paper or foil, and steam for 3 hours. Leave in the basin for a few minutes, then turn out.

Serve with the same warmed jam as used in the recipe.

Mousseline Pudding
See p885.

Newcastle Pudding

6 helpings

25g glacé cherries	a pinch of salt
100g butter **or**	1 × 5ml spoon baking
margarine	powder
100g caster sugar	50ml milk (approx)
2 eggs	fat for greasing
150g plain flour	

Halve the cherries, and use them to decorate the bottom of the basin. Cream the fat and sugar together. Beat the eggs until liquid, and gradually work them into the creamed mixture. Sift together the flour, salt, and baking powder, and stir into the mixture. Add enough milk to make a soft dropping consistency. Put into a greased 750ml basin, cover with greased paper or foil, and steam for 1½–2 hours. Leave in the basin for a few minutes, then turn out.

Serve with Jam Sauce (p726).

Patriotic Pudding

6 helpings

fat for greasing	100g butter **or**
3 × 15ml spoons red jam	margarine
200g plain flour	100g caster sugar
a pinch of salt	1 egg
2 × 5ml spoons baking	75ml milk (approx)
powder	

Grease a 1 litre basin and cover the bottom with the jam. Sift together the flour, salt, and baking powder. Rub the fat into the flour and add the sugar. Beat the egg and milk together, and stir into the dry ingredients, to form a soft dropping consistency. Put the mixture into the basin, cover with greased paper or foil, and steam for 1½–2 hours. Leave in the basin for a few minutes, then turn out.

Serve with the same warmed jam as used in the recipe.

Prince Albert's Pudding

6 helpings

400g prunes	100g butter **or**
500ml water	margarine
grated rind of	100g caster sugar
1 lemon	2 eggs
25g light soft brown	40g rice flour
sugar	100g brown
butter for greasing	breadcrumbs

Sauce

1 × 5ml spoon arrowroot	1 × 10ml spoon
250ml prune liquid (see	granulated sugar
Method)	2–3 drops cochineal

Wash the prunes and soak them in the water overnight. Stew the prunes with half the lemon rind, the water and the brown sugar until soft. Strain, and reserve 250ml of the liquid for the sauce. Stone and halve the prunes. Line a buttered 750ml basin with the prunes, skin sides against the basin. Chop any prunes which are left over.

Cream together well the fat and caster sugar. Separate the eggs and beat the yolks into the creamed mixture. Add the remaining lemon rind, any chopped prunes, the rice flour, and the breadcrumbs. Whisk the egg whites until fairly stiff and fold into the mixture. Put into the basin, cover with greased paper or foil, and steam for 1½–1¾ hours.

Meanwhile, make the sauce. Blend the arrowroot to a smooth paste with some of the reserved prune liquid. Boil the rest of the liquid, and pour it gradually over the blended arrowroot, stirring all the time. Return to the saucepan, and bring to the boil, stirring all the time. Reduce the heat and simmer for 2–3 minutes. Add the sugar and cochineal.

When the pudding is cooked, leave for a few minutes, then turn out on to a serving dish and pour the sauce over it.

BAKED PUDDINGS

Many pastry-based desserts, eg Mrs Beeton's Bake-well Pudding and Apricot Pudding, plus recipes for fruit flans and pies, can be found in the Pastry Making chapter.

Baked Sponge Pudding

Basic recipe

4–6 helpings

100g butter **or** margarine	$\frac{1}{2} \times 2.5ml$ spoon vanilla essence
100g caster sugar	$2 \times 15ml$ spoons milk (approx)
2 eggs	fat for greasing
150g plain flour	
$1 \times 5ml$ spoon baking powder	

Cream the fat and sugar together until light and fluffy. Beat the eggs until liquid, then beat them gradually into the creamed mixture. Sift together the flour and baking powder, and fold them in. Add the essence and enough milk to form a soft dropping consistency. Put into a greased 1 litre pie dish and bake in a moderate oven at 180°C, Gas 4, for 30–35 minutes until well risen and golden-brown.

Serve from the dish with Pouring Cup Custard (p964) or any sweet sauce.

Note If using a pie dish it can be encircled with a pie frill before presenting at table.

VARIATIONS

Jam Sponge

Put $2 \times 15ml$ spoons jam in the bottom of the dish before adding the sponge mixture. Serve with Jam Sauce (p726) made with the same jam.

Orange or Lemon Sponge

Add the grated rind of 1 orange or lemon to the creamed mixture. Serve with Orange or Lemon Sauce (p721).

Spicy Sponge

Sift $1 \times 5ml$ spoon mixed spice, ground ginger, grated nutmeg or cinnamon with the flour. Serve with Ginger Syrup Sauce (p726).

Coconut Sponge

Substitute 25g desiccated coconut for 25g flour. Serve with Apricot Sauce (p723).

Chocolate Sponge

Substitute 50g cocoa for 50g flour. Serve with Chocolate Sauce (p720 or p725).

Baked Jam Roll

6 helpings

300g plain flour	150g shredded suet
$1 \times 5ml$ spoon baking powder	flour for rolling out
a pinch of salt	200–300g jam
	butter for greasing

Sift the flour, baking powder, and salt into a bowl. Add the suet and enough cold water to make a soft, but firm dough. On a lightly floured surface, roll into a rectangle about 5mm thick. Spread the jam almost to the edges, dampen the edges, and roll up lightly. Seal the edges at each end. Grease a baking sheet and place the roll on it, with the sealed edge underneath. Cover loosely with greased paper or foil. Bake in a fairly hot oven at 190°C, Gas 5, for 50–60 minutes until golden-brown.

Serve on a warm platter, sliced, with warmed jam.

VARIATIONS

Instead of the jam, use 200–300g marmalade, or 200g dried fruit mixed with 50g Demerara sugar. Serve with Pouring Cup Custard (p964).

Pineapple Upside-Down Cake

See p1213.

Almond Castles

4–8 helpings

75g butter	1 × 15ml spoon brandy
75g caster sugar	(optional)
3 eggs	150g ground almonds
3 × 15ml spoons single	fat for greasing
cream **or** milk	

Cream together the butter and sugar until light and fluffy. Separate the eggs. Stir the egg yolks, cream or milk, brandy, if used, and ground almonds into the creamed mixture. Whisk the egg whites until just stiff, and fold lightly into the mixture. Three-quarters fill 8 greased dariole moulds. Bake in a warm oven at 160°C, Gas 3, for 20–25 minutes, until the puddings are firm in the centre and golden-brown.

Turn out and serve with Pouring Cup Custard (p964).

Castle Puddings

3–4 helpings

100g butter **or**	100g plain flour
margarine	1 × 5ml spoon baking
100g sugar	powder
2 eggs	fat for greasing
$\frac{1}{2}$ × 2.5ml spoon vanilla	
essence	

Work together the fat and sugar until light and creamy. Beat in the eggs and vanilla essence. Sift together the flour and baking powder, and fold into the creamed mixture. Three-quarters fill 6–8 greased dariole moulds. Bake in a moderate oven at 180°C, Gas 4, for 20–25 minutes, until set and well risen.

Serve with Pouring Cup Custard (p964) or Jam Sauce (p726).

VARIATION

Somerset Puddings

Serve the puddings cold, with the inside scooped out, and the cavity filled with jam or stewed fruit. Serve with whipped cream.

College Puddings

6–8 helpings

100g flour	75g shredded suet
1 × 2.5ml spoon baking	75g caster sugar
powder	50g currants
a pinch of salt	50g sultanas
1 × 2.5ml spoon mixed	2 eggs
spice	100–125ml milk
100g stale white	fat for greasing
breadcrumbs	

Sift together the flour, baking powder, salt, and spice. Add the crumbs, suet, sugar, currants, and sultanas, and mix well. Beat the eggs until liquid and stir into the dry ingredients. Add enough milk to form a soft dropping consistency. Half fill 6–8 greased dariole moulds with the mixture and bake in a fairly hot oven at 190°C, Gas 5, for 20–25 minutes.

Turn out and serve with Pouring Cup Custard (p964) or Lemon Sauce (p721).

Cottage Pudding

5–6 helpings

200g plain flour	75g soft light brown
a pinch of salt	sugar
2 × 5ml spoons baking	100g raisins
powder	1 egg
100g butter **or**	50–75ml milk
margarine	butter for greasing

Sift together the flour, salt, and baking powder. Rub the fat into the flour and add the rest of the dry ingredients. Beat the egg until liquid and stir into the dry ingredients with enough milk to make a soft dropping consistency. Put the mixture into a greased 25 × 20cm baking dish and bake in a fairly hot oven at 190°C, Gas 5, for 35–40 minutes until firm in the centre and golden-brown.

Serve with Pouring Cup Custard (p964) or any sweet sauce.

Devonshire Rum

3–4 helpings

250g (approx) cold Christmas pudding **or** rich fruit cake	250ml milk
	1 × 10ml spoon soft brown sugar
fat for greasing	50ml rum **or** a few drops rum essence
1 egg	
2 × 10ml spoons cornflour	

Cut the pudding or cake into fingers, and arrange in a greased 750ml pie dish. Beat the egg until liquid. Mix the cornflour to a paste with a little of the milk. Heat the remaining milk to scalding point, then pour it slowly on to the cornflour, stirring to prevent lumps forming. Return it to the heat and cook gently for 2 minutes; then stir in the sugar, egg, and rum or rum essence. Pour the mixture over the pudding or cake and bake in a moderate oven at 180°C, Gas 4, for about 30 minutes or until firm.

Serve with Mrs Beeton's Fairy Butter (p1303).

Eve's Pudding

4 helpings

400g cooking apples	fat for greasing
grated rind and juice of 1 lemon	75g butter **or** margarine
75g Demerara sugar	75g caster sugar
1 × 15ml spoon water	1 egg
	100g self-raising flour

Peel, core, and slice the apples thinly. Mix together with the lemon rind and juice, Demerara sugar, and water, and put into a greased 1 litre pie dish. Cream the fat and caster sugar together until light and fluffy. Beat the egg until liquid and beat into the creamed mixture. Fold in the flour lightly and spread the mixture over the apples. Bake in a moderate oven at 180°C, Gas 4, for 40–45 minutes until the apples are soft and the sponge is firm.

Serve with Pouring Cup Custard (p964) or melted apple jelly and single cream.

VARIATIONS
Instead of apples, use 400g apricots, peaches, gooseberries, rhubarb, raspberries or plums.

Exeter Pudding

5–6 helpings

butter for greasing	3 eggs
125g stale white breadcrumbs	2 × 15ml spoons milk
25g ratafias **or** small macaroons	25ml rum **or** to taste (optional)
75g shredded suet	2 individual sponge cakes
50g sago	75g jam (any type)
75g caster sugar	
grated rind and juice of 1 lemon	

Butter a 1 litre pie dish. Coat with some of the crumbs, and cover the bottom with half the ratafias or macaroons. Mix together the remaining crumbs, suet, sago, sugar, lemon rind, and juice. Beat together the eggs, milk, and rum, if used, and stir into the dry ingredients. Slice the sponge cakes. Put some of the mixture into the dish, cover with slices of sponge cake, a layer of jam, and some of the remaining ratafias. Repeat the layers until all the ingredients are used, finishing with a layer of breadcrumb mixture. Bake in a moderate oven at 180°C, Gas 4, for 45–60 minutes.

Serve with Jam Sauce (p726) using the same jam as in the recipe.

Lemon Pudding (2)

4 helpings

50g butter **or** margarine	150g plain flour
100g caster sugar	200ml milk
3 eggs	fat for greasing
grated rind and juice of $1\frac{1}{2}$ lemons	

Cream together the fat and sugar. Separate the eggs and beat the yolks, lemon rind, and juice into the creamed mixture. Fold in the flour and milk. Whisk the egg whites until stiff and carefully fold into the mixture. Put into a greased 1 litre pie dish and bake in a moderate oven at 180°C, Gas 4, for 40–45 minutes until firm and golden-brown.

Serve with Lemon Sauce (p721).

Note For a steamed lemon pudding, see p986.

Puddings, Sweets and Preserves

Fruit Salad is particularly attractive when presented in a scooped-out pineapple (see pp1003–4)

LEFT *Christmas Pudding* (p982) *with Brandy Butter* (p1302)

BELOW *Mrs Beeton's Tipsy Cake* (p1036)

RIGHT *Raspberry Yoghurt Cheesecake* (p1043)

BELOW RIGHT *(back) Hazelnut Meringue Gâteau* (p1045) *(front) Lemon Soufflé* (p1017)

The Versatility of the Apple

LEFT *(clockwise from top)*
Apple Charlotte (p993), *Danish Apple Cake* (p1006),
Baked Apples (p994), *and Glazed Apple Dumplings*
(p995), *Mrs Beeton's Flan of Apples* (p1261), *Apple Pie*
(p1260), *and 3 popular preserves: Apple Butter* (p1123),
Apple Jelly (p1110) *and Apple Chutney* (p1145)

BELOW *Cooking and eating apples*
1 USA Red Delicious
2 Bramley's Seedling
3 Russet
4 Cox's Orange Pippin
5 Granny Smith

LEFT *Knickerbocker Glory* (p1061)

RIGHT *(clockwise from top)* Baked Alaska (p1061), *Lemon Sorbet* (p1055), *Strawberry Ice Cream Layer Gâteau* (p1064), *and Peach Melba* (p1062)

An assortment of sweet and sour preserves

Hot Fresh Fruit Puddings and Desserts

Stewed Fruit

See pp1001–2.

Apple Amber (1)

4 helpings

3 eggs	500ml thick apple purée
1 × 15ml spoon lemon juice	250g caster sugar (approx)

Decoration
glacé cherries   angelica

Separate the eggs. Beat the lemon juice and yolks into the apple purée with about 75g of the sugar. Turn into a 750ml baking dish, cover, and bake in a moderate oven at 180°C, Gas 4, for 15 minutes. Whisk the egg whites until they form stiff peaks. Gradually whisk in 150g of the remaining sugar, adding 1 × 5ml spoonful at a time. Pile the meringue on top of the apple mixture and sprinkle with 1 × 15ml spoon sugar. Return to the oven and bake for a further 15 minutes or until the meringue is pale golden-brown.

Serve at once with Pouring Cup Custard (p964) or single cream.

Note For Apple Amber (2), see p1262.

Apple Charlotte

5–6 helpings

butter for greasing	50–75g butter
400g cooking apples	8–10 large slices white bread, 5mm thick
grated rind and juice of 1 lemon	1 × 15ml spoon caster sugar
100g soft light brown sugar	
a pinch of ground cinnamon	

Grease a 1 litre charlotte mould or 16cm cake tin heavily with butter. Peel, core, and slice the apples.

Simmer the apples, lemon rind and juice with the sugar and cinnamon until the apples soften to a thick purée. Leave to cool.

Melt the butter. Cut the crusts off the bread, and dip 1 slice in the butter. Cut it into a round to fit the bottom of the mould or tin. Fill any spaces if necessary. Dip the remaining bread slices in the butter. Line the inside of the mould with 6 slices, touching one another. Fill the bread case with the cooled purée. Complete the case by fitting the top with more bread slices. Cover loosely with greased paper or foil, and bake in a moderate oven at 180°C, Gas 4, for 40–45 minutes. For serving, turn out and dredge with caster sugar.

Serve with bramble jelly and cream.

VARIATIONS

1) Line the mould or tin with slices of bread and butter, placed buttered side out, instead of dipping bread in melted butter.
2) Instead of lining the sides of the mould or tin, arrange the purée and dipped bread in alternate layers in the mould or tin until all the ingredients are used, ending with a layer of bread.

Apple Crumble

6 helpings

600g cooking apples	75g butter or margarine
100g brown sugar	150g plain flour
50ml water	75g caster sugar
grated rind of 1 lemon	$\frac{1}{2}$ × 2.5ml spoon ground ginger
fat for greasing	

Peel, core, and slice the apples. Cook with the brown sugar, water, and lemon rind in a covered pan until soft. Fill a greased 1 litre pie dish with the apples. Rub the fat into the flour until it resembles fine breadcrumbs. Add the caster sugar and ginger and stir well, sprinkle the mixture over the apples, and press down lightly. Bake in a moderate oven at 180°C, Gas 4, for 30–40 minutes until the crumble is golden-brown.

VARIATION

Instead of apples, use 600g damsons, gooseberries, pears, plums, rhubarb, or raspberries.

Baked Apples

6 helpings

6 cooking apples	*50g Demerara sugar*
filling (see below)	*75ml water*

Wash and core the apples. Cut round the skin of each apple with the tip of a sharp knife two-thirds of the way up from the base. Put into an ovenproof dish, and fill the centres with the chosen filling. Sprinkle the Demerara sugar on top of the apples and pour the water round them. Bake in a moderate oven at 180°C, Gas 4, for 45–60 minutes, depending on the cooking quality and size of the apples.

Serve with Pouring Cup Custard (p964), ice cream or with whipped cream, sweetened and flavoured with brandy.

Fillings

1) Mix together 50g Barbados or other raw sugar and 50g butter.
2) Use blackcurrant, raspberry, strawberry or apricot jam, or marmalade.
3) Chop 75g stoned dates, sultanas, raisins or currants.
4) Mix together 50g soft light brown sugar and 1 × 5ml spoon ground cinnamon.

Baked Apples Stuffed with Rice and Nuts

6 helpings

6 medium-sized cooking apples	*1 egg*
25g flaked almonds or other nuts	*50g sugar or to taste*
40g seedless raisins	*2 × 15ml spoons butter*
25–50g boiled rice (preferably boiled in milk)	*raspberry or blackcurrant syrup*

Wash and core the apples but do not peel them. With a small rounded spoon, hollow out part of the flesh surrounding the core hole. Do not break the outside skin. Mix together the nuts, raisins, and rice, using enough rice to make a stuffing for all the apples. Beat the egg until liquid. Add the sugar to the rice and nuts, and enough egg to bind the mixture; melt and add the butter. Fill the apples with the rice mixture. Place in a baking tray, and add 5mm depth hot water. Bake in a fairly hot oven at 190°C, Gas 5, for 40 minutes or until the apples are tender. Remove from the oven and place on a warmed serving platter. Warm the fruit syrup and pour it over the apples.

Serve with chilled cream or sweetened yoghurt.

Brown Betty

6 helpings

1kg cooking apples	*4 × 15ml spoons golden syrup*
fat for greasing	
150g stale wholemeal breadcrumbs	*100g Demerara sugar*
grated rind and juice of 1 lemon	*2 × 15ml spoons water*

Peel, core, and thinly slice the apples. Coat a greased 1 litre pie dish with a thin layer of breadcrumbs, then fill with alternate layers of apples, lemon rind, and breadcrumbs. Heat the syrup, sugar, water, and lemon juice in a saucepan and pour over the mixture. Bake in a warm oven at 160°C, Gas 3, for 1–1¼ hours until the pudding is brown and the apple cooked.

Serve with single cream or any pouring custard (p964).

Friar's Omelet

4–5 helpings

1kg cooking apples	*2 eggs*
grated rind and juice of 1 lemon	*100g stale white breadcrumbs*
50g butter or margarine	*fat for greasing*
100g granulated sugar	*25g butter*

Peel, core, and slice the apples. Put the apples, lemon rind and juice, fat, and sugar into a saucepan, cover, and cook until the apples are very soft. Remove from the heat, cool slightly, and stir in the eggs; beat the mixture well. Put half the stale breadcrumbs into a greased 1 litre pie dish, cover with the apple mixture, and sprinkle with the remaining crumbs. Dot with butter and bake in a hot oven at 220°C, Gas 7, for 20–25 minutes.

Serve with Simple Custard (p964).

Cherry Pudding

5–6 helpings

400g cooking cherries	50g caster sugar
50ml water	3 eggs
75g soft light brown sugar	grated rind of 1 lemon
50g cornflour	$\frac{1}{2} \times 2.5ml$ spoon ground cinnamon
375ml milk	fat for greasing

Stone the cherries and put into a saucepan with the water and brown sugar. Stew very gently until the fruit is just soft. Leave to cool.

Blend the cornflour with a little of the milk to obtain a smooth paste. Bring the rest of the milk to the boil, and pour it on to the cornflour mixture. Return to the saucepan and bring to simmering point, stirring all the time. Simmer for 2–3 minutes. Stir in the caster sugar, and leave to cool.

Separate the eggs. Add the yolks, lemon rind, and cinnamon to the cornflour sauce. Whisk the egg whites to the same consistency as the sauce and fold them in. Place a layer of cherries in the bottom of a greased 1 litre pie dish, then a layer of the sauce. Continue with the layers until all the sauce has been used. Cover with greased paper or foil and bake in a fairly hot oven at 200°C, Gas 6, for 35–45 minutes or until just set.

Serve with Pouring Cup Custard (p964) or single cream.

Note If liked, the custard or cream can be flavoured with maraschino liqueur or the syrup from a bottle of maraschino cherries.

Glazed Apple Dumplings

6 helpings

300g prepared shortcrust pastry (p1249)	50g brown sugar
	6 cooking apples
flour for rolling out	12 cloves (optional)
$\frac{1}{2} \times 2.5ml$ spoon ground cinnamon	$1 \times 15ml$ spoon milk
	25g caster sugar

Divide the pastry into 6 portions. On a lightly floured surface roll each out into a round. Mix together the cinnamon and brown sugar. Peel and core the apples and put each on a round of pastry. Fill the apple cavity with the sugar mixture, and press 2 cloves into the top of each apple, if liked. Work the pastry round the apple to enclose it, moisten the edges and press well together, leaving the cloves sticking out. Place the dumplings on a baking tray. Brush them with milk and dredge with the caster sugar. Bake in a fairly hot oven at 200°C, Gas 6, for 30–35 minutes or until the apples are tender.

Serve with single cream.

Note For boiled Apple Dumplings, see p981.

Plums with Port

6 helpings

1kg plums	150ml port
100–150g soft light brown sugar	

Cut the plums neatly in half and remove the stones. Put into a baking dish or casserole, sprinkle with the sugar (the amount required will depend on the sweetness of the plums) and pour the port on top. Cover securely with a lid or foil and bake in a cool oven at 150°C, Gas 2, for 45–60 minutes or until the plums are tender. Serve hot, or lightly chilled.

Stuffed Fresh Peaches

4–8 helpings

50g unsalted butter	*2 egg whites*
8 large peaches	*2 drops almond essence*
50g salted butter	*or 1 × 15ml spoon*
125g caster sugar	*anisette liqueur*
125g ground almonds	
125g plain or sponge	
cake crumbs	

Grease a shallow ovenproof dish with the unsalted butter. With the point of a knife, make 2 slits in the skin of each peach. Scald the fruit for 40 seconds, drain and peel. Cut in half and remove the stones carefully without spoiling the shape. Place the peaches on the dish, hollows uppermost. Melt the salted butter. Mix the sugar, ground almonds, and crumbs with most of the melted butter. Add the egg whites and the essence or liqueur and beat the mixture to a creamy consistency. Using a piping bag or spoon, fill the hollow of each peach with the mixture. Brush with the remaining melted butter and bake in a moderate oven at 180°C, Gas 4, for 20 minutes.

Serve hot with Crème Anglaise (p965), ice cream or Zabaglione (p974).

Toffee-topped Grape Cream

4 helpings

225g grapes	*3–4 × 15ml spoons*
fat for greasing	*Demerara sugar*
250ml double cream	
2 × 15ml spoons brandy	
(optional)	

Halve and de-pip the grapes, and put into a greased ovenproof dish. Whip the cream until it holds its shape, then spread it over the grapes. Chill in a refrigerator for at least 8 hours. Just before serving, sprinkle with the brandy and sugar, put under a moderately hot grill, and grill for 3–4 minutes until the sugar melts and bubbles.

Serve at once with Almond Biscuits (p1217) or Mrs Beeton's Savoy Cakes (p1208).

Pears in Wine

4 helpings

100g white sugar	*4 large ripe cooking*
250ml water	*pears (500g approx)*
2 × 15ml spoons red-	*250ml red wine*
currant jelly	*25g blanched almonds*
1 × 2cm piece	*a few drops red food*
cinnamon stick	*colouring (optional)*

Put the sugar, water, redcurrant jelly, and cinnamon stick into a pan and heat gently until the sugar and jelly have dissolved. Peel the pears, leaving the stalks in place. Carefully remove as much of the core as possible without breaking the fruit. Add the pears to the pan, cover, and simmer gently for 15 minutes. Add the wine, and cook, uncovered, for a further 15 minutes. Remove the pears carefully, arrange them on a serving dish and keep warm.

Remove the cinnamon stick. Shred the almonds and add to the pan. Boil the liquid remaining in the pan rapidly until it is reduced to a thin syrup. Add a few drops of red food colouring if the colour is not deep enough. Pour the syrup over the pears and serve warm, with fresh single or double cream.

This dessert can also be served cold. Pour the hot syrup over the pears, leave to cool, then chill before serving.

Note The pears can be baked in a very cool oven at 120°C, Gas $\frac{1}{2}$, for 4–5 hours.

Apple Strudel
See p1267.

Bananas in Rum
See p1450.

Cherries Jubilé
See p1451.

COLD PUDDINGS AND DESSERTS

A plain whipped cream may be served on a glass dish, and garnished with strips of angelica, or pastry leaves, or pieces of bright-coloured jelly: it makes a very pretty addition to the supper-table.

Cold Cereal Sweets

Most cold cereal sweets are moulded desserts or 'shapes' which can be turned out like a jelly. They are made with large grain, ground or powdered cereals, milk, sugar, and flavouring, and sometimes a little gelatine. Properly made, they have a delicate flavour, and can look glamorous, especially if attractively decorated.

MAKING AND MOULDING CEREAL SWEETS

A brief description of different grain cereals is given on p956.

Simmer large grain cereals in the top of a double boiler; sprinkle small grains on to boiling liquid, and stir all the time during cooking; blend powdered cereals with cold liquid before adding the rest of the liquid at boiling point. In all cases, it is important not to allow too much liquid to evaporate during cooking, as the texture of the cereal can then be tough. The consistency of any cereal mixture ready for moulding should be thick, so that a spoonful dropped back on the hot mixture only merges into it when shaken; a cereal shape of a stiffer texture is unpalatable. A knob of butter added during cooking gives any mixture a better flavour and consistency.

Choose china or glass moulds if possible, because the cold surface sets the starch mixture at once, and gives the shape a clean surface when turned out. Pour the mixture into the mould quickly from a height, so that the mixture's own weight drives all the air out of the mould and forces itself into the hollows of the shape. A border or ring mould can be greased with a little butter or oil to make turning out easier.

To turn out, loosen the mixture from the edge of the mould with the point of a knife, place a wetted serving dish over the mould, invert both together, and tap the mould sharply to dislodge it.

BASIC RECIPES

Large and Whole Grain Cereal Sweets
(eg rice, tapioca, barley)

Makes 1 litre (approx)

150g grain	flavouring (p998)
1 litre milk	25g butter
75g sugar	

Wash the grain in cold water and put it into the top of a double boiler with the milk. Simmer gently with the lid on for 2–2½ hours until the grain is tender and the milk almost absorbed. Stir occasionally to prevent the grain from settling on the bottom of the pan. Stir in the sugar, flavouring, and butter. Pour into a wetted 1 litre mould or basin and leave for about 2 hours to set. Turn out and serve with stewed fruit or jam.

VARIATION

Creamed Rice (1)

Fold 125ml single cream into the cooked rice.

Small and Crushed Grain Cereal Sweets

(eg flaked grains, semolina, sago)

Makes 450ml (approx)

500ml milk	*50g caster sugar*
50g grain	*flavouring (see below)*
1 × 10ml spoon gelatine	
2 × 15ml spoons cold water	

Heat the milk to boiling point, sprinkle in the grain and cook gently, stirring all the time, for 15–20 minutes until soft and smooth. Soften the gelatine in the cold water in a small heatproof container, stand the container in a pan of hot water and stir until the gelatine dissolves. Stir into the mixture. Add the sugar and flavouring. Leave to cool, stirring from time to time. When tepid, pour into a wetted 500ml mould and leave for about 2 hours to set. Turn out to serve.

VARIATIONS

Blend 40g cocoa with small or powdered grain, or add 50g grated plain chocolate when the mixture is almost cooked. Extra sugar can be added if required and also a few drops of vanilla, rum or coffee essence.

Creamed Rice(2)

Whip 125–250ml double cream until thick, and fold into the mixture just before moulding. Use a 650ml mould.

Powdered Grain Cereal Sweets

(eg cornflour, custard powder, ground rice, arrowroot)

Makes 1 litre (approx)

75g grain	*50g sugar*
1 litre milk	*flavouring (see below)*

Blend the grain with a little of the cold milk. Bring the rest of the milk to the boil, and pour on to the blended mixture, stirring all the time. Return the mixture to the saucepan, and bring it to simmering point, stirring all the time. Simmer for 5–10 minutes. Add the sugar and flavouring. Pour into a wetted 1 litre mould and leave for about 2 hours to set. Turn out to serve.

Note When made with cornflour, ground rice or arrowroot, and without added colouring, this basic moulded mixture is a blancmange.

VARIATIONS

Ambrosia Mould

Stir 50g melted butter and 125ml sherry into the mixture after it has come to simmering point.

Pink Coconut Mould

Stir 50g desiccated coconut, 50g melted butter, and a few drops of cochineal into the mixture after it has come to simmering point. Use a 1.25 litre mould.

Flavourings for Cereal Sweets

Flavouring essences: Almond, lemon, vanilla or coffee essence can be added to the mixture with the sugar.

Lemon or orange: The grated rind can be stirred into the cooked mixture just before moulding (large grain sweets). Alternatively, thinly cut strips of rind from 1 orange or 1 lemon can be infused in the mixture while cooking (large grain sweets), or in the milk while heating (other cereal sweets). They should be removed before mixing the milk with the grain (small and powdered grain sweets).

OTHER CEREAL SWEETS

Butterscotch Pudding

6 helpings

25g cornflour
500ml milk
2 eggs
125g soft brown sugar

25g butter
1 × 5ml spoon vanilla
    essence

Decoration
25g chopped walnuts

Blend the cornflour with a little of the cold milk. Bring the rest of the milk to the boil, and pour on to the blended cornflour, stirring to prevent lumps forming. Return to the saucepan and bring the mixture to simmering point, stirring all the time. Simmer for 2–3 minutes. Cool for 3–4 minutes.

Separate the eggs and add the yolks to the saucepan. Stir thoroughly, and cook without boiling for a further 2–3 minutes. Melt the sugar in a heavy saucepan, add the butter and, when melted, stir into the cornflour sauce. Whisk the egg whites until fairly stiff and fold lightly into the mixture. Add the essence. Pile into a serving dish and leave for about 1 hour to set. Sprinkle the dessert with the nuts before serving.

Seafoam Pudding

6 helpings

65g cornflour
750ml water
pared rind and juice of
   2 large lemons

100–125g sugar
3 eggs

Blend the cornflour with a little of the water to a thin cream. Put the lemon rind and the rest of the water into a saucepan. Bring to the boil, then remove the rind. Pour the water on to the blended cornflour, stirring all the time. Return to the saucepan and bring the mixture to simmering point, stirring all the time. Simmer for 2–3 minutes. Add the sugar and the lemon juice. Separate the eggs; whisk the whites until stiff and, whisking all the time, gradually work the cornflour mixture into the whites. Pour into a wetted 1.5 litre mould and leave for about 2 hours to set.

Turn out when set and serve with custard made with the egg yolks.

Swiss Cream

4–6 helpings

100g ratafias **or** sponge
   cake
4 × 15ml spoons sweet
   sherry
grated rind and juice of
   1 lemon

500ml basic powdered
   grain mixture made
   with cornflour (p998)
125ml double cream

Decoration
2 × 5ml spoons nibbed
   almonds

4 glacé cherries

Break the biscuits or sponge into small pieces and place in the bottom of a glass dish or individual dishes. Pour over the sherry. Stir the lemon rind and juice into the cornflour mixture. Whip the cream until semi-stiff and stir into the mixture. Pour the mixture over the soaked biscuits and leave for about 2 hours to set. Decorate with nuts and cherries.

Peach Condé

6 helpings

1 litre cold rice pudding (p997)	125ml peach syrup from can
1 × 410g can peach halves	2 drops pink food colouring
2 × 5ml spoons arrowroot	1–2 drops yellow food colouring

Decoration
whipped cream

Divide the rice pudding between 6 sundae glasses. Drain the peaches and arrange 1 half on top of each helping of rice, cut side down. Put the arrowroot into a small saucepan and stir in the syrup. Bring to the boil, stirring all the time, and boil for about 5 minutes until it thickens and clears. Add the colouring and pour over the peaches. Leave to set. Decorate with whipped cream.

VARIATIONS

Apricot or pear halves can be substituted for peaches. Omit the food colouring if pears are used.

Apricot Mould

6 helpings

750ml milk	25g caster sugar
65g ground rice	125ml double cream
1 × 15ml spoon hot water	1 × 15ml spoon apricot liqueur (optional)
4 × 15ml spoons apricot jam	

Bring the milk to boiling point and sprinkle in the ground rice. Cook gently, stirring all the time, for 5–10 minutes, until the mixture is smooth. Mix the hot water and jam together, sieve, and add to the ground rice with the sugar. Pour into a wetted 750ml ring mould and leave for about 2 hours to set. Whip the cream, with the liqueur if used, until just stiff. Turn the mould out on to a serving dish and fill the centre with the cream.

Cold Timbale of Semolina

6–7 helpings

750ml milk	4 × 15ml spoons cold water
100g semolina	250ml double cream
2 × 5ml spoons gelatine	

Filling

2 dessert apples	5 × 15ml spoons apricot jam
2 ripe dessert pears	
juice of 1 lemon	

Heat the milk to boiling point, sprinkle the semolina into it and simmer for 10 minutes in a covered pan, stirring occasionally. Soften the gelatine in the water in a small heatproof container for 5 minutes, stand the container in a pan of hot water and stir until the gelatine dissolves. Stir into the semolina. Remove the saucepan from the heat and leave to cool. Whip the cream until fairly stiff and fold into the cooled mixture. Just before it reaches setting point, when it is thickening, turn the mixture into a wetted 1 litre timbale or ring mould and leave for $1\frac{1}{2}$–2 hours to set.

Meanwhile, make the filling. Peel and core the apples and pears and slice them thinly. Put the fruit, lemon juice, and jam into a saucepan and heat gently until the fruit is just soft. Cool completely. When the timbale is set, turn it out on to a serving plate. Spoon the filling into the centre of the ring.

Serve with whipped cream if liked.

Note For Hot Timbale of Semolina, see p961.

Fruit Desserts

This section illustrates the main ways in which fruit can be used to make attractive and nutritious desserts. Fresh fruit, served just as it is as a dessert, is dealt with on pp1065–76.

Some fruit desserts usually served hot, such as Baked Apples (p994), Pears in Wine (p996), and Plums with Port (p995) can also be served cold.

See also the chapter on Ices and Frozen Desserts.

BASIC FRUIT DESSERTS

Stewed or Poached Fresh Fruit

Fruit can be poached or stewed. If poached, it is cooked in a syrup or other liquid at just below boiling point. The water should just shiver. If stewed, it is cooked at a slightly higher heat in a covered pan.

The syrup is made from sugar and water, or other liquid, with extra flavouring sometimes added. The quantities of sugar and water will depend on the sweetness and ripeness of the fruit; those given below are only rough guides. To make the syrup, put the sugar and liquid into a large saucepan with any solid flavouring. Bring to the boil, reduce the heat, and simmer for 3–4 minutes. Skim and use as required.

The fruit can be cooked either in a saucepan over a direct gentle heat or in a casserole in a moderate to cool oven. The second method takes longer but preserves the shape of the fruit better. The time taken depends on the type of fruit, its size, and ripeness. Most cook in 20 minutes or less in a saucepan, but take twice as long in a casserole. Use a stainless steel, aluminium or enamelled pan or an earthenware casserole. Do not use copper or brass.

When the fruit is cooked, remove it with a perforated spoon, drain well, and transfer to a serving bowl. Discard any solid flavourings from the syrup and boil until it is well reduced. Pour it over the fruit and serve either hot or cold.

Note Individual flavourings are suggested below as appropriate, but any fruit can be stewed in natural or canned juice; brandy or other fortified wine can be added to the syrup.

Apples and pears: Peel, core, and leave whole if small, quarter if large. Make a syrup with 100g sugar and 250ml water (more if the fruit is very hard) per 500g fruit. Flavour with lemon rind, cloves or cinnamon stick. Colour the syrup with cochineal, if liked, or replace some of the water with white wine or cider. Put the prepared fruit into the liquid immediately to preserve its colour; it must be completely covered by the liquid. Stew either in a saucepan or in a casserole in a moderate oven. Cooking pears may take 4–5 hours in the oven.

Currants and other soft berry fruits: Clean and prepare the fruit; remove stalks from currants. Make a syrup with 100g sugar and 125ml water per 500g fruit. Either steep the fruit in the cooled syrup and then poach very gently; or, if it is to be served cold, reduce the syrup by boiling, put the fruit into the hot syrup, and leave it to cool.

Gooseberries: Top and tail, removing a little skin from the tail end to allow the syrup to penetrate; then wash. Make a syrup with 100g sugar and 125–375ml water (depending on the hardness of the fruit) per 500g fruit. Flavour with elderflowers, if available. Poach very gently until the skins crack.

Peaches and apricots: Peel, stone, and halve or quarter the fruit, depending on its size. Make a syrup with 100g sugar and 250ml water per 500g fruit. Flavour with almond or vanilla essence or with a few kernels from the fruit stones. Replace some of the water with white wine if liked.

Plums, greengages, and damsons: Wash the fruit, remove the stalks, and the stones if liked. Make a syrup with 100g sugar and 250ml water per 500g fruit. Flavour with lemon rind, cloves, cinnamon stick, or with a few kernels from the fruit stones. Replace some of the water with red wine, for red plums, if liked. Stew either in a saucepan or in a casserole in a moderate oven.

Rhubarb: String older garden rhubarb, but just wipe young forced fruit. Cut into 2cm lengths, lay in a casserole, and cover with soft light brown sugar. Flavour with lemon rind, root ginger or cinnamon stick. Do not add water. Cover and bake very gently, overnight if possible, in a very cool oven at 110°C, Gas $\frac{1}{4}$.

Apricot Custard Cream

See p1032.

Mrs Beeton's Very Nice Preserve of Damsons

See p1120.

Stewed Dried Fruit

(eg prunes, apricots, peaches, figs, apple rings)

Wash the fruit thoroughly in tepid water. Put it in a large bowl, cover with fresh water or cold tea, allowing 750ml liquid per 500g dried fruit, and leave to soak for 12–24 hours.

Drain, and measure out 250ml liquid (use fresh water if the fruit was soaked in tea) for cooking each 500g soaked fruit. Add sugar as required: 50–100g per 500ml liquid for apricots, peaches, apple rings; 25g per 500ml for other fruit. Add either a strip of lemon rind or a piece of cinnamon stick (for prunes), and bring to the boil. Reduce the heat, simmer for 3–4 minutes, skim, and add the fruit. Simmer until tender, then drain the fruit with a perforated spoon, and transfer to a serving bowl. Discard any solid flavourings from the syrup and boil it until it is well reduced. Pour it over the fruit and serve either hot or cold.

Alternatively, the fruit can be cooked in the liquid without any added sugar. In this case, add the sugar when the syrup is being boiled down.

Fruit Purées

Fruit purées are used for a number of fruit desserts, such as mousses (see p1019) and fools. Hard fruits are generally cooked, but soft fruits such as strawberries, raspberries, peaches, mangoes or melons are simply prepared (ie hulled, peeled, and stoned), then rubbed through a fine nylon sieve, or puréed in an electric blender, and sweetened to taste. Fruit such as raspberries, which contain pips, should be sieved, not blended, to remove all the pips.

Hard fruit should be cooked in as little water as possible. About 4–5 ×15ml spoons should be enough for every 500g fruit; allow slightly less for apples and rhubarb. Put the water in a heavy-bottomed pan, add the fruit, cover, and simmer gently until the fruit is tender. When cooked, remove any stones, then sieve or purée until smooth, and sweeten to taste.

500g fresh fruit will yield about 300ml fruit purée.

Note Apples can also be baked in a moderate oven at 180°C, Gas 4, for 45 minutes–1 hour, then peeled, cored, and sieved or puréed.

Fruit Fool

6 helpings

750g fruit (approx), eg gooseberries, rhubarb, apricots, red, and black currants, raspberries, blackberries, etc
sugar

500ml thick pouring custard (p964) **or** *500ml double cream* **or** *250ml double cream and 250ml custard*

Decoration
ratafias **or** *fresh fruit* **or** *whipped cream*

Purée the fruit (see above), sweeten to taste, and leave to cool. If using cream, whip it until it holds its shape. Fold first the custard, if used, and then the cream into the fruit purée. Turn into a serving bowl and chill before serving. Decorate with ratafias, fresh fruit or whipped cream.

Note Some fruits especially soft berry fruits can be combined to make up the given weight, but as a rule the pure flavour of a single type of fruit is more attractive than mixed flavours.

Strawberry and Apple Fool

See p1406.

Rhubarb and Banana Fool

6–8 helpings

500g rhubarb, preferably forced rhubarb	sugar
6 bananas	250ml thick pouring custard (p964) **or** double cream

Decoration
ratafias **or** *whipped cream*

Cook and purée the rhubarb (p1002). Peel and mash the bananas or purée in a blender. Blend the two purées together and sweeten to taste. Whip the cream, if used, until it just holds its shape; fold either the custard or the cream into the fruit purée. Turn into a serving bowl and decorate with ratafias or piped whipped cream.

Scandinavian Fruit Fool

6 helpings

450g fruit, eg redcurrants and raspberries **or** redcurrants on their own **or** raspberries and strawberries and/or cherries	375ml water 100g sugar (approx) 25g ground sago **or** 1 × 15ml spoon cornflour a little extra caster sugar

Decoration
25g flaked almonds

Prepare and stone the fruit, if necessary. Put it into a pan with the water and simmer gently for about 20 minutes or until very tender. Sieve the fruit, or process in an electric blender and then sieve to remove all the pips; return to the pan. Add sugar to taste. Blend the sago or cornflour with a little of the purée and bring the rest of the purée to the boil. Add the sago or cornflour and bring back to the boil, stirring all the time until the fool thickens. Remove from the heat and turn into 1 large or 6 small serving dishes. Sprinkle with a little extra caster sugar to prevent a skin forming, and then sprinkle on the flaked almonds. Chill well and serve with whipped cream.

Fruit Salad

Always try to include a good selection of fruit with different colours, textures and flavours. Fresh fruit has the most vital flavour, and a portion should always be included, but frozen, canned, and even a few cooked, dried fruits can be added for bulk or variety. Allow about 150g fruit per person and 100ml fruit syrup.

The recipe below is for a basic fruit syrup which can be varied by adding more lemon juice, or sherry, Kirsch, brandy, port, Cointreau, Grand Marnier, white rum etc, to taste.

Basic Fruit Syrup

pared rind and juice of 1 lemon	500ml water 75g sugar

Put the lemon rind and juice into a pan with the water and sugar. Heat gently until the sugar has dissolved, then bring to the boil, and continue boiling until the syrup has been reduced by about half. Remove from the heat, strain, and leave to cool.

Fresh fruit is prepared according to kind as follows:

Apples: Cut into quarters and remove the cores; peel if wished, but if the skins are not too thick they provide an attractive contrast of colour. Cut into thin slices and dip quickly in lemon juice to preserve the colour, or put straight into the fruit syrup if it contains plenty of lemon juice.

Apricots: Cut in half and remove the stones. Cut each half into 2 or 3 pieces and add to the syrup. The stones of the apricots can also be split in half, the kernel removed and added to the fruit salad.

Bananas: Peel the bananas and cut into slices. Dip quickly in lemon juice to preserve the colour, then add to the fruit syrup. Only a few bananas should be added to a fruit salad and they should not be added too long before serving; this is because, even if coated with lemon juice, they will tend to discolour; this also happens if they are chilled in a refrigerator.

Cherries: Stone, cut in halves or leave whole, then add to the syrup.

Chinese gooseberries (kiwi fruit): Peel and cut into slices, and add to the syrup.

Grapes: Cut in half and remove the pips; if wished, grapes can also be peeled, although they provide attractive colour if left unpeeled.

Loganberries: Hull, and add to the syrup shortly before serving. Like other soft fruit they may go soggy or disintegrate if left in the syrup for long, especially if frozen.

Lychees: Peel, halve, remove the stones, and add to the syrup.

Mangoes: Peel, cut into slices, discard the stone, and add to the syrup.

Melons: Cut ripe melons in half, remove the seeds, then cut into cubes or balls with a melon scoop; discard all the peel. Add to the syrup.

Nectarines: As for peaches; the skin may be left on.

Oranges: Using a sharp knife, peel the oranges, removing all the white pith. Carefully cut between the segment skins to remove the flesh alone; do this over a plate to catch any juice and squeeze out all the juice from the remaining pulp. Add to the fruit syrup, together with the juice.

It is easier to remove all the pith if the oranges are put into boiling water for 2 minutes, cooled for another 2 minutes, then peeled while still hot.

Peaches: As for apricots, but cut each half into smaller pieces. Alternatively, slice thinly.

Pears: Peel and core, then cut into thin slices, or cubes. Dip quickly in lemon juice to preserve the colour, then add to the fruit syrup, or put quickly into the fruit syrup if it contains plenty of lemon juice.

Pineapple: Peel the pineapple, and remove all the eyes. Cut in half or quarters lengthways and cut out the hard core. Cut the fruit into small pieces. Add to the syrup.

Plums: Halve, remove the stones, and cut into quarters, if large. Add to the syrup.

Raspberries: Hull, and add to the syrup shortly before serving.

Strawberries: Hull, and add to the syrup shortly before serving.

Note See also the chapter on Fresh Fruit and Nuts.

Serve fruit salad either in a large serving bowl, preferably glass, to emphasize the varied colours of the fruits, or in a scooped-out pineapple or melon.

To scoop out the fruit, remove the top third crossways. Keeping the case intact, cut or scoop out the flesh from the rest of the fruit, leaving about a 1cm rim. Remove the core from the pineapple. Cut the fruit into small pieces, or into balls if using a melon, and add to the rest of the fruit salad. Fill the scooped-out fruit with the salad.

Alternatively, the fruit can be presented in the form of a basket. Prepare as follows:

If using a pineapple, cut off and discard the

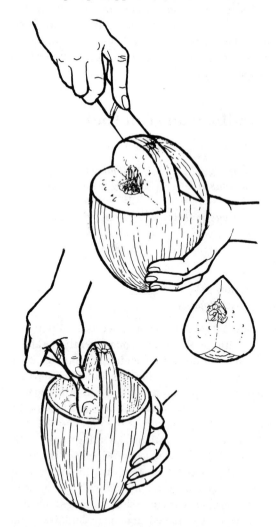

Making a melon basket

green leafy tuft from the top. Keeping the fruit upright, and leaving about a 2cm piece intact in the centre for the handle, cut 2 equal-sized wedges from either side of the top half. Carefully cut out the flesh from the handle, leaving a 1cm rim. Scoop out the flesh from the lower half and continue as above.

Note A pineapple container can also be prepared as for Sweet Pineapple Salad with Kirsch (p1007).

OTHER FRUIT DESSERTS

Frosted Apples

6 helpings

6 cooking apples (750g approx)	1 × 2.5cm piece cinnamon stick
lemon juice	2 cloves
250ml water	2 egg whites
100g granulated sugar	100g caster sugar
1 × 15ml spoon fine-cut marmalade	sugar for dusting

Decoration
125ml double cream	angelica
glacé cherries	

Wash, core, and peel the apples, but leave them whole. Brush all over with the lemon juice to preserve the colour. Put the water, granulated sugar, marmalade, cinnamon stick, cloves, and the apple peelings into a pan. Heat gently until the sugar dissolves, then boil for 2–3 minutes to give a thin syrup. Place the apples in a baking dish and strain the syrup over them. Cover with a lid or foil and bake in a moderate oven at 180°C, Gas 4, for about 30 minutes or until the apples are just tender.

Remove the apples from the syrup carefully, dry well on kitchen paper, then place on a baking tray lined with oiled greaseproof paper or vegetable parchment. Whisk the egg whites until they form stiff peaks, then gradually whisk in the caster sugar, a teaspoon at a time. If using an electric beater, whisk in all the sugar, but if beating by hand, whisk in half the sugar and fold in the rest. Coat each apple completely with the meringue, and dust lightly with caster sugar. Bake in a very cool oven at 120°C, Gas $\frac{1}{2}$, for about $1\frac{1}{2}$ hours or until the meringue is firm and very lightly coloured. Remove from the oven and leave to cool.

Whip the cream until it holds its shape. Pile a spoonful on top of each apple and decorate with small pieces of cherry and angelica. Serve the apples in individual glasses on a bed of whipped cream, or with the cold baking syrup poured over them.

Apple Snow (2)

6 helpings

4 large baking apples (750g approx)	2–3 eggs
juice and pared rind of 1 lemon	50g caster sugar
	1 × 5ml spoon cornflour **or** arrowroot
100g sugar (approx)	4 individual sponge cakes
250ml milk	

Decoration
glacé cherries

Bake and purée the apples (p1002). Add the lemon juice to the purée, sweeten to taste, and leave to cool.

Put the lemon rind into a small pan with the milk and heat gently for 15 minutes, then strain. Separate the eggs and blend the yolks and sugar together with the cornflour or arrowroot. Add the lemon-infused milk. Cook, stirring all the time, in a saucepan for 20–30 minutes or until the custard coats the back of the spoon. Cool.

Split the sponge cakes in half and arrange them in the bottom of a glass dish. Pour the custard over them. Whisk the egg whites until they form stiff peaks, then fold into the apple purée. Pile the mixture on top of the custard and decorate with the glacé cherries.

Note For Apple Snow served hot, see p966.

Banana and Soured Cream Dessert
See p881.

Danish Apple Cake

4–6 helpings

150g dry white
  breadcrumbs
75g granulated sugar

100–125g butter
900g stewed apples
  (p1001)

Decoration (optional)
300ml whipping cream   red jam

Mix the crumbs and sugar together. Melt the butter and fry the mixture until golden. Place alternate layers of crumbs and apples in a glass dish, starting and finishing with the crumbs. Decorate, if liked, with whipped cream and a little red jam.

Summer Pudding

6–8 helpings

1kg soft red fruit,
  eg black and red
  currants, blackberries,
  raspberries, and
  bilberries
100–150g caster sugar

1 strip lemon rind
  (optional)
8–10 slices day-old
  white bread (5mm
  thick)

Pick over and clean the fruit, put into a bowl with sugar to taste and the lemon rind, if used, and leave overnight. Turn the fruit and sugar into a pan, discarding the lemon rind, and simmer for 2–3 minutes until very lightly cooked. Remove from the heat. Cut the crusts off the bread. Cut a circle from 1 slice to fit the bottom of a 1.25 litre pudding basin. Line the base and sides of the basin with bread, leaving no spaces. Fill in any gaps with small pieces of bread. Fill with the fruit and any juice it has made while cooking. Cover with bread slices. Place a flat plate and a 1kg weight on top, and leave overnight, or longer if refrigerated.

Serve turned out, with chilled whipped cream, sweetened if liked.

Note This eighteenth-century pudding was invented (probably at Bath) for spa patients on slimming diets who were not allowed the rich creams and pastries popular at the time. It was then called Hydropathic Pudding. Bilberries are traditionally used in the north.

Banana Snow

6 helpings

6 bananas
  (600g approx)
50g soft light brown
  sugar
1 × 15ml spoon lemon
  juice

125ml double cream
300g natural yoghurt
3 egg whites

Decoration
25g toasted flaked
  almonds (p1185)

Mash the bananas with the sugar and lemon juice, or purée in an electric blender. Whip the cream until it just holds its shape, then fold it into the banana purée with the yoghurt. Whisk the egg whites until they form stiff peaks, then fold into the mixture and pile into 1 large or 6 individual dishes. Sprinkle with the almonds before serving.

Oranges in Caramel Sauce

4 helpings

6 oranges
250ml water
200g sugar

25–50ml chilled orange
  juice

Pare the rind carefully from one of the oranges, and cut it into thin strips. Soak in 125ml of the water for 1 hour, then simmer gently for 20 minutes. Drain. Peel and remove the white pith from all the oranges, and cut the flesh into 7mm thick slices. Place in a glass serving dish. Put the sugar and the remaining 125ml water into a pan. Heat gently, stirring until the sugar has dissolved, then boil rapidly until it is a golden caramel colour. Draw off the heat immediately and add enough orange juice to give the consistency of sauce required. Replace over the heat, stir until just blended, then add the orange rind. Pour the caramel sauce over the oranges and chill for at least 3 hours before serving.

Cherry Compôte

6 helpings

750g red cherries
grated rind and juice of
  1 orange
100ml red wine
3 ×15ml spoons
  redcurrant jelly

1 ×15ml spoon sugar
a pinch of ground
  cinnamon

Stone the cherries and put into a shallow oven-to-table baking dish. Add the orange rind and juice with all the remaining ingredients. Cover securely with a lid or foil and cook in a warm oven at 160°C, Gas 3, for about 30 minutes. Leave to cool, and chill before serving.

Prune Mould

6 helpings

400g prunes
750ml cold water
pared rind and juice of
  1 lemon
75g sugar

1 × 2.5cm piece
  cinnamon stick
2 ×10ml spoons gelatine
a few drops red food
  colouring (optional)

Soak the prunes overnight in the cold water. Put the lemon rind in a pan with the prunes and the liquid in which they have been soaking, the sugar, and the cinnamon stick. Cover the pan, and cook the prunes gently for about 30 minutes or until they are quite tender. Remove from the heat and leave to cool. Remove and discard the lemon rind and the cinnamon stick. Stone the prunes. Sieve the mixture or purée in an electric blender. Put the lemon juice into a heatproof basin and sprinkle the gelatine over it. Leave to soften for 5 minutes, then stand the basin over a pan of hot water and stir until the gelatine has dissolved. Stir into the prune mixture, together with a few drops of red food colouring, if liked. Turn the mixture into a wetted mould and leave in a cool place to set for about 2 hours. Turn out and serve with cream.

VARIATION

Use dried apricots instead of prunes, and omit the cinnamon.

Stuffed Peaches in Brandy

6 helpings

250ml water
100g white sugar
150ml medium-dry **or**
  slightly sweet white
  wine

2 ×15ml spoons brandy
6 large ripe peaches
25g blanched almonds
125ml double cream
50g cut mixed peel

Put the water, sugar, wine, and brandy into a saucepan over low heat until the sugar dissolves. Peel the peaches (if they are difficult to peel, dip them in boiling water for 1 minute first); then poach them gently in the brandy syrup for 15 minutes. Leave to cool completely.

Chop the blanched almonds, and whip the cream until it just holds its shape. Fold the mixed peel and almonds into the cream. Halve the peaches and remove the stones. Put a tablespoonful of the cream mixture in the hollow of 6 halves, then sandwich the peaches together again. Arrange in a shallow serving dish, and pour the syrup over the fruit. Chill until ready to serve.

Sweet Pineapple Salad with Kirsch

4 helpings

2 small pineapples
100g black grapes
1 banana
1 pear
1 ×15ml spoon lemon
  juice

2–3 ×15ml spoons
  Kirsch
sugar

Cut the pineapples in half lengthways. Cut out the core, then scoop out the flesh, using first a knife, then a spoon, but taking care to keep the pineapple cases intact. Discard the core, and chop the flesh. Put into a bowl, together with any pineapple juice. Halve and de-pip the grapes. Peel and slice the banana; peel, core, and slice the pear, and toss both fruits in the lemon juice, before adding to the other fruit in the bowl. Mix all the fruit together, pour the Kirsch over them, and sweeten to taste with the sugar. Pile the fruit back into the pineapple cases and chill until required.

Jellies

Home-made jellies are both simple to make and particularly nutritious, using such ingredients as fruit juice, fruit purée, eggs, milk, water or wine. Like commercially prepared packet jellies, they are set with gelatine. A set jelly should 'shiver' delicately when turned out on to a plate. It must never be rubbery or hard; it is therefore particularly important to weigh the ingredients carefully.

RULES FOR JELLY MAKING

1) Choose a large non-aluminium saucepan as the liquid jelly will rise during making. A thick enamel saucepan is ideal.
2) Use 2 × 10ml spoons powdered gelatine to 500ml water for general purposes, but when a slightly firmer 'set' is required use 3 × 10ml spoons gelatine to 500ml water. The larger amount of gelatine will be required:
   a) in hot weather
   b) if no refrigerator is available
   c) when pieces of fruit are to be set in the jelly and the mould turned out
   d) if the jelly is to be used for lining a mould or chopped for decoration.
3) Always make sure that gelatine is completely dissolved before adding it to other ingredients. Gelatine will dissolve easily if it is sprinkled on to cold water or liquid to soften first. Put the liquid into a small heatproof container, add the gelatine and leave for 5 minutes. Place the container in a saucepan of hot water over low heat and stir, especially round the sides, until the gelatine has completely dissolved.
4) Do not use milk to dissolve gelatine as it will curdle.
5) Do not add a hot gelatine solution to a really cold mixture. It will not mix properly but will set in globules and 'string' as soon as it comes into contact with the cold mixture. The mixture should be at room temperature, tepid, or, ideally, at the same temperature as the gelatine. In any case, the dissolved gelatine should be blended in quickly and thoroughly to prevent it setting in blobs.
6) If the mixture has to be strained, strain through scalded, well-washed, damp butter muslin. The muslin may be held up in a sieve.
7) A jelly mould may be made of glass, china, metal or plastic. When gelatine is included in a recipe, a sharp clean outline to the turned-out shape will be obtained if a metal mould is used. Tin-lined copper moulds are costly but ensure a perfect finish to the jelly. All moulds must be scrupulously clean and rinsed out or wetted with cold water before use. They should be wet inside when the jelly is poured in, although there should be no free water in the bottom.
8) To turn out a jelly, run the tip of a knife or finger round the top of the mould. Dip the mould into hot water for a few seconds, remove, and dry it. Wet a serving plate and place upside-down on the top of the mould. Hold the plate and mould together firmly and turn both over. Shake gently and carefully remove the mould.
9) If using fresh pineapple juice in making a jelly, it must first be boiled for 2–3 minutes. It contains an enzyme, which, if left untreated, destroys the setting power of gelatine.

UNCLEARED JELLIES AND JELLY DESSERTS

These recipes illustrate how to make a simple or fancy jelly dessert using a combination of gelatine and either fruit syrup or purée, wine or liqueurs, milk or a beverage.

Blackcurrant Jelly

2 helpings

125ml blackcurrant syrup, bought **or** *home-made* (p1136)	*25g sugar*
	1 × 10ml spoon gelatine
	125ml cold water

Heat together the syrup and sugar until the sugar has dissolved. Cool. Soften the gelatine in the water in a small heatproof container. Stand the container in a pan of hot water and stir until dissolved. Pour into the cooled syrup. Pour into wetted individual moulds and leave for about 1 hour to set.

Fresh Lemon Jelly

2 helpings

pared rind and juice of 2 lemons	*1 × 10ml spoon gelatine*
175ml water	*2 × 10ml spoons caster sugar*

Put the lemon rind into a saucepan with half the water and simmer for 5 minutes. Cool. Soften the gelatine in the remaining water in a small heatproof container. Stand the container in a pan of hot water and stir until the gelatine has dissolved. Add the lemon juice and sugar. Pour into individual wetted moulds and leave for about 1 hour to set.

VARIATION
Fresh Orange Jelly

Use 2 oranges instead of lemons and only 1 × 10ml spoon of sugar.

Orange Jelly Baskets

6 helpings

500ml water	*2 lemons*
100g sugar	*extra orange juice*
6 oranges	*40g gelatine*

Decoration
6 angelica strips   *125ml double cream*

Put the water and sugar into a saucepan. Pare the rind from three of the oranges. Add the rind to the pan and bring slowly to the boil. Leave to infuse for 10 minutes, keeping the pan covered. Squeeze the juice from the oranges and lemons; make up to 500ml with the extra orange juice if necessary. Reserve the unpeeled orange halves for the baskets. Put 2 × 15ml spoonfuls of fruit juice into a small heatproof container and soften the gelatine in it. Stand the container in a pan of hot water and stir until dissolved. Stir the fruit juice and dissolved gelatine into the sugar syrup. Remove any pulp from the 6 orange halves and put the orange skins into patty tins to keep them rigid. Strain the jelly into the orange shells and leave for about 2 hours until set.

Make handles from the angelica and set them in place with the ends in the set jelly. Whip the cream until stiff. Decorate the baskets with cream.

Black Coffee Jelly

4 helpings

500ml strong black coffee	*2 × 10ml spoons gelatine*
50g sugar	*1 × 15ml spoon rum **or** liqueur*

Decoration
whipped cream

Put the coffee, except for 2 × 15ml spoonfuls, and sugar into a saucepan, and heat until the sugar has dissolved. Cool. Soften the gelatine in the reserved coffee in a small heatproof container. Stand the container in a pan of hot water and stir until dissolved. Add the rum or liqueur. Strain into a wetted mould and leave for 1–2 hours to set. When ready for serving, turn out on to a plate and decorate with whipped cream.

Milk Jelly

2 helpings

250ml milk	*1 × 10ml spoon gelatine*
1 × 15ml spoon caster sugar	*4 × 15ml spoons cold water*
grated rind of 1 lemon	

Heat the milk, sugar, and lemon rind until the sugar has dissolved. Cool. Soften the gelatine in the cold water in a small heatproof container. Stand the container in a pan of hot water and stir until dissolved. Stir the gelatine into the cooled milk, then strain into a basin. Stir from time to time until it is the consistency of thick cream. Pour into a wetted mould and leave for about 1 hour to set.

VARIATIONS
The jelly can be flavoured with vanilla, coffee or other essence, if liked. If coffee essence is used, substitute orange rind for the lemon. Omit the rind if peppermint flavouring is used.

Lemon and Milk Jelly

6 helpings

pared rind and juice of	25g gelatine
3 large lemons	4 × 15ml spoons cold
750ml milk	water
200g sugar	

Put the lemon rind, milk, and sugar into a saucepan and heat until the sugar has dissolved. Leave to cool. Soften the gelatine in the water in a small heatproof container. Stand the container in a pan of hot water and stir until dissolved, then stir into the cooled milk. Stir in the lemon juice and strain into a wetted mould. Leave for about 2 hours to set.

Shaped Apple Jelly

6 helpings

1kg cooking apples	40g gelatine
500ml water	4 × 15ml spoons cold
175g sugar	water
2 cloves	
grated rind and juice of 2	
small lemons	

Wash the apples and cut into pieces. Put into a saucepan with the water, sugar, cloves, lemon rind and juice. Cover, and cook until the apples are soft. Soften the gelatine in the remaining water in a small heatproof container. Stand the container in a pan of hot water and stir until dissolved. Rub the cooked apples through a sieve and stir in the dissolved gelatine. Pour into a wetted mould and leave for 2–3 hours to set.

VARIATION

Gooseberry Jelly

Use 1kg prepared gooseberries instead of apples, and omit the cloves.

Raspberry and Yoghurt Delight
See p877.

Port Wine Jelly (1)

6 helpings

500ml water	25g gelatine
50g sugar	250ml port
2 × 15ml spoons	a few drops cochineal
redcurrant jelly	

Put the water, except for 2 × 15ml spoonfuls, the sugar, and the jelly into a pan and heat until the sugar has dissolved. Soften the gelatine in the rest of the water in a small heatproof container. Stand the container in a pan of hot water and stir until dissolved. Add to the syrup, with the port and the cochineal. Strain through a single thickness of muslin or fine cotton into a wetted mould. Leave for about 2 hours to set.

Note See also p1014 and p1338.

VARIATION

Claret Jelly

Use 250ml claret instead of port.

JELLIES AND JELLY DESSERTS USING EGGS

Amber Jelly (1)

4–6 helpings

375ml water	grated rind of 1 lemon
50ml sherry (optional)	3 egg yolks
125ml lemon juice	25g gelatine
150g lump sugar	

Put 250ml of the water, the sherry, if used, lemon juice, sugar, lemon rind, and egg yolks into a pan, and whisk over a low heat until almost at boiling point. (Do not allow to boil or the eggs will curdle.) Remove from the heat. Soften the gelatine in the remaining water in a small heatproof container. Stand the container in a pan of hot water and stir until dissolved, then whisk it into the saucepan. Strain the jelly through muslin and pour into a wetted mould. Chill for about 1 hour until set.

Note For Amber Jelly (2), see p1338.

Mrs Beeton's Dutch Flummery

4–6 helpings

25g gelatine	4 eggs
125ml cold water	500ml dry sherry
juice and grated rind of 1 lemon	50g caster sugar

Soften the gelatine in the water in a small heatproof container. Stand the container in a pan of hot water and stir until dissolved, then make up with cold water to 500ml. Strain the lemon juice into the gelatine and add the grated rind. Beat the eggs, sherry, and sugar together and add to the mixture. Pour into the top of a double boiler and cook slowly over low heat, stirring all the time, until the mixture coats the back of the spoon. Do not let the mixture boil. Strain the mixture into a wetted 1.5 litre mould and leave for 2–3 hours to set before turning out.

Note Make the day before using if possible.

Lemon Chiffon

4 helpings

3 eggs	3 × 15ml spoons water
150g caster sugar	1 × 10ml spoon gelatine
juice and grated rind of 2 lemons	

Decoration
whipped cream

Separate the eggs. Put the yolks, sugar, and lemon juice (125ml approx) into a heatproof basin, stand it over hot water and whisk the mixture until frothy, pale, and the consistency of single cream. Remove from the heat. Put the water into a heatproof container and sprinkle in the gelatine. Stand the basin in the hot water and stir until the gelatine dissolves. Cool for 5 minutes, then whisk into the yolk mixture. Put the mixture in a cool place, or chill until beginning to set. Stir in the lemon rind. Whisk the egg whites until stiff and fold into the lemon mixture. Spoon into glasses and leave to set in a refrigerator.

Serve chilled, decorated with whipped cream.

Egg Jelly

2 helpings

40g lump sugar	1 × 10ml spoon gelatine
1 large lemon	1 egg

Rub the sugar on the lemon zest. Squeeze and strain the juice from the lemon, and make up to 250ml with water. Put the liquid in a heatproof container, sprinkle on the gelatine and leave to soften. Stand the container in a pan of hot water and stir until dissolved. Separate the egg. Beat the yolk and stir it into the gelatine mixture. Crush and add the sugar. Simmer the mixture for 3 minutes over low heat, stirring all the time. Remove from the heat and leave to cool. Whisk the egg white until stiff and fold it into the mixture. Pour into individual glasses and leave for about 1 hour to set.

Honeycomb Mould

4–6 helpings

2 eggs	2 × 10ml spoons gelatine
25g caster sugar	3 × 15ml spoons cold water
500ml milk	
1 × 5ml spoon vanilla essence	

Filling
375g chopped fresh fruit
  or 1 × 425g can fruit,
  well drained

Separate the eggs. Beat the yolks, sugar and milk together. Pour into the top of a double boiler and cook until the custard coats the back of a spoon, stirring all the time. Do not allow the custard to boil. Add the essence. Soften the gelatine in the water in a small heatproof container. Stand the container in a pan of hot water and stir until dissolved, then pour into the custard. Leave to cool. Whisk the egg whites until just stiff and fold into the custard when it is just beginning to set. Pour into a wetted 1 litre ring mould and leave for 2–3 hours to set. Turn out on to a serving plate and fill the centre with fruit.

Orange Custard Jelly

6 helpings

juice and pared rind of 5 oranges	*3 × 10ml spoons gelatine*
100g sugar	*2 eggs*

Make up the orange juice to 750ml with water, if required. Put the rind, liquid, sugar, and gelatine into a saucepan and heat gently until the sugar and gelatine have dissolved. Leave to cool. Beat the eggs until liquid and add to the pan. Cook again for a few minutes to thicken, stirring all the time, but do not allow to boil. Strain into a wetted mould and leave for about 2 hours to set.

CLEARED JELLIES

Unlike the jellies described on p1008, cleared jelly must be filtered through a foam of coagulated egg whites and crushed egg shells.

General Method

Scald the saucepan, whisk, jelly bag, basins, and jelly mould before use, as the merest trace of grease may cause cloudiness in the finished jelly.

Whisk the egg whites lightly and crush the egg shells before adding to the mixture in the saucepan.

Heat the mixture and whisk constantly until a good head of foam is produced. It should be hot but not boiling. The correct temperature is about 70°C, when the foam begins to set or 'crust'. Care must then be taken not to break up the 'crust' by whisking too long. Remove the whisk but continue to heat the liquid until the 'crust' has risen to the top of the saucepan; the gelatine must *not* boil.

Remove from the heat and let the contents of the saucepan settle in a warm place, covered, for 5–10 minutes.

Strain the settled, clear jelly through a jelly bag into a basin below, while the bag is still hot from scalding. Replace this basin of jelly with another basin and restrain the jelly very carefully by pouring through the foam 'crust' which covers the bottom of the bag, acting as a filter.

If the jelly is not clear when a little is looked at in

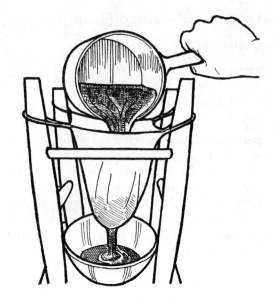

Straining jelly through a jelly bag

a spoon or glass, the filtering must be carried out again.

Filtering is most easily carried out using a jelly bag and stand, but if these are not available, the 4 corners of a clean cloth can be tied to the legs of an upturned stool.

Repeated filtering will cool the jelly, and, if done too often, can result in a poor yield of clear jelly as it will tend to solidify in the cloth.

Note Use lump sugar whenever possible for making a clear jelly; it will give a more brilliant jelly than powdered sugar.

Lining and Decorating a Mould

Pour in just enough jelly to cover the base and sides of the mould, and leave to set completely. If canned fruit is being used, drain well before putting into the mould. Cut pieces of fruit to fit the shape of the mould, and place in a decorative pattern over the set jelly. Each piece of fruit can be dipped in a little liquid jelly, if liked, before being arranged in the mould. Carefully spoon a little liquid jelly over the decoration and allow to set before any other filling is added.

Filling the Mould

Moulds should be filled to the top; this prevents the shape of the mould being broken when it is shaken out. In the case of a cream mixture, liquid jelly may be used to fill the space if there is insufficient mixture.

Note If a jelly is to be set in layers, keep it in a warm place to avoid it setting.

Unmoulding Jellies

See p1008.

Chopping Jelly for Decoration

Clear jelly should be quite firm. It should be coarsely chopped with a wet knife on wet grease-proof paper, so that the light is refracted from the cut surfaces as from the facets of a jewel.

Clear Lemon Jelly

6 helpings

4 lemons	*40g gelatine*
750ml water	*whites and shells of 2*
150g sugar	*eggs*
4 cloves	
1 × 2.5cm piece	
cinnamon stick	

Pare the rind from three of the lemons and squeeze the juice from all four. Make up the juice to 250ml with water, if necessary. Put the rind, juice, water, sugar, cloves, cinnamon stick, and gelatine into a large saucepan. Whisk the egg whites lightly, and crush the shells. Whisk over low heat until just below boiling point. Remove the whisk and allow the liquid to heat until it reaches the top of the pan. Simmer for 5 minutes. Remove from the heat and leave to stand for 5–10 minutes. Strain the liquid carefully through a jelly bag. Pour into a wetted mould and leave for 1–2 hours to set.

Note 2 ×15ml spoons of sherry may be added to the liquid just before filtering.

Marble Jelly

4–6 helpings

750ml clear lemon jelly	*green food colouring*
red food colouring	

Decoration
125ml double cream

Line a mould with a thin layer of lemon jelly and leave to set. Pour 100ml of jelly into 3 basins and colour one red and one green, leaving the third basin with the lemon jelly. Whisk each jelly until frothy and then leave to set. With a small hot spoon, shape the jelly into balls and place round the mould, alternating the colours. When one layer is filled, cover with a little of the remaining lemon jelly and leave to set. Repeat until the mould is filled, finishing with a layer of clear jelly. Leave for 2–3 hours to set. Whip the cream until thick. Turn out the jelly on to a serving plate and decorate with whipped cream.

VARIATION

Neapolitan Jelly

Divide the jelly into 3 equal portions, colour one red, one green and leave the third yellow. Set alternate layers of jelly, of equal thickness, in a mould, allowing 1 layer of jelly to set before the next is poured in. Leave for about 2 hours to set. Turn out and decorate with whipped cream.

Clear Claret Jelly

4–6 helpings

4 lemons	*whites and shells of 2*
625ml water	*eggs*
150g lump sugar	*125ml claret*
40g gelatine	*a few drops cochineal*

Pare the rind from 2 lemons and squeeze the juice from all 4 lemons. Make up the juice to 125ml with water, if necessary. Put the rind, lemon juice, water, sugar, and gelatine into a large saucepan. Whisk the egg whites lightly and crush the shells; add to the saucepan. Whisk over low heat until just below boiling point. Remove the whisk and allow the liquid to heat until it reaches the top of the saucepan. Pour in the claret without disturbing the foam 'crust'. Boil again until it rises to the top of the pan. Remove from the heat, cover and leave for 5 minutes. Strain through a jelly bag. Add the colouring and leave to cool. Remove any froth, pour into a wetted mould, and leave for 1–2 hours to set.

VARIATIONS

Port Wine Jelly (2)

Use 125ml port instead of claret.

Note See also p1010 and p1338.

Cocktail Jelly

Use 75ml brandy and 75ml sherry instead of claret.

Fruit Jelly

6 helpings

fruit eg banana, grapes,	*750ml clear lemon jelly*
cherries, tangerines,	*(p1013)*
apricots, pineapple	

Decoration
125ml chopped jelly (see
  Note)

Prepare enough fruit to decorate the sides of the mould and to make 3–4 layers of fruit in it.

Rinse a mould out with cold water. Pour in just enough jelly to cover the bottom of the mould and allow to set. Cut pieces of fruit to fit the shape of the mould; dip each piece in liquid jelly and place in the mould. Leave to set, then carefully cover the fruit with a little more liquid jelly. Leave to set again and repeat with layers of fruit and jelly, ensuring that each layer is set before the next layer is added, until the mould is full, finishing with a layer of jelly. Leave for about 2 hours to set, then turn out and decorate with chopped jelly.

Note For the decorative chopped jelly, choose a colour and flavour which suits the fruit, eg if using tangerines and grapes, use tangerine jelly.

Candied Fruit Cream Jelly

4 helpings

500ml port wine	*2 strips angelica*
jelly (2)	*(5 ×1cm)*
2 ×10ml spoons gelatine	*50–75g mixture of glacé*
1 ×15ml spoon cold	*cherries, preserved*
water	*ginger, and glacé*
250ml double cream	*pineapple*

Decoration
chopped jelly (p1013)

Rinse a mould in cold water and pour in the jelly to a depth of 1cm. Leave to set. Place a glass in the middle of the mould and pour the remaining jelly into the mould. Leave to set. Soften the gelatine in the water in a small heatproof container. Stand the container in a pan of hot water and stir until dissolved. Whip the cream until just stiff and stir in the dissolved gelatine. Chop the fruits and add to the cream. Carefully remove the glass from the mould by filling it for a minute with hot water. Fill the space with the cream mixture. Leave for about 2 hours to set. Turn out on to a serving dish and decorate with chopped jelly.

WHIPPED JELLIES

Make a basic jelly and allow to set until just thickening; then whisk until thick and foamy. This gives a light texture and refreshing taste. Lightly whisked egg whites can be added to the jelly before whisking. This increases the quantity of jelly made and adds some nutritional value to it. Always add extra flavouring to a whipped jelly; and as they do not turn out satisfactorily set them in individual glass dishes or a large glass serving bowl. Like any glass dish containing a jelly it must be sparklingly clean to set off the jelly.

Blackcurrant Whip

4 helpings

375ml blackcurrant juice	2 ×10ml spoons gelatine
25–50g sugar	3 ×15ml spoons cold water

Put the blackcurrant juice and sugar into a saucepan and heat until the sugar has dissolved. Leave to cool. Soften the gelatine in the water in a small heatproof container. Stand the container in a pan of hot water and stir until dissolved, then add to the saucepan. Pour into a basin and whisk well until thick and foamy. Pile quickly into individual serving dishes and leave for about 45 minutes to set.

VARIATIONS

Damson Whip

Use 375ml damson juice (p1135).

Orange Whip

Use 375ml orange juice.

Pineapple Whip

Use 375ml canned pineapple juice.

Raspberry Whip

Use 375ml raspberry juice (p1135).

Banana Whip Pudding

4–6 helpings

2 ×10ml spoons gelatine	75ml lemon juice
50ml cold water	3 egg whites
375ml boiling water	3 bananas
100g sugar	

Soften the gelatine in the cold water in a small heatproof container. Stand the container in a pan of hot water and stir until dissolved, then add the boiling water and sugar. Stir to dissolve the sugar. Add the lemon juice. Chill until just beginning to set, then whisk until frothy. Whisk the egg whites until just stiff and fold into the jelly. Slice the bananas and arrange them in the bottom of a glass dish. Pile the jelly mixture on top and chill for about 1 hour until firm.

Coffee Whip

4–6 helpings

500ml milk	2 ×15ml spoons cold water
1 ×15ml spoon coffee essence	1 egg white
25g sugar	2 ×10ml spoons gelatine

Decoration
1 ×15ml spoon flaked almonds

Heat together the milk, coffee essence, and sugar. Leave for about 30 minutes to cool. Soften the gelatine in the water in a small heatproof container. Stand the container in a pan of hot water and stir until the gelatine dissolves. Stir into the cooled milk mixture. Whisk the egg white lightly and add to the liquid jelly. Whisk very well until thick and frothy. Pile into a serving dish and decorate with the flaked almonds.

Fruit Yoghurt Whip
See p877.

Cold Sweet Soufflés

Like their hot counterparts (pp975–77), cold soufflés are very light in texture. Unlike them, however, they are held by setting with gelatine rather than by the use of heat.

Cold soufflés can be served in any dish, but they are traditionally presented in a soufflé dish, looking as though they have risen in the manner of a hot soufflé. The dish is prepared in exactly the same way (see pp919–20), with one amendment; it should be stood on a large plate for ease of movement in and out of the refrigerator, and to avoid touching the paper.

Prepare the dish before starting to make the soufflé, and make sure there is space in the refrigerator for it as soon as it is ready.

General Method

Put the water into a heatproof container. Measure the gelatine accurately and sprinkle it slowly on to the water, allowing it to soak in gradually. Try to avoid getting any of the gelatine crystals on the side of the container as these will not dissolve properly. Stand the container in a pan of water which comes half-way up its sides. Heat the water gently until the gelatine has dissolved completely and no crystals are visible; stir all the time to distribute the gelatine. Remove the basin from the water and cool a little.

Separate the eggs. Whisk the yolks, flavouring, and sugar in a heatproof basin over hot water for 10–15 minutes, until very thick and pale. Warmth from the water helps to melt the sugar and lowers the surface tension so that air enters more easily. However, on no account let the basin become really hot as this would cook the egg and make the inclusion of air impossible. The saucepan holding the hot water should be deep enough for the basin to rest firmly on the rim without touching the water.

The mixture is thick enough when the whisk, lifted from the mixture, leaves a visible trail for 2–3 seconds. Remove the basin from the heat and continue whisking until it has cooled slightly.

Add the dissolved gelatine to the yolk mixture; both should be at about the same temperature. First mix 2–3 ×15ml spoons of the cooled yolk mixture into the gelatine, then whisk this into the rest of the yolk mixture. This helps to prevent the gelatine setting in lumps or 'roping'.

Chill the mixture until the consistency is like that of unbeaten egg white, or until the edges show signs of setting. If not sufficiently set at this stage, the mixture will separate and the finished soufflé will have a heavy jelly layer at the bottom.

Whip the cream until it just holds its shape but is still soft. Fold it into the mixture, using a metal spoon. Lastly, whisk the egg whites until stiff but not dry, and fold them into the mixture just before it sets. Add a little whisked white to the mixture first to lighten it, then fold in the rest. It is important that the mixture be evenly blended, but take care not to overmix the soufflé or it will be flat and leathery. Tip the mixture immediately, very gently, into the prepared dish. The mixture should come 1–2cm above the top of the dish.

When the mixture is fully set, after about 2 hours in the refrigerator, remove the paper round the dish. To do this, dip a knife into hot water and run it round the soufflé in an anti-clockwise direction (if right-handed), between the two layers of paper. As the knife moves round the soufflé, gently pull off the paper with your left hand, pulling the paper against the knife.

The sides of the soufflé can then be decorated with chopped nuts, cake crumbs, ratafia crumbs or coconut, toasted or plain. Stand the dish on a piece of paper and press the nuts or crumbs on to the side of the soufflé with a broad-bladed knife or the palms of your hands. Let any loose pieces fall on to the paper. Continue until all the sides are coated.

The top of a sweet soufflé is often decorated with piped, whipped cream, and small pieces of suitable decoration such as crystallized fruit, nuts, angelica or chocolate.

Lemon Soufflé
(Milanaise Soufflé)

Basic recipe

4 helpings

1 × 15ml spoon gelatine	*100g caster sugar*
3 × 15ml spoons water	*125ml double cream*
3 eggs	
grated rind and juice of 2 lemons	

Decoration

finely chopped nuts **or** *cake crumbs*	*crystallized lemon slices* *angelica*
whipped double cream (optional)	

Prepare a 500ml soufflé dish (pp919–20). Soften the gelatine in the water in a small heatproof container. Stand the container in a pan of hot water and stir until dissolved. Cool slightly. Meanwhile, separate the eggs. Put the yolks, lemon rind and juice, and sugar into a heatproof basin and stand it over a pan half-full of hot water over low heat. Do not let the water boil or touch the basin. Whisk the mixture for 10–15 minutes until thick and pale. Remove from the heat and continue whisking until cool. Fold a little of the yolk mixture into the cooled gelatine, then whisk this into the yolk mixture. Put in a cool place until the mixture begins to set.

Whip the cream until it just holds its shape but is still soft. Using a large metal spoon, fold into the mixture until evenly mixed. Whisk the egg whites until stiff, and fold in until evenly blended. Tip the soufflé gently into the dish, and leave to set in a refrigerator for about 2 hours.

Remove the paper carefully as described on p1016. Decorate the sides of the soufflé with chopped nuts or cake crumbs. Pipe whipped cream on top, if liked, and decorate with crystallized lemon slices and small pieces of angelica.

Note For a hot lemon soufflé, see p975.

VARIATIONS
In each of the variations below, omit the lemon rind and juice.

Chocolate Soufflé

Whisk the egg yolks with 2 × 15ml spoons water and 75g caster sugar. Melt 75g grated plain chocolate over a pan of hot water. Add to the yolk mixture with the dissolved gelatine and whisk well.

Chocolate Soufflé de Luxe

Make up the Chocolate Soufflé mixture and add 2 × 15ml spoons brandy, rum, or coffee liqueur with the chocolate.

Coffee Soufflé

Dissolve 2 × 10ml spoons instant coffee in a little hot water, then add more water to make 100ml strong coffee. Whisk with the egg yolks. Decorate with grated chocolate, chopped walnuts, and cream.

Orange Soufflé

Whisk the egg yolks with the finely grated rind and juice of 2 oranges and use 75g caster sugar only. Add 2 × 15ml spoons Grand Marnier or orange curaçao, if liked. Dissolve the gelatine in 1 × 15ml spoon water and 2 × 15ml spoons lemon juice. When set, decorate the soufflé with crystallized orange slices, nuts, and cream.

Praline Soufflé

Prepare 75g praline (p1241) and crush it. Dissolve 1 × 5ml spoon instant coffee in 2 × 15ml spoons hot water, and add 2 × 15ml spoons cold water. Whisk the liquid with the yolks. Add 50g crushed praline to the mixture with the whipped cream. Decorate with the remaining praline and cream.

Raspberry Soufflé

Soften the gelatine in 3 × 15ml spoons of strained fruit syrup from a 440g can of raspberries. Add 1 × 15ml spoon lemon juice and 150ml sieved fruit to the yolk mixture (this can be made up with a little strained syrup, if necessary). Use only 75g sugar and 100ml double cream. Decorate the sides with desiccated coconut, and the top with piped whipped cream and a few reserved raspberries.

Other Fruit Purée Soufflés

Fresh, frozen or canned soft fruits, such as strawberries, blackcurrants or blackberries, can be substituted for raspberries to produce a strongly flavoured soufflé.

Dried apricots also make a delicious soufflé. Soak 50g overnight in just enough water to cover them. Simmer for 15–20 minutes until tender, then process in an electric blender.

Sherry Soufflé

Add 100ml sweet sherry, 1 × 15ml spoon lemon juice, and 75g caster sugar only to the egg yolks. Decorate with mimosa balls, angelica, coconut, and cream.

Milk Chocolate Soufflé

4 helpings

2 eggs	75g milk chocolate
50g sugar	1 × 10ml spoon gelatine
150ml evaporated milk	2 × 15ml spoons water

Decoration

whipped double cream	grated chocolate

Separate the eggs. Put the yolks and sugar in a heatproof basin and stand it over a pan half-full of hot water over low heat. Do not let the water boil or touch the basin. Whisk the mixture for 5–10 minutes until thick and pale. Remove from the heat. Whisk the evaporated milk until thick and whisk into the yolk mixture. Melt the chocolate on a plate over a pan of hot water and whisk into the mixture.

Soften the gelatine in the water in a small heatproof container. Stand the container in a pan of hot water and stir until dissolved. Cool slightly. Add 1–2 spoonfuls of the mixture to the gelatine, then stir into the rest of the mixture. Put in a cool place until the mixture begins to set.

Whisk the egg whites until stiff, and fold carefully into the chocolate mixture until evenly blended. Tip gently into a 1 litre dish or individual glasses and leave to set in a refrigerator for about 2 hours.

Decorate with the cream and the chocolate.

Montelimar Soufflé

4 helpings

1 × 110g jar maraschino cherries	125ml milk
1 × 5ml spoon gelatine	12 marshmallows (100g approx)
2 eggs	

Decoration

whipped double cream	glacé cherries
chopped browned almonds (p1185)	angelica

Drain the cherries and soften the gelatine in some of the juice in a small heatproof container. Stand the container in a pan of hot water and stir until dissolved. Cool slightly. Meanwhile, separate the eggs. Put the yolks, remaining juice from the cherries, milk, and marshmallows into a heatproof basin over a pan of hot water. Cook gently, stirring all the time, for 15–20 minutes, until the mixture is creamy and smooth and the marshmallows have dissolved. Add the dissolved gelatine. Remove from the heat and put in a cool place until the mixture begins to set.

Chop the cherries and stir them in lightly. Whisk the egg whites until stiff, and fold in. Tip into a 650ml dish or individual glasses and leave to set in a refrigerator for 1–2 hours.

Decorate with whipped double cream, chopped browned almonds, glacé cherries, and angelica.

Sweet Mousses

A sweet mousse is a very light, creamy dessert which has as its base a fruit purée or a flavoured custard sauce to which beaten eggs and whipped cream are added. Alternatively, the cream may be used to decorate the mousse. It can be set with gelatine and chilled like a cold sweet soufflé, or frozen, like an ice cream. A frozen mousse mixture is used for making ice cream bombes (p1060).

A mousse can be served in one large serving dish or in individual glasses. Some mixtures can be set in a mould or cake tin, turned out and decorated.

Blackcurrant Mousse

Basic recipe using purée

4 helpings

250g fresh blackcurrants	1 ×10ml spoon gelatine
50g caster sugar	2 ×15ml spoons water
1 ×10ml spoon lemon	125ml double cream
juice	2 egg whites

Decoration
whipped double cream   blackcurrant jam (optional)

Save a few whole blackcurrants for decorating the mousse, if liked; sieve the rest. Make the purée up to 150ml with a little water, if necessary. Put the purée, sugar, and lemon juice in a bowl. Soften the gelatine in the water in a small heatproof container. Stand the container in a pan of hot water and stir until completely dissolved. Cool. Mix in a little of the purée, then stir this mixture into the main purée. Leave in a cool place until beginning to set.

Whip the cream until it just holds its shape, and fold into the mixture using a metal spoon. Whisk the egg whites until fairly stiff and fold in. Make sure that the mixture is fully and evenly blended but do not overmix it. Pour gently into a 500ml dish or wetted mould, or into individual glasses. Leave to set in a refrigerator for 1–2 hours. Turn out, if liked. Decorate with whirls of whipped cream and with either the reserved fruit or jam.

Note Canned or bottled blackcurrants in syrup can also be used; in this case substitute 3 ×15ml spoons of the syrup for the sugar and water. Frozen fruit can also be used; it must be well thawed and drained, and any sugar added must depend on the type and strength of sweetening (if any) used when freezing the fruit.

VARIATIONS
1) Fresh, frozen or canned fruits can be used, eg strawberries, raspberries, blackberries, gooseberries, cherries, apricots, or bananas. The amount of sugar will vary according to the sweetness of the purée.
2) Omit the gelatine; pour the mixture into ice trays and freeze it.

Chocolate Mousse (1)

4 helpings

150g plain chocolate	4 eggs
2 ×15ml spoons water	vanilla essence

Decoration
whipped double cream   chopped walnuts

Break up the chocolate or grate it. Put it into a large heatproof basin with the water and stand over a pan of hot water. Heat gently until the chocolate melts. Remove from the heat and stir until smooth. Separate the eggs. Beat the yolks and a few drops of vanilla essence into the chocolate. Whisk the egg whites until fairly stiff, and fold gently into the mixture until evenly blended. Pour into 4 individual dishes and leave for 1–2 hours to set.

Serve decorated with cream and walnuts.

VARIATIONS
Mocha Mousse

Dissolve 1 ×5ml spoon instant coffee in 2 ×15ml spoons hot water and stir this liquid into the chocolate with the egg yolks and vanilla essence.

Choc-au-Rhum Mousse

Add 1 ×15ml spoon rum to the mixture, or use brandy, Grand Marnier or Tia Maria.

Chocolate Mousse (2)

4 helpings

100g plain chocolate	*3 eggs*
4 × 15ml spoons water	*vanilla essence*
1 × 10ml spoon gelatine	*100ml double cream*

Decoration
whipped double cream   *coarsely grated chocolate*

Break up the chocolate or grate it. Put it into a large heatproof basin with the water. Sprinkle in the gelatine and stand the basin over a pan of hot water. Heat gently until the chocolate has melted and the gelatine dissolved. Remove from the heat and stir until smooth. Separate the eggs. Beat the yolks and a few drops of vanilla essence into the chocolate. Whip the cream until it just holds its shape and fold it into the mixture. Whisk the egg whites until fairly stiff and fold in gently until evenly blended. Pour into a 750ml wetted mould or a deep serving bowl and chill for about 2 hours until set.

If moulded, turn out on to a flat plate. In either case, decorate with the whipped double cream and coarsely grated chocolate.

VARIATION
Chocolate-Orange Mousse

Use the strained juice of 1 orange instead of the same quantity of water.

Coffee Mousse

4 helpings

250ml milk	*50g caster sugar*
1 × 15ml spoon instant	*1 × 10ml spoon gelatine*
coffee	*2 × 15ml spoons water*
2 eggs	*75ml double cream*

Decoration
whipped double cream   *coarsely grated chocolate*

Warm the milk and stir in the coffee. Separate the eggs. Blend the yolks and caster sugar together, then gradually add the warmed milk. Strain through a sieve back into the saucepan and stir

over very gentle heat for about 10 minutes until the custard begins to thicken. Cool slightly.

Soften the gelatine in the water in a small heat-proof container. Stand the container in a pan of hot water and stir until completely dissolved. Cool until it is the same temperature as the custard. Mix a little of the coffee custard into the gelatine, then whisk this into the main custard. Leave in a cool place until beginning to set.

Whip the cream until it just holds its shape, and fold into the mixture. Whisk the egg whites until stiff and fold in. Make sure that the mixture is fully and evenly blended but do not overmix it. Pour into a 500ml dish or wetted mould, or into individual glasses. Leave to set in a refrigerator for 1–2 hours. Turn out, if liked. Decorate with the whipped double cream and coarsely grated chocolate.

VARIATIONS
In each of the variations below omit the instant coffee.

Caramel Mousse

Before making the mousse mixture, warm 100g granulated sugar and 1 × 15ml spoon water in a thick-based saucepan, until the sugar dissolves. Continue heating until the syrup turns a rich brown colour. Add 4 × 15ml spoons hot water and stir quickly until all the caramel is dissolved. Cool. Add 200ml milk to the caramel and heat this with the egg yolks to make the custard for the mousse.

Praline Mousse

Before making the mousse mixture, make and crush 100g praline (p1241). Fold half into the completed mousse mixture. Decorate the top of the mousse with the rest.

Orange Praline Mousse

Make the Praline Mousse; add the finely grated rind of an orange to the custard, and use the juice to dissolve the gelatine.

Syllabubs

A syllabub was originally a sweet, frothy drink made with cider or mead mixed with milk straight from the cow. It is now a rich creamy dessert, often made light and frothy with added egg whites.

Cider Syllabub

4 helpings

grated rind and juice of
½ lemon
50g caster sugar
125ml sweet cider

1 × 15ml spoon brandy
(optional)
250ml double cream

Add the lemon rind and juice to the caster sugar with the cider, and the brandy, if used. Stir until the sugar is dissolved. Whip the cream until it stands in stiff peaks. Fold in the lemon and cider mixture gradually. Pour into stemmed glasses and chill in a refrigerator for about 2 hours. Remove 20 minutes before serving.

Serve with Mrs Beeton's Savoy Cakes (p1208).

Wine Syllabub

4 helpings

200ml double cream
2 egg whites
75g caster sugar

juice of ½ lemon
100ml sweet white wine
or sherry

Decoration
crystallized lemon slices

Whip the cream until it just holds its shape. Whisk the egg whites until they form soft peaks. Fold the sugar into the egg whites, then gradually add the lemon juice and wine or sherry. Fold this mixture into the whipped cream. Pour into glasses and chill in a refrigerator for about 2 hours. Remove 20 minutes before serving. Serve decorated with the lemon slices.

Note The lemon juice and wine will settle in the bottom of the glasses, leaving a frothy top.

Everlasting Syllabub

4 helpings

*8 macaroons **or** 4*
individual sponge cakes
grated rind and juice of
½ lemon

75g caster sugar
2 × 15ml spoons sherry
2 × 15ml spoons brandy
250ml double cream

Crush the macaroons or crumble the sponge cakes; divide between 4 glasses. Add the lemon rind and juice to the sugar, sherry and brandy, and stir until the sugar is dissolved. Whip the cream until it stands up in peaks. Fold in the wine mixture gradually. Pour into the glasses and chill in a refrigerator for about 2 hours. Remove 20 minutes before serving.

Whipped Syllabub

4 helpings

50ml sweet red wine,
*ruby port **or** cream*
sherry
250ml double cream
50ml medium dry sherry

juice of ½ orange
grated rind of ½ lemon
50g caster sugar
a few drops orange food
colouring (optional)

Divide the wine, port or sherry between 4 chilled stemmed glasses, and keep chilled. Whip the cream, adding the remaining ingredients gradually, in order, until the mixture just holds firm peaks. Pile into the chilled glasses, taking care not to mix the cream into the wine; the wine should show clearly in the bottom of the glass. Serve as soon as possible.

Meringue and Meringue Desserts

Meringue is made of stiffly whisked egg whites and sugar or sugar syrup. It is said to have been created by a Swiss pastrycook in about 1720 and made popular by Marie Antoinette. Meringue makes a cheap and attractive dessert and is also a useful way of decorating desserts and gâteaux when cream is lacking. There are 3 varieties:

Swiss Meringue or Chantilly Meringue

This is made with 4 egg whites to 200g fine sugar. Baking powder or cream of tartar is sometimes added to make sure that the meringue shells remain crisp and white. Flavouring such as lemon juice, almond essence (or ground almonds), or a liqueur can also be added.

After cooking and cooling, meringue shells are usually sandwiched together with sweetened whipped cream or butter cream, either flavoured or with added fruit. Large shells are then used as a dessert or for afternoon tea, and smaller shells as party cakes on a buffet table.

This meringue is also used, with less sugar, to top or decorate hot puddings, pies and tarts.

Cooked Meringue or 'Meringue Cuite'

This is made of a similar mixture to Swiss meringue, but the egg whites and sugar are whisked over very gentle heat until very thick. It stays stiffer than Swiss meringue, and is used for making meringue baskets and other small cases, eg for petits fours. It can be flavoured like Swiss meringue.

Italian Meringue

This is made by pouring a sugar syrup boiled to about 140°C on to whisked egg whites and beating it until very thick. It is often used for covering ice cream bombes and other similar desserts such as Baked Alaska (p1061), and also in certain pastries.

BASIC RECIPES

Swiss or Chantilly Meringue
(for shells, toppings, and cakes)

Makes 12–16 medium-sized shells, 24–30 small shells; covers 1 × 20–22cm flan or tart; makes 1 × 20cm case

4 egg whites	*½ × 2.5ml spoon baking*
a pinch of salt	*powder (optional)*
200g caster sugar	

Cream filling (see Method)

125ml double cream	*1 × 5ml spoon caster*
1–2 drops vanilla	*sugar*
essence	

Separate the whites from the yolks very carefully. No trace of yolk must be left, for the fat in them prevents the whites whisking properly. For the same reason the bowl and whisk must be absolutely clean and dry.

Put the whites into a large bowl with the salt. Whisk the whites until they are very stiff and standing up in points. They must be absolutely dry or the meringues will break down in baking. Gradually add half the caster sugar, 1 × 15ml spoonful at a time. Whisk very thoroughly after each addition until the mixture regains its stiffness. The sugar must be blended in very thoroughly or it forms droplets of syrup which brown, and may make the meringues sticky and difficult to remove from the paper. Sprinkle the remaining sugar all at once over the surface together with the baking powder (if used). Fold in very lightly using a metal spoon.

To make the cream filling, whip the cream with the essence and sugar until it just holds its shape.

For *meringue shells*, line a baking sheet with greaseproof paper and rub it lightly with cooking oil, or use vegetable parchment.

Put the meringue mixture into a forcing bag with a 1–2cm nozzle and pipe into rounds on the paper; or shape the mixture using 2 wet dessertspoons – take up a spoonful of the mixture and smooth it with a palette knife, bringing it up into a ridge in the centre. Slide it out with the other spoon on to the tray, with the ridge on top.

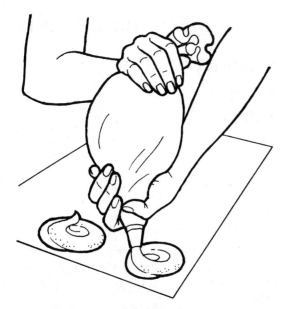

Piping meringue on to a baking tray

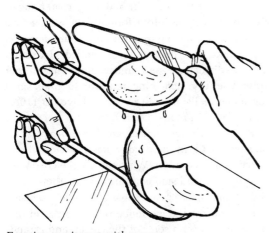

Forming meringues with spoons

Dust the meringues with caster sugar and dry off in a very cool oven at 110°C, Gas $\frac{1}{4}$, for 3–4 hours until they are firm and crisp, but still white. If they begin to brown, prop the oven door open a little. When crisp on the outside, lift the meringues off the tray gently with a palette knife. Turn them on their sides and return them to the oven until their undersides are dry. If the meringues are large, press in the soft centres to dry them out completely.

Put the meringues on a cooling tray until absolutely cold. Sandwich them together with the sweetened flavoured cream not more than 1 hour before they are to be used, or they will go soft. Alternatively, use without the filling to decorate a cold dessert.

For *meringue topping*, use only 25–40g of sugar per egg white. Whisk the whites until stiff and fold the sugar in lightly. Pile the mixture on top of the pudding a few minutes before the end of the cooking time, and spread it out to cover the whole surface. It is more attractive if flicked up into small peaks.

By covering the pudding, the meringue seals it from the heat so that it does not dry out. Sprinkle the top of the meringue with caster sugar. Bake in a very cool oven at 140°C, Gas 1, for 30–40 minutes; or in a hot oven at 220°C, Gas 7, for about 10 minutes. In either case the meringue will be crisp and lightly coloured on the outside, but remain soft inside.

Note A selection of meringue-topped desserts served hot or cold may be found in the chapter on Pastry Making.

For *meringue cases* draw a 20cm circle on a sheet of greaseproof paper or vegetable parchment. Put the paper on a baking sheet. Oil the greaseproof paper very lightly.

Make up the meringue mixture as for shells. Spread some of the meringue all over the circle to form the base of the case. Put the rest of the mixture into a forcing bag and, using a large star vegetable nozzle, pipe it round the edge of the ring in a border 5–6cm high, or use a spoon to make the rim. Bake low down in a very cool oven at 110°C, Gas $\frac{1}{4}$, for 3–4 hours, or until quite dry. Leave to cool on a rack, remove the paper and fill the case with fruit and sweetened whipped cream.

Note If really dried out, meringue shells will keep for 1–2 weeks in an airtight tin.

Nutty Meringues
See p1223.

All-in-one Meringue
See p1420.

Cooked Meringue

(Meringue Cuite)

Makes 4 cases or baskets or 16–20 × 2cm cases for petits fours

4 egg whites
250g icing sugar

2–3 drops vanilla
essence

Whisk the egg whites and sugar together in a basin over a pan of gently simmering water until the mixture is very thick and holds its shape. Flavour with vanilla essence. Bake in a very cool oven at 110°C, Gas ¼, for 1–1½ hours.

To make meringue baskets, line a baking tray as when making a meringue case and make up the meringue mixture. Spoon the meringue on to the tray into 4 portions. Keep them well apart. Hollow out the centres to make neat nest-like shapes.

Alternatively, use a small star vegetable nozzle to make 4 small basket shapes. Bake as for a meringue case.

Make very small meringue cases for use as petits fours in the same way. Make circles 2cm across and hollow out with the tip of a pointed spoon. Then proceed as for meringue baskets. The small cases will, however, dry in 45 minutes– 1 hour.

Italian Meringue

200g granulated sugar
2 × 15ml spoons water

4 egg whites

Put the sugar and water into a small, thick-based saucepan and heat slowly until the sugar has dissolved completely. Stir once or twice to make sure that every grain has dissolved. Increase the heat slightly and continue heating the syrup, without stirring, until it reaches 140°C. Keep the syrup warm. Whisk the egg whites until stiff. Pour the syrup on to the egg whites slowly and steadily, without a pause, while still whisking. (It is easier to get someone else to pour the syrup.) Continue whisking until the meringue is thick and cold. Bake in a very cool oven at 110°C, Gas ¼, for 1–1½ hours.

Use for a vacherin or to cover cold desserts.

OTHER MERINGUE DESSERTS

Raspberry Vacherin

Basic recipe

4 helpings

3 egg whites
a pinch of salt
150g caster sugar
300g fresh raspberries

250ml double cream
1 × 5ml spoon caster
sugar
Kirsch

Decoration
a few angelica leaves

Line 2 baking trays with greaseproof paper or vegetable parchment. Draw a 15cm circle on each one and very lightly oil the greaseproof paper, if used.

Make up a cooked or Italian meringue mixture from the egg whites, salt, and 150g caster sugar. Put the meringue into a forcing bag with a 1cm plain nozzle. Starting from the middle of one circle, pipe round and round to form a coiled, flat round 15cm in diameter. Pipe a similar round on the other tray. Use any remaining mixture to pipe small meringue shells. Bake in a very cool oven at 110°C, Gas ¼, for 1–1½ hours. Leave to cool.

Pick over the raspberries, and leave on a plate for 30 minutes. Clean and pat dry. Reserve a few choice berries for decoration. Whip the double cream until it is thick and stands in firm peaks, then stir in the 1 × 5ml spoon caster sugar and Kirsch to taste.

Place one of the meringue rounds on a serving plate, spread with some of the cream, and arrange half the raspberries on it in a flat layer. (Do not make the cream layer too thick or the vacherin will be difficult and messy to eat and serve.) Put the second meringue on top of the raspberries, arrange the rest of the raspberries in the centre, and pipe rosettes or a decorative edge of cream round the berries. Decorate the sides of the vacherin with the small meringues and angelica leaves.

Serve cut in wedges like a cake, using a flat cake slice to lift the meringue on to the plates.

VARIATIONS

Any fresh fruit or well-drained frozen or canned fruit, such as strawberries, peaches, pineapple, grapes, or clementines can be used to make a similar vacherin.

Hazelnut Meringue Gâteau

See p1045.

Pavlova (1)

4 helpings

3 egg whites	*2 × 5ml spoons cornflour*
150g caster sugar	*filling (see below)*
1 × 2.5ml spoon vinegar	
1 × 2.5ml spoon vanilla essence	

Line a baking sheet with greaseproof paper or vegetable parchment. Draw a 20cm circle on it and very lightly oil the greaseproof paper, if used.

Whisk the egg whites until very stiff. Continue whisking, gradually adding the sugar until the mixture is very stiff again and stands up in peaks. Beat in the vinegar, vanilla essence, and cornflour. Spread the meringue over the circle, piling it up at the edges to form a rim, or pipe the circle and rim from a forcing bag, using a 2cm star nozzle. Bake low down in a cool oven at 150°C, Gas 2, for about 1 hour. The Pavlova should be crisp and tinged a pale coffee colour on the outside and have a texture like marshmallow inside. Leave to cool. Remove the paper very gently and put the Pavlova on a large serving plate.

Note This Pavlova case will not store so it must be made on the day it is to be eaten and filled only just before it is served.

Fillings

1) Whip 250ml double cream until fairly stiff. Skin and slice 400g peaches. Combine the fruit and cream and fill the Pavlova case with the mixture just before serving. Decorate with glacé cherries and angelica.

2) Other fruit such as pineapple, apricots, grapes, strawberries, or raspberries can be used instead of peaches to add to the cream. For a luxury dessert, 1–2 × 15ml spoons of a suitable sweet liqueur can be added to the cream when whipping it.

3) Slice 4 bananas thinly and put into a basin. Add 2 × 15ml spoons brandy and chill for 1 hour, turning the fruit from time to time. Whip 250ml double cream lightly and fold in the bananas and 100g halved, stoned fresh or maraschino cherries. Pile into the Pavlova case and sprinkle generously with grated chocolate and a few chopped nuts.

Pavlova (2)

See p1478.

Strawberry Meringue Torte

4 helpings

4 egg whites	*juice of 1 lemon*
a pinch of salt	*caster sugar*
100g granulated sugar	*125ml double cream* **or**
100g caster sugar	*liqueur-flavoured*
500g fresh **or** *firm frozen strawberries*	*whipped cream using brandy* **or** *Kirsch (p880)*

Make up a cooked (p1024) or Italian (p1024) meringue mixture from the egg whites, salt, granulated and caster sugars. Use most of it to pipe a 15cm meringue case (p1023). Use the rest to pipe small meringue shapes on the paper around the case. Bake in a very cool oven at 110°C, Gas $\frac{1}{4}$; the case will take 3–4 hours, the small shells $1\frac{1}{2}$–2 hours. Leave to cool.

Hull the strawberries, sprinkle with lemon juice and caster sugar and keep chilled until the meringue case is ready. Reserve a few choice berries for decoration. Halve and drain the rest and put them in the meringue case. Whip the cream lightly and cover the fruit. Decorate with the small meringues and strawberries.

Serve quickly or the meringue will go soft. Do not chill before serving.

Creams

There are 3 types of cream:
1) A full cream which consists of double or whipping cream flavoured with an essence, a liqueur, or a little well-flavoured fruit purée.
2) A custard cream or Bavarian cream (Bavarois), which consists of a pouring egg custard (cup or simple custard, see p964), mixed with cream and flavouring. The cream is sometimes omitted.
3) A fruit cream, which is made from more or less equal quantities of a pouring egg custard, cream, and fruit purée.

INGREDIENTS AND GENERAL METHOD

Fresh raw cream gives the best texture and flavour where available; *pasteurized cream* also gives good results. However, other alternatives can be used.

Synthetic cream should be lightly whipped until it just holds its shape; then any sugar that has to be added should be stirred in.

Canned cream should be chilled; the can should then be carefully turned upside-down and opened, and any liquid whey poured off. The remaining thick cream can then be stirred into the dessert unwhipped.

Evaporated milk must be treated before being added to a cream. Either boil the unopened can for 20 minutes, then cool to room temperature and chill until cold; or put the unopened can into a refrigerator for at least 24 hours before using. The evaporated milk will then whip satisfactorily and quite quickly. It will take much longer if taken straight from the store cupboard.

Gelatine must always be dissolved in a little water before being added to a mixture. Sprinkle the carefully measured gelatine on to the water in a heatproof basin. Stand the container in a pan containing a little hot water and heat gently, stirring all the time, until all the gelatine crystals are dissolved. It is important to add the gelatine to the mixture at the right temperature. Ideally, the two mixtures should be at about the same temperature when combined. If hot gelatine is added to a cold mixture, the gelatine will set in hard lumps. Therefore, always cool gelatine before adding it to a cold mixture, but use it while still liquid; do not let it set. Add a few spoonfuls of the main mixture to the liquid gelatine, stir well, then incorporate this into the rest of the main mixture.

Less gelatine is needed to set a cream than a jelly made from fruit juice because the mixture is much thicker.

The lightness and smoothness of any cream depends largely on how easily the various ingredients are blended. If they have the same consistency, they can be blended without clots or lumps forming, which destroy the mixture's airy lightness. Cool the custard until it is just about to set, so that its consistency is like that of a fruit purée. Half whip cream only until it just holds its shape, with soft-tipped peaks. Stir the whipped cream into the mixture just before setting, so that air trapped by the earlier whisking is held in. This helps to lighten the texture of the cream.

Moulds for creams should be made of metal, as these are the best conductors of heat. Since the mould for a rich or party cream is often lined with jelly and decorated before filling, choose a plain charlotte or similar mould, or even a cake tin. For instructions on lining and decorating a mould, see p1012; for turning out a moulded dessert, see p1008.

FULL CREAMS

Velvet Cream

Basic recipe

4 helpings

fresh lemon jelly (p1009) *(optional)*	*50g caster sugar*
glacé cherries (optional)	*2 × 15ml spoons sherry*
angelica (optional)	**or** *a few drops vanilla essence*
3 × 15ml spoons water	*250ml double cream*
1 × 10ml spoon gelatine	*250ml single cream*

If the velvet cream is to be set in a mould, line a 750ml mould with some of the jelly. Cut the cherries into quarters and the angelica into leaf shapes and decorate the mould as described on p1012. Chill the remaining jelly and use to decorate the mould.

To make the cream, put the water into a heat-proof container, sprinkle in the gelatine and leave to soften. Stand the container in a pan of hot water and stir until the gelatine dissolves. Add the sugar and sherry or vanilla essence, and stir until the sugar dissolves completely. Put to one side.

Put the double and single cream into a bowl and whip lightly. Fold the flavoured gelatine into the cream and pour carefully into the prepared mould. Leave to set for about 2 hours.

Turn out on to a flat, wetted plate. Chop the chilled fresh lemon jelly (p1013), and arrange on the plate around the cream.

Note Instead of being poured into a lined mould, the velvet cream can be poured into 4 individual glasses. A thin coating of lemon jelly can then be poured on top and decorated. Leave to set for about 1 hour.

VARIATIONS

In each of the variations below, omit the sherry or vanilla essence.

Almond Cream

Flavour with 1×2.5ml spoon almond essence.

Chocolate Cream

Flavour with 75g melted plain chocolate.

Coffee Cream

Flavour with 1×15ml spoon instant coffee dissolved in 1×15ml spoon hot water. Add 1×15ml spoon rum, if liked.

Highland Cream

Flavour with 1×15ml spoon whisky and serve with a whisky-flavoured apricot sauce.

Lemon and Almond Cream

Flavour with 2×15ml spoons lemon juice, 1×5ml spoon finely grated lemon rind, and 25g ground almonds.

Liqueur Cream

Flavour with 1×15ml spoon brandy, curaçao, Kirsch, or rum.

Pistachio Cream

Blanch, skin, and finely chop 100g pistachio nuts, and fold into the mixture before adding the gelatine. Tint the cream pale green. See also Pistachio Bavarois, p1029.

Raspberry Cream (1)

Use 375ml double cream and fold in 125ml sieved raspberry purée instead of the single cream.

Strawberry Cream (1)

Make as for Raspberry Cream substituting strawberries.

Brandy Cream

4 helpings

400ml double cream	caster sugar (optional)
100ml brandy	ground nutmeg
juice of $\frac{1}{2}$ lemon	

Whip the cream until it just holds its shape with soft-tipped peaks, adding the brandy and the lemon juice gradually and the caster sugar, if used. Spoon into individual glasses. Sprinkle with a little nutmeg and chill before serving.

Caster sugar can be beaten into the cream if desired; add to taste.

Serve with sponge fingers (p1208).

BAVARIAN AND CUSTARD CREAMS

Vanilla Bavarian Cream
(Vanilla Bavarois)

Basic recipe

4 helpings

200ml fresh lemon jelly (p1009)	1 × 2.5ml spoon vanilla essence
angelica (optional)	4 × 15ml spoons water
250ml milk	1 × 10ml spoon gelatine
4 egg yolks **or** 1 whole egg and 2 yolks	125ml double cream
50g caster sugar	125ml single cream

Line a 750ml mould with lemon jelly, cut the angelica into leaf shapes, if used, and decorate the mould as described on p1012. Chill the remaining jelly.

To make the cream, mix the eggs and sugar together until fluffy and pale. Warm the milk, but do not let it boil; slowly stir in the milk. Strain the custard back into the saucepan or into a double boiler or basin held over hot water. (Make sure the water does not touch the upper pan.) Cook over very low heat, until it thickens. Do not let the custard boil.

Strain the thickened custard into a bowl, stir in the vanilla essence, and leave to cool.

Put the water into a heatproof container, sprinkle in the gelatine and leave to soften. Stand the container in a pan of hot water and stir until the gelatine dissolves. Cool until tepid and add to the custard. Leave in a cool place until it thickens at the edges, stirring from time to time to prevent a skin forming.

Put the double and single cream into a bowl and whip lightly. Fold into the custard mixture, and pour into the prepared mould. Leave to set for about 2 hours. Chop the chilled jelly (p1013) and use to decorate the cream. Turn out on to a flat, wetted plate.

VARIATIONS

In each of the variations below omit the vanilla essence.

Caramel Bavarois

Dissolve 100g granulated sugar in 1 × 15ml spoon water and heat until the syrup turns a rich brown colour. Add 4 × 15ml spoons hot water, remove from the heat, and stir until all the caramel dissolves. Stir into the custard.

Chocolate Bavarois

Grate 100g plain chocolate and add with the milk. It will melt in the warm custard. Add 1 × 5ml spoon vanilla essence.

Crème Diplomate(1)

Soak 100g chopped crystallized fruit in 2 × 15ml spoons Kirsch. Pour the vanilla Bavarian cream into the mould to a depth of 1.5cm and leave to set. Spread half the fruit over it and cover with a little of the cream. Leave to set. Continue alternating layers of fruit and cream, finishing with a layer of cream. Allow each layer to set before adding the next.

Crème Diplomate(2)

Divide the mixture into 3 portions. Flavour the first with vanilla essence, the second with chocolate, the third with strawberry purée. Line the mould with vanilla cream in the same way as when lining with jelly (p1012). When this is completely set, fill alternately with equal layers of the chocolate and strawberry creams, allowing each layer to set before adding the next.

Ginger Bavarois

Reduce the sugar to 40g and add 75g chopped preserved ginger and 3 × 15ml spoons ginger syrup from the jar, just before folding in the cream.

Italian Bavarois

Infuse thin strips of rind from 1 lemon in the milk. Add the strained juice of the lemon to the custard with 1×15ml spoon brandy, if liked.

Mocha Bavarois

Melt 75g grated plain chocolate in the milk and add 1×10ml spoon instant coffee dissolved in 1×15ml spoon hot water.

Neapolitan Cream

Line the whole mould with raspberry jelly. Divide the cream into 4 portions: flavour one with vanilla, the second with ratafia essence, colour it green, flavour the third with coffee, and the fourth with strawberry essence, colour it pink. Pour the vanilla cream into the mould and leave it to set, then add the others, allowing each layer to set first.

Orange Bavarois

Infuse thin strips of rind from 2 oranges in the milk. Dissolve the gelatine in the juice from 3 oranges, make up to 250ml with water and strain it into the custard. When nearly set, fold in 125ml lightly whipped double cream.

Ribbon Cream

Divide the mixture into 2 portions, and flavour and colour each half separately; eg with vanilla and chocolate, vanilla and orange, or ginger and chocolate. Do not decorate the mould but oil it lightly. Pour in about 1.5cm of one of the creams, leave to set, then repeat with the second cream. Continue in this way until all the mixture is used.

Pistachio Bavarois

Blanch, skin, and finely chop 100g pistachio nuts. Tint the cream pale green.

Rum Bavarois

Infuse a bay leaf in the milk for a few minutes. Add $2-3 \times 15$ml spoons rum.

Queen Mab's Pudding

4 helpings

oil for greasing	*4 × 15ml spoons water*
400ml milk	*1 × 10ml spoon gelatine*
pared rind of 1 lemon	*50g glacé cherries*
3 eggs	*25g cut mixed peel* **or**
75g caster sugar	*whole citron peel*
a few drops almond	*125ml double cream*
* essence*	

Decoration (optional)
whipped cream   *glacé cherries*

Oil a 750ml mould lightly. Warm the milk with the lemon rind, but do not let it boil. Mix the eggs and sugar together until fluffy and pale, and slowly stir in the milk. Strain the custard back into the pan or into a double boiler or basin held over hot water. (Make sure the water does not touch the upper pan.) Cook over very low heat for 15–20 minutes, stirring all the time, until it thickens. Do not let it come near the boil. Strain the custard into a bowl, stir in the almond essence, and leave to cool.

Put the water into a heatproof container, sprinkle in the gelatine and leave to soften. Stand the container in a pan of hot water and stir until the gelatine dissolves. Cool slightly and add to the custard. Leave in a cool place until it begins to set, stirring from time to time to prevent a skin forming.

Halve the cherries and chop the peel finely. Stir the fruit into the setting custard. Whip the cream until it is semi-stiff and fold in. Pour the pudding into the prepared mould and leave to set for about 2 hours. Turn out on to a flat, wetted plate.

Alternatively, pour the pudding into individual glasses, leave to set for about 1 hour and decorate with whipped cream and glacé cherries.

Marquise Alice

4 helpings

oil for greasing	4 ×15ml spoons water
250ml milk	1 ×10ml spoon gelatine
4 egg yolks **or** 1 whole egg and 2 yolks	5–6 sponge fingers (p1208)
75g caster sugar	4 ×15ml spoons Kirsch
a few drops vanilla essence	125ml double cream
	125ml single cream
50g praline (p1241)	

Decoration

200ml double cream	redcurrant jelly

Oil a plain 750ml mould lightly. Warm the milk, but do not let it come near the boil. Mix the eggs and sugar together until fluffy and pale, and slowly stir in the milk. Strain the custard back into the saucepan, or into a double boiler or basin held over hot water. (Make sure the water does not touch the upper pan.) Cook over very low heat for 15–20 minutes, stirring all the time, until it thickens. Do not let it come near the boil. Strain into a bowl, stir in the vanilla essence, and leave to cool.

Crush the praline if necessary. Put the water into a heatproof container, sprinkle in the gelatine and leave to soften. Add the praline. Stand the container in a pan of hot water until the gelatine and the sugar in the praline dissolve. Stir from time to time. Remove from the heat and cool slightly. Add to the custard and leave in a cool place until it begins to set, stirring from time to time to prevent a skin forming.

Break the sponge fingers into small pieces and put into a basin. Add the Kirsch and leave to soak. Put the double and single cream into a bowl and whip until it just holds its shape. Fold into the setting praline custard. Pour half the mixture into the mould and leave until thickened and beginning to set. Put the soaked sponge fingers in an even layer all over the custard, keeping 5mm at the edge clear, so they will not show when the pudding is turned out. Pour the rest of the mixture over the fingers and leave to set for about 2 hours. Turn out on to a flat, wetted plate.

Whip the double cream for decoration lightly until it just holds it shape. Spread it over the top and sides of the cream, completely masking it. Melt the redcurrant jelly and put into a forcing bag with a fine plain nozzle. Pipe lines of red jelly 1–1.5cm apart across the top of the cream. Pull the point of a skewer at right angles through the centre of the lines. Repeat 4cm to the right and then again 4cm to the left. Turn the pudding right round, through 180°, and draw the skewer across the red lines in the opposite direction to the first time. This gives a very pretty feathered decoration on the top of the Marquise.

VARIATION

Chocolate Marquise (1)

Omit the praline and add 100g grated plain chocolate to the milk so that it melts in the custard. Add 2 ×15ml spoons brandy or Kirsch, if liked.

Chocolate Marquise (2)

6 helpings

150g plain chocolate	6 eggs
200g unsalted butter	

Break up the chocolate or grate it coarsely. Chop the butter into small pieces. Separate the eggs. Put the chocolate into a large basin and stand it over a pan of hot water. Heat gently until the chocolate melts. Beat in the butter gradually, in small pieces, stirring all the time. Stir in the egg yolks, one at a time. When well blended in, remove from the heat. Whisk the egg whites quickly until stiff and fold into the mixture. Pour gently into a glass bowl or 6 individual dishes and chill well before serving.

Note Sugar can be added for a sweet dessert but the rich smoothness of the cream does not really need it.

French Chocolate Creams

(rich)

6 helpings

150ml milk	100g plain chocolate
6 × 10ml spoons caster	100g unsalted butter
sugar	8 egg yolks
a pinch of salt	

Warm the milk, sugar, and salt in a small saucepan, and stir until the sugar dissolves. Put to one side. Grate the chocolate coarsely and chop the butter into small pieces. Put them into a large basin and stand it over a pan of hot water. Heat gently until melted, stirring all the time. When the mixture is quite smooth, add the milk and mix it in thoroughly. Using a balloon whisk if possible, beat in the egg yolks, one at a time; on no account let them curdle. Pour the cream into 6 small pots or ramekins and chill well before serving.

Sherry Custard Cream

4 helpings

4 eggs	3 × 15ml spoons sweet
3 × 15ml spoons caster	sherry
sugar	

Separate the eggs. Put the yolks and sugar into a heatproof basin, stand it over hot water and whisk until thick and creamy. Add the sherry and whisk again until thick. Remove from the heat and cool slightly. Whisk the egg whites until stiff and fold into the yolk mixture. Spoon into glasses, chill and serve.

Crème Brûlée

See pp967–68.

Cold Zabaglione

See p974.

Orange Custard

See p970.

Chocolate Roulade

6 helpings

oil for greasing	butter for greasing
150g bitter-sweet	15g icing sugar
dessert chocolate	175ml double cream
4 eggs	(approx)
125g caster sugar	a few drops vanilla
3 × 15ml spoons hot	essence
water	

Brush a 30 × 42cm baking tray with oil. Line it with a piece of greaseproof paper letting the paper overlap the edge a little. Cut out an extra sheet of greaseproof paper the same size, to cover the roulade after it has been cooked, and have ready a damp cloth with which to cover the baking tray.

Break the chocolate into small pieces and place it in a bowl over a pan of water just taken off the boil. Leave to melt, stirring occasionally. Meanwhile, separate the eggs. Add the caster sugar to the yolks and beat briskly until the mixture is pale and creamy. Add the water to the melted chocolate and beat until well blended. Mix the chocolate into the yolk and sugar mixture, and whisk thoroughly. Whisk the egg whites until fairly stiff, then fold them carefully into the chocolate mixture using a metal spoon. Tip the roulade mixture gently into the prepared tin, and smooth it out evenly. Cook in a fairly hot oven at 190°C, Gas 5, for 20 minutes, until firm on the surface. When cooked, cover immediately with a sheet of buttered greaseproof paper and a damp cloth. Leave to stand overnight.

Next day, remove the cloth. Turn the paper buttered side up, sprinkle with icing sugar and replace sugared side down. Grip the paper and tin and invert both together so that the roulade is upside-down. Lay it down on the paper, and remove the tin. Peel off the lining paper. Whip the cream until very stiff, stir in the vanilla essence and spread evenly over the surface of the roulade. Then, roll the roulade up as you would a Swiss roll, using the paper to help you. Dust with extra icing sugar and chill for several hours before serving.

Note Successful rolling of the roulade depends to a certain extent upon its thickness. Cracks which appear while rolling can be filled with icing sugar.

FRUIT CREAMS

Apricot Custard Cream

Basic recipe

4 helpings

oil for greasing	*50g sugar*
500g fresh apricots **or**	*lemon juice (optional)*
2 × 425g cans apricots	*4 × 15ml spoons water*
200ml milk	*1 × 10ml spoon gelatine*
3 egg yolks **or** *1 whole*	*100ml double cream*
egg and 1 yolk	*100ml single cream*

Oil a 750ml mould lightly. Poach fresh fruit in a little water and sugar if it needs cooking. Process any fruit in an electric blender when tender, or sieve it if it contains seeds (eg berries or currants). Make the purée up to 200ml, if necessary, with a little fruit juice, fruit syrup or water.

Warm the milk, but do not let it come near the boil. Mix together the eggs and 25g of the sugar until fluffy and pale, and slowly stir in the milk. Strain the custard back into the saucepan or into a double boiler or basin held over hot water. (Make sure the water does not touch the upper pan.) Cook over very low heat for 15–20 minutes, stirring all the time, until it thickens. Do not let it come near the boil. Strain the custard into a bowl and leave to cool. Blend together the fruit purée and the cooled custard. Taste, and add more sugar and a little lemon juice if required.

Put the water into a heatproof container, sprinkle in the gelatine and leave to soften. Stand the container in a pan of hot water and stir until the gelatine dissolves. Cool until tepid, and add to the custard. Leave in a cool place until it begins to set, stirring from time to time to prevent a skin forming.

Put all the cream into a bowl and whip lightly. Fold into the setting mixture, and pour gently into the mould. Leave to set for about 2 hours. Turn out on to a flat, wetted plate. Decorate as desired.

VARIATIONS

Blackcurrants, blackberries, damsons, gooseberries, peaches, raspberries, or strawberries also make delicious fruit creams.

Quick Fruit Cream (1)
(using custard powder)

4 helpings

1 × 127g pkt orange	*2 × 15ml spoons custard*
jelly	*powder*
100ml water	*250ml milk*
50ml orange juice	*125ml double cream*

Chop the jelly tablet roughly. Heat the water, add the jelly, and stir until dissolved. Add the juice and leave to cool. Meanwhile, blend the custard powder with a little of the milk. Heat the rest of the milk until it boils. Pour it slowly on to the blended custard powder, stirring all the time. Return to the pan, bring to the boil and boil for 1–2 minutes, stirring all the time, until the custard thickens. Cool slightly and stir into the jelly. Cool until beginning to set. Whip the cream until it leaves a trail and fold into the setting mixture. Pour into individual glasses and chill for about 1 hour. Decorate as desired.

VARIATIONS

Pineapple Cream

Use a pineapple jelly tablet and the juice from a 376g can of crushed pineapple. Fold the fruit into the setting mixture.

Raspberry Cream (2)

Use a raspberry jelly tablet and the juice from a 219g can of raspberries. Fold the fruit into the setting mixture.

Strawberry Cream (2)

Make as for the Raspberry Cream (2).

Tangerine Cream

Use a tangerine jelly tablet and the juice from a 213g can of mandarin oranges. Chop the fruit and fold into the setting mixture.

Quick Fruit Cream (2)

(using ice cream)

4 helpings

1 × 127g pkt orange jelly	100ml water
1 × 300ml block vanilla ice cream	50ml orange juice
	125ml milk
	lemon juice

Chop the jelly tablet roughly, and chop up the ice cream. Heat the water, add the jelly, and stir until dissolved. Add the juice and stir in the ice cream quickly. If the mixture sets at this stage, place the bowl over a pan of hot water and stir until it is liquid again. Add the milk and a little lemon juice as the mixture will be very sweet. Pour into individual glasses and chill for about 1 hour. Decorate as desired.

Lemon Fluff

4 helpings

2 eggs	250ml water
juice and grated rind of 1 large lemon	5 × 15ml spoons caster sugar
2 × 15ml spoons cornflour	125ml single cream

Separate the eggs and keep aside. Blend the lemon juice (2 × 15ml spoons approx) and the cornflour together. Boil the water, then stir a little into the blended cornflour. Return to the heat and bring to the boil, stirring all the time. Boil for 1–2 minutes until the mixture thickens and clears. Stir in 3 × 15ml spoons caster sugar and the lemon rind. Remove the pan from the heat. Add the yolks to the lemon mixture, and stir in vigorously. Cover the mixture with damp greaseproof paper, and cool until tepid.

Stir the cream into the cooled lemon custard. Whisk the egg whites until stiff, add the remaining sugar and whisk until stiff again. Fold the egg whites into the lemon mixture until evenly distributed. Spoon into glasses and chill before serving.

Trifles, Chartreuses, and Charlottes

TRIFLES

Trifle is a very old English dessert, although its direct ancestry is not known and several different traditional desserts are claimed as its forebear.

Like those old dishes, a modern trifle can be varied in many ways. Strictly, it should always include sponge cake, sherry or some other wine or spirit, a rich custard, and whipped cream; but for economy, and when made for children, jam or a strongly flavoured fruit purée often replaces the alcohol. The trifle is usually layered with the jam or purée, and with pieces of fruit. It should be presented in a glass dish.

Apple Trifle

6 helpings

1kg cooking apples	6 individual sponge cakes
grated rind and juice of ½ lemon	375ml thick hot custard (p965)
150g sugar	
2 × 15ml spoons water	

Decoration

175ml double cream	25g flaked browned almonds (p1185)

Peel, quarter, and core the apples. Put with the lemon rind and juice, sugar, and water into a pan and cook gently to a pulp, keeping the pan covered. Slice the sponge cakes, place in a large glass dish and spread with the apple purée. Cover with the custard and leave to cool. Cover with damp greaseproof paper to prevent a skin forming. Whip the cream until stiff and spread it on the custard. Decorate with the almonds. Chill before serving.

VARIATION

Gooseberry Trifle

Use 1kg gooseberries instead of apples.

Apricot Trifle

6 helpings

6 slices jam Swiss roll	2 × 15ml spoons sherry
2 macaroons	500ml thick hot custard
1 × 540g can apricot	(p965)
halves	

Decoration
125ml double cream   25g blanched almonds

Cut the Swiss roll into cubes and break the maca-roons into pieces. Put them in the bottom of a glass dish. Drain the syrup from the can of fruit. Mix together 125ml of the syrup with the sherry and pour it over the cake. Cut up half the apricots and add to the dish. Pour the custard over, cover with damp greaseproof paper and leave for about 30 minutes to set. Whip the cream until stiff and spread it on the custard. Decorate with the remaining apricots and the almonds.

VARIATIONS
Peach Trifle

Use peach slices instead of apricots. Add 1 × 15ml spoon lemon juice to the syrup.

Pineapple Trifle

Use pineapple cubes instead of apricots.

Small Apricot Trifles

6 helpings

12 apricot halves, fresh or canned	2 × 15ml spoons sweetened fruit juice (for fresh fruit)
6 small rounds sponge cake, 2cm thick and 6cm across (see **Note**)	125ml unsweetened fruit juice
1 × 15ml spoon sherry (optional)	25g sugar

Decoration
125ml double cream   6 pistachio nuts

Drain the syrup from the canned apricots if used, and reserve it; or, cut the fresh fruit in half and remove the stones. Place the sponge cake rounds in individual dishes. Mix together the sherry and 2 × 15ml spoons syrup from the can or sweetened juice, and pour it over the sponge cakes. Arrange the fruit on top of the cakes. Heat together the 125ml unsweetened juice and sugar until the sugar has dissolved, then boil for about 10 minutes until it is a thick syrup. Glaze the fruit with the syrup. Leave to cool. Whip the cream until thick. Blanch, skin, dry, and chop the nuts. Decorate the trifles with the cream and nuts. Chill before serving.

Note Small rounds of sponge cake can be cut out with a scone or biscuit cutter from a large layer of Genoese (p1209) or sponge (p1208) cake.

VARIATION
Peach halves or pineapple rings can be used instead of apricots.

Coconut Trifle

6 helpings

6 individual sponge cakes	125ml rum
100g guava jelly	250ml thick hot custard
3 bananas	(p965)
2 × 15ml spoons lemon juice	

Decoration
25g desiccated coconut   glacé cherries

Spread the sponge cakes with some of the jelly and place in a glass dish. Slice the bananas and arrange on top of the cake. Cover the bananas with the remaining jelly. Sprinkle with the lemon juice and rum. Leave to stand for about 30 minutes. Pour the custard over the jelly and leave for about 45 minutes to set. Cover with damp greaseproof paper to prevent a skin forming. Decorate with coconut and cherries.

Individual Trifle (light)
See p1338.

Dean's Cream

8 helpings

6 individual sponge cakes	250ml sherry
raspberry jam	75ml brandy
apricot jam	500ml double cream
100g ratafias	50g caster sugar

Decoration

angelica	crystallized pineapple
glacé cherries	

Cut the sponge cakes in half lengthways, and spread half with raspberry jam and half with apricot jam. Arrange them in a deep glass dish, jam sides upwards. Break the ratafias into pieces and sprinkle on top. Pour the sherry over the cakes and leave to soak for about 30 minutes. Put the brandy, cream, and sugar into a basin and whisk until very thick. Pile into the dish and decorate with angelica, cherries, and crystallized pineapple. Chill well before serving.

Note This dessert was one of the forerunners of the standard modern trifle.

Pear and Chocolate Trifle

6 helpings

6 individual sponge cakes	6 pear halves, fresh **or** canned

Sauce

25g butter	25g sugar
25g cocoa	1 × 10ml spoon gelatine
25g flour	2 × 15ml spoons cold water
500ml milk	

Decoration

125ml double cream	angelica

Place the sponge cakes in individual dishes. If fresh pears are used, peel, halve, and core them. Drain canned pears well. Place a pear half, rounded side uppermost, on each sponge cake.

To make the sauce, melt the butter in a saucepan, add the cocoa and flour and cook for 2 minutes. Stir in the milk gradually, add the sugar and bring the mixture to the boil, stirring all the time. Simmer for 2 minutes. Remove from the heat. Soften the gelatine in the water in a small heatproof container. Stand the container in a pan of hot water and stir until it dissolves, then stir it into the sauce. Leave to cool to a coating consistency. Pour the sauce over the pears and allow some to run into the dish. Leave until cold. Whip the cream until stiff, and use with the angelica to decorate the trifle.

Mrs Beeton's Traditional Trifle

6 helpings

4 individual sponge cakes	grated rind of ½ lemon
raspberry **or** strawberry jam	250ml thick hot custard (p965)
6 macaroons	125ml double cream
12 ratafias	1 egg white
125ml sherry	25g caster sugar
25g blanched shredded almonds	

Decoration

glacé cherries	angelica

Cut the sponge cakes in half and spread one half of each with jam. Sandwich together and arrange in a glass dish. Crush the macaroons and ratafias and put them into the dish. Pour the sherry over them. Sprinkle with the almonds and lemon rind. Cover with the custard and leave for about 30 minutes to cool. Cover with damp greaseproof paper to prevent a skin forming. Whip together the cream, egg white, and sugar until stiff and spread over the dish. Decorate with cherries and angelica.

Walnut Trifle

3–4 helpings

100g walnuts	375ml cold thick custard
150g stale plain cake, eg	(p965)
Madeira, sponge **or**	2 × 15ml spoons
Genoese sponge cake	raspberry jam
2 bananas	

Decoration
angelica   glacé cherries

Reserve a few walnuts for decoration and chop the rest. Crumble the cake to give coarse crumbs. Slice the bananas. Mix together the cake crumbs and enough custard to make a firm paste. Add the bananas, chopped nuts, and jam. Place in a serving dish and cover with the remaining custard. Cover with damp greaseproof paper to prevent a skin forming. Chill for about 1 hour. Decorate with the whole walnuts, angelica, and cherries.

Wine Trifles

6 helpings

grated rind and juice of	1 × 5ml spoon cornflour
½ lemon	375ml sweet white wine
3 eggs	6 individual sponge
100g caster sugar	cakes

Put the lemon rind and juice into a basin with the eggs, sugar, and cornflour and stir well together. Gradually whisk in the wine. Place the basin over a saucepan of hot water and whisk all the time until light and fluffy. The mixture must not be allowed to boil; it can be prepared in the top of a double boiler and will take about 15 minutes to thicken. Remove the basin from the heat and leave to cool slightly. Place the sponge cakes in individual dishes and just before serving, pour over the sauce. Serve either hot or cold.

Mrs Beeton's Tipsy Cake or Brandy Trifle

4–6 helpings

1 × 15cm sponge cake	50g whole blanched
(p1208)	almonds
redcurrant jelly	375ml milk
(optional)	125ml single cream
65–75ml brandy **or**	8 egg yolks
white wine and brandy	75g caster sugar

Put the cake in a glass bowl or dish 16cm in diameter and as deep as the cake. Spread the cake thinly with jelly, if used. Pour over as much brandy or brandy and wine as the cake can absorb. Cut the almonds into spikes lengthways and stick them into the top of the cake all over. Mix the milk and cream. Beat the yolks until liquid, and pour the milk and cream over them. Add the sugar. Cook gently in the top of a double boiler for about 10 minutes or until the custard thickens, stirring all the time. Let the custard cool slightly, then pour it over and around the cake. Cover and chill. When cold, decorate with small spoonfuls of redcurrant jelly.

CHARTREUSES

A chartreuse once meant some kind of vegetable or fruit set in aspic or jelly and presented in the shape of a goblet. It now means either chopped fruit set in jelly with cream in the centre, or fruit layered with jelly in a mould. In this case, the flavour of a commercial jelly tablet can be over-strong, and the jelly is best made with fruit juice set with gelatine. The jelly used in each recipe is assumed to be liquid. Where it is used at different stages, it should be kept in a warm place to prevent setting.

Fruit Juice Jelly for Chartreuses

Makes 250ml (approx)

Dissolve 100g sugar in 250ml hot water, and add the strained juice of 2 lemons and 4 oranges. Dissolve 2 × 10ml spoons gelatine in a little of the liquid, cool, then stir into the remaining liquid.

Banana Chartreuse

4 helpings

250ml fruit juice jelly	*4 × 15ml spoons water*
(p1036)	*1 × 10ml spoon gelatine*
5 bananas	*50g sugar*
angelica	*1 × 15ml spoon lemon*
milk	*juice*
250ml double cream	

Line a 750ml mould with some of the jelly. Chill for 10–20 minutes until set. Slice 1 banana thinly and arrange, overlapping, in a design on the set jelly. Cut the angelica into leaf shapes and arrange over the bananas. Carefully spoon just enough of the remaining jelly (which should still be semi-liquid) over the decoration to cover it. Chill again. When it is set, add enough extra jelly to give a total depth of about 10cm.

Mash the remaining 4 bananas or process them briefly in an electric blender. Add enough milk to make 250ml semi-liquid purée. Whip the cream until soft peaks form and fold in the bananas.

Put the water into a heatproof container, sprinkle in the gelatine and leave to soften. Stand the container in a pan of hot water and stir until the gelatine dissolves. Remove from the heat, and stir in the sugar and lemon juice. When the gelatine mixture is cold but not yet set, stir it into the banana cream. Pour into the mould and leave in a cool place for about 2 hours to set. Turn out on to a wetted serving plate.

VARIATIONS

250ml of any fruit purée can be used instead of bananas and milk, eg apricots, strawberries or raspberries.

Cabinet Pudding (3)

(cold)

6 helpings

250ml clear lemon jelly	*2 × 10ml spoons gelatine*
(p1013)	*2 × 15ml spoons cold*
glacé cherries	*water*
angelica	*a few drops vanilla*
10–12 sponge fingers	*essence*
(p1208)	*125ml double cream*
25g ratafias	
375ml tepid custard	
(p965)	

Line a 750ml soufflé dish with half the jelly, and leave to set. Cut the cherries into quarters and the angelica into leaf shapes, and decorate the pudding as described on (p1012). Decorate the jelly with pieces of cherry and angelica, dipping each piece in liquid jelly before setting in place. Leave to set, then cover with a little more liquid jelly and set again. Chill the remaining jelly. Line the sides of the dish with the sponge fingers, trimming one end so that they stand evenly on the jelly. Trim the fingers level with the top of the tin. Whisk the sponge trimmings and ratafias into the custard so that they are well soaked. Soften the gelatine in the water in a small heatproof container. Stand the container in a pan of hot water and stir until it dissolves, then add the gelatine to the custard. Flavour with the vanilla essence. Whip the cream until just stiff and fold into the crumb custard. Carefully pour into the prepared mould and leave for 1–2 hours to set. Chop the chilled jelly (p1013). Turn the pudding out on to a serving dish and decorate with the chopped jelly.

Note For Cabinet Pudding to be served hot, see p967.

CHARLOTTES

The word 'charlotte' probably comes from the old English *charlyt* which meant 'a dish of custard'. Various French and British dishes have been called charlottes in the past. Today, however, a charlotte is almost always a dish of fruit flavoured cream or a Bavarian cream layered or cased in pre-baked bread or cake. Boudoir biscuits are sometimes used but are less suitable than sponge fingers (p1208) since they break easily when trimmed. Like the chartreuse recipes above, the jelly used is assumed to be liquid, as are the flavoured creams. Prepare the cream whilst the jelly is setting in the mould.

Mrs Beeton's Charlotte Russe

6 helpings

24 sponge fingers (1) (p1208)	1 ×15ml spoon icing sugar **or** to taste
2 ×15ml spoons white glacé icing (p1225)	1 ×15cm round sponge cake (p1208) or Genoese sponge (p1209), 1cm thick
3 ×5ml spoons gelatine	
3 ×15ml spoons water	
500ml single cream	
3 ×15ml spoons any sweet liqueur	

Cut 4 sponge fingers in half, and dip the rounded ends in icing. Line a 15cm soufflé dish with the halved fingers, placing them like a star, with the non-sugared sides uppermost and the iced ends in the centre. Dip one end of each of the remaining biscuits in icing. Line the sides of the dish with them, sugared sides outward, iced ends at the bottom. Trim the biscuits to fit the rim of the dish. Soften the gelatine in the water in a small heatproof container. Stand the container in a pan of hot water and stir until it dissolves. Remove from the heat and whisk together with the cream, liqueur, and sugar until frothy. Stand the mixture in a cool place until it begins to thicken. Fill the charlotte with the mixture, and cover it with the round of sponge cake. Leave in a cool place for 8–12 hours, until firm. Loosen the biscuits from the sides of the dish with a knife, carefully turn out the charlotte on to a plate, and serve.

Charlotte Russe

6 helpings

250ml clear lemon jelly (p1013)	500ml Italian Bavarois (p1029)
20 sponge fingers (p1208)	

Pour enough jelly into the bottom of a 17cm soufflé dish or charlotte mould to give a depth of 5mm. Chill until set. Trim one end of the sponge fingers and dip one long side of each into the remaining liquid jelly; use to line the sides of the mould. Place them sugared side outward and touching each other, with the trimmed end placed on the jelly. The jelly should hold them together. Chill for about $2\frac{1}{2}$ hours until set. Pour the Bavarois into the mould just before it reaches setting point. Chill until fully set. Turn out carefully on to a serving dish, and serve chilled.

Note Kirsch or Cointreau can be used for the Italian Bavarois instead of brandy.

Charlotte St José

8 helpings

250ml clear lemon jelly (p1013)	20 sponge fingers (p1208)
glacé pineapple	750ml pineapple cream (p1032)

Decoration
125ml double cream

Line a 1.25 litre charlotte mould with a thin layer of lemon jelly and leave to set. Decorate the jelly with pieces of pineapple, dipping them in liquid jelly before setting in place. Spoon over a very little jelly and leave to set. Trim one end of each sponge finger and use to line the sides of the mould, placing the trimmed end on to the jelly. Pour the pineapple cream into the prepared mould and leave for 2–3 hours to set. Trim the fingers level with the top of the mould and turn out on to a serving dish. Whip the cream until stiff and use to decorate the charlotte.

VARIATION

Gooseberry Charlotte

Substitute 3 glacé cherries and angelica for the glacé pineapple, and use gooseberry cream (p1032) instead of the pineapple cream.

Apple Charlotte

See p993.

Cream and Chiffon Pies

Many other pies and desserts with a pastry base, eg Fruit Pies and Flans, Jam Tart, Mrs Beeton's Bakewell Pudding, etc can be found in the chapter on Pastry Making.

Peppermint Cream Pie

4 helpings

Pie shell

100g ginger-nuts	*50g butter*
50g plain chocolate	

Filling

2 egg yolks	*2 × 15ml spoons water*
75g caster sugar	*1 × 10ml spoon gelatine*
50ml water	*125ml double cream*
a few drops peppermint	
* essence*	

To make the pie shell, crush the ginger-nuts with a rolling pin (this is best done in a large polythene bag). Melt the chocolate and butter in a basin over hot water. Mix in the crumbs thoroughly. Line a shallow 18cm pie plate with the mixture; press it firmly in an even layer all over the base and sides. Put the shell in a cool place to set.

To make the filling, put the egg yolks, sugar and 50ml water into a heatproof basin, and whisk over simmering water until thick and pale. Whisk in the peppermint essence. Put the water into a small heatproof basin and sprinkle in the gelatine to soften. Stand the basin in hot water and stir until the gelatine dissolves. Cool for 5 minutes, then whisk into the yolk mixture. Whip the cream lightly and fold it in. Turn into the chocolate crumb shell and chill before serving.

Note Peppermint essence is very strong, so add only a drop at a time.

Coconut Cream Pie

4 helpings

Pie shell

100g semi-sweet biscuits	*1 × 15ml spoon sugar*
50g butter	

Filling

300ml milk	*25g butter*
40g cornflour	*a few drops vanilla*
a pinch of salt	* essence*
40g caster sugar	*75g desiccated coconut*
1 egg yolk	

To make the pie shell, crush the biscuits with a rolling pin. Melt the butter and mix in the crumbs and sugar thoroughly. Line a shallow 18cm pie plate with the mixture; press it firmly in an even layer all over the base and sides. Put the shell in a cool place to set.

To make the filling, blend enough milk with the cornflour, salt, and sugar to make a smooth cream. Bring the rest of the milk to the boil. Pour it on to the blended mixture, return to the pan and bring to the boil again slowly, stirring all the time. Cook, stirring vigorously, for 1–2 minutes, until the sauce thickens. Beat in the egg yolk, butter, vanilla essence, and coconut. Cool until tepid, then turn into the pie shell. Chill before serving.

Note The pie shell can be made with plain chocolate digestive biscuits, if preferred. In this case, omit the sugar.

Sherry Cream Pie

4 helpings

Pie shell

150g plain chocolate	*50g butter*
digestive biscuits	

Filling

125ml milk	*2 ×15ml spoons*
2 eggs	*medium dry **or** sweet*
50g sugar	*sherry*
2 ×15ml spoons water	*grated nutmeg*
1 ×10ml spoon gelatine	*125ml double cream*

To make the pie shell, crush the biscuits with a rolling pin. Melt the butter and mix in the crumbs thoroughly. Line an 18cm shallow pie plate with the mixture; press it firmly in an even layer all over the base and sides. Put the shell in a cool place to set.

To make the filling, warm the milk, but do not let it boil. Separate the eggs. Beat the yolks and sugar together lightly. Add the milk. Strain the custard into the pan or a double boiler and cook over low heat, stirring all the time for about 15 minutes or until the custard thickens. Do not let the custard boil or it will curdle. Cool slightly. Put the water into a heatproof container, sprinkle in the gelatine, and leave to soften. Stand the container in a pan of hot water and stir until the gelatine dissolves. Stir from time to time. Remove from the heat, add a little of the custard, stir, and mix into the rest of the custard. Add the sherry a little at a time to prevent the mixture curdling. Add grated nutmeg to taste and put into a cool place until it is on the point of setting.

Whip the double cream until it forms soft peaks, and stir it into the custard. Whisk the egg whites until stiff, and fold in. Pour the custard mixture gently into the pie shell and chill until set.

Coffee Chiffon Pie

4 helpings

Pie shell

75g digestive biscuits	*50g butter*
25g walnuts	*25g caster sugar*

Filling

100g caster sugar	*a pinch of salt*
1 ×10ml spoon gelatine	*1 ×10ml spoon lemon*
2 eggs	*juice*
250ml cold water	
1 ×15ml spoon instant	
coffee	

Decoration
whipped cream

To make the pie shell, crush the biscuits with a rolling pin. Chop the nuts finely. Melt the butter and mix in the crumbs, nuts, and sugar. Line a shallow 18cm pie plate with the mixture; press it firmly in an even layer all over the base and sides. Put into a cool place to set.

To make the filling, mix 50g of the sugar with the gelatine. Separate the eggs. Heat 3 ×15ml spoons of the water. Dissolve the coffee in the hot water, then add the rest of the water to make the liquid up to 250ml. Blend the yolks and black coffee in the pan or basin over a pan of hot water or in a double boiler. Add a pinch of salt and stir in the gelatine and sugar mixture. Cook over gentle heat for about 15 minutes, stirring all the time, until the custard thickens slightly. Do not let it boil. Pour into a cold basin, cover with damp greaseproof paper, and chill until on the point of setting.

Stir the lemon juice into the cooled mixture. Whisk the egg whites until foamy, gradually whisk in the remaining sugar and continue whisking until stiff and glossy. Fold the coffee custard into the meringue, pour into the pie shell and chill for at least 1 hour until set. Serve decorated with whipped cream.

Lemon Chiffon Pie

4 helpings

Pie shell

100g digestive biscuits	*25g caster sugar*
50g butter	

Filling

100g caster sugar	*50ml water*
1 × 10ml spoon gelatine	*juice and grated rind of 2*
3 eggs	*lemons*

To make the pie shell, crush the biscuits with a rolling pin. Melt the butter and mix in the crumbs and sugar thoroughly. Line an 18cm shallow pie plate with the mixture; press it firmly in an even layer all over the base and sides. Put into a cool place to set.

To make the filling, mix 50g of the caster sugar with the gelatine. Separate the eggs. Blend the yolks, water, and lemon juice in a pan or basin over a pan of hot water, or in a double boiler. Stir in the gelatine and sugar mixture. Cook over very gentle heat for about 10 minutes, stirring all the time, until the custard thickens. Do not let it boil. Pour into a cold basin, cover with damp greaseproof paper, and chill until on the point of setting.

Stir the lemon rind into the cooled mixture. Whisk the egg whites until foamy, gradually whisk in the remaining sugar and continue whisking until stiff and glossy. Fold the lemon custard mixture into the meringue, pile into the pie shell and chill for at least 1 hour until set.

VARIATION

Orange Chiffon Pie

Make a pie shell as above. Substitute oranges for the lemons, but use the grated rind of one only. Add 1 × 15ml spoon lemon juice to the orange juice and enough water to make the liquid up to 150ml. Use this to form an orange custard as above with the yolks, gelatine and sugar. Use, however, only 15g sugar with the gelatine, and 40g sugar with the egg whites.

Cheesecakes

Coffee Cheesecake

10–12 helpings

Base

50g butter or margarine	*50g self-raising flour*
50g caster sugar	*1 × 2.5ml spoon baking*
1 egg	*powder*

Filling

75g butter	*2 × 15ml spoons brandy*
100g caster sugar	*1 egg*
2 × 15ml spoons instant	*50g plain flour*
coffee	*75g sultanas*
1 × 15ml spoon boiling	*500g full-fat soft cheese*
water	*250ml double cream*
1 × 15ml spoon orange	
juice	

Beat together all the ingredients for the base until smooth. Spread the mixture over the base of a deep loose-bottomed 20cm cake tin.

To make the filling, cream together the butter and sugar until light and fluffy. Dissolve the coffee in the boiling water and orange juice, and leave to cool. Beat it into the creamed mixture with the brandy and egg. Fold in the flour and sultanas. In a separate bowl, beat the cheese until smooth. Gradually beat in the cream. Fold the cheese mixture carefully into the butter mixture and pour into the prepared tin. Bake in a warm oven at 160°C, Gas 3, for $1\frac{1}{4}$–$1\frac{1}{2}$ hours or until firm. Cool. Remove from the tin and serve cold.

Orange Cheesecake
See p1418.

Cheddar Cheesecake

6–8 helpings

Base

shortcrust pastry (p1249) using 150g flour	flour for rolling out

Filling

150g Cheddar cheese	75g natural yoghurt
1 egg	25g self-raising flour
grated rind and juice of 1 lemon	75g caster sugar
	1 egg white

Roll out the pastry on a lightly floured surface and use it to line a 20cm flan case. Bake blind. Cool completely. Meanwhile, grate the cheese. Separate the egg. Mix together the yolk, lemon rind and juice, yoghurt, flour, and sugar. Add the second egg white to the first, and whisk both together until stiff. Stir 1×15ml spoon of this into the cheese mixture, then fold in the remainder lightly. Turn gently into the cooled pastry case, and bake in a warm oven at 160°C, Gas 3, for 35–45 minutes or until firm in the centre and lightly browned. Serve cold.

Curd Cheesecake (1)

4 helpings

Base

shortcrust pastry (p1249) using 125g flour	flour for rolling out

Filling

curds from 500ml milk (75g approx) (p874) **or** 75g curd cheese	100g sugar
	25g currants
	grated nutmeg
50g butter	1×5ml spoon baking powder
1 egg	
a pinch of salt	

Roll out the pastry on a lightly floured surface and use it to line an 18cm flan ring. Break down the curds with a fork or, if very firm, rub them through a sieve. Melt the butter. Beat the egg until liquid. Mix the butter, egg, salt, sugar, currants, and a little grated nutmeg thoroughly into the curds. Add the baking powder last of all. Put the mixture into the flan case. Bake in a fairly hot oven at 190°C, Gas 5, for 25–30 minutes until the pastry is lightly browned and the filling set. Serve warm or cold.

Curd Cheesecake (2)

4 helpings

fat for greasing	grated rind and juice of $\frac{1}{2}$ lemon
curds from 500ml milk (75g approx) (p874) **or** 75g curd cheese	50g ground almonds
	50g caster sugar
50g butter	2×15ml spoons self-raising flour
2 eggs	

Line and grease an 18cm sandwich tin. Break down the curds with a fork, or, if very firm, rub them through a sieve. Melt the butter. Separate the eggs. Mix the yolks, butter, lemon rind and juice, nuts, and caster sugar thoroughly into the curds. Whisk the whites until stiff. Sift the flour into the curd mixture, and fold in. Fold in the whites. Put the mixture into the tin and bake in a hot oven at 220°C, Gas 7, for 10 minutes; then lower the heat to moderate 180°C, Gas 4, and cook for about 15 minutes until the cake is dry in the centre when tested with a thin heated skewer. If the top is too brown, cover loosely with foil or greaseproof paper.

Lemon Cheesecake

8 helpings

Base

100g digestive biscuits	25g caster sugar
50g butter	

Filling

200g full-fat soft cheese	15g gelatine
75g caster sugar	50ml water
2 eggs	grated rind and juice of 1 lemon
125ml soured cream	

Decoration

whipped cream	crystallized lemon slices

To make the base crush the biscuits finely with a

rolling pin. Melt the butter and mix in the crumbs and sugar. Press the mixture on to the base of a 17cm loose-bottomed cake tin. Put in a cool place to set.

To make the filling, beat the cheese and sugar together. Separate the eggs, and beat the yolks into the cheese mixture. Stir in the soured cream. Soften the gelatine in the water in a small heatproof basin. Stand the basin in a pan of hot water and stir until the gelatine dissolves. Stir the lemon rind, juice, and gelatine into the cheese mixture. Whisk the egg whites until stiff and fold carefully into the mixture. Pour into the prepared tin and chill for 45 minutes–1 hour until firm. Remove from the tin and decorate with whipped cream and crystallized lemon slices.

Raspberry Yoghurt Cheesecake

8–10 helpings

Base

50g butter	25g walnuts
50g caster sugar	50g puffed rice cereal
1 × 15ml spoon golden syrup	fat for greasing

Filling

1 × 15ml spoon gelatine	3 eggs
50ml cold water	250g caster sugar
300g cottage cheese	250ml double cream
125ml raspberry flavoured yoghurt	1 × 175g can raspberries
1 × 15ml spoon lemon juice	

Glaze (optional)

syrup from canned raspberries	1 × 10ml spoon arrowroot
water	a few drops red food colouring

Melt the butter, sugar, and syrup together in a saucepan. Chop the walnuts, and add with the puffed rice cereal to the pan. Stir well and press the mixture on to the base of a greased 20cm loose-bottomed cake tin. Chill for 10 minutes.

Soften the gelatine in the water in a small heatproof basin. Stand the basin in a saucepan of hot water and stir until the gelatine dissolves. Sieve the cottage cheese, add the yoghurt and lemon juice and beat until smooth. Separate the eggs. Mix the yolks and 150g of the sugar in a pan, and cook over low heat, stirring all the time, until the mixture thickens. Remove from the heat, add the gelatine, mix well, and allow to cool until the mixture is beginning to thicken.

Stir the yoghurt and cheese mixture into the cooled gelatine. Whisk the egg whites until stiff, then gradually whisk in the remaining sugar. Whip the cream until it just holds its shape. Fold the whites and cream into the main mixture, and pour it carefully into the prepared tin. Chill for at least 4 hours. If leaving the cake unglazed, remove from the tin, drain the syrup from the can of raspberries and arrange the fruit on top. Chill before serving.

If glazing the cake, make up the syrup to 125ml with water and blend it into the arrowroot in a small saucepan. Bring to the boil, stirring all the time, and simmer for 2–3 minutes until the sauce thickens and clears. Add a few drops of red colouring. Arrange the fruit on top and coat with the glaze. Chill before serving.

VARIATIONS

Use the same quantity of canned or frozen peaches, strawberries, blackcurrants, apricots or black cherries, with the appropriate yoghurt and food colouring.

Cream Cheese Flan

See p899.

Gâteaux, Petits Fours and Friandises

GÂTEAUX

The term *gâteau* is French in origin. In English, it is applied to rich, elaborate cakes, usually served as desserts. They are generally made with layers of thin sponge, pastry or meringue, and fresh whipped cream. They are often decorated with chocolate or nuts and flavoured with a liqueur. A gâteau should be served very fresh, as soon as possible after being made.

For cream pastries suitable as a dessert, see the chapter on Pastry Making.

Black Forest Cherry Gâteau
(Schwarzwälderkirschtorte)

10–12 helpings

1 × 20cm round chocolate sandwich cake (p1205), using 3 eggs	1 × 540g can Morello cherries
250ml double cream	Kirsch
125ml single cream	25g plain chocolate

Cut the cake into 3 layers. Whip together the double and single cream until stiff. Drain and stone the cherries. Reserve the juice and 11 whole cherries. Halve the rest. Gently fold the halved cherries into half the cream. Put to one side. Strain the reserved cherry juice and mix it with Kirsch to taste. Prick the cake layers and sprinkle with the cherry juice and Kirsch until well saturated. Sandwich the layers together using the whipped cream and cherries. When assembled, cover with the remaining cream and use the whole cherries to decorate the top. Grate the chocolate and sprinkle it over the cream.

Apple Strudel
See p1267.

Coffee Gâteau

8–12 helpings

Cake

2 × 10ml spoons instant coffee	150g caster sugar
2 × 10ml spoons boiling water	3 eggs
	150g self-raising flour
150g butter	fat for greasing

Butter cream

2 × 15ml spoons instant coffee	150g butter
3 × 10ml spoons boiling water	450g icing sugar

Decoration

50–75g chopped walnuts	10–12 walnut halves

To make the cake, blend the coffee with the boiling water and leave to cool. Cream the butter and sugar together until very soft and creamy. Beat in the cooled coffee. Beat the eggs lightly and gradually add to the creamed mixture, beating very thoroughly between each addition. Sift the flour and fold it into the creamed mixture, using a metal spoon. Divide the mixture between two 20cm greased and lined sandwich cake tins. Spread evenly in the tins. Bake in a warm oven at 160°C, Gas 3, for 35–40 minutes or until well risen, firm and golden-brown. Leave in the tins for 2–3 minutes, then turn out on to a wire rack to cool.

To make the butter cream, blend the coffee with the boiling water and leave to cool. Cream together the cooled coffee, butter, and half the icing sugar, until soft. Beat in the remaining icing sugar.

Decorate the cake by sandwiching the cakes together using a little of the coffee butter cream. Spread a little more of the butter cream on to the sides of the cake; then roll the cake in the chopped walnuts. Spread most of the remaining butter cream on top of the cake and mark with a fork into an attractive design. Pipe rosettes with any remaining butter cream and decorate with halved walnuts.

Hazelnut Meringue Gâteau

4 helpings

75g hazelnuts	*125ml double cream*
3 egg whites	*1–2 × 5ml spoons caster*
150g caster sugar	*sugar*
2–3 drops vinegar	
2–3 drops vanilla	
essence	

Reserve a few hazelnuts for decorating the gâteau and bake the rest in a moderate oven at 180°C, Gas 4, for 10 minutes. Rub off the skins. Chop the nuts very finely or process briefly in an electric blender or coffee mill.

Line 2 baking trays with greaseproof paper or vegetable parchment. Draw a 15cm circle on each one and very lightly oil the greaseproof paper, if used.

Make up a cooked or Italian meringue mixture (p1024) from the egg whites and caster sugar. Add the vinegar, vanilla essence, and chopped nuts. Spread the meringue inside the marked circles or put the meringue into a forcing bag with a 1cm plain nozzle. If using a forcing bag, start from the middle of one circle and pipe round and round to form a coiled, flat round 15cm in diameter. Pipe a similar round on the other tray. Bake in a moderate oven at 180°C, Gas 4, for 35–40 minutes, until crisp and lightly browned. Leave to cool.

Whip the double cream until it stands in firm peaks, and stir in 1–2 × 5ml spoons caster sugar. Put one of the meringue rounds on a serving plate and spread with most of the cream. (Do not make the cream layer too thick or the gâteau will be difficult and messy to cut and serve.) Put the second meringue round on the cream layer and decorate with the rest of the cream and the reserved hazelnuts.

Note A hazelnut gâteau or vacherin is often filled with cream flavoured with Kirsch or noyau liqueur. The cream can also be richly flavoured with melted chocolate, coffee, or a purée of dried, soaked, and simmered apricots.

For other meringue desserts, see pp1024–25.

Apricot Gâteau

6–8 helpings

1 × 540g can	*125ml apricot juice*
unsweetened apricot	*1 × 250ml pkt lemon*
halves in juice **or** *water*	*jelly*
1 × 15cm round Genoese	*2 × 15ml spoons apricot*
sponge (p1209)	*jam*
2 × 15ml spoons sherry	*375ml double cream*
or *fruit juice*	*25g caster sugar*
24 sponge fingers (p1208)	

Decoration
angelica

Drain the can of apricots. Place the sponge on a serving plate and sprinkle with sherry or fruit juice. Trim the sponge fingers so that the sides and ends are quite straight. Heat the apricot juice. Melt the lemon jelly in the heated juice and leave until cool but not set.

Heat the apricot jam, and sieve it. Brush the non-sugared side of each trimmed sponge finger to a depth of 2cm with apricot jam. Dip one long side of each finger into the liquid jelly, and line the sides of the sponge with the jam-coated sides faced inwards and touching each other. Tie a ribbon 2cm wide round the finished case so that the sponge fingers are held in position. Leave to set.

Reserve 6 apricot halves for decoration and chop the rest. Whip the cream until just stiff and stir in the sugar. Stir the chopped apricots and the rest of the liquid jelly into all but 3 × 15ml spoons of the cream and, when just beginning to set, pour into the prepared case. Leave for about 1 hour to set. Arrange the half apricots on top. Pipe with the remaining cream and decorate with angelica.

Gâteau St Honoré

10–12 helpings

Base

150g prepared shortcrust pastry (p1249)
flour for rolling out

2 beaten eggs for glazing
choux pastry (p1251) using 200g flour

Pastry cream

3 eggs
50g caster sugar
35g plain flour
25g cornflour
a few drops vanilla essence

250ml milk
125ml double cream
50g granulated sugar
3 × 15ml spoons water

Decoration

glacé cherries   angelica

To make the base, roll out the shortcrust pastry on a lightly floured surface into a 20cm round and place on a baking tray. Prick the pastry well and brush with beaten egg. Using a 1cm plain nozzle, pipe a circle of choux paste round the edge of the pastry. Brush with beaten egg. Use the remaining choux to pipe 18–20 small choux buns separately (p1276). Place the circle and buns on a greased baking tray, and brush with beaten egg. Bake in a fairly hot oven at 200°C, Gas 6, for 15 minutes, then reduce to fairly hot, 190°C, Gas 5, for a further 10–15 minutes, or until the choux ring is well risen and golden-brown. Cool on a wire rack.

To make the pastry cream, separate 2 of the eggs. Beat together the yolks, whole egg, and the caster sugar. Stir in the flour, cornflour, and vanilla essence. Heat the milk and gradually beat it into the egg mixture. Return the mixture to the pan, bring to the boil, stirring all the time, and boil for 2–3 minutes. Put the mixture into a clean basin, cover with buttered paper and leave until cold.

Whip the cream until stiff and pipe into the choux buns. Put the sugar and water into a small saucepan, heat until the sugar has dissolved, then boil until a light straw colour. Remove from the heat. Dip the bottom of each bun quickly in the syrup and arrange on the choux round. Spoon a little syrup over each choux bun. Whisk the 2 remaining egg whites until stiff and fold into the pastry cream, with any leftover whipped cream. Fill the centre of the gâteau with the pastry cream. Decorate the buns with glacé cherries and angelica.

Note This gâteau is the traditional birthday cake in France.

Italian Candied Fruit Gâteau

4–6 helpings

150ml double cream
75g caster sugar
250g Ricotta cheese
juice and thinly grated rind of 1 lemon
75ml orange liqueur (Grand Marnier or Cointreau)
50g glacé cherries

50g cut mixed peel
50g angelica
50g crystallized ginger
50g glacé pineapple slices
50g bitter-sweet dessert chocolate
1 × 17cm Victoria sandwich cake (p1205)

Icing

125g plain chocolate
125g icing sugar

125g softened butter
25ml rum

Chill the double cream in the coldest part of the refrigerator for 2 hours. Whip it until soft peaks form and sweeten with 25g of the caster sugar. Chill half for decoration. Sieve the cheese, then blend it with the remaining whipped cream, the lemon juice and rind, and the liqueur. Beat until very smooth and light. Chop the fruits and add to the cheese mixture. Grate the chocolate coarsely, and add with the remaining caster sugar. Split the cake, and fill it with the cream mixture; reserve enough to coat the sides after re-forming the cake. Make smooth and even all round.

Melt the icing ingredients in a bowl over a pan of simmering water. Remove from the heat and beat until smooth. Cool until tepid. Spread all over the top of the sponge. When firm, decorate with the reserved whipped cream. Chill overnight before serving.

Malakoff Gâteau

8–10 helpings

150g butter	*250ml double cream*
4 egg yolks	*30– 32 sponge fingers*
200g caster sugar	*(p1208)*
200g ground almonds	

Decoration

250ml double cream	*canned fruit, eg apricots*
100g caster sugar	*(optional)*

Beat the butter until light and creamy. Mix in the egg yolks one at a time, then add the sugar and ground almonds. Bind with the double cream. Line a 1kg loaf tin with foil. Arrange a layer of sponge fingers along the base of the prepared tin. Spread a layer of filling over them. Repeat the layers until all the ingredients are used, finishing with a layer of sponge fingers. Cover with foil and place heavy weights evenly on top. Chill for 2–3 hours.

Shortly before serving, whip the cream with the sugar until stiff. Turn the gâteau out on to a serving dish and decorate with the cream and fruit, if used. Serve slightly chilled.

Mille-Feuille Gâteau

6–8 helpings

375g prepared puff	*100g raspberry jam*
pastry (p1253)	*(optional)*
flour for rolling out	*glacé icing (p1225) using*
250ml double cream **or**	*100g icing sugar*
confectioners' custard	
(1) (p1237)	

Roll out the pastry on a lightly floured surface 2mm thick and cut into six 15cm rounds. Place on baking trays, prick well, and bake in a very hot oven at 230°C, Gas 8, for 8–10 minutes until crisp and golden-brown. Lift the rounds off carefully and cool them on a wire rack. Whip the cream until thick, if used. Sandwich each layer of pastry together lightly with the jam and cream or confectioners' custard. (If using custard, the jam can be omitted.) Cover the top layer of pastry with the glacé icing.

Strawberry Ice Cream Gâteau

See p1064.

Chocolate Profiteroles

8 helpings

choux pastry (p1251)	*200g chocolate (p1226)*
using 100g flour	**or** *coffee (p1225) glacé*
250ml (approx)	*icing*
Chantilly cream (p880)	
or *confectioners'*	
custard (p1237) **or**	
chocolate butter cream	
(p1236) **or** *see* **Note**	

Use the choux pastry to pipe 24–30 small choux about 2cm in diameter (see p1276). When cooked, open them at the bottom, remove any uncooked paste, and leave to dry out and cool completely. When cold, fill with the desired cream. Glaze the tops with glacé icing, reserving some for assembling the dish. Let the icing harden, then arrange the choux in a pyramid (if possible against the sides of a conical mould). Stick them together with small dabs of icing.

Serve 3 or 4 choux per person, with hot chocolate sauce (p725).

Note The filling can be varied to taste. Sweetened whipped cream flavoured with liqueur can be used, or coffee butter cream (p1236), or mock cream (p1238). If using coffee butter cream, glaze the choux with chocolate glacé icing.

This dessert gâteau, or a variation, is often used as a wedding cake in France where it is called a *croquembouche (p1503).*

Savarin

6–8 helpings

Basic Mixture

75ml milk	$\frac{1}{4} \times 5ml$ spoon salt
15g fresh yeast **or**	$1 \times 10ml$ spoon sugar
$1 \times 10ml$ spoon dried	75g butter
yeast	3 eggs
150g strong white flour	oil for greasing

Rum Syrup

75g lump sugar	$1 \times 15ml$ spoon lemon
125ml water	juice
$2 \times 15ml$ spoons rum	

Glaze

$3 \times 15ml$ spoons apricot	$2 \times 15ml$ spoons water
jam	

Warm the milk until tepid. Blend in the fresh yeast or sprinkle on the dried yeast. Stir in 25g of the flour and leave in a warm place for 20 minutes. Sift the rest of the flour, the salt, and the sugar into a bowl. Rub in the butter. Add the yeast to the mixture, then add the eggs and beat until well mixed. Oil a 20cm ring mould (a savarin mould). Pour the mixture into the tin, cover with a large, lightly oiled polythene bag, and leave in a warm place until the mixture has almost reached the top of the tin. Bake in a fairly hot oven at 200°C, Gas 6, for about 20 minutes or until golden-brown and springy to the touch.

To make the rum syrup, put the sugar and water in a pan and heat until the sugar has dissolved. Bring to the boil and boil steadily for 8 minutes. Add the rum and lemon juice. Turn the warm savarin on to a serving dish, prick all over with a fine skewer, and spoon the rum syrup over it.

To make the glaze, sieve the apricot jam into a saucepan, add the water and bring to the boil, stirring all the time. Brush the glaze all over the soaked savarin.

VARIATIONS

The basic savarin is used for a number of French desserts and cakes. Instead of soaking it in rum syrup it can be filled with various mixtures, such as flavoured whipped cream or fruit purée mixed with rum.

Rum Babas

Makes 12

Make the basic mixture as above but add 50g currants. Grease 12 baba tins. Half fill the tins with the mixture. Place in a large, lightly oiled polythene bag and leave in a warm place for about 20 minutes or until the tins are two-thirds full. Bake in a fairly hot oven at 200°C, Gas 6, for 10–15 minutes or until golden-brown and springy to the touch. While still warm, soak with rum syrup as above.

PETITS FOURS AND FRIANDISES

Petits fours are very small rich cakes and biscuits served at a formal afternoon tea or wedding buffet. They include Miniature Éclairs, Florentines, French cakes, Mrs Beeton's Almond Macaroons, Meringues, Palmiers, Piped Almond Rings and Ratafias. They should be served in a cake basket or similar dish.

Friandises are sweetmeats served with coffee at the end of a formal dinner. The following are suitable: Candied Chestnuts, Candied Fruits, Glacé Fruits, Glazed Fruits, Marzipan Fruits, Stuffed Dates and Walnut Fondants. Petits fours such as Florentines, Ratafias and Almond Macaroons are sometimes included.

Recipes for all of these can be found by reference to the Index.

ICES AND FROZEN DESSERTS

When Raphael paid that memorable visit to Paradise,—which we are expressly told by Milton he did exactly at dinner-time,—Eve seems to have prepared " a little dinner " not wholly destitute of complexity, and to have added ice-creams and perfumes.

WATER ICES

Water ices are made basically from fruit syrup, fruit purée mixed with sugar syrup, or flavoured sugar syrup. The simplest type of water ice is a *granité*, which is not stirred during freezing and has a slightly rougher, more crystalline texture than a standard water ice. A *sorbet* or *sherbet* is also made with a fruit or other flavoured syrup, but generally with the addition of beaten egg whites or a little gelatine.

CREAM ICES

Home-made ice cream can be made wholly of sweetened and flavoured fresh cream or custard, but is more usually made with a mixture of cream and custard. The most common sweet flavourings are based on fruit purée or juice, chocolate, coffee, nuts, liqueurs or essences such as vanilla.

Yoghurt Ice Creams

These are based on yoghurt instead of cream. Yoghurt ice cream can be made at home and is also available commercially.

FROZEN DESSERTS

Mousses and Parfaits

These are iced mixtures which almost always contain whisked egg whites to give them a light and fluffy texture. A mousse may also contain gelatine. The term *parfait* formerly applied only to an iced confection flavoured with coffee, but is now used to describe mixtures made from fruit purées and other flavourings.

Coupes and Sundaes

These are two names for the same dessert. Ice cream is combined with fruit, chocolate or other sweet flavourings, nuts or biscuit crumbs, and whipped cream. Coupes and sundaes are generally served in tall, narrow, fluted glasses.

Moulded Ices

Mousse and parfait mixtures are often frozen in large or small moulds to make iced puddings. The best known pudding of this kind is called a *bombe*. Most bombes consist of two types and flavours of ice mixture, a plain ice cream for the outer layer, and a mousse or parfait mixture for the inside. An Italian *cassata*, which consists of two or more different coloured layers of ice cream for the outer coating and a filling of diced crystallized fruits, nuts or small macaroons, is often moulded in this way.

Ices of different flavours can also be layered in an oblong container to make a *biscuit glacé*; when three flavours and colours are used (normally deep pink, green and white, representing the Italian flag) it is called a *Neopolitan ice cream*. An ice cream mixture containing ground almonds or chestnuts is called a *plombière*. It is either frozen in a single mould, or scooped into small balls, piled into a pyramid and topped with a sweet sauce for serving.

Ice cream can be frozen and layered in rounds with cake or jam between them, like the layers of a sandwich cake, to make ice cream gâteaux.

INGREDIENTS FOR WATER AND CREAM ICES

Sugar

Caster sugar is the sweetening agent most often used in home-made ices, and is frequently added in the form of sugar syrup. For successful freezing it is important to add the right quantity of sugar, especially when making water ices. If the proportion of sugar to liquid is too high, large ice crystals form during freezing and the water ice or ice cream has a gritty texture. If there is too little sugar, the frozen ice is hard and tasteless. Egg white or a little gelatine in a water ice mixture helps to make a smoother texture; so does a little liquid glucose, obtainable from some chemists.

When a *hot* sugar syrup is necessary to the success of a recipe, it is specified in the method. Generally, a hot syrup should be used if flavouring ingredients such as lemon rind are to be infused in it. When syrup is simply to be added to a fruit purée or juice, it is easier to use it cold unless it is newly made or very thick.

Any mixture with hot syrup added must be chilled before freezing. Syrup mixtures must always be cooled before being mixed with cream for an ice cream.

Note If you wish to make water ices regularly, it is worthwhile making up a quantity of stock syrup and storing it in a large bottle or jar, like the syrups used for fruit preserving or making home-made sweets. Add a little liquid glucose to the syrup to prevent it graining.

Cream

Double cream is generally used for ices, as it freezes better than cream with a lower fat content. Single cream can be used if it is combined with a very rich custard base, as in Caramel Ice Cream (p1057). Evaporated milk can be used instead of cream in strongly flavoured ices, if it is processed as for whipping (see p872).

Custard

The richness of the custard depends on the number of egg yolks or whole eggs it contains. Remember that any custard tends to break down when frozen because egg whites and yolks freeze and thaw at different temperatures, so most ice cream mixtures contain at least as much cream or purée as custard, to bind them.

Other Ingredients

These are added to water ices and ice creams to give them body and flavour. The most important feature of these ingredients is that they must be suitable for freezing, and, if solid, must be small and stay soft; chopped glacé cherries and stem ginger can be mixed into ice cream before freezing, but fresh apple should be grated, not diced. Glacé cherries and other fruits freeze much more successfully if they are first washed and dried before adding to an ice mixture.

EQUIPMENT FOR FREEZING ICES

Ices can be frozen in either a freezer or the ice-making compartment of a refrigerator. Whichever method is used, all equipment should be chilled before use.

Freezer

The dial should be set to 'fast freeze' about 1 hour before freezing. Except for *granités*, which are not beaten during freezing, any mixture should, if possible, be packed in a container in which it can be beaten. The mixture is beaten once or twice during freezing to break down the ice crystals and incorporate air. After beating, the mixture is put into its mould, if used, and frozen firm for immediate use, or storage at the freezer's normal temperature. Ices for storage must be sealed, or overwrapped and labelled. For details of storage life for ices, see p1390.

Ice-making Compartment

The dial should be set at the coldest setting at least 1 hour before putting in the ice mixture. If there is room, the mixture should be frozen in a container, as in a home freezer, and beaten in the same way. If there is no room in the compartment, the mixture can be frozen in ice trays with the dividers removed or in similar containers, and either put into another container for beating, or whisked in the trays with a fork. After beating, the ice is returned, covered, to the ice-making compartment until frozen firm, and the dial is then returned to its normal setting.

Electric Ice Cream Maker or Sorbetière

This appliance is placed in the ice-making compartment of a refrigerator, or a home freezer, and beats the mixture steadily until it is frozen, when it ceases automatically; it gives a very smooth texture and more bulk than when the mixture is hand beaten. A spare electric point near the refrigerator or freezer is needed to plug in the sorbetière. Electric churns for use outside the refrigerator are also available; they operate on the same principle as the hand churns described below, and need extra ice and salt to operate.

Churn Freezer

A churn freezer consists of a metal container for the ice cream mixture, placed in an outer churn packed with crushed ice and salt. A 1 litre capacity freezing container needs 3.25kg crushed ice and 1kg common salt or freezing salt (obtainable from most large department stores and fishmongers), for the churn.

Containers

The governing factors in choosing containers must be the size of the freezing space available, and the freezing time you can allow. A deep bowl or box, for example, may not fit into the ice-making compartment of the refrigerator, and a solid block of ice cream takes much longer to freeze than a shallow layer in an ice tray. The larger the quantity of ice mixture the more slowly it freezes, and since quick freezing is generally desirable to prevent the formation of large ice crystals, it is wise to freeze ices in single quantities of 1 litre or less. If it is necessary to freeze more than this amount, use two containers. Rigid plastic, stainless steel, or any similar containers can be used, provided they have lids or can be covered securely with foil. If space allows, it is easier to use rigid plastic bowls with lids to freeze ice mixtures before beating; they can then be beaten in the bowl and transferred to the container in which they are to be served or stored for the final freezing. See also p1383.

Moulds

Large ice cream moulds are exactly like decorative jelly moulds, but have lids. Individual ice creams can be frozen in small fluted jelly moulds which hold about 100ml. Moulds without lids should be covered with foil while the mixture is freezing.

Bombes should be frozen in bell-shaped moulds, or in pudding basins. Use refrigerator ice trays or oblong foil trays for making a *biscuit glacé* or Neapolitan ice cream. Round, flat layers of ice cream for gâteaux can be frozen in deep cake tins, or in sandwich tins or foil dishes.

Other Equipment

An electric or rotary beater makes beating ice mixtures much easier both before and during freezing. A nylon (not metal) sieve for puréeing fruit is also necessary. Fruit can be processed in an electric blender, but fruits such as raspberries or grapes, with pips and skin, have to be sieved to make a really smooth purée. An ice cream scoop for serving individual portions of ice cream or water ices, or for shaping ice cream into small balls for a *plombière* is a useful, though not essential, piece of equipment.

MOULDING ICES

Water ices can be served as 'lollies'. Special moulds are sold with directions for use.

When using a single flavour of ice cream, pour it into a decorative mould after beating, whilst still semi-liquid. Tap the container on the table-top while filling, to knock out any air bubbles. Fill the mould to the brim.

When combining two or more flavours in a *bombe*, first line the mould with one flavoured ice cream, and fill the space in the centre with the other, usually a mousse mixture.

Do this either by filling the mould partially with the first flavour of ice cream when it is still semi-liquid after beating. Place a smaller bowl, large enough to hold the mixture for the centre of the pudding, in the middle of the mould, with the edge

Filling a bombe with two flavours

of the bowl on a level with the brim of the mould. Fill the space between the outer mould and the inner bowl with the first mixture and freeze it until firm; then remove the inner bowl and fill the space with the second mixture.

Alternatively, half fill the mould with the first mixture, and freeze until firm; scoop some of the ice cream out of the centre, leaving a shell at least 2cm thick, and pile up the extra ice cream round the sides; then fill the centre space with the second mixture. This is the easier method if you are using more than two different ice creams, eg for a *cassata*, because the process can be repeated two or three times. Scoop out a smaller centre portion of ice cream each time, leaving two or more complete different ice cream layers surrounding the centre space.

For a layered ice cream, it is a good idea to freeze each layer until firm before adding the next; alternatively, freeze the different layers separately until almost firm before layering them in a suitable container.

FREEZING TIMES

It is not possible to give precise freezing times for ice mixtures because the time depends on several factors:

1) The type of mixture used
2) Whether the mixture is beaten during freezing
3) The quantity frozen in one container and the shape of the container itself
4) Whether the mixture is frozen in a home freezer, the ice-making compartment of a refrigerator, or in a sorbetière or churn.

If a freezing time is given in a recipe it should therefore be regarded only as a broad guideline. When making an ice recipe for the first time it is best to check the condition of the mixture two or three times during the first hour of freezing, particularly if it is to be beaten before freezing completely.

STORING ICES

Any ice mixture stores excellently in a home freezer or the ice-making compartment of a refrigerator, if the container is securely sealed. If water ices and sorbets are to be stored for more than 2–3 days, their keeping quality can be improved by adding 1 × 5ml spoon gelatine to each 500ml of ice mixture during preparation; the gelatine should be softened and then dissolved in 2 × 5ml spoons water, fruit juice or syrup, and stirred into the mixture before freezing. Ices should be stored completely ready to eat; any beating necessary should have been done. Pack the frozen ice into freezer containers, leaving at least 1cm headspace.

SERVING ICES

Very hard ices are difficult to serve, and stun the palate rather than being pleasant to eat. They should therefore be allowed to soften slightly in the refrigerator before serving. Scoop them into stemmed glasses or small dishes, and serve accompanied by sponge fingers or wafer biscuits. An ice cream scoop should be dipped in tepid water before use, and dipped again each time it is used.

Sorbets are generally served only half-frozen, and should be allowed to soften for about 20 minutes in the refrigerator before being served. Traditionally, sorbets were eaten between the entrée and roast courses at a formal dinner to cleanse the palate, but they are now more usually served after the main course as a cold sweet.

If serving a moulded ice, dip the mould in tepid water for a few moments, remove the lid, and invert the mould over the serving dish. The mould should then come away easily.

Water Ices and Granités

POINTS TO NOTE

1) After pouring the mixture into a suitable container, chill if a hot syrup has been used, cover closely, and half freeze unless otherwise directed.
2) Beat the half-frozen mixture thoroughly, scraping off any crystals. Re-cover and freeze completely; label and store.

Note All the recipes in the Water Ice section below can be served as *granités*; they should be frozen completely and the beating omitted.

SYRUPS FOR WATER ICES

Syrup(1)

Makes 1 litre (approx)

1kg caster sugar　　　　　*3 × 2.5ml spoons liquid*
750ml water　　　　　　　*glucose (optional)*

Put the sugar and water in a strong saucepan and dissolve the sugar over gentle heat, without stirring. Bring the mixture to the boil and boil slowly for about 10 minutes or to a temperature of 110°C. Remove the scum as it rises. Strain, cool with a lid on the pan, add the liquid glucose, if used, and store in a glass bottle for use as required. If the syrup is to be used hot, re-heat in a covered pan, and keep covered during any waiting period.

Syrup(2)

Makes 500ml (approx)

200g lump sugar　　　　*500ml water*

Make as for Syrup (1).

Lemon Water Ice

6 helpings

6 lemons	375ml hot syrup (1)
2 oranges	(p1053)

Pare the rind very thinly from the fruit, and put into a basin. Add the hot syrup, cover, and leave to cool. Add the juice of the lemons and oranges to the syrup mixture. Strain through a nylon sieve into a container, chill, and freeze as described on p1053.

VARIATION

Orange Water Ice

Use 6 oranges and 2 lemons, and reduce the syrup quantity to 250ml.

Raspberry or Strawberry Water Ice

6 helpings

450g ripe strawberries, raspberries or loganberries	250ml cold syrup (1) (p1053) juice of 2 lemons

Rub the fruit through a nylon sieve, or process in an electric blender and sieve to make a smooth purée. Add the cold syrup and lemon juice, and mix well. Pour into a suitable container and freeze as described on p1053.

Blackcurrant Water Ice

6–8 helpings

500g blackcurrants	5 × 10ml spoons white rum
100g caster sugar	
375ml water	

Prepare the fruit, and simmer with the sugar and water until soft. Rub through a nylon sieve, or process in an electric blender and sieve to make a smooth purée. Leave to cool. Pour into a suitable container and freeze for 1 hour. Beat until smooth, and stir in the rum. Continue freezing for 2 hours.

Note This ice will not freeze hard.

Tangerine or Mandarin Water Ice

6–8 helpings

50g lump sugar	2 lemons
6 tangerines or mandarins	125ml water
2 oranges	250ml syrup (1) (p1053)

Rub the sugar over the rind of the tangerines or mandarins to extract some of the zest. Put the sugar in a saucepan. Pare the rind thinly from 1 orange and 1 lemon and add to the sugar with the water. Bring to the boil, reduce the heat, and simmer gently for 10 minutes; then add the juice from all the fruit, and the syrup. Bring back to the boil, and strain into a suitable container. Leave to cool, then freeze as described on p1053.

Grape Water Ice

6–8 helpings

300g white grapes	1 × 15ml spoon orange flower water
4 lemons	
250ml very hot syrup (1) (p1053)	

Crush the grapes with a wooden spoon and sieve them, or process in an electric blender and sieve to make a smooth purée. Pare the rind very thinly from 2 lemons and squeeze the juice of all of them. Add the hot syrup to the grape purée, together with the lemon rind and juice. Leave to cool. When cold, strain, and add the orange flower water. Pour into a suitable container, chill, and freeze as described on p1053.

Redcurrant Water Ice

6–8 helpings

400g redcurrants	375ml cold syrup (1)
200g raspberries	(p1053)
	juice of 1 lemon

Prepare the fruit and rub through a nylon sieve, or process in an electric blender and sieve to make a smooth purée. Add the cold syrup and lemon juice, and mix well. Turn into a suitable container and freeze as described on p1053.

Apple Water Ice

8 helpings

250ml hot syrup (1)
  (p1053)
500ml apple purée
2 ×15ml spoons lemon
  juice

*a few drops red or green
food colouring*

Stir the hot syrup into the apple purée and leave until cold. Stir in the lemon juice and a few drops of food colouring. Pour into a container, chill, and freeze as described on p1053.

Liqueur Ice

6 helpings

*4 ×15ml spoons liqueur
 (see Note)*

*500ml cold syrup (2)
(p1053)*

Stir the liqueur into the cold syrup, pour into a suitable container and freeze as described on (p1053).

Note Suitable liqueurs are: Apricot brandy, Calvados, cassis, cherry brandy, curaçao, framboise, Grand Marnier, Kirsch, maraschino or white rum.

Liqueurs may also be added to ices to enhance their flavour, eg curaçao with an orange or tangerine ice, framboise with a raspberry ice, Tia Maria with coffee or chocolate flavour, etc.

Cider Ice

6 helpings

1 large Bramley apple
1 ×15ml spoon water
250ml dry still cider

*250ml syrup (1) (p1053)
juice of 1 large lemon*

Peel, core, and slice the apple. Cook it gently with the water in a covered pan until soft. Rub through a nylon sieve and add all the other ingredients.

Pour into a container and freeze as described on p1053.

Sorbets

Lemon Sorbet(1)

6–8 helpings

2 × 5ml spoons gelatine
250ml water
150g caster sugar
*1 × 2.5ml spoon grated
  lemon rind*

250ml lemon juice
2 egg whites

Soften the gelatine in a little of the water over a pan of hot water. Boil the remaining water and sugar together for 10 minutes. Stir the dissolved gelatine into the syrup, add the lemon rind and juice, and leave to cool. Pour into a suitable container, cover, and freeze for 1 hour. Whisk the egg whites until they hold stiff peaks, beat the half-frozen ice mixture thoroughly, and fold the egg whites into it. Re-cover, and continue freezing for a further 2 hours.

Note This ice will not freeze hard.
  For Lemon Sorbet (2), see p1417.

Pineapple Sorbet

6 helpings

*500ml hot syrup (2)
  (p1053)*
*250ml canned pineapple
  juice*

2 egg whites

Cool the syrup, add the pineapple juice, pour into a suitable container, cover, and half freeze. Whisk the egg whites until they hold stiff peaks, beat the ice mixture until smooth, fold the egg whites into it, re-cover, and freeze completely.

Ice Creams

POINTS TO NOTE

1) Cool hot custard unless required hot.
2) After turning the mixture into a container, chill until thoroughly cold, cover closely and half freeze unless otherwise directed.
3) Beat the mixture well and add any cream, if it has not been added before. Re-freeze until firm; label and store.

Note Ice creams made with an electric ice cream maker are prepared somewhat differently, and the manufacturer's directions should be followed.

CUSTARDS FOR ICE CREAMS

Plain Custard (1)

Makes 500ml (approx)

2 × 15ml spoons custard powder   *500ml milk*
100g caster sugar

Blend the custard powder with a little of the milk. Heat the remaining milk to boiling point and pour on to the blended mixture. Return to the pan and simmer, stirring all the time, until the mixture thickens. Add the sugar, cover, and use hot or cold as required.

Plain Egg Custard (2)

Makes 500ml (approx)

500ml milk   *100g caster sugar*
3 eggs

Heat the milk until almost boiling. Beat the eggs and sugar together and add the hot milk, stirring well. Return the mixture to the pan and cook, without boiling, until the custard coats the back of a wooden spoon. Stir all the time. Strain, cover, and use as required.

Standard Custard (3)

Makes 500ml (approx)

500ml milk   *2 eggs*
8 egg yolks   *100g caster sugar*

Heat the milk until almost boiling. Beat the yolks, eggs, and sugar together until thick and white, and add the hot milk, stirring well. Return the mixture to the pan and cook, without boiling, until the custard thickens, stirring all the time. Strain, cover, and use as required.

Rich Custard (4)

Makes 500ml (approx)

8 egg yolks   *vanilla essence, ground*
100g caster sugar   *spice, liqueur* **or** *other*
500ml single cream   *flavouring*

Beat the yolks and sugar together until very thick. Put the cream in a saucepan and bring slowly to the boil. Pour the cream over the yolks and sugar, stirring well. Return the mixture to the pan and cook, without boiling, until the custard thickens. Stir all the time. Strain, add a few drops of vanilla essence or other flavouring, cover, and use as required.

ICE CREAM RECIPES

Vanilla Ice Cream

6 helpings

125ml double cream   *1 × 5ml spoon vanilla*
500ml cold custard (1)   *essence*

Whip the cream until semi-stiff. Add the cold custard and vanilla essence. Turn into a suitable container, chill, and freeze as described above, beating once while freezing.

Rich Vanilla Ice Cream

6 helpings

250ml double cream
250ml cold custard (2)
 (p1056)

1 × 5ml spoon vanilla
 essence
50g caster sugar

Whip the cream until semi-stiff. Add the cold custard, vanilla essence, and sugar. Turn into a suitable container, chill, and freeze as described on p1056, beating once while freezing.

Apricot Ice Cream

6 helpings

300g fresh apricots
75g caster sugar
125ml water
rind and juice of 1 lemon

yellow food colouring
250ml cold custard (1),
 (2) or (3) (p1056)
125ml double cream

Prepare the apricots. Put into a pan with the sugar, water, lemon rind and juice and a few drops of yellow food colouring. Allow to simmer until the fruit is tender. Rub through a nylon sieve or process in an electric blender, and leave to cool. Add the cold custard and turn into a container. Chill, then freeze for 1 hour. Beat the mixture until smooth, whip the cream lightly, and fold in. Finish freezing as described on p1056.

Blackcurrant Ice Cream

6 helpings

200g ripe blackcurrants
25g caster sugar
125ml water
rind and juice of 1 lemon

red food colouring
250ml cold custard (1),
 (2) or (3) (p1056)
125ml double cream

Put the blackcurrants, sugar, water, lemon rind and juice, and a few drops of red food colouring in a pan, and allow to simmer gently until the fruit is soft. Rub through a nylon sieve. Add the cold custard and turn into a container. Chill, then freeze for 1 hour. Beat the mixture until smooth, whip the cream lightly, and fold in. Finish freezing as described on p1056.

Brown Bread Ice Cream

6–8 helpings

150g brown
 breadcrumbs
500ml double cream

200g caster sugar
4 × 15ml spoons water

Put the breadcrumbs in a very cool oven at 120°C, Gas $\frac{1}{2}$, until dry. Whip the cream until it holds soft peaks, and mix in 150g of the sugar. Put into a refrigerator tray, cover with foil, and freeze for 1 hour. Melt the remaining sugar in the water over low heat, and leave until quite cold. Pour on to the breadcrumbs and fold the breadcrumb mixture into the half-frozen cream. Continue freezing for $1\frac{1}{2}$ hours.

Burnt Almond Ice Cream

6 helpings

50g blanched almonds
50g lump sugar
100ml single cream
750ml hot custard (3) or
 (4) (p1056)

1 × 15ml spoon Kirsch
 (optional)

Shred and bake the almonds until brown. Put the sugar and a few drops of water in a saucepan and boil until a deep golden colour. Add the cream, beat gently, and stir the mixture into the hot custard. Chill, then add the almonds and Kirsch, if used. Freeze as described on p1056, beating once while freezing.

Caramel Ice Cream

6 helpings

50g lump sugar
100ml single cream

750ml hot custard (2),
 (3) or (4) (p1056)

Put the sugar into a small saucepan with a few drops of water and boil until a deep golden colour. Stir in the cream, and when just back at boiling point, stir into the hot custard. Turn into a container, chill, and freeze as described on p1056, beating once while freezing.

Rich Chocolate Ice Cream

6–8 helpings

100g plain chocolate
65ml water
250ml hot custard (3) or
 (4) (p1056)

125ml double cream
1 × 5ml spoon vanilla
 essence

Break up the chocolate roughly and melt it in the water, either in a double saucepan or in a basin over hot water. Add the melted chocolate to the hot custard, and leave to cool. Whip the cream until semi-stiff and fold it into the custard mixture with the vanilla essence. Turn into a container, chill, and freeze as described on p1056, beating once while freezing.

Mocha Ice Cream

6 helpings

50g caster sugar
2 × 15ml spoons water
2 × 15ml spoons instant
 coffee powder

150g plain chocolate
3 egg yolks
250ml double cream

Mix the sugar, water, and coffee powder in a saucepan, bring to the boil, and boil for 1 minute. Break the chocolate into small pieces and melt it in the syrup in the pan. Cool, then stir in the egg yolks. Whip the cream until it holds soft peaks and fold in the chocolate mixture. Put into a refrigerator tray, cover with foil, chill, and freeze as described on p1056, beating once while freezing.

Coffee Ice Cream (1)

6 helpings

250ml double cream
250ml hot custard (1) or
 (2) (p1056)

2 × 15ml spoons strong
 black coffee
50g caster sugar

Whip the cream until semi-stiff. Add the hot custard, the coffee and sugar, and mix well. Turn into a suitable container, chill, and freeze as described on p1056, beating once while freezing.

Coffee Ice Cream (2)

6 helpings

3 × 15ml spoons instant
 coffee powder
65ml hot water

250ml double cream
75g caster sugar

Dissolve the coffee in the hot water and leave to cool. Whip the cream until semi-stiff, and add the sugar. Fold in the dissolved coffee. Turn into a suitable container, chill, and freeze as described on p1056, beating once while freezing.

White Coffee Ice Cream

6 helpings

1–2 × 15ml spoons
 freshly roasted coffee
 beans (to taste)

500ml milk
125ml double cream

Put the coffee beans and milk in a saucepan and bring almost to boiling point. Leave to infuse for 1 hour, keeping the milk hot, but not boiling. Strain, and use the milk to make one of the basic custards described on p1056. Leave the custard to cool. Whip the cream until semi-stiff, and fold into the custard. Turn into a suitable container, chill, and freeze as described on p1056, beating once while freezing.

Ginger Ice Cream

6 helpings

2 × 5ml spoons ground
 ginger
75g preserved ginger in
 syrup

250ml double cream
125ml cold custard (2)
 or (3) (p1056)
50g caster sugar

Dissolve the ground ginger in 65ml of the preserved ginger syrup. Dice the preserved ginger. Whip the cream until stiff and add the custard, ginger, syrup, and sugar. Turn into a suitable container, chill, and freeze as described on p1056, beating once while freezing.

Lemon Ice Cream

6 helpings

8 egg yolks
200g caster sugar
juice of 2 lemons
250ml double cream

Beat the egg yolks until very thick, add the sugar, and beat again. Stir in the lemon juice. Whip the cream until semi-stiff, and add carefully to the egg and sugar mixture. Turn into a suitable container, chill, and freeze for 30 minutes. Beat thoroughly, and finish freezing as described on p1056.

Strawberry or Raspberry Ice Cream

6 helpings

125ml milk
250ml double cream
2 egg yolks
150g caster sugar
400g strawberries **or** *raspberries*
1 × 15ml spoon granulated sugar
1 × 5ml spoon lemon juice
red food colouring

Put the milk and cream in a saucepan and bring almost to boiling point. Beat together the yolks and caster sugar, add to the milk and cream, and return to low heat, stirring all the time, until the mixture thickens. Rub the strawberries or raspberries through a nylon sieve. Fold the granulated sugar into the purée. Mix with the custard, and add lemon juice and a few drops of red food colouring. Turn into a suitable container, chill, and freeze as described on p1056, beating once while freezing.

Tea Ice Cream

6 helpings

250ml hot strong tea
50g caster sugar
65ml single cream
500ml cold custard (1), (2) **or** *(3)* (p1056)

Strain the tea, add the sugar, and leave to cool. Mix together with the cream and cold custard, turn into a suitable container, chill, and freeze as described on p1056, beating once while freezing.

Walnut Ice Cream

6 helpings

100g walnuts
1 × 10ml spoon orange flower water
1 × 5ml spoon vanilla essence
750ml cold custard (2), (3) **or** *(4)* (p1056)

Chop and pound the nuts, gradually adding the orange flower water to prevent them oiling. Add the vanilla essence to the cold custard, turn into a suitable container, chill, and freeze for 1 hour. Beat well, add the walnuts, and finish freezing as described on p1056.

Cottage Yoghurt Ice Cream

4 helpings

1 × 226g carton natural cottage cheese
125g thick natural yoghurt
2 × 15ml spoons clear honey

Sieve the cheese. Stir in the yoghurt and honey very gently, blending thoroughly. Turn into a freezer container with at least 2cm headspace, and leave to stand for 30 minutes. Freeze for 1 hour, or until the mixture is firm at the edges. Mash or beat very thoroughly with a fork. Continue freezing for 2 hours, or until just firm all through.

Note If left in the freezer, the ice cream will get progressively harder. To obtain the right consistency it will have to be thawed for 2–4 hours at room temperature, then refrozen for about 30 minutes.

Bombes

For the method of making bombes, see p1052. Suggested combinations of flavours are:

Bombe Diplomate

Line the mould with vanilla ice cream (p1056). Fill with vanilla iced mousse mixture (below), flavoured with maraschino, and mixed with crystallized fruit soaked in any liqueur.

Bombe Nesselrode

Line the mould with vanilla ice cream (p1056). Fill with vanilla iced mousse mixture (below), mixed with a purée of chestnuts and flavoured with Kirsch.

Bombe Tutti-frutti

Line the mould with strawberry ice cream (p1059). Fill with vanilla iced mousse mixture (below), mixed with chopped crystallized fruit soaked in any liqueur.

Bombe Formosa

Line the mould with vanilla ice cream (p1056). Fill with strawberry flavoured iced mousse mixture (below), and decorate with fresh strawberries.

Bombe Zamora

Line the mould with coffee ice cream (p1058). Fill with vanilla iced mousse mixture (below), flavoured with curaçao.

Bombe Czarine

Line the mould with vanilla ice cream (p1056). Fill with vanilla iced mousse mixture (below), flavoured with kümmel. Decorate with candied flowers.

Fancy Ice Creams and Iced Puddings

Basic Vanilla Iced Mousse Mixture

(for bombes, ice creams, etc)

4 helpings

25g icing sugar
125ml double cream

2 egg whites
vanilla essence

Sift the icing sugar. Whip the cream together with half the sugar. Whisk the egg whites until stiff, and fold in the remaining sugar. Carefully mix the cream and egg whites together, and add the vanilla essence. Turn into a suitable container and freeze.

VARIATIONS

Substitute other essences, spices or liqueurs for the vanilla essence.

Mousse with Glacé Fruit

Add 50g chopped glacé cherries, other glacé fruit or mixed fruit to the mixture with the vanilla essence. Use this mixture for the centre of an Italian *cassata*.

Banana Split

6 helpings

6 bananas
500ml vanilla ice cream
 (p1056)

250ml Melba sauce
 (p724)
50g chopped walnuts

Decoration
125ml double cream
sugar

6 maraschino cherries

Split the bananas in half lengthways and place in small oval dishes. Place 2 small scoops or slices of ice cream between the banana halves. Coat the ice cream with Melba sauce, and sprinkle with the chopped nuts. Whip the cream until stiff and sweeten to taste. Decorate with the cream and cherries.

Baked Alaska

6–8 helpings

3 egg whites
150g caster sugar
1 × 20cm round Genoese
  or *other sponge cake*

500ml vanilla ice cream
  (p1056)

Heat the oven to very hot, 230°C, Gas 8. Whisk the egg whites until very stiff, gradually whisk in half the sugar and fold in the rest. Alternatively, use the whites and sugar to make an Italian meringue (see p1024).

Place the sponge cake round on an ovenproof plate and pile the ice cream on to it, leaving 1cm sponge uncovered all round. Cover quickly with the meringue, making sure that both the ice cream and the sponge are completely covered. Put in the oven for 3–4 minutes until the meringue is just beginning to brown. Serve immediately.

Note The ice cream must be as hard as possible.

VARIATION

This dessert can be made with an oblong piece of sponge cake and a family brick of bought ice cream. Fresh or drained canned fruit can be laid on the sponge base before covering with the ice cream and meringue.

Omelette Soufflée en Surprise

6–8 helpings

1 × 20cm round Genoese
  or *other sponge cake*
1 × 15ml spoon liqueur
1 egg yolk
50g caster sugar
3 egg whites

vanilla essence
1 Nesselrode pudding
  (p1062) **or** *500ml*
  vanilla ice cream
  (p1056)
icing sugar

Decoration
glacé cherries   *angelica*

Place the cake on a silver or flameproof dish and soak with the liqueur. Heat the oven to very hot, 230°C, Gas 8. Whisk the egg yolk and sugar until thick. Whisk the egg whites until very stiff, and fold them into the yolks. Add a few drops of vanilla

essence and place this soufflé mixture in a piping bag with a large rose nozzle. Place the ice cream on top of the cake, and pipe the soufflé mixture over it, covering it completely. Dredge with icing sugar and put in the oven for 3 minutes. Decorate with glacé cherries and angelica, and serve immediately.

Knickerbocker Glory

6 helpings

1 × 500ml pkt yellow
  jelly
1 × 500ml pkt red
  jelly
200g canned peaches
200g canned pineapple
  chunks
150ml double cream

1 × 5ml spoon caster
  sugar
1 litre vanilla ice cream
  (p1056)
500ml Melba sauce
  (p724)
50g chopped mixed nuts

Decoration
6 maraschino cherries

Make the jellies according to the directions on the packet. Leave until set. Drain the peaches and pineapple chunks, chop them, and mix the fruit together. Whip the cream until stiff, and sweeten with the caster sugar. Chop the set jellies with a fork until well broken up.

Put 1 × 15ml spoon of fruit in each of 6 sundae glasses. Cover with 1 × 15ml spoon of yellow jelly, add a scoop of ice cream, and coat with the Melba sauce. Repeat the process using the red jelly. Sprinkle with the chopped nuts, and pipe a rose of whipped cream on top. Decorate each portion with a maraschino cherry.

Note Tall wine glasses can be used instead of sundae glasses.

Nesselrode Pudding

6 helpings

24 chestnuts	*250ml double cream*
250ml milk	*vanilla essence*
4 egg yolks	*50g glacé cherries*
150g caster sugar	

Parboil, shell, and peel the chestnuts (pp766–67). Simmer them in 125ml of the milk until tender. Rub through a fine sieve. Beat the egg yolks until liquid. Heat the rest of the milk almost to boiling point, add the yolks, and cook, stirring all the time, until the custard thickens. Do not let the mixture boil. Stir in the chestnut purée and the sugar. Cool. Whip half the cream until semi-stiff and add to the mixture with a few drops of vanilla essence. Cover, chill, and freeze until nearly set.

Wash, dry, and chop the cherries, whip the rest of the cream until stiff, and stir both into the pudding. Freeze until set, stirring frequently while the mixture freezes. Press into a 750ml mould, cover, and keep frozen until required.

Japanese Plombière

6 helpings

50g apricot jam	*100g macaroons*
lemon juice	*250ml double cream*
100g ground almonds	
500ml hot custard (3) or	
(4) (p1056)	

Decoration
12 ratafias

Make an apricot marmalade by boiling the apricot jam with a few drops of lemon juice until thick. Keep a little aside for decoration, and sieve the rest. Add with the ground almonds to the hot custard, and leave to cool. Crush the macaroons and whip the cream to the consistency of the custard. Add both to the custard. Turn into a suitable container, and chill until cold; then freeze for 2 hours.

To serve, scoop into balls, arrange in a pyramid, cover with the reserved apricot marmalade, and decorate with the ratafias.

Vanilla Plombière

6 helpings

500ml vanilla ice cream	*50g almonds*
(p1056)	*125ml double cream*

Partially freeze the ice cream for 1 hour. Chop the almonds, whip the cream until semi-stiff, and add both to the ice cream. Continue freezing for $1\frac{1}{2}$ hours.

Peach Melba (1)

6–8 helpings

4 firm ripe peaches	*250ml Melba sauce*
150ml vanilla syrup	(p724)
(p1138)	
250ml vanilla ice cream	
(p1056)	

Halve, stone, and peel the peaches; poach them gently in the vanilla syrup until tender. Drain off the syrup, and leave the peaches until completely cold. Line a well-chilled glass dish with a thick layer of ice cream, and arrange the peaches in the middle. Pour over the cold Melba sauce. Place the serving dish inside another dish containing crushed ice, and serve immediately.

Note This is the original dish created by Escoffier for Dame Nellie Melba. Another version can be made as follows:

Peach Melba (2)

6 helpings

500ml vanilla ice cream	*250ml Melba sauce*
(p1056)	(p724)
6 canned peaches	*125ml double cream*

Place a scoop or slice of ice cream in each of 6 sundae glasses. Cover each portion with a peach half. Coat with the Melba sauce. Whip the cream until stiff, and pipe a large rose on top of each portion.

Poire Belle Hélène

4 helpings

4 firm ripe pears
250ml vanilla ice cream
 (p1056)

250ml chocolate sauce (2)
 (p725)
125ml double cream

Decoration
25g crystallized violets

Peel the pears, cut them in half, and remove the cores. Place a scoop or slice of ice cream in each of 4 dishes. Top with the pear halves and mask with chocolate sauce. Whip the cream until stiff, and pipe a large rose on top of each portion. Decorate with the crystallized violets.

Neapolitan Ice

6 helpings

250ml double cream
250ml cold custard (3)
 (p1056)
125ml strawberry **or**
 raspberry purée
75g caster sugar
red food colouring
 (optional)

$\frac{1}{2} \times 2.5$ml spoon almond
 or ratafia essence
green food colouring
2×5ml spoons vanilla
 essence

Whip the cream until semi-stiff and fold into the cold custard. Divide this mixture into 3 equal portions. Mix the fruit purée with one-third of the mixture, and add 25g sugar and a few drops of red food colouring, if necessary. Add the almond or ratafia essence to another third of the mixture with a further 25g sugar and enough food colouring to tint it a bright but not vivid green. Add the vanilla essence and the last 25g sugar to the remaining third of the mixture. Cover, and freeze in separate trays until almost firm; then pack in layers in a suitable square or oblong mould. Cover and freeze until required. Serve cut in slices.

Milk Shakes

See pp1347–48.

Chocolate Freezer Pudding

6 helpings

100g butter
100g drinking chocolate
 powder
100g ground almonds
100g caster sugar

2×15ml spoons water
1 egg
100g Petit Beurre
 biscuits
fat for greasing

Decoration
whipped cream

Cream together the butter and chocolate powder. Work in the ground almonds. Put the sugar and water into a thick saucepan and heat gently until the sugar has melted. Cool, and then work into the butter mixture. Gradually beat in the egg until the mixture is light and creamy. Break the biscuits into small pieces and fold into the chocolate mixture. Pack into a greased freezer container, cover, and freeze.

To serve, thaw at room temperature for 45 minutes, and turn out on to a serving dish. Decorate with whipped cream.

Meringue Glacé Chantilly

8 helpings

250ml vanilla ice cream
 (p1056)
16 small meringue cases

125ml double cream
sugar

Decoration
8 maraschino cherries

Place a scoop or slice of ice cream in each of 8 small oval dishes. Set a meringue case on either side of the ice cream. Whip the cream until stiff and sweeten to taste. Pipe a large rose of the cream on top of the ice cream. Decorate with the maraschino cherries.

Ice Cream Soda

See p1348.

Strawberry Ice Cream Layer Gâteau

8–10 helpings

1 litre strawberry ice cream (p1059)	*25g soft light brown sugar*
1 litre lemon ice cream (p1059)	*250g strawberry jam*
125g digestive biscuits	*4 × 15ml spoons Kirsch*
50g chopped mixed nuts	*200ml double cream*
75g butter	*icing sugar*

Decoration
whole strawberries

Line an 18cm loose-bottomed, deep cake tin with vegetable parchment. Soften both ice creams. Crush the digestive biscuits with a rolling-pin. Put 25g crumbs aside with 25g of the nuts. Melt the butter, and mix in the rest of the crumbs and nuts, and the brown sugar. Press the mixture into the lined cake tin, and chill until firm.

Sieve the jam, and mix with 1 × 15ml spoon of the Kirsch. Mix the strawberries for the decoration with 1 × 15ml spoon Kirsch and a little icing sugar, if liked. Chill for at least 1 hour.

Cover the chilled biscuit crumb base with half the strawberry ice cream, and spread the top with a third of the jam. Sprinkle with one-third of the remaining crumbs and chopped nuts. Freeze until the ice cream is firm. Repeat the process with half the lemon ice cream, then with the rest of the ingredients until alternate layers of ice cream and jam, crumbs, and nuts have been formed. Freeze until each layer of ice cream is firm before adding the next.

Whip the cream until stiff with the remaining Kirsch, and icing sugar to taste. Remove the gâteau from the cake tin, and peel off the vegetable parchment. Put on to a suitable plate, and cover the top layer of lemon ice cream with the whipped cream. Decorate with the strawberries, chill again, and serve.

Note It is easier not to try and detach the crumb base from the bottom of the cake tin; simply put the gâteau on the plate with the bottom of the tin still in place.

Coupe Jacques

6 helpings

50g grapes	*250ml lemon water ice* (p1054) **or** *vanilla ice cream* (p1056)
1 banana	
1 peach	
50g raspberries	*250ml strawberry ice cream* (p1059)
2 × 15ml spoons Kirsch	

Decoration
125ml double cream   *sugar*

Chop and mix the fruit; soak in the Kirsch for 4 hours. Place one portion of each ice in each of 6 sundae glasses. Cover with the soaked fruit. Whip the cream until soft and sweeten to taste. Decorate each portion with the cream.

FRESH FRUIT AND NUTS

Mixed fruits of the larger sort are now frequently served on one dish. This mode admits of the display of much taste in the arrangement of the fruit: for instance, a pine in the centre of the dish, surrounded with large plums of various sorts and colours, mixed with pears, rosy-cheeked apples, all arranged with a due regard to colour, have a very good effect. Again, apples and pears look well mingled with plums and grapes, hanging from the border of the dish in a *négligé* sort of manner, with a large bunch of the same fruit lying on the top of the apples.

This chapter is intended as a brief guide to the use and preparation of fresh fruit and nuts for dessert and basic cookery purposes.

Fruit

The less common fruits available in the UK are described in extra detail, and where different varieties of a particular fruit are suitable for different purposes, as in the case of dessert and cooking apples, some of the most common varieties are listed here.

The preparation of the more usual fruits for stewing and for fruit salad are described in the chapter on Cold Puddings and Desserts; cross-references are given where necessary. Fruit jams, preserves, bottling, and wines are treated in the relevant chapters, and recipes for these can be found by reference to the Index. Freezing techniques are described on pp1393–95.

GLOSSARY OF FRUITS

Apple

Colour and taste vary according to variety: different varieties are available all year round.

Dessert

Varieties: Cox's Orange Pippin, Worcester Permain, Golden Delicious, Egremont, Jonathan, Granny Smith, Russet, Charles Ross, Fortune, James Grieve.

Preparation: Wash, dry, and polish with a soft cloth. For fruit salad, see p1003.

Cooking

Varieties: Bramley's Seedling, Lane's Prince Albert, James Grieve, Blenheim Orange, Lord Derby.

Preparation: For stewing, see p1001. For fritters, see p946.

Apricot

Round, plum-sized, orange-yellow stone fruit, available in late summer.

Dessert

Varieties: Helmskirk, Moorpark, Alfred, and Farmingdale.

Preparation: Wipe, and peel at the table if desired. Choose fruit that is ripe but not over-ripe; under-ripe apricots are hard and tasteless, and if over-ripe the fruit is soft and mushy, with an unpleasant texture. For fruit salad, see p1003.

Cooking

Variety: Clingstone (dessert varieties can also be used).

Preparation: For stewing, see p1001.

Banana

The long, straight, yellow variety most commonly sold in the UK are less sweet than the smaller, curved Canary bananas. Both are available all year round.

Dessert

Preparation: Buy bananas from a bunch rather than loose, and avoid fruit with black spots on the skin. Wipe, and peel at the table. For fruit salad, see p1003; choose under-ripe bananas as they slice more easily.

Cooking

Preparation: Use peeled, whole or sliced. For fritters, see p946.

Bilberry

Blue-black, small, round berries with an acid, slightly bitter taste, available during July–August.

Dessert

Preparation: Not generally used for dessert, but can be eaten raw with cream and sugar. Remove stalks and leaves, and discard any unsound fruit.

Cooking

Preparation: As for dessert. For stewing, see p1001.

Blackberry

Available wild or cultivated during August–September.

Dessert

Preparation: Use cultivated fruit. Remove stalks and leaves, and discard any unsound berries; rinse and pat dry. Use also for fruit salad.

Cooking

Preparation: Use wild or cultivated fruit, and prepare as for dessert. For stewing, see p1001; if cooked for a purée, the fruit must be sieved after cooking.

Blackcurrants

See Currants (p1067).

Blueberry

Similar in appearance and taste to bilberries, but larger. Available wild or cultivated during August–September.

Varieties: Gold Traube, Jersey, Earliblue.

Dessert

Preparation: See Bilberry.

Cooking

Preparation: See Bilberry.

Cherry

According to variety, cherries range in colour from dark red to almost black, or pale yellow with red mottling. Home-grown fruit are available from early June until late July; imported varieties from April until August.

Dessert

Varieties: Bigarreau Napoleon, Early Rivers, Elton Heart, Roundel Heart.
    Preparation: Remove stalks and leaves, and discard any unsound fruit. Rinse and pat dry. For fruit salad, see p1003.

Cooking

Variety: Morello
    Preparation: As for dessert; remove stones if desired. For stewing, see p1001. For fritters see p946.

Cherry Plum

See Plum (p1074).

Chinese Gooseberry

(Kiwi Fruit)

Brown, hairy, sausage-shaped fruit about 5cm long, with green flesh, available July–February. The flavour is similar to that of a ripe gooseberry.

Dessert

Preparation: Rub off the hairs from the outer skin. The fruit is peeled at the table if desired, before scooping out the flesh with a small spoon. For fruit salad, see p1003.

Cooking

Preparation: Peel, and use for chutney.

Cranberry

Cranberries range in colour from pink to deep red; the cherry-sized fruit has an acrid and slightly bitter flavour and is unpleasant eaten raw. Available August–September.

Dessert

Not used.

Cooking

Variety: Early Black.
    Preparation: Rinse, drain, and use for jellies and sauces.

Cumquat

See Orange (p1072).

Currants

Red and white currants are the size of small peas and have a sharp, acid flavour. Blackcurrants are sweeter, with a pleasant smell. All currants are rich in vitamin C. Available June–August.

Varieties: Laxton's No. 1, Red Lake, Random (red); White Versailles (white); Baldwin, Wellington XXX, Boskoop Giant, Tenah (black). These can be used for both dessert and cooking.

Dessert

Preparation: Remove stalks and leaves, and discard any unsound fruit; rinse and pat dry. Blackcurrants must be topped and tailed. Use also for fruit salad.

Cooking

Preparation: As for dessert, but if the fruit is cooked for a purée it must be sieved after cooking to remove the seeds. For fritters, see p946.

Custard Apple

An almost round fruit, up to 10cm across, with a green skin pitted with U-shaped warts. The fruit itself is white, with black seeds, and the flavour is pleasantly acid and aromatic. Available September–February.

Dessert

Preparation: Wipe, and remove skin and seeds at the table.

Cooking

Not used.

Damson

See Plum (p1074).

Date

Brownish-red, sausage-shaped fruit, 2–5cm long, with sweet, firm flesh and a long, narrow stone. Fresh dates are obtainable from September–February, but preserved dates are sold all year round, whole in boxes or in compressed blocks.

Dessert

Preparation: Pick over fresh dates and discard any damaged fruit. Serve whole, with a spoon, and remove skins at the table if desired. Preserved dates in boxes should be served with a fork.

Cooking and other Uses

Preparation: Remove skins from fresh dates if required. Chop stoned preserved dates with a hot, wet knife.

Elderberry

Small, round, black fruit, usually found growing wild in August–September, very rich in vitamin C. Elderberries are not generally eaten raw, but can be cooked (usually with apples) and are used in wine-making. For preparation, see Currants (p1067).

Fig

Pear-shaped, brownish-red, green or purple fruit, with a sweet, juicy flavour when ripe. Fresh figs are available during August–November, and dried figs all year round.

Varieties: Brown Turkey, Negro Lango, White Marseilles.

Dessert

Preparation: Wipe gently, and peel fresh figs at the table. Wash and dry dried figs to remove any dirt.

Cooking and other Uses

Preparation: Peel fresh figs thinly, if liked. Chop dried figs as for dried dates.

Gooseberry

Large, round or oval berry, smooth or hairy according to variety. The colour also varies with the variety and stage of ripeness of the fruit; green, yellow and reddish-green varieties are all common. Available June–August.

Dessert

Varieties: Leveller, Lancashire Lad, Whinham's Industry.

Preparation: Pick over the ripe fruit, avoiding over-ripe, squashy berries, or those with splits and blemishes on the skin. Rinse lightly and pat dry. Top and tail for fruit salad.

Cooking

Varieties: Keepsake, Careless, Whitesmith, Green Gem.

Preparation: For stewing, see p1001. If cooked for a purée, the fruit must be sieved after cooking. For fritters, see p946.

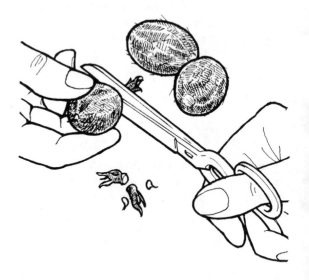

Granadilla

(Passion-fruit)

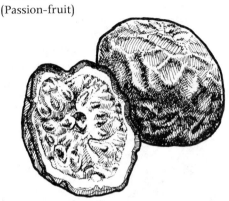

Greenish, oval fruit up to 25 ×15cm in size. The skin deepens in colour to dark purple when ripe, and the flesh is white, with dark seeds which are eaten with the flesh. Available September–January.

Dessert

Preparation: Wipe the fruit. For eating, the fruit is cut open and the flesh and seeds eaten with a spoon.

Cooking and other Uses

Preparation: Split open and scoop out the flesh, for use in jams, etc. The uncooked flesh is also used for flavouring desserts, ice cream, and drinks.

Grape

Grapes can be green, pink or dark purple, according to variety, and the size varies from 1.5–4cm in length. 'White' grapes are, in fact, pale green in colour. Available almost all year round.

Varieties: Black Hamburgh, Muscat of Alexandria, Muscat Hamburgh.

Dessert

Preparation: Pick over, discarding any damaged fruit, and rinse lightly on the bunch without making the leaves sodden. Serve in bunches, with grape scissors for cutting. For fruit salad, see p1003.

Cooking and other Uses

Preparation: Rinse, remove pips with a pin or skewer, or halve and de-pip. Peel if required by covering with boiling water for 5 seconds, draining and covering with cold water. The grapes should then peel easily.

Grapefruit

Large, spherical, yellow citrus fruit, up to 13cm in diameter. There is also a variety with pinkish-yellow skin and delicate pale pink flesh. *Uglis* or *tangelos* are grapefruit-tangerine hybrids, slightly smaller than grapefruit and greenish-yellow, with few pips. Available all year round.

First Course and Dessert

Preparation: See p308.

Cooking

Preparation: Peel, removing all the white pith; then cut out the flesh segments, removing the pips and membranes.

Greengage
See Plum (p1074).

Guava

Round or oval fruit, 4–8cm long, with a thin skin, cream or pinkish flesh, and many small seeds. Available during autumn.

Dessert

Preparation: Wipe, then split the fruit and scoop out the flesh at the table.

Cooking

Preparation: Split, and remove the flesh from the skin. Use to make jelly.

Japanese Wineberry

Small, round, bright orange fruit with a hairy calyx. It is not grown commercially, but is ripe in August–September. For preparation, see Cranberry (p1067).

Kiwi Fruit

See Chinese Gooseberry (p1067).

Lemon

An acid fruit, with smooth, oily skin. Varieties with rougher, thick skins tend to be less juicy. Available all year round.

Dessert

Not used.

Cooking and other Uses

Preparation: Wipe or rinse, and pat dry. Cut in segments or slices, as desired, removing the pips. For decorative lemon garnishes, see pp391–92. Lemon rind, either grated or thinly pared, is used for flavouring. Lemons are also used in making marmalade and preserves.

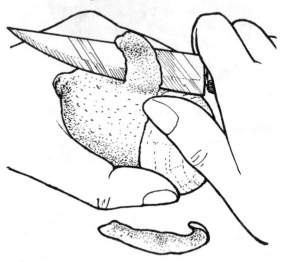

Lime

Similar to a lemon, but smaller and more sharply flavoured, with a thinner, green skin. Available all year round. For preparation, see Lemon.

Loganberry

Burgundy-red, juicy fruit like a large raspberry in shape, but with its own distinctive flavour. Available July–August.

Dessert

Preparation: Pick over and remove stalks, leaves, and any unsound fruit, then hull. For fruit salad, see p1003.

Cooking

Preparation: As for dessert.

Loquat

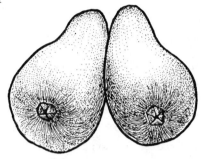

Small, pear-shaped, orange-coloured fruit about 3cm long, with a tart but refreshing flavour. It is seldom available in shops.

Dessert

Preparation: Pick over and serve whole. The skin is removed at the table.

Cooking

Not used.

Lychee

Round, cherry-sized fruit with a thin, hard, scaly outer shell. This is green at first, but gradually turns pink and then brown. Lychees are available fresh in December–February, and canned all year round.

Dessert

Preparation: Pick over. The skin and stones are removed at the table. Lychees are not generally cooked, but are used, skinned and stoned, in uncooked desserts. For fruit salad, see p1003.

Mango

The fruit is oval, about the size of a pear, with a green skin which turns orange-yellow when ripe. The flesh is pale orange. Available January–September.

Dessert

Preparation: Wipe, cut in half, and remove the stone at the table. For fruit salad, see p1003.

Cooking

Preparation: Peel, stone, and use for chutney.

Medlar

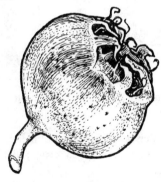

Round, brown fruit, flattened at the top, 3–5cm across. Though seldom available in shops, its season is November. In the UK the fruit is picked when ripe and allowed to become soft before eating.

Dessert

Preparation: Wipe, and serve whole. The flesh is squeezed out into a spoon.

Cooking

Preparation: Squeeze out flesh into a bowl or spoon, or cut up. Use for jellies.

Melon

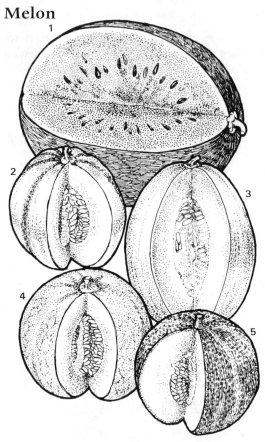

1 Watermelon; 2 Charentais; 3 Honeydew; 4 Ogen; 5 Cantaloup

The most widely available types of melon are:

1) Watermelon – dark green skin, red flesh and black seeds
2) Honeydew – yellow skin, green or pinkish flesh
3) Ogen – yellow to orange skin, marked with pale green stripes, pale yellow flesh
4) Cantaloup – rough greenish-yellow skin, orange-yellow, scented flesh
5) Tiger – a type of Cantaloup, with smooth skin and vivid orange flesh
6) Charentais – slightly rough, greenish-yellow skin, deep orange, faintly scented flesh.
7) Galia – small, with greenish skin and green flesh.

Watermelons are available from May until September, and the other types generally throughout the year, according to variety.

First Course and Dessert

Preparation: See p309. For fruit salad, see p1003.

Cooking and other Uses

Preparation: Remove the peel and seeds, and cut in pieces. Use for marmalade.

Mulberry

Very deep red berries, similar in shape to large loganberries, available in August–September, but not grown commercially. For preparation for dessert and cooking, see Loganberry (p1070).

Nectarine
See Peach (p1073).

Orange and its hybrids

Oranges are available all year round; tangerines and hybrids generally from November–February. The size of the fruit varies according to the variety. *Jaffa* are the largest, with a thick skin and sweet flesh; *Navels* are similar, but smaller. *Valencia* and *Blood* oranges are small and sweet-fleshed, while *Sevilles* are small and bitter, used almost exclusively for making marmalade. *Cumquats* are very small, elongated and slightly bitter, with yellowish skins. *Tangerines* are small, flattish, with loose skins, and are sweet and juicy with many pips. *Naartjes, Mandarins*, and *Satsumas* are similar in appearance and shape, but satsumas have paler skins and no pips. *Clementines* and *Ortaniques* are orange/tangerine hybrids with the same flattened shape, and sweet, juicy flesh.

Dessert

Preparation: Wash, dry, and polish with a soft cloth. The fruit is peeled and the pips and membranes removed at the table. For fruit salad, see p1003.

Cooking and other Uses

Preparation: As for dessert; use segments whole or chopped. The rind, grated or thinly pared, is used for flavouring. For fritters, see p946.

Papaya
(Pawpaw)

Pear-shaped, 15–35cm across, with a greenish skin, turning to yellow when ripe. The flesh is creamy-yellow, with a large seed in the centre. It can be obtained all year round, but is not widely available. For preparation for dessert and cooking, see Melon (p1072).

Passion-fruit
See Granadilla (p1069).

Peach and Nectarine

Round fruit, up to 12cm across, varying in colour from pale green to yellow-red according to variety. Peaches have slightly hairy bloom; nectarines are smooth. Home-grown peaches are available May–October, and nectarines July–September, but imported varieties can be purchased all year round. Popular varieties of peach are: Hales' Early, Peregrine, Rochester. Popular nectarine varieties: Napier, John Rivers. For preparation for dessert and cooking, see Apricot (p1065).

Pear

Shape and colour vary according to variety; different varieties are available all year round.

Varieties: Conference, Doyenne du Comice, William, Bon Chretien (Bartlett).

Dessert

Preparation: See Apple (p1065). For fruit salad, see p1003.

Cooking
Preparation: See Apple (p1065).

Persimmon

Round, pinkish-red fruits, 5–8cm across, with silky hairs on the rind. The flesh is white and firm, with 4 large seeds. Although the flavour is sweet, the smell is unpleasant. Available October–January.

Dessert

Preparation: Wipe. Skin and seeds are removed at the table.

Cooking

Preparation: Remove skin and seeds. The flesh can be pulped if required. Used in jams and jellies.

Pineapple

Similar in shape to a giant fir-cone, with orange-coloured skin divided into segments. The crest of spiky green leaves on the top should be stiff; if wilting, the fruit is over-ripe. Available all year round.

Dessert

Preparation: Cut off the leaf crest in one piece. The fruit is then cut into slices for serving and the skin removed at the table. For fruit salad, and for other ways of preparing a pineapple, see pp1003–05.

Cooking and other Uses

Preparation: Remove leaf crest, skin, and woody 'eyes', then chop the flesh to the size and shape required.

Plum, Damson, Greengage, and Cherry Plum

Plums can be egg-shaped or spherical, and vary widely in colour according to variety. *Greengages* are a type of plum, green in colour and used for dessert cooking; *damsons* and *cherry plums* are generally used only for cooking. Plums, greengages, and damsons are available during July–October, cherry plums during July–September.

Dessert

Varieties: Coe's Golden Drop, Denniston's Superb, Victoria, Pond's Seedling, Quetsche (the last two also used for drying).

   Preparation: Wash, dry, and polish with a soft cloth if large; pat dry if small. The skin and stones are removed at the table. For fruit salad, see p1003.

Cooking

Varieties: Czar, Pershore Yellow Egg, Purple Pershore, Victoria.

   Preparation: For stewing, see p1001.

Pomegranate

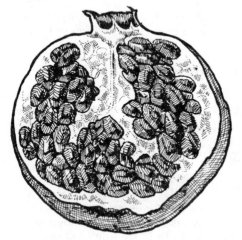

Apple-sized fruit, with a tough, reddish skin and red flesh, containing many seeds. Available October–November.

Dessert

Preparation: Rinse, dry, and polish gently with a soft cloth. The flesh and seeds are generally scooped from the skin with a spoon, and both are eaten.

Cooking and other Uses

Preparation: The skin is removed and the juice and seeds used. Seeds can be used alone for garnishing, and the juice is used to flavour ices, drinks, and grenadine syrup.

Quince

The true quince resembles a large, yellow pear, while the Japanese quince, fruit of the ornamental japonica tree, is smaller and rounded, with yellow or yellowish-green fruit. Quinces ripen in early October, but are not usually available commercially.

Dessert

Quinces are not generally used for dessert, but the true quince can, sometimes, be eaten raw, with cheese.

Cooking

Varieties: Portugal, Vranja.

   Preparation: Peel if desired, cut off the stem end, and cut into suitable portions, or core. Used mainly in preserves and jellies.

Raspberry

Usually a rich red berry, though yellow varieties are sometimes seen. Home-grown fruit are available from June–September, but imported raspberries have a longer season.

Varieties: Glen Cova, Lloyd George, Malling Exploit, Malling Promise, Norfolk Giant, Zeva. These can also be used for cooking.

Dessert

Preparation: See Loganberry (p1070). For fruit salad, see p1003.

Cooking

Preparation: See Loganberry (p1070).

Redcurrants

See Currants (p1067).

Rhubarb

Stem of a herbaceous plant, the leaves of which are poisonous. Forced rhubarb, available from December–March, has slender, pale pink stems and thin skin. Home-grown, outdoor rhubarb, available from March–June, has fatter stems of green suffused with red, and thicker, sometimes stringy, skin.

Dessert

Not used.

Cooking

Preparation: For stewing, see p1001. Also used in jam and wine-making.

Rose-hip

Fruit of the rose. Round or elongated in shape according to the type of rose. The hips are scarlet in colour, smooth, and have a high vitamin C content. Available September–November.

Dessert

Not used.

Cooking

Preparation: Wash, top and tail. Used largely to make jellies and syrup.

Rowan-berry

(Mountain Ash)

Available wild largely in Scotland. Berries are small, round and red, and grow in bunches. At their ripest between September and October.

Dessert

Not used.

Cooking

Preparation: Remove stalks. Use to make jellies.

Sloe

Purple fruit of the blackthorn tree, resembling a bilberry in colour and shape. It is found wild in September.

Dessert

Not used.

Cooking

Preparation: See Bilberry (p1066). Used largely for wine-making.

Strawberry

Round or pointed rich red fruit, 1–8cm across; size, shape, and flavour depend on variety. Imported or forced strawberries are available almost all year round, but home-grown fruit are at their best from May–August.

Dessert

Varieties: Cambridge Favourite, Cambridge Vigour, Grandee, Red Gauntlet, Royal Sovereign, Talisman.

   Preparation: Pick over, removing leaves and any damaged fruit. Hull, and rinse lightly, if necessary. Pat dry and serve whole, sprinkled with sugar, if liked. For fruit salad, see p1003.

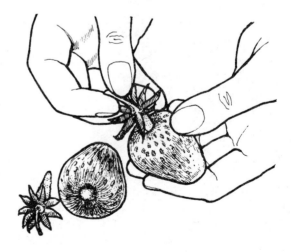

Cooking

Preparation: As for dessert.

Tangelo

See Grapefruit (p1069).

Tangerine

See Orange (p1072).

Ugli

See Grapefruit (p1069).

Youngberry

Similar to Loganberry, but smaller. Available during August–September, but not grown commercially. For preparation for dessert and cooking, see Loganberry (p1070).

Nuts

Nuts can be eaten for dessert, and are also used widely in cooking. The preparation of nuts for cakes, and as garnishes and decorations for savoury and sweet dishes is described in the appropriate chapters; cross-references are given where necessary.

Nuts have a high food value, and are particularly important in vegetarian cookery. Recipes for vegetarian recipes, such as Nut Galantine and Nut Mince, are given in the chapter on Vegetables, and more can be found by reference to the Index.

GLOSSARY OF NUTS

Almond

Almonds come in both bitter and sweet varieties; bitter almonds are considered to be poisonous; sweet almonds are used for cooking. To skin, blanch, split, and roast almonds, see p1185. Almonds are widely used, whole or ground, in confectionery and as a garnish (p394).

Brazil Nut

A three-sided nut with a very hard outer shell and firm, white flesh, imported from South America during November–January. They are generally eaten raw, for dessert, but are also used in confectionery.

Cashew Nut

This white, kidney-shaped nut grows at the base of the small, apple-like fruit of the cashew tree. The nuts, which have a particularly delicate flavour, are imported either canned, or loose, and sold lightly roasted.

Chestnut

A brown, smooth nut, available from October–December, which is one of the most versatile of all nuts. Chestnuts are not usually eaten raw, but can be served for dessert roasted, then peeled at the table. Prick skins with a skewer before roasting, or the nuts will explode in the oven. To prepare, boil, and purée chestnuts for use as a vegetable, see pp766–67. Chestnut purée is also used in sweet recipes, and whole chestnuts are preserved in sugar to make *marrons glacés*.

Cobs, Filberts, and Hazelnuts

Cobs and hazelnuts are round, about 2cm in diameter, and with short husks. A filbert is larger and longer. Available October–January. They are eaten raw for dessert, and used in cakes or as a garnish. To skin, see p1185.

Coconut

A large nut, the size of a baby's head, with a hard shell, white flesh and a hollow centre, which in unripe nuts contains milky juice. Available all year round. To extract the flesh from a fresh coconut, pierce the 'eyes' in the coconut shell with a screwdriver, and drain off the milk. Open the nut with a hammer or saw it in half. Extract the flesh with a sharp knife and pare off the dark skin. Coconut milk can be used as a drink, or for flavouring certain dishes such as curries or soups. The flesh can be dried and shredded to make desiccated coconut, for use in many cakes, puddings, and biscuits. To colour and toast coconut flesh for use as a decoration, see p1235.

Macadamia Nut
(Queensland Nut)

Round, with a hard shell and a firm, white flesh, about 2cm thick, this nut is usually imported in tins; not widely available. It has a delicious flavour, and is eaten raw.

Peanut
(Monkey nut, Groundnut)

The peanut has a wrinkled, straw-coloured, oblong, brittle pod, and the nut itself is red skinned, with a white interior. Available all year round. Serve raw in the shell, or lightly roasted for dessert. Roasted salted peanuts can be bought in packets or cans. To skin and roast peanuts for use in cakes, salads or as a garnish, proceed as for hazelnuts (p1185).

Pine Kernel
(Pignoli)

First popular in Roman times mixed with honey, pine kernels are more frequently used nowadays in the preparation of cakes and sauces. They are very small, are nutty and greasy in texture, and are sold when they have become a creamy white colour.

Pistachio Nut

The pistachio nut is the seed of a tree native to southern Europe, and has a hard shell with a greenish, oval kernel. It can be eaten for dessert, or, if salted, with drinks. It is also widely used as a garnish or decoration, or as a flavouring for ice cream. To blanch and skin pistachio nuts, proceed as for hazelnuts (p1185).

Walnut and Pecan

Walnuts have a round or oval, hard, corrugated shell. Pecans are long, with a smooth shell. Both can be served for dessert. For Pickled Walnuts (p1144), the whole, green nut is used before the shell has begun to form. Chopped or whole walnuts and pecans are also used in confectionery and as a garnish.

HOME-MADE SWEETS

Sugar was first known as a drug, and used by the apothecaries, and with them was a most important article. At its first appearance, some said it was heating; others, that it injured the chest; others, that it disposed persons to apoplexy; the truth, however, soon conquered these fancies, and the use of sugar has increased every day, and there is no household in the civilized world which can do without it.

Many people would like to try their hand at sweet-making but hesitate to do so because they think it is difficult and that elaborate equipment is required. Uncooked sweets are quite easy for even a beginner to make; and for more elaborate ones the only really essential piece of equipment is a sugar boiling thermometer (saccharometer) which takes all the guesswork out of sweet-making. However, if you want to make sweets often or in quantity, it is worthwhile buying some extra equipment.

EQUIPMENT FOR SWEET-MAKING

Sugar boiling thermometer: The markings should be clear and register up to 200°C. The thermometer is usually mounted on a metal frame with a handle at the top, and a movable clip that fits on the side of the saucepan. After buying a thermometer, put it in a saucepan of cold water, heat slowly to boiling point and check that it reads 100°C. Leave the thermometer to cool in the water. When using the thermometer, place it in a jug of warm water while the sugar is dissolving. When placing it in the saucepan, make sure the bulb is wholly covered by the mixture. To get an accurate reading, hold the thermometer at eye level. Once the correct temperature is reached, return the thermometer to the jug of warm water. Always wash it well after use to dissolve any syrup on it.

Saucepan: Choose a strong, thick-based saucepan to prevent sticking and burning. Make sure it is large enough because sugar tends to rise very quickly during cooking. Some older enamel pans are not suitable, as the high temperature of the sugar syrup may damage the surface.

Scraper: This makes the turning of fondant much easier. It is a piece of metal about 10×7cm, with either a wooden handle or a piece of the metal turned over in a curve, to form a handle.

Marble slab: This is expensive to buy and not really necessary since large china or earthenware dishes can be used instead, eg a large meat platter. An enamel tray can be used for cooling fondant syrup, but plastic surfaces should be avoided as they can only withstand a temperature of about 140°C.

Fondant mat: This is a sheet of rubber about 2cm deep, with fancy shapes inset, into which the liquid fondant, jelly or chocolate is poured and then allowed to set. When the sweets are set, they can be removed by bending back the rubber.

Dipping forks: These are metal forks with 2–3 prongs or a loop at the end. They are useful for lifting sweets out of a coating mixture and for decorating the tops of chocolates.

Metal rings: A ring of metal about 1.5cm in diameter and 2cm deep. These rings are used mostly for shaping peppermint creams and setting jelly sweets.

RULES FOR SUGAR BOILING

1) Always put the liquid into the pan first, before the sugar.

2) Always allow the sugar to dissolve completely before bringing the syrup to the boil; one or two grains of undissolved sugar can wholly spoil the texture of a sweet. To speed up the process, tap the bottom of the saucepan with a wooden spoon and draw the spoon through the sugar. Take great care, or the syrup will swirl up, splash on the sides of the saucepan and crystallize.

3) If crystals do form on the sides of the saucepan, brush the sides with a clean pastry brush dipped in cold water. If this is not done, sweets which should be clear and smooth may be sugary and rough when finished.

4) When boiling to a particular temperature, do not stir unless the recipe says so. Where milk or treacle is used, it may need stirring gently to prevent burning. In fudge and caramel mixtures, you will often need to stir near the end of the cooking time to get a grainy consistency.

5) Once the sugar is dissolved and the syrup is brought to the boil, heat very rapidly to the required temperature. As soon as this temperature is reached, remove the pan from the heat and stand the bottom of the saucepan in cold water for a few seconds. This will prevent the temperature rising any further.

Degrees for Sugar Boiling

The different degrees to which sugar is boiled are:

Thread	102°–103°C
Pearl	104°–105°C (seldom used)
Blow	110°–112°C (seldom used)
Soft ball	115°C
Hard ball	120°C
Small crack	140°C
Large crack	155°C
Caramel	177°C

Simple Tests

A sugar boiling thermometer gives exact temperatures, but sugar can be boiled and the degree gauged approximately by using the following tests:

Thread: Dip the handles of two wooden spoons into oil, then into the boiling syrup, then into cold water. If, on immediately separating the handles, the syrup is drawn into a fine thread, the sugar is boiled to the required temperature.

Pearl: Proceed as above but boil the syrup for 2–3 minutes longer before testing. The thread will be pulled a little longer without breaking.

Blow: Dip the top of a metal skewer in the syrup, drain over the saucepan, and blow through the hole. A small bubble should form which floats in the air for a second.

Soft ball: Pour a little of the syrup in a cup of cold water. If it can be rolled into a soft ball with the fingers, the correct temperature has been reached. The temperature can be tested as for the blow but instead of a bubble, the syrup will be blown into small irregular 'feathers'. This is sometimes called the 'feather' stage.

Hard ball: Proceed as above but boil for 2–3 minutes longer. A larger, harder ball will be formed on testing.

Small crack: A few drops of syrup in cold water will soon become brittle and a thin piece will snap.

Large crack: Proceed as above but boil for 2–3 minutes longer. The syrup will be very brittle and will not stick to the teeth when bitten.

Caramel: The syrup changes colour to become 'caramel'; the longer it boils, the darker it becomes. Remove the pan from the heat as soon as the syrup begins to darken, since it can then overcook in seconds. It cannot be used for sweets if it reaches a temperature above 177°C, as it will taste burnt. (Burnt caramel or Black Jack is used as food colouring; see p1081.)

How to 'Pull' Sugar

In some sweet recipes, the boiled sugar mixture is 'pulled' while still warm and pliable, to give it a satiny, shiny look.

When the syrup has reached the correct temperature, pour the mixture on to an oiled, heat-resisting surface. Allow the syrup to settle for a few minutes until a skin has formed, then using two oiled palette knives, turn the mixture sides to the centre until it cools enough to handle. Working quickly, pull the syrup between the hands into a sausage shape, fold in the ends, twist and pull again. Repeat the pulling until the candy has a shiny surface. When it is beginning to harden, shape it into a long rope as thick as needed, and cut quickly into small pieces with oiled scissors. If all the mixture cannot be pulled at once, leave it on an oiled tin in a warm place to keep soft. Several colours can be introduced by dividing the hot sugar mixture into different portions to cool and adding a few drops of colouring to each portion. Pull these separately, then lay them together for the final pulling and shaping. One portion may be left unpulled and clear and added at the final stage of shaping.

Note When working with pulled sugar, it is necessary to oil one's hands well to prevent burning.

INGREDIENTS

Apart from sugar, the following are also used:

Gum Arabic

This is used for mock crystallizing, for giving a bright finish to marzipan sweets and in some jelly-type sweet centres. At one time, it could be bought in crystal form from a chemist, but it is now difficult to obtain except from a specialist supplier, and it is very expensive. To use, dissolve 25g gum arabic in 50ml warm water. Stir, then strain through wet muslin into a screw-top jar. Keep covered. The solution will keep for months, but a mould may appear on the surface. It is quite harmless and can be removed easily before using.

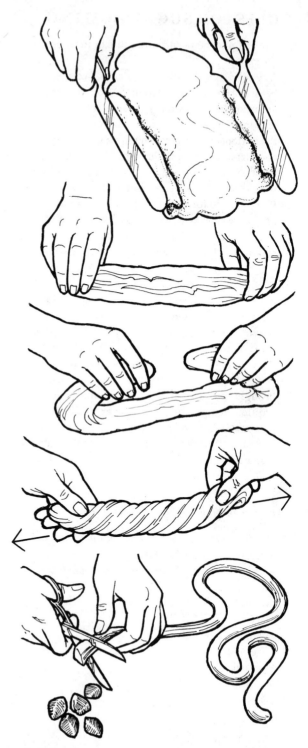

Pulling sugar

Stock Syrup(1)

Stock syrup is added to fondant, when melting, to obtain the correct consistency. It is made by dissolving 400g of granulated sugar in 250ml water. Bring to the boil, and boil to 104°C. Strain through wet muslin or a jelly bag into a wide-mouthed jar with a stopper or screw-top.

Note For Stock Syrup (2), see p1227.

Glucose

The glucose used in sweet-making is a thick colourless liquid; it must not be confused with powdered glucose. When added to sugar syrups, it prevents crystallization. It is obtainable from some chemists. If stored in a screw-top jar, it will keep indefinitely. Cream of tartar or tartaric acid can be used instead of liquid glucose, but the results are not as good.

Burnt Caramel or Black Jack

This is used for colouring. It is made by boiling together 100g lump sugar and 50ml water until they are black. The syrup will become thin and will smoke. At this stage, remove the saucepan from the heat and very gradually pour in another 50ml of hot water. Reboil; the burnt sugar will dissolve into a thin syrup. Leave to cool and pour into a bottle.

SETTING TIMES FOR SWEETS

Sweets vary widely in the time they take to set, depending on their size, shape and thickness, and it is therefore not possible to give accurate setting times in most of the following recipes. As a rule, sweets are best set in a cool place, but not in a refrigerator. Always make sure that they are fully set before packing them; an outer layer or coating may be set, for instance, before the inside is firm.

PACKING AND STORING SWEETS

Careful packing adds to the appeal of sweets. Boiled sweets, toffees, and caramels become sticky when exposed to the air, so should be put in an airtight container, wrapped in waxed paper, transparent cellulose paper or foil. Fudges, fondants, marzipan sweets, and chocolates need no special wrapping, but can be put into small paper sweet cases; they should be stored in an airtight tin lined with waxed paper. Home-made sweets, when attractively packed, make delightful gifts.

USES FOR SWEETS

Some sweets such as barley sugar can provide energy between meals. Others are often offered with after-dinner coffee. Marzipan sweets, truffles and peppermint creams are especially popular as after-dinner sweetmeats.

TOFFEES, CARAMELS AND FUDGES

Simplest Ever Toffee

Makes 400g (approx)

oil for greasing
125ml water
400g lump sugar

a pinch of cream of
tartar

Grease a 15cm square tin. Put the water and sugar into a saucepan and dissolve the sugar, gently stirring occasionally. Bring to the boil, add the cream of tartar, and boil to the small crack stage (140°C). Pour into the prepared tin, leave to cool, then score the surface deeply with a knife, marking into squares. When set, break into squares as marked, wrap in waxed paper, and store in an airtight tin.

Cooking time 20 minutes (approx)

VARIATIONS
Almond Toffee

Add 75g flaked almonds with the water and sugar.

Variations continued over.

Ginger Toffee

Add 1 × 2.5ml spoon ground ginger with the water and sugar.

Lemon Toffee

Add 1 × 2.5ml spoon lemon essence with the cream of tartar.

Vanilla Toffee

Add 1 × 2.5ml spoon vanilla essence with the cream of tartar.

Walnut Toffee

Add 75g chopped walnuts with the water and sugar.

Coconut Toffee

Makes 750g (approx)

oil for greasing	375g granulated sugar
175ml water	125ml liquid glucose
250g Demerara sugar	125g desiccated coconut

Grease a 20cm square tin. Put the water, sugars, and glucose into a saucepan and dissolve the sugar over low heat. Bring to the boil, and boil to the small crack stage (140°C). Remove the saucepan from the heat and stir in the coconut. Return the pan to the heat and boil to the large crack stage (155°C). Pour into the prepared tin, score the surface deeply, marking into squares. When set, cut or break into squares as marked, wrap in waxed paper, and store in an airtight tin.

Cooking time 25 minutes (approx)

Everton Toffee

Makes 325g (approx)

oil for greasing	a pinch of cream of
175ml water	tartar
200g granulated sugar	1 × 10ml spoon lemon
75g soft light brown	juice
sugar	50g butter

Grease a 20cm square tin. Put the water and sugars into a saucepan and dissolve the sugar gently. Add the cream of tartar, bring to the boil, and boil to the small crack stage (140°C). Stir in the lemon juice and the butter, and continue boiling (without stirring) to the large crack stage (155°C). Pour at once into the prepared tin, and when beginning to set score the surface, marking into squares. When set, break into squares as marked, wrap in waxed paper, and store in an airtight tin.

Cooking time 25 minutes (approx)

Russian Toffee

Makes 700g (approx)

oil for greasing	a pinch of cream of
400g granulated sugar	tartar
200g redcurrant jelly	1 × 2.5ml spoon vanilla
100g butter	essence
125ml single cream	

Grease a 20cm square tin. Put the sugar, redcurrant jelly, butter, and cream into a saucepan and dissolve the sugar slowly over low heat. Add the cream of tartar and vanilla essence. Bring to the boil, stirring frequently. (Use a metal trivet, if possible, under the pan as the mixture tends to burn easily.) Boil to the hard ball stage (120°C). Pour at once into the prepared tin, and when beginning to set, score the surface deeply, marking into squares. When set, cut or break into squares as marked, wrap in waxed paper, and store in an airtight tin.

Cooking time 20 minutes (approx)

Treacle Toffee

Makes 300g (approx)

oil for greasing	2 × 15ml spoons water
100g butter	a pinch of cream of
100g black treacle	tartar
150g soft dark brown	
sugar	

Grease a 15cm square tin. Put the butter, treacle, sugar, and water into a saucepan, and dissolve the sugar over low heat. Add the cream of tartar, bring to the boil, and boil to the hard ball stage (120°C). Pour into the prepared tin, and when beginning to set, score the surface deeply, marking into squares. When set, cut or break into squares as marked, wrap in waxed paper, and store in an airtight tin.

Cooking time 20 minutes (approx)

Toffee Apples

Makes 12

12 ripe eating apples　　*2 × 15ml spoons water*
400g granulated sugar　*oil for greasing*
100g butter

Wash and dry the apples and push a large wooden skewer into the centre of each. Put the sugar, butter, and water into a saucepan and dissolve the sugar very slowly. Bring to the boil, and boil to the small crack stage (140°C). Dip the apples, one at a time, into the hot toffee. Put on a well-greased plate and leave to set.

Cooking time 20–30 minutes

Peanut Brittle

Makes 1kg (approx)

oil for greasing　　　*150g golden syrup*
300g unsalted peanuts　*50g butter*
125ml water　　　　　*$\frac{1}{2}$ × 2.5ml spoon*
350g granulated sugar　　*bicarbonate of soda*
150g soft brown sugar

Grease a 20cm square tin. Warm the nuts very gently in the oven. Put the water, sugars and golden syrup into a strong saucepan and dissolve over low heat, stirring all the time. Add the butter, bring to the boil and boil gently to the large crack stage (155°C). Add the bicarbonate of soda and the warmed nuts. Pour into the prepared tin and, when almost set, score the surface, marking into bars.

Cooking time 20–25 minutes

Butterscotch

Makes 225g (approx)

oil for greasing　　　*75ml liquid glucose*
100g caster sugar　　*125ml single cream*
100g butter

Grease a 17cm square tin. Put all the ingredients into a large saucepan and dissolve the sugar very slowly over low heat, stirring all the time. If possible, put a metal trivet under the pan as the mixture tends to burn easily. When the sugar has dissolved, bring to the boil, and boil to the small crack stage (140°C). Pour at once into the prepared tin, and, when beginning to set, score the surface into squares. When set, cut or break into squares as marked, wrap in waxed paper, and store in an airtight tin.

Cooking time 30 minutes (approx)

Candied Popcorn

Makes 75g (approx)

3 × 15ml spoons oil　　*200g caster sugar*
75g popping corn　　　*25g butter*
3 × 15ml spoons water

Put the oil and popping corn into a large saucepan and heat quickly until one corn 'pops'. Immediately remove the pan from the heat for 1 minute, cover, and return to the heat. When the corn starts popping again, shake the pan constantly until the popping stops. Put the water, sugar and butter into a clean saucepan and heat gently until the sugar has dissolved. Bring to the boil and boil to the soft ball stage (115°C). Add the prepared corn and stir briskly until the corn is completely coated. Remove from the heat and continue stirring until cool to prevent the corn from sticking together.

Cooking time 20 minutes (approx)

Note It is particularly important to keep the pan covered when the corn is popping.

Cream Caramels

Makes 400g (approx)

oil for greasing
200g granulated sugar
200g golden syrup
125ml evaporated milk
1 × 2.5ml spoon vanilla
  essence

Grease a 20cm square tin. Put all the ingredients, except the vanilla essence, into a heavy-bottomed saucepan, and dissolve the sugar gently. Bring to the boil, and boil to the hard ball stage (120°C). Stir in the essence and pour the mixture into the prepared tin. When the caramel is cold, score the surface deeply, marking into squares. When set, cut into squares as marked, wrap in waxed paper, and store in an airtight tin.

Cooking time 20 minutes (approx)

Chocolate Caramels

Makes 300g (approx)

oil for greasing
150g caster sugar
1 × 15ml spoon drinking
  chocolate powder
5 × 15ml spoons milk
1 × 15ml spoon liquid
  glucose
100g butter
75ml single cream
1 × 2.5ml spoon vanilla
  essence

Grease a 17cm square tin. Put the sugar, chocolate powder, milk, glucose, and one-third of the butter in a saucepan and dissolve the sugar slowly. Bring to the boil quickly, stirring to prevent burning, and boil to the blow stage (110°C). Stir in half the remaining butter. Continue boiling to the 'large' blow stage (112°C). Remove the saucepan from the heat and quickly stir in the rest of the butter, cream, and vanilla essence. Return the pan to the heat and boil quickly to the soft ball stage (115°C), stirring all the time. Pour into the prepared tin and, when beginning to set, score deeply, marking into squares. When set, cut in squares as marked, wrap in waxed paper, and store in an airtight tin.

Cooking time 20 minutes (approx)

Nut Caramels

Makes 400g (approx)

oil for greasing
50g walnuts
125ml milk
400g granulated sugar
50g golden syrup
25g butter
1 × 5ml spoon vanilla
  essence

Grease a 20cm square tin. Chop the walnuts. Put the milk, sugar, syrup, and butter in a saucepan and dissolve the sugar gently, stirring occasionally. Bring to the boil, and boil to the hard ball stage (120°C). Remove the pan from the heat, and stir in the walnuts and essence. Pour into the prepared tin and, when beginning to set, score deeply, marking into squares. When set, cut into squares as marked, wrap in waxed paper, and store in an airtight tin.

Cooking time 20 minutes (approx)

VARIATION

Chopped almonds or Brazil nuts can be used instead of walnuts.

Simple Fudge

Makes 500g (approx)

oil for greasing
400g granulated sugar
125ml milk
50g butter
1 × 2.5ml spoon vanilla
  essence

Grease an 18cm square tin. Put all the ingredients into a large saucepan and dissolve the sugar gently. Bring to the boil and boil to the soft ball stage (115°C), stirring all the time. Remove the pan from the heat and stir in the essence. Cool for 2 minutes, then beat the mixture until it becomes thick and creamy. Pour into the prepared tin and, when nearly set, score deeply, marking into squares. When set, cut into squares as marked, and store in an airtight tin lined with waxed paper.

Cooking time 15–20 minutes

Chocolate Fudge

Makes 500g (approx)

oil for greasing
400g granulated sugar
50g golden syrup
50g butter

25g cocoa powder
75ml milk
50ml single cream

Grease a 15cm square tin. Put all the ingredients into a heavy saucepan and dissolve the sugar gently. Bring to the boil and boil to the soft ball stage (115°C), stirring all the time. Cool for 5 minutes, then beat until creamy and matt in appearance. Pour the mixture into the prepared tin. Leave until cold before cutting into squares. Pack and store in an airtight tin lined with waxed paper.

Cooking time 15–25 minutes

Chocolate and Walnut Fudge

Makes 900g (approx)

oil for greasing
75g walnuts
500g chocolate polka
    dots **or** *plain chocolate*
1 × 400g can condensed
    milk

a pinch of salt
1 × 2.5ml spoon vanilla
    essence

Grease a 20cm square tin. Chop the walnuts coarsely. Break up plain chocolate, if used, into small pieces. Melt the chocolate in the top of a double boiler over boiling water, stirring occasionally. Remove from the heat. Add the condensed milk, salt, vanilla essence, and walnuts. Beat until smooth. Spread the mixture evenly in the prepared tin. Chill until firm, then cut into squares. Store in an airtight tin lined with waxed paper.

Cooking time 15–25 minutes

Coffee Nut Fudge

Makes 600g (approx)

oil for greasing
400g granulated sugar
125ml milk
50g butter

1 × 15ml spoon instant
    coffee
25ml warm water
50g walnuts

Grease a 15cm square tin. Put the sugar, milk, and butter into a heavy saucepan. Blend the coffee and the water together and add to the pan. Cook over low heat, stirring until the sugar has dissolved. Bring to the boil, and boil to the soft ball stage (115°C), stirring all the time. Remove the pan from the heat. Chop the walnuts and stir into the mixture, then beat until the mixture is thick and creamy. Pour into the prepared tin and score deeply, marking into squares. When set, cut in squares as marked, and store in an airtight tin lined with waxed paper.

Cooking time 20–25 minutes

CANDY

Brown Almond Candy Kisses

Makes 400g (approx)

50g blanched almonds
125ml water
400g Demerara sugar
25g butter

75ml liquid glucose
a few drops caramel
    essence
oil for greasing

Chop the almonds coarsely, then brown them under the grill or in the oven until golden-brown. Put the water and sugar into a saucepan, and dissolve the sugar over low heat. Add the butter and glucose, bring to the boil and boil to the hard ball stage (120°C). Remove the pan from the heat, and stir in caramel essence to taste. Work the syrup with a wooden spoon, pressing it against the sides of the pan to give the candy a grained appearance. When it becomes cloudy, stir in the almonds. When firm enough not to run, put teaspoonfuls of the mixture on to an oiled tray and leave to set. Pack and store in an airtight tin lined with waxed paper.

Cooking time 25–30 minutes

Candy Twist

Makes 350g (approx)

125ml water
375g Demerara sugar
a few drops caramel
  food colouring (gravy
  browning)
a few drops almond
  essence
oil for greasing

Put the water and sugar into a saucepan and dissolve the sugar over low heat. Bring to the boil, and boil to the small crack stage (140°C). Add colouring and flavouring to taste. Pour the syrup on to an oiled, heat-resistant surface and, as the edges cool, fold them over to the centre. When the syrup is cool enough to handle, 'pull' it as described on p1080. Cut into 15cm pieces and twist each into a spiral. Leave until set. Pack and store between layers of waxed paper in an airtight tin.

Cooking time 30–35 minutes

Treacle Candy

Makes 800g (approx)

750g black treacle
300g soft dark brown
  sugar
50g butter
1 × 15ml spoon vinegar
1 × 5ml spoon
  bicarbonate of soda
1 × 10ml spoon hot
  water
oil for greasing

Put the treacle, sugar, butter, and vinegar into a large saucepan and dissolve the sugar over low heat. Bring to the boil, and boil to the hard ball stage (120°C). Remove the pan from the heat. Dissolve the bicarbonate of soda in the hot water and add it to the mixture. Pour it on to an oiled, heat-resistant surface, and, as the edges cool, fold them over to the centre. As soon as the candy is cool enough to handle, 'pull' it as described on p1080 until it is white. Shape into sticks and cut into short lengths. Leave until set. Pack and store between layers of waxed paper in an airtight tin.

Cooking time 20–25 minutes

MARZIPAN AND NUTS

Boiled Marzipan

Makes 350g (approx)

6 × 15ml spoons water
200g granulated sugar
1 × 5ml spoon liquid
  glucose
150g ground almonds
1 egg white
1 × 5ml spoon lemon
  juice
1 × 5ml spoon almond
  essence
icing sugar for dusting

Put the water and sugar in a saucepan and dissolve the sugar gently. Add the glucose, bring the syrup to the boil, and boil to the soft ball stage (115°C). Remove the saucepan from the heat and dip the bottom of the saucepan in a bowl of cold water for a few seconds, to prevent a further rise in temperature. Stir in the ground almonds, then the unbeaten egg white. Return the pan to low heat and cook for 3 minutes, stirring occasionally. Add the lemon juice and almond essence. Turn the mixture on to a board and stir with a wooden spoon in a figure of eight movement, until the mixture is stiff and cool enough to be kneaded with the hands. Knead the marzipan with a little icing sugar until quite smooth. Wrap in waxed paper and store in a polythene bag, in a container, until required.

Note This marzipan is almost white and colours well for cake decorating as well as sweet-making. It is very pliable for moulding. It will keep for months in a cool, dry place, although it may get a little dry on the outside. If this happens, knead lightly with a little egg white.

Cooking time 20 minutes (approx)

VARIATIONS
The following are suitable to serve with after-dinner coffee, or as cake decorations:

Marzipan Apples

Add green food colouring to the marzipan. Divide it into small pieces and shape each piece into a ball. Paint a little red food colouring on each apple for rosiness. Make a leaf from green marzipan, and use a clove as a stalk.

Marzipan Bananas

Add a little yellow food colouring to the marzipan. Divide it into small pieces and shape each piece into a roll, curving it to the shape of a banana. Brush cocoa powder on for shading and stick a clove into one end.

Marzipan Carrots

Add orange food colouring to the marzipan and shape small pieces into rolls, tapered at one end. Make uneven indentations with the point of a knife and put a small piece of angelica at the top as a stalk. Dust with drinking chocolate powder.

Marzipan Lemons

Add yellow food colouring to the marzipan. Divide it into small pieces and shape each piece into an oval with points at each end. Roll lightly on a grater to make indentations.

Marzipan Logs

Add 75–100g melted chocolate to 350g marzipan and roll out into a rectangle 2mm thick. Make a roll of plain marzipan about 1cm in diameter and the same length as the chocolate rectangle. Wrap the chocolate marzipan round the plain roll, and press lightly. Mark the roll lengthways with the back of a knife to represent the bark. Cut into straight or diagonal pieces.

Marzipan Oranges

Add orange food colouring to the marzipan. Divide into small pieces and shape each piece into a ball. Roll on a grater to make indentations and toss in caster sugar. Press a clove into the top of each orange.

Marzipan Peas

Add green food colouring to the marzipan. Roll out a small piece into an oblong and shape to form a pea pod. Make small balls of marzipan and arrange in rows in the pod. Shape a piece of marzipan to make a stalk and place at the closed end of the pod.

Marzipan Potatoes

Use plain marzipan and roll small pieces into oval shapes. Mark some eyes with a skewer and dust with drinking chocolate powder or cocoa powder.

Marzipan Shapes

Cut 350g marzipan into 2, 3, or 4 squares and tint each a different colour. Roll out each square 5mm thick. Brush each with egg white and place one on top of the other. Press lightly together. Brush the top with egg white and sprinkle with caster sugar. Cut through all the layers, making different shapes, such as squares, rectangles, circles, diamonds, and triangles.

Marzipan Strawberries

Add red food colouring to the marzipan. Divide into small pieces and shape each piece into a strawberry shape. Roll each strawberry lightly on a grater to make indentations. Top with a stalk made from a strip of angelica.

Uncooked Marzipan or Almond Paste

Makes 400g (approx)

200g ground almonds	*1 × 2.5ml spoon almond*
200g icing sugar	*essence*
1 egg white	*2 × 5ml spoons lemon*
	juice

Mix the ground almonds and icing sugar together. Beat the egg white lightly and add to the mixture with the almond essence and lemon juice. Work to a firm paste.

Use this marzipan for sweets, fondant, and chocolate centres, or for covering cakes before icing.

Note This marzipan can be kept for 1–2 months. Store wrapped in foil and in a polythene bag in a refrigerator.

Marzipan for Cake Decorating

See p1232.

Marzipan Chestnuts

Makes 300g (approx)

200g chestnuts   *caster sugar for coating*
100g marzipan
  (pp1086–87)

Make a small slit in the shell of each chestnut. Place the chestnuts in a pan of boiling water and boil for 5 minutes. Drain, and remove the shells and skins while they are very hot. Put the peeled chestnuts in a pan and cover with cold water. Bring to the boil, reduce the heat, and simmer gently for about 20 minutes or until tender. Do not let the chestnuts break up. Drain them well and dry with soft kitchen paper. Leave to cool. Cover each chestnut with marzipan, and roll in caster sugar. Put in paper sweet cases.

Buttered Almonds, Walnuts or Brazils

Makes (approx) 50 almonds, 20 walnuts, 15 Brazils

50g blanched almonds   *1 × 10ml spoon liquid*
  or halved walnuts **or**   *glucose*
  whole Brazil nuts   *a pinch of cream of*
oil for greasing   *tartar*
6 × 15ml spoons water   *50g butter*
200g Demerara sugar

Warm the nuts and space them out on an oiled tray. Put the water and sugar into a saucepan and dissolve the sugar, then bring to the boil. Add the glucose, cream of tartar, and butter. Let the butter melt. Boil the syrup to the small crack stage (140°C). Using a teaspoon, pour a little toffee over each nut; it should set very quickly. When cold, remove the nuts from the tray, wrap separately in waxed paper, and store in an airtight container.

Cooking time 25–30 minutes

Almond Rock

Makes 500g (approx)

250ml water   *a few drops almond*
400g lump sugar   *essence*
75ml liquid glucose   *oil for greasing*
100g blanched almonds

Put the water and sugar into a saucepan and dissolve the sugar gently. Add the glucose, bring to the boil, and boil to the small crack stage (140°C). Draw the pan off the heat, add the almonds and essence to taste. Return the pan to the heat and boil for 2–3 minutes until golden-brown. Pour on to an oiled tray and leave to set. Break into pieces, wrap in waxed paper, and store in an airtight tin.

Cooking time 30–35 minutes

Burnt Almonds

Makes 550g (approx)

125ml water   *200g blanched almonds*
400g Demerara sugar   *oil for greasing*

Put the water and sugar into a saucepan and dissolve the sugar over low heat, stirring occasionally. Bring to the boil and boil to the soft ball stage (115°C), without stirring. Add the almonds and stir until the sugar browns slightly, granulates, and has completely coated the almonds. Turn them on to a well greased tray, separate any that may have stuck together and leave to cool completely. Break into pieces, wrap in waxed paper, and store in an airtight container.

Cooking time 20–25 minutes

Candied Chestnuts

Makes 350g (approx)

250g chestnuts   *400g lump sugar*
250ml water   *oil for greasing*

Make a small slit in the shell of each chestnut. Place the chestnuts in a pan of boiling water and boil for 5 minutes. Drain, and remove the shells and skins while they are still very hot. Return them to the pan and cover with cold water. Bring to the boil, reduce the heat, and simmer for 20 minutes or until they are tender but not broken. Drain well and dry; leave to cool. Make a syrup with the water and sugar and boil to the small crack stage (140°C). Dip the chestnuts in the syrup, one at a time as when dipping chocolates (p1096), then place on an oiled tray until set.

Serve with after-dinner coffee.

Cooking time 1 hour (approx)

Stuffed Dates

Makes 24

200g dessert dates
100g whole blanched
* almonds*

25g desiccated coconut

Stone the dates and place an almond in each hollow date. Roll them in coconut and put in paper sweet cases.

VARIATION
Stuff the dates with marzipan and roll in caster sugar.

FRUIT SWEETMEATS

These can be made from surplus fresh fruit, such as cooking apples or quinces, or from dried fruit. No special equipment is required, except a thick-bottomed saucepan to prevent burning. The method is very simple, and fruit can be mixed, depending on what is available.

If cooking apples are not available, the flavour of dessert apples will be improved by adding 1×5ml spoon lemon juice per 100ml purée. Apples combine well with equal quantities of quinces, or double their quantity of pineapple, or half their quantity of plums. Apple improves the texture of plums, peaches, figs, and other fruit weak in pectin. The weight of the fruit should not be less than 1kg because of shrinkage.

Apple Sweetmeat

Blemished apples can be used, providing the damaged parts are removed. Although peeling and coring are not essential, this produces a better result. Cook the peel and cores in a little water until tender. Meanwhile, preserve the whiteness of the cut-up apples by submerging them in water containing 2×5ml spoons of salt per litre. Strain the cooking water from the peel and cores, and use it to cook the fruit until tender; add more water if necessary, but keep the liquid to a minimum.

When the apples are well softened and not too fluid, either sieve them or process in an electric blender. Add 50–60g sugar and 1×5ml spoon salt per 100ml purée, and return to the pan. Stir to dissolve the sugar, then boil the mixture steadily until it is firm and does not stick to the sides or bottom of the pan.

Turn the mixture on to a wooden board or on to muslin over a mesh rack. Spread the mixture about 2cm thick and leave to dry in a warm, sunny place. In a warm, dry atmosphere, it will dry in 2–4 days and can then be cut into cubes or into fancy shapes, and rolled in caster sugar. Leave for 3 more days to continue drying, and then pack into jars or tins with waxed paper to separate the layers.

Various finishes can be used for these sweetmeats. They can be dipped in melted chocolate (p1096) or fondant (p1095) and dried on a rack, or the mixture can be sandwiched between thin layers of fondant and then cut. It can be rolled out to make thin layers and 2 or 3 different kinds put together, then rolled to bind, and cut into pieces.

Dried Fruit Sweetmeats

Any combination of dried fruit or dried fruit and nuts can be used. Remove any seeds, if necessary, and mince the fruit. If the fruit is hard, steam it or soak it in boiling water for a short time, and then mince it. Sweeten with sugar or, to keep the fruit succulent, with honey or syrup. Mix thoroughly and finally sprinkle with minced nuts if liked. Roll out 2cm thick and cut into shapes. These can be finished and stored as for fresh fruit sweetmeats.

Glazed Fruits

Makes 200g (approx)

200g fresh **or** *candied fruit (see Method)*	*200g lump sugar*
50ml water	*a few drops lemon juice*
	oil for greasing

Grapes, mandarins or cherries can be used. Remove the pips but do not peel grapes or cherries; peel mandarins and break into segments. Dry fresh fruit thoroughly; wash candied fruit free from sugar and dry it.

Put the water and sugar into a saucepan and dissolve the sugar gently. Add the lemon juice, bring to the boil, and boil to the small crack stage (140°C). Remove the pan from the heat and place the bottom of the pan in cold water for a minute to prevent further cooking. Dip the prepared fruit in the syrup as when dipping chocolates (p1096). Only dip one piece at a time. Place the glazed fruits on an oiled tray and leave to set.

Serve with after-dinner coffee.

Cooking time 15 minutes (approx)

Candied and Crystallized Fruit

See pp1124–27.

SOFT SUGAR SWEETS

Snowballs

Makes 30–35

25g gelatine	*plain chocolate for coating*
300ml water	*coating*
400g granulated sugar	*desiccated coconut for coating*
1 × 5ml spoon vanilla essence	*coating*

Soften the gelatine in 125ml of the water in a small heatproof container. Stand the container in a pan of hot water and stir until the gelatine dissolves. Dissolve the sugar in the remaining water and boil for 5 minutes. Add the dissolved gelatine and boil for a further 10 minutes. Remove the pan from the heat, add the vanilla essence, and whisk until the mixture is stiff enough to roll into balls. Form into 30–35 small balls. Melt the chocolate in a heatproof bowl over a pan of water and dip the balls in the chocolate as described on p1096. Drain well. Toss the balls in the coconut. Leave to set for 1 hour, then place in paper sweet cases.

Cooking time 25 minutes (approx)

Peppermint Creams(1)

Makes 48 (approx)

400g icing sugar	*icing sugar for dusting*
2 egg whites	
2 × 5ml spoons peppermint essence	

Sift the icing sugar into a bowl, and work in the egg white and peppermint essence. Mix well to a moderately firm paste. Knead well and roll out, on a board dusted with a little icing sugar, to about 5mm thick. Cut into small rounds and put on greaseproof paper. Leave to dry for 12 hours, turning each sweet once. Pack in an airtight container lined with waxed paper.

Note These creams are suitable for coating with chocolate; see p1096.

For Peppermint Creams made with fondant, see p1095.

Raspberry Jellies

Makes 400g (approx)

125ml water	*a few drops red food colouring*
400g lump sugar	*colouring*
25g gelatine	*caster sugar for coating*
a few drops raspberry essence	*coating*

Put 100ml water and the sugar into a saucepan and dissolve the sugar gently. Soften the gelatine in the remaining 25ml water in a small heatproof container. Stand the container in a pan of hot water and stir until the gelatine dissolves. Pour the dissolved gelatine into the saucepan. Stir in the essence and colouring. Strain the liquid through muslin into a wetted 15cm square tin and leave it to set. Cut into shapes such as cubes or crescents, and coat with caster sugar.

Cooking time 10 minutes (approx)

Lemon Quarters

Makes 100g (approx)

125ml lemon juice	6 × 15ml spoons liquid
100g granulated sugar	glucose
25g gelatine	caster sugar for coating

Put the lemon juice and sugar in a saucepan and dissolve the sugar gently. Stir the gelatine into the glucose. Add the glucose and gelatine to the pan and heat until the gelatine dissolves. Wet a 15cm square tin and pour in the mixture. Leave to set. When firm, turn out on to a board and cut into crescent shapes. Roll the sweets in caster sugar.

Cooking time 10 minutes (approx)

VARIATION

Orange Quarters

Substitute 125ml orange juice and use only 75g sugar. Make as above.

Apricotines

Makes 24

1 × 425g can apricots	granulated sugar for
150g granulated sugar	coating
1 × 15ml spoon lemon juice	

Put a sheet of greaseproof paper on a tray and place twenty-four 2cm wetted metal rings on it. Drain the apricots well, reserving the syrup, and sieve the fruit or process briefly in an electric blender to make a purée. Put the purée and about one-third of the syrup into a small saucepan. Add the sugar and lemon juice, and heat until the sugar dissolves. Bring to the boil, stirring frequently. Boil until a little mixture sets when dropped on a plate. The mixture should hold its shape and not spread. Fill the rings with the mixture and leave to set. When set, carefully push the sweets out of the rings. Toss in granulated sugar and put in paper sweet cases. Store in an airtight tin.

Cooking time 10–15 minutes

Note If rings are not available, the mixture can be put into a wetted tin and cut into rounds with a small biscuit cutter when set.

VARIATIONS

Use 1 × 425g can blackcurrants or 1 × 425g can raspberries instead of apricots.

Coconut Ice

Makes 400g (approx)

oil for greasing	100g desiccated coconut
125ml water	a few drops pink food
300g granulated sugar	colouring
1 × 2.5ml spoon liquid glucose	

Grease a 15cm square tin well. Put the water and sugar into a saucepan and dissolve the sugar gently. Add the glucose, bring to the boil, and boil to the soft ball stage (115°C). Remove the saucepan from the heat and add the coconut. Stir as little as possible, but shake the pan to mix the syrup and coconut together. Pour the mixture quickly into the prepared tin and leave to set. Do not scrape any mixture left in the saucepan into the tin as it will be sugary.

Make a second quantity of mixture, adding a few drops of pink food colouring just before 115°C is reached. Pour on top of the set white mixture and leave to set, then cut into squares.

Cooking time 20 minutes (approx)

Note It is advisable to make 2 separate quantities of ice rather than to add colouring to half the first mixture, as the extra stirring will make the mixture 'grain'.

Turkish Delight

Makes 400g (approx)

50g nuts, pistachios, almonds, or walnuts (optional)
250ml water
25g gelatine
400g granulated sugar
½ × 2.5ml spoon citric acid
1 × 2.5ml spoon vanilla essence
2 × 5ml spoons triple-strength rose-water
a few drops pink food colouring (optional)
50g icing sugar
25g cornflour

If using nuts, skin them and chop coarsely. Put the water into a large saucepan, sprinkle in the gelatine and allow to soften. Add the sugar and citric acid. Heat slowly, stirring all the time, until the sugar has dissolved. Bring to the boil, and boil steadily for 20 minutes without stirring. Remove from the heat and leave to stand for 10 minutes. Stir in the vanilla essence, rose-water, and colouring, if used. (Half the mixture can be coloured and half left white, if liked.) Stir the nuts into the mixture. Pour into a wetted 15cm square tin and leave uncovered in a cool place for 24 hours.

Sift the icing sugar and cornflour together and sprinkle on a sheet of greaseproof paper. Turn the Turkish Delight on to the paper, and cut into squares, using a sharp knife. Toss well in the mixture, so that all sides are well coated. Pack in airtight containers lined with waxed paper and dusted with extra icing sugar and cornflour.

Cooking time 30 minutes (approx)

Note Pistachios are used in Greece and Turkey, but almonds or walnuts can be used instead.

Peppermint Turkish Delight

Makes 400g (approx)

250ml water
400g granulated sugar
2 × 15ml spoons gelatine
a few drops green food colouring
1 × 5ml spoon peppermint essence
icing sugar for coating

Put the water, sugar, and gelatine into a saucepan, leave to stand for 5 minutes, then heat gently to dissolve the sugar and gelatine. Bring to the boil, and boil gently for 20 minutes, stirring frequently. Colour pale green, and add the peppermint essence. Pour into a wetted 15cm square tin, and leave uncovered for 24 hours in a cool place to set.

Cut into strips and pull gently out of the tin. Cut into squares and roll in icing sugar. Place on a dry tray in one layer, and leave in a cool place for a further 24 hours. Pack in airtight containers lined with waxed paper and dusted with extra icing sugar.

Cooking time 30 minutes (approx)

White Nougat

Makes 200g (approx)

50g blanched almonds
25g glacé cherries
75g icing sugar
1 × 5ml spoon liquid glucose
50g honey
1 egg white

Line the sides and bottom of a 15 × 10cm tin with rice paper. Chop the almonds and brown them lightly under the grill. Chop the cherries. Put the sugar, glucose, honey, and egg white into a saucepan. Whisk over very low heat for about 20 minutes or until thick and white. Use a metal trivet, if possible, under the pan to prevent browning. Remove the pan from the heat, and stir in the almonds and cherries. Turn the mixture into the prepared tin, and press it down well. Cover with a single layer of rice paper. Place a light, even weight on top and leave until quite cold. Cut into oblong pieces or squares and wrap in waxed paper.

Cooking time 30 minutes (approx)

Brown Nougat

Makes 150g (approx)

oil for greasing
100g blanched almonds
100g icing sugar
1 × 5ml spoon lemon juice

Grease a 12cm square tin. Chop the almonds and brown them lightly under the grill. Put the sugar and lemon juice into a small pan and heat very gently until the sugar turns golden-brown. The sugar must dissolve very slowly. Do not stir it, but, if liked, draw a wooden spoon through it occasionally. Stir in the almonds, and pour quickly into the prepared tin. Mark into squares and leave to set. When set, cut into the squares as marked, and wrap in waxed paper or coat with chocolate (p1096).

Cooking time 10–15 minutes

Marshmallows

Makes 40–44

oil for greasing
250ml water
400g granulated sugar
1 × 15ml spoon golden
 syrup
2 × 15ml spoons gelatine
2 egg whites

1 × 2.5ml spoon vanilla
 or lemon essence
a few drops pink food
 colouring (optional)
50g icing sugar
25g cornflour

Line a 20cm square tin with oiled greaseproof paper. Put 125ml water, the sugar, and golden syrup into a saucepan and dissolve the sugar gently. Bring to the boil, and boil to the hard ball stage (120°C). Meanwhile, soften the gelatine in the rest of the water in a small heatproof container. Stand the container in a pan of water and stir until the gelatine dissolves. When the syrup is ready, remove the pan from the heat, and stir in the gelatine. Whisk the egg whites until stiff, then pour the hot syrup gradually on to the whites, whisking all the time. Add the flavouring and colouring. Continue to whisk the mixture until it is thick and foamy. Pour into the prepared tin and leave at room temperature for 24 hours.

Remove from the tin and cut into squares. Mix the icing sugar and cornflour together and roll each piece of marshmallow thoroughly in the mixture. Leave on a dry tray, in a single layer, at room temperature for 24 hours, then pack and store in boxes lined with waxed paper.

Note All or only part of the mixture may be coloured pink.

Cooking time 25 minutes (approx)

HARD SUGAR SWEETS

Mint Humbugs

Makes 375g (approx)

250ml water
400g granulated sugar
75ml liquid glucose
1 × 2.5ml spoon cream
 of tartar

1 × 2.5ml spoon oil of
 peppermint or to taste
oil for greasing
a few drops green food
 colouring

Put the water, sugar, and glucose into a saucepan and dissolve the sugar over low heat. Add the cream of tartar, bring to the boil, and boil to the small crack stage (140°C). Remove the pan from the heat and add oil of peppermint to taste. Pour on to an oiled surface and divide into 2 portions. Add green colouring to 1 portion. Allow the syrup to cool until workable, then 'pull' each portion separately as described on p1080. When on the point of setting, lay the 2 portions together and 'pull' into a thick rope. Using oiled scissors, cut into 1cm pieces, turning the rope at each cut. When cold and hard, wrap the humbugs individually and store in an airtight tin.

Cooking time 25–30 minutes

Barley Sugar

Makes 350g (approx)

250ml water
400g lump sugar
1 × 2.5ml spoon lemon
 juice

a pinch of cream of
 tartar
oil for greasing

Put the water and sugar into a saucepan and dissolve the sugar gently. Bring to the boil, and boil to the small ball stage (115°C). Add the lemon juice. Continue boiling to the large crack stage (155°C) and add the cream of tartar. Pour the mixture on to a lightly oiled slab or large flat plate. Allow the mixture to cool for a few minutes, then fold the sides to the centre using an oiled palette knife. Cut into strips with oiled scissors, and twist each strip. When cold and set, store in an airtight jar.

Cooking time 20–25 minutes

Fruit Drops

Makes 200g (approx)

fat for greasing
200g granulated sugar
1 × 10ml spoon liquid
  glucose
50ml water

a pinch of cream of
  tartar
flavouring (see **Note***)*
food colouring (see
  Note*)*

Grease metal sweet rings and a tray to put them on, or a shallow 15cm square baking tin. Put the sugar, glucose, and water in a saucepan and dissolve the sugar gently. Add the cream of tartar, bring to the boil, and boil to the hard ball stage (120°C). Remove the pan from the heat and cool for 5 minutes. Add the flavouring and colouring. Stir the syrup with a wooden spoon, pressing a little syrup against the sides of the saucepan to 'grain' it. Pour the syrup at once into the rings or into the tin in a 1cm layer. If the syrup is poured into a tin, mark at once into squares and break into pieces when cold. Wrap in waxed paper and store in an airtight container.

Cooking time 25–30 minutes

Note Flavourings and colourings: Lemon flavour – colour pale yellow; Raspberry or Strawberry flavour – colour pink; Pineapple flavour – colour yellow; Orange or Tangerine flavour – colour orange.

Lemon Acid Drops

Makes 250g (approx)

125ml water
300g lump sugar
½ × 2.5ml spoon cream
  of tartar
oil for greasing

1 × 2.5ml spoon lemon
  essence
1 × 5ml spoon tartaric
  acid
icing sugar for coating

Put the water and sugar into a large saucepan and dissolve the sugar gently. Add the cream of tartar, bring to the boil, and boil to the small crack stage (140°C), when the syrup should be pale yellow in colour. Add the essence. Quickly pour the syrup on to an oiled slab or dish. Sprinkle the tartaric acid over it and work it in well, using a wooden spoon. As soon as the mixture is cool enough to handle,

form into a long roll. Using oiled scissors, cut off pieces about 1cm long, and shape with oiled hands into balls. Coat with sifted icing sugar. Allow to dry thoroughly before storing in an airtight container.

Cooking time 20–25 minutes

Orange Drops

Makes 375g (approx)

oil for greasing
400g lump sugar
2 oranges

250ml water
a few drops yellow food
  colouring

Grease a 15cm square tin. Rub a few sugar lumps over the oranges to obtain the zest. Put all the sugar and water into a saucepan and dissolve the sugar gently. Bring to the boil, and boil to the small crack stage (140°C). Remove the pan from the heat and add a few drops of colouring. Pour the syrup into the prepared tin and mark in small squares. When cold, break into pieces as marked, and store in an airtight container.

Cooking time 25 minutes (approx)

FONDANT SWEETS

Fondant is a solution of sugar and water boiled to the soft ball stage (115°C). It makes soft creamy sweets, forms the basis for other sweets or can be used for chocolate centres. It can be coloured and flavoured to choice. Any fondant left unused can be stored in an airtight jar.

When required, it may be necessary to thin down the fondant using stock syrup (p1081). When adding the syrup to the fondant, work it in well, and place the basin containing the mixture over a pan of hot water. Avoid over-heating the fondant however; it should only be lukewarm. The colder the fondant syrup is before being worked, the smoother the fondant will be. If worked too hot, the grain will be too large and the fondant will feel and taste gritty.

Basic Fondant for Sweets

Makes 300g (approx)

125ml water　　　　　*1 × 5ml spoon liquid*
300g granulated sugar　*glucose*

Put the water and sugar into a large saucepan and dissolve the sugar slowly over low heat. Tap the bottom of the saucepan with a wooden spoon to make sure every grain of sugar is dissolved. Add the glucose, bring to the boil, and boil rapidly to the soft ball stage (115°C). It is very important to brush down the sides of the saucepan with cold water during this process to prevent crystals forming.

Rinse a slab or large meat dish with cold water. Pour the fondant syrup on to it and lightly sprinkle the surface of the syrup with cold water. Do not scrape any syrup from the pan on to the fondant in the dish. Leave the syrup to cool for 20–25 minutes, then work it with a wooden spoon, palette knife or scraper, turning the mixture with a figure of eight movement. With working, the fondant will become dry and white. Gather into a ball and cover with a damp cloth. Leave to rest for about 30 minutes until the fondant softens. Knead into a ball and continue kneading until quite smooth. Store in a jar, covered with waxed paper and an airtight lid or polythene cover.

Cooking time 30 minutes (approx)

Peppermint Creams(2)

Makes 300g

cornflour or icing sugar　　*stock syrup (1)* (p1081)
for dusting　　　　　　　*as required*
300g fondant
a few drops peppermint
essence

Dust a fondant mat with cornflour. Put the fondant into a basin over a saucepan of hot water and let it soften. Do not overheat it. Add the essence and enough stock syrup to make a cream of thick pouring consistency. Pour the fondant into the prepared mat and leave overnight to set.

To remove the sweets, bend back the mat and the sweets will fall out. Leave on a plate for 2 hours to harden. Pack in an airtight container lined with waxed paper.

Note If a fondant mat is not available, roll out the fondant on to a board dusted with icing sugar, cut into rounds or other shapes with small cutters, and leave on a plate to dry for 12 hours, turning once. Pack as above.

For Peppermint Creams (1), see p1090.

Walnut Fondants

Makes 18

100g fondant　　　　　　*a few drops pineapple*
a few drops green food　　*essence*
colouring　　　　　　　*36 walnut halves*

Colour the fondant pale green, and flavour it to taste with pineapple essence. Divide it into 18 equal portions and roll them into balls. Flatten into pieces the same diameter as the walnuts and sandwich between the walnut halves, pressing firmly. Allow the sweets to harden in a dry, warm place. Put in paper sweet cases, and serve with after-dinner coffee.

Fondant Fruits or Nuts

Any firm fruit can be used except those that discolour, eg apple or banana. Clean and dry the fruit, and remove any stones or pips. Divide oranges or mandarins into segments.

Use about 200g fondant to coat 18–20 small fruits such as grapes, or 36–40 nuts.

Put the fondant in a small basin over a saucepan of hot water, and stir until it has the appearance of thick cream. If necessary, add some stock syrup (p1081). Dip any fruits or nuts, one by one, into the fondant. Take care to coat the fruit or nuts thoroughly. Cherries and grapes can be held by the stem, but other fruits and nuts must be immersed and lifted out with a fork, like chocolates (p1096). Place on a plate to dry.

Note These sweets will not keep long.

CHOCOLATES

To Make and Coat Simple Chocolates

A good many of the recipes above are suitable for coating with chocolate, but the process requires time and patience. Couverture chocolate, which is the type used commercially, is not easy to use at home because success depends upon having exact temperatures and controlled atmospheric conditions. Couverture contains a high proportion of cocoa butter and needs to be 'tempered' properly before use (see below). It can be bought in small quantities from a supermarket or delicatessen.

The home chocolate-maker can get quite good results by using a super-fatted commercial dipping chocolate or coating chocolate.

Tempering Couverture Chocolate

Break the chocolate into pieces and put it in the top of a double boiler, or in a basin over a pan of hot water. Be very careful that no steam or condensation gets on to the chocolate, as the slightest drop of moisture will thicken it and make it useless for coating or dipping sweets. The chocolate must be heated over the hot water to a temperature higher than that at which it will be used for coating, usually about 50°C. It should be cooled until it thickens (at about 28°C), then heated again to between 30°–32°C, when it should be just thin enough to use but thick enough to set quickly. If milk couverture is required, the best temperature for using is between 28°–30°C. Frequent stirring and an even temperature is necessary in either case, to keep the cocoa particles well distributed throughout the cocoa butter.

If chocolate other than couverture is used, break it into pieces, put it in a basin over a saucepan of hot water and stir frequently until melted and of a consistency which will coat the chosen centres easily, but will not run into pools when the chocolate is setting.

Centres to Use for Coating

1) Marzipan (p1087), coloured, flavoured, and cut into attractive shapes.
2) Fondant (p1095), coloured, flavoured, shaped, and allowed to dry before coating.
3) Preserved ginger or glacé pineapple cut into small pieces.
4) Blanched almonds, Brazil nuts or walnuts.
5) Caramels, toffee (pp1081–84) or nougat (p1092) cut into squares or rectangles.
6) Coconut ice (p1091); dip completely in the chocolate or just half dip each piece.
7) Maraschino cherries, well drained, and coated with fondant (p1095).
8) Chopped nuts or cornflakes can be mixed with the chocolate in a basin, and spoonfuls of the mixture put into paper cases and allowed to set. These are suitable with after-dinner coffee.

Chocolate Dipping and Marking

Arrange the centres to be coated on a tray, and also any decorations to be used, eg flaked almonds, toasted or nibbed almonds, chopped nuts, crystallized roses or violets. Place a sheet of foil or waxed paper on a flat tray to hold the finished chocolates. Place the bowl of melted chocolate between the centres and the tray for the finished sweets. Beside it place a dipping fork or an ordinary 3–4 pronged table fork for holding and dipping the centres.

When the chocolate is ready, drop in a centre, make sure it is completely covered with the chocolate, then lift it out, right side up, using the fork. Tap the fork on the side of the basin to remove any surplus chocolate. Place the sweet on the tray and gently pull the fork from underneath. Any decoration must be put on each chocolate before another one is dipped. The prongs of the fork can be used for marking the top of the chocolate for a simple decoration. The finished chocolates should be left to dry for several hours before putting them carefully into paper sweet cases.

SIMPLE TRUFFLES

Chocolate Bonbons

Makes 24 (approx)

1 egg white	*75g ground almonds*
75g plain chocolate	*2 × 10ml spoons icing*
100g caster sugar	*sugar*

Beat the egg white lightly until liquid. Grate the chocolate. Mix together the chocolate, caster sugar, ground almonds, and egg white with a wooden spoon. Knead into a stiff paste and shape into small balls. Dredge with icing sugar and leave to dry for several hours before serving.

Serve with after-dinner coffee.

Apricot Truffles

Makes 20 (approx)

100g stale plain cake	*2 × 15ml spoons rum*
100g caster sugar	*chocolate vermicelli for*
100g ground almonds	*coating*
apricot jam	

Rub the cake through a coarse sieve or process briefly in an electric blender to obtain even crumbs. Add the caster sugar and ground almonds. Warm and sieve the apricot jam. Add the rum to the dry ingredients with enough jam to make a stiff paste. Shape the mixture into small balls and leave to dry for 1 hour. Dip each ball in warmed jam and coat with vermicelli. Leave to dry overnight. These can be stored for 1–2 weeks in an airtight container.

Nut Truffles

Makes 20 (approx)

100g stale sponge cake	*1 egg yolk*
100g plain chocolate	*2 × 15ml spoons rum*
50g butter	*100g walnuts*
100g icing sugar	

Rub the cake through a coarse sieve or process briefly in an electric blender to obtain even crumbs. Break the chocolate into small pieces and put in a basin over a pan of hot water. Add the butter and allow to melt. Remove the basin from the pan, add the icing sugar, cake crumbs, egg yolk, and rum. Mix together well. If the mixture is soft, leave for 10 minutes in a cool place. Chop the walnuts finely. Shape the cooled mixture into small balls and coat with the nuts. Leave to harden for 1–2 hours.

Chocolate Truffles

Makes 24 (approx)

50g nibbed almonds	*75g caster sugar*
100g plain chocolate	*a few drops vanilla*
100g ground almonds	*essence*
2 × 15ml spoons double	*grated chocolate or*
cream	*vermicelli for coating*

Brown the nibbed almonds lightly under the grill. Break the chocolate into small pieces and melt it in a basin over a pan of hot water. Remove the basin from the pan. Add all the other ingredients except the coating chocolate and mix to a stiff paste. Roll into small balls, and toss at once in grated chocolate or chocolate vermicelli. Put into paper sweet cases to serve.

Rich Rum Truffles

Makes 15 (approx)

75g plain chocolate	*1 × 5ml spoon*
1 egg yolk	*evaporated milk*
15g butter	*drinking chocolate*
1 × 5ml spoon rum	*powder for coating*

Break the chocolate into small pieces and melt in a basin over a pan of hot water. Add the egg yolk, butter, rum and evaporated milk. Leave the basin over the hot water and beat the mixture until it is thick. Remove from the heat and beat for a further 2–3 minutes. Put the mixture on a board and shape into a roll. Cut off pieces and shape them into balls. Roll in drinking chocolate powder, and leave to harden for 1 hour. Put into paper sweet cases to serve.

Marzipan Truffles

Makes 12 (approx)

25g plain chocolate
100g uncooked marzipan
  (p1087)
25g walnuts
2–3 drops vanilla
  essence

1 ×15ml spoon sweet
  sherry
chocolate vermicelli for
  coating

Break the chocolate into small pieces and melt in a basin over a pan of hot water. Work the melted chocolate into the marzipan. Chop the walnuts finely and add to the marzipan. Mix in the vanilla essence and sherry. Shape into balls and roll in the vermicelli, pressing well to make the coating stick. Leave for 1–2 hours to harden.

CREAM OR GANACHE TRUFFLES

In the following more elaborate truffles, a Ganache Paste is used. This is a mixture of melted chocolate and warm cream, cooled until it hardens. The texture of the paste depends upon the type of cream and chocolate used. Plain chocolate is harder than milk chocolate, so more cream can be used. If any other liquid is used in the recipe, the amount of cream must be reduced accordingly. When the paste is made, it can be moulded and then coated with chocolate (p1096) to help keep it moist. This centre mixture does not keep for more than 2 weeks and the truffles should be kept in a refrigerator.

Basic Vanilla Cream Truffles

Makes 15 (approx)

200g milk chocolate
75ml whipping cream
a few drops vanilla
  essence
4 ×15ml spoons cocoa
  powder

1 ×15ml spoon icing
  sugar
chocolate for coating

Break the chocolate into small pieces and put in a basin over a saucepan of hot water. The water should not be more than 50°C. Stir the chocolate until melted. Put the cream into a small saucepan and bring to the boil, then leave to cool until it is hand-hot. Add the vanilla essence. Pour the cream into the chocolate and stir until well mixed. Leave the mixture to cool, stirring occasionally. The paste should be quite thick but not hard. Beat the mixture with a wooden spoon or an electric hand mixer until pale and light. Leave to cool in a refrigerator until the mixture hardens.

Sift the cocoa and icing sugar together on to a board. Put teaspoonfuls of the cream mixture on the board, coat with the cocoa and sugar, and roll into balls. Do not use more cocoa and sugar than necessary. Return the truffles to the refrigerator to harden again.

Have ready a bowl of melted dipping chocolate (p1096). Spear a truffle centre on a fine skewer and pour a teaspoonful of melted chocolate over it, turning until well coated. Toss each truffle in a little of the cocoa and sugar mixture. Leave for 1–2 hours to set, then put the truffles into paper sweet cases to serve.

VARIATIONS

Orange Cream Truffles

Make as for Vanilla Truffles, substituting plain chocolate, and adding 1 ×15ml spoon concentrated orange juice when the chocolate and cream are stirred together. Use 100ml double cream instead of the whipping cream. Coat the finished truffles with 50g nibbed almonds instead of the sweetened cocoa.

Coffee Cream Truffles

Make as for Vanilla Truffles using 125g milk chocolate and 125g plain chocolate. Substitute 125ml double cream for the whipping cream, and stir in 1 ×15ml spoon instant coffee with the cream. Coat the finished truffles with chocolate vermicelli.

JAMS, JELLIES, MARMALADES, AND OTHER SWEET PRESERVES

Jams require the same care and attention in the boiling as marmalade; the slightest degree of burning communicates a disagreeable empyreumatic taste, and if they are not boiled sufficiently, they will not keep. That they may keep, it is necessary not to be sparing of sugar.

Jams

Jam consists of set fruit and sugar. The quality of the set depends on a balance of pectin (a natural gum-like substance), acid, and sugar, all of which are found to a greater or lesser degree in jam-making fruits. Fruits which are easy to make into a well-set jam are apples, blackcurrants, damsons, gooseberries, plums, and redcurrants. Apricots, blackberries, raspberries, and loganberries are of medium setting quality, while cherries and strawberries are of poor setting quality.

When a fruit is weak in any one constituent, more must be added to obtain good jam. No fruit contains enough sugar to make a preserve, so it is always added. Strawberries and marrow lack acid, so lemon juice must be added. If pectin is lacking, the deficiency can be made up by adding a pectin-rich fruit or its juice, eg apple is added to blackberries, gooseberries to strawberries. Alternatively, commercial or home-made pectin stock can be added. If in doubt about the setting quality of the fruit, test for pectin using the method on p1100.

Pectin Stock
(to add to fruit deficient in pectin)

Prepare cooking apples, gooseberries or redcurrants, and cook with enough water to cover until thoroughly pulped. Crush with a wooden spoon and pour through a scalded jelly bag or double tea-towel. The resulting stock can be added to fruit weak in pectin. The usual allowance is 125ml of stock to 2kg of fruit, but more is required in vegetable jams, such as marrow where there is little natural pectin. For storing, pectin can be bottled in the same way as Fruit Syrups (p1135).

Choice of Fruit for Jams

Choose firm, ripe fruit or a mixture of just ripe and slightly under-ripe fruits. Over-ripe fruit will not give a set and should be used for some other preserve such as syrup or pulp. To retain the natural green colour of gooseberries, really young, under-ripe fruit must be used. Ripe red gooseberries make a fragrant jam, but the skins, like those of blackcurrants, can be tough unless softened by long gentle cooking before the sugar is added.

Choice of a Preserving Pan

Money is well spent on a good quality preserving pan which will give good service without constant fear of burning the jam. Aluminium, stainless steel, and unchipped enamel are good choices. Iron and zinc pans are not suitable as the fruit will react with the metal and spoil the colour and flavour of the preserve. This can also occur with exposed iron in a chipped enamel pan. Copper and brass pans are not recommended. They enhance the colour of jam, especially green gooseberries, but a considerable proportion of the vitamin C in the fruit is destroyed. If copper and brass pans are used for cooking, they must be cleaned with salt and lemon juice and not with metal polish.

It is important to have a large enough pan so that the jam can boil rapidly without it overflowing.

A 6 litre capacity is recommended for yields of 2–3kg.

The inside of the pan can be rubbed with unsalted margarine or butter before use to prevent the jam from sticking. But this is usually unnecessary if a good quality, heavy preserving pan is used.

Preserving pan

GENERAL METHOD FOR MAKING JAM

First, the fruit must be softened and broken down before the sugar is added. For this, water is added to firm fruit to prevent burning. If acid or lemon juice is used, it is also added to the fruit before simmering. The usual quantity of water required is indicated in the recipes but there is no hard and fast rule. A wide shallow pan will need more water than a deep narrow one. The fruit and water should be simmered until the fruit is soft and the bulk is reduced by one-third.

Testing for Pectin

If the setting quality of the fruit is in doubt, a pectin test can be carried out when the fruit is sufficiently softened and reduced, and before any sugar is added.

Take 1×5ml spoon of juice from the cooked-down fruit and put it into a small glass or jar. Leave it to cool and then add 1×15ml spoon methylated spirit. Do not stir but shake gently and leave for 1 minute. Tip the glass and pour off the liquid carefully. If there is plenty of pectin present there will be a single firm clot of jelly; for medium pectin there will be a soft clot or 2 or 3 smaller ones. If there is a feathery clot or no clot at all, pectin stock or some pectin-rich fruit must be added. Alternatively, commercial pectin may be added; this, however, is done after skimming the cooked fruit which is only boiled for a short time. (See Apricot Jam (2) p1102.)

Adding Sugar

Either granulated or preserving sugar can be used for jam-making and it should generally be stirred into the fruit over low heat until thoroughly dissolved. Preserving sugar tends to cause less foaming. Warmed sugar dissolves more quickly than cold sugar. Once the sugar has dissolved, the heat can be increased to give a good rolling boil. When a good quality pan is used, an occasional stir will be enough to prevent burning. Constant stirring tends to produce an excess of foam.

Testing for Setting Point

Start to test for set when the frothing subsides and the jam boils noisily with distinctive heavy plopping bubbles. There is a short period when the jam has a good jellied set. If it is allowed to boil past this point its consistency will become sticky. The 2 usual tests for set are:

Cold plate test: Draw the pan off the heat (to prevent overcooking while testing). Put a small spoonful of the jam on a cold plate or saucer and leave it to cool. Push a fingertip through the cooled jam and if it has reached setting point the surface will wrinkle. If it does not wrinkle, reboil the jam for 3 minutes and test again. With a little experience, it is not difficult to decide if it has reached setting point.

Flake test: Draw the pan off the heat. Dip a clean wooden spoon into the jam, remove it and hold it above the pan for a minute to cool the jam on it. Then hold the spoon at an angle to allow the jam to run off. If setting point has been reached, the cooled jam will hang from the spoon in a curtain and then break off sharply and cleanly in a flake. If setting point has not yet been reached, the cooled jam will run off in a series of drops.

Note The temperature and volume tests below are also sometimes recommended.

Cold plate test

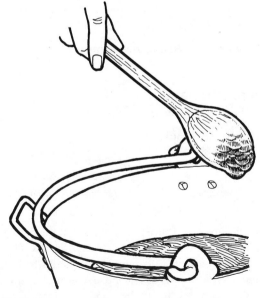

Flake test

Testing for Soluble Solids

If home-made jam is to be sold, it must comply with statutory requirements regarding soluble solids content. One of the 2 following tests should be used as well as a setting test. These can also be used at home as a guarantee of quality.

Temperature test: For this an accurate thermometer marked in degrees up to at least 120°C is required. A sugar boiling thermometer can be used. Its accuracy should be checked occasionally by standing it in a saucepan of cold water. When the water is heated to boiling point the thermometer should register 100°C. If it registers slightly below or above this, then a similar correction must be made when reading the jam temperature. Stand the thermometer in hot water before and after use. Stir the jam to give an even temperature throughout. Hold the thermometer in the jam, ensuring that about 5cm of the stem is immersed and that the bulb is not resting on the base of the pan. Normally a temperature of 104°–105°C indicates that the jam is acceptable for sale.

Volume test: For most jams the final yield is $1\frac{2}{3}$ times the weight of sugar used, ie sugar is 60% of the total yield. The following recipes are based on 1.5kg of sugar which gives a yield of 2.5kg of jam, sufficient to fill 5×450g jars and a small sampling jar. If the volume of jam is measured on a dip-stick principle, the yield can be checked before potting. Fill a 450g jar with water 5 times, pour the water into the preserving pan, and then add water from 1×225g jam jar. Make sure that the pan is standing level. Hold the handle of a wooden spoon carefully upright in the centre of the pan and mark on it the level of the water. Empty the pan and make the jam. Draw the pan off the heat and test for set. When bubbling has subsided, test the level by holding the handle of the wooden spoon upright in the centre of the jam. If the mark is submerged, reboil for a few minutes and test again.

Note If one preserving pan is used consistently, time can be saved if one spoon handle is marked off for different yields or, for jelly making, for different quantities of liquid (a 450g jar holds approximately 300ml of fluid).

Potting and Finishing Jam

When the jam reaches setting point, remove the pan from the heat and remove the scum. This is done most economically with a warm perforated spoon or slice. The scum on jam made from fibrous fruits, eg strawberries or apricots, may be difficult to remove, but for the appearance of the jam it is worth doing well. Where there is very little scum, eg on blackcurrant jam, it can be gently stirred in with the addition of a little butter or margarine. The scum removed can be used to sweeten stewed fruit, or can be served over a steamed pudding. It comprises largely air bubbles, so its flavour, although fruity, is rather weak.

Using a small jar or cup pour the jam while really hot into warm, clean, dry jars, filling them right to the brim (since jam shrinks considerably on cooling). The modern jam jar with a twist-top is ideal for keeping jam in good condition especially in centrally heated homes. The twist-top *must* be put on the preserve as soon as it is potted as it acts as a seal.

Alternatively, with plain-necked jars, a transparent cellulose or waxed disc to fit the surface of the jam should be pressed on the hot preserve. The top cellulose cover can be put on at once while the jam is still very hot, but it is usually easier to wait until the preserve is quite cold. Never put it on *warm* jam as this encourages the growth of mould. Slightly dampen one side of the cover and place that side uppermost over the jam before securing with a rubber band or string.

Label the jars with the type of preserve, the date, and any other details about the fruit or the recipe which will be of interest later. Store preserves in a cool, dry place, preferably dark. The store for jams that are not sealed with twist-tops should have some ventilation.

Because of variations in utensils and ingredients, even a well-tried jam recipe may differ from household to household. The following recipes have been thoroughly tested but yields may vary slightly according to the equipment used.

Note Recipes for jams made using a pressure cooker can be found on pp1437–38.

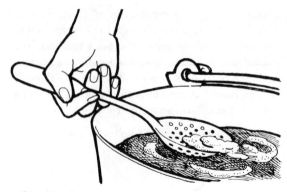

Skimming jam

Apricot Jam(1)
(fresh fruit)

Yield 2.5kg (approx)

1.5kg apricots	*1.5kg sugar*
300ml water	

Wash, halve, and stone the fruit and put it into a preserving pan with the water. If desired, crack a few of the stones, remove and halve the kernels and blanch them by dipping in boiling water. Add the halved kernels to the pan. Simmer until tender and reduced by one-third. Add the sugar and stir over low heat until dissolved. Bring to the boil and boil rapidly until setting point is reached. Remove from the heat, skim, pot, cover, and label.

Cooking time 50 minutes (approx)

Apricot Jam(2)
(with added pectin)

Yield 2.5kg (approx)

1kg ripe apricots	*1.5kg sugar*
200ml water	*½ × 227ml bottle pectin*
3 × 15ml spoons lemon juice	*(generously measured)*

Wash, stone, and slice the apricots. Put the fruit in a preserving pan with the water and lemon juice. Simmer gently for 20 minutes until the fruit is tender. Add the sugar and stir over low heat until dissolved. Bring to the boil and boil rapidly for 1 minute, stirring occasionally. Remove from the heat, skim if required, and stir in the pectin thoroughly. Cool for 5 minutes, then pot and cover immediately before labelling.

Cooking time 30 minutes (approx)

Apricot or Peach Jam
(dried fruit)

Yield 2.5kg (approx)

500g dried apricots **or** *peaches*	*50g blanched almonds (optional)*
1.5 litres water (apricots) **or** *1 litre (peaches)*	*1.5kg sugar*
	2 × 15ml spoons lemon juice

Wash the fruit and cut it up, apricots into 2 or 3 pieces, peaches into 5 or 6 pieces. Put the fruit into a basin with the water and leave to soak for 24–48 hours. Shred the almonds, if used. Transfer the fruit and water to a preserving pan and simmer for about 30 minutes or until tender, stirring occasionally. Add the sugar, lemon juice, and shredded almonds, if used. Stir over low heat until the sugar is dissolved. Bring to the boil and boil rapidly until setting point is reached. Remove from the heat, skim, pot, cover, and label.

Note This can be made in the winter when fresh fruit is scarce.

Cooking time 1 hour (approx)

Apple and Ginger Jam

Yield 2.5kg (approx)

1.5kg apples	*100g crystallized ginger*
25g ginger root	
600ml water	*1.5kg sugar*
juice of 1 lemon (2 × 15ml spoons approx)	

Peel, core, and cut up the apples. Bruise the ginger root. Tie the peel, cores, and bruised ginger loosely in muslin. Put the apples, water, and bag of peel in a preserving pan with the lemon juice and cook slowly until tender. Remove the bag of peel after squeezing it into the preserving pan. Cut the crystallized ginger into neat pieces. Add to the pan with the sugar. Stir over low heat until the sugar has dissolved, then bring to the boil and boil rapidly until setting point is reached. Remove from the heat, skim, pot, cover, and label.

Cooking time 45 minutes (approx)

Blackberry Jam

Yield 2.5kg (approx)

1.5kg blackberries	*1.5kg sugar*
2 × 15ml spoons lemon juice	

Pick over the blackberries and wash gently but thoroughly. Put in a preserving pan with the lemon juice and simmer gently until the fruit is cooked and well softened. Add the sugar and stir over low heat until dissolved. Bring to the boil and boil rapidly until setting point is reached. Remove from the heat, skim, pot, cover, and label.

Cooking time 30–40 minutes (approx)

Blackberry and Apple Jam(1)

Yield 2.5kg (approx)

350g sour apples (peeled and cored)	*1kg blackberries*
300ml water	*1.5kg sugar*

Slice the prepared apples and cook them in half the water until pulped. Pick over the blackberries and wash them gently but thoroughly. Put in another pan with the rest of the water and cook until tender. (If the 2 fruits are cooked together, the apple will not cook to a pulp.) Mix the cooked fruits in a preserving pan and add the sugar. Stir over low heat until the sugar is dissolved, then bring to the boil and boil rapidly until setting point is reached. Remove from the heat, skim, pot, cover, and label.

Cooking time 1 hour (approx)

Note For Blackberry and Apple Jam (2), see p1438.

Seedless Blackberry and Apple Jam

Yield 1.5kg (approx)

1kg blackberries　　　*350g cooking apples*
200–300ml water　　　　*(peeled and cored)*
　　　　　　　　　　　　sugar (see recipe)

Pick over the blackberries and wash them gently but thoroughly. Put them in a pan with half the water and cook over very low heat until tender. Rub through a fine nylon sieve to remove the seeds (at least 500g of pulp should be obtained). Slice the apples and cook them in the rest of the water until soft. Mix the apple pulp with the blackberry pulp and weigh it. Weigh out an equal quantity of sugar. Simmer the pulp until thick, add the sugar and stir over low heat until dissolved, then bring to the boil and boil rapidly until setting point is reached. Remove from the heat, skim, pot, cover, and label.

Cooking time 1 hour (approx)

Blackcurrant Jam

Yield 2.5kg (approx)

1kg blackcurrants　　　*1.5kg sugar*
1 litre water

Remove the currants from the stalks. If the fruit is dirty, wash and drain it thoroughly. Put into a preserving pan with the water, and cook slowly until the skins are soft. This will take at least 30 minutes, probably more. As the pulp thickens, stir frequently to prevent burning. Add the sugar, stir over low heat until dissolved, then bring to the boil and boil rapidly until setting point is reached. (Test for set at intervals after about 10 minutes of rapid boiling.) Remove from the heat, skim, pot, cover, and label.

Cooking time 50 minutes (approx)

Cherry (Morello) Jam (1)

(with redcurrant juice)

Yield 2.5kg (approx)

300ml redcurrant juice　　*1.5kg sugar*
　(see recipe)
1.5kg Morello cherries

To obtain the redcurrant juice, prepare 700g currants and cook in enough water barely to cover until tender. This will take about 1 hour. Strain through a jelly bag or fine nylon sieve, without squeezing. Return the juice to the pan and boil down to 300ml.

Meanwhile, wash the cherries, remove the stones and tie them in a loose muslin bag. Put the cherries and the bag into the redcurrant juice in a preserving pan, and simmer gently until the cherries are very tender. Remove the bag of stones. Add the sugar and stir off the heat until dissolved. Return to the heat, bring to the boil and boil rapidly until setting point is reached. Cool for 7–10 minutes to prevent the fruit from rising in the jars. Skim if required, stir gently, pot, cover, and label.

Cooking time for jam 45 minutes (approx)

Cherry (Morello) Jam (2)

(with added pectin)

Yield 2.5kg (approx)

1kg Morello cherries　　*1.5kg sugar (scant)*
　(stoned)　　　　　　　*1 × 227ml bottle*
200ml water　　　　　　　*pectin*
3 × 15ml spoons lemon
　juice

Wash the cherries and put them in a preserving pan with the water and lemon juice. Cover, and simmer for 15 minutes. Remove the lid, add the sugar and stir over low heat until dissolved. Bring to the boil and boil rapidly for 3 minutes. Remove from the heat, skim if required, and stir in the pectin thoroughly. Cool for 15 minutes, pot, and cover with discs. Tie down and label when cold. Do not use twist-tops.

Cooking time 30 minutes (approx)

Black Cherry Jam

(with added pectin)

Make as above, but add 6 ×15ml spoons lemon juice to the preserving pan and, after adding the pectin, return the pan to the heat to reboil for 1 minute. Then remove and cool for 15 minutes before potting, to prevent the fruit from rising.

Damson Jam

Yield 2.5kg (approx)

1.25kg damsons   1.5kg sugar
500ml water

Remove the stalks, wash the damsons, and put into a preserving pan with the water. Cook slowly until the damsons are well broken down. Add the sugar, stir over low heat until dissolved, then bring to the boil and boil rapidly. Remove the stones as they rise to the surface (a stone basket clipped to the side of the pan is useful for holding the stones, and allows any liquid to drip back into the pan). Continue boiling rapidly until setting point is reached. (Test for set after about 10 minutes of rapid boiling.) Remove from the heat, skim, pot, cover, and label.

Cooking time 45 minutes (approx)

A stone basket clipped to the side of a preserving pan

Gooseberry Jam

Yield 2.5kg (approx)

1–1.25kg gooseberries   1.5kg sugar
500ml water

Use gooseberries which are still green, before they have ripened or turned colour. Top and tail and wash them and put in a preserving pan with the water. Simmer gently until the fruit is soft (this may take 30 minutes or longer). Add the sugar and stir over low heat until dissolved. Bring to the boil and boil rapidly until setting point is reached. (Test for set after about 10 minutes of rapid boiling.) Remove from the heat, skim, pot, cover, and label.

Note This is a good jam for beginners, because it sets very easily. It is especially good served on scones with whipped cream.

Cooking time 50 minutes (approx)

Green Gooseberry Jam

Most gooseberry jam turns a reddish colour as it cooks. If preferred, gooseberry jam can be kept green by taking the following steps:
1) Choose a variety of gooseberry which is green when ripe, eg Careless, Green Gem, Keepsake.
2) Use a copper or brass preserving pan.
3) Once the sugar has been dissolved, give the jam the shortest possible boil in which it will set.

Muscat Flavoured Gooseberry Jam

Put the flowers from 8 heads of elderflowers in a muslin bag and cook with the gooseberries. Squeeze out the juice and remove the bag before the sugar is added.

Greengage Jam

Yield 2.5kg (approx)

1.5kg greengages *1.5kg sugar*
125–250ml water

Remove the stalks, wash the greengages, and put them into a preserving pan with the water. Cook slowly until the fruit is well broken down. Ripe fruit or very juicy varieties will need only a small quantity of water and will be cooked in a few minutes. Firmer varieties may take about 20 minutes to break down, and will need the larger quantity of water. Add the sugar, and stir over low heat until dissolved. Bring to the boil, then boil rapidly, removing the stones as they rise to the surface (a stone basket clipped to the side of the pan is useful for holding the stones, and allows any liquid to drip back into the pan). Test for set after about 10 minutes of rapid boiling. Remove from the heat, skim, pot, cover, and label.

Cooking time 45 minutes (approx)

VARIATION

Plum Jam

Make as for Greengage Jam, but use 250ml water. A few of the raw plums may be stoned, the kernels blanched and added to the pan with the water.

Plum and Apple Jam

Yield 2.5kg (approx)

750g plums *450ml water*
750g apples (peeled and *1.5kg sugar*
* cored)*

Wash the plums and put into a preserving pan with the apples and the water. Cook the fruit slowly until the skins of the plums are softened. Add the sugar, stir over low heat until dissolved, bring to the boil and boil rapidly until setting point is reached. Remove the stones as they rise to the surface (a stone basket clipped to the side of the pan is useful for holding the stones, and allows any liquid to drip back into the pan). Alternatively, the plums may be stoned before cooking. Remove from the heat, skim, pot, cover, and label.

Cooking time 45 minutes (approx)

Peach Jam

Yield 2.5kg (approx)

1.8kg peaches *1 × 5ml spoon tartaric*
300ml water * acid*
* * *1.5kg sugar*

Use small, firm peaches. Dip the fruit into boiling water for 30 seconds, then into cold water, and peel off the skin. Cut up the fruit and put it in a preserving pan with the water and acid. Simmer until the fruit is tender. Add the sugar and stir over low heat until it is dissolved. Bring to the boil and boil rapidly, removing the stones as they rise (a stone basket clipped to the side of the pan is useful for holding the stones, and allows any liquid to drip back into the pan). Test for set after about 10 minutes of rapid boiling. Remove from the heat, skim, pot, cover, and label.

Cooking time 1¼ hours (approx)

Peach Jam
(dried fruit)
See p1103.

Marrow and Ginger Jam
(pulped)

Yield 2.5kg (approx)

1.5kg marrow (peeled *grated rind and juice of*
* and cut up)* * 2 lemons*
100g crystallized ginger *1.5kg sugar*

Put the marrow in a colander over a pan of boiling water, put the pan lid on top of the marrow and steam for 10–20 minutes until it is tender. Drain thoroughly and mash to a pulp. Cut up the crystallized ginger, and put into a preserving pan with the marrow, lemon rind and juice. Bring to the boil, add the sugar and stir over low heat until dissolved.

Continue boiling, stirring frequently, for about 20 minutes or until the marrow is transparent and the preserve is thick. Remove from the heat, skim, pot, cover, and label.

Note This jam does not produce a definite set, but is potted when it reaches the required consistency.

Cooking time 2 hours (approx)

Rhubarb and Ginger Jam

Yield 2.5kg (approx)

1.5kg rhubarb　　　　　*15g ginger root*
1.5kg sugar
3 × 15ml spoons lemon
juice

Wipe or string the rhubarb and cut it into chunks. Put it in a basin, sprinkling on the sugar in layers. Add the lemon juice and leave to stand overnight.

Next day, put the contents of the basin into a preserving pan. Bruise the ginger, tie it in muslin, and add it to the pan. Bring to the boil and boil rapidly until 2.5kg is obtained (use the volume test, p1101). Remove from the heat, skim, pot, cover, and label.

Note This jam is fibrous rather than set. Summer rhubarb is recommended for jam-making as it gives a better texture than spring rhubarb.

Cooking time 20 minutes (approx)

Mulberry and Apple Jam
(sieved)

Yield 2.5kg (approx)

1kg mulberries　　　　*500g apples (peeled and*
250ml water　　　　　　*cored)*
　　　　　　　　　　　1.5kg sugar

Prepare the mulberries and cook in some of the water until soft. Rub through a fine nylon sieve. Cook the apples in a preserving pan in the rest of the water. When the apples are soft, stir in the sieved mulberries and the sugar. Stir over low heat until the sugar is dissolved. Bring to the boil and boil rapidly until 2.5kg jam is obtained (use the volume test, p1101). Remove from the heat, skim, pot, cover, and label.

Cooking time 45 minutes (approx)

Quince Jam

Yield 2.5kg (approx)

1.5kg quinces　　　　*juice of 1 large lemon*
250–500ml water　　　*1.5kg sugar*

Peel, core, and cut up the fruit. If very hard, it can be grated or minced coarsely. Put the fruit with the water (using 500ml if fruit is tough) and the lemon juice in a preserving pan and simmer until soft. Add the sugar and stir over low heat until dissolved. Bring to the boil and boil quickly until setting point is reached. Remove from the heat, skim, pot, cover, and label.

Note This jam has a delicious flavour but is rather solid. Jelly may be preferred (see p1112).

Cooking time 1 hour (approx)

Raspberry Jam
(quick method)

Yield 2.5kg (approx)

1.25kg raspberries　　　*1.5kg sugar*

Do not wash the raspberries unless absolutely necessary; if they have to be washed, drain very thoroughly. Bring the fruit gently to the boil without any added water, then boil rapidly for 5 minutes. Warm the sugar. Draw the pan off the heat, add the warmed sugar, then stir well over low heat until all the sugar has dissolved. Bring to the boil and boil rapidly for 1 minute. Remove from the heat, skim quickly, pot at once, cover, and label.

Note This jam does not set firmly, but it has a delicious fresh flavour.

Cooking time 10 minutes (maximum)

Loganberry Jam

Yield 2.5kg (approx)

1.5kg loganberries   *1.5kg sugar*

Prepare the loganberries and cook very gently without any added water, until the centre core of the fruit is tender. Add the sugar, stir over low heat until it is dissolved, then bring to the boil and boil rapidly until setting point is reached. Remove from the heat, skim, pot, cover, and label.

Cooking time 20–30 minutes (approx)

Strawberry Jam

Yield 2.5kg (approx)

1.5kg strawberries   *juice of 1 lemon*
(hulled)   *1.5kg sugar*

Put the strawberries and lemon juice in a preserving pan. Heat gently for 10 minutes, stirring all the time, to reduce the volume. Add the sugar, stir over low heat until dissolved, then bring to the boil and boil rapidly until setting point is reached. Remove from the heat and skim. Leave the jam undisturbed to cool for about 20 minutes until a skin forms on the surface and the fruit sinks. Stir gently to distribute the strawberries. Pot and cover with discs. Tie down and label when cold. This jam will have cooled too much for the use of a twist-top.

Cooking time 20 minutes (approx)

Whole Strawberry Jam
(with added pectin)

Yield 2.5kg (approx)

1kg small strawberries   *a little butter* **or**
1.5kg sugar   *margarine*
3 × 15ml spoons lemon   *$\frac{1}{2}$ × 227ml bottle pectin*
juice

Hull the strawberries and put them in a preserving pan with the sugar and the lemon juice. Leave to stand for 1 hour, stirring occasionally. Place over low heat and, when the sugar has dissolved, add a small piece of butter or margarine to reduce the foam. Bring to the boil and boil rapidly for 4 minutes. Remove from the heat and stir in the pectin thoroughly. Leave to cool for 20 minutes to prevent the fruit rising. Stir gently, then pot and cover with discs. Tie down and label when the jam is cold. Do not use twist-tops.

Cooking time 1$\frac{1}{2}$ hours (approx)

Jellies

In jelly-making, only the juice extracted from the fruit is used. As no fruit tissue is included to give body to the preserve, the juice must be rich in pectin to ensure a good set. Do not use fruits poor in pectin for making jelly as the extra commercial pectin that must then be added may spoil the flavour of the fruit.

The yield of jelly from a given quantity of fruit is less than for jam so, for economy, wild fruits, such as crab-apple, blackberry (bramble) or the cheaper cultivated fruits, such as damson, are popular for jelly-making. Blackcurrants and redcurrants give a good yield, but raspberries give a poor yield.

GENERAL METHOD FOR MAKING JELLY

Choose fruit which is firm and ripe or slightly under-ripe. Remove any leaves, large stalks, or diseased parts before use. Wash the fruit briefly if necessary; do not leave it soaking to become waterlogged. If the quantity of fruit is small, it is better to use a saucepan rather than a large preserving pan. Either must be bright and clean inside. Put in the required amount of water, add the prepared fruit and any lemon juice or other acid, if required. Simmer until the fruit is tender and well broken down (usually 45 minutes – 1 hour).

Testing for Pectin

A thick, sticky juice indicates good setting quality but it is advisable to take a pectin test (p1100) to check the pectin clot. A firm clot is essential; it is a waste of effort to continue making the jelly without one. To correct a weak clot which may occur from poor quality fruit, either simmer the fruit for a further 20 minutes and then retest, or add a proportion of fruit of good-setting quality, such as apple, and simmer until it is well broken down before retesting.

Straining

While the fruit is cooking, fix a jelly bag or cloth on a stand, or from the legs of an upturned chair or stool. A felt or flannel cloth will give a much clearer jelly than thinner material. Place a bowl under the bag and pour boiling water through the cloth to scald it. Empty the bowl and replace it before pouring the juice from the preserving pan into the cloth. Leave the juice to drip for 45 minutes – 1 hour. Do not squeeze or press the bag as this may make the jelly cloudy. Very little dripping occurs after 1 hour, so there is no advantage in leaving it longer.

Sometimes, with pectin-rich fruit, a second extraction can be made. To do this, return the contents of the bag to the pan after 20 minutes, add about half the original quantity of water, stir, and then simmer for 30 minutes before straining. Mix the 2 extracts together, or make 2 grades of jelly, a richer and fruitier one from the first extraction and a milder blend from the second.

Straining jelly

Adding the Sugar

The amount of sugar required has to be worked out from the strength of the clot and the yield of juice. For an average clot, allow 800g sugar per litre of juice; reduce the sugar to 650g per litre for a less firm clot; increase to 900g for a very firm one. The yield of jelly will be approximately $1\frac{2}{3}$ times the weight of the sugar.

Measure the extract, put it in the cleaned pan and let it simmer. Weigh out the required sugar and stir it into the extract. When dissolved, bring to a steady boil. Very rapid boiling may spoil the clarity of the jelly. After 10 minutes, test for set by either of the methods recommended for jam, and for volume or temperature. The flake test and temperature test are recommended (see pp1100–1).

Potting and Finishing Jelly

Skim very carefully. The last traces of scum can be removed from the surface with the torn edge of a piece of soft kitchen paper. Transfer the jelly gently to clean, warm jars, preferably 225g in size. At first, pour down the side of the tilted jar to avoid including air bubbles. Work quickly to finish potting before the jelly begins to set. Seal or cover at once. Leave the pots of jelly undisturbed, preferably in a warm place, for 24 hours before labelling. Store in a cool, dark cupboard (with some ventilation if the jars are not sealed). Traditionally, jelly is potted into straight-sided jars and turned out for serving. Small jars are recommended because the set begins to 'weep' as soon as a pot of jelly is broken into, so the sooner it is used up the better.

An exact yield of jelly from a particular recipe cannot be given because losses in straining the juice vary. However, the method for calculating an approximate yield from the sugar used is given above. Cooking times in the recipes refer to the time needed to bring the jelly to setting point after straining.

Note Recipes for jellies made using a pressure cooker can be found on pp1438–39.

Apple Jelly

2kg well-flavoured crab-
  apples, cooking apples
  or windfalls
1.5–2 litres water

25g ginger root **or**
  thinly pared rind of
  1 lemon
sugar (see recipe)

Wash and cut up the apples without peeling or coring. If windfalls are used, weigh after removing the damaged parts. Use just enough water to cover, bruise the ginger, if used, add the chosen flavouring and simmer for about 1 hour until tender and well mashed. If the apples do not break down, press them after 30 minutes with a potato masher. Test for pectin (p1100), and if the clot is satisfactory, strain the juice through a scalded jelly bag. Leave to drip for 1 hour, then measure the extract, return it to the cleaned pan, and heat gently. Weigh and add the required sugar (usually 800g for every litre of extract). Stir over low heat until dissolved. Bring the jelly to a steady boil and test for set after 10 minutes. Remove from the heat, skim carefully, pot, cover, and label.

Cooking time 30 minutes (approx)

Rowan-berry and Apple Jelly

1kg rowan-berries
  (mountain ash berries)
1kg apples

2 litres water
sugar (see recipe)

Remove the rowan-berry stalks, and wash and drain the berries. Wash and slice the apples without peeling or coring. Cook them with the rowan-berries and water until soft and broken up. Strain the juice through a scalded jelly bag. Leave to drip for 1 hour, then measure the extract, return it to the cleaned pan, and heat gently. Add 800g sugar for each litre of extract. Stir over low heat until dissolved. Boil steadily until setting point is reached. Remove from the heat, skim, pot, cover, and label.

Note This jelly has the characteristic bitterness of the rowan-berry and would be unpalatable if made without the addition of apple. It is excellent with meat dishes as a change from redcurrant jelly.

Cooking time 30 minutes (approx)

Blackberry and Apple Jelly

1.5kg cooking apples
1.5kg blackberries

1 litre water
sugar (see recipe)

Wash and cut up the apples without peeling or coring. If windfalls are used, weigh after removing the damaged parts. Pick over and rinse the blackberries if necessary. Simmer the fruits separately, giving the larger share of water to the apples. When the fruits are tender, after about 1 hour, mash them and pour both into a scalded jelly bag. Leave to drip for 1 hour, then measure the extract, return it to the clean pan, and heat gently. Add 800g sugar for each litre of extract. Stir over low heat until dissolved. Boil steadily until setting point is reached. Remove from the heat, skim, pot, cover, and label.

Cooking time 30 minutes (approx)

Elderberry and Apple Jelly

1kg apples
1kg elderberries

sugar (see recipe)

Wash and slice the apples without peeling or coring, and cook with enough water to cover the fruit. Cook the elderberries separately with barely enough water to cover. Simmer both fruits until tender and broken up. Mix the 2 pulps, then test for pectin (p1100). If the clot is weak, continue simmering to reduce the quantity. Strain the juice through a scalded jelly bag. Leave it to drip for 1 hour. Measure the extract, return it to the cleaned pan and heat gently. Add 700–800g sugar for each litre of extract. Stir over low heat until dissolved, then boil steadily until setting point is reached. Remove from the heat, skim, pot, cover, and label.

Cooking time 30 minutes (approx)

Cranberry and Apple Jelly

1kg apples
700g cranberries

sugar (see recipe)

Wash the fruit. Slice the apples without peeling or coring, and place in a pan with the cranberries and enough water to cover. Simmer gently until thoroughly mashed. Test for pectin (p1100). Strain through a scalded jelly bag. Leave to drip for 1 hour, then measure the extract, return it to the cleaned pan and heat gently. Weigh and add the required sugar (usually about 800g for each litre of extract). Stir over low heat until dissolved, then boil steadily until setting point is reached. Remove from the heat, skim, pot, cover, and label.

Cooking time 25 minutes (approx)

Damson and Apple Jelly

2kg apples
1kg damsons
2 litres water
sugar (see recipe)

Wash the fruit. Slice the apples without peeling or coring. Add to the damsons and water. Simmer gently until the fruit is thoroughly mashed. Strain through a scalded jelly bag. Leave it to drip for 1 hour. Measure the extract, return it to the cleaned pan and heat gently. Weigh and add the required sugar (usually about 800g for each litre of extract). Stir until dissolved, then boil steadily until setting point is reached. Remove from the heat, skim, pot, cover, and label.

Note If the juice is very thick, a second extraction can be made with another litre of water, and the 2 extracts mixed together.

Cooking time 20 minutes (approx)

Blackcurrant Jelly

2kg blackcurrants
2 litres water
sugar (see recipe)

Remove the leaves and the larger stems, and wash the blackcurrants if necessary. Place in the preserving pan, add 1 litre of the water, and simmer gently until thoroughly tender. Mash well, then strain through a scalded jelly bag, leaving it to drip for at least 15 minutes. Return the pulp left in the jelly bag to the pan, add the rest of the water and simmer for 30 minutes. Strain this pulp through the bag and leave to drip for 1 hour. Mix the 2 extracts

together. Measure the extract, return it to the cleaned pan, and bring to the boil. Add 800g sugar for each litre of extract and stir until dissolved. Boil steadily, without stirring, until setting point is reached. Remove from the heat, skim, pot, cover, and label.

Cooking time 20 minutes (approx)

Gooseberry Jelly

2kg green gooseberries
1.5 litres water
sugar (see recipe)

Wash the gooseberries and place them in the pan without topping and tailing. Add the water and cook until thoroughly tender and broken. Test for pectin (p1100). Strain through a scalded jelly bag. Leave to drip for 1 hour, then measure the extract, and return it to the cleaned pan. Add 700–800g sugar for each litre of extract. Bring to the boil, stirring to dissolve the sugar, and boil steadily until setting point is reached. Remove from the heat, skim, pot, cover, and label.

Note This is a pink-coloured jelly and the addition of the sugar to the cold extract gives a longer boiling time which improves the colour of the preserve.

Cooking time 25 minutes (approx)

Medlar Jelly

1kg ripe medlars
1 litre water
1 small lemon
sugar (see recipe)

Choose very ripe but not rotten fruit. Cut up the medlars, barely cover with the water, and slice and add the lemon. Simmer until soft and mushy, then strain through a scalded jelly bag. Leave it to drip for 1 hour. Measure the extract and return it to the cleaned pan. Add 700–800g sugar for each litre of extract, stir until dissolved, then boil steadily until setting point is reached. Remove from the heat, skim, pot, cover, and label.

Cooking time 30 minutes (approx)

Mint Jelly (1)

1kg green apples
500ml water
a small bunch of fresh
   mint
500ml vinegar

sugar (see recipe)
5 ×10ml spoons
   chopped mint
a few drops green
   colouring (optional)

Wash the apples, cut in quarters and put in a preserving pan with the water and the bunch of mint. Simmer until the apples are soft and pulpy, then add the vinegar and boil for 5 minutes. Strain through a scalded jelly bag and leave to drip for 1–2 hours. Measure the juice and return it to the cleaned pan. Add 800g sugar for each litre of juice, and bring to the boil, stirring until the sugar is dissolved. Boil rapidly until setting point is nearly reached, add the chopped mint and colouring, if used, then boil steadily until setting point is reached. Remove from the heat, pot, and cover immediately. When cold, label and store.

Cooking time 30 minutes (approx)

Note For Mint Jelly (2), see p1438.

Orange Shred and Apple Jelly

1kg crab-apples **or**
   windfalls

peel and juice of
   2 oranges
sugar (see recipe)

Wash the apples and cut into rough pieces, discarding any damaged portions. Place in a preserving pan with enough water barely to cover. Simmer gently for about 1 hour or until the fruit is quite tender. Strain through a scalded jelly bag. Leave it to drip for 1 hour.

Meanwhile, wash the oranges; squeeze out and strain the juice. Cut into quarters and remove the pith. Cook the quarters of peel in 100ml water in a small covered saucepan for about 1 hour, or until tender. Measure the apple extract, the remaining water from the cooked peel, and the juice of the oranges, and put into the preserving pan with 800g sugar for each litre of liquid. Stir over low heat until the sugar is dissolved, then boil fast until setting point is reached. Remove from the heat and skim quickly. Meanwhile, dry the cooked peel in a

cloth and cut into fine shreds. Add these carefully to the jelly immediately after skimming; do not stir. Leave to cool slightly until a skin is formed on the surface of the jelly and then pot, cover, and label.

Note This jelly is rather mild in flavour, but clear and with a delightful colour.

Cooking time 40 minutes (approx)

Quince Jelly

quinces
water

sugar (see recipe)

Wipe the fruit carefully; do not peel. Cut into quarters and put into a preserving pan with enough cold water to cover. Bring slowly to the boil and simmer gently until the quinces are quite tender. Strain through a scalded jelly bag. Leave to drip for 1 hour, then measure the extract, and return it to the cleaned pan. Add 800g sugar for each litre of extract and stir until dissolved, then boil steadily until setting point is reached. Remove from the heat, skim, pot, cover, and label.

Note Only fruit from the quince tree gives the characteristic aromatic flavour, but some ornamental japonicas produce an economical and pleasant jelly.

Cooking time 20 minutes (approx)

Sloe and Apple Jelly

2kg apples
1kg sloes

sugar (see recipe)

Wash and cut up the apples but do not peel or core them. Place in a preserving pan with the sloes, just cover with water and simmer to a pulp. Strain through a scalded jelly bag. Leave to drip for 1 hour. Measure the extract, return it to the cleaned pan, and heat gently. Add 800g sugar for each litre of extract. Stir until dissolved, then boil steadily until setting point is reached. Remove from the heat, skim, pot, cover, and label.

Cooking time 20 minutes (approx)

Redcurrant Jelly

2kg large, juicy
  redcurrants **or**
redcurrants and white
  currants mixed

sugar (see recipe)

Remove the leaves and the larger stems, and wash the fruit if necessary. Put the fruit in a preserving pan, without any water, and heat very gently for about 45 minutes or until the currants are softened and well cooked. Mash, then strain the pulp through a scalded jelly bag. Leave it to drip for 1 hour. Measure the extract, and return it to the cleaned pan. Add 1kg sugar for each litre of extract. Bring to the boil, stirring all the time, then boil, without stirring, for 1 minute. Skim the jelly quickly, and immediately pour it into warmed jars, before it has a chance to set in the pan. Cover and label.

Note The above recipe, using undiluted fruit juice, makes a good full-flavoured jelly. For less experienced cooks, it is easier to add enough water to cover the fruit and to make 2 extractions and then mix them; add 800g sugar for each litre of extract. This will give a larger yield of slightly less robust-flavoured jelly, but it will not set before there is time to pour it into pots.

Cooking time 10 minutes (approx)

Rose-hip and Apple Jelly

1kg apples (preferably
  crab-apples **or**
  windfalls)
500ml water

500g rose-hips
2 ×15ml spoons lemon
  juice
sugar (see recipe)

Wash and cut up the apples roughly, removing any damaged parts. Put the apples in a pan with half the water and simmer until soft. The pan can be covered for this slow cooking. Put the rose-hips in another saucepan with the rest of the water and lemon juice and simmer until soft. After 10 minutes, press down the hips with a wooden spoon to hasten softening. Strain the apples and hips through a scalded jelly bag and leave to drip for 1 hour. Measure the extract, and return it to the cleaned pan. Add 800g sugar for each litre of extract, and

stir until dissolved. Bring to a steady boil and test for set after 5–10 minutes. Remove from the heat, skim, pot, cover, and label.

Note It is important to strain the rose-hips through a closely woven cloth such as flannel or felt to retain the tiny barbed hairs which can cause irritation internally.

Cooking time 1 hour (approx)

Guava Jelly

guavas
water

lime **or** lemon juice
sugar (see recipe)

Choose the fruit carefully, using 3 under-ripe to 1 ripe guava. Cut up the fruit, barely cover with water and simmer until tender and well broken down. Test for pectin (p1100), then strain through a scalded jelly bag. If the pectin test gives a good clot, make another extract with half the original quantity of water and simmer for another 20 minutes. Mix and measure the 2 extracts, add the juice of 1 lime or 1 lemon for each litre and simmer. Add 700–800g sugar for each litre of extract. Stir over low heat until dissolved, then boil steadily until setting point is reached. Remove from the heat, skim, pot, cover, and label.

Cooking time 30 minutes (approx)

Marmalades

Marmalade-making is similar to jam-making and nearly all the same rules apply. As in jam-making, the fruit is first simmered gently, usually in an uncovered pan, until it is thoroughly softened. It is this long, slow cooking which releases the setting agent pectin. After this, the sugar is added and stirred over gentle heat until dissolved. The marmalade is then boiled rapidly, with a full, rolling boil, until setting point is reached. The test for setting point are the same as for jam-making (p1100).

These are the essential differences: the peel of citrus fruit takes longer to soften than the fruit used for jams. For this reason, a pressure cooker can be particularly useful in cutting down cooking time (see p1439).

Because most of the pectin is in the pips and the pith, rather than in the fruit pulp or fruit juice, these are important ingredients in marmalade recipes. The pips and pith should not be discarded (unless they are being replaced by pectin stock) but should be tied loosely in muslin and cooked with the fruit until the pectin has been extracted. If the muslin bag is tied to the handle of the pan, it can easily be removed before adding the sugar. When the bag is removed, squeeze it thoroughly between 2 plates and pour the resulting liquid into the preserving pan.

Because citrus fruit is rich in pectin it requires ample acid and sugar to produce a good result. Many jam recipes use an equal weight of fruit and sugar, whereas with thick marmalades twice as much sugar as fruit can be used.

A muslin bag tied to the handle of a preserving pan

Points to Note

1) All citrus fruits should be only just ripe, and must be used as soon as possible.
2) It is not usually easy for the inexperienced to distinguish between the true Seville orange and other imported bitter oranges. Sevilles have a superior flavour, but ordinary bitter oranges can replace them in the recipes.
3) To peel citrus fruit easily, soak in boiling water for 1–2 minutes to loosen the skin.
4) To cut the peel into shreds, use a very sharp stainless knife and resharpen it from time to

time. Drop the shreds into a bowl of water as soon as they are cut, to prevent them drying out. The peel will swell slightly during cooking. For shredding large quantities, it is worthwhile using a special machine which cuts the peel quickly and easily, although not as evenly as when done by hand.

If a coarse cut marmalade is preferred, use the method on p1115 (Dark Coarse-cut Marmalade). Alternatively, with some other methods, the uncooked fruit can be put through a coarse mincer, but this looks less attractive and gives a paste-like texture.

Shredding peel

5) Many recipes used to recommend soaking the peel, etc for 24–48 hours to soften it before cooking. This is no longer considered necessary, but it may be convenient to do so, if, for instance, the fruit cannot be prepared and cooked on the same day, or if particularly tough skins such as grapefruit are being used. The softening effect of long soaking on the peel is minimal but some pectin is extracted, so setting point is reached more rapidly.
6) The sugar should not be added until the peel will disintegrate when a piece is pressed between thumb and forefinger, and the quantity in the pan has reduced considerably. Stir until the sugar is dissolved, then boil the marmalade briskly until setting point is reached. This should be after 15–20 minutes boiling, but depends to some extent on the quantity and recipe.

Potting and Covering Marmalade

Skim as for jams (p1102) immediately setting point is reached. If the scum is not removed immediately, it subsides on the peel and is then extremely difficult to skim off.

To prevent the peel rising to the top of the pots, leave the skimmed marmalade to cool undisturbed in the pan until a thin skin begins to form on the surface. Then stir to distribute the peel (do this gently to avoid air bubbles). *Do not* stir clear jelly marmalades.

Pour into warm, clean, dry jars, fill to the brim, and continue as for jams (p1102).

Note For recipes for marmalades using a pressure cooker, see p1439.

Clear Shred Orange Marmalade

Yield 4kg (approx)

1.5kg Seville or *bitter oranges*	*1 sweet orange*
2 lemons	*4 litres water*
	sugar (see recipe)

Wash the fruit and cut it in half. Squeeze out and strain the juice, keeping the pulp and pips. Scrape all the white pith from the peel, and put pips, pulp, and pith into a basin with 2 litres of the water. Shred the peel finely and put this into another basin with the remaining water and the juice. Leave both to soak for 24 hours, if liked.

Strain the pips, etc through a muslin bag and tie loosely. Put the bag and strained liquor, the peel, and juice into a preserving pan and bring to simmering point. Simmer for 1½ hours or until the peel is tender. Remove from the heat and squeeze out the muslin bag gently. For a very clear jelly, allow to drip only. Add 800g sugar for each litre of juice and dissolve the sugar completely over low heat. Bring to the boil and boil rapidly for 20–25 minutes or until setting point is reached. Remove from the heat, skim, and cool until a skin forms on the surface. Pot and cover immediately, then label.

Cooking time 2 hours (approx)

Dark Coarse-cut Marmalade

Yield 5kg (approx)

1.5kg Seville oranges	*3kg sugar*
2 lemons	*1 × 15ml spoon black*
4 litres water	*treacle*

Wash the fruit and cut it in half. Squeeze out and strain the juice. Tie the pips and pulp loosely in a muslin bag. Slice the peel into medium-thick shreds, and put into a preserving pan with the juice, muslin bag, and water. Simmer for about 1½–2 hours, or until the peel is tender and the liquid reduced by at least one-third. Remove the bag of pips and squeeze the juice out gently. Remove the pan from the heat, add the sugar and treacle, then stir over low heat until the sugar is dissolved. Bring to the boil and boil rapidly until setting point is reached. Remove from the heat, skim, cool until a skin forms, then stir, pot, cover, and label.

Cooking time 2–2½ hours (approx)

Five Fruit Marmalade

Yield 2.5kg (approx)

1kg fruit: 1 orange,	*2 litres water*
1 grapefruit, 1 lemon,	*1.5kg sugar*
1 large apple, 1 pear	

Wash the citrus fruit, peel it, and shred the peel finely. Scrape off the pith, and chop the flesh coarsely. Put the pips and pith in a basin with 500ml water. Put the peel and chopped flesh in another basin with the remaining water. Soak for 24 hours, if liked. Strain the pips and pith through a muslin bag and tie loosely. Put into a preserving pan with the fruit, peel, and all the liquid. Peel and dice the apple and pear and add to the other fruit. Bring to the boil, reduce the heat and simmer for 1¼ hours until the volume is reduced by one-third. Remove the bag and squeeze out the juice. Add the sugar, and stir over low heat until dissolved. Bring to the boil and boil rapidly for about 30 minutes, or until setting point is reached. Remove from the heat, skim, cool slightly, then stir, pot, cover, and label.

Cooking time 2 hours (approx)

Grapefruit Marmalade

Yield 3.5kg (approx)

1kg grapefruit   *2 litres water*
3 lemons   *2kg sugar*

Wash the fruit and cut it in half. Squeeze out and strain the juice. Remove some of the pith if it is thick, cut it up coarsely and put it with the pips in a muslin bag. Slice the peel finely. Put all the fruit and juice into a basin, add the muslin bag, cover with the water and leave overnight to soften and bring out the flavour.

Next day, put it all into a preserving pan and cook gently for 2 hours or until the peel is soft. Remove the bag and squeeze out the juice, add the sugar, stir until it is dissolved, then boil rapidly until setting point is reached. Remove from the heat, skim, cool slightly, then stir, pot, cover, and label.

Cooking time $2\frac{1}{2}$ hours (approx)

Grapefruit and Pineapple Marmalade

Yield 2.5kg (approx)

500g grapefruit   *juice of 1 lemon*
1.5 litres water   *1.5kg sugar*
1 small pineapple

Wash the grapefruit, peel it, and shred the peel finely. Scrape off the pith and cut up the flesh, putting the pips and coarse tissue to one side. Measure the total quantity, it should be 500ml. Put the flesh and peel into a basin with 1 litre of the water. Put the pips, tissue, and a little of the pith into another basin with the remaining water. Soak for 24 hours, then tie the pips, etc in a muslin bag.

Next day, cut the pineapple into slices, removing skin, eyes, and hard core; chop the flesh into small pieces. Measure the pineapple with the lemon juice; there should be 250ml. Put the pineapple in a preserving pan with the lemon juice, the grapefruit, all the liquid, and the muslin bag. Bring to the boil, reduce the heat, and simmer gently until the volume is reduced by one-third. Remove the

bag and squeeze out the juice. Add the sugar, and stir over low heat until dissolved. Bring to the boil and boil rapidly until setting point is reached. Remove from the heat, skim, cool for 15–20 minutes, then stir, pot, cover, and label.

Note It is important to have the full initial quantity of prepared fruit, ie 750ml total.

Cooking time 2 hours (approx)

Lemon Marmalade

Yield 2.5kg (approx)

750g lemons   *1.5kg sugar*
2 litres water

Wash the lemons and remove the peel. Shred it finely (removing some of the pith if very thick). Cut up the fruit, putting to one side the pips and coarse tissue. Put the fruit and shredded peel in a large basin with half the water. Put the pips, pith, and coarse tissue in another basin and cover with the rest of the water. Leave to soak for 24 hours, if liked.

Next day, tie the pips etc loosely in a muslin bag, and transfer the contents of both basins to the preserving pan. Bring to the boil, reduce the heat and simmer gently for about $1\frac{1}{2}$ hours until the peel is tender and the contents of the pan are reduced by at least one-third. Remove the bag and squeeze out the juice. Add the sugar, stir over low heat until dissolved, then bring to the boil and boil rapidly for about 15–20 minutes or until setting point is reached. Remove from the heat, skim, cool, then stir, pot, cover, and label.

Cooking time 2 hours (approx)

Lemon and Ginger Marmalade

Yield 2.5kg (approx)

750g lemons   *200g crystallized ginger*
2 litres water   *1.5kg sugar*
50g ginger root

Wash the lemons and peel in quarters, shred the peel finely, and place in a large basin. Cut up the fruit finely, putting to one side the pips, pith, and coarse tissue. Add the fruit to the cut peel, and cover with most of the water. Put the pips, pith, and coarse tissue into another basin with the remaining water. Soak for 24 hours, if liked.

Drain the liquid from the pips and tissue and put it in a preserving pan with the rest of the fruit and liquid. Bruise the ginger root. Tie the tissue, pips, and ginger root in a muslin bag and add to the pan. Bring to the boil, reduce the heat, and simmer gently for $1\frac{1}{4}$–$1\frac{1}{2}$ hours until reduced by one-third. Remove the bag and squeeze out the juice. Chop the crystallized ginger finely. Add the sugar and crystallized ginger to the pan and cook over low heat, stirring until the sugar has dissolved. Bring to the boil and boil rapidly for about 20 minutes or until setting point is reached. Remove from the heat, skim, cool for 5–10 minutes, then stir, pot, cover, and label.

Note For economy, use half quantity or less of crystallized ginger, and 75g ginger root.

Cooking time 2–$2\frac{1}{4}$ hours (approx)

Lemon Shred Jelly Marmalade
(with added pectin)

Yield 2kg (approx)

$1 \times 15ml$ spoon very finely shredded lemon peel	250ml lemon juice (4–5 lemons)
500ml water	1.2kg sugar
$\frac{1}{4} \times 5ml$ spoon bicarbonate of soda	$1 \times 227ml$ bottle pectin

Cook the peel in the water and bicarbonate of soda for 10 minutes until softened. Add the lemon juice and sugar and heat gently until the sugar has dissolved, stirring occasionally. Bring to a full rolling boil and boil rapidly for 30 seconds. Remove from the heat and stir in the pectin thoroughly. Reboil for 30 seconds. Remove from the heat, cool slightly to prevent the peel floating, and skim if necessary. Stir, pot, cover, and label.

Cooking time 20 minutes (approx)

Lemon Jelly Marmalade

Yield 2–2.5kg

1kg lemons	1.5kg sugar
2 litres water	

Wash the lemons. Pare off the rind, shred it finely, and tie in a muslin bag. (If marmalade with fewer shreds is preferred, use only half the rind.) Cook the shreds in half the water, in a covered pan, until tender. Meanwhile, roughly cut up the fruit and cook with the remaining water in a preserving pan for 2 hours, keeping the pan covered. Pour off the liquid from the shreds, add it to the cooked fruit and strain it all through a scalded jelly bag. Pour the strained liquid into the cleaned pan, simmer for a few moments if it seems rather thin, add the sugar and stir over low heat until dissolved. Add the shreds and boil rapidly until setting point is reached. Remove from the heat, skim, cool, pot, cover, and label.

Cooking time $2\frac{1}{2}$ hours (approx)

Melon and Lemon Marmalade
(with added pectin)

Yield 2kg (approx)

500g lemons	500g firm, green-fleshed melon (peeled and cubed)
125ml water	
$\frac{1}{4} \times 5ml$ spoon bicarbonate of soda	1.5kg sugar
	$1 \times 227ml$ bottle pectin

Wash the lemons, squeeze out the juice, remove most of the pith, and shred the peel very finely. Pour the water into the pan, add the juice, peel, and bicarbonate of soda. Simmer, covered, for 10 minutes until softened. Add the melon, and simmer until tender and transparent. Add the sugar, and heat gently until dissolved, stirring occasionally. Bring quickly to a full rolling boil and boil for 2 minutes. Remove from the heat and stir in the pectin thoroughly. Leave to cool for a few minutes to prevent the peel rising. Skim if necessary. Stir, pot, cover, and label.

Cooking time 30 minutes (approx)

Seville Orange Marmalade(1)

Yield 3kg (approx)

1kg Seville oranges
3 ×15ml spoons lemon
juice

3 litres water
sugar (see recipe)

Wash the fruit and cut it in half. Squeeze out the juice and the pips. Cut the peel into shreds. Tie the pips in a muslin bag and put it into a basin with the orange and lemon juice, water, and peel. Soak for 24–48 hours. Transfer to a preserving pan and cook gently for about 1½ hours or until the peel is soft. Remove the bag and squeeze out the juice. Draw the pan off the heat, add 800g sugar for each litre (see volume test p1101) and stir until dissolved. Return to the heat, bring to the boil and boil rapidly until setting point is reached. Remove from the heat, skim, cool, then stir, pot, cover, and label.

Cooking time 2½ hours (approx)

Seville Orange Marmalade(2)

Yield 3kg (approx)

1kg Seville oranges
2 litres water

3 ×15ml spoons lemon
juice
2kg sugar

Wash the oranges and, with a sharp knife, shred the whole fruit finely. Tie the pips and pieces of coarse tissue loosely in a muslin bag. Put the fruit, muslin bag, and water in a basin and leave to soak overnight.

Next day, transfer to a preserving pan, bring to the boil, add the lemon juice, and simmer gently for about 1½–2 hours until the peel is soft and the contents of the pan are reduced by at least one-third. Squeeze the muslin bag gently, then remove it. Add the sugar, stir over low heat until dissolved, then bring to the boil and boil rapidly until setting point is reached. Remove from the heat, skim, cool for about 10 minutes, then stir, pot, cover, and label.

Cooking time 2½ hours (approx)

Seville Orange Marmalade(3)

Yield 3kg (approx)

1kg Seville oranges
1.5 litres boiling
water

3 ×15ml spoons lemon
juice
2kg sugar

Wash the fruit and put it whole and unpeeled into a saucepan. Pour on the boiling water, cover and simmer gently for about 2 hours, until the fruit is tender enough to be pierced easily with a fork. Alternatively, the whole fruit and water can be baked in a covered casserole in a very cool oven at about 140°C, Gas 1, until the fruit is soft; this will take about 4–5 hours. When the fruit is tender, cut it in half, remove the pips, then cut it up with a knife and fork, carefully keeping all the juice. Return the pips to the water in which the fruit was cooked, and boil for 5 minutes to extract more pectin. Strain the liquid to remove the pips. Put the sliced fruit with the strained liquid and lemon juice in a preserving pan and bring to the boil. Draw the pan off the heat, add the sugar and stir until dissolved. Bring to the boil and boil rapidly until setting point is reached. Remove from the heat, skim, cool, then stir, pot, cover, and label.

Note This method is simple to do, and is recommended if a fairly coarse-cut marmalade is liked.

Cooking time 2½ hours (approx)

Orange Jelly Marmalade

Yield 2.5kg (approx)

1kg Seville oranges
2.5 litres water

juice of 2 lemons
1.5kg sugar

Wash and peel the oranges, remove the thick pith, and shred finely 100g of the peel. Cook the shreds in 500ml of the water, in a covered pan for about 1½ hours or until tender. Meanwhile, cut up the fruit roughly and put it with the lemon juice and 1.5 litres of water in a preserving pan. Simmer for 2 hours with the lid on the pan. Drain the liquid from the shreds, add it to the cooked fruit and strain it all through a scalded jelly bag. Leave it to drip for 15 minutes, then return the pulp to the preserving pan and add the rest of the water. Simmer for 20 minutes, then strain again through the jelly bag, allowing it to drip undisturbed. Pour the strained extract into the cleaned pan, simmer for a few moments if it seems rather thin, then add the sugar and stir over low heat until dissolved. Add the shreds and boil hard until setting point is reached. Remove from the heat, skim, leave for 15 minutes, then pot, cover, and label.

Cooking time 3 hours (approx)

Orange Shred and Apple Jelly
See p1112.

Three Fruit Marmalade

Yield 2.5kg (approx)

750g fruit (approx):   *2 litres water*
1 grapefruit, 2 lemons,   *1.5kg sugar*
and 1 sweet orange

Wash and peel the fruit, and shred the peel coarsely or finely as preferred. (Remove some of the pith if it is very thick.) Cut up the fruit and tie the pips and any pith or coarse tissue in a muslin bag. Soak the fruit, peel, and muslin bag in the water in a basin for 24 hours.

Next day, transfer to a preserving pan and simmer gently for 1½ hours, or until the peel is tender and the contents of the pan are reduced by about one-third. Remove the bag and squeeze out the juice. Add the sugar and stir over low heat until dissolved. Bring to the boil and boil rapidly until setting point is reached. Remove from the heat, skim, cool, then stir, pot, cover, and label.

Cooking time 2 hours (approx)

Tangerine Marmalade
(with added pectin)

Yield 3kg (approx)

1kg tangerines   *2kg sugar*
1 litre water   *1 × 227ml bottle*
juice of 3 lemons   *pectin*

Wash the tangerines and put into a preserving pan with the water. Simmer gently, covered, for 40 minutes. When cool enough to handle, remove the peel and cut up the fruit, taking out the pips and the coarse tissue. Return the pips and tissue to the liquid and boil hard for 5 minutes. Shred half the peel and discard the rest. Strain the liquid, discarding the pips and tissue, and return to the preserving pan with the pulp, peel, lemon juice, and sugar. Stir over gentle heat until the sugar has dissolved, and then bring to a full rolling boil. Boil hard for 3 minutes. Remove from the heat, stir in the pectin thoroughly, then boil for 1 minute. Remove from the heat, skim if necessary, cool slightly, then stir, pot, cover, and label.

Note Tangerine marmalade is normally difficult to set; the addition of pectin makes this easier. Mandarins or clementines can be used equally well for this recipe.

Cooking time 1 hour (approx)

Other Sweet Preserves

These should be potted and covered in the same way as jams (p1102) unless otherwise indicated.

Mincemeat

Yield 1.8kg (approx)

200g cut mixed peel	50g blanched chopped
200g seedless raisins	almonds
25g preserved stem	a generous pinch each of
ginger	mixed spice, ground
200g cooking apples	ginger, ground
200g shredded suet	cinnamon
200g sultanas	grated rind and juice of
200g currants	2 lemons and 1 orange
200g soft brown	150ml sherry, brandy **or**
sugar	rum

Mince or chop finely the peel, raisins, and ginger. Peel, core, and grate the apples. Combine all the ingredients thoroughly in a large basin. Leave, covered, for 2 days, in a cool place, stirring occasionally. (This prevents fermentation later.) Pot, cover, and label. Store in a cool dry place.

Mrs Beeton's Very Nice Preserve of Damsons

Yield 1kg (approx)

700g firm, ripe	250g granulated **or**
damsons	caster sugar

Remove the stalks from the damsons and discard any that are blemished. Damp the sound fruit slightly with water and put into a large jar; mix with the sugar. Cover loosely and stand in a heavy saucepan with a false bottom (p1131). Cover completely with cold water. Bring the water gradually to the boil, reduce the heat and simmer for about 30 minutes until the fruit is tender. Leave until cold. Pour off the liquid, boil to reduce it by about one-quarter, strain through a scalded jelly bag and pour it over the fruit. Seal securely, label, and keep in a cool place.

Note This very fruity preserve does not set as a jam

but is delicious served with cream or used in a fruit tart. It contains many stones.

Peanut Butter

See p1300.

FRUIT CONSERVES

The following recipes are whole fruit preserves. They have a thick syrup rather than a jam-like set.

Apricot Conserve

Yield 800g (approx)

300ml water	500g stoned, under-ripe
juice of 1 lemon	apricots
500g sugar	

Boil the water, lemon juice, and sugar together for 10 minutes. Skim, then add the fruit. Crack half the stones, skin the kernels, and add them to the syrup. Boil gently for about 45 minutes. Test the syrup on a plate for set and when ready put the conserve into dry, warm pots, cover at once, and label.

Note If the apricots are large, they may be halved or even quartered.

Cooking time 1 hour (approx)

VARIATION

Peach Conserve

Make in the same way but reduce the sugar to 375g and add $\frac{1}{4} \times 5$ml spoon salt. The kernels are not usually included but a few can be added if liked.

Cumquat Conserve

Yield 800g (approx)

500g cumquats
2 × 15ml spoons salt

500g sugar

Wash the fruit, put it into a saucepan with enough water to cover and add the salt. Cook gently until the cumquats are tender, then drain off the water. Cover with fresh water and leave overnight.

Next day, put the sugar in a pan with just enough water to dissolve it. Cook for 5 minutes, without stirring, until a syrup is formed. Drain the fruit carefully, add to the syrup and boil quickly for about 1 hour, taking care to prevent boiling over. Test the syrup on a plate for set, and when ready put the conserve into dry, warm bottles or jars, cover at once, and label.

Cooking time $1\frac{1}{4}$ hours (approx)

Green Fig Conserve

Yield 1.6kg (approx)

1kg fresh green figs
1kg sugar
125ml water

3 × 15ml spoons lemon
   juice **or** cider vinegar

Wipe and slice the fruit. Dissolve the sugar in the water, add the lemon juice or vinegar, and boil for 10 minutes. Add the figs and boil gently for 1 hour. Test the syrup on a plate for set, and when ready put the conserve into dry, warm bottles or jars, cover at once, and label.

Cooking time $1\frac{1}{4}$ hours (approx)

Marrow and Ginger Conserve

Yield 2.5kg (approx)

2kg marrow (peeled and
   cut into 2cm cubes)
1.5kg sugar

50g ginger root
4 × 15ml spoons lemon
   juice

Put the marrow in a colander over a pan of boiling water, put the pan lid on top of the marrow and steam for 10–20 minutes until just cooked and tender. (The time will depend on the ripeness of the marrow and the size of the colander.) Transfer to a basin, cover with the sugar and leave overnight.

Next day, bruise the ginger root and tie it in muslin. Put the bag of ginger into a preserving pan with the marrow and lemon juice. Cook slowly for about 1 hour until the marrow is clear and transparent. This preserve does not give a firm set, so do not cook it for too long. Stop when the correct yield (2.5kg) is obtained (use the volume test p1101). The marrow should be transparent and the syrup thick. Remove the bag of ginger just before the end. Pot, cover, and label.

Cooking time 1 hour (approx)

Pineapple Conserve
(using fresh fruit)

Yield 900g (approx)

4 lemons
500g pineapple (peeled
   and cut into small
   cubes)

150ml water
500g sugar

Strain the juice of the lemons into a basin, put the rind, pith, and pips into a muslin bag. Put the cubes of pineapple, 4 × 15ml spoons lemon juice, the muslin bag, and the water into a preserving pan. Simmer gently until the cubes are completely tender. Remove the muslin bag and the pineapple cubes. Add the sugar and stir until dissolved. Return the pineapple to the syrup and cook until it is clear and the syrup thick. Skim, leave to cool for 5 minutes, then pot, cover, and label.

Cooking time 1 hour (approx)

FRUIT CURDS

These are fruit custards made with citrus fruits, butter and eggs, and used in the same way as jam. They should have a balanced flavour of sharp and sweet, smoothly blended; rind or peel should not be noticeable. If lump sugar is used it can be rubbed on the peel of citrus fruit to remove the zest, but this is a tedious process. The rind can be grated but it is better to pare it off in strips, cook it in the curd, then strain it out.

A double boiler or a basin set over a pan of boiling water is recommended for making any type of curd.

Curd tends to shrink considerably on cooling, especially if the eggs have been whisked, so take care to fill the jars to the brim. Leave to thicken for 24 hours, and use within 1–2 months.

Note Recipes for curds made using a pressure cooker can be found on p1440.

Apricot Curd

Yield 1.5kg (approx)

225g dried apricots	*700g granulated sugar*
grated rind and juice of	*175g butter*
2 lemons	*2 eggs*

Soak the apricots overnight; then cook them until tender, using as little water as possible. The flavour is best if the fruit is cooked in a covered casserole in a very cool oven at 120°C, Gas ½, for 40 minutes. Strain off any excess water, and mash the fruit well; or preferably, sieve or process in an electric blender. Put the fruit into the top of a double boiler or basin over boiling water and with the lemon rind, juice, sugar, and butter. Stir until the sugar has dissolved. Beat the eggs lightly and add them to the mixture. Continue heating and stirring until the curd thickens. Pot, cover and label.

Note For fresh apricots use 700g fruit (unstoned weight).

Cooking time 30 minutes (approx)

Lemon Curd (1)

Yield 300g (approx)

2 lemons	*75g butter*
225g lump **or**	*3 eggs*
granulated sugar	

Wash and dry the lemons. Grate the rind or pare it into strips; squeeze out the juice. Put the rind, juice, and sugar into the top of a double boiler or basin over boiling water. Stir occasionally until the sugar dissolves. Remove from the heat and stir in the butter. Leave to cool. Beat the eggs lightly and pour the cooled mixture over them. Strain it back into the pan or basin and place over gentle heat. Stir frequently with a wooden spoon until the mixture begins to thicken. When it coats the back of the spoon lightly, pour into small jars, taking care to fill to the brim. Cover and label.

Cooking time 30 minutes (approx)

VARIATIONS

Grapefruit Curd

Substitute 2 grapefruit, and use 250g granulated sugar and 100g butter.

Orange Curd (1)

Substitute 2 oranges, and add the juice of 1 lemon. Use only 50g butter and melt it in the double boiler or basin before adding the rind, juices, and sugar.

Note For Lemon and Orange Curd (2), see p1440.

FRUIT BUTTERS

Fruit butters are made from firm fruit pulp and a higher proportion of sugar than is used for jam; this also produces a stiffer consistency. The ratio is 200–300g sugar to every 450g pulp. Butters can be spiced, and are a good way of using up surplus fruit. Apart from spreading on bread and butter, they can be used in desserts or sweet and sour savoury dishes. Use within 1–2 months.

Other fruit butters are made in the same way as the recipe for Apple Butter (1) below.

Apple Butter (1)

Yield 3.25kg (approx)

3kg crab-apples **or**
windfalls

2 litres water **or** *1 litre
water and 1 litre cider*

*granulated sugar (see
recipe)*

*1 × 5ml spoon ground
cloves*

*1 × 5ml spoon ground
cinnamon*

Wash the fruit and cut it up roughly, discarding any damaged parts. Simmer the fruit in the water, or water and cider, until well softened, and then sieve. Weigh the pulp, return it to the pan, and simmer until it thickens. Add three-quarters of the pulp weight in sugar, and the ground spices. Stir until the sugar dissolves, then boil steadily, stirring frequently, until no free liquid runs out when a small sample is cooled on a plate. Pot, cover at once, and label.

Note Apple can be used to extend more expensive fruits.

Cooking time 1–1½ hours

Apple Butter (2)

Yield 2.5–3kg (approx)

2kg cooking apples
400ml apple juice
*300g (approx)
granulated sugar*
*grated rind and juice of
1 lemon*
a pinch of salt
*2 × 5ml spoons ground
cinnamon*

*1 × 2.5ml spoon ground
cloves*
*1 × 2.5ml spoon ground
allspice*
*1 × 2.5ml spoon grated
nutmeg*

Remove the stems from the apples and quarter them; do not peel or core them. Place in a large saucepan and pour over the apple juice. Cover and cook slowly until the apples are broken down to a soft pulp. Remove from the heat and leave to cool completely. When cold, sieve the pulp, and discard the seeds and peel. Add 75g sugar to each 250g pulp, and then add the rest of the ingredients. Return to the heat and stir until the sugar dissolves.

Continue to cook, half covered, until the pulp is the consistency of soft butter. The mixture should be dark brown. Pot in heated jars, leave until the mixture stops bubbling, then cover, cool, and label.

Cooking time 45 minutes (approx)

FRUIT CHEESES

Fruit cheeses contain an even higher proportion of sugar than do butters – an equal quantity of sugar to pulp. They are a more concentrated and stiffer preserve which keeps for 1–2 years. Flavour improves with age. They are best made when there is a glut crop of fruit because the quantity of fruit used is large for the quantity of cheese made.

Damson Cheese

Makes 3.2kg (approx)

2.75kg ripe damsons
250ml water

sugar (see recipe)
glycerine for jars

Remove the stalks and wash the fruit. Put into a heavy-bottomed saucepan, flameproof casserole or (traditionally) an ovenproof earthenware jar. Add the water, cover closely, and either simmer or bake for several hours until the fruit is very tender. (Bake in a very cool oven at 110°–120°C, Gas ¼–½.) Drain, reserving the juice. Sieve the fruit, and weigh the pulp (there should be about 2.3kg). Put into an uncovered pan with a little of the drained juice, and boil gently until very thick. Add 350–450g sugar per 450g pulped fruit and continue cooking, stirring all the time, until the cheese leaves the sides of the pan clean, and a spoon drawn across the bottom of the pan leaves a clean line. Turn at once into small heated jars without shoulders, smeared with glycerine inside; tap the jars on the table-top two or three times while filling to knock out air-holes. Cover while still hot, cool, then label.

Store for several weeks, then use like jam. For a traditional stiff cheese, store for at least a year, then turn out, slice and serve with plain gingerbread, butter, and Cheshire or Lancashire cheese.

Cooking time 1 hour (approx)

FRUIT PRESERVED IN BRANDY

This is a delicious method of preserving luxury fruit, such as dessert apricots, peaches or grapes. Brandy is used because it blends well, but other spirits or liqueurs can be substituted.

Apricots in Brandy

400g sugar　　　　　*1kg firm ripe apricots*
300ml water　　　　　*brandy (see recipe)*

Put 200g of the sugar and the water in a pan, and cook, without stirring, for about 5 minutes until a syrup is formed.

Wash and drain the apricots, prick them with a darning needle, and put them in the boiling syrup. Bring the syrup back to the boil, and remove the riper fruit at once. Firmer fruit should be boiled for 2 minutes, but do not let it become too tender. Pack the fruit into clean, tested bottling jars. Remove the syrup from the heat, and stir in the remaining sugar. When the sugar has dissolved, boil the syrup steadily to 102°C (approx). Leave the syrup to cool, and drain off any syrup which has accumulated in the packed jars. Add 100ml brandy to each 100ml syrup, mix together, and pour into the jars to cover the fruit. Cover the jars and continue as for the Quick Deep Pan method of bottling (p1131), leaving the jars in the pan for 2 minutes after they have simmered at 90°C, and before sealing.

VARIATIONS

Peaches in Brandy

Peel before pricking. Dip the peaches into boiling water for $\frac{1}{2}$–1 minute to loosen the skins, and then submerge them in cold water until they are all peeled. Put into the hot syrup. Continue as above.

Grapes in Brandy

Large, firm grapes must be used. Cut them off the bunch, leaving a little stalk on each. Prick each grape and continue as above, but make the original syrup with 100ml water to 200g sugar, and for bottling allow 150ml brandy to 100ml syrup.

CANDIED AND CRYSTALLIZED FRUIT

Shop-bought candied fruit is a succulent and expensive luxury, but it can be made at home to a professional standard without great skill or special equipment. The main requirement is patience, the process taking about 15 minutes a day for 10–14 days.

To obtain a good result, the water in the fruit must diffuse out slowly to be replaced by syrup. This is achieved by cooking the fruit gently in water, then steeping it in progressively sweeter syrup until it is preserved, plump, and tender. Any attempt to increase the strength of the syrup too quickly will result in tough, hardened, and shrivelled fruit. Sugar alone can be used for syrup making but the fruit's texture is better if part of the sugar is replaced by glucose. Powdered glucose weighs the same as sugar, but if using liquid glucose, increase the weight by one-fifth.

Well-flavoured fruits, fresh or canned, are used, eg apricots, pineapple or large, juicy plums. Very soft fruits, such as raspberries, tend to disintegrate. Fresh fruit should be firm yet ripe. Good quality canned fruit can be used; it lacks some of the full fresh flavour, but the canning process gives a good texture for candying.

The method is given in detail below. Once the details are understood, it should be enough to refer to the charts on p1125 and p1127.

To Candy Fresh Fruit

Note For angelica, orange, grapefruit, and lemon peel, see the special recipes on p1127.

Day 1:
Peaches: Peel and stone.
Pears: Peel, core, and cut into quarters.
Cherries: Stone.
Pineapples: Peel and slice, then cut into wedge-shaped pieces.

Small crab-apples, apricots, fleshy plums, green-gages: Prick several times to the centre with a stainless fork.

Cover the prepared fruit with boiling water and simmer gently until just tender when tested with a fine skewer, 10–15 minutes for firm fruits, only 3–4 minutes for tender fruits. Test often because overcooking at this stage makes the fruit squashy, while undercooking makes it dark and tough.

For each 500g of fruit, make a syrup from 250ml of the water in which the fruit was cooked, plus 50g sugar, and 125g glucose. Alternatively, use 250ml of the water and 150g granulated or pre-serving sugar. Stir until the sugar is dissolved, then bring to the boil.

Drain the fruit and place it in a small bowl, then pour the boiling syrup over it. If there is not enough syrup to cover it, make up some more, using the same proportions. Leave the fruit in the syrup for 24 hours, keeping it below the surface under a plate or saucer.

Day 2: Drain off the syrup into a saucepan, add 50g sugar for each original 250ml (ie add 100g if you originally made up 500ml syrup), bring to the boil and pour the syrup over the fruit in the bowl.

Day 3: Repeat Day 2.
Day 4: Repeat Day 2.
Day 5: Repeat Day 2.
Day 6: Repeat Day 2.
Day 7: Repeat Day 2.

Day 8: Add 75g sugar for every original 250ml syrup, heat and stir until dissolved. Add the drained fruit and boil for 3–4 minutes, then pour it all back into the bowl. (Boiling the fruit in the syrup in these final stages helps to make it plump.) Leave for 48 hours.

Day 10: Repeat Day 8. When the resulting syrup cools, it should then be of the consistency of fairly thick honey. Leave for 4 days. If the syrup is still thin when it cools on Day 10, repeat Day 8 again before leaving to soak for the 4 days.

Day 14: The process is now nearly complete. The fruit may be left at this stage, if liked, as it will keep in this heavy syrup for 2–3 weeks, or for 2 months in a covered jar in the refrigerator. To complete the process, remove the fruit from the syrup, using a fork to lift out. *Do not pierce the fruit.* Place it on a wire cake rack with a plate beneath to catch the drips. Allow the syrup to drain for a few minutes.

Put the rack into a very cool oven (not higher than 50°C). With an electric cooker, use residual

Candied Fresh Fruit Chart

Day	Amount of sweetening per 250ml	Method			Leave soaking for
1	50g sugar + 100g glucose *or* 150g sugar	Dissolve sugar. Bring syrup to boiling point. Pour over the drained cooked fruit.			24 hours
2	50g sugar	,,	,,	,,	24 hours
3	50g sugar	,,	,,	,,	24 hours
4	50g sugar	,,	,,	,,	24 hours
5	50g sugar	,,	,,	,,	24 hours
6	50g sugar	,,	,,	,,	24 hours
7	50g sugar	,,	,,	,,	24 hours
8	75g sugar	Dissolve sugar, add fruit, boil in the syrup for 3–4 minutes. Then return all to the bowl.			48 hours
10	75g sugar	As above. Repeat, if necessary, so that the syrup, when cold, is the consistency of a fairly thick honey.			4 days
14	nil	Dry in a very cool oven, not exceeding 50°C, or in the sunshine.			

heat after cooking. With gas, turn to the lowest glimmer. On some cookers there is a very cool control which can be used. Take care that the rack does not touch the walls of the oven. Candied fruit caramelizes easily and the flavour is then spoilt. Drying should take 3–6 hours if the heat is continuous; it may take 2–3 days if residual heat on several occasions is used. Turn the fruit gently with a fork, until it is no longer sticky to handle. In summer, the fruit can be dried by putting it in the sunshine for a few hours, turning it over at least once.

Pack in cardboard boxes with waxed paper lining the box and separating the layers. Store in a dry, cool place and do not keep for many months as the succulence will be lost.

Candied fruit should have a dry surface. If it remains sticky, the final sugar concentration in the fruit is probably too low. Humid storage conditions should be avoided.

Note Only 1 variety of fruit should be candied in the syrup; if you are candying several fruits at the same time, use separate syrups. Do not waste any surplus syrup; use it for fruit salads or stewed fruit, or for sweetening puddings. Alternatively, use it instead of sugar in fruit chutneys.

To Candy Canned Fruit

Pineapple rings or cubes, plums, peaches sliced or halved, and halved apricots are all recommended. Keep the sizes as uniform as possible. The quantities below are for about 500g drained fruit.

Day 1: Drain off the syrup and put the fruit into a large bowl. Measure the syrup into a pan and make it up to 250ml by adding water if necessary. Add 200g sugar or, better, 100g sugar and 100g glucose. Heat gently and stir until the sugar has dissolved, bring to boiling point, and pour the syrup over the fruit. If there is not enough syrup to cover the fruit, prepare some more by using 225g sugar to 200ml water. The quantity of syrup increases as the process continues, so avoid making extra if possible. Keep the fruit under the syrup with a plate. Leave for 24 hours.

Day 2: Drain the fruit, dissolve 50g sugar in the syrup, bring to the boil and pour over the fruit. Leave for 24 hours.

Day 3: Repeat Day 2.

Day 4: Repeat Day 2.

Day 5: Pour the syrup into a saucepan, add 75g sugar, warm the syrup to dissolve the sugar, and then add the fruit; bring to the boil and boil for 3–4 minutes. Return the fruit and syrup to the bowl. Leave for 48 hours.

Day 7: Repeat Day 5 and let the fruit boil until a little syrup cooled on a plate has the consistency of thick honey. Leave to soak for 3 or 4 days. If the syrup seems thin, add a further 75g sugar, dissolve it and boil the syrup with the fruit for a further few minutes. Leave to soak for 3 or 4 days. These final boilings help to make the fruit plump.

Day 11: Finish the fruit as when candying fresh fruit (Day 14 p1125).

Note Because canned fruit is already in syrup there is no initial cooking and the process is 3 days shorter than for fresh fruit.

Crystallizing Candied Fruit

The simplest method is to have ready some fine granulated sugar on a sheet of polythene, greaseproof paper, or foil. Lift a piece of fruit on a fork, dip it quickly into *boiling* water, allow a moment to drain, and then roll it in the sugar until it is evenly, but not too thickly coated. Pack as for candied fruit.

Making a Glacé Finish

This is used for cherries and some other fruits and gives a smooth, shiny finish.

Dissolve, over gentle heat, 500g granulated sugar in 150ml water, then bring to the boil. Dip each fruit into boiling water for 20 seconds, then drain. Pour a little of the boiling syrup into a warm cup, quickly dip the fruit and place it on a rack. When all the fruit has been dipped, place the rack in a temperature not exceeding 50°C, and turn the fruit often to ensure even drying. Pack as for candied fruit.

The main difficulty in preparing glacé fruits is to

Candied Canned Fruit Chart

Day	Amount of sweetening per 250ml	Method	Leave soaking for
1	100g sugar + 100g glucose *or* 200g sugar	Dissolve sugar. Bring syrup to boiling point and pour over.	24 hours
2	50g	,, ,, ,,	24 hours
3	50g	,, ,, ,,	24 hours
4	50g	,, ,, ,,	24 hours
5	75g	Dissolve sugar, add fruit, boil in the syrup for 3–4 minutes. Return to bowl.	48 hours
7	75g	As above, and boil until cooled syrup has thick honey consistency.	4 days
11	nil	If syrup thin, repeat Day 7. Otherwise, dry fruit in very cool oven, not exceeding 50°C, or in the sunshine.	

prevent the syrup from crystallizing or becoming too diluted. When the syrup in the small cup becomes cloudy, it must be discarded and replaced from the saucepan, which must be kept hot (but not boiling) and closely covered while processing.

Note For those specializing in candying or glacé finishes, it is worthwhile buying a suitable hydrometer to ensure the correct density of syrup.

Candied Angelica

Pick the stalks in April, when they are tender and brightly coloured. Cut off the root ends and leaves. Make a brine with 15g salt in 2 litres water, bring it to the boil and cover the stalks with it. Leave to soak for 10 minutes. Rinse in cold water. Put in a pan of fresh boiling water and boil for 5–7 minutes. Drain. Scrape to remove the outer skin. Continue as for candying fresh fruit pp1125–26, beginning with the instructions for making the syrup, Day 1.

Note Edible green colouring can be added to the syrup if the stalks show signs of losing their fresh colour. A glacé finish is attractive.

Candied Peel

Use oranges, lemons or grapefruit, and wash the fruit thoroughly, scrubbing with a clean brush if necessary. Cut in halves, remove the pulp carefully to avoid damaging the peel. Boil the peel for 1 hour. Give grapefruit peel, which is bitter, several changes of water. Drain, and continue as for candying fresh fruit pp1125–26, beginning with the instructions for making the syrup, Day 1. It is customary to pour some glacé syrup into half peels to set.

Candied Peel

(quick method)

Use oranges, grapefruit or lemons, but soak peel from grapefruit or lemons overnight to extract some of the bitterness. Cut the peel into long strips 5mm wide. Put in a saucepan, cover with cold water and bring slowly to the boil. Drain, add fresh water and bring to the boil again. Drain, and repeat 3 more times. Weigh the cooled peel and place with an equal quantity of sugar in a pan. Just cover with boiling water, and boil gently until the peel is tender and clear. Cool, strain from the syrup, and toss the peel in fine granulated sugar on greaseproof paper. Spread out on a wire rack to dry for several hours. Roll again in sugar if at all sticky. When quite dry, store in covered jars.

Use within 3–4 months.

BOTTLED AND DRIED PRESERVES

Fruits intended for preservation should be gathered in the morning, in dry weather, with the morning sun upon them, if possible; they will then have their fullest flavour, and keep in good condition longer than when gathered at any other time.

Fruit Bottling

Although home food freezers offer an excellent method of preservation for many fruits, there is still a place for bottling. Not every home has got freezing facilities, and some fruits are made more palatable by the bottling process.

Certain principles must, however, be understood. First, the fruit in each bottling jar must be heated to reach a high enough temperature to ensure that all micro-organisms are destroyed and chemical changes inactivated. Second, the jar must be sealed when at its maximum heat to prevent the re-entry of any air and the bacteria it contains. Bottling jars are heated either by immersing them in water which is kept on the boil for a time or by heating them in the oven. A correctly used bottling jar should give an effective seal provided the initial heating is adequate. Large jars and solid packs (fruit which has been packed tightly) will need more heating than small, loose ones; these differences are allowed for in the following instructions.

For a beginner, the more acid fruits are easier to preserve than, say, pears or tomatoes.

TYPES OF BOTTLING JARS

To ensure a seal, a jar must have (1) a gasket, such as a rubber or plastic band or washer, which may be built into the lid or separate, and (2) a sealing device such as a screwband or bail-type clip (on continental jars).

Purpose-made bottling jars with glass lids and separate screwbands are recommended, especially for light-coloured, less acid fruits, but more homely substitutes can be used. The twist-top type of jam jar lid makes a suitable seal if in good condition. This type of lid has an in-built gasket and four lugs which engage in the ridges at the neck of the jar. Twist-top lids can be bought separately to convert the older type of jam jar and some instant coffee jars.

Synthetic skin is sold at some chemists, hardware, and stationery stores, and this can be used for sealing jars for which no lids are available. Paraffin wax is also sold by chemists and makes a satisfactory seal for jars sealed after processing; it can either be melted and poured direct on the bottled fruit or brushed on a clean piece of linen tied over the jar. It is easy and cheap to use.

To Prepare the Jars

It is important to test that the jars are sound and are not chipped at the neck or on the lid as this can affect the seal. Rubber bands must still be elastic and should be soaked in warm water before use. They are comparatively cheap and should only be used once. Metal lids should also be discarded after use, and should certainly never be re-used if scratched or bent.

Corks for syrup, squash, and other bottled liquids should be new if possible. All corks should be boiled for 15 minutes before use.

Jars must be thoroughly clean. Wash them, then rinse in clean water and turn them upside down until required. The fruit will pack more easily if there is a film of water in the jar.

PREPARING THE LIQUID

Any fruit can be bottled in water alone, but the addition of sugar improves the flavour and colour. If sugar must be avoided, bottle the fruit in water and add any permitted sweetening just before use. Many people like to use honey or brown sugar instead of granulated sugar; when first trying this, substitute only half the quantity to test the result, since both honey and brown sugar add their own flavour to that of the fruit.

There is no rule about the quantity of sugar to use when making syrup for fruit bottling, but heavy syrups tend to make the fruit rise in the bottle. This does not matter for everyday use, but will lose points for exhibitors at shows.

Making Syrup

	sugar per litre of water	suitable for
light syrup	200g	apple slices
medium syrup	400–600g	all fruit
heavy syrup	800g	peaches

Heat the water in a saucepan which is light-coloured inside. Stir in the sugar and allow it to boil for 2 minutes only. Place a lid on the pan and remove from the heat. If the syrup is left on the boil longer it evaporates quickly, darkens, and is extravagant to use. A well-made syrup looks bright.

If cold syrup is required quickly, make it up with half the required quantity of water and add the rest cold.

Brine

Brine is used for some tomato preserves. It is very simply prepared by adding 15g salt to 1 litre of water and boiling for 1 minute.

CHOICE AND PACKING OF FRUIT

Select fruit which is fresh, free from blemishes, and just ripe (except for gooseberries, which should be firm and green). Dirty fruit must be washed but good quality fruit is usually clean. Prepare the fruit as described below, grade it by size, and pack it evenly and firmly in the preserving jars.

Solid packs save storage space. To pack the fruit closely but without squashing it, push it into place with a 15cm long stick about 1cm square with a pointed end, or with the handle of a wooden spoon.

PREPARING THE FRUIT

Apples: Peel, core, and cut into slices or rings 5mm thick. To prevent discoloration drop them into brine and keep them under the surface with a plate until ready to use. Drain, rinse, and pack immediately.

Apples – solid pack: After draining from brine, dip the fruit in boiling water for 2 minutes. This shrinks the fruit so that the jar can be tightly filled, with no air-spaces and little or no added liquid.

Apricots: Choose fully ripe fruit, not too soft. Remove stalks, and rinse. Pack whole, or halve by slitting and twisting the fruit; remove stones and pack halves quickly to prevent them browning. Crack some of the stones and add a few kernels to each jar.

Blackberries: Choose large, juicy, fully ripe berries. Remove stalks and leaves and discard any unsound fruit.

Cherries: Use Morello cherries for choice. Any cherries used should have small stones and plump flesh. Remove stalks, and rinse. They can be stoned, but take care not to lose the juice.

Currants (black, red, white): Choose large, firm, juicy, and well-flavoured currants. They should be evenly ripened and unbroken. Remove stalks; rinse if necessary. Red and white currants have large seeds and are best mixed with raspberries.

Damsons: Choose ripe, firm, purple fruit. Remove stalks, and wipe to remove bloom.

Gooseberries: Choose green, hard, and unripe berries. Top and tail and, if preserving in syrup, cut off a *small* slice at either end with a stainless steel knife to prevent the skins shrivelling and toughening.

Greengages: Choose firm, ripe fruit. Remove stalks and wipe to remove bloom. After processing, the fruit will turn greenish-brown and the syrup may become cloudy.

Loganberries: Choose firm, deep red fruit. Handle as little as possible. Remove stalks and leaves, and discard any fruit attacked by maggots.

Mulberries: Choose ripe and really freshly picked fruit. Handle as little as possible. Remove over-ripe and mis-shapen fruit.

Peaches: Choose a free-stone variety (eg Hale) just fully ripe. Dip in a pan of boiling water for 1 minute, then put into cold water; the skin should peel off easily. Halve and stone by slitting and twisting the fruit. Pack quickly.

Pears – dessert: Choose one of the best varieties, eg William's, Bon Chrétien, Conference, Doyenne du Comice, just fully ripe. Peel, halve, and scoop out cores and fibres with a sharp-pointed teaspoon. Place in an acid brine (1 litre water, 1×15ml spoon salt, and 1×5ml spoon citric acid), and keep below the surface with a plate. Rinse when ready for packing. Pack quickly.

Pears – cooking: Prepare as for dessert pears; then stew until tender in sugar syrup (400–600g sugar to 1 litre water). Drain, pack, and cover with the syrup in which they were cooked. Process as for dessert pears. Cooking pears will be darker in colour than dessert fruit.

Pineapples: Remove both ends, the peel, eyes, and centre core. Cut the fruit into rings or cubes. Process in heavy syrup.

Plums: If using Victoria plums, choose them when they are fully grown but firm and just turning pink. Choose purple varieties before the colour has developed, when they are still bright red. Choose yellow varieties when they are firm and lemon-yellow. Remove stalks, and wipe to remove the bloom. Free-stone varieties can be halved; others must be packed whole.

Raspberries: Choose large, firm, bright red, and fully flavoured berries. Pick carefully, putting the fruit gently in shallow baskets to prevent squashing. Remove plugs and damaged fruit. Preserve as soon as possible – it is not usually necessary to rinse the fruit first.

Rhubarb: Bottle rhubarb in the spring when it is tender and needs no peeling. Wipe the stalks and cut into short lengths. Pack immediately (in water or syrup) or after soaking. To soak, pour a hot syrup (400g sugar to 1 litre water) over the prepared rhubarb. Leave to soak and shrink for 8–12 hours; then pack, and cover with syrup.

To avoid a white deposit (unsightly but harmless) use previously boiled or softened water.

Strawberries: Hull the berries and if necessary rinse in cold water. The strawberries should be preshrunk, like rhubarb.

Tomatoes – in their own juice: Dip into boiling water for up to 30 seconds (according to ripeness), then into cold water; the skins should peel off easily. Leave them whole, or pack in halves or quarters if large. Press tightly into the jars, sprinkling the layers with sugar and salt (use 1×5ml spoon sugar, 1×10ml spoon salt, and a pinch of citric acid to each 1kg of tomatoes). No additional liquid is required.

Tomatoes – whole, unskinned: These are best oven-bottled (see below). Remove stalks, rinse tomatoes, and pack into jars. Use a brine (1×15ml spoon salt to 1 litre water and a pinch of citric acid) instead of water or syrup.

See p1134 for recipes for Tomato Purée and Tomato Juice.

Whortleberries: Prepare as for blackcurrants.

Solid pack: For small soft fruit, such as elderberries, blackberries, raspberries, strawberries, and mulberries: roll the fruit in caster sugar, then pack into the jars tightly, without any added liquid. This gives an excellent flavour although the fruit will have shrunk.

METHODS OF BOTTLING

If bottling mixed fruits, the timing and temperature must be based on the fruit which needs the highest temperature.

For bottling using a pressure cooker, see p1442.

Quick Deep Pan Method

1) Have ready a pan deep enough to submerge the bottles. It must have a false bottom, or wooden slats; alternatively layers of newspaper will do. Half fill it with water and heat it to 40°C.
2) Pack the prepared fruit tightly into tested jars. Put rubber rings, if used, to soak in warm water.
3) Fill jars to overflowing with *hot* (about 60°C) syrup or water. For tomatoes use hot brine.
4) Dip the rubber rings in boiling water and put them on the jars, with the lids. Fasten with screwbands, clips or other grips.
5) If using screwbands, tighten them, *then unscrew one-quarter turn to allow for expansion*. Clips are self-adjusting.
6) Stand jars in the pan on the false bottom. See that they do not touch each other or the side of the pan. They should be completely covered with the warm water. Put the lid on the pan.
7) Bring up to *simmering point* (90°C) in 25–30 minutes. Simmer for the time indicated on p1132. Then remove the jars one at a time on to a wooden surface. Use tongs to lift out the jars or, using a cup, empty out sufficient water to enable the jars to be lifted with a cloth.
8) Tighten screwbands. Clips should hold properly without attention. Leave for 24 hours.
9) Next day, remove screwbands or clips. Hold each jar in turn over a basin, and lift it by its lid. If properly sealed, the lid will stay on securely. Label with the date and other details, and store in a cool, dark, dry place. Wash, dry, and grease the screwbands or clips and keep to use again.

If one jar has not sealed, put it in the refrigerator and use the contents within 4–5 days. If a number of jars are unsealed, they must be reprocessed. Check the neck of each jar for chips, use new rubber bands and screwbands, and repeat the whole process.

Processing Times for Quick Deep Pan Method

The following times are for jars up to 1 litre maximum capacity.

Simmer for –

2 minutes: apple rings, blackberries, currants (black, red, white), gooseberries (for pies), loganberries, mulberries, raspberries, rhubarb (for pies), strawberries, whortleberries

10 minutes: apricots, cherries, damsons, gooseberries (for dessert), greengages, plums (whole), rhubarb (for dessert), solid pack of soft fruit (except strawberries)

20 minutes: apples (solid pack), nectarines, peaches, pineapples, plums (halved), solid pack of strawberries

40 minutes: pears, tomatoes (whole)

50 minutes: tomatoes (in own juice).

Slow Deep Pan Method

This is the same as the quick deep pan method, except that:

At step **1)**, do not heat the water in the pan.

At step **3)**, fill the jars with *cold* syrup, water or brine.

At step **7)**, raise the water gradually (ie in 90 minutes) to the temperature indicated below, and maintain it at that temperature for the time stated below.

Processing Times for Slow Deep Pan Method

Raise to 74°C and maintain at that temperature for 10 minutes: apple rings, blackberries, currants (black, red, white), gooseberries (for pies), loganberries, mulberries, raspberries, rhubarb (for pies), strawberries, whortleberries

Raise to 82°C and maintain at that temperature for 15 minutes: apples (solid pack), apricots, cherries, damsons, gooseberries (for dessert), greengages, nectarines, plums (whole or halved), peaches, pineapples, rhubarb (for dessert), solid pack of soft fruit

Raise to 90°C and maintain at that temperature for 30 minutes: pears, tomatoes (whole)

Raise to 90°C and maintain at that temperature for 40 minutes: tomatoes (in own juice).

Oven Method

In the traditional oven method, the fruit is packed into the jars, processed in the oven, then removed and boiling liquid added. However, the dry heat of the oven makes the fruit shrink.

The newer moderate oven method given below is more successful.

1) Fill the warmed jars tightly with the prepared fruit.
2) Fill to within 2cm of the top with boiling syrup or water.
3) Put on the rubber rings and lids (both first dipped in boiling water). Clips and screwbands should not be put on until after processing.
4) Line a baking tray with 3 or 4 layers of newspaper to catch any liquid that boils over during heating. Stand the jars, 5cm apart, on the paper.
5) Heat the oven for 15 minutes to cool, 150°C, Gas 2. Put the jars in the centre of the oven, then process for the times given below. To ensure that the jars are in the centre of the oven, the rack on which they stand should be about one-third of the way up.
6) Remove the jars to a wooden surface. Immediately check that the necks of the jars are free from boiled-out fruit, then fasten clips and screwbands. Leave for 24 hours. Next day, test for fit (see step **9**, Quick Deep Pan Method p1131), label, and store.

Processing Times Using a Moderate Oven

Note 4 × 350ml jars require the same processing time as 2 × 700ml jars.

30–40 minutes (up to 2kg) or 50–60 minutes (2–4.5kg): apple rings, blackberries, currants (black, red, white), gooseberries (for pies), loganberries, mulberries, raspberries, rhubarb (for pies), whortleberries

40–50 minutes (up to 2kg) or 55–70 minutes (2–4.5kg): apricots, cherries, damsons, gooseberries (for dessert), greengages, plums (whole), rhubarb (for dessert)

50–60 minutes (up to 2kg) or 65–80 minutes (2–4.5kg): apples (solid pack), nectarines, peaches, pineapples, plums (halved)

60–70 minutes (up to 2kg) or 75–90 minutes (2–4.5kg): pears, tomatoes (whole)

70–80 minutes (up to 2kg) or 85–100 minutes (2–4.5kg): tomatoes (in own juice).

Note Campden tablets, obtainable from shops selling home winemaking equipment, can be used for bottling fruit. They are useful when quick processing is necessary, eg for a glut crop, or when heating facilities are limited. Use them in the same way as when processing fruit syrups (p1135). Take care that any metal lids and screw caps are protected from the preservative fumes by a layer of wax or oil between the fruit and cover.

Jars suitable for bottling

BOTTLING FRUIT PULP

This is an economical process, as the sound parts of damaged fruits can be used, and fewer bottling jars are required for pulp than for the same weight of bottled whole fruit. Any fruit can be pulped but apples, particularly windfalls, are the most useful and popular. Prepare the fruit as for cooking, removing any stalks or leaves and discarding blemished or damaged parts. As soon as the apples are prepared, immerse them in salted water (1 × 15ml spoon salt to 1 litre water) to prevent browning. Large plums should be stoned, but it is easy to sieve out the stones of small plums or damsons after cooking. Put the prepared fruit into an aluminium, stainless steel or unchipped enamel saucepan with just enough water to prevent burning. Sugar, if required, should be added to taste at this stage. Heat very gently until the fruit begins to soften; increase the heat slightly, and cook until the fruit is of an even, firm, pulped consistency. Have ready a supply of dry, clean, and warm bottling jars and seals on a dry wooden board or on layers of newspaper. Quickly pour the boiling pulp into the jars; then seal them, but not too tightly. Place the filled jars on a false bottom in a pan of water at 90°C (fast simmer). The water must cover the jars. Heat the water to boiling point (100°C) and maintain for 5 minutes. Remove the jars to a dry wooden board or sheets of newspaper, and secure the seals. The following day test the seal, and clean, label, and store the jars as described on p1131.

If fruit is pulped without sweetening and its weight is recorded on the label, it can be converted into jam by heating (with acid if necessary) in a saucepan of suitable size, adding the appropriate amount of sugar, as for making jam.

Tomato Pulp

Choose well-coloured tomatoes; the size and shape are immaterial. It is usual to remove the skins of tomatoes (p1130) before pulping. Cut up the fruit roughly, removing hard cores for really smooth pulp. To each 2kg of prepared tomatoes add 1 × 5ml spoon sugar, 1 × 10ml spoon salt, and $\frac{1}{4}$ × 2.5ml spoon citric acid. Only a very small quantity of water, if any, is needed. Proceed as for fruit pulp but boil the filled bottles for 10 minutes.

When processing tomatoes it is important to carry through the whole job without delay, to achieve a good consistency.

BOTTLING FRUIT PURÉE

Whereas pulp contains fruit skins and seeds, a purée is completely smooth; it is in fact a sieved pulp.

Prepare the fruit by removing leaves, stalks, and blemished parts, but do not bother to peel it or remove stones. However, for a good white apple purée, peel and core the apples, and add a little lemon juice to brighten the colour and enhance the flavour.

Cook the fruit gently with just enough water to prevent burning. When thoroughly softened, press the pulp through a stainless sieve, stir in sugar to taste if liked, re-heat in a clean saucepan, then bottle and finish as for fruit pulp (p1133).

Note For fruit purée made using a pressure cooker, see p1436.

Bottled Tomato Purée

tomatoes

for each 2kg prepared
  tomatoes:

1 × 5ml spoon sugar	*¼ × 2.5ml spoon citric*
1 × 10ml spoon salt	*acid* **or** *4 × 15ml*
	spoons vinegar

Choose well-coloured fruit, cut it up roughly and put in a saucepan with the sugar, salt, and citric acid or vinegar. Add a few spoons of water to prevent the tomatoes burning until the juice begins to run. Heat gently and cook until the fruit is well pulped; press the pulp through a stainless sieve, re-heat in a clean saucepan, then bottle and finish as for Tomato Pulp (p1133).

Bottled Tomato Juice

tomatoes

for each litre of
  prepared juice:

250ml water	*1 × 5ml spoon salt*
25g granulated sugar	*a pinch of pepper*

Choose firm, ripe, red tomatoes, cut them roughly into quarters and heat them in a covered saucepan

until they are soft. Rub through a stainless sieve and measure the juice. Add the water, sugar, salt and pepper in the proportions given above. Stir to mix, re-heat, and bottle, leaving 1cm headspace under the screw cap. Process and finish as for Tomato Pulp (p1133).

Whole Fruit Conserves

See pp1120–21.

Fruit Preserved in Brandy

See p1124.

Canning Fruit

Canning is an excellent method of preserving fruit, but domestic canning equipment is not easily obtainable in the UK.

The canning process is similar to bottling except that after the fruit has been packed into the can, it is covered with boiling syrup and the lid is then sealed on to the can with a special machine. The sealed cans are processed in boiling water, then cooled in cold running water. This treatment would be too drastic for glass jars. Canned fruit tends to taste somewhat fresher than bottled fruit because the heating process and subsequent cooking are completed more quickly.

Bottling Meat and Vegetables

These products are safely prepared commercially under strict control of equipment, method, and hygiene but must not be attempted in the home with domestic equipment. Insufficient processing or any other errors can give rise to a very serious health risk.

Fruit Syrups

Fruit syrups are often considered luxury preserves, but since they are made from fully ripe fruit which is too soft for other processing methods, they can be economical.

MODERN METHOD FOR MAKING FRUIT SYRUPS

The aim is to extract the fruit juice with as little loss of its fresh fruit flavour as possible, then to sweeten and preserve it. Soft fruits are most often used and blackcurrant syrup, correctly made, has a high vitamin C content.

Fruit syrups can be stored in any bottles which have screw-on caps or tight corks; these should be painted with paraffin wax to seal the join. Either kind should be boiled for 15 minutes before use.

Extracting the Juice

Cold Method

The best method is to place the fruit in a china or earthenware bowl, crush it with a wooden spoon, and leave it, covered with a plate, for 4–8 days, repeating the crushing daily. During this period the natural pectin loses its quality and the juice is released. The process can be hastened by using a pectin-decomposing enzyme; this is particularly useful for firmer fruits such as blackcurrants. The enzyme can be bought in small quantities from any shop which sells home winemaking equipment.

If the fruit is very ripe there is a chance that mould may develop; in this case use the following method.

Hot Method

Place the fruit in a bowl over gently boiling water. Crush the fruit and add 600ml water per kg for blackcurrants and 100ml water per kg for blackberries. Other soft fruits do not need any water. Allow the fruit to heat until the juice flows freely, which will take about 1 hour for 3kg of fruit. Take care not to let the saucepan boil dry.

Straining the Juice

With either method, the fruit has to be strained. For a very clear syrup, a scalded felt or flannel bag or cloth should be used and the juice allowed to drip through. Where clarity is less important, scalded muslin or a fine nylon strainer can be used.

Note Strained fruit juice can be used fresh in desserts such as Blackcurrant Whip (p1015). Diluted, and slightly sweetened, the juice makes a good drink, although fruit syrups are more economical for use in beverages (see p1136).

Processing Syrup

Cold Method Using Campden tablets

Measure the juice and steadily stir in 800g sugar per litre, until dissolved. Re-measure the syrup. For strawberry juice, add 10g citric acid per litre. It is not necessary to acidify other fruit juices. For each litre of syrup, crush and dissolve 2 Campden tablets in 2 × 15ml spoons warm water and stir into the syrup with a wooden or plastic spoon. Bottle at once leaving 1cm headspace under the screw caps, which should be tightened. Label and store.

Note The sulphur in the tablets will bleach the syrup, but most of the colour will return when the syrup is exposed to air. If you wish, add a few drops of food colouring.

Cold Method Using Extra Sugar

One continental method of making syrup is to add 1.6kg sugar to each litre of juice, and to stir until dissolved. Some heating is almost essential to dissolve the sugar, but the syrup can then be bottled and will keep without further processing. It is, however, excessively sweet.

Hot Method – Recommended for Home Use

Measure the juice and stir in 600g granulated sugar per litre; use a little heat if necessary to make sure the sugar is dissolved. This quantity of sugar reinforces the fruit flavours so that the syrup can be considerably diluted for use. If less sugar is used the syrup will be less economical in use. Pour the syrup into bottles, leaving 2cm headspace under the screw caps, which should be slightly loosened. Stand the bottles on a false bottom or on layers of newspapers in a deep pan of water. The water should come to the top of the bottles and it will be necessary to wedge them upright with cardboard. Heat the water to 76°C, and maintain for 30 minutes; or heat to simmering point (88°C), and maintain for 20 minutes.

Remove the bottles from the water, then leave to cool. Polish the bottles, label, and store in a dry, preferably cool and dark place.

Uses for Fruit Syrups

Syrups can be diluted with about 4 parts of water, soda water, or other aerated beverage for plain cold drinks. For milk shakes, add the syrup to the milk slowly; stir or whisk briskly to prevent curdling.

Undiluted syrup is delicious on ice cream, natural yoghurt, puddings, batter puddings, and many other desserts. It can be used to make sweet jellies, sauces, and glazes for fruit flans, and is excellent in fruit salads and in sweet-sour savoury dishes.

TRADITIONAL METHOD OF MAKING FRUIT SYRUPS

In this method the fruit juice is boiled before bottling, and so the final product is somewhat different from that made by the more modern process, which strives to retain the fresh flavour of the fruit. For all the recipes below, a little olive oil may be poured on the top of the syrup in the bottle as a seal. The oil must be carefully removed with a clean piece of cotton wool before use. Alternatively, to ensure better keeping quality, all the recipes, except those containing brandy, could be heat-processed as above.

Note The leftover fruit pulp from the following recipes could be used to make fruit cheeses (p1123), although they will not have full food value or flavour.

Apricot Syrup

sound ripe apricots
800g crushed lump sugar
for each litre of juice
olive oil (optional)

Stone and halve the apricots. Three-quarters fill a large jar, or jars, with apricots. Crack half the stones and add the kernels to the jar(s). Stand the jar(s) in a pan of boiling water and simmer until the fruit is quite soft and the juice flows freely. Strain off the liquid through a fine sieve or jelly bag. Measure it carefully and add sugar in the proportion given above. Boil again for 10 minutes, then skim, and pour the hot syrup into clean dry bottles. If screw caps are used, leave at least 2cm headspace; if corks are used, allow for a 2cm space below the cork. As soon as any bubbling ceases, seal securely as described in the general method.

VARIATIONS
Substitute cherries, greengages, peaches, plums or rhubarb for apricots.

Blackberry or Blackcurrant Syrup

blackberries **or**
blackcurrants
1kg crushed **or**
preserving sugar and
1 × 15ml spoon water
for each kg of fruit
100ml brandy for each
litre of syrup

Put the fruit, sugar, and water in a large jar with a close-fitting cover. Stand the jar in a saucepan of boiling water, and cook gently until the juice flows freely. Strain the juice, measure it, put it into a preserving pan or stewpan (preferably enamelled), and boil gently for 20 minutes. Skim, and when the syrup has cooled, add the brandy; then bottle, leaving a headspace, and seal securely as described in the general method.

Cranberry Syrup

sound, ripe cranberries	800g crushed lump sugar for each litre of juice

Crush the fruit in a jar. Stand the jar in a pan of boiling water. Cook gently for 2 hours. Strain off the liquid through a fine sieve, measure carefully, and add sugar in the proportion given above. Bring to the boil again and cook for 15 minutes. Skim when boiling is finished. Leave until quite cold, then pour into bottles, leaving a headspace. Seal securely as described in the general method (p1136).

VARIATIONS

Use gooseberries, raspberries or strawberries.

Damson Syrup

sound, ripe damsons	800g crushed lump sugar for each litre of juice

Put the fruit in an earthenware jar, stand it in a pan of boiling water, and cook until the juice flows freely. Strain off the juice through a fine sieve, measure it carefully and add sugar in the proportion given above. Bring to the boil again and cook for 10 minutes. Skim when boiling is finished, and when quite cold bottle the syrup, leaving a headspace. Seal securely as described in the general method (p1136).

Elderette

sound, ripe elderberries 800g crushed lump sugar, 7 cloves, and 1 × 2cm piece bruised cinnamon stick for each litre of liquid	100ml brandy for each litre of syrup

Crush the elderberries and strain the juice. Mix the juice with an equal quantity of cold water. Add the sugar, cloves, and cinnamon in the proportions given above and boil together for 10 minutes. Strain and measure the syrup. When cool, stir in the brandy. When quite cold, bottle and seal securely as described in the general method (p1136).

Fig Syrup

3 medium-sized lemons 1kg sound, ripe, fresh figs	1.25 litres water 800g crushed lump sugar for each litre of liquid

Pare the lemon rind thinly with a potato peeler; squeeze out the lemon and strain the juice. Slice the figs and put them in an earthenware jar together with the water, lemon rind, and juice. Stand the jar in a pan of boiling water and cook gently for 3 hours. Strain off the liquid through a fine sieve, measure carefully, and stir in sugar in the proportion given above. Boil up again for 10 minutes; skim when boiling is finished. Leave aside until quite cold. Bottle, leaving a headspace, and seal securely as described in the general method (p1136).

Ginger Syrup

1 medium-sized lemon 150g ginger root	1 litre water 800g crushed lump sugar

Pare the lemon rind thinly with a potato peeler; squeeze out the lemon and strain the juice. Bruise the ginger root. Put the ginger into an earthenware jar containing the water. Stand the jar in a pan of boiling water, add the lemon rind, juice, and sugar, and cook for 30 minutes. Skim and strain off the liquid through a fine sieve. When quite cold pour into clean, dry bottles, leaving a headspace. Seal securely as described in the general method (p1136).

Quince Syrup

sound, ripe quinces	800g crushed lump sugar for each litre of juice

Cut up and mash the fruit. Put it into an earthenware jar. Stand the jar in a pan of boiling water, and cook steadily until the fruit is quite soft and the juice flows freely. Strain the liquid off, measure it carefully, and stir in the sugar in the proportion given above. Bring to the boil and cook for 10 minutes, then skim. Leave until quite cold, then bottle, leaving a headspace, and seal securely as described in the general method (p1136).

Pear Syrup

2kg sound, ripe, juicy
  pears
2 lemons
650ml cold water
600g crushed lump sugar
  for each litre of liquid

a few drops strawberry
  essence
100ml brandy for every
  litre of syrup

Peel, core, and slice the pears. Pare the lemon rind thinly with a potato peeler. Put the pears into an earthenware jar and pour on the cold water. Add the lemon rind and stand the jar in a pan of boiling water. Cook gently for 1 hour. Strain off the liquid through a fine sieve, measure carefully and stir in the sugar in the proportion given above. Bring to the boil again and cook for 15 minutes, then skim. Leave aside, and when quite cold, stir in the strawberry essence and the brandy. Bottle, leaving a headspace, and seal securely as described in the general method (p1136).

Rose-hip Syrup

3 litres water
1kg ripe, wild rose-hips

650g preserving sugar

Boil 2 litres of the water. Mince the hips coarsely and put immediately into the boiling water. Bring the water back to the boil, then cool for about 15 minutes. Strain the pulp twice through fine linen or muslin to make sure that all the hairs are removed. Put the liquid obtained to one side. Boil the pulp again with the remaining water, cool for 15 minutes, and strain twice again. Return both extracted liquids to the pan, and boil until the juice is reduced to less than 2 litres. Add the sugar, stirring well. Pour into warmed bottles, leaving a headspace, and seal securely as described in the general method (p1136). Store in a dark cupboard.

Vanilla Syrup

3 vanilla pods **or**
  3 × 5ml spoons vanilla
  essence

800g crushed lump sugar
1 litre water
250ml brandy

Crush the vanilla pods, if used, and break them into small pieces. Put the pods or essence into an enamel pan with the sugar and water. Bring slowly to the boil. Simmer for 20 minutes, skimming from time to time as necessary. Leave to cool. When cold, strain, and add the brandy. Bottle, leaving a headspace, and seal securely as described in the general method (p1136).

Dilute with plain or aerated water when required for use, or use as a concentrated sweet flavouring in cocktails, ice creams, custards, etc.

Fruit Squashes

See p1349.

Pickles, Chutneys, Sauces, and Ketchups

All these preserves depend on vinegar for their keeping quality, although some pickles also need salting first. Both vinegar and salt flavour the food, but there is scope for varying the final taste.

In a pickle the fruit or vegetables remain separate and solid; a chutney is smoother although it may still have solid pieces of fruit or vegetable, while a sauce should be quite smooth and creamy.

Note For relishes, mustards and mustard dressings, see pp402–3.

GENERAL METHOD

1) Vegetables and fruit must be fresh and not over-ripe. Mis-shapen produce of good quality can be used for chutney or sauces.
2) For pickling, most vegetables are treated in salt water to reduce moisture content and to improve texture. They are soaked in brine or dry salt is scattered on them. It is important to allow a good proportion of vinegar when packing them; there should be a depth of 1.5cm above the pickle in the jar, to prevent evaporation.
3) For chutney, the main ingredients should be chopped or finely minced before gentle,

thorough cooking with vinegar and spices. The cooking time depends on the quantity made and the toughness of the vegetables but, as a rule, a chutney using more than 1kg of the main ingredient should be cooked gently for at least 2 hours for a mellow flavour and a smooth consistency. Sugar is not added until the chutney has cooked down well if a light-coloured preserve is wanted; long cooking with sugar darkens the colour. The chutney is ready when no free liquid runs out of a teaspoonful cooled on a plate. Pour into clean jars, then seal or cover with vinegar-proof covers (see **6)** below). When making an unfamiliar recipe, try it out by making a small quantity first, so that the spicing can be adjusted. Remember that freshly made chutney is more spicy than matured chutney.

4) For making sauce, the ingredients should be roughly cut up and cooked in the vinegar with the spices, until soft. They are then sieved and returned to the saucepan to cook with the sugar until they are of a creamy, pouring consistency. Pour into clean bottles and cover securely.

5) Use aluminium, unchipped enamel or stainless steel pans, stainless knives, and stainless or nylon sieves. A special wooden spoon should be kept for stirring vinegar preserves if possible. If not, the spoon must be very thoroughly cleaned and aired before it is returned to general use.

6) Vinegar preserves, especially chutneys, must have acid-proof covers which will prevent evaporation and wasteful drying out. Suitable covers are:

   a) the type of twist-top or screw-on plastic-coated lids used commercially

   b) press-on plastic covers

   c) synthetic skin

   d) a circle of clean card or paper, cut to fit the top of the jar, covered with a piece of linen dipped in melted paraffin wax and tied on

   e) a circle of clean greaseproof paper, cut to fit the surface of the chutney and covered with 2cm of melted paraffin wax. A jam cover should be tied over to keep the wax clean

   f) a boiled cork to fit the bottle and either waxed or covered with greaseproof paper tied securely over (for ketchups and sauces).

Note A chutney will shrink, evaporate, and lose quality quickly if a cellulose tissue jam cover is used.

Pressure cooker method is described on p1440.

Vinegar for Preserving

As vinegar is the main preservative, it is important to buy a good quality product containing at least 5% acetic acid. Malt vinegar has a flavour that blends well with pickles, but distilled or white vinegar is often preferred when colour is important, eg for ripe tomato chutney or sauce.

Pressure cooker method is described on p1440.

Wine vinegar is esteemed for its delicate flavour but as refinement is rarely a feature of pickles, it is wasteful to use it. Cider vinegar gives a good flavour to fruit chutneys and pickled fruits.

Spicing vinegar improves the flavour of pickles. Whole spices are used so that they can be strained out to leave a clear vinegar. If no special spicing is given in a recipe, a good result can be obtained by adding to 1 litre of vinegar, 5–10g of each of the following whole spices: cloves, allspice, cinnamon, white peppercorns, ginger. The smaller quantity will be enough for a mild pickle but for strongly flavoured ones such as onion, the full quantity may be used. Put the spices in a folded cloth and beat them lightly with a rolling-pin to release their flavour. Put the bruised spices into the vinegar and seal the bottle. It may be more convenient to add a double or treble quantity of spices and dilute later with more vinegar, but label the container accordingly if this is done. If time allows, leave the spices in the well-sealed bottle of vinegar for 2 months, shaking daily for the first month. Strain out the spices carefully and re-bottle the vinegar.

For quick use, put the spices and vinegar in a heatproof bowl and cover with a plate. Stand the bowl in a saucepan of cold water, bring the water gently to the boil and draw the pan off the heat. Leave for 2 hours, taking care not to move the plate or flavour will be lost. Strain the vinegar and, if not required immediately, return to the bottle and seal.

PICKLES

Mixed Pickle

mixed vegetables (see Method)
60g cooking salt for each kg of vegetables
spiced vinegar (p1139)

Make a selection of available vegetables. Any of the following are suitable: small cucumbers, cauliflower, small onions, French beans. Prepare the vegetables; only the onions need be peeled, the rest should merely be cut into suitably sized pieces. Weigh the prepared vegetables.

Put all into a large bowl, sprinkle with the required amount of salt, and leave for 24 hours. Rinse, drain thoroughly, and pack into prepared jars. Cover with cold spiced vinegar, and seal with vinegar-proof covers. Leave for at least a month before using.

Bread and Butter Pickles

1.5kg large cucumbers
1.5kg small onions
75g cooking salt
375ml white wine vinegar or distilled malt vinegar
300g light soft brown sugar
1 × 2.5ml spoon turmeric
1 × 2.5ml spoon ground cloves
1 × 15ml spoon mustard seed
1 × 2.5ml spoon celery seed

Wash the cucumbers but do not peel them. Slice thinly. Skin and slice the onions thinly. In a large basin, layer the cucumbers, onions, and salt. Weigh down with a plate and leave for 3 hours.

Rinse the vegetables thoroughly under cold running water; drain and place in a large saucepan. Add the vinegar to the vegetables, and bring to the boil. Simmer gently for 10–12 minutes until the cucumber slices begin to soften. Add the rest of the ingredients, and stir over low heat to dissolve the sugar. Bring to the boil; draw the pan off the heat. Turn the contents of the pan into a large basin and leave until cold. (Do not allow to stand in the hot pan.) Spoon into sterilized jars; seal with vinegar-proof covers.

Piccalilli

1kg mixed vegetables (see Method)
60g cooking salt
700ml vinegar
12 chillies
225g granulated sugar
25g mustard powder
15g turmeric
2 × 15ml spoons cornflour

Cut a variety of vegetables such as cauliflower, cucumber, shallots, and young broad beans into small pieces. They should weigh about 1kg in all when prepared. Put in a large earthenware bowl and sprinkle with the cooking salt. Leave to stand for 24 hours, then rinse, and drain well.

Boil the vinegar and chillies for 2 minutes, leave to stand for 30 minutes, and then strain the vinegar. Mix together the sugar, mustard, turmeric, and cornflour. Blend with a little of the cooled vinegar. Bring the rest of the vinegar back to the boil, pour it over the blended mixture, return to the saucepan and boil for 3 minutes. Remove from the heat and fold in the drained vegetables. Pack into prepared jars and cover at once with vinegar-proof covers.

Pickled Beetroot

beetroot
unspiced or spiced vinegar (p1139).
25g salt for each litre of vinegar

Wash off any soil still clinging to the roots of the beetroot, taking care not to break the skin, since beetroot bleeds easily.

If pickling for immediate use, simmer for $1\frac{1}{2}$–2 hours. When cold, skin and cut into cubes or slices, and cover with unspiced or spiced vinegar.

If pickling for storage, bake in a moderate oven, 180°C, Gas 4, until tender. Cool, then skin and cut into cubes; beetroot packs better that way for keeping. Measure out enough spiced vinegar to cover the beetroot, and add the salt. Bring to the boil. Pack the beetroot into prepared, wide-mouthed jars. Cover with the boiling vinegar. Put on vinegar-proof covers.

Beetroot contains a good deal of sugar, and fermentation is more likely than with other vegetables, so seal carefully to exclude all air.

Pickled Apples and Onions

*equal quantities of
  onions and sour apples
spiced vinegar* (p1139)

*10g salt for each litre of
  spiced vinegar*

Skin the onions and peel and core the apples. Slice them. Mix well together and pack into prepared jars. Measure out and heat as much vinegar as you think you will need to cover the pickles, taking into account the size of the jars and the closeness of the packing. Salt the vinegar. Cover the onions and apples with the hot vinegar. Put on vinegar-proof covers.

This pickle is ready to use as soon as it is cool.

Pickled Artichokes

*Jerusalem artichokes
brine, using 60g salt to
  each litre of water*

spiced vinegar (p1139)

Clean and peel the tubers and boil for about 10 minutes in the brine. (Artichokes have a delicate flavour which strong brining will spoil.) Do not let them get soft or they will fall to pieces in the pickle.

Drain and leave until cold. Pack into prepared, wide-mouthed jars, and cover with boiling, well-spiced vinegar. Put on vinegar-proof covers.

Note Of the 2 kinds of artichoke, globe and Jerusalem, the latter makes the better pickle, but, like all roots, requires cooking and does not keep well.

Pickled Mushrooms

*mushrooms
1 × 5ml spoon salt for
  each 450g mushrooms*

spiced vinegar (p1139)

For pickling, mushrooms need no brining. Put them in layers in a pie dish, sprinkling each layer with salt. Cover with spiced vinegar and cook in a moderate oven, 180°C, Gas 4, until they are quite tender. Pack into prepared jars and pour the hot liquor on top. Put on vinegar-proof covers at once.

Pickled in this way they keep well and the liquor is a useful mushroom ketchup.

Pickled Cauliflower

*cauliflower (see **Note**)
brine, using 225g salt to
  2 litres water*

spiced (p1139) **or**
  *unspiced vinegar
sugar (optional)*

Break the cauliflower into small even-sized florets, but do not use a knife at all (the stalk of cauliflower stains easily, and this is less likely to occur if it is broken and not cut). Steep the florets in the brine for 24 hours; then rinse, drain thoroughly, pack into prepared jars, and cover with cold spiced vinegar. Put on vinegar-proof covers.

If pickling for use later, in other mixed pickles, unspiced vinegar can be used for the temporary pickling.

As a straight pickle, cauliflower is best sweet. Sweetening is done most easily by adding 1–3 × 5ml spoons of sugar (according to size of jar) a couple of days before the pickle is wanted. Turn the jar upside-down 2–3 times during this period to make sure the sugar is dissolved.

Note Cauliflower must not be too mature for pickling, and close-packed heads are best.

Pickled Horseradish

*horseradish roots
1 × 5ml salt to each
  250ml vinegar*

vinegar

Fresh horseradish is best for most culinary purposes, but as it is sometimes difficult to obtain, it can be useful to have a few small jars of pickled roots.

Wash the roots in hot water, scrape off the skin, then either grate or put through a mincer. Horseradish needs no brining, but salt should be added to the vinegar in the proportion given above. Pack the roots loosely in small, prepared jars, and cover with the salted vinegar. Put on vinegar-proof covers.

Pickled Gherkins

small dill cucumbers　　*spiced vinegar (p1139)*
brine, using 225g salt to
　each 2 litres water

The small immature cucumbers that are known as dills or gherkins require longer processing than most vegetables, especially if their deep green colour is to be fixed; they also need partial cooking.

Select gherkins of the same size, put in a saucepan, and cover with the brine. Bring nearly to boiling point. Do not actually boil, but simmer for 10 minutes. Drain and leave until cold, then pack into prepared jars, and cover with spiced vinegar, preferably aromatic. Put on vinegar-proof covers.

VARIATION

Cocktail Gherkins

Many people prefer gherkins sweet; they are especially popular at cocktail parties. These are quite easy to prepare from the ordinary pickled vegetable. Simply add a spoonful of sugar to taste to the jar, shake it up, then leave to stand for 24 hours. It is not advisable to do this too long in advance, as sugar added to a cold pickle in this way may easily start to ferment.

Another way to sweeten gherkins is to turn them out on to a shallow dish in which they will be served and sprinkle with sugar. This can be done a few hours before use.

Pickled Cucumber

cucumbers　　*spiced vinegar (p1139)*
salt

The easiest way to pickle cucumbers is to quarter them lengthways, cut into smaller pieces, and brine with dry salt for 24 hours. Rinse, pack into prepared jars, and cover with cold spiced vinegar. Put on vinegar-proof covers. Like most vegetables, they are best mixed with others.

Pickled Lemons

lemons　　*25–50g mustard seed for*
salt　　　*each jar used*
vinegar　　*2 cloves garlic for each*
whole peppercorns　　*6 lemons used*
ginger root

Select small lemons with thick peel. Slit them lengthways in quarters, but do not cut right through. Rub dry salt sparingly into these cuts and leave the lemons for 5 days, or until all the salt has melted, turning them in the liquor which forms. Drain off this liquor and reserve it. Pack the lemons into prepared jars. Add enough vinegar to the liquor to cover the lemons completely. Boil the liquid with a few whole peppercorns and a small piece of ginger root. Skim well while boiling. Allow the vinegar mixture to cool and pour it over the fruit. Add the mustard seed to each jar. Cut up the garlic and divide between the jars. Put on vinegar-proof covers.

Note No sugar is used, so the pickle is very sharp-flavoured, but it is one of the few that goes well with fish. It is also very hot, so a little goes a long way.

Mustard Pickle
See p1441.

Pickled Melon or Pumpkin

*8 medium-sized melons
  (not watermelons)* **or**
  2 pumpkins
3 litres vinegar
2.5kg sugar
25g celery salt
3 long sticks cinnamon

*1 × 15ml spoon white
  mustard seed*
15 whole cloves
*3 pieces ginger root
  (scraped* **or** *uncoated)*

Cut the melons or pumpkins in small slices. Do not peel them unless the skin is very tough. Boil the vinegar with the sugar and pour it over the sliced fruit. Leave for 24 hours.

Drain, then bring the liquor to the boil and add the celery salt, cinnamon, mustard seed, cloves, and ginger. When boiling, put in the strained fruit, and cook slowly for 3 hours; then pack into prepared jars, pour on the hot vinegar, and put on vinegar-proof covers.

Note Melons and pumpkins belong to the same family and are about 96% water, but each has a distinctive flavour.

Pickled Nasturtium Seeds

nasturtium seeds
*brine, using 225g salt for
  each 2 litres water*

spiced vinegar (p1139)
*tarragon leaves
  (optional)*

Nasturtium seeds when pickled are a good substitute for capers, and add variety to salad dressings. They are rather too small to serve by themselves, but go well in clear mixed pickles.

Gather the seeds while still green on a dry day and steep in the brine for 24 hours. Pack in small prepared jars, and warm in the oven for 10 minutes. Meanwhile, boil enough spiced vinegar to cover the seeds, and pour it over them. Seal with vinegar-proof covers.

It is best to use a hot, spiced mixture for this, and a few leaves of tarragon, if available, are pleasant.

Note It is important to use small jars or bottles, so that the contents can be used at once when opened.

Pickled Onions

pickling onions
water to cover
*1 × 5ml spoon salt
  (approx) for each
  500ml water*

spiced vinegar (p1139)

Use small even-sized pickling onions. Skin with a stainless knife and drop them into a basin of salted water until all have been skinned. Remove from the water, and drain thoroughly before packing into prepared jars or bottles. Cover with cold spiced vinegar and put on vinegar-proof covers. Keep for at least a month before using.

VARIATION

This method prevents one shedding tears:

Put the unskinned onions into a brine made from 225g salt to each 2 litres of water. Leave for 24 hours. Drain and skin the onions, and put them in fresh brine for a further 24 hours. Drain, rinse, and pack into jars as above.

Pickled Pears

*1 × 10ml spoon whole
  cloves*
*1 × 10ml spoon allspice
  berries*
*1 × 5ml spoon crushed
  cinnamon stick*

*a small piece ginger
  root*
250g sugar
300ml vinegar
1kg hard cooking pears

Crush the spices together and tie in a piece of muslin. Put the muslin bag and the sugar into a saucepan with the vinegar and heat gently until the sugar is dissolved. Peel and core the pears, cut into quarters or eighths, and simmer gently in the sweetened spiced vinegar until tender, but not overcooked or broken. Lift out and pack into prepared clean, warm jars. Continue to boil the vinegar until it thickens slightly, then pour it over the pears, filling each jar. Leave until cold, then seal securely with vinegar-proof covers.

Note The pears are best kept for 2–3 months before use.

Pickled Red Cabbage

1 medium-sized red
 cabbage
salt
onions

soft brown sugar (light
 or dark)
spiced vinegar (p1139)

Choose a firm, fresh cabbage. Remove any discoloured outer leaves. Cut the cabbage into quarters and then into shreds. Put layers of the shreds into a large basin or dish, sprinkling each layer with salt. Leave overnight. Next day, drain very thoroughly in a colander, pressing out all the surplus liquid.

Pack a layer of cabbage, about 7cm, into large jars. Cover with a layer of very thinly sliced onion, and sprinkle with 1×5ml spoon brown sugar. Then add another 7cm of cabbage, another layer of onion, and another spoon of sugar. Continue until the jars are filled, ending with the onion and sugar.

Cover with cold spiced vinegar, put on vinegar-proof covers and leave for at least 5 days to a week before opening.

Note Do not make too much of this pickle at one time, because it will lose its crispness after 2 or 3 months' storage.

Pickled Fresh Peaches

2kg fresh peaches
20g whole cloves
20g allspice berries
20g cinnamon sticks

1kg granulated sugar
1 litre distilled malt
 vinegar

Peel the peaches. (Dip them first into boiling water then into cold to make peeling easy.) Halve the fruit. Remove the stones and crack a few; take out the kernels. Blanch the kernels for 1–3 minutes. Tie the spices in muslin and place with the sugar and vinegar in a pan. Bring to the boil and dissolve the sugar. Add the peaches and simmer until just tender, but not overcooked or broken. Lift out and pack into prepared, clean, warm jars with a few of the blanched kernels. Continue to boil the liquid until it thickens, then pour it over the peaches. Put on vinegar-proof covers while hot and store for at least a week before using.

Pickled Shallots

shallots
brine, using 100g salt for
 each litre of water

spiced vinegar (p1139)

Use even-sized shallots. Do not skin them but place straight in the brine. Leave for 12 hours. Remove the shallots from the brine and skin them, using a stainless knife. Cover with fresh brine, making sure that all the shallots are kept below the surface. Leave for a further 24–36 hours; then drain thoroughly. Pack tightly in prepared jars, and cover with cold spiced vinegar. Put on vinegar-proof covers. Keep for 3 months before use.

Pickled Walnuts

soft green walnuts
brine, using 100g salt for
 each litre of water

spiced vinegar (p1139)

Use walnuts whose shells have not begun to form. Prick well with a stainless fork; if the shell can be felt do not use the walnut. The shell begins to form opposite the stalk, about 5mm from the end.

Cover with the brine and leave to soak for about 6 days. Drain, make fresh brine, and leave to soak for a further 7 days. Drain, and spread on a single layer of clean newspaper leaving them exposed to the air, preferably in sunshine, until they blacken (1–2 days). Pack into prepared jars and cover with hot spiced vinegar. Put on vinegar-proof covers when cold. Leave for at least a month before using.

Note To prevent stained hands, always wear gloves when handling walnuts.

CHUTNEYS

Apple Chutney

Yield 5kg (approx)

3kg apples	2 litres vinegar
1kg sultanas	1.5kg sugar
300–400g preserved ginger **or** 30g ground ginger	30g salt
	1 × 5ml spoon ground allspice

Peel, core, and chop the apples into small pieces; chop up the sultanas and preserved ginger. Mix the vinegar, sugar, salt and spice together, and bring to the boil; then add the apples and simmer for 10 minutes before adding the ginger (either preserved or ground) and sultanas. Simmer until the mixture becomes fairly thick. Meanwhile, heat enough jars to hold the chutney. Stand them on a newspaper, to catch any drips. Pour in the chutney and cover as described on p1139. Cool, wipe the jars, label, and store.

Red Tomato Chutney

Yield 3kg (approx)

3kg ripe red tomatoes	a pinch of Cayenne pepper
500g white sugar	
20g salt	300ml spiced white vinegar (p1139)
a pinch of paprika	

Blanch the tomatoes for 30 seconds in fast boiling water. Put into cold water, then skin. Cut up the tomatoes and remove the hard cores. Put into a saucepan with a very little water, bring gently to the boil, then reduce the heat and simmer until thick. Add all the other ingredients, stirring in well. Continue cooking until the whole mixture is thick. Put a spoonful on a cold plate to test its consistency. When ready, pour into hot jars or bottles, and cover at once as described on p1139.

Note The final colour of this chutney depends largely on the redness of the tomatoes and the use of white sugar and vinegar. To give it a good texture, it should be processed without a pause once the tomatoes are blanched.

Green Tomato Chutney(1)

Yield 3kg (approx)

450g cooking apples	450g sultanas
450g onions	15g salt
2kg green tomatoes	$\frac{1}{2}$ × 2.5ml spoon Cayenne pepper
1 × 15ml spoon mustard seed	700ml malt vinegar
1 × 1cm piece ginger root (optional)	450g Demerara sugar

Peel, core, and chop the apples. Skin and chop the onions. Cut up the tomatoes roughly. Tie the mustard seed and ginger root, if used, in a piece of muslin or thin cotton. Put these ingredients with the sultanas, salt, and Cayenne pepper into a large pan, and add just enough vinegar to cover. Bring to simmering point and simmer for 20 minutes. Meanwhile, dissolve the sugar by warming it in the remaining vinegar. Add the mixture to the pan, and boil steadily until the chutney is a good consistency. Pot and cover as described on p1139.

Note For Green Tomato Chutney made using a pressure cooker, see p1440.

Yellow Peach Chutney

Yield 2.5kg (approx)

2kg yellow peaches	225g sugar
2 large onions	1 × 15ml spoon cornflour
2 green peppers	
1 × 15ml spoon coriander seeds	1 × 5ml spoon salt
	1 × 5ml spoon turmeric
3 × 2.5ml spoons allspice berries	1 × 15ml spoon curry powder
750ml vinegar	

Skin and stone the peaches. Skin the onions and de-seed the peppers. Mince together the peaches, onions, and peppers. Tie the coriander seeds and allspice in muslin and simmer in the vinegar for a few minutes. Mix the remaining ingredients together, add to the vinegar, and heat to boiling point. Add the minced peach mixture. Simmer until the chutney thickens. Remove the spices. Bottle and cover immediately as described on p1139.

Banana Chutney

Yield 3kg (approx)

30 bananas	*250g seedless raisins*
60g onions	*50g salt*
25–50g fresh chillies	*50g ground ginger*
1.5 litres white vinegar	*500g brown sugar*

Slice the bananas and onions, and chop the chillies finely. Put all the ingredients into a saucepan and boil gently for 2 hours, stirring occasionally. When the chutney is of a good consistency, pot and cover as described on p1139.

Gooseberry Chutney

Yield 3kg (approx)

50g mustard seed	*750g seedless raisins*
500g onions	*50g ground allspice*
500g light soft brown sugar	*50g salt*
1.5 litres vinegar	*2kg gooseberries*

Bruise the mustard seed gently. Skin and chop the onions finely. Mix the sugar with half the vinegar and boil until a syrup forms; then add the onions, raisins, and spices. Top and tail the gooseberries and boil in the rest of the vinegar until tender; then mix in the sweet spiced vinegar, and cook until the chutney thickens. Pot and cover as described on p1139. Store for 2–3 months if possible before use.

Chinese Gooseberry Chutney

Yield 1kg (approx)

12 Chinese gooseberries	*1 × 10ml spoon salt*
1 large banana	*1 × 5ml spoon ground ginger*
2 lemons	
3 medium-sized onions	*250g brown sugar*
150g sultanas or raisins	*¼ × 5ml spoon pepper*
100g preserved ginger	*300ml vinegar (approx)*

Peel and cut up the gooseberries, bananas, and lemons; skin and grate the onions. Put all the ingredients into a saucepan. The vinegar should just cover the other ingredients. Simmer steadily for 1½ hours, then mash with a potato masher. Continue cooking until fairly thick, then pot and cover as described on p1139.

Dried Apricot Chutney
(Blatjang)

Yield 1.5kg (approx)

500g dried apricots	*1 × 5ml spoon ground ginger*
3–4 large onions	
500g seedless raisins	*1 clove of garlic*
500g light soft brown sugar	*1 litre vinegar*
	50g ground almonds
1 × 5ml spoon Cayenne pepper	*25g salt*

Soak the apricots overnight in enough water to cover them. Cook them in the water until soft. Skin and slice the onions. Soften them in a little simmering water. Mince the raisins. Put all the ingredients into a saucepan and simmer over low heat until the mixture is smooth and firm. A little tested on a plate should not flow when cool. Pot the chutney while hot, and cover at once as described on p1139.

Mango Chutney
See p1441.

SAUCES AND KETCHUPS

Worcestershire Sauce

Yield 1.25 litres (approx)

4 shallots	*4 × 15ml spoons soy sauce*
1 litre good malt vinegar	
6 × 15ml spoons walnut ketchup (p1148)	*1 × 2.5ml spoon Cayenne pepper*
75ml anchovy essence	*salt*

Skin and chop the shallots very finely. Put with all the other ingredients into a large bottle, and cork it tightly. Shake well 3 or 4 times daily for about 14 days, then strain the sauce into small, prepared bottles, leaving a headspace. Cork tightly (p1139), label, and store in a cool, dry place.

Tomato Ketchup (1)

Yield 1.5 litres (approx)

3kg ripe tomatoes
2 × 15ml spoons salt
600ml white vinegar
250g white sugar

1 × 2.5ml spoon each of
ground cloves,
cinnamon, allspice, and
Cayenne pepper

Quarter the tomatoes, place them in a preserving pan with the salt and vinegar, and simmer until they are soft and quite broken up. Rub the mixture through coarse muslin or a fine nylon sieve; then return it to the pan and add the sugar. Simmer until the ketchup starts to thicken, and then add the spices to taste, a little at a time, stirring thoroughly.

Meanwhile, heat enough bottles to hold the ketchup, and prepare seals (p1139). When the ketchup is thick enough, fill the hot bottles, leaving a headspace. Seal immediately, or allow the ketchup to cool slightly; then fill up the bottles, leaving a headspace, and sterilize at 88°C for 30 minutes. Seal immediately. Label when cold.

Note Remember that the ketchup will be thicker when cold, so do not reduce it too much.

For Tomato Ketchup made using a pressure cooker, see p1441.

Tomato Ketchup (2)

Yield 0.5 litres (approx)

12 ripe tomatoes
2 onions
3 × 15ml spoons white
sugar
1 × 10ml spoon each
whole cloves,
cinnamon, allspice

1 × 5ml spoon ground
nutmeg
1 × 2.5ml spoon
Cayenne pepper
1 × 15ml spoon salt
600ml vinegar

Cut the tomatoes into quarters and skin and chop the onions finely. Put all the ingredients into a preserving pan, bring to the boil and cook slowly for 2½ hours. Meanwhile, heat the bottles and prepare seals for the ketchup (p1139). When ready, strain the ketchup through very coarse muslin to remove skins and whole spices. Fill up the bottles, leaving a headspace. Sterilize at 88°C for 30 minutes, and seal immediately. Label when cold.

Tomato Ketchup (3)

Yield 1 litre (approx)

1 × 5ml spoon whole
pickling spices
150ml malt vinegar
100g onions
1.5kg ripe tomatoes
200g apples

125g white sugar
a pinch of Cayenne
pepper
15g salt
1 × 15ml spoon tarragon
vinegar

Bring the pickling spices and the malt vinegar to the boil, and leave to infuse for 2 hours; then strain. Skin the onions, and cut up the tomatoes, onions, and apples (there is no need to peel or core the tomatoes and apples). Put the fruit and vegetables into a pan. Cover and simmer them very slowly; the juice from the tomatoes should be enough to prevent them from burning. When they are thoroughly softened, rub through a fine nylon sieve. Return the pulp to the pan, and add the sugar, pepper, and salt. Boil, with the lid off, until the sauce begins to thicken, stirring occasionally with a wooden spoon. Add the malt and the tarragon vinegars. Boil, with the lid off, until the ketchup is thick and creamy. Heat bottles, and pour the ketchup into the hot bottles. Sterilize in simmering water for 30 minutes and seal immediately (p1139). Label when cold.

Store Sauce (1)

Yield 2 litres (approx)

1.5kg tomatoes
100g onions
250g brown sugar
250g raisins
100g salt (approx)

25g ground ginger
¼ × 2.5ml spoon
Cayenne pepper
1 litre vinegar

Cut up the tomatoes, skin and slice the onions, and put all the ingredients into a saucepan. Simmer until soft. Rub through a nylon or stainless sieve, re-heat and continue cooking until the texture is as thick as required. Bottle, leaving a headspace, and seal at once (p1139). Label when cold.

Note Red tomatoes give a better colour to this brown sauce than green ones, but either can be used.

Store Sauce (2)

Yield 2 litres (approx)

500g onions	25g mixed spice
500g tomatoes	1 lemon
500g apples	1 litre vinegar
25g salt	(preferably white)
250g sultanas	25g cornflour
75g white sugar	

Skin the onions and cut up all the fruit and vegetables roughly. Put into a saucepan with all the other ingredients except the cornflour. Boil gently until thoroughly cooked. Blend the cornflour to a cream with a little cold water. Sieve the cooked mixture and return it to the saucepan. Bring to the boil and stir in the cornflour. Boil for 5 minutes, then bottle, leaving a headspace, and seal at once (p1139). Label when cold.

Walnut Ketchup

Yield 1.5 litres (approx)

100 green walnuts (approx)	15g whole allspice berries
400g onions	1 × 2.5ml spoon whole cloves
2 litres vinegar	
200g salt	1 × 2.5ml spoon ground nutmeg
25g whole peppercorns	

Walnuts must be picked before the shell has hardened. The first week in July is usually the latest time to gather them for pickling.

Skin and chop the onions. Boil all the ingredients together, except the walnuts. Wearing gloves to prevent staining your hands, cut up the walnuts, crush them, and put into a large pan or basin. Pour the boiling vinegar over them, and leave for 14 days, stirring daily. Strain off the liquid and simmer it in a pan for about an hour. Pour it into prepared bottles, leaving a headspace, and seal at once (p1139). Label when cold. Discard the crushed walnuts.

Store Vinegars

Vinegar for pickling is usually well spiced but more delicately flavoured herb vinegars are useful in salad dressings and savoury sauces. Sweetened fruit vinegars are good in sweet-sour dishes and on plain desserts and puddings, or for sore throats!

HERB AND OTHER SAVOURY VINEGARS

The general method of making these is to boil the vinegar with perhaps a little salt and spice, and then to pour it hot over the freshly picked and prepared herb or vegetable, packed in a wide-necked bottle. The bottle is sealed with a vinegar-proof cork or cover, and is then shaken daily for about 10 days. It can then be left for another 10–14 days before the flavoured vinegar is gently poured off and re-bottled for use as required.

Variations on this basic method are given below. Always use good quality, preferably white, vinegar.

Celery Vinegar

250g celery or 15g celery seed	1 × 2.5ml spoon salt
600ml white vinegar (wine vinegar if possible)	

Clean and chop the whole celery, if used. Pack into prepared bottles or divide the seed between the bottles. Boil the vinegar with the salt. Pour the hot vinegar on to the chopped celery or seed, cover, and leave until cold. Seal the bottles and leave the vinegar for 3 weeks; then strain and re-bottle. Seal securely.

Chilli Vinegar

6 fresh chillies	600ml vinegar

Chop the chillies roughly and put into prepared bottles. Boil the vinegar, pour it hot over the chillies, cover, and allow to cool. Seal the bottles and leave the vinegar for 3 weeks; then strain and re-bottle. Seal securely.

VARIATION

Cress Vinegar

Make as for Chilli Vinegar substituting 15g crushed cress seed for the chillies.

Cucumber Vinegar

1 litre vinegar	6 cucumbers
1 × 10ml spoon salt	4 shallots
1 × 10ml spoon white	2 cloves garlic
peppercorns	

Boil the vinegar, salt, and peppercorns together for 20 minutes, then leave to cool completely. Slice the cucumbers (without peeling them) into prepared wide-necked bottles or jars. Skin and add the shallots and garlic. Pour in the cold vinegar. Seal the bottles and leave for 14 days; then strain and re-bottle. Seal securely.

Herb Vinegar

600ml malt vinegar	2 cloves
50g grated horseradish	a sprig each of thyme,
1 × 5ml spoon chopped	basil, savory,
shallot	marjoram, tarragon
rind and juice of	1 bay leaf
½ lemon	

Simmer all the ingredients for 20 minutes. Cool, then strain the vinegar. When cold, bottle, leaving a headspace. Seal securely.

Use a very little, with other vinegar, in salad dressings.

Mint Vinegar or Bottled Mint Sauce

150g chopped mint	25g sugar
(approx)	600ml wine vinegar

Use young, fresh mint. If it is necessary to wash the mint, drain it before chopping. Sprinkle the mint with the sugar. Boil the vinegar, pour it over the mint, and then bottle.

The mint will keep in the vinegar through the winter months, and the vinegar can be strained and used for salad dressings.

Horseradish Vinegar

600ml vinegar	a pinch of Cayenne
50g grated horseradish	pepper
15g chopped shallot	25g sugar
1 × 2.5ml spoon salt	

Boil the vinegar; mix together the other ingredients. Pour the boiling vinegar on to the mixture, and cover. When cool, bottle the mixture and store for 10 days. It may then be used unstrained as horse-radish sauce. To store the vinegar, strain and boil it. Heat some bottles and pour the vinegar into them. Seal securely.

Shallot Vinegar

50g shallots	600ml vinegar or 300ml
	vinegar and 300ml
	white wine

Skin the shallots, and chop them finely. Mix the ingredients, and store them in an airtight bottle for 2 weeks. Strain the vinegar and re-bottle it. Seal securely.

Tarragon Vinegar

50g tarragon leaves	600ml vinegar

Bruise the tarragon leaves slightly. Put them into a bottling jar, pour in the vinegar, and seal. Store for 6 weeks; then strain and re-bottle. Seal securely.

Note If using home-grown tarragon, the leaves should be gathered on a dry day about the end of July, just before the plant begins to bloom.

FRUIT VINEGARS

These traditional preserves are an excellent way of using up over-ripe soft fruit. Discard stalks and any leaves and put the fruit in a china or glass bowl.

Crush with a wooden spoon or vegetable presser and pour the vinegar over it, allowing 500ml vinegar for each 400g of fruit. To obtain a clear, bright colour in fruit such as raspberries, use white vinegar; but malt vinegar is quite suitable for blackcurrants and blackberries.

Cover the bowl with a cloth and leave for 3–5 days, stirring once or twice daily. Strain off the liquid into a pan, using a scalded felt or flannel bag if you want a very clear vinegar; a nylon or stainless strainer will give a less clear vinegar.

Measure the liquid and return it to the pan. Add 800g sugar to each litre of liquid. Granulated sugar gives a better colour, but if you prefer the characteristic flavour of brown sugar, use that instead. Stir the vinegar over gentle heat until the sugar has dissolved, then boil it steadily for 10 minutes. Test a spoonful by pouring it on to a plate. Boil until the vinegar is syrupy. Bottle and seal at once.

If you wish you can use less sugar or none at all at the boiling stage, but it does enhance the fruit flavour and gives a more rounded taste than if sugar is only added just before use.

Raspberries are most often used, but loganberries, blackberries, blackcurrants, mulberries, and strawberries all make pleasant vinegars. These fruit vinegars formerly had their place in the medicine cupboard as gargles and cough cures, but nowadays they are more likely to be used in sweet-sour recipes, or as a sauce to add zest to a plain dessert. It is unusual to use firmer fruit to make vinegar, but the following recipe gives the method.

Stone Fruit Vinegar

fruit with stones (see Method)
1 litre white vinegar for every 3 litres of fruit
800g sugar for each litre of liquid
200ml brandy for each litre of syrup (optional)

Suitable fruits are apricots, cherries, damsons, greengages, peaches, and plums.

Choose good quality, well-ripened fruit, and measure its volume. Halve the fruit (but do not remove the stones) and put into a bowl. Add the vinegar. Cover the bowl with a clean cloth and leave to stand for 6 days, stirring and pressing

down the fruit with a wooden spoon once a day. Finally press the fruit again and pour off the liquid through a fine sieve or jelly bag.

Measure the liquid into a pan and stir in the sugar. Boil steadily for 15 minutes or until the vinegar is syrupy when a small quantity is cooled on a plate. Skim, bottle, and seal at once. Label when cold.

If liked, leave the mixture in the pan until cold, then add the brandy. Stir, bottle, and seal securely.

Cranberry Vinegar

2kg sound ripe cranberries
2.5 litres white wine vinegar
800g sugar for each litre of liquid

Put the fruit in an earthenware bowl, crush it, and pour the vinegar over it. Cover with a clean cloth and leave for 10 days, stirring daily. Strain off the liquid through a fine sieve or jelly bag. Measure it into a saucepan and add the sugar. Boil steadily for 10 minutes or until the vinegar is syrupy when a small quantity is cooled on a plate. Skim, bottle, and seal at once. Label when cold.

VARIATION

Mulberry Vinegar

Make as above using 1kg ripe mulberries, 1.75 litres vinegar and the same proportion of sugar. Leave for 1 week before straining.

Raspberry Vinegar

raspberries
white wine vinegar
water
caster sugar

Clean the fruit thoroughly and put it into a basin. Cover with equal quantities of vinegar and water. Leave to stand overnight. Strain off the liquid through a fine sieve or jelly bag. To each 300ml of liquid, add 200g caster sugar. Pour into a saucepan and boil for 10 minutes. Pour the hot liquid into prepared bottles and seal at once. Label when cold.

Note Diluted with water, this vinegar makes a cooling summer drink.

Drying and Salting

DRYING

1) Use fresh fruits and young, tender vegetables. They usually need to be dried on trays. Special trays can be bought or they can be improvised, eg by covering a wire cake rack or oven rack with a piece of scalded muslin.

2) In good weather it is sometimes possible to dry fruit and vegetables in the sunshine or in a current of warm air by an open window. It is, however, generally better to rely on artificial heat, using a temperature of 50°–70°C. A cool oven can be used, or, on several successive days, the residual heat from the oven; alternatively, use a rack over a hot water tank, night storage heater, central heating boiler or similar warm place. Protect the fruit or vegetables from dust if necessary.

3) The drying can either take several hours or, if intermittent, 2–3 days.

4) It is important to heat fruit very slowly at first to prevent the outside from hardening or the skins from bursting.

5) To store dried fruit and vegetables, leave for 12 hours to cool at ordinary room temperature; then pack fruit in wooden or cardboard boxes lined with greaseproof paper, and vegetables in well-sealed containers. Keep in a dry place.

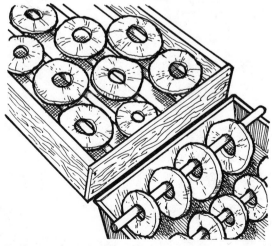

Drying apple rings

Dried Apple Rings

Peel and core the apples and, after removing all blemishes, cut into rings less than 1cm thick. Place immediately in salted water (1 × 15ml spoon salt to 1 litre water). After a few minutes, shake off the water, and thread the rings on sticks. Balance them across a baking tin and put to dry at a temperature of not more than 60°C. If they are dried in continuous heat this may take about 6 hours. When they are dry enough, they should resemble chamois leather in texture. If the centre is pressed with the thumb-nail it should resist the pressure and no juice should ooze out of the apple ring.

This is a suitable method of preserving windfalls and damaged apples. When the blemished parts have been removed it may not be possible to cut rings, but even-sized segments will dry satisfactorily if spread on racks and turned occasionally.

Dried Plums

Use a dark-skinned, fleshy variety, eg Pond's Seedling. Wash if necessary, halve, and stone, then spread out on racks to dry. The temperature must be low at first, 50°C, until the skins begin to shrivel. It can then be raised gradually to 70°C. When the fruit is dry enough, gentle squeezing should neither break the skin of the plum nor produce any juice.

Dried Mushrooms

Use freshly picked mushrooms. Remove the stalks. If the skins are clean and white, it will not be necessary to peel the mushrooms. Spread them on trays to dry. Alternatively, thread them on a string, tying a knot between each, and hang up to dry in a temperature of not more than 50°C, until they are crisp.

Field mushrooms dry well and are very useful in cooking.

Dried Parsley

Wash the parsley and dry in a cloth to remove surplus moisture. Spread on muslin on an oven shelf or tray. Put at the top of a very hot oven, 230°C, Gas 8, until dried – about 1 minute. Crush between the fingers, then sieve to a coarse powder and store in a screwtop jar.

Dried Thyme or Sage

Wash the herbs and shake them; dry in a cloth to remove surplus moisture. Put the bunches on paper in a warm place. As soon as the leaves can be shaken off the stalks, remove them all and store in a jar with a tight-fitting lid.

Note Sage takes longer to dry than thyme, and needs to be rubbed through the fingers and sieved.

Dried Mint and Other Herbs

Wash and dry on a cloth to remove surplus moisture. Tie in a bundle and put into a paper bag, binding the top of the bag with string so that the herbs are enclosed with only the stalks projecting. The paper protects them from dust. Hang in a warm place to dry. Remove the leaves from the stalks, crush, and store in a screwtop jar.

SALTING BEANS

Choose fresh, young, tender French beans or runner beans. Wash and dry them, top and tail, and remove strings. Slice runner beans but leave small French beans whole. Allow one-third of the weight of the beans in salt. Use cooking salt, not free-running table salt. (Weigh accurately and do not use less than this quantity, otherwise the beans will become slimy and will not keep.) Pack a layer of salt into the bottom of a large glass or stoneware jar. On top of this, press down very firmly a layer of beans; add another layer of salt, another layer of beans, and continue until the jar is full, finishing with a layer of salt. Each layer of salt should be about 2cm thick.

Cover the jar and leave it for 3–4 days. At the end of this time, you will find that the salt is drawing moisture from the beans and forming a brine, and that there will be room to fill up with more beans and salt. Press down again very firmly and finish with a layer of salt. When full to the top, cover the jar securely with a stopper, cap or synthetic skin.

Note If using stoneware jars on a stone or concrete floor, stand the jars on wooden blocks.

To Cook Salted Beans

Take out as many as required, wash thoroughly in cold water, then soak them for at least 2 hours in warm water. Do not soak them overnight or they will toughen. Boil in unsalted water until tender.

BREAD AND BREADMAKING

When bread is sufficiently baked, the bottom crust is hard and resonant if struck with the finger, while the crumb is elastic, and rises again after being pressed down with the finger. The bread is, in all probability, baked sufficiently if, on opening the door of the oven, you are met by a cloud of steam which quickly passes away.

Bread is made by baking a mixture of flour, water, and salt which has usually been made light and porous by adding yeast or some other raising agent such as baking powder. Some breads are not aerated and are known as unleavened breads, eg matzos (Jewish), chapattis (Indian), and tortillas (Mexican). These breads are flat and close-textured when cold and often brittle or crisp.

Yeast Breads

Flour

The flour most widely used for breadmaking in Western diets is obtained from wheat. Other cereals such as rye, oats, barley, and maize (cornflour) are used, but generally give better results when combined with wheat flour.

Several types of wheat flour are available. *Wholemeal* and *wholewheat flour* contain the whole of the wheat grain, including all the bran and wheatgerm. This gives wholemeal bread a pleasant nutty texture and flavour but a rather dense and heavy crumb. *Wheatmeal flour* (85–90% of the grain) contains less bran and wheatgerm; it gives a good flavoured bread with a lighter texture. *White flour* (72–74% of the grain) contains no bran or wheatgerm, and so white bread always has a large volume and light texture.

In the UK and elsewhere, the law states that the major nutrients lost in removing the wheatgerm and bran when making white flour must be made good by added nutrients. This means that there is little difference between white and brown bread; substantially only the fibre content differs. Whereas wholewheat and wholemeal breads contain all the fibre present in the wheat grain, brown and wheatmeal breads contain a proportion of the fibre, and white bread contains even less.

The best flour for making standard Western types of bread is a *strong* flour, which has a high gluten content. (A satisfactory result can also be obtained however with an ordinary domestic plain flour.) Gluten is the name given to the elastic substance formed when the wheat proteins in flour combine with water. As a dough is kneaded, the gluten becomes tougher, and an incorporated raising agent blows it up into small 'pockets' which set when heated. Gluten is also toughened by acid, but is softened by fat or sugar.

A *strong* white flour with plenty of gluten absorbs more liquid than a soft (domestic plain) flour, and can be kneaded into a firm elastic dough which gives a larger volume than that obtained with soft flours.

The quantity of flour to buy and store must depend on how much you use. All flours should be stored in cool, dry conditions. Once opened, wholemeal and wheatmeal flours last only about 6 months, due to their fat content. Plain white flour should keep for about 9 months. Self-raising flours can be stored for only about 6 months, however, because of the raising agent they contain.

Yeast

The fermentation method of raising dough involves the use of yeast, which is a living organism. In the presence of warmth, food, and moisture, yeast produces both carbon dioxide gas which raises the dough and alcohols which flavour it. This reaction is retarded, however, by cold, salt, and high concentrations of sugar and fat, and yeast is destroyed by heat. The first yeasts were grown on flour and water pastes which were left uncovered so that wild yeasts present in the air would settle on them. But nowadays special baker's yeast is available in both fresh and dried forms. Whenever yeast is used, twice as much fresh yeast is needed as dried yeast; in other words, 50g fresh yeast = 25g dried yeast.

Fresh Yeast is quick and easy to use but is not always easily obtainable, especially in urban areas. It should be creamy in colour, have a slightly beery smell, be cool to the touch and easy to break. It will store in a polythene bag in a refrigerator for up to a week and will freeze, if well wrapped, for up to 1 month. Fresh yeast should always be blended into a warm liquid rather than creamed with sugar, which tends to give yeasty 'off' flavours in the finished bread.

Dried Yeast, available in packets and tins, has a shelf-life, unopened, of up to 1 year. Once opened, however, it keeps for only 2–3 months, and must be stored in an airtight container.

Before use, dried yeast must be reconstituted. 1 × 5ml spoon of sugar is dissolved in a warm liquid (usually water and/or milk at a temperature of 38°C, ie hand-hot). The dried yeast is sprinkled on the liquid and left in a warm place for 10–15 minutes, or until the yeast has fully dissolved and the mixture is frothy. (This may take longer when using all milk.) If after 30 minutes the mixture has not frothed, the yeast is stale and should be thrown away.

Kneading

Most doughs must be worked after mixing in order to strengthen and develop them and to make them rise well. Very soft doughs are beaten; all others are kneaded.

To hand knead: On a floured surface, fold the dough towards you, then push down and away from you with the heel of your hand. Give the dough a quarter turn and repeat the folding and pushing action, developing a rocking rhythm. Continue until the dough feels firm and elastic and is no longer sticky.

To knead in an electric mixer: Follow the manufacturer's directions for using a dough hook. Place the yeast liquid in the mixer bowl first, then add the dry ingredients. Turn the machine to minimum speed and mix for 1 minute to form the dough. Increase the speed slightly and mix for a further 2 minutes. It may be necessary to hand knead the dough into one piece when it is removed from the mixer bowl.

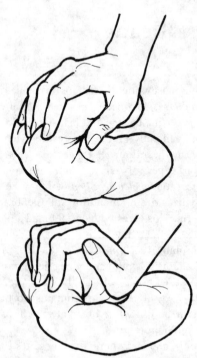

Rising

All yeast doughs must rise at least once before baking. Generally, a dough gives a better flavour and texture if it rises twice, but raising it once makes quite acceptable bread if time is limited. (The second rising is generally called *proving*.)

Rising times vary according to the type of dough and the temperature of the rising place; the warmer the place, the quicker the rise. The rising place must not, however, be too warm or the finished loaf will be dry and will quickly become stale. The dough may also be over-stretched by the yeast working too actively. The bread may collapse in the oven, and the loaf may smell yeasty or sour. As a rough guide, the dough should have risen enough when it has doubled in bulk.

The dough can be left to rise overnight in a refrigerator. In this case, return it to room temperature before shaping. Do not, however, leave rolls to rise in this way. All doughs should be covered during rising to prevent the surface drying out and a skin forming. The most convenient, efficient, and hygienic form of covering is a large polythene bag which has been lightly oiled inside to prevent it sticking to the dough and spoiling the surface of the shaped bread. The dough should only be covered loosely when it is put in the bag; ie some air space should be left above it so that it can rise unimpeded.

Unrisen dough can also be frozen (see p1392).

Baking

All yeasted goods should be baked for at least 10 minutes in a very hot oven to kill the yeast and prevent further rising.

When correctly baked, bread should be well risen, golden-brown and crisp, and should sound hollow when tapped on the bottom.

WHITE BREADS

Basic White Bread

Makes two 800g loaves

800g strong white flour
1 × 10ml spoon salt
1 × 10ml spoon sugar
25g lard
25g fresh yeast **or**
1 × 15ml spoon dried
yeast

500ml warm water
flour for kneading
fat for greasing
beaten egg **or** *milk for*
glazing

Sift together the flour, salt, and sugar into a large bowl. Rub in the lard. Blend the fresh yeast into the warm water or reconstitute the dried yeast. Add the yeast liquid to the flour mixture and mix to a soft dough. Turn on to a floured surface and knead for about 8 minutes or until the dough is smooth, elastic, and no longer sticky. Place the dough in a large, lightly oiled polythene bag and leave in a warm place for about 1 hour or until the dough has doubled in size. Knead the dough again until firm. Cut into 2 equal portions and form each into a loaf shape. Place the dough in 2 greased 23 × 13 × 7cm loaf tins and brush the surface with beaten egg or milk. Place the tins in the polythene bag and leave in a warm place for about 45 minutes or until the dough has doubled in size. Bake in a very hot oven, 230°C, Gas 8, for 35–40 minutes until the loaves are crisp and golden-brown and sound hollow when tapped on the bottom.

VARIATIONS

Milk Bread

Substitute warm milk for the warm water in the above recipe.

For rolls made with Basic White Bread dough, see over.

Scottish Breakfast Rolls
(Baps)

Makes 18

Increase the quantity of lard from 25g to 75g and use 250ml warm milk and 250ml warm water instead of 500ml warm water. Divide the risen dough into 75g pieces. Shape each piece into a ball, then press out to a circle about 12mm thick. Place on a greased sheet, cover with a large, lightly oiled polythene bag, and leave in a warm place for about 30 minutes or until the dough is puffy. Dust the surface of the rolls with flour. Bake in a fairly hot oven, 200°C, Gas 6, for 15–20 minutes until golden-brown.

Fancy Roll Shapes

Makes 26

Divide the risen Basic White Bread dough into 50g pieces and shape as below:

Small Plaits

Divide each piece of dough into 3 equal portions; then shape each of these into a long strand. Plait the 3 strands together, pinching the ends securely.

Small Twists

Divide each piece of dough into 2 equal portions, and shape into strands about 12cm in length. Twist the 2 strands together, pinching the ends securely.

'S' Rolls

Shape each piece of dough into a roll about 15cm in length, and form it into an 'S' shape.

Cottage Rolls

Cut two-thirds off each piece of dough and shape into a ball. Shape the remaining third in the same way. Place the small ball on top of the larger one and push a hole through the centre of both with one finger, dusted with flour, so joining the 2 pieces firmly together.

Huffkins

Shape each piece of dough into an oval about 12mm thick, then make a hole in the centre with one finger, dusted with flour.

Single Knots

Shape each piece of dough into a roll about 15cm in length and tie it into a knot. Place the shaped rolls, spaced well apart, on to greased baking sheets. Brush the surface of each with beaten egg or milk. Place the sheets in a large, lightly oiled polythene bag and leave in a warm place for about 25 minutes or until the rolls have almost doubled in size. Bake as for Basic White Bread (p1155) but reduce the cooking time to 10–15 minutes.

Lardy Cake

Makes 18–20 slices

¼ recipe of risen Basic White Bread dough (p1155) (350g approx)	100g caster sugar
	100g sultanas **or** currants
flour for rolling out	1 × 5ml spoon mixed spice
125g lard	

Glaze

1 × 10ml spoon caster sugar	1 × 15ml spoon water

On a floured surface, roll out the dough to a strip 2cm thick. Place a third of the lard in small pats over the surface of the dough. Sprinkle one-third of the sugar, dried fruit, and spice over it. Fold the dough into three. Repeat the rolling and folding twice more, using the remaining ingredients. Roll out to fit a 20cm square slab cake or baking tin. Score diamond shapes in the surface of the dough with a sharp knife. Place the tin in a large, lightly oiled polythene bag and leave in a warm place for about 45 minutes or until the dough has risen by half. Bake in a fairly hot oven, 200°C, Gas 6, for 40 minutes until crisp and golden-brown.

To make the glaze, boil together the sugar and water until syrupy, and brush over the surface of the warm cake.

Enriched Bread

Makes two 800g loaves

800g strong white flour
1 × 10ml spoon sugar
400ml milk
25g fresh yeast **or**
  1 × 15ml spoon dried
  yeast
1 × 10ml spoon salt

100g butter **or**
  margarine
2 eggs
flour for kneading
fat for greasing
milk for glazing

Sift about 75g of the flour and all the sugar into a large bowl. Warm the milk until hand-hot, then blend in the fresh yeast or stir in the dried yeast. Pour the yeast liquid into the flour and sugar and beat well. Leave the bowl in a warm place for 20 minutes. Sift the remaining flour and salt into a bowl. Rub in the fat. Beat the eggs into the yeast mixture and stir in the flour and fat. Mix to a soft dough. Turn on to a lightly floured surface and knead for about 6 minutes or until the dough is smooth and no longer sticky. Place the dough in a large, lightly oiled polythene bag and leave in a warm place for about 1 hour or until it has doubled in size. Knead again until firm. Cut it into 2 equal portions and form each into a loaf shape. Place in 2 greased 23 × 13 × 7cm loaf tins and cover with the polythene bag. Leave in a warm place for about 30 minutes or until the dough has doubled in size. Brush the surface with milk and bake in a hot oven, 220°C, Gas 7, for 35–40 minutes until the loaves are golden-brown and sound hollow when tapped on the bottom.

VARIATIONS

Bread Plait

Make as for Enriched Bread. Cut the risen dough into 2 equal portions. Cut one of these into 3 equal pieces. Roll each piece into a strand 25–30cm long and plait the strands together. Repeat, using the second portion. Place the plaits on a greased baking tray, cover, rise, and bake as for Enriched Bread.

Cheese Bread Plait

Make as for Bread Plait but add 200g grated Cheddar cheese to the dry ingredients.

Caraway Bread

Make as for Enriched Bread but add 1 × 10ml spoon sage, 1 × 5ml spoon grated nutmeg, and 1 × 15ml spoon caraway seeds to the dry ingredients.

Fruit Bread

Make as for Enriched Bread but add 200g sultanas, currants or raisins to the dough when kneading for the second time.

Nut Bread

Make as for Enriched Bread but add 200g chopped nuts (walnuts, peanuts, etc) to the dough when kneading for the second time.

Poppy Seed Bread

Make as for Enriched Bread but sprinkle poppy seeds thickly over the dough before baking.

Bridge Rolls

Makes 34–38

Make as for Enriched Bread but cut the risen dough into 50g pieces. Roll each piece into a finger shape about 10cm long. Place on a greased baking tray so that the rolls almost touch each other. Dust the surface of the rolls with flour, cover, and leave to rise for about 20 minutes or until the rolls have joined together. Bake as for Enriched Bread but reduce the cooking time to 12–15 minutes.

For further **variations**, see over.

Challah

Makes two 800g loaves

Make as for Enriched Bread (p1157) but substitute water for the milk. Cut the risen dough into 2 equal portions. Cut one of these into 2 equal pieces and roll these into long strands 30–35cm in length. Arrange the 2 strands in a cross on a flat surface. Take the 2 opposite ends of the bottom strand and cross them over the top strand in the centre. Repeat this, using the other strand. Cross each strand alternately, building up the plait vertically, until all the dough is used up. Gather the short ends together and pinch firmly. Lay the challah on its side and place on a greased baking tray. Brush with beaten egg. Repeat, using the second portion. Cover, rise, and bake as for Enriched Bread.

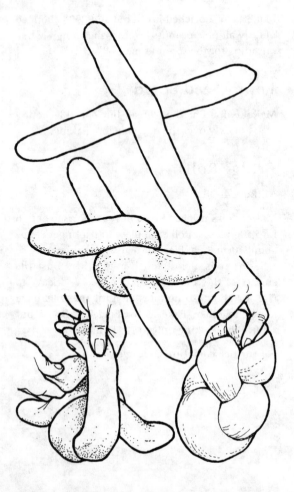

Dinner Rolls

Makes 34–38

Make as for Enriched Bread but cut the risen dough into 50g pieces. Shape each piece into a ball. Place on a greased baking tray 5–8cm apart. Brush with beaten egg, cover, and leave to rise for about 20 minutes or until the rolls have doubled in size. Bake as for Enriched Bread but reduce the cooking time to 12–15 minutes.

Short-time White Bread

Makes two 800g loaves

800g strong white flour	*500ml warm water*
1 × 10ml spoon salt	*25g fresh yeast (see*
1 × 10ml spoon sugar	**Note***)*
25g lard	*flour for kneading*
1 × 25mg tablet ascorbic	*fat for greasing*
acid (see **Note***)*	*beaten egg* **or** *milk for*
	glazing

Sift together the flour, salt, and sugar into a large bowl. Rub in the lard. Crush the ascorbic acid tablet into the warm water, then stir in the fresh yeast. Pour the yeast liquid on to the flour mixture and mix to a soft dough. Turn on to a floured surface and knead for about 8 minutes or until the dough is smooth and elastic and no longer sticky. Cut it into 2 equal portions and form each into a loaf shape. Place in 2 greased 23 × 13 × 7cm loaf tins and brush the surface with beaten egg or milk. Place the tins in a large, lightly oiled polythene bag and leave in a warm place for about 45 minutes or until the dough has doubled in size. Bake in a very hot oven, 230°C, Gas 8, for 35–40 minutes until the loaves are crisp and golden-brown and sound hollow when tapped on the bottom.

Note This dough is best made with fresh yeast rather than dried. Ascorbic acid (vitamin C) tablets are available from chemists.

French Bread

Makes 2 French sticks

*350g plain white flour
  (see **Note**)
50g cornflour
1 × 5ml spoon salt
15g fresh yeast **or**
  1 × 10ml spoon dried
  yeast*

*250ml warm water
flour
beaten egg for glazing*

Sift the flours and salt into a large bowl. Blend the fresh yeast into the warm water or reconstitute the dried yeast. Stir the yeast liquid into the flours and mix to a firm dough. Turn the dough on to a floured surface and knead for about 4 minutes or until it is smooth and no longer sticky. Place the dough in a large, lightly oiled polythene bag and leave in a warm place for about 1 hour or until it has doubled in size. Cut it into 2 equal portions. On a floured surface, roll out 1 piece to an oval 40cm in length. Roll it up like a Swiss roll and place on a well-floured baking sheet. With a sharp knife, slash the top surface at intervals. Brush the surface with beaten egg. Repeat with the other piece of dough. Leave both, *uncovered*, in a warm place for about 30 minutes or until doubled in size.

Meanwhile, place a pan of hot water in the bottom of the oven and heat the oven to hot, 220°C, Gas 7. This is to provide steam to make the French bread expand fully before using dry heat to form the typical crisp crust. Bake the loaves for 15 minutes, remove the pan of water, and continue baking until they are very crisp and well browned.

Note The dough is left uncovered to rise for the second time, so that the surface dries out and a very crisp crust is obtained after the loaf has been 'blown up' by steam heat in the oven. This can be done only when the volume of dough is as small as it is here, otherwise the bread splits open on baking.

Strong flour is not suitable for this bread.

Cooking time 30–35 minutes

BROWN BREADS

Wholemeal Bread

Makes two 800g loaves

*800g wholemeal flour
1 × 10ml spoon sugar
1 × 15ml spoon salt
25g lard
25g fresh yeast **or**
  1 × 15ml spoon dried
  yeast*

*500ml warm water
flour for kneading
fat for greasing
salted water*

Mix together the flour, sugar, and salt in a large bowl. Rub in the lard. Blend the fresh yeast into the warm water or reconstitute the dried yeast. Add the yeast liquid to the flour mixture and mix to a soft dough. Turn on to a lightly floured surface and knead for about 4 minutes or until the dough is smooth and elastic and no longer sticky. Place in a large, lightly oiled polythene bag and leave in a warm place for about 1 hour or until the dough has doubled in size. Knead again until firm. Cut it into 2 equal portions and form each into a loaf shape. Place the dough in 2 lightly greased 23 × 13 × 7cm loaf tins and brush the surface with salted water. Place the tins in the polythene bag and leave in a warm place for about 45 minutes or until the dough has doubled in size. Bake in a very hot oven, 230°C, Gas 8, for 30–40 minutes until the loaves are golden-brown and crisp and sound hollow when tapped on the bottom.

VARIATION

Wholemeal Rolls

Make as for Wholemeal Bread but shape into balls or fancy roll shapes as described on p1156. Bake for 10–15 minutes only.

Malted Brown Bread

Makes two 800g loaves

800g wholemeal flour
1 ×15ml spoon salt
25g fresh yeast **or**
 1 ×15ml spoon dried
 yeast

500ml warm water
2 ×15ml spoons malt
 extract
flour for kneading
fat for greasing

Mix together the flour and salt in a large bowl. Blend the fresh yeast into the warm water or reconstitute the dried yeast. Stir the malt extract into the yeast liquid, add to the flour, and mix to a soft dough. Turn on to a lightly floured surface and knead for about 4 minutes or until the dough is smooth and elastic and no longer sticky. Place it in a large, lightly oiled polythene bag and leave in a warm place for about 1 hour or until the dough has doubled in size. Knead again until firm. Cut it into 2 equal portions and form each into a loaf shape. Place the dough in 2 greased 23 ×13 ×7cm loaf tins and cover with the polythene bag. Leave in a warm place for about 45 minutes or until the dough has doubled in size. Bake in a very hot oven, 230°C, Gas 8, for 35–45 minutes until the loaves are golden-brown and crisp and sound hollow when tapped on the bottom.

Wheatmeal Bread

Makes two 800g loaves

400g wholemeal flour
400g strong white flour
1 ×10ml spoon salt
1 ×10ml spoon sugar
25g lard
25g fresh yeast **or**
 1 ×15ml spoon dried
 yeast

500ml warm water
flour for kneading
fat for greasing
salted water

Mix together the flours, salt, and sugar in a large bowl. Rub in the lard. Blend the fresh yeast into the warm water or reconstitute the dried yeast. Add the yeast liquid to the flour mixture and mix to a soft dough. Turn on to a floured surface, and knead for about 4 minutes or until the dough is smooth and no longer sticky. Cut it into 2 equal

portions and form each into a loaf shape. Place the dough in 2 greased 23 ×13 ×7cm loaf tins, and brush the surface with salted water. Place the tins in a large, lightly oiled polythene bag and leave in a warm place for about 50 minutes or until the dough has doubled in size. Bake in a very hot oven, 230°C, Gas 8, for 30–40 minutes until the loaves are golden-brown and crisp and sound hollow when tapped lightly on the bottom.

Scottish Brown Bread
(oatmeal bread)

Makes two 800g loaves

600g wholemeal flour
200g fine **or** medium
 oatmeal
1 ×10ml spoon sugar
1 ×15ml spoon salt
25g fresh yeast **or**
 1 ×15ml spoon dried
 yeast

500ml warm water
1 × 5ml spoon
 bicarbonate of soda
flour for kneading
fat for greasing

Mix together the flour, oatmeal, sugar, and salt in a large bowl. Blend the fresh yeast into the warm water or reconstitute the dried yeast. Add the bicarbonate of soda to the yeast liquid and stir this into the flour mixture to form a soft dough. Turn on to a lightly floured surface and knead for about 4 minutes or until the dough is smooth and no longer sticky. Place in a large, lightly oiled polythene bag and leave in a warm place for about 1 hour or until the dough has doubled in size. Knead it again until firm. Cut into 2 equal portions and form each into a loaf shape. Place the dough in 2 greased 23 ×13 ×7cm loaf tins and cover with the polythene bag. Leave in a warm place for about 45 minutes or until the dough has doubled in size. Bake in a very hot oven, 230°C, Gas 8, for 20 minutes, then reduce to fairly hot, 190°C, Gas 5 and continue baking until the loaves are crisp and golden-brown and sound hollow when tapped on the bottom.

Cooking time 45–55 minutes

Grant Loaf

(unkneaded bread)

Makes three 400g loaves

800g wholemeal flour	700ml warm water
1 × 10ml spoon sugar	fat for greasing
1 × 15ml spoon salt	
25g fresh yeast **or**	
1 × 15ml spoon dried yeast	

Mix together the flour, sugar, and salt in a large bowl. Blend the fresh yeast into the warm water or reconstitute the dried yeast. Pour the yeast liquid into the flour and stir until the flour is evenly wetted. The resulting dough should be wet and slippery. Spoon it into 3 greased 20 × 10 × 6cm loaf tins. Place the tins in a large, lightly oiled polythene bag and leave in a warm place until the dough has risen by a third. Bake in a fairly hot oven, 190°C, Gas 5, for 50–60 minutes until the loaves are golden-brown and crisp and sound hollow when tapped on the bottom.

Rye Cobs

Makes 4 loaves

900g strong white flour	4 × 5ml spoons salt
25g fresh yeast **or**	4 × 15ml spoons molasses
1 × 15ml spoon dried yeast	
250ml warm water	4 × 15ml spoons cooking oil
450g coarse rye flour	flour for kneading
500ml skimmed milk (from dried milk powder and water)	fat for greasing warm water

Sift the white flour into a large bowl. Blend the fresh yeast into the warm water or reconstitute the dried yeast. Mix the rye flour into the white flour, then add the yeast liquid, skimmed milk, salt, molasses and oil, and knead to a soft dough. Place the mixing bowl inside a large, lightly oiled polythene bag and leave in a warm place for 1½–2 hours until the dough has doubled in size. (Rye bread is slow to rise.) When risen, shape into 4 round loaves. Place on a lightly greased baking sheet or press into 4 greased 15cm sandwich tins. Place again in the polythene bag and leave to rise for 30–45 minutes. Sprinkle with warm water, and bake in a fairly hot oven, 190°C, Gas 5, for about 40 minutes until the loaves sound hollow when tapped on the bottom.

Sour Dough Rye Bread

Makes two 800g loaves

Starter Paste (prepare 4 days before the bulk of the recipe)

100g strong white flour	175ml milk
50g sugar	

500g rye flour	375ml warm water
200g strong white flour	1 × 15ml spoon oil
1 × 10ml spoon salt	fat for greasing
1 × 15ml spoon sugar	

To make the starter paste, sift together the flour and sugar. Warm the milk until hand-hot and then stir it into the flour. Beat to a smooth paste. Place the starter paste in a screw-topped jar and leave in a warm place *for 4 days.*

Put the flours, salt, and sugar in a large bowl. Add the starter paste, warm water and oil, and mix to a slack dough. Beat with a wooden spoon for 3 minutes. Place the dough in 2 greased 23 × 13 × 7cm loaf tins, cover with a large, lightly oiled polythene bag, and leave at room temperature for about 24 hours or until the dough reaches the top of the tins. Bake in a very hot oven, 230°C, Gas 8, for 10 minutes, then reduce to fairly hot, 190°C, Gas 5, and continue baking until the loaves are well browned and sound hollow when tapped on the bottom.

Note To reduce the second rising of the dough to 2 hours, 15g fresh yeast or 1 × 10ml spoon dried yeast can be added when mixing the dough. The fresh yeast should be blended into the warm water and the dried yeast reconstituted.

Cooking time 40–45 minutes

Granary Bread

Makes two 800g loaves

800g granary flour **or** meal	1 × 10ml spoon corn oil flour for kneading
1 × 10ml spoon salt	fat for greasing
1 × 10ml spoon molasses	salted water
500ml warm water	1 × 15ml spoon cracked wheat
25g fresh yeast **or** 1 × 15ml spoon dried yeast	

Mix together the flour and salt in a large bowl. Stir the molasses into the water, and when dissolved, blend in the fresh yeast, or reconstitute the dried yeast. Add the yeast liquid and the oil to the flour and mix to a soft dough. Turn on to a floured surface and knead for about 4 minutes or until it is smooth, elastic, and no longer sticky. Place in a large, lightly oiled polythene bag and leave in a warm place for about 1¼ hours or until doubled in size. Knead the dough again until firm. Cut into 2 equal portions, and form each into a loaf shape. Place the dough in 2 greased 23 × 13 × 7cm loaf tins, brush the surface with salted water, and sprinkle with the cracked wheat. Place the tins in the polythene bag and leave in a warm place for about 45 minutes or until the dough has doubled in size. Bake in a very hot oven, 230°C, Gas 8, for 30–40 minutes until the loaves are browned and crisp and sound hollow when tapped on the bottom.

Wholemeal Fruit Bread

Makes one 800g loaf

400g wholemeal flour	250ml warm water
1 × 2.5ml spoon sugar	flour for kneading
3 × 2.5ml spoons salt	100g stoned prunes
15g lard	grated rind of 1 orange
15g fresh yeast **or** 1 × 10ml spoon dried yeast	25g sugar fat for greasing

Mix together the flour, sugar, and salt in a large bowl. Rub in the lard. Blend the fresh yeast into the warm water or reconstitute the dried yeast. Add the yeast liquid to the flour mixture and mix to a soft dough. Turn on to a floured surface and knead for about 4 minutes or until the dough is smooth and elastic and no longer sticky. Place in a large, lightly oiled polythene bag and leave in a warm place for about 1 hour or until the dough has doubled in size. Meanwhile, chop the prunes roughly. Knead the dough again until firm, incorporating the prunes, orange rind, and sugar. Place the dough in a greased 23 × 13 × 7cm loaf tin, and cover with the polythene bag. Leave in a warm place for about 1 hour or until the dough has doubled in size. Bake in a very hot oven, 230°C, Gas 8, for 30–40 minutes until the loaf is golden-brown and crisp and sounds hollow when tapped on the bottom.

OTHER BAKED GOODS

For Breakfast, Dinner, and Supper

Bagels

Makes 28 rolls

400g strong white flour	1 egg
1 × 5ml spoon salt	flour
2 × 15ml spoons sugar	fat for greasing
50g margarine	poppy seeds
250ml warm water	
15g fresh yeast **or** 1 × 10ml spoon dried yeast	

Sift the flour into a large bowl. Put the salt, sugar, margarine, and half the water in a saucepan and warm gently until the fat has melted. Leave until lukewarm. Blend the fresh yeast with the remaining water or reconstitute the dried yeast. Separate the egg, whisk the white lightly, and add to the flour with the cooled margarine mixture and the yeast liquid. Mix to a soft dough. Place in a large, lightly oiled polythene bag and leave in a warm place for about 1 hour or until the dough has almost doubled in size. Knead it again until firm. Cut it into 25g pieces. Roll each piece into a sausage shape 15–20cm in length; then form this into a ring, pinching the ends securely together. Place the rings on a floured surface and leave for 10 minutes or until they begin to rise. Heat a saucepan of water deep enough to float the bagels, to just under boiling point. Drop in the bagels, a few at a time. Cook them on one side for 2 minutes, then turn them over and cook on the other side for about 2 minutes or until they are light and have risen slightly. Place on a greased baking sheet. Beat the egg yolk, brush it over the top surface of the bagels and sprinkle with poppy seeds. Bake in a fairly hot oven, 190°C, Gas 5, for 20–30 minutes until golden-brown and crisp.

Brioches

Makes 22 brioches

400g strong white flour	4 × 10ml spoons warm
1 × 5ml spoon salt	water
1 × 10ml spoon sugar	2 eggs
50g butter	flour for kneading
25g fresh yeast **or**	fat for greasing
1 × 15ml spoon dried	beaten egg for glazing
yeast	

Sift the flour, salt, and sugar into a large bowl. Rub in the butter. Blend the fresh yeast into the warm water or reconstitute the dried yeast. Beat the eggs into the yeast liquid and stir into the flour to form a soft dough. Turn on to a floured surface and knead for about 5 minutes or until the dough is smooth and no longer sticky. Place in a large, lightly oiled polythene bag and leave in a warm place for about 45 minutes or until doubled in size. Grease twenty-two 7cm brioche or deep bun tins. Knead the dough again until firm and cut into 22 equal pieces. Cut off one-quarter of each piece used. Form the larger piece into a ball and place in a tin. Firmly press a hole in the centre and place the remaining quarter as a knob in the centre. Place the tins on a baking sheet and cover with the polythene bag. Leave in a warm place for about 30 minutes or until the dough is light and puffy. Brush with beaten egg and bake in a very hot oven, 230°C, Gas 8, for 15–20 minutes until golden-brown.

Croissants

Makes 12

400g strong white flour	200ml warm water
1 × 5ml spoon salt	1 egg
100g lard	flour
25g fresh yeast **or**	75g unsalted butter
1 × 15ml spoon dried	beaten egg for glazing
yeast	fat for greasing

Sift the flour and salt into a large bowl. Rub in 25g of the lard. Blend the fresh yeast into the warm water or reconstitute the dried yeast. Beat the egg until liquid. Stir the egg and yeast liquid into the flour and mix to a soft dough. Turn on to a lightly floured surface and knead for about 8 minutes or until the dough is smooth and no longer sticky. Place the dough in a large, lightly oiled polythene bag and leave at room temperature for 15 minutes.

Meanwhile, beat together the rest of the lard and the butter until well mixed; then chill. On a lightly floured surface, roll the dough carefully into an oblong 50 × 20cm. Divide the chilled fat into three. Use one-third to dot over the top two-thirds of the dough, leaving a small border clear. Fold the dough into three by bringing up the plain part of it first, then bringing the top, fat-covered third down over it. Seal the edges together by pressing with the rolling-pin. Give the dough a quarter turn and repeat the rolling and folding twice, using the other 2 portions of fat. Place the dough in the polythene bag and leave in a cool place for 15 minutes.

Repeat the rolling and folding 3 more times. Rest the dough in the polythene bag in a cool place for 15 minutes. Roll it into an oblong 24 × 36cm and then cut it into six 12cm squares. Cut each square into triangles. Brush the surface of the dough with beaten egg and roll each triangle loosely, towards the point, finishing with the tip underneath. Curve into a crescent shape. Place on a greased baking sheet and brush with beaten egg. Place the sheet in the polythene bag again and leave in a warm place for about 30 minutes or until the dough is light and puffy. Bake in a hot oven, 220°C, Gas 7, for 15–20 minutes until golden-brown and crisp.

Grissini

Makes 45 sticks (approx)

400g strong white flour
1 × 5ml spoon salt
1 × 5ml spoon sugar
25g margarine
50ml milk
200ml warm water
15g fresh yeast **or**
 1 × 10ml spoon dried
 yeast

flour for kneading
fat for greasing
beaten egg white **or** milk
 for glazing
sesame seeds, poppy
 seeds **or** salt (optional)

Sift together the flour, salt, and sugar into a large bowl. Rub in the margarine. Warm the milk until hand-hot. Add to the warm water and blend in the fresh yeast or reconstitute the dried yeast. Add the yeast liquid to the flour and mix to a soft dough. Turn on to a lightly floured surface and knead for about 5 minutes or until smooth and no longer sticky. Place in a large, lightly oiled polythene bag and leave in a warm place for about 1 hour or until the dough has doubled in size. Knead again until firm. Cut into 15g pieces. Roll each piece into a strand 32cm long. Place the strands on a greased baking sheet, brush the surface of each with beaten egg white or milk, and sprinkle, if liked, with the seeds or salt. Place the baking sheet in the polythene bag and leave in a warm place for 10 minutes. Bake in a hot oven, 220°C, Gas 7, for 10–15 minutes until golden-brown and very crisp.

Princess Rolls

Makes 18

400g strong white flour
250ml milk
15g fresh yeast **or**
 1 × 10ml spoon dried
 yeast
50g margarine

1 × 15ml spoon caster
 sugar
1 × 5ml spoon salt
flour
150g butter (approx)
fat for greasing

Sift the flour into a large bowl. Warm the milk until hand-hot. Blend half of it with the fresh yeast or reconstitute the dried yeast. Add the margarine, sugar and salt to the remaining milk, and heat until the fat has melted. Leave until lukewarm. Stir with

the yeast liquid into the flour and mix to a soft dough. Turn on to a lightly floured surface and knead for about 6 minutes or until smooth and no longer sticky. Place the dough in a large, lightly oiled polythene bag and leave in a warm place for about 1 hour or until doubled in size. Lightly knead the dough again. Roll out on a floured surface to 8mm thickness. Cut into rounds, using a plain 7cm cutter. Place a small piece of butter on one half of each round. Fold over the other half and pinch the edges firmly together. Place the rolls on a greased baking tray. Put the tray in the polythene bag and leave in a warm place for about 30 minutes or until the rolls have almost doubled in size. Bake in a hot oven, 220°C, Gas 7, for 10–15 minutes until golden-brown.

For Coffee and Tea-Time

Bath Buns

Makes 12

400g strong white flour
1 × 5ml spoon sugar
125ml milk
75ml warm water
25g fresh yeast **or**
 1 × 15ml spoon dried
 yeast
1 × 5ml spoon salt
50g butter

50g caster sugar
150g sultanas
50g chopped mixed peel
2 eggs
fat for greasing
beaten egg for glazing
50g sugar nibs **or** lump
 sugar, coarsely crushed

Sift about 75g of the flour and the 5ml spoon sugar into a large bowl. Warm the milk until hand-hot. Add the water to the milk and blend in the fresh yeast or sprinkle on the dried yeast. Pour the yeast liquid into the flour and sugar and beat well. Leave the bowl in a warm place for 20 minutes. Sift the rest of the flour and the salt into a bowl. Rub in the butter. Add the caster sugar and dried fruit. Beat the eggs into the frothy yeast mixture and add the flour, fat, and fruit mixture. Mix to a very soft dough. Beat with a wooden spoon for 3 minutes. Cover the bowl with a large, lightly oiled polythene bag and leave in a warm place for about 45 minutes or until the dough has almost doubled in size. Beat the dough again for 1 minute. Place 15ml spoonfuls of the mixture on a greased baking sheet leaving plenty of space between them. Place the sheet in the polythene bag and leave in a warm place for about 20 minutes or until the buns have almost doubled in size. Brush the surface of each with beaten egg and sprinkle with the sugar nibs or lump sugar. Bake in a hot oven, 220°C, Gas 7, until golden-brown.

Cooking time 15–20 minutes

VARIATIONS

Hot Cross Buns

Make as for Bath Buns but substitute 100g currants for the sultanas and use only 1 egg. Add 3 × 2.5ml spoons mixed spice, 1 × 2.5ml spoon ground cinnamon, and 1 × 2.5ml spoon grated nutmeg to the flour. After mixing to a soft dough, knead for about 5 minutes on a lightly floured surface until the dough is smooth and no longer sticky. Place in a large, lightly oiled polythene bag and leave to rise for about 1 hour until the dough has almost doubled in size. Knead again until firm. Cut into 12 equal pieces and shape each into a round bun. Place on a floured baking sheet. With a sharp knife, slash a cross on the top of each bun, or make crosses with pastry trimmings or a fairly stiff flour and water paste. Cover with polythene and leave for about 35 minutes until the dough has doubled in size. Bake as for Bath Buns.

Glaze the hot buns by boiling together 2 × 15ml spoons milk, 2 × 15ml spoons water, and 40g caster sugar for 6 minutes and brushing the surface of each with the glaze.

Bun Loaf

Makes one 800g loaf

Make as for Hot Cross Buns but bake the mixture in a greased 23 × 13 × 7cm loaf tin. Increase the cooking time to 30–40 minutes.

Chelsea Buns

Makes 16

400g strong white flour	1 egg
1 × 5ml spoon sugar	flour
200ml milk	1 × 15ml spoon butter
25g fresh yeast **or**	150g currants
1 × 15ml spoon dried yeast	50g chopped mixed peel
	100g soft brown sugar
1 × 5ml spoon salt	fat for greasing
50g butter	honey for glazing

Sift about 75g of the flour and the 5ml spoon of sugar into a large bowl. Warm the milk until hand-hot and blend in the fresh yeast or sprinkle on the dried yeast. Pour the yeast liquid into the flour and sugar and beat well. Leave the bowl in a warm place for 20 minutes. Sift the remaining flour and the salt into a bowl. Rub in the 50g butter. Beat the egg into the frothy yeast mixture and add the flour and fat. Mix to a soft dough. Turn on to a lightly floured surface and knead for about 6 minutes or until smooth and no longer sticky. Place the dough in a large, lightly oiled polythene bag and leave in a warm place for about 1 hour or until the dough has doubled in size. On a floured surface, roll the dough into a 50cm square. Melt the 15ml spoon of butter and brush it all over the surface of the dough. Sprinkle with the dried fruit and sugar. Roll up the dough like a Swiss roll. Cut the roll into 16 equal pieces. Place the buns, about 3cm apart, on a greased baking sheet with the cut side uppermost. Place the baking sheet in the polythene bag and leave in a warm place for about 30 minutes or until the buns have joined together and are light and puffy. Bake in a hot oven, 220°C, Gas 7, for 20–25 minutes until golden-brown. While still hot, brush the buns with honey.

Cornish Splits

Makes 14

400g strong white flour	1 × 5ml spoon salt
50g sugar	50g butter
125ml milk	flour for kneading
125ml water	fat for greasing
15g fresh yeast **or**	
1 × 10ml spoon dried	
yeast	

Sift about 75g of the flour and 1 × 5ml spoon of the sugar into a large bowl. Warm the milk and water until hand-hot. Blend the fresh yeast into the liquid or sprinkle on the dried yeast. Pour the yeast liquid into the flour and sugar and beat until well mixed. Leave the bowl in a warm place for 20 minutes. Sift the rest of the flour and sugar and the salt together. Rub in the butter. Stir into the frothy yeast mixture and mix to form a soft dough. Turn on to a lightly floured surface and knead for about 6 minutes or until smooth and no longer sticky. Place the dough in a large, lightly oiled polythene bag and leave in a warm place for about 1 hour or until it has doubled in size. Knead the dough again until firm. Divide it into 50g pieces and form each into a round bun. Place the buns on a greased baking sheet. Place the sheet in the polythene bag and leave in a warm place for about 30 minutes or until the buns have doubled in size. Bake in a hot oven, 220°C, Gas 7, for 15–20 minutes until golden-brown.

Serve cold, split, and spread with cream and jam.

Crumpets

Makes 10–12

200g strong white flour	a pinch of bicarbonate of
1 × 2.5ml spoon salt	soda
1 × 2.5ml spoon sugar	1 × 15ml spoon warm
100ml milk	water
125ml water	fat for frying
15g fresh yeast **or**	
1 × 10ml spoon dried	
yeast	

Sift together the flour, salt, and sugar into a large bowl. Warm the milk and water until hand-hot.

Blend the fresh yeast into the liquid or reconstitute the dried yeast. Add the yeast liquid to the flour and beat to a smooth batter. Cover with a large, lightly oiled polythene bag and leave in a warm place for about 45 minutes or until the dough has doubled in size. Dissolve the bicarbonate of soda in the 15ml spoon warm water and beat into the batter mixture. Cover and leave to rise again for 20 minutes. Grease a griddle or thick frying pan and heat until a bread cube browns in $\frac{1}{4}$ minute. Grease metal rings, poaching rings or large plain biscuit cutters, about 8cm in diameter. Place the rings on the hot griddle. Pour about 1 × 15ml spoonful of batter into each ring so that the batter is about 3mm deep. Cook until the top is set and the bubbles have burst. Remove the ring and turn the crumpet over. Cook the other side for 2–3 minutes only until firm but barely coloured. Crumpets should be pale on top. Repeat until all the batter has been used up.

Serve toasted, hot, with butter.

VARIATIONS

Welsh Crumpets

These are cooked without rings on a buttered griddle or frying pan. Pour 3–4 × 15ml spoonfuls batter on to the hot surface, and cook the first side until small holes appear on the surface; turn and cook the second side until just golden.

Serve with bacon and chipolata sausages or butter and brown sugar or honey. These griddle cakes are more like small pancakes or thin pikelets.

Pikelets

Pikelets are cooked without rings like Welsh Crumpets. Some experts use double the amount of yeast and slightly more water (about 50ml) than in the basic crumpet batter, but no bicarbonate of soda.

Most pikelets are thinner than crumpets, cook more quickly, and are more like small pancakes. However, in some areas, they can be as thick as muffins. In Yorkshire, Lancashire, and parts of Derbyshire, pikelet is another name for crumpets.

For Durham Pikelets, see p1469.

Ring Doughnuts (1)

Makes 12

200g strong white flour
1 × 2.5ml spoon salt
150g caster sugar
2 eggs
50g butter
15g fresh yeast **or**
  1 × 10ml spoon dried
  yeast

2 × 10ml spoons warm
  water
flour
oil for deep frying
1 × 2.5ml spoon ground
  cinnamon (optional)

Sift the flour, salt, and 50g of the sugar into a large bowl. Beat the eggs until liquid. Melt the butter and leave to cool slightly. Blend the fresh yeast into the warm water or reconstitute the dried yeast. Stir the eggs, butter and yeast liquid into the flour and mix to a soft dough. Turn on to a lightly floured surface and knead for about 5 minutes or until the dough is smooth and no longer sticky. Place the dough in a large, lightly oiled polythene bag and leave in a warm place for about 1 hour or until the dough has almost doubled in size. On a floured surface, roll out the dough to 1cm thickness. Cut into rings, using a 7cm plain cutter for the outside and a 4cm one for the inside. Place on a floured tray and cover with the polythene bag. Leave in a warm place for about 15 minutes or until the dough is light and puffy. Deep fry in hot oil (p303) until crisp and golden-brown, turning frequently. Drain on soft kitchen paper. Toss in the rest of the sugar or in the sugar and cinnamon mixed.

VARIATION

Jam Doughnuts

Cut the rolled-out dough into circles using a 7cm plain cutter. Place a little stiff jam in the centre of each circle and pinch up the edge of the dough to form a ball. Leave to rise, and fry as above.

Ring Doughnuts (2) and (3)
(made without yeast)
See p1191.

Muffins

Makes 20

400g strong white flour
1 × 5ml spoon salt
25g butter **or** margarine
225ml milk
15g fresh yeast **or**
  1 × 10ml spoon dried
  yeast

1 egg
flour
fat for frying

Sift together the flour and salt into a large bowl. Rub in the fat. Warm the milk until hand-hot. Blend the fresh yeast into the milk or reconstitute the dried yeast. Beat the egg into the yeast liquid. Stir the liquid into the flour to make a very soft dough. Beat the dough with your hand or a wooden spoon for about 5 minutes or until smooth and shiny. Put the bowl in a large, lightly oiled polythene bag and leave in a warm place for 1–2 hours, or until the dough has almost doubled in size. Beat again lightly. Roll out on a well floured surface to 1cm thickness. Using a plain 8cm cutter, cut the dough into rounds. Place the rounds on a floured tray, cover with polythene, and leave to rise at room temperature for about 45 minutes or until puffy. Lightly grease a griddle or heavy frying pan and heat until a bread cube browns in $\frac{1}{4}$ minute. Cook the muffins on both sides for about 8 minutes until golden-brown.

To serve, split open each muffin around the edges almost to the centre. Toast slowly on both outer sides so that the heat penetrates to the centre of the muffin. Pull apart, butter thickly, put together again, and serve hot.

Sally Lunn

Makes two 15cm Sally Lunns

400g strong white flour
1 × 5ml spoon salt
1 × 5ml spoon sugar
50g butter
150ml milk

15g fresh yeast **or**
1 × 10ml spoon dried
  yeast
1 egg
fat for greasing

Glaze
1 × 15ml spoon water

1 × 15ml spoon caster
  sugar

Sift together the flour, salt, and sugar into a large bowl. Rub in the butter. Warm the milk until hand-hot. Blend the fresh yeast into the milk or reconstitute the dried yeast. Beat the egg into the yeast liquid and stir into the flour mixture to form a very soft dough. Beat well. Pour the mixture into 2 greased 15cm round cake tins. Place the tins in a large, lightly oiled polythene bag and leave in a warm place for about 1¼ hours or until the dough has doubled in size. Bake in a hot oven, 220°C, Gas 7, for 20–25 minutes until golden-brown.

To make the glaze, boil together the water and sugar until syrupy. Brush the hot glaze over the top of the Sally Lunns.

To serve, split each Sally Lunn crossways into 3 rounds and toast each piece lightly on both sides. Butter thickly or fill with clotted cream, re-form the cake, and cut into slices or wedges.

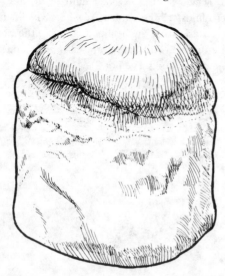

Sweet Almond Bread

Makes one 400g loaf

200g strong white flour
1 × 5ml spoon sugar
100ml milk
15g fresh yeast **or**
  1 × 10ml spoon dried
  yeast
1 × 2.5ml spoon salt

25g butter **or** margarine
1 egg
flour
milk for glazing
fat for greasing
sifted icing sugar for
  dredging

Almond Paste
75g icing sugar
75g ground almonds
1 × 5ml spoon lemon
  juice

a few drops almond
  essence
beaten egg white

Sift about 50g of the flour and the sugar into a bowl. Warm the milk until hand-hot. Blend in the fresh yeast or sprinkle on the dried yeast. Pour the yeast liquid into the flour and sugar and beat well. Leave the bowl in a warm place for 20 minutes. Sift the remaining flour and salt into a bowl. Rub in the fat. Beat the egg into the yeast mixture and stir in the flour and fat. Mix to a soft dough. Turn on to a lightly floured surface and knead for about 5 minutes or until the dough is smooth and no longer sticky. Place in a large, lightly oiled polythene bag and leave in a warm place for about 40 minutes or until the dough has doubled in size. Roll it out on a lightly floured surface to a 25cm circle.

To make the almond paste, sift the icing sugar, and mix together with the ground almonds, lemon juice, almond essence, and enough egg white to bind the mixture together. Spread the paste on to half the circle of dough. Fold the uncovered half of the dough over to cover the paste. Press the edges of dough firmly together. Brush the surface with milk. Place on a greased baking tray, cover with polythene, leave to rise for about 30 minutes, and bake in a hot oven, 220°C, Gas 7, for 10 minutes; then reduce the temperature to fairly hot, 190°C, Gas 5, and bake until golden-brown. When cold, dredge with a little sifted icing sugar.

Cooking time 25–35 minutes

Saffron Bread

Makes one 800g loaf

400g strong white flour	*100ml warm water*
1 × 5ml spoon salt	*50g ground almonds*
125ml milk	*flour for kneading*
75g butter	*50g chopped mixed peel*
a large pinch of	*50g currants*
powdered saffron	*50g raisins*
75g caster sugar	*fat for greasing*
1 egg	*beaten egg for glazing*
25g fresh yeast **or**	*1 × 10ml spoon*
1 × 15ml spoon dried	*granulated sugar*
yeast	*4 blanched almonds*

Sift the flour and salt. Warm the milk and butter together until the fat has melted. Add the saffron and leave to stand for 10 minutes. Beat in the caster sugar and egg. Blend the fresh yeast with the warm water or reconstitute the dried yeast. Add the yeast liquid to the milk and saffron mixture and stir in a third of the flour. Leave in a warm place for 20 minutes. Work in the rest of the flour and ground almonds to form a very soft dough. Turn on to a well floured surface and knead for about 5 minutes or until the dough is smooth. Place it in a large, lightly oiled polythene bag and leave in a warm place for about 2 hours or until it has doubled in size. Work in the dried fruit and form the dough into a loaf shape. Place it in a greased 23 × 13 × 7cm loaf tin. Brush the top with beaten egg. Sprinkle on the granulated sugar. Roughly chop the almonds and sprinkle on the loaf. Place the tin in the polythene bag and leave in a warm place for about 45 minutes or until the dough has doubled in size. Bake in a hot oven, 220°C, Gas 7, for 10 minutes; then reduce the heat to fairly hot, 190°C, Gas 5, and continue baking for a further 30 minutes until golden-brown.

VARIATION

Kulich

Makes two 400g Kulich

Make as for Saffron Bread. After working the fruit into the dough, divide it into 2 equal pieces. Well grease two 450–500g circular tins such as coffee tins. Shape the pieces of dough to fit the tins and put the dough in them. Place them in a large, lightly oiled polythene bag and leave in a warm place for about 35 minutes or until the dough has reached the top of the tins. Bake in a hot oven, 220°C, Gas 7, for 35–40 minutes until golden-brown. When cold, ice with Glacé Icing (p1225).

Cherry Bread

Makes one 400g loaf

200g strong white flour	*25g butter* **or** *margarine*
1 × 5ml spoon sugar	*1 egg*
100ml milk	*flour for kneading*
15g fresh yeast **or**	*75g glacé cherries*
1 × 10ml spoon dried	*fat for greasing*
yeast	*milk for glazing*
1 × 2.5ml spoon salt	

Sift about 50g of the flour and the sugar into a bowl. Warm the milk until hand-hot. Blend in the fresh yeast or sprinkle on the dried yeast. Pour the yeast liquid into the flour and sugar and beat well. Leave the bowl in a warm place for 20 minutes. Sift the remaining flour and salt into a bowl. Rub in the fat. Beat the egg into the yeast mixture and stir in the flour and fat. Mix to a soft dough. Turn on to a lightly floured surface and knead for about 5 minutes or until the dough is smooth and no longer sticky. Place in a large, lightly oiled polythene bag and leave in a warm place for about 40 minutes or until the dough has doubled in size. Chop the cherries roughly and squeeze them into the risen dough until well distributed. Press the dough into a greased 15cm cake tin and brush the surface with a little milk. Place the tin in the polythene bag and leave in a warm place for about 30 minutes or until the dough reaches just above the edge of the tin. Bake in a hot oven, 220°C, Gas 7, for 10 minutes; then reduce the temperature to fairly hot, 190°C, Gas 5, and bake until golden-brown.

Cooking time 25–35 minutes

Quick Breads

Baked goods raised by means other than yeast are useful when bread is needed at short notice, although they have a scone-like texture which is quite different from bread made with yeast. Some are large loaves or bun rounds, others are small baked goods such as scones. Different flours can be used as in making other breads.

Some quick breads are semi-sweet or sweet, and are what Americans call 'coffee breads or cakes'. These keep well and are a useful standby. A coffee cake can also be used in the conventional sense to mean a sweet cake flavoured with coffee.

Quick breads containing fruit are particularly good sliced and buttered for serving with tea or coffee. They can also be sliced, toasted, and buttered.

BASIC BREADS

Basic Quick Bread

Makes 2 bun loaves

400g self-raising flour
  or *a mixture of white*
  and brown self-raising
  flours **or** *400g plain*
  flour and 2 ×10ml
  spoons baking powder

1 × 5ml spoon salt
50g margarine **or** *lard*
250ml milk **or** *water* **or**
  a mixture as preferred
flour for kneading
fat for greasing

Sift the flour, baking powder (if used), and salt into a large bowl. Rub in the fat. Mix in enough liquid to make a soft dough. Turn on to a floured surface, and knead lightly for 1 minute. Shape the dough into 2 rounds and place them on a greased baking sheet. Make a cross in the top of each with the back of a knife. Bake in a fairly hot oven, 200°C, Gas 6, for 30–40 minutes. Cool on a wire rack.

Wholemeal Quick Bread

Substitute 400g wholemeal flour for the plain flour in the basic recipe. Note that wholemeal flour will give a closer-textured loaf.

Nut Bread

Make Wholemeal Quick Bread; add 75g chopped nuts and 50g sugar to the dry ingredients, and add 1 beaten egg to the liquid.

Apricot and Walnut Loaf

Make the basic Quick Bread Mixture but use butter as the fat. Add 100g dried and soaked chopped apricots and 50g chopped walnuts to the dry ingredients, and add 1 beaten egg to the liquid.

Basic Soured Milk Quick Bread

Makes 2 loaves

400g plain flour
1 × 5ml spoon salt
1 ×10ml spoon
  bicarbonate of soda
1 ×10ml spoon cream of
  tartar

250ml soured milk **or**
  buttermilk (approx)
fat for greasing

Sift the flour, salt, bicarbonate of soda, and cream of tartar into a large bowl. Mix to a light spongy dough with the milk. Divide the dough into 2 equal pieces and form each into a round cake. Slash a cross on the top of each loaf with a sharp knife. Place on a greased baking sheet and bake in a hot oven, 220°C, Gas 7, for about 30 minutes until golden-brown. Cool on a wire rack.

Note The keeping quality of this bread is improved by rubbing 50g lard into the sifted flour.

Bran Baking Powder Muffins

Makes 20–24

150g plain flour	*200ml milk*
1 × 5ml spoon baking	*25g butter*
powder	*2 × 15ml spoons golden*
1 × 2.5ml spoon salt	*syrup*
50g sugar	*1 egg*
100g natural wheat bran	*fat for greasing*
1 × 5ml spoon	
bicarbonate of soda	

Sift the flour, baking powder, and salt into a large bowl. Add the sugar and bran. Dissolve the bicarbonate of soda in the milk. Melt the butter and syrup together. Add the milk, syrup and egg to the dry ingredients and mix with a wooden spoon until they are dampened and the mixture is lumpy. Do not over-mix. Spoon the mixture into 20 greased 5–6cm patty tins, filling them only two-thirds full, and bake in a fairly hot oven, 200°C, Gas 6, for about 15–20 minutes or until brown and springy to the touch. Loosen from the pans with a palette knife. Cool on a wire rack. Serve while still just warm, or cold.

VARIATIONS
Apricot Muffins

Add 100g soaked and roughly chopped dried apricots to the dough.

Honey Nut Muffins

Put 1 × 5ml spoon clear honey and 1 × 5ml spoon finely chopped nuts into each patty tin when half filled. Cover with the extra dough required. Serve nut side uppermost.

Griddle Breads

See Griddle Scones (p1177), Inverary Muffins (p1177), Dropped Scones (p1178), Potato Scones (2) (p1179), Welsh Cakes (p1180).

Savoury Rusks

Makes 8 (approx)

200g self-raising flour	*1 × 10ml spoon yeast*
a pinch of salt	*extract*
50g butter **or** *margarine*	*flour for rolling out*
100ml milk	*fat for greasing*

Heat the oven to hot, 220°C, Gas 7. Sift together the flour and salt into a large bowl. Rub in the fat. Mix the milk with the yeast extract and stir into the flour to give a firm dough. Roll out on a floured surface to 1cm thickness. Cut into 6cm rounds. Place on a greased baking sheet and bake for 10 minutes. Using a sharp knife, cut each round in half through the centre. Place cut side downwards on the baking sheet and bake for a further 7 minutes. Cool on the sheet.

SWEET FRUIT AND TEA BREADS

Almond Bread

Makes 12 slices (approx)

75g almonds	*6 × 15ml spoons oil*
250g plain flour	*a few drops almond* **or**
2 × 10ml spoons baking	*vanilla essence*
powder	*flour*
a pinch of salt	*fat for greasing*
2 eggs	*50g caster sugar*
100g granulated sugar	

Blanch and skin the almonds and chop them coarsely. Sift the flour, baking powder, and salt. Beat the eggs and granulated sugar lightly together in a large bowl. Add the oil, flavouring, flour, and almonds, and mix to form a dough. With floured hands, form into a long roll about 8cm wide. Place on a greased and floured baking sheet and bake in a moderate oven, 180°C, Gas 4, for about 30–40 minutes or until lightly browned. Leave until nearly cold, then cut slantways into slices about 1cm thick. Sprinkle lightly with caster sugar and return to a cool oven, 150°C, Gas 2, for about 50–60 minutes, until dry and lightly browned.

American Coffee Bread

Makes 12 slices (approx)

200g plain flour	2 × 15ml spoons butter
100g light soft brown sugar	1 egg
2 × 5ml spoons baking powder	200ml milk
1 × 5ml spoon salt	75g chopped walnuts
	fat for greasing

Sift together the dry ingredients into a large bowl. Melt the butter, add it to the flour mixture with the egg, milk and walnuts, and beat thoroughly. Spread the mixture in a greased 23 × 13 × 7cm loaf tin, level the top, and bake for about 1 hour in a moderate oven, 180°C, Gas 4. Cool on a wire rack.

VARIATIONS

Orange Nut Coffee Bread

Reduce the milk to 100ml. Instead of sugar, use 250g orange marmalade.

Banana Nut Coffee Bread

Reduce the milk to 100ml; add 3 ripe medium-sized bananas, well mashed.

Banana Bread (1)

Makes 12 slices (approx)

300g plain flour	3 eggs
a pinch of salt	3 bananas
1 × 5ml spoon bicarbonate of soda	1 × 15ml spoon strained lemon juice
75g margarine	fat for greasing
100g granulated sugar	

Sift together the flour, salt, and bicarbonate of soda. Cream the margarine and sugar. Beat in the eggs. Mash the bananas with the lemon juice. Add to the creamed margarine and sugar. Work in the dry ingredients. Put the mixture in a greased 23 × 13 × 7cm loaf tin and bake in a fairly hot oven, 190°C, Gas 5, for 50–60 minutes until golden-brown. Cool on a wire rack.

Banana Bread (2)

Makes 12 slices (approx)

3 bananas	125g caster sugar
50g walnuts	75g soft margarine
200g self-raising flour	grated rind of ¼ lemon
1 × 5ml spoon baking powder	2 eggs
½ × 2.5ml spoon bicarbonate of soda	50g seedless raisins
	fat for greasing

Mash the bananas and chop the walnuts. Mix all the ingredients in a large bowl and beat for about 3 minutes by hand using a wooden spoon, or for 2 minutes in a mixer, until smooth. Put the mixture into a greased 19 × 13 × 8cm loaf tin, and bake in a moderate oven, 180°C, Gas 4, for 1 hour 10 minutes or until firm to the touch. Cool on a wire rack.

Apple Loaf

Makes 12 slices (approx)

200g plain flour	200g cooking apples
a pinch of salt	1 × 5ml spoon strained lemon juice
1 × 5ml spoon baking powder	2 eggs
1 × 2.5ml spoon mixed spice	25ml milk
100g butter **or** margarine	fat for greasing
	cold water
150g caster sugar	50g icing sugar
50g currants	1 tart red-skinned eating apple
100g raisins	

Sift the flour, salt, baking powder, and mixed spice into a large bowl. Rub in the fat. Add the sugar and dried fruit. Peel and core the cooking apples, slice thinly, and toss in the lemon juice. Add to the dry mixture. Stir in the eggs and enough milk to make a soft dropping consistency. Put the mixture in a greased 23 × 13 × 7cm loaf tin and bake in a fairly hot oven, 190°C, Gas 5, for about 50–60 minutes until the loaf is golden-brown and a skewer pushed into the centre comes out clean. Allow the loaf to cool on a wire rack.

Add enough cold water to the icing sugar to

make it of brushing consistency. Core the eating apple, cut it into thin segments, and arrange these in a decorative pattern on the loaf. Immediately brush the apple with the icing sugar glaze to prevent discoloration. Leave the glaze to 'set' before serving.

Boston Brown Bread

Makes 12 slices (approx)

200g plain white flour	1 × 5ml spoon
125g cornmeal	bicarbonate of soda
200ml milk	1 × 15ml spoon butter
100g seedless raisins	a pinch of salt
300g molasses	fat for greasing
100ml water	

Mix together the flour, cornmeal, milk, raisins, and molasses in a large bowl. Heat the water to boiling point and dissolve the bicarbonate of soda in it; add to the flour and molasses mixture and mix in thoroughly. Melt the butter and add to the mixture with the salt; mix well. Pour into a greased 1 litre pudding basin, cover securely with greased paper or foil, and steam for 3 hours.

Serve hot with butter, or cold with full-fat soft cheese or butter.

Note A greased 1kg cylindrical coffee tin may be used instead of the pudding basin.

Fatless Fruit Loaf

Makes 12 slices (approx)

300g mixed dried fruit	1 egg
150g dark Barbados sugar	300g self-raising flour
	fat for greasing
200ml strong hot tea	

Put the fruit and sugar in a large bowl. Pour the hot tea over them, cover, and leave overnight.

Next day, beat the egg until liquid and stir it into the tea mixture. Stir in the flour and mix well. Put the mixture into a lined and greased 19 × 13 × 8cm loaf tin and cook in a moderate oven, 180°C, Gas 4, for 1½ hours. Cool on a wire rack. When cold, wrap in foil and store in a tin.

Coconut Bread

Makes 12 slices (approx)

100g butter	1 egg
150g granulated sugar	175ml milk
150g raisins	400g self-raising flour
50g chopped mixed peel	a pinch of salt
250g desiccated coconut	flour for kneading
1 × 5ml spoon vanilla essence	fat for greasing

Cream the butter and sugar. Chop the raisins and add to the creamed mixture. Add the rest of the ingredients and mix well. Turn on to a floured surface and knead until smooth. Put the mixture into a greased 23 × 13 × 7cm loaf tin and bake in a fairly hot oven, 190°C, Gas 5, for 50–60 minutes until golden-brown. Cool on a wire rack.

Date or Raisin Bread

Makes 12 slices (approx)

200g plain flour	25g lard
1 × 15ml spoon baking powder	50g black treacle
1 × 5ml spoon salt	50g dark Barbados sugar
¼ × 2.5ml spoon bicarbonate of soda	150ml milk
100g dates **or** seedless raisins	fat for greasing
50g walnuts **or** almonds, whole **or** chopped	

Sift the flour, baking powder, salt, and bicarbonate of soda into a large bowl. Chop the fruit and nuts finely if necessary, and add them to the dry ingredients. Warm the lard, treacle, sugar, and milk together. The sugar should dissolve, but do not overheat it. Add the liquid to the dry ingredients, and mix to a stiff batter. Pour into a lined and greased 19 × 13 × 8cm loaf tin and bake in a moderate oven, 180°C, Gas 4, for 1½ hours. Cool on a wire rack. When cold, wrap in foil, and store for 24 hours before cutting.

Date and Cheese Bread

Makes 12 slices (approx)

200g stoned dates
125ml boiling water
1 egg
125g mild cheese
175g plain flour
1 × 5ml spoon
  bicarbonate of soda
½ × 2.5ml spoon salt
50g granulated sugar
50g soft brown sugar
fat for greasing
flour

Chop the dates finely. Pour the boiling water on to them. Allow to stand for 5 minutes. Mix in the egg. Grate the cheese and add to the mixture. Sift the flour, bicarbonate of soda, and salt into the date mixture. Add both sugars and mix thoroughly. Put the mixture into a greased and floured 23 × 13 × 7cm loaf tin and bake in a warm oven, 160°C, Gas 3, for about 50 minutes until the loaf is springy to the touch and a skewer pushed into the centre comes out clean. Cool on a wire rack.

Sweet Date Bread

Makes 12 slices (approx)

400g plain flour
a pinch of salt
2 × 10ml spoons
  bicarbonate of soda
150g dark soft brown
  sugar
125g sultanas **or**
  seedless raisins
75g chopped walnuts
400g stoned dates
50g margarine
250ml boiling water
2 eggs
1 × 5ml spoon vanilla
  essence
fat for greasing

Sift together the flour, salt, and bicarbonate of soda into a large bowl. Add the sugar and sultanas or raisins, and then the walnuts. Chop the dates finely. Add the margarine to the dates and pour on the boiling water. Add the date mixture, eggs, and essence to the dry ingredients and mix thoroughly. Put the mixture into a greased 23 × 13 × 7cm loaf tin and bake in a fairly hot oven, 190°C, Gas 5, for 40–50 minutes until the loaf is golden-brown and a skewer pushed into the bread comes out clean. Cool on a wire rack.

Honey Bread

Makes 12 slices (approx)

100g margarine
100g caster sugar
2 eggs
6 × 15ml spoons clear
  honey
250g self-raising flour
  or 250g plain flour and
  1 × 15ml spoon baking
  powder
1 × 5ml spoon salt
125ml milk (approx)
fat for greasing

Cream together the margarine and sugar until pale and fluffy. Beat in the eggs and the honey. Add the dry ingredients alternately with the milk until a soft dropping consistency is obtained. Add the milk carefully as the full amount may not be needed. Put the mixture into a greased 19 × 13 × 8cm loaf tin and bake for 1¼ hours in a moderate oven, 180°C, Gas 4. Cool on a wire rack. When cold, wrap in foil and keep for 24 hours before serving.

Serve sliced and buttered.

Orange Bread

Makes 12 slices (approx)

50g lard
200g granulated sugar
2 eggs
400g plain flour
1 × 10ml spoon baking
  powder
1 × 10ml spoon
  bicarbonate of soda
a pinch of salt
250ml orange juice
1 × 15ml spoon grated
  orange rind
100g chopped mixed
  nuts
fat for greasing

Melt the lard and add to the sugar. Beat in the eggs. Sift together the flour, baking powder, bicarbonate of soda, and salt. Add the flour alternately with the orange juice to the fat and sugar. Stir in the orange rind and nuts. Put the mixture into a greased 23 × 13 × 7cm loaf tin and bake in a fairly hot oven, 190°C, Gas 5, for 50–60 minutes until the loaf is springy to the touch. Cool on a wire rack.

Note This loaf is best left overnight before eating.

Malt Bread

Makes 12 slices (approx)

400g self-raising flour
1 × 10ml spoon
  bicarbonate of soda
100g sultanas **or**
  seedless raisins
250ml milk

4 × 15ml spoons golden
  syrup
4 × 15ml spoons malt
  extract
2 eggs
fat for greasing

Sift the flour and bicarbonate of soda into a large bowl. Add the dried fruit. Warm together the milk, syrup, and malt extract, in a saucepan. Beat in the eggs. Stir the mixture into the flour. Put it into a greased 23 × 13 × 7cm loaf tin and bake in a fairly hot oven, 190°C, Gas 5, for 40–50 minutes until a skewer pushed into the bread comes out clean. Cool on a wire rack.

North Riding Bread

Makes 12 slices (approx)

400g plain flour
1 × 2.5ml spoon salt
1 × 15ml spoon baking
  powder
1 × 2.5ml spoon grated
  nutmeg
100g lard
150g Demerara sugar

150g currants
150g raisins
75g chopped mixed peel
1 × 15ml spoon treacle
1 × 2.5ml spoon almond
  essence
250ml milk
fat for greasing

Sift the flour, salt, baking powder, and nutmeg into a large bowl. Rub in the lard. Add the sugar and dried fruit. Stir the treacle and essence into the milk and mix into the dry ingredients to give a soft dough. Put the mixture into a greased 23 × 13 × 7cm loaf tin and bake in a fairly hot oven, 190°C, Gas 5, for 45–50 minutes until a skewer pushed into the bread comes out clean. Cool on a wire rack.

Note This bread is better if kept in a tin for a week before use.

Gingerbread
See pp1191–93.

Peanut Butter Bread

Makes 12 slices (approx)

400g self-raising flour
a pinch of salt
150g crunchy peanut
  butter

125g sugar
1 egg
250ml milk
fat for greasing

Sift together the flour and salt. Cream the peanut butter and sugar. Add the egg and milk and stir in the flour. Put the mixture into a greased 23 × 13 × 7cm loaf tin and bake in a fairly hot oven, 190°C, Gas 5, for 1–1¼ hours until golden-brown. Cool on a wire rack.

Curled Wiggs
(without yeast)

Makes 2 large wiggs

400g golden syrup (in
  can)
75g unsalted butter
175ml soured milk
450g plain flour
1 × 5ml spoon
  bicarbonate of soda

a pinch of salt
1 × 10ml spoon caraway
  seeds
1 × 10ml spoon ground
  ginger **or** *mixed spice*
fat for greasing

Heat the oven to moderate, 180°C, Gas 4. Warm the can of syrup in the oven, uncovered, to make measuring easier. Measure the syrup, put in a saucepan, and add the butter. Heat together gently until the butter melts. Remove from the heat and add the milk. Sift together the flour, bicarbonate of soda, and salt into a large bowl. Add the seeds and spice. Stir in the syrup mixture. Place two greased 18cm sandwich tins or ovenproof soup plates on a sheet of foil on a baking sheet. Divide the mixture between them. Bake for 25–30 minutes or until the wiggs have risen and curled over the edges of the tins or bowls.

Serve warm, cut in wedges, with butter.

SCONES

A scone used to be a traditional bread, cooked on a bakestone or griddle over an open fire, in the days before ovens were in general use. Today however, most scones are baked in the oven, and a griddle is a piece of equipment not often found in the average kitchen; a strong, thick frying pan or a solid electric cooker plate can be substituted.

Important points to remember when making scones:

1) Because the basic mixture has only a small proportion of fat to flour, it should be mixed to a soft, slightly sticky dough and handled quickly and lightly.
2) Scones are baked in a hot, preheated oven to ensure maximum rising; the top should be brown and the texture open.
3) Cool baked scones on a wire rack so that they are crisp outside. Griddle scones and dropped scones are best cooled in a clean tea-towel so that they keep their traditional softness.
4) Raising ingredients
   When plain flour is used, add either baking powder
   or
   bicarbonate of soda and cream of tartar
   or
   bicarbonate of soda, cream of tartar, and soured milk or buttermilk.
   The exact quantities of the raising ingredients required are given in the recipes.
5) Using a griddle
   Grease or flour the griddle lightly, according to the recipe used, and place over heat until a faint blue haze rises or until the griddle feels comfortably warm if the hand is held about 2cm above it. If the griddle is too hot, the scones brown on the outside before being cooked through to the centre.
   Most griddle scones take about 5 minutes to cook on each side.

Plain Scones (1)

Basic recipe using *plain* **flour**

Makes 10–12

200g plain flour	*125ml fresh milk*
½ × 2.5ml spoon salt	**or**
50g butter **or** *margarine* **and** one of the following raising agents:	*1 × 5ml spoon bicarbonate of soda*
	1 × 5ml spoon cream of tartar
1 × 5ml spoon bicarbonate of soda	*125ml soured milk* **or** *buttermilk*
1 × 10ml spoon cream of tartar	**and**
125ml fresh milk	*flour for rolling out*
or	*fat for greasing*
4 × 5ml spoons baking powder	*milk* **or** *beaten egg for glazing (optional)*

Heat the oven to hot, 220°C, Gas 7. Sift together the flour and salt into a large bowl. Rub in the fat. Sift in the dry raising agents and mix well. Add the milk and mix lightly to form a soft spongy dough. Knead very lightly until smooth. Roll out on a floured surface to 1.5–2cm thickness and cut into rounds, using a 5cm cutter. Re-roll the trimmings, and re-cut. Place the scones on a greased baking sheet and brush the tops with milk or beaten egg, if liked. Bake for 7–10 minutes until well risen and golden-brown. Cool on a wire rack.

Note If preferred, the mixture can be divided into 2 equal portions, each half rolled into a round, 1.5–2cm thick, and each round marked into 6 wedges.

VARIATIONS

Cheese Scones

Add 75g grated cheese to the dry ingredients before mixing in the milk. Cut into finger shapes or squares.

Cheese Whirls

Add 75g grated cheese to the dry ingredients. Roll out the dough into a rectangle. Sprinkle with another 50g grated cheese, then roll up the dough like a Swiss roll. Cut into 1cm slices and lay them flat on greased baking sheets. Brush with milk or egg and bake as in the basic recipe.

Fruit Scones

Add 50g caster sugar and 50g currants, sultanas or other dried fruit to the basic recipe.

Griddle Scones

Add 50g sultanas to the basic dough. Roll out to 5mm–1cm thickness, then cut into 6cm rounds. Cook on a moderately hot, lightly floured griddle or heavy frying pan for 3 minutes or until the scones are golden-brown underneath and the edges are dry. Turn over and cook for about another 2 minutes until golden-brown on both sides. Cool in a linen tea-towel or other similar cloth.

Inverary Muffins

Use only 75ml buttermilk or soured milk to make the dough, and add 25g caster sugar and 1 egg. Roll out 1cm thick, and cut into 8cm rounds. Cook on a griddle or heavy frying pan in the same way as Griddle Scones but for slightly longer.

Nut Scones

Add 50g chopped nuts to the basic recipe.

Oil Scones

Use 3 × 15ml spoons olive oil or corn oil instead of margarine or lard in the basic recipe. Reduce the milk to 75ml and add an egg.

Potato Scones (1)

Use 100g flour and 100g sieved cooked mashed potato. Reduce the milk to 60–65ml.

Note For Potato Scones (2), see p1179.

Rich Scones

Add 25g sugar to the mixed dry ingredients for the basic recipe. Instead of mixing with milk alone, use 1 beaten egg with enough milk to make 125ml.

Syrup or Treacle Scones

Add 2 × 10ml spoons light soft brown sugar, 1 × 2.5ml spoon ground cinnamon or ginger, 1 × 2.5ml spoon mixed spice, and 1 × 15ml spoon warmed golden syrup or black treacle to the basic recipe. Add the syrup or treacle with the milk.

Wheatmeal Scones

Use half wholemeal flour and half plain white flour to make the dough.

Plain Scones (2)

Basic recipe using *self-raising* flour

Makes 12

200g self-raising flour *flour for kneading*
1 × 2.5ml spoon salt *fat for greasing*
25–50g butter or *milk or beaten egg for*
margarine *glazing (optional)*
125ml milk

Heat the oven to hot, 220°C, Gas 7. Sift together the flour and salt into a large bowl. Rub in the fat and mix to a soft dough with the milk, using a round-bladed knife. Knead very lightly on a floured surface until smooth. Roll out to about 1.5cm thickness and cut into rounds, using a 6cm cutter, or divide into 2 equal portions as described for Plain Scones (using plain flour) (p1176). Re-roll the trimmings, and re-cut. Place the scones on a lightly greased baking sheet, and brush the tops with milk or beaten egg, if liked. Bake for 10–12 minutes. Cool on a wire rack.

Note For Plain Scones (3), made with an electric mixer, see p1419.

Sweet Wheatmeal Scones

Makes 10–12

200g wheatmeal flour
½ × 2.5ml spoon salt
1 × 15ml spoon baking
  powder
50g margarine
50g light soft brown
  sugar
50g seedless raisins
1 egg + milk to give
  125ml
flour for rolling out
fat for greasing

Heat the oven to hot, 220°C, Gas 7. Mix together the flour, salt, and baking powder in a large bowl. Rub in the margarine, and stir in the sugar and dried fruit. Beat the egg and milk until liquid. Reserve a little for brushing the tops of the scones and add the rest to the dry ingredients. Mix to a soft dough. Knead lightly, and roll out on a floured surface to just over 1cm thick. Cut into rounds, using a 6cm cutter. Re-roll the trimmings, and re-cut. Place the scones on a lightly greased baking sheet, and bake for 10–15 minutes.

Serve warm or cold, split and buttered.

Note These scones are delicious filled with full-fat soft cheese or butter and spread with honey.

VARIATION

Bran Scones

Use 175g self-raising flour, 1 × 2.5ml spoon salt, 1 × 5ml spoon baking powder, 25g light soft brown sugar, 50g currants or sultanas, instead of the quantities given above. Add 25g bran when mixing the dry ingredients.

Dropped Scones
(Scotch Pancakes)

Makes 24 (approx)

200g plain flour
1 × 5ml spoon salt
25g caster sugar
1 × 10ml spoon cream of
  tartar
1 × 5ml spoon
  bicarbonate of soda
1 egg
175ml milk
fat for greasing

Sift together the dry ingredients 3 times. Add the egg and milk gradually and mix to a smooth thick batter. Heat a lightly greased griddle or a very thick frying pan. Drop 10ml spoonfuls of the mixture on to the griddle or pan. Tiny bubbles will appear and when these burst, turn the scones over, using a palette knife. Cook the underside until golden-brown; then cool the scones in a clean tea-towel on a rack. The scones will take about 3 minutes to cook on the first side and about 2 minutes after turning.

VARIATIONS

Cheese Dropped Scones

Add ½ × 2.5ml spoon dry mustard and 100g finely grated cheese to the basic batter.

Savoury Dropped Scones

Add 2 × 10ml spoons chopped parsley, 1 × 5ml spoon anchovy essence, and 1 × 2.5ml spoon dry mustard to the basic batter.

Potato Scones (2)

Makes 8–10

200g cold boiled potatoes
1 × 15ml spoon butter
 or margarine
salt

75g plain flour (approx)
flour for rolling out
oil for greasing

Mash the potatoes until smooth. Melt the fat and mix it in. Add salt to taste; the quantity will depend on the amount used in cooking the potatoes. Work in as much flour as the potatoes will take up and roll out very thinly (about 4mm thick) on a floured surface. Cut into rounds, using an 8cm cutter. Prick well and cook on a moderately hot greased griddle or heavy frying pan for 3 minutes on each side. Cool in a linen tea-towel or other similar cloth.

Note For Potato Scones (1), see p1177.

Cream Scones

Makes 12 (approx)

200g plain flour
$\frac{1}{2}$ × 2.5ml spoon salt
1 × 5ml spoon
 bicarbonate of soda
1 × 10ml spoon cream of
 tartar

75g butter **or** margarine
65ml milk
4 × 15ml spoons single
 cream
flour for rolling out
fat for greasing

Heat the oven to hot, 220°C, Gas 7. Sift together the dry ingredients 3 times. Rub in the fat and mix to a soft dough with the milk and cream. Knead lightly and roll out on a floured surface to just over 1cm thick. Cut into rounds, using a 6cm cutter. Re-roll the trimmings, and re-cut. Place the scones on a greased baking sheet and bake for 10–12 minutes.

Serve warm or cold, buttered or filled with thick cream and jam.

Singin' Hinnies

Makes 2 hinnies (12–16 scones)

450g plain flour
$\frac{1}{2}$ × 2.5ml spoon salt
$\frac{1}{2}$ × 2.5ml spoon
 bicarbonate of soda
1 × 2.5ml spoon cream
 of tartar
100g butter

100g lard
150g currants (optional)
milk **or** milk and soured
 cream mixed as needed
 (125ml approx)
fat for greasing

Sift the dry ingredients into a large bowl. Rub in the fats. Add the currants, if used. Mix to a stiff dough with milk, or milk and soured cream. Cut the dough into 2 equal portions. Knead each portion lightly until smooth. Roll each into a neat round about 5mm thick. Cook each hinny in turn on a moderately hot greased griddle or heavy frying pan. Cook the first side for 10 minutes until half cooked through and golden-brown underneath. Then turn with a broad knife or slice, adding more fat to the griddle or frying pan, if dry. Lower the heat a little and cook for a further 10 minutes. Turn once more, and cook for 2 minutes to make really hot. Lift off, cut into 6 or 8 wedges, split and butter each, and sandwich them together again. Serve at once in a warmed napkin or serving dish.

Note Instead of turning the hinny a second time, it can be allowed to cool, then cut into wedges, split, and buttered, then re-formed and re-heated in a low oven.

Lardy Johns

Makes 9

200g self-raising flour	*75ml milk (approx)*
1 × 2.5ml spoon salt	*flour for kneading*
100g lard	*fat for greasing*
25g caster sugar	*milk for glazing*
25g currants	

Mix together the flour and salt and rub in the lard. Stir in the sugar and currants. Mix to a soft dough with the milk. Knead the dough lightly on a floured surface until smooth. Turn over, and roll out to an 18cm square. Cut it into nine 3cm squares. Place the squares on a lightly greased baking sheet, and brush the tops with milk. Bake in a hot oven, 220°C, Gas 7, for 10–15 minutes.

Serve while still warm, split and buttered.

Welsh Cakes

Makes 20–24 scones

150g self-raising flour	*50g sugar*
or 150g plain flour and	*50g currants **or** sultanas*
1 × 10ml spoon baking	*1 egg*
powder	*4 × 15ml spoons milk*
1 × 2.5ml spoon salt	*flour*
a pinch of grated nutmeg	
*50g butter **or** margarine*	

Sift the flour, baking powder if used, salt, and nutmeg into a large bowl. Rub in the fat and stir in the sugar and dried fruit. Beat the egg with the milk, and mix into the dry ingredients to make a soft dough. Roll out to 5mm–1cm thickness, and cook on a moderately hot, lightly floured griddle or heavy frying pan for about 6–7 minutes on each side until the scones are golden-brown underneath and the edges are dry. Cool in a linen tea-towel or other similar cloth.

Serve hot or cold, split and buttered.

Note For traditional Welsh Cakes, see p1458.

CAKES, BUNS AND BISCUITS

The heat of the oven is of great importance, especially for large cakes. If the heat be not tolerably fierce, the batter will not rise. If the oven is too quick, and there is any danger of the cake burning or catching, put a sheet of clean paper over the top. Newspaper, or paper that has been printed on, should never be used for this purpose.

GENERAL METHODS OF MAKING CAKES AND BUNS

These vary according to the ingredients used; both the proportions of fat, sugar and eggs to flour and the method of incorporating them, affect the final result.

Rubbing-in method: Rubbing the fat into the flour. Used in recipes where the weight of fat is not more than half that of the flour, eg 100g fat with 200g flour.

Melting method: Melting the fat, as in gingerbread, parkin, some fruit cakes, and sweet or semi-sweet tea breads.

Creaming method: Creaming the fat with the sugar. Used for richer cake recipes, including those where equal weights of fat, sugar, and flour are used.

Whisking method: Whisking the eggs and sugar together for sponge cakes. A true sponge does not include fat but this method is also used for Genoese mixtures which contain melted butter.

All-in-one or one-stage method: All the ingredients are placed together in a bowl, then beaten until the mixture is smooth and creamy. Ideal when using soft tub margarine.

Using oil: A variation of the one-stage method; oil is used instead of margarine. See Gingerbread (p892).

PREPARING TINS FOR BAKING

The best fats to use for greasing are lard, cooking fat or oil. If butter or margarine is used, it must be clarified (p886) first to remove any salt and water which it may contain.

There are 4 principal ways of preparing the insides of cake and bun tins, and the surface of baking sheets for biscuits.

1) Bun and patty tins, and baking sheets for biscuits should be greased; for some biscuits, sheets should be dusted with flour after greasing.
2) For rubbed-in cakes, grease the tin and line the base with greased greaseproof paper or non-stick vegetable parchment.
3) For creamed mixtures, it is advisable to line both the sides and the base of the tins with greased greaseproof paper or vegetable parchment, particularly when the baking time is more than 1 hour. Cake tins for gingerbread should also be lined and greased.
4) For sponge cakes, brush the tin with fat, then coat it with equal quantities of flour and caster sugar, sifted together.

Note Where preparation differs from the above, this is indicated within the recipe in question.

Cake tins, bun tins, and baking sheets are available with special non-stick finishes which do not usually need greasing. Consult the manufacturer's instructions as to whether you need grease the tin or not.

Round and Square Tins

A square tin holds the same amount of mixture as a round tin about 2cm larger in diameter, eg a recipe calling for an 18cm square tin can equally well be baked in a round 20cm tin, provided the tins are the same depth.

The length of time needed for cooking any cake depends on the depth of the mixture. If a smaller tin than specified is used, increase the baking time, and vice versa for a larger tin.

To line a tin – round or square

1) Measure and cut a single or double piece of paper to fit the base of the tin; ensure that it is not bigger than the base or it will spoil the shape of the cake.
2) Measure and cut a strip, single or double, long enough to line the sides of the tin, allowing for a slight overwrap. Make the strip 5cm deeper than the height of the tin.
3) Make a 2cm fold along the bottom of the strip and snip diagonally at 1cm intervals up to the fold.

   Paper for a square tin need only be snipped at the corners.
4) Grease the tin and place the strip round the sides of the tin with the cut edge lying flat against the base. Fit in the round. Grease the lined tin.

Measuring a strip to fit the sides of the tin

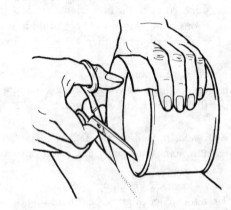

Cutting a strip of paper 5cm deeper than the tin

Measuring paper to fit the base of the tin

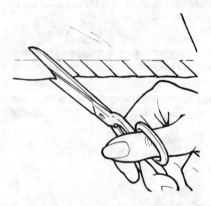

Snipping along bottom edge of strip towards fold

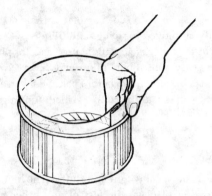

Placing the strip in the tin

To line a Swiss roll tin

1) Cut a piece of paper large enough to fit both the base and sides of the tin. Do not make it higher than the sides of the tin as this may prevent the heat from browning the top.
2) Place the tin on the paper and make a cut on each corner of the paper from the edge to the corner of the tin.
3) Place the paper in the greased tin, folding the corners to give a neat fit. Grease the lined tin.

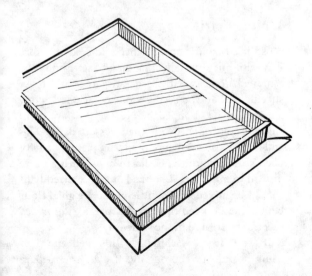

STORING CAKES, BUNS, AND BISCUITS

Wrap very rich cakes and wedding cakes in greaseproof paper and a clean tea-towel. Store in a cool, dry place. Biscuits and other cakes may be stored in a tin but should be used as soon as possible. The prepared dough can be frozen for 2 months (see p1392).

MAIN INGREDIENTS FOR MAKING CAKES, BUNS, AND BISCUITS

Flour

General purpose household flour gives better results in most cases than strong flour, as used for breadmaking. Most flours are fine enough to make sifting unnecessary, unless it is used as a method of mixing several dry ingredients such as spices, cocoa, and salt with the flour.

Self-raising flour is used by many people for cake-making. It produces a more open and lighter texture than plain flour. It should not be used for rich fruit cakes unless the recipe specifies it.

Government regulations concerning self-raising flour lay down a minimum standard for the available carbon dioxide produced by the raising ingredients in the flour, so there is very little variation between one brand and another.

Cornflour is sometimes added to wheat flour to give a softer texture.

Rice flour used to be added to plain flour for shortbread but is now difficult to obtain; ground rice can be substituted.

Raising Ingredients

Baking powder is the raising agent most often used. *Bicarbonate of soda* can be added to darken the crumb, and is often used in cakes made with syrup, eg gingerbread. *Soured milk* is also sometimes added (instead of fresh milk), eg in scones; it gives a light, quick rise.

Bicarbonate of soda and cream of tartar can be used instead of baking powder in the proportion of 1 part bicarbonate of soda to 2 parts cream of tartar. The most suitable raising agent to use is given in the individual recipes.

Fats

Butter gives the best flavour, particularly to rich fruit cakes and shortbread.

Margarine is excellent for general everyday use and is available in several different textures.

Lard which is 100% fat, contributes little colour or flavour; it is sometimes used with spices, treacle, and syrup for gingerbread but is seldom used otherwise in cake-making.

Dripping, being highly flavoured with meat juices, is not suitable for most cakes, but it is used for a few traditional regional ones. It should be clarified (p473) before use.

Other special fats can be used if the manufacturers' instructions are followed.

Sugar

As a general rule, *granulated sugar* is used for rubbed-in and melted mixtures, and *caster sugar* is used for cakes prepared by the creaming method, whisking method, and all-in-one method. Generally, a recipe specifies the most suitable type of sugar to use when it is important for texture or flavour. *Soft dark brown sugar* gives a dark crumb, for instance, to some Christmas and wedding cakes, and to gingerbreads. If in doubt about the type of sugar to use, choose caster rather than granulated for light-coloured and delicately flavoured cakes, and light rather than dark brown sugar for spicy and fruit cakes, and gingerbreads.

Icing sugar is used in some biscuits, but is mainly employed for icings and fillings.

Crushed lump sugar can be used as a topping for some yeast buns. Some cakes may have *Demerara sugar* sprinkled on top before baking; it can also be used to make a baked or grilled topping after baking.

Eggs

These make a cake light and fluffy. The higher the proportion of eggs, the less of any other raising ingredient, such as baking powder, will be needed. Eggs may be added beaten, whole or separated, depending on the type of mixture. Separated egg whites, whisked before being added to a mixture, should be folded in lightly after the other ingredients. A spoonful or two can be stirred into the mixture to lighten it before the rest are folded in.

A little flour added with the eggs to a creamed mixture helps to prevent curdling. Successful meringues cannot be made with truly new-laid eggs; they should be at least 2–4 days old; use the egg whites at room temperature. Provided they whisk up stiffly, good results should be obtained. If the egg whites are old, they will be watery and incapable of holding the necessary air for successful results. For full instructions on making meringues and meringue desserts, see pp1022–25.

Dried Fruit

Most dried fruit is now cleaned and seeded before it is sold, but any stalks that may be left should be removed. *Raisins* with seeds are larger and more succulent than the seedless ones. Packeted block *dates* must be chopped before use, but are more suitable for baked goods than dessert dates. *Figs* and *prunes* also need chopping, and prunes usually need stoning. Fruit is easier to chop with a knife dipped in hot water. Chopped or sticky dried fruit should be mixed with a little of the weighed flour before use, to keep the pieces separate. *Cut mixed peel* can be treated in the same way.

If fruit needs washing, do this well ahead of using it and dry thoroughly. If *glacé cherries* are very sticky or moist, wash and dry them before use, and toss in a little of the weighed flour.

Nuts

Almonds can be bought in their skins or already blanched. Blanched nuts can be bought whole, flaked, split, kibbled (lightly crushed) or as nibs (chopped).

Almonds bought in their skins need blanching for almost all cake recipes. Unless bought ready blanched, use the following procedure: place the almonds in a saucepan with plenty of cold water, bring just to boiling point, drain in a sieve under a running cold tap, pinch off the skins and dry on soft kitchen paper. If the almonds are required split, as for the top of a Dundee cake, do this with a small, sharp knife while the nuts are still warm from blanching.

Browned (or roasted) almonds are often used. They can be browned on a baking tray in a cool oven, or under the grill. If using the oven, almonds should be turned over once or twice during baking. If the grill pan is used, it should be shaken frequently to turn and move the nuts and to prevent dark scorch spots.

Desiccated coconut is used in many cakes, puddings, and biscuits. It can also be used as a decoration on top of jam or icing on a cake. It can be coloured or toasted (see p1235).

Hazelnuts need skinning for most cakes. Place the nuts on a baking tray in the oven, and bake until the skins can be removed by rubbing in a cloth or in a paper bag. Rub off the skins. Alternatively, toast gently under the grill, shaking the pan to turn them over. Chop coarsely, or grind in a nut mill, coffee grinder or in an electric blender, or use whole as a decoration.

Peanuts: skin as for hazelnuts.

Pistachios: skin as for hazelnuts.

Walnuts do not need blanching. They can be bought whole or as roughly chopped pieces.

Brazils, pecans, and other nuts such as *unsalted peanuts* can be used for some cakes, buns, and cookies. Treat pecans like walnuts. *Chopped mixed nuts* are also available in packets. They are a useful substitute for chopped hazelnuts or walnuts.

HINTS FOR SUCCESS IN CAKE-MAKING

1) Check that all the needed ingredients and equipment are ready to hand.
2) Weigh and measure the ingredients carefully; prepare tins as directed.
3) Follow the recipe exactly.
4) When making a cake by the creaming method, beat the fat by itself until it is soft before adding the sugar. Use fat and eggs at room temperature.
5) For the one-stage method, use *all* the ingredients at room temperature.
6) In cakes made by the melting method, only heat the fat, syrup, etc gently for just long enough to melt the fat; do not let it get hot. If the pan becomes too hot for you to hold your hand against the side without discomfort, let the pan cool slightly before using the contents.
7) Do not open the oven door unnecessarily.
8) Test the cake for readiness carefully before taking it out of the oven. Just pull out the oven shelf enough to test it as described below.
9) Allow the cake to cool slightly in the tin so that it can be turned out without breaking. Leave very rich cakes, eg Christmas or wedding cakes, to cool completely in the tin; otherwise, complete cooling on a wire rack.

How to Test when a Cake is Cooked

When fully baked a cake should be evenly browned and have come away from the sides of the tin slightly. If the top crust is pressed very lightly with the finger, the mixture should spring back or, in the case of fruit cakes, feel firm. If a fruit cake feels spongy, cover loosely with greaseproof paper and return to the oven for a short time. Retest before taking the cake out of the oven.

Another way of testing rich cakes is to insert a thin, warmed poultry skewer or thin-bladed knife into the centre of the cake. If it comes out clean the cake is done; if there are crumbs or wet mixture sticking to it, return the cake to the oven for a short time. Retest before taking the cake out of the oven.

How to Turn a Cake on to a Rack to Cool

If the cake tin has been lined, lift out the paper with the cake in it, place on a cooling rack and peel off the paper. Leave the cake to become quite cold. If the tin is unlined, place it on its side and gently ease out the cake. Turn it on to its base on the cooling rack.

Easing the cake from the tin

REASONS FOR SOME COMMON FAULTS IN CAKES

The cake has sunk in the centre

1) Too much raising agent was used.
2) The fat and sugar were over-creamed or too soft a margarine was used.
3) The mixture, before baking, was too soft.
4) The oven door was opened or the cake removed before it was set.
5) It was taken from the oven before it was cooked.

The cake has risen to a peak and may have cracked on top

1) The fat and sugar were not creamed enough.
2) The oven was too hot or the cake was cooked too near the top of it (in a gas oven).
3) The cake tin was too small.

The cake has risen unevenly

1) The mixture was not levelled before baking.
2) The oven had not reached the correct baking temperature when the cake was put in.
3) The cake was placed at one side of the oven.
4) Too much baking powder was used.

The cake is very dry

1) Too much baking powder was used.
2) Not enough eggs or liquid were used.
3) The cake was baked too long.

The texture is coarse and open

1) In a rubbed-in mixture, the fat was not rubbed in finely enough, or a poor quality fat was used.
2) In a creamed mixture, the fat and sugar were under-creamed.
3) Too much baking powder was used.
4) The oven temperature was too high.

The fruit has sunk down towards the bottom of the cake

1) The mixture was too soft before baking.
2) The oven was too cool.
3) Cherries should have been washed, dried and tossed in some of the weighed flour.

The cake has a sugary top crust

1) The fat and sugar were not creamed together enough.
2) The proportion of sugar in the recipe was too high.
3) Too coarse a sugar was used.

Cakes and Buns

For gâteaux, cheesecakes, and meringue-based desserts, see the chapter on Cold Puddings and Desserts. See also the chapter on Pastry Making and Pastry Goods.

PLAIN CAKES AND BUNS
(Fat added by rubbing in)

Plain Cake

Basic recipe

fat for greasing	*50–100g margarine* **or**
200g self-raising flour	*other fat*
or *200g plain flour and*	*75g sugar*
1 × 10ml spoon baking	*2 small eggs*
powder	*125ml milk (approx)*
½ × 2.5ml spoon salt	

Grease a 15cm cake tin and line the base with greased paper. Mix the flour and salt together, cut the fat into small pieces in the flour, and rub in until the mixture resembles fine breadcrumbs. Add the baking powder, if used, and the sugar. Beat the egg with some of the milk and stir into the mixture. Add a little more milk if necessary, to give a consistency which just drops off the end of a wooden spoon. Put the mixture into the cake tin and smooth the top. Bake in a moderate oven, 180°C, Gas 4, for 1–1½ hours.

VARIATIONS

Cherry, Currant or Sultana Cake

Add 100g fruit, cut up if necessary, with the sugar.

Countess or Spice Cake

Use 100g flour, 100g cornflour, 1 × 2.5ml spoon ground ginger, 1½ × 2.5ml spoons ground nutmeg, and 1½ × 2.5ml spoons ground cinnamon. Add 50g currants and 50g seedless raisins after adding the milk.

Lemon or Orange Cake

Add the grated rind of 1 lemon or orange with the sugar. Replace some of the milk with the juice of the fruit.

Boodles Cake

fat for greasing	*75g margarine*
200g self-raising flour	*75–100g sugar*
or *200g plain flour and*	*75g sultanas*
1 × 10ml spoon baking	*75g seedless raisins*
powder	*50g currants*
1 × 2.5ml spoon mixed	*2 small eggs*
spice	*125ml milk (approx)*

Grease a 15cm cake tin and line the base with greased paper. Mix the flour and spice together and rub in the fat. Add the sugar, dried fruit, and baking powder, if used. Beat the eggs with the milk and add to the dry ingredients. Put the mixture into the tin. Bake in a moderate oven, 180°C, Gas 4, for 45 minutes, reduce the temperature to warm, 160°C, Gas 3, and bake for a further 30 minutes.

Date and Walnut Cake

fat for greasing	*75g margarine*
200g self-raising flour	*75g dates*
or *200g plain flour and*	*25g walnuts*
1 × 10ml spoon baking	*75g soft light brown*
powder	*sugar*
a pinch of ground	*2 small eggs*
nutmeg	*125ml milk (approx)*

Grease a 15cm tin and line the base with greased paper. Mix the flour and nutmeg together, and rub in the fat. Chop the dates and walnuts and add to the flour with the sugar and baking powder, if used. Beat the eggs and milk together and mix into the dry ingredients. Bake in a moderate oven, 180°C, Gas 4, for 1¼–1½ hours.

Note For Date and Walnut Loaf using oil, see p1212. For other sweet tea breads, see pp1171–75.

Dripping Cake

fat for greasing
200g self-raising flour
a pinch of salt
$\frac{1}{2} \times 2.5ml$ spoon mixed
  spice
100g beef dripping (see
  Note)

75g granulated sugar
75g seedless raisins
50g currants
1 egg
100ml milk

Grease a 15cm round cake tin and line the base with greased paper. Mix the flour, salt, and spice together. Rub in the dripping, and add the sugar and dried fruit. Beat the egg with the milk and add to the dry ingredients; stir in, then beat until smooth. Put into the tin and smooth the top level. Bake in a moderate oven, 180°C, Gas 4, for 1 hour 10 minutes. Cover the top with greaseproof paper after 1 hour if the cake is already brown enough.

Note Use clarified dripping (p473) which does not have too strong a flavour. If it has been kept in the refrigerator, allow it to come to room temperature.

Fruit Loaf

fat for greasing
200g self-raising flour
a pinch of salt
100g margarine
100g caster sugar
grated rind of 1 orange

200g mixed fruit, eg 25g
  cherries, 25g cut mixed
  peel, 75g sultanas, 75g
  seedless raisins
1 egg
milk

Grease a 23 × 13 × 7cm loaf tin. Line the base with greased paper. Mix the flour and salt together, and rub in the margarine. Stir in the sugar and orange rind. Cut cherries, if used, into 4–6 pieces each, depending on size, and add with the remaining fruit. Beat the egg until liquid and add enough milk to make up to 125ml. Add to the dry ingredients, stir in, then mix well. Put in the tin and smooth the top level. Bake in a moderate oven, 180°C, Gas 4, for about 1 hour or until firm to the touch.

Bran Fruit Cake

fat for greasing
175g self-raising flour
25g natural wheat bran
1 × 2.5ml spoon salt
100g margarine
100g caster sugar **or** soft
  light brown sugar

150g mixed dried fruit
  (currants, sultanas,
  seedless raisins)
2 eggs
2 × 15ml spoons milk

Grease a 15cm cake tin and line the base with greased paper. Mix together the flour, bran and salt, and rub in the margarine. Stir in the sugar and fruit. Beat the eggs with the milk, add to the dry ingredients and mix well. Turn into the tin and bake in a moderate oven, 180°C, Gas 4, for about 1 hour.

Holiday Cake

fat for greasing
200g self-raising flour
$\frac{1}{2} \times 2.5ml$ spoon salt
1 × 2.5ml spoon baking
  powder
75g margarine

75g granulated sugar
100g currants
100g seedless raisins
1 large egg
100ml milk

Grease a 15cm round cake tin and line the base with greased paper. Sift the flour, salt, and baking powder together. Rub in the margarine until the mixture resembles fine breadcrumbs. Stir in the sugar and dried fruit. Beat the egg until liquid and add the milk. Mix into the dry ingredients, and beat to a soft consistency. Put into the tin and bake in a moderate oven, 180°C, Gas 4, for $1\frac{1}{2}$ hours.

Spiced Sultana Cake

fat for greasing
200g self-raising flour
2 × 5ml spoons mixed
  spice
100g margarine

225g sultanas
100g soft light brown
  sugar
1 egg
milk

Grease a 15cm round cake tin and line the base with greased paper. Sift together the flour and spice. Rub in the margarine, then stir in the sultanas and sugar. Beat the egg until liquid and add enough milk to make up to 125ml. Add to the dry ingredients, stir in, then mix well. Put the mixture in the tin and smooth the top level. Bake in a moderate oven, 180°C, Gas 4, for about 1¼ hours or until firm to the touch.

Lunch Cake

fat for greasing
200g plain flour
½ × 2.5ml spoon salt
1 × 10ml spoon mixed
 spice
1 × 2.5ml spoon ground
 cloves
1 × 5ml spoon ground
 cinnamon
1 × 5ml spoon cream of
 tartar

1 × 2.5ml spoon
 bicarbonate of soda
75g lard and margarine
 mixed
100g granulated sugar
75g currants
50g seedless raisins
35g cut mixed peel
2 eggs
4 × 15ml spoons milk

Grease a 15cm round cake tin and line the base with greased paper. Sift together the flour, salt, spices, cream of tartar, and bicarbonate of soda into a bowl. Rub in the fats until the mixture resembles fine breadcrumbs. Add the sugar, dried fruit and peel. Beat the eggs with the milk until blended. Make a hollow in the dry ingredients and pour in the milk mixture. Stir, then beat lightly to a soft consistency. Turn into the prepared tin and bake in a moderate oven, 180°C, Gas 4, for 1¼ hours.

Vinegar Cake

fat for greasing
200g plain flour
½ × 2.5ml spoon salt
75g margarine
75g soft dark brown
 sugar

50g currants
50g sultanas
25g cut mixed peel
1 × 5ml spoon
 bicarbonate of soda
180ml milk
1 × 15ml spoon vinegar

Grease a 15cm round tin and line the base with greased paper. Mix the flour and salt together. Rub in the fat. Stir in the sugar, dried fruit and peel. Dissolve the bicarbonate of soda in 100ml of the milk. Add this with the remaining milk (8 × 10ml spoons) and the vinegar to the dry ingredients and

mix in thoroughly. Bake in a moderate oven, 180°C, Gas 4, for about 1 hour, reduce the heat to warm, 160°C, Gas 3, and bake for a further 30–40 minutes.

Plain Buns

Basic recipe

Makes 12–14

200g self-raising flour
 or 200g plain flour and
 1 × 10ml spoon baking
 powder
½ × 2.5ml spoon salt

75g margarine
75g sugar
1 egg
milk
fat for greasing

Decoration (optional)
glacé icing (p1225)

Heat the oven to fairly hot, 200°C, Gas 6. Sift or mix the flour and salt together. Cut the margarine into small pieces in the flour, and rub in until the mixture resembles fine breadcrumbs. Stir in the baking powder, if used, and the sugar. Beat the egg until liquid and add enough milk to make up to 125ml. Add the liquid to the dry ingredients and mix with a fork to a stiff consistency. This produces a sticky mixture which supports the fork. Divide the mixture into 12–14 portions and form into rocky heaps on a well-greased baking sheet, allowing about 2cm space between each. Bake above the centre of the oven for 15–20 minutes until firm to the touch on the underside.

Coat, if liked, with a spoonful of glacé icing when cool.

Note When small buns are baked in paper cases or greased patty tins, the consistency should be softer than when the buns are put on a baking sheet. Use 1 egg and 125ml milk, or enough to allow the mixture to drop off the spoon with a slight shake. The number of buns obtained will be 14–16, using the same quantity of flour.

For **variations**, see over.

VARIATIONS

Chocolate Buns

Add 50g cocoa to the flour and 1 × 5ml spoon vanilla essence with the milk.

Coconut Buns

Add 75g desiccated coconut with the flour and an extra 2 × 5ml spoons milk.

Lemon or Orange Buns

Add the grated rind of 1 lemon or orange with the flour.

Raspberry Buns

Form the mixture into 12–14 balls with lightly floured hands. Make a deep dent in the centre of each ball and drop 1 × 5ml spoon raspberry jam inside each. Close the mixture over the jam. Brush with egg or milk and sprinkle with sugar.

Rock Buns

Add $\frac{1}{2}$ × 2.5ml spoon ground nutmeg to the flour and 75g mixed fruit (currants, peel, etc, according to taste) with the sugar.

Seed Buns

Add 1 × 15ml spoon caraway seeds with the sugar.

Spice Buns

Add an extra 1 × 5ml spoon mixed spice or 1 × 2.5ml spoon ground cinnamon and 1 × 2.5ml spoon ground nutmeg to the flour.

Ginger Buns

Makes 18–20

150g self-raising flour	25g nibbed almonds
a pinch of salt	1 egg
1 × 5ml spoon ground ginger	2 × 10ml spoons black treacle
$\frac{1}{2}$ × 2.5ml spoon ground cinnamon	2 × 10ml spoons golden syrup
75g butter **or** margarine	2 × 15ml spoons milk
50g soft light brown sugar	fat for greasing (optional)

Heat the oven to fairly hot, 190°C, Gas 5. Sift together the flour, salt, and spices. Rub in the fat, and stir in the sugar and almonds. Beat the egg lightly, mix with the treacle, syrup and milk, and add to the dry ingredients. Beat until smooth. Divide the mixture between 18–20 paper baking cases or greased bun tins. Bake for 15–20 minutes.

VARIATION

Victoria Buns

Substitute a good pinch of ground nutmeg for the ginger, and scatter the almonds over the buns instead of mixing them in.

Honey Buns

Makes 18–20

200g self-raising flour	2 × 15ml spoons clear honey
a pinch of salt	
75g butter **or** margarine	2 × 15ml spoons milk
25g caster sugar	fat for greasing
1 egg	(optional)

Heat the oven to fairly hot, 190°C, Gas 5. Mix together the flour and salt. Rub in the fat, and stir in the sugar. Beat the egg until liquid, and mix it with the honey and milk. Pour into the dry ingredients and beat until well mixed and smooth. Divide between 18–20 paper baking cases or greased bun tins and bake for 15–20 minutes.

Note For Honey Cake, see p1212.

Ring Doughnuts (1)

(with yeast)
See p1167.

Ring Doughnuts (2)

Makes 12 (approx)

200g plain flour	*3 × 15ml spoons sugar*
½ × 2.5ml spoon salt	*1 egg*
a pinch of ground cinnamon or nutmeg	*4 × 15ml spoons milk (approx)*
3 × 2.5ml spoons baking powder	*flour for rolling out*
40g butter or margarine	*fat or oil for deep frying*
	caster sugar

Sift the flour, salt, spice, and baking powder into a bowl. Rub in the fat. Stir in the sugar. Beat the egg lightly. Make a well in the centre of the dry ingredients and add the egg. Gradually work it into the dry ingredients, adding enough milk to make a soft dough. Roll out the dough 1cm thick on a floured board. Heat the fat (p303). Cut the dough into rings using a 6cm and a 3cm cutter. Re-roll and re-cut the trimmings. Fry 1 or 2 doughnuts in the hot fat until light brown underneath; turn and cook the second side. Lift the doughnuts out and drain well. Put some caster sugar in a large paper bag and put in the doughnuts while still hot. Toss them gently until coated. Leave on soft kitchen paper dusted with sugar. Continue until all the doughnuts are fried. Bring the fat back to the correct temperature between each batch.

Serve warm or cold the same day.

Ring Doughnuts (3)

Makes 8–10

150g self-raising flour	*1–2 × 15ml spoons milk*
1 × 2.5ml spoon salt	*flour for rolling out*
50g margarine	*fat or oil for deep frying*
25g sugar	*caster sugar*
1 standard egg	*ground cinnamon*

Mix the flour and salt together. Rub in the fat and stir in the sugar. Beat the egg until liquid and add the milk. Mix into the dry ingredients to make a soft scone-like dough. Roll out 1cm thick on a floured board. Cut into rounds with a 5cm cutter. Remove the centres with an apple corer. Re-roll and re-cut the trimmings. Heat the fat (p303) and fry the doughnuts, turning once when brown on the underside. Drain, and while still hot, toss in caster sugar flavoured with ground cinnamon.

Jam Doughnuts

(with yeast)
See p1167.

CAKES MADE BY THE MELTING METHOD

Gingerbread

Basic recipe

fat for greasing	*50–100g lard*
200g plain flour	*50g brown sugar*
½ × 2.5ml spoon salt	*100g golden syrup or*
2–3 × 5ml spoons ground ginger	*black treacle (or a mixture)*
1 × 2.5ml spoon bicarbonate of soda	*1 egg*
	milk

Grease a 15cm square tin and line with greased paper. Sift together the flour, salt, ginger, and bicarbonate of soda into a bowl. Warm the fat, sugar, and syrup in a saucepan until the fat has melted. Do not allow the mixture to become hot. Beat the egg until liquid and add enough milk to make up to 125ml. Add the melted mixture to the dry ingredients with the beaten egg and milk. Stir thoroughly; the mixture should run easily off the spoon. Pour into the tin and bake in a warm oven, 160°C, Gas 3, for $1\frac{1}{4}$–$1\frac{1}{2}$ hours until firm to the touch.

Note For Golden Syrup Gingerbread Biscuits, see p1218.

For **variations**, see over.

Andrew's Gingerbread or Golden Syrup Gingerbread

Substitute butter or margarine for the fat, and use golden syrup instead of treacle.

Fruit Gingerbread

Add 100–125g dried fruit to the dry ingredients, eg 50g preserved ginger, 25g sultanas or seedless raisins, 25g cut mixed peel, 25g currants.

Nut Gingerbread

Sift $1 \times 10ml$ spoon ground cinnamon with the dry ingredients and add 50g chopped almonds or walnuts.

Country Gingerbread

fat for greasing	*1 × 10ml spoon caraway*
75g plain flour	*seeds*
½ × 2.5ml spoon salt	*75g soft brown sugar*
1 × 15ml spoon ground	*200g golden syrup*
ginger	*75g butter **or** margarine*
1 × 5ml spoon	*1 egg*
bicarbonate of soda	*125ml milk*
125g wholemeal flour	

Grease and line a 20cm square tin. Sift together the plain flour, salt, ginger, and bicarbonate of soda. Add the wholemeal flour, caraway seeds, and sugar. Heat the syrup and fat gently in a saucepan until the fat has melted. Beat the egg and milk together. Add the melted mixture to the dry ingredients with the egg and milk and beat well. Pour into the tin and bake in a warm oven, 160°C, Gas 3, for 50 minutes.

Oatmeal Gingerbread

fat for greasing	*50g butter **or** margarine*
100g plain flour	*50g soft brown sugar*
½ × 2.5ml spoon salt	*2 × 10ml spoons black*
1 × 15ml spoon ground	*treacle*
ginger	*1 egg*
1 × 5ml spoon	*75ml milk **or** soured*
bicarbonate of soda	*milk*
100g fine oatmeal	

Grease and line an 18cm square tin. Sift together the flour, salt, ginger, and bicarbonate of soda. Add the oatmeal. Heat the fat, sugar, and treacle gently in a saucepan until the fat has melted. Beat the egg and milk together. Beat both liquid mixtures into the dry ingredients. Pour into the tin and bake in a moderate oven, 180°C, Gas 4, for $1-1\frac{1}{4}$ hours.

Steamed Gingerbread

Place the prepared mixture in an 18cm cake tin, cover with greased paper or foil and steam for $1\frac{1}{2}$ hours; then bake in a moderate oven, 180°C, Gas 4, for 15–20 minutes to dry the gingerbread.

Dark Gingerbread

fat for greasing	*125g black treacle*
200g plain flour	*75ml milk*
½ × 2.5ml spoon salt	*1 × 5ml spoon*
1 × 15ml spoon ground	*bicarbonate of soda*
ginger	*1 egg*
50g soft brown sugar	
*50g butter, lard **or***	
margarine	

Grease and line an 18cm square tin or a $23 \times 13 \times 7cm$ loaf tin. Sift together the flour, salt, and ginger. Add the sugar. Heat the fat, treacle, and most of the milk gently in a saucepan until the fat has melted. Dissolve the bicarbonate of soda in the rest of the milk. Beat the egg until liquid. Pour the melted mixture into the dry ingredients. Add the egg with the dissolved bicarbonate of soda, and beat well. Pour into the tin and bake in a moderate oven,

180°C, Gas 4, for 20 minutes. Reduce the temperature to cool, 150°C, Gas 2, and bake for a further 30–40 minutes until firm to the touch.

This gingerbread should be kept for at least a week before eating, and is best eaten sliced and spread with butter.

Note For a lighter gingerbread, golden syrup may be used instead of black treacle.

Rich Gingerbread

fat for greasing
200g plain flour
$\frac{1}{2}$ × 2.5ml spoon salt
2 × 5ml spoons ground ginger
$\frac{1}{2}$–1 × 5ml spoon ground cinnamon or nutmeg
1 × 2.5ml spoon bicarbonate of soda

100g lard
100g dark brown sugar
150g black treacle
1 egg
2 × 15ml spoons milk (approx)

Grease and line a 15cm square tin. Sift together the flour, salt, spices, and bicarbonate of soda. Heat the fat, sugar, and treacle gently in a saucepan until the fat has melted. Beat the egg and milk together and add to the dry ingredients, with the melted mixture, to give a soft, dropping consistency. Pour into the tin and bake in a warm oven, 160°C, Gas 3, for $1\frac{1}{4}$–$1\frac{1}{2}$ hours.

VARIATION
Rich Fruit and Nut Gingerbread

Add 100g sultanas and 25g shredded blanched almonds. Use 75g black treacle and 75g golden syrup, and 2 small eggs.

Moist Gingerbread

fat for greasing
200g plain flour
1 × 5ml spoon bicarbonate of soda
$\frac{1}{2}$ × 2.5ml spoon salt
1 × 10ml spoon ground cinnamon
1 × 10ml spoon ground ginger

75g soft dark brown sugar
100g black treacle
100g golden syrup
150g butter or margarine
2 eggs
2 × 15ml spoons milk

Grease and line a 28 × 18cm slab cake or shallow baking tin. Sift together the flour, bicarbonate of soda, salt, cinnamon, and ginger. Add the sugar. Heat the treacle, syrup, and fat gently in a saucepan until the fat has melted. Beat the eggs and milk together. Beat the melted mixture into the dry ingredients, then beat in the eggs and milk. Pour into the tin and bake in a moderate oven, 180°C, Gas 4, for 20 minutes. Reduce the heat to warm, 160°C, Gas 3, and bake for a further 25–35 minutes until firm to the touch.

VARIATION
Moist Fruit and Nut Gingerbread

Add 50g sultanas or seedless raisins, 75g crystallized ginger, and 50g almonds, roughly chopped.

Gingerbread
(made with oil)
See p892.

Westmorland Parkin
See p1467.

Boiled Fruit Cake

fat for greasing
100g mixed dried fruit
50g margarine
25g soft light brown
  sugar
200ml water

grated rind of 1 orange
200g plain flour
1 × 2.5ml spoon mixed
  spice
1 × 2.5ml spoon
  bicarbonate of soda

Grease and line a 15cm cake tin. Put the dried fruit, margarine, sugar, water, and orange rind in a saucepan, bring to the boil, reduce the heat and simmer for 5 minutes. Leave to cool until tepid. Sift the flour, spice, and soda into the fruit mixture and mix well. Put into the tin. Cover with greased paper or foil and steam for 2–2½ hours, or bake in a moderate oven, 180°C, Gas 4, for 1½–2 hours.

Brownies (2)
See p1204.

RICH CAKES
(Fat added by creaming with sugar)

Rich Cake

Basic recipe

fat for greasing
200g plain flour
½ × 2.5ml spoon salt
1 × 2.5ml spoon baking
  powder

4 eggs
150g butter **or**
  margarine
150g caster sugar
1 × 15ml spoon milk

Grease a 15cm round cake tin and line with greased paper. Sift together the flour, salt, and baking powder. Beat the eggs in a basin and stand it in tepid water (or make sure you use eggs at room temperature). Beat the fat until very soft, add the sugar, and cream well together until light and fluffy. Add the eggs gradually, beating well after each addition. If the mixture shows signs of curdling, add a little flour. Fold in the dry ingredients lightly but thoroughly. Add the milk if too stiff. Put into the tin, smooth the top and make a hollow in the centre. Bake in a moderate oven, 180°C, Gas 4,

for 30 minutes, reduce the heat to warm, 160°C, Gas 3, and bake for a further 50 minutes or until firm to the touch.

VARIATIONS
Cherry Cake

Add 125g quartered glacé cherries with the flour.

Cornflour Cake

Use 100g cornflour and 100g plain flour.

Fruit Cake

Add 100g dried fruit (currants, seedless raisins, sultanas), 50g chopped glacé cherries, and 50g cut mixed peel. Bake in a 17cm tin.

Note For One-stage Fruit Cake, see p1211.

Ginger Cake

Add 1 × 5ml spoon ground ginger with the flour and stir in 100g crystallized ginger.

Ground Rice Cake

Use 150g flour and 50g ground rice.

Lemon or Orange Cake

Add the grated rind of 2 lemons or oranges and use fruit juice instead of milk.

Seed Cake

Add 3 × 5ml spoons caraway seeds with the flour.

Applesauce Cake

fat for greasing	1 × 2.5ml spoon ground
400g apples	cloves
1 × 15ml spoon butter	1 × 2.5ml spoon ground
2 × 15ml spoons water	nutmeg
75g sugar	100g margarine
200g self-raising flour	200g caster sugar
¼ × 2.5ml spoon salt	1 egg
1 × 2.5ml spoon ground	100g seedless raisins
cinnamon	100g currants

Icing (optional)
lemon glacé icing (p1225)

Grease and line a 15cm square cake tin. Peel and core the apples and slice them thinly. Melt the butter and add the apples, water, and sugar. Cook gently until soft and fluffy, then beat well. Measure out 250ml of the sauce. Sift the flour, salt, and spices together. Cream the fat and sugar until light and fluffy, beat in the egg, then the apple sauce. Fold in the flour mixture and the dried fruit. Bake in a moderate oven, 180°C, Gas 4, for 30–45 minutes, reduce the heat to warm, 160°C, Gas 3, and bake for a further 20–30 minutes.

When cold, ice the top of the cake with lemon glacé icing, if liked.

Almond Macaroon Cake

fat for greasing	150g caster sugar
150g self-raising flour	3 eggs
a pinch of salt	100g ground almonds
150g butter or	grated rind of 1 lemon
margarine	

Macaroon

1 egg white	1 × 5ml spoon ground
50g ground almonds	rice
75g caster sugar	a few drops almond
	essence

Decoration
25g blanched split
almonds

Grease and line a 15cm cake tin. Make the macaroon mixture first. Whisk the egg white until frothy, then add the rest of the ingredients, beating well.

Mix the flour and salt together. Cream the fat and sugar, add the eggs, one at a time with a spoonful of flour, stir in, then beat well. Fold in the rest of the flour, the ground almonds, and the lemon rind.

Put a layer of the cake mixture, about 2cm thick, at the bottom of the tin. Divide the macaroon mixture into 2 equal portions; put half in the centre of the cake mixture. Add the rest of the cake mixture and spread the rest of the macaroon mixture on top. Cover with the blanched split almonds. Bake in a moderate oven, 180°C, Gas 4, for 1¼ hours, covering with greaseproof paper as soon as the top is pale brown.

Banana and Walnut Cake

fat for greasing	3 large bananas
200g flour	50g walnuts
¼ × 2.5ml spoon baking	100g butter
powder	150g caster sugar
1½ × 2.5ml spoons	2 eggs
bicarbonate of soda	50ml soured milk
a pinch of salt	

Filling
lemon butter icing
(p1227) (for sandwich
cake)

Icing
lemon glacé icing (p1225)

Grease and line either a 20cm ring tin, or two 23cm sandwich tins. Sift the flour, baking powder, soda, and salt. Mash the bananas thoroughly, and chop or crush the walnuts finely. Cream the butter and sugar until light and creamy. Mix in the mashed banana at once, blending well. Add the eggs, one at a time, beating well after each addition. Add the dry ingredients, one-third at a time, alternately with the milk, beating well after each addition. Mix in the walnuts. Bake the ring cake in a moderate oven, 180°C, Gas 4, for about 40 minutes, the sandwich cakes for about 30 minutes.

When cold, fill the sandwich cakes with lemon butter icing; ice either cake with lemon glacé icing.

Birthday Cake

200g mixed dried fruit
65ml milk **or** brandy
fat for greasing
100g butter **or**
  margarine
100g soft light brown
  sugar
35g golden syrup
3 eggs
150g plain flour **or** 125g
  plain flour and 25g
  cocoa

1 × 2.5ml spoon salt
1 × 5ml spoon baking
  powder
1 × 5ml spoon mixed
  spice
50g cut mixed peel **or**
  coarse-cut marmalade
75g glacé cherries
milk

Coating and Icing (optional)
almond paste (p1231)   royal icing (p1234)

Soak the dried fruit in the brandy, if used, for 2 hours before making the cake. Grease and line a 16cm round cake tin. Cream the fat, sugar, and syrup together thoroughly. Beat the eggs lightly. Sift together the flour (or flour and cocoa), salt, baking powder, and spice. Mix 25–50g of the flour with the dried fruit and peel, if used. Chop the glacé cherries and marmalade, if used. Mix the eggs and the flour alternately into the creamed mixture, beating well between each addition. Mix in lightly the floured fruit, cherries, and peel or marmalade. Mix in just enough milk to make a soft dropping consistency. Turn the mixture into the cake tin and bake in a moderate oven, 180°C, Gas 4, for 25 minutes, reduce the heat to cool, 150°C, Gas 2, and bake for another 2–2½ hours. Coat with almond paste and decorate with royal icing, if liked.

VARIATION
Mother's Cake

Make the cake as above and cover it with almond paste and royal icing. When set, prepare some stiff coloured icing. Decorate the rim of the cake with floral decorations and pipe 'Mother' or 'Mother's Day' across the centre with the icing.

Pineapple Birthday Cake

150g sultanas
200g currants
100g glacé cherries
100g glacé pineapple
100g walnut pieces
100g cut mixed peel
50g ground almonds
grated rind of 1 lemon
1 × 15ml spoon brandy
fat for greasing
200g butter

200g soft light brown
  sugar
250g self-raising flour
a pinch of salt
4 eggs
1 × 2.5ml spoon almond
  essence
1 × 2.5ml spoon vanilla
  essence
2 × 15ml spoons black
  treacle **or** golden syrup

Coating and Icing
almond paste (p1231)   glacé icing (p1225)
royal icing (p1234)   (optional)

Put the sultanas and currants in a bowl. Cut the cherries into 4–6 pieces each, depending on size, and add to the dried fruit. Chop the pineapple, and add with the walnuts, peel, ground almonds, and lemon rind. Add the brandy and stir well; cover and leave while preparing the rest of the mixture.

Grease a 23cm round cake tin and line it with doubled greaseproof paper. Cream the butter and sugar until soft and pale. Sift the flour and salt into a second bowl. Add the eggs to the creamed mixture, one at a time, adding a little flour with each. Stir in, then beat well. Beat in the essences, treacle or syrup, and a little more flour. Lastly, stir in the remaining flour, with the fruit and nuts. Put into the tin and bake in a moderate oven, 180°C, Gas 4, for 1 hour, reduce the heat to very cool, 140°C, Gas 1, and continue cooking for 1¾–2 hours until firm. When the cake is sufficiently brown on top, cover it with greaseproof paper. Coat with almond paste and decorate with royal icing; or ice only with glacé icing.

Christmas Cake (1)

fat for greasing
200g plain flour
½ × 2.5ml spoon salt
1–2 × 5ml spoons mixed
  spice
200g butter
200g caster sugar
6 eggs
2–4 × 15ml spoons
  brandy or sherry

100g glacé cherries
50g preserved ginger
50g walnuts
200g currants
200g sultanas
150g seedless raisins
75g cut mixed peel

Coating and Icing
almond paste (p1231)   *royal icing* (p1234)

Grease and line a 20cm cake tin with doubled greaseproof paper and tie a strip of brown paper round the outside.

Sift the flour, salt, and spice together. Cream the butter and sugar together until light and fluffy. Gradually beat in the eggs and the brandy or sherry. Cut up the cherries, chop the ginger and walnuts, and stir with the dried fruit, peel and the flour into the creamed mixture. Put into the tin and make a slight hollow in the centre. Bake in a warm oven, 160°C, Gas 3, for 45 minutes, reduce the heat to cool, 150°C, Gas 2, and bake for a further hour. Reduce the heat to very cool, 140°C, Gas 1, and continue cooking for 45 minutes–1 hour until firm to the touch. Cool in the tin. Cover with almond paste and decorate with royal icing.

Christmas Cake (2)

fat for greasing
250g plain flour
1 × 5ml spoon instant
  coffee
1 × 5ml spoon mixed
  spice
1 × 2.5ml spoon ground
  ginger
1 × 5ml spoon black
  treacle
200g butter
200g dark brown sugar

4 eggs
1 × 5ml spoon vanilla
  essence
2 × 5ml spoons rum or
  lemon juice
grated rind of 1 lemon
25g blanched almonds
25g glacé cherries
200g currants
200g sultanas
200g seedless raisins
25g cut mixed peel

Coating and Icing
almond paste (p1231)   *royal icing* (p1234)

Grease and line a 20cm cake tin with doubled greaseproof paper and tie a strip of brown paper round the outside.

Sift together the flour, instant coffee, spice, and ginger. Put the opened treacle tin in a pan of hot water to make measuring easier. Cream the butter and sugar together until soft and fluffy. Beat in the eggs gradually, then add the treacle, essence, rum or lemon juice, and the lemon rind. Chop the almonds and quarter the cherries. Stir with the flour and the remaining fruit into the creamed mixture. Put into the tin and make a slight hollow in the centre. Bake in a warm oven, 160°C, Gas 3, for 1 hour, reduce the heat to cool, 150°C, Gas 2, and bake for a further 1½–2 hours until firm to the touch. Cool in the tin. Cover with almond paste and decorate with royal icing.

Devil's Food Cake

fat for greasing
plain flour for dusting
100g butter
350g granulated
  sugar
1 × 5ml spoon vanilla
  essence

3 eggs
275ml cold water
250g plain flour
50g cocoa
3 × 2.5ml spoons
  bicarbonate of soda
1 × 5ml spoon salt

Filling and Decoration
Seafoam Frosting (p1229)

Grease and lightly flour three 20cm sandwich tins. Cream the butter with 225g of the sugar until light, then add the vanilla essence. Separate the eggs, and add the yolks, one at a time, to the creamed mixture alternately with the water, beating well after each addition. Beat in the flour, cocoa, soda, and salt. Whisk the egg whites until soft peaks form, add the remaining sugar and continue whisking until stiff peaks form again. Fold the egg whites into the creamed mixture, lightly but thoroughly. Gently pour one-third of it into each sandwich tin. Bake in a moderate oven, 180°C, Gas 4, for 30–35 minutes or until the cakes are firm in the centre, and have shrunk from the sides of the tins. When cold, fill and frost with Seafoam Frosting.

Note For other chocolate cakes, see Chocolate Sandwich Cake (p1205) and American Chocolate Cake (p1211).

Dundee Cake

fat for greasing
200g plain flour
1 × 2.5ml spoon baking
  powder
½ × 2.5ml spoon salt
150g butter
150g caster sugar
4 eggs
100g glacé cherries

150g currants
150g sultanas
100g seedless raisins
50g cut mixed peel
50g ground almonds
grated rind of 1 lemon
50g blanched split
  almonds

Grease and line an 18cm cake tin. Sift together the flour, baking powder, and salt. Cream the butter and sugar together well, and beat in the eggs. Cut the cherries into quarters. Fold the flour, cherries, dried fruit, peel, and ground almonds into the creamed mixture. Add the lemon rind and mix well. Put into the tin and make a slight hollow in the centre. Bake in a moderate oven, 180°C, Gas 4, for 20 minutes, when the hollow should have filled in. Arrange the split almonds on top. Return the cake to the oven, bake for a further 40–50 minutes, then reduce the heat to warm, 160°C, Gas 3, and bake for another hour.

Hazelnut Cake

fat for greasing
75g hazelnuts
75g self-raising flour
¼ × 5ml spoon salt
75g butter **or**
  margarine

75g caster sugar
1 egg
1 × 15ml spoon strong
  coffee
1 egg white

Filling
coffee butter icing (p1227)

Icing
chocolate glacé icing
  (p1226)

Grease and line a 15cm cake tin. Skin and grind the hazelnuts. Sift the flour and salt together. Cream the fat and sugar until light and fluffy. Separate the egg. Beat the coffee and egg yolk into the creamed mixture. Stir in the ground hazelnuts and flour. Whisk the 2 egg whites until stiff, and fold into the mixture. Turn into the tin and bake in a moderate oven, 180°C, Gas 4, for 45 minutes.

When cool, split the cake, sandwich together with coffee butter icing and cover with chocolate glacé icing.

Hazelnut Meringue Gâteau
See p1045.

Madeira Cake

fat for greasing
150g butter **or**
  margarine
150g caster sugar
4 eggs
200g plain flour
2 × 5ml spoons baking
  powder

a pinch of salt
grated rind of 1 lemon
caster sugar for
  dredging
2 thin slices candied **or**
  glacé citron peel

Grease and line a 15cm cake tin. Cream the fat and sugar together until light and fluffy. Beat the eggs until liquid and add gradually to the creamed mixture, beating well after each addition. Sift the flour, baking powder and salt together, and fold into the creamed mixture. Mix in the lemon rind. Mix well. Turn into the tin. Dredge the top with caster sugar. Bake in a moderate oven, 180°C, Gas 4, for 20 minutes, then lay the slices of peel on top. Bake for a further 45–50 minutes.

Mrs Beeton's Nice Useful Cake

fat for greasing
100g butter **or**
  margarine
100g caster sugar
300g plain flour
2 × 5ml spoons baking
  powder

3 eggs
200ml milk
1 × 2.5ml spoon almond
  essence
50g flaked almonds

Grease and line a 15cm cake tin. Cream the fat and sugar until light and fluffy. Sift together the flour and baking powder. Beat the eggs until liquid with the milk. Add the dry ingredients to the creamed mixture in 3 parts, alternately with the egg and milk. Beat well after each addition. Lightly mix in the almond essence and the flaked almonds. Turn lightly into the tin, and smooth the top level. Bake in a warm oven, 160°C, Gas 3, for $1\frac{1}{4}$–$1\frac{1}{2}$ hours.

American Walnut Cake

fat for greasing
200g self-raising
  flour
$\frac{1}{2}$ × 2.5ml spoon salt
75g chopped walnuts

150g butter **or**
  margarine
150g caster sugar
3 eggs
1 × 15ml spoon milk

Filling
butter cream (1) (p1236),
  adding 50g chopped
  walnuts

Icing
American frosting
  (p1228)

Grease and line an 18cm round cake tin. Mix the flour and salt together. Mix the walnuts with the flour. Cream the fat and sugar until light and fluffy. Beat in the eggs gradually, then stir in the flour and nuts, and the milk. Put into the tin, and smooth level. Bake in a moderate oven, 180°C, Gas 4, for $1\frac{1}{4}$–$1\frac{1}{2}$ hours.

When the cake is cold, split into 3 layers and sandwich together with walnut filling. Cover with American frosting.

Cutting a cake into three layers

Twelfth Night Cake

fat for greasing
150g margarine
75g soft dark brown
  sugar
3 eggs
300g plain flour
4 × 15ml spoons milk
1 × 5ml spoon
  bicarbonate of soda
2 × 15ml spoons golden
  syrup

1 × 2.5ml spoon mixed
  spice
1 × 2.5ml spoon ground
  cinnamon
a pinch of salt
50g currants
100g sultanas
100g cut mixed peel
1 dried bean (see **Note**)
1 large dried whole pea
  (see **Note**)

Grease and line a 15cm round cake tin. Cream the fat and sugar until light and fluffy. Beat in the eggs, one at a time, adding a little flour with each. Warm the milk. Dissolve the bicarbonate of soda in the warmed milk and add the syrup. Mix the spices and salt with the remaining flour. Add this to the creamed mixture alternately with the milk mixture. Mix in the dried fruit and peel lightly, until evenly blended. Place half the cake mixture in the tin, lay the bean and pea in the centre, then cover with the rest of the cake mixture. Bake in a moderate oven, 180°C, Gas 4, for about 2 hours.

Note The tradition of the Twelfth Night Cake goes back to the days of the early Christian Church and beyond. In the Middle Ages, whoever found the bean in his cake became the 'Lord of Misrule' or 'King' for the festivities of Twelfth Night, with the finder of the pea as his 'Queen'. Finding the bean was thought to bring luck. The tradition survived until near the end of the nineteenth century.

Simnel Cake

Dundee Cake mixture
(p1198)

Decoration
double quantity of
  almond paste (p1231)
  or 450g prepared
  marzipan
apricot jam

1 egg
white glacé icing (p1225),
  using 50g icing sugar
Easter decorations

Prepare the Dundee cake recipe. Put half the mixture into the lined 18cm tin. Cut off one-third of the almond paste and roll it into a 17cm round about 1cm thick. Place it on the cake mixture lightly, and put the remaining cake mixture on top. Bake in a moderate oven, 180°C, Gas 4, for 1 hour, reduce the heat to warm, 160°C, Gas 3, and bake for a further $1\frac{1}{2}$ hours. Cool in the tin, then turn on to a wire rack.

Warm, then sieve the apricot jam. When the cake is cold, divide the remaining almond paste into 2 equal portions. Roll one-half into a 17cm round. Brush the top of the cake with the apricot jam and press the almond paste lightly on to it. Trim the edge neatly. Beat the egg until liquid. Make small balls from the remaining paste (11 is the traditional number), and place them round the edge of the cake. Brush the balls with beaten egg and brown under the grill. Pour glacé icing into the centre of the cake and decorate with chickens and Easter eggs.

Three Tier Wedding Cake

If possible, prepare the 3 tiers together, using a very large bowl. Cream the butter and sugar, and mix in the other ingredients by hand. Few ovens are large enough to bake the 3 cakes at the same time; leave the cake(s) awaiting baking in a cool place, overnight if necessary.

Make the cakes at least 2 months before covering and icing them with almond paste and royal icing. For instructions on icing and decorating the cakes, see pp1230–34 and p1239.

If liked, the outside of each un-iced cake can be pricked with a skewer when cooled and sprinkled with a little extra brandy.

To store, wrap the cakes in clean greaseproof paper and a clean tea-towel, and keep in a cool, dry place.

If the top tier of a wedding cake is to be kept for some time (for instance to be used as a christening cake), fresh almond paste and royal icing should be applied when it is used.

Small tier

fat for greasing	$\frac{1}{2} \times 2.5ml$ spoon salt
125g currants	1 × 2.5ml spoon mixed
100g sultanas	spice
100g seedless raisins	1 × 2.5ml spoon ground
50g glacé cherries	nutmeg
25g blanched whole	1 × 15ml spoon treacle
almonds	100g butter
25g cut mixed peel	100g soft dark brown
grated rind of 1 small	sugar
orange	2 large eggs
25ml brandy	25g ground almonds
100g plain flour	

Grease and line a 15cm round or 13cm square cake tin with doubled greaseproof paper and tie a strip of doubled brown paper round the outside.

Pick over the dried fruit, removing any stalks. Chop the cherries and almonds coarsely. Put in a bowl with the peel, orange rind, and dried fruit, add the brandy, and stir well. Cover and put to one side while preparing the rest of the cake mixture.

Sift the flour, salt, and spices together in a mixing bowl. Put the opened treacle tin in a pan of hot water to make measuring easier. Cream the butter and sugar well together until pale and fluffy. Beat the eggs until liquid and add one-quarter at a time, together with a little flour, to the creamed mixture; beat well after each addition. Beat in the treacle. Add the rest of the flour, the ground almonds, and the fruit in brandy, and stir until evenly mixed. Put the mixture in the tin and make a slight hollow in the centre. Bake in a very cool oven, 140°C, Gas 1, for $2\frac{3}{4}$–3 hours, until firm to the touch. Cover with ungreased greaseproof paper after $1\frac{1}{2}$ hours. Cool in the tin. Leave for 24 hours before turning out.

Middle tier

250g currants	1 × 2.5ml spoon salt
200g sultanas	1 × 5ml spoon mixed
200g seedless raisins	spice
100g glacé cherries	1 × 5ml spoon ground
50g blanched whole	nutmeg
almonds	2 × 15ml spoons treacle
50g cut mixed peel	200g butter
grated rind of 1 large	200g soft dark brown
orange	sugar
50ml brandy	4 large eggs
200g plain flour	50g ground almonds

Make as for the small tier. Bake in a prepared 20cm round tin or 18cm square tin, in a very cool oven, 140°C, Gas 1, for 4–$4\frac{1}{2}$ hours. Cover the top with ungreased greaseproof paper when the cake is sufficiently brown. Cool as for the small tier.

Large tier

625g currants	1 × 5ml spoon salt
500g sultanas	1 × 10ml spoon mixed
500g seedless raisins	spice
250g glacé cherries	1 × 10ml spoon ground
125g blanched whole	nutmeg
almonds	75ml treacle
125g cut mixed peel	500g butter
grated rind of 2 large	500g soft dark brown
oranges	sugar
125ml brandy	10 large eggs
500g plain flour	125g ground almonds

Line a 28cm round or 25cm square cake tin with doubled greaseproof paper. Tie at least 3 bands of brown paper round the outside of the tin. Make the cake as for the small tier. Bake in a very cool oven, 140°C, Gas 1, for about $5\frac{1}{2}$ hours. After 2 hours cover the top with doubled greaseproof paper, and give the tin a quarter turn, gently. Turn again after each 30 minutes to avoid overbrowning. Cool as for the small tier.

Small Rich Cakes

(Fairy Cakes)

Basic recipe

Makes 12–14

100g self-raising flour	*100g caster sugar*
a pinch of salt	*2 eggs*
100g butter **or**	*fat for greasing*
margarine	

Heat the oven to moderate, 180°C, Gas 4. Mix the flour and salt. Cream the fat and sugar together until light and fluffy. Beat the eggs until liquid, then beat into the mixture gradually. Stir in the flour and salt lightly. Divide the mixture evenly between 12–14 paper cases or greased bun tins, and bake for 15–20 minutes.

Note If using paper cases, place them in dry bun tins before baking.

VARIATIONS

Cherry Cakes

Add 50g chopped glacé cherries with the flour.

Chocolate Cakes

Add 2 × 15ml spoons cocoa with the flour and add 1 × 15ml spoon milk.

Coconut Cakes

Add 50g desiccated coconut with the flour and 1–2 × 15ml spoons milk with the eggs.

Coffee Cakes

Add 2 × 5ml spoons instant coffee, dissolved in 1 × 5ml spoon water, with the eggs. Add cold.

Queen Cakes

Add 100g currants with the flour.

English Madeleines

Make up the basic mixture and bake in 10 well-greased dariole moulds. Turn out when cooked and allow to cool. Trim off the rounded ends if necessary. Stand upright. Brush with warmed, sieved jam and toss in coconut. Decorate the top of each with half a glacé cherry and angelica leaves.

Note A recipe for Madeleines de Commercy can be found on p1503.

Butterfly Cakes

Makes 12–14

basic Small Rich Cakes mixture

Decoration

1 × 5ml spoon caster sugar	*1 × 142ml carton double cream*
½ × 2.5ml spoon vanilla essence	*icing sugar for dusting*

Make and bake the cakes in bun tins as directed, and leave to cool.

Meanwhile, add the caster sugar and the vanilla essence to the cream and whip until stiff. Transfer to a forcing bag with a large star nozzle.

When the cakes are cold, cut a round off the top of each and cut these in half. Pipe a star of cream on each cake. Place the two halves of each round upright, cut side down, in the cream to resemble wings. Dust lightly with icing sugar.

VARIATION

Chocolate Butterflies

Make and bake small chocolate cakes as directed. Pipe with vanilla butter icing, using 50g butter (p1227), then finish as above.

Apricot Baskets

Makes 12–14

basic Small Rich Cakes
  mixture (p1202)

Decoration

1 × 425g can apricot *halves*	*1 × 142ml carton double* *cream*
¼ × 500ml pkt lemon *jelly*	*1 × 5ml spoon caster* *sugar*
1 × 15cm piece angelica	

Make and bake the cakes in bun tins as directed on p1202, and leave to cool.

Meanwhile, drain the apricots and heat 125ml of the syrup to boiling point. Pour it on to the jelly cubes and stir until dissolved. Leave to cool. Soak the angelica in a little hot water until pliable, drain, and pat dry on soft kitchen paper. Cut into strips 5mm wide. Whip the cream and sugar until stiff.

When the cakes are cold and the jelly is just starting to set, place half an apricot on the top of each cake, rounded side uppermost. Coat each apricot with jelly. Using a forcing bag with a small star nozzle, pipe stars of cream around the apricots. Arch the strips of angelica over the cakes to form handles, pushing them into the sides of the cakes.

Cork Cakes

Makes 12–14

basic Small Rich Cakes
  mixture (p1202)

Decoration

15g pistachio nuts	
apricot glaze (p1234)	*1 × 142ml carton double* *cream*
	icing sugar for dusting

Make and bake the cakes in bun tins as directed on p1202.

When cold, remove a small round piece about 1.5cm deep from the centre of each cake, using an apple corer or small cutter. Blanch and chop the pistachio nuts. Brush the tops of the corks with apricot glaze and dip into the chopped nuts. Put the remaining apricot glaze in the hollowed centres of the cakes. Whip the cream until stiff and put it in a forcing bag with a star nozzle about 1.5cm in diameter. Pipe a star of cream on the glaze in the centre of each cake and press the corks lightly into it. Dust with a little icing sugar.

Swiss Shortcakes

Makes 16

150g butter	*a few drops vanilla* *essence*
50g caster sugar	
150g plain flour	

Decoration

glacé cherries	*smooth red jam*
angelica	

Heat the oven to moderate, 180°C, Gas 4. Cream the butter and sugar until light and fluffy. Work in the flour and essence. Place 16 paper cases in dry bun tins, and pipe the mixture in whorls into the cases; use a forcing bag with a large star nozzle. Bake for 15–20 minutes. Decorate with glacé cherries and angelica kept in place with a tiny dab of jam.

VARIATION

Substitute icing sugar for the caster sugar. Use ½ × 2.5ml spoon vanilla essence. Decorate the un-cooked shortcakes with glacé cherries, if liked. Bake in 22–24 paper cases for 20–25 minutes. When cold, dredge with icing sugar.

Piping the cake mixture in whorls

Brown Almond Shortcakes

Makes 8 wedges

75g butter
40g soft dark brown
 sugar
100g wholemeal flour

$\frac{1}{2} \times 2.5ml$ spoon salt
25g ground almonds
fat for greasing

Cream the butter and sugar until light and fluffy. Mix the flour and salt and work it into the creamed mixture with the ground almonds, until the dough is smooth. Press into a greased 15cm round sandwich tin. Bake in a warm oven, 160°C, Gas 3, for 50 minutes. Cut into 8 wedges while still warm. Cool in the tin.

Note For Shortbread, see p1216.

Brownies (1)

Makes 9 (approx)

fat for greasing
150g margarine
150g caster sugar
2 eggs

50g plain flour
2 × 15ml spoons cocoa
100g chopped walnuts

Grease and line a shallow 15cm square tin. Cream the fat and sugar until light and fluffy. Beat in the eggs. Sift together the flour and cocoa, and fold in. Chop the walnuts finely, and add half of them to the mixture. Spread evenly in the tin and bake in a moderate oven, 180°C, Gas 4, for 10 minutes; then sprinkle the rest of the walnuts all over the surface. Bake for a further 15 minutes. Cool in the tin. When cold, cut into squares.

Note The texture of Brownies should be the same as that of a fruit cake. When cooked, the top crust should just be firm to the touch, the inside soft or moist. Do not overbake them.

Brownies (2)

Makes 16–25 (approx)

fat for greasing
125g plain flour
$\frac{1}{2} \times 2.5ml$ spoon baking
 powder
$\frac{1}{2} \times 2.5ml$ spoon salt
100g butter

100g plain chocolate
100g granulated sugar
1 egg
1 × 5ml spoon vanilla
 essence
75g walnut pieces

Grease and line a 20cm square tin. Sift together the flour, baking powder, and salt. Melt the butter and chocolate in a medium-sized pan, remove from the heat and stir in the sugar. Beat the egg until liquid and blend it into the chocolate mixture. Add the vanilla essence. Chop the walnuts and stir in with the dry ingredients; mix well. Spread evenly in the tin. Bake in a moderate oven, 180°C, Gas 4, for 30–40 minutes.

Mushroom Cakes

Makes 12–14

basic Small Rich Cakes
 mixture (p1202)

Decoration
apricot glaze (p1234)
almond paste (p1231),
 using 75g almonds
ground cinnamon for
 dusting

icing sugar for dusting
butter icing (p1227)
 using 50g butter

Make and bake the cakes in bun tins as directed on p1202. Leave until cold.

Brush the sides and tops with apricot glaze. Roll out the almond paste thinly, and cut into rounds large enough to cover the top and sides of the cakes; press them into position. Mix the cinnamon and icing sugar together and place on a sheet of greaseproof paper. Roll the almond paste covered surface of the cakes in this. Put the butter icing in a forcing bag with a small star nozzle, and pipe threads on the flat surface of each cake radiating from the centre to the edge, to represent 'gills'. Use the almond paste trimmings to make tiny 'stalks' and place these in the centre of each cake, making a small hole with a skewer if necessary.

SANDWICH CAKES

Victoria Sandwich Cake (1)

fat for greasing
150g butter **or**
  margarine
150g caster sugar
3 eggs

150g self-raising flour
  or *plain flour and*
  1 × 5ml spoon baking
  powder
a pinch of salt
raspberry **or** *other jam*
  for filling
caster sugar for dredging

Grease and line two 18cm sandwich tins. Cream the fat and sugar together until light and fluffy. Beat the eggs until liquid, and add them gradually, beating well after each addition. Sift together the flour, salt, and baking powder, if used. Stir into the mixture, lightly but thoroughly, until evenly mixed. Divide between the tins and bake in a moderate oven, 180°C, Gas 4, for 25–30 minutes. When cold, sandwich together with jam, and sprinkle the top with caster sugar.

Note The original Victoria Sandwich Cake was oblong, filled with jam or marmalade, and cut into fingers or sandwiches. Now, the basic mixture is used with many different flavourings and fillings, and is served as a single, round cake.

For One-stage Victoria Sandwich Cake see p1211.

For Victoria Sandwich Cake (2) made with a mixer, see p1419.

VARIATIONS

The cake can be baked in a 20cm tin for 40 minutes, cooled, then split and filled. This gives a softer centred cake. All loose crumbs must be brushed off the cut sides before filling. Too moist a filling will seep into the cake.

Chocolate Sandwich Cake

Use 125g self-raising flour and 25g cocoa, and add a few drops of vanilla essence with the eggs. Fill with chocolate butter icing (p1227).

Coffee Sandwich Cake

Add 1 × 15ml spoon instant coffee dissolved in 1 × 10ml spoon water. Fill with coffee butter icing (p1227).

Orange or Lemon Sandwich Cake

Add the grated rind of 1 orange or lemon to the creamed fat and sugar. Fill with orange or lemon butter icing (p1227).

Small Victoria Sandwich Cake

Make the cake in two 15cm sandwich tins. Use only 100g fat, 100g sugar, 2 eggs, 100g self-raising flour, and a pinch of salt.

Iced Sandwich Cake (1)

1 small Victoria
  Sandwich Cake

Filling
butter icing (p1227),
  using 50g butter

colouring
flavouring

Icing
glacé icing (p1225), *using*
  200g icing sugar

Colour and flavour the butter icing as liked, and use just over half to sandwich the 2 layers of the cake together.

Place the cake on a cooling tray over a plate and brush off any loose crumbs with a pastry brush. Make up the glacé icing so that it coats the back of a wooden spoon thickly. Pour it over the top of the cake, starting in the centre and allowing it to run down the sides. If necessary, smooth the icing over the sides with a round-bladed knife dipped in hot water, so that the sides are completely covered. Leave to set, then use the remaining butter icing to decorate the top of the cake.

Iced Sandwich Cake (2)

*1 × 20cm Victoria
  Sandwich Cake (p1205)*

Filling
butter icing (p1227)

Coating
*4 × 15ml spoons sifted,
  dried, lightly browned
  cake crumbs, toasted
  coconut (p1235)* **or**
chopped walnuts

Decoration
*glacé icing (p1225), using
  125g icing sugar*

Cut the cake in half crossways and sandwich the 2 halves together with just less than half the butter icing. Place the crumbs, coconut or nuts on a piece of greaseproof paper. Coat the sides of the cake with the remaining butter icing and roll in the coating, pressing it into place. Make up the glacé icing and surround the cake with a paper band. Pour the icing into the centre of the cake and smooth it all over the top. Leave to set.

Note If liked, decorate the top of the cake with halved walnuts; or make up a little extra butter icing, using 25g butter, and pipe stars round the edge of the cake.

Feather-Iced Sandwich Cake

*1 × 20cm Victoria
  Sandwich Cake (p1205)*

Decoration
*white butter icing
  (p1227), using 50g
  butter
browned cake crumbs*

*glacé icing (p1225), using
  150g icing sugar
food colouring*

Coat the sides of the cake with the butter icing and roll in the browned crumbs as for Iced Sandwich Cake (2). Decorate the cake with Feather Icing (p1225).

Orange Sandwich Cake

*1 Victoria Sandwich
  Cake (p1205)*

Filling and Decoration
*orange butter icing
  (p1227)*

crystallized orange slices

Sandwich the 2 cake layers with just under half the butter icing. Spread the rest of the icing on top of the cake, smooth with a hot, wet knife and decorate with the orange slices.

Note A Lemon sandwich is made in the same way, using lemon butter icing and lemon slices. For a stronger orange or lemon flavour, use the Orange or Lemon Sandwich Cake mixture on p1205.

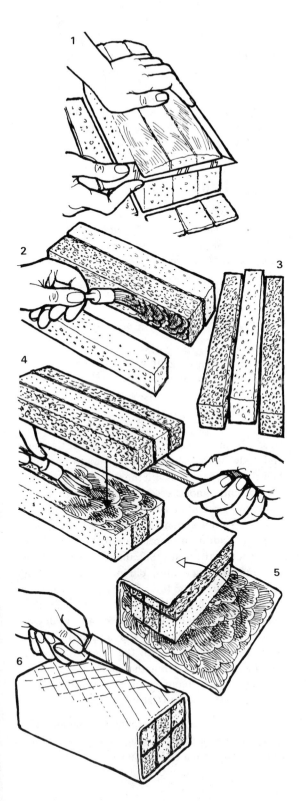

Battenburg Cake

fat for greasing	*2 eggs*
100g self-raising flour	*pink food colouring*
a pinch of salt	*apricot glaze (p1234)*
100g butter **or**	*200g almond paste*
margarine	*(p1231)*
100g caster sugar	

Decoration (optional)
glacé cherries   *angelica*

Grease and line a Battenburg tin, 22 × 18cm, which has a metal divider down the centre; or use a 22 × 18cm tin and cut double greaseproof paper to separate the mixture into 2 parts. Mix the flour and salt together. Cream the fat and sugar together until light and fluffy. Add the eggs, one at a time with a little flour, stir in, then beat well. Stir in the remaining flour lightly but thoroughly. Place half the mixture in one half of the tin. Tint the remaining mixture pink, and place it in the other half of the tin. Smooth both mixtures away from the centre towards the outside of the tin. Bake in a fairly hot oven, 190°C, Gas 5, for 25–30 minutes. Leave the cakes in the tin for a few minutes, then transfer them to a wire rack and peel off the paper. Leave to cool completely.

To finish the cake, cut each slab of cake into 3 strips lengthways. Trim off any crisp edges and rounded surfaces so that all 6 strips are neat and the same size. Arrange 3 strips with 1 pink strip in the middle. Brush the touching sides with the glaze and press together lightly. Make up the other layer in the same way, using 2 pink with 1 plain strip in the middle. Brush glaze over the top of 1 layer and place the other on this.

Roll out the almond paste thinly into a rectangle the same length as the strips and wide enough to wrap round them. Brush it with glaze and place the cake in the centre. Wrap the paste round the cake and press the edges together lightly. Turn so that the join is underneath; trim the ends. Mark the top of the paste with the back of a knife to make a criss-cross pattern. Decorate with glacé cherries and angelica, if liked.

CAKES MADE BY THE WHISKING METHOD

These fall into 2 broad categories: true sponge cakes which contain no fat, and Genoese sponge mixtures which are made with melted fat.

Sponge Cake

Basic recipe

fat for greasing
flour for dusting
caster sugar for dusting
3 eggs
75g caster sugar

75g plain flour
a pinch of salt
a pinch of baking
* powder*

Grease an 18cm round cake tin or two 15cm sandwich tins. Mix small equal quantities of sifted flour and caster sugar and use to dust the sides and base of the tins.

Whisk the eggs and sugar together in a bowl over a pan of hot water, taking care that the base of the bowl does not touch the water. Continue whisking for 10–15 minutes until thick and creamy. Remove the bowl from the pan. Whisk until cold. Sift and fold in the flour, salt, and baking powder, using a metal spoon. Do this lightly, so that the air incorporated during whisking is not lost. Pour the mixture into the prepared tins. Bake in a moderate oven, 180°C, Gas 4, for 40 minutes in an 18cm tin, or for 25 minutes in two 15cm tins. Leave the sponge in the tins for a few minutes, then turn on to a cooling rack and leave until cold.

Note If an electric mixer is used, there is no need to place the bowl over hot water. Whisk at high speed for about 5 minutes until thick. Fold in the flour by hand.

VARIATION

Mrs Beeton's Savoy Cakes or Sponge Fingers (1)

Prepare a baking sheet by greasing and then dredging with caster sugar and flour. Make the sponge mixture and put it in a forcing bag with a 1.5cm plain nozzle. Pipe out about 14 fingers, 8–9cm long. Dredge with caster sugar and bake in a moderate oven, 180°C, Gas 4, for 7–10 minutes.

Note Special sponge finger tins can be used, prepared as above. Fill three-quarters full, dredge with sugar and bake for 10–12 minutes.

For Sponge Fingers (2) see p1223.

Angel Food Cake

flour for dusting
100g plain flour
300g caster sugar
12 egg whites (making
* 300ml egg white when*
* measured)*
3 × 2.5ml spoons cream
* of tartar*

½ × 2.5ml spoon salt
1 × 5ml spoon vanilla
* essence*
1 × 2.5ml spoon almond
* essence*

Decoration
Seafoam Frosting (p1229)
* made with caster sugar*
* **or** Maraschino Glaze*
(p1234)

Dust a 25cm ring cake tin with flour. Sift the flour and 150g of the sugar 6 times; put to one side. Whisk the egg whites with the cream of tartar, salt, vanilla, and almond essence until they form soft peaks but are still moist. Add the remaining 150g sugar, 2 × 15ml spoons at a time, whisking well after each addition; continue whisking until the whites form stiff peaks. Sift about a quarter of the flour over the egg whites; fold in. Repeat the sifting and folding in of the flour 3 more times. Turn the cake mixture into the floured tin and bake in a fairly hot oven, 190°C, Gas 5, for 35–40 minutes, or until the cake is golden on top, and springs back when lightly pressed with the finger. Cool on a wire rack without turning the cake out.

When cold, turn out and decorate with Seafoam Frosting or Maraschino Glaze.

Note If a 25cm ring or tube cake tin or mould is not available, use a greased 450g jam jar set in the centre of an ordinary 25cm cake tin.

Swiss Roll (1)

fat for greasing
3 eggs
75g caster sugar
1 × 2.5ml spoon baking
  powder
75g plain flour

a pinch of salt
jam **or** butter cream
  (p1236)
caster sugar for dusting

Heat the oven to hot, 220°C, Gas 7. Grease and line a Swiss roll tin 20 × 30cm. Whisk the eggs and sugar together in a bowl over a pan of hot water, taking care that the base does not touch the water. Whisk for 10–15 minutes until thick and creamy. Remove from the pan and whisk until cold. Sift the baking powder with the flour and salt, and fold in lightly. Pour into the prepared tin and bake for 10 minutes. Meanwhile, warm the jam, if used.

When the cake is cooked, turn it on to a large sheet of greaseproof paper dusted with caster sugar. Peel off the lining paper. Trim off any crisp edges. Spread the cake with the warmed jam and roll up tightly. Dredge with caster sugar and place on a cooling rack with the cut edge underneath.

Note If the Swiss roll is to be filled with butter cream, cover with greaseproof paper and roll up tightly with the paper inside. Cool completely. When cold, unroll carefully, spread with the filling, and re-roll. Dust with caster sugar.

For Swiss Roll (2) made with a mixer, see p1419.

VARIATION

Chocolate Swiss Roll

Use the recipe for Swiss roll but substitute 1 × 15ml spoon cocoa for 1 × 15ml spoon of flour. When cooked, roll up with greaseproof paper inside. When cold, prepare chocolate butter icing (p1227). Unroll carefully, spread with just over half the butter icing and roll up. Spread the remainder over the top and, if liked, mark with a fork to resemble a log.

For a Yule log, put a robin or sprig of holly on top of the roll.

Genoese Sponge or Pastry (1)

fat for greasing
100g plain flour
1 × 2.5ml spoon salt
75g clarified butter
  (p886) **or** margarine

4 eggs
100g caster sugar

Grease and line a 20 × 30cm Swiss roll tin. Sift together the flour and salt, and put in a warm place. Melt the fat without letting it get hot. Put to one side. Whisk the eggs lightly, add the sugar, and whisk over hot water for 10–15 minutes until thick. Remove from the heat; the fat should be as cool as the egg mixture. Remove from the heat and continue whisking until at blood-heat. Sift half the flour over the eggs, then pour in half the fat in a thin stream. Fold in gently. Repeat, using the remaining flour and fat. Turn gently into the tin, and bake in a moderate oven, 180°C, Gas 4, for 30–40 minutes.

Genoese Sponge or Pastry (2)

Make as for Genoese Sponge (1), using 75g flour, a pinch of salt, 50g clarified butter or margarine, 3 eggs, and 75g caster sugar. Bake in an 18cm square or 15 × 25cm oblong cake tin.

Mayfair Cakes

Makes 18

Genoese Sponge (1)

Decoration
1 × 284ml carton
  double cream
2 × 5ml spoons caster
  sugar

chocolate vermicelli

Cut the cold sponge into about eighteen 4cm rounds. Whip the cream with the sugar until fairly stiff and use to spread the top and sides of each cake. Coat with the chocolate vermicelli, pressing it on lightly with a round-bladed knife. Using a forcing bag with a large rose nozzle, pipe the remaining cream on to each cake in a star.

Cauliflower Cakes

Makes 18 (approx)

Genoese Sponge (1)

Decoration
green food colouring	*1 × 142ml carton double*
almond paste (p1231),	*cream*
using 200g almonds	*1 × 5ml spoon caster*
apricot glaze (p1234)	*sugar*

Cut out about eighteen 4cm rounds from the cold sponge. Work a few drops of green colouring into the almond paste. Roll it out thinly and cut out five 4cm rounds for each cake. Brush the sides of the cakes with apricot glaze, and press the circles of almond paste round the sides of each cake, over-lapping them slightly. Bend the centre top of each piece outward slightly to represent cauliflower 'leaves'. Whip the cream and the sugar until stiff. Using a forcing bag with a small star nozzle, pipe tiny rosettes of cream on top of each to represent the cauliflower head.

Mocha Fingers

Makes 20

Genoese Sponge (2)
baked in a 15 × 25cm
tin

Decoration
50g browned almonds	*icing sugar for dredging*
(p1185)	
coffee butter icing	
(p1227), *using 50g*	
butter	

Shred the browned almonds. Spread the top of the cold sponge with the butter icing. Cover with the browned almonds and press in well. Dredge the top with icing sugar. Cut the cake in half lengthways, then cut each strip into ten 2cm fingers.

French Cakes or Iced Petits Fours

Makes 18–24

Genoese Sponge (1) **or**
(2) baked in an oblong
tin

Filling
jam, lemon curd **or**
butter icing (p1227),
using 50g butter

Icing
glacé icing (p1225)	*food colouring*

Decoration
crystallized violets,
silver balls, glacé
fruits, angelica,
chopped nuts, etc

Cut the cold sponge through the centre crossways; spread with the chosen filling and sandwich to-gether again. Cut the cake into small rounds, tri-angles or squares, and place these small cakes on a wire rack over a large dish. Brush off any loose crumbs. Make up the icing to a coating consistency which will flow easily. Tint some of it with different colourings. Using a small spoon, coat the top and sides of the cakes with the icing or, if preferred, pour it over the cakes, making sure that the sides are coated evenly all over. Place the decorations on the tops and leave to set. The cakes can be served in paper cases.

ONE-STAGE CAKES

The success of this method depends on using all the ingredients at room temperature. Some recipes include extra baking powder; while this increases the volume, it makes the texture drier.

One-stage Victoria Sandwich Cake

fat for greasing
150g self-raising flour
a pinch of salt
150g soft tub margarine
150g caster sugar
3 eggs

Grease two 18cm sandwich tins and line the bases with greaseproof paper. Put all the ingredients in a bowl, stir, then beat until smooth, 2–3 minutes by hand, or 1–1½ minutes with an electric mixer. Divide the mixture evenly between the tins, and smooth level. Bake in a moderate oven, 180°C, Gas 4, for 25–30 minutes until golden-brown and firm to the touch.

Note For a traditional Victoria Sandwich Cake, see p1205.

One-stage Fruit Cake

fat for greasing
100g glacé cherries
200g self-raising flour
1 × 5ml spoon mixed spice (optional)
125g soft tub margarine
100g currants
75g sultanas
25g cut mixed peel
125g soft brown sugar
2 eggs
75ml milk

Grease and line an 18cm round cake tin. Chop the cherries, then mix the flour and spice, if used. Put all the ingredients in a bowl, stir, then beat until smooth, 2–3 minutes by hand or 1–1½ minutes with an electric mixer. Turn the mixture into the tin and smooth level. Bake in a cool oven, 150°C, Gas 2, for 2 hours.

One-stage Cherry Cake

fat for greasing
225g glacé cherries
175g soft tub margarine
175g caster sugar
3 eggs
225g plain flour
1½ × 5ml spoons baking powder
50g ground almonds (optional)

Grease and line an 18cm round cake tin. Wash, dry, and halve the cherries. Put all the ingredients in a bowl and beat for 2–3 minutes until well mixed. Turn into the tin and bake in a warm oven, 160°C, Gas 3, for 1½–1¾ hours.

American Chocolate Cake

fat for greasing
flour for dusting
200g plain flour
300g caster sugar
50g cocoa
2 × 5ml spoons bicarbonate of soda
1 × 5ml spoon salt
100g soft tub margarine
200ml milk
2 eggs
1 × 5ml spoon vanilla essence

Filling
chocolate butter cream
  (p1236)

Grease two 20cm sandwich tins or an oblong tin 33 × 24 × 5cm. Line the base with greaseproof paper and dust with flour.

Sift together all the dry ingredients. Add the margarine and 175ml of the milk. Stir, then beat well until smooth, 2 minutes by hand or 1–1½ minutes with an electric mixer. Add the remaining milk, the eggs and essence, and beat for a further minute. Turn into the tins and bake in a moderate oven, 180°C, Gas 4, for 35–40 minutes in the 2 tins, or 40–45 minutes in the oblong tin. When done, the cakes should be firm to the touch. Leave to cool until firm before turning out on to a cooling rack.

When cold, split the oblong cake into 2 layers crossways, and sandwich together with just under half the butter cream. Sandwich the 2 rounds together in the same way. Swirl the rest of the butter cream on top of the cakes.

Note For other chocolate cakes, see Devil's Food Cake (p1198) and Chocolate Sandwich Cake (p1205).

MISCELLANEOUS CAKES MADE WITH FRUIT OR NUTS

For Apple Strudel, Eccles, Banbury and Sly Cakes, see the chapter on Pastry Making and Pastry Goods.

Danish Almond Cake

fat for greasing	*300g caster sugar*
125g butter	*200g plain flour*
1½ × 15ml spoons top of	*2 × 5ml spoons baking*
the milk	*powder*
4 eggs	

Topping

50g blanched almonds	*1 × 15ml spoon single*
75g unsalted butter	*cream*
75g caster sugar	*1 × 15ml spoon plain*
	flour

Grease and line a 20cm shallow tin. Melt the butter, remove from the heat, and stir in the milk. Leave to cool. Whisk the eggs with the sugar until light and foamy. Mix the flour and baking powder into the eggs, alternately with the melted butter. Pour the mixture into the tin. Bake in a fairly hot oven, 200°C, Gas 6, for 35 minutes.

Meanwhile, make the topping. Chop the almonds coarsely. Mix with the other ingredients in a saucepan. Bring to the boil, then pour over the cake while still hot. (Place a tablespoon on top of the cake first to test whether it can bear the weight.)

Return the cake to the oven and bake for a further 10 minutes.

Mrs Beeton's Coconut Pyramids

Makes 12

fat for greasing	*150g caster sugar*
2 egg whites	*150g desiccated coconut*

Grease a baking sheet and cover with rice paper. Whisk the egg whites until stiff, then fold in the sugar and coconut, using a metal spoon. Divide the mixture into 12 portions and place in heaps on the rice paper. Using a fork, form into pyramid shapes. Bake in a very cool oven, 140°C, Gas 1, for 45 minutes–1 hour until pale brown in colour.

Date and Walnut Loaf

275g plain flour	*2 × 15ml spoons oil*
50g cornflour	*1 large egg*
150g caster sugar	*2 × 5ml spoons*
1 × 5ml spoon salt	*bicarbonate of soda*
50g walnuts	*250ml boiling water*
225g cooking dates	*fat for greasing*

Sift the flour, cornflour, sugar, and salt into a bowl. Chop the walnuts and dates and add to the dry ingredients. Whisk together the oil and egg and add to the flour, fruit, and nuts. Dissolve the bicarbonate of soda in the boiling water, and stir into the other ingredients. Beat well to a soft consistency. Pour into a greased 23 × 13 × 7cm loaf tin and bake in a moderate oven, 180°C, Gas 4, for about 1 hour until firm to the touch. Leave to cool slightly before turning out of the tin.

Serve sliced, spread with butter, if liked.

Note For Date and Walnut Cake, see p1187. For other sweet tea breads, see pp1171–75.

Lekach
(Honey Cake)

fat for greasing	*1 × 5ml spoon ground*
flour for dusting	*ginger*
150g caster sugar	*1 × 5ml spoon*
2 eggs	*bicarbonate of soda*
2 × 15ml spoons corn oil	*1 × 2.5ml spoon mixed*
200g honey or golden	*spice*
syrup	*150ml warm water*
300g plain flour	*100g blanched halved*
1 × 5ml spoon baking	*almonds*
powder	

Grease a 25cm square shallow tin and dust with flour. Beat the sugar and eggs together well. Add the oil and honey or syrup, and mix thoroughly. Sift the flour with all the other dry ingredients and add alternately with the warm water to the honey mixture. Mix in the almonds. Pour into the tin and bake in a moderate oven, 180°C, Gas 4, for 1 hour or until a skewer comes out clean when the cake is pierced.

Mrs Beeton's Nice Yeast Cake

50g butter	*100g soft brown sugar*
2 eggs	*25g fresh yeast*
125ml milk	*150g currants*
300g plain flour	*50g cut mixed peel*

Melt the butter and leave to cool. Add the eggs and milk and whisk until frothy. Put the flour and sugar into a large bowl. Blend the yeast with a little warm water and leave to froth. Make a hollow in the flour mixture and pour in the yeast. Add the butter and egg mixture, and mix well. Knead to a smooth, soft dough. Cover with a damp cloth, and leave to rise for about 1½ hours or until the dough is doubled in size. Add the dried fruit and peel, and knead until it is well distributed. Put into a 15–18cm lined cake tin, and leave to rise for 30 minutes. Bake in a fairly hot oven, 200°C, Gas 6, for 30 minutes. Reduce the temperature to warm, 160°C, Gas 3, and bake for a further 1 hour.

Note Other sweet yeasted recipes, eg Bath Buns, Chelsea Buns, can be found on pp1164–69.

Pineapple Upside-Down Cake

1 × 227g can pineapple rings	*450g self-raising flour*
100g butter	*1 × 5ml spoon ground cinnamon*
275g soft dark brown sugar	*1 × 5ml spoon ground nutmeg*
8 maraschino or glacé cherries	*2 eggs*
	250ml milk

Drain the pineapple rings, reserving the syrup. Melt 50g of the butter in a 20cm square baking tin. Add 125g of the sugar and 1 × 15ml spoon of pineapple syrup; mix well. Arrange the pineapple rings in an even pattern in the bottom of the tin, and place a cherry in the centre of each ring.

Sift together the flour, cinnamon, and nutmeg.

Beat the eggs with the remaining brown sugar. Melt the remaining butter and add to the eggs and sugar with the milk; mix into the spiced flour. Pour this mixture carefully over the fruit in the baking tin without disturbing it. Bake in a moderate oven, 180°C, Gas 4, for 45–50 minutes. Remove the tin from the oven and at once turn upside-down on to a plate; allow the caramel to run over the cake before removing the baking tin.

Serve warm with cream as a dessert, or cold for afternoon tea.

Mousseline Cake
See p885.

Biscuits

Rubbed-in Biscuits

Basic recipe

Makes 24–26

200g plain flour	*1 × 5ml spoon baking powder*
½ × 2.5ml spoon salt	*1 egg yolk*
75–100g butter or margarine	*flour for rolling out*
50g caster sugar	*fat for greasing*

Heat the oven to moderate, 180°C, Gas 4. Mix the flour and salt together. Rub in the fat, stir in the sugar and baking powder. Bind to a stiff paste with the egg yolk. Knead well and roll out just under 1cm thick on a lightly floured surface. Cut into rounds with a 5cm cutter. Re-roll and re-cut any trimmings. Place on a greased baking sheet. Prick the top of each biscuit in 2 or 3 places. Bake for 15–20 minutes or until firm to the touch and pale golden-brown. Leave to stand for a few minutes, then cool on a wire rack.

For **variations**, see over.

VARIATIONS

Plain Chocolate Biscuits

Add 50g powdered drinking chocolate and 2 × 5ml spoons instant coffee dissolved in 3 × 2.5ml spoons water.

Plain Cinnamon or Spice Biscuits

Add 1 × 5ml spoon ground cinnamon or mixed spice to the flour. When cold, sandwich 2 biscuits together with jam, and dredge with icing sugar.

Plain Coconut Biscuits

Use 150g flour and 50g desiccated coconut. As soon as the biscuits are cooked, brush with warm jam glaze (p1234) and sprinkle with coconut.

Almond Fingers

Makes 14 (approx)

150g plain flour	*1 × 5ml spoon baking*
50g ground almonds	*powder*
¼ × 2.5ml spoon salt	*1 egg yolk*
75–100g butter **or**	*flour for rolling out*
margarine	*fat for greasing*
50g caster sugar	

Topping

1 egg white	*50g nibbed almonds*
75g icing sugar	*raspberry jam*

Heat the oven to moderate, 180°C, Gas 4. Mix together the flour, ground almonds, and salt. Rub in the fat, stir in the sugar and baking powder. Bind to a stiff paste with the yolk. Knead well and roll into a strip 8cm wide. Prick the surface well. Transfer to a greased baking sheet and pinch the long edges to decorate. Bake for 15 minutes.

Meanwhile, make the topping. Whisk the egg white until it stands up in peaks, and fold in the sugar and almonds. Remove the baked base from the oven and spread with raspberry jam. Spread the topping over the jam, and return to the oven for 7–10 minutes, until the meringue is set and lightly browned. Cut into fingers while still warm.

Catherine Wheel Biscuits

Makes 24 (approx)

150g plain flour	*a few drops vanilla*
½ × 2.5ml spoon salt	*essence*
1 × 5ml spoon baking	*25ml water*
powder	*1 × 5ml spoon cocoa*
75g butter	*flour for rolling out*
75g caster sugar	*fat for greasing*

Sift together the flour, salt, and baking powder into a mixing bowl. Rub in the butter, and stir in the sugar. Make the mixture into a pliable paste with the essence and water. Divide the paste into 2 equal portions. Put 1 portion back in the mixing bowl. Sprinkle the cocoa over it and work it in evenly, using a fork.

Roll out the plain paste on a lightly floured surface into a rectangle 18 × 22cm. Put to one side. Roll out the chocolate paste to the same size and place it on top of the plain piece. Roll lightly with the rolling-pin to make them stick together. Roll up both pieces from the long side, like a Swiss roll, keeping the join underneath. Chill until firm.

Heat the oven to moderate, 180°C, Gas 4. Cut the paste into slices 1cm thick. Reshape into neat rounds with the hands and place on a greased baking sheet, spaced well apart. Bake for 15–20 minutes until the plain biscuit mixture is golden-brown.

Cinnamon Bars

Makes 20 (approx)

175g plain flour	*fat for greasing*
½ × 2.5ml spoon ground	*25g flaked almonds*
cinnamon	*1 × 15ml spoon*
50g caster sugar	*granulated sugar*
125g butter	

Heat the oven to moderate, 180°C, Gas 4. Sift the flour and cinnamon into a bowl and add the caster sugar. Rub in the butter, and work into a soft dough. Press the mixture into a greased Swiss roll tin. Flatten and level the surface. Sprinkle with the flaked almonds and granulated sugar. Bake for 15–20 minutes until golden-brown. Cut into bars or fingers while still warm.

Coffee Kisses

Makes 12 pairs (approx)

75g butter **or** margarine
150g self-raising flour
50g caster sugar
1 egg yolk

1 × 5ml spoon liquid
  coffee essence
fat for greasing

Filling
coffee butter icing
  (p1227)

icing sugar for dusting
  (optional)

Heat the oven to fairly hot, 190°C, Gas 5. Rub the fat into the flour, then stir in the sugar. Mix the egg yolk with the coffee essence and use to bind the dry ingredients together to a stiff paste. Roll the mixture into balls about the size of a walnut and place on a greased baking sheet. Bake for 10 minutes. When cooked, leave to cool on a wire rack.

Use the coffee butter icing to sandwich the biscuits together in pairs. If liked, dust with icing sugar.

Digestive Biscuits

Makes 12 (approx)

75g wholemeal flour
25g plain white flour
25g fine **or** medium
  oatmeal
1 × 2.5ml spoon baking
  powder
$\frac{1}{2}$ × 2.5ml spoon salt

1 × 15ml spoon soft light
  brown sugar
50g butter **or** margarine
2 × 15ml spoons milk
flour for rolling out
fat for greasing

Heat the oven to moderate, 180°C, Gas 4. Mix all the dry ingredients, sifting the sugar if it is lumpy. Rub in the fat and mix to a pliable dough with the milk. Knead lightly on a floured board and roll out just under 5mm thick. Cut into rounds with a 6cm round cutter, place on a greased baking sheet and prick with a fork. Bake for 15 minutes.

German or Spice Biscuits

Makes 12 (approx)

125g plain flour
50g caster sugar
$\frac{1}{2}$ × 2.5ml spoon mixed
  spice

75g margarine
flour for rolling out
fat for greasing

Heat the oven to warm, 160°C, Gas 3. Mix the flour, sugar, and spice together. Rub in the margarine until the mixture binds together and makes a pliable paste. Roll out on a floured board to 5mm thick, and cut into rounds with a 6cm round cutter. Place on a greased baking sheet. Bake for about 20 minutes until very pale golden-brown.

Jumbles

Makes 20

50g plain flour
a pinch of salt
50g caster sugar
40g butter **or** margarine

1 × 10ml spoon beaten
  egg
flour for rolling out
fat for greasing

Heat the oven to warm, 160°C, Gas 3. Mix the flour, salt, and sugar together. Rub in the fat lightly. Stir in the egg and mix to a soft paste. Roll out with the hands on a floured surface to a long sausage shape about 2cm thick. Divide into 20 pieces, and roll each into an 8cm long sausage. Form into an S shape and place well apart on a greased baking sheet. Bake for 12–15 minutes. Allow the jumbles to cool for a few seconds, then slip a palette knife under each and place on a wire rack to finish cooling.

Oatmeal Biscuits

Makes 22–24

100g medium oatmeal
100g self-raising flour
1 × 2.5ml spoon salt
a pinch of sugar
100g butter **or**
 margarine

2 × 15ml spoons beaten
 egg
2 × 15ml spoons water
flour for rolling out
fat for greasing

Heat the oven to moderate, 180°C, Gas 4. Mix all the dry ingredients together and rub in the fat. Mix the egg with the water and use this to bind the dry ingredients together into a stiff paste. Roll out on a lightly floured surface to just under 1cm thick. Cut into rounds with a 5–6cm cutter. Prick the surface of the biscuits with a fork and place on a greased baking sheet. Bake for 15–20 minutes.

Note For Oatcakes, see p1222.

Shortbread

Makes 8 wedges

100g plain flour
½ × 2.5ml spoon salt
50g rice flour, ground
 rice **or** semolina

50g caster sugar
100g butter
fat for greasing

Mix all the dry ingredients together. Rub in the butter until the mixture binds together to a paste. Shape into a large round about 1cm thick. Pinch up the edges to decorate. Place on an upturned greased baking sheet, and prick with a fork. Bake in a moderate oven, 180°C, Gas 4, for 40–45 minutes. Cut into 8 wedges while still warm.

Note For Brown Almond Shortcakes, see p1204.

VARIATION

Shortbread Biscuits

Roll out the paste on a lightly floured surface to just under 1cm thick. Cut into rounds with a 5–6cm cutter. Prick the surface in several places with a fork. Bake for 15–20 minutes.

Soya Flour Shortbread

Makes 6 wedges

fat for greasing
flour for dusting
125g plain flour

25g soya flour
100g butter
50g caster sugar

Grease and flour a baking sheet and the inside of a 15cm flan ring. Mix together the plain and soya flours. Rub in the butter. Mix in the sugar, and knead the dough until it forms a single mass. Place the ring on the sheet, and press the shortbread dough into it in an even layer. Prick the centre deeply with a fork. Bake in a cool oven, 140–150°C, Gas 1–2, for 45–50 minutes or until very lightly coloured. Leave for 5 minutes. Mark into 6 wedges and leave to cool completely. When cold, remove the flan ring and cut into sections as marked.

Wine Biscuits

Makes 60 (approx)

250g plain flour
½ × 2.5ml spoon salt
½ × 2.5ml spoon ground
 cloves
1 × 5ml spoon ground
 cinnamon
1 × 2.5ml spoon ground
 ginger
150g caster sugar
1 × 2.5ml spoon
 bicarbonate of soda

100g butter
50g ground almonds
2 × 15ml spoons beaten
 egg
25ml white wine
flour for rolling out
halved almonds
 (optional)
fat for greasing

Sift the dry ingredients together, rub in the butter, and add the ground almonds. Beat the egg until liquid and mix with the wine. Add to the dry ingredients and mix to a stiff dough. Leave to stand for several hours or overnight.

Heat the oven to hot, 220°C, Gas 7. Roll out the dough on a lightly floured surface to 3mm thick. Cut into rounds with a 5cm cutter and put them on greased baking sheets. Place half an almond on each biscuit, if liked. Bake for 10 minutes.

Bread, Cakes and Pastry

Breads and Rolls (clockwise from top) Basic White Bread (p1155), *Rye Cobs* (p1161), *Dinner Rolls* (p1158), *Wholemeal Rolls* (p1159), *Bridge Rolls* (p1157) *and Bread Plait* (p1157)

LEFT *A selection of friandises suitable for after dinner coffee (from the centre) Glazed Grapes* (p1090), *Mrs Beeton's Almond Macaroons* (p1223), *Piped Almond Rings* (p1220), *Stuffed Dates* (p1089), *Palmiers* (p1274)

BELOW LEFT *Iced Petits Fours* (p1210), *Flapjacks* (p1221) *and Shrewsbury Biscuits* (p1217)

RIGHT *The technique of feather icing can make the simplest cake look sophisticated* (see p1225)

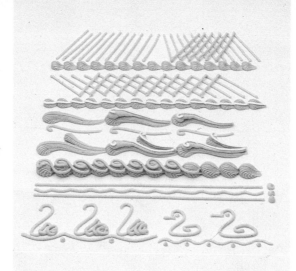

RIGHT *Using 3 very basic icing nozzles, a cake can be transformed out of all proportion*

BELOW *A cake covered with marzipan before and after icing it with royal icing (see pp1230–34)*

EXTREME RIGHT *The finished cake*

LEFT *Different types of Pastry*
At the back, a raised pie (p1250), in front, large, small and cocktail-sized vol-au-vent cases (p1253)

RIGHT *Cream Horns (p1273) and Maids of Honour (p1274)*

BELOW *Treacle Tart (p1266)*

Chocolate Profiteroles (p1047)

Creamed Biscuits

Basic recipe

Makes 26–30

200g plain flour	1 egg yolk **or** ½ beaten
¼ × 2.5ml spoon salt	egg
100–150g butter **or**	flour for rolling out
margarine	fat for greasing
100–150g caster sugar	caster sugar for dredging
	(optional)

Heat the oven to moderate, 180°C, Gas 4. Mix the flour and salt together. Beat the fat until soft, add the sugar, and cream until light and fluffy. Beat the egg into the creamed mixture. Fold in the flour, using a knife and then the fingers. On a lightly floured surface, knead lightly and roll out to 5mm–1cm thick. Cut into rounds with a 6cm cutter. Re-roll and re-cut any trimmings. Prick the surface of the biscuits in 2 or 3 places with a fork. Place on a well-greased baking sheet. Bake for 15–20 minutes. Leave on the baking sheet for 5 minutes before transferring to a cooling rack. Dredge with caster sugar, if liked.

VARIATIONS

Almond Biscuits

Use 150g plain flour and 50g ground almonds instead of 200g flour. When cold, sandwich the biscuits together in pairs with jam and dredge with icing sugar.

Dover or Easter Biscuits

Mix 1 × 2.5ml spoon ground cinnamon with the flour and salt, and add 50g currants. Brush with beaten egg white, and sprinkle with caster sugar 5 minutes before removing from the oven.

Lemon or Orange Biscuits

Add the grated rind of 1 lemon or 1 orange to the flour.

Shrewsbury Biscuits

Use 200g self-raising flour or 200g plain flour and 1 × 5ml spoon baking powder. Omit the salt and use only 100g fat and 100g sugar. Add 1 × 5ml spoon grated lemon rind to the yolk. Bake in a warm oven, 160°C, Gas 3, for 30–40 minutes.

Bourbon Biscuits

Makes 14–16

50g butter **or** margarine	15g cocoa
50g caster sugar	1 × 2.5ml spoon
1 × 15ml spoon golden	bicarbonate of soda
syrup	flour for rolling out
100g plain flour	fat for greasing

Filling	
75g icing sugar	1 × 5ml spoon coffee
50g butter **or** margarine	essence **or** 1 × 2.5ml
1 × 15ml spoon cocoa	spoon instant coffee
	dissolved in 1 × 5ml
	spoon water

Heat the oven to warm, 160°C, Gas 3. Cream the fat and sugar together very thoroughly; beat in the syrup. Sift the flour, cocoa, and bicarbonate of soda together, and work into the creamed mixture to make a stiff paste. Knead well, and roll out on a lightly floured surface into an oblong strip about 5mm thick. Cut into two 6cm fingers. Place on a greased baking sheet covered with greased grease-proof paper. Bake for 15–20 minutes. Cut into equal-sized fingers while still warm. Cool on a wire rack.

Prepare the filling. Sift the icing sugar. Beat the fat until soft, add the sugar, cocoa, and coffee. Beat until smooth. Sandwich the cooled fingers with a layer of filling.

Coconut Biscuits

Makes 28–30

*100g butter **or***
margarine
100g caster sugar
1 egg yolk and a little
egg white if needed
150g self-raising flour
or 150g plain flour and
1 × 5ml spoon baking
powder

a pinch of salt
50g desiccated coconut
flour for rolling out
egg white for glazing
coconut for dusting
fat for greasing

Heat the oven to warm, 160°C, Gas 3. Cream the fat and sugar until light and fluffy. Beat in the egg yolk, then beat in the flour, salt, and coconut, and a little egg white if necessary, to bind together. Roll out 5mm thick, and cut into rounds with a 5–6cm cutter. Prick the biscuits and brush with lightly beaten egg white. Sprinkle with coconut. Place on a greased baking sheet and bake for 15–20 minutes.

Mrs Beeton's Dessert Biscuits

Makes 30–36

100g butter
200g flour
100g caster sugar
3 eggs

1–2 × 2.5ml spoon of
any of the following
flavourings:
ground ginger, ground
cinnamon, grated
*lemon rind **or** a few*
drops lemon essence
fat for greasing

Heat the oven to warm, 160°C, Gas 3. Cream the butter and beat in the flour gradually, incorporating each addition thoroughly. Beat in the sugar, eggs, and flavouring. Place heaped dessertspoonfuls, well apart, on lightly greased baking sheets, flatten slightly, and bake for about 15 minutes. Cool on the baking sheets.

Golden Syrup Gingerbread Biscuits

Makes 16 (approx)

200g plain flour
½ × 2.5ml spoon salt
1 × 10ml spoon ground
ginger
*75g butter **or** margarine*

50g sugar
75g golden syrup
2 eggs
flour for rolling out
fat for greasing

Heat the oven to moderate, 180°C, Gas 4. Sift the flour, salt, and ginger into a bowl. Cream together the fat, sugar, and syrup. Add the dry ingredients. Beat the eggs until liquid, and work enough egg into the mixture to make a stiff dough. Roll out 5mm thick. Cut into squares or rounds using a plain 6cm or 8cm cutter. Place on a greased baking sheet and bake for about 20 minutes.

Melting Moments

Makes 16–20

*100g margarine **or** 50g*
margarine and 50g
white cooking fat
75g caster sugar
25ml beaten egg

125g self-raising flour
a pinch of salt
rolled oats for coating
fat for greasing
4–5 glacé cherries

Heat the oven to moderate, 180°C, Gas 4. Cream the fat and sugar until pale and fluffy. Add the egg, a little flour, and the salt, and beat again. Stir in the remaining flour and shape the mixture into 16–20 round balls with the hands. Place the rolled oats on a sheet of greaseproof paper and toss the balls in them to coat them evenly all over. Place on 2 greased baking sheets. Place a small piece of glacé cherry in the centre of each. Bake for about 20 minutes until pale golden-brown. Leave to cool for a few minutes on the trays, then cool on a wire rack.

Napoleon's Hats

Makes 12

50g margarine
50g caster sugar
2 × 15ml spoons beaten
  egg
100g plain flour

1 × 2.5ml spoon baking
  powder
a pinch of salt
flour for rolling out
fat for greasing

Almond Paste
50g ground almonds
50g caster sugar

2 × 10ml spoons beaten
  egg

Decoration (optional)
glacé icing (p1225),
  using 25g icing sugar

colouring

Cream the fat and sugar until light and fluffy. Beat in the egg. Sift together the flour, baking powder and salt, and work into the creamed mixture. Knead well and roll out 5mm thick on a lightly floured surface. Cut into rounds with an 8cm plain cutter, making 12 biscuits.

Make the almond paste. Mix the almonds and sugar, and work them into a paste with 1 × 10ml spoon beaten egg. Divide the paste into 12 pieces and roll each into a ball. Place one in the centre of each biscuit. Dilute 1 × 10ml spoon egg with a little water. Brush the edges of the biscuits with beaten egg and water, and fold into a hat shape by lifting and pinching the edge of each biscuit at 2 points spaced equally apart. Place the 'hats' on a greased baking tray and bake in a moderate oven, 180°C, Gas 4, for 25 minutes.

When the 'hats' are cold, a little glacé icing can be put on the almond paste, to give them white or coloured 'crowns'.

Palmiers

See p1274.

Orange Peanut Butter Biscuits

Makes 36 (approx)

100g margarine
100g peanut butter
65g caster sugar
75g soft brown sugar
1 × 15ml spoon grated
  orange rind
1 egg

1 × 2.5ml spoon vanilla
  essence
125g plain flour
1 × 2.5ml spoon
  bicarbonate of soda
1 × 2.5ml spoon salt

Cream the margarine and peanut butter with the caster and brown sugars until light and fluffy. Mix in the orange rind. Beat the egg until liquid with the essence, and mix them in. Sift together the flour, soda, and salt. Add to the creamed mixture, and blend in thoroughly. Chill the dough until it can be handled easily.

Heat the oven to moderate, 180°C, Gas 4. Shape the dough into 2cm balls. Lay them well apart on a baking sheet lined with vegetable parchment. Flatten the balls slightly with the palm of the hand. Bake for 15–20 minutes. Leave on the sheet to firm up, then cool on a wire rack.

Peanut Clusters

Makes 20–24

50g soft tub margarine
50g granulated sugar
2 × 15ml spoons beaten
  egg
1 × 2.5ml spoon vanilla
  essence

50g plain flour
a pinch of salt
$\frac{1}{2}$ × 2.5ml spoon
  bicarbonate of soda
50g seedless raisins
50g salted peanuts

Heat the oven to fairly hot, 190°C, Gas 5. Beat the margarine and sugar together until light and fluffy. Beat in the egg and vanilla essence. Sift together the flour, salt, and soda, and beat them into the creamed mixture in 3 portions, blending in well after each addition. Stir in the raisins and nuts. Place small spoonfuls on an ungreased baking sheet, and bake for 9 minutes. Cool on the sheet.

Piped Almond Rings

Makes 24 (approx)

175g butter	1–2 drops vanilla
125g caster sugar	essence
1 egg	2 × 5ml spoons milk
250g self-raising flour	(approx)
50g ground almonds	fat for greasing

Cream the butter and sugar together until light and fluffy. Beat the egg until liquid and add it to the creamed mixture, beating thoroughly. Blend in the flour and ground almonds gradually. Add the vanilla essence and enough milk to give a piping consistency. Leave the mixture to stand for about 20 minutes in a cool place.

Heat the oven to fairly hot, 200°C, Gas 6. Put the mixture into a forcing bag with a medium-sized star nozzle, and pipe small rings on to a well-greased baking sheet. Bake for 10 minutes.

Note These biscuits can be served as petits fours.

Princess Cakes

Makes 10 pairs

100g butter **or**	100g self-raising flour
margarine	grated rind of ½ orange
25g caster sugar	fat for greasing
a pinch of salt	

Filling
orange butter icing
(p1227), using 25g
butter

Heat the oven to moderate, 180°C, Gas 4. Cream the fat and sugar well together. Work in the salt, flour, and orange rind. Place the mixture in a forcing bag with a large star nozzle, and pipe 9cm lengths on to a greased baking sheet, making 20 biscuits. Bake for 15 minutes. Cool on the sheet.

When cool, sandwich together in pairs with orange butter icing.

Ring Cakes

Makes 12

100g margarine	100g plain flour
50g caster sugar	flour for rolling out
1 egg yolk	fat for greasing

Almond Mixture

1 egg white	50g ground almonds
75g caster sugar	

Decoration
4 × 15ml spoons red jam
  or jelly

Cream the fat and sugar together thoroughly. Work in the egg yolk and then the flour. On a lightly floured surface, knead well, then roll out 5mm thick. Cut into 4cm rounds. Place on a greased baking sheet. Heat the oven to moderate, 180°C, Gas 4.

To make the almond mixture, whisk the egg white until frothy, stir in the sugar and the ground almonds. Using a forcing bag with a plain 1cm nozzle, pipe a circle of the almond mixture round the edge of each biscuit. Bake for 15 minutes. Cool on the baking sheet. When cold, fill the centres of the biscuits with jam or jelly.

Anzacs

Makes 36 (approx)

75g rolled oats	3 × 2.5ml spoons
100g plain flour	bicarbonate of soda
150g sugar	2 × 15ml spoons boiling
50g desiccated coconut	water
100g butter	fat for greasing
1 × 15ml spoon golden	
syrup	

Heat the oven to warm, 160°C, Gas 3. Mix the rolled oats, flour, sugar, and coconut together. Melt the butter and syrup gently together. Mix the soda with the water, add to the melted mixture and stir into the dry ingredients. Spoon dessertspoonfuls of the mixture on to a lightly greased baking sheet, leaving plenty of space between them. Bake for 20 minutes. Cool on the sheet.

Brandy Snaps

Makes 14–18

50g plain flour
1 × 5ml spoon ground
  ginger
50g margarine
50g soft dark brown
  sugar
2 × 15ml spoons golden
  syrup

2 × 5ml spoons grated
  lemon rind
1 × 5ml spoon lemon
  juice
fat for greasing

Heat the oven to warm, 160°C, Gas 3. Sift the flour and ginger. Melt the margarine in a small saucepan. Add the sugar and syrup and warm gently but do not allow to become hot. Remove from the heat. Add the sifted ingredients, the lemon rind and juice, and mix well. Put small spoonfuls on to greased baking sheets, spaced well apart to allow the mixture to spread. Do not put more than 6 spoonfuls on a 20 × 25cm baking sheet. Bake for 8–10 minutes.

Remove from the oven and leave to cool for a few moments until the edges begin to firm. Lift with a palette knife and roll loosely round the handle of a greased wooden spoon. Leave to cool before removing the spoon handle. (Several spoon handles will be needed.)

Note If the brandy snaps are to be served at a party or as a dessert, fill at the last moment with fresh whipped cream, confectioners' custard (p1237) or a similar filling. Use either a small spoon or a forcing bag with a large star or rose nozzle.

Ginger Snaps

Makes 56 (approx)

200g self-raising flour
a pinch of salt
1 × 5ml spoon ground
  ginger
100g soft light brown
  sugar

75g margarine
100g golden syrup
1 egg
fat for greasing

Heat the oven to warm, 160°C, Gas 3. Sift together the flour, salt, ginger, and sugar. Melt the margarine

and syrup in a medium-sized saucepan. Beat the egg until liquid. When the fat has melted, add the dry ingredients and egg alternately and beat until smooth and thick. Using 2 teaspoons, place rounds of mixture on to well-greased baking sheets, spaced well apart to allow the mixture to spread. Bake for 15 minutes. Leave on the sheets for a few moments, and finish cooling on a wire rack.

Note The mixture will thicken as it cools. If necessary, wash the sheets for the second and later batches, regrease them and shape the mixture into small balls in the hands. Place on the sheets and bake as before. If the biscuits become too crisp to remove from the sheets easily, put back in the oven for a minute or two.

Crunchies

Makes 20 (approx)

100g margarine
125g rolled oats

75g Demerara sugar
fat for greasing

Melt the margarine and stir in the oats and the sugar. Press into a greased 28 × 18cm tin and bake in a fairly hot oven, 190°C, Gas 5, for 15 minutes. Cut into squares or strips while warm, and leave in the tin until cool.

Flapjacks

Makes 20 (approx)

50g margarine
50g soft light brown
  sugar
2 × 15ml spoons golden
  syrup

100g rolled oats
fat for greasing

Melt the margarine, add the sugar and syrup, and warm gently. Do not boil. Remove from the heat and stir in the oats. Press into a greased 28 × 18cm tin. Bake in a warm oven, 160°C, Gas 3, for 25 minutes or until firm. Cut into fingers while still warm and leave in the tin to cool.

Oatcakes

Makes 16 (approx)

50g bacon fat **or**
 dripping
100g medium oatmeal
1 × 2.5ml spoon salt
½ × 2.5ml spoon
 bicarbonate of soda

boiling water
fine oatmeal for rolling
 out
fat for greasing

Melt the fat and stir in the dry ingredients. Add enough boiling water to make a stiff paste. Knead well. On a surface dusted with fine oatmeal, roll out into a round 5mm thick and cut into wedge-shaped pieces. Place on a greased baking sheet and bake in a warm oven, 160°C, Gas 3, for 20–30 minutes.

Note For Oatmeal Biscuits, see p1216.

Date Surprises

Makes 24–30

200g cooking dates
100g butter **or**
 margarine
150g granulated sugar
½ × 2.5ml spoon salt
1 egg

½ × 2.5ml spoon vanilla
 essence
1 × 15ml spoon milk
50–100g crisp rice cereal
desiccated coconut for
 coating

Chop the dates. Put the fat, sugar, salt, and dates in a saucepan, and cook over gentle heat until the mixture comes to the boil. Cook for 3 minutes, stirring all the time, then remove from the heat. In a mixing bowl, beat together the egg, vanilla essence, and milk until blended. Stir into the date mixture, return to very low heat and cook for 3 minutes, stirring vigorously. Off the heat, stir in the cereal. Pour back the mixture into the mixing bowl, and chill until firm.

When cold, roll into balls, and roll in desiccated coconut.

Florentines

Makes 20–24 (approx)

oil for greasing
25g glacé cherries
100g cut mixed peel
50g flaked almonds
100g chopped almonds
25g sultanas
100g butter **or**
 margarine

100g caster sugar
2 × 15ml spoons double
 cream
100g plain **or** couverture
 chocolate

Heat the oven to moderate, 180°C, Gas 4. Cover 3–4 baking sheets with oiled greaseproof paper. Cut up the glacé cherries and chop the mixed peel a little more finely if necessary. Mix with the flaked and chopped almonds and the sultanas. Melt the fat in a small saucepan, add the sugar, and boil for 1 minute. Remove from the heat and stir in the fruit and nuts. Whip the cream and fold it in. Place small spoonfuls of the mixture on to the baking sheets, leaving room for spreading. Bake for 8–10 minutes. After the biscuits have been in the oven for about 5 minutes, neaten the edges by drawing them together with a plain biscuit cutter. Leave the biscuits to firm up slightly before removing the paper, then cool completely on a wire rack.

To finish, melt the chocolate in a basin over hot water and use to coat the flat underside of the biscuits. Mark into wavy lines with a fork as the chocolate cools.

Canadian Crispies

Makes 12–14

100g plain block
 chocolate
50g crisp rice cereal

25g seedless raisins **or**
 sultanas

Break the chocolate into small pieces and put it in a basin over hot (not boiling) water until it melts and is liquid. Stir in the cereal and the dried fruit. Place in rough heaps in paper cases and leave to cool and set.

Mrs Beeton's Almond Macaroons

Makes 16–20

fat for greasing
2 egg whites
150g caster sugar
100g ground almonds

1 × 10ml spoon ground
rice
split almonds **or** *halved*
glacé cherries

Heat the oven to warm, 160°C, Gas 3. Grease a baking sheet and cover with rice paper. Whisk the egg whites until frothy but not stiff enough to form peaks. Stir in the sugar, ground almonds, and ground rice. Beat with a wooden spoon until thick and white. Place small spoonfuls of the mixture 5cm apart on the paper or pipe them on. Place a split almond or halved glacé cherry on each. Bake for 20 minutes or until pale fawn.

VARIATION

Ratafias

Make as above, but only 2cm in diameter. Omit the almond. Ratafias are used in trifles, to decorate desserts, and as petits fours.

Nutty Meringues

Makes 10–12

oil for greasing if used
50g almonds, walnuts
or hazelnuts

100g icing sugar
2 egg whites
a few drops almond **or**
vanilla essence

Line a baking sheet with oiled greaseproof paper, rice paper or vegetable parchment. Blanch the nuts, and chop them finely. Sift the icing sugar into a bowl. Add the egg whites and stand the bowl over a pan of hot water. Whisk the mixture until it clings stiffly to the whisk. Add a few drops of flavouring and stir in the nuts. Put in small rough heaps on the baking sheet. Bake in a cool oven, 150°C, Gas 2, for 20–30 minutes, until crisp outside, soft inside, and slightly coloured.

Meringues

See p1022–24.

Sponge Fingers (2)

Makes 18

fat for greasing
caster sugar for dusting
3 eggs

100g caster sugar
100g plain flour
a pinch of salt

Heat the oven to warm, 160°C, Gas 3. Grease 18 sponge finger tins and dust with sugar. Separate the eggs. Beat the yolks and sugar together until pale and thick. Sift the flour with the salt. Fold half the flour into the egg mixture very lightly. Whisk the egg whites until stiff. Fold very lightly into the yolk mixture with the rest of the flour. Half fill the tins and bake for 12 minutes. Leave to cool slightly before removing from the tins.

Note For Sponge Fingers (1), see p1208.

ICINGS, FILLINGS AND DECORATIONS

If icing be put on the cakes as soon as they are withdrawn from the oven, it will become firm and hard by the time the cakes are cold. All iced cakes should be kept in a very dry place.

Icings

GLACÉ ICING

Glacé icing is used as a covering and gives a smooth, slightly crisp coating. It is basically a mixture of icing sugar and warm water but may also contain other flavourings and colourings or extra ingredients, eg chocolate glacé icing (p1226).

Points for use: The correct consistency is stiff enough to coat the back of a wooden spoon thickly, otherwise it will run off the surface of the cake.

Glacé icing should be used immediately. If left to stand, even for a short while, it should be covered completely with damp greaseproof paper. Any crystallized icing on the surface should be scraped off before use.

Decorations: Decorations must be put on before the icing sets or it will crack. Do not use decorations liable to melt, run or be damaged by damp. Crystallized flower petals, chocolate decorations and some small sweets should not be used.

To Coat a Cake, Gâteau or Pastries with Glacé Icing

Top: If only the top of a cake or gâteau is to be iced, tie a band of doubled greaseproof paper round it which rises about 1cm higher than the top. This will prevent the icing spilling over the sides.

Top and sides: If the sides as well as the top are to be iced, omit the band, and place the cake, gâteau or pastries on a revolving cake stand (a turntable), on an upturned plate, or on a wire cooling rack with greaseproof paper underneath. Brush any loose crumbs off the surface, using a soft pastry brush.

Pour the icing on to the top of the cake, gâteau or pastries from the centre outwards; spread it lightly if necessary with a hot, wetted palette knife. Tilt the cake or gâteau so that the icing runs down the sides. Spread extra icing over any bare patches.

Decorations: Quickly put on any decorations and leave, undisturbed, to set. Trim off any icing round the base with a sharp knife, and transfer to a serving plate, using a cake slice or fish servers.

A trickling technique called fricking is used mostly for decoration; a coloured coating, eg chocolate, is trickled over a cake on which a white or pale glacé icing coating has been applied to the top and sides and allowed to set. The trickled icing drips over the edges of the cake to contrast with the base coating. Use a thin glacé icing which will spread easily.

Other methods: Very small pieces of Genoese Sponge (or similar cake), when used for petits fours are stuck on skewers and dipped in icing. They should be put immediately on to a wire rack, decorated and left undisturbed to dry.

Glacé icing can also be trickled over pastry desserts such as filled choux. No attempt is made to cover them completely. Éclairs, cream buns, and other dessert pastries are also only partially covered with a single line or cap of icing.

Glacé icing can also be used as a second coat over a base coat of royal icing.

Feather Icing

Enough to coat the top of one 18cm cake

Make up some white glacé icing, using 150g icing sugar. Remove 2 × 15ml spoons and tint it with a few drops of food colouring. Brown is the colour usually chosen as it shows up well.

Coat the top of the cake with the white icing. Place the tinted icing in a piping bag fitted with a fine writing pipe, and pipe parallel lines over the white icing; do this quickly before the coating sets. Then run a cocktail stick or fine skewer lightly across the cake in parallel lines, backwards and forwards at right angles to the piping. Allow to set firmly before cutting.

Feather icing is used on sponge and sandwich cakes, and on some gâteaux.

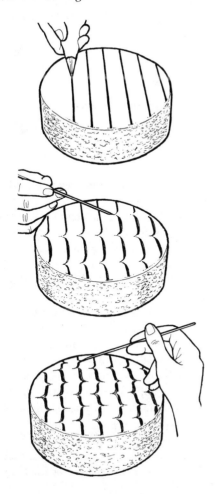

Glacé Icing

Enough to cover the top of one 18cm cake

100g icing sugar	*1 × 2.5ml spoon strained*
2 × 10ml spoons water	*lemon **or** orange juice*
(approx)	*(optional)*
	colouring (optional)

Sift the icing sugar. Put 1 × 15ml spoon water into a small non-stick or enamel saucepan with the icing sugar. If a mild lemon or orange flavour is required add the juice at this stage. Warm very gently, without making the pan too hot to touch on the underside. Beat well with a wooden spoon. The icing should coat the back of the spoon thickly. If it is too thick, add the extra 5ml water; if too thin add a very little extra sifted icing sugar. Add colouring, if liked. Use at once.

Note Icing sugars vary in the amount of liquid they will absorb.

VARIATIONS

Coffee Glacé Icing

Dissolve 1 × 5ml spoon instant coffee in the water.

Lemon or Orange Glacé Icing

Substitute strained lemon or orange juice for the amount of water used.

Note Other fruit flavours can be achieved by using a small quantity of flavouring essence.

Liqueur-flavoured Glacé Icing

Substitute 1 × 10ml spoon liqueur for 1 × 10ml spoon of the water.

Chocolate Glacé Icing (1)

Enough to coat the top of one 18cm cake

50g plain chocolate   *2 ×5ml spoons butter*
1 ×15ml spoon water   *100g icing sugar*

Grate the chocolate into a small, heavy-based pan. Add the water and butter. Warm very gently, stirring thoroughly until the mixture is smooth and creamy. Sift the icing sugar and stir it in, a little at a time, adding a little extra water if necessary to make a coating consistency.

Note The icing will thicken as it cools.

Chocolate Glacé Icing (2)

Enough to coat the top of one 20cm cake

100g plain chocolate   *2 ×15ml spoons water*
2 ×10ml spoons butter   *150g icing sugar*

Break up the chocolate and place it in a heatproof basin. Stand the basin in a pan containing enough hot water to come half-way up its sides. Add the butter and water to the chocolate. Stir over gentle heat until the chocolate and butter melt and become a smooth cream. Cool slightly, then sift in the icing sugar, and beat until the icing is the consistency for easy spreading. Add a few drops of water if it is too thick; it should coat the back of a spoon. Use at once.

FONDANT ICING

Fondant icing is used a great deal commercially because, although soft, it is dry when set and can be handled easily. It can sometimes be obtained from a commercial confectioner or bakers' supplier, or can be made in the home.

To use fondant icing: Put the quantity required in a heatproof bowl with a little water or stock syrup (p1227) and set the bowl over a pan of hot water. Using a wooden spoon, stir the fondant until it is of a creamy spreading consistency, adding more water or syrup if necessary, and any flavouring. Spread the fondant quickly over a large cake in the same way as royal icing (p1232). Let it dry undisturbed on a wire rack. Any fondant which drips off can be scraped up after the cake is dry, moulded into a ball and stored, provided it has no crumbs in it. Fondant icing stores well if kept in an airtight jar, covered with waxed paper and a lid.

Fondant Icing

Enough to cover one 18–20cm cake

450g caster **or** *lump*   *2 ×10ml spoons liquid*
  sugar   *glucose*
150ml water

Put the sugar and water into a heavy-based saucepan which is absolutely free from grease. Heat gently until all the sugar has completely dissolved. Stir very occasionally. Wipe any crystals which form on the sides of the pan with a wet pastry brush. When the sugar has dissolved, add the glucose, and boil to 115°C without stirring. Keep the sides of the pan clean by brushing with the wet brush when necessary. Remove from the heat and allow the bubbles to subside.

Pour the mixture slowly into the middle of a wetted marble slab and allow to cool a little. Work the sides to the middle with a sugar scraper to make a smaller mass. Using a wooden spatula in one hand and the scraper in the other, make a figure of eight with the spatula, keeping the mixture together with the scraper. Work until the mass is completely white. Break off small amounts and knead well, then reknead the small pieces together into one mass. Store in a jar, preferably of stoneware. Cover with waxed paper and a lid.

Fondant Sweets
See pp1094–95.

Stock Syrup (2)
(for diluting fondant)

150g granulated sugar   125ml water

Dissolve the sugar in the water in a saucepan. When it has dissolved, boil without stirring for 3 minutes. Remove any scum as it rises, with a spoon. Allow to cool and strain into a jar with a lid. Store for future use if not required immediately.

Note This syrup can also be kneaded into commercially made almond paste to make the paste more pliable.
For Stock Syrup (1), see p1081.

BUTTER ICING

Butter icing can be used to cover, fill or decorate a cake. Basically, it is a mixture of butter and icing sugar with the addition of hot or cold liquid and flavouring. Sometimes colouring, cream, egg white or yolk are added.

Points for use: The icing must be soft in texture so that it spreads easily or it may drag off loose crumbs which will make the icing look speckled. The butter should be at room temperature and must be softened thoroughly before the sugar is added. If the final consistency is too stiff, place the bowl containing the icing over a pan of warm water and beat well.

Storage: Butter icing hardens as it sets. It can be stored in a refrigerator, but must be returned to room temperature and beaten well before it is used on a cake. Cakes filled or covered with butter icing can be frozen (see p1392).

Butter Icing
Enough for 2 layers in one 18–20cm cake

250g icing sugar   1 × 15ml spoon liquid,
100g softened butter   eg milk, water or
*   fruit juice*

Sift the icing sugar and add gradually to the butter with the liquid, beating until the icing is smooth and of a soft spreading consistency.

Note For Butter Icing (2), see p1421.

VARIATIONS
Chocolate Butter Icing (1)

Grate 50g plain block chocolate. Place it in a basin over hot water with 1 × 15ml spoon milk, stir until dissolved, then cool. Use instead of the liquid in the plain butter icing.

Chocolate Butter Icing (2)

Dissolve 1 × 15ml spoon cocoa in 1 × 15ml spoon hot water. Cool before use. Use instead of the liquid in the plain butter icing.

Coffee Butter Icing

Dissolve 1 × 5ml spoon instant coffee in 1 × 15ml spoon hot water. Cool before use. Use instead of the liquid in the plain butter icing.

Lemon or Orange Butter Icing

Use 1 × 15ml spoon juice and a little grated rind.

Vanilla Butter Icing

Add 1 × 2.5ml spoon vanilla essence with the milk.

Walnut Butter Icing

Add 25g finely chopped walnuts with the milk.

Creamy Butter Icing

Enough to cover two 20cm cakes

50g softened butter **or** *margarine*
½ × 2.5ml spoon salt
450g icing sugar (approx)

75–100ml double cream
1 × 5ml spoon vanilla essence

Cream the butter or margarine with the salt. Sift the icing sugar. Heat the cream to just under boiling point. Beat the sugar and hot cream into the butter alternately, blending well after each addition. Beat in the essence. Continue beating until the icing is cold, creamy, and thick enough to spread.

Note For a stiffer icing, use a little less cream.

VARIATIONS

Browned Butter Icing

Heat the butter or margarine until nut-brown. Remove from the heat and add the salt. Beat in the sugar and cold cream as above. Omit the vanilla essence.

Creamy Lemon Icing

Cream 2 × 5ml spoons grated lemon rind with the butter and salt. Add 1 × 15ml spoon lemon juice with the cream. Omit the vanilla essence.

Creamy Orange Icing

Cream 1 × 5ml spoon grated orange rind with the butter and salt. Use 4 × 15ml spoons orange juice instead of the cream. Omit the vanilla essence.

FROSTING

Frosting is usually spread thickly over a whole cake, the sides as well as the top. It is crisper when set than glacé icing, because the sugar is heated or boiled when making it and sets more firmly. It should be a soft, spreading consistency when applied.

American Frosting (1)

Enough to cover one 15–18cm cake

225g granulated sugar
4 × 15ml spoons water
a pinch of cream of tartar

1 × 2.5ml spoon vanilla essence **or** *a few drops lemon juice (optional)*
1 egg white

Have the cake standing ready to be iced, on a turntable, upturned plate, or wire cooling rack with paper spread underneath. Heat the sugar, water, and cream of tartar gently until the sugar dissolves. Add the flavouring if liked. Heat, without boiling, to 120°C, stirring all the time. Remove the syrup from the heat and leave to cool slightly until it stops swirling. Meanwhile, whisk the egg white until stiff. Pour the syrup on to the egg white in a thin stream, beating with a spoon all the time. Continue beating until the icing is of the required consistency. When thick enough, pour it over the cake and swirl with a round-bladed knife.

American Frosting (2)

Enough to cover one 15cm cake

150g granulated sugar
2 × 15ml spoons water
a pinch of cream of tartar

1 egg white
colouring and flavouring (optional)

Put the sugar and water into a heatproof bowl over a pan of hot water, and stir until dissolved. Add the cream of tartar and the egg white. Bring the water under the bowl to the boil. Whisk the mixture with a rotary or an electric whisk until it forms peaks. (This will take from 4–7 minutes depending on the type of whisk used.) Remove the bowl from the boiling water and add colouring and flavouring if liked. Continue beating until the desired consistency is obtained, either a thick coating mixture or one which stands in peaks.

Seafoam Frosting

Enough to cover the top, sides, and fill one 20cm sandwich cake

2 egg whites	125ml cold water
350g soft light brown sugar	a pinch of salt
$\frac{1}{2}$ × 2.5ml spoon cream of tartar	1 × 5ml spoon vanilla essence

Put all the ingredients, apart from the essence, into the top of a double boiler or heatproof bowl. Beat until blended. Place over boiling water; do not allow the bottom of the top pan or bowl to touch the water. Cook, beating all the time for about 7 minutes, until the frosting forms soft peaks. Do not overcook. Remove from the boiling water, add the vanilla essence, and beat the frosting for about 2 minutes until of spreading consistency.

GRILLED OR BROILED-ON TOPPINGS

These toppings are used on plain and light fruit cakes instead of icing.

Grilled Nut Topping

Enough to cover two 15cm square cakes

50g butter **or** margarine	100g chopped mixed nuts
100g soft light brown sugar	
3 × 15ml spoons single cream	

Cream the fat and sugar together, then beat in the cream. When fully blended, stir in the nuts. Spread the topping on the cake while still warm or just after cooling. Place under gentle grill heat, and grill for 2–3 minutes until the topping is light gold and bubbling. Remove from the heat at once. Leave to cool completely before cutting the cake.

VARIATION

100g finely chopped walnuts can be used instead of the mixed nuts.

Grilled or Broiled Topping

Enough to cover two 15cm square cakes

75g desiccated coconut	3 × 15ml spoons single cream
100g soft light brown sugar	
50g softened butter **or** margarine	

Work the coconut and sugar into the fat with a spoon. Mix in the cream, and beat until all the ingredients are fully blended.

Make sure the top of the cake is fairly level, and brush off any loose crumbs. Spread the topping on the cake while still warm or just after cooling. Place it under gentle grill heat, and grill for 2–5 minutes until the topping is golden-brown.

VARIATION

Orange Coconut Topping

Use 50g butter or margarine, 75g sugar, 3 × 15ml spoons orange juice, and 50g desiccated coconut.

ALMOND PASTE AND MARZIPAN

Both almond paste and marzipan can be used to cover a Battenburg cake, to fill a Simnel cake, or under royal icing on a Christmas or wedding cake. Almond paste and marzipan provide a flat, even surface over which icing will flow in a smooth glossy sheet, and prevent crumbs from the cake mixture spoiling the appearance of the icing.

Marzipan is like almond paste, but is smoother and more malleable. It can be used more easily than almond paste for moulded decorations (pp1239–40) or as petits fours.

To Coat a Cake with Almond Paste or Marzipan

Always level the top of the cake first. If it has risen to a peak in the centre, do not cut it off. Cut out a thin strip of paste and put it round the edge to level the top. Roll it flat.

Brush the cake free of any loose crumbs, then brush it with warm apricot glaze (p1234) or warmed apricot jam. Let it cool. If covering only the top of the cake with paste, do not coat the sides unless you want to cover them with crumbs or chopped nuts (p1235).

To cover the top of a cake only: On a surface lightly dusted with icing sugar, roll out the almond paste or marzipan into a round or square of the required thickness, and 5mm larger than the top of the cake all round. Invert the cake on to the paste. Hold the cake down with one hand and, using a knife, mould and press the paste into the sides of the cake, to give a neat, sharp edge.

Turn the cake the right way up, and roll the top lightly with a rolling-pin dusted with icing sugar. If not level, make it so by rolling, then invert it again and press the excess paste into place on the sides.

To cover the top and sides of a round cake: Roll out the almond paste or marzipan into a circle of the required thickness, and 3–4cm larger than the top of the cake all around. On a cake of average height, this should give an almond paste coating for the sides about half as thick as on top. (If the

cake is more than 8cm high, make the circle a little thicker or larger.)

Invert the cake on to the paste, placing it in the centre of the circle. Using the palms of both hands, mould and press the paste on to the sides of the cake, working it upward to cover them. Press it on firmly and evenly. Press down on the cake to get a sharp edge between the top and sides. Then roll a straight-sided bottle or jar all round the cake to make the paste on the sides an even thickness. Turn the cake the right way up, and check that it is level.

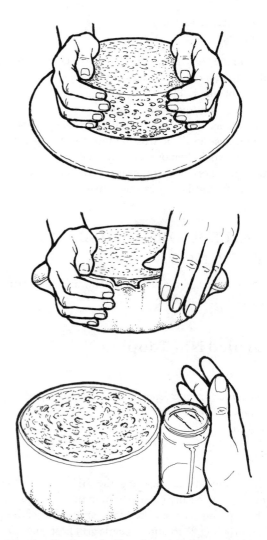

Covering the top and sides of a round cake

To cover the top and sides of a square cake: Cover the sides first. Divide the paste into 2 parts and put 1 aside for the top. Cut the other part into 4 pieces, and roll each into a strip to fit one side of the cake. Lay them on a surface lightly dusted with icing sugar. Up-end the cake, and press each side in turn on to a strip of paste. Trim the edges of the paste with a knife if necessary.

Cover the top of the cake exactly as when covering the top only.

Leave any cake covered with almond paste or marzipan for at least 72 hours, or if possible, a full week, before icing it, to prevent any risk of almond oil from the paste seeping through the icing and staining it.

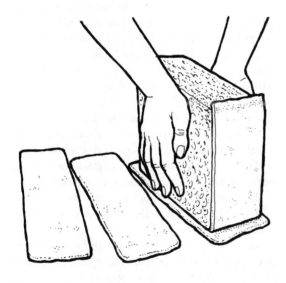

Covering the sides of a square cake before covering the top

Almond Paste

Basic proportions

100g ground almonds
100g icing sugar or 50g icing sugar and 50g caster sugar
1 egg yolk or 1 egg white or ½ beaten standard egg

One of the following flavourings:
1 × 15ml spoon lemon juice or 1 × 2.5ml spoon vanilla essence or 1 × 2.5ml spoon almond essence or 1 × 5ml spoon brandy

Work all the ingredients together to make a pliable paste. For a sweeter paste, increase the quantities of icing and caster sugar equally to give 1½ times the weight of the almonds in sugar; eg when using 100g ground almonds as above, use 75g icing sugar and 75g caster sugar, giving 150g sugar in all.

Note When making almond paste, handle it as little as possible, as the warmth of the hands draws out the oil from the ground almonds.

Quantities to use

For the top only of an 18cm cake, use the basic proportions of ingredients as above.

For the top only of a 20 or 23cm cake, use 150g ground almonds, 150g sugar, enough egg (white, yolk or whole egg) to bind, and flavouring to taste.

For the top only of a 25cm cake, use 200g ground almonds, 200g sugar, 1½–2 egg whites or yolks or 1 egg, and flavouring to taste.

For the top and sides of an 18cm cake, use 200g ground almonds, 200g sugar, 1½–2 egg whites or yolks or 1 egg, and flavouring to taste.

For the top and sides of a 20 or 23cm cake, use 300g ground almonds, 300g sugar, 2 egg whites or yolks or 1½ eggs, and flavouring to taste.

For the top and sides of a 25cm cake, use 400g ground almonds, 400g sugar, 3–4 egg whites or yolks or 2 eggs, and flavouring to taste.

Use the almond paste for covering cakes before applying icing, and for covering or filling some other cakes such as Simnel cake (p1200). If the paste is not to be covered by icing, use egg yolk for binding; it is less brittle, and less likely to flake or crack when dry. The egg whites can be used for making royal icing if they can be stored on the bottom shelf of a refrigerator or a cool place in the larder for 2 days, or in a freezer until the almond paste has dried out.

Marzipan can be used, if preferred.

Marzipan

Basic proportions

200g icing sugar	*200g ground almonds*
1 egg	*flavourings as for*
1 egg white	*almond paste* (p1231)

Sift the icing sugar. Whisk the egg, egg white, and sugar in a heatproof basin over hot water until thick and creamy. Add the ground almonds with the flavourings and mix well. Work in more flavourings if necessary. Knead until smooth.

Use as for almond paste, or for making moulded decorations (pp1239–40).

Uncooked Almond Paste or Marzipan (for sweets)

See p1087.

Boiled Marzipan

(for sweets and moulded decorations)
See p1086.

ROYAL ICING

This classic icing cannot be applied directly to a cake, since it will drag crumbs off the surface. When it is spread on a cake coated with almond paste or marzipan, it should be the consistency of thick cream.

To Ice a Cake with Royal Icing

If an electric mixer is used for beating royal icing, leave the icing to stand for 2–3 hours afterwards, to let any air bubbles escape. Whenever it is left to stand, either during preparation or when fully prepared, cover it with a clean, damp cloth to prevent the surface drying out and forming a crust.

First coat: Put the cake, covered with well-dried almond paste or marzipan, on an upturned plate or on an icing turntable. Take just under half of the icing and put it in the middle of the cake top. Smooth it all over the top quickly with a spatula or palette knife. If necessary, dip the knife into a deep jug of very hot water, shake off surplus water and smooth the surface of the cake with the hot knife.

Smooth the rest of the icing over the sides, lifting a little at a time from the bowl, using a hot wetted knife. Have a fine skewer ready to prick any bubbles gently before the surface sets. See that the top edge is sharp and clean. Do not overwork the icing or it will lose its gloss. Allow the cake to dry, away from dust, for 24 hours.

Second coat: Once the first coating is completely dry, a second, thinner coat of icing can be poured over the cake if the first coat is not perfectly smooth. This second coat should be thick enough to need a little help with a knife to make it flow gently over the top and sides. Extra egg white can be added to make a coating with a very smooth finish. Alternatively, glacé icing (p1225) can be used for this second coat.

Snow scene surface: For a 'snow scene', ie a coating with peaks and swirls, flick up the icing with a knife, making small peaks. If desired, sprinkle the icing, when dry, with sifted icing sugar to represent newly fallen snow.

To Decorate a Cake with Piped Royal Icing

The icing which coats the cake must be completely dry and hard before decorations are applied.

Decorative piping: Icing required for star or rose pipes (see diagram below) needs a little extra sifted icing sugar added so that it is slightly stiffer. When pulled up with a spoon, a 1cm point of icing should hold its shape; the stars will flatten if the icing is too thin. For writing pipes, the icing should be only slightly stiffer than icing for coating a cake, and should pull up into soft points. Beat it very thoroughly before use or it may break in the middle of a line or letter.

A design can be pricked out directly on the cake, using a long clean pin, eg a decorator's pin. However, if the design is to be geometrical or if writing is to be used, it is wise to draw the design on a piece of paper first. If this is done to scale, the paper can be placed on top of the cake and the design pricked through the paper on to the cake with a long clean pin.

To make a paper icing bag or cone: Use greaseproof paper or vegetable parchment. Cut a square about 25cm in diameter, and cut it into 2 triangles, following the diagrams below.

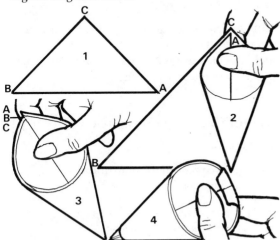

Take 1 triangle and fold A over C as shown. Wrap B round to A and C, and fold in the ends. Cut about 1cm off the point and insert the pipe to be used. Repeat the process, using the other triangle, if a second bag is required.

Greaseproof paper cones can only be used once, but vegetable parchment ones can be wiped and re-used. The same applies to bought nylon icing bags.

Note Metal or plastic syringes can be bought and used for icing.

To fill the bag: After inserting the pipe required, place the bag in a clean jar with the piping tube or nozzle resting on the base of the jar. This will prevent loss of some of the contents while filling. Half fill the bag with icing, using a dessertspoon. Fold over the broad end, and tuck in the sides of the bag. Do not fill the bag more than half full.

For easier filling, the top half of a nylon bag can be folded back before filling; it prevents smears of icing on the part of the bag to be folded over.

Icing pipes to use: Use pipes 1, 2, and 3 (fine, medium, and thick) for straight lines, dots, and writing. These are called writing pipes.

Star or rose pipes may have 5, 6, 8 or more points. They are used for scrolls, shell edgings etc, as well as for rosettes and stars. The size of the decoration will depend on the amount of icing forced through the pipe.

Petal and leaf pipes for flowers and leaves, ribbon pipes for basket work, and many other decorative pipes are also available.

General hints on piping: Practise first on an up-turned plate. If the icing is scraped off before it hardens, it can be re-used.

If possible, place the cake to be decorated on a turntable; it makes turning the cake easier and safer. The end of the pipe should be free of icing before starting. Begin close to, but not touching, the surface to be decorated. Exert an even pressure while forcing icing through the pipe, and stop pressing before lifting the pipe.

Start decorating in the centre of a cake and work outwards. When writing, work from left to right.

Allow all piped-on decorations to dry thoroughly before adding other decorations.

Keep some icing aside for attaching decorations. Cover with a damp cloth to prevent a crust forming.

Royal Icing

450g icing sugar
2 egg whites
1 × 5ml spoon lemon
juice

1 × 5ml spoon glycerine

Sift the icing sugar. Put the egg whites and lemon juice into a bowl and, using a wooden spoon, beat just enough to liquefy the whites slightly. Add half the sugar, a little at a time, and beat for 10 minutes. Add the rest of the sugar gradually, and beat for another 10 minutes until the icing is white and forms peaks when the spoon is drawn up from the mixture. Add the glycerine while mixing.

Quantities to use

The quantities above will cover the top and sides of a 20cm cake. Use half quantities for the top only.

For a 25cm cake, double the quantities above, to cover the top and sides.

GLAZES AND COATINGS

Glazes are used to give a shiny coating to food. Pastry, breads, cakes, and biscuits may be glazed with egg white, egg wash, sugar syrup or warmed jam such as apricot glaze, and then covered with crumbs, ground nuts, coconut, marzipan, almond paste or praline. Fruit flans or tartlets are often coated with a sweet liquid thickened with arrowroot.

Individual recipes usually describe the most suitable type of glaze if one is required.

Apricot Glaze

Enough to coat the top and sides of one 15–18cm cake

200g apricot jam

2 × 15ml spoons water

Heat the jam and the water gently in a saucepan until smooth. Sieve the mixture and return to the cleaned saucepan. Bring slowly to the boil and heat gently until thick.

Note The glaze is used to cover a cake before applying marzipan, almond paste, or a coating of ground or chopped nuts or crumbs. It is slightly thinner than jam used on its own, spreads more easily over a cake, and is therefore less likely to drag crumbs off the surface. It can be stored in a refrigerator for at least 2 weeks.

Maraschino Glaze

Enough to cover one 25cm ring cake or 24 small cakes

175g icing sugar
2 × 15ml spoons
softened butter
2–3 × 15ml spoons milk
1–2 × 5ml spoons
maraschino liqueur **or**
syrup from maraschino
cherries

1–2 drops red food
colouring (optional)

Sift the icing sugar and work it into the butter in a small bowl until thoroughly mixed. Heat the milk until steaming, and mix it gradually into the sugar and butter with the liqueur or syrup. Tint pink if liked. The glaze should be thick enough to spread lightly, yet be able to trickle over the edge of a cake and drip down the sides.

Note An icing sugar glaze of this kind is used most often fricked over an icing of a contrasting colour and flavour (see p1224). Maraschino glaze looks attractive over chocolate icing.

Sweet Coating Glaze for Flans and Tartlets

Enough to cover one 18cm fruit flan or 12–16 tartlets

1 × 5ml spoon arrowroot
125ml fruit syrup from
canned **or** *bottled fruit*
or *125ml water and*
15–25g sugar

1–3 drops food colouring
lemon juice

Blend the arrowroot with a little of the cold fruit syrup or water. Heat the remaining fruit syrup, or water and sugar, to boiling point in a small pan. Pour on to the blended arrowroot, stirring gently. Return to the pan and heat just to boiling point, stirring very gently, to avoid air bubbles (which cloud the glaze). Remove from the heat, add the colouring and lemon juice to taste. Pour or spoon the hot glaze carefully over the flan or tart. Leave to cool and set before serving.

To Apply Coatings over Jam Glaze or Butter Cream

Make sure that any coatings, ie nuts, crumbs or praline are finely crushed or ground, and that the coconut shreds are separated, otherwise they will not stick on the cake. Scatter the coating evenly across a sheet of greaseproof paper. Have ready a fine pastry brush for putting loose crumbs in place.

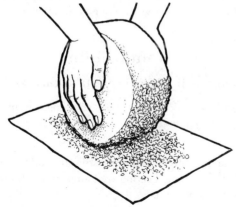

Using jam glaze: Brush any loose crumbs off the cake. Brush the sides with a warm apricot glaze (p1234). Hold the cake on end between your palms, and roll the sides in the coating, pressing gently. Transfer the cake to a plate or wire rack and brush off any surplus crumbs. Brush the top with glaze and distribute the coating evenly over the surface. Use the fine brush to put loose crumbs, nuts, etc in place. Lay a piece of greaseproof paper over the top, and press lightly to make the coating stick.

Using butter cream: The butter cream should be soft enough to spread easily, and should be applied thinly to the cake. Proceed as when applying coatings to a jam glaze.

Glacé icing or whipped cream top: If the sides of a cake are to be coated with butter cream or jam glaze, and the top with glacé icing or whipped cream, ice and coat the sides first. Allow to set before applying the glacé icing. If using butter cream, mould it into a small ridge round the top of the cake to stop the glacé icing spilling over the edge.

Coconut for Coating or Decoration

To colour: Place the coconut in a small bowl, and add a few drops of food colouring. Stir briskly until evenly coloured. Spread the coconut out on a baking tray, and leave to dry in a very cool oven, 120°C, Gas $\frac{1}{2}$. Shake the pan and turn the coconut over to dry it evenly.

To toast: Spread the coconut on the grill pan under very low heat. Shake the pan and turn the coconut over to brown it evenly.

To Coat a Cake, Gâteau or Dessert with Whipped Cream

Flavour the cream and add food colouring, if liked. Whip the cream until very stiff. For a really firm coating, eg if the completed cake, gâteau or dessert must stand in a warm place for a time before being served, add a very little dissolved and cooled gelatine to the cream when whipping; about half the usual setting quantity is enough. Work quickly.

Place the cake on a turntable, an upturned plate or a wire rack. Smooth the whipped cream on the sides first, with a palette knife; then cover the top.

If liked, the cream can be flicked up with a knife, making a 'snow scene' surface like that used for Christmas cakes.

The cake, gâteau or dessert should be coated or decorated before the cream becomes too firm. Avoid decorations which may be spoiled by damp. If possible, chill the cake, gâteau or dessert until required for use.

Whipped Cream Frosting
(blender)
See p1420.

Fillings

Butter Cream (1)

Enough for 2 layers in one 18cm cake

200g icing **or** caster
 sugar
1 egg yolk

100g softened butter
flavouring and colouring
 as required

Sift the icing sugar, if used. Beat the egg yolk, adding the sugar gradually until they are well blended. Beat in the butter, a little at a time. Add the flavouring with the butter and, lastly, stir in any colouring.

Note This filling is richer and slightly less sweet than butter icing (p1227).

Butter Cream (2)

Enough for 2 layers in one 18cm cake

200g icing sugar
2 egg whites
100g butter

flavouring and colouring
 as required

Sift the icing sugar. Whisk the egg whites until stiff. Add the icing sugar, a third at a time, whisking between each addition until the mixture forms peaks. Cream the butter until fluffy and gradually beat in the meringue mixture. Flavour and colour as required.

VARIATIONS

Chocolate Butter Cream (1)

Grate 50g plain block chocolate into a saucepan. Heat gently until the chocolate melts, then cool. Use to flavour the butter cream.

Chocolate Butter Cream (2)

Dissolve 1 × 15ml spoon cocoa in 1 × 15ml spoon hot water, then cool. Use to flavour the butter cream.

Coffee Butter Cream

Dissolve 1 × 5ml spoon instant coffee in 1 × 15ml spoon hot water, then cool. Use to flavour the butter cream.

Coconut Filling

Enough to fill 1 layer in one 15–18cm cake

50g icing sugar
1 egg yolk
1 × 15ml spoon lemon
 juice

25g desiccated coconut

Sift the icing sugar into a heatproof bowl, add the egg yolk and lemon juice and mix to a smooth paste. Place the bowl over a saucepan of hot water over low heat. Cook for 5–7 minutes until thick, stirring all the time. Remove from the heat and stir in the coconut. Leave to cool before using.

Rum and Walnut Filling

Enough to fill 1 layer in one 18–20cm cake

50g butter
75g soft light brown
 sugar

1 × 15ml spoon rum
50g chopped walnuts

Cream the butter and sugar until soft. Add the rum a little at a time, beating well after each addition. Beat in the walnuts.

Use as a filling for spice cakes or Applesauce Cake (p1195).

Cream as a Filling

Sweetened whipped cream, liqueur-flavoured whipped cream (p880), Crème Fraîche (p880), and Chantilly cream (p880) are all used for filling gâteaux, tartlets, pastries, and choux puffs, especially for use as desserts.

Jam as a Filling

Any smooth jam makes a simple, cheap, and pleasant cake or sandwich filling. Avoid using whole fruit jams as they are lumpy and messy to cut and eat.

Lemon curd is also popular for filling cakes and tartlets.

Mincemeat

See p1120.

Sweet Butters as Fillings

Sweet flavoured butters make good cake fillings if they are fairly smooth. See pp1302–3.

CUSTARD FILLINGS

A custard containing flour or cornflour as well as eggs can be thick enough to use as a filling for cakes, choux, éclairs, tarts, and tartlets. It can be savoury or sweet; if sweet, it is called confectioners' custard (*crème patissière*). It can have various flavourings and other additions.

Confectioners' Custard (1)

Makes 250ml (approx)

1 egg	*250ml milk*
1 egg yolk	*a few drops vanilla*
50g caster sugar	*essence*
25g plain flour	

Put the egg, egg yolk, and sugar in a basin and beat with a wooden spoon until light and fluffy. Add the flour and stir in gently. Mix in the milk gradually, keeping the mixture smooth. Transfer to a saucepan, and bring the mixture to the boil, stirring all the time. Add the vanilla essence, pour into a basin, and cover with damp greaseproof paper to prevent a skin forming. Leave to cool.

When cold, use as a filling for cakes, small pastries, and tartlets.

VARIATIONS

Chocolate-flavoured Confectioners' Custard

Dissolve 25g grated chocolate in the milk.

Crème St Honoré

Whisk 4 egg whites until stiff with 1 × 15ml spoon caster sugar. Fold into the hot confectioners' custard. Use as a filling for choux puffs or as an alternative to whipped cream.

Crème Frangipane

Beat 40g melted butter into the hot confectioners' custard, then add 75g crushed almond macaroons or ground almonds and a few drops of almond essence. Use as a tartlet or pancake filling.

Confectioners' Custard (2)

Makes 300ml (approx)

25g cornflour	*1 × 2.5ml spoon vanilla*
250ml milk	*essence* **or** *other essence*
1 egg and 1 egg yolk **or**	**or** *brandy, sherry, rum*
3 egg yolks	**or** *liqueur*
40g caster sugar	

Blend the cornflour to a paste with a little of the milk and beat in the eggs and caster sugar. Heat the remaining milk, but do not let it boil. Pour the hot milk on to the blended cornflour, stirring well. Return to the saucepan and stir over gentle heat until the custard thickens. As soon as the mixture begins to bubble, remove from the heat. Stir in the flavouring. Cover with damp greaseproof paper and leave to cool completely.

Use to fill choux, pastries, and cakes.

Confectioners' Custard or Pastry Cream (made with oil)

See p891.

Mock Cream (1)

Enough to fill 2 layers in one 18cm cake or gâteau

2 × 5ml spoons cornflour　*50g icing **or** caster sugar*
125ml milk　*½ × 2.5ml spoon vanilla*
50g softened butter　*essence*

Blend the cornflour with the milk, bring to the boil in a small saucepan, and cook for 4–5 minutes, stirring all the time, until thick. Cover with damp greaseproof paper, and cool until tepid.

Cream the butter and sugar until it is the same consistency as the cornflour sauce. Add the sauce, a spoonful at a time, beating well after each addition. Beat in the essence and use as required.

Mock Cream (2)

Enough to cover one 18cm cake

2 × 10ml spoons　*25g caster sugar*
*　cornflour*　*a few drops vanilla*
125ml milk　*essence*
25g butter

Blend the cornflour to a smooth paste with a little of the milk, and bring the rest of the milk to the boil. Pour the boiling milk on to the blended cornflour, stirring well. Return the mixture to the pan and cook for 2–3 minutes, stirring all the time as the mixture thickens. Cover with damp greaseproof paper, and cool until tepid.

Cream the butter and sugar until pale. Beat in the cooled cornflour mixture, a little at a time. Add the vanilla essence, and beat well until smooth.

Use as a filling for sponge cakes and pastries, or pipe as a decoration on fancy cakes and desserts.

Decorations

DECORATING DESSERTS

Any decoration on a dessert should contribute to the flavour or texture of the dish as well as to its appearance. It is, however, important not to overshadow the flavour of the dessert or to make it impractical to serve.

Many desserts look attractive on their own and need no extra decoration.

Almost all the recipes in this book suggest decorations to use on the dishes where they are needed. If in doubt about how to decorate any dessert, remember that a few rosettes of whipped cream, a small spoonful of colourful jam, or just sugar is usually enough to complement a dessert.

DECORATING CAKES

Decorations on cakes should never be garish, but they should show up against the background colour on which they are placed.

The sides of a cake can be covered with a decorative band instead of icing, if preferred. Various motifs, leaves, flowers, trees, figures, etc can also be bought ready-made; most are not edible. Edible decorations can, however, be bought quite cheaply: small sweets can be used if care is taken in applying them. The food colouring used for some sweets may run and stain the surface of the cake if the sweets are attached with damp icing. Crystallized or other preserved ginger, and any chocolate decorations should also be used with caution as they may ooze syrup or melt. (A list of edible decorations is given on p1240.)

Christmas and birthday cakes: Christmas cakes are often decorated with a small sprig of holly, figures, or other seasonal emblems. For decorative 'snow scene' icing, see p1232. Birthday cakes for children usually have small candles in holders round the edge of the cake, the number corresponding with the years of the child's age. Holders can be bought in various designs, or icing can be used to stick the candles on the cake. The child's name and a greeting can be written across the centre of the cake before putting on the candles.

Other celebration cakes: Christening, barmitzvah, wedding, silver wedding cakes, etc are decorated in the same general way as other cakes but certain decorations are traditional on particular cakes. A christening cake is usually decorated with white icing only, with flowers and with a model as the most usual added decorations. A wedding cake is the most elaborate, again usually decorated all in white, although gold and silver decorations can be used if liked. Flowers, bells, silver slippers and horseshoes can be used; very often a small vase of flowers is placed in the centre of the top tier of the cake. A paper band is not used. Silver wedding cakes are decorated like wedding cakes but more simply – often just with silver flowers and leaves, and a greeting.

To attach decorations: Scratch the surface of the cake very lightly with a pin in the spot where the decoration will be placed. Put a tiny blob of icing on the underside of the decoration or on the edge of a greeting card if it is to stand upright, and press it lightly into place.

Suggestions for decorating cakes iced with glacé icing are given on pp1224–25. For piping with royal icing see pp1232–33.

Moulded Decorations

Flowers, leaves, fruit, etc can be moulded from small pieces of fondant icing (p1226), moulding icing (p1240) or marzipan (p1232). Marzipan is smoother and easier to use than almond paste. Before adding any moulded decorations to an iced cake or gâteau, let them dry thoroughly.

Knead the icing or marzipan until pliable, working in any flavouring or food colouring desired. Use concentrated confectioners' colours if possible, but do not colour heavily. If very bright decorations are wanted, eg Christmas holly berries, the decorations can be painted with undiluted food colouring when set and dry.

Break off small pieces of the moulding material, roll or pat flat if necessary, and model into the desired shapes.

To make one-piece flowers: Cut out flat circles of the moulding material and pinch up the centres. Make cuts radiating from the pinched-up centres

to the outer edges, to make petals. Pinch and shape the end of each petal and place a mimosa or silver ball in the centre of each flower.

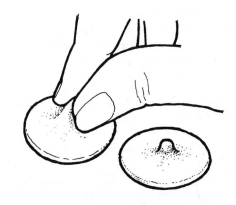

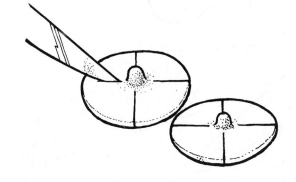

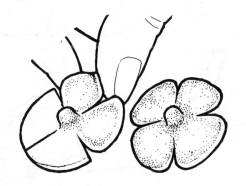

Making one-piece flowers

To make leaves: Cut small ovals or circles using a small pastry cutter. Pinch one side or end to form a stalk. For holly leaves, cut out flat diamonds of moulding material, and scallop the edges with a tiny curved cutter.

Other silhouette shapes: Cut shapes, eg a moon and stars, out of any of the moulding materials. Cut out the shape required in paper, using, for instance, an illustration in a magazine, lay it on the moulding material and cut round it.

Note For moulded marzipan fruits and vegetables, see pp1086–87.

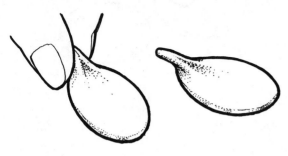

Pinching stalks on marzipan leaves

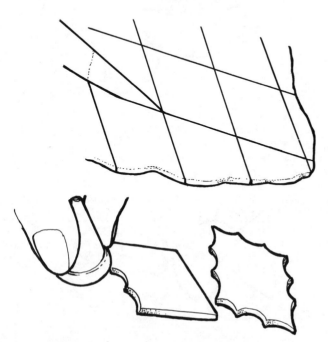

Making marzipan holly leaves

Edible decorations

Angelica leaves	Desiccated coconut
Candied fruit	Fruit, fresh
Chocolate curls or scrolls (p1241)	Fruit, canned
Chocolate vermicelli	Frosting, piped
Chopped or whole crystallized fruit	Hundreds and thousands
Chopped or whole glacé fruit	Icings, piped
Chopped or whole nuts	Jam
Confectioners' custard, piped	Small silver balls
	Small sweets
Cream, piped	Mimosa
Crumbs	Moulded decorations (pp1239–40)
Crystallized flowers	Praline (p1241)
	Shredded chocolate

Moulding Icing for Decorations
(made with gelatine)

Makes 225g (approx)

200g icing sugar
1 × 5ml spoon gelatine
1 × 10ml spoon hot water

1 × 5ml spoon glycerine (scant)
3 × 5ml spoons liquid glucose
food colouring

Sift the icing sugar. Dissolve the gelatine in the hot water, add the glycerine and glucose, and work in the icing sugar. Knead well and work in colouring as required.

Keep the mixture warm while working, and break off small pieces to make leaves, flowers, etc. Leave these to set on waxed paper.

Chocolate Curls or Scrolls

**Makes enough scrolls to decorate
one 20cm cake**

200g plain chocolate   *1 ×15ml spoon salad oil*

Break up the chocolate and put it on a heatproof plate. Place the plate over a pan of simmering water. When the chocolate has melted, work in the salad oil. Remove from the heat and leave to cool slightly, then spread out thinly on the plate. Leave until cold and almost firm. With a round-ended knife held almost parallel with the plate, scrape off bands or curls of chocolate, as wide or narrow as you wish. Place them on soft kitchen paper as you make them, since they are very fragile.

Praline

Makes 200g (approx)

100g caster sugar   *100g browned* **or** *toasted*
½ vanilla pod   *nuts* (p1185) *eg almonds,*
1 ×15ml spoon   *hazelnuts, walnuts*
  water   *oil for greasing*

Heat the sugar, vanilla pod, and water until the sugar is light golden-brown. Stir in the nuts. Turn the mixture immediately on to an oiled marble slab or metal surface, and leave to harden. When hard, crush with a pestle in a mortar, or process in an electric blender. Crush very finely if wanted for flavouring; leave more coarsely crushed for coating or decorating.

Use for flavouring, coating, and decorating cream desserts, ice creams, mousses, soufflés, and gâteaux.

Note Praline powder keeps well in an airtight jar.

PASTRY MAKING AND PASTRY GOODS

The art of making paste requires much practice, dexterity, and skill: it should be touched as lightly as possible, made with cool hands and in a cool place (a marble slab is better than a board for the purpose), and the coolest part of the house should be selected for the process during warm weather.

Pastry Making

All pastry except hot water crust used for raised pies should be as light in texture as possible. Lightness is achieved by incorporating air during making, by using the correct proportion of fat and water to flour, by keeping the ingredients cool, and by handling the pastry as little as possible.

When making flaky, puff, or rough puff pastry, the air is incorporated in thin layers by folding and rolling the dough. In shortcrust and suet crust pastry, air is distributed evenly throughout the dough. Plain flour is almost always used for pastry, the major exception being suet crust pastry which requires a chemical raising agent.

Butter, or butter and lard in equal quantities, give the best results in most pastry-making. Hard block margarine can almost always be substituted for butter. White fat can be used for making flaky or puff pastry, and soft tub margarine and oil are also used in special pastry recipes (see pp889–92).

GENERAL HINTS

1) Work in a cool place, if possible on a stone slab, and keep your hands cool.
2) Always sift the flour and salt after measuring, since this helps to lighten the pastry.
3) When rubbing the fat into the flour, use the finger-tips and lift the hands up from the bowl so that air is trapped as the flour falls back into the bowl.
4) Use cold water and a round-bladed knife for mixing. Flours vary in the amount of water which they absorb, so the quantities given in the recipes can only be approximate. Do not use too much water or the pastry will be hard.
5) Lemon juice strengthens the gluten or protein in flour and helps give a lighter and crisper result when making flaky, puff, or rough puff pastry.
6) Handle the pastry as little and as lightly as possible. Work quickly.
7) Chill the pastry, or leave in a cool place for 15–30 minutes after making.
8) Roll the pastry lightly, quickly, and evenly with short strokes, lifting the rolling-pin between each stroke. Do not roll off the edge of the pastry or the air will be pressed out.
9) Always roll away from yourself, never from side to side, and do not turn the pastry over.
10) Use very little flour for rolling out and remove any surplus flour with a pastry brush.
11) Use the rolled side of the pastry for the outside of a pie case, tart shell or crust.
12) Most pastries are baked in a fairly hot oven; the richer the pastry, the hotter the oven required for cooking. A high temperature is necessary to create steam within the dough and to make the pastry light. It also makes the starch grains burst; the starch then absorbs the fat. Unless the heat is high enough to act on the flour in this way, the melted fat runs out and leaves the pastry heavy and tough, and less rich.

Note Hot water crust and choux pastry are exceptions to these rules.

FAULTS IN PASTRY

Shortcrust and similar Pastry

If the pastry is:

hard and tough:
a) warm fat has been used – either the cook's hands were too warm or the fat was already soft when rubbed in
b) it has been mixed with too much water
c) it has been kneaded too much or rolled out too heavily
d) it has been rolled out with too much flour or has been turned over and rolled on both sides
e) it has been cooked in too cool an oven.

shrunken:
a) it has been stretched in rolling out or shaping
b) it has not been rested long enough before use.

grainy, flaky or blistered:
a) the fat has been badly rubbed in or not rubbed in enough
b) the water has not been fully mixed in or mixed in too slowly
c) the pastry has been badly kneaded or has been rolled out twice, with too much flour.

too short, ie crumbly:
a) it contains too much fat
b) it has been mixed with too little water
c) the fat has been over-rubbed into the flour.

Flaky, Puff, and similar Pastry

If the pastry is:

hard and tough:
a) warm fat has been used
b) it has been mixed with too much water
c) it has been over-kneaded or over-rolled with too much flour
d) it has been cooked in too cool an oven.

unevenly risen:
a) the fat has been mixed in unevenly
b) it has been rolled out unevenly or not folded correctly
c) the pastry edges have not been trimmed
d) it was not rested long enough before use.

too flat, ie not flaky:
a) warm fat has been used in making

b) the fats have been badly mixed.
soggy inside with a hard crust:
it has been cooked in too hot an oven.

Suet Crust Pastry

If the pastry is:

hard and tough:
a) it contains too much water
b) it has been cooked in too slow an oven for too long, or should have been steamed.

too solid or lumpy:
a) it contains too little baking powder or not a high enough proportion of breadcrumbs
b) lumpy suet has been used
c) it has been cooked too quickly so the suet has not melted
d) it has got wet from steam during cooking.

Hot Water Crust Pastry

If the pastry is:

sticky or collapses:
a) it has not been made of an even thickness
b) it has been moulded too thinly in a jar or mould
c) it has been used too warm.

too dry and breakable:
a) it contains too little fat
b) the fat or water or the dough itself have been used too cool.

Choux Pastry

If the pastry is:

too thin:
a) the flour and liquid have not been cooked long enough
b) the mixture has not been beaten sufficiently
c) the liquid has been allowed to cool too much before adding the flour.

too thick:
the liquid has been boiled for too long.

close and solid when cooked:
a) it has not been beaten enough
b) it has been cooked in too hot an oven
c) it has been cooked in too cool an oven.

To Keep Pastry

Pastry which must be kept for several hours or overnight before baking should be wrapped closely in greaseproof paper and kept in a refrigerator or cool place.

USING PASTRY

Open Tarts

Open tarts are usually baked on ovenproof glass or enamel plates. Sweet tarts can be filled with cooked or uncooked fruit, or with jam, syrup or treacle, mincemeat or a custard mixture. For an 18cm plate, pastry using 125g flour will be needed.

Shape the pastry into a ball or round bun shape. Then roll it out into a circle 2cm bigger than the plate all round, and about 2mm thick. Fold the pastry loosely over the rolling-pin and lift it on to the plate. Smooth it carefully with the fingers so that no air is trapped between the pastry and the plate. Take care not to stretch the pastry as it will shrink back during baking, leaving an uneven edge.

If the pastry shell is baked without a filling, prick the bottom well with a fork all over before baking, or bake blind (see p1245).

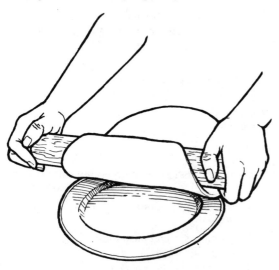

Flans

A flan may be baked in a flan ring, which is a circular, often fluted, hoop of metal without a base. The ring is placed on a flat baking sheet during baking. After baking, the flan ring is lifted off the set pastry shell, which is then transferred to a serving plate.

Alternatively, a flan can be baked in an ovenproof ceramic or metal flan case, like a shallow sandwich tin but with fluted sides. In this case the flan is served from the dish.

To line a flan ring 18cm in diameter, pastry using 125g flour will be needed. Place the flan ring on a baking sheet. Roll the pastry into a round at least 5cm larger than the flan ring and 2mm thick. Lift the pastry with a rolling-pin to prevent it stretching, and lay it in the flan ring. Press the pastry gently down on the baking sheet so that no air bubbles are trapped. Working from the centre outward, press down lightly all over the base. Press the pastry right into the angle where the sides meet the base. Then work up the sides, making sure that the pastry fits into the flutes, and is of even thickness all round. Trim off any surplus pastry with a sharp knife, or roll across the top of the ring with the rolling-pin to cut off the pastry cleanly.

Line a ceramic flan case in the same way.

Double Crust Plate Pies or Tarts

Double crust pies or tarts can be made in ovenproof glass, enamel, metal or foil plates with a raised flat rim or border. A 20cm plate will need pastry made with 225g flour.

Divide the pastry into two portions, form each into a round shape, and roll one portion into a round 2cm larger than the plate and about 2mm thick. Fold it over the rolling-pin and lift on to the plate; smooth to fit the plate without stretching the pastry. Trim off any surplus pastry with a sharp knife. Put in a layer of filling, sprinkle with sugar if required, and cover with another layer of filling. Do not add any extra liquid or the pastry will become soggy.

Roll the remaining piece of pastry into a round slightly larger than the plate. Dampen the edge of the pastry lining the plate with cold water. Lift on the cover and ease it into position without stretching the pastry. Press the edges together firmly and knock up with the back of a knife. Make a small hole in the centre to allow steam to escape.

Deep Pies or Tarts

These can be made with a single top crust or with a double crust. A 750ml pie dish will need pastry made with 150g flour for the top crust. Allow slightly more than double this quantity if the dish is to be lined as well.

Either sweet or savoury fillings, eg stewed fruit, steak and kidney or vegetable, can be used. About 600g filling will be needed for a 750ml pie dish. If the filling is likely to shrink during cooking, or if there is not enough to fill the dish, place a pie funnel or inverted ceramic egg cup in the centre of the dish.

If using fruit, place half of it in the dish, sprinkle with sugar and any flavouring used, then add the remaining fruit, piling it high in the centre. Sugar should not be sprinkled on top of the fruit because it will dissolve and make the top crust soggy. Wet fruit can be dredged lightly with flour, if liked.

If making a double crust pie, line the pie dish in the same way as for a plate pie; then dredge the bottom crust lightly with flour or rolled oats before adding the filling if it is very moist.

For the top crust roll out the pastry 2mm thick and at least 2cm larger than the dish. If the dish has not been lined, cut off a strip of pastry the width and length of the rim of the dish. Dampen the rim of the dish with water, and place the strip of pastry on it. Join the cut ends by pressing them firmly together. Brush the strip of pastry with water.

Lift the pastry lid with the rolling-pin, and lay it over the dish, taking care not to stretch it. Press the two layers of pastry together firmly, trim off any overhanging pastry with a sharp knife, and knock up the edge with the back of the knife. Make a small hole in the centre to allow steam to escape.

Note To line a basin with suet crust pastry, see p979.

Guide to Shortcrust Pastry Quantities

1) To line a flan ring or make a top or bottom crust for a plate pie:

18cm – pastry made with	125g flour
20cm	,,	150g flour
23cm	,,	175g flour
25cm	,,	200g flour

2) To make a double crust plate pie:

18cm	,,	200g flour
20cm	,,	225g flour
23cm	,,	250g flour

3) To make a top crust for a deep oval pie dish:

500ml	,,	125g flour
750ml	,,	150g flour
1 litre	,,	200g flour

Use double these quantities to make a double crust deep pie.

4) Tartlets:

Pastry made with 100g flour will make approximately twelve 7cm tartlets.

Note To make a puff or flaky pastry cover for a 1 litre oval pie dish, use 100g flour.

Baking Blind

In many cases, a tart, flan or patty case must be cooked empty or 'blind' before the filling is added. A partially cooked case is used if the filling will need cooking at a low temperature or for a short time only; a fully baked case is used if the filling will need only brief re-heating or will not be cooked at all.

To bake a case empty or blind, prick the bottom of the case well with a fork. Cover the base with a piece of greaseproof paper, then fill the case with dried beans, bread crusts or rice. Bake the case at the usual temperature for the type of pastry used, for 8–12 minutes if a partially cooked case is needed, ie until the pastry is set, or for 20–30 minutes if a fully cooked case is required. In either case, remove the paper and dry filling, and return the case to the oven for 5–7 minutes to dry out the inside. The dry filling can be stored and re-used many times.

The times given above (p1245) are based on an average cooking temperature of 190°–200°C, Gas 5–6, for shortcrust or similar pastry. The time will however vary with the size of the case and the depth of the dry filling used. Tartlet cases may cook in a shorter time, large tart or flan cases may take a little longer if the dry filling is dense. With partially baked cases, care must be taken that the walls or sides of the case are of uniform thickness all round and are adequately firm before the dry filling is removed, or they may collapse while drying out.

If the top rim of the pastry case is already browned when the dry filling is removed, the case should be dried out at a lower temperature than that used for setting or cooking the pastry.

Pastry Decorations for Flans, Tarts, etc, Baked Blind

Cut out the required shapes in pastry, glaze if liked, and bake beside the main pastry. Cover loosely with foil or remove from the oven if they are cooked and brown before the main pastry.

Greasing Containers

It is not necessary to grease tins, baking sheets, etc when making pastry, unless choux pastry, pâte sucrée or suet crust pastry are used.

If using a container (jam jar, etc) to mould a raised pie, this should be greased and floured.

FINISHES AND DECORATIONS

For Deep Pies or Double Crust Tarts

(using shortcrust, rough puff, flaky or puff pastry)

Edges

Line the edge of a pie dish with a pastry strip, cover, and trim with a sharp knife held at an angle away from the dish to allow for shrinkage during baking. Knock up the edges with the back of a knife.

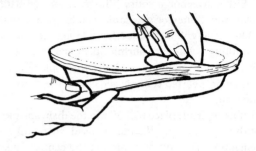

To flute (scallop) edges: Pressing the top with the thumb, draw the edge towards the centre of the pie for about 1cm using the back of a knife. Repeat round the pie edge. For savoury pies, leave about 2cm between the cuts and for sweet pies about 5mm.

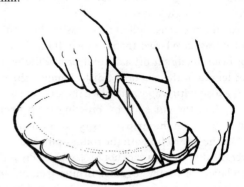

To fork edges: Press the back of a fork into the edge of the pie with the prongs pointed towards the centre. Repeat all round the pie edge.

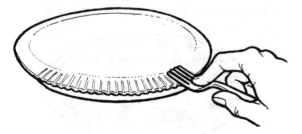

To crimp edges: Pinch the edge between the thumb and first finger of both hands, then twist slightly in opposite directions.

Tops

Make a small hole in the centre of any top pie crust to let the steam out. Decorate savoury pies with pastry leaves, a tassel or a rose. Dampen the shapes lightly before putting them in place.

To make leaves: Roll out a strip of pastry 2–3cm wide. Cut into diamond-shaped pieces. Mark veins on each leaf with the back of a knife. Pinch in one end for a stalk.

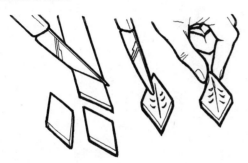

To make a tassel: Roll out a strip of pastry 2 × 15cm. Make 1–2cm cuts every 5mm along the strip. Roll up, place in the centre of the pie, and spread the ends into a fan shape.

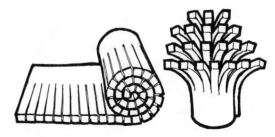

To make a rose: Make a ball of pastry and 2 pastry circles. Place the circles on top of each other and wrap round the ball, pressing the edges together under the ball, to seal. Cut a cross in the top of the ball through the circles with a sharp knife. Open out and turn back the segments to form petals.

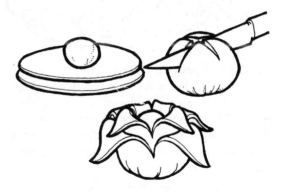

For Open Tarts and Flans
(using shortcrust pastry)

Edges

Use any of the finishes suggested for double crust tarts on pp1246–47, or one of the following:

Twist: Roll pastry trimmings into a long thin strip. Trim to 2cm wide. Moisten the edge of the pastry. Press one end of the strip on to the edge of the tart or flan to secure it, then twist the strip with the right hand and press down gently between the twists with the index finger of the left hand.

Braid: Roll pastry trimmings thinly into a long strip and cut 2 pieces the same length and about 1cm wide. Moisten the edge of the tart or flan. Keeping the strips flat, secure the ends together on the edge, then interweave, pressing the plait down lightly with the finger-tip on the edge of the pastry.

Pastry shapes: Roll out the pastry trimmings thinly and cut into 1cm circles, plain or fluted, or into small triangles or stars. Moisten the edge of the tart or flan, and arrange the shapes on it, overlapping them slightly.

Tops

Plain lattice: Cut thinly rolled pastry strips 5mm–1cm wide. Place in a lattice design on top of the filling, trimming the ends to fit the top neatly.

Twisted lattice: Make as above but twist the pastry strips before laying them on the filling.

Pastry shapes: Cut pastry trimmings into shapes as described above. Use to mark a tart or flan into serving portions or to make a lattice design.

To Glaze Pastry

Meat pies, patties, sausage rolls, etc are usually brushed with well beaten egg before or during baking. If a deeper glaze is desired, the yolk alone is used. If milk or water is beaten with the egg or egg yolk to increase the quantity, the glaze is called an *egg wash*. Salt or sugar in the proportion of 1×2.5ml spoon per egg should be added to make the egg easier to brush on evenly.

Fruit tarts, puffs, etc may be brushed with cold water and dredged with caster sugar before baking. If a thin coating of icing is required, the pastry may be brushed with well whisked egg white and dredged with caster sugar when almost baked.

Types of Pastry

Shortcrust Pastry (1)

(for pies, tarts, etc)

Makes 350g (approx)

200g plain flour
1 × 2.5ml spoon salt
100g fat, eg 50g lard and
  50g butter **or**
  margarine

3 × 15ml spoons cold
  water
flour for rolling out

Sift together the flour and salt into a bowl. Rub the fats into the flour until the mixture resembles fine breadcrumbs. Mix to a stiff dough with cold water. Roll out on a lightly floured surface, and use as required.

Bake in a fairly hot oven, 200°C, Gas 6, until set, then reduce the heat to cook the filling ingredients if necessary.

Shortcrust Pastry (2)

(for pies, tarts, etc)

Makes 350g (approx)

200g plain flour
1 × 2.5ml spoon salt
1 × 5ml spoon baking
  powder
75g lard **or** clarified fat
  (p473)

4 × 15ml spoons cold
  water
flour for rolling out

Sift together the flour, salt, and baking powder into a bowl. Rub in the fat until the mixture resembles fine breadcrumbs. Mix to a stiff paste with cold water. Roll out on a lightly floured surface, and use as required.

Bake in a very hot oven, 230°C, Gas 8, until set, then reduce the heat to cook the filling ingredients, if necessary.

Note Shortcrust Pastry (3), made using a mixer, can be found on p1420.

Wholemeal Shortcrust Pastry

(for pies, tarts, etc)

Makes 350g (approx)

100g plain flour
100g wholemeal flour
1 × 2.5ml spoon salt
50g butter **or** margarine

50g lard
4 × 15ml spoons cold
  water
flour for rolling out

Mix the flours and salt in a bowl and rub in the fats until the mixture resembles fine breadcrumbs. Mix to a soft dough with cold water. Roll out on a lightly floured surface, and use as required.

Bake in a fairly hot oven, 200°C, Gas 6, until set, then reduce the heat to cook the filling ingredients, if necessary.

Sweet Paste or Pâte Sucrée

(for sweet flans, tarts, and tartlets)

Makes 400g (approx)

200g plain flour
$\frac{1}{2}$ × 2.5ml spoon salt
125g butter
50g caster sugar

1 egg yolk
1 × 15ml spoon cold
  water
flour for rolling out

Sift together the flour and salt into a bowl. Cut the butter into small pieces and rub into the flour until the mixture resembles fine breadcrumbs. Mix in the sugar, then the egg yolk, and enough cold water to make a stiff dough. Roll out on a lightly floured surface, and use as required.

Bake in a fairly hot oven, 200°C, Gas 6, until set, then reduce the heat to cook the filling ingredients, if necessary.

Note In warm weather very little water is required.

Suet Crust Pastry

(for meat puddings, dumplings, fruit puddings, roly-poly puddings)

Makes 400g (approx)

200g plain flour
1 × 2.5ml spoon salt
1 × 5ml spoon baking powder

75g shredded suet
125ml cold water

Sift together the flour, salt, and baking powder into a bowl and mix in the suet. Mix to a firm dough with cold water. Bake, boil or steam as directed in the recipe.

Rich Suet Crust Pastry

(for meat and fruit puddings and roly-poly puddings)

Makes 600g (approx)

200g plain flour
1 × 2.5ml spoon salt
1 × 5ml spoon baking powder

75g soft white breadcrumbs
125g shredded suet
175ml cold water

Sift together the flour, salt, and baking powder into a bowl and mix in the breadcrumbs and suet. Mix with cold water to form a dough which is firm but soft enough to roll out easily. Bake, boil or steam as directed in the recipe.

Note This makes a very light, easily digested pudding, but the pastry is liable to break if turned out of the basin.

Hot Water Crust Pastry

(for pork, veal and ham, and raised game pies)

Makes 350g (approx)

200g plain flour
1 × 2.5ml spoon salt

75g lard
100ml milk or water

Sift the flour and salt into a warm bowl, make a well in the centre, and keep the bowl in a warm place. Meanwhile, heat the lard and milk or water together until boiling, then add them to the flour, mixing well with a wooden spoon until the pastry

is cool enough to knead with the hands. Knead thoroughly and mould as required.

Bake in a hot oven, 220°C, Gas 7, until the pastry is set, then reduce the heat to moderate, 180°C, Gas 4, until fully baked.

Note Throughout the mixing, kneading, and moulding, the pastry must be kept warm, otherwise moulding will be extremely difficult. If the pastry is too warm, however, it will be so soft and pliable that it will not retain its shape or support its own weight.

To Mould a Raised Pie

Makes one 13cm diameter pie

hot water crust pastry using 200g flour
fat for greasing flour

The pastry must be raised or moulded while still warm (see **Note** above).

Reserve one-quarter of the pastry for the lid and leave in the bowl in a warm place, covered with a greased polythene bag. Roll out the remainder to about 5mm thick, in a round or oval shape. Shape the pie gently with the hands. If this proves too difficult, use a jar, round cake tin or similar container, as a mould: grease and flour the sides and base of the mould, invert it, lay the pastry over it, and mould the pastry round the sides, taking care not to pull the pastry and making sure that the sides and base are of an even thickness. Leave to cool. When cold, remove the pastry case from the mould and put in the filling. Roll out the pastry reserved for the lid, dampen the rim of the case, put on the lid, and press the edges firmly together. Tie 3 or 4 folds of greaseproof paper round the pie to hold it in shape during baking and to prevent it becoming too brown.

Note If the pie is raised without using a jar, moulding is made easier by firmly pressing some of the filling into the lower part of the pie when it has been raised to the required shape and thickness.

Alternatively, line a hinged raised pie mould with the pastry and bake in the container.

Choux Pastry

(for cream buns, cream puffs, éclairs, etc)

Makes 450g (approx)

100g plain flour	*a pinch of salt*
250ml water	*1 egg yolk*
50g butter **or** *margarine*	*2 eggs*

Sift the flour. Put the water, fat and salt in a saucepan, and bring to the boil. Remove from the heat and add the flour all at once. Return to the heat and beat well with a wooden spoon until the mixture forms a smooth paste which leaves the sides of the pan clean. Remove from the heat, cool slightly, add the egg yolk, and beat well. Add the other eggs, one at a time, beating thoroughly between each addition. Use as required.

Bake in a fairly hot oven, 200°C, Gas 6.

Note This pastry rises better if used while still warm, but if this quantity is not all required at once, raw pastry or baked shells can be successfully frozen (see p1392).

Cheese Pastry

(for savoury pies and canapés)

Makes 450g (approx)

200g plain flour	*100g finely grated cheese*
a pinch of dry mustard	*1 egg yolk*
a pinch of salt	*1–2 × 15ml spoons cold*
a pinch of Cayenne	*water*
pepper	*flour for rolling out*
100–125g butter	
(see **Note**)	

Sift together the flour and seasonings into a bowl. Rub in the butter until the mixture resembles fine breadcrumbs. Add the cheese, egg yolk, and enough cold water to form a stiff dough. Roll out on a lightly floured surface and use as required.

Bake in a fairly hot oven, 200°C, Gas 6, until set, then reduce the heat to cook the filling ingredients, if necessary.

Note Use the smaller quantity of fat if the cheese is fatty and crumbly, the larger if it is fine and dry.

Using a jar to mould a raised pie

Rich Cheese Pastry

(for savoury pies and canapés)

Makes 250g (approx)

100g plain flour	75g grated Parmesan
a pinch of dry mustard	cheese
a pinch of salt	1 egg yolk
a pinch of Cayenne	1 × 10ml spoon cold
pepper	water
75g butter	flour for rolling out

Sift together the flour and seasonings into a bowl. Cream the butter until soft and white, and then add the flour, cheese, egg yolk, and enough cold water to form a stiff dough. Roll out on a lightly floured surface and use as required.

Bake in a fairly hot oven, 200°C, Gas 6, until set, then reduce the heat to cook the filling ingredients, if necessary.

Potato Pastry

(for covering meat or vegetable pies)

Makes 500g (approx)

200g freshly cooked	2 × 5ml spoons beaten
potatoes (see **Note**)	egg
200g plain flour	2 × 15ml spoons warm
25g lard **or** dripping	milk
25g butter	flour for rolling out
$\frac{1}{2}$ × 2.5ml spoon salt	
1 × 5ml spoon baking	
powder	

Mash the potatoes, or rub them through a fine metal sieve. Leave until cold.

Sift the flour. Rub the fats lightly into the flour and add the cold potatoes, salt, and baking powder. Add the beaten egg and enough milk to mix to a smooth dough; the amount of milk needed depends on the type of potato used. Roll out on a lightly floured surface and use as required.

Bake in a fairly hot oven, 200°C, Gas 6, until set, then reduce the heat to cook any filling ingredients, if necessary.

Note Freshly made-up instant potato can be used to make this pastry.

Flaky Pastry

(for pies, tarts, and tartlets)

Makes 450g (approx)

200g plain flour	1 × 2.5ml spoon lemon
$\frac{1}{2}$ × 2.5ml spoon salt	juice
125g butter **or** 75g	125ml cold water
butter and 50g lard	flour for rolling out

Sift together the flour and salt into a bowl. If butter and lard are used, blend them together evenly with a round-bladed knife. Divide the fat into 4 equal portions. Rub one-quarter of the fat into the flour. Mix to a soft dough with lemon juice and cold water. On a lightly floured surface roll the pastry into an oblong strip, keeping the ends square. Divide another quarter of the fat into small knobs, and place them at intervals on the top two-thirds of the pastry. Fold the bottom third up on to the fat and fold the top third down over it. With the rolling-pin, press the edges lightly together to prevent the air escaping. Turn the pastry so that the folded edges are on the left and right. Press the rolling-pin on the pastry at intervals, to make ridges and to distribute the air evenly. Cover the pastry with greaseproof paper and leave to rest in a cool place for 10 minutes. Repeat the rolling and folding 3 more times; the last rolling will be without fat. Leave the pastry to rest between each rolling. Use as required.

Bake in a hot oven, 220°C, Gas 7, until set, then reduce the heat to cook any filling ingredients, if necessary.

Rough Puff Pastry

(for pie crusts, tarts, tartlets, sausage rolls)

Makes 500g (approx)

200g plain flour	1 × 2.5ml spoon lemon
$\frac{1}{2}$ × 2.5ml spoon salt	juice
150g butter **or** 75g	cold water
butter and 75g lard	flour for rolling out

Sift together the flour and salt into a bowl. If butter and lard are used, blend them together evenly with a round-bladed knife. Cut the fat into pieces the size of a walnut and add to the flour. Make a well in the centre of the flour, mix in the lemon juice, then gradually add enough cold water to make an elastic dough. On a lightly floured surface, roll into a long strip keeping the edges square. Fold the bottom third over the centre third, and fold the top third over it. With the rolling-pin, press to seal the edges. Turn the pastry so that the folded edges are on the left and right. Repeat the rolling and folding until the pastry has been folded 4 times. Allow it to rest in a cool place for 10 minutes between the second and third rollings. Use as required.

Bake in a hot oven, 220°C, Gas 7, until set, then reduce the heat to cook any filling ingredients, if necessary.

Puff Pastry

(for pies, tarts, tartlets, bouchées, vol-au-vents, patties, etc)

Makes 500g (approx)

200g plain flour
½ × 2.5ml spoon salt
200g butter
1 × 2.5ml spoon lemon juice
100ml cold water (approx)
flour for rolling out

Sift together the flour and salt into a bowl and rub in 50g of the butter. Add the lemon juice to the flour and mix to a smooth dough with cold water. Shape the remaining butter into a rectangle on greaseproof paper. Roll out the dough on a lightly floured surface into a strip a little wider than the butter and rather more than twice its length. Place the butter on one half of the pastry, fold the other half over it, and press the edges together with the rolling-pin. Leave in a cool place for 15 minutes to allow the butter to harden. Roll out into a long strip. Fold the bottom third up and the top third down, press the edges together with the rolling pin, and turn the pastry so that the folded edges are on the right and left. Roll and fold again, cover, and leave in a cool place for 15 minutes. Repeat this process until the pastry has been rolled out 6 times. Finally, roll out as required and leave in a cool place for 20 minutes before cooking.

Bake in a hot oven, 220°C, Gas 7. Do not open the oven door until the pastry has risen and become partially baked, since a current of cold air may make it collapse.

To Make Vol-au-vent Cases

Makes twenty-four 5cm or twelve 7cm bouchées or eight 9cm or two 15cm vol-au-vent cases

puff pastry using 200g flour
flour for rolling out
beaten egg for glazing

Heat the oven to hot, 220°C, Gas 7. Roll out the pastry about 2cm thick (1cm thick for bouchées) on a lightly floured surface and cut into round or oval shapes as liked. Place on a baking sheet and brush the top of the pastry with beaten egg. With a smaller, floured cutter, make a circular or oval cut in each case, to form an inner ring, cutting through about half the depth of the pastry. Bake until golden-brown and crisp. When baked, remove the inner circular or oval lid, and scoop out the soft inside while still warm.

Note For a better appearance a separate piece of pastry can be baked for the lid instead of using the centre portion of the case.

To Make Patty Cases

Makes twelve 7cm cases

puff or flaky (p1252) pastry using 200g flour
flour for rolling out
beaten egg or milk for glazing

Heat the oven to hot, 220°C, Gas 7. Roll out the puff or flaky pastry about 3mm thick on a lightly floured surface and cut into rounds with a 7cm cutter. Remove the centres from half these rounds with a 3cm or 4cm cutter to use as lids. Moisten the uncut rounds with water and place the rings neatly on top. Prick the centres. Place both cases and lids on a baking sheet and leave to stand for at least 10 minutes in a cool place. Brush the cases and the lids with beaten egg or milk, and bake for 10–15 minutes.

Fleurons of Puff Pastry

See p399.

Genoese Pastry

See p1209.

Crumb Crusts

Biscuit crumbs or similar fine dry crumbs can be used to make a plate pie, flan or tart shell. The method is quick and easy, and is popular for making cheesecakes.

For savoury dishes, cracker crumbs or other unsweetened biscuit crumbs are used, sometimes mixed with a little grated cheese or with grated nuts, and lightly spiced.

For sweet dishes, plain or semi-sweet biscuit crumbs are normally used, eg digestive biscuits (plain or chocolate coated) or ginger-nuts. A small proportion of desiccated coconut can be added.

The exact proportions of fat and sugar used vary with the type of crumbs. The most usual proportions are 100g crumbs, 50g butter, 25g sugar (for sweet shells using plain biscuits). Very dry plain biscuits may need a little more fat. Chocolate melted with a knob of butter can be used instead of butter to bind the crumbs, if liked.

The crumbs should be prepared by crushing the biscuits with a rolling-pin in a polythene bag. Care should be taken to see that the crumbs are fine and even. The fat is melted gently with the sugar if used, cooled slightly, and mixed thoroughly with the crumbs. The mixture is then pressed firmly into the plate, ring or tin. The rim should be levelled by running a sharp knife round it (or over its surface if thick) and any loose crumbs should be brushed off.

The crust can then either be chilled until firm and used as required for a cold filling; or it can be baked in a moderate oven, 180°C, Gas 4, for about 15 minutes until firm, then chilled before filling. A baked case can be rebaked if the filling requires it.

Rolled oats are sometimes used in the same way as biscuit crumbs, and crushed cornflakes can also be used, with a slightly higher proportion of fat and sugar.

Savoury Dishes Using Pastry

The following section contains some examples of different types of savoury pastry dishes. A great many other savoury pies, tarts, tartlets, and canapés are located throughout the book, and can be found by reference to the Index.

Cheese and Onion Pie

6–8 helpings

3 small onions
shortcrust pastry
  (p1249) using 225g
  flour
flour for rolling out
2 × 10ml spoons plain
  flour

salt and pepper
100g Cheddar cheese
3 × 15ml spoons milk

Skin and parboil the onions. Roll out the pastry on a lightly floured surface and use half of it to line a 20cm pie plate. Season the flour with the salt and pepper. Slice the onions, toss them in the seasoned flour, and spread the slices over the base of the lined plate. Grate the cheese and sprinkle it over the onion. Sprinkle with 2 × 15ml spoons of the milk. Dampen the edges of the pastry, and use the remaining pastry to cover the dish, sealing the edges well. Knock up the edge and decorate, if liked. Brush the pastry lid with the remaining milk. Bake in a fairly hot oven, 200°C, Gas 6, for about 40 minutes.

Note If preferred, make the pie as an open tart, using pastry made with 150g flour. Reduce the cooking time to about 30 minutes.

Emmental Flan

4 helpings

shortcrust pastry	*1 egg*
(p1249) using 150g flour	*150ml milk*
flour for rolling out	*50ml double cream*
75g chopped mixed nuts	*3 × 10ml spoons flour*
100g Emmental cheese	*salt and pepper*

Roll out the pastry on a lightly floured surface and use it to line a 20cm tart or cake sandwich tin. Prick the bottom well with a fork. Scatter the nuts in an even layer over the base of the tin. Grate the cheese and spread it on the nuts. Beat the egg into the milk. Mix enough cream with the flour to make a smooth paste, then combine the paste and the remaining cream with the egg and milk, blending smoothly. Season well, then pour the mixture over the cheese in the pastry case. Bake in a fairly hot oven, 190°C, Gas 5, for about 30 minutes until the flan is firm and well browned. Serve hot or cold.

Durham Rabbit Pie

4 helpings

shortcrust pastry	*4 eggs*
(p1249) using 225g flour	*salt and pepper*
flour for rolling out	*beaten egg or milk for*
200g cooked rabbit	*glazing*
50g boiled bacon,	
without rinds	

Roll out the pastry on a lightly floured surface and use half of it to line a 20cm pie plate. Chop the rabbit meat and bacon finely and mix together. Place the mixture on the pastry in the form of a cross, leaving the outside 1cm of pastry uncovered. Break an egg carefully into each uncovered pastry triangle, taking care not to break the yolks. Season well. Dampen the edges of the pastry, cover with the remaining pastry, and glaze with egg or milk. Bake in a fairly hot oven, 200°C, Gas 6, for 30–40 minutes. Serve hot as a supper dish.

Prawn Quiche

4 helpings

shortcrust pastry	*150g Cheddar cheese*
(p1249) using 125g flour	*200g peeled prawns*
flour for rolling out	*juice of ½ lemon*
375ml Béchamel sauce	
(p704)	

Roll out the pastry on a lightly floured surface and use it to line an 18cm flan ring. Bake blind. Meanwhile, make or re-heat the Béchamel sauce and grate the cheese. Add half the cheese and all the prawns to the sauce. Mix well and add the lemon juice. Pour the mixture into the flan shell, and sprinkle with the remaining cheese. Brown under the grill.

Veal and Ham Squares

6 helpings

200g cooked fillet of veal	*salt and pepper*
200g piece of cooked	*a pinch of grated nutmeg*
ham	*shortcrust pastry*
125ml foundation white	*(p1249) using 250g flour*
sauce (p692) made	*flour for rolling out*
with half milk and half	*beaten egg or milk for*
chicken stock	*glazing*
2 hard-boiled eggs	
1 × 15ml spoon chopped	
parsley	

Cut the veal into 2cm cubes. Cut the ham into small pieces. Make the white sauce, using half milk and half stock. Add the cooked veal and the ham to the sauce. Slice the eggs and add them to the sauce with the parsley and seasoning to taste. Leave the mixture to cool. Roll out the pastry on a lightly floured surface and use half of it to line a 15 × 23cm baking tin. Spread the meat filling over it. Cover with the rest of the pastry and seal the edges. Prick the top with a fork and brush with egg or milk. Bake in a fairly hot oven, 190°C, Gas 5, for 30 minutes. Serve hot, cut in squares.

Tomato and Mushroom Patties

Makes 6

300g tomatoes	1 × 5ml spoon chopped
200g mushrooms	basil (optional)
1 small onion	shortcrust pastry
25g butter **or**	(p1249) using 200g
margarine	flour
salt and pepper	flour for rolling out

Skin and slice the tomatoes. Clean and slice the mushrooms. Skin and chop the onion. Melt the fat in a frying pan and fry the onion gently for 5 minutes. Add the mushrooms and cook for a further 10 minutes, then add the tomatoes and cook for a further 5 minutes. Season to taste and add the basil, if liked. Leave to cool.

Roll out the pastry on a lightly floured surface and cut into six 18cm rounds. Drain the vegetable mixture and place in heaps covering half of each round of pastry. Dampen the edges, fold the other half over, and pinch the edges together. Place on a baking tray and bake in a fairly hot oven, 190°C, Gas 5, for 20–30 minutes. Serve hot.

Haddock Boats

Makes 12–14 canapés

shortcrust pastry (p1249)	125g cooked smoked
using 125g flour	haddock
flour for rolling out	2 × 10ml spoons double
1 × 5ml spoon chutney	cream
2 × 5ml spoons mustard	a pinch of pepper
a few drops	6–7 anchovy fillets
Worcestershire sauce	1–2 gherkins
25g butter	

Roll out the pastry thinly on a lightly floured surface and use it to line 12–14 small boat-shaped tins. Bake blind for about 10 minutes, then cool. Mix together the chutney, mustard, and Worcestershire sauce. Spread a thin layer at the bottom of each boat. Cream the butter until light. Flake the haddock very finely and add the butter, cream, and pepper. Mix well and put into the boats. Slice the anchovies and gherkins, and use to top the boats. Serve cold.

Vegetable Flan

6 helpings

wholemeal shortcrust	25g margarine
pastry (p1249) using	25g plain flour
175g flour	250ml milk
flour for rolling out	100g Cheddar cheese
50g young carrots	salt and pepper
100g (approx) frozen **or**	2 × 10ml spoons gelatine
canned sweetcorn	1 × 10ml spoon yeast
kernels	extract
50g shelled peas	250ml tepid water

Roll out the pastry on a lightly floured surface and use it to line a 23cm flan ring. Bake blind, then cool.

Slice the carrots and drain the corn, if necessary. Cook the carrots and peas separately in very little water until just soft. Drain, and season well. Put to one side.

Melt the margarine in a saucepan. Stir in the flour and cook for 2 minutes without colouring. Stir in the milk gradually, bring to the boil, and cook for 2–3 minutes. Remove from the heat. Grate in the cheese, season to taste, stir, and leave to cool under damp greaseproof paper.

Soften the gelatine with the yeast extract in the water in a heatproof container. Stand the container in a pan of hot water and stir until the gelatine dissolves.

Spoon the cheese sauce into the flan shell and spread in an even layer. Arrange the vegetables in sections radiating from the centre of the flan. Brush well with the gelatine mixture to glaze. Leave to set, and serve cold.

Raised Pork Pie

See p589.

Note For other raised pies, see p572 and p1304.

Gougère

(Choux Pastry with Cheese)

6 helpings

fat for greasing
freshly prepared choux
* pastry* (p1251) *using*
* 150g flour*

salt and pepper
150g Gruyère cheese
1 egg yolk

Lightly grease a shallow 18cm pie plate or sandwich tin. Season the pastry well with salt and pepper, and keep it in a warm bowl. Cut half the cheese into 5mm dice and grate the rest. Reserve about 25g of each, and put to one side. Mix the rest lightly into the pastry. Using a small round or oval spoon, place large spoonfuls of the mixture side by side in a circle all round the dish. Make a second circle just inside the first, and repeat until the dish is full. Make the last central choux rather bigger than the rest. Beat the egg yolk with a little water and brush the tops of the choux with it. Sprinkle with the reserved cheese. Bake in a fairly hot oven, 190°C, Gas 5, for 30–35 minutes, until risen and golden-brown. Serve hot or cold.

Note This is the traditional *gougère*. Quite often, the pastry is now used to line a soufflé dish, and is then filled with diced chicken or game in a savoury sauce.

Cheese Éclairs

Makes 20–24

Pastry
50g butter
200ml water
100g plain flour
3 large **or** *4 small eggs*

salt and pepper
a pinch of Cayenne
* pepper*
fat for greasing

Filling
200–250ml thick cheese
* sauce* (p693)

Put the fat and water into a small saucepan and bring to the boil. As soon as the fat melts, tip in all the flour, and stir briskly. Cook until the mixture leaves the sides of the pan clean. Remove from the heat, and cool slightly. Beat in the eggs very thoroughly, one at a time. Add the seasonings with the final egg. The mixture should be stiff enough to pipe easily.

Using a forcing bag with a 1cm nozzle, pipe 5cm lengths of paste on to a lightly greased baking sheet. Bake in a fairly hot oven, 200°C, Gas 6, for 20–30 minutes, until risen and browned. Split open, remove any uncooked paste, and return to the oven for 2–3 minutes. Do not dry out too much. Cool, and fill with the cheese sauce.

Serve as cocktail snacks or at a buffet party.

Cheese Flan

4–6 helpings

cheese pastry (p1251)
* using 150g flour*
flour for rolling out
75g Cheddar cheese

2 eggs
200ml milk
a pinch of salt
Cayenne pepper

Roll out the pastry on a lightly floured surface and use it to line a 20cm flan ring about 2cm deep. Bake blind until set, then cool.

Meanwhile, grate the cheese for the filling. Whisk together with the eggs, milk, and seasonings. Pour into the flan shell, and bake in a fairly hot oven, 190°C, Gas 5, for 25–35 minutes or until firm in the centre and golden-brown.

Cheese Butterflies

See p1291.

Bacon Pasties

6 helpings

potato pastry (p1252)
  using 100g flour
flour for rolling out
200g raw minced steak
150g streaky bacon,
  without rinds

100g lamb's kidney
1 large onion
salt and pepper
1 × 5ml spoon
  Worcestershire sauce
beaten egg for glazing

Roll out the pastry on a lightly floured surface and cut out six 18cm rounds. Put the steak into a bowl. Chop the bacon finely. Skin and core the kidney, and chop it finely. Skin and chop the onion. Mix all these ingredients with the steak, and season with salt, pepper, and Worcestershire sauce. Put a spoonful of mixture in the centre of each pastry round, dampen the edges, and fold up the pastry to form pasties. Crimp the tops with the thumb and forefinger and seal the edges firmly. Brush the pasties with the egg to glaze, place on a baking sheet and bake in a hot oven, 220°C, Gas 7, for 15 minutes. Reduce the temperature to moderate, 180°C, Gas 4, and bake for a further 45 minutes. Serve hot or cold.

Cornish Pasties

See p503, p1305 and p1472.

Wiltshire Pie

6 helpings

4–6 slices cooked breast
  of veal **or** *chicken*
4–6 slices cooked lean
  lamb
4–6 slices boiled bacon
  or *pickled pork*
salt
Cayenne pepper
dripping for greasing

4 hard-boiled eggs
a good pinch of ground
  mace
cooled and jellied stock
  (made from veal bones)
  (p329)
potato pastry (p1252)
  using 100g flour
flour for rolling out

Trim the meat slices, removing any skin and solid fat. Season with salt and Cayenne pepper. Lay half the slices in a greased 1 litre pie dish. Slice the eggs, and arrange them on top of the meat. Sprinkle with seasoning and mace. Cover with the remaining meat slices, filling the dish. Melt the stock, which should be firm and a good clear brown colour, and pour in enough almost to fill the pie dish.

Roll out the pastry on a lightly floured surface and use it to cover the dish. Do not decorate. Make a small hole in the centre of the crust, and from the pastry trimmings make a button of pastry to fit it. Bake the pie in a fairly hot oven, 190°C, Gas 5, for 45 minutes–1 hour until the pastry is crisp and cooked through. Bake the button of pastry blind at the same time. When the pie is cooked, pour in enough extra stock through the hole in the crust to fill the pie completely. Leave until quite cold and firm. Insert the pastry button in the hole. With a sharp knife, loosen the side of the pie from the dish. Turn the pie carefully on to a serving plate so that the pastry is underneath.

Serve cold with salad.

Note Any available cold cooked meat can be used instead of those above.

Anchovy Éclairs

Makes 20 (approx)

puff pastry (p1253)
  using 100g flour
flour for rolling out
12–25 anchovy fillets

milk
3 × 15ml spoons grated
  Parmesan cheese

Heat the oven to fairly hot–hot, 220°–230°C, Gas 7–8. Roll out the pastry thinly on a lightly floured surface and cut it into oblong pieces, slightly longer than the anchovy fillets. Enclose an anchovy fillet in each piece. Dampen the pastry edges with a little milk and press to seal. Sprinkle with cheese and bake for 4–6 minutes until brown and crisp.

Note The éclairs should look like miniature sausage rolls.

VARIATION

Sardine Éclairs

Use well-drained sardines instead of anchovies.

Cheese Strips d'Artois

Makes 8 canapés

puff pastry (p1253)
  using 100g flour
flour for rolling out
1 egg

100g Gruyère cheese or
  mild Cheddar cheese
25g butter
salt and pepper
1 egg yolk

Garnish
chopped parsley

Roll out the pastry thinly into a long rectangular strip on a lightly floured surface. Chill.

Meanwhile, beat the egg until liquid. Grate the cheese, and mix 75g with the egg. Melt the butter, mix into the egg and cheese, and season to taste. Heat the oven to fairly hot, 200°C, Gas 6. Lay the chilled pastry strip out flat and cut in half widthways. Spread the cheese mixture on one half, leaving 1cm uncovered all round the edge. Dampen the uncovered pastry. Cover with the other half of the pastry, and press the edges to seal. Score the top sheet of pastry in strips 2cm wide and 7–8cm long. Brush with the egg yolk and sprinkle with the remaining grated cheese. Place on a baking sheet and bake for 15–20 minutes or until risen, golden-brown, and crisp. Cut into bars through the score lines, pile on to a warmed serving dish, and garnish with parsley.

Chicken Vol-au-vent

(using cooked meat)

4 helpings

150g cooked chicken
  meat
50g cooked ham or
  tongue
50g button mushrooms

250ml Béchamel sauce
  (p704)
a pinch of nutmeg
salt and pepper
one 15cm vol-au-vent
  case (p1253)

Garnish
parsley sprigs or
  mustard and cress

Dice the chicken and the ham or tongue. Clean and slice the mushrooms thinly. Add to the Béchamel sauce, and heat thoroughly, stirring all the time. Add the nutmeg and seasoning.

Meanwhile, re-heat the vol-au-vent case in a warm oven, 160°C, Gas 3, for 10 minutes. Fill with the hot mixture, and serve at once, garnished with parsley or mustard and cress.

Note Small vol-au-vent or patty cases (p1253) can be used instead of the large case. This quantity of filling is enough for twelve 7cm cases. Make as above, heating the baked cases for 6–9 minutes before filling.

For other fillings for vol-au-vent and patty cases, see p1289.

Sausage Rolls

See p1306.

Creamy Onion Tart

6 helpings

puff pastry (p1253)
  using 100g flour
flour for rolling out
1kg onions
100g green bacon
  rashers, without rinds
50g butter or 25g butter
  and 25g lard or 25g
  butter and 25ml oil

25g flour
100ml double cream
100ml soured cream
salt and pepper
a pinch of grated nutmeg
2 eggs

Heat the oven to fairly hot, 200°C, Gas 6. Roll out the pastry 5mm thick on a lightly floured surface. Line a 20cm pie plate or flan ring with the pastry.

Skin the onions and slice them finely. Chop the bacon. Melt the fat in a large frying pan, add the onions and bacon, and simmer over very low heat, covered, for about 12 minutes or until fully softened but not coloured. Stir in the flour and cook for 2 minutes. Stir in the fresh and soured creams, and simmer for 5 minutes. Season well, add a good pinch of nutmeg, and cool. Beat in the eggs. Pour the mixture into the pastry case and bake for 20–25 minutes. Serve hot.

Seafood Flan

6 helpings

Shell

50g butter **or** *margarine*	*100g plain crackers* **or**
a pinch of salt	*water biscuits*
25g finely grated hard	
cheese	

Filling

1 × 10ml spoon gelatine	*2 × 15ml spoons tomato*
3 × 15ml spoons cold	*ketchup*
water	*1 × 5ml spoon chopped*
50g canned salmon **or**	*onion*
tuna	*1 × 5ml spoon chopped*
6 canned sardines	*parsley*
125ml mayonnaise	*salt and pepper*

Garnish

1 hard-boiled egg	*50g peeled prawns*

To make the flan shell, cream together the fat, salt, and cheese. Crush the biscuits and mix with the fat and cheese. Line an 18cm flan ring with the mixture; press it firmly into an even layer all over the base and sides.

To make the filling, soften the gelatine in the cold water. Stand the container in a pan of hot water and stir until the gelatine dissolves. Flake the salmon or tuna and the sardines, removing any bones, then mix together all the ingredients. When beginning to set, pour into the prepared flan shell. Garnish with the hard-boiled egg and prawns.

Desserts Using Pastry

A selection of boiled and steamed puddings using suet crust pastry are on pp981–85 together with some baked puddings. Several of the dessert gâteau on pp1044–47 are made with pastry. A Gâteau St Honoré, for example, uses choux pastry, as do Chocolate Profiteroles. Many of the small, decorated tartlets and pastry cakes at the end of this chapter can also be served as a sweet course, especially for a buffet party.

Apple Pie
(basic deep fruit pie or tart)

6 helpings

shortcrust pastry (p1249)	*6 cloves* **or** *1 × 2.5ml*
using 300g flour	*spoon grated lemon*
flour for rolling out	*rind*
600g cooking apples	*cold water for glazing*
100g sugar	*caster sugar for dredging*

Roll out the pastry on a lightly floured surface and use just over half to line a 750ml pie dish. Peel, core, and slice the apples. Place half in the dish, add the sugar and flavouring, and pile the remaining fruit on top. Cover with the rest of the pastry and seal the edges. Brush the pastry with cold water and dredge with caster sugar. Bake in a fairly hot oven, 200°C, Gas 6, for 20 minutes, then reduce the temperature to moderate, 180°C, Gas 4, and bake for another 20 minutes or until the pastry is golden-brown. Dredge with caster sugar and serve hot or cold.

Note The pastry can be brushed with egg white and sprinkled with sugar before cooking, if liked.

VARIATIONS

Apricot Pie or Tart
(using canned apricots)

Make as for Apple Pie but use two 375g cans apricots instead of apples, and omit the sugar and cloves or lemon rind.

Blackberry and Apple Pie or Tart

Make as for Apple Pie, but use 300g blackberries and 300g apples instead of apples alone.

Damson Pie or Tart

Make as for Apple Pie, but use 600g damsons instead of apples, and omit the cloves or lemon rind.

Gooseberry Pie or Tart

Make as for Apple Pie, but use 600g gooseberries instead of apples. Top and tail the fruit, then wash it thoroughly. Omit the cloves or lemon rind.

Redcurrant and Raspberry Pie or Tart

Make as for Apple Pie, but use 400g redcurrants and 200g raspberries instead of apples. Reduce the sugar to 2 × 15ml spoons. Omit the cloves or lemon rind.

Rhubarb Pie or Tart

Make as for Apple Pie, but use 600g rhubarb cut into 2cm lengths instead of apples.

Basic Fruit Flan

5–6 helpings

shortcrust pastry (p1249)
  using 125g flour
flour for rolling out
1 × 375g can fruit or
  300g fresh fruit
  (strawberries, pears,
  pineapple, cherries,
  apricots, peaches, etc)

25g sugar (optional)
1 × 5ml spoon lemon
  juice
1 × 5ml spoon
  arrowroot

Decoration (optional)
125ml whipped cream

Roll out the pastry on a lightly floured surface and use it to line an 18cm flan ring. Bake blind, then leave to cool. If fresh fruit is used, prepare it, put in a saucepan with 1 × 15ml spoon water, cover, and stew gently until tender. Make up the stewed fruit to 125ml with water. Canned fruit and some fresh fruit, eg strawberries, do not need cooking. Drain the fruit and arrange it in the cold pastry shell. Return most of the liquid to the saucepan, add the sugar, if used, and the lemon juice, and simmer for a few minutes. Blend the arrowroot with the remaining liquid and add it to the hot syrup, stirring all the time. Cook for 3 minutes, still stirring. Cool slightly, and spoon the liquid over the fruit. When cold, decorate with piped whipped cream, if liked.

Mrs Beeton's Flan of Apples

6–7 helpings

6 dessert apples
4 cloves
3 × 15ml spoons
  medium-dry sherry
shortcrust pastry (p1249)
  using 175g flour

flour for rolling out
2 × 15ml spoons soft
  light brown sugar
3 egg whites
5 × 15ml spoons caster
  sugar

Peel and core each apple, and cut it into 8 sections. Place the sections in a heatproof bowl, add the cloves and sherry, cover closely and stand in a deep pan containing boiling water. Cook for about 20 minutes or until the apple sections are tender but not soft enough to break easily.

Meanwhile, roll out the pastry on a lightly floured surface and use it to line a 23cm flan case. Bake blind until the pastry is set. Fill the case with the apple sections arranged in a neat layer, strain 2 × 15ml spoons of the cooking juice over them, and sprinkle with the brown sugar. Whisk the egg whites until stiff with 2 × 5ml spoons of the caster sugar, and spread lightly over the apples. Sprinkle with the remaining caster sugar, and bake in a very cool–cool oven, 140°–150°C, Gas 1–2, for 1 hour. Serve either hot or cold.

Mrs Beeton's Flan of Pineapple

8–9 helpings

shortcrust pastry
  (p1249) using 200g
  flour
flour for rolling out
750g peeled fresh
  pineapple

250ml pineapple juice
25g caster sugar
2 × 5ml spoons
  arrowroot
lemon juice

Roll out the pastry on a lightly floured surface and use it to line a 25cm flan case. Bake blind until the pastry is set. Dice the pineapple, removing all the peel and core. Drain the dice well. Bring the pineapple juice and sugar to the boil, then reduce the heat and simmer for 10 minutes. Mix the arrowroot to a smooth paste with a little lemon juice and stir it into the syrup. Cook gently, still stirring, until it thickens and clears. Put the pineapple dice in an even layer in the flan case, pour the syrup over the fruit, and cool completely.

VARIATIONS

Greengages, plums of all kinds, peaches, currants, raspberries, gooseberries, and strawberries may be used in the same way. Raspberries, gooseberries, and strawberries are improved if a little blackcurrant juice is added to the syrup.

Banana Flan

5–6 helpings

shortcrust pastry
  (p1249) using 125g
  flour
flour for rolling out
250ml cold
  confectioners' custard
  (1) (p1237)

2 × 15ml spoons apricot
  glaze (p1234)
3 bananas

Roll out the pastry on a lightly floured surface and use it to line an 18cm flan ring. Bake blind, then cool completely. When cold, pour in the confectioners' custard. Heat the apricot glaze, if necessary. Slice the bananas and arrange on the custard. Glaze immediately with hot apricot glaze, leave to set, and serve cold.

Apple Amber (2)

6–7 helpings

shortcrust pastry (p1249)
  using 150g flour
flour for rolling out
600g cooking apples
2 × 15ml spoons water

grated rind of 1 lemon
2 eggs
50g butter or margarine
75g brown sugar
50g caster sugar

Decoration (optional)
glacé cherries   angelica

Roll out the pastry on a lightly floured surface and use it to line a 750ml pie dish. Peel, core, and slice the apples. Put into a saucepan with the water and lemon rind, and stew until soft. Sieve, or process in an electric blender. Return the apple to the pan and re-heat slightly. Separate the eggs and add the yolks, fat, and brown sugar to the apple. Mix well. Put the mixture into the lined pie dish and bake in a moderate oven, 180°C, Gas 4 for about 30 minutes or until set. Whisk the egg whites until stiff and fold in the caster sugar. Pile on top of the apple mixture and decorate, if liked, with pieces of glacé cherry and angelica. Bake in a very cool oven, 140°C, Gas 1, for 30–40 minutes or until the meringue is golden-brown. Serve hot or cold.

Note For extra flavour, a good pinch of ground cinnamon and ground cloves can be added to the apples when stewing.

For Apple Amber (1), see p993.

VARIATION
Apple Cheesecakes

Line twelve 7cm patty tins with the pastry. Replace the 75g brown sugar with 50g caster sugar and add the juice of 1 lemon to the apple mixture instead of the water. Bake for 15–20 minutes at 180°C, Gas 4, then for 20–25 minutes at the cooler temperature.

Apricot Pudding

6 helpings

shortcrust pastry (p1249) *using 150g flour*	*1 × 375g can apricots*
	25g sugar
flour for rolling out	*grated rind of 1 lemon*
250ml milk	*2 eggs*
50g bread **or** *plain cake crumbs*	*75g caster sugar*

Roll out the pastry on a lightly floured surface and use it to line a 750ml pie dish. Put the milk in a pan and bring to the boil. Pour it over the bread or cake crumbs. Drain the apricots and sieve, or process in an electric blender. Stir the apricot purée into the milk mixture with the sugar and lemon rind. Separate the eggs and beat the yolks into the milk mixture. Pour the mixture into the pie dish, and bake in a fairly hot oven, 200°C, Gas 6, for 25–30 minutes or until the pastry is golden-brown and the filling is set. Whisk the egg whites until stiff and fold in the caster sugar. Spread the mixture over the filling. Return to a very cool oven, 140°C, Gas 1, and bake for a further 30 minutes or until the meringue is crisp and golden.

VARIATIONS
Chester Pudding

Make as for Apricot Pudding, but increase the sugar to 100g and use 2 × 15ml spoons ground almonds instead of the apricots.

Chestnut Amber

Make as for Apricot Pudding, but use 200g chestnuts instead of the apricots. To peel the chestnuts, bake in a hot oven, 220°C, Gas 7, for 5–10 minutes, then peel off the shells and skins while still hot. Put the chestnuts in a pan with 100ml water and simmer for about 30 minutes or until tender. Drain them, then rub through a sieve.

Gooseberry Pudding

Make as for Apricot Pudding, but use gooseberry purée instead of apricot purée.

Lemon Pudding

Make as for Apricot Pudding, but instead of the apricots, use the grated rind and juice of 2 lemons and increase the sugar to 50g.

Orange Pudding

Make as for Apricot Pudding, but increase the sugar to 50g and use the grated rind of 1 orange and the juice of 4 oranges instead of the apricots and lemon rind.

Coconut Custard Pie

5–6 helpings

shortcrust pastry (p1249) *using 175g flour*	*100g sugar*
	¼ × 2.5ml spoon salt
flour for rolling out	*75g desiccated coconut*
3 eggs	*375ml milk*

Roll out the pastry on a lightly floured surface and use it to line a deep 23cm pie plate. Beat the eggs until liquid and add the rest of the ingredients. Pour into the pastry case and bake in a hot oven, 220°C, Gas 7, for 10 minutes, then reduce the temperature to moderate, 180°C, Gas 4, and bake for another 25–30 minutes or until set.

Mrs Beeton's Bakewell Pudding

4–5 helpings

shortcrust pastry (p1249) using 125g flour
flour for rolling out
jam
50g butter
50g caster sugar
1 egg
50g ground almonds
50g fine plain cake crumbs
a few drops almond essence
icing sugar for dusting

Roll out the pastry on a lightly floured surface and use it to line an 18cm flan ring. Spread over it a good layer of any kind of jam. Beat together the butter and sugar until pale and fluffy. Beat in the egg. Add the almonds, cake crumbs, and essence. Beat until well mixed, then pour the mixture into the flan shell, over the jam, and bake in a fairly hot oven, 200°C, Gas 6, for 30 minutes or until the centre of the pudding is firm. Sprinkle with icing sugar, and serve hot or cold.

VARIATIONS

Bakewell Tart

Make as for Bakewell Pudding, but use raspberry jam, and only 25g breadcrumbs or cake crumbs and 25g ground almonds. Bake for 25 minutes.

Almond Tartlets

Line twelve 7cm patty tins with the pastry. Replace the cake crumbs with another 50g ground almonds, and the almond essence with 1 × 2.5ml spoon lemon juice. Bake for 12–18 minutes. Serve hot or cold.

West Riding Pudding

Line a 500ml pie dish with the pastry. Bake as for Bakewell Pudding but substitute 75g plain flour and 1 × 2.5ml spoon baking powder for the cake crumbs and ground almonds. If the mixture seems stiff, add a little milk. Bake in a fairly hot oven, 190°C, Gas 5, for 1 hour. Serve hot or cold.

Lemon Meringue Pie

6 helpings

shortcrust pastry (p1249) using 175g flour
flour for rolling out
300g granulated sugar
3 × 15ml spoons cornflour
3 × 15ml spoons plain flour
a pinch of salt
300ml water
2 × 15ml spoons butter
1 × 5ml spoon grated lemon rind
75ml lemon juice
3 eggs
75g caster sugar

Roll out the pastry on a lightly floured surface and use it to line a 23cm pie plate. Bake blind until golden-brown, then cool.

Meanwhile, mix the sugar, cornflour, plain flour, and salt in the top of a double boiler. Boil the 300ml water separately, and add it slowly to the dry mixture, stirring all the time. Bring the mixture to the boil, stirring all the time; then place the top of the double boiler over hot water, cover, and cook gently for 20 minutes. Draw the pan off the heat. Add the butter, lemon rind, and lemon juice. Separate the eggs. Beat the yolks until just liquid, and add a little of the cooked mixture. Mix into the cooked ingredients. Replace over heat and cook, stirring all the time, until the mixture thickens. Remove from the heat and leave to cool. Whisk the egg whites until stiff and fold in the caster sugar. Pour the lemon custard into the baked pastry case and top with the meringue, making sure that it covers the top completely. Bake in a moderate oven, 180°C, Gas 4, for 12–15 minutes, until the meringue is lightly browned. Cool before cutting.

Mincemeat Meringue Pie

4–6 helpings

shortcrust pastry (p1249) *using 125g flour*	*2 eggs*
flour for rolling out	*375ml milk*
50g soft white breadcrumbs	*1 × 15ml spoon butter*
2 × 15ml spoons granulated sugar	*1 × 2.5ml spoon vanilla essence*
	250g mincemeat
	75g caster sugar

Roll out the pastry on a lightly floured surface and use it to line an 18cm flan ring. Bake blind, then cool. Place the cooked shell on a baking sheet.

Mix together the breadcrumbs and sugar. Separate the eggs, add the yolks to the crumbs, and mix in well. Warm the milk and butter together in a saucepan until the butter has just melted. Stir this slowly into the breadcrumbs, sugar and yolks, mixing thoroughly. Stir in the essence. Leave to stand for 5 minutes, then pour into the flan shell. Bake in a moderate oven, 180°C, Gas 4, for 35–45 minutes, until the custard is set. When cooked, leave to stand for 4–5 minutes to firm the custard.

Increase the heat to fairly hot, 200°C, Gas 6. Spread the mincemeat over the crumb custard. Whisk the egg whites until very stiff, gradually whisking in about 50g of the caster sugar. Pipe or spoon the meringue on the mincemeat, covering it completely, including the pastry edge. Sprinkle with the remaining sugar. Bake for 5–10 minutes until the meringue is golden.

Serve hot with single cream.

Cranberry Raisin Pie

6 helpings

shortcrust pastry (p1249) *using 250g flour*	*150g sugar*
flour for rolling out	*3 × 10ml spoons flour*
200g cranberries	*½ × 2.5ml spoon salt*
200g seedless raisins	*25g butter*

Roll out the pastry on a lightly floured surface, and use two-thirds of it to line a 23cm pie plate. Mix together the fruits and other dry ingredients. Put the mixture in the pastry case and dot with the butter. Roll out the remaining pastry into an oblong and cut into five 1cm strips. Arrange the strips in a lattice on top of the pie. Bake for 10 minutes in a very hot oven, 230°C, Gas 8, then reduce the heat to moderate, 180°C, Gas 4, and bake for a further 30–40 minutes.

Jam Tart

6 helpings

shortcrust pastry (p1249) *using 150g flour* **or** *puff pastry* (p1253) *using 150g flour*	*flour for rolling out*
	4–6 × 15ml spoons any firm jam (see **Note**)
	beaten egg **or** *milk for glazing (optional)*

Heat the oven to hot, 220°C, Gas 7. Roll out the pastry on a lightly floured surface and use it to line a 20cm pie plate. Decorate the edge with any trimmings. Fill with jam, and glaze the uncovered pastry with beaten egg or milk, if liked. Bake for about 15 minutes or until the pastry is cooked. Serve hot or cold.

Note The larger quantity of jam will be needed if a whole fruit jam is used. Thin syrupy jams containing whole fruits are not suitable for a jam tart. Very firm jams should be lightly covered with greaseproof paper while cooking to prevent scorching.

Treacle Tart

6 helpings

shortcrust pastry (p1249) *using 150g flour*	*50g soft white breadcrumbs*
flour for rolling out	*1 × 5ml spoon lemon*
3 × 15ml spoons golden syrup	*juice or a good pinch of ground ginger*

Roll out the pastry on a lightly floured surface and use most of it to line a 20cm pie plate, reserving a little for decoration. Warm the syrup in a saucepan until melted. Stir in the breadcrumbs and lemon juice or ground ginger, and pour the mixture into the pastry case. Roll out the remaining pastry into an oblong, and cut into 1cm strips. Arrange the strips in a lattice on top of the tart. Bake in a fairly hot oven, 200°C, Gas 6, for about 30 minutes.

Note If preferred, the tart may be baked as a double crust tart (p1244). Use double the amount of pastry and bake for 50 minutes.

Crushed cornflakes can be substituted for the breadcrumbs, if liked.

VARIATION
Treacle Jelly Tart

Use the pastry to line a deep 18cm flan ring. Make as for Treacle Tart, but omit the breadcrumbs and add 1 beaten egg to the syrup. Bake in a moderate oven, 180°C, Gas 4, until golden-brown. When cold, the filling sets like jelly.

Hampshire Pudding

6–7 helpings

puff pastry (p1253) *using 150g flour*	*2 eggs*
flour for rolling out	*1 egg yolk*
2 × 15ml spoons jam	*75g butter*
	75g caster sugar

Roll out the pastry on a lightly floured surface and use it to line a deep 20cm pie plate. Spread the jam over the bottom. Beat the eggs and extra yolk together in a heatproof basin until frothy. Melt the butter in a saucepan. Gradually add the sugar and melted butter to the eggs. Place the basin over a pan of hot water and whisk the mixture until thick. Pour it over the jam and bake in a fairly hot oven, 200°C, Gas 6, for 30 minutes or until firm and golden-brown. If necessary, reduce the heat to moderate, 180°C, Gas 4, after 15–20 minutes to prevent the pastry browning too quickly. Serve hot.

Apple Jalousie

6–7 helpings

250g cooking apples	*puff pastry* (p1253)
50g butter	*using 150g flour*
75g soft light brown sugar	*flour for rolling out*
25g apricot jam	*egg wash* (p1248)
a pinch of ground cinnamon	*icing sugar for glazing*

Peel, core, and slice the apples. Warm the butter and sugar in a saucepan until the butter melts, add the apple slices, and turn them over to coat them with butter. Increase the heat slightly, and simmer for 4 minutes or until the apple slices are half-cooked but not yet soft. Remove from the heat, and mix in the jam and cinnamon. Leave to cool completely.

Heat the oven to fairly hot, 190°C, Gas 5. Roll out the pastry about 4mm thick in a rectangle 18 × 16cm on a lightly floured surface. Cut in half to form two 18 × 8cm rectangles. Dampen a baking sheet, and lay one rectangle in the centre. Cover with the filling mixture, leaving 1cm pastry uncovered all round the edge. Fold the second rectangle in half lengthways, and cut 3cm slits through both thicknesses of pastry from the folded edge inwards. Open out the pastry; it should have 6cm parallel slits across it. Dampen the edges of the base pastry and lay the slit rectangle on top. Press the edges to seal. Brush the egg wash over the jalousie. Bake for 20–25 minutes. Remove from the oven, and dust with icing sugar. Return to the oven for a further 5 minutes to glaze. Cool on the sheet and serve cut in slices.

Apple Strudel

8 helpings

Pastry

200g plain flour	4 × 15ml spoons warm
½ × 2.5ml spoon salt	water
2 × 15ml spoons oil	flour for rolling out
1 egg	

Filling

400g cooking apples	1 × 5ml spoon ground
50g butter	cinnamon
50g soft brown sugar	50g sultanas

To make the pastry, sift the flour and salt into a bowl and add the oil, egg, and warm water. Mix to a firm dough. Cover with foil and leave in a warm place for about 1 hour.

Meanwhile, peel and core the apples, and chop them finely. Melt the butter in a saucepan.

On a floured tea-towel, roll out the dough very thinly to a rectangle 25 × 50cm. Brush with melted butter and sprinkle with the brown sugar, cinnamon, and sultanas. Top with the chopped apple, and roll up the strudel like a Swiss roll. Slide on to a baking sheet and brush the top with more melted butter. Bake in a fairly hot oven, 190°C, Gas 5, for 40 minutes or until golden-brown.

Serve hot or cold.

Linzertorte

5–6 helpings

100g butter	100g plain flour
75g caster sugar	1 × 5ml spoon ground
1 egg yolk	cinnamon
1 × 2.5ml spoon almond	50g ground almonds
essence	flour for rolling out
grated rind of 1 small	200g raspberry jam
lemon	1 × 15ml spoon icing
juice of ½ lemon	sugar

Cream together the butter and sugar until pale and fluffy. Beat in the egg yolk, almond essence, lemon rind and juice. Add the flour, cinnamon and ground almonds, and mix to a smooth dough. Wrap in foil and leave in a cool place for 1 hour. Roll out the dough on a lightly floured surface and use three-quarters of it to line an 18cm flan ring. Spread the jam over the base. Roll out the remaining dough into an oblong 18cm long, and cut into strips about 5mm wide. Arrange the strips in a lattice on top of the jam. Bake in a warm oven, 160°C, Gas 3, for about 1 hour, until golden-brown. Leave to cool, then remove from the flan ring and dredge with icing sugar.

Serve cold with whipped cream.

Note Linzertorte improves in flavour if kept for 2 or 3 days before use.

Stuffed Monkey

Makes 9 squares

Pastry

150g plain flour	1 egg
1 × 2.5ml spoon ground	flour for rolling out
cinnamon	fat for greasing
100g margarine	50g flaked almonds
100g brown sugar	

Filling

3 × 15ml spoons	50g sultanas
margarine	25g sugar
50g cut mixed peel	1 × 2.5ml spoon mixed
50g chopped blanched	spice
almonds	

To make the pastry, sift the flour and cinnamon. Rub in the margarine and add the sugar. Beat the egg until liquid and mix in enough to form a soft dough, reserving a little for glazing. Divide the dough into two equal portions and roll out one portion on a lightly floured surface to fit a greased 18cm square tin. Lay it in the tin.

For the filling, melt the margarine, and mix in all the other ingredients. Cool. Spread the filling over the pastry, leaving 2cm uncovered all round. Dampen the uncovered edge. Roll out the second portion of pastry to fit the first. Lay it on the filling and press the edges to seal. Brush with the reserved beaten egg and sprinkle with the flaked almonds. Bake in a fairly hot oven, 190°C, Gas 5, for 30 minutes. Cool in the tin. Serve cut into squares.

German Apple Tart

6 helpings

Pastry

100g plain flour	*1 ×15ml spoon water,*
½ × 2.5ml spoon salt	*milk* **or** *white wine*
1 × 15ml spoon sugar	*flour for rolling out*
50g butter	*25g rolled oats*
1 egg yolk	

Filling

25g butter	*1 egg*
1 × 15ml spoon flour	*25g ground almonds*
2 × 15ml spoons caster sugar	*1 large cooking apple*
grated rind of ¼ lemon	*1 egg white*
2 × 15ml spoons single cream	

To make the pastry, sift the flour and salt into a bowl, add the sugar and rub in the butter. Mix the pastry to a firm dough with the yolk and water, milk or wine. Roll out the pastry thinly on a lightly floured surface and use it to line an 18cm flan case. Spread a thin layer of rolled oats on the base of the pastry case to prevent the apple juice soaking in.

For the filling, melt the butter in a pan. Stir in the flour, sugar, lemon rind, and cream. Separate the egg and add the yolk to the mixture. Stir in the ground almonds. Peel, core, quarter, and slice the apple, and arrange the slices in circles on the pastry. Whisk both egg whites until stiff, fold into the almond mixture and pour this over the apples. Bake in a fairly hot oven, 190°C, Gas 5, for 45 minutes or until well risen and golden-brown.

Apple and Walnut Tart

6 helpings

Pastry

125g butter	*250g flour*
75g caster sugar	*2 ×5ml spoons baking powder*
1 egg	*flour for rolling out*
1 × 5ml spoon vanilla essence	*fat for greasing*

Filling

750g cooking apples	*1 × 5ml spoon mixed spice*
75g granulated sugar	*50g sultanas*
3 ×15ml spoons water	*50g chopped walnuts*
2 ×15ml spoons light soft brown sugar	*icing sugar for dusting*

Prepare the filling first. Peel, core, and slice the apples. Put them with the granulated sugar in a pan, and add the water. Simmer gently until the apples are tender. Leave to cool.

To make the pastry, melt the butter in a saucepan, add the caster sugar, and heat gently until dissolved. Cool slightly, then stir in the egg and vanilla essence. Sift in the flour and baking powder together. Mix to a smooth dough. Roll out on a lightly floured surface and use two-thirds of the dough to line a greased 18cm loose-bottomed cake tin. Chill the remaining dough in a refrigerator.

Mix the cooked apples with the brown sugar, mixed spice, sultanas, and walnuts. Fill the pastry case with the mixture. Grate the chilled pastry over the apples and bake in a fairly hot oven, 190°C, Gas 5, for 40 minutes. Dust with icing sugar, and serve hot with cream.

Small Pastries and Tartlets

Almond and Apricot Tartlets

Makes 12

shortcrust pastry (p1249) using 100g flour	1 × 15ml spoon ground almonds
flour for rolling out	3 drops almond essence
1 × 10ml spoon apricot jam	2 × 5ml spoons nibbed almonds
50g butter **or** margarine	1 × 15ml spoon apricot glaze (p1234)
50g sugar	2 × 5ml spoons chopped angelica
1 egg	
1 × 15ml spoon plain cake crumbs	

Heat the oven to fairly hot, 190°C, Gas 5. Roll out the pastry on a lightly floured surface and use it to line twelve 7cm patty tins. Put a little apricot jam in each pastry case. Cream together the fat and sugar until pale and fluffy. Gradually beat in the egg. Stir in the cake crumbs, ground almonds, and almond essence. Half fill each pastry case with the mixture and smooth the tops. Sprinkle the nibbed almonds on top. Bake for 15 minutes or until firm to the touch. Leave to cool. Warm the apricot glaze and brush it on the tops of the tartlets, then sprinkle at once with the chopped angelica.

Balmoral Tartlets

Makes 12

shortcrust pastry (p1249) using 100g flour	15g glacé cherries
flour for rolling out	25g plain cake crumbs
50g butter	15g cut mixed peel
50g sugar	1 × 5ml spoon cornflour
1 egg	25g icing sugar

Heat the oven to fairly hot, 200°C, Gas 6. Roll out the pastry on a lightly floured surface and use it to line twelve 7cm patty tins. Cream the butter and sugar together until pale and fluffy. Separate the egg and beat the yolk into the creamed mixture. Chop the cherries and add them to the creamed mixture with the cake crumbs, mixed peel, and cornflour. Mix well. Whisk the egg white until stiff, and fold lightly into the mixture. Fill the pastry cases with the mixture and bake for about 20 minutes. Cool on a wire rack. Sift a little icing sugar over the tartlets before serving.

Cherry Tartlets

Makes 12

shortcrust pastry (p1249) using 100g flour	1 × 10ml spoon lemon juice
flour for rolling out	a drop of red food colouring (optional)
1 × 375g can red cherries in syrup	125ml double cream
25g lump sugar	
1 × 5ml spoon arrowroot	

Roll out the pastry on a lightly floured surface and use it to line twelve 7cm patty tins or small boat-shaped moulds. Bake blind, then cool. Drain and stone the cherries, reserving the syrup. Place a layer of cherries in the pastry cases. Make up the syrup to 125ml with water. Heat the liquid and dissolve the sugar in it, bring to the boil, and boil for 5 minutes. Blend the arrowroot to a smooth paste with the lemon juice and add to the syrup, stirring all the time. Boil for 2 minutes until the syrup is clear and thick. Add the red colouring, if liked. Cool slightly, then pour a little of the glaze over the cherries. Leave to set. Whip the cream until stiff, and pipe a large rosette on each tartlet.

VARIATIONS

Blackcurrant Tartlets

Replace the cherries with 400g blackcurrants stewed in 2 × 15ml spoons water and 4 × 15ml spoons sugar. Omit the food colouring.

Strawberry or Raspberry Tartlets

Fill the tartlets with fresh strawberries or raspberries. Make the glaze using 125ml water instead of fruit syrup.

Cream Tartlets

Makes 12

shortcrust pastry (p1249)
 using 100g flour
flour for rolling out
2 × 15ml spoons smooth
 apricot jam
250ml whipping cream
1 × 15ml spoon icing
 sugar

2 × 15ml spoons finely
 chopped pistachio nuts
or green-tinted
 desiccated coconut
 (p1235)

Roll out the pastry on a lightly floured surface and use it to line twelve 7cm patty tins. Bake blind, then cool completely. When cold, put apricot jam in the bottom of each case. Whip the cream as stiffly as possible, gradually adding the sugar while whipping. Pipe the cream in swirls and peaks over the jam. Sprinkle with nuts or coconut.

Custard Tartlets

Makes 12

shortcrust pastry
 (p1249) using 100g
 flour and 1 × 5ml spoon
 caster sugar
flour for rolling out

1 egg
1 × 15ml spoon caster
 sugar
125ml milk
a pinch of grated nutmeg

Roll out the pastry on a lightly floured surface and use it to line twelve 7cm patty tins. Beat the egg lightly and add the sugar. Warm the milk and pour it on to the egg. Strain the custard into the pastry cases and sprinkle a little nutmeg on top. Bake in a moderate oven, 180°C, Gas 4, until the custard is firm and set. Leave to cool before removing from the tins.

VARIATION

Custard Meringue Tartlets

Make as for Custard Tartlets, but omit the nutmeg and bake for 15 minutes only. Whisk 2 egg whites until stiff and fold in 75g caster sugar. Pile the meringue on to the tartlets and bake in a very cool oven, 140°C, Gas 1, for about 30 minutes or until the meringue is crisp and very slightly browned.

Canadian Cakes

Makes 12

shortcrust pastry (p1249)
 using 100g flour
flour for rolling out
1 egg
100g currants

100g sugar
15g butter
125ml whipping cream
1 × 15ml spoon caster
 sugar

Heat the oven to fairly hot, 200°C, Gas 6. Roll out the pastry on a lightly floured surface and use it to line twelve 7cm patty tins. Beat the egg lightly and add the currants and sugar. Melt the butter in a saucepan and stir into the fruit mixture. Spoon the mixture into the pastry cases and bake for 15–20 minutes. Cool. Whip the cream and sugar together until stiff, and pipe a rosette on each cake.

Filbert Tartlets

Makes 12

shortcrust pastry (p1249)
 using 100g flour
flour for rolling out
75g shelled filberts
3 × 10ml spoons
 cornflour
50ml single cream **or**
 milk

2 eggs
75g caster sugar
25g ground almonds
milk for glazing
 (optional)
caster sugar for glazing
 (optional)

Heat the oven to fairly hot, 200°C, Gas 6. Roll out the pastry on a lightly floured surface and use it to line twelve 7cm patty tins, reserving a little for decoration. Blanch and skin the filberts, and chop them finely. In a saucepan, blend the cornflour with the cream or milk and stir over gentle heat until the mixture boils. Remove from the heat. Beat the eggs and sugar together until pale and fluffy and add the chopped nuts, ground almonds, and cornflour mixture. Put the mixture into the pastry cases. Cut the reserved pastry into thin strips and place 2 strips across each tartlet to form a cross. Brush with milk and dredge with caster sugar to glaze, if liked. Bake for about 20 minutes or until the pastry is golden-brown.

Fruit or Jam Turnovers

Makes 8

*shortcrust pastry
(p1249) using 150g
flour or flaky (p1252),
rough puff (p1252) or
puff (p1253) pastry
using 100g flour*

*flour for rolling out
100g stewed fruit or
2 × 15ml spoons jam
1 × 15ml spoon caster
sugar*

Heat the oven to fairly hot, 200°C, Gas 6. Roll out the pastry 3mm thick on a lightly floured surface and cut into rounds using a 10cm cutter. Place spoonfuls of fruit or jam in the centre of each pastry round. Moisten the edges with water and fold the pastry over the filling. Press the edges well together and crimp or decorate with a fork. Place the turnovers on a baking sheet, brush with water, and dredge with the caster sugar. Bake for about 20 minutes or until golden-brown.

Note These turnovers are called Coventry Turnovers when raspberry jam is used for the filling.

Granville Tartlets

Makes 18

*shortcrust pastry (p1249)
using 200g flour
flour for rolling out
50g butter
75g sugar
50g currants
25g ground rice
25g cut mixed peel*

*75g plain cake crumbs
1 × 15ml spoon single
cream (optional)
4–5 drops lemon essence
2 egg whites
white glacé icing (p1225)
25g desiccated coconut*

Heat the oven to fairly hot, 200°C, Gas 6. Roll out the pastry on a lightly floured surface and use it to line 18 deep 7cm patty tins. Cream together the butter and sugar until pale and fluffy. Add the currants, ground rice, mixed peel, cake crumbs, cream, if used, and lemon essence. Whisk the egg whites until stiff and fold them gently into the creamed mixture. Place spoonfuls of the filling in the pastry cases and bake for 15–20 minutes until golden-brown. Leave to cool. When cold, coat the tartlets with glacé icing and sprinkle with coconut.

Lemon Tartlets

Makes 12

*shortcrust pastry (p1249)
using 100g flour
flour for rolling out
50g butter
50g sugar*

*1 egg
grated rind and juice of
½ lemon
2 × 5ml spoons icing
sugar*

Heat the oven to fairly hot, 200°C, Gas 6. Roll out the pastry on a lightly floured surface and use it to line twelve 7cm patty tins. Cream together the butter and sugar until pale and fluffy. Beat in the egg. Add the lemon rind and juice. Fill the pastry cases with the mixture and bake for 15–20 minutes or until set. Leave to cool. Sift the icing sugar over the tartlets.

VARIATION

To make an orange filling, use 75g butter, 50g sugar, 1 egg yolk, the grated rind of 1 orange, and 2 × 15ml spoons of orange juice.

Parisian Tartlets

Makes 12

*shortcrust pastry (p1249)
using 100g flour
flour for rolling out
50g butter
50g caster sugar
1 egg
1 × 15ml spoon
cornflour
1 × 15ml spoon single
cream or milk*

*25g ground almonds
25g plain cake crumbs
1 × 2.5ml spoon
cinnamon
2 × 5ml spoons lemon
juice
caster sugar for dredging*

Heat the oven to fairly hot, 200°C, Gas 6. Roll out the pastry on a lightly floured surface and use it to line twelve 7cm patty tins. Cream together the butter and sugar until pale and fluffy. Add the egg, and beat well. Blend the cornflour with the cream or milk, stir this into the creamed mixture, and add the ground almonds, cake crumbs, cinnamon, and lemon juice. Fill the pastry cases with the mixture and bake for 15–20 minutes until golden-brown. Dredge with caster sugar when baked.

Lemon Cheesecakes

Makes 12

shortcrust pastry (p1249)   *3 × 15ml spoons lemon*
   using 100g flour   *curd*
flour for rolling out   *25g whole candied peel*

Heat the oven to fairly hot, 200°C, Gas 6. Roll out the pastry on a lightly floured surface and use it to line twelve 7cm patty tins. Half fill each pastry case with the lemon curd. Cut the candied peel into fine strips and use to decorate. Bake for about 20 minutes or until the pastry is golden-brown.

Welsh Cheesecakes

Makes 12

shortcrust pastry (p1249)   *50g caster sugar*
   using 100g flour   *grated rind of ½ lemon*
flour for rolling out   *1 egg*
3 × 15ml spoons   *75g self-raising flour*
   raspberry jam   *milk* **or** *water*
50g butter

Heat the oven to fairly hot, 190°C, Gas 5. Roll out the pastry on a lightly floured surface, and use it to line twelve 7cm patty tins. Put a little jam in each. Cream the butter and sugar until soft and white. Add the lemon rind. Beat the egg lightly, then beat it gradually into the creamed fat. Fold in the flour and add a little milk or water if necessary to give a soft dropping consistency. Half fill the pastry cases with the mixture. Cut any remaining pastry into thin strips and place 2 strips in the form of a cross on top of each tartlet. Bake for 15–20 minutes, until golden and firm in the centre.

Note The term 'cheese' was originally used to describe almost any stiff or set mixture thickened with egg, rennet, acid fruit juice, etc. Custard or egg curds were the commonest form of 'cheese', which is why many custard pies and tartlets today are still called cheesecakes.

Recipes for cheesecakes made with cheese can be found on pp1041–43.

Mince Pies

Makes 12

shortcrust pastry   *flour for rolling out*
   (p1249) *using 300g*   *250g mincemeat*
   flour **or** *flaky* (p1252),   *25g caster* **or** *icing sugar*
   rough puff (p1252) **or**   *for dredging*
   puff (p1253) *pastry*
   using 200g flour

Heat the oven to very hot, 230°C, Gas 8. Roll out the pastry 2mm thick on a lightly floured surface, and use just over half to line twelve 7cm patty tins. Cut out 12 lids from the rest of the pastry. Place a spoonful of mincemeat in each pastry case. Dampen the edges of the cases and cover with the pastry lids. Seal the edges well, brush the tops with water, and dredge with the sugar. Make 2 small cuts in the top of each pie. Bake for 15–20 minutes or until golden-brown.

Raisin Tartlets

Makes 12

shortcrust pastry (p1249)   *6 walnut halves*
   using 100g flour   *1 × 10ml spoon lemon*
flour for rolling out   *juice*
200g seedless raisins   *25g brown sugar*

Heat the oven to fairly hot, 200°C, Gas 6. Roll out the pastry on a lightly floured surface and use it to line twelve 7cm patty tins. Mince the raisins and walnuts or chop very finely. Add the lemon juice and half the brown sugar. Fill the pastry cases with the raisin mixture and sprinkle with the rest of the brown sugar. Bake for 15–20 minutes.

Cream Horns

Makes 8

*puff pastry (p1253)
  using 100g flour*
flour for rolling out
*beaten egg and milk for
  glazing*
*3 × 15ml spoons sieved
  raspberry jam*
*4 × 15ml spoons
  liqueur-flavoured
  whipped cream (p880)*

*2 × 15ml spoons finely
  chopped nuts
  (preferably pistachios)*
or *green-tinted
  desiccated coconut
  (p1235)*

Heat the oven to hot, 220°C, Gas 7. Roll out the pastry 5mm thick on a lightly floured surface and cut into strips 35cm long and 2cm wide. Moisten the strips with cold water. Wind each strip round a cornet mould, working from the point upward, keeping the moistened surface on the outside. Lay the horns on a dampened baking tray, with the final overlap of the pastry strip underneath. Leave

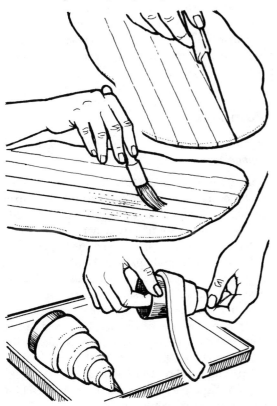

in a cool place for 1 hour. Brush with beaten egg and milk, and bake for 10–15 minutes or until golden-brown. Remove the moulds and return the horns to the oven for 5 minutes. Cool completely on a wire rack. When cold, put a very little jam in the bottom of each horn. Fill the horns with the cream. Sprinkle with the chopped nuts or desiccated coconut.

Note Chantilly Cream (p880) or 2 × 15ml spoons confectioners' custard (p1237) and 2 × 15ml spoons stiffly whipped cream can also be used to fill Cream Horns.

Cream Slices

Makes 8

*puff pastry (p1253)
  using 100g flour*
flour for rolling out
*royal icing (p1234) using
  100g icing sugar*
*2 × 15ml spoons smooth
  seedless jam*

*125ml sweetened
  whipped cream*
*white glacé icing (p1225)
  using 100g icing sugar*

Heat the oven to hot, 220°C, Gas 7. Roll out the pastry 1cm thick on a lightly floured surface into a neat rectangle. Cut it into 8 oblong pieces 10 × 2cm. Place on a baking sheet and spread the tops thinly with royal icing. Bake for 20 minutes or until the pastry is well risen and the icing is slightly browned. Leave to cool completely. When cold, split in half crossways. Spread the top of the bottom half with jam, and the bottom of the top half with cream; then sandwich the halves together again. Spread a little glacé icing on top of each slice, over the browned royal icing.

VARIATION

Vanilla Slices

Make as for Cream Slices but without the royal icing. When the slices are cold, fill with vanilla-flavoured confectioners' custard (p1237) instead of cream. Ice the tops with white glacé icing.

Maids of Honour

Makes 20

puff pastry (p1253) *using*
  200g flour
flour for rolling out
200g ground almonds
100g caster sugar
2 eggs

25g flour
4 × 15ml spoons single
  cream
2 × 15ml spoons orange
  flower water

Heat the oven to fairly hot, 200°C, Gas 6. Roll out the pastry on a lightly floured surface and use it to line twenty 7cm patty tins. Mix together the ground almonds and sugar. Add the eggs, and mix in the flour, cream, and orange flower water. Put the mixture into the pastry cases and bake for about 15 minutes or until the filling is firm and golden-brown.

Mrs Beeton's Fanchonnettes or Custard Tartlets

Makes 12

puff pastry (p1253) *using*
  200g flour
flour for rolling out
25g butter
7 × 10ml spoons icing
  sugar
1 × 15ml spoon flour

3 eggs
250ml milk
a few drops vanilla
  essence
2 × 15ml spoons whole
  fruit strawberry **or**
  blackcurrant jam

Roll out the pastry 5mm thick on a lightly floured surface and leave to rest while preparing the custard.

Cream together the butter and sugar, and mix in the flour until well blended. Whisk the eggs into the milk, add the vanilla essence, and blend the mixture gradually into the butter and sugar, breaking down any lumps. Heat gently in a heavy saucepan, stirring all the time, until the mixture reaches simmering point and is thick. Remove from the heat, cover with damp greaseproof paper, and leave to cool while preparing the pastry cases.

Heat the oven to fairly hot, 190°C, Gas 5. Line twelve 7cm patty tins, about 1cm deep, with the puff pastry, pressing it in well. Put a little of the jam in the bottom of each pastry case. Spoon the custard mixture over the jam, almost filling the cases. Bake for 20–25 minutes until the custard is firm. Cool in the tins. Before serving, decorate each tartlet with a small dab of the jam in the centre.

Apricot Bouchées

Makes 18

puff pastry (p1253) *using*
  200g flour
flour for rolling out
1 × 375g can apricot
  halves

125ml whipping cream
1 × 15ml spoon caster
  sugar

Heat the oven to very hot, 230°C, Gas 8. Roll out the pastry 1cm thick on a lightly floured surface and cut into rounds using a 7cm pastry cutter. Using a 5cm cutter, make a light incision on each round. Bake for 10 minutes, or until well risen and golden-brown. Cool completely. Lift out the top layer of pastry within the ring and scoop out any uncooked paste beneath, making a hollow case. Drain the apricots. Place half an apricot, round side down, in each case. Whip the cream and sugar together until stiff, and pipe a rosette on each apricot.

Palmiers

puff pastry (p1253)
  trimmings

flour for rolling out
caster sugar

Heat the oven to hot, 220°C, Gas 7. Roll out the pastry on a lightly floured surface into a long strip about 30cm wide for large palmiers, 10–12cm wide for petits fours. Sprinkle well with caster sugar. Roll up the pastry from one long side to the centre of the strip. Then roll up, from the other long side so that the two rolls meet in the centre. Chill until firm, then cut the roll in slices; for petits fours, cut thin slices. Sprinkle the slices with more sugar, and place them, sugared side up, on a dampened baking sheet. Bake for 10–12 minutes, depending on the thickness of the slices. Lift off the sheet with a palette knife, and cool on a wire rack.

Serve large palmiers as afternoon tea biscuits, very small ones as petits fours.

Mrs Beeton's Jam Tartlets

puff pastry (p1253) *flour for rolling out*
 trimmings   *jam* **or** *marmalade*

Heat the oven to fairly hot, 200°C, Gas 6. Roll out the pastry 5mm thick on a lightly floured surface and use it to line 7cm patty tins or foil tartlet cases. Bake blind for 7–10 minutes. Dry the empty cases in the oven for another 3–4 minutes. Cool, then fill with jam or marmalade.

Banbury Cakes

Makes 14

rough puff **or** *flaky*   *100g currants*
 (p1252) **or** *puff (p1253)*   *2 × 10ml spoons cut*
 pastry, using 200g flour   *mixed peel*
flour for rolling out   *50g brown sugar*
25g butter **or** *margarine*   *2 × 15ml spoons rum*
3 × 10ml spoons plain   *1 egg white*
 flour   *25g caster sugar*
½ × 2.5ml spoon ground
 nutmeg **or** *ground*
 cinnamon

Heat the oven to hot, 220°C, Gas 7. Roll out the pastry 5mm thick on a lightly floured surface and cut into rounds using a 7cm pastry cutter.

To make the filling, melt the fat in a saucepan and stir in the flour and spice. Cook for 2 minutes. Remove from the heat, and add the fruit, brown sugar, and rum. Place a spoonful of filling in the centre of each pastry round. Dampen the edges of each round with water and gather them up to form a ball; turn the ball over so the join is underneath. Roll or pat each ball into an oval shape, approximately 10 × 6cm. With a sharp knife make 3 cuts in the top. Put the cakes on a baking sheet and bake for 15–20 minutes or until golden-brown.

Whisk the egg white lightly and brush over the hot cakes; dust immediately with caster sugar. Return to the oven for a few minutes to frost the glaze.

Sly Cakes

Makes 16–20

rough puff pastry   *25g cut mixed peel*
 (p1252), using 200g   *50g sugar*
 flour   *1 × 10ml spoon mixed*
flour for rolling out   *spice*
25g butter **or** *margarine*   *beaten egg* **or** *milk for*
1 apple   *glazing*
200g currants   *caster sugar for dusting*

Heat the oven to hot, 220°C, Gas 7. Divide the pastry in half, and roll out each piece on a lightly floured surface into a 15cm square about 2mm thick. Melt the fat. Peel, core, and chop the apple and mix it with the currants, peel, sugar, spice, and melted fat. Spread the mixture on one piece of pastry, lay the other piece on top and seal the edges well. Mark the top into squares or oblongs with the back of a knife, without cutting through the pastry. Glaze with beaten egg or milk. Put on a baking sheet and bake for 20–30 minutes until golden-brown. Cut into squares or oblongs and dust with caster sugar.

Eccles Cakes

Makes 12–14

flaky **or** *rough puff*   *25g cut mixed peel*
 pastry (p1252), using   *½ × 2.5ml spoon mixed*
 200g flour   *spice*
flour for rolling out   *½ × 2.5ml spoon ground*
25g butter **or** *margarine*   *nutmeg*
1 × 15ml spoon sugar   *caster sugar for dusting*
75g currants

Heat the oven to hot, 220°C, Gas 7. Roll out the pastry 5mm thick on a lightly floured surface and cut into rounds using a 10cm pastry cutter. Cream together the fat and the sugar, add the currants, peel and spices, and place spoonfuls of the mixture in the centre of each pastry round. Gather the edges of each round together to form a ball. With the smooth side uppermost, form into a flat cake. Make 2 cuts in the top of each cake with a sharp knife. Brush with water and dust with caster sugar. Put on a baking sheet and bake for 20 minutes or until golden-brown.

Cream Eclairs

Makes 10–12

choux pastry (p1251)
  using 100g flour
fat for greasing
250ml whipping cream
25g caster sugar and
  icing sugar, mixed

3–4 drops vanilla
  essence
chocolate (p1226) **or**
coffee (p1225) glacé
  icing

Make the pastry and use it while still warm. Put it in a forcing bag with a 2cm nozzle, and pipe the mixture in 10cm lengths on to a lightly greased baking sheet. Cut off each length with a knife or scissors dipped in hot water. Bake in a hot oven, 220°C, Gas 7, for 30 minutes. Do not open the oven door while baking. Reduce the heat to moderate, 180°C, Gas 4, and bake for a further 10 minutes. Remove the éclairs from the oven, split them, and remove any uncooked paste. Return to the oven for 5 minutes if still damp inside. Cool completely on a wire rack.

Meanwhile, whip the cream until it holds its shape, adding the mixed sugars gradually. Add the vanilla essence while whipping. Fill the éclairs with the cream, close neatly, and cover the tops with glacé icing.

VARIATIONS

Instead of vanilla-flavoured whipped cream, the éclairs can be filled with Chantilly Cream (p880) or with chocolate-flavoured confectioners' custard (p1237) mixed with an equal quantity of whipped cream.

Cream Buns

Pipe the pastry in 5cm balls, use any of the fillings described above, and sift icing sugar over the tops instead of glacé icing.

Chocolate Meringue Tartlets

Makes 12

pâte sucrée (p1249)
  using 100g flour
flour for rolling out
fat for greasing
1 × 5ml spoon cornflour
1 × 5ml spoon cocoa
125ml milk
2 × 10ml spoons butter
  or margarine

2 × 10ml spoons sugar
2 large egg yolks
a few drops vanilla
  essence
a pinch of ground
  cinnamon
2 large egg whites
75g caster sugar

Decoration
glacé cherries   angelica

Heat the oven to fairly hot, 190°C, Gas 5. Roll out the pastry on a lightly floured surface and use it to line 12 lightly greased 7cm patty tins. Mix together the cornflour and cocoa in a saucepan and blend in the milk. Bring to the boil and cook for 2–3 minutes, stirring all the time. Cool slightly, then stir in the fat, sugar, egg yolks, flavouring and spice. Half fill the pastry cases with the mixture and bake for 10–15 minutes or until set. Reduce the oven temperature to cool, 150°C, Gas 2. Whisk the egg whites until stiff, whisk in 1 × 10ml spoon of the caster sugar, and fold in almost all the rest, using a metal spoon. Pipe the mixture in a spiral or star on the tops of the tartlets. Dredge with the remaining caster sugar and decorate with cherries and angelica. Bake for 15–20 minutes or until the meringue is crisp and very lightly browned.

Beatrice Tartlets

Makes 20

pâte sucrée (p1249)
  using 150g flour
flour for rolling out
butter for greasing
3 bananas
juice of 1 lemon

1 × 15ml spoon caster
  sugar
50g chopped walnuts
125ml double cream
50g plain chocolate

Roll out the pastry on a lightly floured surface and use it to line 20 lightly greased 7cm patty tins. Bake blind, then cool. Chop the bananas and mix with the lemon juice and sugar. Stir the walnuts into the bananas. Pile the mixture into the pastry cases. Whip the cream until stiff, and pipe a large rosette on top of each tartlet. Grate the chocolate finely and sprinkle it over the cream.

Chocolate Nut Tartlets

Makes 12

Pastry

75g margarine	25g cornflour
25g icing sugar	1 egg
100g flour	flour for rolling out
a pinch of salt	

Filling

50g butter **or** margarine	50g caster sugar
50g plain chocolate	1 egg
50g ground almonds	

Decoration

chocolate glacé icing (p1226)	12 walnut halves

Heat the oven to fairly hot, 190°C, Gas 5. To make the pastry, cream together the margarine and icing sugar until well blended. Sift together the flour, salt, and cornflour. Beat the egg until liquid. Add the flour to the creamed mixture and mix to a stiff dough with the egg. Roll out very thinly on a lightly floured surface and use to line twelve 7cm patty tins.

For the filling, cream the fat, grate the chocolate and add it with the ground almonds and caster sugar. Beat the egg until liquid, and mix to a soft dropping consistency with the chocolate mixture. Place spoonfuls of the mixture in each pastry case and bake for 15 minutes until firm. When cold, cover with chocolate glacé icing and place a walnut half in the centre of each tartlet.

Orange Boats

Makes 12

Pastry

100g plain flour	50g butter
$\frac{1}{2} \times 2.5ml$ spoon salt	1 egg yolk
$5 \times 2.5ml$ spoons ground almonds	flour for rolling out

Filling

grated rind of 1 orange	75g caster sugar
50g ground almonds	1 egg white

Decoration

50g icing sugar	$1 \times 15ml$ spoon water
$1 \times 15ml$ spoon orange juice	

To make the pastry, sift the flour and salt into a bowl, and add the ground almonds. Rub the butter into the dry ingredients, then mix to a stiff paste with the egg yolk and a little water, if required. Roll out the pastry on a lightly floured surface and use it to line 12 boat-shaped tartlet tins.

For the filling, mix the orange rind with the ground almonds and caster sugar. Whisk the egg white until stiff, and fold it into the mixture. Fill the pastry cases two-thirds full with the mixture. Bake in a fairly hot oven, 190°C, Gas 5, for 20–30 minutes or until the pastry and filling are golden-brown. Leave to cool completely.

Make a stiff glacé icing (p1225) with the icing sugar, orange juice, and water. When the tartlets are cold, pipe a wavy thread of icing down the centre of each boat.

Note For a children's party, place a wooden cocktail stick upright in each boat as a mast, and attach to it a thin slice of citron peel or a candied orange slice as a sail.

CANAPÉS, SAVOURIES, SANDWICHES, AND FLAVOURED BUTTERS

Anchovy butter makes a pretty dish, if fancifully moulded, for breakfast or supper, and should be garnished with parsley.

Canapés are usually served as small cocktail snacks. As a rule they consist of a round or finger of toast, pastry or a small biscuit, covered with a savoury spread. They can also include larger pieces of toast with more substantial toppings, served as a last-course savoury.

Sandwiches may be savoury or sweet, and, depending on size and filling, are suitable as either a main-course dish, snack or cocktail savoury.

Recipes for rarebits and other similar dishes can be found in the chapter on Breakfasts and Suppers.

Canapés and Savouries

Canapés or croûtes for savouries are neat shapes of toast, fried bread, short or flaky pastry, or crisp biscuits. Their shape can be stamped out with a biscuit cutter.

Toast is the most usual home-made canapé base, but it becomes soft if prepared too far ahead. If fried bread is used it should be very well drained on soft kitchen paper or crumpled tissue paper so that it is dry, not greasy.

Croustades can be made from hollowed-out small bread rolls. These are filled with a savoury mixture either heated through in the oven or eaten cold.

HOT CANAPÉS AND SAVOURIES

Anchovy Croûtes

12 savouries

1 hard-boiled egg
½ × 2.5ml spoon curry paste or 1 × 2.5ml spoon curry powder
50g butter

4 slices toast
12 anchovy fillets
paprika
a few drops lemon juice

Garnish
chopped parsley

Heat the oven to hot, 220°C, Gas 7. Separate the egg yolk from the white and chop the white finely. Rub the yolk through a fine sieve and combine with the curry paste or curry powder, and butter. Mix to a soft paste. Cut the toast into rounds or triangles and spread with the mixture. Arrange an anchovy fillet on each piece of toast and season with paprika. Add 2–3 drops of lemon juice. Place in the oven for 3–4 minutes. Decorate with chopped egg white and parsley just before serving.

Anchovy Fingers

6–9 savouries

butter
2–3 slices toast
1 shallot
parsley sprigs
6–9 anchovy fillets

a few drops lemon juice
Cayenne pepper **or**
 paprika

Heat the oven to fairly hot, 200°C, Gas 6. Butter the toast and cut into fingers. Skin the shallot, chop it finely with the parsley, and sprinkle over the fingers of toast. Place an anchovy fillet on each one. Add a few drops of lemon juice and sprinkle with a little Cayenne pepper or paprika. Place a knob of butter on each finger of toast, and cook for 5–10 minutes in the oven. Serve hot.

Anchovy Toast

8–10 small savouries

1 × 50g can anchovy
 fillets
1 small shallot **or** onion
4 eggs
40g butter

1 × 2.5ml spoon chopped
 parsley
Cayenne pepper
4 slices toast

Drain the anchovy fillets and chop them coarsely. Skin and chop the shallot or onion. Beat the eggs lightly. Heat 25g of the butter in a small saucepan, fry the shallot or onion until lightly browned, then add the anchovies, parsley and eggs, and season with Cayenne pepper. Stir over low heat until the eggs are just set. Butter the toast with the remaining butter and spread the anchovy mixture over it. Cut the toast into fingers.

Angels on Horseback (1)

8 savouries

8 large shelled oysters
8 rashers streaky bacon,
 without rinds

2–3 slices hot toast
butter

Garnish
watercress leaves

Heat the oven (if used) to fairly hot, 200°C, Gas 6. Wrap each oyster in a bacon rasher. Fasten the rolls with small poultry skewers, and grill for 4–6 minutes, or bake for 10 minutes in the oven. Butter the toast and cut into small fingers. Remove the skewers from the 'angels' when cooked, and serve on the fingers of toast. Garnish with watercress.

Angels on Horseback (2)

12 savouries

6 rashers streaky bacon,
 without rinds
1 × 5ml spoon finely
 chopped onion
1 × 2.5ml spoon chopped
 parsley
125ml thick foundation
 white sauce (p692)
1 × 2.5ml spoon lemon
 juice

paprika **or** Cayenne
 pepper
salt
800g canned **or** bottled
 mussels
12 small rounds fried
 bread

Heat the oven to moderate, 180°C, Gas 4. Flatten and spread the bacon, using a knife or small rolling-pin, and cut each piece in half. Stir the onion and parsley into the white sauce, add the lemon juice, and season with the paprika or Cayenne pepper and a little salt to taste. Drain the mussels well and mix with the sauce. Spoon 3 mussels on to each piece of bacon and roll up; secure each bacon roll with a small skewer or cocktail stick if necessary. Place on a baking tray and cook in the oven for 7–8 minutes. Serve hot on fried bread.

Bacon Olives

8 savouries

125g cooked ham **or** tongue
7 × 10ml spoons breadcrumbs
1 × 2.5ml spoon finely chopped onion
1 × 2.5ml spoon finely chopped parsley
a pinch of dried mixed herbs
a pinch of grated nutmeg
salt and pepper
1 egg
8 thin rashers streaky bacon, without rinds
8 small rounds toast **or** pastry canapés

Chop the ham or tongue finely. Mix together with the breadcrumbs, onion, parsley, and herbs, add a pinch of nutmeg, and season to taste with salt and pepper. Beat the egg until liquid, and stir in gradually as much as is needed to bind the mixture. Leave to stand for 30 minutes. Divide the mixture into 8 portions. Form each portion into a cork shape, roll in a rasher of bacon, and secure with string or small skewers. Bake in a fairly hot oven, 190°C, Gas 5, for about 30 minutes. Serve on toast or pastry canapés.

Bengal Croûtes

16 savouries

4 slices toast
butter
100g cooked ham
125ml foundation white sauce (p692)
1 × 15ml spoon double cream
salt and pepper (optional)
3 × 15ml spoons chutney **or** finely chopped piccalilli
3 × 15ml spoons grated hard cheese

Garnish
chopped parsley

Cut off the crusts and butter the toast. Chop the ham finely, and heat for several minutes in the white sauce, adding the cream and seasoning as necessary. Spread the sauce over the toast, then add the chutney or piccalilli. Cover with grated cheese and put under a hot grill for 3–5 minutes until crisp and golden-brown. Cut the toast into fingers, and garnish with the parsley. Serve hot.

Cocktail Sausages

Cooked whole or halved small sausages are popular with most people. If you cannot buy cocktail sausages, use chipolatas instead. Make each into 2 small sausages, squeeze the middle, push the meat to each end, give the casing a good twist, and cut through the twisted casing.

Sausages can be served speared on to cocktail sticks. They are particularly good eaten hot, accompanied by a spicy sauce.

They can also be served on croûtes. Cut the sausages in half lengthways and set each, cut side down, on a small toasted finger-shaped croûte. Put a pat of any savoury butter on top, and garnish with a maraschino cherry, pickled cocktail onion, a tiny cube of cheese or a small chunk of canned pineapple.

Frankfurter sausages can be treated in the same way. Alternatively, split them lengthways, leaving 1 long edge joined. Spread the cut side generously with full-fat soft cheese; then re-form the sausages for serving.

Creamed Lobster Croûtes

8 savouries

25g butter
75g cooked **or** canned lobster meat
1 egg
4 × 15ml spoons double cream
salt and pepper
a pinch of grated nutmeg
8 small rounds toast

Garnish
chopped parsley

Heat the butter and cook the lobster meat gently for 4–5 minutes only; too much cooking will toughen it. Beat the egg lightly and add it to the lobster, together with the cream, seasoning, and nutmeg. Heat the mixture, stirring gently all the time, until it thickens. Put the creamed lobster on the rounds of toast and serve hot, garnished with chopped parsley.

Devilled Chicken Liver Croûtes

8 savouries

4 chicken livers
1 shallot **or** small onion
1 × 2.5ml spoon finely
  chopped parsley
a pinch of Cayenne
  pepper
a pinch of salt
8 small rashers bacon,
  without rinds
4 slices fried bread

Heat the oven (if used) to moderate, 180°C, Gas 4. Cut the livers into halves. Skin the shallot or onion and chop it finely. Mix with the parsley, Cayenne pepper, and salt. Sprinkle this mixture over the livers. Wrap the rashers of bacon round the livers, and fasten them in position with small poultry skewers. Bake in the oven or cook under a moderate grill for 7–8 minutes. Cut each slice of bread in half. Remove the skewers, put a bacon roll on each piece of bread, and serve as hot as possible.

Devilled Herring Roes

8 savouries

200g soft herring roes
1 × 15ml spoon flour
salt and pepper
clarified butter (p886)
  for shallow frying
4 slices toast
anchovy butter (p1297)
25g butter
a squeeze of lemon juice
Cayenne pepper
paprika

Rinse the herring roes gently. Season the flour and roll the roes in it. Fry in the clarified butter, turning over constantly, until golden-brown all over. Drain on soft kitchen paper. Cut the crusts off the toast, cut the slices in half, and spread with anchovy butter. Arrange the roes on the buttered toast and place on a hot dish. Put the 25g butter in the pan and heat until nut-brown and foaming; then add the lemon juice and Cayenne pepper. Pour this mixture over the roes. Dust with paprika and serve very hot.

Cooking time 10 minutes (approx)

Devilled Smoked Salmon Croûtes

9–12 savouries

3–4 slices toast
butter
salt and pepper
150g smoked salmon
  trimmings
curry butter (p1298)

Garnish
parsley sprigs

Heat the oven to fairly hot, 200°C, Gas 6. Cut off the crusts, butter the toast, and sprinkle with pepper and a little salt. Chop the salmon finely, and pound thoroughly to make a fairly smooth mixture which can be spread evenly. Spread the mixture on the toast, and coat with curry butter. Cut each slice into 3 fingers. Heat in the oven for 4–5 minutes. Garnish with sprigs of parsley and serve hot.

Devils on Horseback

8 savouries

butter for shallow frying
1–2 chicken livers **or**
  100g calf's liver
salt and pepper
a pinch of Cayenne
  pepper
8 cooked prunes
8 short thin rashers
  streaky bacon, without
  rinds
8 small bread squares,
  fried in bacon fat

Garnish
4 olives stuffed with
  pimento

Heat the oven to very hot, 230°C, Gas 8. Melt the butter and cook the liver gently, then cut into 8 pieces. Season well and dust with a few grains of Cayenne pepper. Stone the prunes and stuff with the liver. Stretch the bacon to double its size with the flat of a knife. Wrap each prune in a piece of bacon. Place in a baking tin with the bacon edges underneath. Bake in the oven for 8 minutes. Place one 'devil' on each square of fried bread and garnish with olives.

Haddock Croustades

12 savouries

1 small smoked haddock	*25g butter*
2 eggs	*a pinch of grated nutmeg*
2 × 15ml spoons milk	*croustades of bread*
a good pinch of pepper	

Garnish
Cayenne pepper

Cook the haddock in boiling water until just tender. Skin and bone the fish, and flake the flesh. Beat the eggs until liquid with the milk and pepper. Heat the butter in a pan, and when hot, add the eggs, milk, pepper, flaked haddock, and nutmeg. Cook very gently until lightly set. Fill the croustades of bread with the mixture. Garnish with Cayenne pepper.

Cooking time 12 minutes (approx)

Ham Croûtes

8 savouries

150g cooked ham	*2 egg yolks*
25g butter	*a pinch of pepper*
2 × 5ml spoons chopped	*8 round slices fried*
*shallot **or** onion*	*bread **or** toast*

Garnish
chopped parsley

Chop the ham finely. Melt the butter and fry the shallot or onion until lightly browned; then add the ham, and stir until it is hot. Add the egg yolks and season with pepper. Stir until the mixture thickens, spoon it on to the bread, and serve sprinkled with parsley.

Cooking time 10 minutes (approx)

Ham Fingers

8–10 savouries

100g lean cooked ham	*mixed mustard*
1 onion	*1 × 5ml spoon chopped*
25g butter	*parsley*
2 eggs	*fingers of baked cheese*
salt and pepper	*pastry* (p1251) **or** *toast*

Chop the ham finely. Skin and chop the onion finely. Melt the butter and fry the onion without browning. Beat the eggs until liquid. Add the ham and beaten egg to the pan. Stir over gentle heat until the eggs begin to thicken. Add the seasoning, mustard to taste, and half the parsley. Cover the pastry or toast fingers thickly with the mixture, sprinkle with the remainder of the parsley, and serve very hot or quite cold.

Cooking time 10 minutes (approx)

Hot Savoury Toasts

slices of toast	**or**
any firm non-greasy	*mashed sardines*
*meat paste **or** liver*	*seasoned with salt,*
pâté	*pepper and a little*
or	*tomato paste*
cooked sausage, skinned	
and mashed with Dijon	
mustard	

Heat the oven to moderate, 180°C, Gas 4. Cut the crusts off the toast and cut into fingers. Spread with one of the mixtures listed above, place on an ovenproof platter, and cover securely with foil. Heat through for a few minutes in the oven.

Marrow Toast

12 savouries

marrow from 2 beef
  bones
salt
6 slices toast
butter

pepper
chopped parsley,
  chopped olives and a
  few drops lemon juice
  (optional)

Soak the marrow in tepid water for about 2 hours. About 15 minutes before the dish is needed, cut the marrow into small pieces, put into cold water, bring rapidly to the boil, add a good pinch of salt, and cook for 1 minute only. Drain the marrow thoroughly. Heat the oven (if used) to hot, 220°C, Gas 7. Spread the hot toast with butter, and cut each slice in half. Put the marrow on to the slices of toast and season well. Either cook for a few minutes in the oven until the marrow is well melted, or put under a hot grill; take care the marrow does not dry out. Serve at once.

If savoury marrow is preferred, sprinkle with parsley, chopped olives, and lemon juice before serving.

Sardine and Tomato Croûtes

8 savouries

8 large canned sardines
butter
8 fingers toast
2 large tomatoes
1 × 15ml spoon
  cornflour

salt and pepper
2 × 15ml spoons grated
  Parmesan cheese **or**
4 × 15ml spoons grated
  Cheddar cheese

Heat the oven to hot, 220°C, Gas 7. Bone the sardines, making sure that you do not damage their appearance. Butter the toast and keep it hot. Skin and sieve the tomatoes, and put the pulp with the cornflour in a pan. Season well. Cook for 4–6 minutes, adding the cheese after 3 minutes. Spread half the mixture on the pieces of toast, put the sardines on top, and spread with the remaining half. Cover with buttered foil to prevent the mixture from drying out and bake in the oven for 6–8 minutes.

Sardine and Cheese Fingers (1)

12 savouries

100g Cheddar cheese
4 slices toast
2 × 10ml spoons tomato
  ketchup

2 × 125g cans sardines
  in tomato sauce

Garnish
parsley sprigs

Grate the cheese. Cut off the crusts, spread the toast with tomato ketchup, and lay the sardines evenly on the toast. Sprinkle with the cheese and cut into fingers. Grill under a slow heat for about 5 minutes or until the cheese melts. Serve hot, garnished with parsley.

Sardine and Cheese Fingers (2)

8–16 savouries

1 × 125g can sardines in
  oil
salt and pepper
50g Cheddar cheese
50g soft white
  breadcrumbs
1 × 2.5ml spoon made
  English mustard

1 × 5ml spoon
  Worcestershire sauce
soft margarine
4 large slices toast
butter

Garnish
tomato wedges

Drain the sardines but reserve the oil. Season the fish well, and mash thoroughly. Grate the cheese finely, and mix together with the breadcrumbs and a little seasoning. Combine the oil from the fish with the mustard and Worcestershire sauce. Mix into the breadcrumbs and cheese. Add enough soft margarine to make the mixture of spreading consistency. Butter one side of each slice of toast. Spread the mashed sardines all over the buttered sides, and cover with the cheese mixture. Grill under moderate heat for 2–4 minutes until golden-brown. Cut each slice in half lengthways, or into 4 fingers, and place a small wedge of tomato on each finger of toast. Serve at once.

Scotch Woodcock

8–16 savouries

4 slices toast	salt and pepper
75g butter	1 × 50g can anchovy
6 eggs	fillets
3 × 15ml spoons milk	capers

Cut the crusts off the toast. Butter each slice, using half of the butter, and cut each slice in half or quarters. Melt the remaining butter in a pan. Beat the eggs, milk, salt, and pepper together lightly. Pour into the pan, reduce the heat, and cook gently, stirring all the time, until just set and creamy. Divide between the pieces of buttered toast and garnish with small pieces of anchovy fillet and the capers.

Cooking time 15 minutes (approx)

VARIATION

Instead of using anchovy fillets, the toast can be spread with anchovy paste or essence.

Stuffed Cucumber Croûtes

12 savouries

6 slices fried bread	½ × 2.5ml spoon chopped
200g cold meat, eg ham,	mixed herbs
veal, beef, chicken	1 egg
2 large cucumbers	chicken stock
50g butter	salt and pepper
4 × 15ml spoons soft	Worcestershire sauce
white breadcrumbs	(optional)
1 × 15ml spoon chopped	
parsley	

Garnish
parsley sprigs

Cut each slice of bread in half. Mince the cold meat. Peel the cucumbers and cut into 5cm lengths. Scoop out the seeds with an apple corer, or knife. Steam for about 5 minutes until soft. Meanwhile, melt the butter in a saucepan. Stir in the meat, breadcrumbs, parsley, and herbs, and heat thoroughly. Beat the egg lightly, and add it to the mixture together with enough stock to moisten the stuffing. Season well,

and if necessary add Worcestershire sauce for extra flavour. Drain the cucumber and put each piece on a slice of bread. Fill with the hot stuffing, piled up high. Garnish with parsley sprigs.

Cooking time 10 minutes (approx)

VARIATIONS

1) 2 hard-boiled eggs finely chopped and mixed with 150ml thick cheese sauce (p693).
2) 200g macédoine of cooked vegetables (p398) mixed with 150ml very thick foundation white sauce (p692). Water from the vegetables will make the sauce thinner. Add 50g Cheddar cheese.
3) 200g finely chopped cooked mushrooms mixed with chopped onion, parsley, and 6 rashers of cooked, finely chopped bacon mixed with 150ml thick foundation white sauce (p692).

COLD CANAPÉS AND SAVOURIES

Asparagus Rolls

8–10 savouries

thin slices of fresh	mayonnaise **or**
brown bread	Hollandaise sauce
butter	(p712)
1 small bundle cooked **or**	salt and pepper
1 × 300g can	
asparagus tips	

Cut off the crusts and butter the bread. Drain the asparagus and put 1 tip on each piece of bread and butter; add a little mayonnaise or Hollandaise Sauce, and season to taste. Roll up the bread, enclosing the asparagus tip. If the bread is difficult to roll up, flatten it first with a rolling-pin. Keep the rolls under a damp cloth, or cover with foil or clingfilm until required.

VARIATION

The bread and butter can be spread with any full-fat soft cheese.

Aspic Fingers

slices of toast
butter (optional)
anchovy butter (p1297)
 or *creamed savoury*
 butter (p1298) **or**
tomato butter (p1301)

250ml aspic jelly for
 every 6 slices toast

Garnishes
sardines
anchovies
small pieces of smoked
 salmon
prawns

shrimps
sliced hard-boiled egg
asparagus tips
ham

Aspic fingers are small strips of toast, covered with a spread and garnish which are kept in place with a coating of aspic.

Butter the toast or spread it with a flavoured butter. Arrange the garnish on the toast. Pipe a flavoured butter either on the topping before coating with aspic, or later on top of the set aspic. Make the aspic jelly and allow it to cool. When it begins to thicken, spread it over the topping with a knife dipped in hot water or with a pastry brush. It is better to cover the topping with several thin coatings, allowing each layer to set before adding the next, than to try and use too much aspic at one time. Stand the slices on a tray or pastry board when coating with jelly, so that any jelly that drips off can be picked up and used again.

When the jelly is quite set, cut the slices of toast into small fingers with a sharp knife dipped in hot water.

Bread-based Savouries

slices of bread
butter for shallow frying

savoury butter for
 spreading
 (pp1297–1301)

Garnish
chopped green olives **or**
 watercress leaves

Heat the oven to moderate, 180°C, Gas 4. Cut the crusts off the bread and cut it into various shapes, eg hearts, diamonds, squares, and circles, using a pastry cutter. Melt a little butter in a shallow pan, and fry the bread shapes on one side only until golden-brown. Drain. Place, fried side down, on a baking sheet and bake in the oven for 10 minutes. Cool. Spread with any savoury butter. Garnish with green olives or watercress.

Note Leftover plain sandwiches can be used for making the bases.

Burlington Croûtes

12 savouries

100g cooked chicken
2 × 15ml spoons
 mayonnaise
2 tomatoes
salt and pepper

12 rounds fried bread **or**
 crisp biscuits
 butter (optional)
12 stuffed olives

Chop the chicken finely or mince it. Mix with the mayonnaise. Cut the tomatoes into 12 very thin slices, and season them. Drain the fried bread thoroughly or butter the biscuits. Place a slice of tomato on each bread round or biscuit, and pile the chicken mixture on top. Press a stuffed olive into the mixture on top of each croûte.

Celery Stem Savouries

crisp, white celery stalks   *filling (see Method)*
  (enough to produce
  20–25 × 4cm pieces)

Fill the celery stalks with one of the following mixtures before cutting them into 4cm pieces:

Egg Filling: To 3 chopped hard-boiled eggs, add 75ml mayonnaise. Season with salt and pepper and a little finely chopped onion to taste. Fill the celery stalks and sprinkle with chopped parsley.

Low-fat Egg Filling: Chop the whites of 4 hard-boiled eggs finely and rub the yolks through a coarse sieve. Add a few drops of oil and vinegar to the egg yolks, season with salt and pepper, and stir in the egg white. Fill the celery stalks, and garnish with a little chopped parsley or shredded lettuce.

Roquefort Filling: To 100g Roquefort or Danish Blue cheese add 1 × 15ml spoon Worcestershire sauce, 1 × 15ml spoon mayonnaise, salt and pepper. Blend all the ingredients well together and fill the celery stalks. Sprinkle with paprika.

Cheese Cream Croûtes

16–18 savouries

Cheese Cream mixture   *16–18 fingers fried*
  (p321)   *bread*

Garnish
paprika **or** *Cayenne*   *watercress sprigs*
  pepper

Spread the cheese cream mixture thickly on the fingers of fried bread when cool. Garnish with a dusting of paprika or Cayenne pepper and surround with watercress sprigs.

Cheese and Onion Sandwich Croûtes

8 small savouries

25g full-fat soft cheese   *8 pastry bases* **or** *fingers*
1 × 15ml spoon minced   *or rounds of toast* **or**
  onion   *fried bread*
salt and pepper   *paprika*
single **or** *double cream*
  (optional)

Mix the cheese with the onion, and season to taste. If necessary, add cream to moisten the mixture. Spread on the cold pastry or bread bases and sprinkle with paprika.

Cucumber Bonnes-Bouches

10 savouries (approx)

1 large **or** *2 small*   *4 × 15ml spoons aspic*
  cucumbers   *jelly*
75g cooked chicken, veal   *4 × 15ml spoons thick*
  or rabbit   *foundation white sauce*
6 small cooked   *(p692)*
  mushrooms   *4 × 15ml spoons*
25g cooked ham   *whipped cream*
salt and pepper   *brown* **or** *white bread*
a pinch of grated nutmeg   *lemon juice*

Garnish
parsley butter (p1301)

Peel the cucumber, cut into slices 2cm thick, and remove the seeds with an apple corer, potato peeler or knife. Blanch the pieces in salted water for 30 seconds and drain on a cloth. Keep aside. Rub the meat, mushrooms, and ham together through a fine sieve, mince and pound them, or process in an electric blender to make into a fine paste. Season with salt and pepper and a pinch of grated nutmeg.

Blend the aspic jelly with the white sauce while both are still warm. Leave to cool. When the mixture is cool and beginning to thicken, add the whipped cream. Blend in the minced meat and mushroom mixture.

Cut out rounds of bread slightly larger than the cucumber shapes, spread with a little of the purée;

then place a round of cucumber on each piece of bread and fill the centre with the purée piled up high. Season with lemon juice, salt and pepper, and garnish with the parsley butter.

Egg and Prawn Croûtes

8–9 savouries

2 hard-boiled eggs	*a few drops lemon juice*
butter	*Cayenne pepper*
thin slices of bread	*a pinch of salt*
½ shallot or ¼ small	*capers*
onion	*8–9 peeled prawns*

Slice the eggs in thin rings, gently remove the yolks, and put them in a bowl. Butter the slices of bread and cut from them 8–9 rounds about 4cm in diameter. Place a ring of egg white on each bread round. Chop the shallot or onion very finely and add it to the egg yolks together with a little butter and a few drops of lemon juice. Season with Cayenne pepper and a little salt, and blend together. Pile the mixture on the bread. With the point of a skewer make a hollow in the centre of the mixture on each canapé, fill the cavities with capers, and place the prawns on top.

Liver Pâté Croûtes

12 savouries

100g liver pâté	*salt and pepper*
double cream or	*12 rounds fried bread or*
foundation white sauce	*toast*
(p692)	

Garnish
chopped parsley or
paprika

Pound the liver pâté until very smooth, and blend in enough cream or white sauce to make it the consistency of thick whipped cream. Taste, and season if necessary. Spread or pipe the liver mixture on the bread or toast. Garnish with a little finely chopped parsley or sprinkle with paprika.

Foie Gras Croûtes

foie gras	*salt and pepper*
double cream or	*rounds of fried or*
foundation white sauce	*toasted bread*
(p692)	

Pound the foie gras, adding a little cream or white sauce until the consistency is suitable for piping. Rub through a fine sieve, season to taste, and pipe on to the bread, using a piping bag.

Ham Rolls

12 savouries

4 thin slices cooked ham	*2–4 × 10ml spoons*
50ml double cream or	*apricot chutney*
cottage cheese or curd	*small rounds of toast or*
cheese	*pumpernickel*

Lay each slice of ham on a board, and trim off all the fat. Whip the cream lightly, if used; sieve the cottage cheese or mash the curd cheese. Mix together the cream or cheese and the chutney. Spread over the ham and roll up like small Swiss rolls. Cut the slices into 2cm lengths, and place on small rounds of crisp toast or pumpernickel.

Savoury Stuffed Ham Rolls

12 savouries

2 pears	*100g full-fat soft cheese*
juice of 1 lemon	*6 thin slices ham*
25g browned almonds	

Garnish
chopped endive	*half slices of tomato*

Peel, core, and dice the pears. Marinate in lemon juice for 1–2 hours. Chop most of the almonds and combine with the cheese and marinated pears. Reserve the unchopped almonds. Place a little filling on each slice of ham and roll up the ham slices neatly. Cut each roll in half. Arrange on a serving dish and garnish with the endive, tomato, and remaining almonds.

Princess Mushrooms

12 savouries

12 button mushrooms
50g butter
75g full-fat soft cheese
a few drops cochineal
  (optional)
paprika
12 rounds buttered toast
  or fried bread

Remove the stalks from the mushrooms. Melt the butter in a pan and cook the mushrooms and stalks gently for about 10 minutes. Drain thoroughly, and cool. Meanwhile, colour the cheese with a few drops of cochineal, if liked. Pipe a rosette of cheese in the centre of each mushroom. Dust with paprika and put the stalk back in place. Serve on the toast or fried bread.

Note If preferred, the mushrooms can be simmered in water and vinegar for about 10 minutes. Use in the proportion of 2 × 15ml spoons vinegar to 250ml water.

Russian Croûtes

8 savouries

4 × 15ml spoons small
  strips cooked beef
  (2cm × 5mm)
oil
vinegar
pepper
8 rounds fried bread
2 hard-boiled eggs
salt
a little finely grated
  horseradish and
4 × 15ml spoons
  whipped **or** soured
  cream **or** 4 × 15ml
  spoons prepared
  horseradish sauce
Cayenne pepper
a few drops lemon juice

Sprinkle the strips of beef with oil, vinegar and a little pepper, and leave to marinate for 30 minutes. Meanwhile, slice the eggs and use to cover each round of fried bread. Season with salt and pepper. If using fresh horseradish, stir it into the cream. Season with Cayenne pepper and a few drops of lemon juice. Place the strips of beef on the croûtes and coat with the horseradish.

Sardine Cassolettes

8–10 savouries

3 large slices stale bread
  (2cm thick approx)
fat for shallow frying
1 × 65g can sardines
1 × 15ml spoon
  foundation white sauce
  (p692) **or** Fresh
  Tomato sauce (p715)
anchovy essence
  (optional)
salt and pepper
a few drops lemon juice
2 × 5ml spoons grated
  Parmesan cheese **or**
1 × 15ml spoon grated
  Cheddar cheese

Garnish
watercress leaves

Heat the oven to moderate, 180°C, Gas 4. Stamp out 8–10 round shapes of bread with a 5cm biscuit cutter. Using a smaller cutter, about 3cm, make an inner circle, but do not cut right through the bread.

Heat the fat and fry the bread until lightly browned, then drain. With the point of a knife, lift out the inner ring from each shape, to form a hollow case. Put the cases in the oven for a few minutes to crisp the insides. Cool before using.

Mash the sardines thoroughly, and mix with the white or tomato sauce; if using white sauce, add a few drops of anchovy essence. Season, then blend in a few drops of lemon juice and the cheese. Put into the crisp cases and garnish with watercress.

Sardine and Egg Fingers

6–8 savouries

2 hard-boiled eggs
Cayenne pepper
anchovy essence
2 × 10ml spoons butter
1 small gherkin
6–8 sardines
6–8 fingers fried bread

Sieve or mash the egg yolks; chop the whites finely. Add a pinch of Cayenne pepper and a few drops of anchovy essence to the butter and blend well. Chop the gherkin finely. Put 1 well-drained sardine on each finger of bread. Spread a little of the butter on each sardine, and arrange chopped gherkin down the centre of each. Decorate one end with the egg white and the other with the yolk.

PASTRY-CASED AND OTHER SMALL SAVOURIES

Pastry Cases

Vol-au-vents, patty cases, or cornet-shaped cases filled with savoury mixtures are very useful for buffet and cocktail parties. For the latter they should be small enough to eat in one mouthful. They can be served hot or cold. If the filling is put into cold pastry cases, make sure it is quite cold. If, on the other hand, the filling is put into hot pastry cases, heat the filling and the pastry separately, and fill the cases at the last minute so that the filling does not make the pastry soft. If soft cheese is used as the basis of a filling, use it cold, mix it with any hot ingredients and fill into hot cases; the heat of the case and the other ingredients should warm it through.

Directions for making vol-au-vent and patty cases, and cornet shapes are given on p1253 and p1273.

Note Small vol-au-vent cases suitable for cocktail parties can be bought frozen; so can the larger ones for serving at a buffet.

Cocktail Vol-au-vent Fillings

With White Sauce Base

To 250ml foundation white sauce (p692) made with 175ml milk and 75ml single cream add one of the following mixtures:

1) 100g cooked flaked haddock, 100g prawns, 1 × 15ml spoon sherry, 1 × 5ml spoon very finely chopped onion, salt and pepper to taste
2) 100g chopped cooked mushrooms, 100g chopped cooked chicken, 1 × 5ml spoon lemon juice, salt and pepper to taste.

With Soft Cheese Base

Divide 75g full-fat soft cheese into 2 equal portions, and arrange the following mixtures in 2 layers in vol-au-vent cases or in toasted sandwiches:

1) Mix half the cheese with 100g cooked, chopped streaky bacon rashers; mix the other half with 100g finely chopped cooked mushrooms and a little freshly ground pepper.

2) Mix half the cheese with a small onion, finely chopped and gently fried; mix the other half with 100g chopped cooked chicken, adding paprika to taste.

Royal Anchovy Biscuits

12 savouries

Anchovy Pastry

40g butter **or** margarine	a few drops anchovy
75g plain flour	essence
1 egg yolk	flour for rolling out

Anchovy Cream

1 × 50g can anchovy fillets	3 × 15ml spoons double cream
1 hard-boiled egg	a few drops cochineal
25g butter	
a pinch of Cayenne pepper	

Heat the oven to fairly hot, 200°C, Gas 6. Rub the fat into the flour, add the egg yolk, anchovy essence, and enough water to mix to a stiff dough. Roll out thinly on a lightly floured surface, and cut into rounds 3–4cm in diameter. Bake for about 12 minutes until crisp. Cool before using.

Drain the anchovies and pound with the yolk of the hard-boiled egg and the butter until smooth; season with a little Cayenne pepper. Whip the cream until fairly stiff, and fold it in. Add the colouring, drop by drop, until the anchovy cream is pale pink. Pipe rosettes of the mixture on the biscuits.

VARIATION

Anchovy Tartlets

Line 12 very small patty tins with the pastry and prick the bases all over. Bake for 6–8 minutes until crisp, then allow to cool. When cold, fill with anchovy cream. Pile it high in the centre and sprinkle with paprika. Garnish with capers.

Anchovy Eclairs
See p1258.

Rutland Anchovies

12 savouries

cheese pastry (p1251)
 using 75g flour
flour for rolling out
1 hard-boiled egg
1 × 50g can anchovy
 fillets **or** 4 whole
 anchovies
 (boned and filleted)

1 × 15ml spoon double
 cream **or** foundation
 white sauce (p692)
a pinch of Cayenne
 pepper
anchovy essence
cochineal

Garnish
watercress leaves

Heat the oven to fairly hot, 200°C, Gas 6. Roll out the pastry thinly on a lightly floured surface, cut into 3–4cm squares, and bake in the oven until crisp. Cool before using.

Separate the egg yolk and white. Sieve the yolk finely and cut the white into thin strips. Chop the anchovies, and mix with the cream or white sauce, and the sieved yolk. Season lightly with Cayenne pepper, and add a few drops of anchovy essence and cochineal, drop by drop, until a pale pink colour is obtained. Pile the mixture on the pastry biscuits, and garnish with the strips of egg white and the watercress.

Cheese Straws

48–60 straws

rich cheese pastry
 (p1252) using 100g flour

flour for rolling out

Heat the oven to fairly hot, 200°C, Gas 6. Roll out the pastry about 5mm thick on a lightly floured surface and cut into fingers, about 10 × 1cm. From the pastry trimmings make several rings about 4cm in diameter. With a palette knife, lift both rings and straws on to a baking sheet. Bake for 8–10 minutes, or until lightly browned and crisp. Cool on the baking sheet.

To serve, fit a few straws through each ring and lay the bundles in the centre of a plate with any remaining straws criss-crossed around them.

Mrs Beeton's Cheese Straws

48–60 straws

50g butter
50g plain flour
50g soft white
 breadcrumbs
50g Cheshire **or**
 Lancashire cheese

$\frac{1}{2}$ × 2.5ml spoon
 Cayenne pepper
$\frac{1}{2}$ × 2.5ml spoon salt
flour for rolling out

Rub the butter into the flour, and add the breadcrumbs. Grate and add the cheese with the seasonings. Work thoroughly by hand, to make a smooth dough. Chill for 30 minutes.

Heat the oven to moderate, 180°C, Gas 4. Roll out the dough 5mm thick on a lightly floured surface. Cut into thin straws about 3mm × 5cm. Bake for 7–10 minutes. Cool on the baking sheet and serve cold.

Mrs Beeton's Cayenne Cheeses

24–30 savouries

200g butter
200g plain flour
200g Cheshire **or**
 Lancashire cheese

$\frac{1}{2}$ × 2.5ml spoon
 Cayenne pepper
$\frac{1}{2}$ × 2.5ml spoon salt
flour for rolling out

Rub the butter into the flour. Grate and add the cheese with the Cayenne pepper and salt. Work thoroughly by hand, to make a smooth dough. Use a few drops of water if necessary, but the cheeses will be shorter and richer without it. When blended, chill for 30 minutes.

Heat the oven to moderate, 180°C, Gas 4. Roll out the dough 5mm thick on a lightly floured surface, and cut into fingers about 10 × 1cm. Bake for 15–17 minutes. Cool.

Note Do not serve while still warm from the oven as the fingers crumble and break easily. Re-heat gently until warm.

Cheese Butterflies

12–18 savouries

rich cheese pastry
(p1252) using 100g flour
flour for rolling out
100g full-fat soft cheese

a few drops anchovy
essence
a few drops cochineal

Heat the oven to fairly hot, 200°C, Gas 6. Roll out the pastry 2mm thick on a lightly floured surface and cut into rounds about 6cm in diameter. Cut half the rounds across the centre to make 'wings'. With a palette knife, lift on to a baking sheet and bake for 10 minutes. Cool on the baking sheet. Flavour and colour the cheese with the essence and cochineal. When the biscuits are quite cold, pipe a line of cheese across the centre of each full round and press the straight edges of the half-rounds into the cheese in pairs, to make them stand up like wings.

Cheese Meringues
See p899.

Cocktail Sausage Rolls
See p1307.

Haddock Boats
See p1256.

Rissolettes
See p955.

Sandwiches

Sandwiches are a British invention first thought of by the 4th Earl of Sandwich so that he could eat a light meal without having to leave the gaming table. Today, they may be small and fancy for afternoon tea or parties; large and substantial as a lunch-time snack; baked, fried or toasted as a snack or supper dish, or even layered with a variety of fillings and bread to form either a decker or club sandwich.

Bread should be fresh but not too new or soft. White, wholemeal, wheatmeal, rye, malt, fruit or enriched bread can all be used. Rolls or baps make an interesting change from ordinary sliced bread. Instead of the usual butter or margarine, other spreads such as dripping or soft cheese can be used.

Creamed butter is easier to spread than firm butter. It also makes cutting the bread easier. To cream butter, beat it until light with 1×5ml spoon hot water added to each 200g butter. Firm block margarine or hard dripping should be treated in the same way. Soft tub margarine, soft dripping, curd or cream cheese can be used as they are.

Always use a sharp knife for cutting sandwiches, especially fancy shapes.

TYPES OF SANDWICHES

Plain Sandwiches

Use a firm tin loaf rather than a round loaf shape which makes it difficult to remove crusts. If cutting the sandwiches from an unsliced loaf, butter each slice thinly before cutting to avoid crumbling or breaking the bread. Cut each slice not thicker than 5mm and cover the buttered side with the relevant filling which should be prepared in advance. Press an uncovered slice lightly on top, buttered side down, and continue in this way until the required number of sandwiches have been made. Stack 3–4 sandwiches together, remove the crusts, if liked, and cut into triangles, squares or fingers, as required. Bread for fancy sandwiches can also be prepared in this way.

Note Leftover plain sandwiches and crusts need not be wasted. They can be used to make Bread-based Savouries (p1285), Sandwich Croûtons (p1294), or Sandwich Fritters (p1294). Savoury sandwiches can also be crumbled for use in stuffings.

Double or Triple Decker Sandwiches

Use 3 or 4 slices white or brown bread and 2 or 3 different fillings.

Striped Deckers: Alternate slices of brown and white bread, or use different coloured fillings.

Toasted Deckers: Make ordinary decker sandwiches with bread, press the slices firmly together, brush the outsides with melted butter and grill both sides, using moderate heat. Turn each sandwich over to grill the second side as soon as the first is golden-brown. Toasted deckers have a soft untoasted slice of bread in the centre, unlike club sandwiches (see below). Serve with a knife and fork.

Club Sandwiches

Stack 3 slices of hot toast and 2 non-melting fillings. Be generous with the fillings. Cut the sandwiches in large triangles, and spear with cocktail sticks to hold them together. Top each sandwich with a small salad garnish if possible, and serve hot. These are good for using stale bread, as the filling moistens the toast.

Super Club Sandwiches: Cover club sandwiches with a good cheese sauce, and brown gently under a low grill before serving. Serve club or super club sandwiches with a knife and fork.

Open Sandwiches

Use a single large slice of wholemeal, wheatmeal or rye bread with a decorative topping. The attraction of these lies in the arrangement and colours of the ingredients which must be trimmed neatly to form a balanced pattern of colour contrasts.

For party open sandwiches, use 1cm thick slices of white or brown bread or slices of pumpernickel. Cut into fancy shapes, such as triangles, rounds, diamonds or hearts. Spread with creamed butter and suitable sandwich topping. Garnish with stuffed olives, small radishes cut into water lilies (p393), slices of hard-boiled egg, small pieces of tomato, slices of cucumber, gherkins, shredded lettuce, watercress, piped cream cheese, finely sprinkled paprika, etc. Be careful not to overdo the topping or garnish especially if the sandwiches are to be eaten as finger food, eg at an informal buffet, as they will then be unstable or top-heavy, awkward to handle, and may fall off.

Toppings

1) Cover brown bread with a lettuce leaf, with piped rosettes of cream cheese, and chips of apple dipped in lemon juice piled on top. Decorate with thin radish slices.
2) Cover brown bread with mustard-flavoured butter, then with a lettuce leaf. Top with sliced liver sausage, and decorate with crumbled hard-boiled egg yolk.
3) Cover brown bread with cream cheese. Decorate with skinned orange segments and halved cucumber slices (unpeeled). Sprinkle with chopped parsley.
4) Cover brown bread with thin slices of gammon or ham, then lay 2 asparagus spears diagonally across each bread slice, and hold in place with piped rosettes of a savoury butter.
5) Cover brown bread with Brie cheese instead of butter, and decorate with alternate stripes of crumbled hard-boiled egg yolk and finely chopped parsley.

Note For a wider range of toppings, see Smørrebrød (Danish open sandwiches) on p1553.

Fancy or Party Sandwiches

Bread for party sandwiches must be cut very thin, and the crusts removed; amusing and unusual shapes can be cut with pastry or biscuit cutters. For occasions such as cocktail parties and weddings it is usual to serve very small sandwiches, by cutting 6 rather than 4 sandwiches from each round of bread, for instance. Some attractive party sandwiches are given below.

Rolled sandwiches: Use 1 thin white or 1 thin brown slice of bread, cut lengthways from a loaf. Cut off the crusts. Spread thinly with filling, and roll up like a Swiss roll; if necessary secure with a cocktail stick. Wrap in foil, and chill. To serve, cut thin rounds from the roll.

Pinwheel sandwiches: Make as for rolled sandwiches but use 1 thin slice of white and 1 thin slice of brown bread. Spread the white slice very thinly with filling, place the brown slice on top, spread it, and roll up. Chill and serve like the rolled sandwiches.

Pyramid sandwiches: Cut out 5 different sized bread rounds from 2–10cm. Butter, spread with gaily coloured fillings, and stack with the smallest round on top. Vary the colours and flavours of the spreads.

Cornucopia or horn shape sandwiches: Cut thin slices of bread into squares. Spread with butter and filling. Treating one corner of the bread slice as the pointed end of the shell, and the opposite corner as the open end, roll one of the remaining corners over to the centre. Wrap the fourth corner over it, thus forming a cornucopia or horn shape. Add more filling if required.

Ribbon sandwiches: Use a white and a brown loaf. Cut off all the crusts and cut thin slices lengthways from the loaf. Butter the white loaf first, and spread with filling. Repeat the process using the brown loaf. Put white and brown slices together in alternate layers, to build up a new striped loaf. Press the slices together firmly, wrap in clingfilm, and chill. To serve, cut the bread through the layers.

Chequerboard sandwiches: Prepare a ribbon sandwich loaf, cutting all the bread slices 1cm thick. Cut only 4 layers of each bread, and spread the filling evenly. Make up the slices into a loaf. Cut this ribbon loaf into 1cm slices and spread each slice with butter and filling. Pile 4 slices one above the other with the strips of bread all running in the same direction, and with brown strips over white strips and vice versa, making a design of squares when seen from the side. Place the top slice buttered side down. Press the stack firmly together, wrap in clingfilm, and chill well. Repeat this process with all the remaining slices. To serve, cut each stack into slices with a chequerboard design.

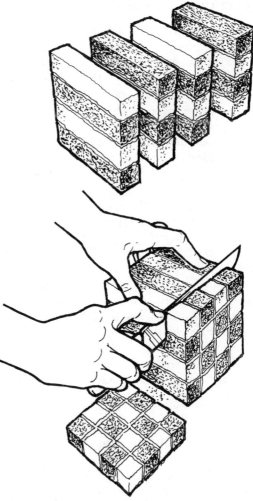

Making rolled sandwiches

Making chequerboard sandwiches

Mosaic sandwiches: Prepare equal numbers of thinly cut white and brown sandwiches, with a smooth filling. Using a small fancy-shaped biscuit cutter, cut out the centres. Exchange these small centre pieces so that all the white sandwiches have brown centres and vice versa.

Sandwich kebabs: Make equal numbers of white and brown sandwiches, using 3 different fillings. Chill for at least 2 hours. Remove the crusts from all the sandwiches, and cut each into 8 or 16 × 1cm squares. Thread 3 mini-sandwiches (2 white and 1 brown or vice versa), each with a different filling, on to thin skewers or cocktail sticks.

Savoury Sandwich Loaf

Trim the crusts off an oblong loaf, and cut the top flat. Cut into slices horizontally, and butter each slice. Then reassemble the loaf, with 2 or 3 different coloured fillings used alternately (see below). Put on the top slice, buttered side down. Press the slices together, wrap closely in clingfilm, and chill. To serve, unwrap, cover with curd or cottage cheese, and decorate with small pieces of gaily coloured salad ingredients.

Fillings

Yellow filling: Blend 75g softened butter with 4 crumbled hard-boiled egg yolks, 25g finely grated Cheddar cheese, and salt and pepper to taste. Add a few drops of yellow food colouring, and work to a smooth paste.

Green filling: Blend 75g softened butter with 100g finely chopped frozen, thawed spinach, well drained, 25g cottage cheese, 2–3 finely chopped spring onions, and salt and pepper to taste. Work together until smooth.

Red filling: Blend 75g softened butter with 1 × 212g can herrings in tomato sauce. Work until smooth.

Sandwich Croûtons

savoury sandwiches   butter for brushing

Cut the sandwiches into cubes. Melt the butter, and brush it over the sandwiches. Toast or fry the sandwiches, turning once, until crisp on both sides. Serve hot with soup, or use as a garnish for any suitable savoury dish.

Sandwich Fritters

savoury sandwiches   100ml milk for every 2
 (see **Note**)   sandwiches
1 egg for every 2   fat for shallow frying
 sandwiches

Cut the crusts off the sandwiches if necessary. Beat the egg with the milk. Lay the sandwiches in a shallow plate, and pour the milk mixture over them. Leave for 10 minutes. Heat the fat, and fry the sandwiches until golden on both sides, turning once. Drain, and serve hot on a paper napkin.

Note Avoid strongly flavoured or oily fillings.

VARIATION

The sandwiches can be dipped in batter and fried in deep fat, if preferred.

Mrs Beeton's Cheese Sandwiches

4 helpings

8 thin slices brown bread   4 slices Cheshire cheese,
butter for spreading   1cm thick and the same
                              size as the bread slices

Heat the oven to fairly hot, 200°C, Gas 6. Butter the bread very lightly, and cut off the crusts. Place the slices of cheese between the bread slices, making 4 sandwiches. Place on a baking sheet, and bake for 7–10 minutes until the top bread slices are crisp and curling at the corners, and the cheese is soft but not yet melted. Serve immediately.

Note These make a last-course savoury or supper snack richer and quite different from ordinary toasted or baked cheese sandwiches.

SANDWICH FILLINGS

Any sandwich filling should consist of:

1) a main nutrient or flavouring ingredient. This may be meat, fish, egg, cheese, a pâté, a cold salad vegetable, fruit, nuts or a flavoured sweetening such as jam.

2) seasoning or flavouring such as salt and pepper, chopped fresh herbs or a spice.

3) a 'binder' to hold the other ingredients together; it may be softened or creamed butter, margarine or another flavoured fat, a savoury or sweet flavoured butter (pp1297–1303). Alternatively, the binder may be used as a spread beneath the main ingredient. If a pâté, soft cheese (either full-fat, medium-fat or cottage cheese), a mayonnaise or other similar sauce, or a stiff pulse purée are used, this will make any butter or margarine unnecessary.

Provided each type of ingredient is used, the possible combinations are a matter of personal choice and are almost endless. It is only important that none of the ingredients is likely to drip or melt, stain, be gritty or hard to chew. If sandwiches are to be toasted or fried, this too will bear a reflection on the filling to be chosen.

Fillings for Plain Sandwiches

The main ingredient should be chopped into very small bits or sliced thinly so that the sandwich can be bitten through cleanly; the filling combination must be fairly firm and dry so that the sandwich does not sag or break apart when picked up.

Some combinations for main and flavouring ingredients are given below as a guide. They should be used with a relevant savoury or sweet binder if one is required.

Savoury Fillings

Use red and strongly flavoured meats such as beef, lamb, tongue, smoked sausage, venison, hare or meat from game birds, with:

1) a chopped, grated or sliced salad vegetable with a cool flavour (eg cucumber, carrot) and a little strong mustard

2) finely chopped gherkin or capers with lemon juice

3) horseradish sauce

4) chopped herbs with a strong flavour, eg rosemary, sage or thyme

5) a freshly ground, strong spice such as juniper, black pepper or allspice

6) sherry, port or Madeira (mixed with the binder).

Use ham, bacon or pickled pork with any of the above, or with:

1) chopped green or red pepper and onion salt

2) finely chopped dried apricots or other dried fruit with freshly ground black pepper

3) chutney or sweet pickles.

Use white meats such as chicken or pork, with:

1) Russian salad (p314)

2) a chopped or sliced well-flavoured salad vegetable such as green pepper, flavoured with lemon juice

3) chopped pineapple or soaked dried fruit with ground black pepper

4) chopped fresh herbs in season

5) a little curry paste or powder, chilli sauce or powder, or paprika mixed into the binder.

Note If a pâté or potted meat is used, any clarified fat from the top should be removed before use. Neither are suitable for toasted or fried sandwiches.

Bought liver sausage can also be used if any outside skin is removed.

Use cooked white fish with:

1) finely chopped canned salmon, or shellfish such as prawns or shrimps

2) canned pimento, capers or dill pickles

3) chopped anchovy fillets or anchovy essence.

Use canned fish, anchovy fillets or smoked fish (cooked if required) with:

1) a chopped, sliced or grated salad vegetable such as cucumber, shallot or chives

2) a coarsely grated fruit such as apple, sprinkled with lemon or orange juice

3) chopped gherkins, capers, fennel or dill stem or seeds

4) hard-boiled egg and ground black pepper.

Note Any fish filling is improved by a few drops of lemon juice among its flavourings.

Use cheese (hard or soft) with:

1) chopped or sliced salad vegetables such as cucumber or celery with ground black pepper
2) chopped olives, gherkin or chives
3) chutney or sweet pickles
4) chopped nuts such as walnuts, peanuts
5) crisply cooked, crumbled bacon
6) sherry, port or Madeira (with hard or blue cheese)
7) concentrated tomato purée, Worcestershire sauce or anchovy essence.

Use eggs (chopped hard-boiled or scrambled) with:

1) finely chopped ham or frankfurters
2) flaked kipper, mashed sardine or lumpfish roe
3) sauerkraut and a few dill or caraway seeds
4) chopped or sliced fresh salad vegetables (eg celery, tomato, green pepper) and soured cream
5) chopped fresh herbs such as spring onion green, mint, chives, parsley.

Use nuts (chopped) with:

1) finely chopped or grated salad vegetables, eg grated carrot, flavoured with lemon juice
2) mashed avocado pear, flavoured with lemon juice to prevent discoloration
3) chopped oranges in a French dressing.

Use cooked or salad vegetables on their own, or mixed with another vegetable and a spicy seasoning, together with a well-flavoured binder.

Sweet Fillings

Use fresh fruit (chopped, mashed or grated), with:

1) chopped dried fruit
2) chopped nuts
3) a well-flavoured jam, eg apricot or plum, or honey.

Always include a few drops of lemon juice to prevent discoloration and to vitalize the flavour. Full-fat soft cheese or cream make an interesting binder.

Fillings for Packed Meal Sandwiches and Rolls

1) sliced Gruyère cheese spread with French mustard, mustard and cress
2) minced cooked chicken and ham or tongue moistened with melted butter and bound with mayonnaise
3) good pâté with thin cucumber slices
4) sliced Cheddar or Cheshire cheese topped with thin slices of tomato and chopped fresh mint
5) sliced boiled ham spread with tomato sauce or chutney
6) sliced cold roast beef topped with slices of tomato and cucumber, with a little horseradish sauce
7) minced turkey or chicken with peanut butter and ordinary butter mixed together
8) cooked skinned sausages split lengthways and spread with apple sauce
9) rasher(s) of fried bacon covered with sautéed mushrooms
10) cooked skinned sausages split lengthways, spread with scrambled egg, and a few drops of anchovy essence.

Fillings for Decker Sandwiches

Choose two of the fillings for plain or packed meal sandwiches, using one salad filling and one meat, fish or cheese filling. As a typical example, use:

1st layer: Sliced cold roast beef, spread with horseradish sauce

2nd layer: Drained, sliced beetroot with vinegar and chopped watercress

or

1st layer: Sliced Cheddar cheese spread with mango chutney

2nd layer: Grated apple mixed with mayonnaise.

Flavoured Butters

Flavoured butters have many uses. If softened, they can be used for spreading on bread, toast or canapés, or, when making sandwiches, they can be used instead of plain butter or margarine. They can also enrich, flavour, and thicken sauces. If melted, a flavoured butter can often serve instead of any other sauce.

If chilled and formed into small cubes or pats, a flavoured butter combines the virtues of providing a garnish for a hot savoury or sweet dish (as it starts to melt) with the succulence of a sauce. Chilled balls or pats of a well-flavoured butter make an equally attractive garnish for a cold savoury dish. Smooth flavoured butters can be piped as a garnish on cold savoury dishes or as a decoration on cold or frozen desserts; and sweet butters also make rich, delicious fillings for meringues, small or large choux, sandwich cakes, biscuits, and party gâteaux.

There are two types of flavoured butter. One is quite smooth because any solid additions are chopped or crushed and then pounded with the butter; these smooth butters can also be sieved before use, for a lighter texture. They are particularly useful for small fancy sandwiches, eg mosaic sandwiches (p1294), and for desserts or gâteaux which require a piped decoration. The second type of flavoured butter still contains fragments of solid flavourings. Although not suitable for piping, they are often more strongly flavoured than a smooth butter, and can be used as a sandwich filling on their own.

Note Slightly salted butter should be used in the following recipes unless unsalted butter is specified.

SAVOURY BUTTERS

Anchovy Butter

50g softened unsalted butter

6 anchovy fillets **or** anchovy essence

lemon juice

pepper

Cream the butter until light. Pound the anchovy fillets, if used, to a paste or process in an electric blender with a little of the butter. Beat the anchovy and seasonings into the butter gradually. Do not over-flavour; the butter becomes stronger as it matures. Leave to stand at room temperature for at least 30 minutes before use. Press into small pots or cartons, tapping while filling to knock out all the air; alternatively, form into pats. Use at once, or cover and chill in a refrigerator. Do not freeze.

Black Butter and Brown Butter
See p715.

Chutney Butter

25g mango chutney
100g softened butter
1 × 5ml spoon French mustard

lemon juice

Chop any large pieces in the chutney very finely, then work with the back of a spoon until smooth. Beat the butter until light, then beat in the chutney and mustard. Add a little lemon juice to taste. Sieve the butter. Use at once, or pot and chill as for Anchovy Butter.

Colbert Butter
See Sole Colbert, p454.

Creamed Savoury Butter

(for sandwiches)

100g unsalted butter	made English mustard
2 × 15ml spoons double cream	salt and pepper
	Cayenne pepper

Beat the butter until soft and creamy. Whip the cream until stiff, and blend it into the butter gradually, using a metal spoon. Season to taste with mustard, salt, pepper, and Cayenne pepper. Use at room temperature.

Note This butter is used mainly for spreading savoury sandwiches as an alternative to plain butter or margarine. It is useful when a bland filling or a mild-flavoured cheese filling is used. If not used at once, it stores well in the refrigerator. Bring to room temperature before use.

Curry Butter

100g softened butter	salt
1 × 5ml spoon curry powder (approx)	a pinch of ground black pepper
1 × 2.5ml spoon lemon juice	

Beat the butter until light. Beat in the curry powder, lemon juice, salt, and pepper. Leave to stand at room temperature for at least 10 minutes, then taste and add extra curry powder if required. Chill to firm up. Use at once, or pot and chill as for Anchovy Butter (p1297)

Devilling Butter

100g softened butter	$\frac{1}{2}$ × 2.5ml spoon curry powder
a good pinch of Cayenne pepper	$\frac{1}{2}$ × 2.5ml spoon ground ginger
a good pinch of white pepper	

Blend all the ingredients together thoroughly, using the back of a spoon, then re-season if required. Shape into pats and chill until firm for use at once, or pot and chill as for Anchovy Butter (p1297).

Derbyshire Butter

50g cooked chicken **or** rabbit	$\frac{1}{2}$ × 2.5ml spoon French mustard
3 anchovy fillets	a few grains Cayenne pepper
75g softened butter	

Garnish (optional)
grated Parmesan cheese

Mince the meat and anchovies, then work with the back of a spoon or process in an electric blender until smooth. Add the butter, mustard and Cayenne pepper, and blend thoroughly. Use at once, or pot and chill as for Anchovy Butter (p1297).

Serve on toast canapés as a cocktail snack or as a cold tartlet or sandwich filling. If using on canapés or in tartlets, sprinkle with Parmesan cheese.

Egg Butter

2 hard-boiled egg yolks	25g softened butter
1 × 2.5ml spoon lemon juice	salt
a few drops Tabasco sauce	a few grains Cayenne pepper

Mash the egg yolks thoroughly. Add the other ingredients, and work with the back of a spoon until well blended. Use at once, or cover and chill. Use within 2 days, as the butter does not store well.

Serve on pastry or toast canapés as a cocktail snack, or use as a sandwich filling.

Epicurean Butter

4 anchovy fillets	1 × 10ml spoon chopped chives
1 × 5ml spoon fresh tarragon	75g softened butter
4 cocktail gherkins	1 × 5ml spoon French mustard
2 hard-boiled egg yolks	

Chop the anchovy fillets, tarragon, and gherkins finely. Mash the egg yolks. Mix these ingredients with the chives. Pound them or process in an electric blender with a little of the butter until smooth. Beat the remaining butter until light, and beat in the mustard. Add the pounded or blended ingredients, and mix in thoroughly. Chill the mixture until firm but still workable. Form into pats. Use at once, or pot and chill as for Anchovy Butter (p1297).

Serve with cheese instead of plain butter or margarine.

Fish Roe Butter (1)

100g softened butter   *lemon juice*
100g cooked soft fish roe *salt and pepper*

Work the butter and roe together with the back of a spoon. Add the lemon juice, a drop at a time. Season to taste. Sieve the mixture. Use at once, or pot and chill as for Anchovy Butter (p1297).

Fish Roe Butter (2)

100g cooked hard fish roe *lemon juice*
  eg *smoked cod's roe*   *salt and pepper*
100g softened butter

Remove the skin and membranes from the roe. Mash thoroughly, then mix with the butter until well blended. Add the lemon juice, a drop at a time. Season to taste. Use at once, or pot and chill as for Anchovy Butter (p1297).

Note This granular butter is not suitable for piping as a garnish, but makes a good sandwich filling.

Green Butter

100g softened butter   *anchovy essence* **or** *paste*
4 × 10ml spoons   *1 × 15ml spoon lemon*
  chopped parsley **or**   *juice*
  more if liked   *salt and pepper*

Beat the butter until light. Beat in the parsley, a little anchovy essence or paste, the lemon juice, and seasoning. Use at once, or pot and chill as for Anchovy Butter (p1297).

Green Herb Butter

Make as for Ravigote Butter (p1301).

Garlic Butter

1 clove of garlic   *50–75g softened butter*

Skin and chop the garlic. Either pound it, grate it, or squeeze it through a garlic press. Mix well with the butter, adjusting the quantity of butter to give the flavour you prefer. Use at once, or pot and chill as for Anchovy Butter (p1297). Use within 2 days.

Ham Butter

100g lean cooked ham   *pepper*
50g softened butter
1 × 15ml spoon double
  cream

Chop the ham finely, discarding any gristle. Mince it twice, then pound it, or process in an electric blender to make a smooth paste. Beat the butter until light, and work in the ham paste and cream lightly but thoroughly. Season to taste. Use at once, or pot and chill as for Anchovy Butter (p1297).

Herb Butter

a good pinch of dried   *50g softened butter*
  parsley   *½ × 2.5ml spoon salt*
a good pinch of dried
  thyme

Work the herbs into the butter lightly. Season to taste. Use at once, or pot and chill as for Anchovy Butter (p1297).

Horseradish Butter

50g softened butter   *lemon juice*
1 × 15ml spoon grated
  fresh **or** *bottled*
  horseradish

Beat the butter until light. Rinse the horseradish, and pat it dry if from a jar. Work it into the butter with the back of a spoon. Add lemon juice to taste, a drop at a time. Use at once, or pot and chill as for Anchovy Butter (p1297). Use within 2 days.

Maître d'Hôtel Butter

2–4 large sprigs parsley
50g softened butter
salt

a small pinch of pepper
a few drops lemon
   juice

Blanch the parsley, and chop it finely. Work it into the butter with the seasonings and lemon juice. Use at once, or pot and chill as for Anchovy Butter (p1297).

See also Parsley Butter (p1301).

Meunière Butter

See p715.

Montpelier Butter

2 ×15ml spoons mixed
   fresh spinach leaves
   plus parsley, chervil,
   cress, tarragon, chives
1 small clove of garlic
1 small cocktail gherkin

a few capers
a few drops anchovy
   essence
1 hard-boiled egg yolk
50g butter

Blanch the vegetables apart from the chervil, dry them well, and chop finely. Squeeze the garlic through a garlic press and add it to the herbs. Chop and add the gherkin and capers, with the anchovy essence and hard-boiled egg yolk. Pound all these ingredients together, adding the butter gradually until a smooth green butter is obtained. Sieve. Use at once, or pot and chill as for Anchovy Butter (p1297).

Mustard Butter (1)

25g softened butter
1 × 2.5ml spoon dry
   mustard

a few drops lemon juice
salt

Beat the butter until light. Beat in the mustard, lemon juice, and salt. If very soft, chill until almost firm but still workable. Form into 2 small pats, and chill until really firm for use at once, or pot and chill as for Anchovy Butter (p1297). Bring to room temperature and form into pats for use when required.

Mustard Butter (2)

50g softened butter

1– 2 × 5ml spoons
   French mustard

Beat the butter until light, gradually adding enough mustard to give the flavour you want. Use at once, or pot and chill as for Anchovy Butter (p1297).

Olive Butter

50g softened butter
2 × 15ml spoons stoned,
   chopped green olives

a few drops onion juice
   (optional)

Beat the butter until light. Pound the olives to a paste, and mix into the butter with the onion juice. Use at once, or pot and chill as for Anchovy Butter (p1297). Do not freeze.

Paprika Butter

50g softened butter
a few drops lemon juice
   or white wine

a pinch of icing sugar
1 × 5ml spoon paprika

Blend together thoroughly the butter, lemon juice or wine, sugar, and paprika. Use at once, or pot and chill as for Anchovy Butter (p1297).

Peanut Butter

100g freshly shelled and
   roasted peanuts, salted
   or unsalted

2 × 5ml spoons
   groundnut oil
salt

Grind the nuts very finely in a nut mill. Put into a bowl, and beat in the oil, drop by drop, using a balloon whisk or wooden spoon. Beat until fully blended and smooth; season to taste.

If using an electric blender, feed the nuts into the goblet slowly, with the motor running. Add the oil in two separate spoonfuls while blending. Blend at high speed for 15 seconds or until smooth. Put into a bowl and season to taste.

Pack into a sterilized dry jar with a screw-topped lid. Store in a cool place, away from strong sunlight.

Parsley Butter

50g softened butter
1 × 10ml spoon chopped
 parsley

a few drops lemon juice
salt and pepper

Cream the butter with the parsley. Leave to stand at room temperature for 10 minutes, then add the lemon juice, and season to taste. Use at once, or pot and chill as for Anchovy Butter (p1297).

See also Maître d'Hôtel Butter (p1301).

Ravigote Butter

2 × 15ml spoons mixed
 fresh herbs (parsley,
 chervil, shallot,
 tarragon, chives)

1 small clove of garlic
25g softened butter
salt and pepper

Chop the herbs finely. If chervil is used it should be chopped separately and not blanched. Crush the garlic clove. Tie the herbs and garlic in a small piece of muslin. Blanch in a little boiling water, then drain and squeeze dry. Work the herbs into the butter with the back of a spoon, and season to taste. Sieve. Use at once, or pot and chill as for Anchovy Butter (p1297). Use within 2 days.

Sardine Butter

75g sardines
a few drops lemon juice

100g softened butter

Drain and mash the sardines, including the bones. Mix with the lemon juice, and work into the butter with the back of a spoon. Sieve if a smooth butter is required. Use at once, or pot and chill as for Anchovy Butter (p1297).

Shallot Butter

25g shallot

100g softened butter

Chop the shallot finely, then pound it to a paste. Work it into the butter thoroughly. Sieve. Use at once, or pot and chill as for Anchovy Butter (p1297).

Shrimp or Prawn Butter

50g peeled shrimps **or**
 prawns

50g softened butter
lemon juice

Chop the shrimps or prawns roughly. Pound them or process in an electric blender until finely shredded. Blend into the butter thoroughly, adding a little lemon juice to taste. Use at once, or pot and chill as for Anchovy Butter (p1297).

Tarragon Butter

sprigs of fresh tarragon
butter

lemon juice

Blanch the tarragon, and take the leaves off the stems. Chop finely. Measure 50g butter for each 5ml spoon chopped tarragon. Chop the butter roughly if firm. Work in the tarragon thoroughly with the back of a spoon, adding lemon juice to taste. Sieve the mixture. Use at once, or pot and chill as for Anchovy Butter (p1297).

Note Use this method to make other fresh herb butters. If using chervil, do not blanch.

Tomato Butter

1 × 5ml spoon
 concentrated tomato
 purée **or** *tomato*
 ketchup

50g softened butter
a few drops lemon juice
 or *vinegar*

Work all the ingredients together until smooth. Use at once, or pot and chill as for Anchovy Butter (p1297).

Watercress Butter

sprigs of watercress
butter

salt

Blanch the watercress, pat dry with soft kitchen paper. Pick off the leaves and chop finely. Measure 25g butter for each 15ml spoon chopped leaves. Chop the butter roughly if firm, and work the leaves into it. Add salt to taste. Do not sieve. Use at once, or pot and chill as for Anchovy Butter (p1297).

SWEET BUTTERS

Almond Butter

100g ground almonds
100g softened butter
4 × 10ml spoons caster
  sugar (approx)

1 × 5ml spoon lemon
  juice (approx)
a few drops almond
  essence

Work the ground almonds into the butter thoroughly, adding the sugar and flavourings gradually. Use at once, or pot and chill as for Anchovy Butter (p1297).

Brandy Butter (1)

50g butter
100g caster sugar

1–2 × 15ml spoons
  brandy

Cream the butter until soft. Beat the sugar gradually into the butter until it is pale and light. Work in the brandy, a little at a time, taking care not to allow the mixture to curdle. Chill before using. If the mixture has separated slightly after standing, beat well before serving.

This sauce is traditionally served with Christmas pudding and mince pies.

Note An egg white whisked until stiff can be stirred into the butter and sugar mixture to give a softer texture.

VARIATIONS

Sherry Butter

Make as for Brandy Butter but substitute sherry for the brandy.

Vanilla Butter

Make as for Brandy Butter but substitute 1 × 5ml spoon vanilla essence for the brandy.

Orange Butter (1)

Cream the grated rind of an orange with the butter and sugar, and then gradually beat in 1 × 15ml spoon orange juice. Omit the brandy.

Lemon Butter

Make as for Orange Butter (1) but substitute the grated rind of half a lemon and 1 × 5ml spoon lemon juice for the orange.

Brandy Butter (2)

100g unsalted butter
75g icing sugar
25g ground almonds

2 × 15ml spoons brandy
a few drops lemon juice

Cream the butter until very light. Sift in the icing sugar, a little at a time, and beat in each addition lightly but thoroughly. Sift in the almonds in 2 or 3 portions, and beat in like the sugar. Lift the fork when beating, to incorporate as much air as possible. Beat in the brandy and lemon juice, a few drops at a time, taking care not to let the mixture separate. Taste, and add extra brandy if liked. Pile the mixture into a dish and leave to firm up before serving; or turn lightly into a jar with a screw-topped lid, without leaving air holes. Cover, and store in a cool place until required. Use within one week, or refrigerate for longer storage. Bring to room temperature before serving.

Chestnut Butter

200g unsweetened
  chestnut purée
200g softened butter

3 × 15ml spoons caster
  sugar (approx)
25ml rum (approx)

Mix the chestnut purée and butter until thoroughly blended. Add the sugar and rum gradually, adjusting the flavour to taste. Chill, then use at once, or pot and chill as for Anchovy Butter (p1297).

Cumberland Rum Butter

100g unsalted butter
100g light soft brown
sugar
2 × 15ml spoons rum
(approx)

1 × 2.5ml spoon grated
orange peel
grated nutmeg

Squeeze and cream the butter with your hand until very soft and light-coloured. Crush any lumps in the sugar. Work it into the butter with your hand until completely blended in. Work in the rum, a few drops at a time, taking care not to let the mixture separate. Mix in the orange peel. Taste, and add extra rum if liked, and a little grated nutmeg. Pile into a dish, and leave to firm up before serving; or turn lightly into a screw-topped jar without leaving air holes, and store in a cool place until required. Use within 4 days, or refrigerate for longer storage. Bring to room temperature before serving.

Mrs Beeton's Fairy Butter

1 × 10ml spoon orange
juice
25g icing sugar
100g softened butter

2 hard-boiled egg yolks
1 × 10ml spoon orange
flower water

Decoration (optional)
1 × 10ml spoon grated
orange rind

Strain the orange juice, and sift the sugar. Sieve the egg yolks. Using a rotary beater, beat in the juice, orange flower water, sugar, and butter alternately until all the ingredients are blended to a smooth paste.

To use, press the fairy butter through a sieve on to a decorative serving plate, in a pile of thin strands. Do not press them down; flick any stray strands into place with a fork. Sprinkle with grated orange rind, if liked. Serve as a rich sweet with small crisp biscuits, or on a trifle or gâteau instead of whipped cream.

Orange Butter (2)

2 oranges
4 sugar lumps
150g softened butter
25g caster sugar
(approx)

1 × 15ml spoon orange
juice
2 × 10ml spoons
Cointreau

Pare the rind of the oranges and grind or grate it with the sugar lumps. Put in a bowl, and work in the butter and caster sugar until well blended. Mix in the juice and liqueur gradually, until fully absorbed. Use at once, or pot and chill as for Anchovy Butter (p1297).

Redcurrant Butter

500g redcurrants
125g raspberries
(optional)

250g icing sugar
(approx)
200g softened butter

Clean, wash, and dry the fruit. Rub it through a sieve. Sift the sugar, and beat most of it with the butter to form a smooth cream. Work in the sieved fruit. Taste, and add more sugar if required. Use at once, or pot and chill as for Anchovy Butter (p1297).

Rum Butter

50g butter
100g light soft brown
sugar

2 × 15ml spoons rum

Cream the butter until soft, beating in the sugar gradually. When light and creamy, work in the rum, a little at a time. Chill before using.

Strawberry Butter

100g softened butter
250g icing sugar

200g fresh strawberries
50g ground almonds

Beat the butter until light. Sift in the sugar and beat it in thoroughly. Crush and add the strawberries with the ground almonds. Mix thoroughly. Use at once.

PACKED AND OUTDOOR MEALS

Things not to be forgotten at a Picnic. A stick of horseradish, a bottle of mint-sauce well corked, a bottle of salad dressing, a bottle of vinegar, made mustard, pepper, salt, good oil, and pounded sugar. If it can be managed, take a little ice. It is scarcely necessary to say that plates, tumblers, wine-glasses, knives, forks, and spoons, must not be forgotten; as also teacups and saucers, 3 or 4 teapots, some lump sugar, and milk, if this last-named article cannot be obtained in the neighbourhood. Take 3 corkscrews.

Packed Meals

Modern food processing and packaging makes it easy to present well-balanced and varied packed meals. Foil or clingfilm can be used to wrap a chicken joint, a meat pie, a chop, a piece of cheese or lettuce leaves, or to wrap sandwiches with fuller fillings than usual. Small cartons, such as the ones in which cream or soft cheese are sold, can be used for pâtés, potted meats, fish, cheese, jellied salads or fruit. A vacuum flask will hold soups or sauced dishes. Packed food should always be kept in the coolest place possible, and items which are likely to deteriorate quickly should not be included in a packed meal or picnic. Insulated boxes, ice packs or simple bags of ice are helpful in keeping food fresh and cool until required.

Various kinds of sandwiches and a selection of fillings are suggested on pp1291–96. The next section of this chapter contains recipes for other lightweight, easily carried dishes, but there are many recipes throughout the book which can be adapted for outdoor meals. Cooked meats, for example, served cold, make excellent picnic food provided the meat can be kept cool until needed. Savoury flans are also easy to serve, as are pâtés and potted foods. Nutritious and easily packed food such as fresh fruit, raw, crisp vegetables and cheese should always be included in an outdoor meal. Refer to the Index for details.

Raised Meat Pie

6–8 helpings

hot water crust pastry (p1250) using 400g flour
600g lean pork (roasting cut) or other meat (see **Note***)*
salt and pepper
200g basic herb forcemeat (p375) or as needed
beaten egg for glazing
250ml white stock (p329)

Line a 20cm round pie mould with three-quarters of the pastry, or use a round cake tin as described on p1250. Use the remaining quarter for the lid. Cut the pork into 1cm cubes, or mince it. Season well. Line the inside of the pastry with some of the forcemeat, put in the meat and cover with a thin layer of forcemeat. Put on the lid, brush with beaten egg and make a hole in the centre to allow steam to escape. Bake in a hot oven, 220°C, Gas 7, for 15 minutes. Reduce to moderate, 180°C, Gas 4, and cook the pie for a further $1\frac{1}{2}$ hours. Remove the mould for the last 30 minutes of the cooking time and brush the top and sides of the pastry with beaten egg.

When cooked, remove from the oven and leave to cool. Funnel the white stock through the hole in the pastry lid until the pie is full, and leave to cool until the stock sets to a jelly.

For a picnic, replace the pie in the mould and wrap it in foil to transport it.

Note Other lean roasting meat such as veal or mildly cured ham, or a mixture of meats, can be used instead of pork.

For Raised Pork Pie, see p589; for Raised Veal, Pork and Egg Pie, see p572.

Cornish Pasties (2)

(economical)

Makes 8

100g raw meat **or** *mince (see* **Note***)*	*shortcrust pastry (p1249) using 200g*
100g potato	*flour* **or** *350g prepared*
50g onion	*pastry*
dried mixed herbs	*flour for rolling out*
salt and pepper	*milk for glazing*
2 × 15ml spoons gravy	
or water	

Mince the meat if required. Peel the potato and cut it into 1cm cubes. Mix the meat and potato together. Skin and chop the onion finely, and add it to the meat with the herbs, seasoning, and gravy or water. Roll out the pastry 5mm thick on a lightly floured surface, and cut it into eight 12cm rounds. Divide the filling between the rounds, making a mound in the centre of each. Moisten the edges of the pastry. Lift them to meet over the filling. Pinch and flute the edges to seal. Prick the pasties with a fork in 2 or 3 places and brush them with milk. Bake in a hot oven, 220°C, Gas 7, for 10 minutes, then reduce to moderate 180°C, Gas 4, and bake for a further 50 minutes. Serve hot or cold.

Wrap the pasties in foil or clingfilm for packed meals.

Note Beef, pork or a mixture of the two can be used. Any bacon joint suitable for boiling can be substituted for the pork.

For Cornish Pasties (1), see p503, and for Cornish Pasties (3), p1472.

Veal and Ham Pie

6–8 helpings

puff (p1253) **or** *flaky (p1252) pastry using 100g flour*	*grated rind of 1 lemon*
	well-flavoured, cooled and jellied stock (pp328–31), as required
500g veal (see **Note***)*	*2 hard-boiled eggs*
250g ham	*flour for rolling out*
salt	*beaten egg for glazing*
1 × 2.5ml spoon pepper	
1 × 2.5ml spoon mixed herbs	
1 × 2.5ml spoon ground mace	

Prepare the pastry and leave to stand in a cool place. Cut the veal and ham into 1cm cubes, and add the seasonings and flavourings. Heat the stock until melted and mix a small amount in with the meat. Slice the hard-boiled eggs. Put half the meat mixture into a 500ml pie dish, cover with the sliced eggs and add the remaining meat. Moisten with the stock, but do not overfill the dish with liquid.

Roll out the pastry on a lightly floured surface, and cut it to fit the top of the pie dish. Dampen the edges of the dish with water. Use some of the trimmings to line the rim of the dish. Dampen the pastry rim, lift the top crust into position, and seal the edge. Make a hole in the centre of the pie, decorate with pastry leaves, and brush with beaten egg. Bake in a hot oven, 220°C, Gas 7, for 15 minutes, then reduce to moderate, 180°C, Gas 4, and bake for $1\frac{1}{2}$ hours. Remove the pie from the oven, make a second hole in the crust and pour in a little more stock. Leave to cool thoroughly, preferably overnight, in a refrigerator.

Serve cold with salads. For a picnic, transport it in the pie dish, securely covered with foil.

Note For quality, choose fillet of veal; for economy use breast or neck.

Veal and Ham Patties

Makes 12

200g cold cooked veal
50–100g cold cooked
  ham **or** gammon (can
  be scraps)
a pinch of mixed herbs
salt and pepper
a pinch of grated nutmeg
a little white stock
  (p329) **or** water

puff (p1253), rough puff
  or flaky (p1252) pastry
  using 200g flour
flour for rolling out
beaten egg **or** milk for
  glazing

Dice the meat finely and mix together with the herbs, seasonings, and spice. Moisten with a little stock or water. Roll out the pastry thinly on a lightly floured surface. With a 7cm cutter, cut out 12 rounds, using about one-third of the pastry. Put these aside for lids. Use the remaining two-thirds to line twelve 7cm patty tins.

Fill the cases with the meat mixture. Dampen the pastry edges and cover with the lids. Press the edges together to seal. Make a small hole in the top of each patty, and decorate with any trimmings. Brush the patties with egg or milk. Bake in a very hot oven, 230°C, Gas 8, for about 10 minutes until the pastry is set and brown, then reduce to moderate, 180°C, Gas 4, and cook for a further 10 minutes.

Wrap in clingfilm for a packed meal.

Chicken and Bacon Patties

Makes 12

150g raw **or** cold cooked
  chicken
50g raw **or** cold cooked
  boiling bacon **or** ham
  (can be scraps)
salt and pepper
a little chicken stock
  (p330) **or** white stock
  (p329) **or** water

shortcrust (p1249) **or**
  puff (p1253) pastry
  using 200g flour
flour for rolling out
beaten egg **or** milk for
  glazing

Dice the chicken meat and the bacon or ham. Season to taste, and moisten with a very little stock or water. Roll out the pastry on a lightly floured surface, and use two-thirds of it to line twelve 7cm patty tins. Divide the filling between the tins. Cover with lids cut from the remaining pastry. Dampen the edges of the pastry and press together to seal. Make a small slit or hole in the top of each patty and decorate with any trimmings. Brush with egg or milk. Bake in a fairly hot oven, 190°C, Gas 5, for 40 minutes if the meat is raw or for 20 minutes if it is cooked. Serve hot or cold.

For packed meals, use shortcrust pastry and wrap in clingfilm for transport.

VARIATION

Substitute rabbit meat for the chicken.

Tomato and Mushroom Patties or Turnovers

See p1256.

Sausage Rolls

Makes 8

200g prepared puff
  (p1253) **or** rough puff
  pastry (p1252)
flour for rolling out

8 sausages **or** 200g
  sausage-meat
1 egg yolk

Roll out the pastry on a lightly floured surface and cut it into 8 equal-sized squares. Skin the sausages if required, or divide the meat into 8 equal portions. Form each portion into a roll the same length as a square of pastry. Place 1 roll of sausage-meat on each pastry square, dampen the edges of the pastry, and fold the pastry over so that they meet. Seal the joined edges and turn the rolls over so the joints are underneath. Leave the ends of the rolls open. Make 3 diagonal slits in the top of each roll. Brush the rolls with egg yolk. Bake in a very hot oven, 230°C, Gas 8, for 10 minutes or until the pastry is well risen and brown. Reduce to moderate, 180°C, Gas 4, and continue baking for 20–25 minutes. Cover loosely with greaseproof paper if the pastry browns too much.

VARIATION
Cocktail Sausage Rolls

Makes 20

Roll the pastry into 1 thin long rectangle or strip. Skin the sausages if required. Form the sausage-meat into 2 long rolls the same length as the strip. Place on the pastry, well apart. Cut the pastry into 2 equal strips, each wide enough to wrap round a roll of meat. Dampen 1 edge of each strip, fold over and press the damp and dry edge of each strip together, forming 2 long rolls. Cut into short lengths, and bake at the higher temperature for 5–7 minutes, then reduce the heat and bake for 15–20 minutes, covering if necessary.

Picnic Pizzas

Makes 4

2 small firm tomatoes	8 anchovy fillets
4 black olives	salt and pepper
200g prepared puff pastry (p1253)	a little olive oil **or** cooking oil
flour for rolling out	
4 slices processed cheese 7cm square and 5mm–1cm thick	

Heat the oven to fairly hot, 200°C, Gas 6. Slice the tomatoes and stone the olives. Roll out the pastry into a 20cm square on a lightly floured surface. Cut it into four 10cm squares and place them on a baking sheet. Prick the centres of the squares with a fork, and turn up the edges, pinching the corners to make them hold.

Place 1 slice of cheese in the centre of each square, and 2 slices of tomato on top. Cross 2 anchovy fillets over each tomato slice. Season well with salt and pepper and place an olive in the centre of each square. Sprinkle the cheese-covered portion of each pizza with oil, and chill for 15–30 minutes. Bake for about 15 minutes or until the pastry is puffed and brown. Serve hot or cold.

For packed meals, wrap in foil or clingfilm.

Cold Stuffed Eggs
See p319.

Note These can be transported in disposable cartons.

Apple and Cheese Picnic Slices

Makes six 8cm squares

100g prepared shortcrust pastry (p1249)	25g cheese (not soft **or** blue cheese)
flour for rolling out	4 ×15ml spoons golden syrup
4 small tart cooking apples	milk for glazing
	Demerara sugar

Divide the pastry into 2 equal-sized portions, and, on a lightly floured surface, roll it out into 2 rectangles to fit a 25 ×17cm shallow baking tin. Lay 1 rectangle in the tin. Core and peel the apples, and slice into thin rounds. Grate the cheese. Warm the syrup until just liquid.

Lay the apple slices over the pastry, leaving 1cm uncovered round the edges. Pour a thin layer of syrup over the apples, being careful not to cover the exposed pastry edges. Reserve any syrup left over. Scatter the cheese over the syrup. Dampen the uncovered edge of the pastry with milk and cover with the second rectangle of pastry. Press the edges together to seal. Brush the surface lightly with milk, and with any remaining golden syrup. Sprinkle lightly with Demerara sugar. Bake in a hot oven, 220°C, Gas 7, for 10 minutes, then reduce to moderate, 180°C, Gas 4, and bake for a further 20 minutes or until the pastry is fully cooked. Cut into 6 squares.

Serve the slices hot or cold. Wrap in clingfilm for a packed meal.

Buttered Picnic Cheesecake

8–10 helpings

Base

75g butter	3 × 2.5ml spoons ground
150g fine dry white	cinnamon
breadcrumbs	
50g caster sugar	

Filling

3 eggs	25g chopped mixed nuts
100g caster sugar	caster sugar and
375g full-fat soft cheese	cinnamon for dusting
grated rind and juice of	butter
1 lemon	
125ml single **or** soured	
cream (see **Note**)	

Melt the butter, add the breadcrumbs, and stir over gentle heat until golden. Remove from the heat, stir in the sugar and cinnamon, and leave to cool. Press about two-thirds of the crumbs over the base of a loose-bottomed 20cm cake tin or foil dish, to form a bottom crust; reserve the rest.

To make the filling, separate the eggs. Beat the yolks until liquid, add the sugar gradually and beat until creamy. Rub the cheese through a sieve and work it in lightly. Add the lemon rind and juice to the mixture with the cream. Whisk the egg whites to a soft foam which will just hold peaks. Stir 2 ×15ml spoons into the cheese mixture, then fold in the rest lightly. Turn the mixture gently into the prepared base. Bake in a moderate oven, 180°C, Gas 4, for 45 minutes. Sprinkle the remaining crumbs and the nuts on top, and bake for a further 15 minutes.

Meanwhile, mix together the sugar and cinnamon for dusting. Remove the cake from the oven and test that it is firm in the centre. Sprinkle with the sugar and cinammon, and dot with butter. Increase the heat to hot, 220°C, Gas 7, and return the cake to the oven for 2–4 minutes or until glazed on top.

Cool in the tin or dish. To transport for a picnic, cover with foil or a lid. Serve on the base.

Note Single cream makes a light cheesecake, soured cream a richer, more tangy one.

For other cheesecake recipes see pp1041–43.

Outdoor Meals

FORMAL AND INFORMAL OUTDOOR MEALS

A formal outdoor meal may be a set buffet for a garden party or a wedding reception held out of doors; or it may be a lunch, tea or dinner party with people seated at a conventionally laid table in the garden or on a patio or verandah.

If hot food is served it should hold its heat well and be served in ceramic or other dishes which hold the heat. Food should be firm, and without delicate garnishes which may be displaced or even blown away in a breeze. Above all, it should be easy to serve and eat.

With reasonable foresight, anyone should be able to choose suitable dishes from the many hundreds in other chapters.

CAMP-FIRE AND BARBECUE MEALS

On these occasions, the food is cooked in the open air, usually over wood or charcoal, normally by grilling, frying or spit-roasting (on a barbecue). As a rule, potatoes baked in their jackets, plain lettuce, tomatoes, rolls, or chunks of bread and butter with cheese, and fresh fruit are enough, besides the main food.

Sources of Heat

The most usual sources of heat for cooking outdoors are:
1) a portable stove burning bottled gas, paraffin or methylated spirit
2) a camp-fire
3) a portable or other barbecue.

Anglers who want to cook their catch at the riverside can use a small portable hot smoker which cooks the fish and gives it a smoked flavour. (These must not be confused with commercial or other cold smoked food products which are pickled before smoking and are not cooked by the smoking process.)

Spirit or gas burning portable stoves are equipped with rings on which a saucepan or frying pan can be placed for cooking, and a limited range of dishes can be cooked in the usual way; the only problem, as a rule, is to ensure that the heat source is adequately protected from sudden gusts of wind and other draughts.

A camp-fire presents the problem of balancing or holding the food over the heat. A large pot can be hung from a tripod over the fire, but a more satisfactory method is to balance a metal grid on bricks or similar supports so that it is suspended over the flames. In this case, a camp-fire can be used for grilling food on the grid, as on a barbecue; or a frying pan or saucepan can be placed on the grid. It is not always necessary to use a grid. Some foods, eg small fish, thin pieces of meat, sausages or slices of bread, can be toasted on toasting forks held close to the flames. Potatoes can be wrapped in foil and baked in the hot ashes.

There are several types of barbecue suitable for family use or for cooking a meal for a larger group. They range from a simple trench 1–2 metres deep to a permanent brick structure with an electrically powered spit. The most widely used is a portable barbecue available in a variety of styles, some with a battery-powered spit. Any barbecue, however, should:

1) be stable and strong so the metal will not warp with the heat.
2) have a means of ventilating and controlling the fire.
3) have adjustable grilling heights.
4) stand at a comfortable working height.

A reasonably good barbecue can be improvised, using a metal wheelbarrow, or a concrete container.

Managing the Fire

Camp-fire cookery and barbecue cooking both need a good fire which should be glowing red-hot, neither flaring nor clogged with ash. The main difference between a camp-fire and barbecue fire is that a camp-fire is usually made with wood, a barbecue fire with charcoal.

In both cases, a good bottom draught is essential, especially when getting the fire started. A camp-fire or a barbecue fire should be lit 30–40 minutes before it is needed. Once well established, the glowing fuel should be raked or spread over the area to be used for cooking. After use, the fire must be put out with old cinders or water. Ashes should be raked into the ground; leftover charcoal can be saved for re-use.

Preparing the barbecue: The bars or mesh of the grilling grid should be well oiled and hot before food is put on it. The time taken for grilling will depend on the heat of the fire, where the food is placed, how thick the food is, and whether it is to be rare or well done.

A semi-portable barbecue with grill

Cooking Equipment

The equipment for camp-fire or barbecue cookery is very simple. The essential items are:
1) heavy gloves
2) tongs for handling fuel and hot food
3) toasting forks or skewers for small items
4) sturdy pots, pans or saucepans
5) foil and soft kitchen paper for wrapping and draining food.

Preparing the Food

Meat: If marinated before grilling, meat should be patted dry with soft kitchen paper. If not marinated, it can be rubbed with Barbecue Spice (p1312) or dried herbs. Do not salt steaks before cooking as this toughens them. The edges of steaks and chops should be snipped to prevent curling. Marinate pork spare ribs in a spicy sauce which can be used for basting. Hamburgers should be brushed with butter or oil, and sausages or frankfurters well pricked and moistened with water. Both grill within 15 minutes. Skin and split kidneys and wrap thick slices of liver in rashers of bacon. Kebabs are ideal for barbecuing; use small pieces of meat.

Fish: Whole oily fish such as trout, mackerel or herring need diagonal slits cut in the skin to prevent them curling open, and should not be salted as this makes the skin peel. Kebabs can be formed by cutting fish into small pieces. Fish can be marinated or well-seasoned and rubbed with lemon juice – this is particularly important for white fish steaks or fillets. Extra flavour can be added by placing a small amount of aromatic herbs, juniper berries, dried fruit wood or vine cuttings on the embers before barbecuing.

Grilling

Steaks and chops should not be more than 3cm thick, and poultry joints should not weigh more than 150g for quick grilling. (Frozen birds must be fully thawed.)

Frying

Food is prepared for frying on a camp-fire in the same way as for grilling except that extra fat or oil will be needed. The food can be fried in an ordinary, heavy frying pan, or it can be fried on a sheet of heavy metal balanced on the fire. Cooking times are approximately the same as for grilling.

Spit-roasting

A large joint or whole bird suitable for a party is usually spiced or otherwise prepared as for grilling. It must then be tied up tightly for spit-roasting. Care must be taken to see that it is not too heavy for the spit and does not unbalance it. Meat must be spitted so the weight falls evenly (this depends on where the bone is); poultry is spitted through the centre parallel to the spine.

The fire should be shovelled to the back of the grill for spit-roasting and a drip pan placed under the food. During roasting it should be basted either with sauce, butter, oil, or the juices which fall into the drip pan.

The cooking time depends on the same factors as for grilling.

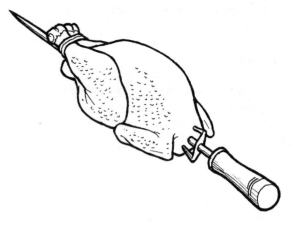

A spitted chicken

Devilling Marinade or Sauce

(for meat, poultry or game)

Makes 200ml (approx)

125ml salad oil
3–4 × 15ml spoons Worcestershire sauce
5 × 15ml spoons tomato ketchup
2 × 10ml spoons French mustard
1 × 15ml spoon made English mustard

1 × 5ml spoon caster sugar
a few drops anchovy essence
salt and pepper
a few grains Cayenne pepper
a pinch of paprika

Mix together all the ingredients, blending thoroughly. Cut raw or cooked meat into serving pieces and score with the sharp point of a kitchen knife, making deep cuts in the flesh. Lay the pieces in the marinade and work it well into the cuts with a spoon. Leave red meat or big pieces of game for several hours or overnight. Small poultry or game bird joints need only 1–2 hours. Drain the meat well when required for use.

Note This marinade keeps well in a refrigerator, and can be re-used.

Other marinades can be found on p730.

Devilled Poultry or Game

3–6 helpings

6 poultry or game bird pieces or joints (thighs, drumsticks, wings)

Devilling Marinade
cooking oil

Soak the meat in Devilling Marinade for 1–2 hours, longer for a stronger flavour. Drain, but reserve the marinade. Pat the meat dry with soft kitchen paper, and brush lightly with oil. If using joints, wrap the bone end of each joint in foil, to make it easier to handle. Place the meat pieces or joints on a grid over a camp-fire or barbecue, and turn as required, until cooked through and golden-brown on all sides. Meanwhile, heat the marinade in a small pan on the grid. Pour off and discard any excess oil from the marinade. Serve the marinade separately in the pan or in a warmed jug as a dip.

Devilled Turkey (2)

4 helpings

2 cold cooked turkey legs
2 × 15ml spoons made English mustard
salt

a few grains Cayenne pepper
chilled pats of butter (optional)

Cut the legs in half at the joints. Score the flesh with lengthways slits cut down to the bone. Rub with the mustard, pressing it well into the slits. Season lightly with the salt and Cayenne pepper. Grill over moderate heat, turning as required, until crisp and brown. Top each joint with a pat of butter if liked, and serve very hot.

Note For Devilled Turkey (1) see p644.

Ash-baked Plugged Potatoes

4 helpings

4 large old potatoes
full fat soft cheese
chopped parsley

4 × 5ml spoons grated hard cheese
oil for greasing
salt and pepper

Cut 4 squares of foil, each of which will enclose one potato completely. With an apple corer, cut a long plug out of each potato. Cut off and reserve 1cm of each plug at the skin end. Mix enough soft cheese and parsley to fill the holes in the potatoes, using 1 × 15ml spoon chopped parsley for each 25g cheese. Add 1 × 5ml spoon grated hard cheese for each potato and blend in. Fill the holes left by the plugs with the cheese mixture. Replace the 1cm plug ends, skin side out. Grease the foil squares well and wrap each potato completely in foil. Bake for about 45 minutes directly on the coals, turning once. Check if done by running a skewer through the foil into the potato. Open the packages, split and season the potatoes, and serve hot.

Note If more convenient, the plugged potatoes can be cooked on the barbecue grill for about 1 hour, turning once.

Barbecue Basting Sauce

Makes 375ml (approx)

200ml tomato juice
100ml water
50ml tomato ketchup
1–2 × 15ml spoons
  Worcestershire sauce
2 × 15ml spoons soft
  dark brown sugar
1 × 15ml spoon paprika

1 × 5ml spoon dry
  mustard
1 × 5ml spoon salt
½ × 2.5ml spoon chilli
  powder
a pinch of Cayenne
  pepper

Mix all the ingredients in a saucepan and simmer for 15 minutes. Use instead of a marinade for meat, especially spare ribs. Baste at intervals for 45 minutes before cooking, and also during cooking. Serve any remaining sauce with the meat.

Barbecued Spare Ribs

6–8 helpings

3 slabs fleshy pork spare
  ribs (at least 1kg each)

Barbecue Basting Sauce

Barbecue Spice
6 × 15ml spoons salt
6 × 15ml spoons soft
  light brown sugar
1 × 15ml spoon grated
  lemon rind

2 × 15ml spoons ground
  black pepper
1 × 15ml spoon paprika

Allow 1 slab of spare ribs for each 2 or 3 people. Do not split them before cooking or they will dry out.

Trim any loose ends off the meat. Mix all the ingredients for the Barbecue Spice together thoroughly and rub well into both sides of the meat, especially the bony side. Brush the meat thoroughly with Barbecue Basting Sauce, and leave for 30 minutes. Repeat the brushing and leave for another 30 minutes. Brush again, then cook on the grid for about 1¼ hours, turning every 20 minutes. Baste with Barbecue Basting Sauce when turning. If the thinner end is cooked first, wrap it in foil until the meat is fully cooked. Serve any remaining Barbecue Basting Sauce with the meat.

If more convenient, the meat can be cooked in a cool oven at 140°–150°C, Gas 1–2, for about 1 hour until nearly cooked. Baste well. It can then be finished off on the grid over the fire. Carve into individual ribs before serving.

Note Any unused Barbecue Spice can be stored in an airtight container for use later.

Barbecue Hamburgers

Makes 8 large or 16 small hamburgers

1 small onion
  (50g approx)
1kg beef mince
1 × 5ml spoon salt
½ × 2.5ml spoon pepper

1 × 2.5ml spoon dried
  mixed herbs
50ml beef stock or milk
  (optional)

Skin and mince the onion. Mix all the ingredients together. Shape the mixture into 8 thick patties or 16 flat small ones. Place on the barbecue grill over hot coals, and barbecue, turning once, for 12–20 minutes, depending on size.

Baste with Barbecue Basting Sauce while cooking, if liked.

Note For the basic hamburger recipe and suggested variations, see p505.

Barbecued Apples

Makes 4

4 cooking apples
50g sultanas
25g soft brown sugar
4 × 15ml spoons golden
  syrup

4 × 15ml spoons butter
4 sprigs mint

Wash and core the apples but do not peel them. Cut 4 squares of foil which will enclose them completely. Place 1 apple in the centre of each square. Mix together the sultanas, sugar and syrup, and fill the core holes of the apples with the mixture. Top each hole with 1 × 15ml spoon butter and a sprig of mint. Wrap the apples completely in the foil. Place on the grid of a camp-fire or barbecue, and cook for 15–20 minutes, turning once. Unwrap and serve hot.

BREAKFASTS AND SUPPERS

The following list of hot dishes may perhaps assist our readers in knowing what to provide for the comfortable meal called breakfast. Broiled fish, such as mackerel, whiting, herrings, dried haddocks, &c.; mutton chops and rump-steaks, broiled sheep's kidneys, kidneys à la maître d'hôtel, sausages, plain rashers of bacon, bacon and poached eggs, ham and poached eggs, omelets, plain boiled eggs, œufs-au-plat, poached eggs on toast, muffins, toast, marmalade, butter, &c. &c.

Breakfasts

Breakfast should provide one-quarter of any individual's daily nutritional requirements. This may be in the form of the traditional British cooked breakfast outlined below but many different, quickly prepared food combinations can provide the nutrients required; for instance, muesli with milk or yoghurt, or a boiled egg, toast and butter, and fruit juice.

The traditional menu varies in town and country, and from area to area, but typically consists of:

1) stewed fruit, or a fresh fruit or juice (usually orange or grapefruit)
2) breakfast cereal, such as porridge, or a cold processed cereal with milk and sugar
3) one hot dish such as:
   a) fried or grilled bacon with fried, poached or scrambled eggs, to which may be added fried bread, grilled or fried sausages, and grilled tomatoes or mushrooms
   b) one or two boiled eggs
   c) grilled herrings, poached haddock (smoked or fresh), kedgeree, or jugged or grilled kippers
   d) grilled or sautéed kidneys
   e) black pudding.
4) toast, butter, and marmalade or honey; or rolls, oatcakes, etc. Hot Cross Buns are usually eaten on Good Friday.
5) tea or coffee.

French croissants may replace the cereal or toast, and yoghurt may be used with a cereal.

Recipes for all these dishes can be found by reference to the Index.

Suppers

A choice of recipes for an informal evening meal is given in this chapter. They include light, easily made dishes for use when the main meal has been taken at midday, and more substantial dishes which are quick to prepare when the cook is tired after a day's work. Dishes suitable for tray meals, eg when watching television, are also included. Many of the recipes make use of cold leftovers. If a second course is wanted, most of these dishes can be followed by fresh fruit, or cheese and biscuits.

In addition to the recipes given in the subsections below, many others from the principal chapters are suitable. Some suggestions are given with each section.

SOUPS

A hearty broth or thick soup containing meat, fish, or pasta, as well as vegetables, makes a good main-course soup. Grated cheese, traditionally sprinkled on many such soups, provides extra nourishment. This may be accompanied by hot bread and rolls, plus perhaps a fresh salad.

Some examples of soups suitable for a main course are Bouillabaisse (p346), Fisherman's Hot Pot (p347), Hotch Potch (p333), Puréed Vegetable Soup (p351) and Vegetable, Cheese and Rice Soup (p365).

FISH DISHES

American Fish Pie

4–5 helpings

200g cooked cod or other
  firm white fish
25g Cheddar cheese
40g butter
250ml foundation white
  sauce (coating
  consistency) (p692)
salt and pepper

a few grains Cayenne
  pepper
1 egg
300–325g cold mashed
  potato
a pinch of grated nutmeg
butter for greasing

Skin, bone, and flake the fish. Grate the cheese. Put the fish into a saucepan with 15g of the butter, the white sauce, and half the cheese. Season to taste, and add the Cayenne pepper. Put to one side.

Beat the egg until liquid, reserve enough for glazing, and stir the rest into the mashed potato. Melt the remaining 25g butter, and mix it into the potato with salt, pepper, and nutmeg to taste. Line a greased 1 litre pie dish with half the potato mixture. Heat the fish mixture until the sauce bubbles and the cheese has melted. Pour it into the lined pie dish, and cover evenly with the rest of the potato. Notch the edge to make the potato look like a pastry crust. Glaze with the remaining egg, and sprinkle with the rest of the cheese. Bake in a fairly hot oven, 190°C, Gas 5, for 8–12 minutes, until well browned.

Cod à la Maître D'Hôtel

See p433.

Crab Salad Toasts

4 helpings

1 × 142g pkt frozen
  crabmeat
2 rashers streaky bacon,
  without rinds
1 × 15ml spoon
  mayonnaise

salt and pepper
4 slices white bread
parsley butter (p1301)

Garnish
shredded lettuce
tomato slices

lemon wedges

Thaw the crabmeat. Grill or fry the bacon until crisp, then crumble it finely. Mix together the crabmeat, bacon and mayonnaise, and season to taste. Remove the crusts and toast the bread lightly on both sides. Spread parsley butter generously on each slice, pile the crabmeat mixture on top, and garnish with lettuce, tomato, and lemon.

Fish Cakes

4 helpings

300g cooked white fish
  (cod, haddock, coley,
  etc)
500g cold boiled potatoes
25g butter
2 × 15ml spoons cream

1 × 15ml spoon finely
  chopped parsley
salt and pepper
flour for coating
fat for shallow frying

Flake the fish and remove all the bones. Mash the potatoes until smooth, and mix in the butter and cream. Add the flaked fish and parsley, and season to taste. Divide the mixture into 8 portions, and shape into flat, round cakes. Season the flour, and dip each cake in it. Shallow fry in butter or oil for 6–8 minutes, turning once.

VARIATION

Instead of coating with flour, dip each cake in beaten egg, coat in breadcrumbs, and deep fry (p303) until crisp and golden-brown.

Fish Pudding

4–5 helpings

400g white fish	*a few drops anchovy*
100g shredded suet	*essence*
50g soft white	*2 eggs*
breadcrumbs	*125ml milk or fish stock*
parsley	*(p330)*
salt and pepper	*butter for greasing*

Skin and fillet the fish, and chop finely. Add the suet with the breadcrumbs, parsley, seasoning, and anchovy essence, and mix well. Beat the eggs lightly, add the milk or stock, and stir into the mixture. Place it in a greased 500ml basin, cover with greased paper or foil, and steam gently for $1\frac{1}{2}$ hours.

Irish Bake

4 helpings

500g potatoes	*salt and pepper*
500g firm white fish	*1 × 298ml can ready-to-*
fillets	*use tomato soup*
1 small onion	*butter for shallow frying*
50g mushrooms	
(optional)	

Garnish
fried parsley (p398)

Peel the potatoes and slice them thinly. Cook for 10 minutes in boiling salted water, then drain well. Meanwhile, skin the fish fillets and cut them into 2cm cubes. Skin and grate the onion. If using mushrooms, remove and chop the stalks. Add the onion and the mushroom stalks to the fish, and place it in a shallow 1.25 litre ovenproof dish, then season to taste. Cover with potato slices, and pour the soup over them. Bake in a fairly hot oven, 200°C, Gas 6, for 30 minutes. Meanwhile, melt the butter and fry the mushrooms, if used. Use them and the parsley to garnish the top of the dish when cooked. Serve very hot.

French Fish Stew

4 helpings

1kg haddock fillets	*150ml single cream*
$\frac{1}{2}$ medium onion or	*1 × 15ml spoon*
1 shallot	*arrowroot*
25g butter	*100ml milk or water*
25ml cooking oil	*salt and pepper*
8 button mushrooms	*a pinch of ground mace*
350ml dry still cider	

Garnish
chopped parsley

Skin the fillets and slice them thinly. Skin and chop the onion or shallot. Heat the butter and oil together in a deep pan, add the onion or shallot and fry gently until soft but not brown. Slice the mushrooms, and add them to the pan; cook for 2 minutes, turning the mushrooms over.

Add the prepared fish, and cook for a further 8 minutes. Remove from the heat and drain off the fat. Add the cider, cover, and return to the heat. Simmer gently for 8 minutes. Stir in the cream, then remove from the heat. Blend the arrowroot with a little of the milk or water. Add to the stew with the rest of the milk or water. Season to taste with salt, pepper, and ground mace. Return the pan to the heat, stirring gently all the time, until the sauce thickens. Sprinkle with chopped parsley just before serving.

Salad Niçoise
See p836.

MEAT DISHES

Beef Scallops

4 helpings

450g cold cooked beef	*250ml brown stock*
1 medium-sized onion	*(p329)*
25g margarine **or**	*margarine* **or** *dripping*
dripping	*dry white breadcrumbs*
25g flour	

Garnish
parsley sprigs

Trim any skin, gristle and surplus fat from the meat, and mince the meat finely. Skin and slice the onion. Melt the fat in a pan, add the onion and fry until soft. Stir in the flour and cook gently until lightly browned. Stir in the stock gradually, reduce the heat, and simmer for 15–20 minutes, until the sauce is well thickened. Strain the sauce, and mix in the meat. Divide the mixture between 4 greased scallop shells, cover well with breadcrumbs and dot with fat. Bake the scallops in a fairly hot oven, 190°C, Gas 5, for 15–20 minutes until well browned. Garnish with sprigs of parsley.

Cannelon of Beef

4–6 helpings

450g cold cooked beef	*salt and pepper*
200g cooked **or** *raw ham*	*1 egg*
or *boiling bacon* **or**	*25g butter, margarine*
cooked pickled pork,	**or** *dripping*
without rinds	*125ml brown stock*
1 × 2.5ml spoon dried	*(p329)*
mixed herbs	*100ml Fresh Tomato*
grated rind and juice of	*sauce* (p715)
½ small lemon	
2 medium-sized cooked	
potatoes	

Trim any skin, gristle and surplus fat from the beef. Chop the meat finely with the ham, bacon or pork. Add the herbs and then the grated lemon rind. Dice or chop the potatoes, and add them; season to taste. Beat the egg lightly, and use it to bind the meat mixture, shaping it into a thick, short roll. Grease a sheet of greaseproof paper with a little of the fat, and use the rest to cover the roll. Wrap it in the greaseproof paper, and place in a roasting tin. Pour the stock round the roll, and bake in a fairly hot oven, 200°C, Gas 6, for 50 minutes. Remove the paper 15 minutes before the end of the cooking time, and baste twice while completing the cooking. Sharpen the tomato sauce with the lemon juice, and heat it.

Serve the meat roll on a warmed dish with the sauce poured round it.

VARIATION
Remains of a roast, baked or braised ox heart can be used instead of beef.

Miroton of Beef

4 helpings

350–400g cold cooked	*1 × 5ml spoon vinegar*
beef	*bouquet garni*
2 medium-sized onions	*salt and pepper*
25g butter, margarine	*browned breadcrumbs*
or *dripping*	*(p375)*
400ml foundation	*butter*
brown sauce	
(p698)	

Garnish
croûtons of fried bread
or *hot diced mixed*
vegetables, sprigs of
cauliflower **or** *peas*

Trim any skin, gristle and surplus fat from the meat. Slice the meat thinly. Skin and slice the onions. Melt the fat in a pan, add the onions, and fry until soft and golden. Add the sauce, vinegar and bouquet garni, and season to taste. Mix together well. Bring to the boil, reduce the heat, and simmer for 30 minutes, stirring and skimming occasionally. Strain, reserving the sauce. Cover the bottom of a shallow ovenproof dish with some of the sauce, place the meat slices in neat layers on top and cover with the remaining sauce. Sprinkle thickly with browned crumbs, and dot with flakes of butter.

Bake in a fairly hot oven, 190°C, Gas 5, for about 20 minutes or until thoroughly heated through.

Garnish with croûtons, hot diced mixed vegetables, sprigs of cauliflower, or peas.

Note The beef may be roasted, pot-roasted or braised whole. Small pieces of stewed meat already cooked slowly in liquor are *not* suitable.

Shepherd's Pie
See p509.

Spaghetti Bolognese
See p856.

Ragoût of Beef

4–6 helpings

650g cold roast rare **or** medium rare beef	500ml beef stock
1 medium-sized onion (100g approx)	salt and pepper
50g margarine **or** dripping	1 × 15ml spoon malt vinegar **or** mushroom ketchup
3 × 15ml spoons plain flour	

Garnish

50g cooked and diced carrot	1 × 15ml spoon chopped parsley
50g cooked and diced turnip	

Cut the meat into neat slices. Prepare the carrot and turnip for the garnish and keep the peelings. Skin and chop the onion coarsely. Melt the margarine or dripping in a saucepan, add the onion, and fry until golden-brown. Sprinkle in the flour, stir, and cook slowly until well browned. Gradually add the stock and stir until boiling. Season with salt and pepper to taste. Add the vegetable peelings and the vinegar or ketchup. Reduce the heat and simmer for 15 minutes. Put in the slices of meat, cover the pan with a tight-fitting lid, and simmer very gently for 1 hour.

Remove the meat from the pan and arrange the slices on a warmed serving dish. Strain the sauce and pour it over the meat. Garnish with the hot diced vegetables and chopped parsley.

Note This recipe is equally suitable for using 'left-over' roast meat, eg brisket, flank, topside and silverside, which must be part-roasted or braised to rare or medium rare before use.

Lamb and Potato Pie

4 helpings

600–650g cold cooked lamb	butter
600g potatoes	salt and pepper
2 medium-sized onions	250ml thin gravy (p727)

Trim any skin, gristle and surplus fat from the meat. Slice the meat thinly. Prepare and slice the potatoes and onions, then parboil them. Line a greased 1.25 litre soufflé or other deep dish with slices of potato, and fill with alternate layers of meat, onion and potato, seasoning each layer to taste. Finish with a layer of potato. Pour in the gravy. Dot the potato with butter, cover with greaseproof paper, and bake in a moderate oven, 180°C, Gas 4, for 1 hour. Remove the paper 15 minutes before the end of the cooking time to let the potatoes brown on top.

Note Roast lamb, pot-roasted lamb, or braised lamb can be used, but stewed lamb which has already cooked slowly in liquor is *not* suitable.

Bordered Lamb
See p546.

Lamb or Mutton Bake

4–6 helpings

500g cold cooked lamb or *mutton*	*a few gherkins*
4–6 slices white bread	*salt and pepper*
butter	*250ml foundation brown sauce* (p698)

Trim any skin, gristle and surplus fat from the meat. Slice the meat neatly. Cut the crusts off the bread and crumble it finely. Line a greased 500ml ovenproof dish with some of the crumbs. Put a layer of meat slices in the bottom, overlapping them slightly. Chop the gherkins and sprinkle some over the meat. Season to taste, and sprinkle with sauce. Repeat the layers until the dish is full, ending with a thick layer of breadcrumbs. Dot with butter. Cover the dish with greaseproof paper, and bake in a moderate oven, 180°C, Gas 4, for about 30 minutes. Uncover 10 minutes before the end of the cooking time. Serve from the dish.

Meat Ragoût with Eggs

6 helpings

400g cold roast veal or *chicken*	*salt and pepper*
40g butter or *margarine*	*juice of ¼ lemon*
40g flour	*2 slices bread*
250ml white (p329) or *chicken stock* (p330)	*fat for shallow frying*
	6 eggs

Garnish
chopped parsley

Trim any skin and gristle off the meat. Mince the meat finely. Melt the fat in a saucepan. Stir in the flour, and cook gently for a few minutes until brown. Draw off the heat, stir in the stock gradually, and season to taste. Return to the heat, and bring to the boil, stirring all the time. Simmer for 5 minutes. Strain the lemon juice into the sauce. Place half the sauce in a basin, and put to one side.

Add the meat to the remaining sauce, and heat for 15 minutes. Fry the bread until golden-brown on both sides, and cut into croûtons or triangles. Poach the eggs and keep them warm. Put the meat mixture in the centre of a warmed dish, arrange the eggs on top, and sprinkle with the croûtons or triangles. Garnish with chopped parsley. Heat the rest of the sauce and serve separately.

Veal Scallops
See p574.

Veal, Salami, and Olive Salad
See p839.

Bacon and Egg Omelet

3–4 helpings

250g back bacon rashers, without rinds	*4 eggs*
1 × 15ml spoon flour	*salt and pepper*
6 × 15ml spoons milk	*15g butter*

Garnish

chopped parsley or *chives*	*tomato wedges*

Place the bacon in the grill pan, and cook for 3–4 minutes until golden-brown and crisp. Meanwhile, blend the flour and milk. Beat in the eggs, and season to taste. Melt the butter in a frying pan, and heat until just turning brown. Pour in the egg mixture, and cook for 5–6 minutes over fairly high heat until set, lifting the edges occasionally. Place the hot bacon rashers on top. Garnish with chopped parsley or chives, and wedges of tomato. Serve from the pan.

Ham Slices with Fruit
See p607.

Jellied Ham Salad
See p838.

Bacon and Apple Savoury

4 helpings

12 rashers streaky bacon, without rinds	75g sugar
6 large, sharp, dessert apples	

Fry the bacon until crisp. Drain, and keep it hot, reserving the fat in the pan. Cut the apples into wedges. Core but do not peel them. Sprinkle with sugar, and fry in the hot bacon fat until soft but not mushy. Put into a warmed serving dish and arrange the bacon rashers on top in overlapping rows.

Serve with rye bread and butter.

Holiday Pork
See p590.

Bubble and Squeak

dripping **or** lard	cold, cooked green vegetables of any kind, as available
thin slices of cold roast **or** braised **or** boiled meat as available	
1 medium-sized onion	salt and pepper
cold mashed potatoes as available	a dash of vinegar (optional)

Heat just enough dripping or lard in a frying pan to cover the bottom. Put in the meat, and fry quickly on both sides until lightly browned. Remove, and keep hot. Skin the onion, slice it thinly, and fry until lightly browned, adding a little more fat to the frying pan if necessary. Mix together the potatoes and green vegetables, season to taste, and add to the frying pan. Stir until thoroughly hot, then add a little vinegar, if liked. Allow to become slightly crusty on the bottom. Turn out on to a warmed dish. Place the meat on top and serve.

Note The name Bubble and Squeak is often given to a dish of re-heated vegetables without meat.

Meatballs in Celeriac Sauce

5–6 helpings

200g lean veal	1 medium-sized onion
200g lean pork	salt and pepper
1 egg	375ml water
5 ×15ml spoons plain flour	1 large celeriac **or** 200g celery
500ml milk	50g butter

Garnish
6 fleurons of puff pastry (p399) **or** triangles of fried bread

Mince the veal and pork together twice. Beat the egg until liquid, and mix with the minced meats. Stir in 3 ×15ml spoons of the flour. Bring the milk to boiling point, and add very gradually to the meat mixture, stirring until it has all been absorbed. Skin and grate the onion, and stir it into the mixture. Season to taste. Form the mixture into small meatballs about 2cm in diameter. Bring the water to boiling point in a large pan. Add a little salt and the meatballs. Boil them for about 5 minutes; then lift them out, and draw the pan off the heat.

Peel and dice the celeriac, if used, and put it into the pan. Return the pan to the heat, and boil the celeriac dice for 15 minutes, or until tender. Remove the celeriac from the water, and reserve both.

If using celery, slice it thinly; then cook until tender, as for the celeriac. Drain, and reserve the cooking water.

Melt the butter in a clean saucepan, and stir in the remaining flour. Cook gently for 3 minutes, stirring all the time. Gradually strain in the water in which the meatballs and celeriac or celery were cooked, stirring all the time. Cook gently until the sauce is thick and smooth. Put the meatballs and celeriac into the sauce and bring to the boil. Season to taste. Serve garnished with small fleurons of puff pastry or triangles of fried bread.

Note Chicken and bacon, or other meat or poultry mixtures, can be used for making these meatballs, provided that at least half is white meat, eg veal, chicken, turkey or rabbit meat.

Meat Polantine

4–6 helpings

400g cold cooked meat	flour for coating
200ml foundation brown	4 firm ripe tomatoes
sauce (p698)	100g butter
salt and pepper	250ml thickened gravy
grated nutmeg	(p727) (optional)
4 medium-sized onions	

Trim any skin, gristle and surplus fat from the meat, and shred the meat finely. Put it into a saucepan, coat with the sauce, and season to taste with salt, pepper, and nutmeg. Put to one side.

Skin the onions, and slice them into rings. Season the flour, and coat the onion rings with it. Slice the tomatoes. Melt the butter in a frying pan, add the onion rings, and fry gently until soft and golden. Remove, drain on soft kitchen paper, and keep warm. Dust the tomato slices with any remaining flour, add them to the fat left in the pan, and fry. Drain the tomato slices well, season lightly, and place in a layer on a warmed serving dish. Heat the meat and sauce until thoroughly hot, and spread the mixture over the tomatoes. Place the onion rings on the meat. Heat the gravy, if used, and serve it in a warmed sauce-boat.

Meat Pancake Stack

4–5 helpings

250ml basic thin batter	1 onion
(p934)	25g butter or margarine
200g (approx) cooked	2 × 10ml spoons flour
meat	125ml stock (see **Note**)
2 × 10ml spoons	salt and pepper
chopped mixed nuts	fat for frying
(optional)	butter

Prepare the batter, and leave to stand. Mince the meat with the nuts, if used. Skin the onion, and chop it finely. Melt the fat in a pan, add the onion, and fry until soft. Stir in the flour, then gradually add the stock, and continue to stir until the mixture thickens. Mix in the minced meat and nuts, and season to taste. Remove from the heat, and put to one side.

Lightly grease a 15cm frying pan, and melt the fat so that it covers the base evenly. Make pancakes with the batter, and place one pancake in a shallow ovenproof dish just large enough to hold it when laid flat. Spread with some of the meat mixture. Alternate the layers of pancake and meat mixture until all the ingredients are used, ending with a pancake. Dot the top pancake with butter. Cover with greaseproof paper, and bake in a moderate oven, 180°C, Gas 4, for 20–25 minutes.

Serve cut into wedges like a cake.

Note Use white (p329) or chicken (p330) stock for white meat, brown stock (p329) for red meats.

Meat Pyramids

6 helpings

300g cooked meat	1 × 5ml spoon Piquant
1 shallot	(p702) or similar
2 mushrooms	savoury brown sauce
25g butter or white fat	salt and pepper
1 egg	6 × 5cm rounds toast or
125ml foundation brown	fried bread
sauce (p698)	

Garnish
chopped parsley

Trim any gristle or skin from the meat, and mince the meat. Peel the shallot and mushrooms, and chop them finely. Melt the fat in a saucepan, add the vegetables, and fry gently for 4–5 minutes. Beat the egg until liquid, and add to the saucepan with the meat, sauces, and seasoning. Cook over low heat for 10–15 minutes, stirring all the time. Pile the mixture on to the rounds of toast or fried bread. Garnish with chopped parsley.

Cold Meat Salad
See p838.

Savoury Sausage Toasts

6 helpings

6 bacon rashers, without
 rinds
12 chipolata sausages
 (300g approx)
2 ripe dessert apples

lemon juice
2 tomatoes
25g butter
6 slices bread

Garnish
parsley sprigs

Roll up the bacon rashers. Prick or moisten the sausages. Core and slice the apples, sprinkle with lemon juice and put to one side. Slice the tomatoes.

Line a grill pan with foil, place the sausages and bacon rolls in it and grill slowly for about 10 minutes, turning once or twice. Meanwhile, melt the butter, and brush the tomato and apple slices with it. Add to the sausages and bacon rolls for the last 5 minutes of the cooking time.

Toast the bread lightly, and cut each slice into a round shape with a pastry cutter. Brush any remaining butter over one side of each round. Place an apple slice on each round, then a tomato slice. Top with 2 sausages, and garnish with a sprig of parsley. Serve the savoury toasts on a dish with the bacon rolls.

Toad-in-the-hole

See p935.

Grilled Kidneys

4 helpings

4 sheep's kidneys
2 ×15ml spoons butter
salt and pepper
4 slices fried bread

chopped parsley
4 pats Maître d'Hôtel
 butter (optional)
 (p1300)

Garnish
bacon rolls (p396)

Skin the kidneys, cut them in half lengthways, and remove the cores. Skewer them with small poultry skewers along their length to keep them flat. Melt the butter, and brush a little on the cut sides of the kidneys. Place them on the grill rack, cut side up, and grill for 5–8 minutes, turning often, and basting with more butter if needed. When cooked through, remove the skewers. Season the kidneys well, and place them cut side up on the slices of fried bread. Sprinkle with parsley, and fill the hollows in the kidneys with Maître d'Hôtel butter, if used. Garnish with bacon rolls.

Note 8 lamb's kidneys can be substituted for the sheep's kidneys.

Kidneys and Scrambled Eggs

6 helpings

3 small calf's kidneys **or**
 4 lamb's kidneys
salt and pepper
1 small onion
100g butter
250ml Espagnole sauce
 (p707)

4 ×15ml spoons sherry
 (optional)
5–6 eggs
125ml milk

Garnish
finely diced sweet red
 pepper

2 ×15ml spoons
 chopped parsley

Skin and core the kidneys, and slice them very thinly. Season to taste. Skin the onion, and chop it finely. Melt 25g of the butter in a pan, add the onion, and fry it lightly. Add the kidneys, and fry quickly, stirring all the time or shaking the pan well, until browned lightly all over. Pour off any excess fat. Pour the Espagnole sauce over the kidneys, add the sherry, if used, and cook gently for 6–8 minutes. Remove the kidneys, place them in a circle on a warmed serving dish, and keep hot. Keep hot the sauce remaining in the pan.

Beat the eggs until liquid, add the milk, and season to taste. Heat the remaining butter in a pan, and scramble the eggs gently until the mixture starts to thicken. Pile the scrambled eggs in the centre of the circle of kidneys, and pour the hot sauce round and over the kidneys. Garnish with red pepper and chopped parsley, and serve at once.

Sautéed Kidneys (1)

4 helpings

4 sheep's kidneys	125ml foundation brown
1 small onion	sauce (p698)
50g butter	salt and pepper
1 × 5ml spoon chopped	4 slices fried bread
parsley	

Garnish
chopped parsley

Skin and core the kidneys, and slice them very thinly. Skin the onion and chop it finely. Melt the butter in a frying pan, and fry the onion until just golden-brown. Add the kidney slices and parsley. Stir, and turn over in the fat for 2–3 minutes until very lightly fried. Add the brown sauce, and season to taste. Bring the sauce just to the boil. Pour the mixture on to a warmed serving dish. Cut the slices of fried bread into triangles, and arrange around the edge of the dish. Garnish with chopped parsley, and serve at once.

Note Lamb's kidneys may be used if sheep's kidneys are difficult to obtain.
For Sautéed Kidneys (2), see p1449.

Kidneys on Croûtes

6 helpings

4 lamb's kidneys	125ml well-flavoured
1 shallot **or** 25g onion	brown stock (p329) **or**
3 × 10ml spoons butter	thin gravy (p727)
1 × 10ml spoon plain	salt and pepper
flour	6 slices bread
4 × 10ml spoons	oil **or** fat for frying
medium-dry sherry **or**	2 × 15ml spoons
Madeira (optional)	chopped parsley

Skin and core the kidneys, and slice as thinly as possible. Skin and chop finely the shallot or onion. Melt the butter in a frying pan, and fry the shallot or onion until browned lightly. Add the sliced kidneys, and toss gently over heat for 3–4 minutes. Remove the kidneys from the pan, and keep warm. Sprinkle the flour into the pan, stir, and cook quickly until brown. Add the sherry or Madeira,

if used, and the stock or gravy; then bring to the boil, stirring all the time. Season to taste. Add the kidneys to the sauce, and put to one side. Cut the crusts off the bread, and fry the croûtes quickly in shallow oil or fat until golden on both sides. Remove from the pan and drain. Re-heat the kidney mixture gently, if necessary. Cover each croûte with kidney mixture, and sprinkle with chopped parsley. Serve at once.

POULTRY AND GAME DISHES

Chicken or Turkey with Celery

4 helpings

3 sticks celery	1 × 5ml spoon fresh
75–100g fat bacon	chopped mixed herbs
scraps	**or** 1 × 2.5ml spoon
250ml foundation white	dried mixed herbs
sauce (coating	salt and pepper
consistency) (p692)	milk
200–300g cooked	200g cooked long-grain
chicken **or** turkey meat	rice

Garnish
watercress sprigs

Wash or wipe the celery, and chop it into 1cm pieces. Dice and fry the bacon scraps in a dry frying pan. When the fat runs, add the celery, reduce the heat, and fry gently for 5–7 minutes, stirring occasionally. Drain, transfer to a saucepan, and add the sauce. Chop the chicken or turkey meat, add it with the herbs to the saucepan, and season to taste. Simmer over gentle heat for 10–15 minutes, adding a little milk if the sauce is very thick. Re-heat the rice for a few minutes in a sieve or steamer over the sauce, or over simmering water. Put in a warmed serving dish, cover with the creamy chicken or turkey, and garnish with sprigs of watercress.

Stuffed Chicken Legs
See p643.

Chicken and Ham Scallops

4–6 helpings

250g cooked chicken	*salt and pepper*
125g cooked ham	*a good pinch of grated*
300ml Béchamel sauce	*nutmeg*
(p704) **or** *foundation*	*25g butter*
white sauce (coating	*6 ×10ml spoons fine dry*
consistency) (p692)	*white breadcrumbs*

Remove any skin and bone from the chicken, and chop the meat coarsely. Chop the ham finely, and add it to the chicken. Moisten the mixture well with some of the sauce, season to taste, and add a good pinch of grated nutmeg. Butter 6 deep scallop shells, fill them with the mixture, sprinkle evenly with breadcrumbs, and flake the rest of the butter on top. Bake in a fairly hot oven, 190–200°C, Gas 5–6, for about 20 minutes until golden-brown. Serve hot.

VARIATIONS

Chicken and Cheese Scallops

Omit the ham, substitute 1 × 5ml spoon lemon juice for the grated nutmeg, and add 1 × 5ml spoon chopped parsley to the mixture. Mix 2 ×10ml spoons grated cheese with the breadcrumbs, and bake as above, or place under moderate grill heat for 4–6 minutes to brown the top.

Browned Chicken Scallops

Heat the chicken and ham mixture gently in a saucepan before putting it into scallop shells. Cover with breadcrumbs and butter, as in the main recipe, then put under moderate grill heat for 4–6 minutes to brown the top.

Note For a more substantial dish, the shells can be garnished with a border of piped mashed potato.

Curried Turkey or Chicken Salad

See p840.

Chicken Pudding

5–6 helpings

500g minced raw	*salt and pepper*
*chicken (see **Note**)*	*75ml chicken stock* **or**
100g soft white	*milk*
breadcrumbs	*fat for greasing*
2 eggs	*crisp dry* **or** *fried*
1 × 2.5ml spoon grated	*breadcrumbs*
lemon rind	
a pinch of powdered	
mace	

Mix all the ingredients together, except the crisp breadcrumbs. Press into a greased 750ml basin or mould, cover with greased paper or foil and steam for 1½ hours. Turn out and coat with fine crisp breadcrumbs. Serve hot or cold.

Note The flesh from the legs and back of the chicken may be used, and the breast kept for a blanquette or fricassée.

Hashed Hare

See p679.

VEGETABLE DISHES

Potato Batter Cakes

4 helpings

100g plain flour	*8 medium-sized potatoes*
375ml milk	*butter, margarine, lard*
1 egg	*or vegetable oil for*
2–3 ×2.5ml spoons salt	*frying*

Blend together the flour and milk, beat in the egg and salt to taste to make a pancake batter. Peel the potatoes, grate them into the batter, and mix well. Heat a knob of fat in a large, shallow frying pan, and pour in 2 ×15ml spoons batter for each cake. Spread the mixture thinly, and fry for 4–6 minutes, turning once, until crisp and golden-brown. Drain on soft kitchen paper.

Serve with fried bacon or sausages, or with Cranberry Sauce.

Cauliflower Cheese

4 helpings

1 medium-sized firm cauliflower	*a pinch of dry mustard*
2 × 15ml spoons butter **or** *margarine*	*a pinch of Cayenne pepper*
4 × 15ml spoons flour	*salt and pepper*
200ml milk	*25g fine dry white breadcrumbs*
125g grated Cheddar cheese	

Prepare the cauliflower. Put the head in a saucepan containing enough boiling salted water to half-cover it. Cover the pan, and cook gently for 20–30 minutes until tender. Drain well, reserving 175ml of the cooking water. Break the head carefully into sections, and place in a warmed ovenproof dish. Keep warm under greased greaseproof paper.

Melt the fat in a medium-sized pan, stir in the flour, and cook for 2–3 minutes, stirring all the time, without letting the flour colour. Mix together the milk and reserved cooking water, and gradually add to the pan, stirring all the time to prevent lumps forming. Bring the sauce to the boil, lower the heat, and simmer until thickened. Remove from the heat, and stir in 100g of the cheese, with the mustard and Cayenne pepper. Season to taste. Stir until the cheese is fully melted, then pour the sauce over the cauliflower. Mix the remaining cheese with the breadcrumbs, and sprinkle them on top. Place in a hot oven, 220°C, Gas 7, for 7–10 minutes, to brown the top. Serve at once.

Note A mixture of 2 × 15ml spoons grated Cheddar cheese and 1 × 15ml spoon grated Parmesan cheese can be used for sprinkling, if liked, or 1–2 crumbled, crisply fried rashers of streaky bacon.

Stuffed Cabbage Leaves
See p760.

Tomato and Onion Pie
See p804.

Parsnip Soufflé

4 helpings

200g parsnips	*100ml milk*
65g butter	*2 × 15ml spoons chopped parsley*
2 × 15ml spoons grated onion	*salt and pepper*
3 × 15ml spoons flour	*a pinch of grated nutmeg*
100ml vegetable stock (p330) or *water in which the parsnips have cooked*	*4 eggs*
	butter for greasing
	125ml Béchamel sauce (p704)

Prepare the parsnips, and cook in a little boiling salted water until tender. Mash and sieve them, working them into a smooth purée. Measure out 150g purée, and keep the rest on one side.

Melt 15g of the butter in a frying pan, and fry the onion gently until soft. Mix it with the parsnip purée.

Heat the oven to fairly hot, 190°C, Gas 5. Put the remaining butter in a saucepan, and melt over low heat. Stir in the flour, and cook together for 3 minutes without colouring. Mix the stock or water and the milk, and stir gradually into the roux. Heat gently, stirring all the time, until the sauce thickens; then simmer for 3 minutes. Stir in the parsnip purée and parsley. Season to taste with salt, pepper, and nutmeg. Remove from the heat, and cool for 5 minutes. Separate the eggs. Beat the yolks lightly, and mix them into the purée one by one. Whisk the whites until stiff, and fold into the mixture. Turn gently into a greased 1 litre soufflé dish, and bake for 25–30 minutes. Meanwhile, mix the remaining purée with the Béchamel Sauce, and heat gently. Serve separately in a warmed sauce-boat.

Chick-pea Casserole
See p787.

DAIRY FOODS AND EGGS

Besides the dishes which follow, any savoury mousse (pp882–84) can be used as a supper dish; so can most recipes in the chapter on Eggs, particularly the soufflés and omelets.

Welsh Rarebit

4 helpings

100–150g Cheddar
cheese
25g butter **or** margarine
1 × 15ml spoon flour
75ml milk **or** 3 × 15ml
spoons milk and
2 × 15ml spoons ale
or beer

1 × 5ml spoon French
mustard
a few drops
Worcestershire sauce
salt and pepper
4 slices bread
butter for spreading

Grate the cheese. Melt the fat in a pan, and stir in the flour. Cook together for 2–3 minutes, stirring all the time; do not let the flour colour. Stir in the milk and blend to a smooth, thick mixture; then stir in the ale or beer, if used, the mustard and Worcestershire sauce. Add the cheese little by little, stir in, and season to taste. Remove from the heat as soon as well blended. Remove the crusts from the bread and toast lightly on both sides. Butter one side well and spread the cheese mixture on the buttered sides. Grill briefly, if liked, using high heat, to brown the surface of the cheese mixture. Serve immediately.

Note The term *rarebit* is generally considered as synonymous with *rabbit*.

VARIATIONS

Buck Rarebit

Make as for Welsh Rarebit, but top each slice with a poached egg. Serve at once.

Yorkshire Rarebit

Make as for Welsh Rarebit, but add 4 rashers of cooked bacon, without rinds.

Irish Rarebit

2 good or 4 light helpings

2 slices bread
butter for spreading
100g mild Cheddar
cheese
4 × 15ml spoons milk
25g butter **or** hard block
margarine

1 × 5ml spoon mild
white vinegar
1 × 5ml spoon made
English mustard
salt and pepper
1 × 10ml spoon chopped
gherkin

Toast the bread lightly on both sides. Butter one side of each slice. Grate the cheese finely. Put the cheese, milk and fat into a saucepan, and cook over gentle heat, stirring all the time, until the cheese has melted and the mixture is well blended and creamy. Mix in the vinegar and mustard, and season to taste. Add the gherkin. Pile the mixture on the buttered side of each slice of toast. Serve as it is, or grill briefly, using moderate heat, to brown the surface.

Note The slices may be cut into three fingers and used as small cocktail savouries.

VARIATIONS

Donegal Rarebit

Use chopped, rinsed anchovy fillets as required, instead of gherkin.

Golden Buck

Substitute Cheshire cheese for Cheddar, light ale for milk, and $\frac{1}{2}$ × 2.5ml spoon red wine vinegar or malt vinegar for white vinegar. Omit the mustard, and use celery salt and Cayenne pepper.

Heat the cheese, butter, and ale in a small saucepan, as in the main recipe. When well blended and creamy, draw off the heat, and stir in 1 × 2.5ml spoon Worcestershire sauce, the vinegar, seasoning, and 2 eggs. Return to the heat and stir briskly until the mixture thickens; do not let it boil. Pour or spread it over the buttered toast. Cut off the crusts, and serve immediately.

Mrs Beeton's Toasted Cheese or Welsh Rarebit

4 helpings

4 slices white bread
butter for spreading
100g Farmhouse English
  Cheshire **or** Double
  Gloucester cheese

a good pinch of dry
  mustard
freshly ground black
  pepper

Remove the crusts from the bread, toast lightly on both sides, and butter one side. Slice or flake the cheese thinly. Lay the cheese on the buttered side of the bread, covering it completely. Sprinkle with the mustard and pepper. Lay the bread slices, cheese side up, on flameproof individual plates which will hold the heat well. Grill very gently, until the cheese just melts. Serve immediately, while still very hot.

VARIATION

Lancashire Rarebit

Substitute Lancashire cheese for English Cheshire or Double Gloucester, and add 1 small onion and 4 rashers of streaky bacon, without rinds. Crumble the cheese, and mix with the skinned and chopped onion and the chopped bacon. Season to taste, and mash or pound to a semi-smooth paste. Spread on the untoasted side of each slice of bread, as in the main recipe, and bake in a fairly hot oven, 190°C, Gas 5, for 10 minutes, until the cheese is crusty and lightly browned. Serve immediately.

Note The cheese mixture will keep for 4–5 days in a refrigerator.

Croque Monsieur

4 helpings

8 slices white bread
butter for greasing and
  spreading

4 thin slices cooked ham
or bacon, without
  rinds
4 slices Gruyère cheese

Remove the crusts from the bread, and butter one side of each slice. Trim the ham or bacon and the cheese to fit the bread, and make four sandwiches with a filling of one thin layer of meat and one of cheese. Spread one side of each sandwich with butter. Grease a shallow baking dish or tin, large enough to hold the sandwiches in one layer. Place the tin in the oven, and heat to moderate, 180°C, Gas 4. Place the sandwiches in the hot tin, buttered side up, and return to the oven. Bake for 10 minutes, until golden and crisp on top.

VARIATION

Fry the sandwiches in butter on one side, turn over and coat the second side with fat, then toast the coated side, using moderate grill heat. Serve fried side uppermost.

Blue Cheese and Apple Slices

4 helpings

75g blue cheese
25g softened butter **or**
  margarine
25g soft white
  breadcrumbs
salt and pepper

1 large **or** 2 small
  cooking apples
flour for dredging
4 large **or** 8 small
  rounds buttered toast
  (optional)

Garnish
Tarragon butter (p1301)
  or 4 × 5ml spoons
  redcurrant jelly

Crumble the cheese, and cream with the fat; then mix in the breadcrumbs, and season lightly. Core the apple or apples, but do not peel them. Cut into four large or eight small thick rounds, trimming the end ones, if used, to make flat slices. Season well, and dredge with flour. Heat the grill rack. Spread one side of each apple slice thickly with the mixture, smoothing the surface. Grill, using moderate heat, until the cheese bubbles and starts to brown. Remove, and leave in a warm place for 2–3 minutes to allow the fat to seep into the apple.

Just before serving, shape the Tarragon butter, if used, into small balls. Garnish each apple slice with one ball, or with a spoonful of redcurrant jelly. Serve on rounds of buttered toast, if liked.

LIGHT DISHES FOR ONE OR TWO

Generally speaking, small dishes only are prepared by broiling; amongst these, the beef-steak and mutton chop of the solitary English diner may be mentioned as celebrated all the world over.

The recipes in this chapter are designed for one or two helpings only; for perhaps an elderly person whose energy requirements are less than those of a younger and more active member of the family, or for a convalescent who is unable to take heavy or rich meals.

It must be stressed, however, that they do not, in themselves, make complete, balanced meals, nor are they designed to meet any special dietary needs; for these, a doctor should be consulted.

Note Each recipe can be adapted to give more helpings by increasing the quantities of ingredients in proportion, except the seasonings, which should be increased slightly less.

Soups

Most consommés and lightly thickened soups, especially vegetable purée soups, are suitable for light meals. They may well precede or replace a main-course dish, provided they contain or are supplemented by protein foods, starchy foods such as pulses, pasta or a slice of bread, and raw or lightly cooked vegetables or fruit. Soups rich in cream, and some shellfish and game meat soups may, however, be rather indigestible, and are not recommended.

Fish Dishes

Dressed Coley

1 helping

100–150g skinned coley fillet
salt and pepper
1 × 5ml spoon French mustard
2 × 10ml spoons natural yoghurt

1 × 5ml spoon apple juice **or** to taste
1 gherkin
$\frac{1}{2}$ sharp eating apple
$\frac{1}{2}$ × 2.5ml spoon dried thyme **or** mixed herbs

Garnish
chopped gherkin   watercress sprigs

Season the fish with salt and pepper. Mix together the mustard, yoghurt, and apple juice. Chop the gherkin. Peel, core, and grate the apple, and mix together. Spoon the yoghurt mixture over the gherkin and fruit, and mix thoroughly. Spread this over the fish, and sprinkle with the thyme or herbs.

Place a clear plastic roasting bag in a roasting tin, and place the fish in it, dressed side up. Close the bag, and make 3–4 slits in the top. Bake in a fairly hot oven, 190°C, Gas 5, for 20 minutes. Slit the bag open, place the fish on a warmed plate, and garnish with chopped gherkin and watercress.

Note If preferred, the fish can be enclosed in foil in the same way as Red Mullet Baked in Foil (p448).

Haddock with Orange

1 helping

2 frozen haddock fillets
fat for greasing
juice of ½ lemon
salt and pepper

a pinch of grated nutmeg
2 × 15ml spoons fresh
 orange juice

Garnish
1 × 5ml spoon grated
 orange rind

Lay the frozen fillets side by side in a lightly greased, shallow foil or ovenproof dish or plate. Sprinkle with the lemon juice, and season lightly with salt, pepper, and nutmeg. Pour the orange juice round them. Cover with a second plate, or with foil. Either steam over a pan of simmering water, or bake in a warm oven, 160°C, Gas 3, for 15–20 minutes. Serve sprinkled with the grated orange rind.

Creamed Fish

1–2 helpings

150g white fish fillet,
 steak or piece
125ml milk or as needed
1 × 15ml spoon butter
 or margarine

2 × 15ml spoons flour
salt and pepper
1 × 5ml spoon chopped
 parsley

Remove any skin and bones from the fish. Wipe it and pat dry. Place in a small saucepan with the milk, and bring to boiling point. Cover, reduce the heat, and simmer gently for 5–8 minutes (depending on the thickness of the fish) or until tender. Strain off the milk, measure it, and make up to 125ml with extra milk, if necessary. Melt the butter or margarine in a small saucepan, stir in the flour, and cook gently for 2–3 minutes. Stir in the milk gradually, and bring to the boil, stirring all the time. Simmer for 3 minutes. Season to taste. Flake the fish, and stir into the sauce with the parsley.

Serve on a slice of toast or with creamed potatoes.

Steamed Fish Pudding

1 helping

75g white fish fillet (eg
 cod, haddock, whiting)
lemon juice
1 × 15ml spoon butter
 or margarine
2 × 15ml spoons flour

75ml milk or as needed
1 egg yolk
2 × 15ml spoons single
 or double cream
salt and pepper
fat for greasing

Garnish
lemon butterfly (p391)

Put the fish into a suitable-sized pan with just enough water to half-cover it; add a few drops of lemon juice. Cover the pan, and poach the fish for 5–7 minutes until tender. Remove the fish but reserve the cooking liquid. Lay the fish on a board, and remove any skin and bones. Pound the flesh, or process in an electric blender, to obtain a smooth paste. Add a very little of the cooking liquid if required. Put to one side.

Melt the fat in a pan, add the flour, and cook for 4 minutes over gentle heat, stirring all the time. Add the milk gradually, or, if preferred, only 50ml milk and 25ml of the fish cooking liquid, stirring all the time, until the mixture thickens smoothly. Remove from the heat, and stir in the fish, egg yolk and cream, blending thoroughly. Season well. Turn the mixture into a greased 250ml heatproof basin. Cover with greased paper or foil, and steam for 45 minutes. Leave it in the basin at room temperature for 4–5 minutes to firm up. To serve, turn out on to a warmed plate and garnish with the lemon butterfly.

VARIATION

Baked Fish Pudding

Prepare the pudding as above, but bake in a warm oven, 160°C, Gas 3, for 45 minutes. Serve from the basin, garnished as above.

Meat, Poultry, and Rabbit Dishes

Beef Jelly

1 helping

1 × 5ml spoon gelatine
2 × 15ml spoons cold
 water

125ml strong beef tea
 (p1339)
salt and pepper

Soften the gelatine in the cold water. Bring the beef tea to simmering point, and pour it on to the softened gelatine; stir until dissolved. Season to taste. Pour into a rinsed individual mould or soup cup, and leave in a cold place to set.

VARIATION

Jellied Egg

Pour only a little of the liquid meat jelly into the mould or soup cup, and chill it until firm. Leave the rest in a warm place to prevent it setting. Put either 1 halved hard-boiled egg or 1 soft-boiled egg in the mould. Fill it up with the remaining jelly, and leave to set.

Beef Tea Custard

See p917.

Wrapped Steak

1 helping

1 × 100g slice braising
 steak, 2cm thick
dry white onion sauce
 mix from pkt for
 sprinkling
1 small carrot

1 stick of celery
1 small potato
1 × 5ml spoon natural
 wheat bran
salt and pepper
1 small tomato

Garnish
parsley sprig

Wipe the steak and trim off any excess fat. Cut a large piece of foil and fold it in half. Place the meat in the centre, and sprinkle well with the sauce mix.

Prepare the carrot, celery and potato. Grate and mix them together; then cover the meat with the mixture. Sprinkle with bran, and season with salt and pepper. Fold the foil over the meat and vegetables to form a sealed parcel and place it in a roasting tin. Bake in a moderate oven, 180°C, Gas 4, for 1¼ hours. Add the tomato to the baking tin for the last 15 minutes of the cooking time. Unwrap the parcel carefully on a warmed plate (the meat makes its own gravy in the parcel). Serve with the tomato and with a parsley sprig on top.

VARIATION

Prepare the foil and the meat slice. Substitute 2 × 15ml spoons finely chopped onion, ½ canned pimento cut into strips, and 2 × 15ml spoons chopped parsley for the sauce mix and root vegetables. Season well. Wrap closely, and cook as above.

Serve with mashed potato instead of tomato.

Simmered Lamb Chop with Vegetables

1 helping

1 lamb chop
125ml general household
 stock (p329) or water
25g onion
salt

1 × 15ml spoon long-
 grain rice or pearl
 barley
75g (approx) frozen
 garden peas or sliced
 green beans

Wipe the chop and trim off most of the fat. Place in a stewpan and add the stock or water. Skin and chop the onion finely and add it to the pan, with salt to taste. Bring to the boil, then cover tightly, reduce the heat, and simmer very gently for 30 minutes. Add the rice or barley, and continue cooking gently for another hour. Fifteen minutes before the end of the hour, add the frozen vegetables and bring to the boil; reduce the heat and continue simmering for the rest of the time.

Serve in a warmed soup plate or bowl, with the rice or barley, vegetables and cooking liquid.

Note This dish may also be cooked in the oven.

Steamed Veal Pudding

2 helpings

50g noodles	*salt and pepper*
150g cold roast veal	*1 egg*
50g ham	*150ml brown stock*
50g dried white	*(p329)* **or** *consommé*
breadcrumbs	*(p335)* **or** *thin gravy*
1 × 2.5ml spoon grated	*(p727)*
lemon rind	*fat for greasing*
a pinch of grated nutmeg	

Cook the noodles in boiling salted water for 10–12 minutes until just tender; drain thoroughly. Meanwhile, remove any skin and gristle from the veal and ham, and mince them finely. Mix together with the breadcrumbs, lemon rind, nutmeg, and salt and pepper. Beat the egg until liquid, and add to the dry ingredients with 2 × 15ml spoons of the stock or other liquid, to bind the mixture.

Arrange some of the noodles in a lattice pattern on the sides and bottom of a greased 275ml heatproof basin. Chop the rest and add to the meat mixture. Press into the basin lightly so that the lattice pattern is not disturbed. Cover the basin with greased paper or foil, and steam the pudding for 40–45 minutes. When the pudding is cooked, leave it to stand at room temperature for 5 minutes; then turn it out on to a warmed plate for serving. While the pudding stands, heat the rest of the stock, consommé or gravy, and serve separately in a warmed jug.

Serve with baked or grilled tomatoes.

Note The pudding can also be made with well-cooked roast beef or lamb. Pork is not suitable.

Liver Mould

1 helping

75g calf's liver	*1 × 5ml spoon*
1 egg	*concentrated tomato*
25g soft white	*purée* **or** *ketchup*
breadcrumbs	*1 × 15ml spoon butter*
1 × 5ml spoon chopped	*salt and pepper*
parsley	*butter for greasing*

Remove the skin and tubes from the liver. Wipe it, then chop or mince it finely. Mix together with the egg, breadcrumbs, parsley, and tomato purée or ketchup. Melt the butter and stir it into the liver mixture. Season to taste. Put into a buttered individual mould or heatproof bowl. Cover with greased paper or foil, and steam for 30 minutes.

Serve with Foundation Brown (p698) or Cucumber Sauce (p705) and with creamed potatoes.

Fricasséed Sweetbreads

1 helping

50g lamb's **or** *calf's*	*a slice of lemon rind*
sweetbreads	*salt and pepper*
1 × 15ml spoon butter	*a pinch of grated nutmeg*
2 × 15ml spoons flour	*1 × 15ml spoon single*
125ml milk	*cream*

Garnish
lemon butterfly (p391)

Prepare the sweetbreads (p553). Put them into a pan and cover with cold water. Bring to the boil, reduce the heat, and simmer gently for 10–15 minutes. Drain off the liquid, and chop the sweetbreads.

Melt the butter in a saucepan, stir in the flour, and cook gently for about 3 minutes. Add the milk and lemon rind, and bring slowly to the boil, stirring all the time. Add the chopped sweetbreads, and season with salt, pepper, and nutmeg. Cover and simmer for 10 minutes. Remove the fricassée from the heat when ready; take out the lemon rind and stir in the cream.

Serve at once on a bed of boiled rice, or a slice of toast, and garnish with the lemon butterfly.

Brains in Parsley Sauce

1 helping

50–75g calf's **or** *lamb's
brains*
salt and pepper
1 × 15ml spoon butter
2 × 15ml spoons flour
100ml milk

*1 × 10ml spoon chopped
parsley*
1 slice of bread
butter

Garnish
a slice of lemon   *a sprig of parsley*

Soak the brains in lightly salted cold water for 30 minutes to remove all traces of blood; then cut off any membranes. Wash thoroughly but very gently. Tie in a small square of muslin, place in a saucepan, cover with cold water, and add a pinch of salt. Bring to the boil, reduce the heat, and simmer gently for 10–15 minutes until tender. Drain the brains, and allow them to cool between two plates with a light weight on top. When cold, remove the muslin and chop the brains finely.

Melt the butter in a saucepan, stir in the flour, and cook gently for 2–3 minutes without colouring. Add the milk gradually, stirring all the time. Bring to the boil, reduce the heat, and cook gently for 2–3 minutes. Add the brains and the parsley, and season to taste with salt and pepper. Remove the crusts from the bread, and toast the bread lightly; then butter it and cut into two pieces. Pile the brains in their sauce on to the hot toast and garnish with the lemon and parsley.

VARIATION

Instead of toasting the bread, cut it into small dice and fry in a little butter until golden.

Baked Fillet of Chicken

1 helping

*1 chicken breast (75g
approx)*
salt and pepper

butter for greasing

Remove any bones from the chicken carefully, keeping the flesh in one piece, if possible. Sprinkle lightly with salt and pepper, and place in a buttered roasting tin. Cover with buttered paper, and bake in a warm oven, 160°C, Gas 3, for 15–20 minutes. Remove from the oven, place on a warmed plate, and slice before serving.

Serve with 50g cooked spinach and 100ml foundation white sauce (p692), if liked.

Coated Chicken

2 helpings

*2 chicken breasts (75g
each approx)*
2 × 15ml spoons corn oil
or *other vegetable oil*
*freshly ground black
pepper*
*25g fine cut orange
marmalade (not jelly
marmalade)*

*1 × 10ml spoon sesame
seeds*
*1 × 15ml spoon natural
wheat bran*

Garnish
*julienne strips of orange
rind* **or** *thin slices of
fresh orange*

watercress sprigs

Wipe the chicken pieces, and dry them well. Brush with oil on both sides, and sprinkle lightly with pepper. Grill under very gentle heat for 15–20 minutes, basting twice with oil. Turn, and grill for a further 15 minutes, basting twice. Remove from the heat, and spread one side of each piece with marmalade. Sprinkle with the sesame seeds and bran. Return to the grill, and cook very gently for 4–5 minutes, taking care that the coating does not burn. Serve hot, garnished with the orange rind or slices, and watercress sprigs.

Chicken and Tomato Mousse

1 helping

1 × 5ml spoon gelatine	*50–75g cooked chicken*
75ml cold chicken stock	*salt and pepper*
1 × 5ml spoon	*1 × 10ml spoon single*
concentrated tomato	*cream (optional)*
purée	*1 egg white*

Garnish
small lettuce leaves	*skinned tomato segments*
chopped hard-boiled egg	*lemon wedge*

Soften the gelatine in 1 × 15ml spoon of the chicken stock. Heat the rest to scalding point, pour it over the gelatine, and stir until the gelatine dissolves. Stir in the tomato purée and leave to cool. Meanwhile, chop the chicken meat and add to the gelatine mixture when tepid; season well. Cool until quite cold but not set. Whip the cream, if used, until semi-stiff, and whisk the egg white until stiff. Fold the cream into the cold chicken mixture; then fold in the whisked egg white lightly but thoroughly. Turn the mixture carefully into an individual serving dish, and leave to set. Serve surrounded by lettuce leaves, with the chopped egg and tomato segments on top. Place the lemon wedge at one side of the dish.

Chicken or Rabbit Charlotte

1 helping

1 large slice of bread	*150ml milk or chicken*
butter	*stock*
50–75g chicken or	*1 egg yolk*
rabbit, finely chopped	*salt and pepper*
or minced (may be	
cooked or raw)	

Garnish
chopped parsley

Remove the crusts, and butter the bread. Cut in half, and put one piece at the bottom of an individual pie dish with the buttered side uppermost. Cover with the chopped or minced meat. Place the second piece of bread and butter on top, buttered side up. Warm the milk or chicken stock. Beat the

egg yolk until liquid, and mix with the warm milk or stock. Season well. Pour into the dish, and stand it in a larger dish of cold water. Bake the cooked meat for 45 minutes, the raw meat for $1\frac{1}{4}$–$1\frac{1}{2}$ hours, in a warm oven, 160°C, Gas 3. Garnish with chopped parsley.

Steamed Chicken or Rabbit Cream

1 helping

75g lightly cooked or	*salt and pepper*
raw chicken or rabbit	*2 × 15ml spoons single*
3 × 15ml spoons milk	*cream or extra milk*
25g butter	*1 egg white*
1 × 10ml spoon soft	*fat for greasing*
white breadcrumbs	

Mince or chop the chicken or rabbit finely. Heat the milk and butter together gently, until the butter melts. Add the breadcrumbs, chicken or rabbit, and seasoning. Stir in the cream or milk. Beat the egg white until stiff, and fold it in. Put into a greased individual mould, and cover with greased paper or foil. Steam for 35 minutes if using cooked meat, or for 50 minutes for raw meat. Place on a warmed plate, and serve with Foundation White (p692) or Fresh Tomato (p715) Sauce.

Mumbled Rabbit or Chicken

2 helpings

2 small rabbit or	*1 hard-boiled egg*
chicken joints	*2 × 15ml spoons butter*
bouquet garni	*salt and pepper*
1 × 5ml spoon anchovy	
essence	

Garnish
chopped parsley

Place the rabbit or chicken joints in a pan of boiling salted water, and simmer with the bouquet garni and anchovy essence for about 40 minutes or until tender. Meanwhile, chop the egg finely. Drain the joints, and discard the bouquet garni. Cut the butter into small pieces. Mix together lightly the rabbit or chicken, chopped egg, butter, and seasoning. Toss briefly over gentle heat to melt the butter, if necessary. Serve garnished with the parsley.

Chicken or Rabbit Fricassée

2 helpings

½ small onion
1 small carrot
3–4 parsley stalks
1 bay leaf
1 whole blade of mace
2 chicken or rabbit
 joints
salt
1 × 15ml spoon butter
 or margarine

2 × 10ml spoons flour
butter for greasing
pepper
a pinch of ground
 allspice
1 egg yolk
1 × 10ml spoon single
 cream
a few drops lemon juice

Garnish
chopped parsley

Prepare the onion and carrot, and tie the parsley stalks, bay leaf, and mace in a small piece of muslin. Put the chicken or rabbit joints in a small stewpan, cover with water, and bring slowly to the boil. Skim well. Add the vegetables and the muslin bag, and season with salt. Simmer gently for 1 hour, or until the joints are tender. Meanwhile, melt the fat in a small pan, stir in the flour, and cook gently for 3 minutes, stirring all the time. Put to one side.

Drain the meat and vegetables, discard the muslin bag, and keep the meat and vegetables warm under buttered paper. Strain the cooking liquid, and reserve 250ml of it. Return the roux to the heat, and gradually stir in the measured liquid. Cook for 3 minutes, stirring all the time. Season to taste with salt, pepper, and allspice. Return the meat and vegetables to the sauce, reduce the heat, and simmer very gently for 5–7 minutes. Beat the egg yolk with the cream, and stir into the sauce. Add a few drops of lemon juice. Continue cooking until thoroughly re-heated, but do not boil. Place in a warmed serving dish, and garnish with the parsley.

Vegetables

Many mildly flavoured, conservatively cooked vegetables are suitable for light meals. Puréed vegetables are particularly valuable for anyone who cannot chew easily, and for very young children.

With a suitable light sauce, and mixed with a protein food such as hard-boiled egg or finely grated or crumbled cheese, green or root vegetables (or a mixture) can make a good main-course dish. Mixed vegetables, including pulses, should be used, if possible. Pulses are rich in protein, and can be used for additional nourishment; soya beans are a good choice, when available.

The recipes below illustrate how small quantities of fresh or processed vegetables and salad onions can be used as the main ingredients in light main-course dishes.

Buttered Carrots

1 helping

500ml water
1 chicken stock cube
a pinch of white sugar
3 small carrots
3 spring onions
1 slice of bread

butter
25g Cheddar cheese
1 × 10ml spoon chopped
 parsley
1 × 10ml spoon butter

Bring the water to the boil in a saucepan, crumble in the stock cube and sugar, then draw off the heat. Prepare the carrots, and cut them into slices 5mm thick. Trim the onions, chop the green parts finely and add to the carrots. Halve and add the bulbs. Return the stock to the heat, add the vegetables, and simmer for 10 minutes; then drain. (Reserve the stock for soup or a drink.) Toast the bread, and butter it. Slice the cheese, and place it on the toast. Pile the vegetables on top, sprinkle with the parsley, and dot with the butter. Serve at once.

Note If liked, the stock can be thickened with about 75g beurre manié, and used as a sauce.

VARIATION
Instead of carrots, use 150–200g cooked swede or turnip cut into 1cm cubes; simmer for 20 minutes.

Mushrooms and Watercress

1 helping

2 large flat mushrooms
25g cottage cheese
1 × 5ml spoon chopped
    watercress
salt and freshly ground
    black pepper
1 slice unpeeled
    cucumber, 1cm thick

1 × 15ml spoon grated
    Emmental cheese
vegetable oil
2 × 15ml spoons
    vegetable stock (p330)
    or thin gravy (p727)

Remove the stalks from the mushrooms. Mix the cheese and watercress and spread on the underside of the caps. Season well. Dice the cucumber, and sprinkle on to the cheese mixture. Re-season lightly. Top with the grated cheese. Place the mushrooms in a small oiled ovenproof or foil dish. Sprinkle lightly with oil, and pour the stock or gravy around the caps. Bake in a warm oven, 160°C, Gas 3, or steam over simmering water, for about 20 minutes, until the mushrooms are tender.

Note This recipe makes two light helpings if served on lightly scrambled egg or boiled chopped spinach.

Steamed Beans with Sage

1 helping

1 × 112g pkt frozen
    sliced green beans
3 large spring onions
salt and pepper
1 × 2.5ml spoon dried
    sage

1 egg
2 × 15ml spoons cottage
    cheese
1 × 15ml spoon grated
    Parmesan cheese
1 × 10ml spoon butter

Use the beans while still frozen. Place them in a steamer. Trim the onions, discard any withered leaves, and chop the fresh green parts over the beans. Quarter the white bulbs and add to the steamer. Season well with salt, pepper, and sage. Cover the steamer.

Bring a saucepan of water to the boil, put in the egg in its shell, and place the steamer on the saucepan. Cook over moderate heat for 10 minutes.

Place the beans on a warmed plate, chop the egg, and mix together. Mix the two cheeses together,

and sprinkle over the beans. Dot with butter and serve at once.

VARIATIONS

1) Shred ¼ small head of firm white cabbage and place in the steamer. Add 1 × 2.5ml spoon caraway seeds, and cook as above, omitting the sage.
2) Instead of chopping the hard-boiled egg, separate the yolk and white. Chop the white, and mix it with the beans. Sieve the yolk over the beans just before serving.

Vegetable Soufflé

2 helpings

1 × 15ml spoon butter
    or margarine
1 × 15ml spoon
    cornflour
½ × 2.5ml spoon salt
a good pinch of pepper

100ml milk
100g finely chopped
    cooked vegetables (see
    Note)
2 large eggs
butter for greasing

Heat the oven to moderate, 180°C, Gas 4. Melt the butter or margarine in a saucepan. Remove from the heat and stir in the cornflour and seasonings; mix until smooth. Stir in the milk slowly to make a smooth mixture. Return to moderate heat, and continue stirring until the mixture comes to the boil and thickens. Remove from the heat and stir in the vegetables. Separate the eggs, and beat the yolks lightly into the vegetable mixture. Whisk the whites until stiff but not dry, and fold them into the mixture. Place in a greased 1 litre soufflé dish, and bake for 1 hour.

Note Use any vegetable or mixture of vegetables which can be chopped or mashed until almost puréed. Spinach or Brussels sprouts mixed with onions, peas or broad beans, Jerusalem artichokes, carrots or turnips are all suitable. Cabbage, kale or celery may have coarse fibres, and should not be used.

Potato Soufflé (2)

2 helpings

225g cold mashed potato
1 × 15ml spoon butter
  or margarine
50ml milk
$\frac{1}{2}$ × 2.5ml spoon salt

a few grains grated
  nutmeg
1 × 5ml spoon chopped
  parsley
2 eggs
butter for greasing

Heat the oven to warm, 160°C, Gas 3. Beat the mashed potato until very smooth; then heat well. With a fork, beat the fat into the potato. Warm the milk, and add it slowly; then mix in the seasonings and parsley. Separate the eggs. Beat the yolks into the potato mixture. Whisk the whites until stiff, and fold lightly into the main mixture. Place in a greased 500ml soufflé dish, and bake for 30 minutes. Serve from the dish.

Note For Potato Soufflé (1), see p923.

Egg and Cheese Dishes

A boiled, baked, poached or scrambled egg can be a good choice for a light meal. Provided fats are not restricted in the diet, cheese also makes a good choice. These recipes show the quantities to use when making certain egg and cheese dishes for one or two people. They are quickly made dishes which can be varied easily by changing a subsidiary ingredient or the flavouring. Many other recipes can be found in the chapters on Dairy Foods and Eggs.

Cardinal Soufflés

2 helpings

100g cottage cheese
a pinch of salt
1 × 5ml spoon flour
1 egg

2 × 5ml spoons tomato
  ketchup
1 × 5ml spoon chopped
  parsley
fat for greasing

Heat the oven to hot, 220°C, Gas 7. Sieve the cheese, and season it with salt. Mix in the flour. Separate the egg, and mix the yolk, ketchup, and parsley

into the cheese. Beat the egg white until stiff. Stir a little of it into the cheese mixture, then fold in the rest. Place the mixture carefully into 2 greased ramekin dishes. Bake for 10–12 minutes until risen and lightly browned. Serve at once.

Cottage Cheese Rarebit

1 helping

1 slice of white bread
25g cottage cheese
1 × 15ml spoon grated
  Edam cheese

salt and pepper
paprika

Remove the crusts, and toast the bread lightly on both sides. Spread it with the cottage cheese, and sprinkle the grated cheese on top. Season with a little salt, pepper, and paprika. Return to a low grill for 2–3 minutes, until the grated cheese bubbles. Serve immediately.

Puddings and Desserts

Almost all milk, light steamed, and similar baked puddings, custards and soufflés are suitable light meals for children, old people or convalescents, as they contain nourishment in the form of eggs, milk or fruit. Suet puddings, and rich puddings containing dried fruit should be avoided. Any jam containing seeds should be sieved before use.

Most light cold desserts are also suitable for light meals. Jellies are a particularly good way of providing the goodness of fruit juices in a palatable, easily eaten form. Cold mousses, although light, may be too rich in cream: a cold custard dish made with milk or skimmed milk powder is more suitable.

The recipes which follow on pp1336–38 show how to reduce the quantities of ingredients to make sweet dishes for one or two helpings if a special dessert is wanted.

Baked Rice Pudding

2 helpings

50g long-grain rice
50g caster sugar
400ml water
7 × 15ml spoons dried
  skimmed milk powder

1 × 15ml spoon butter
a pinch of grated nutmeg
raspberry **or**
  blackcurrant jam

Mix together the rice and sugar. Warm the water until tepid, and mix it gradually into the skimmed milk powder, stirring all the time to prevent lumps forming. Use 1 × 5ml spoon of the butter to grease the inside of a 750ml pie dish. Spread the rice and sugar mixture over the bottom of the dish, and cover with the milk. Dot the remaining butter over the surface, and sprinkle with nutmeg. Bake in a cool oven, 150°C, Gas 2, for 1½ hours. Serve hot with jam.

Note If only one helping is needed, use the remainder as a cold pudding, first removing any skin.

Rice Cream

2 helpings

250ml milk
rind of ½ lemon **or** *a few*
  drops vanilla essence
1 × 10ml spoon sugar

25g long-grain rice
1 × 15ml spoon single
  cream

Heat the milk to scalding point in a double saucepan or a basin over hot water. Add the lemon rind, if used, together with the sugar and rice. Cover, and cook slowly for about 1 hour until the rice is tender. Remove the rind. Beat well, then add the cream and the vanilla essence, if used. Pour into 2 individual dishes.

Serve hot or cold, with redcurrant jelly or fruit purée.

Banana Charlotte

1 helping

1 large banana
50g margarine
2 slices white bread
1 × 113g jar banana
  strained dessert (baby
  food)

1 × 15ml spoon light soft
  brown sugar
ground cinnamon for
  sprinkling

Slice the banana. Melt 25g of the margarine in a frying pan. Add the banana slices and cook gently for 2 minutes, coating each side with fat. Draw off the heat, and push the slices to one side of the pan. Remove the crusts, and cut the bread into 1cm squares. Add the remaining 25g margarine to the pan. Replace on the heat, and fry the bread squares for 3–4 minutes, turning them until brown and crisp on both sides.

Meanwhile, heat the strained banana dessert to simmering point in a small saucepan to make a sauce. Drain any excess fat from the fruit and the bread squares, and mix them in a warmed individual serving dish. Pour the hot sauce over them, sprinkle with sugar and cinnamon, and serve at once.

Plum and Cheese Fool

1 helping

100g cold spiced stewed
  plums (p1337) *and their*
  juice
1 × 5ml spoon gelatine
100g cottage cheese **or**
  unsalted low fat curd
  cheese

1 egg white
a small pinch of salt
caster sugar

Strain the juice from the plums. Put the juice in a small heatproof container, sprinkle the gelatine on it, and leave to soften for 5 minutes. Meanwhile, sieve the fruit into one bowl, and the cheese into another. Whisk the egg white with the salt until just stiff. Stand the container of juice and gelatine in a pan of hot water, and stir until the gelatine dissolves. Pour the mixture into the fruit pulp, stir well, and combine with the cheese, blending lightly but thoroughly. Sweeten to taste with caster sugar. Fold in the whisked egg white. Spoon into a stemmed glass or small glass bowl, and leave to set.

VARIATION

Use the above method for making any other fruit and cheese fool, with 100g fruit pulp and 50–75ml juice. Apricots, gooseberries, peaches, raspberries or strawberries are all suitable, but not pears.

Spiced Stewed Plums

2 helpings

200g ripe plums	*a small pinch of ground*
125ml fresh orange juice	*ginger*
or *bottled natural*	*light soft brown sugar*
orange juice	*single cream (optional)*
a good pinch of ground	
mixed spice	

Place the fruit in a bowl, and pour over the juice. Leave for several hours, or overnight.

Next day, place the fruit in a saucepan, and simmer, uncovered, for 10–15 minutes until soft. The juice should be nearly as thick as a pouring sauce. Add the spices, and sweeten to taste. Pour into a strainer set over a basin, and cover lightly. Leave to cool, then remove the plum stones. Spoon the fruit into 2 bowls with enough juice to moisten each portion well. Top with a trickle of cream, if liked. Serve cold, but not chilled.

Note This method of stewing is suitable for small portions of hard and other stone fruit.

Any leftover juice may be kept for a fruit syrup, milk shake, or for making a jelly.

Prune Whip

1–2 helpings

100g cooked prunes	*1 × 15ml spoon caster*
1 × 15ml spoon lemon	*sugar*
juice	*1 egg white*

Stone the prunes and sieve into a basin. Add the lemon juice, sugar, and egg white. Whisk together until light and fluffy. Pile into 2 individual serving dishes and chill for about 30 minutes before serving.

Fruit Fluff

1–2 helpings

150ml thick fruit purée	*sugar*
(p1002) (eg apples,	*1 egg white*
blackcurrants,	
raspberries,	
strawberries **or**	
blackberries)	

Decoration

whipped cream	*whole fruit*
(optional)	

Sieve the purée if it contains seeds, and add sugar to taste. Whisk the egg white until stiff, and fold it in. Pile into one or two individual glasses, and decorate with whipped cream, if used, and with whole fruit.

Jellied Fruit Mousse

1–2 helpings

200ml thick fruit purée	*sugar*
(p1002) (eg apple,	*1 × 5ml spoon gelatine*
apricot, raspberry,	*2 × 15ml spoons fruit*
blackcurrant **or**	*juice* **or** *water*
rhubarb)	*1 egg white*

Decoration
glacé cherries and
angelica **or** *fresh fruit*

Sieve the purée if it contains seeds, and add sugar to taste. Soften the gelatine in the fruit juice or water in a heatproof container. Stand the container in a pan of hot water and stir until the gelatine dissolves. Stir into the fruit purée and leave to cool. Just before setting point is reached, whisk the egg white until stiff. Fold it into the fruit purée. Spoon the mixture carefully into a serving bowl, and decorate with the cherries and angelica, or with fresh fruit.

Individual Trifle

(light)

1 helping

1 individual sponge cake	*2 × 15ml spoons thick*
1 × 10ml spoon	*fruit purée (p1002)*
redcurrant jelly	*125ml warm thick*
	custard (p965)

Decoration
whipped cream

Cut the sponge cake in half and spread with the jelly. Put into a dish and cover with the fruit purée. Pour the custard over it. Cover with damp grease-proof paper to prevent a skin forming. Leave to set for about 30 minutes. Decorate with a little cream.

Eve's Spanish Cream

1 helping

3 × 2.5ml spoons	*5 drops vanilla essence*
gelatine	*a small pinch of ground*
125ml milk	*cinnamon **or** sugar*
1 egg	*(optional)*
1 × 15ml spoon caster	*single cream (optional)*
sugar	

Soften the gelatine in the milk in a heatproof container. Stand the container in a pan of hot water and stir until the gelatine dissolves. Separate the egg. Beat the yolk with the sugar until liquid, and pour it into the milk and gelatine; stir well. Whisk the egg white until stiff. Pour the milk mixture into a small pan, and heat very gently to boiling point, stirring all the time. Remove from the heat when just at boiling point. Add the essence and fold in the whisked egg white. Spoon gently into a small glass bowl and leave to set. Serve sprinkled with cinnamon or sugar and single cream, if liked.

Fresh Lemon Jelly

See p1009.

Milk Jelly

See p1009.

Amber Jelly (2)

2 helpings

1 lemon	*2 × 15ml spoons dry*
125ml water	*sherry **or** 3 × 15ml*
50g sugar	*spoons medium dry*
1 × 10ml spoon gelatine	*white wine*
1 egg	

Pare off a strip of rind and squeeze the juice from the lemon. Put the rind, juice, water and sugar into a saucepan, and heat until the sugar has dissolved. Remove from the heat and allow to cool until tepid. Sprinkle on the gelatine and stir until dissolved. Beat together the egg and sherry or wine. Whisk the liquid jelly into the egg mixture, strain through muslin into individual dishes, and chill for about 1 hour until set.

Note For Amber Jelly (1), see p1010.

Port Wine Jelly (3)

2 helpings

50ml water	*1 × 15ml spoon cold*
1 × 5ml spoon	*water*
redcurrant jelly	*1 × 15ml spoon gelatine*
1 × 10ml spoon sugar	*50ml port*

Put the water, redcurrant jelly and sugar into a saucepan, and heat until the sugar has dissolved; remove from the heat. Soften the gelatine in the cold water. Stand the container in a pan of hot water and stir until the gelatine dissolves. Add to the saucepan. Add the port and stir well. Pour into individual glasses and allow to set.

Note For other port wine jellies, see p1010 and p1014.

Blackcurrant Jelly

See p1008.

Egg Jelly

See p1011.

Beverages

Beef Tea

2 helpings

*400g shin, flank **or** skirt*   *500ml water*
of beef   *1 × 2.5ml spoon salt*

Wipe the meat and trim off all visible fat; cut into 2cm cubes. Put the meat into an ovenproof casserole or basin, and add the water and salt. Cover the container with a saucer or lid, and cook in a very cool oven, 140°C, Gas 1, for 3 hours.

Strain the liquid through muslin or a fine sieve, and allow to cool. Skim any fat from the top. Reheat, without boiling, and serve as a light soup or beverage, with toast or dry biscuits.

VARIATION

To the basic ingredients, add the following thinly sliced vegetables: 1 small carrot, ⅓ small turnip, and 1 small onion. Add them to the meat and water, with a few sprigs of parsley and 2 bay leaves, and continue cooking as in the basic recipe.

Note Beef tea can be stored in a refrigerator for 2 days. If this is not possible, it must be freshly made each time it is wanted.

Sparkling Mint Tea

2 helpings

2 × 5ml spoons tea   *6 mint leaves*
leaves   *150ml soda water*
300ml boiling water   *ice cubes*
40g caster sugar   *2 slices lemon*

Put the tea leaves into a heatproof jug and add the boiling water. Infuse for 3 minutes. Strain into a clean jug, and stir in the sugar and 2 mint leaves. Cool. Stir in the soda water, and pour into 2 tall glasses. Add ice cubes, a lemon slice and 2 mint leaves per glass. Stir, and serve at once.

Barley Water

See p1349.

Honey and Lemon Drink

1 helping

2 × 10ml spoons clear   *boiling water*
honey   *1 × 2.5ml spoon*
juice of 1 large lemon   *glycerine (optional)*

Mix the honey with the lemon juice in a heatproof mug or glass. Stir in the boiling water and the glycerine, if used. Serve hot or warm.

Blackcurrant Tea

1 helping

2 × 15ml spoons   *1 × 15ml spoon caster*
blackcurrant jam   *sugar **or** to taste*
juice of 1 small lemon   *250ml boiling water*

Mix together all the ingredients in a heatproof jug. Leave in a warm place for 10 minutes, strain, and serve hot or cold.

Switched Egg

2 helpings

1 × 10ml spoon clear   *250ml chilled milk*
*honey **or** to taste*   *a few drops vanilla*
2 eggs   *essence*

Warm the honey so that it flows freely. Whisk the eggs lightly, then whisk in the honey. Mix in the chilled milk, and add the vanilla essence. Strain the mixture into 2 glasses.

Note A switched egg is a quick pick-me-up, or an ideal early morning drink for anyone who does not feel inclined to have solid food.

VARIATIONS

1) To serve hot, warm the honey and milk until just steaming. Remove from the heat, and whisk into the well-beaten eggs. Serve in a heatproof beaker or glass.
2) Sweeten with sugar and flavour with blackcurrant juice, instant coffee or drinking chocolate, if preferred.

BEVERAGES

The beverage called tea has now become a necessary of life. Previous to
the middle of the 17th century it was not used in England, and it was wholly
unknown to the Greeks and Romans. Pepys says, in his Diary,—" September 25th,
1661.—I sent for a cup of tea (a China drink) of which I had never drunk before."

Besides tea, coffee, and chocolate, beverages include other drinks such as milk shakes and fruit drinks.

Tea, coffee, and chocolate have been drunk in Europe for three centuries and have played an important part in the development of Western social life. A good many people in the UK have an early morning cup of tea even before they get up, and at breakfast most Western people drink tea, coffee or hot chocolate. A mid-morning break at work is generally referred to as a 'tea-break' or 'coffee break', even if neither is drunk; and, in the English-speaking world, the dainty sandwiches, cakes, and tea taken in the late afternoon are simply called tea. Throughout Europe and the Middle East, coffee is generally served after both the mid-day and evening meal. Lastly, a cup of tea, mug of cocoa, or a similar beverage is a popular bedtime drink.

One reason why tea, coffee, and cocoa are popular is that they are mild stimulants because they all contain caffeine. Tea or coffee without milk and sugar are also minus kilojoules.

Among other beverages, milk shakes and hot milky drinks are often enjoyed by children who will not drink milk on its own, and are one way of persuading them to drink the milk they need. Fruit or vegetable drinks made with fresh ingredients not only taste refreshing, but are a valuable source of vitamin C.

Cocoa, Chocolate, and Malted Drinks

The Aztec Indians of South America prized cocoa beans so highly that they made them a form of currency. The beans were originally brought to Europe by the Spanish. However, most of our cocoa nowadays comes from Central and West Africa.

Unsweetened cocoa powder has, to quite a large extent, been replaced as a beverage by drinking chocolate and malted drinks, as these are easier to prepare and, in many cases, have a richer flavour. Plain cocoa powder is still used a great deal, however, for baking and for chocolate-based desserts. Instructions on making and serving drinking chocolate are always given on the cans or packets containing these drinks. As a rule, 2–3 × 5ml spoons per cup is recommended for a drink of average strength. Many of the malted and chocolate drinks, which are particularly suitable as 'nightcaps', are fortified with vitamins to give them extra nutritional value.

If using cocoa as a beverage, however, only about 1 × 5ml spoon per cup is generally required. Cocoa does not dissolve readily so it must be mixed to a smooth paste with a little liquid first, and it is important to make it up with boiling water, or milk and water, to cook the starch in it, or the drink will taste bitter and unpleasant.

All these drinks can be made richer by adding single cream, or they can be topped with a swirl of whipped double cream or a spoonful of ice cream.

Hot Cocoa with Rum

2–3 helpings

500ml milk
1 × 2.5ml spoon vanilla essence
a pinch of salt
35g cocoa powder
25g caster sugar

a pinch of ground cinnamon (optional)
1 × 15ml spoon dark rum
4 × 15ml spoons double cream (optional)

Mix together in a saucepan the milk, vanilla essence, and salt. In a bowl, mix the cocoa, sugar, and cinnamon if used. Add just enough of the milk mixture to make the dry ingredients into a smooth paste. Stir into the main milk mixture. Heat gently, stirring all the time, until just on the boil. Stir in the rum. Pour into warmed glasses or mugs and serve topped with double cream, if liked.

Mocha Chocolate

4 helpings

1½ × 15ml spoons instant coffee powder
1 × 15ml spoon drinking chocolate powder
a few grains of salt

500ml milk
250ml water
4 × 15ml spoons grated chocolate

Mix together the instant coffee, drinking chocolate, and salt. Add a little milk and mix the powders to a smooth paste. Put the remaining milk and the water into a small saucepan, and stir in the paste. Heat to just below boiling point. Pour into warmed glasses or mugs, and sprinkle the grated chocolate on top before serving.

Coffee

The origins of coffee drinking are lost in legend, but one thing is certain, once coffee was brought to England in the early seventeenth century, it quickly became the most fashionable drink. Coffee houses were set up all over London and other large towns, and their influence on both the social and business life of their clientele was immense. The most famous coffee house of them all was the one kept by Edward Lloyd in London's Lombard Street, where the shippers and their insurers used to meet; from this humble beginning developed the biggest insurance institution in the world, Lloyds of London.

Although coffee was originally imported into Britain from Arabia and the Far East, the largest single supplier to the UK today is Brazil, followed by various areas in Africa and other parts of Southern and Central America. The bush is beautiful, with white flowers and long sprays of small red fruit which look like small cherries; when crushed, they open to produce two round coffee beans. The fruit is only harvested once a year, and the crop can vary enormously from year to year. This has a considerable effect on the price of coffee, although it is often not felt on the retail market until 18 months to 2 years later.

TYPES OF COFFEE

Ground Coffee

It is only after coffee beans have been roasted that they develop their unique flavour. Although the type of coffee plant and where it is grown are the major influences on its flavour, the way in which it is roasted and then ground are also extremely important. It can be roasted lightly, to medium strength, to a full roast, or to a double roast which makes a strong and bitter coffee suitable for drinking after dinner. The grind can vary from coarse to a very fine powder, depending on how it is to be made; use finely ground coffee for the filter method, and a slightly coarser one for the vacuum and percolator methods (see p1343).

Ideally, coffee beans should be ground and made into coffee immediately after roasting, but obviously this is not always practical. It is, however, essential to use freshly ground beans to obtain a first-class cup of coffee.

Much of the coffee now available is sold ready-ground, and if you do not have a good coffee mill or grinder, this is obviously the most practical way to buy it. Once coffee has been ground, it is important that it is kept in an airtight container, and it should be used as soon as possible once any airtight seal has been broken.

If coffee is sold with additives, eg chicory, figs, etc, these must be listed on the tin; the coffee cannot then be deemed *pure*.

Instant Coffee

Instant coffee is made from a very strong solution of coffee, from which the liquid is then evaporated, leaving a residue of either powder or granules for use. Freeze-dried coffee is, however, made in a slightly different way: strong coffee is first frozen, the liquid is evaporated, and then the resulting block is ground into fairly large granules of soluble coffee, giving a flavour superior to that of ordinary instant coffee. Like ground coffee, additives are sometimes included also.

Coffee Bags

Ground coffee is sometimes sold in small bags like tea bags. Store them in an airtight container so that the bags do not lose their flavour.

Coffee Essence

Coffee essence is a concentrated coffee and chicory extract, sometimes called liquid coffee. It is made from the residual thick liquid left after removing water from infused coffee.

Decaffeinated Coffee

Normally, coffee contains twice as much caffeine as tea. Various brands without caffeine are also available, however. They are of value to people who find caffeine over stimulates them and prevents them from sleeping.

HOW TO MAKE GOOD COFFEE

Quantities

For roasted, ground coffee of average strength, use about $2 \times 15ml$ heaped spoons of coffee per 500ml water, depending on the flavour of the beans, the fineness of the grind, and the method used to make the drink. Use slightly less Brazilian or Jamaican coffee than Kenyan.

When using instant coffee or coffee essence, use $1 \times 5ml$ spoon per cup. Use 1 coffee bag per cup.

Instant Coffee and Coffee Essence

Measure the required amount of instant coffee or coffee essence into individual cups, or a jug or pot. Pour on freshly boiling water, stir well until dissolved and serve at once with milk or cream and sugar to taste.

Coffee Bags

Place the bag in a cup. Pour boiling water over it and leave to steep for 5 minutes, stirring two or three times to extract the maximum flavour.

Jug Method

Warm the jug and add the required amount of medium-ground coffee. Pour on freshly boiling water. Stir and leave to stand for a few minutes; then skim the surface with a spoon to remove any floating grounds. Leave for another minute and pour into cups through a strainer.

Saucepan Method

Heat the measured quantity of medium-ground coffee and water in a saucepan and bring almost to boiling point. Remove from the heat and stir; then cover and leave to stand for a few minutes. Strain into a warm jug and serve at once.

Filter Method

Place a filter paper in a small conical strainer unless the coffee pot has a built-in filter. Warm the jug and measure finely ground coffee into the filter which is placed on top of the jug. Pour on freshly boiling water and allow the water to drip through the coffee and filter into the jug below; do not pour too much water into the filter at once. Electric filter systems often have automatic timing devices. Follow the manufacturer's instructions.

Percolator Method

Most percolators are sold with manufacturers' instructions for use. In general, add the required amount of water to the percolator, measure medium-ground coffee into the special container (the basket), insert into the percolator and put on the lid. Heat and percolate for 6–8 minutes only; then remove the coffee grounds in their container, and serve. Like the filter method, electric percolators may have automatic timing devices.

Vacuum Method

These appliances have a lower glass bowl in which water is heated, and an upper bowl in which fine-ground coffee is placed. When the water in the lower bowl comes to boiling point, it rises up into the upper bowl. Stir and leave on a low heat for 2–3 minutes; then remove from the heat and the coffee will filter back into the lower bowl. Remove the upper bowl and serve the coffee.

Espresso Method

Water is added to the lower container of a vacuum-type coffee maker; high roast, fine-ground coffee is measured into a basket, and the upper container, with the basket, is screwed into the lower container. When heated, the water rises under pressure and is forced through the coffee; this extracts more flavour than the other methods. When all the water has risen into the upper container, it is removed from the heat and the coffee served.

SERVING COFFEE

Milk can be served with coffee, either hot or cold. If heated, be careful not to let it boil as it will then spoil the flavour of the coffee. If serving coffee with cream, use single or whipping cream, or top of the milk.

Irish Coffee

1 helping

6 × 5ml spoons Irish
  whiskey
1 × 5ml spoon brown
  sugar
125ml hot strong black
  coffee

2 × 10ml spoons double
  cream

Warm a 200ml glass, pour in the whiskey and add the brown sugar. Top up to within 2cm of the rim with hot, strong, black coffee and stir to dissolve the sugar. Pour the cream slowly into the glass over the back of a rounded spoon held close to the surface, so that it floats on the top of the coffee. Do not stir after the cream has been added. Serve at once.

Note For the best result, the cream should be very lightly whipped.

VARIATIONS

Liqueurs such as Tia Maria, Kahlua, or Crème de Caçao can be used in place of the whiskey. If vodka is used, it is called Coffee Balalaika.

Coffee with Rum
(Café au Rhum)

1 helping

4 × 5ml spoons white
  rum
1 × 15ml spoon soft dark
  brown sugar **or**
  Demerara sugar

150ml hot strong black
  coffee
1 slice of lemon

Make as for Irish Coffee, but omit the cream and serve with a slice of lemon.

Café Brûlé

6 helpings

50g brown sugar
250ml brandy
6 whole cloves
pared rind of ½ lemon
pared rind of 1 orange

5cm cinnamon stick
1 × 5ml spoon vanilla
  essence
500ml hot black coffee

Put the sugar, brandy, cloves, lemon and orange rind, cinnamon stick, and vanilla essence in a pan and heat gently until it is almost boiling. Add the hot coffee and ignite. When the flames have died down, strain the coffee into 6 cups.

St Clement's Coffee

Put a thin strip of finely pared orange rind and lemon rind into the bottom of a cup. Pour hot black coffee over them and sweeten to taste.

Turkish Coffee

4 helpings

400ml cold water
4 × 10ml spoons very
  finely ground coffee

4 × 10ml spoons caster
  sugar

Turkish coffee must be made with coffee specially ground to a very fine powder; it can be bought from specialist coffee shops. It cannot be made with ordinary ground coffee. It is also more heavily sweetened than ordinary coffee.

Put the water into a saucepan or Turkish coffee pot, and bring to the boil. Add the coffee and sugar and bring back to the boil. Remove from the heat, and tap the base of the saucepan or pot with a metal spoon until the froth subsides. Replace over the heat and bring back to the boil. Repeat this process 3 times in all. After the last boiling, remove from the heat, spoon some of the creamy froth into 4 small coffee cups, and then pour the coffee slowly out of the pan into the cups.

Note Cardamom seeds and other spices are sometimes added to the coffee as it boils and, in the Middle East especially, it is sometimes perfumed.

Iced Coffee (1)

4–6 helpings

250ml strong black
  coffee
50g sugar
500ml milk
a few drops vanilla
  essence

125ml single cream
ice cubes
4 × 15ml spoons ice
  cream (optional)

Mix the coffee with the sugar and stir until it has dissolved. Add the milk and vanilla essence. Chill thoroughly, and stir in the cream. Fill 4–6 large glasses a quarter full with ice cubes, pour the coffee over them, and top with a spoonful of ice cream, if liked.

Iced Coffee (2)

4–6 helpings

3 × 15ml spoons coffee
  essence
750ml chilled milk

100ml double cream
$\frac{1}{2}$ × 2.5ml spoon ground
  cinnamon

Blend the coffee essence into the milk and pour into 4–6 large glasses. Whip the cream lightly, top each glass with a spoonful of cream, and sprinkle with the cinnamon.

Tea

Tea was first imported into England in the seventeenth century, a few years after chocolate and coffee. At first, it was more expensive than either, and only the very wealthy could afford it. However, for them, it became socially important when Charles II's court took it up. Soon tea shops were established as meeting-places for ladies (like coffee houses for men). Tea-drinking became a ritual, with special small cups, a tea-urn or pot, and a sugar-bowl; and it soon became an accepted social routine after dinner.

Tea-gardens were set up in places like the Vauxhall Pleasure Gardens in London, and these were patronized by everyone, not just the wealthy. Tea became cheaper, and more and more popular.

By the mid-eighteenth century, it had become by far the most popular drink in the UK, which, to a large extent, it still is.

There are several hundred varieties of tea bush, and the climate and soil in which they grow have a marked effect on the type of tea they produce. Most of the tea drunk in Britain is grown in India, but Sri Lanka, China, Japan, Kenya, and several other East African countries are also big tea producers.

TYPES OF TEA

There are three basic types of tea; black or fermented tea, green or unfermented tea, and oolong or semi-fermented tea. The most common teas are black teas; some of the best known are Assam and Darjeeling tea from India, Nuwara Eliya tea from Sri Lanka, and Lapsang Suchong from China.

India does produce some green teas although China and Japan are generally thought of as the major producers. For green teas, the leaf is picked without its stalk, and is steamed instead of being allowed to wither and ferment naturally.

Oolong teas are not very common. They are a type between black and green teas in which the tea leaf is allowed to wither slightly before being processed, so that they are slightly fermented.

The Blending of Teas

As the flavour of tea varies so much with the climatic conditions, it is not always possible to produce identical teas from the same estate two years running. Teas are therefore blended to produce, as nearly as is possible, the same flavour in a particular brand each year; and it is not unusual to use 25 types or grades of tea to make a particular flavour or brand of tea.

Tea Bags and Instant Tea

Like coffee, tea is available in small bags and in powdered form. Tea bags are an extremely popular form of packaging for tea because they save one having to dispose of messy, loose tea leaves.

Herbal Teas or Tisanes

The medicinal properties of herbal teas or tisanes have been valued for hundreds of years, and many modern doctors accept their healing properties. Angelica tea is a well known digestive tonic, hyssop tea is helpful for coughs and persistant catarrh, and lemon balm tea is a general pick-me-up (as well as being supposed to prolong life).

HOW TO MAKE GOOD TEA

Quantities

Allow 1 × 5ml spoon per person and 1 extra, ie for 2 people, allow 3 × 5ml spoons and for 4 people, allow 5 × 5ml spoons. If using tea bags in a pot, allow 1 per person and 1 extra. For instant tea, use 1 × 5ml spoon per cup.

Leaf Tea

First bring the water to the boil; just before it boils, pour a little water into the pot to warm it, rinse out, and throw away. Put the required quantity of tea in the pot. When the water boils, pour it over the tea. It is essential that the water is boiling up to the moment it is poured over the tea, or the flavour of the tea will be spoiled and there will be small tea leaves floating on top. Stir the tea once, then leave to infuse for 5 minutes; stir once more, then strain into cups. If milk is used, it can be added to the cups before the tea or afterwards.

Tea Bags and Instant Tea

If using tea bags, make as above, remembering to stir the tea before serving to extract the maximum flavour. It is not necessary to use a strainer.

Use instant tea according to directions on packet.

Herbal Teas or Tisanes

Make tisanes in exactly the same way as ordinary tea, and leave to infuse for 5–10 minutes. If using dried herbs, allow, as a general rule, 1 × 5ml spoon per person and 1 extra, but when using fresh herbs, allow 3 × 5ml spoons and 1 extra. Fresh herbs should be bruised before being put in the pot to extract the maximum flavour.

Tea Liquor for Punches

Cold tea is the basis of a number of excellent drinks, as well as being used for soaking dried fruit and in fruit cakes. Strong Indian tea without milk or sugar is normally used; strain while hot and leave to cool in a covered container. It can be filtered to improve its clarity. For a perfectly clear liquid put 25g dry tea into a bowl with 500ml cold water. Leave to soak overnight, and then strain off the liquid.

Iced Tea Punch
See p1367.

SERVING TEA

In Western countries, tea is either drunk with milk, often with sugar added, or without milk but with a slice of fresh lemon in the cup. Generally, Indian teas are served with milk, while Chinese, Japanese, and other green teas which have a less strong flavour and are usually pleasantly scented, are served plain or with lemon. These light, scented teas are delicious at the end of a meal.

In China and Japan, tea is served in small bowls or cups without handles, and is drunk throughout the meal.

In Russia, the tea is made in a samovar and is then poured into a glass with a slice of lemon and, sometimes, a spoonful of jam.

Spiced Lemon Tea

3 helpings

6 cloves	*750ml freshly made*
6 slices lemon	*China* **or** *weak Indian*
1 cinnamon stick	*tea*
	sugar

Stick 2 cloves into three of the slices of lemon. Put

in a jug with the cinnamon stick. Add the freshly made tea, and sugar to taste. Infuse for 3–4 minutes. Strain into glasses and add a fresh slice of lemon to each.

Orange Tea

1 helping

cracked ice
125ml cold tea liquor
  (p1346)

juice of 1 orange
lemonade

Decoration
1 slice of orange

Put the cracked ice into a glass. Pour in the tea and orange juice, and top up with lemonade. Decorate the glass with a slice of orange.

Peppermint Tea

4–6 helpings

1 litre freshly made
  weak Indian tea
a dash of peppermint
  essence

1 × 15ml spoon caster
  sugar
cracked ice

Decoration
fresh mint leaves

Mix together the tea, peppermint essence, and sugar. Chill well. Pour over cracked ice in tall glasses and serve decorated with mint leaves.

Scotch Mist

2 helpings

100ml hot medium-
  strength Indian tea
75ml whisky

1 × 15ml spoon clear
  honey
1 × 15ml spoon double
  cream

Put the tea, whisky, and honey into a pan, and heat gently until very hot but not boiling. Pour into 2 small cups; then pour in the cream carefully, over a rounded spoon held just above the surface of the hot tea. Serve at once.

Milk Shakes and Other Milk Drinks

Milk shakes can be made quite simply using milk, ice cream, and flavouring.

Home-made fruit syrups (pp1135–38) make an excellent flavouring. There are, however, a number of proprietary brands of powder and syrup for making milk shakes which flavour and sweeten milk quickly and easily. They are useful when children make milk shakes for themselves. Follow the instructions on the packet or bottle, and make sure that the powder or syrup is thoroughly mixed into the milk, which should be well chilled. Processing in an electric blender produces a pleasant frothy effect. For a semi-frozen milk shake, cracked ice can be added; or, for extra nourishment, it can be topped with a spoonful of whipped cream.

Similar milk drinks can also be enriched with eggs. If brandy is added, milk can also make a stimulating hot beverage, (see p1348).

Milk Shake

Basic recipe

2 helpings

500ml milk
2 × 10ml spoons
  concentrated fruit juice
  or fruit syrup

2 scoops ice cream,
  suited to the fruit
  flavour used

Either simply stir the fruit flavouring into the milk, chill, and add the ice cream just before serving; or, mix all the ingredients together and chill well. Then just before serving, whisk thoroughly, or process briefly in an electric blender. Serve while still frothy.

VARIATIONS
Coffee Milk Shake

Substitute 1 × 10ml spoon coffee essence for the fruit flavouring. Use vanilla, chocolate or coffee ice cream.

Ginger Milk Shake

Use ginger syrup from a jar of stem ginger instead of fruit juice. Add 1 × 5ml spoon finely chopped stem ginger to the other ingredients when mixing.

Banana Milk Shake

1 helping

1 banana　　　　　　*1 × 5ml spoon honey*
250ml milk　　　　　 *a pinch of grated*
4 ice cubes　　　　　　*nutmeg*

Peel the banana and chop it roughly. Process in an electric blender for 1 minute with the milk, ice cubes, and honey. Pour into a glass, and sprinkle with the nutmeg before serving.

Ice Cream Soda

Basic recipe

4–6 helpings

200ml fresh fruit purée　　*150g ice cream, suited to*
*　(p1002)*　　　　　　　　*　the fruit flavour used*
150ml milk　　　　　　　*250ml soda water*
*50g caster sugar **or** to*
*　taste (depending on the*
*　sweetness of the fruit)*

Process the fruit purée, milk, and sugar in an electric blender at medium speed until smooth. Add the ice cream and blend for a further 30 seconds. Pour into 4–6 glasses, and top up with the soda water.

Note Use a well-flavoured fruit purée.

Egg Nog

1 helping

1 egg　　　　　　　　*1 × 2.5ml spoon vanilla*
1 × 15ml spoon sugar　*　essence*
150ml milk　　　　　　*a pinch of grated nutmeg*

Beat the egg and sugar together until frothy. Whisk in the milk and vanilla essence. Pour into a glass and sprinkle with the nutmeg before serving.

Hot Brandied Milk

2 helpings

250ml milk　　　　　　*a pinch of ground*
2 × 15ml spoons brandy　*　cinnamon*

Bring the milk almost to boiling point in a small pan. Add the brandy, remove from the heat, and whisk until the mixture is frothy. Pour into 2 mugs and sprinkle with the cinnamon before serving.

Fruit and Vegetable Drinks

With modern appliances, garden and orchard produce can easily be made into fresh fruit and vegetable juices. Firm, ripe fruit with surface blemishes, and surplus vegetables can be used. Home-made fruit juices can be bottled (see pp1135–38) or frozen (see p1394) and have both excellent food value and good flavour. They are especially useful in winter when there is a smaller variety of fresh fruit.

There are also a great many different types of commercial fruit drinks available, of which fruit juice is the purest form. It can be bought canned, bottled, deep-frozen, or pasteurized in cardboard containers. The most common fruit juices are grapefruit, orange, apple, pineapple, and tomato, but combinations of apricot and orange, for example, are also available and some more exotic juices such as passion-fruit. Vegetable juices are also popular. Always carefully follow the manufacturers' instructions concerning storage, since the keeping qualities of juices vary.

Fruit squashes are generally made from only a

small amount of fruit juice, with flavouring added in the form of essence, often made from the skins. These do not have much nutritional value, although some now have added vitamin C.

Fruit syrups are not as popular in the UK as on the Continent where they are used much more than squashes. The two most common fruit syrups used in the UK are rose-hip and blackcurrant; they are often used when feeding infants and young children because of their high vitamin C content.

Other popular drinks include fruit-flavoured soft drinks, carbonated drinks such as tonic water, ginger ale, bitter lemon, and cola. Generally these have little nutritional value, although tonic water contains quinine and some fruit-flavoured drinks have added vitamin C. Many people now make their own soda water, and it is possible to buy concentrates of many of these other drinks.

Vegetable Cocktail

See p1421.

Bottled Tomato Juice

See p1134.

Lemonade

1 large or 2 small helpings

pared rind and juice of   *250ml water*
  1 large lemon
1 × 5ml spoon white
  sugar

Put the lemon rind and juice in a jug with the sugar. Bring the water to the boil, pour into the jug and stir well. Cover and leave until quite cold; then strain and use.

VARIATION

Orangeade

Use 1 large orange instead of the lemon; if the orange is very sweet the sugar can be omitted, otherwise sweeten to taste.

Orange Squash

Makes 1 litre (approx)

4–5 large oranges   *2 segments fresh lemon*
450g sugar   *1 Campden tablet*
450ml water

Grate the rind of 3 oranges finely and put in a saucepan with the sugar, water, and lemon segments. Heat gently, stirring occasionally to dissolve the sugar. Squeeze the juice from the oranges and make up to 300ml with extra juice if necessary. Add the orange juice to the sugar and water, stir, and strain into a clean jug. Discard the lemon segments. Cool. Pour into a bottle, add the Campden tablet, seal tightly, label, and store as for fruit syrup (see pp1135–36).

To serve, dilute to taste with water or soda water.

VARIATIONS

Lemon, lime or grapefruit squash can be made following the instructions above. Use about 8 lemons, 6–8 limes, or 4–5 grapefruit.

Barley Water

3–4 helpings

50g pearl barley   *1 × 5ml spoon lemon*
2–3 lumps sugar   *juice (optional)*
a small pinch of salt *500ml boiling water*
grated rind of 1 small
  lemon

Put the pearl barley in a saucepan and cover with water. Bring to the boil and boil for 2 minutes. Strain. Add the sugar, salt, lemon rind, juice and boiling water to the barley, and pour into a jug. Cover and leave until cold. Strain before using.

Note This makes a nutritious drink. If made without lemon juice, it can also be used to dilute milk.

TABLE WINES AND OTHER DRINKS

In opening wine, let it be done quietly, and without shaking the bottle; if crusted, let it be inclined to the crusted side, and decanted while in that position. In opening champagne, it is not necessary to discharge it with a pop; properly cooled, the cork is easily extracted without an explosion; when the cork is out, the mouth of the bottle should be wiped with the napkin over the footman's arm.

Wines in General

Every cook should have some knowledge of wine: how and where it is made, how to choose, store and serve it, as well as how to use it in cooking.

Wine is produced by the natural fermentation of the sugar in ripe grapes. Alcohol and a number of other chemical substances which give the wine its flavour are produced during this process of fermentation.

Alcoholic beverages familiarly termed 'Wine' can also be made from most other fruits, although, as a rule, extra sugar needs to be added.

HOW THE VINE IS GROWN

The vine will grow successfully between the latitudes 30°–50° North and South. This includes most of Europe, from the Mediterranean to north of the English Channel. Outside Europe, the vine is grown extensively in North and South America, Australia, South Africa, the coast of North Africa, and in the Middle East.

For the production of good-quality wines, the vine is grafted on to a disease-resistant root-stock. In Europe, the vine is severely pruned in the spring (for quantity is inversely proportional to quality). In April, the leaves burst forth and, in May or June, the vine flowers give a heady and unmistakeable scent in the vineyard. The flowers will then set into hard, small, green fruit which will grow and ripen to white or black grapes in the summer sun. Harvesting of the ripe grapes traditionally begins 100 days after the flowering, in late September or early October.

Grape Varieties

A large number of vine varieties are grown, each of which is carefully chosen to suit the particular site, soil and weather in the area of plantation, and will produce wine with its own distinctive flavour. The most important varieties are:

Riesling: White grape, making a medium-dry, fruity wine, eg Moselle and Rhine wines.

Chardonnay: White grape, generally used with the black Pinot Noir, to make Champagne.

Müller-Thurgau: White grape, a hybrid of Riesling and Sylvaner, easy to grow; makes a medium-dry wine.

Cabernet Sauvignon: Black grape, used with others, to make the great clarets. It produces a full red wine.

Gamay: Black grape, producing light fruity red wine, eg Beaujolais.

Sauvignon: White grape that produces crisp, dry, herby white wines, eg from the Loire. When left to become over-ripe, it is used for the sweet white wines of Bordeaux (Sauternes).

Muscat and *Gewürztraminer:* White grapes that produce strongly perfumed white wines.

HOW WINE IS MADE

The Wine-making Process

A ripe grape contains a great deal of water, various acids, pectins and, above all, sugar. Yeasts live on the skins of the grapes, and in the wine-making process, the yeast enzymes convert the sugar in the grape juice into alcohol and carbon dioxide, the latter escaping into the air as gas. This chemical process is known as fermentation. The unfermented grape juice is called 'must'. When the fermentation is complete, the must has become wine.

The young wine, however, needs some time to mature before it is ready for bottling. During this period, it undergoes various treatments, the chief of which are racking, fining, and filtering.

The process of vinification, or wine fermentation, creates substances in the young wine which, as it matures, will settle out as a sediment, or lees. Racking is the removal of wine from one cask to another, to separate it from its lees. Fining is the removal of other substances in the wine, such as proteins, pectins, and dead yeast cells. Finally, the wine is filtered to make it star-bright and to remove any remaining yeasts which could make it ferment in the bottle.

Red Wines, White Wines, and Rosés

The juice of nearly all wine-producing grapes, black or white, is colourless or pale yellow, so, if fermentation is carried out on the grape juice alone, the wine will be white. However, there is a pigment in the skins of black grapes and if the fermentation is carried out with these skins, the wine will be red.

The normal way of producing red wines, therefore, is to crush the grapes lightly, removing the stalks, and to pipe both grapes and skins into a vat where the fermentation can take place. The skins also contain tannin, which helps to give red wines their body and long life. When enough colour and tannin have been produced, the must is separated from the skins and pips by racking and pressing.

In the case of white wines, the grape bunches are pressed through meshes and the must ferments without the skins. Rosé is made in the same way as red wine, but the skins are removed very much sooner, when the wine is a light, pink colour.

Dry and Sweet Wines

If the fermentation of the grapes is allowed to continue until all their sugar has been converted to alcohol, the wine they make will be dry. The exceptions are certain white wines made from grapes whose natural sugar content is very high because they have been picked after the normal period of harvesting, and are over-ripe. The fermentation of these grapes continues until the alcohol level is high enough to kill off the yeasts; it then stops, leaving unfermented sugar which makes the wine naturally sweet.

These 'late harvest' wines are the best sweet wines; they are mostly made in France in the Bordeaux district of Sauternes (in Barsac too – which is part of Sauternes, and has its own appellation), in Hungary and in Germany. Most other sweet wines are normally produced by stopping the fermentation (by filtering out all the yeast cells) before all the sugar is fermented.

While white wines can be sweet, medium or dry, and rosés medium or dry, most red wines are dry.

Still and Sparkling Wines

Naturally made wine is still. A sparkling wine is made by adding sugar and yeasts to a finished wine, causing a second fermentation. The carbon dioxide released by this fermentation is not allowed to escape until the bottle is finally opened at the table, when it rises as millions of tiny bubbles.

This second fermentation can take place either in individual sealed bottles, when it is called the *Méthode Champenoise*, or in tanks under pressure, when it is called the *Méthode Cuve Close*. A third, but inferior, type of sparkling wine can be made by injecting carbon dioxide into wine.

Vintage Wines

The word 'vintage' just means 'harvest'. However, vintage wines, in the sense in which we normally use the term, are wines made from the grapes of one area and one year only. They are chosen and labelled as vintage wines because they are the best and most individual wines produced in a particular year; and, by and large, they are all wines from the classic growing areas discussed below.

Wines obviously vary in quality from year to year in each region, according to the weather. In a 'bad' year, very few wines, or none at all, may be produced which are thought worthy to be vintage wines. However, in all 'good' years, there are poor wines and in every 'bad' year, some surprisingly good wines are made.

Bottles

Most wine areas have their own distinctive bottle shape which can be easily recognised:

MAIN WINE-GROWING AREAS

France

Most of the great red wines of the world, and a lot of the best whites, come from the following main areas of France: Bordeaux, Burgundy, Loire, Rhône, Alsace, and Champagne. The southern areas of Languedoc-Roussillon and Provence produce everyday drinking wines and also some quality wines.

French Quality Labelling

The best French wines are legally defined as *Appellation Contrôlée* (AC) wines (classified as made under strict conditions). Each area has laws covering the type of grape varieties allowed, the methods of

Note Most wines come in bottles holding 70–75cl. Some, especially cheaper wines, are marketed in 1 litre, 1·5 litre or 2 litre bottles.

1) Red and white Bordeaux
2) Red and white Burgundy
3) German wines, Yugoslavia (Alsace bottles are even longer)
-4) Franconia (Germany), Portuguese sparkling rosé
5) Chianti, and other parts of Italy (wines for early drinking)

growing and wine making, and the maximum permitted yield. No wine is entitled to its geographical name unless it has fulfilled these conditions and, in many cases, has passed a tasting test as well.

Next are wines governed by only slightly less stringent regulations; these are called *Vins Délimités de Qualité Supérieure* (VDQS). Then come the *Vins du Pays* (country wines) and, finally, the *Vins Ordinaires* (ordinary wines) for everyday drinking.

Bordeaux

Bordeaux, in south-west France, produces all types of wine but is best known for its reds and whites.

The greatest reds, known in Britain as claret, come from two main regions, Saint-Emilion and the Médoc. Many wines come from individual properties, known as *châteaux*, the best of which have been classified into ranks. These wines are known as *crus classés* (classed growths). Immediately below them are wines, usually a little less expensive, although still good, called *crus bourgeois*.

The Médoc contains the communes or parishes of Saint-Estèphe, Pauillac, Saint-Julien, and Margaux. Near Saint-Emilion are the districts of Pomerol and Fronsac. Across the River Gironde from the Médoc, the main districts for *bourgéois* wines are Bourg and Blaye.

White Bordeaux wines come from the areas of Graves (dry and medium), Entre-deux-Mers (dry and medium), and Sauternes (very sweet).

Burgundy and Beaujolais

This area stretches north from near Lyons to Dijon and produces both red and white wines.

The whites are all dry. They come from the Mâconnais (which includes the village of Pouilly-Fuissé), the Côte de Beaune, round the town of the same name (including villages such as Meursault and Puligny-Montrachet), and Chablis, a district on its own, some 80km to the north-east of Dijon. White wine also comes from Montagny in the Côte Chalonnais.

The best reds come from the Côte d'Or, subdivided into the Côte de Nuits, round the town of Nuits Saint Georges (including such villages as Gevrey-Chambertin, Vosne-Romanée and Vougeot), and the Côte de Beaune (which includes Volnay and Pommard). Similar, but lesser, reds come from the Côte Chalonnais, immediately to the south of the Côte de Beaune, from the villages of Rully, Mercurey and Givry.

At the southernmost end of Burgundy, the Beaujolais region produces a different, lighter style of red wine, the best of which come from individual villages such as Fleurie, Morgon and Moulin-à-Vent.

Dordogne

Wines from this area, east of Bordeaux, include those of the Bergerac region, such as the sweet white Monbazillac and various dryer whites and reds.

Loire

Most Loire wine is white or rosé (though the region also produces some of France's best sparkling wines, notably from Saumur and Vouvray). The river valley contains four major wine areas. Nearest the coast, from round the town of Nantes, come the crisp, dry white wines of Muscadet; then comes Anjou, best known for its medium-dry rosés; the Touraine produces fuller whites, such as Vouvray, which can range from dry to fairly sweet; and, finally, farthest inland, lie the communes of Sancerre and Pouilly, which produce light, fragrant, dry wines.

Rhône

Rhône wines come from that part of the river valley between Lyons and Avignon, and are mainly full, robust reds. In the northern part, the valley is steep and narrow, and the best wines come from the vineyards of Hermitage, Côte Rôtie, and Cornas. In the south, the valley is wider and flatter and the best wine is Château neuf-du-Pape. Full, dry rosé is made at Tavel and a naturally sweet, pinkish Muscat at Beaumes de Venise.

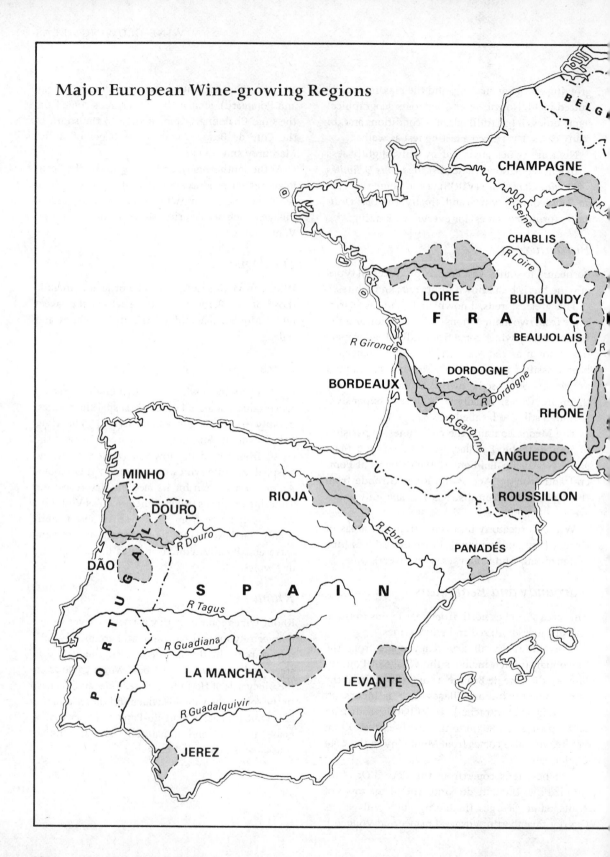

Major European Wine-growing Regions

Alsace

The Alsace vineyards lie on the eastern slopes of the Vosges mountains, adjoining the Rhine and the borders with Germany. Ripe, fruity, dry white wines are made, named after the grape varieties from which they are produced: Riesling, Sylvaner, and Gewürztraminer are the main ones.

Champagne

Champagne, the greatest sparkling wine in the world, comes from the most northerly wine-growing area in France, round the towns of Rheims and Epernay. Vintage Champagne is produced only in the best years. This and other good-quality Champagne is made by the *Méthode Champenoise*, lesser Champagne by the *Méthode Cuve Close*. Dry and extra dry Champagnes are described as *brut*; there are also medium-dry and sweet Champagnes.

South of France

As the wines from the best-known areas of France become increasingly more expensive, more and more wine of excellent value is being produced in the Languedoc-Roussillon region, from such areas as Corbières and Minervois, and in Provence. The best are red, but many dry whites and rosés are also made.

Germany

All well-known German wines are white, and are usually light, fruity, and medium-dry.

Rhine wines come in a tall brown bottle, from four areas of the Rhine valley between Speyer and Koblenz: the Rheingau, Rheinhessen, Nahe, and Palatinate or Pfalz. The best have a honeyed, fruity flavour. Famous wine villages are Johannisberg, Rüdesheim, Nierstein, and Oppenheim. Liebfraumilch is a general name for Rheinhessen wines of a particular style – medium-dry and fruity.

The wines of the Mosel, a tributary of the Rhine, are distinguished in their own right, with lovely bouquets and a refreshing acidity. Well-known names are Bernkastel and Piesport. They are put into tall green bottles.

The district of Franconia on the river Main, around Würzburg, produces the driest of all German wines. These are known as Steinweins, and are bottled in *bockbeutels*.

Many German wine names are formed by adding the suffix 'er' to the name of the village, eg Niersteiner (denoting 'of Nierstein'). The wines' standards are controlled by laws similar to those of France. At the top are the *Qualitätswein mit Prädikat* (QmP) wines, or Quality Wines with Certificate, which guarantees that they come from a defined region and are made in strict accordance with specified conditions. Only these wines can carry additional terms of special status, in ascending order: *Kabinett*, *Spätlese* (made from bunches of grapes picked after the normal harvest), *Auslese* (from specially selected late-picked bunches), *Beerenauslese* (even later, from individually picked over-ripe grapes), and *Trockenbeerenauslese* (the final gathering, from grapes left until they have shrivelled like raisins, giving them a very high concentration of sugar).

The next category is *Qualitätswein bestimmter Anbaugebiete* (QbA). These are wines from a specific area, made from a specified variety of grape. Finally comes the *Tafelwein*, comprising the ordinary table wines. Germany also produces a sparkling wine, known as Sekt, and some interesting red wines.

Italy

Italy is the largest wine-producing country in the world, and its wines are imported in ever increasing quantities to the UK, much of it bottled in 1.5 or 2 litre bottles. Most of the wine in these large bottles is of ordinary quality, but many higher quality wines are also produced.

The Italians have introduced tougher wine laws, and standards have greatly improved. Echoing France's *Appellation Contrôlée* system, their best wines carry the letters DOC on the bottle labels, standing for *Denominazione di Origine Controllata*. Italian wines take their names either from the vineyard region, from the grape variety used or sometimes from past historical associations.

Tuscany

Chianti is a medium-weight red wine, most of which used to be bottled in the traditional wicker flask. Nowadays, though, more and more Chiantis are bottled in Bordeaux-type bottles.

Piedmont

Barolo is the heartiest, fullest Italian red wine, and comes from south of Turin. Other red wines from this area are Barbera and Barbaresco. Asti Spumante, a famous sparkling white wine made from the Muscat grape, is also produced here.

Veneto

Valpolicella and Bardolino are lighter reds, produced at the southern end of Lake Garda, near Verona, in north Italy. Soave is a light, dry white wine produced near Verona.

Lazio

This is a district just south of Rome which produces Frascati, a dry white wine.

Umbria

The area south of Perugia produces Orvieto, a dry white wine.

Marche

A dry white wine called Verdicchio comes from this area on the Adriatic coast at Ancona.

Spain and Portugal

The Iberian Peninsula is most famous for its fortified wines (see pp1358–59), but also produces large quantities of table wine, frequently bottled as cheap branded wine. Some areas produce quality wines; most are red. The best known areas are:

Rioja

This region, in the upper valley of the River Ebro in northern Spain, produces the best reds of Spain, and also some good dry white wines.

Panadés

An area in the hills behind Barcelona in Catalonia which produces white wines both dry and sweet, as well as reds and sparkling wines.

Dão

This area in the central highlands of Portugal, produces the best Portuguese table wines: full, strong reds, and firm, dry whites.

Minho

Vinhos verdes, light white wines, and rosés, which have a slight natural sparkle, come from this area in the north-west of Portugal.

OTHER WINE-PRODUCING AREAS

Australia

A wide range of wines, many of high quality, are made in and exported from South Australia, Victoria, New South Wales, Queensland, and Western Australia. The red claret-type wines predominate. Barossa Valley, Coonawarra, Hunter Valley, and McLaren Vale are well-known district names. A good many wines also carry the names of grape varieties, Shiraz being widely used.

Austria

Like Yugoslavia and Hungary, Austria produces blended wines under various brand names, and some good-quality, medium-dry white wines. These are made largely from the Grüner Veltliner and Riesling grapes.

Cyprus

Cyprus produces table wines (mainly red), a sweet dessert wine called Commandaria and a large range of sherry-style wines.

Hungary

Hungary is best known for its Bull's Blood of Eger, a full, robust red from northern Hungary, and for Tokay, a rich, sweet, white dessert wine, from the slopes of the Carpathian mountains in north-east Hungary. Central Hungary produces the Balatoni Riesling, a similar wine to the Yugoslav Laski Riesling. Other wines are named after the country and grape variety, eg Hungarian Cabernet (red).

Northern Africa

Large quantities of wine, mostly full, rather coarse reds, are produced in Morocco, Algeria, and Tunisia. Many are used for blending.

South Africa

Wine growing started in South Africa three centuries ago and the country now produces both medium and good quality wines, mainly from various districts in the Cape Province. Both white and red wines are made, as well as sherry-style wines, port types and a range of brandies. Controlled by the Co-operative Wine Growers' Association, known as KWV, the quality of standard wine production is high. Constantia, Stellenbosch, Paarl, and Nederburg are all area names of wines, of which Nederburg Rieslings are the best known.

South America

Argentina and Chile both produce wine; indeed Argentina is the fifth largest wine-producing country in the world.

United Kingdom

Since the early 1970s, a large number of commercial English vineyards have been established. These lie across southern England and up into East Anglia. English vineyard owners are experimenting with a number of grapes and blends. At the time of writing (1980), wines from the Müller-Thurgau grape predominate. Almost all the wine is white.

United States

Although wine is made in a number of regions, the centre for quality wine making from European grape varieties is California. American methods are among the most up-to-date and scientific in the whole world, and some wines of outstanding quality have been produced. The leading wine-growing areas are to the north and south of San Francisco in the following counties: Napa, Sonoma, Monterey, and Santa Clara.

Yugoslavia

The biggest selling medium-dry white wine in Britain today is made from the Laski Riesling grape variety, and comes from vineyards in the north-east corner of Yugoslavia.

FORTIFIED WINES

A fortified wine (sherry, port or Madeira, for instance) is one which has grape brandy added at some stage of its manufacture. As a result, it is about twice as strong as a table or unfortified wine, and is usually drunk as an apéritif or digestif. Fortified wines keep well after the bottles have been opened, although it is unwise to keep the lightest and driest types, such as a *fino* sherry, for more than a few weeks.

Sherry

Sherry comes from Jerez in south-western Spain, near the port of Cadiz. The wine is fortified with brandy after fermentation is finished, and derives its unique flavour from being matured entirely in the cask. These casks are never completely filled.

During the fermentation, some of the wine attracts a harmless fungus growth known as *flor*, which lies on the surface of the wine, like a thin layer of cotton wool, and helps to give the dry or *fino* sherries their delicacy and dryness.

Sherry is, initially, a dry wine. *Finos* are left dry and are bottled early, or are allowed to mature into wines with deeper colour and body, and a medium-dry nutty flavour, called *amontillados*. *Olorosos* are normally sweetened, either slightly or heavily, when they become cream sherries. Brown sherries are creams which have had caramel added to make them still heavier and richer. Another sherry name is *manzanilla*; this is a *fino* sherry which has been matured on the coast of Sanlucar, acquiring a characteristic salty tang.

Sherry is matured by what is called the Solera system; this is the progressive topping up of older butts (casks of sherry holding 280 litres approx) with younger wine of the same style. Because of the unusual characteristic that the younger wine gradually takes on the quality of the older wines and eventually becomes indistinguishable from it, the Solera system enables wine of consistent style to be produced year after year. Single vintage sherry is rare.

Sherry-style wines are produced in Cyprus, Australia, South Africa, and at Montilla in southern Spain.

Port

Port is a red fortified wine from the Douro region of Portugal, up-river from the coastal town of Oporto. Unlike sherry, port is fortified during fermentation, as soon as the wine has enough colour. The brandy arrests the fermentation and the wine remains sweet, as not all the natural sugar has been turned into alcohol. Depending on how the wine is matured, it will become one of two essentially different styles of port: vintage or wood.

Vintage port is the best wine of the best years, bottled early, and needing 10–20 years to mature in bottles, during which time it will throw a heavy sediment, or crust. Vintage port will need decanting (see p1363). Some vintage port is left longer in the cask before bottling, and so matures quicker. It is called Late-Bottled Vintage (LBV), or crusted port, if it is a wine of more than one year.

Wood port is port which has spent most of its life in pipes (225 litre casks), and which is bottled when mature. It does not need decanting. Young wood port is called Ruby port, older wine is called Tawny, and is lighter, drier, and more refined in style.

Madeira

Madeira comes from the island of the same name in the Atlantic and derives its character from having been gradually heated in a damp atmosphere and then, more quickly, cooled back to normal temperatures. The result is a wine with a pronounced acidity, together with a mellow, caramelly flavour. The main styles are Sercial (the dryest), Verdelho, Bual, and Malmsey (the sweetest and richest).

Marsala

Marsala is produced in Sicily and is not unlike Madeira. It generally comes in two styles, a medium-dry, often called virgin, and a rich, sweeter type. Flavoured 'liqueur' Marsalas are also available.

VERMOUTHS AND BITTERS

Vermouth is a wine-based apéritif, sweetened and fortified with alcohol, in which assorted herbs and spices have been macerated and/or infused, to extract their flavour. The wine base can be white, from which two styles are produced: a dry and a sweet (*bianco*) vermouth. A particularly stylish dry white vermouth is produced at Chambéry in the French Alps. *Rosso*, or Italian vermouth, is sweet and very spicy and is produced from a red wine base. There is also a pink vermouth based on rosé wine. Vermouths are branded products, and are known by the names of the manufacturing firms: Martini, Cinzano, Noilly Prat, etc.

Other apéritifs are made in a similar way and may include quinine as one of their main flavourings (Dubonnet, Saint Raphael, Byrrh, etc).

Bitters are used either on their own, with soda or as a flavouring for other drinks. They are each made to an individual secret formula. The best known are Angostura, Fernet Branca, Underberg, and Campari.

Spirits and Liqueurs

SPIRITS

Spirits are the result of distillation. A wash of malted cereal and water (for whisky, gin, and vodka) or sugar syrup (rum) or wine (brandy) is distilled. The resulting spirit may be flavoured and matured, and is always blended to make a consistent product.

Aquavit or Akvavit, Schnapps

This is made in Scandinavia and northern Europe from potatoes or grain, flavoured with aromatic herbs and spices. In flavour not unlike gin, it is usually drunk neat.

Brandy

The distillation of wine produces brandy. It is available in all wine-growing areas and countries. The two best brandies, however, come from France: from Cognac, north of the Bordeaux area along the river Charente, and Armagnac, in the department of Gers, south-east of Bordeaux in the foothills of the Pyrenees. Cognac is produced by two separate distillations in a pot still, while Armagnac has a single distillation; after this, both are carefully matured in oak casks and are blended. Most brandy producers describe the age and quality of their blends by a system of stars and letters. 'Three Star' is good basic brandy, suitable as a base for cocktails and long drinks. Very Special Old Pale (VSOP) is older, for after-dinner drinking.

Calvados or Applejack

Calvados is distilled apple wine, and comes from Normandy in northern France. Apple wine made elsewhere is often called Applejack.

Eaux de Vie

These are high-strength, dry, fruit brandies, often based on the crushed kernels of the stones of the fruit. Examples are Kirsch (cherry), and Quetsche and Mirabelle (both different species of plum). Eaux de vie can also be based on other soft fruits.

Gin

Gin is made by redistilling (rectifying) neutral grain spirit together with a number of flavouring ingredients, chief of which is juniper. London gin is dry; Plymouth gin is heavier and more strongly flavoured; Dutch gin or Geneva is a full, heavy spirit with a ripe, malty flavour.

Grappa, Marc

Grappa (Italian) and Marc (French) are types of brandy made from the stalks and stems of grapes left over after the wine-making. Rue is also added.

Ouzo

This is an aniseed-flavoured spirit from Greece.

Pastis, Anis

Aniseed-flavoured spirit is known in France as *pastis* or *anis*. Pernod and Ricard are the best-known names. Both are drunk as 1 part in 5 with water, and turn cloudy or 'milky' with the water.

Rum

Rum is produced by distilling cane-sugar products, chiefly molasses. It can range in style between the light, delicate Cuban rums, such as Bacardi, to golden (Jamaican), and dark (Navy or Demerara) – strong, full-bodied, and flavoured with caramel.

Southern Comfort

A spirit from the USA, flavoured with peaches and other fruits.

Tequila

A colourless Mexican spirit based on the cactus plant, tequila is drunk with lime juice and a pinch of salt.

Vodka

Vodka is a neutral spirit made from grain, potatoes or sugar beet, then filtered through charcoal to remove all traces of colour and flavour.

Whisky

Any cereal can be used to make whisky, but barley is the main ingredient of Irish and Scotch whisky. In the USA, maize (corn) and rye are used, and in Canada, only rye; corn whisky is called bourbon. There are two types of whisky: malt whisky, made in a pot still from malted grain or other starchy product, and grain whisky, made in a patent still from raw grain. Single malt whisky is malt whisky from a single distillery, not a single distillation.

LIQUEURS

Liqueurs are called cordials in the USA and digestifs in France. A liqueur is a sweetened and flavoured spirit. Some of the best known are:

Advocaat

A creamy liqueur based on egg yolks and brandy.

Bénédictine

A brandy-based, sweet herb liqueur from Fécamp in northern France.

Cassis, Crème de

A blackcurrant-flavoured liqueur. Often added to a dry white wine as 1 part in 6 to make Vin Blanc Cassis or Kir.

Chartreuse

Brandy flavoured with herbs, this is marketed in two strengths, 51% (green), and the sweeter 43% (yellow). It is made by the monks at a monastery in Chartreuse, near Grenoble.

Cherry Brandy

Made by macerating cherries in grape brandy.

Curaçao

Based on the distillation of orange peel. *Triple-sec* curaçao is a highly rectified colourless form. Cointreau is the most popular brand of the *triple-sec* curaçaos.

Drambuie, Glen Mist, Glavra

Based on Scotch whisky, herbs, and spices.

Grand Marnier

Based on the distillation of orange peel steeped in Cognac; sweeter than Cointreau.

Kümmel

A neutral spirit, flavoured with caraway seed.

Maraschino

A sweet, colourless liqueur based on Yugoslavian maraschino cherries.

Menthe, Crème de

Heavily sweetened mint or peppermint-flavoured spirit, often coloured green.

Tia Maria and Kahlua

Coffee-flavoured liqueurs.

Van der Hum

Brandy-based liqueur from South Africa with a tangerine-orange flavour.

Purchase, Storage, and Service of Wines and Spirits

PURCHASE OF WINES

What to choose, how much to spend, and from whom to buy wines, need not be difficult decisions. The first thing to remember is the very high amount of fixed cost there is in a bottle of wine. Roughly three-quarters of the selling price of the cheapest bottle of wine is taken up in a fixed duty, the cost of the empty bottle, carton and cork, and the delivery charges from the wine-producing area to the supermarket, high-street shop, bar or specialist wine firm. It follows, therefore, that at the very cheapest level there can be little money left to pay for the wine, and that by paying a little more one will get better value.

The second thing to remember is that one's own tastes are far more important than any rules of etiquette or fashion. Although anyone selling wine should be able to help with advice, and should certainly have tried all his or her cheaper and more popular lines, it is your choice. If you can describe what you have enjoyed before, the seller will be better able to select something for you.

Whether you buy direct from a producer or shipper, from a firm which delivers to your home, or over the counter in a supermarket, store or bar, always try to buy ahead. Jolting during travelling does even cheap wine no good, and ideally it should 'rest' for several days or weeks before being drunk. It is therefore wise to plan your wine purchases carefully, so that you will have a selection of the types you need when you come to drink it. If you do this, you will also save money because you can buy in the best market for your needs instead of in a hurry.

Do not be afraid to experiment when you buy wine, especially at the cheaper end of the scale; you will find that the quality can vary enormously and you may find some surprisingly good cheap wines.

It is also advisable, when you do find something you like very much, to buy it in bulk. If you can, buy a case. Not only will you then be sure of having your wine in stock, but you will often find that you get a discount.

STORAGE

Most wine is ready for drinking as soon as it has recovered from bottling. Many inexpensive wines, especially the whites and rosés, are best drunk as soon as possible, while they are young and fresh, though a few months in a bottle may improve some of the more robust of the cheaper reds. But, like all living things, wines deteriorate after a certain age, and only the finest wines are sturdy enough in the first place to benefit from being kept.

If you want to lay down a cellar of fine wines before they reach maturity, buy from a specialist wine merchant who will be able to tell you when your stock will be ready for drinking. By and large, a wine remains at its peak for drinking for the same number of years as it took to mature. If, therefore, for example, a fine claret was at its best eight years after the vintage date, you will have another eight years in which to drink it.

All wines for long-term storage should be stored on their sides, to keep the cork moist and expanded, and in a dark place free of disturbance and violent changes of temperature. Ideally, the wine should be kept at 10°–12°C, though it will not come to any real harm between 7°–16°C. It is more important that the temperature remains steady.

Wines can be stored in specially constructed racks or bins, available at most stores or through specialist wine merchants, or can even be left in the original carton, if the storage area is dry and the carton is put on its side.

SERVING WINE

Temperature

Red wines should be served at room temperature and white wines should be served chilled. It is important to remember, however, that the term 'room temperature' indicates the temperature of rooms before the days of widespread central heating, and means at about 16° not 20°C, and certainly not 25°C.

A red wine can always be warmed up gently by hand; it is better to be a little on the cool side than over-heated, as the wine may then taste stewed. On no account should red wine be artificially warmed by plunging it in hot water or standing it on the cooker. If necessary, wines can be warmed gently in the airing cupboard. The fuller the red wine, the warmer it can be served. Many people prefer young, light reds, like Beaujolais, at cellar temperature.

The best place to cool white wine is in the milk compartment of a refrigerator, and 30 minutes or so will usually be long enough. However, white wines come to no harm if kept for a week in a refrigerator. If the wine has been kept cold for a long time, however, it is best to allow it to warm up just a little before serving. Too cold a serving temperature muffles the taste. About 6°–8°C is best. The fuller and sweeter the white or rosé wine, the cooler it should be served.

Decanting

Red wines should be uncorked some time (usually about an hour) before being served. Fine old red wines may also need to be decanted.

There are two reasons for decanting: to separate a wine from its sediment – and all good red wines will eventually throw a sediment – and to allow a wine to 'breathe'. It is the act of decanting which lets a wine breathe rather than the length of time it is done before drinking the wine, so there are no hard-and-fast rules about decanting 1 hour or 3 hours before the meal. In most cases, 30 minutes before the meal is quite enough.

An older bottle, which has thrown a sediment, should be stood upright for a few hours before decanting it, to allow the sediment to collect low down in the bottle. The bottle's contents should then be poured into a clean, dry decanter or jug in one movement, carefully holding the neck of the bottle in front of a source of light so that one can see when the sediment is beginning to reach the neck. Muslin can be used as a sieve for wines with a very heavy sediment, such as port. Filter papers should never be used as these taint the wine.

Vintage port often has a wax seal which should be knocked off gently with the end of a corkscrew. Any remains of the wax should be wiped off before removing the cork. Port corks are long, so you will need a long corkscrew to remove them.

If you uncork or decant a bottle of wine and then do not use it as planned, it need not be wasted. Once a bottle has been opened, it will keep for several days in a cool place (for red wines) or in a refrigerator (for white wines). A tapered cork can be purchased very cheaply, with which to recork it. The wine can then be drunk on a later occasion or used for cooking.

To clean a stained decanter, screw up small pellets of newspaper and drop them into the decanter; pour over a little boiling water, and leave for a few minutes, swirling occasionally. The combination of hot water and newsprint will lift the stain. Pour away the water, repeat the process if necessary and rinse thoroughly.

Glasses

Ideally, glasses should be large so that there is plenty of room to swirl the wine and release its aroma; they should hold a full measure without being filled to more than two-thirds capacity. They should be slightly curved inwards – tulip-shaped – at the top, so that the aroma can be concentrated around the nose, and they must be clear so that one can admire the wine's colour. Many ranges offer a smaller size for white to that for red wine; this is not really necessary.

Glasses should be cleaned carefully and rinsed thoroughly, as any residual detergent will taint the wine. Dishwashing machines clean glasses very satisfactorily.

Wine Appreciation

One of the delights of wine is its infinite variety, and the surprising subtlety and complexity of flavour of even very inexpensive wines.

When tasting wine, the first thing to examine is the colour. This should be bright and attractive, not dull or cloudy, and will give an indication of the age and fullness of the wine.

A white wine when young, light and dry, may be anything from greeny-gold or straw to lemon-yellow in colour. The fuller, sweeter and the older the wine is, the deeper will be the colour. Old Sauternes is a rich, deep, gold colour. When a white wine is too old, it turns brownish and loses its pleasant smell.

Red wines, on the other hand, lose colour as they mature. A young, red wine has a purplish hue; as it gets older it changes through crimson to garnet and finally to tawny. A sign of a mature red wine is a hint of brown at the rim of the glass.

The aroma or 'nose' of the wine, otherwise called the bouquet, can be released by gently swirling it around the glass; it should be clean, attractive, and interesting. The smell is no less important than the taste and colour in assessing a wine's beauty, and you should take a good deep sniff of it. Many wines have distinctive smells: a claret may be black-curranty, while a good Moselle may have an aroma of honey and crisp apples, for instance.

These flavours should be confirmed on the palate. A good sip of wine should be allowed to go all the way round the mouth, for one has different sorts of taste buds, responding to different taste sensations, in different parts of the palate. After the wine has been swallowed, one should stop and consider for a minute. Is the 'finish' and the 'after-taste' of the wine interesting and enjoyable? Does the taste linger or is it over quickly? The better the wine, the more complex and longer-lasting the flavour.

Faulty Wines

All wine should have a clean smell and taste. Occasionally, a bottle of wine will prove to be 'off' when opened. If the wine has an unpleasant, rotten smell, or is unnaturally cloudy or fizzy, it should be rejected, refilled as full as possible, recorked, and taken back to where it was bought. It will always be replaced, but it is only fair to take the bottle back as soon as possible to give the seller the chance to assess what is wrong with the wine, as the fault may have affected other bottles in the same batch.

Wine and Food

For information on which wines to serve with which foods, see pp262–63.

Mixed Drinks

Mixed drinks, based on wines and spirits, fall into three main sections:

Hot long drinks: Punches, mulls, and possets
Cold long drinks: Fruit or wine cups
Short drinks: Cocktails, toddies, and nogs.

PUNCHES

Bishop

Fills 12 sherry glasses

12 cloves	*1 bottle port (70–75cl)*
1 large orange	*white sugar*

Press the cloves into the orange, put it into an ovenproof bowl, cover tightly, and roast it in a moderate oven, 180°C, Gas 4, until lightly browned. Cut the orange into 8 pieces and remove the pips. Pour the port into a clean saucepan, add the pieces of orange, and heat gently to simmering point. Sweeten to taste with sugar and simmer for 20 minutes, taking care not to let the liquor boil. Strain the liquid through a fine sieve and serve at once, very hot.

Mulled Ale

Fills 10 wine glasses

1 litre ale
1 × 15ml spoon caster
  sugar
a good pinch of ground
  cloves
a pinch of grated nutmeg

a good pinch of ground
  ginger
1 glass rum or brandy
  (100ml)

Put the ale, sugar, cloves, nutmeg and ginger into a stewpan, and heat almost to boiling point. Add the rum or brandy and more sugar and flavouring, if necessary. Serve at once.

Mulled Wine

Fills 12 wine glasses

500ml water
6 cloves
10g piece of bruised
  cinnamon stick
a pinch of grated nutmeg

finely pared rind of $\frac{1}{2}$
  lemon
1 bottle claret (70–75cl)
white sugar

Put the water in an enamel saucepan and heat gently; then stir in the cloves, cinnamon stick, nutmeg, and lemon rind. Heat to boiling point and simmer for 10 minutes. Strain the liquid into a basin and add the wine. Sweeten to taste with sugar. Return the liquid to the pan and heat without boiling it.

Serve at once with fingers of dry toast.

Negus

Fills 10 wine glasses

100g lump sugar
1 lemon
1 bottle port (70–75cl)
500ml boiling water

$\frac{1}{4}$ small nutmeg
2–3 drops vanilla
  essence

Rub the sugar on the rind of the lemon until all the zest is extracted. Crush it in a basin and pour the port and boiling water over it. Add the nutmeg and the vanilla essence. Serve hot.

Whisky Punch

Fills 15 wine glasses

juice and finely pared
  rind of 3 lemons
1 litre boiling water

1 bottle whisky (75cl)
200g lump sugar

Strain the lemon juice and put it into a basin with the lemon rind. Pour boiling water over them; then add the whisky, and stir in the sugar. When the sugar has dissolved, strain the liquid and serve at once.

Hot Rum Toddy

Fills 2 mugs

2 × 5ml spoons
  Demerara sugar or to
  taste
juice of 1 lemon

50ml rum
2 lemon slices
boiling water

Mix the sugar with the lemon juice and rum. Put 1 lemon slice into each of 2 heated mugs, and pour half the rum mixture into each mug. Add boiling water to give the desired strength of toddy. Taste, and add extra sugar if needed. Serve at once, as hot as possible.

CUPS

Champagne Cup

Fills 12 Champagne glasses

1 bottle Champagne
  (70–75cl)
400ml soda water
a few strips lemon rind
1 × 2.5ml spoon
  maraschino

1 liqueur glass brandy
  (65ml)
1 × 5ml spoon caster
  sugar (optional)

Chill the Champagne and soda water for 1 hour. When ready to serve, put the lemon rind into a large glass jug, and stir in the maraschino, brandy, Champagne, and soda water. Serve at once. If sugar is added, it should be stirred in gradually.

Cider Cup

Fills 12 wine glasses

1 litre cider
500ml soda water
1 liqueur glass brandy
  (65ml)
a few thin strips
  cucumber rind

a few thin strips lemon
  rind
1 × 10ml spoon lemon
  juice
1 × 10ml spoon caster
  sugar (approx)

Chill the cider and soda water for 30 minutes. Put the rest of the ingredients into a large jug, and stir in the chilled cider and soda water. Serve at once.

White Wine Cup

Fills 9 wine glasses

finely pared rind and
  juice of 1 lemon
1 × 15ml spoon caster
  sugar
a few thin slices
  cucumber

2 liqueur glasses curaçao
  (65ml each)
1 bottle Moselle
  (70–75cl)
200ml soda water
a little crushed ice

Put the lemon rind and juice, the sugar, cucumber, curaçao, and wine into a jug. Cover, let it stand for 15–20 minutes, then add the soda water and ice. Serve at once.

Sauternes Cup

Fills 12 wine glasses

1 litre Sauternes
cracked ice
1 liqueur glass
  maraschino (65ml)
1 liqueur glass curaçao
  (65ml)
1 liqueur glass (65ml)
  Cognac **or** *peach*
  brandy

12 large **or** *24 small*
  slices fresh peaches
a few strips lemon rind
a few drops lemon juice
  (optional)
250ml soda water
  (approx)

Decoration
2–3 sprigs fresh mint

Chill the wine for 1 hour. Put the ice in a 2 litre (approx) jug and pour the wine over it. Add the liqueurs, brandy, peach slices, and lemon rind. Add lemon juice if either the wine or fruit is very sweet. Just before serving, pour in the soda water, as required, and decorate with the mint.

Red Wine Cup

Fills 9 wine glasses

1 bottle red wine
  (70–75cl)
a few thin strips lemon
  rind
a few thin strips
  cucumber rind

2 liqueur glasses curaçao
  (65ml each)
200ml soda water
1 × 10ml spoon caster
  sugar (approx)

Pour the wine into a glass jug, add the lemon and cucumber rinds, cover, and chill for 1 hour. Before serving, add the curaçao and soda water, and sweeten to taste with sugar.

Fruit Claret Cup

Fills 12 wine glasses

cracked ice
7 × 5ml spoons brandy
7 × 5ml spoons caster
  sugar
7 × 5ml spoons
  maraschino
6 maraschino cherries
2 × 15ml spoons lemon
  juice

1 sliced lemon
1 sliced orange
6 thin slices fresh
  pineapple
1 litre claret (approx)
175ml soda water
  (approx)

Put some cracked ice into a large jug. Add the brandy, sugar, maraschino, and cherries. Strain the lemon juice and add it. Cut the lemon, orange, and pineapple slices into quarters, and add them. Stir in the claret. Just before serving, add the soda water, and stir once.

Note You can add extra claret or vary the proportions of claret and soda water, if liked.

Sangria

Fills 8 wine glasses

50g sugar	1 bottle red **or** white
50ml water	wine (70–75cl)
1 sliced orange	12 ice cubes
1 sliced lime **or** lemon	

Put the sugar and water in a saucepan and stir over gentle heat until the sugar has dissolved. Pour the syrup over the sliced fruit and leave to cool.

Pour the fruit and the syrup into a jug, and add the wine and ice cubes. Stir well, and serve at once. Put 2–3 slices of fruit in each glass.

NON-ALCOHOLIC CUPS

Fruit Punch

Fills 50 wine glasses

300g caster sugar	1 litre grape juice
(approx)	1 × 227g can crushed
3.5 litres water	pineapple
150ml strong tea,	2 litres ginger ale
without milk	(approx)
juice of 13 lemons	ice cubes
juice of 14 oranges	

Decoration

slices of lemon	1 × 170g bottle
slices of orange	maraschino cherries

Boil the sugar and water together for 6 minutes. Add the tea, leave to cool, then chill. When cold, add the fruit juices and pineapple. Chill for about 2 hours. Just before serving, pour in the ginger ale to taste. Add ice cubes and decorate with the sliced fruit and cherries.

Honey Fruit Cup

Fills 12 wine glasses

2 large oranges	2 litres grape juice
250ml clear honey	(approx)
(approx)	250ml soda water
2 bananas	(approx)
4–6 slices fresh	1 × 15ml spoon lemon
pineapple	juice

Peel the oranges, removing all the pith, and crush the flesh to a pulp, discarding the pips. Mix the pulp with the honey in a large jug. Peel the bananas and pineapple and chop both finely. Add the fruit to the jug and slowly pour in the grape juice and soda water to taste. Add the lemon juice. Leave to stand for 20 minutes, then stir well and serve.

Iced Tea Punch

Fills 6 tumblers

750ml tea liquor (p1346)	juice of 3 oranges
100g caster sugar	cracked ice
juice of 2 lemons	375ml ginger ale

Decoration

6 slices lemon	6 sprigs mint

Strain the tea liquor into a deep jug. Stir in the sugar until dissolved, then add the lemon and orange juices. Stir and chill thoroughly. Put the cracked ice into 6 tumblers, divide the tea between them, and fill up with the ginger ale. Decorate each glass with a slice of lemon and a sprig of mint before serving.

COCKTAILS AND OTHER DRINKS

Besides spirits, wines, liqueurs, bitters, and soft drinks such as quinine tonic, it is necessary to have a source of soda water which can be quickly replenished, and a supply of clean, clear ice. Snowy ice melts quickly.

For serving cocktails and similar 'short' drinks, it is helpful to have the following equipment:

1) *Cocktail shaker*: There are various types, but the most usual consists of a deep container with a perforated screw-on top and an outer lid. The drink and ice are shaken in the deep container with both caps screwed on. The outer cap is then removed, and the drink is poured through the holes of the inner cap. This holds the ice back and prevents it from splashing into the glass. Never fill a cocktail shaker more than four-fifths full, and never shake an effervescent drink. If serving a variety of drinks, keep one shaker for drinks with highly flavoured ingredients and another for milder ones.

2) *Mixing glass and spoon*: This is needed for mixing clear drinks such as dry Martinis.

3) *Ice:* Make ice cubes in the ice making trays in a refrigerator or freezer. Different shaped trays are available to make ice balls, wedges, squares or oblongs. For a party, ice can be made several days in advance and stored in the freezing compartment of a refrigerator, or in a freezer. Tip the ice into a large polythene bag and squirt with soda water to keep the pieces separate, before storing them. Ice cubes are also obtainable from specialist suppliers, or sometimes from fishmongers. To make cracked ice for cocktails, use an ice hammer with a pointed head. For crushed ice, put the cubes into a polythene bag and hammer them hard with a rolling-pin, mallet or rubber-headed hammer. For shaved ice, use a special shaver, which is not unlike a plane.

Decorative ice is attractive in many drinks, especially soft drinks and fruit cups. Fill a 'ball' ice tray with cocktail cherries, inserting cocktail sticks if you wish; top up with water, and freeze. Slices of lemon or orange, sprigs of mint or lemon balm also look attractive set in ice.

Edible food dyes (red, green or yellow) can be used to colour ice shapes; a few drops of yellow dye, a little lemon juice and thin slices of lemon cut to size, make ice cubes both look and taste delicious.

4) *Measures*: Tots and similar measures for cocktails are widely available, and most are marked at the $\frac{1}{4}$, $\frac{1}{2}$ and $\frac{3}{4}$ tot levels. Some measures give 5 tots to 125ml, some give 6 tots.

Cocktail glasses generally hold 50ml, 75ml or 125ml.

Americano

$\frac{2}{3}$ *sweet vermouth*	*soda water*
$\frac{1}{3}$ *Campari*	*a twist of lemon rind*
1 ice cube	

Stir the vermouth and Campari together in a mixing glass, and strain into an 'old fashioned' glass. Add the ice. Top up with soda water. Decorate with the lemon rind.

Black Velvet

$\frac{1}{2}$ *chilled Guinness*	$\frac{1}{2}$ *chilled dry Champagne*

Pour the Guinness and Champagne simultaneously. Do not add ice. Serve in a tumbler or a tankard.

Bloody Mary

ice cubes	*a few drops fresh lemon*
$\frac{1}{3}$ *vodka*	*juice*
$\frac{2}{3}$ *chilled tomato juice*	*salt and pepper*
a few drops	*(optional)*
Worcestershire sauce	

Put the ice cubes in a medium-sized glass. Stir or shake all the ingredients together.

Bronx

½ gin
⅙ dry vermouth
⅙ sweet vermouth
⅙ fresh orange juice

Shake all the ingredients together in a cocktail shaker; then strain into a cocktail glass.

Bucks Fizz

juice of 1 orange
chilled dry Champagne

Strain the orange juice and chill it. Pour into a Champagne glass and top up with the Champagne. Do not add ice.

Champagne Cocktail

1 lump of sugar
a few drops Angostura
 bitters
1 × 5ml spoon
 brandy
chilled Champagne
½ slice orange

Put a lump of sugar in a Champagne glass and soak it in the Angostura bitters. Add the brandy and top up with chilled Champagne. Place the orange slice on top.

VARIATION

Add 1 × 5ml spoon Dubonnet.

Daiquiri

¾ white rum
¼ fresh lime or lemon
 juice
½ × 2.5ml spoon caster
 sugar

Shake all the ingredients together in a cocktail shaker; then strain into a wine or cocktail glass.

VARIATION
Frozen Daiquiri

Shake the ingredients briskly in a cocktail shaker; then pour the liquid over plenty of shaved or crushed ice in a Champagne glass. Do not strain. Drink with a short straw.

Dry Martini

⅔ dry gin
⅓ dry vermouth
cracked ice
a twist of lemon rind

Stir the gin and vermouth together in a mixing glass, and strain into a wine or cocktail glass. Stir in the ice and serve with the lemon rind.

Horse's Neck

1 lemon
ice cubes
4 × 10ml spoons brandy
dry ginger ale
a few drops Angostura
 bitters (optional)

Pare the rind of the lemon in one piece in a spiral. Place one end of the rind over the edge of a tumbler, allowing the remainder to curl inside. Anchor it with 2 cubes of ice at the bottom of the glass. Add the brandy and fill with dry ginger ale. Add a few drops of Angostura bitters, if liked.

Kir

See p1361.

Manhattan

⅔ bourbon whisky
⅓ sweet vermouth
a few drops Angostura
 bitters
cracked ice
1 maraschino cherry

Stir the liquid ingredients together in a mixing glass, and strain into a cocktail glass. Add the ice, and decorate with a cherry.

Negroni

2–3 ice cubes
⅓ dry gin
⅓ sweet vermouth
⅓ Campari
soda water (optional)
1 slice of orange

Put the ice cubes in a tall glass. Pour the spirits over them and top up with soda water, if liked. Decorate with the slice of orange.

Old Fashioned

1 lump of sugar
a few drops Angostura
  bitters
2 × 5ml spoons water
  (approx)

1 measure bourbon
  whisky
ice cubes
1 maraschino cherry
$\frac{1}{2}$ slice of orange

Put a lump of sugar in an 'old fashioned' glass and soak it in the Angostura bitters. Add enough water to dissolve the sugar. Add the whisky and ice cubes, and decorate with a cherry and an orange slice.

Pink Gin

a few drops Angostura
  bitters

1 measure of gin
ice cubes

Shake the Angostura bitters into a wine or cocktail glass and roll it around in the glass. Add the gin, and ice cubes to taste.

Rum Nog

double measure of dark
  rum
1 egg

250ml cold milk
a little sugar
a pinch of grated nutmeg

Mix all the ingredients together thoroughly. Serve in a tumbler.

Screwdriver

$\frac{1}{3}$ vodka
$\frac{2}{3}$ fresh orange juice

ice cubes
1 slice of orange

Stir the liquid ingredients with the ice cubes, in a wine or cocktail glass. Decorate with a slice of orange.

Sidecar

$\frac{1}{2}$ brandy
$\frac{1}{4}$ Cointreau

$\frac{1}{4}$ fresh lemon juice
cracked ice

Shake all the ingredients together in a cocktail shaker; then strain into a wine or cocktail glass.

Vodkatini

$\frac{2}{3}$ vodka
$\frac{1}{3}$ dry vermouth

cracked ice
a twist of lemon rind

Stir the vodka and vermouth together in a mixing glass, and strain into a wine or cocktail glass. Stir in the ice and serve with the lemon rind.

Whisky Mac

$\frac{1}{2}$ whisky

$\frac{1}{2}$ ginger wine

Stir the whisky and ginger wine together in a wine or cocktail glass. Do not add ice.

White Lady

$\frac{1}{2}$ dry gin
$\frac{1}{4}$ Cointreau
$\frac{1}{4}$ fresh lemon juice

ice cubes
$\frac{1}{2}$ × 2.5ml spoon egg
  white

Shake all the ingredients together in a cocktail shaker; then strain into a wine or cocktail glass.

Whisky Sour

4 × 15ml spoons whisky
juice of $\frac{1}{2}$ lemon
1 × 5ml spoon beaten egg
  white

white sugar
cracked ice
soda water

Shake the whisky, lemon juice, egg white, sugar, and ice together in a cocktail shaker; then strain into a wine or cocktail glass. Top up with soda water.

HOME WINE AND BEER MAKING

The elder-berry is well adapted for the production of wine; its juice contains a considerable portion of the principle necessary for a vigorous fermentation, and its beautiful colour communicates a rich tint to the wine made from it. It is, however, deficient in sweetness, and therefore demands an addition of sugar. It is one of the very best of the genuine old English wines; and a cup of it mulled, just previous to retiring to bed on a winter night, is a thing to be " run for," as Cobbett would say.

The Wine-making Process

Making wine at home is no longer the hit-or-miss business of the past. Practised wine-makers have worked out recipes using the right blend of ingredients, a suitable yeast, and the correct control of sugar so that wines can be made which compare favourably with bought wines.

The process of making wine is essentially the fermentation of a sugar solution by the action of enzymes in wine yeast cells. The enzymes in an active colony of yeast cells break down the sugar molecules and convert the sugar in the liquid into alcohol and carbon dioxide. Fruit, vegetables, flowers, herbs and grains provide the flavour.

There are no legal restrictions on the making of wine in the UK, as long as it is for home consumption only. However, it is against the law to sell or raffle home-made wine, even for charity, without a licence. It is also illegal, and indeed potentially dangerous, to try to distil it.

EQUIPMENT

Purpose-made equipment is widely available from specialist suppliers, department stores, and larger chemists. There is a bewildering variety and the beginner is advised to start in a small way, gaining experience with simple equipment before spending a lot of money on the more sophisticated types.

The following is a list of the basic items:

Boiler: For extracting the juice from root vegetables or hard fruit. Purpose-made boilers are available from specialist suppliers and are normally of 12–25 litre capacity. A large stewpan is a practical alternative, as long as it is not made of iron, brass or copper which will impart toxins to the wine. Another method is to use a juice extractor.

Mashing container: For steeping soft fruit and holding the 'must', or fermenting liquor, during the first few days' 'fiery' fermentation. A high density polyethylene (polythene) bin with a tight-fitting lid is ideal, and is readily available from wine-making suppliers. The capacity may vary from 12–25 litres. It is important *not* to use a coloured, low-grade plastic bin which could impart toxins to the wine.

A mashing container

Strainer: For filtering the solid matter, such as fruit residues, from the must. A nylon sieve or bag works well.

Fermentation jars: For holding the must during the main fermentation stage, before the wine is transferred to bottles. The best jars are made of glass, and those with lugs or 'ear' handles are the most popular. The capacity of a fermentation jar is normally 4.5 litres.

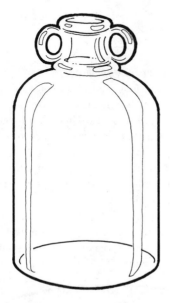

Fermentation traps or air-locks: For allowing carbon dioxide to escape while preventing air entering the must. A trap is fitted to the fermentation jar and filled with sterilizing solution; carbon dioxide bubbles can escape through this, but the must cannot become infected by airborne bacteria.

Wine bottles: For storing the wine after fermentation has ceased and while it is maturing. Use proper wine bottles, rather than squash or sauce bottles, or even returnable tonic and soda water bottles, which are unsuitable and may not be strong enough.

Corks and bungs: For sealing wine bottles and jars. Use new corks rather than old ones, which may be damaged or misshapen and which are difficult to sterilize thoroughly. Plastic and rubber bungs have the advantage of being re-usable and easily sterilized. A corking tool, which is not expensive, is very useful and simplifies bottle sealing.

Siphon tube: For 'racking' or siphoning the wine from the fermentation jars into clean jars or bottles.

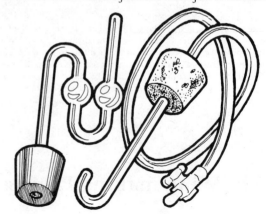

An air-lock (left) and a siphon tube (right)

Hydrometer: For measuring the amount of sugar in the must and for calculating the alcoholic strength of a wine. This instrument, also known as a saccharometer, is not essential, but is most useful in determining how much sugar should be added at any particular stage.

Thermometer: For determining the temperature of the must. The optimum temperature for the initial fermentation is 21°C. Yeast cells are killed at a temperature exceeding 38°C.

Miscellaneous: Also useful are such items as a measuring jug, a plastic or wooden spoon, and a plastic funnel.

Preparation of Equipment

All equipment must be sterilized before use to ensure perfect hygiene, and to prevent infection by organisms such as surface or airborne bacteria.

Each item should be washed thoroughly with hot water; in the case of boilers or stewpans this is sufficient, as the high temperatures to which they are subsequently subjected will kill off any remaining bacteria. The remaining equipment should be sterilized with a solution of 2 Campden tablets and 1×2.5ml spoon citric acid in 500ml cold water. The tablets must be crushed before the addition of water. This solution is used for swirling around the inside and rim of each container; smaller items need only be dipped in it.

BASIC INGREDIENTS

There are four basic ingredients in any wine – flavouring, water, sugar, and yeast.

Flavouring: This is provided by fruit, vegetable, or some form of plant juice. The juice can be fresh, frozen, jammed, canned or derived from dried plants, fruits, grains, herbs or spices. Grape juice produces the finest wine and, as it contains all the nutrients or foods that yeast needs, is the ideal medium for fermentation. The beginner is advised to start with one of the concentrated grape juices that are readily available, before experimenting with the traditional country or hedgerow wines.

Sugar: The amount of sugar used varies with the type of wine desired but, as a very general guide, 250g sugar per 1 litre water gives a dry wine, 300g sugar per 1 litre water a medium wine, and 350g sugar per 1 litre water a sweet one.

Granulated sugar is the type most commonly used and is quite satisfactory for making both red and white wines.

Brown sugar gives a golden colour to white wines, and also adds a slightly caramelized flavour. It should be used only for the richer Madeira-type wines, and never for delicate wines such as those made from flowers.

Yeast: A special wine yeast gives more predictable and satisfactory results than brewers' or bakers' yeast, or the natural yeasts which form the 'bloom' on fruits. Wild yeasts may produce ethyl-acetate, which imparts a vinegary smell, but not taste, to the wine.

Wine yeast has a higher alcohol tolerance than other yeasts and settles out of the wine more readily into a firm sediment. Wine yeasts are available in granule, liquid or tablet form, and in varieties suitable for making particular types of wine. Champagne wine yeast can be used for still wines as well as for sparkling wines.

Other Ingredients

Campden tablets: For killing off wild yeasts and bacteria in the must, before the wine yeast is added, and for sterilizing equipment. They are made from sodium metabisulphite and provide the sterilizing agent, sulphur dioxide, in the right quantities (50 parts per million) when a tablet is dissolved in liquid.

Potassium sorbate: Used in conjunction with Campden tablets to terminate fermentation of low alcohol sweet wines. An extra Campden tablet can be substituted if potassium sorbate is not available.

Yeast nutrient: Unless grape juice, sultanas or raisins are used, the yeast may suffer from a lack of nitrogen. Nitrogen, in the form of di-ammonium phosphate, is readily available in powder or tablet form. Its addition helps to improve fermentation and the production of sufficient alcohol.

Acid: Insufficient acid in the must will inhibit the fermentation and produce a poor-quality, medicinal-tasting wine. As an approximate guide, when a small amount of liquid is tested with acid indicator paper (available from chemists and suppliers of wine-making equipment), a reaction of between pH3.2 and pH3.4 is the desired level.

Some fruits and vegetables, particularly root crops, and flowers, herbs, grains, dates, and figs contain little acid. Acid may be added in the form of lemon juice or citric acid, which is easily obtainable as crystals. Tartaric acid or malic acid may also be used in crystal form. Individual recipes recommend the quantity of acid needed for making a particular wine.

Tannin: The slight dryness in the mouth after tasting red wine comes from the tannin content. It is in the skins, stems, and pips of grapes; lack of it results in a flat, insipid wine whose keeping qualities may also be impaired.

Wines made from ingredients other than grapes, elderberries, and pears will need the addition of grape tannin; the recommended quantities are given in the recipes.

Pectic enzyme: When fruit is crushed to release the juice, the pectin or setting agent is also released, and this can cause a pectin haze in the wine which may be difficult to clear. A pectic (pectolytic) enzyme, available in powder or liquid form, should be added according to the manufacturer's instructions. The enzyme degrades the pectin and should be added to all fruit musts to stimulate the release of the juice.

STEP-BY-STEP GUIDE TO MAKING WINE

Table Wines

The following information outlines the basic method for making most wines. As a general rule, from 1–1.5kg sugar and up to 4.5 litres of water are required for every 2kg of plant material. These proportions will obviously vary with different recipes.

Preparation of ingredients: Scrub vegetables clean of every trace of soil. Top and tail, remove any blemishes, dice and boil them until soft. Leave to cool, strain off the liquor and use this to make the wine. Discard or eat the vegetables.

Gather flowers just before the petals fall on a dry, sunny day. Use only the petals or florets; the leaf, stem, and calyx will make the wine bitter.

Wash fruit, then remove the stalks, stones and blemished parts. Pare citrus fruits very thinly, halve them and squeeze out the juice. Discard the white pith as this gives an unpleasant, bitter flavour.

Preparation of the must: Place the crushed fruit in the mashing container with the water, and stir well. In the case of hard fruit, such as plums and gooseberries, hot water should be added to soften the fruit. When cool, add the citric acid, pectic enzyme and Campden tablet, and any other ingredients, such as raisins, sultanas or grape juice; then stir. At this stage the Campden tablet and pectic enzyme are used together as a sterilizing agent. If the base ingredients are first boiled, eg Parsnip Dessert Wine (p1378), this process is enough to kill any bacteria, and the Campden tablet will not then be required.

Cover the container tightly to prevent infection and leave it for 24 hours in a warm place.

Adding the yeast: The yeast, yeast nutrient, and grape tannin (if included in the recipe) are added the following day, unless otherwise indicated. The optimum temperature for fermentation is 21°C. Small immersion heaters are available from wine-making suppliers, but are not necessary if the container is in a warm place such as near a central heating radiator or in an airing cupboard. It may help to wrap a blanket around the container.

Dried or liquid yeast can be added direct from the container and stirred in, but for a quicker fermentation the yeast is usually activated first. Put it in a sterilized bottle, bowl or jug, with 150ml of the must and the yeast nutrient, according to the manufacturer's instructions; leave the liquid in a warm place until it froths, then add it to the must.

Loosely cover the must and leave for 3–4 days. Remember that the gas must escape, but airborne bacteria and moulds must be kept out. Press the floating fruit pulp down into the must once or twice daily, or keep it submerged with a plate.

Secondary fermentation: Strain the must into a fresh container, through a nylon sieve or bag. If using a hydrometer, this is an opportune time to check the amount of sugar in the must. Pour enough liquid into the trial jar usually sold with the hydrometer, and float the hydrometer in it. Record the specific gravity reading. Stir enough sugar into the must to increase the specific gravity reading to the level which will produce the right amount of alcohol for the particular wine being made (comparative figures are usually given on the hydrometer). Table wines need 10–12% alcohol and dessert wines 15–17%. (The amount of sugar in the recipes which follow is for average-quality fruit, and may need adjusting in the light of hydrometer readings.) After sweetening, pour the must into fermentation jars using a funnel. Fill to 2cm below the top and insert an air-lock containing a little Campden sterilizing liquid. Keep in a warm place as before.

When no more bubbles can be seen, either rising in the jar or passing through the air-lock, the fermentation is finished. The yeast enzymes, having no more sugar to convert or having reached the limit of their alcohol tolerance, have ceased to be active. Put the jar in a cool place for a few days to allow the yeast cells and fruit pulp to settle on the bottom of the jar and form a sediment.

Racking: Siphon the clear wine into a clean fermentation jar which has been washed and rinsed out with Campden sterilizing liquid. Discard the sediment. This process is called racking.

Add 1 Campden tablet per 4.5 litres of wine to prevent infection and oxidation. Top the jar up with similar wine or cold boiled water if necessary, bung it tight and store it in a cool place until the wine is star-bright. Rack again. If the wine is not racked as suggested, the sediment will decompose and give the finished wine a foul flavour.

Bottling: Wine should be left in large jars to mature, but some people prefer to bottle it early since bottles are easier to store. Bottling normally takes place after the wine has been stored for 6 months, although a quantity of red wine over 25 litres can benefit from 8–9 months' storage in a cask. Do not use beer or vinegar casks; they have a taint which cannot be removed and which spoils the wine. Casks with a capacity of less than 25 litres are also unsuitable because their surface to volume ratio is so high that the wine deteriorates through excessive oxidation.

Red wines should be put in dark bottles, otherwise they tend to lose their colour. Sterilize the bottles and corks or bungs before use with the Campden liquid (see p1372). Corks should be soaked for 24 hours to soften them.

Label the bottles with the appropriate name and the date on which the wine was made and bottled.

Storage: Store the bottles on their sides, preferably in a rack or bin in the dark, at a temperature of 13°C. Light white wines are sometimes ready for drinking after 3–4 months, especially wines made from canned gooseberries or apricots. Most red wines need at least one year to mature, and preferably longer.

Sparkling Wine

Make a light wine containing 10% alcohol. Leave it until it is 6 months old and star-bright, then stir in 75g sugar per 4.5 litres wine and an active Champagne yeast. Fit an air-lock and leave the jar in a warm place.

As soon as fermentation starts, pour the wine into sterilized Champagne bottles – no other bottles are strong enough to use safely. Fit hollow-domed, plastic or blister stoppers and wire them on with a cage obtainable from wine-making suppliers. Store the bottles on their sides for at least 6–7 months.

Remove the sediment by first standing the bottles upside-down for 3 weeks, giving them a daily twist and gentle shake to help the sediment slide down the side of the bottles and settle in the stoppers.

Chill the bottles of wine, keeping them inverted.

Crush some ice, mix 1×15ml spoon common salt with it, and stand the neck of the bottle in the ice for 10 minutes until the wine in the stopper is frozen. Remove the cage and stopper. Quickly add 1 or 2 saccharin tablets to sweeten an otherwise very dry wine, and reseal the bottle with a clean and softened stopper. Replace the cage and keep the wine until required.

Dessert Wines

Quite strong dessert wines, similar to port, can be made by feeding the fermentation with extra sugar; this increases the alcohol tolerance of the yeast. Remember to leave room in the jar for the extra sugar when filling it with the must.

Record the specific gravity. When the gravity falls to about 1.010, take out some of the wine. Dissolve half the extra sugar in it and return it to the jar, pouring slowly to prevent frothing. The gravity should increase to 1.020. Add the rest of the sugar in the same way, in two or three equal portions every seventh day until fermentation stops. Dessert wines need more acid than table wines, and tannin to balance the extra alcohol. Red dessert wines also need more tannin. An extra year's storage is needed for the wine to mature.

Apéritif Wines

Sherry-type wine is fermented like dessert wine, but is stored in jars only seven-eighths full. Plug the neck of the jar with cotton wool rather than a bung; air then filters through the cotton wool and helps to develop the sherry flavour.

SERVING HOME-MADE WINES

Home-made wines should be decanted before serving them as they often throw a further deposit during storage. They also look better in a plain decanter. For the technique of decanting, see p1363.

Serve white, golden, rosé, and sparkling home-made wines chilled, remembering however that if they are too cold, their flavour is dimmed. Serve red wines at room temperature.

WINES

Apple Table Wine

Yield six 75cl bottles (4.5 litres)

3 litres cold water
1 × 5ml spoon citric acid
pectic enzyme
Campden tablets
4kg assorted apples
250g sultanas

1 × 2.5ml spoon grape tannin
Champagne wine yeast
1 × 2.5ml spoon yeast nutrient
750g granulated sugar

Pour the cold water into a mashing container with the citric acid, pectic enzyme, and 1 Campden tablet. Wash and chop the apples and sultanas and add them to the liquor immediately, so that the fruit does not turn brown. Continue as described on pp1374–75.

Note Hard pears, crab apples or quinces, up to a total quantity of 1kg, may be added to the 4kg apples for extra flavour.

VARIATION
Pear Table Wine

Make as for Apple Table Wine, using 3kg hard pears instead of the apples. Omit the grape tannin and add an extra 1 × 10ml spoon citric acid. This wine may be effectively sparkled (see p1375).

Elderberry Table Wine

Yield six 75cl bottles (4.5 litres)

3.5 litres cold water
1 × 15ml spoon citric acid
pectic enzyme
Campden tablets
500g ripe elderberries
4 ripe bananas

250g concentrated red grape juice
Bordeaux wine yeast
1 × 2.5ml spoon yeast nutrient
750g granulated sugar

Pour 1.5 litres of the cold water into a mashing container with the citric acid, pectic enzyme, and 1 Campden tablet. Wash and stalk the elderberries; peel and slice the bananas. Heat them both in the remaining water for 20 minutes at a temperature of 80°C. Strain the fruit juice into the container. Cover and leave for 24 hours. Continue as described on pp1374–75.

VARIATION
The wine can be varied by adding 500g mashed blackberries and 250g mashed blackcurrants to the elderberries. In this case, use only 2 bananas and 1 × 10ml spoon citric acid.

Blackberry Dessert Wine

Yield six 75cl bottles (4.5 litres)

3.5 litres cold water
1 × 15ml spoon citric acid
pectic enzyme
Campden tablets
2kg blackberries

4 very ripe bananas
500g concentrated red grape juice
port wine yeast
1 × 5ml spoon yeast nutrient
1kg granulated sugar

Pour the cold water into a mashing container with the citric acid, pectic enzyme, and 1 Campden tablet. Wash, top and tail, and mash the blackberries. Peel and mash the bananas. Add both to the liquor. Continue as described on pp1374–75.

VARIATIONS
Blackcurrant Dessert Wine

Make as for Blackberry Dessert Wine, but use only 1kg blackcurrants and omit the citric acid.

Blackberry and Blackcurrant Dessert Wine

Mix 2kg blackberries and 1kg blackcurrants and double all the other ingredients except the citric acid and yeast. This yields twelve 75cl bottles (9 litres).

Damson or Plum Dessert Wine

Make as for Blackberry Dessert Wine, but substitute 2kg damsons and/or plums for the blackberries.

Damson Table Wine

Yield six 75cl bottles (4.5 litres)

3.5 litres cold water
1 × 10ml spoon citric
  acid
pectic enzyme
Campden tablets
1.5kg ripe damsons
250g concentrated red
  grape juice

1 × 2.5ml spoon grape
  tannin
Burgundy wine yeast
1 × 2.5ml spoon yeast
  nutrient
800g granulated sugar

Pour the cold water into a mashing container with the citric acid, pectic enzyme, and 1 Campden tablet. Wash, stalk, stone, and mash the damsons and add them to the liquor. Continue as described on pp1374–75.

Sparkling Gooseberry Wine

Yield six 75cl bottles (4.5 litres)

1.25kg green
  gooseberries
4 litres boiling water
250g sultanas
1 × 10ml spoon citric
  acid
pectic enzyme

Campden tablets
Champagne wine yeast
1 × 2.5ml spoon yeast
  nutrient
700g granulated sugar

Wash, top and tail the gooseberries and put them into a mashing container. Pour the boiling water over them. Leave for a few hours until the gooseberries are soft, then crush them. Wash and chop the sultanas and add them to the liquor with the acid, pectic enzyme, and 1 Campden tablet. Cover and leave for 24 hours.

Stir in the yeast and nutrient and leave to ferment for 3 days, pressing down the fruit cap twice each day. Strain the must into a fresh container and press the fruit dry. Stir in the sugar and continue as described on pp1374–75.

Note Gooseberries also make a good still wine using a Hock instead of a Champagne wine yeast.

Dandelion Wine

Yield six 75cl bottles (4.5 litres)

1 litre dandelion petals
4.5 litres water
1 × 10ml spoon citric
  acid
Campden tablets
500g concentrated white
  grape juice
1 × 2.5ml spoon grape
  tannin

750g granulated sugar
general purpose wine
  yeast
1 × 2.5ml spoon yeast
  nutrient
1g potassium sorbate

Pick the dandelion petals free from all green and put them into a mashing container. Add 3.5 litres hot water to the petals and crush them against the side of the container with the back of a wooden spoon; leave to cool. Stir in the citric acid and 1 Campden tablet. Cover, and leave for 3 days, macerating the petals against the side of the container daily.

Dissolve the grape juice in the remaining 1 litre of water and strain the flower liquor into it. Stir in the grape tannin, sugar, yeast and nutrient, and pour the liquid into a fermentation jar, leaving some headroom for the first few days of fermentation. Fit an air-lock and leave the jar in a warm place.

When the fermentation becomes steady, top up the jar with cold water. Continue the fermentation until the specific gravity reading on a hydrometer check has fallen to 1.015 (usually in about 2 weeks).

Rack the wine into a sterile jar, add the potassium sorbate and 1 Campden tablet to end the fermentation, and move the jar to a cool place. As soon as a further deposit appears on the bottom of the jar, rack again; then bottle and store (see p1375).

VARIATION

Elderflower or Rose Petal Wine

Make as for Dandelion Wine, but use 1 litre of elderflower or 2 litres of scented rose petals instead of the dandelion petals.

Grape Wines

Campden tablets   pectic enzyme

White Wine
fresh white grapes   *Chablis* **or** *Hock wine yeast*

Red or Rosé Wine
fresh black **or** *blue grapes*   *Burgundy* **or** *Bordeaux wine yeast*

White Wine

Wash, stalk, and crush the white grapes. Place in a mashing container, and add 1 crushed Campden tablet and 1×5ml spoon pectic enzyme per 5kg grapes. Cover, and leave for 24 hours. Strain out the juice and press the pulp dry.

Check the specific gravity with a hydrometer and add enough sugar to increase the gravity to between 1.076 and 1.080. Stir in an active Chablis or Hock wine yeast, pour the must into a fermentation jar, fit an air-lock and continue as described on pp1374–75.

Red Wine

Wash, stalk, and crush the black or blue grapes. Place in a mashing container, and add 1 crushed Campden tablet and 1×5ml spoon pectic enzyme per 5kg grapes. Cover, and leave for 24 hours. Remove some of the juice, check the specific gravity, and add enough sugar to increase the reading to between 1.084 and 1.090. Stir in an active Burgundy or Bordeaux wine yeast and leave to ferment for 10 days, pressing down the fruit cap twice daily and keeping the container well covered.

Strain out and press the pulp dry, pour the must into a fermentation jar, fit an air-lock and continue as described on pp1374–75.

Rosé Wine

Make as for red wine but strain out and press the pulp after 24 hours or as soon as the juice is pink enough. Add enough sugar to increase the specific gravity to 1.080.

Parsnip Dessert Wine

Yield six 75cl bottles (4.5 litres)

2kg fresh parsnips
500g raisins
4 litres water
25g citric acid
1×2.5ml spoon grape tannin
1×2.5ml spoon yeast nutrient
Tokay wine yeast
1kg granulated sugar
Campden tablets

Top and tail the parsnips, scrub them thoroughly, and cut them into small dice. Wash and chop the raisins, and put them in a mashing container. Boil the parsnips in the water until tender, then strain the liquor on to the raisins in the container. Cover and leave to cool, then add the acid, tannin, nutrient, and yeast. Cover, and leave for 7 days, pressing down the floating raisins twice each day. Strain out and press the raisins dry, stir in half the sugar and pour the must into a fermentation jar. Continue as described on pp1374–75.

Note This is a strong, dessert wine with a distinctive flavour like that of Madeira.

Ginger Wine

Yield six 75cl bottles (4.5 litres)

50g ginger root
3.5 litres water
1kg granulated sugar
1×15ml spoon citric acid
1×2.5ml spoon grape tannin
500g concentrated white grape juice
Tokay wine yeast
1×2.5ml spoon yeast nutrient
1g potassium sorbate
Campden tablets

Bruise the ginger root well, and put it into a pan with 2 litres of the water, 500g sugar, and the citric acid. Heat to boiling point, stirring occasionally, reduce the heat and simmer gently for 20 minutes.

Dissolve the tannin and grape juice in the remaining 1.5 litres water in a mashing container. Strain the hot liquor into the container and leave to cool. Add the yeast and nutrient and pour the liquor into a fermentation jar, leaving about 300ml room for the rest of the sugar. Leave for 10 days, then stir in half the remaining sugar. Leave for a further 5 days and add the rest of the sugar.

Check the specific gravity with a hydrometer and when it reaches 1.010 (about another 5 days), rack the wine into a sterile jar and add the potassium sorbate and 1 Campden tablet to end the fermentation. Leave the wine in a cool place until it is clear, then rack again. Keep for 6 months; then bottle and store (p1375) for a further 3 months before use.

Rhubarb Table Wine

Yield six 75cl bottles (4.5 litres)

1 lemon	250g sultanas
3.5 litres water	Chablis wine yeast
pectic enzyme	1 × 2.5ml spoon yeast
Campden tablets	nutrient
2kg fresh rhubarb	900g granulated sugar

Pare the rind of the lemon thinly and squeeze out the juice. Pour the water into a mashing container, add the pectic enzyme, 1 Campden tablet, and the lemon rind and juice. Top, tail, and wipe the rhubarb clean, then chop it into small pieces. Wash and chop the sultanas. Add the rhubarb and sultanas to the liquor. Cover, and leave for 24 hours, then continue as described on pp1374–75.

Mead

Yield six 75cl bottles (4.5 litres)

1.5kg white honey	Maury yeast
3.5 litres warm water	1 × 5ml spoon yeast
2 × 10ml spoons citric	nutrient
acid	honey, sugar or
1 × 5ml spoon grape	saccharin to sweeten
tannin	

Dissolve the honey in the water. Leave to cool and stir in all the other ingredients except the sweetener. Pour into a fermentation jar, fit an airlock and leave in a warm place for 3 days.

Top up the jar with cold water and complete the fermentation. The length of time for this varies between 3 weeks and 6 months. Continue as described on pp1374–75. Sweeten to taste with honey, sugar or saccharin just before serving.

Sloe Dessert Wine

Yield six 75cl bottles (4.5 litres)

1.5kg ripe sloes	1 × 2.5ml spoon grape
4 litres boiling water	tannin
500g raisins	port wine yeast
1 × 15ml spoon citric	1 × 2.5ml spoon yeast
acid	nutrient
pectic enzyme	1kg granulated sugar
Campden tablets	

Stalk and wash the sloes, and put them into a mashing container. Pour the boiling water over them and leave to cool. Crush the sloes. Wash and chop the raisins and add them to the liquor with the citric acid, pectic enzyme, and 1 Campden tablet. Cover, and leave for 24 hours, then continue as described on pp1374–75.

OTHER DRINKS

Sloe Gin

Yield 1.25 litres (approx)

500g ripe sloes	1 litre dry gin
250g caster sugar	

Stalk and wash the sloes and prick them all over with a bodkin. Put them into a jar that can be fitted with an air-tight seal. Dissolve the sugar in the gin and pour it on to the sloes. Seal the jar and store it for 3 months, giving it a gentle shake every few days to extract and distribute the flavour.

Strain, bottle, and store for a further 3 months.

Morello Cherry Brandy

Yield 1 litre (approx)

500g black ripe Morello	1 × 75cl bottle French
cherries	Eau de Vie
250g caster sugar	

Make as for Sloe Gin.

Note The cherries can be used subsequently in an open flan or added to a fruit salad.

Home-brewed Beers

The easiest way to brew beer at home is with a kit of prepared malt extract and hop essence. Kits for making all kinds of beer are available – bitter, brown, stout, lager, barley wine – and all kits include yeast, finings, and full instructions (which may vary slightly from kit to kit). Sugar and water are all that have to be added; and only a high density polyethylene mashing container or bin and beer bottles are needed in the way of equipment. Use only specially strengthened beer bottles for beer (including ginger beer); ordinary soft drink or wine bottles are not strong enough and may explode.

Individual beers can also be made from malt extract, hops, sugar, water, and yeast. Ingredient quantities can be varied to taste.

Home-brewed Beer

Basic recipe

Yield 10 litres (approx)

1kg malt extract
500g granulated sugar
4 litres water

50g Wye Challenger
(Golding) hops
1 sachet dried beer yeast
50g caster sugar

Dissolve the malt extract and sugar in 2 litres warm water in a mashing container. Boil the hops in the remaining 2 litres water for 45 minutes and strain the liquor into the container. Discard the hops. Top up the container to the 10 litre mark with cold water and when the temperature of the 'wort' (as it is called) reaches 20°C, sprinkle the beer yeast over it. Cover, and leave the beer to ferment out.

On the second and third days of fermentation, skim off the yeast head. Leave for about 6 days until fermentation has finished, then siphon the beer into sterilized bottles, leaving room for the priming syrup.

To make the priming syrup, dissolve the caster sugar in 225ml beer and distribute it evenly between the bottles. Fit sterilized stoppers or crown caps for a gas-proof seal. Leave the bottles in a warm place for a week, then store them in a cool place for at least a further 3 weeks before drinking.

VARIATIONS

Brown Ale

Substitute 40g Wye Northdown (Fuggle) hops and 100g chocolate-coloured malt grains for the Golding hops and add 1 × 5ml spoon common salt. Reduce the amount of granulated sugar to 300g. Boil the hops and grains together.

Stout

Substitute 50g Wye Northdown (Fuggle) hops and 100g black malt grains for the Golding hops and add 1 × 5ml spoon common salt. Boil the hops and grains together. For a milk stout, add 200g lactose with the 500g sugar.

Note In soft water areas, omit the salt from these recipes but add some hardening salts when brewing a bitter-style beer, eg the basic recipe. They are available, pre-mixed, in sachets from beer and wine-making suppliers.

Ginger Beer

Yield 5.25 litres (approx)

25g ginger root
2 lemons
500g granulated sugar

3 × 2.5ml spoons cream
of tartar
5 litres hot water
1 sachet dried beer yeast

Bruise the ginger root. Thinly pare the rind of the lemons. Put the ginger, lemon rind, sugar, and cream of tartar in a mashing container and add the hot water. Stir gently until the sugar is dissolved, then leave to cool.

Squeeze out the juice of the lemons, add it to the cooled liquor and sprinkle the yeast over it. Cover and leave in a warm place for 48 hours. Skim off the yeast head after 24 hours, leave until fermentation has finished and then skim again before bottling.

Sterilize enough beer bottles to hold the liquor. Siphon the ginger beer into the bottles, being careful not to disturb the deposit in the container. No priming is required. Seal the bottles tightly and leave in a warm place for 3 days. Serve well chilled.

HOME FREEZING

In June and July, gooseberries, currants, raspberries, strawberries, and other summer fruits, should be preserved.

HIGH QUALITY FOOD PRESERVING

Freezing is a quick method of preserving food safely and in good condition. The activities of micro-organisms are slowed down as food approaches freezing point, and they become dormant at −18°C. Home freezers are designed to bring the food down to this temperature and to maintain it at the same temperature during storage. In some home freezers, the temperature can be reduced still further for fast freezing (which gives a better quality thawed product) but true *deep* freezing is only possible commercially; commercial frozen-food stores are usually maintained at −29°C. Information on types of freezer and their maintenance can be found on pp201–3.

Nearly all fresh foods, and many cooked foods, freeze well, but there are a few items to avoid entirely, or to freeze only with great care. There are also a few foods which cannot be frozen and then eaten raw, although they can be used for cooking.

Foods Not to Freeze

1) hard-boiled eggs (including Scotch eggs, eggs in pies and in sandwiches)
2) soured cream, single cream (less than 40% butterfat), and half-cream which separate
3) yoghurt
4) cottage cheese; this becomes watery
5) custards (including tarts); the custard mixture of eggs and milk can be frozen uncooked, but there is little point in this
6) soft meringue toppings
7) mayonnaise and salad dressings
8) milk puddings
9) royal icing and other icings and frostings without fat; they crumble and chip in the freezer
10) salad vegetables with a high water content, eg lettuce, watercress, radishes
11) old boiled potatoes (potatoes can be frozen mashed, roast, baked or as chips)
12) stuffed poultry
13) food with a high proportion of gelatine
14) whole eggs in shells which will crack

Foods to Freeze with Care

1) Cooked onions, garlic, spices, and herbs. They sometimes get a musty flavour in cooked dishes in the freezer, and recipe quantities should be reduced in such dishes as casseroles; they can be adjusted during re-heating. Careful packing will help to prevent these strong flavours spreading to other foods, but a short time in storage is recommended.
2) Rice, spaghetti, and potatoes should only be frozen without liquid. They become mushy in liquid and should not be frozen in soups or stews.
3) Sauces and gravy are best thickened by reduction, or with a vegetable purée. If flour is used, the sauce or gravy must be re-heated with great care, preferably in a double boiler, to avoid separation. Cornflour can be used but gives a glutinous quality. Egg and cream thickening should only be added after freezing.

1381

4) Apples, pears, avocados, melons, and bananas cannot be successfully frozen whole to eat raw. They can be prepared and frozen for use in various other ways (although pears are never very satisfactory). Bananas are not worth freezing as they are in season at a reasonable price throughout the year.

5) Cabbage cannot be frozen successfully to eat raw, and is not really worth freezing since it occupies a lot of freezer space. Red cabbage may be worth freezing, as it has a short season and is never very plentiful.

6) Celery and chicory cannot be frozen to eat raw. They are useful frozen in liquid to serve as vegetables. Celery can be used in stews or soups.

7) Tomatoes cannot be frozen to eat raw, but are invaluable frozen as purée or juice or to use in soups, stews, and sauces.

8) Milk must be homogenized and packed in waxed cartons. However, it is hardly worth freezing since several types of milk can be stored without refrigeration.

High Quality Storage Life

While frozen food is stored at $-18°C$, slow changes take place in colour, texture, and flavour. The high quality storage life is the longest time food should be stored so that it is still perfect in every way when used. It is important that food stored in the freezer should not remain static; a good turnover should be maintained. Incorrect packaging material, bad packing, and air spaces in the packs will affect the keeping qualities of frozen food. The inclusion of salt, spices, herbs, onion, and garlic, or of fats, also shorten the keeping time of foods as well as affecting their flavour. Cooked dishes in particular should be eaten quickly as they can sometimes suffer badly through changes in their flavour or texture.

Commercial frozen food manufacturers give a shorter recommended storage life for their products than for the equivalent home-frozen product. This allows for storage in warehouses, and for any fluctuations in temperature which may occur during distribution or shop storage.

BUYING FOR THE FREEZER

Most people assume that buying in bulk will lead to the biggest savings. Any savings depend, however, on the number of people involved, on shopping and eating habits, and the accessibility of shops. Freezer owners usually find that they save on such hidden factors as public transport fares or petrol, and on parking charges, and that they save a great deal of shopping time (which represents money). They may also find that, although their overall shopping bills remain the same, they tend to live better, since the price of better cuts of meat or out-of-season vegetables is balanced by freezing cheaper meat or home produce.

It is a mistake to buy in bulk with price as the only consideration. This can result in buying poor quality food; high quality is rarely combined with cheapness. When choosing a source of supply for buying food in bulk, one should consider the quality of the food, the type of service offered, and also the quantity of food one wishes to buy at one time. There is little point in buying a hundred fish fingers for instance, if they will not be eaten within the recommended storage life.

It is also important to know the storage capacity of one's freezer, and to judge how much space will be taken up by bulk purchases compared with other goods one may want to freeze.

It is usually practical to buy fresh food such as fruit and vegetables when they are in season and of good quality. Meat can be bought in bulk but its value must be carefully assessed since it may be better to buy a selection of favourite cuts rather than a complete carcass. Commercially frozen foods such as vegetables, ice cream, and convenience foods represent good value but sample packs should be tasted first. Even if home-grown produce is not available, it may be worth freezing a few seasonal treats such as asparagus or raspberries for winter use.

PREPARING AND PACKING FOOD FOR THE FREEZER

All food for freezing must be processed quickly. Food must be chilled thoroughly before being put in the freezer, to avoid raising the temperature of the food already stored. Any food must be carefully packed to exclude air, and should be clearly labelled for identification. All food should be frozen quickly. This is best done in the fast-freeze section of the freezer which can be adjusted to a much lower temperature than the rest of the cabinet. If there is no fast-freeze section, place the food to be frozen against the coldest part of the freezer, ie the floor or the sides.

Portions

Food should be prepared and packed in usable portions. Most people find it useful to prepare some large packs, and also a number of individual packs for use in single meals. Large packs of fruit and vegetables can be refastened after portions have been removed.

Packaging Materials

All packaging should be moisture and vapour proof, waterproof, and greaseproof, durable and resistant to low temperatures, easily handled, economically stored, and free from smell.

Suitable materials are:

Waxed containers: These are available with airtight lids and with screw-on tops. Waxed cartons are made with fitted lids in square and rectangular shapes, and there are tall containers with tuck-in lids, and special ones with polythene liners which are suitable for food subject to leakage.

Rigid plastic containers: Most branded plastic boxes are suitable for freezer storage. Ones with flexible sides can be lightly pressed to aid removal of contents. Special Swedish freezer boxes are available which can be boiled for sterilization and which stack and save space.

Glass jars: Screw-topped preserving jars, bottles, and honey jars can be used for freezing if tested for resistance to low temperatures first. To test, place an empty jar in a plastic bag in the freezer overnight; if it breaks, the bag will hold the pieces. Jars with shoulders should not be used as this necessitates long thawing before the food can be turned out and used.

Freezer-to-table ware: This is a bad conductor of heat which means that dishes are slow to heat up, but hold their heat for a long time. Allow extra time for water, stock or sauces to reach boiling point, but remove the container from the heat a short while before you would do so for other pans. It is difficult to halt the cooking even after removing the pan from the heat. Sauces tend to solidify or curdle, eggs to harden, and seared meats to burn, if left in the pan for long after cooking.

If other serving dishes are used, they should be tested for resistance to changes of temperature before use, especially if they will be heated after being frozen.

Polythene: Polythene bags are useful for almost all freezer food, and are available in a wide variety of sizes; they should be of the special heavy quality designed for low temperatures. Polythene sheeting is easy to handle for wrapping meat, poultry, and pies, and it makes identification easy.

Special bags designed for freezing and boiling are convenient for stews, one-portion meals, and vegetables.

Foil and freezer paper: Foil dishes are useful for food which is cooked before freezing and is later re-heated, as one container can be used for all the processes. Heavy duty foil sheeting is useful for overwrapping these dishes, and for packing both raw and cooked foods; it should be used with the dull side towards the food. Freezer paper is strong wrapping which is highly resistant to fat and grease, does not puncture easily, and has an uncoated outer surface on which labelling details can be written.

Headspace and Air Exclusion in Packaging

Containers with lids should be packed leaving a headspace of 2–3cm above the surface of the food to allow for expansion. The precise depth varies according to individual foods.

All sheet wrapping or bags must have the air pressed out so that the wrapping adheres closely to the food. When making a parcel, the air can be pressed out with the hands. Air is most easily removed from bags by inserting a drinking straw at the closing and sucking the air out just before sealing.

Sealing

All types of container and sheet wrapping must be firmly sealed. Bags can be closed with fasteners or heat-sealed with a special welding unit, or with a domestic iron used over thick paper. Special freezing tape with gum which is resistant to low temperatures must be used for finishing sheet-wrapped packages and for sealing containers with lids.

Open Freezing

This method is good for berry fruits, peas, and iced cakes or pies which might be damaged by wrapping before freezing. Just put on trays, freeze until hard, and then pack as usual.

Results of Faulty Packaging

Bad packaging causes a number of problems which, while not rendering the food unfit to eat, may cause an unattractive appearance, toughness, dryness, lack of flavour, or unpleasant mingling of flavours from different foods. Some common problems are:

Ice crystals: If too large a headspace is left on liquid foods in containers, a layer of ice crystals may form which will affect storage and flavour. Liquids can be shaken or stirred back into emulsion when heated or thawed. If the problem occurs in meat, fish, vegetables or fruit, it is usually because the food has been frozen too slowly so that the moisture in the cells has expanded, frozen, and broken surrounding tissues. This always results in the loss of juices and flavour.

Dehydration and freezer burn: Long storage or poor wrapping may result in the loss of moisture and juices, particularly from meat. This causes greyish-brown areas on food known as 'freezer burn'.

Oxidation and rancidity: Oxygen from the air which penetrates wrappings can react with fat cells in food to form chemicals which give meat and fish a bad taste and smell. Fried foods and fat meat or fish can suffer from this problem in the freezer. Salt accelerates this rancidity.

Cross-flavouring: Rough handling, sharp edges, brittle wrappings or over-filled containers can cause cracks or breakages which may result in cross-flavouring from strongly flavoured foods. Broken packaging can also cause dehydration and oxidation.

Flabbiness: Limp and flabby fruit and vegetables are caused by slow freezing, and sometimes by using unsuitable varieties; this can only be discovered by trial and error.

Labelling and Recording

All items should be labelled carefully with the contents, weight, date of freezing, and any special instructions for thawing or re-heating. All packs should be recorded on a board or in a book, and a note made when items are used.

Thawing

Thawing speeds up the chemical reactions which have been halted by freezing. It therefore encourages rapid deterioration, so that food is best thawed in a cold atmosphere such as a refrigerator. It must be eaten or cooked immediately after thawing.

Remove food from its wrappings before thawing if possible, unless otherwise directed.

Frozen cooked food must never be thawed and then refrozen. Raw materials should not be thawed and refrozen, but can be made into cooked dishes and then frozen.

FREEZING METHODS

Fish

Only freshly caught fish should be frozen, and this should be done very quickly. Fish bought from a shop is not suitable for freezing. Clean and prepare fish completely and pack in polythene. Separate steaks or fillets with clingfilm, but avoid making packs deeper than 5cm so that fish is frozen quickly. To keep the flavour and colour of white fish, add the juice of a lemon to the water in which it is washed.

Plainly frozen fillets and whole fish (ie uncoated), should be thawed before cooking. Do not place the fish in water or hold it under a tap as this will wash away the natural moisture.

Commercially frozen breaded fish or fish in batter can be fried straight from the freezer, bearing in mind that the temperature of the fat will be reduced by the frozen fish, and this must be allowed for in the overall timing.

Type of fish	Preparation for freezing	High quality storage life	Thawing instructions
Crab, crayfish, and lobster	Cook and cool. Remove flesh and pack in polythene bags or rigid containers	1 month	Thaw in container in refrigerator and serve cold, or add to cooked dishes
Mussels	Scrub and clean thoroughly. Put in a large pan over medium heat for 3 minutes to open. Cool, remove from shells, and pack in rigid containers with juices	1 month	Thaw in container in refrigerator before adding to dishes
Oily fish (eg herring, mackerel, salmon)	Clean well, fillet, cut in steaks or leave whole. Separate pieces of fish with clingfilm. Wrap in polythene, excluding air carefully	2 months	Thaw large fish in refrigerator, but cook small fish from frozen
Oysters	Open and reserve liquid. Wash fish in brine (1 × 5ml spoon salt to 500ml water). Pack in rigid containers in own liquid	1 month	Thaw in container in refrigerator and serve cold, or add to cooked dishes
Prawns and shrimps	Cook and cool in cooking liquid. Remove shells and pack in polythene bags or rigid containers. Shrimps may be covered in melted spiced butter	1 month	Thaw in container in refrigerator and serve cold, or add to cooked dishes
Smoked fish	Pack in polythene bags, wrapping individual fish in clingfilm	6 months	Thaw in refrigerator to eat cold, or cook haddock and kippers from frozen
White fish (eg cod, sole)	Clean, fillet or cut in steaks, or leave whole. Separate pieces of fish with clingfilm. Wrap in polythene, excluding air carefully	3 months	Thaw large fish in refrigerator, but cook small fish from frozen

Meat, Poultry, and Game

If buying a whole carcass, it is best to ask the butcher to freeze this quantity of meat, because it will take 3 or 4 days in a home freezer. Smaller quantities of meat, poultry, and game can be frozen successfully at home. Meat must be frozen quickly and the fast-freeze switch should be turned on well ahead of freezing time so that the cabinet is at the lowest setting.

It is best to freeze meat in the way in which it will be used, such as cubed or minced, as this will save many hours' thawing and preparation time.

Poultry should be plucked, drawn, and jointed if necessary. Most game must be hung for the required time, then plucked or skinned, and drawn. Surplus fat should be removed, and the meat will take up less space if boned and rolled. Any bones should be padded with a twist of foil or paper before the meat is packed in polythene. Pack chops, steaks, and sausages in small quantities, separated by clingfilm. Remember that salted meats have a limited storage life since fat and salt react together in the freezer to cause rancidity.

Type of meat, poultry, and game	Preparation for freezing	High quality storage life	Thawing instructions
Cubed meat	Pack in small quantities in polythene, pressing together tightly	2 months	Thaw in refrigerator for 3 hours
Ham and bacon	Vacuum packed ham or bacon should be frozen sliced or in joints	1 month (sliced) 3 months (joints)	Thaw in wrappings in refrigerator
Offal	Wash and dry well, remove blood vessels and cores. Wrap in polythene, separating pieces with clingfilm	2 months	Thaw in wrappings in refrigerator for 3 hours
Joints	Trim, bone, and roll, if possible. Pack in polythene	12 months (beef) 9 months (lamb and veal) 6 months (pork)	Thaw in refrigerator allowing 4 hours per 500g
Minced meat	Use lean mince and pack in small quantities. Wrap in polythene	2 months	Thaw in refrigerator for 3 hours. If cooked while still frozen, mince may be tough
Sausages and sausage-meat	Pack in small quantities in polythene	1 month	Thaw in refrigerator for 2 hours
Steaks, chops or sliced meat	Pack in small quantities, separating pieces with clingfilm. Wrap in polythene	6–12 months (according to meat)	Cook slowly from frozen, or thaw in refrigerator
Chicken, guinea-fowl or turkey	Hang, pluck, and draw, if necessary. Truss or cut in joints. Chill for 12 hours, pack in polythene bags, excluding giblets. Do not stuff	12 months	Thaw in wrappings in refrigerator. Must be totally thawed before cooking
Giblets	Clean, wash, dry, and chill. Pack in polythene bags	2 months	Thaw in refrigerator for 2 hours
Duck and goose	Hang, pluck, and draw, if necessary. Chill for 12 hours and pack in polythene bags, excluding giblets	6 months	Thaw in wrappings in refrigerator. Must be completely thawed before cooking

Type of meat, poultry, and game	Preparation for freezing	High quality storage life	Thawing instructions
Grouse, partridge, pheasant, pigeon	Hang as liked after removing shot and cleaning wounds. Pluck, draw, and truss, and pad bones. Pack in polythene bags	6 months	Thaw in wrappings in refrigerator
Plover, quail, snipe, woodcock	Prepare as other game but do not draw	6 months	Thaw in wrappings in refrigerator
Hares	Clean shot wounds and hang, bleeding the animal and collecting the blood. Paunch, skin, clean, and cut into joints. Separate joints with clingfilm and pack in polythene bags. Pack blood separately	6 months	Thaw in wrappings in refrigerator
Rabbits	Paunch, skin, clean, and prepare as for hare	6 months	Thaw in wrappings in refrigerator
Venison	Clean, and hang before jointing. Skin, then pack in polythene bags	12 months	Thaw in a marinade in refrigerator

Vegetables

All vegetables for freezing should be young, fresh, and clean, and they should be frozen as soon as possible after picking. Grade vegetables for size and prepare in small quantities (ie 500g is the largest quantity which should be blanched at one time). All vegetables must be blanched by being cooked briefly in boiling water to retard enzymic action and retain colour, flavour, and nutritive value. Use a wire blanching basket in a large saucepan which will hold 4 litres water and has a lid. Vegetables should be put into the boiling water, and the water returned to boiling point as quickly as possible. Timing must be accurate, as under-blanching results in colour change and loss of nutritive value while over-blanching causes loss of flavour and crispness.

After blanching, vegetables must be cooled rapidly in water chilled with ice cubes, not under running tap water which is not cold enough. It should take as long to cool as to blanch each vegetable, and then the vegetables must be well-drained. They may be spread out on open freezing trays and frozen before packing, or packed directly into polythene bags or rigid containers. Vegetables with strong smells, eg onions and garlic, may need overwrapping.

After freezing, vegetables need little cooking. Most vegetables should be put straight into a small quantity of boiling water and cooked until just tender. Vegetables can also be cooked in butter, without any water, in a covered casserole or heavy saucepan, either in the oven or over heat.

For **vegetable freezing chart,** see over.

Vegetable Freezing Chart

Type of vegetable	Preparation for freezing	Blanching time	High quality storage life	Cooking instructions
Artichokes (globe)	Remove outer leaves, stalks, and chokes. Add lemon juice to blanching water	7 minutes	12 months	Cook in boiling water for 10 minutes
Artichokes (Jerusalem)	Peel and slice. Cook in chicken stock and purée	—	3 months	Heat purée and add milk or cream
Asparagus	Clean and grade. Cut in 15cm lengths	2 minutes (thin) 3 minutes (medium) 4 minutes (large)	9 months	Cook in boiling water for 5 minutes
Aubergines	1) Peel and cut into 2cm slices 2) Coat in batter and deep fry	4 minutes —	1) 12 months 2) 2 months	1) Place in boiling water for 5 minutes 2) Heat in warm oven or fry
Avocado pears	Mash pulp with lemon juice (1 × 15ml spoon juice to each pear)	—	2 months	Thaw for 3 hours in refrigerator
Beans (broad)	Shell small young beans	1½ minutes	12 months	Cook in boiling water for 8 minutes
Beans (French)	Top and tail young beans. Leave whole or cut into 2cm chunks	3 minutes (whole) 2 minutes (cut)	12 months	Cook in boiling water for 7 minutes (whole) 5 minutes (cut)
Beans (runner)	Cut in chunks; do not shred	2 minutes	12 months	Cook in boiling water for 7 minutes
Beetroot	Cook very young beet, under 3cm diameter. Peel and leave whole or dice	—	6 months	Thaw for 2 hours, and add dressing
Broccoli	Trim stalks and soak in brine for 30 minutes (1 × 15ml spoon salt to 4 litres water). Wash before blanching	3 minutes (thin) 4 minutes (medium) 5 minutes (thick)	12 months	Cook in boiling water for 8 minutes
Brussels sprouts	Grade and wash well	3 minutes (small) 4 minutes (medium)	12 months	Cook in boiling water for 8 minutes
Cabbage	Shred crisp young cabbage	1½ minutes	6 months	Cook in boiling water for 8 minutes (do not use raw)
Carrots	Use very young carrots. Wash and scrape. Leave whole, dice or slice	3 minutes	12 months	Cook in boiling water for 8 minutes
Cauliflower	Wash and break into florets. Add lemon juice to blanching water	3 minutes	6 months	Cook in boiling water for 10 minutes

Type of vegetable	Preparation for freezing	Blanching time	High quality storage life	Cooking instructions
Celery	Scrub crisp young stalks and cut into 2cm slices	2 minutes	6 months	Cook in stock, or add to soups and stews (do not use raw)
Corn on the cob	Use fresh tender corn and grade for size. Remove husks and silks	4 minutes (small) 6 minutes (medium) 8 minutes (large)	12 months	Thaw in wrappings. Cook in boiling water for 10 minutes
Herbs	Wash and pack whole sprigs or chop into ice cube trays, freeze, and wrap frozen cubes	—	6 months	Thaw and drain, or add herb cubes to dishes
Leeks	Clean and cut into rings	2 minutes	12 months	Cook in boiling water for 8 minutes or add to soups and stews
Marrows and courgettes	1) Cook and mash marrows and freeze purée 2) Cut courgettes into 1cm slices without peeling	3 minutes	2 months	1) Re-heat from frozen in double boiler 2) Fry in oil and season well
Mushrooms	Wipe but do not peel. Pack into bags without blanching	—	3 months	Thaw and cook as fresh
Onions	Skin and chop or slice. Wrap well	2 minutes	2 months	Add to dishes while frozen
Parsnips, turnips, and swedes	Peel and dice	2 minutes	12 months	Cook in boiling water for 15 minutes
Peas	Shell young sweet peas	1 minute	12 months	Cook in boiling water for 5 minutes
Peppers	Remove seeds and membranes	3 minutes (halves) 2 minutes (slices)	12 months	Thaw for 1 hour (halves) or add frozen slices to dishes
Potatoes	Cook and mash, or make into croquettes. Jacket, baked and roast potatoes can be frozen. Slightly under-cook new potatoes, and freeze in bags which can be boiled for re-heating. Fry chips for 4 minutes but do not brown	—	3 months	Re-heat mashed or croquette, roast or jacket potatoes. New potatoes should be kept in bag and heated in boiling water for 10 minutes. Fry chips while frozen
Spinach	Remove any thick stalks and wash leaves very well. Press out moisture after blanching	2 minutes	12 months	Re-heat gently in butter
Tomatoes	Wipe, grade and pack in bags	—	12 months	Thaw for 2 hours (skins will drop off). Do not use raw

Cooked and Other Prepared Dishes

Make dishes to standard recipes, observing one or two special details. Thicken sauce or gravy by reducing, or by adding vegetable purée or cornflour; this is to prevent curdling during re-heating. Add rice, pasta or potatoes to liquid dishes only when re-heating, since they become too soft during freezing. Use onions, garlic, herbs, and spices with care, as flavours can deteriorate during freezing.

Pack cooked foods in freezer containers, or in ordinary dishes which will withstand freezing and heating. Label carefully if additional ingredients have to be included during re-heating. Use cooked foods within 2 months to retain high quality.

Type of dish	Preparation for freezing	High quality storage life	Thawing/re-heating instructions
Casseroles and stews	Slightly undercook vegetables. Do not add rice, pasta or potatoes. Remove surplus fat	2 months	Heat in double boiler, or thaw and bake in casserole in a moderate oven, 180°C, Gas 4 for 1 hour
Flans (sweet and savoury)	Prepare and bake. Open freeze and wrap in foil or polythene	2 months	Thaw at room temperature for 3 hours. Re-heat if required
Ices – fresh fruit purée	Fully prepare	3 months	Serve straight from freezer
– ice cream	Fully prepare	3 months	Allow to soften slightly in refrigerator before serving
– sorbets and water ices	Fully prepare	3 months	Serve straight from freezer
– bombes and other moulded desserts	Wrap in foil	3 months	Unmould on to chilled plate, using cloth wrung out in hot water to release ice cream. Wrap in foil and return to freezer for one hour before serving
– ice cream gâteaux	Pack in rigid containers or wrap in foil	3 months	Place on plate and serve at once. Slice with knife dipped in boiling water
Meat	Do not freeze cooked joints or grilled meats; they can become tough, rancid, and dry 1) Slice cooked meat thinly and separate with clingfilm. Pack tightly in rigid or foil containers 2) Slice meat and pack in gravy or sauce in rigid or foil containers	2 months	Thaw in wrappings in refrigerator for 3 hours. Bake in a moderate oven, 180°C, Gas 4, for 40 minutes
Meat pies	1) Bake and cool. Wrap in foil or polythene	1) 2 months	1) Thaw in refrigerator for 6 hours to eat cold, or bake in a fairly hot oven, 190°C, Gas 5, for 1 hour
	2) Cook meat filling. Cool and cover with pastry. Wrap in foil or polythene	2) 2 months	2) Bake from frozen in a fairly hot oven, 200°C, Gas 6, for 1 hour

Type of dish	Preparation for freezing	High quality storage life	Thawing/re-heating instructions
Mousses	Prepare in freezer-tested serving dishes	1 month	Thaw in refrigerator for 8 hours
Pancakes	Cool and pack in layers with clingfilm. Wrap in greaseproof paper, foil or polythene	2 months	Thaw at room temperature and separate. Heat in a cool oven, 150°C, Gas 2, or on a plate over steam, covered with a cloth
Pasta	Slightly undercook, drain well, cool, and pack in polythene bags	1 month	Put into boiling water, bring back to the boil, and cook for 2–3 minutes until tender
Pasta dishes	Pack pasta and sauce in foil dish with lid	1 month	Remove lid and bake in a fairly hot oven, 200°C, Gas 6, for 45 minutes
Pâté	Cool completely and wrap in foil or polythene. Pâté may also be prepared in freezer-tested dishes	1 month	Thaw in refrigerator for 6 hours
Pizza	Prepare, using fresh herbs, not dried. Do not add anchovies. Bake. Cool and wrap in polythene	1 month	Unwrap and thaw at room temperature for 1 hour. Top with anchovies and bake in a fairly hot oven, 190°C, Gas 5, for 20 minutes
Rice	Slightly undercook, drain well, cool, and pack in polythene bags	1 month	Put into boiling water, bring back to boil, and cook for 2–3 minutes until tender
Rice dishes	Cook completely, but avoid adding hard-boiled eggs. Pack into bags or rigid containers	1 month	Heat in double boiler, stirring well and adding additional ingredients
Sauces (savoury)	Prepare completely, but season sparingly. Pack in rigid containers, leaving headspace. Do not freeze sauces thickened with eggs or cream	1 month	Heat in double boiler and re-season if required
Sauces (sweet)	1) Fresh or cooked fruit sauces should be packed in rigid containers, leaving headspace 2) Thicken pudding sauces with cornflour and pack in rigid containers, leaving headspace	1) 12 months 2) 1 month	1) Thaw in refrigerator for 3 hours to serve cold, or heat in double boiler 2) Heat in double boiler
Soup	Use standard recipes but avoid flour for thickening. Do not include rice, pasta, barley, potatoes, milk or cream. Pack in rigid containers, leaving headspace	2 months	Heat in double boiler, adding additional ingredients
Steamed and baked puddings	Steam or bake puddings in foil containers. Cool and cover with lid, or pack in polythene bag	4 months	Thaw at room temperature for 2 hours, and steam for 45 minutes, or bake from frozen in a fairly hot oven, 190°C, Gas 5, for 45 minutes

Cakes, Pastry, and Breads

Use very fresh ingredients when baking for the freezer. Use butter for good flavour, but margarine for a light texture. Margarine is especially suitable for strongly flavoured cakes such as chocolate and coffee.

Icings and fillings made from fat and sugar can be frozen separately or on cakes. But do not attempt to freeze icings made without fat. Fruit or jam fillings in cakes become soggy after thawing, and are better added just before serving. Decorations are also better added then, since they absorb moisture during thawing and may stain the cake. Sweetened whipped cream can be frozen like a cake filling. Pack cakes carefully to avoid crushing during storage. It is better to open freeze iced cakes before packing to avoid smudging the surfaces.

Type of cake, pastry or bread	Preparation for freezing	High quality storage life	Thawing/baking instructions
Biscuits	Form dough into 2cm diameter roll. Wrap in foil or polythene. **Note** Baked biscuits are best stored in tins without freezing	2 months	Thaw in refrigerator for 45 minutes. Cut in slices and bake in a fairly hot oven, 190°C, Gas 5, for 10 minutes
Bread	Pack in polythene bags. Crusty bread quickly loses its crispness in the freezer	6 weeks	Thaw at room temperature for 4 hours
Breadcrumbs (plain)	Pack in polythene bags	3 months	Thaw in wrappings at room temperature, or sprinkle directly on food to be cooked
Bread dough	Knead dough and put in greased polythene bag without proving	2 months	Unseal bag and tie loosely to allow space for rising. Thaw at room temperature for 6 hours. Knock back, shape, prove, and bake
Brioches and croissants	Pack in rigid containers to prevent crushing, immediately after baking and cooling	2 months	Thaw at room temperature for 30 minutes and heat in oven or under grill
Cakes (uniced)	Cool completely and wrap in foil or polythene	4 months	Thaw at room temperature for 2–3 hours
Cakes (iced)	Fill and ice cake but do not add decorations. Open freeze on tray, and pack in a rigid container	4 months	Thaw at room temperature for 3 hours
Cheesecakes	Make baked or refrigerated variety in cake tin with removable base. Open freeze and pack in rigid container	1 month	Thaw for 8 hours in refrigerator
Choux pastry	Bake but do not fill or ice. Pack in polythene bags or boxes	1 month	Thaw in wrappings at room temperature for 2 hours. Fill and ice
Crumpets and muffins	Pack in polythene bags	6 months	Thaw in wrappings at room temperature for 30 minutes before toasting
Danish pastries	Bake but do not ice. Pack in foil trays with lids, or in rigid containers	2 months	Thaw at room temperature for 1 hour. Heat if liked

Type of cake, pastry or bread	Preparation for freezing	High quality storage life	Thawing/baking instructions
Fruit pies	Brush bottom crust with egg white to prevent sogginess 1) Bake, cool, and pack 2) Use uncooked fruit and pastry, open freeze, and pack	1) 4 months 2) 2 months	1) Thaw to serve cold, or re-heat 2) Bake from frozen in a fairly hot oven, 200°C, Gas 6, for 1 hour
Pastry cases	Freeze baked or unbaked, using foil containers	4 months	Bake frozen cases at recommended temperatures for type of pastry. Re-heat baked cases, or fill with hot filling
Sandwiches	Do not remove crusts. Spread thickly with butter or margarine. Do not use salad fillings, mayonnaise or hard-boiled eggs. Separate sandwiches with clingfilm and pack in foil or polythene	1 month	Thaw at room temperature and remove crusts, or toast under grill while still frozen
Scones and drop scones	Pack in small quantities in polythene bags	2 months	Thaw in wrappings at room temperature for 1 hour. Alternatively, bake frozen scones in a moderate oven, 180°C, Gas 4, for 10 minutes

Fruit

Freeze only fresh, top-quality fruit. Fruit can be frozen dry and unsweetened, with sugar, in syrup, or as purée, and in cooked dishes.

Note As in bottling, white sugar is normally used because it does not colour or flavour the fruit. Other sugar can be used, but Barbados sugar or molasses may develop an unpleasant flavour in storage, and colour the fruit.

Dry Unsweetened Pack

This is best for fruit to be used in pies, puddings, and jams, and for berries and currants to be eaten raw. Do not use it for fruit which discolours badly, since sugar helps to retard the action of the enzymes which cause darkening. Clean any fruit well and open freeze on trays, or pack into bags or rigid containers.

Dry Sugar Pack

Use 1 part sugar to 4 parts fruit, mixing lightly before packing. Sugar draws out juices, and some fruit, eg berries, can become over-soft during thawing.

Sugar Syrup Pack

Use this for non-juicy fruits and those which discolour easily. Make a syrup with white sugar and water, dissolving the sugar completely in boiling water and chilling before use. Three syrup strengths are generally used:

Light syrup	175g sugar to 500ml water
Medium syrup	275g sugar to 500ml water
Heavy syrup	400g sugar to 500ml water

Vitamin C helps to retard discoloration of fruit, and the juice of 1 lemon should be added to each litre of syrup for fruit such as apricots and peaches.

Cover the fruit completely in syrup and crumble a piece of greaseproof paper or clingfilm in the headspace to prevent the fruit rising above the syrup and discolouring.

For **fruit freezing chart** see over.

Fruit Purée

Prepare purée from raw raspberries or strawberries, but cook other fruit in a little water first. Sweeten to taste before freezing and pack with 1.5cm headspace to allow for expansion.

Fruit Juices

Prepare fruit juice and freeze in trays. Wrap frozen cubes individually in foil and store in polythene bags. Apple juice will ferment quickly and should only be stored for a month. Other fruit juices will be at their best for 9 months.

Type of fruit	Preparation for freezing	Method of freezing	High quality storage life	Thawing/cooking instructions
Apples	Peel, core, and slice	1) Dry sugar 2) Medium syrup 3) Cooked purée	12 months 4 months	Cook in puddings or pies, or re-heat purée
Apricots	Skin and cut in halves or slices. Add lemon juice to pack	1) Dry sugar 2) Medium syrup 3) Raw purée	12 months 4 months	Thaw for 4 hours in covered pack in refrigerator
Blackberries and raspberries	Clean and hull	1) Unsweetened 2) Dry sugar 3) Raw or cooked purée	12 months 4 months	Thaw for 3 hours at room temperature
Blueberries	Wash and drain. Crush slightly to soften skins	1) Unsweetened 2) Dry sugar 3) Heavy syrup	12 months	Cook in puddings, pies or jam
Cherries	Chill in water for 1 hour and stone	1) Dry sugar 2) Medium syrup for sweet fruit 3) Heavy syrup for sour fruit	12 months	Thaw for 3 hours at room temperature. Use cold or cook
Cranberries	Wash and drain	1) Unsweetened 2) Cooked whole or purée	12 months 4 months	Cook while frozen, or thaw purée or cooked fruit for $3\frac{1}{2}$ hours at room temperature
Currants (red, white, and black)	Strip fruit from stems	1) Unsweetened 2) Dry sugar 3) Medium syrup 4) Cooked purée	12 months 4 months	Thaw for 2 hours at room temperature
Damsons	Wash, drain, and stone	1) Heavy syrup 2) Cooked purée	12 months 4 months	Thaw for 3 hours at room temperature or cook while frozen
Dried fruit (dates, figs, raisins, currants, sultanas)	Pack in polythene bags	—	12 months	Thaw for 2 hours at room temperature and use in recipes
Figs	Wash ripe figs and remove stems. Do not bruise	1) Unsweetened 2) Light syrup if peeled	12 months	Thaw for 3 hours at room temperature. Eat raw or cooked in syrup
Gooseberries	Clean, top, and tail	1) Unsweetened 2) Medium syrup 3) Cooked purée	12 months 4 months	Thaw for 3 hours at room temperature, or cook while frozen

Type of fruit	Preparation for freezing	Method of freezing	High quality storage life	Thawing/cooking instructions
Grapefruit	Peel, remove pith, and divide into segments	1) Dry sugar 2) Heavy syrup	12 months	Thaw for 3 hours at room temperature
Grapes	Pack seedless grapes whole. Skin, de-seed, and halve large ones	Light syrup	12 months	Thaw for 3 hours at room temperature
Greengages and plums	Cut in half and stone	Medium syrup	12 months	Thaw for 3 hours at room temperature
Lemons and limes	Peel and slice, or slice without peeling and pack for drinks	Light syrup	12 months	Thaw for 1 hour at room temperature, or put in drinks while frozen
Melons	Peel and cut in cubes or shape into balls. Toss in lemon juice	Light syrup	12 months	Thaw for 3 hours in covered pack in refrigerator
Oranges	Peel, remove pith, and divide into segments, or slice	1) Dry sugar 2) Light syrup	12 months	Thaw for 3 hours at room temperature
Peaches and nectarines	Skin, cut in halves or slices, and brush with lemon juice. Alternatively, make a raw purée with 1×15ml spoon lemon juice to 500g fruit	1) Medium syrup 2) Raw purée	12 months 4 months	Thaw for 3 hours in covered pack in refrigerator
Pears	Peel, quarter, and remove cores. Dip pieces in lemon juice. Poach in medium syrup for $1\frac{1}{2}$ minutes, drain, and cool before packing in syrup	Medium syrup	12 months	Thaw for 3 hours at room temperature
Pineapple	Peel and cut in slices or chunks	1) Dry sugar 2) Light syrup	12 months	Thaw for 3 hours at room temperature
Rhubarb	Wash in cold water and trim sticks	1) Unsweetened 2) Medium syrup 3) Cooked purée	12 months 4 months	Thaw purée at room temperature. Cook raw fruit while frozen
Strawberries	Clean and grade for size	1) Unsweetened 2) Dry sugar 3) Medium syrup 4) Raw purée	12 months 4 months	Thaw for 2 hours at room temperature

Dairy Produce

Most cheeses can be frozen successfully but tend to crumble after being frozen. They should be frozen in small pieces, and cut when still slightly hard. Cream cheese tends to separate on thawing. It is best blended with heavy cream before freezing and used as a dip. Cottage cheese tends to separate and should not be frozen. Only homogenized milk in waxed cartons should be frozen, and then only in small quantities which can be used quickly. The texture of frozen cream can be heavy and grainy, but light beating will improve it. If used in hot coffee, the oil will rise to the surface. Only really good thick cream responds well to freezing. Eggs should be very fresh. They should be washed and then broken into a dish to check for quality. They should be frozen already beaten or separated, in rigid containers and sugar or salt added in the proportions below to prevent coagulation.

Dairy produce	Preparation for freezing	High quality storage life	Thawing instructions
Butter and margarine	Overwrap in foil or polythene	6 months (unsalted) 3 months (salted)	Thaw enough for 1 week's use in refrigerator
Cheese – hard	Cut in 200g pieces and wrap in foil or polythene. Pack grated cheese in polythene bags. Pack blue cheeses in polythene and overwrap well	3 months	Thaw in open wrappings at room temperature for 3 hours. Cut while slightly frozen to avoid crumbling
– cream	Blend with heavy cream	3 months	Thaw in container in refrigerator overnight. Blend with fork to restore smoothness
Cream	Freeze all creams in cartons. Do not freeze single, soured or half-cream	6 months	Thaw in carton at room temperature and stir with a fork to restore smoothness
Whipped cream	Sweeten with 2 × 10ml spoons sugar to 500ml cream. Freeze in containers, or open freeze piped rosettes	6 months	Thaw in container at room temperature. Rosettes thaw in 15 minutes at room temperature
Eggs	Do not freeze in shell. 1) Mix yolks and whites, adding 1 × 5ml spoon salt or 1 × 10ml spoon sugar to 5 eggs 2) Mix yolks, adding 1 × 5ml spoon salt or 1 × 10ml sugar to 5 yolks 3) Put whites in containers with no addition	12 months	Thaw in refrigerator but bring to room temperature before use
Milk	Only homogenized milk can be frozen. Leave 2cm headspace	1 month	Thaw at room temperature and use quickly

CONVENIENCE FOODS

At Leith, in the neighbourhood of Edinburgh, at Aberdeen, at Marseilles, and in many parts of Germany, establishments of enormous magnitude exist, in which soup, vegetables, and viands of every description are prepared, in such a manner that they retain their freshness for years. The prepared aliments are inclosed in canisters of tinned iron plate, the covers are soldered air-tight, and the canisters exposed to the temperature of boiling water for three or four hours. The aliments thus acquire a stability, which one may almost say is eternal; and when a canister is opened, after the lapse of several years, its contents are found to be unaltered in taste, colour, and smell.

The term 'convenience food' covers a wide variety of canned, bottled, and vacuum packed foods as well as dry mixes, concentrated, and frozen foods. Recipes throughout this book use various convenience foods such as stock cubes, canned tomatoes and made mustard as standard ingredients, but there are many which in their own right make an interesting meal, or which can be a source of different and interesting foods out of season.

This chapter looks into some unexpected uses for convenience foods. The recipes show how fresh and processed foods can be combined to produce unusual results, and they demonstrate how certain foods can be used to save time or labour in the preparation of complicated dishes such as soufflés, mousses, and pâtés. Additionally it focuses on what to look for when buying convenience foods, and methods and length of storage life.

Buying and Storing

When buying convenience foods it is important to check the packaging for defects.

1) Cans

Do not buy a can that is:
    leaking
    rusty
    distended at the ends
    dented at the seam or ends
Throw away any can with these defects.

2) Other packaging

Check all coated board, paper, foil, and film wrap packaging for rips and small holes. Check the caps of bottles or plastic containers for tightness. Look at the selling dates printed on labels. These dates include a margin for home storage, but the goods should not be kept longer than recommended by the chart on pp1398–99.

Note All convenience foods have a limited storage life and it is not economical to buy more than can be used over a certain period of time.

The content of convenience foods is strictly controlled by the manufacturers. Although some of the nutritional content is lost in the processing, modern methods keep this loss to a minimum. In some instances extra vitamins and minerals are added to the processed food. Most food has to be labelled in detail and this includes a tabulation of the contents in descending order of quantity.

Convenience foods should be stored in a cool, dry larder, store cupboard, refrigerator or freezer, depending on what is being stored. It is a good idea to arrange the store cupboard with the most recently purchased items at the back, moving packs forward as new foods are purchased. Non-metal packs, such as pasta and rice, should be stored in tins or jars. Vacuum packed foods can be stored in a refrigerator or can be frozen.

Once opened, any processed or convenience food must be used as soon as possible. If a can is opened and only part of the contents consumed, the remaining food should be covered with clingfilm or foil and placed in a refrigerator for 2–3 days. Cans of fruit and fruit juice, because of the acidic nature of the juice, should be emptied into a non-metallic container before being placed in the refrigerator.

Canned and bottled foods are already cooked, and should not be cooked again. They need simply to be re-heated either in a saucepan, or in the can, having first removed the lid; stand the can in a pan of boiling water.

Cans which need to be chilled before serving cold, such as consommé, should be kept in a refrigerator for a short time only. Do *not* store cans in the refrigerator as moisture will make them rusty.

Never waste the juice from canned or bottled foods. The liquor from meat, fish, and vegetables can be used in the stock pot or in soups, stews, casseroles, gravy, and sauces. The juice from fruits can be used in jellies, fruit salads, and drinks.

Chart of Storage Life

Food	Method of production/ packaging	Storage life (unopened)
Baby food	Bottled	12–18 months
	Canned	1–2 years
Bread	Dried mix	6 months, 1 month if opened
	Pre-baked loaf	6 months
Cake decorations	Packeted	6 months
Cakes	Dried mix	6 months, 1 month if opened
Carbonated drinks	Canned	6–12 months
Casserole mixes	Dried mix	18 months
Cheeses	Tube	1 year
	Vacuum packed	Date stamped
Coatings	Dried mix	1 year
Coffee, liquid	Bottled	1 year
Coffee, instant	Jars	1 year
	Packeted	1 year
Desserts	Dried mix	18 months
Dessert toppings	Bottled	1 year
	Canned	1 year
	Dried mix	18 months
Fish in brine	Bottled	9–12 months
Fish in oil	Canned	5 years

Food	Method of production/ packaging	Storage life (unopened)
Fish in sauce	Canned	2 years
Flavourings, alcohol base	Bottled	5 years
Flavourings, non-alcoholic	Bottled	18 months
Flours	Packeted	6–9 months
Fruit juices	Bottled	1 year
	Canned	2 years
	Carton	Date stamped
	Concentrated, frozen	6 months
	Dried mix	18 months
Fruit pie fillings	Canned	1–2 years *
Fruits	Bottled	1 year
	Canned	1–2 years
	Dried	2 years
Gelatine	Leaf	6–12 months
	Powdered	6–12 months
Gravies	Canned	1–2 years
	Dried mix	1 year
Ham, pasteurized, above 900g	Canned	6 months, refrigerated **
Ham, sterilized, below 900g	Canned	2–3 years
Jams and marmalades	Bottled	2 years
	Canned	2 years
Jellies	Crystals	12–18 months
	Tablets	1 year
Meat products	Vacuum packed	Date stamped
Meat products, processed	Bottled	2 years
Meat products, solid packed	Canned	5 years
Milk products	Canned	1 year
	Dried	6 months
Pasta	Dried	2 years
Pasta, cook-in sauces	Canned	2 years

Food	Method of production/ packaging	Storage life (unopened)
Pastes	Bottled	6 months
	Canned	1 year
	Tube	1 year
Pastry mixes	Dried mix	6 months, 1 month if opened
Pâtés	Bottled	6 months
	Canned	2 years
Pickles	Bottled	2 years
Porridge oats	Packeted	1 year
Raising agents	Dried	6 months
Rice	Canned	2 years
	Dried	2 years
Sauces	Bottled	6 months
	Canned	2 years
	Dried mix	18 months
Seasonings	Dried mix	6 months
Soups	Canned	2 years
	Dried mix	6–12 months
Stock cubes	Dried mix	1 year
Stuffings	Dried mix	1 year
Sugars	Packeted	5 years
Textured vegetable protein (TVP)	Dried	5 years
Vegetables	Canned	2 years ***
	Dried	1–2 years
Vegetables in brine or water	Bottled	2 years
Yeast extracts	Bottled	2 years
Yeast granules	Dried	1 year

*Rhubarb and prunes should be kept for 1 year only, and gooseberries, plums, blackberries and blackcurrants for 18 months.

**This is an exception to the general guide that cans should not be stored in the refrigerator.

***New potatoes should only be kept for 18 months.

All-in-One Vegetable Soup

4 helpings

1 large onion
1 large potato
3 medium-sized carrots
1 ×15ml spoon cooking oil
750ml water
1 ×15ml spoon concentrated gravy **or** *yeast extract*

50g mince-style textured vegetable protein (TVP)
2 ×15ml spoons dried mixed peppers
1 bouquet garni
salt and pepper

Garnish
1 ×15ml spoon chopped parsley   *grated Parmesan cheese*

Prepare and dice the vegetables. Heat the oil in a large pan and gently fry the vegetables for 3–4 minutes. Add the rest of the ingredients, stirring all the time. Season to taste. Bring the soup to the boil and cover with a tight-fitting lid. Reduce the heat and simmer for 45 minutes. Before serving, remove the bouquet garni. Garnish with parsley and grated Parmesan cheese, and serve with wholemeal bread.

Tomato Soup

4 helpings

1 × 539ml can tomato juice
1 ×170g can evaporated milk
1 ×15ml spoon lemon juice

salt and pepper
3 ×15ml spoons medium dry sherry

Pour the tomato juice and evaporated milk into a large pan. Add the lemon juice, season to taste, and bring to the boil. Remove from the heat and stir in the sherry. Serve at once.

Smooth Pork Pâté

4 helpings

1 × 15ml spoon dried
  mixed peppers
1 × 15ml spoon dried
  onion flakes
125ml water
1 × 198g can pork
  luncheon meat

1 × 17g pkt white sauce
  mix
200ml milk
1 egg
fat for greasing

Garnish
parsley sprigs

Put the dried peppers and onions in a pan with the water and bring to the boil. Reduce the heat and simmer for 5 minutes. Drain the vegetables and mince them with the pork, or rub through a sieve. Make up the white sauce mix as directed using the milk. Beat the egg until liquid. Remove the sauce from the heat and gradually add the beaten egg. Blend the pork and vegetable mixture into the white sauce. Pour the mixture into a greased 500ml pudding basin, and cover with greased paper or foil. Stand the dish in a pan of water coming 3cm up the sides. Bring to the boil, reduce the heat, and simmer for 45 minutes until the mixture is set. Remove the basin from the water and leave to cool; then chill for at least 2 hours.

Turn out and serve garnished with parsley.

Garlic Stuffing

Enough for a 1.5–2kg chicken

1 × 125g German
  teewurst **or** liver
  sausage
150g full fat soft cheese
  with herbs and garlic

1 egg
50g soft white
  breadcrumbs
salt and pepper

Remove and discard any outer skin from the sausage. Put the sausage in a bowl with the cheese, and mix together well. Add the egg and breadcrumbs, and continue to mix until well blended and smooth. Season to taste.

Ham and Tongue Forcemeat Balls

Makes 8

6 × 15ml spoons
  reserved ox tongue and
  ham jelly (p1403)
1 × 15ml spoon warm
  water

3 × 15ml spoons parsley
  and thyme stuffing mix
grated rind of ½ lemon
fat for greasing

Mix the reserved jelly and the water with the stuffing mix and lemon rind. Stir well and leave to stand for 3–5 minutes. Shape the mixture into 8 balls and place on a well-greased baking sheet. Bake in a fairly hot oven, 190°C, Gas 5, for 40 minutes until browned. Remove from the oven and leave to cool for 10 minutes before serving.

Serve with Ham and Tongue en Croûte (p1403).

Artichoke Mousse

6 helpings

3 × 5ml spoons gelatine
2 × 15ml spoons cold
  water
1 × 400g can artichoke
  hearts

125ml double cream
salt and pepper
1 egg white

Soften the gelatine in the cold water. Stand the container in a pan of hot water and stir until the gelatine is dissolved. Drain the artichoke hearts, retaining the liquor, and chop them coarsely. Rub through a sieve, and blend in the cream, dissolved gelatine, and the reserved liquor. Alternatively, process the ingredients in an electric blender. Season to taste. Whisk the egg white until stiff and gently fold into the artichoke mixture. Turn the mousse into a 16cm soufflé dish or into individual ramekin dishes and chill for 2 hours until set.

VARIATION
Substitute the same quantity of well-drained peas or carrots for the artichoke hearts.

Asparagus Cheesecake

6 helpings

50g butter
100g oatcakes
butter **or** *fat for greasing*
3 × 5ml spoons gelatine
2 × 15ml spoons cold water

1 × 298g can condensed asparagus soup
1 × 226g carton plain cottage cheese
pepper

Garnish (optional)
canned asparagus spears   tomato wedges

Melt the butter in a large saucepan, and crush the oatcakes with a rolling-pin. (This is best done in a large polythene bag.) Mix well together until the butter is completely absorbed. Line the base of a greased 18cm flan ring with the mixture and press down firmly so that the mixture is closely packed. Leave to cool for 30 minutes.

Soften the gelatine in the cold water. Stand the container in a pan of hot water and stir until the gelatine is dissolved. In a measuring jug make up the condensed soup to 250ml liquid with cold water. Add the cottage cheese and dissolved gelatine, and mix well. Rub the mixture through a sieve, or process in an electric blender. Season to taste with pepper. Pour the mixture into the prepared flan ring and chill for 1–2 hours until set. Garnish, if liked, with the asparagus spears and tomato wedges.

Note If using canned asparagus spears for the garnish, reserve the drained liquor and add to the condensed soup with the water when making up 250ml liquid.

Brunch Buffet

6 helpings

6 lamb cutlets
6 chicken drumsticks

50g dried breadcrumbs
fat for greasing

Coating for Cutlets
½ × 99g pkt thyme and parsley stuffing mix
½ × 50g pkt Navarin of lamb casserole mix

75ml boiling water

Coating for Drumsticks
1 × 60g pkt instant mashed potato
200ml boiling water

½ × 43g pkt barbecue coating mix

Liver Balls
1 × 125g vacuum packed German liver sausage

1 × 36.5g pkt bread sauce mix
salt and pepper

Garnish
watercress sprigs

Wipe the lamb and chicken with soft kitchen paper and put to one side. Make up the cutlet coating. Mix all the dry ingredients in a bowl, pour on the water, mix well with a fork, and leave to cool.

Make up the drumstick coating. Place the mashed potato mix in a bowl and pour on the water, stirring all the time; add the barbecue coating mix. Leave to cool.

Make the liver balls. Skin the sausage, if necessary, place in a bowl with the bread sauce mix, and mix together well. If the mixture is too stiff, add a little water. Season to taste. Divide into 8 portions and form into balls.

Cover the cutlets and drumsticks first with their special coatings, and then with the breadcrumbs. Roll the liver balls in the crumbs. Place all on a greased baking sheet. Cover loosely with foil and place in a fairly hot oven, 190°C, Gas 5, for 30 minutes. Remove the foil and bake for a further 15–20 minutes.

Arrange the cutlets and drumsticks on a large plate and place a paper ruff over the exposed bones. Arrange the liver balls around the edges and garnish with sprigs of watercress.

Mackerel Croquettes

Makes 8

1 × 200g can mackerel
  in oil **or** brine
1 × 60g pkt instant
  mashed potato
175ml boiling water

2 eggs
salt and pepper
oil for deep frying
50g dried breadcrumbs

Garnish (optional)
parsley sprigs

Drain the fish well and mash it thoroughly with a fork. Make up the packet of instant mashed potato as directed, but use only 175ml boiling water. Add the fish and 1 egg to the potato mixture and mix well. Season to taste. Beat the second egg until liquid. Heat the oil (p303). Shape the fish mixture into 8 croquettes, dip each in the beaten egg, roll in the breadcrumbs until completely coated, and deep fry until golden-brown. Drain the croquettes on soft kitchen paper and serve hot. Garnish, if liked, with sprigs of parsley.

VARIATION

Substitute 1 × 200g can salmon or pilchards for the mackerel, or 1 × 198g can tuna.

Crab Horns

4 helpings

350g puff pastry mix
1 × 170g can crabmeat
1 × 28g pkt Hollandaise
  sauce mix
3 × 15ml spoons double
  cream

1 × 15ml spoon medium
  dry sherry
salt and pepper

Garnish
lettuce leaves

Make up the puff pastry according to the directions on the packet. Prepare and bake 8 puff pastry horns (p1273), and leave to cool on a wire rack. Drain the crabmeat and mash it with a fork. Prepare the Hollandaise sauce mix as directed and leave to cool. Whip the cream and sherry together until stiff, and fold into the Hollandaise sauce. Blend in the crabmeat, and season to taste. Carefully fill the cooled pastry horns with the crab mixture, and place on a bed of lettuce, allowing any excess filling to overflow.

Smoked Fish Balls

Makes 16

150g smoked mackerel
  fillets
1 × 28g pkt parsley and
  lemon sauce mix
200ml milk **or** 200ml
  made-up powdered
  milk

freshly chopped parsley
  (optional)
1 egg
oil for deep frying
50g dried breadcrumbs

Garnish
parsley sprigs

Flake the mackerel. Prepare the parsley and lemon sauce mix as directed but use only 200ml milk. Add the fish, fresh parsley, if used, and mix together well; allow to stand for a few minutes. Divide the mixture into 16 portions. Beat the egg until liquid. Heat the oil (p303). Roll each ball in the beaten egg and then in the breadcrumbs until completely coated. Deep fry the fish balls in two batches until golden-brown. Keep the first batch warm while deep frying the second. Drain on soft kitchen paper. Serve warm, as a cocktail savoury, garnished with parsley.

VARIATION
Salmon Fish Balls

Use 1 × 200g can of salmon in place of the mackerel fillets.

Ham and Tongue en Croûte

6 helpings

1 × 227g can ox tongue
1 × 454g can boneless
  cooked ham
2 thick slices bread
1 egg

6 juniper berries
pepper
225g shortcrust pastry
  mix
flour for rolling out

Garnish
tomato wedges

Drain the jellied liquid from the cans and reserve for use in the recipe for Ham and Tongue Forcemeat Balls (p1400). Mince the tongue and half the ham, and finely chop the bread. Cut the remaining ham into small cubes. Beat the egg until liquid, and mix together with the meat, bread, and juniper berries; season to taste with the pepper.

Make up the shortcrust pastry mix as directed and roll out on a lightly floured surface to about 25cm wide and 16cm long. The pastry should be about 3–4mm thick. Place the meat mixture in the centre of the pastry. Dampen the edges and fold them over the meat so that the mixture is completely covered by the pastry. Pinch the seams together and place the pastry on a baking sheet with the seams underneath. Bake in a fairly hot oven, 190°C, Gas 5, for 40 minutes until the pastry is golden-brown. Remove from the oven and leave to cool for 10 minutes before placing on a wire rack. Leave for 2 hours until completely cold. Transfer to a large serving dish and garnish with tomato wedges.

Serve with Ham and Tongue Forcemeat Balls (p1400).

Stuffed Ham au Gratin

4 helpings

250ml water
2 × 15ml spoons dried
  peppers
2 × 15ml spoons dried
  onions
1 × 85g pkt sage and
  onion stuffing mix
25g Cheddar cheese

1 × 113g can liver pâté
salt and pepper
2 × 113g pkts ham slices
fat for greasing
1 × 35g pkt cheese sauce
  mix
250ml milk
25g breadcrumbs

Bring the water to the boil in a saucepan. Add the dried vegetables, reduce the heat, cover, and simmer for 5 minutes. Add the stuffing mix and stir until well blended. Remove from the heat and leave to stand for a few minutes. Grate the cheese. Add the pâté to the vegetables, season to taste, and mix thoroughly. Spread the mixture on one side of each ham slice and carefully roll up. Arrange in a greased, shallow, ovenproof dish. Make up the cheese sauce as directed, using the milk, and pour it over the ham rolls. Sprinkle with the grated cheese and breadcrumbs, and bake in a hot oven, 220°C, Gas 7, for 20 minutes.

Chicken Soufflé (3)

4 helpings

6 eggs
2 × 298g cans condensed
  cream of chicken soup

black pepper
fat for greasing

Heat the oven to fairly hot, 190°C, Gas 5. Separate the eggs, and beat the yolks, one by one, into the condensed chicken soup. Season to taste with pepper. Whisk the egg whites until stiff. Using a metal spoon, stir 1 spoonful of the whisked egg white into the chicken mixture, then fold in the rest until evenly distributed. Pour the mixture into a greased 20cm soufflé dish, and bake for 30–35 minutes, until well risen and browned on top. Serve immediately.

Note For other chicken soufflé recipes, see p642 and p922.

Turkey and Orange Casserole

4 helpings

600g boned turkey joint
2 × 15ml spoons cooking oil
2 small onions
25g flour
1 × 15ml spoon medium dry sherry

250ml frozen orange juice **or** 2 × 15ml spoons powdered orange juice mix diluted with 250ml water
salt and pepper
150g canned button mushrooms

Garnish
1 × 15ml spoon chopped parsley

Wipe the turkey and cut into cubes. Heat the oil in a large saucepan and cook the turkey until lightly browned. Transfer to an ovenproof dish.

Skin the onions and chop them finely; fry in the remaining oil until golden-brown. Sprinkle the flour over the onions, stir in the sherry and orange juice, and bring to the boil, stirring all the time. When the mixture thickens, season to taste and remove from the heat. Pour the mixture over the turkey and cover with a tight-fitting lid. Cook in a moderate oven, 180°C, Gas 4, for 1 hour. Drain the mushrooms and stir them into the dish; cook for a further 20 minutes. Garnish with parsley.

Serve with rice.

VARIATION

Chicken and Orange Casserole

Use 600g boned chicken in place of turkey.

Paella

4 helpings

1 chicken stock cube
625ml boiling water
100g brown rice
50g mince-style textured vegetable protein (TVP)
1 × 40g pkt quick dried peas
2 × 15ml spoons dried onion flakes
1 × 15ml spoon dried green pepper flakes

a pinch of saffron
1 bay leaf
1 × 2.5ml spoon garlic salt
1 × 2.5ml spoon thyme
1 × 202g can boned, pressed chicken breasts
2 × 50g cartons potted shrimps
salt and pepper

Garnish
chopped parsley

Dissolve the chicken stock cube in the boiling water. Pour into a large pan and add all the ingredients except the chicken, potted shrimps, and the salt and pepper. Stir, and bring to the boil. Reduce the heat and cover with a tight-fitting lid, simmering gently until all the liquid has been absorbed.

Meanwhile, slice the chicken breasts, and add the jelly to the rice mixture in the pan.

Put the chicken and potted shrimps in a pan and heat gently until the butter on the shrimps melts. Shake the pan and heat through, taking care not to cook the chicken and shrimps.

Remove the rice mixture from the heat, season to taste and arrange on a large serving dish. Spoon the chicken and shrimps over the rice and serve hot, garnished with the chopped parsley.

Stuffed Tomatoes

4 helpings

350g frozen **or** canned
  peas
1 × 5ml spoon dried
  mint flakes

salt and pepper
6 large tomatoes
butter

Cook the frozen peas as directed, and drain. If using canned peas, drain only. Rub the peas through a sieve. Add the dried mint, mix well, and season to taste. Halve the tomatoes crossways, remove and discard the pips and juice. Place the tomatoes in a greased ovenproof dish and put a spoonful of the pea mixture in each half. Dot the tops with butter. Bake in a fairly hot oven, 190°C, Gas 5, for 10–15 minutes. Serve hot.

Stuffed Vegetables

4 helpings

1 small marrow **or** 2
  medium-sized
  aubergines

fat for greasing
1 × 127g can tomato
  juice

Stuffing

1 × 452g can tomatoes
1 × 85g pkt parsley and
  thyme stuffing mix

pepper

Garnish

50g softened butter
50g canned pâté

salt and pepper

Make the garnish about 1 hour before preparing the vegetables. Blend the butter into the pâté until the mixture is very smooth; season to taste. Spread the mixture 5mm thick on to a piece of greased paper and chill for 2 hours.

Prepare the marrow or aubergines, slice them in half lengthwise and remove any seeds. Slice the marrow halves again. Blanch the marrow in boiling salted water for 5 minutes, or the aubergines for 10 minutes. Drain well and place in a greased, shallow ovenproof dish, skin side down.

Make the stuffing. Put the tomatoes into a saucepan and bring to the boil. Add the stuffing mix and stir well. Season to taste with pepper and allow to stand for a few minutes. Spoon the mixture into the hollow of the vegetables. Pour the tomato juice over the top and cover with foil. Bake in a fairly hot oven, 190°C, Gas 5, for 45 minutes.

When the pâté has set and is hard, cut it into rounds with a small pastry cutter, and use to garnish the vegetables.

Sautéed Potatoes

3–4 helpings

1 × 539g can new
  potatoes
50g butter
25g fresh chopped
  parsley **or** 1 × 5ml
  spoon dried parsley

25g fresh chopped chives
  or 1 × 5ml spoon dried
  chopped chives
salt and pepper

Drain the potatoes. Melt the butter in a saucepan and stir in the herbs. Sauté the potatoes in the herbs and butter until golden, and season to taste.

Mayonnaise Made with Condensed Milk

Makes 350ml (approx)

75ml sweetened
  condensed milk
125ml salad oil
125ml white vinegar **or**
  lemon juice
2 egg yolks

1 × 2.5ml spoon salt
1 × 5ml spoon dry
  English mustard
a dash of Cayenne
  pepper

Put all the ingredients into a bowl and whisk until thick. Alternatively, put all the ingredients into a screw-topped jar and shake vigorously. Store in a screw-topped jar in a refrigerator.

Serve with salads, vegetables, cold fish or egg dishes.

Baked Apricot Pudding

4 helpings

1 × 15ml spoon flour
1 × 15ml spoon caster
 sugar
1 × 184g pkt sponge cake
 mix
2 eggs

1 × 113g jar apricot
 strained dessert (baby
 food)
1 × 15ml spoon orange
 liqueur
fat for greasing

Heat the oven to fairly hot, 200°C, Gas 6. Put all the ingredients in a large mixing bowl and whisk until smooth. Turn into a greased 18cm square baking tin and bake for 20 minutes until well risen and golden-brown.

Serve with custard.

Strawberry and Apple Fool

4 helpings

3 × 5ml spoons gelatine
2 × 15ml spoons water
1 × 382g can
 strawberries

2 × 15ml spoons dried
 skimmed milk
1 × 113g jar strained
 apple purée (baby food)

Decoration
fresh **or** instant whipped
 cream

Soften the gelatine in the cold water. Stand the container in a pan of hot water and stir until the gelatine is dissolved. Sieve the strawberries with their juice. Add the milk and apple purée, and stir well. Add the dissolved gelatine and mix well, or process in an electric blender. Pour the mixture into individual dessert dishes and chill until set. Decorate with the whipped cream.

Coffee and Hazelnut Ice Cream Sundae

4 helpings

1 × 15ml spoon instant
 coffee
250ml cold milk
25g hazelnuts

2 × 44g pkts powdered
 instant cream topping
2 × 15ml spoons sugar

Decoration
crushed biscuits
crushed chocolate flakes

chocolate sauce

Dissolve the coffee in the milk and pour into a bowl. Chop the hazelnuts. Sprinkle the powdered cream topping over the milk and whisk until soft peaks form. Fold in the sugar and hazelnuts. Turn the mixture into a suitable container and freeze for 3–4 hours.

Serve the sundae in individual dishes sprinkled with crushed biscuits and chocolate flakes. Top with the chocolate sauce.

MIXER, BLENDER, AND PROCESSOR COOKERY

Those who generally digest vegetables with difficulty, should eat them reduced to a pulp or purée, that is to say, with their skins and tough fibres removed. Subjected to this process, vegetables which, when entire, would create flatulence and wind, are then comparatively harmless.

Food Mixers

There are many different models of food mixer, but they fall, basically, into one of three classes:
1) hand mixer
2) bowl mixer
3) large or table mixer.

Hand Mixers: These are designed for use in the hand only, and so have no bowl and stand, although most models are supplied with a wall bracket or can be stood on the flat heel for storage and when pausing during mixing. The machine can be carried to the food to be mixed, eg to whisk mixtures which are cooking, although care must be taken to watch the trailing flex, especially near hot surfaces. The main advantage of this type of mixer, however, is that the style and rate of mixing can be altered instantly while mixing: egg whites, for example, can be whisked with a scooping movement to aerate the mixture.

Bowl Mixers: These mixers can be hand-held, but can also be used on a stand with a specially fitted bowl. Some models are supplied with a stand and bowl; for others these can be obtained separately. All these bowl mixers are quite small and light for easy handling, but are larger, on the whole, than the hand mixers. They can tackle many of the jobs handled by larger table machines, but work most efficiently with smaller quantities and lighter mixtures. Some of them have optional attachments for doing various jobs, but their range is limited. Their motor rating range is about 100–200 watts.

If a bowl mixer is used a lot, it is helpful to have one or two spare bowls and whisks, so that several processes can be carried out without having to dismantle and clean the whisks or transfer the contents of the bowl between each operation.

Table Mixers: These are powerful machines (motors rated about 400–450 watts) which can tackle a wide variety of cookery tasks, and cope easily with large quantities and heavy mixtures. They are valuable if bread is mixed often or if batch baking of cakes is done. Because of their powerful motors, many different attachments can be fitted (see p1409).

It is important to have adequate space on the working surface to stand a table mixer, so that it is always ready for use. It is usually too heavy to lift in and out of a cupboard just for a few moments' use. Some kitchen units are made with a special cupboard or fitted worktop to house the mixer.

As with bowl mixers, it is wise to have two or three bowls, so that several processes can be carried out without having to empty and clean one bowl.

Before buying any mixer, it is wise to check that adequate servicing facilities are available locally, and that replacements or spare parts are easy to obtain. The manufacturer's instructions concerning installation, maintenance, and use should always be followed carefully.

HOW A MIXER WORKS

In hand and bowl mixers the mixer head houses the machine's power unit. The beaters fit into special sockets in the head, and rotate separately. An ejector button in the head is pressed to release the beaters after use. The mixer head also houses the on/off switch and/or speed control switch of the machine. These switches may be in the form of a push button or a dial. In table mixers, the stand usually houses the power unit and control switches combined, so that they cannot be operated independently.

In most bowl and table models, the beaters rotate in the centre of the bowl when the machine is on its stand. Some mixer units have the bowl offset on the stand for greater mixing efficiency, or the two beaters may move round each other as well as rotating independently. Sometimes a single beater revolves round the inside of a fixed bowl.

Most mixers have more than one speed setting, generally three. Some have an electronic speed control which maintains a constant beater speed whatever the load.

USING A FOOD MIXER

The size and power of the machine chosen will dictate what it can do. The lower-powered mixers cream soft mixtures and whip and whisk light ones excellently, but may labour over some other jobs. Care must be taken when using any machine not to overstrain it, as this can burn out the motor.

Generally speaking, any mixer will:

beat cake and pudding mixtures, creamed potatoes, eggs

cream fat and sugar for cakes

mix batters, sauces

rub in fat to flour for biscuits, cakes, pastry or scones

whip cream, cold desserts

whisk egg whites, milk shakes, cocktails.

The optional attachments on a large table mixer will perform many other tasks (see p1409).

Points to remember when using a food mixer:
1) Use the correct beater or other fitting for the job.
2) Use the correct speed for the job. Generally, the lighter the mixture, the higher the speed, and vice versa. As a general guide, use low speed for rubbing in, medium speed for creaming, and high speed for whisking. Remember that it is easy to over-mix and produce a flat-textured, flabby-tasting mixture.
3) Use the correct bowl size. The machine should work in a bowl which allows the mixture to spread in it.
4) Do not overwork the mixer (see above). Usually, a mixer should be rested every 5 minutes or so, to avoid damaging the motor. If the machine shows any sign of labouring, reduce the quantity of mixture being dealt with at once.
5) Stop the machine occasionally while mixing to scrape down any mixture from the sides of the bowl.

CARE AND CLEANING

1) As far as possible, keep the mixer clean and free from spatters and spillages. Scraps of food, especially semi-liquid mixtures, can harden on the casing, in joints, etc, and may be difficult to remove.
2) Always switch off the machine and unplug it before cleaning the casing or parts.
3) Never immerse the motor unit in water. Wipe all metal or plastic parts with a damp cloth only.
4) Wash beaters, bowl, and most attachments in warm soapy water, and dry carefully. Do not use harsh abrasives.
5) Remove and dismantle attachments according to the manufacturer's instructions. Wash and dry thoroughly before storing.

ATTACHMENTS

The following attachments are available for many of the larger mixers, although not every model is equipped with them all. It is important, when choosing optional attachments, to consider which ones will be useful frequently, not just occasionally for a special dish. Attachments which are very seldom used occupy useful space, attract dust, rust and pests, and are liable to deteriorate.

Attachments available include: dough hook, mincer, juice extractor, slicing and/or shredding attachment, can opener, coffee grinder, potato peeler, colander and sieve, juice separator, bean slicer, pea huller, and cream maker. Their mechanisms are described fully in most manufacturers' manuals.

Blenders or Liquidizers

A blender (sometimes called a liquidizer) can be an independent self-contained unit with its own motor, or an attachment to a mixer.

The size and shape of the goblet vary from model to model. It may be made of heat-resistant glass or clear polystyrene. Most have a lip and a handle for pouring, and some are calibrated. Any blender goblet, large or small, has a lid, generally made of plastic, with a removable centre cap so that food can be added during blending. Many have a grinding attachment for grinding solid foods such as nuts.

It is worth checking the jobs that any particular blender will do before purchasing one. Ensure also that it will be large enough. Once installed, it is likely to be used much more than was originally envisaged, so it is worth buying a model with a large capacity. A blender with a capacity of less than 750ml can only handle small quantities of food, and cannot take very stiff mixtures. It may need more liquid added than more powerful types. These small blenders only have a single speed switch as a rule, so an over-large or too stiff a mixture can easily strain the motor. A large quantity of food must therefore be divided and blended in batches (which is wasteful when clearing the goblet), and the machine should be rested between each batch.

Most blenders have a capacity of more than 750ml, and, if independent, have powerful enough motors (200–450 watts) to give the considerable impetus required to set the machine to work. They usually have two or more speeds, and some have fully variable control, ie they can be set at any speed. All the larger blenders can cope with quite big quantities of solid mixture, especially if it is fed into the goblet gradually through the hole in the lid while the machine is running.

Whatever blender is chosen, it must be easy to clean, or a good deal of food may be wasted. A model in which the goblet unscrews from its base is very much easier and more practical to clean than one with a fixed goblet.

HOW A BLENDER WORKS

Set in the base of a blender goblet are sharp cutters which rotate at speeds of up to 28,000 revolutions per minute. The cutter blades are of stainless steel, four being the most usual number. As they rotate, the food mixture is forced up the sides of the goblet, falls into the centre, on to the blades, and the cycle is repeated. In this way the food is turned over and over in the goblet, and is first broken into fragments and then pulverized.

USING A BLENDER

The usual jobs which a blender carries out are:
blending sauces, soups, baby foods, batters, dips
chopping herbs
crumbing bread, biscuits
emulsifying mayonnaise
finely chopping cheese cubes, lemon and orange peel
grinding nuts, coarse sugar
mincing cooked fish and meat for pâtés, pastes, and spreads
pulping fruit and vegetables for chutneys, pickles, and sauces
puréeing fruit and vegetables
shredding vegetables for salads
whipping drinks, milk shakes.

CARE AND CLEANING

1) The manufacturer's instructions and recommendations should be followed carefully. They cover the speed settings to use for the processes described on p1409 and for different mixtures, as well as the running time, handling, and general care of the appliance.

2) The machine must always be switched off and unplugged before being cleaned. After each use, the goblet and base should be removed, and the hollowed top of the motor's casing (if an independent unit) should be wiped out with dry, soft kitchen paper.

3) The motor unit should never be placed in water. It should be wiped over with a clean, damp cloth.

4) After being emptied, the goblet should be half filled with hot water, and a little detergent if liked. It should then be operated at low speed for a few seconds, emptied, rinsed with clean warm water, and turned upside-down to drain.

Food Processors

There are several different models of food processor but all consist of a motor base (rated between 360–650 watts depending on the model) to which is attached a transparent bowl. A cover with a feed tube fits on top. Standard attachments comprise a metal blade for mixing, chopping, and mincing, and two metal discs for grating, slicing, and shredding. Some models also have a plastic blade for mixing softer mixtures like doughs, ice creams, etc. A processor is more compact in size than a mixer, although its range of operations is more limited; whisking, for example, cannot be carried out with any of the standard attachments.

Other attachments such as a juice extractor or whisk can be purchased with some models to extend the range of the machine's operations.

The manufacturer's instruction manual indicates the most efficient use and maintenance of the processor.

HOW A FOOD PROCESSOR WORKS

The engine, housed in the motor base, propels a drive shaft at either one or two speeds depending on the model. Some models have a 'burst' switch which enables the machine to be operated in short sharp bursts, to prevent over-processing. The cover locks shut when the unit is on.

The blades for mixing, chopping and mincing are placed on the base of the drive shaft inside the bowl and ingredients are either dropped through the feed tube on to the rotating blades, or, when mixing cakes, etc, put in the bowl and additions fed through the tube. The metal slicing or shredding disc is placed at the top of the drive shaft, and ingredients are pushed down the tube with a plastic pusher, and sliced or shredded against the rotating disc, falling into the bowl when processed.

USING A FOOD PROCESSOR

The processor is small, so that large quantities must be processed in batches. Always check the instruction manual for quantity guides. As a general guide to the uses of the standard attachments, the metal blade chops, mixes, beats, minces and purées; the metal discs grate, slice and shred.

Points to remember when using a food processor:

1) Handle the sharp blades with care.

2) Never remove the locking cover until the motor has completely stopped.

3) Rest the machine between each operation, and for longer after several consecutive operations.

4) Always feed liquids through the tube while the blades are rotating.

5) Do not put a large amount of liquid in a processor. (For soup, process the solid ingredients and some liquid, not the whole quantity.)

6) Always use the plastic pusher when pushing solid food down the feed tube.

7) Cut food into even-sized pieces before chopping or mincing.

8) Remove the bowl from the base before removing the blades, etc, so that food does not spill through the hole or stick to the drive shaft.

Recipes using a Mixer, Blender or Food Processor

This section gives a selection of typical recipes which can be prepared easily using a mixer, blender or food processor. Some of the recipes are specially designed for the use of these appliances.

Using these recipes as a guide, others can easily be adapted to make full use of a mixer, blender or food processor.

Minestrone (2)

(food processor)

8 helpings

75g haricot beans	225g potatoes
1.7 litres brown stock (p329)	1 clove of garlic
	225g canned tomatoes
100g bacon, without rinds	100g peas
	a pinch of dried rosemary
1 large carrot	salt and pepper
1 onion	75g pasta
¼ cabbage	

Garnish

25g grated Parmesan cheese	chopped parsley

Soak the beans in cold water overnight. Drain, and put into a pan with the stock. Bring to the boil, cover, and simmer for 1 hour. Meanwhile, chop the bacon (metal blade), place the pieces in a pan and cook until golden-brown. Drain, and add to the stock. Prepare the carrot, onion and cabbage, and slice (slicing disc). Peel the potatoes and chop them coarsely (metal blade). Skin and crush the garlic. Add with the tomatoes and their juice, and the rest of the vegetables except the peas to the stock. Cover, and simmer for 35 minutes. Stir in the peas and rosemary, and season to taste. Simmer for 5 minutes. Add the pasta, and cook for 10–12 minutes until tender. Serve hot, garnished with the cheese and parsley.

Note The cheese can be grated using the grating disc and the parsley chopped using the metal blade, if liked.

For Minestrone (1), see p369.

Cold Cucumber Soup

(blender)

4 helpings

1 medium-sized cucumber	1 × 2.5ml spoon salt
	a pinch of pepper
500ml cold milk	

Garnish

chopped parsley

Peel the cucumber and chop it roughly. Process all the ingredients in the blender for 30–45 seconds. Chill thoroughly. Stir, then garnish with chopped parsley before serving.

Crab and Corn Bisque

(blender)

3–4 helpings

salt and pepper	50g flour
500ml milk	1 × 275g can sweetcorn kernels
250g brown and white crabmeat, mixed	75ml double cream
50g butter	

Garnish

chopped parsley

Season the milk lightly with salt and pepper. Put the milk and crabmeat in a saucepan, and simmer for 10 minutes. Process in the blender to make a smooth purée. In the same pan, melt the butter, stir in the flour, and cook together for 2 minutes, stirring all the time. Add the purée gradually to make a sauce, stirring all the time. Bring gently to the boil, reduce the heat, and simmer until thickened. Drain the sweetcorn kernels and add to the purée; simmer for 5 minutes. Remove from the heat, stir in the cream, and serve at once garnished with chopped parsley.

Cream of Watercress Soup (2)
(blender)

4 helpings

1 bunch of watercress	125ml double cream
375ml cold water	1 × 15ml spoon plain
1 chicken stock cube	flour

Wash the watercress. Reserve a few leaves for garnishing. Process all the ingredients in the blender for 30 seconds. Pour the soup into a saucepan and heat, stirring occasionally, until just under boiling point; do not boil. Serve very hot, garnished with the reserved watercress leaves.

Note For Cream of Watercress Soup (1), see p361.

Hot Garlic Dip
(food processor)

Makes 250ml (approx)

5 cloves garlic	150g butter
8 anchovy fillets	1 × 5ml spoon lemon
2 red peppers	juice
150ml olive oil	pepper

Skin the garlic and cut it into small pieces. Cut each anchovy fillet into pieces. De-seed the peppers and cut the flesh into small pieces. Put into the processor bowl with the olive oil and chop very finely (metal blade). Melt the butter and, with the machine still running, pour it into the feed tube until the mixture is creamy. Put into a pan with the lemon juice and pepper to taste. Heat very slowly until the mixture boils; then reduce the heat and simmer for 10 minutes until creamy. Keep hot over a table heater or hotplate.

Serve with crusty bread and a selection of raw vegetables for dipping.

Pork Pâté
(blender)

Makes 1kg pâté (approx)

8 bacon rashers, without rinds	1 × 2.5ml spoon ground mace
200g pig's liver	1 × 5ml spoon crushed
400g lean pork	dried rosemary
125ml cold water	1 × 2.5ml spoon chopped
75g soft white bread	dried sage
¼ small onion	2 × 15ml spoons beaten
salt	egg

Stretch the bacon rashers with a knife. Remove any skin and tubes from the liver. Cut the liver and pork into 2cm cubes. Line the base and sides of a 1kg loaf tin with the rashers, pressing them into place firmly. Put the liver, pork, and water in a saucepan, and simmer for 15 minutes. Cut the bread into 2cm cubes and drop them through the hole in the lid on to the revolving blades of the blender. Tip into a mixing bowl.

Skin the onion and chop it finely. Put with the salt, mace, rosemary, sage and egg in the blender, and process for 15 seconds. Add to the breadcrumbs and mix well. Drain the meat, reserving the liquid, then drop each piece through the hole in the lid of the goblet on to the revolving blades. When the goblet is about one-third full, take out the meat and add to the rest of the ingredients. Continue blending until all the meat has been used. Mix all the ingredients together to a soft consistency. If too firm, add a little of the cooking water from the liver and pork. Put the mixture in the tin, and stand it in a pan of hot water which comes half-way up its sides. Cook in a warm oven, 160°C, Gas 3, for 2 hours. The pâté is cooked when juice pressed out of the centre is clear with no trace of pink.

Remove the tin from the oven, cover with greaseproof paper, and cool under a light weight. Leave to cool completely before turning out. Chill until required.

Turkey Terrine
(food processor)

Makes 750g (approx)

100g white bread	25g butter
4 ×15ml spoons milk	1 egg
350g cooked, light and	salt and pepper
dark turkey meat	a pinch of grated nutmeg
2 ×15ml spoons brandy	a pinch of dried mixed
225g fat pork	herbs
1 onion	fat for greasing

Put the bread in a bowl, pour over the milk, and soak for 10 minutes. Meanwhile, cut the turkey meat into pieces and chop them coarsely (metal blade). Put into a bowl, sprinkle with the brandy and put to one side. Cut the pork into small pieces and chop them finely (metal blade). Skin the onion, cut into quarters and chop finely (metal blade). Melt the butter in a pan and cook the onion until soft and golden. Remove from the heat and add to the pork. Mix together all the ingredients except the turkey meat (metal or plastic blade).

Grease a 1 litre terrine or pie dish. Put in half the mixture, top with a layer of the turkey meat, and cover with the remaining mixture. Cover tightly with a lid or foil, and stand the dish in a pan of hot water which comes half-way up its sides. Bake in a moderate oven, 180°C, Gas 4, for 1¼ hours. When cooked, weight the terrine (p731) and cool it. Leave to stand for 24 hours before serving.

White Sauce
(blender)

Makes 250ml (approx)

250ml milk or cream or	2 ×15ml spoons plain
milk and water	flour
40g butter or margarine	salt

Put all the ingredients in the blender and process for 10 seconds. Pour into a saucepan and cook over medium heat, stirring all the time, until smooth and thickened.

Use at once or treat like white sauce made by the roux method (p692).

Spicy Tomato Sauce
(blender)

Makes 500ml (approx)

¼ green pepper	½ ×2.5ml spoon dried
¼ small onion	oregano
150g concentrated	¼ ×2.5ml spoon dried
tomato purée	basil
1 × 500g can tomatoes	½ ×2.5ml spoon
40g softened butter **or**	Worcestershire sauce
margarine	a few drops Tabasco
3 ×15ml spoons plain	sauce
flour	

De-seed and chop the pepper. Skin and slice the onion. Put all the ingredients in the blender in the order given, and process for 10 seconds. Pour the sauce into a saucepan and cook over medium heat, stirring all the time, until thickened.

Serve over vegetables, fish, croquettes or pasta.

Quick Cheese Sauce
(blender)

Makes 250ml (approx)

50g Cheddar cheese	salt
1 ×170g can evaporated	½ ×2.5ml spoon dry
milk	mustard
1 × 5ml spoon	
Worcestershire sauce	

Dice the cheese, then grate it by dropping it gradually through the hole in the blender lid on to the revolving blades. Add the milk and seasonings, and process for a further 15 seconds. Pour into a saucepan and cook over medium heat for 2–3 minutes, stirring all the time, until thickened.

Serve over vegetables, meat, macaroni or spaghetti.

Sweet Cardinal Sauce

(blender)

Makes 200ml (approx)

200g frozen raspberries	*1 × 15ml spoon Kirsch*
100g caster sugar	*(optional)*
1 × 5ml spoon cornflour	

Thaw the raspberries. Put all the ingredients, including the liquid from the raspberries, in the blender and process for 40 seconds or until smooth. Strain through a sieve and chill.

Serve with any sweet dish.

French Dressing (2)

(blender)

Makes 250ml (approx)

250ml salad oil	*2 × 5ml spoons paprika*
3 × 15ml spoons white	*or 1 × 2.5ml spoon dry*
wine vinegar or lemon	*mustard*
juice	*salt and pepper*
1 slice of onion	
1 × 15ml spoon caster	
sugar	

Put all the ingredients into the blender in the order given, seasoning lightly. Process briefly until thoroughly mixed. Re-season if required.

Note For French Dressing (1), see p849.

VARIATION

Creamy French Dressing

Add 2 × 15ml spoons mayonnaise and 1 × 5ml spoon tomato ketchup before blending.

Mayonnaise (2)

(blender)

Makes 150ml (approx)

1 egg or 2 egg yolks	*1 × 2.5ml spoon salt*
2 × 15ml spoons lemon	*½ × 2.5ml spoon pepper*
juice or white wine	*½ × 2.5ml spoon dry*
vinegar	*mustard*
1 × 2.5ml spoon sugar	*125ml salad oil*

Put all the ingredients apart from the salad oil into the blender and process for 60 seconds. Add the oil, slowly at first, in a steady stream through the hole in the lid while the motor is running. Increase the flow as the mixture begins to thicken.

Note Blender mayonnaise is thicker but less rich than hand-made mayonnaise, especially if a whole egg is used.

For Mayonnaise (1), see p843.

Ham Mousse (2)

(blender)

4–6 helpings

200ml tomato juice	*½ bay leaf*
1 × 15ml spoon gelatine	*½ × 2.5ml spoon salt*
a thin strip of lemon	*200g cooked ham*
rind	*½ × 2.5ml spoon paprika*
1 × 5ml spoon sugar	*250ml double cream*
1 × 10ml spoon chopped	*8 ice cubes*
chives	

Heat the tomato juice, gelatine, lemon rind, sugar, chives, bay leaf, and salt to just under boiling point, stirring all the time. Remove the bay leaf and cool slightly. Dice the ham and put it in the blender with the tomato mixture and the paprika. Process for 20 seconds, stopping and scraping down if required. When the mixture is smooth, pour in the cream and then add the ice cubes through the hole in the lid while the motor is still running. Process for 15 seconds. Pour the mixture into a 1 litre mould and chill. Turn out when completely cold.

Note For Ham Mousse (1), see p883.

Mushroom Soufflé

(mixer and blender)

3–4 helpings

4 eggs	25g flour
200g mushrooms	200ml milk **or** single
50g butter	cream
1 × 5ml spoon grated	salt and pepper
onion	fat for greasing

Separate the eggs. Clean and slice the mushrooms. Melt 1 × 15ml spoon butter in a saucepan and sauté the mushrooms until just cooked. Stir in the grated onion and put to one side. Heat the oven to fairly hot, 190°C, Gas 5. Put the remaining butter, flour, and milk or cream into the blender and process for 30 seconds. Pour this mixture into a saucepan and bring to the boil, stirring all the time. Remove from the heat, then beat in the egg yolks, one at a time, and fold in the mushroom mixture. Season to taste. Whisk the egg whites until stiff, then fold them into the sauce. Put the mixture into a greased 1 litre soufflé dish and bake for 45–50 minutes, until risen, firm, and golden-brown. Serve immediately.

Beef Crumble

(food processor)

4 helpings

350g chuck steak	300ml beef stock
1 large onion	salt and pepper
25g dripping	1 × 10ml spoon chopped
75g plain flour	mixed herbs
1 × 15ml spoon	50g butter
concentrated tomato	50g Cheddar cheese
purée	

Garnish

chopped parsley

Wipe the meat and trim off any excess fat. Cut the steak into pieces and chop finely (metal blade). Skin the onion and chop it finely (metal blade). Heat the dripping and cook the meat and onion over low heat until golden-brown. Add 25g of the flour, the tomato purée, stock, salt and pepper, and a pinch of the herbs. Stir well and simmer for

5 minutes. Put into an ovenproof dish. Put the butter and remaining flour into the processor bowl and mix until like fine breadcrumbs (metal or plastic blade). Grate the cheese (grating disc) and mix with the flour and butter. Add the rest of the herbs and sprinkle over the meat mixture. Cook in a fairly hot oven, 190°C, Gas 5, for 1 hour. Garnish with the chopped parsley before serving.

Note The parsley can be chopped using the metal blade, if liked.

Chicken Croquettes (2)

(blender)

Makes 8

50g bread	$\frac{1}{2}$ × 2.5ml spoon pepper
1 large onion	2 parsley sprigs
125ml milk **or** chicken	300g cooked chicken
stock	1 egg
40g butter **or** margarine	2 × 15ml spoons water
25g plain flour	oil for deep frying
salt	

Cut the bread into cubes and drop them through the hole in the lid on to the revolving blades of the blender. Put to one side. Skin and slice the onion. Put with the milk or stock, the butter, flour, salt, pepper and parsley into the blender, and process for 20 seconds. Pour the mixture into a saucepan and cook over low heat, stirring all the time until very thick. Leave to cool. Dice the chicken, then drop it through the hole in the blender lid on to the revolving blades. Add it to the sauce, mix together very thoroughly, and chill. Shape the mixture into 8 sausages, balls or patties. Chill again for several hours.

About 40 minutes before serving, beat the egg with the water. Dip the croquettes first in the egg, then in the crumbs. Leave to dry for 25 minutes. Heat the oil (p303) and fry the croquettes until golden-brown. Drain on soft kitchen paper.

Serve with Spicy Tomato Sauce (p1413).

Note For Chicken Croquettes (1), see p951.

Sweetcorn Pancakes

(blender)

2–3 helpings

Filling

4 rashers streaky bacon, without rinds	1 × 5ml spoon chopped parsley
1 × 15ml spoon chopped onion	salt and pepper
1 × 198g can creamed sweetcorn	

Batter

250ml milk	1 × 2.5ml spoon salt
1 egg	fat for greasing
100g plain flour	

Make the batter first. Put the milk and egg in the blender, add the flour and salt, and process until smooth. Put to one side.

Chop the bacon roughly. Fry it with the onion until the bacon pieces are crisp and the onion golden. Add the corn, parsley, and seasoning to taste. Cover and keep hot.

Heat a little fat in a frying pan or omelet pan. Pour in some of the batter, and tilt the pan to coat the bottom evenly. Cook for 2–3 minutes until the surface is set and bubbling. Turn the pancake over with a palette knife, and fry the second side until just browned. Remove the pancake to a warmed plate and keep warm. Continue in the same way until all the batter is used. Place about 1 × 15ml spoon of filling in the centre of each pancake, and roll up. Serve hot.

Dessert Crêpes

(blender)

6 helpings

8–10 almond macaroons	1 × 15ml spoon corn oil
250ml milk	3 × 15ml spoons single cream
2 eggs	
100g plain flour	butter for greasing
a pinch of salt	
2 × 15ml spoons caster sugar	

Make crumbs from the macaroons by dropping them through the hole in the lid of the blender on to the revolving blades. Put to one side. Put the milk and eggs into the blender, add all the remaining ingredients apart from the macaroon crumbs, and process until smooth. Let the batter stand for 10–20 minutes. Stir in the macaroon crumbs.

Heat a little butter in a frying pan or omelet pan. Pour in some of the batter, and tilt the pan to coat the bottom evenly. Cook for 2–3 minutes until the surface is set and bubbling. Turn the pancake over with a palette knife, and fry the second side until just browned. Stack the crêpes in a cloth to keep warm and moist. Continue in the same way until all the batter is used. Fill with any suitable filling, and roll up. Serve hot.

Vanilla Custard Ice Cream

(blender)

6 helpings

125ml double cream	*1 × 15ml spoon flour*
250ml single cream	*1 × 2.5ml spoon vanilla*
40g caster sugar	*essence*

Mix together the double and single cream. Put half the mixed cream and the rest of the ingredients into the blender and process for 20 seconds. Pour into a saucepan and cook over medium heat, stirring all the time, until thickened. Cook for 2 minutes. Return the mixture to the blender and pour in the remaining cream through the hole in the lid with the motor running. Blend for 10 seconds. Pour into an ice tray and freeze until mushy but not too firm. Return the mixture to the blender and process for 10 seconds. Return the mixture to the ice tray and freeze until firm.

Lemon Sorbet (2)

(mixer and blender)

4–6 helpings

450ml water	*1 large lemon*
100g caster sugar	*1 egg white*

Put the water and sugar in a heavy-based saucepan and heat slowly until the sugar dissolves, stirring all the time. Bring to the boil and boil without stirring for 5–6 minutes. Leave to cool. Cut the lemon into quarters. Pour the syrup into the blender, add the lemon, and process for about 4 seconds. Strain the liquid into an ice tray and freeze until mushy but not too firm. Whisk the egg white until it forms soft peaks. Remove the frozen mixture from the tray and whisk the egg white into it. Return the mixture to the ice tray and freeze until firm.

Note For Lemon Sorbet (1), see p1055.

Applejack

(mixer and blender)

125g blanched almonds	*1 × 5ml spoon*
or hazelnuts	*bicarbonate of soda*
150g sultanas	*1 × 2.5ml spoon salt*
175g plain flour	*1 × 5ml spoon ground*
150g soft dark brown	*cinnamon*
sugar	*1 × 2.5ml spoon ground*
100g soft tub margarine	*cloves*
1 egg	*margarine for greasing*
200ml thick apple purée	
1 × 15ml spoon	
applejack or Calvados	

Crush the nuts coarsely or process briefly in the blender. Mix with the sultanas and sprinkle with 25g of the flour. Sift the sugar or process in the blender to break up any lumps. Put the sugar, margarine, and egg into the mixer bowl. Mix together the apple purée and applejack or Calvados, and add to the mixer bowl. Mix until smooth and fully blended. Meanwhile, sift together the remaining flour, the bicarbonate of soda, salt, and spices. Add them gradually to the bowl while mixing, and continue mixing until a smooth batter is obtained. Add the nuts and sultanas, and mix in briefly.

Grease a 20cm round springform cake tin and a 450g jam jar. Put the jam jar in the centre of the tin, and spoon the batter round it carefully. Smooth and level the top. Bake in a moderate oven, 180°C, Gas 4, for 50–55 minutes or until the cake shrinks slightly from the sides of the tin. Twist the jar slightly to remove it and release the sides of the tin. Leave to cool for 15 minutes, then remove the base and finish cooling on a wire rack.

VARIATIONS

1) Ice the cake when cold with Lemon Glacé Icing (p1225).
2) For a dessert, fill the centre of the cake with thick sweet apple sauce or stewed apples flavoured with either applejack or Calvados.

Troop Cake

(food processor)

225g sweet biscuits	1 × 15ml spoon golden
50g glacé cherries	syrup
50g walnut halves	50g sultanas
100g butter	fat for greasing
25g sugar	100g plain chocolate
25g cocoa powder	

Break the biscuits into pieces and make the crumbs (metal blade). Put into a bowl. Chop the cherries and walnuts coarsely (metal blade) and add to the crumbs. Cut the butter into small pieces and put into the processor bowl with the sugar, cocoa powder, and syrup. Cream until light and fluffy (metal or plastic blade). Add the crumbs, cherries and nuts, and mix until just blended (metal or plastic blade). Stir in the sultanas. Press the mixture into a greased 18cm square tin about 2cm deep. Chill for 5 hours.

Melt the chocolate in a bowl over hot water, and pour on top of the chilled cake. Leave until set; then cut into squares and remove from the tin.

Orange Cheesecake

(blender)

Makes one 15cm cheesecake

Base

125g digestive biscuits	fat for greasing
40g butter **or** margarine	

Filling

2 eggs	200g full-fat soft cheese
25g gelatine	25g caster sugar
2 × 15ml spoons warm	250ml milk
water	pared rind of 1 orange

Decoration

orange segments	½ glacé cherry

Make crumbs from the digestive biscuits by dropping them through the hole in the blender lid on to the revolving blades. Melt the butter or margarine. Mix the crumbs with the melted fat until very moist. Press them very lightly into the base of a lightly greased 15cm loose-bottomed cake tin.

Separate the eggs. Dissolve the gelatine in the warm water and put into the blender with the rest of the filling ingredients; process for 45 seconds or until smooth. Turn into a bowl. Whisk the egg whites until they form soft peaks, then gently fold them into the blended mixture. Spoon the mixture very gently on to the biscuitcrumb base and chill until firm.

Arrange the orange segments in the form of a flower on the top of the cheesecake and place the cherry in the centre.

Note For other cheesecakes, see pp1041–43.

Chocolate Cake

(mixer and blender)

250g self-raising flour	275g caster sugar
4 × 5ml spoons baking	75g butter **or** margarine
powder	1 × 5ml spoon vanilla
25g cocoa powder	essence
salt	fat for greasing
300ml milk	flour for dusting
2 eggs	

Filling
Whipped Cream
Frosting (p1420) **or** as
desired

Sift the flour, baking powder, cocoa powder, and salt into the mixer bowl. Heat 100ml milk until lukewarm. Put the milk into the blender with the eggs, remaining cold milk, sugar, fat and vanilla essence, and process for 30 seconds. Pour the liquid from the blender into the flour mixture and beat until thoroughly mixed. Pour into two 20cm greased, lined, and floured sandwich tins. Bake in a fairly hot oven, 190°C, Gas 5, for 30 minutes. Cool in the tins for 10 minutes, then turn out on to a wire rack to finish cooling.

Fill and cover with Whipped Cream Frosting or as desired.

Victoria Sandwich Cake (2)

(mixer)

150g butter **or**
  margarine
150g caster sugar
3 eggs

150g self-raising flour
1 × 5ml spoon grated
  lemon rind
fat for greasing

Filling
butter icing (p1227) **or**
  jam

icing sugar for dredging

Warm the mixer bowl and beater. Put the fat and sugar in the bowl and beat on medium speed until light and fluffy. Add the eggs, one at a time, beating thoroughly after each addition. Reduce to minimum speed, sift in the flour, and add the grated lemon rind. Switch off immediately the flour has been incorporated.

Turn the mixture into two 20cm greased and lined sandwich tins and bake in a fairly hot oven, 190°C, Gas 5, for 25–30 minutes. Cool in the tins for a few minutes, then turn out on to a wire rack, and leave to cool completely. Sandwich the cakes together with butter icing or jam, and sprinkle the top with icing sugar.

Note For Victoria Sandwich Cake (1), see p1205.

Swiss Roll (2)

(mixer)

3 eggs
75g caster sugar
75g plain flour

fat for greasing
icing sugar for dredging

Filling
jam **or** freshly whipped
  cream

Heat the oven to hot, 220°C, Gas 7. Warm the mixer bowl and whisk. Put the eggs and sugar into the mixer bowl and whisk on high speed for 5–7 minutes until the mixture is very light and thick. When ready, the mixture should be so thick that the whisk leaves a firm impression. Remove the whisk from the mixer and fold in the flour very carefully. Turn the mixture into a greased and lined 20 × 30cm Swiss roll tin, and bake for 8–10 minutes.

Meanwhile, warm the jam for the filling, if used. Dust a sheet of greaseproof paper with icing sugar, and turn the cooked Swiss roll on to it immediately. Peel off the lining paper and trim off any crisp edges. Spread with the jam, if used, and roll up immediately.

Note If the Swiss roll is to be filled with whipped cream, roll the cake up round a lining of greaseproof paper when it is taken from the oven. Leave to cool, then unroll, spread with cream, and roll it up again.

For Swiss Roll (1), see p1209.

Plain Scones (3)

(mixer)

Makes 12

200g self-raising flour
a pinch of salt
50g butter **or** margarine
25g caster sugar

4 × 15ml spoons milk
flour for rolling out
fat for greasing
milk for glazing

Heat the oven to hot, 220°C, Gas 7. Sift the flour and salt into the mixer bowl. Cut the fat into pieces, add to the bowl, and start mixing on minimum speed. Increase to medium speed, and mix until the mixture resembles fine breadcrumbs. Add the sugar and mix thoroughly. Add the milk, a little at a time, until a soft pliable dough is formed.

Turn out the dough on to a lightly floured surface and knead until smooth. Roll out to 1.5cm thick, then cut into 5cm rounds. Place the scones on a lightly greased baking sheet, and brush the tops with milk. Bake for about 10 minutes until risen and golden-brown on top.

Note For Plain Scones (1) and (2), see p1176 and p1177.

VARIATIONS

1) Add 50g mixed dried fruit with the sugar.
2) Add 1 × 5ml spoon cinnamon with the flour.
3) Add the grated rind of 1 lemon and 1 orange with the sugar.

Spicy Tea-time Loaf
(mixer)

Makes one 500g loaf

150g self-raising flour
3 × 2.5ml spoons ground
  ginger
75g butter **or** margarine
50g walnuts

50g cooking dates
75g soft brown sugar
1 egg
4 × 15ml spoons milk
fat for greasing

Decoration
2 × 10ml spoons soft
  brown sugar

Sift the flour and ginger into the mixer bowl. Cut the fat into pieces, add it to the bowl, and start mixing on minimum speed. Increase to medium speed and mix until the mixture resembles fine breadcrumbs. Chop the walnuts and dates roughly. Add them with the sugar and mix on medium speed. Beat the egg into the milk. When the nuts, fruit, and sugar are evenly distributed, add the liquid to form a stiff dough. Put the mixture in a greased 500g loaf tin and sprinkle with the 2 × 10ml spoons brown sugar. Bake in a moderate oven, 180°C, Gas 4, for 50–60 minutes. Turn out to cool on a wire rack.

Shortcrust Pastry (3)
(mixer)

Makes 300g (approx)

200g plain flour
50g margarine
50g lard

1 × 5ml spoon salt
4 × 10ml spoons cold
  water

Sift the flour. Cut the fat into small pieces. Put the flour and salt in the bowl and add the fat. Start mixing on minimum speed until all the ingredients are incorporated, then increase to medium speed until the mixture resembles fine breadcrumbs. Switch off. Sprinkle the water over the mixture and mix on medium speed. Switch off as soon as the mixture draws together.

Use as required for pies, pastries, etc.

Note For other shortcrust pastry recipes, see p1249.

All-in-one Meringue
(mixer)

Makes nine 5cm meringues

225g icing sugar
4 egg whites

fat for greasing

Sift the icing sugar. Put the egg whites and icing sugar into the mixer bowl and whisk on minimum speed until the ingredients are well blended. Switch to maximum speed and continue to whisk for about 10 minutes or until the meringue mixture is very thick, and the whisk leaves a firm impression on it. If using a hand mixer, whisk the mixture over a saucepan of hot water. The whisking time will then be reduced considerably.

Spoon the meringue lightly into a forcing bag with a 5cm star nozzle. Pipe the mixture on to a lightly greased and lined baking sheet in the shapes required. Cook at the lowest oven setting possible until the meringues are thoroughly dry. (This will take several hours, the exact time depending on the size of the meringues.)

Once thoroughly dry and cool, store the meringues in an airtight tin and use as required.

Whipped Cream Frosting
(blender)

Enough to fill and frost one 20cm cake

2 × 15ml spoons icing
  sugar
250ml double cream
1 × 10ml spoon gelatine
2 × 15ml spoons cold
  water

pared rind and juice of
  $\frac{1}{4}$ lemon
a pinch of salt

Sift the icing sugar. Reserve 2 × 15ml spoons double cream and whip the remainder. Scald the reserved cream and put it into the blender with the gelatine and water. Process for 40 seconds. Add the lemon rind and juice, icing sugar and salt, and process for a further 20 seconds. Pour the mixture into a bowl, and chill until it reaches the consistency of unbeaten egg white. Fold the gelatine mixture into the whipped cream until smooth. Chill until required.

Butter Icing (2)

(mixer)

Makes 225g (approx)

150g icing sugar	*1 × 15ml spoon milk **or***
75g softened butter	*water*

Sift the icing sugar. Put the butter, milk or water in the mixer bowl, and blend on medium speed until well mixed. Reduce to minimum speed and add the icing sugar gradually. Beat until fully blended, then increase the speed for a few moments to make the icing light and fluffy. Use as required.

VARIATIONS

Chocolate: Add 1 × 15ml spoon cocoa and 2 × 15ml spoons boiling water with the icing sugar. Cool the icing before using.

Coffee: Add 1 × 15ml spoon coffee essence or strong black coffee instead of the milk or water.

Lemon: Add 1 × 5ml spoon lemon juice or 1 × 15ml spoon undiluted lemon squash with the milk or water.

Orange: Add 1 × 15ml spoon orange juice or undiluted orange squash with the milk or water.

Note For Butter Icing (1), see p1227.

Vegetable Cocktail

(blender)

1–2 helpings

1 carrot (75g approx)	*juice of ½ lemon*
1 tomato (50g approx)	*125ml water*
1 stick of celery	*1 × 5ml spoon yeast*
1 × 15ml spoon chopped	*extract*
parsley	
salt and freshly ground	
black pepper	

Scrape the carrot, and blanch and skin the tomato. Chop them roughly, with the celery. Process in the blender with all the remaining ingredients until smooth. Strain and chill well before serving.

Cheese and Nut Spread

(mixer)

Makes 175g (approx)

25g flaked almonds	*2 × 5ml spoons*
100g curd cheese	*horseradish cream*
2 × 15ml spoons	*3 × 15ml spoons*
mayonnaise	*chopped gherkin*

Toast the almonds until lightly browned. Put the cheese, mayonnaise, and horseradish cream in the mixer bowl, and mix on medium speed until smoothly blended. Add the almonds and gherkin, and beat them in; switch off as soon as they are incorporated. Chill the mixture before using.

Curried Egg Sandwich Filling

(mixer)

Makes 125g (approx)

2 hard-boiled eggs	*1 × 15ml spoon chopped*
1 × 2.5ml spoon salt	*parsley*
1 × 15ml spoon butter	*1 × 5ml spoon curry*
*1 × 10ml spoon milk **or***	*powder*
mayonnaise	

Crumble the eggs into the mixer bowl, and add all the other ingredients. Begin beating at the lowest speed, then increase the speed and continue beating until the filling is evenly mixed and smooth.

PRESSURE COOKERY

The fire must be watched with great attention during the operation of boiling,
so that its heat may be properly regulated. As a rule, the pot should be kept in a
simmering state; a result which cannot be attained without vigilance.

When foods are cooked in liquid or steam in an
ordinary saucepan, the temperature cannot rise
above the boiling point of the liquid. No matter
how much the heat under the pan is raised, the
food cannot be cooked at a higher temperature or
more quickly. However, if all air can be expelled
from the pan and the steam from the liquid sealed in,
the pressure in the pan will rise, and so will the temperature. This is what happens in a pressure cooker.
Pressurized steam is forced into and through the
food, making the food tender within a very short
span of time, with little loss of nutritive value.

Since food is cooked more quickly in a pressure
cooker, less fuel is used than for ordinary cooking.
A pressure cooker is especially useful where space,
time and fuel are limited, eg in a bed-sitter, on
holiday, or in a boat or caravan.

TYPES OF PRESSURE COOKER

There are two principal types of domestic pressure
cooker; the saucepan and the casserole model,
ranging in capacity from about 3.5 to 10 litres.
Commercial pressure cookers with a capacity of up
to 22 litres are available for large households and
commercial catering.

The saucepan type of pressure cooker is of a
conventional shape, with a long handle on both the
cover and base. According to its size, the cooker
may have a flat or domed cover. The latter allows
room for large joints, tall bottling jars, and for
stacking inner containers. The casserole type has a
small lifting handle on each side, and a flat cover.

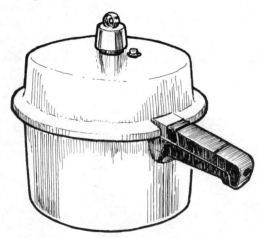

A saucepan pressure cooker

A casserole pressure cooker

In both types, the cover of the cooker 'locks', so that there can be no chance of it lifting as the pressure builds up inside the pan. Most saucepan models have interlocking flanges on the cover and base; the cover is inserted under a rim on the base, and secured with a half-turn of the cover itself. On casserole models the cover is locked by screwing down the central knob on the top. Both types of pressure cooker are made in stainless steel, aluminium or enamelled cast iron.

Other innovations include a manual system for releasing pressure after cooking. This means that the standard process of carrying the cooker to the sink to reduce pressure in cold water is not necessary. By movement of a lever above the handle of the cooker, pressure is released safely and quickly. A second development is the inclusion of a timer on the cooker, which is linked to an automatic release of pressure. Since all cooking in a pressure cooker requires careful timing for good results, this is an advantage. When cooking is complete, a warning bell sounds before pressure is released so that the heat can be turned off.

Most countries have quality and safety regulations laid down for the manufacture of pressure cookers. When choosing one, it is wise to check that it conforms to these.

PARTS OF A PRESSURE COOKER

Any pressure cooker consists of a pan called the base, a lid, known as the cover, and a trivet which fits inside the base. Perforated separators or inner containers are also provided.

The Cover

This is fitted with the following:

A Pressure Control

This is a weight valve placed over the steam vent in the cover, either before the cooker is put on the heat or as soon as steam is seen to escape. When the desired pressure is reached and the heat is correctly adjusted, the pressure control maintains the pressure. If it is a variable control the general guidelines are HIGH pressure for everyday foods, MEDIUM pressure for jams, jellies and marmalades, and LOW pressure for mixtures with raising agents and for bottling fruit. Another type of control is a spring valve, which is closed by lowering a lever. This seals in the steam until the correct pressure is reached.

A Gasket or Sealing Ring

This forms the closure between the cover and the base, to give an air and steam-tight seal. It is usually made from a rubber composition, and is fitted into a ridge or cavity, or under the rim of the cover.

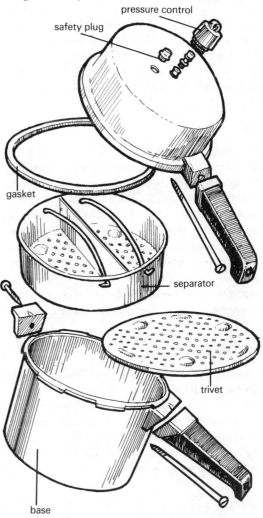

A Safety Plug

Every pressure cooker should have a safety plug already fitted. Each manufacturer has his own variations of this safety device, although the principle remains the same. The safety plug comes into action if excess pressure builds up inside the cooker, or if the cooker is allowed to boil dry. In some cases, the device is in the form of a small metal plug in a rubber surround; in others it is a fusible metal plug. If the pressure rises beyond the valve setting, this plug is forced up, or melts, to allow the excess steam to escape.

The Base

Most pressure cookers can be used on any type of heat, including paraffin stoves and even camp fires. Care must be taken not to damage the rim of the base, since it may cause a leakage of steam from the pan which the gasket cannot seal.

The Trivet

The perforated trivet is provided to allow for the easy circulation of steam. It may have a rim or adjustable feet to keep some foods out of the liquid in the bottom of the cooker. Vegetables, fish, poultry, and meat can be cooked only in steam, and kept dry; they will then require no straining. When reversed or adjusted, the trivet is used as a stand on which to place basins, tins, glass bottling jars, etc. It is not required for liquid cooking, such as stock, soups, stews and milk puddings, or for preserves, where flavours and ingredients must mix together.

Separators

These are perforated or solid containers or baskets designed to fit into the base of the cooker, on top of the trivet, or stacked on top of each other. These accessories are useful for cooking rice, vegetables or other solid foods. The use of several separators allows a variety of foods to be cooked in the same pan, thereby saving time and space.

CARE OF A PRESSURE COOKER

Cleaning

Base and Inserts

These only need ordinary washing-up. Soap and detergents are suitable, but soda should not be used on aluminium pans. Steel wool can be used on discoloured parts, though not on non-stick surfaces, which should only be cleaned with a plastic or nylon pan scrubber. Stains on coloured enamel and painted surfaces should be wiped off as soon as possible with hot water and a cloth; abrasive materials should not be used.

Cover

It is very important to check the steam vent for possible blockages every time the cooker is used. If the vent is blocked, clear it with running water or a thin skewer.

Gasket

This should seldom need removing, but if a liquid has boiled over it or into the rim, it should be washed in warm soapy water, then rinsed and dried thoroughly. Wipe the rim and replace the gasket with as little handling as possible.

Note Neither the base nor the cover should be left standing in water; this dulls the high polish on the surfaces of all types of cooker.

Replacements

Most manufacturers recommend that both gasket and safety plug (if of a rubber composition) should be replaced regularly, usually at least once a year. If steam leaks from around the gasket or the safety plug, these have either stretched or perished, and must be renewed to prevent the cooker from boiling dry. If the safety plug weakens and causes steam to escape, the plug may come into action even before full pressure is built up.

USING A PRESSURE COOKER

The following instructions for using a pressure cooker, together with the pressure cooking times, tables and recipes in the subsequent sections, should be used in conjunction with the manufacturer's booklet supplied with the cooker.

Points to Note

1) The liquid used for pressure cooking must be one which creates steam when it boils, eg water, milk, stock, etc. Fat alone must *not* be used, unless specifically recommended by the manufacturer.
2) Only a very small quantity of liquid is needed. There must, however, be enough to cover the whole base of the pan throughout the cooking time.
3) When cooking solid foods, the pressure cooker should never be more than two-thirds full, to allow room for the steam to circulate. Enough space should be left between the food and the cover to prevent the steam vent from getting blocked. In any model with a flat cover, the top third of the base should be left empty. In models with a domed cover the base can be filled almost to the brim, since the dome provides extra space.
4) When cooking liquid foods, the base must be only half-full when all the ingredients have been added, as the top half of the pan must be left empty in case the liquid boils up, fills the pan and blocks the steam vent.
5) If using an aluminium pressure cooker for recipes to be cooked in a container, eg puddings, bottling, etc, add about $1-2 \times 15$ml spoons lemon juice or vinegar to the cooking liquid in the base to prevent discoloration.

Instructions for Use

1) Prepare the ingredients according to the recipe.
2) Put the correct amount of liquid into the pressure cooker. The minimum amount required is 250ml for the first 15 minutes. Add an extra 125ml for each additional 15 minutes or fraction thereof. Soups, stews, milk puddings, etc, should be cooked with just the quantity required for serving.
3) After the food has been put into the base, close the cover securely, put on the pressure control, and place the cooker over the heat.
4) When cooking solid food, place the pan over *high* heat to boil the liquid and turn it into steam rapidly. Liquids such as soups or milk puddings should, however, be placed over *low* heat so that they do not boil up and block the vent before the pan is filled with steam.
5) The moment there is enough steam in the cooker to give the pressure required, it will start escaping from under the pressure control. This steam, and the loud hissing sound it makes when escaping, is the signal that the calculated pressure cooking time can begin. Lower the heat at once so that it maintains just the right pressure. There should be a continuous slight hiss and a small escape of steam. Raise or lower the heat as required; on a solid fuel stove, use the boiling plate until the pressure cooking time starts, then transfer the cooker to the simmering plate.
6) As soon as the cooking time is up, remove the cooker from the heat. Before taking off the cover, you must reduce the pressure. All cookers which conform to statutory regulations are designed so that it is impossible to open them while there is still any pressure inside.
7) The method of reducing pressure depends on what type of food has been cooked, and is indicated within each section and recipe. Generally speaking, the pressure must be reduced immediately for fish, meat, vegetables and some other solid foods, and slowly for soups, milk and egg dishes, steamed puddings, and when bottling or making jams, jellies or marmalades.

   To reduce pressure immediately, place the cooker in cold water, or, with low-pressure cookers, lift the pressure control slowly. This method reduces the pressure within seconds. If the cooker is of the type mentioned on p1423, which has a lever above the handle to release the pressure, it is not necessary to place the cooker in water; simply move the lever.

To reduce pressure slowly, let the cooker stand at room temperature, away from the heat, until the pressure is fully reduced.

8) To test whether the pressure is fully reduced, the control valve or lever can be lifted slightly. If there is no escape of steam, it can then be removed or opened completely.

Note The recommended pressures and cooking times given in the recipes which follow are for a pressure cooker with a variable control, used up to an altitude of 900 metres above sea level. Above this height, a significant lowering of the boiling point of liquids occurs, and cooking times have to be increased. With a pressure cooker, the necessary adjustments are as follows:

1) Instead of LOW pressure, use MEDIUM.
2) Instead of MEDIUM pressure, use HIGH.
3) With HIGH pressure, increase cooking time by 1 minute for every extra 300 metres.

Adapting Recipes

1) Since pressure cookers vary a good deal in size, recipes often have to be adapted to the capacity of cooker used. The recipes in this chapter are suitable for medium-sized pressure cookers.
2) To adapt ordinary recipes to pressure cooking, check the pressure cooking time for the basic ingredient. Adjust the amount of liquid required by the ordinary recipe, put in the ingredients, and pressure cook for the required time. After reducing the pressure, follow the original recipe to complete the dish.
3) If a pressure cooking time for a particular basic ingredient cannot be found, try using one-third of the normal cooking time. Adjust this if necessary when cooking the same dish again.
4) When adjusting recipes, remember that when food is being timed by weight, the cooking time increases with the weight, and so does the amount of liquid required. If only the total *quantity* of food is increased, and not the *weights* of individual items, no addition need be made to the cooking time or the liquid: eg, if 1.5kg of potatoes are used instead of 400g, no alteration need be made, as each individual potato will still require the same cooking time, but a joint of meat weighing 2kg will require more liquid and a longer cooking time than one weighing 1kg.

FOODS SUITABLE FOR PRESSURE COOKING

As little evaporation takes place in the sealed pan, only a small amount of liquid is required. Vegetables cooked by this method therefore retain more of their colour, flavour and mineral salts, and a higher percentage of those vitamins affected by heat. Dried pulses and vegetables, which do not require overnight soaking, lose less vitamin B, and need only one-third of the normal cooking time. Stock, soups, and steamed or boiled puddings are well suited to pressure cookery, and so are the tougher cuts of meat, often neglected because they need long, slow cooking. If the cooker has adjustable pressures, preserves and fruit bottling are also quickly done.

STOCKS AND SOUPS

Any recipe can be used, but the base of the cooker should not be more than half-full when all the ingredients and liquid have been added. Half the quantity of liquid given in an ordinary recipe will be sufficient. This will give a very concentrated soup, which can be thinned down with extra water, stock or milk before serving.

The trivet is not required. Cook at HIGH pressure, and allow to reduce at room temperature. Cream or any thickening should be added and cooked in the open base just before serving.

Pressure Cooking Times

Household stock containing meat bones	1–2 hours
Cream soups, eg cream of celery	5–10 minutes
Vegetable purée soups, eg leek and potato	10–15 minutes
Meat soups, eg kidney	10–20 minutes
Chicken purée soup	12 minutes
Pulse and dried vegetable soups	15–25 minutes
Lentil soup	12 minutes

Rich Lentil Soup

4 helpings

200g onions	*1 litre white stock*
100g carrots	*(p329)* **or** *2 chicken*
2 large tomatoes	*stock cubes dissolved in*
(optional)	*1 litre water*
margarine **or** *oil for*	*6 black peppercorns*
frying	*salt*
100g lentils	

Garnish
single cream **or** *fresh
chopped parsley* **or**
mint

Skin and chop the onions finely. Scrape and dice the carrots. Skin the tomatoes, if used, and remove the pips. Remove the trivet from the cooker, heat the fat in the base over low heat, and fry the onions gently until golden-brown. Remove from the heat, and stir in the carrots, tomatoes, lentils, stock, and peppercorns. Return to the heat and bring to the boil, stirring all the time. Skim, if necessary. Lower the heat to simmering point, cover, bring to HIGH pressure, and cook for 12 minutes. Allow the pressure to reduce at room temperature. Beat well, or sieve for a very smooth soup. Season to taste, and re-heat just before serving.

Serve in individual cups and garnish each portion with a spoonful of cream, chopped parsley or mint.

FISH

Fish can be pressure cooked on its own for a fish course, or with vegetables to make a complete main-course dish. 250ml liquid (water, milk and water or diluted wine) are required, and the fish should be placed on the greased trivet, seasoned, then covered with buttered paper.

When cooking fish and vegetables together, the fish can be laid in the centre of the trivet with the potatoes piled on each side, and the green vegetables, in perforated separators, placed on top. Alternatively, perforated separators can be filled with different vegetables and put into the cooker first, followed by the trivet or solid separator with the fish placed on top.

There is no need to thaw frozen fish before pressure cooking. Use only half the recommended amount of liquid, as the juices from the fish will make up the full amount. Cook at HIGH pressure and reduce immediately the cooking time is up. The cooking liquid can be used as a base for an accompanying sauce.

Pressure Cooking Times

Fillets of sole, plaice	3 minutes
Steaks of cod, halibut, turbot, haddock, etc.	4 minutes
Herrings, mackerel, whiting:	
whole *or* stuffed	5 minutes
filleted	4 minutes
Salmon: steaks *or* cutlets	4–5 minutes
whole or larger pieces	5–6 minutes per 400g depending on thickness

Salmon Steaks with Cream Sauce

4 helpings

100g cucumber	*lemon juice*
2 large tomatoes	*125ml fish stock* (p330)
50g shallots	**or** *water*
100g button mushrooms	*125ml dry white wine*
4 salmon cutlets	*250ml Hollandaise*
salt and pepper	*sauce* (p712)
butter for frying	*125ml double cream*

Peel and slice the cucumber finely; put into a bowl and cover with boiling water. Prepare and slice the tomatoes and shallots, and clean the mushrooms. Season the salmon well on both sides with salt and pepper.

Remove the trivet from the cooker, melt the butter in the base, and fry the mushrooms for a few seconds, adding a little salt, pepper, and lemon juice. Lift out the mushrooms and drain well. Put a layer of shallots in the base, placing the salmon cutlets on top. Cover with a layer of mushrooms, tomato and the drained cucumber. Pour the stock or water into the base, together with the wine, tilting each piece of salmon to make sure the liquid has run underneath. Cover lightly with greaseproof paper or foil.

Cover the pan, bring to HIGH pressure, and cook for 5 minutes. Reduce the pressure immediately. Drain the salmon and lift it on to a warm, lightly buttered serving dish; cover with greaseproof paper. Boil the remaining liquid in the pan rapidly until reduced by half. Thicken with the Hollandaise sauce and cream, but do not let the sauce boil again. Spoon it over the salmon, brown quickly under a hot grill, and serve immediately.

MEAT

Pressure cooking is ideal for tenderizing meat in a remarkably short time, particularly the coarser, less expensive cuts. The stock or gravy will be concentrated, and full of flavour and nourishment. Pressure cooking is suitable for stewing, braising, boiling and pot-roasting, and meat suet puddings can be cooked in one-third of the normal time.

Stewing or Casseroling

The base of the cooker can be used over low heat for the preparatory frying of meat and vegetables. If the meat has been tossed in flour before frying, it should be lifted out when browned and the pan removed from the heat before adding the hot liquid. The liquid can be stock, water or thin gravy, and only the quantity necessary for serving is required. There will be little loss by evaporation, and the juices from the vegetables and meat themselves will slightly increase the quantity of liquid during cooking. The trivet is not required. Seasoning, and any other thickening of the liquid should be checked after pressure is reduced, just before serving.

Cook at HIGH pressure, and reduce immediately the cooking time is up. The following cooking times apply to cut up meat, eg cubes, etc. It is the size of each piece of meat, not the total amount which is important for stewing, casseroling or braising.

Pressure Cooking Times

Beef	20 minutes
Lamb and mutton	12–15 minutes
Veal	12 minutes
Kidney	12 minutes
Oxtail (allow to stand overnight and skim off fat before re-heating)	40 minutes
Tripe	15 minutes
Mince	7 minutes
Curries: meat, vegetable and fish	10–20 minutes
Leftovers	5–8 minutes

Beef Hot-Pot

4 helpings

500g lean chuck steak	300ml brown stock
salt and pepper	(p329)
flour	chutney **or**
600g potatoes	Worcestershire sauce
300g onions	black pepper
fat **or** oil for frying	25g butter

Wipe the meat and cut it into 2cm cubes. Season the flour and toss the meat lightly in it. Prepare the potatoes and onions, and slice them thickly. Remove the trivet and heat the fat in the base of the cooker. Lightly brown the meat all over and lift it out. Remove the base from the heat, add the stock, stir well to blend in loose flour, and scrape off any frying residue from the base. Arrange the meat, onions, chutney, and two-thirds of the potatoes in layers in the base. If using Worcestershire sauce, sprinkle a little on each layer. Grease the trivet, and put it in the cooker. Arrange the remaining potatoes on it and sprinkle with black pepper.

Cover, bring to HIGH pressure and cook for 15 minutes. Reduce the pressure immediately. Remove the trivet with the potatoes still on it. Place the remaining food in a casserole. Re-season the gravy if required, and add it to the casserole. Arrange the potatoes from the trivet on top of the meat and vegetables. Dot with butter, then brown quickly under a hot grill. Serve immediately.

Braising

Follow the instructions for braising meat given on p473. The liquid added should only just cover the bed of fried vegetables on which the meat is placed. If potatoes are to be served separately, they can be placed on top of the meat, on the trivet. When cooked, remove the potatoes to a separate dish, lift out the trivet, and put the meat in the centre of a serving dish. Mash the remaining vegetables into the liquid in the base to make gravy, or rub them through a sieve. Beat the gravy well, and pour it over the meat.

Cook at HIGH pressure, and reduce immediately the cooking time is up. If braising larger pieces of meat than listed in the following chart, refer to the pressure cooking times for pot-roasting on p1430.

Pressure Cooking Times

Liver	5 minutes
Chops	10–12 minutes
Beef Olives, braised steak	15–20 minutes

Stuffed Sheep's Hearts

4 helpings

4 sheep's hearts	fat **or** oil for frying
50g basic herb stuffing	375ml brown stock
(p375)	(p329)
salt and pepper	flour (optional)
flour	sherry **or** red wine
600g carrots	gravy browning
50g turnips	(optional)

Prepare and stuff the hearts as for Baked Stuffed Sheep's or Lamb's Hearts (p548), season the flour, and toss the hearts in it. Prepare and chop the carrots and turnips roughly. Remove the trivet, heat the fat in the base of the cooker, brown the hearts all over and lift them out. Fry the vegetables gently, then strain off the surplus fat. Heat the stock and add it to the vegetables, stirring well, then replace the hearts. Cover, bring to HIGH pressure and cook for 30 minutes; reduce the pressure immediately.

Place the hearts on a serving dish, and keep warm. Mash the vegetables into the liquid in the base, and thicken this gravy with flour blended in a little stock, if liked. Re-season if required. Add sherry or wine to taste, and gravy browning, if used. Re-heat the gravy, pour it over the hearts, and serve.

Boiling

The trivet is not required. The meat should be covered by the liquid, if possible, remembering that the cooker must never be more than half-full when the meat and vegetables have been added. The liquid can be added to an accompanying sauce later, if required.

Cook at HIGH pressure, and reduce immediately the cooking time is up. If dumplings are cooked, they should be added to the liquid in the base after pressure has been reduced, and cooked for 10–15 minutes, or for the time given in the original recipe, covered only with a large plate or lid.

Pressure Cooking Times

Fresh beef: brisket	12 minutes per 500g
Salt beef: brisket, silverside	15 minutes per 500g
Ham *or* bacon	15 minutes per 500g
Mutton: shoulder, leg, middle neck	15 minutes per 500g
Fresh pork: leg, hand	15 minutes per 500g
Salt pork: belly	20 minutes per 500g
Veal: knuckle	12 minutes per 500g

Pot-Roasting

Only certain meats, and joints weighing less than 1.5kg, are suitable for this type of cooking. The joint should be well seasoned, then browned on all sides in hot fat in the base over low heat. After lifting out the meat, all but a spoonful of fat should be drained off. The required amount of liquid should then be added, and the joint put back on the trivet.

Cook at HIGH pressure, and reduce immediately the cooking time is up. If there is enough room, vegetables for serving separately can be added towards the end of the cooking time. Reduce the pressure, add the vegetables in perforated separators, bring the cooker to pressure again and continue cooking for the required time.

After lifting out the meat and vegetables, re-season if required and re-heat the gravy. If it is to be thickened, add flour blended with a little water to the liquid in the base, and stir while bringing to the boil and cooking.

Pressure Cooking Times

Beef: topside, rump, brisket	12–15 minutes per 500g
Lamb: stuffed breast, middle neck	12–15 minutes per 500g
Veal: best end of neck, stuffed breast	12 minutes per 500g

Meat Puddings and Pies

To ensure the most satisfactory results, pre-cook the meat for suet puddings. This is also a good way to save time and fuel when making covered or plate meat pies. If using an aluminium cooker, use acidulated water in the base.

Steak and Kidney Pudding (2)

4 helpings

400g stewing steak	*flour*
100g ox kidney **or** *2*	*1 medium-sized onion*
sheep's kidneys	*300ml brown stock*
salt and pepper	*(p329)* **or** *water*

Suet crust

200g self-raising flour	*125ml cold water*
salt and pepper	*flour for rolling out*
75g shredded suet	*fat for greasing*

For the cooker
750ml boiling water

Prepare the steak and kidney, and cut into neat pieces. Season the flour, and toss the meat in it. Skin the onion, and chop it finely. Remove the trivet and put in the stock or water, meat, and onion. Cover, bring to HIGH pressure, and cook for 15 minutes. Leave to cool while making the suet crust.

Sift the flour and salt together and mix in the suet. Mix to a firm dough with the water. Cut off one-quarter of the pastry for the lid. Roll out the rest on a lightly floured surface into a round about 5mm thick, and use it to line a greased 750ml pudding basin. Place the meat in the pastry, and add enough of the gravy to half-cover the meat. Roll out the reserved pastry to make the lid. Dampen the edges, put the lid in place, and press the edges together to seal. Cover securely with a double thickness of greased greaseproof paper. Pour the rest of the gravy into a small saucepan.

Wash the base of the cooker, and put in the trivet and boiling water. Stand the pudding on the trivet, and put on the cover. Cook over high heat until steam escapes; then lower the heat, and steam gently for 10 minutes. Raise the heat, bring to LOW pressure, and cook for 35 minutes. Reduce pressure at room temperature. Re-heat the extra gravy, re-season if required, then pour it into the pudding through a hole cut in the crust, or serve separately.

Note For Steak and Kidney Pudding (1), see p503.

VARIATION
Sea Pie (2)

Using the ingredients for Steak and Kidney Pudding, pre-cook the meat and allow to cool. Make the suet crust, roll it out into a circle just smaller than the cooker, then fold it into four. Place the crust on top of the meat in the cooker, unfold it to make a complete topping, then cover with a double circle of greaseproof paper. Steam over low heat for 10 minutes, then cook at LOW pressure for 20 minutes. Reduce pressure at room temperature, and serve direct from the cooker.

Note For Sea Pie (1), see p504.

Meats for a Cold Table

Any suitable recipe can be used; the preparation, ingredients required, and method of serving remain the same. Cook at HIGH pressure, and allow to reduce at room temperature until quite cold.

Pressure Cooking Times

Meat for brawn: pig's head, pig's cheek, cow-heel	35 minutes per 500g
Meat for galantine of beef	35 minutes per 500g
Tongue: ox	15 minutes per 500g
lamb	20 minutes per 500g
Bacon or ham: extra large lean joints, without trivet, covered with water;	15 minutes per 500g
inexpensive fatty cuts, on trivet, with minimum amount of water	15 minutes per 500g

Tongue with Liver Pâté

8–12 helpings

1 ox tongue (1.5–2kg)	100g softened unsalted
2 × 15ml spoons white	butter
vinegar	salt and black pepper
4–6 peppercorns	1 × 15ml spoon aspic
2 cloves	jelly powder or crystals
1 bay leaf	125ml port (optional)
200g liver pâté	125–250ml water

Garnish

watercress sprigs

Prepare the tongue the day before it is required. Weigh it, tie loosely in muslin and put into the cooker without the trivet. Cover with cold water, and bring to the boil in the base. Lift out, rinse under cold water, empty the cooker, then put back the tongue. Cover again with cold water, and add the vinegar and spices. Cover and cook at HIGH pressure for 15 minutes per 500g, then allow to reduce at room temperature. Strip the skin from the cooked tongue, and remove the small bones at the root, together with the surplus fat and gristle. While it is still hot, press the tongue down into a loaf tin so that it will retain its shape. Cover with foil, press down with weights, and leave overnight.

To prepare the tongue for serving, beat the liver pâté with the softened butter, adding salt and freshly ground pepper to taste. Quickly dip the loaf tin in and out of hot water, and turn out the tongue. Cut lengthways into even slices, spread each slice with the pâté mixture, and put them together again to re-form the tongue. Wrap very tightly in foil and leave for an hour or so in a refrigerator.

Make up the aspic jelly according to the directions on the packet, using 125ml port and 125ml water, or 250ml water. Lift the tongue on to the serving dish, and when the aspic is just beginning to thicken, brush it evenly over the tongue and allow to set.

Before serving, use a knife dipped in hot water to lift off the aspic and chop it lightly. Use as a garnish round the tongue with the watercress.

POULTRY AND GAME

Pressure cooking is a quick way of tenderizing boiling fowl and preparing chicken for a variety of casseroles, pie fillings, light dishes, and meals for small children. For boiling fowl, the trivet is not required. Cover the bird with water; add vegetables and rice towards the end of the cooking time, if required. (See Pot-Roasting p1430.) When steaming a chicken or tenderizing it before roasting, the bird should be cooked on the trivet with only the minimum of liquid in the cooker.

Cook at HIGH pressure, and reduce immediately the cooking time is up. If the oven is heated during the pressure cooking time, the cooked chicken can be placed in a pan with a little hot fat, then basted and browned on the top shelf for a further 10 minutes. For braising, use the base of the cooker over low heat to brown chicken, game and vegetables in a small quantity of fat. These can then be used as a braising bed in place of the trivet. Sufficient liquid should be added to cover all but the top layer of vegetables.

Note Frozen chicken, whether whole or in pieces, must be thawed completely before being cooked.

Pressure Cooking Times

Boiling fowl: whole	10–12 minutes per 500g
jointed	10 minutes
Thawed chicken pieces	5–10 minutes
	(depending on size)
Roasting chicken: whole	8 minutes per 500g
Guinea-fowl, partridge	10 minutes
Pheasant	10–12 minutes per 500g

Chicken Gratinée

4 helpings

1 young chicken	*bouquet garni*
(1.25–1.5kg approx)	*salt and pepper*
2 medium-sized carrots	*40g butter*
1 medium-sized onion	*40g flour*
1 leek, white part only	*2 egg yolks*
a stick of celery	*2 × 15ml spoons double*
150g Gruyère cheese	*cream*
fat for frying	*1 × 15ml spoon lemon*
250ml dry white wine	*juice*
250ml water	

Truss the chicken, if liked. Prepare and slice the carrots, onion, leek, and celery. Grate the cheese coarsely.

Remove the trivet, heat the fat in the base and fry the chicken all over without allowing it to brown. Add the wine and water, vegetables, bouquet garni, and seasoning. Cover and cook for 20 minutes at HIGH pressure, then reduce immediately. Lift out the chicken, divide into portions, and arrange on a warmed, buttered serving dish.

Reduce the liquid in the base to 375ml by rapid boiling, and remove any fat from the surface. Strain and set aside. Melt the butter in a clean pan, add the flour and cook for 1–2 minutes without colouring. Remove from the heat and add the strained liquid slowly, beating well. Mix the yolks and cream. Bring the liquid to the boil, stirring briskly. Reduce the heat and gradually whisk in the yolks and cream, without allowing the sauce to boil. Add the lemon juice and re-season if required. When the sauce has cooled a little, spoon it over the chicken pieces, and cover thickly with the cheese. Place in a fairly hot oven, 200°C, Gas 6, and leave for 5–6 minutes or until crisp and brown. Serve immediately.

PULSES, RICE AND PASTA

Pulses require no overnight soaking. Wash, cover with boiling water, and leave for one hour. Cook the beans in the same liquid in which they have soaked, making up the quantity to 1 litre for every 500g pulses before cooking. Season well.

Remove the trivet from the cooker, pour the liquid into the base, and bring to the boil. Add the pulses and any other ingredients, and bring to the boil again. Skim well, lower the heat to simmering point, and bring to HIGH pressure without altering the heat. Cook for the required time, then allow to reduce at room temperature.

Rice cooked on its own requires 750ml of water to each 100g of rice. Remove the trivet, bring the water to the boil, and add 1 × 5ml spoon of salt for each 500ml of water. Sprinkle in the unwashed rice slowly, stir once to prevent it sticking, then cook at HIGH pressure for 5 minutes. Reduce immediately.

Pasta, like rice, needs cooking in plenty of boiling salted water to allow for absorption. Care must be taken that the base of the pan is not more than one-third full, as any pasta tends to froth up, and this may block the vent. When cooking long pasta such as spaghetti and vermicelli, do not break the lengths, but push them into the boiling liquid, a little at a time, as they soften. The trivet is not required. Cook at HIGH pressure, for approximately one-third of the normal cooking time for the type of pasta used, and reduce immediately.

Note When using a pressure cooker with a manual or automatic pressure release, rice and pasta foods should be reduced at room temperature. The cooking times should also be shortened according to the instructions in the manufacturer's booklet.

Pressure Cooking Times

Barley in soups	20 minutes
Beans: haricot	20 minutes
butter	30 minutes
Lentils	15 minutes
Macaroni	4–6 minutes
Noodles	3–4 minutes
Peas: split	15 minutes
whole	20 minutes
Rice: long-grain	5 minutes
Spaghetti	4–6 minutes
Vermicelli	3–4 minutes

Ginger Lamb

4 helpings

150g red kidney beans	*50g butter*
500–750g boned lean lamb	*1 × 5ml spoon ground ginger*
1 medium-sized onion	*1 × 5ml spoon paprika*
1 dessert apple	*500ml dry ginger ale*
2 cloves garlic	*salt and pepper*
25g stem ginger (optional)	*1 × 10ml spoon cornflour*

Garnish
fried apple slices (p395)

Put the beans into a basin, cover with boiling water, and leave for 1 hour, then drain. Wipe the meat, trim off any excess fat, and cut into 2cm cubes. Skin and chop the onion, peel, core, and chop the apple, and skin and crush the garlic. Drain and chop the stem ginger, if used.

Melt the butter in the base of the cooker, and fry the meat, onion and garlic until golden-brown. Remove from the heat, and add the apple, ground ginger, paprika, ginger ale, and salt and pepper to taste. Stir in the soaked beans. Cover, bring to HIGH pressure and cook for 20 minutes; reduce pressure immediately. Return the base to the heat, and stir in the chopped stem ginger, if used; then add the cornflour, blended with a little cold water. Bring to the boil and cook until the gravy thickens, stirring all the time. Re-season if required.

Garnish with fried apple slices, and serve immediately.

FRESH VEGETABLES

The pressure cooking times shown below are average ones, and should be adjusted according to the size and freshness of the vegetables. To obtain the best results, use the shortest possible pressure cooking time.

The trivet or perforated separators should always be used, and at least 250ml liquid must be put into the cooker first. Potatoes or other root vegetables should be cut into suitable sizes so that they require the same cooking time. They should then be piled loosely on the trivet, and sprinkled with salt.

The perforated separators are useful for small vegetables such as peas, beans, shredded cabbage, diced vegetables for a macédoine, etc. To preserve their colour and to make sure they are not over-cooked, green vegetables should be added to the cooker only when the liquid has boiled and the pan is filled with steam. The separators can be placed on top of the other vegetables.

Cook at HIGH pressure, and reduce immediately the cooking time is up.

Pressure Cooking Times

Asparagus: in small bundles	2–4 minutes
Beans: cut French or runner	4 minutes
broad	4 minutes
Beetroot: without trivet, covered with water	
small	10 minutes
medium	20 minutes
large	30 minutes
Brussels sprouts	4 minutes
Broccoli	3 minutes
Cabbage: sliced, green or white	4 minutes
red	4 minutes
Carrots: sliced	4 minutes
new, whole	5–6 minutes
Cauliflower: in florets	4 minutes
Celery: sticks or whole hearts	4–6 minutes
Chicory	5–7 minutes
Corn on the cob: without trivet, with 50g butter added	
small	6 minutes
large	8–10 minutes
Courgettes: whole	4 minutes
Leeks: whole	4–6 minutes
Onions: whole, according to size	6–8 minutes
Peas	3–4 minutes
Potatoes: whole, new, according to size	6–8 minutes
old, quartered or halved	4–6 minutes
Parsnips, swedes, turnips: cubed or cut roughly for mashing	4 minutes
Spinach	1 minute
Vegetable marrows: sliced	4 minutes
halved for stuffing	7 minutes

PUDDINGS

If using an aluminium cooker, use acidulated water in the base when cooking puddings in a basin or other container.

Steamed and Boiled Puddings

When pressure cooking any mixture containing a raising agent, a short 'steaming' time must first be allowed, so that the mixture can rise to give a light, open texture to the pudding. To do this, the valve must be left open and the pudding allowed to steam in the usual way over low heat for the first part of the cooking; the cooker can then be brought to pressure for the rest of the cooking time.

LOW pressure is generally recommended; if a HIGH or fixed pressure has to be used, best results will be obtained if the quantity is divided into individual portions and cooked in small moulds.

Any of the recipes for steamed puddings given in the chapter on Hot Puddings and Desserts can be used. Stainless steel, china, ovenglass, aluminium or heatproof plastic basins are suitable, covered with a double thickness of buttered, greaseproof paper.

Allow 125ml boiling water for each 15 minutes pressure cooking time and 250ml to cover the initial steaming time. The pressure must always be allowed to reduce at room temperature.

Pressure Cooking Times

Plain, rubbed-in mixture based on 150g flour	in one bowl	15 minutes steaming	40 minutes at LOW pressure
	in 4 individual bowls	5 minutes steaming	15 minutes at HIGH pressure

Rich, creamed mixture	in one bowl	15 minutes steaming	25 minutes at LOW pressure
	in 4 individual bowls	5 minutes steaming	10 minutes at HIGH pressure
Suet: 200g suet crust		15 minutes steaming	30 minutes at LOW pressure

Christmas Puddings

Any recipe can be used. The cooking time will depend on the weight of mixture (refer to the table below). Leave 2cm headspace above the mixture in the container. Cook at HIGH pressure and reduce at room temperature. When cold, follow storage instructions on p982.

Pressure Cooking Times

Individual: 150g mixture	750ml water	10 minutes steaming	50 minutes at HIGH pressure
In one bowl: 400g mixture	1.5 litres water	15 minutes steaming	1½ hours at HIGH pressure
In one bowl: 625g mixture	1.75 litres water	20 minutes steaming	2½ hours at HIGH pressure
In one bowl: 850g mixture	2 litres water	30 minutes steaming	3 hours at HIGH pressure

Re-heating Times

Individual	500ml water	10 minutes at HIGH pressure
In one bowl	500ml water	20–30 minutes at HIGH pressure

Milk Puddings

Milk puddings must be cooked with care; if the milk boils up it may block the steam vent. Remove the trivet, melt enough butter or margarine to cover the base of the pan, pour in the milk and bring to the boil as quickly as possible. Stir in the cereal used, and any sugar and flavourings. Let the milk come to the boil again, then lower the heat so that it is still boiling but does not rise in the pan. Cover, bring to HIGH pressure without altering the heat, cook for the required time, and allow to reduce at room temperature. To serve hot, pour into a serving dish, sprinkle with grated nutmeg, dot with butter and brown under a warm grill.

Pressure Cooking Times

50g pudding rice with 500ml milk	12 minutes
50g tapioca, sago, semolina, with 500ml milk	7 minutes

Custard Puddings and Desserts

Egg custards and custard-based desserts are excellent cooked in a pressure cooker. They can be cooked over direct heat and are ready in a few minutes with no danger of curdling. Prepare the custard according to the recipe for Baked Custard on p965, and pour the mixture into a suitable large dish or individual dishes. Cover securely, and stand on the trivet with at least 250ml cold water in the base. Cook at HIGH pressure and reduce at room temperature.

Pressure Cooking Times

For a custard using 500ml milk	5 minutes
In individual portions	3 minutes

Bread and Butter Pudding

For the mixture, follow the recipe on p966. Cover the dish closely. Pour 250ml water into the base and put the dish on the trivet. Bring to HIGH pressure, cook for 6 minutes, then reduce at room temperature. Lift out the dish, remove the cover, sprinkle with brown sugar and grill until crisp.

Queen of Puddings

For the crumb mixture, follow the recipe on p972. Cover the dish closely. Pour 250ml water into the base and put the dish on the trivet. Bring to HIGH pressure, cook for 5 minutes, then reduce at room temperature. Lift out the dish, remove the cover, and spread with jam. Top with meringue, and bake for 20–30 minutes in a cool oven, 150°C, Gas 2, until golden.

CAKES

A watertight container must be used. Light sponge mixtures are best made into small cakes in individual moulds. Allow the mixture to steam gently over low heat for 5–15 minutes before bringing to pressure. Use acidulated water in the base if an aluminium cooker is used.

As with steamed puddings, cook at LOW pressure if available; otherwise divide into individual portions and cook in small moulds at HIGH or fixed pressure. Always allow the pressure to reduce slowly at room temperature.

Fruit Cake

fat for greasing	*1 × 10ml spoon*
65g margarine	*marmalade*
175g self-raising flour	*1 × 2.5ml spoon*
75g granulated sugar	*bicarbonate of soda*
75g currants	*100ml milk*
75g sultanas	*gravy browning*

For the cooker
750ml boiling water

Grease a 15cm round cake or loaf tin which will fit into the cooker, and a double thickness of greaseproof paper.

Rub the margarine into the flour. Stir in the sugar, dried fruit and marmalade. Dissolve the bicarbonate of soda in the milk, and add to the other ingredients to give a slack mixture. Mix well, adding a little gravy browning to give a rich colour. Turn the mixture into the tin, and seal securely with the greaseproof paper. Pour the boiling water into the base. Stand the tin on the trivet, put on the cover and steam gently for 15 minutes. Bring to LOW pressure and cook for 40 minutes. Allow the pressure to reduce at room temperature.

Remove the tin from the cooker, and leave covered until cool. Turn out gently, and when quite cold, store wrapped in foil or clingfilm.

Note This cake can be stored for up to 2 weeks, and improves with keeping.

FRESH FRUITS

These can be cooked successfully in a pressure cooker, either to be kept whole for serving as stewed fruit, or for making into purée.

Soft fruits such as apples, blackberries, gooseberries, rhubarb or cherries should be washed, then packed into a suitable dish and layered with sugar. Do not add any water. Cover the dish securely, stand it on the trivet with 250ml water, and cook at HIGH pressure for 5 minutes; reduce immediately.

Stone fruits such as apricots, greengages and plums are cooked like soft fruit but with the addition of sugar syrup, poured into the container with the fruit. Dessert pears are also cooked this way.

Cooking pears are best heated in a light syrup. Cook at HIGH pressure directly in the base of the cooker and without the trivet, for 8–10 minutes according to hardness. Reduce at room temperature.

Fruits for purées should be prepared, cut up roughly if necessary, and cooked without the trivet in a heavy syrup at HIGH pressure for 3–5 minutes. (Make sure that the base of the cooker is never more than half-full.) The pressure should be allowed to reduce at room temperature.

DRIED FRUIT

Before cooking, wash the fruit and leave to soak in hot water in a covered bowl for 10–30 minutes, allowing 500ml water for each 400g dried fruit. The trivet is not required. Cook at HIGH pressure, using the water in which the fruit has been soaked, with sugar and flavourings to taste. Allow the pressure to reduce at room temperature.

Pressure Cooking Times

Apple rings	6 minutes
Apricots	10 minutes
Figs	10 minutes
Fruit salad	10 minutes
Peaches	5 minutes
Pears	10 minutes
Prunes	10 minutes

Apricot Wine Cups

4 helpings

200g dried apricots	*250ml dry white wine*
75g sugar	*2 eggs*
grated rind and juice of 1 lemon	*1 × 15ml spoon gelatine*
	3 × 15ml spoons water

Decoration

25g toasted flaked almonds	*icing sugar*

Prepare the fruit as described on p1436, soaking it for 30 minutes. Drain, and put in the base with the sugar, lemon rind and juice, and the wine. Bring to HIGH pressure, and cook for 10 minutes; reduce the pressure at room temperature.

When cool, rub the apricots and cooking liquid through a sieve, or process in an electric blender. Separate the eggs. Soften the gelatine in the water in a small heatproof container, stand it in a pan of hot water, and stir until dissolved. Stir into the apricot purée, together with the yolks. Whisk the whites until stiff, and fold them gently into the apricot mixture. Spoon into 4 individual dishes, and chill until set.

Before serving, decorate with the flaked almonds, and dust lightly with icing sugar.

JAMS, JELLIES, MARMALADES, ETC

The advantage of pressure cooking the fruit for jams and jellies is that it can be softened quickly, and marmalades can be cooked thoroughly in a short time. The fruits retain more of their flavour and colour than usual, and provided the instructions are followed carefully, the finished product will be an excellent preserve made with the minimum of time and trouble.

Choose and prepare the fruit in the usual way. Weigh the fruit only after it has been prepared for cooking. The trivet is not required, and the base of the cooker should be no more than half-full when the fruit and water have been put in. Use about one-third of the quantity of water required for an ordinary jam recipe.

Cook fresh fruit jams, jellies and marmalades at MEDIUM pressure. Cooking at HIGH pressure may affect the pectin content of the fruit, and make the jam set less well. The pressure should always be allowed to reduce at room temperature. After cooking the fruit, the base of the cooker can be used as an open pan for boiling the cooked fruit with the sugar. Pressure cooked preserves are potted and labelled like any other preserves (see p1102).

Jams from Fresh Fruit

Yield 1.75kg (approx) from 1kg sugar

Pressure Cooking Times

Apricot	1kg	250ml water 1kg sugar	4 minutes
Blackberry and apple	300g 1kg	125ml water 1.5kg sugar	5 minutes
Blackcurrant	1kg	750ml water 1.5kg sugar	3–4 minutes
Damson	1kg	250ml water 1.5kg sugar	5 minutes
Gooseberry	1kg	250ml water 1.25kg sugar	3 minutes
Melon and pineapple	1kg 200g	juice of 3 lemons 1.5kg sugar	10 minutes
Peach	1kg	250ml water 1.5kg sugar	3–4 minutes
Plum, greengage	1kg	250ml water 1kg sugar	4 minutes
Rhubarb and root ginger or preserved chopped ginger	1.25kg 50g 100g	juice and rind of 2 lemons 1kg sugar (Tie root ginger in muslin)	bring to pressure only

Blackberry and Apple Jam (2)

Yield 2kg (approx)

350g sour apples (peeled   300ml water
  and cored)   1.5kg sugar
1kg blackberries

Slice the prepared apples, pick over the blackberries and wash them gently but thoroughly. Tie
the apple peel and cores in a muslin bag, and put
them in the base with the fruit and water. Cover,
bring to MEDIUM pressure, and cook for 5 minutes.
Allow the pressure to reduce at room temperature.
Remove the bag and squeeze it out gently. Add the
sugar to the fruit, and stir over low heat until the
sugar is dissolved; then bring to the boil and boil
rapidly until setting point is reached. Remove from
the heat, skim, pot, cover, and label.

Note For Blackberry and Apple Jam (1), see p1103.

Jams from Dried Fruit

Dried fruit jams are a useful standby when the
fresh fruit season is over. They are particularly
useful as sauces for steamed puddings and ice
cream, with milk puddings, and as fillings for tarts
and flans.

Dried Apricot Jam

Yield 2.5kg (approx)

500g dried apricots   50g blanched and
1 litre boiling water   shredded almonds
juice of 1 large lemon   (optional)
                              1.5kg sugar

Cut the apricots into small pieces. Put them into the
cooker, pour on the boiling water, cover, and leave
for 1 hour. Bring to HIGH pressure, cook for 10 minutes, then allow the pressure to reduce at room
temperature. Add the lemon juice, almonds and
sugar, and continue the process as when making
fresh fruit jams.

Jellies from Fresh Fruit

Follow the instructions given for jelly making on
pp1108–9. Only the amount of water added, and
the cooking times, need be altered when pressure
cooking as shown below. The yield remains the
same. The trivet is not required; cook at MEDIUM
pressure, and allow to reduce at room temperature.

Pressure Cooking Times

Apple	1.5kg	500ml water	5 minutes
Blackcurrant	1.5kg	1 litre water	5 minutes
Blackberries	1kg	500ml water	3 minutes
		juice of 1 lemon	
Crab-apple	1.5kg	water just to	8 minutes
		show through	
		top layer of fruit	
Gooseberry	1.5kg	500ml water	5 minutes
Redcurrant	1.5kg	water just to	1 minute
		show through	
		top layer of fruit	

Mint Jelly (2)

1kg green gooseberries   fresh, finely chopped
125ml water   mint
sugar (see Method)   green colouring
a bunch of fresh mint   (optional)

Wash the gooseberries, put them in the base with
the water, cover, and cook at MEDIUM pressure for
5 minutes. Allow the pressure to reduce at room
temperature. Mash the gooseberries until well
pulped, and strain through a scalded jelly bag.
Leave it to drip for 1 hour. Measure the extract,
and return it to the base. Add 400g sugar for each
500ml juice, and bring to the boil. Add the bunch
of fresh mint tied with string. When the jelly
shows the first signs of setting, lift out the mint and
continue boiling until setting point is reached.
Allow the jelly to stand until a thin skin forms,
then gently stir in the finely chopped mint, and
colouring if used. Skim, pot, cool, cover, and label.

Note For Mint Jelly (1), see p1112.

Rose-Hip Jelly

1kg well-ripened rose-
hips
750ml water

sugar (see Method)
tartaric acid (see
Method)

Wash, top and tail the fruit, and pass through a coarse mincer. Remove the trivet from the cooker, put in the water and the fruit, cover, and cook for 5 minutes at MEDIUM pressure. Allow to reduce at room temperature.

Mash the fruit thoroughly and strain through a scalded jelly bag. Leave it to drip for 1 hour. Measure the extract, and return it to the base. To each 500ml strained fruit juice, add 400g sugar and 1×2.5ml spoon tartaric acid. Bring to the boil and test for set after 5–10 minutes. Remove from the heat, skim, pot, cover, and label.

Marmalades

Whether the fruit is chopped or sliced before or after cooking will depend on the recipe used, but there is no need to soak the fruit overnight. The pith and pips should always be tied loosely in muslin and cooked with the fruit, to obtain their pectin.

Remove the trivet, put the water and washed fruit into the base of the cooker, bring to MEDIUM pressure, and cook for the time indicated on the following chart. Allow the pressure to reduce at room temperature. Thereafter follow the instructions on p1115.

Pressure Cooking Times

Grapefruit	750g	1 litre water	10 minutes
	200g lemons	2kg sugar	
Lemon	1kg	1 litre water	8 minutes
		2kg sugar	
Seville Orange	1kg	1 litre water	10 minutes
		2kg sugar	
		juice of two	
		lemons	

Three-fruit and other mixed fruit marmalades:

2 oranges, 1 grapefruit	750ml water	10 minutes
2 lemons (1kg total)	2kg sugar	

Jelly Marmalades

These should be made like fruit jellies, but, before cooking, the fruit should be thinly peeled, the peel finely shredded, the pulp cut up, the juice squeezed out and the pulp tied loosely in muslin.

Remove the trivet from the cooker, and put in the water, roughly chopped fruit, and the bag of pulp. Cook at MEDIUM pressure, and allow to reduce at room temperature. Lift out the muslin bag, cool slightly and squeeze well. Strain the marmalade through a jelly bag. Continue the process as when making fruit jellies, but stir in the shreds just at setting point. Pot immediately.

Yield 3.5kg (approx) from 2kg sugar

Pressure Cooking Times

Lemon	1kg	625ml water	8 minutes
Orange	1kg	625ml juice	8 minutes
		2 small lemons	
Tangerine	750g	750ml water	8 minutes
	½ grapefruit		
	2 small lemons		

Lime Jelly Marmalade

Yield 1kg (approx)

500g limes (8 approx)
juice of 1 lemon

750ml water
750g sugar

Wash the limes, pare off the rind, and shred finely. Cut the fruit in half and squeeze out the juice, discarding the pips. Cut up the fruit pulp, tie it in a muslin bag, and put it in the base with the lime and lemon juice, shreds and water. Cover, bring to MEDIUM pressure, and cook for 10 minutes. Reduce the pressure at room temperature. Remove the muslin bag, cool slightly and squeeze well. Strain the liquid through a jelly bag, then simmer the juice for a few moments if too thin. Add the sugar, and stir over gentle heat until dissolved, then boil rapidly until setting point is reached. Add the shreds, then skim, pot, cover, and label.

Note The limes should just be turning yellow, otherwise the marmalade may be bitter.

Curds

These are cooked in a container. Acidulated water should be used in the base of an aluminium cooker to avoid discoloration.

Lemon Curd (2)

Yield 400g (approx)

75g unsalted butter	*rind and juice of 2*
3 eggs	*lemons*
400g caster sugar	

For the cooker
250ml water

Choose a china or ovenproof bowl that will fit into the cooker. Cut the butter into small pieces. Beat the eggs lightly and strain them into the bowl. Stir in the sugar until well mixed. Add the lemon rind and juice, and the butter, and stir well together. Cover the bowl closely. Put the water into the cooker and place the bowl on the trivet. Cover and cook at HIGH pressure for 10 minutes, and allow to reduce at room temperature for 10 minutes. Lift out the bowl, open it, stir well for 1–2 minutes, then pour the curd into a warmed jar. Cover and label.

VARIATION

Orange Curd (2)

Substitute the grated rind of 2 oranges and 2 × 15ml spoons mixed orange and lemon juice for the lemon rind and juice. Follow the same method as for Lemon Curd, but to obtain a smoother consistency, Orange Curd can be sieved when cooked, before potting.

Note For Lemon Curd (1) and Orange Curd (1), see p1122.

CHUTNEYS, PICKLES AND SAUCES

Any basic recipe can be used, since the pressure cooker is only needed for softening the ingredients. The only special care required is to make sure that the base of the cooker is never more than half-full.

Use HIGH pressure, and reduce immediately the cooking time is up.

Pressure Cooking Times

Apple	15 minutes
Apricot	20 minutes
Green tomato	10 minutes
Marrow	8 minutes
Plum	10 minutes

Green Tomato Chutney (2)

Yield 1.75kg (approx)

1.5kg green tomatoes	*15g ginger root* **or**
500g sour apples	*1 × 15ml spoon ground*
100g onions	*ginger*
300g dates **or** *150g*	*500ml malt vinegar*
seedless raisins	*100g brown sugar*
3 × 5ml spoons pickling	*salt and pepper*
spice	

Skin and quarter the tomatoes. Peel, core and cut the apples into small pieces. Skin and chop the onions. Chop the dates, if used. Tie the spices and the root ginger, if used, in muslin. Remove the trivet, put in half the vinegar and the prepared ingredients. Bring to the boil, stirring well. Cover and cook for 10 minutes at HIGH pressure. Reduce immediately. Lift out the muslin bag, add the rest of the vinegar, the ground ginger, if used, and the sugar. Boil in the open base until the correct consistency is obtained, stirring all the time. Add salt and pepper to taste. Pot according to the instructions on pp1138–39.

Note For Green Tomato Chutney (1), see p1145.

Mango Chutney

Yield 1.5kg (approx)

5 slightly under-ripe mangoes	25g ginger root
25g salt	25g whole black peppercorns
375ml spiced vinegar (p1139)	450g Demerara sugar
1 × 5ml spoon Cayenne pepper	

Peel and stone the mangoes, then slice the flesh. Place in a bowl and sprinkle with the salt, then leave to stand overnight. Remove the trivet. Drain and rinse the fruit and put it with 250ml of the vinegar, and the Cayenne pepper, into the base. Bruise the ginger, tie it securely in muslin with the peppercorns, and put them into the base. Bring to the boil, stirring well. Cover and cook for 5 minutes at HIGH pressure. Reduce the pressure immediately. Remove the muslin bag, and squeeze the juices back into the fruit pulp. Add the sugar and the remaining vinegar. Heat gently until the sugar is dissolved, then boil rapidly until the chutney thickens, stirring all the time. Pot and cover immediately, as described on pp1138–39.

Mustard Pickle

Yield 1.75kg (approx)

1.5kg mixed vegetables (see Method)	2 × 15ml spoons ground ginger
1 litre water	2 × 15ml spoons plain flour
100g kitchen salt	2 × 15ml spoons turmeric
500ml white vinegar	
100g brown sugar	
1 × 15ml spoon dry mustard	

Prepare a variety of vegetables such as cucumber, cauliflower, green beans, green tomatoes, marrow and shallots, and cut them into small pieces. Put all the vegetables into the water with the salt, and leave overnight, covered with a weighted plate.

Drain the vegetables and put them into the cooker without the trivet; add three-quarters of the vinegar, the sugar, mustard and ginger. Cover

and cook at HIGH pressure for 1 minute. Reduce immediately. Place a selection of the vegetables into 4 jars, prepared as for making other preserves (see p1138). Blend the flour and turmeric with the rest of the vinegar, add to the liquid, bring to the boil in the base and cook until thick, stirring all the time. Pour an equal amount into each jar. Move the vegetables about with a round-bladed knife, to make sure that the sauce seeps down between them. Cover according to the instructions on p1139.

Tomato Ketchup (4)

Yield 1 litre (approx)

2kg ripe tomatoes	1 × 2.5ml spoon ground mace
250ml white vinegar	200g white sugar
1 × 2.5ml spoon ground ginger	Cayenne pepper
1 × 2.5ml spoon ground cloves	salt

Wash and slice the tomatoes. Remove the trivet, put in the vinegar and tomatoes, cover, and cook at HIGH pressure for 3 minutes. Reduce immediately. Rub the tomatoes through a fine sieve. Return the pulp to the base with the spices and sugar, and bring to the boil. Add Cayenne pepper and salt to taste; stir and cook until thick and creamy.

To seal the jars, follow the bottling instructions on p1139.

Note For Tomato Ketchup (1), (2) and (3), see p1147.

BOTTLING FRUIT

Preparation

The preparation of jars, syrup and fruit for bottling is given in detail on pp1128–30, and the rules given there should be followed when preparing bottled fruit for processing in a pressure cooker. The number and size of bottles that can be processed at one time depends on the size and model of the pressure cooker used, and it is important, therefore, to follow the directions in the manufacturer's instruction booklet.

Soft Fruit: blackberries, loganberries, raspberries, strawberries, etc.
1) Lay the prepared fruit in a single layer in the bottom of a large enamel, glass or china bowl. Do not use a metal container.
2) Prepare a medium syrup (p1129), and pour the boiling syrup over the fruit. Leave to soak overnight.
3) Next morning, drain off the syrup, and reserve it to cover the fruit in the jars.
4) Fill and process the jars following the Basic Pressure Cooker Method given on p1443, and process for the time given in the table for the fruit used.

Hard Fruit: cooking pears, etc.

Prepare the fruit. Pre-cook it in 250ml water in the pressure cooker for 3 minutes at HIGH pressure. Do not use the trivet. Reduce the pressure quickly before putting the fruit into jars.

Fruit Purée: tomatoes, apricots, apples and cranberries, etc.
1) Prepare the fruit for cooking.
2) Remove the trivet. Cover and cook the fruit in 125ml water at HIGH pressure for 2–3 minutes. The base must not be more than half-full.
3) Reduce pressure at room temperature.
4) Sieve, or process the fruit in an electric blender, then re-boil before pouring into warmed jars. Leave 2cm headspace.
5) Continue according to the instructions given in steps 3–10 of the Basic Pressure Cooker Method.

Fruit Salad

Any fruit may be used, but care should be taken not to use too large a proportion of red fruits, such as raspberries or cherries, as the syrup will then be so dark in colour that it will spoil the appearance of the lighter fruits in the mixture. If cooking pears are included, they should be pre-cooked at HIGH pressure for 5 minutes before adding to the other fruits for processing.

Tomatoes

These should be bottled in either a solid pack or a brine solution (see p1130).

Basic Pressure Cooker Method

1) Place clean, warm, tested preserving jars (p1128), into a large bowl of very hot water.

2) Remove the jars one at a time, and pack tightly to the top with prepared fruit. Fill with hot syrup or water to within 5mm of the rim.

3) Dip the rubber rings in boiling water, and put them on the jars with the lids. Fasten with screwbands, clips or other grips. If using screwbands, tighten them, then unscrew them one-quarter turn to allow for expansion. Put the jars back into the bowl of hot water to keep warm until all are packed and fastened.

4) Meanwhile, put the trivet (inverted), and about 750ml water into the cooker. The water should be 2cm deep in the base. Add 1 × 15ml spoon vinegar or lemon juice to the water if using an aluminium cooker to prevent discoloration of the base. Bring to the boil.

5) Place the prepared jars of fruit on the trivet, making sure they do not touch each other or the sides of the pan.

6) Cover and bring to LOW pressure, adjusting the heat so that this process takes about 3 minutes, ie on a medium heat if using an electric cooker.

7) Process according to the times given below. Lower the heat sufficiently to maintain a steady pressure. Fluctuations in pressure must be avoided because they cause loss of liquid from the jars, and the fruit may be under-processed.

8) Remove the pan gently from the heat. Allow pressure to reduce at room temperature for 10 minutes.

9) Lift out the jars, one at a time, on to a wooden surface, tightening the screwbands immediately. Cool for 24 hours, tightening the screwbands further, if necessary. Clips should hold properly without attention.

10) Test, label, and store according to the instructions in Step 9 of the Quick Deep Pan Method, p1131.

Pressure Cooking Times

Apple quarters	1 minute
Apricots	1 minute
Blackberries	1 minute
Cherries	1 minute
Currants: black, red, white	1 minute
Damsons	1 minute
Fruit salad	1 minute
Gooseberries	1 minute
Greengages	1 minute
Plums	1 minute
Rhubarb (not soaked)	1 minute
Fruit purées	1 minute
Loganberries	3 minutes
Peaches	3 minutes
Pineapple	3 minutes
Pears	5 minutes
Tomatoes: whole, halved, puréed	5 minutes
solid pack	7 minutes

TABLE COOKERY

To make pancakes, place a small frying-pan on the fire to get hot; let it be delicately clean, or the pancakes will stick, and, when quite hot, put into it a small piece of butter. By only pouring in a small quantity of batter, and so making the pancakes thin, the necessity of turning them (an operation rather difficult to unskilful cooks) is obviated.

Table-cooked dishes can be divided into two main categories; those cooked, usually at a side table, for the other diners as they wait, and those cooked in a pot, placed on the dining table, from which the guests are served or serve themselves. Most dishes cooked at the table are particularly suitable for a small, informal dinner party.

Although some table cookery, especially *flambé* cookery, can be spectacular, it is not particularly difficult provided that the necessary preparation of food in the kitchen is completed well in advance of the meal, and the food and utensils for the final cooking are carefully assembled and arranged at the table. It is also wise to practise cooking a dish in front of the family before attempting it at the table for a dinner party. Many recipes given in other chapters can be adapted to table cookery in addition to those which follow.

Never attempt to cook more than one dish per meal at the table; the process will seem laborious the second time, and since many table-cooked dishes are rich, one in the meal is usually enough.

Side Table Cookery

Equipment

It is best to place all the necessary ingredients and equipment on a trolley or side table rather than on the dining table. The cook can then work unimpeded and there is less risk of fire or spillage. A portable electric hotplate can be used for the cooking, though a spirit lamp or butane-type gas burner fitted with a trivet allows the cook to regulate the heat most easily.

All the dishes in this section can be cooked in an ordinary heavy metal frying pan, though traditionally a special chafing-dish is used, which consists of two parts, with a lid. The top pan is called the 'blazer', and it can be used over direct heat for quick cooking and frying. It can also be placed on top of the lower pan, which is filled with simmering water, to make a kind of double saucepan in which food can be heated gently without boiling. For stir frying (p1447), a *wok* or similar round-bottomed pan can be used over a spirit lamp or burner with a trivet. An electric frying pan is also suitable for shallow frying and simmering. This is usually a fairly large pan, deeper than a normal frying pan, with an enclosed heating element in the bottom. It is thermostatically controlled, which makes the cooking easier.

Plates and dishes which will be served with the one cooked at the table, can be kept hot on a heated trolley or candle-warmed hotplate. Cooking utensils will be the same as those used in the kitchen. A small stainless steel jug or sauce-boat, or a large ladle is extremely useful for heating alcohol, or for holding small quantities of liqueurs or other ingredients.

DISHES HEATED IN A SAUCE

Lobster Newburg

4 helpings

1 cooked lobster (1kg approx) **or** *2 small cooked lobsters (500g each approx)*	*125ml single cream*
	salt and pepper
	Cayenne pepper
50g butter	*125ml Madeira* **or** *sweet*
2 egg yolks	*sherry*

In the kitchen, split the lobster in half lengthways and remove the head cavity, gills, and intestinal tract. Crack the claws and remove the meat from the shell, keeping the pieces as large as possible. Separate any coral and beat it to a smooth paste with 25g of the butter. Beat the egg yolks lightly, add the cream, and season with salt, pepper, and Cayenne pepper.

At the table, melt the remaining butter in a frying pan or chafing-dish. Add the lobster pieces and heat gently, without browning, for 5 minutes. Pour in the Madeira or sherry and continue cooking for another 5 minutes or until the liquid is reduced by half. Reduce the heat and stir in the egg yolks and cream. Stir very gently and cook until the sauce thickens and coats the back of the spoon. Do not let the sauce boil or it will curdle. Stir in any coral butter.

Serve with boiled rice or hot buttered toast.

Cooking time at table 15 minutes (approx)

Note A little lemon juice can be added at the end to sharpen the flavour of this very rich dish, although the sauce is more likely to curdle.

VARIATION

The lobster can be flamed with 2 ×15ml spoons brandy after it has been heated with the butter. In this case reduce the Madeira or sherry to 100ml.

Devilled Prawns

4 helpings

50g butter	*a few drops Tabasco*
40g flour	*sauce*
400ml milk	*a pinch of Cayenne*
3 × 2.5ml spoons curry powder	*pepper*
	2 egg yolks
1 × 15ml spoon French mustard	*2 ×15ml spoons dry sherry*
2 ×10ml spoons Worcestershire sauce	*300g cooked prawns* **or** *shrimps*
salt and pepper	

In the kitchen, melt the butter in a pan, stir in the flour, and cook for 1 minute. Add the milk gradually and bring to the boil, stirring all the time. Cook for 1–2 minutes, until the sauce has thickened. Remove from the heat, cool, and add the curry powder, mustard, Worcestershire sauce, salt, pepper, Tabasco sauce, and Cayenne pepper. Stir in well. Cover with dampened greaseproof paper until required. Take the sauce and other ingredients to the table.

At the table, pour the sauce into a clean pan and bring to the boil. Remove from the heat, and add the egg yolks and sherry. Stir in the prawns, cover, and allow to stand for 1–2 minutes. Return to the heat and warm gently. Do not let the sauce boil.

Serve immediately with boiled or fried rice.

Cooking time at table 10 minutes (approx)

Beef Stroganoff (1)

4 helpings

250g onions	*3 × 15ml spoons flour*
250g mushrooms	*salt and pepper*
750g thinly sliced rump	*50g butter*
steak	*250ml soured cream*

In the kitchen, prepare and slice the onions and mushrooms thinly. Wipe the steak and trim off any excess fat. Beat the slices with a cutlet bat or rolling-pin, trim, and cut into strips. Season the flour with salt and pepper and toss the meat in it.

At the table, melt 25g of the butter in a pan and fry the onions for about 5 minutes until golden. Add the mushrooms and continue cooking for a further 2–3 minutes. Remove the vegetables from the pan and add the rest of the butter. When the butter has melted, add the meat and fry rapidly for 2–3 minutes, turning frequently. Return the onions and mushrooms to the pan and re-heat for 1 minute. Pour in the soured cream, stir once or twice, and heat for about 1 minute, until warmed through. Do not let the sauce boil once the cream has been added or it will curdle.

Serve with boiled rice or potatoes, and green salad.

Cooking time at table 15 minutes (approx)

Note For Beef Stroganoff (2), see p1552.

Steak Soubise

4 helpings

300g onions	*1 clove of garlic **or** garlic*
50g butter	*powder for sprinkling*
300ml red wine	*2 × 5ml spoons cornflour*
salt and pepper	*125ml single cream*
*4 pieces fillet **or** rump*	
steak (150g each	
approx)	

In the kitchen, skin the onions and slice thinly. Melt 25g of the butter in a blazer or frying pan. Fry the onions for about 5 minutes until golden-brown. Add 150ml of the red wine, and salt and pepper to taste, and simmer for a further 5 minutes until the

onions are very soft. Strain off the liquid and reserve it. Put the onions in a heatproof dish. Take the pan, onions, liquid, and other ingredients to the table. Keep the onions warm on a hotplate.

At the table, rub the steaks with a cut garlic clove, or sprinkle with garlic powder. Melt the remaining butter in the pan, and when it is foaming put in the steaks. Cook quickly, for $1\frac{1}{2}$ minutes on each side if required rare, and 2–3 minutes on each side for medium rare. Remove the steaks from the pan and cover with a plate to keep warm. Blend the cornflour with the reserved onion liquid, and add with the remaining wine, to the pan. Bring to the boil, stirring all the time, and cook until the sauce thickens. Reduce the heat, and stir in the cream. Re-heat the sauce but do not let it boil. Re-season if required. Return the onions and the steaks to the pan and heat through. Serve the steaks with the onions and sauce poured over them.

Cooking time at table 6 minutes (approx)

Spanish Chicken Livers

4 helpings

3 rashers bacon, without	*salt and pepper*
rinds (75g approx)	*a pinch of dried thyme*
50g onion	*200ml red wine*
50g green pepper	*25g stoned black olives*
300g chicken livers	*3 × 15ml spoons*
2 × 15ml spoons flour	*chopped parsley*

In the kitchen, chop the bacon rashers. Prepare and chop the onion and green pepper finely. Remove any skin and tubes from the livers. Cut any large pieces of liver in half. Take all the ingredients to the table.

At the table, put the bacon, onion and green pepper into a blazer or frying pan, and fry gently for 5 minutes, until the bacon is browned and the onion tender. Stir occasionally. Add the chicken livers, flour, salt and pepper, and continue cooking for a further 3 minutes, turning the livers over until they are browned on all sides. Do not overcook the livers; they should be brown outside but slightly pink and tender inside. Stir in the thyme and the wine. Scrape any browned flour from the base of the pan, and when the sauce is smooth add the olives and parsley. Heat for 1–2 minutes.

Serve with savoury or boiled rice or with sliced boiled potatoes.

Cooking time at table 15 minutes (approx)

STIR FRYING

For the technique of stir frying see p932.

Stir-Fried Chicken and Mushrooms

4 helpings

1 whole chicken breast	3 × 15ml spoons
1 thin slice ginger root	cornflour
½ green pepper	1 × 10ml spoon oil
50g button mushrooms	2 × 15ml spoons chicken
a pinch of salt	stock
a pinch of white pepper	

In the kitchen, skin and bone the chicken breast and cut it into 1cm cubes. Mince the ginger. Remove the membranes and seeds from the pepper and cut into 4cm strips. Clean the mushrooms. Mix together the salt, pepper, and 2 × 15ml spoons of the cornflour. Toss the chicken in it until well coated. Carry the ingredients to the table.

At the table, heat the oil in a deep frying pan or *wok* until very hot. Add the ginger root and stir fry for 30 seconds. Add the chicken and stir fry until all traces of pink have disappeared. Remove the chicken from the pan, and keep hot. Add the mushrooms and green pepper and stir fry for 1½ minutes. Mix the remaining cornflour to a smooth paste with the chicken stock. Return the chicken to the pan, add the cornflour mixture, and stir until thickened.

Serve immediately, with rice or noodles.

Cooking time at table 7 minutes (approx)

Stir-Fried Bean Sprouts

4 helpings

350g fresh bean sprouts	a good pinch of salt
½ green pepper	1 thin slice ginger root
½ medium-sized onion	root
3–4 spring onions	2 × 15ml spoons chicken
2 thin slices cooked ham	stock
(75g approx)	2 × 15ml spoons dry
2 × 15ml spoons oil	sherry

In the kitchen, pour boiling water over the bean sprouts and leave them to stand for 20 seconds. Wash in cold running water, drain, and dry on a tea-towel. Shred the other vegetables and the ham. Arrange the ingredients on a plate in the order in which they are to be cooked, and carry them to the table.

At the table, heat the oil in a deep frying pan or *wok*, add the salt and ginger root, and stir fry for 30 seconds. Add the green pepper, onion and spring onions, and stir fry for 1½ minutes. Add the bean sprouts and ham and stir fry for 30 seconds. Add the stock and sherry and bring to the boil. Remove from the heat and serve immediately.

Cooking time at table 4 minutes (approx)

FLAMBÉD OR FLAMED DISHES

Flaming is one of the most spectacular processes of table cookery. Alcohol is added to a dish and set alight, burning off some of the excess fat from round the food and its accompanying sauce, and giving the whole dish a distinctive flavour. Some dishes served in a sauce are *flambéd* or flamed in the kitchen during cooking, but by *flambéd* or flamed dishes we generally mean food cooked or completed at the table in front of the diners.

The alcohol most often used for flaming is brandy. Rum, whisky, and liqueurs can also be used, and sometimes spirits are mixed with wine, usually a fortified wine such as port, sherry or Madeira. Avoid using very sweet wines and liqueurs. Always try to use good quality wines and spirits; cheap ones do not burn as well and do not give dishes such an attractive flavour.

If the dish to be flamed is cooked entirely at the table, use a metal pan because it heats up quickly, but if the dish is cooked in the kitchen and merely brought to the table to be flamed, ceramic or oven-proof dishes are quite suitable. Before flaming, increase the heat under the pan so that it becomes very hot. If the food has very little juice around it, simply tilt the pan, pour in the spirit and light it, using a long match or taper. Stir the spirit into the juice and carefully baste the food so that it absorbs the flavour. The stirring action helps to keep the flame alight; if it dies down too quickly, the alcohol and fat will not have burnt off properly and the flavour may be harsh.

If the pan contains a fair amount of liquid or sauce, warm the spirit separately to make it more volatile. This can be done in a ladle or small pan over heat, or by placing a bowl containing the spirit inside a larger container of very hot water. This method means that the spirit can be warming gently whilst other processes are being carried out, and is perhaps a good idea for someone not quite confident about this kind of cooking. The spirit can then be ignited and poured flaming into the dish, or can be flamed after pouring it over the food. Light the spirit quickly before it mixes with the sauce, since a larger amount of sauce will douse the spirit if it is not lit at once.

Points to note

1) The cooking should not take too long, and the food must therefore be of a quality that needs only brief cooking. Steak and shellfish are ideal. Liver and kidneys, often harmed by overcooking, produce excellent dishes when cooked quickly this way and served immediately.

2) Make sure that the table or trolley on which the food is to be cooked is well clear of any curtains or lampshades. Do not wear full sleeves, or clothing which can come within range of the flames. Remember, too, never to hold your head over the pan when flaming a dish with alcohol, because it can flare up suddenly and singe eyelashes and hair.

Veal Elizabeth

4 helpings

4 veal escalopes (100g each, approx)	50g butter
1 × 15ml spoon flour	200ml medium dry sherry
salt and pepper	1 × 15ml spoon brandy **or** white rum
2 onions (75g each approx)	200ml soured cream
1 clove of garlic	

In the kitchen, wipe the escalopes, place between 2 pieces of greaseproof paper, and beat them until thin with a cutlet bat or rolling-pin. Mix the flour with generous amounts of salt and pepper and coat the escalopes with it. Skin the onions and chop them finely. Take all the ingredients to the table.

At the table, rub a blazer or frying pan with the clove of garlic. Melt the butter, add the onions, and fry over medium heat for about 4 minutes until golden-brown and tender. Increase the heat under the pan and brown the escalopes for about 2 minutes on each side. Reduce the heat and add the sherry. Stir well, scraping any browned flour from the bottom of the pan and, when smooth, allow to simmer for about 3 minutes until the sherry is reduced and thickened slightly. Re-season if required. Add the brandy or rum and light it. Baste the meat until the flames die down. Stir in the cream. Spoon the sauce over the escalopes and serve, accompanied by asparagus.

Cooking time at table 15–18 minutes

Monkey Gland Steak

4 helpings

4 pieces fillet **or** rump steak (150g each approx)	1 onion (100g approx)
	25g butter
	1 × 15ml spoon
salt and pepper	Worcestershire sauce
2 × 5ml spoons French mustard	3 × 15ml spoons brandy
	chopped parsley

In the kitchen, wipe the steaks and trim off any excess fat, then beat them with a cutlet bat or rolling-pin to flatten them. Season, and spread each side with the mustard. Skin the onion and chop it finely. Take all the ingredients to the table.

At the table, melt the butter in a blazer or frying pan, add the chopped onion, and fry gently for about 4 minutes, until soft. Increase the heat, then add the steaks and fry quickly for 2 minutes on each side if required rare, or 3–4 minutes for medium rare. Add the Worcestershire sauce and mix with the onions. Pour in the brandy and light it. Shake the pan and baste until the flames die down.

Sprinkle the steaks with chopped parsley, and serve with potato straws, broccoli or green salad.

Cooking time at table 12–15 minutes

Steak Diane

4 helpings

4 minute, fillet **or** rump steaks (150–200g each)	1 × 5ml spoon caster sugar
1 small onion (50g approx)	Worcestershire sauce
75g unsalted butter	1 × 15ml spoon chopped parsley
grated rind and juice of 1 lemon	2 × 15ml spoons brandy

In the kitchen, wipe the steaks and trim off any excess fat. Beat them flat with a cutlet bat or rolling-pin until they are no more than 6mm thick. Skin the onion and chop it finely. Take all the ingredients to the table.

At the table, melt 50g of the butter in a large, heavy-based frying pan and fry the onion for about 5 minutes until soft. Remove the onion from the pan and keep warm on a plate. Raise the heat under the pan. Using the remaining butter, fry 2 steaks at a time over high heat for 1 minute on each side. Remove from the pan and keep warm. Return the onions to the pan, and add the lemon rind and juice, the sugar, and a few drops of Worcestershire sauce. Stir in the parsley and cook lightly. Warm the brandy. Put the steaks into the pan and flame with the warmed brandy. Serve immediately, with the sauce spooned over them, and with chipped potatoes, grilled mushrooms and/or tomatoes.

Cooking time at table 15–18 minutes

Sautéed Kidneys (2)

4 helpings

12 lamb's kidneys	3 × 15ml spoons brandy
100g mushrooms	salt and pepper
75g onion	1 × 5ml spoon made
2 × 5ml spoons cornflour	English mustard
1 × 15ml spoon water	150ml double cream
25g butter	

In the kitchen, cut the kidneys in half, and remove the skin and cores. Clean and slice the mushrooms. Skin and chop the onion. Blend the cornflour and water. Take all the ingredients to the table.

At the table, melt the butter in a blazer or frying pan, and add the kidneys, mushrooms, and onion. Fry over high heat, stirring all the time for 2–3 minutes, until the kidneys are browned all over. Reduce the heat and cook for a further 3–4 minutes, until the kidneys no longer exude any blood. Care must be taken not to overcook the kidneys, or the flesh shrinks, becomes tough, and exudes a lot of juice. Warm the brandy, add to the pan and light it. When the flame burns out, add the blended cornflour and water, and the salt, pepper, and mustard. Bring to the boil, stirring all the time, and boil for 1 minute. Remove from the heat and stir in the cream. Serve immediately, with boiled rice.

Cooking time at table 10–12 minutes

Note For Sautéed Kidneys (1), see p1322.

Haddock and Fennel Flambé

4 helpings

*1kg thin fillets of
  haddock* **or** *hake
salt and pepper
200g butter*

fresh **or** *dried fennel
  leaves
4 ×15ml spoons brandy
dried fennel stalks*

Garnish
lemon wedges

In the kitchen, wash and dry the fish. Place it on the grid of the grill pan, skin side up. Grill under moderate heat for 5 minutes. Remove the skin carefully. Turn the fillet over, using a fish slice. Season with salt and pepper and dot with 2 × 15ml spoons of butter. Chop a few fennel leaves and sprinkle over the fish. Grill under moderate heat for a further 10 minutes. Melt the remaining butter, and keep it warm. Carry the ingredients to the table.

At the table, warm the brandy. Pile dried fennel stalks on a metal serving dish to a depth of 5cm. Place the cooked fish, still on the grid from the grill pan, over the fennel. Pour the warm brandy over the fish, then light the brandy and dried fennel, using a long match or taper. When the flame has burned out, garnish with lemon wedges and serve with the melted butter and boiled potatoes.

Cooking time at table 5 minutes (approx)

VARIATIONS
1) Small whole haddock can be used. Slash the sides of the fish and put the fennel leaves inside. Season each side, dot with butter, and grill for 10–12 minutes under moderate heat.
2) Mackerel are also good cooked in this way.

Bananas in Rum

4 helpings

*4 large bananas
3 ×15ml spoons soft
  brown sugar
1 ×2.5ml spoon ground
  cinnamon*

*25g butter
3–4 ×15ml spoons rum*

In the kitchen, cut the bananas in half lengthways, and put them flat on a plate. If this is done some time before the dish is cooked, sprinkle the bananas with a little lemon juice to prevent the fruit turning brown. Mix together the soft brown sugar and the cinnamon. Take all the ingredients to the table.

At the table, sprinkle the bananas with the sugar and cinnamon mixture. Melt the butter in a blazer or frying pan, and fry the bananas flat side down for 1–2 minutes until lightly browned underneath. Turn them over carefully, sprinkle with any remaining sugar and cinnamon, and continue frying. When the bananas are soft but not mushy, pour the rum over them. Tilt and baste, then light the rum; baste again. Scrape any caramelized sugar from the base of the pan and stir it into the rum. Shake the pan gently until the flames die down.

Arrange the bananas on warmed serving plates, pour the rum sauce over them and serve with double cream.

Cooking time at table 8–10 minutes

Crêpes Suzette (2)

4 helpings

*12 small, thin pancakes,
 using 350ml cream
 pancake batter* (p937)

Sauce

8 lumps sugar	*2 ×15ml spoons*
2 large coarse-skinned	*Cointreau*
oranges	*2 ×15ml spoons brandy*
75g clarified butter	
(p886) for frying	
2 ×15ml spoons	
strained orange juice	

In the kitchen, rub the lumps of sugar over the oranges until the sugar is soaked with the oil and coloured with the zest. Crush the lumps in a basin with the end of a rolling-pin, or process briefly in an electric blender. Take all the ingredients to the table.

At the table, melt the clarified butter in a metal pan over gentle heat. Add the orange sugar, orange juice and the Cointreau. Stir until the sugar dissolves. Put a pancake into the pan, turn it over, and baste with the sauce. When hot, fold it in half and then in half again, to form a triangle. Push it to one side of the pan. Repeat the process with each of the other pancakes. When all are folded, arrange them in the centre of the pan, spoon the sauce over them once more and turn up the heat. When the pan is hot, tilt it to one side, pour in the brandy and light it. Make sure all the pancakes are coated evenly with the sauce. Quickly put the pancakes on warm plates, stir the remaining sauce to make sure that any caramelized sugar is removed from the bottom of the pan, and spoon it over the pancakes. Serve immediately.

Cooking time at table 10 minutes (approx)

Note To re-heat all the pancakes at once needs a very large pan. If using a suzette pan, make up only half the quantity of sauce at first, and re-heat 6 pancakes; then repeat the process.

For Crêpes Suzette (1), see p942.

VARIATIONS

1) Instead of rubbing the lumps of sugar on the oranges to absorb the flavour, 50g caster sugar and the finely grated rind of 1 large orange can be added to the melted butter. This means that the rind remains in the sauce.
2) The original French recipe did not include orange juice or brandy, and used instead a mixture of 2 ×15ml spoons maraschino, 2 ×15ml spoons Kirsch and 2 ×15ml spoons curaçao. Half this was added to the pan to make the sauce and the other half added at the end and flamed.

Cherries Jubilée

4 helpings

50g sugar	*2 × 5ml spoons*
250ml water	*arrowroot*
500g dark red fresh	*4 ×15ml spoons Kirsch*
cherries	

In the kitchen, make a sugar syrup with the sugar and water. Stone the cherries. Poach them in the syrup until just tender, then drain and cool. Reserve the syrup. Blend the arrowroot with a very little of the syrup, then stir it into the remainder. Pour into a saucepan and bring to the boil, stirring all the time. Boil for 3–5 minutes until thickened and syrupy. Arrange the cherries in individual heat-proof serving bowls and pour the thickened syrup over them. Take the bowls and the Kirsch to the table.

At the table, warm the Kirsch in a small jug or ladle. Pour 1 ×15ml spoon of it over each helping, light it, and serve while still alight if possible.

Cooking time at table 5 minutes (approx)

Note This famous dish was originally created for Queen Victoria's Diamond Jubilee.

Centre-piece Cookery

FONDUE BOURGUIGNONNE

Equipment

Special fondue Bourguignonne sets can be bought at most good stores. A set usually consists of a copper, stainless steel or iron pot which fits over a spirit lamp or burner, and a set of long-handled forks. Since the point of this dish is to cook the meat quickly in very hot oil, the pot must be made of heavy metal to withstand the strong heat and must be deep enough to prevent dangerous splashes from the hot oil. A heatproof or cast iron casserole can be used over a spirit lamp or burner in place of a fondue pot, and it is also possible to keep the oil hot in a thermostatically controlled electric table cooker, but these are sometimes large and not sufficiently attractive for the dining table.

Several small dishes are also needed to hold uncooked food, side dishes, and sauces.

Fondue Bourguignonne

150g good quality fillet **or** *rump steak per person*	*salt and freshly ground black pepper*
garlic (optional)	*oil for deep frying*

Sauces
Agro-dolce sauce (p714)
Béarnaise sauce (p712)
Curry mayonnaise (p844)
Hollandaise sauce (p712)

Cold Horseradish cream (p402)
Tartare sauce (p846)
Tomato mayonnaise (p845)

In the kitchen, wipe the meat and remove any excess fat. Cut the meat into 2cm cubes. Grate or mince a little garlic, if used, and season the meat with the garlic and with salt and pepper. Choose and prepare 4–5 of the sauces. Fill the fondue pot one-third full of oil, and heat it to 190°C. If possible, have a second pot of oil heating so that the first pot, in use on the dining table, can be replaced when it cools. Carry the first pot carefully to the table.

At the table, light the spirit lamp or burner, and put the pot on the trivet. If using an electric table cooker, fill it one-third full of oil, set the thermostat, and heat it up at the table itself. Bring the meat and the sauces to the table, arrange the sauces round the fondue pot in the centre, and place a dish of meat and two long-handled forks in front of each diner. The diner spears a piece of meat on a fork, dips it into the hot oil and holds it there until cooked. After cooking, he transfers the meat to the second, cold fork and dips it into one or other of the sauces before eating.

This dish is given much of its character by the side dishes served with it. Choose accompaniments from among the following: beetroot sliced in vinegar, chopped celery, chopped nuts, cocktail onions, cucumber in soured cream or thick yoghurt sprinkled with dill, green salad with French dressing, sliced gherkins, sliced potato in French dressing, sliced tomato with chives and French dressing. French bread and butter should also be served.

VARIATION
Substitute pork fillets for fillet or rump steak. Cook for at least $2\frac{1}{2}$ minutes per cube to ensure it is fully cooked through.

Vegetable Tempura
See p1536.

SWISS CHEESE FONDUE

Equipment

To make and serve a cheese fondue properly requires a *caquelon*, which is an open ceramic or earthenware pan about 8cm deep. The pan is set on a spirit lamp or burner which can be regulated to keep the cheese mixture at an even, very low heat; if the fondue gets too hot it becomes stringy and inedible. To serve a fondue without a proper *caquelon*, use a shallow casserole or pan set on a burner or hotplate on the dining table. Make the fondue in the casserole in the kitchen, and transfer it to the burner or hotplate for serving.

Swiss Cheese Fondue

4–6 helpings

300–450g white bread	*2 × 5ml spoons fresh*
250–350g Emmental	*lemon juice (approx)*
cheese	*1 × 10ml spoon*
500–750g Gruyère	*cornflour or potato*
cheese	*flour*
1 clove of garlic	*1 × 15ml spoon Kirsch*
350ml light dry white	*white pepper and grated*
wine	*nutmeg*

In the kitchen, cut the bread into 2cm cubes, providing about 75g per person. Put into a basket.

To make the fondue, grate the cheeses. Cut the garlic clove in half, and rub the cut sides over the inside of the *caquelon* or casserole. Warm the wine in the casserole and add lemon juice to taste. Add the cheese in 15ml spoonfuls and bring slowly to the boil, stirring all the time with a whisk. Blend the cornflour or potato flour with the Kirsch to make a smooth paste. Add in 5ml spoonfuls to the cheese mixture, stirring with a figure of eight movement, until the mixture is smooth, thick, and creamy. Season to taste with the pepper and nutmeg. Transfer to the dining table with the basket of bread.

At the table, place the *caquelon* or casserole on the lit burner or hotplate, and eat immediately. Each diner serves himself from the *caquelon* or casserole by spearing bread cubes on a long-handled fork, and dipping them into the fondue mixture.

Plain green salad and Kirsch are the only accompaniments traditionally served with a fondue, although wine can be served instead of Kirsch.

Cooking time in kitchen 30 minutes (approx)

SWEET RECIPES

Equipment

Table Beignets need a pot similar to that used for a Fondue Bourguignonne, set on a trivet over a spirit lamp or burner. For the Crêpes au Choix (p1454), an electric, spirit or candle-warmed hotplate is necessary to keep the pancakes and fillings warm. Strawberry Table Dumplings (p1455) require a large pan set on a spirit lamp or burner.

Table Beignets

4–6 helpings

350–400g prepared	*oil for deep frying*
choux pastry (p1251)	

In the kitchen, make the choux paste. This can be made in advance and rewarmed just before use, if necessary, although it will not puff up as much as when it is freshly made. Fill the fondue pot or heavy casserole one-third full of unflavoured oil.

At the table, place the pot of oil in the centre, over the spirit lamp or burner. When ready to fry, heat the oil until just before smoking point, and bring the warmed choux paste to the table. Lower small spoonfuls of the paste into the hot fat, a few at a time, and fry until puffed and golden-brown. Allow the oil time to regain its original heat before adding another batch. Lift out with a perforated spoon, drain over the pot and serve on to the diners' plates.

Bowls of chocolate sauce (p720), whipped cream, and icing sugar should be arranged around the pot so that diners may help themselves.

Crêpes au Choix

4 helpings

8–12 pancakes, using
  cream pancake batter
  (p937)

fillings (see below)

Toppings

lightly whipped cream

thick custard, mixed
  with a little single
  cream

Lemon sauce (p721)

Orange sauce (p721)

Melba sauce (p724)

smooth fruit purée or
  jam, thinned with a
  little fruit juice **or**
  sweet white wine

Decorations and flavourings (optional)

finely chopped nuts
  mixed with sweet
  biscuit crumbs

Praline (p1241)

grated chocolate

2 or 3 miniature bottles
  of any suitable liqueur

finely chopped glacé
  cherries

mixed peel

strained lemon **or**
  orange juice

In the kitchen, make the pancakes, fillings, and 2 or 3 of the toppings. Prepare the decorations and flavourings, if used. Either keep the pancakes and fillings warm while assembling the toppings, or re-heat them before bringing them to the table. Arrange the pancakes on a warm plate and the fillings in small heatproof dishes or jugs.

At the table, arrange the toppings, decorations and flavourings in small bowls around an electric or similar hotplate placed in the centre. Put the plate of pancakes and the dishes or jugs of fillings on the hotplate.

The diners help themselves to pancakes and fill and top them from the ingredients on the table.

FILLINGS FOR CRÊPES AU CHOIX

Sweet Cheese Filling

40g seedless raisins

250g cottage cheese

3 × 15ml spoons caster
  sugar

½ × 2.5ml spoon grated
  lemon rind

½ × 2.5ml spoon vanilla
  essence

1 × 10ml spoon lemon
  juice

Soak the raisins in warm water for 15–20 minutes until well plumped. Drain thoroughly. Sieve the cheese and work in the sugar, lemon rind, essence, and lemon juice. Mix in the drained raisins. Serve cold, or place in a heatproof jug and warm well in a bain-marie.

Pineapple Filling

1 × 227g can crushed
  pineapple

3 × 15ml spoons smooth
  raspberry jam

2 × 15ml spoons
  cornflour

2–3 drops lemon juice

Drain the can of pineapple and reserve 75ml of the juice. Put the jam and 4 × 15ml spoons of the reserved juice into a saucepan and boil gently for 3 minutes. Blend the cornflour with the remaining 1 × 15ml spoon of juice. Sieve the jam, return it to the pan, and mix in the cornflour paste. Re-heat and simmer for 3 minutes, stirring all the time. Add the lemon juice and crushed pineapple. Keep hot, or turn into a heatproof jug and re-heat in a bain-marie when needed.

Note Chopped fresh or canned fruit, a purée of fresh or stewed fruit, or smooth jam sharpened with a little lemon juice also make good hot or cold pancake fillings. Always choose a well-flavoured fruit such as blackcurrants or raspberries.

Strawberry Table Dumplings

4–6 helpings

750g strawberries, fresh **or** *frozen*	*1 egg yolk*
100g caster sugar	*salt*
1 × 15ml spoon Kirsch (optional)	*100ml water*
2 eggs	*250g flour (approx)* *flour for rolling out*

In the kitchen, hull fresh fruit or thaw frozen fruit. Cover with the sugar and the Kirsch, if used, and leave to stand for 1 hour. Drain thoroughly. Reserve and strain any syrup, if liked. Mash the fruit lightly if still firm and put to one side.

Separate the eggs. Beat the 3 yolks lightly with a pinch of salt; add the water slowly. Beat or mix in gradually enough flour to make a light firm dough. Roll out thinly on a lightly floured surface, and cut into rounds using a 5cm cutter. Brush the edges of each round with egg white. Put about 1 × 2.5ml spoonful of the strawberry filling in the centre of each round, and fold over into small turnovers. Press the edges of each turnover with a fork, to seal.

At the table, have ready a large pan of lightly salted boiling water on a spirit lamp or burner. Lower the dumplings gently into the water, a few at a time, and cook for about 4 minutes until they rise to the surface. Lift out with a perforated spoon, drain over the pan, and serve on to the diners' plates.

A bowl of caster sugar and a sauce-boat containing either the strained fruit syrup, soured cream or melted butter, or soured cream mixed and flavoured with the syrup, should be placed by the pan so that diners can help themselves. The dumplings should be sprinkled with the sugar before having the sauce poured over them.

REGIONAL BRITISH COOKERY

Roast beef has long been a national dish in England. In most of our patriotic songs it is contrasted with the fricasseed frogs, popularly supposed to be the exclusive diet of Frenchmen.

" O the roast beef of old England,
And O the old English roast beef."

Wales

Cawl Cymreig
(Welsh Cawl)

4–6 helpings

1kg cutlets from best end of neck of lamb	1 medium-sized parsnip
salt and pepper	1 small swede
1 large onion	6 small potatoes
3 leeks	2 × 15ml spoons chopped parsley
2 medium-sized carrots	

Wipe and trim the meat and cut it into neat pieces. Put in a large saucepan and cover with cold water. Add salt and pepper and bring to the boil. Reduce the heat and simmer for about 1 hour. Leave to cool, and skim off all the fat.

Skin and slice the onion, wash, trim and slice the leeks. Peel and slice the carrots, parsnip and swede, and add all these vegetables to the pan. Add more water, stir, cover, and cook slowly for a further hour. Peel and halve the potatoes, add with half the parsley, and cook for another 15 minutes. Add the rest of the parsley, re-season if required, and serve hot.

Note Traditionally Cawl was eaten in wooden bowls with wooden spoons; some people served a clear broth first, then the meat and vegetables as a second course.

Pasteiod Cennin
(Leek Pasties or Turnovers)

Makes 10

10 large leeks	1 × 5ml spoon sugar
1 × 5ml spoon salt	125ml single cream
1 × 5ml spoon lemon juice	salt and pepper
	egg wash (p1248)

Pastry

450g flour	100g margarine
1 × 5ml spoon baking powder	125ml cold water (approx)
a pinch of salt	flour for rolling out
100g lard	

Wash and trim the leeks. Remove the green part and slice the white part only into 2cm pieces. Put into a saucepan with just enough boiling water to cover. Add the salt, lemon juice, and sugar. Cook for 5 minutes or until just tender. Drain and leave to cool.

Make the pastry. Sift the flour, baking powder, and salt into a bowl, and rub in the lard and margarine. Mix to a stiff dough with the water. Roll out the pastry on a lightly floured surface to 1cm thick and cut into 10 oblong shapes, about 15 × 10cm. Lay the pieces of leek along the middle of each pastry piece. Moisten with a little cream and season with salt and pepper. Dampen the edges of the pastry and lift them to meet over the filling. Pinch and flute the edges to seal. Brush the pasties with the egg wash and bake in a fairly hot oven, 200°C, Gas 6, for about 20 minutes.

Selsig Morgannwg
(Glamorgan Sausages)

Makes 20 (approx)

150g mature Cheddar cheese	1 × 15ml spoon grated onion
250g soft white breadcrumbs	salt and pepper
1 × 5ml spoon dry mustard	3 eggs
1 × 10ml spoon chopped mixed herbs (as available)	flour for coating
	raspings (p375) for coating
	pork fat **or** oil for shallow frying

Grate the cheese finely. Mix with the soft bread-crumbs, mustard, herbs, and onion. Season well. Separate the eggs, and bind the mixture with the yolks. Form into small sausage shapes (about 20), and roll in flour. Whisk the egg whites until frothy, roll the sausages in the egg white, then coat firmly all over with raspings. Heat the pork fat or oil, and fry the sausages in batches, turning as required, for about 4 minutes until well heated through and brown. Serve immediately.

Swper Mam
(Mother's Supper)

3–4 helpings

8 large bacon rashers, without rinds **or** 8 ham slices	2 medium-sized onions
	100g hard cheese
	pepper

Arrange four of the bacon rashers or ham slices in the bottom of a shallow flameproof dish. Skin and grate the onions and add to the dish. Grate the cheese and sprinkle it over the onion. Season well with pepper. Put the remaining bacon rashers or ham slices on top and cook in a fairly hot oven, 190°C, Gas 5, for about 35 minutes, until the bacon is crisp.

Note Traditionally, this is served with potatoes baked in their jackets.

Bara Brith
(Speckled Bread)

Makes 12 slices

250ml milk	75g soft brown sugar
1 × 5ml spoon sugar	1 × 5ml spoon mixed spice
25g fresh yeast	a pinch of salt
75g lard **or** butter	1 egg
450g strong plain flour	flour for dusting
50g cut mixed peel	oil for greasing
150g seedless raisins	honey for glazing
50g currants	

Warm the milk to tepid with the sugar. Blend the fresh yeast into the milk, and put to one side for 10 to 20 minutes until frothy. Rub the lard or butter into the flour. Stir in the peel, raisins, currants, brown sugar, mixed spice, and salt. Beat the egg until liquid. Make a well in the centre of the dry ingredients and add the yeast mixture and the beaten egg. Mix to a soft dough, place in a large, lightly oiled polythene bag, and leave in a warm place for about 2 hours until the dough has doubled in size.

Turn the dough out on to a floured board and knead well. Put it into a greased 19 × 13 × 8cm loaf tin, pressing it well into the corners. Return to the polythene bag, and leave to rise for a further 30 min-utes. Remove from the bag and bake in a fairly hot oven, 200°C, Gas 6, for 15 minutes. Reduce the heat to warm, 160°C, Gas 3, and bake for about 1¼ hours. Turn out on to a wire rack, and brush the top with clear warm honey while still warm. Serve sliced, spread with butter.

Crempog Ceirch
(Oatmeal Pancakes)

Makes 20 (approx)

300ml milk (approx)	1 egg
15g fresh yeast	pork rind **or** oil for
200g plain flour	greasing
75g fine oatmeal	butter (optional)
1 × 2.5ml spoon salt	

Warm 125ml of the milk to hand-hot and blend the yeast into 2 × 15ml spoons of it. Leave for 10 minutes until frothy. Sift the flour into a large bowl, then mix in the oatmeal and salt. Work in the yeast mixture. Beat the egg lightly and add it. Add the warmed milk to the remaining cold milk and heat until tepid; then add enough to the flour mixture to make a smooth batter of slow dropping consistency.

Place the mixing bowl in a large, lightly oiled polythene bag, and leave in a fairly warm place for about 30 minutes to rise. Check the consistency; if thick, add more warm milk gradually to obtain a batter of dropping consistency. Leave for another 30 minutes. Heat a lightly greased round griddle (Welsh bakestone) or heavy frying pan. Drop heaped 15ml spoonfuls of batter on the hot surface, and fry until lightly browned on each side, turning once.

Spread with butter and eat hot. Alternatively cool, store in an airtight tin, and re-heat when required.

Cacen Gneifio
(Shearing Cake)

butter for greasing	grated rind of ½ lemon
400g plain flour	2 × 10ml spoons
a pinch of salt	caraway seeds
2 × 5ml spoons baking	1 × 5ml spoon grated
powder	nutmeg **or** to taste
200g butter	2 eggs
250g soft light brown	200ml milk
sugar	

Grease and line a 20cm cake tin. Sift together the flour, salt, and baking powder. Rub in the fat, then mix in the sugar, lemon rind, and spices. Beat the egg with the milk lightly, and mix gradually into the dry ingredients. Turn the mixture into the prepared tin, and bake in a moderate oven, 180°C, Gas 4, for 1½ hours. If the cake browns too quickly, cover with a piece of greased paper or foil. Remove from the oven when cooked, cool slightly, then turn on to a wire rack to finish cooling.

Pice ar y Maen
(Welsh Cakes)

Makes 24 (approx)

450g plain flour	100g lard
a pinch of salt	150g caster sugar
1 × 5ml spoon baking	100g currants
powder	2 eggs
1 × 2.5ml spoon mixed	milk
spice	flour for rolling out
100g butter	pork rind for greasing

Sift together the flour, salt, baking powder, and spice. Rub in the fats until the mixture resembles fine crumbs. Add the sugar and currants. Beat the eggs until liquid, and use to bind the mixture, adding enough milk to make a stiff dough. On a lightly floured surface roll out the dough 1cm thick, and cut into rounds about 7cm across. Cook on a moderately hot, lightly greased, round griddle (Welsh bakestone) or frying pan for about 4 minutes on each side until golden-brown. The cakes should be crisp right through, and rough textured.

Scotland

Scots or Scotch Broth

4–6 helpings

500g scrag end of neck of mutton	2 leeks
1 × 5ml spoon salt	1 small turnip
1 litre cold water	1 stick of celery
50g pearl barley	pepper
2 medium carrots	1 × 10ml spoon chopped parsley

Wipe and trim the meat, and cut into 2cm pieces. Put into a deep pan with the bones, salt, and cold water. Heat gently to simmering point. Blanch the barley. Add to the pan, cover and simmer gently for 2 hours. Prepare the vegetables, setting aside one whole carrot and cutting the rest into 5mm dice. Add them to the broth, cover, and simmer for another hour. Grate the whole carrot and add it to the broth 20 minutes before serving. Skim the fat. Remove the bones. Season to taste with pepper and add the chopped parsley just before serving.

Kail Brose or Broth

6–8 helpings

1kg shin of beef or ½ ox head or 2 cow-heels	50g pearl barley or medium oatmeal
2 litres water	1kg kale or cabbage
2 × 5ml spoons salt	salt and pepper
2 leeks (100–200g approx)	

If shin of beef is used, keep it whole, and wipe with a damp cloth. If an ox head is used, it must be thoroughly cleaned and blanched; cow-heels must also be scraped, cleaned, and blanched. Do not have them chopped, split or cut up. Put the meat into a very large pan, and add the water and salt. Wash the leeks thoroughly, cut them into 2cm lengths, and add to the pan. Heat to simmering point, cover, and simmer gently until the meat is tender; this will take 3–4 hours for shin or cow heel, 2–3 hours for ox head. Blanch the pearl barley, if used, and add it to the soup for the last 2 hours of the cooking time. If oatmeal is used, toast it in the oven or under the grill until golden-brown, but only add it to the soup 2–3 minutes before serving. Remove the coarse outer leaves and trim off the stem of the kale or cabbage and shred finely. Add to the broth for the last 20 minutes of the cooking time.

Lift out the meat, cut some of the lean meat into 1cm cubes and return it to the broth. Season to taste with salt and pepper, and serve.

Note The rest of the meat can be used for another dish requiring cooked beef, or can be served as a meat course after the soup. A little of the broth should be reserved to accompany it.

Cock-a-leekie

8 helpings

100g prunes	1kg veal or beef marrow bones (optional)
1 small boiling fowl with giblets (1.5kg approx)	500g leeks
	1.5–2 litres cold water
3 rashers streaky bacon, without rinds (optional)	2 × 5ml spoons salt
	½ × 2.5ml spoon pepper
	bouquet garni

Soak the prunes overnight in cold water; then stone them. Wipe the fowl and wash the giblets. Chop the bacon, if used. Chop the bones into manageable pieces, if used. Wash and trim the leeks and cut them into thin rings. Put the fowl, giblets, marrow bones, and bacon into a deep pan, cover with cold water, add the salt, and heat very slowly to simmering point. Reserve 4 × 15ml spoons of the leeks and add the remaining leeks, the pepper, and bouquet garni to the pan. Cover, and simmer gently for about 3 hours, or until the fowl is tender.

Remove the fowl, carve off the meat and cut it into fairly large serving pieces. Strain the liquid. Return the pieces to the soup with the soaked and stoned prunes and the remaining sliced leeks. Simmer very gently for 30 minutes until the prunes are just tender but not broken. Re-season if required, and serve the soup with the prunes.

Haggis

8–10 helpings

1 sheep's pluck (lungs, heart, and liver)	1 × 5ml spoon ground black pepper
1 sheep's paunch (stomach bag)	2–4 × 5ml spoons salt
500g onions	2 × 5ml spoons crushed dried mixed herbs
125g shredded suet	whisky to taste
500g pinhead oatmeal	

Wash the pluck thoroughly under running water or in several changes of cold water. Place in a large pan with enough boiling water to cover. Hang the windpipe over the side of the pan with a small basin beneath to catch the drips. Boil for 2 hours and leave to cool overnight. Turn the paunch inside out, wash in several changes of fresh water and scrape clean. Steep overnight in cold water.

Drain the pluck and reserve the cooking liquid. Prepare the liver and heart. Mince the liver and finely chop the heart and lungs. Skin and chop the onions finely. Mix all these ingredients with the suet and oatmeal in a large bowl. Add the seasoning and herbs and enough of the cooking liquid to moisten well. Flavour with whisky. Fill the paunch slightly over half-full. Sew with stout thread and prick in a few places to prevent it bursting during boiling. Place in a pan of boiling water, using enough water to cover. Simmer half-covered for 3 hours.

Serve hot, with mashed potatoes and turnips (neeps) and with whisky to drink. Haggis can also be served with Clapshot (p1462).

Note The whole sheep's pluck produces a large quantity of haggis. Although it will keep in a refrigerator for a week or in a freezer for longer, use a lamb's pluck and paunch if a smaller dish is required, and reduce the other ingredients by half.

Howtowdie

(using whole chicken)

6 helpings

1 roasting chicken with giblets (1.75kg approx)	a pinch of ground mace
700ml water	1kg spinach
6 button onions **or** shallots	salt and pepper
75g butter	2 × 5ml spoons cornflour
2 cloves	2 × 15ml spoons double cream (optional)
6 black peppercorns	

Stuffing

50g soft white breadcrumbs	1 × 5ml spoon chopped parsley
milk	salt and pepper
1 small shallot	
1 × 5ml spoon chopped tarragon	

Make the stuffing first. Cover the breadcrumbs with just enough milk to moisten them. Leave to stand for 30 minutes. Skin and chop the shallot finely. Stir it into the breadcrumbs with the herbs, and season the mixture with a little salt and pepper. Place the stuffing in the body of the bird and secure the neck flap with a skewer.

Place the giblets excluding the liver in a pan, cover with the water and simmer while frying the onions and chicken.

Skin and chop the onion or shallots. Melt the butter in a large frying pan and fry the onions gently until lightly browned. Add the chicken and fry it, turning frequently, until lightly browned on all sides; this will take 15–20 minutes.

Put the chicken in a large casserole with the browned onions or shallots, the cloves, peppercorns, mace, and 500ml of the simmered giblet stock. Cover, and cook in a moderate oven, 180°C, Gas 4, for about 1 hour until tender.

Meanwhile, prepare and cook the spinach, drain, season to taste, and keep hot. Remove the chicken from the casserole and keep hot. Strain the stock from the casserole into a saucepan, chop and add the chicken liver, and mash it so that it is blended in. Cook for 5 minutes. Blend the cornflour to a smooth paste with a little water and hot stock. Add the mixture to the pan, bring to the boil, and simmer until the cornflour clears and the sauce thickens. Stir in the cream, if used. Season to taste.

Arrange the spinach on a warmed serving dish, place the chicken on top and pour the sauce over it.

Note If poached eggs are served round the spinach, the dish is called Howtowdie wi' Drappit Eggs – a nineteenth-century recipe.

Tweed Kettle

4 helpings

600g middle cut salmon	*25g butter*
500ml fish stock (p330)	*25g flour*
250ml dry white wine	*25g shallots* **or** *chives*
a pinch of ground mace	*1 × 5ml spoon chopped*
salt and pepper	*parsley*

Put the salmon in a pan and add the fish stock, wine, mace, and seasonings. Poach gently for 10–15 minutes or until just cooked through. Remove the fish, skin and bone it, and place the flesh in a serving dish. Keep hot.

Return the skin and bones to the liquid and simmer gently, uncovered, for 10 minutes, then strain. Return the liquid to the pan, and simmer gently, uncovered, until reduced by half. Work the butter and flour together to make a smooth beurre manié. Skin the shallots, if used, chop them finely, and add them or the chives with the parsley to the fish liquid. Remove from the heat and gradually add the beurre manié in small pieces, stirring all the time. Return to the heat and simmer for another 5 minutes. Season to taste. Pour the sauce over the fish.

Serve with boiled new potatoes and fresh peas.

Partan Bree

4 helpings

1 large cooked crab	*anchovy essence*
50g long-grain rice	*125ml single cream*
500ml milk	*salt and pepper*
500ml water	*milk (optional)*

Garnish
chopped parsley

Remove all the meat from the crab (p423); keep the claw meat separate from the rest. Wash the rice and put it into a pan with the milk and water. Bring to boiling point and simmer for 15–20 minutes until tender. Strain and reserve the liquid. Rub the rice and crabmeat (except the claw meat) through a sieve, or process in an electric blender to obtain a smooth purée. Add to the liquid from the rice. Chop and add the claw meat with anchovy essence to taste, and the cream. Season with salt and pepper, and thin with a little milk, if liked. Heat through and garnish with finely chopped parsley.

Ham and Haddie

4 helpings

600g finnan haddock on	*salt*
the bone	*freshly ground black*
125ml milk	*pepper*
25g butter	*50ml double cream*
4 slices cooked ham	
(125g each approx)	

Put the haddock in a large frying pan and add the milk. Bring to the boil and simmer for 10–20 minutes until the fish is cooked. Remove the fish from the pan. Strain the liquid and reserve it. Skin, bone, and flake the fish.

Heat the butter in a clean pan and put in the ham slices; heat through, turning once. Place the fish on the ham and pour the liquid over them. Season with salt and freshly ground black pepper and pour the cream over the dish. Brown quickly under a hot grill before serving.

Cullen Skink

4 helpings

1 medium onion (100g approx)	*1 litre water*
1 large finnan haddock on the bone (375g approx)	*500g potatoes*
	250ml milk (approx)
	125ml single cream
salt and pepper	*25g butter*

Garnish
chopped parsley

Skin the onion and chop it finely. Put the fish, onion, and seasoning in a large pan, add the water and bring it to boiling point. Simmer for 20 minutes. Lift out the fish, remove the skin and bones, and return these to the stock. Simmer gently for 45 minutes.

Meanwhile, peel the potatoes, boil in slightly salted water until tender, and mash them. Flake the fish roughly.

Strain the fish stock when ready. Add to it the milk, fish and cream, reserving 4 × 10ml spoons cream for a garnish. Mix in the butter and mashed potatoes, and heat through. Add a little extra milk for a thinner soup. Re-season if required.

Serve garnished with chopped parsley and a spoonful of cream on each helping.

Clapshot

4 helpings

500g potatoes	*50g chives*
500g turnips	*50g beef dripping*
salt	*pepper*

Cut very large potatoes in half. Peel the potatoes and turnips, and boil them together in slightly salted water for 20 minutes or until soft. Drain and mash them. Chop the chives finely, and add them with the dripping. Mix well, and season with salt and pepper. Serve hot as a vegetable.

Skirlie

4 helpings

100g beef dripping	*125g coarse oatmeal (approx)*
2 medium-sized onions (100g each approx)	*salt and pepper*

Heat the dripping in a frying pan. Skin and chop the onions finely, and add to the pan. Cook gently for 5 minutes until lightly browned. Add enough oatmeal to absorb the fat, and cook gently for another 10 minutes, stirring occasionally. Season well with salt and pepper.

Note Skirlie is traditionally served with potatoes, as an economical main dish, but it can be served as an accompaniment to any kind of meat, stews, and roasts.

Rumbledethumps

4 helpings

500g cabbage	*125g Dunlop cheese*
750g potatoes	*50g butter*
25g chives or 1 medium-sized onion (100g approx)	*salt and freshly ground black pepper*

Wash the cabbage, remove the coarse outer leaves, trim off the stem, and shred finely. Cook in a little boiling salted water in a covered pan for about 10 minutes or until tender. Drain the cabbage thoroughly.

Peel and boil the potatoes. Drain, and mash well. Chop the chives or skin and chop the onion finely. Grate the cheese. Mix the cabbage, chives or onion, and butter into the mashed potatoes. Season well with salt and pepper. Put the mixture into an ovenproof dish or into 4 individual dishes. Cover with grated cheese and brown under a hot grill or in a hot oven, 220°C, Gas 7, for 7–10 minutes.

Serve as a vegetable or use as a main-course dish with the addition of 125g extra cheese grated and mixed into the cabbage and potatoes.

Cloutie Dumpling

4–6 helpings

50g muscatel raisins
125g shredded suet
300g self-raising flour
125g soft light brown
  sugar
125g sultanas
1 × 5ml spoon baking
  powder
1 × 5ml spoon mixed
  spice
1 × 5ml spoon ground
  ginger

1 × 5ml spoon ground
  cinnamon
50g cut mixed peel
1 × 2.5ml spoon salt
1 medium-sized carrot
  (100g approx) **or**
  eating apple
125g black treacle
200ml milk
1 egg
flour for dusting **or**
  fat for greasing

De-seed the raisins. Mix the suet, dry ingredients and dried fruit together in a large bowl. Peel the apple, if used. Grate the carrot or apple, and add to the dry ingredients. Dissolve the treacle in the milk over low heat. Mix into the dry ingredients to make a fairly soft dropping consistency. Mix in the egg, blending thoroughly.

Put the mixture into a scalded floured cloth, tie with string, allowing room for expansion. Place on a plate in a saucepan and fill up with water to three-quarters of the way up the dumpling. Simmer for 3 hours. Alternatively, steam the dumpling in a 1.5 litre greased basin covered with greased paper or foil.

Serve hot or cold with Pouring Custard (p964).

Cranachan

4 helpings

375ml double cream
125g coarse oatmeal
50g caster sugar

1 × 15ml spoon rum
125g fresh raspberries

Whip the cream until stiff. Toast the oatmeal under a low grill until lightly browned. Shake or stir the pan to brown it evenly. Cool, then mix with the cream. Flavour with the sugar and rum. Hull the raspberries and mix into the cream, or layer with the Cranachan mixture, or serve on top as a decoration. Serve in individual glass dishes.

Atholl Brose Dessert

4 helpings

200g medium oatmeal
125ml water (approx)
4 × 10ml spoons heather
  honey

750ml whisky
250ml double cream
2 egg whites

Decoration
roasted almonds (p1185)

To make the Atholl Brose, put the oatmeal into a small basin and add enough water to make a paste. Leave for 30 minutes, then strain out and reserve the liquid. Press the oatmeal well into the strainer, to squeeze out as much cloudy liquid as possible. Add the honey to the liquid and mix in well. Pour into a bottle and add the whisky. Shake well. Store, and use as required. Always shake well before use.

To make the dessert, pour 1 × 15ml spoon Atholl Brose into 4 individual glass dishes. Whip the cream until stiff and mix in 4 × 15ml spoons Atholl Brose. Whisk the egg whites until stiff and fold them lightly into the cream mixture. Spoon into the 4 glasses on top of the Brose, then chill. Decorate with the almonds.

Oatmeal Porridge

4 helpings

1 litre water
150g coarse **or** fine
  oatmeal

1 × 5ml spoon salt

Bring the water to the boil in a thick pan. Sprinkle in the oatmeal steadily, stirring all the time with a spurtle (porridge stick) or wooden spoon. Cover the pan, reduce the heat, and simmer. Add the salt after 10 minutes. Cook for 20–30 minutes altogether.

Ladle into cold bowls or porringers and serve with a separate bowl of either cream, milk or buttermilk. Dip each spoonful of porridge into this before eating.

Note The cooking time may be shortened by soaking the oatmeal overnight in the water.

Black Bun
(traditional)

400g plain flour
125g blanched whole
  almonds
750g muscatel raisins
200g caster sugar
750g currants
125g cut mixed peel
2 × 15ml spoons ground
  ginger
2 × 15ml spoons ground
  cinnamon
2 × 15ml spoons mixed
  spice

1 × 2.5ml spoon black
  pepper
1 × 5ml spoon
  bicarbonate of soda
1 × 5ml spoon cream of
  tartar
250ml milk
1 × 15ml spoon brandy

Pastry

250g butter
500g plain flour
1 × 5ml spoon baking
  powder

125ml water (approx)
flour for rolling out
beaten egg for glazing

Sift the flour into a large bowl. Chop the almonds roughly. De-seed the raisins. Mix together all the dried fruit and dry ingredients, then moisten with the milk and brandy.

Make the pastry. Rub the butter into the flour and add the baking powder. Mix to a stiff dough with the water. Leave it to rest for a few minutes. Roll out the pastry about 5mm thick on a lightly floured surface. Line a round cake tin, 23cm diameter × 11cm deep with three-quarters of the pastry, leaving a border round the edges for over-lap. Roll out the remaining pastry for the lid. Fill the lined tin with the cake mixture, and turn the edges of the pastry over it. Moisten the edges with water, put on the lid and seal. Decorate the pastry with any trimmings, prick with a fork all over the top and brush with egg. Bake in a fairly hot oven, 200°C, Gas 6, for 1 hour. Reduce the temperature to warm, 160°C, Gas 3, cover the top of the bun loosely with paper or foil and continue baking for another 2 hours.

Leave the bun to cool in the tin for 20 minutes; then remove it from the tin, cool completely, and keep for 1 month in an airtight tin before using.

Ireland

Irish Spiced Beef
(for Christmas)

6–8 helpings

3kg lean boned joint of
  beef
1 × 5ml spoon ground
  allspice
1 × 5ml spoon ground
  cloves

3 carrots
3 medium-sized onions
a bundle of fresh mixed
  herbs **or** bouquet garni
250ml stout

Spicing Mixture

1 × 5ml spoon ground
  cloves
6 blades mace
1 × 5ml spoon
  peppercorns
1 × 5ml spoon allspice

3 × 15ml spoons soft
  light brown sugar
2 × 5ml spoons saltpetre
500g coarse salt
3 bay leaves
1 clove of garlic

Make the spicing mixture first. Mix all the dry ingredients together, then pound in the bay leaves and garlic. Stand the meat in a large earthenware or glass dish, and rub the spicing mixture thoroughly all over it. Repeat every day for a week, taking the spicing mixture from the bottom of the dish. Turn the meat over twice. At the end of the week, wash the meat and tie it into a convenient shape for cooking.

Sprinkle the allspice and cloves over the meat. Prepare and chop the carrots and onions. Make a bed of the vegetables and the herbs in a large saucepan. Put the meat on top. Barely cover with warm water, cover with a lid, and simmer gently for 5 hours. Add the stout for the last hour of the cooking time.

Serve hot or cold. (At Christmas, the beef is usually served cold, in slices.) To serve cold, re-move the hot meat from the cooking liquid, and press between 2 dishes, with a weight on top, until cold.

Dublin Coddle

4 helpings

8 slices raw ham **or** bacon, without rinds (5mm thick)	4 large onions
	1kg potatoes
8 pork sausages	4 × 15ml spoons chopped parsley
1.25 litres boiling water	salt and pepper

Cut the ham or bacon into 5cm squares. Put with the sausages into the boiling water, and boil for 5 minutes. Drain, but reserve the liquid. Put the meat in a large saucepan or in an ovenproof dish with a lid. Skin and slice the onions, peel and slice the potatoes, and add both to the meat. Add the parsley, and season to taste. Pour in just enough of the cooking liquid to cover the ingredients. Lay greaseproof paper on the dish, and cover. Simmer gently, or bake in a very cool oven, 140°C, Gas 1, for about 1 hour, or until the liquid is reduced by half and the ingredients are cooked but not mushy. Serve hot, with the vegetables on top.

Colcannon

4 helpings

500g kale	100ml milk **or** single cream
500g potatoes	
salt	pepper
2 small leeks **or** green onion tops	a pinch of ground mace
	100g butter (approx)

Remove the coarse outer leaves of the kale, and trim off the stems. Peel the potatoes. Cook the kale and the potatoes in slightly salted boiling water until tender. Clean and chop the leeks or onion tops and simmer in the milk or cream until soft. Drain and chop the kale. Drain the potatoes, return to the pan, season well with salt, pepper and mace, and beat or mash them. Add the leeks or onions and milk or cream, and mix well. Beat the kale into the potato mixture over low heat until it is pale green and fluffy. Pile on to a warmed, deep dish, and make a well in the centre. Melt the butter and pour in enough to fill the well. Serve the vegetables with spoonfuls of melted butter.

Irish Soda Bread

Makes one 750g loaf

750g plain flour	250ml buttermilk **or** soured milk **or** fresh milk
1 × 5ml spoon bicarbonate of soda	
1 × 5ml spoon salt	flour for dusting
1 × 5ml spoon cream of tartar (if using fresh milk)	fat for greasing

Mix all the dry ingredients together in a bowl, and make a well in the centre. Add enough milk to make a fairly slack dough, pouring it in almost all at once, not spoonful by spoonful. Mix with a wooden spoon, lightly and quickly. With floured hands, place the mixture on a lightly floured surface, and flatten the dough into a circle about 3cm thick. Turn on to a greased baking sheet, and make a large cross in the surface with a floured knife to make it heat through evenly. Bake in a fairly hot oven, 190°–200°C, Gas 5–6, for about 40 minutes. Pierce the centre with a thin skewer to test for readiness; it should come out clean. Wrap the loaf in a clean tea-towel to keep it soft until required.

Tea Brack

Makes 3 loaves

500g sultanas	1 × 5ml spoon baking powder
500g seedless raisins	
500g soft light brown sugar	1 × 15ml spoon mixed spice (optional)
750ml black tea	fat for greasing
3 eggs	honey for glazing
500g plain flour	

Soak the dried fruit and sugar in the tea overnight. Next day, beat the eggs until liquid. Add to the tea mixture, alternately with the flour in 3 equal parts. Stir in the baking powder, and the spice if used. Turn the mixture into 3 well-greased 20 × 10 × 7cm loaf tins. Bake in a cool oven, 150°C, Gas 2, for 1½ hours or until the loaves sound hollow when tapped underneath. Leave to cool. Melt the honey and brush it on the cooled loaves to glaze them.

English Regions

Many of the dishes in this section are made in several different parts of the country; Fidget or Fitchett Pie is one example. Most of the recipes are similar but each area has developed small, yet significant variations on original themes. The versions given here are the ones generally used in a particular region.

Some traditional regional recipes will be found in other chapters because they have become nationally popular and are widely used.

THE NORTH-WEST

Cumberland Sausage

8–10 breakfast helpings,
4–5 helpings as a main dish

450g lean shoulder of pork	a large pinch of ground mace
150g pork fat	a large pinch of grated nutmeg
1 rasher of smoked bacon, without rind	$\frac{1}{2}$ × 2.5ml spoon dried thyme (optional)
50g wholemeal breadcrumbs	$\frac{1}{4}$ × 2.5ml spoon dried crushed sage (optional)
1 × 5ml spoon salt	lard
1 × 2.5ml spoon pepper	

Chop the pork finely or mince it coarsely with the fat and bacon. Mix in the breadcrumbs, and season well with the salt, pepper, spices, and herbs. Grease a baking sheet with a little lard. Shape or pipe the mixture into a long continuous roll about 2cm thick and coil up on the sheet like a Catherine wheel. Prick well, melt the lard, and brush the sausage very lightly with it. Bake in a warm oven, 160°C, Gas 3, for 30–45 minutes or until the sausage is cooked through. Drain off the fat, and serve cut in short lengths.

Hindle Wakes

6 helpings

1 × 1.5kg chicken	a blade of mace
350ml chicken stock	(optional)
grated rind and juice of $\frac{1}{2}$ lemon	

Stuffing
175g prunes	50g shredded suet
50g onion	1 × 15ml spoon Demerara sugar
125g soft white breadcrumbs	salt and pepper
1 × 5ml dried mixed herbs	1 × 15ml spoon malt vinegar

Garnish
6 soaked prunes (see Method)	lemon slices
	parsley (optional)

Make the stuffing first. Put the prunes in a basin, cover with cold water, and leave to soak overnight. Reserving 6 for the garnish, stone and chop the rest. Skin the onion and chop it finely. Mix it with the prunes, breadcrumbs, mixed herbs, suet, sugar, salt, and pepper. Sprinkle the mixture with the vinegar and mix together. Use the stuffing to fill the body cavity of the chicken.

Truss the chicken and place it in a large saucepan or flameproof casserole. Bring the stock to the boil, add the lemon rind and juice, and a blade of mace. Pour the stock over the chicken. Bring to the boil, reduce the heat, cover, and simmer for $1\frac{1}{2}$ hours until tender. Drain, and garnish with the reserved prunes and lemon slices. Arrange in lines along the back of the chicken, using cocktail sticks to secure the garnish. Parsley sprigs can also be used. Serve with the stuffing and hot lemon stock.

Lancashire Cheese and Onions

4 helpings

5 large onions (125g each approx)	salt and pepper
125ml milk	150g Lancashire cheese
	1 × 15ml spoon butter

Skin the onions, slice them thickly, and put them in a saucepan, with enough water to cover. Boil for

15 minutes or until the slices are tender and the water has almost evaporated. Add the milk and seasonings, and bring to the boil again. Remove from the heat and grate or crumble the cheese into the pan. Add the butter, and leave to stand for 7–10 minutes or until the cheese has fully melted. Stir round once, and re-heat without boiling. Serve at once with hot buttered toast or muffins.

Mrs Beeton's Manchester Pudding

6 helpings

250ml milk	3 × 15ml spoons brandy
2 strips lemon rind	100g prepared puff
75g soft white	pastry (p1253)
breadcrumbs	flour for rolling out
2 eggs	3–4 × 15ml spoons jam
2 egg yolks	extra caster sugar for
50g softened butter	sprinkling
3 × 15ml spoons caster	
sugar	

Heat the milk with the lemon rind and leave to infuse for 30 minutes. Strain the milk on to the breadcrumbs, discarding the rind. Return the mixture to the pan, and simmer for 2–3 minutes or until the crumbs have absorbed all the milk. Beat the eggs and yolks until liquid, and stir into the breadcrumbs with the butter, sugar, and brandy. Mix thoroughly; the butter should melt in the warm mixture. Leave to cool under damp grease-proof paper.

Roll out the pastry on a lightly floured surface and line a 650ml pie dish with it. If liked, cut a strip out of the pastry trimmings, to fit the rim of the pie dish; dampen the rim of the lining, and fit on the extra strip. Spread the jam over the bottom of the pastry. Turn in the cooled breadcrumb mixture and bake in a fairly hot oven, 200°C, Gas 6, for 15 minutes, then reduce the heat to moderate, 180°C, Gas 4, and cook for a further 45–60 minutes or until the pudding is set in the centre. Leave to cool. Serve cold, sprinkled with extra caster sugar.

Westmorland Parkin

fat for greasing	1 × 2.5ml spoon salt
200g butter or clarified	2 × 5ml spoons baking
dripping (p473)	powder
450g black treacle	200g Demerara sugar
450g fine oatmeal	100ml milk
200g plain flour	1 × 5ml spoon
1 × 5ml spoon ground	bicarbonate of soda
allspice	

Grease and line two 20cm square tins. Heat the fat and treacle gently in a saucepan until the fat has melted. Mix together all the dry ingredients, excluding the bicarbonate of soda, and make a well in the centre.

Warm the milk to hand-hot and dissolve the bicarbonate of soda in it. Pour into the dry ingredients. Beat together the melted butter and treacle, then stir them into the dry ingredients. Pour the mixture into the tins and bake in a warm oven, 160°C, Gas 3, for about $1\frac{1}{4}$ hours. Cool in the tins, then cut into squares.

Grasmere Gingerbread

fat for greasing	1 × 2.5ml spoon ground
100g wholemeal flour	ginger
100g plain flour	150g butter
1 × 2.5ml spoon	150g soft dark brown
bicarbonate of soda	sugar
1 × 2.5ml spoon cream	1 × 15ml spoon golden
of tartar	syrup

Grease and line a 20cm square tin. Put the wholemeal flour in a bowl and sift the plain flour, bicarbonate of soda, cream of tartar, and ground ginger in it. Rub in the butter. Mix in the sugar and syrup to form a crumbly mixture. Turn the mixture into the tin and bake in a warm oven, 160°C, Gas 3, for 45 minutes. The gingerbread should be crumbly on top but firm underneath. Do not leave in the tin for longer than 10 minutes after cooking, as it will be too hard to cut. Cut into fingers and finish cooling on a wire rack. When cold, store in an airtight tin.

Westmorland Pepper Cake

fat for greasing
450g self-raising flour
1 × 15ml spoon ground
  ginger
½ × 2.5ml spoon ground
  cloves
½–1 × 2.5ml spoon
  ground black pepper
100g butter

200g caster sugar
100g seedless raisins
100g currants
25g cut mixed peel
200g golden syrup **or**
  golden syrup and
  treacle mixed
2 large eggs
125ml skimmed milk

Grease a deep 18cm square cake tin or a shallower 20cm tin. Sift the flour, spices, and black pepper into a bowl. Rub in the fat. Mix in the sugar, and add the fruit. Warm the syrup, uncovered, in its tin, to make measuring easier. Beat the eggs lightly. Make a well in the flour mixture, pour in the syrup, eggs and milk, and beat lightly.

Turn the mixture into the tin and bake in a warm oven, 160°C, Gas 3, for 2½ hours or until it is firm in the centre and brown, and a skewer pushed into the cake comes out clean. Cool on a wire rack and store for a week before cutting.

Goosnargh Cakes

Makes 36

450g plain flour
  (approx)
300g softened butter
1 × 15ml spoon caraway
  seeds (approx)

50g caster sugar
a pinch of ground
  coriander (optional)
flour for rolling out
fat for greasing

Sift the flour into a bowl. Rub the butter into the flour, a little at a time, until well blended. Mix in the seeds, sugar and spice, if used. Roll out on a well floured surface to 1cm thick, and cut into 36 rounds or squares. Chill or leave in a cool place overnight. Place on a lightly greased baking sheet and bake in a moderate oven, 180°C, Gas 4, for 20 minutes or until cooked through and a deep cream colour. The cakes should not brown.

VARIATION

Mix together the flour and butter, roll out, sprinkle with the seeds, 25g caster sugar, and spice if used.

THE NORTH-EAST

Saltburn Fish Pie

4 helpings

450g haddock fillet
4 × 15ml spoons grated
  onion
salt and pepper
2 × 15ml spoons lemon
  juice
2 large slices raw ham
  or gammon

3 hard-boiled eggs
fat for greasing
2 × 15ml spoons
  chopped parsley
shortcrust pastry (p1249)
  using 150g flour
flour for rolling out

Sprinkle the fish fillet with the onion, and season lightly. Sprinkle lightly with lemon juice. Put the fillet in a frying pan with enough water almost to cover it, and any remaining lemon juice. Heat until just simmering. Simmer for 8–15 minutes, depending on its thickness, until the fish is just tender. Remove from the pan, but reserve the cooking liquid. Remove any fins, bones, and skin from the fish, and flake it. Trim the ham or gammon slices, and cut into 7–8cm squares. Slice the hard-boiled eggs.

Grease a 750ml pie dish. Put in a layer of fish and season lightly with salt. Add a layer of ham or gammon and season with pepper. Cover with a layer of hard-boiled egg slices. Sprinkle with parsley. Continue layering until all the ingredients are used. Moisten with a little of the fish cooking liquid. Roll out the pastry on a lightly floured surface, and use it to cover the dish. Dampen the edge of the dish. Lay the pastry lid on the dish, press down firmly to seal, and bake in a fairly hot oven, 200°C, Gas 6, for 25–30 minutes. Serve hot.

Note Although haddock was originally used, cod or any other firm white fish is suitable.

Cree'd or Frumenty Wheat

375g hulled **or** pearled
  wheat

a pinch of salt
2 litres water (approx)

Put the wheat into a heatproof container with the salt, and cover with cold water. Allow to steep in a very warm place for 24–36 hours, until the starch grains have become a soft mass. It can be put in the plate-warming drawer of an oven or on a radiator or boiler. Add extra water during steeping, if the grain absorbs it all.

Pour off any excess free water, and put the grain in a saucepan. Stir over very gentle heat until the mixture boils and becomes a glutinous mass. Leave to cool, and use for making Frumenty.

Frumenty

6–8 helpings

450g cree'd wheat
75–100g currants **or**
  seedless raisins
300–500ml milk
1 × 15ml spoon flour
  (optional)

sugar, honey **or** treacle
ground allspice **or**
  cinnamon **or** grated
  nutmeg

Prepare the cree'd wheat as in the previous recipe. Meanwhile, soak the dried fruit in enough water to cover; leave until soft and swollen. Put the cree'd wheat into a stewpan with the milk. Drain, and add the dried fruit, and stir over gentle heat until the mixture comes to the boil and is thick and creamy. Thicken the mixture, if liked, by mixing the flour to a cream with a little cold milk and stirring it into the hot frumenty. Sweeten and flavour to taste.

Serve hot like porridge, with 1 × 15ml spoon butter on each helping, or with cream and rum.

Note Frumenty is, by tradition, eaten on Christmas Eve and in some parts of England at mid-Lent and Easter as well. A small cupful is served to each person, and a bowlful is put outside the door for the 'Pharisees' (fairies).

Durham Pikelets

Makes 20–22

200g plain flour
a pinch of salt
40g caster sugar
1 × 5ml spoon
  bicarbonate of soda

275ml buttermilk
50g lard for frying

Sift the flour and salt into a bowl, and mix in the sugar. Mix the bicarbonate of soda into 1 × 15ml spoon of the buttermilk and leave to dissolve. Mix the rest of the buttermilk into the dry ingredients to make a stiff batter. Beat the dissolved bicarbonate of soda in last.

Grease a heavy frying pan with about a quarter of the lard, and heat thoroughly. Drop 10ml spoonfuls of batter on to the hot fat, and spread out. Cook gently until small holes appear on the surface. Turn the pikelets over and cook the second side until the pikelets are golden-brown. Drain on soft kitchen paper. Continue frying until all the mixture is used, adding more fat as required.

Serve hot or still warm, with butter or a local soft curd cheese.

Moggy

Makes one 650g bun

350g flour
a pinch of salt
3 × 2.5ml spoons baking
  powder
75g margarine
75g lard

100g caster sugar
100g golden syrup
50ml milk (approx)
fat for greasing

Sift together the flour, salt, and baking powder. Rub in the fats, then mix in the sugar. Warm the syrup, uncovered, in its tin, to make measuring easier. Mix the syrup with the dry ingredients, adding enough milk to make the mixture into a stiff dough. Shape into a round or oval flat bun about 3cm thick. Place on a lightly greased baking sheet, and bake in a moderate oven, 180°C, Gas 4, for 25–35 minutes until firm and light brown.

Serve warm or cold, cut in wedges or slices, and thickly buttered.

THE MIDLANDS AND EAST ANGLIA

Marsh Pards' Relish

4 helpings

8 rashers smoked streaky bacon, without rinds
4 large ripe tomatoes
50ml water
100g Cheddar or Gouda cheese

Fry the rashers gently until crisp. Drain and keep hot. Chop each tomato into 6 pieces, and simmer in the bacon fat until soft and pulpy. Add the water. Grate the cheese into the pan, stir round, and as the cheese begins to melt, tip the mixture on to the rashers. Serve immediately, with fresh hot rolls (preferably wholemeal) as a supper dish.

Note 'Marsh pard' is a seventeenth-century name for the gypsy-like people living in the Fens. This dish is attributed to them, although they probably used sweet-tasting root vegetables, cooking plums or other fruits, or even fruit pickles in their relish.

Norfolk Dumplings

Makes 30–32

120ml milk
125ml water
1 × 5ml caster sugar
15g fresh yeast
450g plain flour
1 × 2.5ml spoon salt
a pinch of ground black pepper
flour for kneading
oil for greasing

Warm the milk, water and sugar, and blend in the yeast. Leave for 10 minutes until frothy. Sift together the dry ingredients, and stir in the yeast liquid. Turn the mixture on to a floured surface and knead until the dough is smooth, elastic, and no longer sticky.

Place the dough in the bowl, in a lightly oiled polythene bag and leave in a warm place for 2 hours or until it has doubled in size. Shape into 30–32 small balls. Leave for 10 minutes. Drop the dumplings gently into a deep saucepan of boiling water (or stock or soup if serving them with a savoury dish). Boil for 20 minutes, and drain. Serve hot.

Lincolnshire Haslet

Makes 20–24 slices

1 onion (100g approx)
1kg lean boneless pork
200g 2–3 day-old white bread
2 × 15ml spoons salt
1 × 5ml spoon white pepper
1 × 5ml spoon finely chopped sage

Skin the onion. Shred or mince the meat and onion together. Remove the crusts, and cut the bread into 2cm cubes. Cover them with water. Drain as soon as they are thoroughly moistened, and squeeze as dry as possible. Mix together the bread, meat, and onion. Beat with a hand-held rotary whisk or electric beater, and add the seasonings and sage.

Turn the mixture into a deep 1 litre rectangular dish or loaf tin, and press down well. Bake in a fairly hot oven, 190°C, Gas 5, for 1 hour. Pour off any free fat in the tin. Cool the Haslet in the tin under greaseproof paper and a 1kg weight. When cold, turn out and cut in slices.

Serve with salad or use in sandwiches.

Lavenham Buns

Makes 12–16

325g plain white flour
100g ground rice
1 × 10ml spoon baking powder
100g butter
75g caster sugar
2 eggs
milk
75g currants or 35g caraway seeds
flour for rolling out
fat for greasing

Sift together the flour, ground rice, and baking powder. Rub in the butter and stir in the sugar. Beat the eggs until liquid, and use them to bind the dry ingredients to a firm dough. Add a very little milk if required. Mix in the dried fruit or seeds. On a lightly floured surface, pat or roll out the dough to 3cm thick. Cut out in 7cm rounds. Place on a lightly greased baking sheet, and bake in a moderate oven, 180°C, Gas 4, for 20–30 minutes until firm and lightly browned.

Serve hot with butter for tea or supper.

Leicester Cheesecakes

Makes 12

200g prepared puff pastry (p1253)	50g soft white breadcrumbs
flour for rolling out	a pinch of salt
100g low-fat curd (not cottage) cheese	a pinch of grated nutmeg
50g soft tub margarine	grated rind of 1 lemon
50g granulated sugar	1 × 10ml spoon brandy
1 egg	125g mixed currants and sultanas **or** cut mixed peel
1 egg yolk	
1 × 15ml spoon single cream	

Roll out the pastry on a lightly floured surface to about 4mm thick, and use it to line twelve 7cm bun or tartlet tins about 3cm deep. Prick the bottoms, and chill while preparing the filling. Put the cheese, margarine and sugar in a bowl, and mix thoroughly. Beat the egg and egg yolk lightly, then beat them into the mixture, with the cream. Mix in the breadcrumbs, salt, nutmeg, and grated rind. Finally, mix in the brandy and fruit. Fill the pastry shells with the mixture. Bake in a hot oven, 220°C, Gas 7, for 15 minutes, reduce the heat to warm, 160°C, Gas 3, and bake for a further 15 minutes or until the cheesecakes are firm in the centre and well browned. Cool on a wire rack, or serve warm.

Lincolnshire Plum Bread

100g prunes	1 × 2.5ml spoon gravy browning (optional)
fat for greasing	
100g butter	2 eggs
100g soft light brown sugar	1 × 15ml spoons brandy
	100g sultanas
1 × 2.5ml spoon ground mixed spice	100g currants
	175g self-raising flour
1 × 2.5ml spoon ground cinnamon	a pinch of salt

Soak the prunes overnight in cold water. Drain well and pat dry. Remove the stones and chop the prunes finely. Grease and line a 23 × 13 × 7cm loaf tin. Cream the butter and sugar until light and fluffy, then beat in the spices and gravy browning,

if used. Beat the eggs lightly, mix with the brandy, and beat into the creamed mixture. Toss the chopped prunes and other dried fruit in a little of the flour, and mix the rest of the flour with the salt. Fold it into the creamed mixture; then fold in all the dried fruit. Turn the mixture into the prepared tin and level the top. Bake in a very cool oven, 140°C, Gas 1, for 3 hours. Cool in the tin. When cold, turn out and store in an airtight tin.

THE WEST AND SOUTH-WEST

Bath Chap

1 pig's jaw and cheek	raspings (p375)

Ask the butcher to halve the head and remove the halved lower jaw and cheek. To prepare for cooking, remove the tongue and use it for another recipe. Remove any foreign matter from the mouth and clean the teeth before putting the 2 half jaws and cheeks in a pickling brine (p611) or dry salt (p611). A week's salting is usually sufficient.

Cut the jaw bone away, form the meat into the shape of a cornet, and tie with string. Put the meat into a saucepan, cover with cold water and bring to the boil; then drain. Weigh the meat and calculate the cooking time, allowing 1 hour per kg. Return it to the pan, add fresh water and cook gently for the required time.

After cooking, allow to stand for 30 minutes in the cooking water before removing the string and rind. Coat with raspings. A Bath chap is usually served cold.

Note The chap is the lower jaw and cheek of the pig. The half jaw and cheek makes a small joint suitable for 1 or 2 people. For a family, roll the 2 halves together. This makes a fatty joint but it is very tender, and has a delicious characteristic flavour.

Cornish Pasties(3)
(traditional)

Makes 8

Filling

1 large **or** *2 small*	*1 medium-sized onion*
potatoes	*salt and pepper*
1 small turnip	*300g lean chuck steak*

Pastry

500g plain flour	*flour for rolling out*
1 × 5ml spoon salt	*beaten egg for*
150g lard	*glazing*
4 × 15ml spoons	
shredded suet	

Make the pastry first. Sift the flour and salt together. Rub in the lard, and mix in the suet. Moisten with enough cold water to make a stiff dough. Roll out on a lightly floured surface, and cut into eight 16cm rounds.

Peel the potato and turnip, and skin the onion. Slice all the vegetables thinly, mix together, and season well. Divide between the pastry rounds, placing a line of mixture across the centre of each round. Wipe the meat, chop it finely, and place equal amounts on the vegetables. Dampen the pastry edges of each round. Lift them to meet over the filling. Pinch together to seal, and flute the edges. Make small slits in both sides of each pasty near the top. Mark one end of each pasty with the initial of the person who will eat it, either by making small slits, or by pinching up the pastry with thumb and forefinger in the shape of the initial. Place the pasties on a baking sheet, and brush with egg. Bake in a very hot oven, 230°C, Gas 8, for 10 minutes, then reduce the heat to moderate, 180°C, Gas 4, and bake for a further 45 minutes, or until the meat is tender when pierced by a thin, heated skewer through the top of a pasty. Serve hot or cold.

Note See also Cornish Pasties (1) (p503), and Cornish Pasties (2) (p1305).

Fidget or Fitchett Pie

3–4 helpings

3–4 medium-sized	*ground black pepper*
potatoes	*a few grains salt*
3 medium-sized onions	*150ml (approx) general*
3 cooking apples	*household stock (p329)*
200g smoked bacon **or**	*shortcrust pastry*
gammon rashers,	*(p1249) using 150g*
without rinds	*flour*
pork fat for greasing	*flour for rolling out*
1 × 15ml spoon soft light	*beaten egg for glazing*
brown sugar (if needed)	

Peel the potatoes and slice them thickly. Skin the onions and slice thinly. Peel, core, and slice the apples. Cut the bacon or gammon into small strips. Grease a 750ml pie dish with the fat. Put a layer of potatoes and onions into the dish. Dip the apple slices in brown sugar if sour, and place a layer over the potatoes. Cover with strips of meat. Season lightly. Repeat the layers until the dish is very full and all the ingredients are used, ending with a layer of meat. Pour in the stock.

Roll out the pastry on a lightly floured surface to fit the pie dish. Cover the pie with the pastry, and make slits in the crust to let steam escape. Brush with egg and bake in a fairly hot oven, 200°C, Gas 6, for about 20 minutes or until the pastry is set. Reduce the temperature to warm, 160°C, Gas 3, and continue cooking for about 45 minutes until the potatoes and fruit are fully cooked. Test for readiness by piercing the pastry with a skewer to see whether the vegetables are soft. Serve hot.

Stargazey Pie

6 helpings

6 even-sized pilchards
  or herrings
1 small sharp cooking
  apple
1 medium-sized onion
6 × 15ml spoons soft
  white breadcrumbs
salt and pepper
150–175ml dry still
  cider

150g prepared short-
  crust pastry (p1249)
flour for rolling out
2 hard-boiled eggs
2 rashers back bacon,
  without rinds
1 × 10ml spoon cider
  vinegar
cream or top of the milk
  for glazing

Garnish
6 parsley sprigs

Scale and clean the fish. Split them without removing the heads or tails, and ease out the backbones. Peel, core, and chop the apple. Skin the onion, chop it finely, and put 2 × 15ml spoons to one side. Mix the remaining onion and all the apple with the breadcrumbs in a bowl. Season well and add 3–4 × 15ml spoons cider to bind the mixture. Stuff the fish with the mixture and reshape neatly. Reserve any leftover stuffing.

Choose a pie plate or an ovenproof dish that will just hold 2 fish placed end to end across the centre with their tails overlapping in the centre and their heads sticking over the edge of the dish. Roll out the pastry on a lightly floured surface and use just over half of it to line the plate or dish. Arrange the fish in a star shape with heads right on the edge of the plate or dish, their tails overlapping in the centre. Lift the tails and form them into an upright cluster, securing them with wooden cocktail sticks if required. Twist a piece of foil over and round them.

Chop the hard-boiled eggs. Chop the bacon finely. Fill the triangular spaces between the fish with egg, bacon, the reserved onion, and any leftover stuffing. Sprinkle with vinegar. Pour the remaining cider into the dish.

Dampen the edge of the pastry. Trim the remaining pastry to fit over the fish as a pie crust. Make a hole in the centre. Very carefully, lift it and lay it on the pie with the fish tails protruding through the hole. Press the pastry crust between the fish heads; push it back slightly round the heads so that they stick out. Cover the heads with small pieces of foil. Brush the pastry crust lightly with cream or milk. (In Cornwall, they use rich Cornish cream, but any cream will do.) Bake the 'stargazers' in a warm oven, 160°C, Gas 3, for 1 hour. Garnish with sprigs of parsley around the tails, and serve very hot.

Note Mashed potato glazed with egg is sometimes used instead of pastry.

Revel Buns

Makes 12

a large pinch of saffron
  strands or powdered
  saffron
125ml milk
20g fresh yeast
450g plain flour
1 × 2.5ml spoon ground
  cinnamon

a pinch of salt
100g butter
150ml Devonshire cream
2 eggs
100g currants
fat for greasing
beaten egg for glazing
100g caster sugar

Put the saffron in a heatproof jug. Warm the milk until steaming and pour it over the saffron. Leave to infuse for 30 minutes. Strain 4 × 15ml spoons of the milk and leave until hand-hot. Blend in the yeast and leave until frothy. Sift the flour with the cinnamon and salt, then rub in the butter. Strain the remaining saffron-flavoured milk and mix in the cream. Beat the eggs until liquid. Pour the milk and cream into the dry ingredients, with the eggs and yeast mixture. Mix thoroughly, then add the currants. Knead well. Cover, and chill in a refrigerator overnight.

Next day, shape the mixture into 12 buns. Place on a lightly greased baking sheet and leave to rise for 20–30 minutes. Brush the tops with beaten egg, and sprinkle with the sugar. Bake in a fairly hot oven, 190°C, Gas 5, for about 15 minutes.

Serve warm or cold with butter, for tea.

Old English Cider Cake

fat for greasing
200g plain flour
3 × 2.5ml spoons grated
  nutmeg
½ × 2.5ml spoon ground
  cinnamon
1 × 5ml spoon baking
  powder

a pinch of salt
125g butter **or**
  margarine
125g caster sugar
2 eggs
125ml dry still cider

Grease lightly a shallow 20cm square cake tin. Sift the flour with the spices, baking powder, and salt. Beat the fat and sugar together until light and fluffy, then beat in the eggs. Beat half the flour into the creamed fat. Mix in half the cider. Repeat, using the remaining flour and the cider. Turn the mixture into the prepared tin. Bake in a moderate oven, 180°C, Gas 4, for 50–55 minutes until the cake has shrunk slightly from the sides of the tin and springs back when pressed. Cool on a wire rack.

Oldbury Gooseberry Tarts

Makes 4 tarts

200g green gooseberries
450g plain flour
100g butter
100g lard

4 × 15ml spoons boiling
  water
flour for rolling out
175g Demerara sugar

Top and tail the gooseberries. Put the flour in a bowl, and make a well in the centre; chop the butter and lard, and add them. Pour over the boiling water. Stir until the fats dissolve, then mix in the flour gradually to make a warm, waxy-looking, smooth dough.

Cut off one-quarter of the dough. Use just over half to roll out, on a lightly floured surface, into a 15cm circle. Raise the edges 3cm, and mould them to form a case. Fill with a quarter of the gooseberries and sprinkle with a quarter of the sugar. Roll out a second half of the pastry slightly smaller than the case, lay it on the gooseberries, dampen the edges and pinch together to seal firmly. Cut a small hole in the centre to let steam escape. Prepare 3 more tarts in the same way. Place on a baking sheet and leave in a cold place for several hours. Bake in a fairly hot oven, 200°C, Gas 6, for 30–35 minutes.

Damask Cream

4 helpings

600ml single cream
  (approx)
1 blade of mace
1 × 10cm piece
  cinnamon stick

2 × 10ml spoons icing
  sugar
triple-strength rose-
  water
1 × 15ml spoon rennet
  essence

Decoration
deep pink rose-petals **or**
  1 red rose

Pour 500ml of the cream into a saucepan, add the mace and cinnamon stick, and heat almost to boiling point. Remove from the heat and infuse for 20–30 minutes. Meanwhile, sift the icing sugar. Strain the cream into a clean basin, discard the spices, and add 1 × 10ml spoon icing sugar and rose-water to taste. Cool to blood-heat, and stir in the rennet. Pour gently into a decorative 750ml serving bowl and leave to set until cold and firm.

Flavour the remaining cream with rose-water and very gently pour it over the set cream to a depth of 5mm. Sprinkle lightly all over with icing sugar. Strew deep pink rose-petals round the edge of the dish or set one perfect red rosebud in the centre.

Serve with thin, crisp, plain or almond biscuits.

Somerset Cider Syllabub

4 helpings

125ml dry still cider
1 × 15ml spoon brandy
pared rind of 1 lemon
25–50g caster sugar

1 × 2.5ml spoon grated
  nutmeg
250ml double cream
lemon juice (optional)

Mix the cider, brandy, and lemon rind in a basin, and leave overnight. Next day, strain into a large basin. Sift in the sugar and nutmeg. Trickle in the cream, from a height if possible, stirring with a fork all the time. Whisk until the mixture is thick and spongy. Taste, and whisk in a little lemon juice to heighten the flavour if liked. Spoon into small glasses, and chill for at least 6 hours before use. Serve with Shrewsbury Biscuits (p1217).

THE HOME COUNTIES AND SOUTH-EAST

Brown Windsor Soup

6 helpings

150g shin of beef
150g stewing lamb
1 medium-sized onion
 (100g approx)
1 carrot (75g approx)
35g butter
35g flour
1.7 litres beef stock
 or strong general
 household stock (p329)

bouquet garni
salt
a few grains Cayenne
 pepper
75ml brown sherry **or**
 Madeira (optional)
35g boiled rice (optional)

Garnish
toasted croûtons

Cut the beef and lamb into 2–3cm pieces. Skin and slice the onion, and slice the carrot. Heat the butter in a deep heavy saucepan, put in the meat and vegetables, and fry gently until lightly browned. Stir in the flour, and continue cooking until it is well browned. Add the stock gradually, stirring all the time. Heat to boiling point, add the bouquet garni, cover, reduce the heat, and simmer for 2 hours or until the meat is very tender. Season to taste with salt and Cayenne pepper.

Strain the soup into a clean pan. Discard the bouquet garni, and remove any bones, skin and gristle from the meat. Return the meat to the soup, and either rub through a sieve or process in an electric blender to obtain a smooth purée. Return the purée to the pan, add the sherry or Madeira if used, and re-season if required. Just before serving, add the rice if used, and re-heat thoroughly. Serve garnished with croûtons.

Epping Sausages

Makes 18–20

450g boneless lean pork
400g shredded suet
50g soft white
 breadcrumbs
a pinch of grated nutmeg
salt and freshly ground
 black pepper
1 × 15ml spoon grated
 lemon rind

1 × 10ml spoon dried
 crushed herbs (sage,
 thyme, savory **or**
 marjoram)
1 egg
fat for grilling **or**
 shallow frying

Mince the pork. Mix it with the suet and breadcrumbs, and add the other dry ingredients in the order given. Beat the egg until liquid and use it to bind the mixture. Divide the meat into 50g portions, and roll each into a sausage shape. Brush lightly with fat, and grill or fry, using moderate heat for 8–12 minutes or until cooked through; the time will depend on the thickness of the sausages.

Watercress Sauce

Makes 250ml (approx)

100g stale white
 breadcrumbs
4 × 15ml spoons water
125ml single cream
1 bunch of watercress
 (75g approx)

1 × 2.5ml spoon
 tarragon vinegar **or** to
 taste
salt and freshly ground
 black pepper

Soak the crumbs in the water and single cream for 15 minutes. Meanwhile, wash the watercress well, shake to dry, and pick the leaves from the stalks. Mix the leaves with the crumbs. Pound the mixture in a mortar to bruise the leaves, then rub through a fine sieve. Alternatively, process the ingredients in an electric blender until smooth and green. Flavour to taste with the vinegar, salt and pepper. Chill before use.

Serve with cold fish or game.

Sussex Drip Pudding

(with roast beef or lamb)

6 helpings

suet pudding (p980)

Boil the pudding as directed, and leave until tepid. Cut off and discard the rounded ends of the pudding roll. Cut the rest into slices about 1cm thick. Lay the slices in the roasting tin about 30 minutes before the joint is ready, under the meat if on a trivet, or round it. Baste the slices well, and return to the oven for 15 minutes. Turn them over, baste again, and return to the oven to finish cooking.

Serve either with the joint or as a separate course before it, with a rich gravy made from the pan juices.

Hampshire Drops

Makes 24 single or 12 double biscuits

100g butter	*a pinch of salt*
100g caster sugar	*1 × 2.5ml spoon baking*
2 eggs	* powder*
100g plain flour	*fat for greasing*
100g cornflour	*smooth raspberry jam*

Cream the butter, and add in the sugar gradually, beating until light and fluffy. Beat in the eggs, one at a time. Sift together the dry ingredients and blend into the creamed mixture. Drop the mixture on to a greased baking sheet in small spoonfuls; space well apart. Bake in a warm oven, 160°C, Gas 3, for 20–25 minutes. Cool on the sheets. Either decorate with a blob of jam on top, or sandwich the biscuits together with the jam.

Note Bake for 20 minutes for soft 'drops' suitable for sandwiching together. Bake for 25 minutes for crisper 'drops'.

Kentish Well Pudding

8 helpings

450g plain flour	*150g shredded suet*
$\frac{1}{2}$ × 2.5ml spoon salt	*150g currants*
1 × 5ml spoon baking	*flour*
* powder*	*150g chilled butter*

Mix together the flour, salt, baking powder, suet, and currants. Add enough cold water to make a firm dough. Roll out on a lightly floured surface to 1cm thick. Cut off one-third of the dough, and enclose the single block of chilled butter in it, moistening the edges and sealing completely. Place the encased butter in the centre of the remaining dough, joined edge downward. Draw up the edges of the larger piece of dough to cover it. Lay the pudding in a scalded, well-floured pudding cloth and roll up loosely. Tie up the ends of the cloth. Put into a saucepan of fast-boiling water, reduce the heat, and simmer for $2\frac{1}{2}$ hours. Turn out carefully on to a hot dish to make sure it does not break open and let the butter escape. Make a small hole in the top at once, to let steam out and prevent the pudding cracking open. Serve hot, with brown sugar.

VARIATION

Sweet Kentish Well Pudding

This slightly more modern version gives the pudding a centre 'well' of delicious syrup sauce. Use the ingredients as above, but increase the chilled butter to 200g and add 4 × 15ml spoons Demerara sugar.

Make the dough as above, and roll it out to 3cm thick. Grease a 1 litre pudding basin with a little butter, and line it with three-quarters of the dough, leaving a 'well' in the centre which will just hold the chilled butter comfortably. Fill up any spaces round the butter with the Demerara sugar. Cover securely with the remaining dough, then cover tightly with greased foil or greaseproof paper. Steam for 3 hours.

Serve the pudding as above, taking helpings from the top of the pudding, and spooning a little of the syrup sauce from the 'well' over each one.

FOREIGN COOKERY

The French long enjoyed a European reputation for their skill and refinement in the preparing of food. In place of plain joints, French cookery delights in the marvels of what are called made dishes, ragoûts, stews, and fricassées, in which no trace of the original materials of which they are compounded is to be found.

Australia and New Zealand

Cookery in both Australia and New Zealand is largely British in origin and style, although Australian cooking has some American overtones; both countries also have many dishes adapted to the use of local fruits and other products. Meat is cheap and plentiful in Australia and New Zealand, and lamb, in particular, features largely. Pacific fish and shellfish are also popular and widely used.

Tasmanian Scallop Soup   Australia

6 helpings

250g carrots	salt and pepper
3 large onions	150ml dry white wine
100g butter	1.25 litres fish stock
12–16 large scallops	(p330)
1 sprig of thyme	750g potatoes
½ bay leaf	250ml single cream
3 × 15ml spoons	a pinch of Cayenne
chopped parsley	pepper

Prepare and finely chop the carrots and onions. Melt 75g of the butter in a large, heavy saucepan. Chill the rest. Cook the vegetables gently in the butter for 15 minutes. Add the scallops and herbs, and season to taste. Add the wine and fish stock, bring to the boil, reduce the heat, and simmer for 10 minutes. Using a perforated spoon, remove the scallops and keep warm. Peel and dice the potatoes. Add to the soup, and cook until soft. Rub the soup through a sieve, or process in an electric blender; strain if necessary. Transfer to a clean saucepan. Chop the scallops into 2 or 3 pieces each. Add them with the cream to the soup, and heat gently to just under boiling point. Stir in the chilled butter, and sprinkle with Cayenne pepper.

Wellington Salad   New Zealand

4 helpings

375g cooked lamb (from	50g desiccated coconut
leg **or** shoulder)	1 × 5ml spoon curry
1 × 10ml spoon orange	powder
curaçao	4 × 15ml spoons
2 sticks celery	mayonnaise
2 oranges	1 lettuce

Garnish
1 orange

Cut the lamb into 1.5cm cubes and sprinkle with the liqueur. Chop the celery into fine slices. Peel the oranges and divide into segments, removing all the skin, pith, and pips. Mix the orange segments with the lamb and celery. Mix together the coconut, curry powder, and mayonnaise.

Separate the lettuce leaves. Rinse and dry them, if required. Arrange them as a bed in a shallow salad bowl and pile the lamb mixture on top. Coat with the mayonnaise mixture. Cut 4 slices from the remaining orange, halve them, and arrange round the edge of the dish as a garnish.

Baked Murray Cod — Australia

4 helpings

450g cod fillets	milk
oil for greasing	1 bay leaf
1 large onion	salt and pepper
2 rashers fat back	browned breadcrumbs
bacon, without rinds	(p375)

Skin the fish. Grease with oil an ovenproof baking dish just large enough to hold the fish. Skin the onion and chop it finely. Chop the bacon, and put into the dish with the onion; put the fish on top. Pour into a saucepan enough milk almost to cover the fish. Add the bay leaf and bring to the boil. Remove the bay leaf and season the milk lightly. Pour it over the fish, leaving the top surface uncovered. Cover the fish thickly with browned breadcrumbs. Bake in a hot oven, 220°C, Gas 7, for about 20 minutes until the fish is tender.

Note Coarser fish, such as tuna fish, can also be cooked in this way.

Kiwi Eggs — New Zealand

4 helpings

450g lean lamb (from	a few drops
the leg)	Worcestershire sauce
1 large onion	4 hard-boiled eggs
4 × 15ml spoons soft	4 × 15ml spoons dry
white breadcrumbs	white breadcrumbs
2 eggs	oil for deep frying
salt and pepper	

Mince the lamb. Skin and grate the onion. Mix together the lamb, onion, soft breadcrumbs, 1 egg, seasoning, and sauce. Divide the mixture into 4 portions. Mould 1 portion round each hard-boiled egg, enclosing it completely. Beat the second egg until liquid. Roll the coated eggs in beaten egg, then coat in dry breadcrumbs, pressing them on firmly. Heat the oil (p303), and fry the eggs until golden-brown, turning as required. Drain on soft kitchen paper and cool completely. When cold, cut in half lengthways.

Serve with salad.

Carpet-bag Steak — Australia

See p491.

Coolgardie Beef Olives — Australia

See p497.

Pavlova (2) — Australia

4–6 helpings

3 egg whites	1 × 5ml spoon lemon
a pinch of salt	juice
100g caster sugar	filling (see p1479)
1 × 15ml spoon	
cornflour	
2 × 15ml spoons	
granulated sugar	

Whisk the egg whites with the salt until stiff and dry. Add the caster sugar gradually, whisking well after each addition until all the sugar is mixed in. Mix the cornflour and granulated sugar together and fold them into the egg whites with the lemon juice.

Using a forcing bag with a large plain nozzle, pipe a layer of meringue in an 18cm circle on a flat sheet of foil. Pipe extra layers of meringue on the edge of the circle to build up the case. Bake in a cool oven, 150°C, Gas 2, for 40 minutes and leave to cool in the oven. When cold, store in an airtight tin (up to 4 days) until required.

To fill the case, spread a layer of whipped cream all over the bottom. Cover with fruit salad, strawberry cream or a layer of the bananas topped with the passion-fruit. Put the remaining cream in a forcing bag with a large star nozzle, and use it to decorate the filling.

Note For Pavlova (1) see p1025.

FILLINGS

To serve, whip 150–200ml double cream and prepare one of the following fillings. Use as indicated
in the method.

1) Drain 1 × 375g can fruit salad thoroughly.

2) Hull and slice 300g strawberries, reserving a
few whole ones for decoration. Marinate them
in a mixture of 1 × 5ml spoon vodka and 1 × 5ml
spoon lemon juice for 1–2 hours. Drain and mix
with half the whipped cream, mashing the fruit
into the cream until it is tinted pink; do not let
the cream become liquid.

3) Slice 4 bananas. Marinate them in lemon juice
for 1–2 hours. Drain 1 × 250g can passion-fruit
and sweeten slightly.

Pumpkin Scones

Makes 12

*300g well-drained
  cooked pumpkin (see
  Note)
25g softened butter
1 × 15ml spoon caster
  sugar
1 × 15ml spoon golden
  syrup **or** honey
1 egg*

*250g self-raising flour
a pinch of salt
1 × 2.5ml spoon ground
  cinnamon
½ × 2.5ml spoon grated
  nutmeg
50–100ml milk
fat for greasing*

Heat the oven to very hot, 230°C, Gas 8. Mash the
pumpkin. Mix the butter with the sugar and syrup
or honey. Beat the egg until liquid and mix it with
the pumpkin. Add this mixture to the butter and
sugar, mixing thoroughly. Sift the flour, salt and
spices into a bowl, then fold into the pumpkin
mixture, alternately with 50ml milk. Add extra
milk, if required, to make a soft but not sticky
dough. Knead the dough lightly and pat it out to
2cm thick. Cut it into rounds with a 5cm cutter. Put
the scones on a lightly greased baking sheet and
bake for 12–15 minutes until golden-brown.

Note Use leftover steamed or baked pumpkin
cooked without liquid.

Australian Damper   Australia

*flour
1 × 5ml spoon baking
  powder to each 100g
  flour (optional)*

*salt
water
fat for greasing*

Mix all the ingredients together, using salt to taste,
and enough water to give a firm dough. Knead
well. Divide into 50g portions and shape into flat
oval cakes. Place on a lightly greased baking sheet,
and bake in a warm oven, 160°C, Gas 3, for 15–25
minutes or until risen and firm.

Serve warm, with plenty of butter.

Note In Australia's early days of settlement, this
legendary substitute for bread was made from unleavened, coarsely bolted flour, salt and water,
and cooked in the ashes of a camp fire. In later
years, baking powder was added to the flour, and
the dampers were cooked in a camp oven. This is
still the practice, and it produces a light, fragrant,
delicious damper.

Tomato and Passion-fruit Jam

Yield 1.5kg (approx)

*1kg ripe tomatoes
10 passion-fruit*

1.25kg sugar

Skin and chop the tomatoes. Open the passion-fruit
and remove the pulp and seeds. Put half the skins
of the passion-fruit into a saucepan and add enough
water to cover them. Boil for about 1 hour or until
the skins are soft inside. Scoop out any remaining
pulp and discard the skins.

Warm the sugar. Put the tomatoes and uncooked
passion-fruit pulp into a clean saucepan. Add the
pulp from the skins and the sugar. Stir over gentle
heat until the sugar has dissolved. Boil rapidly,
stirring occasionally, for about 50 minutes or until
setting point is reached. Test for set after about 30
minutes of rapid boiling. Remove from the heat,
skim, and pour at once into hot jars. Cover loosely
and cool. Seal and label when cold.

Cumquat Marmalade

Yield 4kg (approx)

1.5kg cumquats   juice of 2 lemons
3 litres water   2.5kg sugar

Wash the cumquats and slice them finely, reserving the pips. Put the fruit in a large saucepan and cover with 2.5 litres of the water. Leave overnight. Cover the pips with the rest of the water and leave overnight as well.

Strain the liquid from the pips, add it to the fruit, and boil until the liquid is reduced by half. Add the lemon juice and sugar. Stir well. Heat gently, stirring until the sugar dissolves, then boil rapidly without stirring for $1\frac{1}{2}$ hours or until setting point is reached. Test for set after about 1 hour. Remove from the heat, skim, and pour at once into hot jars. Cover loosely and cool. Seal and label when cold.

VARIATION

Cumquat Conserve

See p1121.

Central Africa

The staple diet of East, Central, and West Africans is porridge, made from maize, millet or other grain. The grain is husked, then pounded coarsely or finely to make the porridge, of which there are many different kinds, ranging from stiff, solid mixtures to thin gruels. *Putu*, or maize meal porridge, is fairly typical of the porridge served as a main dish, with a spicy vegetable or relish for added flavour.

The choice of other foods is largely determined by climatic conditions, availability and economic and cultural factors. In some societies the diet of adult men consists largely of meat, while in others many different vegetables, fruits, nuts, dried fish, poultry, and even insects, are included in the diet.

Putu

(Mealie Meal Porridge)

4–6 helpings

900ml water   1 × 15ml spoon peanut
1 × 5ml spoon salt   butter
250g mealie meal (white
    polenta)

Bring 600ml of the water to the boil with the salt. Make a paste of the mealie meal and the remaining water. Stir into the boiling water. Cook gently for 20 minutes, stirring occasionally. Stir in the peanut butter, and continue stirring until thoroughly blended in. Cook for a further 10 minutes. Turn into a warmed dish, and serve hot, with sugar.

Note Mealie meal (polenta or maize meal) is usually eaten just as it is, or used (as the Italians use pasta) as a base for a highly seasoned food or spicy sauce. The meal is also made into a semi-liquid gruel which is drunk rather than eaten.

Stewed Chicken

6 helpings

1 chicken (2kg approx)   400ml water
50g butter   salt
2 green peppers   2 × 15ml spoons peanut
150g carrots   butter
1 × 10ml spoon curry
    powder

Joint the chicken (pp619–20). Heat the butter in a frying pan and fry the joints until golden-brown on all sides. Remove the chicken joints and transfer them to a stewpan. De-seed the peppers and chop them. Fry them gently in the remaining fat until it is all absorbed. Add them to the chicken. Scrape and slice the carrots, and add them with the curry powder. Pour in the water, cover, bring to simmering point, and simmer gently for 30–45 minutes or until the chicken joints are tender. Add salt to taste, and the peanut butter. Simmer for a further 10 minutes, and serve hot.

Dried Bean Stew

4 helpings

450g butter **or** haricot
  beans
6 thick slices peeled
  sweet potato
200g green peppers

200g boiled cabbage **or**
  spinach
1 onion
2 × 15ml spoons lemon
  juice

Soak the beans overnight in cold water. Next day, cook them in salted water for 2½–3 hours until very soft. Add the sliced sweet potato and cook for 7 minutes or until the potatoes are tender. De-seed and chop the peppers. Add to the pan with the cabbage or spinach. Skin and chop the onion, and mix it in with the lemon juice and extra salt, if required. Simmer for 10 minutes, and serve hot over plain boiled rice.

Note Pieces of cooked meat can be added to the stew, if liked.

Green Leaves with Nuts

4 helpings

750g shredded green
  leaves (tender young
  leaves of pumpkin,
  turnip, beans, spinach,
  cabbage **or** peas)
200ml water

salt
2 onions
2 tomatoes
1¼ × 15ml spoons
  peanut butter

Rinse and chop the leaves. Bring the water to the boil with the salt. Add the leaves to the boiling salted water, cover closely, and simmer gently for 8–10 minutes until tender. Skin and slice the onions and tomatoes, and add them to the pan 5–6 minutes after the leaves. Work the peanut butter to a soft smooth paste, and stir it into the vegetables. Continue simmering for 5 minutes, stirring once or twice. Serve hot.

Pumpkin with Green Leaves

4 helpings

2 × 15ml spoons grated
  mild cheese
450g cooked mashed
  pumpkin
450g cooked green leaves
  (tender young leaves of
  pumpkin, beans,
  spinach, cabbage **or**
  peas)

2 eggs
salt
fat for greasing

Mix 1 × 15ml spoon grated cheese with the pumpkin and the green leaves. Beat the eggs until liquid, and mix them thoroughly into the vegetables. Add salt to taste. Grease a shallow 18cm baking dish and place the mixture in it; smooth and level the surface. Sprinkle with the remaining cheese. Bake in a moderate oven, 180°C, Gas 4, for 12–15 minutes, or until firm and golden-brown on top. Serve hot.

Sweet Potatoes with Nuts

4 helpings

1kg sweet potatoes
1 large onion
800ml water

salt
2 × 15ml spoons peanut
  butter

Peel the sweet potatoes. Cut into slices 2cm thick. Skin and slice the onion. Bring the water to the boil with the salt. Cook the vegetables in the boiling salted water for 10 minutes or until soft. Add the peanut butter, reduce the heat and simmer for a further 10 minutes. Serve hot.

Green Pawpaw Relish

4 helpings

1kg green pawpaw (papaya)	3 medium-sized tomatoes
1 onion	salt
2 × 15ml spoons cooking oil	200ml water
	100g chopped roasted peanuts

Peel the pawpaw and cut into 3cm cubes. Skin and slice the onion. Heat the oil and fry the onion gently until soft. Skin, slice, and add the tomatoes. Mix in the pawpaw cubes and cook for 3 minutes, stirring all the time. Add salt to taste. Stir in the water and simmer for 5 minutes. Add the nuts and simmer for 3 minutes.

Serve hot over Putu (p1480).

China

Colour, aroma, and taste are the three things to bear in mind when preparing a Chinese meal.

Although there are many regional variations and specialities in Chinese cuisine, the cooking methods are generally similar. Food is cut into small pieces and quick fried, or stir fried in either a wok or large frying pan. The cooking time is short, which improves the texture and preserves the nutritional value of the food.

The meal may be served in various ways according to the number of dishes and the occasion. Each place setting consists of a bowl for rice, one for soup, a medium-sized dish, a small dish for condiments, a porcelain spoon, and a pair of chopsticks. The different courses are placed in the centre of the table, and the guests help themselves.

Most of the ingredients in the following recipes are available in large supermarkets, but some such as the *Szechuan* peppercorns are only obtainable in Chinese grocery stores.

Chinese Chicken Stock

Makes 2.5 litres (approx)

1 chicken (2kg approx)	2 thin slices ginger root
3 litres water	1 × 15ml spoon dry sherry
1 small onion	1 × 5ml spoon salt
3 carrots	
½ celery stick	

Cut the chicken into quarters and put in a heavy saucepan. Add the water and bring to the boil. Skim, reduce the heat, cover, and simmer for 1½ hours. Remove the chicken from the stock and use in another recipe.

Skin the onion and cut it into quarters. Peel and slice the carrot and celery thickly, and add all the vegetables to the stock. Cover, and simmer for 20 minutes. Add the ginger root, sherry and salt, and simmer, covered, for another 10 minutes. Strain the stock, cool, and chill for several hours. Skim off the fat which will have risen to the surface.

Won-ton Soup

Makes 20 won-tons (approx)

1.25 litres Chinese chicken stock

Won-tons

100g plain flour	1 × 15ml spoon milk
salt	2 × 15ml spoons oil
1 egg	flour for rolling out

Stuffing

100g fresh spinach	a small pinch of ground ginger
100g minced pork	
2 × 5ml spoons soy sauce	

Garnish
chopped chives

Make the won-tons first. Mix the flour and salt in a bowl, add the egg, and then the milk and oil. Mix to a firm but pliant dough. Roll out on a lightly floured surface until the dough is paper-thin. Cut into 7cm squares, and cover with a cloth until the stuffing is ready.

For the stuffing, pick over and wash the spinach. Put it into a bowl, pour boiling water over it, and leave for 3 minutes. Drain thoroughly and chop. Mix the pork in a bowl with the soy sauce and ground ginger. Add the chopped spinach and mix thoroughly.

Put 1 × 5ml spoon stuffing in the centre of each square of dough. Fold over one side to form a roll. Fold the two ends of the roll over each other and press together.

Bring the chicken stock to the boil in a large saucepan. Add the won-tons, cover, and simmer for 20 minutes over low heat.

Divide the won-tons between 6 soup plates or bowls, and pour the hot soup over them. Sprinkle with chives, and serve.

Note Won-tons are also good when cooked in salted water, browned quickly in butter, and eaten with hot soup poured over them. Chopped spinach can be used instead of chives to garnish the soup.

Fish Ball Soup

6 helpings (20 fish balls approx)

50g ginger root	*1¼ × 15ml spoons*
1 spring onion	*cornflour*
250ml water	*a pinch of salt*
1 × 15ml spoon dry	*25g lard*
sherry	*1.25 litres Chinese*
1 egg white	*chicken stock (p1482)*
225g firm white fish	
fillet	

Garnish
chopped chives **or** *fresh
coriander leaves*

Finely chop the ginger root and spring onion. Sieve into a bowl of 75ml water and stir briskly, or process in an electric blender. Strain the liquid, discarding any solids. Add another 75ml water to the liquid, with the sherry and the egg white, and whisk until the mixture becomes a smooth purée.

Cut the fish into small pieces and put into a bowl. Add 1 × 15ml spoon of the ginger and onion liquid. Add the cornflour, salt and lard, and mix

thoroughly. Add more of the onion and ginger liquid if required to keep the mixture soft. Form the fish mixture into balls about 4cm in diameter and drop them into a large pan of cold water. Heat the water to boiling point. Reduce the heat and simmer until the fish balls rise to the surface. Remove from the water with a perforated spoon. Heat the chicken stock to boiling point and drop in the fish balls.

Serve immediately in a soup tureen and garnish with the chives or coriander.

Note Uncooked fish balls can be stored in sealed jars of cold water and kept in a refrigerator for 2–3 days, if liked.

Basic Sweet and Sour Sauce

Makes 250ml (approx)

50g granulated sugar	*1½ × 15ml spoons*
125ml distilled vinegar	*cornflour*
2 × 15ml spoons soy	*125ml water* or
sauce	*pineapple juice*
25ml dry sherry	
3 × 15ml spoons tomato	
ketchup **or** *2 × 15ml*	
spoons concentrated	
tomato purée	

Place the sugar, vinegar, soy sauce, sherry, and tomato ketchup or purée in a heavy saucepan. Blend the cornflour with the water or pineapple juice. Bring the sauce to the boil, and add the cornflour mixture, stirring all the time until the sauce is thickened.

Fried Fish in Sweet and Sour Sauce

4 helpings

1kg sea bass **or** *other whole fish*	*4 mushrooms*
250ml Basic Sweet and Sour Sauce (p1483) *(see Method)*	*2 carrots*
	1 clove of garlic
	2 thin slices ginger root
1 medium-sized onion	*2 × 15ml spoons oil*
50g canned **or** *fresh bamboo shoots (optional)*	*a good pinch of salt*
	oil for deep frying
	beaten egg for coating
1 small green pepper	*flour* **or** *cornflour for coating*

Have the fish cleaned and scaled and the head and fins removed. Ask the fishmonger to bone the fish, but to leave the two sides of the fish attached at the tail.

Remove the skin and score the fish lightly on both sides. Prepare the sweet and sour sauce but do not thicken it yet with the cornflour. Keep warm. Skin and slice the onion into 2–4cm slices. Drain the bamboo shoots if canned, or wash and slice fresh ones. Remove the membranes and seeds from the pepper and cut into strips 4 × 1cm. Slice the mushrooms 5mm thick. Cut the carrots diagonally into 3cm pieces and parboil them in salted water for 4–5 minutes. Rinse under cold running water until completely cooled. Pat dry.

Crush the garlic and mince the ginger. Heat the oil in a wok or frying pan. Add the salt and stir fry for about 30 seconds. Add the garlic and ginger, and stir fry for 1 minute. Discard the garlic. Add the vegetables, and stir fry to coat with oil. Stir in half the sweet and sour sauce. Cover, and simmer for about 1½ minutes. Draw off the heat.

Heat the oil for deep frying (p303). Brush the fish inside and out with the beaten egg and coat with flour or cornflour. Fry the fish until golden-brown and tender. Remove with a perforated spoon and drain on soft kitchen paper.

Bring the remaining sweet and sour sauce back to the boil and thicken it with cornflour. Place the fish on a serving dish, pour the sauce over it, and serve immediately, with rice.

Fried Rice

4–6 helpings

350g cold cooked rice	*2 spring onions*
3 eggs	*2 × 15ml spoons oil*
a pinch of salt	*2 × 15ml spoons soy sauce*
3 × 2.5ml spoons water	

Separate the grains of rice with chopsticks or a fork. Beat the eggs lightly with the salt and water. Trim the spring onions and cut into 1cm lengths. Heat the oil in a wok or deep frying pan. Add the spring onions and stir fry for 30 seconds. Add the rice and stir fry until heated through and each grain is coated with oil. Pour in the egg mixture and continue stirring until the egg is nearly set. Add the soy sauce and stir until well mixed into the dish. Serve immediately.

Note Any number of variations can be made to this recipe by adding chopped or thinly sliced vegetables, meat or fish, eg peas, sweetcorn, shredded meat or shrimps. A crushed clove of garlic and a pinch of ground ginger will make a more spicy fried rice.

Eight Jewel Fried Rice

4 helpings

350g cold cooked rice	*75g diced lean pork*
4 eggs	*75g diced boiled ham*
a good pinch of salt	*75g diced chicken breast*
1 × 15ml spoon water	*75g peas*
50ml oil	*1 × 15ml spoon soy sauce*
2 spring onions	
75g mushrooms	*50ml Chinese chicken stock* (p1482)
4 peeled prawns	
3 water chestnuts	

Separate the grains of rice with chopsticks or a fork. Beat the eggs, salt, and water lightly in a small bowl. Heat 1 × 15ml spoon oil in a frying pan, and scramble the eggs until just set. Remove the eggs from the pan and put to one side. Cut the spring onions into 1cm pieces. Finely chop the mushrooms and the prawns, and thinly slice the water chestnuts.

Heat the remaining oil in a wok or deep frying pan. Stir fry the spring onions for 30 seconds, then add the diced pork and stir fry for 2 minutes, or until it has lost any trace of pink. Stir fry the ham, chicken, and the mushrooms for 1 minute. Add the prawns and water chestnuts, and stir fry for another minute. Add the rice and stir fry for a minute to coat the grains. Add the peas, soy sauce, chicken stock, and the scrambled eggs. Stir fry gently until the rice is heated through. Serve immediately.

Crab Foo Yung

4 helpings

4 eggs	2 spring onions
a good pinch of salt	6 medium-sized
a pinch of ground black	mushrooms
pepper	3–4 ×15ml spoons oil
1 ×10ml spoon dry	1 ×15ml spoon finely
sherry	chopped chives
100g fresh or canned	
crabmeat	

Beat the eggs lightly in a bowl. Stir in the salt, pepper, and sherry. Shred the crabmeat, removing any horny pieces, and mix well with the eggs. Trim and finely chop the onions, and slice the mushrooms. Heat 1½ ×15ml spoons oil in a wok or frying pan. Stir fry the spring onions, mushrooms, and chives for 2 minutes over moderate heat. Remove the pan from the heat and allow the mixture to cool for a few minutes. Add the egg mixture to the vegetables in the pan.

Heat 2 ×15ml spoons oil in a frying pan. Add the crabmeat and egg mixture, and cook until just set and lightly browned underneath. Transfer the omelet to a serving dish and serve immediately.

Fried Won-ton with Sweet and Sour Sauce

6 helpings

225g plain flour	cornflour for rolling out
1 × 2.5ml spoon salt	oil for deep frying
1 egg	
3–4 ×15ml spoons	
water	

Stuffing
as for Won-ton Soup
(p1482)

Sift the flour and salt together into a bowl. Make a well in the centre and add the egg and 2 × 15ml spoons water. Mix until well blended. Add the remaining water, a little at a time, using only enough to make the dough hold together. Knead the dough until smooth. Cover the bowl with a damp cloth and chill for 45 minutes. Dust a board lightly with cornflour. Divide the dough into 2 pieces and roll out paper-thin. Cut the dough into 8cm squares. Cover with a damp cloth until ready to use.

Wrap the stuffing for Won-ton soup securely in the squares of dough. Heat the oil in a wok or deep frying pan, and add the won-tons, a few at a time. Lower the heat, and fry until golden-brown, turning the won-tons all the time. Remove with a perforated spoon, and drain on soft kitchen paper.

Serve very hot with Basic Sweet and Sour Sauce (p1483) as a side dish.

Note If preferred, the won-tons can be boiled first, dried thoroughly, and then deep fried.

Soft Fried Noodles

4–6 helpings

450g egg noodles, fresh	*2 spring onions*
*or dried (see **Note**)*	*a good pinch of salt*
4 × 15ml spoons oil	*1 × 5ml spoon soy sauce*

If dried, cook the noodles according to the directions on the packet. If fresh, cook them in boiling salted water for 5–8 minutes.

Drain, rinse under cold running water, and mix with 1 × 15ml spoon of the oil. Trim and cut the spring onions into 1cm lengths. Heat the remaining oil in a wok or deep frying pan until moderately hot. Add the spring onions and stir fry for 30 seconds. Add the noodles and stir fry for 2 minutes, separating the noodles with chopsticks. Add the salt and soy sauce, and stir fry for 1 minute until completely heated through and lightly browned.

Note Chinese noodles are made from various mixtures – wheat flour, rice flour, soya flour (which are transparent), and they can include eggs or other flavourings, eg shrimp or chicken, making them more nutritious.

Pasta comes in different widths and thicknesses, usually sold dried in packets with cooking instructions, although it is sometimes available fresh. If Chinese noodles are difficult to obtain, any similar noodles can be substituted.

Egg Roll Pancakes

Makes 14

225g plain flour	*400ml water*
a good pinch of salt	*oil for frying*
2 eggs	

Sift the flour and salt into a bowl. Make a well in the centre and add the eggs. Stir until well blended. Add the water gradually. Continue stirring with a balloon whisk until the batter is smooth.

Pour 1 × 15ml spoon oil into a 20cm frying pan. Heat until the oil is hot. Drain off the excess oil, leaving a thin film. Pour about 2 × 15ml spoons batter into the pan, tilting it in all directions to spread the batter evenly and thinly over the base. Cook over low heat for about 1–2 minutes until firm but not quite brown. Cook on one side only. Brush the frying pan with a little more oil before cooking each pancake. Stack the pancakes on a plate and wrap them in a clean tea-towel to prevent them drying out. Let the pancakes cool completely before filling.

Egg Rolls

Makes 14

egg roll pancakes	*oil for deep frying*
beaten egg	

Filling

225g lean pork	*3 × 15ml spoons oil*
100g peeled shrimps	*a good pinch of salt*
100g bean sprouts	*1 × 15ml spoon soy*
8 spring onions	*sauce*
65g canned or fresh	*1 × 15ml spoon dry*
bamboo shoots	*sherry*
8 water chestnuts	
3 thin slices ginger root	

Prepare the egg roll pancakes; then make the filling. Cut the pork across the grain into slices 5mm thick and then into thin strips. Chop the strips finely with a sharp knife. Chop the shrimps into small pieces. Rinse the bean sprouts under cold running water, then drain. Chop the spring onions, shred the bamboo shoots, slice the water chestnuts finely, and mince the ginger.

Heat 2 × 15ml spoons oil in a wok or deep frying pan, and add the pork. Stir fry until it loses any trace of pink. Add the shrimps, and stir fry for 45 seconds. Remove the shrimps and pork from the pan and add the remaining oil. Heat until very hot. Add the spring onions, bamboo shoots, water chestnuts, and ginger. Stir fry for 1–2 minutes. Add the bean sprouts and stir fry for 45 seconds. Return the pork and shrimps to the pan. Add the salt, soy sauce and sherry, and heat through. Remove the pan from the heat. Drain the mixture in a colander and cool completely. Divide it into 14 small portions.

Place one portion of filling on each pancake, slightly off centre, and fold over the top of the pancake. Brush two ends with a little of the beaten egg, and tuck them in neatly to enclose the filling from three sides. Brush the remaining open side with more of the egg, and roll the filling towards it to enclose the filling completely and form a roll. Place on a plate, sealed edge down.

Heat the oil (p303) and fry the egg rolls for 3–4 minutes, turning the rolls once to brown them evenly on all sides. Drain, and serve hot.

Chicken Chow Mein

4 helpings

1 small green pepper	2 ×15ml spoons soy
1 small red pepper	sauce
1 small onion	pepper
50g butter	1 ×198g can mushrooms
2 sticks celery	250g cooked chicken
2 ×15ml spoons flour	breasts
250ml Chinese chicken	250g broad Chinese
stock (p1482)	noodles
	oil for shallow frying

Halve the peppers, remove the membranes and seeds, and cut into thin strips. Blanch for 5 minutes in boiling water, then drain. Skin and dice the onion. Melt most of the butter in a frying pan, add the onion and fry lightly. Cut the celery into pieces and add to the frying pan. Sprinkle the flour over the onion and celery. Heat the chicken stock and stir into the pan. Cook until the vegetables are just tender. Season with soy sauce and pepper. Drain the mushrooms. Cut the chicken into neat pieces and add with the pepper strips and mushrooms to the pan. Cover, and simmer gently for 15 minutes.

Meanwhile, cook the noodles for 15 minutes in 1.5 litres lightly salted water. Drain, and rinse with cold water. Put one-third of the noodles to one side, add the remaining butter to the rest, and put into a serving dish. Cover, and keep warm.

Heat the oil for frying. Drain the remaining noodles well, cut into pieces and fry until golden. Drain on soft kitchen paper. Put the chicken pieces and the sauce on the buttered noodles. Alternatively, serve the chicken in its sauce and the garnished buttered noodles separately.

Cantonese Pork

4–6 helpings

1kg lean pork	2 ×15ml spoons olive oil

Marinade

1 clove of garlic	2 ×10ml spoons caster
1 ×15ml spoon soy	sugar
sauce	a pinch of salt
2 ×15ml spoons Chinese	1 ×15ml spoon dry
chicken stock (p1482)	sherry
3 ×15ml spoons clear	
honey	

Wipe the pork with soft kitchen paper and cut into long thin strips.

Make the marinade in a large bowl. Crush the garlic, and mix together with the soy sauce, chicken stock, 1 ×15ml spoon of the honey, the sugar, and sherry.

Pour the marinade over the pork and rub it in well. Cover the bowl and leave to stand for 1 hour. Drain the pork, rub in the oil, and transfer to a heatproof dish. Baste the meat with the marinade, leave uncovered, and bake in a fairly hot oven, 200°C, Gas 6, for 20 minutes. Remove the pork from the oven, brush with the rest of the honey and return to the oven for another 15 minutes.

Serve from the dish with rice, or slice the meat and arrange on a warmed dish with any seasonal vegetable.

Sweet and Sour Pork

4 helpings

600g lean pork

Marinade
1 egg white	*2 × 15ml spoons dry*
35g cornflour	*sherry*
2 × 15ml spoons soy	*salt and pepper*
sauce	

Batter
1 egg	*50ml light beer*
3 × 15ml spoons plain	*a pinch of salt*
flour	*oil for deep frying*
3 × 15ml spoons	
cornflour	

Sauce
1 small red pepper	*3 × 15ml spoons tomato*
1 small green pepper	*ketchup*
1 × 200g can bamboo	*3 × 15ml spoons soy*
shoots	*sauce*
3 rings canned pineapple	*50g caster sugar*
2 × 15ml spoons oil	*salt*
500ml Chinese chicken	*2 × 15ml spoons*
stock (p1482)	*cornflour*
2 × 15ml spoons	
distilled vinegar	

Cut the meat into 2cm cubes. Make the marinade. Beat the egg white in a bowl with the cornflour. Mix in the soy sauce, sherry, and salt and pepper. Marinate the meat cubes for 15 minutes, turning frequently. Remove from the marinade and drain well.

To make the batter, whisk the egg, flour, cornflour, beer and salt in a bowl with a balloon whisk. Heat the oil (p303). Dip the meat cubes into the batter, and fry a few at a time until golden-brown. Remove the meat with a perforated spoon and keep warm until it has all been fried.

Make the sauce. Wash the peppers, halve, deseed, and cut them into thin strips. Drain the bamboo shoots and cut into 1 × 3cm strips. Drain the pineapple rings and cut into small pieces. Heat the oil in a pan, add the peppers, bamboo shoots and pineapple, and fry for 2 minutes, stirring all the time. Add the chicken stock, vinegar, tomato ketchup and soy sauce, and season with sugar and salt. Simmer for 5 minutes. Mix the cornflour to a smooth paste with a little cold water, and add to the sauce, stirring until it thickens. Bring the sauce back to the boil, and pour it over the pieces of meat. Serve at once, with rice or noodles.

Fried Pork with Noodles

4–6 helpings

250g fillet of pork	*1 leek (150g approx)*
2 × 15ml spoons soy	*1 × 200g can bamboo*
sauce	*shoots*
4 × 15ml spoons rice	*150g cooked ham*
*wine **or** dry sherry*	*salt*
2 litres water	*6 × 15ml spoons soy*
250g noodles	*sauce*
100ml groundnut oil	*a pinch of ground ginger*
5 dried mushrooms	*1 × 5ml spoon paprika*

Slice the pork fillet thinly against the grain of the meat. Cut it into strips and place in a bowl. Mix together the soy sauce and 2 × 15ml spoons of the rice wine or sherry, and pour it over the meat. Use it to marinate the meat, turning the meat from time to time while preparing the other ingredients.

Boil the water in a pan, and cook the noodles at a fast boil for 3 to 4 minutes. They should be tender but not quite cooked. Rinse briefly in a sieve under cold water, then drain. Mix 1 × 10ml spoon groundnut oil into the noodles and keep them warm.

Break up the dried mushrooms slightly, pour boiling water over them, and soak for 10 minutes. Clean the leek, and cut it into halves or quarters according to its thickness, then into strips 3cm long. Drain the bamboo shoots, and cut into strips 3cm long. Cut the ham into strips of the same size.

Heat 3 × 15ml spoons groundnut oil in a large frying pan. Take the strips of pork out of the marinade and put into the hot oil. (Reserve the marinade.) Cook briefly, stirring so that the meat does not stick. Add the leek, bamboo shoots, and ham. Drain, and add the mushrooms; stir fry for 4 minutes. Pour in the marinade and bring to the boil. Remove from the heat at once, transfer to another pan or dish, and keep warm.

Clean the frying pan, add the remaining 3 × 15ml spoons oil, and fry the noodles for 10 minutes. Season slightly with salt. Stir together the soy sauce, remaining rice wine or sherry, ginger and paprika, pour it over the noodles, mix together, and cook for a minute or so longer.

Arrange the fried noodles on a warmed dish, and place the meat and vegetables around them.

Peking Duck

4 helpings

1 roasting duck (2.5kg approx)	2.25 litres water
2 bunches spring onions	2 × 15ml spoons honey
4 pieces stem ginger in syrup	

Sauce

1 × 15ml spoon water	50ml soy sauce
1 × 15ml spoon sesame seed oil	2 × 10ml spoons sugar

Pancakes

500g plain flour	flour for kneading
a pinch of salt	2 × 5ml spoons sesame seed oil
125ml boiling water	

Wash the duck in cold water, and pat dry with soft kitchen paper, both inside and out. Tie a string round the duck's neck and hang it in a cool, airy place to dry for 10 hours.

Halve one bunch of spring onions and cut into medium-sized pieces. Chop the second bunch and reserve. Slice the ginger finely. Put the onions into a large saucepan with 2 litres of the water, the honey and sliced ginger, and bring to the boil. Put the duck into the boiling liquid for 10 minutes, turning it occasionally to make sure it is entirely covered. Remove from the pan and hang in a cool airy place for 3 hours.

Meanwhile, make the sauce. Whisk the ingredients together in a small pan. Heat until the sugar has dissolved, then leave to cool.

Bring the remaining water to the boil. Put the duck in a roasting pan, breast upwards, add the hot water and roast the duck in a fairly hot oven, 200°C, Gas 6, for 2 hours. After 1 hour, turn the duck and lower the heat to moderate, 180°C, Gas 4. Roast for another 30 minutes. Finally, turn the heat up again and finish roasting at fairly hot, 200°C, Gas 6, for another 30 minutes.

Take the duck out of the oven, remove the crisp skin and arrange it on a serving dish. Carve the meat and arrange it on a separate serving dish. Reheat the sauce, and serve in a bowl.

During the last 15 minutes of cooking time, prepare the pancakes. Mix the flour and salt with the boiling water until a soft mixture is obtained. Turn it on to a floured surface and knead until it becomes rubbery. Roll out the dough to 1cm thickness, and cut out 6cm rounds. Sandwich the rounds together and between each of them brush a little of the sesame seed oil. Carefully roll out each set of rounds to a diameter of 15cm. Heat the remaining sesame seed oil in a large frying pan and cook each set until the surface bubbles. Turn, and cook the other side for 5–10 seconds. Separate the pancakes and brush the sauce on to the moist side.

Serve the pancakes with the dishes of meat, skin, and remaining sauce. A piece of crisp skin, duck meat, and a little chopped spring onion is placed on each pancake, which is rolled up and eaten in the fingers.

Note The special feature of Peking Duck is the crisp, tender skin, which is served separately with the pancakes. Peking Duck must be roasted neither at too high a heat, or the skin will crumple, become thin and tear, nor at too low a heat, or the skin will not be crisp.

Crispy Szechuan Duck

4 helpings

1 × 5ml spoon Szechuan peppercorns **or** *black peppercorns*	*1 × 15ml spoon soy sauce*
2 sticks cinnamon	*2 egg whites*
2 cloves star anise	*35g cornflour*
25g salt	*1 × 15ml spoon medium-sweet sherry* **or** *sweet white wine*
1 roasting duck (2.5kg approx)	
1 × 2cm piece ginger root	*a pinch of salt*
1 spring onion	*a pinch of granulated sugar*
flour for dredging	*oil for shallow frying*

Garnish (optional)

spring onions   *watercress*

In a dry frying pan, toast the peppercorns, cinnamon, and star anise with the salt. Crush the mixture coarsely. Rub the mixture on both the inside and outside of the duck. Peel the ginger and trim the spring onion. Place the ginger and the spring onion inside the duck and leave to stand overnight.

Dredge the whole duck with flour and place in a heatproof dish in the top of a steamer. Steam for 1½–2 hours until the duck is tender and a fork easily penetrates the flesh. Leave to cool and then rub the skin all over with the soy sauce. If preparing the duck in advance, it can be wrapped in foil at this point, and stored in a refrigerator for 2–3 days.

When ready to cook, combine the egg whites, cornflour, sherry or wine, salt and sugar, and mix to a smooth paste. Coat the outside of the duck with this mixture and leave to stand for 30–45 minutes.

Heat the oil in a wok or deep frying pan until very hot and put in the duck, on its back. Using plenty of hot oil, baste the duck constantly until it is crisp and golden-brown. Garnish with spring onions and watercress, if liked.

Note Szechuan peppercorns and star anise are obtainable from Chinese stores.

Eastern Europe

Eastern Europe is taken to be those countries lying between Germany and Russia, plus the Balkans. These are Poland, Czechoslovakia, Hungary, Rumania, Yugoslavia, Albania, and Bulgaria.

The two dominant influences in their cuisine are the Austrian tradition which has led to an elaborate approach to cooking with many Western-European influences, and the Turkish legacy which has been more basic, with the charcoal grill as its most striking feature.

The picture is far more complex and varied according to each individual national cuisine, local traditions, religious and environmental influences. In this context it is noteworthy that in the mountainous Balkans, pork is rarely used, whereas lamb is common. In Hungary on the other hand, where the pig is better adapted to wooded and watered areas, pork is the national meat and lamb is despised. Religion too has left its mark, notably in the eating of freshwater fish, particularly carp, among the Roman Catholic Czechs and Poles, or the avoidance of pork among Moslem Yugoslavs and Albanians.

The imperial and bourgeois cuisines of Vienna, Prague, Budapest, and Warsaw have been highly influential in establishing gastronomic standards. The peasant influence, however, remains strong, with many traditional dishes using cabbage and dumplings; among Czechs and Poles, ceps mushrooms are very popular.

Gribi v Smetane   Poland
(Mushrooms with Soured Cream)

4 helpings

600g mushrooms	*salt and pepper*
1 large onion	*½ × 2.5ml spoon paprika*
75g butter	
2 × 15ml spoons milk	*350ml soured cream*

Remove the mushroom stalks and slice the caps. Skin and chop the onion. Melt 50g of the butter, add the chopped onion, and fry until the pieces begin to brown. Stir in the milk. Bring to the boil and stir in the mushrooms. Season well with salt, pepper, and paprika. Reduce the heat to simmering point and add 300ml of the cream. Cook gently just below boiling point for 10–15 minutes until the mushrooms are tender.

Serve hot with the remaining cream poured over, and top with the rest of the butter cut into flakes or curls.

Creier cu Ciuperci
Rumania
(Brains with Mushrooms)

6 helpings

1 set of calf's brains **or**	50g butter
2 sets lamb's brains	125ml medium-dry
500g fresh mushrooms	white wine
1 large onion	salt and pepper

Soak the brains in lightly salted water for 30 minutes to remove all traces of blood. Cut off any membranes and wash thoroughly. Heat a pan of lightly salted water to boiling point, add the brains and cook gently for 15 minutes.

Prepare the mushrooms and slice so that the cap and the stem are whole. Skin and finely chop the onion. Melt the butter in a large frying pan and fry the mushrooms for 5 minutes, stirring occasionally. Add the onions and fry together for another minute until lightly glazed. Pour in the wine and season to taste, stirring occasionally. Cover, and simmer for 10 minutes.

Remove the brains with a sieve or large perforated spoon, and drain. Slice finely to about the same thickness as the mushrooms. Add the brains to the vegetables and continue to simmer for 5 minutes until they have reached the same temperature as the mushrooms and onions. Re-season if required. Serve hot as a starter.

Hideg Almaleves
Hungary
(Cold Apple Soup)

6–8 helpings

500g tart apples	500ml milk
$\frac{1}{2}$ lemon	1 × 142ml carton single
a pinch of salt	cream **or** soured cream
2 whole cloves	1 × 15ml spoon flour
a pinch of cinnamon	1 × 15ml spoon brandy
75g caster sugar	**or** Kirsch
500ml medium-dry	
white wine **or** cider	

Peel, core, and finely slice the apples. Place them in a large saucepan over low heat with enough water to cover. Removing only the pips, add the entire lemon to the apples, together with the salt, cloves, cinnamon, and sugar. Stir until blended, and simmer gently for 40 minutes until the apples are tender.

Gradually stir in the wine or cider until blended, then pour in the milk, stirring gently. Simmer over low heat for 5 minutes.

In a separate bowl, whisk together the cream and flour until stiff. Blend into the soup, a little at a time, stirring well to keep the mixture smooth. Heat through for 5 minutes, stirring occasionally, and re-season if required. Remove from the heat and allow to cool for 2 hours. Cover, and chill for 4–5 hours. Just before serving, stir in the brandy or Kirsch.

Bigos
Poland

(Polish Goulash)

6–8 helpings

1kg sauerkraut
125g any boned cut of
   poultry, pork, game,
   bacon **or** gammon
150g smoked pork
   sausages
1 large onion
50g lard
1 × 15ml spoon flour
2 × 15ml spoons
   concentrated tomato
   purée

75ml vodka
75ml medium-dry white
   wine
salt and pepper
1 large green apple
250ml chicken **or** beef
   stock
25g butter

Place the sauerkraut in a sieve or colander and rinse in cold water to wash off the vinegar. Put into a saucepan with enough water to cover, and simmer for 20–30 minutes until tender. Drain, and put to one side.

Wipe the meat, trim off any excess fat, and cut into 2cm cubes. Slice the sausages into pieces 1cm thick. Skin and slice the onion. Melt half the lard in a large frying pan and brown the onion until golden. Add a little of the flour and stir until the mixture is totally blended. Stir in the tomato purée, then the vodka and the wine. Reduce the heat and simmer for 5 minutes. Add all the meats, season to taste, and mix together well. Cover with a tight-fitting lid and cook for 1 hour over low heat until the meats are tender.

Peel, core, and cut the apple into 3–4cm cubes. Put a bed of half the sauerkraut in a large oven-proof dish, followed by a layer of all the meats. Sprinkle with the apple cubes and place a final layer of the remaining sauerkraut on top. Heat the stock and pour half of it over the sauerkraut. Dot with flakes of butter and cook uncovered in a moderate oven, 180°C, Gas 4, for 2 hours.

Ten minutes before the end of cooking time, melt the remaining lard in a frying pan, add the rest of the flour and stir over low heat for 2–3 minutes, without allowing the mixture to colour. Draw the pan off the heat and gradually add the remaining stock, stirring all the time. Return to moderate heat and stir well until the sauce (roux) thickens and is boiling. Simmer for 1–2 minutes, beating briskly. Season to taste.

Pour the roux over the sauerkraut and blend well. Return the dish to the oven and cook uncovered for a further 30 minutes until the top is crisp and golden-brown. Serve very hot.

Note There are many ways of preparing what is in effect Poland's national dish. The essence of all of them is that they should consist of a mixture of sauerkraut and smoked sausage; the other ingredients may be varied.

Marhagulyás
Hungary

(Beef Goulash)

6 helpings

1 kg stewing steak
1 large onion
1 × 5ml spoon salt

1 × 15ml spoon paprika
500g potatoes

Wipe the meat, trim off any excess fat, and cut into 3cm cubes. Skin and slice the onion and place in a large saucepan with the meat cubes. Pour in enough water to cover, and heat to boiling point. Add the salt and one-third of the paprika. Reduce the heat and simmer for 15 minutes.

Meanwhile, peel the potatoes. Add them to the pan and top up with more water. Simmer for 2 hours, keeping the meat and potatoes covered with water at all times. Add the rest of the paprika 10 minutes before the stew has finished cooking, as the first flavour of paprika will have weakened. The meat should be tender when fully cooked. The gravy will be dark and very liquid.

Note *Gulyás*, known in the English-speaking world as 'goulash', is as much a technique as a recipe. It is a very simple and straightforward method of preparing meat, or, indeed, fish.

The word *gulyás* means herdsman, and his method of cooking is ideally adapted to preparing food while looking after cattle or sheep.

Djuvéc   Yugoslavia
(Serbian Rice Hash)

6 helpings

1 large aubergine	75g butter
(450g approx)	250g long-grain rice
2 × 15ml spoons salt	500g ripe tomatoes
1kg braising beef **or**	a pinch of black pepper
pork	a pinch of paprika
1 large onion	water **or** stock as
1 large green pepper	required

Cut the aubergine into 2cm cubes. Lay them on a large dish, sprinkle with some of the salt, and leave for 1 hour; drain, rinse, and dry thoroughly. Wipe the meat, trim off any excess fat, and cut into 3cm cubes. Skin and finely slice the onion. Slice the pepper into thin rounds, discarding the membrane and seeds.

Melt two-thirds of the butter in a large frying pan and fry the onions until golden. Sear the meat on all sides to seal in the juices. Transfer the meat and onions to an ovenproof dish.

Melt a small amount of butter in the frying pan and brown the aubergine cubes. Add them to the meat and onions. Melt the rest of the butter in the pan and brown the rice for 5 minutes. Slice the tomatoes thinly and stir into the rice. Continue stirring until the tomatoes are reduced to a pulp. Season to taste with salt, pepper, and paprika. Add the green pepper to the mixture, which should be fairly liquid. If not, add water or stock to cover. Cover the dish and cook in a warm oven, 160°C, Gas 3, for 2 hours. Remove the lid for the last 20 minutes of the cooking time, and turn up the heat to hot, 220°C, Gas 7, to brown the top. Serve hot as a main course.

Spinaq Top   Albania
(Spinach Dumplings)

6 helpings

500g fresh **or** frozen	salt and pepper
spinach	25g flour
5 white bread rolls	flour for dusting
500ml milk	1.5 litres stock **or** water
75g butter	1 × 15ml spoon grated
2 × 5ml spoons finely	hard cheese
chopped parsley	

Prepare and cook the spinach; drain thoroughly, and mince finely. Drain again and put to one side. Cut the rolls into quarters and soak in the milk for 5 minutes, or until they have absorbed as much milk as possible without crumbling. Remove the rolls with a perforated spoon, drain thoroughly, and squeeze dry with soft kitchen paper. Rub through a sieve until mushy.

Melt 25g of the butter in a large frying pan. Stir in the roll mixture and the parsley. Sauté for 3–5 minutes, and season to taste. Transfer to a large mixing bowl and put to one side.

Make a light roux by melting 25g of the butter in the pan, adding the flour and stirring over low heat for 2–3 minutes, without allowing the mixture to colour. Draw the pan from the heat and gradually add the spinach, stirring all the time. Return to moderate heat and stir until heated through. Add the spinach to the rolls and mix together well. With floured hands, roll the mixture into dumplings about the size and shape of a walnut.

Heat the stock or water to boiling point in a large pan, and gently drop in the dumplings. Reduce the heat and simmer, stirring occasionally to keep the dumplings from sticking to the bottom of the pan. The dumplings are done when they rise to the surface.

Meanwhile, melt the rest of the butter in a small pan and remove from the heat.

Remove the dumplings with a perforated spoon and drain thoroughly. Put them into a large serving dish, sprinkle with grated cheese and pour over the melted butter. Serve immediately as a light, main course.

Liptavský Syr   Czechoslovakia
(Liptauer Cheese)

10–12 helpings

1 × 15ml spoon capers
250g plain cottage cheese
100g softened butter
1 × 142ml carton soured
  cream
1 × 5ml spoon paprika

1 × 5ml spoon made
  English mustard
1 × 5ml spoon caraway
  seeds
salt and pepper

Garnish (optional)
1 × 15ml spoon chopped
  parsley

Finely chop the capers and blend all the ingredients together with a wooden spoon for 10–12 minutes, or process in an electric blender. The mixture will be smooth, thick, and of a pale, brick red colour. Cover, and chill for 3 hours. Garnish, if liked, with the parsley.

    Liptavský Syr is customarily served as a starter with black rye bread and beer.

Dzhuli na Funa   Bulgaria
(Baked Quinces)

6–8 helpings

1kg quinces **or** *1 quince*
  per person
100g shelled walnuts
50g caster sugar

1 × 5ml spoon ground
  cinnamon
150g butter
oil for greasing

Wash the quinces under cold water and leave to drain dry. Remove the stems. Cut the top off each quince. Reserve both cap and base. Pick out and discard the seeds, leaving the pulp.

    Chop the walnuts to a coarse texture, or process in an electric blender. Mix together thoroughly with the sugar and cinnamon. Fill each quince with the mixture. Put a knob of butter on each and replace the caps. Place upright on a lightly oiled baking tin, and bake in a fairly hot oven, 200°C, Gas 6, for 25 minutes. Cool completely and chill for 2 hours. Serve cold as a dessert.

Aranygaluska Borsodoval   Hungary
(Baked Golden Dumplings with Wine Sauce)

8 helpings

400g flour
a pinch of salt
2 × 15ml spoons caster
  sugar
100g softened butter
400ml milk
15g fresh yeast **or**
  1 × 10ml spoon dried
  yeast

3 egg yolks
flour for rolling out
fat for greasing
100g apricot jam
100g ground walnuts

Sauce
2 eggs
50g caster sugar
1 × 5ml spoon flour

250ml medium-sweet
  white wine

Sift together the flour, salt, and sugar into a large bowl. Rub in half the softened butter. Warm one-third of the milk until hand-hot, and blend in the fresh yeast or reconstitute the dried yeast (p1154). Pour the yeast mixture, yolks, and the rest of the milk into the flour mixture, and mix to a soft dough. Turn on to a floured surface and knead for about 10 minutes or until the dough is smooth, elastic, and no longer sticky. Place in a large, lightly oiled polythene bag and leave in a warm place for 1 hour, or until the dough has doubled in size.

    Roll out the dough on a floured surface to about 1cm thickness. Cut out circles with a 5cm pastry cutter. Melt the remaining butter and dip the dough circles in it until completely coated. Place them about 3cm apart in a lightly greased 25cm cake tin. Brush the tops with a layer of jam, and sprinkle with walnuts. Place the cake tin in the polythene bag and leave in a warm place for about 30 minutes, or until the circles have joined together and are light and puffy. Bake in a moderate oven, 180°C, Gas 4, for 35 minutes, until golden-brown.

    Prepare the sauce 5 minutes before the dumplings are done. Whisk together the eggs, sugar, and flour in a large mixing bowl. When the mixture has thickened, pour into a double boiler over heat and slowly add the wine. Continue whisking until the sauce is light and fluffy. Pour immediately over the dumplings and serve hot.

France

The country that produced many of the renowned chefs who perfected an international cuisine of the Western World, fills her own kitchens with the tempting aromas of this distinctive cookery.

The French as a nation take an informed interest in the preparation and presentation of food. The great classic sauces provide the cornerstone of French cookery and are used to enhance ordinary as well as exotic foods with many subtle, blended flavours.

Because each region of this diverse country with its varied climates and products boasts its own unique dishes, French cookery can be considered more regional than national. The names of these specialities often reflect a particular region; Boeuf Bourguignonne, for example, or Salade Niçoise. The dishes vary from region to region, and a recipe prepared in Normandy will be quite unlike one prepared in the Loire district using the same basic ingredients.

The diversity typifying French recipes is also characteristic of the numerous cheeses and wines of France which are essential to the meal itself. Camembert, Chèvre and Brie, like Burgundy, Bordeaux and Champagne – are particular to a region, yet popular everywhere.

Escargots de Bourgogne
(Snails in Garlic Butter)

4 helpings

24 canned snails
  (1 × 125g can)
4 cloves garlic **or** to
  taste
4 × 15ml spoons finely
  chopped shallots
4 × 15ml spoons dry
  white wine
250g butter

3–4 × 15ml spoons
  chopped parsley **or** to
  taste
juice of $\frac{1}{2}$ lemon
salt and freshly ground
  black pepper
2 × 15ml spoons pastis
  (optional)

Open the snails and drain in a nylon sieve or strainer. Chop the garlic finely. Simmer the shallots and garlic in the wine until the liquid has evaporated. Beat the wine mixture into the butter with the parsley, lemon juice, seasoning, and pastis, if used. Put 1 snail in each snail shell, and cover it thickly with flavoured butter (any butter not used can be stored in a refrigerator for use later). Put the shells, open side up, in a snail plate or on a bed of coarse salt, and heat in a fairly hot oven, 200°C, Gas 6, for 5–6 minutes until the butter is melted and very hot. Serve immediately.

Note If more convenient, the snails can be heated in a baking tray designed for petits fours. These trays contain 12 or 24 indentations the same shape as tartlet or bun tins.

Soupe à l'Oignon Gratinée
(French Onion Soup)

6 helpings

50g fat bacon
6 medium-sized onions
  (600g approx)
1 × 2.5ml spoon French
  mustard
750ml consommé (p335)
125ml dry white wine **or**
  cider

salt and pepper
6 slices French bread
50g Gruyère **or**
  Parmesan cheese
butter

Chop the bacon and heat it gently in a deep saucepan until the fat runs freely. Skin the onions and slice them thinly. Add to the bacon fat and fry slowly until golden-brown. Stir in the mustard, consommé, and wine or cider. Heat to boiling point and then simmer gently for 1 hour, or until the onions are quite soft. Season to taste. Toast the bread. Grate the cheese. Butter the toast and spread with the grated cheese. Pour the soup into individual ovenproof soup bowls, float a slice of toast on each, and brown the cheese under the grill or in a very hot oven.

Pot-au-feu

6 helpings of broth and meat plus 750ml stock

*1kg brisket **or** boned top*	*2 small turnips*
*ribs **or** thick flank of*	*(100g approx)*
beef	*1 small parsnip*
200g shin of beef	*(75g approx)*
2 × 5ml spoons salt	*2 leeks (200g approx)*
6 black peppercorns	*¼ small cabbage*
2 litres water	*(100g approx)*
bouquet garni	*2 tomatoes*
4 cloves	*(100g approx)*
4 medium-sized onions	*400g medium-sized*
(400g approx)	*potatoes (optional)*
4 medium-sized carrots	*salt and pepper*
(200g approx)	*6 slices French bread*

Wipe the meat and trim off any excess fat. Tie the meat into a neat shape. Chop the shin of beef into small pieces. Put the meats into a large pan, add the salt, peppercorns and water, and soak for 30 minutes. Heat slowly to boiling point, add the bouquet garni, reduce the heat, and simmer very gently for 1 hour, skimming the surface occasionally.

Meanwhile, prepare the vegetables. Press a clove into each onion. Cut the carrots, turnips, parsnip and leeks into large pieces, and add to the broth with the whole onions. Bring back to simmering point, half cover, and simmer gently for a further 2½ hours, skimming from time to time. Remove the core from the cabbage and shred it finely. Skin, deseed, and chop the tomatoes into small pieces. Add the cabbage and tomatoes to the broth. Peel and add the potatoes, if used, to serve with the meat. Bring back to simmering point, and simmer for a further 30 minutes.

Serve the meat with the potatoes and some of the large pieces of vegetable round it; keep this covered and hot. Discard any bones and the bouquet garni from the broth. Measure 1 litre of the broth into a clean pan. Cut 5mm cubes from the carrot, leek, parsnip and turnip, and put 1 × 15ml spoon of each into the 1 litre broth, and re-heat it. Season to taste. Toast the slices of French bread until golden. Float them in the broth. Serve as a first course, followed by the meat and vegetables.

Quiche Lorraine

(Bacon and Cream Tart)

4–6 helpings

shortcrust pastry (p1249)	*300ml single cream*
using 125g flour	*1 × 2.5ml spoon salt*
flour for rolling out	*a grinding of black*
6 rashers streaky bacon,	*pepper*
without rinds	*a pinch of grated nutmeg*
3 eggs	*25g butter*

Roll out the pastry on a lightly floured surface. Use it to line an 18cm flan ring placed on a baking sheet. Bake blind for 10 minutes until the rim of the pastry is slightly browned but the base still soft.

Cut the bacon rashers in strips 2cm × 5mm. Blanch in boiling water for 3 minutes. Drain well and scatter the strips over the pastry base. Press in lightly. Beat together the eggs, cream, seasoning, and nutmeg until fully mixed. Pour the mixture into the shell, and dot with flakes of butter. Bake in a fairly hot oven, 190°C, Gas 5, for 30 minutes. Serve at once.

Quiche aux Poireaux

(Leek Tart)

8 helpings

8 small leeks	*150ml foundation white*
shortcrust pastry	*sauce (coating*
(p1249) using 125g	*consistency) (p692)*
flour	*salt and pepper*
flour for rolling out	*grated nutmeg*
2 eggs	*25g Gruyère cheese*

Wash and trim the leeks. Use the white parts only. Tie them into 2 bundles with string. Bring a pan of salted water to boiling point, put in the leeks, and cook at a gentle boil for 10 minutes. Drain, and squeeze as dry as possible. Slice the leeks thickly.

Roll out the pastry 5mm thick on a lightly floured surface. Use it to line an 18cm flan ring placed on a baking sheet. Bake blind for 15 minutes. Remove the paper and dry filling, and bake for a further 5 minutes. Cool.

Beat together the eggs and white sauce; season with salt, pepper, and nutmeg. Grate the cheese and blend in half. Put a layer of flavoured sauce in the cooled flan shell, cover with the leeks, then with the remaining sauce. Sprinkle with the rest of the cheese. Bake in a fairly hot oven, 190°C, Gas 5, for 20 minutes or until golden on top.

Filets de Cabillaud Bonne-femme
(Baked Cod Fillets)

4 helpings

4 cod fillets (250g each approx)	150g button mushrooms
25g shallots **or** onion	salt and pepper
25g butter	bouquet garni
2 ×15ml spoons cooking oil	3 ×15ml spoons chopped parsley
1 ×15ml spoon flour	1 ×15ml spoon white wine vinegar
150ml dry white wine	1 ×10ml spoon lemon juice
150ml fish stock (p330)	
butter for greasing	

Skin the fish fillets neatly. Skin the shallots or onion and chop finely. Melt the butter with the oil in a saucepan, and cook the shallot or onion gently until soft but not coloured. Sprinkle in the flour and cook for 1 minute. Add the wine and stock gradually, stirring all the time, and simmer for about 8 minutes to obtain a slightly thickened sauce.

Grease an ovenproof baking dish which will hold the fillets in one overlapping layer. Lay the fillets in the dish. Slice the mushrooms and lay them on top. Season the sauce to taste, and pour it over the fish and mushrooms. Put the bouquet garni into the dish, and tuck it down between the fillets. Cover the dish closely with a lid or foil, and bake in a fairly hot oven, 190°C, Gas 5, for 15–20 minutes, or until the fillets are tender. Sprinkle with parsley, then with the vinegar and lemon juice. Serve from the dish.

Steak Tartare

4 helpings

400–600g lean fillet **or** rump steak **or** topside	1 red **or** green pepper (optional)
salt and freshly ground black pepper	4 ×15ml spoon capers
4 small onions **or** 6 shallots	3 ×15ml spoons chopped parsley
2 cloves garlic (optional)	4 egg yolks (in half shells)

Garnish

8 anchovy fillets (optional)	paprika

Mince the meat finely and season very well. Skin the onions or shallots and the garlic, if used, and chop together. De-seed and chop the pepper, if used. Chop the capers.

Form the meat into 4 thick patties and put each on a separate plate. Arrange small mounds of the onion or shallot mixture, the pepper, capers, and parsley around the meat. Make a hollow in the centre of each patty, and put in it the egg yolk, still in the half shell. Alternatively, cross two anchovy fillets over each yolk if not using the shells. Sprinkle with paprika. Hand oil and vinegar separately, if used.

At the table, the ingredients are mixed together with a fork.

Boeuf Bourguignonne

4–6 helpings

600g chuck steak	3 × 15ml spoons oil
250ml red wine	12 small onions **or**
$\frac{1}{2}$ × 2.5ml spoon black	shallots
pepper	12 button mushrooms
1 × 2.5ml spoon salt	25g flour
bouquet garni	salt and pepper
1 small onion	250ml beef stock
1 small carrot	(approx)
2 cloves garlic	
2 rashers bacon, without	
rinds	

Garnish

sippets of fried bread   chopped parsley

Wipe the steak and cut it into 2cm cubes. Put it in a basin, pour the wine over it, and add the pepper, salt, and bouquet garni. Prepare and finely slice the onion and carrot. Skin and crush the garlic. Add these to the meat and wine, cover, and leave to marinate for about 6 hours.

Cut the bacon into small pieces. Heat most of the oil in a frying pan, add the bacon, and fry lightly, then remove and put to one side. Fry the onions or shallots and the mushrooms in the oil for 3–4 minutes, then remove and put to one side. Drain the meat, reserving the marinade, and pat dry on soft kitchen paper. Season the flour with salt and pepper and coat the meat in the flour. Add a little more oil to the frying pan and fry the meat until sealed all over. Put into a 1.5 litre ovenproof casserole. Stir in the bacon, onions, and mushrooms. Strain the marinade over the meat and add about 250ml stock. Cover, and cook in a warm oven, 160°C, Gas 3, for about 2 hours. Season to taste. Serve garnished with the sippets and chopped parsley.

Navarin d'Agneau Printanier

(Lamb Stew with Vegetables)

8–9 helpings

1.25kg shoulder of lamb	700ml (approx) general
50g flour	household stock (p329)
salt and pepper	1 clove of garlic
1 small onion	250g new potatoes
(50g approx)	250g small young
50ml cooking oil	carrots
4 tomatoes	250g small young
50g concentrated tomato	turnips
purée	125g French beans
bouquet garni	8 button onions
1 × 5ml spoon dried	butter and oil
herbs (basil, mint,	125g fresh peas
oregano)	

Garnish

chopped parsley

Ask the butcher to bone the meat. Cut it into 2–3cm cubes. Season the flour with salt and pepper. Skin and chop the onion. Dust the meat cubes with some of the seasoned flour. Heat the oil in a frying pan and brown the meat cubes on all sides. Add the onion and fry gently for 1 minute. Sprinkle in the remaining flour and cook until it is nut-brown.

Transfer the mixture to a large flameproof casserole. Skin, de-seed, and chop the tomatoes, and add them to the casserole with the purée, bouquet garni, herbs, and stock. Season well. Crush the garlic and add it, with any juices in the frying pan. Bring the mixture gently to the boil, cover closely, reduce the heat, and simmer for $1\frac{1}{2}$ hours. Skim off any excess fat from time to time during cooking.

Meanwhile, cut the potatoes, carrots, and turnips into small oval or cork shapes, and the beans into diamond shapes. Skin the onions. Put the potatoes, carrots, and turnips into boiling salted water, and cook gently for 10 minutes. Add them to the stew 10–20 minutes before the end of the cooking time, so that they will be tender when the meat is ready. Sauté the onions in butter and oil until lightly browned on all sides, and add them to the stew about 15 minutes before the end of the cooking time. Blanch the beans and peas in a little boiling salted water until tender. Drain, and add them to the stew 3–4 minutes before the end of the cooking time, reserving a few peas for garnishing.

When the lamb is ready, skim off any excess fat. Remove any loose bones and the bouquet garni. Transfer the stew to a warmed serving dish. Sprinkle with chopped parsley and the reserved peas just before serving.

Gigot Boulangère
(Roast Leg of Lamb with Baked Potatoes)

12 helpings

1.25kg leg of lamb	150ml general household
2 cloves garlic	stock (p329)
50g butter	250g onions
25g lard	500g potatoes
salt and pepper	bouquet garni

Ask the butcher to cut the knuckle off the leg of lamb. Make 6 small slits in the flesh. Skin the garlic cloves and cut each into 3 slivers. Insert 1 sliver in each slit. Blend together the butter and lard, and spread half the mixture over the joint. Season well. Place the meat in a roasting tin, and roast in a fairly hot oven, 200°C, Gas 6, for 45 minutes. Baste the meat from time to time with some of the stock.

Skin the onions and slice them thinly. Peel and slice the potatoes. Heat the remaining butter and lard in a second roasting tin, and sauté the onions until soft and lightly coloured. Add the potatoes and bouquet garni. Spread the onions and potatoes in the tin. Place the half-roasted meat on top. Reduce the heat to fairly hot, 190°C, Gas 5, and roast for a further 45 minutes, basting from time to time with the juices from the first roasting tin. Remove the joint when fully cooked, and keep hot. Increase the heat to fairly hot, 200°C, Gas 6, and continue cooking the potatoes and onions for about 15 minutes until lightly browned.

Arrange the meat, potatoes, and onions on a serving dish. Discard the bouquet garni. Scrape and pour any juices from both tins into a saucepan. Add any remaining stock. Boil gently for 5 minutes to reduce the sauce, skim, and pour into a warmed sauce-boat. Serve with the meat and vegetables.

Blanquette de Veau à l'Ancienne
(Veal Stew with Mushrooms and Onions)

6 helpings

1kg stewing veal	25g butter
1 large onion	25g flour
2 cloves	50ml double cream
1 large carrot	8–12 button onions
1 clove of garlic	8–12 button mushrooms
salt and pepper	lemon juice
bouquet garni	grated nutmeg

Garnish

chopped parsley	fleurons of puff pastry
	(p399)

Cut the meat into 5cm pieces, discarding any excess fat and gristle. Soak it in cold water for 30 minutes. Skin the onion and press in the cloves. Scrape the carrot and quarter it lengthways. Skin and crush the garlic. Put the meat into fresh cold water, bring to the boil, reduce the heat, and simmer for 10 minutes. Skim well and drain. Transfer the meat to a clean pan with 1 litre water, the onion, carrot, garlic, seasoning, and bouquet garni. Bring gently to the boil, skim, half cover, and simmer very slowly for $1\frac{1}{4}$–$1\frac{1}{2}$ hours, or until the veal is just tender (not soft). Remove the onion, carrot, and bouquet garni. Strain the stock for making the sauce. Cover the pan and keep the meat hot.

Melt the butter in a small saucepan, stir in the flour, and cook together for 3 minutes without colouring the flour. Gradually add the reserved stock from the veal, stirring all the time, and cook gently until the sauce thickens. Add the cream and seasoning if required, and pour the sauce over the meat in the pan.

Skin the button onions, and cook them in lightly salted water for 6 minutes. Drain, and add them to the stew. Simmer the mushrooms separately in water with a little lemon juice for 3 minutes only. Add them with their cooking liquid to the stew. Stir in gently.

Re-heat the stew gently, almost to boiling point. Add the nutmeg, and re-season if required. Serve very hot, sprinkled with chopped parsley and garnished with fleurons of puff pastry.

Tripes à la Mode de Caen
(Tripe with Pork in Cider)

4 helpings

1 calf's foot	*salt and freshly ground*
1 pig's trotter	*black pepper*
500–700g dressed calf's	*Cayenne pepper*
tripe	*bouquet garni*
3 carrots	*6 peppercorns*
75g pickled pork	*375ml dry still cider*
2 large onions	*75ml Calvados or*
4 whole cloves	*brandy*
2 cloves garlic	*cornflour*

Ask the butcher to clean the calf's foot and pig's trotter and to chop them into 2 or 3 pieces each. Wash the tripe, and cut it into pieces about 8cm square. Slice the carrots thinly. Remove the rind from the pork. Put the rind to one side and dice the meat. Skin and halve the onions, and press 1 clove into each half onion. Skin the garlic.

Use a deep pot or casserole, preferably earthenware, which has a tight-fitting lid. In the bottom, put the pork rind, then a layer of carrots, 2 half onions, 1 garlic clove, the calf's foot, the trotter, and half the pork meat. Season well and cover with half the tripe. Put in the rest of the carrots and onions, the second garlic clove, the rest of the pork meat, and the tripe. Add the bouquet garni, peppercorns, and re-season if required. Pour in the cider and Calvados or brandy. Cover the pot very tightly, and cook in a warm oven, 160°C, Gas 3, for 6–7 hours.

Remove the tripe, pork meat and carrots to a warmed serving dish, and keep hot. Strain the stock, discarding the calf's foot and trotter, bouquet garni, peppercorns, onions, and garlic. Measure the liquid. For each 250ml liquid, blend 1×2.5ml spoon cornflour with 1×15ml spoon water. Add a little of the hot liquid. Blend well, stir into the rest of the hot liquid, and stir gently over low heat until the sauce thickens slightly and is very hot. Re-season if required, and pour the sauce over the tripe. Serve immediately.

Pieds de Porç à la Sainte-Menehould
(Grilled Breadcrumbed Trotters)

8 first-course or 4 main-course helpings

8 pig's trotters	*4 × 15ml spoons white*
salt	*wine vinegar*
1 litre water	*300ml dry white wine*
1 medium-sized onion	*200g butter*
2 cloves	*300g (approx) soft white*
2 carrots (75g each	*or browned*
approx)	*breadcrumbs (p375)*
1 clove of garlic	*extra butter*
bouquet garni	

Ask the butcher to clean the trotters. Put them in a large bowl, sprinkle with salt, and leave overnight. Rinse well. Prepare 8 pieces of scalded muslin which will enclose the trotters completely. Wrap each trotter in a piece of muslin and tie the ends of the cloth so that the trotters will keep their shape during cooking.

Put the trotters into a large pan with the water. Skin the onion, press in the cloves, and add it to the pan. Scrape the carrots and skin the garlic. Add to the pan with the bouquet garni and vinegar. Half cover the pan, bring to simmering point, and simmer for 1 hour. Add the wine, and simmer for another $1\frac{1}{2}$ hours or longer, until the trotters are tender when pierced with a skewer through the muslin.

Remove the trotters from the stock. Strain the stock, and put it to one side for making jellied soup or aspic jelly. Unwrap the trotters while still hot or warm. Melt the butter but do not let it get hot. Coat the trotters all over generously with butter, then roll in breadcrumbs, pressing them on to give a thick coating. Transfer to a greased baking tray. Dot with a little extra butter. Bake in a fairly hot oven, 200°C, Gas 6, for 30 minutes until the trotters are well heated through and golden-brown. Alternatively, bake for 15 minutes, then brown the surface of the crumb coating lightly under the grill.

Serve at once, accompanied by mashed or chipped potatoes, if a main course, or with Tartare Sauce (p846), if a first course.

Cassoulet de Toulouse

10–12 helpings

1kg haricot beans	400g lamb and/or pork
1kg goose **or** duck (½ **or**	bones
¼ bird)	4–5 cloves garlic
400g boned pork	6 ×15ml spoons
200g pork rind	concentrated tomato
250–400g boiling bacon	purée
350g onions	500ml dry white wine
1 bouquet garni	1 litre general household
including ½ head	stock (p329)
unpeeled garlic,	pepper
2 cloves, and 2 bay	700g coarse-cut garlic
leaves	sausage
salt	200g dried white
1kg boned well-aged	breadcrumbs **or** as
lamb	needed
4 ×15ml spoons pork,	extra pork, goose **or**
goose **or** duck fat (from	duck fat
roasting bird)	

Soak the haricot beans overnight in cold water. Roast the goose or duck and the boned pork until just cooked. Cool, reserving the cooking juices and fat. Meanwhile, blanch the pork rind in boiling water for 2 minutes, then cut it into 5mm dice, and simmer in fresh water for 15 minutes.

Cut the goose or duck into serving portions. Put the beans and rind into a large stewpan with enough water to cover them. Add the boiling bacon. Skin and slice 100g onions and add them, with the bouquet garni. Season with salt. Bring to the boil, skim well, reduce the heat, and simmer for 2–2½ hours, or until the beans are tender. Add extra boiling water during cooking, if required. Do not cover the pan. Remove the bacon and bouquet garni.

Cut the lamb into 5cm cubes, and pat them dry. Put just enough of the pork, goose or duck fat in a flameproof casserole to cover the bottom to a depth of 5mm. Heat well, and brown the lamb cubes on all sides. Remove, and put to one side. Brown the bones in a little more of the fat, remove, and put to one side. Skin and chop all the remaining onions, and fry them in the same fat for 5 minutes until lightly browned. Return the meat and bones to the casserole. Skin and add the garlic, with the tomato purée, wine, and stock. Season to taste. Bring to simmering point, cover, and simmer for 1½ hours. Remove the meat and discard the bones. Strain the cooking liquid into a bowl, and add any pan juices kept from roasting the goose or duck and boneless pork. Skim off any excess fat, and put to one side.

Cut the sausage into 5cm lengths and the roast pork into 5cm cubes. Slice the boiling bacon. Drain the beans and rind, and add their cooking liquid to the liquid and pan juices in the bowl. Put a layer of beans and rind in the bottom of a very large flameproof casserole or pot. Cover with layers of goose or duck, lamb, bacon, and sausage. Repeat the layers until the ingredients are used, ending with beans. Pour in enough of the cooking liquid from the bowl to cover all but the top layer of beans. Cover thickly with breadcrumbs, and dot with extra fat.

Bring the casserole or pot to simmering point, then bake, uncovered, in a moderate oven, 180°C, Gas 4, for 30 minutes. Break up the breadcrumb crust and baste it with the liquid which wells up. Continue cooking, basting several times, for another 40 minutes. Serve from the casserole.

Note The cassoulet can be kept overnight after boiling the beans and bacon or after cooking the lamb, but extra time must be allowed for reheating.

Poulet Vallée d'Auge
(Chicken in Cider and Cream Sauce)

4 helpings

1 roasting chicken (1kg approx)	2 sticks celery
salt and pepper	2 × 10ml spoons Calvados
grated nutmeg	150ml dry still cider
1 leek (white part only)	150ml chicken stock
1 carrot	bouquet garni
2 small onions	butter for greasing
4 × 10ml spoons butter	2 egg yolks
2 × 10ml spoons cooking oil	1 × 5ml spoon cornflour
	150ml single cream

Garnish

sautéed button mushrooms	lemon juice

Truss the chicken, and season it inside with salt, pepper, and nutmeg. Prepare the leek and carrot and cut into thick slices. Skin and chop the onions. Heat 2 × 10ml spoons butter and all the oil in a frying pan, add the vegetables, cover, and cook over very gentle heat until lightly browned, stirring from time to time. Put the vegetables into a large casserole which will hold the chicken. Spread the remaining butter on the breast of the chicken, and place it in the casserole. Cover, and cook in a fairly hot oven, 190°C, Gas 5, for 20 minutes.

Meanwhile, slice the celery. After 20 minutes, add it to the casserole with the Calvados, cider, stock, and bouquet garni; season to taste. Cover, and cook in the oven for another 30 minutes.

Remove the chicken, and cut it into quarters or serving portions. Place it in an ovenproof baking dish, cover loosely with buttered greaseproof paper or foil and keep hot. Strain the liquid into a saucepan, and bring slowly to the boil. Boil just above simmering point for 10 minutes, or until well reduced. Meanwhile, beat the egg yolks with the cornflour until blended, and stir in the cream. Remove the sauce from the heat, and stir a little of the hot sauce into the egg yolk mixture. Add the egg yolk mixture slowly to the rest of the sauce, beating vigorously. Re-season if required, and pour the sauce over the chicken. Garnish with the mushrooms sprinkled with lemon juice.

Gratin Dauphinois
(Potato and Cheese Bake)

6 helpings

1kg potatoes	25g butter
1 large onion (200g approx)	salt and pepper
200g Gruyère cheese	grated nutmeg
	125ml single cream

Peel the potatoes and onion and slice them thinly. Grate the cheese. Bring a saucepan of water to the boil, put in the potatoes and onions, and blanch for 30 seconds. Drain. Grease a 1.5 litre casserole with some of the butter. Put a layer of potatoes in the bottom of the casserole. Dot with a little of the butter, and sprinkle with some of the onion and cheese, a little salt, pepper, and grated nutmeg. Pour over some of the cream. Repeat the layers until all the ingredients have been used, finishing with a layer of cheese. Pour the remaining cream on top. Cover the casserole and bake in a fairly hot oven, 190°C, Gas 5, for 1 hour. Remove from the oven and place under a hot grill for 5 minutes, or until the top of the cheese is golden-brown and bubbling.

Clafouti aux Cerises
(Cherry Batter Pudding)

6 helpings

450g Morello cherries	75g granulated sugar
2 × 10ml spoons lard	200ml milk
2 × 10ml spoons butter	a pinch of ground cinnamon
125g plain flour	
2 eggs	25g caster sugar
1 egg yolk	1 × 15ml spoon Kirsch

Stone the cherries. Blend the lard and butter together, and use to grease a fluted metal brioche or cake mould about 18cm in diameter (10cm at the base). Sift the flour. Beat together the eggs, yolk, and sugar until light. Heat the milk until steaming. Gradually blend the flour into the egg mixture alternately with a little of the milk, to make a batter. Blend in the remaining milk and flavour with cinnamon. Pour a thin layer of batter into the mould and bake for 5–7 minutes in a fairly hot oven, 200°C, Gas 6, to set the batter. Drain any juice from the cherries. Pour the remaining batter into the mould, add the cherries, and sprinkle with caster sugar. Bake in a fairly hot oven, 200°C, Gas 6, for 10 minutes, then reduce the heat to fairly hot, 190°C, Gas 5, and bake for another 20 minutes. The bottom of the batter should be crusty, and the top soft like confectioners' custard. Serve warm, sprinkled with the Kirsch.

Croquembouche
(Choux Pastry Gâteau)

20 helpings (approx)

1 Madeira cake (20cm in diameter, 6cm high)	apricot glaze (p1234)
200g almond paste (p1231) **or** marzipan (p1232)	white glacé icing (p1225)

Choux

butter for greasing	confectioners' custard
choux pastry (p1251), using 200g flour	(p1237) as required

Caramel

500g granulated sugar	juice of 1 lemon
50ml water	

Decoration
marzipan flowers (p1239)

If the Madeira cake is peaked, cut out a thin strip of paste and put it round the edge of the cake to level the top. Brush off any loose crumbs, then brush the whole cake with warmed apricot glaze. Roll out the rest of the almond paste or marzipan, and use it to cover the top and sides of the cake as described on p1230. Place the cake on a 30cm serving board.

Grease a baking sheet lightly with butter. Put the choux pastry into a forcing bag with a 5mm nozzle and pipe small choux puffs on the sheet. Bake in a fairly hot oven, 190°C, Gas 5, for about 30 minutes. Split open, remove any soft filling, and dry for a few moments in the oven; then cool. When cold, fill with confectioners' custard.

Make a strong paper cone, 30cm high and 15cm diameter at the base.

Make the caramel by boiling together the sugar, water, and lemon juice until golden. Immediately the caramel colours, plunge the bottom of the pan into iced water to prevent further cooking and darkening. Stick the filled choux on the cone by dipping each in caramel and pressing it on to the cone. Begin with a circle of choux at the bottom, and work upwards. At the top, stick on the decorative marzipan flowers, using dabs of caramel.

Leave the caramel to firm up; then lift the cone very carefully on to the Madeira cake.

Ice the exposed sections of the Madeira cake quickly with glacé icing.

Note This gâteau is often used as a wedding cake in France.

If preferred, the cake can be fully iced with royal icing (p1234) before the cone is mounted on it.

See also Profiteroles (p1047).

Madeleines de Commercy

Makes 24

fat for greasing	125g butter
cornflour for dusting	a pinch of salt
4 eggs	2 drops lemon essence
125g caster sugar	2 drops vanilla essence
125g plain flour	25g icing sugar

Grease 24 madeleine moulds (shaped like scallop shells), and dust with cornflour. Separate the eggs. Whisk the yolks with the sugar until very pale and creamy. Whisk in the flour gradually. Meanwhile, warm the butter until just melted but not hot. Pour into a chilled bowl and leave until cool but not solid. Whisk the egg whites with the salt until stiff. Whisk the cooled butter into the cake mixture, and fold in the egg whites at once with the essences.

Fill the moulds with the mixture, and bake in a fairly hot oven, 190°C, Gas 5, for 20 minutes. Cool on a wire rack, and dust the ridged sides with icing sugar before serving.

Coeur à la Crème au Citron

(Lemon-flavoured Sweet Cheese)

6 helpings

125ml double cream	1 × 5ml spoon grated
a pinch of salt	Parmesan cheese
125g low-fat curd cheese	(optional)
50g caster sugar	2 egg whites
grated rind and juice of	
1 lemon	

Line a 375ml heart-shaped mould with greaseproof paper. Whip the cream with the salt until it holds soft peaks. Break up the curd cheese with a fork, and whisk it gradually into the cream with the sugar. Do not let the mixture lose stiffness. Fold the lemon rind and juice into the cream as lightly as possible, adding the Parmesan cheese for extra flavour, if liked. Whisk the egg whites until they hold stiff peaks, and fold them in. Turn the mixture very gently into the mould, filling all the corners, and chill for at least 2 hours.

Serve chilled, with single cream.

VARIATION

For a smooth cheese, dissolve 50g lemon jelly from a packet (crystals or solid) in 150ml hot milk. Cool until cold but not yet set, and whisk into the curd cheese before adding it to the cream.

Paris-Brest

(Ring Gâteau with Praline-flavoured Cream)

6 helpings

butter for greasing	egg wash (p1248)
350g freshly prepared	25g flaked almonds
choux pastry (p1251)	icing sugar for dusting

Praline Cream

50g unblanched	2 × 15ml spoons water
hazelnuts	125ml double cream
125g granulated sugar	125ml single cream

Grease a baking sheet lightly with butter. Put the pastry into a forcing bag with a 1cm nozzle and pipe an 18cm ring of paste on the sheet. Alternatively, pipe it into a flan ring. Brush the top of the ring with egg wash, then sprinkle liberally with the flaked almonds. Bake in a fairly hot oven, 190°C, Gas 5, for 30 minutes. Cool on the sheet.

Make the praline cream. Rub off any loose skins from the hazelnuts. Heat the sugar and water until the sugar is a light golden-brown. Stir in the nuts. Leave to harden on an oiled marble or metal surface. Crush the cooled praline finely. Whisk the double cream until very stiff, gradually whisk in the single cream, then fold in the praline.

Split the choux ring into 2 layers, remove any soft filling inside, and fill with the praline-flavoured cream. The cream will stand up above the pastry casing. Gently put the 2 halves together so that the gâteau is like a sandwich with a very thick filling. Dust the almond-topped surface of the cake with icing sugar. Serve at once.

Gâteau de Pithiviers

8–10 helpings

250g prepared puff	apricot glaze (p1234)
pastry (p1253)	egg wash (p1248)
flour for rolling out	icing sugar

Filling

50g butter	1 egg
50g caster sugar	2 × 10ml spoons plain
1–2 drops almond	flour
essence	50g ground almonds

Make the filling first. Cream the butter and sugar, adding the essence. Mix in the egg and blend smoothly. Mix together the flour and ground almonds, and work them into the butter and sugar mixture to make a smooth pastry cream.

Roll out the pastry on a lightly floured surface and cut two rounds, 18cm and 20cm in diameter. Place the 18cm round on a baking sheet. Cover with apricot glaze to within 1cm of the edge. Spread the glaze with the almond cream in an even layer. Moisten the edge of the pastry. Lay the 20cm layer on top. Press the edges to seal. Make 5 curved cuts in the pastry lid, radiating from the centre at equal intervals. Brush the surface with egg wash. Let the pastry rest for 20 minutes, then bake in a fairly hot oven, 190°C, Gas 5, for 30 minutes or until the pastry is risen and set. Dust the surface with icing sugar and return to the oven for 5 minutes to glaze. Cool on the sheet.

Note If liked, use 1 drop almond essence and 1–2 drops orange liqueur or essence instead of almond essence only.

Bûche de Noël
(Chestnut Christmas Log)

6–8 helpings

Sponge

butter for greasing	*2 × 10ml spoons rum*
100g icing sugar	*65g self-raising flour*
3 eggs	*icing sugar for dusting*

Filling

2 × 440g cans	*125g caster sugar*
unsweetened chestnut	*2 × 15ml spoons rum*
purée	
300g softened butter	

Decorations
marrons glacés **or** *glacé*
  cherries and angelica

Grease a 35 × 25cm Swiss roll tin and line it with greased paper. Warm a mixing bowl with hot water, then dry it. Sift in the icing sugar, and break in the eggs. Beat or whisk vigorously for 5–10 minutes until the mixture is very light and fluffy. Add the rum while beating. When the mixture is like meringue, fold in the flour gently. Turn the mixture into the prepared tin, and bake in a hot oven, 220°C, Gas 7, for 7 minutes. Meanwhile, prepare a sheet of greaseproof paper 40 × 30cm in size and dust it with icing sugar.

Remove the sponge from the oven, loosen the sides from the tin if necessary, and turn it on to the greaseproof paper. Peel off the lining paper. Trim the edges of the sponge if crisp. Roll it up tightly with the greaseproof paper into a Swiss roll shape, beginning either at one long side to make a long thin roll, or at one short end for a thicker, shorter roll. Cool completely.

Meanwhile, prepare the chestnut butter cream for the filling. Turn the purée into a bowl, and beat

in the softened butter; then add the sugar and rum.

When the sponge is cold, unroll it carefully. Minor blemishes and cracks do not matter since they will be covered with butter cream. Cover the underside of the sponge with just over half the butter cream, laying it on thickly at the further edge. When covered, re-roll the sponge, and place it on a sheet of greaseproof paper, with the cut edge underneath. Cover it with the remaining butter cream, either with a knife or using a forcing bag with a ribbon nozzle, imitating the knots and grain of wood. Chill.

Serve chilled, surrounded by marrons glacés or decorated with glacé cherries and angelica.

VARIATIONS
1) Sprinkle the baked roll with the rum while still hot instead of mixing the rum into the sponge.
2) Use chocolate butter icing (p1227) instead of the chestnut filling, and decorate the log with almonds, glacé cherries, angelica, and a sprig of holly.
3) Imitate the grain of wood by scoring it lengthways with the prongs of a fork. Decorate with piped chocolate glacé icing (p1226) on top and at the ends, and serve as a dessert with chocolate sauce.

Germany and Austria

There are many similarities between the cookery of Germany and Austria, with historical and geographical influences of particular significance. Noodles, dumplings, pork, venison, and other wild game are very popular, as are the famous pastries and cakes.

Each country does, however, have its specialities of which a number are included below. A German evening meal is not complete without sausage, smoked or otherwise, and/or bread and cheese, of which there are many varieties. Goose or duck stuffed in various ways and frequently served with pickled red cabbage and dumplings are typical festival dishes, together with *Christstollen* – the German Christmas bread.

Austrian cooking, in particular that of Vienna, has been heavily influenced by the imperial cuisine and is famous for its veal dishes especially Wiener, Holstein, and Paprika Schnitzel. The numerous pastries and cakes – Linzertorte, and many kinds of Strudel – are well known, but Sacher Torte, named after Franz Sacher, chef to Prince Metternich, is perhaps most famous.

Erbsensuppe
(Pea Soup)

Germany

12 helpings

200g dried split yellow or green peas	75g butter
2.5 litres water	50g flour
25g onion	salt and pepper
2 sprigs parsley	1 × 15ml spoon sugar (optional)

Soak the peas overnight in 1 litre of the water in a large saucepan. Grate the onion and chop the parsley. Fry them in 25g of the butter until lightly coloured. Add to the peas and water. Bring to the boil, and simmer gently for about 1 hour until the peas are soft. Rub through a fine sieve, or process in an electric blender to make a smooth purée.

Melt the remaining butter gently in a large saucepan, stir in the flour, and cook gently for 3–4 minutes. Heat 750ml water to boiling point, and add it gradually to the roux, stirring all the time to prevent lumps forming. Pour in the pea purée and the remaining 750ml water. Heat through and blend well together. Season to taste with salt, pepper, and sugar, if liked (sugar enriches the pea flavour).

Serve with small croûtons of fried bread, or cubes of any smoked meat, eg frankfurters. (Frankfurters must not be allowed to boil in the soup as they split and lose their flavour.)

VARIATIONS
1) A thicker consistency may be achieved by adding 2 medium-sized, raw, peeled, and chopped potatoes.
2) The liquid in which a bacon joint has been boiled can be used instead of water in this recipe. It gives a pleasant smoky taste to the soup.

Leberknödelsuppe
(Liver Dumpling Soup)

Germany

8–10 helpings

2.5 litres strong beef stock

Knödel

75g white bread	75g fine dry brown or white breadcrumbs
125g calf's liver	
1 small shallot or onion	1 egg
75g beef dripping or lard	a pinch of dried marjoram
1 × 5ml spoon chopped parsley	salt and pepper

Make the knödel first. Soak the bread in a little cold water. Remove the skin and tubes from the liver, and pat dry. Mince or chop finely, or process in an electric blender. Squeeze the water from the bread, and rub through a fine sieve with the minced liver. Skin and grate the shallot or onion. Heat 1 × 15ml spoon of the fat and fry the shallot or onion until transparent with the parsley. Add to the liver. Melt the remaining dripping or lard, and pour it over the liver and bread mixture. Mix in the breadcrumbs, egg, marjoram, and seasoning to taste. Blend together well, cover, and leave for 30 minutes.

Bring the beef stock to the boil. Roll the mixture into 2cm balls, and drop gently into the boiling beef stock. Cover, and cook for about 10 minutes. Test for readiness before serving; they are cooked when no longer pink inside. Leave for 3–4 minutes longer if not cooked through.

Matjesheringe in Rahmsose

(Matjesherrings in Cream Sauce)   Germany

4–8 helpings

8 plain matjesherring fillets (not spiced)	2–3 eating apples lemon juice
milk **or** water for soaking	½ large Spanish onion

Sauce

125ml soured cream	salt and pepper
5 ×15ml spoons double **or** single cream	1 × 5ml spoon sugar

Clean the herrings and remove any bones. Pat dry. Lay in a glass or enamel bowl and pour over enough milk or water to cover. Put to one side in a cool place for 10–12 hours; this removes much of the saltiness.

Peel, core, and quarter the apples, slice very finely, and sprinkle with lemon juice. Skin the onion and slice it in wafer-thin rings.

Drain the milk or water from the fillets and pat dry. Reserve 2 or 3 onion rings for garnishing. Layer the fillets with the apple slices and onion rings in a flat dish.

To make the sauce, beat the soured cream and double or single cream together until well blended and of a fairly thick consistency; add seasoning and sugar to taste. Pour the sauce over the fillets and decorate with the reserved onion rings. Chill for several hours before serving so that the flavours blend.

Serve with brown bread.

Blauer Karpfen mit Meerrettichsahne

Germany

(Blue Carp with Horseradish Cream)

4–6 helpings

1.5kg mirror carp	250ml dry white wine
1 small onion	a small bunch of parsley
4 cloves	6 peppercorns
3 litres water	2 slices lemon
5 ×15ml spoons salt	300ml white wine vinegar

Sauce

50g fresh horseradish root	salt sugar
250ml double cream	

Ask the fishmonger to clean the carp, but to leave on the head and to avoid damaging the slimy membrane on the outside of the skin, which protects the scales. Tie the carp in a circle by pushing a skewer threaded with string through the nose and tail.

Skin the onion and press the cloves into it. In a pan large enough to hold the carp, combine the rest of the ingredients, apart from the carp and vinegar. Bring gently to the boil. Bring the vinegar to the boil in a separate pan. Lay the fish on a large dish and pour the boiling vinegar over it (this helps the skin to turn blue). Carefully slide the fish into the hot court bouillon; do not add the vinegar. Maintain the liquid at a very gentle simmer; violent boiling will make the skin fall off. Simmer for about 20 minutes, depending on size. Test for readiness; the fish is done when it flakes easily but is still quite moist. Lift it out of the pan on to a serving plate and keep warm.

To make the sauce, wash and dry the horseradish root. Grate very finely and mix with 2 ×15ml spoons of the cream. Whip the remainder of the cream until just stiff. Fold the horseradish mixture gently into the whipped cream with salt and sugar to taste. It should have a clean, strong, and sharp flavour. Chill in a covered container.

Serve the carp with hot melted butter, boiled potatoes, and the horseradish cream.

Hasenrücken
(Saddle of Hare)

Germany

5–6 helpings

1 large young hare
3 juniper berries
salt and pepper
150g bacon for larding
1 carrot
1 stick of celery
½ onion
100g butter **or** lard
1 × 15ml spoon chopped
  parsley
1 × 15ml spoon flour
200ml boiling water **or**
  beef stock
4 × 15ml spoons red
  wine

250ml double cream
20 peppercorns
10 allspice berries
1 bay leaf
a pinch of thyme
1 × 2.5ml spoon grated
  nutmeg
a pinch of ginger
juice of 1 lemon
2 × 15ml spoons wine
  vinegar
1 × 15ml spoon
  redcurrant **or**
  cranberry juice

Skin and clean the hare (pp671–72). Cut away the rib-cage, remove the legs, and keep for another dish. Wash and dry the saddle well. Crush the juniper berries. Rub the hare all over with the juniper berries, salt, and pepper. Lard with the bacon.

Prepare the vegetables. Chop the carrot and celery into 1cm pieces, and chop the onion finely. Melt the butter or lard in a deep, heavy casserole, and fry the vegetables lightly with the parsley. Remove the vegetables.

Lay the larded hare in the pan, turning and basting until browned on all sides to seal in the juices. When the hare is well browned, lift it out of the pan. Return the vegetables, sprinkle in the flour, and blend well with the juices. Pour on the boiling water or stock slowly, stirring to prevent lumps forming, then add the wine and cream. Add all the spices and herbs, the lemon juice, vinegar, and the redcurrant or cranberry juice. Return the hare to the sauce and cover the pan closely. Cook slowly, basting occasionally, for about 1 hour until the meat is tender. The flesh should still be slightly pink. Strain the sauce before serving.

Serve with Spätzli (p1509), rice or noodles, and cranberry or redcurrant sauce.

Königsberger Klops
(Meatballs)

Germany

4–6 helpings

225g beef
225g pork
25g white bread
1 egg
salt and pepper

2 cooked potatoes
1 × 5ml spoon grated
  lemon rind
a pinch of nutmeg
50g butter

Sauce

1 anchovy fillet
50g butter
1 × 15ml spoon chopped
  parsley
1 × 15ml spoon chopped
  chives **or** shallot

50g plain flour
1 bay leaf
juice of ½ lemon
200ml red wine

Trim the beef and pork and mince them finely. Soak the bread in a little water for 5–10 minutes, then squeeze out. Beat the egg until liquid. Break the bread up with a fork, and combine with the beaten egg, minced meats, salt and pepper. Rub the potatoes through a sieve, and mix in with the lemon rind and nutmeg. Mix all the ingredients together thoroughly. Roll the mixture into 12 balls and flatten slightly. Melt the butter in a frying pan, and fry the meat balls gently, turning occasionally.

Meanwhile, crush or chop the anchovy fillet. Melt the butter and lightly fry the parsley with the chives or shallot until transparent. Stir in the flour. Gradually add the bay leaf, lemon juice, wine and anchovy fillet, stirring all the time. Add any juices from the meat balls, and stir thoroughly. Transfer the meat balls to the sauce, stir, and cover tightly. Simmer for about 5 minutes until all the flavours have combined.

Serve with sliced potatoes or Spätzli (p1509).

Paprika Schnitzel

Austria

5–6 helpings

2kg boneless leg of veal or pork	brown stock (p329) or water to cover
salt	200g onion
flour for dredging	1 × 15ml spoon mild paprika
175g fat for shallow frying	1 × 15ml spoon soured cream or yoghurt

Ask the butcher to cut the meat into escalopes about 5mm thick and as large as possible, cut with the grain of the meat. If using pork, cut off all fat. Snip or notch around the edge of each escalope, and pound to about half its thickness with a cutlet bat or rolling-pin. Rub the escalopes with salt, and dredge one side of each with flour. Melt 100g fat in a large frying pan. Fry the escalopes, floured side first, until golden-brown all over. Pour in just enough stock or water to cover, stir around the escalopes, and scrape the bottom of the pan with a fork to loosen all the meat juices; then cover the pan and cook gently for 5 minutes. Lift the meat out of the stock, drain well, and keep hot under buttered paper.

Skin the onion and chop it finely. In a saucepan, melt the remaining fat, and fry the onion gently until soft and just beginning to colour. Dust with flour, add the paprika, and cook gently for a few minutes, stirring all the time. Gradually pour on the stock in which the meat has been cooked, stirring all the time. Simmer for 3–4 minutes, then stir in the soured cream or yoghurt. Re-season if required with salt and paprika. Return the meat to the sauce, and simmer for about 2 minutes to heat the meat in the sauce. Serve very hot.

Wiener Schnitzel

Austria

See p559.

Spätzli

(Noodles)

6–8 helpings

375g plain flour	200ml water
1 × 5ml spoon salt	3 eggs

Sift the flour and salt into a bowl. Mix in the water, taking care to prevent lumps forming. Add the eggs, one at a time, blending well between each addition. Beat the mixture briskly until air bubbles appear; the consistency should be quite soft and loose. (If mixing by hand, let the mixture rest for 1 hour.) Have ready a large pan of boiling salted water. Moisten a wooden board with cold water, and rest it on the top edge of the pan. Spread some of the mixture over the board and, using a large knife, quickly slice off narrow strips, sliding them straight into the boiling water.

The spätzli should boil quite vigorously in an open pan (take care they do not boil over; turn the heat down a little if necessary). After 3 or 4 minutes they will start to rise to the surface. They must not cook too long or they become sticky. Lift them out into a colander, and rinse with hot or cold water, then drain. If they are not to be used immediately, lay them out on a board to cool and dry off. Store in a cool place.

To serve, drop the spätzli into foaming butter, and stir gently over low heat to fry and crisp them lightly. Small cubes of fried ham or bacon can be mixed in to give added flavour.

Note This is a speciality of southern Germany; it is a good accompaniment to rich meat dishes, such as goulash.

Gefüllte Kohlrabi   Germany
(Stuffed Kohlrabi)

4–6 helpings

6 small, young kohlrabi	*butter for greasing*
1 × 10ml spoon sugar	*500ml foundation white*
ham (p375) **or** *calf or*	*sauce (pouring*
chicken liver (p381) **or**	*consistency)* (p692)
sausage-meat (p383)	*made with beef stock*
stuffing	

Wash the kohlrabi, and peel off a thin layer. Cut off the tops and reserve for lids. Hollow out the vegetables with a small sharp knife, leaving a thin but strong wall. Boil the kohlrabi and the lids in a pan of sugared water for 7–10 minutes or until slightly crisp but not too soft. Lift out gently, drain, and fill with the stuffing. Cover with the lids and pack closely in a buttered ovenproof dish. Pour the hot sauce over the kohlrabi. Sprinkle lightly with the remaining sugar, cover loosely with foil, and bake in a moderate oven, 180°C, Gas 4, for 30–40 minutes.

Serve hot as an accompaniment to braised or roast beef and new potatoes.

Note Do not use large kohlrabi as the flesh is tougher.

Mohr im Hemd   Austria
('Moor in a Nightshirt')

6 helpings

fat for greasing	*100g plain chocolate*
caster sugar for dredging	*100g butter*
100g unblanched	*100g caster sugar*
almonds	*6 eggs*

Decoration
250ml double cream	*2 × 15ml spoons sugar*
50ml single cream	

Grease and dust with caster sugar a 24cm deep mould or pudding basin. Grind the almonds with their skins in a nut grinder, or process briefly in an electric blender. Do not overgrind them or their oils will be released. Grate the chocolate finely. Beat the butter and sugar together until light and fluffy. Separate the eggs, and add the yolks to the mixture, one at a time, beating well between each addition. Add the almonds and grated chocolate. Whisk the egg whites until stiff, and gently fold them into the chocolate mixture.

Place the mixture in the prepared mould or pudding basin, and bake in a moderate oven, 180°C, Gas 4, for 1 hour. Cool for a few minutes, then turn out on to a flat round dish and cool completely.

Beat the double and single creams together until thick. Mix in the sugar. Cover the Mohr im Hemd completely with the whipped cream.

Note The cream may be flavoured with rum or vanilla essence, if liked.

Bienenstich   Austria
('Bee Sting')

24 helpings

Pastry Base
10g fresh yeast	*50g butter*
100ml warm milk	*50g caster sugar*
1 × 5ml spoon caster	*1 egg*
sugar	*grated rind of ½ lemon*
250g strong white flour	*fat for greasing*
a pinch of salt	

Almond Layer
50g butter	*2 × 15ml spoons milk*
100g sugar	*(approx)*
125g flaked **or** *nibbed*	
almonds	

Blend the yeast into the warm milk with the sugar, and leave to stand for 10 minutes until frothy. Sift 225g of the flour and the salt into a warmed bowl, and make a well in the centre. Pour in the yeast, mix in a little flour from the sides to make a soft batter, and sprinkle the remaining flour over the top. Cover with a damp cloth, and stand in a warm place for 15–20 minutes, or until bubbles form and the surface cracks.

Cream the butter and sugar together until light and fluffy. Mix the egg and lemon rind together, and add to the yeast dough with the creamed mixture. Work all the ingredients together gently, then knead until the dough leaves the sides of the bowl cleanly and looks shiny. Cover with a large, lightly oiled polythene bag and leave in a warm place until doubled in size. Lightly grease a 34 × 24cm baking tin with 3cm sides. Press the dough lightly into the tin. Leave to rise again for about 20 minutes.

Meanwhile, make the almond layer. Melt the butter in a saucepan, add the sugar, and stir until it has all dissolved. Beat in the almonds, and stir in enough milk to make a stiffish mixture of spreading consistency. Cool, then spread carefully over the risen pastry base. Bake in a moderate oven, 180°C, Gas 4, for 30 minutes until golden-brown. Cut into strips while still warm, and cool before serving.

Linzertorte   Austria
See p1267.

Sacher Torte   Austria

8–12 helpings

125g butter	*fat for greasing*
125g granulated sugar	*flour for dredging*
125g plain chocolate	*50g apricot jam*
6 eggs	*(approx)*
125g self-raising flour	

Filling
25g icing sugar	*40g softened unsalted*
50g plain chocolate	*butter*

Icing
175g plain chocolate	*165ml water*
165g lump sugar	*25g unsalted butter*

Cream the butter and sugar until light and fluffy. Break up or grate the chocolate, melt it in a basin over a pan of hot water, and cool slightly; then stir it into the creamed mixture. Separate the eggs. Beat in the yolks, one by one, until thoroughly blended. Sift the flour. Whisk the egg whites until they hold firm peaks, then fold them into the mixture alternately with the flour; use either a metal spoon or an electric blender on the lowest speed. Pour the mixture into an 18cm loose-bottomed greased and floured cake tin. Set on a baking tray. Make a slight hollow in the centre to ensure even rising.

Bake in a moderate – fairly hot oven, 180°–190°C, Gas 4–5, for about 1½ hours. If the cake shows any sign of browning too much after 1 hour, lower the temperature to warm, 160°C, Gas 3, and continue baking until the cake is fully cooked. Test by inserting a skewer; it will come out clean when the cake is fully baked. Leave in the tin for a few minutes, then turn out on to a wire rack, and cool at room temperature.

Make the filling when the cake is cold. Sift the icing sugar. Break up or grate the chocolate, and melt it in a basin over a pan of hot water. Cream the icing sugar, chocolate, and butter together until very smooth and fully blended.

Split the cold cake in half and spread the filling over the cut surfaces. Sandwich the coated halves together. Warm the apricot jam until liquid, and spread it very thinly over the top and sides.

Make the icing. Break up or grate the chocolate, and melt it in a basin over a pan of hot water. Keep it soft over the hot water while preparing the syrup. Bring the sugar and water to the boil, and boil until they form a thread (103°C). Gradually stir this into the melted chocolate, and beat until the icing coats a wooden spoon thickly, and can be drawn up to a point. Do not overbeat or the mixture will lose its gloss. Stir in the butter. Spread the icing quickly and smoothly over the cake, using a knife dipped in hot water.

Note If Sacher Torte is served as a dessert, it should be accompanied by sweetened whipped cream.

Schwarzwälderkirschtorte
(Black Forest Cherry Gâteau)   Germany
See p1044.

Dresdener Christstollen

(Dresden Christmas Stollen)   Germany

Makes 2 loaves; 24 slices each (approx)

1kg plain flour	*500g raisins*
75g fresh yeast	*225g sultanas*
200ml warm milk	*150g blanched slivered*
350g butter	* almonds*
juice and grated rind of	*100g cut mixed peel*
* 1 lemon*	*flour for dusting*
250g caster sugar	*butter for greasing*
2 egg yolks	*100g unsalted butter*
1 × 5ml spoon salt	*icing sugar for dusting*

Sift the flour. Blend the yeast into the warm milk with 50g of the flour, and leave in a warm place for 10 minutes until frothy. Meanwhile, melt the butter. Cool slightly, and blend into the remaining flour with the lemon juice. Add the milk and yeast, together with the lemon rind, sugar, egg yolks, and salt. Beat well together. Knead until the dough is very firm and elastic, and leaves the sides of the bowl. Cover with a large, lightly oiled polythene bag and leave in a warm place until the dough has doubled in size.

Meanwhile, mix the dried fruit with the nuts and peel. Knock the dough back, pull the sides to the centre, turn it over, and cover once more. Leave to rise for a further 30 minutes. When the dough has doubled its size again, turn it on to a floured surface and knead in the fruit and nut mixture.

Divide the dough in half, and roll each half into a pointed oval shape. Lay each on a buttered baking sheet. Place a rolling-pin along the length of each piece of the dough in the centre. Roll half the dough lightly from the centre outwards. Brush the thinner rolled half with a little water and fold the other half over it, leaving a margin of about 5cm all round which allows the dough to rise. Press well together; the water will bind it. Cover the stollen and leave them to prove in a warm place until doubled in size again. Melt 50g of the unsalted butter and brush it over the stollen.

Bake in a fairly hot oven, 190°C, Gas 5, for about 1 hour until golden. When baked, melt the remaining unsalted butter, brush it over the stollen, and sprinkle with sifted icing sugar. Keep for a day before cutting.

The stollen will remain fresh for many weeks if well wrapped in foil or greaseproof paper and stored in an airtight tin.

Note This is the classic German Christmas bread.

Haselnusstorte   Austria

(Hazelnut Cake)

Makes 12 slices

200g hazelnuts	*grated rind of ½ lemon*
5 eggs	*fat for greasing*
150g caster sugar	*flour for dusting*
Filling	
250ml double cream	*a few drops vanilla*
	* essence*
Decoration	
whole hazelnuts	*grated chocolate*

Roast the hazelnuts on a baking sheet in a moderate oven, 180°C, Gas 4, for 10 minutes, until the skins start to split. While still warm, rub them in a rough cloth to remove the brown skins. Grind coarsely in a nut-mill, or process briefly in an electric blender. Separate the eggs. Beat the yolks and sugar together until light and creamy, and mix in the nuts and lemon rind. Whisk the egg whites until stiff but not dry. Fold them gently and quickly into the nut mixture.

Turn into 2 greased and floured 24cm spring-form or loose-bottomed baking tins, and bake in a moderate oven, 180°C, Gas 4, for 1 hour. Test for readiness; a warmed skewer pushed into the centre should come out dry, and the sides of the cake start to shrink slightly from the edges. Stand the cakes on wire racks to cool, and after a few minutes remove the sides and bases of the tins.

To make the filling, whip the cream with the vanilla essence until stiff. When cold, sandwich the cakes together with some of the cream, and cover the top with the remainder. Decorate with a few whole hazelnuts and a sprinkling of grated chocolate.

Salzburger Nockerl — Austria
(Sweet Dumplings)

4–6 helpings

50g butter	*1 ×15ml spoon plain*
1 ×10ml spoon caster	*flour*
sugar	*125ml milk*
5 eggs	*icing sugar for dredging*

Heat the oven to fairly hot, 200°C, Gas 6. Beat the butter and sugar together until light and fluffy. Separate the eggs, and mix the yolks into the creamed mixture, one at a time. Sift the flour. Whisk the egg whites until stiff, and fold lightly into the rest of the mixture with the flour. Pour the milk into a shallow flameproof dish, and heat gently. Remove from the heat, pour in the batter, smooth it lightly, and bake for about 10 minutes until light brown in colour. Cut out spoonfuls of the nockerl, and arrange on a warmed serving plate. Serve immediately, sprinkled with icing sugar.

Note The nockerl can be cooked in melted butter, instead of milk. Use enough butter to cover the base of the dish.

Kaiserschmarrn — Austria
(Emperor's Pancakes)
See p941.

Greece and the Middle East

Although the following dishes are identified with certain countries, most of them are served, with slight variations, throughout the Middle East. Hummus and Felafel, for instance, are popular dishes everywhere.

Hummus
(Chick-pea Dip)

6–8 helpings

300g cooked chick-peas	*1 clove of garlic*
125ml tahina (sesame	*salt*
seed paste)	*2 ×10ml spoons olive oil*
100ml lemon juice	*chopped parsley*
50ml cooking liquid	
from chick-peas, if	
required	

Grind the chick-peas in a nut-mill, or crush in a pestle and mortar to make a smooth paste. Alternatively, process the chick-peas in an electric blender. In a mixing bowl, blend together the tahina and lemon juice. The mixture should have the consistency of thick cream. If it is too stiff, thin with some of the liquid from cooking the chick-peas. Add the ground chick-peas. Skin and chop the garlic and add to the chick-peas. Stir briskly until well blended. Season with salt. Place the hummus in a shallow serving bowl, trickle the olive oil over it, and sprinkle with chopped parsley.

Serve as a first course with French bread, crispbread or pita bread.

Felafel
(Deep-fried Chick-pea Balls)

Makes 36

Felafel

200g cooked chick-peas
75g fine matzo meal
1 × 5ml spoon salt
2 × 5ml spoons ground
  cumin

$\frac{1}{2}$ × 2.5ml spoon ground
  coriander
$\frac{1}{2}$ × 2.5ml spoon garlic
  powder
oil for deep frying

Tahina Sauce

50g ground sesame seeds
75ml water
$\frac{1}{2}$ × 2.5ml spoon garlic
  powder

$\frac{1}{2}$ × 2.5ml spoon salt
1 × 15ml spoon lemon
  juice
a pinch of pepper

Mince the chick-peas finely or chop and sieve them. Add all the other ingredients for the felafel, and form into small balls. Heat the oil (p302), and fry the felafel until golden-brown.

For the tahina sauce, mix all ingredients together, and sieve to make a smooth purée, or process in an electric blender for a few minutes. Re-season if required.

Serve hot as a first course.

Taramasalata

4 helpings

100g smoked cod's roe.
1 clove of garlic
2 × 15ml spoons lemon
  juice
4 × 15ml spoons olive oil

2 × 15ml spoons cold
  water
freshly ground black
  pepper

Skin the roe and garlic. Pound them in a mortar with the lemon juice until smooth. Add small amounts of oil and water alternately until the mixture is completely blended. Season to taste with black pepper, and serve with pita bread.

Sheleg Chermon   Israel
(Cold Yoghurt Soup with Nuts)

6 helpings

4 cloves garlic
500g cucumber
3 × 2.5ml spoons salt
7 sprigs fresh dill
  (approx)

1kg natural yoghurt
1 × 5ml spoon olive oil
50g ground almonds **or**
  mixed nuts

Garnish

6 sprigs fresh mint

6 ice cubes (optional)

Crush the garlic. Peel the cucumber. Grate it into a bowl, and season well with salt. Chop the leaves of 1 dill sprig finely. Remove the leaves from the stems of the rest, and put to one side. Mix the garlic and chopped dill with the cucumber. Stir in the yoghurt with a few drops of the oil, until well blended. Stir until the yoghurt is liquid; if it is too thick, add a few drops of iced water. Cover, and chill for 10–12 hours.

To serve, fold in the rest of the oil, and the nuts. Pour the soup into 6 bowls. Garnish each bowl with the reserved dill sprigs, a sprig of mint, and an ice cube, if liked. Serve chilled.

Babaghanouj   Egypt
(Aubergine Pâté)

6–8 helpings

1 large aubergine
125ml tahina (sesame
  seed paste)
100ml lemon juice

salt
1 clove of garlic
2 × 10ml spoons olive oil
chopped parsley

Cook the aubergine by placing it over a direct medium-low flame of a gas cooker, or close beneath the grill on either a gas or electric cooker. Cook gently, without breaking the skin, turning the aubergine frequently until brown on all sides, or even beginning to char, and the aubergine feels soft. Put to one side to cool.

In a small bowl, mix the tahina and lemon juice, adding a little salt to taste. The mixture should be the consistency of thick cream. If it is too stiff, thin with a little water. When the aubergine is cool enough to handle comfortably, cut it open and spoon the flesh into a mixing bowl. Chop the garlic finely and add it to the aubergine with the tahina and lemon juice mixture. Stir briskly until well blended. Place in a shallow serving bowl, and trickle the olive oil over it. Sprinkle with chopped parsley.

Serve as a first course with French bread, crispbread or pita bread.

Note In the Middle East, this dish would be prepared on the coals of a charcoal or wood fire.

Moussaka   Greece

4 helpings

1 medium-sized aubergine	1 × 10ml spoon chopped parsley
salt	150ml dry white wine
1 large onion	300ml milk
1 clove of garlic	1 egg
2 medium-sized tomatoes	2 egg yolks
2 × 15ml spoons olive oil	a pinch of grated nutmeg
500g raw lamb **or** beef, minced	75g Kefalotiri **or** Parmesan cheese
pepper	fat for greasing

Cut the aubergine into 1cm slices, sprinkle them with salt and put to one side on a large platter to drain. Chop the onion, grate the garlic, and skin, de-seed, and chop the tomatoes. Heat the olive oil, add the onion and garlic, and sauté gently until the onion is soft. Add the minced meat, and continue cooking, stirring with a fork to break up any lumps in the meat. When the meat is thoroughly browned, add salt, pepper, parsley, and the tomatoes. Mix well, and add the white wine. Simmer the mixture for a few minutes to blend the flavours, then remove from the heat.

In a basin, beat together the milk, egg, egg yolks, salt, and a good pinch of grated nutmeg. Grate the cheese, add about half to the egg mixture, and beat again briefly.

Grease a 20 × 10 × 10cm oven-to-table baking dish. Drain the aubergine slices and pat dry with soft kitchen paper. Place half in the bottom of the casserole and cover with the meat mixture. Lay the remaining aubergine slices on the meat and pour the milk and egg mixture over them. Sprinkle the remaining cheese on top. Bake in a moderate oven, 180°C, Gas 4, for 30–40 minutes, until the custard is set and the top is light golden-brown. Serve from the dish.

Note Moussaka can be made a day ahead, then reheated, covered, in a warm oven.

Souvlakia   Greece
(Lamb Kebabs)

6 helpings

100ml olive oil	1kg boneless lamb
juice of 1 lemon	200g white firm lamb fat
salt and freshly ground pepper	dried crushed oregano

Mix the olive oil, lemon juice, salt and pepper in a basin. Cut the lamb into pieces 2cm square and about 5mm thick. Put the meat and fat in the olive oil mixture. Stir to coat all the pieces with the marinade, and leave to stand for 1 hour, stirring once or twice.

Drain the meat and fat, reserving the marinade. Thread the meat and fat on skewers (about 20cm long), starting with a piece of fat, then 2 or 3 pieces of meat followed by another piece of fat. The last piece on each skewer should be fat.

Grill the meat over glowing coals for 15–20 minutes, turning several times, until done. Dip again into the marinade, then sprinkle liberally with oregano.

Note In Greece the skewers are usually of wood, soaked in water before use, so that they will not char when grilling. Metal skewers are perfectly acceptable.

The souvlakia can be cooked under an ordinary grill, using moderate heat; turn frequently.

Note Another recipe for Lamb Kebabs can be found on p527.

Kibbeh bi Sanieh

Lebanon

(Baked Minced Lamb)

6 helpings

Kibbeh

500g raw lean lamb	2 medium-sized onions
250g burghul (cracked wheat)	salt and pepper
	ground nutmeg
150ml iced water	

Filling

500g raw lean lamb	salt and pepper
1 × 15ml spoon olive oil	ground cumin
2 medium-sized onions	ground cinnamon
50g pine nut kernels or slivered blanched almonds	finely chopped parsley
	25g butter

Sauce

2 medium-sized cucumbers	salt and pepper
	600g natural yoghurt
1 clove of garlic	

Mince the lamb for the kibbeh and for the filling. Keep them separate. Make the kibbeh first.

Soak the burghul for 15 minutes in the iced water, then strain it, and drain well. Reserve the water. Skin and chop the onions. Mix together the chopped onions, the minced lamb, and 50ml of the iced water. Mince very finely 3 times, adding 50ml of the iced water each time. Alternatively, process in an electric blender, adding the water gradually. Add the drained burghul, and a generous amount of salt, pepper, and nutmeg to the prepared meat. Knead the mixture until well blended. Chill for at least 30 minutes.

Meanwhile, make the filling. Heat the olive oil in a frying pan. Skin, chop, and add the onions, and crumble in the minced lamb, stirring to break up any lumps and to let it brown. As soon as the meat begins to brown, stir in the pine kernels or slivered almonds. Cook for 2 minutes longer, then add salt, pepper, ground cumin, ground cinnamon, and parsley to taste. Remove the pan from the heat and put to one side.

To assemble the dish, grease a shallow baking tray, about 30 × 45cm, with half the butter. (In the East, a shallow pan called a sanieh is used.) Spread half the chilled kibbeh evenly over the tray, pressing it down with wet hands. Cover with the filling and layer the remaining half evenly on top.

With a knife, carefully cut through the layered kibbeh diagonally from the left in lines about 5cm apart, then cut again diagonally from the right to make a diamond pattern. Melt the remaining butter, and trickle it evenly over the top. Bake in a moderate oven, 180°C, Gas 4, for 1 hour.

Meanwhile, make the sauce. Dice the cucumbers, skin and chop the garlic. Mix all the ingredients thoroughly. Leave to infuse while the kibbeh cooks.

Remove the kibbeh from the oven and drain off any excess fat. Cut into serving portions and serve with the yoghurt and cucumber sauce.

Moschari Stifado

Cyprus

(Marinated Braised Veal)

6 helpings

1kg lean veal	500ml white stock
300ml olive oil	(p329) or 250ml
a pinch of dried marjoram	chicken and 250ml beef stock
2 cloves garlic	1kg pickling onions
150g concentrated tomato purée	1kg potatoes
	salt and pepper

Marinade

1 small onion	1 bay leaf
4 cloves	a pinch of dried basil
300ml red wine	a pinch of dried thyme
4 × 15ml spoons vinegar	

Garnish

chopped parsley

Make the marinade first. Skin the onion, and press in the cloves. Mix all the ingredients together. Cut the veal into cubes and marinate it for 6–12 hours.

Drain the meat, reserving the marinade. Heat 200ml of the olive oil in a heavy stewpan. Add the meat, and cook over medium heat until browned on all sides. Add the reserved marinade and the marjoram. Skin and chop the garlic, and add it with the tomato purée and stock. Simmer for about $1\frac{1}{2}$ hours until the liquid is reduced by about half.

Heat the remaining olive oil in a frying pan. Skin the pickling onions, and put them into the hot oil. Cook gently, stirring occasionally, until they are browned and tender. If using new potatoes, boil them in their skins until just tender. If using larger, older potatoes, peel and cube them, and boil until tender.

When the meat is cooked, add the prepared onions and potatoes, with salt and pepper to taste. Turn into a warmed serving dish and sprinkle with chopped parsley.

Circassian Chicken   Turkey

4 helpings

1 chicken (1.5kg approx)	*1 bay leaf*
1 large onion	*salt and pepper*
4 cloves	

Walnut Sauce

200g shelled walnuts	*2 × 15ml spoons olive oil*
1 stick day-old French	*salt and pepper*
* bread*	*2 × 15ml spoons paprika*
1 medium-sized onion	

Put the chicken in a flameproof casserole or stew-pan just large enough to hold it. Skin the onion, press in the cloves, then place in the pan with the chicken. Add the bay leaf, salt, and pepper to taste, and enough water just to cover the chicken. Cover, and bring to the boil; then reduce the heat, and simmer for about 1 hour until tender. Meanwhile, blanch the walnuts for the sauce for a few minutes in boiling water, drain and leave to dry.

Remove the chicken from the pan. Strain the chicken stock through a fine sieve into a basin and put to one side. When the chicken is just cool enough to handle, remove the meat from the bones in the largest pieces possible, discarding the skin. Keep hot.

Break apart the French bread, tear the bread away from the crust and put it in a bowl; discard the crust. Add enough chicken stock to moisten the bread thoroughly, and leave until very soft. Reserve the remaining stock.

Skin and chop the onion finely. Heat the olive oil in a small pan over low heat, add the onion, and sauté until quite soft. Turn it into a fairly large bowl, season to taste, add the paprika, and mix well. The mixture should be bright red.

Chop the blanched and dried walnuts fairly finely. Pound them in a mortar until very fine and smooth, or process in an electric blender.

Remove the soaked bread from the bowl, squeeze out any excess liquid, and add it to the walnuts. Mash or blend together, then add them to the onion mixture. Add a little chicken stock, and beat with a rotary beater. Continue to add stock, and beat until the sauce is of the required consistency. Heat until almost boiling.

To serve, place the chicken meat in a ring of Turkish Rice Pilaf (p1518) and pour the walnut sauce over it.

Gareethes me Feta   Greece
(Prawns in Onion and Tomato Sauce)

6 helpings

2 onions	*salt and pepper*
1kg tomatoes	*1kg peeled prawns*
2 cloves garlic	*250g Feta cheese*
100ml olive oil	
1 × 15ml spoon chopped	
* parsley*	

Skin the onions, and cut into thin slices. Skin the tomatoes, de-seed, and chop them. Chop the garlic finely. Heat the olive oil over medium heat in a deep frying pan. Add the prepared vegetables, the parsley, salt, and pepper. Stir the mixture well. Cover the pan and simmer for 1 hour, stirring occasionally.

Put the prawns into 6 scallop shells or individual ovenproof casseroles, cover with the onion and tomato sauce, and crumble the cheese on top. Cook in a very hot oven, 230°C, Gas 8, for 5–7 minutes until the prawns are heated through.

Turkish Rice Pilaf

4 helpings

400ml chicken stock
(made from cooking
Circassian Chicken
(p1517) if possible)

2 × 15ml spoons butter
150g rice

Heat the chicken stock gently to just below boiling point. In a second large pan, melt the butter and stir in the rice, making sure all the grains are coated with butter. Stir frequently until the rice is golden, then pour in the hot chicken stock. Bring to the boil, reduce the heat, cover the pan, and simmer for 20 minutes until all the moisture has been absorbed.

An attractive way to serve this dish is to make a ring of pilaf on a suitable platter, and place pieces of hot cooked chicken meat in the ring. Pour a suitable thick gravy over the chicken and pilaf.

Couscous   Morocco

See p869.

Avgolemono Sauce   Greece

4 helpings

300ml hot stock (see
Method)
3 eggs

50ml lemon juice
salt and pepper

Use stock from the boiled or stewed meat, fish, poultry or vegetables which are to be served with the sauce.

Beat the eggs with the lemon juice until thoroughly blended. Add some of the hot stock gradually, stirring all the time, until 50–60ml of the stock has been used. Put this mixture and the remaining stock in a small saucepan and heat gently, stirring all the time, until the sauce thickens. Do not allow the sauce to boil, or it will curdle. Season to taste.

Serve over meat, fish, poultry or vegetables.

Yuxhni   Syria
(Sauce for Rice)

4 helpings

500g lamb **or** beef
4 × 10ml spoons olive oil
2 medium-sized onions
1 clove of garlic

1 × 5ml spoon salt
pepper
1kg green beans
350ml tomato juice

Cut the meat into 2cm cubes. Heat the olive oil in a large heavy pan over medium heat. Add the meat, and brown it on all sides. Skin, chop, and add the onions. Chop and add the garlic, with salt and pepper to taste, and continue cooking, stirring occasionally, until the onions are golden. Cut the beans into 2cm lengths, add to the meat and onions and stir well. Reduce the heat and cook, stirring occasionally, for about 30 minutes, until the beans are tender. Add the tomato juice, cover the pan, and simmer over low heat for about $1\frac{1}{2}$ hours, until very tender.

Serve over boiled rice.

Summer Salad   Greece

4 helpings

3 tomatoes
1 cucumber
1 onion
6 × 15ml spoons olive oil
2 × 15ml spoons white
  wine vinegar

salt and pepper
200g Feta cheese
20 black olives
chopped fresh **or** dried
  crushed oregano

Cut the tomatoes into large pieces, and cut the cucumber (preferably unpeeled) into small pieces. Skin the onion and cut into 8 or 12 wedges. Place the vegetables on a salad platter. Mix the olive oil, vinegar, salt and pepper together well. Pour the dressing over the salad. Cut the cheese into small chunks, and stone the olives. Sprinkle them both on top of the salad. Sprinkle with oregano, and serve at room temperature, or slightly chilled in very hot weather.

Melopita
Greece

(Honey Pie or Cheesecake)

6 helpings

Filling

700g Myzithra **or**
  cottage cheese

150g caster sugar

2 × 5ml spoons ground
  cinnamon

200g clear honey

5 eggs

Pastry

300g plain flour

3 × 2.5ml spoons baking
  powder

a pinch of salt

125g butter

flour for rolling out

Make the pastry first. Sift the flour, baking powder, and salt together into a bowl. Rub in the butter, and mix to a stiff dough with cold water. Roll out the pastry on a lightly floured surface, and use it to line a 20cm pie plate or flan ring about 5cm deep.

Sieve the cottage cheese, if used. Beat together in a bowl the cheese, sugar, and 1 × 5ml spoon cinnamon. Blend in the honey, then mix in the eggs one by one, beating well after each addition. Sieve the mixture, then turn it into the pastry shell. Bake in a moderate oven, 180°C, Gas 4, for 45 minutes, then increase the heat to hot, 220°C, Gas 7, and bake for another 10–15 minutes until a skewer inserted into the pie comes out clean. Leave to cool in the oven. Sprinkle with the remaining cinnamon before serving. Serve cold.

Imarim Triim be Syrup
Israel

(Fresh Dates in Syrup)

4 helpings

500g fresh dates
  (30–36 dates)

250ml water

125g caster sugar

4–6 cloves

whole blanched almonds
  (1 for each date)

The dates should be ripe but firm. Put them in a saucepan with the water. Bring to the boil, and cook gently for 3–4 minutes until tender. Drain, reserving the water. Skin and stone the dates without spoiling their shape. Scatter a layer of sugar in a saucepan, cover with a layer of dates, and 2–3 cloves. Repeat these layers until all the ingredients are used. Leave to stand overnight.

Next day, remove the dates, scraping off any loose sugar. Add the reserved water to the sugar and cloves in the saucepan, bring to the boil, and cook gently for 7–10 minutes until reduced to a syrup. Meanwhile, stuff each date with an almond. Add the dates to the syrup, and boil gently for 7–10 minutes until very syrupy; there should be enough liquid to half-cover the dates. Leave to cool slightly, then put into heated jars with screw-topped lids. Cover loosely. Cool, screw on the lids tightly, and store for 24 hours or until required.

Serve as a dessert with cream, or as sweetmeats.

Note Do not store for more than 2 weeks.

India

Both the size and the complex history of India have influenced her cookery, which varies enormously from region to region, from family to family, even from cook to cook.

In the recipes below, constant use has been made of some of the main spices which form the basis of many Indian dishes. These are whole garam masala, which is made up from cloves, cardamoms, cinnamon stick, cumin seeds, bay leaves, and peppercorns. Among the ground spices, the most common are cumin, coriander, turmeric, and chilli. Onions are widely used, as well as garlic, ginger, and fresh coriander, which form the basis of Indian sauces and give them colour, body, and flavour.

Although spices and herbs are freshly ground every day in Indian homes, authentic Indian food can be made with ground spices bought in any Indian grocery, supermarket or delicatessen.

An Indian dish is well cooked when the flavour of the spices blends into the other ingredients. The number of spices used is largely a matter of individual taste and regional custom. They should never taste raw or separate, nor should the dish be so over-spiced that its individual character is lost.

Talawa Macchi

(Fried Fish)

4–5 helpings

650g cod **or** hake fillets	1 × 5ml spoon chilli
1½ × 5ml spoons salt	powder
1 × 5ml spoon turmeric	6 × 15ml spoons
	vegetable oil

Cut the fish into 2cm thick slices. Mix the salt and spices to a thick paste with a little water. Rub the fish all over with the mixture and leave to stand for 1 hour.

Heat the oil in a frying pan. Fill the pan with pieces of fish, and fry for about 20 minutes, until golden-brown all over. Repeat until all the fish is cooked.

Serve hot with Pulao Rice (p1523) and Dal (p1522).

Biriani

(Spiced Lamb with Saffron Rice)

4–5 helpings

1 × 2.5ml spoon saffron strands	300g natural yoghurt
4 × 10ml spoons boiling water	300ml vegetable oil
100g fresh **or** frozen peas	4 × 5ml spoons salt
700g leg of lamb	1 × 2.5ml spoon chilli powder
900g onions	3 small green chillies
200g Basmati rice	1 × 5ml spoon ground garam masala
6 cloves garlic	400ml boiling salted water
1 × 5cm piece ginger root	juice of two lemons **or** limes
2 × 15ml spoons fresh coriander leaves	150ml milk

Whole Garam Masala

1 × 5ml spoon cumin seeds	8 cloves
2 × 10cm pieces cinnamon stick	8 whole cardamoms
	8 black peppercorns
	12 bay leaves

Make the whole garam masala first. Add all the spices and herbs together and put to one side in a small bowl. Steep two-thirds of the saffron strands with the 4 × 10ml spoons boiling water in a small cup. Cook the peas, and put to one side. Bone the lamb and cut it into 2cm cubes. Skin the onions, and slice as thinly as possible. Wash and drain the rice thoroughly. Skin and crush the garlic, grate the ginger root, and chop the coriander leaves finely. Beat the yoghurt with a fork until smooth.

Heat the oil in a saucepan, and fry the onions until golden-brown. Drain off any excess oil, with about 200g of the onions, and reserve them. Add the meat to the saucepan with the remaining saffron strands, garlic, ginger, coriander leaves, yoghurt, 2 × 5ml spoons salt, the chilli powder, whole chillies, and the ground garam masala. Add the prepared whole garam masala. Stir the ingredients together, and fry over moderate heat until the meat cubes are browned. Reduce the heat, and simmer for about 40–45 minutes until the meat is three-quarters cooked. The sauce should be thick and well reduced.

Meanwhile, boil the rice for 2 minutes in the 400ml boiling salted water, reduce the heat and simmer, uncovered, for 10 minutes or until the rice is almost cooked. Drain into a warmed dish or bowl. Transfer one-third of the rice to a second bowl, and mix in the soaked saffron and its water.

Put a layer of boiled white rice in a large, oven-to-table flameproof casserole. Cover with a layer of saffron-coloured rice. Sprinkle with the reserved peas and fried onions. Cover with a layer of the spiced lamb mixture. Repeat these layers until all the ingredients are used, ending with a layer of saffron rice. Pour the lemon or lime juice and milk over the dish, and cover with a tight-fitting lid. Cook over high heat for 2 minutes, reduce the heat to simmering point, and cook very gently for 25 minutes or until the rice and meat are cooked through.

Serve hot from the casserole as a main dish, with Raita (p1524) or an onion salad.

Murg Tandori

(Roast Chicken with Spiced Yoghurt)

4–5 helpings

1 roasting chicken (1.25kg approx)	a few drops red food colouring or a pinch of turmeric
1 × 2cm piece ginger root	
4 cloves garlic	juice of 2 lemons
1 × 5ml spoon cumin seeds	1 × 5ml spoon salt
	150g natural yoghurt
1 × 5ml spoon chilli powder	2 × 15ml spoons vegetable oil
1 × 5ml spoon ground garam masala	

Skin the chicken (p620). Keep it whole, or cut into 4 pieces. Grate the ginger. Skin and crush the garlic. Toast the cumin seeds in a small ungreased frying pan over moderate heat for 1 minute. Grind them with a pestle and mortar, or in a pepper mill. Make a paste with all the spices (except the toasted cumin seeds), the garlic, colouring or turmeric, lemon juice, salt, and yoghurt.

Prick the chicken with a fork, and cut a few slits in its legs and breast. Rub the bird with the paste, pressing it deeply into the slits. Marinate for 12 hours or overnight in the paste.

Arrange the chicken on a rack in a shallow roasting tin. Baste it with the oil and any leftover paste. Cook in a moderate oven, 180°C, Gas 4, for 1½–2 hours, basting the chicken with the oil and juices from time to time. When cooked, sprinkle with the toasted cumin seeds.

Serve with a tomato and onion salad.

Keema

(Minced Meat Curry)

4 helpings

2 medium-sized onions (150g approx)	1 × 2.5ml spoon cumin seeds
a small piece of ginger root	4 black peppercorns
	3 bay leaves
3 cloves garlic	2 cloves
75ml vegetable oil	1 whole cardamom
2½ × 5ml spoons ground coriander	1 small stick of cinnamon
1 × 5ml spoon ground turmeric	2 green chillies
	200g lamb bones
1 × 2.5ml spoon chilli powder	450g minced beef or lamb (approx)
1 × 2.5ml spoon ground cumin	200ml water

Skin and slice the onions. Grate the ginger. Skin and crush the garlic. Heat the oil in a saucepan, and fry the onions until they begin to colour. Add the garlic, the spices, and whole chillies, stirring all the time. Cook rapidly for about 2 minutes. Add the meat bones, and fry quickly until brown. Add the minced meat, and stir for about 10–12 minutes, or until all the lumps are broken up and it is evenly fried. Add the water, bring to the boil, reduce the heat, cover, and simmer for 1 hour, adding a little more water if necessary. Discard the bones and whole chillies before serving.

Serve hot as a main course with boiled or Pulao Rice (p1523).

Milamili
(Mixed Vegetable Curry)

4–5 helpings

450g potatoes	2 green chillies
100g carrots	2 × 5ml spoons salt
2 medium-sized onions	2 × 5ml spoons ground
200g aubergines	coriander
2 tomatoes	$\frac{3}{4}$ × 5ml spoon turmeric
a small piece of ginger	1 × 2.5ml spoon ground
root	cumin
2 cloves garlic	1 × 2.5ml spoon chilli
200g firm white cabbage	powder
75ml vegetable oil	200ml hot water
1 × 2.5ml spoon cumin	100g fresh **or** frozen
seeds	peas
6 bay leaves	

Peel the potatoes and scrape the carrots. Skin the onions. Peel the aubergines. Cut the potatoes and aubergines into 2cm cubes, and slice the carrots and onions as thinly as possible. Chop the tomatoes coarsely. Grate the ginger. Skin and crush the garlic. Shred the cabbage.

Heat the oil in a large saucepan and sauté the onions, cumin seeds, and bay leaves. When the onions are lightly browned, add the whole green chillies, tomatoes, salt, garlic, and all the remaining spices. Stir and cook for another 5–7 minutes. Add the carrots and cook for 5 more minutes. Add the cabbage and stir well. Add the hot water. Reduce the heat. After 3 minutes, add the aubergine and fresh peas if used. When the aubergine is half-cooked (6–8 minutes), add the frozen peas, if used. Mix all the vegetables well and cover with a lid. Simmer for 5 minutes until the aromatic spices are absorbed by the vegetables. Remove the chillies before serving.

Serve hot with boiled rice and Raita (p1524) or with Dal.

Dal
(Indian Spiced Lentils)

4–5 helpings

1 small onion	1 × 5ml spoon turmeric
(75g approx)	1 × 5ml spoon ground
1 tomato	coriander
a small piece of ginger	1 × 2.5ml spoon chilli
root	powder
200g red lentils	$\frac{1}{2}$ × 2.5ml spoon ground
400ml water	cumin
2 green chillies	1 × 5ml spoon salt

Sauce

2 cloves garlic	1 × 10cm piece
2 × 15ml spoons	cinnamon stick
vegetable oil	6 dried red chillies
1 × 2.5ml spoon cumin	
seeds	

Skin the onion and slice it thinly. Cut up the tomato. Grate the ginger. Add the lentils and all the remaining ingredients to the water, except those for the sauce. Bring to the boil, reduce the heat, and simmer until the lentils are tender.

Meanwhile, make the sauce. Skin and chop the garlic finely. Heat the oil in a small frying pan, and fry the garlic until golden. Add the cumin seeds, cinnamon stick, and dried chillies. Fry for 2 minutes. Stir this sauce into the lentils and cook for another 10 minutes. The lentils will absorb the fragrance of the spices.

Serve hot with any curry.

Note Another recipe for Spiced Lentils can be found on p776.

Aloo

(Fried Spiced Potatoes)

4–5 helpings

450g potatoes	1 × 5ml spoon ground
1 medium-sized onion	turmeric
(75g approx)	1 × 5ml spoon chilli
1 green chilli	powder
3 × 15ml spoons	1 × 5ml spoon salt
vegetable oil	50ml water
1 × 5ml spoon mustard	2 × 15ml spoons fresh
seeds	lemon juice (optional)

Peel the potatoes. Parboil them, and cut them into pieces. Skin the onion and dice it. Chop the green chilli finely. Heat the oil in a saucepan and fry the onion until soft and transparent. Add the mustard seeds and fry for 1 minute. Add all the other spices, the salt, and chopped green chilli. Fry for 1 minute. Add the parboiled potatoes, and stir until well coated with the spicy mixture. Add the water. Cover with a lid, reduce the heat, and cook gently for 15–20 minutes until the potatoes are cooked through.

Sprinkle with the lemon juice, if liked, and serve hot with Puris, as a lunch dish, first course, or as a side dish at dinner.

Pulao Rice

(Fried Rice)

4–5 helpings

½ small onion	2 bay leaves
200g Basmati rice	4 black peppercorns
1 × 15ml spoon	½ × 2.5ml spoon cumin
vegetable oil	seeds
1 × 2cm piece	450ml water
cinnamon stick	2 × 5ml spoons salt
2 whole cardamoms	

Skin the onion and slice it very thinly. Wash the rice under warm running water, rubbing it between your hands until the water runs clear. Drain and put to one side. Heat the oil in a deep saucepan, and fry the onion until transparent. Add all the spices and fry over medium heat for 2–3 minutes until they give off a fragrant aroma. Add the water and salt. When the water begins to boil, add the rice. Bring back to the boil, then reduce the heat as low as possible. Cover the pan with a tight-fitting lid. Cook for 15 minutes or until the rice is dry.

This rice goes very well with Talawa Macchi (p1520) and Dal (p1522).

Puris

(Deep-fried Unleavened Wholemeal Bread)

Makes 12

225g wholemeal flour	vegetable oil for deep
1 × 2.5ml spoon salt	frying
flour for kneading	

Mix the flour and salt in a bowl. Gradually add enough water to make a soft pliable dough. Turn on to a floured surface and knead until firm. Cover with a damp cloth and leave for 30 minutes. Divide the dough into 12 equal portions. Shape into balls and roll out each one into a thin round pancake about 10cm in diameter.

Heat the oil in a deep frying pan. When it begins to sizzle, drop in a puri. Press it gently with a spoon. It should puff up immediately. Cook for about 10 minutes until golden-brown on both sides, turning once. Remove and drain thoroughly. Keep hot while frying the remaining puris in the same way.

Serve hot with Aloo, or with any meat or vegetable dish.

Fresh Coriander Chutney

4–5 helpings

*2 medium-sized onions
(150g approx)*
1 clove of garlic
1 tomato
1 green chilli
*a small piece of ginger
root*
*1 × 15ml spoon chopped
fresh coriander leaves*

*3 × 15ml spoons tomato
ketchup*
2 × 15ml spoons vinegar
1 × 2.5ml spoon salt
*½ × 2.5ml spoon black
peppercorns*

Skin the onions, garlic, and tomato. Crush the garlic. Chop the tomato and chilli. Grate the ginger and onions. Mix all the ingredients together.

Serve with Pakoras or as an accompaniment to an Indian meal.

Note This chutney will keep for up to 6 days in an airtight jar in a refrigerator.

VARIATION

The ingredients can be processed in an electric blender to make a smooth chutney. In this case, replace the 2 × 15ml spoons vinegar with 150ml water before blending.

Raita

(Yoghurt Sauce with Cucumber)

4–5 helpings

1 clove of garlic
3 black peppercorns
*a very small piece of
ginger root*
¼ cucumber

*1 × 2.5ml spoon cumin
seeds*
600g natural yoghurt
1 × 2.5ml spoon salt

Skin the garlic and crush it with the peppercorns. Grate the ginger and cucumber. Toast the cumin seeds in a small, ungreased frying pan over low heat for 1 minute. Grind them in a peppermill. Beat the yoghurt with a fork until it becomes light and smooth. Add the cucumber and mix thoroughly. Add all the other ingredients except the toasted cumin seeds. Sprinkle these over the sauce.

Serve chilled as an accompaniment.

Pakoras

(Vegetable Fritters)

4–5 helpings

*1 medium-sized potato
(100g approx)*
*1 medium-sized onion
(100g approx)*
*1 medium-sized
aubergine (100g
approx)*
1 green pepper
*200g gram flour (chick-
pea flour)*

*1 × 5ml spoon chilli
powder*
*1 × 5ml spoon ground
turmeric*
1 × 5ml spoon salt
*a pinch of bicarbonate of
soda*
*vegetable oil for deep
frying*

Prepare the potato and onion. Peel the aubergine. Slice them as thinly as possible. De-seed the pepper, and cut it into thin strips. Sift the flour into a mixing bowl. Add the spices, salt, and bicarbonate of soda. Gradually add enough warm water, stirring all the time, until the batter is the consistency of double cream. Heat the oil (p302). Dip a few pieces of the vegetables in the batter and gently drop them into the hot oil. Cook until crisp and golden-brown. Remove with a perforated spoon and drain on soft kitchen paper. Keep hot until all the vegetables are cooked.

Serve hot with Fresh Coriander Chutney as a snack, first course or as part of a main meal.

Shahi Tukra

(Saffron Toasts)

4–5 helpings

*3 medium slices white
bread*
2 cardamoms
*2 whole unblanched
almonds*
*4 whole unblanched
pistachio nuts*
40g ghee or butter

250ml milk
a few strands saffron
3 × 15ml spoons sugar
75ml double cream
*2 × 15ml spoons single
cream*
a pinch of grated nutmeg

Cut the crusts off the bread. Cut each slice into 4 triangular pieces. Peel and crush the cardamoms. Crush the almonds and pistachio nuts with their skins. Heat the ghee or butter in a frying pan, and fry the bread until golden-brown on both sides. Drain on soft kitchen paper. Heat the milk slowly in a shallow pan over medium heat. When it begins to steam, add the saffron strands and sugar. Reduce to very low heat, and cook gently for 20 minutes. Add the double cream and cook for a further 10 minutes. The sauce should be thickened but runny. Drop the fried bread triangles into the sauce. Turn them over after 5 minutes. Cook very slowly until the sauce is absorbed by the fried bread.

Serve hot or cold, covered with single cream and a generous sprinkling of the freshly crushed nuts, cardamom, and a pinch of grated nutmeg.

Sheer Khurma
(Sweet Milk Pudding with Vermicelli)

4–5 helpings

2 × 15ml spoons blanched almonds	1 × 15ml spoon single cream
2 × 15ml spoons pistachio nuts	75g vermicelli
750ml milk	6 × 15ml spoons sugar
	100g desiccated coconut

Chop the almonds. Blanch, skin, and crush the pistachio nuts. Put to one side. Replace 1 × 15ml spoon of the milk with the cream. Boil the milk in a saucepan. Reduce the heat as low as possible, and cook until thickened (30–45 minutes), stirring occasionally. Add the vermicelli and stir for a few minutes. When the vermicelli is half-cooked, after about 7 minutes, add the sugar and increase the heat to give a rolling boil. Boil for 2 minutes, then reduce the heat to simmering. Mix in the coconut, almonds, and pistachios. Simmer over low heat for 30 minutes. Serve hot or cold.

Italy

Almost all Italian cookery is regional. Different specialities and cooking styles are found in each province; the cooking of Tuscany is quite different from that of Lombardy, for instance, and Neapolitan or Sicilian cooking is different again. There are, however, common factors; pasta, cheese, vegetables, and fruit dominate most people's diet. There are hundreds of pasta shapes, presented quite differently in each provincial area. Gnocchi, the small dumplings which date back to the days of ancient Rome are also used widely.

An Italian meal may begin with *antipasti*, often a simple salad of peppers and tomatoes with a few black olives or slices of salami. More lavish ones include fish or shellfish. Pasta may be a starter or main-course dish. The meal usually ends with either cheese and salad or fruit.

Italian ices and ice creams – *gelati, granite,* and *cassata,* are reputedly the best in the world. They are not always served as a dessert, but like Italian pastries, are enjoyed between meals in cafés.

The Italians enjoy their wine and produce many famous varieties including Chianti and Asti Spumante.

Proscuitto con Fichi
(Smoked Ham with Fresh Figs)

4 helpings

250g Parma ham	250g fresh figs
salad oil	8 black olives
4 large lettuce leaves	

The ham should be cut in paper-thin slices. Brush each slice lightly with a little oil and place on the lettuce leaves. Cut a cross in the top of each fig, and open the points out slightly, to imitate the petals of a flower. Arrange the black olives alternately with the figs on the ham.

Fritto Misto al Pescatore
(Deep-fried Seafood and Vegetables)

6 helpings

Fritters

250g frozen scampi
125g cauliflower sprigs
50g flour
salt and pepper

250g fresh sardines **or**
sprats
oil for deep frying
1 large onion
2 courgettes

Batter

1 egg
25ml salad oil
300ml water
125g plain flour

1 × 15ml spoon chopped
parsley
1 clove of garlic
a pinch of salt

Garnish
lemon wedges

Make the batter first. Combine the egg, oil and water, and beat in the flour to make a smooth batter. Leave to stand for 15 minutes. Add the parsley and squeeze in the garlic. Season with salt.

Make the fritters. Thaw the scampi, and parboil the cauliflower sprigs. Season the flour with salt and pepper and use some to coat the sardines or sprats. Heat the oil (p302) and fry the fish. Drain on soft kitchen paper. Drain the thawed scampi and coat with seasoned flour. Dip in the batter, a few at a time, and deep fry at the same temperature. Drain on soft kitchen paper. Coat the cauliflower sprigs with seasoned flour, then dip in the batter, and deep fry. Drain in the same way. Skin the onion, and slice into fine rings. Canelle the courgettes (ie score the skin deeply), but do not peel them. Cut them in half across, then into quarters lengthways; coat with seasoned flour. Dip the onion rings and courgettes in the batter and deep fry (p302). Drain well.

Pile the mixture of fritters on a dish and sprinkle with salt. Serve garnished with lemon wedges.

Scaloppine con Prosciutto e Funghi
(Stuffed Veal Escalopes)

4 helpings

200ml basic thin batter
(p934)
4 thick veal escalopes
(150g each)
4 thin slices Bel Paese
cheese
4 × 25g slices Parma
ham
50g flour
salt and pepper
2 eggs
75ml cooking oil

25g onion
50g mushrooms
1 × 15ml spoon chopped
parsley and dried basil,
mixed
50g butter
50g grated Parmesan
cheese
300ml foundation brown
sauce (p698)
150ml Marsala

Use the batter to make 4 pancakes 16cm in diameter. Put to one side.

Cut a slit in one side of each escalope, and enlarge it to make a pocket. Place 1 slice each of cheese and ham inside. Flatten the escalopes lightly with the palm of the hand to bind the meat and cheese inside. Season the flour with salt and pepper. Coat the escalopes with the seasoned flour. Beat the eggs until liquid, and dip the escalopes in beaten egg, coating each side well. Heat the oil in a large frying pan, and fry the escalopes for 8 minutes, turning once, until golden on both sides. Remove, and leave to cool.

Chop the onion and mushrooms, and sauté with the herbs in the remaining oil for 5 minutes. Spread this mixture over the reserved pancakes. Place 1 escalope on top of each, and wrap the pancake round the escalope.

Melt the butter and use some to grease a shallow ovenproof dish. Place the wrapped escalopes in it in one layer. Brush with more of the melted butter, and sprinkle with the Parmesan cheese. Bake in a fairly hot oven, 190°C, Gas 5, for 10 minutes.

Re-heat the brown sauce with the Marsala. Serve separately in a warmed sauce-boat.

Vitello Tonnata

(Cold Veal with Tuna Sauce)

6–8 helpings

5 anchovy fillets	2 sticks celery
1kg leg of veal, boned	375ml dry white wine
salt and pepper	1 × 99g can tuna fish in
pared rind and juice of	oil
1 lemon	100ml olive oil **or** as
1 onion	needed
2 cloves	1 × 15ml spoon capers
2 bay leaves	
1 medium-sized carrot	
(100g approx)	

Garnish
lemon slices

Drain the anchovy fillets. Remove the thin outer skin and any solid fat from the veal. Place 3 anchovy fillets along the length of the cavity where the bone was removed. Reshape the meat, and tie it into a neat roll about 20 × 14cm. Season the meat. Put it in a stewpan with a strip of lemon rind. Skin the onion, press in the cloves, and add it to the pan with the bay leaves. Slice and add the carrot and celery. Pour in the wine, and add just enough water to cover the meat. Bring to the boil, cover, reduce the heat, and simmer gently for 1½ hours or until the meat is tender. Remove it from the pan and leave to cool completely. (Keep the stock for another dish.)

When the meat is cold, slice it thinly, then re-shape it into the roll. Place it in a deep terrine or serving dish.

Pound the tuna fish with its oil, the lemon juice, and remaining anchovy fillets until smooth. Alternatively, process in an electric blender. When smooth, trickle in the olive oil gradually, as when making mayonnaise, whisking or blending as fast as possible until the mixture thickens. Season to taste. Chop and fold in the capers. Pour the sauce over the meat, cover loosely, and leave to marinate for 12–24 hours. Serve garnished with thin lemon slices.

Ossi Buchi

(Braised Veal Knuckles in Wine)
See p564.

Pollo alla Cacciatora

(Chicken with Tomatoes and Mushrooms)

4 helpings

1 roasting chicken (1.5kg	50ml dry white wine
approx)	75g mushrooms
salt and pepper	2 tomatoes (150g
2 × 15ml spoons flour	approx)
50g butter	2 × 15ml spoons
2 lean bacon rashers	concentrated tomato
(100g approx)	purée
2–3 small onions (100g	1 bay leaf
approx)	150ml chicken stock
1 clove of garlic	
(optional)	

Cut the chicken into small joints (p619–20). Season well with salt and pepper, and coat the joints with flour. Heat half the butter in a frying pan and fry the chicken pieces, turning as required, until lightly browned all over. Cut the bacon into short strips. Skin and slice the onions, and crush the garlic, if used. Heat the rest of the butter in a saucepan and gently fry the bacon strips, onion and garlic, until the onions are soft. Add the chicken pieces and wine. Stir once, then cook quickly until the wine is well reduced.

Slice the mushrooms, and skin and crush the tomatoes. Add them to the pan with the tomato purée and bay leaf. Add the stock and bring to the boil. Reduce the heat, cover, and cook gently for about 45 minutes or until the chicken is tender.

Maccheroni alla Bolognese

(Macaroni with Bolognese Sauce)

4 helpings

250g macaroni **or** other long pasta	50g grated Parmesan cheese
salt and pepper	a pinch of ground mace
50g butter	

Sauce

50g onion	150ml Marsala (optional)
1 clove of garlic	50g concentrated tomato purée
25g celery	
50g carrot	a pinch each of salt, ground mace, dried oregano, ground clove, dried basil, and ground black pepper
150g lean pork	
200g lean beef	
50g chicken's **or** lamb's liver	
50ml oil	25g cornflour
300ml beef stock	150ml single cream

Make the sauce first. Prepare and chop the vegetables, and mince the meats and liver. Heat the oil in a large deep frying pan or saucepan, and fry all the vegetables, including the garlic, for 5 minutes until soft but not very brown. Add the minced meats and liver. Stir well. Cover, and cook gently for 8 minutes, stirring occasionally. Stir in the beef stock, wine if used, tomato purée, and all the seasonings. Bring to the boil, reduce the heat, and simmer for 25 minutes.

Just before the sauce is ready, break the pasta into short lengths. Cook in boiling salted water for 8 minutes. When just tender but still *al dente*, rinse, and drain. Mix in the butter, half the Parmesan cheese, and the mace. Season well with salt and pepper. Keep warm while completing the sauce.

Blend the cornflour into a little of the cream, then blend with the rest of the cream. Stir into the sauce to thicken it. Cook very gently for 5 minutes.

Serve half the sauce on top of the pasta and the rest separately.

Note This is the classic Ragu or Bolognese Sauce. It is used with any kind of pasta, and in many different pasta dishes, both boiled and oven cooked.

Cannelloni alla Romagnola

(Stuffed Pasta with Tomato Sauce)

6 helpings

Cannelloni

1 egg	1 × 2.5ml spoon salt
25ml oil	500g strong plain flour
250ml warm water	flour for rolling out

Filling

50g onion	50g soft white breadcrumbs
1 clove of garlic	25g plain flour
125g lean beef	1 egg
125g lean pork	butter for greasing
50ml oil for frying	300ml Salsa Pomodoro (p1532)
150ml beef stock	
50g concentrated tomato purée	50g grated Parmesan cheese
salt and pepper	
a pinch of ground mace	
1 × 15ml spoon chopped mixed herbs, eg oregano, basil, rosemary, parsley	

Make the cannelloni. Beat the egg until liquid, then mix in the oil, water, and salt. Mix in the flour gradually to form a smooth dough. Knead lightly, and roll into a ball. Leave to stand for 20 minutes.

Roll out the pasta 4mm thick on a lightly floured surface. Cut it into rectangular pieces, 10 × 5cm. Boil the pasta in salted water for 6 minutes. Drain, and lay on a damp tea-towel, side by side, but not touching. Leave to dry.

Meanwhile, make the filling. Skin the onion and the garlic, and chop them finely. Mince all the meat. Heat the oil in a large pan, and fry the onion and garlic for 4 minutes without browning. Add the meat, stir well, cover, and cook for 5 minutes. Mix in the stock, tomato purée, seasoning, and herbs. Cover again and cook gently for 25 minutes. Cool, then blend in the crumbs, flour, and egg to make a stiff filling.

Place a portion of the filling all along one side of each piece of pasta. Roll up the pasta to make stuffed tubes. Put them side by side in a shallow ovenproof dish, well greased with butter. Pour the Salsa Pomodoro over the cannelloni and sprinkle with the Parmesan cheese. Bake in a moderate oven, 180°C, Gas 4, for 25 minutes.

Note If preferred, bought cannelloni can be used. Boil and arrange them as above. When ready to fill them, trickle a little cold water through each tube, to open it up for filling.

Maccheroni alla Carbonara
(Macaroni with Bacon and Egg Sauce)

4 helpings

450g macaroni
100g streaky bacon, without rinds (see **Note**)
1 × 15ml spoon oil
4 eggs
2 × 10ml spoons single cream

salt and freshly ground black pepper
75g grated Pecorino **or** Parmesan cheese

Cook the macaroni in fast boiling salted water until tender but still *al dente*. Meanwhile, cut the bacon into fine strips. Heat the oil in a large frying pan and fry the bacon until the fat is transparent. Draw the pan off the heat. Beat the eggs with the cream, and season with a very little salt, and a generous grinding of pepper.

Drain the cooked macaroni thoroughly, and mix with the bacon. Return to moderate heat, and heat the bacon and macaroni for not more than 2 minutes. Stir the egg mixture rapidly into the pan. As it begins to thicken, tip in the cheese. Do not stir it in. Serve immediately on hot plates.

Note The sauce can be served with any kind of long pasta. Strong Pecorino (sheep's milk) cheese is the traditional cheese to use for any *alla carbonara* dish, but freshly grated Parmesan is a suitable alternative. The sauce must be served as soon as it is made.

De-salted bacon should be used.

Pasta con la Sarde
(Pasta with Sardines)

4–6 helpings

$\frac{1}{2}$ × 2.5ml spoon saffron strands (approx)
50g fennel bulb
400g fresh sardines (approx)
100g onion
2 × 15ml spoons olive oil **or** sunflower oil
3 × 15ml spoons concentrated tomato purée

100g pine nut kernels
75g seedless raisins
450g spaghetti, tagliatelli **or** fettucine
salt and pepper
2 × 15ml spoons chicken stock (optional)
2 × 15ml spoons Marsala

Soak the saffron in 1 × 5ml spoon of water. Blanch the fennel, drain, and separate the fleshy layers. Chop them finely. Cut the fish into 2cm pieces. Skin and chop the onion. Heat the oil in a large frying pan, and sauté the onion gently for 2–3 minutes until tender. Add the fish, tomato purée, pine kernels, raisins, the saffron water, and fennel. Mix well and draw off the heat.

Cook the pasta in fast boiling salted water until just soft. Drain and keep hot. Return the pan of fish to the heat, and simmer for 2–3 minutes, stirring gently. Season well. Add the stock if the mixture seems too dry to coat the pasta, then add the Marsala. Simmer for a further 2–3 minutes. Place the pasta on a heated serving dish, pour the sardine mixture over it, and toss well. Serve very hot.

Note If fresh sardines are not available, use 1 × 425g can pilchards in tomato sauce. Cheese is *not* served with this dish.

Pasticcio di Lasagne Verde
(Baked Green Lasagne with Meat Sauce)

4 helpings

50g onion	*pepper*
1 clove of garlic	*250g tomatoes*
50g celery	*50g red pepper*
50g carrot	*75g walnut pieces*
250g green lasagne	*75g butter and bacon*
50g lean lamb	*fat, mixed*
500g lean beef	*50g sultanas*
50g lard **or** *4 × 15ml*	*150ml cold Béchamel*
spoons oil	*sauce* (p704)
300ml beef stock	*150g grated Parmesan*
50g concentrated tomato	*cheese*
purée	

Prepare and chop the onion, garlic, celery, and carrot. Cook the lasagne in boiling salted water for 15 minutes. Drain, rinse under hot water, and place on a slightly dampened tea-towel, side by side but not touching. Leave to dry.

Mince the lamb and beef. Heat the lard or oil in a frying pan, and sauté the chopped onion, garlic, celery and carrot together for 5 minutes. Add the minced meat and brown it lightly all over. Add the stock, tomato purée, and seasoning. Bring to the boil, reduce the heat, and simmer for 30 minutes. Skin, de-seed, and chop the tomatoes and pepper. Chop the nuts finely.

Grease a shallow ovenproof dish with the bacon fat and butter. Line the bottom with half the pasta and cover with the meat mixture, then sprinkle with nuts, sultanas, tomatoes, and pepper. Cover with the remaining pasta. Coat with thick, cold Béchamel sauce, and sprinkle with the Parmesan cheese. Bake in a moderate oven, 180°C, Gas 4, for 20 minutes.

VARIATION
This dish can also be made with Bolognese Sauce (p1528).

Spaghetti alla Marinara
(Spaghetti with Scampi)

4 helpings

1 clove of garlic	*salt and pepper*
1 × 15ml spoon chopped	*25g flour*
parsley and dried basil,	*250g scampi*
mixed	*25ml oil*
100g butter	*300ml Salsa Pomodoro*
250g spaghetti **or** *other*	*(p1532)*
long pasta	*a pinch of grated*
50g grated Parmesan	*nutmeg*
cheese	

Chop the garlic, and add with the herbs to 50g of the butter. Cream to a smooth paste, and put to one side. Break up the spaghetti into short lengths. Boil in salted water for 15 minutes or until tender. Drain in a sieve or strainer, and rinse with hot water. Turn on to greaseproof paper and pat dry. Put in a pan and re-heat with the remaining butter and half the Parmesan cheese. Season well. Keep hot in a shallow flameproof dish.

Season the flour, and coat the scampi with it, shaking off any surplus. Heat the oil in a frying pan. Shallow fry the scampi for 5 minutes. Drain off the oil, and add the scampi to the spaghetti. Stir in the herb butter. Add the Salsa Pomodoro and nutmeg to taste, and sprinkle with the remaining Parmesan cheese. Brown under a moderate grill for 3–5 minutes.

Tagliatelli con Salsa di Noci
(Ribbon Noodles with Walnut Sauce)

4 helpings

4–6 sprigs marjoram **or**	*salt and pepper*
6–8 sprigs parsley	*450g tagliatelli* **or** *other*
100g walnut pieces	*flat ribbon noodles*
100ml double cream	*50g butter*
olive oil	

Pick the leaves off the marjoram or parsley, and chop finely. Grind the walnuts to a paste in a coffee mill, or mince them; then pound with the leaves to obtain a paste. Alternatively, process in an electric blender with the marjoram or parsley. (It need not be completely smooth.) Mix in the cream slowly, blending thoroughly, then work in just enough oil to make a thick, creamy, pale green purée. Season to taste, and chill.

Boil the noodles in fast boiling salted water until cooked; drain well, and toss with the butter. Place on a heated serving dish, and spoon the cold sauce over the pasta.

Serve grated Parmesan cheese separately.

Gnocchi alla Romana
(Semolina Gnocchi)

4 helpings

600ml water	butter for greasing
125g medium semolina	250g tomatoes
salt and pepper	butter and oil for
a pinch of grated nutmeg	shallow frying
1 clove of garlic	50g grated Parmesan
50ml double cream	cheese
2 egg yolks	

Bring the water to the boil, and sprinkle in the semolina, stirring all the time. Simmer for 10 minutes. Season well with salt, pepper, and nutmeg. Grate in the garlic. Draw the pan off the heat. Blend the cream and egg yolks, and stir them into the semolina. Return the pan to the heat, bring the mixture to simmering point, and cook for 2 minutes, stirring all the time. Remove from the heat. Grease a shallow baking tray thickly with butter. Turn in the hot semolina mixture, smooth the top, and leave to cool and firm up. Meanwhile, skin, de-seed, and chop the tomatoes.

When the gnocchi mixture is cold, cut it into 3cm squares, rectangles or rounds. Heat the butter and oil in a frying pan, and fry the gnocchi gently, until light gold on both sides. Place them in a lightly greased, shallow flameproof dish. Cover with chopped tomatoes, then sprinkle with grated cheese. Brown quickly under a hot grill.

Risotto alla Milanese

4 helpings

50g onion	salt and pepper
25g butter	a good pinch of turmeric
25ml oil	50g salted butter
350g Italian rice	150g grated Parmesan
900ml chicken stock	cheese

Skin the onion and chop it finely. Heat the butter and oil in a large pan, add the onion and fry gently until soft but not brown. Stir in the rice, and cook, stirring, for 2 minutes. Heat the stock to simmering point. Reserve 1 × 15ml spoon stock, and pour the rest into the pan with the rice. Season to taste. Bring to the boil, cover, and cook gently for 20 minutes. Shake the pan from time to time to prevent the rice sticking to the bottom, and add a little extra stock or hot water, if required.

Shortly before the end of the cooking time, when the liquid is almost all absorbed, blend the turmeric into the reserved 1 × 15ml spoon stock, and stir it into the rice. Blend together the butter and grated cheese, and stir into the rice when it is just cooked. Serve as soon as the cheese has melted.

Note In Milan, saffron is always used to colour and flavour this dish. It is steeped for 10 minutes in some of the stock, then strained, and stirred into the rice when it is ready for serving. Turmeric is used for economy in this version.

Additional recipes using pasta, rice, and gnocchi can be found in the chapter on Pasta, Rice and other Grains.

Pizza con Mozzarella

Makes two 25cm pizze

Dough

15g fresh yeast	*3 × 2.5ml spoons olive*
125ml warm water	*oil (approx)*
a few grains caster sugar	*polenta (cornmeal) for*
175g strong white flour	*dusting*
1 × 2.5ml spoon salt	*oil for greasing*

Filling

150ml Salsa Pomodoro	*4 × 15ml spoons olive oil*
200g Mozzarella cheese	*3 × 15ml spoons grated*
4 black olives	*Parmesan cheese*
4 anchovy fillets	

Make the dough. Blend the yeast into a little of the warm water with the sugar, then stir in the remaining water. Leave in a warm place until frothy. Sift the flour and salt into a bowl. Pour in the yeast mixture and oil. Work into a dough and knead well until smooth and elastic. Dust lightly with flour and place in a lightly oiled polythene bag. Leave in a warm place for 1½ hours or until doubled in size. Knock back the dough and divide into two equal portions. Knead lightly. Roll out each portion on a board dusted with polenta into a circle 25cm in diameter and about 5mm thick. Heat the oven to very hot, 230°C, Gas 8.

Pinch up the edge of each dough circle to make a low rim. Pour half the Salsa Pomodoro into each pizza. Crumble half the Mozzarella cheese over the sauce. Halve and stone the olives. Place 2 anchovy fillets in the form of a cross on each pizza, and place the halved olives, cut side down, in the spaces between them. Trickle half the oil over each pizza, and sprinkle the Parmesan cheese on top. Bake on a lightly greased baking sheet for 5 minutes. Reduce the temperature to fairly hot, 200°C, Gas 6, and bake for a further 5 minutes until the dough is lightly browned and the cheese has melted. Serve at once.

Pesto Genovese

(Parmesan and Herb Sauce)

4 helpings

2 cloves garlic	*juice of 1 lemon*
25–40g chopped fresh	*salt and pepper*
basil	*100ml salad oil (approx)*
25g pine nut kernels	
40g grated Parmesan	
cheese	

Chop the garlic and pound it with the herbs, kernels, cheese, lemon juice and seasoning until smooth, or process in an electric blender. While blending, trickle in the oil as when making mayonnaise, until the sauce is a very thick paste.

Serve this sauce with any kind of pasta. Put the pasta in a heated serving bowl or individual bowls, stir in the sauce, and toss the pasta. Serve hot.

Salsa Pomodoro

(Tomato Sauce)

4 helpings

250g tomatoes	*300ml chicken stock*
50g red pepper	*salt and pepper*
50g lean bacon, without	*1 × 10ml spoon thick*
rinds	*honey*
50g bacon fat	*150ml sweet red*
50g onion	*vermouth (optional)*
1 clove of garlic	*1 × 15ml spoon chopped*
25g plain flour	*herbs, eg oregano,*
50g concentrated tomato	*basil, rosemary, mint*
purée	

Skin and de-seed the tomatoes and chop them coarsely. De-seed the pepper. Mince the bacon. Heat the fat in a large pan and sauté the bacon for 2 minutes. Chop the onion, garlic, and pepper. Add them to the bacon, and cook gently for 5 minutes, turning with a spoon. Sprinkle in the flour, stir it in, and add the tomato purée. Cook for 3 minutes. Add the chopped tomatoes, and stir in the chicken stock. Bring to the boil, reduce the heat, and simmer gently for 30 minutes. Season well. Just before serving, stir in the honey, and the vermouth, if used. Sprinkle with the herbs.

Torta di Ricotta
(Sweet Cheese Flan)

8 helpings

Cinnamon Pastry

100g butter	*a pinch of ground*
100g margarine	*cinnamon*
75g icing sugar	*250g plain flour*
2 egg yolks	*flour for rolling out*

Filling

625g Ricotta or cottage	*50g caster sugar*
cheese	*juice and grated rind*
25g grated Parmesan	*of 1 lemon*
cheese	*a pinch of salt*
2 eggs	*a few drops lemon*
25g flour	*essence*
50g natural yoghurt	

Decoration and Sauce

250g fresh raspberries	*4 × 15ml spoons*
1 × 15ml spoon	*maraschino liqueur*
arrowroot	*125ml sweet red*
125ml water	*vermouth*
125ml raspberry jam	

Make the pastry. Cream the fats and sugar until light and fluffy. Blend in the egg yolks, cinnamon, and flour. Knead lightly, and form into a ball. Chill for 20 minutes. Roll out on a lightly floured surface into a round 5mm thick. Line an 18cm flan ring, 4cm deep, with the pastry. Prick the bottom with a fork. Chill until required.

For the filling, cream the cheeses together, and gradually beat in the rest of the filling ingredients. Fill the flan with the mixture. Bake in a cool oven, 150°C, Gas 2, for 30 minutes. Remove from the oven and cut round the pastry edge to separate the filling from the pastry and to prevent the filling from spilling out. Return to the oven for 30 minutes, then leave to cool.

Decorate the cooled flan with the raspberries, and chill while preparing the sauce. Mix together the arrowroot and water. Melt the jam, and when boiling, stir in the arrowroot mixture to thicken it. Flavour with the maraschino liqueur and vermouth. Remove from the heat. When cold, pour the sauce over the raspberries.

Zabaglione (2)

Makes 300ml (approx)

5 egg yolks	*25ml brandy or orange*
1 egg	*liqueur*
50g caster sugar	*juice and thinly grated*
100ml Marsala	*rind of ½ lemon*

Place the egg yolks, whole egg, and sugar in a heatproof bowl. Whisk with a wire balloon whisk for at least 8 minutes until the mixture is light and foamy. Bring a saucepan of water to the boil, and balance the bowl over it. Warm the Marsala and brandy or liqueur, and add to the bowl with the lemon juice and rind. Continue whisking until the custard is thick enough to coat a spoon. Pour into fluted glasses, and serve hot with sponge fingers, small macaroons or shortbread.

Note For Zabaglione (1) see p974.

Spuma Gelata Angelina
(Iced Mousse)

4–6 helpings

300ml Zabaglione (2)	*3 drops orange essence*
2 × 15ml spoons gelatine	*juice of 1 lemon*
200g caster sugar	*5 drops orange food*
150ml water	*colouring (optional)*
300ml double cream	

Decoration
150g peeled orange
  segments

Prepare the Zabaglione as above. Blend the gelatine and 150g of the caster sugar to form jelly crystals. Boil the water, and dissolve the crystals in it. Leave to cool. When cold, but not yet set, blend into the Zabaglione.

Whip the cream until semi-stiff, and fold in the remaining sugar; then fold into the Zabaglione mixture. Add the essence and lemon juice, and the colouring, if liked. Place the mixture in a 1 litre mould and freeze. After 4 hours, unmould and decorate with orange segments.

Japan

The seasons are of great importance in Japanese cooking. Not only are the ingredients seasonal, but their presentation varies with the passing months. Decorations of ice and fresh greenery combine with glass and bamboo tableware to offer cooling refreshment in the summer heat. In winter, earthenware service is used to create an impression of warmth.

The Japanese meal is a balanced composition of taste and appearance. Dishes are presented in a styled harmony of simplicity and subtlety that has been observed for centuries.

The following recipes have been designed to give a basis for experimenting with Japanese cookery. Although these are the traditional meals served in Japanese homes, ingredients which may not be easily available can be omitted without altering the character of the dish.

Dashi
(Japanese Stock)

Makes 1 litre (approx)

15g kombu (seaweed)
1 litre water
15g katsuobushi (dried fish flakes)

50ml mirin (sweet wine)
or *1 × 2.5ml spoon sugar*

Pat the kombu dry with soft kitchen paper. Add to the water with the katsuobushi in a heavy-based saucepan. Allow to stand for 30 minutes, then bring to the boil over medium heat. Draw off the heat immediately, and strain. Return the liquid to the heat and bring to boiling point. Add the mirin or sugar, allowing the stock to boil for one minute; then remove from the heat.

Shime-saba
(Marinated Mackerel)

4 helpings

2 medium-sized fresh mackerel fillets
50–75g salt
150ml wine vinegar
1 lemon

2 × 15ml spoons wasabi (Japanese horseradish)
8 × 15ml spoons soy sauce

Remove the skin from the mackerel fillets, and rub the salt into the flesh. Leave to stand in a refrigerator for 3–4 hours.

Wipe the fillets with soft kitchen paper, place them in a shallow dish, and cover with the vinegar. Slice the lemon and place the slices on top of the fish. Leave to stand for 3–3½ hours.

Before serving, slice the fish at an angle of 45° across the flesh into pieces 2–3cm wide. Serve in individual bowls.

Mix the wasabi to a paste with a little water, and put 1 × 5ml spoon into each bowl with the fish. Provide each person with a small bowl containing about 2 × 15ml spoons soy sauce.

Serve as a starter or accompaniment to a main course.

Note It is most important that any fish used for this or any other of the Japanese recipes should be as fresh as possible.

Saba-no-Teriyaki
(Grilled Mackerel)

4 helpings

150ml soy sauce
3 × 15ml spoons mirin (sweet wine) **or** *3 × 15ml spoons dry sherry with 2 × 5ml spoons sugar added*

a pinch of chilli powder
1 × 15ml spoon grated ginger root
2 cloves garlic
4 medium-sized mackerel fillets

Mix together the soy sauce, mirin or sherry, chilli powder and grated ginger. Crush and add the garlic. Place the mackerel fillets in a shallow dish and pour the mixture over them. Leave to marinate for 2 hours.

Place the mackerel under a hot grill, and cook for 2 minutes on each side, brushing the fillets with the remaining marinade several times during cooking. Serve immediately.

VARIATION

This dish can be also made with herring, salmon, bream or any other oily fish.

Tamago-jiru
(Egg Soup)

4 helpings

2 medium-sized leeks	salt and pepper
1 × 15ml spoon oil	1 egg
1 litre dashi (p1534) or chicken stock	

Garnish
4–5 finely chopped
  spring onions

Trim and finely chop the leeks. Heat the oil in a frying pan, and add the leeks, stirring all the time until they are transparent. Remove the pan from the heat before the leeks begin to brown.

Pour the dashi or chicken stock into a large saucepan. Add the seasoning and boil for 10 minutes, skimming the surface when necessary. Beat the egg until liquid. Stir the soup briskly and remove from the heat while the liquid is swirling. Pour in the well-beaten egg by holding the bowl high above the saucepan and tipping it forward. The egg will solidify into thin shreds upon contact with the hot, swirling soup. Pour into separate bowls and garnish with the spring onions. Serve immediately.

Kenchin-jiru
(Vegetable and Bean Curd Soup)

4 helpings

250g tofu (bean curd cake)	1 × 15ml spoon oil
150g taro potatoes (optional)	1.5 litres dashi (p1534) or chicken stock
100g daikon (white radish)	salt and pepper or
100g carrot	3 × 15ml spoons miso (bean paste)
50g shiitake (dried mushrooms) or fresh mushrooms	

Pat dry the tofu with soft kitchen paper and cut it into 2cm cubes. Peel and cut the potatoes into 2cm cubes also if they are to be included in the recipe. Scrape and finely slice the daikon and the carrot into thin rounds. Quarter each daikon round. Prepare the mushrooms, cut off the stems and slice them finely.

Heat the oil in a large frying pan. Add all the vegetables, and stir fry for 3 minutes, taking care not to brown them. Pour in the stock and bring to the boil, skimming the surface when necessary. Remove from the heat and season to taste. Miso may be substituted for salt. Simmer for 15–20 minutes and serve hot.

Vegetable Tempura

4 helpings

1 medium-sized potato	1 × 2.5ml spoon grated
2 medium-sized carrots	ginger
1 medium-sized parsnip	4 okra
8 heads asparagus	12 French beans
4 small courgettes	4–8 mushrooms
1 small green pepper	12 mange-tout peas
2 × 15ml spoons grated	1–2 sprigs parsley
daikon (white radish)	vegetable oil for deep
	frying

Dipping Sauce

500ml dashi (p1534)	50ml mirin (sweet wine)
75ml soy sauce	or 1 × 15ml spoon
	sugar

Batter

1 egg	a pinch of baking
300ml ice-cold water	powder
300g flour	

Prepare the vegetables, then slice the potato into 5mm pieces, cut the carrots and parsnip into match-sticks, and the asparagus into 10cm pieces. Halve the courgettes and pepper, and cut the pepper into 8 equal-sized pieces. Form a small mound of the grated daikon and a small mound of the grated ginger in each of 4 bowls. Leave the rest of the vegetables whole.

Make the dipping sauce. Heat all the ingredients to boiling point, and boil for 3 minutes. Remove from the heat, and keep warm.

Heat the oil in a strong, thick-based pan and prepare the batter. Beat the egg in a large bowl, pour in the ice-cold water, and mix well. Sift together the flour and the baking powder. Sift again over the surface of the egg and water mixture. Stir gently, but do not mix the ingredients completely. The batter should be lumpy and not sticky.

Test the temperature of the oil by dropping in small bits of batter. The oil is ready if the batter sinks halfway, surfaces and browns in half a minute (approx).

Thinly coat each vegetable with the batter and gently drop them into the oil, a few at a time. Deep fry until golden-brown. Drain on soft kitchen paper, keeping them separate. Keep warm.

Pour the warm sauce into each of the bowls filled with the daikon and ginger, and use as a dip. Arrange the tempura on a large serving dish, and serve warm with the individual bowls of sauce.

Note Buddhist monks, who are vegetarian, created the Vegetable Tempura.

Any tempura recipe can be cooked at the table in a pot similar to that used for Fondue Bourguignonne (p1452).

Tori-no-Takikomigohan
(Chicken and Vegetable Rice)

4 helpings

400g short-grain rice	100g bamboo shoots
3 boned chicken breasts	3 sheets aburage (fried
75g carrots	bean curd)
100g shiitake (dried	2 × 15ml spoons oil
mushrooms) or fresh	1 × 5ml spoon salt
mushrooms	

Soup

375ml water	2 × 15ml spoons sake
75ml soy sauce	(rice wine) (optional)
1 × 15ml spoon sugar	

Garnish

100g cooked peas
2 sheets nori (seaweed)
(optional)

Blend all the ingredients for the soup in a saucepan and heat to boiling point. Remove from the heat and put to one side.

Wash the rice thoroughly and drain well. Skin the chicken and cut it into small pieces about 2cm long and 1cm thick. Scrape the carrots and cut them into matchsticks. Prepare and slice the shiitate and bamboo shoots. Slice the aburage.

Heat the oil in a large pan and fry the vegetables for 3 minutes or until soft. Pour the soup into the pan and simmer for 10 minutes. Add the chicken and simmer for 2–3 minutes. Drain the solids and return the liquid to the heat, adding enough cold water to make up to 400ml liquid. Add the salt and the rice. Cover the pan with a tight-fitting lid, and bring to the boil. Reduce the heat and simmer for

10 minutes, keeping the rice covered, until the water has evaporated.

Remove the pan from the heat and add the drained solids and the peas. Mix the rice gently with the vegetables and the chicken. Transfer the rice to a large serving dish.

Prepare the nori by lightly drying it over low heat until it changes to a green colour. Crumble it into small pieces and sprinkle over the rice. Serve hot.

Sukiyaki
(Fried Meat and Vegetables with Sauce)

6 helpings

1kg sirloin steak	*450g tofu (bean curd*
3 onions	*cake)*
3 leeks	*25g beef fat*
3 carrots	*6 eggs (optional)*
100g mushrooms	
2 packs shirataki	
(transparent noodles)	

Soup

100ml dashi (p1534) **or**	*6 × 15ml spoons sugar*
chicken stock	*3 × 15ml spoons mirin*
200ml soy sauce	*(sweet wine)*

In the kitchen, make the soup in a large mixing bowl with the dashi or chicken stock. Add the soy sauce, sugar and mirin, stir briskly, bring to the boil and remove from the heat. Put to one side.

Wipe the meat and pat dry. Slice into wafer-thin pieces, or let the butcher slice the beef on a meat-slicer. Arrange in a fan shape on a serving dish. Skin and slice the onions into rings, cut the leeks into long strips, slice the carrots lengthwise into 5cm pieces, and halve the mushrooms. Separate the shirataki into 10cm pieces. Drain and cut the tofu into 2cm cubes. Place the vegetables on a separate serving dish in attractive groups.

At the table, melt the beef fat in a large shallow frying pan over a spirit lamp or burner with a trivet. Fry one-quarter of the meat, starting with the smaller pieces, and push to one side of the pan when browned on both sides. In order, fry a small quantity of the onions, leeks, carrots and mushrooms, pushing each to a side of the pan as it cooks through. Do not mix the vegetables. Add the shirataki and the tofu. Lay strips of the cooked meat over the vegetables. Pour in half of the soup to cover, and cook until the meat is tender.

Serve the portions as they are cooked, repeating the process for additional servings until all the ingredients are used up.

Set each place with a small dish containing an unbroken egg which the guest can break and use as a dip to cool the food as it is eaten.

Serve Sukiyaki with plain white rice and Japanese pickles or fresh lettuce.

Teriyaki Steak

4 helpings

4 sirloin steaks

Marinade

3 or 4 cloves garlic	*50ml mirin (sweet wine)*
a pinch of salt	**or** *dry sherry with*
a 7cm piece of ginger	*2 × 10ml spoons sugar*
root (approx)	*added*
a pinch of freshly ground	*6 × 15ml spoons soy*
black pepper	*sauce*

Garnish
5 stems fresh watercress
per person

Wipe the steaks and pat dry. Make the marinade. Skin the garlic, and crush it with a little salt. Grate the ginger, squeeze out the juice, and mix with the garlic in a shallow bowl with the other ingredients.

Rub the steaks with the marinade. Leave for 40 minutes, turning several times. Drain the steaks well. Put them on a rack under a preheated grill. Cook each side for 3 minutes under high heat, brushing each side twice with the sauce. Serve immediately, garnished with the watercress.

Yosenabe

(Mixed Casserole)

4 helpings

500g chicken on the bone
2 leeks
2 medium-sized carrots
*1 pack of shirataki
   (transparent noodles)*
*250g tofu (bean curd
   cake)*

*100g shiitake (dried
   mushrooms) or fresh
   mushrooms*
*1 small head of chinese
   leaves*
200g fresh spinach
500g squid
8 large prawns

Soup

*1 litre dashi (p1534) or
   chicken stock*

*2 × 15ml spoons sake
   (rice wine)*
1 × 15ml spoon salt

Dip

5 small spring onions
150ml rice wine vinegar
*1 × 15ml spoon lemon
   juice*

150ml soy sauce
*a pinch of ground chilli
   pepper*

Make the soup first. In the kitchen, pour the dashi or chicken stock into a large saucepan, add the sake and salt, bring to the boil, stir, and remove from the heat.

Prepare the dip by chopping the onions finely and mixing with the rest of the ingredients in a large bowl. Put to one side.

Cut the chicken into pieces 5cm long and 3cm wide. Trim the leeks and cut them lengthways into 5cm pieces. Cut the carrots into 5cm strips. Separate the shirataki into 10cm pieces. Cut the tofu into 2cm cubes. Remove the stalks from the shiitake, or clean the fresh mushrooms and leave them whole. Wash and drain the Chinese leaves, and chop into 5cm pieces. Wash the spinach and blanch in boiling water. Drain, and chop into 5cm pieces.

Prepare the squid (p428). Halve the heads lengthways and lay the pieces flat. Score the flesh with a sharp knife in a cross-hatched pattern and then cut it into rectangular pieces about 5cm long. Peel the prawns just down to their tails and cut along the underside. Arrange the ingredients on a large serving dish in an attractive fashion.

At the table, pour the soup into a large shallow pan and heat through over a spirit lamp or burner with a trivet. Provide each person with a deep bowl containing about 50ml of the dip. Cook the ingredients in the same order in which they have been prepared, starting with the chicken and ending with the shrimps. The guests should help themselves as each ingredient is cooked.

Oyako Donburi

(Chicken and Egg Omelet)

4 helpings

400g short-grain rice

400ml water

Soup

*2 medium-sized onions
   or leeks*
3 chicken breasts
*200ml dashi (p1534) or
   chicken stock*

1 × 5ml spoon sugar
1 × 5ml spoon salt
75ml soy sauce
3 eggs

Garnish

*1 × 15ml spoon cooked
   peas or 1 × 15ml spoon
   chopped parsley*

Wash and drain the rice thoroughly. Pour the water into a saucepan and add the rice. Cover, and heat to boiling point. Keeping the rice covered, reduce the heat and simmer for 10 minutes until the water has evaporated.

Meanwhile, prepare the soup. Skin the onions, or trim the leeks and halve them lengthwise, then slice the halves. Wipe the chicken and cut it at an angle into small even-sized pieces. Pour the dashi or the chicken stock into a frying pan and heat to boiling point. Add the onions or leeks, sugar, salt, soy sauce, and chicken pieces. Reduce the heat, and simmer for 2–3 minutes until the chicken is cooked through and tender.

Whisk the eggs until liquid, and pour into the pan. Simmer for 2–3 minutes, and remove before the egg has completely hardened.

Serve the rice in 4 bowls. Divide the egg mixture evenly, and place on top with the broth. Garnish with the peas or parsley, and serve immediately.

Jewish

Jewish cooking traditions and food customs are based on dietary laws going back to Biblical times. Many dishes are linked to important Jewish festivals, such as Passover (Pesach), or the Feast of Esther (Purim).

Although the traditions came originally from the land of Israel, the Jewish history of dispersal all over the Middle East and Europe has made it an international cuisine, with distinctive Eastern features.

Jewish dietary laws cover the following main points:

1) Only fish with scales and fins, the forequarters of animals which chew the cud and have cloven hoofs, and only domestic poultry, ie chicken, duck, goose, and turkey may be eaten.
2) Animals must be killed and prepared in a certain way (koshered) to remove the blood.
3) Dishes containing meat and milk must not be served at the same meal. Two sets of utensils for food must be kept – one for preparing, cooking, serving, and washing up meat meals, and the other for milk-based meals.

Those observing Jewish dietary laws will only buy meat from a Jewish butcher who displays an official sign showing Rabbinical approval. Similarly, a list of approved manufactured products and other permitted foods can be obtained from local Rabbinical authorities in different countries.

Orthodox Jews also use separate sets of utensils for meat and for milk during the festival of Passover. These are stored away for the rest of the year. During the eight-day Passover spring festival, which celebrates the flight to freedom of the Jews from Egypt, unleavened bread or matzot is substituted for bread and other products containing yeast or other raising agents.

Smetana Soup
(Soured Cream Soup)

3 helpings

25g radishes	250ml smetana (soured cream)
25g spring onions	1 × 5ml spoon lemon juice
25g cucumber	salt
2–3 × 15ml spoons single cream	

Garnish
1 × 5ml spoon chopped parsley

Chop the vegetables finely. Combine all the ingredients, adding salt to taste. Pour into soup bowls and garnish with the chopped parsley. Serve slightly chilled.

Gefillte Fish

4 helpings

1kg white fish (haddock, cod or whiting)	fish bones and a fish head (if possible)
1 carrot (100g approx)	2 eggs
3 medium-sized onions (200g approx)	3 × 15ml spoons medium matzo meal or soft white breadcrumbs
1 litre water	1 × 5ml spoon caster sugar
2 × 5ml spoons salt	
a pinch of pepper	

Mince the raw fish. Prepare and slice the carrot and 1 onion, and put them in a saucepan with the water, salt, pepper, and fish bones. Cook the stock for 30 minutes, then strain.

Skin, then mince or grate the remaining onions. Beat the eggs lightly, and add to the minced fish, with the matzo meal or breadcrumbs, sugar, onions, and seasoning to taste. Mix together well.

With wet hands, form the fish into 12–14 balls. Heat the fish stock, put in the fish balls, and simmer gently for 1 hour. Remove, drain, and place on a serving plate. Cool. Strain the stock, and cool it. When cold, decorate each fish ball with a slice of cooked carrot. Serve the stock with the fish balls.

Note This mixture can also be used to stuff a whole fish, eg carp, which is then poached whole.

Knaidlach
(Matzo Meal Dumplings)

3–4 helpings

1 small onion (75g approx)	100g medium matzo meal
50g chicken **or** vegetable fat	salt and pepper
	150ml boiling water
	1 egg

Skin and grate the onion. Melt the fat, and fry the onion until lightly browned. Add to the matzo meal, with seasoning to taste. Stir in the boiling water, then leave the mixture to cool. Beat the egg until liquid and mix in.

With wet hands, roll the mixture into small balls. Drop gently into boiling chicken soup or boiling salted water, and simmer for 15 minutes.

Serve with soup or as an accompaniment to meat.

Note The uncooked dumplings will keep for a few days in a refrigerator.

Holishkes
(Stuffed Cabbage)

3–4 helpings

12 large cabbage leaves	25g chicken fat **or** margarine
2 large onions (200g approx)	1 × 15ml spoon golden syrup
500g minced beef	250ml chicken stock **or** water (approx)
2 × 15ml spoons medium matzo meal **or** soft white breadcrumbs	1 × 2.5ml spoon salt
50g long-grain rice	grated rind and juice of 1 lemon
1 carrot (100g approx)	

Wash the cabbage leaves and blanch them in boiling water for 1 minute. Cut out any tough stalks. Skin and mince the onions. Mix together the meat, matzo meal or breadcrumbs, the rice, and 1 onion. Put about 1 × 15ml spoon of the mixture on each cabbage leaf, roll up, and tuck in any loose ends.

Grate the carrot. Melt the fat in a large flame-proof casserole, and fry the remaining onion and the carrot until lightly browned. Add the syrup

and cook for 1–2 minutes. Put in the cabbage parcels, and add just enough stock or water to cover. Sprinkle with the salt, lemon rind and juice. Cover with a tight-fitting lid or foil, and cook in a warm oven, 160°C, Gas 3, for 3 hours.

Potato Latkes

4–6 helpings

500g potatoes	2 × 15ml spoons plain flour
1 small onion (75g approx)	salt and pepper
2 eggs	fat for shallow frying

Peel and grate the potatoes and onion. Drain off all the liquid, and dry well on soft kitchen paper. Turn into a bowl. Beat the eggs until liquid, and add to the potatoes and onion with the flour and seasoning. Mix well. Melt a little fat in a frying pan, and gently drop in spoonfuls of the mixture. Fry slowly for about 10 minutes altogether, browning each side. Drain, and keep hot while frying the remaining latkes.

Cheese Kreplach

3–4 helpings

1 egg	75g plain flour (approx)
salt and pepper	flour for rolling out

Filling
200g curd cheese	50g caster sugar (optional)
1 egg	

Beat the egg with the seasoning. Beat in enough flour to form a stiff dough. Roll out 5mm thick on a lightly floured surface, and leave to rest for 1 hour. Cut into 7cm squares.

Mix all the filling ingredients together. Beat well, and place 1 × 5ml spoon of the mixture on each square. Moisten the pastry edges with water and fold over into a triangle. Leave for 30 minutes. Drop into gently boiling water and simmer for 15 minutes. Drain, and serve with melted butter.

Note The kreplach can be served as a dessert with a little extra sugar sprinkled over them.

Blintzes
See p941.

Bagels
See p1162.

Challah
See p1158.

Lockshen Pudding

3–4 helpings

100g lockshen $\frac{1}{2} \times 2.5ml$ *spoon ground*
(vermicelli)   *cinnamon*
1 × 2.5ml spoon salt   *40g margarine*
1 egg   *fat for greasing*
40g caster sugar   *50g sultanas*

Cook the lockshen in boiling salted water until tender. Drain, and rinse under hot water. Beat the egg with the sugar and cinnamon, and mix into the lockshen. Melt the margarine and add it to the mixture. Turn half of it into a greased, ovenproof dish. Scatter with the sultanas, and cover with the remaining mixture. Bake in a fairly hot oven, 200°C, Gas 6, for 30 minutes.

Cinnamon Balls

Makes 20 (approx)

2 egg whites $\frac{1}{2} \times 5ml$ *spoon mixed*
100g caster sugar   *spice*
200g ground almonds   *fat for greasing*
1 × 15ml spoon ground   *icing sugar for dusting*
cinnamon

Heat the oven to fairly hot, 200°C, Gas 6. Whisk the egg whites until very stiff. Whisk in half the sugar, then fold in the rest with the ground almonds and spices. With wet fingers, roll into small balls. Place on a greased baking sheet, and bake for 15 minutes. While still warm, dust with icing sugar. Cool on a wire rack.

Note This is a speciality of the Passover spring festival.

Plava
(Passover Sponge Cake)

3 eggs   *50g fine matzo meal*
100g caster sugar   *50g potato flour*
grated rind and juice of   *a pinch of salt*
$\frac{1}{2}$ lemon   *fat for greasing*
1 × 15ml spoon water   *icing sugar for dusting*
1 × 15ml spoon corn oil   *(optional)*

Separate the eggs, and whisk the yolks and sugar together until thick and pale. Add the lemon rind and juice, the water and oil, and beat well. Gently fold in the matzo meal and potato flour. Add the salt to the egg whites, whisk until stiff, and fold into the mixture. Grease and line a 25cm cake tin, and pour in the mixture. Bake in a fairly hot oven, 190°C, Gas 5, for 30–35 minutes. Cool on a wire rack. When cold, dust with icing sugar, if liked.

Stuffed Monkey
See p1267.

Hamantaschen

('Haman's Pockets')

Makes 24 (approx)

Pastry

300g plain flour (approx)	100ml corn oil
3 × 2.5ml spoons baking powder	1 × 5ml spoon vanilla essence
2 eggs	flour
125g caster sugar	fat for greasing

Filling

50g mixed dried fruit	2 × 15ml spoons golden syrup
100g poppy seeds	syrup
25g margarine	100ml milk
50g caster sugar	1 × 2.5ml spoon vanilla essence
50g chopped nuts	essence

Make the filling first. Chop the dried fruit with the poppy seeds, and pound in a pestle and mortar. Add all the other ingredients, except the vanilla essence, in the order given. Put in a saucepan, and cook gently for about 5 minutes until thick, stirring all the time. Cover, and leave to cool. When cold, gently stir in the vanilla essence.

Make the pastry. Sift the flour and baking powder into a large bowl. Beat the eggs until liquid. Reserve a little for glazing, then beat the sugar into the eggs with the oil and vanilla essence. Mix into the flour and baking powder, and mix to a soft but manageable dough. Add a little extra flour if necessary. Roll out the pastry to 5mm thickness on a lightly floured surface, and cut into 7cm rounds.

Put 1 × 5ml spoon of filling in the centre of each round. Lift the edges at three equally spaced points, and pinch them together in the centre, over the filling, making a three-cornered hat shape. Pinch together the 3 slits in the top of each pastry to seal. Brush with the reserved egg. Place on lightly greased and floured baking sheets, and bake in a moderate oven, 180°C, Gas 4, for 30 minutes until golden-brown.

Note This is a speciality of the Feast of Esther (Purim).

Latin America

Latin America is the name used to denote all those countries of the Americas and West Indies where Spanish, French or Portuguese is the national language. Geographically, it extends from the US/Mexico border to the southernmost tip of South America and includes most of the West Indies.

There are certain similarities in the cookery of this vast area, although agricultural and geographical elements, together with varied cultural traditions, have deeply affected the character of the local cookery. Fish and shellfish are the common diet for those countries benefiting from the Caribbean, Atlantic and Pacific oceans, while the inland plains of Argentina provide cattle for beef. Within the West Indies, the most widely known dishes are the rice-based jambalayas and gumbos (soups or stews flavoured with okra).

In Latin America on the whole, maize, wheat, and rice provide a basic staple, together with a large variety of tropical fruits and vegetables such as bananas, coconut, pomegranates, and sweet potatoes. Chocolate, strong coffee, and the *Yerba mate* tea from Argentina and Paraguay are also popular. Seasonings tend to be piquant using a variety of mild and hot peppers.

Pumpkin Soup

4–6 helpings

100g pickled pork	600g pumpkin
800ml water	1 × 5ml spoon salt
1 × 5ml spoon chopped thyme or 1 × 2.5ml spoon dried thyme	1 × 5ml spoon pepper
	1 × 2.5ml spoon grated nutmeg
1 bay leaf	

Mince the pork. Put in a deep pan with the water, thyme, and bay leaf. Heat to boiling point, cover, reduce the heat, and simmer for 20 minutes. Remove the seeds, peel the pumpkin and cut the flesh into 1cm cubes. Add to the pan with the salt and pepper. Re-heat to boiling point, cover, and simmer for a further 25 minutes. Rub through a sieve. Return to the pan, and add the nutmeg. Re-season if required. Re-heat and serve hot.

West Indian Peanut Soup

6 helpings

400g shelled peanuts	50g margarine
1 medium-sized onion	25g flour
(100g approx)	400ml milk
2 sticks celery	salt and Cayenne
400ml white stock	pepper
(p329)	

Grind the peanuts. Skin and chop the onion. Wash the celery and slice it thinly. Put the peanuts, onion, and celery in a deep pan with the stock. Heat to boiling point, cover, reduce the heat, and simmer gently for 15 minutes. Melt the margarine in a small pan, stir in the flour and cook for 2–3 minutes without browning. Stir in the milk gradually and heat to boiling point, stirring all the time. Combine the peanut mixture with the white sauce. Season to taste. Simmer for 5 minutes. Rub through a sieve. Re-heat if necessary, and serve.

Fish with Avocado Sauce

6 helpings

1 onion	1 sprig celery leaves
1 clove of garlic	3 sprigs parsley
3 litres water	6 black peppercorns
1 bay leaf	6 × 15ml spoons fresh
1 × 2.5ml spoon dried	unsweetened lime **or**
thyme	lemon juice
1 × 2.5ml spoon dried	1 whole fish (2.3–2.5kg)
oregano	

Sauce

2 avocado pears	1 × 5ml spoon salt
1 × 15ml spoon fresh	freshly ground black
unsweetened lime **or**	pepper
lemon juice	
3 × 15ml spoons oil	

Garnish (optional)

green and black olives	tomato wedges
banana strips dipped in	radishes
lemon juice	parsley sprigs

Skin the onion and slice it. Skin and crush the garlic. Put these ingredients with the water in a deep pan which will just hold the whole fish. Add all the remaining ingredients except the fish. Bring to the boil, reduce the heat, and simmer, half-covered, for 30 minutes. Meanwhile, clean and scale the fish, if required, but leave the head and tail on. Wrap the fish tightly in a piece of muslin.

Cool the cooking liquid until tepid. Put a large plate in the pan, and lay the fish on it. The liquid should cover the fish by at least 3cm. If it does not, add a little extra water. Bring to a bare simmer, cover the pan tightly, and cook for 30–40 minutes until the thickest part of the fish yields slightly when pressed. Lift the fish out of the liquid on to a board. Unwrap the muslin, and skin the fish gently. Turn the fish carefully on to a serving platter, and strip the skin off the second side. Keep the fish warm if it is to be served hot, or leave to cool under a loose cloth covering.

Make the sauce. Discard the avocado stones and skins, and mash the flesh thoroughly with all the other sauce ingredients. Beat until it is the consistency of thick mayonnaise.

Either serve the fish hot with the sauce separately, or use a little of the sauce to mask the fish when cooled, and serve the remaining sauce separately. Garnish a cold fish if liked, with the olives, banana strips, tomato wedges, radishes, and parsley.

Jamaican Caveached Fish

6 helpings

3 green peppers (300g approx)	salt
3 medium-sized onions (250g approx)	350ml water
3 carrots (200g approx)	2 × 15ml spoons groundnut oil
2 bay leaves	6 × 15ml spoons malt vinegar
a 2cm slice of ginger	3 × 15ml spoons oil
8 peppercorns	1kg white fish fillets
1 whole blade of mace	
250g fish bones and trimmings	

Garnish (optional)

green olives	strips of red pepper

De-seed and slice the peppers. Skin and slice the onions, and slice the carrots. Split the bay leaves in half and chop the ginger root finely. Put all these ingredients into a saucepan with the peppercorns, mace, fish bones and trimmings, and salt. Add the water, cover, and simmer for 35 minutes. Add the groundnut oil and vinegar, and simmer for another 2 minutes. Strain and keep warm.

Heat the 3 × 15ml spoons oil in a frying pan, and sauté the fish fillets lightly for 7–8 minutes until just browned on both sides. Drain the fish on soft kitchen paper. Either place in a warmed serving dish, pour the sauce over, and serve hot; or put on a cold dish, cover with sauce, chill, and serve cold. Garnish, if liked, with olives and strips of pepper.

Note The vegetables from the drained sauce can be served as an accompaniment.

Scampi Jambalaya
See p465.

Sausage Jambalaya

4 helpings

175g long-grain rice	200g chorizo sausages
1 large onion	salt and pepper
1 clove of garlic	a pinch of Cayenne pepper
butter for shallow frying	½ small chilli
200g tomatoes	

Cook the rice in boiling salted water until tender, and drain well. Keep hot. Skin and chop the onion and garlic finely, and fry gently in a little butter until a light golden colour. Skin, chop, and add the tomatoes, and mash them well down into the pan.

In a separate deep frying pan, fry the chorizo lightly in butter. When fried, cut into 2–3cm pieces, and return them to the frying pan. Add the rice, onion, garlic, and tomatoes (with the frying butter), and season well with salt, pepper and Cayenne pepper. De-seed and chop the chilli very finely, and add to the pan. Mix well. Cover the pan, heat to simmering point, and simmer for about 15 minutes, stirring from time to time. Serve very hot.

Note Chorizo are Spanish sausages and should be available in delicatessens. Alternatively, use a strongly flavoured German or Italian smoked dried sausage about 3cm thick.

Tamale en Cacerola
(Tamale Pie)

6 helpings

1.25 litres water	2 × 15ml spoons powdered chilli seasoning
250g cornmeal (polenta)	
2 × 5ml spoons salt	
1 large onion (200g approx)	a pinch of Cayenne pepper
1 clove of garlic	1 × 400g can tomatoes
2 × 15ml spoons vegetable oil	beef dripping for greasing
500g minced beef	50g sharp hard cheese

Bring the water to the boil, stir in the cornmeal, and continue stirring until it begins to thicken. Add half the salt, reduce the heat, and simmer, uncovered, for 30 minutes.

Meanwhile, skin the onion and garlic and chop finely. Heat the oil in a large saucepan and fry the onion and garlic until soft. Add the minced beef, and stir until well browned. Add the remaining salt, the chilli seasoning, Cayenne pepper, and the tomatoes with their juice. Cook slowly for 1 hour. Melt the dripping, and use it to grease a 2 litre casserole. Pour in half the cornmeal, spread the meat on top, then cover with the remaining cornmeal. Grate the cheese, and sprinkle over the dish. Bake in a moderate oven, 180°C, Gas 4, for 1 hour.

Note The pie can be prepared ahead of time and chilled or frozen before baking.

Chilli con Carne

See p508.

Chicken Gumbo

6 helpings

1 large boiling fowl	*salt and pepper*
1 thick slice cooked	*a pinch of Cayenne*
gammon (150g approx)	*pepper*
butter or lard for	*a sprig each of thyme*
shallow frying	*and parsley*
1 large onion	*1 bay leaf*
1 litre water	*1 small chilli*
6 tomatoes	*450g okra*

Joint the chicken (pp619–20), and cut the gammon into 2cm cubes. Heat the fat in a large heavy pan, put in the meats, and brown the chicken pieces on all sides. Skin, chop, and brown the onion with the chicken. Heat the water and add it to the chicken. Draw the pan off the heat.

Quarter the tomatoes, and add them to the gumbo, with a little salt and pepper, Cayenne pepper, the herbs, and bay leaf. De-seed the chilli, chop it finely, and sprinkle into the pan. Half cover the pan, return to the heat, and bring to simmering point. Simmer for $1\frac{1}{2}$ hours. Trim the okra at both ends, and add to the pan 30 minutes before the end of the cooking time.

Shortly before serving, remove the chicken joints, and cut off the best pieces of meat. Cut them in 2cm cubes or small slices and return them to the gumbo. (Keep the remaining chicken for another dish.)

Serve from the pan, or from a heated tureen, with plain boiled rice.

Creole Chicken

6 helpings

2 small frying chickens	*2 sprigs each thyme and*
2 × 15ml spoons butter	*parsley*
2 × 15ml spoons cooking	*1 bay leaf*
oil	*3 green peppers (300g*
2 large onions	*approx)*
2 × 15ml spoons flour	*500ml chicken stock*
6 large tomatoes	*salt and pepper*
2 cloves garlic	

Joint the chickens (pp619–20). Melt the butter and oil in a heavy saucepan or flameproof casserole, and brown the chicken pieces on all sides. Lift out on to a plate.

Skin and slice the onions, and add to the pan. Fry until lightly browned. Sprinkle in the flour and let it brown. Draw the pan off the heat. Skin and slice the tomatoes, chop the garlic, take the leaves off the herb sprigs, and de-seed and slice the peppers. Add all these ingredients to the pan, and mix well. Return the chicken to the pan, cover, and simmer for 10 minutes, shaking and stirring the contents from time to time.

Bring the stock to the boil in a separate pan, pour into the first pan, season well, half cover, and simmer for 45 minutes. Put the chicken joints in a hot dish, and cover with the sauce.

Serve with boiled rice.

Pollos Borrachos
(Drunken Chickens)

8 helpings

2 ×1.25kg roasting
  chickens **or** 8 chicken
  quarters **or** large joints
4 ×15ml spoons cooking
  oil
3 medium-sized onions
4–6 ×15ml spoons
  chopped parsley
2 ×15ml spoons sesame
  seeds
4 black peppercorns

1 × 3cm piece cinnamon
  stick
$\frac{1}{2}$ ×2.5ml spoon ground
  cloves
1 bay leaf
2 ×15ml spoons vinegar
50ml dry sherry
16 green olives
2–3 small chillies
salt

Joint whole chickens (p619–20), if used. Put 2 ×15ml spoons of the oil in a heavy flame-proof casserole. Skin and slice the onions and add to the casserole with the parsley, sesame seeds, peppercorns, cinnamon stick, cloves, and bay leaf. Heat gently until the onion is soft. Add the chicken joints, the remaining oil, vinegar, and sherry. Halve, stone, and add the olives. Finely chop and add the chillies. Season to taste with salt, and baste well. Cover the casserole with a tight-fitting lid, and simmer for 1 hour, turning the chicken joints occasionally.

Serve hot with American Spoon Bread (p866).

Pimientos Rellenos
See p789.

Frijoles Refritos
(Refried Beans)

6 helpings

500g borlotti beans **or**
  speckled pink beans
1.25 litres water
1 clove of garlic
3 ×15ml spoons
  (approx) powdered
  chilli seasoning

1 medium-sized onion
  (100g approx)
100g bacon fat
250g Cheddar cheese
1 pickled jalapeno
  pepper (optional)
salt (optional)

Soak the beans overnight in the water. Skin the garlic clove and add it whole to the beans. Add the chilli seasoning. Simmer the beans for about $1\frac{1}{2}$ hours in the water until very soft. Skin the onion and chop it finely. Melt 2 ×15ml spoons of the bacon fat in a large frying pan, and brown the onion lightly.

Drain the beans and discard the garlic, reserving the liquid. Add the beans in small quantities to the bacon fat and onion mixture, mashing the beans into a paste. Add more bacon fat and bean liquid until the beans are quite mushy. Grate the Cheddar cheese, and chop the jalapeno pepper finely, if used. Add the cheese and pepper to the beans, and cook for a further 5 minutes. Season to taste. Add salt if needed and more chilli seasoning for a spicier mixture.

Candied Sweet Potatoes

4–6 helpings

6 sweet potatoes
salt
paprika
butter for greasing
100g soft light brown
  sugar

1 × 2.5ml spoon grated
  lemon rind
2 ×10ml spoons lemon
  juice
2 ×15ml spoons butter

Boil the potatoes in their skins in unsalted water until almost tender. The time will depend on the size and shape of the potatoes. When cool enough to handle, peel thinly, and cut lengthways into slices 1cm thick. Season well with salt and paprika. Grease a shallow ovenproof baking dish, and arrange the potatoes in it in overlapping rows. Sprinkle with the sugar, lemon rind, and juice. Dot with the butter. Bake, uncovered, in a fairly hot oven, 190°C, Gas 5, for 20 minutes.

Serve as a dessert with rum-flavoured custard or as a supper dish with grilled bacon, mild cheese, and fruit chutney.

Buñuelos
(Mexican Fried Pancakes)

Makes 30 (approx)

300g plain flour
1 × 15ml spoon soft light
brown sugar (optional)
1 × 5ml spoon baking
powder
1 × 2.5ml spoon salt

50g butter
200ml milk
4 eggs
100ml water (approx)
flour for rolling out
oil for deep frying

Sauce
200ml liquid honey **or**
brown sugar syrup (see
Method)

ground cinnamon

Sift the dry ingredients into a bowl. Melt the butter and mix with the milk. Beat the eggs lightly. Make a well in the dry ingredients, and add the eggs, butter, and milk. Mix well. Add enough water to make a pliable but not a sticky dough. Knead thoroughly, then form into 3cm balls. Cover with a cloth and leave to stand for 30 minutes. Roll out each ball as thinly as possible into a round on a lightly floured surface. Leave to stand for 10 minutes. Heat the oil (p303) and fry the buñuelos, a few at a time, until light golden on both sides. Drain very well on soft kitchen paper.

For the sauce, either warm the honey and flavour to taste with cinnamon, or make a thin sugar syrup with 200ml water flavoured with brown sugar and cinnamon to taste.

Either serve the buñuelos whole and the sauce separately, or break them into soup bowls and pour the sauce over.

VARIATION
Sopaipillas

Instead of making balls, rest the dough in one piece, then roll out very thinly. Cut into small squares and fry as above.

Serve with a cinnamon-flavoured hot chocolate drink, instead of afternoon tea.

Mango Mousse

6–8 helpings

1kg ripe mangoes
6 × 15ml spoons fresh
unsweetened lime juice
100g caster sugar
1 × 15ml spoon gelatine
3 × 15ml spoons water

2 egg whites
a pinch of salt
100ml double cream
1 × 15ml spoon light
rum

Peel the fruit, and cut the flesh off the stones. Sieve the flesh with the lime juice, or process in an electric blender to obtain a smooth purée. Blend in the sugar. Soften the gelatine in the water in a small heatproof container. Stand the container in a pan of hot water and stir until dissolved. Cool slightly, and stir into the mango purée. Whisk the egg whites with the salt until they hold fairly stiff peaks. Stir 1 × 15ml spoon into the purée, then fold in the rest. Whip the cream lightly with the rum, and fold into the egg white mixture as lightly as possible. Turn into a 1.5 litre serving bowl, and chill for about 3 hours.

Netherlands

Dutch meals are generally plain but ample. Dairy foods are eaten in quantity – Gouda and Edam cheeses have been exported for centuries, and are known all over the world. In Holland, they are eaten for breakfast, with eggs, assorted breads, and plenty of butter. Herring, fresh, pickled or smoked, is the most popular fish, together with smoked or fresh eel. In the days of her Far Eastern empire, Holland imported most of Europe's spices and exotic foods, and her people developed a taste for highly spiced East Indian dishes, and coffee. These still form a large part of the national diet, and the numerous Indonesian restaurants cater both for Holland's immigrant population, and for the Dutch themselves. Beer and flavoured gin (Genever) are very popular, as are liqueurs, of which the best known is probably Advocaat (Dutch egg brandy).

Gestoofde Aal
(Braised Eels)

4 helpings

1kg eels (2cm thick approx)	*100ml dry white wine*
salt	*1 × 2.5ml spoon lemon juice*
freshly ground black pepper	*2 bay leaves*
a pinch of powdered fennel	*1 medium-sized onion*
a pinch of dried thyme	*dry white breadcrumbs*
	butter

Cut the unskinned eels into 7cm lengths and sprinkle with salt. Leave for 5 minutes. Stand the pieces upright in an ovenproof casserole or pot. Sprinkle with pepper, fennel, and thyme. Pour the wine over the fish, then add the lemon juice. Add the bay leaves. Skin the onion, slice it into paper-thin rings, and lay these on top. Sprinkle with breadcrumbs and dot with flakes of butter. Cover, and bake in a very cool–cool oven, 140°–150°C, Gas 1–2, for 15 minutes. Uncover, increase the heat to fairly hot, 200°C, Gas 6, and bake for another 5 minutes. Serve very hot.

Hareng Kaassla
(Herring Salad)

6 helpings

175g fresh peas	*6 sticks celery*
175g Gouda cheese	*salt and pepper*
1 sharp dessert apple	*mayonnaise*
6 gherkins	*6 rollmop herrings*
2 cooked carrots	

Garnish

175g grapes	*chopped parsley*

Cook the peas and leave to cool. Cut the cheese, unpeeled apple, gherkins and carrots into 2–3cm cubes, and mix together. Wash the celery, slice into 2–3cm lengths, and mix in. Add the peas and seasoning to taste. Mix with enough mayonnaise to bind, and pile on a serving platter. Arrange the rollmops on top. Halve and de-pip the grapes, and use to garnish the dish with the parsley.

Nasi Goreng   Indonesia
(Fried Rice)

6 helpings

1 large onion	*200g fillet of pork (optional)*
2 cloves garlic	*200g cooked chicken*
50g butter or 50ml peanut oil	*25g peeled prawns*
1 × 2.5ml spoon chilli powder or Cayenne pepper	*650g cooked long-grain rice*
1 × 15ml spoon soy sauce	

Garnish

3 eggs	*3 × 15ml spoons butter or oil*
1 × 2.5ml spoon salt	*25g salted peanuts*
a pinch of pepper	

Skin and finely chop the onion and garlic. Melt the butter in a large pan, or pour in the peanut oil. Fry the onion and the garlic until transparent. Reserve 1 × 15ml spoon cooked onion for the garnish. Add the chilli or Cayenne pepper, and the soy sauce, and mix well.

Wipe the pork and trim off any excess fat. Cut it

into thin strips and fry with the onion and garlic until browned and tender. Dice the chicken, add to the mixture and heat through. Sprinkle with the prawns. Add the rice, and stir well. Heat through for about 8 minutes, stirring occasionally.

Meanwhile, prepare the garnish. Beat the eggs until liquid and add the salt and pepper. Heat 2 ×15ml spoons of the butter or oil in a frying pan. Pour in the eggs and cook until set and browned underneath. Turn over and cook the top side, then lift out on to a plate. Shred the egg. Fry the peanuts in the remaining fat until golden-brown.

Transfer the rice mixture to a serving dish and garnish with the reserved onion, the egg strips and peanuts. Serve hot as a main course.

Kerst Kranz
(Christmas Ring)

puff pastry (p1253)
  using 100g flour
flour for rolling out
175g ground almonds
175g caster sugar
1 egg

juice of ½ lemon
a few drops almond
  essence
beaten egg yolk for
  glazing

Decoration
apricot jam for glazing
glacé cherries

angelica strips
chopped almonds

Roll out the pastry on a lightly floured surface into a strip approximately 10 × 50cm. Mix together the ground almonds, sugar, egg, lemon juice and almond essence, and knead until well blended. Form into a roll 50cm long, and lay it in the centre of the pastry. Dampen the edges, and fold them over the almond paste to enclose it. Press the edges together to seal. Form the pastry tube into a ring, join the ends, and seal together. Brush with the beaten egg yolk. Place the ring on a baking sheet, and bake in a hot oven, 220°C, Gas 7, for 15–20 minutes. Warm the apricot jam, and brush it over the warm ring. Decorate with the cherries, angelica and almonds before the jam sets.

Russia

Russia extends from the Baltic coast in the west to the borders of China in the east, and from the Arctic circle as far south as the Black Sea. The traditional diet varies immensely, with Asiatic, Scandinavian, and Slavonic trends in cookery. What is generally thought of as typical Russian cookery is in fact the traditional cuisine of central, Caucasian Russia, both before and after the revolution of 1917. It is based on an agricultural peasant diet, making varied use of root and other vegetables, grains, and dairy foods. The exotic dishes of aristocratic Russians under the tzars during the late eighteenth and nineteenth centuries were developed late, and under many diverse foreign influences. Today they are more likely to be found on foreign menus than within Russia itself.

A wide variety of breads are made from millet, oats, rye and buckwheat, and much use is made of dairy foods, especially eggs, soured cream, soft cheeses, and butter. Root vegetables, and hardy green ones such as cabbage, together with mushrooms, cucumbers and some pulses, compose many main-course dishes, although meat and poultry are eaten in plenty by those who can afford them, and when religious customs permit. Dried and salted fish feature largely in Russian recipes, since the only fresh fish available in central Russia in the past were local river fish, which did not keep over the many fast days demanded by the Russian Orthodox church. Pickled fish and vegetables have always been important in Russian cookery for the same reasons.

The most notable feature of the Russian main meal, traditionally a mid-afternoon dinner, are the *zakuski* or hors d'oeuvres, generally followed by soup and *pirog* or *pirozhki* (large or small pies). These are followed by a main course, and sometimes a sweet course. Vodka is the usual drink.

Rassolnik

(Kidney and Cucumber Soup)

4–6 helpings

500g ox kidney	pickling brine from
1 carrot	cucumbers (optional)
1 turnip	sliced sorrel **or** lettuce
1 swede	(optional)
1 onion	salt (optional)
oil for shallow frying	soured cream **or** fresh
4 potatoes	cream
2 pickled cucumbers	

Garnish

chopped parsley **or**
fennel

Skin and core the kidney, and cut into pieces. Put in a saucepan, add enough water to cover, and bring to the boil. Pour off the water. Cover with more water and bring back to the boil. Reduce the heat and simmer very gently for about 1 hour, topping up with extra boiling water as required.

Meanwhile, cut the carrot, turnip, and swede into matchsticks and the onion into rings. Heat the oil in a large saucepan, and fry the vegetables until lightly browned. Remove from the heat. Peel the potatoes and cut them into long chips with the cucumbers. Add to the fried vegetables. Strain in the stock from the kidney, reserving the kidney. Bring the vegetables and stock to the boil, reduce the heat, and simmer for 25–30 minutes.

For sharpness, add the strained cucumber pickling liquid, sliced sorrel or lettuce, and a good pinch of salt 5–10 minutes before the end of the cooking time. Before serving, add the kidney and cream, and sprinkle with chopped parsley or fennel.

VARIATIONS

Rassolnik can be prepared from meat or chicken stock and served with a piece of veal, mutton or chicken instead of using kidneys. The giblets of geese, ducks, turkeys or chickens, washed and chopped, can also be used instead of kidneys. Rassolnik can also be prepared from fish, and served with pieces of boiled perch or sturgeon in it.

Ukrainian Borsch

4 helpings

250g raw beetroot	50g butter
50g lard	25g flour
175g concentrated	400g potatoes
tomato purée	400g cabbage
3 × 2.5ml spoons	salt
vinegar	1 bay leaf
500ml general household	pepper
stock (p329)	a piece of hard pork rind
1 carrot	$\frac{1}{2}$ clove of garlic
1 turnip	1–2 tomatoes
1 swede	150ml soured cream
1 onion	

Garnish

chopped parsley

Peel and slice the beetroot. Put it into a large pan with the lard, tomato purée, vinegar and most of the stock, and simmer for 20–30 minutes. Meanwhile, prepare and slice the carrot, turnip, swede, and onion. Melt the butter, and fry the vegetables lightly. Add the flour, and continue frying until lightly browned. Add the remaining stock gradually, and bring gently to the boil, stirring all the time. Put to one side.

Peel the potatoes and cut into large cubes. Shred the cabbage roughly. Add both to the cooked beetroot, season with salt, and cook for 10–15 minutes. Add the fried vegetables and their sauce, the bay leaf and pepper, and cook until the cabbage and potato are tender. Rub the pork rind with garlic and add to the soup. Cut the tomatoes into wedges and add them. Bring the mixture quickly to the boil, then remove from the heat. Leave to stand for 15–20 minutes. Just before serving, remove the pork rind, add the soured cream, and sprinkle with chopped parsley.

Marinovanaya Riba

(Marinated Fish)

fish (see **Note**)	*flour for coating*
salt and pepper	*vegetable oil*

Marinade

2–3 carrots	*3–5 cloves*
2–3 onions	*1 small piece of*
4 ×15ml spoons	*cinnamon stick*
vegetable oil	*75ml mild malt vinegar*
375g concentrated	*450ml fish stock* (p330)
tomato purée	*salt*
1 sprig of parsley	*sugar*
2 bay leaves	
pepper	

Clean and scale the fish, then sprinkle with salt and a little pepper. Cut into 5cm pieces, if large. Roll in flour, brush with vegetable oil, and grill, turning once, until golden on both sides. Cool.

Make the marinade. Grate the carrots and chop the onions. Heat the oil in a saucepan, add the vegetables, and fry lightly for 3–4 minutes until tender. Add the tomato purée, herbs, seasoning, and spices. Cover, and simmer very gently for 5–10 minutes. Pour in the vinegar and stock, and bring to the boil. Add salt and sugar to taste, and pour the hot mixture over the fish. Cool.

Just before serving, arrange the cooled fish in a deep platter or bowl, with the marinade poured over it.

Note Any kind of fish can be prepared in this way, either in pieces, eg sturgeon or pike, or whole, eg smelts.

This marinated fish is served as *zakuski*.

Gribi Solyanka

(Baked Cabbage and Mushrooms)

4–5 helpings

1kg firm white cabbage	*1–2 ×5ml spoons sugar*
3 ×15ml spoons oil	*salt and pepper*
(approx)	*1 bay leaf*
vinegar	*fine dry white*
1 pickled cucumber	*breadcrumbs for*
100g large flat	*coating*
mushrooms	*oil*
1 onion	
2 ×15ml spoons	
concentrated tomato	
purée	

Garnish

lemon slices **or** *stuffed olives*

Wash and shred the cabbage and put it in a saucepan. Add half the oil, a little water, and vinegar to taste, and simmer for about 1 hour. Meanwhile, slice the pickled cucumber and the mushrooms. Skin and slice the onion. Add the tomato purée, pickled cucumber, sugar, salt, pepper, and bay leaf to the cabbage 15–20 minutes before the end of the cooking time.

In a separate pan, fry the sliced mushrooms in the remaining oil until tender, then remove them. Add extra oil to the pan if required and fry the onion until soft. Mix it with the mushrooms, and season with salt and pepper. Place half the cabbage in a layer in an ovenproof baking dish, lay the mushroom mixture on the cabbage, then place the remaining cabbage on top. Sprinkle with breadcrumbs and oil, and cook in a moderate oven, 180°C, Gas 4, for about 20 minutes. Serve from the dish with a slice of lemon or an olive on each helping.

Beef Stroganoff (2)

4 helpings

500g fillet of beef	*1 × 10ml spoon flour*
1 onion	*250ml soured cream*
3 × 10ml spoons	*1 × 10ml spoon Piquant*
vegetable oil	*sauce (p702)*
salt and pepper	

Garnish
chopped fennel **or**
 parsley

Wipe and trim the meat, cut into small slices, and beat well with a cutlet bat or rolling-pin. Cut into fine slivers. Skin and slice the onion finely. Heat the oil, and fry the onion until softened. Add the sliced meat, season to taste, and fry for 5–6 minutes, stirring slowly with a fork. Sprinkle the meat with the flour, stir, and cook for 2–3 minutes. Add the soured cream, stir, and cook for a further 2–3 minutes. Add the Piquant sauce and salt to taste. Sprinkle both the meat and potatoes with chopped fennel or parsley.

Serve with fried potatoes.

Note For Beef Stroganoff (1), see p1446.

Oladya
(Apple Fritters)

8 helpings

25g fresh yeast	*2 eggs*
500ml warm milk	*1 × 5ml spoon salt*
1 × 15ml spoon caster	*3–4 cooking apples*
sugar	*(450g approx)*
450g flour	*oil for deep frying*
3 × 10ml spoons cooking	
oil	

Blend the yeast into a little of the warm milk with the sugar, and leave in a warm place until frothy. Sift the flour, and beat the oil, eggs, and salt together in a separate basin. Mix the remaining warmed milk and flour into the yeast mixture. Cover, and leave to rise in a warm place for 30 minutes. Mix in the egg and oil mixture, and leave to rise a second time. Meanwhile, peel, core, and slice the apples into thin rings. Coat the slices with the batter. Heat the oil (p303) and fry the fritters, turning once, until golden-brown on both sides.

Serve with sugar.

Vareniki
(Curd Dumplings)

6–8 helpings

450g flour	*flour for rolling out*
1 egg	
3 × 15ml spoons milk **or**	
water (approx)	

Filling

200g curds **or** *curd*	*1 egg*
cheese	*2 × 15ml spoons butter*
sugar	*salt*

Sift the flour twice. Separate the egg. Make a well in the centre of the flour, and put in the egg yolk with a little milk or water. Work into the flour, adding extra milk or water if needed, to make a smooth, firm dough. Roll out thinly on a lightly floured surface, and cut into 7cm squares.

Drain the curds, or mash the curd cheese until very smooth. Mix in the sugar to taste and add the egg. Melt and add the butter. Blend together smoothly. Chill briefly to firm up. Brush the dough squares with the egg white, then place about 1 × 15ml spoonful of filling in the centre of each square. Enclose the filling in the dough, pinching the edges well.

Drop the vareniki gently into rapidly boiling, lightly salted water, and boil until they rise to the surface. Drain well, and pile on a hot serving dish.

Pour melted butter over them, and serve with soured cream or fruit syrup.

Blini
See p942.

Scandinavia

The cookery of the Scandinavian nations is influenced by the climate, and by the fact that they are largely maritime countries. Fish dishes, especially those containing herrings, predominate in everyday meals; often they are salted or pickled in order to last through the long winters. Pickled and salted meats are also widely eaten.

Except in Denmark, dairying is not a major industry, and hardy northern vegetables are the most common, especially pulses. Yellow pea soup is a weekly dish on tables in Norway, Sweden and Denmark alike.

Denmark has the most varied foods. Her open sandwiches and Danish pastries are known and liked far beyond her borders.

Danish Smørrebrød

(Open Sandwiches)

There are hundreds of different toppings for open sandwiches. They may be simple, or vividly coloured compositions, generous and rich enough to be a meal in themselves.

They are generally made on slices of wholegrain or dark rye bread, firm and close-textured so that it can be cut quite thin. Close-textured white bread is sometimes used, and is often toasted. In making a meal of smørrebrød, one starts off with a fish sandwich, proceeds to one made with meat and salad, and finishes with a slice of buttered white bread and Danish cheese. Sweet smørrebrød are made but they are not traditional.

SMØRREBRØD TOPPINGS

Hans Anderson Sandwiches

Butter the bread. Place 2 rashers of crisply fried bacon on each. Cover 1 rasher with a thin slice of liver pâté, and the other with sliced tomato. Top the tomato with grated horseradish and a little firm, chopped aspic jelly.

Aeg ag Sild

(Egg and Herring)

Butter the bread. Arrange thin slices of hard-boiled egg on it, and place one or more boned herring on the egg. Decorate with watercress.

Rejemad

(Shrimp)

Butter the bread. Place a lettuce leaf on each slice, and cover generously with small, peeled shrimps.

Røget Aal og Røraeg

(Smoked Eel and Egg)

Butter the bread. Cut smoked eel into 5cm pieces, and remove the skin and bones. Cover the bread with slices of eel. Top with slices of cold scrambled egg. Sprinkle with chives.

Bøf med Spejlaeg

(Beef, Onions, and Egg)

Butter the bread. Cover each with a thin slice of tender cold roast beef. Fry a few onion rings in deep fat until brown and crisp, drain well, and place on the beef. Fry 1 egg for each slice, place it on the onions, and serve while the egg is still hot.

Swedish Smörgåsbord

The Swedish smörgåsbord is a meal of assorted small hot and cold dishes, served with the spirit *Aquavit*. In the past, it was a cold buffet introducing the main part of a meal, but it has now become the meal itself because of the variety of its dishes. Many of these are herring dishes, notably salted herrings, for which Sweden is famed.

A smörgåsbord may include several courses. The first course usually consists of cheese and herring snacks with hot boiled potatoes to offset the herrings' strong flavour. This is followed by egg and fish dishes, then meats and meat salads, or perhaps a hot dish. Finally, there may be a fresh fruit salad or similar dessert.

Aura Juustokeitto   Finland
(Aura Soup)

6 helpings

1.25 litres brown stock (p329)	100g Finnish Aura cheese **or** Roquefort
50g butter	6 × 15ml spoons double cream
50g plain flour	

Garnish

chopped parsley

Bring the stock almost to the boil. Blend the butter and flour together to a smooth paste. Draw the pan off the heat, and stir in the beurre manié in very small pieces. Return to the heat and stir for 3 minutes. Remove from the heat, and rub the cheese through a sieve into the stock. Stir in the cream. Sprinkle with finely chopped parsley, and serve at once.

Note Do not season with salt as the cheese is fairly salty.

Brun Fiskesuppe   Norway
(Brown Fish Soup)

6 helpings

$\frac{1}{2}$ onion	25g butter
$\frac{1}{4}$ celeriac	1 × 15ml spoon flour
1 leek	salt
2 carrots	100ml dry sherry (approx)
1.5 litres fish stock (p330)	a few small canned fishballs
1 rasher of bacon	
2 × 15ml spoons concentrated tomato purée	

Prepare the vegetables, cut them up roughly, and boil in the fish stock with the bacon until tender. Strain the stock and discard the solids. Add the tomato purée to the liquid and mix well. Heat the butter in the pan, add the flour, and cook until brown. Add the stock gradually, and simmer for 5 minutes, stirring all the time. Add the salt, sherry, and a few small fish balls. Serve at once.

Gul Ärtsoppa   Sweden
(Yellow Pea Soup)

4 helpings

300g whole dried yellow peas	1 onion (optional)
2 litres water	a pinch of dried marjoram **or** thyme (optional)
400g lightly salted pork	salt (optional)

Soak the peas in the water in a large pan for 12 hours or overnight. Bring to the boil in the soaking water, and skim well. Reduce the heat to simmering point. Cube or slice the meat and add it to the soup. Skin and slice the onion and add it to the soup with the herbs and salt, if used. Partly cover the pan, and simmer for $1\frac{1}{4}$ hours until the peas are tender but not broken. Re-season if required. Serve very hot, with mustard.

Note If the meat is sliced, it can be served separately.

Marinerede Stegte Sild   Denmark
(Marinated Fried Herrings)

4 helpings

8 herrings	2 × 15ml spoons flour
1 × 2.5ml spoon salt	butter for shallow frying
1 × 2.5ml spoon pepper	

Marinade

300ml cider vinegar	1 medium-sized onion
300ml water	1 bay leaf
100g sugar	6 peppercorns

Split the herrings and remove the backbones. Mix the salt and pepper with the flour, and coat the fish with it. Melt the butter, and fry the fish for 7–8 minutes until golden-brown on both sides.

Place the vinegar, water, and sugar for the marinade in a saucepan, bring to the boil, and leave to cool. Skin the onion and slice it thinly. Place the fried herrings in a dish with the bay leaf, peppercorns, and onion rings. Pour over the vinegar mixture, and leave for about 6 hours.

Serve cold as a starter with brown bread and butter.

Tomatsild

Norway

(Herring and Tomato Salad)

6 helpings

3 salted herrings

Marinade

2 onions	*3 ×15ml spoons*
12 bay leaves	*concentrated tomato*
2 ×15ml spoons sugar	*purée*
4 ×15ml spoons	*1 ×15ml spoon water*
distilled vinegar	

Clean the herrings and soak for 6 hours in cold water. Cut into small pieces. Make the marinade. Skin and chop the onions and mix with all the remaining ingredients. Marinate the herrings in the mixture for 48 hours before use.

Serve as a starter or as part of a cold buffet.

Note Red herrings can be used but may need longer soaking. If possible, use Scandinavian salted (unsmoked) herrings.

Dillkött

Sweden

(Lamb in Dill Sauce)

4 helpings

*1kg breast **or** best end of*	*1 × 2.5ml spoon white*
neck of lamb (including	*peppercorns*
bone)	*1 bay leaf*
1 onion	*dill sprigs*
2 ×5ml spoons salt for	
each litre water	

Dill Sauce

*25g butter **or** margarine*	*2–3 ×15ml spoons*
2–3 ×15ml spoons plain	*chopped dill*
flour	*1–2 ×15ml spoons*
400ml white stock	*lemon juice*
(p329)	*1 egg yolk*
7 ×15ml spoons single	*salt and pepper*
cream	

Put the meat in a large saucepan with enough water to cover. Bring to the boil and skim. Skin and slice the onion and add to the pan with the salt, peppercorns, bay leaf, and dill. Reduce the heat, cover, and simmer for 1–1½ hours until the meat is tender. Drain the meat and keep hot.

Meanwhile, prepare the sauce. Melt the fat, add the flour and fry for 2–3 minutes. Draw the pan off the heat, slowly add the stock, and 5 ×15ml spoons cream, stirring all the time. Simmer, still stirring, for about 5 minutes. Stir in the dill and lemon juice. Remove from the heat. Blend the egg yolk with the remaining cream, and stir it into the sauce. Season to taste. Carve the boiled meat into slices, place on a warmed shallow serving dish, and pour the sauce over it.

Serve with boiled potatoes.

Stekt Rype

Norway

(Ptarmigan with Soured Cream)

6 helpings

200g butter	*1 ×15ml spoon cold*
4 ptarmigan	*water*
1 × 5ml spoon salt	*gravy browning*
500ml boiling water	*(optional)*
500ml soured cream	
2 slices goat's milk	
cheese	

Heat most of the butter in a large heavy saucepan and brown the birds. Sprinkle with salt, and add the boiling water gradually. Baste frequently, and add a pat of the remaining butter from time to time. Simmer for 30 minutes. Add half the soured cream and simmer for another 45 minutes, basting frequently. When the birds are done, remove them from the sauce. Crumble or shred the cheese. Bring the sauce to a brisk boil, and add the remaining cream, butter, and all the cheese. Add cold water to make the sauce curdle, and a few drops of gravy browning, if liked; do not thicken with flour. Cut the birds in half, arrange on a warmed dish, and pour some of the sauce over them.

Serve with Cranberry sauce, and with sautéed potatoes. Serve the rest of the sauce separately.

VARIATION

Small grouse can be used instead of ptarmigan.

Marinoitu Jänispaisti   Finland
('Marshal Mannerheim's Hare')

6–8 helpings

1 medium-sized hare (2kg approx)	600ml beef stock
8–12 rashers streaky bacon	salt
50g butter	150ml double cream **or** double and single cream, mixed

Marinade
4 large carrots	300ml red wine vinegar
4 onions	20–30 allspice berries
300ml oil	2–3 bay leaves

Make the marinade first. Skin and slice the carrots and onions. Mix all the ingredients together.

Cut the hare into serving pieces. Wrap each piece in a rasher of bacon. Put them into the marinade in a large bowl, and steep for 3 days, turning from time to time.

Drain the hare and vegetables and pat dry. Heat the butter in a large saucepan, and brown the vegetables. Remove them, then brown the pieces of hare. Return the vegetables to the pan, and add the stock and salt to taste. Simmer for $1–1\frac{1}{4}$ hours until the meat is tender. Re-season if required. Remove the vegetables from the saucepan with most of the liquid. Keep hot for serving separately. Add the cream to the hare, and heat through without boiling. (A little hot marinade can also be added if a stronger flavour is desired.)

Serve the hare with the vegetables, and with boiled or fried potatoes or boiled rice.

Note In the winter the Finnish forest hare eats the bark and branches of bushes which gives its flesh a distinctive gamey flavour; this is enhanced by marinating.

Gravad Lax
(Scandinavian Pickled Salmon)
See p451.

Janssons Frestelse   Sweden
('Jansson's Temptation')

4 helpings

2 large onions	200–300ml single cream
6 potatoes	25g butter **or** margarine
butter for greasing	
1 × 65g can anchovy fillets	

Skin the onions and chop or slice them finely. Peel the potatoes and cut into matchsticks. Spread half the potatoes in a buttered flameproof dish. Divide the anchovies and onion evenly over the potato layer. Top with the rest of the potatoes. Pour on half the cream, and a little anchovy liquor from the can. Dot with butter or margarine. Bake in a hot oven, 220°C, Gas 7, for about 20 minutes. Add the remaining cream. Bake for a further 30 minutes or until the potatoes are tender. Serve hot as a first course or supper dish.

Satakuntalainen Ohraryynipuuro   Finland
(Pearl Barley Porridge)

6–8 helpings

600ml water	salt
100g pearl barley	
1.25 litres full-cream milk (approx)	

Bring the water to the boil. Add the pearl barley, cover, and cook very gently for about 1 hour until all the water has been absorbed. Bring the milk to the boil, add it to the barley, and simmer over very low heat for about 4 hours. (Alternatively, the porridge can be baked in a very cool oven, 110°–120°C, Gas $\frac{1}{4}–\frac{1}{2}$, for the same time.) If the porridge begins to stick to the bottom of the pan, add a little more boiling milk. When the porridge is ready, add salt to taste.

Serve each plateful of porridge with a knob of butter in the centre, and with milk.

Note Leftover porridge is delicious fried in butter.

Bruna Bönor

Sweden

(Swedish Brown Beans)

4 helpings

300g brown beans	*2–4 × 15ml spoons corn*
1–1.25 litres water	*syrup or golden syrup*
1½ × 5ml spoons salt	*50ml vinegar*

Wash the beans thoroughly. Soak them in the water for about 12 hours in a large saucepan. Bring to the boil rapidly in the same water, add the salt, then reduce the heat, and simmer for about 1 hour. The beans should be tender, and the mixture thick. Stir occasionally, and add a little water if the beans become too dry. Add the syrup and vinegar, and cook for a further 5–10 minutes, stirring all the time. Season to taste.

Serve with fried pork, meatballs or sausages.

Weinerbrød

Denmark

(Danish Pastries)

Enough for 16 shapes

15g fresh yeast **or**	*200g plain flour*
1 × 10ml spoon dried	*a pinch of salt*
yeast	*25g lard*
75ml warm water	*flour for dusting*
1 egg	*125g softened butter*
1 × 2.5ml spoon caster	
sugar	

Blend the fresh yeast into the water or reconstitute the dried yeast (p1154). Beat the egg until liquid and add to the yeast mixture with the sugar. Sift the flour and salt together. Rub the lard into the flour. Pour in the yeast liquid and mix to a soft dough. Turn on to a floured surface and knead lightly until smooth. Place the dough in a large, lightly oiled polythene bag and leave in a cool place for 10 minutes. Shape the butter into a long rectangle about 1cm thick. Roll out the dough to approximately 25cm square. Place the butter down the centre. Fold the sides of the dough over the middle to overlap about 1cm only. Roll the dough into a strip 45 × 15cm. Fold it evenly into three. Return the dough to the bag and leave for 10 minutes. Roll and fold the dough in the same way twice more, letting it rest for 10 minutes each time. The dough is now ready for making pastries as below. Heat the oven to hot, 220°C, Gas 7, while shaping and proving the pastries.

PASTRY SHAPES

Windmills

Makes 8

Roll out half the dough to approximately 20 × 40cm. Cut into eight 10cm squares and place the squares on a baking sheet. Put a little almond paste (p1231) in the centre of each square (50g in all approximately). Brush the paste lightly with beaten egg. Make a cut from the corners of each square towards the middle. Fold the corners of each triangular piece thus formed towards the centre, and press the points into the almond paste firmly. Brush with beaten egg. Cover the pastries with oiled polythene and prove in a warm place for about 10–15 minutes until puffy. (It is important not to have the temperature too warm or the butter will run out.) Bake for 12–15 minutes. When cool, place a little raspberry jam in the centre of each pastry.

Fruit Snails

Makes 8

Cream together 50g butter, 50g caster sugar, and 2 × 5ml spoons cinnamon. Roll out the second half of the dough into a rectangle 15 × 40cm. Spread with the spiced butter, and scatter 25g sultanas over it. Roll up from the short side to make a fat roll. Cut it into 8 slices and place on a baking sheet. Flatten slightly. Prove and bake as above. Decorate with a little white glacé icing (p1225) when cold.

South Africa

Traditional South African cooking stems from three main sources. The early Dutch settlers brought their national dishes with them, and also adopted those of Malayan slaves brought from their colonial dominions, adding a few basic African dishes, such as maize meal (called mealie meal) porridge. The predominance of sheep-farming over large areas of South Africa has influenced the amount of mutton and lamb used in traditional cookery, and the Malayan influence has led to the widespread use of curries and highly spiced chutneys. A main meal in South Africa is not complete without meat, rice or similar cereal dish, and 3–4 vegetables. Both red and white wines are produced, and locally distilled brandy is a national drink.

Curried Fish

4–6 helpings

1.5kg Cape salmon, Cape cod, King Klip or any other firm white fish
1 ×10ml spoon salt
1 × 2.5ml spoon pepper
4 large onions
25ml oil or 25g fat
4 ×5ml spoons curry powder or to taste
6 peppercorns
6 lemon leaves or 3 bay leaves
5 ×15ml spoons sugar
500ml white wine vinegar and 250ml water (if the vinegar is strong)

Clean the fish and cut into steaks. Sprinkle with half the salt and a little pepper, and fry, bake or steam until cooked. Keep hot. Skin and slice the onions. Heat the oil or fat, and fry the onions until light brown. Add the curry powder, and fry for a further 2–3 minutes. Stir in the remaining ingredients, and simmer for 10–15 minutes.

Pack the hot fish and curry sauce in alternate layers into warmed, dry, sterilized jars, or earthenware or enamel containers. The fish should be completely covered with the sauce. Leave to cool, close the containers, and store in a cool place. The fish is ready for use after 2 days. It should not be kept for more than a week.

VARIATION

Add 1 ×10–15ml spoon finely shredded ginger root to the vinegar, and cook together with the remaining ingredients.

Bobotie

(Curried Minced Lamb)

4–6 helpings

8 dried apricots or 1 tart apple
1 large onion
2 ×15ml spoons lamb fat
1 thick slice of bread
250ml milk
450g boneless lamb
2 ×15ml spoons curry powder
1 ×15ml spoon apricot jam
50ml vinegar or fresh lemon juice
1 × 5ml spoon salt
1 ×2.5ml spoon pepper
75g seedless raisins
4–6 lemon leaves or bay leaves
2 eggs

Soak the apricots overnight if used, then chop them, or peel and grate the apple just before using it. Skin and slice the onion. Heat the lamb fat, and fry the onion gently until browned. Put to one side.

Cut the crusts off the bread, crumble it into 125ml of the milk, and mash with a fork. Mince the meat, and, using a fork, mix lightly with the fruit, onion, bread, curry powder, jam, vinegar or lemon juice, seasoning, and raisins. Turn the mixture into an ovenproof baking dish without pressing it down. Push the lemon leaves or bay leaves into the mixture. Beat the eggs with the rest of the milk, and pour over the meat, lifting the meat lightly with a fork to let the mixture run in. Cover, and bake in a moderate oven, 180°C, Gas 4, for 1 hour. Uncover, and bake for a further 10–15 minutes, until browned on top.

Serve hot, with boiled rice and a fruit chutney.

Sosaties

(Curried Kebabs)

4–6 helpings

½ clove of garlic
1 leg of lamb (1.5kg approx)
3 onions
5 bruised orange or lemon leaves or 2 strips lemon rind
1 × 10ml spoon salt

1 × 2.5ml spoon ground ginger
1 × 2.5ml spoon pepper
1 × 10ml spoon ground coriander (optional)
125ml milk
150g dried apricots

Sauce

6 dried apricots or 3 × 10ml spoons apricot jam
4 large onions
1 red chilli

1 × 5ml spoon turmeric
5 × 15ml spoons sugar
1 × 2.5ml spoon salt
500ml vinegar
flour for thickening

Rub an earthenware bowl with the garlic. Keeping the fat on, cut the meat into 5cm cubes. Skin the onions and chop them into large chunks. Mix all the main ingredients, except the apricots, in the bowl. Leave overnight.

Make the sauce. Soak the 6 dried apricots overnight, if used, then chop them finely. Skin the onions and chop them finely, de-seed and chop the chilli. Mix all the ingredients, except the flour, in a saucepan. Bring to the boil, and boil for 5 minutes, then leave to cool.

Mix the sauce with the meat, and leave to stand for 2–3 days. Soak the 150g apricots in water for 1–2 hours before use.

Thread lean and fat cubes of meat alternately on long skewers, with chunks of onion and whole apricots between them. Grill slowly over charcoal for 15–20 minutes, turning often, until cooked through and brown. Meanwhile, thicken the sauce by sprinkling in a little flour and heating gently. When the sosaties are cooked, serve with the sauce.

Note The sosaties can be oven-baked, if preferred.

Tamatiebredie

(Mutton and Tomato Stew)

4–6 helpings

1kg breast of mutton
25g flour
2 medium-sized onions
1 small chilli
1 × 15ml spoon lamb fat

6 ripe tomatoes
1 × 5ml spoon salt
1 × 2.5ml spoon pepper
5 × 5ml spoons sugar

Cut the meat into serving portions and roll in some of the flour. Skin and slice the onions, de-seed and chop the chilli. Melt the fat in a saucepan, and brown the meat and onion. Sprinkle with the remaining flour, and cook for 2 minutes. Skin and quarter the tomatoes, and add to the meat, with the chopped chilli, salt and pepper. Cover, and simmer for 2–3 hours until the meat is tender and the gravy thick. Add the sugar 15 minutes before serving.

Serve with boiled rice.

VARIATIONS

For other vegetable bredies, use the same quantities of meat, flour, and fat. Brown with or without the onion, and add 500ml water instead of tomatoes. Cook until nearly done, then add one of the following vegetables:

Cabbage or cauliflower: 1 medium-sized chopped cabbage or cauliflower. Add to the meat 30–35 minutes before the bredie is served. Grate a little nutmeg on top.

Green beans: Shred 500g green beans and add 45 minutes before serving the bredie; 1 or 2 medium-sized diced potatoes can also be added.

Koeksisters
(Plaited Doughnuts)

Makes 8–12

250g plain flour	1 egg
a pinch of salt	100ml milk
2 × 5ml spoons baking powder	oil for deep frying
50g butter	flour for rolling out

Syrup

250g sugar	a stick of cinnamon **or**
125ml water	$\frac{1}{2}$ × 2.5ml spoon ground ginger

Make the syrup first. Put all the ingredients into a pan and heat gently, stirring, until the sugar has dissolved. Bring to the boil, and boil for 2 minutes without stirring. Pour into 2 basins, and chill in a refrigerator.

To make the koeksisters, sift the flour, salt, and baking powder into a bowl. Rub in the butter. Beat the egg with the milk. Make a well in the centre of the flour and pour in the egg and milk. Gradually work in the flour to form a soft dough.

Heat the oil (p303). Roll out the dough on a lightly floured surface to 5mm thick. Cut into strips 8cm long and 4cm wide. Cut each strip into three lengthways and plait 7cm of their length. Dampen the ends and press firmly. Drop 3 or 4 koeksisters at a time into the hot oil. Cook until golden-brown underneath, then turn them over and cook for 1 minute on the second side. Lift them out with a perforated spoon and put them immediately into the chilled syrup. Turn them in the syrup with a skewer. Lift out, and place on a cake rack supported by a plate to catch the excess syrup. Return the bowl of syrup to the refrigerator and use for the next batch of koeksisters to be fried.

Note The syrup must be very cold and the koeksisters very hot when dipped.

Blatjang
(Dried Apricot Chutney)
See p1146.

Waatlemoenkonvyt
(Sweet Watermelon Preserve)

watermelon	50–60ml lemon juice
bicarbonate of soda (see Method)	a pinch of salt
1.25kg sugar for each kg watermelon peel	2 small pieces ginger root for each 3kg peel
2 litres water for each kg sugar	

Cut the watermelon into 3cm slices. Cut away and discard the soft pink flesh, and peel off the hard, outer green rind. Prick the fleshy peel just under the rind, very thoroughly, on both sides, then cut into square or rectangular pieces. Weigh the fleshy peel. Put it in boiling water to cover, adding 3 × 15ml spoons bicarbonate of soda for each 5 litres water used. Leave overnight.

Next day, rinse the peel thoroughly and leave in fresh water for 2 hours. Drain. Bring a large pan of water to the boil. Drop the peel gradually into the boiling water, and ensure that the water does not go off the boil. Boil until just tender. At this stage it should be easy to pierce the peel with a blunt match. Measure the sugar and water into a large saucepan in the proportions given above, and make a sugar syrup, together with the lemon juice, salt, and ginger root. Bring to the boil. Put the peel into the boiling syrup, and boil rapidly until the pieces are clear and transparent, and the syrup thick. Pack into dry, hot, sterilized jars, seal immediately, and label.

Note The fruit may be boiled in the syrup over a period of 2 to 3 days. Boil it for 3 minutes the first day, and leave in the syrup to cool. Remove the fruit, bring the syrup to boiling point, then gradually add the fruit so that the syrup does not go off the boil. Boil again for 30–40 minutes. Leave to cool. Repeat the process once more, and then finish boiling.

Watermelon varieties with a firm peel produce a fairly crisp preserve. Some other varieties readily become mushy, and therefore require very little boiling.

VARIATIONS
Use pumpkin, green pawpaw or sweet melon.

Spain and Portugal

Spanish cooking is extremely varied, and reflects the wide contrasts in climate and terrain between the wet and mountainous north and the sun-baked south. Each region has its own specialities. Fish dishes are particularly good. Of the meat dishes, the *ollas* and *cozidos* (stews) from New Castile and the north, and the roast suckling-pig and baby lamb from Old Castile are among the best. Spanish cooking as a whole has been much influenced by the introduction of almonds and spices by the Moors, and by the Conquistadores who brought peppers and tomatoes from South America. Olive oil and wine, both abundant, are used lavishly.

In view of the long coastline, it is not surprising that there is a magnificent variety of fish in Portugal. As in Spain, the main variations in regional cooking are between the mountainous north and the more Mediterranean-like south. The dried *bacalhau* or salt cod is a universal favourite. The north is famous for its *caldo verde* or green soup, and for rich fish and meat stews, while the south makes a range of delicious Moorish-inspired sweetmeats.

Note Although Spanish and Portuguese dishes, like those of Italy or Greece, should properly be cooked in olive oil, a good quality vegetable cooking oil can be used, if preferred.

Caldo Verde   Portugal
(Green Soup)

4–6 helpings

1 onion	*salt and pepper*
450g potatoes	*single cream*
1.25 litres chicken stock	*350g green cabbage*

Garnish
a few slices chouriço **or**
  presunto (see **Note**)

Skin and chop the onion. Peel and slice the potatoes. Heat the chicken stock. Add the onion and potatoes, and simmer for about 20 minutes until tender. Rub through a sieve or process in an electric blender until smooth. Return the purée to the pan, season with salt and pepper, and add cream to taste.

Meanwhile, shred the cabbage finely, and boil it briskly for 5 minutes in an uncovered pan of salted water. Drain, and stir into the purée. Ladle into bowls and sprinkle with a little chopped chouriço or presunto before serving.

Note Chouriço is a sausage spiced with paprika, very like the Spanish chorizo; presunto is a raw, highly cured ham. Parma or Bayonne ham will do just as well.

In Portugal this soup is made with finely shredded *couve*, a tall-growing, dark green type of cabbage.

Sopa de Pescado   Spain
(Fish Soup)

4 helpings

250g angler-fish	*3 ×10ml spoons plain*
250g sea bass	* flour*
250g hake	*1 × 5ml spoon chopped*
500g live mussels	* parsley*
150g onions	*1 ×15ml spoon vinegar*
2 cloves garlic	*1 bay leaf*
1 ×15ml spoon olive oil	*1 litre water*
	salt and pepper

Garnish
*croûtons of bread fried
  in olive oil*

Clean the fish, and cut into small pieces. Wash, scrape, and beard the mussels (p425). Skin the onions, and chop them finely. Crush the garlic. Put the fish into a saucepan, and cover with the olive oil, onions, garlic, flour, parsley, vinegar, and bay leaf. Marinate for 30 minutes. Add the water and a little salt and pepper. Bring to boiling point, and simmer for 15 minutes. Add the mussels, and simmer for another 5 minutes to open them. Serve garnished with croûtons.

Gazpacho Andaluz
(Andalusian Cold Soup)

Spain

4 helpings

4 large tomatoes	*1 litre water*
4 green peppers	*salt and pepper*
½ cucumber	*2 cloves garlic*
150g soft white	*6 ×10ml spoons white*
breadcrumbs	*wine vinegar*
8 ×10ml spoons olive oil	

Skin and chop the tomatoes, de-seed the peppers, and chop finely with the cucumber. Put the breadcrumbs, tomatoes, peppers and cucumbers into a large bowl with the olive oil. Stir in the water and leave for 1 hour. Rub through a sieve or process in an electric blender. Add salt and pepper to taste. Crush the garlic, stir it into the vinegar, and add to the bowl. Cover with foil, and chill well before serving.

Carne de Porco a Alentejana
(Fried Pork with Clams)

Portugal

4–5 helpings

1kg loin of pork	*1kg clams or cockles*
2 ×15ml spoons olive oil	*salt and pepper*

Marinade
1 onion	*1 × 5ml spoon chopped*
1 carrot	*parsley*
2 cloves garlic	*1 × 5ml spoon saffron*
2 ×10ml spoons vinegar	*powder or strands*
150ml dry white wine	*1 sprig fresh coriander*
1 bay leaf	*leaves*

Garnish
chopped parsley

Make the marinade first. Skin the onion and chop it finely. Grate the carrot. Crush the garlic and mix together with the rest of the marinade ingredients. Cut the pork into 2cm cubes and marinate in this mixture for 24 hours. Remove from the marinade with a perforated spoon. Strain the marinade, and reserve the liquid.

Heat the oil in a frying pan, and cook the meat over high heat for 10 minutes, turning it all the time. Reduce the heat to very low, add the clams or cockles, and the liquid from the marinade. Season to taste with salt and pepper, cover, and cook for another 8–10 minutes until the shellfish open. Garnish with chopped parsley and serve with slices of lemon.

VARIATION
This dish can be made with mussels instead of the clams or cockles.

Paella Valenciana

Spain

6–8 helpings

2 spring or grilling	*2 cloves garlic*
chickens or 1 roasting	*75g short-grain Spanish*
chicken (1–1.5kg	*or Italian rice per*
approx)	*person*
flour for coating	*a pinch of saffron*
olive oil for frying	*strands*
1kg live mussels	*salt*

Garnish
50g cooked shellfish per	*strips of canned pimento*
person (prawns,	*green or black olives*
crayfish, lobster or	
crab)	

Joint the chicken (pp619–20) and coat lightly with flour. Heat 4 ×10ml spoons olive oil, and brown the pieces all over. Put to one side. Wash, scrape, and beard the mussels (p425). Put into a large saucepan with very little water. Cover, and heat gently for 5–10 minutes, shaking occasionally until they open. Discard any that do *not* open. Remove the open mussels with a perforated spoon and leave to cool. Reserve the liquid in the pan. Remove the mussels from their shells, retaining the best half-shells. Strain the mussel liquor through muslin, and add it to the liquid in the pan.

Slice half a clove of garlic thinly. Heat some olive oil in a deep frying pan or shallow flameproof oven-to-table casserole. Fry the slices of garlic until golden-brown, then discard them. Add 75g rice per person to the flavoured oil, and fry very gently.

Crush the remaining garlic with the saffron and a little water. Scatter the mixture over the rice, and season with salt. Measure 150ml of the mussel liquid per person (made up with water if necessary), and add to the rice. Heat to simmering point, stirring well. Cook for 5 minutes, still stirring. Add the chicken pieces, and cook them with the rice for a further 15 minutes, until they are tender and the rice is cooked through.

Garnish with the shellfish, pimento, and olives. Replace the mussels in the half-shells, and use as an additional garnish. Remove the pan from the heat, and cover with a cloth for 10 minutes before serving. Serve from the pan.

Note Success depends upon correct cooking of the proper type of Spanish or Italian rice; the grains should be separate and not soggy. There is no need to use expensive shellfish. A well-made paella with chicken and mussels, or even chicken alone, is delicious. Traditionally, very young chicken is used.

Bacalhau Dourado   Portugal
(Golden Bacalhau)

4–6 helpings

450g dried salted cod   *450g potatoes*
  (bacalhau)   *6 eggs*
2 onions   *salt and pepper*
olive oil for shallow
  frying

Garnish
1 × 10ml spoon chopped
  parsley

Soak the fish for 24 hours, changing the water occasionally. Bring to the boil, then drain, skin, bone, and flake the fish. Skin the onions and chop them finely. Fry in olive oil until golden, then add the flaked bacalhau, cook for a few minutes more, and drain off any excess oil. Peel the potatoes, slice them very finely, and fry separately in oil until tender but not crisp. Drain them, add to the bacalhau, and mix thoroughly. Beat the eggs until liquid and add to the pan. Season with salt and pepper.

Continue cooking until the egg mixture just reaches the creamy consistency of scrambled eggs. Turn out on to a serving dish, sprinkle with chopped parsley and serve immediately.

Cocido   Spain
(Spanish Smoked Bacon Stew)
See p612.

Fabada Asturiana   Spain
(Bean and Meat Stew)

6 helpings

1kg butter beans   *225g morcilla* **or**
2 young pig's trotters   *asturiana (Spanish*
500g brisket of beef   *black pudding, see*
1 large onion   **Note***)*
225g chorizo (see **Note***)*   *salt and pepper*

Soak the butter beans in cold water for $1\frac{1}{2}$–2 hours. Wash the trotters, and blanch them for 10–15 minutes in boiling salted water. Rinse well to remove any scum. Put them into a large saucepan. Cut the brisket into 2cm cubes, and add to the trotters. Skin, quarter, and add the onion. Drain and add the butter beans. Cover with water, bring to the boil, and skim well. Reduce the heat, and simmer for 2–3 hours until the meat and beans are very tender. Cut the chorizo and morcilla or asturiana into chunks, season to taste, and add to the stew for the last 30 minutes of the cooking time.

Note Chorizo is a spicy sausage containing paprika, obtainable from many good delicatessens.

If Spanish black pudding is not available, ordinary black pudding can be used.

Perdices Estofadas con Chocolate
(Stewed Partridge with Chocolate) Spain

4 helpings

2 partridges (500g each approx)	125ml dry white wine
1 onion	4 × 10ml spoons white wine vinegar
1 clove	salt and pepper
1 small head of garlic	25g plain chocolate
1 bay leaf	
4 × 10ml spoons olive oil	

Garnish
sautéed potato slices

Put the partridges into a stewpan. Skin and chop the onion, and add to the pan. Stick the clove into the head of garlic, and add to the pan with the bay leaf, olive oil, wine, vinegar, and a little salt and pepper. Bring to the boil, reduce the heat, and simmer for 35 minutes, shaking the pan well at intervals. Remove the partridges, and keep hot on a serving dish.

Grate the chocolate, stir it into the pan, and simmer for a further 10 minutes. Arrange some sliced, sautéed potatoes around the partridges. Rub the chocolate sauce through a sieve, and pour it over them.

Tortilla Espanola
(Spanish Omelet) Spain

4 helpings

750g potatoes	salt
250g onions	6 eggs
olive oil for shallow frying	

Peel and dice the potatoes. Skin and slice the onions, and mix them together. Put enough oil into a large frying pan to cover the bottom by 5mm. Heat the oil until very hot, then add the potatoes and onions, and sprinkle with salt. Fry gently for about 20 minutes until soft but not crisp. Turn over or stir gently from time to time. Remove the vegetables from the pan with a perforated spoon.

Beat the eggs lightly with a pinch of salt, and stir into the fried vegetable mixture. Drain off any oil, clean the pan, and heat 1 × 5ml spoon of oil in it until very hot. Pour in the egg and vegetable mixture, and cook briefly, shaking the pan vigorously to prevent the mixture sticking. Slide the half-cooked omelet on to a large plate, turn it over on to a second plate, then slide it back into the pan, uncooked side down. Cook for another 2–3 minutes to brown the second side, shaking as before.

The finished tortilla should be about 2cm thick, crisp on the outside, and juicy in the middle.

Serve with a green salad.

Cenoura e Laranja
(Carrot and Orange Sweet) Portugal

3–4 helpings

2 medium-sized carrots	5 × 2.5ml spoons Bagaceira (see **Note**)
grated rind and juice of 1 large orange	
4 × 10ml spoons caster sugar (approx)	

Grate the carrots finely. Mix all the ingredients together in a small saucepan. Simmer for 10 minutes until the liquid is absorbed. Taste, and add a little more sugar if required. Shape into ovals between 2 small rounded spoons, and cool on a plate. Serve cold.

Note Bagaceira is a Portuguese spirit much like Marc de Bourgogne brandy. Grand Marnier can be used instead.

Churros
(Fritters) Spain

4 helpings

500ml water	olive oil for shallow frying
1 × 5ml spoon salt	caster sugar for dusting
400g plain flour	
2 eggs	

Bring the water and salt to the boil in a large saucepan. Sift in the flour, and beat vigorously with a wooden spoon until the dough cleanly leaves the sides of the pan. Remove the pan from the heat, add the eggs, and stir until completely blended, and the dough is smooth. Place in a forcing bag with a large nozzle.

Heat enough oil in a frying pan to cover the base to a depth of 5mm. Squeeze the dough into the very hot oil in figure-of-eight shapes. Fry for 15–20 minutes, turning once until the churros are golden-brown. Remove with a perforated spoon, drain on soft kitchen paper to absorb any excess oil, and sprinkle with sugar. Serve while still hot.

Note These light fritters are a favourite breakfast dish in Spain, where they are often dunked in coffee or hot chocolate.

Switzerland

Swiss cooking is German, French or Italian in style, depending on the region, although many dishes have acquired a national identity, usually through the use of Swiss products and mountain herbs. Swiss food is rich by most European standards; dairy foods such as butter, eggs and cheese are used lavishly. Recipes are straightforward on the whole; meat and root vegetables predominate, often in a plainly flavoured cream sauce.

Papet Vaudois
(Bacon, Sausage and Vegetable Hot Pot)

4 helpings

2 small onions	3 large potatoes (600g
1kg leeks	approx)
1 × 10ml spoon butter	100ml white stock
salt and pepper	(p329)
200g smoked bacon	100ml dry white wine
rashers, thickly sliced	200g cervelat **or** other
and without rinds	smoked sausage (in one
	piece)

Skin and slice the onions. Wash the leeks and cut the white parts into 4cm long pieces. Melt the butter in a large deep pan, and cook the onions in it until soft but not coloured. Add the leeks and

continue cooking for a few minutes. Season well with salt and pepper. Add the bacon to the pan and cook gently for 10 minutes.

Meanwhile, peel the potatoes, and cut them into 1cm cubes. Add to the pan with the wine and stock, cover again, and cook for another 10 minutes. Prick the sausage well in several places, add to the pan, cover, and simmer for 20 minutes.

To serve, remove the bacon and sausage and cut the sausage into 4 or 8 slices. Put the vegetables into a warmed, shallow serving dish, and place the bacon and sausage on top. Serve hot.

Züri Gschnätlets
(Veal in Cream Sauce)

4–6 helpings

600g lean boneless veal	salt and pepper
or 450g veal and 150g	200ml dry white wine
calf's kidney	200ml single cream
4 shallots **or** 1 small	1 × 10ml spoon chopped
onion	parsley
3 × 10ml spoons butter	
1 × 10ml spoon flour	
(approx)	

Wipe the meat, trim off any excess fat, and cut into small thin strips. Skin the kidney, if used, remove the core, and cut into strips like the meat. Skin and chop the shallots or onion. Melt the butter in a frying pan, add the meat and kidney if used, and sear on all sides. Remove at once before any juices run. Keep warm.

Reduce the heat, add the shallots or onion, and fry gently until soft. Dust with the flour, add seasoning to taste, and stir in the wine. Simmer, uncovered, until the wine is reduced by half. Stir in the cream. Continue simmering until the sauce thickens. Re-season if required. Return the meat to the pan, heat for 30 seconds–1 minute, place on a well warmed serving dish, and sprinkle with chopped parsley. Serve at once, with Rösti (p1566).

Rösti
(Fried Potato Cake)

6 helpings

1kg potatoes	*150g unsalted butter*
100g smoked bacon, without rinds	*2 × 10ml spoons milk*
1 onion (100g approx)	*salt and pepper*

Boil the potatoes in their skins until tender but not soft. Drain, cool, and leave overnight.

Peel the potatoes and grate coarsely. Chop the bacon finely. Chop the onion and mix together with the potatoes. Melt the butter in a frying pan. Put in the potato mixture, and press down with the back of a spoon to form a thick flat cake covering the bottom of the pan. Sprinkle with the milk, season lightly, and cover. When the cake starts to sizzle, reduce the heat to very low, and cook for 30 minutes without removing the lid. The cake should be golden-brown underneath. Turn on to a warmed serving plate and serve with the golden-brown side on top.

Aargauer Rüeblitorte
(Carrot Cake)

5 eggs	*4 × 10ml spoons plain flour and 1 × 5ml*
300g caster sugar	*spoon baking powder*
grated rind of ½ lemon	*or 4 × 10ml spoons*
300g ground almonds	*self-raising flour*
300g carrots (weighed after grating)	*a pinch of salt*
1 × 2.5ml spoon ground cinnamon	*2 × 10ml spoons rum, Kirsch or lemon juice*
a pinch of ground cloves	*fat or oil for greasing*

Icing

150g icing sugar	*2 × 10ml spoons Kirsch*
1 × 15ml spoon egg white	*or lemon juice*
	apricot glaze (p1234)

Separate the eggs. Beat the yolks until liquid, add the sugar, and beat together until pale and creamy. Add the lemon rind. Beat the almonds into the creamed mixture. Grate the carrots, weigh them, and stir into the mixture. Mix together the spices, flour and salt, and stir in. Add the rum, Kirsch or lemon juice.

Whisk the egg whites until stiff but not dry. Stir 2 × 15ml spoonfuls into the carrot mixture, then fold in the rest lightly with a metal spoon. Turn the mixture gently into a greased shallow 25cm cake tin or pie dish. Bake in a fairly hot oven, 190°C, Gas 5, for 1–1½ hours, or until a thin hot skewer inerted in the centre comes out clean.

Meanwhile, make the icing. Mix together the sugar, egg white, and Kirsch or lemon juice to make a fairly stiff icing. Warm the apricot glaze and spread it on the warm cake. Put the icing into a forcing bag with a 5mm plain nozzle, and pipe a pattern of concentric rings on the cake. Leave to cool, and serve as a dessert or party cake.

Swiss Cheese Fondue
See p1453.

USA and Canada

The cookery of the United States has been developed and influenced by people of many nations. The first traditional Thanksgiving Day dinner of roast turkey, cornbread and pumpkin pie, dates from 1621, when English pilgrims were taught by the native American Indians how to grow maize and survive in a new land.

Although dishes such as grilled steak, hamburgers, hot dogs and apple pie are characterized as all-American, the East Coast chowders and baked beans, the Southern chillies and gumbos are just as all-American, and their origins are English, Spanish and French.

Throughout the USA there are many ethnic quarters where the traditional cuisines of the Chinese, Russian, Polish, Jewish, Greek, Italian, Armenian, and other nationalities are the daily fare for American families.

Canada's rich agricultural resources provide a basis for a national cuisine that is predominantly French. The Tourtière is perhaps one of the most popular dishes. But, as with the USA, Canada's cookery has enjoyed the influences of other settlers, namely, the English, Irish, Scottish and German.

Rumaki

Makes 36 pieces

250g chicken liver
50g butter
1 × 350g can whole
  water chestnuts

500g streaky bacon,
  without rinds

Cut the chicken liver into medium-sized pieces. Melt the butter and sauté the liver gently for 2–3 minutes. Remove from the pan and drain on soft kitchen paper. Drain the water chestnuts and cut them into 2cm strips. Cut each piece of bacon in half. Roll each half rasher round a piece of chicken liver and water chestnut. Fasten with a wooden cocktail stick. Grill, turning frequently, for 3–5 minutes under moderate heat, until the bacon is crisp. Serve hot.

Fish and Corn Chowder

6 helpings

325g sweetcorn kernels,
  canned or frozen
250g potatoes
500g white fish
2 × 15ml spoons salt
½ × 2.5ml spoon ground
  white pepper
3 rashers streaky bacon,
  without rinds

1 medium-sized onion
  (100g approx)
3 sticks celery
25g plain flour
500ml milk
50g butter

Drain the canned corn, or thaw the frozen corn. Put to one side. Peel the potatoes and cut into 2cm cubes, then boil for 5 minutes in enough salted water to cover. Cut the fish into 6cm pieces and add to the potatoes with the salt and pepper. Simmer, covered, for 12 minutes.

Meanwhile, chop the bacon finely and fry separately until just crisp, then remove from the pan. Thinly slice the onion and celery. Cook together in the bacon fat until the onion is golden. Remove the onion and celery with a perforated spoon, and add to the fish mixture with the bacon. Reserve the fat in the pan. Add the flour to the bacon fat and mix well. Cook gently for 2–3 minutes, without colouring; then add the milk gradually, stirring all the time until thick. Add to the fish. Add the corn and butter, and cook for 5 minutes longer. Serve hot.

VARIATIONS
Clam Chowder

1) 1 × 500g can clams or 500g fresh clams can be substituted for the white fish.
2) To make Manhattan Clam Chowder, add 1 × 396g can tomatoes with their liquid to the clam chowder.

Corn Chowder

Increase the quantity of sweetcorn to 1kg, and omit the fish.

Note Other chowders can be found in the chapter on Soups.

Cornbread Stuffing

Enough for a 1.5kg chicken or a 3kg turkey

100g stale white bread
200g Texas cornbread
  (p1570)
1 medium-sized onion
  (100g approx)
3 sticks celery
1 × 5ml spoon salt

¼ × 2.5ml spoon ground
  black pepper
1 × 5ml spoon dried
  crushed sage
100g butter
375ml chicken or turkey
  stock (approx)

Crumble the white bread and the cornbread into a large basin. Chop the onion and celery finely. Add with the salt, pepper, and dried sage to the crumb mixture. Melt the butter, and pour it over the bread and seasonings. Slowly add just enough chicken or turkey stock, to make a damp but not liquid mixture.

Steaks with Barbecue Sauce

6 helpings

6 rump **or** *porterhouse*
steaks, approx 2cm
thick and well-marbled
with fat

Barbecue Sauce

1 ×15ml spoon salt	*2 ×15ml spoons*
1 × 2.5ml spoon ground	*Worcestershire sauce*
black pepper	*200ml water*
3 ×15ml spoons soft	*2 ×15ml spoons chilli*
dark brown sugar	*sauce*
50ml tomato ketchup	*100ml red wine vinegar*
3 ×15ml spoons mixed	*200ml corn oil*
English mustard	

Make the sauce first. Mix all the ingredients together in a saucepan, using a balloon whisk. When well blended, simmer slowly until slightly thickened, then cool.

Marinate the steaks in the sauce for at least 6 hours before cooking. Grill either over charcoal or under moderate grill heat for about 10 minutes, or until cooked to taste; turn at least once. Brush well with the sauce on both sides while cooking. Serve with any sauce left over.

New England Boiled Dinner

6 helpings

1.5kg salted silverside	*1 large swede*
or *other salt beef*	*1 large cabbage*
1 bay leaf	*6 medium-sized carrots*
4 peppercorns	*6 small potatoes*
1 clove of garlic	*6 small onions*

Trim the beef, and tie or skewer it into a neat shape. Put into a large pan with a lid, and cover with boiling water. Add the bay leaf, peppercorns, and garlic clove. Boil for 15 minutes, skimming off any excess fat as it rises. Reduce the heat, cover, and simmer gently for 2½ hours until the meat is tender.

Meanwhile, cut the swede into 4cm cubes. Cut the cabbage into 6 pieces, and cut out the hard stalk and core. Peel the carrots, potatoes, and onions.

When the meat is tender, add the swede and carrots, and cook for 15 minutes. Pour about 250ml of the cooking liquid into a second pan, and put in the cabbage. Cover, and simmer until tender. Add the potatoes and onions to the meat and vegetables, and cook for another 25–30 minutes until all the vegetables are tender. For the last 30 minutes of the cooking time, check that the beef does not dry out; add extra water if required. When the dish is ready, the beef should still have enough well-flavoured broth with it to serve as a sauce.

To serve, place the beef on a large carving dish or serving platter, and surround with the vegetables. Serve the broth separately in a warmed sauce-boat.

Boston Baked Beans with Pork

6–8 helpings

400g haricot beans	*1 ×15ml spoon black*
1 litre water	*treacle*
2 ×5ml spoons dry	*1 ×15ml spoon golden*
mustard	*syrup*
1 ×15ml spoon salt	*50g soft brown sugar*
1 × 2.5ml spoon ground	*250g salt belly of pork*
black pepper	
3 medium-sized onions	
(300g approx)	

Wash the beans in several changes of water, then soak them overnight in 500ml of the water.

Mix the mustard, salt, and pepper with the remaining water in a large casserole. Pour in the beans with their liquid. Skin the onions and cut them into quarters. Add them to the casserole with the treacle, syrup, and brown sugar. Cover with a tight-fitting lid, and cook in a very cool oven, 120°C, Gas ½, for 6–8 hours.

Half-way through the cooking, put the pork into a saucepan, cover with cold water and soak for 1 hour; then bring to boiling point, reduce the heat, and simmer for 10 minutes. Drain. Remove the rind from the pork and cut it into thin strips 5 ×3cm (approx). Place both the meat and the strips of rind in the casserole over the beans, replace the lid, and continue cooking for about 1 hour or until the meat is tender. If necessary, add extra water at the same time as the pork. Remove the lid for the last 30 minutes of the cooking time. Transfer the meat to a carving dish for serving. Serve the beans from the casserole.

Tourtière

6 helpings

1 × 500g can chopped pork	1 bay leaf
1 small onion	150ml water
1 clove of garlic	100g breadcrumbs
dried savory	shortcrust pastry (p1249)
a pinch of ground cloves	using 225g flour
	flour for rolling out

Mince the pork. Skin the onion and dice it finely. Crush the garlic. Mix the pork, onion, and garlic with the herbs and water in a saucepan. Bring to the boil, reduce the heat, and simmer for 20 minutes, or until the meat is light brown and the water has evaporated. The mixture should be damp but not wet. Remove from the heat and add the breadcrumbs gradually until all the fat is absorbed from the surface. Leave to cool.

Roll out the pastry on a lightly floured surface and use just over half to line a 20cm pie plate. Use the other half to make a lid. Put in the meat mixture, dampen the edge and cover with the pastry lid. Seal the edges and make a small hole in the centre to let the steam escape. Bake in a moderate oven, 180°C, Gas 4, for 20 minutes or until the crust is golden-brown.

Note This is the famous Quebec pie associated with the Christmas *reveillon*.

Southern Fried Chicken with Cream Gravy

4–6 helpings

1 roasting chicken or 4 chicken quarters (1–1.5kg)	1 × 2.5ml spoon ground black pepper
50g plain flour	2 eggs
1 × 5ml spoon salt	vegetable oil for frying

Cream Gravy

375ml milk	a pinch of ground black pepper
3 × 15ml spoons plain flour	3 × 15ml spoons chicken fat or dripping
1 × 5ml spoon salt	

Cut the chicken into serving pieces. Mix the flour, salt, and pepper. Beat the eggs lightly. Dip each piece of chicken, first in the beaten egg, then in the flour. Allow to dry slightly, then dip into the egg and flour a second time. Heat enough oil in a large frying pan to fill half its depth. Brown the chicken pieces quickly on both sides. Cover the pan closely, reduce the heat, and cook until tender (20 minutes approx). Turn the chicken pieces occasionally. Uncover the pan for the last 10 minutes of the cooking time to crisp the coating.

To make the gravy, shake together the milk, 2 × 15ml spoons of the flour, the salt, and pepper in a screw-topped jar. Heat the chicken fat or dripping in a small saucepan, and stir in the remaining flour. Cook gently for 2–3 minutes, stirring all the time until it browns. Add the milk mixture, and cook slowly for a further 5 minutes. Re-season if required. Serve separately with the chicken.

Note If using fat left over from frying the chicken, leave any sediment in the pan as it adds a distinctive chicken flavour to the gravy.

Stuffed Acorn Squash

8 helpings

4 medium-sized acorn squash (750g approx)	250g sausage-meat
butter for greasing	½ × 2.5ml spoon dried crushed sage
1 small onion (50g approx)	salt

Halve the squash and take out the seeds. Butter a shallow baking tin, place the squash in it, cut side down, and bake in a moderate oven, 180°C, Gas 4, for 35–40 minutes. Meanwhile, skin and chop the onion very finely. Combine the sausage-meat, onion, and sage.

When the squash are cooked, remove from the oven, turn cut sides up, and sprinkle with salt. Fill the cavities in the squash with the sausage-meat mixture. Return to the oven and bake for another 20 minutes until the sausage-meat is cooked through.

Note Thick rings of vegetable marrow can be used instead of the halved squash.

Crookneck Squash

See p808.

Sunshine Salad

4 helpings

1 × 127g pkt lemon jelly	1 carrot
1 × 75g can crushed pineapple	a pinch of salt

Garnish

lettuce leaves	mayonnaise

Prepare the jelly in a small basin according to the directions on the packet. Allow it to thicken slightly. Drain the pineapple. Scrape the carrot and grate it coarsely. Fold the pineapple, carrot, and salt into the partially set jelly. Turn into a wetted 650ml mould or glass bowl, and chill. Leave until set. Unmould before serving, if liked. Serve on a bed of lettuce leaves, garnished with piped, stiff mayonnaise.

Green Goddess Dressing

Makes 300ml (approx)

1 egg yolk	1 × 15ml spoon onion salt
1 × 2.5ml spoon salt	
2 × 15ml spoons tarragon vinegar	a few grains garlic salt
2 × 15ml spoons anchovy essence	2 × 15ml spoons chopped chives
200ml vegetable oil	2 × 15ml spoons chopped parsley
50ml soured cream	
1 × 15ml spoon lemon juice	

Mix together in a small basin the egg yolk, salt, vinegar, and anchovy essence. Beat in the vegetable oil, 1 × 15ml spoonful at a time, until the mixture is the same consistency as mayonnaise. Stir in the rest of the ingredients. Re-season if required. Serve over green salad.

Texas Cornbread

Makes 200g (approx)

125g bacon fat **or** beef dripping	1 × 2.5ml spoon bicarbonate of soda
125g cornmeal (polenta)	200ml buttermilk **or** fresh milk with a squeeze of lemon juice
50g plain flour	
1 × 5ml spoon salt	
1 × 5ml spoon baking powder	2 eggs
	fat for greasing

Melt the bacon fat or dripping, and leave to cool slightly. Mix together the cornmeal, flour, salt, baking powder, and bicarbonate of soda in a bowl. Add the buttermilk or milk, the eggs, and the melted fat or dripping. Mix well. Turn into a greased 20cm cake tin and bake in a very hot oven, 230°C, Gas 8, for 30 minutes. The bread should be firm to the touch when done. Serve warm.

Breakfast Pancakes

See p940.

Plain Muffins

Makes 12

200g plain flour
1 × 15ml spoon baking
  powder
1 × 2.5ml spoon salt
50g granulated sugar

50g butter
1 egg
200ml milk
butter for greasing

Heat the oven to fairly hot, 200°C, Gas 6. Sift the flour, baking powder, salt, and sugar into a basin. Melt the butter. Mix with the egg and milk in a separate basin. Pour the liquid mixture over the dry ingredients. Stir only enough to dampen the flour; the mixture should be lumpy. Butter twelve 6cm muffin tins or deep bun tins. Fill each tin, as lightly as possible, only two-thirds full. Bake for about 15 minutes. Cool in the tins for 2–3 minutes, then turn out on to a wire rack to finish cooling.

Note Unlike English muffins, American muffins are quick breads. They are light savoury or sweet buns made with a slightly more puffed, richer dough than scones. They are very popular breakfast breads.

VARIATIONS

Bramble Muffins

Increase the sugar to 100g. Reserve 50g of the flour. Sprinkle it over 250g drained blackberries. Stir into the mixture last.

Jam Muffins

Before baking, top each muffin with 1 × 5ml spoon sharp-flavoured jam.

Walnut Muffins

Increase the sugar to 100g. Add 75g chopped walnuts before adding the liquids. After filling the muffin tins, sprinkle with a mixture of sugar, cinnamon, and extra, finely chopped walnuts.

Raisin Muffins

Add 50g seedless raisins before adding the liquids.

Wholemeal Muffins

Substitute 100g wholemeal flour for 100g of the plain flour. Do not sift the wholemeal flour, but add it after sifting the plain flour with the other ingredients.

Blueberry Pie

6 helpings

shortcrust pastry
  (p1249) using 300g
  flour
flour for rolling out
1kg fresh blueberries **or**
  bilberries
200g caster sugar
3 × 15ml spoons plain
  flour

1 × 5ml spoon grated
  lemon rind
1 × 2.5ml spoon ground
  cinnamon
a pinch of salt
1 × 15ml spoon lemon
  juice
1 × 15ml spoon butter

Roll out the pastry on a lightly floured surface and use just over half to line a 25cm pie plate. Use the other half to make a lid. Wash the berries. Mix them with the sugar, flour, lemon rind, cinnamon, and salt.

Fill the pie plate with the berries. Sprinkle with lemon juice and dot with butter. Dampen the edge and cover with the pastry lid. Seal the edge, making 3 or 4 slits in the top to let steam escape. Bake in a fairly hot oven, 200°C, Gas 6, for 35–40 minutes. Serve hot or cold.

Pumpkin Pie

6 helpings

shortcrust pastry (p1249)
using 200g flour
flour for rolling out
1 × 500g can pumpkin
or *500g cooked mashed*
pumpkin
150g soft dark brown
sugar
3 × 2.5ml spoons ground
cinnamon

1 × 2.5ml spoon salt
1 × 5ml spoon ground
ginger
1 × 2.5ml spoon grated
nutmeg
3 eggs
250ml milk
125ml evaporated milk

Roll out the pastry on a lightly floured surface, and use it to line a 25cm pie plate; chill in a refrigerator.

Mix the pumpkin with the sugar, cinnamon, salt, ginger, and nutmeg. Beat the eggs in another basin, add both milks, and mix well. Mix the eggs and milk into the pumpkin mixture and pour into the pastry case. Bake in a fairly hot oven, 200°C, Gas 6, for about 50 minutes, or until a knife inserted in the centre comes out clean. Cool before serving.

Southern Pecan Pie

6 helpings

shortcrust pastry (p1249)
using 200g flour
flour for rolling out
50g butter
200g soft light brown
sugar
3 eggs
225g whole shelled pecan
nuts

150g white corn syrup
or *molasses* **or** *golden*
syrup
1 × 15ml spoon dark
rum **or** *a few drops*
vanilla essence
1 × 2.5ml spoon salt

Roll out the pastry on a lightly floured surface and use it to line a 25cm pie plate. Prick the base well, and bake in a very hot oven, 230°C, Gas 8, for 5 minutes, then cool. Reduce the heat to moderate, 180°C, Gas 4. Cream the butter and the sugar. Beat in the eggs, one at a time. Stir in the rest of the ingredients. Fill the pastry case with the mixture, and bake for about 40 minutes until a knife inserted in the centre comes out clean. Serve warm or cold with double cream.

Maple Mousse

4 helpings

200ml pure maple syrup
(see **Note**)
4 egg yolks

200ml whipping cream

Pour the maple syrup into a saucepan. Beat the egg yolks lightly, and stir them into the syrup. Cook over very low heat, stirring all the time with a wooden spoon, until the mixture thickens enough to coat the back of the spoon thinly. Remove from the heat and leave to cool, covered with dampened greaseproof paper. Stir once or twice while cooling.

When cold, cover and chill. Shortly before serving, whip the cream to the same consistency as the custard and fold it in. Turn very gently into a chilled serving bowl and chill until required.

Note If 'maple flavoured' syrup is substituted for pure maple syrup, it will have to be thickened with gelatine.

Fudge Nut Topping
(for ice cream or cake)

6 helpings

200g sugar
200ml water
175g golden syrup
75g unsweetened
chocolate (see **Note**)

1 × 5ml spoon vanilla
essence
100ml evaporated milk
50g walnut pieces

Mix the sugar, water, and golden syrup in a medium-sized saucepan. Boil to the small ball stage (115°C), stirring all the time; then remove from the heat. Break up the chocolate, add it to the hot syrup, and stir briskly until the chocolate is completely melted. Add the vanilla essence and beat well. Add the evaporated milk slowly, beating all the time. Add the walnuts and mix in thoroughly. Cool either under dampened greaseproof paper, or serve hot over ice cream or sponge cake.

Note Use baking or cooking chocolate, or unsweetened couverture chocolate; do not use processed chocolate sold for making icings, frostings, and fillings.

MENUS

The nation which knows how to dine has learnt the leading lesson of progress. It implies both the will and the skill to reduce to order, and surround with idealisms and graces, the more material conditions of human existence; and wherever that will and that skill exist, life cannot be wholly ignoble.

Successful meals require careful menu planning as well as good cooking.

All meals should be nutritionally well balanced to provide an adequate supply of protein, carbohydrates, vitamins, etc (see the chapter on Nutrition and Diet). Other points then follow as a matter of course, ie personal preferences, whether it is to be a midday or evening meal, a formal or informal occasion, the time of year (although imported, packaged and frozen foods have created a greater flexibility).

Variations of flavour, colour, and texture in each course are important. You should not follow a soup with a liquid stew or casserole, a savoury flan with a pastry-based dessert, a tomato soup with grilled tomatoes as a vegetable, or a rich, creamy main course with a cream-based dessert.

Plan your menu around the main course; this will make the choice of first course and dessert, accompanying vegetables or salad much easier. Bear in mind the number of rings on top of your cooker, and do not attempt to cook two dishes in the oven at the same time if they require different temperatures.

A set of menus has been selected to complement the seasons. The dinner menus have been given as three-course meals, but they can be extended to four courses by offering cheese, either before or after the dessert. This section is followed by menus suitable for other occasions.

Spring

Lunch

Consommé Julienne

Seafood Flan
Beetroot and Celery Salad
Tossed Green Salad

Fresh Orange Jelly

Lunch

Carrot Salad

Haddock Florentine
Creamed Potatoes

Orange Pancakes

Lunch

Cheese Soufflé

Rabbit with Tomato and Lemon
Boiled Noodles
Boiled Spinach

Fresh Fruit

Lunch

Eggs in Cocottes with Spinach

Boiled Ham
New Potatoes
French Beans

Rhubarb Fool

Sunday Lunch

Grapefruit Cocktail

Roast Leg of Lamb
Mint Sauce
Roast Potatoes
Spring Cabbage

Chocolate Soufflé

Supper

Bean Salad with Tuna

Lamb Shish Kebab
Boiled Rice
Grilled Tomatoes and Mushrooms

Cheese

Supper

Spring Purée Soup

Chicken Salad
Spinach Salad
Cooked Cauliflower Salad

Fruit Flan

Dinner

Herring Roe Pâté

Coq au Vin
Sautéed Potatoes
Broccoli

Milanaise Soufflé

Dinner

Avocado Pears with Prawns

Beef Olives
Creamed Potatoes
Spinach

Lemon Water Ice

Dinner

Terrine of Duck

Turbot Dugléré
New Potatoes
Mixed Salad

Banana Flan

Summer

Lunch

Prawn Bisque

Boiled Ox Tongue (pressed)
Cucumber Salad
Pepper Salad
Rice Salad with Apricots

Lemon Meringue Pie

Lunch

Broad Bean Salad

Fricandeau of Veal
Boiled Rice
Fried Aubergines

Linzertorte

Lunch

Potted Ham

Crab au Gratin
New Potatoes
Tossed Green Salad

Cherry Compôte

Lunch

Eggs Baked in Tomatoes

Raised Pork Pie
Caesar Salad
Plain Watercress Salad

Scandinavian Fruit Fool

Sunday Lunch

Stuffed Tomato Salad

Roast Chicken with Herb Stuffing
New Potatoes
Buttered Peas

Apricot Ice Cream

Supper

Melon

Noisettes of Lamb Jardinière
Summer Cabbage

Coffee Ice Cream

Supper

Veal, Salami and Olive Salad

Smoked Haddock Soufflé
Spinach
Sautéed Potatoes

Plums with Port

Dinner

Cucumber in Soured Cream

Stuffed Boned Duck
Orange Sauce
Petits Pois à la Française
Plain Boiled Brown Rice

Stuffed Peaches in Brandy

Dinner

Hot Asparagus with Butter

Cold Poached Salmon Trout
Green Mayonnaise
Tossed Green Salad
German Potato Salad
Tomato Salad

Strawberry Soufflé

Dinner

Chilled Avocado Soup

Fillet of Beef en Croûte
Potatoes Lyonnaise
Runner Beans

Raspberry Vacherin

Autumn

Lunch

Chicory Salad

Braised Beef with Peppers
Potato Croquettes
Marrow

Damson Pie

Lunch

Eggs Rémoulade

Scampi Provençale
Boiled Rice
Tossed Green Salad

Cheese

Lunch

Aubergine Pâté

Roast Chicken with Honey and Almonds
Roast Potatoes
Runner Beans

Wine Syllabub

Lunch

Courgettes à la Grecque

Emmental Flan
Apple, Celery, and Nut Salad
Fennel and Cucumber Salad

Orange Water Ice

Sunday Lunch

Cream of Tomato Soup

Roast Pork with Apple and Celery Stuffing
Roast Potatoes
Courgettes

Fresh Fruit Salad

Supper

Russian Salad

Devilled Kidneys
Celeriac and Potato Purée
Cabbage

Mrs Beeton's Flan of Apples

Supper

Beetroot and Celery Salad

Mrs Beeton's Steak Pie
Creamed Potatoes
Cauliflower

Toffee Topped Grape Cream

Dinner

Liver Pâté

Chicken Chasseur
Potatoes Savoyarde
Carrots

Creme Brûlée

Dinner

Globe Artichokes with Butter

Leg of Lamb Provençale
Roast Potatoes
Salsify au Gratin

Pears in Wine

Dinner

Coquilles St. Jacques Mornay *

Normandy Partridges
Potato Puffs
Broccoli

Sweet Pineapple Salad with Kirsch

*Follow recipe on p464, but put under a moderate grill

Winter

Lunch

Cooked Leek Salad

Beef Goulash
Boiled Rice
Braised Celery

Lemon Delicious Pudding

Lunch

Sweet and Sour Cabbage Soup

Cheese Pudding
Endive Salad with Bacon
Tomato and Onion Salad

Fresh Fruit

Lunch

Celeriac in Mustard Dressing

Lamb Cutlets en Papillotes
Red Cabbage
Jacket Potatoes

Chocolate Mousse

Lunch

Celery Soup

Rabbit Terrine
Red Cabbage and Apple Salad
Potato Salad

Pineapple Fritters

Sunday Lunch

Prawn Cocktail

Roast Beef
Horseradish Sauce
Yorkshire Pudding
Roast Potatoes
Roast Parsnips
Winter Cabbage

Snowdon Pudding

Supper

Spiced Grapefruit

Pigeon or Rabbit Pudding
Brussels Sprouts
Creamed Potatoes

Potted Stilton

Supper

Eggs Maître D'Hôtel
Lasagne with Tomatoes, Meat, and Cheese
Tossed Green Salad

Rich Chocolate Ice Cream

Dinner

Moules Marinière

Pork Fillets Stuffed with Prunes
Boiled Noodles
Leeks

Black Forest Cherry Gâteau

Dinner

Consommé Jardinière

Sole with Prawns
Creamed Potatoes
French Beans

Oranges in Caramel Sauce

Dinner

Waldorf Salad

Jugged Hare
Potato Puffs
Brussels Sprouts

Coupe Jacques

Hot Buffet Menu (1)

Jellied Chicken Liver Pâté
or
Eggs Courtet

Blanquette of Lamb
Oven-cooked Rice
Glazed Carrots
or
Prawn Celeste
Boiled Rice
Chicory Salad

Apricot Trifle
or
Cider Syllabub

Cold Buffet Menu (1)

Salmon Mousse
or
Chicken Mousse

Jellied Ham Salad
or
Galantine of Veal
Rice Salad with Apricots
Cucumber Salad
French Bean and Tomato Salad

Chocolate Profiteroles
or
Fruit Salad

Hot Buffet Menu (2)

Prawn Quiche
or
Cheese Flan

Carbonnade of Beef with Scalloped Potatoes
or
Chicken with Curried Rice
Green Salad

Raspberry Mousse
or
Pineapple Sorbet

Cold Buffet Menu (2)

Liver Pâté with Mushrooms
or
Smoked Mackerel Pâté

Veal and Tuna Salad
or
Chicken Salad
Apple, Celery, and Nut Salad
Spinach Salad
Potato and Bacon Salad

Lemon Chiffon Pie
or
Rhubarb and Banana Fool

Hot Buffet Menu (3)

Baked Hare Pâté
or
Ham and Egg Tartlets

Casserole of Veal with French Mashed Potatoes
or
Scampi Jambalaya
Green Salad

Charlotte Russe
or
Blackcurrant Ice Cream

Cold Buffet Menu (3)

Cold Stuffed Eggs
or
Avocado and Cheese Slices

Chaudfroid of Chicken
or
Poached Salmon
Carrot and Pineapple Salad
Potato Salad
Spanish Salad

Strawberry Tartlets
or
Beatrice Tartlets

Gala Dinner Menu

Grapefruit Baskets
or
Marinated Melon

Fillets of Sole Bonne Femme

Duckling in Red Wine
Duchesse Potatoes
Peas
Cauliflower

Strawberry Ice Cream Layer Gâteau

PARTY FOOD

Where small rooms and large parties necessitate having a standing supper, many things in the bill of fare may be placed on the buffet. Dishes for these suppers should be selected which may be eaten standing without any trouble.

Whatever kind of party you are giving, your choice of menu will depend largely on your budget and cooking capabilities and upon the season of the year (see the chapter on Menus). The principles of menu planning apply just as much to buffet party food as they do to a sit-down meal. Attractive presentation and contrasts of flavour, texture, and colour are important. There should not be too many rich dishes, particularly if there are elderly people amongst your guests. Remember – or try to find out – if there are some foods which any of your guests cannot eat, and plan accordingly.

If you are cooking for eight or more people, the size of your oven may restrict you to using it for one course only. Hot food will need to be kept warm at the table, so do not plan to serve more than your hot-plates or heated trolley will hold. If the numbers are more than you usually cater for, you may have to hire extra or larger sized kitchen equipment.

For both formal dinners and buffets it is better not to plan elaborate dishes or ones which need finishing off at the last minute unless you have help in the kitchen.

If you have a home freezer, it can save a great deal of trouble and last-minute cooking for a party. Check how much spare space you can manage to have in it. Your choice of dishes will be widened immensely if, ahead of time, you can prepare and freeze soup, main dishes, creamy desserts, or pastry and other baked goods, breads or sandwiches. When planning to use frozen foods for a party, select dishes which freeze really well, and package them in portions small enough to thaw out quickly.

Remember that big casseroles need at least 30 minutes extra heating time if put into the oven still frozen. Most desserts need some last-minute preparation when thawed, so allow time for this as well.

Cooking in Quantity

For party menus, see pp1577–78.

There are a number of important factors to bear in mind when catering in quantity. If you are planning to scale up a favourite recipe, you must first look at it carefully to see if it contains any strong flavourings. These do not need to be scaled up in the same proportions as the meat or vegetable content of the recipe, as a small amount of flavouring will penetrate quite large quantities of food. Spices, garlic, strong herbs, and proprietary sauces all need to be handled with care.

The liquid content of the dish also needs to be looked at carefully. A fish dish with sauce, for example, will not need as much sauce when produced in quantity. Stews and casseroles, too, may not need the same proportion of liquid.

As well as the logical reasons for these differences when increasing quantities, there is also a psychological reason. When dishes are prepared for four or six people, the cook wishes the food not only to be sufficient but to look sufficient, and very often enough food is made for five or seven. Unless this factor is taken into account when scaling up, the resultant recipe for fifty would actually feed sixty or more people.

The simplest way of estimating the right quantity of food to prepare for a number of people is to allow so much of the major elements of a meal per person. Here are some general guidelines:

Quantities of Basic Foods to Allow per Person (approx)

Bread

French bread	2 slices (with dinner; more may be eaten with salad)
	3–4 slices (served with just wine and cheese)
Sliced bread	1–2 slices (with dinner)
Rolls	2
Butter	25g
Cheese	100g (served at wine and cheese party)
	50g (served as last course of dinner)
Pâté	50g (as first-course dish)
Soup	150ml
Meat	
on the bone	150–225g (main course: depending on whether used in casserole with vegetables or on its own)
off the bone	100–150g (main course: depending on whether used in casserole with vegetables or on its own)
Chicken	
on the bone	150–225g (main course: depending on whether used in casserole with vegetables or on its own)
off the bone	100–150g (main course: depending on whether used in casserole with vegetables or on its own)
Fish fillet or steak	100–150g (depending on whether main or subsidiary course)
Vegetables	100g (served with one other vegetable and potatoes as accompaniment to main course)
Rice	25–50g (uncooked)
Pasta	50–100g (depending on whether main course or subsidiary)
Gravy/sauces	80–100ml (served with main dish)
Salad dressings	15–20ml (smaller quantity for French dressing, larger for mayonnaise)

Desserts

ice cream	50–75ml (depending on richness, whether an accompaniment, etc)
fruit	150g (for fruit salad)
pouring cream	75ml
Tea	1 × 5ml spoon per person
	125ml milk for 4 people
Coffee	125ml per person
	125ml cream for 4 people

For finger buffets and cocktail canapés, check by making a mental picture of one of each of all the items you are planning to serve set out together on a plate. This will give you an idea of the quantity allowed for each person.

Quantities of Drink to Serve at Parties

If possible, always buy wine, beer and other liquors on a sale or return basis; this allows you to have ample supplies even if they are not all used.

Most people tend to drink at least half a 70–75cl bottle of wine, and it may be worth buying litre bottles if you are entertaining a large number of people. When beer is served as an alternative to wine, allow at least 1.5 litres per person.

A 75cl bottle of spirits will give about twenty-five 25ml measures; a 70cl bottle of sherry or vermouth will give about twelve measures. Two 500ml bottles of tonic or soda water should be provided for each 75cl bottle of spirits.

For instructions on making and storing ice in quantity, see p1368.

Large-scale Menu Quantities

The tables on the following pages show the quantities of ingredients required to make some of the dishes which appear in the party menus on pp1577–78, for twelve, twenty-five or fifty people.

	Ingredients	50 helpings	25 helpings	12 helpings
Prawn Quiche (p1255)	shortcrust pastry	2kg	1kg	375g
	flour for rolling out	as required	as required	as required
	Béchamel sauce	5 litres	2.5 litres	1.2 litres
	Cheddar cheese	2kg	1kg	450g
	peeled prawns	2.6kg	1.3kg	600g
	lemon juice	6 lemons (makes six 28cm flans)	3 lemons (makes three 28cm flans)	1½ lemons (makes three 18cm flans)
Salmon Mousse (3) (p883)	canned red or pink salmon	2.5kg catering pack	6 × 200g cans	3 × 200g cans
	butter	200g	90g	45g
	flour	200g	90g	45g
	milk	2.5 litres	1.2 litres	600ml
	eggs	25	12	6
	concentrated tomato purée	150ml	75ml	3 × 15ml spoons
	lemon juice **or** cider vinegar	150ml	75ml	3 × 15ml spoons
	dry mustard	1 × 5ml spoon	1 × 2.5ml spoon	½ × 2.5ml spoon
	salt and pepper	to taste	to taste	to taste
	double cream	1.2 litres	600ml	300ml
	pink food colouring (optional)	½ × 2.5ml spoon	¼ × 2.5ml spoon	a few drops
	gelatine	12 × 15ml spoons	6 × 15ml spoons	3 × 15ml spoons
	water	250ml	180ml	100ml
	GARNISH			
	aspic jelly	300ml	200ml	150ml
	cucumber slices	as required	as required	as required
	mustard and cress	as required	as required	as required
Fillets of Sole Bonne Femme (p454)	lemon sole fillets	100	50	24
	butter for greasing	as required	as required	as required
	mushrooms	1kg	500g	300g
	shallots	8	4	2
	chopped parsley	4 × 15ml spoons	2 × 15ml spoons	1 × 15ml spoon
	salt and pepper	to taste	to taste	to taste
	dry white wine	1 litre	600ml	300ml
	Velouté sauce (p708)	1 litre	600ml	300ml
	butter	175g	100g	50g

	Ingredients	50 helpings	25 helpings	12 helpings
Scampi Jambalaya (p465)	butter	200g	100g	50g
	cooking oil	100ml	4 × 15ml spoons	2 × 15ml spoons
	onions	3kg	1.5kg	700g
	ham	1.2kg	600g	300g
	tomatoes	2kg	1kg	500g
	green peppers	12	6	3
	garlic	3 cloves	2 cloves	1 clove
	bay leaves	3	2	1
	thyme	1 × 5ml spoon	1 × 2.5ml spoon	½ × 2.5ml spoon
	salt and pepper	to taste	to taste	to taste
	Cayenne pepper	1 × 2.5ml spoon	½ × 2.5ml spoon	a pinch
	Worcestershire sauce	3 × 15ml spoons	1½ × 15ml spoons	3 × 5ml spoons
	long-grain rice	2.5kg	1.3kg	700g
	chicken stock	1.3 litres	650ml	350ml
	peeled scampi shelled, cooked	5kg	2.5kg	1.3kg
	mussels	1.2kg	600g	300g
	medium-dry sherry	400ml	200ml	100ml
Duckling in Red Wine (p651)	ducklings	13	7	3
	salt and pepper	to taste	to taste	to taste
	onions	1.2kg	600g	300g
	bay leaves	3	2	1
	red wine	3 litres	1.5 litres	750ml
	bacon	400g	300g	200g
	cooking oil	2 × 15ml spoons	2 × 10ml spoons	1 × 15ml spoon
	stock	2.5 litres	1.75 litres	1 litre
	carrots	1kg	6 carrots	3 carrots
	celery	10 sticks	6 sticks	4 sticks
	grated orange rind	3 oranges	2 oranges	1 orange
	button mushrooms	750g	500g	250g
Carbonnade of Beef (p495)	stewing steak	6kg	3kg	1.4kg
	dripping	175g	125g	75g
	onions	1.4kg	700g	350g
	garlic	3 cloves	2 cloves	1 clove
	plain flour	8 × 15ml spoons	4 × 15ml spoons	2 ×15ml spoons
	beef stock	1 litre	600ml	375ml
	brown ale	1.2 litres	800ml	550ml
	salt and pepper	to taste	to taste	to taste
	bouquet garni	1	1	1
	nutmeg	½ × 2.5ml spoon	a pinch	a pinch
	light soft brown sugar	1 × 5ml spoon	1 × 2.5ml spoon	½ × 2.5ml spoon
	red wine vinegar	1 × 15ml spoon	1 × 10ml spoon	1 × 5ml spoon
	French bâton loaves	12 thin slices	10 thin slices	8 thin slices
	dry mustard	2 × 15ml spoons	2 × 10ml spoons	1 × 5ml spoon

	Ingredients	50 helpings	25 helpings	12 helpings
Galantine of Veal (p570)	breasts of veal	8	4	2
	salt and pepper	to taste	to taste	to taste
	sausage-meat	2.5kg	1.2kg	600g
	streaky bacon without rinds	24 rashers	12 rashers	6 rashers
	hard-boiled eggs	16	8	4
	mace	1 × 2.5ml spoon	½ × 2.5ml spoon	a pinch
	nutmeg	1 × 2.5ml spoon	½ × 2.5ml spoon	a pinch
	white stock (p329), chicken stock (p330), or water	Cook 2 breasts at a time in a large pan with 2 litres liquid		
	onions	4	4	4
	turnips	2	2	2
	carrots	2	2	2
	peppercorns	10	10	10
	meat glaze	as required	as required	as required
	GARNISH			
	sprigs of parsley	as liked	as liked	as liked
Duchesse Potatoes (p793)	old potatoes	4–4.5kg	2–2.5kg	1kg
	butter or margarine	200g	100g	50g
	eggs	8	4	2
	salt and pepper	to taste	to taste	to taste
	nutmeg (optional)	to taste	to taste	to taste
	margarine for greasing	as required	as required	as required
	beaten eggs for brushing	2	1	a little
Oven-cooked Rice (p863)	onions	1.4kg	700g	350g
	margarine	4 × 15ml spoons	3 × 15ml spoons	2 × 15ml spoons
	long-grain rice	1.6kg	800g	400g
	water or white stock (p329)	3.2 litres	1.6 litres	800ml
	salt	3 × 5ml spoons	2 × 5ml spoons	1 × 5ml spoon
Spanish Salad (p830)	firm tomatoes	4kg	2kg	1kg
	cooked potatoes	2.5kg	1.3kg	700g
	cooked or canned red peppers	750g	400g	200g
	cooked French beans	2kg	1kg	500g
	salt and pepper	to taste	to taste	to taste
	French dressing	200ml	150ml	100ml

	Ingredients	50 helpings	25 helpings	12 helpings
Chocolate Profiteroles (p1047)	choux pastry (p1251)	600g flour	300g flour	150g flour
	Chantilly cream (p880), or confectioners' custard (p1237) **or** chocolate butter cream (p1236)	1.5 litres	750ml	375ml
	chocolate (p1226) **or** coffee (p1225) glacé icing	1.2kg	600g	300g
Cider Syllabub (p1021)	lemon juice and grated rind	6 lemons	3 lemons	1½ lemons
	caster sugar	600g	300g	150g
	sweet cider	1.5 litres	750ml	375ml
	brandy (optional)	175ml	90ml	45ml
	double cream	3 litres	1.5 litres	750ml

INDEX

Note All recipe entries are in italic, eg *Alma pudding 987*

NOTES

NOTES